UNIVERSITY CASEBOOK SERIES

CASES AND MATERIALS

Prosser, Wade and Schwartz's
TORTS

TENTH EDITION

by

Victor E. Schwartz
Adjunct Professor of Law, University of Cincinnati Law School
Senior Partner, Crowell & Moring
Washington, D.C.

Kathryn Kelly
Associate Professor of Law,
The Catholic University of America

David F. Partlett
Dean and Professor of Law,
Washington and Lee School of Law

NEW YORK, NEW YORK
Foundation Press

2000

TEXT IS PRINTED ON 10% POST
CONSUMER RECYCLED PAPER

To our dear colleague
whose wisdom and grace was shared with so many
and whose insight lives on in this text,
Dean John W. Wade

PREFACE

This edition marks the 50th anniversary of a work first published in 1951, authored then by one of the most insightful minds in the law of torts during the 20th Century, William Lloyd Prosser. He established a tradition of excellence in scholarship combined with ease of use. That tradition was continued and enhanced for almost three decades by our late colleague, Dean John W. Wade. Each of them contributed not just to the learning of countless students through their work on this casebook, but also to the development of the law through their scholarly writings and service as reporters to the American Law Institute Restatement of Torts (Second).

The casebook has benefitted from the half century of learning from many other sources and we, the current authors, Victor Schwartz, Kathryn Kelly, and David Partlett, felt a special sense of responsibility in editing its 10th Edition. As we worked on this edition, we did more than read cases (thousands of cases), statutes, and law review articles. We consulted with law professors who have adopted our book in the past, as well as with those who had not, about how it could be improved. Through e-mails, letters, and telephone calls, they sent us their thoughts. Some of their ideas were broad and conceptual, others were technical, and a few were chastising; the book benefitted from all of them. We sought comments from students who have studied from our book, including former students, now practicing lawyers, who took time from their busy law practices to send us cases, comment on the trends they observe from the frontlines of tort law, and share their reflections on the best ways to prepare for the practice of tort law.

With that goal and all of those suggestions in mind, we eliminated cases that were deemed overbearing and unproductive; we pruned cases that were thought too lengthy; we added cases, not for the purpose of "change," but to make the subject more interesting and to assure that current and vital issues are discussed. Since the publication of the 9th Edition in 1994, the law has seen many changes and this edition reflects those changes. We would like to highlight three of them. First, a new Restatement of Torts (Third) is being published by the American Law Institute in segments. Victor Schwartz has served as an Adviser to all three sections. The first major step has been Restatement (Third) of Torts: Products Liability. The Products Liability chapter includes a focus on the new Restatement. It presents controversies that surrounded both its making and its content. Second, while fully respecting the traditional common law development of torts, we have focused on the role of the modern legislature in creating tort law and the response of the state judiciary to that phenomenon by reorganizing material and adding cases so that a chapter is now devoted to the law of torts in the age of statutes. The outcome of this struggle between the courts and the legislature over the shaping of America's tort law is yet to be written. Finally, we have appreciated the growing role of so-called "business torts." Most punitive damage awards, for example, do not occur in the area of personal injury but in commercial tort disputes. Commercial tort disputes occupy much of the time of many practicing lawyers in the field. The cases on misrepresentation have been revamped and the tort of interference with business relationships is examined through several recent cases, including a key one from the California Supreme Court.

Throughout the text, we have held fast to a cardinal principle that has been a hallmark of this text for five decades: the casebook is not used to present any particular philosophy or ideology of tort law. We leave that to the law reviews, the Congressional testimony, and the *amicus* briefs. This casebook aspires to provide teachers with the raw material to inform and challenge students to learn the law and to think critically about it.

While the size and breadth of this casebook may give pause to some, we believe that all students should be given an opportunity, if they wish, to peruse topics that there may not be time to cover in class. The casebook easily can be adapted for use in a first-year course of different credit hours and in optional advanced courses.

As in previous editions of this casebook, the deletion of a part of the text from a published opinion is indicated by the use of lacunae (***). When only citations are omitted, the letter "c" is used for "citation." To indicate that several citations have been deleted, "cc" is used. The letter is capitalized or not, depending on whether the citation was placed in the middle of a sentence or started a new sentence.

Those of you learning torts from this casebook will make the law in the 21st Century. That is an important undertaking. We hope that you will find the first step of that undertaking, learning torts from this 10th Edition, challenging and enjoyable.

VICTOR SCHWARTZ
KATHRYN KELLY
DAVID PARTLETT

April 2000

WILLIAM L. PROSSER
Late Professor of Law, University of California,
Hastings College of Law

JOHN W. WADE
Late Dean and Distinguished Professor of Law,
Vanderbilt University School of Law

*

ACKNOWLEDGMENTS

1. *Pictures*. Grateful acknowledgment is made to the following for their kind assistance in locating or their courtesy in supplying or granting permission to publish pictures:

Picture of Dean John W. Wade. Mary Moody Wade.

Picture of Dean William L. Prosser. Hastings College of Law.

The Far Side Cartoon. FarWorks, Inc.

Palsgraf pictures. William J. Pallas, Assistant General Counsel, Long Island Railroad.

Wagon Mound pictures. John Fairfax & Sons, Ltd., Sydney, N.S.W., Australia.

St. Francis Hotel picture. The hotel.

MacPherson Buick Model. Buick Motor Division of General Motors Corporation.

Pictures of New York Court of Appeals and of some individual Justices. Professor Robert J. Tyman, Albany Law School.

Pictures of California Supreme Court and of individual Justices. Professor T.A. Smedley, Hastings Law School.

Pictures of Supreme Court of Oregon. Retired Justice Ralph M. Holman.

Pictures of the parties and house in Katko v. Briney. Bruce A. Palmer, Esq., Oskaloosa, Iowa.

Pictures of the bridge in Dillon v. Twin State Gas and Electric Co. Peter H. Bornstein, Esq., Berlin, New Hampshire.

Pictures of Judge Andrews in *Palsgraf* case. Retired Judge Francis Bergan.

Picture of Justice Francis in *Henningsen* case. Rutgers Law Review.

Picture of the New Jersey Supreme Court. Stephen W. Townsend, Clerk of the Court.

Especial appreciation is due to Ms. Bernice Loss, in charge of the Art Collection at Harvard Law School, for her courtesy in making available the following pictures: Lords Abinger, Blackburn, Cairns, Ellenborough and Herschell, Lord Justice Bowen, Chief Baron Pollock, Chief Justices Holt, Shaw and Tindall, Justices Cardozo and Holmes, Judge Learned Hand, and Dean Bohlen.

2. *Reprints.* Appreciative acknowledgment is also made to the following for permission to include the indicated selections:

American Law Institute. Certain sections from the Restatement, Second, Torts and from the Restatement of the Law, Third, Torts: Products Liability.

National Conference of Commissioners on Uniform State Laws. Certain Uniform and Model Acts.

Matthew Bender & Co. Three paragraphs from A. Larson, The Law of Workmen's Compensation.

RAND—The Institute for Civil Justice. Several pages from a report, No–Fault Approaches to Compensating People Injured in Automobile Accidents, by S.J. Carroll, et al.

SUMMARY OF CONTENTS

*

TABLE OF CONTENTS

*

TABLE OF CASES

Principal cases are in bold type. Non-principal cases are in roman type. References are to Pages.

CASES AND MATERIALS

PROSSER, WADE AND SCHWARTZ'S
TORTS

*

CHAPTER I

DEVELOPMENT OF LIABILITY
BASED UPON FAULT

"Tort" comes from the Latin word "tortus," which means twisted, and the French word "tort," which means injury or wrong. A tort is a civil wrong, [other than a breach of contract,] for which the law provides a remedy. This area of law imposes duties on persons to act in a manner that will not injure other persons. A person who breaches a tort duty has committed a tort and may be liable in a lawsuit brought by a person injured because of that tort.

Over the years, tort law has normally been a part of the common law, developed by the courts through the opinions of the judges in the cases before them. In some areas, however, statutes have long been common— e.g., trespass to real property, limitation of actions; and statutes have been more frequently used in recent years.

Modern Tort Law—Beyond the Casebooks Into the Field of Public Debate. From the time this casebook began with its first edition in the early 1950's, tort law was of concern primarily to law students, law professors and attorneys who practiced in the field. The public, in general, knew very little, if anything, about the subject. In the past couple of decades, however, this has changed quite dramatically. Prior to coming to law school, you probably read about so-called "liability crises"; about nurse-midwives "struggling" to obtain malpractice insurance; about product manufacturers going out of business or declining to put new and useful products on the market, all because of problems in the area of "tort law."

Both the Federal Government and state governments have studied these "crises." Legislation affecting tort law has multiplied in recent years. As you study the law of torts, you may find that you will be reading news stories about the subject from a new perspective. You may decide that many stories oversimplify the tort system and perhaps miss important points. It is important to pay attention to these stories, however, for the subject you are studying is very live, very real and at the center of major public policy debates.

In studying the subject, you should consider the major purposes of tort law: (1) to provide a peaceful means for adjusting the rights of parties who might otherwise "take the law into their own hands"; (2) to deter wrongful conduct; (3) to encourage socially responsible behavior; and (4) to restore injured parties to their original condition, insofar as the law can do this, by compensating them for their injury. Should people always be compensated when they have been injured by the action of another? If your answer to this question is in the affirmative, think about whether it is always

1

necessary to have a trial, with a plaintiff, a defendant and lawyers. On the other hand, if tort law should not compensate every person who is injured by another, what are appropriate rules and standards to determine whom to compensate and under what circumstances? This is the primary problem to which the law of torts addresses itself.

It is important to remember, also, that in back of the tort system is an insurance system. Even non-lawyers know that most people who are sued in tort law have some form of liability insurance. The "crises" that have occurred in tort law often have been precipitated by difficulty in obtaining or affording liability insurance. These difficulties, in turn, may lead to problems that more directly affect the public—a fireworks display is not held, a physician no longer delivers babies, a useful product is not market-ed, an injured person remains uncompensated by a liable but insolvent tortfeasor.

The casebook will explore the system that has been accused of having caused these crises. Evaluate it carefully, and remember that you are not only learning a legal subject, but also becoming an educated citizen who can and should participate in the debate about the direction tort law should take now and into the next century.

Historical Origins. Historians have differed as to how the law of torts began. There is one theory that it originated with liability based upon "actual intent and actual personal culpability," with a strong moral tinge, and slowly formulated external standards that took less account of personal fault. O. Holmes, The Common Law, Lecture I (1881). It seems quite likely that the most flagrant wrongs were the first to receive redress.

Another, and more generally accepted theory, is that the law began by imposing liability on those who caused physical harm, and gradually developed toward the acceptance of moral standards as the basis of liability. Wigmore, Responsibility for Tortious Acts: Its History, 7 Harv.L.Rev. 315, 383 & 441 (1894). Ames, Law and Morals, 22 Harv.L.Rev. 97 (1908). An alternative theory is that there has been no steady progression from liability without fault to liability based on fault. The difference between no-fault periods and fault-based periods is, rather, one of degree. Isaacs, Fault and Liability, 31 Harv.L.Rev. 954, 965 (1918).

Certainly at one time the law was not very much concerned with the moral responsibility of the defendant. "The thought of man shall not be tried," said Chief Justice Brian, in Y.B. 7 Edw. IV, f. 2, pl. 2 (1468), "for the devil himself knoweth not the thought of man." The courts were interested primarily in keeping the peace between individuals by providing a substitute for private vengeance, and the party injured was just as likely to take the law into his own hands when the injury was an innocent one. The person who hurt another by unavoidable accident or in self-defense was required to make good the damage inflicted. "In all civil acts," it was said, in Lambert v. Bessey, T.Raym. 421, 83 Eng.Rep. 220 (K.B.1681), "the law doth not so much regard the intent of the actor, as the loss and damage of the party suffering."

Forms of action. In the early English law, after the Norman conquest, remedies for wrongs were dependent upon the issuance of writs to bring the defendant into court. In the course of the thirteenth century, the principle was established that no one could bring an action in the King's common law courts without the King's writ. As a result of the jealous insistence of the nobles and others upon the prerogatives of their local courts, the number of writs that the King could issue was limited, and their forms were strictly prescribed. There were, in other words, "forms of action," and unless the plaintiff's claim could be fitted into the form of some established and recognized writ, the plaintiff could not seek money damages in the King's courts. The result was a highly formalized system of procedure that governed and controlled the law as to the substance of the wrongs that might be remedied. You may learn more about how the forms of action affected the law of procedure in your civil procedure classes.

Two common law writs are the genesis of tort law—the writ of trespass and the writ of trespass on the case, often called action on the case.

The form of action in trespass originally had a criminal character. It would lie only in cases of forcible breaches of the King's peace, and it was only on this basis that the royal courts assumed jurisdiction over the wrong. The purpose of the remedy was at first primarily that of punishment of the crime; but to this there was added later the satisfaction of the injured party's claim for redress. If the defendant was found guilty, damages were awarded to the successful plaintiff, and the defendant was imprisoned, and allowed to purchase his release by payment of a fine. What similarity remains between tort and crime is to be traced to this common beginning. See Woodbine, The Origin of the Action of Trespass, 33 Yale L.J. 799 (1923), 34 Yale L.J. 343 (1934); F. Maitland, The Forms of Action at Common Law, 65 (1941).

(handwritten margin note: kind of like criminal law ↗ crimes against the state)

The writ of trespass on the case developed out of the practice of applying to the Chancellor, in cases in which no writ could be found in the Register to cover the plaintiff's claim, for a special writ, in the nature of trespass, drawn to fit the particular case. Historians have differed as to the origin of this practice. Attempts to trace it are found in C. Fifoot, History and Sources of the Common Law: Tort and Contract, 66–74 (1949), and Kiralfy, The Action on the Case, Chapter I (1951).

Whatever may have been its origin, it was through this action on the case, rather than through trespass, that most of the modern law of both tort and contract developed. Thus, in the field of tort law, actions for nuisance, conversion, deceit, defamation, malicious prosecution, interference with economic relations and the modern action for negligence all developed out of the action on the case.

The distinction between trespass and case lay in the direct and immediate application of force to the person or property of the plaintiff. Trespass would lie only for direct and forcible injuries; case, for other tangible injuries to person or property. The classic illustration of this distinction is that of a log thrown into the highway. A person struck by the rolling log could maintain trespass against the thrower, since the injury was direct and immediate; but one who came along later and was hurt by stumbling over the stationary log in the road could maintain only an action on the case. Leame v. Bray, 3 East 593, 102 Eng.Rep. 724 (1802).

Note that the distinction was not one between intentional and negligent conduct. The emphasis was upon the causal sequence, rather than the character of the defendant's wrong. Trespass would lie for all forcible, direct injuries, whether or not they were intended, while the action on the case might be maintained for injuries intended but not forcible or not direct. There were two additional significant points of difference between the two actions. Trespass, because of its quasi-criminal character, required no proof of any actual damage, since the invasion of the plaintiff's rights by the criminal conduct was regarded as a tort in itself; while in the action on the case, which developed purely as a civil remedy, there could ordinarily be no liability unless actual damage was proved. Also, in its earlier stages trespass was identified with the view that liability might be imposed without regard to the defendant's fault, while case from the beginning required proof of culpability: either a wrongful intent or wrongful conduct (negligence).

The criminal aspect of trespass disappeared in 1697, when the statute of 5–6 William & Mary, c. 12, abolished the fine, and left the action as an exclusively civil remedy. Out of adherence to precedent, however, the courts continued to allow the action even though no real injury was suffered. They were, however, disinclined to extend the scope of trespass beyond the existing precedents, perhaps because of the belief that punishment was primarily the function of the criminal law and the civil action should be used only to compensate for harm done. This explains why in modern law there is a requirement of proving actual damages except in cases of assault, offensive but harmless battery, false imprisonment, and trespass to land. If harm was done, the injured party could still sue in case and recover, even though the defendant's wrong did not amount to a trespass. If no harm was done, the recovery of punitive damages in a civil action was limited to the most flagrant types of cases, where the criminal law did not apply or was not effective as a deterrent.

Anonymous

King's Bench, 1466.
Y.B. 5 Edw. IV, folio 7, placitum 18.

BRIAN. In my opinion if a man does a thing he is bound to do it in such a manner that by his deed no injury or damage is inflicted upon others. As in the case where I erect a building, and when the timber is being lifted a piece of it falls upon the house of my neighbor and bruises his house, he will have a good action, and that, although the erection of my house was lawful and the timber fell without my intent.

Similarly, if a man commits an assault upon me and I cannot avoid him if he wants to beat me, and I lift my stick in self-defense in order to prevent him, and there is a man in back of me and I injure him in lifting my stick, in that case he would have an action against me, although my lifting the stick was lawful to defend myself and I injured him without intent.

[handwritten: he would have an action — doesn't mean he would actually file or surely win]

NOTES AND QUESTIONS

1. This passage, translated from the Norman French, is one of the few bits and fragments of the early English law of torts that have come down to us. Although Brian, who became Chief Justice of the Court of Common Pleas in 1471, was apparently only arguing as counsel in this case, he appears to have been summarizing accepted law.

Weaver v. Ward

[handwritten: plaintiff — defendant]

King's Bench, 1616.
Hobart 134, 80 Eng.Rep. 284.

Weaver brought an action of trespass of assault and battery against Ward. The defendant pleaded, that he was amongst others by the commandment of the Lords of the Council a trained soldier in London, of the band of one Andrews captain; and so was the plaintiff, and that they were skirmishing with their muskets charged with powder for the exercise in re militari [in a military matter], against another captain and his band; and as they were so skirmishing the defendant casualiter & per infortunium & contra voluntatem suam [accidentally and by misfortune and against his will] in discharging his piece did hurt and wound the plaintiff, which is the same, & c. absque hoc [without this], that he was guilty aliter sive alio modo [otherwise or in another manner].

[handwritten: manslaughter?]

And upon demurrer by the plaintiff, judgment was given for him; for though it were agreed, that if men tilt or turney in the presence of the King, or if two masters of defence playing their prizes kill one another, that this shall be no felony, or if a lunatick kill a man, or the like, because felony must be done animo felonico [with a felonious mind]; yet in trespass, which tends only to give damages according to hurt or loss, it is not so; and therefore if a lunatick hurt a man, he shall be answerable in trespass; and therefore no man shall be excused of a trespass (for this is in the nature of an excuse, and not of a justification, prout ei bene licuit [as is properly permitted to him]), except it may be judged utterly without his fault.

[handwritten: motion to dismiss = insufficient facts for a case — Holding — Rule of law]

[handwritten: removed intent => homicide ⇂ manslaughter]

As if a man by force take my hand and strike you, or if here the defendant had said, that the plaintiff ran cross his piece when it was discharging, or had set forth the case with the circumstances, so as it had appeared to the Court that it had been inevitable and that the defendant had committed no negligence to give occasion to the hurt.

[handwritten: case says not always strict liability → has to be negligence]

[handwritten: man must pay but not so severely only as redress not as punishment]

NOTES AND QUESTIONS

1. This is the earliest known case in which it was clearly recognized that a defendant might not be liable, even in a trespass action, for a purely accidental injury occurring entirely without his fault. Note that the burden rests upon the defendant to plead and prove his freedom from all fault.

2.   The next two centuries see a gradual blurring of the distinction between trespass and case. The procedural distinction is now long antiquated, although some vestige of it still remains in jurisdictions retaining common law pleading in a modified form. Modern law has almost entirely abandoned the artificial classification of injuries as direct and indirect, and looks instead to the intent of the wrongdoer or his negligence.

3.   The first step was taken when the action on the case was held to cover injuries that were merely negligent but were directly inflicted, as in Williams v. Holland, 10 Bing. 112, 131 Eng.Rep. 848 (1833). Although this left the plaintiff an election between trespass and case, the action of case came to be used quite generally in all cases of negligence, whether direct or indirect, while trespass remained as the remedy for intentional injuries inflicted by acts of violence. Terms such as battery, assault and false imprisonment, which were varieties of trespass, gradually came to be associated only with intent, and negligence emerged as a separate tort. The shift was a slow one, and the courts seem to have been quite unconscious of it at the time. When in the nineteenth century the old forms of action were replaced in most jurisdictions by the modern code procedure, the new classification remained. Prichard, Trespass, Case and the Rule in Williams v. Holland, Cambridge L.J. 234 (1964). There was occasional confusion, and some talk, for example, of a negligent battery, as in Anderson v. Arnold's Ex'r, 79 Ky. 370 (1881), but, in general, these old trespass terms are now restricted to actions involving intent.

4.   Although we no longer have "forms of action," it usually is helpful from the vantage point of advocacy to place one's claim under a tort "label" that will be familiar to the court: e.g., "battery," "assault," "defamation," "nuisance."

5.   With certain exceptions, actions for injuries to the person, or to tangible property, now require proof of an intent to inflict them, or of failure to exercise proper care to avoid them. As to the necessity of proving actual damage, the courts have continued the distinctions found in the older actions of trespass and case. Whether the damage is essential to the existence of a cause of action for a particular tort depends largely upon its ancestry in terms of the old procedure.

6.   The story of the change in the law is narrated in Goodhart and Winfield, Trespass and Negligence, 49 L.Q.Rev. 358 (1933); Gregory, Trespass to Negligence to Absolute Liability, 37 Va.L.Rev. 359 (1951); Roberts, Negligence: Blackstone to Shaw to ? An Intellectual Escapade in a Tory Vein, 50 Cornell L.Q. 191 (1964); Kretzmer, Transformation of Tort Liability in the 19th Century, 4 Oxf.J.Leg.Stud. 46 (1984). A thoughtful perspective on the problems of this chapter is Malone, Ruminations on the Role of Fault in the History of the Common Law of Torts, 31 La.L.Rev. 1 (1970).

Brown v. Kendall

Supreme Judicial Court of Massachusetts, 1850.
60 Mass. (6 Cush.) 292.

This was an action of trespass for assault and battery. * * * [Two dogs, owned by plaintiff and defendant, were fighting. Defendant tried to separate them by beating them with a stick. In doing so he backed up toward the plaintiff, and in raising his stick over his shoulder, hit plaintiff in the eye, and injured him.]

Whether it was necessary or proper for the defendant to interfere in the fight between the dogs; whether the interference, if called for, was in a proper manner, and what degree of care was exercised by each party on the occasion; were the subject of controversy between the parties, upon all the evidence in the case * * *

[The trial judge, refusing to give requested instructions to the contrary, instructed the jury that if beating the dogs was a necessary act which defendant was under a duty to do, defendant was required to use only ordinary care in doing it; but if it were only a proper and permissible act, defendant was liable unless he exercised extraordinary care; and that the burden of proving the extraordinary care was on the defendant.]

The jury under these instructions returned a verdict for the plaintiff; whereupon the defendant alleged exceptions.

Chief Justice Shaw

SHAW, C.J. * * * The facts set forth in the bill of exceptions preclude the supposition, that the blow, inflicted by the hand of the defendant upon the person of the plaintiff, was intentional. The whole case proceeds on the assumption, that the damage sustained by the plaintiff, from the stick held by the defendant, was inadvertent and unintentional; and the case involves the question how far, and under what qualifications, the party by whose unconscious act the damage was done is responsible for it. We use the term "unintentional" rather than involuntary, because in some of the cases, it is stated, that the act of holding and using a weapon or instrument, the movement of which is the immediate cause of hurt to another, is a voluntary act, although its particular effect in hitting and hurting another is not within the purpose or intention of the party doing the act.

It appears to us, that some of the confusion in the cases on this subject has grown out of the long-vexed question, under the rule of the common law, whether a party's remedy, where he has one, should be sought in an action of the case, or of trespass. This is very distinguishable from the question, whether in a given case, any action will lie. The result of these cases is, that if the damage complained of is the immediate effect of the act of the defendant, trespass *vi et armis* lies; if consequential only, and not immediate, case is the proper remedy. [Cc]

In these discussions, it is frequently stated by judges, that when one receives injury from the direct act of another, trespass will lie. But we think this is said in reference to the question, whether trespass and not case will lie, assuming that the facts are such, that some action will lie. These *dicta* are no authority, we think, for holding, that damage received by a direct act of force from another will be sufficient to maintain an action of trespass, whether the act was lawful or unlawful, and neither wilful, intentional, or careless. * * *

We think, as the result of all the authorities, the rule is correctly stated by Mr. Greenleaf, that the plaintiff must come prepared with evidence to show either that the *intention* was unlawful, or that the defendant was *in fault;* for if the injury was unavoidable, and the conduct of the defendant was free from blame, he will not be liable. 2 Greenl. Ev. §§ 85 to 92; [c]. If, in the prosecution of a lawful act, a casualty purely accidental arises, no action can be supported for an injury arising therefrom. [Cc] In applying these rules to the present case, we can perceive no reason why the instructions asked for by the defendant ought not to have been given; to this effect, that if both plaintiff and defendant at the time of the blow were using ordinary care, or if at that time the defendant was using ordinary care, and the plaintiff was not, or if at that time, both the plaintiff and defendant were not using ordinary care, then the plaintiff could not recover.

In using this term, ordinary care, it may be proper to state, that what constitutes ordinary care will vary with the circumstances of cases. In general, it means that kind and degree of care, which prudent and cautious men would use, such as is required by the exigency of the case, and such as is necessary to guard against probable danger. A man, who should have occasion to discharge a gun, on an open and extensive marsh, or in a forest, would be required to use less circumspection and care, than if he were to do the same thing in an inhabited town, village, or city. To make an accident, or casualty, or as the law sometimes states it, inevitable accident, it must be such an accident as the defendant could not have avoided by the use of the kind and degree of care necessary to the exigency, and in the circumstances in which he was placed.

exigency — a demand for immediate action or performance arising from a circumstance or condition

We are not aware of any circumstances in this case, requiring a distinction between acts which it was lawful and proper to do, and acts of legal duty. There are cases, undoubtedly, in which officers are bound to act under process, for the legality of which they are not responsible, and perhaps some others in which this distinction would be important. We can have no doubt that the act of the defendant in attempting to part the fighting dogs, one of which was his own, and for the injurious acts of which he might be responsible, was a lawful and proper act, which he might do by proper and safe means. If, then, in doing this act, using due care and all proper precautions necessary to the exigency of the case, to avoid hurt to others, in raising his stick for that purpose, he accidentally hit the plaintiff in his eye, and wounded him, this was the result of pure accident, or was involuntary and unavoidable, and therefore the action would not lie. * * *

The court instructed the jury, that if it was not a necessary act, and the defendant was not in duty bound to part the dogs, but might with propriety interfere or not as he chose, the defendant was responsible for the consequences of the blow, unless it appeared that he was in the exercise of extraordinary care, so that the accident was inevitable, using the word not in a strict but a popular sense. This is to be taken in connection with the charge afterwards given, that if the jury believed, that the act of interference in the fight was unnecessary, (that is, as before explained, not a duty incumbent on the defendant,) then the burden of proving extraordinary care on the part of the defendant, or want of ordinary care on the part of the plaintiff, was on the defendant.

should he or should he have not used the stick?

must either have been necessary interference or defendant used extraordinary care in either defendant wins → no action

The court are of opinion that these directions were not conformable to law. If the act of hitting the plaintiff was unintentional, on the part of the defendant, and done in the doing of a lawful act, then the defendant was not liable, unless it was done in the want of exercise of due care, adapted to the exigency of the case, and therefore such want of due care became part of the plaintiff's case, and the burden of proof was on the plaintiff to establish it. [Cc]

otherwise → action against him

said defendant didn't use proper care

Perhaps the learned judge, by the use of the term extraordinary care, in the above charge, explained as it is by the context, may have intended nothing more than that increased degree of care and diligence, which the exigency of particular circumstances might require, and which men of ordinary care and prudence would use under like circumstances, to guard against danger. If such was the meaning of this part of the charge, then it does not differ from our views, as above explained. But we are of opinion, that the other part of the charge, that the burden of proof was on the defendant, was incorrect. Those facts which are essential to enable the plaintiff to recover, he takes the burden of proving. The evidence may be offered by the plaintiff or by the defendant; the question of due care, or want of care, may be essentially connected with the main facts, and arise from the same proof; but the effect of the rule, as to the burden of proof, is this, that when the proof is all in, and before the jury, from whatever side it comes, and whether directly proved, or inferred from circumstances, if it appears that the defendant was doing a lawful act, and unintentionally hit and hurt the plaintiff, then unless it also appears to the satisfaction of the jury, that the defendant is chargeable with some fault, negligence, carelessness, or want of prudence, the plaintiff fails to sustain the burden of proof, and is not entitled to recover.

New trial ordered.

NOTES AND QUESTIONS

1. Why a new trial? Why not simply a judgment for the defendant?

2. What has gone on in the law since the Anonymous Case in 1466? How would Justice Shaw have decided Weaver v. Ward?

3. This decision is the earliest clear statement of the rule commonly applied: liability must be based on legal fault.

4. While Brown v. Kendall dealt with a defendant who was separating dogs, most tort defendants in Massachusetts at the time were industrial employers. Does this fact, plus the social policy of the time, have a bearing on the legal change reflected in the opinion? See Schwartz, The Character of Early American Tort Law, 36 U.C.L.A. L. Rev. 641, 667–670 (1989).

5. In some jurisdictions, the old distinction between trespass and case survived until comparatively recent dates, in the form of decisions holding that if the injury is one for which trespass would lie, the defendant must sustain the burden of proving that he was not at fault, while if only case would lie the burden of proving fault is on the plaintiff. The distinction was not finally abandoned in England until Fowler v. Lanning, [1959] 1 Q.B. 426.

Cohen v. Petty

Court of Appeals of the District of Columbia, 1933.
62 App.D.C. 187, 65 F.2d 820.

GRONER, ASSOCIATE JUSTICE. Plaintiff's declaration alleged that on December 14, 1930, she was riding as a guest in defendant's automobile; that defendant failed to exercise reasonable care in its operation, and drove it at a reckless and excessive rate of speed so that he lost control of the car and propelled it off the road against an embankment on the side of the road, as the result of which plaintiff received permanent injuries. The trial judge gave binding instructions [directed a verdict], and the plaintiff appeals.

There were four eyewitnesses to the accident, namely, plaintiff and her sister on the one side, and defendant and his wife on the other. All four were occupants of the car. Defendant was driving the car, and his wife was sitting beside him. Plaintiff and her sister were in the rear seat. * * * After passing the Country Club, and when somewhere near Four Corners and five or six miles from Silver Spring, the automobile suddenly swerved out of the road, hit the abutment of a culvert, and ran into the bank, throwing plaintiff and her sister through the roof of the car onto the ground.

Plaintiff's sister estimated the speed of the car just before the accident somewhere between thirty-five and forty miles an hour, and plaintiff herself, who had never driven a car, testified she thought it was nearer forty-five. The place of the accident was just beyond a long and gradual curve in the road. Plaintiff testified that just before the accident, perhaps a minute, she heard the defendant, who, as we have said, was driving the car, exclaim to his wife, "I feel sick," and a moment later heard his wife exclaim in a frightened voice to her husband, "Oh, John, what is the matter?" Immediately thereafter the car left the road and the crash occurred. Her sister, who testified, could not remember anything that occurred on the ride except that, at the time they passed the Country Club, the car was being driven about thirty-five or forty miles an hour and that the occupants of the car were engaged in a general conversation. The road was of concrete and was wide. Plaintiff, when she heard defendant's wife exclaim, "What is the matter?" instead of looking at the driver of the car, says she continued to look down the road, and as a result she did not see and does not know what subsequently occurred, except that there was a collision with the embankment.

Defendant's evidence as to what occurred just before the car left the road is positive and wholly uncontradicted. His wife, who was sitting beside him, states that they were driving along the road at the moderate rate of speed when all of a sudden defendant said, "Oh, Tree, I feel sick"— defendant's wife's name is Theresa, and he calls her Tree. His wife looked over, and defendant had fainted. "His head had fallen back and his hand had left the wheel and I immediately took hold of the wheel with both hands, and then I do not remember anything else until I waked up on the road in a strange automobile." The witness further testified that her husband's eyes were closed when she looked, and that his fainting and the collision occurred in quick sequence to his previous statement, "Oh, Tree, I feel so sick." The defendant himself testified that he had fainted just before the crash, that he had never fainted before, and that so far as he knew he was in good health, that on the day in question he had had breakfast late, and had had no luncheon, but that he was not feeling badly until the moment before the illness and the fainting occurred. * * *

The sole question is whether, under the circumstances we have narrated, the trial court was justified in taking the case from the jury. We think its action was in all respects correct.

It is undoubtedly the law that one who is suddenly stricken by an illness, which he had no reason to anticipate, while driving an automobile, which renders it impossible for him to control the car, is not chargeable with negligence. [Cc]

In the present case the positive evidence is all to the effect that defendant did not know and had no reason to think he would be subject to an attack such as overcame him. Hence negligence cannot be predicated in this case upon defendant's recklessness in driving an automobile when he knew or should have known of the possibility of an accident from such an event as occurred.

As the plaintiff wholly failed to show any actionable negligence prior to the time the car left the road, or causing or contributing to that occurrence, and as the defendant's positive and uncontradicted evidence shows that the loss of control was due to defendant's sudden illness, it follows the action of the lower court was right. Even if plaintiff's own evidence tended more strongly than it does to imply some act of negligence, it would be insufficient to sustain a verdict and judgment upon proof such as the defendant offered here of undisputed facts, for in such a case the inference must yield to uncontradicted evidence of actual events.

Affirmed.

NOTES AND QUESTIONS

1. Defendant, asleep on the rear seat of an automobile, unconsciously pushed with his foot against the front seat in which plaintiff, the driver, was sitting. Plaintiff's arms were forced off the wheel, the car crashed into a culvert and overturned, and plaintiff was injured. Is defendant liable? Lobert v. Pack, 337 Pa. 103, 9 A.2d 365 (1939) (defendant not liable because he did not act with volition).

2. Defendant, driving an automobile, fell asleep at the wheel. The car went into the ditch and injured the plaintiff. Is defendant liable for his conduct while he is asleep? What if he knew that he was getting sleepy and continued to drive? Is this not always the case? At least one court has found that falling asleep at the wheel of a car is negligence unless the driver was suddenly overcome with illness. Bushnell v. Bushnell, 103 Conn. 583, 131 A. 432 (1925). Defendant became so frightened when she realized that her brakes were not working that she fainted and was thus unconscious when she collided with plaintiff's car. Liability? Kohler v. Sheffert, 250 Iowa 899, 96 N.W.2d 911 (1959) (fact that she was unconscious at time of collision did not excuse previous negligence in causing the situation that frightened her).

3. Defendant, knowing that he was subject to epileptic seizures, drove an automobile. He had a seizure while driving and lost control of the car, which ran into the plaintiff and injured him. Is defendant liable? Eleason v. Western Casualty & Surety Co., 254 Wis. 134, 35 N.W.2d 301 (1948). What if he had never had a seizure before? Moore v. Capital Transit Co., 226 F.2d 57 (D.C.Cir.1955), cert. denied, 350 U.S. 966 (1956).

4. A patient was given prescription drugs (Prolixin, Decanoate and Thorazine) and discharged from the hospital, without being warned that they would impair his mental and physical abilities. The patient drove his automobile, lost control and struck a tree, injuring his passenger. Is the driver liable to his passenger? Is his doctor? Is the manufacturer of the drugs? Cf. Kirk v. Michael Reese Hospital and Medical Center, 136 Ill.App.3d 945, 91 Ill.Dec. 420, 483 N.E.2d 906 (1985), rev'd, 117 Ill.2d 507, 111 Ill.Dec. 944, 513 N.E.2d 387 (1987).

5. Do you agree with the result of the principal case? What about the argument that anyone who drives an automobile should bear the risk that others will be injured if he suffers a heart attack while driving, and should make good their loss? In a case where an epileptic had an unanticipated seizure, plaintiff's counsel

argued most strongly that since defendant had liability insurance, he should bear the risk. Was the argument a good one? See Hammontree v. Jenner, 20 Cal.App.3d 528, 97 Cal.Rptr. 739 (1971). The court rejected this contention.

6. See Kaufman and Kantrowitz, The Case of the Sleeping Motorist, 25 N.Y.U. L.Q.Rev. 362 (1950).

if you get into a car knowing a someone is epileptic, you take some of the burden yourself

Spano v. Perini Corp.

Court of Appeals of New York, 1969.
25 N.Y.2d 11, 250 N.E.2d 31, 302 N.Y.S.2d 527, on remand,
33 A.D.2d 516, 304 N.Y.S.2d 15 (1969).

FULD, CHIEF JUDGE. The principal question posed on this appeal is whether a person who has sustained property damage caused by blasting on nearby property can maintain an action for damages without a showing that the blaster was negligent. Since 1893, when this court decided the case of Booth v. Rome, W. & O.T.R.R. Co., 140 N.Y. 267, 35 N.E. 592, 24 L.R.A. 105, it has been the law of this State that proof of negligence was required unless the blast was accompanied by an actual physical invasion of the damaged property—for example, by rocks or other material being cast upon the premises. We are now asked to reconsider that rule.

The plaintiff Spano is the owner of a garage in Brooklyn which was wrecked by a blast occurring on November 27, 1962. There was then in that garage, for repairs, an automobile owned by the plaintiff Davis which he also claims was damaged by the blasting. Each of the plaintiffs brought suit against the two defendants who, as joint venturers, were engaged in constructing a tunnel in the vicinity pursuant to a contract with the City of New York. The two cases were tried together, without a jury, in the Civil Court of the City of New York, New York County, and judgments were rendered in favor of the plaintiffs. The judgments were reversed by the Appellate Term and the Appellate Division affirmed that order, granting leave to appeal to this court.

It is undisputed that, on the day in question (November 27, 1962), the defendants had set off a total of 194 sticks of dynamite at a construction site which was only 125 feet away from the damaged premises. Although both plaintiffs alleged negligence in their complaints, no attempt was made to show that the defendants had failed to exercise reasonable care or to take necessary precautions when they were blasting. Instead, they chose to rely, upon the trial, solely on the principle of absolute liability * * *

The concept of absolute liability in blasting cases is hardly a novel one. The overwhelming majority of American jurisdictions have adopted such a rule. [Cc] Indeed, this court itself, several years ago, noted that a change in our law would "conform to the more widely (indeed almost universally) approved doctrine that a blaster is absolutely liable for any damages he causes, with or without trespass". [C]

We need not rely solely however upon out-of-state decisions in order to attain our result. Not only has the rationale of the *Booth* case [c] been overwhelmingly rejected elsewhere but it appears to be fundamentally inconsistent with earlier cases in our own court which had held, long before *Booth* was decided, that a party was absolutely liable for damages to neighboring property caused by explosions. (See, e.g., Hay v. Cohoes Co., 2 N.Y. 159; Heeg v. Licht, 80 N.Y. 579.) In the *Hay* case (2 N.Y. 159, supra), for example, the defendant was engaged in blasting an excavation for a canal and the force of the blasts caused large quantities of earth and stones to be thrown against the plaintiff's house, knocking down his stoop and part of his chimney. The court held the defendant *absolutely* liable for the damage caused * * *

Although the court in *Booth* drew a distinction between a situation—such as was presented in the *Hay* case—where there was "a physical invasion" of, or trespass on, the plaintiff's property and one in which the damage was caused by "setting the air in motion, or in some other unexplained way," [c], it is clear that the court, in the earlier cases, was not concerned with the particular manner by which the damage was caused but by the simple fact that any explosion in a built-up area was likely to cause damage. Thus, in Heeg v. Licht, 80 N.Y. 579, the court held that there should be absolute liability where the damage was caused by the accidental explosion of stored gunpowder, even in the absence of a physical trespass (p. 581):

"The defendant had erected a building and stored materials therein, which from their character were liable to and actually did explode, causing injury to the plaintiff. The fact that the explosion took place tends to establish that the magazine was dangerous and liable to cause damage to the property of persons residing in the vicinity. * * * The fact that the magazine was liable to such a contingency, which could not be guarded against or averted by the greatest degree of care and vigilance, evinces its dangerous character, * * * In such a case, the rule which exonerates a party engaged in a lawful business, when free from negligence, has no application."

Such reasoning should, we venture, have led to the conclusion that the *intentional* setting off of explosives—that is, blasting—in an area in which it was likely to cause harm to neighboring property similarly results in absolute liability. However, the court in the *Booth* case rejected such an extension of the rule for the reason that "[t]o exclude the defendant from blasting to adapt its lot to the contemplated uses, at the instance of the plaintiff, would not be a compromise between conflicting rights, but an extinguishment of the right of the one for the benefit of the other" [c]. The court expanded on this by stating, "This sacrifice, we think, the law does not exact. Public policy is sustained by the building up of towns and cities and the improvement of property. Any unnecessary restraint on freedom of action of a property owner hinders this."

This rationale cannot withstand analysis. The plaintiff in *Booth* was not seeking, as the court implied, to "exclude the defendant from blasting" and thus prevent desirable improvements to the latter's property. Rather, he was merely seeking compensation for the damage which was inflicted upon his own property as a result of that blasting. The question, in other words, was not *whether* it was lawful or proper to engage in blasting but *who* should bear the cost of any resulting damage—the person who engaged in the dangerous activity or the innocent neighbor injured thereby. Viewed in such a light, it clearly appears that *Booth* was wrongly decided and should be forthrightly overruled * * *

[The court here considered the evidence of causation of the plaintiffs' damage, and concluded that it was sufficient.]

Even though the proof was not insufficient as a matter of law, however, the Appellate Division affirmed on the sole ground that no negligence had been proven against the defendants and thus had no occasion to consider the question whether, in fact, the blasting caused the damage. That being so, we must remit the case to the Appellate Division so that it may pass upon the weight of the evidence. [Cc]

The order appealed from should be reversed, with costs, and the matter remitted to the Appellate Division for further proceedings in accordance with this opinion.

NOTES AND QUESTIONS

1. The early common law strict liability of the type of Weaver v. Ward has persisted most stubbornly in connection with trespass to real property and has been exorcised only in contemporary times. Thus, in Randall v. Shelton, 293 S.W.2d 559 (Ky.1956), defendant's truck ran over a small stone in the gravel highway and the tire cast it out so that it hit plaintiff, who was standing in her yard, and injured her. The appellate court found no negligence and held that the defendant's motion for judgment notwithstanding the verdict should have been granted. To do this, it had to overrule an earlier Kentucky case in which a runaway street car invaded plaintiff's property and did damage. The special rule for trespass explains some of the early New York cases discussed in the opinion of the principal case.

2. The procedural distinction long made in New York, between an action of trespass for blasting causing physical invasion by casting rocks on the plaintiff's land, for which there was strict liability, and the action of nuisance for vibration or concussion which shook plaintiff's house to pieces, which would require proof of negligence, has long been denounced as a marriage of procedural technicality with scientific ignorance. This distinction has lost its significance in states that apply strict liability to blasting operations because blasting is an abnormally dangerous activity. See, e.g., Stocks v. CFW Construction Co., Inc., 472 So.2d 1044 (Ala.1985). The question of strict liability for damage to land by blasting and other activities that have been deemed extrahazardous is considered at greater length in Chapter 14, on strict liability.

3. For the present, it is sufficient to note that this case represents one type of situation in which strict liability may be applied, without any showing of intent or negligence, by the majority of the courts that have considered the question. This has sometimes been called absolute liability, or liability without fault. The first Restatement of Torts § 519 conferred the name of "ultrahazardous activity" upon these cases. The drafters of Restatement (Second) of Torts concluded that a better name is "abnormally dangerous activities," since the emphasis is more upon the abnormal character of what the defendant does in relation to its surroundings than upon the high degree of danger.

4.   Strict liability also has been imposed upon manufacturers of products when defects in their wares have caused injury. This position is now generally followed when the defect causing the injury is due to an error in the manufacturing process. There is less agreement as to the application of strict liability for failure to use a safer design or to warn of dangers.

5.   Strict liability involves a good many issues that are to be considered later in Chapters 14 and 15. For present purposes, note merely that there are three possible bases of tort liability:

① A.   Intentional conduct.

② B.   Negligent conduct that creates an unreasonable risk of causing harm.

③ C.   Conduct that is neither intentional nor negligent but that subjects the actor to strict liability because of public policy.

6.   These will be considered in turn, which will carry us through Chapter 15. The remainder of this book covers particular fields of case law in which special problems arise, and in most of which intent, negligence, and strict liability are all involved and intermingled as possible bases for recovery.

CHAPTER II

INTENTIONAL INTERFERENCE WITH PERSON OR PROPERTY

1. INTENT

Garratt v. Dailey

Supreme Court of Washington, 1955.
46 Wash.2d 197, 279 P.2d 1091.

HILL, JUSTICE. The liability of an infant for an alleged battery is presented to this court for the first time. Brian Dailey (age five years, nine months) was visiting with Naomi Garratt, an adult and a sister of the plaintiff, Ruth Garratt, likewise an adult, in the back yard of the plaintiff's home, on July 16, 1951. It is plaintiff's contention that she came out into the back yard to talk with Naomi and that, as she started to sit down in a wood and canvas lawn chair, Brian deliberately pulled it out from under her. The only one of the three present so testifying was Naomi Garratt. (Ruth Garratt, the plaintiff did not testify as to how or why she fell.) The trial court, unwilling to accept this testimony, adopted instead Brian Dailey's version of what happened, and made the following findings:

"III. * * * that while Naomi Garratt and Brian Dailey were in the back yard the plaintiff, Ruth Garratt, came out of her house into the back yard. Some time subsequent thereto defendant, Brian Dailey, picked up a lightly built wood and canvas lawn chair which was then and there located in the back yard of the above described premises, moved it sideways a few feet and seated himself therein, at which time he discovered the plaintiff, Ruth Garratt, about to sit down at the place where the lawn chair had formerly been, at which time he hurriedly got up from the chair and attempted to move it toward Ruth Garratt to aid her in sitting down in the chair; that due to the defendant's small size and lack of dexterity he was unable to get the lawn chair under the plaintiff in time to prevent her from falling to the ground. That plaintiff fell to the ground and sustained a fracture of her hip, and other injuries and damages as hereinafter set forth.

"IV. That the preponderance of the evidence in this case establishes that when the defendant, Brian Dailey moved the chair in question *he did not have any wilful or unlawful purpose* in doing so; that *he did not have any intent to injure the plaintiff, or any intent to bring about any unauthorized or offensive contact with her person* or any objects appurtenant thereto; that the circumstances which immediately preceded the fall of the plaintiff established that the defendant, *Brian Dailey, did not have purpose,*

17

intent or design to perform a prank or to effect an assault and battery upon the person of the plaintiff.'' (Italics ours, for a purpose hereinafter indicated.)

It is conceded that Ruth Garratt's fall resulted in a fractured hip and other painful and serious injuries. To obviate the necessity of a retrial in the event this court determines that she was entitled to a judgment against Brian Dailey, the amount of her damage was found to be $11,000. Plaintiff appeals from a judgment dismissing the action and asks for the entry of a judgment in that amount or a new trial.

The authorities generally, but with certain notable exceptions, [c] state that when a minor has committed a tort with force he is liable to be proceeded against as any other person would be. * * *

In our analysis of the applicable law, we start with the basic premise that Brian, whether five or fifty-five, must have committed some wrongful act before he could be liable for appellant's injuries. * * *

It is urged that Brian's action in moving the chair constituted a battery. A definition (not all-inclusive but sufficient for our purpose) of a battery is (the intentional infliction of a harmful bodily contact upon another.)* * *

We have in this case no question of consent or privilege. We therefore proceed to an immediate consideration of intent and its place in the law of battery. In the comment on clause (a) of § 13, the Restatement says:

"*Character of Actor's Intention.* In order that an act may be done with the intention of bringing about a harmful or offensive contact or an apprehension thereof to a particular person, either the other or a third person, the act must be done for the purpose of causing the contact or apprehension or with knowledge on the part of the actor that such contact or apprehension is substantially certain to be produced.'' [C]

We have here the conceded volitional act of Brian, i.e., the moving of a chair. Had the plaintiff proved to the satisfaction of the trial court that Brian moved the chair while she was in the act of sitting down, Brian's action would patently have been for the purpose or with the intent of causing the plaintiff's bodily contact with the ground, and she would be entitled to a judgment against him for the resulting damages. [Cc]

The plaintiff based her case on that theory, and the trial court held that she failed in her proof and accepted Brian's version of the facts rather than that given by the eyewitness who testified for the plaintiff. After the trial court determined that the plaintiff had not established her theory of a battery (i.e., that Brian had pulled the chair out from under the plaintiff while she was in the act of sitting down), it then became concerned with whether a battery was established under the facts as it found them to be.

In this connection, we quote another portion of the comment on the "Character of actor's intention,'' relating to clause (a) of the rule from [Restatement, (First) Torts, 29, § 13]:

"It is not enough that the act itself is intentionally done and this, even though the actor realizes or should realize that it contains a very grave risk of bringing about the contact or apprehension. Such realization may make the actor's conduct negligent or even reckless but unless he realizes that to a substantial certainty, the contact or apprehension will result, the actor has not that intention which is necessary to make him liable under the rule stated in this section."

A battery would be established if, in addition to plaintiff's fall, it was proved that, when Brian moved the chair, he knew with substantial certainty that the plaintiff would attempt to sit down where the chair had been. If Brian had any of the intents which the trial court found, in the italicized portions of the findings of fact quoted above, that he did not have, he would of course have had the knowledge to which we have referred. The mere absence of any intent to injure the plaintiff or to play a prank on her or to embarrass her, or to commit an assault and battery on her would not absolve him from liability if in fact he had such knowledge. [C] Without such knowledge, there would be nothing wrongful about Brian's act in moving the chair and, there being no wrongful act, there would be no liability.

While a finding that Brian had no such knowledge can be inferred from the findings made, we believe that before the plaintiff's action in such a case should be dismissed there should be no question but that the trial court had passed upon that issue; hence, the case should be remanded for clarification of the findings to specifically cover the question of Brian's knowledge, because intent could be inferred therefrom. If the court finds that he had such knowledge the necessary intent will be established and the plaintiff will be entitled to recover, even though there was no purpose to injure or embarrass the plaintiff. [C] If Brian did not have such knowledge, there was no wrongful act by him and the basic premise of liability on the theory of a battery was not established.

It will be noted that the law of battery as we have discussed it is the law applicable to adults, and no significance has been attached to the fact that Brian was a child less than six years of age when the alleged battery occurred. The only circumstance where Brian's age is of any consequence is in determining what he knew, and there his experience, capacity, and understanding are of course material.

From what has been said, it is clear that we find no merit in plaintiff's contention that we can direct the entry of a judgment for $11,000 in her favor on the record now before us.

Nor do we find any error in the record that warrants a new trial. * * *

The cause is remanded for clarification, with instructions to make definite findings on the issue of whether Brian Dailey knew with substantial certainty that the plaintiff would attempt to sit down where the chair which he moved had been, and to change the judgment if the findings warrant it. * * *

Remanded for clarification.

[On remand, the trial judge concluded that it was necessary for him to consider carefully the time sequence, as he had not done before; and this resulted in his finding "that the arthritic woman had begun the slow process of being seated when the defendant quickly removed the chair and seated himself upon it, and that he knew, with substantial certainty, at that time that she would attempt to sit in the place where the chair had been." He entered judgment for the plaintiff in the amount of $11,000, which was affirmed on a second appeal in Garratt v. Dailey, 49 Wash.2d 499, 304 P.2d 681 (1956).]

NOTES AND QUESTIONS

1.   The trial court judge found that plaintiff suffered damages in the amount of $11,000. For most intentional torts, plaintiff need not prove actual damages in order to recover. The court will award nominal damages even if no actual damages were proved. Of course, if the plaintiff does prove actual damages, as she did in this case, defendant is liable for those actual damages. How would Ms. Garratt's lawyer prove actual damages? See Chapter 10, Damages.

2.   Note that the trial judge was the finder of fact at both trials. Why do you think his findings of fact were different the second time? Might he have been influenced by the appellate court's view of the facts as well as its view of the law?

3.   Can a child five years and nine months old have an intent to do harm to another? And if so, how can that intent be "fault"? Suppose that a boy of seven, playing with a bow and arrow, aims at a girl of five and hits her, and she is injured. Is he liable? Weisbart v. Flohr, 260 Cal.App.2d 281, 67 Cal.Rptr. 114 (1968). See generally Restatement (Second) of Torts § 8A.

4.   Can a two-year-old child who bites an infant be liable for an intentional tort? See Fromenthal v. Clark, 442 So.2d 608 (La.App.1983), cert. denied, 444 So.2d 1242 (1984).

5.   Can a young child commit a tort requiring a "malicious" state of mind? Ortega v. Montoya, 97 N.M. 159, 637 P.2d 841 (1981). Some states have parental responsibility statutes, making parents liable for their child's malicious torts.

✠ Spivey v. Battaglia

Supreme Court of Florida, 1972.
258 So.2d 815.

Dekle, Justice. * * * Petitioner (plaintiff in the trial court) and respondent (defendant) were employees of Battaglia Fruit Co. on January 21, 1965. During the lunch hour several employees of Battaglia Fruit Co., including petitioner and respondent, were seated on a work table in the plant of the company. Respondent, in an effort to tease petitioner, whom he knew to be shy, intentionally put his arm around petitioner and pulled her head toward him. Immediately after this "friendly unsolicited hug," petitioner suffered a sharp pain in the back of her neck and ear, and sharp pains into the base of her skull. As a result, petitioner was paralyzed on the left side of her face and mouth.

An action was commenced in the Circuit Court of Orange County, Florida, wherein the petitioners, Mr. and Mrs. Spivey, brought suit against respondent for, (1) negligence, and (2) assault and battery. Respondent, Mr. Battaglia, filed his answer raising as a defense the claim that his "friendly unsolicited hug" was an assault and battery as a matter of law and was barred by the running of the two-year statute of limitations on assault and battery. Respondent's motion for summary judgment was granted by the trial court on this basis. The district court affirmed on the authority of McDonald v. Ford, [223 So.2d 553 (Fla.App.1969)].

The question presented for our determination is whether petitioner's action could be maintained on the negligence count, or whether respondent's conduct amounted to an assault and battery as a matter of law, which would bar the suit under the two-year statute (which had run).

In *McDonald* the incident complained of occurred in the early morning hours in a home owned by the defendant. While the plaintiff was looking through some records, the defendant came up behind her, laughingly embraced her and, though she resisted, kissed her hard. As the defendant was hurting the plaintiff physically by his embrace, the plaintiff continued to struggle violently and the defendant continued to laugh and pursue his love-making attempts. In the process, plaintiff struck her face hard upon an object that she was unable to identify specifically. With those facts before it, the district court held that what actually occurred was an assault and battery, and not negligence. The court quoted with approval from the Court of Appeals of Ohio in Williams v. Pressman, 113 N.E.2d 395, at 396 (Ohio App.1953):

"* * * an assault and battery is not negligence, for such action is intentional, while negligence connotes an unintentional act."

The intent with which such a tort liability as assault is concerned is not necessarily a hostile intent, or a desire to do harm. Where a reasonable man would believe that a particular result was *substantially certain* to follow, he will be held in the eyes of the law as though he had intended it. It would thus be an assault (intentional). However, the knowledge and appreciation of a *risk,* short of substantial certainty, is not the equivalent of intent. Thus, the distinction between intent and negligence boils down to a matter of degree. "Apparently the line has been drawn by the courts at the point where the known danger ceases to be only a foreseeable risk which a reasonable man would avoid (negligence), and becomes a substantial certainty." In the latter case, the intent is legally implied and becomes an assault rather than unintentional negligence.

The distinction between the unsolicited kisses in McDonald, supra, and the unsolicited hug in the present case turns upon this question of intent. In McDonald, the court, finding an assault and battery, necessarily had to find initially that the results of the defendant's acts were "intentional." This is a rational conclusion in view of the struggling involved there. In the instant case, the DCA must have found the same intent. But we cannot agree with that finding in these circumstances. It cannot be said that a reasonable man in this defendant's position would believe that the bizarre *no intent — no assault*

results herein were "substantially certain" to follow. This is an unreasonable conclusion and is a misapplication of the rule in *McDonald*. This does not mean that he does not become liable for such unanticipated results, however. The settled law is that a defendant becomes liable for reasonably foreseeable consequences, though the exact results and damages were not contemplated.

Acts that might be considered prudent in one case might be negligent in another. Negligence is a relative term and its existence must depend in each case upon the particular circumstances which surrounded the parties at the time and place of the events upon which the controversy is based.

The trial judge committed error when he granted summary final judgment in favor of the defendant. The cause should have been submitted to the jury with appropriate instructions regarding the elements of negligence. Accordingly, certiorari is granted; the decision of the district court is hereby quashed and the cause is remanded with directions to reverse the summary final judgment.

It is so ordered.

NOTES AND QUESTIONS

1. Distinguish:

A. The intent to do an act. The defendant fires a gun or drives an automobile in excess of the speed limit.

Intended to fire gun? or drive in excess?

B. The intent to harm someone. The bullet or the car hits someone. It is the intent to act, not the intent to harm, that is critical in determining whether there is an intentional tort. See Etcher v. Blitch, 381 So.2d 1119 (Fla.App.1979), cert. denied, 386 So.2d 636 (1980) (defendant fired gun through car window, not intending to hit plaintiff, but only to frighten him).

2. Distinguish:

no action — trespassing

A. The defendant does not act. He is carried onto plaintiff's land against his will. Smith v. Stone, Style 65, 82 Eng.Rep. 533 (1647).

B. He acts intentionally, but under fear or threats. Twelve armed men compel him to enter plaintiff's land and steal a horse. Gilbert v. Stone, Style 72, 82 Eng.Rep. 539 (1648). *still action against him — he can find one against them*

liable for negligence — not intent

C. He acts intentionally, but without any desire to affect the plaintiff, or any certainty that he will do so. He rides a horse, which runs away with him and runs the plaintiff down. Gibbons v. Pepper, 1 Ld.Raym. 38, 91 Eng.Rep. 922 (1695).

D. He acts with the desire to affect the plaintiff, but for an entirely permissible or laudable purpose. He shoots the plaintiff in self-defense, or while a soldier defending his country. *intent   liability?*

3. For a discussion of the treatment of intent in English and American tort law, see Finnis, John, "Intention in Tort Law" in Philosophical Foundations of Tort Law 229 (Clarenden Press 1995).

4. It may not seem important to distinguish between negligent and intentionally wrongful conduct: the defendant usually will be held liable to the plaintiff in either situation. Nevertheless, the distinction may be legally significant. Consider the following:

A. Will defendant be liable for punitive damages? See Chapter 10, Section 3.

B. Will the defense of contributory negligence be available to defendant? See page 590, note 7.   *not to an intentional tort*

C. Will defendant's employer be liable under the doctrine of *respondeat superior*? See page 663, note 4.   *could be in either intentional or negligent*

D. How far will the law trace the consequences of defendants' wrongful act? See Tate v. Canonica, 180 Cal.App.2d 898, 5 Cal.Rptr. 28 (1960) (liability for causing suicide) and RD v. WH, 875 P.2d 26 (Wyo.1994) (higher degree of responsibility for those who commit intentional act).

E. Will the defendant be reimbursed by a liability insurance policy? See Allstate Ins. Co. v. Hiseley, 465 F.2d 1243 (10th Cir.1972); Cloud v. Shelby Mut. Ins. Co., 248 So.2d 217 (Fla.App.1971). Pryor, The Stories We Tell: Intentional Harm and the Quest for Insurance Funding, 75 Tex.L.Rev. 1721 (1997).

F. Has the state statute of limitations run? See the principal case. *intent changes that*

G. Will an employer be subject to liability to an employee in spite of a general worker compensation immunity shield? Some state worker compensation statutes provide an exception to the immunity for intentional wrongdoing. Does an employer's intentional failure to train an employee to perform a dangerous task supply the requisite intent to injure under the workers' compensation intentional injury exception? See Reed Tool Co. v. Copelin, 689 S.W.2d 404 (Tex.1985). What about an employer's deliberate exposure of employees to dangerous products? See Millison v. E.I. du Pont de Nemours & Co., 101 N.J. 161, 501 A.2d 505 (1985) and Bardere v. Zafir, 102 A.D.2d 422, 477 N.Y.S.2d 131, aff'd, 63 N.Y.2d 850, 472 N.E.2d 37, 482 N.Y.S.2d 261 (1984) (plaintiff must show "specific acts [by the employer] directed at causing harm to particular employees").

H. Will the plaintiff be able to bring a cause of action against the United States, which may be liable for the negligent acts of its employees, but not for their intentional acts? See page 653.   *not if intent can be proved*

5. Do you think that a court's characterization of a defendant's conduct as "negligent" or "intentional" sometimes might be influenced by the legal effect of its finding? Since the court is not bound by either party's characterization of the events, such influence could occur, but only in close cases. At the receiving dock of a meatpacking plant, plaintiff was unloading a truck when a government meat inspector leapt out at him, screamed "boo," pulled his wool stocking cap over his eyes, and jumped on his back to ride him piggyback. Plaintiff fell forward and struck his face on some meat hooks, severely injuring his mouth and teeth. Plaintiff's complaint was for negligent conduct, apparently because the defendant's employer, the United States, would not be liable for its employee's battery. Cf. Lambertson v. United States, 528 F.2d 441 (2d Cir.1976), cert. denied, 426 U.S. 921 (1976) (court did not permit plaintiff to recover by "dressing up the substance" of battery in the "garments" of negligence).

☆ Ranson v. Kitner

Appellate Court of Illinois, 1889.
31 Ill.App. 241.

CONGER, J. This was an action brought by appellee against appellants to recover the value of a dog killed by appellants, and a judgment rendered for $50.

The defense was that appellants were hunting for wolves, that appellee's dog had a striking resemblance to a wolf, that they in good faith believed it to be one, and killed it as such.

Many points are made, and a lengthy argument failed to show that error in the trial below was committed, but we are inclined to think that no material error occurred to the prejudice of appellants.

The jury held them liable for the value of the dog, and we do not see how they could have done otherwise under the evidence. Appellants are clearly liable for the damages caused by their mistake, notwithstanding they were acting in good faith.

We see no reason for interfering with the conclusion reached by the jury, and the judgment will be affirmed.

NOTES AND QUESTIONS

1. Did the defendant intend to kill the dog? The court calls it "mistake." Why not accident? *there was intent to. as wolf kill the animal not the dog*

2. Defendant fuel oil distributor had a contract to deliver oil to a residence. One day, during the delivery, the oil overflowed and damaged surrounding lawn and shrubberies. The tank overflowed because it already had been filled by another company, hired by the new owner. The previous owner apparently had not canceled his contract when he moved. Is the fuel oil distributor liable for trespass? Serota v. M. & M. Utilities, Inc., 55 Misc.2d 286, 285 N.Y.S.2d 121 (1967) (reasonable mistake no defense to trespass). *no*

3. Does the mistake negate intent to affect the person or property in question? Defendant shoots at an animal, not knowing whose or what it is. Does he intend to kill it? Defendant, seeking to confront the driver who frightened his horses the previous day, pushed back the hat of the wrong man. Does he intend to touch him? Seigel v. Long, 169 Ala. 79, 53 So. 753 (1910). What if a surgeon operates on the wrong patient? Gill v. Selling, 125 Or. 587, 267 P. 812 (1928). Generally, mistake as to the identity of the person or animal does not negate intent. Will the mistake protect the defendant against liability for the result he intended to cause? There is general agreement that it does not where the defendant by mistake appropriates property of the plaintiff. If he is not held liable for his mistake, he would be unjustly enriched. Perry v. Jefferies, 61 S.C. 292, 39 S.E. 515 (1901) (cutting and removing timber from plaintiff's land under a reasonable belief that defendant owned it); Dexter v. Cole, 6 Wis. 319, 70 Am.Dec. 465 (1857) (driving off plaintiff's sheep, believed to be defendant's).

4. On the other hand, some of the defendant's privileges depend, not upon the existence of a fact, but upon the reasonable belief that the fact exists. Defendant, seeing the plaintiff reach for a handkerchief in his pocket, reasonably believes that he is reaching for a gun, and attacks plaintiff to defend himself. See page 102. Mistakes as to the existence of a privilege are dealt with below in connection with the privilege itself.

5. See generally Whittier, Mistake in the Law of Torts, 15 Harv.L.Rev. 335 (1902).

✮ McGuire v. Almy

Supreme Judicial Court of Massachusetts, 1937.
297 Mass. 323, 8 N.E.2d 760.

QUA, JUSTICE. This is an action of tort for assault and battery. The only question of law reported is whether the judge should have directed a verdict for the defendant.

The following facts are established by the plaintiff's own evidence: In August, 1930, the plaintiff was employed to take care of the defendant. The plaintiff was a registered nurse and was a graduate of a training school for nurses. The defendant was an insane person. Before the plaintiff was hired she learned that the defendant was a "mental case and was in good physical condition," and that for some time two nurses had been taking care of her. The plaintiff was on "24 hour duty." The plaintiff slept in the room next to the defendant's room. Except when the plaintiff was with the defendant, the plaintiff kept the defendant locked in the defendant's room. * * *

On April 19, 1932, the defendant, while locked in her room, had a violent attack. The plaintiff heard a crashing of furniture and then knew that the defendant was ugly, violent and dangerous. The defendant told the plaintiff and a Miss Maroney, "the maid," who was with the plaintiff in the adjoining room, that if they came into the defendant's room, she would kill them. The plaintiff and Miss Maroney looked into the defendant's room, "saw what the defendant had done," and "thought it best to take the broken stuff away before she did any harm to herself with it." They sent for a Mr. Emerton, the defendant's brother-in-law. When he arrived the defendant was in the middle of her room about ten feet from the door, holding upraised the leg of a low-boy as if she were going to strike. The plaintiff stepped into the room and walked toward the defendant, while Mr. Emerton and Miss Maroney remained in the doorway. As the plaintiff approached the defendant and tried to take hold of the defendant's hand which held the leg, the defendant struck the plaintiff's head with it, causing the injuries for which the action was brought.

The extent to which an insane person is liable for torts has not been fully defined in this Commonwealth. * * *

Turning to authorities elsewhere, we find that courts in this country almost invariably say in the broadest terms that an insane person is liable for his torts. As a rule no distinction is made between those torts which would ordinarily be classed as intentional and those which would ordinarily be classed as negligent, nor do the courts discuss the effect of different kinds of insanity or of varying degrees of capacity as bearing upon the ability of the defendant to understand the particular act in question or to make a reasoned decision with respect to it, although it is sometimes said that an insane person is not liable for torts requiring malice of which he is incapable. Defamation and malicious prosecution are the torts more commonly mentioned in this connection. * * * These decisions are rested more upon grounds of public policy and upon what might be called a popular

Public Policy
Rules
Liability
for
Persons insanity

view of the requirements of essential justice than upon any attempt to apply logically the underlying principles of civil liability to the special instance of the mentally deranged. Thus it is said that a rule imposing liability tends to make more watchful those persons who have charge of the defendant and who may be supposed to have some interest in preserving his property; that as an insane person must pay for his support, if he is financially able, so he ought also to pay for the damage which he does; that an insane person with abundant wealth ought not to continue in unimpaired enjoyment of the comfort which it brings while his victim bears the burden unaided; and there is also a suggestion that courts are loath to introduce into the great body of civil litigation the difficulties in determining mental capacity which it has been found impossible to avoid in the criminal field.

The rule established in these cases has been criticized severely by certain eminent text writers both in this country and in England, principally on the ground that it is an archaic survival of the rigid and formal mediaeval conception of liability for acts done, without regard to fault, as opposed to what is said to be the general modern theory that liability in tort should rest upon fault. Notwithstanding these criticisms, we think, that as a practical matter, there is strong force in the reasons underlying these decisions. They are consistent with the general statements found in the cases dealing with the liability of infants for torts, [cc] including a few cases in which the child was so young as to render his capacity for fault comparable to that of many insane persons, [cc]. Fault is by no means at the present day a universal prerequisite to liability, and the theory that it should be such has been obliged very recently to yield at several points to what have been thought to be paramount considerations of public good. Finally, it would be difficult not to recognize the persuasive weight of so much authority so widely extended.

But the present occasion does not require us either to accept or to reject the prevailing doctrine in its entirety. For this case it is enough to say that where an insane person by his act does intentional damage to the person or property of another he is liable for that damage in the same circumstances in which a normal person would be liable. This means that in so far as a particular intent would be necessary in order to render a normal person liable, the insane person, in order to be liable, must have been capable of entertaining that same intent and must have entertained it in fact. But the law will not inquire further into his peculiar mental condition with a view to excusing him if it should appear that delusion or other consequence of his affliction has caused him to entertain that intent or that a normal person would not have entertained it. * * *

Coming now to the application of the rule to the facts of this case, it is apparent that the jury could find that the defendant was capable of entertaining and that she did entertain an intent to strike and to injure the plaintiff and that she acted upon that intent. See American Law Institute Restatement, Torts, §§ 13, 14. We think this was enough. * * *

[The rest of the opinion holds that whether the plaintiff consented to the attack or assumed the risk of it is an issue to be left to the jury. There was no evidence that the defendant had previously attacked any one or made any serious threat to do so. The plaintiff had taken care of the defendant for fourteen months without being attacked. When the plaintiff entered the room the defendant was breaking up the furniture, and it could be found that the plaintiff reasonably feared that the defendant would do harm to herself. Under such circumstances it cannot be ruled as a matter of law that the plaintiff assumed the risk.]

Judgment for the plaintiff on the verdict.

NOTES AND QUESTIONS

1. Can someone who is mentally ill have an intent to do harm to another? And if so, how can such an intent be "fault"? How does the insane person differ from the automobile driver who suffers a heart attack, in Cohen v. Petty, page 10?

2. Note that this is different from criminal law standards for the responsibility of the mentally ill for their actions. Polmatier v. Ross, 206 Conn. 229, 537 A.2d 468 (1988) (defendant liable for battery of plaintiff's decedent even though he was found not guilty by reason of insanity in criminal case arising out of same incident).

3. The American decisions are unanimous in their agreement with the principal case. The result has, however, been much criticized. See, e.g., Bohlen, Liability in Tort of Infants and Insane Persons, 23 Mich.L.Rev. 9 (1924); Curran, Tort Liability of the Mentally Ill and Mentally Deficient, 21 Ohio St.L.J. 52 (1960). Good discussions of the whole problem include Fridman, Mental Incompetency, 79 Law Q.Rev. 502 (1963), 80 Law Q.Rev. 84 (1964); and Splane, Tort Liability of the Mentally Ill in Negligence Actions, 93 Yale L.J. 153 (1983).

4. Several jurisdictions have carved out a narrow exception to this general rule, holding that an institutionalized mentally disabled patient who cannot control or appreciate the consequences of his conduct cannot be held liable for injuries caused to those employed to care for the patient. The jurisdictions that have addressed this issue have done so both in the context of intentional torts and negligence. Gould v. American Family Mutual Ins. Co., 198 Wis.2d 450, 543 N.W.2d 282 (1996) (negligence action brought against patient with Alzheimer's); Creasy v. Rusk, 696 N.E.2d 442 (Ind.App.1998) (same); Anicet v. Gant, 580 So.2d 273 (Fla.App.1991) (assault and battery against twenty-three year old man suffering from "irremediable mental difficulties" who was unable to control himself from acts of violence).

5. It has been held that the insanity may prevent the specific kind of intent necessary for certain torts, such as deceit that requires the plaintiff to prove that the defendant knew that he was not speaking the truth. See Irvine v. Gibson, 117 Ky. 306, 77 S.W. 1106 (1904); Chaddock v. Chaddock, 130 Misc. 900, 226 N.Y.S. 152 (1927); Beaubeauf v. Reed, 4 La.App. 344 (1926).

6. Even if a mentally ill person lacks the ability to form the intent to commit a tort, an action may lie against persons responsible for caring for the mentally ill person, based on negligent supervision. See Rausch v. McVeigh, 105 Misc.2d 163, 431 N.Y.S.2d 887 (1980) (cause of action for negligent supervision against parents of 22–year-old autistic son who attacked his therapist).

7. *Intoxication*. What if the defendant is intoxicated? Does intoxication pre-clude a showing of intent? Bar patron passed out or fell asleep at bar and other patrons agreed to drive him home. Bar employee helped him from bar and was putting him into the back seat of a car when he began shouting obscenities and kicked the employee in the face, seriously injuring him. Sufficient intent for battery? Janelsins v. Button, 102 Md.App. 30, 648 A.2d 1039 (1994) (voluntary intoxication does not vitiate intent).

Talmage v. Smith
Supreme Court of Michigan, 1894.
101 Mich. 370, 59 N.W. 656.

MONTGOMERY, J. The plaintiff recovered in an action of trespass. The case made by plaintiff's proofs was substantially as follows: * * * Defendant had on his premises certain sheds. He came up to the vicinity of the sheds, and saw six or eight boys on the roof of one of them. He claims that he ordered the boys to get down, and they at once did so. He then passed around to where he had a view of the roof of another shed, and saw two boys on the roof. The defendant claims that he did not see the plaintiff, and the proof is not very clear that he did, although there was some testimony from which it might have been found that he was within his view. Defendant ordered the boys in sight to get down, and there was testimony tending to show that the two boys in defendant's view started to get down at once. Before they succeeded in doing so, however, defendant took a stick, which is described as being two inches in width, and of about the same thickness, and about 16 inches long, and threw it in the direction of the boys; and there was testimony tending to show that it was thrown at one of the boys in view of the defendant. The stick missed him, and hit the plaintiff just above the eye with such force as to inflict an injury which resulted in the total loss of the sight of the eye. * * * George Talmage, the plaintiff's father, testifies that defendant said to him that he threw the stick, intending it for Byron Smith,—one of the boys on the roof,—and this is fully supported by the circumstances of the case. * * *

The circuit judge charged the jury as follows: "If you conclude that Smith did not know the Talmage boy was on the shed, and that he did not intend to hit Smith, or the young man that was with him, but simply, by throwing the stick, intended to frighten Smith, or the other young man that was there, and the club hit Talmage, and injured him, as claimed, then the plaintiff could not recover. If you conclude that Smith threw the stick or club at Smith, or the young man that was with Smith,—intended to hit one or the other of them,—and you also conclude that the throwing of the stick or club was, under the circumstances, reasonable, and not excessive, force to use towards Smith and the other young man, then there would be no recovery by this plaintiff. But if you conclude from the evidence in this case that he threw the stick, intending to hit Smith, or the young man with him,—to hit one of them,—and that that force was unreasonable force, under all the circumstances, then [the defendant] would be doing an unlawful act, if the force was unreasonable, because he had no right to use it. He would be liable then for the injury done to this boy with the stick. * * *" [The jury rendered a verdict for the plaintiff.]

We think the charge is a very fair statement of the law of the case. * * * The right of the plaintiff to recover was made to depend upon an intention on the part of the defendant to hit somebody, and to inflict an unwarranted injury upon some one. Under these circumstances, the fact that the injury resulted to another than was intended does not relieve the defendant from responsibility. * * *

[handwritten: Holding]

[handwritten: Rule of Law]

The judgment will be affirmed, with costs.

NOTES AND QUESTIONS

1. This doctrine of "transferred intent" was derived originally from the criminal law, and goes back to the time when tort damages were awarded as a side issue in criminal prosecutions. It is familiar enough in the criminal law, and has been applied in several tort cases where the defendant has shot at A, or thrown a rock at him, and has unintentionally hit B instead. See, for example, Lopez v. Surchia, 112 Cal.App.2d 314, 246 P.2d 111 (1952) (shooting); Carnes v. Thompson, 48 S.W.2d 903 (Mo.1932) (striking); Singer v. Marx, 144 Cal.App.2d 637, 301 P.2d 440 (1956) (throwing a rock).

2. The doctrine is discussed in Prosser, Transferred Intent, 45 Tex.L.Rev. 650 (1967). The conclusion there is that it applies whenever both the tort intended and the resulting harm fall within the scope of the old action of trespass—that is, where both involve direct and immediate application of force to the person or to tangible property. There are five torts that fell within the trespass writ: battery, assault, false imprisonment, trespass to land, and trespass to chattels. When the defendant intends any one of the five, and accidentally accomplishes any one of the five, the doctrine applies and the defendant is liable.

3. Thus he is liable when he shoots to frighten A (assault) and the bullet unforeseeably hits a stranger (battery). Brown v. Martinez, 68 N.M. 271, 361 P.2d 152 (1961); Hall v. McBryde, 919 P.2d 910 (Colo.App.1996) (firing at passing car and hitting neighbor). Or when he shoots at a dog (trespass to chattels) and hits a boy scout (battery). Corn v. Sheppard, 179 Minn. 490, 229 N.W. 869 (1930). What if defendant, believing a house to be empty, intends arson (trespass to chattels) and accomplishes battery (sleeping man killed by smoke inhalation)? Cf. Lewis v. Allstate Ins. Co., 730 So.3d 65 (Miss. 1998).

4. On the other hand, when either the tort intended or the one accomplished does not fall within the trespass action, the doctrine does not apply. Clark v. Gay, 112 Ga. 777, 38 S.E. 81 (1901) (defendant committed murder in plaintiff's house and plaintiff sought value of house because his family refused to live there after the murder); McGee v. Vanover, 148 Ky. 737, 147 S.W. 742 (1912) (defendant inflicted beating on A, causing mental distress to plaintiff bystander).

2. BATTERY

⚖ Cole v. Turner

Nisi Prius, 1704.
6 Modern Rep. 149, 90 Eng.Rep. 958.

At Nisi Prius, upon evidence in trespass for assault and battery, Holt, C.J., declared:

1.   That the least touching of another in anger is a battery.

2.   If two or more meet in a narrow passage, and without any violence or design of harm, the one touches the other gently it will be no battery.

3.   If any of them use violence against the other, to force his way in a rude inordinate manner, it is a battery; or any struggle about the passage, to that degree as may do hurt, is a battery.

NOTES AND QUESTIONS

1.   In United States v. Ortega, 4 Wash.C.C. 531, 27 Fed.Cas. 359 (E.D.Pa. 1825), defendant, in an offensive manner, approached the plaintiff, took hold of the breast of his coat, and said that he demanded satisfaction. Is this a battery?

2.   What about spitting in the plaintiff's face? Alcorn v. Mitchell, 63 Ill. 553 (1872). Or forcibly removing his hat? Seigel v. Long, 169 Ala. 79, 53 So. 753 (1910). Or an attempted search of his pockets? Piggly–Wiggly Alabama Co. v. Rickles, 212 Ala. 585, 103 So. 860 (1925). Or touching her private parts? Skousen v. Nidy, 90 Ariz. 215, 367 P.2d 248 (1961). Cf. Gates v. State, 110 Ga.App. 303, 138 S.E.2d 473 (1964) (stranger touching woman on the buttocks). Yes

3.   What about tapping plaintiff on the shoulder to attract his attention? "Pardon me, sir, could you direct me, etc."? Coward v. Baddeley, 4 H. & N. 478, 157 Eng.Rep. 927 (1859). no

4.   With the modern shift of emphasis to intent and negligence, as distinguished from trespass and case, "battery" has become exclusively an intentional tort. Thus there is no battery when defendant negligently, or even recklessly, drives his car into plaintiff and injures him, without intending to hit him. Cook v. Kinzua Pine Mills Co., 207 Or. 34, 293 P.2d 717 (1956). The same shift of emphasis accounts for the modern cases allowing recovery when the contact inflicted is not direct and immediate, but indirect.

RESTATEMENT (SECOND) OF TORTS (1965)

"§ 13. Battery: Harmful Contact

"An actor is subject to liability to another for battery if

"(a) he acts intending to cause a harmful or offensive contact with the person of the other or a third person, or an imminent apprehension of such a contact, and

"(b) a harmful contact with the person of the other directly or indirectly results."

"§ 18. Battery: Offensive Contact

"(1) An actor is subject to liability to another for battery if

"(a) he acts intending to cause a harmful or offensive contact with the person of the other or a third person, or an imminent apprehension of such a contact, and *to whom?*

"(b) an offensive contact with the person of the other directly or indirectly results.

"(2) An act which is not done with the intention stated in Subsection (1, a) does not make the actor liable to the other for a mere offensive contact with the other's person although the act involves an unreasonable risk of inflicting it and, therefore, would be negligent or reckless if the risk threatened bodily harm."

NOTES AND QUESTIONS

1. Has the "black letter" law of battery undergone any substantial changes since Cole v. Turner in 1704? *yes now only intentional*

2. When defendant intentionally causes plaintiff to undergo an offensive contact and the resulting injuries are more extensive than a reasonable person might have anticipated, the defendant will still be liable for those injuries. See Baldinger v. Banks, 26 Misc.2d 1086, 201 N.Y.S.2d 629 (1960) (six-year-old boy shoves four-year-old girl). A similar case is Harrigan v. Rosich, 173 So.2d 880 (La.App.1965), where defendant, wishing to get rid of the plaintiff, pushed him with his finger, and said, "Go home, old man."

3. In Vosburg v. Putney, 80 Wis. 523, 50 N.W. 403 (1891), one schoolboy, during a class hour, playfully kicked another on the shin. He intended no harm, and the touch was so slight that the plaintiff actually did not feel it. It had, however, the effect of "lighting up" an infection in the leg from a previous injury, and as a result the plaintiff suffered damages found by the jury to be $2,500. Is there liability for battery? The case is entertainingly and exhaustively discussed in Zile, Vosburg v. Putney: A Centennial Story, [1992] Wis.L.Rev. 877 (1992). See also Reynolds, Tortious Battery: Is "I Didn't Mean Any Harm" Relevant?, 37 Okla.L.Rev. 715 (1984).

intent to kick but the extent of the injury could not be reasonably anticipated

4. Does it make any difference that the defendant is trying to help the plaintiff? In Clayton v. New Dreamland Roller Skating Rink, Inc., 14 N.J.Super. 390, 82 A.2d 458 (1951), cert. denied, 13 N.J. 527, 100 A.2d 567 (1953), plaintiff fell at a skating rink and broke her arm. Over the protests of plaintiff and her husband, defendant's employees proceeded to manipulate the arm in an attempt to set it. Is this battery? *no intent to cause harm*

5. Can the plaintiff by prohibiting a contact that would not be offensive to a reasonable person, such as a tap on the shoulder to attract attention, make the defendant liable for that touch? The Restatement (Second) of Torts § 19, leaves the question open. See Richmond v. Fisk, 160 Mass. 34, 35 N.E. 103 (1893), where defendant, against orders, entered plaintiff's bedroom and woke him up to present a milk bill. This was held to be battery, but no doubt it would be offensive to a reasonable person.

6. Can there be liability for battery for a contact of which plaintiff is unaware at the time? Did Sleeping Beauty have a cause of action against Prince Charming? Or an unauthorized surgical operation is performed while plaintiff is under an anaesthetic? Does it make any difference whether the operation is harmful or beneficial? See Mohr v. Williams, page 91.

it could be battery possibly yes if unconsented touching/contact

7. Is the transmission of a disease, such as herpes, through sexual activity a battery? Does consent to the sexual activity operate as a defense? See Doe v. Johnson, 817 F.Supp. 1382 (W.D.Mich.1993) (battery action alleged in transmission of HIV; consent to intercourse does not bar action). Liability in Tort for the Sexual

if D was notified of disease?

Transmission of Disease: Genital Herpes and the Law, 70 Cornell L.Rev. 101 (1984); Baruch, AIDS In the Courts: Tort Liability for the Sexual Transmission of Acquired Immune Deficiency Syndrome, 22 Tort & Ins. L.J. 165 (1987).

8.   Does a mortician who embalms a body unaware that it was infected with the AIDS virus have a cause of action for battery? Cf., Funeral Services by Gregory v. Bluefield Community Hospital, 186 W.Va. 424, 413 S.E.2d 79 (1991). What about the patients of a dentist who does not disclose he has AIDS? What if the dentist always wore gloves during treatment procedures? Would the reasonable person find such touching offensive? See Brzoska v. Olson, 668 A.2d 1355 (Dela. 1995).

Fisher v. Carrousel Motor Hotel, Inc.

Supreme Court of Texas, 1967.
424 S.W.2d 627.

[Action for assault and battery. Plaintiff, a mathematician employed by NASA, was attending a professional conference on telemetry equipment at defendant's hotel. The meeting included a buffet luncheon. As plaintiff was standing in line with others, he was approached by one of defendant's employees, who snatched the plate from his hand, and shouted that a "Negro could not be served in the club." Plaintiff was not actually touched, and was in no apprehension of physical injury; but he was highly embarrassed and hurt by the conduct in the presence of his associates. The jury returned a verdict for $400 actual damages for his humiliation and indignity, and $500 exemplary (punitive) damages in addition. The trial court set aside the verdict and gave judgment for the defendants notwithstanding the verdict. This was affirmed by the Court of Civil Appeals. Plaintiff appealed to the Supreme Court.]

GREENHILL, JUSTICE * * * Under the facts of this case, we have no difficulty in holding that the intentional grabbing of plaintiff's plate constituted a battery. The intentional snatching of an object from one's hand is as clearly an offensive invasion of his person as would be an actual contact with the body. "To constitute an assault and battery, it is not necessary to touch the plaintiff's body or even his clothing; knocking or snatching anything from plaintiff's hand or touching anything connected with his person, when done in an offensive manner, is sufficient." Morgan v. Loyacomo, 190 Miss. 656, 1 So.2d 510 (1941).

Such holding is not unique to the jurisprudence of this State. In S.H. Kress & Co. v. Brashier, 50 S.W.2d 922 (Tex.Civ.App.1932, no writ), the defendant was held to have committed "an assault or trespass upon the person" by snatching a book from the plaintiff's hand. The jury findings in that case were that the defendant "dispossessed plaintiff of the book" and caused her to suffer "humiliation and indignity."

The rationale for holding an offensive contact with such an object to be a battery is explained in 1 Restatement (Second) of Torts § 18 (Comment p. 31) as follows:

"Since the essence of the plaintiff's grievance consists in the offense to the dignity involved in the unpermitted and intentional invasion of the inviolability of his person and not in any physical harm done to his body, it is not necessary that the plaintiff's actual body be disturbed. Unpermitted and intentional contacts with anything so connected with the body as to be customarily regarded as part of the other's person and therefore as partaking of its inviolability is actionable as an offensive contact with his person. There are some things such as clothing or a cane or, indeed, anything directly grasped by the hand which are so intimately connected with one's body as to be universally regarded as part of the person.''

We hold, therefore, that the forceful dispossession of plaintiff Fisher's plate in an offensive manner was sufficient to constitute a battery, and the trial court erred in granting judgment notwithstanding the verdict on the issue of actual damages. * * *

[handwritten: Holding]

Damages for mental suffering are recoverable without the necessity for showing actual physical injury in a case of willful battery because the basis of that action is the unpermitted and intentional invasion of the plaintiff's person and not the actual harm done to the plaintiff's body. Restatement (Second) of Torts § 18. Personal indignity is the essence of an action for battery; and consequently the defendant is liable not only for contacts which do actual physical harm, but also for those which are offensive and insulting. [Cc]. We hold, therefore, that plaintiff was entitled to actual damages for mental suffering due to the willful battery, even in the absence of any physical injury. [The court then held that the defendant corporation was liable for the tort of its employee.]

[handwritten: Rule of Law]

[handwritten: Holding]

The judgments of the courts below are reversed, and judgment is here rendered for the plaintiff for $900 with interest from the date of the trial court's judgment, and for costs of this suit.

NOTES AND QUESTIONS

[handwritten: still battery]   *[handwritten: not battery]*

1. What if the plate had been snatched without a racial epithet? Or, suppose the waiter had not touched plaintiff's plate, but said in a loud voice, "Get out, we don't serve Negroes here!"? What if the doorman at the hotel shouted a racial epithet and kicked plaintiff's car when he was about to leave. Battery? Cf. Van Eaton v. Thon, 764 S.W.2d 674 (Mo.App.1988) (defendant struck horse plaintiff was riding).

[handwritten: does car count as person?]

2. Does the utilization of the tort of battery confuse things? Why not characterize what happened as "intentional infliction of emotional harm"? See Browning v. Slenderella Systems, 54 Wash.2d 440, 341 P.2d 859 (1959) and Contreras v. Crown Zellerbach Corp., 88 Wash.2d 735, 565 P.2d 1173 (1977). Might the case be regarded as one of imaginative lawyering, assuming the state was not ready to recognize intentional infliction of emotional harm as a tort? What other remedies might have been available to plaintiff? Compare this with the *State Rubbish Collectors* case, page 47.

[handwritten: racial discrimination, trespass on his person?]

3. Defendant, unreasonably suspecting the plaintiff of shoplifting, forcibly seized a package from under her arm and opened it. Morgan v. Loyacomo, 190 Miss. 656, 1 So.2d 510 (1941). Defendant deliberately blew pipe smoke in plaintiff's face, knowing she was allergic to it. Richardson v. Hennly, 209 Ga.App. 868, 434 S.E.2d 772 (1993).

[handwritten: Defendant is liable → battery]

4. A is standing with his arm around B's shoulder, and leaning on him. C, passing by, violently jerks B's arm, as a result of which A falls down. To whom is C liable for battery? Reynolds v. Pierson, 29 Ind.App. 273, 64 N.E. 484 (1902).

5. For general treatments of battery, see Carpenter, Intentional Invasion of Interest of Personality, 13 Or.L.Rev. 227, 275 (1934); Vold, The Legal Allocation of Risk in Assault, Battery and Imprisonment, 17 Neb.L.Rev. 149 (1938); Restatement (Second) of Torts §§ 13–20 (1966); 1 Harper and James, Torts §§ 3.1–3.3 (2d ed. 1986); Prosser and Keeton on Torts (5th ed. 1984) § 11. (Hereafter no general references to treatises will be given.)

3. ASSAULT

I de S et ux. v. W de S

At the Assizes, 1348.
Y.B.Lib.Ass. folio 99, placitum 60.

I de S and M, his wife, complain of W de S concerning this, that the said W, in the year, etc., with force and arms did make an assault upon the said M de S and beat her. And W pleaded not guilty. And it was found by the verdict of the inquest that the said W came at night to the house of the said I and sought to buy of his wine, but the door of the tavern was shut and he beat upon the door with a hatchet which he had in his hand, and the wife of the plaintiff put her head out of the window and commanded him to stop, and he saw and he struck with the hatchet but did not hit the woman. Whereupon the inquest said that it seemed to them that there was no trespass since no harm was done.

THORPE, C.J. There is harm done and a trespass for which he shall recover damages since he made an assault upon the woman, as has been found, although he did no other harm. Wherefore tax the damages, etc. And they taxed the damages at half a mark. Thorpe awarded that they should recover their damages, etc., and that the other should be taken. And so note that for an assault a man shall recover damages, etc.

NOTES AND QUESTIONS

1. This is the great-grandparent of all assault cases. Why allow the action if "no harm was done"?

Western Union Telegraph Co. v. Hill

Court of Appeals of Alabama, 1933.
25 Ala.App. 540, 150 So. 709.

Action for damages for assault by J.B. Hill against the Western Union Telegraph Company. From a judgment for plaintiff, defendant appeals.

SAMFORD, JUDGE. The action in this case is based upon an alleged assault on the person of plaintiff's wife by one Sapp, an agent of defendant in charge of its office in Huntsville, Ala. The assault complained of consisted of an attempt on the part of Sapp to put his hand on the person of plaintiff's wife coupled with a request that she come behind the counter in defendant's office, and that, if she would come and allow Sapp to love and pet her, he "would fix her clock."

The first question that addresses itself to us is, Was there such an assault as will justify an action for damages? * * *

While every battery includes an assault, an assault does not necessarily require a battery to complete it. What it does take to constitute an assault is an unlawful attempt to commit a battery, incomplete by reason of some intervening cause; or, to state it differently, to constitute an actionable assault there must be an intentional, unlawful, offer to touch the person of another in a rude or angry manner under such circumstances as to create in the mind of the party alleging the assault a well-founded fear of an imminent battery, coupled with the apparent present ability to effectuate the attempt, if not prevented. * * *

What are the facts here? Sapp was the agent of defendant and the manager of its telegraph office in Huntsville. Defendant was under contract with plaintiff to keep in repair and regulated an electric clock in plaintiff's place of business. When the clock needed attention, that fact was to be reported to Sapp, and he in turn would report to a special man, whose duty it was to do the fixing. At 8:13 o'clock p.m. plaintiff's wife reported to Sapp over the phone that the clock needed attention, and, no one coming to attend the clock, plaintiff's wife went to the office of defendant about 8:30 p.m. There she found Sapp in charge and behind a desk or counter, separating the public from the part of the room in which defendant's operator worked. The counter is four feet and two inches high, and so wide that, Sapp standing on the floor, leaning against the counter and stretching his arm and hand to the full length, the end of his fingers reaches just to the outer edge of the counter. The photographs in evidence show that the counter was as high as Sapp's armpits. Sapp had had two or three drinks and was "still slightly feeling the effects of whisky; I felt all right; I felt good and amiable." When plaintiff's wife came into the office, Sapp came from towards the rear of the room and asked what he could do for her. She replied: "I asked him if he understood over the phone that my clock was out of order and when he was going to fix it. He stood there and looked at me a few minutes and said: 'If you will come back here and let me love and pet you, I will fix your clock.' This he repeated and reached for me with his hand, he extended his hand toward me, he did not put it on me. I jumped back. I was in his reach as I stood there. He reached for me right along here (indicating her left shoulder and arm)." The foregoing is the evidence offered by plaintiff tending to prove assault. Per contra, aside from the positive denial by Sapp of any effort to touch Mrs. Hill, the physical surroundings as evidenced by the photographs of the locus tend to rebut any evidence going to prove that Sapp could have touched plaintiff's wife across that counter even if he had reached his hand in her direction unless she was leaning against the counter or Sapp should have stood upon something so as to elevate him and allow him to reach beyond the counter. However, there is testimony tending to prove that, notwithstanding the width of the counter and the height of Sapp, Sapp could have reached from six to eighteen inches beyond the desk in an effort to place his hand on Mrs. Hill. The evidence as a whole presents a question for the jury. This was the view taken by the trial judge, and in the several rulings bearing on this question there is no error. * * *

[Reversed on the ground that Sapp had not acted within the scope of his employment.]

NOTES AND QUESTIONS

1. Defendant, standing three or four feet from plaintiff, made a "kissing sign" at her by puckering his lips and smacking them. He did not touch her, and made no effort to kiss her, or to use any force. Is this an assault? Fuller v. State, 44 Tex.Crim. 463, 72 S.W. 184 (1903). Defendant Ku Klux Klan members dressed in KKK robes and carrying guns rode around in a shrimp boat on Galveston Bay from dock to dock frightening Vietnamese fishermen and their families. What would the family members have to prove to recover for assault? See, Vietnamese Fishermen's Ass'n v. Knights of the K.K.K., 518 F.Supp. 993 (S.D.Tex.1981).

2. Defendant, a hundred yards from plaintiff, starts running toward him, throwing rocks as he runs. At what point does this become an assault? Cf. State v. Davis, 23 N.C. (1 Ired.) 125, 35 Am.Dec. 735 (1840); Grimes v. State, 99 Miss. 232, 54 So. 839 (1911).

3. What about mere preparation, such as bringing a gun along for an interview? Penny v. State, 114 Ga. 77, 39 S.E. 871 (1901).

4. Must the plaintiff be put in fear, as distinguished from mere apprehension of contact? Suppose Ms. Hill had a black belt in karate? Assault? Cf. Brady v. Schatzel, [1911] Q.St.R. 206, 208. Why might a lawyer plead and try to prove fear if it is not a necessary element of the tort?

5. Is there an assault if defendant threatens the plaintiff with an unloaded gun? See Allen v. Hannaford, 138 Wash. 423, 244 P. 700 (1926). Suppose the gun remains on defendant's lap? See Castiglione v. Galpin, 325 So.2d 725 (La.App.1976).

6. In State v. Barry, 45 Mont. 598, 124 P. 775 (1912), it was held that there was no assault where the plaintiff did not know that a gun was aimed at him with intent to shoot him until it was all over. The Restatement (Second) of Torts § 22, has agreed.

7. A major distinction between a criminal assault and an assault in tort is that for a criminal assault, a victim need not have an apprehension or fear of contact. A criminal assault occurs if the defendant intends to injure the victim and has the ability to do so. Commonwealth v. Slaney, 345 Mass. 135, 185 N.E.2d 919 (1962). For the tort of assault, the victim must have an apprehension of contact, and it is not necessary that the defendant have the actual ability to carry out the threatened contact. Depending upon the jurisdiction, a defendant could be subject to either criminal prosecution or civil damages, or both.

8. What if the threat is not imminent? Brower v. Ackerley, 88 Wash. App. 87, 943 P.2d 1141, 1145 (1997) (threats of future action—"I'm going to find out where you live and kick your ass" and "you're finished; cut you in your sleep"—not imminent enough to state cause of action for assault.) Does a complaint state a cause of action for assault if one paragraph of the complaint asserts that the defendants threatened to strike the plaintiffs with blackjacks and that the threats

placed the plaintiffs in fear that a battery will be committed against them and a subsequent paragraph asserts that the defendants showed the plaintiffs that the defendants were carrying blackjacks? Cucinotti v. Ortmann, 399 Pa. 26, 159 A.2d 216 (1960) ("words in themselves, no matter how threatening, do not constitute an assault").

9. What if these words are accompanied by a threatening gesture? Assault? *possibly if you can prove intent*

A. With his hand upon his sword, "If it were not assize-time, I would not take such language from you." Tuberville v. Savage, 1 Modern Rep. 3 (1669).

B. "Were you not an old man, I would knock you down." State v. Crow, 23 N.C. (1 Ired.) 375 (1841).

C. "If it were not for your gray hairs, I would tear your heart out." Commonwealth v. Eyre, 1 Serg. & Rawle 347 (Pa.1815).

D. "I have a great mind to hit you." State v. Hampton, 63 N.C. 13 (1868).

E. "If you do not pay me my money, I will have your life"? Keefe v. State, 19 Ark. 190 (1857).

10. Can words make an assault out of conduct that would otherwise not be sufficient for the tort? Suppose that while defendant and plaintiff are engaged in a violent quarrel, defendant reaches for his hip pocket. Does it make any difference whether he says, "I'll blow your brains out," or "Pardon me, I need a handkerchief"?

11. What about words that threaten harm from an independent source? "Look out! There is a rattlesnake behind you!"

4. FALSE IMPRISONMENT

Big Town Nursing Home, Inc. v. Newman
Court of Civil Appeals of Texas, 1970.
461 S.W.2d 195.

Nursing Home appeals for actual & exemplary damages

McDONALD, CHIEF JUSTICE. This is an appeal by defendant Nursing Home from a judgment for plaintiff Newman for actual and exemplary damages in a false imprisonment case. *(compensatory damages) punitive*

Plaintiff Newman sued defendant Nursing Home for actual and exemplary damages for falsely and wrongfully imprisoning him against his will from September 22, 1968 to November 11, 1968. * * *

Plaintiff is a retired printer 67 years of age, and lives on his social security and a retirement pension from his brother's printing company. He has not worked since 1959, is single, has Parkinson's disease, arthritis, heart trouble, a voice impediment, and a hiatal hernia. He has served in the army attaining the rank of Sergeant. He has never been in a mental hospital or treated by a psychiatrist. Plaintiff was taken to defendant nursing home on September 19, 1968, by his nephew who signed the admission papers and paid one month's care in advance. Plaintiff had been arrested for drunkenness and drunken driving in times past (the last time in 1966) and had been treated twice for alcoholism. Plaintiff testified he was not intoxicated and had nothing to drink during the week prior to admission to the nursing home. The admission papers provided that patient will not be forced to remain in the nursing home against his will for any length of time." Plaintiff was not advised he would be kept at the nursing home against his will. On September 22, 1968, plaintiff decided he wanted to leave and tried to telephone for a taxi. Defendant's employees advised plaintiff he could not use the phone, or have any visitors unless the manager knew them, and locked plaintiff's grip and clothes up. Plaintiff walked out of the home, but was caught by employees of defendant and brought back forceably, and thereafter, placed in Wing 3 and locked up. Defendant's Administrator testified Wing 3 contained senile patients, drug addicts, alcoholics, mentally disturbed, incorrigibles and uncontrollables, and that "they were all in the same kettle of fish." Plaintiff tried to escape from the nursing home five or six times but was caught and brought back each time against his will. He was carried back to Wing 3 and locked and taped in a "restraint chair", for more than five hours. He was put back in the chair on subsequent occasions. He was not seen by the home doctor for some 10 days after he was admitted, and for 7 days after being placed in Wing 3. The doctor wrote the social security office to change payment of plaintiff's social security checks without plaintiff's authorization. Plaintiff made every effort to leave and repeatedly asked the manager and assistant manager to be permitted to leave. The home doctor is actually a resident studying pathology and has no patients other than those in two nursing homes. Finally, on November 11, 1968, plaintiff escaped and caught a ride into Dallas, where he called a taxi and was taken to the home of a friend. During plaintiff's ordeal he lost 30 pounds. There was never any court proceeding to confine plaintiff. * * *

False imprisonment is the direct restraint of one person of the physical liberty of another without adequate legal justification. There is ample evidence to sustain [the jury's finding that plaintiff was falsely imprisoned]. * * *

Defendant placed plaintiff in Wing 3 with insane persons, alcoholics and drug addicts knowing he was not in such category; punished plaintiff by locking and taping him in the restraint chair; prevented him from using the telephone for 51 days; locked up his clothes; told him he could not be released from Wing 3 until he began to obey the rules of the home; and detained him for 51 days during which period he was demanding to be released and attempting to escape. * * *

Defendant may be compelled to respond in exemplary damages if the act causing actual damages is a wrongful act done intentionally in violation of the rights of plaintiff. [Cc]

Defendant acted in the utter disregard of plaintiff's legal rights, knowing there was no court order for commitment, and that the admission agreement provided he was not to be kept against his will. * * *

[The court of appeals found that the amount of damages was excessive and offered plaintiff a remittitur. Plaintiff subsequently agreed to the remittitur and the judgment below, so reformed, was affirmed.]

[handwritten top margin: some claim but not false imprisonment]

NOTES AND QUESTIONS

[handwritten: defendent owns it say he can say who enters]

1. Plaintiff has a ticket to enter defendant's race track. Defendant refuses to admit him. Is this false imprisonment? Marrone v. Washington Jockey Club, 35 App.D.C. 82 (1910). Suppose the exclusion is on the basis of race. See 42 U.S.C.A. § 2000a, page 71, at note 5.

[handwritten right margin: does refused admittance qualify as someone depriving someone of liberty Directly?]

2. In Cullen v. Dickenson, 33 S.D. 27, 144 N.W. 656 (1913), the defendant prevented plaintiff from entering a dance hall, under the mistaken belief that she was under eighteen years of age. It was held that under modern code procedure this was a tort for which plaintiff could recover damages, although not false imprisonment.

3. Can there be false imprisonment in a moving automobile? Cieplinski v. *[handwritten: if person won't stop?]* Severn, 269 Mass. 261, 168 N.E. 722 (1929). In an entire city? Allen v. Fromme, 141 App.Div. 362, 126 N.Y.S. 520 (1910). In the state of Rhode Island? Texas? Cf. Albright v. Oliver, 975 F.2d 343 (7th Cir.1992) (in dicta, court notes that actionable confinement could be "as large as an entire state"). When plaintiff is not permitted to leave the United States? *[handwritten: if state, why not country?]*

4. If one exit of a room or a building is locked with plaintiff inside, but another reasonable means of exit is left open, there is no imprisonment. Davis & Allcott Co. v. Boozer, 215 Ala. 116, 110 So. 28 (1926); Furlong v. German–American Press Ass'n, 189 S.W. 385, 389 (Mo.1916) ("If a way of escape is left open which is available without peril of life or limb, no imprisonment"). See also the classic case of Bird v. Jones, 7 A. & E., N.S., 742, 115 Eng.Rep. 668 (1845).

5. The Restatement (Second) of Torts § 36, comment *a*, treats the means of escape as unreasonable if it involves exposure of the person (plaintiff in the water and defendant steals his clothes), material harm to the clothing, or danger of substantial harm to another. Plaintiff would not be required to make his escape by crawling through a sewer.

6. A means of escape is not a reasonable one if the plaintiff does not know of its existence, and it is not apparent. Talcott v. National Exhibition Co., 144 App.Div. 337, 128 N.Y.S. 1059 (1911).

7. If the only means of escape could cause physical danger to plaintiff, and he could remain "imprisoned" without any risk of harm, he may not recover for injuries he suffers in making his escape. See Sindle v. New York City Transit Authority, 33 N.Y.2d 293, 307 N.E.2d 245, 352 N.Y.S.2d 183 (1973) (plaintiff jumped from window of moving bus).

8. Along with battery and assault, false imprisonment has now become exclusively an intentional tort. The Restatement (Second) of Torts § 35, comment *h*, points out, however, that for negligence resulting in the confinement of another a negligence action will lie, but only if some actual damage results. Cf. Mouse v. Central Sav. & Trust Co., 120 Ohio St. 599, 7 Ohio L.Abs. 334, 167 N.E. 868 (1929). What would be the result if defendant double-parks his automobile and thus prevents plaintiff from driving to an important business meeting? *[handwritten: negligence—no punitive no intent]*

[handwritten right margin: if intentional then false imprisonment]

[handwritten left margin: establishes requirement of knowledge for f.i.]

—Parvi v. City of Kingston
Court of Appeals of New York, 1977. *[handwritten: supreme]*
41 N.Y.2d 553, 362 N.E.2d 960, 394 N.Y.S.2d 161.

[Police, responding to a complaint, found two brothers engaged in a noisy quarrel in an alley behind a commercial building. Plaintiff was with them, apparently trying to calm them. According to police testimony, all three were showing "the effects of alcohol." Plaintiff told the police he had no place to go, so rather than arrest him, they took him outside the city limits to an abandoned golf course to "dry out." There was conflicting testimony as to whether he went willingly. Within an hour, plaintiff had wandered 350 feet and onto the New York State Thruway, where he was struck by a car and severely injured. On cross-examination, he admitted he had no recollection of what happened that night.

Action for false imprisonment. The trial court dismissed the case and the Appellate Division affirmed.]

FUCHSBERG, JUSTICE. * * * [The element of] consciousness of confinement is a more subtle and more interesting subissue in this case. On that subject, we note that, while respected authorities have divided on whether awareness of confinement by one who has been falsely imprisoned should be a *sine qua non* for making out a case, [cc] *Broughton* [v. State of New York], 37 N.Y.2d p. 456, 373 N.Y.S.2d p. 92, 335 N.E.2d p. 313 has laid that question to rest in this State. Its holding gives recognition to the fact that false imprisonment, as a dignitary tort, is not suffered unless its victim knows of the dignitary invasion. Interestingly, the Restatement (Second) of Torts § 42 too has taken the position that there is no liability for intentionally confining another unless the person physically restrained knows of the confinement or is harmed by it.

However, though correctly proceeding on that premise, the Appellate Division, in affirming the dismissal of the cause of action for false imprisonment, erroneously relied on the fact that Parvi, after having provided additional testimony in his own behalf on direct examination, had agreed on cross that he no longer had any *recollection* of his confinement. In so doing, that court failed to distinguish between a later recollection of consciousness and the existence of that consciousness at the time when the imprisonment itself took place. The latter, of course, is capable of being proved though one who suffers the consciousness can no longer personally describe it, whether by reason of lapse of memory, incompetency, death or other cause. Specifically, in this case, while it may well be that the alcohol Parvi had imbibed or the injuries he sustained, or both, had had the effect of wiping out his recollection of being in the police car against his will, that is a far cry from saying that he was not conscious of his confinement at the time when it was actually taking place. And, even if plaintiff's sentient state at the time of his imprisonment was something less than total sobriety, that does not mean that he had no conscious sense of what was then happening to him. To the contrary, there is much in the record to support a finding that the plaintiff indeed was aware of his arrest at the time it took place. By way of illustration, the officers described Parvi's responsiveness to their command that he get into the car, his colloquy while being driven to Coleman Hill and his request to be let off elsewhere. At the very least, then, it was for the jury, in the first instance, to weigh credibility, evaluate inconsistencies and determine whether the burden of proof had been met. * * *

Reversed.

BREITEL, Chief Judge (dissenting). * * * [P]laintiff has failed even to make out a prima facie case that he was conscious of his purported confinement, and that he failed to consent to it. His memory of the entire incident had disappeared; at trial, Parvi admitted that he no longer had any independent recollection of what happened on the day of his accident, and that as to the circumstances surrounding his entrance into the police car, he only knew what had been suggested to him by subsequent conversations. In light of this testimony, Parvi's conclusory statement that he was ordered into the car against his will is insufficient, as a matter of law, to establish a prima facie case. * * *

[handwritten: insufficient proof of consciousness]

NOTES AND QUESTIONS *[handwritten: yes]*

1. In addition to the false imprisonment claim, could plaintiff have filed a negligence claim based on the police officers' conduct? For a more recent case with eerily similar facts, see Deuser v. Vecera, 139 F.3d 1190 (8th Cir.1998) (plaintiff's decedent who had been briefly detained by park rangers for public drunkenness, but not arrested, was released in a parking lot and wandered onto interstate where he was killed by motorist).

2. The mother of a 16–year–old boy, who is disoriented and ill, instructed a police officer to take her son to a particular hospital. Is there false imprisonment if the officer intentionally takes the boy to a different hospital? Cf. Haisenleder v. Reeder, 114 Mich.App. 258, 318 N.W.2d 634 (1982). Or what if the plaintiff, a sufferer from diabetes who is unconscious from insulin shock, is wrongfully arrested and confined in jail overnight in the belief that he is drunk, but is released before he regains consciousness. Is there a tort? See Prosser, False Imprisonment: Consciousness of Confinement, 55 Colum.L.Rev. 847 (1955); Restatement (Second) of Torts § 42.

[handwritten: not unless the boy has consciousness it is quite possible that he doesn't]
[handwritten: battery? mistake liability]
[handwritten: possibly, but not for false imprisonment]

3. Called upon to make an emergency evaluation, a doctor diagnoses a person as mentally ill and has her detained in a mental institution. Is this false imprisonment? See Williams v. Smith, 179 Ga. App. 712, 348 S.E.2d 50 (1986) (no false imprisonment if statutory commitment procedures were followed even if doctor was negligent in diagnosis); Foshee v. Health Mgt. Assocs., 675 So.2d 957 (Fla.App.1996) (false imprisonment if statutory commitment procedures were not followed by nurse who physically prevented patient from leaving a psychiatric facility and coerced her into signing voluntary admission papers). What if a hospital detains a woman for two hours while its staff initiates involuntary commitment proceedings because she is agitated and threatened suicide? Riffe v. Armstrong, 197 W.Va. 626, 477 S.E.2d 535 (1996) (justification for hospital to proceed in good faith and for good reason).

►Hardy v. LaBelle's Distributing Co.

Supreme Court of Montana, 1983.
203 Mont. 263, 661 P.2d 35.

GULBRANDSON, JUSTICE. * * * Defendant, LaBelle's Distributing Company (LaBelle's) hired Hardy as a temporary employee on December 1, 1978. She was assigned duty as a sales clerk in the jewelry department.

On December 9, 1978, another employee for LaBelle's, Jackie Renner, thought she saw Hardy steal one of the watches that LaBelle's had in stock. Jackie Renner reported her belief to LaBelle's showroom manager that evening.

On the morning of December 10, Hardy was approached by the assistant manager of LaBelle's jewelry department and told that all new employees were given a tour of the store. He showed her into the showroom manager's office and then left, closing the door behind him.

There is conflicting testimony concerning who was present in the showroom manager's office when Hardy arrived. Hardy testified that David Kotke, the showroom manager, Steve Newsom, the store's loss prevention manager, and a uniformed policeman were present. Newsom and one of the policemen in the room testified that another policeman, instead of Kotke, was present.

Hardy was told that she had been accused of stealing a watch. Hardy denied taking the watch and agreed to take a lie detector test. According to conflicting testimony, the meeting lasted approximately from twenty to forty-five minutes.

Hardy took the lie detector test, which supported her statement that she had not taken the watch. The showroom manager apologized to Hardy the next morning and told her that she was still welcome to work at LaBelle's. The employee who reported seeing Hardy take the watch also apologized. The two employees then argued briefly, and Hardy left the store.

Hardy brought this action claiming that defendants had wrongfully detained her against her will when she was questioned about the watch.

On appeal Hardy raises basically two issues: (1) Whether the evidence is sufficient to support the verdict and judgment and (2) Whether the District Court erred in the issuance of its instructions.

The two key elements of false imprisonment are the restraint of an individual against his will and the unlawfulness of such restraint. [Cc] The individual may be restrained by acts or merely by words which he fears to disregard. [Cc]

Here, there is ample evidence to support the jury's finding that Hardy was not unlawfully restrained against her will. While Hardy stated that she felt compelled to remain in the showroom manager's office, she also admitted that she wanted to stay and clarify the situation. She did not ask to leave. She was not told she could not leave. No threat of force or otherwise was made to compel her to stay. Although she followed the assistant manager into the office under pretense of a tour, she testified at trial that she would have followed him voluntarily if she had known the true purpose of the meeting and that two policemen were in the room. Under these circumstances, the jury could easily find that Hardy was not detained against her will. [Cc] See also, Meinecke v. Skaggs (1949), 123 Mont. 308, 213 P.2d 237, and Roberts v. Coleman (1961), 228 Or. 286, 365 P.2d 79. * * *

[The court also found that the District Court did not err in issuance of jury instructions on the law of false imprisonment, and affirmed the District Court's judgment in favor of defendants.]

NOTES AND QUESTIONS

1. An employee is suspected of stealing property from her employer and is told a trip to her home is necessary to recover the property. If the employee feels mentally compelled for fear of losing her job to go in an automobile with her supervisor to her home, has she been confined involuntarily? What if she agrees to go along, but during the automobile trip she asks to stop and call her husband and is denied permission to do so? See Faniel v. Chesapeake & Potomac Tel. Co., 404 A.2d 147 (D.C.App.1979).

2. Retention of plaintiff's property sometimes may provide the "restraint" necessary to constitute false imprisonment. See Fischer v. Famous–Barr Co., 646 S.W.2d 819 (Mo.App.1982), where plaintiff set off the security alarm when exiting a store because the salesperson forgot to remove the sensor tag from an article of clothing she had purchased. Because an employee of the store took possession of the bag containing her purchases, plaintiff felt she had to follow the employee back to the fourth floor where she had made her purchase. Compare Marcano v. Northwestern Chrysler–Plymouth Sales, Inc., 550 F.Supp. 595 (N.D.Ill.1982), where plaintiff went to a car dealership to discuss a dispute over payments on her loan and voluntarily gave her keys to the dealer so he could inspect the car. The dealer locked the car and kept the keys. Plaintiff stayed at the dealership for five hours because she had no other way to get home. The court held that there was no false imprisonment because she could have left and because the defendant did not intend to confine her personally, but only to keep the car.

3. False imprisonment has not been extended beyond such direct duress to person or to property. If the plaintiff submits merely to persuasion, and accompanies the defendant to clear himself of suspicion, without any implied threat of force, the action does not lie. Hunter v. Laurent, 158 La. 874, 104 So. 747 (1925); James v. MacDougall & Southwick Co., 134 Wash. 314, 235 P. 812 (1925). Suppose the defendant says to the plaintiff, "You must remain in this room, or I will never speak to you again"? Compare Fitscher v. Rollman & Sons Co., 31 Ohio App. 340, 167 N.E. 469 (1929), where defendant threatened to make a scene on the street unless plaintiff remained.

4. It is generally agreed that false imprisonment resembles assault, in that threats of future action are not enough. Thus the action does not lie where the defendant merely threatens to call the police and have the plaintiff arrested unless he remains. Sweeney v. F.W. Woolworth Co., 247 Mass. 277, 142 N.E. 50 (1924); Priddy v. Bunton, 177 S.W.2d 805 (Tex.Civ.App.1943).

5. On the shopkeeper's privilege to detain a suspected thief, see Bonkowski v. Arlan's Department Store, page 113.

Enright v. Groves

Colorado Court of Appeals, 1977.
39 Colo.App. 39, 560 P.2d 851.

SMITH, JUDGE. Defendants Groves and City of Ft. Collins appeal from judgments entered against them upon jury verdicts awarding plaintiff $500 actual damages and $1,000 exemplary damages on her claim of false imprisonment * * *.

The evidence at trial disclosed that on August 25, 1974, Officer Groves, while on duty as a uniformed police officer of the City of Fort Collins, observed a dog running loose in violation of the city's "dog leash" ordinance. He observed the animal approaching what was later identified as the residence of Mrs. Enright, the plaintiff. As Groves approached the house, he encountered Mrs. Enright's eleven-year-old son, and asked him if the dog belonged to him. The boy replied that it was his dog, and told Groves that his mother was sitting in the car parked at the curb by the house. Groves then ordered the boy to put the dog inside the house, and turned and started walking toward the Enright vehicle.

Groves testified that he was met by Mrs. Enright with whom he was not acquainted. She asked if she could help him. Groves responded by demanding her driver's license. She replied by giving him her name and address. He again demanded her driver's license, which she declined to produce. Groves thereupon advised her that she could either produce her driver's license or go to jail. Mrs. Enright responded by asking, "Isn't this ridiculous?" Groves thereupon grabbed one of her arms, stating, "Let's go!" * * *

She was taken to the police station where a complaint was signed charging her with violation of the "dog leash" ordinance and bail was set. Mrs. Enright was released only after a friend posted bail. She was later convicted of the ordinance violation. * * *

Appellants contend that Groves had probable cause to arrest Mrs. Enright, and that she was in fact arrested for and convicted of violation of the dog-at-large ordinance. They assert, therefore, that her claim for false imprisonment or false arrest cannot lie, and that Groves' use of force in arresting Mrs. Enright was permissible. We disagree.

False arrest arises when one is taken into custody by a person who claims but does not have proper legal authority. W. Prosser, Torts § 11 (4th ed.). Accordingly, a claim for false arrest will not lie if an officer has a valid warrant or probable cause to believe that an offense has been committed and that the person who was arrested committed it. Conviction of the crime for which one is specifically arrested is a complete defense to a subsequent claim of false arrest. [Cc]

Here, however, the evidence is clear that Groves arrested Mrs. Enright, not for violation of the dog leash ordinance, but rather for refusing to produce her driver's license. This basis for the arrest is exemplified by the fact that he specifically advised her that she would either produce the license or go to jail. We find no statute or case law in this jurisdiction which requires a citizen to show her driver's license upon demand, unless, for example, she is a driver of an automobile and such demand is made in that connection. * * *

Here, there was no testimony that Groves ever even attempted to explain why he was demanding plaintiff's driver's license, and it is clear that she had already volunteered her name and address. Groves admitted that he did not ask Mrs. Enright if she had any means of identification on her person, instead he simply demanded that she give him her driver's license.

We conclude that Groves' demand for Mrs. Enright's driver's license *[Holding]* was not a lawful order and that refusal to comply therewith was not therefore an offense in and of itself. Groves was not therefore entitled to use force in arresting Mrs. Enright. Thus Groves' defense based upon an arrest for and conviction of a specific offense must, as a matter of law, fail. * * *

Judgment affirmed. *trial court did not err as Groves did not have right to arrest for failure to produce license*

NOTES AND QUESTIONS

1. Is it necessary that the defendant be an officer? Suppose a filling station attendant asserts legal authority to detain the plaintiff, and plaintiff submits? *If plaintiff submits, no f.i.* Daniel v. Phillips Petroleum Co., 229 Mo.App. 150, 73 S.W.2d 355 (1934). Plaintiff, attempting to leave defendant's train, fell and broke his leg. A cab was called to take him to the hospital. Defendant's conductor told plaintiff that the law required him to remain and fill out a statement about the accident. Plaintiff did so, and the cab was held for fifteen or twenty minutes, during which plaintiff was in considerable pain, while the statement was filled out and signed. This was held to be false imprisonment. Whitman v. Atchison, T. & S.F.R. Co., 85 Kan. 150, 116 P. 234 (1911).

2. A private citizen who aids a policeman in making a false arrest can be held liable to plaintiff for false imprisonment. If, however, the police officer requests *unless* assistance, the private citizen will not be liable unless he knows the arrest is an unlawful one. See Restatement (Second) of Torts § 45A and 139.

3. Regardless of the unreasonableness of the arrest, no action for false imprisonment will lie if the plaintiff actually committed the crime. See Taco Bell, Inc. v. Saleme, 701 S.W.2d 78 (Tex.App.1985).

Whittaker v. Sandford

Supreme Judicial Court of Maine, 1912.
110 Me. 77, 85 A. 399.

[Plaintiff was a member and her husband was a minister of a religious sect, of which defendant was the leader. The sect had a colony in Maine and at Jaffa (now Tel Aviv), the latter of which plaintiff had joined. Plaintiff decided to abandon the sect and to return to America. While she and her four children were awaiting passage from Jaffa on a steamer, defendant offered her passage back to America on his yacht. When plaintiff told defendant that she was afraid that he would not let her off the yacht until she was "won to the movement again," defendant assured her repeatedly that under no circumstances would she be detained on board. Plaintiff accepted this assurance and sailed for America on the yacht. On arrival in port, defendant refused to furnish her with a boat so that she could leave the yacht, saying it was up to her husband whether she could leave. When plaintiff raised the issue with her husband, he said it was up to defendant, the leader of the sect and the owner of the yacht. She remained on board for nearly a month, during which time defendant and plaintiff's husband attempted to persuade her to rejoin the sect. On several occasions, plaintiff, always in the company of her husband, was allowed to go ashore to the mainland and to various islands. She was not allowed to leave the yacht unaccompanied. She finally obtained her release and that of her four children with the assistance of the sheriff and a writ of habeas corpus. She then brought this action for false imprisonment. The jury returned a verdict in her favor for $1100. Defendant excepted to the court's instructions, and appealed from an order denying his motion for a new trial.

SAVAGE, J. * * * The court instructed the jury that the plaintiff to recover must show that the restraint was physical, and not merely a moral influence; that it must have been actual physical restraint, in the sense that one intentionally locked into a room would be physically restrained but not necessarily involving physical force upon the person; that it was not necessary that the defendant, or any person by his direction, should lay his hand upon the plaintiff; that if the plaintiff was restrained so that she could not leave the yacht Kingdom by the intentional refusal to furnish transportation as agreed, she not having it in her power to escape otherwise, it would be a physical restraint and unlawful imprisonment. We think the instructions were apt and sufficient. If one should, without right, turn the key in a door, and thereby prevent a person in the room from leaving, it would be the simplest form of unlawful imprisonment. The restraint is physical. The four walls and the locked door are physical impediments to escape. Now is it different when one who is in control of a vessel at anchor, within practical rowing distance from the shore, who has agreed that a guest on board shall be free to leave, there being no means to leave except by rowboats, wrongfully refuses the guest the use of a boat? The boat is the key. By refusing the boat he turns the key. The guest is as effectually locked up as if there were walls along the sides of the vessel. The restraint is physical. The impassable sea is the physical barrier. * * *

A careful study of the evidence leads us to conclude that the jury were warranted in finding that the defendant was guilty of unlawful imprisonment. This, to be sure, is not an action based upon the defendant's failure to keep his agreement to permit the plaintiff to leave the yacht as soon as it should reach shore. But his duty under the circumstances is an important consideration. It cannot be believed that either party to the agreement understood that it was his duty merely to bring her to an American harbor. The agreement implied that she was to go ashore. There was no practical way for her to go ashore except in the yacht's boats. The agreement must be understood to mean that he would bring her to land, or to allow her to get to land, by the only available means. The evidence is that he refused her a boat. His refusal was wrongful. The case leaves not the slightest doubt that he had the power to control the boats, if he chose to exercise it. It was not enough for him to leave it to the husband to say whether she might go ashore or not. She had a personal right to go on shore. If the

[Margin annotations: "Facts"; "Issue — court right in jury instructions? jury right in finding f?"; "Prima facie elements — breach in duty (elements for tort)"; "Holding — D's refusal of means for P to get off boat constitutes false imprisonment"]

defendant personally denied her the privilege, as the jury might find he did, it was a wrongful denial.

NOTES AND QUESTIONS

1. A woman tells her boyfriend she does not want to see him anymore, but agrees to ride with him just to the store and back. When they return to her parents' house and she opens the car door, the boyfriend suddenly starts the car off, making it dangerous for her to exit the moving vehicle. False imprisonment? See Noguchi v. Nakamura, 2 Haw. App. 655, 638 P.2d 1383 (1982). *yes*

2. In Talcott v. National Exhibition Co., 144 App.Div. 337, 128 N.Y.S. 1059 (1911), plaintiff was one of a crowd seeking admission to the baseball game between the Chicago Cubs and the New York Giants that played off the tie for the 1908 National League pennant. This was necessary because of a one-to-one tie in an earlier game between the same teams, produced when Fred Merkle of the Giants pulled his famous "bonehead play" in failing to touch second base. For two fascinating accounts of that game told by other players in it, see L. Ritter, The Glory of Their Times 98–100 and 124–218 (1966); the book has a picture of the after-game crowd in the Polo Grounds at page 126. The Giants, who would have won the pennant except for the Merkle error, lost the playoff game. Plaintiff succeeded in entering an enclosure where tickets were sold, but found that he could not get in to the stands. Defendant closed the entrance gates behind him to prevent injuries from the crush. There was another exit, of which defendant failed to inform plaintiff, and he remained within the enclosure for more than an hour. In his action for false imprisonment, a verdict and judgment in his favor were affirmed. It was held that while the defendant might have been justified in closing the gates, it was then under a duty to inform plaintiff of the other exit. *knowledge*

3. Members of a religious cult are abducted by their relatives and subjected to deprogramming. Is this false imprisonment? Eilers v. Coy, 582 F.Supp. 1093 (D.Minn.1984). *yes! even ● if done in good faith / for good reason*

4. Plaintiff boarded a plane in Washington, D.C., for a flight to New York where he was to attend a reception at the United Nations. After sitting on the tarmac for over an hour waiting for his flight to take off, plaintiff realized he had missed the reception and demanded to be returned to the terminal. Is the airline liable for failing to allow him to leave the airplane after it had pulled away from the gate? After it had sat on the tarmac for an hour? Somewhere above New Jersey? See Abourezk v. New York Airlines, 895 F.2d 1456 (D.C.Cir.1990) (no duty to release passenger until plane reached New York absent exigent circumstances not present in the case).

5. Intentional Infliction of Mental Distress

State Rubbish Collectors Ass'n v. Siliznoff

Physical confinement / detention of contracting party's property

Threats

Supreme Court of California, 1952.
38 Cal.2d 330, 240 P.2d 282.

law presumes it follows from type of wrong committed

[The State Rubbish Collectors Association sued Siliznoff to collect on certain notes. Siliznoff counterclaimed, asking that the notes be cancelled because of duress and want of consideration. In addition, he sought general and punitive damages because of alleged "assaults" made on him. The evidence was that Siliznoff had collected the trash from the Acme Brewing *facts*

threat used to compel someone to do something recognized + a tort

defense against his will

Company, which the Association regarded as within the territory of another member of the Association named Abramoff. The defendant was called before the Association and ordered to pay over the collected money to Abramoff, as a result of which he signed the notes in question. Further facts appear in the opinion.

The jury returned a verdict for Siliznoff on the original complaint and on the counterclaim. Siliznoff obtained a judgment against the Association for $1,250 general and special damages and $4,000 punitive damages. The Association appealed the judgment.]

TRAYNOR, J. * * * Plaintiff's primary contention is that the evidence is insufficient to support the judgment. Defendant testified that: * * *

Andikian [an inspector of the Association] told defendant that " 'We will give you up till tonight to get down to the board meeting and make some kind of arrangements or agreements about the Acme Brewery, or otherwise we are going to beat you up.' * * * He says he either would hire somebody or do it himself. And I says, 'Well, what would they do to me?' He says, well, they would physically beat me up first, cut up the truck tires or burn the truck, or otherwise put me out of business completely. He said if I didn't appear at that meeting and make some kind of an agreement that they would do that, but he says up to then they would let me alone, but if I walked out of that meeting that night they would beat me up for sure." Defendant attended the meeting and protested that he owed nothing for the Acme account and in any event could not pay the amount demanded. He was again told by the president of the association that "that table right there [the board of directors] ran all the rubbish collecting in Los Angeles and if there was any routes to be gotten that they would get them and distribute them among their members * * *." After two hours of further discussion defendant agreed to join the association and pay for the Acme account. He promised to return the next day and sign the necessary papers. He testified that the only reason "they let me go home, is that I promised that I would sign the notes the very next morning." The president "made me promise on my honor and everything else, and I was scared, and I knew I had to come back, so I believe he knew I was scared and that I would come back. That's the only reason they let me go home." Defendant also testified that because of the fright he suffered during his dispute with the association he became ill and vomited several times and had to remain away from work for a period of several days.

Plaintiff contends that the evidence does not establish an assault against defendant because the threats made all related to action that might take place in the future; that neither Andikian nor members of the board of directors threatened immediate physical harm to defendant. [C] We have concluded, however, that a cause of action is established when it is shown that one, in the absence of any privilege, intentionally subjects another to the mental suffering incident to serious threats to his physical well-being, whether or not the threats are made under such circumstances as to constitute a technical assault.

In the past it has been frequently stated that the interest in emotional and mental tranquillity is not one that the law will protect from invasion in its own right. [Cc] As late as 1934 the Restatement of Torts took the position that "The interest in mental and emotional tranquillity and, therefore, in freedom from mental and emotional disturbance is not, as a thing in itself, regarded as of sufficient importance to require others to refrain from conduct intended or recognizably likely to cause such a disturbance." Restatement, Torts, § 46, comment *c*. The Restatement explained the rule allowing recovery for the mere apprehension of bodily harm in traditional assault cases as an historical anomaly (§ 24, comment c), and the rule allowing recovery for insulting conduct by an employee of a common carrier as justified by the necessity of securing for the public comfortable as well as safe service (§ 48, comment c).

The Restatement recognized, however, that in many cases mental distress could be so intense that it could reasonably be foreseen that illness or other bodily harm might result. If the defendant intentionally subjected the plaintiff to such distress and bodily harm resulted, the defendant would be liable for negligently causing the plaintiff bodily harm. Restatement, Torts, §§ 306, 312. Under this theory the cause of action was not founded on a right to be free from intentional interference with mental tranquillity, but on the right to be free from negligent interference with physical well-being. A defendant who intentionally subjected another to mental distress without intending to cause bodily harm would nevertheless be liable for resulting bodily harm if he should have foreseen that the mental distress might cause such harm.

The California cases have been in accord with the Restatement in allowing recovery where physical injury resulted from intentionally subjecting the plaintiff to serious mental distress. [Cc]

The view has been forcefully advocated that the law should protect emotional and mental tranquillity as such against serious and intentional invasions, [cc] and there is a growing body of case law supporting this position. [Cc] In recognition of this development the American Law Institute amended section 46 of the Restatement of Torts in 1947 to provide:

"One who, without a privilege to do so, intentionally causes severe emotional distress to another is liable (a) for such emotional distress, and (b) for bodily harm resulting from it."

In explanation it is stated that "The interest in freedom from severe emotional distress is regarded as of sufficient importance to require others to refrain from conduct intended to invade it. Such conduct is tortious. The injury suffered by the one whose interest is invaded is frequently far more serious to him than certain tortious invasions of the interest in bodily integrity and other legally protected interests. In the absence of a privilege, the actor's conduct has no social utility; indeed it is anti-social. No reason or policy requires such an actor to be protected from the liability which usually attaches to the wilful wrongdoer whose efforts are successful." (Restatement of the Law, 1948 Supplement, Torts, § 46, comment d.)

There are persuasive arguments and analogies that support the recognition of a right to be free from serious, intentional and unprivileged invasions of mental and emotional tranquillity. If a cause of action is otherwise established, it is settled that damages may be given for mental suffering naturally ensuing from the acts complained of [cc], and in the case of many torts, such as assault, battery, false imprisonment and defamation, mental suffering will frequently constitute the principal element of damages. [C] In cases where mental suffering constitutes a major element of damages it is anomalous to deny recovery because the defendant's intentional misconduct fell short of producing some physical injury.

It may be contended that to allow recovery in the absence of physical injury will open the door to unfounded claims and a flood of litigation, and that the requirement that there be physical injury is necessary to insure that serious mental suffering actually occurred. The jury is ordinarily in a better position, however, to determine whether outrageous conduct results in mental distress than whether that distress in turn results in physical injury. From their own experience jurors are aware of the extent and character of the disagreeable emotions that may result from the defendant's conduct, but a difficult medical question is presented when it must be determined if emotional distress resulted in physical injury. [C] Greater proof that mental suffering occurred is found in the defendant's conduct designed to bring it about than in physical injury that may or may not have resulted therefrom. * * *

In the present case plaintiff caused defendant to suffer extreme fright. By intentionally producing such fright it endeavored to compel him either to give up the Acme account or pay for it, and it had no right or privilege to adopt such coercive methods in competing for business. In these circumstances liability is clear. * * *

The judgment is affirmed.

NOTES AND QUESTIONS

1.   Why not assault? Why not false imprisonment? Assuming neither tort occurred, how many attorneys in 1952 would have thought of bringing a cross-complaint in this case for "intentional infliction of emotional harm"? How many judges would have adopted it?

2.   But what form of tort has been unleashed? Is it as definite in character as those that arose out of the writ of trespass? What result in the main case if the Association had only threatened to close down Siliznoff's business, but had not made threats to his physical well-being? Do you agree that the jury can more easily determine whether conduct is outrageous than whether physical injury resulted from emotional harm? If so, does this fact suggest that a claim should be allowed?

3.   The seminal case to allow recovery for the intentional infliction of mental distress as a distinct tort was Wilkinson v. Downton, [1897] 2 Q.B. 57, in which a practical joker amused himself by telling the plaintiff that her husband had been smashed up in an accident, was lying at The Elms in Leytonstone with both legs broken, and that she was to go to him at once in a cab with two pillows to fetch him home. The shock to her nervous system caused serious physical illness with

permanent consequences, and at one time threatened her reason. Why the defendant was held liable is unclear to the reader of the opinion and apparently to the court as well.

4. Unlike California in the principal case, some states recognize the tort but restrict its application to situations in which plaintiff has suffered "physical consequences." See Duty v. General Fin. Co., 154 Tex. 16, 273 S.W.2d 64 (1954); Clark v. Associated Retail Credit Men, 105 F.2d 62 (D.C.Cir.1939). Others, like California, rely upon the outrageous nature of the conduct rather than requirements of physical impact or physical manifestation to guard against fraudulent claims. Sacco v. High Country Independent Press, Inc., 271 Mont. 209, 896 P.2d 411 (1995).

5. There are now numerous decisions in which, upon the basis of extreme outrage, the recovery has been allowed. Recovery for mental distress without physical injury is allowed if the defendant's conduct exceeds the "limits of social toleration." Some states call the tort "outrage." Consider the following: Wilson v. Wilkins, 181 Ark. 137, 25 S.W.2d 428 (1930) (mob threat to harm plaintiff if he was not out of town by nightfall); Savage v. Boies, 77 Ariz. 355, 272 P.2d 349 (1954) (police decoyed plaintiff into confinement by telling her that her husband and child were injured and in the hospital); Young v. Stensrude, 664 S.W.2d 263 (Mo.App. 1984) (during a business meeting at a university medical center, defendant showed what he announced was an educational film but which turned out to be a pornographic film to plaintiff and four men while making obscene remarks to plaintiff).

6. As the principal case indicates, § 46 of the Restatement of Torts was changed in the 1948 Supplement to recognize the cause of action for the intentional infliction of severe emotional distress, and to allow recovery "(a) for such emotional distress, and (b) for bodily harm resulting from it." This has been retained by the Restatement (Second) of Torts, § 46, where it is said that liability exists when the defendant's conduct is "extreme and outrageous," and leaves open the possibility of further expansion.

7. Is it necessary that the defendant intended to cause the mental disturbance, or that it be substantially certain to follow, within the rule stated in Garratt v. Dailey, page 17? What if there is merely a high degree of probability, and the defendant acts in conscious disregard of it, so that his conduct is "wilful," "wanton," or "reckless"? See Restatement (Second) of Torts § 46.

►Slocum v. Food Fair Stores of Florida

Supreme Court of Florida, 1958.
100 So.2d 396.

DREW, JUSTICE. This appeal is from an order dismissing a complaint for failure to state a cause of action. Simply stated, the plaintiff sought money damages for mental suffering or emotional distress, and an ensuing heart attack and aggravation of pre-existing heart disease, allegedly caused by insulting language of the defendant's employee directed toward her while she was a customer in its store. Specifically, in reply to her inquiry as to the price of an item he was marking, he replied: "If you want to know the price, you'll have to find out the best way you can * * * you stink to me." She asserts, in the alternative, that the language was used in a malicious or grossly reckless manner, ["or with intent to inflict great mental and emotional disturbance to said plaintiff."]

No great difficulty is involved in the preliminary point raised as to the sufficiency of damages alleged, the only direct injury being mental or emotional with physical symptoms merely derivative therefrom. [C] While that decision would apparently allow recovery for mental suffering, even absent physical consequences, inflicted in the course of other intentional or malicious torts, it does not resolve the central problem in this case, i.e. whether the conduct here claimed to have caused the injury, the use of insulting language under the circumstances described, constituted an actionable invasion of a legally protected right. Query: does such an assertion of a deliberate disturbance of emotional equanimity state an independent cause of action in tort?

Appellant's fundamental argument is addressed to that proposition. The case is one of first impression in this jurisdiction, and she contends that this Court should recognize the existence of a new tort, an independent cause of action for intentional infliction of emotional distress.

A study of the numerous references on the subject indicates a strong current of opinion in support of such recognition, in lieu of the strained reasoning so often apparent when liability for such injury is predicated upon one or another of several traditional tort theories. * * *

A most cogent statement of the doctrine covering tort liability for insult has been incorporated in the Restatement of the Law of Torts, 1948 supplement, sec. 46, entitled "Conduct intended to cause emotional distress only." It makes a blanket provision for liability on the part of "one, who, without a privilege to do so, intentionally causes severe emotional distress to another," indicating that the requisite intention exists "when the act is done for the purpose of causing the distress or with knowledge * * * that severe emotional distress is substantially certain to be produced by [such] conduct." Comment (a), Sec. 46, supra. Abusive language is, of course, only one of the many means by which the tort could be committed.

However, even if we assume, without deciding, the legal propriety of that doctrine, a study of its factual applications shows that a line of demarcation should be drawn between conduct likely to cause mere "emotional distress" and that causing "severe emotional distress," so as to exclude the situation at bar. [C] "So far as it is possible to generalize from the cases, the rule which seems to be emerging is that there is liability only for conduct exceeding all bounds which could be tolerated by society, of a nature especially calculated to cause mental damage of a very serious kind." [C] And the most practicable view is that the functions of court and jury are no different than in other tort actions where there is at the outset a question as to whether the conduct alleged is so legally innocuous as to present no issue for a jury. [C]

This tendency to hinge the cause of action upon the degree of the insult has led some courts to reject the doctrine in toto. [C] Whether or not this is desirable, it is uniformly agreed that the determination of whether words or conduct are actionable in character is to be made on an objective rather than subjective standard, from common acceptation. The unwarranted intrusion must be calculated to cause "severe emotional distress" to a person of ordinary sensibilities, in the absence of special knowledge or notice. There is no inclination to include all instances of mere vulgarities, obviously intended as meaningless abusive expressions. While the manner in which language is used may no doubt determine its actionable character, appellant's assertion that the statement involved in this case was made to her with gross recklessness, etc., cannot take the place of allegations showing that the words were intended to have real meaning or serious effect.

[handwritten margin note: Holding — there is no action as facts do not support the fact that the words were intended to have "real meaning" or "serious effect"]

A broader rule has been developed in a particular class of cases, usually treated as a distinct and separate area of liability originally applied to common carriers. Rest.Torts, per. ed., sec. 48. The courts have from an early date granted relief for offense reasonably suffered by a patron from insult by a servant or employee of a carrier, hotel, theater, and most recently, a telegraph office. The existence of a special relationship, arising either from contract or from the inherent nature of a non-competitive public utility, supports a right and correlative duty of courtesy beyond that legally required in general mercantile or personal relationships. [Cc]

In view of the concurrent development of the cause of action first above described, there is no impelling reason to extend the rule of the latter cases. Their rationale does not of necessity cover the area of business invitees generally, where the theory of respondeat superior underlying most liabilities of the employer would dictate some degree of conformity to standards of individual liability. This factor, together with the stringent standards of care imposed in a number of the carrier cases [c], may have influenced the treatment of the subject by editors of the Restatement, where the statement of the carrier doctrine is quite limited in scope and classified separately from the section covering the more general area of liability under consideration. But whether or not these rules are ultimately adopted in this jurisdiction, the facts of the present case cannot be brought within their reasonable intendment.

Affirmed.

NOTES AND QUESTIONS

1. Why is the intentional infliction of mental disturbance by the insult not a tort in itself? *[handwritten: unless "severe distress" can be proved ⟹ no action (tort)]*

2. "Against a large part of the frictions and irritations and clashing of temperaments incident to participation in community life, a certain toughening of the mental hide is a better protection than the law could ever be. * * * Of course there is danger of getting into the realm of the trivial in this matter of insulting language. No pressing social need requires that every abusive outburst be converted into a tort; upon the contrary, it would be unfortunate if the law closed all the safety valves through which irascible tempers might legally blow off steam." Magruder, Mental and Emotional Disturbance in the Law of Torts, 49 Harv.L.Rev. 1033, 1035, 1053 (1936).

3. A South Carolina gentleman, incensed at his inability to get a telephone number, so far forgets his chivalry as to call the operator a God damned woman, and to say that if he were there he would break her God damned neck. The unprecedented experience, according to her allegations, causes her extreme mental disturbance, and leaves her a nervous wreck. Does this state a cause of action? Brooker v. Silverthorne, 111 S.C. 553, 99 S.E. 350 (1919). *possibly an assault*

4. Compare Halliday v. Cienkowski, 333 Pa. 123, 3 A.2d 372 (1939) ("Scotch bitch," "bastard," and "bum"); Atkinson v. Bibb Mfg. Co., 50 Ga.App. 434, 178 S.E. 537 (1935) (foreman cursing discharged woman, with open knife in his hand); Kramer v. Ricksmeier, 159 Iowa 48, 139 N.W. 1091 (1913) (profanity and abuse over the telephone, with threats of future violence); Barry v. Baugh, 111 Ga.App. 813, 143 S.E.2d 489 (1965) ("crazy").

5. Insult statutes in Mississippi, Virginia and West Virginia, which had their origin as part of anti-dueling codes, provide an action for "all words which from their usual construction and acceptation are considered as insults, and lead to violence and breach of the peace." They are treated in Wade, Tort Liability for Abusive and Insulting Language, 4 Vand.L.Rev. 63 (1950), which discusses liability in general.

The constitutionality of these statutes is questionable. In criminal cases, they are deemed valid only when the words used are likely to incite an immediate breach of the peace. See Gooding v. Wilson, 405 U.S. 518, 523 (1972). Virginia has merged its insult statute into the state's law of libel with the result that truth is an absolute defense and defendant's comments may be privileged. See Old Dominion Branch v. Austin, 213 Va. 377, 192 S.E.2d 737 (1972), rev'd on other grounds, 418 U.S. 264 (1974).

6. Common carriers and innkeepers have been held to a higher standard of conduct and may be liable for using insulting language to their passengers and patrons. See, e.g., Lipman v. Atlantic Coast Line R.R. Co., 108 S.C. 151, 93 S.E. 714 (1917) (carrier); Emmke v. De Silva, 293 F. 17 (8th Cir.1923) (hotel). But cf. Wallace v. Shoreham Hotel Corp., 49 A.2d 81 (D.C.Mun.App.1946) (restaurant patron did not state cause of action based on waiter's insult) and Bethel v. N.Y.C. Transit Authority, 92 N.Y.2d 348, 703 N.E.2d 1214 (1998) (abolishing higher standard of care for common carriers).

▸ Harris v. Jones

Court of Appeals of Maryland, 1977.
281 Md. 560, 380 A.2d 611.

MURPHY, CHIEF JUDGE. * * * The plaintiff, William R. Harris, a 26–year–old, 8–year employee of General Motors Corporation (GM), sued GM and one of its supervisory employees, H. Robert Jones, in the Superior Court of Baltimore City. The declaration alleged that Jones, aware that Harris suffered from a speech impediment which caused him to stutter, and also aware of Harris' sensitivity to his disability, and his insecurity because of it, nevertheless "maliciously and cruelly ridiculed * * * [him] thus causing tremendous nervousness, increasing the physical defect itself and further injuring the mental attitude fostered by the Plaintiff toward his problem and otherwise intentionally inflicting emotional distress." It was also alleged in the declaration that Jones' actions occurred within the course of his employment with GM and that GM ratified Jones' conduct.

The evidence at trial showed that Harris stuttered throughout his entire life. While he had little trouble with one syllable words, he had great difficulty with longer words or sentences, causing him at times to shake his head up and down when attempting to speak.

During part of 1975, Harris worked under Jones' supervision at a GM automobile assembly plant. Over a five-month period, between March and August of 1975, Jones approached Harris over 30 times at work and verbally and physically mimicked his stuttering disability. In addition, two or three times a week during this period, Jones approached Harris and told him, in a "smart manner," not to get nervous. As a result of Jones' conduct, Harris was "shaken up" and felt "like going into a hole and hide."

On June 2, 1975, Harris asked Jones for a transfer to another department; Jones refused, called Harris a "troublemaker" and chastised him for repeatedly seeking the assistance of his committeeman, a representative who handles employee grievances. On this occasion, Jones, "shaking his head up and down" to imitate Harris, mimicked his pronunciation of the word "committeeman," which Harris pronounced "mmitteeman." * * *

Harris had been under the care of a physician for a nervous condition for six years prior to the commencement of Jones' harassment. He admitted that many things made him nervous, including "bosses." Harris testified that Jones' conduct heightened his nervousness and his speech impediment worsened. He saw his physician on one occasion during the five-month period that Jones was mistreating him; the physician prescribed pills for his nerves.

Harris admitted that other employees at work mimicked his stuttering. Approximately 3,000 persons were employed on each of two shifts, and Harris acknowledged the presence at the plant of a lot of "tough guys," as well as profanity, name-calling and roughhousing among the employees. He said that a bad day at work caused him to become more nervous than usual. He admitted that he had problems with supervisors other than Jones, that he had been suspended or relieved from work 10 or 12 times, and that after one such dispute, he followed a supervisor home on his motorcycle, for which he was later disciplined.

On this evidence, * * * the jury awarded Harris $3,500 compensatory damages and $15,000 punitive damages against both Jones and GM. [This was reversed by the Court of Special Appeals.]

In concluding that the intentional infliction of emotional distress, standing alone, may constitute a valid tort action, the Court of Special Appeals relied upon Restatement (Second) of Torts, ch. 2, Emotional Distress, § 46 (1965), which provides, in pertinent part:

"§ 46. Outrageous Conduct Causing Severe Emotional Distress

"(1) One who by extreme and outrageous conduct intentionally or recklessly causes severe emotional distress to another is subject to liability for such emotional distress, and if bodily harm to the other results from it, for such bodily harm."

The court noted that the tort was recognized, and its boundaries defined, in W. Prosser, Law of Torts § 12, at 56 (4th ed. 1971), as follows:

"So far as it is possible to generalize from the cases, the rule which seems to have emerged is that there is liability for conduct exceeding all bounds usually tolerated by decent society, of a nature which is especially calculated to cause, and does cause, mental distress of a very serious kind."

The trend in other jurisdictions toward recognition of a right to recover for severe emotional distress brought on by the intentional act of another is manifest. Indeed, 37 jurisdictions appear now to recognize the tort as a valid cause of action. * * *

[F]our elements * * * must coalesce to impose liability for intentional infliction of emotional distress:

(1) The conduct must be intentional or reckless;

(2) The conduct must be extreme and outrageous;

(3) There must be a causal connection between the wrongful conduct and the emotional distress;

(4) The emotional distress must be severe. * * *

[The intermediate Court of Special Appeals had found that the first two elements were established but reversed on the ground that the last two elements were not.]

Whether the conduct of a defendant has been "extreme and outrageous," so as to satisfy that element of the tort, has been a particularly troublesome question. Section 46 of the Restatement, comment d, states that "Liability has been found only where the conduct has been so outrageous in character, and so extreme in degree, as to go beyond all possible bounds of decency, and to be regarded as atrocious, and utterly intolerable in a civilized community." The comment goes on to state that liability does not extend, however: "to mere insults, indignities, threats, annoyances, petty oppressions, or other trivialities. The rough edges of our society are still in need of a good deal of filing down, and in the meantime plaintiffs must necessarily be expected and required to be hardened to a certain amount of rough language, and to occasional acts that are definitely inconsiderate and unkind. * * *"

In determining whether conduct is extreme and outrageous, it should not be considered in a sterile setting, detached from the surroundings in which it occurred. [C] The personality of the individual to whom the misconduct is directed is also a factor. "There is a difference between violent and vile profanity addressed to a lady, and the same language to a Butte miner and a United States marine." Prosser, Intentional Infliction of Mental Suffering: A New Tort, 37 Mich.L.Rev. 874, 887 (1939). * * *

It is for the court to determine, in the first instance, whether the defendant's conduct may reasonably be regarded as extreme and outrageous; where reasonable men may differ, it is for the jury to determine whether, in the particular case, the conduct has been sufficiently extreme and outrageous to result in liability. * * *

While it is crystal clear that Jones' conduct was intentional, we need not decide whether it was extreme or outrageous, or causally related to the emotional distress which Harris allegedly suffered.[2] The fourth element of the tort—that the emotional distress must be severe—was not established by legally sufficient evidence justifying submission of the case to the jury. That element of the tort requires the plaintiff to show that he suffered a *severely* disabling emotional response to the defendant's conduct. The severity of the emotional distress is not only relevant to the amount of recovery, but is a necessary element to any recovery. * * *

Assuming that a causal relationship was shown between Jones' wrongful conduct and Harris' emotional distress, we find no evidence, legally sufficient for submission to the jury, that the distress was "severe" within the contemplation of the rule requiring establishment of that element of the tort. The evidence that Jones' reprehensible conduct humiliated Harris and caused him emotional distress, which was manifested by an aggravation of Harris' pre-existing nervous condition and a worsening of his speech impediment, was vague and weak at best. * * * While Harris' nervous condition may have been exacerbated somewhat by Jones' conduct, his family problems antedated his encounter with Jones and were not shown to be attributable to Jones' actions. Just how, or to what degree, Harris' speech impediment worsened is not revealed by the evidence. Granting the cruel and insensitive nature of Jones' conduct toward Harris, and considering the position of authority which Jones held over Harris, we conclude that the humiliation suffered was not, as a matter of law, so intense as to constitute the "severe" emotional distress required to recover for the tort of intentional infliction of emotional distress.

Judgment affirmed; costs to be paid by appellant.

NOTES AND QUESTIONS

1. How culpable must defendant's conduct be before it reaches the level of being extreme enough to be deemed tortious? Some guidelines can be found in decided cases. Thus, it is generally held that the mere solicitation of a woman to illicit intercourse is not only not an assault but does not give rise to any other cause of action. Reed v. Maley, 115 Ky. 816, 74 S.W. 1079 (1903). "The view being, apparently, that there is no harm in asking." Magruder, Mental and Emotional Disturbance in the Law of Torts, 49 Harv.L.Rev. 1033, 1055 (1936). Jones v. Clinton, 990 F.Supp. 657, 677 (E.D.Ark.1998) (applying Arkansas law) ("While the Court will certainly agree that plaintiff's allegations describe offensive conduct, the Court, as previously noted, has found that the Governor's alleged conduct does not constitute sexual assault. Rather, the conduct as alleged by plaintiff describes a mere sexual proposition or encounter, albeit an odious one.... The Court is not

2. The fact that Harris may have had some pre-existing susceptibility to emotional distress does not necessarily preclude liability if it can be shown that the conduct intensified the pre-existing condition of psychological stress. [Cc]

aware of any authority holding that such a sexual encounter or proposition of the type alleged in this case, without more, gives rise to a claim of outrage.")

In Samms v. Eccles, 11 Utah 2d 289, 358 P.2d 344 (1961), a married woman was hounded by continued telephone calls from May to December, some of them late at night; and on one occasion defendant came to her home and made an indecent exposure of his person. The court said that under usual circumstances such solicitation would not be actionable ("It seems to be a custom of long standing and one which in all likelihood will continue"), but found such "aggravated circumstances" in this case as to make the defendant liable. See also Ford v. Revlon, Inc., 153 Ariz. 38, 734 P.2d 580 (1987) (employer liable for intentional infliction of emotional distress of plaintiff due to co-employee's actions in repeatedly subjecting plaintiff to physical assaults and vulgar remarks).

2.   Courts are reluctant to subject either internal family disputes or petty but strongly felt antagonisms to the sanctions of tort law. However, when conduct exceeds all reasonable bounds of behavior tolerated by society, courts are likely to find that a claim has been stated. Cf. Miller v. Currie, 50 F.3d 373 (6th Cir.1995) (applying Ohio law) (plaintiff's brother and sister-in-law and the employees of a nursing home prevented her from seeing her ninety-eight-year old mother); Halio v. Lurie, 15 A.D.2d 62, 222 N.Y.S.2d 759 (1961) (man who had jilted a woman wrote her jeering verses and taunting letters); Jackson v. Brown, 904 P.2d 685 (Utah 1995) (last minute cancellation of wedding not enough for outrage, but courting woman, proposing, making arrangements for wedding including applying for license while married to someone else may be); Flamm v. Van Nierop, 56 Misc.2d 1059, 291 N.Y.S.2d 189 (1968) (defendant constantly drove behind plaintiff at a "dangerously close distance," phoned him unnecessarily at his home and business and either hung up or remained on the line in silence, and "dashed" at him in public places).

3.   Is filing a frivolous lawsuit against someone sufficiently outrageous to permit recovery for intentional infliction of emotional distress? After being injured in a fight in a parking lot that was poorly lit, crowded, and chaotic, plaintiff identified a man as her assailant even though she only had a vague impression of the physical characteristics of the person responsible for breaking her leg and someone else had apologized for causing her injury. Even though he had been found not guilty on the criminal charges arising out of her identification, plaintiff filed a civil suit against the man. He counterclaimed for intentional infliction of emotional distress. Davis v. Currier, 704 A.2d 1207 (Maine 1997) (no cause of action for intentional infliction of emotional distress.) What if a juror, found in contempt for failing to show up one day two weeks into the trial of someone accused of torturing and killing six people, was placed alone in a jail cell with the alleged murderer, was questioned and berated by the alleged murderer, and was laughed at by the jailors who placed her there? Johnson v. Wayne County, 213 Mich. App. 143, 540 N.W.2d 66 (1995) (states a cause of action).

4.   Many cases, like the principal case, arise out of workplace behavior. Anderson v. Oklahoma Temp. Svcs., Inc., 925 P.2d 574 (Okla. App. 1996) (supervisor's use of profanity, smoking around employee after being asked to stop, and vulgar behavior not enough to state a cause of action for extreme and outrageous conduct).

5.   What if a hospital had a policy of placing patients infected with the HIV virus in the same rooms as patients who were not, without disclosing that fact? Patient accidentally used his roommate's razor to shave and was then informed by the roommate that roommate was infected with HIV. Patient alleges that the hospital's conduct is outrageous and the he suffered severe emotional distress as a

result. Liability? What other information would you like to have before deciding this issue? Bain v. Wells, 936 S.W.2d 618 (Tenn.1997).

6. Is there any common theme or set of similar factors running through the following cases?

A. State Rubbish Collectors Association v. Siliznoff, page 47.

B. Defendant, a private detective, representing that he was a police officer, threatened to charge the plaintiff, a resident alien, with espionage unless she turned over to him certain private letters in her possession. She suffered severe mental disturbance, and was made seriously ill. The defendant was held liable. Janvier v. Sweeney, [1919] 2 K.B. 316.

C. Defendants, school authorities, called a high school girl to the school office, and bullied and badgered her for a considerable length of time, threatening her with prison and with public disgrace for herself and her family, unless she confessed to immoral conduct with various men. They succeeded in extorting from her a confession of misconduct, of which she was innocent. She suffered severe mental disturbance, and resulting illness. Defendants were held liable. Johnson v. Sampson, 167 Minn. 203, 208 N.W. 814 (1926).

D. *Collecting Agencies.* While reasonable attempts to collect a debt lead to no liability, even though they may be expected to, and do, cause serious mental distress—Berrier v. Beneficial Finance, Inc., 234 F.Supp. 204 (N.D.Ind.1964); Passman v. Commercial Credit Plan of Hammond, Inc., 220 So.2d 758 (La.App.1969)— more excessive conduct may produce a different result. Defendant, a creditor, had plaintiff called to the telephone of her neighbor, with the message that it was an emergency call. Defendant began the conversation by telling plaintiff that "this is going to be a shock; it is as much of a shock to me to have to tell you as it will be to you." When plaintiff said that she was prepared for the message, the defendant let her have it: "This is the Federal Outfitting Company—why don't you pay your bill?" Plaintiff suffered severe nervous shock and resulting serious illness. A complaint alleging these facts was held to state a cause of action. Bowden v. Spiegel, Inc., 96 Cal.App.2d 793, 216 P.2d 571 (1950). A veterinarian and an animal hospital threaten to "do away with" plaintiffs' dog unless plaintiffs paid in cash a bill for treating the dog for injuries suffered when struck by an automobile. See Lawrence v. Stanford and Ashland Terrace Animal Hospital, 655 S.W.2d 927 (Tenn.1983).

E. There are similar cases involving the outrageous tactics of insurance adjusters seeking to force a settlement. Continental Cas. Co. v. Garrett, 173 Miss. 676, 161 So. 753 (1935). See also, as to refusal of a liability insurer to settle a claim, Fletcher v. Western Nat. Life Ins. Co., 10 Cal.App.3d 376, 89 Cal.Rptr. 78 (1970). When the insurance company is reasonable in its refusal to settle a claim, it will not be held liable simply because its client happened to be an excessive worrier about fiscal problems. See Rossignol v. Noel, 289 A.2d 691 (Me.1972).

F. Other cases have involved evicting landlords, Kaufman v. Abramson, 363 F.2d 865 (4th Cir.1966), and even high pressure salesmen. See Turner v. ABC Jalousie Co., 251 S.C. 92, 160 S.E.2d 528 (1968).

7. The plaintiff's sensitivities may be a factor in deeming defendant's conduct extreme and outrageous. Cf. Korbin v. Berlin, 177 So.2d 551 (Fla.App.1965), where defendant approached a six-year-old girl and said to her: "Do you know that your mother took a man away from his wife? Do you know that God is going to punish them? Do you know that a man is sleeping in your mother's room? God will punish them." It was alleged that the child suffered serious mental distress and resulting physical injury. Should a demurrer to a complaint pleading these facts be overruled? Cf. Delta Fin. Co. v. Ganakas, 93 Ga.App. 297, 91 S.E.2d 383 (1956) (eleven-year-old child home alone frightened by threats she would be taken to jail if she did not open

door for defendant seeking to repossess television set). Drejza v. Vaccaro, 650 A.2d 1308 (D.C.App.1994) (outrageousness of police officer's conduct while interviewing rape victim must be evaluated in light of the fact that it occurred only an hour after the rape, when she would be expected to be more susceptible to emotional distress).

8.   Should abuse of plaintiff's sensitivity for race or religion be similarly regarded? In Alcorn v. Anbro Eng'g Inc., 2 Cal.3d 493, 468 P.2d 216, 86 Cal.Rptr. 88 (1970), plaintiff was employed by defendant as a truck driver and was also shop steward for the local union. Defendant's foreman discharged him for pointing out that an employee who was not a member of the union could not drive a truck to a jobsite, shouting "You goddam 'niggers' are not going to tell me about the rules." A claim was allowed. In Contreras v. Crown Zellerbach Corp., 88 Wash.2d 735, 736, 565 P.2d 1173, 1174 (1977), plaintiff alleged that he suffered severe emotional distress after being subjected to "continuous humiliation and embarrassment by reason of racial jokes, slurs and comments made in his presence" by coworkers and supervisors. Held to state a claim.

9.   Should special protection be accorded to pregnant women? When a creditor came to the house of a woman seven months pregnant and screamed profanity, abuse and accusations of dishonesty in the presence of others and she suffered severe emotional disturbance which resulted in a miscarriage, she was allowed to recover in Kirby v. Jules Chain Stores Corp., 210 N.C. 808, 188 S.E. 625 (1936). See Bartow v. Smith, 149 Ohio St. 301, 78 N.E.2d 735 (1948), a holding that otherwise was overruled by Yeager v. Local Union 20, 6 Ohio St.3d 369, 453 N.E.2d 666 (1983).

10.   Other physical conditions that affect plaintiff may be taken into account when defendant is aware of them. Plaintiff was suffering from arterial hypertension, as a result of which he had lost his sight, but was slowly recovering. Knowing his condition, the defendants, representing a creditor to whom plaintiff owed $61.80, wrote him three letters in which they threatened suit, attachment and garnishment and permanent ruination of his credit unless he paid the bill, which he was unable to do. Worry over these letters aggravated plaintiff's condition, and caused him to suffer a relapse and severe attacks of hypertension. Defendants were held liable. Clark v. Associated Retail Credit Men, 105 F.2d 62 (D.C.Cir.1939).

11.   Should protection also be given to the hypersensitive or idiosyncratic plaintiff? In one early landmark case protection was allowed. Plaintiff, an eccentric elderly woman, believed that a pot of gold had been buried in her back yard, and was constantly digging for it. Defendant buried a pot with other contents where she would dig it up. When she did so, he caused her to be escorted by a procession in triumph to the city hall, where she opened the pot under circumstances of extreme public humiliation. She suffered acute mental distress, with resulting serious illness, which apparently further unsettled her reason and contributed to her early death. The "pot of gold" came in the form of a judgment, but only to her heirs. Nickerson v. Hodges, 146 La. 735, 84 So. 37 (1920). Certain emotional human weaknesses for potentially harmful goods may be exploited by sellers of alcohol and tobacco. Should they be liable under an emotional harm theory? See White, Intentional Exploitation of Man's Known Weaknesses, 9 Hous.L.Rev. 889 (1972).

▸ Taylor v. Vallelunga

District Court of Appeal of California, 1959.
171 Cal.App.2d 107, 339 P.2d 910.

O'DONNELL, JUSTICE pro tem. * * * In the first count, plaintiff Clifford Gerlach alleges that on December 25, 1956, defendants struck and beat him causing him bodily injury for which he seeks damages. In the second count, plaintiff and appellant Gail E. Taylor incorporates by reference the charging allegations of the first count and proceeds to allege that she is the daughter of plaintiff Clifford Gerlach, that she was present at and witnessed the beating inflicted upon her father by defendants, and that as a result thereof, she suffered severe fright and emotional distress. She seeks damages for the distress so suffered. It is not alleged that any physical disability or injury resulted from the mental distress. A general demurrer to the second count of the complaint was interposed by defendants. The demurrer was sustained and appellant was granted ten days leave to amend. Appellant failed to amend and judgment of dismissal of the second count was entered. The appeal is from the judgment of dismissal.

The California cases have for some time past allowed recovery of damages where physical injury resulted from intentionally subjecting the plaintiff to serious mental distress. [C] In the Siliznoff case [page 47] the Supreme Court extended the right of recovery to situations where no physical injury follows the suffering of mental distress, saying that "a cause of action is established when it is shown that one, in the absence of any privilege, intentionally subjects another to the mental suffering incident to serious threats to his physical well-being, whether or not the threats are made under such circumstances as to constitute a technical assault." [C] In arriving at this result the court relied in substantial part upon the development of the law in this field of torts as traced by the American Law Institute, and it quotes with approval [c] section 46, as amended, of the Restatement of Torts, (Restatement of the Law, 1948 Supplement, Torts, § 46) which reads: "One who, without a privilege to do so, intentionally causes severe emotional distress to another is liable (a) for such emotional distress, and (b) for bodily harm resulting from it." In explanation of the meaning of the term "intentionally" as it is employed in said section 46, the Reporter says in subdivision (a) of that section: "An intention to cause severe emotional distress exists when the act is done for the purpose of causing the distress or with knowledge on the part of the actor that severe emotional distress is substantially certain to be produced by his conduct. See Illustration 3." Illustration 3 referred to reads as follows: "A is sitting on her front porch watching her husband B, who is standing on the sidewalk, C, who hates B and is friendly to A, *whose presence is known to him*, stabs B, killing him. C is liable to A for the mental anguish, grief and horror he causes." [Emphasis added.]

The failure of the second count of the complaint in the case at bar to meet the requirements of section 46 of the Restatement of Torts is at once apparent. There is no allegation that defendants knew that appellant was present and witnessed the beating that was administered to her father; nor is there any allegation that the beating was administered for the purpose of causing her to suffer emotional distress, or, in the alternative, that defendants knew that severe emotional distress was substantially certain to be produced by their conduct. * * *

Judgment affirmed.

NOTES AND QUESTIONS

1. California has continued to require that the conduct not only be intentional and outrageous, but also directed at the plaintiff or take place in the presence of the plaintiff, with the defendant's awareness. Family members filed suit against mortuaries and crematoria, alleging that the remains of their relatives had been mishandled, by having organs harvested from them, by disposing of them in the kiln of a ceramics company, and by comingling the remains of many bodies. Complaint did not state a cause of action for intentional infliction of emotional distress because plaintiffs did not allege that the conduct was directed primarily at the family members or done to cause them emotional distress. Christensen v. Superior Court of Los Angeles Cty., 54 Cal.3d 868, 820 P.2d 181 (1991).

2. Why not "transferred intent," as in Talmage v. Smith, page 28? There is one case, Lambert v. Brewster, 97 W.Va. 124, 125 S.E. 244 (1924), in which it was mentioned by way of analogy when plaintiff recovered for mental disturbance at the peril of another. Is it desirable to extend the liability to every one who may be shocked or frightened at conduct directed at a third person? What if three million people witness an assassination of a President on television? Defendant plays a practical joke on a neighbor that humiliates him and produces physical illness. This result produces severe emotional disturbance in members of his family. How far does liability extend?

3. A case allowing recovery when plaintiff was present is Hill v. Kimball, 76 Tex. 210, 13 S.W. 59 (1890), where defendant inflicted a violent, bloody battery upon two people in the presence of a pregnant woman and she suffered a miscarriage as the result of her mental disturbance. See also Rogers v. Williard, 144 Ark. 587, 223 S.W. 15 (1920).

4. In Knierim v. Izzo, 22 Ill.2d 73, 174 N.E.2d 157 (1961), defendant threatened a woman that he would murder her husband and then, out of her presence, carried out the threat. Her claim was upheld. How did it differ from the main case?

5. When a five-year-old girl was molested by a teenage baby sitter, the child's mother who learned about it later was allowed a claim against the sitter but not against his parents for the emotional distress she suffered from learning about what had happened. See Schurk v. Christensen, 80 Wash.2d 652, 497 P.2d 937 (1972). How might this case be distinguished from the main case?

6. A number of courts have required that plaintiff be present at the time. Thus, recovery was denied in Koontz v. Keller, 52 Ohio App. 265, 3 N.E.2d 694 (1936), where defendant murdered plaintiff's sister, and she later discovered the body, and in Ellsworth v. Massacar, 215 Mich. 511, 184 N.W. 408 (1921), where plaintiff made a later discovery of an attack on her husband. Should this be a "black letter" requirement? What if she were to learn of it ten years later? The Restatement has included it as a restriction, but has supplied a "caveat. See Restatement (Second) of Torts § 46(2).

7. *Dead Bodies.* A good many cases have allowed recovery for mental distress at the intentional mutilation or disinterment of a dead body, or for interference with proper burial. See, for example, Alderman v. Ford, 146 Kan. 698, 72 P.2d 981 (1937); Gostkowski v. Roman Catholic Church, 262 N.Y. 320, 186 N.E. 798 (1933); Papieves v. Lawrence, 437 Pa. 373, 263 A.2d 118 (1970). In most of these cases, the courts have talked of a property right in the body, said to be in the next of kin or a group of close relatives, which serves as a foundation for the action for mental disturbance. See, for example, Whaley v. County of Tuscola, 58 F.3d 1111 (6th Cir.1995) (applying Michigan law) and Brotherton v. Cleveland, 923 F.2d 477 (6th

Cir.1991) (applying Ohio law) (both cases involving unauthorized removal of corneas and eyeballs by coroner). Apart from the difficulty of deciding who owns it, this is at best an unsatisfactory kind of property, which cannot be sold or conveyed unless it should happen to be willed to a hospital, can be used only for the one purpose of burial, and not only has no pecuniary value but is a source of liability for funeral expenses. But suppose an eye from the body had been willed to X, a blind person who might be able to see again. Y, who hated X, mutilated the eye. What should be the basis, if any, of X's claim against Y? → *Some sort of destruction of property?*

In Gadbury v. Bleitz, 133 Wash. 134, 233 P. 299 (1925), where the body was held without burial with demand for payment of another debt, the court avoided difficulties surrounding right of ownership by recognizing that the tort was in reality the intentional infliction of mental distress upon the survivors by extreme outrage. In accord is Stephens v. Waits, 53 Ga.App. 44, 184 S.E. 781 (1936).

8. The classic article on the infliction of mental distress is Magruder, Mental and Emotional Distress in the Law of Torts, 49 Harv.L.Rev. 1033 (1936). For general review of this Section, see Prosser, Insult and Outrage, 44 Calif.L.Rev. 40 (1956); Wade, Tort Liability for Abusive and Insulting Language, 4 Vand.L.Rev. 63 (1950); Partlett, Tort Liability and the American Way: Reflections on Liability for Emotional Distress, Am.J. Comp.L. 601 (1997).

6. TRESPASS TO LAND

Dougherty v. Stepp

Supreme Court of North Carolina, 1835.
18 N.C. 371.

action to recover damages from unlawful or visibly enclosed entry enclosed land

whereas he or she the broke close

This was an action of trespass quare clausum fregit, tried at Buncombe on the last Circuit, before his Honor Judge Martin. The only proof introduced by the plaintiff to establish an act of trespass, was, that the defendant had entered on the unenclosed land of the plaintiff, with a surveyor and chain carriers, and actually surveyed a part of it, claiming it as his own, but without marking trees or cutting bushes. This, his Honor held not to be a trespass, and the jury (under his instructions,) found a verdict for the defendant, and the plaintiff appealed. * * *

Holding: judge erred in his instruction to the jury

RUFFIN, CHIEF JUSTICE. In the opinion of the Court, there is error in the instructions given to the jury. The amount of damages may depend on the acts done on the land, and the extent of injury to it therefrom. But it is an elementary principle, that every unauthorized, and therefore unlawful entry, into the close of another, is a trespass. From every such entry against the will of the possessor, the law infers some damage; if nothing more, the treading down the grass or herbage, or as here, the shrubbery.

Rule of Law: any unauthorized entrance onto closed land is a trespass

Judgment reversed, and new trial ordered.

NOTES AND QUESTIONS

1. We are here concerned only with intentional trespass to land. There may be negligent trespass, but it is governed by the ordinary rules applicable to negligence actions. One of these is that when the entry upon the land is merely negligent, proof of some actual damage is essential to the cause of action. Thus, the word trespass may be used to describe the kind of interest that defendant has invaded. Tradition-

ally, that interest has been described as the right to exclusive possession of land. Restatement (Second) of Torts § 165.

2. Is the trespass intentional when the defendant enters the land in the honest and reasonable belief that it is his own? See Glade v. Dietert, 156 Tex. 382, 387, 295 S.W.2d 642, 645 (1956) (dictum). Cf. Ranson v. Kitner, page 23 and Serota v. M. & M. Utilities, Inc., 55 Misc.2d 286, 285 N.Y.S.2d 121 (1967), page 24, note 2.

3. In addition to a cause of action for trespass, the plaintiff might have a cause of action for ejectment. Ejectment would lie if the defendant was in possession of the land, rather than just having been on it temporarily. A judgment in her favor would entitle plaintiff to the sheriff's help in removing the defendant from her land. If the plaintiff is in possession of the land, but the defendant is claiming to own it, a quiet title action would lie.

4. In a trespass action, plaintiff will be awarded nominal damages if there are no actual (compensatory) damages. Why nominal damages when the trespass does no harm? Why bother? The explanation sometimes given is that the action of trespass is frequently either a suit intended to try title or is directed at the vindication of the legal right, without which the defendant's conduct, if repeated, might ripen into a prescriptive right. Hence there is no room for the application of the maxim, *de minimis non curat lex*. See 1 T. Street, Foundations of Legal Liability, 25 (1906). On the other hand, if the law declared that there was no cause of action for invasions that caused only nominal damages, it would not be possible to acquire a "prescriptive" right. At common law, one reason underlying the rule was to keep the peace. Is the rule justified today? What about punitive damages? Should they be available if only nominal damages were awarded? See Jacques v. Steenberg Homes, Inc., 209 Wisc.2d 605, 563 N.W.2d 154 (1997)(upholding punitive damages award even though no compensatory damages were proved where defendant had bulldozed a path in the snow across plaintiff's field to deliver a mobile home despite plaintiff's repeated refusals to permit the defendant to cross his land to make the delivery).

5. When a trespassory invasion is found, the fact that defendant's conduct was socially useful or even beneficial to plaintiff does not affect liability. See Harmony Ditch Co. v. Sweeney, 31 Wyo. 1, 222 P. 577 (1924); Longenecker v. Zimmerman, 175 Kan. 719, 267 P.2d 543 (1954).

6. Of course, if the plaintiff does suffer compensatory damages, those too are recoverable in the trespass action. What about emotional distress damages? Defendant landlord, seeking to persuade tenants to vacate a townhouse, entered the premises without their consent, changed the locks on the garage, blocked the driveway, and repeatedly threatened and harassed the tenants. Johnson v. Marcel, 251 Va. 58, 465 S.E.2d 815 (1996)(where alleged trespass is deliberate and accompanied by aggravating circumstances, emotional distress damages may be recovered even in the absence of physical injury).

Bradley v. American Smelting and Refining Co.

Supreme Court of Washington, 1985.
104 Wash.2d 677, 709 P.2d 782.

CALLOW, JUSTICE. This comes before us on a certification from the United States District Court for the Western District of Washington. [The parties had filed cross motions for summary judgment with the trial court judge.]

Plaintiffs, (landowners on Vashon Island,) had sued for damages in trespass and nuisance from the deposit on their property of microscopic, airborne particles of heavy metals which came from the American Smelting and Refining Company (ASARCO) copper smelter at Ruston, Washington. * * * Plaintiff's property is located some 4 miles north of defendant's smelter. Defendant's primary copper smelter (also referred to as the Tacoma smelter), has operated in its present location since 1890. * * * As a part of the industrial process of smelting copper at the Tacoma smelter, various gases such as sulfur dioxide and particulate matter, including arsenic, cadmium and other metals, are emitted. Particulate matter is composed of distinct particles of matter other than water, which cannot be detected by the human senses. * * *

Facts

The insistence that a trespass involve an invasion by a "thing" or "object" was repudiated in the well known (but not particularly influential) case of Martin v. Reynolds Metals Co., [221 Or. 86, 342 P.2d 790 (1959)], which held that gaseous and particulate fluorides from an aluminum smelter constituted a trespass for purposes of the statute of limitations: "[L]iability on the theory of trespass has been recognized where the harm was produced by the vibration of the soil or by the concussion of the air which, of course, is nothing more than the movement of molecules one against the other." The view recognizing a trespassory invasion where there is no "thing" which can be seen with the naked eye undoubtedly runs counter to the definition of trespass expressed in some quarters. [Citing the Restatement of Torts and Prosser]. It is quite possible that in an earlier day when science had not yet peered into the molecular and atomic world of small particles, the courts could not fit an invasion through unseen physical instrumentalities into the requirement that a trespass can result only for a direct invasion. But in this atomic age even the uneducated know the great and awful force contained in the atom and what it can do to a man's property if it is released. In fact, the now famous equation $E = MC^2$ has taught us that mass and energy are equivalents and that our concept of "things" must be reframed. If these observations on science in relation to the law of trespass should appear theoretical and unreal in the abstract, they become very practical and real to the possessor of land when the unseen force cracks the foundation of his house. The force is just as real if it is chemical in nature and must be awakened by the intervention of another agency before it does harm. * * *

[*Martin*] was an action in trespass brought against the defendant corporation for causing gases and fluoride particulates to settle on the plaintiffs' land making it unfit for livestock. * * * The court stated: "Trespass and private nuisance are separate fields of tort liability relating to actionable interference with the possession of land. They may be distinguished by comparing the interest invaded; and actionable invasion of a possessor's interest in the exclusive possession of land is a trespass; an actionable invasion of a possessor's interest in the use and enjoyment of his land is a nuisance."

def. trespass to land & nuisance

Martin v. Reynolds held: actionable invasion of a possessor's interest in exclusive poss of land is a trespass

in use/enjoyment of his land is nuisance

We hold that theories of trespass and nuisance are not inconsistent, that the theories may apply concurrently, and that the injured party may proceed under both theories when the elements of both actions are present. * * *

Having held that there was an intentional trespass, we adopt, in part, the rationale of Borland v. Sanders Lead Co., 369 So.2d 523, 529 (Ala.1979), which stated in part: "Although we view this decision as an application, and not an extension, of our present law of trespass, we feel that a brief restatement and summary of the principles involved in this area would be appropriate. Whether an invasion of property interest is a trespass or a nuisance does not depend upon whether the intruding interest is 'tangible' or 'intangible.' Instead, an analysis must be made to determine the interest interfered with. If the intrusion interferes with the right to exclusive possession of property, the law of trespass applies. If the intrusion is to the use and enjoyment of property, the law of nuisance applies. As previously observed, however, the remedies of trespass and nuisance are not necessarily mutually exclusive. * * *"

We accept and approve the elements of trespass by airborne pollutants as set forth in the Borland case. * * *

When airborne particles are transitory or quickly dissipate, they do not interfere with a property owner's possessory rights and, therefore, are properly denominated as nuisances. [Cc] When, however, the particles or substance accumulates on the land and does not pass away, then a trespass has occurred. [Cc] While at common law any trespass entitled a landowner to recover nominal or punitive damages for the invasion of his property, such a rule is not appropriate under the circumstances before us. No useful purpose would be served by sanctioning actions in trespass by every landowner within a hundred miles of a manufacturing plant. Manufacturers would be harassed and the litigious few would cause the escalation of costs to the detriment of many. The elements that we have adopted for an action in trespass from Borland require that a plaintiff has suffered actual and substantial damages. Since this is an element of the action, the plaintiff who cannot show that actual and substantial damages have been suffered should be subject to dismissal of his cause upon a motion for summary judgment. * * *

The United States District Court for the Western District of Washington shall be notified for such further action as it deems appropriate.

[The trial court judge then granted ASARCO's motion for summary judgment on the trespass count, finding that the concentrations of cadmium and arsenic in plaintiffs' soil were not harmful and thus plaintiffs could not establish a necessary element of their environmental trespass claim, actual and substantial damage to the property itself. Bradley v. American Smelting & Refining Co., 635 F.Supp. 1154 (W.D.Wash.1986).]

NOTES AND QUESTIONS

1. Since the tort protects plaintiff's alleged right to exclusive possession of his land, traditionally there has been a requirement that the invasion be a physical one,

which usually must be accomplished by a tangible mass. See Ryan v. Emmetsburg, 232 Iowa 600, 4 N.W.2d 435 (1942). Thus, in Amphitheaters, Inc. v. Portland Meadows, 184 Or. 336, 198 P.2d 847 (1948), it was held to be no trespass where race track lights were reflected onto plaintiff's outdoor movie theater. Would any other action lie? *nuisance because lights interfere w/ use/enjoyment of property*

2. Trespass has often been contrasted with the tort of nuisance that protects plaintiff's use and enjoyment of the land. In an action for nuisance, courts usually require some actual damage, do not require a physical invasion of land, and take into account the social utility of defendant's activity. See Chapter 16, Nuisance.

Herrin v. Sutherland

Supreme Court of Montana, 1925.
74 Mont. 587, 241 P. 328.

* * * [T]he defendant, while engaged in hunting ducks and other migratory game birds, and while standing on the lands of another, repeatedly discharged a Winchester shotgun at water fowl in flight over plaintiff's said premises * * * "to plaintiff's damage in the sum of $10." *Facts:*
* * *

After defendant's general demurrer * * * was overruled, he declined to answer, and his default was entered. Upon the suggestion of counsel for plaintiff that only nominal damages would be demanded, the court rendered judgment in favor of the plaintiff for damages in the sum of $1. From this judgment the defendant has appealed.

CALLAWAY, C.J. * * * It must be held that when the defendant, although standing upon the land of another, fired a shotgun over plaintiff's premises, dwelling and cattle, he interfered with the "quiet, undisturbed, peaceful enjoyment of the plaintiff," and thus committed a technical trespass at least. The plaintiff was the owner of the land. "Land," says Blackstone, "in its legal significance has an indefinite extent, upwards as well as downwards; whoever owns the land possesses all the space upwards to an indefinite extent; such is the maxim of the law." * * *

Issue! whether there is still an action of trespass for objects passing over the land but never actually touching it

Sir Frederick Pollock, in the tenth edition of his valuable work on Torts, page 363, observes that it has been doubted whether it is a trespass to pass over land without touching the soil, as one may in a balloon, or to cause a material object as a shot fired from a gun, to pass over it. * * * Continuing, he observes:

"As regards shooting, it would be strange if we could object to shots being fired point blank across our land only in the event of actual injury being caused, and the passage of the foreign object in the air above our soil being thus a mere incident and a distinct trespass to person or property."

But he concludes that when taking into account the extreme flight of projectiles fired from modern artillery which may pass thousands of feet above the land, the subject is not without difficulty. That shortly it will become one of considerable importance is indicated by the rapid approach of the airplane as an instrumentality of commerce, as is suggested in a valuable note found in 32 Harvard Law Review, 569. However, it seems to be the consensus of the holdings of the courts in this country that the air space, at least near the ground, is almost as inviolable as the soil itself. * * * It is a matter of common knowledge that the shotgun is a firearm of short range. To be subjected to the danger incident to and reasonably to be anticipated from the firing of this weapon at water fowl in flight over one's dwelling house and cattle would seem to be far from inconsequential, and while plaintiff's allegations are very general in character, it cannot be said that a cause of action is not stated, for nominal damages at least. * * *

The judgment is affirmed.

NOTES AND QUESTIONS

1.   A, disturbed at night by the howling of a cat on the roof of B's adjoining house, shoots the cat. The bullet remains in the cat, and neither bullet nor cat touches the ground. Is this a trespass to B's land? Davies v. Bennison, 22 Tasmanian L.Rep. 52 (1922).

2.   During a dispute between neighbors over a backyard fence, one of them extends her arm over the fence, without touching it. Is this a trespass? Hannabalson v. Sessions, 116 Iowa 457, 90 N.W. 93 (1902). What about a scaffold that hangs over plaintiff's property? See Geller v. Brownstone Condominium Ass'n, 82 Ill. App.3d 334, 37 Ill.Dec. 805, 402 N.E.2d 807 (1980).

3.   *"Cujus est solum, ejus est usque ad coelum et ad inferos."* [Whose is the soil, his it is also unto the sky and the depths.] Coke, Littleton, 4a. How practical a rule today?

4.   The Restatement of Torts, §§ 159, 194, had provided that air travel was a trespass but may be privileged. For historical treatment, see R. Wright, The Law of Air Space (1968); Sweeny, Adjusting the Conflicting Interests of Landowner and Aviator in Anglo–American Law, 3 J.Air L. & Com. 329 and 531 (1932); Thurston, Trespass to Air Space, in Harvard Legal Essays, 501 (1934). The Restatement (Second) of Torts § 159, now provides that air travel is a trespass only if it "enters into immediate reaches of the air space next to the land, and * * * interferes substantially with the others' use and enjoyment of the land." This is essentially the position in Hinman v. Pacific Air Transport, 84 F.2d 755 (9th Cir.1936); Freeman v. United States, 167 F.Supp. 541 (D.Okl.1958) ("immediate reaches").

5.   In effect, the Restatement approach changes a fundamental aspect of the tort of trespass (see Dougherty v. Stepp, page 63). Some courts have been more explicit in doing so and have held that flight by aircraft is never trespassory and plaintiff's remedy lies in negligence or nuisance. See Atkinson v. Bernard, Inc., 223 Or. 624, 355 P.2d 229 (1960); Nestle v. Santa Monica, 6 Cal.3d 920, 496 P.2d 480, 101 Cal.Rptr. 568 (1972). What is the advantage to plaintiff in these approaches?

6.   When government overflights have substantially affected habitability of the land below, a court may find a "taking" within the meaning of the Fifth Amendment to the United States Constitution and the government will be required to compensate the owner. See, for example, Brown v. United States, 73 F.3d 1100 (Fed.Cir.1996) (owners of recreational ranch sought compensation for taking based on noise from low overflights by Air Force planes doing touch and go exercises at adjacent airstrip in remote West Texas, near Mexican border). See also, R. Epstein, Takings: Private Property and the Power of Eminent Domain, pp. 41–49 (1985). Local government is subject to the same constitutional responsibility. See Griggs v. Allegheny County, 369 U.S. 84 (1962) (county operated airport).

7.   For treatment of noise and vibration as a nuisance and of the application of inverse condemnation, see Boomer v. Atlantic Cement Co., Inc., 26 N.Y.2d 219, 257 N.E.2d 870, 309 N.Y.S.2d 312 (1970), page 819. Remedies for ground damage as the result of airline crashes are considered in the chapters on negligence and strict liability.

8.   The interest in the possession of land also extends below the surface, and may present similar problems there. The question frequently arises in connection with mining law. It is held by most jurisdictions that it is a trespass to mine under another's land. North Jellico Coal Co. v. Helton, 187 Ky. 394, 219 S.W. 185 (1920); Chartiers Block Coal Co. v. Mellon, 152 Pa. 286, 25 A. 597 (1893). In many of the western states, however, the miner is permitted to follow the vein wherever it may lead, so long as it is unbroken.

9.   In Edwards v. Sims, 232 Ky. 791, 24 S.W.2d 619 (1929), the plaintiff owned a tract of land on a hill. Defendant discovered on his adjoining land the entrance to a cave, which extended a considerable distance under plaintiff's land. Defendant developed the cave, advertised it, and conducted tourists through it. Plaintiff brought suit to compel a survey of the cave and an accounting, claiming that the repeated entries by defendant and his tourists were trespasses upon plaintiff's land and that defendant was accountable to plaintiff for a portion of the profits he had made. Plaintiff also asked an injunction preventing further trespasses on that part of the cave under his land. The trial court ordered the survey. The Court of Appeals refused to prohibit it, relying on the maxim "cujus est solum," and saying: "the owner of realty * * * is entitled to the free and unfettered control of his own land above, upon, and beneath the surface. So whatever is in a direct line between the surface of the land and the center of the earth belongs to the owner of the surface." Both an injunction and damages were awarded. The dissenting opinion of Logan, J., is well worth reading as a piece of literature. But cf. Boehringer v. Montalto, 142 Misc. 560, 254 N.Y.S. 276 (1931) (sewer line at depth of 150 feet).

◄ Rogers v. Board of Road Com'rs for Kent County

Supreme Court of Michigan, 1947.
319 Mich. 661, 30 N.W.2d 358.

REID, JUSTICE. Plaintiff instituted this suit to recover damages because of the death of her husband, Theodore Rogers, which plaintiff claims was caused by the trespass and negligence of the defendant board of county road commissioners. Defendant filed a motion to dismiss, based on the pleadings and on the ground of governmental immunity. The lower court granted defendant's motion and dismissed the cause. Plaintiff appeals from the judgment of dismissal of her cause.

Plaintiff claims that for two winter seasons previous to the date of the fatal injury to her husband the defendant board of road commissioners had obtained a license to place a snow fence in decedent's field parallel to the roadway past decedent's farm. Plaintiff claims in her declaration that the placing of the snow fence there was with the distinct understanding and agreement between the defendant and decedent that all of the fence together with the anchor posts should be removed by defendant at the end of each winter season when the necessity for snow fences for that season no longer existed. [The defendant failed to remove an anchor post, and plaintiff's husband, driving his mowing machine, was thrown to the ground when the bar of the machine struck the post, and received injuries that caused his death.] * * *

The court dismissed plaintiff's cause of action, ruling that the action was plainly an action based upon negligence, that there was no basis for any finding of trespass and that the defense of governmental immunity applied to the facts set forth in plaintiff's declaration.

Failure to remove the anchor stake upon expiration of the license to have it on defendant's land was a continuing trespass and is alleged by plaintiff to have been a proximate cause of the damage for which she seeks to recover.

"§ 160. Failure to remove a thing placed on the land pursuant to a license or other privilege

"A trespass, actionable under the rule stated in § 158, may be committed by the continued presence on the land of a structure, chattel or other thing which the actor or his predecessor in legal interest therein has placed thereon

"(a) with the consent of the person then in possession of the land, if the actor fails to remove it after the consent has been effectively terminated, or

"(b) pursuant to a privilege conferred on the actor irrespective of the possessor's consent, if the actor fails to remove it after the privilege has been terminated, by the accomplishment of its purpose or otherwise." Restatement of the Law, Torts, p. 368. * * *

The judgment of the court dismissing the cause of action is reversed and the cause remanded for such further proceedings as shall be found necessary.

NOTES AND QUESTIONS

1. A privileged entry onto the land of another may be limited not only by time and space, but also by purpose. In Brown v. Dellinger, 355 S.W.2d 742 (Tex.Civ.App. 1962), two children, who had been permitted to play in their neighbor's yard, on one occasion improperly ignited a charcoal burner in the garage and caused $28,000 worth of damages. They were treated as trespassers. In Copeland v. Hubbard Broadcasting, Inc., 526 N.W.2d 402 (Minn.App.1995), the Copelands gave permission to their veterinarian to bring with him to their home a student who said she was considering a career in veterinary medicine. She did not disclose that she was an employee of a local television station doing a report on their veterinarian's practice. While in plaintiffs' home, she secretly videotaped the treatment of their cat. When the videotape of their home was broadcast as part of the report, the Copelands sued for trespass. The court found that there was a trespass because the entrant moved beyond the scope of the Copelands' invitation by using the visit for something other than educational or vocational purposes.

2. At common law trespass would not lie unless defendant entered the land illegally (breaking of the close). As the principal case reflects, the distinction between trespass and case is no longer controlling, and a trespass can arise today

when a visitor who entered land with the consent of the possessor "overstays" his welcome. Of course, the visitor must be aware that he no longer has the possessor's consent to remain.

3. Should the possessor have the right to revoke the welcome mat for any reason? Suppose he simply does not like the visitor's looks? See Mitchell v. Mitchell, 54 Minn. 301, 55 N.W. 1134 (1893); Davis v. Stone, 120 Mass. 228 (1876). See generally Gibson, Visitor's Refusal to Leave Premises, 21 Clev.St.L.Rev. 154 (1972).

4. *Consequences of Trespass.* Note that in the principal case the defendant is held liable to the wife for the death of her husband resulting from the trespass, without any question of negligence in failing to remove the anchor post. See Prosser, Transferred Intent, 45 Tex.L.Rev. 650, 658–671 (1967). Compare the following:

A.   Defendant, a trespasser, entered plaintiff's blacksmith shop, and built a fire in the forge. After he left, and without any showing of negligence on the part of defendant, the shop caught fire and was destroyed. Defendant was held liable for the loss of the shop on the basis of the trespass. Wyant v. Crouse, 127 Mich. 158, 86 N.W. 527 (1901).

B.   Defendant's employee, delivering a package at plaintiff's residence, entered a side door into a sun porch, left the door open, and crossed the porch to knock at an inner door. Plaintiff's child, whom defendant did not see, fell through the open door and was injured. The jury were permitted to find that he was a trespasser, and to return a verdict against defendant. Keesecker v. G.M. McKelvey Co., 141 Ohio St. 162, 47 N.E.2d 211 (1943).

C.   Plaintiffs, husband and wife, arrived home to find a parked car blocking their driveway. Defendants, neighbors of the plaintiffs, were loading the trunk with tools that they had just used to dig a trench across plaintiffs' driveway. Defendants and plaintiffs argued about the trench. Plaintiff went into the house to call the police. When she returned three minutes later, she found her husband lying face-down in a mud puddle and saw the defendants driving away. Husband was pronounced dead from a heart attack in the Emergency Room. Court held that damages (heart attack) caused by a trespasser need not be foreseeable to be compensable. Baker v. Skymkiv, 6 Ohio St.3d 151, 451 N.E.2d 811 (1983).

5. *Restrictions on Right to Exclude Persons from Premises.* Some of the federal civil rights acts require certain landowners and possessors of land to make their premises open to the public without discrimination, and the Constitution has been held to impose other restrictions.

A.   *Anti-discrimination Statutes.* The Federal Civil Rights Act of 1964, 42 U.S.C.A. § 2000a, requires all places of public accommodation whose business affects interstate commerce to serve customers "without discrimination or segregation on the ground of race, color, religion, or national origin." Members of protected groups may enter a restaurant and demand service, and remain to insist upon it after they are ordered to leave. They cannot be prosecuted for criminal trespass when they do so. Hamm v. Rock Hill, 379 U.S. 306 (1964), rehearing denied, 379 U.S. 995. In accord is Dilworth v. Riner, 343 F.2d 226 (5th Cir.1965), as to a civil suit for trespass. Cf. Restatement (Second) of Torts § 886.

B.   *Freedom of Speech.* A private individual may control territory so extensive that it may become "public" for the purposes of First Amendment freedom of speech. See Marsh v. Alabama, 326 U.S. 501 (1946) (company town). This limits the owner's power to restrict entry and expression upon his land; he would have the same responsibility as the government to allow peaceful picketing. See also Hudgens

v. N.L.R.B., 424 U.S. 507 (1976) (private property would be deemed public for First Amendment purposes if the landowner had virtually supplanted a municipal government.) In PruneYard Shopping Center v. Robins, 447 U.S. 74 (1980), the Supreme Court found that a provision in the California constitution that allows individuals to exercise their free speech rights on the property of a privately-owned shopping center does not violate the owner's property rights. Nuances of this topic are usually treated in Constitutional Law. See generally Schwartz, A Landholder's Right to Possession of Property Versus A Citizen's Right of Free Speech: Tort Law As A Resource For Conflict Resolution, 45 U.Cin.L.Rev. 1 (1976).

7.   TRESPASS TO CHATTELS

Glidden v. Szybiak

Supreme Court of New Hampshire, 1949.
95 N.H. 318, 63 A.2d 233.

Actions at law under the provisions of R.L. c. 180, §§ 23, 24, to recover for a dog bite sustained by the plaintiff Elaine Glidden upon September 29, 1946, and for medical expenses incurred by her father, Harold Glidden. Trial by the Court, with verdicts for the plaintiffs. The plaintiff Elaine Glidden, who was four years old at the time of the occurrence here involved, left her home about noon on the day of her injury, to go to a neighborhood store for candy. On the porch of the store Elaine encountered a dog named Toby and engaged in play with him. She eventually climbed on his back and pulled his ears. The dog snapped at her and bit her nose, inflicting wounds for which a recovery is sought. She was treated by two physicians and a successful result obtained. Such scars as were left are "in no way disfiguring but discernible on close view." The dog Toby was owned by the defendant Jane Szybiak, an unmarried daughter of the other two defendants, 26 years of age at the time of the trial, living with her parents. * * * The defendants also excepted to the denial of their motions for judgment at the close of the evidence. The Court also made the following finding: "Elaine is found to have been of such tender years as to be incapable of being guilty of contributory negligence in her conduct toward the dog Toby. If she was too young to be guilty of negligence, she cannot be found to have been guilty of a trespass or a tort at the time she received her injury." To this finding the defendants duly excepted.

BRANCH, CHIEF JUSTICE. The statute under which these actions were brought reads as follows: "23. Liability of owner. Any person to whom or to whose property damage may be occasioned by a dog not owned or kept by him shall be entitled to recover such damage of the person who owns or keeps the dog, or has it in possession, unless the damage was occasioned to him while he was engaged in the commission of a trespass or other tort."

It is the contention of the defendants that the plaintiff Elaine was engaged in the commission of a trespass at the time of her injury and is, therefore, barred from recovery under the statute. The law in regard to a trespass to chattels is thus summarized in the Restatement of the Law of Torts, s. 218: "One who without consensual or other privilege to do so, uses or otherwise intentionally intermeddles with a chattel which is in possession of another is liable for a trespass to such person if, (a) the chattel is impaired as to its condition, quality or value, or (b) the possessor is deprived of the use of the chattel for a substantial time, or (c) bodily harm is thereby caused to the possessor or harm is caused to some person or thing in which the possessor has a legally protected interest." In comment (f) to clauses (a) and (b), it is pointed out that "the interest of a possessor of a chattel in its inviolability, unlike the similar interest of a possessor of land, is not given legal protection by an action for nominal damages for harmless intermeddlings with the chattel. * * * Sufficient legal protection of the possessor's interest in the mere inviolability of his chattel is afforded by his privilege to use reasonable force to protect his possession against even harmless interference."

No claim was advanced at the trial that the dog Toby was in any way injured by the conduct of the plaintiff Elaine. Consequently she could not be held liable for a trespass to the dog. Consequently her conduct did not constitute a trespass which will prevent her recovery under the statute here invoked. * * *

Judgment on the verdict against the defendant Jane. * * *

NOTES AND QUESTIONS

1. Might plaintiff have avoided defendant's argument on this issue altogether? What did the New Hampshire legislature mean by "trespass"?

2. The earliest cases in which trespass was applied to chattels involved asportation, or carrying off, and a special form of the writ, known as trespass de bonis asportatis ("d.b.a.") was developed for such situations. Later the action was extended to cases where the chattels were damaged but not taken, as where animals were killed or beaten. It at last became applicable to any physical interference with a chattel in the possession of the plaintiff. Thus Parker v. Mise, 27 Ala. 480, 62 Am.Dec. 776 (1855) (shooting dog); Bruch v. Carter, 32 N.J.L. 554 (1867) (moving horse from one place to another); Cole v. Schweer, 159 Ill.App. 278 (1910) (releasing fish).

3. Trespass to chattels is now quite universally limited to intentional interferences with them. Thus in Mountain States Tel. & Tel. Co. v. Horn Tower Const. Co., 147 Colo. 166, 363 P.2d 175 (1961), it was held that there was no trespass when defendant unintentionally severed plaintiff's telephone conduit. An action would lie for negligent interference that causes damage, but that action has been absorbed into the general field of negligence actions, and no longer is called trespass.

4. As in the case of trespass to land, the conduct is treated as intentional even though the defendant acts under an innocent mistake, as where he drives off the plaintiff's sheep, believing that they are his own. Dexter v. Cole, 6 Wis. 319, 70 Am.Dec. 465 (1857).

5. The only doubtful question as to trespass to chattels is whether the action will lie without proof of any actual damage to the chattel. If there is actual dispossession, as in Wintringham v. Lafoy, 7 Cow. 735 (N.Y.1827), where an officer by mistake levied execution upon goods belonging to the plaintiff, the deprivation of possession is regarded as damage in itself, and no other is required. But where there is merely interference with the chattel, as by laying hands on a horse or an automobile, the few American decisions have held that the action cannot be

maintained without proof of actual damages. Marentille v. Oliver, 2 N.J.L. 379 (1808); Paul v. Slason, 22 Vt. 231, 54 Am.Dec. 75 (1850); Graves v. Severens, 40 Vt. 636 (1868). In accord is the Restatement (Second) of Torts, § 218. What should be the result if defendant places a bumper sticker for the Texas Beef Council on Oprah Winfrey's car?

6.   English writers have contended that the analogy of trespass to land should apply to trespass to chattels, and that there is a real necessity for an action for nominal damages to protect property from intermeddlers. See Salmond and Heuston, Torts 89–90 (20th ed. 1992), citing several British cases apparently holding this, including Thurston v. Charles, 21 T.L.R. 659 (K.B.1905), holding liability for showing a private letter to an unauthorized person (£400 damages).

7.   The development of the action of trover, and the tort of conversion, provided a convenient substitute for trespass to chattels, and has made that action unnecessary in many cases. It survives as a possible remedy for interferences when the plaintiff wants to keep the chattel and sue for the harm. See, for example, Van Eaton v. Thon, 764 S.W. 2d 674 (1988) (diminution in value of horse, which became "head-shy" after incident in which defendant struck it in jaw with his fist) and the next principal case.

CompuServe Inc. v. Cyber Promotions, Inc.

United States District Court, Southern District of Ohio, 1997.
962 F.Supp. 1015.

GRAHAM, DISTRICT JUDGE. This case presents novel issues regarding the commercial use of the Internet, specifically the right of an online computer service to prevent a commercial enterprise from sending unsolicited electronic mail advertising to its subscribers.

Plaintiff CompuServe Incorporated ("CompuServe") is one of the major national commercial online computer services. It operates a computer communication service through a proprietary nationwide computer network. In addition to allowing access to the extensive content available within its own proprietary network, CompuServe also provides its subscribers with a link to the much larger resources of the Internet. This allows its subscribers to send and receive electronic messages, known as "e-mail," by the Internet. Defendants Cyber Promotions, Inc. and its president Sanford Wallace are in the business of sending unsolicited e-mail advertisements on behalf of themselves and their clients to hundreds of thousands of Internet users, many of whom are CompuServe subscribers. CompuServe has notified defendants that they are prohibited from using its computer equipment to process and store the unsolicited e-mail and has requested that they terminate the practice. Instead, defendants have sent an increasing volume of e-mail solicitations to CompuServe subscribers. CompuServe has attempted to employ technological means to block the flow of defendants' e-mail transmission to its computer equipment, but to no avail.

This matter is before the Court on the application of CompuServe for a preliminary injunction which would extend the duration of the temporary restraining order issued by this Court on October 24, 1996 and which would in addition prevent defendants from sending unsolicited advertisements to CompuServe subscribers. * * *

Internet users often pay a fee for Internet access. However, there is no per-message charge to send electronic messages over the Internet and such messages usually reach their destination within minutes. Thus electronic mail provides an opportunity to reach a wide audience quickly and at almost no cost to the sender. It is not surprising therefore that some companies, like defendant Cyber Promotions, Inc., have begun using the Internet to distribute advertisements by sending the same unsolicited commercial message to hundreds of thousands of Internet users at once. Defendants refer to this as "bulk e-mail," while plaintiff refers to it as "junk e-mail." In the vernacular of the Internet, unsolicited e-mail advertising is sometimes referred to pejoratively as "spam."[1] * * *

Over the past several months, CompuServe has received many complaints from subscribers threatening to discontinue their subscription unless CompuServe prohibits electronic mass mailers from using its equipment to send unsolicited advertisements. CompuServe asserts that the volume of messages generated by such mass mailings places a significant burden on its equipment which has finite processing and storage capacity. CompuServe receives no payment from the mass mailers for processing their unsolicited advertising. However, CompuServe's subscribers pay for their access to CompuServe's services in increments of time and thus the process of accessing, reviewing and discarding unsolicited e-mail costs them money, which is one of the reasons for their complaints. CompuServe has notified defendants that they are prohibited from using its proprietary computer equipment to process and store unsolicited e-mail and has requested them to cease and desist from sending unsolicited e-mail to its subscribers. Nonetheless, defendants have sent an increasing volume of e-mail solicitations to CompuServe subscribers.

In an effort to shield its equipment from defendants' bulk e-mail, CompuServe has implemented software programs designed to screen out the messages and block their receipt. In response, defendants have modified their equipment and the messages they send in such a fashion as to circumvent CompuServe's screening software. Allegedly, defendants have been able to conceal the true origin of their messages by falsifying the point-of-origin information contained in the header of the electronic messages. Defendants have removed the "sender" information in the header of their messages and replaced it with another address. Also, defendants have developed the capability of configuring their computer servers to conceal their true domain name and appear on the Internet as another computer, further concealing the true origin of the messages. By manipulating this data, defendants have been able to continue sending messages to CompuServe's equipment in spite of CompuServe's protests and protective efforts. Defendants assert that they possess the right to continue to send these

---

1. This term is derived from a skit performed on the British television show Monty Python's Flying Circus, in which the word "spam" is repeated to the point of absurdity in a restaurant menu.

communications to CompuServe subscribers. CompuServe contends that, in doing so, the defendants are trespassing upon its personal property. * * *

This Court will now address the * * * aspect of plaintiff's motion in which it seeks to enjoin defendants Cyber Promotions, Inc. and its president Sanford Wallace from sending any unsolicited advertisements to any electronic mail address maintained by CompuServe.

CompuServe predicates this aspect of its motion for a preliminary injunction on the common law theory of trespass to personal property or to chattels, asserting that defendants' continued transmission of electronic messages to its computer equipment constitutes an actionable tort.

Trespass to chattels has evolved from its original common law application, concerning primarily the asportation of another's tangible property, to include the unauthorized use of personal property: Its chief importance now, is that there may be recovery ... for interferences with the possession of chattels which are not sufficiently important to be classed as conversion, and so to compel the defendant to pay the full value of the thing with which he has interfered. Trespass to chattels survives today, in other words, largely as a little brother of conversion. Prosser & Keeton, Prosser and Keeton on Torts, § 14, 85–86 (1984). * * *

Both plaintiff and defendants cite the Restatement (Second) of Torts to support their respective positions. In determining a question unanswered by state law, it is appropriate for this Court to consider such sources as the restatement of the law and decisions of other jurisdictions. [Cc]

The Restatement § 217(b) states that a trespass to chattel may be committed by intentionally using or intermeddling with the chattel in possession of another. Restatement § 217, Comment e defines physical "intermeddling" as follows: ... intentionally bringing about a physical contact with the chattel. The actor may commit a trespass by an act which brings him into an intended physical contact with a chattel in the possession of another[.] Electronic signals generated and sent by computer have been held to be sufficiently physically tangible to support a trespass cause of action. [Cc] It is undisputed that plaintiff has a possessory interest in its computer systems. Further, defendants' contact with plaintiff's computers is clearly intentional. Although electronic messages may travel through the Internet over various routes, the messages are affirmatively directed to their destination.

Defendants, citing Restatement (Second) of Torts § 221, which defines "dispossession," assert that not every interference with the personal property of another is actionable and that physical dispossession or substantial interference with the chattel is required. Defendants then argue that they did not, in this case, physically dispossess plaintiff of its equipment or substantially interfere with it. However, the Restatement (Second) of Torts § 218 defines the circumstances under which a trespass to chattels may be actionable: One who commits a trespass to a chattel is subject to liability to the possessor of the chattel if, but only if, (a) he dispossesses the other of the chattel, or (b) the chattel is impaired as to its condition, quality, or value, or (c) the possessor is deprived of the use of the chattel for a substantial time, or (d) bodily harm is caused to the possessor, or harm is caused to some person or thing in which the possessor has a legally protected interest. Therefore, an interference resulting in physical dispossession is just one circumstance under which a defendant can be found liable. Defendants suggest that "unless an alleged trespasser actually takes physical custody of the property or physically damages it, courts will not find the 'substantial interference' required to maintain a trespass to chattel claim." * * * To support this rather broad proposition, defendants cite only two cases which make any reference to the Restatement. In Glidden v. Szybiak, 95 N.H. 318, 63 A.2d 233 (1949), the court simply indicated that an action for trespass to chattels could not be maintained in the absence of some form of damage. The court held that where plaintiff did not contend that defendant's pulling on her pet dog's ears caused any injury, an action in tort could not be maintained. 63 A.2d at 235. In contrast, plaintiff in the present action has alleged that it has suffered several types if injury as a result of defendants' conduct. In Koepnick v. Sears Roebuck & Co., 158 Ariz. 322, 762 P.2d 609 (1988) the court held that a two-minute search of an individual's truck did not amount to a "dispossession" of the truck as defined in Restatement § 221 or a deprivation of the use of the truck for a substantial time. It is clear from a reading of Restatement § 218 that an interference or intermeddling that does not fit the § 221 definition of "dispossession" can nonetheless result in defendants' liability for trespass. * * *

* * * In the present case, any value CompuServe realizes from its computer equipment is wholly derived from the extent to which that equipment can serve its subscriber base. Michael Mangino, a software developer for CompuServe who monitors its mail processing computer equipment, states by affidavit that handling the enormous volume of mass mailings that CompuServe receives places a tremendous burden on its equipment. * * * Defendants' more recent practice of evading CompuServe's filters by disguising the origin of their messages commandeers even more computer resources because CompuServe's computers are forced to store undeliverable e-mail messages and labor in vain to return the messages to an address that does not exist. * * * To the extent that defendants' multitudinous electronic mailings demand the disk space and drain the processing power of plaintiff's computer equipment, those resources are not available to serve CompuServe subscribers. Therefore, the value of that equipment to CompuServe is diminished even though it is not physically damaged by defendants' conduct.

Next, plaintiff asserts that it has suffered injury aside from the physical impact of defendants' messages on its equipment. Restatement § 218(d) also indicates that recovery may be had for a trespass that causes harm to something in which the possessor has a legally protected interest. Plaintiff asserts that defendants' messages are largely unwanted by its subscribers, who pay incrementally to access their e-mail, read it, and discard it. Also, the receipt of a bundle of unsolicited messages at once can require the subscriber to sift through, at his expense, all of the messages in order to find the ones he wanted or expected to receive. These inconveniences decrease the utility of CompuServe's e-mail service and are the foremost subject in recent complaints from CompuServe subscribers. * * * Many subscribers have terminated their accounts specifically because of the unwanted receipt of bulk e-mail messages. * * * Defendants' intrusions into CompuServe's computer systems, insofar as they harm plaintiff's business reputation and goodwill with its customers, are actionable under Restatement § 218(d). * * *

Defendants argue that plaintiff made the business decision to connect to the Internet and that therefore it cannot now successfully maintain an action for trespass to chattels. Their argument is analogous to the argument that because an establishment invites the public to enter its property for business purposes, it cannot later restrict or revoke access to that property, a proposition which is erroneous under Ohio law. * * *

Based on the foregoing, plaintiff's motion for a preliminary injunction is GRANTED. The temporary restraining order filed on October 24, 1996 by this Court is hereby extended in duration until final judgment is entered in this case. Further, defendants Cyber Promotions, Inc. and its president Sanford Wallace are enjoined from sending any unsolicited advertisements to any electronic mail address maintained by plaintiff CompuServe during the pendency of this action. It is so ORDERED.

NOTES AND QUESTIONS

1. You probably will run into cases in your other classes, as well as in Chapter 17, Defamation, page 867 where you will see the courts struggling with the application of traditional legal concepts to the new frontier of the Internet. Notice that both plaintiffs and defendants used the Restatement (Second) of Torts to support their arguments that defendant's conduct was trespass to chattels *vel non*. If you had been CompuServ's lawyer, would you have remembered the *Glidden* case and thought to apply its principles to your client's problem with spam?

2. What if a disgruntled former worker barrages a company's e-mail system with messages that go to all 30,000 of its employees? Trespass to chattels? Could a CompuServ subscriber bring her own cause of action for trespass to chattels against Cyber Promotions for interference with her own computer?

8. CONVERSION

(A) NATURE OF THE TORT

► Pearson v. Dodd

United States Court of Appeals, District of Columbia Circuit, 1969.
410 F.2d 701, cert. denied, 395 U.S. 947, 89 S.Ct. 2021, 23 L.Ed.2d 465 (1969).

J. SKELLY WRIGHT, CIRCUIT JUDGE: This case arises out of the exposure of the alleged misdeeds of Senator Thomas Dodd of Connecticut by newspaper columnists Drew Pearson and Jack Anderson. The District Court has granted partial summary judgment to Senator Dodd, appellee here, finding liability on a theory of conversion. At the same time, the court denied *appeal that occurs before trial court's ruling on entire case*

partial summary judgment on the theory of invasion of privacy. Both branches of the court's judgment are before us on interlocutory appeal. We affirm the District Court's denial of summary judgment for invasion of privacy and reverse its grant of summary judgment for conversion.

Holding

The undisputed facts in the case were stated by the District Court as follows: " * * * [O]n several occasions in June and July, 1965, two former employees of the plaintiff, at times with the assistance of two members of the plaintiff's staff, entered the plaintiff's office without authority and unbeknownst to him, removed numerous documents from his files, made copies of them, replaced the originals, and turned over the copies to the defendant Anderson, who was aware of the manner in which the copies had been obtained. The defendants Pearson and Anderson thereafter published articles containing information gleaned from these documents."

published info from unlawfully obtained source

[For another part of this case involving the tort of invasion of privacy, see page 944].

The District Court ruled that appellants' receipt and subsequent use of photocopies of documents which appellants knew had been removed from appellee's files without authorization established appellants' liability for conversion. We conclude that appellants are not guilty of conversion on the facts shown.

Dean Prosser has remarked that "[c]onversion is the forgotten tort." That it is not entirely forgotten is attested by the case before us. History has largely defined its contours, contours which we should now follow except where they derive from clearly obsolete practices or abandoned theories.

Conversion is the substantive tort theory which underlay the ancient common law form of action for trover. A plaintiff in trover alleged that he had lost a chattel which he rightfully possessed, and that the defendant had found it and converted it to his own use. With time, the allegations of losing and finding became fictional, leaving the question of whether the defendant had "converted" the property the only operative one.

The most distinctive feature of conversion is its measure of damages, which is the value of the goods converted. The theory is that the "converting" defendant has in some way treated the goods as if they were his own, so that the plaintiff can properly ask the court to decree a forced sale of the property from the rightful possessor to the converter.

Because of this stringent measure of damages, it has long been recognized that not every wrongful interference with the personal property of another is a conversion. Where the intermeddling falls short of the complete or very substantial deprivation of possessory rights in the property, the tort committed is not conversion, but the lesser wrong of trespass to chattels.

Rule of law

The Restatement (Second) of Torts has marked the distinction by defining conversion as: " * * * [A]n intentional exercise of dominion or control over a chattel which so seriously interferes with the right of another to control it that the actor may justly be required to pay the other

Definition of conversion

the full value of the chattel." Less serious interferences fall under the Restatement's definition of trespass.

The difference is more than a semantic one. The measure of damages in trespass is not the whole value of the property interfered with, but rather the actual diminution in its value caused by the interference. More important for this case, a judgment for conversion can be obtained with only nominal damages, whereas liability for trespass to chattels exists only on a showing of actual damage to the property interfered with. Here the District Court granted partial summary judgment on the issue of liability alone, while conceding that possibly no more than nominal damages might be awarded on subsequent trial. Partial summary judgment for liability could not have been granted on a theory of trespass to chattels without an undisputed showing of actual damages to the property in question.

It is clear that on the agreed facts appellants committed no conversion of the physical documents taken from appellee's files. Those documents were removed from the files at night, photocopied, and returned to the files undamaged before office operations resumed in the morning. Insofar as the documents' value to appellee resided in their usefulness as records of the business of his office, appellee was clearly not substantially deprived of his use of them.

This of course is not an end of the matter. It has long been recognized that documents often have value above and beyond that springing from their physical possession. They may embody information or ideas whose economic value depends in part or in whole upon being kept secret. The question then arises whether the information taken by means of copying appellee's office files is of the type which the law of conversion protects. The general rule has been that ideas or information are not subject to legal protection, but the law has developed exceptions to this rule. Where information is gathered and arranged at some cost and sold as a commodity on the market, it is properly protected as property. Where ideas are formulated with labor and inventive genius, as in the case of literary works or scientific researches, they are protected. Where they constitute instruments of fair and effective commercial competition, those who develop them may gather their fruits under the protection of the law.

The question here is not whether appellee had a right to keep his files from prying eyes, but whether the information taken from those files falls under the protection of the law of property, enforceable by a suit for conversion. In our view, it does not. The information included the contents of letters to appellee from supplicants, and office records of other kinds, the nature of which is not fully revealed by the record. Insofar as we can tell, none of it amounts to literary property, to scientific invention, or to secret plans formulated by appellee for the conduct of commerce. Nor does it appear to be information held in any way for sale by appellee, analogous to the fresh news copy produced by a wire service. * * *

Because no conversion of the physical contents of appellee's files took place, and because the information copied from the documents in those files has not been shown to be property subject to protection by suit for conversion, the District Court's ruling that appellants are guilty of conversion must be reversed.

So ordered.

NOTES AND QUESTIONS

1. Conversion is a tort whose detailed complications exceed the time that can conveniently be allotted to it in any Torts course. There are thousands of conversion cases, but most of them have been concerned only with settling the title to disputed goods, and there are relatively few in which the tort itself has been in issue. The topic of conversion has tended to be shunted back and forth between the courses in Torts and Property and so to be covered in neither. Many of the practical problems relating to title and conversion are covered in Article 2 of the Uniform Commercial Code and law school courses in sales or commercial law.

2. The hand of history lies heavily on the tort. It is the lineal descendant of the old common law action of trover and for that reason is commonly listed under the heading "Trover and Conversion." (You may have seen a reference to it this way in your Civil Procedure course. Because it developed out of a common law writ, parties are entitled to a jury trial in such actions brought in federal courts.) Trespass and trover were both actions founded upon possession, and for some centuries they remained as alternative remedies for the wrongful taking or damaging of chattels. There was, however, one important difference between them, as to the measure of damages. The theory of trespass to chattels was that the plaintiff remained the owner of the chattel, with possession merely interrupted or interfered with, so that when the chattel was returned, the owner had to accept it and recovery was limited to damages to the chattel, or to reimbursement for the time it was missing. The theory of trover was that the defendant, by "converting" the chattel to the defendant's use had appropriated the plaintiff's property, for which he was required to make compensation—generally computed as market value at the time and place of conversion. The defendant did not have the option of simply returning the chattel and paying damages.

3. In each of the following cases, was the interference with the plaintiff's chattel serious enough to warrant an action for conversion?

A. Plaintiff and defendant owned a house as tenants in common. During a dispute over ownership, defendant notified plaintiff that if he did not remove his furniture she would have it removed. She did so, informing him of the location. Zaslow v. Kroenert, 29 Cal.2d 541, 176 P.2d 1 (1946) (no conversion, trespass to chattels for which plaintiff may recover only actual damages suffered by reason of the loss of use of the property).

B. The same facts, except that defendant removes the furniture to a warehouse at a distance, so that plaintiff is subject to substantial inconvenience and expense in recovering it. This is a conversion. Forsdick v. Collins, 1 Starkie 173, 171 Eng.Rep. 437 (1816); and cf. Electric Power Co. v. Mayor of New York, 36 App.Div. 383, 55 N.Y.S. 460 (1899).

C. The same facts, except that defendant does not notify plaintiff. This is a conversion. McGonigle v. Victor H. Belleisle Co., 186 Mass. 310, 71 N.E. 569 (1904); Borg & Powers Furniture Co. v. Reiling, 213 Minn. 539, 7 N.W.2d 310 (1942).

D. The same facts, except that defendant stores the furniture in his own name, with the intent to keep it for himself. This is a conversion. Hicks Rubber Co., Distributors v. Stacy, 133 S.W.2d 249 (Tex.Civ.App.1939).

E.   The same facts, except that while the furniture is in the warehouse, and before plaintiff can remove it, it is destroyed by fire. This is a conversion. McCurdy v. Wallblom Furniture & Carpet Co., 94 Minn. 326, 102 N.W. 873 (1905).

4.   What would be the elements of damage in an action of trespass d.b.a.?

5.   A conversion may occur when one who is authorized to use a chattel uses it in a manner exceeding the authorization. See Swish Mfg. Southeast v. Manhattan Fire & Marine Ins., 675 F.2d 1218 (11th Cir.1982) (lease permitted use of aircraft for transporting passengers and lessee used aircraft for transportation of contraband). A type of case that once was common is Doolittle v. Shaw, 92 Iowa 348, 60 N.W. 621 (1894). Defendant rented a horse from plaintiff, to be driven to Manchester and back. Defendant drove the horse six or seven miles into the country beyond Manchester, without damaging it. It was held that this was not a conversion. But if the horse had been seriously injured in an accident while it was beyond Manchester, with or without the defendant's fault, there would have been a conversion. Palmer v. Mayo, 80 Conn. 353, 68 A. 369 (1907); Baxter v. Woodward, 191 Mich. 379, 158 N.W. 137 (1916).

One of the minor mysteries of the law is why there have been no similar cases involving automobiles. In Grossman Chevrolet Co. v. Enockson, 86 N.W.2d 644 (N.D.1957), a car rental dealer sued a sublessee of an automobile when the vehicle had been kept beyond the rental period and badly damaged in an accident. Plaintiff was permitted to recover for damage to the car, but the theory was based on negligence. Could there have been recovery on any basis if the bailee had not been negligent in having the accident?

6.   Is a human body part "property" that can be converted? Plaintiff's spleen was removed as part of his treatment for cancer. Later, plaintiff discovered that his doctors had used cells from the removed spleen to develop a cell line for which they obtained a patent. The patent was then licensed for commercial development. Does plaintiff have a conversion action against the doctors and the commercial developer? See Moore v. Regents of the University of California, 51 Cal.3d 120, 793 P.2d 479, 271 Cal.Rptr. 146 (1990), page 188. Do the next of kin have a property interest in the body parts of the deceased? See Whaley v. County of Tuscola, 58 F.3d 1111 (6th Cir.1995) (unauthorized removal of corneas and eyes during autopsies).

The Restatement (Second) of Torts has undertaken to identify the factors that influence courts in determining if a conversion has taken place when there has been interference with a chattel. It provides:

"§ 222A. What Constitutes Conversion

"(1) Conversion is an intentional exercise of dominion or control over a chattel which so seriously interferes with the right of another to control it that the actor may justly be required to pay the other the full value of the chattel.

"(2) In determining the seriousness of the interference and the justice of requiring the actor to pay the full value the following factors are important:

"(a) the extent and duration of the actor's exercise of dominion or control;

"(b) the actor's intent to assert a right in fact inconsistent with the other's right of control;

"(c) the actor's good faith;

"(d) the extent and duration of the resulting interference with the other's right of control;

"(e) the harm done to the chattel;

"(f) the inconvenience and expense caused to the other."

The ways in which an actor may convert a chattel—i.e., intentionally exercise dominion and control over it that so seriously interferes with the owner's right to control it that it is just to require the actor to pay its full value—include the following:

(1) acquiring possession of it—e.g., stealing the chattel;

(2) damaging or altering it—e.g., intentionally running over an animal and killing it;

(3) using it—e.g., a bailee seriously violates the terms of the bailment;

(4) receiving it—e.g., obtaining possession after a purchase from a thief;

(5) disposing of it—e.g., a bailee wrongfully sells the chattel;

(6) misdelivering it—e.g., delivery to wrong person by mistake so that the chattel is lost; and

(7) refusing to surrender it—e.g., bailee refuses to return the chattel.

See Restatement (Second) of Torts § 223 and following sections.

(B) Effect of Good Faith

An individual may be subject to liability for conversion although he was not subjectively at fault. This can occur in at least two ways:

1. When the defendant intends to affect the chattel in a manner inconsistent with the plaintiff's right of control, the fact that he acted in good faith, and under a mistake, does not prevent liability for conversion. Thus, if a bailee delivers goods to an imposter or on the basis of a forged document, he is liable to the bailor or owner. See Baer v. Slater, 261 Mass. 153, 158 N.E. 328 (1927) (defendant delivers goods to imposter); Potomac Ins. Co. v. Nickson, 64 Utah 395, 231 P. 445 (1924) (garage delivers car to person who presented a stolen duplicate parking ticket); Suzuki v. Small, 214 App.Div. 541, 212 N.Y.S. 589 (1925) (steel sent to wrong company). Compare Ranson v. Kitner, page 23.

Some special rules have developed at common law for the protection of bailees and servants who deal with the chattels of third persons under directions from their bailors or employers. These are rules of commercial convenience and the reason underlying them is clearly the practical necessity of permitting someone to receive goods for storage or safekeeping or transportation, without inquiry as to the title of the person from whom they are received. If, for example, a garage accepting an automobile for overnight parking were to be held liable for conversion when it turned out to be a stolen car, there would be few people willing to operate a parking garage.

A owns goods. B steals them from him, and turns them over to C, a carrier, for shipment to a distant point. Neither the receipt of the stolen goods nor the transportation nor the redelivery to B, the thief, will make C liable to A for conversion of the goods, so long as C acts in good faith, without notice of A's claim to the goods. This is also true if C delivers the goods at destination to D in accordance with B's directions. The rules are also applied to an employee who receives the goods from the employer.

This privilege does not extend to a case in which the goods are in the hands of the bailee or servant, and they are claimed from him by both the bailor or employer and the true owner. In this case, the bailee or servant is required, at his peril, to see that he delivers to the right person, and he becomes liable for conversion if he delivers to the wrong one. His remedy is to interplead the claimants, or under modern statutes to deposit the goods in court.

2. The other major area in which an innocent conversion may take place concerns good faith purchasers. An innocent purchaser cannot obtain a title from a thief. The purchaser acts at her peril and may be sued in conversion by the true owner.

Complications arise when A induces B to sell goods by fraud. In this case, title passes to A, but the equity courts permitted B to rescind the transaction because of the fraud and recover back goods. At a later stage, the law courts took over the equitable principle and permitted B to rescind the transaction of his own motion, and recover from A as if consent never had been given. This meant that B could maintain trover against A. The remedy remained essentially the equitable one of rescission even after it was taken over by the law courts. The plaintiff must act promptly, must himself do equity and must in all other respects conform to equitable principles. See, for example, Thurston v. Blanchard, 39 Mass. (22 Pick.) 18 (1839).

Because a bona fide purchase cuts off equitable rights, this right to rescind for fraud is terminated when a bona fide purchaser acquires both title and possession from the defrauding party. There is thus a distinction between stolen goods, as to which the legal title does not pass and a bona fide purchaser is therefore not protected, and goods obtained by fraud, as to which the title does pass, subject to an equity of rescission, which is cut off by a bona fide purchase.

(C) NECESSITY OF DEMAND; RETURN OF CHATTEL

Demand. Some states have followed the rule that possession by a bona fide purchaser or other innocent converter is not in itself a sufficiently serious defiance of the owner's rights, and hold that the possessor is liable only if refusing to return the goods on demand. In most states, however, a conversion occurs as soon as the defendant takes dominion and control over the goods in a manner inconsistent with plaintiff's ownership. In these states, there may be a separate act of conversion for an initial taking of possession and for a later refusal to return on demand, and the owner can elect between them. Restatement (Second) of Torts § 229.

Return. When a converter offers to return the converted goods and the owner accepts, the return does not bar the action for conversion, but it must be taken into account to reduce the damages recovered. If the chattel is in the same condition as when it was taken, has not changed in value and the plaintiff has suffered no special damage through being deprived of possession, the effect may be to reduce his recovery to nominal damages.

When the plaintiff refuses to accept the offered return, the older rule was that the defendant could not force the goods back upon him in reduction of the damages. The plaintiff could insist upon the full value of the goods as the measure of damages, and the defendant had to keep them. In Professor Warren's phrase, defendant had "bought something."

The English courts and some American jurisdictions have held that when the conversion is an innocent one committed under an honest mistake, the court may require the plaintiff to take back the goods and credit the defendant with their value, in any case in which the goods are undamaged and there has been no change in the plaintiff's position. The matter is within the sound discretion of the trial court, and even in these jurisdictions there is no absolute right to the return as a matter of law. See Rutland & W.R. Co. v. Bank of Middlebury, 32 Vt. 639 (1860). The Restatement (Second) of Torts has followed this approach in § 922.

Payment of the chattel's value by a converter to the original owner effectuates a common law forced sale of the chattel and precludes the original owner's further recovery of damages for subsequent conversions. Baram v. Farugia, 606 F.2d 42 (3d Cir.1979) (Trainer of race horse gave horse to defendants as payment of debt. Plaintiff, owner of race horse, filed a conversion action against defendants and was awarded value of horse and punitive damages. On appeal, court found that because plaintiff already had collected the full value of the horse from trainer, the acceptance of that payment was a "forced sale" to trainer and thus plaintiff did not have a conversion action against defendants.) Is a judgment for plaintiff sufficient for this purpose too?

(D) DAMAGES

The measure of damages for conversion is the value of the property converted. Usually, this is the market value—what the property could have been sold for in the open market by a willing seller to a willing buyer. For elaboration on this and indication of other recoverable damages, see Restatement (Second) of Torts § 927.

The market value is determined at the time and place of the conversion. The theory is that if the chattel is available on the market, the owner should mitigate damages by purchasing another chattel. This need not be done at the very moment of the conversion. While some courts would give him the highest intermediate value between the time of conversion and the time of the suit or the judgment, the rule approved by most commentators is the highest intermediate value between the time of conversion and a reasonable time for making a replacement. If there is no market value, other methods may be used, such as manufacturing cost, less depreciation. See Restatement (Second) of Torts § 911.

Sometimes the property destroyed or damaged has little market worth, but has a peculiar value to the owner. Damages cannot be recovered for sentiment alone, but if defendant's conduct is outrageous, plaintiff may be able to recover damages for emotional harm suffered from the loss. See La Porte v. Associated Independents, Inc., 163 So.2d 267 (Fla.1964) (pet dachshund). See also Windeler v. Scheers Jewelers, 8 Cal.App.3d 844, 88 Cal.Rptr. 39 (1970) (plaintiff told jeweler of great sentimental value of ring; recovery allowed in claim for negligence).

Punitive damages may be allowed when the conversion was malicious but not when it was done innocently.

(E) WHAT MAY BE CONVERTED

Because of its origin as an action against the finder of lost goods, trover was limited to the conversion of things that were capable of being lost and found. It would lie for any chattel, but not for land, which in the eyes of the law could not be lost. Hence the dispossession or withholding of real property could not be a conversion. Nor could the severance of timber, minerals, crops or fixtures attached to the land. Once there was severance, however, the goods became chattels and the plaintiff could bring trover for their removal from the land. These rules are still applied.

Since intangible rights, such as those of a stockholder in a corporation, could not be lost and found, the original common law rule was that they could not be the subject of a conversion. This has been considerably modified. See Rubin, Conversion of Choses in Action, 10 Fordham L.Rev. 415 (1941). It was first held that damages could be recovered for the conversion of intangible rights when they were merged and identified with a special instrument, such as a promissory note, a check, a bill of lading or a stock certificate, and that instrument itself was converted. This has now been generally extended to permit recovery for the conversion of rights of a kind customarily merged with such an instrument, such as those of a stockholder, without any conversion of the stock certificate itself. Herrick v. Humphrey Hardware Co., 73 Neb. 809, 103 N.W. 685 (1905) (refusal to register a transfer on the books of the corporation, depriving the new owner of his rights as a stockholder).

What if an attorney who is leaving a law firm takes with her the files of seventy of the firm's clients? Is she liable for conversion of the files? Is the law firm who becomes her new employer? See Parker v. Kowalsky & Hirshorhorn, 124 Md. App. 447, 722 A.2d 441, 447 (1999) ("While we agree with the lower court's conclusion that [first law firm] stated a viable cause of action in conversion against [attorney], we do not believe that this allegation demonstrates that [first law firm] had a possessory interest in the fees that were received by [second law firm, from work performed for clients whose files had been converted.]")

(F) WHO MAY MAINTAIN THE ACTION

Trover, like trespass, was founded upon the plaintiff's possession. From this has come the rule that anyone in possession of a chattel at the time of a conversion can maintain an action for it. Thus a finder can recover for conversion. See Aigler, Rights of Finders, 21 Mich.L.Rev. 664, 57 Am.L.Rev. 511 (1928); Moreland, Rights of Finders, 16 Ky.L.J. 1 (1927). The same is true of a bailee to whom the chattel is loaned, although he has no other interest in it, or a sheriff who has seized it on execution.

Recovery has been permitted even when the plaintiff's possession is wrongful, and in defiance of the true owner. Thus one converter may recover from another. Jeffries v. Great Western R. Co., 5 El. & Bl. 802, 119 Eng.Rep. 680 (1856). In this case, however, the plaintiff usually has had some colorable claim of right to the chattel; and it has been held that in the absence of such a claim there is no recovery. Turley v. Tucker, 6 Mo. 583, 35 Am.Dec. 449 (1840); Rexroth v. Coon, 15 R.I. 35, 23 A. 37 (1885).

Trover was also extended to permit recovery by one who did not have possession, but had the immediate right to it, as in the case of a bailor at will who was entitled to possession on demand. Manders v. Williams, 4 Exch. 339, 154 Eng.Rep. 1242 (1849). Or a mortgagee after default. Nichols & Shepard Co. v. Minnesota Thresher Mfg. Co., 70 Minn. 528, 73 N.W. 415 (1897). This, too, has carried over into the modern law of conversion.

a finder (not the true owner) can recover for conversion

CHAPTER III

PRIVILEGES

1. CONSENT

O'Brien v. Cunard S.S. Co.

Supreme Judicial Court of Massachusetts, 1891.
154 Mass. 272, 28 N.E. 266.

Tort, for an assault, and for negligently vaccinating the plaintiff, who was a steerage passenger on the defendant's steamship. The trial court directed a verdict for the defendant, and the plaintiff brings exceptions. [Plaintiff alleged that she suffered ulceration at the site and blistering all over her body due either to contamination of the vaccine or of the vaccination site. There was conflicting medical expert testimony as to the cause of her injuries]]

KNOWLTON, J. * * * To sustain the first count, which was for an alleged assault, the plaintiff relied on the fact that the surgeon who was employed by the defendant vaccinated her on ship-board, while she was on her passage from Queenstown to Boston. On this branch of the case the question is whether there was any evidence that the surgeon used force upon the plaintiff against her will. In determining whether the act was lawful or unlawful, the surgeon's conduct must be considered in connection with the surrounding circumstances. If the plaintiff's behavior was such as to indicate consent on her part, he was justified in his act, whatever her unexpressed feelings may have been. In determining whether she consented, he could be guided only by her overt acts and the manifestations of her feelings. [Cc] It is undisputed that at Boston there are strict quarantine regulations in regard to the examination of emigrants, to see that they are protected from small-pox by vaccination, and that only those persons who hold a certificate from the medical officer of the steam-ship, stating that they are so protected, are permitted to land without detention in quarantine, or vaccination by the port physician. It appears that the defendant is accustomed to have its surgeons vaccinate all emigrants who desire it, and who are not protected by previous vaccination, and give them a certificate which is accepted at quarantine as evidence of their protection. Notices of the regulations at quarantine, and of the willingness of the ship's medical officer to vaccinate such as needed vaccination, were posted about the ship in various languages, and on the day when the operation was performed the surgeon had a right to presume that she and the other women who were vaccinated understood the importance and purpose of vaccination for those who bore no marks to show that they were protected. By the plaintiff's testimony, which, in this particular, is undisputed, it appears that about

88

200 women passengers were assembled below, and she understood from conversation with them that they were to be vaccinated; that she stood about 15 feet from the surgeon, and saw them form in a line, and pass in turn before him; that he "examined their arms, and, passing some of them by, proceeded to vaccinate those that had no mark;" that she did not hear him say anything to any of them; that upon being passed by they each received a card, and went on deck; that when her turn came she showed him her arm; he looked at it, and said there was no mark, and that she should be vaccinated; that she told him she had been vaccinated before, and it left no mark; "that he then said nothing; that he should vaccinate her again;" that she held up her arm to be vaccinated; that no one touched her; that she did not tell him she did not want to be vaccinated; and that she took the ticket which he gave her, certifying that he had vaccinated her, and used it at quarantine. She was one of a large number of women who were vaccinated on that occasion, without, so far as appears, a word of objection from any of them. They all indicated by their conduct that they desired to avail themselves of the provisions made for their benefit. There was nothing in the conduct of the plaintiff to indicate to the surgeon that she did not wish to obtain a card which would save her from detention at quarantine, and to be vaccinated, if necessary, for that purpose. Viewing his conduct in the light of the surrounding circumstances, it was lawful; and there was no evidence tending to show that it was not. The ruling of the court on this part of the case was correct. * * *

Exceptions overruled.

NOTES AND QUESTIONS

1. Suppose that in the course of an argument defendant announces that he is going to punch plaintiff in the nose. Plaintiff stands his ground but says and does nothing, and defendant punches him. Is there consent?

2. On a park bench in the moonlight, a young man informs his fiancée that he is going to kiss her. She says and does nothing, and he kisses her. Is he liable for battery? What if it's their first date? What if he is a stranger who has just sat down next to her when he makes his announcement?

3. With the principal case, contrast Mulloy v. Hop Sang, 1 W.W.R. 714 (Alberta C.A.) (1935) (appellate court does not accept that consent was given to medical procedure when patient with limited English did not reply or make objections to surgeon's statement that he would do what was necessary after administering anesthesia).

◥ Hackbart v. Cincinnati Bengals, Inc.

United States Court of Appeals, Tenth Circuit, 1979.
601 F.2d 516, cert. denied, 444 U.S. 931, 100 S.Ct. 275, 62 L.Ed.2d 188 (1979).

WILLIAM E. DOYLE, CIRCUIT JUDGE. The question in this case is whether in a regular season professional football game an injury which is inflicted by one professional football player on an opposing player can give rise to liability in tort where the injury was inflicted by the intentional striking of a blow during the game.

The injury occurred in the course of a game between the Denver Broncos and the Cincinnati Bengals, which game was being played in Denver in 1973. The Broncos' defensive back, Dale Hackbart, was the recipient of the injury and the Bengals' offensive back, Charles "Booby" Clark, inflicted the blow which produced it. * * *

The trial court's finding was that Charles Clark, "acting out of anger and frustration, but without a specific intent to injure * * * stepped forward and struck a blow with his right forearm to the back of the kneeling plaintiff's head and neck with sufficient force to cause both players to fall forward to the ground." Both players, without complaining to the officials or to one another, returned to their respective sidelines since the ball had changed hands and the offensive and defensive teams of each had been substituted. Clark testified at trial that his frustration was brought about by the fact that his team was losing the game. * * *

Despite the fact that the defendant Charles Clark admitted that the blow which had been struck was not accidental, that it was intentionally administered, the trial court ruled as a matter of law that the game of professional football is basically a business which is violent in nature, and that the available sanctions are imposition of penalties and expulsion from the game. Notice was taken of the fact that many fouls are overlooked; that the game is played in an emotional and noisy environment; and that incidents such as that here complained of are not unusual. * * *

Indeed, the evidence shows that there are rules of the game which prohibit the intentional striking of blows. Thus, Article 1, Item 1, Subsection C, provides that: "All players are prohibited from striking on the head, face or neck with the heel, back or side of the hand, wrist, forearm, elbow or clasped hands." Thus the very conduct which was present here is expressly prohibited by the rule which is quoted above.

The general customs of football do not approve the intentional punching or striking of others. That this is prohibited was supported by the testimony of all of the witnesses. They testified that the intentional striking of a player in the face or from the rear is prohibited by the playing rules as well as the general customs of the game. Punching or hitting with the arms is prohibited. Undoubtedly these restraints are intended to establish reasonable boundaries so that one football player cannot intentionally inflict a serious injury on another. Therefore, the notion is not correct that all reason has been abandoned, whereby the only possible remedy for the person who has been the victim of an unlawful blow is retaliation. * * *

In sum, having concluded that the trial court did not limit the case to a trial of the evidence bearing on defendant's liability but rather determined that as a matter of social policy the game was so violent and unlawful that valid lines could not be drawn, we take the view that this was not a proper issue for determination and that plaintiff was entitled to have the case tried on an assessment of his rights and whether they had been violated. * * *

Reversed and remanded for a new trial.

NOTES AND QUESTIONS

1. What about one player clipping another in a football game? In order to recover, plaintiff must show that the act was intentional, not just that it violated the game's safety rules. See Gauvin v. Clark, 404 Mass. 450, 537 N.E.2d 94 (1989) (jury found college hockey player did not act willfully in striking other player in abdomen). Greer v. Davis, 921 S.W.2d 325 (Tex.App.1996) (question for jury whether base runner acted intentionally or merely negligently in colliding with catcher rather than sliding or stepping out of baseline to avoid the tag).

2. Plaintiff and defendant were opposing players in a family softball game. *possibly negligence (accident)* Defendant, sliding into second base, knocked the plaintiff down and broke two bones in his ankle. Is there liability? Tavernier v. Maes, 242 Cal.App.2d 532, 51 Cal.Rptr. 575 (1966). What other facts do you want to know about the game to decide if the plaintiff consented to the contact? Would it make a difference if the conduct occurred while players were warming up rather than during the game? Cf. Savino v. Robertson, 273 Ill.App.3d 811, 652 N.E.2d 1240 (1995) (no difference).

3. What about a course of rough-house practical joking between the parties in the past? Wartman v. Swindell, 54 N.J.L. 589, 25 A. 356 (1892). *negligence maybe not intentional*

4. Defendant taps plaintiff on the shoulder to attract his attention for a reasonable purpose. May consent be assumed? Wiffin v. Kincard, 2 Bos. & P.N.R. 471, 127 Eng.Rep. 713 (1807); Coward v. Baddeley, 4 Hurl. & N. 478, 157 Eng.Rep. 927 (1859). Is this a battery, to begin with? *if offensive unsolicited contact*

5. Local custom permits the public to take fish from small lakes and ponds. Defendant passes over plaintiff's property to reach such a lake. Consent? See Marsh v. Colby, 39 Mich. 626 (1878). *NO*

Mohr v. Williams

Supreme Court of Minnesota, 1905.
95 Minn. 261, 104 N.W. 12.

[Plaintiff consulted defendant, an ear specialist, concerning trouble with her right ear. On examining her, he found a diseased condition of the right ear, and she consented to an operation upon it. When she was unconscious under the anaesthetic, defendant concluded that the condition of the right ear was not serious enough to require an operation; but he found a more serious condition of the left ear, which he decided required an operation. Without reviving the plaintiff to ask her permission, he operated on the left ear. The operation was skillfully performed, and was successful. Plaintiff nevertheless brought an action for battery. In the court below the jury returned a verdict in favor of the plaintiff for $14,322.50. The trial judge denied defendant's motion for judgment notwithstanding the verdict, but granted a new trial on the ground that the damages were excessive. Both parties appeal.] *judgment entered for one party even though jury verdict has been rendered for other party*

facts

BROWN, J. * * * The evidence tends to show that, upon the first examination of plaintiff, defendant pronounced the left ear in good condition, and that, at the time plaintiff repaired to the hospital to submit to the operation on her right ear, she was under the impression that no difficulty existed as to the left. In fact, she testified that she had not previously experienced any trouble with that organ. It cannot be doubted that ordinarily the patient must be consulted, and his consent given, before a physician may operate upon him. * * *

The physician impliedly contracts that he possesses, and will exercise in the treatment of patients, skill and learning, and that he will exercise reasonable care and exert his best judgment to bring about favorable results. The methods of treatment are committed almost exclusively to his judgment, but we are aware of no rule or principle of law which would extend to him free license respecting surgical operations. Reasonable latitude must, however, be allowed the physician in a particular case; and we would not lay down any rule which would unreasonably interfere with the exercise of his discretion, or prevent him from taking such measures as his judgment dictated for the welfare of the patient in a case of emergency. If a person should be injured to the extent of rendering him unconscious, and his injuries were of such a nature as to require prompt surgical attention, a physician called to attend him would be justified in applying such medical or surgical treatment as might reasonably be necessary for the preservation of his life or limb, and consent on the part of the injured person would be implied. And again, if, in the course of an operation to which the patient consented, the physician should discover conditions not anticipated before the operation was commenced, and which, if not removed, would endanger the life or health of the patient, he would, though no express consent was obtained or given, be justified in extending the operation to remove and overcome them. But such is not the case at bar. The diseased condition of plaintiff's left ear was not discovered in the course of an operation on the right, which was authorized, but upon an independent examination of that organ, made after the authorized operation was found unnecessary. Nor is the evidence such as to justify the court in holding, as a matter of law, that it was such an affection as would result immediately in the serious injury of plaintiff, or such an emergency as to justify proceeding without her consent. She had experienced no particular difficulty with that ear, and the questions as to when its diseased condition would become alarming or fatal, and whether there was an immediate necessity for an operation, were, under the evidence, question of fact for the jury.

The contention of defendant that the operation was consented to by plaintiff is not sustained by the evidence. At least, the evidence was such as to take the question to the jury. This contention is based upon the fact that she was represented on the occasion in question by her family physician; that the condition of her left ear was made known to him, and the propriety of an operation thereon suggested, to which he made no objection. It is urged that by his conduct he assented to it, and that plaintiff was bound thereby. It is not claimed that he gave his express consent. It is not disputed but that the family physician of plaintiff was present on the occasion of the operation, and at her request. But the purpose of his presence was not that he might participate in the operation, nor does it appear that he was authorized to consent to any change in the one originally proposed to be made. Plaintiff was naturally nervous and fearful of the consequences of being placed under the influence of anaesthetics, and the presence of her family physician was requested under the impression that it would allay and calm her fears. The evidence made the question one of fact for the jury to determine.

The last contention of defendant is that the act complained of did not amount to an assault and battery. This is based upon the theory that, as plaintiff's left ear was in fact diseased, in a condition dangerous and threatening to her health, the operation was necessary, and having been skillfully performed at a time when plaintiff had requested a like operation on the other ear, the charge of assault and battery cannot be sustained; that, in view of these conditions, and the claim that there was no negligence on the part of defendant, and an entire absence of any evidence tending to show an evil intent, the court should say, as a matter of law, that no assault and battery was committed, even though she did not consent to the operation. In other words, that the absence of a showing that defendant was actuated by a wrongful intent, or guilty of negligence, relieves the act of defendant from the charge of an unlawful assault and battery. We are unable to reach that conclusion, though the contention is not without merit. It would seem to follow from what has been said on the other features of the case that the act of defendant amounted at least to a technical assault and battery. If the operation was performed without plaintiff's consent, and the circumstances were not such as to justify its performance without, it was wrongful; and, if it was wrongful, it was unlawful. As remarked in 1 Jaggard on Torts, 437, every person has a right to complete immunity of his person from physical interference of others, except in so far as contact may be necessary under the general doctrine of privilege; and any unlawful or unauthorized touching of the person of another, except it be in the spirit of pleasantry, constitutes an assault and battery. In the case at bar, as we have already seen, the question whether defendant's act in performing the operation upon plaintiff was authorized was a question for the jury to determine. If it was unauthorized, then it was, within what we have said, unlawful. It was a violent assault, not a mere pleasantry; and, even though no negligence is shown, it was wrongful and unlawful. The case is unlike a criminal prosecution for assault and battery, for there an unlawful intent must be shown. But that rule does not apply to a civil action, to maintain which it is sufficient to show that the assault complained of was wrongful and unlawful or the result of negligence. [C]

The amount of plaintiff's recovery, if she is entitled to recover at all, must depend upon the character and extent of the injury inflicted upon her, in determining which the nature of the malady intended to be healed and the beneficial nature of the operation should be taken into consideration, as well as the good faith of the defendant.

you can get nominal damages in intentional / no punitive in negligence

there was no negligence

Order affirmed.

[Reference to the records of the District Court of Ramsey County, Minnesota, discloses that on the second trial the plaintiff received a verdict and judgment for $39. There was no appeal.]

NOTES AND QUESTIONS

1. Why did plaintiff's attorney sue under a theory of battery instead of ordinary negligent medical malpractice? Should there be recovery if defendant used all reasonable care in the operation? Cf. Rogers v. Board of Road Commissioners, page 69. *Yes- no consent ⇒ no emergency ⇒ no privilege*

2. Plaintiff, a boy 15 years of age, was run over by a train and his foot was crushed. When he arrived at the hospital he was unconscious and slowly bleeding to death. Defendant, the house surgeon, concluded that immediate amputation of the foot was necessary to save the boy's life. Finding no relatives present, he performed the operation. Is he liable? Why? Luka v. Lowrie, 171 Mich. 122, 136 N.W. 1106 (1912). *No ⇒ grave emergency*

3. Medical care providers may act in the absence of express consent if (1) the patient is unable to give consent (unconscious, intoxicated, mentally ill, incompetent); (2) there is a risk of serious bodily harm if treatment is delayed; (3) a reasonable person would consent to treatment under the circumstances; and (4) this patient would consent to treatment under the circumstances. See, e.g., Kozup v. Georgetown U. Hosp., 851 F.2d 437 (D.C.Cir.1988) (parents' consent to baby's transfusion was not implied simply because it was necessary to save baby's life where there was no showing that there was no time to seek consent).

4. What if the plaintiff had remained conscious, and had insisted on prohibiting the operation, saying that he would rather die than lose his foot? See Mulloy v. Hop Sang, 1 W.W.R. 714 (Alberta C.A.) (1935). Construction worker, believing that he saw "666, the sign of the devil" on his hand cut it off with a power saw. His co-workers rushed him and his severed hand, packed in ice, to the hospital. A hand surgeon was standing by ready to attempt to reattach it. Patient refused permission, saying it was against his religion. What should surgeon do? See "Man Who Lost Hand Loses Lawsuit," The Richmond Times Dispatch, Sept. 14, 1997 at C4.

5. The principal case has been regarded for years as the leading case on unauthorized operations. It is still sound law. Today, most surgery is performed in hospitals, which have their own rules and standardized practices, including broad consent forms. In many cases, it has been found that the consent is sufficiently general in its terms to justify the physician in doing whatever he thinks necessary in the course of the operation. See for example Rothe v. Hull, 352 Mo. 926, 180 S.W.2d 7 (1944); Baxter v. Snow, 78 Utah 217, 2 P.2d 257 (1931). Further, many hospitals today use specialized consent forms drafted with legal assistance. What should they say? What if an obstetrician who has privileges at a hospital fails to obtain consent for a blood transfusion? The obstetrician would be liable. Would the hospital? Ward v. Lutheran Hospitals & Homes Soc. of Am., Inc., 963 P.2d 1031 (Alaska 1998) (noting that overwhelming weight of authority holds that hospital does not owe duty to patient to obtain consent for treatment when patient is under care of independent physician).

6. What if the plaintiff specifically insists that the operation shall go thus far, and no further? For example, she consents to an incision and an examination of her stomach under ether, but expressly and emphatically forbids anything more. If the

surgeon goes ahead and removes a tumor found there, is he liable? Schloendorff v. Society of New York Hospital, 211 N.Y. 125, 105 N.E. 92 (1914). What if patient limits her consent to female health care providers, explaining that her religious beliefs prohibit her from being seen unclothed by a member of the opposite sex? During surgery, a male nurse sees and touches her as part of proper medical treatment. Liability for battery? Cohen v. Smith, 269 Ill.App.3d 1087, 648 N.E.2d 329 (1995) (violation of plaintiff's right to bodily integrity by unconsented to touching is the essence of battery). What if a patient withdraws her consent during the procedure? Schreiber v. Physicians Ins. Co. of Wisconsin, 223 Wis.2d 417, 588 N.W.2d 26 (1999) (withdrawal of consent means that physician must conduct new informed consent discussion, cannot continue to rely on previously given consent).

7. May a competent, informed adult refuse medical treatment that is necessary to preserve life? Thor v. Superior Court, 5 Cal.4th 725, 855 P.2d 375, 21 Cal.Rptr.2d 357 (1993) (right to refuse treatment not limited to those who are suffering from terminal conditions).

8. Brother Joseph Fox, an 83–year–old member of a Roman Catholic order, had previously expressed a desire not to have his life artificially prolonged by extraordinary means of treatment if there was no reasonable hope for recovery. During surgery to repair a hernia, he suffered permanent brain damage due to cardiac arrest. Was his refusal of extraordinary means of treatment (a respirator) still effective after he became incompetent? Matter of Storar, 52 N.Y.2d 363, 438 N.Y.S.2d 266, 420 N.E.2d 64, cert. denied, 454 U.S. 858 (1981). This issue is resolved in many jurisdictions by statutory provisions for "living wills" or "advance directives" that state the patient's consent and limitations on treatment. In many states there are also statutes that protect physicians from claims for damages based on their failure to withdraw life-sustaining medical care. See, for example, Duarte v. Chino Community Hosp., 72 Cal. App. 4th 849, 85 Cal.Rptr. 2d 521 (1999) (discussing California's statute).

9. What happens if health care personnel ignore a "do not resuscitate order"? If the patient (or his family) has a cause of action for battery, what is the measure of damages? Anderson v. St. Francis–St. George Hospital, Inc., 77 Ohio St.3d 82, 671 N.E.2d 225 (1996) (where the battery was physically harmless, plaintiff entitled only to nominal damages, not compensatory damages for wrongful living or wrongful prolongation of life.) See also, Milani, Better Off Dead Than Disabled?: Should Courts Recognize a "Wrongful Living" Cause of Action When Doctors Fail to Honor Patients' Advance Directives?, 54 WASH. & LEE L. REV. 149 (1997).

10. When plaintiff refused to consent to a transfusion on religious grounds, the court in Application of the President and Directors of Georgetown College, 331 F.2d 1000 (D.C.Cir.1964), granted a declaratory judgment to proceed, with the judge who issued the emergency order finding that the patient felt that it would not be her responsibility if the judge ordered the transfusion. A similar request was denied in In re Osborne, 294 A.2d 372 (D.C.App.1972), where a bedside record disclosed that the patient would regard a transfusion under any circumstances as violative of his religious beliefs. See also Stamford Hospital v. Vega, 236 Conn. 646, 674 A.2d 821 (1996) (patient competent to make decisions entitled to refuse blood transfusion even if that decision is fatal).

11. In the case of a minor child, consent of the parent is necessary to any major surgical operation, except in an emergency. Zoski v. Gaines, 271 Mich. 1, 260 N.W. 99 (1935) (9½ years); Bonner v. Moran, 126 F.2d 121 (D.C.Cir.1941) (15 years). A minor 17 or 18 years of age, however, has been held capable of legally consenting, at least to minor operations. Gulf & S.I.R. Co. v. Sullivan, 155 Miss. 1, 119 So. 501

(1928); Lacey v. Laird, 166 Ohio St. 12, 139 N.E.2d 25 (1956). Is consent from a parent necessary to prescribe a contraceptive pill? Must a minor female have parental consent for an abortion? Ballard v. Anderson, 4 Cal.3d 873, 484 P.2d 1345, 95 Cal.Rptr. 1 (1971).

12. When a parent refuses on religious or other grounds to allow a hospital to provide medical treatment for a child, courts are likely to grant a hospital's application to overrule the parent if the treatment is life threatening, but not if it only will improve the child's comfort or appearance. Compare In re Sampson, 29 N.Y.2d 900, 328 N.Y.S.2d 686, 278 N.E.2d 918 (1972) (approving) with In re Green, 448 Pa. 338, 292 A.2d 387 (1972) (disallowing).

13. Can parents "consent" on behalf of their child to be a donor in a transplant operation for the benefit of a sibling? See Hart v. Brown, 29 Conn.Supp. 368, 289 A.2d 386 (1972). Can a guardian consent to an incompetent's donation of an organ? See Strunk v. Strunk, 445 S.W.2d 145 (Ky.1969). Does the mother's consent to an abortion prevent the child who was injured by the failed abortion from bringing a personal injury action against the physician? Vandervelden v. Victoria, 177 Wis.2d 243, 502 N.W.2d 276 (App.1993).

De May v. Roberts

Supreme Court of Michigan, 1881.
46 Mich. 160, 9 N.W. 146.

MARTSON, C.J. The declaration in this case in the first count sets forth that the plaintiff was at a time and place named a poor married woman, and being confined in child-bed and a stranger, employed in a professional capacity defendant De May who was a physician; that defendant visited the plaintiff as such, and against her desire and intending to deceive her wrongfully, etc., introduced and caused to be present at the house and lying-in room of the plaintiff and while she was in the pains of parturition the defendant Scattergood, who intruded upon the privacy of the plaintiff, indecently, wrongfully and unlawfully laid hands upon her and assaulted her, the said Scattergood, which was well known to defendant De May, being a young unmarried man, a stranger to the plaintiff and utterly ignorant of the practice of medicine, while the plaintiff believed that he was an assistant physician, a competent and proper person to be present and to aid her in her extremity. * * *

The evidence on the part of the plaintiff tended to prove the allegations of the declaration. On the part of the defendants evidence was given tending to prove that Scattergood very reluctantly accompanied Dr. De May at the urgent request of the latter; that the night was a dark and stormy one, the roads over which they had to travel in getting to the house of the plaintiff were so bad that a horse could not be rode or driven over them; that the doctor was sick and very much fatigued from overwork, and therefore asked the defendant Scattergood to accompany and assist him in carrying a lantern, umbrella and certain articles deemed necessary upon such occasions; that upon arriving at the house of the plaintiff the doctor knocked, and when the door was opened by the husband of the plaintiff, De May said to him "that I had fetched a friend along to help carry my things;" he, plaintiff's husband, said all right, and seemed to be perfectly satisfied. They were bid to enter, treated kindly and no objection whatever made to the presence of defendant Scattergood. That while there Scattergood, at Dr. De May's request, took hold of plaintiff's hand and held her during a paroxysm of pain, and that both of the defendants in all respects throughout acted in a proper and becoming manner actuated by a sense of duty and kindness. * * *

Dr. De May therefore took an unprofessional young unmarried man with him, introduced and permitted him to remain in the house of the plaintiff, when it was apparent that he could hear at least, if not see all that was said and done, and as the jury must have found, under the instructions given, without either the plaintiff or her husband having any knowledge or reason to believe the true character of such third party. It would be shocking to our sense of right, justice and propriety to doubt even but that for such an act the law would afford an ample remedy. To the plaintiff the occasion was a most sacred one and no one had a right to intrude unless invited or because of some real and pressing necessity which it is not pretended existed in this case. The plaintiff had a legal right to the privacy of her apartment at such a time, and the law secures to her this right by requiring others to observe it, and to abstain from its violation. The fact that at the time, she consented to the presence of Scattergood supposing him to be a physician, does not preclude her from maintaining an action and recovering substantial damages upon afterwards ascertaining his true character. In obtaining admission at such a time and under such circumstances without fully disclosing his true character, both parties were guilty of deceit, and the wrong thus done entitles the injured party to recover the damages afterwards sustained, from shame and mortification upon discovering the true character of the defendants. * * *

Judgment for plaintiff affirmed.

NOTES AND QUESTIONS

1. Defendant gives plaintiff some chocolate candy, which contains an irritant poison. In ignorance of this fact, plaintiff eats the candy, and is made ill. Is there liability for a battery? Cf. Commonwealth v. Stratton, 114 Mass. 303, 19 Am.Rep. 350 (1873). Defendant calls on plaintiff, a woman with an artificial leg, in her house. Representing himself to be a doctor, he induces her to remove her dress, expose her person, and to permit him to touch her. He is in fact a doctor, but of theology. Battery? Cf. Commonwealth v. Gregory, 132 Pa.Super. 507, 1 A.2d 501 (1938). On the effect, in general, of fraud and mistake on consent, see Restatement (Second) of Torts § 892B; Fischer, Fraudulently Induced Consent to Intentional Torts, 46 U.Cin.L.Rev. 71 (1977).

2. Suppose that A consents to sexual intercourse with B, in ignorance of the fact that B has a sexually transmitted disease. A contracts the disease. Has she an action against B? Kathleen K. v. Robert B., 150 Cal.App.3d 992, 198 Cal.Rptr. 273 (1984). Crowell v. Crowell, 180 N.C. 516, 105 S.E. 206 (1920); cf. De Vall v. Strunk, 96 S.W.2d 245 (Tex.Civ.App.1936). A woman consents to sexual intercourse with a man only after he assured her that "I can't possibly get anyone pregnant," knowing that the statement was false. She then suffers an ectopic pregnancy and must

undergo surgery, which saves her life but makes her sterile. Liability? Barbara A. v. John G., 145 Cal.App.3d 369, 193 Cal.Rptr. 422 (1983). Does it make a difference if he also does not know? See McPherson v. McPherson, 712 A.2d 1043 (Me.1998) (no liability because husband who infected wife with venereal disease neither knew nor had reason to know that he was infected). A wife consents to sexual intercourse with her husband, in ignorance of the fact that he is having an affair. After learning of the affair, she sues him for battery, claiming that her consent was obtained by fraud. Liability? Neal v. Neal, 125 Idaho 617, 873 P.2d 871 (1994).

3. Note that most of the "consent induced by fraud" cases involve battery. What if the underlying tort is trespass? Compare these two cases against ABC, which broadcasts PrimeTime Live. Plaintiff, an ophthalmic surgeon who owned several clinics, was approached by a producer of PrimeTime Live and told the show was doing a segment on cataract operations. The producer told plaintiff that the segment would not involve ambush interviews or undercover surveillance and would be fair and balanced. Plaintiff cooperated by permitting film crews and interviews of doctors, patients, and technicians at his clinic in Chicago. Unbeknownst to plaintiff, the producer also had dispatched seven undercover test "patients" equipped with concealed cameras to other clinic locations owned by plaintiff. The resulting show was very critical of the clinics. Plaintiff sues for trespass, claiming the consent given to the seven test patients with concealed cameras was induced by fraud. Liability? Desnick v. Am. Broadcasting Co., Inc., 44 F.3d 1345 (7th Cir.1995) (applying Illinois law) (no trespass because not an interference with the ownership or possession of land). Plaintiff, the Food Lion grocery store chain, was the target of a PrimeTime Live exposé on meat handling. Employees of ABC created false identities and applied for work at several Food Lion stores. While working for Food Lion, they filmed various activities with hidden cameras. Food Lion sued for trespass, claiming its consent to the ABC employees' presence in its deli and meatpacking departments was obtained by fraud. Food Lion, Inc. v. Capital Cities/ABC, Inc., 194 F.3d 505 (applying North and South Carolina law) (4th Cir. 1999) (jury verdict of trespass affirmed). See also Copeland v. Hubbard Broadcasting, Inc., 526 N.W.2d 402 (Minn.App.1995) (reporter posing as student interested in observing veterinarian liable in trespass to pet owners who allowed her in their home to observe). For a discussion of the invasion of privacy claims in these cases, see Chapter 18, Privacy.

4. Plaintiff is in a bar, so intoxicated that he does not know what he is doing when he agrees to "Indian wrestle" with defendant. Valid consent? Cf. Hollerud v. Malamis, 20 Mich.App. 748, 174 N.W.2d 626 (1969) (consent ineffective if plaintiff incapable of expressing rational will).

5. Plaintiff consents to an operation under a general anesthetic only on condition that her own physician is present during the operation. He was not present. Is the consent vitiated? Pugsley v. Privette, 220 Va. 892, 263 S.E.2d 69 (1980). What is the effect of allowing a resident physician to perform the operation under the supervision of the designated surgeon? Suppose the designated surgeon is not present at all.

6. "Informed Consent." The doctrine of "informed consent" requires a physician or surgeon to disclose to the patient the risks of proposed medical or surgical treatment. If she does not do so, she may be liable when injury results from the treatment. In early cases, this liability was placed on the ground of battery, by analogy to De May v. Roberts, and the cases in the preceding notes. Among the cases so holding have been Bang v. Charles T. Miller Hospital, 251 Minn. 427, 88 N.W.2d 186 (1958); Gray v. Grunnagle, 423 Pa. 144, 223 A.2d 663 (1966). Around 1960, the failure to disclose the risk began to be treated as a breach of the doctor's

professional duty, and hence as a matter of negligence. The cases now generally proceed on that basis. The matter is therefore treated in Chapter 4, Negligence. When the physician exceeds the boundaries of consent, the matter is still treated as battery as set forth in Mohr v. Williams. Some courts have attempted to broaden the battery theory in these types of situations. See Shultz, Informed Choice to Patient Choice: A New Protected Interest, 95 Yale L.J. 219 (1985).

Hart v. Geysel

Supreme Court of Washington, 1930.
159 Wash. 632, 294 P. 570.

MAIN, J. This action was brought by the administrator of the estate of Hamilton I. Cartwright, deceased, who died as the result of a blow received in a prize fight. To the amended complaint, which will be referred to as the complaint, each of the defendants interposed a demurrer which was sustained. The plaintiff refused to plead further and elected to stand upon the complaint. A judgment was entered dismissing the action, from which the plaintiff appeals.

February 5, 1929, Hamilton I. Cartwright and Cecil Geysel engaged in a prize fight in the city of Seattle, during which Cartwright received a blow which caused his death. In the complaint there are no facts showing that the mutual combat was engaged in in anger, that there was malicious intent to seriously injure, or that there was excessive force.

The controlling question is whether the action can be maintained for wrongful death when the encounter, though unlawful, was entered into with the consent of both parties.

Section 2556, Rem.Comp.Stat., makes prize fighting unlawful and provides that one engaging therein shall be guilty of a gross misdemeanor, with a proviso which is not here material. * * *

Upon the question stated, the adjudicated cases, as well as the text-writers, are in conflict. One line supports what is known as the majority rule, and the other, the minority. The majority rule has been stated as follows:

"Where the parties engage in mutual combat in anger, each is civilly liable to the other for any physical injury inflicted by him during the fight. The fact that the parties voluntarily engaged in the combat is no defense to an action by either of them to recover damages for personal injuries inflicted upon him by the other." [Cc]

The minority rule has been stated as follows:

"Where parties engage in a mutual combat in anger, the act of each is unlawful and relief will be denied them in a civil action; at least, in the absence of a showing of excessive force or malicious intent to do serious injury upon the part of the defendant." * * *

In each of the cases which support the majority rule, the combat was entered into in anger, with a malicious intent to seriously injure, and in some of them the question of excessive force was present as bearing upon the question of damages. In the cases which support the minority rule, the encounter, or fist fight, as it may be called, was entered into in anger, from which it would be necessarily inferred that there was an intent to do injury.

The majority rule carries into a civil action, where one party sues the other for damages for something which has been done in violation of positive law, the principle applied in criminal prosecutions by the state to the effect that the consent of one or both of the parties does not prevent such a prosecution. The minority rule does not apply this principle when a civil action is brought by one of the parties against the other for damages which have been sustained in a combat consented to by both parties, but which was in violation of positive law. The authorities supporting the majority rule recognize that if the thing done is not one prohibited by positive law, for which a penalty is imposed, then consent is a complete defense in a civil action for damages. The majority rule is an exception to two generally well-recognized and accepted principles of law: (a) That one who has consented to suffer a particular invasion of his private right has no right to complain; and (b) that no one shall profit by his own wrongdoing. The minority rule recognizes and applies these principles.

The facts in the case now before us do not bring it within the authorities supporting the majority rule, because here there are no facts which show anger, malicious intent to injure, or excessive force. It may be stated that the facts of this case do not contain one element of the minority rule, that of anger. It is unnecessary, as we view it, in the present case to adopt either rule. It is sufficient to say that in our opinion one who engages in prize fighting, even though prohibited by positive law, and sustains an injury, should not have a right to recover any damages that he may sustain as the result of the combat, which he expressly consented to and engaged in as a matter of business or sport. To enforce the criminal statute against prize fighting, it is not necessary to reward the one that got the worst of the encounter at the expense of his more fortunate opponent. This view is supported by the rule tentatively adopted by the American Law Institute [and now § 60 of the First and Second Restatements of Torts.]

The appellant cites a number of cases which hold that consent to an abortion by a patient is no defense to a subsequent action for damages against the doctor for performing the operation in a negligent manner, but if that be the rule in such cases it is not necessarily applicable to the facts now before us. We here distinctly do not express any opinion upon whether consent to an abortion precludes a right of recovery for the negligent act of the doctor in performing the operation.

The judgment will be affirmed.

NOTES AND QUESTIONS

1. The question of when plaintiff's consent should be invalidated because defendant violated a criminal statute is not free from difficulty. Some of the considerations include (a) the policy of denying compensation to an intentional wrongdoer who himself may have committed a crime and been injured as a result of it; (b) the effect of deterring him, and others like him, by denying him recovery if he

gets hurt; (c) the effect of potential liability in deterring defendant, and others like him; (d) the fact that plaintiff has after all been intentionally battered by defendant; (e) the policy expressed by the maxim, *In pari delicto potior est conditio defendentis* [In equal guilt, the position of the defendant is the stronger].

2. A growing number of courts and the Restatement (Second) of Torts § 892C have followed the position espoused in Hudson v. Craft, 33 Cal.2d 654, 204 P.2d 1 (1949). Plaintiff's consent will be nullified if the defendant's conduct violated a criminal statute designed to protect a class of persons to which plaintiff belongs. Under that theory, how would the following cases be decided?

A. Plaintiff, a 15–year–old girl, consents to intercourse with a 50–year–old man in a state with criminal penalties for men who have sexual relations with children that age. Most courts have held plaintiff's consent to be ineffective. See Gaither v. Meacham, 214 Ala. 343, 108 So. 2 (1926). A competent adult woman, however, cannot maintain an action for her own seduction when she has consented, even if intercourse between unmarried adults is illegal in the state. Defendant's overpowering personality or extraordinary powers of persuasion are not tantamount to "duress" that would nullify consent. See Rouse v. Creech, 203 N.C. 378, 166 S.E. 174 (1932).

B. Defendant provides plaintiff's decedent with sleeping pills, knowing he intends to use them to commit suicide. The state's criminal law prohibits both aiding and abetting suicide and attempted suicide. Schwartz, Civil Liability for Causing Suicide: A Synthesis of Law and Psychiatry, 24 Vand.L.Rev. 217, 220–222 (1971), evaluating the factors set forth in note 1, suggests that a claim should be allowed. Would family members of those who commit suicide using the Kevorkian suicide machine have a cause of action against Dr. Kevorkian?

C. Defendant physician provides plaintiff with an abortion at a period in her pregnancy when the action is illegal. Prior to Roe v. Wade, 410 U.S. 113 (1973), which limited the power of states to regulate abortions, courts were about evenly divided on the question of whether the consent of the woman upon whom the operation was performed barred her recovery. One line of cases, as in Miller v. Bennett, 190 Va. 162, 56 S.E.2d 217 (1949), held that the consent is a bar. Another, as in Milliken v. Heddesheimer, 110 Ohio St. 381, 144 N.E. 264 (1924), held that it is not.

3. The classic article on the general subject is Bohlen, Consent as Affecting Civil Liability for Breaches of the Peace, 24 Colum.L.Rev. 849 (1924).

2. Self-Defense

The privilege of self-defense is normally covered in Criminal Law, and detailed discussion must be left to that course. Cases involving tort liability are infrequent. When they arise, the criminal law rules are carried over and applied without much variation. The following brief summary will indicate how self-defense fits into the tort picture:

1. *Existence of Privilege*. Anyone is privileged to use reasonable force to defend himself against a threatened battery on the part of another. The recognition of this privilege came as late as about 1400, and it always has been an affirmative defense to be pleaded and proved by the defendant. In some jurisdictions, the burden of proof is reversed if the defendant is a police officer. Then, plaintiff would have to show as his prime facie battery case that the use of force was unreasonable (and thus not privileged). See,

for example, Edson v. City of Anaheim, 63 Cal. App. 4th 1269, 74 Cal. Rptr. 2d 614 (1998), collecting cases from other jurisdictions. The trial court judge will make the initial determination whether a self-defense instruction is warranted by the facts. See, for example, Goldfuss v. Davidson, 79 Ohio St. 3d 116, 679 N.E.2d 1099 (1997) in which the Supreme Court of Ohio approved the trial court judge's refusal to give a jury instruction on self-defense where defendant shot from his kitchen window at two men who had broken in to his pole barn. Defendant and his family were inside the house with all the doors locked, the police had been called, the pole barn was a hundred feet from the house, and the men were running away when defendant fired.

2. *Retaliation.* The privilege is one of defense against threatened battery, and not one of retaliation. When the battery is no longer threatened, the privilege terminates; and thereafter the original victim himself becomes liable for battery. Germolus v. Sausser, 83 Minn. 141, 85 N.W. 946 (1901) (defendant had grabbed a whip away from plaintiff and then knocked him unconscious); cf. Drabek v. Sabley, 31 Wis.2d 184, 142 N.W.2d 798 (1966) (battery and false imprisonment of boy who had thrown a snowball).

Even if a person initially was an aggressor, once he has retreated he has a right to self-defense against the person he initially threatened. Edgar v. Emily, 637 S.W.2d 412 (Mo.App.1982) (After coming to his sister's house armed with a stick, defendant walked back to his car intending to leave. At that point, the sister's husband came out of the house and grabbed defendant's shirt sleeve, which ripped as he tried to leave. The two men began fighting and the sister came at defendant with a hatchet or hammer and hit him in the face with her fist. He then hit his sister with the stick).

3. *Reasonable Belief.* The privilege exists when the defendant reasonably believes that the force is necessary to protect himself against battery, even though there is in fact no necessity. This is an instance in which a reasonable mistake on the part of the actor will protect him. The reason that the rule in Ranson v. Kitner, page 23, is not applied is apparently the importance attached by the courts to "self-preservation as the first law of nature." Smith v. Delery, 238 La. 180, 114 So.2d 857 (1959) (newspaper delivery boy shot while retrieving his dog from the back of defendant's house); Bunten v. Davis, 82 N.H. 304, 133 A. 16 (1926) (defendant fired at plaintiff and his companions who were out riding around on the Fourth of July setting off fireworks).

A. Plaintiff and defendant were on bad terms. They met in the highway, and defendant accosted plaintiff, asking why plaintiff had been slandering him. Plaintiff, who had a reputation for shooting people, suddenly put his hand into his pocket. Defendant, believing that he was about to draw a revolver, struck him on the head with a cane and knocked him down. It was held that the jury should have been instructed that defendant was liable only if he had no reasonable grounds to fear an immediate attack by plaintiff. Keep v. Quallman, 68 Wis. 451, 32 N.W. 233 (1887).

B. Defendant ejected from a dance an intoxicated individual named Noble, who had not paid his admission fee. Defendant was then informed that Noble was outside, "getting some bricks." Defendant stepped into the doorway, looking out into the darkness for Noble. At this moment, plaintiff, arriving late for the dance, came running rapidly up the steps, which were dimly lighted. Defendant, believing that he was being attacked by Noble, struck plaintiff and knocked him down the steps. Defendant was held not liable. Crabtree v. Dawson, 119 Ky. 148, 83 S.W. 557 (1904).

4. *Provocation.* Should insults, verbal threats, or opprobrious language justify the exercise of self-defense? Almost every court that has passed upon the question has held that they do not. See Crotteau v. Karlgaard, 48 Wis.2d 245, 179 N.W.2d 797 (1970) ("Get out of the way, you dumb son of a bitch"); Prell Hotel Corp. v. Antonacci, 86 Nev. 390, 469 P.2d 399 (1970) ("hateful, degrading name"). For a long time, some Louisiana courts permitted this line of defense, but that state has joined the others. See Morneau v. American Oil Co., 272 So.2d 313 (La.1973), noted in 34 La.L.Rev. 137 (1973). In many states, the offending words can be introduced on the issue of punitive damages, and in some states they may reduce compensatory damages.

Although the general rule of law is relatively clear, its application in the context of disputes is not. Thus, if the abusive words are accompanied by an actual threat of physical violence reasonably warranting an apprehension of imminent bodily harm, one may be privileged to defend, see Silas v. Bowen, 277 F.Supp. 314 (D.S.C.1967); and one does not have to wait for the blow to fall before acting. See Martin v. Estrella, 107 R.I. 247, 266 A.2d 41 (1970). Further, when accompanied by an overt hostile act, oral abuse may amount to a challenge to fight and constitute consent. Restatement (Second) of Torts § 69.

5. *Amount of Force.* The privilege is limited to the use of force that is or reasonably appears to be necessary for protection against a threatened battery. Differences in age, size and relative strength are proper considerations. Thus, a 5'6", 135–pound middle-aged man was permitted to ward off a 6'6", 230–pound young athlete with a shot aimed near his feet. Silas v. Bowen, 277 F.Supp. 314 (D.S.C.1967) (it missed and hit plaintiff). Similarly a small ten-year-old was permitted to throw a broom at a larger ten-year-old in McDonald v. Terrebonne Parish School Bd., 253 So.2d 558 (La.App. 1971), cert. denied, 260 La. 128, 255 So.2d 353 (1971) (it missed and took out plaintiff's eye). But a teenage boy engaged in a fistfight with another was not justified in using a baseball bat to protect himself from the threatened injury in Andrepont v. Naquin, 345 So.2d 1216 (La.App.1977). To justify resistance with a deadly weapon, defendant must have a reasonable apprehension of loss of life or great bodily injury. See Greenberg v. Mobil Oil Corp., 318 F.Supp. 1025 (N.D.Tex.1970). Generally, defendant has the burden of proving that the use of force was reasonable under the circumstances, although some jurisdictions shift the burden to the plaintiff if the defendant is a police officer. See, for example, Edson v. City of

Anaheim, 63 Cal. App. 4th 1269, 74 Cal. Rptr. 2d 614 (1998), collecting cases from other jurisdictions.

6. *Retreat.* One basic disagreement in approach to the privilege of self-defense focuses on whether the defendant must retreat if he can do so without increasing his danger, rather than stand his ground and use force. It is settled that he may stand his ground and use any force short of that likely to cause serious injury. The common law rule was that, rather than kill his assailant or seriously wound him, defendant must "retreat to the wall." A minority of the American courts still apply this rule, and it is adopted by the Restatement (Second) of Torts § 65. Even the Restatement, however, does not require retreat within one's own home. The majority have insisted upon a higher importance of the dignity and honor of the individual and have held that the defendant may stand his ground and use deadly force, and even kill his assailant. Since it is usually difficult or impossible to retreat safely from an assailant with a gun, the question no longer has the importance that it once had, particularly since the Restatement provides that the victim may use deadly force if there is the slightest doubt, if reasonable, that the retreat can be safely made, and "in determining whether his doubt is reasonable every allowance must be made for the predicament in which his assailant has placed him." Restatement (Second) of Torts § 65, comment *g*.

7. *Injury to Third Party.* A small number of cases have dealt with the situation in which the defendant, defending himself against A, unintentionally shoots B instead. So far as "transferred intent" is concerned, the privilege of self-defense is carried over, and the defendant is held not to be liable to B in the absence of some negligence toward him. And in determining whether there is negligence, the emergency, and the necessity of defense against A, are still to be considered. Morris v. Platt, 32 Conn. 75 (1864); Shaw v. Lord, 41 Okl. 347, 137 P. 885 (1914). Cf. Thompson v. Beliauskas, 341 Mass. 95, 167 N.E.2d 163 (1960) (defense of property).

3.   DEFENSE OF OTHERS

1. *Nature of Privilege.* A privilege similar to that of self-defense is recognized for the defense of third persons. The early common law recognized a feudal privilege in the master of the household to defend members of his family and his servants against attack. Most of the cases have involved members of the same family defending one another, or the relation of master and servant, as in Frew v. Teagarden, 111 Kan. 107, 205 P. 1023 (1922), but the privilege is not so limited.

As in the case of self-defense, the closest questions concern whether defendant used reasonable force in the circumstances. For cases upholding the privilege, see e.g., Boyer v. Waples, 206 Cal.App.2d 725, 24 Cal.Rptr. 192 (1962) (plaintiff, who had previously made serious threats to members of defendant's family and was seen outside the defendant's home at night with an object in hand that looked like dynamite, but was, in fact, a flashlight, was shot and wounded); McCullough v. McAnelly, 248 So.2d 7 (La.App.1971), cert. denied, 259 La. 748, 252 So.2d 451 (1971) (three teenaged boys attacked defendant's son and would not desist when warned; father shot and wounded one). Compare Lopez v. Surchia, 112 Cal.App.2d 314, 246 P.2d 111 (1952) (defendant shot boy who was fighting with defendant's son on front lawn—force exceeded privilege).

2. *Reasonable Mistake.* One question over which the courts have differed is that of the effect of a reasonable mistake as to the necessity for taking action. Some courts hold that the intervenor steps into the shoes of the person he is defending, and is privileged only when that person would be privileged to defend himself. If it turns out that he has intervened to help the aggressor, he is liable. Robinson v. Decatur, 32 Ala.App. 654, 29 So.2d 429 (1947). Other courts hold that the defendant is privileged to use reasonable force to defend another even when he is mistaken in his belief that intervention is necessary, so long as his mistake was reasonable. The Restatement (Second) of Torts § 76, has adopted this position.

4. DEFENSE OF PROPERTY

Katko v. Briney

Supreme Court of Iowa, 1971.
183 N.W.2d 657.

MOORE, CHIEF JUSTICE. The primary issue presented here is whether an owner may protect personal property in an unoccupied boarded-up farm house against trespassers and thieves by a spring gun capable of inflicting death or serious injury.

We are not here concerned with a man's right to protect his home and members of his family. Defendants' home was several miles from the scene of the incident to which we refer infra.

Plaintiff's action is for damages resulting from serious injury caused by a shot from a 20–gauge spring shotgun set by defendants in a bedroom of an old farm house which has been uninhabited for several years. Plaintiff and his companion * * * had broken and entered the house to find and steal old bottles and dated fruit jars which they considered antiques. * * *

The jury returned a verdict for plaintiff and against defendants for $20,000 actual and $10,000 punitive damages.

After careful consideration of defendants' motions for judgment notwithstanding the verdict and for new trial, the experienced and capable trial judge overruled them and entered judgment on the verdict. Thus we have this appeal by defendants. * * *

[The house was inherited from Mrs. Briney's grandparents and had been unoccupied for some time. There had been a series of intrusions and thefts.] Defendants through the years boarded up the windows and doors in an attempt to stop the intrusions. They had posted "no trespass" signs on the land several years before 1967. The nearest one was 35 feet from the house. On June 11, 1967 defendants set "a shotgun trap" in the north

Mr. and Mrs. Edward Briney in front of their vacant farmhouse near Oskaloosa, Iowa

bedroom. After Mr. Briney cleaned and oiled his 20–gauge shotgun, the power of which he was well aware, defendants took it to the old house where they secured it to an iron bed with the barrel pointed at the bedroom door. It was rigged with wire from the doorknob to the gun's trigger so it would fire when the door was opened. Briney first pointed the gun so an intruder would be hit in the stomach but at Mrs. Briney's suggestion it was

Plaintiff Marvin E. Katko

lowered to hit the legs. He admitted he did so "because I was mad and tired of being tormented" but "he did not intend to injure anyone." He gave no explanation of why he used a loaded shell and set it to hit a person already in the house. Tin was nailed over the bedroom window. The spring gun could not be seen from the outside. No warning of its presence was posted. * * *

[Plaintiff] entered the old house by removing a board from a porch window which was without glass. * * * As he started to open the north bedroom door the shotgun went off striking him in the right leg above the ankle bone. Much of his leg, including part of the tibia, was blown away. Only by * * * assistance [from his accomplice] was plaintiff able to get out of the house and after crawling some distance was put in his vehicle and rushed to a doctor and then to a hospital. He remained in the hospital 40 days. * * *

There was undenied medical testimony plaintiff had a permanent deformity, a loss of tissue, and a shortening of the leg. * * *

The main thrust of defendants' defense in the trial court and on this appeal is that "the law permits use of a spring gun in a dwelling or warehouse for the purpose of preventing the unlawful entry of a burglar or thief." * * *

Instruction 6 stated: "An owner of premises is prohibited from willfully or intentionally injuring a trespasser by means of force that either takes life or inflicts great bodily injury; and therefore a person owning a premise is prohibited from setting out 'spring guns' and like dangerous devices which will likely take life or inflict great bodily injury, for the purpose of harming trespassers. The fact that the trespasser may be acting in violation of the law does not change the rule. The only time when such conduct of setting a 'spring gun' or a like dangerous device is justified would be when the trespasser was committing a felony of violence or a felony punishable by death, or where the trespasser was endangering human life by his act." * * *

The overwhelming weight of authority, both textbook and case law, supports the trial court's statement of the applicable principles of law. * * *

Restatement of Torts § 85, 180, states: "The value of human life and limb, not only to the individual concerned but also to society, so outweighs the interest of a possessor of land in excluding from it those whom he is not willing to admit thereto that a possessor of land has, as is stated in § 79, no privilege to use force intended or likely to cause death or serious harm against another whom the possessor sees about to enter his premises or meddle with his chattel, unless the intrusion threatens death or serious bodily harm to the occupiers or users of the premises. * * * A possessor of land cannot do indirectly and by a mechanical device that which, were he present, he could not do immediately and in person. Therefore, he cannot gain a privilege to install, for the purpose of protecting his land from intrusions harmless to the lives and limbs of the occupiers or users of it, a mechanical device whose only purpose is to inflict death or serious harm upon such as may intrude, by giving notice of his intention to inflict, by mechanical means and indirectly, harm which he could not, even after request, inflict directly were he present." * * *

The facts in Allison v. Fiscus, 156 Ohio St. 120, 100 N.E.2d 237, decided in 1951, are very similar to the case at bar. There plaintiff's right to damages was recognized for injuries received when he feloniously broke a door latch and started to enter defendant's warehouse with intent to steal. As he entered a trap of two sticks of dynamite buried under the doorway by defendant owner was set off and plaintiff seriously injured. The court held the question whether a particular trap was justified as a use of reasonable and necessary force against a trespasser engaged in the commission of a felony should have been submitted to the jury. The Ohio Supreme Court recognized plaintiff's right to recover punitive or exemplary damages in addition to compensatory damages. * * *

In addition to civil liability many jurisdictions hold a landowner criminally liable for serious injuries or homicide caused by spring guns or other set devices. [Cc] * * *

[The court declined to rule on whether punitive damages were allowable in this type of case because defendant's attorney had not raised that issue in the trial court.]

Study and careful consideration of defendants' contentions on appeal reveal no reversible error.

Affirmed.

LARSON, JUSTICE [dissented, noting that the trial judge's instructions "failed to tell the jury it could find the installation was not made with the intent or purpose of striking or injuring the plaintiff," and that the principle espoused by the court had never been applied to a burglar, but only "in the case of a mere trespasser in a vineyard."]

NOTES AND QUESTIONS

1. Katko pled guilty to petty larceny and received a 30–day suspended sentence and a $50 fine. The Brineys had to sell 80 acres of their 120–acre farm in order to pay the judgment in this case. A strange development later arose between the parties. When the 80 acres were put up for judgment sale and there were no bids above the minimum price of $10,000, three neighbors borrowed money to purchase the land for a dollar more, expecting to hold it for the Brineys until they won their appeal. When they did not win, the neighbors leased the land back to them for enough to pay taxes and interest costs on the money the neighbors had borrowed. Several years later when land values rose, the neighbors offered to sell it back to Brineys at a price they could not afford. One of the neighbors then bought the property from the others for $16,000 and sold it to his son for $16,500. The Brineys and Katko, to whom the Brineys still owed money from the judgment, then sued the neighbors, arguing that the land was being held in trust for the Brineys and that they were entitled to the profit from the increase in value. Just before the case came to trial, it was settled for a sum large enough to pay the remainder of

Brineys' judgment to Katko. Further background about the case can be found in Palmer, Katko v. Briney: A Study in American Gothic, 56 Iowa L.Rev. 1219 (1971).

2. The United Press International (UPI) reported the results of the trial court decision in this case, stating in part that Katko was "shot and seriously injured in the *home* of Mr. and Mrs. Edward Briney." (Emphasis added.) A public outcry about the decision resulted in the introduction of "Briney Bills" in several state legislatures. The Nebraska Legislature enacted a self-defense act that provided in part that "no person * * * shall be placed in * * * jeopardy * * * for protecting, by any means necessary, himself, his family, or his real or personal property * * *." The statute was held to be unconstitutional by the Supreme Court of Nebraska on the ground of improper delegation of sentencing authority. See State v. Goodseal, 186 Neb. 359, 183 N.W.2d 258 (1971), cert. denied, 404 U.S. 845 (1971).

Unlike in the case of self-defense, a reasonable mistake as to the existence of the privilege will not protect the defendant. That is, he acts at his own peril in defending property and will be liable if the invader is on the land as a matter of right.

4. As in the case of self-defense, the privilege to defend property is limited to the use of force reasonably necessary to the situation as it appears to the defendant. What constitutes reasonable force is normally a question for the jury, but there are several recognized limitations. When the invasion is peaceful and occurs in the presence of the possessor, the use of any force at all will be unreasonable unless a request has been made to depart. Chapell v. Schmidt, 104 Cal. 511, 38 P. 892 (1894) (defendant caned elderly person who was picking flowers); Emmons v. Quade, 176 Mo. 22, 75 S.W. 103 (1903) (mill worker used a club on a twelve-year-old boy who was trying to scoop up grain that had been left in a railroad car after it was unloaded). A request does not have to be made, however, when the conduct of the intruder would indicate to a reasonable person that it would be useless or that it could not safely be made in time. See Higgins v. Minaghan, 78 Wis. 602, 47 N.W. 941 (1891).

5. *Use of Force Calculated to Cause Death or Serious Injury.* The principal case caused a good deal of re-thinking about when, if ever, force calculated to cause death or serious injury may be utilized to defend property. It is one of the few cases in which a burglar or a thief was able to recover civil damages from his intended victim.

A. When the invader threatens the personal safety of the defendant or his family (self-defense), the defendant may use deadly force if it is necessary in the circumstances. This is likely to occur when the invader attempts to enter the homestead at night. See Tipsword v. Potter, 31 Idaho 509, 174 P. 133 (1918); Coleman v. New York & N.H.R. Co., 106 Mass. 160 (1870).

B. There also is a privilege to use reasonable force to prevent the commission of a crime. With a serious felony like burglary the amount of permissible force is greater, and some courts have permitted a deadly force. See Scheuermann v. Scharfenberg, 163 Ala. 337, 50 So. 335 (1909) (uninhabited warehouse); Gray v. Combs, 30 Ky. 478 (1832) (same). Do you think a court would make the same decision in those cases today? What if the property was a government laboratory where deadly biological agents were stored for research?

C. In Ilott v. Wilkes, 3 B. & Ald. 304, 106 Eng.Rep. 674 (1820), it was held that a landowner who placed spring guns on his land to keep off poachers was not liable to a trespasser who was shot. The result of this decision was a storm of public disapproval, which led to an act of Parliament making the setting of such devices a crime. In Bird v. Holbrook, 4 Bing. 628, 130 Eng.Rep. 911 (1824), a case which arose before the statute was passed, but was decided afterward, the court overruled the *Ilott* case and a defendant who set a spring gun was held liable to a trespasser.

D.   Most American courts, including the Iowa Supreme Court, and the Restatement (Second) of Torts § 85 have followed Bird v. Holbrook. Many jurisdictions have placed the restrictions on the use of deadly force in their state statutory codes. See statutes collected in Posner, Killing or Wounding to Protect a Property Interest, 14 J.L. & Econ. 201, 228–232 (1971). Some statutes and some cases appear to allow the use of deadly force against serious invasions of property, such as burglary. There is also some authority that the right of peaceful habitation may be protected by the use of deadly force. See Model Penal Code § 3.06(d)(i) (1962). Compare Bramble v. Thompson, 264 Md. 518, 287 A.2d 265 (1972) (German Shepherd).

E.   The general rule prohibiting deadly force is modified in some states if defendant gives the plaintiff clear notice of the danger. See Starkey v. Dameron, 92 Colo. 420, 21 P.2d 1112 (1933) (dictum); State v. Marfaudille, 48 Wash. 117, 92 P. 939 (1907). This is especially likely to occur when defendant's use of force involved a vicious dog. See Hood v. Waldrum, 58 Tenn.App. 512, 434 S.W.2d 94 (1968); Sappington v. Sutton, 501 P.2d 814 (Okl.1972). Compare Loomis v. Terry, 17 Wend. 496, 31 Am.Dec. 306 (N.Y.1837) (no warning, defendant liable). Barbed wire may give notice in and of itself. See Quigley v. Clough, 173 Mass. 429, 53 N.E. 884 (1899). What privilege is operating in these cases? In most jurisdictions, even posted warnings will not protect the landholder if he would not be privileged to use this amount of force were he there in person. See State v. Plumlee, 177 La. 687, 149 So. 425 (1933); State v. Childers, 133 Ohio St. 508, 14 N.E.2d 767 (1938).

F.   What if the landholder claims that he intended only to frighten and not to injure the intruder? How does this correlate with the doctrine of transferred intent? See Allison v. Fiscus, 156 Ohio St. 120, 100 N.E.2d 237 (1951) (defendant argued that he did not think the two sticks of dynamite buried in the floor of tool shed would injure anyone). In Goldfuss v. Davidson, 79 Ohio St. 3d 116, 679 N.E.2d 1099 (1997), defendant yelled at men he saw running away from his pole barn and fired from his kitchen window warning shots "over their heads" to try to get them to stop until the police arrived. One of the men was killed by the shots and his father filed a wrongful death action against defendant. The court found no prejudicial error in the trial court judge's instruction that the jury was to determine whether defendant's discharge of a firearm was reasonably necessary to prevent the theft of his property. The jury awarded $150,000 to the estate of the thief.

6.   The limitations on the possessor's privilege may also restrict his power to eject the plaintiff from his property into a position of unreasonable physical danger. Thus a teenager stealing a ride on a railroad train cannot be thrown off at thirty miles an hour. Chesapeake & O. Ry. Co. v. Ryan Adm'r, 183 Ky. 428, 209 S.W. 538 (1919). In Depue v. Flateau, 100 Minn. 299, 111 N.W. 1 (1907), plaintiff, a travelling cattle buyer, called at defendant's farmhouse on a cold winter evening, and was asked to stay for dinner. After dinner plaintiff was overcome by a "fainting spell," and became very weak and seriously ill. He asked permission to stay over night, which was refused. Defendant led him out to his sleigh, put him into it, adjusted the robes around him, and threw the reins, which he was too weak to hold, over his shoulders. Defendant then started the horses on the road to town. Plaintiff was found the following morning by the side of the road about three-quarters of a mile away, badly frost-bitten, and nearly frozen to death. Case was permitted to go to the jury. Suppose the landowner places a drunken guest in his car to go home?

7. On the other hand, if the plaintiff's presence endangers the personal safety of those on the premises, the privilege of self-defense, or that of defense of third persons, may justify the ejection. In Tucker v. Burt, 152 Mich. 68, 115 N.W. 722 (1908), plaintiff, the mother-in-law of the janitor of an apartment house, fell ill with a highly contagious disease. Defendant, the owner of the building, ejected her. It was held that defendant was not liable. One of the interesting facts about Tucker v. Burt is that the plaintiff's description of her trip from her daughter's apartment (from which she was ejected by defendant landlord) to her own apartment includes walking a block to the street car stop, two street car rides (including a transfer), and then walking two blocks to her apartment. She obviously exposed many more people to her illness during the trip than she would have had she stayed put at her daughter's apartment. How could that point be used in the case to support a public policy argument in favor of plaintiff's recovery from her daughter's landlord?

8. See Bohlen and Burns, The Privilege to Protect Property by Dangerous Barriers and Mechanical Devices, 35 Yale L.J. 535 (1926); Hart, Injuries to Trespassers, 47 Law Q.Rev. 92, 101–105 (1931).

5. RECOVERY OF PROPERTY

Hodgeden v. Hubbard

Supreme Court of Vermont, 1846.
18 Vt. 504, 46 Am.Dec. 167.

[Trespass for assault and battery, and for taking and carrying away a stove. Plaintiff buyer had purchased the stove on credit at the warehouse of defendants, and carried it away. Defendants discovered almost at once that plaintiff had misrepresented his assets and credit and that he was financially irresponsible. They immediately started out in pursuit, and overtook the plaintiff about two miles away, where they took the stove away from him by force. His resistance was such that the defendants used violence and applied force to his person with "great rudeness and outrage." Plaintiff drew a knife, and he was then forcibly held by one of the defendants while the other took possession of the stove.

The court charged the jury that, although plaintiff was guilty of misrepresentation and fraud in obtaining the stove, the defendants were still not justified in forcibly taking it from him, or using force against his person, but must resort to redress by legal process; and that if they found that the force was used, the defendants would be liable. Verdict for plaintiff for $1.00 damages. Exceptions by defendants.]

WILLIAMS, CH. J. It is admitted, in this case, that the property in the stove did not pass to the plaintiff, that, though the plaintiff obtained possession of the stove, yet it was by such means of falsehood and fraud, criminal in the eye of the law, as made the possession unlawful, and that, although the consent of the owner was apparently obtained to the delivery of the possession to the plaintiff, yet, as it respects the plaintiff, and so far as the right of property was concerned, no such consent was given. * * *

In the present case the defendants had clearly a right to retake the property, thus fraudulently obtained from them, if it could be done without unnecessary violence to the person, or without breach of the peace. * * *

[handwritten margin notes: "① Rule of law: ∆ can take back property as long as he used unreasonable force"]

[handwritten margin notes: "② Holding: as Plaintiff resisted and (with drawn knife) defendants justified in using force"]

In this case before us it is stated, that it did not appear "how much force was used, or its character," before the defendants were assaulted by the plaintiff. To obtain possession of the property in question no violence to the person of the plaintiff was necessary, or required, unless from his resistance. * * * The plaintiff had no lawful possession, nor any right to resist the attempt of the defendants to regain the property, of which he had unlawfully and fraudulently obtained the possession. By drawing his knife he became the aggressor, inasmuch as he had no right thus to protect his fraudulent attempt to acquire the stove, and the possession of the same, and it was the right of the defendants to hold him by force, and, if they made use of no unnecessary violence, they were justified; if they were guilty of more, they were liable. * * *

The judgment of the county court is reversed.

NOTES AND QUESTIONS

1. The privilege of an owner dispossessed of a chattel to use force to recapture it appears to have been first recognized in cases in which there was only a momentary interruption of his possession, so that it was easy to regard him as in effect defending his original possession rather than interfering with that of another. This was extended later to situations in which the wrongdoer had obtained the chattel by force or fraud, and had made his escape with it, but the pursuit was "fresh." These limitations have continued to be applied to the privilege. As to the requirement of force or fraud, see Watson v. Rheinderknecht, 82 Minn. 235, 84 N.W. 798 (1901).

2. Fresh pursuit is limited to prompt discovery of the dispossession, and prompt and persistent efforts to recover the chattel. Any undue lapse of time during which the pursuit has not been commenced, or has come to a halt, will mean that the owner is no longer privileged to fight himself back into possession, but must resort to the law. Restatement (Second) of Torts § 103.

3. The privilege is limited to force reasonable under the circumstances. As in the case of the defense of possession, it is not reasonable to use force calculated to inflict serious bodily harm to protect a property interest. Gortarez v. Smitty's Super Value, Inc., 140 Ariz. 97, 680 P.2d 807 (1984) (shopowner's use of a choke hold on teenage boy after chasing him in parking lot because of suspected shoplifting was not reasonable). Restatement (Second) of Torts § 106. If the wrongdoer resists, the owner may use any force reasonably required to defend his own person. Gyre v. Culver, 47 Barb. (N.Y.) 592 (1867); Hamilton v. Barker, 116 Mich. 684, 75 N.W. 133 (1898). A resort to any force at all will not be justified until a demand has been made for the return of the property; but this is not required when it reasonably appears that demand would be useless or dangerous. Restatement (Second) of Torts § 104.

4. The few cases dealing with the point indicate that this privilege differs from the privilege of defending the original possession, in that the loss due to a reasonable mistake must fall on the one who makes it. Estes v. Brewster Cigar Co., 156 Wash. 465, 287 P. 36 (1930); Restatement (Second) of Torts § 100, comment *d*, adding "unless the mistake was induced by the other."

5. The question frequently arises in cases of conditional sales of such things as automobiles, pianos, refrigerators and television sets, where the buyer has purchased on the installment plan, has been given possession, and has defaulted in his

payments. Title has remained in the seller, and upon such default he is entitled to possession; and if he can retake the chattel peaceably he may do so without liability. On the other hand, since he has voluntarily surrendered possession in the first place, he has no privilege to recapture it by force; and if the buyer will not give up the chattel, he must resort to his legal remedy. Roberts v. Speck, 169 Wash. 613, 14 P.2d 33 (1932). There have been quite a few cases—not all in agreement—dealing with what constitutes the use of force (for example, the use of a skeleton key).

6.   The courts are not agreed as to whether a clause in the contract giving the seller the privilege to use force is effective. A few of the older decisions have held that it is. Lambert v. Robinson, 162 Mass. 34, 37 N.E. 753 (1894); W.T. Walker Furniture Co. v. Dyson, 32 App.D.C. 90 (1908). The prevailing view of the later decisions is that the clause is void as inviting a breach of the peace. Girard v. Anderson, 219 Iowa 142, 257 N.W. 400 (1934), is one of the best decisions. Is the problem one of the scope of the privilege of recapture or whether consent should be invalidated?

7.   The retaking of possession by a seller under a conditional sale, on default by the buyer, is now controlled by § 9–503 of the Uniform Commercial Code, which provides that "unless otherwise agreed a secured party has on default the right to take possession of the collateral. In taking possession a secured party may proceed without judicial process if this can be done without breach of the peace."

Bonkowski v. Arlan's Department Store

Court of Appeals of Michigan, 1968.
12 Mich.App. 88, 162 N.W.2d 347.

NEAL E. FITZGERALD, JUDGE. This appeal from a jury verdict for false arrest and slander, rendered against the defendant store whose agent stopped and questioned the plaintiff whom he suspected of larceny, surprisingly presents questions that are novel to the appellate courts of this jurisdiction.

The plaintiff, Mrs. Marion Bonkowski, accompanied by her husband, had left the defendant's Saginaw, Michigan store about 10:00 p.m. on the night of December 18, 1962 after making several purchases, when Earl Reinhardt, a private policeman on duty that night in the defendant's store, called to her to stop as she was walking to her car about 30 feet away in the adjacent parking lot. Reinhardt motioned to the plaintiff to return toward the store and when she had done so, Reinhardt said that someone in the store had told him the plaintiff had put three pieces of costume jewelry into her purse without having paid for them. Mrs. Bonkowski denied she had taken anything unlawfully, but Reinhardt told her he wanted to see the contents of her purse. On a cement step in front of the store, plaintiff emptied the contents of her purse into her husband's hands. The plaintiff produced sales slips for the items she had purchased, and Reinhardt, satisfied that she had not committed larceny, returned to the store.

Plaintiff brought this action against Earl Reinhardt and Arlan's Department Store, seeking damages on several counts. She complains that as a result of defendant's tortious acts she has suffered numerous psychosomatic symptoms, including headaches, nervousness, and depression. Arlan's Department Store filed a third-party complaint against Earl Reinhardt's employer, Gerald Kaweck, doing business as Michigan Security Police Service, who defaulted. On the counts of false arrest and slander the case went to the jury, who returned a verdict of $43,750. The defendant's motions for judgment notwithstanding the verdict, remittitur, and new trial were denied by the trial court. * * *

We conclude the plaintiff established a case entitling her to go to the jury on a charge of false arrest. [The court first concluded that the private policeman Reinhardt was the agent of defendant department store, which was responsible for his acts.]

To the common-law tort of false arrest, privilege is a common-law defense, and we recognize as applicable here a privilege similar to that recognized by the American Law Institute in the Restatement (Second) of Torts. In section 120A, the Institute recognizes a privilege in favor of a merchant to detain for reasonable investigation a person whom he reasonably believes to have taken a chattel unlawfully. We adopt the concept embodied in section 120A, and we state the rule for this action as follows: if defendant Arlan's agent, Earl Reinhardt, reasonably believed the plaintiff had unlawfully taken goods held for sale in the defendant's store, then he enjoyed a privilege to detain her for a reasonable investigation of the facts.

The Commissioners' [sic; Institute's] comment states the strong reason behind recognizing such a privilege:

"The privilege stated in this section is necessary for the protection of a shopkeeper against the dilemma in which he would otherwise find himself when he reasonably believes that a shoplifter has taken goods from his counter. If there were no such privilege, he must either permit the suspected person to walk out of the premises and disappear, or must arrest him, at the risk of liability for false arrest if the theft could not be proved." 1 Restatement (Second) of Torts, page 202.

That the problem of shoplifting, faced by merchants, has reached serious dimensions is common knowledge, and we find compelling reason to recognize such a privilege, similar to that recognized in other jurisdictions. [Cc]

In Montgomery Ward & Co., Inc., v. Freeman, the United States Court of Appeals for the Fourth Circuit, in a case arising in Virginia and involving a detention considerably longer than the detention here of [Mrs.] Bonkowski, reversed a verdict for the plaintiff because of the trial court's too narrow instruction on the point of justifiable detention and sent the case back, stating that "the instruction should submit the reasonableness of the detention to the jury and should set out the facts which, if found, would constitute reasonable grounds for the defendant's conduct." 199 F.2d 720, 724.

The privilege we recognize here goes beyond that set forth in the Restatement, for the Commissioners [sic] there stated a caveat that "the Institute expresses no opinion as to whether there may be circumstances under which this privilege may extend to the detention of one who has left the premises but is in their immediate vicinity." 1 Restatement (Second) of Torts page 202.

In their comment, the Commissioners [sic] state that, by their caveat, in the absence of express authority, they intended to leave the question open. 1 Restatement (Second) of Torts page 204. We think the privilege should be so extended here because we think it entirely reasonable to apply it to the circumstances of the case at bar, for the reason that a merchant may not be able to form the reasonable belief justifying a detention for a reasonable investigation before a suspected person has left the premises. In *Montgomery Ward*, supra, the court recognized the privilege as applicable even though the plaintiff was stopped by a manager after she had left the store.

On remand, on the cause for false arrest, therefore, it will be the duty of the jury to determine in accordance with the rule we have set down, whether or not the defendant's agent, Earl Reinhardt, reasonably believed the plaintiff had unlawfully taken any goods held for sale at the defendant's store. If the jury finds the defendant's agent did so reasonably believe, then it must further determine whether the investigation that followed was reasonable under all the circumstances. If the jury finds the defendant does not come within this privilege, then from the facts as discussed above, it could find a false arrest. * * *

Reversed and remanded for new trial in accordance with this opinion. The award of costs to await final determination of the cause.

[In Bonkowski v. Arlan's Department Store, 383 Mich. 90, 174 N.W.2d 765 (1970), the Supreme Court of Michigan dismissed the false imprisonment claim on the ground that there was insufficient evidence that defendant intended to take plaintiff into custody. In dictum, the court affirmed the existence of the privilege.]

NOTES AND QUESTIONS

1. Shoplifting is a major problem for merchants. It costs them, in the aggregate, millions of dollars every year, which the public of course pays. It puts the merchant in the dilemma that, if he has the suspected person arrested he may be liable for false imprisonment if there was no theft or if a jury fails to convict, while if he does nothing, and permits the suspect to walk out, the merchandise and all hope of proof will disappear forever.

2. Although some states have adopted this privilege by case law (see Collyer v. S.H. Kress Co., 5 Cal.2d 175, 54 P.2d 20 (1936)), it is statutory in many jurisdictions. The scope of the privilege differs in the various states and it is hazardous for an attorney to advise a client about the privilege without researching the current state law. The more important variables include the following:

A. Whether force can be utilized and, if so, how much? The Restatement would allow reasonable force short of bodily harm. A "request" to stay must be made if it is practicable to do so. See Restatement (Second) of Torts § 120A, comment *k*. If the merchant is not allowed to use force, is the privilege of any real benefit?

B. What constitutes "reasonable grounds" or "probable cause" to detain a shopper and whether that issue is to be decided by the court or a jury? See Moore v. Pay'N Save Corp., 20 Wash.App. 482, 581 P.2d 159 (1978); Turner v. Hudson Salvage, Inc., 709 So.2d 425 (Miss.1998) (unreasonable for second employee to detain plaintiff after first employee had questioned her and determined she had not stolen shoes).

C. What constitutes a reasonable time or manner of detention? The Virginia statute specifies that the detention cannot exceed an hour. Va. Code § 18.2–105 (1996). Most courts would agree that defendant is liable when he demands a signed confession, and says that he will detain the plaintiff until it is signed. Moffatt v. Buffums', Inc., 21 Cal.App.2d 371, 69 P.2d 424 (1937); W.T. Grant Co. v. Owens, 149 Va. 906, 141 S.E. 860 (1928). Defendant also is liable when he threatens to detain the plaintiff until he pays. Cox v. Rhodes Avenue Hospital, 198 Ill.App. 82 (1916).

D. Whether the privilege should extend beyond the premises? Should the answer to this problem vary with the type of business in which the defendant is engaged?

E. Who is entitled to the privilege? Some states have extended the privilege beyond merchants to suppliers of services when defendant has failed to pay. See Standish v. Narragansett S.S. Co., 111 Mass. 512, 15 Am.Rep. 66 (1873).

3. The merchant's privilege usually does not extend to protection against an action for defamation. See Chapter 17.

Re-entry Upon Real Property

4. May one use force to retake possession of real property? A minority of states permit an individual who has the legal right to immediate possession of land to attempt to retake possession by use of reasonable force short of causing death or serious injury. See Shorter v. Shelton, 183 Va. 819, 33 S.E.2d 643 (1945).

5. Most states provide the lawful owner with a quick and inexpensive remedy usually called "Forcible Entry and Detainer." This fact has led a growing number of courts to hold that the rightful owner can retake possession of his land only if he does not use force. Further, the party in peaceful possession may have a claim for assault and battery or trespass to his goods occurring in the course of a forcible entry. See Lobdell v. Keene, 85 Minn. 90, 88 N.W. 426 (1901). A claim for intentional infliction of emotional harm has been allowed when the invading owner's conduct was extreme and outrageous. See Daluiso v. Boone, 71 Cal.2d 484, 455 P.2d 811, 78 Cal.Rptr. 707 (1969).

6. The basic policy decision inherent in these cases can be traced to a 1381 statute, 5 Richard II, c. 2, which made it a criminal offense for one entitled to possession of land to enter and recover it by force. Aside from a temporary aberration in Newton v. Harland, 1 Man. & G. 644, 133 Eng.Rep. 490 (1840), however, the English courts did not utilize the statute to allow the party in peaceful possession a civil claim against the invader. See Turner v. Meymott, 1 Bing. 158, 130 Eng.Rep. 64 (1823), and Hemmings v. Stoke Poges Golf Club, [1920] 1 K.B. 720. The English law is thus contrary to the majority American rule.

7. If a tenant consents in the lease to a forcible entry by the landlord in the case of non-payment of rent, should that agreement shield the landlord from liability based on an invasion? See Princess Amusement Co. v. Smith, 174 Ala. 342, 56 So. 979 (1911); Goshen v. People, 22 Colo. 270, 44 P. 503 (1896); Backus v. West, 104 Or. 129, 205 P. 533 (1922).

6. NECESSITY

☛Surocco v. Geary

Supreme Court of California, 1853.
3 Cal. 69, 58 Am.Dec. 385.

MURRAY, CHIEF JUSTICE. This was an action, commenced in the court below, to recover damages for blowing up and destroying the plaintiffs' house and property, during the fire of the 24th of December, 1849.

Geary, at that time Alcalde of San Francisco, justified, on the ground that he had authority, by virtue of his office, to destroy said building, and also that it had been blown up by him to stop the progress of the conflagration then raging.

It was in proof, that the fire passed over and burned beyond the building of the plaintiffs', and that at the time said building was destroyed, they were engaged in removing their property, and could, had they not been prevented, have succeeded in removing more, if not all of their goods.

The cause was tried by the court sitting as a jury, and a verdict rendered for the plaintiffs, from which the defendant prosecutes this appeal under the Practice Act of 1850.

The only question for our consideration is, whether the person who tears down or destroys the house of another, in good faith, and under apparent necessity, during the time of a conflagration, for the purpose of saving the buildings adjacent, and stopping its progress, can be held personally liable in an action by the owner of the property destroyed. * * *

The right to destroy property, to prevent the spread of a conflagration, has been traced to the highest law of necessity, and the natural rights of man, independent of society or civil government. "It is referred by moralists and jurists to the same great principle which justifies the exclusive appropriation of a plank in a shipwreck, though the life of another be sacrificed; with the throwing overboard goods in a tempest, for the safety of a vessel; with the trespassing upon the lands of another, to escape death by an enemy. It rests upon the maxim, *Necessitas inducit privilegium quod jura privata*" [Necessity provides a privilege for private rights].

The common law adopts the principles of the natural law, and places the justification of an act otherwise tortious precisely on the same ground of necessity. [C]

This principle has been familiarly recognized by the books from the time of the saltpetre case, and the instances of tearing down houses to prevent a conflagration, or to raise bulwarks for the defense of a city, are made use of as illustrations, rather than as abstract cases, in which its exercise is permitted. At such times, the individual rights of property give way to the higher laws of impending necessity.

A house on fire, or those in its immediate vicinity, which serve to communicate the flames, becomes a nuisance, which it is lawful to abate, and the private rights of the individual yield to the considerations of general convenience, and the interests of society. Were it otherwise, one stubborn person might involve a whole city in ruin, by refusing to allow the destruction of a building which would cut off the flames and check the progress of the fire, and that, too, when it was perfectly evident that his building must be consumed. * * *

The counsel for the respondent has asked, who is to judge of the necessity of the destruction of property?

This must, in some instances, be a difficult matter to determine. The necessity of blowing up a house may not exist, or be as apparent to the owner, whose judgment is clouded by interest, and the hope of saving his property, as to others. In all such cases the conduct of the individual must be regulated by his own judgment as to the exigencies of the case. If a building should be torn down without apparent or actual necessity, the parties concerned would undoubtedly be liable in an action of trespass. But in every case the necessity must be clearly shown. It is true, many cases of hardship may grow out of this rule, and property may often in such cases be destroyed, without necessity, by irresponsible persons, but this difficulty would not be obviated by making the parties responsible in every case, whether the necessity existed or not.

The legislature of the State possess the power to regulate this subject by providing the manner in which buildings may be destroyed, and the mode in which compensation shall be made; and it is to be hoped that something will be done to obviate the difficulty, and prevent the happening of such events as those supposed by the respondent's counsel.

In the absence of any legislation on the subject, we are compelled to fall back upon the rules of the common law.

The evidence in this case clearly establishes the fact, that the blowing up of the house was necessary, as it would have been consumed had it been left standing. The plaintiffs cannot recover for the value of the goods which they might have saved; they were as much subject to the necessities of the occasion as the house in which they were situate; and if in such cases a party was held liable, it would too frequently happen, that the delay caused by the removal of the goods would render the destruction of the house useless.

The court below clearly erred as to the law applicable to the facts of this case. The testimony will not warrant a verdict against the defendant.

Judgment reversed.

NOTES AND QUESTIONS

1. Defendant is fighting a forest fire that threatens an entire county. From an airplane he sprays fire-retardant chemicals onto plaintiff's land, which damage plaintiff's timber. Is defendant liable? Cf. Stocking v. Johnson Flying Service, 143 Mont. 61, 387 P.2d 312 (1963). During the floods of 1993 along the Mississippi River, the town of Prairie du Rocher, Illinois blew up one levee deliberately flooding a plain north of town to relieve pressure on another levee protecting the historic town. According to newspaper reports, the dynamiting of the levee saved the town

but ruined farmland above the town because the floodwaters carried away the rich topsoil. Could the owner of the farm recover for the loss to that property? See Lev, " 'Trap' Appears to Hold Back Flood From Town," Chicago Tribune (Aug. 5, 1993).

2.   Defendant, a public officer, burns the clothing worn by a person who has died of smallpox. Is he liable to the heir, the new owner of the clothing? Cf. Seavey v. Preble, 64 Me. 120 (1874); State v. Mayor of Knoxville, 80 Tenn. 146, 47 Am.Rep. 331 (1883). Putnam v. Payne, 13 Johns. (N.Y.) 312 (1816) (shooting mad dog in the street). South Dakota Dept. of Health v. Heim, 357 N.W.2d 522 (S.D.1984) (state destroyed plaintiff's herd of elk, which were suffering from a contagious disease).

3.   In December, 1941, the United States Army destroyed stored petroleum, terminal facilities, and vital parts of the plant of an oil company in Manila, in order to prevent them from falling into the hands of the advancing Japanese army. It was held that this was privileged, and not a compensable taking for public use, the theory of the majority being that it was not the Army's conduct but an act of war that was the cause of the destruction. See United States v. Caltex, Inc., 344 U.S. 149 (1952). Contra, that the Crown has no such privilege, Burmah Oil Co., Ltd. v. Lord Advocate, [1964] 2 All E.R. 348.

4.   To be privileged, must the defendant be a public officer? In Harrison v. Wisdom, 54 Tenn. 99 (1872), private citizens of the town of Clarksville, Tenn., destroyed all the liquor in the town just before the entry of the Union army. It was held that the court properly charged the jury that if they found that there was imminent danger, and a real public necessity, this was privileged. To the same effect is Restatement (Second) of Torts §§ 196 and 262. Suppose it only appeared to be necessary?

5.   Even if the "champion of the public" is not liable, should not the city or other community, whose interests he protects, be required to make compensation to the plaintiff? See Hall and Wigmore, Compensation for Property Destroyed to Stop the Spread of a Conflagration, 1 Ill.L.Rev. 501 (1907), written just after the San Francisco earthquake of 1906 and Wegner v. Milwaukee Mutual Ins. Co., 479 N.W.2d 38 (Minn.1991) (holding municipality liable for damage done to plaintiff's house by SWAT team using tear gas and "flash-bang" grenades to force out suspected felon who had taken refuge there).

In the past, governmental immunity has prevented liability, but as indicated in Chapter 12, that doctrine is rapidly disappearing from the law. When governmental immunity is abrogated the state is usually deemed liable "in the same manner and to the same extent as a private individual under like circumstances." See 28 U.S.C.A. § 2674 (Federal Tort Claims Act). Is this approach sensible in regard to the privilege of public necessity?

Some jurisdictions have provided for compensation by statute.

6.   Do the constitutional provisions against taking private property for public use without due compensation have any application here? See, e.g.,Customer Co. v. City of Sacramento, 10 Cal.4th 368, 895 P.2d 900, 41 Cal.Rprt.2d 658 (1995) (owner of convenience store substantially damaged by SWAT team attempting to flush out fugitive sought recovery under just compensation clause of California constitution).

What about fire insurance? For years the policies excepted destruction of property to prevent spread of fire. The Standard Fire Insurance Policy now provides that the policy does not apply to destruction by order of public authorities, except to prevent spread of fire caused by a reason not excluded. Does this take care of the problem?

➤Vincent v. Lake Erie Transp. Co.

Supreme Court of Minnesota, 1910.
109 Minn. 456, 124 N.W. 221.

Action by R.C. Vincent and others against the Lake Erie Transportation Company. Verdict for plaintiffs. From an order denying a new trial, defendant appeals.

O'BRIEN, J. The steamship Reynolds, owned by the defendant, was for the purpose of discharging her cargo on November 27, 1905, moored to plaintiff's dock in Duluth. While the unloading of the boat was taking place a storm from the northeast developed, which at about 10 o'clock p.m., when the unloading was completed, had so grown in violence that the wind was then moving at 50 miles per hour and continued to increase during the night. There is some evidence that one, and perhaps two, boats were able to enter the harbor that night, but it is plain that navigation was practically suspended from the hour mentioned until the morning of the 29th, when the storm abated, and during that time no master would have been justified in attempting to navigate his vessel, if he could avoid doing so. After the discharge of the cargo the Reynolds signaled for a tug to tow her from the dock, but none could be obtained because of the severity of the storm. If the lines holding the ship to the dock had been cast off, she would doubtless have drifted away; but, instead, the lines were kept fast, and as soon as one parted or chafed it was replaced, sometimes with a larger one. The vessel lay upon the outside of the dock, her bow to the east, the wind and waves striking her starboard quarter with such force that she was constantly being lifted and thrown against the dock, resulting in its damage, as found by the jury, to the amount of $500.

We are satisfied that the character of the storm was such that it would have been highly imprudent for the master of the Reynolds to have attempted to leave the dock or to have permitted his vessel to drift away from it. * * * Nothing more was demanded of them than ordinary prudence and care, and the record in this case fully sustains the contention of the appellant that, in holding the vessel fast to the dock, those in charge of her exercised good judgment and prudent seamanship. * * *

The appellant contends by ample assignments of error that, because its conduct during the storm was rendered necessary by prudence and good seamanship under conditions over which it had no control, it cannot be held liable for any injury resulting to the property of others, and claims that the jury should have been so instructed. An analysis of the charge given by the trial court is not necessary, as in our opinion the only question for the jury was the amount of damages which the plaintiffs were entitled to recover, and no complaint is made upon that score.

The situation was one in which the ordinary rules regulating property rights were suspended by forces beyond human control, and if, without the direct intervention of some act by the one sought to be held liable, the property of another was injured, such injury must be attributed to the act of God, and not to the wrongful act of the person sought to be charged. If during the storm the Reynolds had entered the harbor, and while there had become disabled and been thrown against the plaintiffs' dock, the plaintiffs could not have recovered. Again, if while attempting to hold fast to the dock the lines had parted, without any negligence, and the vessel carried against some other boat or dock in the harbor, there would be no liability upon her owner. But here those in charge of the vessel deliberately and by their direct efforts held her in such a position that the damage to the dock resulted, and, having thus preserved the ship at the expense of the dock, it seems to us that her owners are responsible to the dock owners to the extent of the injury inflicted. * * *

In Ploof v. Putnam, 81 Vt. 471, 71 A. 188 (1908), the Supreme Court of Vermont held that where, under stress of weather, a vessel was without permission moored to a private dock at an island in Lake Champlain owned by the defendant, the plaintiff was not guilty of trespass, and that the defendant was responsible in damages because his representative upon the island unmoored the vessel, permitting it to drift upon the shore, with resultant injuries to it. If, in that case, the vessel had been permitted to remain, and the dock had suffered an injury, we believe the shipowner would have been held liable for the injury done.

Theologians hold that a starving man may, without moral guilt, take what is necessary to sustain life; but it could hardly be said that the obligation would not be upon such person to pay the value of the property so taken when he became able to do so. And so public necessity, in times of war or peace, may require the taking of private property for public purposes; but under our system of jurisprudence compensation must be made.

Let us imagine in this case that for the better mooring of the vessel those in charge of her had appropriated a valuable cable lying upon the dock. No matter how justifiable such appropriation might have been, it would not be claimed that, because of the overwhelming necessity of the situation, the owner of the cable could not recover its value.

This is not a case where life or property was menaced by any object or thing belonging to the plaintiff, the destruction of which became necessary to prevent the threatened disaster. Nor is it a case where, because of the act of God, or unavoidable accident, the infliction of the injury was beyond the control of the defendant, but is one where the defendant prudently and advisedly availed itself of the plaintiff's property for the purpose of preserving its own more valuable property, and the plaintiffs are entitled to compensation for the injury done.

Order affirmed.

[The dissenting opinion of Lewis, J. is omitted.]

NOTES AND QUESTIONS

1. The cases all appear to be in agreement with the principal case. See Newcomb v. Tisdale, 62 Cal. 575 (1881); Bohlen, Incomplete Privilege to Inflict Intentional Invasions of Interests of Property and Personality, 39 Harv.L.Rev. 307

(1926). See also Restatement (Second) of Torts, §§ 197 and 263. If defendant has not been at fault, why should he pay? For one view, see Fletcher, Fairness and Utility in Tort Doctrine, 85 Harv.L.Rev. 537, 546 (1972). Might the same approach be followed in regard to other privileges, such as self-defense?

2. What result in the principal case if it was necessary to moor the vessel to allow crewmen to escape onto land? See Mouse's Case, 12 Co.Rep. 63, 77 Eng.Rep. 1341 (1609).

3. A traveler upon the public highway is normally held to be privileged to turn out to avoid an obstruction, and to pass over the abutting land. Morey v. Fitzgerald, 56 Vt. 487, 48 Am.Rep. 811 (1884); Irwin v. Yeagar, 74 Iowa 174, 37 N.W. 136 (1888). See also Dodwell v. Missouri Pac. R. Co., 384 S.W.2d 643 (Mo.1964) (boy crawling through train that blocked crossing).

4. An extortioner arrives at the office of business tycoon and threatens to drop a package of explosives if not paid $1 million. Business tycoon attempts to placate him, but when the negotiations fail, the extortioner drops the package. Is the Tycoon liable if he leaps behind the plaintiff and is protected? If he pulls the plaintiff in front of himself? Cf. Laidlaw v. Sage, 158 N.Y. 73, 52 N.E. 679 (1899).

5. Should the necessity privilege ever extend to the taking of life? In criminal law the answer has generally been "No." Thus, in Arp v. State, 97 Ala. 5, 12 So. 301 (1893), the court affirmed the trial court's refusal to allow the defendant to be excused on the basis that two other men armed with shotguns had been present and threatened to kill him unless he murdered the deceased. On the other hand, § 2.09 of the Model Penal Code permits duress as a defense if the force or threat of force was such that a person "of reasonable firmness in his situation would be unable to resist." Which is the better approach in tort law?

6. In Regina v. Dudley, 15 Cox C.C. 624, 14 Q.B.D. 273 (1884), four survivors of a shipwreck were adrift in an open boat, a thousand miles from land, and dying of hunger. Three of them killed the fourth, a boy, and ate him. They were held criminally liable for his death. See Simpson, Cannibalism and the Common Law (1984) for an interesting exploration of the social mores of the time and how those mores influence the law and vice versa. In United States v. Holmes, 1 Wall.Jr. 1, 26 Fed.Cas. 360 (E.D.Pa.1842), after a passenger ship had hit an iceberg and sunk, nine members of her crew and thirty-two passengers were adrift in a badly overloaded lifeboat. The wind freshened, the sea began to rise, and the boat was in imminent danger of being swamped. The crew then threw overboard six of the passengers to lighten the boat. The following morning the survivors were rescued by a passing ship. Holmes, who had taken a leading part in throwing the passengers over, was tried for manslaughter, convicted and sentenced to hard labor for a long term, which the court subsequently reduced to six months. The president later remitted the sentence. The story is told in full in Hicks, Human Jettison (1927). What should be the position of tort law in these situations?

7. For an exhaustive and most stimulating discussion about the theoretical jurisprudence of many of these problems, see Fuller, The Case of the Speluncean Explorers, 62 Harv.L.Rev. 616 (1949).

THE FAR SIDE By GARY LARSON

"Fair is fair, Larry . . . We're out of food, we drew
straws — you lost."

7. AUTHORITY OF LAW

The defense of legal authority is a subject for a course, a casebook or a text in itself. It can only be touched on here.

If the defendant is duly commanded or authorized by law to do what he does, he is of course not liable for doing it. The problem is to discover how far the legal sanction extends. A case illustrating how easily a physician can fall into error and be subject to liability when he attempts to justify his conduct under a state commitment statute is Stowers v. Wolodzko, 386 Mich. 119, 191 N.W.2d 355 (1971). A good study of the matter is Jennings, Tort Liability of Administrative Officers, 21 Minn.L.Rev. 263 (1937); see also Restatement (Second) of Torts § 895D.

A distinction is commonly made between acts (1) that call for administrative judgment, such as those of a prosecuting attorney in deciding whether to seek an indictment, or a school board dismissing a pupil, which are called "discretionary" or "quasi-judicial," and ② those requiring less personal judgment, such as remitting a prisoner to jail or dipping sheep, which are called "ministerial" only.

This subject is treated further in Chapter 12, Section 3(F).

Arrest

One common form of action under authority of law is arrest of the person, which consists of taking him into the custody of the law. An arrest may be made under a warrant, which is a signed order issued by a court directing that the person in question be arrested; or it may be made without a warrant.

Arrest under a warrant, or the seizure of goods under civil process, to which the same rules apply, is an act generally considered to be "ministerial," so that the officer is liable if he acts improperly. If the court issuing the warrant is entirely without jurisdiction to do it, it is commonly held that the invalid order affords the officer no protection. Warren v. Kelley, 80 Me. 512, 15 A. 49 (1888); Smith v. Hilton, 147 Ala. 642, 41 So. 747 (1906). But if the court has general jurisdiction to issue similar process, it is generally held that the officer is privileged if the warrant is "fair on its face," even though there may be errors and irregularities in its issue that affect the jurisdiction of the court in the particular case. Vittorio v. St. Regis Paper Co., 239 N.Y. 148, 145 N.E. 913 (1924); David v. Larochelle, 296 Mass. 302, 5 N.E.2d 571 (1936).

Even if the warrant is entirely valid, however, it does not protect the officer unless he carries out the order given him, even though he makes a perfectly reasonable mistake in good faith. Thus an officer who has a warrant for the arrest of A, and who reasonably believes B to be A and arrests him, is liable to B for false arrest.

Arrest without a warrant normally is covered in the course in criminal law. It may be made by a police officer, or by a private citizen. The common law imposed limitations upon the authority of each, with that of the private citizen, as might be expected, more narrowly restricted. The original common law rules concerning arrest without a warrant were as follows:

1. Either an officer or a citizen may arrest without a warrant to prevent a felony, or a breach of the peace that is being committed or reasonably appears about to be committed, in his presence.

2. An officer may make an arrest if he has information that affords reasonable grounds for thinking that a felony has been committed and that he has the right criminal.

3. The citizen may arrest without a warrant if a felony has in fact been committed, and he has reasonable grounds to suspect the man he arrests; but his authority depends upon the fact of the crime, and he must take the full risk if none has been committed.

4.) For a past breach of the peace that is not a felony, an officer or a citizen may arrest without a warrant only if the offense was committed in his presence and he is in fresh pursuit.

5.) For mere misdemeanors the old common law rule was that neither the officer nor the citizen could arrest without a warrant. This has now been modified in some jurisdictions to extend the power to an officer when the misdemeanor is committed in his presence.

These common law rules have been extensively changed by the modern penal codes, and, for any particular jurisdiction, reference must be made to the statutes.

6. Assuming that an arrest would be lawful, an officer may also be subject to liability if he uses excessive force in the process of apprehending the suspect.

8. DISCIPLINE

Parent and Child. There are a number of relations in which the necessity of some orderly discipline gives persons who have the control of others the privilege of exercising reasonable force and restraint upon them. One of the most important examples of this privilege is that given to a parent or one who is deemed to stand in place of a parent. See Clasen v. Pruhs, 69 Neb. 278, 95 N.W. 640 (1903); Fortinberry v. Holmes, 89 Miss. 373, 42 So. 799 (1907) (one caring for a child). The scope of the privilege was rarely tested for many years because parents were held to be immune from suits by their children. Interestingly enough, this very immunity arose in a case where a court may have been unwilling to delineate the scope of the privilege. See Hewlett v. George, 68 Miss. 703, 9 So. 885 (1891) (claim of false imprisonment).

Recently, a growing number of courts have abandoned the concept of tort immunity between parent and child, especially in the area of intentional torts. (For details, see Chapter 12, Section 3(A).) More cases dealing with the scope of this privilege may therefore arise in the future. In Gillett v. Gillett, 168 Cal.App.2d 102, 335 P.2d 736 (1959), an aunt who stood *in loco parentis* to a young child was held liable when she inflicted serious bodily injuries on the child in the course of disciplining her for an act of minor misbehavior. Are there practical reasons why there may not be too many cases of a child suing a parent even when immunity has been abolished?

While some decisions have stated that a parent delegates his authority to discipline his child to a teacher when the youngster is in school, the teacher's privilege to discipline is more properly predicated on the need to maintain reasonable order in the classroom. See LaFrentz v. Gallagher, 105 Ariz. 255, 462 P.2d 804 (1969); Suits v. Glover, 260 Ala. 449, 71 So.2d 49 (1954). Thus discipline may be exercised even though the parent objects. Most litigation has concerned the scope of the privilege. It is not defined with precision.

First, there is some uncertainty as to whether it extends to activities conducted away from school that have only a slight connection with the educational program.

Second, an instructor will be subject to liability for using "excessive" force. See Johnson v. Horace Mann Mut. Ins. Co., 241 So.2d 588 (La.App. 1970). Significant variables gleaned from the cases include (1) the nature of the punishment, (2) the conduct of the student, (3) the age and physical condition of the student, and (4) the motive of the instructor, e.g., did he act in anger or out of dislike, rather than in an attempt to discipline. See Story v. Martin, 217 So.2d 758 (La.App.1969); Tinkham v. Kole, 252 Iowa 1303, 110 N.W.2d 258 (1961).

Local school regulations may limit the teacher's privilege. See Simms v. School Dist. No. 1, 13 Or.App. 119, 508 P.2d 236 (1973).

Corporal punishment has been held not to violate the due process clause or the Eighth Amendment privilege against cruel and unusual punishment. See Baker v. Owen 395 F.Supp. 294 (M.D.N.C.), aff'd, 423 U.S. 907 (1975) and Ingraham v. Wright, 430 U.S. 651 (1977).

Others. Other examples of the privilege of discipline are those of military and naval officers over their subordinates, which are largely governed by military law and dealt with by courts martial; and the authority of the master of a ship over both the crew and the passengers. Again the privilege, in the latter case, is limited to force reasonable under the circumstances; and the captain will be liable if he puts a passenger in irons for calling him the landlord of a floating hotel. King v. Franklin, 1 F. & F. 360, 175 Eng.Rep. 764 (1858).

9. JUSTIFICATION

Sindle v. New York City Transit Authority

New York Court of Appeals, 1973.
33 N.Y.2d 293, 307 N.E.2d 245, 352 N.Y.S.2d 183.

JASEN, JUDGE. At about noon on June 20, 1967, the plaintiff, then 14 years of age, boarded a school bus owned by the defendant, New York City Transit Authority, and driven by its employee, the defendant Mooney. It was the last day of the term at the Elias Bernstein Junior High School in Staten Island and the 65 to 70 students on board the bus were in a boisterous and exuberant mood. Some of this spirit expressed itself in vandalism, a number of students breaking dome lights, windows, ceiling panels and advertising poster frames. There is no evidence that the plaintiff partook in this destruction.

The bus made several stops at appointed stations. On at least one occasion, the driver admonished the students about excessive noise and damage to the bus. When he reached the Annadale station, the driver discharged several more passengers, went to the rear of the bus, inspected the damage and advised the students that he was taking them to the St. George police station.

The driver closed the doors of the bus and proceeded, bypassing several normal stops. * * *

The plaintiff, joined with his father, then commenced an action to recover damages for * * * false imprisonment. * * * At the close of the plaintiffs' case, the court denied defendants' motion to amend their answers to plead the defense of justification. The court also excluded all evidence bearing on the justification issue.

We believe that it was an abuse of discretion for the trial court to deny the motion to amend and to exclude the evidence of justification. It was the defendants' burden to prove justification—a defense that a plaintiff in an action for false imprisonment should be prepared to meet—and the plaintiffs could not have been prejudiced by the granting of the motion to amend. The trial court's rulings precluded the defendants from introducing any evidence in this regard and were manifestly unfair. Accordingly, the order of the Appellate Division must be reversed and a new trial granted.

In view of our determination, it would be well to outline some of the considerations relevant to the issue of justification. In this regard, we note that, generally, restraint or detention, reasonable under the circumstances and in time and manner, imposed for the purpose of preventing another from inflicting personal injuries or interfering with or damaging real or personal property in one's lawful possession or custody is not unlawful. (Cf. Penal Law, §§ 35.20, 35.25; see, also, General Business Law, § 218, which affords a retail merchant a defense to an action for false arrest and false imprisonment where a suspected shoplifter is reasonably detained for investigation or questioning.) Also, a parent, guardian or teacher entrusted with the care or supervision of a child may use physical force reasonably necessary to maintain discipline or promote the welfare of the child. (Penal Law, § 35.10.)

Similarly, a school bus driver, entrusted with the care of his student-passengers and the custody of public property, has the duty to take reasonable measures for the safety and protection of both—the passengers and the property. In this regard, the reasonableness of his actions—as bearing on the defense of justification—is to be determined from a consideration of all the circumstances. At a minimum, this would seem to import, a consideration of the need to protect the persons and property in his charge, the duty to aid the investigation and apprehension of those inflicting damage, the manner and place of the occurrence, and the feasibility and practicality of other alternative courses of action. * * *

For the reasons stated, the order of the Appellate Division should be reversed and the case remitted for a new trial.

NOTES AND QUESTIONS

1. What privileges did the court rely on "by analogy"? Are there others—not mentioned by the court—that might be relevant? For a case that relied on *Sindle*, see Matter of Malone, 105 A.D.2d 455, 480 N.Y.S.2d 603 (1984) (attorney raised

defense of justification in that he had been acting in his "official" capacity as Inspector General when he advised client to testify falsely).

2. Can you think of other examples of conduct that might "justify" an apparent intentional tort although they do not fit within the traditional common law privileges discussed in this chapter? See, e.g., Rice, Issues Raised by the Abortion Rescue Movement, 23 Suffolk U.L. Rev. 15 (1989) (exploring the use of justification as a defense to the intentional tort of trespass in cases involving Operation Rescue participants).

3. In Peterson v. Sorlien, 299 N.W.2d 123 (Minn.1980), cert. denied, 450 U.S. 1031 (1981), the Supreme Court of Minnesota held that the parent-child relationship justified limitations the defendant parents placed upon their adult child's mobility during "deprogramming" that would otherwise support a judgment of false imprisonment. See LeMoult, Deprogramming Members Of Religious Sects, 46 Fordham L.Rev. 599, 635 (1978). On the other hand, good intentions would not justify the unlawful restraint of a young girl even though the defendant sincerely believed that the girl's best interests would be served by the discipline imposed in a cloister. Gallon v. House of Good Shepherd, 158 Mich. 361, 122 N.W. 631 (1909). Cf. Smith v. Sisters of Good Shepherd, 87 S.W. 1083 (Ky.1905).

CHAPTER IV

NEGLIGENCE

1. HISTORY

Negligence was scarcely recognized as a separate tort before the earlier part of the nineteenth century. Prior to that time, the word had been used in a very general sense to describe the breach of any legal obligation, or to designate a mental element, usually one of inadvertence or inattention or indifference, entering into the commission of other torts. As a result, some writers once maintained that negligence was merely one way of committing any tort, just as some courts, for example, spoke occasionally of a negligent "battery."

One of the earliest appearances of what we now know as the tort of negligence was in the liability of those who professed to be competent in certain "public" callings. A carrier, an innkeeper, a blacksmith, or a surgeon was regarded as holding himself out to the public as one in whom confidence might be reposed, and hence as assuming an obligation to give proper service, for the breach of which, by any negligent conduct, he might be liable. But in other fields such as trespass and nuisance the idea developed, thinly disguised, that there might be liability for negligence; and in later years the action on the case produced a large, undigested group of situations in which negligence was the essence of the tort.

Somewhere around the year 1825, negligence began to emerge out of the action on the case, and to be recognized as a separate basis of tort liability, independent of other causes of action. Its rise coincided to a marked degree with the Industrial Revolution in England. "It was probably stimulated a good deal by the enormous increase of industrial machinery in general and by the invention of railways in particular. At that time railway trains were notable neither for speed nor for safety. They killed any object from a Minister of State to a wandering cow, and this naturally reacted upon the law." P. Winfield, Law of Tort 404 (5th ed. 1950).

The separate recognition of negligence was undoubtedly greatly encouraged by the disintegration of the old forms of action, and the disappearance of the distinction between direct and indirect injuries, found in trespass and case. Intentional injuries, whether direct or indirect, began to be grouped as a distinct field of liability, and negligence took separate form as the basis for unintended torts. Today, it is no longer disputed that distinct problems and principles, as well as distinct questions of policy, arise in negligence cases.

For the history of negligence in early law, and its development as an independent tort, see Winfield, The History of Negligence in the Law of

Torts, 42 L.Q.Rev. 184 (1926); Wigmore, Responsibility for Tortious Acts: Its History, 7 Harv.L.Rev. 315, 441, 453 (1894).

2.   ELEMENTS OF CAUSE OF ACTION

"Negligence" is the word used to describe the conduct of the person or company being evaluated. But a cause of action for negligence requires more than negligent conduct. The traditional formula for the elements necessary to the cause of action includes the following:

1.   A **duty** to use reasonable care. This is an obligation recognized by the law, requiring the actor to conform to a certain standard of conduct, for the protection of others against unreasonable risks.

2.   A failure to conform to the required standard. This is commonly called **breach** of the duty. These two elements go to make up what the courts usually have called negligence; but the term frequently is applied to the second alone. Thus it may be said that the defendant was negligent, but is not liable because he was under no duty to the plaintiff to use reasonable care.

3.   A reasonably close causal connection between the conduct and the resulting injury. This is commonly called **causation.** Causation involves a combination of two elements—causation in fact and legal or "proximate" causation. They receive separate treatment in Chapters 5 and 6.

4.   Actual loss or **damage** resulting to the interests of another. The action for negligence developed chiefly out of the old form of action on the case; and it retained the rule of that action that pleading and proof of damage was an essential part of the plaintiff's case. It is clear that nominal damages to vindicate a technical right cannot be recovered in a negligence action if no actual damage has occurred. If defendant's risk-creating negligent conduct threatens but does not harm plaintiff, however, he may be able to obtain an injunction and stop the activity as a "nuisance." While the modern law of torts has retained the requirement that proof of damage is an essential part of the law of negligence, the question of what constitutes damage is less certain than it once was. Has the plaintiff suffered damage if the wrongful act causes her to fear that she will develop a disease in the future or reduces her chance of surviving a disease?

Although the negligence formula is useful in segregating and drawing attention to the elements of the cause of action the courts require, it is misleading to view the elements as discrete. None of the elements can really be defined except by reference to the others. Another commonly used rubric for negligence is conduct that falls below the standard of care established by law for the protection of others against the unreasonable risk of harm.

Most of the cases in this chapter involve the allegedly negligent conduct of the defendant from whom the plaintiff is seeking compensatory damages. Sometimes, however, it is the *plaintiff's* conduct that is being measured against the standard of the reasonable person because the defendant has pled the affirmative defense of contributory negligence: the defendant is claiming the plaintiff's conduct was negligent and that the plaintiff's negligent conduct also contributed to the cause of plaintiff's injuries. Chapter 12, Defenses, will explore this affirmative defense in detail. For now, keep in mind that the standard—reasonable care under the circumstances—applies to all parties, whether they are plaintiffs or defendants in a particular case.

3. A NEGLIGENCE FORMULA

➤Lubitz v. Wells

Superior Court of Connecticut, 1955.
19 Conn.Sup. 322, 113 A.2d 147.

TROLAND, JUDGE. The complaint alleges that James Wells was the owner of a golf club and that he left it for some time lying on the ground in the backyard of his home. That thereafter his son, the defendant James Wells, Jr., aged eleven years, while playing in the yard with the plaintiff, Judith Lubitz, aged nine years, picked up the golf club and proceeded to swing at a stone lying on the ground. In swinging the golf club, James Wells, Jr., caused the club to strike the plaintiff about the jaw and chin.

Negligence alleged against the young Wells boy is that he failed to warn his little playmate of his intention to swing the club and that he did swing the club when he knew she was in a position of danger.

In an attempt to hold the boy's father, James Wells, liable for his son's action, it is alleged that James Wells was negligent because although he knew the golf club was on the ground in his backyard and that his children would play with it, and that although he knew or "should have known" that the negligent use of the golf club by children would cause injury to a child, he neglected to remove the golf club from the backyard or to caution James Wells, Jr., against the use of the same.

The demurrer challenges the sufficiency of the allegations of the complaint to state a cause of action or to support a judgment against the father, James Wells.

It would hardly be good sense to hold that this golf club is so obviously and intrinsically dangerous that it is negligence to leave it lying on the ground in the yard. The father cannot be held liable on the allegations of this complaint. [Cc]

The demurrer is sustained.

NOTES AND QUESTIONS

1. Is a householder negligent for leaving in his backyard an object such as a baseball bat, or a hose with a nozzle, which one child might pick up and swing at another? What if the object had been a hoe? A loaded shotgun?

2. Why might the boy be found negligent if the father was not? What result if plaintiff had tripped over the golf club? Cf. Johnson v. Krueger, 36 Colo.App. 242, 539 P.2d 1296 (1975).

3. A twelve-year-old boy lost his eye from a pellet from a slingshot fired by his eleven-year-old playmate. Was it negligence to sell the slingshot? See Moning v. Alfono, 400 Mich. 425, 254 N.W.2d 759 (1977). *[handwritten] x an 11 y old.*

4. Defendant, facing a clear fairway, drove a golf ball from the tee without crying "Fore!" The ball hooked badly, curved, and struck the plaintiff, who was playing on another fairway 125 yards away. Is this negligence? Rose v. Morris, 97 Ga.App. 764, 104 S.E.2d 485 (1958). Is it negligence not to cry "Fore!" when the defendant sees the ball begin to hook?

5. Defendant parks his car on the edge of a city street without a curb, in front of a house where a mother and a 13–month old toddler are sitting on a front porch. He goes across the street to visit a friend there. He comes back in 5 minutes, gets in the car and drives off. There is a bump that he thought was a paving stone, but that turned out to be the toddler who had crawled under the car. Was he negligent? Williams v. Jordan, 208 Tenn. 456, 346 S.W.2d 583 (1961).

[handwritten margin note] the mother was to let her kid crawl under the car

Blyth v. Birmingham Waterworks Co.

Court of Exchequer, 1856.
11 Exch. 781, 156 Eng.Rep. 1047.

[Defendants had installed water mains in the street, with fire plugs at various points. The plug opposite the plaintiff's house sprung a leak during a severe frost, because the connection between the plug and the water main was forced out by the expansion of freezing water. As a result, a large quantity of water escaped through the earth and into plaintiff's house, causing damage. The apparatus had been laid down 25 years ago, and had worked well during that time. The trial court left the question of defendant's negligence to the jury, which returned a verdict for plaintiff. Judgment was entered on the verdict, and defendant appealed.]

ALDERSON, B. I am of opinion that there was no evidence to be left to the jury. The case turns upon the question, whether the facts proved show that the defendants were guilty of negligence. Negligence is the omission to do something which a reasonable man, guided upon those considerations which ordinarily regulate the conduct of human affairs, would do or doing something which a prudent and reasonable man would not do. The defendants might have been liable for negligence, if unintentionally, they omitted to do that which a reasonable person would have done, or did that which a person taking reasonable precautions would not have done. A reasonable man would act with reference to the average circumstances of the temperature in ordinary years. The defendants had provided against such frosts as experience would have led men, acting prudently, to provide against; and they are not guilty of negligence, because their precautions proved insufficient against the effects of the extreme severity of the frost of 1855, which penetrated to a greater depth than any which ordinarily occurs south of the polar regions. Such a state of circumstances constitutes a contingency against which no reasonable man can provide. The result was an accident for which the defendants cannot be held liable.

Verdict to be entered for the defendants.

[The concurring opinions of MARTIN, B., and BRAMWELL, B., are omitted.]

NOTES AND QUESTIONS

1. In 1951, plaintiff's goods, in freight cars in the yards of defendant railroad company at Topeka, were destroyed by a flood that swept over the yards. There never had been any prior flood that had come anywhere near the yards; and when defendant first learned that the water was likely to reach them, it was too late to move the cars. Is defendant negligent in not moving them sooner? Ismert–Hincke Milling Co. v. Union Pacific R. Co., 238 F.2d 14 (10th Cir.1956). *no*

2. Is a contractor building a skyscraper in Chicago required to take precautions against an earthquake? In San Francisco? *yes*

3. Could it be negligence to fail to take precautions against a stroke of lightning near an oil storage tank? Tex–Jersey Oil Corp. v. Beck, 292 S.W.2d 803 (Tex.Civ.App.1956). On a golf course? Compare Hames v. State of Tennessee, 808 S.W.2d 41 (Tenn.1991) with Maussner v. Atlantic City Country Club, Inc., 299 N.J.Super. 535, 691 A.2d 826 (1997). What else would you like to know before deciding this? *did they know for a fact the lightning was coming or was there a higher occurrence of lightning in general in that area*

▶Gulf Refining Co. v. Williams

Supreme Court of Mississippi, 1938.
183 Miss. 723, 185 So. 234.

Action by Willie Williams against the Gulf Refining Company and others for injuries allegedly resulting from defect in gasoline container which caused a fire. From a judgment for plaintiff, defendants appeal.

GRIFFITH, JUSTICE. Appellants are the distributors of petroleum products, including gasoline. Shortly before the injury here complained of, appellants, from their station at Canton, sold and delivered to a planter in that vicinity a drum of gasoline for use in farm tractors. Appellee was the planter's employee and was engaged in operating a tractor. The drum of gasoline had been taken to the field, but no attempt had been made to use it, until for the first time since its delivery, appellee undertook to remove the bunghole cap from the drum in order to replenish the fuel in the tractor, whereupon there was a sudden outburst of fire, caused, as the jury was justified in concluding upon the evidence, by a spark which was produced by the condition of unrepair in the threads of the bung cap, as will be later mentioned.

Facts!

Appellee was severely burned by the sudden fire, and recovered judgment in an action therefor, from which judgment this appeal is prosecuted.

The chief argument of appellants is that the proof shows that an explosion or fire in drawing gasoline from a drum, when, or on account of, taking off the bung cap is an unusual, extraordinary and improbable occurrence, so much so that some of the witnesses say that no such happening had ever before been heard of by them; and that, therefore, appellant cannot be held liable as for a failure to anticipate the danger of any such improbable occurrence. And appellants call attention to language used by the courts wherein the declaration is made that there is no liability when the occurrence is unusual, extraordinary, and improbable. * * *

This general language has led to the occasional misunderstanding as to what may be termed the degree of probability which is meant by these expressions, as used in the law of negligence; and it is sometimes supposed and argued that unless such a foreseeable consequence is one which is more likely to happen than not to happen there can be no liability. * * *

When the inquiry is upon an issue whether a certain alleged fact existed or happened in the past, it is not sufficient to prove only or no more than a possibility, however substantial the possibility may be, so long as it is only a possibility. There the proof must establish the fact as a probability, using that word in its ordinary and common acceptation. * * * But when the inquiry is one of foreseeability, is as regards a thing that may happen in the future and to which the law of negligence holds a party to anticipation as a measure of duty, that inquiry is not whether the thing is to be foreseen or anticipated as one which will probably happen, according to the ordinary acceptation of that term, but whether it is likely to happen, even though the likelihood may not be sufficient to amount to a comparative probability. * * *

The test as respects foreseeability is not the balance of probabilities, but the existence, in the situation in hand, of some real likelihood of some damage and the likelihood is of such appreciable weight and moment as to induce, or which reasonably should induce, action to avoid it on the part of a person of a reasonably prudent mind.

The drum, or gasoline container, involved herein was of standard material, construction and manufacture, and of the kind in general use; and had it been in reasonably good repair there would, of course, be no liability. But the proof is that the drum had been in use nine years; that the threads in the bung plug or bung cap were broken, bent and jagged; that this condition had been brought about by repeated hammering on the bung cap during the course of its use,—a condition which had attracted the attention of one of appellants' employees before the container was sent out on this occasion. There is no adequate proof to show that appellee had equal knowledge or appreciation of the significance of this fact, or any knowledge which was sufficient to put the use at his risk as by the so-called assumption thereof, as contended for by appellants,—leaving aside whether, if the facts were otherwise, there would be assumption of risk, rather than contributory negligence. [C] The proof is sufficient to show that a person of ordinary prudence, and mindful of the duty of cautious care with which appellants were charged, should have known of the condition aforesaid and should reasonably have anticipated, as a likelihood of weight and moment, that a sudden fire or explosion would be caused by the stated condition of unrepair; and hence appellants are liable for the injury to appellee which resulted.

Affirmed.

NOTES AND QUESTIONS

1. In Tullgren v. Amoskeag Mfg. Co., 82 N.H. 268, 133 A. 4 (1926), defendant escorted an employee with a "sick headache" home and left her to walk about 700

feet over a difficult road. On reaching her home she died. On motion for rehearing after reversing a directed verdict for defendant, the court said in part: "For a person to be careless it is not necessary that damage as a more rather than a less probable result should be anticipated. * * * Danger consists in the risk of harm, as well as the likelihood of it, and a danger calling for anticipation need not be of more probable occurrence than less. If there is some probability of harm sufficiently serious that ordinary men would take precautions to avoid it, then failure to do so is negligence. That the danger will more probably than otherwise not be encountered on a particular occasion does not dispense with the exercise of care. One who crosses a railroad track may not reasonably anticipate that a train will in fact be met but, by reason of the risk that one may be, he is called upon to do what is reasonably required to find out. In going around a sharp turn on a highway, where the view is obstructed, a driver may be careless toward opposite travel in speed or other ways, though the probabilities may be against meeting any one. If the chance is so great that ordinary men would drive differently, then it is careless not to do so. * * * The test is not of the balance of probabilities, but of the existence of some probability of sufficient moment to induce action to avoid it on the part of a reasonable mind."

2. An electric power company strung a copper wire along irregularly spaced poles. The wire blended into the autumn countryside. Should the company be liable when the wire is struck by a helicopter? See Arizona Public Service Co. v. Brittain, 107 Ariz. 278, 486 P.2d 176 (1971).

3. In Pease v. Sinclair Refining Co., 104 F.2d 183 (2d Cir.1939), plaintiff, a high school science teacher, wrote to defendant requesting an advertised free "science exhibit," consisting of bottles of petroleum products. Defendant sent him the exhibit and plaintiff, in preparation for an experiment, poured what was labeled "kerosene" onto metallic sodium to preserve it. Unfortunately, the bottle actually contained water, which caused an explosion seriously injuring the teacher. Was the petroleum company negligent in failing to label the bottle "water" rather than "kerosene"?

4. In Paris v. Stepney Borough Council, [1951] A.C. 367, plaintiff, a man with one eye, was employed by defendant at garage work that required him on occasion to hammer on metal. Defendant did not supply him with goggles for the work. While he was hammering to drive out a rusty bolt, a chip flew off the bolt, struck him in the eye, and blinded him. Was this negligence? Suppose he had both eyes and one was blinded. Johnson v. Wichita Valley R. Co., 104 S.W.2d 128 (Tex.Civ.App. 1937).

5. The toilet to a railway coach car was heated by steam passing through an uninsulated iron pipe that went around the corner under the lavatory. Plaintiff, a passenger, fainted and fell with her face against the pipe, seriously burning it. Is the railroad negligent? Hauser v. Chicago, Rhode Island & Pacific Ry., 205 Iowa 940, 219 N.W. 60 (1928).

Chicago, B. & Q.R. Co. v. Krayenbuhl

Supreme Court of Nebraska, 1902.
65 Neb. 889, 91 N.W. 880.

[Action to recover for personal injuries sustained by plaintiff, a child four years old, in playing on a railroad turntable maintained by defendant.

The trial resulted in a verdict and judgment for plaintiff, and defendant brings error.

The turntable was located between two branches of defendant's line. A path or footway, in common use by the general public and by plaintiff's family, passed within about 70 feet of the turntable. The turntable had a movable bolt by which it could be held in position and was provided with a padlock. The defendant's rules required its employees to keep the turntable locked when not in use, but there was evidence that this rule was frequently disregarded and that one of the staples was so loose that the turntable could be unfastened without difficulty. Plaintiff, in company with other young children, found the turntable unlocked and unguarded. Plaintiff got on the turntable, and when the other children set it in motion, plaintiff's foot was caught between the rails and severed at the ankle joint.

The court first held that the fact that the children were trespassers on the defendant's property did not deprive them of the right to enforce defendant's duty to use reasonable care to make its premises safe. As to this, see pages 481–485.]

ALBERT, C. * * * It is true, as said in Loomis v. Terry, 17 Wend. 497, 31 Am.Dec. 306, "the business of life must go forward"; the means by which it is carried forward cannot be rendered absolutely safe. * * * The business of life is better carried forward by the use of dangerous machinery; hence the public good demands its use, although occasionally such use results in the loss of life or limb. It does so because the danger is insignificant, when weighed against the benefits resulting from the use of such machinery and for the same reason demands its reasonable, most effective, and unrestricted use, up to the point where the benefits resulting from such use no longer outweigh the danger to be anticipated from it. At that point the public goods demands restrictions. For example, a turntable is a dangerous contrivance, which facilitates railroading; the general benefits resulting from its use outweigh the occasional injuries inflicted by it; hence the public good demands its use. We may conceive of means by which it might be rendered absolutely safe, but such means would so interfere with its beneficial use that the danger to be anticipated would not justify their adoption; therefore the public good demands its use without them. But the danger incident to its use may be lessened by the use of a lock which would prevent children, attracted to it, from moving it; the interference with the proper use of the turntable occasioned by the use of such lock is so slight that it is outweighed by the danger to be anticipated from an omission to use it; therefore the public good, we think demands the use of the lock. The public good would not require the owner of a vacant lot on which there is a pond to fill up the pond or inclose the lot with an impassable wall to insure the safety of children resorting to it, because the burden of doing so is out of proportion to the danger to be anticipated from leaving it undone. [C] But where there is an open well on a vacant lot, which is frequented by children, of which the owner of the lot has knowledge, he is liable for injuries sustained by children falling into the well, because the danger to be anticipated from the open well, under the circumstances, outweighs the

slight expense or inconvenience that would be entailed in making it safe.
* * *

Hence, in all cases of this kind in the determination of the question of negligence, regard must be had to the character and location of the premises, the purpose for which they are used, the probability of injury therefrom, the precautions necessary to prevent such injury, and the relations such precautions bear to the beneficial use of the premises. The nature of the precautions would depend on the particular facts in each case. In some cases a warning to the children or the parents might be sufficient; in others, more active measures might be required. But in every case they should be such as a man of ordinary care and prudence would observe under like circumstances. If, under all the circumstances, the owner omits such precautions as a man of ordinary care and prudence, under like circumstances, would observe, he is guilty of negligence. * * *

[The judgment was reversed for error in instructions to the jury amounting to improper comment on the evidence.]

NOTES AND QUESTIONS

1.   There are risks associated with the operation of trains, airplanes, automobiles, snowmobiles. How does the jury decide whether the risk is an unreasonable one (negligence) or not?

2.   Defendant, excavating in the highway, set out an open flare pot at night to give warning of the excavation. It left the flare pot until 10:00 a.m. in a street in which it knew that children were accustomed to play. A child meddled with the flare pot and was seriously burned. Should defendant be liable? Why? Would it make a difference if the child was injured at 10:00 a.m. or 10:00 p.m.? Ott v. Washington Gas Light Co., 205 F.Supp. 815 (D.D.C.1962), aff'd, 317 F.2d 138 (D.C.Cir.1963).

Davison v. Snohomish County

Supreme Court of Washington, 1928.
149 Wash. 109, 270 P. 422.

BEALS, J. Plaintiffs instituted this action against Snohomish county as defendant, seeking to recover damages alleged to have been suffered by them as the result of negligence of defendant in the construction and maintenance of the elevated approach to a bridge known as the Bascule bridge across Ebey slough. In the southwesterly approach to this bridge there is a right angle turn towards the south just easterly of the slough, and at this point the causeway or approach to the bridge is at quite an elevation above the ground level. The bridge itself is approximately 18 feet wide; the approach leading to the bridge proper at the curve just to the east of the bridge increases in width to a maximum of 30.9 feet, narrowing again to 18 feet at the end of the turn.

At about 8 o'clock in the evening of November 11, 1926, plaintiffs were driving their Ford automobile toward the city of Snohomish, and proceeded to cross the bridge from the west to east at a low rate of speed. Plaintiff Edwin F. Davison was driving, and, as the car rounded the curve to the east of the slough, he lost control, the car skidded, struck the railing on the east or outer edge of the approach just around the curve, broke through the railing, and, with plaintiffs, fell to the ground. Both plaintiffs suffered severe and painful injuries, and the automobile was wrecked; for all of which damage plaintiffs prayed for judgment in a large amount.

Defendant answered plaintiffs' complaint, denying all the allegations of negligence on its part and affirmatively pleading contributory negligence on the part of plaintiffs. The action came on regularly for trial, and resulted in a verdict in plaintiffs' favor in the sum of $2,500. Defendant seasonably moved for judgment in its favor notwithstanding the verdict, or, in the alternative, for a new trial. Both of these motions were denied by the trial court, which thereupon entered judgment upon the verdict, from which judgment defendant appeals. * * *

[Respondents contended that the bridge was unsafe because of] the insufficiency of the railing or guard to prevent respondents' automobile from skidding off the approach * * *.

The use of the automobile as a means of transportation of passengers and freight has, during recent years, caused certain changes in the law governing the liability of municipalities in respect to the protection of their roads by railings or guards. A few years ago, when people traveled either on foot or by horse-drawn vehicles, a guardrail could to a considerable extent, actually prevent pedestrians or animals drawing vehicles from accidentally leaving the roadbed; but as a practical proposition, municipalities cannot be required to protect long stretches of roadway with railings or guards capable of preventing an automobile, moving at a rapid rate, from leaving the road if the car be in any way deflected from the roadway proper and propelled against the railing. As was said by this court in the case of Leber v. King County, 69 Wash. 134, 124 P. 397:

"Roads must be built and traveled, and to hold that the public cannot open their highways until they are prepared to fence their roads with barriers strong enough to hold a team and wagon when coming in violent contact with them, the condition being the ordinary condition of the country, would be to put a burden upon the public that it could not bear. It would prohibit the building of new roads and tend to the financial ruin of the counties undertaking to maintain the old ones."

This principle applies with special force to elevated causeways constructed of wood, such as the approach from which respondents' automobile fell, as upon such a structure the railing can be anchored or secured only to the deck of the causeway. Upon the ground, in situations of special danger, strength can be given to a guard or railing by driving posts into the earth, and a guard of any desired strength can be constructed in that manner. A concrete viaduct can be constructed with side walls of considerable resisting power; but the same degree of protection cannot be expected from a guard or railing along the side of an elevated frame causeway or viaduct. Respondents introduced some testimony to the effect that the posts which supported the railing were, to some extent, rotted. We have carefully considered this testimony, and, for the purposes of this opinion, assume that it was true; but we still do not think that it was sufficient to take the case to the jury upon the question of appellant's negligence in connection with the condition of the railing at the time of the accident. * * *

The judgment is reversed, with directions to dismiss the action.

NOTES AND QUESTIONS

1. Compare a later decision of the same court in Bartlett v. Northern Pacific R. Co., 74 Wash.2d 881, 447 P.2d 735 (1968). With almost identical facts the trial court had granted summary judgment to the defendant on the basis of the Davison case. The Supreme Court reversed and remanded, saying: "The reasoning in *Davison* * * * was based on the impracticality as a matter of engineering and on prohibitive costs. We do not consider the ideas of the court, expressed 40 years ago, as necessarily authoritative on the engineering and financial phases of the same problem today. We are satisfied that the parties should have the opportunity of presenting their evidence as to the practicality (cost wise or otherwise) of guardrails or barriers on dangerous or misleading roadways to stop slow-moving vehicles."

2. Defendant constructed its railway track so that it approached and crossed a public highway at a narrow acute angle, with the track close beside the highway for a considerable distance before the crossing. While plaintiff was riding his horse on the highway, the horse took fright at the approach of a train, as a result of which plaintiff was injured. The train was operated with due care. Is defendant liable for negligence in the construction of the track? Beatty v. Central Iowa R. Co., 58 Iowa 242, 12 N.W. 332 (1882).

3. In determining whether a choice of alternatives is reasonable, must the risk of harm to third persons be taken into account? Defendant's engineer, operating a train, unexpectedly finds a truck load of furniture on a crossing ahead of him. He can stop the train abruptly and avoid the collision, but if he does he will almost certainly throw his passengers about and injure them. What is he to do? Lucchese v. San Francisco–Sacramento R. Co., 106 Cal.App. 242, 289 P. 188 (1930).

4. Defendant, driving a truck heavily loaded with pipe, is suddenly confronted with a situation requiring him to stop suddenly or injure the plaintiff's intestate. If he stops the pipe may be expected to shift forward and crush him to death. What is he to do? Thurmond v. Pepper, 119 S.W.2d 900 (Tex.Civ.App.1938). Who decides?

United States v. Carroll Towing Co.

United States Circuit Court of Appeals, Second Circuit, 1947.
159 F.2d 169.

[Libel in admiralty for the sinking of libelant's barge, the *Anna C*. The *Anna C* was owned by the Conners Co. and had been chartered to the Pennsylvania Railroad Co., which had loaded it with a cargo of flour that belonged to the United States. The charter required that the Conners Co. provide a bargee between the hours of 8:00 a.m. and 4:00 p.m. Carroll Towing Co. was the owner of a tug whose servants negligently shifted the *Anna C*'s mooring lines, causing her to break free from her pier. After the *Anna C* broke away, she drifted up against a tanker at the next pier down the North River. Unbeknownst to those in the harbor responding to the problem, the tanker's propeller apparently broke a hole in the *Anna C* at or near her bottom. She careened, dumped her cargo of flour belonging to the United States, and sank. The United States sought compensation for the flour and Conners Co. sought compensation for the barge. Carroll Towing Co. argued that the barge could have been kept afloat and her cargo saved if it had been known that she had been damaged by the propeller, but because her bargee had gone ashore, there was no one on board to observe that she was leaking. The trial court divided the damages, according to the admiralty rule, because it found Conners Co. partly responsible for the loss of the cargo and the barge in not having a custodian on board the barge at the time.]

Judge Learned Hand

LEARNED HAND, CIRCUIT JUDGE. * * * [The court reviewed a number of decisions in other cases involving absentee bargees.] It appears from the foregoing review that there is no general rule to determine when the absence of a bargee or other attendant will make the owner of the barge liable for injuries to other vessels if she breaks away from her moorings. However, in any cases where he would be so liable for injuries to others, obviously he must reduce his damages proportionately, if the injury is to his own barge. It becomes apparent why there can be no such general rule, when we consider the grounds for such a liability. Since there are occasions when every vessel will break from her moorings, and, since, if she does, she becomes a menace to those about her, the owner's duty, as in other similar situations, to provide against resulting injuries is a function of three variables: (1) The probability that she will break away; (2) the gravity of the resulting injury, if she does; (3) the burden of adequate precautions. Possibly it serves to bring this notion into relief to state it in algebraic terms: if the probability be called P; the injury L; and the burden B; liability depends upon whether B is less than L multiplied by P; i.e., whether B is less than PL.

Rule of Law (contd.)

Applied to the situation at bar, the likelihood that a barge will break from her fasts, and the damage she will do, vary with the place and time; for example, if a storm threatens, the danger is greater; so it is, if she is in a crowded harbor where moored barges are constantly being shifted about. On the other hand, the barge must not be the bargee's prison, even though he lives aboard; he must go ashore at times. * * * We hold that it is not in all cases a sufficient answer to a bargee's absence without excuse, during working hours, that he has properly made fast his barge to a pier, when he leaves her. In the case at bar the bargee left at five o'clock on the afternoon of January 3rd, and the flotilla broke away at about two o'clock in the afternoon of the following day, twenty-one hours afterwards. The bargee had been away all the time, and we hold that his fabricated story was affirmative evidence that he had no excuse for his absence. At the locus in quo—especially during the short January days and in the full tide of war activity—barges were being constantly drilled in and out. Certainly it was not beyond reasonable expectation that, with the inevitable haste and bustle, the work might not be done with adequate care. In such circumstances we hold—and that is all that we do hold—that it was a fair requirement that the should have a bargee aboard (unless he had some excuse for his absence), during the working hours of daylight.

Holding

[Conners Co. was found partly responsible for the losses.]

NOTES AND QUESTIONS

1. In Conway v. O'Brien, 111 F.2d 611, 612 (2d Cir.1940), Judge Learned Hand stated in part: "The degree of care demanded of a person by an occasion is the resultant of three factors: the likelihood that his conduct will injure others, taken with the seriousness of the injury if it happens, and balanced against the interest which he must sacrifice to avoid the risk. All these are practically not susceptible of any quantitative estimate, and the second two are generally not so, even theoretically. For this reason a solution always involves some preference, or choice between incommensurables, and it is consigned to a jury because their decision is thought most likely to accord with commonly accepted standards, real or fancied." Is this statement consistent with the approach taken in the principal case? Is a court well equipped to weigh these considerations? A jury?

2. In California, some of the considerations that courts have employed in various contexts to determine the existence and scope of duty are the foreseeability of harm to the plaintiff, the degree of certainty that the plaintiff suffered injury, the closeness of the connection between the defendant's conduct and the injury suf-

fered, the moral blame attached to the defendant's conduct, the policy of preventing future harm, the extent of the burden to the defendant and consequences to the community of imposing a duty to exercise care with resulting liability for breach, and the availability, cost, and prevalence of insurance for the risk involved. See Rowland v. Christian 69 Cal. 2d 108, 113, 70 Cal. Rptr. 97, 443 P.2d 561 (1968).

3. An urban electric utility fails to insulate its high tension wires and the decedent is electrocuted when his ladder comes in contact with a wire. Negligence? Amici curiae "complain of the increased costs of more adequate insulation. When the likelihood of danger to human life is to be balanced against the costs of insulation, we do not think the latter is a good argument." Kingsport Util. v. Brown, 201 Tenn. 393, 299 S.W.2d 656 (1955).

4. Is it negligence to fail to design an automobile hood so that if it flies up while the car is going it will not block all vision and produce a wreck? Evidence showed that there were 6 or 7 such happenings in 7 or 8 years and that it would cost up to $10 to make a change. Cf. Roach v. Kononen, 269 Or. 457, 525 P.2d 125 (1974).

5. A five-year-old boy toboggans down a hill in his parents' yard and collides head first with a snowmobile left there by his eight-year-old brother. He was seriously injured by a metal bracket on the underside of the snowmobile when he slid between the skis. Was it negligence for the manufacturer not to install some sort of guard to prevent someone from sliding underneath the snowmobile? Whiteford v. Yamaha Motor Corp., 582 N.W.2d 916 (Minn.1998)(danger too remote to impose duty on Yamaha).

RESTATEMENT (SECOND) OF TORTS (1965)

§ 291. Unreasonableness; How Determined; Magnitude of Risk and Utility of Conduct

Where an act is one which a reasonable man would recognize as involving a risk of harm to another, the risk is unreasonable and the act is negligent if the risk is of such magnitude as to outweigh what the law regards as the utility of the act or of the particular manner in which it is done.

§ 292. Factors Considered in Determining Utility of Actor's Conduct

In determining what the law regards as the utility of the actor's conduct for the purpose of determining whether the actor is negligent, the following factors are important:

(a) the social value which the law attaches to the interest which is to be advanced or protected by the conduct;

(b) the extent of the chance that this interest will be advanced or protected by the particular course of conduct;

(c) the extent of the chance that such interest can be adequately advanced or protected by another and less dangerous course of conduct.

§ 293. Factors Considered in Determining Magnitude of Risk

In determining the magnitude of the risk for the purpose of determining whether the actor is negligent, the following factors are important:

(a) the social value which the law attaches to the interests which are imperiled;

(b) the extent of the chance that the actor's conduct will cause an invasion of any interest of the other or of one of a class of which the other is a member;

(c) the extent of the harm likely to be caused to the interests imperiled;

(d) the number of persons whose interests are likely to be invaded if the risk takes effect in harm.

4. THE STANDARD OF CARE

(A) THE REASONABLE PRUDENT PERSON

➡ Vaughan v. Menlove

Court of Common Pleas, 1837.
3 Bing. (N.C.) 467, 132 Eng.Rep. 490.

[Defendant built a hay rick near the boundary of his land not far from the plaintiff's cottages. It was alleged that the rick was likely to ignite, thereby endangering the plaintiff's cottages, of which the defendant had notice; that the defendant was negligent in maintaining the rick in this dangerous condition; and that the rick did ignite and the fire spread to plaintiff's land, burning his cottages. Defendant denied that he was negligent.]

At the trial it appeared that the rick in question had been made by the defendant near the boundary of his own premises; that the hay was in such a state when put together, as to give rise to discussions on the probability of fire; that though there [were] conflicting opinions on the subject, yet during a period of five weeks, the defendant was repeatedly warned of his peril; that his stock was insured; and that upon one occasion, being advised to take the rick down to avoid all danger, he said, "he would chance it." He made an aperture or chimney through the rick; but in spite, or perhaps in consequence of his precaution, the rick at length burst into flames from the spontaneous heating of its materials; the flames communicated to the defendant's barn and stables, and thence to the plaintiff's cottages, which were entirely destroyed.

Patterson, J., before whom the cause was tried, told the jury that the question for them to consider, was, whether the fire had been occasioned by gross negligence on the part of the defendant; adding, that he was bound to proceed with such reasonable caution as a prudent man would have exercised under such circumstances.

A verdict having been found for the plaintiff, a rule nisi for a new trial was obtained, on the ground that the jury should have been directed to

Chief Justice Tindal

Issue: were the jury instructions correct?

consider, not, whether the defendant had been guilty of gross negligence with reference to the standard of ordinary prudence, a standard too uncertain to afford any criterion; but whether he had acted bona fide to the best of his judgment; if he had, he ought not to be responsible for the misfortune of not possessing the highest order of intelligence. The action under such circumstances, was of the first impression.

Principle (Rule)

TINDAL, C.J. I agree that this is a case primae impressionis; but I feel no difficulty in applying to it the principles of law as laid down in other cases of a similar kind. * * * [T]hough the defendant did not himself light the fire, yet mediately, he is as much the cause of it as if he had himself put a candle to the rick; for it is well known that hay will ferment and take fire if it be not carefully stacked. It has been decided that if an occupier burns weeds so near the boundary of his own land that damage ensues to the property of his neighbor, he is liable to an action for the amount of injury done, unless the accident were occasioned by a sudden blast which he could not foresee. * * *

It is contended, however, that the learned Judge was wrong in leaving this to the jury as a case of gross negligence, and that the question of negligence was so mixed up with reference to what would be the conduct of a man of ordinary prudence that the jury might have thought the latter the rule by which they were to decide; that such a rule would be too uncertain to act upon; and that the question ought to have been whether the defendant had acted honestly and bona fide to the best of his own judgment. * * * The care taken by a prudent man has always been the rule laid down; and as to the supposed difficulty of applying it, a jury has always been able to say whether, taking that rule as their guide, there has been negligence on the occasion in question.

Instead, therefore, of saying that the liability for negligence should be co-extensive with the judgment of each individual, which would be as variable as the length of the foot of each individual, we ought rather to adhere to the rule which requires in all cases a regard to caution such as a man of ordinary prudence would observe. That was in substance the criterion presented to the jury in this case, and therefore the present rule must be discharged.

[The concurring opinions of PARK and VAUGHAN, JJ., are omitted. GASLEE, J., concurred in discharging the rule.]

NOTES AND QUESTIONS

1. How can an honest mistake in judgment be "fault"? Based on the evidence as summarized by Chief Justice Tindal, what other argument could defendant's lawyer have made on behalf of his client?

2. "If, for instance, a man is born hasty and awkward, is always hurting himself or his neighbors, no doubt his congenital defects will be allowed for in the courts of Heaven, but his slips are no less troublesome to his neighbors than if they sprang from guilty neglect. His neighbors accordingly require him, at his peril, to come up to their standard, and the courts which they establish decline to take his personal equation into account." Holmes, The Common Law 108 (1881). See also Seavey, Negligence—Subjective or Objective? 41 Harv.L.Rev. 1 (1927).

3. The standard formula for instructing the jury has been that of "a reasonable man of ordinary prudence." Variations on this have, however, been upheld, if they obviously mean the same thing. Thus the "ordinarily prudent man," Osborne v. Montgomery, 203 Wis. 223, 234 N.W. 372 (1931); the "typical prudent man," Warrington v. New York Power & Light Corp., 252 App.Div. 364, 300 N.Y.S. 154 (1937); the "average person of ordinary prudence," Charbonneau v. MacRury, 84 N.H. 501, 153 A. 457 (1931).

"The 'reasonable man' has been described by Greer, L.J. as 'the man in the street' or 'the man in the Clapham omnibus', or, as I recently read in an American author, 'the man who takes the magazines at home, and in the evening pushes the lawn mower in his shirt sleeves.' " Hall v. Brooklands Club, [1933] 1 K.B. 205, 224. For whimsical treatments, see A. Herbert, Uncommon Law 1–6 (7th ed. 1952); R. Megarry, The Clapham Omnibus, in Miscellany-at-Law 260 (1955).

4. The courts have quite jealously guarded the integrity of the instruction to the jury, and in particular the entirely hypothetical character of the "reasonable

man." Thus in Freeman v. Adams, 63 Cal.App. 225, 218 P. 600 (1923), it was held reversible error to charge the jury that:

"In determining what a reasonable and prudent man would do under the circumstances, you will remember that presumably a jury is composed of such reasonable and prudent persons, and you may each ask yourself, Did the defendants do, or fail to do, anything which, under the circumstances, I would not have done or would have done?"

Courts have traditionally referred to this mythical person in the masculine gender. Obviously, this form of description is now outdated. The form used here and in the jury instructions in most jurisdictions is the reasonable, prudent person.

"* * * In applying the universally accepted standard of care: that of the ordinary, reasonable and prudent man under the circumstances, the term 'ordinary' should be given its true meaning by not requiring the conduct of an extraordinarily careful person. Such an 'ordinary' man is not necessarily a supercautious individual devoid of human frailties and constantly preoccupied with the idea that danger may be lurking in every direction about him at any time. We appreciate that to require such constant apprehension of danger from every possible source would indeed be beyond normal conduct and would be too exacting a standard." Whitman v. W.T. Grant Co., 16 Utah 2d 81, 395 P.2d 918, 920 (1964).

6. See Seavey, Negligence—Subjective or Objective, 41 Harv.L.Rev. 1 (1927); Green, The Negligence Issue, 37 Yale L.J. 1029 (1928), reprinted in Green, Judge and Jury 153 (1930); James, The Qualities of the Reasonable Man in Negligence Cases, 16 Mo.L.Rev. 1 (1951); Reynolds, The Reasonable Man of Negligence Law: A Health Report on the "Odious Creature," 23 Okla.L.Rev. 410 (1970).

Delair v. McAdoo

Supreme Court of Pennsylvania, 1936.
324 Pa. 392, 188 A. 181.

KEPHART, CHIEF JUSTICE. Plaintiff brought an action in trespass to recover for damages to his person and property sustained as a result of a collision between his automobile and that owned by the defendant. The accident occurred when defendant, proceeding in the same direction as plaintiff, sought to pass him. As defendant drew alongside of plaintiff, the left rear tire of his car blew out, causing it to swerve and come into contact with the plaintiff's car. The latter's theory at trial was that defendant was negligent in driving with defective tires. The jury found for plaintiff in the sum of $7,500. The court below granted defendant a new trial on the ground that the verdict was excessive, but refused his motion for a judgment n.o.v. Its ruling on the latter motion is here for review. * * *

It has been held in other states that the question whether a particular person is negligent in failing to know that his tires are in too poor a condition for ordinary operation on the highways is a question of fact for the jury. [Cc] In the instant case the testimony relative to the defect was as follows: A witness for the plaintiff stated that the tire "was worn pretty well through. You could see the tread in the tire—the inside lining." The witness later described this inside lining as the "fabric." The fact that the tire was worn through to and into the fabric over its entire area was corroborated by another witness. The repairman who replaced the tire which had blown out stated that he could see "the breaker strip" which is just under the fabric of a tire. This testimony was contradicted by the defendant.

A jury is just as well qualified to pass judgment as to the risk of danger in the condition of an article in universal use under a given state of facts as experts. We have in this state more than a million automobiles and trucks, approximately two for every three families. Their daily use over the highways is common, and requires a certain amount of knowledge of the movable parts, particularly the tires; it is imperative that a duty or standard of care be set up that will be productive of safety for other users of the highways. Any ordinary individual, whether a car owner or not, knows that when a tire is worn through to the fabric, its further use is dangerous and it should be removed. When worn through several plies, it is very dangerous for further use. All drivers must be held to a knowledge of these facts. An owner or operator cannot escape simply because he says he does not know. He must know. The hazard is too great to permit cars in this condition to be on the highway. It does not require opinion evidence to demonstrate that a trigger pulled on a loaded gun makes the gun a dangerous instrument when pointed at an individual, nor could one escape liability by saying he did not know it was dangerous. The use of a tire worn through to the fabric presents a similar situation. The rule must be rigid if millions are to drive these instrumentalities which in a fraction of a second may become instruments of destruction to life and property. There is no series of accidents more destructive or more terrifying in the use of automobiles than those which come from "blow-outs." The law requires drivers and owners of motor vehicles to know the condition of those parts which are likely to become dangerous where the flaws or faults would be disclosed by a reasonable inspection. It will assume they do know of the dangers ascertainable by such examination.

Order affirmed.

NOTES AND QUESTIONS

1. This case is sent back for a new trial. In the light of the opinion, how should the trial judge instruct the jury?

2. Compare Michigan City v. Rudolph, 104 Ind.App. 643, 12 N.E.2d 970 (1938), holding that the driver is held to the knowledge that an automobile will go out of control if it is driven fast through loose sand. What if the driver is a teenager who has just obtained her license?

3. Are there any facts that every mentally competent adult knows? The law of gravity—something dropped will fall? Seaboard Air Line R. Co. v. Hackney, 217 Ala. 382, 115 So. 869 (1928). The principle of leverage—one end of a balanced board will fly up if the other is trod on? Cf. City of Huntingburg v. First, 15 Ind.App. 552, 43 N.E. 17 (1896). The fact that wood and paper will burn? Lillibridge v. McCann, 117 Mich. 84, 75 N.W. 288 (1898).

4. Suppose the individual has led a life that has not brought him into contact with information common in the particular community. A city dweller who never

has seen a bull or a mule, or heard anything about their characteristics, visits a friend in the country, and makes a misguided attempt to fraternize with the animals. Tolin v. Terrell, 133 Ky. 210, 117 S.W. 290 (1909). A Notre Dame law student from Southern California drives to the library in the midst of a lake effect snow storm. Reasonable conduct?

5. Distinguish ignorance from the breach of a duty to find out. A stranger in a town is suddenly confronted with a purple traffic light. Can she continue to drive across town without stopping to find out what the light means? In Gobrecht v. Beckwith, 82 N.H. 415, 135 A. 20 (1926), defendant, a landlord, installed a gas heater in a closed and almost unventilated bathroom, in ignorance of the fact that it would fill the room with carbon monoxide. Plaintiff, a tenant, used the bathroom, lighted the heater, and was poisoned. It was held that it was unreasonable (negligent) for defendant not to make an inquiry or investigation as to the safety of the heater, but reasonable (not negligent) for plaintiff not to make an inquiry and to rely on the landlord.

6. Suppose persons who do not hold themselves out as having superior knowledge or training do actually have them. Should they be required to exercise those superior skills to avoid harm to others? For example, in the principal case, suppose the defect was a latent one, but defendant could easily have discovered it because his hobby was auto mechanics. Should he be held liable? The Restatement (Second) of Torts suggests an affirmative answer in § 289(b), and in comment *m*. But see Fredericks v. Castora, 241 Pa. Super. 211, 360 A.2d 696 (1976) (court refused to impose higher standard on truck driver despite twenty years experience).

7. It is commonly held that the reasonable person will not forget what is actually known, and that forgetfulness does not excuse negligence. But when distracted attention, lapse of time or other similar factors make it reasonable to forget, it can be found that there is no negligence. See Ferrie v. D'Arc, 31 N.J. 92, 155 A.2d 257 (1959), rev'g, 55 N.J.Super. 65, 150 A.2d 83 (1959).

Trimarco v. Klein

Court of Appeals of New York, 1982.
56 N.Y.2d 98, 436 N.E.2d 502, 451 N.Y.S.2d 52.

FUCHSBERG, JUDGE. After trial by jury in a negligence suit for personal injuries, the plaintiff, Vincent N. Trimarco, recovered a judgment of $240,-000. A sharply divided Appellate Division, 82 A.D.2d 20, 441 N.Y.S.2d 62, having reversed on the law and dismissed the complaint, our primary concern on this appeal is with the role of the proof plaintiff produced on custom and usage. The ultimate issue is whether he made out a case.

The controversy has its genesis in the shattering of a bathtub's glass enclosure door in a multiple dwelling in July, 1976. Taking the testimony most favorably to the plaintiff, as we must in passing on the presence of a prima facie case, we note that, according to the trial testimony, at the time of the incident plaintiff, the tenant of the apartment in which it happened, was in the process of sliding the door open so that he could exit the tub. It is undisputed that the occurrence was sudden and unexpected and the injuries he received from the lacerating glass most severe.

The door, which turned out to have been made of ordinary glass variously estimated as one sixteenth to one quarter of an inch in thickness, concededly would have presented no different appearance to the plaintiff and his wife than did tempered safety glass, which their uncontradicted testimony shows they assumed it to be. Nor was there any suggestion that defendants ever brought its true nature to their attention. * * *

As part of his case, plaintiff, with the aid of expert testimony, developed that, since at least the early 1950's, a practice of using shatterproof glazing materials for bathroom enclosures had come into common use, so that by 1976 the glass door here no longer conformed to accepted safety standards. This proof was reinforced by a showing that over this period bulletins of nationally recognized safety and consumer organizations along with official Federal publications had joined in warning of the dangers that lurked when plain glass was utilized in "hazardous locations", including "bathtub enclosures". * * * And, on examination of the defendants' managing agent, who long had enjoyed extensive familiarity with the management of multiple dwelling units in the New York City area, plaintiff's counsel elicited agreement that, since at least 1965, it was customary for landlords who had occasion to install glass for shower enclosures, whether to replace broken glass or to comply with the request of a tenant or otherwise, to do so with "some material such as plastic or safety glass".

In face of this record, in essence, the rationale of the majority at the Appellate Division was that, "assuming that there existed a custom and usage at the time to substitute shatterproof glass" and that this was a "better way or a safer method of enclosing showers[c] unless prior notice of the danger came to the defendants either from the plaintiff or by reason of a similar accident in the building, no duty devolved on the defendants to replace the glass either under the common law or under section 78 of the Multiple Dwelling Law. * * *

Our analysis may well begin by rejecting defendants' contention that the shower door was not within the compass of section 78 of the Multiple Dwelling Law. From early on, it was understood that this statute was enacted in recognition of the reality that occupants of tenements in apartment houses, notwithstanding their control of the rented premises, as a practical matter looked to their landlords for the safe maintenance of the tenanted quarters as well. The result was that, if responsibility for keeping "every part thereof * * * in good repair" was not placed on the landlords, defects would remain unremedied [cc]. * * *

Which brings us to the well-recognized and pragmatic proposition that when "certain dangers have been removed by a customary way of doing things safely, this custom may be proved to show that [the one charged with the dereliction] has fallen below the required standard" [c]. Such proof, of course, is not admitted in the abstract. It must bear on what is reasonable conduct under all the circumstances, the quintessential test of negligence.

It follows that, when proof of an accepted practice is accompanied by evidence that the defendant conformed to it, this may establish due care [c] and, contrariwise, when proof of a customary practice is coupled with a showing that it was ignored and that this departure was a proximate cause of the accident, it may serve to establish liability. [c]. Put more conceptually, proof of a common practice aids in "formulat[ing] the general expectation of society as to how individuals will act in the course of their undertakings, and thus to guide the common sense or expert intuition of a jury or commission when called on to judge of particular conduct under particular circumstances" (Pound, Administrative Application of Legal Standards, 44 ABA Rep, 445, 456–457).

The source of the probative power of proof of custom and usage is described differently by various authorities, but all agree on its potency. Chief among the rationales offered is, of course, the fact that it reflects the judgment and experience and conduct of many (2 Wigmore, Evidence [3d ed], § 461; Prosser, Torts [4th ed], § 33). Support for its relevancy and reliability comes too from the direct bearing it has on feasibility, for its focusing is on the practicality of a precaution in actual operation and the readiness with which it can be employed (Morris, Custom and Negligence, 42 Col.L.Rev. 1147, 1148). Following in the train of both of these boons is the custom's exemplification of the opportunities it provides to others to learn of the safe way, if that the customary one be. (See Restatement (Second) Torts § 295A, Comments *a, b.*)

From all this it is not to be assumed customary practice and usage need be universal. It suffices that it be fairly well defined and in the same calling or business so that "the actor may be charged with knowledge of it or negligent ignorance" (Prosser, Torts [4th ed], § 33, p. 168; Restatement (Second) Torts § 295A, p. 62, Comment *a*).

However, once its existence is credited, a common practice or usage is still not necessarily a conclusive or even a compelling test of negligence (1 Shearman & Redfield, Negligence [rev ed], § 10). Before it can be, the jury must be satisfied with its reasonableness, just as the jury must be satisfied with the reasonableness of the behavior which adhered to the custom or the unreasonableness of that which did not [c]. After all, customs and usages run the gamut of merit like everything else. That is why the question in each instance is whether it meets the test of reasonableness. As Holmes' now classic statement on this subject expresses it, "[w]hat usually is done may be evidence of what ought to be done, but what ought to be done is fixed by a standard of reasonable prudence, whether it usually is complied with or not" (Texas & Pacific Ry. Co. v. Behymer, 189 U.S. 468, 470, 23 S.Ct. 622, 622–23, 47 L.Ed. 905).

So measured, the case the plaintiff presented, even without the [evidence concerning a statute which applied only to construction after 1973 which the court held should not have been admitted], was enough to send it to the jury and to sustain the verdict reached. The expert testimony, the admissions of the defendant's manager, the data on which the professional and governmental bulletins were based, the evidence of how replacements were handled by at least the local building industry for the better part of two decades, these in the aggregate easily filled that bill. Moreover, it was also for the jury to decide whether, at the point in time when the accident occurred, the modest cost and ready availability of safety glass and the dynamics of the growing custom to use it for shower enclosures had transformed what once may have been considered a reasonably safe part of the apartment into one which, in the light of later developments, no longer could be so regarded.

Furthermore, the charge on this subject was correct. The Trial Judge placed the evidence of custom and usage "by others engaged in the same business" in proper perspective, when, among other things, he told the jury that the issue on which it was received was "the reasonableness of the defendant's conduct under all the circumstances". He also emphasized that the testimony on this score was not conclusive, not only by saying so but by explaining that "the mere fact that another person or landlord may have used a better or safer practice does not establish a standard" and that it was for the jurors "to determine whether or not the evidence in this case does establish a general custom or practice".

Nevertheless, we reverse and order a new trial because the General Business Law sections [concerning the statute which did not apply] should have been excluded. * * *

Order reversed, with costs, and case remitted to Supreme Court, Bronx County, for a new trial in accordance with the opinion herein.

NOTES AND QUESTIONS

1. Who is interested in introducing evidence of the custom, plaintiff or defendant? Why? Do you see that industry custom is one way to show the jury what a reasonable person would do under the circumstances?

2. Defendant, driving an automobile on a private road, where no statute is applicable, violates the custom in the United States by driving on the left side of the road. In the absence of special circumstances, can he be found negligent in doing so? Cf. Eamiello v. Piscitelli, 133 Conn. 360, 51 A.2d 912 (1947) (walking on wrong side of road). What about special circumstances? Suppose the right side of the road is full of dangerous potholes? Compare Texas & Pacific R. Co. v. Behymer, 189 U.S. 468 (1903), quoted in the principal case, where it was railway custom to make up a train by bumping cars together with brakemen standing on top of them; and this was done on one occasion when the cars were covered with a sheet of ice.

3. What if the custom of the industry is a careless one? Defendant's tug boats were towing plaintiff's barges loaded with coal up the coast from Norfolk, Virginia to New York when they were lost in an easterly gale off the Jersey Coast. The tugs were not equipped with a radio that would have allowed them to receive a warning from the Weather Bureau in time to pull into safety in the Delaware Breakwater. Defendants proved that it was the custom of the barge lines not to provide radio receiving sets to the crews. In upholding the verdict against the defendants, Learned Hand wrote an oft-quoted passage, which summarizes the law in this area: "[I]n most cases reasonable prudence is in fact common prudence; but strictly it is never its measure; a whole calling may have unduly lagged in the adoption of new and available devices. It never may set its own tests, however persuasive be its usages. Courts must in the end say what is required; there are precautions so

imperative that even their universal disregard will not excuse their omission." The T.J. Hooper, 60 F.2d 737 (2d Cir.1932).

4. What if a custom violates a statute? Suppose everyone in town habitually jaywalks, crossing the street in the middle of the block? Cf. Fowler v. Key System Transit Lines, 37 Cal.2d 65, 230 P.2d 339 (1951).

5. Are there customs that are so clearly unreasonable that they are not even to be admitted as evidence of due care? In Mayhew v. Sullivan Mining Co., 76 Me. 100 (1884), defendant mining company did not guard or even light ladder-holes in the platforms in its mine. A workman fell through such a hole and was injured. Barrow, J.: "If the defendants had proved that in every mining establishment that has existed since the days of Tubal Cain, it has been the practice to cut ladder-holes in their platforms, situated as this was while in daily use for mining operations, without guarding or lighting them, and without notice to contractors or workmen, it would have no tendency to show that the act was consistent with ordinary prudence or a due regard for the safety of those who were using their premises by their invitation."

6. The classic article on this topic is Morris, Custom and Negligence, 42 Colum.L.Rev. 1147 (1942), reprinted in Morris, Studies in the Law of Torts 214 (1952). See also James, Particularizing Standards of Conduct in Negligence Trials, 5 Vand.L.Rev. 697, 709–714 (1952).

Cordas v. Peerless Transportation Co.

City Court of New York, New York County, 1941.
27 N.Y.S.2d 198.

CARLIN, JUSTICE. This case presents the ordinary man—that problem child of the law—in a most bizarre setting. As a lonely chauffeur in defendant's employ he became in a trice the protagonist in a breath-bating drama with a denouement almost tragic. It appears that a man, whose identity it would be indelicate to divulge, was feloniously relieved of his portable goods by two nondescript highwaymen in an alley near 26th Street and Third Avenue, Manhattan; they induced him to relinquish his possessions by a strong argument ad hominem couched in the convincing cant of the criminal and pressed at the point of a most persuasive pistol. Laden with their loot, but not thereby impeded, they took an abrupt departure, and he, shuffling off the coil of that discretion which enmeshed him in the alley, quickly gave chase through 26th Street toward 2d Avenue, whither they were resorting "with expedition swift as thought" for most obvious reasons. Somewhere on that thoroughfare of escape they indulged the stratagem of separation ostensibly to disconcert their pursuer and allay the ardor of his pursuit. He then centered on for capture the man with the pistol, whom he saw board the defendant's taxicab which quickly veered south toward 25th Street on 2d Avenue, where he saw the chauffeur jump out while the cab still in motion, continued toward 24th Street; after the chauffeur relieved himself of the cumbersome burden of his fare the latter also is said to have similarly departed from the cab before it reached 24th Street.

The chauffeur's story is substantially the same except that he states that his uninvited guest boarded the cab at 25th Street while it was at a standstill waiting for a less colorful fare; that his "passenger" immediately advised him "to stand not upon the order of his going but go at once," and added finality to his command by an appropriate gesture with a pistol addressed to his sacroiliac. The chauffeur in reluctant acquiescence proceeded about fifteen feet, when his hair, like unto the quills of the fretful porcupine, was made to stand on end by the hue and cry of the man despoiled, accompanied by a clamorous concourse of the law-abiding who paced him as he ran; the concatenation of "stop thief," to which the patter of persistent feet did maddingly beat time, rang in his ears as the pursuing posse all the while gained on the receding cab with its quarry therein contained. The hold-up man sensing his insecurity suggested to the chauffeur that in the event there was the slightest lapse in obedience to his curt command that he, the chauffeur, would suffer the loss of his brains, a prospect as horrible to an humble chauffeur as it undoubtedly would be to one of the intelligentsia.

[margin note: threatened chauffeur's life]

The chauffeur, apprehensive of certain dissolution from either Scylla, the pursuers, or Charybdis, the pursued, quickly threw his car out of first speed in which he was proceeding, pulled on the emergency, jammed on his brakes and, although he thinks the motor was still running, swung open the door to his left and jumped out of his car. He confesses that the only act that smacked of intelligence was that by which he jammed the brakes in order to throw off balance the hold-up man, who was half-standing and half-sitting with his pistol menacingly poised. Thus abandoning his car and passenger the chauffeur sped toward 26th Street and then turned to look; he saw the cab proceeding south toward 24th Street, where it mounted the sidewalk. The plaintiff-mother and her two infant children were there injured by the cab, which, at the time, appeared to be also minus its passenger, who, it appears, was apprehended in the cellar of a local hospital where he was pointed out to a police officer by a remnant of the posse, hereinbefore mentioned. He did not appear at the trial. The three aforesaid plaintiffs and the husband-father sue the defendant for damages, predicating their respective causes of action upon the contention that the chauffeur was negligent in abandoning the cab under the aforesaid circumstances. Fortunately the injuries sustained were comparatively slight. * * *

[margin note: said chauffeur was negligent]

Negligence has been variously defined but the common legal acceptation is the failure to exercise that care and caution which a reasonable and prudent person ordinarily would exercise under like conditions or circumstances. * * * Negligence is "not absolute or intrinsic," but "is always relevant to some circumstances of time, place or person." In slight paraphrase of the world's first bard it may be truly observed that the expedition of the chauffeur's violent love of his own security outran the pauser, reason, when he was suddenly confronted with unusual emergency which "took his reason prisoner." The learned attorney for the plaintiffs concedes that the chauffeur acted in an emergency, but claims a right to recovery upon the following proposition taken verbatim from his brief: "It is respectfully submitted that the value of the interest of the public at large to be immune from being injured by a dangerous instrumentality such as a car unattended while in motion is very superior to the right of a driver to abandon same while it is in motion, even when acting under the belief that his life is in danger and by abandoning same he will save his life.''

To hold thus under the facts adduced herein would be tantamount to a repeal by implication of the primal law of nature written in indelible characters upon the fleshy tablets of sentient creation by the Almighty Law-giver, ''the supernal Judge who sits on high.'' There are those who stem the turbulent current for bubble fame, or who bridge the yawning chasm with a leap for the leap's sake, or who ''outstare the sternest eyes that look, outbrave the heart most daring on the earth, pluck the young sucking cubs from the she-bear, yea, mock the lion when he roars for prey'' to win a fair lady, and these are the admiration of the generality of men; but they are made of sterner stuff than the ordinary man upon whom the law places no duty of emulation. The law would indeed be fond if it imposed upon the ordinary man the obligation to so demean himself when suddenly confronted with a danger, not of his creation, disregarding the likelihood that such a contingency may darken the intellect and palsy the will of the common legion of the earth, the fraternity of the ordinary man—whose acts or omissions under certain conditions make the yardstick by which the law measures culpability or innocence, negligence or care. * * *

Returning to our chauffeur. If the philosophic Horatio and the martial companions of his watch were ''distilled almost to jelly with the act of fear'' when they beheld ''in the dead vast and middle of the night'' the disembodied spirit of Hamlet's father stalk majestically by ''with a countenance more in sorrow than in anger,'' was not the chauffeur, though unacquainted with the example of these eminent men-at-arms more amply justified in his fearsome reactions when he was more palpably confronted by a thing of flesh and blood bearing in its hand an engine of destruction which depended for its lethal purpose upon the quiver of a hair? When Macbeth was cross-examined by Macduff as to any reason he could advance for his sudden dispatch of Duncan's grooms he said in plausible answer, ''Who can be wise, amazed, temperate and furious, loyal and neutral in a moment? No man.'' * * *

Kolanko v. Erie Railroad Co., 215 App.Div. 82, 86, 212 N.Y.S. 714, 717, says: ''The law in this state does not hold one in an emergency to the exercise of that mature judgment required of him under circumstances where he has an opportunity for deliberate action. He is not required to exercise unerring judgment, which would be expected of him, were he not confronted with an emergency requiring prompt action.'' The circumstances provide the foil by which the act is brought into relief to determine whether it is or is not negligent. If under normal circumstances an act is done which might be considered negligent, it does not follow as a corollary that a similar act is negligent if performed by a person acting under an emergency, not of his own making, in which he suddenly is faced with a patent danger with a moment left to adopt a means of extrication.

The chauffeur—the ordinary man in this case—acted in a split second in a most harrowing experience. To call him negligent would be to brand him coward; the court does not do so in spite of what those swaggering heroes, "whose valor plucks dead lions by the beard", may bluster to the contrary. The court is loathe to see the plaintiffs go without recovery even though their damages were slight, but cannot hold the defendant liable upon the facts adduced at the trial. Motions, upon which decision was reserved, to dismiss the complaint are granted, with exceptions to plaintiffs. Judgment for defendant against plaintiffs dismissing their complaint upon the merits.

NOTES AND QUESTIONS

1. Compare Vincent v. Lake Erie Transp. Co., page 120. Why a different result? Would it make any difference if plaintiff in the principal case had been killed or seriously injured? Should it? Some legal scholars have observed that society tends to prevent direct taking of life while permitting indirect, but statistically certain, deaths. See Calabresi, Reflections on Medical Experiments in Humans, 98 Daedalus 387 (1969).

2. In the principal case, unlike in most negligence cases, the judge acted as a trier of fact. In cases where the jury acts as the fact-finder, legal disputes surrounding the emergency doctrine arise in regard to whether a judge should have instructed a jury about "the reasonable person in an emergency." See Miller v. Reilly, 21 Md.App. 465, 319 A.2d 553 (1974) (failure to apply emergency brake). Since the jury is usually instructed to view the reasonable person "in the circumstances," why insist upon a separate instruction? Lockhart v. List, 542 Pa. 141, 665 A.2d 1176 (1995) (reaffirming that separate sudden emergency instruction should be given to explain context for judging behavior in light of circumstances).

3. Does the emergency excuse the actor from the standard of the reasonable person? What if the actor's conduct is found to be unreasonable even in the light of the emergency?

4. There is general agreement that if the emergency is created by the negligence of the actor, the emergency doctrine does not apply. See for example Lunzer v. Pittsburgh & L.E.R. Co., 296 Pa. 393, 145 A. 907 (1929); Frisby v. Agerton Logging, Inc., 323 Ark. 508, 915 S.W.2d 718 (1996). It has been said, however, that it is not the conduct after the emergency has arisen that the law does not excuse, but the negligent conduct that brought it about. Windsor v. McKee, 22 S.W.2d 65 (Mo.App.1929).

5. Are there situations in which one may be required to anticipate an emergency, and be prepared to meet it? What if defendant is driving past a school, and a child suddenly comes darting out of a driveway on a bicycle? Lederer v. Connecticut Co., 95 Conn. 520, 111 A. 785 (1920); Conery v. Tackmaier, 34 Wis.2d 511, 149 N.W.2d 575 (1967).

6. See Reynolds, Put Yourself in an Emergency—How Will You Be Judged? 62 Ky.L.J. 366 (1973); Evans, the Standard of Care in Emergencies, 31 Ky.L.J. 207 (1943).

Roberts v. State of Louisiana

Court of Appeal of Louisiana, 1981.
396 So.2d 566.

LABORDE, JUDGE. In this tort suit, William C. Roberts sued to recover damages for injuries he sustained in an accident in the lobby of the U.S.

Post Office Building in Alexandria, Louisiana. Roberts fell after being bumped into by Mike Burson, the blind operator of the concession stand located in the building.

Plaintiff sued the State of Louisiana, through the Louisiana Health and Human Resources Administration, advancing two theories of liability: respondeat superior and negligent failure by the State to properly supervise and oversee the safe operation of the concession stand. The stand's blind operator, Mike Burson, is not a party to this suit although he is charged with negligence.

[The trial court ordered plaintiff's suit dismissed.]

We affirm the trial court's decision for the reasons which follow.

On September 1, 1977, at about 12:45 in the afternoon, operator Mike Burson left his concession stand to go to the men's bathroom located in the building. As he was walking down the hall, he bumped into plaintiff who fell to the floor and injured his hip. Plaintiff was 75 years old, stood 5÷6″ and weighed approximately 100 pounds. Burson, on the other hand, was 25 to 26 years old, stood approximately 6÷ and weighed 165 pounds. * * *

Even though Burson was not joined as a defendant, his negligence or lack thereof is crucial to a determination of the State's liability. Because of its importance, we begin with it.

Plaintiff contends that operator Mike Burson traversed the area from his concession stand to the men's bathroom in a negligent manner. To be more specific, he focuses on the operator's failure to use his cane even though he had it with him in his concession stand.

In determining an actor's negligence, various courts have imposed differing standards of care to which handicapped persons are expected to perform. Professor William L. Prosser expresses one generally recognized modern standard of care as follows:

"As to his physical characteristics, the reasonable man may be said to be identical with the actor. The man who is blind ... is entitled to live in the world and to have allowance made by others for his disability, and he cannot be required to do the impossible by conforming to physical standards which he cannot meet. ... At the same time, the conduct of the handicapped individual must be reasonable in the light of his knowledge of his infirmity, which is treated merely as one of the circumstances under which he acts ... It is sometimes said that a blind man must use a greater degree of care than one who can see; but it is now generally agreed that as a fixed rule this is inaccurate, and that the correct statement is merely that he must take the precautions, be they more or less, which the ordinary reasonable man would take if he were blind." W. Prosser, *The Law of Torts*, Section 32, at Page 151–52 (4th ed. 1971).

A careful review of the record in this instance reveals that Burson was acting as a reasonably prudent blind person would under these particular circumstances.

Mike Burson is totally blind. Since 1974, he has operated the concession stand located in the lobby of the post office building. It is one of twenty-three vending stands operated by blind persons under a program funded by the federal government and implemented by the State through the Blind Services Division of the Department of Health and Human Resources. Burson hired no employees, choosing instead to operate his stand on his own. * * *

On the date of the incident in question, Mike Burson testified that he left his concession stand and was on his way to the men's bathroom when he bumped into plaintiff. He, without hesitancy, admitted that at the time he was not using his cane, explaining that he relies on his facial sense which he feels is an adequate technique for short trips inside the familiar building. Burson testified that he does use a cane to get to and from work.

Plaintiff makes much of Burson's failure to use a cane when traversing the halls of the post office building. Yet, our review of the testimony received at trial indicates that it is not uncommon for blind people to rely on other techniques when moving around in a familiar setting. For example George Marzloff, the director of the Division of Blind Services, testified that he can recommend to the blind operators that they should use a cane but he knows that when they are in a setting in which they are comfortable, he would say that nine out of ten will not use a cane and in his personal opinion, if the operator is in a relatively busy area, the cane can be more of a hazard than an asset. * * *

The only testimony in the record that suggests that Burson traversed the halls in a negligent manner was that elicited from plaintiff's expert witness, William Henry Jacobson. Jacobson is an instructor in peripathology, which he explained as the science of movement within the surroundings by visually impaired individuals. Jacobson, admitting that he conducted no study or examination of Mike Burson's mobility skills and that he was unfamiliar with the State's vending program, nonetheless testified that he would require a blind person to use a cane in traversing the areas outside the concession stand. * * *

Upon our review of the record, we feel that plaintiff has failed to show that Burson was negligent. Burson testified that he was very familiar with his surroundings, having worked there for three and a half years. He had special mobility training and his reports introduced into evidence indicate good mobility skills. He explained his decision to rely on his facial sense instead of his cane for these short trips in a manner which convinces us that it was a reasoned decision. Not only was Burson's explanation adequate, there was additional testimony from other persons indicating that such a decision is not an unreasonable one. Also important is the total lack of any evidence in the record showing that at the time of the incident, Burson engaged in any acts which may be characterized as negligence on his part. For example, there is nothing showing that Burson was walking too fast, not paying attention, et cetera. Under all of these circumstances, we conclude that Mike Burson was not negligent.

Our determination that Mike Burson was not negligent disposes of our need to discuss liability on the part of the State.

For the above and foregoing reasons, the judgment of the trial court dismissing plaintiff's claims against defendant is affirmed and all costs of this appeal are assessed against the plaintiff-appellant.

Affirmed.

NOTES AND QUESTIONS

1.   Accord, as to the other physical characteristics: Otterbeck v. Lamb, 85 Nev. 456, 456 P.2d 855 (1969) (deafness); Stephens v. Dulaney, 78 N.M. 53, 428 P.2d 27 (1967) (no sense of smell); Mahan v. State of New York to Use of Carr, 172 Md. 373, 191 A. 575 (1937) (short stature, unable to see over hood of automobile); Storjohn v. Fay, 246 Neb. 454, 519 N.W. 2d 521 (1994) (epilepsy); Burgess v. Shreveport, 471 So.2d 690 (La.1985), reh'g denied (age); Hodges v. Jewel Cos., 72 Ill.App.3d 263, 28 Ill.Dec. 571, 390 N.E.2d 930 (1979) (paralysis caused by polio).

2.   Is a blind person negligent in going out on the street unaccompanied? See Hill v. Glenwood, 124 Iowa 479, 100 N.W. 522 (1904), where a blind man was the injured party. Suppose he had gone out without a cane. Smith v. Sneller, 147 Pa.Super. 231, 24 A.2d 61, 63 aff'd, 345 Pa. 68, 26 A.2d 452 (1942). ("A blind man may not rely wholly upon his other senses to warn him of danger but must use the devices usually employed, to compensate for his blindness.")

3.   Will the reasonable person with a physical disability always exercise more care than one without it? Should it make any difference if the party with a physical disability is a plaintiff or a defendant?

4.   Suppose that instead of being physically disabled, the actor has superior endowments—he is stronger, can see farther or is wiser. Is it sufficient for him to exercise ordinary abilities or must he exercise his superior ones? See Restatement (Second) of Torts § 289(b) and comment m.

5.   What about the obligation of the defendant to take the possibility of such a disability as blindness into account? See Fletcher v. Aberdeen, 54 Wash.2d 174, 338 P.2d 743 (1959).

6.   See ten Broek, The Right to Live in the World: The Disabled in the Law of Torts, 54 Cal.L.Rev. 841 (1966); Weisiger, Negligence of the Physically Infirm, 24 N.C.L.Rev. 187 (1945).

7.   The Americans With Disabilities Act ("ADA"), 42 U.S.C.A. §§ 12101–12213 (1990), designed to require accommodations in all areas (employment, public service, public accommodation, telecommunication) where a disabled person might encounter unnecessary difficulties went into full effect in 1994. In what ways might the ADA affect tort law?

8.   *Intoxication.* Although intoxication arguably could be classified as a physical disability, the courts have consistently refused to make any allowance for it where it is "voluntary," or even negligent. Why? Is voluntary intoxication negligence in itself? What if the defendant indulged in any other drug that impairs physical abilities? Cf. Janelsins v. Button, 102 N.W. App. 30, 648 A.2d 1039 (1994) (voluntary intoxication). For treatment of the numerous problems see McCoid, Intoxication and its Effect Upon Civil Responsibility, 42 Iowa L.Rev. 38 (1956).

9.   What is defendant's obligation toward one who is intoxicated? One of the most famous judicial utterances is in Robinson v. Pioche, Bayerque & Co., 5 Cal.

460 (1885): "A drunken man is as much entitled to a safe street as a sober one, and much more in need of it."

Robinson v. Lindsay — Standard of care for reasonable minors

Supreme Court of Washington, 1979.
92 Wash.2d 410, 598 P.2d 392.

UTTER, CHIEF JUSTICE. [Billy Anderson, age 13 years, was driving a snowmobile belonging to defendant Lindsay, pulling plaintiff Kelly Robinson on an innertube attached to the snowmobile. Plaintiff's thumb was severed when it was caught in the tow rope. The thumb was reattached, but still not fully functional at the time of trial. Plaintiff filed suit against Billy Anderson and Lindsay, the owner of the snowmobile.] An action seeking damages for personal injuries was brought on behalf of Kelly Robinson who lost full use of a thumb in a snowmobile accident when she was 11 years of age. The petitioner, Billy Anderson, 13 years of age at the time of the accident, was the driver of the snowmobile. After a jury verdict in favor of Anderson, the trial court ordered a new trial.

The single issue on appeal is whether a minor operating a snowmobile is to be held to an adult standard of care. The trial court failed to instruct the jury as to that standard and ordered a new trial because it believed the jury should have been so instructed. We agree and affirm the order granting a new trial.

The trial court instructed the jury under WPI 10.05 that: "In considering the claimed negligence of a child, you are instructed that it is the duty of a child to exercise the same care that a reasonably careful child of the same age, intelligence, maturity, training and experience would exercise under the same or similar circumstances." Respondent properly excepted to the giving of this instruction and to the court's failure to give an adult standard of care.

The question of what standard of care should apply to acts of children has a long historical background. Traditionally, a flexible standard of care has been used to determine if children's actions were negligent. Under some circumstances, however, courts have developed a rationale for applying an adult standard.

In the courts' search for a uniform standard of behavior to use in determining whether or not a person's conduct has fallen below minimal acceptable standards, the law has developed a fictitious person, the "reasonable man of ordinary prudence." That term was first used in Vaughan v. Menlove, 132 Eng.Rep. 490 (1837).

Exceptions to the reasonable person standard developed when the individual whose conduct was alleged to have been negligent suffered from some physical impairment, such as blindness, deafness, or lameness. Courts also found it necessary, as a practical matter, to depart considerably from the objective standard when dealing with children's behavior. Children are traditionally encouraged to pursue childhood activities without the same burdens and responsibilities with which adults must contend. [C] As a result, courts evolved a special standard of care to measure a child's negligence in a particular situation.

In Roth v. Union Depot Co., 13 Wash. 525, 43 P. 641 (1896), Washington joined "the overwhelming weight of authority" in distinguishing between the capacity of a child and that of an adult. As the court then stated, at page 544, 43 P. at page 647: "[I]t would be a monstrous doctrine to hold that a child of inexperience—and experience can come only with years—should be held to the same degree of care in avoiding danger as a person of mature years and accumulated experience."

The court went on to hold, at page 545, 43 P. at page 647: "The care or caution required is according to the capacity of the child, and this is to be determined, ordinarily, by the age of the child. * * * [A] child is held * * * only to the exercise of such degree of care and discretion as is reasonably to be expected from children of his age."

* * * In the past we have always compared a child's conduct to that expected of a reasonably careful child of the same age, intelligence, maturity, training and experience. This case is the first to consider the question of a child's liability for injuries sustained as a result of his or her operation of a motorized vehicle or participation in an inherently dangerous activity.

Courts in other jurisdictions have created an exception to the special child standard because of the apparent injustice that would occur if a child who caused injury while engaged in certain dangerous activities were permitted to defend himself by saying that other children similarly situated would not have exercised a degree of care higher than his, and he is, therefore, not liable for his tort. Some courts have couched the exception in terms of children engaging in an activity which is normally one for adults only. See, e.g., Dellwo v. Pearson, 259 Minn. 452, 107 N.W.2d 859 (1961) (operation of a motorboat). We believe a better rationale is that when the activity a child engages in is inherently dangerous, as is the operation of powerful mechanized vehicles, the child should be held to an adult standard of care.

Such a rule protects the need of children to be children but at the same time discourages immature individuals from engaging in inherently dangerous activities. Children will still be free to enjoy traditional childhood activities without being held to an adult standard of care. Although accidents sometimes occur as the result of such activities, they are not activities generally considered capable of resulting in "grave danger to others and to the minor himself if the care used in the course of the activity drops below that care which the reasonable and prudent adult would use * * *." Daniels v. Evans, 107 N.H. 407, 408, 224 A.2d 63, 64 (1966).

Other courts adopting the adult standard of care for children engaged in adult activities have emphasized the hazards to the public if the rule is otherwise. We agree with the Minnesota Supreme Court's language in its decision in Dellwo v. Pearson, supra, 259 Minn. at 457–58, 107 N.W.2d at 863:

"Certainly in the circumstances of modern life, where vehicles moved by powerful motors are readily available and frequently operated by immature individuals, we should be skeptical of a rule that would allow motor vehicles to be operated to the hazard of the public with less than the normal minimum degree of care and competence."

Dellwo applied the adult standard to a twelve-year-old defendant operating a motor boat. Other jurisdictions have applied the adult standard to minors engaged in analogous activities. Goodfellow v. Coggburn, 98 Idaho 202, 203–04, 560 P.2d 873 (1977) (minor operating tractor); Williams v. Esaw, 214 Kan. 658, 668, 522 P.2d 950 (1974) (minor operating motorcycle); Perricone v. DiBartolo, 14 Ill.App.3d 514, 520, 302 N.E.2d 637 (1973) (minor operating gasoline-powered minibike); Krahn v. LaMeres, 483 P.2d 522, 525–26 (Wyo.1971) (minor operating automobile). The holding of minors to an adult standard of care when they operate motorized vehicles is gaining approval from an increasing number of courts and commentators. [C]

The operation of a snowmobile likewise requires adult care and competence. Currently 2.2 million snowmobiles are in operation in the United States. 9 Envir.Rptr. (BNA) 876 [1978 Current Developments]. Studies show that collisions and other snowmobile accidents claim hundreds of casualties each year and that the incidence of accidents is particularly high among inexperienced operators. [C]

At the time of the accident, the 13-year-old petitioner had operated snowmobiles for about 2 years. When the injury occurred, petitioner was operating a 30-horsepower snowmobile at speeds of 10–20 miles per hour. The record indicates that the machine itself was capable of 65 miles per hour. Because petitioner was operating a powerful motorized vehicle, he should be held to the standard of care and conduct expected of an adult.

The order granting a new trial is affirmed.

NOTES AND QUESTIONS

1. The standard used by a majority of jurisdictions usually is stated to be "what it is reasonable to expect of children of like age, intelligence and experience." See Restatement (Second) of Torts § 283A; Cleveland Rolling–Mill Co. v. Corrigan, 46 Ohio St. 283, 20 N.E. 466 (1889). What significance should be attached to a child's testimony that he understood the danger associated with his conduct? See Norfolk & Portsmouth Belt Line R. v. Barker, 221 Va. 924, 275 S.E.2d 613 (1981).

2. This means that more may be required of a child of superior intelligence. Compare Jones v. Firemen's Ins. Co. of Newark New Jersey, 240 So.2d 780 (La.App.1970), with Robertson v. Travis, 393 So.2d 304 (La.App.1980).

3. The question is normally one for the jury; but if the conclusion is that the child has behaved unreasonably in view of the child's estimated capacity, the judge may direct a verdict against the child.

4. A few courts use arbitrary age limits. See Price v. Kitsap Transit, 125 Wash.2d 456, 886 P.2d 556 (1994) (declining to abandon conclusive presumption that children under six are incapable of negligence); Kuhns v. Brugger, 390 Pa. 331, 135 A.2d 395 (1957). For example, a child under the age of seven may be, as a

matter of law, incapable of any negligence; one between seven and 14 may be presumed incapable, but may be proved capable; one over 14 maybe presumed capable, but may be proved incapable. These arbitrary rules have been taken over from the common law rules as to the capacity of children to commit crime. They were originally derived from the civil law which goes back to the Bible, with its emphasis upon multiples of the mystic number seven. Even the courts that refuse to hold that a child under seven is not capable of negligence will still hold that extremely young children are without the capacity. See, for example, Mastland, Inc. v. Evans Furniture, Inc., 498 N.W.2d 682 (Iowa 1993) (child under three who started fire playing with cigarette lighter in his crib was not capable of negligence as a matter of law even though Iowa had rejected the per se rules on the capacity of children for negligence).

5.   The maximum age to which the special rule as to children has been applied appears to be seventeen, in Charbonneau v. MacRury, 84 N.H. 501, 153 A. 457 (1931). In Atlanta Gas Light Co. v. Brown, 94 Ga.App. 351, 94 S.E.2d 612 (1956), it was "presumed" that a 20–year–old was as capable as an adult.

6.   As reflected in the decision in the principal case, the Restatement (Second) of Torts has taken the position that the special rule should not be applied when the actor engages "in an activity which is normally undertaken only by adults, and for which adult qualifications are required." What activities fit within this rule? Thus far it has been deemed applicable when a child was driving an automobile, Nielsen v. Brown, 232 Or. 426, 374 P.2d 896 (1962); a motorboat, Dellwo v. Pearson, 259 Minn. 452, 107 N.W.2d 859 (1961); a motorcycle, Harrelson v. Whitehead, 236 Ark. 325, 365 S.W.2d 868 (1963) and Daniels v. Evans, 107 N.H. 407, 224 A.2d 63 (1966); a motor scooter, Adams v. Lopez, 75 N.M. 503, 407 P.2d 50 (1965); and when a teen-ager was playing golf, Neumann v. Shlansky, 58 Misc.2d 128, 294 N.Y.S.2d 628 (1968), aff'd, 63 Misc.2d 587, 312 N.Y.S.2d 951 (1970) (Gullota, J., dissenting), aff'd, 36 A.D.2d 540, 318 N.Y.S.2d 925 (1971). The rule was not applied to plaintiffs who were bicycle riding, Williams v. Gilbert, 239 Ark. 935, 395 S.W.2d 333 (1965) and Bixenman v. Hall, 251 Ind. 527, 242 N.E.2d 837 (1968); deer hunting, Purtle v. Shelton, 251 Ark. 519, 474 S.W.2d 123 (1971); building a fire outdoors, Farm Bureau Ins. Group v. Phillips, 116 Mich.App. 544, 323 N.W.2d 477 (1982); or downhill skiing, Goss v. Allen, 70 N.J. 442, 360 A.2d 388 (1976).

7.   The court in Dellwo v. Pearson, note 6, said in dictum that: "There may be a difference between the standard of care that is required of a child in protecting himself against hazards and the standard that may be applicable when his activities expose others to hazards." This distinction was rejected in Dunn v. Teti, 280 Pa.Super. 399, 421 A.2d 782 (1980), where the court held that a child's conduct should be judged by the same standard whether he is plaintiff or a defendant.

8.   See Shulman, The Standard of Care Required of Children, 33 Yale L.J. 617 (1927); Bohlen, Liability in Tort of Infants and Insane Persons, 23 Mich.L.Rev. 9 (1924); Gray, The Standard of Care for Children Revisited, 45 Mo.L.Rev. 597 (1980).

9.   There are some decisions in which a similar allowance has been made for the physical and mental deficiencies of old age, but all have involved plaintiffs and have tended to focus on particular infirmities rather than age itself. Tobia v. Cooper Hospital University Med. Ctr., 136 N.J. 335, 643 A.2d 1 (1994) (holding that infirmities, including those caused by age, should be taken into account in determining whether comparative negligence instruction is appropriate in case where eighty-five year-old patient fell while getting off a gurney in emergency room). LaCava v. New Orleans, 159 So.2d 362 (La.App.1964); Johnson v. St. Paul City R. Co., 67 Minn. 260, 69 N.W. 900 (1897); Kitsap County Transp. Co. v. Harvey, 15

F.2d 166 (9th Cir.1926). See Note, Negligence and the Elderly: A Proposal for a Relaxed Standard of Care, 17 J.Mar.L.Rev. 874 (1984).

Breunig v. American Family Ins. Co.

Supreme Court of Wisconsin, 1970.
45 Wis.2d 536, 173 N.W.2d 619.

[Action for personal injuries received by plaintiff when his truck was struck by an automobile driven on the wrong side of the highway by Mrs. Erma Veith. The action was brought against Mrs. Veith's automobile insurance company under Wisconsin procedure which permits direct action against a liability insurer. The jury returned a verdict for plaintiff, and defendant appealed.]

HALLOWS, CHIEF JUSTICE. There is no question that Erma Veith was subject at the time of the accident to an insane delusion which directly affected her ability to operate her car in an ordinarily prudent manner and caused the accident. * * *

The evidence established that Mrs. Veith, while returning home after taking her husband to work, saw a white light on the back of the car ahead of her. She followed this light for three or four blocks. Mrs. Veith could not remember anything else except landing in a field, lying on the side of the road, and people talking. She recalled awaking in the hospital.

The psychiatrist testified Mrs. Veith told him she was driving on a road when she believed that God was taking ahold of the steering wheel and was directing her car. She saw the truck coming and stepped on the gas in order to become air-borne because she knew she could fly because Batman does it. To her surprise she was not air-borne before striking the truck, but after the impact she was flying. * * * The psychiatrist testified Erma Veith was suffering from "schizophrenic reaction, paranoid type, acute." He stated that from the time Mrs. Veith commenced following the car with the white light and ending with the stopping of her vehicle in the cornfield, she was not able to operate the vehicle with her conscious mind, and that she had no knowledge or forewarning that such illness or disability would likely occur. * * *

The case was tried on the theory that some forms of insanity are a defense to and preclude liability for negligence. [C] Not all types of insanity vitiate responsibility for a negligent tort. The question of liability in every case must depend upon the kind and nature of the insanity. The effect of the mental illness or mental hallucination must be such as to affect the person's ability to understand and appreciate the duty which rests upon him to drive his car with ordinary care, or if the insanity does not affect such understanding and appreciation, it must affect his ability to control his car in an ordinarily prudent manner. And in addition, there must be an absence of notice or forewarning to the person that he may be suddenly subject to such a type of insanity or mental illness. * * *

Public policy reasons for not considering insanity [handwritten margin note]

The policy basis of holding a permanently insane person liable for his tort is: (1) Where one of two innocent persons must suffer a loss it should be borne by the one who occasioned it; (2) to induce those interested in the estate of the insane person (if he has one) to restrain and control him; and (3) the fear an insanity defense would lead to false claims of insanity to avoid liability. * * *

The cases holding an insane person liable for his torts have generally dealt with pre-existing insanity of a permanent nature and the question here presented was neither discussed nor decided. The plaintiff cites Sforza v. Green Bus Lines (1934) 150 Misc. 180, 268 N.Y.S. 446; Shapiro v. Tchernowitz (1956) 3 Misc.2d 617, 155 N.Y.S.2d 1011; Johnson v. Lambotte (1961) 147 Colo. 203, 363 P.2d 165, for holding insanity is not a defense in negligence cases. *Sforza* and *Shapiro* are New York trial court decisions which do not discuss the question here presented and are unconvincing. In *Johnson,* the defendant was under observation by order of the county court and was being treated in a hospital for "chronic schizophrenic state of paranoid type." On the day in question, she wanted to leave the hospital and escaped therefrom and found an automobile standing on a street with its motor running a few blocks from the hospital. She got into the car and drove off, having little or no control of the car. She soon collided with the plaintiff. Later she was adjudged mentally incompetent and committed to a state hospital. *Johnson* is not a case of sudden mental seizure with no forewarning. The defendant knew she was being treated for mental disorder and hence would not come under the nonliability rule herein stated.

Rule of Law [handwritten margin note]

We think the statement that insanity is no defense is too broad when it is applied to a negligence case where the driver is suddenly overcome without forewarning by a mental disability or disorder which incapacitates him from conforming his conduct to the standards of a reasonable man under like circumstances. These are rare cases indeed, but their rarity is no reason for overlooking their existence and the justification which is the basis of the whole doctrine of liability for negligence, i.e., that it is unjust to hold a man responsible for his conduct which he is incapable of avoiding and which incapability was unknown to him prior to the accident.

We need not reach the question of contributory negligence of an insane person or the question of comparative negligence as those problems are not now presented. All we hold is that a sudden mental incapacity equivalent in its effect to such physical causes as a sudden heart attack, epileptic seizure, stroke, or fainting should be treated alike and not under the general rule of insanity.

An interesting case holding this view in Canada is Buckley & Toronto Transp. Comm'n v. Smith Transport, Ltd. [1946] Ont.Rep. 798, 4 Dom. L.Rep. 721, which is almost identical on the facts with the case at bar. There, the court found no negligence when a truck driver was overcome by a sudden insane delusion that his truck was being operated by remote control of his employer and as a result he was in fact helpless to avert a collision.

Holding

[The court then considered whether Mrs. Veith had any warning or knowledge that would reasonably lead her to believe that hallucinations would occur and be such as to affect her driving an automobile. It concluded that, notwithstanding the testimony of the psychiatrist that in his opinion she did not, there was sufficient evidence of her past conduct to permit the jury to conclude that she believed she had a special relationship to God and was the chosen one to survive at the end of the world, and that she could believe that God would take over the direction of her life to the extent of driving her car. The question was held therefore to be properly left to the jury. Various other questions were also considered.]

Judgment affirmed. *left to the jury*

NOTES AND QUESTIONS

1. Most courts do not make any allowance for the mental illness of the defendant—the defendant is judged by the standard of the reasonable person. See, for example, Johnson v. Lambotte, 147 Colo. 203, 363 P.2d 165 (1961); Cross v. Kent, 32 Md. 581 (1870); Williams v. Hays, 143 N.Y. 442, 38 N.E. 449 (1894); Ellis v. Fixico, 174 Okl. 116, 50 P.2d 162 (1935). This been true even in the case of "sudden insanity." See Kuhn v. Zabotsky, 9 Ohio St.2d 129, 224 N.E.2d 137 (1967).

2. Is this policy in accord with current understanding of mental illness? Does an "insane" defendant actually "know" about his condition and have the ability to make a rational decision not to drive? Cf. C.T.W. v. B.C.G., 809 S.W.2d 788 (Tex.App.1991) (pedophile negligent for failing to seek professional help and to avoid situations where he would be alone with children). Should an exception be made for someone who is in treatment? See Shuman, Therapeutic Jurisprudence and Tort Law: A Limited Subjective Standard of Care, 46 SMU L.Rev. 409 (1992) (suggesting adoption of limited subjective standard of care for the mentally ill defendant who initiated treatment prior to allegedly negligent conduct). Should an exception be made for someone who is institutionalized and has injured a paid caretaker? See note 4, page 27, re jurisdictions that have carved out a narrow exception for institutionalized mentally disabled patients unable to control or appreciate the consequences of their conduct, which results in injury to a paid caretaker. *like Durrenmatt*

3. Who was the actual "defendant" in the principal case? What bearing does that have on the problem? *insurance company* *Erma actually*

4. What if the defendant is suffering from Alzheimer's Disease? Should that be treated as a mental illness (no exception made, defendant held to the reasonable person standard) or a physical condition (defendant held to standard of reasonable person with Alzheimer's)? See Gould v. American Family Mutual Ins. Co., 198 Wis.2d 450, 543 N.W.2d 282 (1996). What if someone's mental capacity is so limited that he is more like a child than an adult? Compare Restatement (Second) § 283(B) (no allowance is made for "lack of intelligence") with Lynch v. Rosenthal, 396 S.W.2d 272 (Mo.App.1965) (expert testimony that farm hand's IQ of 65 meant that his mental ability was less than that of a 10–year-old child considered in evaluating contributory negligence).

5. Why treat the diminished capacity of mentally disabled adults differently from the diminished capacity of children? At least one court has departed from the traditional view and found that mental capacity, whether in a child or adult, should

be taken into account in determining what duty they owe. Creasy v. Rusk, 696 N.E.2d 442 (Ind.App.1998).

6.   There are a few cases on the contributory negligence of insane plaintiffs. They appear to allow more flexibility in evaluating the insane person's conduct and to excuse the conduct if the insanity prevented the plaintiff from understanding the danger and taking action. Emory Univ. v. Lee, 97 Ga.App. 680, 104 S.E.2d 234 (1958); De Martini v. Alexander Sanitarium, 192 Cal.App.2d 442, 13 Cal.Rptr. 564 (1961); Johnson v. Texas & Pac. R. Co., 16 La.App. 464, 135 So. 114 (1931). Stacy v. Jedco Const. Co., 119 N.C.App. 115, 120, 457 S.E.2d 875, 879 (1995) ("one whose mental faculties are diminished, not amounting to total insanity, is capable of contributory negligence, but is not held to the objective reasonable person standard. Rather, such a person should be held only to the exercise of such care as he was capable of exercising, i.e., the standard of care of a person of like mental capacity under similar circumstances.").

7.   In most of the cases we have read on the standard for negligence, the courts are considering the conduct of the defendant; some are considering the conduct of the plaintiff in order to determine whether the plaintiff's own negligence contributed to the cause of the accident. The effect of such a finding will be explored in more detail in Chapter 12, Defenses. The courts have consistently stated that the determination whether the reasonable person standard was met is the same, whether the actor is a defendant or a plaintiff, despite some argument that it should be different. See James and Dickinson, "Accident Proneness and Accident Law," 63 HARV. L. REV. 769, 782–791 (1950).

8.   See Alexander and Szasz, Mental Illness as an Excuse for Civil Wrongs, 43 Notre Dame Law. 24 (1967); Bohlen, Liability in Tort of Infants and Insane Persons, 23 Mich.L.Rev. 9 (1924); Green, Public Policy Underlying the Law of Mental Incompetency, 38 Mich.L.Rev. 1189 (1940).

(B)   THE PROFESSIONAL

➤ Heath v. Swift Wings, Inc.

Court of Appeals of North Carolina, 1979.
40 N.C.App. 158, 252 S.E.2d 526.

On 3 August 1975 a Piper 180 Arrow airplane crashed immediately after takeoff from the Boone–Blowing Rock Airport. * * * [On board the plane were the pilot, Fred Heath, his wife, their son, and a family friend, Vince Smathers. All were killed in the crash. This action alleges that the negligence of the pilot Fred Heath caused the crash. It was brought by the estates of the wife and son against the estate of the pilot (their husband and father) and Swift Wings, the owner of the airplane.]

Plaintiff's evidence, except to the extent it is quoted from the record, is briefly summarized as follows: Mary Payne Smathers Curry, widow of Vance Smathers, observed the takeoff of the Piper aircraft shortly after 5:00 o'clock on 3 August 1975. She observed Fred Heath load and reload the passengers and luggage, apparently in an effort to improve the balance of the aircraft. He also "walked around [the airplane] and looked at everything * * *. She remembers seeing him and thinking that he's doublechecking it to be sure no one has slashed the tires." The airplane engine started promptly and the plane was taxied to the end of the runway where it paused for approximately five minutes before takeoff. The airplane came very close to the end of the runway before takeoff. However "[t]he engine sounded good the entire time, and she did not recall hearing the engine miss or pop or backfire." After takeoff, the airplane "gained altitude but it didn't go up very high" and then "leveled off pretty low". * * *

William B. Gough, Jr., a free-lance mechanical engineering consultant and pilot, testified concerning the operation and flight performance of the Piper 180 Arrow. He testified concerning the many factors affecting the takeoff capabilities of the Piper and the calculations to be made by the pilot before takeoff, utilizing flight performance charts. He testified that in his opinion, according to his calculations, the pilot should have used flaps to aid in the takeoff. Furthermore, he stated that in his opinion the reasonably prudent pilot should have made a controlled landing in the cornfield shortly after takeoff if he were experiencing difficulty attaining flight speed, and that if he had done so [he, his wife and son, and Smathers] would have survived. * * *

After the customary motions at the conclusion of all the evidence, the case was submitted to the jury upon voluminous instructions by the trial court. The jury returned a verdict answering the following issue as indicated: "1. Was Fred Heath, Jr., negligent in the operation of PA–28R 'Arrow' airplane on August 3, 1975 as alleged in the complaint?" Answer: "No". Plaintiff appeals assigning error to the exclusion of certain evidence and to the charge to the jury. * * *

MORRIS, CHIEF JUDGE. * * * Assignment of error No. 4 is directed to the trial court's charge concerning the definition of negligence and the applicable standard of care:

"Negligence, ladies and gentlemen of the jury, is the failure of someone to act as a reasonably and careful and prudent person would under the same or similar circumstances. Obviously, this could be the doing of something or the failure to do something, depending on the circumstances. With respect to aviation negligence could be more specifically defined as the failure to exercise that degree of ordinary care and caution, which an ordinary prudent pilot having the same training and experience as Fred Heath, would have used in the same or similar circumstances."

It is a familiar rule of law that the standard of care required of an individual, unless altered by statute, is the conduct of the reasonably prudent man under the same or similar circumstances. [Cc] While the standard of care of the reasonably prudent man remains constant, the quantity or degree of care required varies significantly with the attendant circumstances. [Cc]

The trial court improperly introduced a subjective standard of care into the definition of negligence by referring to the "ordinary care and caution, which an ordinary prudent pilot *having the same training and experience as Fred Heath,* would have used in the same or similar circumstances." (Emphasis added.) We are aware of the authorities which support the application of a greater standard of care than that of the ordinary prudent man for persons shown to possess special skill in a particular endeavor. See generally Prosser, Law of Torts (4th ed.) § 32. Indeed, our courts have long recognized that one who engages in a business, occupation, or profession must exercise the requisite degree of learning, skill, and ability of that calling with reasonable and ordinary care. See e.g., Insurance Co. v. Sprinkler Co., 266 N.C. 134, 146 S.E.2d 53 (1966) (fire sprinkler contractor); Service Co. v. Sales Co., 261 N.C. 660, 136 S.E.2d 56 (1964) (industrial designer); Hunt v. Bradshaw, 242 N.C. 517, 88 S.E.2d 762 (1955) (physician); Hodges v. Carter, 239 N.C. 517, 80 S.E.2d 144 (1954) (attorney). Furthermore, the specialist within a profession may be held to a standard of care greater than that required of the general practitioner. [C] Nevertheless, the professional standard remains an objective standard. For example, the recognized standard for a physician is established as "the standard of professional competence and care customary in similar communities among physicians engaged in his field of practice." Dickens v. Everhart, 284 N.C. at 101, 199 S.E.2d at 443.

Such objective standards avoid the evil of imposing a different standard of care upon each individual. The instructions in this case concerning the pilot's standard of care are misleading at best, and a misapplication of the law. They permit the jury to consider Fred Heath's own particular experience and training, whether outstanding or inferior, in determining the requisite standard of conduct, rather than applying a minimum standard generally applicable to all pilots. The plaintiff is entitled to an instruction holding Fred Heath to the objective minimum standard of care applicable to all pilots. * * *

This matter was well tried by both counsel for plaintiff and counsel for defendants, and several days were consumed in its trial. Nevertheless, for prejudicial errors in the charge, there must be a

New trial.

HARRY C. MARTIN and CARLTON, JJ., concur.

NOTES AND QUESTIONS

1.   A growing proportion of negligence litigation involves persons rendering services. The basic principles involved are relatively uncomplicated: the reasonable prudent person takes on the profession of the actor and an objective standard is applied. See The Germanic, 196 U.S. 589 (1905) (shipmaster—"external standard" applied by Justice Holmes).

2.   The standard is expressed in objective form—the knowledge, training and skill (or ability and competence) of an ordinary member of the profession in good standing. See, e.g., Centman v. Cobb, 581 N.E.2d 1286 (Ind.App.1991) (defendant who had just graduated from medical school and was doing an internship at hospital held to same standard of care as a physician). "Average" member is incorrect instruction because this would literally mean that half of the members could not meet the standard. See, e.g., Nowatske v. Osterloh, 198 Wis.2d 419, 543 N.W.2d 265 (1996) (finding that "average" should be eliminated from pattern jury instruction).

Cf. Gridley v. Johnson, 476 S.W.2d 475 (Mo.1972) (phrase "in good standing" held to be too vague).

3. The "professional" usually (contracts) to render services, but the suit is usually in tort for damage caused by negligence. There is no need to contract specifically to exercise the normal skill of the professional—the law imposes the duty. Ordinarily, the professional is liable only for negligence, because the service performed does not have a guaranteed result. The service provider may choose to provide a guarantee, which would be enforceable through contract law. Absent such an express contract for a particular result, the cause of action is in tort. See, e.g., Sciacca v. Polizzi, 403 So.2d 728 (La.1981) (cause of action for injuries caused by IUD sounded in tort rather than contract despite plaintiff's explicit wording in complaint because no specific guarantees were made by physician); Sullivan v. O'Connor, 363 Mass. 579, 296 N.E.2d 183 (1973) (plastic surgeon promised plaintiff Heddy Lamar's nose); Haase v. Starnes, 323 Ark. 263, 915 S.W.2d 675 (1996) (ads promised a full, growing head of hair for life).

You can warrant a product and you can warrant your services

4. *Expert Testimony*. When the professional is engaged in work that is technical in nature—not a matter of "common knowledge"—a lay jury is not in a position to understand without explanation the nature of the work or the application of the standard of care to this work. For practical reasons, a plaintiff must offer expert evidence on these matters or the judge may well decide that the jury does not have sufficient evidence on which to make a determination as to negligence and will direct a verdict for the defendant. As a general rule this is the extent of the requirement of expert testimony. See Aetna Ins. Co. v. Hellmuth, Obata & Kassabaum, Inc., 392 F.2d 472 (8th Cir.1968). But for one profession—medicine—the courts usually have laid down a "rule of law" that expert testimony is required.

—because lay jury will not understand

5. Professional negligence is now commonly called malpractice. On the subject in general, see D. Partlett, Professional Negligence (1985); Restatement (Second) of Torts § 299A.

6. Representative treatments of negligence for the major professions include the following:

Attorneys. Mallen & Smith, Legal Malpractice (3rd ed. 1989); Wade, The Attorney's Liability for Negligence, 12 Vand.L.Rev. 735 (1959).

Doctors and Veterinarians. Danzon, Medical Malpractice: Theory, Evidence, and Public Policy (1985); Weiler, Medical Malpractice on Trial (1991). For a discussion of psychiatric malpractice, see Nurcombe & Partlett, Child Mental Health & the Law (1994), Chapter 8. See also Price v. Brown, 545 Pa. 216, 680 A.2d 1149 (1996) (distinguishing veterinary malpractice from bailment in case involving death of pet).

The American Law of Medical Malpractice Harvey Waxman

Architects and Engineers. Bell, Professional Negligence of Architects and Engineers, 12 Vand.L.Rev. 711 (1959); Seybold, Liability of Architects or Engineers to Their Clients, in Defense Research Institute, Liability of Architects and Engineers 3 (1969); Peck & Hock, Liability of Engineers for Structural Design Errors: State of the Art Considerations in Defining the Standard of Care, 30 Villanova L.Rev. 403 (1985).

Designer of group health insurance plan; professional malpractice. Coyne & Delany Co. v. Selman, 98 F.3d 1457 (4th Cir.1996) (applying Virginia law).

Teachers. Some commentators and parties have argued for a new form of potential malpractice has arisen called "educational malpractice." See, for example, Elson, Common Law Remedies for the Educational Harms Caused by Incomplete or Careless Teaching, 33 Notre Dame Law. 306 (1977); Foster, Educational Malpractice: A Tort for The Untaught?, 19 U.B.C.L.Rev. 161 (1985); Donohue v. Copiague Union Free School Dist., 47 N.Y.2d 440, 391 N.E.2d 1352, 418 N.Y.S.2d 375 (1979). The courts generally have rejected the arguments, however, partly because of difficulties in determining why the student failed to learn, partly because it would be difficult to choose among various educational theories to set the standard, and partly because of problems in financing an award. Brantley v. District of Columbia, 640 A.2d 181, 183 (D.C.App.1994)("There is thus overwhelming judicial authority for the proposition that public school authorities' failure to educate students, or to assign them to the correct school or program, does not give rise to a suit for money damages.") For well written opinions discussing the policy issues involved, see Ross v. Creighton University, 957 F.2d 410 (7th Cir.1992) and Tolman v. CenCor Career Colleges, Inc., 851 P.2d 203 (Colo.App.1992). See also Wade, An Overview of Professional Negligence, 17 Mem.St.L.Rev. 465 (1987).

Accountants. Defense Research Institute, Professional Liability; Liability of Accountants (1972); Brodsky and Swanson, The Expanded Liability of Accountants for Negligence, 12 Sec.Reg.L.J. 252 (1984). See also pages 1032–1045.

Clergy. Within the last decade, several plaintiffs have attempted to persuade their jurisdictions to recognize a separate tort for clergy malpractice, although none of them has yet succeeded. See, for example, Nally v. Grace Com. Church of the Valley, 47 Cal. 3d 278, 763 P.2d 948, 253 Cal. Rptr. 97 (1988), cert. denied 490 U.S. 1007 (1989); Destefano v. Grabrian, 763 P.2d 275 (Colo.1988); Byrd v. Faber, 57 Ohio St.3d 56, 565 N.E.2d 584 (1991); Schieffer v. Catholic Archdiocese, 244 Neb. 715, 508 N.W.2d 907 (1993); Bladen v. First Presbyterian Church, 857 P.2d 789 (Okla.1993); Cherepski v. Walker, 323 Ark. 43, 913 S.W.2d 761 (1996); F.G. v. MacDonnell, 150 N.J. 550, 696 A.2d 697 (1997). Most of the cases involve allegations that the cleric engaged in consensual sexual relations with the parishioner, with some of the complaints also alleging that the parishioner was receiving marital counseling from the cleric. Others allege that the consent was obtained through intimidation or fraud. The courts appear reluctant to recognize a new cause of action where the alleged acts already give rise to an existing cause of action (counseling malpractice or battery) or where such a recognition would entangle the court in defining reasonable conduct within the context of religious tenets.

7. The standard is appropriately modified for specialists in a particular profession holding themselves out to have higher skills. Aves v. Shah, 997 F.2d 762 (10th Cir.1993) (physician who held herself out as a specialist in obstetrics could not object to jury instruction that held her to the higher standard of care of a specialist); Duffey Law Office v. Tank Transport, Inc., 194 Wis.2d 674, 535 N.W.2d 91 (App. 1995) (attorney who held himself out as specialist in labor law held to higher standard).

8. The standard is not modified for professionals providing their services *pro bono.* See Becker v. Janiski, 15 N.Y.S. 675, 677 (1891) ("Whether the patient be a pauper or a millionaire, whether he be treated gratuitously or for reward, the physician owes him precisely the same measure of duty, and the same degree of skill and care.")

[handwritten: lawyer malpractice suit]

► Hodges v. Carter

Supreme Court of North Carolina, 1954.
239 N.C. 517, 80 S.E.2d 144.

Civil action to recover compensation for losses resulting from the alleged negligence of defendant D.D. Topping and H.C. Carter, now deceased, in prosecuting, on behalf of plaintiff, certain actions on fire insurance policies.

On 4 June 1948 plaintiff's drug store building located in Bellhaven, N.C., together with his lunch counter, fixtures, stock of drugs and sundries therein contained, was destroyed by fire. At the time plaintiff was insured under four policies of fire insurance against loss of, or damage to, said mercantile building and its contents. He filed proof of loss with each of the four insurance companies which issued said policies. The insurance companies severally rejected the proofs of loss, denied liability, and declined to pay any part of the plaintiff's losses resulting from said fire.

H.C. Carter and D.D. Topping were at the time attorneys practicing in Beaufort and adjoining counties. As they were the ones from whom plaintiff seeks to recover, they will hereafter be referred to as the defendants. * * *

On 3 May 1949 defendants, in behalf of plaintiff, instituted in the Superior Court of Beaufort County four separate actions—one against each of the four insurers. Complaints were filed and summonses were issued, directed to the sheriff of Beaufort County. In each case the summons and complaint, together with copies thereof, were mailed to the Commissioner of Insurance of the State of North Carolina. The Commissioner accepted service of summons and complaint in each case and forwarded a copy thereof by registered mail to the insurance company named defendant therein.

Thereafter each defendant [insurance company] made a special appearance and moved to dismiss the action against it for want of proper service of process for that the Insurance Commissioner was without authority, statutory or otherwise, to accept service of process issued against a foreign insurance company doing business in this State. The statute provided that the Insurance Commissioner could *be served*. At that time, service meant personal delivery; there was no statutory authorization for service by mail. The attorneys followed a local custom of mailing the summons instead of having it served personally on the Insurance Commissioner. The insurance companies argued that the Insurance Commissioner did not have the authority to accept service by mail.] When the special appearance and motion to dismiss came on for hearing at the February Term 1950, the judge presiding concluded that the acceptance of service of process by the Insurance Commissioner was valid and served to subject the movants to the jurisdiction of the court. Judgment was entered in each case denying the motion therein made. Each defendant excepted and appealed. This Court reversed. Hodges v. New Hampshire Fire Insurance Co., 232 N.C. 475, 61 S.E.2d 372. See also Hodges v. Home Insurance Co., 233 N.C. 289, 63 S.E.2d 819.

On 4 March 1952 plaintiff instituted this action in which he alleges that the defendants were negligent in prosecuting his said actions in that they failed to (1) have process properly served, and (2) sue out alias summonses at the time the insurers filed their motions to dismiss the actions for want of proper service of summons, although they then had approximately sixty days within which to procure the issuance thereof.

Defendants, answering, deny negligence and plead good faith and the exercise of their best judgment.

At the hearing in the court below the judge, at the conclusion of plaintiff's evidence in chief, entered judgment of involuntary nonsuit. Plaintiff excepted and appealed.

BARNHILL, CHIEF JUSTICE. * * * Ordinarily when an attorney engages in the practice of the law and contracts to prosecute an action in behalf of his client, he impliedly represents that (1) he possesses the requisite degree of learning, skill, and ability necessary to the practice of his profession and which others similarly situated ordinarily possess; (2) he will exert his best judgment in the prosecution of the litigation entrusted to him; and (3) he will exercise reasonable and ordinary care and diligence in the use of his skill and in the application of his knowledge to his client's cause. [Cc]

An attorney who acts in good faith and in an honest belief that his advice and acts are well founded and in the best interest of his client is not answerable for a mere error of judgment or for a mistake in a point of law which has not been settled by the court of last resort in his State and on which reasonable doubt may be entertained by well-informed lawyers. [Cc]

Conversely, he is answerable in damages for any loss to his client which proximately results from a want of that degree of knowledge and skill ordinarily possessed by others of his profession similarly situated, or from the omission to use reasonable care and diligence, or from the failure to exercise in good faith his best judgment in attending to the litigation committed to his care. [Cc]

When the facts appearing in this record are considered in the light of these controlling principles of law, it immediately becomes manifest that plaintiff has failed to produce a scintilla of evidence tending to show that defendants breached any duty the law imposed upon them when they accepted employment to prosecute plaintiff's actions against his insurers or that they did not possess the requisite learning and skill required of an attorney or that they acted otherwise than in the utmost good faith.

The Commissioner of Insurance is the statutory process agent of foreign insurance companies doing business in this State, G.S. § 58–153, Hodges v. New Hampshire Insurance Co., 232 N.C. 475, 61 S.E.2d 372, and when defendants mailed the process to the Commissioner of Insurance for his acceptance of service thereof, they were following a custom which had prevailed in this State for two decades or more. [The custom was to mail the summons to the Insurance Commissioner rather than have it personally served.] Foreign insurance companies had theretofore uniformly ratified such service, appeared in response thereto, filed their answers, and made their defense. The right of the Commissioner to accept service of process [by mail] in behalf of foreign insurance companies doing business in this State had not been tested in the courts. Attorneys generally, throughout the State, took it for granted that under the terms of G.S. § 58–153 such acceptance of service was adequate. And, in addition, the defendants had obtained the judicial declaration of a judge of our Superior Courts that the acceptance of service by the Commissioner subjected the defendants to the jurisdiction of the court. Why then stop in the midst of the stream and pursue some other course?

Doubtless this litigation was inspired by a comment which appears in our opinion on the second appeal, Hodges v. Home Insurance Co., 233 N.C. 289, 63 S.E.2d 819. However, what was there said was pure dictum, injected—perhaps ill advisedly—in explanation of the reason we could afford plaintiff no relief on that appeal. We did not hold, or intend to intimate, that defendants had been in any wise neglectful of their duties as counsel for plaintiff.

The judgment entered in the court below is

Affirmed.

NOTES AND QUESTIONS

1. The dictum in the Hodges v. Home Ins. Co. case, referred to in the last major paragraph of the principal case, reads as follows: "At the time defendant entered its motion to dismiss the original action, the plaintiff still had more than sixty days in which to sue out an alias summons and thus keep his action alive. He elected instead to rest his case upon the validity of the service had. The unfortunate result is unavoidable." The statute of limitations had run and no new suit could be brought. As a result the loss fell on the insured. Is this where it should fall?

2. Note that the principal case lists three areas in which an attorney's conduct may be questioned. *Possession of knowledge or skill.* Defendant attorney, representing a wife in a divorce proceeding, failed to claim for his client her interests under the California community property law in her husband's retirement benefits. He mistakenly believed that they were not subject to the claim. The trouble was that he failed to research the topic and would have found the law relatively clear that the retirement rights were community property. The court upheld a judgment for $100,000. Smith v. Lewis, 13 Cal.3d 349, 530 P.2d 589, 118 Cal.Rptr. 621 (1975). Professionals are not expected to know everything, just what the ordinary member of the profession does. See, Lucas v. Hamm, 56 Cal.2d 583, 364 P.2d 685, 15 Cal.Rptr. 821 (1961), where a will had trust provisions that violated the rule against perpetuities and the rule on restraint on alienation. Of these topics, it was said that "few, if any, areas of the law have been more fraught with more confusion or concealed traps for the unwary draftsman," and the court held the attorney not liable.

3. *Exercise of Best Judgment.* While most treatments of the standard of care for professionals have been confined to the element of knowledge and skill, there are, as the opinion in this case indicates, two other significant elements. The first is the exercise of a discerning judgment in the exercise of a reasonable discretion. It is usually expressed by saying that a doctor or lawyer is not liable for a "mere error of judgment." Crosby v. Jones, 705 So.2d 1356 (Fla.1998)(good faith tactical decisions or decisions made on debatable point of law are not actionable so long as attorney exercises best judgment). She is, however, required to exercise her own best judgment. For lawyers, it may include the recommendation to settle. Thomas v. Bethea, 351 Md. 513, 718 A.2d 1187 (1998). The same language is used for doctors, particularly in the use of discretion in making a diagnosis. See Blankenship v. Baptist Memorial Hosp., 26 Tenn.App. 131, 168 S.W.2d 491 (1942).

4. *Use of Due Care*. The other element involves the professional's use of due care in the application of the professional's skill and knowledge. This element describes steps that are mechanical rather than discretionary and hence because such steps implicate no professional judgment, courts are more willing to find liability. A prime illustration of this type of negligence for lawyers is failure to file a suit before the running of the statute of limitations. Lally v. Kuster, 177 Cal. 783, 171 P. 961 (1918); Watkins v. Sheppard, 278 So.2d 890 (La.App.1973). For doctors it would be failure to obtain the requisite data on which to exercise trained discretion to develop a diagnosis. Butts v. Watts, 290 S.W.2d 777 (Ky.1956); Merchants Nat'l Bank & Trust Co. v. United States, 272 F.Supp. 409 (D.N.D.1967).

5. While engaged in litigation, an attorney may run into problems involving all three aspects of the standard care. See the treatment in the important case of Woodruff v. Tomlin, 616 F.2d 924 (6th Cir.1980), alleging negligence in the conduct of personal injury litigation arising out of an automobile accident.

6. Just as the patient-plaintiff in a medical malpractice case must show that the patient would have recovered, in attorney negligence cases the plaintiff-client must show that but for the attorney's negligence the client would have been successful in prosecuting or defending the claim. See Togstad v. Vesely, Otto, Miller & Keefe, 291 N.W.2d 686 (Minn.1980). On this causation issue, do you think it would be more difficult for a plaintiff-client to bring a successful attorney-negligence case where the claim is that the attorney inadequately prepared for trial or where the claim is that the attorney missed the statute of limitations?

7. An attorney appointed to represent an indigent defendant in a criminal trial is not entitled to any degree of immunity from suit for malpractice brought by that defendant. Ferri v. Ackerman, 444 U.S. 193 (1979).

Boyce v. Brown

Supreme Court of Arizona, 1938.
51 Ariz. 416, 77 P.2d 455.

LOCKWOOD, JUDGE. Berlie B. Boyce and Nannie E. Boyce, his wife, hereinafter called plaintiffs, brought suit against Edgar H. Brown, hereinafter called defendant, to recover damages for alleged malpractice by the defendant upon the person of Nannie E. Boyce. The case was tried to a jury and, at the close of the evidence for plaintiffs, the court granted a motion for an instructed verdict in favor of the defendant, on the ground that there was no competent testimony that he was guilty of any acts of commission or omission sufficient, as a matter of law to charge him with malpractice. Judgment was rendered on the verdict, and, after the usual motion for new trial was overruled, this appeal was taken. * * *

The sole question for our consideration, therefore, is whether, taking the evidence as strongly as is reasonably possible in support of plaintiffs' theory of the case, as we must do when the court instructs a verdict in favor of defendant, there was sufficient evidence to sustain a judgment in favor of plaintiffs. * * *

About September 1, 1927, plaintiffs engaged the services of defendant, who for many years had been a practicing physician and surgeon in Phoenix, to reduce a fracture of Mrs. Boyce's ankle. This was done by means of an operation which consisted, in substance, of making an incision at the point of fracture, bringing the broken fragments of bone into apposition, and permanently fixing them in place by means of a metal screw placed in the bone. Defendant continued to attend Mrs. Boyce for three or four weeks following such operation until a complete union of the bone had been established, when his services terminated. There is no serious contention in the record that defendant did not follow the approved medical standard in the treatment of the fractured bone up to this time. No further professional relations existed between the parties until seven years later, in November, 1934, when Mrs. Boyce again consulted him, complaining that her ankle was giving her considerable pain. He examined the ankle, wrapped it with adhesive tape, and then filed the edge of an arch support, which he had made for her seven years before, and which, from use, had grown so thin that the edge was sharp. About a week later he removed the bandage. Her ankle, however, did not improve after this treatment, but continued to grow more painful until January, 1936, some two years later. At this last-mentioned time she returned to defendant, who again examined the ankle. A few days later she went to visit Dr. Kent of Mesa, who, on hearing the history of the case, and noticing some discoloration and swelling, caused an X-ray of the ankle to be made. This X-ray showed that there had been some necrosis of the bone around the screw. Dr. Kent operated upon Mrs. Boyce, removing the screw, and she made an uneventful recovery, the ankle becoming practically normal.

There are certain general rules of law governing actions of malpractice, which are almost universally accepted by the courts, and which are applicable to the present situation. We state them as follows: (1) One licensed to practice medicine is presumed to possess the degree of skill and learning which is possessed by the average member of the medical profession in good standing in the community in which he practices, and to apply that skill and learning, with ordinary and reasonable care, to cases which come to him for treatment. If he does not possess the requisite skill and learning, or if he does not apply it, he is guilty of malpractice. [C] (2) Before a physician or surgeon can be held liable as for malpractice, he must have done something in his treatment of his patient which the recognized standard of good medical practice in the community in which he is practicing forbids in such cases, or he must have neglected to do something which such standard requires. [C] (3) In order to sustain a verdict for the plaintiffs in an action for malpractice, the standard of medical practice in the community must be shown by affirmative evidence, and, unless there is evidence of such a standard, a jury may not be permitted to speculate as to what the required standard is, or whether the defendant has departed therefrom. [Cc] (4) Negligence on the part of a physician or surgeon in the treatment of a case is never presumed, but must be affirmatively proven, and no presumption of negligence nor want of skill arises from the mere fact that a treatment was unsuccessful, failed to bring the best results, or that the patient died. [C] (5) The accepted rule is that negligence on the part of a physician or surgeon, by reason of his departure from the proper standard of practice, must be established by expert medical testimony, unless the negligence is so grossly apparent that a layman would have no difficulty in recognizing it. [Cc] (6) The testimony of other physicians that they would have followed a different course of treatment than that followed by the defendant is not sufficient to establish malpractice unless it also appears that the course of treatment followed deviated from one of the methods of treatment approved by the standard in that community. [C]

With these principles of the law governing the relation of physician and patient, and malpractice actions arising out of that relation as a guide, let us consider the record to see whether plaintiffs presented sufficient evidence to sustain a judgment in their favor. Two questions present themselves to us: (a) What was the treatment which defendant gave Mrs. Boyce in November, 1934? and (b) What was the medical standard which he was required to conform to, under all the circumstances, in giving her treatment at that time? The treatment given, according to her own testimony, consisted in an ordinary examination of the ankle, the smoothing of an arch support which she was then wearing, and the wrapping of the ankle with adhesive tape, with the suggestion that the tape be left on for a few days. About a week later Mrs. Boyce returned and the tape was taken off. The evidence does not show that she ever came back to defendant for further treatment in November, 1934, or, indeed, until January, 1936. The next question is whether the examination and treatment given by defendant departed from the established standard for cases like that of Mrs. Boyce. The only testimony we have which, in any manner, bears upon medical standards or the proper treatment of Mrs. Boyce in November, 1934, is that of Dr. Kent, who performed the operation on the ankle in January, 1936, and of defendant. The latter testified that he did what was required by Mrs. Boyce's condition as it existed then. Dr. Kent's testimony as to the condition he found in 1936, and what he did, is clear and distinct. He was asked as to how long prior to that time the screw should have been removed, and stated that he could not answer; that, if the ankle was in the same condition as it was when he operated, he would say that the screw should have been removed, but that it was impossible for him to testify as to when the condition justifying removal arose. He was questioned more fully and answered substantially that his first conclusion, if he had been in the position of defendant, when Mrs. Boyce called on the latter in November, 1934, would have been that arthritis in the ankle joint was causing the pain, but that he would not have been fully satisfied without having an X-ray made of the ankle. On cross-examination he testified that the method of uniting bone used by defendant was a standard one, and that the screw was not removed, as a rule, unless it made trouble. Nowhere, however, did Dr. Kent testify as to what was the proper standard of medical care required at the time defendant treated Mrs. Boyce in 1934, or as to whether, in his opinion, the treatment given deviated from that standard. The nearest he came to such testimony was the statement that he personally would have had an X-ray taken, but he did not say the failure to do so was a deviation from the proper standard of treatment.

Counsel for plaintiffs, in their oral argument, apparently realized the weakness of their evidence on the vital point of what the proper medical standard required in 1934, and based their claim of negligence almost entirely upon the failure of defendant to take an X-ray of Mrs. Boyce's ankle at that time. They urge that this comes within the exception to the general rule, in that a failure to do so is such obvious negligence that even a layman knows it to be a departure from the proper standard. We think this contention cannot be sustained. It is true that most laymen know that the X-ray usually offers the best method of diagnosing physical changes of the interior organs of the body, and particularly of the skeleton, short of an actual opening of the body for ocular examination, but laymen cannot say that in all cases where there is some trouble with the internal organs that it is a departure from standard medical practice to fail to take an X-ray. Such things are costly and do not always give a satisfactory diagnosis, or even as good a one as other types of examination may give. In many cases the taking of an X-ray might be of no value and put the patient to unnecessary expense, and, in view of the testimony in the present case as to the arthritis which Mrs. Boyce had, and which Dr. Kent testified would have been his first thought as to the cause of Mrs. Boyce's pain in 1934, we think it is going too far to say that the failure to take an X-ray of Mrs. Boyce's ankle at that time was so far a departure from ordinary medical standards that even laymen would know it to be gross negligence. Since, therefore, there was insufficient evidence in the record to show that defendant was guilty of malpractice, under the rules of law above set forth, the court properly instructed a verdict in favor of the defendant.

The judgment of the superior court is affirmed.

NOTES AND QUESTIONS

1. In the principal case, do you suppose that the defendant was not negligent or just not proved to be negligent? Did plaintiff lose because her attorney failed to ask the right questions of Dr. Kent or because Dr. Kent really did not believe that Dr. Brown violated the standard of care in failing to take the x-ray? Why didn't Mrs. Boyce's attorney choose a different expert witness?

2. *Customary Practice (Violation of).* It is not enough that an expert witness testify that he would not personally follow the defendant's practice; he must also testify that the practice was not recognized as valid.

3. Proof that a professional violated the standard of care usually must be established by expert testimony, unless the negligence is so obvious that it is within the common knowledge and experience of lay jurors. See, e.g., Welte v. Bello, 482 N.W.2d 437 (Iowa 1992) (during surgery on her nose, patient suffered third-degree burns on her arm caused by anesthesia that escaped from vein into surrounding tissue); Dickerson v. Fatehi, 253 Va. 324, 484 S.E.2d 880 (1997) (following surgery on her neck, patient had severe pain in her right arm and hand and 20 months later it was discovered that surgeon had failed to remove a hypodermic needle with a plastic attachment from the surgical site). See also res ipsa loquitur cases, pages 237-238.

4. *Customary Practice (Compliance with).* For the professions in general, evidence as to customary practice is admissible and may prove very influential. For the medical profession, it is usually found to be controlling and the jury are usually told that the plaintiff cannot recover unless the plaintiff proves that the defendant's

conduct was not in accord with recognized medical practice. There are very few cases where the plaintiff has been allowed to recover despite the fact that the defendant health care provider complied with the customary practice of the profession. See Helling v. Carey, 83 Wash.2d 514, 519 P.2d 981 (1974) (ophthalmologist held negligent as a matter of law for failing to routinely test patients under age 40 for glaucoma despite expert testimony from both sides that the standards of the profession did not require such testing of patients that age; decision based on balancing court's perception of seriousness of potential risk against cost of test). This decision has been criticized by the commentators and reversed by the legislature. See e.g., King, In Search of a Standard of Care for the Medical Profession: The "Accepted Practice" Formula, 28 Vand.L.Rev. 1213 (1975) and Keeton, Medical Negligence—The Standard of Care, 10 Tex.Tech.L.Rev. 351 (1979). For an interesting pair of cases with opposite results on this issue in the context of the obligation of a blood bank to do surrogate testing to screen for the AIDS virus before the AIDS antibody test was available, see Osborn v. Irwin Memorial Blood Bank, 5 Cal. App.4th 234, 7 Cal.Rptr.2d 101 (1992) ("professional prudence is defined by actual or accepted practice within a profession, rather than theories about what 'should' have been done"; j.n.o.v. for blood bank upheld) and United Blood Services v. Quintana, 827 P.2d 509 (Colo.1992) (applicable standard of care adopted by a profession, as established by expert testimony, is presumed to constitute due care for those practicing in that profession, but that presumption may be rebutted; plaintiffs entitled to new trial and opportunity to prove universal practice of blood banks was negligent).

Morrison v. MacNamara

District of Columbia Court of Appeals, 1979.
407 A.2d 555.

[Appellant Morrison reported to appellee medical laboratory in Washington, D.C., for a urethral smear test, which was physically invasive, for trichomonas, a urinary tract infection. The test was administered while Morrison was standing. Morrison had an adverse reaction to the test—he fainted and struck his head on a metal blood pressure stand and on the floor, causing permanent loss of his senses of smell and taste, among other injuries.

At trial, Morrison presented an expert witness from Michigan who testified that the test often causes the patient to feel faint and that the "national standard of care" requires that the patient sit or lie down during the test. The trial court refused to allow the testimony, holding that expert witnesses in medical malpractice cases must come from the same community as the defendant. Morrison appeals that ruling. Appellees presented expert witnesses from Washington area laboratories who testified that they always administered the test with the patient standing.]

NEWMAN, CHIEF JUDGE: * * * At the close of all the evidence, appellant submitted several jury instructions which were based on the national standard of care. Appellant maintained that in view of the national certification of the laboratory, the laboratory was under a duty to adhere to nationally accepted standards for administering the urethral smear test, and that the jury should be so instructed. Appellees argued that the laboratory owed only the duty to adhere to that standard of medical care recognized in the Washington, D.C. metropolitan area. The trial court agreed with appellees.

* * * In medical malpractice, a term referring to ordinary negligence concepts in the area of medical diagnosis, treatment, and the like, the duty of care is generally formulated as that degree of reasonable care and skill expected of members of the medical profession under the same or similar circumstances. * * *

The locality rule states that the conduct of members of the medical profession is to be measured solely by the standard of conduct expected of other members of the medical profession in the same locality or the same community. [Cc]

This doctrine is indigenous to American jurisprudence and appears to have developed in the late nineteenth century. [Cc] The rule was designed to protect doctors in rural areas who, because of inadequate training and experience, and the lack of effective means of transportation and communication, could not be expected to exhibit the skill and care of urban doctors. * * *

In addition, it was argued that in view of the ability of urban areas to attract the most talented doctors, a rule which would hold rural doctors to urban standards of care would precipitate the departure of doctors from rural areas and thereby leave rural communities without sufficient medical care. [Cc] In sum, the locality rule was premised on the notion that the disparity in education and access to advances in medical science between rural and urban doctors required that they be held to different standards of care.

The cases in this jurisdiction exhibit a lack of uniformity on the issue of the geographic area in which the conduct of members of the medical profession is to be measured. For example, a number of cases state that members of the medical profession are held to the skill and learning exercised by members of their profession in the District of Columbia. [Cc] In other cases, the standard is referred to as that degree of care exercised by other members of the medical profession in the District or a similar locality. [Cc] Finally, a number of cases have articulated the medical standard of care without referring to any geographic limitation whatsoever. [Cc] Since courts in this jurisdiction were never directly presented with this issue, the empirical validity of the assumptions behind the locality rule has not previously been examined.

Even a cursory analysis of the policy behind the locality doctrine reveals that whatever relevance it has to the practice of medicine in remote rural communities, it has no relevance to medical practice in the District of Columbia. Clearly the nation's capital is not a community isolated from recent advances in the quality of care and treatment of patients. Rather, it is one of the leading medical centers in quality health care. * * *

Moreover, any purported disparity between the skills of practitioners in various urban centers has for the most part been eliminated. Unlike the diversified and often limited training that was available a hundred years ago, medical education has been standardized throughout the nation through a system of national accreditation. [Cc] Moreover, the significant improvements in transportation and communication over the past hundred years cast further doubt on continued vitality of the doctrine. * * * In sum, the major underpinnings of the locality doctrine no longer obtain. The locality rule has been quite properly criticized as a relic of the nineteenth century which has no relevance to the realities of modern medical practice. [Cc]

Quite apart from the locality rule's irrelevance to contemporary medical practice, the doctrine is also objectionable because it tends to immunize doctors from communities where medical practice is generally below that which exists in other communities from malpractice liability. [Cc] Rather than encouraging medical practitioners to elevate the quality of care and treatment of patients to that existing in other communities, the doctrine may serve to foster substandard care, by testing the conduct of medical professionals by the conduct of other medical professionals in the same community.

The locality rule is peculiar to medical malpractice. Architects are not held to a standard of conduct exercised by other architects in the District or a similar locality. [C] Moreover, the conduct of lawyers is not measured solely by the conduct of other lawyers in the District or a similar community. [Cc]

Despite these criticisms, the locality rule is still followed in several jurisdictions. * * *

Courts which have abandoned the locality rule have taken different approaches in defining the geographical boundary within which the conduct of a medical practitioner is to be measured. For example, a number of courts have modified the locality rule by extending the geographical reference group of the standard of care to include that of "the same or similar localities." [Cc]

This approach has been criticized because of the difficulty in determining whether two communities are similar. [Cc] In addition, the similar locality formulation has been criticized for containing the same deficiencies as the traditional locality rule, *i.e.*, if the standard of conduct in a similar community is substandard, the similar locality rule would immunize those medical professionals whose conduct conforms to the substandard medical practice in a similar community. [Cc]

Other courts, noting that medical standards have been nationalized largely through a system of national board certification, have adopted a national standard of care, and accordingly have eliminated any reference to a geographically defined area in their formulation of the standard of care applicable to medical professionals. [Cc] The import of these decisions is that health care professionals who are trained according to national standards and who hold themselves out to the public as such, should be held to a national standard of care.

We are in general agreement with those courts which have adopted a national standard of care. Varying geographical standards of care are no longer valid in view of the uniform standards of proficiency established by national board certification. * * *

Although we have found no cases which address the issue of the standard of care applicable to a clinical laboratory, the same reasons which justify the application of a national standard of care to physicians and hospitals appear to apply with equal validity to medical laboratories. Medical laboratories are often staffed and operated by doctors who undergo the same rigorous training as other physicians. The opportunities for keeping abreast of medical advances that are available to doctors are equally available to clinical laboratories. Indeed medical laboratories are often an integral part of a hospital. [C] Moreover, clinical laboratories generally conduct many of the routine tests that would normally be performed by physicians and hospitals. Accordingly, they owe similar duties in their care and treatment of patients. [C]

Thus we hold that at least as to board certified physicians, hospitals, medical laboratories, and other health care providers, the standard of care is to be measured by the national standard. It follows that an instruction which compares a nationally certified medical professional's conduct exclusively with the standard of care in the District or a similar community is erroneous.

In the present case, appellees concede that they are a nationally certified medical laboratory and that they hold themselves out to the public as such. Appellant's expert witness testified at trial that the proper procedure to be employed in conducting a urethral smear test, according to national standards, is with the patient in a sitting or prone position. Appellees' expert witnesses who were all from the Washington metropolitan area testified that they were not aware of any national standards for conducting the test and that they always conducted the test with the patient in a standing position. However, the trial court instructed the jury that the appellees' conduct is to be compared solely with the standard of care prevailing in Washington, D.C. Thus, in effect the jury was instructed to ignore the testimony of appellant's expert witness on the standard of care. This instruction was error. The conflict in expert testimony was for the jury to resolve. Accordingly, we vacate the judgment in favor of appellees and order a new trial. * * * Reversed.

NOTES AND QUESTIONS

1. It was traditional with the medical profession to state the standard of knowledge and skill in terms of a practitioner in good standing in the local community in which the defendant practices. This is sometimes known as the "strict locality" rule. This apparently arose in the days in which medical education was not standardized and there was wide variance in the knowledge and skill of doctors in different parts of the country, particularly between rural and urban areas. As the principal case suggests, the locality rule has not been generally followed in regard to the other professions. See, e.g., Russo v. Griffin, 147 Vt. 20,

510 A.2d 436 (1986) (adopting statewide standard of care in attorney malpractice case).

2.   Critics charged that the strict locality rule reinforced the status quo of care in any given community, served as a disincentive for the elevation of the standard of care, and sometimes made it difficult for the plaintiff to locate an expert witness because physicians within the same community were reluctant to testify against each other. See, e.g., McGulpin v. Bessmer, 241 Ia. 1119, 43 N.W.2d 121 (1950) (criticizing requirement of expert testimony of physician from same community). Most jurisdictions now have adopted a "similar community in similar circumstances" test, which is designed to balance the need to avoid evaluating a general practitioner in a rural area by the same standards as a specialist in an urban teaching hospital with the need of the plaintiff for access to expert testimony. But see Vergara v. Doan, 593 N.E.2d 185 (Ind.1992) (standard of care does not focus on locality but uses it as one of factors to be considered, along with advances in profession, availability of facilities, and whether health care provider was specialist or general practitioner). Some jurisdictions have gone further and adopted a "national standard," especially for specialists who are certified by a national board within their specialty areas. See, e.g., Shilkret v. Annapolis Emergency Hosp. Ass'n., 276 Md. 187, 349 A.2d 245 (1975) (because "medical profession itself recognizes national standards for specialists that are not determined by geography, the law should follow suit"); Hall v. Hilbun, 466 So.2d 856 (Miss.1985) (adopting a nationwide standard for care and skill but not for resources); and Jordan v. Bogner, 844 P.2d 664 (Colo.1993) ("family practice" specialist who delivered baby in rural area held to national standard because specialist); Sheeley v. Memorial Hospital, 710 A.2d 161 (R.I.1998) (abandoning "same or similar" community test for national standard).

3.   As the critics of the strict locality rule had pointed out, the locality rule can create serious injustice in some situations. Does the rule in the principal case create injustice for the medical profession? Suppose it spawns "professional experts" who travel from city to city, testifying in medical malpractice cases against doctors.

Scott v. Bradford

Supreme Court of Oklahoma, 1979.
606 P.2d 554.

DOOLIN, JUSTICE. This appeal is taken by plaintiffs in trial below, from a judgment in favor of defendant rendered on a jury verdict in a medical malpractice action.

Mrs. Scott's physician advised her she had several fibroid tumors on her uterus. He referred her to defendant surgeon. Defendant admitted her to the hospital where she signed a routine consent form prior to defendant's performing a hysterectomy. After surgery, Mrs. Scott experienced problems with incontinence. She visited another physician who discovered she had a vesico-vaginal fistula which permitted urine to leak from her bladder into the vagina. This physician referred her to an urologist who, after three surgeries, succeeded in correcting her problems.

Mrs. Scott, joined by her husband, filed the present action alleging medical malpractice, claiming defendant failed to advise her of the risks involved or of available alternatives to surgery. She further maintained had she been properly informed she would have refused the surgery.

The case was submitted to the jury with instructions to which plaintiffs objected. The jury found for defendant and plaintiffs appeal. * * *

P objected to jury instructions

The issue involved is whether Oklahoma adheres to the doctrine of informed consent as the basis of an action for medical malpractice, and if so did the present instructions adequately advise the jury of defendant's duty.

 Issue

Anglo–American law starts with the premise of thoroughgoing self-determination, each man considered to be his own master. This law does not permit a physician to substitute his judgment for that of the patient by any form of artifice. The doctrine of informed consent arises out of this premise.

Consent to medical treatment, to be effective, should stem from an understanding decision based on adequate information about the treatment, the available alternatives, and the collateral risks. This requirement, labeled "informed consent," is, legally speaking, as essential as a physician's care and skill in the *performance* of the therapy. The doctrine imposes a duty on a physician or surgeon to inform a patient of his options and their attendant risks. If a physician breaches this duty, patient's consent is defective, and physician is responsible for the consequences.

If treatment is completely unauthorized and performed without any consent at all, there has been a battery. However, if the physician obtains a patient's consent but has breached his duty to inform, the patient has a cause of action sounding in negligence for failure to inform the patient of his options, regardless of the due care exercised at treatment, assuming there is injury. * * *

The first buds of court decisions heralding this new medical duty are found in Salgo v. Leland Stanford, Jr., University Board of Trustees, 154 Cal.App.2d 560, 317 P.2d 170 (1957). That court grounded the disclosure requirement in negligence law, holding a physician violates a duty to his patient and subjects himself to liability if he withholds any facts which are necessary to form the basis of an intelligent consent by the patient to the proposed treatment. The court strongly suggested a physician is obligated not only to disclose *what* he intends to do, but to supply information which addresses the question of *whether* he should do it. This view was a marked divergence from the general rule of "professional standard of care" in determining what must be disclosed. Under that standard, earlier decisions seemed to perpetuate medical paternalism by giving the profession sweeping authority to decide unilaterally what is in the patient's best interests. Under the "professional standard of care" a physician needed only to inform a patient in conformance with the prevailing medical practice in the community.

More recently, in perhaps one of the most influential informed consent decisions, Canterbury v. Spence, 150 U.S.App.D.C. 263, 464 F.2d 772 (D.C.Cir.1972), cert. den. 409 U.S. 1064, the doctrine received perdurable impetus. Judge Robinson observed that suits charging failure by a physician adequately to disclose risks and alternatives of proposed treatment were not innovative in American law. He emphasized the fundamental concept in American jurisprudence that every human being of adult years and sound mind has a right to determine what shall be done with his own body. True consent to what happens to one's self is the informed exercise of a choice. This entails an opportunity to evaluate knowledgeably the options available and the risks attendant upon each. It is the prerogative of every patient to chart his own course and determine which direction he will take.

The decision in *Canterbury* recognized the tendency of some jurisdictions to turn this duty on whether it is the custom of physicians practicing in the community to make the particular disclosure to the patient. That court rejected this standard and held the standard measuring performance of the duty of disclosure is conduct which is reasonable under the circumstances: "[We can not] ignore the fact that to bind disclosure obligations to medical usage is to arrogate the decision on revelation to the physician alone." We agree. A patient's right to make up his mind whether to undergo treatment should not be delegated to the local medical group. What is reasonable disclosure in one instance may not be reasonable in another. We decline to adopt a standard based on the professional standard. We, therefore, hold the scope of a physician's communications must be measured by his patient's need to know enough to enable him to make an intelligent choice. In other words, full disclosure of all *material risks* incident to treatment must be made. There is no bright line separating the material from the immaterial; it is a question of fact. A risk is material if it would be likely to affect patient's decision. When non-disclosure of a particular risk is open to debate, the issue is for the finder of facts.

This duty to disclose is the first element of the cause of action in negligence based on lack of informed consent. However, there are exceptions creating a privilege of a physician not to disclose. There is no need to disclose risks that either ought to be known by everyone or are already known to the patient. Further, the primary duty of a physician is to do what is best for his patient and where full disclosure would be detrimental to a patient's total care and best interests a physician may withhold such disclosure, for example, where disclosure would alarm an emotionally upset or apprehensive patient. Certainly too, where there is an emergency and the patient is in no condition to determine for himself whether treatment should be administered, the privilege may be invoked.

The patient has the burden of going forward with evidence tending to establish prima facie the essential elements of the cause of action. The burden of proving an exception to his duty and thus a privilege not to disclose, rests upon the physician as an affirmative defense.

The cause of action, based on lack of informed consent, is divided into three elements, the duty to inform being the first, the second is causation, and the third is injury. The second element, that of causation, requires that plaintiff patient would have chosen no treatment or a different course of treatment had the alternatives and material risks of each been made known to him. If the patient would have elected to proceed with treatment had he been duly informed of its risks, then the element of causation is missing. In other words, a causal connection exists between physician's breach of the duty to disclose and patient's injury when and only when disclosure of material risks incidental to treatment would have resulted in a decision against it. A patient obviously has no complaint if he would have submitted to the treatment if the physician had complied with his duty and informed him of the risks. This fact decision raises the difficult question of the correct standard on which to instruct the jury.

The court in Canterbury v. Spence, supra, although emphasizing principles of self-determination permits liability only if non-disclosure would have affected the decision of a fictitious "reasonable patient," even though actual patient testifies he would have elected to forego therapy had he been fully informed.

Decisions discussing informed consent have emphasized the *disclosure* element but paid scant attention to the consent element of the concept, although this is the root of causation. Language in some decisions suggest the standard to be applied is a subjective one, i.e., whether that particular patient would still have consented to the treatment, reasonable choice or otherwise. [Cc]

Although the *Canterbury* rule is probably that of the majority, its "reasonable man" approach has been criticized by some commentators as backtracking on its own theory of self-determination. The *Canterbury* view certainly severely limits the protection granted an injured patient. To the extent the plaintiff, given an adequate disclosure, would have declined the proposed treatment, and a reasonable person in similar circumstances would have consented, a patient's right of self-determination is *irrevocably lost*. This basic right to know and decide is the reason for the full-disclosure rule. Accordingly, we decline to jeopardize this right by the imposition of the "reasonable man" standard.

If a plaintiff testifies he would have continued with the proposed treatment had he been adequately informed, the trial is over under either the subjective or objective approach. If he testifies he would not, then the causation problem must be resolved by examining the credibility of plaintiff's testimony. The jury must be instructed that it must find plaintiff would have refused the treatment if he is to prevail.

Although it might be said this approach places a physician at the mercy of a patient's hindsight, a careful practitioner can always protect himself by insuring that he has adequately informed each patient he treats. If he does not breach this duty, a causation problem will not arise.

The final element of this cause of action is that of injury. The risk must actually materialize and plaintiff must have been injured as a result of submitting to the treatment. Absent occurrence of the undisclosed risk, a physician's failure to reveal its possibility is not actionable.

In summary, in a medical malpractice action a patient suing under the theory of informed consent must allege and prove:

(1) defendant physician failed to inform him adequately of a material risk before securing his consent to the proposed treatment;

(2) if he had been informed of the risks he would not have consented to the treatment;

(3) the adverse consequences that were not made known did in fact occur and he was injured as a result of submitting to the treatment.

As a defense, a physician may plead and prove plaintiff knew of the risks, full disclosure would be detrimental to patient's best interests or that an emergency existed requiring prompt treatment and patient was in no condition to decide for himself.

Because we are imposing a new duty on physicians, we hereby make this opinion prospective only, affecting those causes of action arising after the date this opinion is promulgated.

The trial court in the case at bar gave rather broad instructions upon the duty of a physician to disclose. The instructions objected to did instruct that defendant should have disclosed material risks of the hysterectomy and feasibility of alternatives. Instructions are sufficient when considered as a whole they present the law applicable to the issues. Jury found for defendant. We find no basis for reversal.

Affirmed. * * *

BARNES, JUSTICE, concurring in part, dissenting in part: I concur with the majority opinion in all respects except I would adopt the reasonable man test set out in Canterbury v. Spence, 150 U.S.App.D.C. 263, 464 F.2d 772 (D.C.Cir.1972), cert. den. 409 U.S. 1064.

NOTES AND QUESTIONS

1.   The doctrine of informed consent has had a very checkered career. Developed first as a basis for vitiating the consent and holding that an action of battery would lie, it proved to be too strong a remedy for the evil it purported to cure. The battery theory is now generally abandoned, except, of course, where the physician has not obtained any consent at all. See, e.g., Mohr v. Williams, page 91. Pennsylvania is one of a few jurisdictions that continues to categorize informed consent as a battery action. Thus, it applies only to surgery or other invasive procedures, and not to the prescribing of drugs. Morgan v. Rose, 550 Pa. 202, 704 A.2d 617 (1997) (reaffirming battery basis for action but noting statute extends informed consent requirement to radiation, chemotherapy, blood transfusions, and experimental drug therapy).

2.   With the abandonment of the battery theory, the courts held that the question was whether the doctor was negligent in failing to disclose the nature, consequences, risks, and alternatives of any proposed treatment. This brought into play the doctrine of customary practice and the need of having expert medical testimony concerning the practice of a physician using customary care. Thus, if the cause of action is for informed consent, the plaintiff, like the plaintiff in the principal case, usually needs an expert witness, while she does not need an expert witness if the cause of action is for battery. Because of gum disease, plaintiff was advised to have her teeth extracted. Her dentist anesthetized her entire oral cavity and began a full extraction of all thirty-two of her teeth. Plaintiff says dentist never

told her he was planning to extract all her teeth at one visit and never obtained her consent. Dentist, arguing that the case was based on lack of informed consent, moved for summary judgment because plaintiff did not have an expert witness to establish the standard—the usual and customary information given to patients to procure consent in similar situations. The Tennessee Supreme Court found the case was for medical battery, not lack of informed consent, and did not require an expert witness: "Lack of informed consent in a medical malpractice action under Tenn. Code Ann. § 29–16–118 operates to negate a patient's authorization for a procedure thereby giving rise to a cause of action for battery. [C] There is, however, no prior authorization or consent in a medical battery case to be negated by expert testimony. The primary consideration in a medical battery case is simply whether the patient knew and authorized a procedure. This determination does not require the testimony of an expert witness." Blanchard v. Kellum, 975 S.W.2d 522, 524 (Tenn.1998).

3. This traditional, professional standard, which focuses on what physicians usually tell patients about a particular procedure, continues to be the rule in many jurisdictions. Some jurisdictions, however, have changed the test from what the *reasonable physician* would disclose to what the *reasonable patient* would want to know. See Culbertson v. Mernitz, 602 N.E.2d 98 (Ind.1992) for a discussion of the competing policy concerns present in the alternative standards. The principal case goes one step further and allows the patient to prove that even if the *reasonable patient* would not have refused the procedure, this patient would have. Does that mean the patient's testimony would be determinative as to the effect of the failure to inform? If a state adopts the "reasonable patient" standard, does the patient still need expert testimony to establish a prima facie case? Carr v. Strode, 79 Haw. 475, 904 P.2d 489 (1995) (plaintiff retains the burden of providing expert medical testimony as to the nature of risks inherent in a particular treatment, the probabilities of therapeutic success, the frequency of the occurrence of particular risks, and the nature of available alternatives to treatment).

4. Note that the physician is required to inform about "material" risks. What does that mean? Is a 1–3 percent possibility material? Martin v. Richards, 192 Wis.2d 156, 531 N.W.2d 70 (1995) (in light of serious consequences, including death, a 1–3 percent possibility is not remote). Canterbury v. Spence, 464 F.2d 772 (D.C.Cir.1972) (although the risk of a complication may be small, such risk may be significant to a patient's decision in light of the potentially severe consequences).

5. Most informed consent cases involve whether to disclose particular risks of treatment or particular alternatives to treatment. What if the physician fails to tell the patient that she could do nothing at all and the condition might disappear on its own? Wecker v. Amend, 22 Kan.App.2d 498, 918 P.2d 658 (1996) (if doing nothing is medically acceptable alternative, which was contested in case, then patient must be so informed). What if the physician fails to tell the patient of the risks of refusing a diagnostic test? Truman v. Thomas, 27 Cal.3d 285, 611 P.2d 902, 165 Cal. Rptr. 308 (1980) (physician liable for failing to warn patient of risk of refusing pap smear test). What if the physician fails to inform the patient of the availability of an alternative diagnostic test? Martin v. Richards, 192 Wis.2d 156, 531 N.W.2d 70 (1995) (physician liable for failing to inform parents of child who suffered head injury in bicycle accident of availability of CAT scan). What if physician fails to inform patient of psychological (not physical) risks of a procedure? Curtis v. MRI Imaging Services II, 327 Or. 9, 956 P.2d 960 (1998) (physician may be liable for failing to inform patient of possible claustrophobic effects of MRI procedure).

6.   Most informed consent cases are against physicians. If the treating physician with privileges at a hospital fails to obtain consent to a blood transfusion, does the hospital have a duty to obtain consent? Does the blood bank that provided the blood? Ward v. Lutheran Hospitals & Homes Soc. of Am., Inc., 963 P.2d 1031 (Alaska 1998) (noting that overwhelming weight of authority holds that hospital does not owe duty to patient to obtain consent for treatment when patient is under care of independent physician and finding that neither hospital not blood bank owed patient a duty).

☛ Moore v. The Regents of the University of California

Supreme Court of California, 1990.
51 Cal.3d 120, 793 P.2d 479, 271 Cal.Rptr. 146.

Opinion by PANELLI, J.:

[Plaintiff, John Moore, first visited UCLA Medical Center in October 1976, shortly after being diagnosed with hairy-cell leukemia. Defendant Golde, his treating physician at UCLA, withdrew blood, bone marrow, and other bodily substances to test them. Dr. Golde then recommended that Moore's spleen be removed. Based upon Dr. Golde's representation that the removal of the spleen was necessary to slow down the progress of the disease, Moore consented to the recommended surgery. Moore alleged that Dr. Golde "formed the intent and made the arrangements to obtain portions of his spleen following the removal" to use them in research which was unrelated to Moore's medical care. Moore returned to UCLA Medical Center several times between November 1976 and September 1983 at Dr. Golde's direction and based on Dr. Golde's representations that the follow up was necessary for his treatment. After relocating to the Seattle area, Moore continued to return to UCLA because he had been told the procedures could only be performed there. In fact, Dr. Golde and some colleagues had discovered that Moore's cells were unusually useful in the genetic research they were performing. Dr. Golde and others developed and patented a cell line from Mr. Moore's cells and then licensed it for commercial development to Genetics Institute and Sandoz Pharmaceuticals, also named as defendants in the action.

Plaintiffs filed a complaint containing thirteen causes of action, including inter alia, conversion and lack of informed consent and breach of fiduciary duty for failing to disclose the financial interest of the defendants. The trial court sustained a demurrer to the conversion count and then dismissed the entire complaint without ruling on the other counts because of its view that the other counts simply repeated the inadequate allegations of the conversion count. The Court of Appeal reversed on the conversion count, holding that it did state a cause of action for conversion, agreed that the informed consent count against the commercial defendants was not adequate but directing the trial court to give Moore leave to amend, and directed the trial court to consider the remaining causes of action that had not been ruled upon. This appeal followed.]

* * *

A. Breach of Fiduciary Duty and Lack of Informed Consent

Moore repeatedly alleges that Golde failed to disclose the extent of his research and economic interests in Moore's cells before obtaining consent to the medical procedures by which the cells were extracted. These allegations, in our view, state a cause of action against Golde for invading a legally protected interest of his patient. This cause of action can properly be characterized either as the breach of a fiduciary duty to disclose facts material to the patient's consent or, alternatively, as the performance of medical procedures without first having obtained the patient's informed consent.

Our analysis begins with three well-established principles. First, "a person of adult years and in sound mind has the right, in the exercise of control over his own body, to determine whether or not to submit to lawful medical treatment." [Cc] Second, the patient's consent to treatment, to be effective, must be an informed consent." [C] Third, in soliciting the patient's consent, a physician has a fiduciary duty to disclose all information material to the patient's decision. [Cc]

These principles lead to the following conclusions: (1) a physician must disclose personal interests unrelated to the patient's health, whether research or economic, that may affect the physician's professional judgment; and (2) a physician's failure to disclose such interests may give rise to a cause of action for performing medical procedures without informed consent or breach of fiduciary duty.

To be sure, questions about the validity of a patient's consent to a procedure typically arise when the patient alleges that the physician failed to disclose medical risks, as in malpractice cases, and not when the patient alleges that the physician had a personal interest, as in this case. The concept of informed consent, however, is broad enough to encompass the latter. "The scope of the physician's communication to the patient * * * must be measured by the patient's need, and that need is whatever information is material to the decision." [C]

Indeed, the law already recognizes that a reasonable patient would want to know whether a physician has an economic interest that might affect the physician's professional judgment. As the Court of Appeal has said, "[c]ertainly a sick patient deserves to be free of any reasonable suspicion that his doctor's judgment is influenced by a profit motive." * * *

It is important to note that no law prohibits a physician from conducting research in the same area in which he practices. Progress in medicine often depends upon physicians, such as those practicing at the university hospital where Moore received treatment, who conduct research while caring for their patients.

Yet a physician who treats a patient in whom he also has a research interest has potentially conflicting loyalties. This is because medical treatment decisions are made on the basis of proportionality—weighing the benefits to the patient against the risks to the patient. As another court has said, "the determination as to whether the burdens of treatment are worth enduring for any individual patient depends upon the facts unique in each case," and "the patient's interests and desires are the key ingredients of the decision-making process." [C] A physician who adds his own research interests to this balance may be tempted to order a scientifically useful procedure or test that offers marginal, or no, benefits to the patient. The possibility that an interest extraneous to the patient's health has affected the physician's judgment is something that a reasonable patient would want to know in deciding whether to consent to a proposed course of treatment. It is material to the patient's decision and, thus, a prerequisite to informed consent. [C]

Golde argues that the scientific use of cells that have already been removed cannot possibly affect the patient's medical interests. The argument is correct in one instance but not in another. If a physician has no plans to conduct research on a patient's cells at the time he recommends the medical procedure by which they are taken, then the patient's medical interests have not been impaired. In that instance the argument is correct. On the other hand, a physician who does have a preexisting research interest might, consciously or unconsciously, take that into consideration in recommending the procedure. In that instance the argument is incorrect: the physician's extraneous motivation may affect his judgment and is, thus, material to the patient's consent.

We acknowledge that there is a competing consideration. To require disclosure of research and economic interests may corrupt the patient's own judgment by distracting him from the requirements of his health. But California law does not grant physicians unlimited discretion to decide what to disclose. Instead, "it is the prerogative of the patient, not the physician, to determine for himself the direction in which he believes his interests lie." [C] "Unlimited discretion in the physician is irreconcilable with the basic right of the patient to make the ultimate informed decision * * *." [C]

However, we made that statement in the context of a physician-patient relationship unaffected by possible conflicts of interest. Cobbs v. Grant, supra, permits a physician acting solely in the patient's best interests to consider whether excessive disclosure will harm the patient. Disclosure of possible conflicts of interest raises different considerations. To illustrate, a physician who orders a procedure partly to further a research interest unrelated to the patient's health should not be able to avoid disclosure with the argument that the patient might object to participation in research. In some cases, however, a physician's research interest might play such an insignificant role in the decision to recommend a medically indicated procedure that disclosure should not be required because the interest is not material. By analogy, we have not required disclosure of "remote" risks [c] that "are not central to the decision to administer or reject [a] procedure." [C]

Accordingly, we hold that a physician who is seeking a patient's consent for a medical procedure must, in order to satisfy his fiduciary duty and to obtain the patient's informed consent, disclose personal interests unrelated to the patient's health, whether research or economic, that may affect his medical judgment.

* * *

[The court then discussed the specific allegations of the complaint relating to each of the medical procedures. First, Moore did not state a cause of action with respect to the original drawing of blood and tissue samples because Dr. Golde did not yet know of the rare nature of Moore's cells. Second, Moore stated a cause of action with respect to the surgical removal of the spleen even though the surgery had therapeutic value for Moore because Moore alleged that Dr. Golde planned to keep the removed spleen for scientific research but did not disclose that to Moore. Third, the postoperative takings of bodily tissues were done at a time when Dr. Golde had an undisclosed financial interest in them and even though they had no therapeutic purpose. Thus the complaint stated a cause of action against Dr. Golde for those procedures.

The court found that the remaining defendants could be liable to Moore for a failure of informed consent if they were vicariously liable for Dr. Golde's actions and ruled that Moore could amend his complaint to attempt to state a lack of informed consent cause of action against them.

On the conversion issue, see Chapter 2, the Court decided that the traditional common law doctrine of conversion did not cover Moore's cells and that the court should not expand the common law doctrine to cover this kind of case.]

The decision of the Court of Appeal is affirmed in part and reversed in part. The case is remanded to the Court of Appeal, which shall direct the superior court to: (1) overrule Golde's demurrers to the causes of action for breach of fiduciary duty and lack of informed consent; (2) sustain, with leave to amend, the demurrers of the [commercial defendants] to the purported causes of action for breach of fiduciary duty and lack of informed consent; (3) sustain, without leave to amend, all defendants' demurrers to the purported cause of action for conversion; and (4) hear and determine all defendants' remaining demurrers.

[The concurring and dissenting opinions are omitted.]

NOTES AND QUESTIONS

1. Note that California uses the *reasonable patient* rather than the *reasonable physician* test for informed consent. Do you think the court would have made the same ruling on the informed consent issue if California followed the *reasonable physician* test?

2. What will happen next in the case? If the jury finds for the plaintiff on the informed consent cause of action, what would the damages be? Will Moore share in the profits of the cell line started by his spleen?

3. Most risks that must be disclosed relate to the therapy or procedure. What about risks relating to the physician and the physician's capacity to perform? See, e.g., Faya v. Almaraz, 329 Md. 435, 620 A.2d 327 (1993). (HIV status of surgeon); Hidding v. Williams, 578 So.2d 1192 (La.App.1991) (alcoholism); Johnson v. Kokem-

oor, 199 Wis.2d 615, 545 N.W.2d 495 (1996) (comparative morbidity/mortality rates
for the procedure between surgeons experienced in procedure and those inexperienced like himself); Bray v. Hill, 517 N.W.2d 223 (Iowa App.1994) (that Board of
Medical Examiners had placed surgeon on probationary status for three years). Cf.
Shea v. Esensten, 107 F.3d 625 (8th Cir.1997) (that doctor's contract with HMO
contained financial incentives to influence doctor not to refer patient to specialist).

4. *Causation*? Informed consent raises one problem that can be only mentioned at this early point in the course. Liability is being imposed even though there
was no other negligence in performing the operation or administering the treatment. If so, it must be on the basis that if the risk had been disclosed the patient
would not have agreed to be subjected to the risk by undergoing the operation or
the treatment. How do we know? Can we rely on the patient's testimony after the
risk has manifested itself? Can we resort to the reasonable prudent person again? Is
that true causation? See also note 2, page 262.

5.   Other causation problems can arise with professional services. If an attorney negligently lets the statute run without filing suit, what is he liable for? The
value of the suit? How can we tell what, if anything, it was worth without trying it?
Does the client then have to win two separate suits in one? See pages 267–268.

6.   Can you think of ways in which the doctrine of informed consent could be
applied to attorney malpractice cases? In declining to take a personal injury case on
a contingent fee basis, the attorney may be obligated to warn the plaintiff about the
statute of limitations. See, e.g., Togstad v. Vesely, Otto, Miller & Keefe, 291 N.W.2d
686 (Minn.1980).

Some of the professional-services cases involve another problem to be taken
up later. Is the defendant liable to people who were not clients of the defendant? A
lawyer draws up a will that is invalid. Can the intended beneficiary of a legacy
recover after the testator dies? Hesser v. Central National Bank & Trust Co., 956
P.2d 864 (Okla.1998) (lawyer erred in will's execution so heirs at law challenged
validity of will's bequest to plaintiff). Cf. Prudential Ins. Co. v. Dewey, Ballantine,
Bushby, Palmer & Wood, 80 N.Y.2d 377, 590 N.Y.S.2d 831, 605 N.E.2d 318 (1992)
(law firm may be liable to non-client who relied on opinion letter). But see Bily v.
Arthur Young & Co., 3 Cal.4th 370, 11 Cal.Rptr.2d 51, 834 P.2d 745 (1992) (no
liability to non-client of accounting firm). A physician negligently advises a patient
exposed to hepatitis that if she remains symptom free for six weeks she has not
contracted the disease and is not contagious. The advice should have been six
months rather than six weeks. Patient refrains from sexual intercourse for eight
weeks after the exposure and then resumes sexual intercourse with plaintiff. Both
patient and plaintiff are diagnosed with hepatitis. Does plaintiff have a medical
malpractice cause of action against the physician? See DiMarco v. Lynch Homes,
525 Pa. 558, 583 A.2d 422 (1990) (yes). Physician administers oral polio vaccine to
infant and fails to inform parents that they might contract polio from infant. Does
father have negligence case against physician? Tenuto v. Lederle Labs., 90 N.Y.2d
606, 687 N.E.2d 1300, 665 N.Y.S.2d 17 (1997) (yes). Physician treats patient for
disease that is genetically transferable. Physician does not tell patient to warn her
children that they too may develop the disease. Does patient's adult daughter have
a medical malpractice cause of action against physician? Pate v. Threlkel, 661 So.2d
278 (Fla.1995) (maybe, if standard of care can be shown to include warning patient).
Physician treats patient for epilepsy, which is controlled by medication for years.
Patient then has a seizure even while on medication. Physician fails to warn him
not to drive. Patient has seizure while driving and kills the plaintiff's intestate.
Does the family of the woman who was killed in the car accident caused by the

seizure have a cause of action against physician? Praesel v. Johnson, 967 S.W.2d 391 (Tex.1998)(no).

**The "Medical Malpractice Crisis" and Statutory
Change in the Common Law.**

In the latter part of the 1970's and again in the mid–1980's, an increase in the number of medical malpractice suits produced sudden sharp rises in the premiums for, and in some instances, unavailability, of malpractice liability insurance. This in turn produced alarm within the profession and insistent demands that the state legislatures find ways of alleviating the "crisis" caused by the burden of the malpractice insurance premiums and the unavailability of insurance. Much of the blame was placed by the lobbyists on the law of negligence, and various modifications of the substantive law of torts were rushed through the legislatures. See Logue, Toward a Tax Based Explanation of the Liability Insurance Crisis, 82 Va.L.Rev. 895 (1996). Almost every state passed legislation of some sort. The statutes have varied considerably and there is no particular pattern to them. (See Sanders & Joyce, "Off to the Races": the 1980's Tort Crisis and the Law Reform Process, 27 Hous.L.Rev. 207 (1990).) Changes were made in the standard of care, the doctrine of informed consent (see page 182), the doctrine of res ipsa loquitur (see page 229), the collateral source rule (see page 539), the statute of limitations (see page 613), imposing limits on the amount that could be received for pain and suffering or on the total amount recovered in a malpractice action, and prohibiting the setting forth in a complaint of the amount of the relief requested. Many states required submission of the case to a screening board before bringing action, others required submission to arbitration and others sought to impose restrictions on the contingent-fee system. The impact of the reform initiatives are difficult to discern. Viscusi and Born, Medical Malpractice in the Wake of Liability Reform, 24 J.Legal Stud. 463 (1995).

Some individual doctors brought malicious prosecution or abuse of process suits against the patient (or his attorney) for bringing unwarranted civil actions (see page 998). This latter device did not prove to be very successful, and state supreme courts held a number of the statutory provisions to be unconstitutional for various reasons; but most of the states still have some of the statutory modifications in effect. An attorney must therefore carefully research state statutes as well as common law in this area. See, for example, Smith v. Schulte, 671 So.2d 1334 (Ala.1995) (cap on damages in medical malpractice cases violates state constitutional guarantees of equal protection and right to jury trial); Redish, Legislative Response to the Medical Malpractice Insurance Crisis: Constitutional Implications, 55 Tex.L.Rev. 759 (1977); Smith, Battling a Tort Frontier: Constitutional Attacks on Medical Malpractice Laws, 38 Okla.L.Rev. 195 (1985).

(C) AGGRAVATED NEGLIGENCE

1. *"Degrees" of Care.* It is obvious, and elementary, that the care required by the standard of the reasonable person will vary according to the risk. As the danger increases, the actor is required to exercise caution commensurate with it, and so to be more careful. Those who deal with things that are *known to be dangerous*, such as explosives or electricity, must exercise more care than one who is merely walking down the street. Likewise, those who have accepted a special responsibility toward others, as in the case of *a common carrier* responsible for the safety of passengers, must exercise more care in accordance with the duty undertaken. On many occasions, this has been expressed in instructions to the jury, approved on

appeal, that the carrier, or the person dealing with special danger, must exercise "the highest degree of care," or "the utmost caution characteristic of very careful prudent persons." See, for example, Bayer v. Crested Butte Mountain Resort, Inc., 960 P.2d 70 (Colo.1998) (ski lift operator must exercise highest degree of care commensurate with the lift's practical operation); Peck v. Fanion, 124 Conn. 549, 1 A.2d 143 (1938); Pennsylvania Co. v. Roy, 102 U.S. 451 (1880). On "reasonable care" vs. "extraordinary care" regarding the use of firearms, see the opinions in Everette v. New Kensington, 262 Pa.Super. 28, 396 A.2d 467 (1978).

There are many other decisions in which this type of instruction has been held to be error, on the ground that there are no "degrees" of care recognized by the law, but merely amounts of care, greater or less; that the care required of the actor is always the same under the traditional formula, that of a reasonable person under like circumstances; and that the greater danger, or the greater responsibility, are merely circumstances that require a greater amount of care. See Flowers v. Torrance Memorial Hospital Med. Ctr., 8 Cal.4th 992, 884 P.2d 142, 35 Cal.Rptr.2d 685 (1994) ("There are no 'degrees' of care as a matter of law; there are only different amounts of care, as a matter of fact"); Bethel v. N.Y.C. Transit Authority, 92 N.Y.2d 348, 355, 703 N.E.2d 1214,Union Traction 1218 (1998) ("we conclude that the rule of a common carrier's duty of extraordinary care is no longer viable. Rather, a common carrier is subject to the same duty of care as any other potential tortfeasor—reasonable care under all of the circumstances of the particular case.").

2.   *"Degrees" of Negligence.* A different attempt, carried to considerable lengths in the last century, has been to distinguish "degrees" of negligence, breaking it down into different kinds of conduct, with different legal consequences. This idea was lifted from the Roman law by Chief Justice Holt in a bailment case, Coggs v. Bernard, 2 Ld.Raym. 909, 92 Eng.Rep. 107 (1704). As it developed, the distinction was made between "slight" negligence, defined as a failure to use great care; ordinary negligence, or failure to use reasonable care; and "gross" negligence, which is failure to exercise even slight care. See Green, High Care and Gross Negligence, 23 Ill.L.Rev. 4 (1928); Elliott, Degrees of Negligence, 6 So.Cal. L.Rev. 91 (1932).

These distinctions were subjected to a good deal of criticism almost from the start. In Wilson v. Brett, 11 M. & W. 113, 152 Eng.Rep. 737 (1843), Baron Rolfe made a much quoted statement that gross negligence is merely the same thing as ordinary negligence, "with the addition of a vituperative epithet." In some of the very early cases, this was true. "Gross negligence" was an expression used to mean nothing more than negligence. See, for example, Vaughan v. Menlove, page 143. But when it is intended to mean more, "gross" negligence is readily understood by the ordinary person as involving an extreme departure from ordinary standards of conduct, and it is very probable that Judge Magruder's students at the Harvard Law School knew what he meant when he explained "Chief Justice Rugg's famous distinctions among negligence, gross negligence and recklessness as being the distinctions among a fool, a damned fool, and a God-damned fool." Harvard Law Record, April 16, 1959.

In practice, however, it proved extraordinarily difficult to set any lines of demarcation, and these distinctions filled the courts with vexatious appeals in which they were asked to rule upon particular conduct as a matter of law. During the latter half of the nineteenth century, the courts of Illinois and Kansas were deluged with appeals, as a result of their adoption of a rule that contributory negligence was not a defense when the negligence of the defendant was found to be "gross," and that of the plaintiff "slight" in comparison. Both courts finally threw up their hands and threw out the distinctions, declaring that henceforth only one kind of negligence, measured by the standard of the reasonable person, was to be recognized. The story is told in Malone, The Formative Era of Contributory Negligence, 41 Ill.L.Rev. 151 (1946).

Since then, "gross" and "slight" negligence have been under a cloud, and discredited with the courts. They have largely lost their significance in the common law, both in England and in most states. Some vestiges still remain in the law of bailments, where some courts still hold that a gratuitous bailee owes his bailor only the duty of slight care, and so is liable only for gross negligence in looking after the goods. See, for example, Altman v. Aronson, 231 Mass. 588, 121 N.E. 505 (1919). The words "gross negligence" occasionally appear as words of art in automobile guest statutes. In that context, they have been construed to mean "the absence of slight care." See, for example, Hennon v. Hardin, 78 Ga.App. 81, 50 S.E.2d 236 (1948). On occasion they have been treated as synonyms for "recklessness." See Jackson v. Edwards, 144 Fla. 187, 197 So. 833 (1940).

(3) *Willful, wanton, and reckless conduct.* Another distinction is made by some courts based on defendant's state of mind. The effect is to establish an intermediate class of conduct, between negligence (including gross negligence) and intentional torts, which in some respects takes on the character of each. This type of conduct usually is defined as consisting of a deliberate and conscious disregard for a known high degree of probability of harm to another. Restatement (Second) of Torts § 500 (1965). This level of conduct is the threshold for punitive damages in many jurisdictions (see Chapter 10, Damages) and for particular causes of action in others. See, for example, Hickingbotham v. Burke, 140 N.H. 28, 662 A.2d 297 (1995) (recognizing cause of action for social host liability if service of alcohol was reckless) and Crawn v. Campo, 136 N.J. 494, 643 A.2d 600 (1994) (noting that majority of jurisdictions require plaintiff injured in recreational sports activity to prove that defendant's conduct was reckless, not merely negligent, in order to recover).

Automobile Guest Statutes

The use of the expressions "recklessness," "gross negligence" and "willful and wanton conduct" evolved for the most part in connection with statutes providing that the driver of an automobile is liable only for some form of aggravated misconduct to one who is riding as a guest in a car.

The principle of limiting the duty that a driver owes to an automobile guest originated in the Massachusetts case of Massaletti v. Fitzroy, 228

Mass. 487, 118 N.E. 168 (1917). The court derived the principle from what it regarded as an analogous situation—the relationship between a gratu-itous bailee and his bailor. While the *Massaletti* decision had only a minor impact on the case law of other states, it had an enormous impact on state legislatures. Over half the states adopted guest statutes, with quite a bit of variation in their categories and exceptions.

The many legislatures that followed *Massaletti* were persuaded by a persistent lobby on the part of some liability insurance companies. Ratio-nales included the possibility of collusion between host and injured guest in manufacturing a claim against the host's insurer, a fair allocation of a limited insurance fund to pedestrians and persons in other cars in prefer-ence to "guests," and savings in fuel by encouraging car pools.

The statutes filled the courts with cases, in which a good many knotty little problems of interpretation arose; and the efforts of many courts to get around the statute in cases of manifest hardship led to some rather peculiar law. First of all, who was a "guest"? What was the effect of sharing expenses, of the host's business interest in offering the ride, of an employer's order prohibiting the driver from taking free riders, of stow-aways, of a passenger's demand to be let out of the car? Once each state had settled those questions, there was the further problem of whether the driver's conduct in the particular case fit into the state's definition of "gross negligence," "recklessness," or "willful and wanton." A major subissue was whether or not plaintiff needed to prove that the defendant had actual knowledge of the risk involved. Compare Bailey v. Brown, 34 Ohio St.2d 62, 63 Ohio Op.2d 92, 295 N.E.2d 672 (1973) with Williamson v. McKenna, 223 Or. 366, 354 P.2d 56 (1960).

In Brown v. Merlo, 8 Cal.3d 855, 506 P.2d 212, 106 Cal.Rptr. 388 (1973), the Supreme Court of California held that the California guest statute denied "equal protection of the laws" to nonpaying automobile guests. See also Ramey v. Ramey, 273 S.C. 680, 258 S.E.2d 883 (1979) (South Carolina guest statute unconstitutional). Other state supreme courts found their guest statutes unconstitutional under state or federal constitutional provisions, and many state legislatures have repealed their guest statutes, recognizing their incompatibility with modern notions of risk distribution. See Woods, Goodbye and Good Riddance, 16 Cumb.L.Rev. 263 (1986) for a history of automobile guest statutes.

The legacy of the guest statutes is each state's definition of aggravated negligence, which today most often arises when juries decide whether to award punitive damages. See Chapter 10, Damages.

5. RULES OF LAW

Pokora v. Wabash Ry. Co.

Supreme Court of the United States, 1934.
292 U.S. 98, 54 S.Ct. 580, 78 L.Ed. 1149.

[Plaintiff, driving a truck, approached a level railroad crossing at which defendant had four tracks. Because of boxcars standing on the first track,

five or ten feet to the north of the crossing, he could not see the tracks to
the north. He stopped, looked as well as he could, and listened, but heard
no bell or whistle. He then drove slowly ahead, and when he reached the
main track was struck by a passenger train from the north, coming at a
speed of about thirty miles an hour. The trial court directed a verdict for
defendant, on the ground that plaintiff's conduct was contributory negligence as a matter of law, and this was affirmed by the Circuit Court of
Appeals. Certiorari was granted by the Supreme Court.]

Facts:

Mr. Justice Cardozo delivered the opinion of the Court. * * * The Circuit
Court of Appeals (one judge dissenting) affirmed, resting its judgment on
the opinion of this court in B. & O.R. Co. v. Goodman, 275 U.S. 66, 48 S.Ct.
24, 72 L.Ed. 167. * * *

The argument is made, however, that our decision in B. & O.R. Co. v.
Goodman, supra, is a barrier in the plaintiff's path, irrespective of the
conclusion that might commend itself if the question were at large. There is
no doubt that the opinion in that case is correct in its result. Goodman, the
driver, traveling only five or six miles an hour, had, before reaching the
track, a clear space of eighteen feet within which the train was plainly
visible. With that opportunity, he fell short of the legal standard of duty
established for a traveler when he failed to look and see. This was decisive
of the case. But the court did not stop there. It added a remark, unnecessary upon the facts before it, which has been a fertile source of controversy.
"In such circumstances it seems to us that if a driver cannot be sure
otherwise whether a train is dangerously near he must stop and get out of
his vehicle, although obviously he will not often be required to do more
than to stop and look."

Rule in B.&O.R Co. v. Goodman

There is need at this stage to clear the ground of brushwood that may
obscure the point at issue. We do not now inquire into the existence of a
duty to stop, disconnected from a duty to get out and reconnoitre. The
inquiry, if pursued, would lead us into the thickets of conflicting judgments. Some courts apply what is often spoken of as the Pennsylvania rule,
and impose an unyielding duty to stop, as well as to look and listen, no
matter how clear the crossing or the tracks on either side. * * *

Other courts, the majority, adopt the rule that the traveler must look
and listen, but that the existence of a duty to stop depends upon the
circumstances, and hence generally, even if not invariably, upon the judgment of the jury. * * * The subject has been less considered in this court,
but in none of its opinions is there a suggestion that at any and every
crossing the duty to stop is absolute, irrespective of the danger. Not even in
B. & O. R. Co. v. Goodman, supra, which goes farther than the earlier cases,
is there support for such a rule. To the contrary, the opinion makes it clear
that the duty is conditioned upon the presence of impediments whereby
sight and hearing become inadequate for the traveler's protection.

Choice between these diversities of doctrine is unnecessary for the
decision of the case at hand. Here the fact is not disputed that the plaintiff
did stop before he started to cross the tracks. If we assume that by reason
of the box cars, there was a duty to stop again when the obstructions had

Issue: contributory negligence of the plaintiff

been cleared, that duty did not arise unless a stop could be made safely after the point of clearance had been reached. * * * For reasons already stated, the testimony permits the inference that the truck was in the zone of danger by the time the field of vision was enlarged. No stop would then have helped the plaintiff if he remained seated on his truck, or so the triers of fact might find. His case was for the jury, unless as a matter of law he was subject to a duty to get out of the vehicle before it crossed the switch, walk forward to the front, and then, afoot, survey the scene. We must say whether his failure to do this was negligence so obvious and certain that one conclusion and one only is permissible for rational and candid minds.

Standards of prudent conduct are declared at times by courts, but they are taken over from the facts of life. To get out of a vehicle and reconnoitre is an uncommon precaution, as everyday experience informs us. Besides being uncommon, it is very likely to be futile, and sometimes even danger-ous. If the driver leaves his vehicle when he nears a cut or curve, he will learn nothing by getting out about the perils that lurk beyond. By the time he regains his seat and sets his car in motion, the hidden train may be upon him. * * * Often the added safeguard will be dubious though the track happens to be straight, as it seems that this one was, at all events as far as the station, about five blocks to the north. A train traveling at a speed of thirty miles an hour will cover a quarter of a mile in the space of thirty seconds. It may thus emerge out of obscurity as the driver turns his back to regain the waiting car, and may then descend upon him suddenly when his car is on the track. Instead of helping himself by getting out, he might do better to press forward with all his faculties alert. So a train at a neighboring station, apparently at rest and harmless, may be transformed in a few seconds into an instrument of destruction. At times the course of safety may be different. One can figure to oneself a roadbed so level and unbroken that getting out will be a gain. Even then the balance of advantage depends on many circumstances and can be easily disturbed. Where was Pokora to leave his truck after getting out to reconnoitre? If he was to leave it on the switch, there was the possibility that the box cars would be shunted down upon him before he could regain his seat. The defendant did not show whether there was a locomotive at the forward end, or whether the cars were so few that a locomotive could be seen. If he was to leave his vehicle near the curb, there was even stronger reason to believe that the space to be covered in going back and forth would make his observations worthless. One must remember that while the traveler turns his eyes in one direction, a train or a loose engine may be approaching from the other.

Illustrations such as these bear witness to the need for caution in framing standards of behavior that amount to rules of law. The need is the more urgent when there is no background of experience out of which the standards have emerged. They are then, not the natural flowerings of behavior in its customary forms, but rules artificially developed, and imposed from without. Extraordinary situations may not wisely or fairly be subjected to tests or regulations that are fitting for the commonplace or

Justice Holmes

normal. In default of the guide of customary conduct, what is suitable for the traveler caught in a mesh where the ordinary safeguards fail him is for the judgment of a jury. * * * The opinion in Goodman's Case has been a source of confusion in the federal courts to the extent that it imposes a standard for application by the judge, and has had only wavering support in the courts of the states. We limit it accordingly.

The judgment should be reversed, and the cause remanded for further proceedings in accordance with this opinion.

It is so ordered.

NOTES AND QUESTIONS

1. In Baltimore & Ohio R. Co. v. Goodman, 275 U.S. 66 (1927), Justice Holmes concluded his opinion with: "It is true * * * that the question of due care very generally is left to the jury. But we are dealing with a standard of conduct, and when the standard is clear it should be laid down once and for all by the courts."

Do you think that Justice Holmes really intended to declare a rule to which there could be no possible exceptions? How would he handle exceptional circumstances?

2. The decision created something of a furor. See Note, Aftermath of the Supreme Court's Stop, Look and Listen Rule, 43 Harv.L.Rev. 926 (1930). The rule stated has had something of a checkered history. In Green, The Duty Problem in Negligence Cases, 29 Colum.L.Rev. 255, 275 (1929), there is a short account of the economic background. When the railroads were new and poverty-stricken, it was considered more reasonable to put the burden of protecting himself upon the vehicle driver by an ironclad rule. Is there still the same justification?

3. Notwithstanding all the criticism, the general rule still has held up. In nearly all jurisdictions, it is still usually negligence as a matter of law not to look and listen when approaching a known railroad crossing, and not to slow down or even stop when obstructed vision or something else in the situation calls for it. See, for example, Chicago, R.I. & P.R. Co. v. McFarlin, 336 F.2d 1 (10th Cir.1964).

4. But over the years too many cases arose in which special circumstances made the rule an unreasonable one. Thus crossing gates were left open, as in Wabash R. Co. v. Glass, 32 F.2d 697 (6th Cir.1929). Or the driver relied on the absence of a customary flagman or flasher signal, as in Wabash R. Co. v. Walczak, 49 F.2d 763 (6th Cir.1931). Or it was clear that the conduct specified would have added nothing to the driver's safety, as in Torgeson v. Missouri–Kansas–Texas R. Co., 124 Kan. 798, 262 P. 564 (1928).

5. A similar fate has overtaken similar "rules of law," formerly stated by a good many courts as absolute, such as the rule that it is always negligence to drive an automobile at such a speed that it is impossible to stop within the range of vision. See, for example, Tapp v. Blackmore Ranch, Inc., 254 Neb. 40, 575 N.W.2d 341 (1998). Usually this is true. But the "rule" has had to give way when the driver is suddenly blinded by the lights of an approaching car, as in Emerson v. Bailey, 102 N.H. 360, 156 A.2d 762 (1959). Or a car ahead with a visible tail-light turns out to be backing up. Cerny v. Domer, 13 Ohio St.2d 117, 235 N.E.2d 132 (1968). Or there is a dense fog, and a sudden obstacle of an entirely unusual and unexpected kind turns up, such as the house being moved in the middle of the street in Morehouse v. Everett, 141 Wash. 399, 252 P. 157 (1926).

6. Compare the "rule" that a pedestrian crossing the street must continue to look all the way across. McKinney v. Yelavich, 352 Mich. 687, 90 N.W.2d 883 (1958) contains an excellent discussion of reducing negligence to fixed rules in this situation.

6. VIOLATION OF STATUTE

Osborne v. McMasters

Supreme Court of Minnesota, 1889.
40 Minn. 103, 41 N.W. 543.

Action for damages by M. Osborne, administrator, against S.R. McMasters, for the death of plaintiff's intestate, resulting from the use of poison sold without a label by defendant's clerk in the course of his employment. Judgment for plaintiff, and defendant appeals.

MITCHELL, J. Upon the record in this case it must be taken as the facts that defendant's clerk in his drug-store, in the course of his employment as such, sold to plaintiff's intestate a deadly poison without labeling it "Poison," as required by statute; that she, in ignorance of its deadly qualities, partook of the poison which caused her death. * * * It is now well settled, certainly in this state, that where a statute or municipal ordinance imposes upon any person a specific duty for the protection or benefit of others, if he neglects to perform that duty he is liable to those for whose protection or benefit it was imposed for any injuries of the character which the statute or ordinance was designed to prevent, and which were proximately produced by such neglect. * * * It is immaterial whether the duty is one imposed by the rule of common law requiring the exercise of ordinary care not to injure another, or is imposed by a statute designed for the protection of others. In either case the failure to perform the duty constitutes negligence, and renders the party liable for injuries resulting from it. The only difference is that in the one case the measure of legal duty is to be determined upon common-law principles, while in the other the statute fixes it, so that the violation of the statute constitutes conclusive evidence of negligence, or, in other words, negligence *per se.* The action in the latter case is not a statutory one, nor does the statute give the right of action in any other sense, except that it makes an act negligent which otherwise might not be such, or at least only evidence of negligence. All that the statute does is to establish a fixed standard by which the fact of negligence may be determined. The gist of the action is still negligence, or the non-performance of a legal duty to the person injured. * * *

Judgment affirmed.

NOTES AND QUESTIONS

1. Compare the remarks of Traynor, J. in Clinkscales v. Carver, 22 Cal.2d 72, 136 P.2d 777 (1943): "A statute that provides for a criminal proceeding only does not create a civil liability; if there is no provision for a remedy by civil action to persons injured by a breach of the statute it is because the Legislature did not contemplate one. A suit for damages is based on the theory that the conduct inflicting the injuries is a common-law tort, in this case the failure to exercise the care of a reasonable man at a boulevard stop. The significance of the statute in a civil suit for negligence lies in its formulation of a standard of conduct that the court adopts in the determination of such liability. (See Holmes, The Common Law, 120–129 (1881); Morris, The Relation of Criminal Statutes to Tort Liability, 46 Harv.L.Rev. 453 (1932).) The decision as to what the civil standard should be still rests with the court, and the standard formulated by a legislative body in a police regulation or criminal statute becomes the standard to determine civil liability only because the court accepts it. In the absence of such a standard the case goes to the jury, which must determine whether the defendant has acted as a reasonably prudent man would act in similar circumstances. The jury then has the burden of deciding not only what the facts are but what the unformulated standard is of reasonable conduct. When a legislative body has generalized a standard from the

experience of the community and prohibits conduct that is likely to cause harm, the court accepts the formulated standards and applies them.''

2.   Why give any effect at all in a civil action for negligence to a statute which merely specifies a crime, and provides for a criminal penalty? What about the following arguments?

A.   The reasonable person will always obey the criminal law. Is this true? Should it be a question for the jury? What about a statute such as the legendary one providing that when two railroad trains approach a crossing each shall stop and neither shall move forward until the other has passed by?

B.   The legislature intended, or is ''presumed'' to have intended, a civil remedy for the violation. What is the probability as to the state of mind of the legislature: (1) it did intend to provide a civil remedy, but did not say so; (2) it intended not to provide one and therefore omitted it; (3) it never thought about the matter at all?

C.   The statute gives rise to a right. A right without a remedy is useless and the court supplies an appropriate remedy. *Ubi ius ibi remedium.*

D.   The court adopts the standard of conduct from the criminal statute and lays it down as a rule of law in the civil action. See the preceding section. See Chapter 23, Torts in the Age of Statutes, on the effect of statutes on torts other than negligence.

3.   What if a criminal statute is invalid for criminal prosecutions? For example, an ordinance establishing an arterial stop sign, and requiring drivers to stop under criminal penalty, was never properly published, as required for the adoption of such ordinances. Does this prevent the court, in a negligence action, from adopting the stop as a required standard of conduct? A number of cases say, no. See Lewis v. Miami, 127 Fla. 426, 173 So. 150 (1937); Ponca City v. Reed, 115 Okl. 166, 242 P. 164 (1925); Clinkscales v. Carver, 22 Cal.2d 72, 136 P.2d 777 (1943). What if the statute is that of a neighboring jurisdiction where the violation took place? Cf. Gaines–Tabb v. ICI Explosives, USA, Inc., 160 F.3d 613 (10th Cir.1998) (victims of bombing of Oklahoma City federal building filed negligence per se claim based on violation of Kansas fertilizer labeling statute against manufacturer of ammonium nitrate, which was used to construct the bomb).

4.   Must the court accept the statute's definition of reasonable conduct as controlling? See the next three cases.

(A) APPLICABILITY OF STATUTE

Stachniewicz v. Mar–Cam Corp.

Supreme Court of Oregon, 1971.
259 Or. 583, 488 P.2d 436.

HOLMAN, JUSTICE. The patron of a drinking establishment seeks to recover against the operator for personal injuries allegedly inflicted by other customers during a barroom brawl. The jury returned a verdict for defendant. Plaintiff appealed.

From the evidence introduced, the jury could find as follows:

A fight erupted in a bar between a group of persons of American Indian ancestry, who were sitting in a booth, and other customers who were at an adjacent table with plaintiff. One of plaintiff's friends had refused to allow a patron from the booth to dance with the friend's wife because the stranger was intoxicated. Thereafter, such threats as, "Hey, Whitey, how big are you?" were shouted from the booth at plaintiff and his companions. One of the persons at the table, after complaining to the bartender, was warned by him, "Don't start trouble with those guys." Soon thereafter, those individuals who had been sitting in the booth approached the table and one of them knocked down a person who was talking to a member of plaintiff's party. With that, the brawl commenced.

After a short melee, someone shouted "Fuzz!" and those persons who had been sitting in the booth ran out a door and into the parking lot, with one of plaintiff's friends in hot pursuit. Upon reaching the door, the friend discovered plaintiff lying just outside with his feet wedging the door open.

Plaintiff suffered retrograde amnesia and could remember nothing of the events of the evening. No one could testify to plaintiff's whereabouts at the time the band in the booth went on the warpath or to the cause of the vicious head injuries which plaintiff displayed when the brawl was ended.

The customers in the booth had been drinking in defendant's place of business for approximately two and one-half hours before the affray commenced.

The principal issue is whether, as plaintiff contends, violations of ORS 471.410(3) and of Oregon Liquor Control Regulation No. 10–065(2) constitute negligence as a matter of law. The portion of the statute relied on by plaintiff reads as follows:

"(3) No person shall give or otherwise make available any alcoholic liquor to a person visibly intoxicated * * *."

The portion of the regulation to which plaintiff points provides:

"(2) No licensee shall permit or suffer any loud, noisy, disorderly or boisterous conduct, or any profane or abusive language, in or upon his licensed premises, or permit any visibly intoxicated person to enter or remain upon his licensed premises."

The trial court held that a violation of either the statute or the regulation did not constitute negligence per se. It refused requested instructions and withdrew allegations of negligence which were based on their violation.

A violation of a statute or regulation constitutes negligence as a matter of law when the violation results in injury to a member of the class of persons intended to be protected by the legislation and when the harm is of the kind which the statute or regulation was enacted to prevent. [Cc] The reason behind the rule is that when a legislative body has generalized a standard from the experience of the community and prohibits conduct that is likely to cause harm the court accepts the formulation. Justice Traynor in Clinkscales v. Carver, 22 Cal.2d 72, 136 P.2d 777 (1943).

However, in addition, it is proper for the court to examine preliminarily the appropriateness of the standard as a measure of care for civil litigation under the circumstances presented. F. James, Jr., "Statutory

Standards and Negligence in Accident Cases," 11 La.L.Rev. 95, 111–12 (1950–51); Restatement (Second) of Torts § 286, comment *d* (1965). The statute in question prevents making available alcohol to a person who is *already visibly intoxicated.* This makes the standard particularly inappropriate for the awarding of civil damages because of the extreme difficulty, if not impossibility, of determining whether a third party's injuries would have been caused, in any event, by the already inebriated person. Unless we are prepared to say that an alcoholic drink given after visible intoxication is the cause of a third party's injuries as a matter of law, a concept not advanced by anyone, the standard would be one almost impossible of application by a factfinder in most circumstances. * * *

The regulation promulgated by the commission is an altogether different matter. * * *

ORS 471.030, entitled "Purpose of Liquor Control Act," provides, in part, as follows:

"(1) The Liquor Control Act shall be liberally construed so as:

"(a) To prevent the recurrence of abuses associated with saloons or resorts for the consumption of alcoholic beverages." * * *

An examination of the regulation discloses that it concerns matters having a direct relation to the creation of physical disturbances in bars which would, in turn, create a likelihood of injury to customers. A common feature of our western past, now preserved in story and reproduced on the screen hundreds of times, was the carnage of the barroom brawl. No citation of authority is needed to establish that the "abuses associated with saloons," which the Liquor Control Act seeks to prevent, included permitting on the premises profane, abusive conduct and drunken clientele (now prohibited by the regulation) which results in serious personal injuries to customers in breach of the bar owner's duty to protect his patrons from harm. We find it reasonable to assume that the commission, in promulgating the regulation, intended to prevent these abuses, and that they had in mind the safety of patrons of bars as well as the general peace and quietude of the community. In view of the quoted purpose of the Act and of the history of injury to innocent patrons of saloons, we cannot assume otherwise.

In addition, we see no reason why the standard is not an appropriate one for use in the awarding of civil damages. Because plaintiff was within the class of persons intended to be protected by the regulation and the harm caused to him was the kind the statute was intended to prevent, we hold that the trial court erred in (not) treating the alleged violations of the regulation as negligence as a matter of law. * * *

We believe it would be fair for the jury to infer, in the circumstances set forth in the statement of the facts, that plaintiff was injured by one of the persons in the booth who had created the disturbance and that the injuries would not have occurred except for defendant's violation of the commission's regulation, as alleged.

The judgment of the trial court is reversed and the case is remanded for a new trial.

NOTES AND QUESTIONS

1. Why does the opinion identify the "ancestry" of the bar patrons sitting in the booth?

2. What is the basis upon which a court seeks to select or reject a criminal statute as a standard of care in a particular tort suit? This is not a readily solvable problem. The court must determine that

A. The party seeking to charge the other with violation of the statute is a member of the class the legislature intended to protect. See Thomas v. Baltimore & O.R. Co., 19 Md.App. 217, 310 A.2d 186 (1973) (plaintiff who knew of location of railway crossing not in class to be protected by regulation requiring warning); Erickson v. Kongsli, 40 Wash.2d 79, 240 P.2d 1209 (1952) (abutting landowner's property damaged when defendant made an illegal left turn—not in class to be protected); Distad v. Cubin, 633 P.2d 167 (Wyo.1981) (violation of regulations on emergency treatment not negligence per se when plaintiff did not appear to need emergency care—not in class to be protected); Lockhart v. Loosen, 943 P.2d 1074 (Okla.1997) (plaintiff, who had contracted herpes from her husband after his extramarital affair with defendant, could not use negligence per se to prove her case because she was not in the class of persons the legislature intended to protect in passing legislation that prohibited diseased persons from marrying or otherwise exposing others to venereal disease).

What result in the principal case if an employee of the drinking establishment had been injured in the melee?

B. The hazard that occurred was one the legislature intended to prevent. The leading case on the "different hazard" is Gorris v. Scott, L.R. 9 Ex. 125 (1874), where a contagious diseases act required that animals shipped by boat be kept in pens, to avoid the spread of disease. Plaintiff's sheep were washed overboard from defendant's boat during a storm, because they were not in pens. It was held that the violation of the statute did not make the defendant liable for the loss of the sheep.

What result in the principal case if plaintiff had been injured when an intoxicated person had stumbled and fallen upon him?

C. Whether it is appropriate to impose tort liability for violations of the statute. See Stevens v. Luther, 105 Neb. 184, 180 N.W. 87 (1920) (six mile an hour speed limit); Stafford v. Chippewa Valley Electric R. Co., 110 Wis. 331, 85 N.W. 1036 (1901) (requirement that a street bell be rung continuously); Ridge v. Cessna Aircraft Co., 117 F.3d 126 (applying Virginia law) (4th Cir. 1997) (FAA regulations for general guidelines and standards of conduct for pilots too general to warrant application as negligence standard).

3. The Restatement (Second) of Torts spells out in greater detail these requirements in § 287, and it states in § 288:

"The court will not adopt as the standard of conduct of a reasonable man the requirements of a legislative enactment or an administrative regulation whose purpose is found to be exclusively

"(a) to protect the interests of the state or any subdivision of it as such, or

"(b) to secure to individuals the enjoyment of rights or privileges to which they are entitled only as members of the public, or "(c) to impose upon the actor the performance of a service which the state or any subdivision of it undertakes to give the public, or

"(d) to protect a class of persons other than the one whose interests are invaded, or

"(e) to protect another interest than the one invaded, or

"(f) to protect against other harm than that which has resulted, or

"(g) to protect against any other hazards than that from which the harm has resulted."

4.   Because state legislative history may be scanty and also difficult to obtain, there may be wide latitude for a court to decide who is in the "class" or what was the "hazard" that the legislature had in mind. On occasion the court may rely on the title or the preamble of the statute. Compare Kelly v. Henry Muhs Co., 71 N.J.Law 358, 59 A. 23 (1904) with Drake v. Fenton, 237 Pa. 8, 85 A. 14 (1912).

5.   *Federal statutes and regulations.* There is no "doctrine" of negligence per se in federal law. If there is no general federal common law of negligence as a result of Erie R. Co. v. Tompkins, 304 U.S. 64 (1938), the federal courts are in no position to adopt a criminal statutory rule of conduct as a civil rule of conduct replacing the general standard of care. The result is that they find it necessary to "imply" a civil action from the criminal statute, thus placing the responsibility for the action on the Congress. See Chapter 23. Should violation of a federal statute be a basis for finding negligence per se in a state court? Surprisingly, there is very little consideration of this issue. See Steagall v. Dot Mfg. Corp., 223 Tenn. 428, 446 S.W.2d 515 (1969), where the court assumed that violation of the Federal Hazardous Substances Act might be negligence per se but found no proximate cause. In a case of first impression in Idaho, a state court found that violation of Occupational Safety and Health Administration regulations constituted negligence per se as a matter of state law. Sanchez v. Galey, 112 Idaho 609, 733 P.2d 1234 (1986). In diversity cases where they are applying state law, federal courts have sometimes assumed, without careful consideration, that the state court would apply negligence per se to a federal statute or regulation. See Orthopedic Equip. Co. v. Eutsler, 276 F.2d 455 (4th Cir.1960) (Federal Food, Drug & Cosmetic Act—Virginia law); Gober v. Revlon, Inc., 317 F.2d 47 (4th Cir.1963) (same—California law); Ridge v. Cessna Aircraft Co., 117 F.3d 126 (4th Cir.1997) (FAA regulations—Virginia law; inapplicable for other reasons).

6.   *Ordinances.* Generally, ordinances have been treated in the same manner as statutes. A few states give a lesser effect to ordinances than they do to statutes.

7.   *Administrative regulations.* Unlike the principal case, regulations promulgated under the authority of administrative agencies are sometimes given lesser effect than statutes. See, e.g., Chambers v. St. Mary's School, 82 Ohio St.3d 563, 697 N.E.2d 198 (1998) (violation of administrative rule does not constitute negligence per se, but may be admissible as evidence of negligence); Elliott v. S.D. Warren Co., 134 F.3d 1 (1st Cir.1998) (applying Maine law) (OSHA regulation, at best, is on par with statute and thus evidence of negligence under Maine law); Hassan v. Stafford, 472 F.2d 88 (3d Cir.1973); Morris, The Role of Administrative Safety Measures in Negligence Actions, 28 Tex.L.Rev. 143 (1949). Is an OSHA regulation that applies to employers admissible against the manufacturer of an allegedly defective machine used in the workplace? See Hansen v. Abrasive Engineering and Mfg., Inc., 317 Or. 378, 856 P.2d 625 (1993) (admitted and given same weight as industry custom).

8. *Advisory codes, voluntary industry standards.* Advisory safety codes promulgated by governmental authority, industry or voluntary associations may be admissible, though not binding, on the issue of negligence if properly identified and shown through expert testimony to have general acceptance in the industrial community. See Lemery v. O'Shea Dennis, Inc., 112 N.H. 199, 291 A.2d 616 (1972); Philo, Use of Safety Standards, Codes and Practices in Tort Litigation, 41 N.D.Law. 1 (1965). Many jurisdictions will not admit them, however, on the ground that their use by an expert does not cure the hearsay problem.

Ney v. Yellow Cab Co.

Illinois Supreme Court, 1954.
2 Ill.2d 74, 117 N.E.2d 74.

MAXWELL, JUSTICE. * * * The Appellate Court here affirmed the trial court's judgment fixing liability on the defendant for violation of a section of the Uniform Traffic Act. The plaintiff charged that defendant, by its servant, negligently permitted its taxicab to remain unattended on a Chicago street without first stopping the engine or locking the ignition or removing the key, contrary to a section of said act. The undisputed facts reveal that a thief stole the taxicab and while in flight ran into plaintiff's vehicle causing property damage. Defendant's motion to dismiss the complaint was based on the theory that the acts or omissions of the defendant did not constitute actionable negligence, nor the proximate cause of the damage. Briefly stated, plaintiff contended that the defendant's violation of the statute was negligence and the proximate cause of the damage.

The statute in question, section 92 of article XIV of the Uniform Traffic Act, provides: "(a) No person driving or in charge of a motor vehicle shall permit it to stand unattended without first stopping the engine, locking the ignition and removing the key, or when standing upon any perceptible grade without effectively setting the brake thereon and turning the front wheels to the curb or side of the highway. (b) No person shall operate or drive a motor vehicle who is under fifteen years of age." Ill.Rev.Stat.1953, chap. 95½, par. 189; Jones Ann.Stat. 85.221.

The defendant takes the position that this particular statute is not an antitheft measure but is a traffic regulation, the violation of which could impose no liability on the owner or operator of the vehicle for the misconduct of a thief, for the reason that, under such circumstances, the violation of the statute is not actionable negligence in that the misconduct is neither negligence with relation to the resulting injury, nor its proximate cause. The plaintiff, on the other hand, contends that the statute is a safety measure for the benefit of the public; that its violation is prima facie evidence of negligence; and that reasonable persons might reasonably foresee that its violation could result in the consequences which occurred here. The plaintiff further contends that irrespective of the statute there would be a common-law liability under the same circumstances, and that in either event the questions of negligence and proximate cause are, under the facts alleged and admitted here, questions of fact and not questions of law.
* * *

We have carefully studied the reasoning of our Appellate Courts and the courts of the other jurisdictions, in the light of these distinctions, and conclude that the issue presented requires our determination of the following questions: (a) What was the legislative intention? (b) Is the violation of the statute the proximate cause of the injury? (c) Is the act of the thief an intervening, independent, efficient force which breaks the causal connection between the original wrong and the injury?

Labeling of the statute does not solve the problem. Defendant urges that the statute is a traffic regulation and not an antitheft measure, and from this premise reasons to a conclusion of nonliability. It seems to argue that if it were an antitheft measure liability would attach in this case. * * * We think the key to the construction of the statute with regard to the legislative intention appears in the statute itself. The requirement that the brakes be set and the wheels turned to the curb on a grade is no material theft deterrent. The second subparagraph of the section prohibiting persons under fifteen years of age from operating a motor vehicle indicates to us that the legislature was thinking about the danger to the public in permitting persons lacking in experience, judgment, knowledge and maturity to operate such vehicles. We cannot but conclude that this entire section is a public safety measure. This being so, what harm did the legislature foresee and attempt to prevent by prohibiting the leaving of an unattended motor vehicle with the key in the ignition? The motor vehicle with the key in its ignition in itself could obviously do no harm.

Consequently, there enters into our consideration the question of foreseeability as to intervention of outside agencies not under the control of the person in charge of the motor vehicle. The drawing of lines of demarcation in problems of cause and effect is often difficult in the study of formal logic and these difficulties are not minimized in the field of jurisprudence. We cannot say that the legislature intended to distinguish between certain types of outside agencies without expressing such distinction. Such a distinction would be too tenuous a ground to serve as a basis for decision in view of the broad general sweep of the statutory language employed. The legislature has here used clear and express terms making it the duty of persons in charge of motor vehicles to do certain acts upon leaving their vehicles unattended. The motivation of such legislation is not the State's desire to punish but rather its interest in public welfare for protection of life, limb and property by prevention of recognized hazards.

The violation of the statute is prima facie evidence of negligence under the prevailing rule of this State. [Cc] This in itself creates no liability. The injury must have a direct and proximate connection with the violation of the statute before liability will be held to exist. It is the existence of this cause and effect relationship which makes the negligence of the defendant actionable.

Where an independent agency intervenes, the solution of the problem becomes aggravated. * * *

A further problem is presented when the independent agency is an illegal or criminal act. Wrongful acts of independent third persons, not actually intended by the defendant, are not regarded by the law as natural consequences of his wrong, and he is not bound to anticipate the general probability of such acts, any more than a particular act by this or that individual. The rule applies a fortiori to criminal acts. The intervention of a criminal act, however, does not necessarily interrupt the relation of cause and effect between negligence and an injury. If at the time of the negligence, the criminal act might reasonably have been foreseen, the causal chain is not broken by the intervention of such act. * * *

The speed and power of automobiles have increased to the extent that safety experts are now showing keen awareness of their potentials even in the hands of rightful owners and careful operators. Incidents of serious havoc caused by runaway thieves or irresponsible juveniles in stolen or "borrowed" motor vehicles frequently shock the readers of the daily press. With this background must come a recognition of the probable danger of resulting injury consequent to permitting a motor vehicle to become easily available to an unauthorized person through violation of the statute in question. The percentage of cases of this nature or the incidence of injury done where an independent force has intervened after such violation, however, is not the standard or measure of liability. We are here concerned only with the question as to whether or not this intervening force is without or within the range of reasonable anticipation and probability. * * *

* * * [W]e recall the reasoning of Justice Cardozo, that the range of reasonable apprehension is at times for the court, and at times, if varying inferences are possible, a question for the jury. The possibility of varying inferences in a case such as the one before us has been amply demonstrated. * * *

We are in agreement with the court below in our belief that reasonable men might differ on the question where there were special circumstances surrounding the defendant's violation of the statute which may be the proximate cause of the damage that followed. We * * * believe that under the circumstances as presented in the case before us we find no persuasive authority and no impelling reasoning for this court to hold, *as a matter of law,* that no actionable negligence can exist.

Holding

Questions of negligence, due care and proximate cause are ordinarily questions of fact for a jury to decide. The right of trial by jury is recognized in the Magna Charta, our Declaration of Independence and both our State and Federal constitutions. It is a fundamental right in our democratic judicial system. Questions which are composed of such qualities sufficient to cause reasonable men to arrive at different results should never be determined as matters of law. The debatable quality of issues such as negligence and proximate cause, the fact that fair-minded men might reach different conclusions, emphasize the appropriateness and necessity of leaving such questions to a fact-finding body. The jury is the tribunal under our legal system to decide that type of issue. To withdraw such questions from the jury is to usurp its function. [C]

For the foregoing reasons, it is our opinion that the Appellate Court was correct in affirming the judgment of the municipal court of Chicago.

Judgment affirmed.

HERSHEY, J., dissenting. The majority opinion is contradictory within itself. It first concludes that section 92 of article XIV of the Uniform Traffic Act [C] is not an antitheft statute, but is, in fact, a public safety measure. Although the opinion fails to answer in specific fashion its question as to what harm the legislature foresaw and attempted to prevent by the passage of this act, it does ultimately determine that the statute was to prevent accidents caused by a thief in stealing the vehicle. This determination is manifest by the majority's adoption of the Appellate Court determination. The majority thus finds the statute, or at least that part of the statute rendering it unlawful to fail to remove the keys from a parked vehicle, to be an antitheft measure. * * *

The majority concludes that all parts of this statute, except that portion referring to the keys, indicate an intention on the part of the legislature to prevent harm to the public by an inadvertent or negligent movement of a parked vehicle, or through its being driven by a young person devoid of experience, judgment, knowledge, or maturity. It finds that the legislature's purpose in relation to those portions of the statute was not to deter theft. However, the majority then concludes that the portion directing the removal of the keys from the vehicle was to prevent the operation of the vehicle and possible public harm by a thief in flight. The slightest experience renders everyone cognizant of the fact that the removal of automobile ignition keys is only a minor deterrent, if any, to the theft of an automobile and a subsequent flight from detection and pursuit. Consequently, it is only reasonable and logical to construe the legislature's intention in the passage of this portion of the statute in the same light as is attributed to the remainder of the section. One can only conclude, therefore, that the legislature required the removal of the key to prevent a mere negligent or inadvertent starting of the automobile and an ensuing uncontrolled movement thereof. Obviously the legislature could not presume by such legislation to prevent a wilful movement of the vehicle by an unauthorized person. It is generally recognized that one may leave a motor vehicle standing unattended in a public street temporarily, without being guilty of negligence, provided he takes the ordinary precautions of securing it by the appliances with which it is equipped for that purpose, and that if it is thereafter set in motion by the wilful or negligent act of a third person, such wilful or negligent act will be deemed the proximate cause of the accident or injury resulting therefrom and the owner will not be liable. * * *

This section, not being an antitheft measure, and not making the failure to remove the key an absolute act of negligence, cannot constitute the proximate cause of this injury. But for the intervention of the theft the failure to remove the key could not have caused this injury. Moreover, unless the thief was in immediate flight from the scene of his theft, the act of thievery could not even be a factor contributing to the injury. * * *

NOTES AND QUESTIONS

1. The principal case illustrates how much discretion a court may have in determining the purpose of a statute. Was the purpose of this key-in-the-car statute to prevent theft of the car, with resulting loss to the owner and his insurance company and an increased burden on the police? Cf. Anderson v. Theisen, 231 Minn. 369, 43 N.W.2d 272 (1950). To prevent the car from being started up by children or other irresponsible people? Cf. Bouldin v. Sategna, 71 N.M. 329, 378 P.2d 370 (1963). To prevent joy-riding teenagers from "taking it out for a spree"? Cf. Kozicki v. Dragon, 255 Neb. 248, 583 N.W.2d 336 (1998) (statute is for protection of users of public streets; teenage thief testified that four or five of the cars she had previously stolen had ended up wrecked). To prevent it from being stolen by a tense thief, endangering people in the vicinity while trying to make his getaway?

2. Observe how the two opinions in this case argue for a single purpose. May there not be more than one purpose? Cf. Hines v. Foreman, 243 S.W. 479 (Tex.Com.App.1922). The statute prohibited use of a "cut-out" in the exhaust pipe leading to the muffler, in order to make a zooming or roaring noise. Plaintiff had his cut-out open driving down the streets of a Texas city. He approached a railroad track, and unknown to him because of the noise of the cut-out, there was a train coming and he was engaged in a race that ended in a tie. The issue was whether he was contributorily negligent, and he claimed that the statute was irrelevant because its purpose was to prevent harassing noises. Held, it had a double purpose, and one of them was to eliminate noises preventing him from hearing traffic hazards.

3. The statute at issue in the principal case is part of the Uniform Vehicle Code prepared and revised by the National Committee on Uniform Traffic Laws and Ordinances and continuously monitored and revised. It is in a chapter on safety provisions and committee members have stated that it was intended as a safety measure. Is this relevant? For a strong case holding that the purpose includes a thief making a getaway, with the opinion written by Judge Edgerton, a former torts teacher, see Ross v. Hartman, 139 F.2d 14 (D.C.Cir.1943).

4. Who makes the decision as to the purpose of the statute—judge or jury?

5. Both opinions in the principal case became heavily involved in the problem of proximate cause. In theory, there should be no problem of proximate cause if the event is within the hazard that the statute is intended to avert. By deciding the purpose of the statute, the court implicitly finds proximate cause. See Ross v. Hartman, note 3. Is there an element of begging the question by following this procedure? But it may simplify some of the difficulties of proximate cause. Look for it later when the subject of proximate cause is taken up.

6. A statute requires that a seller of a "deadly weapon receive positive identification" of the purchaser from two residents of the state, and keep a record of name, age, address and other details. Defendant sells a gun without complying, and the purchaser uses it on the plaintiff in the course of an armed robbery. Should the defendant be liable? Cf. Hetherton v. Sears, Roebuck & Co., 593 F.2d 526 (3d Cir.1979), second appeal, 652 F.2d 1152 (3d Cir.1981). Fertilizer manufacturer sells ammonium nitrate, allegedly in violation of various federal and state labeling statutes. Terrorist uses it to construct bomb. Should the manufacturer be liable? Gaines–Tabb v. ICI Explosives, USA, Inc., 160 F.3d 613 (10th Cir.1998) (case brought by victims of bombing of Oklahoma City federal building dismissed due to lack of causal link between alleged statutory violations and injury).

►Perry v. S.N. and S.N.

Texas Supreme Court, 1998.
973 S.W.2d 301.

PHILLIPS, CHIEF JUSTICE. * * * This is a suit for injuries arising out of the abuse of children at a day care center. Plaintiffs filed suit individually and as next friends of their two children, alleging that defendants witnessed the abuse and failed to report it to the police or child welfare officials. The sole issue before us is whether plaintiffs may maintain a cause of action for negligence per se based on the Family Code, which requires any person having cause to believe a child is being abused to report the abuse to state authorities and makes the knowing failure to do so a misdemeanor. See TEX. FAM. CODE §§ 261.101(a), 261.109 (formerly TEX. FAM. CODE §§ 34.01, 34.07). The trial court granted summary judgment for defendants, but the court of appeals reversed and remanded plaintiffs' negligence per se and gross negligence claims for trial. [C] We reverse the judgment of the court of appeals and render judgment that plaintiffs take nothing. Because plaintiffs did not preserve their common law negligence claims, we do not decide whether there should be a common law duty to report child abuse in some circumstances.

B.N. and K.N. attended a day care center operated by Francis Keller and her husband Daniel Keller from March 25, 1991, to August 28, 1991. Their parents, S.N. and S.N., allege that during that period, Daniel Keller regularly abused B.N. and K.N. and other children at the center both physically and sexually. Mr. and Mrs. N. brought suit against the Kellers and three of the Kellers' friends, Douglas Perry, Janise White, and Raul Quintero. Plaintiffs claim that Francis Keller confided in White at an unspecified time that Daniel Keller had "abusive habits toward children." They further allege that on one occasion in August 1991, while visiting the Kellers, defendants Perry, White, and Quintero all saw Daniel Keller bring a number of children out of the day care center into the Kellers' adjoining home and sexually abuse them. The record does not indicate whether B.N. and K.N. were among these children. According to plaintiffs, Perry, White, and Quintero did not attempt to stop Daniel Keller from abusing the children or report his crimes to the police or child welfare authorities. * * *

Mr. and Mrs. N. alleged only that Perry, White, and Quintero were negligent per se because they violated a statute requiring any person who "has cause to believe that a child's physical or mental health or welfare has been or may be adversely affected by abuse" to file a report with the police or the Department of Protective and Regulatory Services. [C] Plaintiffs also asserted gross negligence and common law negligence claims. They claimed that Perry, White, and Quintero's failure to report the abuse proximately caused them harm by permitting the day care center to remain open, thus enabling Daniel Keller to continue abusing the children at the center. They sought damages for pain, mental anguish, and medical expenses, as well as loss of income when they could not work outside the home because of B.N. and K.N.'s injuries.

Perry, White, and Quintero moved for summary judgment on the sole ground that plaintiffs failed to state a cause of action. * * *

The trial court granted Perry, White, and Quintero's motions for summary judgment and severed plaintiffs' claims against those three defendants from their suit against the Kellers, which is not before us. * * * When the ground for the trial court's decision is that plaintiffs failed to state a cause of action, we must take the allegations in the pleadings as true in determining whether a cause of action exists. [C]

The court of appeals affirmed the summary judgment on plaintiffs' common law negligence claims but reversed and remanded for trial on the issues of negligence per se and gross negligence, holding that a violation of the Family Code's child abuse reporting requirement is negligence per se. [C] Mr. and Mrs. N. have not appealed the court of appeals' judgment affirming the summary judgment against them on common law negligence. Therefore, the question of whether Texas should impose a new common law duty to report child abuse on the facts of this case is not before us.* * *

"It is fundamental that the existence of a legally cognizable duty is a prerequisite to all tort liability." Graff v. Beard, 858 S.W.2d 918, 919 (Tex.1993). The court of appeals found a duty in the [mandatory child abuse reporting statute.] * * *

All persons have a duty to obey the criminal law in the sense that they may be prosecuted for not doing so, but this is not equivalent to a duty in tort. See, e.g., Smith v. Merritt, 940 S.W.2d 602, 607–08 (Tex.1997) (statute making it a crime to furnish alcohol to persons under age 21 did not impose a tort duty on social hosts). "It is well-established that the mere fact that the Legislature adopts a criminal statute does not mean that this court must accept it as a standard for civil liability." [C] "The considerations which warrant imposing tort liability are not identical with those which warrant criminal conviction," Morris, The Role of Criminal Statutes in Negligence Actions, 49 COLUM. L. REV. 21, 22–23 (1949), and we will not apply the doctrine of negligence per se if the criminal statute does not provide an appropriate basis for civil liability. * * *

Before we begin our analysis of whether section 261.109 of the Family Code is an appropriate basis for tort liability, we emphasize that we must look beyond the facts of this particular case to consider the full reach of the statute. We do not decide today whether a statute criminalizing only the type of egregious behavior with which these defendants are charged—the failure of eyewitnesses to report the sexual molestation of preschool children—would be an appropriate basis for a tort action. That is not the statute the Legislature passed. Rather, the issue before us is whether it is appropriate to impose tort liability on any and every person who "has cause to believe that a child's physical or mental health or welfare has been or may be adversely affected by abuse or neglect and knowingly fails to report." [C] Cf. Leonard, The Application of Criminal Legislation to Negligence Cases: A Reexamination, 23 SANTA CLARA L. REV. 427, 457–66

(1983) (contrasting the rigidity of statutory standards with the flexibility of case-by-case common law determinations of duty and breach).

The threshold questions in every negligence per se case are whether the plaintiff belongs to the class that the statute was intended to protect and whether the plaintiff's injury is of a type that the statute was designed to prevent. [Cc] Texas's first mandatory child abuse reporting statute, from which Family Code section 261.101(a) is derived, stated that "the purpose of this Act is to protect children who ... are adversely affected by abuse or neglect." [C] Similarly, the current Family Code provision governing the investigation of reports of child abuse states that "the primary purpose of the investigation shall be the protection of the child." [C]

B.N. and K.N. are within the class of persons whom the child abuse reporting statute was meant to protect, and they suffered the kind of injury that the Legislature intended the statute to prevent. [Footnote omitted.] But this does not end our inquiry. [C] The Court must still determine whether it is appropriate to impose tort liability for violations of the statute. [C] This determination is informed by a number of factors, some discussed by the court of appeals in this case and others derived from past negligence per se decisions of Texas courts and from scholarly analysis. These factors are not necessarily exclusive, nor is the issue properly resolved by merely counting how many factors lean each way. Rather, we set out these considerations as guides to assist a court in answering the ultimate question of whether imposing tort liability for violations of a criminal statute is fair, workable, and wise.

We first consider the fact that, absent a change in the common law, a negligence per se cause of action against these defendants would derive the element of duty solely from the Family Code. At common law there is generally no duty to protect another from the criminal acts of a third party or to come to the aid of another in distress. [Cc] Although there are exceptions to this no-duty rule, see, e.g., Lefmark Management Co. v. Old, 946 S.W.2d 52, 53 (Tex.1997) (noting that under some circumstances, person in control of premises has duty to protect invitees from crime), this case does not fall within any of the established exceptions, and Mr. and Mrs. N. have not asked this Court to impose on persons who are aware of child abuse a new common law duty to report it or take other protective action.

In contrast, the defendant in most negligence per se cases already owes the plaintiff a pre-existing common law duty to act as a reasonably prudent person, so that the statute's role is merely to define more precisely what conduct breaches that duty. [Cc] For example, the overwhelming majority of this Court's negligence per se cases have involved violations of traffic statutes by drivers and train operators—actors who already owed a common law duty to exercise reasonable care toward others on the road or track. [Cc]

When a statute criminalizes conduct that is also governed by a common law duty, as in the case of a traffic regulation, applying negligence per se causes no great change in the law because violating the statutory standard of conduct would usually also be negligence under a common law reasonableness standard. [Cc] But recognizing a new, purely statutory duty "can have an extreme effect upon the common law of negligence" when it allows a cause of action where the common law would not. In such a situation, applying negligence per se "brings into existence a new type of tort liability." Burnette v. Wahl, 284 Ore. 705, 588 P.2d 1105, 1109 (Or.1978). The change tends to be especially great when, as here, the statute criminalizes inaction rather than action.

Some commentators contend that the term "negligence per se" does not even apply when the statute on which civil liability is based corresponds to no common law duty. See Keeton et al., Prosser & Keeton on the Law of Torts § 36, at 221 n.9; Forell, The Statutory Duty Action in Tort: A Statutory/Common Law Hybrid, 23 IND. L. REV. 781, 782 (1990). While our definition has never been so restrictive, this Court in fact has created a new duty by applying negligence per se on only one occasion. * * * Thus, based on both this Court's past practice and the observations of noted scholars, we conclude that the absence of a relevant common law duty should be considered in deciding whether to apply negligence per se to the Family Code's reporting provision.

The court of appeals in this case listed several factors to consider in deciding whether to apply negligence per se. [Cc] According to the court of appeals, the principal factors favoring negligence per se are that the Legislature has determined that compliance with criminal statutes is practicable and desirable and that criminal statutes give citizens notice of what conduct is required of them. [C] As considerations against negligence per se, the court of appeals cautioned that some penal statutes may be too obscure to put the public on notice, may impose liability without fault, or may lead to ruinous monetary liability for relatively minor offenses. [C] The first of these factors is not helpful because it points the same way in every case: the very existence of a criminal statute implies a legislative judgment that its requirements are practicable and desirable. The court of appeals' remaining factors, however, are pertinent to our analysis.

On the question of notice, this Court has held that one consideration bearing on whether to apply negligence per se is whether the statute clearly defines the prohibited or required conduct. [Cc] The Family Code's reporting requirement is triggered when a person "has cause to believe that a child's physical or mental health or welfare has been or may be adversely affected by abuse or neglect." [C] In this case, defendants allegedly were eyewitnesses to sexual abuse. Under these facts, there is no question that they had cause to believe abuse was occurring, and thus that the statute required them to make a report. In many other cases, however, a person may become aware of a possible case of child abuse only through second-hand reports or ambiguous physical symptoms, and it is unclear whether these circumstances are "cause to believe" that such conduct "may be" taking place.[1] [C] A statute that conditions the requirement to report on

---

1. Determining whether abuse is or may be occurring in a particular case is likely to be especially difficult for untrained laypersons. Texas is one of a minority of states that these difficult judgment calls does not clearly define what conduct is required in many conceivable situations. (Footnote omitted.)

The next factor the court of appeals considered was whether applying negligence per se to the reporting statute would create liability without fault. [C] We agree with the court of appeals that it would not, because the statute criminalizes only the "knowing" failure to report. * * * This characteristic of the statute weighs in favor of imposing civil liability.

Our next consideration is whether negligence per se would impose ruinous liability disproportionate to the seriousness of the defendant's conduct. In analyzing this factor, the court of appeals treated child abuse as the relevant conduct. [C] ("The abuse of children has become notorious."). The conduct criminalized by section 261.109, however, is not child abuse but the failure to report child abuse. Through its penal laws, the Legislature has expressed a judgment that abuse and non-reporting deserve very different legal consequences. * * * [The Court contrasted the severe penalty for the offense committed by the abuser, five to ninety-nine years in prison and a fine of up to $10,000, with the penalty provided for failure to report, no more than six months in jail and a $2,000 fine.] This evidence of legislative intent to penalize non-reporters far less severely than abusers weighs against holding a person who fails to report suspected abuse civilly liable for the enormous damages that the abuser subsequently inflicts. The specter of disproportionate liability is particularly troubling when, as in the case of the reporting statute, it is combined with the likelihood of "broad and wide-ranging liability" by collateral wrongdoers * * *

Finally, in addition to the factors discussed by the court of appeals, we have also looked to whether the injury resulted directly or indirectly from the violation of the statute. * * * [T]he indirect relationship between violation of such a statute and the plaintiff's ultimate injury is a factor against imposing tort liability * * *

We conclude by noting that for a variety of reasons, including many of those we have discussed, most other states with mandatory reporting statutes similar to Texas's have concluded that the failure to report child abuse is not negligence per se. [Cc]

* * * Because a decision to impose negligence per se could not be limited to cases charging serious misconduct like the one at bar, but rather would impose immense potential liability under an ill-defined standard on a broad class of individuals whose relationship to the abuse was extremely indirect, we hold that it is not appropriate to adopt Family Code section 261.109(a) as establishing a duty and standard of conduct in tort. Therefore, Mr. and Mrs. N. and their children may not maintain a claim for

require any person who suspects child abuse to report it. See O'Brien & Flannery, The Pending Gauntlet to Free Exercise: Mandating that Clergy Report Child Abuse, 25 Loy. L.A. L. Rev. 1, 24–25 & n.127 (1991) (collecting statutes). Most states place such a requirement only on professionals who may be expected to know more than the average person about recognizing child abuse and who have a professional relationship with and responsibility for children. * * *

negligence per se or gross negligence based on defendants' violation of the child abuse reporting statute. Because plaintiffs did not appeal the court of appeals' adverse decision on their common law negligence claims, we do not consider whether Texas should impose a common law duty to report or prevent child abuse.

For the foregoing reasons, we reverse the judgment of the court of appeals and render judgment that plaintiffs take nothing.

NOTES AND QUESTIONS

1. Generally, if the plaintiff is not permitted to use the statute to prove the standard of conduct, the plaintiff's case defaults to the reasonable person standard and may still succeed if the plaintiff can prove that the defendant failed to act as the reasonable person would act. Why did the plaintiffs in this case not have the chance to argue to the jury that the defendants failed to act as a reasonable person would act under the circumstances? *because they did not appeal their negligence claims*

2. Who makes the decision whether the provision of the Family Code can be used as the basis for negligence per se—judge or jury?

3. What if the day care center in the principal case had been operating without a license required by statute? Could that serve as the basis for a negligence per se jury instruction? Most courts have refused to use licensing statutes to establish the standard of care. Brown v. Shyne, 242 N.Y. 176, 151 N.E. 197 (N.Y. 1926) (chiropractor not licensed to practice medicine); Hertz Driv–Ur–Self System v. Hendrickson, 109 Colo. 1, 121 P.2d 483 (1942) (violation of statute prohibiting renting of car to someone who did not have operator's permit); Fuller v. Sirois, 97 N.H. 100, 82 A.2d 82 (1951) (driving motor vehicle after operator's license was suspended for reckless driving). See generally Gregory, Breach of Criminal Licensing Statutes in Civil Litigation, 36 Cornell L.Q. 622 (1951). Plaintiff is injured by fireworks that had been brought into the state in violation of a state statute. May defendant use the violation of the statute to show the plaintiff's contributory negligence? Hortstmeyer v. Golden Eagle Fireworks, 534 N.W.2d 835 (N.D.1995) (violation of statute does not establish negligent conduct because, by analogy to licensing cases, the violation did not cause the harm).

Relationship of violation + injury important

4. The fact that a statute is inapplicable, because it is not intended for the protection of the class of persons in which the plaintiff is included, or because it was not intended for protection against the particular risk, or because it's otherwise inappropriate for such use, does not necessarily rule it out entirely as evidence bearing on the issue of negligence. Thus in Hansen v. Kemmish, 201 Iowa 1008, 208 N.W. 277 (1926), a statute, intended only to prevent the misbreeding of animals, provided that hogs should be confined by fences of specified strength. Defendant fenced his hogs with a fence of less strength; one of them broke through the fence, escaped into the highway, and wrecked plaintiff's car. It was held that, while the statute did not define a standard of conduct to be adopted as a matter of law, the jury could consider it as bearing on the kind of fence necessary for the proper confinement of hogs.

5. The effect of the violation of criminal (and other) statutes and regulations on the law of torts is not confined by any means to the tort of negligence and the doctrine of negligence per se. It has been generally recognized that in furtherance of the purpose of particular legislation and to insure its effectiveness, a court may, despite the absence of a provision to this effect, supply a civil action for damages

according relief to a person for whose benefit conduct of another was either proscribed or required by the legislation. Restatement (Second) of Torts § 874A. The usual explanation is that the right is "implied" from the legislation. See Chapter 23, Torts in the Age of Statutes.

(B) EFFECT OF STATUTE

Martin v. Herzog

Court of Appeals of New York, 1920.
228 N.Y. 164, 126 N.E. 814.

CARDOZO, J. The action is one to recover damages for injuries resulting in death.

Plaintiff and her husband, while driving toward Tarrytown in a buggy on the night of August 21, 1915, were struck by the defendant's automobile coming in the opposite direction. They were thrown to the ground, and the man was killed. At the point of the collision the highway makes a curve. The car was rounding the curve when suddenly it came upon the buggy, emerging, the defendant tells us, from the gloom. Negligence is charged against the defendant, the driver of the car, in that he did not keep to the right of the center of the highway [c]. Negligence is charged against the plaintiff's intestate, the driver of the wagon, in that he was traveling without lights [c]. There is no evidence that the defendant was moving at an excessive speed. There is none of any defect in the equipment of his car. The beam of light from his lamps pointed to the right as the wheels of his car turned along the curve toward the left; and looking in the direction of the plaintiff's approach, he was peering into the shadow. The case against him must stand, therefore, if at all, upon the divergence of his course from the center of the highway. The jury found him delinquent and his victim blameless. The Appellate Division reversed, and ordered a new trial. [Plaintiff now appeals to the Court of Appeals.]

* * * We think the unexcused omission of the statutory signals is more than some evidence of negligence. It is negligence in itself. Lights are intended for the guidance and protection of other travelers on the highway. Highway Law, § 329a. By the very terms of the hypothesis, to omit, willfully or heedlessly, the safeguards prescribed by law for the benefit of another that he may be preserved in life or limb, is to fall short of the standard of diligence to which those who live in organized society are under a duty to conform. That, we think, is now the established rule in this state. [Cc]

In the case at hand, we have an instance of the admitted violation of a statute intended for the protection of travelers on the highway, of whom the defendant at the time was one. Yet the jurors were instructed in effect that they were at liberty in their discretion to treat the omission of lights either as innocent or as culpable. They were allowed to "consider the default as lightly or gravely" as they would (Thomas, J., in the court below). They might as well have been told that they could use a like discretion in holding a master at fault for the omission of a safety appliance prescribed by positive law for the protection of a workman. [Cc] Jurors have no dispensing power, by which they may relax the duty that one traveler on the highways owes under the statute to another. It is error to tell them that they have. The omission of these lights was a wrong, and, being wholly unexcused, was also a negligent wrong. No license should have been conceded to the triers of the facts to find it anything else.

*Rule of Law
jury should be so instructed*

We must be on our guard, however, against confusing the question of negligence with that of the causal connection between the negligence and the injury. A defendant who travels without lights is not to pay damages for his fault, unless the absence of lights is the cause of the disaster. A plaintiff who travels without them is not to forfeit the right to damages, unless the absence of lights is at least a contributing cause of the disaster. To say that conduct is negligence is not to say that it is always contributory negligence. "Proof of negligence in the air, so to speak, will not do." Pollock Torts (10th Ed.) p. 472.

We think, however, that evidence of a collision occurring more than an hour after sundown between a car and an unseen buggy, proceeding without lights, is evidence from which a causal connection may be inferred between the collision and the lack of signals. [Cc] If nothing else is shown to break the connection, we have a case, prima facie sufficient, of negligence contributing to the result.

Holding

We are persuaded that the tendency of the charge, and of all the rulings, following it, was to minimize unduly, in the minds of the triers of the facts, the gravity of the decedent's fault. Errors may not be ignored as unsubstantial, when they tend to such an outcome. A statute designed for the protection of human life is not to be brushed aside as a form of words, its commands reduced to the level of cautions, and the duty to obey attenuated into an option to conform.

The order of the Appellate Division should be affirmed, and judgment absolute directed on the stipulation in favor of the defendant, with costs in all courts.

[The dissenting opinion of HOGAN, J., is omitted.]

NOTES AND QUESTIONS

1. Who used violation of a statute to establish the standard of care in this case, plaintiff or defendant? *defendant*

2. The great majority of the courts take the position stated by Cardozo in this case, that when a statute applies to the facts, an *unexcused* violation is "negligence per se," which must be declared by the court and not left to the jury.

3. A few states treat violation of a statute as giving rise to a "presumption" of negligence, which becomes negligence as a matter of law unless the presumption is rebutted. Since it can be rebutted only by showing an excuse for the violation, this appears to come out at much the same place as the "negligence per se" rule.

4. A minority of states hold that the violation is only evidence of negligence, which the jury may accept or reject as it sees fit.

5.   The California court had quite a workout on all this in Satterlee v. Orange Glenn School District, 29 Cal.2d 581, 177 P.2d 279 (1947), with Traynor, Edmonds and Carter, JJ., each writing an opinion, and taking a different one of the foregoing three positions. Edmonds carried the majority of the court with his "presumption" theory. The case has a good exposition of the arguments.

Zeni v. Anderson

Supreme Court of Michigan, 1976.
397 Mich. 117, 243 N.W.2d 270.

WILLIAMS, JUSTICE. * * * The accident which precipitated this action occurred one snowy morning, March 7, 1969, when the temperature was 11% F, the sky was clear and the average snow depth was 21 inches. Plaintiff Eleanor Zeni, then a 56–year–old registered nurse, was walking to her work at the Northern Michigan University Health Center in Marquette. Instead of using the snow-covered sidewalk, which in any event would have required her to walk across the street twice to get to her job, she traveled along a well-used pedestrian snowpath, with her back to oncoming traffic.

Defendant Karen Anderson, a college student, was driving within the speed limit in a steady stream of traffic on the same street. Ms. Anderson testified that she had turned on the defroster in the car and her passenger said she had scraped the windshield. An eyewitness whose deposition was read at trial, however, testified that defendant's windshield was clouded and he doubted that the occupants could see out. He also testified that the car was traveling too close to the curb and that he could tell plaintiff was going to be hit.

Defendant's car struck the plaintiff on the driver's right side. Ms. Anderson testified she first saw the plaintiff between a car parked on the right-hand side of the road and defendant's car, and that she did not hear nor feel her car strike Ms. Zeni. The eyewitness reported seeing plaintiff flip over the fender and hood. He said when he went over to help her his knees were on or inside the white line delineating a parking space. A security officer observed blood stains on the pavement approximately 13 feet from the curb.

Ms. Zeni's injuries were serious and included an intra-cerebral subdural hematoma which required neurosurgery. She has retrograde amnesia and therefore, because she does not remember anything from the time she began walking that morning until sometime after the impact, there is no way to determine whether she knew defendant was behind her. Following an extended period of convalescence, plaintiff, still suffering permanent disability, could return to work on only a part-time basis.

Testimony at trial indicated that it was common for nurses to use the roadway to reach the Health Center, and a security officer testified that in the wintertime it was safer to walk there than on the one sidewalk. Apparently, several days before the accident, Ms. Zeni had indeed fallen on the sidewalk. Although she was not hurt when she fell, the Director of University Security was hospitalized when he fell on the walk.

Defendant, however, maintained that plaintiff's failure to use that sidewalk constituted contributory negligence because, she said, it violated M.C.L.A. § 257.655; M.S.A. § 9.2355, which requires:

"Where sidewalks are provided, it shall be unlawful for pedestrians to walk upon the main traveled portion of the highway. Where sidewalks are not provided, pedestrians shall, when practicable, walk on the left side of the highway facing traffic which passes nearest." * * *

[There was a jury verdict for plaintiff in the trial court. The court of appeals reversed because of instructions on the subject of last clear chance. Discussion of last clear chance is omitted.]

A. *Violation of Statute as Rebuttable Presumption.* In a growing number of states, the rule concerning the proper role of a penal statute in a civil action for damages is that violation of the statute which has been found to apply to a particular set of facts establishes only a prima facie case of negligence, a presumption which may be rebutted by a showing on the part of the party violating the statute of an adequate excuse under the facts and circumstances of the case. The excuses may not necessarily be applicable in a criminal action, since, in the absence of legislatively-mandated civil penalties, acceptance of the criminal statute itself as a standard of care in a civil action is purely discretionary. See Comment and Illustrations, 2 Restatement (Second) of Torts § 288A, pp. 33–37.

Michigan cases have in effect followed this rule. For example, over a 65 year period, cases concerning the effect in a negligence action of violation of the statute requiring vehicles to keep to the right side of the road have almost consistently adopted a rebuttable presumption approach, even though the language of the statute is not written in terms of a presumption. * * *

We think the test of the applicable law was well stated by our brother Justice Fitzgerald when he was a judge on the Court of Appeals. In Lucas v. Carson, 38 Mich.App. 552, 196 N.W.2d 819 (1972), he analyzed a case where, in spite of defendant's precautions, her vehicle "inexplicably slid into the rear of plaintiff's stopped car" where plaintiff was waiting at a traffic signal. * * *

First, in analyzing whether the presumption of negligence attributed to a rear-end collision had been rebutted in the case before them, the Court of Appeals acknowledged that the usual grounds for rebuttal, sudden emergency, did not appear in this case. In effect accepting defendant's contention that the doctrine of sudden emergency was not the sole basis for rebutting a presumption of negligence, the Court held:

"The general rule appears to be that evidence required to rebut this presumption *as a matter of law* should be positive, unequivocal, strong, and credible. In the case at bar, defendant driver contended that she was at all times driving in a reasonable and prudent manner. * * * [T]here was sufficient evidence at least to generate a jury question regarding rebutting of the presumption." * * *

This is the approach we follow today. * * *

[An] attraction of this approach is that it is fair. "If there is sufficient excuse or justification, there is ordinarily no violation of a statute and the statutory standard is inapplicable." Satterlee v. Orange Glenn School Dist. of San Diego County, 29 Cal.2d 581, 594, 177 P.2d 279, 286 (1947) (dissenting in part). It would be unreasonable to adhere to an automatic rule of negligence "where observance would subject a person to danger which might be avoided by disregard of the general rule." Tedla v. Ellman, 280 N.Y. 124, 131–132, 19 N.E.2d 987, 991 (1939).

The approach is logical. Liability without fault is not truly negligence, and in the absence of a clear legislative mandate to so extend liability, the courts should be hesitant to do so on their own. Because these are, after all, criminal statutes, a court is limited in how far it may go in plucking a statute from its criminal milieu and inserting it into the civil arena. The rule of rebuttable presumption has arisen in part in response to this concern, and in part because of the reluctance to go to the other extreme and in effect, discard or disregard the legislative standard. * * *

B. Violation of Statute as Negligence Per Se. While some Michigan cases seem to speak of negligence per se as a kind of strict liability, Holbert v. Staniak, 359 Mich. 283, 290, 102 N.W.2d 186 (1960), an examination indicates that there are a number of conditions that attempt to create a more reasonable approach than would result from an automatic application of a per se rule.

[Reference is made here to the court's construing the statute, determining its purpose and applying principles of proximate cause.]

Despite such limitations, the judge-made rule of negligence per se has still proved to be too inflexible and mechanical to satisfy thoughtful commentators and judges. It is forcefully argued that no matter how a court may attempt to confine the negligence per se doctrine, if defendant is liable despite the exercise of due care and the availability of a reasonable excuse, this is really strict liability, and not negligence. Prosser, The Law of Torts (4th ed.), § 36, p. 197. Since it is always possible that the Legislature's failure to deal specifically with the question of private rights was not accidental, and that there might have been no legislative intent to change the law of torts, such treatment of the statute may well be a gross perversion of the legislative will. It is troublesome, too, that "potentially ruinous civil liability" may follow from a "minor infraction of petty criminal regulations", [c] or may, in a jurisdiction burdened by contributory negligence, serve to deprive an otherwise deserving plaintiff of a much-needed recovery. * * *

C. Violation of Statute as Evidence of Negligence. Just as the rebuttable presumption approach to statutory violations in a negligence context apparently arose, at least in part, from dissatisfaction with the result of a mechanical application of the per se rule, a parallel development in our state with respect to infractions of ordinances and of administrative regulations, has been that violations of these amount to only evidence of negligence. [Cc]

We have not, however, chosen to join that small minority which has decreed that violation of a statute is only evidence of negligence. In view of the fairness and ease with which the rebuttable presumption standard has been and can be administered, we believe the litigants are thereby well served and the Legislature is given appropriate respect.

D. Application of Statutory Standard to This Case. We have seen, therefore, that while some of our Michigan cases seem to present negligence per se as an unqualified rule, the fact of the matter is that there are a number of qualifications which make application of this rule not really a per se approach at all. Not only must the statutory purpose doctrine and the requirement of proximate cause be satisfied, but the alleged wrongdoer has an opportunity to come forward with evidence rebutting the presumption of negligence.

An accurate statement of our law is that when a court adopts a penal statute as the standard of care in an action for negligence, violation of that statute establishes a prima facie case of negligence, with the determination to be made by the finder of fact whether the party accused of violating the statute has established a legally sufficient excuse. If the finder of fact determines such an excuse exists, the appropriate standard of care then becomes that established by the common law. Such excuses shall include, but shall not be limited to, those suggested by the Restatement (Second) of Torts § 288A, and shall be determined by the circumstances of each case.

In the case at bar, moreover, the statute itself provides a guideline for the jury, for a violation will not occur when it is impracticable to use the sidewalk or to walk on the left side of a highway. This is ordinarily a question for the finder of fact, [c] and thus the statute itself provides not only a legislative standard of care which may be accepted by the court, but a legislatively mandated excuse as well. * * *

* * * [W]e find the jury was adequately instructed as to the effect of the violation of this particular statute on plaintiff's case. * * *

The Court of Appeals is reversed and the trial court is affirmed. Costs to plaintiff.

NOTES AND QUESTIONS

1. Section 288A of the Second Restatement, referred to in the principal case, reads as follows:

"(1) An excused violation of a legislative enactment or an administrative regulation is not negligence.

"(2) Unless the enactment or regulation is construed not to permit such excuse, its violation is excused when

"(a) the violation is reasonable because of the actor's incapacity;

"(b) he neither knows nor should know of the occasion for compliance;

"(c) he is unable after reasonable diligence or care to comply;

"(d) he is confronted by an emergency not due to his own misconduct;

"(e) compliance would involve a greater risk of harm to the actor or to others."

This list is "not intended to be exclusive."

2.   The principal case classifies the approaches to the question of what effect to give to the violation of a statute into three groups: (1) negligence per se, (2) prima facie negligence and (3) some evidence of negligence. Most commentators would agree with this classification. But there may be disagreement on the content of the first two groups. The Restatement espouses the negligence per se approach, but it also permits excuses as indicated in § 288A. The two concepts are regarded as fitting together in an accurate delineation of the per se approach. The second classification (prima facie negligence) would then apply to jurisdictions in which the issue goes to the jury even when there is no credible evidence of a recognized excuse, but merely testimony that the defendant acted with due care. It is in this situation alone that a distinction exists between the two classes. These differing classifications, of course, are merely a matter of semantics. What significance do they have on the content of an instruction to the jury?

3.   In light of the Restatement (Second) of Torts and the principal case, how might the following situations be decided?

A.   A statute provides that no vehicle shall be driven on the highway at night without a tail light. Without any fault or knowledge of defendant, his tail light goes out while he is driving at night, and as a result plaintiff is injured in a collision with him. Brotherton v. Day & Night Fuel Co., 192 Wash. 362, 73 P.2d 788 (1937). What if defendant discovered that the light was out, but continued to drive carefully to a near-by filling station? Taber v. Smith, 26 S.W.2d 722 (Tex.Civ.App.1930).

B.   A statute prohibits automobile drivers from passing at an intersection. Defendant approaches an intersection concealed from view and not marked by any warning sign, of whose existence he is ignorant, and as he reaches it attempts to pass. Hullander v. McIntyre, 78 S.D. 453, 104 N.W.2d 40 (1960).

C.   A child, too young to know or appreciate the statute, crosses a street in the middle of the block? Morby v. Rogers, 122 Utah 540, 252 P.2d 231 (1953); Maker v. Wellin, 214 Or. 332, 327 P.2d 793 (1958). Suppose an adult does not know of the jaywalking statute?

D.   Defendant drives on the left side of the road to avoid hitting a child who has darted out from the right. Burlie v. Stephens, 113 Wash. 182, 193 P. 684 (1920); Sims v. Eleazer, 116 S.C. 41, 106 S.E. 854 (1921). Would it be negligence *not* to violate the statute? But see Monreal v. Tobin, 61 Cal.App.4th 1337, 72 Cal.Rptr.2d 168 (1998) (driver who was traveling at posted speed limit did not owe a duty to speed up or move to a slower lane when approached from rear by vehicle traveling 25 m.p.h. in excess of posted speed limit even though there was testimony that "normal" speed on that stretch of interstate was at least 10 m.p.h. in excess of speed limit).

4.   Certain types of statutes are commonly interpreted to make the defendant liable without regard to any excuse for the violation. They include

A.   Child labor acts, providing under criminal penalty that no minor under a minimum age shall be employed in certain occupations, as in Krutlies v. Bulls Head Coal Co., 249 Pa. 162, 94 A. 459 (1915); Blanton v. Kellioka Coal Co., 192 Ky. 220, 232 S.W. 614 (1921).

B.   Pure Food Acts that prohibit the commercial sale of adulterated food. Doherty v. S.S. Kresge Co., 227 Wis. 661, 278 N.W. 437 (1938); Bolitho v. Safeway Stores, 109 Mont. 213, 95 P.2d 443 (1939).

C.   The Federal Safety Appliance Act, requiring that railway cars used in interstate commerce be equipped with automatic couplers and other safety devices, in good operating condition. O'Donnell v. Elgin, J. & E.R. Co., 338 U.S. 384 (1949). Accord, St. Louis S.W.R. Co. v. Williams, 397 F.2d 147 (5th Cir.1968) (Boiler Inspection Act).

D.   "Safe place" statutes, requiring lights and other protection in tenement houses, or premises open to the public. Monsour v. Excelsior Tobacco Co., 115 S.W.2d 219 (Mo.App.1938); Smulczeski v. City Center of Music and Drama, 3 N.Y.2d 498, 146 N.E.2d 769 (1957).

E.   Statutes prohibiting the sale of firearms and other dangerous objects to minors.

5.   When liability without fault is imposed because no excuse is permitted, it often is held that the legislative purpose cannot be given full effect unless the defenses of contributory negligence and assumption of risk are made unavailable to the defendant.

6.   *Reasonable Care Per Se.* Suppose defendant shows that he complied with all applicable statutes and administrative regulations. Should his conduct be deemed "reasonable care per se"? See Raymond v. Riegel Textile Corp., 484 F.2d 1025 (1st Cir.1973) (Flammable Fabrics Act); Black v. Pub. Serv. Elec. & Gas Co., 56 N.J. 63, 265 A.2d 129, 136 (1970) (evidence of care); Wilson v. Piper Aircraft Corp., 282 Or. 61, 577 P.2d 1322 (1978). Should the answer depend on how completely the product or activity is regulated by government? See preemption discussion, Chapters 15 and 23.

7. PROOF OF NEGLIGENCE

(A) COURT AND JURY: CIRCUMSTANTIAL EVIDENCE

Goddard v. Boston & Maine R.R. Co.

Supreme Judicial Court of Massachusetts, 1901.
179 Mass. 52, 60 N.E. 486.

Action by Wilfred H. Goddard against the Boston & Maine Railroad Company for personal injuries received by falling upon a banana skin lying upon the platform at defendant's station at Boston. The evidence showed that [plaintiff] was a passenger who had just arrived, and was about the length of the car from where he alighted when he slipped and fell. There was evidence that there were many passengers on the platform. Verdict directed for defendant, and plaintiff excepts.

HOLMES, C.J. The banana skin upon which the plaintiff stepped and which caused him to slip may have been dropped within a minute by one of the persons who was leaving the train. It is unnecessary to go further to decide the case.

Exceptions overruled.

Anjou v. Boston Elevated Railway Co.

Supreme Judicial Court of Massachusetts, 1911.
208 Mass. 273, 94 N.E. 386.

Action by Helen G. Anjou against the Boston Elevated Railway Company. Verdict was directed for defendant, and the case reported.

Rugg, J. The plaintiff arrived on one of defendant's cars on the upper level of the Dudley Street terminal; other passengers arrived on the same car, but it does not appear how many. She waited until the crowd had left the platform, when she inquired of one of defendant's uniformed employés the direction to another car. He walked along a narrow platform, and she, following a few feet behind him toward the stairway he had indicated, was injured by slipping upon a banana peel. It was described by several who examined it in these terms: It "felt dry, gritty, as if there were dirt upon it," as if "trampled over a good deal," as "flattened down, and black in color," "every bit of it was black, there wasn't a particle of yellow," and as "black, flattened out and gritty." It was one of the duties of employés of the defendant, of whom there was one at this station all the time, to observe and remove whatever was upon the platform to interfere with the safety of travelers. These might have been found to be the facts.

The inference might have been drawn from the appearance and condition of the banana peel that it had been upon the platform a considerable period of time, in such position that it would have been seen and removed by the employés of the defendant if they had been reasonably careful in performing their duty. Therefore there is something on which to base a conclusion that it was not dropped a moment before by a passenger, and Goddard v. Boston & Maine R.R., 179 Mass. 52, 60 N.E. 486 is plainly distinguishable. The obligation rested upon the defendant to keep its station reasonably safe for its passengers. It might have been found that the platform was suffered to remain in such condition as to be a menace to those rightfully walking upon it. Hence there was evidence of negligence on the part of the defendant, which should have been submitted to the jury. [Cc]

In accordance with the terms of the report, let the entry be:

Judgment for the plaintiff for $1,250 with costs.

[Normally, this case would have been reversed for a new trial. For some reason (perhaps to avoid expense of a new trial), defense counsel apparently agreed to an entry of judgment against his client if he lost on appeal.]

Joye v. Great Atlantic and Pacific Tea Co.

United States Court of Appeals, Fourth Circuit, 1968.
405 F.2d 464.

Craven, Circuit Judge: Willard Joye slipped and fell on a banana in defendant's A & P supermarket. In his diversity suit in the district court the jury returned a verdict for him in the amount of $10,000 and defendant appeals. We reverse because we are unable to find in the record sufficient evidence to present a jury issue as to constructive notice to defendant of a dangerous condition. Without such notice, in the context of the case, and under South Carolina law which we must apply, the district court should have granted defendant's Rule 50(b) motion for judgment n.o.v. * * *

There was no evidence that the A & P (1) put the banana on the floor or (2) had actual notice of its presence. Thus plaintiff's case turns on the sufficiency of the evidence to establish constructive notice. [C]

Plaintiff offered no direct evidence below as to how long the banana had been on the floor before the accident. The circumstantial evidence taken most favorably to the plaintiff shows that the floor may not have been swept for as long as 35 minutes. No one saw the banana until *after* Joye fell on it. It was then described as dark brown in color, having dirt and sand on it. There was dirt on the floor near the banana, and the banana was sticky around the edges. From this evidence we think the jury could not tell whether the banana had been on defendant's floor for 30 seconds or 3 days. * * *

P offered no evidence as to reasonable amt. of time for dangerous condition

Because it cannot be determined from the evidence how long (even the broadest range of approximation) the banana may have been on the floor, we reverse the judgment of the district court and remand to that court with instructions to enter judgment in favor of the defendant, The Great Atlantic & Pacific Tea Company.

Reversed.

—Jasko v. F.W. Woolworth Co.

exception to general rule of slip & fall - slipped on a piece of Pizza

Supreme Court of Colorado, 1972.
177 Colo. 418, 494 P.2d 839.

[Plaintiff was injured when she slipped on a piece of pizza that was on the terrazzo floor near the "pizza-hoagie counter" in defendant's store.]

GROVES, JUSTICE. * * * We address ourselves solely to the necessity of notice of the specific condition, which under the facts of this case is of first impression in this court. * * *

In her attempt to meet the requirement of notice, plaintiff did not claim or show that the alleged pizza was placed or dropped on the floor directly by the defendant or its employees, or that defendant knew of its presence. [C] Rather, it was her contention that defendant's method of selling pizza was one which leads inescapably to such mishaps as her own, and that in such a situation conventional notice requirements need not be met. We agree.

The dangerous condition was created by the store's method of sale. The steps taken to constantly clean the floor show that the store owner recognized the danger.

The practice of extensive selling of slices of pizza on waxed paper to customers who consume it while standing creates the reasonable probability that food will drop to the floor. Food on a terrazzo floor will create a dangerous condition. In such a situation, notice to the proprietor of the specific item on the floor need not be shown.

P unable to show time period but could show practice of selling food eaten while standing creates dangerous condition

The basic notice requirement springs from the thought that a dangerous condition, when it occurs, is somewhat out of the ordinary. * * * In such a situation the storekeeper is allowed a reasonable time, under the circumstances, to discover and correct the condition, unless it is the direct result of his (or his employees') acts. However, when the operating methods of a proprietor are such that dangerous conditions are continuous or easily foreseeable, the logical basis for the notice requirement dissolves. Then, actual or constructive notice of the specific condition need not be proved. * * *

The ruling of the Court of Appeals is reversed and the cause remanded to it for further remand to the trial court and new trial.

NOTES AND QUESTIONS

1. Can these cases be reconciled?

2. Why not require the defendant to prove that it was not negligent—that is, that it was not responsible for the substance plaintiff slipped on? Plaintiff has no information, and can get none, as to what defendant's employees have or have not done; defendant knows, or can perhaps find out.

3. To what extent is plaintiff's disadvantage remedied by modern discovery procedure that provides both parties access to relevant information, including that within the possession of the other party.

4. Plaintiff has three separate burdens of proof on the issue of negligence—the burden of pleading, the burden of coming forward with enough evidence to avoid a directed verdict against him and, if he hurdles that, the burden of persuading the trier of fact to find in his favor. In most situations, plaintiff discharges the first burden by alleging sufficient facts in his complaint, the second by convincing the judge that reasonable jurors could find on a more-probable-than-not basis that plaintiff's contention is correct. Generally speaking, issues of negligence, either the defendant's or the plaintiff's, are not susceptible to summary adjudication and must be resolved by the jury. Only rarely is it appropriate for the judge to direct a verdict in favor of one party or the other on the issue of negligence. See, e.g., Bell v. Leatherwood, 206 Ga.App. 550, 425 S.E.2d 679 (1992). Plaintiff must then persuade the jury that the preponderance of the evidence is in his favor.

5. What kind of evidence has plaintiff introduced in these cases? How reliable is it? There are footprints in the mud, and a hundred eyewitnesses testify on oath that they sat there the whole time and no one passed by. Can the jury find that some one did? Would you expect them to? Cf. Phoenix Refining Co. v. Powell, 251 S.W.2d 892 (Tex.Civ.App.1952) (tire skid marks); Macfie v. Kaminski, 219 Neb. 524, 364 N.W.2d 31 (1985) (proof of skid).

6. Think about how you would prove negligence in some of the other cases you have read. Suppose an employee leaves a company-sponsored banquet at which alcohol was served and then rear ends another car at a stoplight. Plaintiff files suit against the employee and the employer, alleging that the employer served the employee when she was obviously intoxicated. Against the employee you could probably use eyewitness testimony to establish the fact that she had rear ended the plaintiff's car and a rule of law or negligence per se or the reasonable person standard to establish that such conduct was negligent. What about the case against the employer? Perhaps you could find an eyewitness to say employee was visibly intoxicated at the banquet. What if the police officer called to the scene of the accident would testify that she was visibly intoxicated there? Is that enough? Cf. Fairbanks v. J.B. McLoughlin Co., Inc., 131 Wash.2d 96, 929 P.2d 433 (1997)

("[Employer] relies on the [testimony] from those attending the banquet which uniformly state that [employee] did not appear intoxicated. Nonetheless, [employee] appeared obviously intoxicated to both Fairbanks and to Officer Asheim. Officer Asheim in particular noted that she smelled of alcohol, slurred her speech, stumbled as she got out of the car, and staggered when she walked. A police officer's subjective observation that the employee was obviously intoxicated shortly after leaving the banquet may raise an inference that she was obviously intoxicated when the employer served her, provided that the employee did not consume any alcohol after leaving the banquet and provided that no time remains unaccounted for between the banquet and the subsequent observation. [C] Because a reasonable jury could find based on [employee]'s own testimony that she left the banquet at 10:30 p.m. and was involved in the accident just 20 minutes later, Fairbanks' and Officer Asheim's observations were sufficient to raise a factual issue as to whether she was obviously intoxicated at the banquet.")

7. What if the product that plaintiff claims was negligently designed or manufactured disappears after the accident? How does plaintiff prove that it was made by defendant? Plaintiff was injured by a multipiece truck rim that was reassembled and then either used on another truck or placed against the wall. No one could identify it by the time the suit was filed and at least six different companies manufacture three-piece rims. Healey v. Firestone Tire & Rubber Co., 640 N.Y.S.2d 860, 87 N.Y.2d 596, 663 N.E.2d 901 (1996) (identity of manufacturer may be established by circumstantial evidence if product itself is destroyed after use, but there was insufficient circumstantial evidence available in this case to do so).

[margin note: if defective product disappeared after accident how to prove?]

8. What if there is enough circumstantial evidence to identify the part and its manufacturer, but the part itself has disappeared and the manufacturer argues that it cannot defend itself without being able to examine the part to ascertain whether it failed, why it failed, or if its failure caused the accident? Bachmeier v. Wallwork Truck Ctrs., 544 N.W.2d 122 (N.D.1996) (summary judgment for manufacturer upheld where plaintiff had failed to preserve truck hub that allegedly failed due to a faulty design where manufacturer argued that failure might have been due to negligent maintenance). What if one of the parties actually destroys the evidence? Vodusek v. Bayliner Marine Corp., 71 F.3d 148 (4th Cir.1995) (expert retained by plaintiff destroyed boat while conducting his accident investigation; trial court judge acted within his discretion to instruct jury that it could draw negative inference from loss of evidence for which party was responsible). See also Chapter 23, Torts in the Age of Statutes.

9. Problems involved in proving facts in tort cases, as any competent trial lawyer will affirm, are often more difficult than developing the relevant rules of law. Although a Torts course can only introduce the students to problems of proof, it is important for them to have a continuing sensitivity to the problems throughout the law school career. This awareness will be developed in courses in evidence, trial practice, and clinics, as well as in continuing legal education programs after graduation from law school.

(B) Res Ipsa Loquitur

➡Byrne v. Boadle

Court of Exchequer, 1863.
2 H. & C. 722, 159 Eng.Rep. 299.

[Action for negligence. The plaintiff's evidence was that he was walking in a public street past the defendant's shop, and that a barrel of flour fell upon him from a window above the shop, knocked him down, and seriously injured him. There was no other evidence. The Assessor was of the opinion that there was no evidence of negligence for the jury, and nonsuited the plaintiff, reserving leave to him to move the Court of Exchequer to enter the verdict for him for £50 damages. Plaintiff obtained a rule nisi.]

Facts

ruling that holds unless other party shows up to argue why it shouldn't

Charles Russell now shewed cause. First, there was no evidence to connect the defendant or his servants with the occurrence. * * * It is consistent with the evidence that the purchaser of the flour was superintending the lowering of it by his servant, or it may be that a stranger was engaged to do it without the knowledge or authority of the defendant. [Pollock, C.B. The presumption is that the defendant's servants were engaged in removing the defendant's flour; if they were not it was competent to the defendant to prove it.]

No causal connection

Secondly, assuming the facts to be brought home to the defendant or his servants, these facts do not disclose any evidence for the jury of

Chief Baron Pollock

negligence. The plaintiff was bound to give affirmative proof of negligence. But there was not a scintilla of evidence, unless the occurrence is of itself evidence of negligence. There was not even evidence that the barrel was being lowered by a jigger-hoist as alleged in the declaration. [Pollock, C.B. There are certain cases of which it may be said res ipsa loquitur, and this seems one of them. In some cases the Courts have held that the mere fact of the accident having occurred is evidence of negligence, as, for instance, in the case of railway collisions.]

POLLOCK, C.B. We are all of opinion that the rule must be absolute to enter the verdict for the plaintiff. The learned counsel was quite right in saying that there are many accidents from which no presumption of negligence can arise, but I think it would be wrong to lay down as a rule that in no case can a presumption of negligence arise from the fact of an accident. Suppose in this case the barrel had rolled out of the warehouse and fallen on the plaintiff, how could he possibly ascertain from what cause it occurred? It is the duty of persons who keep barrels in a warehouse to take care that they do not roll out, and I think that such a case would, beyond all doubt, afford prima facie evidence of negligence. A barrel could not roll out of a warehouse without some negligence, and to say that a plaintiff who is injured by it must call witnesses from the warehouse to prove negligence seems to me preposterous. * * * The present case upon the evidence comes to this, a man is passing in front of the premises of a dealer in flour, and there falls down upon him a barrel of flour. I think it apparent that the barrel was in the custody of the defendant who occupied the premises, and who is responsible for the acts of his servants who had the control of it; and in my opinion the fact of its falling is prima facie evidence of negligence, and the plaintiff who was injured by it is not bound to show that it could not fall without negligence, but if there are any facts inconsistent with negligence it is for the defendant to prove them.

[The concurring opinions of BRAMWELL, B., CHANNELL, B., and PIGOTT, B., are omitted.]

NOTES AND QUESTIONS

1. What kind of evidence of defendant's negligence has plaintiff offered? How persuasive is it? What about the possibility that some trespasser entered the premises and rolled the barrel out of the window? Suppose the defendant in the principal case was merely a deliverer of flour and not the owner of the shop? Cf. Hake v. George Wiedemann Brewing Co., 23 Ohio St.2d 65, 52 Ohio Op.2d 366, 262 N.E.2d 703 (1970).

2. *Res Ipsa Loquitur.* ("The thing speaks for itself.") This is an old phrase, found in Cicero and other ancient writers; and it has been used from time to time in other connections in the law. Chief Baron Pollock was an English gentleman, with a classical education, as was counsel to whom he spoke. Just what did he mean by it? This question has been put in Latin: Res ipsa loquitur, sed quid in infernos dicet?

3. There has been considerable denunciation of the use of the phrase in negligence cases. See, for example, Bond, C.J., dissenting in Potomac Edison Co. v. Johnson, 160 Md. 33, 152 A. 633 (1930): "It adds nothing to the law, has no meaning which is not more clearly expressed for us in English, and brings confusion

to our legal discussions. It does not represent a doctrine, is not a legal maxim, and is not a rule." Also Lord Shaw, in Ballard v. North British R. Co., [1923] Sess.Cas.H.L. 43, 56: "If that phrase had not been in Latin, nobody would have called it a principle."

4. The first attempt to state the rule of Byrne v. Boadle was that of Chief Justice Erle in Scott v. London & St. Katherine Docks Co., 3 H. & C. 596, 159 Eng.Rep. 665 (1865): "There must be reasonable evidence of negligence; but where the thing is shown to be under the management of the defendant or his servants, and the accident is such as in the ordinary course of things does not happen if those who have the management use proper care, it affords reasonable evidence, in the absence of explanation by the defendants, that the accident arose from want of care." These remain the two core requirements of the doctrine, although you will sometimes see a third requirement listed in opinions. Some jurisdictions added a requirement that the event not have been brought about by the actions of the plaintiff. Usually, however, the conduct of the plaintiff is considered when evaluating causation and comparative negligence, which will be discussed later in Chapters 5 and 12. See, for example, Giles v. New Haven, 228 Conn. 441, 455, 636 A.2d 1335, 1341 (1994) (res ipsa loquitur applies even if plaintiff's conduct contributed to injuries; jury to apply comparative negligence principles to account for plaintiff's conduct).

5. Shortly after 1870, this principle became entangled and confused with an older and quite different rule. In Christie v. Griggs, 2 Camp. 79, 170 Eng.Rep. 1088 (1809), the axle of a stagecoach broke and a passenger was injured. Sir James Mansfield declared that the burden lay upon the common carrier to prove that the injury was not caused by its negligence. Later decisions explained this on the basis of the special responsibility which the carrier had undertaken under its contract to transport the passenger safely.

6. The two principles became intermingled and ultimately merged in cases of injuries to passengers under the name of "res ipsa loquitur"; and much of the confusion that has surrounded the doctrine is due to this merger.

7. On "res ipsa loquitur" generally, see Atiyah, Res Ipsa Loquitur in England and Australia, 35 Mod.L.Rev. 337 (1972); Carpenter, The Doctrine of Res Ipsa Loquitur, 1 U.Chi.L.Rev. 519 (1934); Malone, Res Ipsa Loquitur and Proof by Inference, 4 La.L.Rev. 70 (1941); Morris, Res Ipsa Loquitur in Texas, 26 Tex.L.Rev. 257, 761 (1948); Prosser, Res Ipsa Loquitur in California, 37 Cal.L.Rev. 183 (1949), reprinted in Prosser, Selected Topics on the Law of Torts 302 (1954); James, Proof of the Breach in Negligence Cases, 37 Val.U.L.Rev. 179 (1951).

McDougald v. Perry

Supreme Court of Florida, 1998.
716 So. 2d 783.

WELLS, J. * * * Lawrence McDougald sued Henry Perry and Perry's employer, C & S Chemical, Inc., (collectively referred to as respondents), for personal injuries sustained in an accident which occurred on July 26, 1990, on U.S. Highway 60 West, in Bartow, Florida. On July 26, McDougald was driving behind a tractor-trailer which was driven by Perry. The trailer was leased by C & S from Ryder Truck Rentals, Inc. As Perry drove over some railroad tracks, the 130–pound spare tire came out of its cradle underneath the trailer and fell to the ground. The trailer's rear tires then ran over the spare, causing the spare to bounce into the air and collide the windshield of McDougald's Jeep Wagoneer.

The spare tire was housed in an angled cradle underneath the trailer and was held in place by its own weight. Additionally, the tire was secured by a four to six-foot long chain with one-inch links, which was wrapped around the tire. Perry testified that he believed the chain to be the original chain that came with the trailer in 1969. Perry also stated that, as originally designed, the chain was secured to the body of the trailer by a latch device. At the time of the accident, however, the chain was attached to the body of the trailer with a nut and bolt.

Perry testified that he performed a pretrip inspection of the trailer on the day of the accident. This included an inspection of the chain, although Perry admitted that he did not check every link in the chain. After the accident, Perry noticed that the chain was dragging under the trailer. Perry opined that one of the links had stretched and slipped from the nut which secured it to the trailer. [Footnote omitted.] The judge instructed the jury on the doctrine of res ipsa loquitur. The jury subsequently returned a verdict in McDougald's favor.

On appeal, the district court reversed with instructions that the trial court direct a verdict in respondents' favor. The district court concluded that the trial court erred by * * * [instructing the jury on res ipsa loquitur.] For the reasons expressed herein, we quash the decision below and approve the Fifth District's application of res ipsa loquitur to the circumstances of a wayward automobile wheel accident.

* * * In Marrero [v. Goldsmith, 486 So. 2d 530 (Fla.1986)], we stated:

> Res ipsa loquitur is a Latin phrase that translates "the thing speaks for itself." Prosser and Keaton, Law of Torts § 39 (5th ed. 1984). It is a rule of evidence that permits, but does not compel, an inference of negligence under certain circumstances. "The doctrine of res ipsa loquitur is merely a rule of evidence. Under it an inference may arise in aid of the proof." [C] In Goodyear [Tire & Rubber Co. v. Hughes Supply, Inc., 358 So.2d 530 (Fla. 1982)], a products liability case, we explained the doctrine as follows:

> It provides an injured plaintiff with a common-sense inference of negligence where direct proof of negligence is wanting, provided certain elements consistent with negligent behavior are present. Essentially the injured plaintiff must establish that the instrumentality causing his or her injury was under the exclusive control of the defendant, and that the accident is one that would not, in the ordinary course of events, have occurred without negligence on the part of the one in control. [Cc]

In concluding that it was reversible error for the trial court to give the res ipsa loquitur instruction, the Second District determined that "McDougald failed to prove that this accident would not, in the ordinary course of events, have occurred without negligence by the defendants." [C] The court explained that, "the mere fact that an accident occurs does not support the application of the doctrine." Id. In support of the Second District's conclusion, respondents cite to Burns v. Otis Elevator Co., 550 So. 2d 21 (Fla.App.1989), in which the Third District stated:

To prevail at trial, plaintiff must still present sufficient evidence, beyond that of the accident itself, from which the jury may infer that the accident would not have occurred but for the defendants' breach of due care. [C] Respondents assert that this language means that res ipsa loquitur did not apply in this case because "there was no expert or other testimony or evidence that the failure of the safety chain and the spare tire's exit onto the roadway would not ordinarily occur in the absence of [respondents'] negligence." [C]

The Second and Third Districts misread and interpret too narrowly what we stated in Goodyear. We did not say, as those courts conclude, that "the mere fact that an accident occurs does not support the application of the doctrine." Rather, we stated:

An injury standing alone, of course, ordinarily does not indicate negligence. The doctrine of res ipsa loquitur simply recognizes that in rare instances an injury may permit an inference of negligence if coupled with a sufficient showing of its immediate, precipitating cause. [C] (emphasis added).

Goodyear and our other cases permit latitude in the application of this common-sense inference when the facts of an accident in and of themselves establish that but for the failure of reasonable care by the person or entity in control of the injury producing object or instrumentality the accident would not have occurred. On the other hand, our present statement is not to be considered an expansion of the doctrine's applicability. We continue our prior recognition that res ipsa loquitur applies only in "rare instances."

The following comments in section 328D of Restatement (Second) of Torts (1965) capture the essence of a proper analysis of this issue:

c.   Type of event. The first requirement for the application of the rule stated in this Section is a basis of past experience which reasonably permits the conclusion that such events do not ordinarily occur unless someone has been negligent. There are many types of accidents which commonly occur without the fault of anyone. The fact that a tire blows out, or that a man falls down stairs is not, in the absence of anything more, enough to permit the conclusion that there was negligence in inspecting the tire, or in the construction of the stairs, because it is common human experience that such events all too frequently occur without such negligence. On the other hand there are many events, such as those of objects falling from the defendant's premises, the fall of an elevator, the escape of gas or water from mains or of electricity from wires or appliances, the derailment of trains or the explosion of boilers, where the conclusion is at least permissible that such things do not usually happen unless someone has been negligent. To such events res ipsa loquitur may apply.

d. Basis of conclusion. In the usual case the basis of past experience from which this conclusion may be drawn is common to the community, and is a matter of general knowledge, which the court recognizes on much the same basis as when it takes judicial notice of facts which everyone knows. It may, however, be supplied by the evidence of the parties; and expert testimony that such an event usually does not occur without negligence may afford a sufficient basis for the inference. Such testimony may be essential to the plaintiff's case where, as for example in some actions for medical malpractice, there is no fund of common knowledge which may permit laymen reasonably to draw the conclusion. On the other hand there are other kinds of medical malpractice, as where a sponge is left in the plaintiff's abdomen after an operation, where no expert is needed to tell the jury that such events do not usually occur in the absence of negligence.

Restatement (Second) of Torts § 328D cmts. c-d (1965).

We conclude that the spare tire escaping from the cradle underneath the truck, resulting in the tire ultimately becoming airborne and crashing into McDougald's vehicle, is the type of accident which, on the basis of common experience and as a matter of general knowledge, would not occur but for the failure to exercise reasonable care by the person who had control of the spare tire. As the Fifth District noted, the doctrine of res ipsa loquitur is particularly applicable in wayward wheel cases. * * * [C]ommon sense dictates an inference that both a spare tire carried on a truck and a wheel on a truck's axle will stay with the truck unless there is a failure of reasonable care by the person or entity in control of the truck. Thus an inference of negligence comes from proof of the circumstances of the accident.

Furthermore, we do not agree with the Second District that McDougald failed to establish this element because "other possible explanations exist to explain the failure of the chain." [C] Such speculation does not defeat the applicability of the doctrine in this case. As one commentator has noted:

Holding

> The plaintiff is not required to eliminate with certainty all other possible causes or inferences.... All that is required is evidence from which reasonable persons can say that on the whole it is more likely that there was negligence associated with the cause of the event than that there was not.

W. Page Keeton, et al., Prosser and Keaton on the Law of Torts, § 39, at 248 (5th ed. 1984). * * *

Accordingly, we quash the decision below, and remand this case with directions that the district court reinstate the trial court's judgment as to respondents' liability based upon the jury's verdict and for further proceedings consistent with the district court's decision on issues related to damages.

It is so ordered.

HARDING, C.J., and OVERTON, SHAW, KOGAN and PARIENTE, JJ., concur.

ANSTEAD, J., concurring.

I fully concur in the majority opinion, and write separately to note that this case presents a classic scenario whereby an aged appellate opinion giving rise to a legal doctrine in the distant past still illuminates and informs today's society. The thread of common sense in human experience ties today's decision to an opinion voiced by Baron Pollock in the 1863 decision in Byrne v. Boadle, 2 Hurlet & C. 722, 159 Eng. Rep. 299 (Ex. 1863). In Byrne a pedestrian was struck by a barrel which fell from a window of the defendant's flour business. In reversing a directed verdict against the plaintiff, Pollock declared for the Court:

> We are all of opinion that the rule must be absolute to enter the verdict for the plaintiff. The learned counsel was quite right in saying that there are many accidents from which no presumption of negligence can arise, but I think it would be wrong to lay down as a rule that in no case can presumption of negligence arise from the fact of an accident. Suppose in this case the barrel had rolled out of the warehouse and fallen on the plaintiff, how could he possibly ascertain from what cause it occurred? It is the duty of persons who keep barrels in a warehouse to take care that they do not roll out, and I think that such a case would, beyond all doubt, afford prima facie evidence of negligence. A barrel could not roll out of a warehouse without some negligence, and to say that a plaintiff who is injured by it must call witnesses from the warehouse to prove negligence seems to me preposterous. So in the building or repairing a house, or putting pots on the chimneys, if a person passing along the road is injured by something falling upon him, I think the accident alone would be prima facie evidence of negligence. Or if an article calculated to cause damage is put in a wrong place and does mischief, I think that those whose duty it was to put it in the right place are prima facie responsible, and if there is any state of facts to rebut the presumption of negligence, they must prove them. The present case upon the evidence comes to this, a man is passing in front of the premises of a dealer in flour, and there falls down upon him a barrel of flour. I think it apparent that the barrel was in the custody of the defendant who occupied the premises, and who is responsible for the acts of his servants who had the control of it; and in my opinion the fact of its falling is prima facie evidence of negligence, and the plaintiff who was injured by it is not bound to shew that it could not fall without negligence, but if there are any facts inconsistent with negligence it is for the defendant to prove them.

We can hardly improve upon this explanation for our decision today. The common law tradition is alive and well.

NOTES AND QUESTIONS

1.   How does the court know that this accident would be unlikely to occur in absence of negligence on the part of defendant? How could an attorney persuade the court that this was true? What other possible explanations for the failure of the

chain could defendant have argued? What about the possibility that the chain had been tampered with at a truck stop?

2. What would you expect the rule to be when an airplane crashed without explanation? See Wilson v. Colonial Air Transport, 278 Mass. 420, 180 N.E. 212 (1932); Herndon v. Gregory, 190 Ark. 702, 81 S.W.2d 849 (1935); Cox v. Northwest Airlines, Inc., 379 F.2d 893 (7th Cir.1967). What if a plane, flying through smooth air, suddenly and without any warning strikes a "bump," and a passenger is thrown from his seat? Cudney v. Midcontinent Airlines, 363 Mo. 922, 254 S.W.2d 662 (1953); Ness v. West Coast Airlines, Inc., 90 Idaho 111, 410 P.2d 965 (1965). Or hot tea is spilled into his lap from a tray? Lazarus v. Eastern Air Lines, 292 F.2d 748 (D.C.Cir.1961). See generally McLarty, Res Ipsa Loquitur in Airline Passenger Litigation, 37 Va.L.Rev. 55 (1951).

3. How persuasive is the inference of negligence in the following cases?

(A) When a television set catches fire and burns, the manufacturer was negligent. See Gast v. Sears Roebuck & Co., 39 Ohio St.2d 29, 68 Ohio Op.2d 17, 313 N.E.2d 831 (1974).

[handwritten margin notes: could have been other causes / TV exclusive in control of manufacturer? / No]

(B) When the doors of a self-service elevator close on a person, the owner of the building is at fault. Isaacs v. Warren Terrace, Inc., 60 Ohio Op.2d 214, 277 N.E.2d 88 (1971).

(C) When a human body falls upon a work of art, the person who fell was negligent. See Krebs v. Corrigan, 321 A.2d 558 (D.C.App.1974).

(D) When an automobile leaves the travelled portion of a highway and over-turns or crashes into a stationary object, the driver was at fault. See Badela v. Karpowich, 152 Conn. 360, 206 A.2d 838 (1965).

(E) When a single automobile crashes, the driver is at fault. Mets v. Granrud, 606 P.2d 1384 (Mont.1980).

(F) When a fertilizer plant explodes, the person in control of the plant was negligent. Collins v. N–Ren Corp., 604 F.2d 659 (10th Cir.1979).

(G) When an escalator comes to a sudden stop, the company responsible for its manufacture and maintenance is at fault. Compare the majority and dissenting opinions in Barretta v. Otis Elevator Co., 242 Conn. 169, 698 A.2d 810 (1997) (no res ipsa instruction because no evidence such a malfunction ordinarily does not happen in the absence of negligence; such evidence not necessary because ordinary, common experience is enough to suggest it).

(H) When cattle escape onto the highway, the rancher is at fault. Roberts v. Weber & Sons, 248 Neb. 243, 533 N.W.2d 664 (1995) (agreeing with courts that have found res ipsa instruction appropriate, but noting an even split among jurisdictions that have faced the issue).

4. Note that in the principal case the defendant had argued that the plaintiff needed expert witness testimony to support his argument that the accident would not normally have occurred in the absence of negligence. Although the court rejected the argument in that case, there may be times when it is not within common knowledge that the event would not ordinarily occur in the absence of negligence, for example, when professional malpractice is at issue. In which of the following cases would the trial court judge find that what happened does not ordinarily happen in the absence of negligence?

A. Patient continues to experience complications three months after surgery, so a second operation is performed and a laparotomy sponge, left in her during the first surgery, is removed. Coleman v. Rice, 706 So.2d 696 (Miss.1997).

B. Plaintiff undergoes a surgical operation. Afterward she is returned to her hospital room, and left in an unconscious condition for an hour. When she recovers consciousness, she has a second-degree burn on her stomach in the exact shape of a hot water bottle. Cf. Timbrell v. Suburban Hosp., 4 Cal.2d 68, 47 P.2d 737 (1935).

C. After surgery for a tumor of the spinal cord, plaintiff begins to hemorrhage. Defendant surgeon, having failed in other efforts to stop the bleeding, reopens the incision and packs the wound with a cellulosic material and sews it up. Plaintiff wakes up paralyzed below the incision. Brannon v. Wood, 251 Or. 349, 444 P.2d 558 (1968).

D. A few days after abdominal surgery to enhance her chances to become pregnant, plaintiff loses function in her left leg. Connors v. University Assocs., 4 F.3d 123 (2d Cir.1993).

E. Shortly after undergoing a bilateral mastectomy, plaintiff experiences numbness in her right arm, which was subsequently diagnosed as ulnar neuropathy, degenerative nerve damage affecting her right hand. Mireles v. Broderick, 117 N.M. 445, 872 P.2d 863 (1994).

F. Plaintiff has permanent paralysis of her vocal cord after surgery to remove her thyroid. Hightower–Warren v. Silk, 548 Pa. 459, 698 A.2d 52 (1997).

5. The courts found only the first two of the above to be within common experience. Suppose that in all the other cases, the plaintiff has an expert that will testify that the injury is one that does not ordinarily occur in the absence of negligence. Should that expert be permitted to testify? Wouldn't the use of expert witness testimony in a res ipsa loquitur case be contradictory? After all, the "thing" is hardly speaking for itself if an expert is involved. Most, but not all, courts permit the plaintiff to use expert witness testimony. See, for example, Mireles v. Broderick, 117 N.M. 445,448, 872 P.2d 863, 866 (1994) ("the central issue is not whether common knowledge alone is sufficient to establish an inference of negligence. Rather, the issue is whether there is a factual predicate sufficient to support an inference that the injury was caused by the failure of the party in control to exercise due care. The requisite probability of negligence may exist independently of the common knowledge of the jurors. The common-knowledge exception to the expert testimony rule may inform but does not delimit the application of res ipsa loquitur.") Is the requirement of expert witness testimony on the subject whether the accident would have happened in the absence of negligence peculiar to malpractice cases? See Fricke, The Use of Expert Evidence in Res Ipsa Loquitur Cases, 5 Vill.L.Rev. 59 (1959). Cf. Newell v. Westinghouse Electric Corp., 36 F.3d 576 (7th Cir.1994) (applying Indiana law) (plaintiff permitted to present expert witness testimony that particular elevator failure would not ordinarily happen in the absence of negligent maintenance).

6. As part of medical malpractice reform legislation (see page 193), a number of states have codified the res ipsa loquitur doctrine, limiting its application to specific types of medical mishaps. One statute allows a "rebuttable inference of negligence" only for foreign bodies unintentionally left in the body following surgery, an explosion or fire originating in a substance used for treatment, or a surgical procedure on the wrong patient or the wrong part of the body. 18 Del.Code Ann. tit. 18, § 6853 (1992).

Larson v. St. Francis Hotel

District Court of Appeal of California, 1948.
83 Cal.App.2d 210, 188 P.2d 513.

BRAY, JUSTICE. The accident out of which this action arose was apparently the result of the effervescence and ebullition of San Franciscans in their exuberance of joy on V–J day, August 14, 1945. Plaintiff (who is not included in the above description), while walking on the sidewalk on Post

The St. Francis Hotel, viewed from Union Square.
Post Street runs to the right of the Hotel

Facts

Street adjoining the St. Francis Hotel, just after stepping out from under the marquee, was struck on the head by a heavy, over-stuffed arm chair, knocked unconscious, and received injuries for which she is asking damages from the owners of the hotel. Although there were a number of persons in the immediate vicinity, no one appears to have seen from whence the chair came nor to have seen it before it was within a few feet of plaintiff's head, nor was there any identification of the chair as belonging to the hotel. However, it is a reasonable inference that the chair came from some portion of the hotel. For the purposes of this opinion, we will so assume, in view of the rule on nonsuit cases that every favorable inference fairly deducible from the evidence must be drawn in favor of plaintiff, and that all the evidence must be construed most strongly against the defendants. [C]

★ *Issue*

does res ipsa loquitur hold true/ apply in this case?

At the trial, plaintiff, after proving the foregoing facts and the extent of her injuries, rested, relying upon the doctrine of res ipsa loquitur. On motion of defendant the court granted a nonsuit. The main question to be determined is whether under the circumstances shown, the doctrine applies. The trial court correctly held that it did not.

In Gerhart v. Southern California Gas Co., 56 Cal.App.2d 425, 132 P.2d 874, 877, cited by plaintiff, the court sets forth the test for the applicability of the doctrine. " * * * for a plaintiff to make out a case entitling him to the benefit of the doctrine, *he must prove* (1) that there was an accident; (2) that the thing or instrumentality which caused the accident was at the time of and prior thereto under the *exclusive* control and management of the defendant; (3) *that the accident was such that in the ordinary course of events, the defendant using ordinary care, the accident would not have happened. * * ** The doctrine of res ipsa loquitur applies only where the cause of the injury is shown to be under the exclusive control and management of the defendant and can have no application * * * to a case having a divided responsibility where an unexplained accident may have been attributable to one of several causes, for some of which the defendant is not responsible, and when it appears that the injury was caused by one of two causes for one of which defendant is responsible but not for the other, plaintiff must fail, if the evidence does not show that the injury was the result of the former cause, or leaves it as probable that it was caused by one or the other." [Emphasis added.]

★ *Rule of Law*

Applying the rule to the facts of this case, it is obvious that the doctrine does not apply. While, as pointed out by plaintiff, the rule of exclusive control "is not limited to the actual physical control but applies to the right of control of the instrumentality which causes the injury" it is not clear to us how this helps plaintiff's case. A hotel does not have exclusive control, either actual or potential, of its furniture. Guests have, at least, partial control. Moreover, it cannot be said that with the hotel using ordinary care "the accident was such that in the ordinary course of events * * * it would not have happened." On the contrary, the mishap would quite as likely be due to the fault of a guest or other person as to that of defendants. The most logical inference from the circumstances shown is that the chair was thrown by some such person from a window. [It thus appears that this occurrence is not such as ordinarily does not happen without the negligence of the party charged, but, rather, one in which the accident ordinarily might happen despite the fact that the defendants used reasonable care and were totally free from negligence. To keep guests and visitors from throwing furniture out windows would require a guard to be placed in every room in the hotel, and no one would contend that there is any rule of law requiring a hotel to do that. * * *

The judgment appealed from is affirmed.

NOTES AND QUESTIONS

1. Must the possibility that the event has been caused by the conduct of a third person, for which defendant is not responsible, be entirely eliminated? Defendant parks on the side of a hill. Shortly afterward, without explanation, the automobile runs away down the hill and injures plaintiff. What are the possibilities? Can plaintiff get to the jury? Glaser v. Schroeder, 269 Mass. 337, 168 N.E. 809 (1929); Borg & Powers Furniture Co. v. Clark, 194 Minn. 305, 260 N.W. 316 (1935). A court allowed plaintiff's case to be heard by the jury although there was a four-hour lapse of time after defendant parked her car. See Hill v. Thompson, 484 P.2d 513 (Okl.1971). An escalator comes to a sudden halt, injuring plaintiff who sues the department store owner. Holzhauer v. Saks & Co., 346 Md. 328, 697 A.2d 89 (1997) (res ipsa not applicable because evidence showed emergency stop buttons were accessible to patrons and thus escalator was not in exclusive control of defendant).

2. A television catches fire in plaintiff's home. How does he persuade a court to invoke res ipsa loquitur against the manufacturer when the set left the factory several months before the incident in question? See Gast v. Sears Roebuck & Co., 39 Ohio St.2d 29, 68 Ohio Op.2d 17, 313 N.E.2d 831 (1974). Generally, what should the plaintiff do to eliminate his own conduct as a cause of the accident? Is it enough that he testifies that he did nothing unusual, and only made use of the thing furnished him by defendant for the purpose for which it was furnished?

3. Hot water escapes through a ruptured fitting on a radiator in a tenant's apartment, causing personal injury and damaging property. Should defendant landlord's "right to control" the instrumentality be sufficient to invoke res ipsa loquitur? See Niman v. Plaza House, Inc., 471 S.W.2d 207 (Mo.1971), noted 38 U.Mo.L.Rev. 371 (1973); Errico v. LaMountain, 713 A.2d 791 (R.I.1998) (landlord had statutory right to enter premises; tenant entitled to res ipsa loquitur jury instruction after balcony railing gave way when she leaned against it). Some of the older cases required that defendant have "exclusive control." Thus, in Kilgore v. Shepard Co., 52 R.I. 151, 158 A. 720 (1932), plaintiff sat down on a chair in defendant's store, and it collapsed and injured him. Recovery was denied because plaintiff, and not defendant, was in "control" of the chair at the time. Contra: Gow v. Multnomah Hotel, 191 Or. 45, 224 P.2d 552 (1950); Rose v. Melody Lane of Wilshire, 39 Cal.2d 481, 247 P.2d 335 (1952). Modern cases tend to focus more on the Restatement (Second) § 328(D)(1)(b) language that "other responsible causes, including the conduct of the plaintiff and third persons, are sufficiently eliminated by the evidence" rather than strictly on the traditional "exclusive control" language. See, for example, Errico v. LaMountain, 713 A.2d 791 (R.I.1998) (noting that Rhode Island has disavowed the earlier requirement of exclusive control in favor of the Restatement formulation).

4. *Defendant's Superior Knowledge.* It has sometimes been said that the basis of res ipsa loquitur is the defendant's superior knowledge, or ability to obtain evidence, as to just what has occurred; or in other words, that the purpose of the rule is to "smoke out" evidence that the defendant has or can get, and the plaintiff cannot. See Reese v. Memorial Hospital, 955 P.2d 425, 427 (Wyo.1998) ("If the circumstances do not show or suggest that defendant should have superior knowledge, or if the plaintiff himself possesses equal or superior means of explaining the occurrence, the rule may not properly be invoked.") This has often been stated as an additional reason for applying res ipsa loquitur when it was otherwise applicable, or for refusing to apply it when it was otherwise inapplicable, as in Hughes v. Jolliffe, 50 Wash.2d 554, 313 P.2d 678 (1957). Several writers have contended that defendant's superior knowledge is the primary, if not the sole, purpose of the rule. This is the thesis of the book by Shain, Res Ipsa Loquitur (1945). The late Professor Carpenter was a vigorous advocate of this position. Carpenter, The Doctrine of Res Ipsa Loquitur in California, 10 So.Cal.L.Rev. 166 (1937); Carpenter, Res Ipsa Loquitur, 10 So.Cal.L.Rev. 467 (1937). Most of the cases hold that res ipsa loquitur applies, even though the defendant's knowledge is not superior to that of the plaintiff. See, for example, Johnson v. Foster, 202 So.2d 520 (Miss.1967) (car unaccountably leaves highway and overturns; both parties dead); Nicol v. Geitler, 188 Minn. 69, 247 N.W. 8 (1933) (similar; guest dead, driver disappeared); Burkett v. Johnston, 39 Tenn.App. 276, 282 S.W.2d 647 (1955) (similar; both dead); Haasman v. Pacific Alaska Air Express, 100 F.Supp. 1 (D.Alaska 1951), aff'd, 198 F.2d 550 (9th Cir.1952) (lost plane); Judson v. Giant Powder Co., 107 Cal. 549, 40 P. 1020 (1895) (nitroglycerin factory blew up; the "witnesses who saw and knew, like all things else around, save the earth itself, were scattered to the four winds").

5. *Car Leaving Highway.* There is general agreement that the fact that an automobile leaves the traveled portion of the highway and overturns, or crashes into a stationary object, is enough, in the absence of explanation, to make out a res ipsa loquitur case against the driver. Badela v. Karpowich, 152 Conn. 360, 206 A.2d 838 (1965); Bavis v. Fonte, 241 Md. 123, 215 A.2d 739 (1966); Tanski v. Jackson, 269 Minn. 304, 130 N.W.2d 492 (1964); Bagby v. Commonwealth, 424 S.W.2d 119 (Ky.1968).

Ybarra v. Spangard

Supreme Court of California, 1944.
25 Cal.2d 486, 154 P.2d 687.

Action by Joseph Roman Ybarra against Lawrence C. Spangard and others for injuries resulting from allegedly improper treatment by physicians and nurses. From a judgment of nonsuit, plaintiff appeals. Reversed.

GIBSON, CHIEF JUSTICE. This is an action for damages for personal injuries alleged to have been inflicted on plaintiff by defendants during the course of a surgical operation. The trial court entered judgments of nonsuit as to all defendants and plaintiff appealed.

On October 28, 1939, plaintiff consulted defendant Dr. Tilley, who diagnosed his ailment as appendicitis, and made arrangements for an appendectomy to be performed by defendant Dr. Spangard at a hospital owned and managed by defendant Dr. Swift. Plaintiff entered the hospital, was given a hypodermic injection, slept, and later was awakened by Drs.

Tilley and Spangard and wheeled into the operating room by a nurse whom he believed to be defendant Gisler, an employee of Dr. Swift. Defendant Dr. Reser, the anesthetist, also an employee of Dr. Swift, adjusted plaintiff for the operation, pulling his body to the head of the operating table and, according to plaintiff's testimony, laying him back against two hard objects at the top of his shoulders, about an inch below his neck. Dr. Reser then administered the anesthetic and plaintiff lost consciousness. When he awoke early the following morning he was in his hospital room attended by defendant Thompson, the special nurse, and another nurse who was not made a defendant.

Plaintiff testified that prior to the operation he had never had any pain in, or injury to, his right arm or shoulder, but that when he awakened he felt a sharp pain about half way between the neck and the point of the right shoulder. He complained to the nurse, and then to Dr. Tilley, who gave him diathermy treatments while he remained in the hospital. The pain did not cease but spread down to the lower part of his arm, and after his release from the hospital the condition grew worse. He was unable to rotate or lift his arm, and developed paralysis and atrophy of the muscles around the shoulder. He received further treatments from Dr. Tilley until March, 1940, and then returned to work, wearing his arm in a splint on the advice of Dr. Spangard. * * *

Plaintiff's theory is that the foregoing evidence presents a proper case for the application of the doctrine of res ipsa loquitur, and that the inference of negligence arising therefrom makes the granting of a nonsuit improper. Defendants take the position that, assuming that plaintiff's condition was in fact the result of an injury, there is no showing that the act of any particular defendant, nor any particular instrumentality, was the cause thereof. They attack plaintiff's action as an attempt to fix liability "en masse" on various defendants, some of whom were not responsible for the acts of others; and they further point to the failure to show which defendants had control of the instrumentalities that may have been involved. Their main defense may be briefly stated in two propositions: (1) that where there are several defendants, and there is a division of responsibility in the use of an instrumentality causing the injury, and the injury might have resulted from the separate act of either one of two or more persons, the rule of res ipsa loquitur cannot be invoked against any one of them; and (2) that where there are several instrumentalities, and no showing is made as to which caused the injury or as to the particular defendant in control of it, the doctrine cannot apply. We are satisfied, however, that these objections are not well taken in the circumstances of this case. * * *

The present case is of a type which comes within the reason and spirit of the doctrine more fully perhaps than any other. The passenger sitting awake in a railroad car at the time of a collision, the pedestrian walking along the street and struck by a falling object or the debris of an explosion, are surely not more entitled to an explanation than the unconscious patient on the operating table. Viewed from this aspect, it is difficult to see how the doctrine can, with any justification, be so restricted in its statement as to become inapplicable to a patient who submits himself to the care and custody of doctors and nurses, is rendered unconscious, and receives some injury from instrumentalities used in his treatment. Without the aid of the doctrine a patient who received permanent injuries of a serious character, obviously the result of someone's negligence, would be entirely unable to recover unless the doctors and nurses in attendance voluntarily chose to disclose the identity of the negligent person and the facts establishing liability. [Cc] If this were the state of the law of negligence, the courts, to avoid gross injustice, would be forced to invoke the principles of absolute liability, irrespective of negligence, in actions by persons suffering injuries during the course of treatment under anesthesia. But we think this juncture has not yet been reached, and that the doctrine of res ipsa loquitur is properly applicable to the case before us.

The condition that the injury must not have been due to the plaintiff's voluntary action is of course fully satisfied under the evidence produced herein; and the same is true of the condition that the accident must be one which ordinarily does not occur unless some one was negligent. We have here no problem of negligence in treatment, but of distinct injury to a healthy part of the body not the subject of treatment, nor within the area covered by the operation. The decisions in this state make it clear that such circumstances raise the inference of negligence and call upon the defendant to explain the unusual result.

The argument of defendants is simply that plaintiff has not shown an injury caused by an instrumentality under a defendant's control, because he has not shown which of the several instrumentalities that he came in contact with while in the hospital caused the injury; and he has not shown that any one defendant or his servants had exclusive control over any particular instrumentality. Defendants assert that some of them were not the employees of other defendants, that some did not stand in any permanent relationship from which liability in tort would follow, and that in view of the nature of the injury, the number of defendants and the different functions performed by each, they could not all be liable for the wrong, if any.

We have no doubt that in a modern hospital a patient is quite likely to come under the care of a number of persons in different types of contractual and other relationships with each other. For example, in the present case it appears that Drs. Smith, Spangard and Tilley were physicians or surgeons commonly placed in the legal category of independent contractors; and Dr. Reser, the anesthetist, and defendant Thompson, the special nurse, were employees of Dr. Swift and not of the other doctors. But we do not believe that either the number or relationship of the defendants alone determines whether the doctrine of res ipsa loquitur applies. Every defendant in whose custody the plaintiff was placed for any period was bound to exercise ordinary care to see that no unnecessary harm came to him and each would be liable for failure in this regard. Any defendant who negligently injured him, and any defendant charged with his care who so neglected him as to allow injury to occur, would be liable. The defendant employers would be liable for the neglect of their employees; and the doctor in charge of the operation would be liable for the negligence of those who became his temporary servants for the purpose of assisting in the operation. * * *

It may appear at the trial, that, consistent with the principles outlined above, one or more defendants will be found liable and others absolved, but this should not preclude the application of the rule of res ipsa loquitur. The control at one time or another, of one or more of the various agencies or instrumentalities which might have harmed the plaintiff was in the hands of every defendant or of his employees or temporary servants. This, we think, places upon them the burden of initial explanation. Plaintiff was rendered unconscious for the purpose of undergoing surgical treatment by the defendants; it is manifestly unreasonable for them to insist that he identify any one of them as the person who did the alleged negligent act. * * *

[I]f we accept the contention of defendants herein, there will rarely be any compensation for patients injured while unconscious. A hospital today conducts a highly integrated system of activities, with many persons contributing their efforts. There may be, e.g., preparation for surgery by nurses and interns who are employees of the hospital; administering of an anesthetic by a doctor who may be an employee of the hospital, an employee of the operating surgeon, or an independent contractor; performance of an operation by a surgeon and assistants who may be his employees, employees of the hospital, or independent contractors; and post surgical care by the surgeon, a hospital physician, and nurses. The number of those in whose care the patient is placed is not a good reason for denying him all reasonable opportunity to recover for negligent harm. It is rather a good reason for re-examination of the statement of legal theories which supposedly compel such a shocking result.

We do not at this time undertake to state the extent to which the reasoning of this case may be applied to other situations in which the doctrine of res ipsa loquitur is invoked. We merely hold that where a plaintiff receives unusual injuries while unconscious and in the course of medical treatment, all those defendants who had any control over his body or the instrumentalities which might have caused the injuries may properly be called upon to meet the inference of negligence by giving an explanation of their conduct.

The judgment is reversed.

[On the second trial, each of the defendants except the owner of the hospital gave evidence, and each testified that while he was present he saw nothing occur that could have produced the injury to plaintiff's arm and shoulder. The trial court, without a jury, found that this did not overcome the inference of negligence, and found against all of them. This was affirmed, on the basis of the above opinion, in Ybarra v. Spangard, 93 Cal.App.2d 43, 208 P.2d 445 (1949).]

NOTES AND QUESTIONS

1. This decision was approved and followed, upon similar facts, in Frost v. Des Moines Still College of Osteopathy, 248 Iowa 294, 79 N.W.2d 306 (1956) and Beaudoin v. Watertown Memorial Hosp., 32 Wis.2d 132, 145 N.W.2d 166 (1966). On the other hand it was rejected in Rhodes v. De Haan, 184 Kan. 473, 337 P.2d 1043 (1959); and Talbot v. Dr. W.H. Groves' Latter–Day Saints Hosp., Inc., 21 Utah 2d 73, 440 P.2d 872 (1968). The case is criticized in Seavey, Res Ipsa Loquitur: Tabula in Naufragio, 63 Harv.L.Rev. 643 (1950). A good article is Thode, The Unconscious Patient; Who Should Bear the Risk of Unexplained Injuries to a Healthy Part of His Body?, 1969 Utah L.Rev. 1. Compare a situation where plaintiff brought a claim against one physician but did not eliminate, as a cause of her harm, another physician who participated in the operation. Jones v. Harrisburg Polyclinic Hosp., 496 Pa. 465, 437 A.2d 1134 (1981). What if the patient sues the hospital that is responsible for the conduct of the nurses, but does not include the surgeon and the anesthesiologist? Darrah v. Bryan Memorial Hospital, 253 Neb. 710, 571 N.W.2d 783 (1998) (summary judgment for hospital because plaintiff did not eliminate surgeon and anesthesiologist as possible sources of injury).

2. How far is the decision to be explained on the basis of the special responsibility undertaken by the defendants toward the plaintiff? By the refusal of the potential witnesses to testify? In Gobin v. Avenue Food Mart, 178 Cal.App.2d 345, 2 Cal.Rptr. 822 (1960), the court explained the *Ybarra* case as based upon the special obligation of the medical defendants to their patient, and refused to extend it by applying res ipsa loquitur against the manufacturer, wholesaler and retailer of a defective dart gun that injured the purchaser.

3. Courts have applied res ipsa loquitur against multiple defendants in only a few special situations. In Loch v. Confair, 372 Pa. 212, 93 A.2d 451 (1953), and Nichols v. Nold, 174 Kan. 613, 258 P.2d 317 (1953), it was applied against the bottler and the retailer of bottled beverages that exploded. Both states then imposed strict liability, in the form of a "warranty" to the consumer, upon sellers of food products.

In Gilbert v. Korvette, Inc., 457 Pa. 602, 327 A.2d 94 (1974), plaintiff was injured by an escalator in a Korvette's store. The court found that the rule of res ipsa loquitur supported the conclusion that both the store operator and escalator operator were responsible causes of the injury and that each may be subjected to liability.

In Dement v. Olin–Mathieson Chem. Corp., 282 F.2d 76 (5th Cir.1960), defendant A manufactured dynamite and sold it to defendant B, which resold it together with a cap of its own manufacture. The dynamite and cap exploded prematurely, and injured a workman. The court applied res ipsa loquitur against both A and B, stressing the fact that each had cooperated to contribute to the final unified product.

4. In several states all this may be affected by statutes that permit the plaintiff to join defendants in one action and plead that they are liable in the alternative. It has been held that in order to carry out the purpose of these statutes, they must be interpreted to mean that the plaintiff, by showing that one or the other is liable, can get by a motion for nonsuit or dismissal and can get to the jury if defendants offer no evidence. Hummerstone v. Leary, [1921] 2 K.B. 664; S. & C. Clothing Co. v. United States Trucking Corp., 216 App.Div. 482, 215 N.Y.S. 349 (1926); Thermoid Rubber Co. v. Baird Rubber & Trading Co., 124 Misc. 774, 209 N.Y.S. 277 (1925). But if, at the close of the whole case, there is not sufficient

evidence against any defendant, a verdict must still be directed against the plaintiff. Julius Klugman's Sons v. Oceanic Steam Nav. Co., 42 F.2d 461 (S.D.N.Y.1930).

5. Nine members of the Wauwatosa High School Band Mothers individually cooked turkeys in their own homes from which turkey salad was made at a church kitchen by some of them. Plaintiff ate the turkey salad and suffered food poisoning. Should res ipsa loquitur be invoked against all of them? Does the situation differ from the principal case? See Samson v. Riesing, 62 Wis.2d 698, 215 N.W.2d 662 (1974).

6. _Collisions Between Vehicles_. There is general agreement that when plaintiff's car collides with defendant's, neither driver has a res ipsa loquitur case against the other. Why? When the collision injures a third person, such as a bystander on the sidewalk, most of the decisions have held that he does not have a _res ipsa_ case against either driver. Busch v. Los Angeles Ry. Corp., 178 Cal. 536, 174 P. 665 (1918); Union Traction Co. v. Alstadt, 195 Ind. 389, 143 N.E. 879 (1924).

7. _Common Carriers_. When one of the vehicles is operated by a common carrier, and the injury is to its passenger, some courts apply res ipsa loquitur against the carrier alone. See Capital Transit Co. v. Jackson, 80 U.S.App.D.C. 162, 149 F.2d 839 (1945). But see Reardon v. Boston Elevated R. Co., 247 Mass. 124, 141 N.E. 857 (1923) and Bethel v. N.Y.C. Transit Authority, 92 N.Y.2d 348, 355, 703 N.E.2d 1214, 1218 (1998) (abandoning higher duty for common carriers in part because it results in different standards applying to different parties involved in the same accident). Why res ipsa loquitur against the carrier, but not against the other driver, when the evidence against each is the same? The reason sometimes given is that, since the carrier is held to the highest degree of care, it is more probable that the collision was due to some negligence on the part of the carrier than of the other driver. See James, Proof of the Breach in Negligence Cases, 37 Va.L.Rev. 179 (1951); and cf. Simpson v. Gray Line Co., 226 Or. 71, 358 P.2d 516 (1961), holding that a tire blowout on a bus creates a res ipsa case against the carrier. A better explanation may be simply that this is a survival of the older rule which once placed the burden of proof upon the carrier; and that its basis is the special responsibility undertaken toward the passenger.

8. There is a good discussion of the whole problem of multiple defendants in McCoid, Negligence Actions Against Multiple Defendants, 7 Stan.L.Rev. 480 (1955).

Sullivan v. Crabtree

Court of Appeals of Tennessee, 1953.
36 Tenn.App. 469, 258 S.W.2d 782.

FELTS, JUDGE. Plaintiffs sued for damages for the death of their adult son, Robert Sullivan, who was killed while a guest in a motor truck which swerved off the highway and overturned down a steep embankment. Suit was brought against both the owner and the driver of the truck, but a nonsuit was taken as to the owner, and the case went to trial against the driver alone. There was a verdict and judgment in his favor, and plaintiffs appealed in error.

The truck was a large trailer-tractor truck * * *. Its driver Crabtree * * * permitted Sullivan to ride with him as a guest in the cab of the truck.

The road on which he was driving was a paved first-class Federal-state highway (U.S. 41, Tenn. 2), but coming down the mountain from Monteagle to Pelham it had a number of moderate grades and pretty sharp curves. It was midafternoon, and the weather was dry and clear. As Crabtree was approaching a curve another truck overtook and passed him, and just after it did so, Crabtree's truck suddenly swerved from his right side over to his left, ran off the left shoulder, overturned down a steep embankment, and crushed Sullivan to death.

Defendant testified that there was some loose gravel on the road, which had perhaps been spilled there by trucks hauling gravel, and the pavement was broken a little on the right-hand side; and that when he "hit the edge of the curve on the right-hand side" he "lost control of the truck," and it turned from his right side across to the left, and ran off the shoulder of the highway. On cross-examination he further said:

"Q. Can you tell the Jury now what caused you to lose control of the truck and permit it to run off the road down the embankment? A. No. The brakes could have gave way, or the brakes could have grabbed or it could have been a particular wheel grabbed, because on a tractor, if the brakes happen to grab on it, the load is so much heavier than the tractor, it whips either way and takes control of the tractor and you have nothing to do with it.

"Q. Did that happen in this case? A. It is possible. * * *

"Q. You can't tell us just what did cause the accident or cause you to lose control of the truck? A. Probably hitting the edge of the pavement or it could have been several different things. Like one going off the mountain, if it is pulled out with the wrecker, you don't know whether a hose got connected up in there and when you turned the curve break a hose, cut it or break it loose. The brakes are cut on and off with a catch there like that, and it is easy for a hose to get loose."

Such being the undisputed facts, plaintiffs contend that defendant was guilty, as a matter of law, of negligence causing the death sued for, and that there was no evidence to support a verdict for defendant. They show a duty of care owing by defendant to the deceased under our rule that a driver must use ordinary care for the safety of his guest [c] and to make out a breach of that duty, or proximate negligence, they invoke the rule of res ipsa loquitur.

They insist that the facts of this case brought it within the rule of res ipsa loquitur requiring a finding of negligence, in the absence of an explanation disproving negligence; that since there was no such explanation, since defendant did not know why he lost control of the truck or what caused the accident, the jury were bound to find that it was caused by his negligence and could not reasonably render a verdict in his favor. * * *

The maxim res ipsa loquitur means that the facts of the occurrence evidence negligence; the circumstances unexplained justify an inference of negligence. In the principle of proof employed, a case of res ipsa loquitur does not differ from an ordinary case of circumstantial evidence. Res ipsa loquitur is not an arbitrary rule but rather "a common sense appraisal of the probative value of circumstantial evidence." Boykin v. Chase Bottling Works, 32 Tenn.App. 508, 520–523, 222 S.W.2d 889, 896.

This maxim does not generally apply to motor vehicle accidents but it may apply to such an accident where the circumstances causing it were within the driver's control and the accident was such as does not usually occur without negligence. So where a motor vehicle, without apparent cause, runs off the road and causes harm, the normal inference is that the driver was negligent, and res ipsa loquitur is usually held to apply. * * *

So we agree with learned counsel for plaintiffs that the facts of this case brought it within the maxim res ipsa loquitur. The accident was such as does not usually occur without negligence, and the cause of it was in control of the driver, or rather it resulted from his loss of control of the truck, which he could not explain.

While we agree that these facts made a case of res ipsa loquitur, we do not agree that they, though unexplained, required an inference or finding of negligence, or that the jury could not reasonably refuse to find negligence and return a verdict for defendant, or that there was no evidence to support their verdict for him.

It is true there has been confusion in the cases as to the procedural effect of res ipsa loquitur, some cases giving it one and some another of these three different effects:

(1) It warrants an *inference* of negligence which the jury may draw or not, as their judgment dictates. [Cc]

(2) It raises a *presumption* of negligence which requires the jury to find negligence if defendant does not produce evidence sufficient to rebut the presumption. [Cc]

(3) It not only raises such a presumption but also *shifts the ultimate burden of proof* to defendant and requires him to prove by a preponderance of all the evidence that the injury was not caused by his negligence. [Cc]

The effect of a case of res ipsa loquitur, like that of any other case of circumstantial evidence varies from case to case, depending on the particular facts of each case; and therefore such effect can no more be fitted into a fixed formula or reduced to a rigid rule than can the effect of other cases of circumstantial evidence. The only generalization that can be safely made is that, in the words of the definition of res ipsa loquitur, it affords "reasonable evidence," in the absence of an explanation by defendant, that the accident arose from this negligence.

The weight or strength of such "reasonable evidence" will necessarily depend on the particular facts of each case, and the cogency of the inference of negligence from such facts may of course vary in degree all the way from practical certainty in one case to reasonable probability in another.

In exceptional cases the inference may be so strong as to require a directed verdict for plaintiff, as in cases of objects falling from defendant's premises on persons in the highway, such as Byrne v. Boadle (1863), 2 H. &

C. 720, 159 Eng.Reprint 299 (a barrel of flour fell from a window of defendant's warehouse); McHarge v. M.M. Newcomer & Co., 117 Tenn. 595, 100 S.W. 700, 9 L.R.A.N.S. 298, N.S., 298 (an awning roller fell from defendant's building); and Turnpike Co. v. Yates, supra (a toll gate or pole fell on a traveler); cf. Annotation, 153 A.L.R. 1134.

In the ordinary case, however, res ipsa loquitur merely makes a case for the jury—merely permits the jury to choose the inference of defendant's negligence in preference to other permissible or reasonable inferences. [Cc]

We think this is true in the case before us. The cause of the death sued for was defendant's loss of control of the truck. This may have been due to his own negligence, or it may have been due to no fault of his—an unavoidable accident resulting from the brakes giving way or the breaking of some part of the control mechanism of the truck. Since such conflicting inferences might be reasonably drawn from the evidence, it was for the jury to choose the inference they thought most probable; and we cannot say that there was no evidence to support their verdict for defendant. * * *

All the assignments of error are overruled and the judgment of the Circuit Court is affirmed.

NOTES AND QUESTIONS

1.   Most cases are in accord with the principal case as to the procedural effect of res ipsa loquitur: it warrants the *inference* of negligence that the jury may draw or not, as its judgment dictates. See George Foltis, Inc. v. New York, 287 N.Y. 108, 38 N.E.2d 455 (1941). Others hold that res ipsa creates a rebuttable presumption and some that it shifts the burden of proof to the defendant.

2.   Suppose plaintiff, the guardian of her sister who was confined to a nursing home, proved at trial that her sister had gone into a coma because she received an overdose of a drug used to treat diabetes. The patient did not have diabetes and her chart did not indicate the administration of any medication other than sterile water as a placebo when she complained of pain. Is this enough evidence to warrant a res ipsa jury instruction? Now suppose that defendant nursing home proves that it did not have that drug in its pharmacy because no patient in its care used it, that patient frequently was visited by her family and had visited her sister's home two weeks before the overdose, that her sister was diabetic and had the drug in her home for her own treatment, and that patient had become addicted to prescription drugs and was a "known drug seeker." Think about this case in the context of each possible effect of res ipsa. Could the jury draw an inference of negligence on the part of the nursing home? Did defendant nursing home rebut a presumption of negligence on the part of the nursing home? Did defendant nursing home prove that its negligence did not cause patient's overdose? See Harder v. F.C. Clinton, Inc., 948 P.2d 298 (Okla.1997).

3.   There may be exceptional cases where the inference of negligence will be so compelling that the jury cannot be permitted to reject it, and a verdict must be directed for the plaintiff in the absence of evidence to explain it away. One such case is the head-on collision of two trains on the same track in Moore v. Atchison, T. & S.F.R. Co., 28 Ill.App.2d 340, 171 N.E.2d 393 (1960). "The time will probably never come when a collision resulting from an attempt to have two trains going at

full speed, in opposite directions, pass each other, on the same track, will not be held to be negligence in law." Rouse v. Hornsby, 67 Fed. 219, 221 (8th Cir.1895).

4. Some courts have given res ipsa loquitur a greater procedural effect when the action is brought by an injured passenger against his carrier. See, for example, Greyhound Corp. v. Brown, 269 Ala. 520, 113 So.2d 916 (1959), and Transcontinental Bus System v. Simons, 367 P.2d 160 (Okla.1961), shifting the burden of proof to the defendant. This is obviously a carry-over from the original rule that, because of the special responsibility undertaken by the carrier, it had the burden of proof.

5. *Effect of Pleading Specific Acts of Negligence.* No less than four positions have been taken by the courts, as to whether the plaintiff, by his specific pleading of negligence, is precluded from relying upon *res ipsa loquitur:* (a) that he cannot rely on it at all; (b) that he may take advantage of *res ipsa loquitur* to the extent that the inference of negligence to be drawn supports the specific allegations; (c) that he may rely on *res ipsa* only if the specific pleading is accompanied by a general allegation of negligence; and (d) that it is available without regard to the form of the pleading. Which is the best rule? Do you see how each of the positions might impact on the plaintiff in a particular case? See discussion in Vogreg v. Shepard Ambulance Co., 47 Wash.2d 659, 289 P.2d 350 (1955).

6. Similar positions have been taken as to the effect of the introduction of specific evidence of negligent conduct. What if the plaintiff's specific evidence tells the complete story of how the accident happened and just what the defendant did? Is there any room for the application of *res ipsa loquitur*? See Augspurger v. Western Auto Supply Co., 257 Iowa 777, 134 N.W.2d 913 (1965); Dover Elevator Co. v. Swann, 334 Md. 231, 638 A.2d 762 (1994) (expert's opinion as to the specific cause of the elevator misleveling precluded reliance on *res ipsa*). Compare the following: "When the plaintiff shows that the railway car in which he was a passenger was derailed, there is an inference that the defendant railroad has somehow been negligent. When the plaintiff goes further and shows that the derailment was caused by an open switch, the plaintiff destroys any inference of other causes; but the inference that the defendant has not used proper care in looking after its switches is not destroyed, but considerably strengthened. If the plaintiff goes further still and shows that the switch was left open by a drunken switchman on duty, there is nothing left to infer; and if the plaintiff shows that the switch was thrown by an escaped convict with a grudge against the railroad, the plaintiff has proven himself out of court." W. Prosser and W. Keeton, Torts, 260 (5th ed. 1984).

CHAPTER V

CAUSATION IN FACT

[handwritten: "But for..." causation (but for D's conduct, P would not have been injured)]

1. SINE QUA NON

Perkins v. Texas and New Orleans Ry. Co.

Supreme Court of Louisiana, 1962.
243 La. 829, 147 So.2d 646.

SANDERS, JUSTICE. This is a tort action. Plaintiff, the 67-year-old widow of Tanner Perkins, seeks damages for the death of her husband in the collision of an automobile, in which he was riding, with a train of the defendant railroad. The district court awarded damages. The Court of Appeal affirmed. We granted certiorari to review the judgment of the Court of Appeal.

[handwritten: Facts]

The tragic accident which gave rise to this litigation occurred at the intersection of Eddy Street and The Texas and New Orleans Railroad Company track in the town of Vinton, Louisiana, at approximately 6:02 a.m., after daylight, on September 28, 1959. At this crossing Eddy Street runs north and south, and the railroad track, east and west. Involved was a 113–car freight train pulled by four diesel engines traveling east and a Dodge automobile driven by Joe Foreman in a southerly direction on Eddy Street. Tanner Perkins, a guest passenger, was riding in the front seat of the automobile with the driver.

Located in the northwest quadrant of the intersection of the railroad track and Eddy Street was a warehouse five hundred feet long. A "house track" paralleled the main track on the north to serve the warehouse. This warehouse obstructed the view to the west of an automobile driver approaching the railroad crossing from the north on Eddy Street. It likewise obstructed the view to the north of trainmen approaching the crossing from the west. Having previously served on this route, the engineer and brakeman were aware of this obstruction.

To warn the public of the approach of trains, the defendant railroad had installed at the crossing an automatic signal device consisting of a swinging red light and a bell. At the time of the accident, this signal was operating. A standard Louisiana railroad stop sign and an intersection stop sign were also located at the crossing.

Proceeding east, the train approached the intersection with its headlight burning, its bell ringing, and its whistle blowing.

The engineer, brakeman, and fireman were stationed in the forward engine of the train. The engineer was seated on the right or south side, where he was unable to observe an automobile approaching from the left of the engine. The brakeman and fireman, who were seated on the left or north side of the engine, were looking forward as the train approached the intersection. These two crewmen saw the automobile emerge from behind the warehouse. At that time the front wheels of the automobile were on or across the north rail of the house track. The fireman estimated that the train was approximately 60 feet from the crossing when the automobile emerged from behind the warehouse. The brakeman, however, estimated that the train was 30 to 40 feet from the crossing at the time the automobile came into view. Both crewmen immediately shouted a warning to the engineer, who applied the emergency brakes. The train struck the right side of the automobile and carried it approximately 1250 feet. The two occupants were inside the automobile when it came to rest. Both were killed.

The speed of the automobile in which Tanner Perkins was riding was variously estimated from 3–4 miles per hour to 20–25 miles per hour.

The plaintiff and defendant railroad concede in their pleadings that Joe Foreman, the driver of the automobile, was negligent in driving upon the track in front of the train and that his negligence was a proximate cause of the death of Tanner Perkins.

It is conceded that the railroad's safety regulations imposed a speed limit of 25 miles per hour on trains in the town of Vinton. The plaintiff has conceded in this Court that this self-imposed speed limit was a safe speed at the crossing. The train was in fact traveling at a speed of 37 miles per hour.

Applicable here is the rule that the violation by trainmen of the railroad's own speed regulations adopted in the interest of safety is evidence of negligence. * * *

We find, as did the Court of Appeal, that the trainmen were negligent in operating the train 12 miles per hour in excess of the speed limit.

* * * [T]he prime issue in this case is whether the excessive speed of the train was a cause in fact of the fatal collision.

It is fundamental that negligence is not actionable unless it is a cause in fact of the harm for which recovery is sought. It need not, of course, be the sole cause. Negligence is a cause in fact of the harm to another if it was a substantial factor in bringing about that harm. Under the circumstances of the instant case, the excessive speed was undoubtedly a substantial factor in bringing about the collision if the collision would not have occurred without it. On the other hand, if the collision would have occurred irrespective of such negligence, then it was not a substantial factor. [Cc]

In the instant case the train engineer testified that at a speed of 25 miles per hour he would have been unable to stop the train in time to avoid the accident. Other facts of record support his testimony in this regard. With efficient brakes, the mile-long train required 1250 feet to stop at a speed of 37 miles per hour. It is clear, then, that even at the concededly safe speed of 25 miles per hour, the momentum of the train would have, under the circumstances, carried it well beyond the crossing. This finding, of course, does not fully determine whether the collision would have been averted at the slower speed. The automobile was also in motion during the crucial period. This necessitates the further inquiry of whether the automobile would have cleared the track and evaded the impact had the train been moving at a proper speed at the time the trainmen observed the automobile emerge from behind the warehouse. Basic to this inquiry are the speed of the automobile and the driving distance between it and a position of safety. [C]

The testimony of the witnesses is in hopeless conflict as to the speed of the automobile at the time of the collision.

* * * Despite these deficiencies in the evidence, the plaintiff argues that had the train been traveling at a proper speed the driver of the automobile would "conceivably" have had some additional time to take measures to avert disaster and the deceased would have had some additional time to extricate himself from danger. Hence, the plaintiff reasons, the collision and loss of life "might not" have occurred.

On the facts of this case, we must reject the escape theory advanced in this argument. Because of the deficiencies in the evidence which we have already noted, it is devoid of evidentiary support. The record contains no probative facts from which the Court can draw a reasonable inference of causation under this theory. In essence, the argument is pure conjecture.

Based upon the evidence of record, it appears almost certain that the fatal accident would have occurred irrespective of the excessive speed of the train. It follows that this speed was not a substantial factor in bringing about the accident.

We conclude that the plaintiff has failed to discharge the burden of proving that the negligence of the defendant was a cause in fact of the tragic death. The judgment in favor of plaintiff is manifestly erroneous.

For the reasons assigned, the judgment of the Court of Appeal is reversed, and the plaintiff's suit is dismissed at her cost.

NOTES AND QUESTIONS

1. In the principal case, if the collision was a cause of the plaintiffs' deaths, why should the defendant have avoided liability?

2. Driver is driving 30 m.p.h. in a 25 m.p.h. zone in a thunderstorm. Her speed causes her car to be passing under a tree just as it is struck by lightning and falls onto the car, injuring passenger. Does passenger have a negligence cause of action against driver? 43 ATL 240   Tenn. Supreme Court

3. Defendant truck driver negligently failed to signal for a left turn. Plaintiff crashed into the truck. Can defendant win the case by establishing that plaintiff was not looking and would not have seen the signal if it had been given? Rouleau v. Blotner, 84 N.H. 539, 152 A. 916 (1931) ("if he were a deaf man, the failure to sound whistle, bell or horn would be immaterial").

4. Defendant excavates a hole in the sidewalk, and leaves it unguarded and unlighted. Plaintiff, a traveler on the sidewalk, accidentally falls into it in the dark. Is defendant's negligence a cause of his injury? What if a third person negligently

yes

bumps into plaintiff, and knocks him into the hole? Village of Carterville v. Cook, 129 Ill. 152, 22 N.E. 14 (1889). Suppose the third person intentionally shoves him into it? Milostan v. Chicago, 148 Ill.App. 540 (1909).

No third person liable — *intentional tort*

5.   The mate of defendant's steam trawler falls overboard, and disappears immediately. Defendant's lifeboat is lashed to the deck instead of being suspended from davits, and is equipped with only one oar. Is this negligence a cause of his death? Ford v. Trident Fisheries Co., 232 Mass. 400, 122 N.E. 389 (1919). *maybe*

D was negligent but not necessarily cause of P death

6.   Defendant, cutting ice on a lake, was negligent in failing to fence the opening as required by statute, in failing to give warning of its location, and in not having ropes or other appliances at hand to rescue anyone who fell in. Plaintiff's horses ran away, plunged into the opening, and were drowned. The evidence was that the horses were uncontrollable and could not have been stopped or directed, and that they went under the ice and could not have been rescued. Is defendant's negligence a cause of their loss? Stacy v. Knickerbocker Ice Co., 84 Wis. 614, 54 N.W. 1091 (1893). See also Haft v. Lone Palm Hotel, 3 Cal.3d 756, 478 P.2d 465, 91 Cal.Rptr. 745 (1970), where a motel operator failed to fulfill a statutory obligation to provide either a lifeguard for a motel pool or post a suitable warning that no lifeguard was present. A father and son, last seen playing in the pool, were found at the bottom. Was the motel operator's negligence a cause of the deaths? Would the presence of a lifeguard have prevented the drownings? Would the presence of a sign warning that there was no lifeguard have prevented the drownings?

sign no, lifeguard possibly

7.   In Technical Chemical Co. v. Jacobs, 480 S.W.2d 602 (Tex.1972), defendant failed to put a warning on a can of refrigerant. Plaintiff started using it without reading the instructions. Was defendant's failure to warn a cause of plaintiff's injury? See also Nelson v. Ford Motor Co., 150 F.3d 905 (8th Cir.1998) (applying Missouri law) (since plaintiff did not read owner's manual or other instructions before using jack, he did not show that modified or additional warnings would have prevented accident).

8.   Defendant railroad violated a statute in failing to display a warning sign at a railroad crossing. Plaintiff, who was injured at the crossing, knew from prior experience of the danger. Was defendant's negligence a cause in fact of plaintiff's injuries? See Thomas v. Baltimore & Ohio R. Co., 19 Md.App. 217, 310 A.2d 186 (1973).

9.   Can this be reduced to a rule? For an attempt, see Strachan, Scope and Application of the "But For" Causal Test, 33 Mod.L.Rev. 386 (1970). Three excellent articles on causation in fact are Malone, Ruminations on Cause–In–Fact, 9 Stan.L.Rev. 60 (1958); Zwier, "Cause in Fact" in Tort Law—A Philosophical and Historical Examination, 31 DePaul L.Rev. 769 (1982); Wright, Causation in Tort Law, 73 Cal.L.Rev. 1735 (1985). Two elaborate books are Becht and Miller, The Test of Causation in Fact (1961); and Hart and Honoré, Causation (2d ed. 1985). The latter deals with the philosophical and legal aspects of both cause in fact and "proximate cause."

2.   PROOF OF CAUSATION

Gentry v. Douglas Hereford Ranch, Inc.

Supreme Court of Montana, 1998.
290 Mont. 126, 962 P.2d 1205.

[Defendant Bacon was planning to hunt deer on his wife's grandmother's ranch while his wife and a friend of theirs, Barbara Gentry, painted the interior of the grandmother's new house. After trying unsuccessfully to start the furnace at the new house, Bacon started a fire in the fireplace and then left to go get his rifle from where he had parked his car. He then returned to the new house to get the ranch pickup, holding his rifle on his shoulder with his right hand. As he was approaching a wooden deck adjacent to the house and accessed by two wooden steps, Barbara Gentry came out of the house to get a radio from the pickup. Bacon stumbled and his rifle discharged, the bullet struck Barbara Gentry in the head, and she died several weeks later from the head injury. Her husband brought wrongful death and survival actions against Bacon, the ranch company owned by the grandmother, and a cattle company that leased part of the ranch. The complaint alleged that Bacon had been negligent in his handling of the rifle and that the ranch and cattle company defendants had been negligent in maintaining the deck stairs in a dangerous condition and that their combined negligence had caused the injury. After Bacon sought bankruptcy protection, he was dismissed from the case. The trial court judge entered summary judgment in favor of the ranch company defendants and plaintiff appealed on several grounds.]

TRIEWEILER, J. * * *

ISSUE 1

Did the District Court err when it concluded as a matter of law that the [ranch company] defendants were not negligent? * * *

A negligence action requires proof of four elements: (1) existence of a duty; (2) breach of the duty; (3) causation; and (4) damages. If the plaintiff fails to offer proof of one of these elements, the action in negligence fails and summary judgment in favor of the defendant is proper. [C] The causation element requires proof of both cause in fact and proximate cause. * * *

In Busta v. Columbus Hospital Corp. (1996), 276 Mont. 342, 916 P.2d 122, 139, we held that:

In those cases which do not involve issues of intervening cause, proof of causation is satisfied by proof that a party's conduct was a cause-in-fact of the damage alleged. As stated in Prosser and Keeton on Torts § 41, at 266 (5th ed. 1984), a party's conduct is a cause-in-fact of an event if "the event would not have occurred but for that conduct; conversely, the defendant's conduct is not a cause of the event, if the event would have occurred without it."

* * * We limit our discussion, however, to our conclusion that Gentry failed to prove cause in fact.

Gentry alleged that the ranch company [defendants] ... were negligent by failing to maintain the stairs to the deck adjoining the "new house" in a reasonably safe condition. He contended that the bottom stair was unstable and that the area leading to it was cluttered by debris, including a drain pipe, electric wires, and rocks. However, the defendants' motions for summary judgment were based on Bacon's testimony that he was unable to attribute his fall to any of those conditions. When he was deposed on May 2, 1997, he gave the following testimony in response to the following questions:

Q: Do you remember stumbling as you started up the steps?

A: I don't remember hardly anything.

. . .

Q: And you don't remember exactly where you were when you began to stumble; is that right?

A: That's correct.

Q: And you don't know whether it was—whether there was even some object that caused you to slip or stumble; is that right?

A: I don't remember anything.

. . .

Q: You don't remember where you were?

A: No.

Q: And from the time after the rifle discharged, you don't know exactly where you were when you fell or what caused you to fall; is that right?

A: Correct.

. . .

Q: And you don't recall if you had even reached the steps at the time that you fell; is that right?

A. That's correct.

. . .

Q: Did you want to add something?

A: Yes. I've stated umpteen numerous times that I don't remember if I tripped or if I was just clumsy or if I missed the step or hit it or whatever. I've stated that and stated that, and I don't recall.

Bacon also testified that while he had stumbled climbing those same steps prior to the incident in question, he had done so as the result of his own clumsiness, and not because of the condition of the steps.

In response to Bacon's deposition testimony, which was cited to the District Court in support of the defendants' motions for summary judgment, Gentry cited the District Court, and now cites this Court, to the following statement made by Bacon during an interview with investigators on November 16, 1995.

TW: Okay. So, you remember stumbling, and you don't remember on what?

BB: No, I don't remember if I went to step up on the step or if . . . there's a rock there also underneath the step to keep it level. I don't think it was that, I think it was the step.

Gentry contends that based on this isolated statement a reasonable finder of fact could infer that it was the step which caused Bacon's fall. However, earlier in the same interview, he was asked the following question and gave the following answer:

TW: Do you remember what you stumbled on?

BB: No I don't.

Furthermore, when asked in his deposition whether, at the time of his November 16 statement, he had remembered what caused him to fall, he testified that he had not. That testimony was consistent with his statement on the date of the incident in which he stated that he did not know how he fell.

Finally, even the isolated statement relied on by Gentry does not support the contention that it was the condition of the step or the area surrounding the step which caused Bacon to stumble and fall. The most that could be inferred was that he was about to ascend the stairs when he did stumble and fall. Why he stumbled and fell would still require speculation. In the context of summary judgment proceedings, we have previously held that neither a suspicion nor speculation is sufficient to defeat a motion for summary judgment. In Benson v. Diehl (1987), 228 Mont. 199, 203, 745 P.2d 315, 317, we held that:

> A suspicion, regardless of how particularized it may be, is not sufficient to sustain an action or to defeat a motion for summary judgment. Unsupported conclusory or speculative statements do not raise a genuine issue of material fact. The trial court has no duty to anticipate possible proof. [C]

The facts presented in this case are similar to those presented in Krone v. McCann (1982), 196 Mont. 260, 638 P.2d 397, overruled on other grounds by Richardson v. Corvallis Public School Dist. (Mont. 1997), 286 Mont. 309, 950 P.2d 748, 754, 758 Mont. St. Rep. 1422, 1428. In that case, the plaintiff sought damages for injuries she sustained while walking on property owned by the defendant. She was injured when she stumbled over some object on the property. However, she was unable to identify what it was that caused her to stumble. We affirmed summary judgment for the defendant for the following reasons:

> More importantly, the fact is undisputed that the appellant cannot describe what caused her injury. She does not know if it was merely a mound of dirt or an old corral pole.
>
> In an action for negligence, a plaintiff must produce evidence from which it can be reasonably inferred that negligent conduct on the part of the defendant or its agents was the proximate cause of the plaintiff's injuries. [C] Here, the appellant simply does not know exactly what caused her injury. As noted above, the respondents cannot be the

insurers of the appellant and held liable for her injury merely because an accident happened on their land. [C]

Likewise, Gentry has offered no substantial evidence that any condition on the property owned by the ranch company and leased by the cattle company caused Bacon to stumble and fall immediately before his rifle discharged and struck the decedent, Barbara Gentry. Therefore, we conclude that cause in fact cannot be proven as a matter of law, and the District Court did not err when it held that the [ranch company] defendants ... were not negligent in a manner that contributed to the injuries and death of Barbara Gentry. * * *

Holding

[The court then ruled that the ranch company defendants were not vicariously responsible for Bacon's negligent handling of the rifle since he was not an employee or agent of the ranch companies.]

We affirm the judgment of the District Court.

NOTES AND QUESTIONS

1. In the principal case, if the steps were negligently maintained, why did the court affirm the trial court's entry of judgment in favor of the ranch company defendants? As you read the next principal case, Reynolds v. Texas & Pac. Ry. Co., think about what change in the facts would have been enough to get the principal case to the jury.

they were not the cause of injury necessarily

2. What happened to Bacon? Why doesn't he have to compensate plaintiff? Wasn't his negligent handling of the rifle a cause in fact of the injury to plaintiff's wife?

3. Notice the court's allusion to cause in fact and proximate cause as two separate analyses. Proximate cause will be discussed in Chapter 6.

4. A woman on board a cruise ship stepped into the bathtub in her cabin to take a shower. She slipped and injured herself. The bathtub had four anti-skid strips running parallel to each other from the middle to the back of the tub. After the accident, she noticed that there was sufficient space between the strips so that her foot could just fit between them. She does not know where her feet were when she slipped. Assuming that she could prove that the placement of the anti-skid strips was negligent, is the cruise ship liable for her injures? Fedorczyk v. Caribbean Cruise Lines, Ltd., 82 F.3d 69, 75 (3d Cir.1996) ("Even though we must draw all legitimate inferences in Fedorczyk's favor, the inference that she was standing between the strips at the time of the accident, because her feet could fit between the strips, is not an appropriate inference to be drawn. The possibility of the existence of an event does not tend to prove its probability.")

Reynolds v. Texas & Pac. Ry. Co.

Court of Appeals of Louisiana, 1885.
37 La.Ann. 694.

[Plaintiff and his wife sought damages against defendant company for injuries she suffered when she fell down a stairway.]

FENNER, J. * * * The train was behind time. Several witnesses testify that passengers were warned to "hurry up." Mrs. Reynolds, a corpulent woman, weighing two hundred and fifty pounds, emerging from the bright light of the sitting-room, which naturally exaggerated the outside darkness, and hastening down these unlighted steps, made a misstep in some way and was precipitated beyond the narrow platform in front and down the slope beyond, incurring the serious injuries complained of. [The trial court, without a jury, gave judgment to the plaintiffs for $2,000 damages. Defendant appealed.]

[Defendant] contends that, even conceding the negligence of the company in [failing to light the stairway or provide a handrail], it does not follow that the accident to plaintiff was necessarily caused thereby, but that she might well have made the misstep and fallen even had it been broad daylight. We concede that this is possible, and recognize the distinction between post hoc and propter hoc. But where the negligence of the defendant greatly multiplies the chances of accident to the plaintiff, and is of a character naturally leading to its occurrence, the mere possibility that it might have happened without the negligence is not sufficient to break the chain of cause and effect between the negligence and the injury. Courts, in such matters, consider the natural and ordinary course of events, and do not indulge in fanciful suppositions. The whole tendency of the evidence connects the accident with the negligence. * * *

Judgment affirmed.

NOTES AND QUESTIONS

1. If a life preserver had been thrown to a drowning man, would he have caught it and been saved? Kirincich v. Standard Dredging Co., 112 F.2d 163 (3d Cir.1940). Would an adequate number of campus police have prevented trespassing boys from shooting a student in the eye with an air rifle? Stockwell v. Board of Trustees of Leland Stanford Junior University, 64 Cal.App.2d 197, 148 P.2d 405 (1944). How are these questions to be decided? Who should decide them?

Kramer Service, Inc. v. Wilkins

Supreme Court of Mississippi, 1939.
184 Miss. 483, 186 So. 625.

[The plaintiff, a guest in the defendant's hotel, received a cut on his forehead from a piece of glass that fell from a broken transom when the plaintiff opened the door. There was evidence that the condition of disrepair had existed long enough to charge defendant with notice of it. The wound did not heal, and two years after the injury plaintiff went to a specialist in skin diseases, who found that at the point of the injury a skin cancer had developed, which was not fully cured at the time of the trial, some three years after the original injury. The defendant appeals a jury verdict for the plaintiff.]

GRIFFITH, JUSTICE. * * * Appellant requested an instruction to the effect that the cancer or any prolongation of the trouble on account thereof should not be taken into consideration by the jury, but this instruction was refused.

Two physicians or medical experts, and only two, were introduced as witnesses, and both were specialists in skin diseases and dermal traumatisms. One testified that it was possible that a trauma such as appellee suffered upon his temple, could or would cause a skin cancer at the point of injury, but that the chances that such a result would ensue from such a cause would be only one out of one hundred cases. The other testified that there is no causal connection whatever between trauma and cancer, and went on to illustrate that if there were such a connection nearly every person of mature age would be suffering from cancer. * * *

There is one heresy in the judicial forum which appears to be Hydra-headed, and although cut off again and again, has the characteristic of an endless renewal. That heresy is that proof that a past event possibly happened, or that a certain result was possibly caused by a past event, is sufficient, in probative force to take the question to a jury. Such was never the law in this state, and we are in accord with almost all of the other common-law states. * * * It is not enough that negligence of one person and injury to another coexisted, but the injury must have been caused by the negligence. Post hoc ergo propter hoc is not sound as evidence or argument. Nor is it sufficient for a plaintiff, seeking recovery for alleged negligence by another toward the plaintiff, to show a possibility that the injury complained of was caused by negligence. Possibilities will not sustain a verdict. It must have a better foundation. * * *

Taking the medical testimony in this case in the strongest light in which it could be reasonably interpreted in behalf of the plaintiff, this testimony is that as a possibility a skin cancer could be caused by an injury such as here happened, but as a probability the physicians were in agreement that there was or is no such a probability.

And the medical testimony is conclusive on both judge and jury in this case. That testimony is undisputed that after long and anxious years of research the exact cause of cancer remains unknown—there is no dependably known origin to which it can be definitely traced or ascribed. If, then, the cause be unknown to all those who have devoted their lives to a study of the subject, it is wholly beyond the range of the common experience and observation of judges and jurors, and in such a case medical testimony when undisputed, as here, must be accepted and acted upon in the same manner as is other undisputed evidence; otherwise the jury would be allowed to resort to and act upon nothing else than the proposition post hoc ergo propter hoc, which, as already mentioned, this Court has long ago rejected as unsound, whether as evidence or as argument.

In all other than the exceptional cases now to be mentioned, the testimony of medical experts, or other experts, is advisory only; but we repeat that where the issue is one which lies wholly beyond the range of the experience or observation of laymen and of which they can have no appreciable knowledge, courts and juries must of necessity depend upon and accept the undisputed testimony of reputable specialists, else there would be no substantial foundation upon which to rest a conclusion. * * *

Affirmed as to liability; reversed and remanded on the issue of the amount of the damages [in allowing recovery for the skin cancer in addition to the original cut on the forehead].

NOTES AND QUESTIONS

1.   Why not decide this case on the basis of Reynolds v. Texas & Pacific Ry. Co.? How much is proved by the fact that, out of a good many square inches of skin on the human body, the cancer developed at the exact point of the unhealed cut? Compare Emery v. Tilo Roofing Co., 89 N.H. 165, 195 A. 409 (1937), where a fire started at a place on a roof where workmen had been smoking cigarettes, shortly after they had left it. What if a woman develops breast cancer after bruising her breast in a fall precipitated by defendant's negligence? Cf. Daly v. Bergstedt, 267 Minn. 244, 126 N.W.2d 242 (1964). A woman develops a rare and fatal lung disease after taking an overdose of a drug that had been negligently prescribed by her doctor. The lung disease had not been linked to exposure to the drug in any other patient; very few women had ever received such a high dose. Her expert testified that the onset and progression of her symptoms matched those of others who had developed the lung disease when exposed to other drugs (mainly anti-cancer chemotherapy) known to induce pulmonary disease. She had been exposed to no other known causes of the lung disease. Is this enough to prove causation? Zuchowicz v. United States, 140 F.3d 381, 390 (2d Cir.1998) (applying Connecticut law in a Federal Tort Claims Act case) (upholding trial court judge's finding of causation based on expert's testimony).

2.   Cases dealing with informed consent, pages 182–193, can present a special problem in the area of cause in fact. Assume that patient proves that doctor failed to inform him of a material risk, that the applicable standard of care (whether physician or patient based) was violated, and that the risk manifested itself. How does patient prove causation? Should plaintiff patient be able to hurdle the issue if he testifies that he would not have undergone the medical procedure if defendant physician had informed him of the risk? Sard v. Hardy, 281 Md. 432, 379 A.2d 1014, 1025 (1977), quoting Canterbury v. Spence, 150 U.S.App.D.C. 263, 464 F.2d 772, 791 (1972), ("Such a test puts the physician in 'jeopardy of the patient's hindsight and bitterness.' ") Some courts have said that an objective test is preferable, i.e., what would a prudent person in the patient's position have decided if adequately informed of the peril? Aronson v. Harriman, 321 Ark. 359, 901 S.W.2d 832 (1995) (plaintiff's failure to testify that he would not have undergone the surgery if he had been informed of the risk of paralysis did not defeat his claim; test is what a reasonable person would have decided if adequately informed). Others have insisted that the test must be subjective in order to fully protect the underlying concept of bodily integrity. Flanagan v. Wesselhoeft, 712 A.2d 365, 370 (R.I.1998) ("The essential inquiry then is not which course of treatment the trial justice, expert medical professionals, or even a reasonable person might elect. Rather, 'the patient's right to make his decision in the light of his [or her] own individual value judgment is the very essence of his freedom of choice' "). See also Hartke v. McKelway, 707 F.2d 1544 (D.C.Cir.1983) (discussing proof problems that could arise under either objective or subjective tests) and Schreiber v. Physicians Ins. Co., 223 Wis.2d 417, 588 N.W.2d 26 (1999) (reaffirming objective test for most informed consent cases, but applying subjective test where patient, in midst of labor, had withdrawn consent to vaginal delivery and expressed preference for Cesarean section delivery).

3. Should a broadcasting company be held liable for airing scenes of violent acts on television, when those scenes may incite others to perform similar acts? See Olivia N. v. National Broadcasting Co., Inc., 74 Cal.App.3d 383, 141 Cal.Rptr. 511 (1977), cert. denied, 435 U.S. 1000 (1978) (nine-year-old girl "artificially raped" with a bottle by her attackers, also minors, who had watched a similar incident depicted in a television drama); McCollum v. CBS, Inc., 202 Cal.App.3d 989, 249 Cal.Rptr. 187 (1988) (no liability for suicide of teenager listening to rock music that parents claimed incited suicide) (collecting cases attempting to impose liability on media defendants for inciting various illegal and violent acts). See also, note 4, page 459. Putting aside for the moment the First Amendment issues surrounding the imposition of tort liability on media defendants, what problems in proving causation would a plaintiff encounter?

Wilder v. Eberhart

United States Court of Appeals, First Circuit, 1992.
977 F.2d 673.

[Plaintiff Wilder was being treated by Dr. Eberhart for obesity. Dr. Eberhart performed surgery on Ms. Wilder that involved stapling her stomach. Following surgery, Ms. Wilder suffered serious complications arising from tears in her lower esophagus. Plaintiff's expert witness testified that the sole cause of the esophagal injury was mobilization of the esophagus during surgery. Defendants' experts were planning to testify that there were other possible causes of the injury and that the least likely of the possible causes was mobilization of the esophagus by Dr. Eberhart. The trial court judge excluded the testimony of the defendant's experts because their opinions could not be expressed in terms of "probability" rather than "mere possibility." From a jury verdict for plaintiff of $685,-000, defendants appealed.]

TORRUELLA, CIRCUIT JUDGE. * * *

It is well settled under New Hampshire law that the burden of proof with respect to causation in a medical malpractice case rests and remains with the plaintiff. [C] Moreover, proximate causation between negligence and the injury complained of in a medical malpractice case must be established by expert testimony. [C] On the other hand, the defendant need not disprove causation. Rather, he must produce credible evidence which tends to discredit or rebut the plaintiff's evidence. [C] As the New Hampshire Supreme Court recently stated in Tzimas, the plaintiff in a negligence action bears the burden of producing evidence "to prove that it is more likely than not that [plaintiff's] injury was" caused by the defendant's negligence. [C] Defendant need not prove another cause, he only has to convince the trier of fact that the alleged negligence was not the legal cause of the injury. Id. In proving such a case, a defendant may produce other "possible" causes of the plaintiff's injury. These other possible causes need not be proved with certainty or more probably than not. To fashion such a rule would unduly tie a defendant's hands in rebutting a plaintiff's case, where as here, plaintiff's expert testifies that no other cause could have caused plaintiff's injury. The burden would then shift and defendant would then bear the burden of positively proving that another specific cause, not the negligence established by plaintiff's expert, caused the injury. Certainly, this is much more than what should be required of a defendant in rebutting a plaintiff's evidence.

Were we to accept plaintiff's argument that once a plaintiff puts on a prima facie case, a defendant cannot rebut it without proving another cause, the resulting inequities would abound. For example if ninety-nine out of one hundred medical experts agreed that there were four equally possible causes of a certain injury, A, B, C and D, and plaintiff produces the one expert who conclusively states that A was the certain cause of his injury, defendant would be precluded from presenting the testimony of any of the other ninety-nine experts, unless they would testify conclusively that B, C, or D was the cause of injury. Even if all of defendant's experts were prepared to testify that any of the possible causes A, B, C or D, could have equally caused plaintiff's injury, so long as none would be prepared to state that one particular cause, other than that professed by plaintiff more probably than not caused plaintiff's injury, then defendant's experts would not be able to testify at all as to causation. * * *

Under the circumstances of this case, Dr. Eberhart was prejudiced by the granting of the Second Motion in Limine [excluding his experts' testimony], and this prejudice constituted reversible error. Thus, the judgment in favor of plaintiff is vacated and remanded for a new trial.

Vacated and remanded.

NOTES AND QUESTIONS

1. How does this case differ from Reynolds v. Texas & Pacific Ry. Co.?

2. What is a motion in limine?

3. In a medical malpractice case, if the patient can show that the doctor violated the standard of care by failing to order particular diagnostic procedures, what else does she have to show to recover? That the tests would have revealed a problem? That knowledge of the problem would have enabled the doctor to treat it? That the results would have been better? Gardner v. Pawliw, 150 N.J. 359, 696 A.2d 599 (1997) (patient need only show to a reasonable degree of medical probability that the failure to give the test increased the risk of harm, which may be established even if such tests are helpful in only a small proportion of cases).

Herskovits v. Group Health Cooperative of Puget Sound

Supreme Court of Washington, 1983.
99 Wash.2d 609, 664 P.2d 474.

Dore, Justice. This appeal [from the trial court's action in granting defendant's motion for summary judgment] raises the issue of whether an estate can maintain an action for professional negligence as a result of failure to timely diagnose lung cancer, where the estate can show probable reduction in statistical chance for survival but cannot show and/or prove that with timely diagnosis and treatment, decedent probably would have lived to normal life expectancy.

Both counsel advised that for the purpose of this appeal we are to *assume* that the respondent Group Health Cooperative of Puget Sound and Dr. William Spencer negligently failed to diagnose Herskovits' cancer on his first visit to the hospital and *proximately* caused a 14 percent reduction in his chances of survival. It is undisputed that Herskovits had less than a 50 percent chance of survival at all times herein.

The main issue we will address in this opinion is whether a patient, with less than a 50 percent chance of survival, has a cause of action against the hospital and its employees if they are negligent in diagnosing a lung cancer which reduces his chances of survival by 14 percent. * * *

We are persuaded by the reasoning of the Pennsylvania Supreme Court in Hamil v. Bashline, 481 Pa. 256, 392 A.2d 1280 (1978). While *Hamil* involved an original survival chance of greater than 50 percent, we find the rationale used by the *Hamil* court to apply equally to cases such as the present one, where the original survival chance is less than 50 percent. The plaintiff's decedent was suffering from severe chest pains. His wife transported him to the hospital where he was negligently treated in the emergency unit. The wife, because of the lack of help, took her husband to a private physician's office, where he died. In an action brought under the wrongful death and survivorship statutes, the main medical witness testified that if the hospital had employed proper treatment, the decedent would have had a substantial chance of surviving the attack. The medical expert expressed his opinion in terms of a 75 percent chance of survival. It was also the doctor's opinion that the substantial loss of a chance of recovery was the result of the defendant hospital's failure to provide prompt treatment. The defendant's expert witness testified that the patient would have died regardless of any treatment provided by the defendant hospital.

The *Hamil* court distinguished the facts of that case from the general tort case in which a plaintiff alleges that a defendant's act or omission set in motion a force which resulted in harm. In the typical tort case, the "but for" test, requiring proof that damages or death probably would not have occurred "but for" the negligent conduct of the defendant, is appropriate. In *Hamil* and the instant case, however, the defendant's act or omission failed in a *duty* to protect against harm from *another source*. Thus, as the *Hamil* court noted, the fact finder is put in the position of having to consider not only what *did* occur, but also what *might have* occurred. *Hamil* states at p. 271: "Such cases by their very nature elude the degree of certainty one would prefer and upon which the law normally insists before a person may be held liable. Nevertheless, in order that an actor is not completely insulated because of uncertainties as to the consequences of his negligent conduct, Section 323(a) [of the Torts Restatement] tacitly acknowledges this difficulty and permits the issue to go to the jury upon a less than normal threshold of proof." (Footnote omitted.) The *Hamil* court held that once a plaintiff has demonstrated that the defendant's acts or omissions have increased the risk of harm to another, such evidence furnishes a basis for the jury to make a determination as to whether such increased risk was in turn a substantial factor in bringing about the resultant harm.] * * *

Where percentage probabilities and decreased probabilities are submitted into evidence, there is simply no danger of speculation on the part of the jury. More speculation is involved in requiring the medical expert to testify as to what would have happened had the defendant not been negligent.

Both counsel have agreed for the purpose of arguing this summary judgment, that the defendants were negligent in failing to make a diagnosis of cancer on Herskovits' initial visit in December 1974, and that such negligence was the proximate cause of reducing his chances of survival by 14 percent. It is undisputed that Herskovits had less than a 50 percent chance of survival at that time. Based on this agreement and Dr. Ostrow's deposition and affidavit, a prima facie case is shown. We reject Group Health's argument that plaintiffs *must show* that Herskovits "probably" would have had a 51 percent chance of survival if the hospital had not been negligent. We hold that medical testimony of a reduction of chance of survival from 39 percent to 25 percent is sufficient evidence to allow the proximate cause issue to go to the jury.

Causing reduction of the opportunity to recover (loss of chance) by one's negligence, however, does not necessitate a total recovery against the negligent party for all damages caused by the victim's death. Damages should be awarded to the injured party or his family based only on damages caused directly by premature death, such as lost earnings and additional medical expenses, etc.

We reverse the trial court and reinstate the cause of action.

[This opinion was concurred in by only one other judge. ROSELLINI, J. Three judges dissented, urging that the traditional proximate cause standard should be maintained. The concurring opinion of PEARSON, J., joined by three judges, differed from Dore's in urging that the issues should be framed by looking at the injury as the reduced chance of survival, *not* as the death as Dore viewed it. Damages would then be calculated based on that loss.]

NOTES AND QUESTIONS

1.   Washington, through the principal case, was one of the first jurisdictions to find a way to allow the plaintiff to recover in a medical malpractice case even though the plaintiff could not prove that it was more likely than not that the malpractice had caused the death of the patient. Notice that it does so by allowing the case to go to the jury as long as the plaintiff shows some reduction in the chance of survival. Some jurisdictions permit recovery in such cases only if the lost chance was a substantial factor in producing the harm. See, e.g., McKellips v. St. Francis Hosp., Inc., 741 P.2d 467, 471 (Okla.1987) ("An evolving trend has developed to relax the standard for sufficiency of proof of causation ordinarily required of a plaintiff to provide a basis upon which the jury may consider causation in the 'lost chance of survival' cases.") and Evers v. Dollinger, 95 N.J. 399, 413, 471 A.2d 405,

413 (1984) ("Courts have come to recognize that the difficulties of identifying, defining, and proving injury in certain types of medical malpractice cases justifies the application of a standard of causation that is more flexible than that used in conventional tort claims.") In such a case, how should the jury assess damages? If the jury finds that the malpractice was a substantial factor in bringing about the patient's death, does the physician pay the full amount of the wrongful death damages? See DeBurkarte v. Louvar, 393 N.W.2d 131 (Iowa 1986) (criticizing those jurisdictions that permit the plaintiff to collect the full amount of the damages).

2. Other jurisdictions have analyzed the issue by viewing the patient's injury as the loss of the opportunity, rather than as the death. In those jurisdictions, the patient is permitted to recover damages, but only a proportion of the full amount. See, e.g., Roberts v. Ohio Permanente Medical Group, Inc., 76 OhioSt.3d 483, 668 N.E.2d 480 (1996); Delaney v. Cade, 255 Kan. 199, 873 P.2d 175 (1994); Scafidi v. Seiler, 119 N.J. 93, 574 A.2d 398 (1990); and Falcon v. Memorial Hosp., 436 Mich. 443, 462 N.W.2d 44 (Mich. 1990) (Michigan has since reverted to traditional causation by act of legislature).

3. Some jurisdictions have refused either to relax the traditional causation requirement or recognize a cause of action for a reduced chance of recovery. See, e.g., Jones v. Owings, 318 S.C. 72, 456 S.E.2d 371 (1995) (less than 50% chance of surviving lung cancer reduced to 20% chance of survival); Fennell v. Southern Maryland Hosp. Center, 320 Md. 776, 580 A.2d 206 (1990) (40% chance of surviving acute bacterial meningitis lost due to failure to do lumbar puncture after CT Scan suggested inflammatory process); Gooding v. University Hosp. Bldg., Inc., 445 So.2d 1015 (Fla.1984) (answering certified question by refusing to expand liability to include loss of a chance to survive).

4. Those jurisdictions that have in some way permitted recovery in loss of chance cases must decide whether to extend the doctrine beyond medical malpractice cases. Hardy v. Southwestern Bell Telephone Co., 910 P.2d 1024 (Okla.1996) (declining to extend loss of chance doctrine to negligence action against telephone company for design flaw in 911 system that made it impossible for woman to reach 911 during her husband's heart attack due to volume of calls seeking purchase of Garth Brooks concert tickets); Lowmack v. Century Products Co., 139 F.3d 890 (4th Cir.1998) (upholding trial court judge's prediction that Virginia would not extend loss of chance doctrine to negligent design claim against child car seat manufacturer).

5. For a general discussion of this area of law, see King, Causation, Valuation, and Chance in Personal Injury Torts Involving Preexisting Conditions and Future Consequences, 90 Yale L.J. 1353 (1981) (cited in concurring opinion of principal case) and King, "Reduction of Likelihood" Reformulation and Other Retrofitting of the Loss-of-a-Chance Doctrine, 28 Mem. St. U.L. Rev. 492 (1998) (author's proposed reformulation of doctrine after fifteen years of its development in the courts).

6. *Attorney Malpractice Cases.* Establishing causation in fact can be a substantial burden in a suit against an attorney for professional negligence. An attorney fails to file a suit for his client before the statute of limitations runs. What must the client prove besides negligence? That the client would have won the original lawsuit? The amount of the damages the jury would have awarded in the original lawsuit? That the award in the original lawsuit was collectible? See Kituskie v. Corbman, 552 Pa. 275, 714 A.2d 1027 (1998) (noting that a majority of jurisdictions require plaintiff to prove that he would have won the case, how much the award would have been, and that the award was collectible, but agreeing with minority that defendant must plead and prove uncollectibility of judgment as affirmative

defense) and Klump v. Duffus, 71 F.3d 1368 (7th Cir.1995) (applying Illinois law) (accord except that burden of proving award collectible is placed on plaintiff). But see Vahila v. Hall, 77 Ohio St.3d 421, 674 N.E.2d 1164 (1997) (recognizing that proof of causation often dictates that plaintiff prove merits of underlying litigation, but declining to adopt rule that plaintiff must show that she would have won and recognizing that plaintiff could show that she suffered the damages of a less favorable result).

7.   Suppose the attorney was negligent in failing to cite to a court relevant cases that might have avoided jail for his client. What must the client prove in an action against the attorney? See Martin v. Hall, 20 Cal.App.3d 414, 97 Cal.Rptr. 730 (1971). Would the attorney be liable for the client's death if the client committed suicide in jail after being wrongfully convicted due to the attorney's malpractice? See McLaughlin v. Sullivan, 123 N.H. 335, 461 A.2d 123 (1983) (denying liability) and McPeake v. William T. Cannon, 381 Pa.Super. 227, 553 A.2d 439 (1989) (accord).

8.   A company co-signed a ten-year lease on a building for one of its wholly owned subsidiaries. A couple of years later, it sold that subsidiary to another company. Client claims that it instructed the lawyers who represented it in the sale to negotiate to eliminate its contingent liability for rent on the building the subsidiary was using. Lawyers failed to do so, former subsidiary went bankrupt, and client was forced to pay $2.6 million dollars under the lease. How does the client prove that the lawyer's failure to try to negotiate the elimination of the contingent liability caused its loss? "Proof of causation is often difficult in legal malpractice cases involving representation in litigation—the vast majority of such cases— because it is so difficult, yet vital, to estimate what difference a lawyer's negligence made in the actual outcome of a trial or other adversary proceeding. [Cc] How many criminal defendants, required as they are to prove that their lawyer's ineffective assistance prejudiced them, succeed in overturning their convictions on this ground? Proof of causation is even more difficult in a negotiating situation, because while there is (at least we judges like to think there is) a correct outcome to most lawsuits, there is no 'correct' outcome to a negotiation. Not only does much depend on the relative bargaining skills of the negotiators, on the likely consequences to each party if the negotiations fall through, and on luck, so that the element of the intangible and the unpredictable looms large; but there is no single 'right' outcome in a bargaining situation even in principle. Every point within the range bounded by the lowest offer that one party will accept and the highest offer that the other party will make is a possible transaction or settlement point, and none of these points is 'correct' or 'incorrect.'" Nicolet Instrument Corp. v. Lindquist & Vennum, 34 F.3d 453, 455 (7th Cir.1994) (applying Wisconsin law).

9.   Do you see parallels between the medical loss of a chance cases and the attorney malpractice cases? See Kramer v. Lewisville Memorial Hospital, 858 S.W.2d 397 (Tex.1993) (if court were to adopt the loss of chance doctrine in the context of this medical malpractice action, "it is doubtful that there is any principled way we could prevent its application to similar actions involving other professions. If, for example, a disgruntled or unsuccessful litigant loses a case that he or she had a less than 50 percent chance of winning, but is able to adduce expert testimony that his or her lawyer negligently reduced this chance by some degree, the litigant would be able to pursue a cause of action for malpractice under the loss of chance doctrine.") (Citations and footnote omitted.)

Daubert v. Merrell Dow Pharmaceuticals, Inc.

United States Court of Appeals, Ninth Circuit, 1995.
43 F.3d 1311.

KOZINSKI, J. On remand from the United States Supreme Court, we undertake "the task of ensuring that an expert's testimony both rests on a reliable foundation and is relevant to the task at hand." Daubert v. Merrell Dow Pharmaceuticals, Inc., 125 L. Ed. 2d 469, 113 S. Ct. 2786, 2799 (1993).

I

A. Background

Two minors brought suit against Merrell Dow Pharmaceuticals, claiming they suffered limb reduction birth defects because their mothers had taken Bendectin, a drug prescribed for morning sickness to about 17.5 million pregnant women in the United States between 1957 and 1982. [Footnote omitted][Cc] This appeal deals with an evidentiary question: whether certain expert scientific testimony is admissible to prove that Bendectin caused the plaintiffs' birth defects.

For the most part, we don't know how birth defects come about. We do know they occur in 2–3% of births, whether or not the expectant mother has taken Bendectin. [C] Limb defects are even rarer, occurring in fewer than one birth out of every 1000. [C] But scientists simply do not know how teratogens (chemicals known to cause limb reduction defects) do their damage: They cannot reconstruct the biological chain of events that leads from an expectant mother's ingestion of a teratogenic substance to the stunted development of a baby's limbs. * * *

Not knowing the mechanism whereby a particular agent causes a particular effect is not always fatal to a plaintiff's claim. Causation can be proved even when we don't know precisely *how* the damage occurred, if there is sufficiently compelling proof that the agent must have caused the damage *somehow*. One method of proving causation in these circumstances is to use statistical evidence. If 50 people who eat at a restaurant one evening come down with food poisoning during the night, we can infer that the restaurant's food probably contained something unwholesome, even if none of the dishes is available for analysis. This inference is based on the fact that, in our health-conscious society, it is highly unlikely that 50 people who have nothing in common except that they ate at the same restaurant will get food poisoning from independent sources.

It is by such means that plaintiffs here seek to establish that Bendectin is responsible for their injuries. * * *

The opinions proffered by plaintiffs' experts do not, to understate the point, reflect the consensus within the scientific community. The FDA—an agency not known for its promiscuity in approving drugs—continues to approve Bendectin for use by pregnant women because "available data do not demonstrate an association between birth defects and Bendectin." U.S. Department of Health and Human Services News, No. P80–45 (Oct. 7,

1980). Every published study here and abroad—and there have been many—concludes that Bendectin is not a teratogen. In fact, apart from the small but determined group of scientists testifying on behalf of the Bendectin plaintiffs in this and many other cases, there doesn't appear to be a single scientist who has concluded that Bendectin causes limb reduction defects.

It is largely because the opinions proffered by plaintiffs' experts run counter to the substantial consensus in the scientific community that we affirmed the district court's grant of summary judgment the last time the case appeared before us. The standard for admissibility of expert testimony in this circuit at the time was the so-called *Frye* test: Scientific evidence was admissible if it was based on a scientific technique generally accepted as reliable within the scientific community. * * * We found that the district court properly applied this standard, and affirmed. The Supreme Court reversed, holding that *Frye* was superceded by Federal Rule of Evidence 702, 113 S. Ct. at 2794, and remanded for us to consider the admissibility of plaintiffs' expert testimony under this new standard.

B.   Procedural Issues

* * *

[The Court decided the case did not need to be remanded to the trial court judge to make an initial determination of admissibility under the standard newly articulated by the Supreme Court and that the admissibility of one of the defendant's expert's affidavits, challenged by plaintiffs, was irrelevant.]

II

A.   Brave New World

Federal judges ruling on the admissibility of expert scientific testimony face a far more complex and daunting task in a post-*Daubert* world than before. The judge's task under *Frye* is relatively simple: to determine whether the method employed by the experts is generally accepted in the scientific community. [C] Under *Daubert*, we must engage in a difficult, two-part analysis. First, we must determine nothing less than whether the experts' testimony reflects "scientific knowledge," whether their findings are "derived by the scientific method," and whether their work product amounts to "good science." [C] Second, we must ensure that the proposed expert testimony is "relevant to the task at hand," [c], i.e., that it logically advances a material aspect of the proposing party's case. The Supreme Court referred to this second prong of the analysis as the "fit" requirement. [C]

The first prong of *Daubert* puts federal judges in an uncomfortable position. The question of admissibility only arises if it is first established that the individuals whose testimony is being proffered are experts in a particular scientific field; here, for example, the Supreme Court waxed eloquent on the impressive qualifications of plaintiffs' experts. [C] Yet something doesn't become "scientific knowledge" just because it's uttered by a scientist; nor can an expert's self-serving assertion that his conclusions were "derived by the scientific method" be deemed conclusive * * *

The task before us is more daunting still when the dispute concerns matters at the very cutting edge of scientific research, where fact meets theory and certainty dissolves into probability. As the record in this case illustrates, scientists often have vigorous and sincere disagreements as to what research methodology is proper, what should be accepted as sufficient proof for the existence of a "fact," and whether information derived by a particular method can tell us anything useful about the subject under study.

Our responsibility, then, unless we badly misread the Supreme Court's opinion, is to resolve disputes among respected, well-credentialed scientists about matters squarely within their expertise, in areas where there is no scientific consensus as to what is and what is not "good science," and occasionally to reject such expert testimony because it was not "derived by the scientific method." Mindful of our position in the hierarchy of the federal judiciary, we take a deep breath and proceed with this heady task.

B. Deus ex Machina

* * *

Which raises the question: How do we figure out whether scientists have derived their findings through the scientific method or whether their testimony is based on scientifically valid principles? Each expert proffered by the plaintiffs assures us that he has "utilized the type of data that is generally and reasonably relied upon by scientists" in the relevant field, see, e.g., [c], and that he has "utilized the methods and methodology that would generally and reasonably be accepted" by people who deal in these matters, see, e.g., [c]. The [Supreme] Court held, however, that federal judges perform a "gatekeeping role," *Daubert*, 113 S. Ct. at 2798; to do so they must satisfy themselves that scientific evidence meets a certain standard of reliability before it is admitted. This means that the expert's bald assurance of validity is not enough. Rather, the party presenting the expert must show that the expert's findings are based on sound science, and this will require some objective, independent validation of the expert's methodology.

While declining to set forth a "definitive checklist or test," id. at 2796, the Court did list several factors federal judges can consider in determining whether to admit expert scientific testimony under Fed. R. Evid. 702: whether the theory or technique employed by the expert is generally accepted in the scientific community; whether it's been subjected to peer review and publication; whether it can be and has been tested; and whether the known or potential rate of error is acceptable. Id. at 2796–97. [Footnote omitted.] We read these factors as illustrative rather than exhaustive; similarly, we do not deem each of them to be equally applicable (or applicable at all) in every case. [Footnote omitted.] Rather, we read the

Supreme Court as instructing us to determine whether the analysis under-girding the experts' testimony falls within the range of accepted standards governing how scientists conduct their research and reach their conclusions.

One very significant fact to be considered is whether the experts are proposing to testify about matters growing naturally and directly out of research they have conducted independent of the litigation, or whether they have developed their opinions expressly for purposes of testifying. That an expert testifies for money does not necessarily cast doubt on the reliability of his testimony, as few experts appear in court merely as an eleemosynary gesture. But in determining whether proposed expert testimony amounts to good science, we may not ignore the fact that a scientist's normal workplace is the lab or the field, not the courtroom or the lawyer's office. [Footnote omitted.] * * *

We have examined carefully the affidavits proffered by plaintiffs' experts, as well as the testimony from prior trials that plaintiffs have introduced in support of that testimony, and find that none of the experts based his testimony on preexisting or independent research. While plaintiffs' scientists are all experts in their respective fields, none claims to have studied the effect of Bendectin on limb reduction defects before being hired to testify in this or related cases.

If the proffered expert testimony is not based on independent research, the party proffering it must come forward with other objective, verifiable evidence that the testimony is based on "scientifically valid principles." One means of showing this is by proof that the research and analysis supporting the proffered conclusions have been subjected to normal scientific scrutiny through peer review and publication. [Footnote omitted.] [C]

Peer review and publication do not, of course, guarantee that the conclusions reached are correct; much published scientific research is greeted with intense skepticism and is not borne out by further research. But the test under *Daubert* is not the correctness of the expert's conclusions but the soundness of his methodology. * * * That the research is accepted for publication in a reputable scientific journal after being subjected to the usual rigors of peer review is a significant indication that it is taken seriously by other scientists, i.e., that it meets at least the minimal criteria of good science. *Daubert*, 113 S. Ct. at 2797 ("scrutiny of the scientific community is a component of 'good science' "). If nothing else, peer review and publication "increase the likelihood that substantive flaws in methodology will be detected."[7]

Bendectin litigation has been pending in the courts for over a decade, yet the only review the plaintiffs' experts' work has received has been by judges and juries, and the only place their theories and studies have been

---

7. For instance, peer review might well have brought to light the more glaring arithmetical errors in the testimony presented by plaintiffs' experts in other Bendectin cases. See DeLuca v. Merrell Dow Pharmaceuticals, Inc., 791 F. Supp. 1042, 1048 (D.N.J.1992), aff'd, 6 F.3d 778, (3d Cir.1993).

published is in the pages of federal and state reporters. [Footnote omitted.]
None of plaintiffs' experts has published his work on Bendectin in a
scientific journal or solicited formal review by his colleagues. Despite the
many years the controversy has been brewing, no one in the scientific
community—except defendant's experts—has deemed these studies worthy
of verification, refutation or even comment. It's as if there were a tacit
understanding within the scientific community that what's going on here is
not science at all, but litigation.[9]

Establishing that an expert's proffered testimony grows out of pre-
litigation research or that the expert's research has been subjected to peer
review are the two principal ways the proponent of expert testimony can
show that the evidence satisfies the first prong of Rule 702. [Footnote
omitted] Where such evidence is unavailable, the proponent of expert
scientific testimony may attempt to satisfy its burden through the testimony of its own experts. For such a showing to be sufficient, the experts must
explain precisely how they went about reaching their conclusions and point
to some objective source—a learned treatise, the policy statement of a
professional association, a published article in a reputable scientific journal
or the like—to show that they have followed the scientific method, as it is
practiced by (at least) a recognized minority of scientists in their field. [C][11]

Plaintiffs have made no such showing. * * * We've been presented
with only the experts' qualifications, their conclusions and their assurances
of reliability. Under *Daubert*, that's not enough. * * *

Were this the only question before us, we would be inclined to remand
to give plaintiffs an opportunity to submit additional proof that the
scientific testimony they proffer was "derived by the scientific method."
Daubert, however, establishes two prongs to the Rule 702 admissibility

---

9. There may well be good reasons why
a scientific study has not been published. For
example, it may be too recent or of insufficiently broad interest. [C] These reasons do
not apply here. Except with respect to the
views expressed in this litigation, plaintiffs'
experts have been well-published, see, e.g.,
Crescitelli Aff. at 3 (authored 125 formal
papers, 80–100 short notes or abstracts, a
half-dozen reviews, and articles concerning
antihistamines and related compounds), and
the opinions they proffer, if supported by
sound methodology, would doubtless be
greedily devoured by the machinery of peer
review. A conclusion that Bendectin causes
birth defects would be of significant public
interest both in this country (where millions
of women have taken Bendectin and the FDA
continues to approve its use) and abroad
(where Bendectin is still widely used). That
plaintiffs' experts have been unable or unwilling to publish their work undermines
plaintiffs' claim that the findings these ex-

perts proffer are "grounded in the methods
and procedures of science" and "derived by
the scientific method." [C]

11. This underscores the difference between *Daubert* and *Frye*. Under *Frye*, the
party proffering scientific evidence had to
show it was based on the method generally
accepted in the scientific community. The
focus under *Daubert* is on the reliability of
the methodology, and in addressing that
question the court and the parties are not
limited to what is generally accepted; methods accepted by a minority in the scientific
community may well be sufficient. However,
the party proffering the evidence must explain the expert's methodology and demonstrate in some objectively verifiable way that
the expert has both chosen a reliable scientific method and followed it faithfully. Of
course, the fact that one party's experts use a
methodology accepted by only a minority of
scientists would be a proper basis for im-
peachment at trial.

inquiry. [C] We therefore consider whether the testimony satisfies the second prong of Rule 702: Would plaintiffs' proffered scientific evidence "assist the trier of fact to ... determine a fact in issue"? Fed. R. Evid. 702.

C. No Visible Means of Support

In elucidating the second requirement of Rule 702, *Daubert* stressed the importance of the "fit" between the testimony and an issue in the case: "Rule 702's 'helpfulness' standard requires a valid scientific connection to the pertinent inquiry as a precondition to admissibility." 113 S. Ct. at 2796. Here, the pertinent inquiry is causation. In assessing whether the proffered expert testimony "will assist the trier of fact" in resolving this issue, we must look to the governing substantive standard, which in this case is supplied by California tort law.

Plaintiffs do not attempt to show causation directly; instead, they rely on experts who present circumstantial proof of causation. Plaintiffs' experts testify that Bendectin is a teratogen because it causes birth defects when it is tested on animals, because it is similar in chemical structure to other suspected teratogens, and because statistical studies show that Bendectin use increases the risk of birth defects. Modern tort law permits such proof, but plaintiffs must nevertheless carry their traditional burden; they must prove that their injuries were the result of the accused cause and not some independent factor. In the case of birth defects, carrying this burden is made more difficult because we know that some defects—including limb reduction defects—occur even when expectant mothers do not take Bendectin, and that most birth defects occur for no known reason.

California tort law requires plaintiffs to show not merely that Bendectin increased the likelihood of injury, but that it more likely than not caused their injuries. [C] In terms of statistical proof, this means that plaintiffs must establish not just that their mothers' ingestion of Bendectin increased somewhat the likelihood of birth defects, but that it more than doubled it—only then can it be said that Bendectin is more likely than not the source of their injury. Because the background rate of limb reduction defects is one per thousand births, plaintiffs must show that among children of mothers who took Bendectin the incidence of such defects was more than two per thousand.[13]

None of plaintiffs' epidemiological experts claims that ingestion of Bendectin during pregnancy more than doubles the risk of birth defects. * * * While plaintiffs' epidemiologists make vague assertions that there is

---

13. No doubt, there will be unjust results under this substantive standard. If a drug increases the likelihood of birth defects, but doesn't more than double it, some plaintiffs whose injuries are attributable to the drug will be unable to recover. There is a converse unfairness under a regime that allows recovery to everyone that may have been affected by the drug. Under this regime, all potential plaintiffs are entitled to recover, even though most will not have suffered an injury that can be attributed to the drug. One can conclude from this that unfairness is inevitable when our tools for detecting causation are imperfect and we must rely on probabilities rather than more direct proof. In any event, this is a matter to be sorted out by the states, whose substantive legal standards we are bound to apply. [C]

a statistically significant relationship between Bendectin and birth defects, none states that the relative risk is greater than two. These studies thus would not be helpful, and indeed would only serve to confuse the jury, if offered to prove rather than refute causation. A relative risk of less than two may suggest teratogenicity, but it actually tends to disprove legal causation as it shows that Bendectin does not double the likelihood of birth defects. [Footnote omitted.]

With the exception of Dr. Palmer, whose testimony is inadmissible under the first prong of the Rule 702 analysis, * * * the remaining experts proffered by plaintiffs were equally unprepared to testify that Bendectin caused plaintiffs' injuries; they were willing to testify only that Bendectin is "capable of causing" birth defects. [Cc] * * * But what plaintiffs must prove is not that Bendectin causes some birth defects, but that it caused their birth defects. To show this, plaintiffs' experts would have had to testify either that Bendectin actually caused plaintiffs' injuries (which they could not say) or that Bendectin more than doubled the likelihood of limb reduction birth defects (which they did not say).

As the district court properly found below, "the strongest inference to be drawn for plaintiffs based on the epidemiological evidence is that Bendectin could possibly have caused plaintiffs' injuries." 727 F. Supp. at 576. * * * Plaintiffs do not quantify this possibility, or otherwise indicate how their conclusions about causation should be weighted, even though the substantive legal standard has always required proof of causation by a preponderance of the evidence. [Footnote omitted.] Unlike these experts' explanation of their methodology, this is not a shortcoming that could be corrected on remand; plaintiffs' experts could augment their affidavits with independent proof that their methods were sound, but to augment the substantive testimony as to causation would require the experts to change their conclusions altogether. Any such tailoring of the experts' conclusions would, at this stage of the proceedings, fatally undermine any attempt to show that these findings were "derived by the scientific method." Plaintiffs' experts must, therefore, stand by the conclusions they originally proffered, rendering their testimony inadmissible under the second prong of Fed. R. Evid. 702.

Conclusion

The district court's grant of summary judgment is AFFIRMED.

NOTES AND QUESTIONS

1. Before you tackle the substantive issues in this case, make sure you understand its procedural posture. What is the question before the Ninth Circuit? What route did the case take to get to this point? What happens next in the case?

2. *Daubert* was one of the most closely watched cases on the issue of the admissibility of scientific causation evidence that has arisen in the last three decades. What courts (besides the Ninth Circuit) are bound by the Supreme Court's decision in the case? Does the court's gatekeeper function apply only to novel scientific theories? In Kumho Tire Co. v. Carmichael, 119 S.Ct. 1167 (1999), the

Supreme Court resolved a split among the circuits and ruled that the gatekeeper function applied to all expert testimony, not just scientific testimony. Thus, in that case, the trial court judge had to decide whether the opinion of a tire failure analyst was based on reliable methodology.

3. Why does the opinion talk about California tort law?

4. Notice the parallel between the proposed testimony of some of plaintiffs' experts in this case and the plaintiff's expert in Kramer Service, Inc. v. Wilkins, page 260: Bendectin or a cut *could* cause the harm, not it *did* cause the harm.

5. In footnote 13, the opinion alludes to another issue with which the courts have been struggling. In cases involving exposure to other drugs or chemicals, unlike in the principal case, there may be clear evidence that a particular substance increases the risk of harm. That is, the experts generally agree that exposure to the substance increases the incidence of a particular disease. Application of the preponderance rule to such mass exposure cases may result in unfairness to both plaintiffs and defendants. Do you see why? Suppose expert testimony established that the incidence of a particular birth defect in the general population was 4 births per 1000 and that it was 5 births per 1000 in the population of those exposed to a toxic substance. Assume that the testimony would show that this is a statistically significant difference. A plaintiff with a birth defect would have difficulty proving to the court that his particular birth defect was caused by the toxic substance and was not one of the four naturally occurring. On the other hand, if the tort system requires the defendant to compensate each person born with a birth defect, the defendant is paying for five times the risk created by producing the toxic substance. See Rubanick v. Witco Chemical Corp., 125 N.J. 421, 593 A.2d 733 (1991) (adopting a broadened standard for determining the reliability and admissibility of scientific theories of causation in toxic tort cases). See also, Rosenberg, The Causal Connection in Mass Exposure Cases: A "Public Law" Vision of the Tort System, 97 Harv.L.Rev. 851 (1984) and 2 A.L.I., Reporter's Study, Enterprise Responsibility for Personal Injury, Approaches to Legal and Institutional Change, pp. 369–375 (1991) urging the courts to move away from traditional tort doctrine in mass exposure cases.

6. Generally, a plaintiff in a tort case must establish causation by a preponderance of the evidence. In claims made in no-fault systems like worker compensation or in proceedings setting governmental safety standards, however, the burden of establishing causation may be lower than preponderance of the evidence. See, e.g., McAllister v. Workmen's Compensation Appeals Bd., 69 Cal.2d 408, 445 P.2d 313, 71 Cal.Rptr. 697 (1968) ("reasonable probability" enough to show that firefighter's lung cancer was caused by repeated inhalation of smoke during career) and Industrial Union Dept., AFL–CIO v. American Petroleum Inst., 448 U.S. 607, 655–656 (1980) (OSHA "has no duty to calculate the exact probability of harm" or "to support its finding that a significant risk exists with anything approaching scientific certainty" in setting standards for workplace exposure to toxic substances).

3. CONCURRENT CAUSES

Hill v. Edmonds

Supreme Court of New York, Appellate Division, 1966.
26 A.D.2d 554, 270 N.Y.S.2d 1020.

MEMORANDUM BY THE COURT. In a negligence action to recover damages for personal injury, plaintiff appeals from a judgment of the Supreme Court,

Queens County, entered June 21, 1965, which dismissed the complaint as against defendant Bragoli upon the court's decision at the close of plaintiff's case upon a jury trial. * * *

At the close of plaintiff's case the court dismissed the complaint against the owner of a tractor truck who on a stormy night left it parked without lights in the middle of a road where the car in which plaintiff was a passenger collided with it from the rear. From the testimony of the driver of the car the court concluded that she was guilty of negligence and was solely responsible for the collision. That testimony was that she saw the truck when it was four car lengths ahead of her and that she saw it in enough time to turn. At other points, however, she indicated that she did not know just what happened, that she swerved to avoid the truck, "and the next thing I knew I woke up. I was unconscious." Assuming, *arguendo,* that she was negligent, the accident could not have happened had not the truck owner allowed his unlighted vehicle to stand in the middle of the highway. Where separate acts of negligence combine to produce directly a single injury each tortfeasor is responsible for the entire result, even though his act alone might not have caused it. [Cc] Accordingly, the complaint against the truck owner must be reinstated and a new trial had.

Facts

Rule of law

NOTES AND QUESTIONS

1. As a horse-drawn street car stopped for a railroad crossing, the railroad's employee negligently raised the crossing gates, although a train was approaching. The street car driver negligently proceeded onto the crossing without looking, whereupon the railroad lowered the gates, shutting in the street car on the railroad track. Passengers on the street car, seeing the train coming, stampeded in panic, and plaintiff, one of the passengers, was pushed off of the car and injured. Who is liable? Washington & Georgetown R. Co. v. Hickey, 166 U.S. 521 (1897).

2. Plaintiff's horse fell into an excavation made by a traction company and left unguarded at night. It scrambled out, and promptly fell into a second and adjoining excavation, left in the street by the town authorities. After it climbed out again, and in consequence of both falls, the horse took fright and ran away. The horse was injured and the wagon was broken. The traction company and the town were acting entirely independently. Are they each liable for the entire damage? Carstesen v. Stratford, 67 Conn. 428, 35 A. 276 (1896).

Joint and several liability — both D's are liable for the full amount of the injury

▸Anderson v. Minneapolis, St. P. & S. St. M. R.R. Co.

Supreme Court of Minnesota, 1920.
146 Minn. 430, 179 N.W. 45.

LEES, C. This is a fire case brought against the defendant railway company. * * * Plaintiff had a verdict. The appeal is from an order denying a motion in the alternative for judgment notwithstanding the verdict or for a new trial. * * *

[A forest fire, which originated in a bog and was found by the jury to have been caused by the negligence of the defendant, swept over a large area. It merged with another fire of independent and uncertain origin, and the combined fires burned over plaintiff's property. The defendant contends that the following instruction to the jury was in error:]

"If the plaintiff was burned out by some fire other than the bog fire, which other fire was not set by one of the defendant's engines, then, of course, defendant is not liable. * * * If plaintiff was burned out by fire set by one of the defendant's engines in combination with some other fire not set by any of its engines, then it is liable.

"If you find that other fire or fires not set by one of defendant's engines mingled with one that was set by one of the defendant's engines, there may be difficulty in determining whether you should find that the fire set by the engine was a material or substantial element in causing plaintiff's damage. If it was, the defendant is liable, otherwise it is not. * * *

"If you find that the bog fire was set by the defendant's engine and that some greater fire swept over it before it reached the plaintiff's land, then it will be for you to determine whether that bog fire * * * was a material or substantial factor in causing plaintiff's damage. If it was * * * the defendant is liable. If it was not, the defendant is not liable."

The following proposition is stated in defendant's brief and relied on for reversal:

"If plaintiff's property was damaged by a number of fires combining, one * * * being the fire pleaded * * * the others being of no responsible origin, but of such sufficient or superior force that they would have produced the damage to plaintiff's property regardless of the fire pleaded, then defendant was not liable."

This proposition is based on Cook v. Minneapolis, St. P. & S.S.M. Ry. Co., 98 Wis. 624, 74 N.W. 561. * * * If the Cook case merely declares that one who negligently sets a fire is not liable if another's property is damaged, unless it is made to appear that the fire was a material element in the destruction of the property, there can be no question about the soundness of the decision. But if it decides that if such fire combines with another of no responsible origin, and after the union of the two fires they destroy the property, and either fire independently of the other would have destroyed it, then irrespective of whether the first fire was or was not a material factor in the destruction of the property, there is no liability, we are not prepared to adopt the doctrine as the law of this state. If a fire set by the engine of one railroad company unites with a fire set by the engine of another company, there is joint and several liability, even though either fire would have destroyed plaintiff's property. But if the doctrine of the Cook case is applied and one of the fires is of unknown origin, there is no liability. * * * [T]here [should] be liability in such a case. We, therefore hold that the trial court did not err in refusing to instruct the jury in accordance with the rule laid down in the Cook case. * * *

We find no error requiring a reversal, and hence the order appealed from is affirmed.

NOTES AND QUESTIONS

1. As plaintiff was driving his horse and wagon down a narrow road, two motorcycles, independently operated by two defendants, roared past him, one on each side. The horse took fright and ran away, and plaintiff was injured. Either motorcycle alone would have been sufficient to frighten the horse. Who is liable? *both* Corey v. Havener, 182 Mass. 250, 65 N.E. 69 (1902).

2. A stabs B with a knife. C then fractures B's skull with a rock. Either injury would be fatal. B dies from the effect of both. Who is liable for his death? Wilson v. *both* State, 24 S.W. 409 (Tex.Cr.App.1893); People v. Lewis, 124 Cal. 551, 57 P. 470 (1899). Should the answer be the same in criminal and tort law?

3. A car rental company rents a car with defective brakes. The driver negligently fails to see the plaintiff and hits him. Who, if anyone, is liable? See Prosser and Keeton, Torts 267, n. 27 (5th ed. 1984).

4. While plaintiff is suffering from terminal cancer, he is negligently hit by defendant's automobile and killed. How does this case differ from the principal case and those cited in note 2? See Follett v. Jones, 252 Ark. 950, 481 S.W.2d 713 (1972).

5. The "substantial factor" test would retain "but for" causation as an essential precondition except in situations, such as the principal case, in which two or more actively operating forces, for only one of which the defendant was responsible, combine to bring about the harm, while each alone would have been sufficient to bring about the harm. See Restatement (Second) of Torts §§ 431–433 (1965). "Substantial factor" was taken by the trial judge in the *Anderson* case from an article by Jeremiah Smith, Legal Cause in Actions of Tort, 25 Harv.L.Rev. 103, 223, 229 (1911). It obviously has the advantage of eliminating cases in which the defendant has made a proved, but insignificant, contribution to the result—as where he throws a lighted match into a forest fire. See generally Fischer, Causation in Fact in Omission Cases, 1992 Utah L.Rev. 1335 (discussing difficult proof problems in cases involving a party's failure to act to prevent harm).

6. California has eliminated the "but for" language in favor of "substantial factor" in its jury instruction on causation, even in cases involving one cause. Mitchell v. Gonzales, 54 Cal.3d 1041, 819 P.2d 872, 1 Cal.Rptr.2d 913 (1991). See also Horton v. Harwick Chemical Corp., 73 Ohio St. 3d 679, 653 N.E.2d 1196 (Ohio 1995) (in context of asbestos case with multiple defendants, court adopts the Restatement definition of substantial factor: " 'substantial' is used to denote the fact that the defendant's conduct has such an effect in producing the harm as to lead reasonable men to regard it as a cause, using that word in a popular sense, in which there always lurks the idea of responsibility, rather than the so-called 'philosophical sense,' which includes every one of the great number of events without which any happening would not have occurred.")

4. PROBLEMS IN DETERMINING WHICH PARTY CAUSED THE HARM

➤ Summers v. Tice

Supreme Court of California, 1948.
33 Cal.2d 80, 199 P.2d 1.

Actions by Charles A. Summers against Harold W. Tice and against Ernest Simonson for negligently shooting plaintiff while hunting. From judgments for plaintiff, defendants appeal, and the appeals were consolidated pursuant to stipulation.

[Plaintiff and the two defendants were members of a hunting party. Both defendants negligently fired, at the same time, at a quail and in the plaintiff's direction. Plaintiff was struck in the eye by a shot from one gun. There was no other satisfactory evidence.]

CARTER, J. * * * The problem presented in this case is whether the judgment against both defendants may stand. It is argued by defendants that they are not joint tort feasors, and thus jointly and severally liable, as they were not acting in concert, and that there is not sufficient evidence to show which defendant was guilty of the negligence which caused the injuries—the shooting by Tice or that by Simonson. * * * The one shot that entered plaintiff's eye was the major factor in assessing damages and that shot could not have come from the gun of both defendants. It was from one or the other only.

It has been held that where a group of persons are on a hunting party, or otherwise engaged in the use of firearms, and two of them are negligent in firing in the direction of a third person who is injured thereby, both of those so firing are liable for the injury suffered by the third person, although the negligence of only one of them could have caused the injury. * * *

These cases speak of the action of defendants as being in concert as the ground of decision, yet it would seem they are straining that concept and the more reasonable basis appears in Oliver v. Miles, 144 Miss. 852, 110 So. 666. There two persons were hunting together. Both shot at some partridges and in so doing shot across the highway injuring plaintiff who was traveling on it. The court stated they were acting in concert and thus both were liable. The court then stated: "We think that * * * each is liable for the resulting injury to the boy, although no one can say definitely who actually shot him. *To hold otherwise would be to exonerate both from liability, although each was negligent, and the injury resulted from such negligence.*" [Emphasis added.] * * *

When we consider the relative position of the parties and the results that would flow if plaintiff was required to pin the injury on one of the defendants only, a requirement that the burden of proof on that subject be shifted to defendants becomes manifest. They are both wrongdoers—both negligent toward plaintiff. They brought about a situation where the negligence of one of them injured the plaintiff, hence it should rest with them each to absolve himself if he can. The injured party has been placed by defendants in the unfair position of pointing to which defendant caused the harm. If one can escape the other may also and plaintiff is remediless. Ordinarily defendants are in a far better position to offer evidence to determine which one caused the injury. This reasoning has recently found favor in this Court. [The court refers here to its earlier holding in Ybarra v. Spangard, page 242].

[T]he same reasons of policy and justice shift the burden to each of defendants to absolve himself if he can—relieving the wronged person of the duty of apportioning the injury to a particular defendant, apply here where we are concerned with whether plaintiff is required to supply evidence for the apportionment of damages. If defendants are independent tort feasors and thus each liable for the damage caused by him alone, and, at least, where the matter of apportionment is incapable of proof, the innocent wronged party should not be deprived of his right to redress. The wrongdoers should be left to work out between themselves any apportionment. * * *

Holding

The judgment is affirmed.

NOTES AND QUESTIONS

1. In accord, on similar facts, Cook v. Lewis, [1952] 1 Dom.L.Rep. 1, [1951] B.C.Rep. 830. The Restatement (Second) of Torts, § 433B, has approved the rule. See also Bowman v. Redding & Co., 449 F.2d 956 (D.C.Cir.1971). What is the relation of this case to Ybarra v. Spangard, page 242?

2. As plaintiff got out of her car to purchase some tomatoes, she was approached by two dogs, both of which barked and snapped at her. Trying to get away and into her car, she turned her back and was bitten by one of them. The incident took place on the common driveway between the homes of next door neighbors who allowed their two dogs, which were of similar size and appearance, to run freely between their two properties. Plaintiff filed suit against both dog owners, but is unable to testify as to which dog bit her. Should the trial court judge enter summary judgment for the owners? Hood v. Hagler, 606 P.2d 548 (Okla.1979) (court relied upon principal case to shift burden of proof to defendant owners to prove that his dog was not the one.) Suppose the defendants produce evidence that the neighbor across the street has two dogs of a similar breed that they have had to chase away from their property on numerous occasions? How does the burden of proof apply?

alternative liability theory (Summers v. Tice)

3. Two automobiles, negligently driven by A and B, collide. Immediately, a car negligently driven by C piles into the wreck. Somewhere in the process plaintiff, a passenger in A's car, is killed. There is no other evidence. What result? Cummings v. Kendall, 41 Cal.App.2d 549, 107 P.2d 282 (1940); Murphy v. Taxicabs of Louisville, Inc., 330 S.W.2d 395 (Ky.1959); cf. Petersen v. Parry, 92 Idaho 647, 448 P.2d 653 (1968) (two cars collide; all occupants killed).

4. A number of defendants spew pollution into the air and damage plaintiff's property, but he cannot show which one caused what damage. Is this enough to apply the principal case? See Michie v. Great Lakes, page 390. Worker's job is to reclaim and recondition fifty-five gallon drums that had been used to transport petroleum products and other chemicals. Neither his employer nor the owners of the drums warned him of the risks associated with inhaling fumes from the drums. He developed stomach and liver cancer. His expert witness will testify that several of the chemicals to which he was exposed are carcinogens, each of which could have caused his cancer. Is this enough to shift the burden to the defendants? James v. Bessemer Processing Co., Inc., 155 N.J. 279, 714 A.2d 898 (1998).

5. Should it make any difference in the principal case if plaintiff sues only one defendant, without joining the other? What if there had been ten hunters in the principal case and plaintiff only joined two?

depends on the jurisdiction

if they can prove one of the other 8 did it

Sindell v. Abbott Laboratories

Supreme Court of California, 1980.
26 Cal.3d 588, 607 P.2d 924, 163 Cal.Rptr. 132, cert. denied,
449 U.S. 912, 101 S.Ct. 285, 66 L.Ed.2d 140 (1980).

MOSK, JUSTICE. This case involves a complex problem both timely and significant: may a plaintiff, injured as the result of a drug administered to her mother during pregnancy, who knows the type of drug involved but cannot identify the manufacturer of the precise product, hold liable for her injuries a maker of a drug produced from an identical formula?

[Plaintiff alleged that her mother ingested a drug, diethylstilbestrol (DES), which was marketed by the defendants, five drug companies. The drug also was marketed by approximately 195 other companies, not joined as defendants. The drug, a synthetic estrogen, was given to plaintiff's mother while she was pregnant with plaintiff to prevent miscarriage. Plaintiff, now an adult, alleged that she developed cancer as a result of her exposure to the drug. She also indicated that she could not identify the manufacturer of the drug. The trial court dismissed the action.

This court held that (1) Summers v. Tice did not apply because not all the defendants were before the court, and (2) there was no "concert of action" among the defendants. See page 279].

A third theory upon which plaintiff relies is the concept of industry-wide liability, or according to the terminology of the parties, "enterprise liability." This theory was suggested in Hall v. E.I. Du Pont De Nemours & Co., Inc. (E.D.N.Y.1972) 345 F.Supp. 353. In that case, plaintiffs were 13 children injured by the explosion of blasting caps in 12 separate incidents which occurred in 10 different states between 1955 and 1959. The defendants were six blasting cap manufacturers, comprising virtually the entire blasting cap industry in the United States, and their trade association. There were, however, a number of Canadian blasting cap manufacturers which could have supplied the caps. The gravamen of the complaint was that the practice of the industry of omitting a warning on individual blasting caps and of failing to take other safety measures created an unreasonable risk of harm, resulting in the plaintiffs' injuries. The complaint did not identify a particular manufacturer of a cap which caused a particular injury.

The court reasoned as follows: there was evidence that defendants, acting independently, had adhered to an industry-wide standard with regard to the safety features of blasting caps, that they had in effect delegated some functions of safety investigation and design, such as labelling, to their trade association, and that there was industry-wide cooperation in the manufacture and design of blasting caps. In these circumstances, the evidence supported a conclusion that all the defendants jointly controlled the risk. Thus, if plaintiffs could establish by a preponderance of the evidence that the caps were manufactured by one of the defendants, the burden of proof as to causation would shift to all the defendants. The court noted that this theory of liability applied to industries composed of a small number of units, and that what would be fair and reasonable with regard to an industry of five or ten producers might be manifestly unreasonable if applied to a decentralized industry composed of countless small producers. * * *

We decline to apply this theory in the present case. At least 200 manufacturers produced DES; *Hall*, which involved 6 manufacturers representing the entire blasting cap industry in the United States, cautioned against application of the doctrine espoused therein to a large number of producers. (345 F.Supp. at p. 378.)

Moreover in *Hall*, the conclusion that the defendants jointly controlled the risk was based upon allegations that they had delegated some functions relating to safety to a trade association. There are no such allegations here, and we have concluded above that plaintiff has failed to allege liability on a concert of action theory. * * *

If we were confined to the theories of *Summers* and *Hall*, we would be constrained to hold that the judgment must be sustained. Should we require that plaintiff identify the manufacturer which supplied the DES used by her mother or that all DES manufacturers be joined in the action, she would effectively be precluded from any recovery. As defendants candidly admit, there is little likelihood that all the manufacturers who made DES at the time in question are still in business or that they are subject to the jurisdiction of the California courts. There are, however, forceful arguments in favor of holding that plaintiff has a cause of action.

In our contemporary complex industrialized society, advances in science and technology create fungible goods which may harm consumers and which cannot be traced to any specific producer. The response of the courts can be either to adhere rigidly to prior doctrine, denying recovery to those injured by such products, or to fashion remedies to meet these changing needs. * * *

The most persuasive reason for finding plaintiff states a cause of action is that advanced in *Summers*: as between an innocent plaintiff and negligent defendants, the latter should bear the cost of the injury. Here, as in *Summers*, plaintiff is not at fault in failing to provide evidence of causation, and although the absence of such evidence is not attributable to the defendants either, their conduct in marketing a drug the effects of which are delayed for many years played a significant role in creating the unavailability of proof.

From a broader policy standpoint, defendants are better able to bear the cost of injury resulting from the manufacture of a defective product. As was said by Justice Traynor in *Escola* [v. Coca Cola Bottling Co.], "[t]he cost of an injury and the loss of time or health may be an overwhelming misfortune to the person injured, and a needless one, for the risk of injury can be insured by the manufacturer and distributed among the public as a cost of doing business." (24 Cal.2d 462, 150 P.2d 441; see also Rest.2d Torts, § 402A, com. c, 349–350.) The manufacturer is in the best position to discover and guard against defects in its products and to warn of harmful effects; thus, holding it liable for defects and failure to warn of harmful effects will provide an incentive to product safety. [Cc] These considerations are particularly significant where medication is involved, for the consumer is virtually helpless to protect himself from serious, sometimes permanent, sometimes fatal, injuries caused by deleterious drugs.

Where, as here, all defendants produced a drug from an identical formula and the manufacturer of the DES which caused plaintiff's injuries cannot be identified through no fault of plaintiff, a modification of the rule of *Summers* is warranted. As we have seen, an undiluted *Summers* rationale is inappropriate to shift the burden of proof of causation to defendants because if we measure the chance that any particular manufacturer supplied the injury-causing product by the number of producers of DES, there is a possibility that none of the five defendants in this case produced the offending substance and that the responsible manufacturer, not named in the action, will escape liability.

But we approach the issue of causation from a different perspective: we hold it to be reasonable in the present context to measure the likelihood that any of the defendants supplied the product which allegedly injured plaintiff by the percentage which the DES sold by each of them for the purpose of preventing miscarriage bears to the entire production of the drug sold by all for that purpose. Plaintiff asserts in her briefs that Eli Lilly and Company and 5 or 6 other companies produced 90 percent of the DES marketed. If at trial this is established to be the fact, then there is a corresponding likelihood that this comparative handful of producers manufactured the DES which caused plaintiff's injuries, and only a 10 percent likelihood that the offending producer would escape liability.

If plaintiff joins in the action the manufacturers of a substantial share of the DES which her mother might have taken, the injustice of shifting the burden of proof to defendants to demonstrate that they could not have made the substance which injured plaintiff is significantly diminished.

* * *

The presence in the action of a substantial share of the appropriate market also provides a ready means to apportion damages among the defendants. Each defendant will be held liable for the proportion of the judgment represented by its share of that market unless it demonstrates that it could not have made the product which caused plaintiff's injuries.

* * *

Under this approach, each manufacturer's liability would approximate its responsibility for the injuries caused by its own products. Some minor discrepancy in the correlation between market share and liability is inevitable; therefore, a defendant may be held liable for a somewhat different percentage of the damage than its share of the appropriate market would justify. It is probably impossible, with the passage of time, to determine market share with mathematical exactitude. * * * As we said in *Summers* with regard to the liability of independent tortfeasors, where a correct division of liability cannot be made "the trier of fact may make it the best it can." (33 Cal.2d at 88, 199 P.2d at 5.)

We are not unmindful of the practical problems involved in defining the market and determining market share, but these are largely matters of proof which properly cannot be determined at the pleading stage of these proceedings. Defendants urge that it would be both unfair and contrary to public policy to hold them liable for plaintiff's injuries in the absence of proof that one of them supplied the drug responsible for the damage. Most of their arguments, however, are based upon the assumption that one manufacturer would be held responsible for the products of another or for those of all other manufacturers if plaintiff ultimately prevails. But under the rule we adopt, each manufacturer's liability for an injury would be approximately equivalent to the damages caused by the DES it manufactured.

The judgments are reversed.

BIRD, C.J., and NEWMAN and WHITE, JJ., concur.

RICHARDSON, CLARK and MANUAL, JJ., dissent.

NOTES AND QUESTIONS

1.   Five state supreme courts have chosen to retain in DES cases the traditional common law requirement that the plaintiff prove the identity of the tortfeasor in order to recover. Zafft v. Eli Lilly and Co., 676 S.W.2d 241, 247 (Mo.1984); Mulcahy v. Eli Lilly and Co., 386 N.W.2d 67 (Iowa 1986); Smith v. Eli Lilly and Co., 137 Ill.2d 222, 560 N.E.2d 324, 148 Ill.Dec. 22 (1990); and Gorman v. Abbott Lab., 599 A.2d 1364 (R.I.1991); Sutowski v. Eli Lilly & Co., 82 Ohio St.3d 347, 696 N.E.2d 187 (1998).

2.   California and the five state supreme courts that have followed its lead and fashioned some theory to allow a DES plaintiff to recover even if she cannot identify the manufacturer of the drug that injured her have done so in a variety of ways.

A.   California requires the plaintiff to bring before the court defendants representing a "substantial share" of the market. A defendant is dismissed from the case if it can prove that it did not manufacture the drug taken by the plaintiff's mother. Assuming that the plaintiff can prove her case, each of the remaining defendants is severally liable for only that portion of the plaintiff's damages that corresponds to the percentage of its share of the market. Brown v. Superior Crt., 44 Cal.3d 1049, 751 P.2d 470, 245 Cal.Rptr. 412 (1988).

B.   New York has not specified how many of the defendants need to be joined in order to use a market share theory of recovery. It does not allow a defendant to exculpate itself by proving that it did not manufacture the drug taken by the plaintiff's mother. As in California, each of the defendants is severally liable for only that portion of the plaintiff's damages that corresponds to the percentage of its share of the market. There is no joint and several liability. Market is defined as the national market. Hymowitz v. Eli Lilly and Co., 73 N.Y.2d 487, 539 N.E.2d 1069, 541 N.Y.S.2d 941 (1989).

C.   Washington and Florida require the plaintiff to file suit against only one defendant, with that defendant then impleading others, if it so chooses. A defendant is dismissed from the case if it can prove that it did not manufacture the drug taken by the plaintiff's mother. The remaining defendants are then presumed to have an equal share of the entire DES market and the burden of proof shifts to each defendant to prove its actual share of the market. If a defendant succeeds in proving that its actual share is less than its presumptive share, it is only liable for that portion of plaintiff's damages that corresponds to its actual market share. The remaining defendants (those unable to prove their actual market shares) have their presumptive shares adjusted upward to again reflect 100% of the market. If there are no defendants unable to prove their actual market share, and plaintiff has not joined all defendants, the plaintiff may be unable to collect the full amount of her damages. Martin v. Abbott Labs., 102 Wash.2d 581, 689 P.2d 368 (1984); Conley v. Boyle Drug Co., 570 So.2d 275 (Fla.1990).

D. Wisconsin adopted a "risk contribution theory," requiring the plaintiff to file suit against only one defendant, with that defendant impleading others. A defendant is dismissed from the case if it can prove that it did not manufacture the drug taken by the plaintiff's mother. The jury, using comparative negligence principles, assigns to the remaining defendants shares of liability based on the amount of "risk" they contributed rather than their market share. Market share is only one of several factors considered by the jury in its assessment of risk. Collins v. Eli Lilly and Co., 116 Wis.2d 166, 342 N.W.2d 37 (1984).

E. Michigan has applied alternative liability (like Summers v. Tice). If plaintiff can join all possible manufacturers as defendants, the burden of proof is shifted to each defendant to prove that it did not make the DES that injured the plaintiff. Any defendants who cannot exculpate themselves are jointly and severally liable, apparently on a per capita rather than a market share basis. Abel v. Eli Lilly and Co., 418 Mich. 311, 343 N.W.2d 164 (1984).

3. The alternative theories of liability rarely have been extended beyond the DES context. See, e.g., Sheffield v. Eli Lilly and Co., 144 Cal.App.3d 583, 192 Cal.Rptr. 870 (1983) (vaccine); Goldman v. Johns–Manville Sales Corp., 33 Ohio St.3d 40, 514 N.E.2d 691 (1987) (asbestos); Lee v. Baxter Healthcare Corp., 721 F.Supp. 89 (D.Md.1989), aff'd, 898 F.2d 146 (4th Cir.1990) (breast implants); City of Philadelphia v. Lead Industries Ass'n., Inc., 994 F.2d 112 (3d Cir.1993) (lead paint); Rogers v. AAA Wire Products, Inc., 182 Wis.2d 263, 513 N.W.2d 643 (1994) (wire bread cart in grocery store); Bly v. Tri–Continental Indust. Inc., 663 A.2d 1232 (D.C.App.1995) (benzene in gasoline); Skipworth v. Lead Indust. Assn. Inc., 547 Pa. 224, 690 A.2d 169 (Pa. 1997) (lead paint). But see Smith v. Cutter Biological, Inc., 72 Haw. 416, 823 P.2d 717 (1991) (blood clotting protein) and King v. Cutter Labs., 714 So.2d 351 (Fla.1998) (sending blood clotting protein case back for full evidentiary hearing to determine whether products manufactured by various defendants were sufficiently uniform in risk of infection to justify application of market share theory).

4. Those of you writing for a law review and wondering if anyone reads your efforts should know that the Sindell decision itself was based on a student law review contribution. See Comment, DES and a Proposed Theory of Enterprise Liability, 46 Fordham L.Rev. 963 (1978). See also, Twerski, Market Share—A Tale of Two Centuries, 55 Brooklyn L.Rev. 869 (1989).

5. Courts that have adopted one of the alternative liability theories have had to decide how many of the defendants must be before the court (all? a substantial share? one?), what the plaintiff must prove about her efforts to identify the manufacturer of the DES that injured her (nothing? some effort? due diligence?), whether a defendant can avoid liability by proving that it did not manufacture the DES taken by the plaintiff's mother (plaintiff's mother remembers round green pills, defendant marketed red capsules), who will absorb the shares of defendants who are not present or who are judgment proof (plaintiff? all defendants who were sued by plaintiff? defendants impled by other defendants? defendants who are

unable to prove they were not the manufacturer?), how the defendants will share the liability (per capita? risk contribution? market share?), what the relevant market is (plaintiff's state? region where plaintiff's mother took DES? suppliers of the pharmacy at which her mother filled her prescription? all DES manufacturers? only those who made small red pills?). Would the legislature be a more desirable forum to work out causational proof problems in mass tort cases? For an in-depth discussion of this alternative, see Schwartz and Mahshigian, Failure to Identify the Defendant in Tort Law: Towards a Legislative Solution, 73 Calif.L.Rev. 941 (1985).

6.   The complaint in *Sindell* contained allegations of strict liability, breach of warranty, and fraud, as well as negligence. Should the underlying theory of recovery make a difference as to whether the court relaxes the traditional burden of proof for causation? See Brown v. Superior Court, 44 Cal.3d 1049, 751 P.2d 470, 245 Cal.Rptr. 412 (1988) (strict liability, breach of warranty, and fraud not available in DES market share case) and King v. Cutter Labs., 714 So.2d 351 (Fla.1998) (reiterating that market share applies only in negligence actions).

7.   Compare the plaintiffs in the Bendectin litigation (*Daubert*) and in the DES litigation (*Sindell*). Both faced difficulty in proving causation under traditional negligence principles. How did their experiences differ?

(handwritten margin notes: causation in fact, probability vs possibility, foreseeability)

PROXIMATE OR LEGAL CAUSE

Atlantic Coast Line R. Co. v. Daniels

Court of Appeals of Georgia, 1911.
8 Ga.App. 775, 70 S.E. 203.

POWELL, J. * * * Cause and effect find their beginning and end in the limitless and unknowable. Therefore courts, in their finitude, do not attempt to deal with cause and effect in any absolute degree, but only in such a limited way as is practical and as is within the scope of ordinary human understanding. Hence arbitrary limits have been set, and such qualifying words as "proximate" and "natural" have come into use as setting the limits beyond which the courts will not look in the attempt to trace the connection between a given cause and a given effect. A plaintiff comes into court alleging, as an effect, some injury that has been done to his person or to his property. He shows that antecedent to the injury a wrongful act of another person occurred, and that, if this wrongful act had not occurred, the injury complained of would not (as human probabilities go) have occurred. We then say, in common speech, that the wrong was a cause of the injury. But to make such a standard (that, if the cause had not existed, the effect would not have occurred) the basis of legal responsibility would soon prove very unsatisfactory; for a *reductio ad absurdum* may be promptly established by calling to mind that, if the injured person had never been born, the injury would not have happened. So the courts ask another question: Was the wrongful act the proximate cause? * * *

NOTES AND QUESTIONS

1. For "proximate," we are indebted to Francis Bacon, Lord Chancellor, who in his time committed other sins. His maxim was: *In jure non remota causa, sed proxima, spectatur.* [In law, not the remote cause but the nearest one, is looked to.] According to the Random House Dictionary of the English Language (unabridged edition), proximate means "1. next; nearest; immediately before or after in order * * * 2. close, very near * * *" How important is the matter of physical distance between defendant's conduct and plaintiff's injury? See the discussion of the *Kinsman* cases, page 9, note 313.

2. What about nearness or remoteness as to time? In City of Brady, Texas v. Finklea, 400 F.2d 352, 357 (5th Cir.1968), an electrician was electrocuted by wires suspended from a transformer cross arm that had been negligently installed by the city over 28 years before. The court stated that "lapse of time is but one element to be considered along with all relevant facts in the case." Cf. Bradler v. Craig, 274 Cal.App.2d 466, 79 Cal.Rptr. 401 (1969) (house built 18 years earlier).

3.   The Restatement (Second) of Torts § 431 has substituted the term "legal cause" for proximate cause. Is this a more descriptive term? Is it more helpful in understanding the nature of proximate cause? Thus far, most courts have been inclined to retain the terminology of "proximate cause." Both terms are often used to include cause in fact, a necessary predicate to an inquiry about proximate cause. If cause in fact is not present, then there is no need to inquire whether there is proximate cause.

4.   Articles, notes and comments on "proximate cause" are legion. The topic has had a peculiar fascination for legal writers, and most of them have used it as a springboard to launch their own theories as to the proper basis of legal liability. At one extreme, there have been attempts to reduce it all to definite mechanical rules, as in Beale, The Proximate Consequences of an Act, 33 Harv.L.Rev. 633 (1920). At the other extreme, there has been a rejection of all rules, and the position that the court must decide each case according to its ideas of "justice," as in Edgerton, Legal Cause, 72 U.Pa.L.Rev. 211, 343 (1924).

Among the principal landmarks of discussion have been the book by Leon Green, The Rationale of Proximate Cause (1927); Bohlen, The Probable or the Natural Consequences as a Test of Liability in Negligence, 40 U.Pa.L.Rev. 79, 148 (1901); Smith, Legal Cause in Actions of Tort, 25 Harv.L.Rev. 103, 223, 303 (1911); Green, Are There Dependable Rules of Causation? 77 U.Pa.L.Rev. 601 (1929); Goodhart, The Unforeseeable Consequences of a Negligent Act, 39 Yale L.J. 532 (1930); Campbell, Duty, Fault and Legal Cause, 1938 Wis.L.Rev. 402; Gregory, Proximate Cause in Negligence—A Retreat from "Rationalization," 6 U.Chi.L.Rev. 36 (1938). See also the books by Robert Keeton, Legal Cause in the Law of Torts (1963), and Hart and Honoré, Causation in the Law of Torts (2d ed. 1985).

Some efforts by law review writers include Seidelson, Some Reflections on Proximate Cause, 19 Duq.L.Rev. 1 (1980); Shavell, Analysis of Causation and the Scope of Liability in the Law of Torts, 9 J.Legal Stud. 463 (1980); King, Causation, Valuation, and Chance in Personal Injury Torts Involving Preexisting Conditions and Future Consequences, 90 Yale L.J. 1353 (1981); Wright, Actual Causation vs. Probabilistic Linkage: The Bane of Economic Analysis, 14 J.Leg.Stud. 435 (1985); Twerski, Informed Decision Making and the Law of Torts: The Myth of Justiciable Causation, 1988 U.Ill.L.Rev. 607; Kelley, Proximate Cause in Negligence Law: History, Theory and the Present Darkness, 69 Wash.U.L.Q. 49 (1991). For economic applications and ramifications of proximate cause, see Landes & Posner, Causation in Tort Law: An Economic Approach, 12 J.Legal Stud. 109 (1983); and Grady, Proximate Cause and the Law of Negligence, 69 Iowa L.Rev. 363 (1984).

5.   Here is a recent articulation of the difference between cause in fact and proximate cause from the Tennessee Supreme Court: "The distinction between cause in fact and proximate, or legal, cause is not merely an exercise in semantics. The terms are not interchangeable. Although both cause in fact and proximate, or legal, cause are elements of negligence that the plaintiff must prove, they are very different concepts. Cause in fact refers to the cause and effect relationship between the defendant's tortious conduct and the plaintiff's injury or loss. Thus, cause in fact deals with the 'but for' consequences of an act. The defendant's conduct is a cause of the event if the event would not have occurred but for that conduct. In contrast, proximate cause, or legal cause, concerns a determination of whether legal liability should be imposed where cause in fact has been established. Proximate or legal cause is a policy decision made by the legislature or the courts to deny liability for otherwise actionable conduct based on considerations of logic, common sense, policy, precedent and 'our more or less inadequately expressed ideas of what justice

demands or of what is administratively possible and convenient.' " Snyder v. LTG Lufttechnische, GmbH, 955 S.W.2d 252 (Tenn.1997) (citations omitted).

6.   As you read the cases in this chapter, remember that proximate cause is a concept that cuts off liability even though there is cause in fact.

1.   UNFORESEEABLE CONSEQUENCES

Ryan v. New York Central R.R. Co.

Court of Appeals of New York, 1866.
35 N.Y. 210, 91 Am.Dec. 49.

HUNT, J. On the 15th day of July, 1854, in the city of Syracuse, the defendant, by the careless management, or through the insufficient condition of one of its engines, set fire to its woodshed, and a large quantity of wood therein. The plaintiff's house, situated at a distance of one hundred and thirty feet from the shed, soon took fire from the heat and sparks, and was entirely consumed, notwithstanding diligent efforts were made to save it. A number of other houses were also burned by the spreading of the fire. The plaintiff brings this action to recover from the railroad company the value of his building thus destroyed. The judge at the Circuit nonsuited the plaintiff, and the General Term of the fifth district affirmed the judgment.

The question may be thus stated: A house in a populous city takes fire, through the negligence of the owner or his servant; the flames extend to and destroy an adjacent building: Is the owner of the first building liable to the second owner for the damage sustained by such burning?

It is a general principle that every person is liable for the consequences of his own acts. He is thus liable in damages for the proximate results of his own acts, but not for remote damages. It is not easy at all times to determine what are proximate and what are remote damages. * * *

If an engineer upon a steamboat or locomotive in passing the house of A., so carelessly manages its machinery that the coals and sparks from its fires fall upon and consume the house of A., the railroad company or the steamboat proprietors are liable to pay the value of the property thus destroyed. [C] Thus far the law is settled and the principle is apparent. If, however, the fire communicates from the house of A. to that of B., and that is destroyed, is the negligent party liable for his loss? And if it spreads thence to the house of C., and thence to the house of D., and thence consecutively through the other houses until it reaches and consumes the house of Z., is the party liable to pay the damages sustained by these twenty-four sufferers? The counsel for the plaintiff does not distinctly claim this, and I think it would not be seriously insisted that the sufferers could recover in such case. Where then is the principle upon which A. recovers and Z. fails? * * *

I prefer to place my opinion upon the ground that in the one case, to-wit, the destruction of the building upon which the sparks were thrown by the negligent act of the party sought to be charged, the result was to have been anticipated the moment the fire was communicated to the building;

that its destruction was the ordinary and natural result of its being fired. In the second, third or twenty-fourth case, as supposed, the destruction of the building was not a natural and expected result of the first firing. That a building upon which sparks and cinders fall should be destroyed or seriously injured must be expected, but that the fire should spread and other buildings be consumed is not a necessary or an usual result. That it is possible, and that it is not infrequent, cannot be denied. The result however depends, not upon any necessity of a further communication of the fire, but upon a concurrence of accidental circumstances, such as the degree of the heat, the state of the atmosphere, the condition and materials of the adjoining structures and the direction of the wind. These are accidental and varying circumstances. The party has no control over them, and is not responsible for their effects.

My opinion therefore is, that this action cannot be sustained, for the reason that the damages incurred are not the immediate but the remote result of the negligence of the defendants. The immediate result was the destruction of their own wood and sheds; beyond that, it was remote. * * *

To sustain such a claim as the present, and to follow the same to its legitimate consequences, would subject to a liability against which no prudence could guard, and to meet which no private fortune would be adequate. * * * A man may insure his own house or his own furniture, but he cannot insure his neighbor's building or furniture, for the reason that he has no interest in them. To hold that the owner must not only meet his own loss by fire, but that he must guarantee the security of his neighbors on both sides, and to an unlimited extent, would be to create a liability which would be the destruction of all civilized society. No community could long exist under the operation of such a principle. In a commercial country each man, to some extent, runs the hazard of his neighbor's conduct, and each, by insurance against such hazards, is enabled to obtain a reasonable security against loss. To neglect such precaution, and to call upon his neighbor on whose premises a fire originated, to indemnify him instead, would be to award a punishment quite beyond the offense committed. It is to be considered also that if the negligent party is liable to the owner of a remote building thus consumed, he would also be liable to the insurance companies who should pay losses to such remote owners. The principle of subrogation would entitle the companies to the benefit of every claim held by the party to whom a loss should be paid. * * *

The remoteness of the damage, in my judgment, forms the true rule on which the question should be decided, and which prohibits a recovery by the plaintiff in this case.

Judgment should be affirmed.

NOTES AND QUESTIONS

1. New York then modified the rule to allow recovery of the first adjoining landowner, as distinct from the first building. Webb v. Rome, W. & O.R. Co., 49 N.Y. 420, 10 Am.Rep. 389 (1872). Or the first property to which the fire jumps, although it is not adjoining. Homac Corp. v. Sun Oil Co., 258 N.Y. 462, 180 N.E. 172

(1932). The New York Court of Appeals has said that the *Ryan* case "should not be extended beyond the precise facts that appear therein," (Frace v. N.Y.L.E. & W.R. Co., 143 N.Y. 182, 189, 38 N.E. 102 (1894)), but on occasion the shadow of the old rule has barred a nonadjacent landowner's claim. See Rose v. Pennsylvania R. Co., 236 N.Y. 568, 142 N.E. 287 (1923). Other courts have rejected the "first building" test. Most of the decisions on fires spreading for a substantial distance have held the defendant liable. See, for example, Smith v. London & S.W.R. Co. [1870] L.R. 6 C.P. 14; Hoyt v. Jeffers, 30 Mich. 181 (1874); E.T. & H.K. Ide v. Boston & Maine R. Co., 83 Vt. 66, 74 A. 401 (1909).

2.   At the opposite extreme from the principal case is Atchison, T. & S.F.R. Co. v. Stanford, 12 Kan. 354, 15 Am.Rep. 362 (1874), where a railroad that negligently set a fire next to its tracks was held liable to the owner of a farm nearly four miles away, to whose property the fire spread. Kansas had, at the time of the decision, many miles of uninsured grain, and its community attitude toward railroads is not necessarily the same as that of New York. Do these factors account for the difference in opinions? Is there any reason why the two states should have the same rule? What if the same railroad operates in both states?

3.   Policy considerations weighed heavily in the principal case. How important was insurance? Could the defendant railroad have purchased liability insurance to cover this situation? Should the fact that the plaintiff could easily have purchased accident or fire insurance be utilized to restrict the liability of a negligent defendant to consequences that are less than reasonably foreseeable? Why? The mention of "insurance" as a decisional factor, in the opinion of the principal case, has sustained academic interest for over 100 years. For examples, see Green & Smith, No–Fault and Jury Trial II, 50 Tex.L.Rev. 1297, 1303 (1972); Smith, The Miscegenetic Union of Liability Insurance and the Tort Process in the Personal Injury Claims System, 54 Cornell L.Rev. 645, 666 (1969); Ehrenzweig, Negligence Without Fault, 54 Calif.L.Rev. 1422, 1448, 1452 (1966); Weinreb, Causation & Wrongdoing, 63 Chi.-Kent L.Rev. 407 (1987).

Bartolone v. Jeckovich

Supreme Court of New York, 1984.
103 A.D.2d 632, 481 N.Y.S.2d 545.

DENMAN, JUSTICE. On October 4, 1976 plaintiff was involved in a four-car chain reaction collision in Niagara Falls for which defendants were found liable. Plaintiff sustained relatively minor injuries consisting of whiplash and cervical and lower back strain for which he was treated with muscle relaxants and physical therapy but was not hospitalized. Subsequently, however, he suffered an acute psychotic breakdown from which he has not recovered. The theory on which plaintiff's case was tried was that the accident aggravated a pre-existing paranoid schizophrenic condition which has totally and permanently disabled him. * * *

At the time of the accident, plaintiff was a 48 year old man who lived alone in one room and worked out of a union hall as a carpenter. He was very proud of his physique and his strength, spending on the average of four hours daily at the local YMCA engaged in body building. On weekends, in order to conserve his strength, he pursued nonphysical interests such as painting and sculpture, singing and playing the guitar and trombone. Since the accident, plaintiff has been in a degenerative psychotic condition in which he is withdrawn, hostile, delusional, hears voices and sees shadows, refuses to cut his hair, shave or bathe and no longer participates in any of his former interests. In the words of his treating psychiatrist, he is "a life lost."

Three psychiatrists and one neurosurgeon testified on behalf of plaintiff. From their testimony a strange and sad profile emerged: Plaintiff's mother had died of cancer when he was a very young boy. His sister had also died of cancer. Probably as a consequence, plaintiff had developed a fear and dislike of doctors and engaged in body building in order to avoid doctors and ward off illness. His bodily fitness was extremely important to him because it provided him with a sense of control over his life so that he was able to function in a relatively normal way. * * * Because he had such an intense emotional investment in his body, his perception of this impairment made him incapable of his former physical feats and he was thus deprived of the mechanism by which he coped with his emotional problems. As a consequence, he deteriorated psychologically and socially as well. * * *

Defendants' expert, who had never seen the plaintiff, even at trial, agreed that plaintiff suffered from schizophrenia but stated that, in his opinion, it had not been exacerbated by the accident and that defendant was merely attempting to make money. The jury, who had an opportunity to see the plaintiff and hear his testimony, returned a verdict of $500,000. The court set that verdict aside stating that there was no basis on which the jury could conclude that plaintiff's total mental breakdown could be attributed to a minor accident.

We find, to the contrary, that there was ample proof in the record to support the jury's verdict. There is precedent for such determination. In *Bonner v. U.S.*, 339 F.Supp. 640, plaintiff was a passenger in a car which was rear-ended. She received a whiplash injury resulting in cervical spasms and lumbar-sacral strain for which she was treated with muscle relaxants and physiotherapy. She later developed numbness, headaches, hearing difficulties, inability to keep her eyes open, deteriorated personal hygiene, degeneration in appearance, facial tics and jerking and twitching of her head, all of which were determined to be of a psychological rather than neurological origin. The psychiatric testimony established that she had a pre-existing underlying psychotic illness with which she was able to cope until the accident but that the accident had precipitated a chronic psychosis which was totally disabling.

In *Steinhauser v. Hertz Corp.*, 421 F.2d 1169 (2d Cir.), plaintiff, a 14 year old girl, was riding as a passenger in a car with her parents when it was struck by another vehicle. The occupants did not suffer any bodily injuries. Within minutes after the accident, plaintiff began to behave in a bizarre manner. After a series of hospitalizations, she was diagnosed as suffering from a "schizophrenic reaction—acute—undifferentiated." The other evidence at trial was similar to the evidence in the case before us. Prior to the accident she had a " 'prepsychotic' personality" and displayed a predisposition to abnormal behavior. * * * Nevertheless, there was testimony that, had it not been for the accident, she might have been able to lead a normal life and that the accident was the precipitating cause of her psychosis. The trial court did not allow plaintiff's counsel to elicit testimony as to whether the accident could have been an aggravating cause of her condition. In reversing a verdict of no cause for action, the United States Court of Appeals for the Second Circuit stated that the evidence made clear that plaintiff had some degree of pathology which was activated into schizophrenia by the emotional trauma connected with the accident and that she was entitled to have that issue fairly weighed by a jury.

The circumstances of those cases as well as those of the case before us illustrate the truth of the old axiom that a defendant must take a plaintiff as he finds him and hence may be held liable in damages for aggravation of a pre-existing illness (see McCahill v. New York Transp. Co., 201 N.Y. 221, 94 N.E. 616). Nor may defendants avail themselves of the argument that plaintiff should be denied recovery because his condition might have occurred even without the accident. [Cc]

The record presents ample evidence that plaintiff, although apparently suffering from a quiescent psychotic illness, was able to function in a relatively normal manner but that this minor accident aggravated his schizophrenic condition leaving him totally and permanently disabled.

Accordingly, the order should be reversed and the jury's verdict reinstated.

Order unanimously reversed with costs, motion denied and verdict reinstated.

NOTES AND QUESTIONS

1. The seminal American opinion on the rule that a defendant must take a plaintiff as he finds him is McCahill v. New York Transp. Co., 201 N.Y. 221, 94 N.E. 616 (1911). One of the illustrations running through the English cases, originating in Dulieu v. White, [1901] 2 K.B. 669, 679, is that of the man with the thin skull, who suffers death when an ordinary man would have had only a bump on the head.

2. The courts are agreed upon the rule stated in this case, when unforeseeable consequences follow from a *physical* injury to the person of the plaintiff. Keegan v. Minneapolis & St. L.R. Co., 76 Minn. 90, 78 N.W. 965 (1899) (death from inflammation of the heart resulted from a sprained ankle); Ominsky v. Charles Weinhagen & Co., 113 Minn. 422, 129 N.W. 845 (1911) (loss of hair from fright); Thompson v. Lupone, 135 Conn. 236, 62 A.2d 861 (1948) (obesity of 261–pound woman delayed recovery from normal period of two weeks to eight months: "The defendants took her as they found her"); Lockwood v. McCaskill, 262 N.C. 663, 138 S.E.2d 541 (1964) (amnesia due to plaintiff's predisposition).

3. A few courts have applied the doctrine only to pre-existing *physical* conditions. Munn v. Algee, 924 F.2d 568, 576 (5th Cir.1991) (stating that Mississippi has applied the "eggshell skull" rule only to pre-existing physical conditions and declining to extend its scope to cover the plaintiff's religious beliefs, which had prevented her from undergoing a blood transfusion); Ragin v. Harry Macklowe Real Estate Co., 6 F.3d 898 (2d Cir.1993) (in housing discrimination case, upholding the trial court judge's decision not to consider as part of emotional damages the effect of the discrimination in light of plaintiffs' past traumatic experiences with race

discrimination). Most courts, however, include the fragile psyche as well as the fragile skull. In addition to the principal case, see Steinhauser v. Hertz Corp., 421 F.2d 1169 (2d Cir.1970) (schizophrenia triggered by car accident).

⚡ Note that the doctrine applies only to the proximate cause issue, not to the determination of reasonable care (negligence) or defect (strict liability). Those determinations are made in light of the ordinary consumer. See Vaughn v. Nissan Motor Corp., 77 F.3d 736, 738 (4th Cir.1996) (applying South Carolina law) ("The tortfeasor's duty of care is measured by the ordinary person, but the plaintiff's injuries may not be. In short, if Nissan breached its objective duty of care, it must take its victim as it finds her.")

In re Arbitration Between Polemis and Furness, Withy & Co., Ltd.

Court of Appeal, [1921] 3 K.B. 560.

BANKES, L.J. By a time charter party dated February 21, 1917, the respondents chartered their vessel to the appellants. * * * The vessel was employed by the charterers to carry a cargo to Casablanca in Morocco. The cargo included a quantity of benzine or petrol in cases. While discharging at Casablanca a heavy plank fell into the hold in which the petrol was stowed, and caused an explosion, which set fire to the vessel and completely destroyed her. The owners claimed the value of the vessel from the charterers, alleging that the loss of the vessel was due to the negligence of the charterers' servants. The charterers contended * * * that the damages claimed were too remote. The claim was referred to arbitration and the arbitrators stated a special case for the opinion of the Court. Their findings of fact are as follows: The arbitrators found that the ship was lost by fire; that the fire arose from a spark igniting the petrol vapor in the hold; that the spark was caused by the falling board coming into contact with some substance in the hold; and that the causing of the spark could not reasonably have been anticipated from the falling of the board, though some damage to the ship might reasonably have been anticipated, and stated the damages at £ 196, 165 1s. 11d. * * *

In the present case the arbitrators have found as a fact that the falling of the plank was due to the negligence of the defendants' servants. The fire appears to me to have been directly caused by the falling of the plank. Under these circumstances I consider that it is immaterial that the causing of the spark by the falling of the plank could not have been reasonably anticipated. The appellants' junior counsel sought to draw a distinction between the anticipation of the extent of damage resulting from a negligent act and the anticipation of the type of damage resulting from such an act. He admitted that it could not lie in the mouth of a person whose negligent act had caused damage to say that he could not reasonably have foreseen the extent of the damage, but he contended that the negligent person was entitled to rely upon the fact that he could not reasonably have anticipated the type of damage which resulted from his negligent act. I do not think that the distinction can be admitted. Given the breach of duty which constitutes the negligence, and given the damage as a direct result of that negligence, the anticipations of the person whose negligent act has produced the damage appear to me to be irrelevant. I consider that the damages claimed are not too remote. * * *

SCRUTTON, L.J. * * * The second defense is that the damage is too remote from the negligence, as it could not be reasonably foreseen as a consequence. * * * [I]f the act would or might probably cause damage, the fact that the damage it in fact causes is not the exact kind of damage one would expect is immaterial, so long as the damage is in fact directly traceable to the negligent act, and not due to the operation of independent causes having no connection with the negligent act, except that they could not avoid its results. Once the act is negligent, the fact that its exact operation was not foreseen is immaterial. * * * In the present case it was negligent in discharging cargo to knock down the planks of the temporary staging, for they might easily cause some damage either to workmen, or cargo, or the ship. The fact that they did directly produce an unexpected result, a spark in an atmosphere of petrol vapor which caused a fire, does not relieve the person who was negligent from the damage which his negligent act directly caused.

For these reasons the experienced arbitrators and the judge appealed from came, in my opinion, to a correct decision, and the appeal must be dismissed with costs.

Appeal dismissed.

[The concurring opinion of WARRINGTON, L.J., is omitted.]

NOTES AND QUESTIONS

1.   The "rule" of this case has had considerable support in the United States. See, e.g., Christianson v. Chicago, St. P., M. & O.R. Co., 67 Minn. 94, 69 N.W. 640 (1896) ("consequences which follow in unbroken sequence, without an intervening efficient cause, from the original negligent act are natural and proximate"); Ramsey v. Carolina–Tennessee Power Co., 195 N.C. 788, 143 S.E. 861 (1928). What is the reason underlying the rule? Is the rule similar in nature to the early common law distinction between trespass and case? See page 3. What supported that rule?

2.   Was the petrol vapor in the hold an independent cause? Was the entire chain of events foreseeable? Was it negligence to start to unload with petrol vapor permeating the hold?

3.   Distinguish between unforeseeability of the result that has occurred and unforeseeability of the manner in which it is brought about. It is quite generally agreed that the latter will not relieve the defendant of responsibility. A remarkable illustration is Bunting v. Hogsett, 139 Pa. 363, 21 A. 31 (1891), where negligent operation of defendant's industrial "dinky" engine caused a collision with a train on a crossing. Just before the collision the engineer reversed the engine, shut off the steam, and jumped. The collision jarred loose the throttle, and the engine backed up, gathering momentum, and traveled around a loop to a second crossing, where there was a second collision with the train. Plaintiff, a passenger on the train, was injured in the second collision. Defendant was held liable. See also Colonial Inn Motor Lodge, Inc. v. Gay, 288 Ill.App.3d 32, 680 N.E.2d 407 (1997) (driver who negligently backed into building, severing natural gas line of air conditioning unit, was responsible for explosion that destroyed building even though he might not

have foreseen the exact manner in which damage from his negligent driving would occur).

4. *Intentional Torts*. In Derosier v. New England Tel. & Tel. Co., 81 N.H. 451, 130 A. 145 (1925), the court made the following statement of policy, which has been much quoted: "In determining how far the law will trace causation and afford a remedy, the facts as to the defendant's intent, his imputable knowledge, or his justifiable ignorance are often taken into account. The moral element is here the factor that has turned close cases one way or the other. For an intended injury the law is astute to discover even very remote causation. For one which the defendant merely ought to have anticipated it has often stopped at an earlier stage of the investigation of causal connection. And as to those where there was neither knowledge nor duty to foresee, it has usually limited accountability to direct and immediate results."

This is undoubtedly true, although, it has represented a general and often unexpressed tendency, rather than any clear and definite lines of demarcation. There have, however, been a few decisions in which liability for intended injury has been clearly carried farther than for the same injury negligently inflicted. See, for example, as to suicide resulting from intentional misconduct, the cases cited, pages 23 and 331.

Overseas Tankship (U.K.) Ltd. v. Morts Dock & Engineering Co., Ltd. "Wagon Mound No. 1"

Privy Council, 1961.
[1961] A.C. 388.

[Plaintiff Morts Dock operated a wharf for shipbuilding and ship repairing in the Port of Sydney, Australia. The freighter Wagon Mound, owned by the defendants, was moored about 600 feet away. She carelessly discharged into the harbor a large quantity of furnace oil, which spread across the surface. The oil came in contact with the slipways of plaintiffs' wharf, and interfered with their use, thus causing minor damage, which was so slight that plaintiffs made no claim for it. The oil was ignited when cotton waste floating on its surface was set fire by molten metal dropped from the wharf by plaintiff's workmen. The fire seriously damaged the wharf, as well as two ships docked alongside of it. The trial court specifically found that defendants "did not know and could not reasonably be expected to have known" that the oil (which was stated by counsel to have a flash point of about 170° F.) was capable of being set afire when spread on water. Judgment was given for the plaintiff, which was affirmed by the Supreme Court of New South Wales. Defendants appealed to the Privy Council, where the decision was reversed. After reviewing In re Polemis, page 295, and a number of subsequent British decisions, the court continued:]

Morts Dock after the fire

Morts Dock was never rebuilt

Viscount Simonds: * * * [I]t does not seem consonant with current ideas of justice or morality that for an act of negligence, however slight or venial, which results in some trivial foreseeable damage the actor should be liable for all consequences however unforeseeable and however grave, so long as they can be said to be "direct." It is a principle of civil liability, subject only to qualifications which have no present relevance, that a man must be considered to be responsible for the probable consequences of his act. To demand more of him is too harsh a rule, to demand less is to ignore that civilized order requires the observance of a minimum standard of behaviour. * * *

[I]f it is asked why a man should be responsible for the natural or necessary or probable consequences of his act (or any other similar description of them) the answer is that it is not because they are natural or necessary or probable, but because, since they have this quality, it is judged by the standard of the reasonable man, that he ought to have foreseen them. Thus it is that over and over again it has happened that in different judgments in the same case and sometimes in a single judgment liability for a consequence has been imposed on the ground that it was reasonably foreseeable or alternatively on the ground that it was natural or necessary or probable. The two grounds have been treated as coterminous, and so they largely are. * * *

It is not the act but the consequences on which tortious liability is founded. Just as (as it has been said) there is no such thing as negligence in the air, so there is no such thing as liability in the air. Suppose an action brought by A for damage caused by the carelessness (a neutral word) of B, for example a fire caused by the careless spillage of oil. It may of course become relevant to know what duty B owed to A, but the only liability that is in question is the liability for damage by fire. It is vain to isolate the liability from its content and to say that B is or is not liable and then to ask for what damage he is liable. For his liability is in respect of that damage and no other. If, as admittedly it is, B's liability (culpability) depends on the reasonable foreseeability of the consequent damage, how is that to be determined except by the foreseeability of the damage which in fact happened—the damage in suit? And, if that damage is unforeseeable so as to displace liability at large, how can the liability be restored so as to make compensation payable?

But, it is said, a different position arises if B's careless act has been shown to be negligent and has caused some foreseeable damage to A. Their Lordships have already observed that to hold B liable for consequences however unforeseeable of a careless act, if, but only if, he is at the same time liable for some other damage however trivial, appears to be neither logical nor just. This becomes more clear if it is supposed that similar unforeseeable damage is suffered by A and C but other foreseeable damage, for which B is liable, by A only. A system of law which would hold B liable to A but not to C for the similar damage suffered by each of them could not easily be defended. Fortunately, the attempt is not necessary. For the same fallacy is at the root of the proposition. It is irrelevant to the question whether B is liable for unforeseeable damage that he is liable for foreseeable damage, as irrelevant as would the fact that he had trespassed on Whiteacre be to the question whether he had trespassed on Blackacre. Again suppose a claim by A for damage by fire by the careless act of B. Of what relevance is it to that claim that he has another claim arising out of the same careless act? It would surely not prejudice his claim if that other claim failed; it cannot assist it if it succeeds. Each of them rests on its own bottom and will fail if it can be established that the damage could not reasonably be foreseen. * * * As Lord Denning said in King v. Phillips, [1953] 1 Q.B. 429 at p. 441, there can be no doubt since Bourhill v. Young that the test of *liability for shock* is foreseeability of *injury by shock.* Their Lordships substitute the word "fire" for "shock" and endorse this statement of the law. * * *

[The appeal was allowed, and the action for damages caused by negligence dismissed. The case was remanded to the Full Court of New South Wales for disposition of an alternative claim for liability on the basis of nuisance, since their Lordships thought that it would not be proper for them to come to any conclusion upon the material before them. The plaintiffs decided not to proceed further with the nuisance liability, and their litigation ended with this decision of the Privy Council.]

NOTES AND QUESTIONS

1.   The rule of this case has been the underlying premise of many decisions in the United States. See, e.g., Mauney v. Gulf Refining Co., 193 Miss. 421, 9 So.2d 780 (1942) ("The area within which liability is imposed is that which is within the circle of reasonable foreseeability").

A.   When defendant served "foul smelling" shrimp, he risked causing patron to become ill, but not causing someone else to trip on her vomit. Crankshaw v. Piedmont Driving Club, 115 Ga.App. 820, 156 S.E.2d 208 (1967).

B.   When defendant bus driver drove at an unreasonable speed in a snowstorm, he risked a collision with another vehicle, but not creating a snow-swirl that would blind another driver who followed in his wake. Metts v. Griglak, 438 Pa. 392, 264 A.2d 684 (1970).

C.   When defendant manufacturer supplied a defective metal ring on a dog collar, it risked causing the owner to lose his dog, but not causing the plaintiff to be bitten by the dog. Oehler v. Davis, 223 Pa.Super. 333, 298 A.2d 895 (1972) (products liability case applying proximate cause principles of negligence law).

D.   When defendant allowed a rug to remain on the floor after the wind had blown its edge up, he risked that a customer would trip over it, but not that the wind would wrap it around the legs of a customer using another door. Lyvere v. Ingles Markets, Inc., 36 N.C.App. 560, 244 S.E.2d 437 (1978).

E.   When defendant day care center allowed a child to consume rat poison, it risked the child becoming ill, but not that the relatives with whom the child was residing would lose custody of the child because the child's subsequent minor bruises would become accentuated by the effects of the poison and be mistaken for the results of child abuse. Lewis v. Kehoe Academy, 346 So.2d 289 (La.App.1977).

2.   Professor (now Judge) Robert E. Keeton has suggested a general rule that helps to explain Wagon Mound I and other cases that espouse its approach to proximate cause. One of his three formulations of the rule is: "A negligent actor is

legally responsible for that harm, and only that harm, of which the negligent aspect of his conduct is a cause in fact." R. Keeton, Legal Cause in the Law of Torts, 9 (1963). How helpful is this formulation? Is it similar to the rationale of the Palsgraf case, page 303? Compare it to the rule as to violation of statutes intended to protect plaintiffs against a particular risk. See page 205 note 2B. Should the same rule apply when there is no statute, and the defendant's conduct creates only a particular risk? Or do the written law and the policy of strict statutory construction afford a reason to make a distinction?

3. Since the Privy Council was the highest appellate court for the Commonwealth and its decisions not binding in England, there was initially some doubt whether the case would be accepted by the English courts. This was finally set to rest in Doughty v. Turner Mfg. Co., [1964] 1 Q.B. 518, where an asbestos cement cover was knocked into a vat filled with an extremely hot solution of sodium cyanide, which might have been expected to splash some of the molten substance upon anyone standing nearby. Although no injuries were sustained when the cover was initially knocked into the vat, the molten liquid erupted a short time later and caused injury to the plaintiff. His recovery in the trial court was reversed, because there was no reason for anyone to expect the eruption.

4. Other English decisions have made it clear that there are some limits on the requirement of foreseeability laid down in Wagon Mound No. 1. Thus the way in which the event occurs need not be foreseeable, so long as the event itself is to be anticipated. Hughes v. Lord Advocate, [1963] A.C. 837. And the rule as to the thin skull, where the consequences of an actual personal injury are unforeseeable, continues to be applied. Smith v. Leech Brain & Co., [1962] 2 Q.B. 405.

➤Overseas Tankship (U.K.) Ltd. v. Miller Steamship Co. "Wagon Mound No. 2"

Privy Council, 1966.
[1967] 1 A.C. 617.

[The accident facts are the same as in the preceding case, but this action was brought, on the grounds of nuisance and negligence, by the owners of the two ships docked at the wharf. The trial court, Walsh, J., made more elaborate findings on the issue of foreseeability, as follows:

"(1) Reasonable people in the position of the officers of the *Wagon Mound* would regard the furnace oil as very difficult to ignite upon water. (2) Their personal experience would probably have been that this had very rarely happened. (3) If they had given attention to the risk of fire from the spillage, they would have regarded it as a possibility, but one which could become an actuality only in very exceptional circumstances. (4) They would have considered the chances of the required exceptional circumstances happening whilst the oil remained spread on the harbour waters as being remote. (5) I find that the occurrence of damage to the plaintiff's property as a result of the spillage not reasonably foreseeable by those for whose acts the defendant would be responsible. * * * (8) Having regard to those findings, and because of finding (5), I hold that the claim of each of the plaintiffs, framed in negligence, fails."

Judgment for the defendants was affirmed by the Supreme Court of New South Wales, and plaintiffs appealed to the Privy Council.]

LORD REID [after holding that the count in nuisance added nothing, since it must be a nuisance founded upon negligence]. It is now necessary to turn to the respondents' submission that the trial judge was wrong in holding that damage from fire was not reasonably foreseeable. * * *

In *The Wagon Mound (No. 1)* the Board were not concerned with degrees of foreseeability because the finding was that the fire was not foreseeable at all. So Lord Simonds had no cause to amplify the statement that the "essential factor in determining liability is whether the damage is of such a kind as the reasonable man should have foreseen." But here the findings show that some risk of fire would have been present to the mind of a reasonable man in the shoes of the ship's chief engineer. So the first question must be what is the precise meaning to be attached in this context to the words "foreseeable" and "reasonably foreseeable."

[The court here referred to Bolton v. Stone, [1951] A.C. 850, where the risk that a cricket ball would be driven out of the grounds and strike a plaintiff on an unfrequented public road was held to be "so small that in the circumstances a reasonable man would have been justified in disregarding it and taking no steps to eliminate it."]

But it does not follow that, no matter what the circumstances may be, it is justifiable to neglect a risk of such a small magnitude. A reasonable man would only neglect such a risk if he had some valid reason for doing so, e.g., that it would involve considerable expense to eliminate the risk. He would weigh the risk against the difficulty of eliminating it. * * *

In the present case there was no justification whatever for discharging the oil into Sydney Harbour. Not only was it an offence to do so, but it involved considerable loss financially. If the ship's engineer had thought about the matter, there could have been no question of balancing the advantages and disadvantages. From every point of view it was both his duty and his interest to stop the discharge immediately.

It follows that in their Lordships' view the only question is whether a reasonable man having the knowledge and experience to be expected of the chief engineer of the *Wagon Mound* would have known that there was a real risk of the oil on the water catching fire in some way; if it did, serious damage to ships or other property was not only foreseeable but very likely. * * *

The findings show that he ought to have known that it is possible to ignite this kind of oil on water, and that the ship's engineer probably ought to have known that this had in fact happened before. The most that can be said to justify inaction is that he would have known that this could only happen in very exceptional circumstances. But this does not mean that a reasonable man would dismiss such a risk from his mind and do nothing when it was so easy to prevent it. If it is clear that the reasonable man would have realized or foreseen and prevented the risk, then it must follow that the appellant is liable in damages. * * *

Appeal (of the ship owners) allowed.

NOTES AND QUESTIONS

1. What is the difference between Wagon Mound No. 1 and No. 2? Is the law applied different or is there a difference in the facts before the court? Do you suppose the attorneys representing the ship plaintiffs benefitted from the experience of the attorneys representing Morts Dock?

2. Has *Polemis* come in again by the back door, in the guise of foreseeability of the remotely possible? Are there many events which the reasonable person would not recognize as possible, with a slight degree of risk?

3. Compare the formula of Learned Hand in United States v. Carroll Towing Co., page 139. How does it relate to this case? *risk-utility*

4. There are good discussions of Wagon Mound No. 2 in Goodhart, The Brief Life Story of the Direct Consequence Law in English Tort Law, 53 Va.L.Rev. 857 (1967); Smith, The Limits of Tort Liability in Canada: Remoteness, Foreseeability and Proximate Cause, included in Linden, Studies in Canadian Tort Law (1968); Green, The Wagon Mound No. 2—Foreseeability Revisited, 1967 Utah L.Rev. 197. Dean Green, in the article above, suggests that "foreseeability" is being "overloaded." Is he right?

➤Palsgraf v. Long Island R.R. Co.

Court of Appeals of New York, 1928.
248 N.Y. 339, 162 N.E. 99.

CARDOZO, C.J. Plaintiff was standing on a platform of defendant's railroad after buying a ticket to go to Rockaway Beach. A train stopped at the station, bound for another place. Two men ran forward to catch it. One of the men reached the platform of the car without mishap, though the train was already moving. The other man, carrying a package, jumped aboard the car, but seemed unsteady as if about to fall. A guard on the car, who had held the door open, reached forward to help him in, and another guard on the platform pushed him from behind. In this act, the package was dislodged, and fell upon the rails. It was a package of small size, about fifteen inches long, and was covered by a newspaper. In fact it contained fireworks, but there was nothing in its appearance to give notice of its contents. The fireworks when they fell exploded. The shock of the explosion threw down some scales at the other end of the platform many feet away. The scales struck the plaintiff, causing injuries for which she sues. *Facts*

The conduct of the defendant's guard, if a wrong in its relation to the holder of the package, was not a wrong in its relation to the plaintiff, standing far away. Relatively to her it was not negligence at all. Nothing in the situation gave notice that the falling package had in it the potency of peril to persons thus removed. Negligence is not actionable unless it involves the invasion of a legally protected interest, the violation of a right. "Proof of negligence in the air, so to speak, will not do." Pollock, Tort (11th Ed.) p. 455 * * *. *Issue — is it actionable?*

Monday 8:45

Chief Judge Cardozo   Judge Andrews

The plaintiff, as she stood upon the platform of the station, might claim to be protected against intentional invasion of her bodily security. Such invasion is not charged. She might claim to be protected against unintentional invasion by conduct involving in the thought of reasonable men an unreasonable hazard that such invasion would ensue. These, from the point of view of the law, were the bounds of her immunity, with perhaps some rare exceptions, survival for the most part of ancient forms of liability, where conduct is held to be at the peril of the actor. [C] If no hazard was apparent to the eye of ordinary vigilance, an act innocent and harmless, at least to outward seeming, with reference to her, did not take to itself the quality of a tort because it happened to be a wrong, though apparently not one involving the risk of bodily insecurity, with reference to some one else. "In every instance, before negligence can be predicated of a given act, back of the act must be sought and found a duty to the individual complaining, the observance of which would have averted or avoided the injury." McSherry, C.J., in West Virginia Central & P.R. Co. v. State, 96 Md. 652, 666, 54 A. 669, 671. [Cc]

"The ideas of negligence and duty are strictly correlative." Bowen, L.J., in Thomas v. Quartermaine, 18 Q.B.D. 685, 694. The plaintiff sues in her own right for a wrong personal to her, and not as the vicarious beneficiary of a breach of duty to another.

Scales of the type involved in *Palsgraf*

Scene of *Palsgraf* accident, taken a few years later
but with no change in features

A different conclusion will involve us, and swiftly too, in a maze of
contradictions. A guard stumbles over a package which has been left upon a
platform. It seems to be a bundle of newspapers. It turns out to be a can of
dynamite. To the eye of ordinary vigilance, the bundle is abandoned waste,

which may be kicked or trod on with impunity. Is a passenger at the other end of the platform protected by the law against the unsuspected hazard concealed beneath the waste? If not, is the result to be any different, so far as the distant passenger is concerned, when the guard stumbles over a valise which a truckman or a porter has left upon the walk? The passenger far away, if the victim of a wrong at all, has a cause of action, not derivative, but original and primary. His claim to be protected against invasion of his bodily security is neither greater nor less because the act resulting in the invasion is a wrong to another far removed. In this case, the rights that are said to have been violated, the interests said to have been invaded, are not even of the same order. The man was not injured in his person or even put in danger. The purpose of the act, as well as its effect, was to make his person safe. If there was a wrong to him at all, which may very well be doubted, it was a wrong to a property interest only, the safety of his package. Out of this wrong to property, which threatened injury to nothing else, there has passed, we are told, to the plaintiff by derivation or succession a right of action for the invasion of an interest of another order, the right to bodily security. The diversity of interests emphasizes the futility of the effort to build the plaintiff's right upon the basis of a wrong to some one else. Even then, the orbit of the danger as disclosed to the eye of reasonable vigilance would be the orbit of the duty.
* * *

The argument for the plaintiff is built upon the shifting meanings of such words as "wrong" and "wrongful," and shares their instability. What the plaintiff must show is "a wrong" to herself; i.e., a violation of her own right, and not merely a wrong to some one else, nor conduct, "wrongful" because unsocial, but not "a wrong" to any one. * * * The risk reasonably to be perceived defines the duty to be obeyed and risk imports relation; it is risk to another or to others within the range of apprehension. [C] This does not mean, of course, that one who launches a destructive force is always relieved of liability, if the force, though known to be destructive, pursues an unexpected path. "It was not necessary that the defendant should have had notice of the particular method in which an accident would occur, if the possibility of an accident was clear to the ordinarily prudent eye." Munsey v. Webb, 231 U.S. 150, 156. [Cc] Some acts, such as shooting are so imminently dangerous to any one who may come within reach of the missile however unexpectedly, as to impose a duty of prevision not far from that of an insurer. Even today, and much oftener in earlier stages of the law, one acts some times at one's peril. [Cc] Under this head, it may be, fall certain cases of what is known as transferred intent, an act willfully dangerous to A resulting by misadventure in injury to B. [Cc] These cases aside, wrong is defined in terms of the natural or probable, at least when unintentional. [Cc] The range of reasonable apprehension is at times a question for the court, and at times, if varying inferences are possible, a question for the jury. Here, by concession, there was nothing in the situation to suggest to the most cautious mind that the parcel wrapped in newspaper would spread wreckage through the station. If the guard had thrown it down knowingly and willfully, he would not have threatened the plaintiff's safety, so far as appearances could warn him. His conduct would not have involved, even then, an unreasonable probability of invasion of her bodily security. Liability can be no greater where the act is inadvertent.

Negligence, like risk, is thus a term of relation. Negligence in the abstract, apart from things related, is surely not a tort, if indeed it is understandable at all. * * *

The law of causation, remote or proximate, is thus foreign to the case before us. The question of liability is always anterior to the question of the measure of the consequences that go with liability. If there is no tort to be redressed, there is no occasion to consider what damage might be recovered if there were a finding of a tort. We may assume, without deciding, that negligence, not at large or in the abstract, but in relation to the plaintiff, would entail liability for any and all consequences, however novel or extraordinary. [Cc]

There is room for argument that a distinction is to be drawn according to the diversity of interests invaded by the act, as where conduct negligent in that it threatens an insignificant invasion of an interest in property results in an unforeseeable invasion of an interest of another order, as, e.g., one of bodily security. Perhaps other distinctions may be necessary. We do not go into the question now. The consequences to be followed must first be rooted in a wrong.

The judgment of the Appellate Division and that of the Trial Term should be reversed, and the complaint dismissed, with costs in all courts.

ANDREWS, J. (dissenting). Assisting a passenger to board a train, the defendant's servant negligently knocked a package from his arms. It fell between the platform and the cars. Of its contents the servant knew and could know nothing. A violent explosion followed. The concussion broke some scales standing a considerable distance away. In falling, they injured the plaintiff, an intending passenger.

Upon these facts, may she recover the damages she has suffered in an action brought against the master? The result we shall reach depends upon our theory as to the nature of negligence. Is it a relative concept—the breach of some duty owing to a particular person or to particular persons? Or, where there is an act which unreasonably threatens the safety of others, is the doer liable for all its proximate consequences, even where they result in injury to one who would generally be thought to be outside the radius of danger? This is not a mere dispute as to words. We might not believe that to the average mind the dropping of the bundle would seem to involve the probability of harm to the plaintiff standing many feet away whatever might be the case as to the owner or to one so near as to be likely to be struck by its fall. If, however, we adopt the second hypothesis, we have to inquire only as to the relation between cause and effect. We deal in terms of proximate cause, not of negligence. * * *

But we are told that "there is no negligence unless there is in the particular case a legal duty to take care, and this duty must be one which is owed to the plaintiff himself and not merely to others." Salmond Torts (6th

Ed.) 24. This I think too narrow a conception. ~~Where there is the unreasonable act, and some right that may be affected there is negligence whether damage does or does not result~~. That is immaterial. Should we drive down Broadway at a reckless speed, we are negligent whether we strike an approaching car or miss it by an inch. The act itself is wrongful. It is a wrong not only to those who happen to be within the radius of danger, but to all who might have been there—a wrong to the public at large. Such is the language of the street. Such the language of the courts when speaking of contributory negligence. * * *

Due care is a duty imposed on each one of us to protect society from unnecessary danger, not to protect A, B, or C alone.

It may well be that there is no such thing as negligence in the abstract. "Proof of negligence in the air, so to speak, will not do." In an empty world negligence would not exist. It does involve a relationship between man and his fellows, but not merely a relationship between man and those whom he might reasonably expect his act would injure; rather, a relationship between him and those whom he does in fact injure. If his act has a tendency to harm some one, it harms him a mile away as surely as it does those on the scene. * * *

The proposition is this: Every one owes to the world at large the duty of refraining from those acts that may unreasonably threaten the safety of others. Such an act occurs. Not only is he wronged to whom harm might reasonably be expected to result, but he also who is in fact injured, even if he be outside what would generally be thought the danger zone. There needs be duty due the one complaining, but this is not a duty to a particular individual because as to him harm might be expected. Harm to some one being the natural result of the act, not only that one alone, but all those in fact injured may complain. We have never, I think, held otherwise. * * * Unreasonable risk being taken, its consequences are not confined to those who might probably be hurt. * * * An overturned lantern may burn all Chicago. We may follow the fire from the shed to the last building. We rightly say the fire started by the lantern caused its destruction.

A cause, but not the proximate cause. What we do mean by the word "proximate" is that, because of convenience, of public policy, of a rough sense of justice, the law arbitrarily declines to trace a series of events beyond a certain point. This is not logic. It is practical politics. Take our rule as to fires. Sparks from my burning haystack set on fire my house and my neighbor's. I may recover from a negligent railroad. He may not. Yet the wrongful act as directly harmed the one as the other. We may regret that the line was drawn just where it was, but drawn somewhere it had to be. We said the act of the railroad was not the proximate cause of our neighbor's fire. Cause it surely was. The words we used were simply indicative of our notions of public policy. Other courts think differently. * * *

Take the illustration given in an unpublished manuscript by a distinguished and helpful writer on the law of torts. A chauffeur negligently collides with another car which is filled with dynamite, although he could not know it. An explosion follows. A, walking on the sidewalk nearby, is killed. B, sitting in a window of a building opposite, is cut by flying glass. C, likewise sitting in a window a block away, is similarly injured. And a further illustration: A nursemaid, ten blocks away, startled by the noise, involuntarily drops a baby from her arms to the walk. We are told that C may not recover while A may. As to B it is a question for court or jury. We will agree that the baby might not. Because, we are again told, the chauffeur had no reason to believe his conduct involved any risk of injuring either C or the baby. As to them he was not negligent.

But the chauffeur being negligent in risking the collision, his belief that the scope of the harm he might do would be limited is immaterial. His act unreasonably jeopardized the safety of any one who might be affected by it. C's injury and that of the baby were directly traceable to the collision. Without that, the injury would not have happened. C had the right to sit in his office, secure from such dangers. The baby was entitled to use the sidewalk with reasonable safety.

The true theory is, it seems to me, that the injury to C, if in truth he is to be denied recovery, and the injury to the baby, is that their several injuries were not the proximate result of the negligence. And here not what the chauffeur had reason to believe would be the result of his conduct, but what the prudent would foresee, may have a bearing—may have some bearing, for the problem of proximate cause is not to be solved by any one consideration. It is all a question of expediency. There are no fixed rules to govern our judgment. There are simply matters of which we may take account. * * * There is in truth little to guide us other than common sense.

There are some hints that may help us. The proximate cause, involved as it may be with many other causes, must be, at the least, something without which the event would not happen. The court must ask itself whether there was a natural and continuous sequence between cause and effect. Was the one a substantial factor in producing the other? Was there a direct connection between them, without too many intervening causes? Is the effect of cause on result not too attenuated? Is the cause likely, in the usual judgment of mankind, to produce the result? Or, by the exercise of prudent foresight, could the result be foreseen? Is the result too remote from the cause, and here we consider remoteness in time and space. [C] Clearly we must so consider, for the greater the distance either in time or space, the more surely do other causes intervene to affect the result. When a lantern is overturned, the firing of a shed is a fairly direct consequence. Many things contribute to the spread of the conflagration—the force of the wind, the direction and width of streets, the character of intervening structures, other factors. We draw an uncertain and wavering line, but draw it we must as best we can.

* * * Once again, it is all a question of fair judgment, always keeping in mind the fact that we endeavor to make a rule in each case that will be practical and in keeping with the general understanding of mankind.

Here another question must be answered. In the case supposed, it is said, and said correctly, that the chauffeur is liable for the direct effect of the explosion, although he had no reason to suppose it would follow a collision. "The fact that the injury occurred in a different manner than that which might have been expected does not prevent the chauffeur's negligence from being in law the cause of the injury." But the natural results of a negligent act—the results which a prudent man would or should foresee—do have a bearing upon the decision as to proximate cause. We have said so repeatedly. What should be foreseen? No human foresight would suggest that a collision itself might injure one a block away. On the contrary, given an explosion, such a possibility might be reasonably expected. I think the direct connection, the foresight of which the courts speak, assumes prevision of the explosion, for the immediate results of which, at least, the chauffeur is responsible.

It may be said this is unjust. Why? In fairness he should make good every injury flowing from his negligence. Not because of tenderness toward him we say he need not answer for all that follows his wrong. We look back to the catastrophe, the fire kindled by the spark, or the explosion. We trace the consequences, not indefinitely, but to a certain point. And to aid us in fixing that point we ask what might ordinarily be expected to follow the fire or the explosion.

This last suggestion is the factor which must determine the case before us. The act upon which defendant's liability rests is knocking an apparently harmless package onto the platform. The act was negligent. For its proximate consequences the defendant is liable. If its contents were broken, to the owner; if it fell upon and crushed a passenger's foot, then to him; if it exploded and injured one in the immediate vicinity, to him also as to A in the illustration. Mrs. Palsgraf was standing some distance away. How far cannot be told from the record—apparently 25 or 30 feet, perhaps less. Except for the explosion, she would not have been injured. We are told by the appellant in his brief, "It cannot be denied that the explosion was the direct cause of the plaintiff's injuries." So it was a substantial factor in producing the result—there was here a natural and continuous sequence—direct connection. The only intervening cause was that, instead of blowing her to the ground, the concussion smashed the weighing machine which in turn fell upon her. There was no remoteness in time, little in space. And surely, given such an explosion as here, it needed no great foresight to predict that the natural result would be to injure one on the platform at no greater distance from its scene than was the plaintiff. Just how no one might be able to predict. Whether by flying fragments, by broken glass, by wreckage of machines or structures no one could say. But injury in some form was most probable.

Under these circumstances I cannot say as a matter of law that the plaintiff's injuries were not the proximate result of the negligence. That is all we have before us. The court refused to so charge. No request was made to submit the matter to the jury as a question of fact, even would that have been proper upon the record before us.

The judgment appealed from should be affirmed, with costs.

POUND, LEHMAN and KELLOGG, JJ., concur with CARDOZO, C.J.

ANDREWS, J., dissents in opinion in which CRANE and O'BRIEN, JJ., concur.

Judgment reversed, etc.

NOTES AND QUESTIONS

1. Plaintiff on a motion for reargument pointed out that Mrs. Palsgraf stood much closer to the scene of the explosion than the majority opinion would suggest. Would this fact be likely to alter Judge Cardozo's decision in the case? See Palsgraf v. Long Island R. Co., 249 N.Y. 511, 164 N.E. 564 (1928).

2. A study of the record in this case indicates that as described in the opinions, the event could not possibly have happened. These were apparently ordinary fireworks, and not bombs. Firecrackers were heard exploding; there was a "ball of fire" (from a Roman candle?), and a "mass of black smoke." All this happened in the pit below the edge of the platform, which would have protected the scale. No one testified to seeing it fall over. An appreciable interval elapsed after the first noise and smoke, during which Mrs. Palsgraf said to her daughter, "Elizabeth, turn your back." Then "the scale blew and hit me in the side." The platform was crowded, and there was no evidence of any other damage to anybody or anything. Plaintiff's original complaint, before amendment, alleged that the scale was knocked over by a stampede of frightened passengers. If that is what happened, would Judge Cardozo allow Mrs. Palsgraf to recover for her injuries? Would Judge Andrews?

The news story in the New York Times for August 25, 1924, p. 1, col. 4, differs in numerous details. It lists 13 persons injured, including Helen Polsgraf [sic], whose injury was "shock." It describes the events as happening at 11:25 a.m. at the East New York station, under the Atlantic Avenue stations, and a transfer point. There was a large crowd of excursionists, "jostling and pushing" to board a Jamaica express train. Three men, each carrying a large package, sought to board the train and a package fell to the tracks below. A large explosion rocked the car and tore away part of the platform and "overthrew a penny weighing machine more than ten feet away," smashing the glass and wrecking its mechanism. The police surmised that the three men, who disappeared, were Italians "bound for an Italian celebration somewhere on Long Island, where fireworks and bombs were to play an important role." The police decided that the event was an accident, with the man dropping the exploding package being jostled by the crowd. One of the other men dropped his parcel in the station as he fled, and it was found to contain fireworks of various kinds.

Further discussion of the facts is to be found in Prosser, Palsgraf Revisited, 52 Mich.L.Rev. 1 (1953); J. Noonan, Persons and Masks of the Law, c. 4 (1976); and Palsgraf Kin Tell Human Side of Famed Case, 66 Harv.L.Record [No. 8] 1 (Apr. 14, 1978). On the relationship of the case to the Restatement of Torts, see Prosser and Noonan, supra, and R. Keeton, A Palsgraf Anecdote, 56 Tex.L.Rev. 513 (1978).

3. Accepting the facts as stated, Mrs. Palsgraf was a passenger. She had bought her ticket, and started her trip by going upon the platform. Did the defendant owe her no duty? Was there no relation between them? This is ignored by both opinions. See Goldberg and Zipursky, The Moral of *MacPherson*, 146 U. Pa. L. Rev. 1733 (1998) (critiquing Prosser's influence on tort law through his treatment of the duty concept in proximate cause cases like *Palsgraf*).

4. If the "scale" in question could be toppled over by the explosion of fireworks some distance away, it may not have been steadily anchored to the railroad platform. Does this suggest an argument that might have allowed plaintiff to prevail under the language and rationale of Judge Cardozo's opinion?

5. How does the decision square with In re Polemis, page 295? The Restatement of Torts approved both cases, in § 281, and in § 433, comment *e*. Are they consistent?

6. Both opinions in *Palsgraf* have been cited scores of times; almost every practicing lawyer knows the case by name and it has served as a stimulus for legal writers to work out their own ideas, and endeavor to line up "duty" and "proximate cause." See, among many others, Green, The Palsgraf Case, 30 Colum.L.Rev. 789 (1930), reprinted in L. Green, Judge and Jury, ch. 8 (1930); 48 Yale L.J. 390 (1939), 39 Colum.L.Rev. 20 (1939); Ehrenzweig, Loss–Shifting and Quasi–Negligence: A New Interpretation of the Palsgraf Case, 8 U.Chi.L.Rev. 729 (1941); Prosser, Palsgraf Revisited, 52 Mich.L.Rev. 1 (1953), reprinted in Prosser, Selected Topics on the Law of Torts, 191 (1953); James, Scope of Duty in Negligence Cases, 47 Nw.U.L.Rev. 778 (1953).

7. How important is all this as a practical matter? How often will a case involve direct causation and an unforeseeable plaintiff? In a recurring situation, a vehicle negligently strikes someone whose body then strikes plaintiff who had been in a position of apparent safety. Is plaintiff "unforeseeable"? A number of courts have allowed recovery. See Kommerstad v. Great N.R. Co., 120 Minn. 376, 139 N.W. 713 (1913); Alabama Great S.R. Co. v. Chapman, 80 Ala. 615, 2 So. 738 (1887); Wolfe v. Checker Taxi Co., 299 Mass. 225, 12 N.E.2d 849 (1938). On the other hand, the Supreme Court of Pennsylvania has twice declared that this fact pattern presents an "unforeseeable" plaintiff. See Wood v. Pennsylvania R. Co., 177 Pa. 306, 35 A. 699 (1896) (train); Dahlstrom v. Shrum, 368 Pa. 423, 84 A.2d 289 (1951) (bus). A child toboggans down a hill in his parents' yard, collides head first with a snowmobile left there by his brother, and is seriously injured by a metal bracket on the underside of the snowmobile. Is the child an unforeseeable plaintiff? Whiteford v. Yamaha Motor Corp., 582 N.W.2d 916 (Minn.1998) (danger too remote to impose duty on snowmobile manufacturer).

8. For some cases following *Palsgraf,* see Busta v. Columbus Hospital Corp., 276 Mont. 342, 916 P.2d 122, 133 (1996) ("Any discussion of foreseeability as it relates to liability law begins with the oft-cited decision of the Court of Appeals of New York in Palsgraf v. Long Island Railroad Co."); Edwards v. Honeywell, Inc., 50 F.3d 484 (7th Cir.1995) (Indiana, which follows Palsgraf's exclusion of the unforeseeable victim, would not permit firefighter's widow to recover in case against alarm company whose negligence caused a delay in the notification of the fire department); Tucker v. Collar, 79 Ariz. 141, 285 P.2d 178 (1955) (defective machinery supplied by defendant to a tenant started a fire which burned the landlord's building); Diamond State Tel. Co. v. Atlantic Refining Co., 205 F.2d 402 (3d Cir.1953) (defendant negligently collided with a boat, and damaged plaintiff's cable, which defendant had no reason to expect to be attached to the boat); Radigan v. W.J. Halloran Co., 97 R.I. 122, 196 A.2d 160 (1963) (defendant negligently brought a crane into contact with an uninsulated high tension power line, and electricity passed through the crane, through an electrical conduit in the ground, and burned a hole in a gas main, which ultimately resulted in explosion of gas on the third floor of a fire station).

Palsgraf has been rejected by other cases. See Jackson v. B. Lowenstein & Bros., 175 Tenn. 535, 136 S.W.2d 495 (1940); Pfeifer v. Standard Gateway Theater, 262 Wis. 229, 55 N.W.2d 29 (1952). In the Jackson case, a customer in a department store fell on a defective mat at the top of the stairway. Her potential rescuer jostled another customer who fell and injured plaintiff who was around the corner of the stairs.

9. With the pair of *Wagon Mound* cases, compare the pair of *Kinsman* cases. Petition of Kinsman Transit Co., 338 F.2d 708 (2d Cir.1964) ("Kinsman No. 1"), arose out of a "series of misadventures" that happened during the night of January 21, 1959. Employees of Kinsman Transit Company improperly moored a ship, the *Shivas*, at a dock operated by the Continental Grain Company, in the Buffalo River, at a point nearly three miles above a lift bridge maintained by the City of Buffalo. The river, winding and about 200 feet wide, was full of floating ice, which was moving with a rapid current. Ice and debris accumulated, building a wedge between the ship and the dock. Pressure from the wedge snapped the mooring lines and pulled out an improperly anchored mooring block.

The *Shivas* broke loose and drifted downstream. She collided with another ship, the *Tewksbury*, which had been properly moored at its dock. The collision broke the *Tewksbury* loose, and the two ships went on down the river together. Frantic telephone calls to city workers at the bridge to have them raise it in time went unanswered because one bridge crew had gone off duty, and another was late in coming on. By the time the second crew began to raise the drawbridge, it was too late. The ships crashed into the center of the bridge and caused it to collapse. Ice jammed in behind the wreckage; the river backed up, and property on the banks of the Buffalo River flooded as far upstream as the Continental dock.

On some twenty claims for such property damage, the trial court found negligence and liability on the part of Kinsman, Continental, and the City of Buffalo, and entered its decree accordingly. Affirming the trial court's decision, the Court of Appeals (Friendly, J.) stated:

"The weight of authority in this country rejects the limitation of damages to consequences foreseeable at the time of the negligent conduct when the consequences are 'direct,' and the damage, although other and greater than expectable, is of the same general sort that was risked. [Cc] Other American courts, purporting to apply a test of foreseeability to damages, extend that concept to such unforeseen lengths as to raise serious doubt whether the concept is meaningful; indeed, we wonder whether the British courts are not finding it necessary to limit the language of the Wagon Mound as we have indicated." Id. at 724–25.

The court also noted that as long as the actor's risk, no matter how small, was "of the same general sort, from the same forces, and to the same class of persons," id. at 725, then the actor would be liable if he failed to exercise due care.

The court realized, however, that there must be some limitation to this. "Somewhere a point will be reached when courts will agree that the link has become too tenuous—that what is claimed to be consequence is only fortuity." Id. Finally, the court echoed the words of Judge Andrews dissenting in *Palsgraf*, at page 309, ___: "It is all a question of expediency, * * * of fair judgment, always keeping in mind the fact that we endeavor to make a rule in each case that will be practical and in keeping with the general understanding of mankind."

Four years after the first *Kinsman* decision, the same court heard another complaint based upon the same incident. Petition of Kinsman Transit Co. ("Kinsman No. 2"), 388 F.2d 821 (2d Cir.1968). This claim, however, was brought by owners of wheat stored aboard a ship berthed in the Buffalo harbor below the bridge. Because of the accident, the ship could not be moved and unloaded at the shipper's grain elevators located above the collapsed bridge; and the shipper was put to considerable additional expense for extra transportation and storage costs and for the purchase of replacement wheat.

Affirming the lower court's ruling, the Second Circuit (Kaufman, J.) held that "the injuries to [the shippers] were too 'remote' or 'indirect' a consequence of defendant's negligence." Id. at 824. In effect, the Court was stating that the facts in the *Kinsman* No. 2 case had reached a point at which the consequences were too "tenuous" for liability.

The Court noted, however, that the trial judge had reached the same result by differentiating between damage to property, involved in *Kinsman No. 1* and economic loss in *Kinsman No. 2*. The former type of damages is recoverable in tort law, the latter is not. See State of Louisiana ex rel. Guste v. M/V Testbank, Chapter 8, page 435. Do you find the distinction valid? Useful?

➤ Yun v. Ford Motor Co.

Superior Court of New Jersey, Appellate Division, 1994.
276 N.J. Super. 142, 647 A.2d 841.

VILLANUEVA, J. * * *

I.

On November 27, 1988, between 11:10 p.m. and 11:40 p.m., Chang was a passenger in a 1987 Ford van owned and driven by his daughter, Yun Cho Shim (Yun), northbound in the local lanes of the Garden State Parkway (Parkway). While driving on the Parkway returning from Atlantic City, Yun heard a "rattling type" noise coming from the rear of the van. * * * [T]he plastic cover and spare tire and part of the support bracket which was screwed to the rear of the van landed directly behind Yun's van and then rolled across both lanes of traffic or were pushed there by another vehicle, ultimately coming to a rest against the wooden guard rail separating the Parkway lanes.

Yun safely drove the van onto the right berm of the highway and stopped. Chang, a rear seat passenger who was sixty-five years old at the time, exited the vehicle, then ran across two lanes of the dark, rain-slicked Parkway and retrieved the spare tire and some of the other parts. During the course of returning back to the Ford van across the Parkway, Chang was struck by the vehicle operated by defendant Precious Linderman. * * *

[Yun, as representative of her father's estate, sued Ford, the manufacturer of the van; Miller, the manufacturer of the spare tire assembly; Universal, which converted the chasis and installed the spare tire assembly; Castle, the dealer; the Lindermans, the driver and owner of the car; and Kim's Mobile Service Center, which had changed the oil about a month before the accident and pointed out to Ms. Yun that the spare tire assembly was bent. She instructed Kim not to fix it because it had been damaged in an accident and she was waiting for the other driver's insurance company to handle having it repaired.]

II.

With a broad brush, plaintiffs seek to reverse the summary judgment granted to all defendants except Lindermans [who had settled]. Plaintiffs in their appellate argument do not even mention any of the defendants by name or capacity, rather they assert that the issue of proximate cause is a question for the jury.

Plaintiffs abandoned their claim against Ford apparently because the evidence showed that the spare tire assembly was not part of the vehicle when it left Ford's factory. At the motion for summary judgment the plaintiffs' attorney specifically told the court that he did "not oppose the motion made by Ford Motor Company." Having so stated, plaintiffs have no standing to appeal against Ford. [Cc]

III.

Kim, in its motion for summary judgment, relied upon the lack of proximate cause argument made by the other defendants but also asserted that there was no legal basis for plaintiffs' claim against Kim. Furthermore, plaintiffs' expert did not impute any negligence against Kim. Rather, he opined that the defect was weld failure with which Kim had nothing to do.

Kim alerted Chang and Yun to the problem but Chang and Yun told Kim that they did not want Kim to repair it. Kim had no duty to repair and therefore did not breach any duty. [C] An order or judgment will be affirmed on appeal if it is correct, even though the judge gave the wrong reasons for it. [Cc] This is true even if the judge erroneously declined to reach the merits of the issue. [C]

IV.

Because the initial complaint was filed on May 17, 1990, it falls within the scope of the Products Liability Act * * * The Act does not affect the requirement of causation, which is an essential element of an action based in either strict liability or negligence. [Cc]

Accordingly, plaintiffs must prove that the alleged defect in the spare tire bracket assembly proximately caused the injuries sustained by Chang. [C] Proximate cause is "any cause which in the natural and continuous sequence, unbroken by an efficient intervening cause, produces the result complained of and without which the result would not have occurred." [Cc]

Proximate cause has been described as a standard for limiting liability for the consequences of an act based "upon mixed considerations of logic, common sense, justice, policy and precedent." [Cc] Proximate cause "must be limited to those causes which are so closely connected with the result and of such significance that the law is justified in imposing liability." [C] Under the most liberal interpretation, conduct constituting proximate cause "need only be a cause which sets off a foreseeable sequence of consequences, unbroken by any superseding cause, and which is a substantial factor in producing the particular injury." [C] Thus, our focus must be on whether Chang's conduct was reasonably foreseeable versus "highly extraordinary," thereby breaking the chain of causation. [C]

The present case presents extraordinary circumstances. After Ford manufactured a van, spare tire assembly was attached to the van by Universal. Assuming plaintiffs' allegations are true, an alleged defect in the spare tire assembly caused the spare tire and other parts to fall off the van and roll across the Parkway. Because the van in which Chang was traveling came safely to rest at the side of the Parkway, his actions were "highly extraordinary." Chang's attempt to retrieve the parts involved crossing the Parkway in both directions—an activity which cannot be described as anything short of extraordinarily dangerous, if not suicidal, as the action proved. In the process of returning from the middle of the Parkway, Chang was struck by Mrs. Linderman and fatally injured. Although cited in the context of the foreseeability of a person's emotional reaction to a given event, the New Jersey Supreme Court aptly noted in Caputzal [v. The Lindsay Co., 48 N.J. 69, 222 A.2d 513 (1966)], supra: "Generally a defendant's standard of conduct is measured by the reaction to be expected of normal persons. . . ." [C]

Logic and fairness dictate that liability should not extend to injuries received as a result of Chang's senseless decision to cross the Parkway under such dangerous conditions. Common sense should have persuaded Chang, who was only a passenger, to wait for assistance or abandon the bald tire and damaged assembly. The van could have been driven safely home. * * *

[T]he alleged defect in the spare tire assembly did not injure Chang. The driver of the van was able to pull the vehicle to the side of the road safely and without incident. Chang's injury occurred after he decided to leave the vehicle and cross the Parkway and return where he was struck. At most, the presence of the spare tire created a "condition upon which the subsequent intervening force acted" and in such case there is no proximate cause relationship between the defective product and the injury. [Cc]

A tortfeasor will be held responsible for his negligent conduct if it is a "substantial factor" in bringing about plaintiff's injuries. [C] Where, however, concurrent forces are involved, the manufacturer of a defective product may negate strict liability upon a showing of an intervening, superseding cause or the existence of another "sole proximate cause" of the resulting injury. [Cc] Assuming, arguendo, that the spare tire assembly was a substantial factor in causing Chang's injuries, Chang's highly extraordinary and dangerous actions in crossing the Parkway twice with complete disregard for his own personal safety clearly constitute a superseding and intervening cause of his own injuries. * * * The danger involved in crossing a busy highway at night should be apparent to an adolescent, let alone an adult sixty-five years of age.

The allegedly defective product (the spare tire carrier) did not cause Chang's injuries. Chang's and Yun's joint decision, thirty days before this accident, not to repair the allegedly defective assembly and Chang's flagrant disregard for his personal safety by crossing the Parkway late at night and the injuries he received when struck by Linderman's vehicle constitute intervening superseding causes. Logic, common sense, justice and fairness dictate that the alleged product defect was not a proximate cause of Chang's injury.

Usually, the issue of proximate cause is reserved for the jury's determination. [Cc] In certain cases, however, the issue of proximate cause has been held so intertwined with issues of policy as to be treated as a matter of law for the court to determine. [C] This is especially true where the manner or type of harm caused to the plaintiff is unexpected. As the Supreme Court stated in Caputzal: "the idea of non-liability for the highly extraordinary consequence as a question of law for the court has already been recognized in this state." [C] This position is consistent with that of the Restatement (Second) Torts § 435(2) (1965): The actor's conduct may be held not to be a legal cause of harm to another where after the event and looking back from the harm to the actor's negligent conduct, it appears to the court highly extraordinary that it should have brought about the harm. * * *

In Jensen v. Schooley's Mountain Inn, 216 N.J. Super. 79, 522 A.2d 1043 (App.Div.), certif. denied, 108 N.J. 181 (1987), the defendant bar served alcoholic beverages to Jensen while he allegedly was visibly intoxicated. After leaving the bar, Jensen drove eight miles, where he "parked his car and, for some unknown reason, began climbing a tree." Id. at 80. The branches of the tree apparently could not support Jensen's weight and one broke, causing Jensen to fall twenty feet to the river bank. Jensen either fell or rolled into the river and drowned. Accepting as true plaintiffs' allegations that the defendant negligently and wrongfully served Jensen, we nonetheless affirmed the trial court's granting of summary judgment in favor of the defendant. We stressed: [L]egal responsibility for the consequences of an act cannot be imposed without limit. The events here transgress the judicial line beyond which liability should not be extended as a matter of fairness or policy. [Id. at 82, 522 A.2d 1043 (citations omitted).]

That principle is equally applicable herein. It was not reasonably foreseeable to defendants that if the spare wheel assembly was defective, and the driver-owner of the car and Chang refused to have it repaired and later while they were driving on the Parkway at night, it fell off but they safely brought the car to a stop on a berm, that Chang would then violate the law by twice crossing the Parkway to go to the median to retrieve the parts and be killed by a passing car. Furthermore, reasonable people could not differ that the continued driving for thirty days with knowledge of the defect and the senseless, and illegal crossing of the Parkway were intervening superseding causes of the accident which broke the chain of causation.

Affirmed.

BAIME, J., concurring and dissenting: I agree that the judgment in favor of Ford Motor Company should be affirmed because plaintiffs offered no opposition to that defendant's motion for a dismissal of the complaint. [Cc] So too, my careful review of the record fails to disclose facts sufficient to support a negligence claim against Kim's Mobile Service Center. Consequently, the judgment in favor of that defendant should also be affirmed. [C] However, I part company with my colleagues in their affirmance of the

Law Division's judgment as to the remaining defendants. I believe that plaintiff's submissions relating to proximate cause were sufficient to defeat the defendants' motion for summary judgment. * * *

Ordinarily, questions of proximate cause are left to the jury for its factual determination. [Cc] Likewise, questions of intervening cause are generally within the jury's domain. [Cc] Prosser and Keeton have instructed that: if reasonable persons could differ, either because relevant facts are in dispute or because application of the legal concept of "proximate cause" to the case at hand is an evaluative determination as to which reasonable persons might differ, the issue of "proximate cause" is submitted to the jury with appropriate instructions on the law.

Thus, in any case where there might be reasonable difference of opinion as to the foreseeability of a particular risk, the reasonableness of the defendant's conduct with respect to it, or the normal character of an intervening cause, the question is for the jury, subject of course to suitable instructions from the court as to the legal conclusion to be drawn as the issue is determined either way. By far the greater number of the cases which have arisen have been of this description; and to this extent it may properly be said that "proximate cause is ordinarily a question of fact for the jury, to be solved by the exercise of good common sense in the consideration of the evidence of each particular case." [Prosser and Keeton on Torts § 45 at 321 (5th ed. 1984).]

Applying these principles, I am convinced that reasonable persons might differ regarding whether the plaintiff's death was proximately caused by the defective spare tire assembly. A jury could find that it was reasonably foreseeable the tire would dislodge and fall onto the roadway while the van was in operation and that the operator or passenger might sustain injuries in his or her attempt to retrieve it. Indeed, some might think it odd if the operator or passenger were to abandon the tire and drive off, especially where, as shown by the record here, traffic is "very light," and "visibility [is] good." And if the operator or passenger were negligent in his or her attempt to retrieve the tire, this would be reflected within the calculus of comparative fault. In other words, the entire incident could reasonably be viewed within an "objective 'realm of foreseeability.' " [C] A jury could also reasonably find that the harm that resulted was not proximately caused by the defective assembly and that fairness and logic demand that defendants be absolved from responsibility. I am of the view that the issue is reasonably debatable and one that should be submitted to the jury for its determination.

I note one final point before leaving the subject. While I recognize the power and duty of a trial judge to bar the jury from considering the question of proximate cause where the consequences of a negligent act are so extraordinary that as a matter of law they cannot be considered "natural," that authority should be exercised sparingly. We judges are strange creatures. It is not that we are less brave than others, but rather by reason of our training, if not our nature, we tend to the conservative. For most of us, prudence and caution are the watchwords. We are rarely rewarded for taking risks. But the rest of the population does not always act the way we do. What may appear strange to judges might seem rather ordinary to others. It thus generally makes sense to have lay people, not judges, make decisions on the question of proximate cause, grounded as that concept is in considerations of foreseeability and fairness. And in that context, a jury might well find it rather ordinary for a person to venture on to the highway on a clear night when there is little traffic in order to retrieve a spare tire that has become dislodged from his vehicle. I would thus reverse as to all defendants except Ford Motor Company and Kim's Mobile Service Center.

[The New Jersey Supreme Court issued a per curiam opinion, reversing the appellate division for the reasons expressed in Judge Baime's dissent. That decision too drew a dissenting opinion. Yun v. Ford Motor Co., 143 N.J. 162, 669 A.2d 1378 (1996).]

NOTES AND QUESTIONS

1. What happens to the case after the New Jersey Supreme Court opinion?

2. The trial court judge, a majority of the panel at the appellate division, and one of seven New Jersey supreme court judges found no proximate cause as a matter of law. One dissenting judge at the appellate division and six supreme court judges thought a reasonable jury could find in plaintiff's favor against some of the defendants. What do you think? Note Justice Baime's point about the difficulty inherent in a judge making decisions about what the reasonable person would do. Do you find that argument persuasive?

3. As in Palsgraf, there are slight differences in the recitation of the facts in the two opinions. For example, the majority calls the Garden State Parkway "dark, rain-slicked," while the dissent notes that traffic was "very light," and "visibility good." Do you see other examples?

4. If you were representing one of the parties in this case, what would say to your client about proximate cause and how it was likely to be viewed by the judge or jury? How would you advise your client on whether to settle the case or take it to trial?

5. Dealer negligently failed to tighten lug bolts on the wheels of Hairston's newly purchased automobile. A wheel fell off and Hairston brought the car safely to a stop on a bridge. A van stopped behind Hairston's auto, and the driver offered to assist Hairston. Hairston got out and was standing behind his car when Alexander's flatbed truck rammed into the van stopped behind Hairston, propelling the van into Hairston, who was killed. The court held the dealer liable even though the conduct of the driver of the flatbed truck was "inexcusable." His conduct, however, was not "so highly improbable and extraordinary an occurrence in this series of events as to bear no reasonable connection to the harm threatened" by the dealer's original negligence. The intervening act of Alexander's negligent driving was therefore in the "area of risk created by the negligence" of dealer not tightening the lug bolts. Hairston v. Alexander Tank and Equipment Co., 310 N.C. 227, 311 S.E.2d 559, 567 (1984).

6. In addition to unforeseeable consequences, the doctrine of proximate cause may be used to cut off liability even though there is cause in fact, in cases involving

other acts that intervene in the causal link between the defendant's act and the plaintiff's injury.

2. INTERVENING CAUSES

Derdiarian v. Felix Contracting Corp.

New York Court of Appeals, 1980.
51 N.Y.2d 308, 414 N.E.2d 666, 434 N.Y.S.2d 166.

[Defendant Felix Contracting Corporation, in performing a contract to install an underground gas main in Mount Vernon, N.Y., had excavated a worksite in the street. Plaintiff Derdiarian, employee of a subcontractor, was engaged in sealing a gas main.]

COOKE, CHIEF JUDGE. * * * On the afternoon of November 21, 1973, defendant James Dickens suffered an epileptic seizure and lost consciousness, allowing his vehicle to careen into the work site and strike plaintiff with such force as to throw him into the air. When plaintiff landed, he was splattered over his face, head and body with 400 degree boiling hot liquid enamel from a kettle struck by the automobile. The enamel was used in connection with sealing the gas main. Although plaintiff's body ignited into a fire ball, he miraculously survived the incident.

At trial, plaintiff's theory was that defendant Felix had negligently failed to take adequate measures to insure the safety of workers on the excavation site. * * *

To support his claim of an unsafe work site, plaintiff called as a witness Lawrence Lawton, an expert in traffic safety. According to Lawton, the usual and accepted method of safeguarding the workers is to erect a barrier around the excavation. Such a barrier, consisting of a truck, a piece of heavy equipment or a pile of dirt, would keep a car out of the excavation and protect workers from oncoming traffic. The expert testified that the barrier should cover the entire width of the excavation. He also stated that there should have been two flagmen present, rather than one, and that warning signs should have been posted advising motorists that there was only one lane of traffic and that there was a flagman ahead.

* * * Defendant Felix now argues that plaintiff was injured in a freakish accident, brought about solely by defendant Dickens' negligence, and therefore there was no causal link, as a matter of law, between Felix' breach of duty and plaintiff's injuries.

The concept of proximate cause, or more appropriately legal cause, has proven to be an elusive one, incapable of being precisely defined to cover all situations * * *.

Where the acts of a third person intervene between the defendant's conduct and the plaintiff's injury, the causal connection is not automatically severed. In such a case, liability turns upon whether the intervening act is a normal or foreseeable consequence of the situation created by the defendant's negligence. [Cc] If the intervening act is extraordinary under the circumstances, not foreseeable in the normal course of events, or independent of or far removed from the defendant's conduct, it may well be a superseding act which breaks the causal nexus. [Cc] Because questions concerning what is foreseeable and what is normal may be the subject of varying inferences, as is the question of negligence itself, these issues generally are for the fact finder to resolve.

There are certain instances, to be sure, where only one conclusion may be drawn from the established facts and where the question of legal cause may be decided as a matter of law. Those cases generally involve independent intervening acts which operate upon but do not flow from the original negligence. Thus, for instance, we have held that where an automobile lessor negligently supplies a car with a defective trunk lid, it is not liable to the lessee who, while stopped to repair the trunk, was injured by the negligent driving of a third party. [C] Although the renter's negligence undoubtedly served to place the injured party at the site of the accident, the intervening act was divorced from and not the foreseeable risk associated with the original negligence. And the injuries were different in kind than those which would have normally been expected from a defective trunk. In short, the negligence of the renter merely furnished the occasion for an unrelated act to cause injuries not ordinarily anticipated. [C]

By contrast, in the present case, we cannot say as a matter of law that defendant Dickens' negligence was a superseding cause which interrupted the link between Felix' negligence and plaintiff's injuries. From the evidence in the record, the jury could have found that Felix negligently failed to safeguard the excavation site. A prime hazard associated with such dereliction is the possibility that a driver will negligently enter the work site and cause injury to a worker. That the driver was negligent, or even reckless, does not insulate Felix from liability. [Cc] Nor is it decisive that the driver lost control of the vehicle through a negligent failure to take medication, rather than a driving mistake. [C] The precise manner of the event need not be anticipated. The finder of fact could have concluded that the foreseeable, normal and natural result of the risk created by Felix was the injury of a worker by a car entering the improperly protected work area. An intervening act may not serve as a superseding cause, and relieve an actor of responsibility, where the risk of the intervening act occurring is the very same risk which renders the actor negligent.

In a similar vein, plaintiff's act of placing the kettle on the west side of the excavation does not, as a matter of law, absolve defendant Felix of responsibility. Serious injury, or even death, was a foreseeable consequence of a vehicle crashing through the work area. The injury could have occurred in numerous ways, ranging from a worker being directly struck by the car to the car hitting an object that injures the worker. Placement of the kettle, or any object in the work area, could affect how the accident occurs and the extent of injuries. That defendant could not anticipate the precise manner of the accident or the exact extent of injuries, however, does not preclude liability as a matter of law where the general risk and character of injuries are foreseeable. * * *

For the foregoing reasons, the order of the Appellate Division should be affirmed, with costs.

NOTES AND QUESTIONS

1. Why does the opinion focus on the contractor? What about the driver? Shouldn't he be liable? *possibly*

2. Note that when courts have decided that the intervening act should cut off liability, it is labelled a "superseding" cause.

3. *Foreseeability of Intervening Force.* The test for determining whether an intervening force constitutes a superseding cause is often couched in terms of foreseeability. See Restatement (Second) of Torts § 477 (1965). A person must foresee the normal consequences of his conduct, but is not responsible for extraordinarily negligent intervening acts of third persons. On considerations important in determining whether an intervening force is a superseding cause, see Restatement of Torts § 442. Consider whether the defendant should be liable in the cases that follow.

is the cause so extraordinary/bizarre that it could not be foreseeable?

4. A wrecking company failed to secure a condemned house during salvage, prior to demolition. Trespassers using the house for shelter accidentally started a fire that spread to the building next door. Testimony established that the neighborhood was one frequented by "vagrants" and that it was the custom of the industry to lock and board up buildings during salvage to keep trespassers out. Aetna Ins. Co. v. 3 Oaks Wrecking and Lumber Co., 65 Ill.App.3d 618, 382 N.E.2d 283, 21 Ill.Dec. 919 (1978) (jury verdict for plaintiff affirmed).

5. Defendant sets off an auto alarm at 4:00 a.m. while attempting to repossess a car. In the resulting confusion, a neighbor is shot. Is the negligent handling of a rifle foreseeable under those circumstances or one that interrupts the causal link? Griffith v. Valley of Sun Recovery & Adjustment Bureau, Inc., 126 Ariz. 227, 613 P.2d 1283 (1980) (question of fact for jury).

6. Defendant parks his car in violation of parking regulations and a negligently driven fire truck on its way to a fire collides with it and a pedestrian on the adjacent sidewalk is injured. Cf. Falk v. Finkelman, 268 Mass. 524, 168 N.E. 89 (1929) (no liability, too remote).

7. Around 9:30 p.m., a man, distraught because he recently had been fired by the power company, climbed up a 34,000–volt power pole and threatened to electrocute himself. A crowd formed. About midnight, the police chief of the city ordered the power shut off, the power company complied, and portions of the city went dark. Around 1:00 a.m., two teenagers on their way home from a concert were driving through the city. Driver noticed about 100 yards before an intersection that streetlights and traffic lights were out. He drove through the intersection without stopping because he "wasn't quite up on the rules of the road." His car collided with another car in the intersection and his passenger sued both drivers, the city, the power company, and the man who had threatened suicide. Who should be liable? Quirke v. City of Harvey, 266 Ill. App. 3d 664, 639 N.E.2d 1355 (1994). *contributory negligence*

8. Defendant, under an obligation to furnish a safe place to work, set plaintiff, its employee, at cleaning a coin-operated machine with gasoline in a small room in which there was a lighted gas heater with an open flame. While he was working, a rat escaped from the machine and ran to take refuge under the heater, where its fur, impregnated with gasoline fumes, caught fire from the flame. The rat "returned in haste and flames to its original hideout," and exploded the gasoline vapor

flaming rat case!

inside the machine, injuring the plaintiff. Is defendant liable? United Novelty Co. v. Daniels, 42 So.2d 395 (Miss.1949).

9. A rock radio station with an extensive teenage audience conducted a contest that rewarded the first contestant to locate a peripatetic disc jockey. Two minors driving in separate automobiles attempted to follow the disc jockey's automobile to its next stop. In the course of their pursuit, at speeds up to 80 m.p.h., one of the minors negligently forced a car off the highway, killing the driver. Wrongful death action against the radio station. What result? Weirum v. RKO Gen., Inc., 15 Cal.3d 40, 539 P.2d 36, 123 Cal.Rptr. 468 (1975). On April Fool's Day, defendant encouraged his child to call a friend of his and pretend that she was home alone and frightened. The friend, concerned about the child, jumped into his pick-up truck to go the child. In his haste, he ran a stop sign and collided with plaintiff's motorcycle. Plaintiff was seriously injured and sued the driver and the instigator of the practical joke. Who should be liable? Kolar v. Bergo, 280 Mont. 262, 929 P.2d 867 (1996).

10. Note that a plaintiff's own conduct can constitute an intervening cause that breaks the causal connection between defendant's negligence and the injury. However, in order to be a superseding cause, plaintiff's conduct must be more than contributory negligence that would be relevant in apportioning negligent conduct. For example, in Mesick v. State of New York, 118 A.D.2d 214, 504 N.Y.S.2d 279 (1986), plaintiff's conduct was not a superseding cause of his injuries when he swung himself from a rope tied to a tree branch out into a water hole and fell onto jagged rocks. There was evidence that the defendant, State of New York, was aware that the rope had been tied to the tree and was used by people who swam at the water hole. In addition to being foreseeable, it must rise to such a level of culpability as to replace defendant's negligence as the legal cause of the injury.

11. Two or more intervening acts may combine to form a superseding cause. Wagner v. Clark Equipment Co., Inc., 243 Conn. 168, 700 A.2d 38 (1997) (jury question whether negligence of forklift driver who backed into plaintiff, plaintiff's employer, and plaintiff combined to supersede the negligence of the forklift manufacturer in causing plaintiff's injury).

12. *Act of God.* One standard type of "intervening force" is called an "act of God," "vis major" or "force of nature." In Kimble v. Mackintosh Hemphill Co., 359 Pa. 461, 59 A.2d 68, 71–72 (1948), defendant was not relieved of liability when a section of a negligently maintained roof crashed, falling onto and killing plaintiff. The defendant claimed that the roof collapsed as a result of extremely high winds. The court stated, "We cannot say that the intervening cause [of the high winds] was vis major. One who fails in his duty to remedy a defective or dangerous condition is liable for injuries resulting therefrom, although the immediate cause of the injury is the wind. [Cc] The causal connection is not broken, and the original wrongdoer is liable for the injury sustained." Note how the issue in *Kimble* differs from Blyth v. Birmingham Waterworks Co., page 132. Is it consistent in principle with the *Anderson* "twin fires" case, page 277? The Restatement § 450 defines force of nature, and § 451 outlines the consideration that will make the force of nature a superseding cause. In which of these situations does the intervening force of nature interrupt the causal link between defendant's act and plaintiff's injury?

A. Defendant did not inspect a telephone pole for 14 years and it is felled during a 12–inch snowfall and injures plaintiff. Bowman v. Columbia Tel. Co., 406 Pa. 455, 179 A.2d 197 (1962).

B.   In the dead of winter, defendant ships plaintiff's apples in an unheated car through the state of Maine. A cold spell sets in, and the apples are frozen. Fox v. Boston & Maine R. Co., 148 Mass. 220, 19 N.E. 222 (1889).

C.   Defendant's negligence damages canvas coverings designed to protect plaintiff's pineapple plants from frost. Before they can be replaced, the plants are killed by a frost. Benedict Pineapple Co. v. Atlantic Coast Line R. Co., 55 Fla. 514, 46 So. 732 (1908).

D.   Defendant charter plane company negligently fails to supply one of its vehicles with sufficient fuel. The pilot is forced to make an emergency landing on a small island in the Pacific. A volcano erupts and kills a passenger. Cf. Doss v. Big Stone Gap, 145 Va. 520, 134 S.E. 563 (1926).

13.   Remember that there may be more than one proximate cause of an injury and, therefore, more than one defendant may be held jointly and severally liable. Do you see why it would be prejudicial to the plaintiff to instruct the jury that the defendant's negligence must be "the" proximate cause of the injury?

Watson v. Kentucky & Indiana Bridge & R.R. Co.

Court of Appeals of Kentucky, 1910.
137 Ky. 619, 126 S.W. 146.

[Through the negligence of the defendant railroad, a tank car full of gasoline was derailed and its valve broken, so that the gasoline ran into the street. One Duerr struck a match, igniting the gasoline vapor, and an explosion followed, injuring plaintiff, a bystander. Duerr testified that he struck the match to light a cigar, and that when he dropped the match the explosion occurred before it reached the ground. Other witnesses testified that Duerr had said to a companion, "Let's go set the damn thing on fire," that he struck the match against a fence and deliberately threw it into the gasoline vapor. The trial court directed a verdict for the defendant, and plaintiff appealed.]

SETTLE, J. * * * The lighting of the match by Duerr having resulted in the explosion, the question is, was that act merely a contributing cause, or the efficient and, therefore, proximate cause of appellant's injuries? The question of proximate cause is a question for the jury. In holding that Duerr in lighting or throwing the match acted maliciously or with intent to cause the explosion, the trial court invaded the province of the jury. There was, it is true, evidence tending to prove that the act was wanton or malicious, but also evidence conducing to prove that it was inadvertently or negligently done by Duerr. It was therefore for the jury and not the court to determine from all the evidence whether the lighting of the match was done by Duerr inadvertently or negligently, or whether it was a wanton and malicious act. * * *

If the presence on Madison street in the city of Louisville of the great volume of loose gas that arose from the escaping gasoline was caused by the negligence of the appellee Bridge & Railroad Company it seems to us that the probable consequence of its coming in contact with fire and causing an explosion was too plain a proposition to admit of doubt. Indeed, it was most probable that some one would strike a match to light a cigar or for other purposes in the midst of the gas. In our opinion, therefore, the act of one lighting and throwing a match under such circumstances cannot be said to be the efficient cause of the explosion. It did not of itself produce the explosion, nor could it have done so without the assistance and contribution resulting from the primary negligence, if there was such negligence, on the part of the appellee Bridge & Railroad Company in furnishing the presence of the gas in the street. This conclusion, however, rests upon the theory that Duerr inadvertently or negligently lighted and threw the match in the gas.

If, however, the act of Duerr in lighting the match and throwing it into the vapor or gas arising from the gasoline was malicious, and done for the purpose of causing the explosion, we do not think appellees would be responsible, for while the appellee Bridge & Railroad Company's negligence may have been the efficient cause of the presence of the gas in the street, and it should have understood enough of the consequences thereof to have foreseen that an explosion was likely to result from the inadvertent or negligent lighting of a match by some person who was ignorant of the presence of the gas or of the effect of lighting or throwing a match in it, it could not have foreseen or deemed it probable that one would maliciously or wantonly do such an act for the evil purpose of producing the explosion. Therefore, if the act of Duerr was malicious, we quite agree with the trial court that it was one which the appellees could not reasonably have anticipated or guarded against, and in such case the act of Duerr, and not the primary negligence of the appellee Bridge & Railroad Company, in any of the particulars charged, was the efficient or proximate cause of appellant's injuries. The mere fact that the concurrent cause or intervening act was unforeseen will not relieve the defendant guilty of the primary negligence from liability, but if the intervening agency is something so unexpected or extraordinary as that he could not or ought not to have anticipated it, he will not be liable, and certainly he is not bound to anticipate the criminal acts of others by which damage is inflicted and hence is not liable therefor.

For the reasons indicated, the judgment is * * * reversed as to the Bridge & Railroad Company, and the cause remanded for a new trial consistent with the opinion.

NOTES AND QUESTIONS

1. *Intervening Criminal Acts.* The principal case continues to be cited frequently, although the Kentucky Supreme Court has noted that criminal conduct no longer automatically interrupts the causal link in Kentucky. Britton v. Wooten, 817 S.W.2d 443, 451 (1991) (whether the spark that ignited trash negligently accumulated next to building was ignited accidentally, negligently, intentionally, or even criminally, it may still have been foreseeable and thus would not cut off liability).

2. Under ordinary circumstances, is it reasonably to be expected that someone will criminally tamper with a railroad track? Deyo v. New York Central R. Co., 34 N.Y. 9, 88 Am.Dec. 418 (1865). What if there is a strike in progress, with a record of continued violence on the part of the strikers? Int'l & G.N.R. Co. v. Johnson, 23

Tex.Civ.App. 160, 203, 55 S.W. 772 (1900). In the absence of any special circumstances, should the defendant anticipate forgery of a check? Benenson v. National Surety Co., 260 N.Y. 299, 183 N.E. 505 (1932). Assault upon a railway passenger? Hoff v. Public Service R. Co., 91 N.J.L. 641, 103 A. 209 (1918). A baseball umpire? Toone v. Adams, 262 N.C. 403, 137 S.E.2d 132 (1964).

3. It is probably impossible to state any comprehensive rule as to when a defendant will be liable for the intervening criminal act of a third person. See Restatement (Second) of Torts §§ 448–449 (1965). Some of the more common situations in which liability has been found are the following:

A. Defendant, by contract or otherwise, is under a duty to protect plaintiff against criminal misconduct, and fails to do so. See, e.g., Silva v. Showcase Cinemas Concessions of Dedham, Inc., 736 F.2d 810, 813 (1st Cir.1984), cert. denied, 469 U.S. 883 (1984), where the court held that a jury could reasonably find that a proximate cause of plaintiff's being stabbed to death was the theatre's failure adequately to patrol its premises. See also Cherry, Liability of Business Property Owners for Injury to Customers in Parking Lots by Criminal Attacks From Third Parties, 13 Real Est.L.J. 141 (1984). Similar liability may be imposed upon lessors and their duty to protect lessees, and a government's obligation to its citizens.

Sixth grade class was taken to nearby park for a drug awareness program. Student did not appear at the meeting place to return to school and teacher left without her. Walking home alone, she was accosted by students from a nearby junior high school and raped. Bell v. Bd. of Educ. of the City of New York, 90 N.Y.2d 944, 687 N.E.2d 1325, 665 N.Y.S.2d 42 (1997) (question of fact for jury whether intervening act of another is itself the foreseeable harm that shaped the duty imposed and thus defendant who failed to guard against such conduct would not be relieved of liability).

B. Defendant's affirmative act destroys or defeats a protection that plaintiff has placed around his person or property to guard them against crime. Defendant, who has leased floor space in plaintiff's jewelry store, goes to the store on a holiday, and leaves the key in the front door. Garceau v. Engel, 169 Minn. 62, 210 N.W. 608 (1926). Cf. Southwestern Bell Tel. Co. v. Adams, 199 Ark. 254, 133 S.W.2d 867 (1939) (defendant left windows of plaintiff's warehouse open).

C. Defendant brings into association with plaintiff a person whom he knows or should know to be peculiarly likely to commit crime, under circumstances creating a recognizable unreasonable risk that he will do so. The security agency for an apartment building hired a security guard with a violent record. The guard used his passkey to gain access to plaintiff's apartment, where he assaulted her. Easley v. Apollo Detective Agency, 69 Ill.App.3d 920, 26 Ill.Dec. 313, 387 N.E.2d 1241 (1979).

Compare Hines v. Garrett, 131 Va. 125, 108 S.E. 690 (1921), where a railroad carried an 18 year-old past her station, and put her off the train near a place known locally as "Hoboes' Hollow," which the court described as known to be frequented by hoboes, tramps, and questionable characters. On her way back to town, she was raped by two different unidentified persons. Is the railroad company liable?

D. Defendant has taken custody of a person of dangerous criminal tendencies, and fails to restrain him. Matron held liable for policeman's death when he was shot by juveniles who escaped from a youth center. Christensen v. Epley, 36 Or.App. 535, 585 P.2d 416 (1978). Contra, and much criticized, was Henderson v. Dade Coal Co., 100 Ga. 568, 28 S.E. 251 (1897), where a company using convict labor negligently guarded a brutal and vicious convict with a record of sexual offenses, and he escaped and raped the plaintiff. What if the convict were only a forger, with no

[handwritten margin note: Should D have been on notice of prior criminal acts / Should D be under a higher duty of care]

record of violence, and he held up plaintiff with a gun in the course of his escape? Williams v. State, 308 N.Y. 548, 127 N.E.2d 545 (1955).

4. The following cases will help to test one's understanding of the rules and policy implications involved with regard to intervening criminal acts:

A. The State of New York was negligent in having only one attendant in a maximum-security closed ward. This led to the escape of a known dangerous psychotic. Some four hours after this occurred the escapee chanced upon an automobile with the keys in it, drove away and collided with plaintiff's automobile. Should the State be liable for this consequence? Dunn v. State, 29 N.Y.2d 313, 277 N.E.2d 647, 327 N.Y.S.2d 622 (1971).

B. Defendant insurance company issued a policy on the life of a child, payable to her aunt as beneficiary. Under state law the policy was prohibited because the aunt did not have an insurable interest in the life of the child. The aunt murdered the child in the hope of collecting the life insurance. Should the company be liable to the child's parents in a wrongful death action? See Liberty Nat'l Life Ins. Co. v. Weldon, 267 Ala. 171, 100 So.2d 696 (1957); cf. Galanis v. Mercury International Ins. Underwriters, 247 Cal.App.2d 690, 55 Cal.Rptr. 890 (1967) (suicide-bent person buys insurance at airport vending machine and causes plane to crash). See also Tarasoff v. Regents of The University of California, page 429.

C. Promoters of a gun show were negligent in providing security and several minors were able to gain admission and steal handguns and ammunition. Later than night, while deliberately skidding their car on snow-covered roads to slide into trash cans, they were confronted by plaintiffs. One of the teenagers shot both of the plaintiffs with a gun stolen from the gun show. Should the promoters be liable? Pavlides v. Niles Gun Show, Inc., 93 Ohio App.3d 46, 637 N.E.2d 404 (1994).

D. Plaintiff was driving home when a fifteen-year-old dropped a twenty-pound chunk of concrete from an overpass onto her car, killing her. Her family filed suit against the highway department, alleging that the negligence of its employees in inadequately fencing the overpass, allowing loose pieces of concrete to be left there, and failing to light it properly caused the death. Should the highway department be liable? State ex rel. Missouri Hwy. and Transp. Com. v. Dierker, 961 S.W.2d 58 (Mo.1998).

E. Defendant manufactured ammonium nitrate, a chemical used in fertilizer, and sold it through several intermediaries to a terrorist who mixed it with fuel oil and used it to blow up the Murrah Federal Building in Oklahoma City. Plaintiffs, who were injured or whose family members were killed in the blast, allege that the chemical was negligently mislabeled as fertilizer grade rather than explosive grade. Should the manufacturer or the farm co-op that sold the chemical be liable? Gaines–Tabb v. ICI Explosives, USA, Inc., 160 F.3d 613, 620 (1998) (applying Oklahoma law) ("When the intervening act is intentionally tortious or criminal, it is more likely to be considered independent.") See also Port Authority of N.Y. and N.J. v. Arcadian Corp., 189 F.3d 305 (3d Cir.1999) (applying New York and New Jersey law) (accord, World Trade Center bombing).

5. *Keys Left in Car.* One fairly common proximate-cause puzzle involves an intervening criminal act and subsequent negligence by the intervenor. This occurs when defendant leaves keys in the ignition of his unlocked automobile. A thief drives off with the vehicle and negligently injures plaintiff in a subsequent collision. See, for example, Kozicki v. Dragon, 255 Neb. 248, 583 N.W.2d 336 (1998) (teenage thief testified that four or five of the cars she had previously stolen had ended up wrecked and police officer submitted affidavit that stolen vehicles are more likely to be involved in accidents). For treatment when a statute or ordinance is involved, see

Ney v. Yellow Cab Co., page 207 and notes. When there is no statute or ordinance involved, most courts have declined to impose liability unless the vehicle has been left in an area where the crime is especially likely to happen. See Hergenrether v. East, 61 Cal.2d 440, 393 P.2d 164, 39 Cal.Rptr. 4 (1964). The fact that the vehicle is an extraordinarily dangerous one may also be a circumstance that suggests liability. See Richardson v. Ham, 44 Cal.2d 772, 285 P.2d 269 (1955) (26–ton bulldozer left unlocked and unguarded at construction site). What is the likelihood that a motor vehicle thief will be involved in an accident? See Peck, An Exercise Based Upon Empirical Data—Liability for Harm Caused by Stolen Vehicles, 1969 Wis.L.Rev. 909. If an owner of a vehicle is liable in this context, should an automobile manufacturer also be liable if a thief is able to "jump the wires" to start a vehicle? See Dean v. General Motors Corp., 301 F.Supp. 187 (E.D.La.1969). the 4" find says

6. *Intervening Intentional Misconduct.* What if the conduct in not necessarily criminal, but at least intentional? Defendant service station attendant sold a small amount of gasoline to six-year-old Penny Jones. Penny falsely told the attendant that her mother had requested it. Later that day, Penny's four-year-old half-sister Candy threw a lighted match into the gasoline and the ensuing flames ignited her legs and dress. Is defendant liable? Can the principal case be distinguished? See Jones v. Robbins, 289 So.2d 104 (La.1974). See also, Kush v. City of Buffalo, 59 N.Y.2d 26, 449 N.E.2d 725, 462 N.Y.S.2d 831 (1983) (plaintiff was injured by chemicals negligently stored by defendant and then stolen by two teenagers).

7. In Village of Carterville v. Cook, 129 Ill. 152, 22 N.E. 14 (1889), defendant excavated a hole in the sidewalk and a third person negligently jostled the plaintiff into it. Defendant was held liable. What if the third person had deliberately pushed plaintiff into the hole? Alexander v. New Castle, 115 Ind. 51, 17 N.E. 200 (1888); Milostan v. Chicago, 148 Ill.App. 540 (1909).

8. Defendant left the door of its elevator shaft unlocked and unguarded. A stranger, impersonating an elevator boy, politely ushered plaintiff through the door. She fell down the shaft and was injured. Is defendant liable? Cole v. German Savings & Loan Society, 124 Fed. 113 (8th Cir.1903).

9. In Parness v. Tempe, 123 Ariz. 460, 600 P.2d 764 (1979), a young boy was pushed to the ground by two others at a neighborhood recreation center. The center did not provide adequate supervision. Should it be liable for the intentional conduct of others? In Stevens v. Des Moines Independent Cnty. School Dist., 528 N.W.2d 117 (Iowa 1995) the school failed to adequately supervise the corridors at a middle school and plaintiff was beaten by another student. Is the student's intentional act a superseding cause?

10. Defendant engaged in an extramarital affair with plaintiff's husband. Plaintiff alleges that defendant knew or should have known that she had a sexually transmitted disease and failed to warn plaintiff's husband that she was infectious. Plaintiff contracted the disease from her husband and filed suit against defendant for damages. Is the conduct of plaintiff's husband an intentional act that is a superseding cause? Lockhart v. Loosen, 943 P.2d 1074 (Okla.1997) (superseding cause if husband knew because defendant's silence—which could have been a proximate cause of plaintiff's injury—would then be a mere condition).

Fuller v. Preis

New York Court of Appeals, 1974.
35 N.Y.2d 425, 322 N.E.2d 263, 363 N.Y.S.2d 568.

BREITEL, CHIEF JUDGE. Plaintiff executor, in a wrongful death action, recovered a jury verdict for $200,000. The Appellate Division set aside the verdict and judgment in favor of plaintiff executor and dismissed the complaint. In doing so, that court noted that even if it were not to dismiss the complaint, it would set the verdict aside as contrary to the weight of the credible evidence. Plaintiff executor appeals.

Chief Judge Breitel

Decedent, Dr. Lewis, committed suicide some seven months after an automobile accident from which he had walked away believing he was uninjured. In fact he had suffered head injuries with consequences to be detailed later. The theory of the case was that defendants, owner and operator of the vehicle which struck decedent's automobile, were responsible in tort for the suicide as a matter of proximate cause and effect. The issue is whether plaintiff's evidence of cause of the suicide was sufficient to withstand dismissal of the complaint.

There should be a reversal of the order of the Appellate Division and a new trial ordered. * * *

[An] act of suicide, as a matter of law, is not a superseding cause in negligence law precluding liability. An initial tort-feasor may be liable for the wrongful acts of a third party if foreseeable (see Restatement (Second) of Torts § 442A). * * *

Thus, there is neither public policy nor precedent barring recovery for suicide of a tortiously injured person driven "insane" by the consequence of the tortious act. [Cc] * * *

[T]his case was tried for all purposes in accordance with the prevailing law. Indeed, the jury was instructed, primarily, upon the theory of liability for a suicide by an accident victim suffering from ensuing mental disease, who was unable to control the "irresistible impulse" to destroy himself. The theory of the trial, therefore, determines the rule to be applied on the appeal.

Dr. Lewis was physically and mentally healthy immediately prior to the automobile accident in which he struck his head against the interior of his own vehicle. After the accident he suffered several epileptic seizures, often with unconsciousness. Before the accident he had never suffered a seizure. For seven months between the accident and his death, Dr. Lewis experienced no fewer than 38 separate seizures. * * *

The only authentic issue is whether the suicide was an "irresistible impulse" caused by traumatic organic brain damage. * * *

On the day of the suicide, only seven months after the accident, when Dr. Lewis had had three seizures, his daughter tried to speak with him but he did not respond. After the third seizure he seemed unable to recognize his wife, had a strange look, and locked himself in the bathroom. Twenty minutes later, his wife heard him mutter, "I must do it, I must do it", and then a gunshot rang out. Dr. Lewis had shot himself in the head and died the following day. * * *

In tort law, as contrasted with criminal law, there is recognition that one may retain the power to intend, to know, and yet to have an irresistible impulse to act and therefore be incapable of voluntary conduct. * * *

The issue in this case was, precisely, whether Dr. Lewis, who obviously knew what he was doing and intended to do what he did, nevertheless, was, because of mental derangement, incapable of resisting the impulse to destroy himself. Precedents and modern knowledge say that that could have been. The jury found that it was so. * * *

Of course, there may be and undoubtedly have been cases where the causal nexus becomes too tenuous to permit a jury to "speculate" as to the proximate cause of the suicide. * * *

A suicide is a strange act and no rationalistic approach can fit the act into neat categories of rationality or irrationality. When the suicide is preceded by a history of trauma, brain damage, epileptic seizures, aberrational conduct, depression and despair, it is at the very least a fair issue of fact whether the suicide was the rational act of a sound mind or the irrational act or irresistible impulse of a deranged mind evidenced by a physically damaged brain. It would be illogical to conclude otherwise. Consequently, although the Appellate Division in exercise of its supervisory power to review the facts could set the jury verdict aside, it was impermissible for it to dismiss the complaint.

Since the Appellate Division, in reversing, stated that in any event it would have set the verdict aside as contrary to the weight of the evidence, the verdict in favor of plaintiff may not be reinstated and a new trial is required.

Accordingly, the order of the Appellate Division should be reversed, with costs, and a new trial directed.

NOTES AND QUESTIONS

1. If a suicide is a deliberate, intentional act by an individual, how can one individual be liable for the suicide of another?

2. Early decisions steadfastly denied claims based on causing suicide as long as the decedent had even the slightest awareness of what he was doing. See Scheffer v. Railroad Co., 105 U.S. 249 (1881); Brown v. American Steel and Wire Co., 43 Ind.App. 560, 88 N.E. 80 (1909); Daniels v. New York, N.H. & H.R. Co., 183 Mass. 393, 67 N.E. 424 (1903). Courts followed the view from ecclesiastical and early common law that a person who knowingly committed suicide was a culpable wrongdoer. Even when defendant had engaged in extreme and outrageous conduct highly likely to cause severe emotional distress, decedent's cognitive recognition of his act would be deemed a superseding cause and bar any claim. Lancaster v. Montesi, 216 Tenn. 50, 390 S.W.2d 217 (1965) (sadistic physical and emotional torture). Some courts have allowed a claim in this type of situation although decedent was aware of his own conduct. See R.D. v. W.H., 875 P.2d 26 (Wyo.1994); State for Use and Benefit of Richardson v. Edgeworth, 214 So.2d 579 (Miss.1968); Tate v. Canonica, 180 Cal.App.2d 898, 5 Cal.Rptr. 28 (1960); Cauverien v. De Metz, 20 Misc.2d 144, 188 N.Y.S.2d 627 (Sup.Ct.1959).

3. Liability for negligently caused suicide was broadened when some courts stated that a wrongful death claim would be allowed not only when the decedent was unaware of what he was doing, but also when the decedent's injury caused an irresistible impulse to commit suicide. Padula v. State, 48 N.Y.2d 366, 398 N.E.2d 548, 422 N.Y.S.2d 943 (1979); Wallace v. Bounds, 369 S.W.2d 138 (Mo.1963); Long v. Omaha & C.B. St. R. Co., 108 Neb. 342, 187 N.W. 930 (1922). Most courts found an irresistible impulse only when decedent acted in a sudden frenzy; when he left a note or purchased poison the courts found control. In one decision, the court relied on the efficient manner in which the decedent cut his throat to deny recovery. Brown v. American Steel and Wire Co., 43 Ind.App. 560, 88 N.E. 80 (1909).

The principal case is one of the few giving a broader interpretation of the irresistible impulse test. For a good review of the cases on this issue, see Grant v. F.P. Lathrop Constr. Co., 81 Cal.App.3d 790, 146 Cal.Rptr. 45 (1978).

4. Some worker's compensation cases have allowed a claim when a work-related accident was a substantial factor in the decedent's becoming incapable of normal judgment and committing suicide. See Delaware Tire Center v. Fox, 411 A.2d 606 (Del.Super.1980); Graver Tank & Mfg. Co. v. Industrial Commission, 97 Ariz. 256, 399 P.2d 664 (1965); Burnight v. Industrial Accident Commission, 181 Cal.App.2d 816, 5 Cal.Rptr. 786 (1960). Studies suggest that this test comports better with the psychiatric understanding of the cause of suicide than the irresistible impulse formula. See Schwartz, Civil Liability for Causing Suicide: A Synthesis of Law and Psychiatry, 24 Vand.L.Rev. 217, 232–236 (1971). Is it an appropriate one for tort law?

5. An affirmative duty to use care to prevent suicide is sometimes imposed by tort law upon certain classes of defendants. Problems of proximate cause may still arise. As to hospitals, see Meier v. Ross General Hospital, 69 Cal.2d 420, 445 P.2d 519, 71 Cal.Rptr. 903 (1968). Jacoves v. United Merchandising Corp., 9 Cal.App.4th 88, 11 Cal.Rptr.2d 468 (1992). As to psychiatrists, see Fernandez v. Baruch, 52 N.J. 127, 244 A.2d 109 (1968); McNamara v. Honeyman, 546 N.E.2d 139 (Mass.1989); and White v. Lawrence, 975 S.W.2d 525 (Tenn.1998) (question for jury whether suicide of patient was superseding negligence in case where physician had directed alcoholic patient's wife to secretly administer drug Antabuse to him and he committed suicide the next day). What if defendant negligently sells a gun, ammunition, or drugs to plaintiff who uses it to commit suicide? Scoggins v. Wal–Mart Stores, Inc., 560 N.W.2d 564 (Iowa 1997) (ammunition sold to minor; plaintiff's act is superseding cause) (collecting cases); Runyon v. Reid, 510 P.2d 943 (Okla.1973) (barbiturates sold without refill authorization; plaintiff's act is superseding cause). The cases suggest that the result might have been otherwise if defendants had had any reason to suspect the intent of the purchaser. Compare the cases on liability of a seller of liquor, page 343.

McCoy v. American Suzuki Motor Corp.

Supreme Court Washington, 1998.
136 Wash.2d 350, 961 P.2d 952.

SANDERS, J. * * * At 5:00 p.m. on a cold November evening James McCoy drove eastbound on Interstate 90 outside Spokane as the car which preceded him, a Suzuki Samurai, swerved off the roadway and rolled. McCoy stopped to render assistance, finding the driver seriously injured. Shortly thereafter a Washington State Patrol trooper arrived on the scene and asked McCoy to place flares on the roadway to warn approaching vehicles. McCoy did so, but concerned the flares were insufficient, continued further and positioned himself a quarter-mile from the accident scene with a lit flare in each hand, manually directing traffic to the inside lane.

By 6:50 p.m., almost two hours after the accident, the injured driver and passenger of the Suzuki were removed and the scene was cleared, leaving only the trooper and McCoy on the roadway. McCoy walked back on the shoulder of the roadway to his car with a lit flare in his roadside hand. When McCoy was within three or four car-lengths of the trooper, the trooper pulled away without comment. Moments later McCoy was struck from behind while still walking on the roadway's shoulder by a hit-and-run vehicle.

McCoy and his wife filed a multicount complaint against the driver of the Suzuki for negligent driving; the passenger of the Suzuki for negligently grabbing the steering wheel when the car was fishtailing, further causing it to lose control; the State for the negligence of the trooper; and American Suzuki Motor Corporation and its parent corporation, Suzuki Motor Company, Ltd., for its allegedly defective Samurai which allegedly caused the wreck in the first place. We presently consider only McCoy's claim against Suzuki. * * *

Suzuki moved for summary judgment asserting: (1) the rescue doctrine does not apply to product liability actions; and (2) even if it does, McCoy must still, but cannot, prove Suzuki proximately caused his injuries. The trial court found the rescue doctrine applies to product liability actions but concluded any alleged defect in the Suzuki was not the proximate cause of McCoy's injuries and, accordingly, granted summary judgment of dismissal. * * *

[McCoy appealed the dismissal and the Court of Appeals reversed, finding the rescue doctrine applies in product liability actions just as it does in negligence actions, but that an injured rescuer need not prove the defendant proximately caused his injuries. Instead the court concluded the rescuer need only prove the defendant proximately caused the danger and that the rescuer was injured while rescuing.]

The Rescue Doctrine

The rescue doctrine is invoked in tort cases for a variety of purposes in a variety of scenarios. The doctrine, as here asserted, allows an injured rescuer to sue the party which caused the danger requiring the rescue in the first place. [C] As Justice Cardozo succinctly summarized, the heart of this doctrine is the notion that "danger invites rescue." Wagner v. International Ry. Co., 232 N.Y. 176, 133 N.E. 437, 437, 19 A.L.R.1 (1921). This doctrine serves two functions. First, it informs a tort-feasor it is foreseeable a rescuer will come to the aid of the person imperiled by the tort-feasor's actions, and, therefore, the tort-feasor owes the rescuer a duty similar to the duty he owes the person he imperils. [Cc] Second, the rescue doctrine negates the presumption that the rescuer assumed the risk of injury when he knowingly undertook the dangerous rescue, so long as he does not act rashly or recklessly. [C]

To achieve rescuer status one must demonstrate: (1) the defendant was negligent to the person rescued and such negligence caused the peril or appearance of peril to the person rescued; (2) the peril or appearance of peril was imminent; (3) a reasonably prudent person would have concluded such peril or appearance of peril existed; and (4) the rescuer acted with reasonable care in effectuating the rescue. [C] The Court of Appeals found McCoy demonstrated sufficient facts of rescuer status to put the issue of whether he met the four requirements * * * to the jury. [C] Suzuki does not question this finding. Nor will we.

Does the Rescue Doctrine Apply in Product Liability Actions?

Suzuki argues the rescue doctrine may not be invoked in product liability actions. Suzuki contends the [Washington product liability statute] supplants all common law remedies and contends the rescue doctrine is nothing more than a common law remedy. We disagree. The rescue doctrine is not a common law remedy. Rather, it is shorthand for the idea that rescuers are to be anticipated and is a reflection of a societal value judgment that rescuers should not be barred from bringing suit for knowingly placing themselves in danger to undertake a rescue. We can conceive of no reason why this doctrine should not apply with equal force when a product manufacturer causes the danger. * * * We adopt the Court of Appeals analysis on this point and conclude the rescue doctrine may be invoked in product liability actions just as it may in ordinary negligence actions.

Must Plaintiff Show Proximate Causation Under the Rescue Doctrine?

McCoy argues the rescue doctrine relieves the rescuer-plaintiff of proving the defendant's wrongdoing proximately caused his injuries. McCoy asserts a rescuer may prevail in a suit by showing the defendant proximately caused the danger and that, while serving as rescuer, the plaintiff was injured. The Court of Appeals agreed stating the rescue doctrine "varies the ordinary rules of negligence." McCoy, 86 Wash. App. at 110 (citing Solgaard v. Guy F. Atkinson Co., 6 Cal. 3d 361, 491 P.2d 821, 99 Cal. Rptr. 29 (1971)).

The Court of Appeals erred on this point. * * * [The rescuer, like any other plaintiff, must still show the defendant proximately caused his injuries.]

In Maltman [v. Sauer, 84 Wash.2d 975, 530 P.2d 254 (1975)] a rescue helicopter was called to the scene of an auto accident to transport one of the injured to the hospital. However, the rescue helicopter crashed on the way to the scene killing the entire crew. A wrongful death suit was brought on behalf of the deceased crew members under the rescue doctrine against the party which allegedly caused the car accident in the first place. We * * * concluded, as a matter of law, the car accident was not the proximate cause of the helicopter crash and, accordingly, dismissed. [C]

We adhere to *Maltman* noting its requirement that a rescuer show the defendant proximately caused his injuries is in keeping with general principles of liability.

Did Suzuki Proximately Cause McCoy's Injuries?

Concluding that the rescue doctrine may apply to a product liability action and that the rescuer must show the defendant proximately caused his injuries, we question whether McCoy has demonstrated Suzuki proximately caused his injuries. * * *

Here, Suzuki argues, it was totally unforeseeable that a rescuer such as McCoy would be injured by a third vehicle under these particular facts and, accordingly, Suzuki asks us to rule in its favor on this issue as a matter of law. We find the issue of foreseeability of the intervening cause is sufficiently close that it should be decided by a jury, not the court. A jury might consider the position of the rescuer, the negligence of the oncoming motorist, if any, and many other factors.

McCoy cites In re Estate of Keck v. Blair, 71 Wash. App. 105, 108–09, 856 P.2d 740 (1993). In Keck a rescuer aided a driver who had been drinking and who caused an accident. As the rescuer escorted the driver across the highway to safety, a car approached and the rescuer had barely enough time to push the person he was rescuing to safety but was himself hit and instantly killed. The Court of Appeals allowed the decedent's estate to bring suit against the person he was rescuing under the rescue doctrine. The court held it could not say as a matter of law whether the original accident was the proximate cause of decedent's injuries and accordingly remanded the case for jury determination. The facts of the present case are not sufficiently different from those of Keck to take the issue from the jury.

In the present case, if the Suzuki Samurai is found to be defective the jury could find it foreseeable that the Suzuki Samurai would roll and that an approaching car would cause injury to either those in the Suzuki Samurai or to a rescuer, depending on the specific facts to be proved. We note sister jurisdictions have reached the same conclusion under similar facts. * * *

if reasonable people can differ on proximate cause issue, it should be a question of fact for the jury

As numerous cases illustrate, the court often exercises its gatekeeper function by dismissing an action without trial for lack of legal cause if the defendant's actions are too remote a cause of plaintiff's injuries. In *Malt-man* we dismissed the action, reasoning the party causing the principal accident should not be liable for the subsequent crash of a rescue helicopter hundreds of miles away because the helicopter crash was simply too remote a result of the principal accident. In *Hartley* [v. State, 103 Wash.2d 768, 698 P.2d 77 (1985)] the estate of a decedent killed by a drunk driver sued the State for failing to revoke the drunk driver's license. There we similarly dismissed reasoning the State should not be held liable for injuries caused by a driver simply because the State failed to revoke that driver's license. [C] Such fault on the State's behalf was again too remote a cause of the ensuing injury to impose liability.

Here, we do (not) find the alleged fault of Suzuki, if proved, to be so remote from these injuries that its liability should be cut off as a matter of law. Certainly the alleged fault of Suzuki is not as remote as the fault of the defendants in *Maltman* and *Hartley* and, thus, we must distinguish their results. Accordingly, we will (not) dismiss this case for lack of legal causation. Instead we remand the case for trial consistent with this opinion. * * *

Holding

NOTES AND QUESTIONS

1.   What happens to the case after the Washington Supreme Court opinion? What must McCoy prove at trial in order to recover from Suzuki? *that defective suzuki was proximate cause of injuries*

2.   The opinion quotes Judge Cardozo's famous pronouncement in Wagner v. International Ry. Co., 232 N.Y. 176, 180, 133 N.E. 437, 437–38 (1921): "Danger invites rescue." In that opinion, he went on to say "[t]he cry of distress is the summons to relief. The law does not ignore these reactions of the mind in tracing conduct to its consequences. It recognizes them as normal. It places their effects within the range of the natural and probable. The wrong that perils life is a wrong to the imperiled victim; it is a wrong also to his rescuer.... The risk of rescue, if only it be not wanton is born of the occasion. The emergency begets the man. The wrongdoer may not have foreseen the coming of a deliverer. He is accountable as if he had."

3.   A few of the numerous legal problems raised by the "rescue doctrine" are listed here. By his efforts the rescuer may injure himself, as in *McCoy* and *Wagner*, or the rescued person, or a third person. Are the issues the same? Should the defendant be liable for all of these injuries?

4.   House caught fire because water heater was installed negligently too close to insulation. Passerby saw smoke and stopped to assist family in escaping. Husband broke bedroom window and lowered child to passerby. Husband was then trying to clear away more glass to make wider opening when wife pushed him aside and dove head first out window. Passerby was injured trying to break her fall. Passerby sued installer of water heater and wife. Rescue doctrine applies to installer. Does it also apply to rescuee wife? See Williams v. Foster, 281 Ill. App. 3d 203, 666 N.E.2d 678 (1996) (court raised but did not reach issue because it found wife was not negligent in jumping from burning building). See also In re Estate of Keck v. Blair, 71 Wash. App. 105, 108–09, 856 P.2d 740 (1993) (cited in the principal case) (permitting case against rescuee); Lowrey v. Horvath, 689 S.W.2d 625 (Mo.1985) (rescue doctrine extends to plaintiff's decedent killed while trying to rescue defendant from well). Suppose the rescuee was in the act of taking his own life and clearly did not want to be rescued? See Talbert v. Talbert, 22 Misc.2d 782, 199 N.Y.S.2d 212 (1960).

5.   What if the attempt at rescue is utterly foolish? A passenger about to alight from defendant's train hands her baby to a man on the platform. The train unexpectedly starts up and carries her away. A bystander heroically snatches up the child and runs after the train. He runs the length of the platform, losing ground steadily, and stumbles over a baggage truck at the far end. The child is injured. Liability? Atchison, T. & S.F.R. Co. v. Calhoun, 213 U.S. 1 (1909). Cf. Robinson v. Butler, 226 Minn. 491, 33 N.W.2d 821 (1948) (excited passenger seizing steering wheel of automobile). Suppose the rescuer was mistaken and the rescuee was not actually in danger? Cf. Ellmaker v. Goodyear Tire & Rubber Co., 372 S.W.2d 650 (Mo.App.1963).

6.   What if plaintiff is injured while rescuing his own property? Defendant starts a fire that burns toward plaintiff's house, and plaintiff is burned while trying to put it out. Illinois Central R. Co. v. Siler, 229 Ill. 390, 82 N.E. 362 (1907). Plaintiff is injured trying to rescue his dog from his burning house. Govich v. North American Systems, Inc., 112 N.M. 226, 814 P.2d 94 (1991). Suppose he tries to rescue the property of a third person? Stewart v. Jefferson Plywood Co., 255 Or. 603, 469 P.2d 783 (1970); Burnett v. Conner, 299 Mass. 604, 13 N.E.2d 417 (1938). The property of the defendant? Rushton v. Howle, 79 Ga.App. 360, 53 S.E.2d 768 (1949); Green v. Britton, 22 Conn.Super. 71, 160 A.2d 497 (1960).

7.   Suppose the lawsuit is based on product liability rather than negligence? In addition to the principal case, see Dillard v. Pittway Corp., 719 So.2d 188 (Ala.1998) (smoke detector manufacturer liable to neighbor who was injured trying to rescue elderly residents from boarding house fire) and Govich v. North American Systems, Inc., 112 N.M. 226, 814 P.2d 94 (1991) (manufacturer of coffee maker that started house fire may be liable to plaintiffs).

8.   What about the rescuer of a rescuer? Richards v. Kansas Electric Power Co., 126 Kan. 521, 268 P. 847 (1928); Brown v. Ross, 345 Mich. 54, 75 N.W.2d 68 (1956); Richardson v. United States, 248 F.Supp. 99 (E.D.Okl.1965); Govich v. North American Systems, Inc., 112 N.M. 226, 814 P.2d 94 (1991) (mother injured rescuing adult son from his burning home, which he had entered to rescue his dog).

9. Suppose the injured rescuer is a professional—a police officer, a firefighter, a lifeguard, a paramedic. Some states do not permit recovery by professionals, at least against the property owner, under the so-called "firefighter's rule," which is premised on the theory that those professionals already have been compensated for their potentially hazardous duty. See, e.g., Walters v. Sloan, 20 Cal.3d 199, 571 P.2d 609, 142 Cal.Rptr. 152 (1977) (police officer). The rule operates to preclude recovery only if the risk created was the type of risk reasonably anticipated by the job. Compare Smith v. Tully, 665 A.2d 1333 (R.I.1995) (police officer injured in altercation with an intoxicated person armed with a knife in a bar after responding to call from bar employee barred by firefighter's rule) with Solgaard v. Guy F. Atkinson Co., 6 Cal.3d 361, 491 P.2d 821, 99 Cal.Rptr. 29 (1971) (doctor who had agreed to provide medical services at construction site not barred when he was injured in seeking to reach injured person trapped in landslide). The firefighter's rule has been limited or abolished in some jurisdictions. See, e.g., Mahoney v. Carus Chemical Co., 102 N.J. 564, 510 A.2d 4 (1986) (not applicable when defendant's act was intentional in exposing firefighter to risk) and Christensen v. Murphy, 296 Or. 610, 678 P.2d 1210 (1984) (abolishing rule).

10. *Attempt to Escape from Danger Created by Defendant.* The cases generally agree that the defendant who caused the danger will be liable to someone who is injured trying to escape from it. The classic decision is Tuttle v. Atlantic City R. Co., 66 N.J.L. 327, 49 A. 450 (1901), where a freight car jumped a track and lunged across the street. Plaintiff, on the sidewalk, ran from the car, fell and injured her knee. She was allowed to recover. See also Kroeger v. Safranek, 161 Neb. 182, 72 N.W.2d 831 (1955); Thornton v. Weaber, 380 Pa. 590, 112 A.2d 344 (1955).

11. *Attempt to Alleviate Harm Caused by Defendant.* The primary example of this is the case in which a physician treats the plaintiff's injuries and negligently aggravates them. Is the original defendant liable for the aggravation? The usual answer is in the affirmative. Weber v. Charity Hosp., 475 So.2d 1047 (La.1985) (plaintiff contracted hepatitis from blood transfusions to treat injuries she received in automobile accident for which defendant was responsible); Jess Edwards, Inc. v. Goergen, 256 F.2d 542 (10th Cir.1958); Thompson v. Fox, 326 Pa. 209, 192 A. 107 (1937). Suppose the injured party is being taken by an ambulance to the hospital for treatment. An accident en route causes additional injuries. Should it make any difference whether the second collision was caused by (1) the speed of the ambulance because of the emergency, (2) the negligence of the driver though no emergency was involved, or (3) the negligence of a third party in running into the ambulance? Atherton v. Devine, 602 P.2d 634 (Okla.1979). The intervening negligence may be so unusual that the court holds it to be superseding, as in Purchase v. Seelye, 231 Mass. 434, 121 N.E. 413 (1918), where the hospital made a mistake and operated on the wrong patient.

12. *Second Injury Caused by Weakened Condition Resulting from First Injury.* There are some recurrent patterns falling into this classification, in which the cases have indicated a more or less crystallized response, holding the first defendant liable for the second injury. The first involves the onset of a disease likely to attack one in a weakened condition—for example, the pneumonia in Beauchamp v. Saginaw Mining Co., 50 Mich. 163, 15 N.W. 65 (1883), or the hemolytic streptococcus infection in Wallace v. Ludwig, 292 Mass. 251, 198 N.E. 159 (1935). An earlier distinction depending on the time when the germs invaded the body has been abandoned, but it may still make a difference whether the disease was of a type that would attack a healthy person and produce the same result. See, e.g., Case of Upham, 245 Mass. 31, 139 N.E. 433 (1923) (appendicitis).

Another type of case involves a second breaking of a limb that had not fully recovered its original strength. The plaintiff usually recovers for the second injury. Squires v. Reynolds, 125 Conn. 366, 5 A.2d 877 (1939); Mitchell v. Legarsky, 95 N.H. 214, 60 A.2d 136 (1948). Factors that may affect the holding, however, include the length of time between the accidents, the location and nature of the second injury, the reasonableness of the plaintiff's conduct and the character of the second accident. See Linder v. Payette, 64 Idaho 656, 135 P.2d 440 (1943); Vance, Liability for Subsequent Injuries, 42 Tex.L.Rev. 86 (1963).

13.   *Legal Concepts Affecting These Cases.* In the notes above, fact patterns for classifying the cases have been suggested. Running through some of these fact patterns with varying significance are several legal concepts that may affect the determination of legal cause. Consider how the following sets of contrasting concepts apply to the patterns above:

(A) Dependent vs. independent intervening cause. "A dependent intervening cause is one which operates in response to or is a reaction to the stimulus of a situation for which the actor has made himself responsible by his negligent conduct." Restatement (Second) of Torts § 441, Comment *c.* It is less likely to be held to be superseding than an independent intervening cause.

(B) Extent of liability vs. existence of liability. If tort liability already exists between the parties, the court may be more ready to extend it to additional or augmented harm than if there had been no liability.

(C) Normal intervening force vs. extraordinary intervening force. A normal intervening force is defined in the Restatement (Second) as "a normal consequence of a situation created by the actor's negligent conduct." § 443. "It means that the court or jury, looking at the matter after the event, and therefore knowing the situation which existed when the new force intervened does not regard its intervention as so extraordinary as to fall outside of the class of normal events." Id., Comment *b.* This is obviously based on a hindsight approach, but the concept can also be used with the foresight approach. Thus, one would assume knowledge of the initial incident and then ask himself what subsequent intervening forces would be readily foreseeable. In his dissenting opinion in the *Palsgraf* case, Judge Andrews expressed a similar idea in a different context. "I think the direct connection, the foresight of which the courts speak, assumes prevision of the explosion * * * And surely, given such an explosion as here, it needed no great foresight to predict that the natural result would be to injure one on the platform at no greater distance than the plaintiff." Supra, page 310. Is he talking about the same thing?

3.   Public Policy

Kelly v. Gwinnell

Supreme Court of New Jersey, 1984.
96 N.J. 538, 476 A.2d 1219.

[Defendant Gwinnell, after having driven co-defendant Zak home, spent an hour or two at Zak's home before leaving to return to his own home. During that time, Gwinnell consumed two or three drinks of scotch on the rocks with Zak and his wife. Later, Zak accompanied Gwinnell outside to his car, chatted with him, and watched as Gwinnell drove off to go home. On the way home, Gwinnell was involved in a head-on collision with an automobile operated by plaintiff Marie Kelly, who was seriously injured. Kelly sued Gwinnell and Gwinnell's employer, and those defendants in turn sued the Zaks in a third party action. Thereafter, plaintiff amended her complaint to include the Zaks as direct defendants. The trial court granted the Zaks' motion for summary judgment holding that as a matter of law a host is not liable for the negligence of an adult social guest who has become intoxicated at the host's home. The appellate court affirmed, noting that New Jersey has no Dram Shop Act imposing liability on the provider of alcoholic beverages and that New Jersey common law liability had been extended to a social host only when the guest was a minor.]

WILENTZ, C.J. This case raises the issue of whether a social host who enables an adult guest at his home to become drunk is liable to the victim of an automobile accident caused by the drunken driving of the guest. Here the host served liquor to the guest beyond the point at which the guest was visibly intoxicated. We hold the host may be liable under [certain] circumstances. * * *

"Negligence is tested by whether the reasonably prudent person at the time and place should recognize and foresee an unreasonable risk or likelihood of harm or danger to others." [Cc] When negligent conduct creates such a risk, setting off foreseeable consequences that lead to plaintiff's injury, the conduct is deemed the proximate cause of the injury. "[A] tortfeasor is generally held answerable for the injuries which result in the ordinary course of events from his negligence and it is generally sufficient if his negligent conduct was a substantial factor in bringing about the injuries." [Cc]

Under the facts here defendant provided his guest with liquor, knowing that thereafter the guest would have to drive in order to get home. Viewing the facts most favorably to plaintiff (as we must, since the complaint was dismissed on a motion for summary judgment), one could reasonably conclude that the Zaks must have known that their provision of liquor was causing Gwinnell to become drunk, yet they continued to serve him even after he was visibly intoxicated. By the time he left, Gwinnell was in fact severely intoxicated. A reasonable person in Zak's position could foresee quite clearly that this continued provision of alcohol to Gwinnell was making it more and more likely that Gwinnell would not be able to operate his car carefully. Zak could foresee that unless he stopped providing drinks to Gwinnell, Gwinnell was likely to injure someone as a result of the negligent operation of his car. * * *

[T]he only question remaining is whether a duty exists to prevent such risk or, realistically, whether this Court should impose such a duty. * * *

When [a] court determines that a duty exists and liability will be extended, it draws judicial lines based on fairness and policy. In a society where thousands of deaths are caused each year by drunken drivers, where the damage caused by such deaths is regarded increasingly as intolerable, where liquor licensees are prohibited from serving intoxicated adults, and where long-standing criminal sanctions against drunken driving have recently been significantly strengthened to the point where the Governor notes that they are regarded as the toughest in the nation, see Governor's Annual Message to the N.J. State Legislature, Jan. 10, 1984, the imposition of such a duty by the judiciary seems both fair and fully in accord with the State's policy. * * *

We therefore [expand our prior decisions that limited liability to licensees who served liquor for profit or social hosts who served liquor to a minor and] hold that a host who serves liquor to an adult social guest, knowing both that the guest is intoxicated and [that he] will thereafter be operating a motor vehicle, is liable for injuries inflicted on a third party as a result of the negligent operation of a motor vehicle by the adult guest when such negligence is caused by the intoxication. We impose this duty on the host to the third party because we believe that the policy considerations served by its imposition far outweigh those asserted in opposition. While we recognize the concern that our ruling will interfere with accepted standards of social behavior; will intrude on and somewhat diminish the enjoyment, relaxation, and camaraderie that accompany social gatherings at which alcohol is served; and that such gatherings and social relationships are not simply tangential benefits of a civilized society but are regarded by many as important, we believe that the added assurance of just compensation to the victims of drunken driving as well as the added deterrent effect of the rule on such driving outweigh the importance of those other values. * * * We therefore reverse the [summary] judgment in favor of the defendants Zak and remand the case. * * *

Garibaldi (dissenting). * * * The majority need not parade the horrors that have been caused by drunk drivers to convince me that there is always room for stricter measures against intoxicated drivers. I too am concerned for the injured victim of a drunken driver. However, the almost limitless implications of the majority's decision lead me to conclude that the Legislature is better equipped to effectuate the goals of reducing injuries from drunken driving and protecting the interests of the injured party, without placing such a grave burden on the average citizen of this state. * * *

My reluctance to join the majority is not based on any exaggerated notion of judicial deference to the Legislature. Rather, it is based on my belief that before this Court plunges into this broad area of liability and imposes high duties of care on social hosts, it should carefully consider the ramifications of its actions. * * *

[T]his Court has, in the past, imposed civil liability on commercial licensees who serve alcoholic beverages to intoxicated patrons. Commercial licensees are subject to regulation by both the Alcoholic Beverage Commission (ABC) and the Legislature. It is reasonable to impose tort liability on licensees based on their violation of explicit statutes and regulations.

I have no quarrel with the imposition of such liability because of the peculiar position occupied by the licensee. A social host, however, is in a different position. * * *

A significant difference between an average citizen and a commercial licensee is the average citizen's lack of knowledge and expertise in determining levels and degrees of intoxication. Licensed commercial providers, unlike the average citizen, deal with the alcohol-consuming public every day. This experience gives them some expertise with respect to intoxication that social hosts lack. A social host will find it more difficult to determine levels and degrees of intoxication. * * *

The nature of home entertaining compounds the social host's difficulty in determining whether a guest is obviously intoxicated before serving the next drink. In a commercial establishment, there is greater control over the liquor; a bartender or waitress must serve the patron a drink. Not so in a home when entertaining a guest. At a social gathering, for example, guests frequently serve themselves or guests may serve other guests. Normally, the host is so busy entertaining he does not have time to analyze the state of intoxication of the guests. * * * Furthermore, the commercial bartender usually does not drink on the job. The social host often drinks with the guest, as the Zaks did here. * * *

Further, it is not clear from the Court's opinion to what lengths a social host must go to avoid liability. Is the host obligated to use physical force to restrain an intoxicated guest from drinking and then from driving? Or is the host limited to delay and subterfuge tactics short of physical force? What is the result when the host tries to restrain the guest but fails? Is the host still liable? The majority opinion is silent on the extent to which we must police our guests.

The most significant difference between a social host and a commercial licensee, however, is the social host's inability to spread the cost of liability. The commercial establishment spreads the cost of insurance against liability among its customers. The social host must bear the entire cost alone. * * *

[The social host] may not have sufficient insurance to cover the limitless liability that the Court seeks to impose. These people may lose everything they own if they are found liable as negligent social hosts under the Court's scheme. The individual economic cost to every New Jersey citizen should be weighed before today's result is reached. * * *

NOTES AND QUESTIONS

1. The New Jersey legislature later modified the decision by statute to limit liability in several ways. Under the statute, liability extends only to third parties (i.e., not the intoxicated person); there is an irrebuttable presumption that anyone whose blood alcohol level tested at less than 0.10% was not visibly intoxicated and a rebuttable presumption that anyone whose blood alcohol level is between 0.10% and 0.15% was not visibly intoxicated; and the social host is not jointly and severally liable, which means the social host would pay only a portion of the judgment, even if the driver is insolvent.

2. The traditional common law view was that the drinker's voluntary consumption was the sole "proximate" cause of the third party's injury and that a person who sold or gave liquor to an intoxicated adult drinker was not liable for subsequent injuries caused by his intoxication. A seminal decision is Cruse v. Aden, 127 Ill. 231, 20 N.E. 73 (1889) where a wife filed suit against her husband's friend

for giving her husband two drinks while he was a guest at the friend's house. While returning home on horseback, the husband was thrown from the horse and died. The Illinois Supreme Court refused to impose liability, finding no cause of action for giving "a glass of intoxicating liquor to a friend as a mere act of courtesy and politeness." Illinois recently reaffirmed this decision, holding that for "over one century, this court has spoken with a single voice to the effect that no social host liability exists in Illinois." Charles v. Seigfried, 165 Ill.2d 482, 651 N.E.2d 154 (1995). See also Ferreira v. Strack, 652 A.2d 965 (R.I.1995). Almost all state supreme courts ruling on this issue have declined to impose liability on a social host when the recipient of the alcohol is an adult. See, e.g., Klein v. Raysinger, 504 Pa. 141, 470 A.2d 507, 510 (1983) ("Thus, the great weight of authority supports the view that in the case of an ordinary able-bodied man it is the consumption of the alcohol, rather than the furnishing of the alcohol, which is the proximate cause of any subsequent occurrence").

3. Why no liability? Could the social hosts argue that the consequences of their serving alcohol was not foreseeable? "The paucity of cases in this country imposing social host liability cannot be explained solely on the ground that a social host does not, as a matter of law, create a reasonably foreseeable risk of harm to highway travelers in serving an alcoholic drink to a drunken guest. The risk created by serving liquor to an intoxicated person who is about to operate a motor vehicle is far too apparent to permit the conclusion that the social host's act could not have been the 'proximate' cause of a third person's injury. The reluctance of courts to impose liability in these circumstances has been founded, rightly or wrongly, on policy considerations, particularly consideration of the effect that a rule of social host liability would have on a multitude of personal relationships in a variety of social settings." McGuiggan v. New England Telephone & Telegraph Co., 398 Mass. 152, 496 N.E.2d 141, 145 (1986).

4. New Hampshire, however, imposes liability if the social host's service of alcohol was reckless. Hickingbotham v. Burke, 140 N.H. 28, 662 A.2d 297 (1995) (expressed as highly unreasonable conduct, involving an extreme departure from ordinary care, in a situation where a high degree of danger is apparent). In dicta, Massachusetts has hinted it would impose liability under the appropriate circumstances. McGuiggan v. New England Telephone & Telegraph Co., 398 Mass. 152, 496 N.E.2d 141 (1986) (no liability in this case because no evidence that guest was obviously intoxicated).

5. In contrast to almost universal rejection of social host liability for serving adult guests, many jurisdictions have imposed liability on those who serve alcohol to minors. See Wiener v. Gamma Phi Chapter of Alpha Tau Omega Fraternity, 258 Or. 632, 485 P.2d 18 (1971) (fraternity found negligent for serving beer to minor who subsequently injured third party in automobile accident); Congini by Congini v. Portersville Valve Co., 504 Pa. 157, 470 A.2d 515 (1983); cf. Sutter v. Hutchings, 254 Ga. 194, 327 S.E.2d 716 (1985) (defendant mother who purchased keg of beer for consumption at party for high school friends of defendant daughter, may be liable to estate of driver who was killed by minor party guest who ran a red light leaving party); Hansen v. Friend, 118 Wash.2d 476, 824 P.2d 483 (1992) (two adult companions held liable to estate of minor who drowned while intoxicated after defendants had provided minor with alcohol on overnight fishing trip). But see Smith v. Merritt, 940 S.W.2d 602 (Tex.1997) and Charles v. Seigfried, 165 Ill.2d 482, 651 N.E.2d 154 (1995) (both declining to impose liability even where guest is minor). Why are courts more willing to impose liability when a minor is involved? What if the social host is also a minor? Kapres v. Heller, 536 Pa. 551, 640 A.2d 888 (1994) (declining to impose liability on social host who is a minor).

6. _Commercial Dispensers of Liquor._ A legislative response to early common law liability insulation of commercially licensed vendors was the Dram Shop Act. These acts generally provided a civil cause of action (as well as criminal sanctions) against furnishers of alcohol for damages resulting from a consumer's intoxicated state. In addition, states that have repealed or are otherwise without a Dram Shop Act have enacted alcohol-beverage control laws, the violation of which will usually constitute negligence per se, as it did in the case of Stachniewicz v. Mar–Cam Corp., 259 Or. 583, 488 P.2d 436 (1971), page 202. It is clear that licensed vendors' supplying of liquor to patrons has become widely recognized as a proximate cause of injuries attributable to intoxicated persons. See Ontiveros v. Borak, 136 Ariz. 500, 667 P.2d 200 (1983). But see Ling v. Jan's Liquors, 237 Kan. 629, 703 P.2d 731 (1985) (listing twelve jurisdictions that do not recognize such liability.) Courts have consistently been unwilling to extend liability on these grounds to a social host. What are the policy considerations and tort law principles differentiating a licensee and a social host? See Page, The Law of Premises Liability § 12.2–24 (2d ed. 1988 & Supp. 1994).

7. _Employers._ Some courts also have imposed liability on employers where employees became intoxicated at work or at a work-related social event and then injured someone while driving intoxicated. See, e.g., Dickinson v. Edwards, 105 Wash.2d 457, 716 P.2d 814 (1986) (alcohol served at employer-sponsored "banquet"); Otis Engineering Corp. v. Clark, 668 S.W.2d 307 (Tex.1983) (employee sent home because discovered by supervisor to be intoxicated at work); Slade v. Smith's Management Corp., 119 Idaho 482, 808 P.2d 401 (1991) (employee struck and killed pedestrian on way home from company party). But see, Overbaugh v. McCutcheon, 183 W.Va. 386, 396 S.E.2d 153 (1990) (no liability for employer of driver who struck another car on way home from office Christmas party) and Johnston v. KFC National Management Co., 71 Haw. 229, 788 P.2d 159, 162 (1990) (employee injured someone after office Christmas party, "we find no clear judicial trend toward modifying the traditional common law, nor any statutory enactment or policy which leads this court to conclude that a change in the common law is appropriate at this time.")

8. _Entrustment._ A car owner lends his vehicle to a person who is obviously intoxicated. The driver negligently runs into plaintiff. Should the owner be liable? See Deck v. Sherlock, 162 Neb. 86, 75 N.W.2d 99 (1956). K–Mart sells a gun to a visibly intoxicated person who shoots the plaintiff. Should K–Mart be liable? Kitchen v. K–Mart, 697 So.2d 1200 (Fla.1997). Suppose the bailee is not intoxicated at the time but is a known alcoholic. See Powell v. Langford, 58 Ariz. 281, 119 P.2d 230 (1941). What if a borrower returns the car to its intoxicated owner? See Lombardo v. Hoag, 237 N.J.Super. 87, 566 A.2d 1185 (1989). Should it make any difference that the automobile is given outright rather than loaned? Estes v. Gibson, 257 S.W.2d 604 (Ky.1953). What if the defendant loaned money to her grandson to buy a car knowing that he had a drinking problem? What if the car dealer from whom the grandson purchased the car was also aware of the problem? Cf. Vince v. Wilson, 151 Vt. 425, 561 A.2d 103 (1989). Many courts have recognized the analogy between negligent sale of alcohol and the tort of negligent entrustment. See Buchanan v. Merger Enterprises, Inc., 463 So.2d 121, 126 (Ala.1984).

➤Enright v. Eli Lilly & Co.

Court of Appeals of New York, 1991.
77 N.Y.2d 377, 570 N.E.2d 198, 568 N.Y.S.2d 550.

[Plaintiff Karen Enright's grandmother ingested DES as a miscarriage preventive during a pregnancy that resulted in the birth of plaintiff

Patricia Enright in 1960. Plaintiff Patricia Enright alleges that she developed abnormalities of her reproductive system due to her in utero exposure to DES and that these abnormalities resulted in several miscarriages and the premature birth of plaintiff Karen Enright. Karen suffers from cerebral palsy and other disabilities that plaintiffs attribute to her premature birth and thus to her grandmother's ingestion of DES. Karen Enright's claims were dismissed by the trial court and she appealed. The appellate division affirmed the dismissal of the causes of action based on negligence, breach of warranty and fraud, but reinstated the strict liability count, holding that the strong public policy in favor of providing a remedy for DES victims justified recognizing a strict products liability cause of action. Patricia Enright's claim for her own injuries and her husband's derivative claim for loss of consortium were not affected by the trial court's ruling and were still pending.

WACHTLER, CHIEF JUDGE. * * *

The tragic DES tale is well documented in this Court's decisions and need not be recounted here (see, e.g., Hymowitz v. Lilly & Co., supra; Bichler v. Lilly & Co., 55 N.Y.2d 571, 450 N.Y.S.2d 776, 436 N.E.2d 182). It is sufficient to note that between 1947 and 1971, the drug, a synthetic estrogen-like substance produced by approximately 300 manufacturers, was prescribed for use and ingested by millions of pregnant women to prevent miscarriages. In 1971, the Food and Drug Administration banned the drug's use for the treatment of problems of pregnancy after studies established a link between in utero exposure to DES and the occurrence in teen-age women of a rare form of vaginal and cervical cancer. Plaintiffs allege that in utero exposure to DES has since been linked to other genital tract aberrations in DES daughters, including malformations or immaturity of the uterus, cervical abnormalities, misshapen Fallopian tubes and abnormal cell and tissue growth, all of which has caused in this population a marked increase in the incidence of infertility, miscarriages, premature births and ectopic pregnancies.

The Legislature and this Court have both expressed concern for the victims of this tragedy by removing legal barriers to their tort recovery—barriers which may have had their place in other contexts, but which in DES litigation worked a peculiar injustice because of the ways in which DES was developed, marketed and sold and because of the insidious nature of its harm.

For example, prior to 1986, the long-standing rule in this State was that a cause of action for personal injuries caused by a toxic substance accrued and the limitations period began to run upon exposure to the substance [c]. The Legislature, recognizing that under this rule claims for injuries caused by exposure to DES and other toxic substances were often time barred before the harmful effects of the exposure could be discovered, changed the law to provide that the limitations period in exposure cases begins to run upon discovery of the injury [c]. At the same time, the Legislature revived for one year previously time-barred causes of action based on exposure to DES and four other toxic substances [c].

More recently, this Court responded to the fact that—for a variety of reasons unique to the DES litigation context—a DES plaintiff generally finds it impossible to identify the manufacturer of the drug that caused her injuries. We held that liability could be imposed upon DES manufacturers in accordance with their share of the national DES market, notwithstanding the plaintiff's inability to identify the manufacturer particularly at fault for her injuries [c].

In the present case, we are asked to do something significantly different. We are asked, not to remove some barrier to recovery that presents unique problems in DES cases, but to recognize a cause of action not available in other contexts simply (or at least largely) because this is a DES case.

In Albala v. City of New York, 54 N.Y.2d 269, 271, 445 N.Y.S.2d 108, 429 N.E.2d 786, *supra,* we were presented with the question "whether a cause of action lies in favor of a child for injuries suffered as a result of a preconception tort committed against the mother". There, the mother suffered a perforated uterus during the course of an abortion. Four years later, she gave birth to a brain-damaged child, whose injuries were allegedly attributable to the defendants' negligence in perforating the mother's uterus. We declined, as a matter of policy, to recognize a cause of action on behalf of the child, believing that to do so would "require the extension of traditional tort concepts beyond manageable bounds" [c]. Among other things, we were concerned with "the staggering implications of any proposition which would honor claims assuming the breach of an identifiable duty for less than a perfect birth" and the difficulty, if such a cause of action were recognized, of confining liability by other than artificial and arbitrary boundaries [c].

The case now before us differs from *Albala* only in that the mother's injuries in this case were caused by exposure to DES instead of by medical malpractice. A different rule is justified, therefore, only if that distinction alters the policy balance we struck in *Albala.*

The primary thrust of plaintiffs' argument and the Appellate Division's decision is that DES itself alters that balance. From the Legislature's actions in modifying the applicable Statute of Limitations and reviving time-barred DES cases and from our adoption of a market-share liability theory in *Hymowitz,* plaintiffs perceive a public policy favoring a remedy for DES-caused injuries sufficient to overcome the countervailing policy considerations we identified in *Albala.* The implication, of course, is that the public interest in providing a remedy for those injured by DES is stronger than the public interest in providing a remedy for those injured by other means—medical malpractice, for example. We do not believe that such a preference has been established.

To be sure, recent developments demonstrate legislative and judicial solicitude for the victims of DES, but they do not establish DES plaintiffs as a favored class for whose benefit all traditional limitations on tort liability must give way. To the extent that special rules have been fashioned, they are a response to unique procedural barriers and problems of proof peculiar to DES litigation. * * * [The Court discusses the public policy rationale for the change in the statute of limitations and in the adoption of market share liability.]

In the present case, however, neither plaintiffs, the Appellate Division, nor the dissent has identified any unique feature of DES litigation that justifies the novel proposition they advance—recognition of a multigenerational cause of action that we have refused to recognize in any other context. The fact that this is a DES case does not by itself justify a departure from the *Albala* rule.

Closer to the mark, though still falling short, is plaintiffs' second argument. They note that *Albala* was a negligence case and that we left open the question whether a different result might obtain under a strict products liability theory, because of the potentially different policy considerations in such a case [c]. Having now examined the question in the context of this particular strict products liability claim, we find no basis for reaching a different conclusion than we did in *Albala*.

On one hand, weighing somewhat more heavily in favor of recovery in a strict products liability action than in ordinary negligence actions is the policy of diverting the burden of product-caused injuries from the innocent victim to the manufacturer. The product manufacturer is generally in a better position than an individual tort-feasor to distribute this burden by passing the costs along to customers in the cost of the product. This is one justification offered for holding manufacturers of defective products strictly liable for injury caused by their products without regard to privity, foreseeability or due care [c].

Of course, imposing liability on the manufacturer in such circumstances also serves to encourage the development of safer products [c], but this rationale is not a distinctive feature of strict products liability theory, since imposition of liability on a negligent tort-feasor is also based in part on a policy of deterrence [c]. This factor, therefore, does not appear to add anything new to the mix of policy considerations that was not also present in *Albala*. We recognize, however, that a widely distributed product, if defective, presents a risk to a broad range of potential victims. For that reason, although the need for deterrence is not unique to the products liability context, it may have added weight there.

Despite these considerations, the countervailing ones remain strong enough to preclude us from recognizing a cause of action here. To begin, the concerns we identified in *Albala* are present in equal measure here. The nature of the plaintiffs' injuries in both cases—birth defects—and their cause—harm to the mothers' reproductive systems before the children were conceived—are indistinguishable for these purposes. They raise the same vexing questions with the same "staggering implications" [c]. As in *Albala*, the cause of action plaintiffs ask us to recognize here could not be confined without the drawing of artificial and arbitrary boundaries. For all we know, the rippling effects of DES exposure may extend for generations. It is our duty to confine liability within manageable limits (see, Tobin v. Grossman, 24 N.Y.2d 609, 619, 301 N.Y.S.2d 554, 249 N.E.2d 419; Prosser, Palsgraf

Revisited, 52 Mich.L.Rev. 1, 27). Limiting liability to those who ingested [*solution*] the drug or were exposed to it in utero serves this purpose.

At the same time, limiting liability in this fashion does not unduly impair the deterrent purposes of tort liability. The manufacturers remain amenable to suit by all those injured by exposure to their product, a class whose size is commensurate with the risk created. In addition, we note that the tort system is not the only means of encouraging prescription drug safety; the Federal Food and Drug Administration has primary responsibility for that task (*see,* Note, A Question of Competence: The Judicial Role in the Regulation of Pharmaceuticals, 103 Harv.L.Rev. 773). We do not suggest, as some have (*see, id.*), that for this reason the judicial system should abandon its traditional role. But in light of the FDA's responsibility in this area, the need for the tort system to promote prescription drug safety is at least diminished.

That the product involved here is a prescription drug raises other considerations as well. First, as in most prescription drug cases (*see,* Vinson & Slaughter, Products Liability: Pharmaceutical Drug Cases, at 123–140), liability here is predicated on a failure to warn of dangers of which the manufacturers knew or with adequate testing should have known. Such a claim, though it may be couched in terms of strict liability, is indistinguishable from a negligence claim [c]. Concepts of reasonable care and foreseeability are not divorced from this theory of liability, as they may be under other strict products liability predicates. Thus, the effort to distinguish this case from *Albala* is strained.

More important, however, is recognition that public policy favors the availability of prescription drugs even though most carry some risks (see, Brown v. Superior Ct., 44 Cal.3d 1049, 245 Cal.Rptr. 412, 751 P.2d 470, 478–479; Restatement [Second] of Torts § 402A, comment *k;* [c]. That is not to say that drug manufacturers should enjoy immunity from liability stemming from their failure to conduct adequate research and testing prior to the marketing of their products. They do not enjoy such immunity, as evidenced by our recognition of liability in favor of those who have been injured by ingestion or in utero exposure to DES. But we are aware of the dangers of overdeterrence—the possibility that research will be discouraged or beneficial drugs withheld from the market. These dangers are magnified in this context, where we are asked to recognize a legal duty toward generations not yet conceived.

The dissent would have us believe that this case involves nothing but application of straightforward strict products liability doctrine. But this case is fundamentally different in the same way that *Albala* was fundamentally different from other negligence cases. In neither this case nor *Albala* was the infant plaintiff exposed to the defendants' dangerous product or negligent conduct; rather, both were injured as a consequence of injuries to the reproductive systems of their mothers. * * *

In sum, the distinctions between this case and *Albala* provide no basis for a departure from the rule that an injury to a mother which results in injuries to a later-conceived child does not establish a cause of action in favor of the child against the original tort-feasor. For this reason, we decline to recognize a cause of action on behalf of plaintiff Karen Enright.

Holding

* * *

NOTES AND QUESTIONS

1.   Note that the appellate court had found that proximate cause would extend further in a strict liability action than in an negligence action. Should there be such a distinction? See Chapters 14 and 15.

2.   In a comparable case, Ohio also found no liability because of the remoteness in time and causation. Grover v. Eli Lilly & Co., 63 Ohio St. 3d 756, 591 N.E.2d 696 (1992).

3.   The day after he performed surgery on a twelve-year-old girl, doctor learned that the blood with which she was transfused was contaminated with HIV antibodies. He did not tell her or her parents until she was seventeen and was diagnosed with AIDS. In the meantime, she had infected her boyfriend. He sued physician for failing to inform the patient or her parents of the exposure, the risk that she might develop AIDS, and the risk to her sexual partners. Is the boyfriend a foreseeable plaintiff? See Reisner v. UCLA, 37 Cal.Rptr.2d 518, 31 Cal.App.4th 1195 (1995) (appellate court reversed judgment on the pleadings, allowing boyfriend's case to proceed). What if he infected someone else before he found out? What if the woman he infected had a baby with AIDS?

4.   A drug company failed to warn physicians of possible risks associated with prescribing a drug for children under particular circumstances. Child suffered permanent damage after taking drug. Parents sued pediatrician and drug company. Can pediatrician recover for his pain and suffering caused by knowing the child was injured by the drug he prescribed and by the litigation itself? Cf. Washington State Physicians Ins. Exch. & Assn., 122 Wash.2d 299, 858 P.2d 1954 (1993) (drug company argued that physician's damages were too remote; case decided on narrower grounds).

5.   Plaintiff is wounded by gunmen who also killed his father. He learned the gunmen had been hired by a business associate of his father's through a "Gun for Hire" ad in a magazine for mercenaries. Plaintiff seeks compensation for his gunshot wounds and, along with his brother, for the wrongful death of his father from the publisher of the magazine, claiming that the publisher should have foreseen that the ad would result in violent criminal activity. How might plaintiffs prove that the result was foreseeable to the publisher? How far should courts go in imposing liability? Compare Braun v. Soldier of Fortune Magazine, Inc., 968 F.2d 1110 (11th Cir.1992), cert. denied, 506 U.S. 1071 (1993) (upholding liability) and Eimann v. Soldier of Fortune Magazine, 880 F.2d 830 (5th Cir.1989), cert. denied, 493 U.S. 1024 (1990) (denying liability). Soldier of Fortune magazine has stopped accepting personal ads and narrowly avoided bankruptcy in the wake of the *Braun* case. How far should the courts go to protect the First Amendment rights of the publisher?

6.   James Perry brutally murdered an eight-year-old quadriplegic, his mother, and his private duty nurse. Perry had been hired by the boy's father who was after the $2 million that his son had received in settlement for the injuries that had left him paralyzed for life. In negotiating with the father, planning the murders, and executing them, Perry had followed the detailed instructions and advice of the book

Hit Man: A Technical Manual for Independent Contractors, published by Paladin Enterprises. Is Paladin a proximate cause of the deaths? Should the First Amendment preclude liability? Rice v. Paladin Enterprises, Inc., 128 F.3d 233 (4th Cir.1997).

7. Defendants went on a shooting spree, during which they killed someone and seriously injured plaintiff, a clerk in a convenience store. Plaintiff's complaint alleges that the killers were trying to emulate characters in the movie *Natural Born Killers*, which they watched repeatedly on videotape, sometimes under the influence of mind-altering drugs. Warner Brothers and Oliver Stone also are among the defendants named. Plaintiff claims they used violent imagery that was intended to cause its viewers to imitate it. If plaintiff can prove her allegations, should Warner Brothers and Oliver Stone be liable? Byers v. Edmonson, 712 So.2d 681 (La.App. 1998).

BY WAY OF SYNTHESIS

The problem involved in the cases in this chapter is whether defendant's liability to plaintiff should be cut off even though the defendant's conduct was both negligent and a factual cause of the plaintiff's injury. Is there a system by which this problem can be handled and a test by which to make the determination?

1. It may first be suggested that the problem can be raised and treated by the court in connection with any one of the four elements of a negligence case—duty, breach of duty, causation or damage. The duty approach, for example, is espoused in the majority opinion in *Palsgraf* and is rather frequently used in cases of the unforeseeable plaintiff. Certain types of damage may be held not to be the basis of recovery. Negligence may be held not to be directed to the plaintiff. But most courts have treated the question in the causation element.

The problem is a difficult one, but the length of the treatment in this casebook and the amount of time allotted it in most courses may perhaps give an exaggerated impression of its importance. In the great majority of negligence cases, the problem does not arise at all; it comes up only in the fraction of negligence actions that involve unusual fact situations. How is it to be handled when it does arise?

There are many legal tests that have been devised by the courts and legal scholars—some rather precise and almost mechanical and some very broad and general. The more precise ones give an illusion of certainty. As a matter of fact, almost every jurisdiction has two distinct and apparently unrelated lines of authority—one with a broad scope of liability and the other with a narrow scope. They do not help the court especially to reach a decision on a case before it, but they do help substantially in explaining the decision after it has been reached.

This is not a situation, however, in which precision and certainty are essential. Neither party to the action engaged in his conduct in reliance upon a "rule" of proximate cause. The principal task of the court is to do justice as between these parties in their present situation. For this purpose, a weighing, evaluative process is required, rather than a clear-cut rule of law. This suggests the use of a standard similar to the one for determining whether a person was negligent (what a reasonable, prudent person would do under the same or similar circumstances). A standard allows the taking into consideration of competing factors or policy elements. Often these policy elements are not articulated or brought out into the open. For an analysis of some of them, see L. Green, Judge and Jury, Ch. 4, 5 (1930).

2.   There are two general approaches to the problem of proximate cause—the hindsight, or direct-causation, approach and the foreseeability approach. Practically every jurisdiction has used both, at one time or another. In many instances they would be likely to produce the same result, but not always. In theory the foresight approach would produce a smaller ambit of liability.

But foreseeability is an accordion concept, depending upon the detail and precision with which foresight is required. Many torts teachers have found it helpful to express foreseeability in terms of the risk idea. "This position has been justified as more rational, since the factors which define negligence should also limit liability for negligence; as easier to administer, since it fixes the nearest thing to a definite boundary of liability which is possible; and more just, since negligence may consist of only a slight deviation from the community standard of conduct, and even be free from all moral blame, while its consequences may be catastrophic, and out of all proportion to the fault." Prosser and Keeton, Torts 282 (5th ed. 1984), citing Pollock, Liability for Consequences, 38 Law Q.Rev. 165 (1922); Goodhart, The Unforeseeable Consequences of a Negligent Act, 38 Yale L.J. 449 (1930); Seavey, Mr. Justice Cardozo and the Law of Torts, 52 Harv. L.Rev. 372 (1939), 48 Yale L.J. 390 (1939), 39 Colum.L.Rev. 20 (1939); Foster, Grant and Green, The Risk Theory and Proximate Cause, 32 Neb.L.Rev. 72 (1952); Wilson, Some Thoughts About Negligence, 2 Okla. L.Rev. 275 (1949); R. Keeton, Legal Cause in the Law of Torts (1963).

There is much force in these arguments, but they suggest far more in the way of certainty and precision than the test warrants. Consider a single illustration, adapted from Judge Magruder's opinion in Marshall v. Nugent, 222 F.2d 604 (1st Cir.1955).

Suppose that a truck is driven at excessive speed. It is relatively easy to say that the total risk, made up of the aggregate of all of the possibilities of harm, whether they are very probable or fantastic, is so great that the reasonable man of ordinary prudence would not do this, and therefore the driver is negligent. How easy is it, by a process of fragmentation of the risk, to separate out particular consequences and intervening factors, and to say that they are, or are not, significant parts of the original total foreseeable risk? Is it "foreseeable," in any sense that the reasonable driver could have the possibility in mind, and so take precautions against it, that

(a) The driver will hit another car and kill someone?

(b) The car with which he collides will be thrown out of control, and hit a third car, or even a fourth? Springer v. Pacific Fruit Exchange, 92 Cal.App. 732, 268 P. 951 (1928).

McCoy, danger invites rescue

(c) He will endanger a child in the street, and a person who tries to rescue her will sustain a broken arm? Wagner v. International R. Co., note 2, page 335.

(d) The truck will narrowly miss a pregnant woman, who will be frightened into a miscarriage? Cf. Mitnick v. Whalen Bros., 115 Conn. 650, 163 A. 414 (1932).

negligent infliction of emotional distress

(e) He will hit a pedestrian, who will be left helpless in the street, and be run over by another car? Bunda v. Hardwick, 376 Mich. 640, 138 N.W.2d 305 (1965).

(f) He will cause a collision, which will leave wrecked cars blocking the highway, and another driver will run into the wreckage? Holmberg v. Villaume, 158 Minn. 442, 197 N.W. 849 (1924).

(g) He will hit a pedestrian, and while the pedestrian is unconscious, his watch will be stolen? Cf. Brauer v. New York Central R. Co., 91 N.J.L. 190, 103 A. 166 (1918).

take the plaintiff as you find him

(h) The person he injures will contract pneumonia because of his weakened condition, and die of it? Wallace v. Ludwig, page 337, 198 N.E. 159, note 12.

(i) The injured person may suffer a second accident six months later while he is walking on crutches? Squires v. Reynolds, page 338, note 12, 5 A.2d 877.

if reasonable people differ, send it to the jury

(j) The person he injures will receive negligent medical treatment, and die or be further injured because of it? Jess Edwards, Inc. v. Goergen, page 337, note 11.

(k) The truck will knock a car up against a stone wall. The wall is weakened and, as a result, a stone falls off the top a day later and injures a pedestrian. Cf. In re Guardian Casualty Co., 253 App.Div. 360, 2 N.Y.S.2d 232 (1938).

All of these things have happened and there have been holdings that each was "proximate." Is it perhaps overloading the risk concept to make it the basis for determining each of these situations?

Like the purpose-of-the-statute test (see note 3, page 205), from which it is derived, the risk test often approaches a begging of the question. One decides how broadly or narrowly to express the purpose of the criminal statute or the scope of the risk of an act of common law negligence with an awareness of what the result of that decision will be and with the decision perhaps influenced by it.

And yet, despite all of these difficulties, the risk approach, viewed entirely as an approach rather than as a definitive test, can be very helpful. It poses the problem in a way that can help to direct the line of thought of the decision-maker. If the idea is expressed in terms of a reasonably close relation between the harm threatened (or the risk created) and the injury incurred, then it is put in the form of a standard instead of a rule, and the need to exercise discretion in its application is made apparent. See Prosser, Selected Topics on the Law of Torts, 191, 233, 242 (1954); Wade, Book Review, 8 Vand.L.Rev. 657, 660–663 (1955).

3.   For an interesting case in which the court expressly used the risk approach, see Hill v. Lundin & Associates, Inc., 260 La. 542, 256 So.2d 620 (1972), where defendant contractor left an aluminum ladder standing against the side of a house after making emergency repairs following a hurricane, an unidentified third person moved it to the ground in the back yard, and plaintiff tripped over it in rushing to protect a small child from the ladder. Said the court, in part:

* * * "The same policy considerations which would motivate a legislative body to impose duties to protect from certain risks are applied by the court in making its determination. 'All rules of conduct, irrespective of whether they are the product of a legislature or are a part of the fabric of the court-made law of negligence, exist for purposes. They are designed to protect *some* persons under *some* circumstances against *some* risks. Seldom does a rule protect every victim against every risk that may befall him, merely because it is shown that the violation of the rule played a part in producing the injury. The task of defining the proper reach or thrust of a rule in its policy aspects is one that must be undertaken by the court in each case as it arises. How appropriate is the rule to the facts of this controversy? This is a question that the court cannot escape.' Malone, Ruminations on Cause–In–Fact, 9 Stanford L.Rev. 60, 73 (1956).

"This defendant's alleged misconduct, its alleged breach of duty was in leaving the ladder leaning against the house unattended. The risk encountered by the plaintiff which caused her harm was the ladder lying on the ground where it was placed by another, over which she tripped as she moved to protect the child. The record is devoid of any evidence tending to establish that the defendant could have reasonably anticipated that a third person would move the ladder and put it in the position which created this risk, or that such a 'naked possibility' was an unreasonable risk of harm. [C]

"A rule of law which would impose a duty upon one not to leave a ladder standing against a house does not encompass the risk here encountered. We are of the opinion that the defendant was under no duty to protect this plaintiff from the risk which gave rise to her injuries. The plaintiff has failed to establish legal and actionable negligence on the part of the defendant." 256 So.2d at 623.

What was the risk created by the defendant's conduct? Is the court responding to this by defining "the risk encountered by the plaintiff"? Might the risk have been defined broadly enough to cover the plaintiff's injury? How would the case be decided under the hindsight approach? By talking in terms of a superseding cause? Was the defendant negligent here? Is that the major issue?

4. From the consideration of the cases in this chapter, you should have obtained a "feel" for the problem, so that it is possible to tell promptly whether the answer is clear or so difficult that litigation may be warranted. You are not expected to be sure of the answer for all cases, but you should identify fact patterns in which application of the principles of proximate cause have become fairly well crystallized—for example, the thin-skull and rescue situations.

You should have become acquainted with the various legal tests and their ramifications and be able (1) to use or respond to them in argument, (2) to present a lucid and logical legal argument for a particular result, and (3) to utilize or respond to such modifying adjectives for the word "cause" as active, efficient, natural and probable, foreseeable or unforeseeable, proximate, nearest and superseding and such terms as risk, unbroken sequence, just or expedient result, or dependent or independent intervening cause.

You ought to know how to argue the facts as well as the law. A few illustrations may be helpful in this regard. In Hines v. Morrow, 236 S.W. 183 (Tex.Civ.App.1921), defendant negligently left a mudhole in a highway. A's car drove into it and got stuck. B, a man with a wooden leg, attempted to pull A's car out of the mud with a tow rope. His wooden leg got stuck in the mud, and in order to extricate himself B took hold of the tail gate of the tow truck. As the truck moved, a loop in the tow rope lassoed his good leg and broke it. Clarence Morris in Proximate Cause in Minnesota, 34 Minn.L.Rev. 185 (1950), attributes the "peg leg" decision in the *Hines* case to the summary of the facts in plaintiff's brief, as follows: "The case stated in briefest form, is simply this: Appellee was on the highway, using it in a lawful manner, and slipped into this hole, created by appellant's negligence, and was injured in attempting to extricate himself."

If the plaintiff had used the same approach in stating the issue in Koehler v. Waukesha Milk Co., 190 Wis. 52, 208 N.W. 901 (1926), he would have said that the defendant left a glass milk bottle on the plaintiff's doorstep with a slight chip near the top, and the decedent perished as a result—with the consequence that he would probably have lost the case. Instead, he explained that the decedent had picked the bottle up and scratched a finger. The scratch had become infected, the infection had gone into blood poisoning (before the advent of penicillin) and the decedent died.

5. If a trial court decides "as a matter of law" that the defendant's conduct was not a proximate cause of the plaintiff's injury, it dismisses the complaint, grants summary judgment, or directs a verdict for the defendant. This has happened in many of the cases in this chapter. If there is an issue of proximate cause in the case and the trial court decides to let it go to the jury, it must instruct the jury as to the nature of the problem that it is to decide. What does the court say? There is no consensus. Model instructions from two different states illustrate the variety.

Arkansas. Model Jury Instructions (1989). AMI 501. "When I use the expression 'proximate cause,' I mean a cause which, in a natural and continuous sequence, produces damage and without which the damage would not have occurred."

"[This does not mean that the law recognizes only one proximate cause of damage. To the contrary, if two or more causes work together to produce damage, then you may find that each of them was a proximate cause.]"

AMI 503. "_____ contends and has the burden of proving that following any act or omission on his part, an event intervened which in itself caused any damage completely independent of his conduct. If you so find, then his act or omission was not a proximate cause of any damage resulting from the intervening event."

Texas Pattern Jury Charges. 2.4. "Proximate cause means that cause which, in a natural and continuous sequence, produces an event, and without which cause such event would not have occurred. In order to be a proximate cause, the act or omission complained of must be such that a person using ordinary care would have foreseen the event, or some similar event, which might reasonably result therefrom. There may be more than one proximate cause of an event."

Are these instructions meaningful to the average jury? Is that necessary? Would they do as the test for the court to apply? Would they produce the same result in such cases as _Palsgraf,_ Derdiarian v. Felix Contracting Co. and Fuller v. Preis? Is it better for them to be complex and accurate, or simple and understandable? Do they suggest that the court should be more ready to decide the case itself or turn it over to the jury? See Mikell, Jury Instructions and Proximate Cause: An Uncertain Trumpet in Georgia, 27 Ga. St.B.J. 60 (1990) for a discussion of several empirical studies concerning the jury's understanding of the instruction on proximate cause.

4. SHIFTING RESPONSIBILITY

Usually, when the defendant has negligently created a risk of harm to the plaintiff, the failure of a third person to intervene and take some action to prevent the risk from being realized, that is, to prevent the harm, will not affect the liability of the defendant when the harm in fact occurs. If, for example, the defendant negligently sets a grass fire that is burning toward the plaintiff's building, the failure of someone else to put out the fire does not relieve the defendant. Wiley v. West Jersey R. Co., 44 N.J.L. 247 (1882). The fact that the third person was under a duty to the plaintiff to extinguish the fire, and would be liable to the plaintiff for his failure to do so, makes no difference to the defendant's liability.

Thus in Diehl v. Fidelity Philadelphia Trust Co., 159 Pa.Super. 513, 49 A.2d 190 (1946), the defendant Metropolitan negligently discharged steam onto the sidewalk in front of a building owned by Fidelity. The steam condensed and froze, forming a coating of invisible ice on the pavement. With notice of the situation, Fidelity failed to clean off the ice although it was under a duty to do so. Plaintiff, a pedestrian, slipped on the ice, fell, and was injured. It was held that the failure of Fidelity to perform its duty did not relieve Metropolitan of liability, and that the two were liable as joint tortfeasors.

This is unquestionably the usual conclusion in situations of this nature. There are, however, a few cases in which the conduct of the third person, whether action or inaction, has been held to relieve the defendant because the responsibility has been shifted from his shoulders. One fact pattern in which this has occurred involves defendant construction companies that have left dynamite caps lying about. They are found by a child who takes them home; the child's parent discovers them, knows what they are, and takes them away. Parent subsequently leaves them lying where child finds them, plays with them and is injured. The responsibility is held to have shifted to the parent, relieving the originally negligent defendant. See Peterson v. Martin, 138 Minn. 195, 164 N.W. 813 (1917); Pittsburg Reduction Co. v. Horton, 87 Ark. 576, 113 S.W. 647 (1908); Calkins v. Albi, 163 Colo. 370, 431 P.2d 17 (1967).

Although it may be said in these cases that the risk created by the defendant has terminated, the risk is still there, and very much alive. What has happened is that another person has taken control of it. When should that fact shield the original wrongdoer? It is probably not possible to find any general principle that will determine when the risk will be found to have shifted.

CHAPTER VII

JOINT TORTFEASORS

1. LIABILITY AND JOINDER OF DEFENDANTS

Bierczynski v. Rogers

Supreme Court of Delaware, 1968.
239 A.2d 218.

HERRMANN, JUSTICE. This appeal involves an automobile accident in which the plaintiffs claim that the defendant motorists were racing on the public highway, as the result of which the accident occurred.

The plaintiffs Cecil B. Rogers and Susan D. Rogers brought this action against Robert C. Race and Ronald Bierczynski, ages 18 and 17 respectively, alleging concurrent negligences in that they violated various speed statutes and various other statutory rules of the road, and in that they failed to keep a proper lookout and failed to keep their vehicles under proper control. The jury, by answer to interrogatories in its special verdict, expressly found that Race and Bierczynski were each negligent and that the negligence of each was a proximate cause of the accident. Substantial verdicts were entered in favor of the plaintiffs against both defendants jointly. The defendant Bierczynski appeals therefrom. The defendant Race does not appeal; rather, he joins with the plaintiffs in upholding the judgment below.

[The evidence justified a finding that the automobiles driven by Bierczynski and Race engaged in a speed contest, as they came down a hill side-by-side at twice the legal speed. Ahead of them was the car of the plaintiffs, in the westbound lane. As they approached it, Race tried to get his car back into the eastbound lane. He lost control of it, and careened sideways, at about 70 miles per hour, into the front of plaintiffs' car. Bierczynski remained in the proper lane at all times, and brought his car to a stop in it, about 35 feet from the area of collision. It did not come in contact with the plaintiffs' vehicle.]

In many States, automobile racing on a public highway is prohibited by statute, the violation of which is negligence per se. [Cc] Delaware has no such statute. Nevertheless, speed competition in automobiles on the public highway is negligence in this State, for the reason that a reasonably prudent person would not engage in such conduct. This conclusion is in accord with the general rule, prevailing in other jurisdictions which lack statutes on the subject, that racing motor vehicles on a public highway is negligence. [Cc]

It is also generally held that all who engage in a race on the highway do so at their peril, and are liable for injury or damage sustained by a third person as a result thereof, regardless of which of the racing cars directly inflicted the injury or damage. The authorities reflect generally accepted rules of causation that all parties engaged in a motor vehicle race on the highway are wrongdoers acting in concert, and that each participant is liable for harm to a third person arising from the tortious conduct of the other, because he has induced and encouraged the tort. [Cc]

We subscribe to those rules; and hold that, as a general rule, participation in a motor vehicle race on a public highway is an act of concurrent negligence imposing liability on each participant for any injury to a non-participant resulting from the race. If, therefore, Race and Bierczynski were engaged in a speed competition, each was liable for the damages and injuries to the plaintiffs herein, even though Bierczynski was not directly involved in the collision itself. Bierczynski apparently concedes liability if a race had, in fact, been in progress. Clearly there was ample evidence to carry to the jury the issue of a race—and with it, implicit therein, the issue of proximate cause as to Bierczynski. * * *

We find no error as asserted by the appellant. The judgments below are affirmed.

NOTES AND QUESTIONS

1. Defendant Bierczynski is held liable to the plaintiffs even though his car did not come into contact with them because he acted in concert with defendant Race to cause injury to plaintiffs. Observe that there is also a civil procedure issue lurking beneath the holding of this case. The civil procedure rule of joinder governs whether the causes of action that the plaintiffs have against each of the two defendants can be joined together in a single lawsuit.

2. *Joinder.* Originally, English law permitted joinder in the same lawsuit of multiple defendants only if those defendants had acted in concert as in the principal case. Thus, under the old common law rules of joinder, Race and Bierczynski could have been joined as defendants, but defendants who had not acted in concert could not be joined in the same action. See Sadler v. Western Ry. Co., [1896] A.C. 450 (two trucks, acting independently, blocked both ends of a street, preventing access to plaintiff's land—separate actions required). Modern procedural codes or rules of court are based on principles of convenience and provide that joinder is permitted when the plaintiff's claims arise from "the same transaction, occurrence, or series of transactions or occurrences and if any question of law or fact common to all defendants will arise in the action." See Fed.R.Civ.Proc. 20(a) and its state law counterparts. Joinder, therefore, is now permitted when the defendants acted in concert, when the defendants acted independently to cause the same harm, and even when the defendants acted independently to cause different harms.

3. Most jurisdictions, while *permitting* the plaintiff to join multiple defendants in the same action, do not *require* that the plaintiff do so. The plaintiff has the right to sue one tortfeasor alone, without joining others who may also be liable. If the plaintiff does, the defendant cannot, over the plaintiff's objection, compel the joinder of the others. See Sox v. Hertz Corp., 262 F.Supp. 531 (D.S.C.1967) and Magnuson v. Kelsey–Hayes Co., 844 S.W.2d 448 (Mo.App.1992) (defendant cannot prevent the voluntary dismissal of co-defendant by plaintiff if defendant had not

[handwritten margin note: P has right to sue only one of joint tortfeasors (joint tortfeasors have option of contribution indemnity)]

filed a cross-claim against co-defendant). Although the defendant cannot affect the cause of action between the plaintiff and other potential defendants, the defendant can enforce whatever right to contribution or indemnity the defendant may have against another potential defendant by impleading that other party or by bringing a separate lawsuit for contribution or indemnity against the other party. See Knell v. Feltman, page 378.

4. *Liability.* "Joint and several liability" means that each of several tortfeasors is liable jointly with the others for the amount of the judgment against them, and that each is also individually liable for the full amount. The plaintiff can collect from any one of them or any group.

5. There are three types of factual situations in which joint and several liability usually is imposed. The instant case illustrates the first—that in which the tortfeasors acted in concert. The classic discussion is Prosser, Joint Torts and Several Liability, 25 Calif.L.Rev. 413 (1937); and see Jackson, Joint Torts and Several Liability, 17 Tex.L.Rev. 399 (1939).

A. Three defendants, acting in concert, set upon the plaintiff. One held him, which was false imprisonment; another battered him; the third stole his silver buttons. All three were held liable for the entire damages. Smithson v. Garth, 3 Lev. 324, 83 Eng.Rep. 711 (1691). Cf. Garrett v. Garrett, 228 N.C. 530, 46 S.E.2d 302 (1948) and the echoes of Romeo and Juliet in Tricoli v. Centalanza, 100 N.J.L. 231, 126 A. 214 (1924).

B. Suppose that X attacks and beats the plaintiff. Defendant takes no part in the attack, but encourages X to go ahead and prevents others from interfering. Is defendant liable? Hilmes v. Stroebel, 59 Wis. 74, 17 N.W. 539 (1883); Thompson v. Johnson, 180 F.2d 431 (5th Cir.1950). What if he merely stands by and approves, but does nothing active?

C. Did the principal case involve an express or implied agreement to injure plaintiff? If not, why are defendants deemed joint tortfeasors? Did they participate in the joint creation of a negligent risk? See Lemons v. Kelly, 239 Or. 354, 360–61, 397 P.2d 784, 787 (1964).

D. Suppose, in the principal case, that Race and Bierczynski had not been drag racing, but had entered a contest to see which one could get first from one point in the city to another, with each selecting his own route. Race was speeding and hit the plaintiffs. Should Bierczynski, who went by a different route, be liable? Would it make any difference whether Bierczynski was also speeding? Whether the point of the contest was to see who could drive the fastest or who picked the shortest route?

6. Four friends (Woods, Cole, Hill, and Carrera) decided to travel to a farm belonging to Cole's grandfather to go shooting. On the way, Woods fell asleep. Cole hatched a plan to frighten Woods. He persuaded Hill and Carrera to load their guns so that they would fire only one shell or bullet. Upon arrival at the farm, the pickup truck was driven into a barn, Woods was left asleep in the truck, and the guns were prepared. Following the plan, all three of them fired their guns into the ground near the truck, awakening plaintiff. They then pointed their guns at plaintiff, saying "it's time to die," and pulled the triggers. Cole's and Carrera's guns produced a click as Cole had planned, but Hill's gun discharged, killing Woods. His representative filed suit against Cole, alleging that he had acted in concert with Hill to negligently injure Woods. Would Cole be liable under traditional common law rules of joint and several liability? What if the jurisdiction has amended its common law rule to provide for apportionment of liability and otherwise limiting joint and several

liability? Woods v. Cole, 181 Ill.2d 512, 693 N.E.2d 333 (1998) (no indication that legislature intended to abolish well-established principle of common law that those who act in concert are jointly and severally liable). See also Restatement (Third) of Torts: Apportionment of Liability § 25.

7.   The second situation in which joint and several liability may be imposed is that in which defendants fail to perform a common duty to the plaintiff. Included in this category are cases involving the liability of two parties based on their relationship to each other, e.g., the liability of a master for acts of the servant, the liability of an employer for the acts of the employee, the liability of the retailer for a defect in the product. Marcon v. Kmart Corp., 573 N.W.2d 728 (Minn.App.1998) (under Minnesota statute governing joint and several liability, Kmart liable for entire $8 million award based on jury's finding that sled was defective because bankrupt manufacturer had failed to warn of risks of kneeling on sled). See Chapters 13 and 15 for discussions of vicarious liability and liability of seller of product.

8.   The third category of cases imposing joint and several liability, and the last of the three to be recognized by the law, is that involving defendants who acted independently to cause an indivisible harm. As you read the cases that follow, keep in mind that the defendants might have acted either simultaneously or concurrently. Does this make a difference? Should it?

Coney v. J.L.G. Industries, Inc.

Supreme Court of Illinois, 1983.
97 Ill.2d 104, 454 N.E.2d 197, 73 Ill.Dec. 337.

[This is a wrongful death action brought by Coney as administrator of the estate of Clifford M. Jasper. Jasper died while operating a hydraulic aerial work platform, manufactured by defendant, and the action is based on strict products liability. Defendant argued that Jasper had committed contributory negligence and that his employer, V. Jobst & Sons, also had contributed to the plaintiff's injuries by failing to provide a "groundman," and by failing to "instruct and train Jasper on the operation of the platform." These three questions were certified to the Supreme Court:

"Whether the doctrine of comparative negligence or fault is applicable to actions or claims seeking recovery under products liability or strict liability in tort theories?

Whether the doctrine of comparative negligence or fault eliminates joint and several liability?

Whether the retention of joint and several liability in a system of comparative negligence or fault denies defendants equal protection of the laws in violation of the Federal and state constitutions?

The court's answer to the first question was in the affirmative. This issue will be considered in more detail in the chapters on Defenses and Product Liability.]

THOMAS J. MORAN, JUSTICE: * * * The common law doctrine of joint and several liability holds joint tortfeasors responsible for the plaintiff's entire injury, allowing plaintiff to pursue all, some, or one of the tortfeasors responsible for his injury for the full amount of the damages. [Cc]

Defendant asserts joint and several liability is a corollary of the contributory negligence doctrine. Prior to *Alvis* [v. Ribar, 85 Ill.2d 1, 421 N.E.2d 886, 52 Ill.Dec. 23 (1981), judicially adopting pure comparative negligence,] a plaintiff who was guilty of even slight contributory negligence was barred from recovery. Defendant maintains that joint and several liability balanced this inequity by permitting a faultless plaintiff to collect his entire judgment from any defendant who was guilty of even slight negligence. With the adoption of comparative negligence where damages are apportioned according to each party's fault, defendant argues it is no longer rational to hold a defendant liable beyond his share of the total damages. * * *

The vast majority of jurisdictions, however, which have adopted comparative negligence have retained joint and several liability as a part of their comparative negligence doctrine [citing authorities from 16 states].

Generally, four reasons have been advanced for retaining joint and several liability:

(1) The feasibility of apportioning fault on a comparative basis does not render an indivisible injury "divisible" for purposes of the joint and several liability rule. A concurrent tortfeasor is liable for the whole of an indivisible injury when his negligence is a proximate cause of that damage. In many instances, the negligence of a concurrent tortfeasor may be sufficient by itself to cause the entire loss. The mere fact that it may be possible to assign some percentage figure to the relative culpability of one negligent defendant as compared to another does not in any way suggest that each defendant's negligence is not a proximate cause of the entire indivisible injury.

(2) In those instances where the plaintiff is not guilty of negligence, he would be forced to bear a portion of the loss should one of the tortfeasors prove financially unable to satisfy his share of the damages.

(3) Even in cases where a plaintiff is partially at fault, his culpability is not equivalent to that of a defendant. The plaintiff's negligence relates only to a lack of due care for his own safety while the defendant's negligence relates to a lack of due care for the safety of others; the latter is tortious, but the former is not.

(4) Elimination of joint and several liability would work a serious and unwarranted deleterious effect on the ability of an injured plaintiff to obtain adequate compensation for his injuries. [Cc]

In adopting comparative negligence, this court eliminated the total bar to recovery which a plaintiff had faced under contributory negligence. In return for allowing a negligent plaintiff to recover, this court said fairness requires that a plaintiff's damages be "reduced by the percentage of fault *attributable to him*." (Emphasis added.) (Alvis v. Ribar (1981), 85 Ill.2d 1, 25, 52 Ill.Dec. 23, 421 N.E.2d 886.) Were we to eliminate joint and several liability as the defendant advocates, the burden of the insolvent or immune defendant would fall on the plaintiff; in that circumstance, plaintiff's damages would be reduced beyond the percentage of fault *attributable to him.* We do not believe the doctrine of comparative negligence requires this further reduction. Nor do we believe this burden is the price plaintiffs must pay for being relieved of the contributory negligence bar. The *quid pro quo* is the reduction of plaintiff's damages. What was said in American Motorcycle Association v. Superior Court (1978), 20 Cal.3d 578, 590, 578 P.2d 899, 906, 146 Cal.Rptr. 182, 189, is applicable here: "[F]airness dictates that the 'wronged party should not be deprived of his right to redress,' * * * '[t]he wrongdoers should be left to work out between themselves any apportionment.' " * * *

Now, under *Alvis,* damages are allocated according to fault. As such, defendant argues, *Alvis* mandates that a tortfeasor should be liable only to the extent that his negligent acts or omissions produced the damages.

We find nothing in *Alvis* which mandates either a shift in who shall bear the risk of the insolvent defendant or the elimination of joint and several liability. Defendant has not cited nor have we found persuasive judicial authority for the proposition that comparative negligence compels the abolition of joint and several liability. On the contrary, most jurisdictions which have adopted comparative negligence have retained the doctrine. Therefore, we hold that our adoption of comparative negligence in *Alvis* does not change the longstanding doctrine of joint and several liability. * * *

Prospective application of a new doctrine or rule of law does not violate the equal protection of laws under either the Federal or Illinois constitution. [Cc]

Therefore, in response to the questions posed, we conclude that (1) comparative fault is applicable to strict products liability actions; (2) comparative fault does not eliminate joint and several liability; and (3) retention of joint and several liability does not deny defendants equal protection of the laws. * * *

Affirmed and remanded, with directions.

Bartlett v. New Mexico Welding Supply, Inc.

Court of Appeals of New Mexico, 1982.
98 N.M. 152, 646 P.2d 579, cert. denied, 98 N.M. 336, 648 P.2d 794.

WOOD, JUDGE * * * The automobile accident involved three vehicles. The car in front of plaintiffs' car signaled a right hand turn. This lead car turned into and then pulled out of a service station in a very fast motion. Plaintiff Jane Bartlett slammed on her brakes to avoid hitting the lead car. Defendant's truck was behind plaintiffs' car. Defendant's driver applied his brakes; however, the truck skidded into the rear of plaintiffs' car.

The driver of the lead car is unknown. Plaintiffs sued defendant on a theory of negligence. Defendant contended that the negligence of the unknown driver "caused or contributed to cause" the accident and resulting damages. * * *

The jury answered "special questions." It determined that plaintiffs' damages were $100,000.00, that plaintiffs were not negligent, that defendant was negligent, that defendant's negligence contributed to the accident and plaintiffs' damages to the extent of 30%, that the unknown driver was negligent and this negligence contributed to the accident and plaintiffs' damages to the extent of 70%.

Plaintiffs moved that judgment be entered in their favor in the amount of $100,000.00. This motion was not granted. Instead, the trial court ordered a new trial. * * *

We granted defendant's application for an interlocutory appeal.

In this case, in using the term "joint and several liability," we mean that either of two persons whose concurrent negligence contributed to cause plaintiffs' injury and damage may be held liable for the entire amount of the damage caused by them.

It is not disputed that this is a common law rule which existed in New Mexico prior to Scott v. Rizzo, 96 N.M. 682, 634 P.2d 1234 (1981), which adopted the opinion of the Court of Appeals in Claymore v. City of Albuquerque. In *Claymore,* this Court adopted pure comparative negligence. * * *

The question is whether, in a comparative negligence case, a concurrent tortfeasor is liable for the entire damage caused by concurrent tortfeasors. * * * The premise for the question to be answered is that, under the common law rule, either the defendant or the unknown driver could be held liable for the damage caused by their combined negligence.

The question has been answered in several states; most of these decisions are not helpful because the answer depended upon the contents of a comparative negligence statute. [The court discusses rulings in a number of states.]

The foregoing discussion shows that joint and several liability, for concurrent tortfeasors, has been retained by judicial decision in pure comparative negligence states. We recognize that this retention accords with 2 Restatement (Second) of Torts § 433A (1965). *See,* Comment h to § 433A. Retention also accords with the Uniform Comparative Fault Act, § 2.

The retention of joint and several liability ultimately rests on two grounds; neither ground is defensible.

The first ground is the concept that a plaintiff's injury is "indivisible." The California Supreme Court, in American Motorcycle Ass'n [v. Superior Court, 20 Cal.3d 578, 146 Cal.Rptr. 182, 578 P.2d 899 (1978)] supra, followed this ground when it stated: "[T]he simple feasibility of apportioning fault on a comparative negligence basis does not render an indivisible injury 'divisible' for purposes of the joint and several liability. * * * In other words, the mere fact that it may be possible to assign some percentage figure to the relative culpability of one negligent defendant as compared to another does not in any way suggest that each defendant's negligence is not a proximate cause of the entire indivisible injury."

Thus, under the California Supreme Court decision, a concurrent tortfeasor, 1% at fault, is liable for 100% of the damage caused by concurrent tortfeasors, on the basis that the tortfeasor, 1% at fault, caused the entire damage. A practical answer, in this case, is that the jury found that defendant was 30% at fault and caused 30% of the damage.

Prosser, Law of Torts, 4th Edition, § 41, p. 241, states: "The law of joint tortfeasors rests very largely upon recognition of the fact that each of two or more causes may be charged with a single result."

Prosser, "Joint Torts and Several Liability," 25 Cal.L.Rev. 413 (1936–37), states that the rule holding a concurrent tortfeasor for the entire loss "grew out of the common law concept of the unity of the cause of action; the jury could not be permitted to apportion the damages, since there was but one wrong." The "unity" concept, in turn was based on common law rules of pleading and joinder. * * *

Joint and several liability is not to be retained in our pure comparative negligence system on a theory of one indivisible wrong. The concept of one indivisible wrong, based on common law technicalities, is obsolete, and is not to be applied in comparative negligence cases in New Mexico. [C]

The second ground is that joint and several liability must be retained in order to favor plaintiffs; a plaintiff should not bear the risk of being unable to collect his judgment. We fail to understand the argument. Between one plaintiff and one defendant, the plaintiff bears the risk of the defendant being insolvent; on what basis does the risk shift if there are two defendants, and one is insolvent? In our case, the risk factor arises because the concurrent tortfeasor, 70% at fault, is unknown. * * *

Joint and several liability is not to be retained in our pure comparative negligence system on the basis that a plaintiff must be favored.

We hold that defendant is not liable for the entire damage caused by defendant and the unknown driver. Defendant, as a concurrent tortfeasor, is not liable on a theory of joint and several liability. * * *

The trial court properly instructed the jury to consider the negligence and damage resulting from the negligence of the unknown driver.

The order granting a new trial is reversed. The cause is remanded with instructions to enter judgment in favor of plaintiffs, against defendant, for the 30% of plaintiffs' damages caused by defendant.

NOTES AND QUESTIONS

1. In these two cases, the negligent conduct of more than one actor combines to produce a particular injury to the plaintiff. The negligence of each of them is found to be a proximate cause of that injury. The injury has therefore been treated as indivisible and this has commonly been regarded as the third situation in which the principle of joint and several liability should be applied. But this doctrine of joint and several liability originally was based upon two other major tort principles

that have been changing. One principle involves contributory negligence, which at common law barred plaintiff's recovery but has been changed in all but a few states so that it now has the effect of diminishing the amount of plaintiff's recovery (details in Chapter 12, Section 1). A second principle involves contribution among joint tortfeasors, which was not allowed at common law but is now generally permitted, usually by statute. A joint tortfeasor paying more than his share of the plaintiff's damages may recover from the other joint tortfeasors on either a pro-rata basis or a comparative-fault basis (this Chapter, Section 3). The question being asked by many courts is whether the doctrine of joint and several liability, which was premised on these two principles, also should change. See, e.g., McIntyre v. Balentine, 833 S.W.2d 52, 58 (Tenn.1992) (adopting comparative negligence and abolishing joint and several liability). See also Twerski, The Joint Tortfeasor Legislative Revolt: A Rational Response to the Critics, 22 U.C. Davis L.Rev. 1125 (1989). But see Wright, Allocating Liability Among Responsible Causes: A Principled Defense of Joint and Several Liability, Actual Harm as Risk Exposure, 21 U.C. Davis L.Rev. 1141 (1988); Wright, Throwing Out the Baby with the Bathwater: A Reply to Professor Twerski, 22 U.C. Davis L.Rev. 1147 (1989). For a collection of scholarly opinions, see Comparative Negligence Symposium, 23 MEM. ST.U.L.REV. (1992). See also Restatement (Third) of Torts: Apportionment of Liability § 20 for an extensive discussion of the various ways in which the states have resolved these questions.

2. It is now being urged that the concept of comparative negligence should be applied to compare the negligence of the defendants to each other as well as to compare the negligence of the defendants to the plaintiff and that each defendant be responsible for only that part of the injury that the percentage of fault apportioned to him bears to the total negligence of all tortfeasors. Otherwise, it is claimed, he will not be treated fairly. If each tortfeasor is identifiable (unlike the driver of the "lead" car in the *Bartlett* case), not protected by immunity (unlike the employer in the *Coney* case), subject to the jurisdiction of the court, and solvent, this form of liability will produce exactly the same result as the traditional system of joint and several liability, aided by contribution among joint tortfeasors, would produce. Contribution would be unnecessary if there was no joint and several liability.

3. The principal difference between the two systems arises when the shares of one or more tortfeasors cannot be collected from them. Under joint and several liability, the plaintiff can collect from one (or more) of the tortfeasors (sometimes called the "Deep Pocket") and leave it up to that defendant either to obtain contribution from the others or to bear the loss alone. Under several liability, each tortfeasor pays no more than his apportioned share, and the injured party bears the loss of any uncollectible share. Which is the fairer method? Some courts have found that the public policy reasons for requiring tortfeasors rather than injured persons to bear the burden of uncollectible portions of the damages continue even with the adoption of comparative negligence. See, e.g., American Motorcycle Assn. v. Superior Crt., 20 Cal.3d 578, 578 P.2d 899, 146 Cal.Rptr. 182 (1978); Kaeo v. Davis, 68 Haw., 447, 719 P.2d 387 (1986).

4. The Uniform Comparative Fault Act continues joint and several liability but provides for the determination of each party's "equitable share of the obligation" in accordance with his percentage of fault. Then, in case one party's share is uncollectible, it provides for a reallocation of that share among the other parties (including the plaintiff, if he is at fault) according to their respective percentages of fault. Does this seem fair? Suppose the plaintiff is not at fault?

5.   How should an immune or unidentifiable actor be treated? Note that in the *Bartlett* case, the 70% tortfeasor was a "hit and run" driver, and therefore not a party to the action. Is it appropriate to determine the percentage attributable to a nonparty? Chronister v. Bryco Arms, 125 F.3d 624 (8th Cir.1997) (applying Missouri law) (noting that neither legislature nor courts have addressed issue whether fault can be apportioned to a nonparty). Do you see why it might affect the nonparty? One court has found that assigning a share of comparative responsibility to a nonparty violates the due process rights of the nonparty. Plumb v. Fourth Judicial District Court, 927 P.2d 1011 (Mont.1996) (in slip and fall case against shopping center, shopping center sought to reduce its liability by proving nonparty physician's malpractice in treating plaintiff).

6.   If the unidentifiable tortfeasor should later be found and sued, would the determination of fault in the prior case be binding? Would the plaintiff or any of the tortfeasors be able to use collateral estoppel to prevent relitigation of the allocation of fault?

7.   What if the nonparty is an intentional tortfeasor and the party was negligent in failing to protect the plaintiff? How should the nonparty's intentional conduct be compared to the party's negligent conduct? Hutcherson v. City of Phoenix, 192 Ariz. 51, 961 P.2d 449 (1998) (in case where 911 operator's negligence in categorizing call caused shooting death of two people being attacked by former boyfriend of one of them, jury found that City was 75% at fault and killer was 25% at fault); Welch v. Southland Corp., 134 Wash.2d 629, 952 P.2d 162 (1998) (in case brought by patron who was shot by thief at 7–11 convenience store, statute did not permit jury to compare intentional conduct of thief to negligence of owners); Ozaki v. Assn. of Apartment Owners of Discovery Bay, 87 Haw. 273, 954 P.2d 652 (App.), rev'd on other grounds, 954 P.2d 644 (1998) (in case where woman was murdered in her apartment by her paramour, negligent conduct of condominium complex security could be compared to intentional conduct of murderer, but condominium association would be subject to joint and several liability for murderer's share). See also Restatement (Third) of Torts: Apportionment of Liability § 24 for an extensive discussion of the cluster of issues arising in cases involving negligent failure to protect against intentional conduct.

8.   What if the nonparty is immune from suit by the plaintiff? Should that be treated differently from nonparties who were not joined for other reasons? Worker is injured when he reaches into a cotton bailor to clear some loose cotton away from a protective switch. The opening through which he reached should have been covered by a plate that had been bolted on by the manufacturer of the bailor. Worker sues manufacturer. The manufacturer argues that the employer, who permitted the protective plate to be removed in violation of manufacturer's instructions, is at least partially at fault for the injury. Should the jury be permitted to allocate a percentage of fault to the employer, immune from a suit by the worker through the exclusive remedy provision of the state worker compensation law? Snyder v. LTG Lufttenchnische, 955 S.W.2d 252 (Tenn.1997) (jury may consider actions of employer in deciding whether manufacturer is liable, but may not assess fault against the employer).

9.   During the last decade, the traditional common law doctrine of joint and several liability for all joint tortfeasors has been changed in some way in most jurisdictions (including Illinois, the jurisdiction of one of the principal cases) by either legislative enactments as part of "tort reform" movements or by judicial decisions. Some jurisdictions have abolished joint and several liability. See, e.g., Alaska and Wyoming. Others have modified it so that it does not apply 1) to

noneconomic damages like pain and suffering or emotional distress (see, e.g., California and Connecticut); 2) to defendants whose percentage of fault is below a certain threshold (see e.g., Iowa and Montana); 3) to certain types of defendants (see e.g., Michigan, for municipalities); 4) to certain types of actions (see, e.g., Idaho, which still applies joint and several liability only to cases involving intentional torts, hazardous wastes, medical and pharmaceutical products). There are many other variables and some of the jurisdictions combine more than one element of change. Which is preferable? Do they all address the same "problem"? Restatement (Third) of Torts: Apportionment of Liability § 27 takes no position as to whether joint and several liability, several liability, or some combination thereof should govern the liability of tortfeasors whose independent acts cause an indivisible injury. Instead, it leaves that to be determined by local law and then proposes several alternative tracks for addressing related issues, depending on the resolution of the basic question.

10.   Would it be desirable to have the judge explain to the jury the consequences of their decision in setting the percentage of fault? See Kaeo v. Davis, 68 Haw. 447, 719 P.2d 387 (1986). (City wanted jury told that it would have to pay the whole verdict even if only 1% of fault was allocated to it by jury because codefendant driver who had run into utility pole, injuring plaintiff passenger, was insolvent).

11.   See generally Restatement (Third) of Torts: Apportionment of Liability (2000).

2.   SATISFACTION AND RELEASE

Bundt v. Embro

Supreme Court of New York, Queens County, 1965.
48 Misc.2d 802, 265 N.Y.S.2d 872.

[Action by five plaintiffs, who were passengers in one or the other of two automobiles that collided. The actions were against the owners and drivers, as well as a contractor who was repairing the highway and who had negligently obstructed the view of a stop sign. Defendants moved to amend their answers to interpose the defense of discharge and satisfaction when plaintiffs recovered a judgment for the same injuries against the State of New York in the Court of Claims and this judgment had been satisfied.]

WILLIAM B. GROAT, JUSTICE. * * * "[I]t is elementary law that one who has been injured by the joint wrong of several parties may recover his damages against either or all; but, although there may be several suits and recoveries, there can be but one satisfaction. [Cc] The reason of the rule is that while there may be many perpetrators of a wrongful act, each of whom is separately liable, yet the act and its consequences are indivisible, and the injured person is, therefore, limited to a single satisfaction." [C] * * *

Nor does this court agree with plaintiffs' argument that the rule that the satisfaction of the judgment against one joint tort feasor discharges the others has no application to a Court of Claims judgment. Section 8 of the Court of Claims Act states:

"The state hereby waives its immunity from liability and action and hereby assumes liability and consents to have the same determined in accordance with the same rules of law as applied to actions in the supreme court against individuals or corporations, provided the claimant complies with the limitations of this article."

"By the adoption of such section the State places itself as to those making claims against the State, in the same position as a private individual or a corporation would be for his or its negligence." [C]

The Court of Claims determined that the state was negligent and the plaintiffs were awarded judgments for the injuries sustained. If defendants are joint tort feasors with the state, the fact that the judgment satisfied is a Court of Claims judgment should not prevent application of a rule which prevents double recovery for a single injury.

The state may also be a joint tortfeasor [c]. While the sovereign has always been immune from suit at common law, " '[w]hen, however, the state confers upon a court jurisdiction to hear and determine all claims against it, or all claims of a particular class, the situation in that court is the same as if the claim were against a private individual or corporation.' " [Cc]

Therefore, if the trial court shall determine that the defendants were in fact joint tort feasors with the state, the satisfaction of a judgment against the state would operate as a discharge of the defendants.

Accordingly, leave to amend is granted to the defendants.

NOTES AND QUESTIONS

1. The original English mandatory joinder rule, now altered by statute, was that the plaintiff could obtain but one judgment against one or more "joint tortfeasors." Only those who acted in concert or were vicariously liable for each other's actions were called "joint tortfeasors" at that time. Since the act of each was the act of all, it was considered that there was only one cause of action against all of them, which was "merged" in the judgment, so that the judgment against one alone, even though unsatisfied, barred any later action against another. This rule is now repudiated everywhere in the United States, and it is held that the plaintiff may bring a series of separate actions against defendants liable for the same damage, and take each to judgment. Why would the plaintiff want to do that? Can you think of examples, other than the one in the principal case involving suit against governmental entity in a designated court?

2. Suppose the plaintiff is unhappy with the amount of damages set by the first court and does not collect on that judgment? Cf. Nielson v. Spanaway General Med. Clinic, Inc., 135 Wash.2d 255, 956 P.2d 312 (1998) (plaintiff's dissatisfaction with the amount of damages may be the basis for an appeal, but it does not prevent the application of collateral estoppel in the second action, requested by the second set of defendants to estop the plaintiffs from relitigating the amount of the damages).

3. A quite distinct principle developed in England, and carried over to the United States, that the plaintiff was entitled to only one compensation, and that *full satisfaction* of his claim, by full payment, would prevent its further enforcement. It is obvious that this rule is equitable in its nature, and that its purpose is to prevent unjust enrichment. It is this principle that is being applied in the principal case.

4.   A necessary corollary to the rule that there be only one full satisfaction of a claim through satisfaction of the judgment was that any *partial satisfaction* of the claim must be credited to the other parties who are also liable. All states provide for a credit against the judgment for partial satisfaction of the judgment. The judgment is reduced dollar for dollar by the amount of any partial satisfaction, often referred to as a *pro tanto reduction*, or reduced on a percentage basis. See, e.g., Va. Code Ann. § 8.01–35.1 (Michie 1992) ("reduced by any amount stipulated by the covenant or the release, or in the amount of the consideration paid for it, whichever is the greater."); Jones v. Ahlberg, 489 N.W.2d 576 (N.D.1992) (non-settling defendant receives credit for percentage of fault that the settling defendant represents). Restatement (Third) of Torts: Apportionment of Liability § 26, recognizing that each possibility has its advantages and disadvantages, recommends a percentage credit based on comparative responsibility. Think about how each scheme would influence the parties' settlement negotiations under different factual scenarios.

5.   What if the claim is reduced to a judgment against one tortfeasor (like the principal case), but the amount of the damages is agreed by the parties rather than adjudicated by the court (unlike the principal case)? Plaintiff, a teenage minor, was riding in the front seat of a truck when the door flew open while the driver was turning a corner. Plaintiff fell out and was injured. His mother filed suit against the driver of the truck and obtained a consent judgment against him in the amount of his automobile liability policy. Later, plaintiff sued Chrysler, the manufacturer of the truck, alleging that the truck door flew open due to defective design or manufacture. Chrysler sought summary judgment, arguing that the previous (consent) judgment, which had been satisfied, operated to discharge Chrysler. Plaintiff argued that the prior judgment was not a full compensation for his injuries even if it was a full satisfaction of the consent judgment. Abandoning previous decisions that had treated all judgments the same, whether they were the result of consent or adjudication, Oklahoma concluded that satisfaction of a consent judgment should be treated like a settlement and release (partial satisfaction) and not like a judgment (full satisfaction). Kirkpatrick v. Chrysler Corp., 920 P.2d 122 (Okla.1996). If New York had made such a ruling, would it change the result in the principal case?

6.   What if the jury's allocation of fault does not match the amount of the settlement? Kiss v. Jacob, 138 N.J. 278, 650 A.2d 336 (1994) (if plaintiff makes a particularly good bargain in settlement and the ultimate percentage of negligence attributed to the settling defendant would have resulted in a judgment for less than the amount of the settlement, plaintiff will benefit by the excess amount, just as plaintiff runs the risk of a low settlement).

7.   Suppose the trial occurs in a jurisdiction that reduces the amount of the plaintiff's recovery by the percentage of the plaintiff's comparative negligence. (See Chapter 12.) Does the trial court judge first subtract the amount of the settlement and then reduce it by the percentage of plaintiff's fault or vice versa? Whalen v. Kawasaki Motors Corp., 680 N.Y.S.2d 435, 92 N.Y.2d 288, 703 N.E.2d 246 (1998) (subtracting amount of settlement from judgment and then reducing it by percentage of fault attributed by jury to plaintiff, noting that New York's adoption of the settlement-first method is in accord with prevailing trend). Suppose the trial occurs in a jurisdiction that places a cap on the amount of the damages. (See Chapter 10.) Does the trial court judge first reduce the jury verdict to the cap and then credit the amount of a settlement or vice versa? Compare Fairfax Hosp. Sys., Inc., v. Nevitt, 249 Va. 591, 457 S.E.2d 10 (1995) (reducing to amount of cap and then subtracting amount of settlement) with Teeter v. Mo. Hwy. and Transp. Com., 891 S.W.2d 817 (Mo. 1995) (subtracting amount of settlement first and then reducing to amount of cap applicable to actions against state highway department).

8. Suppose the trial occurs in a jurisdiction that has eliminated joint and several liability. Would the nonsettling defendant still be entitled to a setoff? Neil v. Kavena, 176 Ariz. 93, 859 P.2d 203 (App. 1993) (setoff not applicable if settling and nonsettling defendants are not jointly and severally liable). Suppose the trial occurs in a jurisdiction that has limited joint and several liability to economic damages only. Would the nonsettling defendant be entitled to a setoff for the economic damages? How would the settlement be allocated between economic and non-economic losses? Wells v. Tallahassee Memorial Regional Medical Ctr., Inc., 659 So.2d 249 (Fla.1995) (nonsettling defendant entitled to setoff for economic damages only, with settlement proceeds to be divided between economic and noneconomic damages in the same proportion as the jury's award.)

9. Payments made by the tortfeasor's liability insurance company are of course made on the tortfeasor's behalf and therefore credited against the judgment. Payments that were not made by, or on behalf of, the tortfeasor are not credited to the benefit of the tortfeasors, even though this means plaintiff may receive double compensation for some losses. If, for example, a plaintiff's medical treatment is provided for free by plaintiff's relative or paid for by some source collateral to the defendant, such as a relative, employer or health insurance company, the defendant should not "be permitted to profit by any gratuity extended to his victim, and consequently, the reasonable value of said services should be recoverable." Burke v. Byrd, 188 F.Supp. 384 (N.D.Fla.1960) (plaintiff entitled to reasonable value of medical treatment provided free to him as member of military). This—the so-called collateral-source rule—applies to insurance policies maintained by the injured party, to gratuities to him, to employment benefits and to benefits from social legislation. Approximately half of the states have modified the common law collateral source rule by statute, usually as part of "tort reform" statutes. See Chapter 10.

Cox v. Pearl Investment Co.

Supreme Court of Colorado, 1969.
168 Colo. 67, 450 P.2d 60.

HODGES, JUSTICE. This is a negligence case which terminated in the trial court with a summary judgment in favor of the defendant on a showing that a purported release had been executed by the plaintiffs in favor of a joint tort-feasor. The common law rule of law that the release of one tort-feasor releases all others who may have liability was applied by the trial court.

As plaintiffs in the trial court, Mr. and Mrs. Cox sought recovery of damages for injuries which Mrs. Cox sustained when she fell on property owned by the defendant Pearl Investment Company. * * * When the summary judgment motion was considered by the trial court, it was shown that the tenant, Goodwill Industries, had previously paid the plaintiffs $2500 in consideration of the plaintiffs' execution of a document entitled "Covenant Not to Proceed with Suit." * * *

[The court found against the plaintiffs on an alleged error relating to a procedural issue.]

The plaintiffs' second assignment of error, however, does bring into focus another important issue concerning the legal effect to be given to the "Covenant Not to Proceed with Suit" involved here. The trial court denominated it a release and, without ascribing any dignity to the expressed words that the plaintiffs reserved "the right to sue any other person or persons against whom they may have or assert any claim on account of damages arising out of the above described accident," ruled that it therefore barred any action against the defendant as a joint tort-feasor.

Although Price v. Baker, 143 Colo. 264, 352 P.2d 90 supports the trial court, we no longer deem it advisable to further impose on our body of law the harshness and rigidity of the rule and rationale of *Price.* * * * In our present analysis of this issue, we are drawn toward only one conclusion. We can no longer countenance the continuation of a rule of law which is not only harsh and illogical, but which gives refuge and absolution to wrongdoers by depriving a litigant under these circumstances of probable just and full compensation for his injuries caused by wrongdoers. It is not possible to visualize any reasonable or compelling justification for persisting in the application of this harsh and unrealistic rule except on the basis of ancient formalisms, the reasons for which no longer prevail. * * *

In *Price,* we declared "this state has long followed the universal rule that the release of one joint tort-feasor is a release of all." We hereby confirm this to be still the rule in Colorado. Also, we agree with the proposition that a joint tort-feasor is not ipso facto released by a covenant not to sue. We do, however, now state that the instrument involved in Price v. Baker, which is substantially identical to the writing involved in the case at bar, was improvidently interpreted to be an absolute and full release of all joint tort-feasors.

The manifest intent of the parties to a contract should always be given effect unless it be in violation of law or public policy. This is fundamental in contract law. Where a contract has the effect of releasing one joint tort-feasor but expressly reserves the right to sue others who may be liable, it should not in law be treated otherwise. The expressed reservation in this instrument of the right to sue other joint tort-feasors evinces a clear-cut manifestation that the plaintiffs were not receiving full compensation; and if this is borne out, their right to bring an action against others who were the cause of their damages should not be foreclosed. The danger of over compensation or double compensation is no excuse for barring a claim against joint tort-feasors. Obviously, no court would permit the accomplishment of this possible contingency. And certainly, the non-settling joint tort-feasor is not prejudiced, but rather, he is benefited for he would be entitled to have the amount of the judgment reduced by the amount paid by his co-tortfeasor. * * *

To be particularly noted is the early case of Matheson v. O'Kane, 211 Mass. 91, 97 N.E. 638. The facts therein are quite similar to the facts of the instant case in that the released parties were authorized to plead the instrument in bar to any action filed by the plaintiffs. It was held that this did not constitute a release of other defendants and further stated:

" * * * But where it is evident that the consideration paid to the plaintiff was not intended to be full compensation for his injuries, and the agreement signed by him although in form a release was clearly intended to preserve the liability of those who were not parties to it, many of the courts have sought to give effect to that intention by construing the agreement as in legal effect a covenant not to sue and not a technical release." 4 Restatement of Torts § 885 which is modeled after numerous cases like *Matheson,* supra, provides that a release will be construed as a covenant not to sue where the right to proceed against the remaining tort-feasors is expressly reserved. This section emphasizes the importance of the expressed intent of the contracting parties.

In the supplemental brief of the defendant, it is urged that *Price,* supra, establishes the rule in Colorado that the document involved there which is essentially identical to the instrument here is an absolute release of all joint tort-feasors and therefore, should not now be repudiated under the doctrine of stare decisis. This doctrine is assiduously followed by this court. However, when, as here, a prior decision is adverse to the rules of fundamental law and initiates a harsh and unrealistic rule, we believe it becomes incumbent upon us at the first opportunity presented to make a necessary change.

Accordingly, the judgment is reversed and the cause remanded to the trial court for further proceedings not inconsistent with the views expressed herein.

NOTES AND QUESTIONS

1. Distinguish between judgment and satisfaction of the judgment. Plaintiffs may proceed to judgment against as many tortfeasors as they wish, as long as they are not affected by res judicata or collateral estoppel. Satisfaction is receiving full compensation for the injury, based either on the plaintiff's valuation of the case (settlement) or the jury's (verdict). A plaintiff's claim is satisfied when the judgment is actually paid after the trial or when a settlement reflecting the full amount of plaintiff's claim is actually paid. A plaintiff may receive only one satisfaction for an injury.

2. Distinguish between satisfaction and release. Satisfaction is acceptance of full compensation for the injury. A release is a surrender of the plaintiff's claim, which may be for only partial compensation or be for no compensation at all. Releases in the early common law were under seal, which disposed of the question of consideration.

3. Distinguish between a release and a covenant not to sue. The theory of the covenant is that plaintiff does not surrender the cause of action, but contracts not to sue on it. The right is retained, but there is agreement not to enforce it. The protection to the defendant is that if the plaintiff sues, he will have a counterclaim or cross-claim for breach of the covenant, in which the damages will equal any recovery by the plaintiff plus the expenses of defending the suit. This is well set out in Pellett v. Sonotone Corp., 26 Cal.2d 705, 160 P.2d 783 (1945). It is generally recognized by the courts that the covenant is a mere procedural device, invented by the ingenuity of counsel to get around the traditional effect of a release at common law.

4. In early common law the only "joint tortfeasors" were those who acted in concert. Because the act of one was the act of all, a release to one of them was held to release the others, since there was but one cause of action, which was surren-

dered. Confusion as to the meaning of "joint tortfeasors" carried this rule over in the early American decisions to those who acted independently but could be joined in the same lawsuit because they were liable for the same damages. In addition, perhaps because of abolition of the seal, release was confused with satisfaction. See Abb v. Northern Pacific R. Co., 28 Wash. 428, 68 P. 954 (1902) (a release, even with express reservation of rights against other tortfeasors, is "conclusive evidence of satisfaction"). The result was, almost everywhere, an original American rule that a release of one tortfeasor releases all who are liable for the same damages, regardless of compensation paid or reservation of rights.

5. That original rule to the effect that the release of one joint tortfeasor releases all has been extensively changed, by decision or by statute.

(a) Some states distinguish between a release and a covenant not to sue, and hold that the release necessarily releases other tortfeasors, but the covenant does not unless full compensation has been paid.

(b) Some states hold that a release with express reservation of rights against other tortfeasors is to be treated as a covenant not to sue, regardless of words of release.

(c) Some states hold that even a release without such a reservation does not release other tortfeasors unless it shows an intention to do so or full compensation has been paid.

(d) Statutes in some states have provided that a release with an express reservation of rights against other tortfeasors does not release them. For example, the Uniform Joint Obligations Act, § 4. Or that they are released only when the terms so provide. Uniform Contribution Among Tortfeasors Act, § 4(a). A release usually is a separate document, but does not need to be. Bank drafts (checks) from insurance companies frequently have a general release printed on them. See Cupidon v. Alexis, 335 Md. 230, 643 A.2d 385 (1994) (language on face of drafts constitutes release).

See Payne, "Release of One Joint Tortfeasor as Discharging Liability of Others under Uniform Contribution Among Tortfeasors Act and Other Statutes Expressly Governing Effect of Release," 6 A.L.R.5th 883 (1999).

6. In some jurisdictions, a release of the negligent agent (like the driver in an automobile accident or the doctor in a medical malpractice action) also releases the principal who is vicariously liable for the agent's conduct (like the employer of the driver or the doctor). Compare Anne Arundel Medical Ctr., Inc. v. Condon, 102 Md. App. 408, 649 A.2d 1189 (1994) (release of doctor also discharges hospital employer) with JFK Medical Ctr. v. Price, 647 So.2d 833 (Fla.1994) (release of doctor does not release hospital employer).

7. Driver negligently runs into the plaintiff and breaks his leg. Physician negligently treats the break, with the result that the leg is permanently shorter. Suppose that plaintiff accepts a payment from driver for the original injury and releases him, expecting to hold physician liable for the aggravation. When he sues physician, physician relies on the common law rule as to the effect of the release of one joint tortfeasor. Assuming that driver's liability extends to the total injury (see page 359), some cases have held that physician was released by the release of driver. Thompson v. Fox, 326 Pa. 209, 192 A. 107 (1937). The booby-trap aspect of this application has led a number of courts to decline to apply the rule to successive tortfeasors in a situation like this. Derby v. Prewitt, 12 N.Y.2d 100, 187 N.E.2d 556, 236 N.Y.S.2d 953 (1962); Fieser v. St. Francis Hosp. & School of Nursing, 212 Kan.

35, 510 P.2d 145 (1973). Other courts resort to construction of the "release" as a means of avoiding the consequences of the plain language.

8. Suppose there is only one tortfeasor. A release is signed on the basis of assumed injuries. It turns out that the injuries are actually much more extensive than assumed. What can the injured party do? Ordinarily he must seek to set the release aside on the ground of fraud, mistake, duress, or undue influence. Most courts will not permit plaintiff to avoid the terms of the release if the mistake is about the extent of the injury or its consequences. Mack v. Albee Press, 32 N.Y.S.2d 231 (1942), aff'd without opinion, 288 N.Y. 623, 42 N.E.2d 617 (1942) (plaintiff settles claim for bruised toe, only to develop gangrene and suffer the amputation of his leg). Some courts have set aside releases where the plaintiff believed she had no personal injury (having settled her property damage claim), when in fact her injuries were serious. Williams v. Glash, 789 S.W.2d 261 (Tex.1990). This issue is explained in other courses, such as Restitution or Remedies. For treatment, see D. Dobbs, Remedies, § 11.9 (2d ed. 1993); Havighurst, The Effect upon Settlement of Mutual Mistake as to Injuries, 12 Defense L.J. 1 (1963).

9. Some courts will still enforce a *general release* ("any and all other persons who are or may be liable for injuries arising out of said accident") even in favor of joint tortfeasors who did not participate in the settlement that generated the release. Enos v. Key Pharmaceuticals, Inc., 106 F.3d 838 (8th Cir.1997) (applying South Dakota law) (general release executed as part of settlement with physicians in medical malpractice case by parents of minor who suffered brain damage while taking asthma medication operated to release drug manufacturers in later suit based on product liability and fraud). But see Russ v. General Motors Corp., 111 Nev. 1431, 906 P.2d 718 (1995) (general release executed as part of settlement with driver in negligence case operates to release car manufacturer in later suit based on product liability against automobile manufacturer only if parties to release intended such a result).

10. Should an attorney be liable (in professional malpractice) for failing to advise a client that a general release forecloses lawsuits against other tortfeasors? See Collas v. Garnick, 425 Pa.Super. 8, 624 A.2d 117 (1993) (alleging client lost opportunity to sue tortfeasor because attorney failed to advise her of the effect of signing a general release as part of a settlement; malpractice action allowed).

11. For a practical perspective, see Kemp, Strategy of Remaining Codefendant(s); When the Plaintiff Settles With One Codefendant, 36 Fed.Ins. & Corp. Couns.Q. 41 (1985) and Kelly, "It's Not Over Until It's Over Or How to Avoid the Pitfalls of the Case That Wouldn't Stay Settled," I Product Liability: Cases and Trends (P–H No. 22, October 1988) (discussing issues related to finalizing settlements, including releases).

Elbaor v. Smith

Supreme Court of Texas, 1992.
845 S.W.2d 240.

[As a result of an automobile accident, plaintiff Smith suffered serious injuries, including a compound fracture of her left ankle. Dr. Syrquin treated her in the emergency room of Dallas/Fort Worth Medical Center ("D/FW Medical Center") on the night of the accident and then eight days later she was transferred to Arlington Community Hospital ("ACH") where she was treated by Drs. Elbaor (an orthopedic surgeon), Stephens (a plastic surgeon), and Gatmaitan (an infectious disease specialist). Ms. Smith received treatment at other facilities from other specialists over the next few years and ultimately, her ankle joint was fused. She filed a medical malpractice action against Dr. Syrquin and D/FW Medical Center and against Drs. Elbaor, Stephens, and Gatmaitan and ACH. Prior to trial, Ms. Smith settled and dismissed her claims against D/FW Medical Center and non-suited her claim against Dr. Gatmaitan. She also entered into "Mary Carter" settlement agreements with Dr. Syrquin, Dr. Stephens, and ACH. Those agreements provided that they would pay her a total of $425,010, remain as defendants, participate in the trial of the case, and be paid back all or part of the settlement money paid to Ms. Smith out of the recovery against the remaining defendant, Dr. Elbaor. Dr. Elbaor requested that the Mary Carter agreements be voided as against public policy or, alternatively, that the settling defendants be dismissed from the trial. The trial court denied this request, the case proceeded to trial, and the jury awarded Ms. Smith damages in the amount of $2,253,237, allocating responsibility between Dr. Elbaor (88%) and Dr. Syrquin (12%). After deducting the credits for the settlements, the trial court entered a judgment against Dr. Elbaor for $1,872,848. The court of appeals affirmed.]

GONZALEZ, JUDGE * * *

Although the Mary Carter agreements were not entered into evidence, the trial judge was troubled by them and he took remedial measures to mitigate their harmful effects by reapportioning the peremptory challenges, changing the order of proceedings to favor Dr. Elbaor, allowing counsel to explain the agreements to the jury, and instructing the jury regarding the agreements.

During the trial, the settling defendants' attorneys, who sat at the table with Dr. Elbaor's attorneys, vigorously assisted Ms. Smith in pointing the finger of culpability at Dr. Elbaor. This created some odd conflicts of interest and some questionable representations of fact. For example, although Ms. Smith's own experts testified that Dr. Syrquin committed malpractice [by closing the wound too soon], her attorney stated during voir dire and in her opening statement that Dr. Syrquin's conduct was "heroic" and that Dr. Elbaor's negligence caused Ms. Smith's damages. And during her closing argument, Ms. Smith's attorney urged the jury to find that Dr. Syrquin had not caused Ms. Smith's damages. This is hardly the kind of statement expected from a plaintiff's lawyer regarding a named defendant. ACH and Drs. Syrquin and Stephens had remained defendants of record, but their attorneys asserted during voir dire that Ms. Smith's damages were "devastating," "astoundingly high," and "astronomical." Furthermore, on cross examination they elicited testimony from Ms. Smith favorable to her and requested recovery for pain and mental anguish. The settling defendants' attorneys also abandoned their pleadings on Ms. Smith's contributory negligence, argued that Ms. Smith should be awarded all of her alleged damages, and urged that Dr. Elbaor was 100 percent liable.

The term "Mary Carter agreement" has been defined in different ways by various courts and commentators.[13]

* * *

A Mary Carter agreement exists, under our definition, when the plaintiff enters into a settlement agreement with one defendant and goes to trial against the remaining defendant(s). The settling defendant, who remains a party, guarantees the plaintiff a minimum payment, which may be offset in whole or in part by an excess judgment recovered at trial. [Cc] This creates a tremendous incentive for the settling defendant to ensure that the plaintiff succeeds in obtaining a sizable recovery, and thus motivates the defendant to assist greatly in the plaintiff's presentation of the case (as occurred here). Indeed, Mary Carter agreements generally, but not always, contain a clause requiring the settling defendant to participate in the trial on the plaintiff's behalf.

Given this Mary Carter scenario, it is difficult to surmise how these agreements promote settlement. Although the agreements do secure the partial settlement of a lawsuit, they nevertheless nearly always ensure a trial against the non-settling defendant. [Cc] Mary Carter agreements frequently make litigation inevitable, because they grant the settling defendant veto power over any proposed settlement between the plaintiff and any remaining defendant. [C] Thus, "only a mechanical jurisprudence could characterize Mary Carter arrangements as promoting compromise and discouraging litigation—they plainly do just the opposite." [C] * * *

Many jurisdictions have decided to tolerate the ill effects of Mary Carter agreements, presumably because they believe that the agreements promote settlement. Some have sought to mitigate the agreements' harmful skewing of the trial process by imposing prophylactic protections. Indeed, Texas previously has taken such an approach [c] Smithwick, 724 S.W.2d at 8–12 (Spears, J., concurring).[19] These protective measures generally seek to remove the secrecy within which Mary Carter agreements traditionally have been shrouded. See Slusher v. Ospital, 777 P.2d 437, 440 (Utah 1989) (secrecy is the essence of a Mary Carter agreement).

Justice Spears rightly noted in Smithwick the falsity of the premise upon which the prophylactic protection approach is founded, namely, the promotion of equitable settlements. *Id. at 8.* Mary Carter agreements

---

13. The majority of cases and commentators define "Mary Carter agreement" as one in which the settling defendant possesses a financial stake in the outcome of the case and the settling defendant remains a party to the litigation. [Cc] Many cases also describe other requisite elements of a Mary Carter agreement, such as secrecy. [C] Other cases and commentators argue that a Mary Carter agreement exists any time the settling defendant possesses a financial interest in the plaintiff's recovery. [Cc]

19. The guidelines provided in the Smithwick concurrence require that Mary Carter agreements: (1) are discoverable; (2) should be fully disclosed "to the trial court before trial or immediately after the agreement is formed;" (3) should be considered by the trial court in allowing jury strikes and ruling on witness examination; and (4) should be fully disclosed to the jury at the start of the trial. Smithwick, 724 S.W.2d at 8–11.

instead: present to the jury a sham of adversity between the plaintiff and one co-defendant, while these parties are actually allied for the purpose of securing a substantial judgment for the plaintiff and, in some cases, exoneration for the settling defendant. [Cc] The agreements pressure the "settling" defendant to alter the character of the suit by contributing discovery material, peremptory challenges, trial tactics, supportive witness examination, and jury influence to the plaintiff's cause. [C] These procedural advantages distort the case presented before a jury that came "to court expecting to see a contest between the plaintiff and the defendants [and] instead sees one of the defendants cooperating with the plaintiff." Smithwick, 724 S.W.2d at 9 (Spears, J., concurring). Mary Carter agreements not only allow plaintiffs to buy support for their case, they also motivate more culpable defendants to "make a 'good deal' [and thus] end up paying little or nothing in damages." [Cc] Remedial measures cannot overcome nor sufficiently alleviate the malignant effects that Mary Carter agreements inflict upon our adversarial system. No persuasive public policy justifies them, and they are not legitimized simply because this practice may continue in the absence of these agreements. The Mary Carter agreement is simply an unwise and champertous device that has failed to achieve its intended purpose.

* * *

As a matter of public policy, this Court favors settlements, but we do not favor partial settlements that promote rather than discourage further litigation. And we do not favor settlement arrangements that skew the trial process, mislead the jury, promote unethical collusion among nominal adversaries, and create the likelihood that a less culpable defendant will be hit with the full judgment. The bottom line is that our public policy favoring fair trials outweighs our public policy favoring partial settlements.

This case typifies the kind of procedural and substantive damage Mary Carter agreements can inflict upon our adversarial system. Thus, we declare them void as violative of sound public policy.

* * *

[Reversed and remanded for new trial.] Dissenting opinion by Justice Doggett, joined by Justices Mauzy and Gammage.

* * *

In the instant case the trial court took great care to safeguard procedurally the adversarial nature and fairness of its proceedings. Nothing about the agreements now under attack was hidden from anyone. The court appropriately solicited and welcomed suggestions from Elbaor and the other parties as to what and when to tell the jury about the Mary Carter agreements. At voir dire, the court informed prospective jury members that ACH and Syrquin, by participating in the trial, could recover all or a portion of the amounts paid in settlement to Smith, depending on the size of the verdict. An additional warning was extended regarding the possibility of witness bias arising from the agreements. The implications of the agreements were also explored by various counsel during voir dire.

To offset any disadvantage to Elbaor resulting from the agreements, the trial court gave him the same number of peremptory challenges as those of Smith and the three settling defendants together. Recognizing that these settling parties effectively were no longer aligned against one another, the trial court denied them the customary right of an opponent to lead each other's witnesses. Finally, the order of presentation was changed to guarantee that Elbaor always had the final opportunity to present evidence and examine witnesses. While Elbaor specifically complains of a lack of forcefulness in Smith's assertion of her claim against Syrquin, her counsel criticized Syrquin beginning in voir dire, though crediting his efforts to save Smith's life. Since in some multi-party suits co-defendants become aligned against one another, Elbaor might have found Syrquin and Stephens blaming him for Smith's injury even in the absence of the Mary Carter agreements. Despite Elbaor's concession that "the trial court [correctly] followed Texas law when it disclosed the Mary Carter agreements and implemented the other procedures to protect [him]," the majority rejects these procedures as "missing the point," thereby renewing its commitment to limit the role of the jury in the truth-seeking process. [C] Simply because jurors may initially expect the plaintiff to have interests adverse to all defendants does not mean that they are incapable of understanding that certain defendants have an incentive for the plaintiff to succeed. Indeed the same may occur in some multiparty litigation where no Mary Carter agreement is involved. The trial cannot be a "sham of adversity," when the jury, as here, is fully aware of this shift in alliances. Nor does the trial become less adversarial merely because some of the parties have switched sides—the names may have changed but the struggle is left intact. So long as at least two parties with antagonistic interests remain, the likelihood that the truth will emerge is not diminished.

Accordingly, most jurisdictions allow Mary Carter agreements when trial courts implement similar procedural safeguards to those adopted here. [Cc] In rejecting the full disclosure approach, today's opinion embraces a decidedly minority view accepted in only "a couple of states" that have previously chosen to prohibit such agreements. [C]

* * *

The elitist view that ordinary people acting as jurors are incapable of determining the facts after full disclosure has once again prevailed. While protecting the litigation process from deleterious agreements, this court should avoid precipitous action with uncertain consequences for so many litigants, particularly when, as here, the parties have exercised considerable care and the trial court has conscientiously monitored the proceedings.

NOTES AND QUESTIONS

1. As the opinion in the principal case suggests, Mary Carter agreements were named after an agreement discussed in the case of Booth v. Mary Carter Paint Co.,

202 So.2d 8 (Fla.App.1967), and sometimes are called Gallagher covenants, Loan Receipt Agreements, or High/Low agreements. As the dissent pointed out, some courts allow the agreements, others allow them as long as they are not secret, and a few, like Texas in the principal case, have found them void as against public policy even when disclosed. Carter v. Tom's Truck Repair, Inc., 857 S.W.2d 172, 176 (Mo.1993) ("There is a strong public policy against allowing secret agreements to work a fraud on either the nonsettling defendant(s), the jury, or the trial court. However, there are also strong public policy considerations in favor of allowing plaintiffs to control their own cases and settle with defendants as they choose. This court finds no reason that these policies cannot coexist, even in the presence of a Mary Carter Agreement, so long as the other defendant is not deceived. [C] Like the court of appeals, we are convinced that the appropriate solution is to examine these troublesome agreements on a case-by-case basis rather than brand them all as outcasts.") Interestingly, Florida, the home of the case that gave the agreement its name, has followed the lead of the principal case and no longer permits such agreements, even if they are disclosed. Dosdourian v. Carsten, 624 So.2d 241 (Fla.1993). See also Bernstein and Klerman, "An Economic Analysis of Mary Carter Settlement Agreements," 83 Geo.L.J. 2215 (1995).

2. The case is a good illustration of the ways in which strategy in a multiparty case can cause shifting alliances even where there is no Mary Carter agreement. See also Newman v. Ford Motor Co., 975 S.W.2d 147 (Mo.1998).

3. Note Justice Doggett's dissenting opinion chides the majority for "once again" allowing an "elitist view" of the jury system to prevail. What does that tell you about the process of decision making at the Texas Supreme Court?

3. CONTRIBUTION AND INDEMNITY

Knell v. Feltman

United States Court of Appeals, District of Columbia, 1949.
85 U.S.App.D.C. 22, 174 F.2d 662.

WILBUR K. MILLER, CIRCUIT JUDGE. On May 19, 1945 Evelyn Langland and her husband were guest passengers in an automobile owned and operated by Kenneth E. Knell. At 12th Street and Pennsylvania Avenue, in the District of Columbia, the car in which they were riding collided with a taxicab owned by Ralph L. Feltman and operated by his employee, as a result of which Mrs. Langland was seriously injured. She and her husband sued Feltman to recover damages. After answering, Feltman filed a third-party complaint against Knell, asserting the collision was caused by the contributing or sole negligence of Knell.

[The jury found, in answer to special interrogatories, that both Feltman's servant and Knell were negligent, that the negligence of each contributed to the collision, and that plaintiffs' damages were $11,500. The court then awarded judgment in favor of plaintiffs against Feltman for $11,500, and upon payment of this by Feltman, judgment in favor of Feltman against Knell for $5,750.]

Is Feltman to be denied contribution because the Langlands neither asked nor obtained judgment against Knell? The gist of Knell's argument on this question is that the right to contribution exists only between tortfeasors liable in common to the plaintiff; that his liability to the plaintiff was not established by a judgment against him in favor of the plaintiffs; that, therefore, his and Feltman's common liability to the Langlands was not established, and that consequently Feltman cannot have contribution from him. * * *

In addition to being balked by Rule 14(a) [of the Federal Rules of Civil Procedure, which provides that a defendant may bring into the action another person who may be liable to him for all or any part of the damages, even though the plaintiff does not seek a judgment against him], the appellant's theory that there can be no contribution unless the plaintiff has first obtained a judgment against both wrongdoers is untenable for still another reason. The right to seek contribution belongs to the tortfeasor who has been forced to pay, and the existence of the right cannot logically depend upon a selection of defendants made by the plaintiff. If it did so depend, the caprice or whim of the plaintiff, or his deliberate intention to fasten liability on one defendant alone, could preclude that defendant from having contribution to which he might otherwise be entitled. Moreover, such an application of the contribution doctrine would open the way to collusion between a plaintiff, and one against whom he has a cause of action to impose liability solely upon another against whom he has a cause of action for the same wrong.

For these reasons, we see no substance in the suggestion that contribution between concurrent tortfeasors can be enforced only if both are judgment debtors of the plaintiff.

We come now to consider whether the fact that Knell personally participated in the commission of the tort takes this case out of the ruling in George's Radio, [Inc. v. Capital Transit Co., 75 U.S.App.D.C. 187, 126 F.2d 219 (1942),] where both wrongdoers were "vicariously" negligent.

This consideration logically leads to an examination of the interesting history of the no-contribution doctrine, which is conventionally said to begin with Merryweather v. Nixan, 8 Term Rep. 186, 101 Eng.Rep. 1337 (K.B.1799). The plaintiff and defendant in that case had injured a mill by taking or damaging its machinery and the plaintiff, having satisfied the judgment of the mill owner, sued for contribution. The trial judge nonsuited on the ground that "no contribution could by law be claimed as between joint wrongdoers." On appeal, affirming the trial court, Kenyon, C.J., stated "that he had never before heard of such an action having been brought, where the former recovery was for a tort." In 1799, the word "tort" was used only to describe wrongs of a wilful or intentional character.

Due to the brevity of the report and a misleading headnote, the Merryweather case has often been cited in support of the sweeping proposition that no contribution can be had between joint tortfeasors. It is plain, however, that the ruling of the case was limited to the denial of contribution between wilful or intentional wrongdoers.

Nevertheless, after a period of adherence to the true Merryweather holding, the majority of American courts have long flatly said there can be no contribution between joint or concurrent tortfeasors, without distinguishing between those who are intentional wrongdoers and those whose unpurposed negligence results in a tort.

Widespread revulsion against that rule, which Chief Justice Groner said "is not sustainable upon any fair basis of reasoning, is wrong, and should be overruled", was demonstrated when the legislatures of some fifteen states enacted alleviating statutes in one form or another. Dissatisfaction with the rule is further shown by the fact that many courts have "riddled it with exceptions." * * *

We conclude that when a tort is committed by the concurrent negligence of two or more persons who are not intentional wrongdoers, contribution should be enforced; that a joint judgment against such tort-feasors is not a prerequisite to contribution between them, and it is immaterial whether they were, or any of them was, personally negligent. In other words, we adopt for the District of Columbia, without exception or reservation, the rule stated by Chief Justice Groner in the George's Radio case "that when the parties are not intentional and wilful wrongdoers, but are made so by legal inference or intendment, contribution may be enforced." * * *

Affirmed.

NOTES AND QUESTIONS

1. As the opinion in the principal case notes, the rule that there can be no contribution among joint tortfeasors had its origin in 1799 in the case of Merryweather v. Nixan, 8 T.R. 186, 101 Eng.Rep. 1337 [K.B.1799]. There is a very meager report of the case, but it seems clear that there had been a joint judgment against two defendants in an action for conversion and that they had acted in concert, since they were joined at a time when joinder was possible only on this basis. One defendant was denied contribution from the other, apparently on the ground that he had acted intentionally and his claim rested upon what was, in the eyes of the law, entirely his own wrong.

2. The early American cases denied contribution in cases of wilful misconduct, but allowed it when the tort committed by the claimant was a matter of negligence or mistake. But once the door was thrown open to joinder in one action of those tortfeasors who had acted independently to cause the same harm, the origin of the rule and the reason for it were lost to sight, and contribution was denied among all "joint tortfeasors." This was the majority common law rule in the United States through the first half of the twentieth century.

3. Most of the early twentieth century commentators advocated contribution, at least when the claimant is not an intentional wrongdoer, on the ground that it is unfair to saddle the entire burden of a loss, for which two are responsible, upon one alone, while the other goes scot free. See Bohlen, Contribution and Indemnity Between Tortfeasors, 21 Cornell L.Q. 522 (1936), 22 id. 569 (1937); Leflar, Contribution and Indemnity Between Tortfeasors, 81 U.Pa.L.Rev. 130 (1932); Hodges, Contribution and Indemnity Among Tortfeasors, 26 Tex.L.Rev. 150 (1947); Gregory, Contribution Among Joint Tortfeasors: A Uniform Practice, 1938 Wis.L.Rev. 365.

4. The common law rule prohibiting contribution among joint tortfeasors has been extensively changed. A substantial majority of the states now permit contribu-

tion, either by statute or judicial decision. See, e.g., Safeway Stores, Inc. v. Raytown, 633 S.W.2d 727 (Mo.1982). The Restatement (Third) of Torts: Apportionment of Liability § 33 has adopted this position. Three successive uniform acts have provided for it. See Uniform Contribution Among Tortfeasors Act (1939), Uniform Contribution Among Tortfeasors Act (1955), and Uniform Comparative Fault Act (1979). The basic alternatives are as follows:

(a) The traditional common law rule of no contribution—long the majority rule but now in a minority and diminishing. (b) Contribution allowed between joint tortfeasors but only if a joint judgment has been obtained against them—a statutory rule adopted in a few states. (c) Contribution generally allowed among negligent tortfeasors.

5. Keep in mind that contribution is neither necessary nor permitted in jurisdictions that have eliminated joint and several liability. After a single car accident, passenger sued driver and driver's employer. Before trial, passenger settled with defendants. Settling defendants then filed a contribution claim against the State, arguing that its negligence in maintaining the road contributed to the accident. Washington had limited joint and several liability by statute and its scope did not include this situation. Thus, settling defendants were not entitled to contribution. Kottler v. State of Washington, 136 Wash.2d 437, 449, 963 P.2d 834, 841 (1998) (settling defendants "settled in the eyes of the law only for their proportionate shares of total liability. Absent joint and several liability[,] they simply have no claim for contribution under the statute.")

6. The common law rule that contribution is not permitted among intentional wrongdoers has persisted, and there seems little inclination to change it. It is specifically enacted in several statutes. But see Southern Pacific Transp. Co. v. State of California, 115 Cal.App.3d 116, 171 Cal.Rptr. 187 (1981), where the court concluded that willful misconduct does not bar contribution among joint tortfeasors. A limitation to the general rule of not permitting contribution among joint tortfeasors occurs in admiralty cases and fraud in securities actions. See, e.g., Musick, Peeler & Garrett v. Employers Insurance of Wausau, Ins., 508 U.S. 286 (1993) (contribution allowed in cases where defendants violated Rule 10b–5 of Securities Exchange Act).

7. The traditional rule, by analogy to contribution among sureties, used an equal-division basis—half and half if there are two tortfeasors, by thirds if there are three, and so on. With the advent of comparative negligence, most jurisdictions make the division according to the relative fault of the parties. In accord, the Uniform Comparative Fault Act and Restatement (Third) of Torts: Apportionment of Liability § 33(b) cmt. e.

Yellow Cab Co. of D.C., Inc. v. Dreslin

United States Court of Appeals, District of Columbia Circuit, 1950.
86 U.S.App.D.C. 327, 181 F.2d 626.

PROCTOR, CIRCUIT JUDGE. The question here concerns contribution between tortfeasors where the judgment creditor is the wife of the tortfeasor against whom contribution is sought.

A taxicab of appellant (hereafter called "Cab Co."), driven by its agent, and an automobile, driven by appellee (hereafter called "Dreslin"), collided. Dreslin's wife and others in his car were injured. They sued the Cab Co. for damages. Dreslin joined with them, claiming for loss of consortium, medical expenses for Mrs. Dreslin and damages to his automobile. Among its defenses, the Cab Co. pleaded contributory negligence of Dreslin. It also cross-claimed against him for damages to the taxicab and for contribution for any sums recovered by the other plaintiffs against it. The jury's verdict established the collision to have been caused by concurrent negligent operation of the two cars. Accordingly judgments for varying amounts were entered in favor of all plaintiffs except Dreslin. In addition a declaratory judgment was entered allowing the Cab Co. contribution against Dreslin upon the several judgments except that of Mrs. Dreslin. This was disallowed because, as the Court held, "the right to contribution arises from a joint liability," and as Dreslin was not liable in tort to his wife, there was no joint liability between him and the Cab Co. as to her. This appeal is confined to that single question.

We agree with the conclusion of the trial court. Neither husband nor wife is liable for tortious acts by one against the other. That is the common law rule. It prevails today in the District of Columbia. * * *

The rights of contribution arise out of a common liability. The rule "hinges on the doctrine that general principles of justice require that in the case of a common obligation, the discharge of it by one of the obligors without proportionate payment from the other, gives the latter an advantage to which he is not equitably entitled." [C] Contribution, then, depends upon joint liability. An injured party plaintiff in the suit from which a right of contribution develops must have had a cause of action against the party from whom contribution is sought. Here there was no liability by Dreslin to his wife,—no right to action against him and the Cab Co., hence nothing to which a right of contribution could attach.

The argument that it would be inequitable to allow Mrs. Dreslin to be "enriched" at the sole expense of the Cab Co., permitting her husband, equally at fault, to escape any of the burden, overlooks the fact that preservation of domestic peace and felicity is the policy upon which the rule of immunity between husband and wife is based. * * *

The judgment is affirmed.

NOTES AND QUESTIONS

1. This is the majority rule. Non-immune tortfeasors may not seek contribution or indemnity from those who are immune. See Sears, Roebuck & Co., v. Hsu-Nan Huang, 652 A.2d 568 (Dela. 1995) (owner and manufacturer of escalator could not seek contribution from parent whose failure to supervise child contributed to injury); Bond v. Pittsburgh, 368 Pa. 404, 84 A.2d 328 (1951) (charitable immunity). See Hertz, The Tort Triangle: Contribution from Defendants When Plaintiff Cannot Sue, 32 Me.L.Rev. 83 (1980). See Chapter 12, Section 3, Immunities.

2. A similar problem arises in connection with worker's compensation statutes, which prevent the employee from suing the employer in tort. Most courts have construed their state's statute as cutting off all possible liability, but a few courts have disagreed. For a stimulating discussion of this controversial issue, see 7 Larson's, Workers' Compensation Law, § 76 (1999); Ramsden & Bowen, Workmen's

Compensation: The Continuing Dilemma of Third–Party Actions, 21 Idaho L.Rev. 57 (1985). Restatement (Third) of Torts: Apportionment of Liability takes no position on this. See § 33 comment *j*.

3. What if the plaintiff does not file against one tortfeasor before the statute of limitations has run? Can the other tortfeasor, against whom the plaintiff did file in time and who has paid a judgment, collect contribution even though the tortfeasor is protected by the statute of limitations against any action by the injured person? Keleket X–Ray Corp. v. United States, 275 F.2d 167 (D.C.Cir.1960); Cooper v. Philadelphia Dairy Products Co., 34 N.J.Super. 301, 112 A.2d 308 (1955). See Kutner, Contribution Among Tortfeasors: The Effects of Statutes of Limitations and Other Time Limitations, 33 Okla.L.Rev. 203 (1980). Restatement (Third) of Torts: Apportionment of Liability permits contribution under these circumstances. See § 33, comment *k*.

4. In most jurisdictions, a party who is sued for negligence may file a cross-claim for contribution if plaintiff joined both tortfeasors, may join (implead) another person as a third-party defendant from whom he is seeking contribution, or may bring a separate action for contribution. Some states permit the claim for contribution to be made as a motion for contribution even though no cross-claim had been filed. See, for example, Lerman v. Heeman, 347 Md. 439, 701 A.2d 426 (1997).

5. *Contribution sought by settling defendant:* Most states permitting contribution do not require that a judgment be obtained against a tortfeasor before he pays and seeks contribution. He may settle out of court with the injured party and then obtain contribution. Of course, in addition to proving that the other party is a joint tortfeasor, he has the burden of proving that the settlement was reasonable. This position is endorsed by Restatement (Third) of Torts: Apportionment of Liability. See § 33 comment *h*.

6. *Contribution sought by nonsettling defendant*: A is injured by the combined negligence of B and C. A accepts $100,000 from B and gives him a covenant not to sue (or release retaining rights). A proceeds to trial against C and obtains a judgment for $500,000. In a jurisdiction that gives C a percentage setoff against the judgment, C would pay only his share and no contribution would be necessary. In a jurisdiction that provides for a *pro tanto* (dollar for dollar) setoff against the judgment, C pays $400,000 ($500,000 minus the credit for the partial satisfaction of the claim, see note 4, page 368.) Can C obtain contribution from B? See the next case and the notes that follow it.

Slocum v. Donahue

Court of Appeals of Massachusetts, 1998.
44 Mass.App.Ct. 937, 693 N.E.2d 179.

After Robert Donahue pleaded guilty to motor vehicle homicide in the death of their [the Slocums'] eighteen month old son, the Slocums filed a civil action against the Donahues alleging negligence and gross negligence. The Donahues then filed a third-party complaint against Ford Motor Company (Ford), denying negligence and [seeking contribution and indemnity,] alleging that Ford was negligent and was in breach of warranties of merchantability and fitness for a particular use. The Donahues claim that, when Robert Donahue was in the car prior to the accident, he inadvertently pushed the floor mat on the driver's side, under the throttle. When he later started to back the car down his driveway, the engine began to race and, although he repeatedly stepped on the brakes, his car continued to acceler- ate. The car's rear wheels hit the curb across the street from his house, became airborne, turned, and then hit a fence. When he got out of the car, he saw Todd Slocum lying on the lawn. The Donahues' expert would testify at trial that the floor mat was defective, permitting it to interfere with the operation of the vacuum booster which caused the power brakes to fail to function.[4]

Prior to trial, the Slocums and Ford signed a settlement agreement providing that Ford would pay $150,000 to the Slocums in exchange for a release of any claim. Ford then moved for summary judgment as to the Donahues' claims and on the grounds that the settlement was made in good faith and, pursuant to G.L. c. 231B, § 4, that all claims for contribution were thereby extinguished, and that there was no basis for the Donahues' claims for indemnity. * * * The Donahues appeal from the final judgment dismissing their third-party complaint against Ford.[5] We affirm.

1.   Right to contribution. Under G.L. c. 231B, § 4, as inserted by St.1962, c. 730, § 1, "When a release ... is given in good faith to one of two or more persons liable in tort for the same injury: ... (b) It shall discharge the tortfeasor to whom it is given from all liability for contribu- tion to any other tortfeasor." The Donahues argue on appeal that the settlement between Ford and the Slocums was not made in good faith and was collusive both because the amount of the settlement was for less than the value of the case and because Ford allegedly told the Slocums that Ford would allow them to use its experts so that the Donahues' attempt to attribute liability to Ford at trial would be unsuccessful.

The seminal Massachusetts case construing this statute in this context, Noyes v. Raymond, 28 Mass.App.Ct. 186, 548 N.E.2d 196 (1990), controls the instant case in material respects. * * *

As in Noyes, there were facts before the judge showing that the settlement between Ford and the Slocums was fair and reasonable. It was reasonably predictable that damages would be high and that a jury would find liability on the part of Robert Donahue, in view of the fact that he pleaded guilty in the criminal case and on the basis of his admission in his deposition that, prior to the accident, he was drinking from a bottle of vodka that he kept under the driver's seat in a brown bag. Given these facts, it was not unreasonable to think that a jury might not find any liability on the part of Ford.

According to the Donahues' attorney, in February of 1995, counsel for Ford notified the Donahues' attorney that Ford was proposing a settlement offer totaling $300,000 with $150,000 to be contributed by Ford, $125,000

---

4. Robert Donahue claims that he pleaded guilty in the criminal case because he feared receiving the maximum sentence if he proceeded to trial.

5. After the entry of judgment in the third-party action in the lower court, the case of the Slocums against Robert Donahue pro- ceeded to trial. The jury returned a verdict against Donahue.

by Liberty Mutual Insurance Company (the policy limits of the Donahues' insurance carrier), and $25,000 by the Donahues personally.[6] The Donahues' attorney responded that she would discuss the matter with her clients, but that $25,000 was not an amount that her clients would be financially able to contribute to the settlement. Apparently the subsequent negotiations between the Slocums and Ford occurred without the Donahues' participation. In May, 1995, the Slocums settled with Ford for $150,000. Noyes instructs that the purpose of the contribution statute is to promote settlement, that a low settlement figure alone is not evidence of "bad faith," and that settlements should be routinely approved without extended hearings if the purpose of the statute is to be served. Further, the court in Noyes observed that lack of good faith was evidenced by "collusion, fraud, dishonesty, and other wrongful conduct." [C] In these circumstances Ford's settlement with the Slocums for an amount contemplated as its contribution to a total settlement package does not indicate bad faith or collusion.

As to the Donahues' contention that the Slocums' use of experts originally retained by Ford is evidence of collusion, we disagree. [Footnote omitted.] In Commercial Union Ins. Co. v. Ford Motor Co., 640 F.2d 210 (9th Cir.), cert. denied, 454 U.S. 858 (1981), cited by the Donahues, the court found that the settlement was collusive because, to some extent, it was "dictated by the tactical advantage of removing a deep-pocket defendant because of the experts it could produce" and, therefore, "[was] not made in 'good faith' consideration of the relevant liability of all parties." Id. at 214. [Footnote omitted.] The Donahues' argument suggests that there was bad faith here because the Slocums were not interested in the deep pocket of Ford, but settled with Ford because they believed that Ford was not responsible for the death of their son. Such a speculation does not trigger the necessity for a more extensive hearing on the issue of good faith. See McDermott, Inc. v. AmClyde, 511 U.S. 202, 213 n. 16, 216–217 (1994) (while recognizing "the cursory nature of most good-faith hearings," also noted "the large potential for unfairness" in "the pro tanto rule untamed by good-faith hearings"). The motion for summary judgment was properly allowed.

2.   Right to indemnity. "Under G.L. c. 231B, contribution is allowed between joint tortfeasors who cause another, by reason of their wrongdoing, to incur injury or damage. In addition, ... the statute permits a plaintiff to settle with one joint tortfeasor and still have recourse against remaining tortfeasors (subject to the limitations stated in the statute). The right to contribution, unlike the right to indemnity, is based on the shared fault of the joint tortfeasors. Indemnity, on the other hand, allows someone who is without fault, compelled by operation of law to defend himself against the wrongful act of another, to recover from the wrongdoer the entire amount of his loss, including reasonable attorney's fees." [C] "[I]ndemnity is permitted only when the would-be indemnitee does not join in

---

6. Counsel for the Slocums had earlier indicated to Ford's counsel that they would consider settling this matter with all parties for a total settlement package of $400,000.

the negligent act." [Cc] "This right to indemnity is limited to those cases in which the would-be indemnitee is held derivatively or vicariously liable for the wrongful act of another." [C]

If the claim against Ford had gone to trial and Ford had been found liable to the Donahues,[9] it would have been as a result of its negligence or breach of warranty. [Footnote omitted.] "Such liability will not be derivative or vicarious in nature, nor will it be constructive rather than actual. Accordingly, the third-party plaintiffs are not entitled to indemnification...." [C]

Once Ford settled with the Slocums, the sole question for the fact finder was whether Todd Slocum's death was caused by defendant Robert Donahue's negligence. [Footnote omitted.] Robert Donahue was free to claim that he was not negligent and that Todd Slocum's death was caused by Ford's negligence in selling a defective product. Under no set of circumstances could the jury properly have held the Donahues liable to the Slocums for the conduct of Ford. Further, in holding Robert Donahue negligent (as they did; see note 5, supra) the jury concluded that he was solely negligent (or was a joint tortfeasor with Ford). His liability is not vicarious and he is not entitled to indemnification from Ford. If Ford had remained in the case, any liability on its part would have been as a joint tortfeasor, and contribution would have been required. Indemnity would not have been appropriate.[12] "Contribution and indemnity are mutually exclusive remedies." Callahan v. A.J. Welch Equip. Corp., 36 Mass.App.Ct. 608, 613, 634 N.E.2d 134 (1994). Summary judgment on the issue of indemnification was appropriate. * * *

Judgment affirmed.

NOTES AND QUESTIONS

1.   *Contribution.* The Massachusetts statute providing for no contribution from settling defendants is based on the 1955 Uniform Act, § 4. It is also endorsed by Restatement (Third) of Torts: Apportionment of Liability. See § 33 comment *i*.

2.   Not all jurisdictions protect a settling defendant from contribution; some permit the nonsettling defendant to seek contribution from the settling defendant. This is the position of the 1939 Uniform Act, § 4. Do you see why this approach might discourage settlement? Lavoie v. Celotex Corp., 505 A.2d 481, 483 (Me.1986) (Although encouraging settlement to help reduce the burden upon the judicial system is an important principle, it should not be followed to the detriment of nonsettling defendants.)

3.   Note that in Massachusetts, and other jurisdictions following the position of the 1955 Uniform Act, a settlement with the plaintiff protects the settling defendant from a contribution claim brought by a nonsettling defendant, as long as the settlement is in good faith. How is good faith to be determined? See Kornhauser and

---

9. The Slocums never made a direct claim against Ford.

12. If, as the Donahues claimed, any damages sustained by the Slocums were caused not by the negligence or gross negligence of the Donahues (but, rather, solely as a result of Ford's breach of warranty) this would have constituted an absolute defense to the Slocum's action but would not provide the basis for an indemnity claim. [C]

Revesz, "Settlements Under Joint and Several Liability," 68 N.Y.U.L.Rev. 427 (1993) (collecting cases and noting that courts are divided on whether a "good faith" determination should involve only an inquiry concerning the absence of collusion or also should include a determination of the adequacy of the settlement).

4. *Indemnity.* The opinion in the principal case also explains the difference between contribution and indemnity. Although the terms are frequently linked in a phrase and both may be pleaded in a complaint, as in the principal case, they are actually distinct concepts. Traditionally, while contribution allowed a tortfeasor to be partially reimbursed for money paid in judgment or settlement, indemnity was available to shift the entire cost of the judgment or settlement from a tortfeasor whose liability to the plaintiff was not based on its own wrongful conduct, but imposed on it by law because of its relationship with the tortfeasor whose wrongful conduct caused the injury. For example, the employer's liability for its employee's conduct, the owner's liability for a driver's conduct, the retailer's liability for the manufacturer's product would give rise to a cause of action for indemnity, or full reimbursement for the liability to the injured party. (See Chapters 13 and 15). In addition, the right to indemnity can arise through agreement, sometimes referred to as a "hold harmless" clause in a contract. See also Restatement (Third) of Torts: Apportionment of Liability § 32.

5. In some states, a doctrine of "equitable indemnity" developed, usually to avoid restrictive contribution statutes that provided for pro rata contribution even though one of the tortfeasors was substantially more culpable than the other. In those jurisdictions, indemnity was sometimes permitted if the indemnitor was "actively" negligent while the indemnitee was "passively" negligent or if the indemnitor was "primarily" liable while the indemnitee was "secondarily" liable. Cf. Field v. Boyer Co., 952 P.2d 1078 (Utah 1998) (owner of premises liable to woman who was assaulted in parking lot had common law indemnity action against assailant). With the development of comparative responsibility principles, this form of indemnity has been curtailed in many states. Tolbert v. Gerber Indus., Inc., 255 N.W.2d 362 (1977) (in light of Minnesota's adoption of comparative negligence, contribution rather than indemnity is appropriate vehicle for allocating loss between negligent manufacturer and negligent installer); Owens v. Truckstops of America, 915 S.W.2d 420 (Tenn.1996) (claim for indemnity can no longer be based on active-passive negligence because that distinction subsumed into newly adopted doctrine of comparative fault).

4. APPORTIONMENT OF DAMAGES

Bruckman v. Pena

Colorado Court of Appeals, 1971.
29 Colo.App. 357, 487 P.2d 566.

DWYER, JUDGE. * * * Plaintiff was injured on July 21, 1964, when the car in which he was riding collided with a truck driven by the defendant Bruckman and owned by the defendant Armored Motors Service. On June 11, 1965, plaintiff was injured in a second collision and certain injuries he had sustained in the first collision were aggravated. This action was commenced on June 25, 1965, and the only defendants named in the action are the owner and driver of the truck involved in the first collision.

[The jury returned a verdict in favor of plaintiff William Pena in the sum of $50,000.]

In seeking reversal, defendants assert that the court was in error in one of its instructions to the jury. * * *

The instruction complained of concerns the amount of damages recoverable from the defendants. The first part of the instruction, which is a proper statement of the law applicable to the case, is as follows:

"If you find that after the collision complained of Plaintiff, William Pena, had an injury which aggravated the ailment or disability received in the collision complained of, the Plaintiff is entitled to recover for the injury or pain received in the collision complained of; but he is not entitled to recover for any physical ailment or disability which he may have incurred subsequent to the collision.

"Where a subsequent injury occurs which aggravated the condition caused by the collision, it is your duty, if possible, to apportion the amount of disability and pain between that caused by the subsequent injury and that caused by the collision."

In addition to this correct statement of the law, the court further instructed the jury: "But if you find that the evidence does not permit such an apportionment, then the Defendants are liable for the entire disability." Defendants argue that this last statement in the instruction is in error. * * *

It is the general rule that one injured by the negligence of another is entitled to recover the damages proximately caused by the act of the tortfeasor, and the burden of proof is upon the plaintiff to establish that the damages he seeks were proximately caused by the negligence of the defendant. In accordance with this general rule, we hold that the instruction is in error because it permits the plaintiffs to recover damages against the defendants for injuries which the plaintiff received subsequent to any act of negligence on the part of the defendants and from causes for which the defendants were in no way responsible. The instruction erroneously places upon the defendants the burden of proving that plaintiff's disability can be apportioned between that caused by the collision here involved and that caused by the subsequent injury in order to limit their liability to the damages proximately caused by their negligence. Counsel for plaintiffs argues that the rules concerning apportionment of disability announced by our Supreme Court in Newbury v. Vogel, 151 Colo. 520, 379 P.2d 811, should also apply here. In *Newbury,* the Court stated:

"We find the law to be that where a pre-existing diseased condition exists, and where after trauma aggravating the condition disability and pain result, and no apportionment of the disability between that caused by the pre-existing condition and that caused by the trauma can be made, in such case, even though a portion of the present and future disability is directly attributable to the pre-existing condition, the defendant, whose act of negligence was the cause of the trauma, is responsible for the entire damage."

The pre-existing condition in the *Newbury* case was of non-traumatic origin, but the rules there announced also apply where the pre-existing condition was caused by trauma. [C] The reasons for the adoption of the *Newbury* rules are not present here. It is one thing to hold a tort-feasor who injures one suffering from a pre-existing condition liable for the entire damage when no apportionment between the pre-existing condition and the damage caused by the defendant can be made, but it is quite another thing to say that a tort-feasor is liable, not only for the damage which he caused, but also for injuries subsequently suffered by the injured person. We hold that the defendants here cannot be held liable for the plaintiff's subsequent injury and this is so whether or not such damage can be apportioned between the two injuries.

The plaintiffs also rely on the case of Maddux v. Donaldson, 362 Mich. 425, 108 N.W.2d 33, 100 A.L.R.2d 1. This case involved a chain-type collision, and plaintiff's injuries resulted from successive impacts which to all intents and purposes were concurrent. The court there held that where independent concurring negligent acts have proximately caused injury and damage which cannot be apportioned between the tort-feasors, each tort-feasor is jointly and severally liable for all of the injury and damage. This rule is not applicable where, as here, the second injury or aggravation of the first injury is attributable to a distinct intervening cause without which the second injury or aggravation would not have occurred. * * *

Judgments reversed and cause remanded for a new trial on the issues of damages alone.

NOTES AND QUESTIONS

1. *Concurrent Tortfeasors*. A and B, driving separate cars, negligently collide. One car bounces over on the sidewalk, hits C and injures him. C's injury is indivisible and therefore not apportionable. A and B are each liable for the full injury. Seattle First Nat'l Bank v. Shoreline Concrete Co., 91 Wash.2d 230, 588 P.2d 1308 (1978). See also Maddux v. Donaldson, 362 Mich. 425, 108 N.W.2d 33 (1961) (chain reaction collision in which successive impacts were all but concurrent).

2. If A and B separately hit the plaintiff and the combined effect of the two accidents is that C dies, the death is treated as an indivisible result for which each is liable. Glick v. Ballentine Produce Inc., 396 S.W.2d 609 (Mo.1965). So, also, if insanity results from the combined effect of the two accidents. Rooney v. New York, N.H. & H.R. Co., 173 Mass. 222, 53 N.E. 435 (1899).

3. *Successive Tortfeasors (unrelated accidents)*. What if, unlike in the principal case, it had been the second tortfeasor who was the defendant? Plaintiff suffered injury to his right elbow in March and was under a physician's care because of continued pain and swelling when, about a month later, he was in an automobile accident in which his elbow again was injured. In an action based on the automobile accident, the trial court judge found no basis for apportioning damages to the elbow between the March and April accidents. Lovely v. Allstate Ins. Co., 658 A.2d 1091 (Me.1995) (second tortfeasor liable for whole injury where damages could not be apportioned). See also Montalvo v. Lapez, 77 Haw. 282, 884 P.2d 345 (1994) (noting that whether plaintiff recovered could depend upon which unrelated tortfeasor is before the court).

4. *Successive Tortfeasors (related accidents).* In the principal case, the court found that plaintiff had the burden of proving what damages plaintiff had suffered in the first accident, for which defendants were responsible, and that defendants could not be held responsible for the second, independent accident. What if the second incident was not independent? Driver negligently strikes pedestrian, breaking his leg. While pedestrian is lying helpless in street, bicyclist negligently runs over his arm. At the hospital, pedestrian is treated negligently by physician, aggravating his leg injury. Driver would be responsible for all injuries. Bicyclist would be responsible for arm injury. Physician would be responsible for aggravation of leg injury. See note 11, page 337.

5. A comment on the principal case in 49 Den.L.J. 115 (1972), indicates that there was testimony in the trial below that plaintiff had suffered permanent brain damage in each of the accidents and that it was impossible to apportion the damage between them. How can the jury apportion? Compare McAllister v. Pennsylvania R. Co., 324 Pa. 65, 187 A. 415 (1936), where plaintiff suffered, six months apart, an injury to each leg, with some combined effect on the back. The doctor treating the first injury had died. The court held that there is a "reasonable basis of apportionment" when there is "some evidence to sustain the apportionment made, even though, due to circumstances of the particular case, the proofs do not attain the degree of precision which would make possible an exact dividing line between the injuries." In Loui v. Oakley, 50 Haw. 260, 438 P.2d 393 (1968), involving four accidents, the court held that the jury should be told to make a "rough estimate" and if that were impossible, "to apportion the damages equally among the various accidents."

6. For a particularly challenging factual scenario, see Montalvo v. Lapez, 77 Haw. 282, 884 P.2d 345 (1994) (apportionment of damages in case involving injury to plaintiff's back during rear-end chain reaction automobile accident in which plaintiff had a congenital condition that made him more susceptible to back injuries, previously had been injured in an another automobile accident, had been the victim of assaults that included blows to his spine and face, and had himself engaged in activities (boogey boarding and pushing a car with a flat tire) that exacerbated his back injuries). See also Restatement (Third) of Torts: Apportionment of Liability § 50.

Michie v. Great Lakes Steel Division, Nat'l Steel Corp.

United States Court of Appeals, Sixth Circuit, 1974.
495 F.2d 213.

EDWARDS, CIRCUIT JUDGE. This is an ~~interlocutory~~ appeal from a District Judge's denial of a motion to dismiss filed by three corporations which are defendants-appellants herein. * * *

Appellants' motion to dismiss was based upon the contention that each plaintiff individually had failed to meet the requirement of a $10,000 amount in controversy for diversity jurisdiction set forth in 28 U.S.C.A. § 1332 (1970).

The facts in this matter, as alleged in the pleadings, are somewhat unique. Thirty-seven persons, members of thirteen families residing near LaSalle, Ontario, Canada, have filed a complaint against three corporations which operate seven plants in the United States immediately across the

Detroit River from Canada. Plaintiffs claim that pollutants emitted by plants of defendants are noxious in character and that their discharge in the ambient air violates various municipal and state ordinances and laws. They assert that the discharges represent a nuisance and that the pollutants are carried by air currents onto their premises in Canada, thereby damaging their persons and property. Each plaintiff individually claims damages ranging from $11,000 to $35,000 from all three corporate defendants jointly and severally. There is, however, no assertion of joint action or conspiracy on the part of defendants. * * *

We believe the principal question presented by this appeal may be phrased thus: Under the law of the State of Michigan, may multiple defendants, whose independent actions of allegedly discharging pollutants into the ambient air thereby allegedly create a nuisance, be jointly and severally liable to multiple plaintiffs for numerous individual injuries which plaintiffs claim to have sustained as a result of said actions, where said pollutants mix in the air so that their separate effects in creating the individual injuries are impossible to analyze. * * *

In Maddux v. Donaldson, 362 Mich. 425, 108 N.W.2d 33 the Michigan Supreme Court cites Landers v. East Texas Salt Water Disposal Company, 151 Tex. 251, 248 S.W.2d 731, a pollution case, in support of the above stated proposition. The court indicated that

" * * * [i]t is clear that there is a manifest unfairness in 'putting on the injured party the impossible burden of proving the specific shares of harm done by each. * * * Such results are simply the law's callous dullness to innocent sufferers. One would think that the obvious meanness [sic] of letting wrongdoers go scot free in such cases would cause the courts to think twice and to suspect some fallacy in their rule of law'." * * *

It is the opinion of this court that the rule of *Maddux,* supra, and *Landers,* supra, cited therein is the better, and applicable rule in this air pollution case.

On this point we affirm the decision of the District Judge. This complaint appears to have been filed under the diversity jurisdiction of the federal courts. All parties have agreed that Michigan law alone controls.

Like most jurisdictions, Michigan has had great difficulty with the problems posed in tort cases by multiple causes for single or indivisible injuries. * * *

We believe that the issue was decided in the lengthy consideration given by the Michigan court in the *Maddux* case. There Justice Talbot Smith (now Senior Judge, United States District Court for the Eastern District of Michigan, Southern Division) in an opinion for the court majority (joined by the writer of this opinion) held:

"It is our conclusion that if there is competent testimony, adduced either by plaintiff or defendant, that the injuries are factually and medically separable, and that the liability for all such injuries and damages, or parts thereof, may be allocated with reasonable certainty to the impacts in turn, the jury will be instructed accordingly and mere difficulty in so doing will not relieve the triers of the facts of this responsibility. This merely follows the general rule that 'where the independent concurring acts have caused distinct and separate injuries to the plaintiff, or where some reasonable means of apportioning the damages is evident, the courts generally will not hold the tort-feasors jointly and severally liable.]

"But if, on the other hand, the triers of the facts conclude that they cannot reasonably make the division of liability between the tort-feasors, this is the point where the road of authority divides. Much ancient authority, not in truth precedent, would say that the case is now over, and that plaintiff shall take nothing. Some modern courts, as well, hold that his is merely the case of the marauding dogs and the helpless sheep relitigated in the setting of a modern highway. The conclusion is erroneous. Such precedents are not apt. When the triers of the facts decide that they cannot make a division of injuries we have, by their own finding, nothing more or less than an indivisible injury, and the precedents as to indivisible injuries will control. They were well summarized in Cooley on Torts in these words: 'Where the negligence of two or more persons concur in producing a single, indivisible injury, then such persons are jointly and severally liable, although there was no common duty, common design, or concert action.'" Maddux v. Donaldson, 362 Mich. 425, 432–433, 108 N.W.2d 33, 36 (1961). * * *

We recognize, of course, that the *Maddux* [case] involves multiple collisions causing allegedly indivisible injuries. Hence, appellants are free to argue that the rule stated does not necessarily apply to the nuisance category of torts with which we deal here. Indeed, appellants call our attention to what appears to be a contrary rule applicable to nuisance cases referred to in the *Maddux* opinion. Restatement of Torts § 881.

In the latest Restatement, however, both the old and the newer rule are recognized and as the Michigan court held in *Maddux,* the question of whether liability of alleged polluters is joint or several is left to the trier of the facts. Where the injury itself is indivisible, the judge or jury must determine whether or not it is practicable to apportion the harm among the tortfeasors. If not, the entire liability may be imposed upon one (or several) tortfeasors subject, of course, to subsequent right of contribution among the joint offenders.

Perhaps the best summary of the rationale for such a rule is found in Harper and James:

"In the earlier discussion of the substantive liability of joint tort-feasors and independent concurring wrongdoers who have produced indivisible harm it was indicated that there were four categories into which these parties may be placed: situations in which (1) the actors knowingly join in the performance of the tortious act or acts; (2) the actors failed to perform a common duty owed to the plaintiff; (3) there is a special relationship between the parties (e.g., master and servant or joint entrepreneurs); (4) although there is no concerted action nevertheless the independent acts of several actors concur to produce indivisible harmful consequences. * * *

"While the Restatement of Torts contains a short and apparently simple statement of the rule in category four, this type of situation has caused a great deal of disagreement in the courts. Here joint and several liability is sometimes imposed for the harm caused by the independent concurring acts of a number of persons. In all the situations in which such recovery is permitted the court must find first that the harm for which the plaintiff seeks damages is 'indivisible.' This can mean that the harm is not even theoretically divisible (as death or total destruction of a building) or that the harm, while theoretically divisible, is single in a practical sense so far as the plaintiff's ability to apportion it among the wrongdoers is concerned (as where a stream is polluted as a result of refuse from several factories). In the first type of case almost uniformly courts will permit entire recovery from any or all defendants. There is conflict, however, in the second situation, with some well-reasoned recent cases recognizing that the plaintiff's right to recover for his harm should not depend on his ability to apportion the damage but that this is a problem which is properly left with the defendants themselves." 1 F. Harper & F. James, The Law of Torts § 10.1 at 697–98, 701–02 (1956). * * *

Assuming plaintiffs in this case prove injury and liability as to several tort-feasors, the net effect of Michigan's new rule is to shift the burden of proof as to which one was responsible and to what degree from the injured party to the wrongdoers. The injustice of the old rule is vividly illustrated in an early Michigan case, Frye v. City of Detroit, 256 Mich. 466, 239 N.W. 886 (1932). There a pedestrian was struck by an automobile, thrown in the path of a street car and struck again. Since his widow could not establish which impact killed him, a verdict was directed against her case. * * *

In this diversity case Michigan law is not finally and conclusively declared. The District Judge, under Erie R. Co. v. Tompkins, 304 U.S. 64, 58 S.Ct. 817, 82 L.Ed. 1188 (1938), had to seek to establish what the Supreme Court of Michigan would do with this case on the basis of what it has already decided. Like the District Judge, we believe that the Michigan courts would apply the *Maddux* principles to the case at bar. Under *Maddux,* each plaintiff's complaint should be read as alleging $11,000 or more in damages against each defendant. Therefore, the principle of Zahn v. International Paper Co., 414 U.S. 291, 94 S.Ct. 505, 38 L.Ed.2d 511 (1973), which would disallow aggregation of plaintiffs' claims for the purpose of establishing diversity jurisdiction, does not apply to this case. * * *

As modified [in regard to punitive damages], the judgment of the District Court is affirmed.

NOTES AND QUESTIONS

1. How does the problem in the principal case differ from the *Sindell* and *Bierczynski* cases supra? Recognize the difference between identifying a possible tortfeasor and apportioning responsibility.

2. Did you notice the opinion's allusion to "the marauding dogs and the helpless sheep"? It refers to a collection of cases involving a scenario that apparent-

ly was quite common at the time. Several vicious dogs, having separate owners, invade a field and kill sheep belonging to plaintiff. Consider the following means of handling the legal problems: (a) plaintiff can recover only for sheep whose death he can prove was caused by a particular dog, see Nohre v. Wright, 98 Minn. 477, 108 N.W. 865, 8 Ann.Cas. 1071 (1906); King v. Ruth, 136 Miss. 377, 101 So. 500 (1924) (nominal damages only); (b) each owner may be held liable for a proportionate share of the sheep, cf. Anderson v. Halverson, 126 Iowa 125, 101 N.W. 781 (1904); Wilbur v. Hubbard, 35 Barb. 303 (N.Y.1861); (c) each owner is liable for all the sheep except those which he can prove his dog did not kill, cf. Nelson v. Nugent, 106 Wis. 477, 82 N.W. 287 (1900) ("circumstance that another dog was engaged in the same act does not lessen the liability unless we are able to apportion the damage done by each dog"); (d) the dogs acted in concert and each owner is liable for all sheep, cf. Stephens v. Schadler, 182 Ky. 833, 207 S.W. 704 (1919); (e) this was an indivisible result since the dogs may have combined on individual sheep, cf. Inhabitants of Worcester County v. Ashworth, 160 Mass. 186, 35 N.E. 773 (1893) ("practically impossible to tell what part of the damage was done by one dog"—statute). Should the resolution of the marauding dogs and helpless sheep cases provide guidance to the courts in pollution cases?

3. Earlier cases were inclined to be slow to find an indivisible result and to require the plaintiff to prove the source of his injury so that the jury might make a finding. See, e.g., Johnson v. Fairmont, 188 Minn. 451, 247 N.W. 572 (1933) (stream pollution); Chipman v. Palmer, 77 N.Y. 51 (1879) (same); Grzybowski v. Connecticut Co., 116 Conn. 292, 164 A. 632 (1933) (successive injuries); Frye v. Detroit, 256 Mich. 466, 239 N.W. 886 (1932) (same—see discussion in opinion of principal case). The principal case, however, indicates the attitude of many of the more recent decisions in finding the defendants each liable for the total damage. Two different legal means are used to accomplish this result: (a) to find that the injury is indivisible and therefore not apportionable as a matter of substantive law, and (b) to hold that the burden of proof is upon the defendants to show factual basis for apportionment, with the result that apportionment is unavailable as a practical matter. Illustrations of the first approach are Holtz v. Holder, 101 Ariz. 247, 418 P.2d 584 (1966) (chain collision); Ruud v. Grimm, 252 Iowa 1266, 110 N.W.2d 321 (1961) (same); Landers v. East Texas Salt Water Disposal Co., 151 Tex. 251, 248 S.W.2d 731 (1952) (pollution). Illustrations of the second approach are Murphy v. Taxicabs of Louisville, 330 S.W.2d 395 (Ky.1959) (chain collision); Maddux v. Donaldson, 362 Mich. 425, 108 N.W.2d 33 (1961) (same); Phillips Petroleum Co. v. Hardee, 189 F.2d 205 (5th Cir.1951) (pollution); Finnegan v. Royal Realty Co., 35 Cal.2d 409, 218 P.2d 17 (1950) (aggravation of injuries caused by failure to supply exit doors).

4. In jurisdictions that apportion liability among defendants based on comparative responsibility, how should the cases governing apportioning of damages be treated? One Friday on his way to work, Plaintiff was rear-ended while stopped to let pedestrians cross the street. He called his doctor about pain in his neck and upper back, but was unable to see her that morning. On his way to lunch that same day, plaintiff's car was again hit from the rear and he again called his doctor. Plaintiff finally saw his doctor on Monday. Neither she nor any other doctor were able to attribute any particular part of plaintiff's injuries to one accident or the other. Plaintiff sued both drivers. Arizona has abolished joint and several liability and requires the court to allocate responsibility among all responsible actors, whether or not they are present in the action. Is either driver liable? Both? On what basis? Piner v. Superior Court, 192 Ariz. 182, 962 P.2d 909 (1998) (burden of proof to attempt to apportion damages is on defendants; if damages are indivisible, fault

is apportioned and defendants are severally liable). See also Campione v. Soden, 150 N.J. 163, 695 A.2d 1364 (1997) (allocation of damages and of responsibility in case involving two impacts in jurisdiction with modified joint and several liability) and Restatement (Third) of Torts: Apportionment of Liability § 50, which takes the position that the damages should first be divided into indivisible component parts and then liability should be separately apportioned for each.

Dillon v. Twin State Gas & Electric Co.

Supreme Court of New Hampshire, 1932.
85 N.H. 449, 163 A. 111.

Action by Henry Dillon, administrator, against the Twin State Gas & Electric Company, transferred to the Supreme Court on defendant's exception to the denial of its motion for directed verdict.

Action for negligently causing the death of the plaintiff's intestate, a boy of 14. A jury trial resulted in a disagreement.

The defendant maintained wires to carry electric current over a public bridge in Berlin. In the construction of the bridge there were two spans of girders on each side between the roadway and footway. In each span the girders at each end sloped upwards towards each other from the floor of the bridge until connected by horizontal girders about nineteen feet above the floor.

The wires were carried above the framework of the bridge between the two rows of girders. To light the footway of the bridge at its center a lamp was hung from a bracket just outside of one of the horizontal girders and crossing over the end of the girder near its connection with a sloping girder. Wires ran from a post obliquely downward to the lamp and crossed the horizontal girder a foot or more above it. The construction of the wire lines over and upon the bridge is termed aerial. The wires were insulated for weather protection but not against contact.

The decedent and other boys had been accustomed for a number of years to play on the bridge in the daytime, habitually climbing the sloping girders to the horizontal ones, on which they walked and sat and from which they sometimes dived into the river. No current passed through the wires in the daytime except by chance.

The decedent, while sitting on a horizontal girder at a point where the wires from the post to the lamp were in front of him or at his side, and while facing outwards from the side of the bridge, leaned over, lost his balance, instinctively threw out his arm, and took hold of one of the wires with his right hand to save himself from falling. The wires happened to be charged with a high voltage current at the time and he was electrocuted.

ALLEN, J. [after holding that the defendant was under a duty to the decedent to exercise reasonable care, and that the question of its negligence was for the jury]:

Two views of the bridge over the Androscoggin River in Berlin, N.H.

The circumstances of the decedent's death give rise to an unusual issue of its cause. In leaning over from the girder and losing his balance he was entitled to no protection from the defendant to keep from falling. Its only liability was in exposing him to the danger of charged wires. If but for the current in the wires he would have fallen down on the floor of the bridge or into the river, he would without doubt have been either killed or seriously injured. Although he died from electrocution, yet, if by reason of his preceding loss of balance he was bound to fall except for the intervention of the current, he either did not have long to live or was to be maimed. In such an outcome of his loss of balance, the defendant deprived him, not of a life of normal expectancy, but of one too short to be given pecuniary allowance, in one alternative, and not of normal, but of limited, earning capacity, in the other.

If it were found that he would have thus fallen with death probably resulting, the defendant would not be liable, unless for conscious suffering found to have been sustained from the shock. In that situation his life or earning capacity had no value. To constitute actionable negligence there must be damage, and damage is limited to those elements the statute prescribes.

If it should be found that but for the current he would have fallen with serious injury, then the loss of life or earning capacity resulting from the electrocution would be measured by its value in such injured condition. Evidence that he would be crippled would be taken into account in the same manner as though he had already been crippled.

His probable future but for the current thus bears on liability as well as damages. Whether the shock from the current threw him back on the girder or whether he would have recovered his balance, with or without the aid of the wire he took hold of, if it had not been charged, are issues of fact, as to which the evidence as it stands may lead to different conclusions.

Exception overruled.

NOTES AND QUESTIONS

1. Plaintiff is suffering from a fatal illness, such as cancer, which will inevitably shorten his life. Defendant negligently kills him. The value of his life is to be measured by his anticipated future earnings, along with other factors. Is his illness to be taken into account? See Follett v. Jones, 252 Ark. 950, 481 S.W.2d 713 (1972); Fortner v. Koch, 272 Mich. 273, 261 N.W. 762 (1935); Denman v. Johnston, 85 Mich. 387, 48 N.W. 565 (1891).

2. Plaintiff's house is on fire, and the firemen are delayed in reaching it because the defendant railroad has wrongfully blocked the highway. The house is completely destroyed. For what damages is defendant liable? Felter v. Delaware & Hudson R. Corp., 19 F.Supp. 852 (M.D.Pa.1937), aff'd, 98 F.2d 868 (3d Cir.1938) (jury verdict for roughly half of value of house upheld).

3. Plaintiff is standing in the path of an avalanche when defendant negligently shoots him. Or plaintiff is about to embark for Europe on a ship, when defendant negligently shoots him; a week later the ship runs into an iceberg and sinks with everyone on board. Is the result the same?

4. See Peaslee, Multiple Causation and Damage, 47 Harv.L.Rev. 1127 (1934); King, Causation, Valuation and Chance in Personal Injury Torts Involving Preexisting Conditions and Future Consequences, 90 Yale L.J. 1353 (1981).

CHAPTER VIII

DUTY OF CARE

In Heaven v. Pender, 11 Q.B.D. 503 (C.A.1883), Brett, M.R., declared, "The proposition * * * is that whenever one person is by circumstances placed in such a position with regard to another that every one of ordinary sense * * * would at once recognize that if he did not use ordinary care and skill in his own conduct with regard to those circumstances, he would cause danger of injury to the person or property of the other, a duty arises to use ordinary care and skill to avoid such danger."

This is a noted passage much quoted by courts and writers, notwithstanding the fact that ten years later, in Le Lievre v. Gould, [1893] 1 Q.B. 491 (C.A.), Brett, who had become Lord Esher, was forced to retreat from his own words.

As a general proposition, applicable in the ordinary negligence case, where the defendant has taken some affirmative action such as driving an automobile, it holds good. That is to say, that whenever the automobile driver should reasonably foresee that his conduct will involve an unreasonable risk of harm to other drivers or to pedestrians, he is then under a duty to them to exercise the care of a reasonable person as to what he does or does not do.

There are, however, some defendants and some situations for which a duty does not arise. In other words, the defendant is under no legal obligation toward the plaintiff to act with the care of a reasonable person and is not liable even though his conduct falls short of that standard and the other is injured as a result. And this is true although the danger is obvious and the risk entirely unreasonable, considered merely as a risk. We have already met two such situations. One is that of the common law rule that a gratuitous bailee is liable only for gross negligence in looking after the goods, supra page 195. The other is that of the statutes making the driver liable to a gratuitous guest in his car only for aggravated misconduct, supra page 195.

Recall from *Palsgraf* supra page 303 that duty is a relative concept: negligence cannot be committed "in the air". A person must build her case upon a duty owed to herself and not to another. That person must be within the class of persons who foreseeably will be injured as a result of the defendant's act. The principle may be stated, with few exceptions, that "a person is guilty of the tort of negligence, and therefore liable to pay compensation, for *physical* damage to the person or property of another, caused by *affirmative* negligent conduct on his part." (Peter Cane, Atiyah's Accidents, Compensation and the Law (4th ed. 1987), p. 63. Professor Atiyah, former Professor of English Law at Oxford University, then states:

The doubtful areas of the law are nearly all concerned with two principal questions: first, the extent of liability for damages of a kind other than physical injury, for instance, mental distress or pecuniary loss; secondly, the extent of liability for omissions as opposed to affirmative conduct.

To these two, a third may be added: the extent of liability owed where no existing *person* is injured, for instance injuries to a fetus and losses surrounding birth and conception. The view reflects that of the reporters of the Restatement (Third) of the Law, Torts: General Principles (Council Draft No. 1, 1998), at 82–83, who describe duty as a "non-issue." The draft defines negligence liability at § 3: "An actor is subject to liability for negligent conduct that is a legal cause of physical harm." See id. at 37. While duty is usually viewed in modern law as a mechanism for limiting the range of liability (an empty vessel for policy), other commentators submit that Cardozo, the case law, and a proper conception of negligence, require a judicial determination that defendant's unreasonable conduct constituted a breach of duty owed to persons in a class to which plaintiff belonged. See Goldberg & Zipursky, The Moral of *MacPherson*, 146 U. Pa. L. Rev. 1733 (1998).

However this debate concludes, it is within the concept of duty that the frontier arenas of negligence are recognized and the courts are put to the test of how far to expand the domain of negligence.

1. Privity of Contract

Historically, the contract action developed considerably later than the tort liability. Along with it, it remained possible to maintain the old tort action on the case in any situation where it had already been recognized. The result was a distinction, generally recognized, between "nonfeasance," where the defendant had done no more than make a promise and break it, and "misfeasance," where he had attempted performance but done the wrong thing.

Nonfeasance. In general, when there is only the promise and the breach, only the contract action will lie, and no tort action can be maintained. A good illustration is Louisville & Nashville R. Co. v. Spinks, 104 Ga. 692, 30 S.E. 968 (1898), where the defendant invited plaintiff to come to Cincinnati for employment, and promised that if it did not employ him, it would furnish him with transportation back to Atlanta. He came, fell ill, and was not employed. Defendant refused to give him a ticket to Atlanta, and he was forced to walk the whole way, suffering "much from pain, weariness and blistered feet." It was held that his only remedy was an action on the contract, and no tort action would lie. See also Newton v. Brook, 134 Ala. 269, 32 So. 722 (1902), where defendants contracted to prepare a body for shipment by a certain train, and then did nothing. Again it was held that there was no tort remedy.

To this general rule there are a few recognized exceptions. One is that a common carrier, or other public utility, which has undertaken the duty of serving the public, becomes liable in tort when it fails to do so, whether or not it has made a contract. See, for example, Nevin v. Pullman Palace–Car Co., 106 Ill. 222, 46 Am.Rep. 688 (1883); Zabron v. Cunard S.S. Co., 151 Iowa 345, 131 N.W. 18 (1911). Another is that a defendant who makes a contract without the intention to perform it is regarded as committing a form of misrepresentation, or fraud, for which a tort action of deceit will lie. See Burgdorfer v. Thielemann, page 1058. Promises or undertakings may form the foundation of a special relationship sufficient to impose a duty to take affirmative action to protect a person from harm. See Section 2.

Misfeasance. When the defendant misperforms the contract, the possibility of recovery in tort is greatly augmented. In some instances this is merely the survival of the older tort action, as when a carrier remains liable in tort, as well as for breach of contract, for negligent injury to a passenger, or for loss of his baggage. In the United States this has gradually been extended to virtually any type of contract. One of the leading cases is Flint & Walling Mfg. Co. v. Beckett, 167 Ind. 491, 79 N.E. 503 (1906), where the defendant negligently installed a windmill on the plaintiff's barn, and it collapsed and wrecked the barn. In all these cases the question may arise whether the defendant has gone so far in his performance, as distinguished from mere preparation for it, as to have undertaken a tort duty.

Two good cases discussing all this are Hart v. Ludwig, 347 Mich. 559, 79 N.W.2d 895 (1956), and Kozan v. Comstock, 270 F.2d 839 (5th Cir.1959).

Election and Gravamen. In many cases it is thus possible to maintain an action in either contract or tort. When this is true, a number of questions may arise as to different rules of law applicable to the two actions. For example, a particular court may have jurisdiction over one type of action, but not the other, or certain remedies, such as summary judgment, attachment, or arrest of the defendant, may be available in one action but not the other. Different statutes of limitations may apply. Different rules as to the damages may prevail, especially in regard to punitive damages or for emotional harm. Some defenses, such as infancy or the statute of frauds, may be set up against one action and not the other.

In these situations the courts have proceeded along two different lines. One is to permit the plaintiff to choose the theory of his action, and dispose of the particular question accordingly. Thus in Doughty v. Maine Cent. Transp. Co., 141 Me. 124, 39 A.2d 758 (1944), an action for personal injuries received by a passenger through the negligence of the carrier would be barred by the statute of limitations if the action were in tort, but not if it were in contract. It was held that the plaintiff, having elected to treat his action as one for breach of contract, was not barred by the tort statute.

On the other hand, some courts will not give plaintiff this latitude. Rather, the court will determine the "gravamen" or "gist" of the action, which is to say the essential facts on which the plaintiff's claim rests. Thus in Webber v. Herkimer & Mohawk St. R. Co., 109 N.Y. 311, 16 N.E. 358 (1888), another case of a passenger injured by a carrier's negligence, it was held that the action was essentially founded on the negligence, and that it was governed by the tort rather than the contract statute of limitations. See also the ample discussion of the tort versus contract cause of action problem in Victorson v. Bock Laundry Mach. Co., 37 N.Y.2d 395, 335 N.E.2d 275, 373 N.Y.S.2d 39 (1975), overruling Mendel v. Pittsburgh Plate Glass Co., 25 N.Y.2d 340, 253 N.E.2d 207, 305 N.Y.S.2d 490 (1969) (personal injury—breach of implied warranty).

The liability of professionals directly raises the issue because plaintiff and defendant are usually in a contractual relationship. Can a client sue his attorney for negligently caused losses in both tort and contract? In most instances the courts have not restricted the cause of action to breach of contract, Collins v. Reynard, 154 Ill.2d 48, 607 N.E.2d 1185,180 Ill.Dec. 672 (1992) (reversing appellate court that found lawyer malpractice cognizable in contract but not in tort).

As these cases suggest, there is little consistency in the decisions, even in a single state, although many courts have tended to look to the policy underlying the particular rule of law or statute to be applied in order to assist themselves in making the characterization.

The famous discussion of this topic is Prosser, The Borderland of Tort and Contract, in W. Prosser, Selected Topics on the Law of Torts, 380, at 429–450 (1954).

Winterbottom v. Wright

Exchequer of Pleas, 1842.
10 M. & W. 109, 152 Eng.Rep. 402.

[Defendant Wright, a manufacturer and repairer of mail coaches, contracted with the Postmaster General, Mr. Atkinson, to keep the coaches in a safe and secure condition. Defendant failed to comply with his promise and plaintiff Winterbottom, a mail coach driver, was seriously injured when a vehicle broke down due to lack of repair.]

Lord Abinger, C.B. I am clearly of opinion that the defendant is entitled to our judgment. We ought not to permit a doubt to rest upon this subject, for our doing so might be the means of letting in upon us an infinity of actions. * * * There is no privity of contract between these parties; and if the plaintiff can sue, every passenger, or even any person passing along the road, who was injured by the upsetting of the coach, might bring a similar action. Unless we confine the operation of such contracts as this to the parties who entered into them, the most absurd and outrageous consequences, to which I can see no limit, would ensue. Where a party becomes responsible to the public, by undertaking a public duty, he is liable, though the injury may have arisen from the negligence of his servant or agent. So, in cases of public nuisances, whether the act was done by the party as a servant, or in any other capacity, you are liable to an action at the suit of any person who suffers. Those, however, are cases where the real ground of the liability is the public duty, or the commission of the public nuisance.

Lord Abinger

There is also a class of cases in which the law permits a contract to be turned into a tort; but unless there has been some public duty undertaken, or public nuisance committed, they are all cases in which an action might have been maintained upon the contract. Thus, a carrier may be sued either in assumpsit or case; but there is no instance in which a party, who was not privy to the contract entered into with him, can maintain any such action. The plaintiff in this case could not have brought an action on the contract; if he could have done so, what would have been his situation, supposing the Postmaster–General had released the defendant? That would, at all events, have defeated his claim altogether. By permitting this action, we should be working this injustice, that after the defendant had done everything to the satisfaction of his employer, and after all matters between them had been adjusted, and all accounts settled on the footing of their contract, we should subject them to be ripped open by this action of tort being brought against him.

ALDERSON, B. I am of the same opinion. The contract in this case was made with the Postmaster–General alone; and the case is just the same as if he had come to the defendant and ordered a carriage, and handed it at once over to Atkinson. If we were to hold that the plaintiff could sue in such a case, there is no point at which such actions would stop. The only safe rule is to confine the right to recover to those who enter into the contract: if we go one step beyond that, there is no reason why we should not go fifty. The only real argument in favour of the action is, that this is a case of hardship; but that might have been obviated, if the plaintiff had made himself a party to the contract. * * *

ROLFE, B. The breach of the defendant's duty stated in this declaration, is his omission to keep the carriage in a safe condition, and when we examine the mode in which that duty is alleged to have arisen, we find a statement that the defendant took upon himself, to wit, under and by virtue of the said contract, the sole and exclusive duty, charge, care, and burden of the repairs, state and condition of the said mail-coach, and, during all the time aforesaid, it had become and was the sole and exclusive duty of the defendant, to wit, under and by virtue of his said contract, to keep and maintain the said mail-coach in a fit, proper, safe, and secure state and condition. The duty, therefore, is shewn to have arisen solely from the contract; and the fallacy consists in the use of that word "duty." If a duty to the Postmaster–General be meant, that is true; but if a duty to the plaintiff be intended (and in that sense the word is evidently used), there was none. This is one of those unfortunate cases in which there certainly has been damnum, but it is damnum absque injuriâ; it is, no doubt, a hardship upon the plaintiff to be without a remedy, but by that consideration we ought not to be influenced. Hard cases, it has been frequently observed, are apt to introduce bad law.

Judgment for the defendant.

NOTES AND QUESTIONS

1. Although the principal case involved nonfeasance, it was universally interpreted as applying to any negligence of the defendant, including misfeasance; and this resulted in many decisions holding that the seller of a chattel was under no liability, in contract or in tort, to anyone other than his immediate buyer. The first major service rendered by Professor Bohlen to the law was to point out this error in his article, The Basis of Affirmative Obligations in the Law of Tort, 44 Am.L.Reg., N.S., 209, 280–285, 289–310 (1905), also in F. Bohlen, Studies in the Law of Torts, 33 (1926). This same point is made by Stapleton, Duty of Care and Economic Loss: A Wider Agenda, 107 L.Q.Rev. 249, 250 (1991).

MacPherson v. Buick Motor Co.

Court of Appeals of New York, 1916.
217 N.Y. 382, 111 N.E. 1050.

Action by Donald C. MacPherson against the Buick Motor Company. From a judgment of the Appellate Division (160 App. Div. 55, 145 N.Y.

Supp. 462), affirming a judgment of the Supreme Court for plaintiff, defendant appeals.

CARDOZO, J. The defendant is a manufacturer of automobiles. It sold an automobile to a retail dealer. The retail dealer resold to the plaintiff. While the plaintiff was in the car it suddenly collapsed. He was thrown out and injured. One of the wheels was made of defective wood, and its spokes crumbled into fragments. The wheel was not made by the defendant; it was bought from another manufacturer. There is evidence, however, that its defects could have been discovered by reasonable inspection, and that inspection was omitted. There is no claim that the defendant knew of the defect and willfully concealed it. * * * The charge is one, not of fraud, but of negligence. The question to be determined is whether the defendant owned a duty of care and vigilance to any one but the immediate purchaser.

Judge Cardozo

[The court discusses competing lines of precedents. One group of cases suggested that the manufacturer owed a duty of care to ultimate purchasers only when the product was "inherently dangerous." Some courts confined this classification to guns, poisons or other products whose normal function it was to injure or destroy. Other decisions suggested that a manufacturer would breach a duty of care to a foreseeable user of the product if the product was likely to cause injury if negligently made.]

We hold * * * that * * * [I]f the nature of a thing is such that it is reasonably certain to place life and limb in peril when negligently made, it is then a thing of danger. Its nature gives warning of the consequences to be expected. If to the element of danger there is added knowledge that the thing will be used by persons other than the purchaser, and used without new tests, then, irrespective of contract, the manufacturer of this thing of danger is under a duty to make it carefully. That is as far as we are required to go for the decision of this case. There must be knowledge of a danger, not merely possible, but probable. It is possible to use almost anything in a way that will make it dangerous if defective. That is not enough to charge the manufacturer with a duty independent of his contract. Whether a given thing is dangerous may be sometimes a question for the court and sometimes a question for the jury. There must also be knowledge that in the usual course of events the danger will be shared by others than the buyer. Such knowledge may often be inferred from the nature of the transaction. But it is possible that even knowledge of the danger and of the use will not always be enough. The proximity or remoteness of the relation is a factor to be considered. We are dealing now with the liability of the manufacturer of the finished product, who puts it on the market to be used without inspection by his customers. If he is negligent, where danger is to be foreseen, a liability will follow. * * * We have put aside the notion that the duty to safeguard life and limb, when the consequences of negligence may be foreseen, grows out of contract and nothing else. We have put the source of the obligation where it ought to be. We have put its source in the law.

There is nothing anomalous in a rule which imposes upon A., who has contracted with B., a duty to C. and D. and others according as he knows or does not know that the subject-matter of the contract is intended for their use. We may find an analogy in the law which measures the liability of landlords. If A. leases to B. a tumbledown house, he is not liable, in the absence of fraud, to B.'s guests who enter it and are injured. This is because B. is then under the duty to repair it, the lessor has the right to suppose that he will fulfill that duty, and, if he omits to do so, his guests must look to him. Bohlen, Affirmative Obligations in the Law of Torts, 44 Am. Law Reg., N.S., 341. But if A. leases a building to be used by the lessee at once as a place of public entertainment, the rule is different. There injury to persons other than the lessee is to be foreseen, and foresight of the consequences involves the creation of a duty. [C]

In this view of the defendant's liability there is nothing inconsistent with the theory of liability on which the case was tried. It is true that the court told the jury that "an automobile is not an inherently dangerous vehicle." The meaning, however, is that danger is not to be expected when the vehicle is well constructed. The court left it to the jury to say whether the defendant ought to have foreseen that the car, if negligently constructed, would become "imminently dangerous." Subtle distinctions are drawn by the defendant between things inherently dangerous and things imminently dangerous, but the case does not turn upon these verbal niceties. If danger was to be expected as reasonably certain, there was a duty of vigilance, and this whether you call the danger inherent or imminent. In varying forms that thought was put before the jury. We do not say that the court would not have been justified in ruling as a matter of law that the car was a dangerous thing. If there was any error, it was none of which the defendant can complain.

We think the defendant was not absolved from a duty of inspection because it bought the wheels from a reputable manufacturer. It was not merely a dealer in automobiles. It was responsible for the finished product. It was not at liberty to put the finished product on the market without subjecting the component parts to ordinary and simple tests. [C] Under the charge of the trial judge nothing more was required of it. The obligation to inspect must vary with the nature of the thing to be inspected. The more probable the danger the greater the need of caution. * * *

The judgment should be affirmed with costs.

[The dissenting opinion of WILLARD BARTLETT, C.J., is omitted.]

NOTES AND QUESTIONS

1. The privity limitation lasted longer with regard to those who perform services. It is clear today, however, that an individual who undertakes to make a repair owes a duty to use care to those who may be foreseeably injured in case the repair is negligently made. See Lee v. Rowland, 11 N.C.App. 27, 180 S.E.2d 445 (1971) (failure properly to repair broken axle on a truck, defendant liable to those he should expect to be in the vicinity of the vehicle); Nagy v. McEachern, 28 Mich.App. 439, 184 N.W.2d 556 (1970) (failure adequately to repair safety catch on rifle).

2. The main dispute today in failure-to-repair cases focuses on whether there was any actual undertaking by the contractor. In Wroblewski v. Otis Elevator Co., 9 A.D.2d 294, 193 N.Y.S.2d 855 (3d Dept.1959), an inspection of the elevator was enough for the court to find an undertaking and misfeasance. If the repairer had done nothing at all, the case might have been deemed one of nonfeasance and the privity limitation might have applied. See Hanson v. Blackwell Motor Co., 143 Wash. 547, 255 P. 939 (1927) (repair shop took no steps to fix vehicle). When there is an assurance to an owner that a repair has been made even though nothing has in fact been done, many modern courts have found misfeasance and thus a breach of duty even to third parties. See Moody v. Martin Motor Co., 76 Ga.App. 456, 46 S.E.2d 197 (1948).

3. If defendant does begin performance and then fails to act, he is liable. See Waters v. Anthony, 252 Ala. 244, 40 So.2d 316 (1949); Landreth v. Phillips Petroleum, 74 F.Supp. 801 (W.D.Mo.1947).

4. A physician prescribes a drug to a patient without warning her of its soporific effect. The patient takes the drug, falls asleep at the wheel of her automobile, and thereby injures a third party. Is the physician liable to the third party? Joy v. Eastern Maine Medical Center, 529 A.2d 1364 (Me.1987) (duty of care); Kirk v. Michael Reese Hospital & Medical Center, 136 Ill.App.3d 945, 483 N.E.2d 906, 91 Ill.Dec. 420 (1985), rev'd, 117 Ill.2d 507, 513 N.E.2d 387, 111 Ill.Dec. 944 (1987) (no duty of care); Petersen v. State of Washington, 100 Wash.2d 421, 671 P.2d 230 (1983) (duty of care).

H.R. Moch Co. v. Rensselaer Water Co.

Court of Appeals of New York, 1928.
247 N.Y. 160, 159 N.E. 896.

CARDOZO, C.J. The defendant, a waterworks company under the laws of this state, made a contract with the city of Rensselaer for the supply of water during a term of years. Water was to be furnished to the city for sewer flushing and street sprinkling; for service to schools and public buildings; and for service at fire hydrants, the latter service at the rate of $42.50 a year for each hydrant. Water was to be furnished to private takers within the city at their homes and factories and other industries at reasonable rates, not exceeding a stated schedule. While this contract was in force a building caught fire. The flames, spreading to the plaintiff's warehouse near by, destroyed it and its contents. The defendant, according to the complaint, was promptly notified of the fire, "but omitted and neglected after such notice, to supply or furnish sufficient or adequate quantity of water, with adequate pressure to stay, suppress, or extinguish the fire before it reached the warehouse of the plaintiff, although the pressure and supply which the defendant was equipped to supply and furnish, and had agreed by said contract to supply and furnish, was adequate and sufficient to prevent the spread of the fire to and the destruction of the plaintiff's warehouse and its contents." By reason of the failure of the defendant "to fulfill the provisions of the contract between it and the city of Rensselaer," the plaintiff is said to have suffered damage, for which judgment is demanded. A motion, in the nature of a demurrer, to dismiss the complaint, was denied at Special Term. The Appellate Division reversed by a divided court. * * *

We think the action is not maintainable as one for a common-law tort. * * *

If conduct has gone forward to such a stage that inaction would commonly result, not negatively merely in withholding a benefit, but positively or actively in working an injury, there exists a relation out of which arises a duty to go forward. [C] So the surgeon who operates without pay is liable, though his negligence is the omission to sterilize his instruments * * *; the engineer though his fault is in the failure to shut off steam * * *; the maker of automobiles, at the suit of some one other than the buyer, though his negligence is merely in inadequate inspection [c]. The query always is whether the putative wrongdoer has advanced to such a point as to have launched a force or instrument of harm, or has stopped where inaction is at most a refusal to become an instrument for good. * * *

The plaintiff would have us hold that the defendant, when once it entered upon the performance of its contract with the city, was brought into such a relation with every one who might potentially be benefited through the supply of water at the hydrants as to give to negligent performance, without reasonable notice of a refusal to continue, the quality of a tort. * * * We are satisfied that liability would be unduly and indeed indefinitely extended by this enlargement of the zone of duty. The dealer in coal who is to supply fuel for a shop must then answer to the customers if fuel is lacking. The manufacturer of goods, who enters upon the performance of his contract must answer, in that view, not only to the buyer, but to those who to his knowledge are looking to the buyer for their own sources of supply. Every one making a promise having the quality of a contract will be under a duty to the promisee by virtue of that promise, but under another duty, apart from contract, to an indefinite number of potential beneficiaries when performance has begun. The assumption of one relation would mean the involuntary assumption of a series of new relations, inescapably hooked together. Again we may say in the words of the Supreme Court of the United States, "The law does not spread its protection so far." Robins Dry Dock & Repair Co. v. Flint, 275 U.S. 303. * * *

We think the action is not maintainable as one for the breach of a statutory duty. * * *

The judgment should be affirmed, with costs.

NOTES AND QUESTIONS

1.   What if the city's own property were destroyed by fire because of lack of sufficient water pressure? Town of Ukiah v. Ukiah Water & Improvement Co., 142 Cal. 173, 75 P. 773 (1904); Inhabitants of Milford v. Bangor Ry. & Elec. Co., 106 Me. 316, 76 A. 696 (1909).

2.   What about the arguments:

A.   That the defendant, by undertaking to supply water, has induced the city and the plaintiff to rely upon such protection, and to forego other protection to which they might have resorted?

B.   That defendant has actually entered upon the performance of its undertaking and has performed it negligently?

C.   That by entering upon performance the defendant has become a public utility, and so has entered into a relation with members of the general public that imposes a duty?

3.   The principal case represents the majority rule. It was applied in an accident caused by the great New York power failure of 1977. The plaintiff, the tenant of a building, had fallen in a dark stairwell, Strauss v. Belle Realty Co., 65 N.Y.2d 399, 482 N.E.2d 34, 492 N.Y.S.2d 555 (1985). Con. Ed., in another fall on dark stairs case, succeeded again in arguing it owed no duty of care to the tenant of a building, Goldstein v. Consolidated Edison Co. of New York, 115 A.D.2d 34, 499 N.Y.S.2d 47 (1 Dept.1986). But cf. Hall v. Consolidated Edison Co., 104 Misc. 2d

565, 428 N.Y.S.2d 837 (N.Y.Sup.Ct.1980) (liability where plaintiff fell in darkened hallway after defendant cut off power without notice). Some cases have allowed recovery. Harlan Water Co. v. Carter, 220 Ky. 493, 295 S.W. 426 (1927), did so on the theory that plaintiff is a third-party beneficiary of the contract with the city. In Fisher v. Greensboro Water Supply Co., 128 N.C. 375, 38 S.E. 912 (1901), and Mugge v. Tampa Water Works Co., 52 Fla. 371, 42 So. 81 (1906), the theory was one of tort for breach of a duty undertaken. In Doyle v. South Pittsburgh Water Co., 414 Pa. 199, 199 A.2d 875 (1964), the defendant was held to have entered on performance.

Both sides of the argument were presented at length in Reimann v. Monmouth Consol. Water Co., 9 N.J. 134, 87 A.2d 325 (1952), which, by a vote of 4–2, adhered to the majority rule.

4. If defective water is in fact supplied under a contract with the city, the defendant may be liable to an individual for resulting injury, such as typhoid fever. Hayes v. Torrington Water Co., 88 Conn. 609, 92 A. 406 (1914).

5. There is much the same difference of opinion on the failure of a telephone company to render service under a contract with a private individual, as a result of which a third party is injured. See, for example, Mentzer v. New England Tel. & Tel. Co., 276 Mass. 478, 177 N.E. 549 (1931) (no liability); McLeod v. Pacific Tel. Co., 52 Or. 22, 94 P. 568 (1908) (liability).

Clagett v. Dacy

Court of Special Appeals of Maryland, 1980.
47 Md.App. 23, 420 A.2d 1285.

WILNER, JUDGE. Appellants were the high bidders at a foreclosure sale, but because the attorneys conducting the sale failed to follow the proper procedures, the sale was set aside. This occurred twice. Ultimately, the debtor discharged the loan, thus "redeeming" his land, and appellants lost the opportunity to acquire the property and make a profit on its resale. They sued the attorneys in the Circuit Court for Prince George's County to recover their loss, alleging that the attorneys in question owed them, as bidders, a duty to use care and diligence and to conduct the sale "properly and carefully." By sustaining the attorneys' demurrer without leave to amend, the court concluded that no such duty existed—at least not one from which an action for damages will arise; and, by affirming that order, we shall indicate our concurrence with the court's conclusion. * * *

Although [Prescott v. Coppage, 266 Md. 562, 296 A.2d 150 (1972)] has a most unusual factual setting, it does seem to suggest a modest relaxation of the strict privity requirement to the extent of allowing a true third party beneficiary to sue an attorney as he could sue any other defaulting or tortious party to a contract made for his benefit. This extension is not unique to Maryland. [C]

It is, however, a limited one with a special utility. It is most often seen and applied in actions based on drafting errors in wills and other such documents or on erroneous title reports—errors that, by their very nature, will likely have a long or delayed effect and will most probably impact upon persons other than the attorney's immediate employer, [cc] although it has been applied in other contexts as well. See Donald v. Garry, 19 Cal.App.3d 769, 97 Cal.Rptr. 191 (1971) (creditor who assigned claim to collection agency for collection allowed to sue agency's attorney for negligence in prosecuting his claim).

The *Coppage* Court made clear that only those persons who qualify under the normal rules for determining third party beneficiaries will be afforded the privileged status *vis à vis* attorney defendants; i.e., creditor beneficiaries. [Cc] This would seem to limit the extension to actions based upon contract, to which the third party beneficiary theory is peculiarly applicable, and would not supply a basis for permitting third parties to sue attorneys on a pure negligence theory—violation of some general duty arising in the absence of an underlying contractual attorney-client relationship.

In Donald v. Garry, supra, the California court utilized the concept expressed in Restatement (Second) of Torts § 324A, to support a third party action, concluding that "[a]n attorney may be liable for damage caused by his negligence *to a person intended to be benefited by his performance* irrespective of any lack of privity of contract between the attorney and the party to be benefited." (Emphasis supplied.) The context of this, as noted above, was an action by the true creditor against the collection agency attorney, and the court was careful to mention that "the transaction in which the respondent's negligence occurred was intended primarily for the benefit of [the creditor]. Respondent was retained to collect an account due him."

It will, moreover, take more than general conclusory allegations to satisfy that requirement. Attorneys are not quite the free agents as some others are in the world of commerce. There are well-recognized limitations, judicially imposed and enforced, upon how they may conduct themselves, and who they may, and may not, represent in certain situations. Except in very limited circumstances, they may not represent or act for conflicting interests in a transaction; their manifest duty of loyalty to their employer/client forbids it. See, for example, Code of Professional Responsibility, Canon 5, EC5–14, 5–15, 5–16, 5–19, 5–22; DR5–105.

These limitations, predominant but not necessarily exclusive with attorneys, must, of necessity, be taken into account when dealing with actions founded upon an implied duty owed by an attorney to a person who is not his direct employer/client, or upon an employment relationship alleged to arise by implication rather than by express agreement. Thus, the duties or obligations inherent in an attorney-client relationship will not be presumed to flow to a third party and will not be presumed to arise by implication when the effect of such a presumption would be tantamount to a prohibited or improbable employment, absent the clearest exposition of facts from which such an employment may be fairly and rationally inferred.

When judged against these principles, it becomes clear that the Declaration at issue here has failed to state a cause of action. It does not sufficiently allege a proper standing on the part of appellants to sue the appellee attorneys; nor, from what *is* alleged, could it do so. Appellees were engaged to represent the mortgagee (deed of trust beneficiary), not the bidders, whose interest would likely be in conflict with that of the mortgagee. The mortgagee's economic interest, and legal obligation, is to secure the highest possible price for the property, whereas the bidders' goal is to pay as little as possible. It is evident, in that circumstance, that an attorney could not lawfully represent both the mortgagee and the bidder in the transaction; and it will not be lightly presumed or inferred that appellees did so.

Nor may the prohibited employment be inferred from an allegation that appellees' fees would ultimately be paid from the proceeds of sale. The mere fact that those fees, along with the other costs of the proceeding, may be taken from the purchase price paid by the successful bidder does not mean that the purchaser is actually paying the fees. Quite the contrary. The debtor/mortgagor ultimately pays the fees and all other costs, for he gets only the net surplus (if any) available after all such fees and costs are discharged. The bidder pays only for the property, not the cost of selling it; and he is not, therefore, the client (express or implied) of the attorney engaged to sell the property.

Judgment affirmed; appellants to pay the costs.

NOTES AND QUESTIONS

1. One place in which the privity limitation is still significant is the area of professional relationships.

2. *Attorneys.* As the principal case reflects, the privity duty limitation has also been utilized by attorneys when they have committed an act of professional negligence. In many jurisdictions the privity limitation is still strictly applied.

3. The first major inroad on the privity rule as applied to attorneys occurred in California in Biakanja v. Irving, 49 Cal.2d 647, 320 P.2d 16 (1958), where a notary public acting as an attorney prepared a will for his "client," but negligently failed to have the will properly attested: the exception to the privity requirement was formulated along the lines of the principal case; cf. Brammer v. Taylor, 175 W.Va. 728, 338 S.E.2d 207 (1985). In Lucas v. Hamm, 56 Cal.2d 583, 364 P.2d 685, 15 Cal.Rptr. 821 (1961), cert. denied, 368 U.S. 987 (1962), the court indicated that the new rule would be applied to an actual attorney; however, the court found that the defendant was not negligent in drafting a will provision that ran afoul of the rule against perpetuities.

Connecticut followed this lead in Licata v. Spector, 26 Conn.Supp. 378, 225 A.2d 28 (1966). New York disagreed; see Victor v. Goldman, 74 Misc.2d 685, 344 N.Y.S.2d 672 (1973), aff'd, 43 A.D.2d 1021, 351 N.Y.S.2d 956 (1974).

4. Cases in which attorneys have been held liable to third parties generally have involved beneficiaries of wills. See Heyer v. Flaig, 70 Cal.2d 223, 449 P.2d 161, 74 Cal.Rptr. 225 (1969), where an attorney neglected to advise his client that her pending marriage would affect her intent to have all of her property flow to her daughters. But, whenever an attorney's work product is primarily for the benefit of a third party, potential liability can arise. See Donald v. Garry, 19 Cal.App.3d 769, 97 Cal.Rptr. 191 (1971) (attorney hired by collection agency liable to individual creditor). Vereins–Und Westbank v. Carter, 691 F.Supp. 704 (S.D.N.Y.1988) (attorney's opinion letter, written at client's request but with plaintiff's reliance in mind).

Should it matter that an attorney intentionally drafted a will in such a way that testator failed to receive what was owed her? See Kirgan v. Parks, 60 Md.App. 1, 478 A.2d 713 (1984).

5. Although California courts have formulated a "rule" almost twenty years ago, they still struggle when it must be applied in specific fact situations. For example, should an attorney be liable to an apparently intended beneficiary charitable organization when his client gave him an incorrect name of the group and this voided that provision of the will? See Ventura County Humane Society v. Holloway, 40 Cal.App.3d 897, 115 Cal.Rptr. 464 (1974). See also Roberts v. Ball, Hunt, Hart, Brown and Baerwitz, 57 Cal.App.3d 104, 128 Cal.Rptr. 901 (1976); and Goodman v. Kennedy, 18 Cal.3d 335, 556 P.2d 737, 134 Cal.Rptr. 375 (1976), both holding for the defendant. For discussion see Partlett, Professional Negligence (1985) pp. 78–85. Liability in the cases generally does not depend upon the plaintiff's reasonable reliance.

6. Most courts have been punctilious in not undermining the prime obligation owed by attorney to client, see Ross v. Caunters [1980] Ch. 297 (weighing this in finding a duty of care owed by attorney to disappointed beneficiary under a negligently drawn will); One National Bank v. Antonellis, 80 F.3d 606 (1st Cir.1996) (applying Massachusetts law, holding that defendant attorney owes no duty of care in negligence to a nonclient who relies on attorney's certificate of good title; the rationale was the potential conflict with the duty attorney owed the client). Accordingly, physicians have had little success in arguing that attorneys bringing malpractice actions against them on behalf of clients, owe the physician a duty of care. Weaver v. Superior Court, 95 Cal.App.3d 166, 156 Cal.Rptr. 745 (1979) (applying Goodman v. Kennedy, supra).

7. A leases from B space to operate a restaurant in an airplane terminal. B contracts with C to upgrade the facility. C's negligence in carrying out work for the upgrade causes A's restaurant to close for some weeks. Does A have a good cause of action against C for the lost revenue? J'Aire v. Gregory, 24 Cal. 3d 799, 598 P.2d 60, 157 Cal. Rptr. 407 (1979); Junior Books v. Veitchi (1983) 1 A.C. 520 (House of Lords (Eng.)). Are there reasons to doubt the legitimacy of the holdings?

2. FAILURE TO ACT

Hegel v. Langsam

Court of Common Pleas of Ohio, 1971.
29 Ohio Misc. 147, 55 Ohio Ops.2d 476, 273 N.E.2d 351.

BETTMAN, JUDGE. This matter is before the Court on defendant's motion for judgment on the pleadings. The gravamen of plaintiff's position is that the defendants permitted the minor plaintiff, a seventeen year old female student from Chicago, Illinois, enrolled at the University, to become associated with criminals, to be seduced, to become a drug user and further allowed her to be absent from her dormitory and failed to return her to her parents' custody on demand.

In our opinion plaintiffs completely misconstrue the duties and functions of a university. A university is an institution for the advancement of knowledge and learning. It is neither a nursery school, a boarding school nor a prison. No one is required to attend. Persons who meet the required qualifications and who abide by the university's rules and regulations are permitted to attend and must be presumed to have sufficient maturity to conduct their own personal affairs.

We know of no requirement of the law and none has been cited to us placing on a university or its employees any duty to regulate the private lives of their students, to control their comings and goings and to supervise their associations.

We do not believe that O.R.C. 3345.21 requiring a university to maintain "law and order" on campus, nor O.R.C. 2151.41, making it a crime to contribute to the delinquency of a child, have any bearing on the fact situation before us.

For these reasons we hold that plaintiffs have failed to state a cause of action and defendants' motion for judgment on the pleadings should be granted. * * *

NOTES AND QUESTIONS

1. Compare with the instant case, Duarte v. State, 84 Cal.App.3d 729, 148 Cal.Rptr. 804 (1978), holding a university liable for rape and murder in a student dormitory. Reconcilable?

Although a governmental unit was technically the defendant in this case, the court applied the same fundamental tort principles that have been applied to private parties. Thus:

A. Bigan enticed his friend Yania, a competent adult, to jump into a large open trench in a strip mining area. The trench contained water 8 to 10 feet in depth and Yania drowned. Bigan made no rescue effort. Should he be liable to Yania's widow? Yania v. Bigan, 397 Pa. 316, 155 A.2d 343 (1959).

[handwritten margin note: common law says no duty you put unless that person in peril]

B. Siegrist and Farwell drove around town stopping at various restaurants and drive-ins. At one stop a gang beat up Farwell; Siegrist escaped injury. Should he have a duty to obtain medical aid for his friend? Farwell v. Keaton, 396 Mich. 281, 240 N.W.2d 217 (1976).

[handwritten margin note: legally no]

2. The view of the common law is stated nicely by Justice Deane of the High Court of Australia in Jaensch v. Coffey, 155 Comm.L.R. 549, 578 (1984):

> [T]he common law has neither recognised fault in the conduct of the feasting Dives nor embraced the embarrassing moral perception that he who has failed to feed the man dying from hunger has truly killed him.

Do you consider the common law's stance appropriate? An array of opinion has developed, see articles listed in note 5 infra.

3. Should the status of the defendant impose a duty of care?

Assuming that "governmental tort immunity" is not applicable (see pages 635–636), how far should government agencies be liable for a failure to rescue or protect imperiled citizens? Some cases are discussed, and many cited, by Professor Barbara E. Armacost, Affirmative Duties, Systemic Harms, and the Due Process Clause, 94 Mich. L. Rev. 982, 1009–1025 (1996). A few of the many pertinent cases are, Simpson's Food Fair, Inc. v. Evansville, 149 Ind.App. 387, 272 N.E.2d 871 (1971) (failure to provide police protection to grocer); Riss v. City of New York, infra page 640 (individual who was threatened did not obtain requested police protection); Florence v. Goldberg, 44 N.Y.2d 189, 375 N.E.2d 763, 404 N.Y.S.2d 583 (1978) (police patrolling crossing but none on the day of the accident); Sinthasomphone v. Milwaukee, 785 F.Supp. 1343 (E.D.Wis.1992) (action by parents of murder victim who was returned by defendant police to Jeffrey Dahmer after report by neighbor that victim was in distress on street); and Kircher v. Jamestown, 74 N.Y.2d 251, 543 N.E.2d 443, 544 N.Y.S.2d 995 (1989) (action by victim of assault and rape after police failed to follow up report of suspicious event in parking lot).

4. Should professionals be under an obligation to assist an individual in need of their services? Although the American Medical Association's Principles of Medical Ethics, Number 5 provides that, in an emergency, a physician should render service to the best of his ability, tort law places no such obligation on the profession. See Hurley v. Eddingfield, 156 Ind. 416, 59 N.E. 1058 (1901).

Originally, before the idea of contract obligations had developed, those engaged in "public callings" were held to have undertaken an obligation to serve the public, which made them liable for failure to do so. This survives today in the rule that common carriers, innkeepers, and public utilities generally, are liable for failure to render service. See, for example, Nevin v. Pullman Palace–Car Co., 106 Ill. 222, 46 Am.Rep. 688 (1883), where the defendant was held liable for failure to provide a sleeping car berth.

5. Several European countries have provisions in their penal codes imposing a duty to rescue. Typical is the Dutch Penal Code, Art. 450: "One who, witnessing the danger of death with which another is suddenly threatened, neglects to give or furnish him such assistance as he can give or procure without reasonable fear of danger to himself or to others, is to be punished, if the death of the person in distress follows, by a detention of three months at most, and an amende of three hundred florins at most." Cf. Vt.Stat.Ann. tit. 12, § 579 (1973); see Franklin, Vermont Requires Rescue: A Comment, 25 Stan.L.Rev. 51 (1972). For others, see Rudzinski, The Duty to Rescue: A Comparative Analysis, in Ratcliffe, The Good Samaritan and the Law, 91 (1966). The common law "no duty" rule is severely criticized in Bender, A Lawyer's Primer on Feminist Theory and Tort, 38 J. of Legal Ed. 3 (1988)—"a consequence of a legal system devoid of care and responsiveness to the safety of others."

6. The President signed the "Volunteer Protection Act of 1997" (Public Law 105–19) on June 18, 1997. Congress found that the percentage of American volunteers declined in the years leading up to 1997. Congress also found that the budgets of nonprofit entities were increasingly burdened by high insurance premiums related to a rise in the amount of tort claims that the entities were forced to defend. The purpose of the Act was to eliminate the number of tort claims and reduce damages by immunizing volunteers from personal liability for torts they commit in the scope of their service. Congress reasoned that the Act would promote a rebound in national volunteer rates.

Specifically, the Act limits the personal tort liability of volunteers as long as they are: (1) acting in the scope of their responsibilities for a nonprofit or government entity at the time of the act or omission, (2) properly licensed, certified or authorized to perform the activity causing harm by the State where the injury occurred, (3) not acting with intent to commit harm or criminal negligence, and (4) not driving a vehicle that the State requires a license or insurance to operate. The Act absolves volunteers from punitive damages unless they commit harm in a manner that would constitute criminal conduct. The Act also limits a volunteer's liability for noneconomic loss to that which is proportional to the volunteer's responsibility for the harm. As a final caveat, the Act contains a preemption and election section that allows states: (1) to pass laws that extend further protections to volunteers or (2) opt out of the Act through legislation that mentions the Act by name.

L.S. Ayres & Co. v. Hicks

Supreme Court of Indiana, 1942.
220 Ind. 86, 40 N.E.2d 334.

[Plaintiff, a boy six years old, accompanied his mother to defendant's department store while she was shopping. Plaintiff fell, and got his fingers caught in defendant's escalator. Defendant unreasonably delayed stopping the escalator, as a result of which plaintiff's injuries were aggravated. Judgment for plaintiff, and a new trial denied. Defendant appeals.]

SHAKE, C.J. [after holding that there was no negligence in the construction of the escalator]. It may be observed, on the outset, that there is no general duty to go to the rescue of a person who is in peril. So, in Hurley, Adm'r, v. Eddingfield, 1901, 156 Ind. 416, 59 N.E. 1058, it was held that a physician was not liable for failing without any reason to go to the aid of one who was violently ill and who died from want of medical attention which was otherwise unavailable. The effect of this rule was aptly illustrated by Carpenter, C.J., in Buch v. Amory Mfg. Co., 1897, 69 N.H. 257, 260, 44 A. 809, 810, as follows:

"With purely moral obligations the law does not deal. For example, the priest and Levite who passed by on the other side were not, it is supposed, liable at law for the continued suffering of the man who fell among thieves, which they might, and morally ought to have prevented or relieved."

There may be principles of social conduct so universally recognized as to be demanded that they be observed as a legal duty, and the relationship of the parties may impose obligations that would not otherwise exist. Thus, it has been said that, under some circumstances, moral and humanitarian considerations may require one to render assistance to another who has been injured, even though the injury was not due to negligence on his part and may have been caused by the negligence of the injured person. Failure to render assistance in such a situation may constitute actionable negligence if the injury is aggravated through lack of due care. [C] The case of Depue v. Flatau, 1907, 100 Minn. 299, 111 N.W. 1, lends support to this rule. It was there held that one who invited into his house a cattle buyer who called to inspect cattle which were for sale owed him the duty, upon discovering that he had been taken severely ill, not to expose him to danger on a cold winter night by sending him away unattended while he was in a fainting and helpless condition.

After holding that a railroad company was liable for failing to provide medical and surgical assistance to an employee who was injured without its fault but who was rendered helpless, by reason of which the employee's injuries were aggravated, it was said with the subsequent approval of this court, in Tippecanoe Loan, etc., Co. v. Cleveland, etc., R. Co., 1915, 57 Ind.App. 644, 649, 650, 104 N.E. 866, 868.

"In some jurisdictions the doctrine has been extended much further than we are required to do in deciding this case. It has been held to apply to cases where one party has been so injured as to render him helpless by an instrumentality under the control of another, even though no relation of master and servant, or carrier and passenger, existed at the time. It has been said that the mere happening of an accident of this kind creates a relation which gives rise to a legal duty to render such aid to the injured party as may be reasonably necessary to save his life, or to prevent a serious aggravation of his injuries, and that this subsequent duty does not depend on the negligence of the one party, or the freedom of the other party from contributory negligence, but that it exists irrespective of any legal responsibility for the original injury."

From the above cases it may be deduced that there may be a legal obligation to take positive or affirmative steps to effect the rescue of a person who is helpless or in a situation of peril, when the one proceeded against is a master or invitor, or when the injury resulted from use of an instrumentality under the control of the defendant. Such an obligation may exist although the accident or original injury was caused by the negligence of the plaintiff or through that of a third person and without any fault on the part of the defendant. Other relationships may impose a like obligation, but it is not necessary to pursue that inquiry further at this time.

In the case at bar the appellee was an invitee and he received his initial injury in using an instrumentality provided by the appellant and under its control. Under the rule stated above and on the authority of the cases cited this was a sufficient relationship to impose a duty upon the appellant. Since the duty with which we are presently concerned arose after the appellee's initial injury occurred, the appellant cannot be charged with its anticipation or prevention but only with failure to exercise reasonable care to avoid aggravation. * * *

Since the appellee was only entitled to recover for an aggravation of his injuries, the jury should have been limited and restricted in assessing the damages to the injuries that were the proximate result of the appellant's actionable negligence. * * *

The judgment is reversed with directions to sustain the appellant's motion for a new trial.

NOTES AND QUESTIONS

1. *Special Relations.* The maritime law developed the rule that a ship master was required to make reasonable efforts to rescue a seaman who fell overboard. Harris v. Pennsylvania R. Co., 50 F.2d 866 (4th Cir.1931). There are a good many cases in which this has been extended to other employers, in situations where the employee has suffered sunstroke and the like. See, for example, Carey v. Davis, 190 Iowa 720, 180 N.W. 889 (1921); Rival v. Atchison, T. & S.F.R. Co., 62 N.M. 159, 306 P.2d 648 (1957); Anderson v. Atchison, T. & S.F.R. Co., 333 U.S. 821 (1948).

2. The employer's duty is limited to situations where the employee is evidently unable to look after himself. It is also limited to the course of employment, and there is no duty to aid an employee who has stepped out on his own time for a beer.

Allen v. Hixson, 111 Ga. 460, 36 S.E. 810 (1900); Matthews v. Carolina & N.W.R. Co., 175 N.C. 35, 94 S.E. 714 (1917).

3. Other special relations that have been held to impose a duty to take reasonable affirmative action to aid are:

A. Common carrier and passenger. See, for example, Middleton v. Whitridge, 213 N.Y. 499, 108 N.E. 192 (1915); Yu v. New York, N.H. & H.R. Co., 145 Conn. 451, 144 A.2d 56 (1958).

B. Innkeeper and guest, at least to the extent of aiding the guest to escape from a fire in the hotel. Dove v. Lowden, 47 F.Supp. 546 (W.D.Mo.1942).

C. Temporary legal custodian and his charge. For example, jailor and prisoner, Thomas v. Williams, 105 Ga.App. 321, 124 S.E.2d 409 (1962). The custody and control relationship may create a duty on a grade school teacher to make a reasonable effort to obtain medical aid for a pupil. See Pirkle v. Oakdale Union Grammar School Dist., 40 Cal.2d 207, 253 P.2d 1 (1953). A duty of care has been imposed on a school to protect their students from the torts of peers. Rupp v. Bryant, 417 So. 2d 658 (Fla.1982), among other cases, was cited with approval by the Supreme Court in Davis v. Monroe County Board of Education, 526 U.S. 629 (1999) (finding student-on-student harassment actionable under a Title IX damages action on a showing of "deliberate indifference").

4. The relationship established between occupier and entrant onto land may, as the principal case exemplifies, create an affirmative duty on the occupier to protect the entrant. Connelly v. Kaufmann & Baer Co., 349 Pa. 261, 37 A.2d 125 (1944); Larkin v. Saltair Beach Co., 30 Utah 86, 83 P. 686 (1905). See cases listed in Chapter 9 infra. Does an airport authority have a duty to rescue the pilot of an airplane crashing near the airport? Traudt v. City of Chicago, 98 Ill.App.2d 417, 240 N.E.2d 188 (1968).

5. In California, bar owners or employees have no duty to make an emergency call to police to protect a person threatened outside their establishment. They do have a duty, however, to allow a good samaritan the use of a public telephone on the premises. See Soldano v. O'Daniels, 141 Cal.App.3d 443, 190 Cal.Rptr. 310 (1983). Should it make a difference if it is a long-distance call? What should be the result if the good samaritan is injured, after defendant refuses to permit him use of telephone, in attempting to rush the victim of the defendant's negligence to hospital? Day v. Waffle House, Inc., 743 P.2d 1111 (Okl.App.1987).

6. There may be other relations. Two likely ones are those between husband and wife, and parent and child, where a duty to aid has been recognized by the criminal law, as in Rex v. Smith, 2 C. & P. 449, 172 Eng.Rep. 203 (1826). Cf. State v. Zobel, 81 S.D. 260, 134 N.W.2d 101 (1965). Assuming that intrafamily immunity has been abolished in a state, should tort law impose a duty on a parent to make a reasonable effort to protect or rescue his child? See Holodook v. Spencer, 36 N.Y.2d 35, 324 N.E.2d 338, 364 N.Y.S.2d 859 (1974).

7. *Negligent Injury by Defendant.* When the defendant by his own negligence injures another, there is general agreement that he is then under a duty to take reasonable affirmative action to aid him. Parrish v. Atlantic Coast Line R. Co., 221 N.C. 292, 20 S.E.2d 299 (1942).

8. *Innocent Injury by Defendant.* When defendant, without negligence, creates a dangerous condition in the highway, it is agreed that he is under a duty to take reasonable precautions against injury to persons using it. Thus in Hardy v. Brooks, 103 Ga.App. 124, 118 S.E.2d 492 (1961), the defendant innocently hit a cow and

killed it. He was held under a duty to use reasonable care to remove it from the highway, give warning, or otherwise protect other drivers. Accord: Simonsen v. Thorin, 120 Neb. 684, 234 N.W. 628 (1931) (trolley pole knocked over into street); Montgomery v. National Convoy & Trucking Co., 186 S.C. 167, 195 S.E. 247 (1938) (truck stalled on icy road at night); Buchanan v. Rose, 138 Tex. 390, 159 S.W.2d 109 (1942) (truck without negligence breaks down portion of bridge).

9. When the defendant, or his instrumentality, innocently injures the plaintiff, there are older cases holding that he is under no duty to do anything about it. Thus a railroad company which, without any negligence, ran over a trespasser, was held to be under no obligation to do anything at all to keep him from bleeding to death. Union Pac. R. Co. v. Cappier, 66 Kan. 649, 72 P. 281 (1903). Or even to remove the train from his body. Griswold v. Boston & Maine R. Co., 183 Mass. 434, 67 N.E. 354 (1903).

It appears unlikely that these rather appalling cases would be followed today. See Pridgen v. Boston Hous. Auth., 364 Mass. 696, 308 N.E.2d 467, 477 n. 7 (1974). The Restatement (Second) of Torts has changed the rule of its § 322 to impose a duty to act. In accord are Whitesides v. Southern R. Co., 128 N.C. 229, 38 S.E. 878 (1901); and apparently Ward v. Morehead City Sea Food Co., 171 N.C. 33, 87 S.E. 958 (1916).

10. "Hit and run driver" statutes, requiring an automobile driver involved in an accident to stop and give aid, have been held in a number of states to mean that a failure to do so is negligence per se. Brumfield v. Wofford, 143 W.Va. 332, 102 S.E.2d 103 (1958).

11. A duty to act may be imposed whenever the defendant assumes a responsibility to act and such undertaking increases the risk of such harm, or is relied upon by the plaintiff to her detriment. The Restatement (Second) of Torts §§ 323–324. Thus while employers generally owe no duty to their prospective employees to ascertain whether they are physically fit, where an employer assumes such a duty he is liable if performed negligently. Coffee v. McDonnell–Douglas Corp., 8 Cal.3d 551, 503 P.2d 1366, 105 Cal.Rptr. 358 (1972) (failure reasonably to disclose disease in physical examination for job purposes). See DeLong v. Erie County, infra page 643 (911 rescue call) and Florence v. Goldberg, supra (reliance upon police patrol at children's school crossing); Kleinknecht v. Gettysburg College, 989 F.2d 1360 (3d Cir.1993) (duty on college to provide appropriate assistance to athlete member of intercollegiate lacrosse team when engaged in school-sponsored intercollegiate athletic activity). For cases that fit more comfortably with the Restatement see Kirshenbaum v. General Outdoor Advertising Co., 258 N.Y. 489, 180 N.E. 245 (1932); Kuchynski v. Ukryn, 89 N.H. 400, 200 A. 416 (1938). Contra: Cummings v. Henninger, 28 Ariz. 207, 236 P. 701 (1925); Bluhm v. Byram, 193 Wis. 346, 214 N.W. 364 (1927).

12. When does the defendant enter upon an "undertaking" by affirmative action? Defendant sees a swimmer drowning in a river; he cries, "Courage, my good fellow, I will save you!"; he starts running to a shed where there is a rope; he gets the rope; he returns to the bank; he casts the rope once and it falls short; he casts it again and the swimmer catches hold; he pulls the swimmer five feet nearer the shore; he then decides that it is all just too much trouble, and abandons the whole thing; the swimmer drowns. Suppose that there is no one else within a mile. At the end of the whole sequence, would you expect any court to hold that there is no liability? Where should the line be drawn?

13. The duty to act affirmatively to protect another may be seen to spring from a defendant's voluntary undertaking and the plaintiff's detrimental reliance upon it. Where the defendant's omission in such circumstances causes the plaintiff personal injury the courts have widely recognized the duty. The undertaking may be, as in the following cases, to guard a person against the negligent or, indeed, criminal acts of others:

A. Crowley v. Spivey, 285 S.C. 397, 329 S.E.2d 774 (1985), the defendant grandparents of the decedent children undertook to the father to supervise and safeguard the children when they visited their mother, whom they knew had a history of mental disease. The mother, left alone with the children, shot and killed them. The court affirmed the trial court's judgment finding the grandparents liable.

B. In Morgan v. Yuba County, 230 Cal.App.2d 938, 41 Cal.Rptr. 508 (1964), a county sheriff's department failed to warn Mrs. Helen Morgan (as it had promised) that a dangerous prisoner was about to be released. Mrs. Morgan had played a part in the prisoner's original arrest. After the prisoner killed Mrs. Morgan, her husband brought a wrongful death claim against the county. The court held that plaintiff could state a claim if the county had induced reliance on the part of Mrs. Morgan and she had, in fact, relied on its promise. See also Williams v. United States, 450 F.Supp. 1040 (D.S.D.1978).

C. In Dudley v. Victor Lynn Lines, Inc., 48 N.J.Super. 457, 138 A.2d 53 (1958), rev'd on other grounds, 32 N.J. 479, 161 A.2d 479 (1960), a truck driver took ill while at work. He appeared to be suffering only from a bad cold, and apparently was quite able to look after himself. His helper called his wife, who was unable to come and take him home. She asked the assistant warehouse foreman to call a doctor; he promised to do so and did not. The illness turned out to be a heart attack and the man died. After rejecting any liability on the basis of the duty of an employer, on the ground that there was no apparent necessity for aid, the court held defendant liable in tort for breach of the promise, relied on to the man's detriment. Should a casual promise to make a phone call create liability?

D. In Marsalis v. La Salle, 94 So.2d 120 (La.App.1957), a cat bit plaintiff during a rabies scare. The cat owner promised plaintiff to keep the cat indoors while a physician determined whether plaintiff was infected with rabies. The cat escaped from the owner's yard; plaintiff sued and won medical expenses due to defendant's failure to act with reasonable care.

E. In Dykema v. Gus Macher Enterprises, Inc., 196 Mich.App. 6, 492 N.W.2d 472 (1992), the Court found no special relationship subsisted between the organizer of an outdoor basketball tournament and a spectator to impose a duty to warn of an approaching thunderstorm. Plaintiff had not entrusted himself to the control and protection of defendant, with consequent loss of self-protective capacity. Same for golfer, Hames v. State, 808 S.W.2d 41 (Tenn.1991). But what of spectator at U.S. Open Golf Tournament where a system of warning is provided?

If the interest trenched upon is not physical but economic, the courts have been slow to recognise a duty of care. See Chapter 21.

14. Often the undertaking and reliance are implied or attenuated. In *Coffee supra* it is impossible to discern an express undertaking or reliance. This is the case with numbers of authorities, including an important group of cases relating to the liability of hospitals running emergency facilities. In Wilmington General Hospital v. Manlove, 54 Del. (4 Storey) 15, 174 A.2d 135 (1961), the Delaware Supreme Court found a common law duty on the hospital to provide emergency care:

It may be conceded that a private hospital is under no legal obligation to the public to maintain an emergency ward * * *. If a person, seriously hurt, applies for such aid at an emergency ward, relying on the established custom to render it, is it still the right of the hospital to turn him away without any reason?

Such a set of circumstances is analogous to the case of the negligent termination of gratuitous services, which create a tort liability. (at 139)

Other cases have relied on statutes creating a public policy to render emergency services, see Thompson v. Sun City Community Hospital, Inc., 141 Ariz. 597, 688 P.2d 605 (1984). Such statutes may provide a statutory cause of action, see Consolidated Omnibus Budget Reconciliation Act of 1985 (COBRA), Pub.L. 99–272, 100 Stat. 82 (1986) (codified at 42 U.S.C.A. § 1395dd, otherwise called the "Federal Antidumping" Act).

Some courts have not based their reasoning on a broad duty to render emergency care but on the establishment of a duty once a person is present in the emergency room, see New Biloxi Hospital, Inc. v. Frazier, 245 Miss. 185, 146 So.2d 882 (1962), cf. Hurley v. Eddingfield, supra.

15. *Statutes.* Doctors, who are called on much more than anyone else in such emergencies, are much disturbed about this. While liability is aimed at deterring negligence, it has the unfortunate side effect of deterring doctors from providing emergency medical assistance. The doctors are concerned about potential malpractice suits, especially when they are obliged to work on the scene of an emergency without any equipment, without proper sanitation, and without any assistance. To encourage doctors to help, states have enacted good samaritan laws, relieving them of some liability. Every state and the District of Columbia have a form of the protective statute, despite the absence of empirical studies demonstrating any beneficial impact of the legislation. Note, Imposing Duties on Witnesses to Child Sexual Abuse: A Futile Response to Bystander Indifference, 67 Fordham L. Rev. 3169, 3180 (1999).

California was the first in 1959. The statute in its relevant part states:

No licensee, who in good faith renders emergency care at the scene of an emergency, shall be liable for any civil damages as a result of any acts or omissions by such person in rendering emergency care.

"The scene of an emergency" as used in this section shall include, but not be limited to, the emergency rooms of hospitals in the event of a medical disaster. (West's Ann.Cal.Bus. & Prof.Code § 2395)

The California statute has been found applicable to emergency situations in hospitals where a doctor is called from his duties elsewhere in the hospital, McKenna v. Cedars of Lebanon Hospital, 93 Cal.App.3d 282, 155 Cal.Rptr. 631 (1979). See also Gordin v. William Beaumont Hospital, 180 Mich.App. 488, 447 N.W.2d 793 (1989). For a case outside the hospital setting see, McCain v. Batson, 233 Mont. 288, 760 P.2d 725 (1988) (physician on vacation sutures a hiker's wound in his condominium).

16. Tort claims parallel claims stemming from deprivation of constitutional rights. In DeShaney v. Winnebago County Department of Social Services, 489 U.S. 189 (1989), the mother of an abused child sued the state of Wisconsin. She alleged that the failure of state welfare officers to protect her child from repeated beatings (at the hands of his father) breached her child's constitutionally protected due process rights under the 14th Amendment. The court found, however, that due process conferred "no affirmative right to government aid * * * [thus] the State

cannot be held liable * * * for injuries that could have been averted had it chosen to provide them." If, however, the state officers had acted to protect the child and had failed to do so, his due process rights would have been implicated. The distinction was put by Judge Posner as whether the state is the "doer of harm rather than merely an inept rescuer, just as the Roman state was a doer of harm when it threw Christians to lions." K.H. Through Murphy v. Morgan, 914 F.2d 846, 849 (7th Cir.1990). Thus, "once the state assumes custody of a person, it owes him a rudimentary duty of safekeeping no matter how perilous his circumstances when he was free." The distinction tracks tort law—there is no duty to rescue but, having effected it, the "rescuer" is "not entitled to harm the person whom he has rescued."

J.S. and M.S. v. R.T.H.

Supreme Court of New Jersey, 1998.
155 N.J. 330, 714 A.2d 924.

HANDLER, J., delivered the unanimous opinion of the Court.

In this case, two young girls, ages 12 and 15, spent substantial periods of recreational time with their neighbor at his horse barn, riding and caring for his horses. Betraying the trust this relationship established, the neighbor, an older man, sexually abused both girls for a period of more than a year. Following the man's conviction and imprisonment for these sexual offenses, the girls, along with their parents, brought this action against the man and his wife for damages, contending that the wife's negligence rendered her, as well as her husband, liable for their injuries. The man conceded liability for both the intentional and negligent injuries that he inflicted on the girls by his sexual abuse. His wife, however, denied that, under the circumstances, she could be found negligent for the girls' injuries.

This case presents the issue of whether a wife who suspects or should suspect her husband of actual or prospective sexual abuse of their neighbors' children has any duty of care to prevent such abuse. And, if there is such a duty, does a breach of that duty constitute a proximate cause of the harm that results from sexual abuse.

Defendants R.T.H. and R.G.H., husband and wife (called "John" and "Mary" for purposes of this litigation), moved into a house in Vineland, New Jersey, and became next-door neighbors of plaintiffs, J.S. and M.S. and their two daughters, C.S. and M.S.

John, 64 years old, was charged with sexually assaulting the two sisters over a period of more than a year. He pled guilty to endangering the welfare of minors and was sentenced to eighteen months in state prison. Plaintiffs, as the natural parents and guardians ad litem of their two daughters, filed a complaint against John alleging intentional, reckless, and/or negligent acts of sexual assault against each of the two girls. In an amended complaint, plaintiffs added Mary as a defendant, alleging that she "was negligent in that she knew and/or should have known of her husband's proclivities/propensities" and that as a result of her negligence the two girls suffered physical and emotional injury.

Defendants filed a joint answer in which they denied plaintiffs' allegations. In an amended answer, Mary offered the defenses that she owed no duty to plaintiffs, that any alleged negligence on her part was not the proximate cause of any injuries or damages sustained by plaintiffs, and that any damages sustained by plaintiffs were the result of actions by a third party over whom she exercised no control. Mary also filed a crossclaim for contribution and indemnification against John, alleging that even if plaintiffs' allegations were proven, John was the primary, active, and sole culpable cause of any injuries to the plaintiffs.

* * *

The trial court entered summary judgment on behalf of Mary. On appeal, the Appellate Division reversed the order and remanded for entry of an order granting plaintiffs extended discovery. [C]

This Court granted defendant's petition for certification. [C]

* * *

In determining whether a duty is to be imposed, courts must engage in a rather complex analysis that weighs and balances several, related factors, including the nature of the underlying risk of harm, that is, its foreseeability and severity, the opportunity and ability to exercise care to prevent the harm, the comparative interests of, and the relationships between or among, the parties, and, ultimately, based on considerations of public policy and fairness, the societal interest in the proposed solution. See Hopkins v. Fox & Lazo Realtors, 132 N.J. 426, 439, 625 A.2d 1110 (1993).

Foreseeability of the risk of harm is the foundational element in the determination of whether a duty exists. [C] The "ability to foresee injury to a potential plaintiff" is "crucial" in determining whether a duty should be imposed. [C]

Foreseeability as a component of a duty to exercise due care is based on the defendant's knowledge of the risk of injury and is susceptible to objective analysis. [C] That knowledge may be an actual awareness of risk. [C] Such knowledge may also be constructive; the defendant may be charged with knowledge if she is "in a position" to "discover the risk of harm." [C] In some cases where the nature of the risk or the extent of harm is difficult to ascertain, foreseeability may require that the defendant have a "special reason to know" that a "particular plaintiff" or "identifiable class of plaintiffs" would likely suffer a "particular type" of injury. See People Express Airlines, Inc. v. Consolidated Rail Corp., 100 N.J. 246, 262, 263, 495 A.2d 107 (1985). Further, when the risk of harm is that posed by third persons, a plaintiff may be required to prove that defendant was in a position to "know or have reason to know, from past experience, that there [was] a likelihood of conduct on the part of [a] third person[]" that was "likely to endanger the safety" of another. Clohesy v. Food Circus Supermarkets, Inc., 149 N.J. 496, 507, 694 A.2d 1017 (1997).

"The question whether there is a 'duty' merely begs the more fundamental question whether the plaintiff's interests are entitled to legal protection against the defendant's conduct." [C] The imposition of a duty thus requires an evaluation and a balancing of the conflicting interests of the respective parties. Portee v. Jaffee, 84 N.J. 88, 101, 417 A.2d 521 (1980). That assessment necessarily includes an examination of the relationships between and among the parties. Also implicated in this analysis is an assessment of the defendant's "responsibility for conditions creating the risk of harm" and an analysis of whether the defendant had sufficient control, opportunity, and ability to have avoided the risk of harm. Kuzmicz v. Ivy Hill Apts., Inc., 147 N.J. 510, 515, 688 A.2d 1018 (1997); Carvalho [v. Toll Bros. And Developers, 143 N.J. 565, 573, 675 A.2d 209, 212].

Ultimately, the determination of the existence of a duty is a question of fairness and public policy. Clohesy, supra, 149 N.J. at 502. In fixing the limits of liability as a matter of public policy, courts must draw on "notions of fairness, common sense, and morality." Hopkins, supra, 132 N.J. at 443. Public policy must be determined in the context of contemporary circumstances and considerations. See, e.g., Kelly v. Gwinnell, 96 N.J. 538, 544–45, 476 A.2d 1219 (1984) (noting that in a society growing increasingly intolerant of drunken driving, the imposition of a duty on social hosts "seems both fair and fully in accord with the State's policy"). Thus, " 'duty' is not a rigid formalism" that remains static through time, but rather is a malleable concept that "must of necessity adjust to the changing social relations and exigencies and man's relation to his fellows." Wytupeck v. Camden, 25 N.J. 450, 462, 136 A.2d 887 (1957).

The Court, in its determination whether to impose a duty, must also consider the scope or boundaries of that duty. [C] The scope of a duty is determined under "the totality of the circumstances," Clohesy, supra, 149 N.J. at 514, and must be "reasonable" under those circumstances, id. at 520. Factors to be taken into consideration include the risk of harm involved and the practicality of preventing it. Id. at 519–20; see also Hopkins, supra, 132 N.J. at 447 (noting that "negligence has often been defined as the failure to take precautions that cost less than the damage wrought" by the harm). When the defendant's actions are "relatively easily corrected" and the harm sought to be prevented is "serious," it is fair to impose a duty. Kelly, supra, 96 N.J. at 549–50. In the final analysis, the "reasonableness of action" that constitutes such a duty is "an essentially objective determination to be made on the basis of the material facts" of each case. [C]

Here, a man criminally sexually assaulted unrelated, adolescent children whom he had befriended. The defendant is the spouse of the wrongdoer. The abuse occurred on her own property over an extended period of time. The tortious, assaultive conduct is of a type that is extremely difficult to identify, anticipate, and predict. While these considerations bear on all of the factors that are relevant in determining whether a duty of care should be recognized and imposed on the spouse, they bear materially on the primary element of foreseeability.

Although conduct involving sexual abuse is often secretive, clandestine, and furtive, a number of factors are relevant when determining whether or not it is foreseeable to a wife that her husband would sexually abuse a child. These include whether the husband had previously committed sexual offenses against children; the number, date, and nature of those prior offenses; the gender of prior victims; the age of prior victims; where the prior offenses occurred; whether the prior offense was against a stranger or a victim known to the husband; the husband's therapeutic history and regimen; the extent to which the wife encouraged or facilitated her husband's unsupervised contact with the current victim; the presence of physical evidence such as pornographic materials depicting children and the unexplained appearance of children's apparel in the marital home; and the extent to which the victims made inappropriate sexual comments or engaged in age-inappropriate behavior in the husband and wife's presence. See, e.g., Pamela L. v. Farmer, 112 Cal. App. 3d 206, 169 Cal. Rptr. 282 (Ct. App. 1980) (finding that foreseeability of harm is great where the sexual assault occurred in the marital home, the child victims were expressly invited into the home by the wife, the wife knew that the husband had molested children in the past, and the wife left the children in the unsupervised presence of her husband); Doe v. Franklin, 930 S.W.2d 921 (Tex. Ct. App. 1996) (ruling that foreseeability requirement is met where wife had knowledge that her husband was a pedophile, wife invited child victim into home, child tried to tell the wife of the molestation, and wife left child in the unsupervised presence of the husband); T.A. v. Allen, 447 Pa. Super. 302, 669 A.2d 360, 372 (Pa. Super. Ct. 1995) (Ford Elliot, J., dissenting) (stating that wife owed duty to children where she allowed them to enter into the marital home where she knew that the husband kept a studio devoted to sexual experiments on children), appeal denied, 544 Pa. 661, 676 A.2d 1201 (1996); see also In re Registrant G.B., 147 N.J. 62, 70–71, 685 A.2d 1252 (1996) (listing factors that the Legislature has identified as indicative of the likelihood of a pedophile's re-offense); In re Registrant C.A., 146 N.J. 71, 81–83, 679 A.2d 1153 (1996) (same); Doe v. Poritz, 142 N.J. 1, 15, 662 A.2d 367 (1995) (noting that there is a 10–29% recidivism rate for offenders who sexually assault little girls and a 13–40% recidivism rate for offenders who sexually assault little boys).

Moreover, there is some empirical support for the conclusion that sexual abuse of a child, while extremely difficult to detect or anticipate, is a risk that can be foreseen by a spouse. This evidence indicates that an extremely high percentage of child sexual molesters are men, many of whom are married. U.S. Dept. of Justice, Bureau of Justice Statistics, Child Victimizers: Violent Offenders and Their Victims 5 (March 1996). The vast majority of child victims are female and many child victims fall prey to an immediate relative or a family acquaintance; most of these sexual assaults are committed either in the offender's home or the victim's home. [C] Given those factors, the wife of a sexual abuser of children is in a unique position to observe firsthand telltale signs of sexual abuse. A wife may well be the only person with the kind of knowledge or opportunity to know that a particular person or particular class of persons is being sexually abused or is likely to be abused by her husband. Cf. Franklin, supra, 930 S.W.2d at 928 (concluding that once wife assumed the task of caring for her child and inviting the child into her home, the wife had a duty not to leave the child alone with her pedophiliac husband); Chaney v. Superior Ct., 39 Cal. App. 4th 152, 46 Cal. Rptr. 2d 73 (Ct. App. 1995) (indicating that where a child is sexually assaulted in marital home by husband, wife has a duty of reasonable care if husband's behavior was "reasonably foreseeable").

These considerations warrant a standard of foreseeability in this case that is based on "particular knowledge" or "special reason to know" that a "particular plaintiff" or "identifiable class of plaintiffs" would suffer a "particular type" of injury. [Cc] "Particularized foreseeability" in this kind of case will conform the standard of foreseeability to the empirical evidence and common experience that indicate a wife may often have actual knowledge or special reason to know that her husband is abusing or is likely to abuse an identifiable victim and will accommodate the concerns over the inherent difficulties in predicting such furtive behavior. That test of foreseeability will also ensure that the wife is not subject to a broad duty that may expose her to liability to every child whom her husband may threaten and harm. Foreseeability under that definitional standard is neither unrealistic nor unfair.

The nature of the parties' interests bears on the need to recognize a duty of care. "There can be no doubt about the strong policy of this State to protect children from sexual abuse and to require reporting of suspected child abuse." That policy is so obvious and so powerful that it can draw little argument. It is an interest that is massively documented.

The Legislature has dealt comprehensively with the subject of child abuse and has enacted a plethora of statutes designed to prevent the sexual abuse of children. For example, N.J.S.A. 9:6–8.10 requires any person having reasonable cause to believe that a child has been subject to abuse to report the abuse immediately to the Division of Youth and Family Services. The duty to report is not limited to professionals, such as doctors, psychologists, and teachers, but is required of every citizen. [C] Indeed, friends or neighbors are often in the best position to fulfill this statutory duty because they are the people "who frequently hear or observe acts of child abuse." Id. at 357.

* * *

"Megan's Law," N.J.S.A. 2C:7–1 to–11, provides yet more evidence of the State's intolerance of sexual abuse of children. In affirming the constitutionality of the community notification and registration requirements of Megan's Law for convicted sex offenders, this Court recognized the enormous public interest in protecting society from the threat of potential molestation, rape, or murder of women and children. [C]

While the interest in protecting children from sexual abuse is great, this Court must also take into consideration defendants' interests in a stable marital relationship and in marital privacy. [C] That interest traditionally found expression in the common-law doctrine of interspousal immunity wherein one spouse could not sue or be sued by another, [c] and the testimonial disqualification wherein one spouse was not permitted to testify for or against the other [c]. Both courts and scholars, however, increasingly questioned whether the doctrine of marital immunity actually succeeded in promoting the marital tranquility and privacy it was designed to serve. [C]

Moreover, the societal interest in enhancing marital relationships cannot outweigh the societal interest in protecting children from sexual abuse. The child-abuse reporting statute itself has mandated that balance— it applies to every citizen, including a spouse. [Cc]

Considerations of fairness and public policy also govern whether the imposition of a duty is warranted. [C] Public policy considerations based in large measure on the comparative interests of the parties support over-whelmingly the recognition of a duty of care in these circumstances. This Court has recognized that the sexual abuse of children not only traumatizes the victims, but also exacts a heavy toll on society:

Recent research indicates that a number of psychosocial problems— including chronic depression and anxiety, isolation and poor social adjust-ment, substance abuse, suicidal behavior, and involvement in physically or sexually abusive relationships as either aggressor or victim—are more common among adults molested as children than among those with no such childhood experiences. Victims of sexual abuse can suffer an impaired ability to critically evaluate the motives and behavior of others, making them more vulnerable to revictimization. An especially disturbing finding about child sexual abuse is its strong intergenerational pattern; in particu-lar, due to the psychological impact of their own abuse, sexually abused boys have been found to be more likely than non-abused boys to turn into offenders against the next generation of children, and sexually abused girls are more likely to become mothers of children who are abused. And studies show that adult male aggressive behavior, particularly sexual aggression, is associated with the trauma of childhood sexual abuse. Thus, apart from the substantial personal trauma caused to the victims of such crimes, sexual crimes against children exact heavy social costs as well.

Considerations of fairness implicate the scope as well as the existence of a duty. In defining the duty to be imposed, the court must weigh the ability and opportunity of the defendant to exercise reasonable care. Defendant contends that the imposition of a duty to prevent her husband from engaging in sexual abuse of another person would be unfair. She argues that sexual offenses are extremely difficult to combat and that she did not necessarily have the power, the ability, or the opportunity to control her husband and should not be expected or required to police his conduct continuously. However, fairness concerns in these circumstances can be accommodated by a flexible duty of care that requires a spouse, when there is particularized foreseeability of harm of sexual abuse to a child, to take reasonable steps to prevent or warn of the harm. See Franklin, supra, 930 S.W.2d at 928–29 (holding that "a duty exists to not place a child in a situation in which the risk of sexual abuse is heightened and in which the risk is foreseeable" and that therefore a wife who "knew or should have known of her husband's proclivities, [] should have taken steps to ensure that [the grandchild] would not be placed in harm's way or to otherwise ensure that her husband would not be in a position to act on his temptations"); Phillips v. Deihm, 213 Mich. App. 389, 541 N.W.2d 566 (Mich.Ct.App.1995) (finding that victim of sexual abuse had cause of action against pedophile's wife who was allegedly aware of, but failed to prevent, the abuse that occurred in the marital home and pickup truck); Pamela L., supra, 169 Cal. Rptr. 282 (finding that children who suffered sexual abuse stated valid cause of action against pedophile's wife, where the complaint alleged that the wife knew her husband had molested children in the past, she encouraged and invited the children to be alone with her husband in the family pool when she was at work, and she unreasonably exposed the children to harm); Chaney, supra, 46 Cal. Rptr. 2d at 76 (noting that "public policy requires that where a child is sexually assaulted in the defendant wife's home by her husband, the wife's duty of reasonable care to the injured child depends on whether the husband's behavior was reasonably foreseeable"); see also T.A. v. Allen, supra, 669 A.2d at 364–65 (Olszewski, J., dissenting) (arguing that where step-grandmother knew or had reason to know of her husband's pedophilia, she had a duty to warn the children of the danger posed by their grandfather); id. at 372 (Ford Elliott, J., dissenting) (arguing that wife in those circumstances had duty to protect the children from a known child abuser, not simply to warn them of the danger); cf. Arvanitis v. Hios, 307 N.J. Super. 577, 705 A.2d 355 (App.Div.1998) (citing Appellate Division decision in this case and holding that layperson, a wife, owes duty of reasonable care under the circumstances to her nephew who was injured while assisting her in convincing her husband, whom she knew to have violent tendencies, to take his medication); Tarasoff [v. Regents of the University of California, 17 Cal. 3d 425, 431, 551 P.2d 334, 340, 131 Cal. Rptr. 14, 20] (imposing duty of reasonable care when defendant knew that a third person posed a risk of harm to the victim).

Considerations of foreseeability, the comparative interests and relationships of the parties, and public policy and fairness support the recognition of a duty of care. Based in large measure on the strong public policy of protecting children from sexual abuse, we conclude that there is a sound, indeed, compelling basis for the imposition of a duty on a wife whose husband poses the threat of sexually victimizing young children.

Closely-related to the recognition of a duty, however, is the issue of proximate causation, which must also be considered in determining whether any liability may be allowed for the breach of such a duty. Proximate causation is "that combination of 'logic, common sense, justice, policy and precedent' that fixes a point in the chain of events, some foreseeable and some unforeseeable, beyond which the law will bar recovery." People Express, supra, 100 N.J. at 264 (quoting Powers v. Standard Oil Co., 98 N.J.L. 730, 734, 119 A. 273 (Sup. Ct.), aff'd o.b., 98 N.J.L. 893, 121 A. 926 (E. & A. 1923)); accord Prosser, Torts § 41 at 236–37 (3rd ed. 1964) ("As a practical matter, legal responsibility must be limited to those causes which are so closely connected with the result and of such significance that the law is justified in imposing liability.'').

It does not seem highly extraordinary that a wife's failure to prevent or warn of her husband's sexual abuse or his propensity for sexual abuse would result in the occurrence or the continuation of such abuse. The harm from the wife's breach of duty is both direct and predictable. There is little question, here, that the physical and emotional injuries allegedly suffered by the girls are hardly an extraordinary result of John's acts of molestation and that their victimization is not an extraordinary consequence of Mary's own negligence. Mary's negligence could be found to be a proximate cause of plaintiffs' injuries. [C]

Accordingly, we hold that when a spouse has actual knowledge or special reason to know of the likelihood of his or her spouse engaging in sexually abusive behavior against a particular person or persons, a spouse has a duty of care to take reasonable steps to prevent or warn of the harm. Further, we hold that a breach of such a duty constitutes a proximate cause of the resultant injury, the sexual abuse of the victim.

It may be found that the relationship between the next-door neighbors' in this case had been close. Mary knew that the neighbors' adolescent girls were visiting at her home nearly every day and that they spent considerable amounts of time there alone with her husband. Moreover, she never "confronted" her husband about the unsupervised time he was spending with the girls. At both the trial level and on appeal, Mary conceded for the purposes of argument that "at all relevant times" she "knew or should have known of her husband's proclivities/propensities." Thus, it may be determined that it was particularly foreseeable that John was abusing the young girls. Further, the evidence at trial could support a finding of negligence on Mary's part. It is inferable, as explained by the Appellate Division, that Mary could have discharged her duty by confronting her husband and warning him, by insisting or seeing that the girls were not invited to ride or care for the horses, by keeping a watchful eye when she knew the girls to be visiting with her husband, by asking the girls' parents to ensure that the children not visit when she was not present, or by warning the girls or their parents of the risk she perceived. [C] Finally, the evidence may be found sufficient to support the determination that the harm suffered by the girls was not a highly extraordinary result of the breach of that duty.

We affirm the judgment of the Appellate Division.

NOTES AND QUESTIONS

1.   Putting aside those cases, supra where the duty is generated by a voluntary undertaking and reliance upon it, the duty to take affirmative action to control the conduct of a third person may arise in two different ways. Under the first, the defendant stands in a special relation to the plaintiff that requires him to exercise affirmative care to protect him against the conduct of the third person. Thus the duty of a common carrier to its passengers may require it to take steps to prevent personal attack upon them, theft of their property, or even negligent conduct which

threatens to injure them. Kinsey v. Hudson & Manhattan R. Co., 130 N.J.L. 285, 32 A.2d 497 (1943).

2.   In the other type of case the defendant stands in a special relation to the third person, that gives him a power of control over that person's actions. He is then required to use reasonable care to exercise that control to prevent the third person from injuring the plaintiff. Relationships include parent and child, employer and employee, automobile owner and driver, and persons who have taken charge of dangerous lunatics, criminals and persons with contagious diseases. In Otis Engineering Corp. v. Clark, 668 S.W.2d 307 (Tex.1983), a drunken employee, after being told to go home, killed the plaintiff's husband in an automobile accident. The court grounded the duty on the defendant employer's ability to control the intoxicated employee. An interesting case is Connolly v. Nicollet Hotel, 254 Minn. 373, 95 N.W.2d 657 (1959), where a convention in the defendant's hotel got out of hand and started menacing everybody and everything in the vicinity, and the management was held to be under a duty to make reasonable efforts to control it. Does a passenger in an automobile who is aware that the driver has been drinking heavily have an affirmative duty to warn other passengers who do not realize the driver's potentially impaired condition? See VanHaverbeke v. Bernhard, 654 F.Supp. 255 (S.D.Ohio 1986). Cf. Pulka v. Edelman, 40 N.Y.2d 781, 358 N.E.2d 1019, 390 N.Y.S.2d 393 (1976) (automobile garage and customers driving out over a sidewalk outside the exit).

3.   Again, in all these cases, the defendant is liable only for failure to exercise the care of a reasonable person under the circumstances. In Capps v. Carpenter, 129 Kan. 462, 283 P. 655 (1930), it was held that the parent was not liable merely because the child was incorrigible, exhibited a mean disposition and had been badly reared when the child did something that he never had done before. But in Bieker v. Owens, 234 Ark. 97, 350 S.W.2d 522 (1961), repeated attacks on other children were held to be enough. Compare the principal case.

4.   In Schurk v. Christensen, 80 Wash.2d 652, 497 P.2d 937 (1972), defendants' son, while acting as a baby-sitter, sexually molested a neighbor's five-year-old daughter. The neighbors suffered severe emotional harm when they learned about this fact from their daughter and they sued defendants. What should be the major legal and factual issues in the case? Distinguish this case from Haselhorst v. State, 240 Neb. 891, 485 N.W.2d 180 (1992), where the plaintiff parents suffered emotional distress when they discovered that their children had been sexually assaulted by a foster child placed with them by the Nebraska Department of Social Services. In Randi W. v. Muroc Joint Unified School District, 14 Cal. 4th 1066, 929 P.2d 582 (1997), the California Supreme Court held that a former employer of a teacher had a duty owed to a molested student not to misrepresent the fitness of that teacher to a school district proposing to hire him. The defendant former employer knew of charges and complaints of sexual misconduct by the employee-teacher. After being hired, the teacher molested plaintiff.

Tarasoff v. Regents of University of California

Supreme Court of California, 1976.
17 Cal.3d 425, 551 P.2d 334, 131 Cal.Rptr. 14.

[Posenjit Poddar was an out-patient under the care of a psychologist, Dr. Lawrence Moore, at Cowell Memorial Hospital of the University of California. During the course of treatment, Dr. Moore learned from Poddar that he intended to kill Tatiana Tarasoff because she had spurned Poddar's romantic advances.

On the basis of this information, Dr. Moore had the campus police detain Poddar, apparently at the hospital. Poddar was released shortly afterward. Despite disagreement among the psychiatrists the final decision was that no further action should be taken to confine Poddar. This judgment proved to be mistaken; two months later Poddar shot and then repeatedly stabbed Tatiana. Plaintiffs, Tatiana's parents, brought a wrongful death claim against the four psychiatrists. Plaintiffs claimed that they should be liable because they failed to confine Poddar. The court rejected this claim because California Government Code Section 856 cloaked the doctors with tort immunity with regard to this type of decision. Plaintiffs also claimed that defendants should be liable for Tatiana's death because they failed to warn her or them about Poddar's threat.]

TOBRINER, JUSTICE. * * * The second cause of action can be amended to allege that Tatiana's death proximately resulted from defendants' negligent failure to warn Tatiana or others likely to apprise her of her danger. Plaintiffs contend that as amended, such allegations of negligence and proximate causation, with resulting damages, establish a cause of action. Defendants, however, contend that in the circumstances of the present case they owed no duty of care to Tatiana or her parents and that, in the absence of such duty, they were free to act in careless disregard of Tatiana's life and safety. * * *

Although * * * under the common law, as a general rule, one person owed no duty to control the conduct of another [cc], nor to warn those endangered by such conduct [cc], the courts have carved out an exception to this rule in cases in which the defendant stands in some special relationship to either the person whose conduct needs to be controlled or in a relationship to the foreseeable victim of that conduct (see Rest.2d Torts, supra, §§ 315–320). * * *

Although plaintiffs' pleadings assert no special relation between Tatiana and defendant therapists, they establish as between Poddar and defendant therapists the special relation that arises between a patient and his doctor or psychotherapist. Such a relationship may support affirmative duties for the benefit of third persons. Thus, for example, a hospital must exercise reasonable care to control the behavior of a patient which may endanger other persons. A doctor must also warn a patient if the patient's condition or medication renders certain conduct, such as driving a car, dangerous to others.

Although the California decisions that recognize this duty have involved cases in which the defendant stood in a special relationship *both* to the victim and to the person whose conduct created the danger, we do not think that the duty should logically be constricted to such situations. Decisions of other jurisdictions hold that the single relationship of a doctor to his patient is sufficient to support the duty to exercise reasonable care to protect others against dangers emanating from the patient's illness. The courts hold that a doctor is liable to persons infected by his patient if he negligently fails to diagnose a contagious disease [c] or, having diagnosed the illness, fails to warn members of the patient's family. * * *

Defendants contend, however, that imposition of a duty to exercise reasonable care to protect third persons is unworkable because therapists cannot accurately predict whether or not a patient will resort to violence. In support of this argument amicus representing the American Psychiatric Association and other professional societies cites numerous articles which indicate that therapists, in the present state of the art, are unable reliably to predict violent acts; their forecasts, amicus claims, tend consistently to overpredict violence, and indeed are more often wrong than right. Since predictions of violence are often erroneous, amicus concludes, the courts should not render rulings that predicate the liability of therapists upon the validity of such predictions. * * *

We recognize the difficulty that a therapist encounters in attempting to forecast whether a patient presents a serious danger of violence. Obviously we do not require that the therapist, in making that determination, render a perfect performance; the therapist need only exercise "that reasonable degree of skill, knowledge, and care ordinarily possessed and exercised by members of [that professional specialty] under similar circumstances." * * *

In the instant case, however, the pleadings do not raise any question as to failure of defendant therapists to predict that Poddar presented a serious danger of violence. On the contrary, the present complaints allege that defendant therapists did in fact predict that Poddar would kill, but were negligent in failing to warn.

Amicus contends, however, that even when a therapist does in fact predict that a patient poses a serious danger of violence to others, the therapist should be absolved of any responsibility for failing to act to protect the potential victim. In our view, however, once a therapist does in fact determine, or under applicable professional standards reasonably should have determined, that a patient poses a serious danger of violence to others, he bears a duty to exercise reasonable care to protect the foreseeable victim of that danger. * * *

The risk that unnecessary warnings may be given is a reasonable price to pay for the lives of possible victims that may be saved. We would hesitate to hold that the therapist who is aware that his patient expects to attempt to assassinate the President of the United States would not be obligated to warn the authorities because the therapist cannot predict with accuracy that his patient will commit the crime.

Defendants further argue that free and open communication is essential to psychotherapy [c]; that "unless a patient * * * is assured that * * * information [revealed by him] can and will be held in utmost confidence, he will be reluctant to make the full disclosure upon which diagnosis and treatment * * * depends." (Sen.Com. on Judiciary, comment on Evid.Code, § 1014.) The giving of a warning, defendants contend, constitutes a breach of trust which entails the revelation of confidential communications.

We recognize the public interest in supporting effective treatment of mental illness and in protecting the rights of patients to privacy [c] and the consequent public importance of safeguarding the confidential character of psychotherapeutic communication. Against this interest, however, we must weigh the public interest in safety from violent assault. The Legislature has undertaken the difficult task of balancing the countervailing concerns. In Evidence Code section 1014, it established a broad rule of privilege to protect confidential communications between patient and psychotherapist. In Evidence Code section 1024, the Legislature created a specific and limited exception to the psychotherapist-patient privilege: "There is no privilege * * * if the psychotherapist has reasonable cause to believe that the patient is in such mental or emotional condition as to be dangerous to himself or to the person or property of another and that disclosure of the communication is necessary to prevent the threatened danger." * * *

Our current crowded and computerized society compels the interdependence of its members. In this risk-infested society we can hardly tolerate the further exposure to danger that would result from a concealed knowledge of the therapist that his patient was lethal. If the exercise of reasonable care to protect the threatened victim requires the therapist to warn the endangered party or those who can reasonably be expected to notify him, we see no sufficient societal interest that would protect and justify concealment. The containment of such risks lies in the public interest. For the foregoing reasons, we find that plaintiffs' complaints can be amended to state a cause of action against defendants Moore, Powelson, Gold, and Yandell and against the Regents as their employer, for breach of a duty to exercise reasonable care to protect Tatiana. * * *

[WRIGHT, C.J., and SULLIVAN and RICHARDSON, JJ., concurred and dissented in part; and CLARK and McCOMB, JJ., dissented.]

NOTES AND QUESTIONS

1. In his dissent Justice Clark agreed with the majority that when a psychiatrist in terminating a patient increases the risk of his violence toward a particular individual, a duty to warn should arise. However, he could find neither precedent nor reason to support a duty to warn solely based on the psychiatrist-patient relationship. Other courts have agreed that the relationship does not ground a duty to warn. The Virginia Supreme Court in Nasser v. Parker, 249 Va. 172, 455 S.E.2d 502 (1995), found that the principal case "is at odds with [its] interpretation of the Restatement's provisions relating to one's duty to control the conduct of a third person." Id. at 177, 504. Plaintiff must show defendant had "taken charge" of third person within the meaning of Restatement § 319, id. at 178, 504. This was not the case in Tarasoff, nor in this case where defendants had released the victim's former boyfriend from hospital without warning victim of the release. The degree of control necessary to generate a duty of care was raised in Estate of Morgan v. Fairfield Family Counseling Center, 77 Ohio St. 3d 284, 673 N.E.2d 1311 (1997). In this case, the victim's son had been in outpatient care of the defendants. Their negligent misdiagnosis and treatment of the patient's schizophrenia led to the patient shooting and killing his parents and wounding his sister. Defendant's control over the patient was attenuated. In itself a want of close control, the court found, does not determine that a duty should not be imposed. Rather, the court insisted on a balancing of factors: "(1) the psychotherapist's ability to control the outpatient; (2) the public's interest in safety from violent assault; (3) the difficulty inherent in

attempting to forecast whether a patient represents a substantial risk of physical harm to others; (4) the goal of placing the mental patient in the least restrictive environment and safeguarding importance of maintaining the confidential nature of psychotherapeutic communications." Id. at 297, 1322.

2. Some courts have deemed it tortious for a psychotherapist to reveal a patient's confidential communication, infra Chapter 18: Breach of Confidentiality. Where does the principal case leave the psychotherapist? See generally Fleming and Maximov, The Patient or His Victim: The Therapist's Dilemma, 62 Calif.L.Rev. 1025 (1974) (an article influential in the court's decision); Stone, The *Tarasoff* Decision: Suing Psychotherapists to Safeguard Society, 90 Harv.L.Rev. 358 (1976) (criticizing the rationale in *Tarasoff*).

3. Describe the duty that should be imposed on a physician who finds that her patient is HIV positive. Should she warn the patient's sexual partners? See, In Estate of Behringer (M.D.) v. Medical Center at Princeton, 249 N.J.Super. 597, 592 A.2d 1251 (1991) (dicta). It has been held that physicians owe a duty to unidentified third persons, but may fulfill duty by informing patient of risks of transmission of AIDS. See Reisner v. Regents of Univ. of Cal., 37 Cal. Rptr. 2d 518 (Cal.Ct.App. 1995); but see Santa Rosa Health Care Corp. v. Garcia, 964 S.W.2d 940 (Tex.1998) (reversing court of appeals holding that physicians owed a duty to inform patient's wife of probable HIV risk); Gostin & Hodge, Piercing the Veil of Secrecy in HIV/AIDS and Other Sexually Transmitted Diseases: Theories of Privacy and Disclosure in Partner Notification, 5 Duke J. Gender L. & Pol'y 9, n.171 (1998). Case law may increasingly favor a duty to require professionals to warn third persons who may have been exposed to HIV. Wavle, Comment, HIV and AIDS Test Results and the Duty to Warn Third Parties: A Proposal for Uniform Guidelines for Texas Professionals, 28 St. Mary's L.J. 783, 800 & n.78 (1997) (footnote cites several recent cases and an article). The issue has legal and ethical dimensions. Ainslie, Questioning Bioethics: AIDS, Sexual Ethics, and the Duty to Warn, The Hastings Center Report Sept.-Oct. 1999, at 26. Should a physician be liable where she gives medical advice to her infected patient, who, in reliance upon that advice, acts as to infect a third party with that communicable disease? Troxel v. A. I. Dupont Inst., 675 A.2d 314 (Pa. Super. Ct. 1996); Ellis v. Peter, 627 N.Y.S.2d 707, 211 A.D.2d 353 (1995) (communication of tuberculosis).

4. The duty to protect subsumes a duty to warn. Does it include a duty to commit or retain custody? Currie v. United States, 644 F.Supp. 1074 (M.D.N.C. 1986); Lipari v. Sears, Roebuck & Co., 497 F.Supp. 185 (D.Neb.1980); Hamman v. County of Maricopa, 161 Ariz. 58, 775 P.2d 1122 (1989); and Perreira v. State, 768 P.2d 1198 (Colo.1989); Estate of Morgan v. Fairfield Family Counseling Center, 77 Ohio St. 3d 284, 673 N.E.2d 1311 (1997) (stating that a fear of undue confinement caused by the imposition of a duty has no reliable statistical support). Other actions may be called for, e.g. in Lundgren v. Fultz, 354 N.W.2d 25 (Minn.1984), blocking return of guns to paranoid schizophrenic patient obsessed with weapons.

5. In the principal case the duty was owed to an identified victim. When the threat is not pointed but general the authorities are split. In Thompson v. County of Alameda, 27 Cal.3d 741, 614 P.2d 728, 167 Cal.Rptr. 70 (1980), James, a juvenile offender, was released into his mother's custody even though it was known that he had a history of violence and had indicated that, if released, he would take the life of a young child in the neighborhood. Within twenty-four hours, he had carried out his threat, killing the plaintiff's son. The court agreed with the trial court that no duty of care obtained in these circumstances. The extent of warning, with its adverse impact on the rehabilitation of the patient and its probable ineffectuality as a guard against violence, convinced the majority of the court to distinguish the principal case. Accord: Brady v. Hopper, 570 F.Supp. 1333 (D.Colo.1983), aff'd, 751

F.2d 329 (10th Cir.1984) (suit against John Hinckley's psychiatrist by victims of the attempted assassination of President Reagan); Rousey v. United States, 115 F.3d 394 (6th Cir.1997) (applying Maine law, holding that duty to warn requires identification of victims). Cf. Petersen v. State, 100 Wash.2d 421, 671 P.2d 230 (1983); Nova Univ., Inc. v. Wagner, 491 So.2d 1116 (Fla.1986).

6. In the principal case it was assumed, for the purposes of the appeal, that the defendant clinicians had predicted Poddar's dangerousness. This issue, however, is often live. Although it is rare for mental health clinicians to be liable, by reason of failure to reasonably predict violence, those professionals have remained anxious lest courts too readily conclude that violence can be accurately predicted. For discussion see Hedlund v. Superior Court of Orange County, 34 Cal.3d 695, 669 P.2d 41, 194 Cal.Rptr. 805 (1983); note Justice Mosk's concerns in dissent, at 48–49, 194 Cal.Rptr. at 812–13. See also White v. United States, 780 F.2d 97 (D.C.Cir. 1986), and Tamsen v. Weber, 166 Ariz. 364, 802 P.2d 1063 (App.1990). A comprehensive empirical study on accuracy of predictions shows that clinicians did pick out a statistically more violent group and that violence was serious in comparison with the control group. However, the judgments were relatively inaccurate predictors of violence especially in respect of violence in women. Lidz, Mulvey, Gardner, The Accuracy of Predictions of Violence to Others, 269 JAMA 1007 (1993).

7. Professional anxiety, on the last issue, in particular, and on the balancing of confidentiality against protection of the public, in general, in a changing legal background, has produced a legislative response based on a model propounded by the American Psychiatric Association's Council on Psychiatry and Law. See, for example, Colo.Rev.Stat. § 13–21–117 (1986); Idaho Code § 6–1902 (1991); Ind.Code § 34–4–12.4–2 (1987); Ky.Rev.Stat.Ann. § 202A.400 (1986); La.Rev.Stat.Ann. § 9:2800.2 (West 1986); Mass.Gen.L. ch. 112 § 129A (1989); Mich.Comp.Laws § 330.1946 (1989); Minn.Stat. § 148.975 (1986); N.H.Rev.Stat.Ann. § 330–A:22 (1987); Tenn.Code Ann. § 33–10–302 (1989). The California legislation provides that psychotherapists are immune from liability to warn "except where the patient has communicated to the psychotherapist a serious threat of physical violence against a reasonably identifiable victim or victims"; Cal.Civil Code § 43.92. The act goes on to prescribe the means by which the duty to warn may be discharged. From the viewpoint of the psychotherapist's comfort do you consider that this provision is entirely satisfactory? How does it fall short? Some states provide a statutory exception to psychotherapist-patient confidentiality for serious threats of imminent harm to the patient or third persons. Harris, The Dangerous Patient Exception to the Psychotherapist–Patient Privilege: The Tarasoff Duty and the Jaffee Footnote, 74 Wash. L. Rev. 33, 42 (1999) (citing CT, RI, SC, TN, WV, and WY). The precision permitted by legislation favors this approach. Almason, Comment, Personal Liability Implications of the Duty to Warn are Hard Pills to Swallow: From Tarasoff to Hutchinson v. Patel and Beyond, 13 J. Contemp. Health L. & Pol'y 471, 481 (1997).

8. In Bellah v. Greenson, 81 Cal.App.3d 614, 146 Cal.Rptr. 535 (1978), the court found no duty to warn when a psychiatrist had failed to alert a patient's parents that the patient had suicidal propensities and was running risks by consorting with heroin addicts. Likewise, in Nally v. Grace Community Church of the Valley, 47 Cal.3d 278, 763 P.2d 948, 253 Cal.Rptr. 97 (1988), a religious counsellor was found to owe no duty to refer a suicidal young man to a mental health professional. In contrast, school counsellors owed a duty to warn the parents of a thirteen-year-old girl of a suicidal statement made at school. The dangers were acute and the burdens of warning the parents light. Eisel v. Board of Education of Montgomery County, Md., 324 Md. 376, 597 A.2d 447 (1991).

9. An attorney's client has violent tendencies towards identified persons. Does she have a duty to warn? See Hawkins v. King County, Dept. of Rehabilitative

Services, Div. of Involuntary Treatment Services, 24 Wash.App. 338, 602 P.2d 361 (1979). Attorney had a duty to warn of client's threat to cause judge serious harm. See State v. Hansen, 862 P.2d 117, 122 (Wash.1993) (instant case distinguished from *Hawkins* because threatened party did not have notice of the potential danger).

10. What of a student who overhears a plan to rob a grocery store? Duty to warn? If a person knowing of the danger of rape in an area fails to warn a victim? If we find a duty to warn, would that be consistent with our finding of no duty to rescue when the defendant is uniquely positioned and could offer help without risking his own life? For example, doesn't the student have the same relationship with the grocer that a man on shore with a life preserver has to a drowning man? Is it like warning the rape victim of impending danger?

3. Pure Economic Loss

The citadel of privity has now been vanquished. In most cases the fact that *A* was in a contractual relationship with *B* alone cannot defeat a claim that a duty was owed by *A* to *C* to prevent causing *C* foreseeable physical injury. A last bastion survives, however. If the harm is pure economic loss the courts take more seriously the claim that liability should be restricted. Pure economic loss arises when a person suffers pecuniary loss not consequent upon injury to his person or property. The cases fall into two categories:

(1) Negligent misrepresentation or misstatement causing economic loss; and

(2) Negligent acts causing economic loss.

The former category is treated in detail in Chapter 21. The paradigmatic cases relate to auditor or accountant liability. An auditor retained by a corporation completes a negligent audit which is then relied upon by a third person to his detriment. Does that third person have a cause of action against the negligent auditors? Does privity describe the limits of liability or does the auditor owe a duty to a class of persons outside privity of contract? Benjamin Cardozo, the champion of the assault on the privity citadel, held back from imposing a duty of care in negligence. Ultramares Corporation v. Touche, infra page 1043. The courts, nevertheless, have found duties of care to parties outside privity of contract, sometimes narrowly, sometimes broadly, in a way reminiscent of the hesitation that has surrounded the scope of the duty in negligence for emotional distress.

The latter category—negligent acts causing economic loss—held firmly against the proponents of wider tort liability.

State of Louisiana Ex Rel. Guste v. M/V Testbank

United States Court of Appeals, Fifth Circuit (en banc), 1985.
752 F.2d 1019, cert. denied, 477 U.S. 903 (1986).

Higginbotham, Circuit Judge: We are asked to abandon physical damage to a proprietary interest as a prerequisite to recovery for economic loss in cases of unintentional maritime tort. We decline the invitation.

I. In the early evening of July 22, 1980, the M/V Sea Daniel, an inbound bulk carrier, and the M/V Testbank, an outbound container ship, collided at approximately mile forty-one of the Mississippi River Gulf outlet. At impact, a white haze enveloped the ships until carried away by prevailing winds, and containers aboard Testbank were damaged and lost overboard. The white haze proved to be hydrobromic acid and the contents of the containers which went overboard proved to be approximately twelve tons of pentachlorophenol, PCP, assertedly the largest such spill in United States history. The United States Coast Guard closed the outlet to navigation until August 10, 1980 and all fishing, shrimping, and related activity was temporarily suspended in the outlet and four hundred square miles of surrounding marsh and waterways. * * * [Numerous lawsuits, representing various interests,] were filed and consolidated before the same judge in the Eastern District of Louisiana. * * *

Defendants moved for summary judgment as to all claims for economic loss unaccompanied by physical damage to property. The district court granted the requested summary judgment as to all such claims except those asserted by commercial oystermen, shrimpers, crabbers and fishermen who had been making a commercial use of the embargoed waters. * * *

On appeal a panel of this court affirmed, concluding that claims for economic loss unaccompanied by physical damage to a proprietary interest were not recoverable in maritime tort. 728 F.2d 748 (5th Cir.1984). The panel, as did the district court, pointed to the doctrine of Robins Dry Dock & Repair Co. v. Flint, 275 U.S. 303 (1927), and its development in this circuit. Judge Wisdom specially concurred, agreeing that the denial of these claims was required by precedent, but urging reexamination en banc. We then took the case en banc for that purpose. After extensive additional briefs and oral argument, we are unpersuaded that we ought to drop physical damage to a proprietary interest as a prerequisite to recovery for economic loss. To the contrary, our reexamination of the history and central purpose of this pragmatic restriction on the doctrine of foreseeability heightens our commitment to it. Ultimately we conclude that without this limitation foreseeability loses much of its ability to function as a rule of law. * * *

III. The meaning of Robins Dry Dock v. Flint, 275 U.S. 303 (1927) (Holmes, J.) is the flag all litigants here seek to capture. We turn first to that case and to its historical setting.

Robins broke no new ground but instead applied a principle, then settled both in the United States and England, which refused recovery for negligent interference with "contractual rights." Stated more broadly, the prevailing rule denied a plaintiff recovery for economic loss if that loss resulted from physical damage to property in which he had no proprietary interest. *See, e.g.,* Byrd v. English, 117 Ga. 191, 43 S.E. 419 (1903); Cattle v. Stockton Waterworks Co., 10 Q.B. 453, 457 (C.A.1875). See also James, Limitations on Liability for Economic Loss Caused by Negligence: A Pragmatic Appraisal, 25 Vand.L.Rev. 43, 44–46 (1972) (discussing history of the rule); Carpenter, Interference with Contract Relations, 41 Harv.L.Rev. 728

(1928). Professor James explains this limitation on recovery of pure economic loss: "The explanation * * * is a pragmatic one: the physical consequences of negligence usually have been limited, but the indirect economic repercussions of negligence may be far wider, indeed virtually open-ended." James, *supra,* at 45.

Decisions such as *Stockton* illustrate the application of this pragmatic limitation on the doctrine of foreseeability. The defendant negligently caused its pipes to leak, thereby increasing the plaintiff's cost in performing its contract to dig a tunnel. The British court, writing fifty-two years before *Robins,* denied the plaintiff's claim. The court explained that if recovery were not contained, then in cases such as Rylands v. Fletcher, L.R. 1 Ex. 265 (1866), the defendant would be liable not only to the owner of the mine and its workers "but also to * * * every workman and person employed in the mine, who in consequence of its stoppage made less wages than he would otherwise have done." *Id.* at 457. [C]

1. In *Robins,* the time charterer of a steamship sued for profits lost when the defendant dry dock negligently damaged the vessel's propeller. The propeller had to be replaced, thus extending by two weeks the time the vessel was laid up in dry dock, and it was for the loss of use of the vessel for that period that the charterer sued. The Supreme Court denied recovery to the charterer, noting: " * * * no authority need be cited to show that, as a general rule, at least, a tort to the person or property of one man does not make the tort-feasor liable to another merely because the injured person was under a contract with that other unknown to the doer of the wrong. The law does not spread its protection so far * * * " 275 U.S. at 309. * * *

2. The principle that there could be no recovery for economic loss absent physical injury to a proprietary interest was not only well established when *Robins Dry Dock* was decided, but was remarkably resilient as well. * * * Indeed this limit on liability stood against a sea of change in the tort law. Retention of this conspicuous bright-line rule in the face of the reforms brought by the increased influence of the school of legal realism is strong testament both to the rule's utility and to the absence of a more "conceptually pure" substitute. The push to delete the restrictions on recovery for economic loss lost its support and by the early 1940's had failed. *See* W. Prosser, *Law of Torts* § 129, at 938–940 (4th ed. 1971). In sum, it is an old sword that plaintiffs have here picked up.

3. Plaintiffs would confine *Robins* to losses suffered for inability to perform contracts between a plaintiff and others, categorizing the tort as a species of interference with contract. When seen in the historical context described above, however, it is apparent that *Robins Dry Dock* represents more than a limit on recovery for interference with contractual rights. Apart from what it represented and certainly apart from what it became, its literal holding was not so restricted. If a time charterer's relationship to its negligently injured vessel is too remote, other claimants without even the connection of a contract are even more remote. * * *

The language and the cases the *Robins* Court pointed to as "good statement[s]" of the principle make plain that the charterer failed to recover its delay claims from the dry dock because the Court believed them to be too remote. Notably, although the dry dock company did not know of the charter party when it damaged the propeller, delay losses by users of the vessel were certainly foreseeable. Thus, *Robins* was a pragmatic limitation imposed by the Court upon the tort doctrine of foreseeability.

In a sense, every claim of economic injury rests in some measure on an interference with contract or prospective advantage. It was only in this sense that profits were lost in *Byrd v. English* when the electrical power to plaintiffs printing plant was cut off. The printing company's contractual right to receive power was interfered with, and in turn, its ability to print for its customers was impinged. That the printing company had a contract with the power company did not make more remote the relationship between its loss of profits and the tortious acts. To the contrary, the contract reduced this remoteness by defining an orbit of predictable injury smaller than if there were no contract between the power company and the printer. When the loss is economic rather than physical, that the loss caused a breach of contract or denied an expectancy is of no moment. If a plaintiff connected to the damaged chattels by contract cannot recover, others more remotely situated are foreclosed *a fortiori*. Indisputably, the *Robins Dry Dock* principle is not as easily contained as plaintiff would have it. * * *

4.   This circuit has consistently refused to allow recovery for economic loss absent physical damage to a proprietary interest. [The court discusses in detail its own decisions and those of other circuits. It gives particular attention to Petition of Kinsman Transit Co., 388 F.2d 821 (2d Cir.1968) (Kinsman II, described in this casebook, supra page 313); and Union Oil Co. v. Oppen, 501 F.2d 558 (9th Cir.1974)].

IV.   Plaintiffs urge that the requirement of physical injury to a proprietary interest is arbitrary, unfair, and illogical, as it denies recovery for foreseeable injury caused by negligent acts. At its bottom the argument is that questions of remoteness ought to be left to the trier of fact. Ultimately the question becomes who ought to decide—judge or jury—and whether there will be a rule beyond the jacket of a given case. * * *

Those who would delete the requirement of physical damage have no rule or principle to substitute. Their approach fails to recognize limits upon the adjudicating ability of courts. We do not mean just the ability to supply a judgment; prerequisite to this adjudicatory function are preexisting rules, whether the creature of courts or legislatures. Courts can decide cases without preexisting normative guidance but the result becomes less judicial and more the product of a managerial, legislative or negotiated function.

Review of the foreseeable consequences of the collision of the [two ships in this case] demonstrates the wave upon wave of successive economic consequences and the managerial role plaintiffs would have us assume. The vessel delayed in St. Louis may be unable to fulfill its obligation to haul from Memphis, to the injury of the shipper, to the injury of the buyers, to the injury of their customers. Plaintiffs concede, as do all who attack the requirement of physical damage, that a line would need to be drawn—

somewhere on the other side, each plaintiff would say in turn, of its recovery. Plaintiffs advocate not only that the lines be drawn elsewhere but also that they be drawn on an ad hoc and discrete basis. The result would be that no determinable measure of the limit of foreseeability would precede the decision on liability. We are told that when the claim is too remote, or too tenuous, recovery will be denied. Presumably then, as among all plaintiffs suffering foreseeable economic loss, recovery will turn on a judge or jury's decision. There will be no rationale for the differing results save the "judgment" of the trier of fact. Concededly, it can "decide" all the claims presented, and with comparative if not absolute ease. The point is not that such a process cannot be administered but rather that its judgments would be much less the products of a determinable rule of law. In this important sense, the resulting decisions would be judicial products only in their draw upon judicial resources.

The bright line rule of damage to a proprietary interest, as most, has the virtue of predictability with the vice of creating results in cases at its edge that are said to be "unjust" or "unfair." Plaintiffs point to seemingly perverse results, where claims the rule allows and those it disallows are juxtaposed—such as vessels striking a dock, causing minor but recoverable damage, then lurching athwart a channel causing great but unrecoverable economic loss. The answer is that when lines are drawn sufficiently sharp in their definitional edges to be reasonable and predictable, such differing results are the inevitable result—indeed, decisions are the desired product. But there is more. The line drawing sought by plaintiffs is no less arbitrary because the line drawing appears only in the outcome—as one claimant is found too remote and another is allowed to recover. The true difference is that plaintiffs' approach would mask the results. The present rule would be more candid, and in addition, by making results more predictable, serves a normative function. It operates as a rule of law and allows a court to adjudicate rather than manage.[12]

V.   That the rule is identifiable and will predict outcomes in advance of the ultimate decision about recovery enables it to play additional roles. Here we agree with plaintiffs that economic analysis, even at the rudimentary level of jurists, is helpful both in the identification of such roles and the essaying of how the roles play. Thus it is suggested that placing all the consequence of its error on the maritime industry will enhance its incentive for safety. While correct, as far as such analysis goes, such *in terrorem* benefits have an optimal level. Presumably, when the cost of an unsafe condition exceeds its utility there is an incentive to change. As the costs of an accident become increasing multiples of its utility, however, there is a point at which greater accident costs lose meaning, and the incentive curve

---

12. Fuller, The Forms and Limits of Adjudication, 92 Harv.L.Rev. 353, 396 (1978). This case illustrates how our technocratic tradition masks a deep difference in attitudes toward the roles of a judiciary. The difference between the majority and dissenting opinions is far more than a choice between competing maritime rules. The majority is driven by the principle of self ordering and modesty for the judicial role; the dissent accepts a role of management which can strain the limits of adjudication.

flattens. When the accident costs are added in large but unknowable amounts the value of the exercise is diminished.

With a disaster inflicting large and reverberating injuries through the economy, as here, we believe the more important economic inquiry is that of relative cost of administration, and in maritime matters administration quickly involves insurance. Those economic losses not recoverable under the present rule for lack of physical damage to a proprietary interest are the subject of first party or loss insurance. The rule change would work a shift to the more costly liability system of third party insurance. For the same reasons that courts have imposed limits on the concept of foreseeability, liability insurance might not be readily obtainable for the types of losses asserted here. As Professor James has noted, "[s]erious practical problems face insurers in handling insurance against potentially wide, open-ended liability. From an insurer's point of view it is not practical to cover, without limit, a liability that may reach catastrophic proportions, or to fix a reasonable premium on a risk that does not lend itself to actuarial measurement." James, *supra,* at 53. By contrast, first party insurance is feasible for many of the economic losses claimed here. Each businessman who might be affected by a disruption of river traffic or by a halt in fishing activities can protect against that eventuality at a relatively low cost since his own potential losses are finite and readily discernible. Thus, to the extent that economic analysis informs our decision here, we think that it favors retention of the present rule. * * *

VI.   Plaintiffs seek to avoid the *Robins* rule by characterizing their claims as damages caused by a public nuisance. They suggest that when a defendant unreasonably interferes with public rights by obstructing navigation or negligently polluting a waterway he creates a public nuisance for which recovery is available to all who have sustained "particular damages." * * *

* * * With economic losses such as the ones claimed here the problem is to determine who among an entire community that has been commercially affected by an accident has sustained a pecuniary loss so great as to justify distinguishing his losses from similar losses suffered by others. Given the difficulty of this task, we see no jurisprudential advantage in permitting the use of nuisance theory to skirt the *Robins* rule. * * *

VII.   In conclusion, having reexamined the history and central purpose of the doctrine of *Robins Dry Dock* as developed in this circuit, we remain committed to its teaching. Denying recovery for pure economic losses is a pragmatic limitation on the doctrine of foreseeability, a limitation we find to be both workable and useful. Nor do we find persuasive plaintiffs' arguments that their economic losses are recoverable under a public nuisance theory, as damages for violation of federal statutes, or under state law.

Accordingly, the decision of the district court granting summary judgment to defendants on all claims for economic losses unaccompanied by physical damage to property is affirmed.

GEE, CIRCUIT JUDGE, with whom CLARK, CHIEF JUDGE, joins, concurring: * * *
It is my thesis that the dispute-resolution systems of courts are poorly
equipped to manage disasters of such magnitude and that we should be
wary of adopting rules of decision which, as would that contended for by
the dissent, encourage the drawing of their broader aspects before us. * * *
Such a system as ours works tolerably well in the traditional case for which
it was developed, where the stakes are limited to who owns the farm or to
some other finite benefit. Its deficiencies become immediately and painfully
apparent, however, when the consideration of factors inherently extraneous
to the dispute becomes necessary or desirable to resolving it. Of these
factors, perhaps the most often encountered is that of financial reality.
* * *

Extending theories of liability may not always be the more moral
course, especially in such a case as this, where the extension, in the course
of awarding damages to unnumbered claimants for injuries that are unavoidably speculative, may well visit destruction on enterprise after enterprise, with the consequent loss of employment and productive capacity
which that entails.

[GARWOOD and WILLIAMS, JJ., concurred specially in separate opinions.]

WISDOM, CIRCUIT JUDGE, with whom ALVIN B. RUBIN, POLITZ, TATE, and JOHNSON,
CIRCUIT JUDGES, join, dissenting.

Robins is the Tar Baby of tort law in this circuit. And the brierpatch is
far away. This Court's application of *Robins* is out of step with contemporary tort doctrine, works substantial injustice on innocent victims, and is
unsupported by the considerations that justified the Supreme Court's 1927
decision. * * *

The * * * bar for claims of economic loss unaccompanied by any
physical damage conflicts with conventional tort principles of foreseeability
and proximate cause. I would analyze the plaintiffs' claims under these
principles, using the "particular damage" requirement of public nuisance
law as an additional means of limiting claims. Although this approach
requires a case-by-case analysis, it comports with the fundamental idea of
fairness that innocent plaintiffs should receive compensation and negligent
defendants should bear the cost of their tortious acts. Such a result is
worth the additional costs of adjudicating these claims, and this rule of
liability appears to be more economically efficient. Finally, this result would
relieve courts of the necessity of manufacturing exceptions totally inconsistent with the expanded *Robins* rule of requiring physical injury as a
prerequisite to recovery. * * *

II. THE INAPPLICABILITY OF *Robins Dry Dock* TO THIS CASE. Whatever the
pragmatic justification for the original holding in *Robins*, the majority has
extended the case beyond the warrant of clear necessity in requiring *a
physical injury* for a recovery of economic loss in cases such as the one
before the court. *Robins* prevented plaintiffs who were neither proximately
nor foreseeably injured by a tortious act or product from recovering solely
by claiming a contract with the injured party. The wisdom of this rule is

apparent. This rule, however, has been expanded now to bar recovery by plaintiffs who would be allowed to recover if judged under conventional principles of foreseeability and proximate cause. * * *

Robins held only that if a defendant's negligence injures party *A,* and the plaintiff suffers loss of expected income or profits because it had a contract with *A,* then the plaintiff has no cause of action based on the defendant's negligence. * * *

It is a long step from *Robins* to a rule that requires *physical damage* as a prerequisite to recovery in maritime tort. The majority believes that the plaintiff's lack of any contractual connection with an injured party, taken with the *Robins* rule, forecloses liability: "If a plaintiff connected to the damaged chattels by contract cannot recover, others more remotely situated are foreclosed *a fortiori.*"

This conclusion follows readily from the reasoning that if uninjured contracting parties are barred from recovery, and if contracting parties have a closer legal relationship than non-contracting parties, then a party who is not physically injured and who does not have a contractual relation to the damage is surely barred.

This argument would be sound in instances where the plaintiff suffered no loss *but for a contract* with the injured party. We would measure a plaintiff's connection to the tortfeasor by the only line connecting them, the contract, and disallow the claim under *Robins.* In the instant case, however, some of the plaintiffs suffered damages whether or not they had a contractual connection with a party physically injured by the tortfeasor. These plaintiffs do not need to rely on a contract to link them to the tort. The collision proximately caused their losses, and those losses were foreseeable. These plaintiffs are therefore freed from the *Robins* rule concerning the recovery of those who suffer economic loss because of an injury to a party with whom they have contracted.

Because *Robins* provides an overly restrictive bar on recovery, courts have over the years developed a number of exceptions. The traditional exceptions allow recovery for certain husband-wife claims, recovery for negligent interference with contract when the interference results from a tangible injury to the contractor's person or property, and recovery for persons employed on fishing boats to recover for lost income when the employment contract is disrupted by a third party's negligent injury to the ship or equipment. * * * [The opinion discusses other cases.]

One cannot deny that *Robins*'s policy of limiting the set of plaintiffs who can recover for a person's negligence and damage to physical property provides a "bright line" for demarcating the boundary between recovery and nonrecovery. Physical harm suggests a proximate relation between the act and the interference. At bottom, however, the requirement of a tangible injury is artificial because it does not comport with accepted principles of tort law. Mrs. Palsgraf, although physically injured, could not recover. Many other plaintiffs, although physically uninjured, can recover. * * *

With deference to the majority, I suggest, notwithstanding their well reasoned opinion, that the utility derived from having a "bright line" boundary does not outweigh the disutility caused by the limitation on recovery imposed by the physical-damage requirement. *Robins* and its progeny represent a wide departure from the usual tort doctrines of foreseeability and proximate cause. Those doctrines, as refined in the law of public nuisance, provide a rule of recovery that compensates innocent plaintiffs and holds the defendants liable for much of the harm proximately caused by their negligence.

III. An Alternate Rule of Recovery. Rather than limiting recovery under an automatic application of a physical damage requirement, I would analyze the plaintiffs' claims under the conventional tort principles of negligence, foreseeability, and proximate causation. I would confine *Robins* to the "factual contours" of that case: A plaintiff's claim may be barred only if the claim is derived solely through contract with an injured party. The majority's primary criticism of this approach to a determination of liability is that it is potentially open ended. Yet, there are well-established tort principles to limit liability for a widely-suffered harm. Under the contemporary law of public nuisance, courts compensate "particularly" damaged plaintiffs for harms suffered from a wide-ranging tort, but deny recovery to more generally damaged parties. Those parties who are foreseeably and proximately injured by an oil spill or closure of a navigable river, for example, and who can also prove damages that are beyond the general economic dislocation that attends such disasters, should recover whether or not they had contractual dealings with others who were also damaged by the tortious act. The limitation imposed by "particular" damages, together with refined notions of proximate cause and foreseeability, provides a workable scheme of liability that is in step with the rest of tort law, compensates innocent plaintiffs, and imposes the costs of harm on those who caused it.

* * *

IV. Advantages of the Alternate Rule of Recovery. The advantages of this alternate rule of recovery are that it compensates damaged plaintiffs, imposes the cost of damages upon those who have caused the harm, is consistent with economic principles of modern tort law, and frees courts from the necessity of creating a piecemeal quilt of exceptions to avoid the harsh effects of the *Robins* rule. * * *

If tort law fails to compensate plaintiffs or to impose the cost of damages on those who caused the harm, it should be under a warrant clear of necessity. When a rule of law, once extended, leads to inequitable results and creates principles of recovery that are at odds with the great weight of tort jurisprudence, then that rule of law merits scrutiny. A strict application of the extension denies recovery to many plaintiffs who should be awarded damages. Conventional tort principles of foreseeability, proximate causation, and "particular" damages would avoid such unfairness.

It is true that application of foreseeability and proximate causation would necessitate case-by-case adjudication. But I have a more optimistic assessment of courts' ability to undertake such adjudication than the majority.[38] Certainly such an inquiry would be no different from our daily task of weighing such claims in other tort cases.

The majority opinion also states that the *Robins* rule, being free from the vagaries of factual findings in a case-by-case determination, serves an important normative function because it is more predictable and more "candid." Normative values would also be served, however, by eliminating a broad categorical rule that is insensitive to equitable and social policy concerns that would support allowing the plaintiffs' claims in many individual cases. In assessing "normative concerns", the courts' compass should be a sense of fairness and equity, both of which are better served by allowing plaintiffs to present their claims under usual tort standards. It is not clear, moreover, that a jury's finding of negligence in a case-by-case determination is "less the product of a determinable rule of law" when the finder of fact is guided in its determination by rules of law. The jury's finding of liability in this case would be no more "lawless" than a finding of proximate cause, foreseeability, and particular damages in a physical damage case. * * *

The economic arguments regarding allocation of loss that purportedly favor the *Robins* rule of nonliability are not as clear to me as they appear to be to the majority. It is true that denial of recovery may effectively spread the loss over the victims. It is not certain, however, that victims are generally better insurers against the risk of loss caused by tortious acts having widespread consequences. Although the victims do possess greater knowledge of their circumstances and their potential damages, we do not know whether insurance against these types of losses is readily available to the businesses that may be affected. We do know that insurance against this kind of loss is already available for shippers. Imposition of liability upon the shippers helps ensure that the potential tortfeasor faces incen-

---

38. The majority criticizes foreseeability because it necessitates a case-by-case determination of liability. But this criticism of "foreseeability" as the criterion for judgment applies with equal force to well-established tort law for physical injury. The unquestioned concepts of foreseeability and proximate cause as established in *Palsgraf* and its progeny are open to the same condemnation that the majority makes of a rule of liability that would abandon *Robins:* "The result would be that no determinable measure of the limit of foreseeability would precede the decision on liability. We are told that where a claim is too remote, or too tenuous, recovery will be denied. Presumably then, as among all plaintiffs suffering foreseeable economic loss, recovery will turn on a judge['s] or jury's decision. * * * The point is not that

such a process cannot be administered but rather that its judgments would be much less the product of a determinable rule of law." [C]

The majority opinion favors a bright line rule, as opposed to a case-by-case determination of liability, because it enables courts to "adjudicate" rather than to "manage." A bright line rule such as the one the majority proposes, however, requires no adjudication whatsoever. Judges need merely to preside over a self-executing system of limited liability where recovery is predicated upon an easily determined physical injury. The application of such a rule, rather than a case-by-case determination, seems more "management" than adjudication.

tives to take the proper care. The majority's point is well taken that the incentives to avoid accidents do not increase once potential losses pass a certain measure of enormity. But in truth we have no idea what this measure is: Absent hard data, I would rather err on the side of receiving little additional benefit from imposing additional quanta of liability than err by adhering to *Robins'* inequitable rule and bar victims' recovery on the mistaken belief that a "marginal incentive curve" was flat, or nearly so. If a loss must be borne, it is no worse if a "merely" negligent defendant bears the loss than an innocent plaintiff absorb the damages.

V. Conclusion. The *Robins* approach restricts liability more severely than the policies behind limitations on liability require and imposes the cost of the accident on the victim, who is usually not in a superior position to obtain insurance to cover this loss. I would apply a rule of recovery based on conventional tort principles of proximate cause and foreseeability and limit eligibility only by the requirement that a claimant prove "particular" damages.

Alvin B. Rubin, Circuit Judge, with whom Wisdom, Politz and Tate, Circuit Judges, join, dissenting. * * * *Robins* should not be extended beyond its actual holding and should not be applied in cases like this, for the result is a denial of recompense to innocent persons who have suffered a real injury as a result of someone else's fault. We should not flinch from redressing injury because Congress has been indifferent to the problem.

NOTES AND QUESTIONS

1. The principal case follows the clear majority rule. But disagreement in the opinions in the case indicates the current ferment. The case is discussed by Atiyah, Economic Loss in the United States, 5 Ox.J. of Leg.Stud. 485 (1985). For a strong case holding liability, see People Express Airlines, Inc. v. Consolidated Rail Corp., 100 N.J. 246, 495 A.2d 107 (1985) (tank car accident producing toxic fumes requiring evacuation of plaintiff's offices at Newark Airport, resulting in economic loss).

2. The foundational authority in the Common Law world establishing no duty is Justice Holmes's opinion in Robins Dry Dock & Repair Co. v. Flint, supra. But see Goldberg, Recovery of Pure Economic Loss in Tort: Another Look at Robins Dry Dock v. Flint, 20 J.Leg.Stud. 249 (1991), noting that "[t]ort law is under constant pressure to extend the boundaries of what constitutes a compensable injury" and that *Robins* is inapposite in many contexts in which it has been employed to deny liability. He finds a requirement for "some intellectual apparatus for evaluating the myriad of claims for recovery of mere economic loss."

3. Australian and Canadian courts, faced with the *Robins* rule denying recovery, have crafted exceptions allowing limited recovery: Norsk Pacific Steamship Co. Ltd. v. Canadian National Railway Co. [1992] 1 S.C.R. 1021 (owner of barge which negligently damaged bridge required to compensate plaintiff railway for losses incurred in rerouting traffic over another bridge); Caltex Oil (Aust.) Pty. Ltd. v. The Dredge "Willemstad," 136 C.L.R. 529 (1976) (Austl.) (owner of dredge which severed a pipeline required to compensate plaintiff refinery for extra cost of transporting oil while the pipe was being repaired). Although often applied in the admiralty context in the United States, it is a traditional common law rule that is

traceable to Cattle v. Stockton Waterworks Co., 10 Q.B. 453 (1895): In re Ballard Shipping Co. v. Beach Shellfish, 32 F.3d 623 (1st Cir.1994) (finding that the rule in *Robins* did not preempt Rhode Island legislation affording expanded state law remedies for oil pollution).

4. Sometimes the loss will arise from the defectiveness of a good or structure. In East River Steamship Corp. v. Transamerica Delaval, Inc., 476 U.S. 858 (1986), the manufacturers of defective turbine engines owed no duty of care to the charterer of a supertanker, who suffered loss when the turbine had to be replaced because the low pressure turbine had been damaged by faulty installation of a valve. The plaintiff's claim, being for damage to the product itself, is economic and "most naturally understood as a warranty claim" (p. 872). How is the damage to be characterized in these cases:

(A) the defective engine explodes causing the ship to sink; liability to the injured crew, the ship's owner for her loss?

(B) design defect in a fishing vessel's hydraulic system causes her to catch fire and sink; the accident destroys, in addition to the vessel, equipment added after the initial sale, namely a skiff, a fishing net, and spare parts: Saratoga Fishing Co. v. J. M. Martinac & Co., 520 U.S. 875 (1997)?

(C) the defective engine threatens to explode necessitating drydocking and repairs and resulting in wasted hire charges and a loss of profits?

(D) the defective engine does not work at all when the manufacturer knew the purpose to which the engine would be put?

In respect of goods these issues become acute when liability in tort imposes strict liability, in our example on the manufacturer of the engine. See Moorman Manufacturing Co. v. National Tank Co., 91 Ill.2d 69, 435 N.E.2d 443, 61 Ill.Dec. 746 (1982). See generally Chapter 15:5 Interests Protected.

5. The courts do not always restrict liability via the duty issue. In Petitions of Kinsman Transit Co., 388 F.2d 821 (2d Cir.1968), supra Chapter 6, Kaufman J. employed a proximate cause analysis to deny recovery for economic losses suffered by wheat owners when Buffalo harbor was blocked due to the defendant's negligence.

4. MENTAL DISTURBANCE AND RESULTING INJURY

Daley v. LaCroix

Supreme Court of Michigan, 1970.
384 Mich. 4, 179 N.W.2d 390.

T.M. KAVANAGH, JUDGE. * * * On July 16, 1963, about 10:00 p.m., defendant was traveling west on 15 Mile Road near plaintiffs' farm in Macomb county. Defendant's vehicle left the highway, traveled 63 feet in the air and 209 feet beyond the edge of the road and, in the process, sheared off a utility pole. A number of high voltage lines snapped, striking the electrical lines leading into plaintiffs' house and caused a great electrical explosion resulting in considerable property damage.

Plaintiffs claimed, in addition to property damage, that Estelle Daley suffered traumatic neurosis, emotional disturbance and nervous upset, and that Timothy Daley suffered emotional disturbance and nervousness as a result of the explosion and the attendant circumstances. * * *

The Court of Appeals (13 Mich.App. 26, 163 N.W.2d 666) affirmed the trial court's grant of a directed verdict upon the ground that Michigan law denies recovery for negligently caused emotional disturbance absent a showing of physical impact. * * *

Recovery for mental disturbance caused by defendant's negligence, but without accompanying physical injury or physical consequences or any independent basis for tort liability, has been generally denied with the notable exception of the *sui generis* cases involving telegraphic companies and negligent mishandling of corpses. * * *

[However], compensation for a purely mental component of damages where defendant negligently inflicts an *immediate physical injury* has always been awarded as "parasitic damages." * * *

The final bastion against allowing recovery [for negligent infliction of emotional harm] is the requirement of some impact upon the person of the plaintiff. It is this doctrine and its continued vitality in our State which we must now consider. * * *

In the landmark decision of Victorian Railways Commissioners v. Coultas, 13 A.C. 222 (1888), recovery for a much disputed damage to plaintiff's nervous system caused by defendant's oncoming train was denied upon the ground that:

"Damages arising from mere sudden terror unaccompanied by any actual physical injury, but occasioning a nervous or mental shock, cannot under such circumstances, their Lordships think, be considered a consequence which, in the ordinary course of things, would flow from the negligence of the gate-keeper. If it were held that they can, it appears to their Lordships that it would be extending the liability for negligence much beyond what that liability has hitherto been held to be. Not only in such a case as the present, but in every case where an accident caused by negligence had given a person a serious nervous shock, there might be a claim for damages on account of mental injury. The difficulty which now often exists in case of alleged physical injuries of determining whether they were caused by the negligent act would be greatly increased, and a wide field opened for imaginary claims."

As a further hedge against fraudulent or fancied claims and the feared flood of litigation, a large number of American courts in adopting the Victorian Railways Commissioners rule superimposed the additional requirement of a contemporaneous physical impact. * * *

The leading American authority of Mitchell v. Rochester Ry. Co. (1896), 151 N.Y. 107, 45 N.E. 354, with "remorseless logic" stated the position as follows (pp. 109, 110, 45 N.E. p. 354):

"Assuming that fright cannot form the basis of an action, it is obvious that no recovery can be had for injuries resulting therefrom. That the result may be nervous disease, blindness, insanity, or even a miscarriage, in no way changes the principle. These results merely show the degree of fright, or the extent of the damages. * * * Therefore the logical result of the respondent's concession would seem to be, not only that no recovery can be had for mere fright, but also that none can be had for injuries which are the direct consequences of it. * * * These considerations lead to the conclusion that no recovery can be had for injuries sustained by fright occasioned by the negligence of another, where there is no immediate personal injury." * * *

The life of the law, however, has not been logic but experience. Bowing to the onslaught of exceptions[9] and the growing irreconcilability between legal fact and decretal fiction, a rapidly increasing majority of courts have repudiated the "requirement of impact" and have regarded the physical consequences themselves or the circumstances of the accident as sufficient guarantee.

Pertinently, the New York Court of Appeals in Battalla v. State (1961), 10 N.Y.2d 237, 219 N.Y.S.2d 34, 176 N.E.2d 729, expressly overruled its Mitchell v. Rochester Ry. Co., decision, supra, observing at p. 239, 219 N.Y.S.2d at p. 36, 176 N.E.2d at p. 730:

"Before passing to a resume of the evolution of the doctrine in this State, it is well to note that it has been thoroughly repudiated by the English courts which initiated it, rejected by a majority of American jurisdictions, abandoned by many which originally adopted it, and diluted, through numerous exceptions, in the minority which retained it. Moreover, it is the opinion of the scholars that *the right* to bring an action should be enforced."

Based upon close scrutiny of our precedential cases and the authority upon which they rested and cognizant of the changed circumstances relating to the factual and scientific information available, we conclude that the "impact" requirement of the common law should not have a continuing effect in Michigan and we therefore overrule the principle to the contrary contained in our previous cases.

We hold that where a definite and objective physical injury is produced as a result of emotional distress proximately caused by defendant's negligent conduct, the plaintiff in a properly pleaded and proved action may

9. The divergent approaches of the courts to find an exception to the Rochester Ry. Co. rule is excellently summarized by Prosser, Torts (3d Ed.), pp. 350, 351:

"Apart from some quite untenable notions of causal connection, the theory seems to be that the 'impact' affords the desired guarantee that the mental disturbance is genuine. But the same courts have found 'impact' in minor contacts with the person which play no part in causing the real harm, and in themselves can have no importance whatever. 'Impact' has meant a slight blow, a trifling burn or electric shock, a trivial jolt or jar, a forcible seating on the floor, dust in the eye, or the inhalation of smoke. The requirement has even been satisfied by a fall brought about by a faint after a collision, or the plaintiff's own wrenching of her shoulder in reaction to the fright. 'The magic formula "impact" is pronounced; the door opens to a full joy of a complete recovery.' A Georgia circus case has reduced the whole matter to a complete absurdity by finding 'impact' where the defendant's horse 'evacuated his bowels' into the plaintiff's lap."

recover in damages for such physical consequences to himself notwithstanding the absence of any physical impact upon plaintiff at the time of the mental shock.

The rule we adopt today is, of course, subject to familiar limitations.

Generally, defendant's standard of conduct is measured by reactions to be expected of normal persons. Absent specific knowledge of plaintiff's unusual sensitivity, there should be no recovery for hypersensitive mental disturbance where a normal individual would not be affected under the circumstances. * * *

Further, plaintiff has the burden of proof that the physical harm or illness is the *natural result* of the fright proximately caused by defendant's conduct. In other words, men of ordinary experience and judgment must be able to conclude, after sufficient testimony has been given to enable them to form an intelligent opinion, that the physical harm complained of is a natural consequence of the alleged emotional disturbance which in turn is proximately caused by defendant's conduct. * * *

In view of the above holding it becomes necessary to discuss another issue raised by plaintiffs—whether, considering the evidence in the light most favorable to plaintiffs, sufficient evidence was presented to create a jury question. Denying plaintiffs' motion for a new trial which sought to set aside the directed verdict against plaintiffs Timothy and Estelle Daley, the trial court reasoned:

"There was no expert or medical testimony offered on behalf of the minor, Timothy. Extremely vague lay testimony was offered to the effect he was nervous. It was so vague and uncertain it did not, in the court's opinion, reach the dignity of possessing any evidentiary value whatever. It afforded the jury nothing into which the jury could put its 'damage-assessment teeth'." Vachon v. Todorovich, 356 Mich. 182 [, 97 N.W.2d 122].

"On behalf of Estelle Daley, Dr. Goldin, a psychiatrist, testified. Direct and cross examination were extensive. He testified clearly that she had been neurotic since childhood and the incident complained of did not cause her neurosis. Dr. Goldin indicated the incident could have broken down her 'balances' somewhat although she did not consult him until a year after the accident.

"The lay testimony was of the same type as was given in Timothy's claim. It was vague and uncertain and indefinite."

From an examination of the evidence presented on behalf of Timothy Daley, we believe that, even though the question is a close one, on favorable view, he presented facts from which under our new rule as announced in this case, a jury could reasonably find or infer a causal relation between defendant's alleged negligence and the injuries alleged. We conclude that Timothy Daley should be given an opportunity to prove his alleged cause of action, if he can do so, at a new trial.

Plaintiff Estelle Daley's claim that she suffered physical consequences naturally arising from the fright proximately caused by defendant's conduct is amply supported by the record. Her sudden loss of weight, her inability to perform ordinary household duties, her extreme nervousness and irritability, repeatedly testified to by plaintiffs, are facts from which a jury could find or infer a compensable physical injury.

The plaintiffs' testimony is also supported by the medical expert witness, who diagnosed plaintiff Estelle Daley as "a chronic psychoneurotic * * * in partial remission," and who attributed this state or condition to the explosion directly caused by defendant's acts:

"Q. I want to ask one more question, from everything that you know about this case, Doctor, do you feel there is a causal relationship between the explosion of July, 1963 and the symptoms that she has shown that you have reported?

"A. Yes, the trauma is the triggering point for her breaking the balance in her.

"Q. By trauma?

"A. Any trauma, may be emotional trauma or physical trauma, in this case having this explosive sound that she heard and the fears that were attendant with the explosive sounds."

We hold * * * that this record presents sufficient facts from which a jury could reasonably find, or infer therefrom, a causal relationship between the fright occasioned by defendant's negligence and the injuries alleged in plaintiffs' complaint. The trial court erred in taking plaintiff Estelle Daley's case from the jury. [Cc] It follows that the trial court also erred in striking plaintiff Leonard H. Daley's claim for medical expenses.

The order of the trial court granting directed verdicts against plaintiffs Estelle Daley and Timothy Daley and the Court of Appeals' affirmance thereof are reversed and the causes remanded for new trials. * * *

Costs shall abide the final result.

DETHMERS, T.G. KAVANAGH, ADAMS and BLACK, JJ., concurred with T.M. KAVANAGH.

BRENNAN, CHIEF JUSTICE (dissenting). If this were a case where a definite and objective physical injury was produced without impact by the negligent act of the defendant, it might be appropriate to adopt the rule set forth in the Restatement (Second) of Torts § 436(2).

This is not such a case. Plaintiffs did not suffer definite and objective physical injury. Plaintiffs suffered, if anything, indefinite and subjective injury. Traumatic neurosis, emotional disturbance and nervous upset are the very type of complaints which ought to be eliminated by restricting "no impact" cases to those in which a definite and objective physical injury occurs.

I would affirm the trial court's grant of directed verdict.

KELLY, J., concurred with BRENNAN, C.J.

NOTES AND QUESTIONS

1. The "impact" rule once predominated. Is it completely devoid of sense? Are you quite sure that within the past two years you have not almost hit someone with an automobile? Can you swear that you have not frightened anyone? What if you were sued on a claim that you had caused a miscarriage? A few courts still retain the impact rule. E.g., Champion v. Gray, 478 So.2d 17 (Fla.1985), and Brown v. Cadillac Motor Car Div., 468 So.2d 903 (Fla.1985).

2. The policy reasons for and against allowing recovery despite the absence of an impact are vigorously and colorfully expounded in the dissenting opinions in two Pennsylvania cases. In Bosley v. Andrews, 393 Pa. 161, 169, 142 A.2d 263, 267 (1958), Musmanno, J., dissented against the continued application of the impact rule. In Niederman v. Brodsky, 436 Pa. 401, 413, 261 A.2d 84, 90 (1970), Bell, C.J., dissented against the overruling of the impact rule. The uninhibited language more readily used in a dissenting opinion makes entertaining reading.

3. Where the plaintiff has narrowly escaped imminent and serious harm to his own physical well being, the courts have readily allowed recovery upon a demonstration of ensuing mental disturbance. See Falzone v. Busch, 45 N.J. 559, 214 A.2d 12 (1965) (pedestrian almost struck by automobile).

4. When plaintiff's alleged emotional suffering stems from other causes, the cases are more difficult to decide. Thus:

A. Defendant sold plaintiff a water softener that caused a rusty discoloration of the water in plaintiff's home. Plaintiff noticed the discoloration after she drank a cup of coffee made from this water, and claimed she suffered a heart attack as a result of her shock. The court denied her claim. See Caputzal v. Lindsay Co., 48 N.J. 69, 222 A.2d 513 (1966). Is the denial of a claim best placed on the ground of proximate cause or duty? In the most famous and foundational case of English and Commonwealth tort law, Donoghue v. Stevenson, [1932] A.C. 562, the House of Lords decided that the relationship of the manufacturer of ginger beer and eventual consumer gave rise to a duty of care. Mrs. Stevenson claimed she had suffered severe shock as a result of witnessing the decomposed remains of a snail emerge from a bottle of ginger beer made by Donoghue, some of which she had already drunk.

B. Mrs. Donoghue's American "cousin," Ms. Ellington, was more imaginative thinking that the Coca–Cola she was drinking contained a worm. It was in fact a piece of Good–N–Plenty candy that did not touch her lips. Should she be able to recover for her emotional distress? See Ellington v. Coca Cola Bottling Co., 717 P.2d 109 (Okl.1986). Is it appropriate to insist on a standard of normality? How would this comport with the thin skull cases?

C. A person has been exposed to asbestos and incurs asbestosis (scarring of the lung). In addition to damages for this injury, can he also recover damages for his fear of contracting lung cancer? See Jackson v. Johns–Manville Sales Corp., 781 F.2d 394 (5th Cir.1986), cert. denied, 478 U.S. 1022 (1986). Suppose there has been exposure to asbestos but no illness has yet occurred?

5. Should fear of becoming ill or dying at a later date be compensable? The question arises today in litigation over toxic torts and latent diseases. See, e.g., Gideon v. Johns–Manville Sales Corp., 761 F.2d 1129 (5th Cir.1985) (asbestos-related cancer); Mauro v. Raymark Indus., 116 N.J. 126, 561 A.2d 257 (1989) (asbestos); Payton v. Abbott Laboratories, 386 Mass. 540, 437 N.E.2d 171 (1982) (diethylstilbestrol); Hagerty v. L & L Marine Services, Inc., 788 F.2d 315 (5th Cir.1986) (seaman soaked in toxic chemicals; recovery for "serious mental distress arising from fear of developing cancer where fear is reasonable and causally related

to the defendant's negligence"). What criteria should be applied? Is the impact rule really a problem here? Metro–North Commuter Railroad Company v. Buckley, 117 S.Ct. 2113 (1997) (asbestos action under Federal Employers' Liability Act); Majca v. Beekil, 183 Ill. 2d 407, 701 N.E.2d 1084 (1998) (damages for fear of contracting AIDS from scalpel left in wastebasket; collecting and relying on cases requiring proof of actual exposure to HIV). But cf. Williamson v. Waldman, 150 N.J. 232, 696 A.2d 14 (1997) (same claim; rejecting the actual exposure test and substituting a test based upon the reasonableness of the emotional distress, but measured by "a level of knowledge of the disease that is then-current, accurate, and generally available to the public"). The toxic tort cases introduce a plethora of problems—numerosity, wide distribution of claims, long latency periods, indeterminate proof of harm and multiple sources of responsibility. See 2 American Law Institute, Reporters' Study Enterprise Responsibility for Personal Injury (1991) at 385.

6. How should a court determine what is or is not a "physical injury" for the purposes of this rule? Should it be left to the jury to decide the question on the basis of conflicting expert testimony? Is there any viable alternative to the "physical injury threshold"? Consider the statement of Judge McEntee in Petition of the United States, 418 F.2d 264 (1st Cir.1969): "The term 'physical' is not used in its ordinary sense for purposes of applying the 'physical consequences' rule. Rather, the word is used to indicate that the condition or illness for which recovery is sought must be one susceptible to objective determination. Hence, a definite nervous disorder is a 'physical injury' sufficient to support an action for damages for negligence." See also Wallace v. Coca–Cola Bottling Plants, Inc., 269 A.2d 117 (Me.1970): "The mental and emotional suffering to be compensable must be substantial and manifested by objective symptomatology." In accord, see Ford v. Aldi, Inc., 832 S.W.2d 1 (Mo.App.1992). In Johnson v. Ruark Obstetrics & Gynecology Assoc., 327 N.C. 283, 303–4, 395 S.E.2d 85, 97 (1990), the court held that recovery depended upon proof of "severe emotional distress" which meant "any emotional or mental disorder, such as, for example, neurosis, psychosis, chronic depression, phobia, or any other type of severe and disabling emotional or mental condition which may be generally recognized and diagnosed by professionals trained to do so."

7. Uncertainties of tracing causation from defendant's conduct to plaintiff's injuries have formed a basic rationale for adhering to the impact rule. The Supreme Court of Virginia has sponsored a procedural safeguard on this issue: plaintiff must prove causation in fact by "clear and convincing" evidence. Womack v. Eldridge, 215 Va. 338, 210 S.E.2d 145 (1974). Yet the courts have often pointed to medical scientific knowledge as a reason for extending liability, e.g.:

> There is * * * nothing unusual or peculiar in the recognition by the law that compensable injury may be caused just as much by a direct assault upon the mind or the nervous system as by direct physical contact with the body. This is no more than the natural and inevitable result of the growing appreciation by modern medical science of recognizable causal connections between shock to the nervous system and physical or psychiatric illness.

Alcock v. Chief Constable of the South Yorkshire Police, [1992] 1 A.C. 310, at 406–407 (House of Lords) per Lord Oliver.

Thing v. La Chusa

Supreme Court of California, In Bank 1989.
48 Cal.3d 644, 771 P.2d 814, 257 Cal.Rptr. 865.

EAGLESON, JUSTICE.

The narrow issue presented by the parties in this case is whether the Court of Appeal correctly held that a mother who did not witness an accident in which an automobile struck and injured her child may recover damages from the negligent driver for the emotional distress she suffered when she arrived at the accident scene. The more important question this issue poses for the court, however, is whether the "guidelines" enunciated by this court in Dillon v. Legg (1968) 68 Cal.2d 728, 69 Cal.Rptr. 72, 441 P.2d 912, are adequate, or if they should be refined to create greater certainty in this area of the law.

[In *Dillon*, the court had enunciated a test based upon whether defendant should have reasonably foreseen the injury to plaintiff, the victim's mother, who had suffered emotional distress. This foreseeability test of duty demanded courts "take in account such factors as the following: (1) Whether plaintiff was located near the scene of the accident as contrasted with one who was a distance away from it. (2) Whether the shock resulted from a direct emotional impact upon plaintiff from the sensory and contemporaneous observance of the accident, as contrasted with learning of the accident from others after its occurrence. (3) Whether plaintiff and the victim were closely related, as contrasted with an absence of any relationship or the presence of only a distant relationship."]

* * *

On December 8, 1980, John Thing, a minor, was injured when struck by an automobile operated by defendant James V. La Chusa. His mother, plaintiff Maria Thing, was nearby, but neither saw nor heard the accident. She became aware of the injury to her son when told by a daughter that John had been struck by a car. She rushed to the scene where she saw her bloody and unconscious child, whom she believed was dead, lying in the roadway. Maria sued defendants, alleging that she suffered great emotional disturbance, shock, and injury to her nervous system as a result of these events, and that the injury to John and emotional distress she suffered were proximately caused by defendants' negligence.

The trial court granted defendants' motion for summary judgment, ruling that, as a matter of law, Maria could not establish a claim for negligent infliction of emotional distress because she did not contemporaneously and sensorily perceive the accident.

* * *

[N]egligence cases permitting recovery of damages for emotional distress had developed in California at the time *Siliznoff* [supra Chapter II], [C], was decided. Initially, however, in negligence cases the right to recover for emotional distress had been limited to circumstances in which the victim was himself injured and emotional distress was a "parasitic" item of damages, or if a plaintiff who had been in the "zone of danger" did not suffer injury from impact, but did suffer physical injury as a result of the emotional trauma. (See Webb v. Francis J. Lewald Coal Co. (1931) 214 Cal.

182, 184, 4 P.2d 532; Lindley v. Knowlton (1918) 179 Cal. 298, 301–302, 176 P. 440.)

* * *

* * * [I]n Amaya v. Home Ice, Fuel & Supply Co., supra, * * * the court had declined the opportunity to broaden the right to recover for emotional distress.

* * * [A]fter confirming that the "impact rule" making a contemporaneous physical impact a prerequisite to recovery for negligently induced fright or shock was not applicable in California, [the court] held damages could not be recovered by persons outside the zone of danger created by the defendant's negligence even when that shock was reflected in physiological symptoms.

* * *

The *Amaya* view was short lived, however. Only five years later, the decision was overruled in *Dillon v. Legg,* supra.

In *Dillon* * * *, the issue was limited. The mother and sister of a deceased infant each sought damages for "great emotional disturbance and shock and injury to her nervous system" which had caused them great mental pain and suffering. Allegedly these injuries were caused by witnessing the defendant's negligently operated vehicle collide with and roll over the infant as she lawfully crossed a street. The mother was not herself endangered by the defendant's conduct. The sister may have been. The trial court had therefore granted the defendant's motion for judgment on the pleadings as to the mother, but had denied it with respect to the sister of the decedent. Faced with the incongruous result demanded by the "zone of danger" rule which denied recovery for emotional distress and consequent physical injury unless the plaintiff himself had been threatened with injury, the court overruled *Amaya.*

* * *

The difficulty in defining the limits on recovery * * * was rejected as a basis for denying recovery, but the court did recognize that "to limit the otherwise potentially infinite liability which would follow every negligent act, the law of torts holds defendant amenable only for injuries to others which to defendant at the time were reasonably foreseeable." [C] * * * Thus, while the court indicated that foreseeability of the injury was to be the primary consideration in finding duty, it simultaneously recognized that policy considerations mandated that infinite liability be avoided by restrictions that would somehow narrow the class of potential plaintiffs. But the test limiting liability was itself amorphous.

In adopting foreseeability of the injury as the basis of a negligent actor's duty, the *Dillon* court identified the risks that could give rise to that duty as both physical impact and emotional disturbance brought on by the conduct. Having done so, the *Dillon* court conceded: "We cannot now predetermine defendant's obligation in every situation by a fixed category;

no immutable rule can establish the extent of that obligation for every circumstance of the future." [C] * * *

* * *

The expectation of the *Dillon* majority that the parameters of the tort would be further defined in future cases has not been fulfilled. Instead, subsequent decisions of the Courts of Appeal and this court, have created more uncertainty. And, just as the "zone of danger" limitation was abandoned in *Dillon* as an arbitrary restriction on recovery, the *Dillon* guidelines have been relaxed on grounds that they, too, created arbitrary limitations on recovery. Little consideration has been given in post-*Dillon* decisions to the importance of avoiding the limitless exposure to liability that the pure foreseeability test of "duty" would create and towards which these decisions have moved.

Both the physical harm and accident or sudden occurrence elements were eliminated, however, in Molien v. Kaiser Foundation Hospitals, 27 Cal.3d 916, 167 Cal.Rptr. 831, 616 P.2d 813, at least as to those plaintiffs who could claim to be "direct victims" of the defendant's negligence. The court held in *Molien* that a defendant hospital and doctor owed a duty directly to the husband of a patient who had been diagnosed erroneously as having syphilis, and had been told to so advise the husband in order that he could receive testing and, if necessary, treatment.

In finding the existence of a duty to the husband of the patient, the court reasoned that the risk of harm to the husband was reasonably foreseeable, and that the tortious conduct was directed to him as well as the patient. [C] The status of the plaintiff mother in *Dillon* was distinguished as she suffered her injury solely as a "percipient witness" to the infliction of injury on another. She was therefore a "bystander" rather than a "direct victim." * * * The limitations on recovery for emotional distress that had been suggested in the *Dillon* "guidelines" were not applicable to "direct" victims of a defendant's negligence.

The subtleties in the distinction between the right to recover as a "bystander" and as a "direct victim" created what one Court of Appeal has described as an "amorphous nether realm" [Cc] * * *

"The problem * * * is: how are we to distinguish between 'direct victim' cases and 'bystander' cases? * * * The inference suggested is that a 'direct victim' is a person whose emotional distress is a reasonably foreseeable consequence of the conduct of the defendant. This does not provide criteria which delimit what counts as reasonable foreseeability. It leads into the quagmire of novel claims which the Supreme Court foresaw as an unacceptable consequence of a 'pure' foreseeability analysis * * *." * * * [C]

"[F]oreseeability," the court noted later in Newton v. Kaiser Foundation Hospitals, 184 Cal.App.3d 386, 391, 228 Cal.Rptr. 890, "is endless because foreseeability, like light, travels indefinitely in a vacuum." *Molien*, supra, thus, left to future cases the "unenviable tasks of distinguishing bystander from direct victim cases and establishing limits for the latter * * * with a 'foreseeable' diversity of results."

* * * In order to avoid limitless liability out of all proportion to the degree of a defendant's negligence, and against which it is impossible to insure without imposing unacceptable costs on those among whom the risk is spread, the right to recover for negligently caused emotional distress must be limited.

We acknowledged and addressed one aspect of this problem in Elden v. Sheldon (1988) 46 Cal.3d 267, 250 Cal.Rptr. 254, 758 P.2d 582, holding that cohabitation, without formal marriage, did not constitute the close relationship contemplated by the *Dillon* guidelines and that foreseeability of injury alone does not justify imposition of liability for negligently caused emotional distress. In so doing, we again recognized that policy considerations justify restrictions on recovery for emotional distress notwithstanding the sometimes arbitrary result, and that the court has an obligation to establish those restrictions. *Elden* confirmed that those policy considerations include both the burden on the courts in applying vaguely defined criteria and the importance of limiting the scope of liability for negligence. If the consequences of a negligent act are not limited an intolerable burden is placed on society. A "bright line in this area of the law is essential." [C] * * *

The issue resolved in *Elden* was too narrow to create that "bright line" * * * This case, however, presents a broader question and thus affords the court a better opportunity to meet its obligation to create a clear rule under which liability may be determined. In so doing we balance the impact of arbitrary lines which deny recovery to some victims whose injury is very real against that of imposing liability out of proportion to culpability for negligent acts. We also weigh in the balance the importance to the administration of justice of clear guidelines under which litigants and trial courts may resolve disputes.

* * *

The impact of personally observing the injury-producing event in most, although concededly not all, cases distinguishes the plaintiff's resultant emotional distress from the emotion felt when one learns of the injury or death of a loved one from another, or observes pain and suffering but not the traumatic cause of the injury. Greater certainty and a more reasonable limit on the exposure to liability for negligent conduct is possible by limiting the right to recover for negligently caused emotional distress to plaintiffs who personally and contemporaneously perceive the injury-producing event and its traumatic consequences.

Similar reasoning justifies limiting recovery to persons closely related by blood or marriage since, in common experience, it is more likely that they will suffer a greater degree of emotional distress than a disinterested witness to negligently caused pain and suffering or death. Such limitations are indisputably arbitrary since it is foreseeable that in some cases unrelated persons have a relationship to the victim or are so affected by the traumatic event that they suffer equivalent emotional distress. As we have observed, however, drawing arbitrary lines is unavoidable if we are to limit liability and establish meaningful rules for application by litigants and lower courts.

No policy supports extension of the right to recover * * * to a larger class of plaintiffs. Emotional distress is an intangible condition experienced by most persons, even absent negligence, at some time during their lives. Close relatives suffer serious, even debilitating, emotional reactions to the injury, death, serious illness, and evident suffering of loved ones. These reactions occur regardless of the cause of the loved one's illness, injury, or death. That relatives will have severe emotional distress is an unavoidable aspect of the "human condition." The emotional distress for which monetary damages may be recovered, however, ought not to be that form of acute emotional distress or the transient emotional reaction to the occasional gruesome or horrible incident to which every person may potentially be exposed in an industrial and sometimes violent society. Regardless of the depth of feeling or the resultant physical or mental illness that results from witnessing violent events, persons unrelated to those injured or killed may not now recover for such emotional upheaval even if negligently caused. Close relatives who witness the accidental injury or death of a loved one and suffer emotional trauma may not recover when the loved one's conduct was the cause of that emotional trauma. The overwhelming majority of "emotional distress" which we endure, therefore, is not compensable.

Unlike an award of damages for intentionally caused emotional distress which is punitive, the award * * * simply reflects society's belief that a negligent actor bears some responsibility for the effect of his conduct on persons other than those who suffer physical injury. In identifying those persons and the circumstances in which the defendant will be held to redress the injury, it is appropriate to restrict recovery to those persons who will suffer an emotional impact beyond the impact that can be anticipated whenever one learns that a relative is injured, or dies, or the emotion felt by a "disinterested" witness. The class of potential plaintiffs should be limited to those who because of their relationship suffer the greatest emotional distress. When the right to recover is limited in this manner, the liability bears a reasonable relationship to the culpability of the negligent defendant.

The elements which justify and simultaneously limit an award of damages for emotional distress caused by awareness of the negligent infliction of injury to a close relative are * * * the traumatic emotional effect on the plaintiff who contemporaneously observes both the event or conduct that causes serious injury to a close relative and the injury itself. Even if it is "foreseeable" that persons other than closely related percipient witnesses may suffer emotional distress, this fact does not justify the imposition of what threatens to become unlimited liability for emotional distress on a defendant whose conduct is simply negligent. Nor does such abstract "foreseeability" warrant continued reliance on the assumption that the limits of liability will become any clearer if lower courts are permitted to continue approaching the issue on a "case-to-case" basis some 20 years after *Dillon.*

We conclude, therefore, that a plaintiff may recover damages for emotional distress caused by observing the negligently inflicted injury of a third person if, but only if, said plaintiff: (1) is closely related to the injury victim; (2) is present at the scene of the injury-producing event at the time it occurs and is then aware that it is causing injury to the victim; and (3) as a result suffers serious emotional distress—a reaction beyond that which would be anticipated in a disinterested witness and which is not an abnormal response to the circumstances. * * * Experience has shown that, contrary to the expectation of the *Dillon* majority, * * * there are clear judicial days on which a court can foresee forever and thus determine liability but none on which that foresight alone provides a socially and judicially acceptable limit on recovery of damages for that injury.

The undisputed facts establish that plaintiff was not present at the scene of the accident in which her son was injured. She did not observe defendant's conduct and was not aware that her son was being injured. She could not, therefore, establish a right to recover for the emotional distress she suffered when she subsequently learned of the accident and observed its consequences. The order granting summary judgment was proper.

The judgment of the Court of Appeal is reversed.

Each party shall bear its own costs on appeal.

LUCAS, C.J., and PANELLI and ARGUELLES, JJ., concur. JUSTICE KAUFMAN concurred but disagreed with the reasoning of the majority and dissent, finding that *Dillon* ought to be overruled and liability be confined to those in the zone of danger put in fear of their *own* safety. JUSTICE BROUSSARD dissented.

NOTES AND QUESTIONS

1.   The principal case traces a distinction between direct and bystander victims. The distinction is treated more satisfactorily by Justice Mosk in his dissent. The "direct victim" cases are denoted by a "special relationship" between the plaintiff and defendant. In *Molien,* supra, defendant physician had plaintiff directly in mind when giving advice to his patient, plaintiff's husband. In Marlene F v. Affiliated Psychiatric Medical Clinic, Inc., 48 Cal. 3d 583, 588–592, 770 P.2d 278, 281–293 (Cal. 1989), court held that plaintiff's mother had a good cause of action against defendant therapist who had allegedly molested their children. The mother and children were in family therapy. The unique connection between mother and her baby allows mother a *direct* claim for emotional distress caused by false information that her baby was stillborn when it was born alive. The father's claim, however, was limited by the *indirect* bystander requirements: Carey v. Lovett, 132 N.J. 44, 622 A.2d 1279 (1993). Similarly, in Burgess v. Superior Court, 2 Cal.4th 1064, 831 P.2d 1197, 9 Cal.Rptr.2d 615 (1992), mother suffered emotional distress because of defendant physician's negligent delivery of child. She was a patient of the defendant and thus regarded as a direct victim. But cf. Schwarz v. Regents of University of California, 226 Cal.App.3d 149, 276 Cal.Rptr. 470 (1990), rejecting a father's claim for emotional distress as a result of negligent psychiatric treatment of his child; the father was not involved in the treatment.

2. A woman in therapy recovers memories of sexual abuse perpetrated upon her by her father years before when she was a child. The woman accuses her father, who, protesting his innocence, suffers emotional distress. Father believes that the memories were induced by the therapy. Does the therapist owe a duty of care to the father? The growing body of case law is contradictory. Flanders v. Cooper, 706 A.2d 589 (Me.1998) (finding no duty of care because the duty might restrict treatment choices of health care professionals and hence intrude on professional patient relationship); Doe v. McKay, 700 N.E.2d 1018 (Ill.1998); but see Sawyer v. Midelfort, 595 N.W.2d 423 (Wis.1999) (finding a duty of care to those accused of abuse for emotional injuries caused).

3. Most states retain the physical manifestation requirement, but two exceptions are well recognized. The death-telegram rule (recovery for emotional harm resulting from negligent transmission by a telegraph company of a message announcing death) is a minority rule but followed by a number of the states. See Johnson v. State, 37 N.Y.2d 378, 334 N.E.2d 590, 372 N.Y.S.2d 638 (1975); Mentzer v. Western Union Tel. Co., 93 Iowa 752, 62 N.W. 1 (1895); Western Union Tel. Co. v. Redding, 100 Fla. 495, 129 So. 743 (1930); Camper v. Minor, 915 S.W.2d 437, 443 (Tenn.1996) (recognizing the exception); Oswald v. LeGrand, 453 N.W.2d 634, 639 (Iowa 1990) (recognizing the exception). The Federal rule allows recovery if physical harm results. Kaufman v. Western Union Tel. Co., 224 F.2d 723 (5th Cir.1955), cert. denied, 350 U.S. 947 (1956); O'Brien v. Western Union Tel. Co., 113 F.2d 539 (1st Cir.1940).

majority rule for n.i.e.d. requirement

The second exception involves negligent interference with dead bodies. See Lott v. State, 32 Misc.2d 296, 225 N.Y.S.2d 434 (1962); Christensen v. Superior Court, 230 Cal.App.3d 798, 271 Cal.Rptr. 360 (1990), superseded, 54 Cal.3d 868, 820 P.2d 181, 2 Cal.Rptr.2d 79 (1991) (defendant mortuaries and crematoriums mishandling of about 16,000 decedents); Mokry v. University of Texas Health Science Center, 529 S.W.2d 802 (Tex.Civ.App.1975) (eyeball); Dufour v. Westlawn Cemeteries, Inc., 639 So. 2d 843 (La.Ct.App., 1994); Contreraz v. Michelotti–Sawyers, 271 Mont. 300, 896 P.2d 1118 (1995); but see Gonzalez v. Metropolitan Dade County Public Health Trust, 651 So. 2d 673, 675 (Fla.1995) (holding a plaintiff must prove physical injury or that the defendant acted willfully or wantonly to maintain an action for mental anguish based on negligent handling of a dead body); cf. Corso v. Crawford Dog and Cat Hosp., 97 Misc.2d 530, 415 N.Y.S.2d 182 (1979) (substitution in casket of cat for beloved pet dog); Campbell v. Animal Quarantine Station, 63 Haw. 557, 632 P.2d 1066 (1981) (dog).

4. As the principal case shows, the twists and turns in bystander liability have been manifold. Some have adopted the foreseeability test: Ramsey v. Beavers, 931 S.W.2d 527 (Tenn.1996) (foreseeability requiring consideration of relevant factors, position of plaintiff, degree of injury, relationship to injured party, and proof of severe emotional injury); Clohessy v. Bachelor, 237 Conn. 31, 675 A.2d 852 (1996) (adopting a rule of "reasonable foreseeability if bystander satisfies the following conditions: (1) he or she is closely related to the injury victim, such as the parent or the sibling of the victim; (2) emotional injury of the bystander is caused by the contemporaneous sensory perception of the event or conduct that causes the injury, or by arriving on the scene soon thereafter and before substantial change has occurred in the victim's condition or location; (3) injury of the victim must be substantial, resulting in his or her death or serious physical injury; and (4) bystander's emotional injury must be serious, beyond that which would be anticipated in a disinterested witness and which is not the result of an abnormal response.)"; Gabaldon v. Jay–Bi Property Management, Inc., 122 N.M. 393, 925 P.2d 510 (1996) (adopting contemporaneous sensory perception as a requirement;

mother called to scene of son's near drowning in wave pool arrived too late to fall within class of persons owed a duty of care); Bowen v. Lumbermens Mutual Casualty Co., 183 Wis. 2d 627, 517 N.W.2d 432 (1994) (rejecting the zone of impact rule and adopting a framework that "should be free of artificial, vague and inconsistent rules," and hence articulating a rule that guards against false claims and overdue burdens on actors: factors employed are (1) victim's serious injury or death, (2) close familial relationship, (3) direct perception of accident or coming immediately upon its aftermath).

Others have criticized the *Dillon* foreseeability test as too broad in imposing sweeping liability. In New York a zone of danger test has been adopted: Tobin v. Grossman, 24 N.Y.2d 609, 249 N.E.2d 419, 301 N.Y.S.2d 554 (1969) and Bovsun v. Sanperi, 61 N.Y.2d 219, 461 N.E.2d 843, 473 N.Y.S.2d 357 (1984). Elsewhere in the common law world the *Dillon* foreseeability test predominates, e.g., Alcock v. Chief Constable of the South Yorkshire Police [1992] 1 A.C. 310 the House of Lords dealt with a number of emotional distress claims arising from a soccer riot at Hillsborough Stadium, Sheffield. The defendant police allowed an excessively large number of spectators to enter a section of the ground. In the resulting crush 95 people were killed and over 400 injured. The scene was broadcast live on television. The plaintiffs suffered psychiatric illness when persons with whom they were related were killed in the meleé. Some of the plaintiffs had witnessed the event on television, others from another section of the ground. Note Lord Keith's speech, [1992] 1 A.C. 310, 397, dismissing the plaintiffs' appeals:

> As regards the class of persons to whom a duty may be owed to take reasonable care to avoid inflicting psychiatric illness through nervous shock sustained by reason of physical injury or peril to another, I think it sufficient that reasonable foreseeability should be the guide. I would not seek to limit the class by reference to particular relationships such as husband and wife or parent and child. The kinds of relationship which may involve close ties of love and affection are numerous, and it is the existence of such ties which leads to mental disturbance when the loved one suffers a catastrophe. They may be present in family relationships or those of close friendship, and may be stronger in the case of engaged couples than in that of persons who have been married to each other for many years. It is common knowledge that such ties exist, and reasonably foreseeable that those bound by them may in certain circumstances be at real risk of psychiatric illness if the loved one is injured or put in peril. The closeness of the tie would, however, require to be proved by a plaintiff, though no doubt being capable of being presumed in appropriate cases. The case of a bystander unconnected with the victims of an accident is difficult. Psychiatric injury to him would not ordinarily, in my view, be within the range of reasonable foreseeability, but could not perhaps be entirely excluded from it if the circumstances of a catastrophe occurring very close to him were particularly horrific.

5.   Should the following recover for emotional distress? Police or others who attempted to resuscitate victims of the Hillsborough Football Stadium disaster, supra note 3. Those who came later moved and attempted to revive victims. Those who had stripped and labeled bodies and dealt with distraught relatives. In Frost v. Chief Constable of South Yorkshire Police, [1997] 1 All E.R. 504 (Court of Appeal), a majority of the Lord Justices held the first two categories of plaintiffs could recover, but not the third.

6.   The California law has not stood still since *Thing*. Its limits were tested in In re Air Crash Disaster, 967 F.2d 1421 (9th Cir.1992), where the plaintiff, having

left her house shortly before, returned to find her house ablaze with her husband and two children inside; part of an Aeromexico jetliner had crashed into it. See also Wilks v. Hom, 2 Cal.App.4th 1264, 3 Cal.Rptr.2d 803 (1992) in which the "sensory and contemporaneous observance of the accident" requirement was satisfied when an explosion severely injured the plaintiff's daughter and blew the plaintiff out of the house. She did not see her daughter being injured but was contemporaneously aware of that fact.

7. Should it make any difference if the defendant is a doctor or a psychologist? Suppose a therapist decides to "date" a patient's sexual companion, having learned of the companion through the course of psychotherapy with his patient—now a plaintiff. See Rowe v. Bennett, 514 A.2d 802 (Me.1986). Should other special relationships deserve special treatment?

5. Unborn Children

Endresz v. Friedberg

New York Court of Appeals, 1969.
24 N.Y.2d 478, 248 N.E.2d 901, 301 N.Y.S.2d 65.

Fuld, Chief Judge. * * * The plaintiff, Janice Endresz, seven months pregnant, was injured in an automobile accident in the winter of 1965 and two days later was delivered of stillborn twins, a male and a female. Four actions in negligence were brought against the persons assertedly responsible for the accident. In the first two actions—one for the wrongful death of each child—the plaintiff Steve Endresz, Janice's husband, suing as administrator, seeks damages of $100,000 by reason of the distributees' "loss of anticipated * * * care, comfort and support during the minority and majority" of each infant and for "medical, hospital and funeral expenses incurred by reason of the death" of the children. * * *

On motion of the defendants, the court at Special Term * * * dismissed the first two suits for wrongful death. * * *

This court has already decided that a wrongful death action may not be maintained for the death of an unborn child. [Cc] This view is held by a number of other jurisdictions and, although there is authority to the contrary, further study and thought confirm the justice and wisdom of our earlier decisions.

Section 5–4.1 of the EPTL (L.1966, ch. 952, eff. Sept. 1, 1967), * * * declares, insofar as pertinent, that "The personal representative * * * of a decedent who is survived by distributees may maintain an action to recover damages for a wrongful act, neglect or default which caused the decedent's death against a person who would have been liable to the decedent by reason of such wrongful conduct if death had not ensued." Before there may be a "decedent", there must, perforce, be birth, a person born alive, and, although the statute, enacted in 1847 (L.1847, ch. 450), is silent on the subject, it is fairly certain that the Legislature did not intend to include an "unborn" foetus within the term "decedent". Indeed, it was not until 1951, more than 100 years later, that this court—overruling a long-standing

Chief Justice Fuld

decision (Drobner v. Peters, 232 N.Y. 220, 133 N.E. 567, 20 A.L.R. 1503
[1921])—decided that "a child viable but *in utero,* if injured by tort, should,
when born, be allowed to sue." (Woods v. Lancet, 303 N.Y. 349, 353, 102
N.E.2d 691, 693, 27 A.L.R.2d 1250.) If, before *Woods,* a child so injured had
no right of action, still less was such an action intended to lie on behalf of
one who, never seeing the light of day, was deprived of life while still in its
mother's womb.

Our decision in the *Woods* case (303 N.Y. 349, 102 N.E.2d 691, supra)
does not require us, as suggested, to reinterpret the wrongful death statute
to provide compensation to the distributees of a stillborn foetus for "pecuniary injuries" resulting from its death apart from those sustained by the
mother and father in their own right. The *Woods* decision, as the court
recognized in Matter of Logan, 3 N.Y.2d 800, 166 N.Y.S.2d 3, 144 N.E.2d
644, supra, simply brought the common law of this State into accord with
the demand of natural justice which requires recognition of the legal right
of every human being to begin life unimpaired by physical or mental
defects resulting from the negligence of another. The considerations of
justice which mandate the recovery of damages by an infant, injured in his
mother's womb and born deformed through the wrong of a third party, are

absent where the foetus, deprived of life while yet unborn, is never faced with the prospect of impaired mental or physical health.

In the latter case, moreover, proof of pecuniary injury and causation is immeasurably more vague than in suits for prenatal injuries. * * *

Beyond that, since the mother may sue for any injury which she sustained in her own person, including her suffering as a result of the stillbirth, and the father for loss of her services and consortium, an additional award to the "distributees" of the foetus would give its parents an unmerited bounty and would constitute not compensation to the injured but punishment to the wrongdoer. [Cc]

A leading law review article on the subject has clearly pointed up the differences in the two situations (Gordon, The Unborn Plaintiff, 63 Mich. L.Rev. 579, 594–595):

"The hardship of many of the decisions denying relief [in prenatal injury cases] lay in the fact that they required an infant to go through life * * * bearing the seal of another's fault. There is no such justification in the wrongful death situation. * * *

"A fundamental basis of tort law is the provision for compensation of an innocent plaintiff for the loss he has suffered. Tort law is not, as a general rule, premised upon punishing the wrongdoer. It is not submitted that the tortious destroyer of a child in utero should be able to escape completely by killing instead of merely maiming. But it is submitted that to compensate the parents any further than they are entitled by well-settled principles of law and to give them a windfall through the estate of the fetus is blatant punishment."

* * * Even if, as science and theology teach, the child begins a separate "life" from the moment of conception, it is clear that, "except in so far as is necessary to protect the child's own rights" (Matter of Roberts, 158 Misc. 698, 699, 286 N.Y.S. 476, 477), the law has never considered the unborn foetus as having a separate "juridical existence" (Drabbels v. Skelly Oil Co., 155 Neb. 17, 22, 50 N.W.2d 229) or a legal personality or identity "until it sees the light of day." (Matter of Peabody, 5 N.Y.2d 541, 547, 186 N.Y.S.2d 265, 270, 158 N.E.2d 841, 844, 845.) * * *

It is argued that it is arbitrary and illogical to draw the line at birth, with the result that the distributees of an injured foetus which survives birth by a few minutes may have a recovery while those of a stillborn foetus may not. However, such difficulties are always present where a line must be drawn. To make viability rather than birth the test would not remove the difficulty but merely relocate it and increase a hundredfold the problems of causation and damages. Thus, one commentator aptly observed that (Wenger, Developments in the Law of Prenatal Wrongful Death, 69 Dickinson L.Rev. 258, 268), "since any limitation will be arbitrary in nature, a tangible and concrete event would be the most acceptable and workable boundary. Birth, being a definite, observable and significant event, meets this requirement."

In light of all these considerations, then, we do not feel that, on balance and as a matter of public policy, a cause of action for pecuniary loss should accrue to the distributees of a foetus stillborn by reason of the negligence of another; the damages recoverable by the parents in their own right afford ample redress for the wrong done. Decidedly applicable here is the rule that "[l]iability for damages caused by wrong ceases at a point dictated by public policy or common sense." [C] * * *

The order appealed from should be affirmed, without costs.

BURKE, JUDGE (dissenting in part). * * * The illogicalness of the majority's position was aptly demonstrated by the Supreme Court of Wisconsin, in the analogous case of Kwaterski v. State Farm Mut. Auto. Ins. Co., 34 Wis.2d 14, 20, 148 N.W.2d 107, 110, in these terms: "If no right of action is allowed, there is a wrong inflicted for which there is no remedy. Denying a right of action for negligent acts which produce a stillbirth leads to very incongruous results. For example, a doctor or midwife whose negligent acts in delivering a baby produced the baby's death would be legally immune from a lawsuit. However, if they badly injured the child they would be exposed to liability. Such a rule would produce the absurd result that an unborn child who was badly injured by the tortious acts of another, but who was born alive, could recover while an unborn child, who was more severely injured and died as the result of the tortious acts of another, could recover nothing." * * *

In summary, I am of the opinion that it is both illogical and unreasonable to distinguish between injuries wrongfully inflicted upon a viable foetus which result in death just prior to the infant's separation from the mother and those which cause either permanent injuries or death itself, but at some short interval after birth has occurred. I, therefore, dissent from that portion of the majority opinion which affirms the dismissal of the wrongful death actions by the personal representatives of these stillborn foetus.

KEATING, J., concurred.

NOTES AND QUESTIONS

1. The question of whether any duty is owed to unborn children has undergone substantial change in the law and still is not free from controversy. At one time, the answer was a simple one: no claim was allowed. See, e.g., Dietrich v. Inhabitants of Northampton, 138 Mass. 14, 52 Am.Rep. 242 (1884).

2. The reasons for denial of recovery were threefold: First, it was assumed that the fetus had no separate existence from its mother. This hypothesis was later found to be inaccurate as a matter of medical science.

Second, it was thought that the problems of proving causation in fact would be overwhelming. Medical science was of assistance here also, although highly speculative questions about causation still arise. For example, can physical trauma to a mother cause a child to be born with Down's Syndrome? Compare Sinkler v. Kneale, 401 Pa. 267, 164 A.2d 93 (1960) (allowing plaintiff to attempt to prove a case), with Puhl v. Milwaukee Auto. Ins. Co., 8 Wis.2d 343, 99 N.W.2d 163 (1959) (finding that plaintiff had not met her burden of proof after trial).

Third, damages were thought to be too speculative. How could the jury accurately estimate a new born baby's loss of earning power? In spite of the difficulties involved, is it clear that the child has suffered a loss and would often need medical treatment in the future? Is this a sufficient reason to allow a claim?

3.   Beginning in 1946 with the case of Bonbrest v. Kotz, 65 F.Supp. 138 (D.D.C.1946), an overwhelming majority of jurisdictions has held that the reasons supporting the denial of a claim were no longer persuasive and has allowed a cause of action for prenatal injuries when they were inflicted on a viable fetus who was subsequently born alive.

4.   Suppose plaintiff alleges that defendant's wrongful conduct adversely affected the mother's ability to produce normal children prior to conception? Recovery has been allowed in several cases. See Bergstreser v. Mitchell, 577 F.2d 22 (8th Cir.1978) (negligent performance of caesarean—subsequent child had birth difficulties producing brain damage); Renslow v. Mennonite Hosp., 67 Ill.2d 348, 10 Ill.Dec. 484, 367 N.E.2d 1250 (1977) (wrong Rh-type blood transfusion to a 13–year–old produced injury to her child years later); Lazevnick v. Gen. Hosp., 499 F.Supp. 146 (M.D.Pa.1980) (similar); Walker v. Rinck, 604 N.E.2d 591 (Ind.1992) (similar). The New York Court of Appeals was scathing in its condemnation of Renslow, Albala v. City of New York, 54 N.Y.2d 269, 429 N.E.2d 786, 445 N.Y.S.2d 108 (1981).

5.   The major controversy today focuses on the situation in the principal case. A majority of states uphold a civil claim for the wrongful death of an unborn child. See, e.g., Volk v. Baldazo, 103 Idaho 570, 651 P.2d 11 (1982); Vaillancourt v. Medical Center Hosp., Inc., 139 Vt. 138, 425 A.2d 92 (1980); but the authorities are not consistently in favor of liability, e.g., Milton v. Cary Medical Center, 538 A.2d 252 (Me.1988); Witty v. American General Capital Dist., Inc., 727 S.W.2d 503 (Tex.1987); and Peters v. Hospital Authority of Elbert County, Georgia, 265 Ga. 487, 458 S.E.2d 628 (1995). Some states also sustain criminal claims. In some jurisdictions courts have done little more than decide that the words "death of a person" in the state wrongful death statute were only intended to include individuals who were born alive. See Kilmer v. Hicks, 22 Ariz.App. 552, 529 P.2d 706 (1974); Carroll v. Skloff, 415 Pa. 47, 202 A.2d 9 (1964). In Wartelle v. Women's and Children's Hospital, Inc., 704 So. 2d 778 (La.1997), the court held that a survival action could not be sustained for a stillborn birth upon a construction of the meaning of "person" under the prevailing statute. Id. at 780. A wrongful death action was available. Id. at 781. As the principal case reflects, other courts have gone beyond the matter of legislative intent (was there any?) and weighed policy considerations that support the grant or denial of a claim. Suppose the child dies during the delivery process? Duncan v. Flynn, 342 So.2d 123 (Fla.App.1977).

6.   As the principal case predicts, if a wrongful death action is available for the death of an unborn fetus, the issue then is posed of whether the action should extend beyond independent viability of the fetus. Thibert v. Milka, 419 Mass. 693, 646 N.E.2d 1025 (1995) (holding that a fetus with a gestational age of sixteen weeks was not viable and thus could not recover under a wrongful death action).

7.   Should a pregnant woman owe a duty of care to take reasonable precautions to protect her fetus from harm? Grodin v. Grodin, 102 Mich.App. 396, 301 N.W.2d 869 (1980) (liability of mother taking an antibiotic while pregnant that discolored the infant's teeth); but cf. Stallman v. Youngquist, 125 Ill.2d 267, 531 N.E.2d 355, 126 Ill.Dec. 60 (1988) (fetus subsequently born alive has no cause of action against mother for unintentional infliction of prenatal injuries (injuries sustained in auto accident)). The split in authority is reflected in more recent case law: Chenault v. Huie, 989 S.W.2d 474 (Tex.App.1999) (holding in an action arising

from injuries to child allegedly caused by mother's drug and alcohol use during pregnancy; Texas law recognizes no general legal duty owed by a mother to her fetus). But cf. Bonte v. Bonte, 136 N.H. 286, 616 A.2d 464 (N.H. 1992) ("recognizing a child born alive has a cause of action against his or her mother for negligent conduct that results in prenatal injury"). See Finley, A Breach in the Silence: Including Women's Issues in a Torts Course, 1 Yale J. of L. & Feminism 41 (1989).

Procanik by Procanik v. Cillo

Supreme Court of New Jersey, 1984.
97 N.J. 339, 478 A.2d 755.

POLLOCK, J. The primary issue on this appeal is the propriety of a grant of a partial summary judgment dismissing a "wrongful life" claim brought by an infant plaintiff through his mother and guardian *ad litem*. That judgment, which was granted on the pleadings, dismissed the claim because it failed to state a cause of action upon which relief may be granted. [C]

Justices Daniel J. O'Hern, Alan B. Handler, Robert L. Clifford,
Robert Wilentz, Sidney M. Schreiber, Stewart G. Pollock
and Marie L. Garibaldi.

The infant plaintiff, Peter Procanik, alleges that the defendant doctors * * * negligently failed to diagnose that his mother, Rosemary Procanik, had contracted German measles in the first trimester of her pregnancy. As a result, Peter was born with congenital rubella syndrome. Alleging that the doctors negligently deprived his parents of the choice of terminating the pregnancy, he seeks general damages for his pain and suffering and for "his parents' impaired capacity to cope with his problems." He also seeks special damages attributable to the extraordinary expenses he will incur for medical, nursing, and other health care. The Law Division granted defendants' motion to dismiss, and the Appellate Division affirmed. * * *

We granted certification, 95 N.J. 176, 470 A.2d 403 (1983). We now conclude that an infant plaintiff may recover as special damages the extraordinary medical expenses attributable to his affliction, but that he may not recover general damages for emotional distress or for an impaired childhood. * * * Accepting as true the plaintiff's allegations, [c] the complaint discloses the following facts. * * *

On June 9, 1977, during the first trimester of her pregnancy with Peter, Mrs. Procanik consulted the defendant doctors and informed Dr. Cillo "that she had recently been diagnosed as having measles but did not know if it was German measles." Dr. Cillo examined Mrs. Procanik and ordered "tests for German Measles, known as Rubella Titer Test." The results "were 'indicative of past infection of Rubella.'" Instead of ordering further tests, Dr. Cillo negligently interpreted the results and told Mrs. Procanik that she "had nothing to worry about because she had become immune to German Measles as a child." In fact, the "past infection" disclosed by the tests was the German measles that had prompted Mrs. Procanik to consult the defendant doctors.

Ignorant of what an accurate diagnosis would have disclosed, Mrs. Procanik allowed her pregnancy to continue, and Peter was born on December 26, 1977. Shortly thereafter, on January 16, 1978, he was diagnosed as suffering from congenital rubella syndrome. As a result of the doctors' negligence, Mr. and Mrs. Procanik were deprived of the choice of terminating the pregnancy, and Peter was "born with multiple birth defects," including eye lesions, heart disease, and auditory defects. The infant plaintiff states further that "he has suffered because of his parents' impaired capacity to cope with his problems," and seeks damages for his pain and suffering and for his "impaired childhood."

In April 1983, while this matter was pending in the Appellate Division, Peter moved to amend the first count to assert a claim to recover, as special damages, the expenses he will incur as an adult for medical, nursing, and related health care services. In its opinion, the Appellate Division denied without prejudice leave to amend. * * *

In this case we survey again the changing landscape of family torts. *See Schroeder v. Perkel,* 87 *N.J.* 53, 71, 432 A.2d 834 (1981). Originally that landscape presented a bleak prospect both to children born with birth defects and to their parents. If a doctor negligently diagnosed or treated a pregnant woman who was suffering from a condition that might cause her to give birth to a defective child, neither the parents nor the child could maintain a cause of action against the negligent doctor. *Gleitman v. Cosgrove,* 49 *N.J.* 22, 227 A.2d 689 (1967).

Like the present case, *Gleitman* involved a doctor who negligently treated a pregnant woman who had contracted German measles in the first trimester of her pregnancy. Reasoning from the premise that the doctor did not cause the infant plaintiff's birth defects, the *Gleitman* Court found it impossible to compare the infant's condition if the defendant doctor had not been negligent with the infant's impaired condition as a result of the negligence. Measurement of "the value of life with impairments against the nonexistence of life itself" was, the Court declared, a logical impossibility. [C] Consequently, the Court rejected the infant's claim.

The Court denied the parents' claim for emotional distress and the costs of caring for the infant, because of the impossibility of weighing the intangible benefits of parenthood against the emotional and monetary injuries sustained by them. Prevailing policy considerations, which included a reluctance to acknowledge the availability of abortions and the mother's right to choose to terminate her pregnancy, prevented the Court from awarding damages to a woman for not having an abortion. Another consideration was the Court's belief that "[i]t is basic to the human condition to seek life and hold on to it however heavily burdened." [C]

In the seventeen years that have elapsed since the *Gleitman* decision, both this Court and the United States Supreme Court have reappraised, albeit in different contexts, the rights of pregnant women and their children. The United States Supreme Court has recognized that women have a constitutional right to choose to terminate a pregnancy. Roe v. Wade, 410 *U.S.* 113 (1973). Recognition of that right by the high court subsequently influenced this Court in Berman v. Allan, 80 *N.J.* 421, 404 *A.*2d 8 [1979].

In *Berman,* the parents sought to recover for their emotional distress and for the expenses of raising a child born with Down's Syndrome. Relying on *Roe v. Wade,* the Court found that public policy now supports the right of a woman to choose to terminate a pregnancy. [C] That finding eliminated one of the supports for the *Gleitman* decision—*i.e.,* that public policy prohibited an award for depriving a woman of the right to choose whether to have an abortion. Finding that a trier of fact could place a dollar value on the parents' emotional suffering, the *Berman* Court concluded "that the monetary equivalent of this distress is an appropriate measure of the harm suffered by the parents." [C]

Nonetheless, the Court rejected the parents' claim for "medical and other expenses that will be incurred in order to properly raise, educate and supervise the child." [C] The Court reasoned that the parents wanted to retain "all the benefits inhering in the birth of the child—*i.e.,* the love and joy they will experience as parents—while saddling defendants with enormous expenses attendant upon her rearing." *Id.* Such an award would be disproportionate to the negligence of the defendants and constitute a windfall to the parents. *Id.*

The *Berman* Court also declined to recognize a cause of action in an infant born with birth defects. Writing for the Court, Justice Pashman reasoned that even a life with serious defects is more valuable than nonexistence, the alternative for the infant plaintiff if his mother chose to have an abortion. [C]

More recently we advanced the parents' right to compensation by permitting recovery of the extraordinary expenses of raising a child born with cystic fibrosis, including medical, hospital, and pharmaceutical expenses. Schroeder v. Perkel, 87 N.J. at 68–69, 432 A.2d 834. No claim on behalf of the infant was raised in that case, [c] and we elected to defer consideration of such a claim until another day. [C] That day is now upon us, and we must reconsider the right of an infant in a "wrongful life" claim to recover general damages for diminished childhood and pain and suffering, as well as special damages for medical care and the like.

The terms "wrongful birth" and "wrongful life" are but shorthand phrases that describe the causes of action of parents and children when negligent medical treatment deprives parents of the option to terminate a pregnancy to avoid the birth of a defective child. See Schroeder v. Perkel, supra, 87 *N.J.* at 75–76, 432 A.2d 834 (Handler, J., concurring and dissenting). In the present context, "wrongful life" refers to a cause of action brought by or on behalf of a defective child who claims that but for the defendant doctor's negligent advice to or treatment of its parents, the child would not have been born. "Wrongful birth" applies to the cause of action of parents who claim that the negligent advice or treatment deprived them of the choice of avoiding conception or, as here, of terminating the pregnancy. [Cc]

Both causes of action are distinguishable from the situation where negligent injury to a fetus causes an otherwise normal child to be born in an impaired condition. [Cc] In the present case, the plaintiffs do not allege that the negligence of the defendant doctors caused the congenital rubella syndrome from which the infant plaintiff suffers. Neither do plaintiffs claim that the infant ever had a chance to be a normal child. The essence of the infant's claim is that the defendant doctors wrongfully deprived his mother of information that would have prevented his birth.

Analysis of the infant's cause of action begins with the determination whether the defendant doctors owed a duty to him. The defendant doctors do not deny they owed a duty to the infant plaintiff, and we find such a duty exists. [Cc] In evaluating the infant's cause of action, we assume, furthermore, that the defendant doctors were negligent in treating the mother. Moreover, we assume that their negligence deprived the parents of the choice of terminating the pregnancy and of preventing the birth of the infant plaintiff.

Notwithstanding recognition of the existence of a duty and its breach, policy considerations have led this Court in the past to decline to recognize any cause of action in an infant for his wrongful life. The threshold problem has been the assertion by infant plaintiffs not that they should not have been born without defects, but that they should not have been born at all. [Gleitman] The essence of the infant's cause of action is that its very life is wrongful. [Berman] Resting on the belief that life, no matter how burdened, is preferable to non-existence, the Berman Court stated that the infant "has not suffered any damage cognizable at law by being brought into existence." [C] Although the premise for this part of the *Berman* decision was the absence of cognizable damages, the Court continued to be troubled, as it was in *Gleitman,* by the problem of ascertaining the measure of damages. [C]

The courts of other jurisdictions have also struggled with the issues of injury and damages when faced with suits for wrongful life. Although two intermediate appellate courts in New York and California recognized an infant's claim for general damages, those decisions were rejected by the courts of last resort in both jurisdictions. * * *

Other courts have uniformly found that the problems posed by the damage issues in wrongful life claims are insurmountable and have refused to allow the action on behalf of the infant. [Cc]

Even when this Court declined to recognize a cause of action for wrongful life in *Gleitman* and *Berman,* dissenting members urged recognition of that claim. * * *

Recently we recognized that extraordinary medical expenses incurred by parents on behalf of a birth-defective child were predictable, certain, and recoverable. [*Schroeder*] * * *

When a child requires extraordinary medical care, the financial impact is felt not just by the parents, but also by the injured child. As a practical matter, the impact may extend beyond the injured child to his brothers or sisters. Money that is spent for the health care of one child is not available for the clothes, food, or college education of another child.

Recovery of the cost of extraordinary medical expenses by either the parents or the infant, but not both, is consistent with the principle that the doctor's negligence vitally affects the entire family. * * *

Law is more than an exercise in logic, and logical analysis, although essential to a system of ordered justice, should not become a instrument of injustice. Whatever logic inheres in permitting parents to recover for the cost of extraordinary medical care incurred by a birth-defective child, but in denying the child's own right to recover those expenses, must yield to the injustice of that result. The right to recover the often crushing burden of extraordinary expenses visited by an act of medical malpractice should not depend on the "wholly fortuitous circumstance of whether the parents are available to sue." [Cc]

The present case proves the point. Here, the parents' claim is barred by the statute of limitations. Does this mean that Peter must forego medical treatment for his blindness, deafness, and retardation? We think not. His claim for the medical expenses attributable to his birth defects is reasonably certain, readily calculable, and of a kind daily determined by judges and juries. We hold that a child or his parents may recover special damages for extraordinary medical expenses incurred during infancy, and that the infant may recover those expenses during his majority. * * *

In restricting the infant's claim to one for special damages, we recognize that our colleagues, Justice Schreiber and Justice Handler, disagree with us and with each other. From the premise that "man does not know whether non-life would have been preferable to an impaired life," [c] Justice Schreiber concludes that a child does not have a cause of action for wrongful life and, therefore, that "it is unfair and unjust to charge the doctors with the infant's medical expenses." [C] Justice Handler reaches a diametrically opposite conclusion. He would allow the infant to recover not only his medical expenses, but also general damages for his pain and suffering and for his impaired childhood.

We find, however, that the infant's claim for pain and suffering and for a diminished childhood presents insurmountable problems. The philosophical problem of finding that such a defective life is worth less than no life at all has perplexed not only Justice Schreiber, but such other distinguished members of this Court as Chief Justice Weintraub, [c] Justice Proctor, [c] and Justice Pashman, [c]. We need not become preoccupied, however, with these metaphysical considerations. Our decision to allow the recovery of extraordinary medical expenses is not premised on the concept that non-life is preferable to an impaired life, but is predicated on the needs of the living. We seek only to respond to the call of the living for help in bearing the burden of their affliction.

Sound reasons exist not to recognize a claim for general damages. Our analysis begins with the unfortunate fact that the infant plaintiff never had a chance of being born as a normal, healthy child. Tragically, his only choice was a life burdened with his handicaps or no life at all. The congenital rubella syndrome that plagues him was not caused by the negligence of the defendant doctors; the only proximate result of their negligence was the child's birth.

The crux of the problem is that there is no rational way to measure non-existence or to compare non-existence with the pain and suffering of his impaired existence. Whatever theoretical appeal one might find in recognizing a claim for pain and suffering is outweighed by the essentially irrational and unpredictable nature of that claim. Although damages in a personal injury action need not be calculated with mathematical precision, they require at their base some modicum of rationality.

Underlying our conclusion is an evaluation of the capability of the judicial system, often proceeding in these cases through trial by jury, to appraise such a claim. Also at work is an appraisal of the role of tort law in compensating injured parties, involving as that role does, not only reason, but also fairness, predictability, and even deterrence of future wrongful acts. In brief, the ultimate decision is a policy choice summoning the most sensitive and careful judgment.

From that perspective it is simply too speculative to permit an infant plaintiff to recover for emotional distress attendant on birth defects when that plaintiff claims he would be better off if he had not been born. Such a claim would stir the passions of jurors about the nature and value of life, the fear of non-existence, and about abortion. That mix is more than the judicial system can digest. We believe that the interests of fairness and justice are better served through more predictably measured damages—the cost of the extraordinary medical expenses necessitated by the infant plaintiff's handicaps. Damages so measured are not subject to the same wild swings as a claim for pain and suffering and will carry a sufficient sting to deter future acts of medical malpractice.

As speculative and uncertain as is a comparison of the value of an impaired life with non-existence, even more problematic is the evaluation of a claim for diminished childhood. The essential proof in such a claim is that the doctor's negligence deprives the parents of the knowledge of the condition of the fetus. The deprivation of that information precludes the choice of terminating the pregnancy by abortion and leaves the parents unprepared for the birth of a defective child, a birth that causes them emotional harm. The argument proceeds that the parents are less able to love and care for the child, who thereby suffers an impaired childhood. [Cc]

Several considerations lead us to decline to recognize a cause of action for impaired childhood. At the outset, we note the flaw in such a claim in those instances in which the parents assert not that the information would have prepared them for the birth of the defective child, but that they would have used the information to prevent that birth. Furthermore, even its advocates recognize that a claim for "the kind of injury suffered by the child in this context may not be readily divisible from that suffered by her wronged parents." Berman v. Allan, supra, 80 N.J. at 445, 404 A.2d 8 (Handler, J., concurring and dissenting). We believe the award of the cost of the extraordinary medical care to the child or the parents, when combined with the right of the parents to assert a claim for their own emotional distress, comes closer to filling the dual objectives of a tort system: the compensation of injured parties and the deterrence of future wrongful conduct. * * *

The judgment of the Appellate Division is affirmed in part, reversed in part, and the matter is remanded to the Law Division. The infant plaintiff shall have leave to file an amended complaint asserting a claim for extraordinary medical, hospital, and other health care expenses.

[The gist of the separate partially dissenting opinions of HANDLER and SCHREIBER, JJ., is described in the majority opinion.]

NOTES AND QUESTIONS

1. In Smith v. Cote, 128 N.H. 231, 513 A.2d 341 (1986), the court dealt with a factually similar case: the defendants, obstetricians and gynecologists, had not tested their patient for rubella early in the pregnancy when she had an untrammelled right to an abortion. The child was born with congenital rubella syndrome. In a thorough analysis, Justice Batchelder found that suits of this kind, by parents and children, had been spawned by scientific advances in detection of abnormalities in fetus and in the pregnancy risk factors and the Supreme Court's decision in Roe v. Wade, 410 U.S. 113 (1973). (The Supreme Court in Planned Parenthood of Southeastern Pennsylvania v. Casey, 505 U.S. 833 (1992), refused to overrule Roe v. Wade, supra, but substituted that decision's trimester division with the more

flexible criterion that the state may regulate provided a woman's right to choose an abortion is not unduly burdened.) Taking the actions separately, he supported the wrongful birth action—the parents' action—as comporting with accepted tort doctrine. The difficulty of measuring damages could not undermine the action. As to damages, the court found, they should be limited to extraordinary costs even beyond the age of majority. This figure could include extraordinary maternal care, susceptible to valuation, made necessary by the child's condition. Also recoverable were the parent's pecuniary losses resulting from the emotional distress, in seeking medical help or counselling. However, general emotional distress was not compensable. But cf. Greco v. U.S., 893 P.2d 345 (Nev.1995) (holding that emotional distress suffered as a result of the birth should be allowed). Some courts have remained unmoved in disallowing an action. Etkind v. Suarez, 271 Ga. 352, 519 S.E.2d 210 (1999).

After an examination of the law supporting the wrongful life action, including the principal case, the court, nevertheless, for the following reasons, was not moved to allow the child a wrongful life action.

A. Distinguishing the right to die cases (see Cruzan by Cruzan v. Director, Missouri Dept. of Health, 497 U.S. 261 (1990)) the issue is "not protection of the impaired child's right to choose nonexistence over life but whether legal injury has occurred as a result of the defendant's conduct * * * [The court] has no business in declaring that among the living are people who should never have been born." Id., 249.

B. Recognition of the claim would stigmatize the child's life as wrongful, cutting against policies of removing social disabilities.

C. The contingent nature of the loss valuation is beyond the capacity of the courts proceeding by way of predictable rules.

On the last point, the principal case fashioned a pragmatic compromise—special damages for extraordinary expenses. The New Hampshire Court referred to Justice Schreiber's opinion, dissenting in part from the majority's opinion in the principal case:

> The position that a child may recover special damages despite the failure of his underlying theory of wrongful life violates the moral code underlying our system of justice from which the fundamental principles of tort law are derived.

Procanik v. Cillo, 97 N.J. 339, 370, 478 A.2d 755, 772 (1984).

2. An older but related line of cases concern situations where a woman has conceived or become pregnant due to the tortious action of the defendant. In these cases the child is not necessarily handicapped but the pregnancy was not wanted. Generally, the cause of action is in negligence for: (1) lack of informed consent, or (2) negligent performance of a sterilization operation. Burke v. Rivo, 406 Mass. 764, 551 N.E.2d 1 (1990), is an example of the former (failure to advise plaintiff of the risks of recanalization in sterilization operation) and Marciniak v. Lundborg, 153 Wis.2d 59, 450 N.W.2d 243 (1990), an example of the latter (negligence in performance of "laparoscopy with bilateral fallopian tube cautery"). Both cases accepted the legitimacy of the cause of action and addressed the issue of the measure of damages. Damages flowing directly from the operation and pregnancy were readily recoverable: these include, cost of the operation and corrective surgery, loss of earnings during pregnancy, medical expenses surrounding pregnancy and hospitalization, and husband's loss of consortium. Pain and suffering and emotional distress are usually recoverable. The difficult issue was whether the costs of rearing the child should be recoverable. Against a strong dissent supported by weighty authority, the majority in *Burke* decided that "the cost of rearing a normal healthy but (at

least initially) unwanted child [were recoverable if the parents'] reason for seeking sterilization was founded on economic and financial considerations." The same arguments rejected by the majority in *Rivo* were also dismissed in *Marciniak:* the awarding of damages for the costs of child rearing would not psychologically harm the child nor "debase the sanctity of human life." The argument that the plaintiffs had not mitigated their damages by putting the child out to adoption or by aborting met the same fate: it was not reasonable to force this choice on the plaintiffs. On the issue of offsetting the benefits of the child against the detriments the court turned to § 920 Restatement of Torts (Second) (1979), embodying the principle that damages resulting from an invasion of one interest are not diminished by showing another interest has been benefited. Thus emotional benefit could not be set off against financial detriments.

Are you concerned in drawing a distinction on the grounds of motivation for the operation?

3.   Few jurisdictions allow actions for wrongful life. The most poignant cases result from a negligent failure to detect the genetic disease, Tay–Sachs Syndrome, a devastating disease characterized by severe mental retardation and physical disability limiting life to a few painful years. In Schloss v. Miriam Hospital, No. C.A. 98–2076, 1999 WL 41875 (R.I.Super., Jan.11, 1999), the Rhode Island court allowed a wrongful birth action but rejected the wrongful life claim where the child was born with Tay–Sachs after negligent genetic testing. The court found the moral issues beggared their judicial ability, and unlike the few cases in California, Washington, and New Jersey that had recognized the claim, here the wrongful birth action accorded compensation for the injury. In the few that recognize wrongful life, the damages have been curtailed as to include only extraordinary expenses arising from the condition with which the child is afflicted. No general damages for pain and suffering are awarded. Turpin v. Sortini, 31 Cal.3d 220, 643 P.2d 954, 182 Cal.Rptr. 337 (1982). The California Supreme Court in Curlender v. Bio–Science Laboratories, 106 Cal.App.3d 811, 165 Cal.Rptr. 477 (1980), allowed pain and suffering damages, where the plaintiff's parents had obtained blood tests from the defendant lab in order to ascertain whether their offspring was likely to suffer from Tay–Sachs disease. The lab was negligent in performing the blood tests. In *Sortini* the court found that general damages were not awardable since no principles were available to discern whether an injury was suffered in being born rather than not, or that the balancing of incommensurable elements in general damages, the joy of life versus the pain of it made the calculus too speculative. Extraordinary expenses, on the other hand, could have been estimated with some certainty and no setoff of highly subjective elements would be allowable under the § 920 Restatement of Torts (Second) principle. The majority's reasoning was savaged by Justice Mosk dissenting. Do you consider that the plaintiff ought to be precluded from recovery of pain and suffering in *Curlender?*

4.   The grounding of wrongful life and birth actions on the missed opportunity to abort the fetus has proved controversial. North Carolina and Missouri courts have refused to recognize actions thus premised, see Peters, Rethinking Wrongful Life: Bridging the Boundary Between Tort and Family Law, 67 Tul.L.Rev. 397, 415 (1992) (also listing various state legislation proscribing such claims). Recently the Court of Appeals of Michigan in Taylor v. Kurapati, 236 Mich. App. 315, 600 N.W.2d 670 (Mich. App. 1999), took the extraordinary step of repudiating its past recognition of the wrongful birth action. It found that it had developed a "misshapen jurisprudence" in its recognition of the action but total rejection of the wrongful life action and its partial rejection of the wrongful conception action. Such a tort, it found, must be expressed through legislative action.

5. What actions may be available if the abortion is performed but was unnecessary? Parent's action, Martinez v. Long Island Jewish Hillside Medical Center, 70 N.Y.2d 697, 512 N.E.2d 538, 518 N.Y.S.2d 955 (1987). Fetus's action?

6. Should parents be liable in a wrongful life action? In Zepeda v. Zepeda, 41 Ill.App.2d 240, 190 N.E.2d 849 (1963), a child sued his father for wrongfully begetting him as an illegitimate child by deceiving his mother that he would marry her when in fact he was already married. Recovery denied. What of an institution that fails to protect a vulnerable patient from being raped? Does the child have an action? The answer was "no" in Williams v. State of New York, 18 N.Y.2d 481, 223 N.E.2d 343, 276 N.Y.S.2d 885 (1966) and again "no," after a lower court "yes," in Cowe v. Forum Group, Inc., 541 N.E.2d 962, 964 (Ind.App.1989), aff'd in part and vacated in part, 575 N.E.2d 630 (Ind.1991). In *Curlender,* supra note 3, the court suggested that parents may be liable for a conscious decision to conceive and allow to be born a seriously impaired infant. The California legislature quickly responded by relieving the parents of liability. § 43.6 Civil Code, 1981.

7. *A,* a broker for surrogate mother contracts, engages *B* to have a baby for *C*. *B* is artificially inseminated with *C*'s semen. *C*'s semen carries a disease that causes birth defects to (a) the offspring or (b) *B*'s child by her husband. Does *A* owe a duty to reasonably protect *C? B?* And the offspring? See Stiver v. Parker, 975 F.2d 261 (6th Cir.1992), finding an affirmative duty to *C* and *B* by dint of the "special relationship" between the brokers and the parties to the arrangement (supra); the court emphasized the commercial aspects of the arrangement in finding the duty. The duty to the "offspring" was not discussed; should a duty to the surrogate offspring be imposed?

8. In Canesi ex rel. Canesi v. Wilson, 730 A.2d 805 (N.J.1999), the parents of a child born with bilateral limb reduction brought an action against two obstetricians involved with the mother's pregnancy. Plaintiffs alleged that the defendants were negligent in failing to warn them of the risks posed by the drug Provera and to take diagnostic measures to ascertain the presence of the defect. Two possible causes arose, the first in informed consent and the second in wrongful birth. The court held that for the former, plaintiffs must prove that the negligence caused the bilateral limb reduction. For the latter—the wrongful birth action—such proof was unnecessary. The appropriate inquiry was "whether the defendant's negligence was the proximate cause of the parents' loss of the option to make an informed and meaningful decision either to terminate the pregnancy or to give birth to a potentially defective child." Id. at 818. In other words, medical causation is not essential in a wrongful birth action. The majority reasoning is criticized by Pollock, J. dissenting, who finds the "majority's result is unprecedented in any jurisdiction." Id. at 825.

CHAPTER IX

OWNERS AND OCCUPIERS OF LAND

1. OUTSIDE THE PREMISES

Taylor v. Olsen

Supreme Court of Oregon, 1978.
282 Or. 343, 578 P.2d 779.

LINDE, JUSTICE. Plaintiff sued for damages for injuries she sustained when her car, on a dark and windy January evening, struck a tree which shortly before had splintered and fallen across a * * * road. The trial court directed verdicts for * * * Marion Olsen, the adjoining landowner who was alleged to be in possession of the location. Plaintiff appeals from the judgment entered on the directed verdict for Olsen. * * *

We think * * * that, except for extreme situations, the question of the landowner's or possessor's attention to the condition of his roadside trees under a general standard of "reasonable care to prevent an unreasonable risk of harm" is to be decided as a question of fact upon the circumstances of the individual case. The extent of his responsibility either to inspect his trees or only to act on actual knowledge of potential danger cannot be defined simply by categorizing his land as "urban" or "rural." Surely it is not a matter of zoning or of city boundaries but of actual conditions. No doubt a factfinder will expect more attentiveness of the owner of an ornamental tree on a busy sidewalk [cc] than of the United States Forest Service * * *, but the great variety of intermediate patterns of land use, road use, traffic density, and preservation of natural stands of trees in urban and suburban settings prevents a simple "urban-rural" classification.

* * * [T]he onus on a homeowner of inspecting a few trees in his yard is modest, but the "practical difficulty of continuously examining each tree in the untold number of acres of forests" or in "sprawling tracts of woodland adjacent to or through which a road has been built [can be] so potentially onerous as to make property ownership an untenable burden. This would be particularly true for an absentee landowner." [C] It is less obviously true, however, for one who is engaged in logging or in actively developing the land. * * *

In this case, the road in question was a two-lane blacktop highway serving a number of communities * * *. There was testimony that it was used by an average 790 vehicles a day; in other words, a fallen tree might encounter a vehicle within an average of about two minutes, depending on the time of day. Defendant had purchased the land adjoining the road in

1973 for logging purposes, and during the five or six weeks before the accident he had logged about half the timber on his land. This included the trees adjacent to the tree on the county's right-of-way that eventually fell onto the road. Under these circumstances we conclude * * * that it would be a jury question whether defendant had taken reasonable care to inform himself of the condition of this tree, provided there was evidence that an inspection would have disclosed its hazardous condition.

The evidence is that after the tree broke and fell onto the road, the center of the tree at the point of the break proved to be decayed. However, the decay did not extend through the bark, or even to the surface below the bark except perhaps in a few places. Only by chopping or boring into the trunk of the tree would there have been a substantial chance of discovering the decay. Thus the question is not so much whether defendant had some responsibility to give his attention to the safety of this tree left behind by his logging operations as, rather, how far that responsibility extends.

There was no evidence to suggest that chopping or drilling into the trunk would have been a normal or expected way to examine a standing tree in the absence of external indications that it might not be structurally sound. * * *

It requires some evidence either that the defendant should have been on notice of possible decay in this tree, or that cutting through the bark to the trunk is a common and ordinary method of examining trees generally. In the absence of such evidence, it was not error to direct a verdict for the defendant.

Affirmed.

NOTES AND QUESTIONS

1. This chapter, like Chapter 8, considers the state of the law in an area that traditionally has involved limited duties. It specifically deals with the duty that owners of land owe to persons on and off the premises.

2. With regard to most conditions on land that arise in the state of nature, most courts have held that there is no duty upon the landholder to protect persons outside the premises. See Roberts v. Harrison, 101 Ga. 773, 28 S.E. 995 (1897) (foul swamp); Brady v. Warren, [1909] 2 Ir.Rep. 632 (rabbits).

3. This rule has been extended in a number of cases where the owner of rural land has been held not liable for the growth and spread of weeds, on the ground that they were the "natural growth of the soil," even though the cultivation was a contributing cause. Langer v. Goode, 21 N.D. 462, 131 N.W. 258 (1911) (wild mustard). The fine-spun distinction between hazards naturally arising (no liability) and those caused by human agency (liability) is "not only inconvenient, but also lacks * * * any logical foundation." Goldman v. Hargrave [1967] 1 A.C. 645 (Privy Council) (liability for bush fire in the hot Australian summer).

4. An exception has evolved with regard to trees, and there is agreement that the landowner is liable for negligence if he knows that the tree is defective and fails to take reasonable precautions. Turner v. Ridley, 144 A.2d 269 (Mun.App.D.C.1958); Plesko v. Allied Inv. Co., 12 Wis.2d 168, 107 N.W.2d 201 (1961). Constructive notice

is sufficient but the "decay" must be readily observable: Ivancic v. Olmstead, 66 N.Y.S.2d 349, 350–51, 488 N.E.2d 72, 73, 497 N.Y.S.2d 326, 327 (1985).

5.   The rule was clear at one time that the owner of land abutting on a rural highway is under no duty to inspect it to discover defects in trees. Chambers v. Whelen, 44 F.2d 340 (4th Cir.1930); O'Brien v. United States, 275 F.2d 696 (9th Cir.1960). The trend is toward decisions like the principal case. See Medeiros v. Honomu Sugar Co., 21 Haw. 155 (1912); Brandywine Hundred Realty Co. v. Cotillo, 55 F.2d 231 (3d Cir.1931); Hensley v. Montgomery County, 25 Md.App. 361, 334 A.2d 542 (1975).

6.   In Sprecher v. Adamson Cos., 30 Cal.3d 358, 636 P.2d 1121, 178 Cal.Rptr. 783 (1981), however, the landowner's general immunity for harm outside the premises caused by natural conditions was abolished, and an uphill landowner was found to owe a duty of care to a downhill landowner to control a landslide condition. This decision was followed in Moeller v. Fleming, 136 Cal.App.3d 241, 186 Cal.Rptr. 24 (1982), where a landowner could be sued by a pedestrian who slipped on an irregular break in the sidewalk that was caused by tree roots from the landowner's adjacent property. In the English decision of Leakey v. National Trust for Places of Historic Interest or Natural Beauty [1980] 1 Q.B. 485 (CA), the landowner, the National Trust, was found liable for destruction wrought by the collapse of the steep bank of the Burrow Mump, a famous conical hill. Natural weather conditions had caused the Mump to slide piling up detritus against the wall of the plaintiff's kitchen. The duty owed was governed by reasonableness, taking account of degree of fault, resources and magnitude of hazard; the rule distinguishing natural and artificial hazards was repudiated. Also, compare the First Restatement of Torts, § 363(2) [promulgated in 1963–64], with Restatement (Second) of Torts, § 840(2) [promulgated in 1977]; see also, id., § 840, comment c.

7.   Some states recognize a "self-help" rule, under which a landowner can resort to self-help and cut off tree branches and roots intruding onto his property from adjoining property. See, e.g., Melnick v. C.S.X. Corp., 68 Md.App. 107, 510 A.2d 592 (1986), limiting remedy to "self-help" for incidents of healthy trees, as the most efficient and equitable way to resolve the problem.

Salevan v. Wilmington Park, Inc.

Superior Court of Delaware, 1950.
45 Del. (6 Terry) 290, 72 A.2d 239.

WOLCOTT, JUDGE. The plaintiff brings suit for personal injuries received when struck in the back by a baseball while walking on East Thirtieth Street in the City of Wilmington, past the ball park of the defendant.

The defendant is the owner of land * * * on which is located the ball park in question. The business of the defendant is the maintenance and renting of the ball park and its facilities and has been carried on by the defendant for over eight years. * * *

[I]t appears that in the course of an average ball game, 16 to 18 foul balls come from inside the park into Thirtieth Street and, of them, an average of 2 or 3 foul balls come from within the park over the 10–foot fence and into the area along Thirtieth Street through which the plaintiff was passing at the time of the injury. The manager of the defendant testified that, on an average, 68 baseball games were played at Wilmington Park during the baseball season.

The plaintiff does not contend that the defendant is an insurer of persons lawfully using the highways and sidewalks adjacent to its ball park, but does contend that the defendant, as a landowner, has the duty to exercise reasonable care in the use of its land so as to prevent injury to travelers lawfully using the highways adjacent thereto. The plaintiff contends that the defendant had notice of the passage of baseballs outside of its park into East Thirtieth Street to the danger of persons using that public street, and that the failure of the defendant to take reasonable precautions to safeguard the public was negligence. * * *

It is clear that the public has a right to the free and unmolested use of the public highways, and that abutting landowners may not so use their land as to interfere with the rights of persons lawfully using the highways. * * *

The inherent nature of the game of baseball * * * is such as to require the landowner to take reasonable precautions for the protection of the traveling public. What precautions are reasonable must depend upon the facts and circumstances of the particular case. Only those precautions are required which the inherent nature of the game and its past history in the particular location make necessary for the protection of a person lawfully using the highways. * * *

While the defendant has shown that consideration was given by it to the protection of the public at the time the park was first built, the fact remains that despite the precautions taken, baseballs went out of its park into the public highway and that the defendant either knew that baseballs went out of its park or, under the circumstances, should have known. The evidence is not seriously contradicted that baseballs went out of the park into Thirtieth Street within the area through which the plaintiff was passing at the time of her injury two or three times in each game played in the defendant's park.

Under the circumstances, it seems clear to me that while the defendant took precautions to protect people passing along Thirtieth Street, those precautions were insufficient. It further seems clear that the defendant knew, or should have known, that the precautions taken initially were insufficient to protect the public engaged in its lawful right, that is, using the highways. This circumstance puts the case at bar squarely within the rule I have drawn from the reported decisions, and if this were a jury trial, would be sufficient to submit the case to the jury and would compel, in my opinion, the jury to return a verdict for the plaintiff. Accordingly, my conclusion is that judgment should be entered for the plaintiff.

Judgment being entered for the plaintiff, it remains to determine in what amount that judgment should be. Under the circumstances, I believe the sum of $2500.00 will adequately compensate the plaintiff for the injuries received as a result of the negligence of the defendant.

NOTES AND QUESTIONS

1. Once a landowner alters a condition of his land, it becomes an "artificial" one for the purposes of tort law and the owner must exercise reasonable care for the

protection of those outside of the premises. Thus Towaliga Falls Power Co. v. Sims, 6 Ga.App. 749, 65 S.E. 844 (1909) (damming a stream to form a malarial pond); Ettl v. Land & Loan Co., 122 N.J.L. 401, 5 A.2d 689 (1939) (piling sand where the wind may blow it). This obligation will also arise with regard to a condition that may appear, on the surface, to be a natural one. See, e.g., Coates v. Chinn, 51 Cal.2d 304, 332 P.2d 289 (1958) (cultivated trees).

2.   The landowner is not liable for the normal flow of surface water, which is regarded as a "natural" condition. Livezey v. Schmidt, 96 Ky. 441, 29 S.W. 25 (1895); Middlesex County v. McCue, 149 Mass. 103, 21 N.E. 230 (1889). On the same principle, it is generally held that an abutting owner is under no duty to remove snow and ice that falls naturally upon the highway. Ainey v. Rialto Amusement Co., 135 Wash. 56, 236 P. 801 (1925); Norville v. Hub Furniture Co., 59 App.D.C. 29, 32 F.2d 420 (1929).

3.   Ordinances requiring the property owner to remove snow and ice from abutting sidewalks usually are construed to create a duty only to the municipality, and not to any private individual. Hanley v. Fireproof Bldg. Co., 107 Neb. 544, 186 N.W. 534 (1912); Griswold v. Camp, 149 Wis. 399, 135 N.W. 754 (1912). Usually, however, these ordinances provide that the owner must remove the snow and ice or pay the cost of removal, and are held to indicate an intent to protect the city.

4.   Some courts, though, have extended an owner's responsibility for abutting sidewalks. Stewart v. 104 Wallace St., Inc., 87 N.J. 146, 432 A.2d 881 (1981) (owner liable for failing to maintain abutting sidewalks in reasonably good condition), and Cogliati v. Ecco High Frequency Corp., 92 N.J. 402, 456 A.2d 524 (1983) (current owner and predecessor in title liable for poorly maintained public sidewalks).

5.   If the owner has altered the condition of the premises so that surface water or snow is discharged upon the highway, he may be directly held liable for negligence or nuisance. Tremblay v. Harmony Mills, 171 N.Y. 598, 64 N.E. 501 (1902); Adlington v. Viroqua, 155 Wis. 472, 144 N.W. 1130 (1914). See De Graff, Snow and Ice, 21 Cornell L.Q. 436 (1936); Note, 21 Minn.L.Rev. 703 (1937).

6.   Suppose the plaintiff is injured outside the premises by something subject to the control of the owner of the premises? Compare Blake v. Dunn Farms, Inc., 274 Ind. 560, 413 N.E.2d 560 (1980) (horse runs out on highway), with Weber v. Madison, 251 N.W.2d 523 (Iowa 1977) (geese on highway). Cf. Leary v. Lawrence Sales Corp., 442 Pa. 389, 275 A.2d 32 (1971) (food dropped on shopping-center mall two feet from defendant's premises). What if the condition of premises gives criminals an opportunity to mug passersby? Hutchins v. 1001 Fourth Avenue Associates, 116 Wash.2d 217, 802 P.2d 1360 (1991) (no duty of care owed by occupier of premises to provide security measures to protect passersby from the risk of criminal assault on the premises); Waters v. New York City Housing Authority, 69 N.Y.2d 225, 505 N.Ed.2d 922, 513 N.Y.S.2d 356 (1987) (no duty to prevent assault on member of public).

7.   A large body of caselaw has developed concerning the obligation of land-owners to users of the highway. In Hayes v. Malkan, 26 N.Y.2d 295, 258 N.E.2d 695, 310 N.Y.S.2d 281 (1970), the plaintiff's automobile crashed into a utility pole owned by the defendant situated on private land. Distinguishing the law relating to objects near the highway placed on public land, the court found that to require a duty of reasonable care on private property owners would place an "intolerable burden on the property owner." Liability would subsist for a trap that may injure persons deviating from the highway, but a utility pole was not a trap. Is this consistent with Bigbee v. Pacific Tel. & Tel. Co., 34 Cal.3d 49, 665 P.2d 947, 192 Cal.Rptr. 857 (1983), wherein a telephone booth user, injured when the booth was struck by an automobile that had jumped the curb, sued the telephone company for

dangerously locating the booth in a parking lot 15 feet from the side of a major thoroughfare and near a driveway? But compare Justice v. CSX Transp., Inc., 908 F.2d 119 (7th Cir.1990), wherein an action was brought for the death of a truck driver at a railroad crossing. The driver's view was obstructed by the placement of the defendant's railroad cars. Although the cause was confined to an obstruction on the defendant's land and merely blocked a view, the defendant nevertheless owed a duty to avoid "the creation of visual obstacles that unreasonably imperil the users of adjacent public ways * * *" (per Posner J.).

8. Most courts agree that a landholder owes a duty to a traveler who accidentally falls into excavations on land immediately adjoining the highway. Downes v. Silva, 57 R.I. 343, 190 A. 42 (1937), where created or maintained by the landowner; Zens v. Chicago, Milwaukee, St. Paul & Pac.R.R. Co., 386 N.W.2d 475 (S.D.1986). Also to those who inadvertently stray a short distance from the highway. Puchlopek v. Portsmouth Power Co., 82 N.H. 440, 136 A. 259 (1926) (slip); Durst v. Wareham, 132 Kan. 785, 297 P. 675 (1931).

9. The rule has even been extended, in several cases, to those who deviate intentionally from the highway for some casual purpose connected with travel. Weidman v. Consolidated Gas, E.L. & P. Co., 158 Md. 39, 148 A. 270 (1930) (stepping out to avoid crowd); Gibson v. Johnson, 69 Ohio App. 19, 42 N.E.2d 689 (1941) (stepping out to allow others to pass); Lacanfora v. Goldapel, 37 A.D.2d 721, 323 N.Y.S.2d 990 (1971) (knobless door close to sidewalk opened when child leaned on it, precipitating him to 12–foot drop).

10. In Murray v. McShane, 52 Md. 217 (1879), plaintiff, walking along the public sidewalk, sat down on defendant's doorstep to tie his shoe, and was injured when a brick fell on him out of the doorway. He was allowed to recover. In Foley v. H.F. Farnham Co., 135 Me. 29, 188 A. 708 (1936), where the plaintiff met a friend and sat down to talk to him, recovery was denied. What is the difference?

11. There is no liability as to dangers a considerable distance from the highway. Hardcastle v. South Yorkshire R. & R.D.R. Co., 4 H. & N. 67, 157 Eng.Rep. 761 (1859). In Flint v. Bowman, 42 Tex.Civ.App. 354, 93 S.W. 479 (1906), plaintiff was driving along a highway obliterated by fifteen inches of snow. He missed a right turn, and continued on across the defendant's land for nearly half a mile until he drove into an abandoned and unguarded well. Is the defendant liable to him?

12. When the land has a deceptive appearance of being a continuation of the public way, a duty may be imposed on the landholder to guard a trap or excavation even though the hazard is actually a considerable distance within private property. See Louisville & Nashville R. Co. v. Anderson, 39 F.2d 403 (5th Cir.1930); Holmes v. Drew, 151 Mass. 578, 25 N.E. 22 (1890). In such a case the entrant on the land may be deemed to be invited and not a trespasser. Is this inconsistent with the rule of Ranson v. Kitner, supra page 23?

2. ON THE PREMISES

(A) TRESPASSERS

Sheehan v. St. Paul & Duluth Ry. Co.

United States Circuit Court of Appeals, Seventh Circuit, 1896.
76 Fed. 201.

[Action for damages for personal injury. While plaintiff was walking on defendant's railroad track, his foot slipped and became caught between the rail and a cattle guard. He was unable to extricate his shoe, or to get at it to untie it. Defendant's train approached, and ran over his foot. Defendant's train crew did not see him until the train was almost upon him, and it was too late to stop it. The trial court directed a verdict for defendant, on the ground that "upon the undisputed facts of the case, this injury did not occur through any wrongful action upon the part of the defendant." Plaintiff appeals.]

SEAMAN, DISTRICT JUDGE. * * * The plaintiff, at the time of his injury, was neither in the relation of passenger nor of one in a public crossing or place in which the public were licensed to travel, but, upon the undisputed facts, was a mere intruder on the tracks of the defendant,—technically, a trespasser; and this record excludes any of the elements of implied license or invitation to such use which have given rise to much discussion and diversity of views in the courts. Therefore the inquiry is here squarely presented: What is the duty which a railway company owes to a trespasser on its tracks, and how and when does the duty arise? The decisions upon this subject uniformly recognize that the trespasser cannot be treated as an outlaw; and, at the least, that, if wantonly injured in the operation of the railroad, the company is answerable in damages. Clearly, then, an obligation is placed upon the company to exercise some degree of care when the danger becomes apparent. Is it, however, bound to foresee or assume that rational beings will thus enter as trespassers in a place of danger, and to exercise in the running of its trains the constant vigilance in view of that probability which is imposed for public crossings? There are cases which would seem to hold this strict requirement [cc]; but by the great preponderance of authority, in this country, and in England, the more reasonable doctrine is pronounced, in effect, as follows: That the railroad company has the right to a free track in such places; that it is not bound to any act or service in anticipation of trespassers thereon; and that the trespasser who ventures to enter upon a track for any purpose of his own assumes all risks of the conditions which may be found there, including the operation of engines and cars. * * *

The well-established and just rule which holds the railroad company to the exercise of constant and strict care against injury through its means is applicable only to the relation on which it is founded, of an existing duty or obligation. This active or positive duty arises in favor of the public at a street crossing or other place at which it is presumable that persons or teams may be met. It is not material, so far as concerns this inquiry, whether the place is one for which a lawful right of passage exists, as it is the fact of notice to the company, arising out of its existence and the probability of its use, which imposes the positive duty to exercise care; the requirement of an extreme degree of care being superadded because of the hazards which attend the operations of the company. The case of a trespasser on the track, in a place not open to travel, is clearly distinguishable in the absence of this notice to the company. There is no constructive notice upon which to base the obligation of constant lookout for his presence there, and no actual notice up to the moment the trainmen have discovered the fact of his peril. As that peril comes wholly from his unauthorized act and temerity, the risk, and all positive duty of care for his safety, rests with the trespasser. The obligation of the company and its operatives is not, then, pre-existing, but arises at the moment of discovery, and is negative in its nature,—a duty, which is common to human conduct, to make all reasonable effort to avert injury to others from means which can be controlled. This is the issue presented here. It excludes all inquiry respecting the character of the roadbed, cattle guard, locomotive, brake appliances, or other means of operation, or of the speed or manner of running the train up to the moment of notice, because no breach of positive duty is involved. It is confined to the evidence relating to the discovery by the engineer and fireman of the plaintiff's peril, and to the efforts then made to avert the injury, and, out of that, to ascertain whether, in any view which may justly be taken, it is shown that these men, or the engineer, in disregard of the duty which then confronted them, neglected to employ with reasonable promptness the means at hand for stopping the train. * * *

The court was clearly justified in directing a verdict for the defendant, and the judgment is affirmed.

NOTES AND QUESTIONS

1. How valid are the following explanations, commonly given for the nonliability to the trespasser:

A. His presence is not reasonably to be anticipated. Suppose a railroad company, as well as everyone else, knows that people do habitually trespass on its right of way?

B. The trespasser assumes the risk. What if he does not know there is any risk or is a child too young to assume it? See Santora v. New York, N.H. & H.R. Co., 211 Mass. 464, 98 N.E. 90 (1912), where a child 27 months old got onto a railroad track and was run over.

C. He is contributorily negligent or is himself a wrongdoer not entitled to legal protection. Again, suppose that he is a child too young to be negligent? Or that under the rule of the last clear chance there would be liability to one not a trespasser even though he were negligent? Newman v. Louisville & N.R. Co., 212 Ala. 580, 103 So. 856 (1925); Dyrcz v. Missouri Pac. R. Co., 238 Mo. 33, 141 S.W. 861 (1911).

What is the explanation of the rule?

2. The rule stated in the principal case is commonly applied to a wide variety of dangerous conditions on the land, including dangerous machinery and defective construction.

3. The landowner's immunity toward trespassers extends to the members of his household. Sohn v. Katz, 112 N.J.L. 106, 169 A. 838 (1934). It does not extend to adjoining landowners. Fitzpatrick v. Penfield, 267 Pa. 564, 109 A. 653 (1920).

4. The courts have not favored the immunity to trespassers, and have tended to erode it with exceptions. The first exception is that of a trespasser whose presence has been discovered. Frederick v. Philadelphia Rapid Transit Co., 337 Pa. 136, 10 A.2d 576 (1940) (plaintiff fell from subway platform onto track, train

automatically stopped by "tripper," crew drove on without making adequate inspection).

A. The earliest cases finding liability to a trespasser were those of spring guns or traps deliberately set for him. From these cases the rule developed that the defendant was not allowed to injure the trespasser negligently by an act specifically directed at him, as in Palmer v. Gordon, 173 Mass. 410, 53 N.E. 909 (1899); Magar v. Hammond, 183 N.Y. 387, 76 N.E. 474 (1906); or recklessly by conduct in conscious disregard of his danger, as in Aiken v. Holyoke St. Ry. Co., 184 Mass. 269, 68 N.E. 238 (1903); Trico Coffee Co. v. Clemens, 168 Miss. 748, 151 So. 175 (1933).

B. From such decisions the rule developed that the defendant is liable for injury to a trespasser for conduct that is "wilful or wanton." Thus in Bremer v. Lake Erie & W.R. Co., 318 Ill. 11, 148 N.E. 862 (1925), the defendant was held liable when its engineer recklessly ran past a signal and injured a trespasser on the train who had not been discovered.

C. In a number of states it is still held that there is no liability even to a discovered trespasser unless the defendant's conduct is wilful or wanton. Some of these jurisdictions have defined "wilful and wanton," as in the principal case, to include a failure to use ordinary care after discovery of the trespasser's presence. Cf. Sloniker v. Great N.R. Co., 76 Minn. 306, 79 N.W. 168 (1899).

D. The great majority of the courts have now discarded "wilful and wanton" as a limitation, and have held that when the presence of the trespasser is discovered there is a duty to use ordinary care to avoid injuring him by active operations. This duty includes the control of operating forces, such as machinery already in motion, or a warning against it. Maldonado v. Jack M. Berry Grove Corp., 351 So.2d 967 (Fla.1977).

E. Cases involving passive conditions on the land, as distinguished from active operations, have been infrequent. It was once held, in Buch v. Amory Mfg. Co., 69 N.H. 257, 44 A. 809 (1898), that the defendant was under no duty even to cry a warning to a trespasser whom he saw walking into a concealed danger. This apparently has now given way to the rule that he must at least warn the trespasser. Martin v. Jones, 122 Utah 597, 609, 253 P.2d 359,(1953); Restatement (Second) of Torts § 337.

5. The second exception is that of frequent trespassers on a very limited area of the land. The defendant is required to anticipate the trespassers and to exercise reasonable care in his activities for their protection. In Imre v. Riegel Paper Corp., 24 N.J. 438, 132 A.2d 505 (1957), the existence of a well-defined path across the land was held to be sufficient evidence of frequent trespass.

6. The third exception is that of *tolerated intruders*. This is sometimes explained or justified on the theory that the defendant's continued toleration of the trespasses amounts to permission to use the land, so that the plaintiff becomes a licensee. In most cases, however, the mere fact that a railway company or other defendant has failed to take steps to prevent trespassing, which would be burdensome, expensive, and perhaps futile, is not in itself any indication that it consents to the entry. See Restatement (Second) of Torts § 330, comment c; Bohlen, The Duty of a Landowner Toward Those Entering His Premises of Their Own Right, 69 U.Pa.L.Rev. 142, 237 (1921).

7. Other exceptions include dangerous conditions obvious to an owner, Restatement (Second) of Torts §§ 342–343 (1965); and trapped trespassers in peril. Pridgen v. Boston Hous. Auth., 364 Mass. 696, 308 N.E.2d 467 (1974).

8. In a few jurisdictions, the courts have developed in railroad cases a special rule requiring the defendant to be on the lookout for trespassers where their presence is foreseeable and the activity carried on involves a high degree of danger to them. Pickett v. Wilmington & W.R. Co., 117 N.C. 616, 23 S.E. 264 (1895); Gulf, C. & S.F.R. Co. v. Russell, 125 Tex. 443, 82 S.W.2d 948 (1935).

9. There is a division of authority over whether a defendant using the land by permission of the owner shares the immunity of the owner toward trespassers. See, e.g., Humphrey v. Twin State Gas & Electric Co., 100 Vt. 414, 139 A. 440 (1927). Thus gratuitous licensees, invitees and holders of easements have been held liable in some cases and not in others. The Restatement (Second) of Torts §§ 383–386, has endeavored to resolve the conflict with the statement that persons on the premises who are doing work or creating artificial conditions *on behalf* of the possessor are subject to the same liability, and entitled to the same immunity, as the possessor; but that other persons on the land with his permission have no such immunity. This offers a logical approach, and serves to explain the greater number of the cases, although by no means all. See, Dzenutis v. Dzenutis, 200 Conn. 290, 304, 512 A.2d 130, 137 (1986); Muckey v. Dittoe, 235 Neb. 250, 454 N.W.2d 682 (1990).

10. Elsewhere in the Common Law world the law relating to trespassers has gone through similar contortions. The English House of Lords attempted to state a definitive rule in British Railways Board v. Herrington [1972] A.C. 877; the duty owed to trespassers is one of "common humanity." The rule was not a panacea and legislation was enacted, see infra Section E, note 2.

(B) LICENSEES

Barmore v. Elmore

Appellate Court of Illinois, Second District, 1980.
83 Ill.App.3d 1056, 403 N.E.2d 1355, 38 Ill.Dec. 751.

LINDBERG, JUSTICE. Plaintiff, Leon Barmore ("plaintiff"), appeals from an order of the Circuit Court of Winnebago County directing a verdict in favor of defendants, Thomas Elmore, Sr., and Esther Elmore ("defendants").

On August 8, 1977, at approximately 5:30 or 6:00 p.m., plaintiff came to the defendants' home. Both plaintiff and Thomas Elmore, Sr. ("Thomas, Sr.") were officers of a Masonic Lodge and plaintiff's purpose in making the visit was to discuss lodge business. During the course of plaintiff's visit, codefendant, Thomas Elmore, Jr., ("Thomas, Jr."), the defendants' 47–year old son, entered the living room with a steak knife. Thomas, Jr. said "You've been talking about me," and advanced toward plaintiff. Thomas, Sr. tried to restrain his son while plaintiff left the house. However, Thomas, Jr. was able to get away from his father, and he followed plaintiff out of the house where he stabbed the plaintiff several times in the chest area. Thomas, Sr. followed his son out of the house and, when he saw that plaintiff had been injured, he summoned help.

Based on this incident, plaintiff filed suit against [defendants.] * * * [P]laintiff's basic contention is that defendants, as landowners, were negligent in failing to protect him from a dangerous condition upon their premises—namely their son who had a history of mental illness. The extent of defendants' duty in this regard is based in part on whether the plaintiff had the status of an invitee or of a licensee at the time he visited the premises of the defendants.

* * * In order for a person to be classified as an invitee it is sufficient that he go on the land in furtherance of the owner's business. It is not necessary that the invited person gain an advantage by his entry on the land. [C] A social guest is considered a licensee and has been defined as one who enters the premises of the owner by permission, but for the licensee's own purposes. Therefore, a social guest is a person who goes on another's property for companionship, diversion, or entertainment. [C]

The duty owed by the owner of premises towards an invitee is greater than that owed towards a licensee. [C] A social guest as a licensee, generally must take the premises of his host as he finds them. However, the owner of the premises has a duty to warn the licensee of any hidden dangers which are unknown to his guest, of which he, the owner, has knowledge, and to refrain from injuring his guest willfully or wantonly. [Cc] Towards an invitee, the owner of the premises has a duty to exercise reasonable care in keeping the premises reasonably safe for use by the invitee. [C] There may be circumstances by which this duty is extended to include the responsibility to protect the invitee from criminal attacks by third parties. [C]

Plaintiff asserts that sufficient evidence was presented at trial to establish his status as an invitee at the time of the incident. Specifically, plaintiff argues that Illinois courts have recognized that the transaction of business of a fraternal organization carries with it such a status. * * *

Here, although there is evidence that Thomas, Sr. permitted lodge members to come to his home to pay their dues, the primary benefit of this service ran not to the defendant himself, but rather to the fraternal organization of which both parties were members. In sum, we conclude that plaintiff is best categorized as a licensee—social guest and thus the only duty owed to the plaintiff by the defendants was to warn him of hidden dangers unknown to the plaintiff of which the defendants had knowledge.

There is no question that defendants failed to warn plaintiff of the danger that their son might attack a house guest before the attack was underway. Thus the issue becomes whether under the facts of this case defendants had a duty to do so. Plaintiff contends that he presented sufficient evidence by which a jury could have concluded that the defendants had knowledge of previous incidents which would charge them with a duty to anticipate the criminal acts of their son toward the plaintiff. We disagree. [The Court summarizes the evidence.]

Verdicts should be directed and judgments n.o.v. entered "only in those cases in which all of the evidence, when viewed in its aspect most favorable to the opponent, so overwhelmingly favors movant that no contrary verdict based on that evidence could ever stand." [C] In our view, the evidence so overwhelmingly established that the defendants did not know or have reason to know of the possibility that Thomas, Jr. would commit a criminal act toward plaintiff that no contrary verdict could ever stand. Although they did know that their son had a history of mental problems and had been hospitalized several times, and also that approximately ten years before the present incident their son had been involved in what could be characterized as two or three violent incidents, the length of time which had passed would not give them reason to know that their son would engage in violent behavior in August, 1977. This conclusion is buttressed by the fact that plaintiff had previous contact with Thomas, Jr. without incident.

Accordingly, the judgment * * * is affirmed.

NOTES AND QUESTIONS

1. As in the case of trespassers, it was at first held that there was no duty to a licensee except to refrain from inflicting wilful or wanton injury; and there are still courts which hold this. Duff v. United States, 171 F.2d 846 (4th Cir.1949) (Maryland law); Hill v. Baltimore & Ohio R. Co., 153 F.2d 91 (7th Cir.1946) (Illinois law). Courts often define "wilful or wanton" to include a failure to exercise ordinary care after the presence of the licensee has been discovered, or should reasonably have been expected. Atlantic Coast Line R. Co. v. Heath, 57 Ga.App. 763, 196 S.E. 125 (1938); Jackson v. Pennsylvania R. Co., 176 Md. 1, 3 A.2d 719 (1939).

2. Most of the courts now have overruled older decisions, and hold that the defendant, in conducting active operations, is under a duty of reasonable care toward licensees. This duty extends not only to licensees who are discovered, but to those whose presence might reasonably be anticipated. Babcock & Wilcox Co. v. Nolton, 58 Nev. 133, 71 P.2d 1051 (1937); Szafranski v. Radetzky, 31 Wis.2d 119, 141 N.W.2d 902 (1966) (handling gun powder).

3. If defendant landholder knows about a dangerous, latent condition on his premises that a visitor is likely to encounter, he is under a duty to warn the licensee about it. Laube v. Stevenson, 137 Conn. 469, 78 A.2d 693 (1951), involving a dangerous condition on a stairwell, is an excellent case illustrating difference in result between a defendant who knew and one who did not know about the hazard. See also Barry v. Cantrell, 150 Ga.App. 439, 258 S.E.2d 61 (1979) (hammock tied to dead tree); Rushton v. Winters, 331 Pa. 78, 200 A. 60 (1938) (defective porch railing).

The Restatement (Second) of Torts § 342 subjects the landholder to liability if he had "reason to know" about the unsafe condition. Even in this modern age when householder's liability insurance is common, this extension has not always met with approval.

4. In some jurisdictions the licensee category is broken down into two sub-groups, the ordinary licensee and the "bare" licensee. The latter group includes salespersons, canvassers and social visitors who "drop in" without an express invitation. As might be expected, the duty owed to "bare" licensees is less than that owed to ordinary licensees. See Kight v. Bowman, 25 Md.App. 225, 333 A.2d 346, 350 (1975); Wilson v. Goodrich, 218 Iowa 462, 252 N.W. 142 (1934); cf. Scheibel v. Lipton, 156 Ohio St. 308, 102 N.E.2d 453 (1951). In other states, the word "bare" is simply an uncomplimentary epithet applied to all licensees.

5. *Social Guests.* Ever since Southcote v. Stanley, 1 H. & N. 247, 156 Eng.Rep. 1195 (1856), the decisions have been essentially uniform in holding that a social

guest, although he is invited, and even urged to come, is not in law an invitee but is to be treated as merely a licensee. See, for example, Stevens v. Dovre, 248 Md. 15, 234 A.2d 596 (1967); Zuther v. Schild, 224 Kan. 528, 581 P.2d 385 (1978).

6.   As the principal case reflects, there is general agreement that the fact that the guest renders some incidental service to his host, such as washing the dishes or repairing a broken shelf, does not change his status. And it has been held that an economic motive in inviting the defendant's employer to dinner does not make him an invitee. Cf. Hall v. Duke, 513 S.W.2d 776 (Tenn.1974).

7.   Should the rule be changed? Does a social guest anticipate that the premises will be made reasonably safe for his benefit? What about the uninvited social guest, salesperson or canvasser? Does the host receive a "benefit" from a purely social guest? Is it enough to impose a duty of reasonable care? For an incisive analysis of the rule relating to social guests see Burrell v. Meads, 569 N.E.2d 637 (Ind.1991) (holding that social guests are entitled to a standard of reasonable care from host landowners because social guests are invitees).

8.   Should the host be liable for protecting third parties from acts of intoxicated guests? See Kelly v. Gwinnell, 96 N.J. 538, 476 A.2d 1219 (1984), supra page ___; where parents leave teenagers "home alone" and a drunken guest injures plaintiff in motor vehicle accident after leaving the party? See Morella v. Machu, 235 N.J.Super. 604, 563 A.2d 881 (App.Div.1989).

9.   The few cases that raise the question of strict liability to licensees all have involved dangerous animals. In all of them, the strict liability has been held to extend to the licensee. See, for example, Parker v. Cushman, 195 Fed. 715 (8th Cir.1912); Marquet v. La Duke, 96 Mich. 596, 55 N.W. 1006 (1893).

(C) INVITEES

Campbell v. Weathers

Supreme Court of Kansas, 1941.
153 Kan. 316, 111 P.2d 72.

[Defendant, as tenant of a part of a building in the city of Wichita, operated a lunch counter and cigar stand. Plaintiff entered defendant's place of business, loitered in the front part of the premises for fifteen or twenty minutes without making any purchase, and then went to the back part of the building to use the toilet. He stepped into an open trap door in a dark hallway, and was injured. In his action for negligence, the trial court sustained defendant's demurrer to the evidence and plaintiff appeals.]

WEDELL, J. * * * The first issue to be determined is the relationship between plaintiff and the lessee. Was plaintiff a trespasser, a licensee or an invitee? The answer must be found in the evidence. A part of the answer is contained in the nature of the business the lessee conducted. It is conceded lessee operated a business which was open to the public. Lessee's business was that of selling cigars and lunches to the public. It was conceded in oral argument, although the abstract does not reflect it, that the lessee also operated a bar for the sale of beer, but that beer was not being sold on Sunday, the day of the accident. Plaintiff had been a customer of the lessee for a number of years. He resided in the city of Wichita. He was a switchman for one of the railroads. He stopped at the lessee's place of business whenever he was in town. He had used the hallway and toilet on numerous occasions, whenever he was in town, and had never been advised that the toilet was not intended for public use. * * *

That the public had a general invitation to be or to become lessee's customers cannot be doubted. * * * Can we say, as a matter of law, in view of the record in this particular case, appellant had no implied invitation to use the toilet simply because he had not made an actual purchase before he was injured? * * *

The evidence of lessee's own employees was that the toilet was not regarded as a private toilet. * * * In a densely populated business district such a privilege may have constituted a distinct inducement to bring, not only old customers like appellant, but prospective customers into lessee's place of business. * * * But we need not rest our conclusion that appellant was an invitee upon the fact that according to the unqualified evidence, not only customers but everybody was permitted to use the toilet.

The writer cannot subscribe to the theory that a regular customer of long standing is not an invitee to use toilet facilities required by law to be provided by the owner of a restaurant, simply because the customer had not actually made a purchase on the particular occasion of his injury, prior to his injury. It would seem doubtful whether such a doctrine could be applied justly to regular customers of a business which the law does not specifically require to be supplied with toilet facilities, but which does so for the convenience or accommodation of its guests. Women do a great deal of shopping. They sometimes shop all day in their favorite stores and fail to make a single purchase. Shall courts say, as a matter of law, they were not invitees of the business simply because on a particular occasion they had not yet made a purchase? No business concern would contend that they were not invitees unless perchance an injury had occurred. Men frequently, during spare moments, step into a place of business, which they patronize regularly, where drinks, cigars and lunches are sold. They may not have intended definitely to presently make a purchase. They may, nevertheless, become interested, for example, in a new brand of cigars on display which they may purchase then or on some future occasion. Would the owner or operator of the business contend that they were not invitees? We do not think so. Then why should courts arbitrarily say so, as a matter of law? * * *

Manifestly this does not imply that a trespasser or a mere licensee who enters the premises on a personal errand for the advancement of his own interest or benefit is entitled to the protection due to an invitee. In the case of Kinsman v. Barton & Co., 141 Wash. 311, 251 P. 563, that court had occasion to determine what constituted an invitee, and said:

"An invitee is one who is either expressly or impliedly invited onto the premises of another in connection with the business carried on by that other. * * * If one goes into a store with a view of then, or at some other time, doing some business with the store, he is an invitee." * * *

Of course, if it appears that a person had no intention of presently or in the future becoming a customer he could not be held to be an invitee, as there would be no basis for any thought of mutual benefit. * * *

The order sustaining the demurrer of the lessee is reversed.

NOTES AND QUESTIONS

1.   In Indermaur v. Dames, L.R. 1 C.P. 274 (1866), a journeyman gasfitter came to defendant's sugar refinery to test a patent gas regulator installed there by his employer. He fell down an open and unguarded shaft in the floor, and was injured. It was held that the defendant owed him a duty of reasonable care to make the premises safe for him, because he came "on business which concerns the occupier, and upon his invitation, express or implied."

From this case, those who enter premises "upon business which concerns the occupier" acquired the name of invitees. The early cases left it doubtful whether "business" was used in a commercial sense, to refer to a profit motive, or whether it meant to the courts only the defendant's affairs or concerns, as when we say the thing is my own business, and none of yours. Most of the early decisions did not mention any commercial motive behind the invitation, and were decided solely upon the ground that the defendant had thrown his premises open and "invited" the plaintiff to use them. See Corby v. Hill, 4 C.B., N.S., 556 (1858); Sweeney v. Old Colony & Newport R. Co., 10 Allen (Mass.) 368, 87 Am.Dec. 644 (1865); Gillis v. Pennsylvania R. Co., 59 Pa. 129, 87 Am.Dec. 644 (1868).

The Restatement of Torts, in § 332, discarded the term "invitees," and referred instead to "business visitors." The theory adopted was that the duty of affirmative care to make the premises safe is the price that the occupier must pay for the present or prospective economic benefit to be derived from the visitor's presence. It appears to have originated in Campbell, Law of Negligence 63–64 (2d ed. 1878) and, was espoused by the Reporter of the First Restatement in Bohlen, The Basis of Affirmative Obligations in the Law of Tort, 44 Am.L.Reg., N.S., 209, 227 (1905); Bohlen, The Duty of a Landowner Towards Those Entering His Premises of Their Own Right, 69 U.Pa.L.Rev. 142, 340, 342 (1920).

2.   Actual or potential pecuniary benefit is easily made out in the case of customers who intend to buy, or who are merely "shopping." How valid is the attempt to find it in the following situations:

A.   Children accompany parents to stores or other places of business, where nothing is to be bought for the child. Anderson v. Cooper, 214 Ga. 164, 104 S.E.2d 90 (1958). Or adult friends accompany the customer. Goldsmith v. Cody, 351 Mich. 380, 88 N.W.2d 268 (1958).

B.   Friends meet passengers at a railway station, or see them off. McCann v. Anchor Line, 79 F.2d 338 (2d Cir.1935). Or a potential passenger has not yet obtained a ticket on an airline. Suarez v. Trans World Airlines, Inc., 498 F.2d 612 (6th Cir.1974).

C.   Tourists are invited to go through factories. Gilliland v. Bondurant, 51 S.W.2d 559 (Mo.App.1932), aff'd, 332 Mo. 881, 59 S.W.2d 679 (1933).

3.   In all of the following instances the plaintiff has been held to be an invitee:

A.   Those attending free public meetings. Bunnell v. Waterbury Hosp., 103 Conn. 520, 131 A. 501 (1925) (Salvation Army); Howe v. Ohmart, 7 Ind.App. 32, 33

N.E. 466 (1893) (literary society); Geiger v. Simpson M.E. Church, 174 Minn. 389, 219 N.W. 463 (1928) (social meeting at church).

B. Spectators at public amusements, entering on a free pass. Recreation Centre Corp. v. Zimmerman, 172 Md. 309, 191 A. 233 (1937); Mesa v. Spokane World Exposition, 18 Wash.App. 609, 570 P.2d 157 (1977).

C. Free use of a telephone provided for the public. Randolph v. Great Atl. & Pac. Tea Co., 2 F.Supp. 462 (W.D.Pa.1932), aff'd, 64 F.2d 247 (3d Cir.1933); Ward v. Avery, 113 Conn. 394, 155 A. 502 (1931).

D. Entering a bank to get change for a $20 bill. First Nat'l Bank of Birmingham v. Lowery, 263 Ala. 36, 81 So.2d 284 (1955).

E. Coming to get things advertised to be given away. Roper v. Commercial Fibre Co., 105 N.J.L. 10, 143 A. 741 (1928) (ashes and boxes); Edwards v. Gulf Oil Corp., 69 Ga.App. 140, 24 S.E.2d 843 (1943) (comic books at filling station).

F. Use of state or municipal land open to the public. Caldwell v. Village of Island Park, 304 N.Y. 268, 107 N.E.2d 441 (1952) (park); Lowe v. Gastonia, 211 N.C. 564, 191 S.E. 7 (1937) (golf course); Ashworth v. City of Clarksburg, 118 W.Va. 476, 190 S.E. 763 (1937) (swimming pool).

G. Visitors in national parks. Adams v. United States, 239 F.Supp. 503 (E.D.Okl.1965); Smith v. United States, 117 F.Supp. 525 (N.D.Cal.1953) (camper).

4. Most courts have rejected the old rule that plaintiff's status on public land depends on whether he was entering the premises for the purpose for which they were open to the public (invitee) or whether he entered the premises for an unintended purpose (licensee). See Home Ins. Co. v. Spears, 267 Ark. 704, 590 S.W.2d 71 (1979). In other words, on public land the state, city or county owes to persons coming on the premises a duty to all persons to use reasonable care to keep the premises safe.

5. What about loafers, loiterers, and those who enter merely to get out of the rain, upon premises open for business? Dye v. Rule, 138 Kan. 808, 28 P.2d 758 (1934); Murry Chevrolet Co. v. Cotten, 169 Miss. 521, 152 So. 657 (1934). Or a man who takes a short cut through the defendant's premises? Baird v. Goldberg, 283 Ky. 558, 142 S.W.2d 120 (1940); Cook v. 177 Granite St., 95 N.H. 397, 64 A.2d 327 (1949).

6. In Guilford v. Yale Univ., 128 Conn. 449, 23 A.2d 917 (1942), plaintiff attended a class reunion on the Yale campus. Late at night, seeking to urinate, he proceeded into a dark area, fell over a low retaining wall to a level ten feet below, and was injured. It was held that he was an invitee, without regard to any question of "mutual benefit." Is this one of the purposes for which Old Eli invites its alumni to return to the hallowed elms?

Whelan v. Van Natta

Court of Appeals of Kentucky, 1964.
382 S.W.2d 205.

[Plaintiff came into defendant's grocery store, and purchased some cigarettes. He then asked about a box for his son. Defendant, who was busy behind the counter, replied, "Go back in the backroom. You will find some back there." Plaintiff went to the rear of the store, and opened the door of the storage room. The room was dark, and the light was not turned on. In hunting around for a box, plaintiff fell into an unseen stair well, and was injured. The defendant testified that he did not warn plaintiff of the existence of the stair well, that the light in the room had been on that morning, and that he did not know whether it was still on when the plaintiff fell.

On these facts, the court gave judgment for the defendant, and plaintiff appealed.]

MONTGOMERY, JUDGE. * * * The trial court held that appellant was a licensee at the time of his fall, to whom appellee owed no duty to provide a safe place, save and except to have abstained from doing any intentional or willful act endangering his safety or knowingly letting appellant run upon a hidden peril. [C] Appellant contends that he entered the store on business with appellee and thus had the status of an invitee and that he still occupied this status when he fell and was injured. The question is: "Did the status of appellant change from invitee to licensee after he made his purchase and went into the storage room to obtain the box?" The status of appellant determines the degree of responsibility of appellee.

Pertinent discussion of the scope of the invitation is contained in Torts, Restatement of the Law, Second, Chapter 13, Section 332, page 67 as follows:

"The possessor of land is subject to liability to another as an invitee only for harm sustained while he is on the land within the scope of his invitation. Thus an invitee ceases to be an invitee after the expiration of a reasonable time within which to accomplish the purpose for which he is invited to enter, or to remain. Whether at the expiration of that time he becomes a trespasser or a licensee will depend upon whether the possessor does or does not consent to his remaining on the land.

"Likewise, the visitor has the status of an invitee only while he is on the part of the land to which his invitation extends—or in other words, the part of the land upon which the possessor gives him reason to believe that his presence is desired for the purpose for which he has come. In determining the area included within the invitation, the purpose for which the land is held open, or the particular business purpose for which the invitation is extended is of great importance. * * *

"If the invitee goes outside of the area of his invitation, he becomes a trespasser or a licensee, depending upon whether he goes there without the consent of the possessor, or with such consent. Thus one who goes into a shop which occupies part of the building, the rest of which is used as the possessor's residence, is a trespasser if he goes into the residential part of the premises without the shopkeeper's consent; but he is a licensee if the shopkeeper permits him to go to the bathroom, or invites him to pay a social call."

Judgment affirmed.

NOTES AND QUESTIONS

1. A toilet is provided for the use of customers, as is usual in theatres, department stores and railway stations. The customer makes use of it, and is

injured while doing so. What is his status? Knapp v. Connecticut Theatrical Corp., 122 Conn. 413, 190 A. 291 (1937); Bass v. Hunt, 151 Kan. 740, 100 P.2d 696 (1940).

2.   What if the toilet is kept for the use of the occupier and his employees, and is not intended for the public, as is usual in groceries and drug stores; and the customer uses it by permission? Liveright v. Max Lifsitz Furniture Co., 117 N.J.L. 243, 187 A. 583 (1936).

3.   What if the visitor is invited to go to an unusual part of the premises, such as a stock room, to make his own selection of goods? Bullock v. Safeway Stores, 236 F.2d 29 (8th Cir.1956). Cf. Lavitch v. Smith, 224 Or. 498, 356 P.2d 531 (1960) (salesman invited into private office); Crown Cork & Seal Co. v. Kane, 213 Md. 152, 131 A.2d 470 (1957) (truck driver's helper forced to wait, going to smoking room).

4.   What if the visitor is injured taking a shortcut to the parking lot? Nicoletti v. Westcor, Inc., 131 Ariz. 140, 639 P.2d 330 (1982).

Wilk v. Georges

Supreme Court of Oregon, 1973.
267 Or. 19, 514 P.2d 877.

HOWELL, JUSTICE. Plaintiff filed this action for damages for injuries sustained when she slipped and fell on defendant's premises. A jury returned a verdict for the defendant, and plaintiff appeals.

The defendant operates a garden supply and nursery business in southeast Portland. On December 13, 1969, plaintiff and her husband went to defendant's nursery to purchase a live Christmas tree [and plaintiff slipped and fell on a plank walkway].

Defendant testified that he knew the bare planks were "slippery and dangerous" when wet, and for that reason he placed the asphalt material on them. Defendant also testified that he had placed a warning sign by the gate and one on each side of the building. The signs stated (verbatim):

"Please watch where you are going. This is a nursery where plants grow. There is four seasons: summer and winter, cold and hot, rain, icey spots. Flower petals always falling on the floor, leaves always on the floor.

"We are dealing with nature and we are hoping for the best. We are not responsible for anyone get hurt on the premises.

"Thank you."

The plaintiff and her husband testified that they did not see the signs.
* * *

Plaintiff's primary assignment of error on this appeal is that the court erred in giving the following instruction:

"If a customer coming on the premises knows of a dangerous condition or if this condition is obvious, there is no duty on the part of the owner to correct or warn of the condition unless, despite the fact that the danger is known or obvious, the owner should anticipate that the dangerous condition will cause physical harm to the customer."

The plaintiff contends that the instruction was erroneous because it stated that a mere warning of a dangerous condition would satisfy the defendant's legal obligation to plaintiff. However, the defendant contends that the instruction is correct because if a prudent landowner should anticipate that an unreasonably dangerous condition will cause harm to a customer even though the danger is known or obvious, he may either (1) correct the condition, or (2) warn the customer and satisfy his duty. * * *

Under the 2 Restatement (Second) 218, Torts § 343A, comment *f*, if the possessor should anticipate that the dangerous condition will cause harm to the invitee despite the latter's knowledge, the possessor's duty of reasonable care *may* require him "to warn the invitee, *or* to take other reasonable steps to protect him * * *." (Emphasis ours.)

Dean Prosser, in the Law of Torts, discusses situations when a warning may or may not be sufficient. He points out that in the usual case there is no obligation to protect the invitee from dangers known to the invitee because it is expected that the visitor will protect himself. Under these circumstances reasonable care will require nothing more than a warning of the danger. However, where the possessor should anticipate an unreasonable risk of harm to the invitee notwithstanding his knowledge or a warning, "something more in the way of precaution may be required." Examples are situations where the invitee's attention may be distracted or conditions such as icy steps which cannot be negotiated with reasonable safety. "In all such cases the jury may find that obviousness, warning or even knowledge is not enough." Prosser, Torts (4th ed.) 394, 395, § 61. * * *

The jury should have been instructed that if they found that the condition that existed was unreasonably dangerous—a condition which cannot be encountered with reasonable safety even if the danger is known and appreciated—the owner of the premises is obligated to do more than post warning signs; he must take reasonable and feasible steps to obviate the danger. * * *

There was evidence in the instant case from which the jury could have found that the defendant as a reasonable man should have anticipated an unreasonable risk or harm to plaintiff notwithstanding the posted signs. He placed the asphalt material on most of the walkways because, as he testified, he knew that the planks were slippery and dangerous when wet. Both the bare planks and the asphalt cover were green in color, which could be misleading to one traversing a walkway looking around for a particular tree or shrub. Under these circumstances slipping and falling by a customer was easily foreseeable. * * *

Reversed and remanded.

NOTES AND QUESTIONS

1. As the principal case reflects, even though the danger is known to the plaintiff, the defendant may be found to be negligent if it is not too difficult to eliminate the danger and he should reasonably anticipate that the plaintiff might

still be injured by it. See, e.g., Hechler v. McDonnell, 42 Cal.App.2d 515, 109 P.2d 426 (1941).

2. A common type of case is that in which the attention of a customer is distracted, as the defendant should reasonably expect it to be, by goods on display, and she fails to observe an entirely obvious obstacle left in the aisle, and falls over it. Is the defendant liable? Jaudon v. F.W. Woolworth Co., 303 F.2d 61 (4th Cir.1962); Yuma Furniture Co. v. Rehwinkel, 8 Ariz.App. 576, 448 P.2d 420 (1968).

3. When an obvious hazard is also a natural one such as snow, ice or rainwater, a number of jurisdictions hold that the invitor owes no duty to any invitee who slips or falls because of the hazard. See Luebeck v. Safeway Stores, Inc., 152 Mont. 88, 446 P.2d 921 (1968); Sidle v. Humphrey, 13 Ohio St.2d 45, 233 N.E.2d 589 (1968). But cf. Schoondyke v. Heil, Heil, Smart & Golee, Inc., 89 Ill.App.3d 640, 411 N.E.2d 1168, 44 Ill.Dec. 802 (1980) (company maintaining a condominium).

4. As elsewhere the duty is not confined to injuries caused solely because of the condition of the premises. A much litigated line of cases concerns the liability of an invitor's duty to an invitee injured at the hands of third-party criminal elements. Injured parties assert either that (1) the invitor has failed to take reasonable measures to reduce the likelihood of dangerous criminal activity posing a danger to invitees or that (2) the invitor's actions (or those of her servant) in face of the crime negligently endangered the invitee. In the former category, the courts have sometimes found a duty to protect entrants as in Erickson v. Curtis Investment Co., 447 N.W.2d 165 (Minn.1989), wherein a duty of care was imposed on the operator or owner of a parking ramp facility toward a customer who was raped in her parked car. The court stressed the particular focus and opportunity for criminals and their criminal activities in structures of this kind. The duty was expressed in terms of reasonable care to deter, requiring the jury to weigh "the likelihood of the risk with the financial and practical feasibility of the means to meet that risk * * *." A Canadian case of similar import is Allison v. Rank City Wall, 6 D.L.R. (4th) 144 (Ont.1984). Past experience of crime may call for measures to protect entrants vulnerable to harm, see Kelly v. Kroger Co., 484 F.2d 1362 (10th Cir.1973), installation of silent alarm may unduly endanger persons in store when police arrive. In contrast, the Michigan Supreme Court in Williams v. Cunningham Drug Stores, Inc., 429 Mich. 495, 418 N.W.2d 381 (1988), found that the proprietor of a drug store owed no duty to hire armed guards to deter robberies and associated violence in a high crime area. The defendant was found not to have sufficient control and any duty would be difficult to operationalize. On the issue of "reasonable care" see Preuss v. Sambo's of Arizona, Inc., 130 Ariz. 288, 635 P.2d 1210, 1211 (1981); cf. Restatement (Second) of Torts, §§ 343, 343A. The duty to use care may apply to discovery of the dangerous criminal, cf. Townsley v. Cincinnati Gardens, Inc., 39 Ohio App.2d 5, 68 Ohio Op.2d 72, 314 N.E.2d 409 (1974) (dictum); to becoming aware of his dangerous character, cf. Repka v. Rentalent Inc., 477 P.2d 470 (Colo.App.1970); or to giving a warning of the danger, cf. Sinn v. Farmers' Deposit Sav. Bank, 300 Pa. 85, 150 A. 163 (1930).

In respect of the latter category—the invitor's actions in the face of a crime—the courts have shown a disinclination to second guess actions taken in the exigencies of an ongoing crime. In Boyd v. Racine Currency Exchange, Inc., 56 Ill.2d 95, 306 N.E.2d 39 (1973), the plaintiff's decedent was shot by a robber when a teller, behind a bullet-proof shield, refused to comply with the robber's demand for money or access to a restricted area. The court found that to impose a duty of compliance would benefit criminals and endanger "future business invitees."

5. A landowner may be liable for injuries sustained by an invitee for the intentional acts of others falling short of criminal behavior. Reasonable precautions must be taken to prevent an intoxicated patron from harming another, McFarlin v. Hall, 127 Ariz. 220, 619 P.2d 729 (1980). Recall Morella v. Machu, above. Similarly, a duty extends to taking reasonable precautions to maintain order in a movie theater to forestall reasonably foreseeable violence to a patron in the parking lot following the movie. Silva v. Showcase Cinemas Concessions of Dedham, Inc., 736 F.2d 810 (1st Cir.1984), cert. denied, 469 U.S. 883 (1984). The duty may also extend to adjacent property, particularly entrances to the business premises if the business is aware of a dangerous condition and fails to warn invitees or take precautions. Banks v. Hyatt Corp., 722 F.2d 214 (5th Cir.1984). For fact variations, see Merhi v. Becker, 164 Conn. 516, 325 A.2d 270 (1973) (violent conduct at union picnic, host failed to protect guest); F.W. Woolworth v. Kirby, 293 Ala. 248, 302 So.2d 67 (1974) (duty to control unruly crowd); Jacobsma v. Goldberg's Fashion Forum, 14 Ill. App.3d 710, 303 N.E.2d 226 (1973) (invitee attempted to apprehend felon and was injured); Jenness v. Sheraton–Cadillac Properties, Inc., 48 Mich.App. 723, 211 N.W.2d 106 (1973) (hotel guest picks up prostitute in lobby and is assaulted by her in his room).

(D) PERSONS OUTSIDE THE ESTABLISHED CATEGORIES

(1) CHILDREN

Courts have been reluctant to apply to child trespassers or licensees the same limited-duty rules that would be applicable to adults. By various legal devices, most of them have imposed on landowners the duty to exercise a higher standard of care toward children. A principal reason for this is society's interest in protecting children from serious injury. See Green, Landholders' Responsibility to Children, 27 Tex.L.Rev. 1 (1948).

The Attractive Nuisance Doctrine. The first major inroad serving to raise the duty owed to child trespassers and licensees developed over a hundred years ago—it was known as the "attractive nuisance" or "turntable" doctrine. See Sioux City & Pac. R. Co. v. Stout, 84 U.S. (17 Wall.) 657 (1873); Keffe v. Milwaukee & St. Paul R. Co., 21 Minn. 207, 18 Am.Rep. 383 (1875). These cases arose when a young child entered on railroad property and was seriously injured while playing on an unlocked turntable. The courts decided that when a landholder sets before young children a temptation that he has reason to believe will lead them into danger, he must use ordinary care to protect them from harm. The courts relied on English precedents where defendants who set traps baited with strong smelling meat on their land were held liable when dogs were lured upon the land and killed in the traps.

On the basis of the turntable decisions, the doctrine acquired the misleading name "attractive nuisance." The word "nuisance" was used because of a supposed analogy to conditions dangerous to children outside the premises. The word "attractive" was applied because courts regarded it as essential that the child be lured or enticed onto the premises.

The development of the doctrine received a set-back from Justice Holmes in United Zinc & Chemical Co. v. Britt, 258 U.S. 268 (1922). In this case, two children trespassed on defendant's land and then discovered a pool of water, apparently clear but actually poisoned with sulfuric acid. The children went into the water and were harmed. Justice Holmes held that the attractive-nuisance doctrine did not apply because the children were not attracted onto the land and induced to trespass in the first instance by the thing that injured them. While at first receiving a favorable response, the *Britt* case was later rejected by a substantial majority of states.

Dean Francis Bohlen
Reporter for the First Restatement of Torts

Restatement of Torts § 339. The question of what duty should be owed to child trespassers or licensees occupied considerable time and thought in the preparation of the First Restatement of Torts. The result of these efforts was § 339, which became one of the most influential provisions of the entire Restatement. The authors abandoned the fictitious language of "attractive nuisance" and substituted the title "Artificial Conditions Highly Dangerous to Trespassing Children." As readopted, with only a few modifications, in the Restatement (Second) of Torts, it reads:

"A possessor of land is subject to liability for physical harm to children trespassing thereon caused by an artificial condition upon the land if

(a) the place where the condition exists is one upon which the possessor knows or has reason to know that children are likely to trespass, and

(b) the condition is one of which the possessor knows or has reason to know and which he realizes or should realize will involve an unreasonable risk of death or serious bodily harm to such children, and

(c) the children because of their youth do not discover the condition or realize the risk involved in intermeddling with it or in coming within the area made dangerous by it, and

(d) the utility to the possessor of maintaining the condition and the burden of eliminating the danger are slight as compared with the risk to children involved, and

(e) the possessor fails to exercise reasonable care to eliminate the danger or otherwise to protect the children.''

As one can see, the Restatement rejected the *Britt* case. It is not essential that the child be attracted, lured or enticed on the premises by the thing that injures him. Nevertheless, plaintiff must show that there is a condition upon the land that would cause the possessor to know or at least have reason to know that children will appear. In Dzenutis v. Dzenutis supra (note 9, Sect. A) defendant's prior observation support the conclusion that defendant had reason to know that children were likely to trespass. Thus, if children had never previously entered the premises and there was no reason to anticipate that they would, recovery may be denied. See Goll v. Muscara, 211 Pa.Super. 93, 235 A.2d 443 (1967).

Assuming that the owner knows that children are present or trespass in the area, it is not every hazardous condition that will subject him to liability. It must be one that will involve ''an unreasonable risk of death or serious bodily harm to the children.'' Further, the plaintiff must establish that because of his youth he did not ''discover the condition or realize the risk involved in meddling with it or coming within an area made dangerous by it.'' See Pocholec v. Giustina, 224 Or. 245, 355 P.2d 1104 (1960). Naturally, as a child gets older, proof of this becomes more difficult. A nine-year-old, it was found, would perceive a moving train as a danger so obvious that he would ''readily discover it and realize the risk on coming within the area made dangerous by it'': Holland v. Baltimore & O.R. Co., 431 A.2d 597 (D.C.App.1981). Cf. Dzenutis v. Dzenutis, supra, tar heated to 360%F a danger not ''fully realized.''

Most of the cases allowing recovery have involved children under the age of twelve. A few courts have fixed an arbitrary age limit of fourteen—a rule taken over from decisions relating to the presumed incapacity of children under that age for contributory negligence. On the other hand, a good many decisions have permitted recovery by teenagers when persons of that age might not be expected to appreciate the danger.

Plaintiff must also show that the ''utility to the possessor of maintaining the condition and burden of eliminating the danger are slight as compared with the risk for children involved.'' There has been little careful discussion of this aspect of Restatement of Torts § 339 in the cases. Rather, courts have relied on general language. For example, it is frequently said that "the defendant cannot be an insurer of children's safety."

Finally, the landholder is required to exercise only reasonable care to protect children from the hazard. This means, in many cases involving children who are able to read, that a clear and precise warning about the hazard will discharge the landholder's duty.

See generally Prosser, Trespassing Children, 47 Calif.L.Rev. 427 (1959).

Special Limitations on the Rules Protecting Children. There are two limitations that some jurisdictions have placed on rules that create a special duty to trespassing children.

First, some courts have eliminated "common hazards" on the ground that any child of sufficient age to be allowed at large by his parents, and so to be likely to trespass, can be expected as a matter of law to appreciate the danger and avoid it, or at least make his own reasonable and intelligent choice. Hazards to which the limitation has most often been applied include drowning in water, dangers of fire, fall from a height or into an excavation, moving vehicles, ordinary visible machinery in motion, sliding or caving soil, and piles of lumber and similar materials. In some jurisdictions, the limitation has not been applied when the defendant knows or has reason to know that the children who are likely to trespass are so young that they cannot be expected to appreciate the danger. King v. Lennen, 53 Cal.2d 340, 348 P.2d 98, 1 Cal.Rptr. 665 (1959); Shaw v. Petersen, 169 Ariz. 559, 821 P.2d 220 (App.1991) (both cases relating to toddlers and swimming pools); Cockerham v. R.E. Vaughan, Inc., 82 So.2d 890 (Fla.1955) (2½ years, excavation); and the Restatement (Second) of Torts takes this position.

The common-hazard limitation has also been eliminated where there is some special and concealed danger, even though an older child is injured. Cooper v. Reading, 392 Pa. 452, 140 A.2d 792 (1958) (deep hole in muddy pool); Cicero State Bank v. Dolese & Shepard Co., 298 Ill.App. 290, 18 N.E.2d 574 (1939) (scum over pool, looking like solid ground).

The present tendency is to discard this concept as a fixed rule, and to include all these conditions with the others. The fact that the condition is one which any child likely to trespass can be expected to understand and appreciate is, however, still important, and may often defeat recovery.

A second and more enduring limitation eliminates hazards that arise in the state of nature. Courts have expressed a continuing reluctance to place a burden on the landholder to protect children from these conditions. An example is Loney v. McPhillips, 268 Or. 378, 521 P.2d 340 (1974) (wind-swept ocean cave particularly dangerous at high tide). See also Fitch v. Selwyn Village, 234 N.C. 632, 68 S.E.2d 255 (1951); Anneker v. Quinn–Robbins Co., 80 Idaho 1, 323 P.2d 1073 (1958). The Restatement (Second) of Torts expressed "no opinion" on whether § 339 should apply to natural conditions.

Child Licensees. While most of the cases concerning the attractive nuisance doctrine or the Restatement of Torts § 339 involve child trespassers, there are some cases that focus upon child licensees. The special rules may provide added protection for them. Thus, there may be an obligation to inform a child licensee about a risk when there would be no duty with regard to an adult. Equally important, if the child licensee is very young, a court may deem a mere warning an insufficient protection in a context when it would be sufficient if the victim were an adult. See Shannon v. Butler Homes, Inc., 102 Ariz. 312, 428 P.2d 990 (1967); Di Gildo v. Caponi, 18 Ohio St.2d 125, 47 Ohio Ops.2d 282, 247 N.E.2d 732 (1969); Restatement (Second) of Torts § 343B, Comment b.

(2) PERSONS PRIVILEGED TO ENTER IRRESPECTIVE OF LANDOWNER'S CONSENT

Public employees or officials do not fit very well into any of the categories that the law has established for the classification of visitors. They are not trespassers, since they are privileged to enter. This privilege is independent of any permission, consent or license of the occupier; they would be privileged to enter and could insist upon doing so even if the landholder made an active objection. They normally do not come for any of the purposes for which the premises are held open to the public, and frequently they do not enter for any benefit of the occupier, or under circumstances which would justify any expectation that the place has been prepared to receive them.

Many courts have still struggled to place public officers and employees within the category of invitees. Some public officers enter for a purpose connected with defendant's business, and are essential to it, since without them it could not legally be carried on. This is true, for example, of sanitary and safety inspectors, who are commonly held to be invitees. Swift & Co. v. Schuster, 192 F.2d 615 (10th Cir.1951); Atchley v. Berlen, 87 Ill.App.3d 61, 408 N.E.2d 1177, 42 Ill.Dec. 468 (1980). Economic advantage may also be made out in the case of a garbage collector, a city water-meter reader or a postman. Finnegan v. Fall River Gas–Works Co., 159 Mass. 311, 34 N.E. 523 (1893); Paubel v. Hitz, 339 Mo. 274, 96 S.W.2d 369 (1936). Some courts have found an economic advantage to the landholder operative in a visit from a tax collector. Wilson v. Union Iron Works Dry Dock Co., 167 Cal. 539, 140 P. 250 (1914); Anderson & Nelson Distilling Co. v. Hair, 103 Ky. 196, 44 S.W. 658 (1898).

On the other hand, both firemen and policemen have generally been held to enter under a bare license conferred by the law, and so to be no more than licensees. This means, however, that if defendant knows they are present, he must warn them of known dangers which they are unlikely to discover. James v. Cities Serv. Oil Co., 66 Ohio App. 87, 31 N.E.2d 872 (1939), aff'd, 140 Ohio St. 314, 23 Ohio Ops. 571, 43 N.E.2d 276 (1942); Rogers v. Cato Oil & Grease Co., 396 P.2d 1000 (Okl.1964).

One factor having some influence in the refusal to include firemen and policemen in the invitee category has been the fact that they are usually covered either by worker's compensation or by pension funds and thus will be compensated for their injuries. See Scheurer v. Trustees of Open Bible Church, 175 Ohio St. 163, 192 N.E.2d 38 (1963).

A practical reason for treating policemen and firemen as licensees is that they often appear at unexpected times and in unexpected places, and it might place an inordinate burden on the landholder to provide for their safety. Rosa v. Dunkin' Donuts of Passaic, 122 N.J. 66, 73, 583 A.2d 1129, 1132 (1991). Is the rule justified to any extent by the doctrine of voluntary assumption of risk?

The general frustration with categorizing policemen and firemen into common law categories has prompted some courts to abandon the category system as applied to public officers and simply apply a general reasonable-care, negligence standard. See Mounsey v. Ellard, 297 N.E.2d 43 (Mass. 1973); Armstrong v. Mailand, 284 N.W.2d 343 (Minn.1979). Recently, Michigan refused to adopt the firemen's rule in Kreski v. Modern Whole-sale Elec. Supply Co., 151 Mich.App. 376, 390 N.W.2d 244 (1986); and Oregon abolished it in Christensen v. Murphy, 296 Or. 610, 678 P.2d 1210 (1984).

At least five different answers have been given to the question of how public officials are to be treated. They have been: (1) classified as licensees, (2) classified as invitees, (3) held as entitled to the duty owed to licensees or invitees depending upon the highest duty which the landowner already owed to some other person at that place and time, (4) given a separate classification, with a special duty owed to it, and (5) held entitled to reasonable care under all the circumstances.

After all this you may sympathize with Lord Bridge in Ogwo v. Taylor, [1988] A.C. 431, 449, who after examining varying opinions displayed in Walters v. Sloan, 20 Cal.3d 199, 571 P.2d 609, 142 Cal.Rptr. 152 (1977), concluded that he was "left in no doubt whatever that the American 'fireman's rule' has no place in English law."

Private Persons. The same kinds of problems, with some additional complications, exist in regard to private individuals who come on the premises for self-protection or to rescue or aid someone. They may be privileged as a matter of law to enter, regardless of the landowner's consent. Should the duty owed to them be derivative, depending upon the classification of the person being rescued? What would be the effect of that person's contributory negligence? If the duty owed is an independent one owed to the rescuer in his own right, do all of the possible answers listed in the previous paragraph apply? Perhaps all of this is an appropriate introduction to the next Section.

(E) Rejection or Merging of Categories

Rowland v. Christian

Supreme Court of California, 1968.
69 Cal.2d 108, 443 P.2d 561, 70 Cal.Rptr. 97.

Peters, Justice. Plaintiff appeals from a summary judgment for defendant Nancy Christian in this personal injury action.

[The evidence was that plaintiff was a social guest in defendant's apartment; that he asked to use the bathroom; and that while there he was injured when a cracked handle of the cold water faucet on the basin broke and severed tendons and nerves on his right hand. Also that defendant had known for two weeks that the handle was cracked and had complained to the manager of the building, but that she did not say anything to the plaintiff as to its condition.]

One of the areas where this court and other courts have departed from the fundamental concept that a man is liable for injuries caused by his carelessness is with regard to the liability of a possessor of land for injuries to persons who have entered upon that land. It has been suggested that the special rules regarding liability of the possessor of land are due to historical considerations stemming from the high place which land has traditionally held in English and American thought, the dominance and prestige of the landowning class in England during the formative period of the rules governing the possessor's liability, and the heritage of feudalism. [C]

[The court reviewed the various confusing rules and exceptions that had been applied in California to licensees.]

California Supreme Court
Front row: McComb, Traynor, C.J., Peters
Back row: Burke, Tobriner, Mosk, Sullivan

The cases dealing with the active negligence and the trap exceptions are indicative of the subtleties and confusion which have resulted from application of the common law principles governing the liability of the possessor of land. Similar confusion and complexity exist as to the definitions of trespasser, licensee, and invitee. [C]

In refusing to adopt the rules relating to the liability of a possessor of land for the law of admiralty, the United States Supreme Court stated: "The distinctions which the common law draws between licensee and invitee were inherited from a culture deeply rooted to the land, a culture which traced many of its standards to a heritage of feudalism. In an effort to do justice in an industrialized urban society, with its complex economic and individual relationships, modern commonlaw courts have found it necessary to formulate increasingly subtle verbal refinements, to create subclassifications among traditional commonlaw categories, and to delineate fine gradations in the standards of care which the landowner owes to each. Yet even within a single jurisdiction, the classifications and subclassifications bred by the common law have produced confusion and conflict. As new distinctions have been spawned, older ones have become obscured. Through this semantic morass the common law has moved, unevenly and with hesitation, towards 'imposing on owners and occupiers a single duty of reasonable care in all circumstances.'" (Footnotes omitted.) (Kermarec v. Compagnie Generale, 358 U.S. 625, 630–631.) * * *

There is another fundamental objection to the approach to the question of the possessor's liability on the basis of the common law distinctions based upon the status of the injured party as a trespasser, licensee, and invitee, the immunities from liability predicated upon where the underlying principles governing liability are based upon proper considerations. Whatever may have been the historical justifications for the common law distinctions, it is clear that those distinctions are not justified in the light of our modern society and that the complexity and confusion which has arisen is not due to difficulty in applying the original common law rules—they are all too easy to apply in their original formulation—but is due to the attempts to apply just rules in our modern society within the ancient terminology.

Without attempting to labor all of the rules relating to the possessor's liability, it is apparent that the classifications of trespasser, licensee, and invitee, the immunities from liability predicated upon those classifications, and the exceptions to those immunities, often do not reflect the major factors which should determine whether immunity should be conferred upon the possessor of land. Some of those factors, including the closeness of the connection between the injury and the defendant's conduct, the moral blame attached to the defendant's conduct, the policy of preventing future harm, and the prevalence and availability of insurance, bear little, if any, relationship to the classifications of trespasser, licensee and invitee and the existing rules conferring immunity.

Although in general there may be a relationship between the remaining factors and the classifications of trespasser, licensee, and invitee, there are many cases in which no such relationship may exist. Thus, although the foreseeability of harm to an invitee would ordinarily seem greater than the foreseeability of harm to a trespasser, in a particular case the opposite may be true. The same may be said of the issue of certainty of injury. The burden to the defendant and consequences to the community of imposing a duty to exercise care with resulting liability for breach may often be greater with respect to trespassers than with respect to invitees, but it by no means follows that this is true in every case. In many situations, the burden will be the same, i.e., the conduct necessary upon the defendant's part to meet the burden of exercising due care as to invitees will also meet his burden with respect to licensees and trespassers. The last of the major factors, the cost of insurance, will, of course, vary depending upon the rules of liability adopted, but there is no persuasive evidence that applying ordinary principles of negligence law to the land occupier's liability will materially reduce the prevalence of insurance due to increased cost or even substantially increase the cost.

Considerations such as these have led some courts in particular situations to reject the rigid common law classifications and to approach the issue of the duty of the occupier on the basis of ordinary principles of negligence. [Cc] And the common law distinctions after thorough study have been repudiated by the jurisdiction of their birth. (Occupiers' Liability Act, 1957, 5 and 6 Eliz. 2, ch. 31.)

A man's life or limb does not become less worthy of protection by the law nor a loss less worthy of compensation under the law because he has come upon the land of another without permission or with permission but without a business purpose. Reasonable people do not ordinarily vary their conduct depending upon such matters, and to focus upon the status of the injured party as a trespasser, licensee, or invitee in order to determine the question whether the landowner has a duty of care, is contrary to our modern social mores and humanitarian values. The common law rules obscure rather than illuminate the proper considerations which should govern determination of the question of duty. * * *

Once the ancient concepts as to the liability of the occupier of land are stripped away, the status of the plaintiff relegated to its proper place in determining such liability, and ordinary principles of negligence applied, the result in the instant case presents no substantial difficulties. As we have seen, when we view the matters presented on the motion for summary judgment as we must, we must assume defendant Miss Christian was aware that the faucet handle was defective and dangerous, that the defect was not obvious, and that plaintiff was about to come in contact with the defective condition, and under the undisputed facts she neither remedied the condition nor warned plaintiff of it. Where the occupier of land is aware of a concealed condition involving in the absence of precautions an unreasonable risk of harm to those coming in contact with it and is aware that a person on the premises is about to come in contact with it, the trier of fact can reasonably conclude that a failure to warn or to repair the condition constitutes negligence. Whether or not a guest has a right to expect that his host will remedy dangerous conditions on his account, he should reasonably be entitled to rely upon a warning of the dangerous condition so that he, like the host, will be in a position to take special precautions when he comes in contact with it. * * *

The judgment is reversed.

Burke, J. I dissent. In determining the liability of the occupier or owner of land for injuries, the distinctions between trespassers, licensees and invitees have been developed and applied by the courts over a period of many years. They supply a reasonable and workable approach to the problems involved, and one which provides the degree of stability and predictability so highly prized in the law. The unfortunate alternative, it appears to me, is the route taken by the majority in their opinion in this case; that such issues are to be decided on a case by case basis under the application of the basic law of negligence, bereft of the guiding principles and precedent which the law has heretofore attached by virtue of the relationship of the parties to one another.

Liability for negligence turns upon whether a duty of care is owed, and if so, the extent thereof. Who can doubt that the corner grocery, the large department store, or the financial institution owes a greater duty of care to one whom it has invited to enter its premises as a prospective customer of its wares or services than it owes to a trespasser seeking to enter after the close of business hours and for a nonbusiness or even an antagonistic purpose? I do not think it unreasonable or unfair that a social guest (classified by the law as a licensee, as was plaintiff here) should be obliged to take the premises in the same condition as his host finds them or permits them to be. Surely a homeowner should not be obliged to hover over his guests with warnings of possible dangers to be found in the condition of the home (e.g., waxed floors, slipping rugs, toys in unexpected places, etc., etc.). Yet today's decision appears to open the door to potentially unlimited liability despite the purpose and circumstances motivating the plaintiff in entering the premises of another, and despite the caveat of the majority that the status of the parties may "have some bearing on the question of liability * * *," whatever the future may show that language to mean.

In my view, it is not a proper function of this court to overturn the learning, wisdom and experience of the past in this field. Sweeping modifications of tort liability law fall more suitably within the domain of the Legislature, before which all affected interests can be heard and which can enact statutes providing uniform standards and guidelines for the future.

I would affirm the judgment for defendant.

McComb, J., concurred.

NOTES AND QUESTIONS

1. Criticism of the categories as a vehicle for determining the duty a possessor of land owes to a visitor or intruder is not new. See Bohlen, The Duty of a Landholder Towards Those Entering His Premises of Their Own Right, 69 U.Pa. L.Rev. 142 (1921), also in F. Bohlen, Studies in the Law of Torts, 136, 163 (1926); Lord Denning in Dunster v. Abbott, [1953] 2 All E.R. 1572, 1574 (C.A.).

2.   In 1957, as the result of a Report of the Law Reform Committee, the Occupiers' Liability Act, 5 & 6 Eliz. II, c. 31, was adopted in England. The Act declared the occupier's common duty of care to all lawful visitors (thus excluding trespassers) upon his land, and enumerated various factors to be considered in determining whether that duty had been discharged. The English law was subsequently supplemented by a duty to treat all trespassers with "common humanity." See British Railways Board v. Herrington, [1972] A.C. 877 (House of Lords). Eventually statutory reform came in Occupiers' Liability Act, 1984, to provide a duty owed to unlawful entrants where: (1) the occupier is aware of the danger or has reasonable grounds to believe that it exists; (2) he knows or has reasonable grounds to believe that the other is in, or may come into, the vicinity of the danger; and (3) the risk is one against which, in all the circumstances of the case, he may reasonably be expected to offer the other some protection. Cf. Restatement § 339 discussed above. In Scotland a duty had extended to both lawful and unlawful from the outset of statutory reform. Occupiers' Liability (Scotland) Act, 1960.

3.   In Hopkins v. Fox & Lazo Realtors, 132 N.J. 426, 625 A.2d 1110 (1993), the court held that a real estate broker owed a duty to a person inspecting the house during an open-house. The duty was one to take reasonable care in preventing foreseeable harm to its open-house customers. The duty was owed in addition to that of the owner to the entrant. The court applied the principal case finding that approximately fourteen jurisdictions had completely abrogated the various categories of entrants, while "many others" had eliminated the distinction between licensees and business invitees. Other jurisdictions, however, have reaffirmed the retention of the categories. Whaley v. Lawing, 352 So.2d 1090 (Ala.1977); Bailey v. Pennington, 406 A.2d 44 (Del.1979); Huyck v. Hecla Mining Co., 101 Idaho 299, 612 P.2d 142 (1980); Gerchberg v. Loney, 223 Kan. 446, 576 P.2d 593 (1978); Murphy v. Baltimore Gas & Elec. Co., 290 Md. 186, 428 A.2d 459 (1981) (trespassers only); Buchanan v. Prickett & Son, Inc., 203 Neb. 684, 279 N.W.2d 855 (1979); Moore v. Denune & Pipic, Inc., 26 Ohio St.2d 125, 269 N.E.2d 599 (1971); Younce v. Ferguson, 106 Wash.2d 658, 724 P.2d 991 (1986). Other courts have not directly confronted the issue, but retain the common law classifications. E.g., Nicoletti v. Westcor, Inc., 131 Ariz. 140, 639 P.2d 330 (1982); Champlin v. Walker, 249 N.W.2d 839 (Iowa 1977); Taylor v. Baker, 279 Or. 139, 566 P.2d 884 (1977).

4.   While there is considerable agreement that the general negligence standard should be applied to all persons invited or permitted on the premises, there is less accord as to how the trespasser should be handled. Some cases deliberately apply it to a trespasser. In Mark v. Pacific Gas & Elec. Co., 7 Cal.3d 170, 496 P.2d 1276, 101 Cal.Rptr. 908 (1972), a college student was electrocuted when he attempted to unscrew a street lamp located outside his apartment bedroom window. The Supreme Court of California reaffirmed that the negligence standard would be applied to trespassers. Many of the cases adopting *Rowland* have not involved trespass, and in some that have raised the issue the courts have not extended the duty to the benefit of trespassers: Wood v. Camp, 284 So.2d 691 (Fla.1973) and Younce v. Ferguson, 106 Wash.2d 658, 724 P.2d 991 (1986).

3.   LESSOR AND LESSEE

Borders v. Roseberry

Supreme Court of Kansas, 1975.
216 Kan. 486, 532 P.2d 1366.

PRAGER, JUSTICE. * * * The sole point raised on this appeal by the plaintiff, Gary D. Borders, is that the trial court committed reversible error in concluding as a matter of law that a landlord of a single-family house is under no obligation or duty to a social guest of his tenant to repair or remedy a known condition whereby water dripped from the roof onto the front steps of a house fronting north, froze and caused the social guest to slip and fall.

Traditionally the law in this country has placed upon the lessee as the person in possession of the land the burden of maintaining the premises in a reasonably safe condition to protect persons who come upon the land. It is the tenant as possessor who, at least initially, has the burden of maintaining the premises in good repair. [Cc]

The relationship of landlord and tenant is not in itself sufficient to make the landlord liable for the tortious acts of the tenant. [Cc]

When land is leased to a tenant, the law of property regards the lease as equivalent to a sale of the premises for the term. The lessee acquires an estate in the land, and becomes for the time being the owner and occupier, subject to all of the responsibilities of one in possession, both to those who enter onto the land and to those outside of its boundaries. Professor William L. Prosser in his Law of Torts, 4th Ed. § 63, points out that in the absence of agreement to the contrary, the lessor surrenders both possession and control of the land to the lessee, retaining only a reversionary interest; and he has no right even to enter without the permission of the lessee. There is therefore, as a general rule, no liability upon the landlord, either to the tenant or to others entering the land, for defective conditions existing at the time of the lease.

The general rule of non-liability has been modified, however, by a number of exceptions which have been created as a matter of social policy. Modern case law on the subject today usually limits the liability of a landlord for injuries arising from a defective condition existing at the time of the lease to six recognized exceptions. These exceptions are as follows:

1. Undisclosed dangerous conditions known to lessor and unknown to the lessee.

This exception is stated in Restatement (Second) of Torts § 358 as follows:

"§ 358. Undisclosed Dangerous Conditions Known to Lessor

"(1) A lessor of land who conceals or fails to disclose to his lessee any condition, whether natural or artificial, which involves unreasonable risk of physical harm to persons on the land, is subject to liability to the lessee and others upon the land with the consent of the lessee or his sublessee for physical harm caused by the condition after the lessee has taken possession, if

"(a) the lessee does not know or have reason to know of the condition or the risk involved, and

"(b) the lessor knows or has reason to know of the condition, and realizes or should realize the risk involved, and has reason to expect that the lessee will not discover the condition or realize the risk.

"(2) If the lessee [sic] actively conceals the condition, the liability stated Subsection (1) continues until the lessee discovers it and has reasonable opportunity to take effective precautions against it. Otherwise the liability continues only until the vendee has had reasonable opportunity to discover the condition and to take such precautions." * * *

It should be pointed out that this exception applies [in Kansas] only to latent conditions and not to conditions which are patent or reasonably discernible to the tenant. [C]

2. Conditions dangerous to persons outside of the premises.

This exception is stated in Restatement (Second) of Torts § 379 as follows:

"§ 379. Dangerous Conditions Existing When Lessor Transfers Possession

"A lessor of land who transfers its possession in a condition which he realizes or should realize will involve unreasonable risk of physical harm to others outside of the land, is subject to the same liability for physical harm subsequently caused to them by the condition as though he had remained in possession."

The theory of liability under such circumstances is that where a nuisance dangerous to persons outside the leased premises (such as the traveling public or persons on adjoining property) exists on the premises at the time of the lease, the lessor should not be permitted to escape liability by leasing the premises to another. * * *

3. Premises leased for admission of the public. [§ 359]

The third exception arises where land is leased for a purpose involving the admission of the public. The cases usually agree that in that situation the lessor is under an affirmative duty to exercise reasonable care to inspect and repair the premises before possession is transferred, to prevent any unreasonable risk or harm to the public who may enter. * * *

4. Parts of land retained in lessor's control which lessee is entitled to use. [§§ 360, 361]

When different parts of a building, such as an office building or an apartment house, are leased to several tenants, the approaches and common passageways normally do not pass to the tenant, but remain in the possession and control of the landlord. Hence the lessor is under an affirmative obligation to exercise reasonable care to inspect and repair those parts of the premises for the protection of the lessee, members of his family, his employees, invitees, guests, and others on the land in the right of the tenant. * * *

5. Where lessor contracts to repair. [§ 357]

At one time the law in most jurisdictions and in Kansas was that if a landlord breached his contract to keep the premises in good repair, the only remedy of the tenant was an action in contract in which damages were limited to the cost of repair or loss of rental value of the property. Neither the tenant nor members of his family nor his guests were permitted to recover for personal injuries suffered as a result of the breach of the agreement. [C] In most jurisdictions this rule has been modified and a cause of action given in tort to the injured person to enable him recovery for his personal injuries. * * *

In Steele v. Latimer, 214 Kan. 329, 521 P.2d 304, we held that the provisions of a municipal housing code prescribing minimum housing standards are deemed by implication to become a part of a lease of urban residential property, giving rise to an implied warranty on the part of the lessor that the premises are habitable and safe for human occupancy in compliance with the pertinent code provisions and will remain so for the duration of the tenancy. Such an implied warranty creates a contractual obligation on the lessor to repair the premises to keep them in compliance with the municipal housing standards as set forth in a municipal housing code.

6.   Negligence by lessor in making repairs. [§ 362]

When the lessor does in fact attempt to make repairs, whether he is bound by a covenant to do so or not, and fails to exercise reasonable care, he is held liable for injuries to the tenant or others on the premises in his right, if the tenant neither knows nor should know that the repairs have been negligently made. * * * [The court found the first five exceptions not applicable in this case.]

[Exception six] comes into play only when the lessee lacks knowledge that the purported repairs have not been made or have been negligently made. Here it is undisputed that the tenant had full knowledge of the icy condition on the steps created by the absence of guttering. It seems to us that the landlord could reasonably assume that the tenant would inform his guest about the icy condition on the front steps. We have concluded that the factual circumstances do not establish liability on the landlord on the basis of negligent repairs made by him.

In his brief counsel for the plaintiff vigorously argues that the law should be changed to make the landlord liable for injuries resulting from a defective condition on the leased premises where the landlord has knowledge of that condition. He has not cited any authority in support of his position, nor does he state with particularity how the existing law pertaining to a landlord's liability should be modified. We do not believe that the facts and circumstances of this case justify a departure from the established rules of law discussed above.

The judgment of the district court is affirmed.

NOTES AND QUESTIONS

1.   The principal case presents a reasonably accurate picture of the law in most states in regard to the duty in tort of a lessor toward his lessee and the lessee's guests: a general rule of "no duty," modified by a series of exceptions.

2.   All courts agree that the lessor must disclose concealed dangerous conditions existing at the time of the transfer of possession, of which he has knowledge.

The liability extends not only to the tenant, and the members of his family, but to his employees, his social guests and others on the premises in his right, and to a subtenant to whom he leases the premises. Most of the courts have said that it is sufficient that the lessor has information that would lead a reasonable person to conclude that the danger may exist, and that if he does he must disclose such information to the tenant. See Cesar v. Karutz, 60 N.Y. 229, 19 Am.Rep. 164 (1875) ("reasonable notice"); Cutter v. Hamlen, 147 Mass. 471, 18 N.E. 397 (1888) ("should have known"); Rhoades v. Seidel, 139 Mich. 608, 102 N.W. 1025 (1905) ("ought to have known").

3.   Until about 1965, a majority of the courts that had considered the question held that when a landlord's covenant or contract to repair is broken, the only remedy is a contract action for the breach. An increasing number of the courts worked out a liability in tort for the lessor's failure to perform a contract to repair. The lessor thus becomes liable for resulting injuries to the tenant and also to members of his family, and to others, such as his guests, who are on the premises in the right of the tenant, and even to those outside of the land. The First Restatement of Torts, § 357, adopted the minority position, and this has been continued in the Second Restatement. It is now the majority position.

4.   Several states now have statutes, such as the Tenement Act in Michaels v. Brookchester, Inc., 26 N.J. 379, 140 A.2d 199 (1958), which require the owners of certain types of dwellings to keep them in repair. The New York Multiple Dwelling Law, § 78, expressly provides for civil liability for injuries resulting from failure to repair. Even in the absence of an express provision, the statutes may be construed to result in civil liability. Compare Daniels v. Brunton, 9 N.J.Super. 294, 76 A.2d 73 (1950), aff'd, 7 N.J. 102, 80 A.2d 547 (1951), with Johnson v. Carter, 218 Iowa 587, 255 N.W. 864 (1934). See Restatement (Second) of Property § 17.6, providing for liability in this situation.

5.   An important exception to the no-duty rule is the obligation on the landlord to use reasonable care to maintain common facilities and areas within his control. This usually includes common stairways, front steps and other passage ways. However, it may also encompass other "common facilities" under the lessor's control such as water pipes and air conditioning units. See Coleman v. Steinberg, 54 N.J. 58, 253 A.2d 167 (1969). Should the lessor owe this same duty to a social guest of a lessee? What about the argument that this would make the lessor's duty to the social guest greater than the lessee's? See Taneian v. Meghrigian, 15 N.J. 267, 104 A.2d 689 (1954).

6.   When premises are leased in an existing condition that is dangerous to persons on the highway, the lessor is under a duty that he cannot delegate to the tenant. See, for example, Isham v. Broderick, 89 Minn. 397, 95 N.W. 224 (1903). This is also true when the condition is a private nuisance. McLean v. Wunder, 134 Pa. 334, 19 A. 749 (1890) (cesspool); Mylander v. Beimschla, 102 Md. 689, 62 A. 1038 (1906) (downspout).

7.   What if the lessor does in fact repair, and does it negligently? See Bartlett v. Taylor, 351 Mo. 1060, 174 S.W.2d 844 (1943).

Pagelsdorf v. Safeco Ins. Co. of America

Supreme Court of Wisconsin, 1979.
91 Wis.2d 734, 284 N.W.2d 55.

CALLOW, JUSTICE. We dispose of this appeal by addressing the single issue of the scope of a landlord's duty toward his tenant's invitee who is injured as a result of defective premises. Abrogating the landlord's general cloak of immunity at common law, we hold that a landlord must exercise ordinary care toward his tenant and others on the premises with permission.

The defendant Richard J. Mahnke owned a two-story, two-family duplex. There were four balcony porches: one in front and one in back of each flat. Mahnke rented the upper unit to John and Mary Katherine Blattner. * * *

[Plaintiff Pagelsdorf was assisting Mrs. Blattner move some furniture. He leaned against the railing for the second-floor front balcony, and it collapsed with him. The railing had a dryrot condition and should have been replaced. The trial court put the case to the jury in terms of plaintiff's being a licensee of Mahnke, the landlord, and the jury found by special verdict that he had no knowledge of the defective condition of the railing. Judgment was entered on the verdict, dismissing the complaint.]

The question on which the appeal turns is whether the trial court erred in failing to instruct the jury that Mahnke owed Pagelsdorf a duty to exercise ordinary care in maintaining the premises.

Prior to December 10, 1975, the duty of an occupier of land toward visitors on the premises was determined in Wisconsin law on a sliding scale according to the status of the visitor. * * * In Antoniewicz v. Reszcynski, 70 Wis.2d 836, 854–55, 236 N.W.2d 1, 10 (1975), we abolished, prospectively, the distinction between the different duties owed by an occupier to licensees and to invitees. * * *

The classification of visitors identified the degree of duty of the possessor or occupier of the premises. [C] When the property is leased, the duty of the landlord was controlled by a different rule: That, with certain exceptions, a landlord is not liable for injuries to his tenants and their visitors resulting from defects in the premises. [C] The general rule of nonliability was based on the concept of a lease as a conveyance of property and the consequent transfer of possession and control of the premises to the tenant. [Cc]

There are exceptions to this general rule of nonliability. * * * The rule of nonliability persists despite a decided trend away from application of the general rule and toward expansion of its exceptions. [Cc]

None of the exceptions to the general rule are applicable to the facts of this case. * * *

Therefore, if we were to follow the traditional rule, Pagelsdorf was not entitled to an instruction that Mahnke owed him a duty of ordinary care. We believe, however, that the better public policy lies in the abandonment of the general rule of nonliability and the adoption of a rule that a landlord is under a duty to exercise ordinary care in the maintenance of the premises.

Such a rule was adopted by the New Hampshire court in Sargent v. Ross, 113 N.H. 388, 308 A.2d 528 (1973). The plaintiff's four-year-old child fell to her death from an outdoor stairway of a residential building owned by the defendant. In a wrongful death action against the landlord, the plaintiff claimed the stairs were too steep and the railing inadequate. The jury awarded the plaintiff damages, and the landlord appealed from a judgment entered on the verdict. After eliminating the established exceptions to the rule of nonliability, the court concluded that the rule had nothing to recommend itself in a contemporary, urban society and ought to be abandoned. Instead, general principles of negligence should apply. The court stated that the " 'quasi-sovereignty of the landowner' " had its genesis in "agrarian England of the dark ages." [C] Whatever justification the rule might once have had, there no longer seemed to be any reason to except landlords from a general duty of exercising ordinary care to prevent foreseeable harm. The court reasoned that the modern trend away from special immunities in tort law and the recognition of an implied warranty of habitability in an apartment lease transaction argued in favor of abolishing the common law rule of nonliability. Accordingly, a landlord's conduct should be appraised according to negligence principles. Questions of control, hidden defects, and common use would be relevant only as bearing on the general determination of negligence, including foreseeability and unreasonableness of the risk of harm.

In *Antoniewicz,* [c] we cited *Sargent* as one of many cases whose reasoning supported the abolition of the common law distinctions between licensees and invitees. The policies supporting our decision to abandon these distinctions concerning a land occupier's duty toward his visitors compel us, in the instant case, to abrogate the landlord's general cloak of immunity toward his tenants and their visitors. Having recognized that modern social conditions no longer support special exceptions for land occupiers, it is but a short step to hold that there is no remaining basis for a general rule of nonliability for landlords. Arguably, the landlord's relinquishment of possession, and consequently control of the premises, removes this case from the sweep of the policies embodied in *Antoniewicz.* We are not so persuaded. One of the basic principles of our tort law is that one is liable for injuries resulting from conduct foreseeably creating an unreasonable risk to others. [C] Public policy limitations on the application of this principle are shrinking. [Cc]

The modern-day apartment lease is regarded as a contract, not a conveyance. Pines v. Perssion, 14 Wis.2d 590, 111 N.W.2d 409 (1961). In *Pines* we determined that modern social conditions called for judicial recognition of a warranty of habitability implied in an apartment lease. * * *

It would be anomalous indeed to require a landlord to keep his premises in good repair as an implied condition of the lease, yet immunize him from liability for injuries resulting from his failure to do so. We conclude that there is no remaining justification for the landlord's general cloak of common law immunity and hereby abolish the general common law principle of nonliability of landlords toward persons injured as a result of their defective premises. * * *

At trial plaintiffs' counsel requested the jury be instructed that Mahnke owed Pagelsdorf, as his invitee, a duty of ordinary care. Pagelsdorf's proposed special verdict inquired whether Mahnke was "negligent in failing to keep the guardrail in question in a reasonably good state of repair." Thus Pagelsdorf preserved the assigned error for appeal. We simply reach the result he seeks by a different means. [C] * * *

Generally, a decision overruling or repudiating other cases is given retrospective operation. [C] The rule of landlords' nonliability was riddled with many exceptions; thus reliance on the rule could not have been great. [C] We find no reason to depart from the general rule of retrospective operation of the mandate herein.

In conclusion, a landlord owes his tenant or anyone on the premises with the tenant's consent a duty to exercise ordinary care. If a person lawfully on the premises is injured as a result of the landlord's negligence in maintaining the premises, he is entitled to recover from the landlord under general negligence principles. Issues of notice of the defect, its obviousness, control of the premises, and so forth are all relevant only insofar as they bear on the ultimate question: Did the landlord exercise ordinary care in the maintenance of the premises under all the circumstances?

Judgment reversed and cause remanded for proceedings consistent with this opinion.

NOTES AND QUESTIONS

1. Except for early holdings in Tennessee—e.g., Wilcox v. Hines, 100 Tenn. 538, 46 S.W. 297 (1898)—Sargent v. Ross, 113 N.H. 388, 308 A.2d 528 (1973), set forth in the principal case, is the first to apply the general negligence principle to lessors. See also Brennan v. Cockrell Inv. Co., 35 Cal.App.3d 796, 111 Cal.Rptr. 122 (1973); Young v. Garwacki, 380 Mass. 162, 402 N.E.2d 1045 (1980); Mansur v. Eubanks, 401 So.2d 1328 (Fla.1981); Stephens v. Stearns, 106 Idaho 249, 678 P.2d 41 (1984); Turpel v. Sayles, 101 Nev. 35, 692 P.2d 1290 (1985); Favreau v. Miller, 156 Vt. 222, 591 A.2d 68 (1991). But cf. Francis v. Pic, 226 N.W.2d 654 (N.D.1975). The new rule has gradually collected adherents. What is your opinion of the ultimate outcome? Is it Rowland v. Christian revisited, or are the problems materially different?

2. As indicated in the principal case, a number of courts in recent years have utilized an "implied warranty of habitability" to create a duty on the part of the lessor to deliver the premises in a habitable condition. See Knight v. Hallsthammar, 29 Cal.3d 46, 623 P.2d 268, 171 Cal.Rptr. 707 (1981); Lemle v. Breeden, 51 Haw. 426, 462 P.2d 470 (1969); Marini v. Ireland, 56 N.J. 130, 265 A.2d 526 (1970). These decisions provided tenants only with a defense to an eviction action or a right to withhold rent until repairs were made. They did not necessarily mean that the general limitation on a landlord's duty in tort was abolished. And see Restatement (Second) of Property § 17.6.

3. In Becker v. IRM Corp., 38 Cal. 3d 454, 698 P.2d 116 (1985), the California Supreme Court took the next step imposing strict liability to landlords for injuries caused by latent structural defects in the premises. The decision attracted a firestorm of criticism and was repudiated in Peterson v. Superior Court of Riverside

County, 10 Cal. 4th 1185, 899 P.2d 905 (1995) (holding that a tenant could not reasonably expect a landlord to have eliminated defects of which the landlord was unaware and which would have not been disclosed by a reasonable inspection).

4. Efforts by lessors to immunize themselves against liability through exculpatory clauses in leases have been held to be void as against public policy, at least insofar as they seek to immunize lessors against damages caused by negligence in maintaining common areas. Cappaert v. Junker, 413 So.2d 378 (Miss.1982).

5. What damages should be available to lessees for lessor's negligence? In Simon v. Solomon, 385 Mass. 91, 431 N.E.2d 556 (1982), the court upheld damages to the tenant for emotional distress caused by the landlord's substandard maintenance of her apartment, after evidence showed that water and sewage from an adjoining area flooded her basement apartment approximately 30 times. In a similar vein, see 49 Prospect Street Tenants Ass'n v. Sheva Gardens, 227 N.J. Super. 449, 547 A.2d 1134 (App.Div.1988), affirming jury award for emotional distress where the landlord of rent controlled premises failed to maintain utility services, rid the building of vermin, repair broken windows and evict squatters. Do you see an appropriate role for tort law in these circumstances?

Kline v. 1500 Massachusetts Ave. Apartment Corp.

United States Court of Appeals, District of Columbia Circuit, 1970.
141 U.S.App.D.C. 370, 439 F.2d 477.

[Plaintiff Sarah B. Kline, a lessee of defendant, sustained serious injuries when she was criminally assaulted and robbed at approximately 10:15 P.M. while she was in the common hallway of a large (585–unit) combination office-apartment building. Although a doorman had been employed in the past, the entrances to the building were left unguarded at the time plaintiff was assaulted. This procedure was followed in spite of the fact that defendant lessor had notice of an increasing number of assaults, larcenies and robberies being perpetrated against the tenants in and from the common hallways of the building.]

WILKEY, CIRCUIT JUDGE. The appellee apartment corporation states that there is "only one issue presented for review * * * whether a duty should be placed on a landlord to take steps to protect tenants from foreseeable criminal acts committed by third parties". The District Court as a matter of law held that there is no such duty. We find that there is, and that in the circumstances here the applicable standard of care was breached. We therefore reverse and remand to the District Court for the determination of damages for the appellant. * * *

In this jurisdiction, certain duties have been assigned to the landlord because of his *control* of common hallways, lobbies, stairwells, etc., used by all tenants in multiple dwelling units. * * *

While [prior cases have] dealt with a physical defect in the building leading to plaintiff's injury, the rationale as applied to predictable criminal acts by third parties is the same. The duty is the landlord's because by his control of the areas of common use and common danger he is the only party who has the *power* to make the necessary repairs or to provide the necessary protection.

As a general rule, a private person does not have a duty to protect another from a criminal attack by a third person. We recognize that this rule has sometimes in the past been applied in landlord-tenant law, even by this court. Among the reasons for the application of this rule to landlords are: judicial reluctance to tamper with the traditional common law concept of the landlord-tenant relationship; the notion that the act of a third person in committing an intentional tort or crime is a superseding cause of the harm to another resulting therefrom; the oftentimes difficult problem of determining foreseeability of criminal acts; the vagueness of the standard which the landlord must meet; the economic consequences of the imposition of the duty; and conflict with the public policy allocating the duty of protecting citizens from criminal acts to the government rather than the private sector.

But the rationale of this very broad general rule falters when it is applied to the conditions of modern day urban apartment living, particularly in the circumstances of this case. The rationale of the general rule exonerating a third party from any duty to protect another from a criminal attack has no applicability to the landlord-tenant relationship in multiple dwelling houses. The landlord is no insurer of his tenants' safety, but he certainly is no bystander. And where, as here, the landlord has notice of repeated criminal assaults and robberies, has notice that these crimes occurred in the portion of the premises exclusively within his control, has every reason to expect like crimes to happen again, and has the exclusive power to take preventive action, it does not seem unfair to place upon the landlord a duty to take those steps which are within his power to minimize the predictable risk to his tenants. * * *

[I]nnkeepers have been held liable for assaults which have been committed upon their guests by third parties, if they have breached a duty which is imposed by reason of the innkeeper-guest relationship. By this duty, the innkeeper is generally bound to exercise reasonable care to protect the guest from abuse or molestation from third parties, be they innkeeper's employees, fellow guests, or intruders, if the attack could, or in the exercise of reasonable care, should have been anticipated.

Liability in the innkeeper-guest relationship is based as a matter of law either upon the innkeeper's supervision, care, or control of the premises, or by reason of a contract which some courts have implied from the entrustment by the guest of his personal comfort and safety to the innkeeper. In the latter analysis, the contract is held to give the guest the right to expect a standard of treatment at the hands of the innkeeper which includes an obligation on the part of the latter to exercise reasonable care in protecting the guest.

Other relationships in which similar duties have been imposed include landowner-invitee, businessman-patron, employer-employee, school district-pupil, hospital-patient, and carrier-passenger. In all, the theory of liability is essentially the same: that since the ability of one of the parties to provide for his own protection has been limited in some way by his submission to the control of the other, a duty should be imposed upon the one possessing control (and thus the power to act) to take reasonable precautions to protect the other one from assaults by third parties which, at least, could reasonably have been anticipated. * * *

As between tenant and landlord, the landlord is the only one in the position to take the necessary acts of protection required. He is not an insurer, but he is obligated to minimize the risk to his tenants. Not only as between landlord and tenant is the landlord best equipped to guard against the predictable risk of intruders, but even as between landlord and the police power of government, the landlord is in the best position to take the necessary protective measures. * * *

We * * * hold in this case that the applicable standard of care in providing protection for the tenant is that standard which this landlord himself was employing in October 1959 when the appellant became a resident on the premises at 1500 Massachusetts Avenue. * * * [W]e hold that the same relative degree of security should have been maintained. * * *

Having said this, it would be well to state what is not said by this decision. We do not hold that the landlord is by any means an insurer of the safety of his tenants. His duty is to take those measures of protection which are within his power and capacity to take, and which can reasonably be expected to mitigate the risk of intruders assaulting and robbing tenants. The landlord is not expected to provide protection commonly owed by a municipal police department; but as illustrated in this case, he is obligated to protect those parts of his premises which are not usually subject to periodic patrol and inspection by the municipal police. We do not say that every multiple unit apartment house in the District of Columbia should have those same measures of protection which 1500 Massachusetts Avenue enjoyed in 1959, nor do we say that 1500 Massachusetts Avenue should have precisely those same measures in effect at the present time. Alternative and more up-to-date methods may be equally or even more effective. * * *

The landlord is entirely justified in passing on the cost of increased protective measures to his tenants, but the rationale of compelling the landlord to do it in the first place is that he is the only one who is in a position to take the necessary protective measures for overall protection of the premises, which he owns in whole and rents in part to individual tenants.

Reversed and remanded to the District Court for the determination of damages.

[MACKINNON, J., dissented.]

NOTES AND QUESTIONS

1. How important is the fact that the assault occurred in a common passage-way? Suppose the attacker had waited outside Mrs. Kline's apartment, forced his way in and attacked her in the living room. Liability? Cf. Wassell v. Adams, 865 F.2d 849 (7th Cir.1989) (plaintiff assaulted when she opened her motel door late at

night). How does *Kline* differ from those holding a landlord liable when a tenant trips on a defective condition in a common hallway?

2. Prior to the 1970s, the courts would find no duty obligation in the instant case. See Goldberg v. Hous. Auth. of Newark, 38 N.J. 578, 186 A.2d 291 (1962); Bass v. New York, 38 A.D.2d 407, 330 N.Y.S.2d 569 (1972), aff'd, 32 N.Y.2d 894, 300 N.E.2d 154, 346 N.Y.S.2d 814 (1973) (municipally-owned dwelling treated as privately owned); Daniels v. Shell Oil Co., 485 S.W.2d 948 (Tex.Civ.App.1972). Some courts adhere to the no duty rule, unless the landlord actively "assumes a duty": Feld v. Merriam, 506 Pa. 383, 485 A.2d 742 (1984). The main arguments against imposing that duty are stated in the principal case. Also, it is said that a tenant makes a choice as to where to live and in effect "assumes the risk" of injury from criminal elements in a low security building. What about the contention that the *Kline* decision places the cost of crime on those who can least afford it—the rent-paying tenants? Who is in the better position to take measures against these criminal activities?

3. Today there are several decisions finding the landlord liable to tenant or its employee or agent for an attack by a third person when the attack was foreseeable and reasonable steps to increase security would have prevented it. See Graham v. M. & J. Corp., 424 A.2d 103 (D.C.App.1980); Holley v. Mt. Zion Terrace Apts., 382 So.2d 98 (Fla.1980); Jardel Co. v. Hughes, 523 A.2d 518 (Del.1987); and Lay v. Dworman, 732 P.2d 455 (Okl.1986). A few courts have extended the warranty of habitability to include security. See Trentacost v. Brussel, 82 N.J. 214, 412 A.2d 436 (1980); Secretary of HUD v. Layfield, 88 Cal.App.3d Supp. 28, 152 Cal.Rptr. 342 (1978); Brownstein v. Edison, 103 Misc.2d 316, 425 N.Y.S.2d 773 (1980). In Isaacs v. Huntington Memorial Hospital, 38 Cal.3d 112, 695 P.2d 653, 211 Cal.Rptr. 356 (1985), evidence of similar incidents in order to establish foreseeability, although relevant, was found not to be essential. But cf. Ann M. v. Pacific Plaza Shopping Center, 6 Cal.4th 666, 863 P.2d 207, 25 Cal.Rptr.2d 137 (1993) (reinterpreting *Isaacs* to require that a duty be predicated upon "a high degree of foreseeability."). However, the Kansas Supreme Court in Seibert v. Vic Regnier Buildings, Inc., 253 Kan. 540, 856 P.2d 1332 (1993), adopted the *Isaacs* test that the duty should turn on foreseeability as drawn from the totality of the circumstances. *Seibert* was followed by the Supreme Court of Tennessee in another parking lot shooting case, McClung v. Delta Square Ltd. Pshp. 937 S.W.2d 891 (1996) (holding that an important ingredient in the foreseeability test is the magnitude of the risk and the steps that may be taken against it).

4. If a duty to protect tenants is established, an obvious problem is defining the extent of that obligation. What was defendant supposed to do in the principal case? In Johnston v. Harris, 387 Mich. 569, 198 N.W.2d 409 (1972), an elderly tenant was assaulted as he reached for the doorknob to his apartment in defendant's four-unit apartment building. The building was located in a high crime area. In Sherman v. Concourse Realty Corp., 47 A.D.2d 134, 365 N.Y.S.2d 239 (1975), the landlord of a 200–tenant multiple dwelling removed a lock cylinder from the building's security buzzer system which had been installed as a condition for a rent increase. Plaintiff-tenant was assaulted by an intruder.

5. Should the liability imposed on landlords be extended to condominium boards and their members? See Frances T. v. Village Green Owners Ass'n, 42 Cal.3d 490, 723 P.2d 573, 229 Cal.Rptr. 456 (1986).

CHAPTER X

DAMAGES

Many law students take a separate course in Remedies that will cover the issues in this chapter in more detail and will cover other damages issues not relevant to tort law. For additional discussion of damages topics see Dobbs, The Law of Remedies (2d ed. 1993). Because the valuation of the plaintiff's injuries is integral to the operation of the tort system, it is important to at least get an overview of some of the specific damages issues in tort litigation.

Proof of damages is an essential part of plaintiff's causes of action in negligence and strict liability, stemming historically from the actions on the case. In these actions, damage is the gist of the action. Recall that elsewhere, in actions based on trespass—the intentional torts—the cause of action is complete upon showing an invasion of the protected interest. Nevertheless, whether the plaintiff's skull was fractured by a deliberate blow, an act of negligence, or a product that was defectively designed, the amount of damages the defendant will have to pay to compensate the plaintiff for the skull fracture is the same.

The question of how much damage plaintiff suffered is often at the heart of the dispute between plaintiff and defendant. In the course of settlement negotiations, defendant may be willing to concede the issue of liability, but vigorously dispute the amount plaintiff is claiming for damages. Also, a good deal of trial time and effort is devoted to the topic of how much plaintiff should recover.

Some matters already considered in the chapter on duty (such as the question whether plaintiff can recover for negligent infliction of emotional harm) and the chapters on causation (was the injury for which plaintiff seeks compensation caused by the defendant) also can be viewed as damages questions. In this chapter, it is assumed that a duty has been breached, that plaintiff has been injured, and that the law would allow some monetary recovery. The question here is deceptively simple: how much?

As part of the "tort reform" movement during the decade of the 1980's, over half the states passed legislation affecting the common law of damages in some way. In order to understand and appreciate the effect of this legislation, you must first consider the traditional scheme of tort damages. Let us begin with some basic vocabulary and some underlying themes.

NOTES AND QUESTIONS

There are three basic kinds of damages in tort law:

1. *Nominal Damages.* These consist of a small sum of money awarded to the plaintiff in order to vindicate rights, make the judgment available as a matter of record in order to prevent the defendant from acquiring prescriptive rights, and carry a part of the costs of the action. The amount of the award, so long as it is trivial, is unimportant.

2. *Compensatory Damages.* These are intended to represent the closest possible financial equivalent of the loss or harm suffered by the plaintiff, to make the plaintiff whole again, to restore the plaintiff to the position the plaintiff was in before the tort occurred. Most of this chapter is concerned with these damages.

3. *Punitive Damages.* These are an additional sum, over and above the compensation of the plaintiff, awarded in order to punish the defendant, to make an example of defendant, and to deter defendant and others engaging in similar tortious conduct.

4. As you read the next two principal cases, think about how the lawyers used the discovery process to develop the information on damages and how it was presented, through the testimony of lay and expert witnesses.

1. PERSONAL INJURIES

maximum recovery rule

Anderson v. Sears, Roebuck & Co.

United States District Court, Eastern District of Louisiana, 1974.
377 F.Supp. 136.

[Plaintiff Helen Britain, a young child, was severely burned when her home was completely consumed by fire. The blaze was triggered by a heater that was found to be negligently manufactured by defendant Sears and defendant Controls Company of America. The jury awarded plaintiff $2,000,000 in compensatory damages and defendants moved for a remittitur of that verdict.]

CASSIBRY, DISTRICT JUDGE. The legal standard on which to gauge a jury verdict for remittitur purposes is the "maximum recovery rule". [Cc] This rule directs the trial judge to determine whether the verdict of the jury exceeds the maximum amount which the jury could reasonably find and if it does, the trial judge may then reduce the verdict to the highest amount that the jury could properly have awarded. Functionally, the maximum recovery rule both preserves the constitutionally protected role of the jury as finder of facts and prevents the predilections of the judge from infecting the jury's determination. Thus, the court's task is to ascertain, by scrutinizing all of the evidence as to each element of damages, what amount would be the maximum the jury could have reasonably awarded. In this case there are five cardinal elements of damages; past physical and mental pain; future physical and mental pain; future medical expenses; loss of earning capacity and permanent disability and disfigurement.

Past Physical and Mental Pain. The infant child Helen Britain, was almost burned to death in the tragic fire that swept her home. She was burned over forty per cent of her entire body; third degree burns cover eighty per cent of her scalp and second and third degree burns of the trunk and of her extremities account for the remainder. Helen Britain's immediate post-trauma treatment required hospitalization for twenty-eight days, during which time the child developed pneumonia, required numerous transfusions, suffered fever, vomiting, diarrhea, and infection, and underwent skin graft surgery, under general anesthesia, to her scalp, which was only partially successful. Keloid scarring caused webbing and ankylosis of the child's extremities and severely limited their motion. The child's fingers became adhered together; scarring bent the arm at the elbow in a burdensome, fixed position; and thick scarring on the thighs and on the side of and behind the knees impaired walking.

This child had to undergo subsequent hospitalizations for further major operations and treatment. The second major operation under general anesthesia was undertaken to graft new skin from the back and stomach to the remaining bare areas of the scalp. The third operation under general anesthesia was an attempt to relieve the deformity of her left hand caused by the webbing scars which bound down the fingers of that hand. A fourth operation under general anesthesia was performed to reduce scars which had grown back on the left hand again webbing the fingers. I cannot envisage the breadth and intensity of the pain experienced by Helen Britain throughout this ordeal.

The undisputed testimony reveals that one of the most tragic aspects of this case is that the horrible mental and emotional trauma caused to this child occurred at an age which medical experts maintain is crucial to a child's entire psyche and personality formation. Helen Britain's persistent emotional and mental disturbance is evidenced by bed wetting, nightmares, refusing to sleep alone, withdrawal, and speech impediments. Dr. Cyril Phillips, a psychiatrist, and Dr. Diamond both indicated that the child manifested to them, even at this early age, emotional illness and retarded mental growth.

The evidence reflects that an award of six hundred thousand dollars for this element of damages alone would not be unreasonable.

Future Physical and Mental Pain. There is clear evidence that the stretching, pulling, and breaking down of scars inherent in growth will continue to cause severe pain and a crippling limitation of motion in varying degrees to all of Helen Britain's upper and lower extremities. Very little can be done to improve the condition of the scalp which will never be able to breathe, sweat or grow hair. There will be risks, trauma and pain, both physical and mental, with each of the recommended twenty-seven future operations which will extend over most of the child's adult life, if she is in fact fortunate enough to be able to risk undergoing these recommended surgeries. Furthermore, Helen Britain must vigilantly guard against irritation, infection and further injury to the damaged and abnormal skin, scars and grafts because any injury, however slight, can generate cancer in these adynamic areas.

The inherent stresses and tensions of each new phase of life will severely tax this little girl's debilitated and delicate mental and emotional capacity. Throughout her future life expectancy of seventy-five years, it is reasonable to expect, that she will be deprived of a normal social life and that she will never find a husband and raise a family. On top of this, Helen Britain will always be subjected to rejection, stares and tactless inquiries from children and adults.

The court concludes that an award of seven hundred fifty thousand dollars for this element of damages alone would not be excessive.

Future Medical Expenses. A large award for future medical expenses is justified. The uncontradicted testimony was that Helen Britain would need the guidance, treatment and counseling of a team of doctors, including plastic surgeons, psychiatrists and sociologists, throughout her lifetime. Add to this the cost of the twenty-seven recommended operations and the cost of private tutoring necessitated by the child's mental and emotional needs and the jury could justifiably award a figure of two hundred and fifty thousand dollars to cover these future expenses.

Loss of Earning Capacity. The evidence of Helen Britain's disabilities both physical, mental and emotional was such that this court holds that the jury could properly find that these disabilities would prevent her from earning a living for the rest of her life. Not only do the physical impairments to her extremities disable her but her emotional limitations require avoiding stress and the combined effect is the permanent incapacity to maintain serious employment.

The jury was provided with actuarial figures which accurately calculated both the deduction of interest to be earned and the addition of an inflationary buffer, on any award made for future loss of earning capacity. [Italics added.] In view of these incontrovertible projections at trial, it was within the province of the jury to award as much as $330,000.00 for the loss of earning capacity.

Permanent Disability and Disfigurement. The award for this element of damage must evaluate in monetary terms the compensation due this plaintiff for the permanent physical, mental and emotional disabilities and disfigurements proved by the evidence adduced at trial. A narration treating Miss Britain's permanent disabilities and disfigurements would be lengthy and redundant; therefore, I resort to listing.

1. The complete permanent loss of 80% of the scalp caused by the destruction of sweat glands, hair follicles and tissue—all of which effects a grotesque disfigurement and freakish appearance.

2. The permanent loss of the normal use of the legs.

3. The permanent impairment of the left fingers and hand caused by recurring webbing and resulting in limited motion.

4. The permanent impairment of the right hand caused by scars and webbing of the fingers.

5. The permanent injury to the left elbow and left arm with ankylosis and resulting in a crippling deformity.

6. The permanent destruction of 40% of the normal skin. As a result of this a large portion of the body is covered by "pigskin." Pigskin resembles the dry, cracked skin of an aged person and is highly susceptible

to irritation from such ordinary things as temperature changes and washing.

7.   Permanent scars over the majority of the body where skin donor sites were removed.

8.   The permanent impairment of speech.

9.   The loss of three years of formative and impressionable childhood.

10.   Permanently reduced and impaired emotional capacity.

11.   The permanent impairment of normal social, recreational and educational life.

12.   The permanent imprint of her mother's hand on her stomach.

Considering each of the foregoing items, the court concludes that the jury had the prerogative of awarding up to $1,100,000 for this element of damages.

By totaling the estimated maximum recovery for each element of damages, the jury's actual award is placed in proper perspective. According to my calculations the maximum jury award supported by the evidence in this case could have been $2,980,000. Obviously, the jury's $2,000,000 verdict is well within the periphery established by the maximum award test.

[Defendants] argue that the introduction of photographs of the plaintiff was inflammatory. Since a part of plaintiff's claim for damages is for disfigurement and the humiliation and embarrassment resulting therefrom, I hold that these photographs were properly admitted to show the condition of the plaintiff as she appeared to others, at the time they were taken. [Cc]

The defendants suggest that the presence of the child in the courtroom and in the corridors of the courthouse in some way inflamed or prejudiced the jury. This allegation is unfounded; the defendants have not pointed out any wrongful conduct on the part of Helen Britain, her parents, or counsel for plaintiffs. Helen Britain was well behaved and quiet the entire time she was in the courtroom.

Accordingly I hold that there was not any bias, prejudice, or any other improper influence which motivated the jury in making its award.

The defendants' motions for a remittitur are denied.

Richardson v. Chapman

Supreme Court of Illinois, 1997.
175 Ill. 2d 98, 676 N.E.2d 621.

MILLER, J. * * * [Plaintiff Keva Richardson was the driver of a car with plaintiff Ann McGregor as a passenger. While they were stopped at a traffic light, their car was struck from behind by a semi-trailer driven by defendant Chapman who was employed by defendant Tandem/Carrier. At the trial, the judge directed a verdict in favor of the plaintiffs and against Chapman and his employer on the question of liability. Determining only the plaintiffs' damages, the jury returned verdicts against them in favor of Richardson and McGregor in the amounts of $22,358,814 and $102,215, respectively. The intermediate appellate court rejected the defendants' challenges to the amounts of damages awarded by the jury.]

In their initial challenge to the damages verdicts, the defendants complain of certain testimony introduced by plaintiff Richardson concerning the calculation of the present value of her future economic losses. The defendants maintain that Professor Charles Linke, who testified as Richardson's economist, improperly used non-neutral, actual figures in describing to the jury the calculation of present cash value. Richardson's life expectancy at the time of trial, in May 1990, was 54.5 years. Relying on information and figures supplied by Richardson's primary physician, Professor Linke testified that the present cash value of her future medical expenses had a lower bound of $7,371,914 and an upper bound of $9,570,-034. The lower bound figure assumed a discount rate one percentage point higher than the growth rate; the upper bound figure assumed that the two rates would be equal. The difference between the two numbers was based on different assumptions concerning future growth rates and interest rates. Professor Linke also provided testimony regarding the present cash value of Richardson's lost future earnings. Assuming a work history of 27.5 years, Professor Linke found that the present cash value of Richardson's lost income was between $854,107 and $971,944; using a longer work history of 35.8 years, Professor Linke arrived at a range of $1,068,343 to $1,265,363. Again, the differences between the two ranges were based on the witness' different assumptions regarding future growth and interest rates. * * *

In a further objection to Professor Linke's testimony, the defendants also briefly argue that the economist erroneously included inflation and real growth in reducing Richardson's economic damages to their present cash value. As we have noted, Professor Linke testified to what he termed "lower bound" and "upper bound" figures in computing the future medical expenses and lost earnings. The "lower bound" figure assumed that the prevailing interest rate would be one percentage point higher than the growth rate of wages and prices, while the "upper bound" figure assumed that the two rates would be equal. In this way, Professor Linke attempted to avoid having to predict the exact rates that would prevail; as Professor Linke explained in his testimony, it is not the absolute levels of the interest rate and growth rate that determine present cash value, but the difference between them. * * *

We conclude that Professor Linke's approach was a reasonable one; by using a differential between the two rates, he did not have to make a prediction of future growth and inflation rates. Professor Linke was consistent in his treatment of inflation, and he did not adopt a method that would undercompensate or overcompensate the plaintiff. [Cc]

The defendants next contend that the damages awarded to the plaintiffs are excessive. Before resolving this question, we will briefly summarize the evidence presented at trial regarding the two women's injuries.

Keva Richardson was 23 years old at the time of the accident. She grew up in Pampa, Texas, and received a bachelor's degree in elementary education in May 1987 from Texas Tech University. While in college, she participated in a number of athletic activities and was, by all accounts, a popular, happy person. After graduating from college, Keva obtained a position as a flight attendant with American Airlines. She planned to work in that capacity for several years before returning to school to gain a post-graduate degree in education; her ultimate goal was to teach. Keva met Ann McGregor in the flight attendant training program, and the two decided to room together upon completion of their training. At the conclusion of the program, they were assigned to the Chicago area, and they had moved there just several days before the accident occurred.

Following the accident, Keva was initially taken to Highland Park Hospital for treatment. Because of the seriousness of her injuries, however, Keva was transferred that morning to Northwestern Memorial Hospital. Dr. Giri Gereesan, an orthopedic surgeon specializing in spinal surgery, determined that Keva had incurred a fracture of the fifth cervical vertebra, which severely damaged her spinal cord and resulted in incomplete quadriplegia. Dr. Gereesan performed surgery on Keva on December 1, 1987, to stabilize her spine so that she would be able to support her head; the surgery did not repair the damage to her spinal cord, and no treatment exists that could do so.

Keva was transferred to the Rehabilitation Institute of Chicago in December 1987, where she came under the care of Dr. Gary Yarkony. Keva was initially dependent on others in all aspects of her daily life. At the Rehabilitation Institute she learned how to perform a number of basic tasks, such as sitting in a wheelchair, transferring from a bed to a wheelchair, brushing her teeth, washing her face, and putting on loose-fitting tops. Keva's initial stay at the Rehabilitation Institute lasted until April 1988, when she moved to her parents' home in Texas. Keva returned to the Rehabilitation Institute in 1988 and in 1989 for follow-up visits. Keva also required hospitalization in Texas on three subsequent occasions for treatment of conditions arising from the accident.

Testifying in Keva's behalf at trial, Dr. Gary Yarkony, who had served as her primary physician at the Rehabilitation Institute, described Keva's current condition. He explained that she cannot use her legs and that she has only limited functioning in her arms, with loss of control of her fingers and fine muscles in her hands. She suffers pain in her legs and shoulders. Her chest and abdomen are paralyzed, and she has restrictive pulmonary disease. In addition, she has no control over her bladder or bowel functions and requires assistance in emptying them. As a consequence of her physical condition, she is at risk for bladder infections, pneumonia, and pressure ulcers. Keva also suffered a number of facial injuries in the accident. Some of these scars were later repaired through plastic surgery, but others remain.

At trial, Keva's mother, Dixie Richardson, described her daughter's current activities and the level of care necessary to assist her in her daily routine. Keva requires help in taking a shower and getting dressed. She cannot put on underwear, socks, or pants by herself but is able to put on pullover shirts and sweaters. With assistance, she can brush her teeth, apply makeup, and put in her contact lenses. She is unable to cut food or button a sweater. She can push her wheelchair on a smooth, level surface but otherwise needs assistance. In her own testimony, Keva said that she is self-conscious about her appearance now and the impression she makes on others. She said that the thing she misses most is just being able to get up in the morning and begin her day; now she requires the assistance of others, throughout the day.

The jury awarded Richardson a total of $22,358,814 in damages, divided among the following six elements: $258,814 for past medical care; $11,000,000 for future medical care; $900,000 for past and future lost earnings; $3,500,000 for disability; $2,100,000 for disfigurement; and $4,600,000 for pain and suffering. In challenging Richardson's award of damages, the defendants first argue that the sum of the future medical costs found by the jury-$11,000,000–is not supported by the evidence, for it exceeds even the larger of the two figures supplied by Professor Linke, $9,570,034. The defendants contend that the decision to award Richardson nearly $1.5 million more illustrates the jury's failure to properly determine damages in this case.

In response, Richardson argues that the larger award may simply be attributable to the jury's decision to make an award of expenses that she is likely to incur in the future but that were not specifically included in the calculations performed by Professor Linke. Richardson notes that Dr. Yarkony, in compiling for Linke's use the list of likely future medical costs, did not assign specific values to certain items, such as the expenses of future hospitalizations and the costs of wheelchairs and a specially equipped van. Richardson thus argues that the jury's decision to award an amount for future medical costs greater than Professor Linke's higher estimate might simply reflect the jury's desire to compensate her for those unspecified but likely expenses. We agree with Richardson that the trier of fact enjoys a certain degree of leeway in awarding compensation for medical costs that, as shown by the evidence, are likely to arise in the future but are not specifically itemized in the testimony. [Cc] In the present case, however, the amount awarded by the jury for future medical costs is nearly $1.5 million more than the higher of the two figures claimed at trial by Richardson. Notably, Professor Linke did not rely on the projections by the General Accounting Office (GAO) of the growth of future medical care costs, mentioned in the partial concurrence. Professor Linke explained that the GAO's study included a large number of technology-based items, while the main expense to be incurred by Richardson will be wages for attendant care. Given the disparity between the trial testimony and the jury's eventual award, we will not attribute the entire difference between those sums simply to miscellaneous costs Richardson is likely to incur in the future. For these reasons, we conclude that it is appropriate, by way of remittitur, to reduce by $1 million the nearly $1.5 million differential between the award for Richardson's future medical expenses and the higher figure presented in the testimony. This adjustment allows Richardson recovery for expected future medical costs for which no specific estimates were introduced, yet is not so large that it represents a departure from the trial testimony.

We do not agree with the defendants, however, that the remainder of the award of damages to Richardson, including the sums for pain and suffering, disability, and disfigurement, is duplicative or excessive or lacks support in the record. The determination of damages is a question reserved to the trier of fact, and a reviewing court will not lightly substitute its opinion for the judgment rendered in the trial court. [Cc] An award of damages will be deemed excessive if it falls outside the range of fair and reasonable compensation or results from passion or prejudice, or if it is so large that it shocks the judicial conscience. [C] When reviewing an award of compensatory damages for a nonfatal injury, a court may consider, among other things, the permanency of the plaintiff's condition, the possibility of future deterioration, the extent of the plaintiff's medical expenses, and the restrictions imposed on the plaintiff by the injuries. [C]

Here, it was the jury's function to consider the credibility of the witnesses and to determine an appropriate award of damages. We cannot say that the present award to Richardson is the result of passion or prejudice, "shocks the conscience," or lacks support in the evidence. The record shows that Richardson suffered devastating, disabling injuries as a consequence of the accident. The defendants urge us to compare Richardson's damages with amounts awarded in other cases. Courts in this state, however, have traditionally declined to make such comparisons in determining whether a particular award is excessive [cc], and we do not believe that such comparisons would be helpful here.

The defendants also contend that the jury's award of damages to Ann McGregor is excessive. McGregor was 22 years old at the time of the accident. She grew up in Houston, Texas, and graduated from Southern Methodist University in May 1987 with a degree in psychology. Like Keva Richardson, McGregor was accepted after graduation for a position as a flight attendant with American Airlines. As mentioned earlier, the two women met while enrolled in the flight attendant training program and were sharing an apartment in the Chicago area at the time of the accident. Following the accident, McGregor was taken to Highland Park Hospital, where she was treated and released that day; she was then off work for about two weeks. A laceration she suffered on her forehead eventually healed, with only minimal scarring. At trial McGregor testified that she continues to suffer from nightmares about the accident. The jury awarded McGregor a total of $102,215 in damages, divided among the following components: $1,615 for past medical expenses, $600 for lost earnings, and $100,000 for pain and suffering.

* * * [W]e believe that the award of $100,000 for pain and suffering is, in these circumstances, excessive. McGregor was not seriously injured in the accident, incurring a laceration on her forehead, which left only a slight scar. The jury declined to award McGregor any compensation for disfigure-

ment; rather, the bulk of her recovery consisted of compensation for pain and suffering. We conclude that a more appropriate figure for pain and suffering would be $50,000, which would reduce her total damages to $52,215. By way of remittitur, we accordingly reduce the judgment entered in favor of McGregor and against Tandem/Carrier and Chapman to that amount.

[The court then ruled on various matters relating to contribution and indemnity issues among the defendants.]

For the reasons stated, the judgment of the appellate court is affirmed in part, reversed in part, and vacated in part, and the judgment of the circuit court of Cook County is affirmed in part, reversed in part, and vacated in part. * * * In the absence of consent to the entry of a remittitur by each plaintiff within 21 days of the filing of this opinion or any further period in which the mandate is stayed, her individual action will be remanded to the circuit court of Cook County for a new trial on the question of damages. * * *

McMorrow, J., concurring in part and dissenting in part: I concur in the opinion of my colleagues in all but one respect: I do not agree with the majority that it is proper to order a remittitur of the jury's award of damages to Keva Richardson for present cash value of future medical expenses or the jury's award to Ann MacGregor for pain and suffering.

In determining the total verdict awarded to Richardson, the jury considered extensive evidence relating to six separate components of damages. As noted by the majority, Richardson "suffered devastating, disabling injuries." The appellate court majority's unpublished opinion describes her condition: "After the collision, doctors determined that the communication connection between Richardson's brain and the rest of her body had become severed and she was rendered a quadriplegic. Richardson was soon placed in traction with tongs affixed to her skull by driving screws into the side of her head. She was also placed in a roto-rest bed with 25 pounds weights attached to her body for traction. Eventually, Richardson underwent surgery to stabilize her spine so it could support the weight of her head which hung like a rag doll's head. In that operation, bone from her hips was grafted to her cervical spine with the use of metal plates and screws. The surgery did not repair the injury to Richardson's spinal cord, nor does medical technology yet exist to rectify the injury."

Other evidence related Richardson's need for assistance every six hours to empty her bladder by catheterization and daily assistance to empty her bowel, over which she permanently lacks control. She has lost the use of her legs, fingers, and the fine muscles of her hand. Her chest and abdomen are paralyzed. She is subject to risk of serious infections and other conditions and, according to the evidence, having a child would be life-threatening. The appellate court opinion further stated that Richardson "may expect to be hospitalized on a regular basis for the balance of her life."

The jury awarded $11 million to compensate Richardson for her future medical needs. To this sum the majority applies a remittitur of $1 million, based on the majority's observation that the jury's award for this element of damages exceeded by $1.5 million the testimony of economist Charles Linke regarding the "upper bound" of the present cash value of Richardson's future medical needs. Linke explained that he calculated a "lower bound" present value ($7.4 million) and an "upper bound" present value ($9.5 million). His figures were derived from different assumptions regarding the relationship of the rate of interest to the rate of growth. In explaining his economic assumptions and methods, Linke also noted that there were different accounting methods that could be used to calculate Richardson's future medical needs. The one he employed yielded a more conservative figure for medical care than that used by the General Accounting Office, which, according to Linke, would yield the conclusion that "the present value of Keva Richardson's care needs would be approximately 12.1 million dollars."

In assuming that the $9.5 million "upper bound" figure represents the maximum amount that is sustained by the evidence with respect to Richardson's future medical expenses, the majority opinion fails to acknowledge that the information upon which Linke based his calculation of present cash value of future medical expenses represented Richardson's minimum care needs for the rest of her life. Dr. Yarkony, upon whose testimony Linke's economic analysis was based, detailed the specific types of medical expenses that Richardson would be expected to need in the coming years. Dr. Yarkony testified, "This is the basic minimum care not covering any hospital admissions for emergencies, complications, and the like." He further testified that in his opinion Richardson would continue to require hospitalizations in the future caused by complications related to her spinal cord injury, including infections, pressure sores, pneumonia, and blood clots.

Notwithstanding the above testimony of Linke and Dr. Yarkony, the majority determines that the jury improperly affixed damages for future medical costs in an amount exceeding the experts' estimates by $1.5 million. The majority concedes that the jury could properly compensate Richardson for medical costs not otherwise included in the experts' calculations. The majority permits one third of the excess award to stand, and concludes that $500,000, rather than $1.5 million, represents the appropriate additional sum the jury could award in excess of Linke's upper bound estimate of $9.5 million. In so holding, the majority usurps the jury's function and substitutes its own judgment regarding what is reasonable and fairly supported by the expert economic and medical evidence with respect to the present value of Richardson's future medical costs. The majority's application of remittitur in the case at bar thereby operates as an arbitrary limitation on the jury's ability to assess the evidence. * * *

Nothing in the record or the itemized jury verdict indicates that the jury departed from its customary duty to weigh the evidence and assess damages that would fairly compensate Richardson for her permanent and disabling injuries. The jury's award for future medical expenses, which arguably exceeded certain testimony, does not warrant the conclusion that the jury's determination was a departure from the flexible range of damages that was reasonably supported by the facts. There is no indication that the jury's award was the product of passion or prejudice. In fact, with respect to a different component of damages, i.e, Richardson's past and future lost earnings, the jury awarded a sum that was $1.265 million less than the higher of the testimonial estimates presented for that item of damages. If experts' estimates of a person's future income losses or medical expenses were an exact science capable of mathematical precision, there would be no need to have a jury make the final determination of proven damages. * * *

Similarly, I depart from the majority's holding that Ann MacGregor's damages award of $100,000 for pain and suffering was excessive. The majority orders a remittitur of $50,000 as a "more appropriate figure for pain and suffering." [C] The majority appears to base its conclusion on the relatively minor injury MacGregor sustained, noting that she suffered a laceration on her forehead that healed with only minimal scarring. Although the majority views the award of $100,000 as overly generous for a facial laceration that did not result in permanent disfigurement, the majority substitutes its own subjective judgment for the jury's evaluation of the evidence. The record indicates that MacGregor's lacerated forehead took six months to heal. The record further indicates that she suffered ongoing trauma, including recurrent nightmares resulting from the rear-end collision that left the other occupant of the car a quadriplegic. The jury, as finder of fact, had the superior ability to assess the evidence, including MacGregor's testimony relating to her traumatic and painful experience. I am aware of no sound reason to nullify the function of the jury and arbitrarily reduce MacGregor's award for pain and suffering to $50,000. Therefore, I cannot concur in the reasoning or result of the majority with respect to the reduction by remittitur of both plaintiffs' verdicts.

For the reasons stated, I concur in part and dissent in part from the judgment of the majority.

JUSTICE FREEMAN joins in this partial concurrence and partial dissent.

NOTES AND QUESTIONS

1. The principal cases present a catalogue of many of the major elements of damages in a personal injury case. How much time and thought did plaintiff's attorney devote to developing proof of these items? See O'Quinn, Common Elements of Recovery in Personal Injury Cases, 18 S.Tex.L.J. 179 (1977). Although both cases were based on negligence, similar items of damage can occur in actions based on intentional torts or strict liability.

2. The court in the *Anderson* case rejected defendants' argument that the child's presence inflamed or prejudiced the jury. Generally, a party is entitled to attend the trial and will be excluded only if there is disruptive conduct. Cary v. Oneok, Inc., 940 P.2d 201 (Okla.1997) (new trial ordered in case involving six-year-

old burn victim who had been excluded from the courtroom during the liability phase of the case).

3.   In the *Richardson* case, note the difference in detail between the majority's and the dissent's description of plaintiffs' injuries and treatment. The dissent added detail from the appellate court opinion which, in turn, was gleaned from the trial transcript. Keep in mind when you are reading appellate opinions that their summary of testimony below is often cooler and more detached than the way it actually was given at the trial court level. In terms of strategy, do you think plaintiff McGregor benefitted from joining her claim with plaintiff Richardson or would she have been better off bringing it separately?

4.   Note the courts' recitation of the standard in each of the jurisdictions for granting a new trial based on the amount of the damages. See notes 21–23.

5.   *Evidence of Damages.* Proof of damages is an essential part of plaintiff's cause of action, whether based on intentional conduct, negligence, or strict liability. There have been extensive developments over the past few decades in techniques for presenting this proof. For example, attorneys have made growing use of what is called "demonstrative evidence." This form of evidence consists of tangible items such as charts, photographs, motion pictures and models. The purpose of this evidence is to bring home to the jury the total extent of plaintiff's injury. Much of this was set in motion by San Francisco attorney Melvin M. Belli, who empirically showed how demonstrative evidence might greatly enlarge the amount of a plaintiff's verdict. See Belli, Demonstrative Evidence and the Adequate Award, 22 Miss.L.J. 284 (1951). This development has not gone without criticism, and some observers believe that demonstrative evidence often has the effect of misleading rather than assisting the jury. See, e.g., Milwid, The Misuse of Demonstrative Evidence, 28 Ins.Couns.J. 435 (1961).

In addition, trial lawyers have made a growing use of experts in proving damages. Experts may be used to project earnings, to detail plaintiff's medical difficulties, both physical and psychological, and in a variety of other ways. This is treated in more detail in courses in Evidence and Trial Practice.

6.   It has become customary to divide damages in a personal injury case into separate categories. One classification is between "special" and "general" damages; another is between "economic" and "non-economic" damages. The two classifications are not always coterminous, but in personal injury cases lost earnings and medical and other expenses are treated as special damages subject to objective measurement of the economic loss, while pain and suffering and emotional distress are treated as general damages whose loss is fundamentally non-economic. You will sometimes hear attorneys discussing a case ask, as a preliminary question, how much the "specials" are. The specials are all of the plaintiff's out of pocket expenses.

Economic Losses

7.   *Medical Expenses.* As the principal cases indicate, the plaintiff is compensated for reasonable medical expenses. Medical expenses may include bills for hospitals, doctors (including psychiatrists), physical therapists, nurses, medication, x-rays, crutches, wheel chairs, braces, travel to a different climate, etc. Past medical expenses are proved at trial by submitting the bills into evidence or through testimony. Future medical expenses (e.g., surgery that the plaintiff will need or medication plaintiff takes) must be proved by expert testimony establishing the anticipated need and predicted cost. Note that in the *Richardson* case the future medical expenses were proved by the testimony of two experts. Plaintiff's treating

physician testified as to the medical care she was likely to need and an economist testified as to the likely cost of those procedures, based on assumptions about the rise in medical care costs over the time period in issue. Plaintiff will be able to recover unless the costs incurred were not related to the tortious injury, were unnecessary (trips to three medical specialists where one would have been reasonable), or excessively high (hourly fees higher than reasonable).

8. If the plaintiff has no physical illness or disease but alleges that the defendant negligently exposed the plaintiff to a toxic substance that increased the plaintiff's risk of contracting a disease in the future, may the plaintiff recover for the increased risk itself? (Petriello v. Kalman, 215 Conn. 377, 576 A.2d 474 (1990)); for the cost of medical monitoring in order to detect disease early if it develops? (Compare Metro–North Commuter Railroad Co. v. Buckley, 521 U.S. 424 (1997) (not permitted in FELA case) with Bower v. Westinghouse, Corp., 522 S.E.2d 424 (W.Va.1999) (recovery permitted), (page 1209)); for the fear of developing the disease? (Simmons v. Pacor, Inc., 543 Pa. 664, 674 A.2d 232 (1996); Majca v. Beekil, 183 Ill.2d 407, 701 N.E.2d 1084 (1998) (collecting AIDS cases)). See McCarter, Medical Sue–Veillance: A History and Critique of the Medical Monitoring Remedy in Toxic Tort Litigation, 45 Rutgers L.Rev. 227 (1993); A.L.I. Reporter's Study, Enterprise Responsibility for Personal Injury, Approaches to Legal and Institutional Change (1991), suggesting a threshold standard of probability of risk, a requirement that funds be placed in a trust, abolition of the collateral source rule, and requirement of proof that medical intervention would cure the disease. What is the reason for each of these criteria? Should this cause of action be recognized with these criteria? At all?

9. *Lost Wages.* If the plaintiff was employed at a fixed wage at the time of injury, the wages lost during the time of injury are relatively easy to calculate. For example, if an attorney who works for the Department of Justice loses two months from work because of an injury suffered in an automobile accident, she will be able to recover from the defendant responsible for her injury for two months' pay. The damages calculation is more complicated if the plaintiff was not employed at the time of the injury. For example, if the attorney was at home caring for two small children at the time of the injury, damages probably would be calculated on the basis of the cost of replacement care for her two children. See Johnson, Calculating the Economic Value of Lost Homemaker Services in Wrongful Death/Personal Injury Litigation, 29 Trial Law. Guide 136 (1985).

10. *Loss or Impairment of Future Earning Capacity.* If the injury is one from which the plaintiff does not recover and reenter the workforce, the measure of damages will be for loss of earning capacity (sometimes called loss of future earnings) or impairment of earning capacity. First, the jury must be persuaded that the injury is permanent. See, e.g., Byrum v. Maryott, 26 Md.App. 130, 337 A.2d 142 (1975) (discussion of adequacy of expert witness testimony re permanency of injury). Then, expert testimony is needed to assist the jury in estimating what the plaintiff would have earned during the plaintiff's lifetime. As indicated in the *Anderson* case, even a very young plaintiff who would not be expected to engage in employment until the distant future may recover for the loss of future earnings. So may a plaintiff who was temporarily unemployed or voluntarily out of the workforce (e.g., while caring for family members or going to school in preparation to starting a new career). The jury is assisted in its estimate of lifetime earnings by the presentation of expert testimony on issues like life expectancy. The jury is instructed that it is to rely on the tables only as a general guideline in determining how long plaintiff might be expected to live. The jury may consider how much individual factors such as plaintiff's "sex, prior state of health, nature of daily employment

and its perils, manner of living, personal habits, and individual characteristics" will affect the life expectancy figure provided by a mortality table. See Volz v. Dresser, 150 Pa.Super. 371, 28 A.2d 493 (1942). Moreover, it is loss of earning capacity that is being calculated and most people do not continue to earn money for their entire lives. Thus, the jury may consider the prospects for change in plaintiff's earning capacity, taking into account not only the nature of the person's employment, but also the fact that in growing older the person may be expected to earn more, and that a point is ultimately reached at which an older person will earn less or nothing at all. Note that in the *Richardson* case the economist calculated lost earnings based on two different work life expectancies (27.5 years and 35.8 years). Why did he do that? See Fisher, Use of an Economist To Prove Future Economic Losses, 18 S.Tex.L.J. 403 (1977); Hadley & Rapp, Estimating Future Lost Earnings: Some Common Problems, 21 Trial [No. 1] 28 (Feb. 1985); Zabel, A Plain English Approach to Loss of Future Earning Capacity, 24 Washburn L.J. 253 (1985).

11. *Damage Calculation: Present Value.* In personal injury actions, a plaintiff is awarded a lump sum to compensate for all future pecuniary losses, such as loss of future wages or future medical expenses. Most jurisdictions require that the lump sum award for future losses be reduced to its "present value." That is, the jury is instructed to award the amount of money in a lump that will produce for the plaintiff the amount the plaintiff would have earned or will need for a future operation. For example, plaintiff is a child whose back was injured. The back injury requires surgery, but not until the child has stopped growing. Thus, the medical testimony is that the child will need an operation ten years from the time of trial and that the cost of that operation in ten years is estimated to be $5,000. The jury must award the child enough money (principal) at the time of trial so that the principal plus the interest it will earn will equal $5,000 in ten years. Similarly, if the plaintiff is an adult who had been earning $50,000 a year and had a worklife expectancy of 10 years at the time of trial, the jury must award the adult enough money (principal) at the time of trial so that the adult will have an earnings stream of $50,000 a year for the next ten years with no principal remaining at the end of the 10 years. The present value is computed by formula or by reference to tables once it has been determined at what interest rate to assume the plaintiff will be able to invest the lump sum (principal). Expert witnesses frequently differ as to the predicted interest rate, usually called the "discount rate" in this context, that should be used. In addition to the *Richardson* opinion, see generally, Restatement (Second) of Torts § 913A; Jarrell and Pulsinelli, Obtaining the Ideal Discount Rate in Wrongful Death and Injury Litigation, 32 Defense L.J. 191 (1983).

12. *Future Inflation.* In recent years plaintiffs' attorneys have argued that the jury should not merely reduce lump sum awards to present value, but also should consider the countervailing effect of future inflation. They contend that an upward price movement is probable and that valuing future damages in terms of present prices does not fully compensate the victim. To continue the examples we used earlier, it may be argued at trial that although the back operation costs $5,000 today, inflation will make its cost $6,000 in ten years and that today's $50,000 a year salary will be $52,000 next year. Most jurisdictions have recognized the need to adjust for expected future inflation in some way. Differences have arisen, however, with respect to the proper means to account for inflation, and how to mesh calculations for inflation with those for discount for present value. Three general methods have dominated the discussion: (a) the "inflation-discount method," which seeks to avoid undercompensation by increasing expected future earnings to account for inflation, and then discounting to present value by the market interest rate. Turcotte v. Ford Motor Co., 494 F.2d 173 (1st Cir.1974); (b) the "real interest

method," whereby the "real" interest rate is perceived to be stable (between one percent and three percent) regardless of the level of inflation. Doca v. Marina Mercante Nicaraguense, S.A., 634 F.2d 30 (2d Cir.1980); and (c) the "total offset method," which assumes as a matter of law that the market interest rate normally used to discount damage awards is completely offset by inflation in computing lost future income. Beaulieu v. Elliott, 434 P.2d 665 (Alaska 1967); State v. Guinn, 555 P.2d 530 (Alaska 1976); Kaczkowski v. Bolubasz, 491 Pa. 561, 421 A.2d 1027 (1980).

In Jones & Laughlin Steel Corp. v. Pfeifer, 462 U.S. 523 (1983), the Supreme Court reviewed various approaches and concluded that it should not establish one method as the exclusive federal rule for use in federal causes of action in federal courts. The Court observed that there are two stages in calculating damages (estimation of the lost stream of income or the cost of the surgery in the future and selection of an appropriate discount rate) and found that inflation should be included in both stages. Although the Court declined to establish any one method as the federal rule, it did note the attractiveness of the total offset method. This would amount to no discounting at all. Such a system would be easy to administer, but would it be fair? Is this a problem arising out of the highly inflationary decade of the 1970's with no real impact now? To return to the example, would the court allow a party to demonstrate that there are different inflation rates for medical services than for the general inflation index? Note that the economist in the *Richardson* case testified that he had modified the GAO's projections for the cost of future medical services because he thought they were too focused on technology-based items and that Ms. Richardson's needs would primarily be for attendant care. The topic is treated in Fisher & Hartnett, Admissibility of Economic Testimony on Future Inflation (1977); Winer, Adjusting Damage Awards for Future Inflation, 1982 Wis.L.Rev. 397.

13. *Federal Income Tax.* Plaintiff's award for personal injuries is not subject to the federal income tax. Under Section 104(a)(2) of the Internal Revenue Code, a tort victim can exclude from gross income the amount of compensatory damages received on account of personal injuries. Punitive damages, however, are considered income. O'Gilvie v. United States, 519 U.S. 79 (1996). A problem arises when the award, or a part of it, is to compensate for a loss that would have been subject to income tax. The primary instance is compensation for lost wages. If no reduction is made in the award, the injured plaintiff receives more for wages than if he had not been injured. For this reason, some courts have held that the "tax-free" nature of the award must be taken into account in setting the amount of the award. Caldwell v. Haynes, 136 N.J. 422, 643 A.2d 564 (N.J. 1994) (plaintiff has burden of producing evidence of net income for lost future wages); Floyd v. Fruit Indus., 144 Conn. 659, 136 A.2d 918 (1957); Maus v. New York, C. & St. L.R. Co., 165 Ohio St. 281, 135 N.E.2d 253 (1956). Other authorities have taken the position that to deduct the anticipated tax saving from the recovery would nullify the tax benefit conferred by Congress. Spencer v. A–1 Crane Svc., Inc., 880 S.W.2d 938 (Tenn.1994). See also Dodge, Taxes and Torts, 77 Cornell L.Rev. 143 (1992); Yorio, The Taxation of Damages: Tax and Non–Tax Policy Considerations, 62 Cornell L.Rev. 701 (1977).

Most courts have refused to take into account the "tax-free" nature of the award because of concern about the speculative character of the amount of a potential deduction, at least insofar as it applies to future earnings. There is no way of telling what the tax rates will be in the future, nor what exemptions, deductions and other income the plaintiff would have, so as to determine what tax bracket he would have been in; and the whole matter is affected by possible future inflation. For these reasons, most courts have been inclined toward the position that in the case of the average taxpayer no deduction should be made, and the plaintiff should receive the benefit of the windfall. In fact, most jurisdictions do not tell the jury that the award is tax free. But see Norfolk & Western Ry. Co. v. Liepelt, 444 U.S. 490 (1980) (Supreme Court in Federal Employers' Liability Act case allows jury to be told that award is tax exempt). There is a good debate on the pertinent policy issues between Judges Friendly and Lumbard in McWeeney v. New York, N.H. & H.R. R. Co., 282 F.2d 34 (2d Cir.1960), cert. denied, 364 U.S. 870 (1960).

14. *Interest.* Tort damages for personal injuries are generally unliquidated—that is, no precise sum of damages is sought by the complaint. The jury must set a value on the loss suffered by plaintiff. Consequently, courts traditionally have not permitted the plaintiff to collect interest on the award until judgment is entered or until a verdict is reached. Potter v. Hartzell Propeller, Inc., 291 Minn. 513, 189 N.W.2d 499 (1971), noted in 56 Minn.L.Rev. 739 (1972). This rule has been criticized as discouraging settlements because it is to defendant's advantage to keep the money as long as possible without having to pay interest on it. See Moore–McCormack Lines, Inc. v. Amirault, 202 F.2d 893 (1st Cir.1953). For this reason, legislatures in a number of states have enacted statutes that provide for interest on the amount of the award from the date of the injury, the date of a demand of payment from the plaintiff, the date the cause of action was filed, or the date the expense actually was incurred by the plaintiff. See, e.g., Nev.Rev.Stats.Ann. § 17.130 (1999); N.H.Rev.Stat.Ann. §§ 524:1–a, 524:1–b (1999). The plaintiff must pay federal income tax on the pre-judgment interest. Brabson v. United States, 73 F.3d 1040 (10th Cir.1996).

What is your view? Should plaintiff be paid interest on his claim? If so, when should interest obligations begin? Should interest cover both special and general damages? Even in the absence of statute, the jury may consider the time that has elapsed between the harm and the time of determining the amount of damages. See In re Air Crash Disaster Near Chicago, 644 F.2d 633 (7th Cir.1981) (although the relevant statute did not specify that prejudgment interest could be awarded, it could be allowed as one element of "fair and just compensation"). On interest in general, see Restatement (Second) of Torts § 913.

Non–Economic Losses

15. *Physical Pain and Suffering, Mental Anguish.* In an action for a personal injury the plaintiff may recover damages for general or non-economic damages. They include not only suffering prior to the trial, but also any suffering reasonably certain to result from the injury in the future. Since pain, suffering and mental anguish are not capable of being reduced to any precise equivalent in money, there can be no fixed standard by which damages for them can be measured. The best that can be done is to leave the question to the jury, subject to control by the court, to fix a reasonable amount as compensation. It is reversible error if the jury does not make an award for pain and suffering. American States Ins. Co. v. Audubon Country Club, 650 S.W.2d 252 (Ky.1983) (reversible error to accept a verdict for medical expenses with no recovery for pain and suffering); Bowers v. Sprouse, 254 Va. 428, 492 S.W.2d 637 (1997) (jury award for exact amount of specials is inadequate as a matter of law, even if those damages were controverted; plaintiff experienced pain, suffering, and inconvenience and is entitled to be compensated for that). See also, Red Lake Band of Chippewa Indians v. United States, No. 81–3193,1990 WL 515095 (D.D.C. March 22, 1990), rev'd on other grounds, 936 F.2d 1320 (D.C.Cir.1991) (In assessing damages in a bench trial in a suit against the United States under the Federal Tort Claims Act, the court noted that plaintiff "spoke little of his emotional distress and inconvenience or annoyance. Indeed, he gave sparse testimony on this. The court takes note of [plaintiff's] stoic nature. It

also is aware of [plaintiff's] age, schooling, and health, and recognizes that he had to speak English in court, when this may not be his tongue of choice. Stoics unwilling or unable to orate on their anger, fear, worry, or pain feel these no less keenly than the voluble. When the law entitles a man to damages he should not be penalized for his reserve. The court has kept all this in mind when finding facts about damages * * *.") But see Warren v. Ballard, 266 Ga. 408, 467 S.E.2d 891 (1996) (no recovery for anxiety about paying medical bills after automobile accident).

The general damages portion of the award may consist of several different elements. The most common is the physical pain caused by the injury. This may be of relatively short duration and be over by the time of trial (past pain and suffering) or it may be a chronic symptom that the medical experts predict plaintiff will always have (future pain and suffering). Plaintiff must be conscious to recover for this element of damages. Thus, whether the plaintiff was conscious after the accident but before death may be a hotly contested issue in some cases. How might the plaintiff's attorney prove conscious pain and suffering? Ghotra v. Bandila Shipping, Inc., 113 F.3d 1050 (9th Cir.1997) (affidavit from doctor opining that it was "highly likely" that decedent was conscious for ten seconds following accident not enough to overcome defendant's motion for summary judgment on the issue of pain and suffering where eyewitness testimony and autopsy report indicated that decedent was not conscious after injury and prior to death).

Loss of Function or Appearance. Plaintiff also may be able to recover for other types of loss. For example, there are holdings that allow a jury to award a recovery for the loss of sense of taste and smell, Purdy v. Swift & Co., Indus. Indem. Exch., 34 Cal.App.2d 656, 94 P.2d 389 (1939); incontinence, Thoren v. Myers, 151 Neb. 453, 37 N.W.2d 725 (1949); impotency and loss of desire for sexual intercourse, Sullivan v. City and County of San Francisco, 95 Cal.App.2d 745, 214 P.2d 82 (1950); change of personality and change of attitude towards others, Fjellman v. Weller, 213 Minn. 457, 7 N.W.2d 521 (1942); insomnia and inability to drive a car, Napier v. DuBose, 45 Ga.App. 661, 165 S.E. 773 (1932); fear of injury to an unborn child, Domenico v. Kaherl, 160 Me. 182, 200 A.2d 844 (1964); scars and other disfigurements, Gray v. Washington Water Power Co., 30 Wash. 665, 71 P. 206 (1903).

Emotional Distress. Should plaintiff be entitled to pain and suffering damages in a legal malpractice action? Lickteig v. Alderson, Ondov, Leonard & Sween, 556 N.W.2d 557 (Minn.1996) (emotional distress may be an element of damages only if plaintiff suffers physical injury; if plaintiff was exposed to physical injury due to the negligence of another and develops physical symptoms after emotional distress; or if emotional distress results from a direct invasion of plaintiff rights such as in slander, libel, malicious prosecution, seduction or other willful, wanton, or malicious conduct). See also Chapter 8.

Litigation-Induced Stress. Should plaintiff be able to recover for the anxiety and stress that accompanies litigation? Most courts have not recognized it as a separate component of damages. School Dist. v. Nilsen, 271 Or. 461, 534 P.2d 1135 (1975) (this type of stress inherent in most litigation); Buoy v. ERA Helicopters, Inc. 771 P.2d 439 (Ala. 1989) (litigation-induced depression); Stoleson v. United States, 708 F.2d 1217, 1223 (7th Cir.1983) (alleged tortfeasor should have the right to defend himself without thereby multiplying his damages); Picogna v. Bd. of Education, 143 N.J. 391, 671 A.2d 1035 (1996) (not appropriate element of pain and suffering damages).

16. *Loss of Enjoyment of Life.* As the cases in note 15 illustrate, most jurisdictions allow plaintiffs to recover for the loss of specific aspects of their lives as

part of the recovery for pain and suffering. This is sometimes called "hedonic damages." How does the jury determine the amount of damages for this type of injury? Should the jury be aided by the testimony of an economist on how to calculate a value? Plaintiffs have been largely unsuccessful in persuading the courts to permit expert testimony on this issue. Wilt v. Buracker, 191 W.Va. 39, 443 S.E.2d 196 (1993) (loss of enjoyment of life damages not subject to economic calculation and therefore economist's testimony concerning calculation of award based on willingness-to-pay studies was not admissible); Montalvo v. Lapez, 77 Haw. 282, 884 P.2d 345 (1994) (economist no more expert at valuing pleasure of life than average juror); Loth v. Truck–A–Way Corp., 70 Cal. Rptr.2d 571, 60 Cal.App.4th 757 (1998) (method of computing hedonic damages is not matter for which expert testimony is admissible because not sufficiently beyond common experience of trier of fact). Generally, courts have required that the plaintiff must be conscious, that is aware of the loss, in order to recover for loss of enjoyment of some aspect of life. See McDougald v. Garber, 73 N.Y.2d 246, 536 N.E.2d 372, 538 N.Y.S.2d 937 (1989). Some jurisdictions have recognized a separate, though related, element of damages for loss of enjoyment of life that is characterized as a "thing" and therefore the plaintiff is entitled to recover for its diminished value even though the plaintiff is not conscious of the loss. See, e.g., Eyoma v. Falco, 247 N.J.Super. 435, 589 A.2d 653 (1991) (jury may award loss of enjoyment of life damages to comatose patient).

17. _Per-diem Argument._ A controversial technique of counsel for the plaintiff in arguing to the jury has been to break physical and mental suffering down into days, hours, or even minutes, set a value on each unit, and multiply it by the total number of the units that pain and suffering has lasted and may be expected to last. Although the practice is no doubt quite old, it originated, so far as publication is concerned, with Belli, The Use of Demonstrative Evidence in Achieving "The More Adequate Award," 32–35 (1951). It is not permitted in some jurisdictions because it tends to give the appearance of mathematical precision, through the use of a formula, to something that is by its nature neither mathematical nor precise and because it ignores the fact that once the "threshold" of pain is crossed, the body tends to adjust to it and the suffering to diminish. See, e.g., Affett v. Milwaukee & Suburban Transport Corp., 11 Wis.2d 604, 106 N.W.2d 274 (1960); Reid v. Baumgardner, 217 Va. 769, 232 S.E.2d 778 (1977). A majority of jurisdictions, however, permit the argument, assuming that defendant's counsel can point out any flaws in the argument and that the jury will not be misled. See, e.g., Weeks v. Holsclaw, 306 N.C. 655, 295 S.E.2d 596 (1982); Debus v. Grand Union Stores of Vermont, 159 Vt. 537, 621 A.2d 1288 (1993).

18. Assuming that plaintiff is awarded damages for future pain and suffering, should that amount be capitalized at its present value? Most courts have held that since damages for pain and suffering do not have a precise market value, they are not reduced to present value. See Texas & Pac. R. Co. v. Buckles, 232 F.2d 257 (5th Cir.), cert. denied, 351 U.S. 984 (1956). A few courts have indicated that a rough attempt at reduction is better than no effort at all. See In re Millard's Estate, 251 Iowa 1282, 105 N.W.2d 95 (1960); Abbott v. Northwestern Bell Tel. Co., 197 Neb. 11, 246 N.W.2d 647 (1976). A California court has left the decision to the discretion of the jury. Garfoot v. Avila, 213 Cal.App.3d 1205, 261 Cal.Rptr. 924 (1989). For a general discussion see O'Connell & Carpenter, Payment for Pain and Suffering through History, 50 Ins. Couns.J. 411 (1983).

19. The idea of awarding money damages for pain and suffering is not without its critics. Do these damages do any good? Do they help plaintiff bear the pain? A legal-medical study concluded that damages should be allowed only for pain that has a physiological basis. See Peck, Compensation for Pain: A Reappraisal in Light of

New Medical Evidence, 72 Mich.L.Rev. 1355 (1974). Professor Jeffrey O'Connell has concluded that the awarding of damages for pain and suffering is a wasteful process that is a creation of lawyers, unknown and unimportant to most of the public. See J. O'Connell and R. Simon, Payment for Pain and Suffering: Who Wants What, When and Why? (1972). See also the criticisms of Traynor, J., dissenting in Seffert v. Los Angeles Transit, 56 Cal.2d 498, 364 P.2d 337, 15 Cal.Rptr. 161 (1961). What of the argument that an award for pain and suffering is an indirect way of taking care of the plaintiff's attorney's fees, thus allowing the plaintiff the full amount of the pecuniary loss? See page 538 re legislative alterations to common law recovery for pain and suffering.

20. *Reduced Life Expectancy.* Traditionally, American authority has denied any damages for the shortening of the plaintiff's life expectancy itself, as distinguished from loss of prospective earnings. There have been three major factors responsible for this (a) the belief that the common law rule against compensating for loss of life except as provided by statute must preclude compensation for shortening life; (b) the fear that duplication of damages may result; and (c) unwillingness to enter a field filled with incalculable variables. See Farrington v. Stoddard, 115 F.2d 96 (1st Cir.1940); O'Leary v. United States Lines Co., 111 F.Supp. 745 (D.Mass.1953); Rhone v. Fisher, 224 Md. 223, 167 A.2d 773 (1961); and Paladino v. Campos, 145 N.J.Super. 555, 368 A.2d 429 (1976).

English authorities have held that the shortening of life expectancy is itself a compensable harm, constituting a distinct element of damages. See Flint v. Lovell, [1935] 1 K.B. 354 (C.A.); Yorkshire Elec. Bd. v. Naylor, [1968] A.C. 529. In Downie v. United States Lines Co., 359 F.2d 344 (3d Cir.1966), cert. denied, 385 U.S. 897 (1966), the court agreed with this position. There is an excellent discussion of the entire problem, including survival of actions and wrongful death, in Fleming, The Lost Years: A Problem in the Computation and Distribution of Damages, 50 Calif.L.Rev. 598 (1962).

Judicial Control of Amounts Recovered

21. A trial judge (through a motion for a new trial) or an appellate panel (on appeal) can disturb the jury's finding on the amount of the damages only if the verdict is so excessive or so inadequate as to demonstrate that the jury acted contrary to the law—in passion or prejudice rather than according to their instructions. The test for disturbing a jury award on the amount of damages is expressed in various ways. The principal case referred to the "maximum amount which the jury could reasonably find." Other courts have used terms like "grossly" excessive or inadequate, "inordinate," "shocking to the judicial conscience," or "outrageous."

22. If the judicial review of the verdict concludes that the award was grossly excessive or grossly inadequate, the judge(s) must then decide whether to set aside the verdict and grant a new trial on both liability and damages, or to allow the liability portion of the verdict to stand and to grant a new trial on damages alone. Maier v. Santucci, 697 A.2d 747 (Dela. 1997) (new trial on damages ordered where jury, in rear-end collision, back injury case, awarded $0 damages to plaintiff after trial court judge had directed a verdict for plaintiff on liability). Usually, a whole new trial is granted. A partial new trial, on damages only, is the appropriate remedy only if the judge is persuaded that whatever influenced the jury to act inappropriately in setting the amount of damages did not also taint the liability verdict.

23. *Remittitur and Additur.* If the judge decides to grant a new trial on damages alone, the judge may make the grant conditional. To avoid the expense, inconvenience and delay of new trials in these cases, trial courts frequently, in cases

remittur

additur

of excessive verdicts, grant a motion for a new trial that is conditioned upon the refusal of the plaintiff to accept a lesser amount. This order is called a remittitur and was at issue in both principal cases. When the verdict is inadequate, the trial judge, much less frequently, may grant the motion for a new trial conditioned on the defendant's refusal to pay a larger sum set by the court. This order is called an additur or an increscitur. It has generally been held that remittitur does not violate the guaranty of jury trial contained in the federal and state constitutions. On the other hand the power of additur has been denied to the federal courts by a 5–4 decision of the Supreme Court, Dimick v. Schiedt, 293 U.S. 474 (1935). The decisions as to the constitutionality of additur under state constitutions are split, with some courts interpreting their state constitutions to permit additur and others finding that additur violates their state constitutions as the Supreme Court had found that it violates the Seventh Amendment.

In the *Richardson* case, what happens after the Illinois Supreme Court decision? Will there be a new trial?

Legislative Control of Amounts Recovered

24.   In response to the tort reform efforts of the 1980's, about half of the state legislatures passed laws that in some way limited the amount of damages recoverable. Many of these statutes applied to only particular types of claims (e.g., medical malpractice claims, claims against the government), while others covered all tort actions seeking recovery for personal injury, but applied only to non-economic injuries. Compare Va.Code Ann. § 8.01–581.15 (1999) (medical malpractice only, $1,000,000 total recovery) with Md.Cts. & Jud.Proc.Code Ann. § 11–108 (1992) (all personal injury actions, $350,000 for non-economic damages).

25.   Some of the state schemes have been found unconstitutional, particularly those limited to certain causes of action, but many have survived constitutional scrutiny. Compare Best v. Taylor Machine Works, 179 Ill.2d 367, 689 N.E.2d 1057 (1997) (cap on compensatory damages for noneconomic injuries is unconstitutional special legislation) and Ray v. Anesthesia Assocs., 674 So.2d 525 (Ala.1995) (cap on wrongful death actions against health care providers violates right to jury trial and right to equal protection of law under state constitution) with Fein v. Permanente Medical Group, 38 Cal.3d 137, 695 P.2d 665, 211 Cal.Rptr. 368 (1985) (legislature may expand or limit recoverable damages so long as its action is rationally related to a legitimate state interest) and Johnson v. St. Vincent Hospital, Inc., 273 Ind. 374, 404 N.E.2d 585 (1980) ($500,000 cap in medical malpractice cases does not violate due process or equal protection guarantees).

26.   In addition to the question whether the caps will survive constitutional challenges, the legislative alterations of the common law raise other issues. Is the jury to be told of the cap? How does the cap apply to multiple causes of action arising out of the same incident? Where comparative negligence reduces the verdict by a percentage, which is to be applied first, the percentage reduction or the cap?

27.   How do you think the calculation of intangible damages should be handled? What about a standard schedule that would guarantee and limit the award to a certain range depending on the particular physical injury and age of the claimant? See, e.g., Bovbjerg, Sloan, and Blumstein, Valuing Life and Limb in Tort: Scheduling "Pain and Suffering," 83 Nw.U.L.Rev. 908 (1989); Geistfeld, Placing a Price on Pain and Suffering: A Method for Helping Determine Tort Damages for Nonmonetary Injuries, 83 Calif. L. Rev. 773 (1995).

Montgomery Ward & Co., Inc. v. Anderson

Supreme Court of Arkansas, 1998.
334 Ark. 561, 976 S.W.2d 382.

NEWBERN, J. * * * On November 14, 1994, appellee Shirley Anderson was badly injured in a fall while shopping in appellant's Montgomery Ward store in Little Rock. Montgomery Ward personnel sent her to the hospital at the University of Arkansas for Medical Sciences ("UAMS") to be treated. Ms. Anderson had surgical and other medical-services expenses at UAMS totaling $24,512.45. Montgomery Ward moved in limine to prohibit Ms. Anderson from presenting the total amount billed by UAMS as proof of her medical expenses and asked that her evidence be limited to the actual amount for which she would be responsible to pay. In response, Ms. Anderson stated that, through her attorney, she had reached an agreement with UAMS that UAMS would discount the bill by fifty per cent. Ms. Anderson asserted that the collateral-source rule would prohibit Montgomery Ward from introducing evidence of the discount.

The Trial Court denied the motion in limine, ruling that the negotiated discount with UAMS was a collateral source, and allowed evidence of the entire amount billed by UAMS. Montgomery Ward urges that the ruling and the denial of the motion for new trial made on the same basis were erroneous. * * *

We have held that the collateral-source rule applies unless the evidence of the benefits from the collateral source is relevant for a purpose other than the mitigation of damages. [C] The issue, then, is whether the forgiveness of a debt for medical services is a collateral source to be sheltered by the rule. There is no Arkansas authority dealing directly with that precise issue, but our cases explaining the policy behind the rule support the Trial Court's ruling. * * *

Although those cases [relied on by the trial court judge] do not directly answer the question in this case, they deal with analogous situations and explain the policy behind the collateral-source rule. A trial court must "exclude evidence of payments received by an injured party from sources 'collateral' to ... the wrongdoer, such as private insurance or government benefits...." Bell v. Estate of Bell, 318 Ark. 483, 490, 885 S.W.2d 877, 880 (1994). [Cc] Recoveries from collateral sources "do not redound to the benefit of a tortfeasor, even though double recovery for the same damage by the injured party may result." Bell v. Estate of Bell, 318 Ark. at 490, 885 S.W.2d at 880; [c].

In the Bell case, we recognized that commentators had criticized the rule as being "incongruous with the compensatory goal of the tort system" and that some jurisdictions had modified or abrogated the rule. * * *

We also noted that the rule had been extended to cases in other areas of the law, such as unemployment compensation received during a period later held to have resulted from a wrongful discharge under the Teacher Fair Dismissal Act. [C] In a later case, [c], a defendant argued that the collateral-source rule was inequitable because it resulted in a windfall to the plaintiff. We disposed of the argument by explaining the policy behind the rule as follows: "Whether she received the money from her employer or from an insurance policy, she, rather than the alleged tortfeasor, is entitled to the benefit of the collateral source, even though in one sense a double recovery occurs. [C] The law rationalizes that the claimant should benefit from the collateral source recovery rather than the tortfeasor, since the claimant has usually paid an insurance premium or lost sick leave, whereas to the tortfeasor it would be a total windfall." [East Texas Motor Freight Lines, Inc. v. Freeman,] 289 Ark. 539, at 548, 713 S.W.2d 456, at 462, (1986). That statement of policy and the cases cited favor including discounted and gratuitous medical services within the shelter of the collateral-source rule. There is no evidence of record showing that Montgomery Ward had anything to do with procuring the discount of Ms. Anderson's bill by UAMS. The rationale of the rule favors her, just as it would had she been compensated by insurance for which she had arranged. * * *

We recognize four situations in which the rule does not apply.... They are cases in which a collateral source of recovery may be introduced (1) to rebut the plaintiff's testimony that he or she was compelled by financial necessity to return to work prematurely or to forego additional medical care; (2) to show that the plaintiff had attributed his condition to some other cause, such as sickness; (3) to impeach the plaintiff's testimony that he or she had paid his medical expenses himself; (4) to show that the plaintiff had actually continued to work instead of being out of work, as claimed. [Cc] This Court has also allowed evidence of collateral sources when the plaintiff opens the door to his or her financial condition. [Cc] The Trial Court ruled that none of the exceptions applied to the facts at hand, and an examination of the abstract indicates that ruling was correct. There is no testimony by the plaintiff that arguably invokes any of the exceptions.

The Restatement (Second) of Torts § 920A(2) provides guidance on this issue and explains that the general rule is that "[p]ayments made to or benefits conferred on the injured party from other sources are not credited against the tortfeasor's liability, although they cover all or a part of the harm for which the tortfeasor is liable." Comment b to that Restatement section explains that, if the plaintiff is responsible for the benefit received, the law allows the plaintiff to keep it. Further, if the benefit was a gift to the plaintiff from a third party or established for the plaintiff by law, the plaintiff should not be deprived of the advantage that it confers. Another way to state the rule is to say that "it is the tortfeasor's responsibility to compensate for all harm that he [or she] causes, not confined to the net loss that the injured party receives." Restatement (Second) of Torts § 920A cmt. b. Comment c (3) indicates that gratuities of cash or services are collateral sources that are not subtracted from a plaintiff's recovery. The comment gives the example of a doctor who does not charge for medical services.

Other authority indicates that a substantial number of jurisdictions addressing the issue have held that the plaintiff may recover the reasonable value of nursing care or services rendered gratuitously for the plaintiff's benefit. [C] The primary issue remaining today is how to value the services, [c], but that issue is determined in this case by the total medical bill submitted to Ms. Anderson by UAMS.

Montgomery Ward cites cases from Massachusetts, New York, and Illinois for the proposition that gratuitous medical services may not be an item of recovery because the policy behind the collateral-source rule does not apply where the plaintiff has incurred no expense or obligation for the services needed. Peterson v. Lou Bachrodt Chev. Co., 76 Ill.2d 353, 29 Ill.Dec. 444, 392 N.E.2d 1 (1979); Coyne v. Campbell, 11 N.Y.2d 372, 230 N.Y.S.2d 1, 183 N.E.2d 891 (1962); Daniels v. Celeste, 303 Mass. 148, 21 N.E.2d 1 (1939). We are, however, persuaded by cases holding that gratuitous medical services do fall under the collateral-source rule. [C] See also Joshmer v. Fred Weber Contractors, Inc., 294 S.W.2d 576 (Mo.App.1956), which held that contributions received by the injured party as a direct result of being injured are not to be taken into consideration in assessing damages.

We choose to adopt the rule that gratuitous or discounted medical services are a collateral source not to be considered in assessing the damages due a personal-injury plaintiff. It is the rule recommended by the Restatement (Second) of Torts, and it is consistent with our oft-stated policy of allowing the innocent plaintiff, instead of the tortfeasor defendant, to receive any windfall associated with the cause of action. Accordingly, we hold that the Trial Court did not err by excluding evidence of the UAMS discount as a collateral source.

Affirmed.

NOTES AND QUESTIONS

1. *Collateral Source Rule.* As the principal case suggests, the collateral source or collateral benefits rule is applied when the plaintiff receives compensation from any source collateral to the tortfeasor. Those sources may include health or medical insurance, life insurance, disability insurance, employee benefits (sick leave, vacation pay), or governmental benefits (free care at Veteran's Hospital or through Medicare). Helfend v. Southern Cal. Rapid Transit Dist., 2 Cal.3d 1, 465 P.2d 61, 84 Cal.Rptr. 173 (1970). But see Washington v. Barnes Hospital, 897 S.W.2d 611 (Mo.1995) (availability of free public school special education and therapy services admissible in case where plaintiff's expert had testified about the cost of private school education because plaintiff did not pay for or bargain for free services and services were not contingent on plaintiff's financial need or special status as some government programs are). The rule does not apply, however, to payments made by the defendant or by a joint tortfeasor or one who mistakenly thinks he is a tortfeasor, or by an insurance company or other person who makes payment on behalf of a tortfeasor. See, in general, Restatement (Second) of Torts § 920A and note 4, page 368.

2. When benefits are conferred upon the plaintiff gratuitously, as when a plaintiff is nursed without charge by the spouse, the prevailing rule is that plaintiff is entitled to recover the reasonable value of the services from the defendant, since they are a gift to the plaintiff, and not to the defendant, and should not reduce the liability of the latter. Strand v. Grinnell Auto. Garage Co., 136 Iowa 68, 113 N.W.

exceptions to the rule

criticism to collateral source rule

defenses of it as well

488 (1907); Wells v. Minneapolis Baseball & Athletic Ass'n, 122 Minn. 327, 142 N.W. 706 (1913). A minority rule, however, does not permit the plaintiff to recover for the value of services provided without charge to plaintiff. See Coyne v. Campbell, 11 N.Y.2d 372, 183 N.E.2d 891, 230 N.Y.S.2d 1 (1962) and other cases cited in the principal case.

3. As the principal case states, plaintiff may recover double when the collateral source rule is applied. This is not usually the case, however. Paid sick leave will reduce the amount of sick leave the plaintiff has to use for other injuries. Health insurance contracts and government programs providing benefits typically provide that the insured must pay back benefits provided from the proceeds of a judgment or settlement with a tortfeasor.

4. There has been criticism of the collateral source rule. See American Law Institute Reporters' Study, "Enterprise Responsibility for Personal Injury," vol. II, pp. 161–182 (1991) (recommending an elimination of the common law collateral benefits rule except with respect to life insurance); Schwartz, Tort Law Reform: Strict Liability and the Collateral Source Rule Do Not Mix, 39 Vand.L.Rev. 569 (1986); J. O'Connell, Ending Insult to Injury 141–147 (1975); Fleming, The Collateral Source Rule and Loss Allocation in Tort Law, 54 Calif.L.Rev. 1478 (1966); Maxwell, The Collateral Source Rule in the American Law of Damages, 46 Minn. L.Rev. 669 (1962); James, Social Insurance and Tort Liability, 27 N.Y.U.L.Rev. 537 (1952). The rule is vigorously defended in Lambert, The Case for the Collateral–Source Rule, 3 Trial Law.Q. 52 (1965).

5. Over half of the states have modified the common law collateral source rule by statute, usually as part of "tort reform" movements. Some of the modifications apply only to particular causes of action (e.g., medical malpractice). About half of those provide that the information concerning the collateral source is admissible in evidence (see e.g., Ariz.Rev.Stat. § 12–565 (1999)) without indicating what the jury is to do with that information, while others specify that the award is to be reduced by the amount of the collateral source (see, e.g., N.Y. McKinney's Civ.Prac.L. & R. § 4545(c) (1999)). Some of these statutes have been found unconstitutional, while others have survived constitutional challenge. Compare Carson v. Maurer, 120 N.H. 925, 424 A.2d 825 (1980) and American Legion Post 57 v. Leahey, 681 So.2d 1337 (Ala.1996) (unconstitutional) with Barme v. Wood, 37 Cal.3d 174, 689 P.2d 446, 207 Cal.Rptr. 816 (1984) and Reid v. Williams, 964 P.2d 453 (Alaska 1998) (constitutional). The Kansas legislature has tried three times (1976, 1986, and 1992) to limit the common law collateral source rule and each time the Kansas Supreme Court found the statute unconstitutional. See Thompson v. KFB Insurance Co., 252 Kan. 1010, 850 P.2d 773 (1993).

6. *Loss of Consortium.* Most states recognize a claim by the spouse of an injured person for loss of conjugal relations, society, companionship, household services, etc. during the time period that the injured person is recovering or for a permanent loss. The claim is derivative of the injured person's and in most states must be joined in the same cause of action as the injured person's. Should loss of consortium be available for relationships not formalized by marriage? Should loss of consortium be available for damage to the parent child relationship? See a more detailed discussion of these issues in Chapter 22, Section 2, Family Relations.

7. *Expenses of Litigation.* Under the English practice, the winning party, whether plaintiff or defendant, recovers his expenses of litigation, including attorney's fees. This is not the practice in the United States in regard to litigation in general, or tort litigation in particular, except in Alaska. Alaska Civil Rule 82. See Restatement (Second) of Torts § 914. It is sometimes suggested that in a personal-injury case, as a practical matter, the award for pain and suffering may have the

effect of allowing the plaintiff to pay the attorney and still retain compensation for pecuniary loss. Punitive damages, also, are regarded as a means of covering plaintiff's attorney's fees. Schlein v. Smith, 160 F.2d 22 (D.C.Cir.1947).

Chapter 21, Misuse of Legal Procedure, covers the tort action for bringing a suit held to be frivolous or for using legal procedure for an improper purpose—"abuse of process." It also treats statutes and Rules of Court providing for the trial judge to impose a sanction—usually payment of attorney's fees—for conduct of this nature.

8.   *The Contingent Fee.* Lawyers who represent plaintiffs in personal injury litigation are usually paid on the basis of a contingent fee contract. Under this arrangement, the lawyer agrees to render professional services for a fee that is based on a percentage of the amount the client recovers in the case. If there is no recovery, the lawyer receives no fee. The percentage of the contingent fee varies, sometimes depending upon whether the case is settled or litigated, or on the size of recovery. A common contingent fee is 30%–40%. If for some reason no figure is set by attorney and client, or there is later a dispute about the amount of the figure, an attorney may bring an action against the former client for a *quantum meruit* recovery. See e.g., Nugent v. Downs, 230 So.2d 597 (La.App.1970) (fixing a fee of 30%). In certain situations the amount of the contingent fee may be fixed by statute. For example, the Federal Torts Claims Act makes it a crime for an attorney to obtain a contingent fee greater than 25% of the judgment (20% of a settlement) for a suit against the United States Government. 28 U.S.C. § 2678. Jurors are not informed about the contingent fee and they are not to add that fee to their verdict. Thus, it is a basic part of the tort damage system that plaintiff absorbs the costs of bringing a law suit.

As one might anticipate, the contingent fee has been criticized. See M.T. Bloom, The Trouble With Lawyers (1968); Kraut, Contingent Fee: Champerty or Champion?, 21 Clev.St.L.Rev. 15 (1972); Brickman, Contingent Fees Without Contingencies: Hamlet Without the Prince of Denmark?, 37 UCLA L.REV. 29 (1989); Horowitz, Making Ethics Real, Making Ethics Work: A Proposal for Contingency Fee, 44 EMORY L.J. 173 (1995). The contingent fee does come close to the borderline of champerty and maintenance, practices that have long been forbidden by common law. It is not champerty because the client theoretically retains control over the case and can dismiss the lawyer at any time. It does not represent maintenance because the client must pay for the out-of-pocket expenditures connected with the suit. Nevertheless, the contingent fee may result in an attorney being compensated far beyond or far below what would be a "reasonable fee" for the effort expended. Also, it may create a conflict of interest between attorney and client as to whether to accept a settlement. Contingent–Fee Lawyers and Their Clients: Settlement Expectations, Settlement Realities, and Issues of Control in the Lawyer–Client Relationship, 23 LAW & SOC. INQUIRY 795 (1998). The lawyer, of course, is obligated to place the interests of the client first. On the other hand, the contingent fee system has allowed poor persons to obtain good legal services when they are injured. Karsten, Enabling the Poor to Have Their Day in Court: The Sanctioning of Contingency Fee Contracts, A History to 1940, 47 DePaul L.Rev. 231 (1998). Also, individual "fees" look less exorbitant when one considers that plaintiff attorneys also lose cases, thus receiving no compensation for the work on those cases. Schwartz and Mitchell, An Economic Analysis of the Contingent Fee in Personal Injury Litigation, 22 Stan.L.Rev. 1125 (1970) (suggesting that the client be given a choice of fee systems: traditional contingent fee, hourly contingent fee or an hourly rate); Symposium: Contingency Fee Financing of Litigation in America, Third Annual Clifford Seminar on Tort Law and Social Policy, 47 DePaul L.Rev. 227 (1998).

Retainer billed on hourly basis

9. *The Hourly Fee.* In contrast to lawyers who represent plaintiffs, most lawyers who represent defendants are paid for their services based on an hourly fee for the work done. In many of the cases you have read, the payments to the lawyer for the defendant are actually made by the defendant's liability insurance carrier. In others, the defendant had no insurance or was self-insured and made the payments. Attorneys working under this system are sometimes accused of doing more work than is necessary to prepare the case for trial or of delaying settlement talks to keep the case, and their payments for services rendered in the meantime, alive. Such conduct would be a violation of the rules of professional conduct.

10. *Periodic Payment of Damages.* When an injury is very serious, large damages are likely to be involved. The traditional common law treatment is to provide for lump-sum damages, with the money to go to the injured party to spend or invest as he sees fit. The lump sum is paid after a jury verdict to satisfy the judgment or before a trial as part of a settlement agreement. During the last 30 years, attorneys have begun using structured settlements to settle some cases. A structured settlement is any settlement that provides that payments are to be made periodically instead of in a lump sum. The periodic payments can be tailored to meet the individual plaintiff's needs (e.g., monthly income for someone unable to work, four annual payments to begin when a minor reaches college age). The primary advantage of the structured settlement is its favorable tax treatment. As long as the agreement meets certain requirements, the income earned on the principal is tax free. 26 U.S.C.A. § 130. If the money had been paid in a lump sum, the principal would not be taxable income to the plaintiff but the interest earned on the principal would be. For example, under a properly structured settlement agreement, the defendant may pay $50,000 to purchase an annuity that would pay the plaintiff $380 per month for life with fifteen years guaranteed. Thus, the plaintiff would receive $68,400 guaranteed and would receive $192,000 if the plaintiff lived out his life expectancy. This has led to much interest in utilizing structured settlements. See Hindert, Periodic Payment of Personal Injury Damages, 31 Fed.Ins.Couns.Q. 3 (1980); Krause, Structured Settlements for Tort Victims, 66 A.B.A.J. 1527 (1980); Stone, Explaining Structured Settlements, 21 Trial 96 (Feb. 1985); Vaughan, Tax Issues of Personal Injury and Wrongful Death Awards, 19 Tulsa L.J. 702 (1984); Wells, Tax Consequences of Damages, 12 Colo.Law. 53 (1983); Harrison, The Ethics of Structuring Settlements, 34 Drake L.Rev. 1045 (1985).

There has been interest in arranging for periodic payments after a judgment has been awarded and many states have enacted some form of periodic payment legislation to permit, or in some instances require, periodic payment of damages. See, e.g., Fla.Stat. § 768.78 (1999) and Md.Cts. & Judic.Proc. § 11–109 (1999). Constitutional challenges to statutes regarding periodic payment of punitive damages have met with mixed success. Compare Salgado v. Cty. of Los Angeles, 19 Cal.4th 629, 967 P.2d 585, 80 Cal. Rptr.2d 46 (1998) (periodic payment of judgment statute constitutional) with Galayda v. Lake Hospital Systems, Inc., 71 Ohio St.3d 421, 644 N.E.2d 298 (1994) (unconstitutional deprivation of right to jury trial and due process). See generally, Henderson, Designing a Responsible Periodic Payment System for Tort Awards, 32 Ariz.L.Rev. 21 (1990).

P's duty × mitigate damages

Zimmerman v. Ausland

Supreme Court of Oregon, 1973.
266 Or. 427, 513 P.2d 1167.

[Plaintiff suffered a torn semilunar cartilage in her knee as the result of an automobile accident caused by the negligence of defendant. She obtained a jury verdict for $7,500, which included damages for "permanent injury" in that she would no longer be able to engage in strenuous physical education activities. She had previously engaged in these activities in her work as a substitute teacher.

Defendant introduced a physician's expert testimony that if plaintiff had the torn cartilage "surgically excised," she "should recover completely." At the time of trial, plaintiff had not undergone the operation and she gave no indication that she would do so in the future.]

TONGUE, JUSTICE. * * * Defendant contends that the trial court erred in submitting to the jury the issue whether plaintiff sustained a permanent injury, as alleged in her complaint, and in instructing the jury on plaintiff's life expectancy, after taking judicial notice of the Standard Mortality Tables. * * *

It is * * * well established that the plaintiff in a personal injury case cannot claim damages for what would otherwise be a permanent injury if the permanency of the injury could have been avoided by submitting to treatment by a physician, including possible surgery, when a reasonable person would do so under the same circumstances. [Cc]

In this case defendant did not request an instruction on mitigation of damages, with the result that this question was not submitted to the jury. Nevertheless, if the facts are such that the court must hold, as a matter of law, that the plaintiff failed to mitigate her damages by submission to surgery when a reasonable person would have done so, the plaintiff would not be entitled to claim damages for what might otherwise be a permanent injury. It would also follow, in such an event, that defendant would be correct in contending that it was error to submit the issue of permanent injury to the jury, including consideration of the mortality tables.

In general * * * the test to be applied in determining whether a plaintiff has unreasonably failed or refused to mitigate his damages by submitting to a surgical operation is whether, under the circumstances of the particular case, an ordinarily prudent person would do so, i.e., the duty to exercise reasonable care under the circumstances. [Cc]

* * * Conversely, if under the circumstances, a reasonable person might well decline to undergo a surgical operation, a failure to do so imposes no disability against recovering full damages. [C]

The factors to be considered for this purpose ordinarily include the risk involved (i.e., the hazardous nature of the operation), the probability of success, and the expenditure of money or effort required. [C] Some courts also consider the pain involved as a factor, but no such question is presented for decision in this case. * * *

[I]t has been held that there must be evidence relating to the extent of the risk involved in a particular type of surgical operation before a jury may properly consider the contention that a plaintiff acted unreasonably in declining to submit to a surgical operation. * * *

No case has been cited to us in which it has been held that a plaintiff with a torn cartilage in the knee must submit to surgery to remove the damaged cartilage or be barred, as a matter of law, from seeking damages for an otherwise permanent injury, at least in the absence of such evidence. * * *

We hold * * * that under the facts and circumstances of this case the evidence supporting defendant's contention that plaintiff was required to submit to surgery upon her knee and the related contention that, for failure to do so, she is barred from claiming damages for a permanent injury to her knee, were not so clear and conclusive as to make it proper for the court to decide those questions in this case as a matter of law. This is not to say, of course, that defendant was not entitled to offer evidence of these questions and have them submitted to the jury under appropriate instructions. After examining the record in this case we also hold that testimony was offered by plaintiff from which, if believed by the jury, it could properly find that plaintiff has suffered a permanent injury, and one which interferes with her normal and usual activities, including those relating to her work as a substitute teacher. It follows that the trial court did not err in submitting that issue to the jury or in instructing it on life expectancy tables. The verdict of the jury was supported by substantial evidence and the judgment of the trial court is affirmed.

McALLISTER, J., concurs in the result.

NOTES AND QUESTIONS

1. The so-called duty to mitigate damages in tort law, sometimes called the doctrine of avoidable consequences, actually is merely a rule that does not allow recovery of those damages that plaintiff could have avoided by reasonable conduct on the part of the plaintiff after a legal wrong has been committed by defendant. It is distinguished from the defense of contributory negligence, which is unreasonable conduct on the part of plaintiff that contributes to the happening of the accident or injury in the first place. See Restatement (Second) of Torts § 918.

2. Most decisions are in accord with the principal case in that defendant must prove that plaintiff's unreasonable conduct prevented the diminution of the injuries. See Roy v. Robin, 173 So.2d 222 (La.App.1965) cert. denied, 247 La. 877, 175 So.2d 110 (1965); Colton v. Benes, 176 Neb. 483, 126 N.W.2d 652 (1964). But see Barretto v. Akau, 51 Haw. 383, 463 P.2d 917 (1969). There is division as to whether the matter must be specifically pleaded by defendant. What would be the advantage of that requirement? See Moulton v. Alamo Ambulance Serv., Inc., 414 S.W.2d 444 (Tex.1967).

3. The failure to submit to surgery that a reasonable person would undergo to mitigate injury can limit plaintiff's damages for both loss of wages and pain and suffering. See Young v. American Export Isbrandtsen Lines, Inc., 291 F.Supp. 447 (S.D.N.Y.1968) (failure to remove ruptured cartilage). See generally, Failure to Mitigate Damages by Showing Plaintiffs Failed to Follow Doctors' Orders, 31 Current Med. 16 (1984); Kelley, Refusal of Surgery in Mitigation of Damages, 10 Clev.Mar.L.Rev. 421 (1961). The mere fact that there is some risk involved, even with a chance of fatality, may not bar the application of the avoidable consequences rule. See Bowers v. Lumbermens Mut. Casualty Co., 131 So.2d 70 (La.App.1961).

See also Hayes v. United States, 367 F.2d 340 (2d Cir.1966). Is this inconsistent with the principle inherent in the law of battery that individuals should have the right to decide whether another person can violate their physical being? Why impose an obligation to mitigate damages?

4. In some cases, the plaintiff's failure to undergo reasonable medical treatment is motivated by the plaintiff's religious beliefs. How should this affect the doctrine? Some courts would not admit evidence of the plaintiff's religious beliefs while others permit the jury to consider it as part of their determination of reasonableness. How might the First Amendment affect the application of the tort doctrine? See Munn v. Algee, 924 F.2d 568 (5th Cir. 1991); Williams v. Bright, 658 N.Y.S.2d 910 (1997); Note, Medical Care, Freedom of Religion, and Mitigation of Damages, 87 Yale L.J. 1466 (1978) and Note, Reason, Religion, and Avoidable Consequences: When Faith and the Duty to Mitigate Collide, 67 N.Y.U.L. Rev. 1111 (1992) and cases cited therein.

2. PHYSICAL HARM TO PROPERTY

Damages for physical harm to land or chattels is closely tied in with the concept of value, or in other words, what the property is worth. If a chattel is completely destroyed, or is converted, the measure of damages is its entire value at the time and place of the tort. If it is damaged, but not destroyed or converted, the damages are measured by the difference in value before and after the injury. If there is merely deprivation of use, as in the case of dispossession for a limited time, the damages consist of the value of the use of which the plaintiff has been deprived.

Value necessarily involves the idea of some standard by which it can be determined. What we are looking for is the financial equivalent of the property, or the harm to it. In the vast majority of the cases, whether the harm is to chattels or to land, the standard set for value is the market value of the property. The theory underlying this is that the plaintiff, given this financial equivalent, can go out on the open market and replace the property by buying other property freely offered for sale. See, generally, Restatement (Second) of Torts § 911.

Market value usually is defined as what the property in question could probably have been sold for on the open market, in the ordinary course of voluntary sale by a leisurely seller to a willing buyer. Thus it is not the cost to the seller, or the asking price, nor is it what could be obtained on a forced sale. Since value must be looked at from the point of view of one who is complaining of being deprived of the thing valued, it is the highest price that could have been realized, and not the lowest price at which there could reasonably have been a sale. Also, the market value of property must be taken as a whole; and if, for example, there is conversion of a stock of goods or a tract of land, it is the wholesale price of the stock of goods that is to be considered, since that is the only price at which it could have been sold in its entirety, and is the price of the land as a tract, rather than as subdivided into lots, that must be considered.

Market value ordinarily is determined on the basis of the market at the place where the wrong occurred. When there is no available market at that place, there is resort to the nearest market, with allowance made for the costs of transportation to and from it. If the goods were intended by the plaintiff for use, these costs will be added to the market price; but if they were intended for sale, they will be deducted.

Market value also is ordinarily determined as of the time of the wrong. There is, however, one group of cases in which subsequent increases in value have been taken into account. These arise where there is conversion of goods of the kind commonly dealt in on exchanges, such as stocks and bonds, and commodities such as grain. The same exception is made as to cases of breach of contract to sell such goods to the plaintiff. Even here, some courts refuse to consider subsequent increase in value, and adhere strictly to the value at the time of the wrong. Most of the American courts have made some kind of allowance for an increase. The leading cases on this are Galigher v. Jones, 129 U.S. 193 (1889) and Schultz v. Commodity Futures Trading Comm'n, 716 F.2d 136 (2d Cir.1983).

Assuming that some allowance is to be made for subsequent increase, or in other words, for successful speculation, the courts have not agreed as to just what is to be allowed. One group of cases has allowed as damages the highest value which the goods have reached during the period from the time of the wrong to the trial of the action. This is called the "rule of the highest intermediate value." It has been criticized because it assumes that the plaintiff would have sold the goods at the peak reached during that entire period and because the longer the delay until trial the longer the time during which the plaintiff may benefit from a rise in the market. In partial response to these criticisms, some courts require that the plaintiff's action be prosecuted with reasonable diligence, while others permit recovery only of the highest intermediate value up to the commencement of the action.

Many courts follow the rule originated in New York, which, as the great commercial center, has received considerable respect in all matters concerning exchanges. The New York rule has been that the plaintiff may recover the highest market value between the time of conversion and a reasonable period within which he could have replaced the goods by purchase on the market. This is commonly known as the "highest replacement value" rule. The time for replacement does not begin at the time of the defendant's wrong, but at the time the plaintiff learns of it. The "reasonable time" for replacement is kept from being extended too far by the jury, by the view, at least in many courts, that where the facts are not in dispute, it is for the judge to say how long is a "reasonable time." See Restatement (Second) of Torts § 927.

Occasionally, chattels have no market value, simply because they are not salable. More often the market value clearly would not be adequate compensation. In these cases, there may be recovery of the value to the owner, as distinguished from value to others. This is true of family heirlooms and other articles that have a purely personal value, to the plaintiff and no one else. It is also true, in general, of clothing, books, pictures, furniture and household goods, which will be worth more to the owner than their value to a second-hand store. The "personal value" so awarded is determined by consideration of whatever factors may be relevant, such as original cost of the property, the use made of it, and its condition at the time of the wrong. See, for example, Campins v. Capels, 461 N.E.2d 712 (Ind.App.1984) ("those items generally capable of generating sentimental feelings, not just emotions peculiar to the owner"); Shaffer v. Honeywell, Inc., 249 N.W.2d 251 (S.D.1976) (trophies won at horse shows); Brown v. Frontier Theatres, Inc., 369 S.W.2d 299 (Tex.1963) (grandmother's wedding veil); Brousseau v. Rosenthal, 110 Misc.2d 1054, 443 N.Y.S.2d 285 (1980) (dog); Southern Express Co. v. Owens, 146 Ala. 412, 41 So. 752 (1906) (unpublished manuscript).

When the property is not destroyed or converted, but only damaged, the measure becomes one of the difference in value before and after the wrong. The cost of repairing the land or chattel is admissible in evidence, on the assumption that it amounts to a restoration of the original value; but it is not conclusive, and may be challenged by either side as excessive or inadequate for the purpose. Restatement (Second) of Torts § 928. The cost of repairs may not exceed the value of the chattel prior to the injury. See Smith v. Brooks, 337 A.2d 493 (D.C.App.1975).

When there is only temporary deprivation of use, as by dispossession for a limited period, the measure becomes one of the rental value of the property for that period—or in other words, the amount which the owner could have obtained in the market by renting out the property, or the cost to him of renting similar property for the specified time. See Brownstein, What's the Use? A Doctrinal and Policy Critique of the Measurement of Loss of Use Damages, 37 Rutgers L.Rev. 433 (1985).

Consequential damages may be recovered for the conversion of property, or for harm to it, when they are "proximately" caused. These might include, for example, the reasonable expense of trying to recover possession of the property, or loss of a profitable bargain resulting from deprivation of the goods, and the like. Parroski v. Goldberg, 80 Wis. 339, 50 N.W. 191 (1891); Preble v. Hanna, 117 Or. 306, 244 P. 75 (1926); Universal Credit Co. v. Wyatt, 56 S.W.2d 487 (Tex.Civ.App.1933). An interesting case in which market value, consequential damages and punitive damages all were recovered is Glass v. Brunt, 157 Kan. 27, 138 P.2d 453 (1943).

3. Punitive Damages

Punitive damages, sometimes called exemplary or vindictive damages, or "smart money," consist of an additional sum, over and above the compensation of the plaintiff for the harm suffered, that are awarded for the purpose of punishing the defendant, of admonishing the defendant not to do it again, and of deterring others from following defendant's example. They originated in England in the days of George III, in cases of outrageous abuses of authority by government officers, such as Huckle v. Money, 2 Wils.K.B. 205, 95 Eng.Rep. 768 (1763), and were then adopted in the United States.

The policy of awarding punitive damages in tort cases has been a subject of much dispute. It has been condemned as undue compensation to the plaintiff beyond his just deserts, in the form of a criminal fine that should be paid to the state if to anyone and is indeed fixed by the caprice of the jury, without any standards, and without any of the usual safeguards of criminal procedure, such as proof of guilt beyond a reasonable doubt, the privilege against self-incrimination, and even the rule against double jeopardy—since, in most places, the defendant may still be punished for the crime after he has been mulcted in the tort action.

Punitive damages have been defended as a salutary method of discouraging evil motives, as a partial remedy for the refusal of American civil procedure to allow compensation for the expenses of litigation including counsel fees, as a way of diverting plaintiff's desire for revenge into peaceful channels, and as an incentive to bring into court and redress a long array of petty cases of outrage and oppression, which in practice escape the notice of busy prosecuting attorneys occupied with serious crime and which a private individual would otherwise find not worth the trouble and expense of a lawsuit.

" 'Punitive damages' is a legal term of art that has a widely accepted common-law meaning; 'punitive damages have long been a part of traditional state tort law.' [C] Although the precise nature and use of punitive damages may have evolved over time, and the size and frequency of such awards may have increased, this Court's decisions make clear that the concept of 'punitive damages' has a long pedigree in the law. 'It is a well-established principle of the common law, that in actions of trespass and all actions on the case for torts, a jury may inflict what are called exemplary, punitive, or vindictive damages upon a defendant, having in view the enormity of his offense rather than the measure of compensation to the plaintiff.' [C]" Molzof v. United States, 502 U.S. 301, 306 (1992).

Gryc v. Dayton–Hudson Corp.

Supreme Court of Minnesota, 1980.
297 N.W.2d 727, cert. denied, 449 U.S. 921 (1980).

TODD, JUSTICE. On December 8, 1969, Lee Ann Gryc, then 4 years of age, was clothed in pajamas made from a cotton material manufactured by defendant Riegel Textile Corporation (Riegel). The material was commercially known as "flannelette." It was not treated but did meet the minimum federal standards of product flammability. Lee Ann reached across the electric stove in her home to shut off a timer. Her pajamas were instantly ignited and she received severe burns over her upper body. The jury found Riegel liable for these injuries and awarded Lee Ann $750,000 in compensatory damages and $1,000,000 in punitive damages. We affirm. * * *

At trial, plaintiffs contended and presented evidence which tended to prove that the fabric used in the Gryc pajamas was defective. They claimed and their evidence tended to show that: (1) the cotton flannelette was unreasonably dangerous for use in children's sleepwear because of its highly flammable characteristics; (2) there were commercially available durable flame retardant chemicals which could have significantly increased the safety of the product; (3) there were inherently flame retardant synthetics which could have been used for children's sleepwear instead of cotton flannelette; (4) garment manufacturers, sellers, and consumers should have been warned of the flammable characteristics of the cotton flannelette; and (5) consumers should have been instructed of a simple home remedy which could have been used to flame retard the fabric after each washing. * * *

Riegel * * * contends that the trial court, in instructing the jury on the issue of punitive damages, applied an incorrect legal standard and burden of proof. Riegel argues that a "reckless disregard" standard was improperly applied and that the burden of proof on this issue should have been one of "clear and convincing evidence" rather than a "preponderance of the evidence." Riegel presents these arguments for the first time on appeal. These arguments were not raised at trial or in Riegel's post-trial motions.

* * * [W]e hold that the trial court's instructions cannot now be attacked by Riegel. The instructions constitute the law of the case and Riegel's subsequent arguments will be reviewed on the basis of the legal standard imposed by the trial court.[6]

In instructing the jury on the issue of punitive damages, the court listed several factors which the jury was to take into account in determining whether Riegel had acted in willful or reckless disregard of plaintiffs' rights:

1. The existence and magnitude of the product danger to the public;

2. The cost or feasibility of reducing the danger to an acceptable level;

3. The manufacturer's awareness of the danger, the magnitude of the danger, and the availability of a feasible remedy;

4. The nature and duration of, and the reasons for, the manufacturer's failure to act appropriately to discover or reduce the danger;

5. The extent to which the manufacturer purposefully created the danger;

6. The extent to which the defendants are subject to federal safety regulation;

7. The probability that compensatory damages might be awarded against defendants in other cases; and, finally,

8. The amount of time which has passed since the actions sought to be deterred.

We have reviewed the entire record and, after taking into consideration the above-listed factors, have concluded that there was sufficient, in fact substantial, evidence for the jury to find that Riegel acted in willful,

---

6. We note that 1978 Minn.Laws c. 738, § 4, which subsequently changed the law with respect to the legal standard for punitive damages, is not applicable in this case.

wanton and/or malicious disregard of the rights of others in marketing its flannelette. * * *

Riegel contends that various policy considerations dictate against an award of punitive damages in this case. It argues that, in products liability cases where there is a potential for multiple plaintiffs, over-severe admonition and severe economic hardship may result if punitive damages awards are allowed. This same criticism was made by Judge Friendly in the case of Roginsky v. Richardson–Merrell, Inc., 378 F.2d 832, 838–9 (2d Cir.1967). However, this argument has been consistently rejected by other courts and commentators who have considered this issue. * * *

Moreover, since Riegel's wealth or poverty and the degree to which it has already been punished was relevant in this case and will be relevant in future actions against it, Riegel is adequately protected against being overly punished for its misconduct.

Riegel also argues that there is no need for the deterrent of punitive damages in this case. Riegel contends that compensatory damages and loss of sales and reputation act as an adequate deterrent. Riegel also posits that since it no longer manufactures cotton flannelette and since the Flammable Fabrics Act presently has more stringent standards for children's sleepwear, no deterrent is needed. This argument ignores the fact that Riegel was shown to have acted in reckless disregard of the public for purely economic reasons in the past. A punitive damages award serves to deter Riegel from acting in a similar manner with respect to other products manufactured by it in the future. Furthermore, since the potential of compensatory damages awards and loss of sales and reputation did not serve to deter Riegel in the past, Riegel cannot now argue that these considerations act as an adequate deterrent.

Riegel also overlooks the fact that one of the functions of a punitive damages award is to punish past misconduct. This function is well served by a punitive damages award in this case.

Riegel contends that the punitive damages award of $1,000,000 was clearly excessive. This court has stated that it will not disturb a punitive damages award unless it appears that the award was actuated by passion and prejudice and is so excessive as to be deemed unreasonable. [C] We have reviewed the record in this case and find that the punitive damages award is not unreasonable in light of the evidence presented.

The evidence shows that Riegel created a substantial danger to the public by marketing its highly flammable cotton flannelette. Riegel continued to market this product even though there were economically feasible measures which could have been taken to reduce this danger to a fairly acceptable level. The evidence also showed that Riegel was aware of the danger and the means for reducing this danger. Furthermore, Riegel is a multi-million dollar corporation which reaped substantial profits through the sale of its highly flammable cotton flannelette. We, therefore, do not find that the punitive damages award was excessive as a matter of law. * * *

[The Court also determined that the defendant's compliance with the Flammable Fabrics Act, P.L. 90–189 § 6, 81 Stat. 568, did not preempt the jury's right to award punitive damages.]

The judgment is, therefore, affirmed.

NOTES AND QUESTIONS

1. *Intentional Torts.* Punitive damages are generally permitted when defendant has committed an intentional tort such as assault, battery, false imprisonment, conversion, trespass, malicious prosecution or intentional infliction of emotional harm. Defendant's conduct need not be motivated by personal hatred; it is enough if it has the character of "outrage." Jones v. Fisher, 42 Wis.2d 209, 166 N.W.2d 175 (1969). But, there are still times when a technically intentional tort may be committed innocently. For example, a defendant innocently buys a stolen article or falsely imprisons a person whom he reasonably believes to have stolen his property. In those cases the absence of ill will or malice may bar a claim for punitive damages.

2. *Negligent Torts.* Conduct short of intentional wrongdoing may be sufficient to justify punitive damages in most jurisdictions. Courts use a variety of formulas to spell this out, including "reckless disregard for the rights of others," Allman v. Bird, 186 Kan. 802, 353 P.2d 216 (1960); or "willful misconduct, wantonness, recklessness, or want of care indicative of indifference to consequences," In re Air Crash Disaster Near Chicago, 644 F.2d 594 (7th Cir.1981), cert. denied, 454 U.S. 878 (1981). Conduct that is merely negligent, even if it causes severe damage, is insufficient to justify punitive damages. This is usually held to be true of "grossly negligent" conduct when those terms are used as a synonym for "extreme carelessness" as opposed to "recklessness." But see Williams v. Wilson, 972 S.W.2d 260 (Ky.1998) (new statutory punitive damages standard, which required "subjective awareness" that conduct would result in human death or bodily harm, violated state constitutional jural rights doctrine because recovery for conduct that was grossly negligent was well-established common law right). See page 1218.

3. *Strict Liability in Tort.* Should punitive damages be available in a cause of action based on strict liability? In addition to the principal case, see Fischer v. Johns–Manville Corp., 103 N.J. 643, 512 A.2d 466 (1986) (defendant unsuccessfully argued that the concept of strict liability for products that theoretically focuses on the condition of the product rather than the conduct of the manufacturer, is incompatible with the concept of punitive damages, which is based on the defendant's malicious conduct); Owens–Illinois, Inc. v. Zenobia, 325 Md. 420, 601 A.2d 633 (1992) (evidence necessary to sustain punitive damages award goes far beyond that necessary to sustain a compensatory damages award in a strict liability claim, but such an approach is open to plaintiff; "actual malice" requirement is satisfied in product liability case by showing of actual knowledge of the defect and conscious or deliberate disregard of the foreseeable harm resulting from the defect).

4. *Estate as Defendant.* Should punitive damages be available against the estate of a deceased tortfeasor? How are the goals of punishment and deterrence served in that situation? Plaintiff's former boyfriend distributed photocopies of sexually explicit photographs of her that he had taken during their relationship. The photocopies contained her address and telephone number and captions that implied that she was a prostitute. The photocopies were distributed throughout the community, including places that would ensure that they would be seen by plaintiff's minor children, her mother, her brother, and her employer. The distribution finally stopped when plaintiff filed a complaint including counts of defamation,

you can get punitive for strict liability actions

Punitive if
no compensation
courts split

intentional infliction of emotional distress, and false light invasion of privacy. The tortfeasor committed suicide before the trial and his sister, the executrix of his estate, was substituted as a defendant. Should the jury award of punitive damages be upheld? G.J.D. v. Johnson, 552 Pa. 169, 713 A.2d 1127 (1998) (permitting award of punitive damages against estate, but noting that the majority of jurisdictions do not). See Chapter 11, Wrongful Death and Survival.

5. Can the plaintiff recover punitive damages if she has suffered no compensable harm? Some courts have held that an award of compensatory damages is required, although others have deemed it sufficient that the plaintiff prove the elements of her underlying cause of action, even if the jury does not actually award compensatory damages. Clark v. McClurg, 215 Cal. 279, 9 P.2d 505 (1932). Can award of nominal damages support an award of punitive damages? Jacque v. Steenberg Homes, Inc., 209 Wis.2d 605, 563 N.W.2d 154 (1997) (general rule that compensatory damages are required for award of punitive damages does not apply in case of intentional tort of trespass; defendant had bulldozed a path in the snow across plaintiff's field to deliver a mobile home despite plaintiff's repeated refusals to give permission to defendant to cross his land to make the delivery).

6. In a medical malpractice action, jury found that patient's medical records had been altered in a way that made it more difficult for her to prove her case. The alteration in the records did not, however, affect her treatment so it did not cause any of her damages. Does a showing of actual malice permit the imposition of punitive damages if the malicious conduct did not cause compensable harm? Moskovitz v. Mt. Sinai Medical Ctr., 69 Ohio St.3d 638, 635 N.E.2d 331 (1994) (not necessary that malicious intent necessary to sustain an award of punitive damages must itself have proximately caused compensable harm as long as plaintiff also proves compensable harm in suit). See also note 2, page 1006.

7. The decisions usually hold that punitive damages are a windfall to the plaintiff, not a right and that the jury has complete discretion to refrain from awarding them in any case. Harrison v. Ely, 120 Ill. 83, 11 N.E. 334 (1887); Petrey v. Liuzzi, 76 Ohio App. 19, 61 N.E.2d 158 (1945); Luke v. Mercantile Acceptance Corp., 111 Cal.App.2d 431, 244 P.2d 764 (1952).

BMW of North America, Inc. v. Gore

Supreme Court of the United States, 1996.
517 U.S. 559, 116 S.Ct. 1589, 134 L.Ed.2d 809.

JUSTICE STEVENS delivered the opinion of the Court.

The Due Process Clause of the Fourteenth Amendment prohibits a State from imposing a " 'grossly excessive' " punishment on a tortfeasor. TXO Production Corp. v. Alliance Resources Corp., 509 U.S. 443, 454, 125 L. Ed. 2d 366, 113 S. Ct. 2711 (1993) (and cases cited). The wrongdoing involved in this case was the decision by a national distributor of automobiles not to advise its dealers, and hence their customers, of predelivery damage to new cars when the cost of repair amounted to less than 3 percent of the car's suggested retail price. The question presented is whether a $2 million punitive damages award to the purchaser of one of these cars exceeds the constitutional limit.

I

In January 1990, Dr. Ira Gore, Jr. (respondent), purchased a black BMW sports sedan for $40,750.88 from an authorized BMW dealer in Birmingham, Alabama. After driving the car for approximately nine months, and without noticing any flaws in its appearance, Dr. Gore took the car to "Slick Finish," an independent detailer, to make it look " 'snazzier than it normally would appear.' " [C] Mr. Slick, the proprietor, detected evidence that the car had been repainted [to repair damage done by acid rain while the car was in transit from Germany]. Convinced that he had been cheated, Dr. Gore brought suit against petitioner BMW of North America (BMW), the American distributor of BMW automobiles. Dr. Gore alleged, inter alia, that the failure to disclose that the car had been repainted constituted suppression of a material fact. (Footnotes omitted.) * * *

At trial, BMW acknowledged that it had adopted a nationwide policy in 1983 concerning cars that were damaged in the course of manufacture or transportation. If the cost of repairing the damage exceeded 3 percent of the car's suggested retail price, the car was placed in company service for a period of time and then sold as used. If the repair cost did not exceed 3 percent of the suggested retail price, however, the car was sold as new without advising the dealer that any repairs had been made. Because the $601.37 cost of repainting Dr. Gore's car was only about 1.5 percent of its suggested retail price, BMW did not disclose the damage or repair to the Birmingham dealer.

* * *

[Dr. Gore asserted that his repainted car was worth less than a car that had not been refinished. At trial, he used the testimony of a former BMW dealer, who estimated that the value of a repainted BMW was approximately 10 percent less than the value of a new car that had not been damaged and repaired, $4000 in this case. To support his claim for punitive damages, Dr. Gore introduced evidence that since 1983 BMW had sold 983 refinished cars as new, including 14 in Alabama, without disclosing that the cars had been repainted before sale at a cost of more than $300 per vehicle. Using the actual damage estimate of $4,000 per vehicle, Dr. Gore argued that a punitive award of $4 million would provide an appropriate penalty for selling approximately 1,000 cars for more than they were worth. In defense of its disclosure policy, BMW argued that it was under no obligation to disclose repairs of minor damage to new cars and that Dr. Gore's car was as good as a car with the original factory finish. It disputed Dr. Gore's assertion that the value of the car was impaired by the repainting and argued that this good-faith belief made a punitive award inappropriate. BMW also maintained that transactions in jurisdictions other than Alabama had no relevance to Dr. Gore's claim.

The jury returned a verdict finding BMW liable for compensatory damages of $4,000, and assessing $4 million in punitive damages. The trial judge denied BMW's post-trial motion to set aside the punitive damages award, holding, among other things, that the award was not "grossly excessive" and thus did not violate the Due Process Clause of the Fourteenth Amendment. BMW had filed a post-trial motion and introduced evidence that established that its nondisclosure policy was consistent with the laws of roughly 25 States defining the disclosure obligations of automobile manufacturers, distributors, and dealers. The most stringent of these statutes required disclosure of repairs costing more than 3 percent of the suggested retail price; none mandated disclosure of less costly repairs. Relying on these statutes, BMW contended that its conduct was lawful in these States and therefore could not provide the basis for an award of punitive damages. The Alabama Supreme Court reduced the award to $2 million on the ground that, in computing the amount, the jury had improperly multiplied Gore's compensatory damages by the number of similar sales in all States, not just those in Alabama.]

II

Punitive damages may properly be imposed to further a State's legitimate interests in punishing unlawful conduct and deterring its repetition. [Cc] In our federal system, States necessarily have considerable flexibility in determining the level of punitive damages that they will allow in different classes of cases and in any particular case. Most States that authorize exemplary damages afford the jury similar latitude, requiring only that the damages awarded be reasonably necessary to vindicate the State's legitimate interests in punishment and deterrence. [Cc] Only when an award can fairly be categorized as "grossly excessive" in relation to these interests does it enter the zone of arbitrariness that violates the Due Process Clause of the Fourteenth Amendment. [C] For that reason, the federal excessiveness inquiry appropriately begins with an identification of the state interests that a punitive award is designed to serve. We therefore focus our attention first on the scope of Alabama's legitimate interests in punishing BMW and deterring it from future misconduct. No one doubts that a State may protect its citizens by prohibiting deceptive trade practices and by requiring automobile distributors to disclose presale repairs that affect the value of a new car. But the States need not, and in fact do not, provide such protection in a uniform manner. Some States rely on the judicial process to formulate and enforce an appropriate disclosure requirement by applying principles of contract and tort law. (Footnote omitted). Other States have enacted various forms of legislation that define the disclosure obligations of automobile manufacturers, distributors, and dealers. (Footnote omitted.) The result is a patchwork of rules representing the diverse policy judgments of lawmakers in 50 States.

That diversity demonstrates that reasonable people may disagree about the value of a full disclosure requirement. Some legislatures may conclude that affirmative disclosure requirements are unnecessary because the self-interest of those involved in the automobile trade in developing and maintaining the goodwill of their customers will motivate them to make voluntary disclosures or to refrain from selling cars that do not comply with self-imposed standards. The legislatures that do adopt affirmative disclosure obligations may take into account the cost of government regulation, choosing to draw a line exempting minor repairs from such a requirement. * * *

We think it follows from these principles of state sovereignty and comity that a State may not impose economic sanctions on violators of its laws with the intent of changing the tortfeasors' lawful conduct in other States. Before this Court Dr. Gore argued that the large punitive damages award was necessary to induce BMW to change the nationwide policy that it adopted in 1983. But by attempting to alter BMW's nationwide policy, Alabama would be infringing on the policy choices of other States. To avoid such encroachment, the economic penalties that a State such as Alabama inflicts on those who transgress its laws, whether the penalties take the form of legislatively authorized fines or judicially imposed punitive damages, must be supported by the State's interest in protecting its own consumers and its own economy. Alabama may insist that BMW adhere to a particular disclosure policy in that State. Alabama does not have the power, however, to punish BMW for conduct that was lawful where it occurred and that had no impact on Alabama or its residents. Nor may Alabama impose sanctions on BMW in order to deter conduct that is lawful in other jurisdictions. (Footnotes omitted.)

* * *

III

Elementary notions of fairness enshrined in our constitutional jurisprudence dictate that a person receive fair notice not only of the conduct that will subject him to punishment, but also of the severity of the penalty that a State may impose. (Footnote omitted.) Three guideposts, each of which indicates that BMW did not receive adequate notice of the magnitude of the sanction that Alabama might impose for adhering to the nondisclosure policy adopted in 1983, lead us to the conclusion that the $2 million award against BMW is grossly excessive: the degree of reprehensibility of the nondisclosure; the disparity between the harm or potential harm suffered by Dr. Gore and his punitive damages award; and the difference between this remedy and the civil penalties authorized or imposed in comparable cases. We discuss these considerations in turn.

Degree of Reprehensibility

Perhaps the most important indicium of the reasonableness of a punitive damages award is the degree of reprehensibility of the defendant's conduct. (Footnote omitted.) As the Court stated nearly 150 years ago, exemplary damages imposed on a defendant should reflect "the enormity of his offense." [Cc] (Footnote omitted.) This principle reflects the accepted view that some wrongs are more blameworthy than others. Thus, we have said that "nonviolent crimes are less serious than crimes marked by violence or the threat of violence." [C] Similarly, "trickery and deceit," [C], are more reprehensible than negligence. * * *

In this case, none of the aggravating factors associated with particularly reprehensible conduct is present. The harm BMW inflicted on Dr. Gore was purely economic in nature. The presale refinishing of the car had no effect on its performance or safety features, or even its appearance for at least nine months after his purchase. BMW's conduct evinced no indifference to or reckless disregard for the health and safety of others. To be sure, infliction of economic injury, especially when done intentionally through affirmative acts of misconduct, [c], or when the target is financially vulnerable, can warrant a substantial penalty. But this observation does not convert all acts that cause economic harm into torts that are sufficiently reprehensible to justify a significant sanction in addition to compensatory damages. Dr. Gore contends that BMW's conduct was particularly reprehensible because nondisclosure of the repairs to his car formed part of a nationwide pattern of tortious conduct. Certainly, evidence that a defendant has repeatedly engaged in prohibited conduct while knowing or suspecting that it was unlawful would provide relevant support for an argument that strong medicine is required to cure the defendant's disrespect for the law. [C] Our holdings that a recidivist may be punished more severely than a first offender recognize that repeated misconduct is more reprehensible than an individual instance of malfeasance. [C]

* * *

* * * We do not think it can be disputed that there may exist minor imperfections in the finish of a new car that can be repaired (or indeed, left unrepaired) without materially affecting the car's value. (Footnote omitted.) There is no evidence that BMW acted in bad faith when it sought to establish the appropriate line between presumptively minor damage and damage requiring disclosure to purchasers. For this purpose, BMW could reasonably rely on state disclosure statutes for guidance. In this regard, it is also significant that there is no evidence that BMW persisted in a course of conduct after it had been adjudged unlawful on even one occasion, let alone repeated occasions. (Footnote omitted.)

Finally, the record in this case discloses no deliberate false statements, acts of affirmative misconduct, or concealment of evidence of improper motive, such as were present in [other cases.] [Cc] We accept, of course, the jury's finding that BMW suppressed a material fact which Alabama law obligated it to communicate to prospective purchasers of repainted cars in that State. But the omission of a material fact may be less reprehensible than a deliberate false statement, particularly when there is a good-faith basis for believing that no duty to disclose exists. That conduct is sufficiently reprehensible to give rise to tort liability, and even a modest award of exemplary damages does not establish the high degree of culpability that warrants a substantial punitive damages award. Because this case exhibits none of the circumstances ordinarily associated with egregiously improper conduct, we are persuaded that BMW's conduct was not sufficiently reprehensible to warrant imposition of a $2 million exemplary damages award.

Ratio

The second and perhaps most commonly cited indicium of an unreasonable or excessive punitive damages award is its ratio to the actual harm inflicted on the plaintiff. [Cc] The principle that exemplary damages must bear a "reasonable relationship" to compensatory damages has a long pedigree. (Footnote omitted.) Scholars have identified a number of early English statutes authorizing the award of multiple damages for particular wrongs. Some 65 different enactments during the period between 1275 and 1753 provided for double, treble, or quadruple damages. (Footnote omitted.) Our decisions in both [Pacific Mut. Life Ins. Co. v.] *Haslip* [, 499 U.S. 1 (1991)] and *TXO* endorsed the proposition that a comparison between the compensatory award and the punitive award is significant.

In *Haslip* we concluded that even though a punitive damages award of "more than 4 times the amount of compensatory damages" might be "close to the line," it did not "cross the line into the area of constitutional impropriety." [C] *TXO*, following dicta in *Haslip*, refined this analysis by confirming that the proper inquiry is " 'whether there is a reasonable relationship between the punitive damages award and the harm likely to result from the defendant's conduct as well as the harm that actually has occurred.' " [C] Thus, in upholding the $10 million award in *TXO*, we relied on the difference between that figure and the harm to the victim that would have ensued if the tortious plan had succeeded. That difference suggested that the relevant ratio was not more than 10 to 1. (Footnote omitted.)

The $2 million in punitive damages awarded to Dr. Gore by the Alabama Supreme Court is 500 times the amount of his actual harm as determined by the jury. (Footnote omitted.) Moreover, there is no suggestion that Dr. Gore or any other BMW purchaser was threatened with any additional potential harm by BMW's nondisclosure policy. The disparity in this case is thus dramatically greater than those considered in Haslip and *TXO*. (Footnote omitted.)

Of course, we have consistently rejected the notion that the constitutional line is marked by a simple mathematical formula, even one that compares actual and potential damages to the punitive award.[C] Indeed, low awards of compensatory damages may properly support a higher ratio than high compensatory awards, if, for example, a particularly egregious act has resulted in only a small amount of economic damages. A higher ratio may also be justified in cases in which the injury is hard to detect or the monetary value of noneconomic harm might have been difficult to determine. It is appropriate, therefore, to reiterate our rejection of a categorical approach. Once again, "we return to what we said . . . in Haslip: 'We need not, and indeed we cannot, draw a mathematical bright line between the constitutionally acceptable and the constitutionally unacceptable that would fit every case. We can say, however, that [a] general concer[n] of reasonableness . . . properly enter[s] into the constitutional calculus.' " [C] In most cases, the ratio will be within a constitutionally acceptable range, and remittitur will not be justified on this basis. When the ratio is a breathtaking 500 to 1, however, the award must surely "raise a suspicious judicial eyebrow." [C]

Sanctions for Comparable Misconduct

Comparing the punitive damages award and the civil or criminal penalties that could be imposed for comparable misconduct provides a third indicium of excessiveness. As Justice O'Connor has correctly observed, a reviewing court engaged in determining whether an award of punitive damages is excessive should "accord 'substantial deference' to legislative judgments concerning appropriate sanctions for the conduct at issue." * * * [The Court noted that the maximum civil penalty authorized by the Alabama Legislature for a violation of its Deceptive Trade Practices Act is $2,000.]

The sanction imposed in this case cannot be justified on the ground that it was necessary to deter future misconduct without considering whether less drastic remedies could be expected to achieve that goal. The fact that a multimillion dollar penalty prompted a change in policy sheds no light on the question whether a lesser deterrent would have adequately protected the interests of Alabama consumers. In the absence of a history of noncompliance with known statutory requirements, there is no basis for assuming that a more modest sanction would not have been sufficient to motivate full compliance with the disclosure requirement imposed by the Alabama Supreme Court in this case.

IV

We assume, as the juries in this case and in the *Yates* case [a 1993 Alabama case arising out of the same BMW policy] found, that the undisclosed damage to the new BMW's affected their actual value. Notwithstanding the evidence adduced by BMW in an effort to prove that the repainted cars conformed to the same quality standards as its other cars, we also assume that it knew, or should have known, that as time passed the repainted cars would lose their attractive appearance more rapidly than other BMW's. Moreover, we of course accept the Alabama courts' view that the state interest in protecting its citizens from deceptive trade practices justifies a sanction in addition to the recovery of compensatory damages. We cannot, however, accept the conclusion of the Alabama Supreme Court that BMW's conduct was sufficiently egregious to justify a punitive sanction that is tantamount to a severe criminal penalty. The fact that BMW is a large corporation rather than an impecunious individual does not diminish its entitlement to fair notice of the demands that the several States impose on the conduct of its business. Indeed, its status as an active participant in the national economy implicates the federal interest in preventing individual States from imposing undue burdens on interstate commerce. While each State has ample power to protect its own consumers, none may use the punitive damages deterrent as a means of imposing its regulatory policies on the entire Nation. As in Haslip, we are not prepared to draw a bright line marking the limits of a constitutionally acceptable punitive damages award. Unlike that case, however, we are fully convinced that the grossly excessive award imposed in this case transcends the constitutional limit. (Footnote omitted.) Whether the appropriate remedy requires a new trial or merely an independent determination by the Alabama Supreme Court of the award necessary to vindicate the economic interests of Alabama consumers is a matter that should be addressed by the state court in the first instance.

The judgment is reversed, and the case is remanded for further proceedings not inconsistent with this opinion.

It is so ordered.

(Justice Breyer's concurring opinion, in which Justice O'Connor and Souter joined, is omitted. Justice Scalia's dissenting opinion, in which Justice Thomas joined, is omitted. Justice Ginsburg's dissenting opinion, in which the Chief Justice joined, is omitted.).

NOTES AND QUESTIONS

1. On remand, the Alabama Supreme Court ordered a remittitur of the punitive damages to $50,000 and Dr. Gore accepted. 701 So. 2d 507, 515 (Ala.1997) ("After carefully reconsidering this case, analyzing the Hammond–Green Oil factors in the light of the United States Supreme Court's opinion in BMW, and incorporating the guideposts articulated therein, we agree that the $2 million award of punitive damages against BMW was grossly excessive.")

2. *Calculation of Amount.* There is a strong tradition in many jurisdictions of requiring that the punitive damages award bear some reasonable relation to the compensatory award. This usually is expressed in terms of a factor to be considered by the jury, although some jurisdictions have set firmer guidelines by statute. Fla. Stat. §§ 768.73(1)(a) and (b) (1999 Supp.) (three times compensatory); Colo. Rev. Stat. §§ 31–21–102(1)(a) and (3) (1999 Supp.) (one times compensatory or three times compensatory under specified circumstances). Some jurisdictions have imposed a cap on the amount of punitive damages. N.J. Stat.§ 2A:15–5.14 (1999 Supp.) (greater of five times compensatory damages or $350,000); Va. Code Ann. § 8.01–38.1 (1992) ($350,000).

3. Within the limits set by a cap or ratio, what factors should the jury consider in setting the amount of punitive damages? In California, the jury may consider "the character of defendant's act, the nature and extent of the harm to the plaintiff and the wealth of the defendant." See Coats v. Constr. & Gen. Laborers Local #185, 15 Cal.App.3d 908, 93 Cal.Rptr. 639 (1971). Oregon advises the jury to consider the likelihood that serious harm would arise from the misconduct, the degree of defendant's awareness of the misconduct, the profitability of the misconduct, the duration of the misconduct and any concealment of it, the attitude and conduct of defendant upon discovery of the misconduct, the financial condition of the defendant, and the total deterrent effect of other punishment imposed for the same conduct. Ore. Rev. Stat. § 30.925 (1997). South Carolina directs the jury to consider the degree of culpability, the duration of the conduct, the awareness or concealment of conduct, the existence of similar past conduct, the likelihood that the award will deter defendant or other, whether the award is reasonably related to the harm likely to result, the defendant's ability to pay, and any other factors deemed appropriate. Atlas Food Sys. And Svcs., Inc. v. Crane Nat. Vendors, Inc., 99 F.3d 587 (4th Cir.1996). The fact that the defendant's wealth is considered may justify

different awards against two defendants who engaged in equally culpable conduct. See Joab, Inc. v. Thrall, 245 So.2d 291 (Fla.App.1971).

4.   Where defendant's wealth is relevant to the determination of the amount of punitive damages, who has the burden of producing that evidence? Compare Anderson v. Latham Trucking Co., 728 S.W.2d 752 (Tenn.1987) (either plaintiff or the defendant may offer proof of the financial condition of defendant but it is not essential or mandatory that the record contain any such evidence to sustain an award of punitive damages) with Adams v. Murakami, 54 Cal.3d 105, 813 P.2d 1348, 284 Cal.Rptr. 318 (1991) (plaintiff has burden). Where defendant's wealth is not relevant, financial records are neither admissible nor discoverable. Corbetta v. Albertson's, Inc., 975 P.2d 718 (Colo.1999) (because punitive damages tied to amount of compensatory damages, no discovery of financial records permitted). How is the defendant's financial status to be measured? By net worth or annual sales or profits? Barnett v. Turbomeca, 963 S.W.2d 639 (Mo.App.1997) (permitting evidence of gross yearly sales as well as of net worth and finding $26,500,000 is appropriate punitive damages award against helicopter manufacturer after accident that killed two people and seriously injured two others).

5.   Some courts permit the defendant to show that he has been criminally punished for the same wrong or punished in an earlier civil suit in an effort to lower the amount of punitive damages imposed. Compare Hanover Ins. Co. v. Hayward, 464 A.2d 156 (Me.1983) (fact-finder may consider whether criminal liability has been imposed as one factor in determining whether an award of damages would serve as a meaningful deterrent) with Owens–Illinois, Inc. v. Zenobia, 325 Md. 420, 601 A.2d 633 (1992) (after discussing proof problems associated with such a proffer, court declined to "impose this onerous burden on the trial court"). See also Ore. Rev. Stat. § 30.925(3)(g) (1997) and Owens–Corning Fiberglas Corp. v. Malone, 972 S.W.2d 35 (Tex.1998) (evidence of paid punitive damages awards and past settlements that specified amounts for punitive damages relevant when offered in mitigation of punitive damages). Are there tactical reasons why defense counsel may decline this opportunity?

6.   *Procedural Issues.* Most jurisdictions permit the jury to consider evidence, like the wealth of the defendant, in awarding punitive damages that would be irrelevant and unduly prejudicial on the liability and compensatory damages aspects of the case. Therefore, many jurisdictions have developed various safeguards to protect against the misuse of that evidence. Some require that the plaintiff make a prime facie showing of entitlement to punitive damages before permitting discovery of financial information. Others require that the trial be bifurcated so that the jury does not hear evidence of defendant's financial status until after it has ruled on liability, compensatory damages, and liability for punitive damages. Campen v. Stone, 635 P.2d 1121 (Wyo.1981) (adopting bifurcation procedure through case law); Cal. Civ. Code Ann. § 3295(d) (1997) (requiring bifurcation on request of defendant in case seeking punitive damages); Kan. Stat. Ann. § 60–3701(a)–(b) (1994) (trier of fact determines liability for punitive damages, then court determines amount). But see Life Ins. Co. of Ga. v. Johnson, 701 So.2d 524 (Ala.1997) (previously ordered bifurcation proceeding found no longer to be necessary in light of BMW of No. America, Inc. v. Gore, 517 U.S. 559 (1996)).

7.   As the opinion in *Gryc* indicates, the applicable burden of proof for establishing entitlement to punitive damages in Minnesota was preponderance of the evidence. It is now clear and convincing evidence. Minn.Stat. § 549.20.1(a) (1999 Supp.). This higher standard, between "preponderance of the evidence" and the criminal standard "beyond a reasonable doubt" is in effect in many of the

jurisdictions that permit punitive damages. See Rodgriguez v. Suzuki Motor Corp., 936 S.W.2d 104 (Mo.1996) (adopting the higher standard because punitive damages are extraordinary and harsh and listing twenty-four jurisdictions that adopted the higher standard by statute and seven other jurisdictions that adopted it by judicial decision).

8. Some jurisdictions have directed that a portion of the punitive damages award be paid to a state fund. Ga. Code Ann. § 51–12–5.1(e) (1999 Supp.) (three-quarters of punitive damages award, less proportionate share of costs and attorneys' fees, must be paid to state treasury); Iowa Code § 668A.1(2)(b) (1998) (in certain circumstances, 75% of punitive damages, after payment of costs and counsel fees, goes to civil reparations trust fund); Ore.Rev.Stat. § 18.540 (1997) 60% to compensation fund for crime victims). Georgia has upheld the constitutionality of that requirement. State of Georgia v. Moseley, 263 Ga. 680, 436 S.E.2d 632 (1993) (provision requiring payment of punitive damages to state treasury does not violate right to jury trial or right to choice provisions of Georgia constitution). What if all of the award went to a state fund? What would be the incentive for the claimant and the claimant's attorney to pursue the punitive damages case? Should the jury be told that a portion of the punitive damages goes to the state? Honeywell v. Sterling Furniture Co., 310 Or. 206, 797 P.2d 1019 (1990) (no because jury might be encouraged to award damages for improper reason–to enhance state account); Ford v. Uniroyal Goodrich Tire Co., 267 Ga. 226, 476 S.E.2d 565 (1996) (no because it is irrelevant to jury's consideration who will be compensated by the award or how much plaintiff will ultimately receive).

9. *Vicarious Liability for Punitive Damages.* Some courts take the position that a party can be liable for punitive damages only for the party's own conduct and not vicariously liable for the acts of others, like agents or employees. Others take the position that when the agent or employee commits an act that makes the agent liable for punitive damages, the principal or employer should be liable as well. An especially vigorous opinion to this effect is found in Goddard v. Grand Trunk Ry., 57 Me. 202, 2 Am.Rep. 39 (1869). A majority of courts take the middle position of the Restatement (Second) of Torts § 909 (1965) and hold that the principal (whether an individual or corporation) is liable only if the principal authorized or ratified the act, was reckless in employing or retaining the agent, or the agent was employed in a managerial capacity and was acting in the scope of employment. See, e.g., American Society of Mechanical Engineers, Inc. v. Hydrolevel Corp., 456 U.S. 556 (1982); Miles v. Melrose, 882 F.2d 976 (5th Cir.1989); Chuy v. Philadelphia Eagles Football Club, Inc., 595 F.2d 1265 (3d Cir.1979); and Purvis v. Prattco, Inc., 595 S.W.2d 103 (Tex.1980) (a compelling story of facts that should justify an imposition of punitive damages if ever they are to be awarded). See also Owen, Problems in Assessing Punitive Damages Against Manufacturers of Defective Products, 49 U.Chi.L.Rev. 1 (1982); Walden, The Publicly Held Corporation and the Insurability of Punitive Damages, 53 Fordham L.Rev. 1383 (1985).

10. For a collection of articles focusing on issues arising out of punitive damages litigation, see generally Punitive Damages Symposium, 40 Ala.L.Rev. (1989).

Price v. Hartford Accident and Indemnity Co.

Supreme Court of Arizona, 1972.
108 Ariz. 485, 502 P.2d 522.

[Gary Gardner was seriously injured as a result of a drag race between Charles Price and another young man. Gardner brought a claim against

Price for $100,000 compensatory and $25,000 punitive damages. Price's liability insurance company asserted that it had no duty to defend or indemnify him for the punitive-damage claim. Price's liability insurance policy issued by defendant promised to pay for "all sums" he might become liable to pay as damages "arising out of the ownership, maintenance and use" of the automobile in question. The policy had a $1,000,000 limit. In this suit, Charles Price and his mother sought a declaratory judgment that the policy included coverage for punitive damages.]

HAYS, CHIEF JUSTICE. * * * The clear, unequivocal language of the policy requires the insurance company to defend the action and pay the judgment. The only issue, therefore, is whether the public policy of the state makes the insurance contract illegal insofar as it relates to punitive damages. On this issue there is a conflict of opinion among the several states, and the matter has never been determined by this court.

The arguments favoring the view that it is against public policy to allow a defendant to insure his liability for punitive damages are well expressed in Northwestern National Casualty Co. v. McNulty, 307 F.2d 432, in which the court used the following language:

"Considering the theory of punitive damages as punitory and as a deterrent and accepting as common knowledge the fact that death and injury by automobile is a problem far from solved by traffic regulations and criminal prosecutions, it appears to us that there are especially strong public policy reasons for not allowing socially irresponsible automobile drivers to escape the element of personal punishment in punitive damages when they are guilty of reckless slaughter or maiming on the highway. * * * The delinquent driver must not be allowed to receive a windfall at the expense of the purchasers of insurance, transferring his responsibility for punitive damages to the very people—the driving public—to whom he is a menace. * * *

"If [the wrongdoer] were permitted to shift the burden to an insurance company, punitive damages would serve no useful purpose. Such damages do not compensate the plaintiff for his injury, since compensatory damages already have made the plaintiff whole. And there is no point in punishing the insurance company; it has done no wrong. In actual fact, of course, and considering the extent to which the public is insured, the burden would ultimately come to rest not on the insurance companies but on the public, since the added liability to the insurance companies would be passed along to the premium payers. Society would then be punishing itself for the wrong committed by the insured."

These arguments, at first blush, seem to have merit, but a careful analysis of them reveals several weaknesses. First, even though a driver is insured for punitive damages he cannot engage in wanton conduct with impunity. In the instant case, drag racing would subject him to criminal penalties. His insurance rates would soar. Hartford argues that the assigned risk provisions of the Arizona system would prevent them from soaring. However, the assigned risk procedure would not enable him to procure more than the minimum coverage of $15,000/30,000, and in order to replace his $1,000,000.00 limits, his premium would be tremendous. Second, Hartford has voluntarily covered its insured's liability for punitive damages, and since its premiums were based on its exposure, it may be presumed that holding it liable for what it has promised to pay would not result in additional burdens on the driving public. Third, the criminal penalties include possible loss of the driver's license and compulsory attendance at the traffic school. Fourth, punitive damages are not only designed to punish the offender but are also designed to serve as a deterrent to others. Since it is common knowledge that the vast majority of drivers do not carry million dollar liability policies, the possibility that punitive damages will exceed their policy limits will exercise a deterrent effect on them. Fifth, there is no evidence that those states which deny coverage have accomplished any appreciable effect on the slaughter on their highways. Sixth, the state of Arizona has more than one public policy. Such policy appears in many fields. One such public policy is that an insurance company which admittedly took a premium for covering *all* liability for damages, should honor its obligation. * * *

It is our holding that the premium has been paid and accepted and the protection has been tendered, and that under the circumstances public policy would be best served by requiring the insurance company to honor its obligation.

Reversed and remanded to the Superior Court for further proceedings consistent with this opinion.

NOTES AND QUESTIONS

1. Jurisdictions have split on this issue. Compare Allen v. Simmons, 533 A.2d 541 (R.I.1987) (burden of satisfying punitive damage award should remain with wrongdoer and not be spread upon the blameless through higher insurance premiums) with Whalen v. On–Deck, Inc., 514 A.2d 1072 (Del.1986) (wrongdoer who is insured would still be punished through higher insurance premiums or loss of insurance) and Hensley v. Erie Ins. Co., 168 W.Va. 172, 283 S.E.2d 227 (1981) (increased cost of insurance has some deterrent effect and punishment not only use of punitive damages; additional compensation to plaintiff is part of reason for award).

2. As the opinion in the principal case reflects, the issue before the court is a very close one. What would be the view of Gary Gardner (the party injured by Price's alleged recklessness) on this issue?

3. If you were house counsel for a liability insurance company that did business in Arizona, how would you advise your employer on the matter of punitive damages? See Abbie Uriguen Oldsmobile Buick, Inc. v. United States Fire Ins. Co., 95 Idaho 501, 511 P.2d 783 (1973).

[handwritten margin note: cannot get punitives for ordinary negligence]

CHAPTER XI

WRONGFUL DEATH AND SURVIVAL

1. WRONGFUL DEATH

Moragne v. States Marine Lines, Inc.

Supreme Court of the United States, 1970.
398 U.S. 375, 90 S.Ct. 1772, 26 L.Ed.2d 339.

MR. JUSTICE HARLAN delivered the opinion of the Court. We brought this case here to consider whether The Harrisburg, 119 U.S. 199, in which this Court held in 1886 that maritime law does not afford a cause of action for wrongful death, should any longer be regarded as acceptable law.

The complaint sets forth that Edward Moragne, a longshoreman, was killed while working aboard the vessel Palmetto State in navigable waters within the State of Florida. Petitioner, as his widow and representative of his estate, brought this suit in a state court against respondent States Marine Lines, Inc., the owner of the vessel, to recover damages for wrongful death and for the pain and suffering experienced by the decedent prior to his death. The claims were predicated upon both negligence and the unseaworthiness of the vessel. * * *

The Court's opinion in *The Harrisburg* acknowledged that the result reached had little justification except in primitive English legal history—a history far removed from the American law of remedies for maritime deaths. * * *

One would expect, upon an inquiry into the sources of the common-law rule, to find a clear and compelling justification for what seems a striking departure from the result dictated by elementary principles in the law of remedies. Where existing law imposes a primary duty, violations of which are compensable if they cause injury, nothing in ordinary notions of justice suggests that a violation should be nonactionable simply because it was serious enough to cause death. On the contrary, that rule has been criticized ever since its inception, and described in such terms as "barbarous." [Cc] Because the primary duty already exists, the decision whether to allow recovery for violations causing death is entirely a remedial matter. It is true that the harms to be assuaged are not identical in the two cases: in the case of mere injury, the person physically harmed is made whole for his harm, while in the case of death, those closest to him—usually spouse and children—seek to recover for their total loss of one on whom they depended. This difference, however, even when coupled with the practical difficulties of defining the class of beneficiaries who may recover for death, does not seem to account for the law's refusal to recognize a wrongful killing as an actionable tort. One expects, therefore, to find a persuasive, independent justification for this apparent legal anomaly.

Legal historians have concluded that the sole substantial basis for the rule at common law is a feature of the early English law that did not survive into this century—the felony-merger doctrine. [Cc] According to this doctrine, the common law did not allow civil recovery for an act that constituted both a tort and a felony. The tort was treated as less important than the offense against the Crown, and was merged into, or pre-empted by, the felony. [Cc] The doctrine found practical justification in the fact that the punishment for the felony was the death of the felon and the forfeiture of his property to the Crown; thus, after the crime had been punished, nothing remained of the felon or his property on which to base a civil action. Since all intentional or negligent homicide was felonious, there could be no civil suit for wrongful death.

The first explicit statement of the common-law rule against recovery for wrongful death came in the opinion of Lord Ellenborough, sitting at *nisi prius,* in Baker v. Bolton, 1 Camp. 493, 170 Eng.Rep. 1033 (1808). That opinion did not cite authority, or give supporting reasoning, or refer to the felony-merger doctrine in announcing that "[i]n a Civil court, the death of a human being could not be complained of as an injury." Ibid. Nor had the felony-merger doctrine seemingly been cited as the basis for the denial of recovery in any of the other reported wrongful-death cases since the earliest ones, in the 17th century. [Cc] However, it seems clear from those first cases that the rule of Baker v. Bolton did derive from the felony-merger doctrine, and that there was no other ground on which it might be supported even at the time of its inception. * * *

The historical justification marshaled for the rule in England never existed in this country. In limited instances American law did adopt a vestige of the felony-merger doctrine, to the effect that a civil action was delayed until after the criminal trial. However, in this country the felony punishment did not include forfeiture of property; therefore, there was nothing, even in those limited instances, to bar a subsequent civil suit. [Cc]

Nevertheless, despite some early cases in which the rule was rejected as "incapable of vindication," [cc] American courts generally adopted the English rule as the common law of this country as well. * * *

It was suggested by some courts and commentators that the prohibition of nonstatutory wrongful-death actions derived support from the ancient common-law rule that a personal cause of action in tort did not survive the death of its possessor [c], and the decision in Baker v. Bolton itself may have been influenced by this principle. [C] However, it is now universally recognized that because this principle pertains only to the victim's own personal claims, such as for pain and suffering, it has no bearing on the question whether a dependent should be permitted to recover for the injury he suffers from the victim's death. [Cc]

We need not, however, pronounce a verdict on whether *The Harrisburg,* when decided, was a correct extrapolation of the principles of decisional law then in existence. A development of major significance has intervened, making clear that the rule against recovery for wrongful death is sharply out of keeping with the policies of modern American maritime law. * * *

[L]egislatures both here and in England began to evidence unanimous disapproval of the rule against recovery for wrongful death. The first statute partially abrogating the rule was Lord Campbell's Act, 9 & 10 Vict., c. 93 (1846), which granted recovery to the families of persons killed by tortious conduct, "although the Death shall have been caused under such Circumstances as amount in Law to Felony."

In the United States, every State today has enacted a wrongful-death statute. See Smith, supra, 44 N.C.L.Rev. 402. The Congress has created actions for wrongful deaths of railroad employees, Federal Employers' Liability Act, 45 U.S.C.A. §§ 51–59; of merchant seamen, Jones Act, 46 U.S.C. § 688; and of persons on the high seas, Death on the High Seas Act, 46 U.S.C.A. §§ 761, 762. Congress has also, in the Federal Tort Claims Act, 28 U.S.C.A. § 1346(b), made the United States subject to liability in certain circumstances for negligently caused wrongful death to the same extent as a private person. [C]

These numerous and broadly applicable statutes, taken as a whole, make it clear that there is no present public policy against allowing recovery for wrongful death. The statutes evidence a wide rejection by the legislatures of whatever justifications may once have existed for a general refusal to allow such recovery. This legislative establishment of policy carries significance beyond the particular scope of each of the statutes involved. The policy thus established has become itself a part of our law, to be given its appropriate weight not only in matters of statutory construction but also in those of decisional law. See Landis, Statutes and the Sources of Law, in Harvard Legal Essays 213, 226–227 (1934).

Professor Landis has said, "much of what is ordinarily regarded as 'common law' finds its source in legislative enactment." Landis, supra, at 214. It has always been the duty of the common-law court to perceive the impact of major legislative innovations and to interweave the new legislative policies with the inherited body of common-law principles—many of them deriving from earlier legislative exertions.

[The court then concluded that it was sometimes the duty of the common law court to bend to the weight of legislative authority and noted that Congress by its failure to enact a specific remedy did not intend to forestall recovery for wrongful death in admiralty and that the doctrine of *stare decisis* does not preclude a change in law.]

Respondents argue that overruling *The Harrisburg* will necessitate a long course of decisions to spell out the elements of the new "cause of action." We believe these fears are exaggerated, because our decision does not require the fashioning of a whole new body of federal law, but merely removes a bar to access to the existing general maritime law. In most respects the law applied in personal-injury cases will answer all questions that arise in death cases. * * *

The one aspect of a claim for wrongful death that has no precise counterpart in the established law governing nonfatal injuries is the determination of the beneficiaries who are entitled to recover. General maritime law, which denied any recovery for wrongful death, found no need to specify which dependents should receive such recovery. On this question, petitioner and the United States argue that we may look for guidance to the expressions of Congress, which has spoken on this subject in the Death on the High Seas Act, the Jones Act, and the Longshoremen's and Harbor Workers' Compensation Act. Though very similar, each of these provisions differs slightly in the naming of dependent relatives who may recover and in the priority given to their claims. * * *

We do not determine this issue now, for we think its final resolution should await further sifting through the lower courts in future litigation. For present purposes we conclude only that its existence affords no sufficient reason for not coming to grips with *The Harrisburg*. If still other subsidiary issues should require resolution, such as particular questions of the measure of damages, the courts will not be without persuasive analogy for guidance. Both the Death on the High Seas Act and the numerous state wrongful-death acts have been implemented with success for decades. The experience thus built up counsels that a suit for wrongful death raises no problems unlike those that have long been grist for the judicial mill.

In sum, in contrast to the torrent of difficult litigation that has swirled about *The Harrisburg* * * * and the problems of federal-state accommodation [it] occasioned, the recognition of a remedy for wrongful death under general maritime law can be expected to bring more placid waters. That prospect indeed makes for, and not against, the discarding of *The Harrisburg.*

We accordingly overrule *The Harrisburg,* and hold that an action does lie under general maritime law for death caused by violation of maritime duties. The judgment of the Court of Appeals is reversed, and the case is remanded to that court for further proceedings consistent with this opinion. It is so ordered.

Reversed and remanded.

NOTES AND QUESTIONS

1. American admiralty law was the last island for the common law rule that "the death of a human being could not be complained of as an injury." Baker v. Bolton, 1 Camp. 493, 170 Eng.Rep. 1033 (N.P.1808). Lord Ellenborough did not supply reasons for his rule, but later sympathizers with his result have given at least two. First, allowing a claim would lead jurors to award runaway damages and, second, it is "immoral" to place a monetary value on a human life.

2. The principal case is most unusual in making a major change away from the common law rule by the process of judicial decision, rather than by action of the legislature. In its subsequent decision of Sea–Land Services, Inc. v. Gaudet, 414 U.S. 573 (1974), the Supreme Court elaborated on its holding that there is a

maritime common law cause of action for wrongful death. It held that the fact that the decedent had previously recovered damages for loss of wages, pain and suffering, and medical expenses did not interfere with the independent common law cause of action for wrongful death resulting from the original injury, so that the later action was not precluded by res judicata. Recovery for wrongful death was held to cover damages for (1) "loss of support, * * * [including] all the financial support that the decedent would have made to his dependents had he lived," (2) "the monetary value of services the decedent provided and would have continued to provide but for his wrongful death * * * [including] the nurture, training, education, and guidance that a child would have received had not the parent been wrongfully killed * * * [plus] services the decedent performed at home or for his spouse," (3) "compensation for loss of society * * *, [embracing] a broad range of mutual benefits each family member receives from the others' continued existence, including love, affection, care, attention, companionship, comfort and protection," and (4) "damages for funeral expenses * * * in circumstances where the decedent's dependents have either paid for the funeral or are liable for its payment." The potential for double liability coming from the awards to the decedent for loss of future wages and to the dependents for loss of support was held to be controlled by the law of collateral estoppel, but it has continued to be a cause of concern to some courts. See Alfone v. Sarno, 87 N.J. 99, 432 A.2d 857 (1981) for a discussion of duplication of damages in such cases.

3. All fifty states have some form of statutory action for the recovery of the wrongful death of another. Most of the statutes were modeled after Lord Campbell's Act, mentioned by Justice Harlan. These statutes vary in many important respects and the material considered in this Chapter is necessarily only introductory in nature. Lawyers do have the benefit of an excellent treatise on the subject that treats the statutes individually and has been kept up to date. See S. Speiser, Recovery for Wrongful Death and Injury (3rd ed. 1992). The topic of wrongful death therefore differs from many others in the law of torts because it is statutory. Courts must engage in the process of statutory construction and fathoming legislative intent. This is not an easy process with regard to wrongful death statutes because there is rarely much legislative history and most statutes are over one hundred years old.

4. Representative wrongful death statutes from two states provide as follows:

South Carolina

"*Civil Action for Wrongful Act Causing Death.* Whenever the death of a person shall be caused by the wrongful act, neglect or default of another and the act, neglect or default is such as would, if death had not ensued, have entitled the party injured to maintain an action and recover damages in respect thereof, the person who would have been liable, if death had not ensued, shall be liable to an action for damages, notwithstanding the death of the person injured, although the death shall have been caused under such circumstances as make the killing in law a felony. In the event of the death of the wrongdoer, such cause of action shall survive against his personal representative." S.C.Code § 15–51–10 (1998).

"*Beneficiaries of Action for Wrongful Death; By Whom Brought.* Every such action shall be for the benefit of the wife or husband and child or children of the person whose death shall have been so caused, and, if there be no such wife, husband, child or children, then for the benefit of the parent or parents, and if there be none such, then for the benefit of the heirs of the person whose death shall have been so caused. Every such action shall be brought by or in the name of the executor or administrator of such person." Id. § 15–51–20 (1998).

Kentucky

"*Action for Wrongful Death—Personal Representative to Prosecute—Distribution of Amount Recovered.* (1) Whenever the death of a person results from an injury inflicted by the negligence or wrongful act of another, damages may be recovered for the death from the person who caused it, or whose agent or servant caused it. If the act was willful or the negligence gross, punitive damages may be recovered. The action shall be prosecuted by the personal representative of the deceased. (2) The amount recovered, less funeral expenses and the cost of administration and costs of recovery including the attorney fees, not included in the recovery from the defendant, shall be for the benefit of and go to the kindred of the deceased in the following order: (a) If the deceased leaves a widow or husband, and no children or their descendants, then the whole to the widow or husband. (b) If the deceased leaves a widow and children or a husband and children, then one-half (1/2) to the widow or husband and the other one-half (1/2) to the children of the deceased. (c) If the deceased leaves a child or children, but no widow or husband, then the whole to the child or children. (d) If the deceased leaves no widow, husband or child, then the recovery shall pass to the mother and father of the deceased, one (1) moiety each, if both are living; if the mother is dead and the father is living, the whole thereof shall pass to the father; and if the father is dead and the mother living, the whole thereof shall go to the mother. In the event the deceased was an adopted person, 'mother' and 'father' shall mean the adoptive parents of the deceased. (e) If the deceased leaves no widow, husband or child, and if both father and mother are dead, then the whole of the recovery shall become a part of the personal estate of the deceased, and after the payment of his debts the remainder, if any, shall pass to his kindred more remote than those above named, according to the law of descent and distribution." Ky. Rev. Stat. § 411.130 (1998).

5. Note that both of these statutes provide that the action is to be brought by the personal representative of the deceased for the benefit of the named beneficiaries. Some statutes provide that the action can be brought by the beneficiaries themselves. In a jurisdiction that provides that the wrongful death action for a minor child must be brought by his "surviving mother or father," can his grandmother bring the action? The child lived with the grandmother and she alleged that she was his "psychological" or "de facto" mother and that the parents had agreed to her bringing the action. Goodleft v. Gullickson, 556 N.W.2d 303 (N.D.1996) (grandmother not entitled to bring claim even though she was in loco parentis; trial court should have given parents thirty days to substitute themselves as parties).

Beneficiaries

6. The original Lord Campbell's Act specified that the action was for the benefit of the husband, wife, parent or child of the deceased, and many American acts have limited recovery to a similar group. Interpretation problems often arise.

7. *Spouse.* All of the states provide that the lawful spouse is a designated beneficiary. Lewis v. Allis–Chalmers Corp., 615 F.2d 1129 (5th Cir.1980) (applying Louisiana law) (but former wife may not recover). The cases have been consistent in refusing to extend the definition of spouse to unmarried cohabitants. See, e.g., Nieto v. City of Los Angeles, 138 Cal.App.3d 464, 188 Cal.Rptr. 31 (1982); Raum v. Restaurant Assocs., Inc., 675 N.Y.S.2d 343 (App. Div. 1998) (unmarried couples

living together, whether heterosexual or homosexual, are not "spouses" within the wrongful death statute and thus have no cause of action).

8. *Child.* Most jurisdictions provide that children of the decedent are beneficiaries, although some put them in a different category from spouses and allow them to recover only if there is no surviving spouse.

9. *Stepchild.* Did the legislature intend to cover stepchildren? Most cases have held no. See, e.g., in Steed v. Imperial Airlines, 12 Cal.3d 115, 524 P.2d 801, 115 Cal.Rptr. 329 (1974) (statute later amended to cover stepchildren who were financially dependent on decedent) and Klossner v. San Juan County, 21 Wash.App. 689, 586 P.2d 899 (1978), aff'd, 93 Wash.2d 42, 605 P.2d 330 (1980) (unadopted stepchildren not beneficiaries under wrongful death statute unless statute provides for recovery to "persons to whom the deceased stood in loco parentis").

10. *Child born out of wedlock.* Until the late 1960's a majority of American courts held that children born out of wedlock were not intended beneficiaries under the statute, unless the statute said so. Contra, Armijo v. Wesselius, 73 Wash.2d 716, 440 P.2d 471 (1968) (child permitted to bring a claim for the death of his natural father when the latter had both acknowledged and contributed to the support of the child). The Supreme Court has held that the Louisiana Wrongful Death Statute constituted a denial of equal protection of the laws when it precluded a child born out of wedlock from bringing a wrongful death claim upon the death of her mother. Levy v. Louisiana, 391 U.S. 68 (1968). The court also struck down a Louisiana provision that barred the claim of a mother for the wrongful death of her child born out of wedlock. See Glona v. American Guarantee & Liability Ins. Co., 391 U.S. 73 (1968). Although some jurisdictions require that a father have acknowledged paternity or that paternity have been adjudicated before the death in order for a wrongful death action to be brought, most permit the showing to be made after the death. Brookbank v. Gray, 74 Ohio St.3d 279, 658 N.E.2d 724 (1996) (citing cases from other jurisdictions). Washington's requirement that the father have contributed regularly to financial support of the child in order to recover for the child's wrongful death was found to violate Washington's Equal Rights Amendment since the same requirement was not imposed on the mother. Guard v. Jackson, 132 Wash.2d 660, 940 P.2d 642 (1997).

11. *Unborn child.* Should parents be able to obtain recovery for the death of an unborn child? Every jurisdiction has a cause of action for prenatal injuries to a viable unborn child who is born alive. Some, however, will not allow recovery if the child is stillborn. See e.g., Wilson v. Kaiser Foundation Hospitals, 141 Cal.App.3d 891, 190 Cal.Rptr. 649 (1983) (a stillborn child is not a person within the meaning of the wrongful death statute); Tanner v. Hartog, 696 So.2d 705 (Fla.1997) (same, but parents have cause of action for their pain and suffering and for medical expenses). Others will not allow recovery if the child was not viable at the time of injury, even if born alive. Miller v. Kirk, 120 N.M. 654, 905 P.2d 194 (1995). But see Connor v. Monkem Co., Inc., 898 S.W.2d 89 (Mo.1995) and Farley v. Sartin, 195 W.Va. 671, 466 S.E.2d 522 (1995) (both permitting wrongful death action for unborn child even when injured prior to viability). See also Chapter 8, page 461.

12. *Parent.* In most jurisdictions, a parent is a beneficiary when a child dies without a spouse or children. For a discussion of the measure of damages when the decedent is a minor child, see the next principal case.

13. *Next of kin.* Some statutes provide that the next of kin is the beneficiary, as long as that person can show financial loss. A Roman Catholic nun who belonged to the order the Sisters of St. Ursula was killed when the car she was driving was

struck by a drunk driver who ran a stop sign. She had been a member of the Convent for almost forty years and had taken a vow of poverty that meant that she gave all her income to the Convent for the common good. At the time of her death, she was earning $18,000 a year, so her community lost about $250,000 that she would have earned over the rest of her lifetime. Is the Convent her next of kin and therefore a beneficiary under the wrongful death statute? Buchert v. Newman, 90 Ohio App.3d 382, 629 N.E.2d 489 (1993) (Convent not next of kin under statute even though community showed financial dependency on decedent).

14. In most jurisdictions, if no designated beneficiaries are living at the time of the wrongful death, the action fails. A problem of statutory interpretation occurs if the beneficiary dies after the person has been wrongfully killed, but before an action has begun or even after commencement of the action, but before judgment. How are courts to decide these things? Compare Murrell v. Springdale Memorial Hospital, 952 S.W.2d 153 (Ark.1997) (summary judgment for medical malpractice defendants is appropriate upon death of widower of patient) and Thomas v. Eads, 400 N.E.2d 778 (Ind.App.1980) (no award for wrongful death unless at the commencement of the action, and also at the time of awarding damages, there be living some person or persons in the class of beneficiaries set by statute) with Gray v. Goodson, 61 Wash.2d 319, 378 P.2d 413 (1963)(once a right of action for wrongful death has accrued, the subsequent death of a beneficiary does not abate the action, but the benefit of the action survives to the beneficiary's estate, with the measure of damages recoverable to the estate limited to the amount of loss sustained by the beneficiary prior to his death) and McDaniel v. Bullard, 34 Ill.2d 487, 216 N.E.2d 140 (1966) (cause of action for wrongful death accrues at time of death and survives death of sole beneficiary, whose estate may maintain the cause of action).

15. *Allocation of proceeds among beneficiaries.* Most jurisdictions provide for some formal mechanism by which the court can allocate the proceeds among the beneficiaries. California, for example, provides that there is only one cause of action for wrongful death and that if one of the beneficiaries chooses not to join in the action, he can be made a nominal defendant. The court has jurisdiction to adjudicate the claim even if not all beneficiaries are present. Patient died, allegedly as a result of medical malpractice, and his widow and minor children brought a wrongful death action, naming his adult daughter from a previous marriage as a nominal defendant. She was never served, however, and did not learn about the settlement with the malpractice defendants until the proceeds had been distributed to the widow and minor children. Does she have a cause of action against the malpractice defendants? Against the widow for a share of the proceeds? Ruttenberg v. Ruttenberg, 53 Cal.App.4th 801, 62 Cal. Rptr.2d 78 (1997) (no cause of action against medical malpractice defendants because court had power to adjudicate that action; no cause of action for share of proceeds because that amount represented only their loss; cause of action for omitting her from wrongful death action, thereby causing her to lose her opportunity to prove damages in that action).

Selders v. Armentrout

Supreme Court of Nebraska, 1973.
190 Neb. 275, 207 N.W.2d 686.

McCown, Justice. * * * Three minor children (aged 15, 13, and 9) were killed in an automobile accident due to the negligent conduct of defendants. Their parents brought these wrongful death actions. The sole issue on this appeal involves the proper elements and measure of damages in a tort action in Nebraska for the wrongful death of a minor child. The [trial] court essentially instructed the jury that except for medical and funeral expenses, the damages should be the monetary value of the contributions and services which the parents could reasonably have expected to receive from the children less the reasonable cost to the parents of supporting the children.

The defendants contend that the measure of damages is limited to pecuniary loss and that the instructions to the jury correctly reflect the measure and elements of damage. The plaintiffs assert that the loss of the society, comfort, and companionship of the children are proper and compensable elements of damage, and that evidence of amounts invested or expended for the nurture, education, and maintenance of the children before death is proper. * * *

[A] broadening concept of the measure and elements of damages for the wrongful death of a minor child has been in the development stage for many years. [Cc] Following a discussion of the rigid common law rules limiting recovery for wrongful death to the loss of pecuniary benefits, Prosser states: "Recent years, however, have brought considerable modification of the rigid common law rules. It has been recognized that even pecuniary loss may extend beyond mere contributions of food, shelter, money or property; and there is now a decided tendency to find that the society, care and attention of the deceased are 'services' to the survivor with a financial value, which may be compensated. This has been true, for example, not only where a child has been deprived of a parent, * * * but also where the parent has lost a child * * *." Prosser, Law of Torts (4th Ed.), § 127, p. 908.

The original pecuniary loss concept and its restrictive application arose in a day when children during minority were generally regarded as an economic asset to parents. Children went to work on farms and in factories at age 10 and even earlier. This was before the day of child labor laws and long before the day of extended higher education for the general population. A child's earnings and services could be generally established and the financial or pecuniary loss which could be proved became the measure of damages for the wrongful death of a child. Virtually all other damages were disallowed as speculative or as sentimental.

The damages involved in a wrongful death case even today must of necessity deal primarily with a fictitious or speculative future life, as it might have been had the wrongful death not occurred. For that reason, virtually all evidence of future damage is necessarily speculative to a degree. The measure and elements of damage involved in a wrongful death case, however, have been excessively restrictive as applied to a minor child in contrast to an adult. Modern economic reality emphasizes the gulf between the old concepts of a child's economic value and the new facts of modern family life. To limit damages for the death of a child to the monetary value of the services which the next of kin could reasonably have expected to receive during his minority less the reasonable expense of maintaining and educating him stamps almost all modern children as worthless in the eyes of the law. In fact, if the rule was literally followed, the average child would have a negative worth. This court has already held that contributions reasonably to be expected from a minor, not only during his minority but afterwards, may be allowed on evidence justifying a reasonable expectation of pecuniary benefit. [Cc] Even with that modification, the wrongful death of a child results in no monetary loss, except in the rare case, and the assumption that the traditional measure of damages is compensatory is a pure legal fiction.

Particularly in the last decade, a growing number of courts have extended the measure of damages to include the loss of society and companionship of the minor child, even under statutes limiting recovery to pecuniary loss or pecuniary value of services less the cost of support and maintenance, or similar limitations. [Cc]

In this state, the statute has not limited damages for wrongful death to pecuniary loss but this court has imposed that restriction. For an injury to the marital relationship, the law allows recovery for the loss of the society, comfort, and companionship of a spouse. This court has allowed such a recovery for the wrongful death of a wife. [C] There is no logical reason for treating an injury to the family relationship resulting from the wrongful death of a child more restrictively. It is no more difficult for juries and courts to measure damages for the loss of the life of a child than many other abstract concepts with which they are required to deal. We hold that the measure of damages for the wrongful death of a minor child should be extended to include the loss of the society, comfort, and companionship of the child. To the extent this holding is in conflict with prior decisions of this court, they are overruled. * * *

The judgment of the trial court as to liability is affirmed, the judgment as to damages is reversed and the cause remanded for trial on the issue of damages only, consistent with our holding in this opinion.

WHITE, CHIEF JUSTICE (dissenting). * * * I submit that the majority opinion, which arbitrarily and in one stroke, after 50 years of settled law and without public hearing or consideration of the different interests and policies involved, and in violation of the 1945 legislative policy clearly announced in the statute, and unrepealed, simply throws open a death claim for a minor child to a sympathy and sentiment contest in the award of money, and is a serious mistake for us to make.

NOTES AND QUESTIONS

1. There is little doubt that the original Lord Campbell's Act and wrongful death legislation in the United States patterned after that law were intended to limit damages to "pecuniary" losses caused by the death of a loved one. This was to meet concerns of common law judges that awards made for emotional losses arising from another's death would know no bounds. In most states pecuniary loss is measured by having the trier of fact attempt to determine the monetary contribution that decedent would have made during his lifetime to the plaintiff beneficiary. This is frequently referred to as a loss-to-survivors statute. As in the case of permanent injuries discussed in Chapter 10, the trier of fact is aided by mortality

tables, income projections, and expert testimony. Pecuniary loss also may include the market value of any services that the decedent performed for the beneficiary. Most states measure the economic loss by calculating the "joint life expectancy" of the decedent and each beneficiary, i.e., the period of loss is the life expectancy of the decedent or the life expectancy of the beneficiary, whichever is shorter. See, e.g., Runyon v. District of Columbia, 463 F.2d 1319 (D.C.Cir.1972) (interpreting District of Columbia's statute). Beginning in early 19th century cases and continuing today, most jurisdictions recognized that the economic loss suffered by a child due to the death of a parent includes loss of training, education, guidance, and nurture as well as direct financial support. See, e.g., McKay v. New England Dredging Co., 92 Me. 454, 43 A. 29 (1899) (education and training that children receive from parent "are of actual and commercial value to them").

2. Although most states measure the damages based on the loss to the beneficiaries, some use the loss to the decedent's estate. This is frequently referred to as a loss-to-estate statute. In those jurisdictions, how should lost earnings be calculated? Should the jury award the probable worth of the decedent's gross earnings through his worklife expectancy? Should an estimate of the decedent's own living expenses be deducted and the net amount awarded to the beneficiaries? See Wehner v. Weinstein, 191 W.Va. 149, 444 S.E.2d 27 (1994) (choosing to permit jury to award gross amount, but recognizing that most jurisdictions require the deduction of decedent's projected living expenses).

3. In Alabama, damages are based on the extent of the defendant's culpability. The plaintiff's pecuniary loss is immaterial.

4. As the principal case reflects, the pecuniary-loss limitation has caused problems when a minor child has been killed and his parents bring a wrongful death claim. In many states that adhere to the pecuniary-loss standard, substantial damages have been upheld on the theory that the child eventually would have made a corresponding monetary contribution to the parents.

5. A growing number of courts have taken the route of the principal case and allowed recovery for "loss of companionship" or consortium of a deceased family member. Some do so by finding that loss of society and companionship is an element of pecuniary damages. Smith v. Detroit, 388 Mich. 637, 202 N.W.2d 300 (1972). Also, some states have amended their wrongful death statutes to provide for loss of companionship in all cases, not just those involving the death of a minor child. See, e.g., Hawaii Rev.Stat. § 663–3 (1999) ("pecuniary injury and loss of love and affection"). Some jurisdictions have a built-in protection against runaway damages by placing a ceiling on damages for loss of companionship. See Kan.Stat. Ann. § 60–1903 (1998) ($250,000); Me.Rev.Stat.Ann. tit. 18A, § 2–804 (1998) ($150,000 limit).

6. What elements of proof would be required in a jurisdiction permitting recovery for loss of companionship damages? Where it is the spouse who is seeking recovery, evidence of happiness or discord in the marriage is admissible on the issue of damages. Consider the court's summary of parents' proof on this issue after the death of their child in Anderson v. Lale, 88 S.D. 111, 216 N.W.2d 152, 159 (1974): "The record in this case shows that the decedent was seven years of age and a bright, affectionate, kindly child who did well in school and church activities. She was an energetic, active, obedient, helpful child and an integral part of a close-knit family."

7. Some states go beyond damages for "loss of companionship" and also provide for damages based on "grief." See, e.g., Ark. Stat. Ann. § 16–62–102 (1997)

("When mental anguish is claimed as a measure of damages under this section, mental anguish will include grief normally associated with the loss of a loved one."); Kan.Stat.Ann. § 60–1904 (1998) ("mental anguish, suffering or bereavement").

8. Note that courts generally do not allow recovery for purely emotional harm where the plaintiff has suffered no physical injury. See Chapter 8, Section 4. How does this comport with awarding "grief" damages to beneficiaries in wrongful death cases?

9. Almost half of the wrongful death statutes as originally enacted contained restrictions on the maximum amount that could be awarded. They represented a response to the concern that the new cause of action would create unlimited liability and the possibility of runaway jury verdicts. The limitations ranged from $5,000 to $20,000. Over time the limitations were raised and then eliminated. No modern American jurisdiction limits recovery for pecuniary losses, although some do limit recovery for non-pecuniary losses. See note 5 and Chapter 10, page 538. Do the "tort reform" statutory caps on non-economic damages apply to wrongful death actions? United States v. Streidel, 329 Md. 533, 620 A.2d 905 (1993) (Maryland cap applicable to "personal injury actions" does not apply to wrongful death action); Cole v. Sullivan, 110 Md.App. 79, 676 A.2d 85 (1996) (legislature then amended statute to extend cap to wrongful death actions). Another important limit is the Warsaw Convention, an international agreement limiting liability for personal injury or death occurring during international air travel to $75,000. See Zicherman v. Korean Air Lines Co., 516 U.S. 217 (1996) (interpreting applicability of treaty).

10. Should punitive damages be awarded to the beneficiary in cases involving reckless or intentional conduct? About half of the states permit punitive damages to be awarded in a wrongful death action. Some of those jurisdictions have statutes that specifically authorize punitive damages; others have interpreted their statutes, although silent on the subject, to permit an award of punitive damages. See S. Speiser, Recovery for Wrongful Death and Injury § 3A:4 (3rd ed. 1992). Oklahoma has a separate statute that covers the wrongful death of a minor child. 12 Okl. St. § 1055 (1998). It does not list punitive damages as a permissible element of recovery even though the general wrongful death statute does. 12 Okl. St. § 1053 (1998). The mother of three minor children killed in a head on collision with a drunk driver on the wrong side of the road filed suit against the driver and the bars where he had been drinking. She sought both compensatory damages and punitive damages. Should punitive damages be permitted? Roach v. Jimmy D. Enters., 912 P.2d 852 (Okla.1996) (yes because general wrongful death statute and statute for death of minor child should be read in conjunction with each other).

11. A controversy has arisen on whether the trier of fact should be informed that a plaintiff has remarried since the death of decedent spouse. Most courts have held that this information should be withheld from the jury. In one case, plaintiff spouse, whose name was different from the decedent's because she had remarried, changed her name back to the decedent's name solely for the purpose of bringing the wrongful death suit. Should the jury be told this? See Bell Aerospace Corp. v. Anderson, 478 S.W.2d 191 (Tex.Civ.App.1972).

2. SURVIVAL

Murphy v. Martin Oil Co.

Supreme Court of Illinois, 1974.
56 Ill.2d 423, 308 N.E.2d 583.

[Suit for negligently causing the death of plaintiff's husband. The husband was injured in a fire on defendant's premises, survived for nine days, and then died from the injuries. The claim was in two counts: (1) under the Wrongful Death Statute and (2) under the Survival Statute. The trial court dismissed the second count. The intermediate appellate court allowed the claim in part. Both parties appealed to the State Supreme Court.]

WARD, JUSTICE. Count I of the complaint claimed damages for wrongful death under the Illinois Wrongful Death Act. * * * The language of section 1 of the statute is:

"Whenever the death of a person shall be caused by wrongful act, neglect or default, and the act, neglect or default is such as would, if death had not ensued, have entitled the party injured to maintain an action and recover damages in respect thereof, then and in every such case the person who or company or corporation which would have been liable if death had not ensued, shall be liable to an action for damages, notwithstanding the death of the person injured, and although the death shall have been caused under such circumstances as amount in law to felony." * * *

The second count of the complaint asked for damages for the decedent's physical and mental suffering, for loss of wages for the nine-day period following his injury and for the loss of his clothing worn at the time of injury. These damages were claimed under the common law and under our survival statute, which provides that certain rights of action survive the death of the person with the right of action. (Ill.Rev.Stat.1971, ch. 3, par. 339.) The statute states:

"In addition to the actions which survive by the common law, the following also survive: actions of replevin, actions to recover damages for an injury to the person (except slander and libel), actions to recover damages for an injury to real or personal property or for the detention or conversion of personal property, actions against officers for misfeasance, malfeasance, or nonfeasance of themselves or their deputies, actions for fraud or deceit, and actions provided in Section 14 of Article VI of 'An Act relating to alcoholic liquors', approved January 31, 1934, as amended."

On this appeal we shall consider: (1) whether the plaintiff can recover for the loss of wages which her decedent would have earned during the interval between his injury and death; (2) whether the plaintiff can recover for the destruction of the decedent's personal property (clothing) at the time of the injury; (3) whether the plaintiff can recover damages for conscious pain and suffering of the decedent from the time of his injuries to the time of death.

This State in 1853 enacted the Wrongful Death Act and in 1872 enacted the so-called Survival Act (now section 339 of the Probate Act). This court first had occasion to consider the statutes in combination in 1882 in Holton v. Daly, 106 Ill. 131. The court * * * held that the Wrongful Death Act provided the exclusive remedy available when death came as a result of given tortious conduct. In considering the Survival Act the court stated that it was intended to allow for the survival of a cause of action only when the injured party died from a cause other than that which caused the injuries which created the cause of action. Thus, the court said, an action for personal injury would not survive death if death resulted from the tortious conduct which caused the injury.

This construction of the two statutes persisted for over 70 years. [Cc] Damages, therefore, under the Wrongful Death Act were limited to pecuniary losses, as from loss of support, to the surviving spouse and next of kin as a result of the death. [C] Under the survival statute damages recoverable in a personal injury action, as for conscious pain and suffering, loss of earnings, medical expenses and physical disability, could be had only if death resulted from a cause other than the one which gave rise to the personal injury action. * * *

In Prosser, Handbook of the Law of Torts (4th ed. 1971), at page 901, it is said: "[T]he modern trend is definitely toward the view that tort causes of action and liabilities are as fairly a part of the estate of either plaintiff or defendant as contract debts, and that the question is rather one of why a fortuitous event such as death should extinguish a valid action. Accordingly, survival statutes gradually are being extended; and it may be expected that ultimately all tort actions will survive to the same extent as those founded on contract." And at page 906 Prosser observes that where there have been wrongful death and survival statutes the usual holding has been that actions may be concurrently maintained under those statutes. The usual method of dealing with the two causes of action, he notes, is to allocate conscious pain and suffering, expenses and loss of earnings of the decedent up to the date of death to the survival statute, and to allocate the loss of benefits of the survivors to the action for wrongful death.

As the cited comments of Prosser indicate, the majority of jurisdictions which have considered the question allow an action for personal injuries in addition to an action under the wrongful death statute, though death is attributable to the injuries. Recovery for conscious pain and suffering is permitted in most of these jurisdictions. [Citing cases from 21 different jurisdictions.]

Too, recovery is allowed under the Federal Employers' Liability Act for a decedent's conscious pain and suffering provided it was not substantially contemporaneous with his death. [Cc]

We consider that those decisions which allow an action for fatal injuries as well as for wrongful death are to be preferred to this court's holding in Holton v. Daly that the Wrongful Death Act was the only remedy available when injury resulted in death.

The holding in *Holton* was not compelled, we judge, by the language or the nature of the statutes examined. The statutes were conceptually separable and different. The one related to an action arising upon wrongful death; the other related to a right of action for personal injury arising during the life of the injured person.

The remedy available under *Holton* will often be grievously incomplete. There may be a substantial loss of earnings, medical expenses, prolonged pain and suffering, as well as property damage sustained, before an injured person may succumb to his injuries. To say that there can be recovery only for his wrongful death is to provide an obviously inadequate justice. Too, the result in such a case is that the wrongdoer will have to answer for only a portion of the damages he caused. Incongruously, if the injury caused is so severe that death results, the wrongdoer's liability for the damages before death will be extinguished. It is obvious that in order to have a full liability and a full recovery there must be an action allowed for damages up to the time of death, as well as thereafter. Considering "It is more important that the court should be right upon later and more elaborate consideration of the cases than consistent with previous declarations" [c], we declare *Holton* and the cases which have followed it overruled. * * *

[T]he judgment of the appellate court is affirmed insofar as it held that an action may be maintained by the plaintiff for loss of property and loss of wages during the interval between injury and death, and that judgment is reversed insofar as it held that the plaintiff cannot maintain an action for her decedent's pain and suffering.

NOTES AND QUESTIONS

1. Under English common law as it was received by American courts, personal tort actions died with the person of the plaintiff or the defendant. For the historical background of this rule see W. Prosser & W. Keeton, Torts 940 (5th Ed. 1984) and materials cited.

2. In almost every jurisdiction today survival statutes have modified these rules. At the very least, these statutes provide that causes of action for injury to all tangible property survive the death of either party. The majority of statutes also allow personal injury actions to survive. Only a few states permit claims for intangible interests of personalty (such as intentional infliction of emotional harm or defamation) to survive.

3. Two survival statutes are presented below. What are the important differences between them?

South Carolina

"*Survival of Right of Action.* Causes of action for and in respect to any and all injuries and trespasses to and upon real estate and any and all injuries to the person or to personal property shall survive both to and against the personal or real representative, as the case may be, of a deceased person and the legal representative of an insolvent person or a defunct or insolvent corporation, any law or rule to the contrary notwithstanding." S.C.Code § 15–5–90 (1998).

Kentucky

"*What Action Shall Survive.* No right of action for personal injury or for injury to real or personal property shall cease or die with the person injuring or injured, except actions for slander, libel, criminal conversation, and so much of the action for malicious prosecution as is intended to recover for the personal injury. For any other injury an action may be brought or revived by the personal representative, or against the personal representative, heir or devisee, in the same manner as causes of action founded on contract." Ky. Rev. Stat. 411.140 (1998).

4. Generally, survival actions are brought by the executor or administrator of the estate and a recovery becomes an asset of that estate, with the recovery subject to the claims of creditors of the estate and the net proceeds distributed with the rest of the estate to the heirs under the will or intestacy statute. Damages are based on loss to the estate rather than on loss to the dependents or survivors. See S. Speiser, Recovery for Wrongful Death and Injury § 14.1 (3rd ed. 1992).

5. The only major argument against survival statutes is that they may result in a windfall to distant relatives who cared very little about the decedent and were not in any way dependent on the decedent. Do you find the argument persuasive? Obviously, the survival action may be the only recourse for someone who is not named as a beneficiary in the wrongful death statute. See, e.g., Warner v. McCaughan, 77 Wash.2d 178, 460 P.2d 272 (1969) (parents of college student who could not recover under wrongful death act because they were not financially dependent on decedent college student could bring survival action because they were heirs to her estate).

6. Many states have both survival and wrongful death statutes. There are then two causes of action that may be maintained separately or concurrently to successful judgment. But see ACandS, Inc. v. Redd, 703 So.2d 492 (Fla.App.1997) (in Florida, personal injury cause of action abates with death of claimant and recovery is through wrongful death action) (holding that spouse's loss of consortium claim also abates with death of primary claimant). The problem courts face in this connection is to control the damages in each action so as to avoid holding the defendant liable twice for the same elements of recovery. A good case struggling with the problem is Pezzulli v. D'Ambrosia, 344 Pa. 643, 26 A.2d 659 (1942).

7. Funeral and burial expenses paid by the survivors, are normally allocated to the death action. The physical and mental pain and suffering of the decedent are allocated to the survival action, as are medical expenses. Decedent's loss of potential earnings during normal life expectancy is also assigned to the survival action. But since it is out of these future earnings that decedent would have been expected to provide support for family, or to have made contributions to them, it is obvious that there would be a double recovery to the extent that they were allowed to recover for the loss when both actions are maintained. A frequent solution has been to allow in the survival action the potential earnings of the decedent during life expectancy, reduced to their present value, and to deduct the probable cost of maintenance of family, which must be recovered in the death action. See, for example, First Nat'l Bank in Greensburg v. M. & G. Convoy, Inc., 106 F.Supp. 261 (W.D.Pa.1952); and Wetzel v. McDonnell Douglas Corp., 491 F.Supp. 1288 (E.D.Pa.1980). See also Martin, Measuring Damages in Survival Actions for Tortious Death, 47 Wash.L.Rev. 609 (1972).

8. Recovery for pain and suffering is allowed only if the decedent was conscious of it. See, e.g., Schlichte v. Franklin Troy Trucks, 265 N.W.2d 725 (Iowa 1978). Thus, courtroom battles between medical experts have developed over this factual issue when the decedent lived only a short time after injury. Compare Fialkow v. DeVoe Motors, Inc., 359 Mass. 569, 270 N.E.2d 798 (1971) (evidence of gasping, gurgling and heavy breathing insufficient to show consciousness) with Campbell v. Leach, 352 Mass. 367, 225 N.E.2d 594 (1967) (evidence that decedent cried out sufficient to support an award).

9. Should the claim include pain and suffering that occurred before the physical injury, sometimes called "pre-impact fright"? Several courts have permitted recovery in the context of airplane crashes. See, e.g., Shu–Tao Lin v. McDonnell Douglas Corp., 742 F.2d 45 (2d Cir.1984) (applying New York law). A few have

applied it in other contexts. Beynon v. Montgomery Cablevision Ltd. Partnership, 351 Md. 460, 718 A.2d 1161 (1998) (jury verdict of $1,000,000 for pre-impact fright of 2 seconds based on evidence of 71' skidmarks left by plaintiff's vehicle before it rear ended tractor trailer, killing plaintiff instantly) (collecting cases from other jurisdictions).

10.   Should a claim for punitive damages survive the death of the claimant? Most jurisdictions permit the estate to recover for all damages, including punitive damages, that the decedent would have had. But see Froud v. Celotex Corporation, 98 Ill.2d 324, 456 N.E.2d 131 (1983) (In Illinois, punitive damages ablate with the death of the claimant.). Should a claim for punitive damages survive the death of the tortfeasor? Who would be punished? Tortfeasor distributed photocopies of sexually explicit photographs of his former girlfriend throughout the community, particularly where her mother, minor children, and employer would see them. She filed suit against him to stop the distribution and seeking compensatory and punitive damages. The tortfeasor committed suicide before the trial and his sister, the executrix of his estate, was substituted as a defendant. Should the estate be liable for punitive damages? G.J.D. v. Johnson, 552 Pa. 169, 713 A.2d 1127 (1998) (permitting award of punitive damages against estate, but noting that the majority of jurisdictions do not). See Chapter 10, Section 3, Punitive Damages.

11.   See Smedley, Some Order Out of Chaos in Wrongful Death Law, 37 Vand.L.Rev. 273 (1984), for an incisive analysis of the problems arising under the various types of statutes in the several states and a careful evaluation of reform proposals, including the Uniform Law Commissioners' Model Survival and Death Act.

A Note on Defenses

The interrelationship of wrongful death and survival statutes and defenses, although presented at this point, will be better appreciated by the reader after completion of Chapter 12 on Defenses. The discussion is based on W. Prosser & W. Keeton, Torts 954–60 (5th ed. 1984).

12.   *Defenses Based on Conduct or Status of the Decedent.* Since the survival type of death statute merely continues the decedent's own cause of action beyond his death and enhances it with damages for the death, any defenses that might have been set up against decedent if decedent had lived are still available to the defendant. The contrary might perhaps have been expected of the wrongful death acts, which create a separate and independent cause of action, founded upon the death itself, for the benefit of the designated beneficiaries. The original Lord Campbell's Act, however, contained an express provision limiting the death action to those cases in which the deceased might have recovered damages if he had lived; and this provision has been carried over into most of the American acts, or has been read into them by implication when it does not expressly appear. It obviously is intended at least to prevent recovery for death when the decedent could never at any time have maintained an action, as where there was simply no tortious conduct toward him.

On the same theoretical basis, but with less manifest justification, there has been general agreement denying recovery when the defendant's conduct has been tortious toward the decedent and has caused his death, thus causing loss to the innocent beneficiaries, but the defendant would have had a defense available against the decedent. This has been true of contributory negligence, assumption of risk or consent to the defendant's conduct, as well as privileges such as self-defense or defense of property. See also Restatement (Third) of Torts: Apportionment of

Liability § 6 (2000). Many of the courts that have considered the question have given the same effect to the immunity of one member of a family for torts against another, although there is a strong minority view to the contrary, based upon the theory that death destroys the reason for the immunity.

13. *Defenses Based on Conduct of the Beneficiaries.* Defenses available against the beneficiaries themselves offer a still more troublesome problem, on which the courts have not agreed. When the action is brought under a survival act, it is in theory still on behalf of the decedent, and the contributory negligence of even a sole beneficiary has been held not to prevent recovery. The same conclusion has been reached under wrongful death acts where the damages are recoverable on behalf of the decedent's estate, on the ground that the estate is distinct from the beneficiary. Under the usual death act, the recovery is for the beneficiaries, and the contributory negligence or the consent or assumption of risk of a sole beneficiary or of all beneficiaries generally is held to preclude the action, on the same principle that would bar any other plaintiff in interest. A few statutes have been construed to the contrary.

When only one of several beneficiaries is contributorily negligent, the prevailing view is that the action is not barred for those who were not negligent, but that recovery is diminished to the extent of the damages of the negligent beneficiary, who is denied all share in the proceeds. The same conclusion has been reached for assumption of risk. See also Restatement (Third) of Torts: Apportionment of Liability § 6 (2000). About all that remains of the barred action is the antique rule in a small number of states which "imputes" the negligence of one parent to the other when the action is for the death of a child. Except when it can be justified on the basis that the damages recovered will be community property, this, too, has generally been rejected as a survival of a discarded concept of marital unity. See, for example, Teeter v. Mo. Hwy. and Transp. Com., 891 S.W.2d 817 (1995) (mother's contributory fault in driving vehicle in which her passenger daughter was killed cannot be attributed to father where both mother and father are wrongful death beneficiaries). Although the death acts usually are construed to provide that only one action may be maintained for the death, it has been held that a release from one beneficiary will not prevent recovery by others and even that the statute of limitations may run against recovery on behalf of one, but not others.

14. *Comparative Negligence.* Under comparative negligence systems, there is the possibility of having the jury consider both the negligence of a beneficiary and the decedent since the negligence of either one—standing alone—may not automatically bar a claim. The process is not as complicated as it may appear: the jury simply allocates a percentage of negligence to the beneficiary and the decedent and then reduces the award to the beneficiary by that total amount. In modified comparative negligence systems, recovery by that beneficiary is precluded as soon as the threshold is reached. See also Restatement (Third) of Torts: Apportionment of Liability § 6 (2000).

15. *Effect of Personal Injury Action Brought Before Death.* A majority of the courts have held that a judgment for or against the decedent in an action for his injuries commenced during his lifetime, or the compromise and release of the action, will operate as a bar to any subsequent suit founded upon his death. This has the effect of placing in the decedent's hands the power to sell out the claim of the beneficiaries before it has come into existence. Their action is regarded as "derivative," arising out of and dependent upon the wrong done to him. The courts undoubtedly have been influenced by a fear of a double recovery. This is of course possible in any jurisdiction where the decedent would be allowed to recover for the

prospective earnings lost through his diminished life expectancy, out of which any benefits receivable by the beneficiaries would be expected to come.

Opposed to this possibility is the counter-danger of an improvident settlement by an optimistic individual, confident that he is not going to die, which takes no account of shortened life expectancy or of the interests of the survivors. Because of this, there is a substantial minority view that neither a judgment in his action nor his release of his claim will bar the action for wrongful death. See, for example, Thompson v. Wing, 70 Ohio St.3d 176, 637 N.E.2d 917 (1994) (medical malpractice judgment during patient's lifetime did not bar subsequent wrongful death claim by her beneficiaries because it is an independent claim; court notes that this is minority view). See also Brown v. Drillers, Inc., 630 So.2d 741 (La.1994) (release signed by personal injury claimant and his wife releases subsequent claim by wife as wrongful death beneficiary only if release unequivocally reflects that parties contemplated a release of future wrongful death claims). The possibility of double compensation either has been ignored, on the ground that legally it could not arise, or has been met by a deduction from the award to the death beneficiaries, of the amount found to have been paid to the decedent covering the permanent destruction of his earning capacity, or the suggestion that the expectancy of the survivors be deducted from the probable earnings in the decedent's own action. No satisfactory systematic solution to the whole problem has yet been found.

On the defense of the statute of limitations, which is distinguishable only in that it does not involve the danger of double compensation, some jurisdictions have held that the statute runs against the death action only from the date of death, even though at that time the decedent's own action would have been barred while he was living. See, e.g., Evans v. Southern Ohio Medical Ctr., 103 Ohio App.3d 250, 659 N.E.2d 326 (1995) (wrongful death claim not barred even though underlying medical malpractice action was). Others hold that it runs from the time of the original injury and consequently that the death action may be lost before it ever has accrued. See, e.g., Russell v. Ingersoll–Rand Co., 841 S.W.2d 343 (Tex.1992) (wrongful death action, because it is dependent on underlying personal injury action, may not be brought if statute of limitations expired on personal injury action before decedent's death); Edwards v. Fogarty, 962 P.2d 879 (Wyo.1998) (accord, noting that this is the majority rule).

16. *Statutes of Limitation.* The wrongful death statutes of most states contain their own time period within which to bring the action for wrongful death. In those states, that time limit rather than the general statute of limitations controls the wrongful death action. Because the action is a creature of statute rather than of the common law, filing within the limitation period is an essential element of the cause of action. Rosier v. Garron, Inc., 156 W.Va. 861, 199 S.E.2d 50 (1973) (creates a condition precedent for bringing action). It is not subject to the tolling provisions of the general statute of limitations. See, e.g., Cofer v. Ensor, 473 So.2d 984 (Ala.1985) (not subject to tolling provision of infancy); Taylor v. Black & Decker Mfg. Co., 21 Ohio App.3d 186, 486 N.E.2d 1173 (1984) (not tolled by beneficiary's minority). In jurisdictions whose wrongful death statutes do not contain a separate time limit and in jurisdictions who provide a wrongful death remedy through an expanded survival action, the statute of limitations for personal injury is applied. In those jurisdictions, the tolling provisions of the general statute of limitations (e.g., infancy, discovery) usually are applied.

The accrual of the cause of action (when does the statute begin to run?) is dependent on the wording of the wrongful death statute. Some specify that the cause of action accrues at death. Of those statutes that do not specify the accrual of the cause of action, some have interpreted their statutes as providing that the cause of action accrues at death while others have held that the action accrues at the time of injury.

17. *Two Separate Actions*. Most jurisdictions have both wrongful death and survival actions and most of the time those two actions are joined. That is not always the case, however, and it is important to keep in mind that they are two distinct causes of action, each with its own requirements. Motorist was injured in a collision with another vehicle. Doctors who treated him at the hospital failed to diagnose fractures in his vertebrae. He and his wife filed suit against the driver of the other vehicle for his personal injuries. He died while that lawsuit was pending. His representative then filed a wrongful death action against both the driver and the doctors and tried to amend the personal injury complaint against the driver to include a claim against the doctors. Because the Alabama survival statute provides that unfiled tort claims do not survive the death of the claimant, the doctors sought to dismiss the estate's claim against them. The estate's representative argued that the amended complaint should relate back to the filing of the original complaint, before patient's death. Should it? Malcolm v. King, 686 So.2d 231 (Ala.1996) (medical malpractice claim against doctors is distinct claim from negligence claim against driver and does not relate back; no survival cause of action against medical malpractice defendants). In wrongful death action against tobacco company, beneficiaries sought to prove that cigarettes caused decedent's lung cancer and that the cancer caused his death. Tobacco company argued that his death was caused by a blood clot that lodged in his heart and was a complication of surgery that he had undergone to treat urinary tract problems unrelated to the lung cancer. Jury returned a verdict that found that the death was unrelated to lung cancer or pulmonary disease. Beneficiaries, who were also the heirs, argued that they should at least be able to recover for damages suffered by decedent during his lifetime. Neither smoker during his lifetime nor his heirs after his death had filed a survival action, however, so the judgment for the tobacco company on the wrongful death action was affirmed. Wilks v. American Tobacco Co., 680 So.2d 839 (Miss.1996).

CHAPTER XII

DEFENSES

1. PLAINTIFF'S CONDUCT

(A) CONTRIBUTORY NEGLIGENCE

Butterfield v. Forrester

King's Bench, 1809.
11 East 60, 103 Eng.Rep. 926.

This was an action on the case for obstructing a highway, by means of which obstruction the plaintiff, who was riding along the road, was thrown down with his horse, and injured, & c. At the trial before Bayley J. at Derby, it appeared that the defendant, for the purpose of making some repairs to his house, which was close by the road side at one end of the town, had put up a pole across this part of the road, a free passage being left by another branch or street in the same direction. That the plaintiff left a public house not far distant from the place in question at 8 o'clock in the evening in August, when they were just beginning to light candles, but while there was light enough left to discern the obstruction at 100 yards distance: and the witness, who proved this, said that if the plaintiff had not been riding very hard he might have observed and avoided it: the plaintiff however, who was riding violently, did not observe it, but rode against it, and fell with his horse and was much hurt in consequence of the accident; and there was no evidence of his being intoxicated at the time. On this evidence Bayley J. directed the jury, that if a person riding with reasonable and ordinary care could have seen and avoided the obstruction; and if they were satisfied that the plaintiff was riding along the street extremely hard, and without ordinary care, they should find a verdict for the defendant: which they accordingly did.

Vaughan Serjt. now objected to this direction, on moving for a new trial; and referred to Buller's Ni.Pri. 26(a), where the rule is laid down, that "if a man lay logs of wood across a highway; though a person may with care ride safely by, yet if by means thereof my horse stumble and fling me, I may bring an action."

BAYLEY, J. The plaintiff was proved to be riding as fast as his horse could go, and this was through the streets of Derby. If he had used ordinary care he must have seen the obstruction; so that the accident appeared to happen entirely from his own fault.

LORD ELLENBOROUGH, C.J. A party is not to cast himself upon an obstruction which has been made by the fault of another, and avail himself of it, if he

Lord Ellenborough

do not himself use common and ordinary caution to be in the right. In cases of persons riding upon what is considered to be the wrong side of the road, that would not authorize another purposely to ride up against them. One person being in fault will not dispense with another's using ordinary care for himself. Two things must concur to support this action, an obstruction in the road by the fault of the defendant, and no want of ordinary care to avoid it on the part of the plaintiff.

PER CURIAM. Rule refused.

NOTES AND QUESTIONS

1. Consider the basic options available to the law in connection with how to treat the fact that plaintiff's negligence contributed to the happening of the accident. First, the law could completely bar plaintiff's claim. This approach, called contributory negligence, was taken by the court in *Butterfield*. What does it have to recommend it?

Second, the law could completely ignore plaintiff's culpable conduct. This is the approach taken under most Workers' Compensation Acts and No–Fault Automobile Accident Reparation Systems. The advantage to the plaintiff is obvious. Do you also see its philosophical underpinnings?

Third, the law could adopt one of the first two options as a general rule and then set up other rules making exceptions for designated situations. This is what the common law later did—generally adopting option 1, but allowing exceptions to it. Note that this is still an all-or-nothing approach to the individual case; the fact that the cases may average out as a whole provides cold comfort to the parties to the particular case. Would it be desirable to leave to the jury the question of whether to allow the plaintiff to recover all or nothing? This may have been the practice prior to the principal case. See Cruden v. Fentham, 2 Esp. 685, 170 Eng.Rep. 496 (N.P.1799); Clay v. Wood, 5 Esp. 44, 170 Eng.Rep. 732 (N.P.1803).

Fourth, the law could compare plaintiff's fault with that of defendant and reduce plaintiff's damages according to the measure of fault. This approach, called comparative negligence, has now been expressly adopted in 46 states, by statute or judicial decision. In only four states (Alabama, Maryland, Virginia, North Carolina) and the District of Columbia, contributory negligence continues to be a complete bar to recovery.

What are the advantages and disadvantages of each approach?

2. In 1854 a Pennsylvania judge reflected the feelings of many of his brethren when he called the defense of contributory negligence a "rule from time immemorial" and ventured to guess that it was "not likely to be changed for all time to come." Pennsylvania R. Co. v. Aspell, 23 Pa. 147, 149 (1854). While the judge was a poor historian (a form of comparative negligence was applied by English Admiralty Courts long before the *Butterfield* decision), he did rather well as a prognosticator of the law into the Twentieth Century. The defense had great appeal and sticking power in the United States. It was even adopted in Louisiana—a state that could easily have utilized its code and civil law tradition to adopt a comparative negligence approach. See Malone, Comparative Negligence—Louisiana's Forgotten Heritage, 6 La.L.Rev. 125 (1945).

3. The following theories all have been advanced from time to time in explanation or justification of the defense. Which of them are valid?

A. The defense has a penal basis, and plaintiff is denied recovery as punishment for misconduct. See Barker v. Kallash, 63 N.Y.2d 19, 468 N.E.2d 39, 479 N.Y.S.2d 201 (1984) (teenager, who was injured while building a pipe bomb, filed suit against nine-year-old who had sold him the firecrackers from which he extracted the gun powder for the pipe bomb).

B. Plaintiff is required to come into court with "clean hands," and the court will not aid one whose own fault has participated in causing his injury.

C. A rule of negligence is designed to encourage optimal care by both interacting parties. Usually, primary liability will suffice in promoting that level of care, but it may be inadequate where one party acts negligently and the other has an opportunity to avoid the accident. Without the defense of contributory negligence, the injured party may face a diluted incentive to take due care and the system may incur more administrative costs as well. See Landes & Posner, The Economic Structure of Tort Law 73–77 (1987).

D. Plaintiff's negligence is an intervening, superseding cause, which makes the defendant's negligence no longer "proximate." What if two negligently driven automobiles collide and injure both drivers and a pedestrian who was in no way negligent. The pedestrian could recover from either driver, but neither driver could recover from the other. Does the "proximate cause" analysis vary as applied to each of the potential plaintiffs? The plaintiff's negligence can be viewed as an act that stops the defendant's responsibility for the wrongful conduct. Without the intervention of the plaintiff's action, corrective justice notions would demand that the defendant rectify the wrong toward the plaintiff. For an examination of corrective justice issues, see Symposium, Corrective Justice and Formalism: The Care One Owes One's Neighbors, 77 Iowa L.Rev. 403 (1992).

4. The defense of contributory negligence should be distinguished from the rule on avoidable consequences or mitigation of damages, discussed in Chapter 10, Damages. The doctrine of avoidable consequences becomes material *after* plaintiff has been injured.

5. The common law rule of contributory negligence often produced results that a court or jury regarded as unjust. Whenever a rule of law regularly produces unjust results or lags behind social and economic developments, courts develop ameliorating practices and a group of exceptions for avoiding its application. This tenet of judicial behavior, which might be called the Erosion Principle, has occurred in a number of important areas in the law of torts. Can you think of some other illustrations? Over the years, the courts created a number of judicial devices to ameliorate the harsh effects of the rule of contributory negligence as a complete bar to recovery.

A. *Burden of Proof.* The burden of pleading and proving contributory negligence is on the defendant. See e.g., Brown v. Piggly–Wiggly Stores, 454 So.2d 1370 (Ala.1984) (contributory negligence is an affirmative defense). This is also true of comparative negligence. See Restatement (Third) of Torts: Apportionment of Liability § 4 (2000).

B. *Leaving the Question of Contributory Negligence to the Jury.* Courts have been very reluctant to take the issue of contributory negligence away from the jury through summary judgment or judgment as a matter of law. See e.g., Lazar v. Cleveland Electric Illuminating Co., 43 Ohio St.2d 131, 331 N.E.2d 424 (1975) (plaintiff grabbed an uninsulated high tension wire) and Urban v. Wait's Supermarket, Inc., 294 N.W.2d 793 (S.D.1980) (plaintiff tripped over a watermelon in a store aisle). It has been suggested that the effect of all this is to create a *de facto* comparative negligence system in which the jury applies *sub silentio* a rule of comparative negligence and apportions damages. See Ulman, A Judge Takes the Stand, 30–34 (1933). Does this eliminate the need for comparative negligence? Is it good policy to rely on a lay jury to correct an undesirable condition of the law?

C. *Causation in Fact.* Plaintiff's negligence stands on the same footing as defendant's and will bar recovery only if it is a substantial factor in bringing about the result. See, for example, Bahm v. Pittsburgh & Lake Erie R. Co., 6 Ohio St.2d 192, 217 N.E.2d 217 (1966) (jury instruction that plaintiff's recovery was barred if his conduct directly and proximately contributed "in any degree" to bring about the accident was error; quoted phrase must be eliminated so it is clear that plaintiff's conduct must be a substantial factor in bringing about the accident); Hofstrom v. Share, 295 N.J. Super. 186, 684 A.2d 981 (1996) (negligence of plaintiff in failing to follow emergency room physician instructions to return immediately if condition worsened not relevant because defendant's experts did not establish that her conduct affected her injuries).

D. *Proximate Cause.* Courts have subtly confined the defense by narrowly limiting the scope of proximate cause as applied to risks that plaintiff exposed himself to by his act of negligence. Prime examples are Furukawa v. Uoshio Ogawa, 236 F.2d 272 (9th Cir.1956) (negligence as to danger of falling, but not of falling upon a hook) and Smithwick v. Hall & Upson Co., 59 Conn. 261, 21 A. 924 (1890) (negligence as to danger of slipping off an unguarded icy ledge, but not of wall collapsing on plaintiff). What should happen to these cases once a jurisdiction adopts comparative negligence?

6. *Dual Standards of Care.* Professor Fleming James has argued that the different treatment of plaintiff's contributory negligence as compared with defendant's negligence should be recognized as a formal rule, but the courts steadfastly have refused to do so. See Restatement (Third) of Torts: Apportionment of Liability § 3 cmt. a (2000). See also James, Contributory Negligence, 62 Yale L.J. 691 (1953); James and Dickinson, Accident Proneness and Accident Law, 63 Harv.L.Rev. 769 (1950).

Applicability of Contributory Negligence in Particular Circumstances

7. *Defendant Engaged in Intentional, Wanton or Wilful or Reckless Conduct.* It is standard hornbook law that contributory negligence is not a defense to an intentional tort. See W. Prosser & W. Keeton, Torts 462 (5th ed. 1984). Thus, one cannot defend against a battery by arguing that the plaintiff was negligent in failing to duck. The same general rule has been extended in almost every jurisdiction to situations in which defendant engaged in "wanton and willful" or reckless conduct. It is said that this conduct differs from negligence not only in degree, but also in kind and, therefore, the defense of contributory negligence is inapplicable. See, e.g., Kasanovich v. George, 348 Pa. 199, 34 A.2d 523 (1943) and Adkisson v. City of Seattle, 42 Wash.2d 676, 258 P.2d 461, 467 (1953) ("Wanton misconduct is not negligence, since it involves intent rather than inadvertence, and is positive rather than negative.")

8. *Strict Liability.* On this, see Chapter 15 pages 770–777.

9. *Defendant Violates a Statute.* Generally, contributory negligence is still held to be a defense although defendant was negligent *per se* because of violation of a statute. See Brown v. Derry, 10 Wash.App. 459, 518 P.2d 251 (1974) (motorist transported individual on outside of vehicle). Certain statutes, however, are deemed to abrogate the defense.

A. *Statutes Explicitly Abolishing the Defense in Limited Situations.* Sometimes the legislature explicitly abolishes the contributory negligence defense in a limited situation. An example is under the F.E.L.A. when defendant has violated a federal safety standard and that caused the injury. See 45 U.S.C.A. § 53.

B. *Statutes "Intended" to Protect a Plaintiff Unable to Protect Himself.* Statutes prohibiting child labor, the sale of firearms to minors, the sale of liquor to intoxicated persons, and those that require safety devices to protect factory workers, have been held to be in this category. The court must determine that the "statute [was] enacted to protect a class of persons from their inability to exercise self-protective care." Restatement (Second) of Torts § 483.

C. See generally Prosser, Contributory Negligence as Defense to Violation of Statute, 32 Minn.L.Rev. 105 (1948).

Davies v. Mann

Exchequer, 1842.
10 M. & W. 547, 152 Eng.Rep. 588.

At the trial, before Erskine, J., at the last Summer Assizes for the county of Worcester, it appeared that the plaintiff, having fettered the fore feet of an ass belonging to him, turned it into a public highway, and at the time in question the ass was grazing on the off side of the road about eight yards wide, when the defendant's waggon, with a team of three horses, coming down a slight descent, at what the witness termed a smartish pace, ran against the ass, knocked it down, and the wheels passing over it, it died soon after. The ass was fettered at the time, and it was proved that the driver of the waggon was some little distance behind the horses. The learned Judge told the jury, that though the act of the plaintiff, in leaving the donkey on the highway so fettered as to prevent his getting out of the way of carriages travelling along it, might be illegal, still, if the proximate cause of the injury was attributable to the want of proper conduct on the part of the driver of the waggon, the action was maintainable against the defendant; and his Lordship directed them, if they thought that the accident might have been avoided by the exercise of ordinary care on the part of the driver, to find for the plaintiff. The jury found their verdict for the plaintiff, damages 40s.

Godson now moved for a new trial, on the ground of misdirection.

LORD ABINGER, C.B. I am of opinion that there ought to be no rule in this case. The defendant has not denied that the ass was lawfully in the highway, and therefore we must assume it to have been lawfully there; but even were it otherwise, it would have made no difference, for as the defendant might, by proper care, have avoided injuring the animal, and did not, he is liable for the consequences of his negligence, though the animal may have been improperly there.

PARKE, B. * * * [A]lthough the ass may have been wrongfully there, still the defendant was bound to go along the road at such a pace as would be likely to prevent mischief. Were this not so, a man might justify the driving over goods left on a public highway, or even over a man lying asleep there, or the purposely running against a carriage going on the wrong side of the road.

NOTES AND QUESTIONS

1. "The groans, ineffably and mournfully sad, of Davies' dying donkey, have resounded around the earth. The last lingering gaze from the soft, mild eyes of this docile animal, like the last parting sunbeams of the softest day in spring, has appealed to and touched the hearts of men. There has girdled the globe a band of sympathy for Davies' immortal 'critter.' Its ghost, like Banquo's ghost, will not down at the behests of the people who are charged with inflicting injuries, nor can

its groanings be silenced by the ranting and excoriations of carping critics. The law as enunciated in that case has come to stay." McLain, J., in Fuller v. Illinois Cent. R. Co., 100 Miss. 705, 717, 56 So. 783 (1911).

2.   Later commentators have rationalized the holding in the principal case into what has come to be known as the doctrine of last clear chance. As the title indicates, the thought is that if the defendant had the opportunity to avoid the accident after the opportunity was no longer available to the plaintiff, the defendant is the one who should bear the loss. Note that under this doctrine the whole loss is still placed on one party or the other. Does this accomplish justice between the parties?

3.   Which of the following explanations for the doctrine of last clear chance are satisfactory?

A.   The later negligence of defendant is an intervening, superseding cause, breaking the connection between plaintiff's prior negligence and plaintiff's injury. See Ackerman v. James, 200 N.W.2d 818 (Iowa 1972) (collecting cases). Is this view sound?

B.   The later negligence of defendant must necessarily be the greater fault: "the assumption is that he is the more culpable whose opportunity to avoid the injury was later." Kansas City S.R. Co. v. Ellzey, 275 U.S. 236 (1927). Suppose plaintiff is lying unconscious in the street, and defendant, properly driving an automobile, sees him there and excitedly steps on the accelerator instead of the brake? Cf. Smith v. Connecticut R. & L. Co., 80 Conn. 268, 67 A. 888 (1907).

C.   The doctrine arises out of dislike of the defense of contributory negligence, and represents a retreat from its application in a group of cases where an excuse can be found. MacIntyre, The Rationale of Last Clear Chance, 53 Harv.L.Rev. 1225 (1940).

4.   The jurisdictions that still following the common law rule of contributory negligence apply the exception of last clear chance in at least one of its many forms. Application of the doctrine may depend on whether the plaintiff is (1) helpless, unable to avoid the danger, or (2) merely inattentive. The Restatement (Second) of Torts §§ 479, 480, groups the patterns around the nature of the plaintiff's conduct. The whole doctrine of last clear chance is one of fearful and wonderful complexity. For a trio of modern cases in which the courts struggle to untangle its many threads to find the one applicable to the facts of the cases, see Belton v. WMATA, 20 F.3d 1197 (D.C.Cir.1994) (Plaintiff, dressed in a Batman cape and roaming the streets of Georgetown taunting motorists, banged on a bus door as the driver turned the corner. He slid under the bus and was injured.); Williams v. Harrison, 255 Va. 272, 497 S.E.2d 467 (1998) (Plaintiff and defendant and two of their friends were driving their four cars through a suburban neighborhood at a speed of 60 m.p.h. when the second and third cars in the line collided with each other.); WMATA v. Johnson, 699 A.2d 404 (D.C.App.1997) (on certified question from federal court, court rules that the last clear chance doctrine applies in case where parents of woman who committed suicide by jumping into path of oncoming subway train sought recovery from transit authority for subway train operator's failure to stop in time).

5.   The last clear chance doctrine has been called a "transitional doctrine," a way station on the road to some other remedy, such as comparative negligence. James, Last Clear Chance: A Transitional Doctrine, 47 Yale L.J. 704 (1938). Its effect, for many years, however, was to freeze the transition rather than to speed it. The opinion in the next principal case recounts the transition from contributory

negligence as a complete bar to recovery to comparative negligence in the various jurisdictions in the United States

(B) COMPARATIVE NEGLIGENCE

McIntyre v. Balentine

Supreme Court of Tennessee, 1992.
833 S.W.2d 52.

DROWOTA, J.

In this personal injury action, we granted Plaintiff's application for permission to appeal in order to decide whether to adopt a system of comparative fault in Tennessee. * * *

In the early morning darkness of November 2, 1986, Plaintiff–Harry Douglas McIntyre and Defendant–Clifford Balentine were involved in a motor vehicle accident resulting in severe injuries to Plaintiff. The accident occurred in the vicinity of Smith's Truck Stop in Savannah, Tennessee. As Defendant–Balentine was traveling south on Highway 69, Plaintiff entered the highway (also traveling south) from the truck stop parking lot. Shortly after Plaintiff entered the highway, his pickup truck was struck by Defendant's Peterbilt tractor. At trial, the parties disputed the exact chronology of events immediately preceding the accident.

Both men had consumed alcohol the evening of the accident. After the accident, Plaintiff's blood alcohol level was measured at .17 percent by weight. Testimony suggested that Defendant was traveling in excess of the posted speed limit.

Plaintiff brought a negligence action against Defendant–Balentine and [the lessee of the truck]. Defendants answered that Plaintiff was contributorily negligent, in part due to operating his vehicle while intoxicated. After trial, the jury returned a verdict stating: "We, the jury, find the plaintiff and the defendant equally at fault in this accident; therefore, we rule in favor of the defendant."

* * *

[After judgment was entered for Defendants, Plaintiff brought an appeal alleging the trial court erred by refusing to instruct the jury regarding the doctrine of comparative negligence. The Court of Appeals affirmed, holding that comparative negligence is not the law in Tennessee.]

I.

The common law contributory negligence doctrine has traditionally been traced to Lord Ellenborough's opinion in Butterfield v. Forrester, 11 East 60, 103 Eng.Rep. 926 (1809). There, plaintiff, "riding as fast as his horse would go," was injured after running into an obstruction defendant had placed in the road. Stating as the rule that "one person being in fault will not dispense with another's using ordinary care," plaintiff was denied recovery on the basis that he did not use ordinary care to avoid the obstruction. [C]

The contributory negligence bar was soon brought to America as part of the common law, see Smith v. Smith, 19 Mass. 621, 624 (1825), and proceeded to spread throughout the states. See H.W. Woods, The Negligence Case: Comparative Fault § 1:4 (1978). This strict bar may have been a direct outgrowth of the common law system of issue pleading; issue pleading posed questions to be answered "yes" or "no," leaving common law courts, the theory goes, no choice but to award all or nothing. See J.W. Wade, W.K. Crawford, Jr., and J.L. Ryder, Comparative Fault In Tennessee Tort Actions: Past, Present and Future, 41 Tenn.L.Rev. 423, 424–25 (1974). A number of other rationalizations have been advanced in the attempt to justify the harshness of the "all-or-nothing" bar. Among these: the plaintiff should be penalized for his misconduct; the plaintiff should be deterred from injuring himself; and the plaintiff's negligence supersedes the defendant's so as to render defendant's negligence no longer proximate. [Cc]

In Tennessee, the rule as initially stated was that "if a party, by his own gross negligence, brings an injury upon himself, or contributes to such injury, he cannot recover;" for, in such cases, the party "must be regarded as the author of his own misfortune." [C] In subsequent decisions, we have continued to follow the general rule that a plaintiff's contributory negligence completely bars recovery. [Cc]

Equally entrenched in Tennessee jurisprudence are exceptions to the general all-or-nothing rule: contributory negligence does not absolutely bar recovery where defendant's conduct was intentional, [cc]; where defendant's conduct was "grossly" negligent, [cc]; where the defendant had the "last clear chance" with which, through the exercise of ordinary care, to avoid plaintiff's injury, [cc]; or where plaintiff's negligence may be classified as "remote." [Cc]

In contrast, comparative fault has long been the federal rule in cases involving injured employees of interstate railroad carriers, [c], and injured seamen. [Cc] See generally V. Schwartz, Comparative Negligence § 1.4(A) (2d ed. 1986).

Similarly, by the early 1900s, many states, including Tennessee, had statutes providing for the apportionment of damages in railroad injury cases. See V. Schwartz, supra, at § 1.4. While Tennessee's railroad statute did not expressly sanction damage apportionment, it was soon given that judicial construction. * * * This system of comparative fault was utilized for almost a century until 1959 when, trains no longer unique in their "astonishing speeds," the statute was overhauled, its strict liability provision being replaced by negligence per se and the common law contributory negligence bar. [Cc]

Between 1920 and 1969, a few states began utilizing the principles of comparative fault in all tort litigation. [C] Then, between 1969 and 1984, comparative fault replaced contributory negligence in 37 additional states. [C] In 1991, South Carolina became the 45th state to adopt comparative fault, see Nelson v. Concrete Supply Co., 303 S.C. 243, 399 S.E.2d 783 (1991), leaving Alabama, Maryland, North Carolina, Virginia, and Tennessee as the only remaining common law contributory negligence jurisdictions.

Eleven states have judicially adopted comparative fault. Thirty-four states have legislatively adopted comparative fault.

* * *

II.

Over 15 years ago, we stated, when asked to adopt a system of comparative fault:

> We do not deem it appropriate to consider making such a change unless and until a case reaches us wherein the pleadings and proof present an issue of contributory negligence accompanied by advocacy that the ends of justice will be served by adopting the rule of comparative negligence.

Street v. Calvert, 541 S.W.2d [576] at 586 [Tenn.1976]. Such a case is now before us. After exhaustive deliberation that was facilitated by extensive briefing and argument by the parties, amicus curiae, and Tennessee's scholastic community, we conclude that it is time to abandon the outmoded and unjust common law doctrine of contributory negligence and adopt in its place a system of comparative fault. Justice simply will not permit our continued adherence to a rule that, in the face of a judicial determination that others bear primary responsibility, nevertheless completely denies injured litigants recompense for their damages.

We recognize that this action could be taken by our General Assembly. However, legislative inaction has never prevented judicial abolition of obsolete common law doctrines, especially those, such as contributory negligence, conceived in the judicial womb. See Hanover v. Ruch, 809 S.W.2d 893, 896 (Tenn.1991) (citing cases). Indeed, our abstinence would sanction "a mutual state of inaction in which the court awaits action by the legislature and the legislature awaits guidance from the court," Alvis v. Ribar, 85 Ill.2d 1, 421 N.E.2d 886, 896, 52 Ill.Dec. 23 (1981), thereby prejudicing the equitable resolution of legal conflicts.

Nor do we today abandon our commitment to stare decisis. While "confidence in our courts is to a great extent dependent on the uniformity and consistency engendered by allegiance to stare decisis, * * * mindless obedience to this precept can confound the truth and foster an attitude of contempt." Hanover, 809 S.W.2d at 898.

III.

Two basic forms of comparative fault are utilized by 45 of our sister jurisdictions, these variants being commonly referred to as either "pure" or "modified." In the "pure" form[5] a plaintiff's damages are reduced in

---

5. The 13 states utilizing pure comparative fault are Alaska, Arizona, California, Florida, Kentucky, Louisiana, Mississippi, Missouri, Michigan, New Mexico, New York, proportion to the percentage negligence attributed to him; for example, a plaintiff responsible for 90 percent of the negligence that caused his injuries nevertheless may recover 10 percent of his damages. In the "modified" form[6] plaintiffs recover as in pure jurisdictions, but only if the plaintiff's negligence either (1) does not exceed ("50 percent" jurisdictions) or (2) is less than ("49 percent" jurisdictions) the defendant's negligence. See generally V. Schwartz, supra, at §§ 3.2, 3.5.

Although we conclude that the all-or-nothing rule of contributory negligence must be replaced, we nevertheless decline to abandon totally our fault-based tort system. We do not agree that a party should necessarily be able to recover in tort even though he may be 80, 90, or 95 percent at fault. We therefore reject the pure form of comparative fault.

We recognize that modified comparative fault systems have been criticized as merely shifting the arbitrary contributory negligence bar to a new ground. See, e.g. Li v. Yellow Cab Co., 13 Cal.3d 804, 532 P.2d 1226, 119 Cal.Rptr. 858 (1975). However, we feel the "49 percent rule" ameliorates the harshness of the common law rule while remaining compatible with a fault-based tort system. Accord Bradley v. Appalachian Power Co., 163 W.Va. 332, 256 S.E.2d 879, 887 (1979). We therefore hold that so long as a plaintiff's negligence remains less than the defendant's negligence the plaintiff may recover; in such a case, plaintiff's damages are to be reduced in proportion to the percentage of the total negligence attributable to the plaintiff.

In all trials where the issue of comparative fault is before a jury, the trial court shall instruct the jury on the effect of the jury's finding as to the percentage of negligence as between the plaintiff or plaintiffs and the defendant or defendants. Accord Colo.Rev.Stat. § 13–21–111.5(5) (1987). The attorneys for each party shall be allowed to argue how this instruction affects a plaintiff's ability to recover.

IV.

Turning to the case at bar, the jury found that "the plaintiff and defendant [were] equally at fault." Because the jury, without the benefit of proper instructions by the trial court, made a gratuitous apportionment of fault, we find that their "equal" apportionment is not sufficiently trustworthy to form the basis of a final determination between these parties. Therefore, the case is remanded for a new trial in accordance with the dictates of this opinion.

Rhode Island, and Washington. See V. Schwartz, supra, at § 2.1.

6. The 21 states using the "50 percent" modified form: Connecticut, Delaware, Hawaii, Illinois, Indiana, Iowa, Massachusetts, Minnesota, Montana, Nevada, New Hampshire, New Jersey, Ohio, Oklahoma, Oregon, Pennsylvania, South Carolina, Texas, Vermont, Wisconsin, and Wyoming. The 9 states using the "49 percent" form: Arkansas, Colorado, Georgia, Idaho, Kansas, Maine, North Dakota, Utah, and West Virginia. Two states, Nebraska and South Dakota, use a slight-gross system of comparative fault. See V. Schwartz, supra, at § 2.1.

V.

We recognize that today's decision affects numerous legal principles surrounding tort litigation. For the most part, harmonizing these principles with comparative fault must await another day. However, we feel compelled to provide some guidance to the trial courts charged with implementing this new system.

First, and most obviously, the new rule makes the doctrines of remote contributory negligence and last clear chance obsolete. The circumstances formerly taken into account by those two doctrines will henceforth be addressed when assessing relative degrees of fault.

Second, in cases of multiple tortfeasors, plaintiff will be entitled to recover so long as plaintiff's fault is less than the combined fault of all tortfeasors.

Third, today's holding renders the doctrine of joint and several liability obsolete. Our adoption of comparative fault is due largely to considerations of fairness: the contributory negligence doctrine unjustly allowed the entire loss to be borne by a negligent plaintiff, notwithstanding that the plaintiff's fault was minor in comparison to defendant's. Having thus adopted a rule more closely linking liability and fault, it would be inconsistent to simultaneously retain a rule, joint and several liability, which may fortuitously impose a degree of liability that is out of all proportion to fault.[7]

Further, because a particular defendant will henceforth be liable only for the percentage of a plaintiff's damages occasioned by that defendant's negligence, situations where a defendant has paid more than his "share" of a judgment will no longer arise, and therefore the Uniform Contribution Among Tort-feasors Act, T.C.A. §§ 29–11–101 to 106 (1980), will no longer determine the apportionment of liability between codefendants.

Fourth, fairness and efficiency require that defendants called upon to answer allegations in negligence be permitted to allege, as an affirmative defense, that a non-party caused or contributed to the injury or damage for which recovery is sought. In cases where such a defense is raised, the trial court shall instruct the jury to assign this nonparty the percentage of the total negligence for which he is responsible. However, in order for a plaintiff to recover a judgment against such additional person, the plaintiff must have made a timely amendment to his complaint and caused process to be served on such additional person. Thereafter, the additional party will be required to answer the amended complaint. The procedures shall be in accordance with the Tennessee Rules of Civil Procedure.

Fifth, until such time as the Tennessee Judicial Conference Committee on Civil Pattern Jury Instructions promulgates new standard jury instruc-

---

7. Numerous other comparative fault jurisdictions have eliminated joint and several liability. See, e.g., Alaska Stat. § 09.17.080(d) (Supp.1991); Colo.Rev.Stat. § 13–21–111.5(1) (1987); Kan.Stat.Ann. § 60–258a(d) (Supp.1991); N.M.Stat.Ann. § 41–3A–1 (1989); N.D.Cent.Code § 32–03.2–02 (Supp.1991); Utah Code Ann. § 78–27–38,–40 (1992); Wyo.Stat.Ann. § 1–1–109(d) (1988).

tions, we direct trial courts' attention to the suggested instructions and special verdict form set forth in the appendix to this opinion.

VI.

The principles set forth today apply to (1) all cases tried or retried after the date of this opinion, and (2) all cases on appeal in which the comparative fault issue has been raised at an appropriate stage in the litigation.

* * *

For the foregoing reasons, the judgment of the Court of Appeals is reversed in part and affirmed in part [on another issue on appeal], and the case is remanded to the trial court for a new trial in accordance with the dictates of this opinion. The costs of this appeal are taxed equally to the parties.

NOTES AND QUESTIONS

1. Note the court's discussion of the history of the shift from contributory negligence to comparative negligence and of the policy issues underlying each of the doctrines.

2. Only four states (Alabama, Maryland, North Carolina, and Virginia) and the District of Columbia continue to apply the common law doctrine that contributory negligence is a complete bar to recovery. Williams v. Delta International Mach. Corp., 619 So.2d 1330 (Ala.1993) ("We have heard hours of oral argument; we have read numerous briefs; we have studied cases from other jurisdictions and law review articles; and in numerous conferences we have discussed in depth this issue and all of the ramifications surrounding such a change. After this exhaustive study and these lengthy deliberations, the majority of the Court, for various reasons, has decided that we should not abandon the doctrine of contributory negligence, which has been the law in Alabama for approximately 162 years.")

3. As the principal case tells you, most of the 46 jurisdictions that have adopted comparative negligence have done so by legislation with only a dozen doing so by judicial decision. Even in some jurisdictions that first adopted comparative negligence by decision, the legislature has since acted to establish a statutory scheme. See, e.g., Goetzman v. Wichern, 327 N.W.2d 742 (Iowa 1982) and Iowa Code Ann. § 668.3 (1997); Alvis v. Ribar, 85 Ill.2d 1, 421 N.E.2d 886, 52 Ill.Dec. 23 (1981) and 735 Ill. Comp. Stat. 5/2–1116 (1999).

4. Do you think that the behavior of persons will differ according to whether contributory negligence or some form of comparative negligence is the rule? The law and economics literature has explored this issue. The comparative negligence rule also has been advocated by reference to game theory. Orr, The Superiority of Comparative Negligence, 20 J. Legal Stud. 119 (1991). What about litigation costs? Do you think that more litigation, more hotly contested, and less susceptible to settlement, would be generated under comparative fault? Is "fairness" enough to justify comparative negligence even if it is less efficient? See also, Cane, Atiyah's Accidents, Compensation and the Law 124–125 (4th ed. 1987).

5. Note that the Tennessee Supreme Court in adopting comparative negligence had to make a number of other decisions. What type of comparative negligence? What about the continuing effect of ameliorating doctrines like last clear chance? In multiple defendant cases, does the jury compare the fault of the plaintiff

to each defendant or to all of the defendants combined? Should joint and several liability survive the adoption of comparative negligence? Should the fault of a non-party be considered by the jury? What should the jury be told about the impact of its allocation of fault? When should the new rules take effect? The notes that follow discuss how these and other issues have been resolved in jurisdictions adopting comparative negligence.

6. *Types of Comparative Negligence.* After deciding against the "all or nothing" approach of contributory negligence, the court or legislature must decide the effect of the plaintiff's contributory negligence on plaintiff's recovery.

A. Pure. About a dozen jurisdictions (e.g., Arizona, California, Florida, Michigan, and New York) and several federal statutes (e.g., F.E.L.A., Jones Act) have adopted the pure comparative negligence approach. In those jurisdictions, the plaintiff's recovery is reduced by the percentage fault attributable to the plaintiff. See also Restatement (Third) of Torts: Apportionment of Liability § 7 (2000).

B. Modified (plaintiff "not as great as"). About a dozen jurisdictions (e.g., Arkansas, Colorado, Georgia, Nebraska, and Tennessee) have adopted a modified form of comparative negligence in which the plaintiff's recovery is reduced by the percentage of fault attributable to the plaintiff as long as the plaintiff's fault is "not as great as" the defendant's. If the plaintiff's fault is equal to or greater than the defendant's, the plaintiff is completely barred from recovery. Maine's statute authorizes the jury to reduce the damages to "such extent as the jury thinks just and equitable having regard to the claimant's share in the responsibility for the damage," without actually requiring that it be proportional. Thus, the jury may reduce the amount of damages by more than the percentage of fault attributable to the plaintiff. Pelletier v. Fort Kent Golf Club., 662 A.2d 220 (Maine 1995) (interpreting 14 Maine Rev.Stat. § 156 (1998)).

C. Modified (plaintiff "not greater than"). About twenty jurisdictions (e.g., Connecticut, Illinois, Ohio, Pennsylvania, and Wisconsin) have adopted a modified form of comparative negligence in which the plaintiff's recovery is reduced by the percentage of fault attributable to the plaintiff as long as the plaintiff's fault is "not greater than" the fault of the defendant's. If the plaintiff's fault is greater than the defendant's, the plaintiff is completely barred from recovery.

The two modified forms of comparative negligence produce a different result only in the 50/50 case. Although this distinction may not seem very important in theory, it is important as a practical matter because a 50/50 apportionment is an appealing one to juries.

D. Slight/Gross. South Dakota is the only remaining jurisdiction that apportions damages so long as plaintiff's negligence "was slight in comparison with the negligence of the defendant."

7. *What is Being Compared?* In comparative negligence jurisdictions, what is the jury being asked to compare? Should fault be apportioned according to the nature of the parties' conduct (whose conduct was worse) or the proximity of the causal relationship between the conduct and the injuries (whose conduct contributed more to the cause of the injury) or some combination of the two? Eaton v. McLain, 891 S.W.2d 587 (Tenn.1994) (cataloguing the approaches of various jurisdictions).

8. *Mechanics of Apportionment.* Some statutes use a special verdict or special interrogatory procedure by which the jurors inform the court as to (1) what percentage of fault was attributable to each party and (2) how much damage each claimant suffered. The court then computes the damages. Is this procedure better or

is it better to let the jury return a general verdict? See, for example, In re Asbestos Litigation Pusey Trial Group, 669 A.2d 108 (Dela. 1995) (establishing order of questions for jury to consider re effect of plaintiffs' smoking in lung cancer cases brought against asbestos defendants).

9. *Burden of Proof.* The burden of proof is on the defendant to show both that the plaintiff was negligent and that the plaintiff's negligent conduct was a proximate cause of the plaintiff's injuries. See Restatement (Third) of Torts: Apportionment of Liability § 4 (2000).

10. *Should the Jury Be Instructed as to the Legal Consequences of Their Verdict?* For example, in a modified comparative negligence jurisdiction, a percentage change of a single point may make a complete difference as to whether the plaintiff can recover or not. See Kaeo v. Davis, 68 Haw. 447, 719 P.2d 387 (1986) (jury should be told). See also Restatement (Third) of Torts: Apportionment of Liability § 7 cmt. n (2000) and Reporters' Notes thereto; Brown, Federal Special Verdicts: The Doubt Eliminator, 44 F.R.D. 338 (1968); Smith, Comparative Negligence Problems With the Special Verdict: Informing the Jury of the Legal Effects of Their Verdicts, 10 Land & Water L.Rev. 199 (1975).

11. *Multiple Parties.* In a modified comparative negligence system, if there are several defendants, should plaintiff's negligence be compared with that of each defendant individually or with all of them together? See Restatement (Third) of Torts: Apportionment of Liability § 7 cmt. n (2000).

12. *Application to Persons Not Made Party to the Action.* Should their proportion of the fault be assessed and taken into consideration? Cf. Brown v. Keill, 224 Kan. 195, 580 P.2d 867 (1978) and Consolidated Freightways Corp. v. Osier, 185 Mont. 439, 605 P.2d 1076 (1979). Should the fault of an immune party be considered? Snyder v. LTG Lufttenchnische, 955 S.W.2d 252 (Tenn.1997) (jury may consider actions of immune employer in deciding whether manufacturer of product used by worker is liable, but may not assess fault against the employer); Sears, Roebuck & Co. v. Huang, 652 A.2d 568 (Dela. 1995) (accord, parental negligence in supervising child who was injured by escalator); YH Investments, Inc. v. Godales, 690 So.2d 1273 (Fla.1997) (jury, in assessing fault against owner of apartment building responsible for guardrail that was in violation of statute, could consider fault of mother of two-year-old plaintiff).

13. *Relationship to Contribution.* What should be done if a separate statute provides for pro rata contribution?

14. *Should Joint and Several Liability Be Abolished?* As the principal case indicates, some states have eliminated joint and several liability after adopting comparative negligence, while others have retained it. See also Fernanders v. Marks Construction of S.C., Inc., 330 S.C. 470, 499 S.E.2d 509 (1998) (declining to abolish joint and several liability in wake of adoption of comparative negligence and collecting cases and statutes from other jurisdictions). See the cases and notes at pages 359–366.

15. *Effect of Comparative Negligence on Certain Common Law Doctrines.* (a) *Last clear chance.* Some courts have found that the doctrine is no longer necessary under comparative negligence, while others have retained it even after switching to comparative negligence. See Restatement (Third) of Torts: Apportionment of Liability § 3 cmt. b (2000). (b) *Res ipsa loquitur.* Should it still be necessary for the plaintiff to present evidence that no negligent conduct on his part contributed to the injury? (c) *Negligence per se.* The conduct of either plaintiff or defendant may violate a statute. Should either of these affect the percentage of negligence? (d)

Imputed negligence. (e) ~~*Punitive damages.*~~ (f) *Avoidable consequences.* (g) *Trial Judge's Control of Jury* (remittitur or additur).

16. *Types of Defendant's Conduct Subject to Application of Comparative Fault.* Comparative fault is, of course, applicable to negligence. What about an intentional tort? If defendant swings at plaintiff, should the damages be reduced because of plaintiff's negligent failure to duck? The answer would normally be no in a contributory negligence jurisdiction. What about recklessness? Willful and wanton misconduct? Compare Blazovic v. Andrich, 124 N.J. 90, 590 A.2d 222 (1991) (various types of conduct differ in degree, not in kind and jury should compare even intentional conduct of defendant with that of plaintiff) with Burke v. 12 Rothschild's Liquor Mart, Inc., 148 Ill.2d 429, 170 Ill.Dec. 633, 593 N.E.2d 522 (1992) (qualitative difference between negligence and willful/wanton conduct means that they cannot be compared and comparative negligence is thus not a defense to intentional or willful/wanton conduct). Violation of a "higher degree of care" imposed on a common carrier? Strict liability for abnormally dangerous activities (Chapter 14), or for products liability based on strict liability or breach of warranty (Chapter 15)? Defendant maintains a nuisance (Chapter 16); should all nuisances be treated alike? He makes a misrepresentation that plaintiff relies upon to his detriment (Chapter 21); are intentional and negligent misrepresentations treated alike?

17. *Extent to Which Plaintiff's Condition or the Nature of His Conduct Affects the Application of Comparative Fault.* Assume plaintiff is a minor or aged, or is mentally or physically impaired; or is an automobile guest in a state that has a different standard of care for them; he is a trespasser or licensee on defendant's land; or acted recklessly (all problems treated in earlier chapters). What if plaintiff has "assumed the risk" (next Section) or has "misused" a product manufactured by the defendant (Chapter 15). What if plaintiff acted intentionally (to take his own life) in a situation where the intentional conduct was the foreseeable risk created by the negligent tortfeasor? White v. Lawrence, 975 S.W.2d 525 (Tenn.1998) (patient's intentional suicide should not be compared to the negligence of physician in determining fault).

18. See V. Schwartz, Comparative Negligence (3d ed. 1994); H. Woods, The Negligence Case: Comparative Fault (3d ed. 1993); Comparative Negligence Symposium, 23 Mem. St. U.L.Rev. (1992).

(C) ASSUMPTION OF RISK

(1) EXPRESS

➤ Winterstein v. Wilcom

Court of Special Appeals of Maryland, 1972.
16 Md.App. 130, 293 A.2d 821.

[Plaintiff Roland Winterstein was seriously injured when his vehicle hit a 36″ long, hundred-pound cylinder head that was lying on a drag racetrack owned by defendant. At the time plaintiff was participating in a speed contest. For this opportunity he paid defendant an entry fee.

Defendant's employees were stationed in a tower to watch "for any hazards on the track," but negligently failed to do so. Plaintiff Roland Winterstein brought a claim for his personal injuries and his wife, Barbara, brought a claim for loss of consortium. Prior to participating in the race, both plaintiffs signed releases drafted by defendant that stated in part:

"*Request and Release.* I, the undersigned, hereby request permission to enter the premises * * * and participate in auto timing and acceleration runs, tests, contests and exhibitions to be held this day. I have inspected the premises and I know the risks and dangers involved in the said activities, and that unanticipated and unexpected dangers may arise during such activities and I assume all risks of injury to my person and property that may be sustained in connection with the stated and associated activities, in and about the premises.

In consideration of the permission granted to me to enter the premises and participate in the stated activities, and in further consideration of the provisions of an insurance medical plan, I do hereby, for myself, my heirs, administrators and assigns, release, remise and discharge the owners, operators, and sponsors of the said premises, of the activities, of the vehicles, and of the equipment therein, and their respective servants, agents, officers, and officials, and all other participants in the stated activities of and from all claims, demands, actions, and causes of action of any sort, for injuries sustained by my person and/or property during my presence in said premises and participation in the stated activities due to negligence or any other fault."

Plaintiffs conceded that the risk that injured Roland fell within the terms of the release, but they contended that the release should be invalidated as a matter of "public policy." The trial court did not accept this argument and dismissed both claims. Plaintiffs appealed.]

ORTH, J. * * * In the absence of legislation to the contrary, the law, by the great weight of authority, is that there is ordinarily no public policy which prevents the parties from contracting as they see fit, as to whether the plaintiff will undertake the responsibility of looking out for himself. "It is quite possible for the parties expressly to agree in advance that the defendant is under no obligation of care for the benefit of the plaintiff, and shall not be liable for the consequences of conduct which would otherwise be negligent." Prosser, Law of Torts, 3rd Ed. (1964) § 67, p. 456. In other words, the parties may agree that there shall be no obligation to take precautions and hence no liability for negligence. * * *

There is a proviso to the general rule. The relationship of the parties must be such that their bargaining be free and open. When one party is at such an obvious disadvantage in bargaining power that the effect of the contract is to put him at the mercy of the other's negligence, the agreement is void as against public policy. The proviso is applicable on this basis between employer and employee.

It is also against public policy to permit exculpatory agreements as to transactions involving the public interest, as for example with regard to public utilities, common carriers, innkeepers and public warehousemen. Prosser feels that there has been a definite tendency to expand the exception raised by the proviso to other professional bailees who are under no public duty but deal with the public, such as garagemen, owners of parking lots, and parcel checkrooms, because the indispensable need for their services deprives the customer of all real equal bargaining power. He finds decisions divided as to other private bailees for hire, the decision likely to turn upon the extent to which it is considered that the public interest is involved. [C]

Generally, exculpatory agreements otherwise valid are not construed to cover the more extreme forms of negligence—wilful, wanton, reckless or gross. Nor do they encompass any conduct which constitutes an intentional tort. [C] And, of course, it is fundamental that if an agreement exempting a defendant from liability for his negligence is to be sustained, it must appear that its terms were known to the plaintiff, and "if he did not know of the provision in his contract and a reasonable person in his position would not have known of it, it is not binding upon him, and the agreement fails for want of mutual consent." [C] * * *

Because an exculpatory provision may not stand if it involves the public interest, see 175 A.L.R. 8 (1948), our inquiry turns to what transactions are affected with a public interest. In Tunkl v. Regents of the University of California, 60 Cal.2d 92, 383 P.2d 441, 32 Cal.Rptr. 33 (1963) the Supreme Court of California, in bank, found that in placing particular contracts within or without the category of those affected with a public interest, the courts have revealed a rough outline of that type of transaction in which exculpatory provisions will be held invalid. "Thus the attempted but invalid exemption involves a transaction which exhibits some or all of the following characteristics It concerns a business of a type generally thought suitable for public regulation. The party seeking exculpation is engaged in performing a service of great importance to the public, which is often a matter of practical necessity for some members of the public. The party holds himself out as willing to perform this service for any member of the public who seeks it, or at least for any member coming within certain established standards. As a result of the essential nature of the service, in the economic setting of the transaction, the party invoking exculpation possesses a decisive advantage of bargaining strength against any member of the public who seeks his services. In exercising a superior bargaining power the party confronts the public with a standardized adhesion contract of exculpation, and makes no provision whereby a purchaser may pay additional reasonable fees and obtain protection against negligence. Finally, as a result of the transaction, the person or property of the purchaser is placed under the control of the seller, subject to the risk of carelessness by the seller or his agents." [C]

We note a further refinement. Although the traditional view has been that where the defendant's negligence consists of the violation of a statute, the plaintiff may still assume the risk, there is a growing tendency to the contrary where a safety statute enacted for the protection of the public is violated. The rationale is that the obligation and the right so created are public ones which it is not within the power of any private individual to waive. [Cc]

It is clear that the exculpatory provisions involved in the case before us whereby Winterstein expressly agreed in advance that Wilcom would not be liable for the consequences of conduct which would otherwise be negligent were under the general rule recognizing the validity of such provisions. There was not the slightest disadvantage in bargaining power between the parties. Winterstein was under no compulsion, economic or otherwise, to race his car. He obviously participated in the speed runs simply because he wanted to do so, perhaps to demonstrate the superiority of his car and probably with the hope of winning a prize. This put him in no bargaining disadvantage.

The business operated by Wilcom had none of the characteristics of one affected with the public interest. The legislature has not thought it suitable for public regulation for it has not sought to regulate it. Wilcom is not engaged in performing a service of great importance to the public which is a matter of practical necessity for any member of the public. Wilcom does not hold himself out as willing to perform the service for any member of the public coming within certain established standards; we see nothing to indicate that he may not arbitrarily refuse to permit any person to participate in the speed runs. Since the service is not of an essential nature Wilcom had no decisive advantage of bargaining strength against any member of the public seeking to participate. Nor was Winterstein so placed under the control of Wilcom that he was subject to the risk of carelessness by Wilcom or his agents; Winterstein was under no obligation whatsoever to race his car.

We do not believe that any safety statute of this State, enacted for the protection of the public, was involved. Our attention has not been called to, nor are we aware of, such a statute dealing with activities of the nature conducted by Wilcom.

We observe that Winterstein did not allege that the negligence he attributed to Wilcom was other than simple negligence; he characterized Wilcom's omissions and commissions as careless, not wilful, wanton, reckless or gross; he does not say that he was wronged by an intentional tort.

The short of it is that as to the releases here the effect of the exemptive clauses upon the public interest was nil. We find that each release was merely an agreement between persons relating entirely to their private affairs. In the absence of a legislative declaration, we hold that they were not void as against public policy. * * *

Judgment affirmed with costs.

NOTES AND QUESTIONS

1. There are two basic issues involved when defendant asserts that plaintiff expressly assumed a risk. The first concerns whether the risk that injured plaintiff fell within the terms of the agreement. Suppose in the instant case plaintiff had been injured when an employee of defendant had become angry and knocked him down. Would defendant have been protected by the release? Cf. Brown v. Moore, 247 F.2d 711 (3d Cir.1957); Feigenbaum v. Brink, 66 Wash.2d 125, 401 P.2d 642 (1965). How should a release be drafted to cover that risk? Plaintiff signed a release

concerning inherent risks involved in horseback riding. Her own horse behaved well, but the guide's horse kicked her. Is that within the scope of the release? Wright v. Loon Mtn. Rec. Corp., 140 N.H. 166, 663 A.2d 1340 (1995) (question of fact for jury). Must the release actually mention the word "negligence"? Compare Witt v. Dolphin Research Ctr., Inc., 582 So.2d 27 (Fla.App.1991) (yes) with Boehm v. Cody Country Chamber of Commerce, 748 P.2d 704 (Wyo.1987) ("hold harmless and release * * * all claims" language is adequate). Restatement (Third) of Torts: Apportionment of Liability § 2 cmt. c (2000) (word "negligence" not necessary if language is otherwise clear and unequivocal).

2. The second issue is whether the contract itself violates public policy and therefore should not be enforced. The principal case is one of the most comprehensive in setting forth the considerations that underlie that determination. In light of those principles, how should a court rule on the validity of a document in which

A. A patient agreed to assume all risks that had been explained to her in connection with medical diagnosis and treatment in a hospital. Meiman v. Rehabilitation Center, Inc., 444 S.W.2d 78 (Ky.1969); Cudnik v. William Beaumont Hosp., 207 Mich. App. 378, 525 N.W.2d 891 (1994) (joining the "overwhelming majority" of jurisdictions that have found exculpatory agreements for providing of medical treatment invalid and unenforceable). Suppose the patient did not have to pay for medical services. Should that make a difference? Tunkl v. Regents of Univ. of California, 60 Cal.2d 92, 383 P.2d 441, 32 Cal.Rptr. 33 (1963) (no).

B. An express assumption of risk clause is written into a contract of sale between two industrial giants. See Delta Air Lines, Inc. v. McDonnell Douglas Corp., 503 F.2d 239 (5th Cir.1974).

C. A passenger is given the opportunity to ride free on a common carrier, but he must relieve it of all liability to him for negligent acts committed in the course of transportation. See Gonzales v. Baltimore & Ohio R. Co., 318 F.2d 294 (4th Cir.1963). Suppose the passenger paid for the ticket? See New York Cent. R. Co. v. Lockwood, 84 U.S. (17 Wall.) 357 (1873).

D. A parent signs an assumption of the risk form on behalf of a minor child so that the child may attend ski-racing lessons or play recreational soccer. Is the agreement enforceable against the parent who signed the agreement? against the other parent? against the child? Compare Scott v. Pacific West Mountain Resort, 119 Wash.2d 484, 834 P.2d 6 (1992) (parents can waive their own rights but not their minor child's) with Zivich v. Mentor Soccer Club, Inc., 82 Ohio St.3d 367, 696 N.E.2d 201 (1998) (mother waived her rights, and child's rights, and father's rights).

E. In the principal case, both Mr. Winterstein and his wife signed releases. What if Mrs. Winterstein had not signed a release? Would her loss of consortium claim be barred by her husband's express assumption of the risk? See Huber v. Hovey, 501 N.W.2d 53 (Iowa 1993).

3. In any case involving express assumption of risk, an attorney must research not only tort law but also appropriate regulatory laws that may affect the validity of the documents. See, e.g., N.Y.Gen.Oblig.Law § 5–321 (1999) (declaring exculpatory clauses in rental of real property void).

4. Must the agreement be in writing in order to constitute express assumption of the risk? See Boyle v. Revici, 961 F.2d 1060 (2d Cir.1992) (applying New York law) (assumption of the risk of unconventional treatment for cancer need not be in writing).

5.   As indicated in a later case, comparative negligence statutes may affect implied assumption of risk, but they do not affect an express assumption of risk. See Gilson v. Drees Bros., 19 Wis.2d 252, 120 N.W.2d 63, 67 (1963).

(2) IMPLIED

Rush v. Commercial Realty Co.

Supreme Court of New Jersey, 1929.
7 N.J.Misc. 337, 145 A. 476.

PER CURIAM. The case for the plaintiffs was that they were tenants of the defendant, which controlled the house wherein they lived and also the adjoining house, and provided a detached privy for the use of both houses; that Mrs. Rush having occasion to use this privy, went into it and fell through the floor, or through some sort of trap door therein, descended about nine feet into the accumulation at the bottom, and had to be extricated by use of a ladder. * * * The two grounds of appeal are that the trial court erred in refusing a nonsuit, and erred in refusing to direct a verdict for the defendant.

Taking the facts as the jury were entitled to find them, most favorably for the plaintiffs, the situation was that of a building under the control of the landlord for the use of tenants generally, and maintained by the landlord; a consequent duty of care in maintenance; a defective condition in the floor which the jury might say was due to negligent maintenance by the defendant; and an accident resulting therefrom. In such a situation it would seem that the argument for a nonsuit or for a direction must be restricted to the questions of contributory negligence and assumption of risk. In dealing with these, it should be observed that Mrs. Rush had no choice, when impelled by the calls of nature, but to use the facilities placed at her disposal by the landlord, to wit, a privy with a trap door in the floor, poorly maintained. We hardly think this was the assumption of a risk; she was not required to leave the premises and go elsewhere. Whether it was contributory negligence to step on a floor, which she testified was in bad order, was a question for the jury to solve according to its finding of the conditions and her knowledge of them, or what she should have known of them; it does not seem to be a court question.

We conclude that there was no error in denying motions to take the case from the jury, and the judgment will accordingly be affirmed.

NOTES AND QUESTIONS

1.   Is implied assumption of risk virtually the same as the consent defense to intentional torts? Assumption of risk, in the sense of consent, is sometimes called *volenti*, after the Latin maxim, *Volenti non fit injuria* [To the willing, there is no injury]. It requires actual knowledge of the particular risk, appreciation of its magnitude, and voluntary encountering of the risk.

2.   In a number of states the defense of assumption of risk has been carried beyond the concept of consent and applied to any factual situation where the plaintiff consciously and voluntarily places himself in a position where he is subject

to a known risk. The relationship of this type of assumption of risk to contributory negligence has given much trouble. Sometimes the distinction is drawn by saying that the "essence of contributory negligence is carelessness; of assumption of risk, venturousness. Thus an injured person may not have acted carelessly, may have exercised the utmost care, yet may have assumed, voluntarily, a known hazard." Hunn v. Windsor Hotel Co., 119 W.Va. 215, 193 S.E. 57 (1937) (plaintiff deliberately walked down defective steps when others, not greatly more inconvenient, were also available). Assumption of the risk involves the meeting of a subjectively known risk; contributory negligence may involve a plaintiff exposing himself to a danger of which he was subjectively unaware but which would have been apparent had he used due care. Robinson v. BF Goodrich Tire Co., 664 A.2d 616 (Pa.Super.1995) (distinguishing assumption of the risk and contributory negligence). This approach gives the defendant two separate defenses for the same conduct, which is what the trial court did in the principal case.

3. Distinguish the following. Which defense or defenses would be available to defendant in each?

A. Plaintiff voluntarily enters into a relation with defendant, which he knows to involve some not unreasonable risk. He teaches a beginner to drive an automobile. Le Fleur v. Vergilia, 280 App.Div. 1035, 117 N.Y.S.2d 244 (1952).

B. Plaintiff, entering defendant's premises in the dark, does not know that they are dangerous, and fails to exercise ordinary caution to find out.

C. Plaintiff knows that defendant's activity, or a condition created by him, involves some danger, but quite reasonably concludes that he can safely encounter it and proceeds. In an amusement park, he buys a ride on a moving belt that upsets the riders. See Judge Cardozo's terse opinion in Murphy v. Steeplechase Amusement Co., 250 N.Y. 479, 166 N.E. 173 (1929).

D. Plaintiff, fully aware of an unreasonable risk, voluntarily proceeds to encounter it. He consents to ride with a drunken driver on a dark night. Cf. Sutherland v. Davis, 286 Ky. 743, 151 S.W.2d 1021 (1941).

4. Assuming that plaintiff was contributorily negligent, why might the defense of assumption of risk have practical importance? Consider

A. If defendant has been reckless, contributory negligence is usually avoided, see page 601, but assumption of risk will remain. One can assume the risk of reckless conduct. See Evans v. Holsinger, 242 Iowa 990, 48 N.W.2d 250 (1951).

B. Some courts have held that assumption of risk will bar recovery in an action founded on strict liability, while plaintiff's ordinary negligence may not. See Gomes v. Byrne, 51 Cal.2d 418, 333 P.2d 754 (1959) (abnormally dangerous activity). What problems would be created by the application of this distinction?

5. As the principal case indicates, it is essential that defendant show that plaintiff knew of the risk. The best way to show this, of course, is to secure a direct admission from plaintiff or someone who heard him. See Vanderlei v. Heideman, 83 Ill.App.3d 158, 403 N.E.2d 756, 38 Ill.Dec. 525 (1980) (horseshoer testified he knew of risk of being kicked because he had been kicked several times before). But circumstantial evidence may be adequate. Cf. Wyly v. Burlington Indus., 452 F.2d 807 (5th Cir.1971) (plaintiff contestant in "National Lap Sitting Contest" promoting wrinkle-free slacks must have been aware of risk of chair collapsing when 14 college students sat on his lap). Suppose plaintiff is rendered incompetent by the accident. How can it be determined if he assumed the risk? See Farley v. M.M. Cattle Co., 549 S.W.2d 453 (Tex.Civ.App.1977).

6. The scope of the risk assumed must be addressed. Courts, unfavorably disposed to assumption of risk, place a narrow or specific gloss on "risk," and thereby do a great deal to undermine the practical utility of the defense. See Hawthorne v. Gunn, 123 Cal.App. 452, 11 P.2d 411 (1932) (woman sitting on man's lap in a moving car assumes certain risks, but a collision is not among them). Does a hockey fan assume the risk of being struck in face by an errant puck? Even if she deliberately buys a ticket for a seat low in the stands behind the plexiglass shield? Cf. Moulas v. PBC Prods., Inc., 570 N.W.2d 739 (Wis.App.1997), aff'd 576 N.W.2d 929 (1998) (no recovery for plaintiff). Does a football fan who holds season tickets for seats in the end zone assume the risk that a ball might soar over the net and hit him? That unruly fans might trample him while attempting to relieve him of a ball he caught? Cf. Telega v. Security Bureau, Inc., 719 A.2d 372 (Pa.Super.1998) (being trampled by unruly fans not a risk inherent in or an ordinary part of football).

7. Apart from knowledge of the risk, plaintiff must proceed to encounter it "voluntarily." How much latitude does this concept give a court to define the scope of the defense?

8. Defendant negligently maintains a highway, leaving a large mudhole in it. Plaintiff, knowing the condition of the highway, attempts to drive past the mudhole, and while keeping to the extreme edge of the road slides off into the ditch and is injured. Should it make any difference whether (1) plaintiff is away from home and has to get back or (2) there is a reasonably short and convenient detour at hand, in good condition? Pomeroy v. Westfield, 154 Mass. 462, 28 N.E. 899 (1891); Campion v. Rochester, 202 Minn. 136, 277 N.W. 422 (1938). Defendant's negligent operation of a train endangers a child on the track. Plaintiff dashes on the track to save the child and is himself injured. Does he assume the risk? Bond v. Baltimore & Ohio R. Co., 82 W.Va. 557, 96 S.E. 932 (1918); Eckert v. Long Island R. Co., 43 N.Y. 502 (1871). Suppose he dashes into a burning building to save his hat? On his own property, plaintiff was bitten by a vicious boar owned by a neighbor. The plaintiff had knowledge of the vicious propensities of the boar and yet left his house and exposed himself to the risk. See Marshall v. Ranne, 511 S.W.2d 255 (Tex.1974) (not voluntary because his only choices were to remain prisoner in his own house or to try to make it past the boar to his pickup truck).

9. *Plaintiff's Protests.* The fact that plaintiff has protested against the defendant's conduct is of course important evidence that he does not consent to assume the risk. But having protested, he may thereafter, even though reluctantly, accept the situation, and as the courts have sometimes put it, "waive" the protest. Whether he does so is a question of fact, and usually a question for the jury. Often it will turn upon the existence of some reasonable alternative to the plaintiff's course. Compare Young v. Wheby, 126 W.Va. 741, 30 S.E.2d 6 (1944), with Ridgway v. Yenny, 223 Ind. 16, 57 N.E.2d 581 (1944).

➤ Blackburn v. Dorta

Supreme Court of Florida, 1977.
348 So.2d 287.

[Several cases in the Florida District Court of Appeal had reached differing decisions on the issue of whether "the doctrine of assumption of risk is still viable as an absolute bar to recovery subsequent to adoption of the rule of comparative negligence in Hoffman v. Jones, 280 So.2d 431

(Fla.1973)." Three of them were consolidated by the state supreme court under its "conflict certiorari jurisdiction."]

SUNDBERG, JUSTICE. * * * Since our decision in Hoffman v. Jones, supra, contributory negligence no longer serves as a complete bar to plaintiff's recovery but is to be considered in apportioning damages according to the principles of comparative negligence. We are now asked to determine the effect of the *Hoffman* decision on the common law doctrine of assumption of risk. If assumption of risk is equivalent to contributory negligence, then *Hoffman* mandates that it can no longer operate as a complete bar to recovery. However, if it has a distinct purpose apart from contributory negligence, its continued existence remains unaffected by *Hoffman*. This question was expressly reserved in *Hoffman* as being not ripe for decision. 280 So.2d 431, 439.

At the outset, we note that assumption of risk is not a favored defense. There is a puissant drift toward abrogating the defense. The argument is that assumption of risk serves no purpose which is not subsumed by either the doctrine of contributory negligence or the common law concept of duty. It is said that this redundancy results in confusion and, in some cases, denies recovery unjustly. * * * The issue is most salient in states which have enacted comparative negligence legislation. Those statutes provide that the common law defense of contributory negligence no longer necessarily acts as a complete bar to recovery. The effect of these statutes upon the doctrine of assumption of risk has proved to be controversial. Joining the intensifying assault upon the doctrine, a number of comparative negligence jurisdictions have abrogated assumption of risk. Those jurisdictions hold that assumption of risk is interchangeable with contributory negligence and should be treated equivalently. Today we are invited to join this trend of dissatisfaction with the doctrine. For the reasons herein expressed, we accept the invitation.

At the commencement of any analysis of the doctrine of assumption of risk, we must recognize that we deal with a potpourri of labels, concepts, definitions, thoughts, and doctrines. The confusion of labels does not end with the indiscriminate and interchangeable use of the terms "contributory negligence" and "assumption of risk." In the case law and among text writers, there have developed categories of assumption of risk. Distinctions exist between *express* and *implied;* between *primary* and *secondary;* and between *reasonable* and *unreasonable* or, as sometimes expressed, *strict* and *qualified.* It will be our task to analyze these various labels and to trace the historical basis of the doctrine to unravel what has been in the law an "enigma wrapped in a mystery."

It should be pointed out that we are not here concerned with express assumption of risk which is a contractual concept outside the purview of this inquiry and upon which we express no opinion herein. * * *

The breed of assumption of risk with which we deal here is that which arises by implication or *implied* assumption of risk. Initially it may be divided into the categories of *primary* and *secondary*. The term primary assumption of risk is simply another means of stating that the defendant was not negligent, either because he owed no duty to the plaintiff in the first instance, or because he did not breach the duty owed. Secondary assumption of risk is an affirmative defense to an established breach of a duty owed by the defendant to the plaintiff. [C]

The concept of primary assumption of risk is the basis for the historical doctrine which arose in the master-servant relationship during the late nineteenth century. * * *

It is apparent that no useful purpose is served by retaining terminology which expresses the thought embodied in primary assumption of risk. This branch (or trunk) of the tree of assumption of risk is subsumed in the principle of negligence itself. * * * An example of this concept is presented in the operation of a passenger train. It can be said that a passenger assumes the risk of lurches and jerks which are ordinary and usual to the proper operation of the train, but that he does not assume the risk of extraordinary or unusual lurches and jerks resulting from substandard operation of the train. The same issue can be characterized in terms of the standard of care of the railroad. Thus, it can be said that the railroad owes a duty to operate its train with the degree of care of an ordinary prudent person under similar circumstances which includes some lurching and jerking while a train is in motion or commencing to move under ideal circumstances. So long as the lurching or jerking is not extraordinary due to substandard conduct of the railroad, there is no breach of duty and, hence, no negligence on the part of the railroad. The latter characterization of the issue clearly seems preferable and is consistent with the manner in which the jury is instructed under our standard jury instructions.

Having dispensed with *express* and *primary-implied* assumption of risk, we recur to *secondary-implied* assumption of risk which is the affirmative defense variety that has been such a thorn in the judicial side. The affirmative defense brand of assumption of risk can be subdivided into the type of conduct which is reasonable but nonetheless bars recovery (sometimes called *pure* or *strict* assumption of risk), and the type of conduct which is unreasonable and bars recovery (sometimes referred to as *qualified* assumption of risk). [C] Application of pure or strict assumption of risk is exemplified by the hypothetical situation in which a landlord has negligently permitted his tenant's premises to become highly flammable and a fire ensues. The tenant returns from work to find the premises a blazing inferno with his infant child trapped within. He rushes in to retrieve the child and is injured in so doing. Under the pure doctrine of assumption of risk, the tenant is barred from recovery because it can be said he voluntarily exposed himself to a known risk. Under this view of assumption of risk, the tenant is precluded from recovery notwithstanding the fact that his conduct could be said to be entirely reasonable under the circumstances. [C] There is little to commend this doctrine of implied-pure or strict assumption of risk, and our research discloses no Florida case in which it has been applied. Certainly, in light of Hoffman v. Jones, supra, there is no reason supported by law or justice in this state to give credence to such a principle of law.

There remains, then, for analysis only the principle of implied-qualified assumption of risk, and it can be demonstrated in the hypothetical recited above with the minor alteration that the tenant rushes into the blazing premises to retrieve his favorite fedora. Such conduct on the tenant's part clearly would be unreasonable. Consequently, his conduct can just as readily be characterized as contributory negligence. It is the failure to exercise the care of a reasonably prudent man under similar circumstances. It is this last category of assumption of risk which has caused persistent confusion in the law of torts because of the lack of analytic difference between it and contributory negligence. If the only significant form of assumption of risk (implied-qualified) is so readily characterized, conceptualized, and verbalized as contributory negligence, can there be any sound rationale for retaining it as a separate affirmative defense to negligent conduct which bars recovery altogether? In the absence of any historical imperative, the answer must be no. We are persuaded that there is no historical significance to the doctrine of implied-secondary assumption of risk. * * *

We find no discernible basis analytically or historically to maintain a distinction between the affirmative defense of contributory negligence and assumption of risk. The latter appears to be a viable, rational doctrine only in the sense described herein as implied-qualified assumption of risk which connotes unreasonable conduct on the part of the plaintiff. This result comports with the definition of contributory negligence appearing in Restatement (Second) of Torts § 466 (1965). Furthermore, were we not otherwise persuaded to elimination of assumption of risk as a separate affirmative defense in the context herein described, the decision of this Court in Hoffman v. Jones, supra, would dictate such a result. As stated therein:

" * * * A primary function of a court is to see that legal conflicts are equitably resolved. In the field of tort law, the most equitable result that can ever be reached by a court is the equation of liability with fault. Comparative negligence does this more completely than contributory negligence, and we would be shirking our duty if we did not adopt the better doctrine." 280 So.2d 431, 438.

Is liability equated with fault under a doctrine which would totally bar recovery by one who voluntarily, but reasonably, assumes a known risk while one whose conduct is unreasonable but denominated "contributory negligence" is permitted to recover a proportionate amount of his damages for injury? Certainly not. Therefore, we hold that the affirmative defense of implied assumption of risk is merged into the defense of contributory negligence and the principles of comparative negligence enunciated in Hoffman v. Jones, supra, shall apply in all cases where such defense is asserted. * * *

It is so ordered.

NOTES AND QUESTIONS

1. Assumption of risk is not favored by the courts; and it has been cordially disliked by the friends of the plaintiff, because of its long history of defeating

recovery in cases of genuine hardship—particularly in those of injuries to employees before the workers' compensation acts. The first cases to refuse to recognize the defense involved the violation of statutes that were found to be enacted to protect a particular class of persons against their own consent; and it was declared that the purpose of the statute would be defeated if the defense were allowed. Child labor acts afford the obvious example. Lenahan v. Pittston Coal Mining Co., 218 Pa. 311, 67 A. 642 (1907); Terry Dairy Co. v. Nalley, 146 Ark. 448, 225 S.W. 887 (1920).

2. *Comparative Negligence.* A growing number of courts are in accord with the holding of the principal case that implied assumption of risk does not remain an affirmative defense separate and apart from contributory negligence. As the principal case reflects, the advent of comparative negligence is prompting courts to implement a merger of the defenses of contributory negligence and implied assumption of risk. What are the reasons for this? Some comparative negligence statutes have treated assumption of risk the same as contributory negligence, but the merger may occur even if the comparative negligence statute is completely silent about assumption of risk. See Kopischke v. First Continental Corp., 610 P.2d 668 (Mont.1980) and Monk v. Virgin Islands Water & Power Authority, 53 F.3d 1381 (3d Cir.1995) (applying Virgin Islands law) (distinguishing primary assumption of risk and collecting cases and statutes from other jurisdictions). See also Restatement (Third) of Torts: Apportionment of Liability § 3 cmt. c (2000) (conduct of plaintiff who is actually aware of risk and voluntarily encounters it is evaluated under comparative negligence standard).

But see Neb. Rev. Stat. § 25–21,185.12 (1992) (codifying assumption of the risk as a separate affirmative defense). Which approach do you prefer? See also Diamond, Assumption of Risk After Comparative Negligence: Integrating Contract Theory into Tort Doctrine, 52 Ohio St.L.J. 717 (1991).

3. *Failure of Plaintiff to Take Advance Precaution Against Extent of Injury.* Plaintiff negligently fails to wear his seatbelt and is more seriously injured than he would have been if he had worn it. Should plaintiff's failure to wear a seatbelt be considered in his case against the other driver? against the vehicle manufacturer? See Restatement (Third) of Torts: Apportionment of Liability § 3 cmt. b, illus. 3 (2000) (unless there is a statute precluding consideration, such conduct should be taken into account in assigning percentage of fault). See also Restatement (Third) of Torts: Products Liability § 16 cmt. f (1998) (Reporters' Note lists jurisdictions that have statutes that do not permit plaintiff's damages to be reduced by failure to wear a seatbelt and those that do). In a case where the jury found that the plaintiff was 90% at fault for her injuries due to her failure to use the shoulder harness of her seatbelt, should her damages award be reduced by 5% as provided by the seatbelt statute or 90% as provided by the comparative fault statute? Klinke v. Mitsubishi Motors Corp., 458 Mich. 582, 581 N.W.2d 272 (1998) (5% cap on reduction applicable only against another driver, not against a product manufacturer).

4. The conceptual problem underlying the seatbelt cases is not new. Many tort law students of the 1930's and 1940's spent hours studying the case of Mahoney v. Beatman, 110 Conn. 184, 147 A. 762 (1929). Plaintiff drove an automobile at excessive speed and defendant negligently crossed over the median and collided with it. The proof was clear that plaintiff's speed was not responsible for the collision, but it did increase his damages. How should the court have decided the case? See Green, Mahoney v. Beatman: A Study in Proximate Cause, 39 Yale L.J. 532 (1930); Gregory, Judge Maltbie's Dissent in Mahoney v. Beatman, 24 Conn.B.J. 78 (1950). Would this case be easier to handle today? Cf. East Hampton Dewitt Corp. v. State Farm Mut. Auto. Ins. Co., 490 F.2d 1234 (2d Cir.1973).

5. Suppose plaintiff motorcyclist fails to wear a helmet in violation of state criminal law. Defendant negligently crashes into him. Should the court allow defendant to show that plaintiff's injuries would have been less severe if he wore the helmet? Cf. Thurel v. Varghese, 207 A.D.2d 220, 621 N.Y.S.2d 633 (N.Y. App. 1995). See Rogers v. Frush, 257 Md. 233, 262 A.2d 549 (1970). What if a parent does not secure a child in a child safety seat in violation of state law? In what other situations might there be a duty imposed on plaintiff to take self-precaution against the negligence of others? Should neighbors have to wear masks in an area polluted by a factory? Should they have to wear hard hats when walking near a negligently maintained construction site? Where should the line be drawn?

6. On the seatbelt defense, see generally LeBel, Reducing the Recovery of Avoidable "Seat–Belt Damages": A Cure for the Defects of Waterson v. General Motors Corporation, 22 Seton Hall L.Rev. 1 (1992); Ackerman, The Seat Belt Defense Reconsidered: A Return to Accountability in Tort Law?, 16 N.M.L.Rev. 221 (1986); Schwartz, The Seat Belt Defense and Mandatory Usage: Law, Ethics, and Economics, 24 Idaho L.Rev. 275 (1988).

2. STATUTES OF LIMITATIONS AND REPOSE

Teeters v. Currey

Supreme Court of Tennessee, 1974.
518 S.W.2d 512.

HENRY, JUSTICE. This malpractice action essentially involves a determination of whether the statute of limitation begins to run from the date of the injury or from the date of the discovery of the injury.

The admitted facts are that on June 5, 1970, plaintiff gave birth to a normal child. Defendant was the attending physician. Following delivery, because of edema anemia and other medical complications, he recommended that plaintiff have a bilateral tubal ligation, the purpose of which was to avoid future pregnancies. Defendant performed this surgery on June 6, 1970, and her recovery was uneventful.

On December 6, 1972 she was hospitalized at Newell Clinic and was attended by Dr. Edgar Atkin. Dr. Atkin discovered that she was pregnant. He so advised her and referred her to other physicians for obstetrical care.

On March 9, 1973 plaintiff was delivered of a premature child and there were severe complications. Pursuant to medical advice, another bilateral tubal ligation was performed on March 11, 1973.

Plaintiff instituted suit on November 15, 1973, three years, five months and nine days after the operation, but approximately eleven months after discovering her pregnancy.

Plaintiff alleges that during the course of this latter surgery it was discovered that the earlier surgery performed by the defendant was negligently and inadequately done and was not performed in accordance with proper standards of care and good medical practice.

Specifically, she charges that defendant failed to properly or completely sever the left fallopian tube in a manner which would assure sterility and prevent future pregnancies. Further, she charges that he failed to identify the right fallopian tube in a manner which would assure sterility and prevent future pregnancies. Further, she charges that he failed to cut, sever or ligate this tube in any manner.

The defendant's answer pleads the statute of limitations and denies that he was guilty of any act of negligence. * * *

Section 28–304, T.C.A. applies to malpractice suits and provides that the action be "commenced within one (1) year after cause of action accrued."

When does the cause of action accrue?

In Bodne v. Austin, 156 Tenn. 366, 2 S.W.2d 104 (1928) the Court said: " * * * we have been referred to no authority holding that mere ignorance and failure to discover the existence of the cause of action, or the consequential damages resulting from the breach of duty or wrongful act, can prevent the running of the statute of limitations."

But this was in 1927 almost half a century ago.

In Albert v. Sherman, 167 Tenn. 133, 67 S.W.2d 140 (1934), the Court followed *Bodne*.

This was forty years ago. * * *

The time has come for us to re-examine the past holdings of our Appellate Courts in the light of contemporary standards of justice and of the holdings of the courts of last resort in other American jurisdictions. * * *

We recognize that statutes of limitations are statutes of repose designed to promote stability in the affairs of men and to avoid the uncertainties and burdens inherent in defending stale claims.

In recognition of this, traditionally our courts have held that a right of action accrues immediately upon the infliction or occurrence of injury and that mere ignorance or failure of plaintiff to discover his cause of action or the subsequent resulting damage does not toll the statute. Bodne v. Austin, supra.

That this is a harsh and an oppressive rule there can be little doubt. To counter the casualties it has produced the courts have fashioned the so-called "discovery doctrine," under which the statute does not begin to run until the negligent injury is, or should have been, discovered.

This concept has been adopted by judicial interpretation in at least a majority of the American states. [C] Some of these jurisdictions limit the application of the doctrine to "foreign objects"; the majority apply it to all medical malpractice cases. * * *

As evidence of the rapidity with which the various jurisdictions have embraced this equitable doctrine, the main volume of 80 A.L.R.2d, published in *1961*, at page 388, lists *seven (7) states* as having adopted the discovery rule, viz., California, Colorado, Louisiana, Missouri, North Carolina, Pennsylvania and Texas.

The main volume of the appropriate Later Case Service, published in *1968*, lists *twelve (12) additional states,* Arizona, Delaware, Hawaii, Idaho, Iowa, Maryland, Michigan, Montana, Nebraska, New Jersey, Utah and West Virginia.

The *1974* supplement lists *nine (9) more states,* Georgia, Illinois, Kansas, Kentucky, North Dakota, Oklahoma, Oregon, Rhode Island and Washington.

This brings the total to twenty-eight (28) states.

Add Tennessee to the list.

We adopt as the rule of this jurisdiction the principle that in those classes of cases where medical malpractice is asserted to have occurred through the negligent performance of surgical procedures, the cause of action accrues and the statute of limitations commences to run when the patient discovers, or in the exercise of reasonable care and diligence for his own health and welfare, should have discovered the resulting injury. All cases contra are overruled.

In the instant case the cause of action accrued when plaintiff discovered that she was pregnant, or in the exercise of reasonable care and diligence, she should have so discovered.

We add, in meticulous fairness to the trial judge, that in ruling as he did, he properly relied upon our precedents.

We here merely recede from prior cases in order to establish a rule which we are convinced will be productive of results more nearly consonant with the demands of justice and the dictates of ethics and morality.

Reversed and remanded. Appellee will pay all costs incident to this appeal.

HARBISON, JUSTICE, concurred in a separate opinion.

NOTES AND QUESTIONS

1. The statute of limitations is a complete bar to actions that do not meet its time limits. It is in no way dependent on the merits of the case. All states have some statute of limitation, although the time period within which the action must be brought varies in length. For actions sounding in tort, most states impose a two or three year limitation. Even within each state, there is variation depending on the type of action that is brought. Statutes of limitations in tort law may vary in length, depending upon the basis of liability, the general subject matter of the claim, and the type of interest invaded. One of the first points a lawyer ascertains on undertaking a claim is what is the appropriate statute of limitations. It may be malpractice not to do so.

2. *Classification of Action for the Purpose of the Statutes of Limitations.* A good deal of judicial prose has been spent in classifying actions for the purpose of the statute of limitations. Is the action based on "intent" or "negligence?" See Spivey v. Battaglia, page 20. Is an action for breach of warranty a matter of tort or contract? See, e.g., Heavner v. Uniroyal, Inc., 118 N.J.Sup. 116, 286 A.2d 718 (1972) and cases collected in Banks and Curp, Products Liability: Use of Identity to Determine the Applicable Statute of Limitations, 3 Ohio North.L.Rev. 1 (1973). Is

negligent conduct ordinary negligence or professional malpractice? J.B. v. Sacred Heart Hosp., 635 So.2d 945 (Fla.1994) (plaintiff contracted AIDS because hospital failed to tell him his brother had AIDS and how to care for him while transporting him to another medical facility; court found failure was ordinary negligence rather than medical malpractice). Cases that have defined the terms "contract," "tort," "intent" or "malpractice" in other legal contexts are not always helpful in solving classification problems involving the statute of limitations. Why?

3. ~~Accrual.~~ Most statutes of limitation provide that the time within which to file begins to run when the cause of action "accrues," leaving to the courts to fix that point. Since damage is an essential part of a cause of action based on negligence, most courts have held that the statute begins to run when there has been an actual injury to plaintiff's person or property. In most cases, that is easy to determine and not a subject of dispute between the parties. Some categories of cases have arisen, however, where the date of injury is not easily ascertainable or where the strict application of the time-of-injury rule works an apparent injustice. For example, in the principal case, when did the cause of action accrue? That is, when did "injury" occur? At the time the surgery was performed negligently or at the time of conception of the baby? See Nunnally v. Artis, 254 Va. 247, 492 S.E.2d 126 (1997) (on facts similar to principal case, court finds injury occurs at conception of baby). Note that logically the court should reach this question first and then decide whether to recognize a discovery rule to toll the running of the statute of limitations.

4. ~~Continuing Tort.~~ In some medical malpractice cases, courts have found that the statute of limitations did not begin to run until the course of treatment was complete. See, e.g., Justice v. Natvig, 238 Va. 178, 381 S.E.2d 8 (1989). This is sometimes referred to as a continuing tort. Should this concept be extended to other areas of the law? Plaintiff lived with defendant in an abusive relationship for ten years. The statute of limitations for assault and battery is one year. Plaintiff argues that "battered women's syndrome" prevented her from leaving the relationship. How should the courts treat the statute of limitations issue? Cusseaux v. Pickett, 279 N.J. Super. 335, 652 A.2d 789 (1994) (recognizing a cause of action and treating it as a continuing tort for statute of limitations purposes).

5. The fact that a latent defect in a building may not manifest itself for years or even decades affects the application of the statute of limitations to builders, architects, and engineers. How long should these professionals be subject to liability? Is it reasonable to begin the running of the statute when the construction of the building is completed and the parties' professional relationship terminated? The client then can inspect the building and determine if the structure is sound. Compare Sosnow v. Paul, 43 A.D.2d 978, 352 N.Y.S.2d 502 (1974) (time of construction), with Malesev v. Board of County Rd. Comm'rs, 51 Mich.App. 511, 215 N.W.2d 598 (1974) (time of discovery). A number of state legislatures have enacted special statutes of limitations dealing with malpractice by builders, architects and engineers. See Knapp & Lee, Application of Special Statutes of Limitations Concerning Design and Construction, 23 St. Louis U.L.J. 351 (1979). If these classes of defendants are given special protection without any rational basis, the special statute of limitation may be found to be unconstitutional because it denies equal protection. Kallas Millwork Corp. v. Square D Co., 66 Wis.2d 382, 225 N.W.2d 454 (1975).

6. Problems with the time-of-damage rule also have arisen with regard to negligent acts of other professionals. When should the statute of limitations begin to run with regard to an attorney who has committed an act of malpractice? See

Grunwald v. Bronkesh, 131 N.J. 483, 621 A.2d 459 (1993) (limitations period begins to run when the client suffers actual damage and discovers the damage was attributable to the attorney's negligent advice). Draper v. Brennan, 713 A.2d 373 (N.H.1998) (where attorney commits malpractice in prosecution or defense of claim that results in litigation, statute of limitations on malpractice action is not tolled by appeal of adverse ruling).

See generally R. Mallen and Smith, Legal Malpractice (4th ed. 1996).

7. _Tolling._ Statutes of limitation contain within them provisions that toll or stop the running of the time within which to file for various reasons. The most common of these are provisions that toll the statute for minors until they have reached their majority and for those legally insane or incompetent. In addition, many jurisdictions recognize equitable tolling where, for example, the defendant fraudulently concealed the injury from the plaintiff or concealed his own identity. See, e.g., Lakeman v. La France, 102 N.H. 300, 156 A.2d 123 (1959) (doctor allegedly concealed medical malpractice during surgery from patient) and Bernson v. Browning–Ferris Indus. of Cal., Inc., 30 Cal. Rptr.2d 440, 873 P.2d 613, 7 Cal.4th 926 (1994) (statute of limitations for libel tolled because defendants allegedly concealed their identity by anonymously publishing defamatory "dossier" on member of City Council). Such equitable tolling is not available, however, if it is another entity that concealed the identity of the defendant. Renaud v. Sigma–Aldrich Corp., 662 A.2d 711 (R.I.1995) (worker injured on job by chemical spill claimed that her employer and supplier of chemical misled her as to identity of manufacturer of container, causing her to miss the statute of limitations in claim against that manufacturer).

8. _Discovery Rule._ As the principal case reflects, the time-of-damage rule can lead to difficulty in certain types of actions for medical malpractice. Some legislatures have specifically dealt with the problem and adopted a time-of-discovery rule for medical malpractice cases. See Conn.Gen.Stat., § 52–584 (1999); R.S.Mo., § 516.105 (1999). In other jurisdictions, the discovery rule is a creature of the courts. Chase v. Sabin, 445 Mich. 190, 516 N.W.2d 60 (1994) (discovery rule applied to plaintiff who discovered that the loss of his eye, which had occurred 26 years previously after cataract surgery, was caused by negligence of nurse anesthetist). Some courts have limited the application of the time-of-discovery rule to situations where surgeons have left sponges, scalpels or other objects in the patient's body. They apply the time-of-damage rule to cases of negligent diagnosis or ingestion of a drug or toxic substance. A few states, in adopting a discovery rule, have placed an outside limit on claims. See, e.g., Ohio Rev. Code, § 2305.11(B) (1999) (six years after the act of malpractice).

9. The discovery rule, first developed in medical malpractice cases like the principal case, has been extended in many jurisdictions to apply to any action based on a latent injury. See, e.g., Perlov v. G.D. Searle & Co., 621 F.Supp. 1146 (D.Md.1985) ("Although ordinarily that statute begins to run at the time of injury, in this case the Maryland 'discovery rule' should be utilized to determine when the cause of action accrued which is when the statute begins to run. Under this rule, the delayed filing of an action is tolerated for causes of action which are inherently unknowable, so the cause of action accrues only when 'the claimant in fact knew or reasonably should have known of the alleged wrongs.' ") But see Hing–Har Lo v. Burke, 249 Va. 311, 455 S.E.2d 9 (1995) (Virginia does not recognize discovery rule).

10. The discovery rule itself can be narrow or broad depending on _what_ the plaintiff has to discover. The injury? That the injury was caused by defendant's conduct or product? That the defendant's conduct was negligent or its product

defective? What about a child abuse case where the plaintiff only became aware through psychotherapy after becoming an adult that the actions of the defendant were tortious and that those actions caused the plaintiff's emotional problems? Pritzlaff v. Archdiocese of Milwaukee, 194 Wis.2d 302, 533 N.W.2d 780 (1995) (noting that many states recognize a special discovery rule for cases involving incest and other forms of child sexual abuse). Because fixing the time that plaintiff "should have discovered" something usually is dependent on fact finding by the jury, the discovery rule makes it difficult for the defendant to obtain summary judgment based on the statute of limitations. Tucker v. Baxter Healthcare Corp., 158 F.3d 1046 (9th Cir.1998) (applying California law) (summary judgment precluded because question of fact as to when plaintiff suspected or should have suspected that her breast implants were likely cause of autoimmune disease).

11. _Res judicata and the Second Disease_. Sometimes, plaintiff will develop a second, more serious illness after initial, less serious symptoms were noted. A patient is told by her doctor that she has pelvic inflammatory disease ("PID") in 1977 and that it probably was caused by an intrauterine device ("IUD"). In 1980, after months of difficulty trying to become pregnant, she is diagnosed as infertile due to the PID. In her case against the manufacturer of the IUD, when did the statute of limitations begin to run? See, e.g., Gnazzo v. G.D. Searle & Co., 973 F.2d 136 (2d Cir.1992) (applying Connecticut law) (statute begins to run when plaintiff discovers some form of actionable harm, not the fullest manifestation thereof); Klempka v. G.D. Searle & Co., 963 F.2d 168 (8th Cir.1992) (applying Minnesota law) (plaintiff who is aware of both her injury and the likely cause of her injury is not permitted to circumvent the statute of limitations by waiting for a more serious injury to develop from the same cause); Kemp v. G.D. Searle & Co., 103 F.3d 405 (5th Cir. 1997) (applying Mississippi law) (infertility is merely a sequella of PID and not a separate disease). See also Shadle v. Pearce, 287 Pa.Super. 436, 430 A.2d 683 (1981) (dental malpractice cause of action accrued when patient first injured, not two years later when patient developed incapacitating complication); Golla v. General Motors Corp., 167 Ill.2d 353, 657 N.E.2d 894 (1995) (cause of action against car manufacturer based on alleged design defect of car seat accrued on day of accident, not a year later when plaintiff was diagnosed with reflex sympathetic dystrophy, a condition she alleged was caused by the design defect). But what if the claimant, pressured by the statute of limitations, files suit, her case is adjudicated and _then_ she develops a more serious disease? Traditional claim preclusion principles may bar her second action because a plaintiff is not permitted to split her claim. See, e.g., Gideon v. Johns–Manville Sales Corp., 761 F.2d 1129 (5th Cir.1985) (under Texas law, only one suit may be brought from all injuries caused by asbestos exposure) and Joyce v. A.C. and S., Inc., 785 F.2d 1200 (4th Cir.1986) (applying Virginia law). What if the plaintiff claims that the second injury is a new, separate injury rather than a complication of the first injury? In asbestos cases, a majority of jurisdictions have permitted a second action for cancer where the first disease was a non-malignant disease like asbestosis. See, e.g., Marinari v. Asbestos Corp., Ltd., 417 Pa.Super. 440, 612 A.2d 1021 (1992) (collecting cases).

12. _Notice-of-Claim Statutes_. Statutes that provide a limited waiver of sovereign immunity to allow tort claims against governmental entities frequently provide that a notice-of-claim must be made within a particular time frame, in addition to a statute of limitation. The time period for the filing of the notice-of-claim may be very short. See, e.g., D.C. Code § 12–309 (1999) (6 months); N.M. Stat. Ann. § 41–4–16(A) (1999) (90 days); Va. Code Ann. § 8.01–195.6 (1999) (one year).

13. _Statutes of Repose_. A statute of limitation limits the time during which a cause of action can be brought. A statute of repose limits potential liability by

limiting the time during which a cause of action can arise. Statutes of repose, which are substantive rather than procedural in nature, stem from the equitable concept that a time should arrive when a person is no longer responsible for a past act. Statutes of repose have been enacted primarily in the areas of product liability and liability for architects and engineers. For example, after a certain number of years from the sale or delivery of the product, no claim can arise against the manufacturer. If a product has operated without incident for 20 years, is it fair to assume that any injury occurring after that time was due to something other than an original defect in the product? What about the possibility that the product has been improperly maintained, repaired, or altered? In addition to the fact that the time period may run even before a person is injured, the statutes create a number of problems, especially for victims of conditions with a long latency period. A few states have made special exceptions for particular products such as asbestos or diethylstilbestrol (DES). Some state courts have declared statutes of repose unconstitutional based on equal protection or "open courts" provisions in state constitutions. See, e.g., DeYoung v. Providence Medical Ctr., 136 Wash.2d 136, 960 P.2d 919 (1998) (medical malpractice); Hazine v. Montgomery Elevator Co., 176 Ariz. 340, 861 P.2d 625 (1993); Lankford v. Sullivan, Long & Hagerty, 416 So.2d 996 (Ala.1982); Bolick v. American Barmag Corp., 306 N.C. 364, 293 S.E.2d 415 (1982). Other courts have upheld the statutes. See, e.g., Love v. Whirlpool Corp., 264 Ga. 701, 449 S.E.2d 602 (1994) (products liability statute of repose); Damiano v. McDaniel, 689 So.2d 1059 (Fla.1997) (medical malpractice statute); Jones v. Five Star Eng'g, Inc., 717 S.W.2d 882 (Tenn.1986); Arsenault v. Pa–Ted Spring Co., Inc., 203 Conn. 156, 523 A.2d 1283 (1987).

14. See generally Corman, Limitation of Actions (1991) and the bibliography therein.

3. IMMUNITIES

An immunity differs from a privilege, or justification or excuse, although the difference is largely one of degree. A privilege avoids liability for tortious conduct only under particular circumstances, and because those circumstances make it just and reasonable that the liability should not be imposed. An immunity, on the other hand, avoids liability in tort under all circumstances, within the limits of the immunity itself. It is conferred, not because of the particular facts, but because of the status or position or relation of the favored defendant. It does not deny the tort, but the resulting liability. The immunity does not mean that conduct that would amount to a tort on the part of other defendants is not still equally tortious in character, but merely that for the protection of the particular defendant, or of interests that the defendant represents, absolution from liability is granted. The "absolute privilege" to publish defamation in the course of judicial, legislative or executive proceedings (pages 923–926), for example, is really an immunity of those engaged in the proceedings, conferred because of the public interest in protecting them from suit. Judicial immunity may extend to those operating in quasi-judicial capacities as long as their actions were integral to the judicial process. Prosecuting attorneys, court-appointed guardians ad litem, and court-appointed psychiatrists may be protected by immunity. See, for example, Muzingo v. St. Luke's Hospital, 518 N.W.2d 776 (Iowa 1994) (court-appointed psychiatrist and hospital immune from suit brought by woman injured by bomb planted in her car by her husband who had been examined by psychiatrist pursuant to involuntary commitment proceeding).

Immunities are today very much upon the wane, as the result of years of attack from numerous legal writers, and expressed doubts on the part of many courts. On the other hand, the abolishment of immunities has produced a new and challenging question—what is to be the scope of the duty owed by defendants who were previously immune from suit.

(A) FAMILIES

Freehe v. Freehe

Supreme Court of Washington, 1972.
81 Wash.2d 183, 500 P.2d 771.

NEILL, ASSOCIATE JUSTICE. Plaintiff, Clifford Freehe, seeks compensation for personal injuries allegedly sustained due to defendant's negligent maintenance of a tractor and failure to warn plaintiff of the tractor's unsafe condition. The claim for relief would be just the normal action in tort for personal injury but for the fact that the defendant is the wife of the plaintiff, thus bringing into issue the doctrine of interspousal tort immunity.

The farm on which the accident took place is the separate property of defendant, doing business under the name of Hazel Knoblauch. The tractor involved in this accident, together with all other assets and income of the farm, were and remain the separate property of defendant. The business of the farm is carried on separately from any community business of the parties. Plaintiff has no interest in the farming operation. Neither was he employed by defendant.

The trial court granted defendant's motion for summary judgment solely on the basis of interspousal tort immunity. Plaintiff appeals. * * *

The rule of interspousal immunity or disability is of common law origin, court made and court preserved. * * * Our cases have referred to the historical arguments supporting the common law disability. One is the "supposed unity of husband and wife." [Cc]

The "supposed unity" of husband and wife * * * is not a reference to the common nature or loving oneness achieved in a marriage of two free individuals. Rather, this traditional premise had reference to a situation, coming on from antiquity, in which a woman's marriage for most purposes rendered her a chattel of her husband.

"It has been said, whether humorously or not, that at common law husband and wife were one person, and that person was the husband. * * * [A]s to her personal and property rights, the very legal existence of the wife was regarded as suspended for the duration of the marriage, and merged into that of the husband, so that she lost the capacity to contract for herself, or to sue or be sued without joining the husband as a plaintiff or defendant. The husband acquired the right to possession and use of his wife's real and personal property, and he was entitled to all of her choses in action, provided that he 'reduced them to possession' during marriage by some act by which he appropriated them to himself, such as collecting the money or obtaining judgment in a suit in his own name. In turn he became liable for the torts of his wife, committed either before or during the marriage." (footnotes omitted) W.L. Prosser, Torts ch. 23, § 122 (4th ed. 1971) at 859–60. At old common law, with the husband entitled to the chose in action for his own torts and liable to himself for his wife's torts against him, the rule of interspousal disability made sense.

Things have changed. * * * Neither spouse is liable for the separate debts of the other. RCW 26.16.200. * * * [E]ither spouse may sue the other for invasion of separate property rights. RCW 26.16.180. [Cc] Spouses are no longer individually liable for each other's torts unless they would be jointly liable if unmarried.

Modern realities do not comport with the traditional "supposed unity" of husband and wife. In our view, this concept of legal identity is no longer a valid premise for a rule of this interspousal disability.

A second major reason given for the disability is the notion that to allow a married person to sue his or her spouse for tort damages would be to destroy the peace and tranquility of the home. On reflection, we are convinced that this is a conclusion without basis. If a state of peace and tranquility exists between the spouses, then the situation is such that either no action will be commenced or that the spouses—who are, after all, the best guardians of their own peace and tranquility—will allow the action to continue only so long as their personal harmony is not jeopardized. If peace and tranquility is nonexistent or tenuous to begin with, then the law's imposition of a technical disability seems more likely to be a bone of contention than a harmonizing factor. * * *

A third reason advanced in support of maintaining the common law rule of disability is the suggestion that the injured spouse has an adequate remedy through the criminal and divorce laws. It has been observed that neither of these alternatives actually compensates for the damage done, or provides any remedy for nonintentional (negligent) torts. Prosser, supra, at pages 862–63. * * * To these reflections we add the observation that limiting the injured party to a divorce or criminal action against his or her tort-feasor spouse is quite inconsistent with any policy of preserving domestic tranquility. Thus, the argument based on suggested legal alternatives simply does not withstand analysis.

It has also been argued that to permit litigation between spouses over personal torts would flood the courts with a burdensome amount of trivial matrimonial disputes. * * * [T]his theoretical problem has not materialized elsewhere. Furthermore, should the courts find this possibility to be materializing, there is nothing to prevent application of established notions of "consent" or "assumption of risk" to minor annoyances associated with the ordinary frictions of wedlock. [C]

Respondent also suggests that another argument in favor of the disability rule is that to permit suits between spouses would encourage collusion and fraud where one or both of the spouses carries liability insurance. * * * In * * * Borst v. Borst, 41 Wash.2d at page 653, 251 P.2d at page 155, we stated:

"The courts may and should take cognizance of fraud and collusion when found to exist in a particular case. However, the fact that there may be greater opportunity for fraud or collusion in one class of cases than another does not warrant courts of law in closing the door to all cases of that class. Courts must depend upon the efficacy of the judicial processes to ferret out the meritorious from the fraudulent in particular cases. [C] If those processes prove inadequate, the problem becomes one for the legislature. [C] Courts will not immunize tort feasors from liability in a whole class of cases because of the possibility of fraud, but will depend upon the legislature to deal with the problem as a question of public policy."

We there cited, as an example of the ability of the legislature to cope with such a problem should it arise, the enactment of host-guest statutes (RCW 46.08.080, –.085, –.086) in automobile personal injury cases. We conclude that this possibility is not a valid premise for the common law disability rule.

Respondent also suggests that any change in the marital disability rule is a matter for the legislature * * * This argument ignores the fact that the rule is not one made or sanctioned by the legislature, but rather is one that depends for its origins and continued viability upon the common law. * * *

[The court then decided that the state's community property laws imposed no barrier to abandoning interspousal immunity.]

We are cognizant of the long standing nature of the common law rule of interspousal tort immunity. But we find more impelling the fundamental precept that, absent express statutory provision, or compelling public policy, the law should not immunize tort-feasors or deny remedy to their victims. With this in mind, we have reviewed the stated reasons for the common law rule, and have found all of them to be insufficient. Therefore, the rule of interspousal disability in personal injury cases is hereby abandoned. * * *

Reversed and remanded.

NOTES AND QUESTIONS

1. *General Abrogation.* The movement toward complete abrogation of interspousal immunity began with a dissenting opinion of the first Justice Harlan in Thompson v. Thompson, 218 U.S. 611 (1910). It is now the majority rule. Waite v. Waite, 618 So.2d 1360 (Fla.1993) (abolishing doctrine and noting that thirty-two other states already had completely abrogated the doctrine of interspousal immunity). See generally Restatement (Second) of Torts § 895F.

2. Some decisions that have taken this step have placed heavy reliance on the state's married women's property act. See, e.g., Gilman v. Gilman, 78 N.H. 4, 95 A. 657 (1915); Fitzmaurice v. Fitzmaurice, 62 N.D. 191, 242 N.W. 526 (1932). These

statutes, enacted in the mid–1800's, abrogated the common law disabilities of wives to sue or be sued in their own name and to buy, own or sell property. Other decisions have construed the statutes as having no intent to affect interspousal immunity. See, e.g., Oken v. Oken, 44 R.I. 291, 117 A. 357 (1922). These latter decisions may be correct in measuring legislative intent. As the principal case reflects, policies that allegedly support interspousal tort immunity are not necessarily related to legal restrictions on the rights of women.

3. *Partial Abrogation.* Many of the courts that still recognize the immunity have limited it. They refuse to apply it in one or more specific situations where they are certain that no good reason supports it.

A. After divorce or marital dissolution, spouses are permitted a claim for torts that occurred prior to and, in some jurisdictions, during the marriage. See, e.g., Gaston v. Pittman, 224 So.2d 326 (Fla.1969) (prior); Sanchez v. Olivarez, 94 N.J.Super. 61, 226 A.2d 752 (1967) (during). Claims also are permitted if either spouse is dead at the time the action is brought. Asplin v. Amica Mut. Ins. Co., 121 R.I. 51, 394 A.2d 1353 (1978).

B. When the tort occurred prior to the marriage some states allow the claim. See, e.g., Childress v. Childress, 569 S.W.2d 816 (Tenn.1978); Berry v. Harmon, 329 S.W.2d 784 (Mo.1959). The reason given for allowing the claim is that the spouse should not lose a property right because of entering into a marriage.

C. When the tort is an intentional one such as battery, assault or false imprisonment, many states allow the claim. See Lusby v. Lusby, 283 Md. 334, 390 A.2d 77 (1978) (husband and two accomplices forced wife's car off road by threatening her with rifle, kidnaped her, raped her, and threatened to kill her if she told anyone).

4. The facts of the principal case are somewhat unusual as compared with most tort suits between spouses. The overwhelming majority of these cases have involved automobile accidents, and a number of courts have expressly limited their repeal of the immunity in negligence actions to those situations. See Digby v. Digby, 120 R.I. 299, 388 A.2d 1 (1978); Richard v. Richard, 131 Vt. 98, 300 A.2d 637 (1973).

5. Suppose a wife sues her husband in tort for the injury she suffered because he prepared her food in a careless and unsanitary manner. Does she have a claim? Suppose the wife alleges that she suffered serious medical injury because her husband was negligent in his selection of a family doctor. Would she then have a claim? In Beaudette v. Frana, 285 Minn. 366, 173 N.W.2d 416 (1969), the Supreme Court of Minnesota abolished interspousal immunity, but it also observed in dictum that: "There is an intimate sharing of contact within the marriage relationship, both intentional and unintentional, that is uniquely unlike the exposure among strangers. The risks of intentional contact in marriage are such that one spouse should not recover damages from the other without substantial evidence that the injurious contact was plainly excessive or a gross abuse of normal privilege. The risks of negligent conduct are likewise so usual that it would be an unusual case in which the trial court would not instruct the jury as to the injured spouse's peculiar assumption of risk." What if the husband alleges that the wife infected him with a sexually transmitted disease? Does the outcome depend on whether the conduct was intentional or negligent? What if the husband alleges that the wife intentionally inflicted emotional distress on him by engaging in an affair during their entire marriage and falsely telling him that he was the father of two of their three children? Doe v. Doe, 122 Md. App. 295, 712 A.2d 132 (1998).

6.   The history of the immunity is well described in Kahn–Freund, Inconsistencies and Injustices in the Law of Husband and Wife, 15 Mod.L.Rev. 133 (1952); and Williams, The Legal Unity of Husband and Wife, 10 Mod.L.Rev. 16 (1947). See generally McCurdy, Personal Torts Between Spouses, 4 Vill.L.Rev. 521 (1959); Herskowitz, Tort Liability Between Husband and Wife, 21 U.Miami L.Rev. 423 (1966); Tobias, Interspousal Tort Immunity in America, 23 Ga.L.Rev. 359 (1989).

Renko v. McLean

Court of Appeals of Maryland, 1997.
346 Md. 464, 697 A.2d 468.

KARWACKI, J. In Warren v. Warren, 336 Md. 618, 650 A.2d 252 (1994), and Frye v. Frye, 305 Md. 542, 505 A.2d 826 (1986), this Court declined to create an exception to the parent-child immunity doctrine in motor tort cases based upon the existence of compulsory automobile liability insurance coverage. We are asked in this case to reexamine those decisions. Having done so, we shall reaffirm the vitality of the parent child-immunity doctrine in this State and affirm the judgment of the Circuit Court for Anne Arundel County.

I.

The facts of this case are brief and undisputed. On December 8, 1992, Natasha Renko suffered serious injuries when her biological mother, Teresa Kaylor McLean, negligently drove the car both women were occupying into the rear of another vehicle. At the time, Natasha Renko was seventeen years old. * * *

[Following her eighteenth birthday, Renko filed suit against her mother, alleging negligence in the operation of the motor vehicle. Her mother filed a motion to dismiss based on parent-child immunity and Renko beseeched the court to recognize an exception to the parent-child immunity doctrine and allow emancipated children to file actions against their parents for injuries sustained in motor vehicle accidents occurring in minority between fifteen and eighteen years of age. The trial court declined to do so and entered judgment in favor of defendant. Renko appealed.]

II.

For nearly seventy years, the parent-child tort immunity doctrine has been, with few exceptions,[4] a salient feature of Maryland law. [C][5] It remains so today.

---

4. We have departed from this rule on only two occasions. First, when a child has suffered cruel or unusually malicious conduct at the hands of a parent, an action for monetary damages may be maintained. [C] Second, a child may sue a parent's business partner for negligence committed in the operation of the partnership. * * *

5. The first formulation of the parent-child immunity doctrine was adopted by the Supreme Court of Mississippi in Hewllette v. George, 68 Miss. 703, 9 So. 885 (1891). Mississippi has since repudiated the doctrine in motor tort cases. [C]

Once an absolute bar to tort actions between parents and their minor children,[6] the parent-child immunity doctrine grew out of an abiding belief that it served the compelling public interest in preserving, under normal circumstances, the internal harmony and integrity of the family unit and parental authority in the parent-child relationship. [Cc] In fact, the special relationship, with its reciprocal duties and obligations, that the minor child shares with his or her parents forms a major component of the foundation upon which the parent-child immunity doctrine is built—a relationship recognized both at common law (footnote omitted) and by the General Assembly (footnote omitted). Other justifications offered for the rule include the prevention of fraud and collusion among family members to the detriment of third-parties, and the threat that intrafamilial litigation will deplete family resources. [C]

Nevertheless, the parent-child immunity doctrine has never stood static where historical experience and common sense dictated that it must yield. Indeed, "the parent[-]child immunity rule ... was a creature of the common law. It was judicially conceived, judicially adopted in Maryland, judicially changed in certain significant aspects, and otherwise judicially nurtured and applied in this jurisdiction[.]" Frye, 305 Md. at 566, 505 A.2d at 839; see also n.4, supra. But our acknowledgment that circumstance sometimes severs the doctrine from its rationale and reason in no way detracts from our fundamental belief that "the parent-child immunity rule [is still] essential to the maintenance of discipline and to the stability of family harmony." Frye, 305 Md. at 561, 505 A.2d at 836; [c].

In Frye, *supra*, we exhaustively surveyed the creation and refinement of the parent-child immunity doctrine both in this State and across our Country. Despite the growing chorus of criticism surrounding the doctrine,[9] we determined that the parent-child relationship had changed little, if at all, in the ensuing years since our predecessors first recognized parent-child immunity. We thus concluded that "today's parent-child relationship, as recognized by this Court and the Legislature, furnishes no compelling reason to abrogate the rule." Id. at 561, 505 A.2d at 836; [c].

III.

Renko nonetheless mounts a three-pronged attack upon the parent-child immunity doctrine. She asserts that (1) adult children should be

6. The immunity does not apply to tort actions between parents and their adult children arising beyond minority. [C]

9. See, e.g., Pipino, In Whose Best Interest? Exploring the Continuing Validity of the Parent Child Immunity Doctrine?, 3 Ohio St. L.J. 1111 (1992); W. Prosser & W.P. Keeton, The Law of Torts § 122 (5th ed. 1984); Comment, Parent–Child Tort Immunity: Time for Maryland to Abrogate an Anachronism, 11 U.Balt. L. Rev. 435 (1982); Hollister, Parent–Child Immunity: A Doctrine in Search of Justification, 50 Fordham L. Rev. 489 (1982); Comment, The Demise of Parent–Child Immunity, 12 Willamette L. J. 605 (1976); Comment, Time to Abolish Parent–Child Tort Immunity: A Call to Repudiate Mississippi's Gift to the American Family, 4 Nova L.J. 25 (1980); McCurdy, Torts Between Parent and Child, 5 Vill. L. Rev. 521 (1960); McCurdy, Torts Between Persons in Domestic Relation, 43 Harv. L. R. 1030, 1077–1081 (1930).

allowed to maintain actions against their parents for injuries occurring in their minority; (2) no contemporary justification exists to apply the doctrine to the facts of the case sub judice in light of compulsory motor vehicle liability insurance; and (3) any such application is violative of Articles 19 and 24 of the Maryland Declaration of Rights and of the Fourteenth Amendment to the United States Constitution. We shall address each of these contentions in turn.

a.

Renko correctly points out that we have permitted suits between parents and their minor children in limited circumstances. For instance, we have held that a minor child may maintain an action against a father's business partner for alleged negligence arising out of the operation of the partnership. [C] That decision was predicated upon our belief that the parent-child relationship, so important to the parent-child immunity rule, would remain inviolate in a suit against the father's business partner. * * *

Recognizing that reality sometimes belies the ideal of family life, our predecessors also deemed permissible a suit by a minor child against her father's estate for alleged injuries she sustained when, within the span of one week, the father both murdered the child's mother and committed suicide in the child's presence. Mahnke v. Moore, 197 Md. 61, 77 A.2d 923 (1951). The Court reasoned that "in these circumstances, there can be no basis for the contention that the daughter's suit against her father's estate would be contrary to public policy, for the simple reason that there is no home at all in which discipline and tranquility are to be preserved. . . . When . . . the parent is guilty of acts which show complete abandonment of the parental relation, the rule giving him immunity from suit by the child, on the ground that discipline should be maintained in the home, cannot logically be applied, for when he is guilty of such acts he forfeits his parental authority and privileges, including his immunity from suit. . . . Justice demands that a minor child shall have a right of action against a parent for injuries resulting from cruel and inhuman treatment or for malicious and wanton wrongs." Id. at 67–68, 77 A.2d at 926.

Renko contends that since this Court has already permitted children to maintain actions against their parents for acts occurring after the child reaches the age of majority, see Waltzinger v. Birsner, 212 Md. 107, 128 A.2d 617 (1957), we should take the logical step of allowing otherwise adult children to sue their parents for wrongful acts that occur during minority. We see no such logic. In fact, Renko's proffered solution to her particular dilemma would result in a de facto abrogation of the parent-child immunity doctrine in its entirety.

Maryland Code (1995 Repl. Vol., 1996 Supp.), § 5–201 (footnote omitted) of the Courts & Judicial Proceedings Article permits minors to bring tort actions for injuries sustained in minority at the hands of another within three years after reaching the age of majority. Thus, an injured minor child could simply wait until reaching the age of majority before initiating a suit that is otherwise barred in his or her infancy. In that circumstance, the parent-child immunity doctrine would serve not as a bar to actions between parent and child, but rather as an obstacle easily overcome with the passage of time. The looming specter of a lawsuit is as surely detrimental to family peace and harmony and parental authority as is the actual suit itself. Given this Court's long commitment to the parent-child immunity doctrine, we refuse to create an exception that would effectively negate the rule and open courthouse doors to every conceivable dispute between parent and child. [C] Indeed, the rule was fashioned to prevent just that.

b.

Renko alternatively contends that "with mandatory automobile insurance creating universal coverage for auto torts, there can be no rational objection to recovery by an emancipated child in" the case sub judice. * * *

We recognized in Warren and Frye, supra, that an overwhelming majority of jurisdictions have abrogated the parent-child immunity doctrine in whole or in part. [Cc]

At the time we issued the Warren opinion, "only eight states, including Maryland, continued to adhere to the doctrine of parent-child immunity without exception for motor torts." 336 Md. at 621 n.1, 650 A.2d at 254 n.1. Those same jurisdictions continue to stand their ground.[12]

Other jurisdictions, however, have found persuasive arguments calling for the abolition of the parent-child immunity doctrine in motor tort cases. The seminal decision in this area is Sorensen v. Sorensen, 369 Mass. 350, 339 N.E.2d 907 (1975). There, the Supreme Judicial Court of Massachusetts observed: "In dealing with an automobile accident in which two passengers, one an unemancipated minor child of the defendant driver and the other a minor who had no familial relationship to the defendant driver, are injured, it would be incongruous to permit recovery against a parent and the parent's insurance company by the unrelated child but to deny recovery to the parent's child when culpability is admitted or established." Id. at 360, 339 N.E.2d at 913. Noting the basis of the parent-child immunity doctrine, the court commented that "the primary disruption to harmonious filial relations is not the lawsuit brought for damages after the injury but the injury itself, resulting from the misconduct of a parent. [C] When the wrong has been committed, the harm to the basic fabric of the family has already been done and the source of rancor and discord already introduced into family relations. [Cc] It can hardly aid family reconciliation to deny the injured child access to the courts and, through them, to any liability insurance which the family might maintain." Id. at 360, 339 N.E.2d at 913.

---

12. See La. Rev. Stat. § 9:571 (West 1997); Mitchell v. Davis, 598 So. 2d 801 (Ala. 1992); Robinson v. Robinson, 323 Ark. 224, 914 S.W.2d 292 (Ark. 1996); Terror Mining Co. v. Roter, 866 P.2d 929 (Colo.1994); Mo- horn v. Ross, 205 Ga. App. 443, 422 S.E.2d 290 (1992); Vaughan v. Vaughan, 161 Ind. App. 497, 316 N.E.2d 455 (1974); Pullen v. Novak, 169 Neb. 211, 99 N.W.2d 16 (1959).

Considering the same issue, the Supreme Court of Delaware concluded, that with the almost universal existence of motor vehicle liability insurance, "the domestic tranquility argument is, at best, hollow. Liability insurance impersonalizes the suit and negates the possible disruption of family harmony by easing the financial repercussions of the accident. In short 'when insurance is involved, the action between parent and child is not truly adversary; both parties seek recovery from the insurance carrier to create a fund for the child's medical care and support without depleting the family's other assets.' " Williams v. Williams, 369 A.2d 669, 672 (Del.1976) (citing Sorensen, 369 Mass. at 362–63, 339 N.E.2d at 914); see also Schneider v. Coe, 405 A.2d 682 (Del.1979) (affirming abrogation of parent-child immunity in auto tort cases where insurance coverage exists). Stated otherwise, "domestic peace and harmony may be more threatened by denying the cause of action than by permitting one, especially where there is insurance." Glaskox v. Glaskox, 614 So. 2d 906, 911 (Miss.1992). Thus, the argument goes, abrogating parent-child immunity where automobile liability insurance exists furthers the objectives of the rule by relieving the family of the financial burden of an adverse judgment while at the same time providing a means of recovery for the injured child. Numerous other jurisdictions concur in this view. (Footnote omitted.)

The Delaware court added that the "domestic-tranquility justification" also lacked merit in light of the fact that other courts have permitted various types of intrafamilial litigation, including, inter alia, suits between siblings. Williams, 369 A.2d at 672 (citing Midkiff v. Midkiff, 201 Va. 829, 113 S.E.2d 875 (1960)) (suit brought by a minor against his unemancipated brother for injuries sustained in a motor vehicle accident); [c].

The fraud-collusion justification for the parent-child immunity doctrine too has suffered its critics, among them, the Mississippi Supreme Court— the birthplace of the parent-child immunity doctrine. See Hewlett v. George, 68 Miss. 703, 9 So. 885 (1891). In Glaskox, supra, the court majority observed that " 'the possibility of collusion exists to a certain extent in any case. Every day we depend on juries and trial judges to sift evidence in order to determine the facts and arrive at proper verdicts. Experience has shown that the courts are quite adequate for this task. In litigation between parent and child, judges and juries would naturally be mindful of the relationship and would be even more on the alert for improper conduct.' " 614 So. 2d at 912 (quoting Nocktonick v. Nocktonick, 227 Kan. 758, 768–69, 611 P.2d 135, 142 (1980)). In a similar vein, the Supreme Court of Pennsylvania has added: "In the last analysis it is much to be preferred that we depend upon the efficacy of the judicial process to ferret out the meritorious from the fraudulent rather than using a broad broom to sweep away a class of claims, a number of which are admittedly meritorious." Falco v. Pados, supra, 444 Pa. at 381, 282 A.2d at 356.

Recognizing the continuing need to protect parental authority and family harmony, some jurisdictions have attempted to limit immunity to negligent conduct arising out of an "exercise of parental authority . . . [or] an exercise of ordinary parental discretion with respect to the provision of food, clothing, housing, medical and dental services, and other care." Goller v. White, 20 Wis. 2d 402, 413, 122 N.W.2d 193, 198 (1963); [cc].

California and New York have adopted their own unique brands of parent-child immunity. California courts apply a "reasonable parent" standard to determine the viability of tort actions between parent and child. [C] New York, on the other hand, seems to permit all such actions, except those arising out of a parent's failure to properly supervise the child. Under New York law, parents owe no legal duty to their children to supervise them properly. [C]

Despite the majority trend, even those most critical of the rule must acknowledge that its abrogation is not a panacea. At least with respect to motor tort cases, the argument for abrogation suffers from several infirmities.

In a normal case, liability insurance becomes relevant only after an insured's liability is fixed in an appropriate legal proceeding. Yet as between parent and child, it becomes the raison d'etre of the suit. Thus, unlike a true adversarial proceeding, an insurer is forced into the unenviable position of attempting to defend a suit that its insured has every incentive to lose. (Footnote omitted.) * * *

Further, many families carry medical insurance that would necessarily compensate the injured child, and therefore, his or her family, for injury-related expenses. Allowing children then to proceed to court and recover for pain and suffering and other noneconomic damages, which often far exceed medical costs, might potentially saddle a family with a judgment that they can ill-afford to pay because, as previously indicated, it exceeds available insurance. * * *

In light of the foregoing observations and on balance, we remain convinced that the parent-child immunity rule "is still in the best interests of both children and parents to retain . . . [and that] abrogating immunity would result only in further discord within the family and would interfere with the exercise of parental discretion in raising and disciplining children." Warren, 336 Md. at 626, 650 A.2d at 255.

c.

Renko lastly contends that the parent-child immunity doctrine as applied in motor vehicle torts is "irrational and arbitrary and violates Articles 19 and 24 of the Maryland Declaration of Rights, and the Equal Protection and Due Process Clauses of the [Fourteenth Amendment to the] United States Constitution." (Footnotes omitted from quotation.) We find these assertions to be meritless. * * *

Judgment affirmed, with costs.

NOTES AND QUESTIONS

1. Unlike the interspousal immunity doctrine, which was part of the common law of England, the immunity between parent and child is a homegrown product. In Hewlett v. George, 68 Miss. 703, 9 So. 885 (1891), the court applied the doctrine to

bar a minor daughter's claim for false imprisonment against her mother, who had wrongfully committed her to an insane asylum. Other states soon adopted the rule, applying it to actions for negligence as well as intentional torts. See, e.g., Mesite v. Kirchstein, 109 Conn. 77, 145 A. 753 (1929); Roller v. Roller, 37 Wash. 242, 79 P. 788 (1905) (15–year–old girl attempting to bring a tort claim against her father for rape). The fact that the doctrine was not announced by any of the writers of common law did not seem to trouble courts because "it was unmistakably and indelibly carved upon the tablets of Mount Sinai." Small v. Morrison, 185 N.C. 577, 585–86, 118 S.E. 12, 16 (1923).

2. *General Abrogation*. Abolition of the parent-child immunity has lagged behind the abolition of interspousal immunity, perhaps because of the absence of any statute to trigger the change as the married women's property acts did for interspousal immunity. For opinions abandoning the immunity in all cases, see Gibson v. Gibson, 3 Cal.3d 914, 479 P.2d 648, 92 Cal.Rptr. 288 (1971); Anderson v. Stream, 295 N.W.2d 595 (Minn.1980); and Broadbent v. Broadbent, 184 Ariz. 74, 907 P.2d 43 (1995) (all abolishing parental immunity and adopting reasonable and prudent parent standard).

3. *Partial Abrogation*. As in the case of interspousal immunity and as in the principal case, some states developed one or more exceptions to the general rule when they believed that the policies supporting it were inapplicable or were outweighed by the benefit of allowing a tort claim. Some of the more common exceptions include

A.   When the action is for personal injury inflicted intentionally, or is "willful" or "wanton." The usual explanation has been that that conduct is so foreign to the relation as to take the case out of it. In Rodebaugh v. Grand Trunk W.R. Co., 4 Mich.App. 559, 145 N.W.2d 401 (1966), the court added gross negligence and in Oldman v. Bartshe, 480 P.2d 99 (Wyo.1971), the court added willful disregard for the well-being of a child. Henderson v. Woolley, 230 Conn. 472, 644 A.2d 1303 (1994) (answering certified question from federal court) (immunity doctrine does not bar action for sexual abuse, sexual assault, or sexual exploitation); Eagan v. Calhoun, 347 Md. 72, 698 A.2d 1097 (1997) (parent-child immunity does not apply in case where children filed wrongful death action against father who had committed voluntary manslaughter of mother).

B.   When the relation has been terminated before suit by the death of the parent or child or both. MFA Mut. Ins. Co. v. Howard Constr. Co., 608 S.W.2d 535 (Mo.App.1980). This includes action for the wrongful death of the child through the negligence of the parent. Bonner v. Williams, 370 F.2d 301 (5th Cir.1966) (Alabama law); Mosier v. Carney, 376 Mich. 532, 138 N.W.2d 343 (1965).

C.   When the action is for the wrongful death of the other parent. Johnson v. Ottomeier, 45 Wash.2d 419, 275 P.2d 723 (1954).

D.   When the defendant is a step-parent or other person standing in loco parentis. Gillett v. Gillett, 168 Cal.App.2d 102, 335 P.2d 736 (1959); Xaphes v. Mossey, 224 F.Supp. 578 (D.Vt.1963). But see McGee v. McGee, 936 S.W.2d 360 (Tex.App.1996) (step-parent protected by immunity if was in loco parentis to child).

E.   When the child has been legally emancipated. Fitzgerald v. Valdez, 77 N.M. 769, 427 P.2d 655 (1967); Carricato v. Carricato, 384 S.W.2d 85 (Ky.1964). There is a good discussion of what constitutes emancipation in Gillikin v. Burbage, 263 N.C. 317, 139 S.E.2d 753 (1965); Small v. Rockfeld, 66 N.J. 231, 330 A.2d 335 (1974).

F.   Many jurisdictions have abolished the immunity in the context of automobile accident cases, where the relationship is coincidental to the conduct. See, e.g.,

Broadwell v. Broadwell, 871 S.W.2d 471 (Tenn.1994) (in context of automobile accident case, parental immunity was limited to conduct that constitutes the exercise of parental authority, the performance of parental supervision, and the provision of parental care and custody.).

4. _Liability Insurance._ The existence or availability of liability insurance has served as an important justification for the abolishment of the parent-child immunity. Nevertheless, some courts have been steadfast in holding that the existence of insurance cannot "create liability or reduce the need for the immunity." In addition to the principal case, see Maxey v. Sauls, 242 S.C. 247, 130 S.E.2d 570 (1963) and Squeglia v. Squeglia, 234 Conn. 259, 661 A.2d 1007 (1995) (plaintiff's reliance on the existence of liability insurance as a basis for discarding the doctrine is misplaced both as a matter of law and public policy). A few courts have even turned the insurance argument against the plaintiff and have said that its existence is a reason to uphold the immunity because it creates an opportunity for fraud and collusion against the insurance company. The insurance company does receive some protection against this possibility from the "failure to cooperate" clause that appears in the standard liability insurance policy. At least one court has abolished the immunity in negligence cases to the extent that the parent is protected by liability insurance. See Williams v. Williams, 369 A.2d 669 (Del.1976).

5. _Beyond Immunity: What Standard?_ Once an immunity is abolished courts face novel questions regarding the extent of the duty owed by a brand new class of defendants. If the parent is alleged to have negligently injured the child while operating an automobile, the standard is what the reasonable driver would have done under the circumstances. But what if the allegation, like the ones in the principal case, are for negligent supervision of the child. What is the standard? The reasonable person? The reasonable parent? Is there a difference? See e.g., Hartman v. Hartman, 821 S.W.2d 852 (Mo.1991) (parents not required to meet an idealized standard). For a good discussion of the issues and other factual examples, see Holodook v. Spencer, 36 N.Y.2d 35, 324 N.E.2d 338, 364 N.Y.S.2d 859 (1974) ("parents have always had the right to determine how much independence, supervision and control a child should have, and to best judge the character and extent of development of their child"); Shoemake v. Fogel, Ltd., 826 S.W.2d 933 (Tex.1992) ("The discharge of parental responsibilities, such as the provision of a home, food and schooling, entails countless matters of personal, private choice. In the absence of culpability beyond ordinary negligence, those choices are not subject to review in court."); and Squeglia v. Squeglia, 234 Conn. 259, 661 A.2d 1007 (1995) ("The decision to maintain a dog in the home is an example of parental discretion, and permitting a minor child to be exposed to the dog is within the parental supervisory function. This maintenance of the home environment typifies the day-to-day exercise of parental discretion that the state would rather not disrupt."). What result if the child alleges that he suffered emotional harm because the parent failed to perform general parental duties? See Burnette v. Wahl, 284 Or. 705, 588 P.2d 1105 (1978). Is this a matter that should be addressed by tort law? Can an older sibling be liable for negligent supervision? See Smith v. Sapienza, 52 N.Y.2d 82, 417 N.E.2d 530, 436 N.Y.S.2d 236 (1981).

6. _Parent Sues Minor Child._ What if it is the parent who sues the child? Should the parent-child immunity protect the child? Most courts that have considered the issue have found that because the underlying policy reasons would apply equally to such a case, immunity, to the extent recognized and including whatever exceptions have been recognized, should be reciprocal. See Ales v. Ales, 650 So.2d 482 (Miss.1995) (collecting cases).

immunity of charitable institutions

(B) CHARITIES

Abernathy v. Sisters of St. Mary's

Supreme Court of Missouri, 1969.
446 S.W.2d 599.

motion for summary judgment sustained.

Judgment entered for D

T appeals

HENLEY, CHIEF JUSTICE. This is an action by a patient against a hospital for $35,000 damages for personal injuries allegedly suffered as a result of negligence of defendant. Defendant moved for summary judgment, alleging that it is, and operates the hospital as, a benevolent, religious, nonprofit corporation and charitable institution and, therefore, is immune from liability for its torts. The motion was sustained, judgment was entered for defendant, and plaintiff appealed.

[Plaintiff alleged that defendant's employee negligently failed to assist him as he moved from his bed to the bathroom. Plaintiff fell and suffered multiple injuries.]

The doctrine of immunity of charitable institutions from liability for tort was adopted in this state in 1907 by a decision of the Kansas City Court of Appeals in Adams v. University Hospital, 122 Mo.App. 675, 99 S.W. 453. * * *

Policy argument

[T]he court said, in effect, that it is better that the individual suffer injury without compensation from the negligent charitable institution than to risk the judicially assumed probability that the public and state would be deprived of the benefits of the charity; that the interest of the latter is so supreme that the former must be sacrificed to it. * * *

There can be no doubt that at the time of its adoption the exception was a rule of expediency justifiable then, and for some time thereafter, to encourage and protect charity as vital to the growth and development of the state, but the reasons for the exception to the rule do not exist today. * * * "Today charity is big business. It often is corporate both in the identity of the donor and in the identity of the donee who administers the charity. Tax deductions sometimes make it actually profitable for donors to give to charity. Organized corporate charity takes over large areas of social activity which otherwise would have to be handled by government, or even by private business. Charity today is a large-scale operation with salaries, costs and other expenses similar to business generally. It makes sense to say that this kind of charity should pay its own way, not only as to its office expenses but as to the expense of insurance to pay for torts as well." [C] Today public liability insurance is available to charitable institutions to indemnify them against losses by way of damages for their negligence, and it is common knowledge that most charitable institutions carry such insurance and pay the premiums thereon as a part of their normal cost of operation.[12] In the states where immunity has not been accorded charity,

Rule

---

12. We do not make the existence of liability insurance the criterion of liability, as some states have done; we merely emphasize its availability and widespread use as a fact and circumstance that did not exist when the doctrine was adopted. We have held that the experience has shown that the apprehension expressed here and elsewhere that the purses of donors would be closed and the funds of charity depleted if these institutions were not granted immunity was (not) well founded. In the quarter century since the doctrine began its decline, there has been no indication in the states which have abolished immunity that its withdrawal has discouraged donations or that the funds of these institutions have been depleted resulting in their demise. * * *

The public is doubtless still interested in the maintenance of charitable institutions and we acknowledge society's debt to them and recognize their right to every benefit and assistance which the law can justly allow. But the day has arrived when these institutions must acknowledge the injustice of denying compensation to a person injured as a result of their negligence or the negligence of their agents or employees; when they must acknowledge that all persons, organizations and corporations stand equal before the law and must be bound or excused alike. They must recognize that " * * * immunity fosters neglect and breeds irresponsibility, while liability promotes care and caution * * *."

[The court then discussed two of the principal arguments utilized to support charitable immunity—the "implied waiver" and "trust fund" theories.]

The theory of "implied waiver," namely, that he who accepts the benefit of charity impliedly agrees he will not assert against the institution any right of recourse for wrong done him is a mere fiction. The fiction is based upon impossibility in many instances. It is impossible to say that a conscious or unconscious grievously injured accident victim carried to the emergency room of a charitable hospital, or an ill person received at such hospital unconscious, or a conscious ill person who enters such hospital by arrangement of others waives his rights by accepting its benefits. To say that an insane person, a minor or babe in arms waives his rights when he receives or there is administered to him the benefits of *any* charitable institution does violence to the facts; such persons have no legal capacity to will away their rights. The waiver theory obviously cannot be applied alike to all persons and this fact points up the fallacy in relying upon it to support immunity as a rule of public policy.

The "trust fund" theory as support for the doctrine of immunity rests on an illogical, and therefore weak, foundation. The essence of the theory is that the institutions' funds, given and held for charitable purposes, cannot be used to *pay* judgments resulting from tort claims. Thus, the rationale of the theory is identified solely with the right to *satisfaction* of a judgment, rather than to the fundamental question of whether an injured person has a right to maintain an action and secure a judgment. If it is reasonable to say, and it is, that the existence of liability insurance does not create liability where none exists, then it is also reasonable to say that the existence of liability insurance is immaterial on the issue of liability and adhere to that decision. * * *

inability to have satisfaction of a judgment does not create or support exemption from liability where exemption does not otherwise exist. * * *

Defendant and amici curiae recognize that the court has the authority to abolish or modify the doctrine of charitable immunity, but insist the doctrine as public policy is so deeply and firmly embedded in our law that if it is to be modified or abolished the change should be made by the legislature rather than the court.

It is neither realistic nor consistent with the common law tradition to wait upon the legislature to correct an outmoded rule of case law. Nor is legislative silence as instructive or persuasive. * * *

[L]egislative indifference to remedies for private wrongs may be common enough in times when the assembly is occupied with a multitude of matters of grave public concern, but failure to enact a bill is not one of the constitutional methods by which the assembly makes law. * * *

For the reasons stated, we hold that a nongovernmental charitable institution is liable for its own negligence and for the negligence of its agents and employees acting within the scope of their employment.

Having abolished the doctrine of charitable immunity, it remains for us to determine the point of departure from precedent. We are cognizant of the fact that retrospective application of our decision could result in great hardship to those institutions which have relied on our prior decisions upholding the doctrine of charitable immunity. Therefore, feeling that justice will best be served by prospective application of the decision announced today, we hold that the new rule shall apply to this case and to all future causes of action arising after November 10, 1969, the date of the filing of this opinion.

The judgment is reversed and the cause remanded for further proceedings.

DONNELLY, J., concurs in result in separate concurring opinion filed.

NOTES AND QUESTIONS

1.   Charitable immunity originated in England in 1846, in Feoffees of Heriot's Hospital v. Ross, 12 C. & F. 507, 8 Eng.Rep. 1508 (1846). It was later repudiated in Mersey Docks Trustees v. Gibbs, 11 H.L.Cas. 686 (1866). It was, however, taken up by Massachusetts in McDonald v. Massachusetts Gen. Hosp., 120 Mass. 432, 21 Am.Rep. 529 (1876), which was followed in the United States. Prior to 1942, the immunity was accepted, sometimes with various minor limitations, by all but two or three of the American courts. In that year, Judge Rutledge, in what has become a landmark opinion, abolished the immunity for the District of Columbia. See President and Directors of Georgetown College v. Hughes, 130 F.2d 810 (D.C.Cir. 1942). A substantial majority of the states now follow the decision, see Rabon v. Rowan Memorial Hosp. Inc., 269 N.C. 1, 152 S.E.2d 485 (1967) (collecting cases). Are these decisions consistent in policy with federal and state tax laws that grant exemptions to qualified charitable organizations? The immunity, at least on a qualified basis, is not without its defenders. See Moore v. Warren, 250 Va. 421, 463 S.E.2d 459 (1995) (public policy considerations underlie doctrine of charitable immunity that precludes action by beneficiary against charity so long as charity

exercised due care in hiring and retention of agents); Abramson v. Reiss, 334 Md. 193, 638 A.2d 743 (1994) (charitable immunity doctrine based on trust fund theory precludes action against Jewish Community Center).

2. Some jurisdictions have made one or more inroads on the immunity, but have not abolished it completely. The more common incursions include (1) abolishing the immunity to charitable hospitals but retaining it as to religious institutions and other charities, (2) limiting the immunity to recipients of the benefits of the charity, and (3) abolishing the immunity to the extent that the defendant is covered by liability insurance or to the extent that the judgment can be satisfied out of other nontrust fund assets.

3. New Jersey, by statute, provides immunity for negligent acts as to any "beneficiary" of the works of the charity. N.J.S.A. 2A:53A–7 (1999). Does "beneficiary" include a paying patient at a hospital? A pedestrian walking past a church who is struck by a falling stone from a negligently maintained steeple? Some states provide limited charitable immunity tied to liability insurance coverage. See, e.g., Md. Cts. & Jud. Proc. § 5–632 (1999) (liability of charitable hospital limited to $100,000 if hospital obtains liability insurance in that amount). Do charities of any kind deserve special treatment under tort damage rules? What if the tort is intentional? Should a religious organization be immune from punitive damages? See Mrozka v. Archdiocese of St. Paul & Minneapolis, 482 N.W.2d 806 (Minn.App.1992) (punitive damages against religious organization that allegedly placed known child molester in positions where he would have contact with children).

4. During the last two decades, the general expansion of tort liability combined with the tight insurance market of the 1980's raised concerns about the ability of some charitable organizations to continue to provide services. Thus, some state legislatures acted to extend partial immunity to some charitable organizations. See, e.g., N.H.Rev.Stat.Ann. § 508:17 (1999) (limiting liability of charitable organization to $250,000 in action based on alleged negligence of volunteer). What if an individual volunteer is sued rather than or in addition to the organization? N.H. Rev. Stat. Ann. § 508:17 (1999) (immunity for volunteer so long as certain conditions met); Moore v. Warren, 250 Va. 421, 463 S.E.2d 459 (1995) (volunteer driver who was providing transportation to plaintiff was protected by the immunity of the charitable organization, the American Red Cross).

5. See generally Feezer, The Tort Liability of Charities, 77 U.Pa.L.Rev. 191 (1928); Fisch, Charitable Liability for Tort, 10 Vill.L.Rev. 71 (1964); Tremper, Compensation for Harm from Charitable Activity, 76 Cornell L.Rev. 401 (1991); Restatement (Second) of Torts § 895E, and Appendix.

☞(C) Employer Immunity

Worker Compensation statutes in effect in all jurisdictions provide that employees may recover from their employers for work-related injuries without having to show any fault on the part of the employer. This alternative compensation system is described in more detail in Chapter 24, Compensations Systems as Substitutes for Tort Law. It is a complex area. The one aspect that is critical at this juncture is that because the statutes provide an alternative to the tort system, they confer immunity from tort liability on the employer. Thus, under most circumstances, an employee who is injured on the job cannot file a tort claim against his employer even if the employer was negligent.

(D) STATE AND LOCAL GOVERNMENTS

►Ayala v. Philadelphia Board of Public Education

Supreme Court of Pennsylvania, 1973.
453 Pa. 584, 305 A.2d 877.

ROBERTS, JUSTICE. Appellants, William Ayala and William Ayala, Jr., instituted this action to recover damages for injuries suffered by William, Jr., when his arm was caught in a shredding machine in the upholstery class of the Carrol School in Philadelphia. As a result of these injuries, the 15 year old student's arm was amputated.

Appellants alleged that appellee school district, through its employees, was negligent in failing to supervise the upholstery class, in supplying the machine for use without a proper safety device, in maintaining the machine in a dangerous and defective condition, and in failing to warn the children of the dangerous condition. Appellee, the Philadelphia Board of Public Education, interposed preliminary objections asserting the defense of governmental immunity. These objections were sustained and the Superior Court affirmed in a per curiam order. [C] We granted allocatur.

We now hold that the doctrine of governmental immunity—long since devoid of any valid justification—is abolished in this Commonwealth. In so doing, we join the ever-increasing number of jurisdictions which have judicially abandoned this antiquated doctrine. [The court cited decisions from Alaska, Arizona, Arkansas, California, Colorado, the District of Columbia, Florida, Idaho, Illinois, Indiana, Kentucky, Michigan, Minnesota, Nebraska, New Jersey, Nevada, Rhode Island and Wisconsin.]

It is generally agreed that the historical roots of the governmental immunity doctrine are found in the English case of Russell v. Men of Devon, 2 T.R. 667, 100 Eng.Rep. 359 (1788). [Cc] There, the court, in extending immunity to an unincorporated county, expressed the fear that if suits against such political subdivisions were permitted, there would be "an infinity of actions." Russell v. Men of Devon, supra at 672, 100 Eng.Rep. at 362. That court was also influenced by the absence of a fund "out of which satisfaction is to be made." Id. Finally, Justice Ashurst, expressing the eighteenth century societal evaluation of the individual and local governmental interests, observed that "it is better that an individual should sustain an injury than that the public should suffer an inconvenience." Id.

While some attribute the immunity of municipal corporations and quasi-corporations to an extension of the theory that "the King can do no wrong", it has been noted that in Russell v. Men of Devon there is no mention of that phrase. * * *

Additionally, it has been suggested that the doctrine of governmental immunity was a result of the English courts' difficulties with the principle of respondeat superior. * * *

"*Respondeat superior* had caused difficulties as early as the nineteenth century in England, when the question arose whether the King, who by that time could be sued in contract whenever 'right should be done,' should be held for his officers' torts. The courts denied such relief, reasoning that *respondeat superior* was based on the identity of principal and agent, because the King could not himself commit a tort, the attribution failed for want of a competent principal." Jaffe, Suits Against Governments and Officers: Damage Actions, 77 Harv.L.Rev. 209, 210 (1963) (footnote omitted).

Whatever may have been the actual basis for Russell v. Men of Devon, the doctrine it advanced was soon applied in the United States. * * *

Governmental immunity can no longer be justified on "an amorphous mass of cumbrous language about sovereignty. * * * Leflar and Kantrowitz, Tort Liability of the States, 29 N.Y.U.L.Rev. 1363, 1364 (1954). As one court has stated:

" ' * * * it is almost incredible that in this modern age of comparative sociological enlightenment, and in a republic, the medieval absolutism supposed to be implicit in the maxim, "the King can do no wrong," should exempt the various branches of the government from liability for their torts, and that the entire burden of damage resulting from the wrongful acts of the government should be imposed upon the single individual who suffers the injury, rather than distributed among the entire community constituting the government, where it could be borne without hardship upon any individual, and where it justly belongs.' Barker v. City of Santa Fe, 47 N.M. 85, 136 P.2d 480, 482. * * * " Molitor v. Kaneland Community Unit Dist. No. 302 (1959) 18 Ill.2d 11, 21–22, 163 N.E.2d 89, 94. * * *

We must also reject the fear of excessive litigation as a justification for the immunity doctrine. Empirically, there is little support for the concern that the courts will be flooded with litigation if the doctrine is abandoned. * * *

Equally unpersuasive is the argument advanced in Russell v. Men of Devon * * * that immunity is required because governmental units lack funds from which claims could be paid. It is argued that funds would be diverted to the payment of claims and the performance of proper governmental functions would be obstructed. Initially, we note our disagreement with the assumption that the payment of claims is not a proper governmental function. "As many writers have pointed out, the fallacy in [the no-fund theory] is that it assumes the very point which is sought to be proved i.e., that payment of damage claims is not a proper purpose." [C]

Additionally, the empirical data does not support the fear that governmental functions would be curtailed as a result of liability for tortious conduct. * * *

The availability of public insurance removes what was the underlying reason for *Men of Devon.* [C]

[In a prior case, the court abrogated governmental immunity when a municipality engaged in a "proprietary" as compared with a "governmental" function. The court's discussion of the validity of that distinction follows.]

[T]he distinction between governmental and proprietary functions "is probably one of the most unsatisfactory known to the law, for it has caused confusion not only among the various jurisdictions but almost always within each jurisdiction." Davis, Administrative Law Treatise § 25.07 at 460 (1958). * * *

In now rejecting the immunity doctrine and the "legalistic distinctions that have only remote relationship to the fundamental considerations of municipal tort responsibility" [c], we recognize, as did Dean Prosser, that:

"Virtually all writers have agreed that no one of these reasons for denying liability is sound, and all of them can be found to have been rejected at one time or another in the decided cases. The current of criticism has been that it is better that the losses due to tortious conduct should fall upon the municipality rather than the injured individual, and that the torts of public employees are properly to be regarded, as in other cases of vicarious liability, as a cost of the administration of government, which should be distributed by taxes to the public." Prosser, supra at 1004– 05 (footnotes omitted).

Imposition of tort liability will, thus, be more responsive to current concepts of justice. Claims will be treated as a cost of administration and losses will be spread among all those benefited by governmental action. [Cc]

Moreover, "where governmental immunity has had the effect of encouraging laxness and a disregard of potential harm, exposure of the government to liability for its torts will have the effect of increasing governmental care and concern for the welfare of those who might be injured by its actions." [C]

[The court then determined that it need not defer to the legislature to change "this court made rule" and that the doctrine of *stare decisis* did not bind the court to "perpetuating error." Finally, it declined to accept appellee's argument that the ruling be made totally prospective and not apply to the instant case.]

Having concluded that local governmental units—municipal corporations and quasi-corporations—are no longer immune from tort liability, the order sustaining appellee's preliminary objections is reversed and the record remanded for proceedings consistent with this opinion.

MANDERINO, J., joins in this opinion and filed a concurring opinion.

JONES, C.J., and EAGEN and O'BRIEN, JJ., dissent.

NOTES AND QUESTIONS

1. The origin of the idea of governmental immunity at common law seems to have lain in the theory, allied with the divine right of kings, that "the King can do no wrong," together with the feeling that it was necessarily a contradiction of his sovereignty to allow him to be sued as of right in his own courts. The explanations for the initial acceptance of this feudal and monarchistic doctrine in the democracy of this country are quite obscure.

2. *Federal Government.* Sovereign immunity was first recognized on the purely procedural basis that the federal government could not be sued without its consent. When justifications were finally offered, they were consistent with this procedural rule. The explanation most commonly quoted is that of Justice Holmes, in Kawananakoa v. Polyblank, 205 U.S. 349, 353 (1907).

"A sovereign is exempt from suit, not because of any formal conception of obsolete theory, but on the logical and practical ground that there can be no legal right as against the authority that makes the law on which the right depends." With the passage of time, the idea of substantive immunity, as distinct from the denial of the right to sue, began to appear in the federal decisions, until in Gibbons v. United States, 75 U.S. (8 Wall.) 269 (Ct.Cl.1868), it was held that the federal government was immune from all liability in tort. The United States waived its sovereign immunity for tort claims under certain circumstances through the Federal Tort Claims Act of 1946, discussed pages 646–655.

3. *State Governments.* The immunity of state governments from tort liability has the same origin as that of the United States, in feudal notions that the King could do no wrong and that it was a denial of his sovereignty to permit him to be sued in his own courts without his consent. The immunity was given firmer underpinning in some state statutes and in a few state constitutions that required legislative consent for the state to be liable in tort. Even when consent to suit was given, some state courts held that this was not "consent to liability" and they continued to apply the immunity. The immunity was held to extend to state agencies, such as prisons, hospitals, educational institutions, state fairs, and commissions for public works—although a definite tendency developed to find a legislative intent in creating the agency that it should be subject to liability.

4. *Municipal Corporations.* Municipal corporations, such as cities, school districts, and the like have a rather curious dual character. On the one hand, they are subdivisions of the state, acting as local governments. On the other, they are corporate bodies, capable of much the same acts and having much the same special interests and relations as private corporations. The absence of any constitutional or statutory provisions requiring consent to suit made it much easier than in the case of state immunities to develop exceptions to the rule of immunity. The principal exception was for activities that were deemed "proprietary" or "private" as contrasted with "governmental" functions. Courts imposed liability when the city or town engaged in activity that normally was carried out by the private sector of the economy. As the principal case indicates, the distinction produced a morass of confusion and inconsistency—nevertheless, a number of jurisdictions still make the attempt to apply it. See, e.g., Steelman v. New Bern, 279 N.C. 589, 184 S.E.2d 239 (1971) (public street lighting governmental rather than proprietary). Casey v. Wake County, 45 N.C.App. 522, 263 S.E.2d 360 (1980) (county health department dispensing of IUD contraceptive device is governmental function).

5. As with charitable immunity, when the state has authorized a municipal corporation to purchase liability insurance, a number of courts have held that action to be an implied waiver of the immunity to the extent of the insurance. See, e.g., Ballew v. Chattanooga, 205 Tenn. 289, 326 S.W.2d 466 (1959); Bollinger v. Schneider, 64 Ill.App.3d 758, 381 N.E.2d 849, 21 Ill.Dec. 522 (1978).

6. *Abrogation.* Beginning in 1957 with Hargrove v. Cocoa Beach, 96 So.2d 130 (Fla.1957), there have been a number of decisions abrogating the immunity of municipal corporations even for governmental functions. See the principal case, Merrill v. Manchester, 114 N.H. 722, 332 A.2d 378 (1974); Kitto v. Minot Park Dist., 224 N.W.2d 795 (N.D.1974); and Oroz v. Board of County Comm'rs of Carbon

County, 575 P.2d 1155 (Wyo.1978) (except for judicial and legislative functions). Other courts have held that the matter should be left to the legislature. See O'Dell v. School Dist. of Independence, 521 S.W.2d 403 (Mo.1975); Crowder v. Department of State Parks, 228 Ga. 436, 185 S.E.2d 908 (1971); Mayor and City Council of Baltimore v. Austin, 40 Md.App. 557, 392 A.2d 1140 (1978). Judicial respect for governmental immunity has been greater in regard to state government than for municipal corporations. See, e.g., Henry v. Oklahoma Turnpike Auth., 478 P.2d 898 (Okl.1970). When there has been no state constitutional barrier, some courts have abrogated the immunity. See, e.g., Stone v. Arizona Highway Comm'n, 93 Ariz. 384, 381 P.2d 107 (1963); Smith v. State, 93 Idaho 795, 473 P.2d 937 (1970) ("proprietary" functions only); Hicks v. State, 88 N.M. 588, 544 P.2d 1153 (1975); Jones v. State Highway Comm'n, 557 S.W.2d 225 (Mo.1977) (except in legislative, judicial and executive functions); Bulman v. Hulstrand Construction Co., 521 N.W.2d 632 (N.D.1994) (abrogation of immunity is prospective only, to allow Legislature to implement and plan in advance by securing liability insurance or by creating funds for self-insurance).

7. State and municipal immunities also may be abrogated by legislation. Legislation regulating the matter may be enacted after judicial abrogation. Some statutes are modeled on the Federal Torts Claims Act, discussed page 646. Others broadly provide that the state shall be liable to the same extent as any private individual. Rather complex "codes" have been worked out in several states. See, e.g., Cal.Gov't Code §§ 810 et seq. (West 1999); N.J.Stat.Ann. §§ 59:1–1 et seq. (1999); Utah Code Ann. §§ 63–30–1 et seq. (1999). Today, almost all states have limited sovereign immunity to some extent. Most state schemes preserve some special privileges to the state as well as placing various procedural limits on the enforcement of the claims. For example, the state may cap the total amount of damages for which it is liable, create special courts of claims, or impose additional "notice of claim" requirements (see page 618). See generally Civil Actions Against State and Local Government, Its Divisions, Agencies, and Officers (Shepard's 2d ed. 1992); Restatement (Second) of Torts §§ 895B (states), 895C (local governments); the Reporter's Note in the Appendix to these sections carries a compilation showing the position of each state on both state and local government immunity.

8. Generally, even those states that have eliminated or limited governmental immunity have retained immunity for the judicial and legislative functions of the government. This immunity also extends to the agents of the government. Thus, a legislator may not be sued for how he voted or a judge for how she ruled.

9. As in the states where other immunities, like parental immunity, were abolished or limited, states that abolished or limited governmental immunity then grappled with how to define the duty owed to its citizens. In the next two principal cases, the court is faced with determining the duty owed by the government in its provision of emergency protective services.

Riss v. New York

New York Court of Appeals, 1968.
22 N.Y.2d 579, 240 N.E.2d 860, 293 N.Y.S.2d 897.

[The description of the facts in this case is taken from the dissenting opinion of Judge Keating:

"Linda Riss, an attractive young woman, was for more than six months terrorized by a rejected suitor well known to the courts of this State, one

Burton Pugach. This miscreant, masquerading as a respectable attorney, repeatedly threatened to have Linda killed or maimed if she did not yield to him: 'If I can't have you, no one else will have you, and when I get through with you, no one else will want you.' In fear for her life, she went to those charged by law with the duty of preserving and safeguarding the lives of the citizens and residents of this State. Linda's repeated and almost pathetic pleas for aid were received with little more than indifference. Whatever help she was given was not commensurate with the identifiable danger. On June 14, 1959 Linda became engaged to another man. At a party held to celebrate the event, she received a phone call warning her that it was her 'last chance.' Completely distraught, she called the police, begging for help, but was refused. The next day Pugach carried out his dire threats in the very manner he had foretold by having a hired thug throw lye in Linda's face. Linda was blinded in one eye, lost a good portion of her vision in the other, and her face was permanently scarred. After the assault the authorities concluded that there was some basis for Linda's fears, and for the next three and one-half years, she was given around-the-clock protection."]

BREITEL, J. This appeal presents, in a very sympathetic framework, the issue of the liability of a municipality for failure to provide special protection to a member of the public who was repeatedly threatened with personal harm and eventually suffered dire personal injuries for lack of such protection. * * * The issue arises upon the affirmance by a divided Appellate Division of a dismissal of the complaint, after both sides had rested but before submission to the jury. * * *

[T]his case involves the provision of a governmental service to protect the public generally from external hazards and particularly to control the activities of criminal wrongdoers. [Cc] The amount of protection that may be provided is limited by the resources of the community and by a considered legislative-executive decision as to how those resources may be deployed. For the courts to proclaim a new and general duty of protection in the law of tort, even to those who may be the particular seekers of protection based on specific hazards, could and would inevitably determine how the limited police resources of the community should be allocated and without predictable limits. This is quite different from the predictable allocation of resources and liabilities when public hospitals, rapid transit systems, or even highways are provided.

Before such extension of responsibilities should be dictated by the indirect imposition of tort liabilities, there should be a legislative determination that that should be the scope of public responsibility. * * *

When one considers the greatly increased amount of crime committed throughout the cities, but especially in certain portions of them, with a repetitive and predictable pattern, it is easy to see the consequences of fixing municipal liability upon a showing of probable need for and request for protection. To be sure these are grave problems at the present time, exciting high priority activity on the part of the national, State and local governments, to which the answers are neither simple, known, or presently within reasonable controls. To foist a presumed cure for these problems by judicial innovation of a new kind of liability in tort would be foolhardy indeed and an assumption of judicial wisdom and power not possessed by the courts.

* * *

For all of these reasons, there is no warrant in judicial tradition or in the proper allocation of the powers of government for the courts, in the absence of legislation, to carve out an area of tort liability for police protection to members of the public. Quite distinguishable, of course, is the situation where the police authorities undertake responsibilities to particular members of the public and expose them, without adequate protection, to the risks which then materialize into actual losses (Schuster v. City of New York, 5 N.Y.2d 75).

Accordingly, the order of the Appellate Division affirming the judgment of dismissal should be affirmed.

KEATING, JUDGE (dissenting). It is not a distortion to summarize the essence of the city's case here in the following language: "Because we owe a duty to everybody, we owe it to nobody." * * * To say that there is no duty is, of course, to start with the conclusion. The question is whether or not there should be liability for the negligent failure to provide adequate police protection.

The foremost justification repeatedly urged for the existing rule is the claim that the State and the municipalities will be exposed to limitless liability. The city invokes the specter of a "crushing burden" * * *.

The fear of financial disaster is a myth. The same argument was made a generation ago in opposition to proposals that the State waive its defense of "sovereign immunity". The prophecy proved false then, and it would now. * * *

Another variation of the "crushing burden" argument is the contention that, every time a crime is committed, the city will be sued and the claim will be made that it resulted from inadequate police protection. Here, again, is an attempt to arouse the "anxiety of the courts about new theories of liability which may have a far-reaching effect" * * *.

The instant case provides an excellent illustration of the limits which the courts can draw. No one would claim that, under the facts here, the police were negligent when they did not give Linda protection after her first calls or visits to the police station in February of 1959. The preliminary investigation was sufficient. If Linda had been attacked at this point, clearly there would be no liability here. When, however, as time went on and it was established that Linda was a reputable person, that other verifiable attempts to injure her or intimidate her had taken place, that other witnesses were available to support her claim that her life was being threatened, something more was required—either by way of further investigation or protection—than the statement that was made by one detective to

Linda that she would have to be hurt before the police could do anything for her. * * *

More significant, however, is the fundamental flaw in the reasoning behind the argument alleging judicial interference. It is a complete over-simplification of the problem of municipal tort liability. What it ignores is the fact that indirectly courts are reviewing administrative practices in almost every tort case against the State or a municipality, including even decisions of the Police Commissioner * * *.

DeLong v. Erie County

New York Supreme Court, 1982.
89 A.D.2d 376, 455 N.Y.S.2d 887.

HANCOCK, JUSTICE: * * * Before her death, Amalia DeLong, her husband, and their three young children resided at 319 Victoria Boulevard in the Village of Kenmore, a suburb of Buffalo located in Erie County. In October, 1976, the Village of Kenmore was one of the four communities outside of Buffalo fully served by the 911 emergency telephone system operated by the Central Police Services, an agency of Erie County, with the active assistance and cooperation of the Buffalo Police Department. The system was located in the 911 room in Buffalo Police Headquarters in downtown Buffalo. At 9:29:29 in the morning of October 25, 1976 Amalia DeLong dialed 911 on her telephone and was immediately connected to the 911 room. The transcript of her call is as follows:

9:29:29—Caller:		"Police?"
	—Complaint Writer:	"911."
	—Caller:	"Police, please come, 319 Victoria right away."
	—Complaint Writer:	"What's wrong?"
	—Caller:	"There's a burglar."
9:29:34—Complaint Writer:		"In there now?"
	—Caller:	"I heard a burglar; I saw his face in the back; he was trying to break in the house; please come right away."
	—Complaint Writer:	"Okay, right away."
9:29:43—Caller:		"Okay."

The complaint writer recorded the address on the complaint card as "219 Victoria"—not "319 Victoria". The call had lasted 14 seconds. [The evidence regarding police response time indicated that the decedent's life might have been saved if the police had not been misdirected to a nonexistent address.] As a result of the failure of proper police response, Amalia DeLong had received seven knife wounds: to the left side of the neck, the left side of the head, the second finger of the right hand, the nail of the third finger on the left hand, the thumb of the left hand, and a wound to the left shoulder. The laceration on the neck was fatal. It was deep and had severed the jugular vein and carotid artery on the left. The cuts on the fingers were described as being of a "defensive type".

The police in searching the house found evidence of a savage attack.
* * *

The purpose of the 911 emergency or "hot line" system is to assist in the delivery of police services to the people in the communities served (determined by whether the telephone exchanges in the communities are such that dialing 911 will give an automatic connection with the 911 room at Buffalo police headquarters). * * *

On the morning of October 25, the complaint writer, in addition to mistakenly recording the address on the complaint card as 219 instead of 319 Victoria, failed to follow the instructions in four respects: (1) he did not ask the name of the caller; (2) he did not determine the exact location of the call; (3) he did not address the caller by name; (4) he did not repeat the address.

The operating procedures in effect on October 25, 1976 also called for follow-up action if, as with the DeLong call, the report came back to the dispatcher: "No such address." In such event, the dispatcher was required to notify the complaint writer or the 911 lieutenant (the Buffalo police lieutenant on duty in the 911 room) so that the tape recording of the call could be replayed, the Haines Directory and the street guides consulted, and other communities having street names identical or similar to the street name given by the caller immediately notified. On Amalia DeLong's call, no follow-up of any kind took place. The call was treated as a fake.

Our discussion of the questions raised concerning liability must start with Riss v. City of New York, 22 N.Y.2d 579, 293 N.Y.S.2d 897, 240 N.E.2d 860, in which the court found no legal responsibility for the tragic consequences of the city's failure to furnish police protection despite proof of Linda Riss' repeated and agonized pleas for assistance. In an opinion by then Associate Judge Breitel, the court, with one dissent, concluded: "[T]here is no warrant in judicial tradition or in the proper allocation of the powers of government for the courts, in the absence of legislation, to carve out an area of tort liability for police protection to members of the public. Quite distinguishable, of course, is the situation where the police authorities undertake responsibilities to particular members of the public and expose them, without adequate protection, to the risks which then materialize into actual losses [cc]. This fundamental rule remains the law [cc] when a relationship is created between the police and an individual which gives rise to a special duty, the municipality loses its governmental immunity and liability may result. Courts have found such a special duty to be owing "to informers [c], undercover agents [c], persons under court orders of protection [c], and school children for whom the municipality has assumed the responsibility of providing crossing guards [cc]. * * *

It is not the establishment of the emergency call system to serve the Village of Kenmore, standing alone, which creates the duty. It is the holding out of the 911 number as one to be called by someone in need of assistance, Amalia DeLong's placing of the call in reliance on that holding out, and her further reliance on the response to her plea for immediate help: "Okay, right away." This is not a mere failure to furnish police protection owed to the public generally but a case where the municipality has assumed a duty to a particular person which it must perform "in a nonnegligent manner, [although without the] voluntary assumption of that duty, none would have otherwise existed" [c]. The complaint writer's acceptance of the call, his transmittal of the complaint card to the dispatcher and the dispatcher's radio calls to the police cars were affirmative actions setting the emergency machinery in motion. This voluntary assumption of a duty to act carried with it the obligation to act with reasonable care [c].

But, defendants remind us, failing to fulfill an undertaking to provide police protection does not result in municipal liability unless it be shown that the police conduct in some way increased the risk [c]. They maintain that the evidence does not establish that the conduct had "gone forward to such a stage that inaction would commonly result, not negatively merely in withholding a benefit, but positively or actively in working an injury" [c]. In other words, defendants argue, although the hand may have been set to the task and withdrawn [c], it has resulted in no harm. We disagree.

While there could in this case be no direct evidence that Amalia DeLong relied to her ultimate detriment on the assurance of police assistance, the circumstantial evidence strongly suggests that she did so. Instead of summoning help from the Village police or from her neighbors (one of whom was a captain in the Kenmore Police Department), she waited for the response to her 911 call. Instead of taking her baby and going out the front door where she would have been safe, she remained defenseless in the house. * * *

Finally, contrary to the city's contentions, we view the evidence as supporting the jury's conclusion that the city and county were equally at fault. We find no merit in defendants' other arguments on the liability issue.

[The court found that the jury's award of $200,000 for pain and suffering was "within reasonable bounds." The period of time of decedent's fatal encounter with her assailant was between 9:30 and 9:42 a.m.]

Accordingly, the judgment insofar as it awards damages for conscious pain and suffering, should be affirmed.

Judgment affirmed with costs.

[Concurring and dissenting opinions omitted.]

NOTES AND QUESTIONS

1. Do you agree with Judge Keating's dissent in the *Riss* case? Has New York decided that because the state government owes a duty to protect everyone it owes no duty to a particular crime victim? At what point does Ms. Riss move from being a member of the general public to being a particular person, like Ms. DeLong, to whom the government has assumed a duty? Suppose the state never inspects a chicken processing plant during its eleven years of operation and thus fails to find numerous fire safety violations. A fire there killed 25 workers and injured 55 others whose escape from the burning building was prevented or hindered by the fire safety violations. Does the state owe a duty to the workers? Stone v. North Caroline

Dept. of Labor, 347 N.C. 473, 495 S.E.2d 711 (1998) (obligation to inspect runs to public at large, not individuals, and thus there is no liability). Suppose two children report that they are being sexually abused by their stepfather but state social workers, after promising to take action, do nothing to protect them. Sabia v. State of Vermont, 164 Vt. 293, 669 A.2d 1187 (1995) (obligation to protect children where report of abuse has been made runs to those children and state may be liable if it was negligent in not providing protection).

2. Many states and the federal government continue immunity for discretionary functions, but have eliminated it for ministerial acts. Discretionary functions are those where the government is acting to establish policy. Ministerial acts are those that implement or effectuate the policies. Do you see why the government is more appropriately held accountable for discretionary decisions through elections and the political process? Court review of discretionary decisions would interfere with democratic choices: how much money to spend on the police force, how many snow plows to buy, whether to build a new middle school or provide internet access in public libraries. Ministerial decisions, on the other hand, are not manifestations of public policy decisions and therefore can subject the government to liability if they are performed negligently. For example, the government may be liable if one of its agents negligently drives a car, negligently fails to maintain government premises, or negligently fails to maintain public roads. Although some actions are easily categorized as discretionary or ministerial, many actions are not so easily characterized. The next principal case raises that issue in the context of the Federal Tort Claims Act, the federal government's statutory waiver of immunity.

3. For those who may be interested, here is a side note on the subsequent history of the personalities in the *Riss* case. Burton Pugach, the attorney who hired the "three thugs" who partially blinded Ms. Riss, served 14 years and one month in prison for his crime. Six months after his release he proposed to Ms. Riss. She accepted and the couple were married on November 27, 1974. See N.Y. Times Nov. 28, 1974, at 1, col. 4. In 1990, they were still happily married and Pugach was working as a paralegal while attempting to have his disbarment lifted so that he could again practice law. See Agus, City Legend: What They Did for Love, Newsday April 26, 1990, at 4. The disbarment was never lifted. In 1996, a nurse with whom Pugach had been having a five-year long extramarital affair reported to the police that he had threatened her when she attempted to end their affair. She claimed he said "It's 1959 all over again" and "I have tremendous contacts. All I have to do is tell them to do a job." Pugach admitted the affair, but denied that he had made any threats. He acted as his own lawyer at the criminal trial and his wife (the former Ms. Riss) testified as a character witness. See Donohue and Kennedy, "Lover Lawyer Grills His Ex," Daily News April 22, 1997, at 8. Pugach was acquitted of several charges, but convicted of one count of harassment. He and his wife then filed a lawsuit against the nurse, alleging malicious prosecution based on the criminal charges and breach of confidentiality based on the nurse's disclosure of medical data about Linda (Riss) Pugach. Pugach v. Borja, 175 Misc.2d 683, 670 N.Y.S.2d 718 (1998).

(E) THE UNITED STATES

Deuser v. Vecera

United States Court of Appeals, Eighth Circuit, 1998.
139 F.3d 1190.

BOWMAN, CIRCUIT JUDGE. * * * On July 3–6, 1986, the event known as the Veiled Prophet (or VP) Fair was held on the grounds of the Jefferson

National Expansion Memorial in St. Louis, Missouri (the site of the Gateway Arch). Because the Expansion Memorial is a national park (a special use permit was issued to the city of St. Louis for the Fair), the Secretary of the Interior is responsible for maintaining the park and its facilities and for providing services to visitors, functions generally carried out by the National Park Service. [C] The park is within the jurisdiction of the National Park Rangers. On the evening of July 4, 1986, many thousands of people were in attendance at the Fair, including Larry Deuser. Rangers David Vecera and Edward Bridges observed Deuser grabbing women on the buttocks, to the obvious outrage of the victims and others. The rangers warned Deuser, and continued to keep an eye on him. When he urinated in public, the rangers arrested him. As the rangers made their way to their tent with Deuser, he was argumentative with them and continued making rude comments to female visitors.

After conferring with chief ranger Dennis Burnett, the rangers elected to turn Deuser over to St. Louis police. But the police department was overwhelmed with the additional workload created by the Fair, and officers were unable or unwilling to process Deuser's arrest. At this point, the rangers, together with St. Louis police officer Lawrence King, decided to release Deuser, but away from the park so that he would not return to the Fair that evening.

There is some dispute between the parties about where Deuser was released, and also some question of the timing of the events that occurred that night. It is sufficient for our purposes to know the undisputed facts: Deuser was freed in a parking lot somewhere in St. Louis, alone and with no money and no transportation. At some time after that, he wandered onto an interstate highway and was struck and killed by a motorist. Deuser's blood alcohol level was 0.214 at the time of his death, well above the legal limit for intoxication. [Deuser's survivors brought several state and federal claims against municipal and federal actors. This wrongful death action against the United States under the Federal Tort Claims Act ("FTCA") based on the allegedly negligent acts of the park rangers was dismissed by the trial court judge. The survivors appealed.] * * *

II.

By enacting the FTCA, Congress opted to waive the sovereign immunity to civil suit enjoyed by the United States, and to give consent to be sued "for money damages ... for injury or loss of property, or personal injury or death caused by the negligent or wrongful act or omission of any employee" of the United States acting within the scope of his employment. 28 U.S.C.A. § 1346(b)(1) (Supp.1997). The federal courts have subject matter jurisdiction over such claims "under circumstances where the United States, if a private person, would be liable to the claimant in accordance with the law of the place where the act or omission occurred." Id. But, as is true in other cases where Congress on behalf of the United States has waived sovereign immunity, amenability to suit is not without exception.

The exception relevant here is commonly known as the discretionary function exception. It is statutory and shields the government from civil liability for claims "based upon the exercise or performance ... [of] a discretionary function or duty on the part of a federal agency or an employee of the Government, whether or not the discretion involved be abused." 28 U.S.C. § 2680(a) (1994). The exception "marks the boundary between Congress' willingness to impose tort liability upon the United States and its desire to protect certain governmental activities from exposure to suit by private individuals." [C]

To determine whether the discretionary function exception applies here to protect the rangers and the United States from suit, we engage in a two-step inquiry.

A.

First, we must consider whether the actions taken by the rangers as regards Deuser were discretionary, that is, "a matter of choice." Berkovitz [v. United States], 486 U.S. [531] at 536, [1988]. "[C]onduct cannot be discretionary unless it involves an element of judgment or choice." Id. It is axiomatic that a government employee has no such discretion "when a federal statute, regulation, or policy specifically prescribes a course of action for an employee to follow." Id. If the rangers had a policy they were to follow in releasing Deuser, as the appellants contend, "then there is no discretion in the conduct for the discretionary function exception to protect." Id. * * *

[The court then described the written Standard Operating Procedure ("SOP") for an arrest and the VP Fair Operations Handbook.] The opening paragraph of the Handbook's General Enforcement Guidelines makes it clear that the guidelines are in fact quite general and are for use by the rangers "in enforcement contacts[,] but in no way should [they] be construed as a substitute for sound judgement and discretionary action on the part of the Ranger." The guidelines then cover the areas of concern for enforcement by rangers during the Fair: traffic control; liquor law violations; city ordinances in effect for the duration of the Fair concerning alcoholic beverages, glass containers, and pets; access to the Arch; and a variety of crimes against persons from simple assault to murder. The Enforcement section of the Handbook then wraps up with a paragraph that makes it clear the rangers have wide latitude in making enforcement decisions:

> This will be a busy weekend and our holdover facilities at the 4th District may or may not be available per our existing agreement. Transport of federal prisoners to either St. Clair in Illinois or Cape Giraudeau [sic] in Missouri will tie up rangers that we can ill afford and create an extreme workload on the 7th of July [the first business day after the Fair] when we can least afford it. That does not mean we will not take appropriate action, only that our actions will be tempered with reality and arrests will only be on a "last resort" basis.

* * * The Handbook was intended to provide guidance to the rangers on the extent to which certain laws should be enforced during the Fair. Read as a whole, the Handbook suggests that enforcement in many circumstances might be relaxed during the event, so that arrests would be kept to a minimum. The rangers' "sound judgement and discretionary action" was to be exercised in the context of making decisions on whether to make an arrest at all; the Handbook never touches on the procedure to be followed in the event an arrest is made (except to note that holding facilities and rangers will be busy during the Fair). The Handbook did not override the standard operating procedures. [Footnote omitted.] Based on the record before us, it appears the SOP for processing arrestees remained unchanged during the Fair. Still, that conclusion does not mean that the rangers were required to complete an arrest, that is, to charge and incarcerate a suspect, once he was in custody.

We know that Deuser was arrested by the rangers. The SOP to be followed when a person is arrested by a ranger at the Expansion Memorial is precise and, as to the salient points, mandatory. Appellants are correct that there was very little discretion to be exercised, at least for as long as Deuser was under arrest. And it seems that the rangers initially followed the prescribed procedure: they searched Deuser and handcuffed him before transporting him. After that, it is true that the SOP was not followed—but when Deuser was released in the parking lot, the arrest was terminated. He was free to go, and further arrest procedures—booking the prisoner and so forth—were irrelevant. Deuser was not charged with a crime, so there was no reason to follow the procedures for incarceration.

The question remains whether a ranger's decision to terminate an arrest made at the park during the Fair would require the same sort of judgment and choice as would the initial decision to make the arrest. We think that it would. There is nothing in either the SOP or the Handbook that sets forth a policy—whether discretionary or otherwise—for terminating an arrest. But we conclude that this is because the decision to terminate an arrest is closely akin to the decision to make the arrest in the first place. Law enforcement decisions of the kind involved in making or terminating an arrest must be within the discretion and judgment of enforcing officers. See, e.g., Redmond v. United States, 518 F.2d 811, 816–17 (7th Cir.1975) ("It cannot be denied that the Government has a duty to maintain law and order, but how best to fulfill this duty is wholly within the discretion of its officers ..."). It would be impossible to put into a manual every possible scenario a ranger might encounter, and then to decide in advance for the ranger whether an arrest should be made and, once made, under what circumstances an arrest could be terminated. Just as the rangers had discretion to decide (within constitutional limits, of course) when and whether to make an arrest, so they had—and here exercised—discretion to terminate an arrest without charging the suspect. Under the terms of the Handbook, that discretion became even broader during the Fair.

We hold that terminating Deuser's arrest, that is, releasing him without charging him with a crime, was a discretionary function reserved to the judgment of the rangers.

B.

We move now to the second part of our inquiry. Notwithstanding the judgment involved in terminating Deuser's arrest, we must ask "whether that judgment is of the kind that the discretionary function exception was designed to shield." Berkovitz, 486 U.S. at 536, 108 S.Ct. at 1959. To be protected, the rangers' conduct must be "grounded in the social, economic, or political goals" of the Handbook's discretionary enforcement guidelines. United States v. Gaubert, 499 U.S. 315, 323, 111 S.Ct. 1267, 1274, 113 L.Ed.2d 335 (1991). * * *

We think the conduct of the rangers here is the classic example of a "permissible exercise of policy judgment." Berkovitz, 486 U.S. at 539, 108 S.Ct. at 1960. Social, economic, and political goals—all three—were the basis for the actions taken by the rangers.

An important function of the rangers during the Fair, according to the Handbook, was to serve and protect visitors to the park. Clearly, the decision to remove Deuser from the park served the social goals of protecting innumerable other fairgoers and ensuring that their enjoyment of the festivities was not diminished by the obnoxious and offensive behavior of a fellow attendee. Further, the decision to release Deuser, rather than to charge him for the offenses he committed, may have prevented a night of revelry that obviously was out of control from becoming a criminal conviction. And the rangers who otherwise would have spent considerable time booking Deuser were free to return to the Fair, possibly to prevent more serious or more dangerous crimes from being committed, or to apprehend the perpetrators of graver offenses, thereby continuing to further the goal of visitor protection.

The economic goals of the guidelines are clear, and are spelled out in some detail in the Handbook. Law enforcement manpower was expected to be stretched thin, both during the Fair and on the first business day following the Fair, when arrestees would have to be transported for court appearances. (In fact, the SOP tells rangers to expect the process to take all day, even under ordinary circumstances.) There were simply not enough officers to arrest and to charge all persons who might commit a crime at the park during the four-day Fair. The rangers' colleagues, St. Louis police department officers, were expected to be equally taxed with their own enforcement duties. Moreover, it was anticipated that the nearest holdover facility would be overcrowded with arrestees, meaning more miles and more manpower to transport suspects to alternative holdover facilities and to see to their arraignments. Releasing Deuser without charging him preserved already scarce law enforcement resources.

The political goals to be served by the guidelines concern law enforcement "territories." The Fair was not a National Park Service event. The Handbook acknowledges that "[t]he St. Louis Police Department is the lead agency for law enforcement." VP Fair 1986 Operations Handbook—Overview and Hindsight para. 6. As the chief ranger stated in the Handbook, the federal park rangers' "primary role is defined as resource protection followed by the things we do best, visitor services and visitor care." Id. When the police opted not to process Deuser's arrest, the rangers appropriately decided not to override the decision of "the lead agency for law enforcement." The Fair's success depended in part on all enforcement agencies involved working together toward a common goal, and the rangers acted properly to preserve that cooperation by releasing Deuser in this situation. Further, the Fair was designed to be an enjoyable event for the city, and it would have been unfortunate if overzealous federal law enforcement had dampened the festivities. * * *

[We hold that the conduct of the officers here was grounded in the social, economic, and political policies of the Handbook.]

The judgment of the District Court is affirmed.

NOTES AND QUESTIONS

1. Governmental immunity has barred tort suits against the United States for the greater part of its history. Consent to be sued began to appear in the form of private bills by Congress authorizing particular plaintiffs to sue on particular claims. Apart from the obvious possibility of political influence, this of necessity involved considerable delay and inconvenience, as well as inflicting a considerable burden upon the time of Congress. In 1855 it was largely replaced by a statute setting up a Court of Claims to hear contract cases. This was initially merely an advisory court making recommendations to Congress; but in 1863 the Court of Claims was given the power to render effective judgments. There were also a number of minor statutes permitting suit upon particular types of claims, and in a few instances some of these even authorized some relief in tort. The great majority of the tort claims against the United States remained, however, without any redress. The inconvenience caused by private bills pressured Congress to provide for a general tort remedy. Between 1919 and 1946, some 18 proposals were considered. Finally, the specter of hundreds and possibly thousands of private bills flooding Congress as servicemen returned from World War II (only to be hit by postal trucks), proved too much. On August 2, 1946 the Federal Tort Claims Act was enacted. It applied to all claims accruing on and after January 1, 1945. In effect, it represented the first judicial remedy of general application available to persons who suffered tortious injury to their person or property caused by employees of the United States Government.

2. Tort claims against the Federal Government are a major source of tort litigation today. As an author of a three-volume treatise on the subject has observed: "[L]awsuits against the United States under the Federal Tort Claims Act pending before the federal courts at one time involve[d] claims of approximately $5 billion. New suits are filed at the rate of more than 1,500 each year * * * This large volume * * * is understandable when you consider that the United States employs more than 5 million people * * * It operates more than a half a million * * * vehicles. It employs * * * more than 85,000 * * * medical personnel. * * * [M]otor vehicle and pedestrian accidents comprise a little over half of the litigation under the Act * * * [T]he remainder covers virtually the entire field of torts * * *." L. Jayson, Handling Federal Tort Claims 1, 8–9 (1993).

3.   The Federal Tort Claims Act is a subject for separate study. Only a few major issues under the Act will be noted here. It is of paramount importance to remember that a lawyer cannot assume that matters will be handled in "the ordinary way" under the Act. Here are a few examples:

A.   A person seeking recovery must present his claim to the "appropriate Federal agency" before instituting suit. 28 U.S.C.A. § 2675.

[handwritten margin note: must give notice]

B.   When a claim is made, it must be filed in the United States district court in the district where the plaintiff resides or wherein the act complained of occurred. 28 U.S.C.A. § 1402.

[handwritten margin note: can't file in state court]

C.   The suit will be tried by a judge and not a jury. 28 U.S.C.A. § 2402.

D.   The plaintiff's attorney's contingent fee is subject to express regulation and imposition of a higher fee constitutes a federal crime. 28 U.S.C.A. § 2678. (25% of any judgment or settlement made after commencement of the action and 20% of any settlement through the administrative procedure before filing suit is the maximum amount permitted.)

4.   Two major sections of the Act are the jurisdiction and general liability sections. They are quoted below:

The federal district courts "shall have exclusive jurisdiction of civil actions on claims against the United States, for money damages, accruing on or after January 1, 1945, for injury or loss of property, or personal injury or death caused by the negligent or wrongful act or omission of any employee of the Government while acting within the scope of his office or employment, under circumstances where the United States, if a private person, would be liable to the claimant in accordance with the law of the place where the act or omission occurred." 28 U.S.C.A. § 1346(b).

"The United States shall be liable, respecting the provisions of this title relating to tort claims, in the same manner and to the same extent as a private individual under like circumstances, but shall not be liable for interest prior to judgment or for punitive damages.

[handwritten margin note: must be negligence; strict liability claims cannot be brought under these rules]

"If, however, in any case wherein death was caused, the law of the place where the act or omission complained of occurred provides, or has been construed to provide, for damages only punitive in nature, the United States shall be liable for actual or compensatory damages, measured by the pecuniary injuries resulting from such death to the persons respectively for whose benefit the action was brought, in lieu thereof." 28 U.S.C.A. § 2674.

A.   What problems of statutory interpretation can you glean from each section? Why do you think Congress did not enact a complete code of federal tort law rather than rely on the "law of the place where the tort occurred"? Should the liability of the federal government vary from state to state?

B.   Would the United States be subject to strict liability under the Act? Suppose it engaged in an "abnormally dangerous" activity or manufactured a "defective" product? This matter would appear to have been finally put to rest in Laird v. Nelms, 406 U.S. 797 (1972) (sonic boom), where the Supreme Court held that the Act did not authorize suit against the government based on strict or absolute liability. Nevertheless, could you make an argument the other way based on language of the Act itself?

C.   Many claims have arisen on the issue of whether a government officer or employee was "acting within his office or employment" for the purpose of the Act. Should this be decided as a matter of state or federal law? If a government employee's negligent operation of a vehicle does come under the Act, he is shielded by it and the plaintiff's only possible cause of action is against the United States. 28 U.S.C.A. § 2679(b). This exclusive remedy provision shields the government employee even if another provision means that the United States also is immune. United States v. Smith, 499 U.S. 160 (1991) (claimant allegedly injured by medical malpractice of military doctor stationed in Italy has no cause of action against the doctor because of the exclusive remedy provision even though the FTCA provides no remedy because the cause of action arose outside of the United States).

5. The Act contains 13 specific exceptions to the waiver of immunity in 28 U.S.C.A. § 2680. Most of them deal with specific activities of the government, such as the transmission of mail, the assessment or collection of customs duties, the imposition of quarantines, the fiscal operations of the Treasury, and the like, and in particular the combatant activities of military and naval forces in time of war. The Supreme Court of the United States has adhered to the proposition that it will not "extend the waiver of sovereign immunity more broadly than has been directed by Congress." United States v. Shaw, 309 U.S. 495, 502 (1940). Three of the most important exceptions are for

A. "Any claim based upon an act or omission of an employee of the Government, exercising due care, in the execution of a statute or regulation, whether or not such statute or regulation be valid, or based upon the exercise or performance or the failure to exercise or perform a discretionary function or duty on the part of a federal agency or an employee of the Government, whether or not the discretion involved be abused." 28 U.S.C.A. § 2680(a). This was the issue in the principal case.

Problems regarding the interpretation of this section are not dissimilar from those that have arisen in suits against municipalities after judicial abrogation of governmental immunity. In Berkovitz v. United States, 486 U.S. 531 (1988), cited in the principal case, plaintiff was a child who was left paralyzed and unable to breathe without a respirator when he contracted polio from a dose of oral polio vaccine. His parents filed suit against the manufacturer of the vaccine and against the United States alleging that the United States (through the Office of Biologics of the Food and Drug Administration) had wrongfully licensed the manufacturer to produce the vaccine and had wrongfully approved the release of the particular lot that had injured the plaintiff. The United States moved to dismiss, invoking the discretionary function exception and arguing that it applied to all regulatory activities. Justice Marshall delivered the unanimous opinion of the Court, holding that the discretionary function exception applied to only those activities that involve an element of judgment or choice and that are based on public policy considerations. Because plaintiff had alleged that the FDA had knowingly released that lot to the public without testing it for compliance with safety standards, there was no discretion involved and the United States would be liable if plaintiff could prove his allegations. Justice Marshall noted that the FDA could have adopted a policy of testing only some batches and that decision would not be reviewable. Having made the decision to test all batches, however, the FDA had no discretion not to test each batch. See also United States v. S.A. Empresa (Varig Airlines), 467 U.S. 797 (1984) (FAA decision to certify airplanes as airworthy without inspecting each one and only "spot-checking" them for compliance with safety standards is a discretionary function decision that cannot subject the United States to liability) and Irving v. United States, 162 F.3d 154 (1st Cir.1998) (OSHA's failure to inspect machine that then injured plaintiff is within discretionary function exception to liability).

B. "Any claim arising out of assault, battery, false imprisonment, false arrest, malicious prosecution, abuse of process, libel, slander, misrepresentation, deceit, or interference with contract rights: Provided, That, with regard to acts or omissions of investigative or law enforcement officers of the United States Government, the provisions of this chapter and section 1346(b) of this title shall apply to any claim arising, on or after the date of the enactment of this proviso, out of assault, battery, false imprisonment, false arrest, abuse of process, or malicious prosecution. For the purpose of this subsection, 'investigative or law enforcement officer' means any officer of the United States who is empowered by law to execute searches, to seize evidence, or to make arrests for violations of Federal law." 28 U.S.C.A. § 2680(h).

Do you see why the plaintiff in the principal case, unlike the plaintiff in Parvi v. City of Kingston, page 39, could not make a claim for false arrest? Do you see why the plaintiff in United States v. Lambertson, page 23, characterized his cause of action as one for negligence rather than battery when he was injured by a government meat inspector who leapt out at him, screamed "boo," pulled his wool stocking cap over his eyes, and jumped on his back to ride him piggyback?

This section contains many familiar words from tort law. Should they be construed by looking to local state or federal common law? In Moos v. United States, 225 F.2d 705 (8th Cir.1955), the plaintiff underwent an operation in a veteran's hospital, and the surgeon mistakenly, and negligently, operated on the wrong hip and leg. It was held that there was no liability under the Act, because under the law of Minnesota this was technically a battery. What does "arising out of" mean? An off duty U.S. Navy Corpsman fired rifle shots into a car passing by outside the hospital where he worked. Plaintiff alleged that other U.S. Naval employees knew he was intoxicated and brandishing a rifle and negligently failed to take steps to prevent the battery. Liability? See Sheridan v. United States, 487 U.S. 392 (1988) (claim does not "arise out of" a battery and thus is not barred).

C. 28 U.S.C.A. § 2680(j) provides that the Federal Tort Claims Act does not apply to any "claim arising out of the combatant activities of the military or naval forces, or the Coast Guard, during time of war." Moreover, the Supreme Court has held that the Federal Tort Claims Act does not permit recovery for claims arising out of or in the course of activity incident to any active duty service. Feres v. United States, 340 U.S. 135 (1950). Rationales for the doctrine include the need for uniformity of law, the health and welfare benefits provided to servicemen and their dependents, the absence of private liability in like circumstances, and the potential for disrupting military discipline. The definition of "incident to service" has been exhaustively litigated over the past fifty years. Although most of the cases involve soldiers struck by government vehicles while on varying degrees of leave, others raise more interesting policy issues. See, e.g., United States v. Stanley, 483 U.S. 669 (1987) (plaintiff injured by LSD experiment conducted by government without informing him of the risks was precluded from suit because experiments were "incident to service"); Kitowski v. United States, 931 F.2d 1526 (11th Cir.1991) (military trainer's holding a recruit underwater until he died was within bar of Feres doctrine); Minns v. United States, 155 F.3d 445 (4th Cir.1998) (claims brought by wives and children of Gulf War veterans for birth defects allegedly caused by inoculations and exposure to various toxins dismissed because injuries had their genesis in injuries to soldiers incident to service). Cases are collected in 1 L. Jayson, Personal Injury: Handling Federal Tort Claims, Chapter 5A (1999). The Feres doctrine was extended to shield the government against contribution or indemnity claims brought by manufacturers of products who could be sued by service personnel. Stencel Aero Eng'g Corp. v. United States, 431 U.S. 666 (1977), reh'g denied, 434 U.S. 882 (1977).

6. If a claimant is unsuccessful under the Federal Tort Claims Act, all is not necessarily lost. It is still possible to obtain relief by private bill. This is a difficult procedure requiring full cooperation of a Representative, plus tremendous persistence by an attorney.

(F) PUBLIC OFFICERS

Public officers are subject to personal liability for tortious conduct committed in the course of their official duties. Claims against them may be predicated on the common law of torts, special statutes (a prime example being the Civil Rights Act of 1871, 42 U.S.C.A. § 1983), or a provision of the United States Constitution. See Bivens v. Six Unknown Named Agents, 403 U.S. 388 (1971), page 1159.

In each of these situations the public official may be shielded from liability if the official's conduct comes within common law official immunity—a doctrine that is separate and apart from governmental immunity. Thus, even if governmental immunity has been abolished, official immunity still may protect a public official. Conversely, when the state has not consented to be sued on a matter (for example, the intentional torts exempted from coverage in the Federal Tort Claims Act), a public official may be liable if the conduct does not come within the immunity discussed in this section.

It should be noted here that sometimes when the legislature has waived governmental immunity, it has granted immunity to a public employee whose negligent conduct will now be paid for by the state. An example can be found in the Federal Tort Claims Act. 28 U.S.C.A. § 2679(b) provides that the remedy against the United States for negligent operation of motor vehicles is exclusive of any remedy against a driver employee. See also Agnew v. Porter, 23 Ohio St.2d 18, 260 N.E.2d 830 (1970) (construing state statute that protected policemen from tort claims based on their operation of motor vehicles while responding to emergency calls). If this makes sense, should it be extended to other types of torts committed by government employees?

The common law immunity for public officers would appear to be based "not so much [on a] desire to protect an erring officer as * * * [on] a recognition of the need of preserving independence of action, without deterrence or intimidation by the fear of personal liability and vexatious suits." Restatement (Second) of Torts § 895D, comment b; see the classic statement of Learned Hand, J., in Gregoire v. Biddle, 177 F.2d 579 (2d Cir.1949) (federal prosecutor).

Legislators and judges have been granted absolute immunity for acts committed within the scope of their office even if they acted in bad faith. See, e.g., Tenney v. Brandhove, 341 U.S. 367 (1951) (legislators); Pierson v. Ray, 386 U.S. 547 (1967) (judges).

Federal executive officers, even at lower levels, appear also to benefit from the immunity. See Barr v. Matteo, 360 U.S. 564 (1959).

The President of the United States is absolutely immune for acts within the scope of his office. Nixon v. Fitzgerald, 457 U.S. 731 (1982). But presidential aides are entitled only to a qualified immunity. Harlow v. Fitzgerald, 457 U.S. 800 (1982).

State executive officers in some states also have the benefit of absolute immunity with regard to common law torts committed in the course of their official duties. In other states, the immunity is qualified; in some, it depends upon whether the harmful action was taken in good faith, and in others it depends on whether the official had a reasonable basis for taking the action.

When the immunity is qualified, it becomes similar in an operative sense to a "privilege," see page 619, and perhaps the major reason to preserve the label of "immunity" is to signify that it applies to negligent as well as intentional conduct.

A qualified immunity appears to be the standard developed with respect to violations of the Civil Rights Act of 1871 (42 U.S.C.A. § 1983). See Harlow v. Fitzgerald, 457 U.S. 800 (1982) (adopting objective test to determine "good faith."); Wood v. Strickland, 420 U.S. 308 (1975). A state official may be deemed to have violated the act if he knew or reasonably should have known that his conduct would violate plaintiff's constitutional rights or if he took the action in bad faith. On the other hand, a prosecuting attorney is held to have absolute immunity under the Act. See Imbler v. Pachtman, 424 U.S. 409 (1976). Why should a prosecutor be distinguished from officials in the executive branch of the government?

Official immunity is applied only with respect to acts that are "discretionary" as opposed to "ministerial" in nature. This distinction, which we have seen evolving in the area of governmental immunity, has not been an easy one to apply. Obviously, if the official was engaged in formulating policy at a high level in government, the conduct will be deemed "discretionary." Can you think of examples? How would you classify the conduct of a police chief in regard to his method of training officers? See Carter v. Carlson, 144 U.S.App.D.C. 388, 447 F.2d 358 (1971), rev'd on other grounds sub nom., District of Columbia v. Carter, 409 U.S. 418 (1973). Comment f to Section 895D of Restatement (Second) of Torts sets forth most of the factors courts have looked to when they have attempted to classify an official's conduct as "discretionary" or "ministerial."

While there has been little litigation on the point, the doctrine of vicarious liability would not appear to be applicable to hold public officials liable for torts committed by lower echelon employees, at least when the officials in no way personally participated in the wrongdoing. See, e.g., Carter v. Allan, 94 Idaho 190, 484 P.2d 739 (1971) (suit against mayor and city council for injuries caused by negligently constructed sidewalk).

See Restatement (Second) of Torts § 895D; Civil Actions Against State and Local Government, Its Divisions, Agencies, and Officers (Shepard's 2d ed. 1992).

CHAPTER XIII

VICARIOUS LIABILITY

A is negligent; B is not; C is injured by A's negligence. "Imputed negligence" means that, by reason of some relationship between A and B, B is liable to C for A's actions, although B has played no part in it, has done nothing to aid or encourage it, and in fact may have done all that he possibly could to prevent it. The result may be that B, in an action against C for his own injuries, is barred from recovery because of A's negligence, to the same extent as if he had been negligent himself. This is commonly called "imputed contributory negligence." Or the result may be that B, in C's action against him, becomes liable as a defendant for C's injuries, to the same extent as if he had been negligent himself. This is sometimes called "imputed negligence." More often it is called vicarious liability or *respondeat superior*, which may be freely translated, "look to the person higher up." The topic is covered in depth in a course in Agency. Only highlights closely related to torts are presented in this Chapter.

1. RESPONDEAT SUPERIOR

Lundberg v. State

Court of Appeals of New York, 1969.
25 N.Y.2d 467, 255 N.E.2d 177, 306 N.Y.S.2d 947.

SCILEPPI, JUDGE.

John H. Lundberg, claimant's husband, was killed on the morning of February 14, 1966 when his car was struck by an auto owned and operated by John Sandilands, an employee of New York State. There is no dispute as to the facts and there is no question that the death was caused solely by the negligence of Sandilands. The only issue raised by this appeal is whether Sandilands' negligence can be imputed to his employer, the State of New York, the defendant in this action.

* * *

On Monday, February 14, 1966, at 7:30 a.m. Sandilands was driving back to the reservoir [his assigned job site near which he stayed in a hotel during the week] from Buffalo [his residence 80 miles away] after a holiday weekend. While attempting to pass a truck, his car skidded and struck the car driven by Lundberg, head on. Lundberg died as a result of the injuries he sustained in the accident.

Sandilands applied for and was granted Workmen's Compensation benefits for the injuries which he suffered in the accident. Claimant, Lundberg's widow, brought * * * wrongful death and survival actions against Sandilands and * * * the State, as Sandilands' employer. The action against Sandilands was settled for $20,000. The one against the State went to trial and resulted in a judgment for more than $73,000. The Appellate Division, Fourth Department, unanimously affirmed and the State is appealing by permission of this court from the order of affirmance.

The sole issue presented by this appeal is whether the State of New York should be held liable, pursuant to the doctrine of *respondeat superior,* for the pain and suffering and wrongful death caused by its employee's negligence. It is our opinion that Sandilands was not acting in the scope of his employment while driving from Buffalo to his work site and that, therefore, the complaint against the defendant State should have been dismissed.

Under the doctrine of *respondeat superior,* an employer will be liable for the negligence of an employee committed while the employee is acting in the scope of his employment [c]. An employee acts in the scope of his employment when he is doing something in furtherance of the duties he owes to his employer and where the employer is, or could be, exercising some control, directly or indirectly, over the employee's activities [cc]. As a general rule, an employee driving to and from work is not acting in the scope of his employment [cc]. Although such activity is work motivated, the element of control is lacking. An exception to this rule is, that an employee who uses his car in furtherance of his work is acting in the scope of his employment while driving home from his last business appointment, since such a person is working, and is under his employer's control, from the time he leaves the house in the morning until he returns at night [cc]. In the instant case, however, the employee was not driving his car in further-ance of his work at the time of the accident. He was engaged in an independent personal activity over which the State had no control. Thus, the general rule applies. * * *

[I]n the instant case it is our opinion that it has been established, as a matter of law, that Sandilands was not acting in the scope of his employ-ment. Firstly, Sandilands was not driving to satisfy an obligation he owed to his employer but solely to satisfy his personal desire to visit his home in Buffalo. Moreover, the State clearly did not have the power to control Sandilands' activities after the close of work on Friday until the commence-ment of work on Monday. During these hours, Sandilands was free to do as he pleased. He could have chosen to remain in Salamanca or in the alternative to travel by any available means, to any place he desired, including Buffalo. In our opinion the mere fact that the State had agreed to pay Sandilands' travel expenses, in the form of a mileage allowance [because he had to travel 80 miles to the worksite], did not bestow in it any right of control. To hold that by simply paying his travel expenses to his home the State opened itself to liability for any tortious act he might commit while traveling between Buffalo and the work site would be patently unfair and beyond the scope of the doctrine of *respondeat superior* (Restatement, 2d Agency, § 239; see 52 A.L.R.2d 290, 325). * * *

Accordingly, the order of the Appellate Division should be reversed and the claim against the defendant dismissed.

BURKE, JUDGE (dissenting). * * * Of particular relevance in this case, as distinguished from the vague and theoretical question of "right to control", is the test for liability posited by former Chief Judge Cardozo in Matter of Marks v. Gray, 251 N.Y. 90, 93–94, 167 N.E. 181, 183: "The test in brief is this: If the work of the employee creates the necessity for travel, he is in the course of his employment, though he is serving at the same time some purpose of his own" [c]. The undisputed facts in the present case clearly indicate that that test has been met. Sandilands' temporary employment at a work site 80 miles from his permanent station and home in Buffalo created the necessity for his travel between Buffalo and the work site. While so traveling, he was clearly acting in furtherance of his employment * * *. The mere fact that his traveling back and forth was motivated by his desire to see his family occasionally in no way detracts from the fact that the trips would not have been made at all had it not been for his assignment to a distant work site.

In addition, it should be recognized that the fact that the State paid Sandilands' travel expenses for these trips is significant not because it has any relation to some theoretical "right to control" but precisely because it indicates that the State recognized that Sandilands' employment necessitated such travel and acquiesced in his use of his own automobile for that travel. * * * Accordingly, the order of the Appellate Division should be affirmed.

Fruit v. Schreiner

Supreme Court of Alaska, 1972.
502 P.2d 133.

[Clay Fruit, a life insurance salesman, was required to attend a sales convention conducted by his employer, The Equitable Life Assurance Society. Fruit drove his own car, but was reimbursed for his expenditures. The convention included social as well as business events, and he was "encouraged to mix freely" with out-of-state insurance experts in order "to learn as much as possible about sales techniques." On the second evening of the convention, after all business-related activities and scheduled social events were long over, Fruit drove to the Waterfront Bar and Restaurant in order to look for some out-of-state colleagues. Finding none, he drove back toward the convention center. On this journey, at approximately 2:00 a.m., he skidded across a highway and struck a disabled vehicle. John Schreiner was standing in front of that vehicle and his legs were crushed in the impact. Schreiner brought a personal injury claim against both Fruit and his employer. The jury found that Fruit was negligent and awarded Schreiner $635,000.]

BOOCHEVER, JUSTICE. * * * The jury found that Fruit was an employee acting within the course and scope of his employment for Equitable at the time and place of the accident. Under the doctrine of *respondeat superior* (which simply means "let the employer answer") Equitable would thus be liable for Fruit's acts of negligence despite lack of fault on Equitable's part.

Equitable argues, however, that the evidence was insufficient to establish that Fruit was acting within the course and scope of his employment. Equitable contends that any business purpose was completed when Fruit left the Waterfront Bar and Restaurant. It cites cases holding that an employee traveling to his home or other personal destination cannot ordinarily be regarded as acting in the scope of his employment. But Fruit was not returning to his home. He was traveling to the convention headquarters where he was attending meetings as a part of his employment.

In addition, Equitable seeks to narrow the scope of *respondeat superior* to those situations where the master has exercised control over the activities of employees. Disposition of this issue requires an analysis of the doctrine of *respondeat superior,* one of the few anomalies to the general tort doctrine of no liability without fault.

The origins of the principle whereby an employer may be held vicariously liable for the injuries wrought by his employee are in dispute. Justice Holmes traces the concept to Roman law while Wigmore finds it to be of Germanic origin. The doctrine emerged in English law in the 17th Century. Initially a master was held liable for those acts which he commanded or to which he expressly assented. This was expanded to include acts by implied command or authority and eventually to acts within the scope of employment. The modern theory evolved with the growth of England's industry and commerce.

A truly imaginative variety of rationales have been advanced by courts and glossators in justification of this imposition of liability on employers. Among the suggestions are the employer's duty to hire and maintain a responsible staff of employees, to "control" the activities of his employees and thus to insist upon appropriate safety measures; the belief that the employer should pay for the inherent risks which result from hiring others to carry on his business; the observation that the employer most often has easier access to evidence of the facts surrounding the injury; and the metaphysical identification of the employer and employee as a single "persona" jointly liable for the injury which occurred in the context of the business.

Baty more cynically states: "In hard fact, the reason for the employers' liability is the damages are taken from a deep pocket." Baty, Vicarious Liability 11 (1916).

The two theories which carry the greatest weight in contemporary legal thought are respectively, the "control" theory which finds liability whenever the act of the employee was committed with the implied authority, acquiescence or subsequent ratification of the employer, and the "enterprise" theory which finds liability whenever the enterprise of the employer would have benefitted by the context of the act of the employee but for the unfortunate injury.

Since we are dealing with vicarious liability, justification may not be found on theories involving the employer's personal fault such as his failure to exercise proper control over the activities of his employees or his failure to take proper precautions in firing or hiring them. Lack of care on the employer's part would subject him to direct liability without the necessity of involving *respondeat superior.* * * *

The aspect of the relationship most commonly advanced to delimit the theory is the "scope of employment" of the employee-tortfeasor. While the factual determination generally is left to the jury, many cases lying in the penumbras of "scope of employment" have produced confusing and contradictory legal results in the development of an otherwise worthy doctrine of law. To assist in delineating the areas of tortious conduct imposing liability, it is helpful to consider what we believe to be the correct philosophical basis for the doctrine.

There was a time when the artisans, shopkeepers and master craftsmen could directly oversee the activities of their apprentices and journeymen. * * * But in the present day when hundreds of persons divide labors under the same corporate roof and produce a single product for market to an unidentified consumer, the communal spirit and shared commitment of enterprises from another age is sacrificed to other efficiencies. At the same time, the impersonal nature of such complex enterprises and their mechanization make third parties considerably more vulnerable to injury incidentally arising from the pursuit of the business. Business corporations are granted a personal identification in legal fiction to limit liability of the investors, but not to insulate the corporate entity itself from liability for the unfortunate consequences of its enterprise.

"Scope of employment" as a test for application of *respondeat superior* would be insufficient if it failed to encompass the duty of every enterprise to the social community which gives it life and contributes to its prosperity. * * *

The basis of *respondeat superior* has been correctly stated as "the desire to include in the costs of operation inevitable losses to third persons incident to carrying on an enterprise, and thus distribute the burden among those benefitted by the enterprise." [C]

The desirability of the result is readily discernible when an employee obviously engaged in his employer's business causes injury to a third party as a result of the employee's negligence. * * * Insurance is readily available for the employer so that the risk may be distributed among many like insureds paying premiums and the extra cost of doing business may be reflected in the price of the product.

The principle has been recognized by every state in the enactment of workmen's compensation laws whereby employees may recover compensation for injuries arising out of and in the course of their employment without reference to negligence on the part of employers. The costs to the employers are distributed to the public in the price of the product. * * *

The rule of *respondeat superior,* however, has not been extended to that length and is limited to requiring an enterprise to bear the loss incurred as a result of the employee's negligence. The acts of the employee need be so connected to his employment as to justify requiring that the employer bear that loss.

Although not usually enunciated as a basis for liability, in essence the enterprise may be regarded as a unit for tort as opposed to contract liability purposes. Employees' acts sufficiently connected with the enterprise are in effect considered as deeds of the enterprise itself. Where through negligence such acts cause injury to others it is appropriate that the enterprise bear the loss incurred.

Consistent with these considerations, it is apparent that no categorical statement can delimit the meaning of "scope of employment" once and for all times. Applicability of *respondeat superior* will depend primarily on the findings of fact in each case. In this particular case, Clay Fruit's employment contract required that he attend the sales conference. Each employee was left to his own resources for transportation, and many of the agents, including Fruit, chose to drive their own automobiles. By the admission of Equitable's agency manager, the scope of the conference included informal socializing as well as formal meetings. Social contact with the out-of-state guests was encouraged, and there is undisputed evidence that such associations were not limited to the conference headquarters * * *.

Because we find that fair-minded men in the exercise of reasonable judgment could differ as to whether Fruit's activities in returning from [the Waterfront Bar] to the convention headquarters were within the scope of his employment, we are not disposed to upset the jury's conclusion that liability for damages may be vicariously imputed to Equitable. * * *

The judgment below is affirmed.

NOTES AND QUESTIONS

1. The various rules that have imputed the negligence of one person to another in order to impose vicarious liability upon him as a defendant all have one thing in common. Each rule has involved an effort, sometimes openly declared by the court, more often unexpressed or tacitly assumed, to find a financially responsible defendant. The plaintiff is injured; his life may be utterly ruined if he is left without compensation. The person who has injured him is, or is likely to be, unable to pay that compensation. There is another who stands in such a relation to the wrongdoer that it is not unreasonable to make the responsibility his; and that other is more likely to be able to pay. So, without exonerating the wrongdoer, who remains liable to the plaintiff and will be required to indemnify the other to the extent that he is able to do so, the liability is imposed upon both.

In one sense this is strict liability, since the new person who is held liable is without any fault of his own and becomes liable only by reason of his relation to the actual wrongdoer. In another it is not. The foundation of vicarious liability is still negligence or other fault on the part of someone; and what the law does is to broaden the liability for that fault by imposing it upon an additional defendant who is himself without fault.

2. A prime example of vicarious liability is the doctrine of *respondeat superior* as discussed in the principal cases. It is triggered by the employee acting "within the scope of his employment." There have been literally thousands of cases

exploring this issue. See Prince v. Atchison, Topeka and Santa Fe Ry. Co., 76 Ill.App.3d 898, 395 N.E.2d 592, 32 Ill.Dec. 362 (1979), aff'd, 95 Ill.App.3d 856, 51 Ill.Dec. 323, 420 N.E.2d 737 (1981), where the court used a two-pronged test to determine whether an employee who went on a "frolic" had reentered the scope of his employment. (The phrase was first uttered in 1834 by Baron Parke in Joel v. Morrison, 6 C. & P. 501, 172 Eng.Rep. 1338 to label actions of the employee taken for the employee's own benefit and not for the benefit of the employer.) As the principal cases note, an employee's commuting to and from work is generally not considered within the scope of his employment. It is not always easy to predict the particular actions courts will find to be within the scope of employment. Mauk v. Wright, 367 F.Supp. 961 (M.D.Pa.1973), (football player on his own "free time" during training camp could still be deemed "within the scope of employment"); Harris v. Trojan Fireworks Co., 120 Cal.App.3d 157, 174 Cal.Rptr. 452 (1981), aff'd, 155 Cal.App.3d 830, 202 Cal.Rptr. 440 (1984) (intoxicated employee on way home from office Christmas party injured plaintiff); Edgewater Motels, Inc. v. Gatzke, 277 N.W.2d 11 (Minn.1979) (employee's negligent handling of cigarette led to plaintiff's injury); Valdiviez v. United States, 884 F.2d 196 (5th Cir.1989) (serviceman who donated blood contaminated with the AIDS virus while on duty was not acting in the scope of his employment and thus his employer, the United States, was not vicariously liable to the patient who contracted AIDS from a transfusion of contaminated blood).

3. Courts agree that the employer cannot insulate himself from liability by imposing safety rules or by instructing his employees to proceed carefully—no matter how specific and detailed his orders may be. See Limpus v. London Gen. Omnibus Co., 1 H. & C. 526, 158 Eng.Rep. 993 (1862); Cosgrove v. Ogden, 49 N.Y. 255 (1872).

4. *Vicarious Liability for Intentional Torts (Compensatory Damages). Respondeat superior* is not limited to negligent torts. An employer may be held liable for the intentional torts of his employee when they are reasonably connected with the employment and so within its "scope." Thus the master may be liable for assault and battery on the part of an employee trying to collect a debt, because the employee is acting in furtherance of the employer's business; and the same may be true of false imprisonment, malicious prosecution, defamation, deceit or intentional infliction of emotional distress. See Chuy v. Philadelphia Eagles Football Club, 595 F.2d 1265 (3d Cir.1979). But when the employee acts from purely personal motives, as for example out of a desire to revenge the seduction of his wife, or in a quarrel in no way connected with the master's interests, he is considered to have departed from his employment and the master is not liable. The courts have had difficulty applying this test. What should be the result: When a professional baseball pitcher intentionally "beans" a heckling spectator? Manning v. Grimsley, 643 F.2d 20 (1st Cir.1981). When an employee in a bar gives a customer a "hot foot"? Sullivan v. Crowley, 307 Mass. 189, 29 N.E.2d 769 (1940). When a gas station attendant shoots a customer who refused to pay cash? Jefferson v. Rose Oil Co. of Dixie, 232 So.2d 895 (La.App.1970). When a minister sexually assaults a parishioner? Byrd v. Faber, 57 Ohio St.3d 56, 565 N.E.2d 584 (1991); Gibson v. Brewer, 952 S.W.2d 239 (Mo.1997). When a health care provider sexually assaults a patient during treatment? Lisa M. v. Henry Mayo Newhall Mem. Hosp., 12 Cal.4th 291, 907 P.2d 358, 48 Cal.Rptr.2d 510 (1995); Porter v. Harshfield, 329 Ark. 130, 948 S.W.2d 83 (1997). When the college debate coach kills one of his students? Copeland v. Samford University, 686 So.2d 190 (Ala.1996). When a nurse, who learned that an acquaintance of her teenage daughter's had genital herpes through her employment at a

doctor's office, reveals this to her teenage daughter and the daughter tells all their friends. Jones v. Baisch, 40 F.3d 252 (8th Cir.1994) (applying Nebraska law).

5. *Vicarious Liability for Intentional Torts (Punitive Damages)*. A majority of courts follow the position of the Restatement (Second) of Torts § 909 (1965) that the principal (whether an individual or corporation) is liable only if the principal authorized or ratified the act, was reckless in employing or retaining the agent, or the agent was employed in a managerial capacity and was acting in the scope of employment. See Chapter 10, note 9, page 563. See also College Hospital, Inc. v. Superior Court, 8 Cal.4th 704, 882 P.2d 894, 34 Cal.Rptr.2d 898 (1994) (punitive damages not assessed on respondeat superior basis, evidence of fault by the employer itself must be shown.)

6. *Negligence in Hiring or Retention of Employee*. To be distinguished are cases in which the employer is liable for its own negligence in hiring or retaining an employee without adequately checking the employee's background or failing to properly train the employee. Suppose the employer retains an employee who had previously shot a patron of employer's discotheque. Later the employee shoots another patron. Should the employer be liable? See Freeman v. Bell, 366 So.2d 197 (La.App.1978). See also F & T Co. v. Woods, 92 N.M. 697, 594 P.2d 745 (1979) (employer retained an alleged rapist to deliver and repair home appliances and was sued by a rape victim); Glomb v. Ginosky, 366 Pa.Super. 206, 530 A.2d 1362 (1987) (parents liable for retaining babysitter despite child's bruises and fears). What if the employer knew the employee had been convicted of a felony and hired him as a part of a rehabilitation program?

7. In some situations, a master can seek indemnity from either a servant or an independent contractor who has assets of his own. See pages 378–387.

2. INDEPENDENT CONTRACTORS

Murrell v. Goertz

Court of Appeals of Oklahoma, 1979.
597 P.2d 1223.

REYNOLDS, JUDGE. Mrs. C.L. Murrell, plaintiff in the trial court, appeals the order sustaining the motion for summary judgment in favor of co-defendant Oklahoma Publishing Company (appellee), in a suit for damages resulting from an alleged assault and battery by co-defendant Bruce Goertz.

On August 27, 1976, Bruce Goertz was making monthly collections for the delivery of appellant's morning newspaper, the Daily Oklahoman, which is published by appellee. Appellant questioned Goertz concerning damage to appellant's screen door caused by the newspaper carrier throwing the newspaper into it. An argument ensued culminating in appellant slapping Goertz who in turn struck appellant. As a result thereof, appellant was allegedly injured, requiring medical treatment and subsequent hospitalization. Appellant filed suit in the District Court of Oklahoma County seeking a total of $52,500 for past and future medical expenses, pain and suffering, and exemplary damages.

Appellant's petition contends that Goertz was a servant of appellee either by agreement between the co-defendants, or by appellee creating the apparent belief in appellant that Goertz was a servant by allowing Goertz to deliver the paper, advertise that product, and to collect for accounts due. Both appellee and Goertz answered denying that Goertz was appellee's servant. * * *

The line of demarcation between an independent contractor and a servant is not clearly drawn. An independent contractor is one who engaged to perform a certain service for another according to his own methods and manner, free from control and direction of his employer in all matters connected with the performance of the service except as to the result thereof. [C] The parties agree that the decisive test for determining whether a person is an employee or an independent contractor is the right to control the physical details of the work. [C] * * *

Appellant contends that the distribution of papers and the collection of money therefor is an integral part of appellee's business. Appellant cites the following factors as indicative of the high degree of control appellee possesses over the physical details of the work: ultimate control over the territorial boundaries of Goertz's route; appellee set a standard policy that paper deliveries be completed by 6 a.m.; appellee set policy that all papers were to be held by rubber bands; customers who were missed by the carrier called appellee to report it; complaints concerning the service were lodged with appellee; and new subscribers called appellee to initiate newspaper service.

Appellee submits that the affidavit of Russell Westbrook and Goertz's deposition reveal that Goertz had no contact with appellee. Westbrook stated that he was an independent newspaper distributor for appellee and that he employed Bruce Goertz as an independent carrier salesman. Westbrook further stated that Goertz was responsible only to him for the delivery of the newspapers and was in no way under the supervision, dominion, and control of appellee. By the terms of Westbrook's contract, he was an independent contractor and likewise not subject to the supervision, dominion, and control of appellee as to the manner and method of performing his job. Appellee further cites the statements of Westbrook and Goertz that Goertz was collecting money for Westbrook at the time of the incident with appellant, and that appellee received money only from Westbrook.

From a review of the record we conclude that the evidence is reasonably susceptible of but one inference. Bruce Goertz was hired as an independent carrier salesman by his friend Russell Westbrook, who was himself an independent contractor. Appellee had no input into the decision to hire Goertz and had no knowledge of his employment. Goertz had no direct contract with appellee in his business operations. While appellee established certain policies and standards to which all distributors and carriers were to adhere, such policies and standards do not rise to that level of supervision, dominion, and control over Goertz's day to day activities as to make him appellee's servant.

Affirmed.

NOTES AND QUESTIONS

1.   According to a "general rule" that developed both in English and American law, one who arranged for work to be done by an independent contractor is not vicariously liable for the contractor's torts. The distinction between a servant and an independent contractor has been said to lie in the fact that the latter does the work on his own time, in his own way, and under no one's directions but his own, so that the employer has no control or right of control over the manner in which it is done. It is therefore to be regarded as the contractor's own enterprise, and he, rather than the one who retained his services, is the proper party to be charged with the risk. Also, no doubt, there is in the picture, although not often expressed, the fact that, taken as a class, independent contractors are in the main financially responsible parties, at least to a far greater extent than employees.

2.   Should the state be vicariously liable for the actions of foster parents when a foster child is injured due to the negligence of the foster parents? Mitzner v. State, 257 Kan. 258, 891 P.2d 435 (1995) (foster parents are independent contractors and state is not liable). Should the state be vicariously liable for the medical malpractice of those with whom it arranged to provide medical care to prisoners? Herbert v. District of Columbia, 716 A.2d 196 (D.C.App.1998) (state not liable for actions of independent contractors because duty may be delegated).

3.   The "general rule" remains. But so many exceptional situations have been recognized in which vicarious liability is imposed, that it has been observed that "the rule is now primarily important as a preamble to the catalog of its exceptions." Pacific Fire Ins. Co. v. Kenny Boiler & Mfg. Co., 201 Minn. 500, 277 N.W. 226 (1937).

Maloney v. Rath

Supreme Court of California, 1968.
69 Cal.2d 442, 445 P.2d 513, 71 Cal.Rptr. 897.

[Defendant's automobile collided with a car driven by plaintiff. The accident was caused by a brake failure. The trial court found that defendant had no reason to know the brakes were defective. Three months prior to the accident, defendant had her brakes overhauled by a mechanic, Peter Evanchik. The trial court determined that Evanchik's negligent repair effort was the cause of the accident and rendered a judgment in favor of defendant. Plaintiff appealed.

The Supreme Court of California first stated that it would not hold a motorist strictly liable for damage caused by brake failure. Although the state vehicle code required that brakes be maintained "in good working order," a failure to comply could be excused by the owner's exercise of "ordinary prudence," and the court found that defendant had met that standard of care. It then discussed the question of whether defendant vehicle owner could delegate the responsibility of making a brake repair to an independent contractor.]

TRAYNOR, JUSTICE. * * * Unlike strict liability, a nondelegable duty operates, not as a substitute for liability based on negligence, but to assure that when a negligently caused harm occurs, the injured party will be compensated by the person whose activity caused the harm and who may therefore properly be held liable for the negligence of his agent, whether his agent was an employee or an independent contractor. To the extent that recognition of nondelegable duties tends to insure that there will be [a] financially responsible defendant available to compensate for the negligent harms caused by that defendant's activity, it ameliorates the need for strict liability to secure compensation. * * *

[W]e have found nondelegable duties in a wide variety of situations and have recognized that the rules set forth in the Restatement of Torts with respect to such duties are generally in accord with California law. Such duties include those imposed by a public authority as a condition of granting a franchise [cc], the duty of a condemning agent to protect a severed parcel from damage [c], the duty of a general contractor to construct a building safely [c], the duty to exercise due care when an " * * * independent contractor is employed to do work which the employer should recognize as necessarily creating a condition involving an unreasonable risk of bodily harm to others unless special precautions are taken" [cc], the duty of landowners to maintain their property in a reasonably safe condition [cc], and to comply with applicable safety ordinances [cc], and the duty of employers and suppliers to comply with the safety provisions of the Labor Code [cc].

Restatement (Second) of Torts § 423 provides that "One who carries on an activity which threatens a grave risk of serious bodily harm or death unless the instrumentalities used are carefully * * * maintained, and who employs an independent contractor to * * * maintain such instrumentalities, is subject to the same liability for physical harm caused by the negligence of the contractor in * * * maintaining such instrumentalities as though the employer had himself done the work of * * * maintenance." Section 424 provides that "One who by statute or by administrative regulation is under a duty to provide specified safeguards or precautions for the safety of others is subject to liability to the others for whose protection the duty is imposed for harm caused by the failure of a contractor employed by him to provide such safeguards or precautions." Both of these sections point to a nondelegable duty in this case. The statutory provisions regulating the maintenance and equipment of automobiles constitute express legislative recognition of the fact that improperly maintained motor vehicles threaten "a grave risk of serious bodily harm or death." The responsibility for minimizing that risk or compensating for the failure to do so properly rests with the person who owns and operates the vehicle. He is the party primarily to be benefitted by its use; he selects the contractor and is free to insist upon one who is financially responsible and to demand indemnity from him; the cost of his liability insurance that distributes the risk is properly attributable to his activities; and the discharge of the duty to exercise reasonable care in the maintenance of his vehicle is of the utmost importance to the public.

In the present case it is undisputed that the accident was caused by a failure of defendant's brakes that resulted from her independent contractor's negligence in overhauling or in thereafter inspecting the brakes. Since her duty to maintain her brakes in compliance with the provisions of the Vehicle Code is nondelegable, the fact that the brake failure was the result of her independent contractor's negligence is no defense.

The judgment and the order denying the motion for judgment notwithstanding the verdict on the issue of liability are reversed and the case is remanded to the trial court for a new trial on the issue of damages only.

NOTES AND QUESTIONS

1. How does the imposition of liability on the theory of a nondelegable duty differ from strict liability?

2. There are several situations where the selection of an independent contractor will not insulate the party choosing the independent contractor from liability:

A. *Negligence in the Selection of the Contractor.* If a company is negligent in selecting the contractor or in giving improper directions or equipment or in failing to stop any unnecessarily dangerous practices that come to its attention, the company will be held liable for its own negligence, which has combined with that of the contractor. See Posner v. Paul's Trucking Serv., Inc., 380 F.2d 757 (1st Cir.1967). This, of course, is not vicarious liability at all, but ordinary concurrent negligence.

B. *Nondelegable Duties.* There are certain responsibilities that courts will not permit an employer to delegate to an independent contractor. *Maloney* contains a broad, but not totally complete, list of examples. There is no obvious criterion by which it can be determined whether a duty is "delegable" or not. In the last analysis, the cases represent *ad hoc* decisions that, as a matter of public policy, one cannot avoid particular responsibilities by hiring someone else to discharge them, because of the importance of the duty. See Westby v. Itasca County, 290 N.W.2d 437 (Minn.1980), where the court held the county vicariously liable for an independent contractor's failure to clear the road of mud from an exploded beaver dam. See also Jackson v. Power, 743 P.2d 1376 (Alaska 1987) (general acute care hospital's duty to provide emergency room care nondelegable and therefore facility liable for actions of independent physician in emergency room). Simmons v. Tuomey Regional Med. Ctr., 330 S.C. 115, 498 S.E.2d 408 (App. 1998) (duty to emergency room patients is absolute and is incapable of being delegated). But see Baptist Memorial Hospital System v. Sampson, 969 S.W.2d 945 (Tex.1998) (declining invitation of court of appeals to find a nondelegable duty for hospital emergency room); Broussard v. United States, 989 F.2d 171 (5th Cir.1993) (in F.T.C.A. case, hospital not liable for actions of emergency room physicians who were independent contractors), and Estates of Milliron v. Francke, 243 Mont. 200, 793 P.2d 824 (1990) (no nondelegable duty to provide radiology services).

C. *Apparent Authority.* One who expressly or impliedly represents that another party is his servant or agent may be held vicariously liable for the latter's negligent acts to the extent of that representation. This result may occur even though the negligent party is an independent contractor or even when there is no employment relationship whatsoever between the negligent actor and the party making the representation.

This theory, called apparent authority, apparent agency, or agency by estoppel, allows an injured party who reasonably relies on the representation to hold the party who made the misrepresentation liable. See Restatement (Second) of Agency, §§ 228, 229 (1957). The theory has been utilized to hold franchisors vicariously liable for the negligent conduct of their independent contractor franchisees. See Singleton v. International Dairy Queen, Inc., 332 A.2d 160 (Del.1975); Wood v. Holiday Inns, Inc., 508 F.2d 167 (5th Cir.1975); Gizzi v. Texaco, Inc., 437 F.2d 308 (3d Cir.), cert. denied, 404 U.S. 829 (1971) (Texaco's advertising and other representations sufficient for a jury to determine that the company had vested "apparent authority" in a dealer who sold a van on his own behalf). The theory also has been applied in cases holding hospitals vicariously liable for the medical malpractice of independent physicians practicing medicine on their premises. See, e.g., Seneris v. Haas, 45 Cal.2d 811, 291 P.2d 915 (1955) ("record reveals defendant did nothing to put [patient] on notice that the X-ray laboratory was not an integral part of the institution, and it cannot seriously be contended that [patient] should have inquired whether the individual actors who examined him were employees"); Clark v. Southview Hosp. & Family Health Ctr., 68 Ohio St.3d 435, 444, 628 N.E.2d 46, 53 (1994) ("A hospital may be held liable under the doctrine of agency by estoppel for the negligence of independent medical practitioners practicing in the hospital if it holds itself out to the public as a provider of medical services and in the absence of notice or knowledge to the contrary, the patient looks to the hospital, as opposed to the individual practitioner, to provide competent medical care.") But see Raglin v. HMO Illinois, Inc., 230 Ill.App.3d 642, 595 N.E.2d 153, 172 Ill.Dec. 90 (1992) (HMO not vicariously liable for the medical malpractice of independent physicians with which it had contracted to provide health services because HMO had no apparent authority over physicians); Baptist Memorial Hospital System v. Sampson, 969 S.W.2d 945 (Tex.1998) (emergency room patient failed to establish apparent authority because written consent form signed by patient before treatment explained that all physicians were independent contractors and not employees of hospital); O'Banner v. McDonald's Corp., 173 Ill.2d 208, 670 N.E.2d 632 (1996) (customer who was injured in slip and fall accident in bathroom did not show the justifiable reliance necessary to hold franchisor liable through apparent agency). See generally, Reed, Expanding Theories of Hospital Liability: A Review, 21 J. Health & Hosp. L. 217 (1988).

D. *"Inherently" or "Intrinsically" Dangerous Activities.* Originally this came from Bower v. Peate, [1876] 1 Q.B.D. 321, where the foundation of plaintiff's building was undermined by an excavation. It never has been limited to activities (such as blasting) that involve an extraordinarily high degree of danger and are classified as "abnormally dangerous" for the purposes of imposing strict liability on the actor. See Chapter 14. Rather, the exception is applicable when the activity involves a peculiar risk of harm that calls for more than ordinary precaution. This would be the case, for example, if the contractor were engaged to transport giant logs, six feet in diameter, over the highway, in which case an obvious special danger to others arises unless the logs are properly anchored and secured. Risley v. Lenwell, 129 Cal.App.2d 608, 277 P.2d 897 (1954). Or to mark traffic lines on a busy street, where special precautions are required to keep traffic proceeding in another lane. Van Arsdale v. Hollinger, 68 Cal.2d 245, 437 P.2d 508, 66 Cal.Rptr. 20 (1968). Or to sell ice cream to small children from an ice cream vending truck on a busy street. Wilson v. Good Humor Corp., 757 F.2d 1293 (D.C.Cir.1985).

Collateral Negligence. This exception does not apply when the independent contractor's negligence is deemed "collateral" to the risk: in other words, not recognizable in advance as particularly likely to occur or as calling for special precaution. This is sometimes referred to as the "peculiar risk" exception. Clausen v. R.W. Gibert Construction Co., 309 N.W.2d 462 (Iowa 1981). The question of what is a collateral risk cannot be answered mechanically. For example, how should a court classify negligence on the part of contractor's employee in operating a wrecking crane? See Garczynski v. Darin & Armstrong Co., 420 F.2d 941 (6th Cir.1970). This general topic is well discussed in Smith, Collateral Negligence, 25 Minn.L.Rev. 399 (1941).

E.   *"Illegal Activities."* One who contracts for performance of an illegal act is vicariously liable for any damage even if the agent is an independent contractor. See King v. Loessin, 572 S.W.2d 87 (Tex.Civ.App.1978).

3.   JOINT ENTERPRISE

Popejoy v. Steinle

Supreme Court of Wyoming, 1991.
820 P.2d 545.

GOLDEN, JUSTICE. * * *On the morning of May 8, 1986, Connie Steinle, accompanied by her seven-year-old daughter and a niece, left the family ranch for Douglas, Wyoming. The purpose of the trip was to purchase a calf for the daughter to raise on the ranch. While en route to Douglas, the truck Connie was driving collided with a vehicle driven by Ronald Popejoy. Connie died as a result of the accident and Ronald sustained injuries initially diagnosed as a muscle strain. As a result of his injuries, Ronald received outpatient medical treatment at a local hospital. * * *

Approximately fifteen months after the accident Ronald Popejoy began experiencing severe pain in his neck and back. Because other treatments failed to correct the problem, he underwent two separate neurosurgeries to fuse cervical vertebrae. Following the second surgical procedure, Ronald attempted unsuccessfully to reopen Connie Steinle's estate which had been probated and closed more than a year earlier. The Popejoys then filed a creditor's claim against the estate [of Connie's husband, William,] as he had died in the interim following Connie's death. After the Popejoys' creditor's claim was rejected, they filed a complaint against the personal [the] representatives of William's estate. The complaint was premised on the theory that William and Connie Steinle were engaged in a joint venture when Connie embarked on her May 8, 1986 "business trip" to pick up the daughter's calf.

* * *

[The trial court granted the Estate's motion for summary judgment, finding that a careful reading of the depositions and affidavits submitted to support the motion showed that Mr. Steinle had no financial or other interest in the purpose of the trip to town, such that vicarious liability could be imposed upon him based on the alleged negligence of his wife. This appeal followed.]

The Popejoys seek to impute Connie Steinle's alleged negligence to her husband William's estate by claiming that the Steinles were engaged in a joint venture relationship at the time of the accident. "The burden of establishing the existence of a joint venture is upon the party asserting that the relationship exists." [Cc] Consequently, the Popejoys are required to demonstrate each of the elements of a joint venture relationship in order to prevail. They must also show that the joint venture relationship existed at the time of Connie's alleged negligent conduct. [C]

This court has never set forth a specific "test" of elements necessary to prove existence of a joint venture. The parties in this case and many courts from other jurisdictions frequently use the terms "joint venture" and "joint enterprise" interchangeably and the two terms are conceptually closely related. It has been stated that "[t]he term joint enterprise is often used interchangeably with joint venture, and it has been stated that when the term joint enterprise is used to describe a business or commercial undertaking, no significant differences between the terms may be drawn." 48A C.J.S. *Joint Ventures* § 3 at 395 (1981).

* * *

Although the Restatement [(Second) of Torts § 491 comment c at 548 (1965)] does not define elements of a joint venture, it does define the four elements of a joint enterprise as:

(1) an agreement, express or implied, among the members of the group; (2) a common purpose to be carried out by the group; (3) a community of pecuniary interest in that purpose, among the members; and (4) an equal right to a voice in the direction of the enterprise, which gives an equal right of control.

Id.

In *Holliday* [v. Bannister, 741 P.2d 89 (Wyo.1987)], we considered among several issues a claim that a father and son were engaged in a joint enterprise while together on a hunting trip. The plaintiff in *Holliday,* as personal representative for the estate of a hunter accidently shot and killed by the son, asserted that the father was vicariously liable for his son's negligence.

In Part II of the *Holliday* opinion and the cases and authorities cited therein, we emphasized the commercial and profit motive aspects of the "community of pecuniary interest" element of a joint enterprise or joint venture relationship. For example, in citing *Easter v. McNabb,* 97 Idaho 180, 541 P.2d 604 (1975), this court said:

[T]he Idaho Supreme Court concluded that, by limiting the doctrine of joint enterprise to those having a business or pecuniary purpose, it avoided the imposition of a basically commercial concept, derived from the law of partnership and principles of agency, to non-commercial situations which are more often matters of friendly or family cooperation and accommodation.

Holliday, 741 P.2d at 94. [Cc] We then concluded by stating:

We are convinced by the foregoing line of authority that the pecuniary, commercial and business aspects of a joint enterprise are the missing elements necessary to create vicarious liability in the appellee. * * * There was absent the contract, a profit motive and equal right of control found in and required by the business relationship of a joint enterprise. Any attempt to warp such a relationship to fit a social event would be unbecoming of the law.

Holliday, 741 P.2d at 94 (footnote omitted). Thus, in affirming summary judgment for the defendant father in *Holliday,* this court concluded that in addition to other elements of a joint enterprise the hunting trip lacked the requisite element of business, commercial or profit motive and, therefore, summary judgment was proper. *Holliday,* 741 P.2d at 94[.] [Cc]

The Popejoys' claim in this case is premised on a theory of joint venture and the contention that William and Connie Steinle were engaged in securing an appreciable business asset for their family business at the time of the accident. In the type of business activity being alleged by the Popejoys, there are no significant differences between a joint venture and a joint enterprise. Thus, in determining the existence or nonexistence of a joint venture relationship in this case, we apply the same four-pronged joint enterprise test in *Holliday,* 741 P.2d at 93.

In support of its * * * motion for summary judgment, the Estate submitted several affidavits, depositions and other materials. The Steinle daughter who was accompanying her mother at the time of the accident and who was the intended recipient of the calf they were on their way to buy submitted an affidavit stating that her father did not ordinarily have any ownership interest in the cattle that she, her sisters and mother raised and owned. She also stated that she, her mother and sisters were primarily responsible for caring for the "pets" and other domestic animals raised on the ranch.

Carl Steinle, William's brother and one of two personal representatives of the Estate, submitted an affidavit indicating that Connie and the Steinle daughters regularly kept numerous farm animals as their own and that William would not have had any interest in the calf that was to be purchased. Further, he stated that the purpose of the trip was to purchase a calf for the daughter to raise as her own. A second Steinle daughter also submitted an affidavit confirming the purpose of the trip.

Other materials submitted with the motion supplemented the affidavits described above and included the affidavit and deposition of Roger Wesnitzer, a certified public accountant. After reviewing Steinle tax records, ranch journal books, bank records, livestock sales receipts and the other affidavits and depositions, Wesnitzer stated that other livestock raised by the Steinle daughters in the past had been given directly to the children by the parents. Further, he stated that while William Steinle bore the costs of raising such livestock on his ranch, sale proceeds went directly to the children. Similar "nonranch" cattle owned by the Steinle daughters in the past had been separately identified by brands owned by the daughters and sale proceeds had gone directly to the children. He stated that William and Connie did not share in any portion of livestock sale proceeds of their daughters' cattle. He concluded that it was his professional opinion that the trip in which Connie was killed and Ronald was injured did not involve a joint venture between William and Connie Steinle.

* * *

Taken as a whole, this evidence satisfied the threshold requirement of establishing the nonexistence of any genuine issue of material fact as to whether William and Connie Steinle were engaged in a joint venture at the time of Connie's accident. "The burden then shifts to the party opposing the motion for summary judgment to present specific facts showing the existence of a genuine issue of material fact." In the Matter of the Estate of Zona R. Loomis, 810 P.2d 126, 128 (Wyo.1991). Thus, we examine the affidavits, deposition excerpts and other materials submitted by the Popejoys in opposition to the motion for summary judgment to determine whether the evidence supports existence of the requisite elements of the joint venture test.

In attempting to demonstrate existence of a joint venture relationship, the Popejoys relied extensively on the affidavits provided by Ted Grooms, a certified public accountant. Grooms stated in his first affidavit that William and Connie Steinle did not separate their income and expenses with respect to their ranching activities and that Connie did much of the work around the ranch because of William's poor health. In his second affidavit, Grooms maintained that after reviewing all the depositions, affidavits, business and tax records submitted by the Steinles for the years 1982–1986 he was convinced that William and Connie were involved in a joint venture at the time of Connie's trip on May 8, 1986. Grooms stated that William's eventual purchase of the calf for his daughter a week after the accident, his efforts in raising and selling the calf, and the fact that the calf bore the brand of the daughter's older sister led him to the conclusion that a joint venture relationship existed between Connie and William. Finally, and significantly, he stated that it was his understanding that only a pecuniary interest and not an interest in profit was needed to show existence of a joint venture.

Noticeably missing from Grooms' testimony is any evidence that proceeds from the sale of the calf that Connie and the daughter were on their way to purchase on May 8, 1986, would not have gone solely to the daughter. Along the same lines, he found no evidence that proceeds from the actual sale of the calf that was eventually purchased for the daughter following the accident went to anyone other than the daughter. Thus, it appears that only the daughter had an actual pecuniary or financial interest in the profits of the sale of the calf that was to be purchased at the time of the accident.

The record in this case shows that Connie's trip to Douglas to purchase a calf for the couple's seven-year-old daughter was a family undertaking.
* * *

In *Holliday,* this court adopted and applied a narrow definition of joint enterprise. *See, e.g.,* W. Keeton, *Prosser and Keaton on the Law of Torts* § 72 (5th ed. 1984). By limiting the application of the doctrine to a venture having a distinct business or pecuniary purpose, we avoid the imposition of a basically commercial concept upon relationships not having this characteristic. [C] With our decision in this case, we reaffirm our holding in *Holliday* and continue to restrict application of the joint venture/joint enterprise doctrine in Wyoming.

After a careful review of the record, we hold that the Popejoys failed to demonstrate the existence of a genuine issue of material fact which would preclude summary judgment as a matter of law. William and Connie Steinle were not engaged in a joint venture when Connie attempted to drive to Douglas to purchase the calf for their daughter.

The decision of the trial court is affirmed.

NOTES AND QUESTIONS

1. The joint enterprise theory was developed by American courts to impose liability vicariously upon one person who is engaged in the same activity with another person committing the tortious act. The Restatement (Second) of Torts § 491, comment *c*, quoted in the principal case, sets out four elements required for liability to be imposed. Because of these elements, each member of the joint enterprise is held to be the agent of the other; each may therefore be held liable for the acts of the other.

2. This theory as a means of imposing vicarious liability is most commonly applied in automobile accident cases. It has been applied occasionally in other contexts. See, e.g., Cullinan v. Tetrault, 123 Me. 302, 122 A. 770 (1923) (one party purchases liquor for a party); see Shell Oil Co. v. Prestidge, 249 F.2d 413 (9th Cir.1957) (parties prospecting for oil). It generally does not apply to parties who take pleasure trips or other nonbusiness journeys together. Fugate v. Galvin, 84 Ill.App.3d 573, 406 N.E.2d 19, 22, 40 Ill.Dec. 318 (1980) (travel arrangements to meet a mutual friend not a joint venture); Lovell v. Brock, 330 Ark. 206, 952 S.W.2d 161 (1997) (hunting party). As in the principal case, joint ownership without more usually is not enough to impose vicarious liability; there must be some business purpose involved. The person subjected to liability also must have a right to control operation of the vehicle, even when there is a common purpose for the trip and a community of business interest, such as when parties commute to and from work. See Spradley v. Houser, 247 S.C. 208, 146 S.E.2d 621 (1966).

4. BAILMENTS

Shuck v. Means

Supreme Court of Minnesota, 1974.
302 Minn. 93, 226 N.W.2d 285.

KELLY, JUSTICE. * * * On March 27, 1967, an automobile owned by Hertz, leased to one George A. Codling, and driven by Means, collided with an automobile in which plaintiff Shuck was a passenger. Means was uninsured at the time of the accident and the parties later stipulated that he had been negligent. * * * [These facts present for] our consideration only the following issue: Whether a car rental agency is liable under the Minnesota Safety Responsibility Act when one of its cars is leased by one person, but operated by another in violation of the rental agreement.

The applicable owner-consent statute, Minn.St.1965, § 170.54, provides as follows: "Whenever any motor vehicle * * * shall be operated upon any public street or highway of this state, by any person other than the owner, with the consent of the owner, express or implied, the operator thereof shall in case of accident, be deemed the agent of the owner of such motor vehicle in the operation thereof."

This provision, enacted as part of the Safety Responsibility Act, was intended to make the owners of motor vehicles liable to those injured by their operation where no such liability would otherwise exist, giving such injured persons more certainty of recovery by encouraging owners to obtain appropriate liability insurance. And to that end, the statute is to be given a liberal construction. [C]

This court, in Foster v. Bock, 229 Minn. 428, 39 N.W.2d 862 (1949), was asked to decide whether a vehicle owner was liable under the owner-consent statute where a subpermittee was driving at the time of the accident, the permittee remaining in the vehicle only as a passenger. In imposing liability on the owner, the court quoted with approval the following language used in Kerns v. Lewis, 246 Mich. 423, 425, 224 N.W. 647, 648 (1929) by the Supreme Court of Michigan in construing a similar statute:

" * * * Does the essential consent mentioned in the statute relate to the *driver*, or to the vehicle, 'being driven'? The statute makes the owner liable if the 'motor vehicle is being driven with his or her express or implied consent or knowledge,' and we cannot read into it the restriction that the particular driver must be known by and his driving consented to by the owner." 229 Minn. 435, 39 N.W.2d 866.

In Granley v. Crandall, 288 Minn. 310, 180 N.W.2d 190 (1970), the restriction referred to in the above quotation was sought to be expressly imposed by the owner. The court held that notwithstanding a parent's explicit instructions to her child forbidding the operation of her automobile by anyone else, the parent is deemed to have given her consent under Minn.St. 170.54 when the car is driven by a third person with the child's permission and under its direction if the child is actually a passenger in the car.

The court [has gone] a step further in * * * holding that the presence of the permittee as a passenger in an automobile being driven by a subpermittee is not a necessary condition to liability of the owner under § 170.54.

Proving lack of consent in these situations requires a strong showing that the car was being used by the permittee without the owner's knowledge and contrary to his explicit instructions, or that the subpermittee was driving without the permission of the first permittee under conditions which approach the status of conversion or a theft. [C]

Neither of these situations is shown by the facts of the instant case, and the trial court's finding that implied consent existed is justified under the aforementioned cases unless the holdings of those cases are confined to situations involving permittees who are minor children of the owners. Such a narrow application of those cases would be inappropriate in light of the purpose of the owner-consent statute and the commercial nature of the transaction here involved.

Accordingly, the trial court was correct in concluding that Means was operating the vehicle with the implied consent of Hertz.

Affirmed.

NOTES AND QUESTIONS

1.   Under the common law in most states, a bailment does not make a bailor vicariously liable for the acts of the bailee in the use of the chattel. Suppose you loan your car to a friend at law school, who gets drunk with a stranger—the stranger robs the friend and steals your car. The thief then causes an accident. Are you liable as owner of the car? See Cherokee Enterprises, Inc. v. Rogers, 451 So.2d 553 (Fla.App.1984).

2.   The common law rule on bailments has been altered by decision and, as in the principal case, by statute with respect to automobiles.

A. *Presumption That Owner Controls the Vehicle.* Some older cases held that the mere presence of the owner in the car establishes his right of control over the driving, so that the owner becomes responsible for the acts of the driver as if the driver were the agent of the owner. See, for example, Boker v. Luebbe, 198 Neb. 282, 252 N.W.2d 297 (1977). In a number of states courts have retreated from this position even when the parties are close relatives because it is unrealistic and may encourage dangerous back-seat driving, Bauer v. Johnson, 79 Ill.2d 324, 38 Ill.Dec. 149, 403 N.E.2d 237 (1980); Reed v. Hinderland, 135 Ariz. 213, 660 P.2d 464 (1983) (the mere presence of the owner in an automobile driven by another does not create any presumption of a master-servant relationship or joint enterprise; existence of such a relationship must be proved by the party asserting it in the same manner as any other issue in the case). This does not relieve the owner of a duty to object to or otherwise interfere with negligent driving as soon as becoming aware of it. The breach of that duty would trigger liability based on primary negligence on the part of the driver, not vicarious liability. See Sherman v. Korff, 353 Mich. 387, 91 N.W.2d 485 (1958).

B. *The Family Purpose Doctrine.* The "family purpose" or "family car" doctrine is a court-created legal fiction by which the owner of an automobile is held vicariously liable when the car is negligently driven by a member of the immediate household. The fiction is predicated on the assumption that the driver is implementing a "family purpose," even if the driver is only using the automobile for his own pleasure or convenience. The car must be driven with the permission of the owner, but this may be inferred from very general circumstances. The doctrine has many nuances, exceptions and complications. In general, it is limited to automobiles, but the court in Stewart v. Stephens, 225 Ga. 185, 166 S.E.2d 890 (1969), extended it to a "family motorboat." Who should be primarily liable as between a father or mother? What if the mother has custody of the child? See Flannigan v. Valliant, 400 So.2d 225 (La.App.1981), cert. denied, 406 So.2d 611 (1981).

C. *Automobile Consent Statutes.* Many states have statutes that make the owner of an automobile vicariously liable for injury caused by the negligent operation of the vehicle. Problems of statutory construction arising under those statutes include what constitutes "consent"; what happens when the scope of the consent is exceeded; and whether "owner" includes conditional sellers who have legal title but no power to control the vehicle. What if a parent co-signed on a car loan but was not listed as a co-owner on the title?

3.   The need for automobile consent statutes has been considerably lessened because of the "omnibus clause" in standard automobile liability insurance policies. This clause provides that liability insurance for the designated automobile applies to the named insured, any member of the insured's household, and to any person using the automobile with the insured's permission, provided the use was within the scope of permission. How does this differ from the consent statutes?

4.   Do the policies that support an application of vicarious liability to owners of automobiles apply to any other bailors? Some attorneys have made enterprising, but unsuccessful, attempts to apply the same rule to private aircraft. See McCord v. Dixie Aviation Corp., 450 F.2d 1129 (10th Cir.1971); Broadway v. Webb, 462 F.Supp. 429 (W.D.N.C.1977) (summarizing cases). See also, McDaniel v. Ritter, 556 So.2d 303 (Miss.1989) (in granting summary judgment to owner, court notes nothing in Tennessee law that would change the common law rule of no vicarious liability for bailor).

5.   There are other, occasional, instances of statutes creating vicarious liability. Some states have imposed the liability on owners of private aircraft. See Kreindler, Aviation Accident Law § 4.02 (1993). Some states impose vicarious liability on municipalities for certain acts committed by a mob through so-called "anti-lynching" statutes. Finally, some states impose vicarious liability on parents for certain torts committed by their children.

6.   *Distinguish Negligent Entrustment.* All of the vicarious liability circumstances should be carefully distinguished from cases in which the plaintiff is arguing that the employer/owner/bailor/hospital was itself negligent in some way. Just as the employer may be negligent in hiring an employee (see note 6, page 664), the owner/bailor may be liable in entrusting the chattel to the bailee. This is frequently referred to as "negligent entrustment." See Wery v. Seff, 136 Ohio St. 307, 16 Ohio Ops. 445, 25 N.E.2d 692 (1940) (unlicensed minor driver); Snowhite v. State, 243 Md. 291, 221 A.2d 342 (1966) (owner knew driver was frequently intoxicated); Kahlenberg v. Goldstein, 290 Md. 477, 431 A.2d 76 (1981) (father funded purchase of automobile for son whom he knew to be an irresponsible driver); Vince v. Wilson, 151 Vt. 425, 561 A.2d 103 (1989) (evidence that defendant who provided funding to grandnephew to purchase car knew he did not have driver's license, had failed driver's test several times, and abused alcohol and other drugs was sufficient to get negligent entrustment case to jury). This may occur not only with automobiles, but also with other chattels. See McBerry v. Ivie, 116 Ga.App. 808, 159 S.E.2d 108 (1967) (shotgun given to a young child); Miles v. Harrison, 223 Ga. 352, 155 S.E.2d 6 (1967) (power mower); LaFaso v. LaFaso, 126 Vt. 90, 223 A.2d 814 (1966) (cigarette lighter).

5.   Imputed Contributory Negligence

Smalich v. Westfall

Supreme Court of Pennsylvania, 1970.
440 Pa. 409, 269 A.2d 476.

Eagen, Justice. Two automobiles collided in Westmoreland County. One of the vehicles, owned by Julia Smalich, was operated by Felix Rush Westfall. Julia Smalich [was a] passenger in this automobile at the time. The other vehicle involved was operated by Stephanna Louise Blank. Julia Smalich suffered injuries in the collision which caused her death. * * *

The estate of Julia Smalich sought damages [against both Westfall and Blank] in both a wrongful death action and a survival action. * * *

The trial jury found that Westfall's negligent operation of the Smalich automobile was a proximate cause of the collision. That the trial record amply supports this finding is not and cannot be questioned. After trial, the court en banc ruled that, under the facts, the contributory negligence of Westfall must be imputed to the owner of the automobile [Smalich] as a matter of law and this precluded recovery by the Smalich Estate against defendant Blank. * * *

[A] plaintiff ought not to be barred from recovery against a negligent defendant by the contributory negligence of a third person unless the relationship between the plaintiff and the third person is such that the plaintiff would be vicariously liable as a defendant for the negligent acts of the third person: Prosser, The Law of Torts § 73 (3d ed. 1964). See also, Restatement (Second) Torts §§ 485, 486 and 491 (1965). Placed in the context of this case, a driver's negligence will not be imputed to a passenger, unless the relationship between them is such that the passenger would be vicariously liable as a defendant for the driver's negligent acts * * *. The relationship between the passenger and the driver is therefore a very critical one, worthy of careful analysis and consideration. * * * We therefore now state unequivocally that only a master-servant relationship or a finding of joint enterprise will justify the imputation of contributory negligence.

We have serious doubt that, in the ordinary situation, the mutual understanding of the owner-passenger and the driver is that the owner-passenger reserves a right to control over the physical details of driving or that the driver consents to submit himself to the control of a "back-seat driver." It seems more reasonable that the mutual understanding is that the driver will use care and skill to accomplish a result, retaining control over the manner of operation yet subject to the duty of obedience to the wishes of the owner-passenger as to such things as destination. Such would only constitute an agency relationship and not one of master-servant, although there are undoubtedly situations where the understanding might well be such as to constitute a master-servant relationship. * * *

The jury rendered a verdict for the plaintiffs against defendant Blank, and therefore, must have determined that Julia Smalich had relinquished her right to control her automobile to defendant Westfall. On the facts, such a conclusion is justified under the law as we have now stated it. Judgments n.o.v. should not, therefore, have been entered in favor of defendant Blank and against the Smalich Estate. These judgments are vacated, and the record remanded with directions to enter judgments in favor of the Smalich Estate and against defendant Blank in accordance with the jury's verdict. * * *

ROBERTS, JUSTICE, concurring. I am pleased that the Court today partially repudiates the imputed contributory negligence doctrine. I am unable to join the majority's opinion, however, because I believe that in adopting a limited "both ways" test, it falls short of accomplishing the degree of reform necessary in this area. I am particularly disturbed that the majority, in continuing to apply the doctrine to the master-servant relationship, places so much weight on the physical control a master has over a servant. I therefore can only concur in the result.

The imputed contributory negligence doctrine has been criticized on two grounds. For one, it is quite obvious that the doctrine is based on the absurd fiction that the owner-passenger has the "right" to control the vehicle. In the real world, however, a passenger can in no safe way exercise operational control over the vehicle in which he rides, even if he is the owner. * * *

A second weakness in the doctrine of imputed contributory negligence arises from the fact that courts have often failed to discern the difference between using the fiction of control to impute negligence when the owner-passenger is the defendant, and using it to impute contributory negligence when the owner-passenger is the plaintiff. The assumption has been that if the driver's negligence is imputed, it is only logical to likewise impute his contributory negligence. But there is no justification for imputing contributory negligence, other than "the strong psychological appeal of all rules case in the form of balanced and logical symmetry." * * *

[T]he "both-ways test" has been strongly criticized. In 1932 it was written that "[c]ourts seem unaware that the policies involved in granting or denying the defensive plea may be different from those controlling the responsibility in damages of a master for the conduct of his servant, and that the latter are probably concerned simply with providing a financially responsible defendant." Gregory, Vicarious Responsibility and Contributory Negligence, 41 Yale L.J. 831, 833 (1932). * * *

The Supreme Court of Minnesota re-examined the whole problem of imputed contributory negligence recently in a well-reasoned opinion that deserves close study. See Weber v. Stokley–Van Camp, Inc., 274 Minn. 482, 144 N.W.2d 540 (1966). There the court repudiated the application of the doctrine to the master-servant relation in automobile negligence cases, stressing the absurdity of the control argument, and the absence of need for a solvent defendant, unlike vicarious liability cases where the master properly is held accountable for the negligence of his servant.

I look forward to the day when this Court completes its reform in this area.

NOTES AND QUESTIONS

1. "Imputed contributory negligence" has acquired a bad reputation in the law, because of a set of rules that developed in the latter part of the nineteenth century, under which entirely innocent persons, seriously injured without any fault of their own, were barred from recovery against one person who negligently injured

them, because they were charged with the negligence of another who had contributed to the injury. The result was that, of the three persons involved, the entire loss fell upon the only one who was free from all negligence. Most of this is now thoroughly discredited and obsolete. For a court decision that "completed the reform" in a well-reasoned decision, see Bibergal v. McCormick, 101 Misc.2d 794, 421 N.Y.S.2d 978 (1979). It has been largely rejected in the following areas:

A. *Driver and Passenger.* An early English decision, Thorogood v. Bryan, 8 C.B. 115, 137 Eng.Rep. 452 (1849), "imputed" negligence of the driver of an omnibus to a passenger who was injured in a collision, so as to prevent recovery by the passenger against the other driver. The decision has long since been overruled in England. Although some decisions in United States jurisdictions followed it for a time, those cases also have been overruled. As the principal case suggests, however, a passenger in an automobile can be charged with contributory negligence of his own. While older cases imposed a rather harsh duty on the passenger to keep a "look out," most cases today allow a passenger to rely upon a driver whom he reasonably believes to be competent. What is reasonable under the circumstances often becomes a question for the jury.

B. *Husband and Wife.* At common law a married woman's separate legal identity was merged with that of her husband. One result of this legal fiction was that if her spouse contributed to the happening of an accident, his negligence could be imputed to her and would bar any claim against a negligent third party. All this is ancient history. Today, the result is that, except in community property jurisdictions, the contributory negligence of one spouse is no longer imputed to bar a recovery by the other, on the basis of the marital relation alone.

C. *Parent and Child.* The common law had no similar rule of legal identity as between parent and child. The child always has been held to be entitled to the separate ownership of his own property, to the enforcement of his causes of action, and to be liable as an individual for his own torts. Consequently no statutes have been necessary to affect the situation. On occasion a parent's negligence will be so substantial in regard to the accident that a court will treat his conduct as a superseding cause and bar the child's claim against the third party. Modern courts may be reluctant to accept this argument and will regard it as an end run attempt to restore the old rules imputing contributory negligence. See, e.g., Caroline v. Reicher, 269 Md. 125, 304 A.2d 831 (1973), noted in 34 Md.L.Rev. 155 (1975) (parent's failure to supervise child will not relieve landlord of liability for child's consumption of paint containing lead). But see Lash v. Cutts, 943 F.2d 147 (1st Cir.1991) (applying Maine law), where a child was injured when he rode his bicycle down a neighbor's driveway into the path of a speeding car. The combined negligence of the child and the mother (in failing to properly supervise the child), which was imputed to the child was greater than the negligence of the defendant driver, so the child collected nothing under Maine's modified comparative negligence scheme.

2.   A general rule developed in many jurisdictions that contributory negligence will not be imputed unless negligence could be imputed. Many courts then accepted the converse of this proposition: if negligence can be imputed, contributory negligence will be also. This is the so-called "both-ways test." The both-ways test has been under a slow, but steady attack. This first occurred in connection with automobile consent statutes where some courts construed the legislation as intended only to impose vicarious liability. See page 674, note 2. A few courts have taken the same approach in regard to the family purpose doctrine. See White v. Yup, 85 Nev. 527, 458 P.2d 617 (1969).

3. The "both-ways" test remains viable in several areas. See generally Restatement (Third) of Torts: Apportionment of Liability § 5 (2000). The contributory negligence of the employee will be imputed to the corporate plaintiff employer. After an accident involving a delivery truck and a motorcycle, the company that owned the delivery truck and employed the driver filed suit against the driver of the motorcycle to recover for the damage to the truck and the worker compensation benefits paid to its driver. The jury found both the truck driver and the motorcycle driver negligent and assessed percentages of fault to each of them. The percentage of fault of the truck driver was imputed to his employer, the plaintiff. See, e.g., Thomas Oil, Inc. v. Onsgaard, 298 Minn. 465, 215 N.W.2d 793 (1974). What if the employee is the defendant in an indemnity or contribution action brought by the employer? The contributory negligence of one member of a joint venture or partnership will be attributed to the others.

4. *Derivative Claims.* When a claim is held to be derivative in nature, the contributory negligence of an injured party usually will be imputed to the plaintiff. The most common example of this is a wrongful death action. See page 582. Other examples include claims for loss of consortium, or for negligent infliction of emotional harm based on the claimant's observation of a physical injury inflicted on a close relative. The imputation of contributory negligence is not based on principles of vicarious liability, but on the judgment of a court or legislature that plaintiff's claim is not independent in nature but is derived from and dependent on another party's claim.

5. How much does the so-called "deep-pocket" theory explain the doctrines discussed in this chapter? Put another way, is the doctrinal basis of imputed negligence actually based on courts trying to find a solvent defendant? The next two chapters explore a more direct route for this result—strict and products liability.

CHAPTER XIV

STRICT LIABILITY

When a court imposes "strict liability" on a defendant, it is saying that the defendant must pay damages although the defendant neither intentionally acted nor failed to live up to the objective standard of reasonable care that traditionally has been at the root of negligence law. Some courts and textwriters call this process "absolute liability." This description overstates the case because there are numerous defenses to an action for strict liability and sometimes, especially in the so-called "strict products liability" area (Chapter 15), fault creeps back into the system. Some other textwriters and courts group the cases in this chapter under the rubric "liability without fault." This description suggests that negligence and intentional tort causes of action are always based on fault, but there are many examples of imposition of liability without fault under the negligence and intentional tort bases of liability. Can you recall some?

As Dean Prosser observed: "Once the legal concept of 'fault' is divorced, as it has been, from the personal standard of moral wrongdoing, there is a sense in which liability with or without 'fault' must beg its own conclusion. The term requires such extensive definition, that it seems better not to make use of it at all, and to refer instead to strict liability, apart from either wrongful intent or negligence." W. Prosser & W. Keeton, Torts 538 (5th ed. 1984).

Thus far we have seen that most activities are judged on the basis of intent or negligence. This chapter focuses on activities that have been selected by judges over the past two centuries to bear the burden of strict liability. Observe the rationales that underlie their judgments. Are they consistent? Are they sound? Should they be extended?

1. ANIMALS

One of the first areas selected by courts for the imposition of strict liability focused on the care and maintenance of particular animals in certain situations. Keep in mind that the liability that is being imposed, whether it is strict liability or negligence, is imposed on those who keep, possess, or harbor the animal, not just the owner. See, e.g., Snow v. Birt, 968 P.2d 177 (Colo.App.1998) (owners of house where child was bitten responsible even though dog belonged to their adult son who resided with them). See also Restatement (Second) of Torts § 514 (1977). Worldwide Primates is a breeder of monkeys and other primates operating in southern Florida. During Hurricane Andrew, the primate cages were damaged and many escaped. A macaque monkey was captured by Mr. Gomez who sold it to Mr. Martinez who sold it to the plaintiff (a photographer whose specialty was photographing people with exotic animals) whom the monkey bit.

Photographer sued Worldwide Primates for negligence in letting the monkey escape and strict liability for possessing a wild animal. Should Worldwide Primates be strictly liable? Scorza v. Martinez, 683 So.2d 1115 (Fla.App.1996) (strict liability not available against owner of escaped animal once someone else has taken possession of it).

Trespassing Animals. Somewhere around the middle of the fourteenth century, the courts began to recognize a rule making the owner of cattle liable when his animals trespassed upon the plaintiff's land. The origin of the rule is somewhat obscure. It has been attributed to a fiction that the trespass of the animals was to be attributed to the owner, because he was in some way identified with them, and responsible for what they did. According to Glanville Williams, Liability for Animals 127–34 (1939), there was no such fiction, and the early cases were those in which the owner intentionally put his cattle upon the land of the plaintiff. Liability for mere escape originated as a deliberate extension designed to remedy a gap in the law; and because it came before the full development of the action on the case, it was identified with trespass, although the invasion was an indirect one. Out of this there developed the rule that the owner of animals of a kind likely to roam and do damage is strictly liable for their trespasses.

The kinds of animals for whose trespasses their owner would be liable were limited, and they had a definite barnyard pattern. They included cattle, horses, sheep, hogs and goats, as well as such common errant fowl as turkeys, in McPherson v. James, 69 Ill.App. 337 (1896), and chickens, in Adams Bros. v. Clark, 189 Ky. 279, 224 S.W. 1046 (1920), or even pigeons, in Taylor v. Granger, 37 A. 13 (1896).

On the other hand, such household favorites as dogs and cats were not included. Olson v. Pederson, 206 Minn. 415, 288 N.W. 856 (1939); McDonald v. Castle, 116 Okl. 46, 243 P. 215 (1925); Buckle v. Holmes, [1926] 2 K.B. 125; Bischoff v. Cheney, 89 Conn. 1, 92 A. 660 (1914). The reason formerly given was that dogs and cats were of no value, which is of course clearly wrong; and that their trespasses were likely to be trivial and do no serious harm. This last, of course, is unlikely to appeal to the owners of flowerbeds and poultry. A better explanation may be that of Glanville Williams, Liability for Animals 145–146 (1939), that dogs and cats are very difficult to confine or restrain, and the general custom of the community has permitted them to roam at large. In other words, the keeping of these household pets is so far sanctioned by general usage that an exception is made in their favor. Cf. Baker v. Howard County Hunt, 171 Md. 159, 188 A. 223 (1936) (trespass rule applied to pack of hunting dogs).

An early and well established exception to the rule of strict liability for trespassing cattle and the like was the case of animals straying from a highway on which they were lawfully being driven. Tillett v. Ward, L.R. 10 Q.B. 17 (1882). This obviously arose out of the necessity of getting the animals to market. It was explained as in the nature of a servitude to which owners of lands adjoining the highway were subject; and it did not apply to other lands. Thus when cattle strayed from the highway across the lands of

A, and thence onto the land of B, B could use strict liability even though A could not. Wood v. Snider, 187 N.Y. 28, 79 N.E. 858 (1907).

In the United States the rule as to strict liability for animal trespass has had something of a checkered history. In the early days many of the courts, particularly in the western part of the country where cattle were customarily permitted to graze at large on open range, rejected the common law rule, as not suitable to the conditions of the country and established local custom. See for example Delaney v. Errickson, 10 Neb. 492, 6 N.W. 600 (1880); Beinhorn v. Griswold, 27 Mont. 79, 69 P. 557 (1902). These cases are among the leading authorities for the proposition that, under state reception statutes, the common law of England is to be followed only when it is suitable and appropriate.

As the country became more settled, some states began to enact "fencing out" statutes, which provided that if the plaintiff fenced his land properly there was strict liability when the animals broke through the fence. Otherwise, there was liability only if their owner was negligent. See for example Buford v. Houtz, 133 U.S. 320 (1890); Garcia v. Sumrall, 58 Ariz. 526, 121 P.2d 640 (1942); Hart v. Meredith, 196 Ill.App.3d 367, 553 N.E.2d 782, 143 Ill.Dec. 75 (1990) (application of fencing out statute to impose strict liability on farmer whose bull broke through fence and bred two of plaintiff's purebred Angus cows, causing plaintiff to lose the services of the cows in plaintiff's embryo transplant breeding operation).

As the country became still more settled, the conflict between the grazing interests and developing agricultural interests—or, in other words, as the motion pictures would have it, between the range men and the "nesters" along the creek bed—resulted in many states in "fencing in" statutes, which required the owner of the animals to fence them in or otherwise restrain them, and made the owner strictly liable if he did not do so. Plaintiff's pickup truck hit a black cow standing in a dark road at midnight. Florida has a fencing in statute that requires the plaintiff to show defendant's intent or negligence in order to recover if animals escape onto the highway. The only evidence is that defendant's gate could only be opened by human hands, that defendant himself had secured the gate the day before, that defendant had had no visitors after that, and that he did not know how the gate had been opened. Liability? Fisel v. Wynns, 667 So.2d 761 (Fla.1996) (summary judgment in favor of owner approved).

Finally, some states, particularly in the eastern part of the country, apply the common law rule. See King v. Blue Mountain Forest Ass'n, 100 N.H. 212, 123 A.2d 151 (1956).

A common type of statute today permits a county to choose the rule it wishes to apply. Thus in some states animals are permitted to run at large unless a county adopts a "fencing in" or a "fencing out" ordinance. Others permit counties to employ the fiction of designating the boundary lines of lots or tracts as lawful fences, which automatically results in a rule of strict liability. There are states in which all four variants of the rule—strict liability, fencing out, fencing in, and no liability without fault—can be found in different counties.

Wild Animals. Under the common law of England, the owner or possessor of a nondomesticated animal (collectively referred to by courts as "wild animals" or animals *"ferae naturae"*) was subject to strict liability if the animal injured anyone. See May v. Burdett, 9 Q.B. 101 (1846) (monkey bite); Filburn v. People's Palace and Aquarium Co., Ltd., 25 Q.B.Div. 258 (C.A.1890) (attacking elephant); Johnson v. Swain, 787 S.W.2d 36 (Tex. 1989) (gored by bull elephant). On the other hand the owner of a domestic animal such as a cat, dog, sheep, or horse was subject to strict liability only if the owner knew or had reason to know that the animal had vicious propensities.

This led to interesting problems of classification. Obviously lions, tigers, and bears were deemed "wild animals." What about deer? Congress & Empire Spring Co. v. Edgar, 99 U.S. 645 (1878); Briley v. Mitchell, 238 La. 551, 115 So.2d 851 (1959). A pet raccoon? Andrew v. Kilgour, 19 Man.L.Rep. 544 (1910). A hive of bees? Ammons v. Kellogg, 137 Miss. 551, 102 So. 562 (1925). A boar? Marshall v. Ranne, 511 S.W.2d 255 (Tex.1974). A bird able to open its own cage and startle people? See Neagle v. Morgan, 360 Mass. 864, 277 N.E.2d 482 (1971).

The customs of the community apparently influence the determination. In Burma an elephant is regarded as a domesticated animal, for which there is no strict liability. Maung Kayn Dun v. Ma Kyian, 2 Upper Burma Rulings, Civ. 570 (1900). Suppose an elephant is brought from Burma to England to perform in a circus. Behrens v. Bertram Mills Circus, Ltd., [1957] 2 Q.B. 1. How about a camel, which is now domesticated virtually everywhere it is found? McQuaker v. Goddard, [1940] 1 K.B. 687. A ferret? Gallick v. Barto, 828 F.Supp. 1168 (M.D.Pa.1993) (finding that ferret is a wild animal even though evidence showed that approximately one million are kept as pets in United States).

The majority American position has followed the rule of strict liability in regard to wild animals. See Isaacs v. Powell, 267 So.2d 864 (Fla.App. 1972) (chimpanzee); Franken v. Sioux Center, 272 N.W.2d 422 (Iowa 1978) (tiger); Whitefield v. Stewart, 577 P.2d 1295 (Okl.1978) (monkey). But see Wisconsin, which has not adopted strict liability for wild animals but instead applies a negligence standard that is modified slightly by the fact that the owner is charged with the knowledge of the animal's "natural traits and habits." See Ollhoff v. Peck, 177 Wis.2d 719, 503 N.W.2d 323 (1993) (negligence standard applied to musky).

Some courts have applied a negligence standard with regard to the liability of persons who display wild animals to the public, although the standard of care is often raised to one of extreme caution. See Hansen v. Brogan, 145 Mont. 224, 400 P.2d 265 (1965) (buffalo); Vaughan v. Miller Bros. "101" Ranch Wild West Show, 109 W.Va. 170, 153 S.E. 289 (1930) ("ape"). The trend is more pronounced with regard to public zoos, although some of the decisions are based on the fact that the legislature authorized the activity. See, e.g., City and County of Denver v. Kennedy, 29 Colo.App. 15, 476 P.2d 762 (1970). Contra: City of Mangum v. Brownlee, 181 Okl.

515, 75 P.2d 174 (1938). What about wild animals that roam freely in animal parks where visitors drive their cars?

Domestic Animals. As for domestic animals, the canard is often repeated that the common law rule is that a domestic animal such as a dog (or cat) is entitled to one bite. The cases do not bear this out. If the owner knows or has reason to know (scienter) that a domestic animal has vicious propensities, this is sufficient to classify that animal with wild ones and strict liability is imposed. See Andrews v. Smith, 324 Pa. 455, 188 A. 146 (1936); Barger v. Jimerson, 130 Colo. 459, 276 P.2d 744 (1954); Harris v. Williams, 160 Okl. 103, 15 P.2d 580 (1932). Many of the cases show interesting and imaginative efforts on the part of plaintiff's counsel to prove that the animal had such a temperament and that the owner was aware of it. See, e.g., Walters v. Grand Teton Crest Outfitters, Inc., 804 F.Supp. 1442 (D.Wyo.1992) (whether plaintiff had proved mule had vicious propensities by showing it had thrown two previous riders and had rolled on its back before plaintiff had mounted it was question of fact for the jury); Zarek v. Fredericks, 138 F.2d 689 (3d Cir.1943) (dog snarled at guests and was almost always accompanied by his owners); Frederickson v. Kepner, 82 Cal.App.2d 905, 187 P.2d 800 (1947); and Perkins v. Drury, 57 N.M. 269, 258 P.2d 379 (1953) (children warned to stay away from dog); Hill v. Moseley, 220 N.C. 485, 17 S.E.2d 676 (1941) (dog had bad reputation in the neighborhood). Can an entire breed of animal be classified as "vicious by nature"? Cf. Rolen v. Maryland Casualty Co., 240 So.2d 42 (La.App.1970) (German shepherds); Slack v. Villari, 59 Md.App. 462, 476 A.2d 227 (1984) (mere fact that dog belongs to a breed (Doberman pinscher) with an unsavory reputation not enough to prove owner had knowledge of that particular dog's dangerous propensities); Briscoe v. Graybeal, 95 Md.App. 670, 622 A.2d 805 (1993) (cannot make showing of propensity based solely on fact that horse was thoroughbred). Note that although many of the cases use the term "vicious," the test is really whether the animal has a "dangerous propensity abnormal to its class." Restatement (Second) of Torts § 509, comment *c* (1977) (large dog that owner knows has a tendency to "fawn violently" would be strictly liable for harm done by dog's playfulness or demonstrative show of affection). See also Bauman v. Auch, 539 N.W.2d 320 (S.D.1995) (testimony that horse was flighty, high-strung, and spirited, not mean or vicious, enough to create jury question on issue whether strict liability should apply).

If the plaintiff is unable to prove that the owner knew or should have known of a domestic animal's dangerous propensities, then strict liability does not apply and the plaintiff must prove negligence in order to recover. See, e.g., Duren v. Kunkel, 814 S.W.2d 935 (Mo.1991) (plaintiff not entitled to strict liability because failed to show that Limousin bull had any dangerous propensity different from any other bull of its breed or class, but was entitled to go to jury on question of owner's negligence in failing to protect plaintiff from animal).

In many states the common law regarding liability for dog bites has been changed by statute. These statutes usually do away with the necessity

Prior knowledge/intention

of plaintiff's proving scienter in order to recover. The statutes may also list defenses—e.g., plaintiff committing a trespass or presence of warning sign. See, for example, the New Hampshire statute quoted in Glidden v. Szybiak, page 72.

Liability is also affected by statutory provisions requiring dogs to be muzzled or leashed. If a person is injured due to the failure of the owner to comply with the ordinance, the owner is "negligent per se" and so liable for the damages. Wistafka v. Grotowski, 205 Ill.App. 529 (1917). As in all negligence per se cases, causation still must be proved. If the muzzling of the dog would not have prevented the injury, as where the dog does not bite the plaintiff but knocks him down, there is no causal connection, and plaintiff must prove negligence. Kennet v. Sossnitz, 260 App.Div. 759, 23 N.Y.S.2d 961 (1940), aff'd, 286 N.Y. 623, 36 N.E.2d 459 (1941).

In Florida, statutory immunity is created for a dog owner who displays an easily readable sign that says "BAD DOG" in a prominent place in his premises. Suppose an owner who displays such a sign says to an invitee, "Rex can be bad, but he can also be good." Rex is bad that day. See Noble v. Yorke, 490 So.2d 29 (Fla.1986). An animal receiving a lot of press attention because of its occasional viciousness is the pit bull dog. Should a landlord have a duty to tell a potential tenant that a neighbor owns a pit bull dog? See Wylie v. Gresch, 191 Cal.App.3d 412, 236 Cal.Rptr. 552 (1987) ("a vicious dog is a danger one might expect to encounter anywhere in our society").

2. ABNORMALLY DANGEROUS ACTIVITIES

Rylands v. Fletcher

In the Exchequer, 3 H. & C. 774, 159 Eng.Rep. 737, 1865.
In the Exchequer Chamber, L.R. 1 Ex. 265, 1866.

In the House of Lords, L.R. 3 H.L. 330, 1868.

[Action brought in 1861 and tried at the Liverpool Summer Assizes (1862). A verdict was found for the plaintiff subject to the award of an arbitrator, who was afterwards empowered by a court order to state a special case instead of making an award. The material facts in the special case stated by the arbitrator were as follows:

Facts:

The defendants were the owners of a mill. In order to supply it with water they constructed upon the nearby land of Lord Wilton, with his permission, a reservoir. The plaintiff under lease from Lord Wilton was working certain coal mines under lands close to but not adjoining the premises on which the reservoir was constructed. They worked their mine in the direction of the reservoir until they came upon certain old workings, part of which at least had been made and abandoned at a time beyond living memory. These workings consisted of horizontal passages and vertical shafts, the latter apparently filled with rubbish and marl similar to that of the solid earth surrounding them. The defendant employed a competent engineer and competent contractors to plan and construct the reservoir, and it was so planned and constructed solely by them upon a site, in the choice of which the defendants were guilty of no personal fault. In fact, the old mine workings lay beneath it and, continuing under the intermediate lands, communicated, at the point to which the plaintiff had pushed its workings in that direction, with the workings of the plaintiff. The contractors in excavating for the bed of the reservoir came upon five of the above mentioned vertical shafts; the sides or walls of these were of timber, but, because they were filled with soil of the same kind as that composing the surrounding ground, neither the contractors nor the defendants suspected that they were abandoned mine shafts. The arbitrator found that the defendants were guilty of no personal negligence or fault, but that the engineer and contractors had not in fact exercised proper care, with reference to the shafts discovered, to provide for the sufficiency of the reservoir to bear the pressure that it was designed to bear when in use.

The reservoir was completed in December, 1860, and the defendants had it partly filled. Within a few days, one of the shafts that had been met while excavating gave way and burst downward, letting the water into the abandoned workings beneath, through which it flowed, through the communications that the plaintiffs in working their mine had made between the two, into the plaintiffs' workings, flooding their mine.

The question for the opinion of the Court was whether the plaintiff was entitled to recover damages from the defendant by reason of the matters thus stated by the arbitrator.

In the Exchequer, judgment was given for the defendants by a 2–to–1 vote. Martin, B., said there was no trespass, because the damage was not "immediate," but "mediate or consequential." There was no nuisance, because the defendants were doing a lawful and reasonable act. The same rule must be applied to real property as to personal property, that there must be negligence on the part of the defendant to make him responsible. The plaintiff brought error to the Exchequer Chamber.]

BLACKBURN, J. * * * It appears from the statement in the case, that the plaintiff was damaged by his property being flooded by water which, without any fault on his part, broke out of a reservoir constructed on the defendants' land by the defendants' orders, and maintained by the defendants. * * *

The plaintiff, though free from all blame on his part, must bear the loss, unless he can establish that it was the consequence of some default for which the defendants are responsible. The question of law therefore arises, what is the obligation which the law casts on a person who, like the defendants, lawfully brings on his land something which though harmless whilst it remains there, will naturally do mischief if it escape out of his land. It is agreed on all hands that he must take care to keep in that which he has brought on the land and keeps there, in order that it may not escape and damage his neighbors; but the question arises whether the duty which the law casts upon him, under such circumstances, is an absolute duty to keep it in at his peril, or is, as the majority of the Court of Exchequer have thought, merely a duty to take all reasonable and prudent precautions, in order to keep it in, but no more. If the first be the law, the person who has brought on his land and kept there something dangerous, and failed to keep it in, is responsible for all the natural consequences of its escape. If the second be the limit of his duty, he would not be answerable except on proof of negligence, and consequently would not be answerable for escape arising from any latent defect which ordinary prudence and skill could not detect. * * *

Lord Blackburn

We think that the true rule of law is that the person who for his own purposes brings on his lands and collects and keeps there any thing likely to do mischief if it escapes, must keep it in at his peril, and if he does not do so, is prima facie answerable for all the damage which is the natural consequence of its escape. He can excuse himself by showing that the escape was owing to the plaintiff's default; or perhaps that the escape was the consequence of vis major, or the act of God; but as nothing of this sort exists here, it is unnecessary to inquire what excuse would be sufficient. The general rule, as above stated, seems on principle just. The person whose grass or corn is eaten down by the escaping cattle of his neighbor, or whose mine is flooded by the water from his neighbor's reservoir, or whose cellar is invaded by the filth of his neighbor's privy, or whose habitation is made unhealthy by the fumes and noisome vapors of his neighbor's alkali works, is damnified without any fault of his own; and it seems but reasonable and just that the neighbor, who has brought something on his own property which was not naturally there, harmless to others so long as it is confined to his own property, but which he knows to be mischievous if it gets on his neighbor's, should be obliged to make good the damage which ensues if he does not succeed in confining it to his own property. But for his act in bringing it there no mischief could have accrued, and it seems but just that he should at his peril keep it there, so that no mischief may accrue, or answer for the natural and anticipated consequences. And upon authority, this we think is established to be the law, whether the things so brought be beasts, or water, or filth, or stenches.

The case that has most commonly occurred and which is most frequently to be found in the books, is as to the obligation of the owner of cattle which he has brought on his land to prevent their escaping and doing mischief. The law as to them seems to be perfectly settled from early times; the owner must keep them in at his peril, or he will be answerable for the natural consequences of their escape; that is, with regard to tame beasts, for the grass they eat and trample upon, though not for an injury to the person of others, for our ancestors have settled that it is not the general nature of horses to kick, or bulls to gore; but if the owner knows that the beast has a vicious propensity to attack man, he will be answerable for that too. * * *

Judgment for the plaintiff.

Rylands and Horrocks brought error to the House of Lords against the judgment of the Exchequer Chamber, which had reversed the judgment of the Court of Exchequer.

THE LORD CHANCELLOR (LORD CAIRNS). * * * My Lords, the principles in which this case must be determined appear to me to be extremely simple. The defendants, treating them as the owner or occupiers of the close on which the reservoir was constructed, might lawfully have used that close for any purpose for which it might in the ordinary course of the enjoyment of land be used; and if, in what I may term the natural user of that land, there had been any accumulation of water, either on the surface or underground, and if, by the operation of the laws of nature, that accumulation of water had passed off into the close occupied by the plaintiff, the plaintiff could not have complained that that result had taken place. If he had desired to guard himself against it, it would have been lain upon him to have done so, by leaving, or by interposing, some barrier between his close and the close of the defendants in order to have prevented that operation of the laws of nature.

Lord Cairns

As an illustration of that principle, I may refer to a case which was cited in the argument before your Lordships, the case of Smith v. Kendrick, in the Court of Common Pleas, 7 C.B. 515.

On the other hand, if the defendants, not stopping at the natural use of their close, had desired to use it for any purpose which I may term a non-natural use, for the purpose of introducing into the close that which in its natural condition was not in or upon it, for the purpose of introducing water either above or below ground in quantities and in a manner not the result of any work or operation on or under the land; and if in consequence of their doing so, or in consequence of any imperfection in the mode of their doing so, the water came to escape and to pass off into the close of the plaintiff, then it appears to me that that which the defendants were doing they were doing at their own peril; and, if in the course of their doing it the evil arose to which I have referred, the evil, namely, of the escape of the water and its passing away to the close of the plaintiff and injuring the plaintiff, then for the consequence of that, in my opinion, the defendants would be liable. As the case of Smith v. Kendrick is an illustration of the first principle to which I have referred, so also the second principle to which I have referred is well illustrated by another case in the same Court, the case of Baird v. Williamson, 15 C.B.N.S. 317, which was also cited in the argument at the bar. * * *

Judgment of the Court of Exchequer Chamber affirmed.

[The concurring opinion of LORD CRANWORTH is omitted.]

NOTES AND QUESTIONS

1. Why not liability simply for trespass to land? Or nuisance? The contractor who did the work was negligent in not discovering the abandoned mine shafts and blocking them up. Why was defendant not liable for the negligence of the person with whom he contracted to do the work? Would he be liable today? Was defendant negligent in having the reservoir at all? If not negligent, was he still at fault? See Keeton, Conditional Fault in the Law of Torts, 72 Harv.L.Rev. 401 (1959).

2. Professor Simpson, in Legal Liability for Bursting Reservoirs: The Historical Context of Rylands v. Fletcher, 13 J.Leg.Stud. 209 (1984), states that bursting dams were a particular problem at the time and that events had prompted public inquiries and legislation concerning the liability of dam owners. The reservoir in this case was located in a part of Lancashire devoted to coal mining. The American equivalent would be a reservoir in the immediate vicinity of Scranton, Pa. Has this any significance?

3. Professor Bohlen, in The Rule in Rylands v. Fletcher, 59 U.Pa.L.Rev. 298 (1911), first advanced a "materialistic" explanation of the principal case, to the effect that the judges who wrote the opinions belonged to the landed gentry, and were seeking to protect that class against the encroachments of industry. This was refuted by the painstaking biographies of the judges in Molloy, Fletcher v. Rylands: A Re-examination of Juristic Origins, 9 U.Chi.L.Rev. 266 (1942).

4. How far does the opinion of Lord Cairns limit that of Blackburn in *Rylands?* What does he mean by a "natural use" of land? Something like trees, in a state of nature? Note that he relies on Smith v. Kendrick, 7 C.B. 515, 137 Eng.Rep. 205 (1849), where defendant's normal and usual mining operations resulted in the flow of percolating water from springs into plaintiff's adjoining mine, and defendant was held not liable. A parallel case is Zampos v. United States Smelting R. & M. Co., 206 F.2d 171 (10th Cir.1953). He relies also upon Baird v. Williamson, 15 C.B. (N.S.) 376, 143 Eng.Rep. 831 (1863), where defendant pumped the water from his mine to a higher level, from which it flowed into plaintiff's mine, and was held liable.

5. Subsequent decisions in England have followed the distinction between "natural" and "nonnatural" uses of land made by Lord Cairns. In determining what is a nonnatural use, the English courts have looked not only to the character of the thing or activity in question, but also to the place and manner in which it is maintained, and its relation to its surroundings. Thus water collected in large tanks in dangerous proximity to plaintiff's land has been held to be a matter for strict liability; but water in a cistern, in household pipes, in a water closet, or in a barnyard tank supplying cattle, has not, provided there was no negligence. Fire in a fireplace, or in an authorized railway engine, is a natural use; but a traction engine shooting out sparks on the highway is not. Although the automobile is dangerous, and fatal to thousands annually, it is held to be "natural"; but a ten ton traction engine or a steam roller that crushes conduits under the street is not. See

Stallybrass, Dangerous Things and the Non–Natural User of Land, 3 Cambridge L.J. 376 (1929); Newark, Non–Natural Use and Rylands v. Fletcher, 24 Mod.L.Rev. 447 (1961). How would you state the English rule?

6. In Read v. J. Lyons & Co. Ltd., [1947] A.C. 156, where a government inspector was injured by an explosion in defendant's munitions plant, the court further limited Rylands v. Fletcher by holding that the rule would apply only when something "escaped" from defendant's land. The decision is said to have stunted the growth of strict liability in English law.

7. In the United States, Rylands v. Fletcher started out with approval in Ball v. Nye, 99 Mass. 582, 97 Am.Dec. 56 (1868) (percolation of filthy water), and Cahill v. Eastman, 18 Minn. 324, 10 Am.Rep. 184 (1872) (water escaping from a tunnel). The case then was rejected in its entirety by three leading American courts in three years. Losee v. Buchanan, 51 N.Y. 476, 10 Am.Rep. 623 (1873); Marshall v. Welwood, 38 N.J.L. 339 (1876); Brown v. Collins, 53 N.H. 442, 16 Am.Rep. 372 (1873). The first two of these involved the explosion of ordinary steam boilers, and the third a runaway horse. They were clearly cases of customary, natural uses, to which the English courts would certainly never have applied the rule. In each case the attack was directed at Blackburn's broad statement in the intermediate court, and the decision in the House of Lords was given little or no attention. Rylands v. Fletcher was treated as holding that the defendant is absolutely liable whenever anything whatever escapes from his control and causes damage. In other words, the rule of the case was misstated, and as misstated was rejected, in cases in which it had no proper application in the first place.

8. These decisions gave Rylands v. Fletcher a bad name, and it was rejected in several jurisdictions, such as Maine, New Hampshire, New York, Oklahoma, Rhode Island, Texas and possibly Wyoming. For a time a majority of the courts that considered the case by name rejected it. In recent years the American trend has been very much in favor of approval of the case, and a majority now favor the case. What factors may have influenced recent courts to accept the *Rylands* principle? Have there been changes in society that made courts more willing to impose strict liability for hazardous activities? See Cities Service Co. v. State, 312 So.2d 799 (Fla.App.2d Dist.1975).

9. Many of the courts rejecting Rylands v. Fletcher by name have accomplished much the same result in many cases by calling the defendant's activity or condition an "absolute nuisance." See page 811. Also Prosser, Nuisance Without Fault, 20 Tex.L.Rev. 399 (1942).

10. Rylands v. Fletcher has been a favorite topic of legal writers. See Bohlen, The Rule in Rylands v. Fletcher, 59 U.Pa.L.Rev. 298 (1911); Thayer, Liability Without Fault, 29 Harv.L.Rev. 801 (1916); Morris, Hazardous Enterprises and Risk–Bearing Capacity, 61 Yale L.J. 1172 (1952); Stallybrass, Dangerous Things and the Non–Natural User of Land, 3 Cambridge L.J. 376 (1929); Carpenter, The Doctrine of Green v. General Petroleum Corp., 5 So.Cal.L.Rev. 263 (1932); Prosser, The Principle of Rylands v. Fletcher, in his Selected Topics on the Law of Torts 135 (1953); Baker, An Eclipse of Fault Liability, 40 Va.L.Rev. 273 (1954); Lemmon, the Developing Doctrine of *Rylands v. Fletcher*: Hazardous Waste Remediation Contractors Beware, 42 LOY. L. REV. 287 (1996); Claus, Oregon's Development of Absolute Liability under the *Rylands* Doctrine: a Case Study, 53 WASH. U. J. URB. & CONTEMP. L. 171 (1998).

⌐ Bridges v. The Kentucky Stone Co., Inc.

Supreme Court of Indiana, 1981.
425 N.E.2d 125.

HUNTER, J. This action stems from an allegedly intentional and malicious explosion of dynamite at the home of plaintiff Charles Bridges in Johnson County, Indiana, on February 10, 1975. In the explosion, Bridges's twelve year old son was killed; a second son and Bridges both were injured in the blast * * *.

Bridges subsequently filed suit against Kentucky Stone and co-defendant Webb to recover damages for the injuries sustained in the blast. Bridges's claim against William Webb rested on the allegation that he had set and ignited the explosives at Bridges's home. Kentucky Stone was named as a defendant on the basis that it had "negligently kept and stored" dynamite and other ultra-hazardous explosives at its Tyrone plant, thereby permitting Webb to obtain the explosives ultimately used at the Bridges's home in Johnson County.

The trial court held (as a matter of law) that the assumed negligent storage of dynamite by Kentucky Stone was (not) the proximate cause of the explosion and injuries to Bridges. On this basis, Kentucky Stone was granted summary judgment.

The Court of Appeals * * * reversed the summary judgment * * *.

In Yukon Equipment, Inc. v. Fireman's Fund Insurance, [585 P.2d 1206 (Alaska 1978),] thieves broke into an explosives storage magazine located in the suburbs of Anchorage and ignited 80,000 pounds of explosives, damaging homes within a two-mile radius. Notwithstanding the cause of the blast and the fact that the magazine was located on land which, by federal order, was devoted to the storage of explosives, the Alaska Supreme Court imposed absolute liability on the operators of the storage magazine. The per se rule of liability imposed stemmed from the Court's conclusion that the storage of dynamite was in and of itself an "ultra-hazardous activity."

We do (not) share that opinion. Rather, we are persuaded that whether the storage of dynamite in any particular circumstance is an "ultra-hazardous activity" must be determined on a case-by-case basis, as per the various factors outlined by the American Law Institute in Restatement (Second) of Torts § 520 (1977).[2] But * * * we reject the per se rule of liability adopted in Alaska. * * *

Here, unlike Yukon Equipment, Inc. v. Fireman's Fund Insurance, supra, the consequence of the assumed negligent storage was not contemporaneous damage to the inhabitants and property of the area surrounding the storage site. Rather, the blast occurred nearly three weeks subsequent to the theft at a location over one hundred miles from the storage site. The

---

2. [The note quotes § 520, which is discussed in detail in the next case, and then continues:]

The storage of dynamite, we note is distinguished from the use and explosion of dynamite, the latter activity being one to which this jurisdiction accords absolute liability. Enos Coal Mining Co. v. Schuchart (1963) 243 Ind. 692, 188 N.E.2d 406.

disappearance of the dynamite was reported to federal authorities within twenty-four hours of its discovery, as required by federal regulations 27 C.F.R. 181.127 and 181.130. The discovery and reporting occurred within twenty-four to forty-eight hours after the theft and nearly three weeks prior to the blast. In the face of these circumstances, we hold the theft of the explosive materials, the transporting of them from Tyrone to Johnson County, the preparation necessary to the discharge, and the eventual trespass and detonation at the Bridges's residence was a superseding cause of the blast precluding liability for any supposed negligence of Kentucky Stone. * * * We expressly limit our decision to the facts before us. * * * [T]he opinion of the Court of Appeals is vacated, and the judgment of the trial court is affirmed. * * * DeBruler, J. dissents with opinion * * *.

NOTES AND QUESTIONS

1. The first Restatement of Torts had used the term "ultrahazardous" and applied it to an activity that "necessarily involves a risk of serious harm to the persons, land or chattels of others which cannot be eliminated by the exercise of the utmost care and * * * is not a matter of common usage." § 520. The definition is categoric. If an activity is ultrahazardous, it would be so regarded no matter where it took place. This was the approach taken by the Alaska court regarding storage of explosives in the *Yukon Equipment* case, described in the opinion in the principal case. That case carried the approach so far that it held liability on the part of the company storing the explosives, even though they were stolen by the other defendant and deliberately set off to produce the explosion. (This situation is the subject of a caveat in the Restatement.)

2. The Second Restatement, on the other hand, uses the term "abnormally dangerous" and makes the decision depend on the nature of the location where the activity takes place. Consider, for example, whether a hardware store in a small town, keeping a small amount of dynamite for the benefit of farmers clearing fields of stumps, would be subject to strict liability. Cf. Barnes v. Zettlemoyer, 25 Tex.Civ.App. 468, 62 S.W. 111 (1901). What would the Alaska court hold?

3. A majority of the courts impose strict liability for blasting if it is done in an urban or residential area. Some state that the nature of the location is important in determining whether the activity is ultrahazardous, while others impose strict liability for use but not storage. See Otero v. Burgess, 84 N.M. 575, 505 P.2d 1251 (1973); cf. Chavez v. Southern Pac. Transp. Co., 413 F.Supp. 1203 (E.D.Cal.1976) (keeping 18 bomb-loaded box cars in railroad yard near town). Sometimes strict liability is accomplished by calling the activity a nuisance, as in Gossett v. Southern R. Co., 115 Tenn. 376, 89 S.W. 737 (1905). Some courts, stressing the comparative safety with which it can be carried on by the exercise of due care, hold that strict liability is not applicable and there is liability only for negligence. Reynolds v. W.H. Hinman Co., 145 Me. 343, 75 A.2d 802 (1950); Wadleigh v. Manchester, 100 N.H. 277, 123 A.2d 831 (1956).

Indiana Harbor Belt R.R. Co. v. American Cyanamid Co.

United States Court of Appeals, Seventh Circuit, 1990.
916 F.2d 1174.

Posner, J.

American Cyanamid Company, the defendant in this diversity tort suit governed by Illinois law, is a major manufacturer of chemicals, including acrylonitrile, a chemical used in large quantities in making acrylic fibers, plastics, dyes, pharmaceutical chemicals, and other intermediate and final goods. On January 2, 1979, at its manufacturing plant in Louisiana, Cyanamid loaded 20,000 gallons of liquid acrylonitrile into a railroad tank car that it had leased from the North American Car Corporation. The next day, a train of the Missouri Pacific Railroad picked up the car at Cyanamid's siding. The car's ultimate destination was a Cyanamid plant in New Jersey served by Conrail rather than by Missouri Pacific. The Missouri Pacific train carried the car north to the Blue Island railroad yard of Indiana Harbor Belt Railroad, the plaintiff in this case, a small switching line that has a contract with Conrail to switch cars from other lines to Conrail, in this case for travel east. The Blue Island yard is in the Village of Riverdale, which is just south of Chicago and part of the Chicago metropolitan area.

The car arrived in the Blue Island yard on the morning of January 9, 1979. Several hours after it arrived, employees of the switching line noticed fluid gushing from the bottom outlet of the car. The lid on the outlet was broken. After two hours, the line's supervisor of equipment was able to stop the leak by closing a shut-off valve controlled from the top of the car. No one was sure at the time just how much of the contents of the car had leaked, but it was feared that all 20,000 gallons had, and since acrylonitrile is flammable at a temperature of 30 degrees Fahrenheit or above, highly toxic, and possibly carcinogenic [c], the local authorities ordered the homes near the yard evacuated. The evacuation lasted only a few hours, until the car was moved to a remote part of the yard and it was discovered that only about a quarter of the acrylonitrile had leaked. Concerned nevertheless that there had been some contamination of soil and water, the Illinois Department of Environmental Protection ordered the switching line to take decontamination measures that cost the line $981,022.75, which it sought to recover by this suit.

One count of the two-count complaint charges Cyanamid with having maintained the leased tank car negligently. The other count asserts that the transportation of acrylonitrile in bulk through the Chicago metropolitan area is an abnormally dangerous activity, for the consequences of which the shipper (Cyanamid) is strictly liable to the switching line, which bore the financial brunt of those consequences because of the decontamination measures that it was forced to take.

[The trial court judge found that strict liability applied and granted summary judgment in favor of the plaintiff on that count.]

* * *

The question whether the shipper of a hazardous chemical by rail should be strictly liable for the consequences of a spill or other accident to the shipment en route is a novel one in Illinois[.]

* * *

The parties agree that the question whether placing acrylonitrile in a rail shipment that will pass through a metropolitan area subjects the shipper to strict liability is, as recommended in Restatement (Second) of Torts § 520, comment 1 (1977), a question of law, so that we owe no particular deference to the conclusion of the district court. They also agree * * * that the Supreme Court of Illinois would treat as authoritative the provisions of the Restatement governing abnormally dangerous activities. The key provision is section 520, which sets forth six factors to be considered in deciding whether an activity is abnormally dangerous and the actor therefore strictly liable.

The roots of section 520 are in nineteenth-century cases. The most famous one is Rylands v. Fletcher, 1 Ex. 265, aff'd, L.R. 3 H.L. 300 (1868), but a more illuminating one in the present context is Guille v. Swan, 19 Johns. (N.Y.) 381 (1822). A man took off in a hot-air balloon and landed, without intending to, in a vegetable garden in New York City. A crowd that had been anxiously watching his involuntary descent trampled the vegetables in their endeavor to rescue him when he landed. The owner of the garden sued the balloonist for the resulting damage, and won. Yet the balloonist had not been careless. In the then state of ballooning it was impossible to make a pinpoint landing.

Guille is a paradigmatic case for strict liability. (a) The risk (probability) of harm was great, and (b) the harm that would ensue if the risk materialized could be, although luckily was not, great (the balloonist could have crashed into the crowd rather than into the vegetables). The confluence of these two factors established the urgency of seeking to prevent such accidents. (c) Yet such accidents could not be prevented by the exercise of due care; the technology of care in ballooning was insufficiently developed. (d) The activity was not a matter of common usage, so there was no presumption that it was a highly valuable activity despite its unavoidable riskiness. (e) The activity was inappropriate to the place in which it took place—densely populated New York City. The risk of serious harm to others (other than the balloonist himself, that is) could have been reduced by shifting the activity to the sparsely inhabited areas that surrounded the city in those days. (f) Reinforcing (d), the value to the community of the activity of recreational ballooning did not appear to be great enough to offset its unavoidable risks.

These are, of course, the six factors in section 520. They are related to each other in that each is a different facet of a common quest for a proper legal regime to govern accidents that negligence liability cannot adequately control. The interrelations might be more perspicuous if the six factors were reordered. One might for example start with (c), inability to eliminate the risk of accident by the exercise of due care. [C] The baseline common law regime of tort liability is negligence. When it is a workable regime, because the hazards of an activity can be avoided by being careful (which is to say, nonnegligent), there is no need to switch to strict liability. Sometimes, however, a particular type of accident cannot be prevented by taking care but can be avoided, or its consequences minimized, by shifting the activity in which the accident occurs to another locale, where the risk or harm of an accident will be less ((e)), or by reducing the scale of the activity in order to minimize the number of accidents caused by it ((f)). [Cc] By making the actor strictly liable—by denying him in other words an excuse based on his inability to avoid accidents by being more careful—we give him an incentive, missing in a negligence regime, to experiment with methods of preventing accidents that involve not greater exertions of care, assumed to be futile, but instead relocating, changing, or reducing (perhaps to the vanishing point) the activity giving rise to the accident. [C] The greater the risk of an accident ((a)) and the costs of an accident if one occurs ((b)), the more we want the actor to consider the possibility of making accident-reducing activity changes; the stronger, therefore, is the case for strict liability. Finally, if an activity is extremely common ((d)), like driving an automobile, it is unlikely either that its hazards are perceived as great or that there is no technology of care available to minimize them; so the case for strict liability is weakened.

The largest class of cases in which strict liability has been imposed under the standard codified in the Second Restatement of Torts involves the use of dynamite and other explosives for demolition in residential or urban areas. Restatement, supra, § 519, comment d; [c]. Explosives are dangerous even when handled carefully, and we therefore want blasters to choose the location of the activity with care and also to explore the feasibility of using safer substitutes (such as a wrecking ball), as well as to be careful in the blasting itself. Blasting is not a commonplace activity like driving a car, or so superior to substitute methods of demolition that the imposition of liability is unlikely to have any effect except to raise the activity's costs.

Against this background we turn to the particulars of acrylonitrile. Acrylonitrile is one of a large number of chemicals that are hazardous in the sense of being flammable, toxic, or both; acrylonitrile is both, as are many others. A table in the record, drawn from Glickman & Harvey, Statistical Trends in Railroad Hazardous Material Safety, 1978 to 1984, at pp. 63–65 (Draft Final Report to the Environmental & Hazardous Material Studies Division of the Association of American Railroads, April 1986) (tab. 4.1), contains a list of the 125 hazardous materials that are shipped in highest volume on the nation's railroads. Acrylonitrile is the fifty-third most hazardous on the list. Number 1 is phosphorus (white or yellow), and among the other materials that rank higher than acrylonitrile on the hazard scale are anhydrous ammonia, liquified petroleum gas, vinyl chloride, gasoline, crude petroleum, motor fuel antiknock compound, methyl and ethyl chloride, sulphuric acid, sodium metal, and chloroform. The plaintiff's lawyer acknowledged at argument that the logic of the district court's opinion dictated strict liability for all 52 materials that rank higher than acrylonitrile on the list, and quite possibly for the 72 that rank lower as well, since all are hazardous if spilled in quantity while being shipped by rail. Every shipper of any of these materials would therefore be strictly liable for the consequences of a spill or other accident that occurred while the material was being shipped through a metropolitan area. The plaintiff's lawyer further acknowledged the irrelevance, on her view of the case, of the fact that Cyanamid had leased and filled the car that spilled the acrylonitrile; all she thought important is that Cyanamid introduced the product into the stream of commerce that happened to pass through the Chicago metropolitan area. Her concession may have been incautious. One might want to distinguish between the shipper who merely places his goods on his loading dock to be picked up by the carrier and the shipper who, as in this case, participates actively in the transportation. But the concession is illustrative of the potential scope of the district court's decision.

* * *

Cases * * * that impose strict liability for the storage of a dangerous chemical provide a potentially helpful analogy to our case. But they can be distinguished on the ground that the storer * * * has more control than the shipper.

So we can get little help from precedent, and might as well apply section 520 to the acrylonitrile problem from the ground up. To begin with, we have been given no reason * * * for believing that a negligence regime is not perfectly adequate to remedy and deter, at reasonable cost, the accidental spillage of acrylonitrile from rail cars. * * * [A]lthough acrylonitrile is flammable even at relatively low temperatures, and toxic, it is not so corrosive or otherwise destructive that it will eat through or otherwise damage or weaken a tank car's valves although they are maintained with due (which essentially means, with average) care. No one suggests, therefore, that the leak in this case was caused by the inherent properties of acrylonitrile. It was caused by carelessness—whether that of the North American Car Corporation in failing to maintain or inspect the car properly, or that of Cyanamid in failing to maintain or inspect it, or that of the Missouri Pacific when it had custody of the car, or that of the switching line itself in failing to notice the ruptured lid, or some combination of these possible failures of care. Accidents that are due to a lack of care can be prevented by taking care; and when a lack of care can * * * be shown in court, such accidents are adequately deterred by the threat of liability for negligence.

* * *

The district judge and the plaintiff's lawyer make much of the fact that the spill occurred in a densely inhabited metropolitan area. Only 4,000 gallons spilled; what if all 20,000 had done so? Isn't the risk that this might happen even if everybody were careful sufficient to warrant giving the shipper an incentive to explore alternative routes? Strict liability would supply that incentive. But this argument overlooks the fact that, like other transportation networks, the railroad network is a hub-and-spoke system. And the hubs are in metropolitan areas. Chicago is one of the nation's largest railroad hubs. In 1983, the latest date for which we have figures, Chicago's railroad yards handled the third highest volume of hazardous-material shipments in the nation. East St. Louis, which is also in Illinois, handled the second highest volume. Office of Technology Assessment,

Transportation of Hazardous Materials 53 (1986). With most hazardous chemicals (by volume of shipments) being at least as hazardous as acrylonitrile, it is unlikely—and certainly not demonstrated by the plaintiff—that they can be rerouted around all the metropolitan areas in the country, except at prohibitive cost. Even if it were feasible to reroute them one would hardly expect shippers, as distinct from carriers, to be the firms best situated to do the rerouting.

* * *

The difference between shipper and carrier points to a deep flaw in the plaintiff's case. Unlike Guille * * * and unlike the storage cases, beginning with Rylands itself, here it is not the actors—that is, the transporters of acrylonitrile and other chemicals—but the manufacturers, who are sought to be held strictly liable. [C] A shipper can in the bill of lading designate the route of his shipment if he likes, [c] but is it realistic to suppose that shippers will become students of railroading in order to lay out the safest route by which to ship their goods? Anyway, rerouting is no panacea. Often it will increase the length of the journey, or compel the use of poorer track, or both. When this happens, the probability of an accident is increased, even if the consequences of an accident if one occurs are reduced; so the expected accident cost, being the product of the probability of an accident and the harm if the accident occurs, may rise. Glickman, Analysis of a National Policy for Routing Hazardous Materials on Railroads (Department of Transportation, Research and Special Programs Administration, Transportation Systems Center, May 1980). It is easy to see how the accident in this case might have been prevented at reasonable cost by greater care on the part of those who handled the tank car of acrylonitrile. It is difficult to see how it might have been prevented at reasonable cost by a change in the activity of transporting the chemical. This is therefore not an apt case for strict liability.

* * *

In emphasizing the flammability and toxicity of acrylonitrile rather than the hazards of transporting it, as in failing to distinguish between the active and the passive shipper, the plaintiff overlooks the fact that ultrahazardousness or abnormal dangerousness is, in the contemplation of the law at least, a property not of substances, but of activities: not of acrylonitrile, but of the transportation of acrylonitrile by rail through populated areas. [C] Natural gas is both flammable and poisonous, but the operation of a natural gas well is not an ultrahazardous activity. [C] Whatever the situation under products liability law (section 402A of the Restatement), the manufacturer of a product is not considered to be engaged in an abnormally dangerous activity merely because the product becomes dangerous when it is handled or used in some way after it leaves his premises, even if the danger is foreseeable. [Cc] The plaintiff does not suggest that Cyanamid should switch to making some less hazardous chemical that would substitute for acrylonitrile in the textiles and other goods in which acrylonitrile is used. Were this a feasible method of accident avoidance, there would be an argument for making manufacturers strictly liable for accidents that occur during the shipment of their products (how strong an argument we need not decide). Apparently it is not a feasible method.

The relevant activity is transportation, not manufacturing and shipping. This essential distinction the plaintiff ignores. But even if the plaintiff is treated as a transporter and not merely a shipper, it has not shown that the transportation of acrylonitrile in bulk by rail through populated areas is so hazardous an activity, even when due care is exercised, that the law should seek to create—perhaps quixotically—incentives to relocate the activity to nonpopulated areas, or to reduce the scale of the activity, or to switch to transporting acrylonitrile by road rather than by rail, perhaps to set the stage for a replay of Siegler v. Kuhlman. It is no more realistic to propose to reroute the shipment of all hazardous materials around Chicago than it is to propose the relocation of homes adjacent to the Blue Island switching yard to more distant suburbs. It may be less realistic. Brutal though it may seem to say it, the inappropriate use to which land is being put in the Blue Island yard and neighborhood may be, not the transportation of hazardous chemicals, but residential living. The analogy is to building your home between the runways at O'Hare.

The briefs hew closely to the Restatement, whose approach to the issue of strict liability is mainly allocative rather than distributive. By this we mean that the emphasis is on picking a liability regime (negligence or strict liability) that will control the particular class of accidents in question most effectively, rather than on finding the deepest packet and placing liability there. At argument, however, the plaintiff's lawyer invoked distributive considerations by pointing out that Cyanamid is a huge firm and the Indiana Harbor Belt Railroad a fifty-mile-long switching line that almost went broke in the winter of 1979, when the accident occurred. Well, so what? A corporation is not a living person but a set of contracts the terms of which determine who will bear the brunt of liability. Tracing the incidence of a cost is a complex undertaking which the plaintiff sensibly has made no effort to assume, since its legal relevance would be dubious. We add only that however small the plaintiff may be, it has mighty parents: it is a jointly owned subsidiary of Conrail and the Soo line.

* * *

The judgment is reversed (with no award of costs in this court) and the case remanded for further proceedings, consistent with this opinion, on the plaintiff's claim for negligence.

Reversed and remanded, with directions.

NOTES AND QUESTIONS

1. Some other activities held subject to strict liability:

A. *Toxic Chemicals and Inflammable Liquids* transported or stored in quantity in an urban area. Zero Wholesale Gas Co. v. Stroud, 264 Ark. 27, 571 S.W.2d 74 (1978) (propane gas); Northglenn v. Chevron U.S.A., Inc., 519 F.Supp. 515 (D.Colo. 1981) (service station stored large amounts of gasoline underground near a residential area and its sewer lines). Contra: Hudson v. Peavey Oil Co., 279 Or. 3, 566 P.2d 175 (1977) (filling stations common in residential areas).

B. *Pile Driving,* setting up excessive vibration. Vern J. Oja & Associates v. Washington Park Towers, Inc., 89 Wash.2d 72, 569 P.2d 1141 (1977).

C. *Crop Dusting.* Langan v. Valicopters, Inc., 88 Wash.2d 855, 567 P.2d 218 (1977). Contra, requiring negligence: Lawler v. Skelton, 241 Miss. 274, 130 So.2d 565 (1961). Accord, Koos v. Roth, 55 Or.App. 12, 637 P.2d 167 (1981) aff'd, 293 Or. 670, 652 P.2d 1255 (1982) (agricultural field burning also subject to strict liability under same rationale as crop dusting).

D. *Poisonous Gases.* Luthringer v. Moore, 31 Cal.2d 489, 190 P.2d 1 (1948) (fumigation); Langlois v. Allied Chemical Corp., 258 La. 1067, 249 So.2d 133 (1971). Contra: Fritz v. E.I. du Pont Denemours & Co., 45 Del. 427, 75 A.2d 256 (1950).

E. *Rockets.* Defendants testing rocket fuel have been held subject to strict liability in Smith v. Lockheed Propulsion Co., 247 Cal.App.2d 774, 56 Cal.Rptr. 128 (1967) and Berg v. Reaction Motors Div., 37 N.J. 396, 181 A.2d 487 (1962).

F. *Fireworks Display.* Klein v. Pyrodyne Corp., 117 Wash.2d 1, 810 P.2d 917 (1991) (4th of July celebration). Contra, Cadena v. Chicago Fireworks Mfg. Co., 297 Ill.App.3d 945, 697 N.E.2d 802 (1998) (court, using same §§ 519–520 analysis, reaches opposite result).

G. *Hazardous Waste Disposal Site.* Cf. Village of Wilsonville v. SCA Services, Inc., 86 Ill.2d 1, 55 Ill.Dec. 499, 426 N.E.2d 824 (1981); Bauer, Love Canal: Common Law Approaches to a Modern Tragedy, 11 Envtl.L.Nw.U. 133 (1980); Hurley–Bruno, The Development of a Strict Liability Cause of Action for Personal Injuries Resulting from Hazardous Waste, 16 N.Eng.L.Rev. 543 (1981). Does the defendant have to know that the material of which it is disposing is hazardous in order for strict liability to apply? See State Dept. of Environmental Protection v. Ventron, 94 N.J. 473, 468 A.2d 150 (1983) (strict liability applied to unknowing disposal of PCB's).

H. *Oil Wells.* Green v. General Petroleum Corp., 205 Cal. 328, 270 P. 952 (1928). Contra: Turner v. Big Lake Oil Co., 128 Tex. 155, 96 S.W.2d 221 (1936) (salt water reservoir).

I. *Water Escape.* Branch v. Western Petroleum, Inc., 657 P.2d 267 (Utah 1982); Clark–Aiken Co. v. Cromwell–Wright Co., 367 Mass. 70, 323 N.E.2d 876 (1975); Smith v. Board of County Comm'rs, 5 Mich.App. 370, 146 N.W.2d 702 (1966); Thorson v. Minot, 153 N.W.2d 764 (N.D.1967); cf. Doundoulakis v. Hempstead, 42 N.Y.2d 440, 368 N.E.2d 24, 398 N.Y.S.2d 401 (1977) (hydraulic landfill).

2. Note that these activities involve the use of property. Can the abnormally dangerous or ultrahazardous activity theory be used to establish strict liability for other activities not involving the use of land? See Perkins v. F.I.E. Corp., 762 F.2d 1250 (5th Cir.1985) (marketing of handguns—theory not applied); Tompson v. Mindis Metals, Inc., 692 So.2d 805 (Ala.1997) (sale of batteries to recycling facility—theory not applied). What about maintenance of a frequently used device that may cause injury without fault on the part of a proprietor? Cf. Brown v. Sears, Roebuck & Co., 136 Ariz. 556, 667 P.2d 750 (1983) (frayed electric cord). What about committing suicide by running automobile in closed garage of duplex? Laterra v. Treaster, 17 Kan.App.2d 714, 844 P.2d 724 (1992) (strict liability applied where plaintiff's decedent was asphyxiated by carbon monoxide that leaked from defendant's decedent's garage).

3. *Aviation—Ground Damage.* In early stages of commercial aviation, airlines were held strictly liable for ground damage resulting from a crash. This view is no longer justified by the character of the planes and their accident records if the basis is an ultrahazardous or abnormally dangerous activity; and a number of courts have retreated to a negligence standard. See Crosby v. Cox Aircraft Co., 109 Wash.2d 581, 746 P.2d 1198 (1987) (noting "modern trend" away from strict liability to negligence standard for ground damage from aviation accident). Does it make sense that as an industry becomes stronger economically or technologically it is shifted to a less stringent basis of liability? The law review discussions do not deal directly with this point. After considerable wavering by the American Law Institute, a rule of strict liability was adopted in § 520A of the Second Restatement. Is there any other basis on which strict liability can be justified?

4. *"Matter of Common Usage."* Automobile accidents kill and injure more people and damage more property than any of the other activities listed. Why is driving an automobile not an abnormally dangerous activity subject to strict liability? What about driving an automobile under the influence of alcohol? See Goodwin v. Reilley, 176 Cal.App.3d 86, 221 Cal.Rptr. 374 (1985) (rejecting the application of strict liability). What about engaging in sexual intercourse while infected with a sexually transmitted disease? See Doe v. Johnson, 817 F.Supp. 1382 (W.D.Mich.1993) (in action seeking damages for transmission of HIV, the virus that causes AIDS, plaintiff's strict liability count was dismissed). Similarly, the transmission of electricity and natural gas are considered matters of common usage and thus not subject to strict liability. See, e.g., Voelker v. Delmarva Power & Light Co., 727 F.Supp. 991 (D.Md.1989).

5. *"Inappropriate for the Location."* Many of the differences in the holdings of the cases cited in Note 1 can be explained on the basis of the location of the activity. See also the Reporter's Note to § 520 of the Restatement, classifying the cases according to the location of the activity.

6. Professor Seavey suggested that a nuclear reactor would be a nonnatural use of land no matter where it was located. See Seavey, Torts and Atoms, 46 Calif.L.Rev. 3, 9 (1958). Compare Carolina Environmental Study Group, Inc. v. United States Atomic Energy Comm'n, 431 F.Supp. 203 (D.N.C.1977), rev'd sub nom., Duke Power Co. v. Carolina Study Group, Inc., 438 U.S. 59 (1978). Damages arising from accidents caused by nuclear reactors are covered by federal legislation called the Price–Anderson Act (Atomic Energy Damages), 42 U.S.C.A. § 2210. The underlying premise of Price–Anderson is that where strict liability is to be imposed in a situation where there may be massive harm, the amount of damages paid should be *limited.* There have been Congressional debates under Price–Anderson about who should pay. Assuming no negligence on the part of a defendant, should the harm be a private or public cost? What about other activities discussed in this chapter?

7. *Policy Behind the Imposition of Strict Liability.* Strict liability is "founded upon a policy of the law that imposes upon anyone who for his own purposes creates an abnormal risk of harm to his neighbors, the responsibility of relieving against that harm when it does in fact occur. The defendant's enterprise, in other words, is required to pay its way by compensating for the harm it causes because of its special, abnormal and dangerous character." Restatement (Second) of Torts § 519, comment *d.* The liability "is applicable to an activity that is carried on with all reasonable care, and that is of such utility that the risk involved in it cannot be regarded as so great or so unreasonable as to make it negligence merely to carry it

on." Id., § 520, comment *b*. Observe also, that the decision whether an activity is subject to strict liability is for the court, not the jury, to make. Id.

In other words, this liability is analogous to negligence per se, but it is not called negligence because a court makes a judgment that value to the community is sufficiently great that the mere participation in the activity is not to be stigmatized as wrongdoing in the negligence sense. The activity is simply required to pay its own way, without that stigma, but it does pay with full tort damages, including pain and suffering damages when personal injury is involved. Does it make for sound social policy to make a "non-negligent" defendant pay the same as a "negligent" one? Should courts, as contrasted with legislatures, make judgments as to which activities should be subject to "strict liability"? What practical difference would such judgments entail?

Of course, one who carries on an abnormally dangerous activity may also be negligent in the way in which he conducts it and therefore subject to liability on both bases.

3. LIMITATIONS ON STRICT LIABILITY

Foster v. Preston Mill Co.

Supreme Court of Washington, 1954.
44 Wash.2d 440, 268 P.2d 645.

HAMLEY, JUSTICE. Blasting operations conducted by Preston Mill Company frightened mother mink owned by B.W. Foster, and caused the mink to kill their kittens. Foster brought this action against the company to recover damages. His second amended complaint, upon which the case was tried, sets forth a cause of action on the theory of absolute liability * * *.

After a trial to the court without a jury, judgment was rendered for plaintiff in the sum of $1,953.68. The theory adopted by the court was that, after defendant received notice of the effect which its blasting operations were having upon the mink, it was absolutely liable for all damages of that nature thereafter sustained. * * *

The primary question presented by appellant's assignments of error is whether, on these facts, the judgment against appellant is sustainable on the theory of absolute liability.

[The court pointed out that in Washington there is strict liability in blasting cases whether the damage is caused by trespassory or non-trespassory invasions.]

However the authorities may be divided on the point just discussed, they appear to be agreed that strict liability should be confined to consequences which lie within the extraordinary risk whose existence calls for such responsibility. [Cc] This limitation on the doctrine is indicated in the italicized portions of the rule as set forth in Restatement of Torts, § 519:

> "Except as stated in §§ 521–4, one who carries on an ultrahazardous activity is liable to another whose person, land or chattels the actor should recognize as likely to be harmed by the unpreventable miscarriage of the activity for harm resulting thereto *from that which*

makes the activity ultrahazardous, although the utmost care is exercised to prevent the harm." (Italics supplied.)

This restriction which has been placed upon the application of the doctrine of absolute liability is based upon considerations of policy. * * * " * * * It is one thing to say that a dangerous enterprise must pay its way within reasonable limits, and quite another to say that it must bear responsibility for every extreme of harm that it may cause. The same practical necessity for the restriction of liability within some reasonable bounds, which arises in connection with problems of 'proximate cause' in negligence cases, demands here that some limit be set. * * * This limitation has been expressed by saying that the defendant's duty to insure safety extends only to certain consequences. More commonly, it is said that the defendant's conduct is not the 'proximate cause' of the damage. But ordinarily in such cases no question of causation is involved, and the limitation is one of the policy underlying liability." Prosser on Torts, 457, § 60.

Applying this principle to the case before us, the question comes down to this: Is the risk that any unusual vibration or noise may cause wild animals, which are being raised for commercial purposes, to kill their young, one of the things which make the activity of blasting ultrahazardous?

We have found nothing in the decisional law which would support an affirmative answer to this question. The decided cases, as well as common experience, indicate that the thing which makes blasting ultrahazardous is the risk that property or persons may be damaged or injured by coming into direct contact with flying debris, or by being directly affected by vibrations of the earth or concussions of the air. * * *

The relatively moderate vibration and noise which appellant's blasting produced at a distance of two and a quarter miles was no more than a usual incident of the ordinary life of the community. See 3 Restatement of Torts 48, § 522, comment a. The trial court specifically found that the blasting did not unreasonably interfere with the enjoyment of their property by nearby landowners, except in the case of respondent's mink ranch.

It is the exceedingly nervous disposition of mink, rather than the normal risks inherent in blasting operations, which therefore must, as a matter of sound policy, bear the responsibility for the loss here sustained. We subscribe to the view expressed by Professor Harper (30 Mich.L.Rev. 1001, 1006, supra) that the policy of the law does not impose the rule of strict liability to protect against harms incident to the plaintiff's extraordinary and unusual use of land. This is perhaps but an application of the principle that the extent to which one man in the lawful conduct of his business is liable for injuries to another involves an adjustment of conflicting interests. * * *

It is our conclusion that the risk of causing harm of the kind here experienced, as a result of the relatively minor vibration, concussion, and noise from distance blasting, is not the kind of risk which makes the activity of blasting ultrahazardous. The doctrine of absolute liability is therefore inapplicable under the facts of this case, and respondent is not entitled to recover damages.

The judgment is reversed.

NOTES AND QUESTIONS

1. Suppose defendant had been found negligent in making unnecessary noise with heavy equipment, knowing of the possibility that plaintiff's mink might be frightened and kill their kittens. Should defendant be held liable? See Summit View, Inc. v. W.W. Clyde & Co., 17 Utah 2d 26, 403 P.2d 919 (1965). Suppose the defendant could postpone his blasting activity until the one-month-danger period for the mink (whelping season) was over. Under the rationale of the principal case, should that make a difference? What about liability in negligence? See MacGibbon v. Robinson, [1953] 2 D.L.R. 689; Mason v. Grandel, [1952] 1 D.L.R. 516. Should it make any difference that these cases arose in a portion of Canada where the raising of mink was an important part of the economy?

2. In accord with the principal case, upon similar facts, are Madsen v. East Jordan Irrigation Co., 101 Utah 552, 125 P.2d 794 (1942); and Gronn v. Rogers Constructors, Inc., 221 Or. 226, 350 P.2d 1086 (1960). Compare Uvalde Const. Co. v. Hill, 142 Tex. 19, 175 S.W.2d 247 (1943), where the blasting frightened a cow, which bounded against a milkmaid.

3. Without any negligence on the part of the defendant, his cow trespasses in plaintiff's garden. Plaintiff tries to drive the cow out, and the cow attacks and injures her. Strict liability? Troth v. Wills, 8 Pa.Super. 1 (1897); Nixon v. Harris, 15 Ohio St.2d 105, 238 N.E.2d 785 (1968). What about the miscegenation of the scrub bull and the pedigreed heifer? The court had some fun with this in Kopplin v. Quade, 145 Wis. 454, 130 N.W. 511 (1911). What if the cow wanders into plaintiff's barn and breaks through a rotten place in the floor; and plaintiff, entering the barn in the dark falls into the hole and is injured? Hollenbeck v. Johnson, 79 Hun 499, 29 N.Y.S. 945 (1894).

4. Defendant parades his circus elephants through the streets of a city. Plaintiff's skittish horse, seeing a large object pass at a distance of a city block, takes fright and runs away, and plaintiff is injured. Is there strict liability? Schribner v. Kelly, 32 Barb. 14 (N.Y.1862); Bostock–Ferari Amusement Co. v. Brocksmith, 34 Ind.App. 566, 73 N.E. 281 (1905).

5. Defendant keeps a vicious dog that he knows has in the past attacked human beings. This dog, trotting peacefully down the street, accidentally runs into plaintiff and knocks him down. Strict liability? Koetting v. Conroy, 223 Wis. 550, 270 N.W. 625 (1936). What if the dog's owner knows that the animal has attacked other dogs and fought with them but it has never attacked a human being? Is there strict liability when it does so? Cf. Ewing v. Prince, 425 S.W.2d 732 (Ky.1968). See also Martinez v. Modenbach, 396 So.2d 471 (La.App.1981) (chasing dog away, plaintiff slips on the wet grass and falls).

6. In Behrens v. Bertram Mills Circus Ltd., [1957] 2 Q.B. 1, defendant's elephant became frightened by a dog and knocked over a tent. One occupant was injured and the other was frightened. Under English precedent, elephants were deemed hazardous because they attacked man. Should it make any difference that this elephant had no desire to attack but only to avoid the fearsome canine?

Golden v. Amory

Supreme Judicial Court of Massachusetts, 1952.
329 Mass. 484, 109 N.E.2d 131.

Lummus, Justice. The defendants owned a hydroelectric plant in Ludlow in the Red Bridge area. As a result of the hurricane of September 21, 1938, the Chicopee River overflowed and damaged the real estate of the several plaintiffs. In these actions of tort the first count of the several declarations alleged that no permit or decree or approval of the county commissioners was secured by the defendants for the construction, maintenance, and operation of the Alden Street dike. The second count alleged negligence in the maintenance of that dike. The judge directed verdicts for the defendants on the first count, and on the second count, after verdicts for the plaintiffs, entered verdicts for the defendants under leave reserved. To that action, as well as to the exclusion of certain evidence offered by the plaintiffs, the plaintiffs excepted.

The plaintiffs rely upon the rule stated in Fletcher v. Rylands, L.R., 1 Ex. 265, 279, and affirmed in Rylands v. Fletcher, L.R., 3 H.L. 330, 339–340, that "the person who for his own purposes brings on his lands and collects and keeps there anything likely to do mischief if it escapes, must keep it in at his peril, and, if he does not do so, is prima facie answerable for all the damage which is the natural consequence of its escape." That rule is the law of this Commonwealth. [Cc] But that rule does not apply where the injury results from "vis major, the act of God * * *, which the owner had no reason to anticipate." Gorham v. Gross, 125 Mass. 232, 238; Bratton v. Rudnick, 283 Mass. 556, 560–561, 186 N.E. 669. In the present case the flood, as disclosed by the evidence, was plainly beyond the capacity of any one to anticipate, and was clearly an act of God. [Citation] For this reason the rule under discussion does not apply, and the defendants cannot be held liable for injury caused by the flood waters.

Upon the whole case, we find no error, either in the rulings of the judge or in his exclusion of evidence offered by the plaintiffs.

Exceptions overruled.

NOTES AND QUESTIONS

1. In accord are Nichols v. Marsland, L.R. 2 Ex.Div. 1 (1876) (dam washed out by extraordinary rainfall); Bratton v. Rudnick, 283 Mass. 556, 186 N.E. 669 (1933) (same); Murphy v. Gillum, 73 Mo.App. 487 (1898) (see page from dam embankment caused by unprecedented frost). Cf. Carstairs v. Taylor, L.R. 6 Ex. 217 (1871) (rat gnawed a hole in defendant's water box).

2. What if defendant's reservoir overflows because the owner of another reservoir upstream releases suddenly a large quantity of water? Box v. Jubb, 4 Ex.Div. 76 (1879). Cf. Rickards v. Lothian, [1913] A.C. 263 (malicious third person plugged up defendant's lavatory basin and turned the water on full); Kaufman v. Boston Dye House, 280 Mass. 161, 182 N.E. 297 (1932) (petroleum product ignited by third person's gasoline engine); Perry v. Kendricks Transport, Ltd., [1956] 1 W.L.R. 85 (petrol in automobile tank, held to fall within Rylands v. Fletcher, exploded when boys deliberately threw lighted matches into it); Kleebauer v.

Western Fuse & Explosives Co., 138 Cal. 497, 71 P. 617 (1903) (alleged murderer, pursued by police, took refuge in defendant's powder magazine and committed suicide by blowing it up). Cf. Baker v. Snell, [1908] 2 K.B. 352, 825. Defendant, the owner of a dog that he knew to be vicious, entrusted it to his servant. The servant deliberately incited it to attack the plaintiff. Two of the judges, with a third dissenting, thought there would be strict liability even if the servant were not acting within the scope of his employment.

3.   See Harper, Liability Without Fault and Proximate Cause, 30 Mich.L.Rev. 1001 (1932). On the effect of an intervening act of God or of a third party, compare the provisions in Restatement (Second) of Torts §§ 504(3)(c) (livestock), 510 (wild or dangerous animals) and 522 (abnormally dangerous activities). Compare the treatment of the hurricane in this case with that of Hurricane Andrew in Scorza v. Martinez, 683 So.2d 1115 (Fla.App.1996), pages 682–683. Why the difference? Should the rule be applied any differently when the defendant has been negligent?

Sandy v. Bushey

Supreme Judicial Court of Maine, 1925.
124 Me. 320, 128 A. 513.

STURGIS, J. In the summer of 1923, the plaintiff turned his mare and colt out in the pasture of a neighbor. Other horses occupied the pasture during the season, including the defendant's three-year old colt. On July 14, 1923, the plaintiff went to the pasture to grain his mare, and, while so doing, was kicked by the defendant's horse and seriously injured. This action on the case is brought to recover damages for such injuries and, after verdict for the plaintiff, is before this court on a general motion.

By the common law the owners or keepers of domestic animals are not answerable for an injury done by them in a place where they have a right to be, unless the animals in fact, and to the owners' knowledge, are vicious. If, however, a person keeps a vicious or dangerous animal which he knows is accustomed to attack and injure mankind, he assumes the obligation of an insurer against injury by such animal, and no measure of care in its keeping will excuse him. His liability is founded upon the keeping of such an animal when he has knowledge of its vicious propensities, and his care or negligence is immaterial. In an action for an injury caused by such an animal, the plaintiff has only to allege and prove the keeping, the vicious propensities, and the scienter. Negligence is not the ground of liability, and need not be alleged or proved. This rule of liability of keepers of domestic animals finds its origin in the ancient common law and, except as modified by statute in case of injuries by dogs, is retained as the rule of law in this class of cases in this state. [Cc]

A careful consideration of the evidence discloses facts which fairly tend to establish that the defendant's horse had exhibited a vicious and ugly disposition at various times prior to the day on which the plaintiff was injured, and notice of the animal's vicious propensities had been brought home to the defendant. Upon these issues the jury's verdict in favor of the plaintiff was fully warranted.

The defendant, however, says that the plaintiff was guilty of contributory negligence and cannot, therefore, recover in this action. We are unable to sustain this contention under the rule of liability adopted by this court. In those jurisdictions which have departed from the ancient common-law rule and declared negligence to be the ground of liability in actions for injuries by animals, the defense of contributory negligence has been recognized, and the injured party's failure to exercise due care will defeat his action. [Cc] In this state, however, the negligence doctrine has not been accepted, and contributory negligence in the strict sense of that term cannot be held to constitute a defense to the action. Exclusion of negligence as the basis of liability forbids the inclusion of contributory negligence as a defense. Something more than slight negligence or want of due care on the part of the injured party must be shown in order to relieve the keeper of a vicious domestic animal known to be such from his liability as an insurer.

In Muller v. McKesson, 73 N.Y. 195, 29 Am.Rep. 123, which may be fairly accepted as the leading case in this country upon the question of contributory negligence as a defense to an action of this character, Church, C.J., in stating the opinion of the court, says:

"If a person with full knowledge of the evil propensities of an animal wantonly excites him, or voluntarily and unnecessarily puts himself in the way of such an animal, he would be adjudged to have brought the injury upon himself, and ought not to be entitled to recover. In such a case it cannot be said, in a legal sense, that the keeping of the animal, which is the gravamen of the offense, produced the injury. * * * But as the owner is held to a rigorous rule of liability on account of the danger to human life and limb, by harboring and keeping such animals, it follows that he ought not to be relieved from it by slight negligence or want of ordinary care. To enable an owner of such an animal to interpose this defense, acts should be proved with notice of the character of the animal, which would establish that the person injured voluntarily brought the calamity upon himself." * * *

We are convinced that the principle announced by Chief Justice Church correctly defines the degree of responsibility which must be fixed upon the injured party in order to relieve the keeper of a known vicious animal from his liability as an insurer with which he is charged in this state. The fact must be established that the injury is attributable, not to the keeping of the animal, but to the injured party's unnecessarily and voluntarily putting himself in a way to be hurt knowing the probable consequences of his act, so that he may fairly be deemed to have brought the injury upon himself.

Applying this rule to the facts in the case before us, we are of the opinion that the prima facie case against the defendant, established by the evidence, is not rebutted by the plaintiff's acts or omissions. The plaintiff led his mare away from the other horses in the pasture and started to grain her, when the defendant's horse approached in a threatening manner. The plaintiff drove him away and turned to continue feeding the mare. The colt's return was silent and swift and his attack unexpected. It cannot be said that the plaintiff voluntarily put himself in a way to be injured by the defendant's horse, knowing the probable consequences of his act. The defendant is liable, as found by the jury.

Motion overruled.

NOTES AND QUESTIONS

1.   In accord is Marshall v. Ranne, 511 S.W.2d 255 (Tex.1974), where plaintiff was taunted and tormented periodically by his neighbor's wild boar. One day the boar made good on his threats and bit plaintiff.

2.   The Restatement (Second) of Torts also has adopted the rule for both wild animals and abnormally dangerous activities. See §§ 515, 523, 524. Is this a logical rule? If ordinary contributory negligence is a defense when defendant is negligent, why is it not a defense when he is not even negligent?

3.   Most states have adopted comparative negligence rules, reducing a plaintiff's damages by the plaintiff's percentage of negligence. If a plaintiff's negligence is no longer a complete bar to recovery, should it be a defense in strict liability cases as well as negligence cases? Is it true that conduct constituting negligence and conduct forming the basis for strict liability cannot be rationally compared? Plaintiff, who had been around cattle all his life, attempted to move a newborn calf away from the danger of a muddy river bank, with its mother unsecured and only a few feet away. She attacked as he put the calf down and injured him. Should plaintiff's actions completely bar his recovery? See Andrade v. Shiers, 564 So.2d 787 (La.App. 1990) (plaintiff's fault compared to owners' strict liability; 80% of fault allocated to plaintiff).

4.   Defendant keeps a bear in a cage at a circus. Plaintiff crawls under the rope in front of the cage and goes within six inches of the bars. The bear slaps at him through the bars hitting him in the face and putting out his eye. Is defendant liable? Cf. Ervin v. Woodruff, 119 App.Div. 603, 103 N.Y.S. 1051 (1907); Heidemann v. Wheaton, 72 S.D. 375, 34 N.W.2d 492 (1948). A customer at a service station put his hand in an unlocked box of snakes kept for public display at a service station. He was bitten by a rattlesnake. Is his claim barred? See Keyser v. Phillips Petroleum Co., 287 So.2d 364 (Fla.App.1973). Defendant raises exotic animals on her farm, including Siberian tigers. A man who is visiting the tenant who lives above her garage goes into defendant's backyard to pet a tiger through the fence. The tiger grabs his arm and pulls it through the fence. His injury requires multiple surgeries. Is the owner strictly liable? Can she argue assumption of the risk as a defense? Plaintiff had visited the tenant on the farm about the thirty times before the incident. Irvine v. Rare Feline Breeding Ctr., 685 N.E.2d 120 (Ind.App.1997) (strict liability applies to wild animals; question of fact for jury whether defendant proved assumption of risk).

5.   Defendant is conducting blasting operations in dangerous proximity to a highway. He stations a flagman to stop traffic when a blast is about to be set off. Plaintiff drives past the flagman, and is injured by the blast. Should it make any difference whether plaintiff does not see the flagman because he is not looking, or sees him and deliberately drives past? See Worth v. Dunn, 98 Conn. 51, 62, 118 A. 467, 471 (1922); Wells v. Knight, 32 R.I. 432, 80 A. 16 (1911).

6.   *Immunity Created by Legal Sanction.* Statutory sanction for defendant's conduct has frequently been held to confer immunity from strict liability, on the ground that the defendant cannot be held liable for doing properly what the law has

authorized him to do, although he will still of course be liable for any negligence. Thus the custodian of a public zoo may be held not subject to strict liability for harm done by the animals kept in it. Jackson v. Baker, 24 App.D.C. 100 (1904); Guzzi v. New York Zoological Society, 192 App.Div. 263, 182 N.Y.S. 257 (1920), aff'd, 233 N.Y. 511, 135 N.E. 897 (1922). This has been held to be true for gas or electric conduits laid in the street under legislative authority. Gould v. Winona Gas Co., 100 Minn. 258, 111 N.W. 254 (1907). Also for common carriers required by law to ship wild animals or explosives. Actiesselskabet Ingrid v. Central R. Co. of N.J., 216 Fed. 72 (2d Cir.1914); Pope v. Edward M. Rude Carrier Corp., 138 W.Va. 218, 75 S.E.2d 584 (1953).

The rule has also been extended to a contractor doing such work as blasting for the state. Nelson v. McKenzie–Hague Co., 192 Minn. 180, 256 N.W. 96 (1934); Pumphrey v. J.A. Jones Const. Co., 250 Iowa 559, 94 N.W.2d 737 (1959). There has been a strong challenge to the proposition that a government contract alone should shield the contractor from strict liability. While such a privilege may result in lower costs to government, that saving is acquired at the expenditure of denying recovery to an innocent victim. In light of the abrogation of governmental immunity itself, modern courts may be inclined to give more consideration to the injured party and impose strict liability on the contractor who engages in an abnormally dangerous activity. There is a good discussion in Smith v. Lockheed Propulsion Co., 247 Cal.App.2d 774, 56 Cal.Rptr. 128, 139–142 (1967).

7. The next chapter addresses the development of strict liability for "unreasonably dangerous" products. Is this analogous to the principle of strict liability for abnormally dangerous activities? See Arlington Forest Assoc. v. Exxon Corp., 774 F.Supp. 387 (E.D.Va.1991) (under § 519, strict liability attaches only to abnormally dangerous activities, not substances); Indiana Harbor Belt R.R. Co. v. American Cyanamid Co., 916 F.2d 1174 (7th Cir.1990) ("ultrahazardousness or abnormal dangerousness is, in the contemplation of the law at least, a property not of substances, but of activities").

CHAPTER XV

PRODUCTS LIABILITY

"Products liability" is the umbrella term for the liability of a manufacturer, seller, or other supplier of chattels, to one with whom he is not in privity of contract, who suffers physical harm caused by the chattel. The liability may rest upon the supplier's negligence or upon a warranty, or it may be based on strict liability in tort. Strict liability theories have become the paramount basis of liability for manufacturers of products, although negligence and breach of warranty remain important as well.

Some jurisdictions have extended the theories supporting the imposition of strict liability against manufacturers of products onto other classes of defendants. Thus retailers, lessors of chattels, builders and developers of real property, and even providers of services may be subject to strict liability.

This "revolution" in the common law of torts is not as radical as it may initially seem. Developments in negligence and warranty law foreshadowed the adoption of strict liability in many jurisdictions. Moreover, elements of the law of negligence, especially the "reasonableness" standard, have crept back into the strict liability basis. Courts have continued to assert that strict liability is not absolute liability, but some decisions have come close to that outer mark.

The law set forth in this chapter represents a significant intellectual achievement whose influence runs far beyond the borders of the United States as Europe and other common law countries have utilized it as a model for their own efforts. See, e.g., the Product Liability Directive for the European Economic Community (85/374/EEC). The law initially developed through the courts, largely around the organizing principle of the Restatement (Second) of Torts, which had its intellectual roots in the views of some of the great scholars of tort law—Fleming James, William Prosser, Roger Traynor, and John Wade. The achievement has been a controversial one. Manufacturers have claimed that the application of strict liability for design and warnings cases have kept good products off the market, inhibited product development, and created an unreasonable "tort tax" on products. Consumer groups and plaintiffs' lawyers deny these claims and argue that strict liability has acted as a surrogate policeman to make products safer. To add to the confusion, each side is not always defining "strict liability" in the same way. As you will discern from this chapter, courts have had a great deal of difficulty in defining strict liability in the context of design and warning cases. See Henderson & Eisenberg, The Quiet Revolution in Products Liability: An Empirical Study of Legal Change, 37 U.C.L.A.L.Rev. 479 (1990); Henderson and Twerski, Closing the American Product Liability Frontier: The Rejection of Liability Without Defect, 66 N.Y.U.L.Rev. 1263 (1991); G. Schwartz, The Beginning and the

Possible End of the Rise of Modern American Tort Law, 26 Ga.L.Rev. 601 (1992) and V. Schwartz, The Death of "Super Strict Liability": Common Sense Returns to Tort Law, 27 Gonz.L.Rev. 179 (1992). Legislative bodies at the state level have become involved in shaping the law, sometimes intervening to alter common law doctrines. Congress has heard and "reheard" about the need for federal legislation, but thus far has not acted except in very limited areas. See Chapter 24. The American Law Institute has promulgated Restatement (Third) of Torts: Products Liability (1998).

As you work your way through this chapter, think about the rationale for the system. Why is a liability rule necessary to assure product safety? Is the market a viable mechanism for weeding out unsafe products? Why not? If the market fails, should product safety be assured by government regulation given the institutional advantage of government in broad information gathering, cost-benefit evaluation, predictability and uniformity? Should the questions asked be confined to ones of efficiency or should justice also be considered? See Owen, The Moral Foundations of Products Liability Law: Toward First Principles, 68 Notre Dame L.Rev. 427 (1993).

The topic of products liability has sufficient material to support a separate law school course. Two major treatises, both regularly supplemented, cover the field. See R. Hursh and Bailey, American Law of Products Liability (3d ed. 1987); L. Frumer and Friedman, Products Liability (Rev. ed. 1993). See also CCH Products Liability Reporter and BNA Products Safety and Liability Reporter. What follows is a taste of some of the common issues and basic theories of this burgeoning area of the law.

1. DEVELOPMENT OF THEORIES OF RECOVERY

(A) NEGLIGENCE

MacPherson v. Buick Motor Co.

Court of Appeals of New York, 1916.
217 N.Y. 382, 111 N.E. 1050.

Action, by Donald C. MacPherson against the Buick Motor Company. From a judgment of the Appellate Division (160 App.Div. 55, 145 N.Y.Supp. 462), affirming a judgment of the Supreme Court for plaintiff, defendant appeals.

CARDOZO, J. The defendant is a manufacturer of automobiles. It sold an automobile to a retail dealer. The retail dealer resold to the plaintiff. While the plaintiff was in the car it suddenly collapsed. He was thrown out and injured. One of the wheels was made of defective wood, and its spokes crumbled into fragments. The wheel was not made by the defendant; it was bought from another manufacturer. There is evidence, however, that its defects could have been discovered by reasonable inspection, and that inspection was omitted. There is no claim that the defendant knew of the

Buick Model 10 Runabout (1909)
(The model Mr. MacPherson purchased)

defect and willfully concealed it. * * * The charge is one, not of fraud, but of negligence. The question to be determined is whether the defendant owed a duty of care and vigilance to any one but the immediate purchaser.

[The court discusses competing lines of precedents. One group of cases suggested that the manufacturer owed a duty of care to ultimate purchasers only when the product was "inherently dangerous." Some courts confined this classification to guns, poisons or other products whose normal function it was to injure or destroy. Other decisions suggested that a manufacturer would breach a duty of care to a foreseeable user of the product if the product was likely to cause injury if negligently made.]

We hold * * * that * * * [i]f the nature of a thing is such that it is reasonably certain to place life and limb in peril when negligently made, it is then a thing of danger. Its nature gives warning of the consequences to be expected. If to the element of danger there is added knowledge that the thing will be used by persons other than the purchaser, and used without new tests, then, irrespective of contract, the manufacturer of this thing of danger is under a duty to make it carefully. That is as far as we are required to go for the decision of this case. There must be knowledge of a danger, not merely possible, but probable. It is possible to use almost anything in a way that will make it dangerous if defective. That is not enough to charge the manufacturer with a duty independent of his contract. Whether a given thing is dangerous may be sometimes a question for the court and sometimes a question for the jury. There must also be knowledge that in the usual course of events the danger will be shared by others than the buyer. Such knowledge may often be inferred from the nature of the transaction. But it is possible that even knowledge of the danger and of the use will not always be enough. The proximity or remoteness of the relation is a factor to be considered. We are dealing now with the liability of the manufacturer of the finished product, who puts it on the market to be used without inspection by his customers. If he is negligent, where danger is to be foreseen, a liability will follow. * * * We have put aside the notion that the duty to safeguard life and limb, when the consequences of negligence may be foreseen, grows out of contract and nothing else. We have put the source of the obligation where it ought to be. We have put its source in the law.

There is nothing anomalous in a rule which imposes upon A., who has contracted with B., a duty to C. and D. and others according as he knows or does not know that the subject-matter of the contract is intended for their use. We may find an analogy in the law which measures the liability of landlords. If A. leases to B. a tumbledown house, he is not liable, in the absence of fraud, to B.'s guests who enter it and are injured. This is because B. is then under the duty to repair it, the lessor has the right to suppose that he will fulfill that duty, and, if he omits to do so, his guests must look to him. Bohlen, Affirmative Obligations in the Law of Torts, 44 Am.Law Reg., N.S., 341. But if A. leases a building to be used by the lessee at once as a place of public entertainment, the rule is different. There injury to persons other than the lessee is to be foreseen, and foresight of the consequences involves the creation of a duty. [C]

In this view of the defendant's liability there is nothing inconsistent with the theory of liability on which the case was tried. It is true that the court told the jury that "an automobile is not an inherently dangerous vehicle." The meaning, however, is that danger is not to be expected when the vehicle is well constructed. The court left it to the jury to say whether the defendant ought to have foreseen that the car, if negligently constructed, would become "imminently dangerous." Subtle distinctions are drawn by the defendants between things inherently dangerous and things imminently dangerous, but the case does not turn upon these verbal niceties. If danger was to be expected as reasonably certain, there was a duty of vigilance, and this whether you call the danger inherent or imminent. In varying forms that thought was put before the jury. We do not say that the court would not have been justified in ruling as a matter of law that the car was a dangerous thing. If there was any error, it was none of which the defendant can complain.

We think the defendant was not absolved from a duty of inspection because it bought the wheels from a reputable manufacturer. It was not merely a dealer in automobiles. It was responsible for the finished product. It was not at liberty to put the finished product on the market without subjecting the component parts to ordinary and simple tests. [C] Under the charge of the trial judge nothing more was required of it. The obligation to inspect must vary with the nature of the thing to be inspected. The more probable the danger the greater the need of caution. * * *

The judgment should be affirmed with costs.

[The dissenting opinion of WILLARD BARTLETT, C.J., is omitted.]

NOTES AND QUESTIONS

1.   The early development of liability of a manufacturer or seller of chattels to third parties was strongly influenced by Winterbottom v. Wright, 10 M. & W. 109, 152 Eng.Rep. 402 (1842), page 401. The case was misinterpreted to state a general rule of nonliability of any contractor, including any supplier of a product, to third parties, whether in contract or in tort, and whether for nonfeasance or misfeasance. This misinterpretation was first pointed out by Professor Bohlen in a noted article in 1905. Bohlen, The Basis of Affirmative Obligations in the Law of Torts, 44 Am.L.Reg. (N.S.) 209, 280–85, 289–310 (1905). Nevertheless, most courts clung to the general rule while carving out a few exceptions for "inherently dangerous" products.

2.   The principal case became a leading case, and a new point of departure. It is now accepted in all of the American jurisdictions, although one or two of them, such as Mississippi in State Stove Mfg. Co. v. Hodges, 189 So.2d 113 (Miss.1966), jumped over negligence to the strict liability base.

3.   For a time some of the courts continued to use the language "inherently dangerous," although it was clear from the opinions that this meant no more than that substantial harm is to be anticipated if the chattel should be defective. This seems to have faded out almost entirely. What finally emerged is a general rule imposing negligence liability upon all sellers of chattels—whether damage is to person or property, whether the manufacturer produced the whole product or a significant component part, whether the injured person was the immediate purchaser or not.

4.   Even with the advent of alternative means of recovery such as breach of warranty and strict liability, negligence continues to be an important cause of action for plaintiffs injured by products. Almost every cause of action for product liability contains a negligence count. Most plaintiffs' lawyers still try to prove negligence. Why? An experienced practitioner has observed: "More plaintiffs would prefer to present their respective cases to a jury on a negligence, rather than on a

strict liability, basis. In McLuhanesque terms negligence is 'hot' and strict liability is 'cold.' It is easier to prevail by showing that the defendant did something wrong than that there is something technically defective about the product." Rheingold, The Expanding Liability of the Product Supplier: A Primer, 2 Hofstra L.Rev. 521, 531 (1974). Can the theory affect a jury's willingness to award damages? Why?

(B) WARRANTY

The action by the buyer of goods against the seller for breach of warranty is a freak hybrid, "born of the illicit intercourse of tort and contract," and partaking the characteristics of both. It is unique in the law. Originally the action was in tort, in an action of trespass on the case for breach of an assumed duty, and the wrong was conceived to be a form of misrepresentation, in the nature of deceit, and not at all clearly distinguished from it. Ames, History of Assumpsit, 2 Harv.L.Rev. 1, 8 (1888). In the latter part of the seventeenth century, decisions such as Cross v. Gardiner, 1 Show.K.B. 68, 89 Eng.Rep. 453 (1689), and Medina v. Stoughton, 1 Ld.Raym. 593, 91 Eng.Rep. 1297 (1700), established the fact that the tort action would lie for a mere affirmation of fact ("express warranty") made without knowledge of its falsity or negligence. As a result warranty became a form of strict liability in tort.

In Stuart v. Wilkins, 1 Doug. 18, 99 Eng.Rep. 15 (1778), it was first held that assumpsit would lie for breach of an express warranty as a part of the contract of sale. After that decision, and over a period of more than a century, warranties gradually came to be regarded as express or implied terms of the contract of sale, and the action on the contract became the usual remedy for any breach.

Warranty has, however, never entirely lost its original tort character. There are numerous decisions holding that a tort action can be maintained for the breach, without proof of either intentional misrepresentation or negligence. See, for example, Shippen v. Bowen, 122 U.S. 575 (1887). Nor is this entirely a procedural matter. Even when the action is in form one for breach of contract, its basic tort character has sometimes been recognized by the application of tort rules, such as that for survival of actions in Gosling v. Nichols, 59 Cal.App.2d 442, 139 P.2d 86 (1943). Or the statute of limitations. Rubino v. Utah Canning Co., 123 Cal.App.2d 18, 266 P.2d 163 (1954). Or the more liberal tort rule as to damages. Despatch Oven Co. v. Rauenhorst, 229 Minn. 436, 40 N.W.2d 73 (1949). And several jurisdictions allow recovery for wrongful death arising out of breach of warranty, when the action would not lie for a pure breach of contract. See for example Greco v. S.S. Kresge Co., 277 N.Y. 26, 12 N.E.2d 557 (1938); Kelley v. Volkswagenwerk Aktiengesellschaft, 110 N.H. 369, 268 A.2d 837 (1970).

The question began to be asked: if warranty is a matter of tort as well as contract and it can arise without any intent to make it a matter of contract, why should it require a contract between the parties? Why should it not arise, in tort, between parties who have not dealt at all with one another—or in other words, without privity of contract?

(1) EXPRESS WARRANTIES

Baxter v. Ford Motor Co.

Supreme Court of Washington, 1932.
168 Wash. 456, 12 P.2d 409.

HERMAN, J. During the month of May, 1930, plaintiff purchased a model A Ford town sedan from defendant St. John Motors, a Ford dealer, who had acquired the automobile in question by purchase from defendant Ford Motor Company. Plaintiff claims that representations were made to him by both defendants that the windshield of the automobile was made of nonshatterable glass which would not break, fly, or shatter. October 12, 1930, while plaintiff was driving the automobile through Snoqualmie pass, a pebble from a passing car struck the windshield of the car in question, causing small pieces of glass to fly into plaintiff's left eye, resulting in the loss thereof. Plaintiff brought this action for damages for the loss of his left eye and for injuries to the sight of his right eye. The case came on for trial, and, at the conclusion of plaintiff's testimony, the court took the case from the jury and entered judgment for both defendants. From that judgment, plaintiff appeals. * * *

The principal question in this case is whether the trial court erred in refusing to admit in evidence, as against respondent Ford Motor Company, the catalogues and printed matter furnished by that respondent to respondent St. John Motors to be distributed for sales assistance. Contained in such printed matter were statements which appellant maintains constituted representations or warranties with reference to the nature of the glass used in the windshield of the car purchased by appellant. A typical statement, as it appears in appellant's exhibit for identification No. 1, is here set forth:

"Triplex Shatter–Proof Glass Windshield. All of the new Ford cars have a Triplex shatter-proof glass windshield—so made that it will not fly or shatter under the hardest impact. This is an important safety factor because it eliminates the dangers of flying glass—the cause of most of the injuries in automobile accidents. In these days of crowded, heavy traffic, the use of this Triplex glass is an absolute necessity. Its extra margin of safety is something that every motorist should look for in the purchase of a car— especially where there are women and children."

Respondent Ford Motor Company contends that there can be no implied or express warranty without privity of contract, and warranties as to personal property do not attach themselves to, and run with, the article sold.

[The court here referred at length to Mazetti v. Armour & Co., 75 Wash. 622, 135 P. 633 (1913), in which a restaurant keeper was permitted to recover for damage to his business resulting when a customer was served defective canned food manufactured by the defendant.]

In the case at bar the automobile was represented by the manufacturer as having a windshield of nonshatterable glass "so made that it will not fly or shatter under the hardest impact." An ordinary person would be unable to discover by the usual and customary examination of the automobile whether glass which would not fly or shatter was used in the windshield. In that respect the purchaser was in a position similar to that of the consumer of a wrongly labeled drug, who has bought the same from a retailer, and who has relied upon the manufacturer's representation that the label correctly set forth the contents of the container. For many years it has been held that, under such circumstances, the manufacturer is liable to the consumer, even though the consumer purchased from a third person the commodity causing the damage. Thomas v. Winchester, 6 N.Y. 397, 57 Am.Dec. 455. The rule in such cases does not rest upon contractual obligations, but rather on the principle that the original act of delivering an article is wrong, when, because of the lack of those qualities which the manufacturer represented it as having, the absence of which could not be readily detected by the consumer, the article is not safe for the purposes for which the consumer would ordinarily use it.

The vital principle present in the case of Mazetti v. Armour & Co., supra, confronts us in the case at bar. In the case cited the court recognized the right of a purchaser to a remedy against the manufacturer because of damages suffered by reason of a failure of goods to comply with the manufacturer's representations as to the existence of qualities which they did not in fact possess, when the absence of such qualities was not readily discoverable, even though there was no privity of contract between the purchaser and the manufacturer.

Since the rule of caveat emptor was first formulated, vast changes have taken place in the economic structures of the English speaking peoples. Methods of doing business have undergone a great transition. Radio, billboards, and the products of the printing press have become the means of creating a large part of the demand that causes goods to depart from factories to the ultimate consumer. It would be unjust to recognize a rule that would permit manufacturers of goods to create a demand for their products by representing that they possess qualities which they, in fact, do not possess, and then, because there is no privity of contract existing between the consumer and the manufacturer, deny the consumer the right to recover if damages result from the absence of those qualities, when such absence is not readily noticeable.

"An exception to a rule will be declared by courts when the case is not an isolated instance, but general in its character, and the existing rule does not square with justice. Under such circumstances a court will, if free from the restraint of some statute, declare a rule that will meet the full intendment of the law." Mazetti v. Armour & Co., supra.

We hold that the catalogues and printed matter furnished by respondent * * * Ford Motor Company for distribution and assistance in sales were improperly excluded from evidence, because they set forth representations by the manufacturer that the windshield of the car which appellant bought contained Triplex nonshatterable glass which would not fly or shatter. The nature of nonshatterable glass is such that the falsity of the representations with reference to the glass would not be readily detected by a person of ordinary experience and reasonable prudence. Appellant, under the circumstances shown in this case, had the right to rely upon the representations made by respondent Ford Motor Company relative to qualities possessed by its products, even though there was no privity of contract between appellant and respondent Ford Motor Company. * * *

The trial court erred in taking the case from the jury and entering judgment for respondent Ford Motor Company. It was for the jury to determine under proper instructions, whether the failure of respondent Ford Motor Company to equip the windshield with glass which did not fly or shatter was the proximate cause of appellant's injury. * * *

Reversed, with directions to grant a new trial with reference to respondent Ford Motor Company; affirmed as to respondent St. John Motors.

[The second trial resulted in a verdict for plaintiff, and defendant Ford Motor Company appealed. In Baxter v. Ford Motor Co., 179 Wash. 123, 35 P.2d 1090 (1934), judgment entered on the verdict was affirmed. HOLCOMB, J., said in part:

"A new point arising out of the last trial, claimed as error, was in excluding testimony of an expert witness on behalf of appellant to the effect that there was no better windshield made than that used in respondent's car and in sustaining the objection to appellant's offer of proof on that point.

"No authorities are cited by appellant to sustain this claim, and we know of none. Indeed, it would seem that whether there was any better make of shatter-proof glass manufactured by any one at that time would be wholly immaterial, under the law as decided by us on the former appeal. Since it was the duty of appellant to know that the representations made to purchasers were true. Otherwise it should not have made them. If a person states as true material facts, susceptible of knowledge, to one who relies and acts thereon to his injury, if the representations are false, it is immaterial that he did not know they were false, or that he believed them to be true. * * *

"The court charged the jury that 'there is no proof of fraud in this case.' It has become almost axiomatic that false representations inducing a sale or contract constitute fraud in law. * * * However, the instruction, if it was error against respondent, was cured by the verdict of the jury favorable to respondent."]

NOTES AND QUESTIONS

1. Is this an extension of a contract warranty to one who has made no contract with the defendant, or is it strict liability in tort for an innocent misrepresentation made to the plaintiff? Most of the cases have talked of "express warran-

ty." But in Ford Motor Co. v. Lonon, 217 Tenn. 400, 398 S.W.2d 240 (1966), the court reverted to the theory of misrepresentation. It relied on the Restatement (Second) of Torts § 402B, which states the strict liability without using the word "warranty." The section reads:

"One engaged in the business of selling chattels who, by advertising, labels, or otherwise, makes to the public a misrepresentation of a material fact concerning the character or quality of a chattel sold by him is subject to liability for physical harm to a consumer of the chattel caused by justifiable reliance upon the misrepresentation, even though (a) it is not made fraudulently or negligently, and (b) the consumer has not bought the chattel from or entered into any contract relation with the seller."

See Sales, Innocent Misrepresentation Doctrine: Strict Tort Liability Under Section 402B, 16 Hous.L.Rev. 239 (1979); Green, Strict Liability Under Sections 402A and 402B: A Decade of Litigation, 54 Tex.L.Rev. 1185 (1976). Tennessee later limited the *Lonon* innocent misrepresentation cause of action to cases involving personal injury, leaving plaintiffs with only economic losses to seek redress on breach of contract theories. First Nat'l. Bank of Louisville v. Brooks Farms, 821 S.W.2d 925 (Tenn.1991).

2. The principal case generally has been followed for express statements as to quality made in advertising, on labels, in brochures or other literature accompanying the product, or documents supplied to be transmitted to the ultimate purchaser. See Wade, Strict Liability of Manufacturers, 19 Sw.L.J. 5, 13 (1965). It has been extended to apply to property damage as well as personal injury. See Randy Knitwear, Inc. v. American Cyanamid Co., 11 N.Y.2d 5, 181 N.E.2d 399, 226 N.Y.S.2d 363 (1962). Should contributory negligence or plaintiff's fault be a defense?

3. Should the plaintiff be required to demonstrate reliance upon the representation, either in making the purchase or in using the product? Randall v. Goodrich–Gamble Co., 238 Minn. 10, 54 N.W.2d 769 (1952); Dobbin v. Pacific Coast Coal Co., 25 Wash.2d 190, 170 P.2d 642 (1946). Most courts require this, but some have not. Plaintiff, a minor, was seriously injured while driving intoxicated. He filed a breach of warranty claim against defendant beer manufacturer arguing that its advertising campaign induced him to purchase and consume beer and to drive while intoxicated. Liability? See Smith v. Anheuser–Busch, Inc., 599 A.2d 320 (R.I.1991) (upholding trial court's dismissal of complaint on ground that plaintiff could not demonstrate reasonable reliance on alleged representation in media advertising that driving while intoxicated is safe or acceptable). Plaintiff bought a mace gun that was advertised to "instantly stop and subdue entire groups * * *." It failed to stop an intruder who shot plaintiff after he had sprayed him. See Klages v. General Ordnance Equip. Co., 240 Pa.Super. 356, 367 A.2d 304 (1976) (manufacturer's argument that representations were mere puffery and that the plaintiff did not justifiably rely upon them rejected). See Restatement (Third) of Torts: Products Liability § 9 (1998).

4. What result if a tire manufacturer advertises, "If it saves your life once, it's a bargain," and plaintiff's decedent is killed when the product "blows out"? See Collins v. Uniroyal, Inc., 64 N.J. 260, 315 A.2d 16 (1974). Suppose the manufacturer of a grinding disc states that the product is "stronger, sharper, and longer-lived than ever before available anywhere." The wheel breaks and injures plaintiff. See Jakubowski v. Minnesota Mining & Mfg., 80 N.J.Super. 184, 193 A.2d 275 (1963), rev'd on other grounds, 42 N.J. 177, 199 A.2d 826 (1964). Courts have stated that the promise of safety must be a specific one. What about old cigarette advertising

such as "not a cough in a carload" or "more doctors smoke our brand"? Do they constitute express warranties? Cf. Cipollone v. Liggett Group, Inc., 893 F.2d 541 (3d Cir.1990), affirmed in part and reversed in part, 112 U.S. 2608 (1992) (breach of express warranty allegations based on cigarette advertising). What if the plaintiff buys a cream to remove age spots on her skin that is labeled "safe," but that causes a severe irritation? Spiegel v. Saks 34th Street, 43 Misc.2d 1065, 252 N.Y.S.2d 852 (1964), aff'd mem., 272 N.Y.S.2d 972 (1966) (breach of express warranty). There is a trend in recent case law to allow violation of more generalized statements to be actionable. See Schwartz, Violation of Express Warranty: A Useful Tort That Must Be Kept Within Rational Boundaries, 3 Prod. Liab. J. 147 (May 1992).

(2) IMPLIED WARRANTIES

Henningsen v. Bloomfield Motors, Inc.

Supreme Court of New Jersey, 1960.
32 N.J. 358, 161 A.2d 69.

[Plaintiff Mrs. Henningsen was badly injured while driving a 1955 Plymouth automobile, when "something went wrong" with the steering gear, and the car turned sharply to the right into a wall. The automobile had been manufactured by defendant Chrysler Corporation, and sold by it to defendant Bloomfield Motors, a retail dealer. Mr. Henningsen purchased it from Bloomfield, and gave it to his wife for Christmas.

When he purchased the car, Mr. Henningsen signed a contract, without reading 8½ inches of fine print on the back of it. Included in this fine print was a "warranty" clause, which provided that the manufacturer and the dealer gave no warranties, express or implied, except that they would make good at the factory any parts which became defective within 90 days after delivery of the car to the original purchaser, or before the car had been driven 4,000 miles, whichever event should first occur. In plaintiff's action against both defendants, negligence counts were dismissed by the trial court, and the cause was submitted to the jury solely on the issues of implied warranty of merchantability. Verdicts were returned for plaintiff against both defendants. Defendants appealed, and the appeal was certified directly to the Supreme Court.]

FRANCIS, J. * * * In the ordinary case of sale of goods by description an implied warranty of merchantability is an integral part of the transaction. R.S. 46:30–20, N.J.S.A. If the buyer, expressly or by implication, makes known to the seller the particular purpose for which the article is required and it appears that he has relied on the seller's skill or judgment, an implied warranty arises of reasonable fitness for that purpose. R.S. 46:30–21(1), N.J.S.A. The former type of warranty simply means that the thing sold is reasonably fit for the general purpose for which it is manufactured and sold. [Cc] As Judge Cardozo remarked in Ryan v. Progressive Grocery Stores (1931) 255 N.Y. 388, 175 N.E. 105, the distinction between a warranty of fitness for a particular purpose and of merchantability in many instances is practically meaningless. * * *

Justice John J. Francis

The uniform [sales] act codified, extended and liberalized the common law of sales. The motivation in part was to ameliorate the harsh doctrine of caveat emptor, and in some measure to impose a reciprocal obligation on the seller to beware. The transcendent value of the legislation, particularly with respect to implied warranties, rests in the fact that obligations on the part of the seller were imposed by operation of law, and did not depend for their existence upon express agreement of the parties. And of tremendous significance in a rapidly expanding commercial society was the recognition of the right to recover damages on account of personal injuries arising from a breach of warranty. [Cc] The particular importance of this advance resides in the fact that under such circumstances strict liability is imposed upon the maker or seller of the product. Recovery of damages does not depend upon proof of negligence or knowledge of the defect. [Cc]

As the Sales Act and its liberal interpretation by the courts threw this protective cloak about the buyer, * * * many manufacturers took steps to avoid these ever increasing warranty obligations. Realizing that the act governed the relationship of buyer and seller, they undertook to withdraw from actual and direct contractual contact with the buyer. They ceased selling products to the consuming public through their own employees and making contracts of sale in their own names. Instead, a system of independent dealers was established; their products were sold to dealers who in turn dealt with the buying public, ostensibly solely in their own personal capacity as sellers. In the past in many instances, manufacturers were able to transfer to the dealers burdens imposed by the act and thus achieved a large measure of immunity for themselves. * * *

There is no doubt that under early common-law concepts of contractual liability only those persons who were parties to the bargain could sue for a breach of it. In more recent times a noticeable disposition has appeared in a number of jurisdictions to break through the narrow barrier of privity when dealing with sales of goods in order to give realistic recognition to a universally accepted fact. The fact is that the dealer and the ordinary buyer do not, and are not expected to, buy goods, whether they be foodstuffs or automobiles, exclusively for their own consumption or use. Makers and manufacturers know this and advertise and market their products on that assumption; witness, the "family" car, the baby foods, etc. The limitations of privity in contracts for the sale of goods developed their place in the law when marketing conditions were simple, when maker and buyer frequently met face to face on an equal bargaining plane and when many of the products were relatively uncomplicated and conducive to inspection by a buyer competent to evaluate their quality. [C] With the advent of mass marketing, the manufacturer became remote from the purchaser, sales were accomplished through intermediaries, and the demand for the product was created by advertising media. In such an economy it became obvious that the consumer was the person being cultivated. Manifestly, the connotation of "consumer" was broader than that of "buyer." He signified such a person who, in the reasonable contemplation of the parties to the sale, might be expected to use the product. Thus, where the commodities sold are such that if defectively manufactured they will be dangerous to life or limb, then society's interests can only be protected by eliminating the requirement of privity between the maker and his dealers and the reasonably expected ultimate consumer. In that way the burden of losses consequent upon use of defective articles is borne by those who are in a position to either control the danger or make an equitable distribution of the losses when they do occur. As Harper & James put it, "The interest in consumer protection calls for warranties by the maker that *do* run with the goods, to reach all who are likely to be hurt by the use of the unfit commodity for a purpose ordinarily to be expected." 2 Harper & James, Torts, 1571, 1572. * * *

Most of the cases where lack of privity has not been permitted to interfere with recovery have involved food and drugs. [Cc] In the fact, the rule as to such products has been characterized as an exception to the general doctrine. But more recently courts, sensing the inequity of such limitation, have moved into broader fields. [Cc] * * *

Under modern conditions the ordinary layman, on responding to the importuning of colorful advertising, has neither the opportunity nor the capacity to inspect or to determine the fitness of an automobile for use; he must rely on the manufacturer who has control of its construction, and to some degree on the dealer who, to the limited extent called for by the manufacturer's instructions, inspects and services it before delivery. In such a marketing milieu his remedies and those of persons who properly claim through him should not depend "upon the intricacies of the law of sales." The obligation of the manufacturer should not be based alone on privity of contract. It should rest, as was once said, upon "the demands of social justice." [C] "If privity of contract is required," then, under the circumstances of modern merchandising, "privity of contract exists in the consciousness and understanding of all right-thinking persons." [C]

Accordingly, we hold that under modern marketing conditions, when a manufacturer puts a new automobile in the stream of trade and promotes its purchase by the public, an implied warranty that it is reasonably suitable for use as such accompanies it into the hands of the ultimate purchaser. * * *

In the light of these matters, what effect should be given to the express warranty in question which seeks to limit the manufacturer's liability to replacement of defective parts, and which disclaims all other warranties, express or implied? In assessing its significance we must keep in mind the general principle that, in the absence of fraud, one who does not choose to read a contract before signing it, cannot later relieve himself of its burdens. [C] And in applying that principle, the basic tenet of freedom of competent parties to contract is a factor of importance. But in the framework of modern commercial life and business practices, such rules cannot be applied on a strict, doctrinal basis. The conflicting interests of the buyer and seller must be evaluated realistically and justly, giving due weight to the social policy evinced by the Uniform Sales Act, the progressive decisions of the courts engaged in administering it, the mass production methods of manufacture and distribution to the public, and the bargaining position, occupied by the ordinary consumer in such an economy. * * *

In a society such as ours, where the automobile is a common and necessary adjunct of daily life, and where its use is so fraught with danger to the driver, passengers and the public, the manufacturer is under a special obligation in connection with the construction, promotion and sale of his cars. Consequently, the courts must examine purchase agreements closely to see if consumer and public interests are treated fairly. * * *

[W]arranties originated in the law to safeguard the buyer and not to limit the liability of the seller or manufacturer. It seems obvious in this instance that the motive was to avoid the warranty obligations which are normally incidental to such sales. The language gave little and withdrew much. In return for the delusive remedy of replacement of defective parts at the factory, the buyer is said to have accepted the exclusion of the maker's liability for personal injuries, arising from the breach of the warranty, and to have agreed to the elimination of any other express or

implied warranty. An instinctively felt sense of justice cries out against such a sharp bargain. But does the doctrine that a person is bound by his signed agreement, in the absence of fraud, stand in the way of any relief?
* * *

The traditional contract is the result of free bargaining of parties who are brought together by the play of the market, and who meet each other on a footing of approximate economic equality. In such a society there is no danger that freedom of contract will be a threat to the social order as a whole. But in present-day commercial life the standardized mass contract has appeared. It is used primarily by enterprises with strong bargaining power and position. "The weaker party, in need of the goods or services, is frequently not in a position to shop around for better terms, either because the author of the standard contract has a monopoly (natural or artificial) or because all competitors use the same clauses. His contractual intention is but a subjection more or less voluntary to terms dictated by the stronger party, terms whose consequences are often understood in a vague way, if at all." Kessler, "Contracts of Adhesion—Some Thought About Freedom of Contract," 43 Colum.L.Rev. 629, 632 (1943). * * *

The warranty before us is a standardized form designed for mass use. It is imposed upon the automobile consumer. He takes it or leaves it, and he must take it to buy an automobile. No bargaining is engaged in with respect to it. In fact, the dealer through whom it comes to the buyer is without authority to alter it; his function is ministerial—simply to deliver it. The form warranty is not only standard with Chrysler but, as mentioned above, it is the uniform warranty of the Automobile Manufacturers Association. * * *

The gross inequality of bargaining position occupied by the consumer in the automobile industry is thus apparent. There is no competition among the car makers in the area of the express warranty. Where can the buyer go to negotiate for better protection? Such control and limitation of his remedies are inimical to the public welfare and, at the very least, call for great care by the courts to avoid injustice through application of strict common-law principles of freedom of contract. Because there is no competition among the motor vehicle manufacturers with respect to the scope of protection guaranteed to the buyer, there is no incentive on their part to stimulate good will in that field of public relations. Thus, there is lacking a factor existing in more competitive fields, one which tends to guarantee the safe construction of the article sold. Since all competitors operate in the same way, the urge to be careful is not so pressing. See "Warranties of Kind and Quality," 57 Yale L.J. 1389, 1400 (1948). * * *

The task of the judiciary is to administer the spirit as well as the letter of the law. On issues such as the present one, part of that burden is to protect the ordinary man against the loss of important rights through what, in effect, is the unilateral act of the manufacturer. * * * In the framework of this case, illuminated as it is by the facts and the many decisions noted, we are of the opinion that Chrysler's attempted disclaimer of an implied warranty of merchantability and of the obligations arising therefrom is so inimical to the public good as to compel an adjudication of its invalidity. * * *

[The court then held that the dealer, Bloomfield Motors, would not be permitted to disclaim an implied warranty of fitness with respect to personal injuries caused by the automobile in question. The problem of whether retailers should be subject to strict liability is discussed at page 785.]

NOTES AND QUESTIONS

1. The first case to extend an implied warranty of the seller beyond privity of contract was Mazetti v. Armour & Co., 75 Wash. 622, 135 P. 633 (1913), which was a bad food case. It came upon the heels of a prolonged nation-wide agitation about dangerous food, and the political overturn of 1912. The decision was promptly followed in Mississippi and Kansas, and then in other states. There was a period of some twenty years during which the courts struggled to evolve various ingenious theories, most of them with an obvious element of fiction—such as agencies of the dealer to buy for the consumer or to sell for the manufacturer, or third party beneficiary contracts and the like. Finally, in Coca–Cola Bottling Works v. Lyons, 145 Miss. 876, 111 So. 305 (1927), the Mississippi court came up with the idea of an implied warranty running with the goods, by analogy to a covenant running with the land; and subsequent cases until 1963 all adopted some theory of warranty to the consumer. By 1960 nearly half of the courts had accepted the special rule as to food, and five more reached the same result under pure food statutes. The whole development is traced in Prosser, The Assault Upon the Citadel, 69 Yale L.J. 1099 (1960).

2. A gradual extension beyond food began not long after 1950, with other products for what might be called intimate bodily use, such as hair dye and clothing. Although there was an earlier case in a lower Ohio Court, which was overruled, the first decision that went the whole way was Spence v. Three Rivers Builders & Masonry Supply, Inc., 353 Mich. 120, 90 N.W.2d 873 (1958), in which the court leaped completely over food products, and applied the manufacturer's warranty to cinder building blocks when the consumer's house collapsed. Seven or eight other decisions followed, but the *Henningsen* decision has come to be regarded as the leading case.

3. The Uniform Sales Act, discussed in the principal case, was promulgated in 1906. Its warranty provisions were intended to apply only to buyer and seller. The Uniform Sales Act has now been superseded by the Uniform Commercial Code (UCC). Article 2, which contains the warranty provisions, has been adopted in every state except Louisiana. While the UCC's implied-warranty provisions are similar to those in the Uniform Sales Act (UCC §§ 2–314 and 315), the Code has extended warranties to certain third parties in Section 2–318. This is one area, however, in which the Uniform Commercial Code is not uniform. State legislatures are given three alternatives to choose from:

Alternate A. A seller's warranty whether express or implied extends to any natural person who is in the family or household of his buyer or who is a guest in his home if it is reasonable to expect that such person may use, consume or be affected by the goods and who is injured in person by breach of the warranty. A seller may not exclude or limit the operation of this section.

Alternate B. A seller's warranty whether express or implied extends to any natural person who may reasonably be expected to use, consume or be affected by the goods and who is injured in person by breach of the warranty. A seller may not exclude or limit the operation of this section.

Alternate C. A seller's warranty whether express or implied extends to any person who may reasonably be expected to use, consume or be affected by the goods and who is injured by breach of the warranty. A seller may not exclude or limit the operation of this section with respect to injury to the person of an individual to whom the warranty extends. As amended 1966.

The official comment to this Section states in part: "The first alternative expressly includes as beneficiaries within its provisions the family, household and guests of the purchaser. Beyond this, the section in this form is neutral and is not intended to enlarge or restrict the developing case law on whether the seller's warranties, given to his buyer who resells, extend to other persons in the distributive chain. The second alternative is designed for states where the case law has already developed further and for those that desire to expand the class of beneficiaries. The third alternative goes further, following the trend of modern decisions as indicated by Restatement of Torts (Second) § 402A * * * in extending the rule beyond injuries to the person."

4. *Disclaimers.* The UCC, unlike the Uniform Sales Act, deals directly with the problem of disclaimers. The most important sections include 2–302, 2–316, and 2–719. Subsection (3) of the latter section is of particular interest in regard to the disclaimer problem: "Consequential damages may be limited or excluded unless the limitation or exclusion is unconscionable. Limitation of consequential damages for injury to the person in the case of consumer goods is prima facie unconscionable but limitation of damages where the loss is commercial is not." In addition, some states have amended their version of the UCC to prohibit the exclusion or modification of implied warranties as to consumer goods and services. See, e.g., Me.Rev.Stat.Ann., Tit. 11, § 2–316(5); Mass.Gen.Laws Ann., Ch. 106, § 2–316A.

5. *Notice.* Could the principal case have been decided the same way within the framework of the UCC? How? The UCC and its predecessor, the Uniform Sales Act, have a number of stumbling blocks in the way of a strict liability recovery in tort law. One of them is UCC § 2–607, which requires that a buyer must "within a reasonable time after he discovers or should have discovered the breach [of warranty] notify the seller or be barred from any remedy." The analogue Uniform Sales Act provision and the whole problem of the utility of warranty as a tort law remedy confronted Justice Traynor in the next case.

6. *Federal Acts.* The abuses discussed in the principal case have become the subject of federal regulation.

A. *The "Magnuson–Moss Warranty–Federal Trade Commission Improvement Act,"* 15 U.S.C.A. §§ 2301–12, created a comprehensive regulatory system governing the form and to some degree the content of written warranties and warranties implied by state law. The Act applies to warranties offered to "consumers" by "suppliers" of "consumer products." The Act does not require that a warranty be given; rather, it regulates the scope of warranties that are provided. While it does not affect state personal injury actions, it will affect the nature and scope of disclaimers in the sale of most consumer products that are sold with a "warranty" in the United States.

in addition to state acts

B. *The Consumer Product Safety Act.* The Consumer Product Safety Act, 15 U.S.C.A. §§ 2051 et seq., created a new federal agency, the Consumer Product Safety Commission, that has regulatory power over consumer products that are not already subject to safety regulation by other federal agencies (such as the F.D.A.). The Commission is empowered to establish and enforce uniform safety standards for consumer products and to ban products from the market if they create an "unreasonable risk" of injury to the consumer. Section 2072 of the Act provides a federal tort remedy to persons who are injured as a result of a knowing violation of a safety standard, or a rule of the Commission.

C. *Other Federal Regulation.* The trend toward increased federal involvement with product safety began with the National Traffic and Motor Vehicle Safety Act of 1966, which required the Secretary of Transportation to establish motor vehicle safety standards. See 15 U.S.C.A. §§ 1381 et seq. Some of the other important federal regulatory acts relating to products include the Occupational Safety and Health Act (OSHA), 29 U.S.C.A. §§ 651 et seq., the Federal Hazardous Substances Act, 15 U.S.C.A. §§ 1261 et seq., the Poison Prevention Packaging Act, 15 U.S.C.A. §§ 1471 et seq., the Flammable Fabrics Act, 15 U.S.C.A. §§ 1191 et seq., and the Refrigerator Safety Act, 15 U.S.C.A. §§ 1211 et seq. While none of these acts creates specific civil tort remedies, violation of a specific standard issued under them may subject a defendant to liability on a negligence per se or implied tort theory. See note 5, page 206; note 5, page 217.

7. What implications does this growing body of federal regulation have for state tort law?

(C) STRICT LIABILITY IN TORT

Greenman v. Yuba Power Products, Inc.

Supreme Court of California, 1963.
59 Cal.2d 57, 377 P.2d 897, 27 Cal.Rptr. 697.

TRAYNOR, JUSTICE. Plaintiff brought this action for damages against the retailer and the manufacturer of a Shopsmith, a combination power tool that could be used as a saw, drill, and wood lathe. He saw a Shopsmith demonstrated by the retailer and studied a brochure prepared by the manufacturer. He decided he wanted a Shopsmith for his home workshop, and his wife bought and gave him one for Christmas in 1955. In 1957 he bought the necessary attachments to use the Shopsmith as a lathe for turning a large piece of wood he wished to make into a chalice. After he had worked on the piece of wood several times without difficulty, it suddenly flew out of the machine and struck him on the forehead, inflicting serious injuries. About ten and a half months later, he gave the retailer and the manufacturer written notice of claimed breaches of warranties and filed a complaint against them alleging such breaches and negligence.

After a trial before a jury, the court ruled that there was no evidence that the retailer was negligent or had breached any express warranty and that the manufacturer was not liable for the breach of any implied warranty. Accordingly, it submitted to the jury only the cause of action alleging breach of implied warranties against the retailer and the causes of

trial court said No evidence of negligence or breach of express warr.

only to jury on implied w

Judge Traynor

jury verdict for retailer against P & for P against manufacturer

action alleging negligence and breach of express warranties against the manufacturer. The jury returned a verdict for the retailer against plaintiff and for plaintiff against the manufacturer in the amount of $65,000. The trial court denied the manufacturer's motion for a new trial and entered judgment on the verdict. * * *

Plaintiff introduced substantial evidence that his injuries were caused by defective design and construction of the Shopsmith. His expert witnesses testified that inadequate set screws were used to hold parts of the machine together so that normal vibration caused the tailstock of the lathe to move away from the piece of wood being turned permitting it to fly out of the lathe. They also testified that there were other more positive ways of fastening the parts of the machine together, the use of which would have prevented the accident. The jury could therefore reasonably have concluded that the manufacturer negligently constructed the Shopsmith. The jury could also reasonably have concluded that statements in the manufacturer's brochure were untrue, that they constituted express warranties, and that plaintiff's injuries were caused by their breach.

The manufacturer contends, however, that plaintiff did not give it notice of breach of warranty within a reasonable time and that therefore his cause of action for breach of warranty is barred by section 1769 of the Civil Code. Since it cannot be determined whether the verdict against it was based on the negligence or warranty cause of action or both, the manufacturer concludes that the error in presenting the warranty cause of action to the jury was prejudicial.

Section 1769 of the Civil Code provides: "In the absence of express or implied agreement of the parties, acceptance of the goods by the buyer shall not discharge the seller from liability in damages or other legal remedy for breach of any promise or warranty in the contract to sell or the sale. But, if after acceptance of the goods, the buyer fails to give notice to the seller of the breach of any promise or warranty within a reasonable time after the buyer knows, or ought to know of such breach, the seller shall not be liable therefor."

Like other provisions of the uniform sales act (Civ.Code, §§ 1721–1800), section 1769 deals with the rights of the parties to a contract of sale or a sale. It does not provide that notice must be given of the breach of a warranty that arises independently of a contract of sale between the parties. Such warranties are not imposed by the sales act, but are the product of common-law decisions that have recognized them in a variety of situations. [Cc]

It is true that in many of these situations the court has invoked the sales act definitions of warranties (Civ.Code, §§ 1732, 1735) in defining the defendant's liability, but it has done so, not because the statutes so required, but because they provided appropriate standards for the court to adopt under the circumstances presented. [Cc]

The notice requirement of section 1769, however, is not an appropriate one for the court to adopt in actions by injured consumers against manufacturers with whom they have not dealt. [Cc] "As between the immediate parties to the sale, [the notice requirement] is a sound commercial rule, designed to protect the seller against unduly delayed claims for damages. As applied to personal injuries, and notice to a remote seller, it becomes a booby-trap for the unwary. The injured consumer is seldom 'steeped in the business practice which justifies the rule,' [cc] and at least until he has had legal advice it will not occur to him to give notice to one with whom he has had no dealings." [Cc] It is true that in [four prior California cases cited] the court assumed that notice of breach of warranty must be given in an action by a consumer against a manufacturer. Since in those cases, however, the court did not consider the question whether a distinction exists between a warranty based on a contract between the parties and one imposed on a manufacturer not in privity with the consumer, the decisions are not authority for rejecting the rule. [Cc] We conclude, therefore, that even if plaintiff did not give timely notice of breach of warranty to the manufacturer, his cause of action based on the representations contained in the brochure was not barred.

Moreover, to impose strict liability on the manufacturer under the circumstances of this case, it was not necessary for plaintiff to establish an express warranty as defined in section 1732 of the Civil Code. A manufacturer is strictly liable in tort when an article he places on the market, knowing that it is to be used without inspection for defects, proves to have a defect that causes injury to a human being. Recognized first in the case of unwholesome food products, such liability has now been extended to a variety of other products that create as great or greater hazards if defective. [Cc]

Although in these cases strict liability has usually been based on the theory of an express or implied warranty running from the manufacturer to the plaintiff, the abandonment of the requirement of a contract between them, the recognition that the liability is not assumed by agreement but imposed by law [cc], and the refusal to permit the manufacturer to define the scope of its own responsibility for defective products [cc], make clear that the liability is not one governed by the law of contract warranties but by the law of strict liability in tort. Accordingly, rules defining and governing warranties that were developed to meet the needs of commercial transactions cannot properly be invoked to govern the manufacturer's liability to those injured by their defective products unless those rules also serve the purposes for which such liability is imposed.

We need not recanvass the reasons for imposing strict liability on the manufacturer. * * * The purpose of such liability is to insure that the costs of injuries resulting from defective products are borne by the manufacturers that put such products on the market rather than by the injured persons who are powerless to protect themselves. Sales warranties serve this purpose fitfully at best. [C] In the present case, for example, plaintiff was able to plead and prove an express warranty only because he read and relied on the representations of the Shopsmith's ruggedness contained in the manufacturer's brochure. Implicit in the machine's presence on the market, however, was a representation that it would safely do the jobs for which it was built. Under these circumstances, it should not be controlling whether plaintiff selected the machine because of the statements in the brochure, or because of the machine's own appearance of excellence that belied the defect lurking beneath the surface, or because he merely assumed that it would safely do the jobs it was built to do. It should not be controlling whether the details of the sales from manufacturer to retailer and from retailer to plaintiff's wife were such that one or more of the implied warranties of the sales act arose. [C] "The remedies of injured consumers ought not to be made to depend upon the intricacies of the law of sales." [Cc] To establish the manufacturer's liability it was sufficient that plaintiff proved that he was injured while using the Shopsmith in a way it was intended to be used as a result of a defect in design and manufacture of which plaintiff was not aware that made the Shopsmith unsafe for its intended use. * * *

The judgment is affirmed.

NOTES AND QUESTIONS

1. The *Greenman* decision, which might be characterized as the *MacPherson* of a later day, appeared two years before the final published draft of the Restatement (Second) of Torts § 402A:

§ 402A. Special Liability of Seller of Product for Physical Harm to User or Consumer

codified greenman

(1) One who sells any product in a defective condition unreasonably dangerous to the user or consumer or to his property is subject to liability for physical harm thereby caused to the ultimate user or consumer, or to his property, if

(a) the seller is engaged in the business of selling such a product, and

(b) it is expected to and does reach the user or consumer without substantial change in the condition in which it is sold.

(2) The rule stated in Subsection (1) applies although

(a) the seller has exercised all possible care in the preparation and sale of his product, and

(b) the user or consumer has not bought the product from or entered into any contractual relation with the seller.

It should be noted in passing that the law was moving so fast that this Section was actually drafted three times—first as applicable only to food and drink, next, as extended also to include products for "intimate bodily use," and finally, as applicable to all products.

2. Section 402A literally swept the country. Only a couple of jurisdictions still do not recognize a cause of action for strict liability for personal injury caused by a product. See, Sensenbrenner v. Rust, Orling & Neale, 236 Va. 419, 374 S.E.2d 55 (1988) and Smith v. Fiber Controls Corp., 300 N.C. 669, 268 S.E.2d 504 (1980).

3. Now that almost all jurisdictions have followed the lead of the principal case and the Restatement (Second) and recognized some form of strict liability, should breach of implied warranty still survive as a separate cause of action? Compare Denny v. Ford Motor Co., 87 N.Y.2d 248, 662 N.E.2d 730, 736 (1995) (as long as the legislature, through enactment of UCC, is the source of authority for a breach of implied warranty claim, "we are not free to merge the warranty cause of action with its tort-based sibling regardless of whether, as a matter of policy, the contract-based warranty claim may fairly be regarded as a historical relic that no longer has any independent substantive value") with Restatement (Third) of Torts: Products Liability § 2 cmt. n (1998) (Restatement "contemplates that a well-coordinated body of law governing liability for harm to persons or property arising out of the sale of defective products requires a consistent definition of defect, and that the definition properly should come from tort law, whether the claim carries a tort label or one of implied warranty of merchantability").

4. Whether the liability rests upon negligence, warranty or strict liability in tort, it appears clear by this time, that it applies to all types of products. Whatever limitations there may once have been as to food and drink, intimate bodily use, "inherent danger" or a high degree of danger, all have gone by the boards. The product need not even be dangerous to human beings, or injure them; and such things as animal foods that may foreseeably cause harm only to property, are within the liability. Kassab v. Central Soya, 432 Pa. 217, 246 A.2d 848 (1968); Franklin Serum Co. v. Hoover & Son, 418 S.W.2d 482 (Tex.1967) (animal serum).

5. Also gone by the boards is a rather foolish distinction that used to plague the food cases, between the product itself and the container in which it is sold. The two are now treated as one, and if a bottled beverage explodes, it no longer makes any difference whether it is due to a defect in the bottle. Kroger Co. v. Bowman, 411 S.W.2d 339 (Ky.1967); Vallis v. Canada Dry Ginger Ale, Inc., 190 Cal.App.2d 35, 11 Cal.Rptr. 823 (1961). Would strict liability apply to the manufacturer of Tylenol for failure to make its packaging tamper proof? Cf. Elsroth v. Johnson & Johnson, 700 F.Supp. 151 (S.D.N.Y.1988) (cyanide poisoning due to breach of tamper resistant packaging by unknown third party).

6. With warranty language out of the way, a number of problems (including the notice requirement confronting the court in *Greenman*) disappear. For example, courts have held that a tort and not a contract statute of limitations applies to plaintiff's claim. See Patterson v. Her Majesty Indus., 450 F.Supp. 425 (E.D.Pa. 1978); Victorson v. Bock Laundry Mach. Co., 37 N.Y.2d 395, 335 N.E.2d 275, 373 N.Y.S.2d 39 (1975). Further, plaintiff can file suit under both wrongful death and survival statutes. Suppose the tort law statute of limitations has run, but the UCC statute of limitations has not run? See Redfield v. Mead, Johnson & Co., 266 Or. 273, 512 P.2d 776 (1973).

The court in Greeno v. Clark Equip. Co., 237 F.Supp. 427, 429 (N.D.Ind.1965), stated that strict liability in tort is "hardly more than what exists under implied warranty when stripped of the contract doctrines of privity, disclaimer, requirements of notice of defeat, and limitation through inconsistencies with express warranties." To the court's list might be added any limitations arising from the UCC in terms of when the direct warranties from the seller to the buyer arise.

6. Should a seller be able to disclaim liability under Restatement (Second) of Torts § 402B (discussed Note 1, page 720) after making an express warranty that the user has relied on? See First Nat'l. Bank of Louisville v. Brooks Farms, 821 S.W.2d 925 (Tenn.1991) (Tennessee would not give effect to disclaimer where jury found that statements in sales brochures about product performance were fraudulent.) See generally Metzger, Disclaimers, Limitations of Remedy, and Third Parties, 48 U.Cin.L.Rev. 663 (1979).

7. A number of rationales have been advanced by legal writers in support of strict liability in tort. Which do you regard as sound?

A. The consumer finds it too difficult to prove negligence against the manufacturer.

B. Strict liability provides an effective and necessary incentive to manufacturers to make their products as safe as possible.

C. Res ipsa loquitur is in fact applied, in some cases, to impose liability upon producers who have not in fact been negligent; therefore negligence should be dispensed with.

D. Reputable manufacturers do in fact stand behind their products, replacing or repairing those which prove to be defective; and many of them issue express agreements to do so. Therefore all should be responsible when an injury results from a normal use of the product.

E. The manufacturer is in a better position to protect against harm, by insuring against liability for it, and, by adding the cost of the insurance to the price of his product, to pass the loss on to the general public.

F. Strict liability already can be accomplished by a series of actions, in which the consumer first recovers from the retailer on a warranty, and liability on warranties is then carried back through the intermediate dealers to the manufacturer. The process is time-consuming, expensive, and wasteful; there should be a short-cut.

G.   By placing the product on the market, the seller represents to the public that it is fit; and he intends and expects that it will be purchased and consumed in reliance upon that representation. The distributors and retailers are no more than a conduit, a mechanical device through which the thing sold reaches the consumer.

H.   The costs of accidents should be placed on the party best able to determine whether there are means to prevent that accident. When those means are less expensive than the costs of such accidents, responsibility for implementing them should be placed on the party best able to do so.

8.   What about the danger of deterring manufacturers from introducing new products, or improving old ones? And what about the danger of fictitious claims? "The rats of Hamlin were as nought in comparison with that horde of mice which has sought refreshment within Coca–Cola bottles and died of a happy surfeit." Spruill, Privity of Contract as a Requisite for Recovery on Warranty, 19 N.C.L.Rev. 551, 566 (1941). Assuming that there will be frivolous claims, are there ways the manufacturer can be protected from those claims without eliminating strict liability?

9.   *Beyond Restatement (Second).* When the American Law Institute's (ALI) Restatement (Second) 402A was drafted, a decision was made to use a singular definition of defect to cover all cases of product liability: "any product in a defective condition unreasonably dangers to the user or consumer." Following this model, when the European EC Product Liability Directive was drafted, although the words were slightly modified, a single definition of defect was utilized. As Restatement (Second) 402A was applied by the courts, it became clearer that a single definition standard was being used to address very different types of defects.

The first type of defect, and the focus of the Drafters of Restatement (Second), is a manufacturing defect. Such a defect occurs when a product that injures a person does so because there is a flaw that is not in the general product line. It is a failure in quality control. As the cases suggest, strict product liability for this type of defect had been evolving for a substantial period of time. The second type, which is very different, is a defect attributable to failure of design. Here, an entire product line is challenged. The singular definition provided little or no guidelines to courts as to how liability should be imposed: Should fault be a basis? Should it be strict liability or absolute liability? Where was the line to be drawn? The third type is a defect due to failure to warn. Restatement (Second) did not separate this type of defect in its Black Letter rule, but did address it separately in comment *j*, suggesting a fault predicate for failure to warn.

In the 30 years that followed the publication of Restatement (Second) § 402A, literally thousands of cases wrestled with the problem of a singular definition of defect. As each jurisdiction struggled with its standard for liability in the context of each of the types of defect, it became apparent that the monolithic approach was such in name (strict liability) or number (§ 402A) only. In reality, the standards for each type of defect were somewhat different. In 1993, the American Law Institute began work on a new Restatement of Torts, with a specific focus on products liability. See Henderson and Twerski, A Proposed Reform of Section 402A of the Restatement (Second) of Torts, 77 Cornell L.Rev. 1512 (1992). The process through which it was developed is told below and the critical section shifting the paradigm of Restatement (Second) § 402A is then reprinted.

2. PRODUCT DEFECTS

The five year process of the development of Restatement (Third) of Torts: Products Liability began with a draft prepared by its Reporters, Professor Aaron Twerski of Brooklyn Law School and Professor James Henderson of Cornell Law School. They were assisted by a 20–person Advisory Committee composed of judges, law professors, and practicing attorneys. The decision to once again "restate" the law of products liability was the result of an ALI study entitled "Enterprise Liability." That study appreciated that case law interpreting 402A had produced many new and challenging issues that called out for resolution. These issues were not anticipated in the early 1960's when Restatement (Second) 402A was drafted.

After the Reporters produced an initial draft, it went through an intensive review process by the Advisory Committee, a Members Consultative Group, interest groups that were not members of the ALI, the ALI's Governing Council, and finally the ALI membership itself. A multiplicity of drafts went through the same process until May 1998 when the Final Draft was approved overwhelmingly by the ALI membership. The process is described in Schwartz, The Restatement (Third) of Torts: Products Liability: The American Law Institute's Process of Democracy and Deliberation, 26 Hofstra L.Rev. 743 (1998). Both the process by which the new Restatement was developed and the final product that was approved have been subject to strong criticism. See Shapo, In Search of the Law of Products Liability: The ALI Restatement Project, 48 Vand. L. Rev. 631 (1995) and Popper, Tort Reform Policy More Than State Law Dominates Section 2 of the Third Restatement, 8 Kan. J.L. & Pub. Pol'y 38 (1998). The decision to abandon the single definition approach and to replace it with separate functional rules for manufacturing defects, design defects, and defects due to failure to warn was its most fundamental change. There were some members of the ALI who believed that Restatement (Second) had it right, that judges needed latitude to shape the law, and that any further definition of defect would restrict them. Other ALI members supported the functional model, but differed as to whether the Reporters had arrived at the correct approach in defining each of the three separate categories. Only time will tell whether the new Restatement receives the general acceptance that ultimately met the Restatement (Second) 402A. Here is the basic text defining product defectiveness from Restatement (Third) of Torts: Products Liability (1998):

TOPIC 1. PRODUCT DEFECTIVENESS

§ 1. Liability of Commercial Seller or Distributor for Harm Caused by Defective Products

(a) One engaged in the business of selling or otherwise distributing products who sells or distributes a defective product is subject to liability for harm to persons or property caused by the defect.

a true restatement

§ 2. Categories of Product Defect

VERY IMPORTANT!

A product is defective when, at the time of sale or distribution, it contains a manufacturing defect, is defective in design, or is defective because of inadequate instructions or warnings. A product:

(a) contains a manufacturing defect when the product departs from its intended design even though all possible care was exercised in the preparation and marketing of the product;

(b) is defective in design when the foreseeable risks of harm posed by the product could have been reduced or avoided by the adoption of a reasonable alternative design by the seller or other distributor, or a predecessor in the commercial chain of distribution, and the omission of the alternative design renders the product not reasonably safe;

(c) is defective because of inadequate instructions or warnings when the foreseeable risks of harm posed by the product could have been reduced or avoided by the provision of reasonable instructions or warnings by the seller or other distributor, or a predecessor in the commercial chain of distribution, and the omission of the instructions or warnings renders the product not reasonably safe.

"reasonable alternative safer design"

As you review the cases in the rest of this chapter, consider whether the monolithic approach of Restatement (Second) § 402A (1965) or the functional approach of Restatement (Third) of Torts: Products Liability (1998) better serves the goals of tort law.

(A) MANUFACTURING DEFECT

Rix v. General Motors Corp.

Supreme Court of Montana, 1986.
222 Mont. 318, 723 P.2d 195.

WEBER, J.

In 1978, Michael Rix was injured when the pickup he was driving was hit from behind by a 1978 General Motors Corporation (GMC) two ton chassis-cab, which had been equipped with a water tank after sale by the GMC dealer. Plaintiff sued GMC on a theory of strict liability in the Yellowstone County District Court. Following a jury verdict for GMC, plaintiff appeals. * * *

jury verdict for GMC

1. Did the trial court properly instruct the jury on strict liability?

ISSUE

* * *

Plaintiff contends he was injured by an unreasonably dangerous 1978 two ton chassis-cab, which had been placed in the stream of commerce by GMC. Premised on a theory of strict liability, he maintains the product was unreasonably dangerous because of both manufacturing and design defects.

The parties stipulated that the accident occurred because of brake failure. Expert testimony from both parties established that the fluids necessary to the braking system had escaped when a brake tube came out of a nut where it fastened to the top of the Hydrovac, a booster unit.

Facts

Witnesses also testified that the brake tube came out of the nut either because the tube broke or was improperly flared.

Plaintiff contends that the tube broke because there was a manufacturing defect in the tube, basically a bad flare, when the truck came off the assembly line. Plaintiff also contends that the brake system on the truck, a single system, was defectively designed, and argues that GMC's knowledge of available technology coupled with the foreseeable use of the vehicle should have mandated a dual braking system, which provides extra braking power. Plaintiff maintains the accident would have been less severe or would not have happened had the truck been equipped with a dual system.

GMC agreed that the brake tube was defective, but contended that the tube had been altered after it left the GMC assembly line, so that the defective tube was not GMC's responsibility. GMC also contended that the single system was neither a design defect nor unreasonably dangerous, and that the accident would have occurred even if the truck had been equipped with a dual brake system.

Did the trial court properly instruct the jury on strict liability?

* * *

INSTRUCTION NO. 10

I will now define the doctrine of strict liability to you. Keep in mind that this is only a general definition, and must be considered along with the specific instructions on the same topic which follow. The general principle of strict liability as it applies in the State of Montana is:

(1) One who sells any product in a defective condition unreasonably dangerous to the user or consumer or to his property is subject to liability for physical harm thereby caused to the ultimate user or consumer, or to his property, if:

(a) the seller is engaged in the business of selling such a product, and

(b) it is expected and does reach the user or consumer without substantial change in the condition in which it is sold.

(2) The rule stated in Subsection (1) applies although

(a) the seller has exercised all possible care in the preparation and sale of his product, and

(b) the user or consumer has not bought the product from or entered into any contractual relation with the seller.

INSTRUCTION NO. 11

The plaintiff must establish three essential elements in order to recover under his theory of strict liability. They are as follows:

First, that the defendant General Motors Corporation manufactured and sold a product which at the time General Motors sold it was in a defective condition unreasonably dangerous to the consumer or user;

Second, that the product was expected to and did reach the ultimate consumer without substantial change in the condition it was in at the time it was sold; and

Third, that the defective condition in the product proximately caused injury to the plaintiff.

Jury instruction #10 is the same as Section 402A Restatement (Second) of Torts (1965). Plaintiff did not make an objection at the time the instruction was offered. Plaintiff objected to jury instruction #11 "on the grounds that the second standard improperly states Montana law regarding tracing requirement back to the manufacturer."

* * *

We will now discuss strict liability under a manufacturing defect theory. Under a manufacturing defect theory, the essential question is whether the product was flawed or defective because it was not constructed correctly by the manufacturer:

Issue in manufacturing defect strict liability

"[M]anufacturing defects, by definition, are imperfections that inevitably occur in a typically small percentage of products of a given design as a result of the fallibility of the manufacturing process. A [defectively manufactured] product does not conform in some significant aspect to the intended design, nor does it conform to the great majority of products manufactured in accordance with that design.' (Henderson, Judicial Review of Manufacturers' Conscious Design Choices: The Limits of Adjudication, 73 Col.L.Rev. 1531, 1543). Stated differently, a defectively manufactured product is flawed because it is misconstructed without regard to whether the intended design of the manufacturer was safe or not. Such defects result from some mishap in the manufacturing process itself, improper workmanship, or because defective materials were used in construction." [C]

Rule

Restatement (Second) of Torts, Section 402A (1965) has been adopted by this Court as the applicable law with regard to strict liability under a manufacturing defect theory. The Restatement view is continued in Instruction #10, previously quoted in this opinion. In the context of strict liability under a manufacturing defect theory, we conclude that instructions #10 and #11, as given by the District Court, are adequate. * * *

* * *

We reverse and remand [on other grounds] for a new trial in conformity with this opinion.

NOTES AND QUESTIONS

1. The distinction between defect in design and defect in manufacture (or construction) was not well developed in early strict liability cases. See, e.g., Greenman v. Yuba Power Prods., Inc., page 729; Mosier v. American Motors Co., 303 F.Supp. 44 (S.D.Tex.1967). Today, the distinction may be quite important in terms of strict liability theory. If a product has a material defect in construction that causes a personal injury to the user, strict liability usually will be imposed. The

important distinction between defect in design / defect in manufacture plaintiff's main problems will be in the area of factual proof—a topic developed at page 764. On the other hand, when plaintiff contends that the product is defectively designed or was accompanied by inadequate warnings, the test for defect varies by jurisdiction.

2.   Note that the plaintiff has to prove that the product deviated from the seller's design or from the seller's other products of the same design, not what specific conduct of the manufacturer led to that defect. In the context of the principal case, the plaintiff only needs to show that the brakes failed because of a manufacturing defect in the tube (strict liability), not what assembly line actions led to that defect (negligent conduct of the manufacturer). What if the manufacturer could show that it had the best quality control procedures in the entire industry, that only one out of every one million tubes came off the assembly line with a defect, and that there was no way to detect those defects? That would constitute reasonable care and thus no liability under a negligence standard. Under a strict liability standard, however, the manufacturer would be liable. See also Restatement (Third) of Torts: Products Liability § 2(a) (1998).

3.   The manufacturer in this case was claiming that the defect was not present when it left the assembly line, but was introduced by someone else who later altered the product. If the manufacturer can prove this at trial, the manufacturer would not be liable. No doubt anticipating this possibility, the plaintiff also has alleged a design defect—that the manufacturer should have provided for a dual braking system, which would have prevented the accident. Very few cases contain only a manufacturing defect claim. Based on the principal case, do you see why it would be to the plaintiff's advantage to bring a design defect claim in addition to the manufacturing defect claim? Do you see why there is almost always a design defect claim arising out of a manufacturing defect case?

(B) DESIGN DEFECT

Prentis v. Yale Mfg. Co.
Supreme Court of Michigan, 1984.
421 Mich. 670, 365 N.W.2d 176.

BOYLE, JUSTICE. This products liability action arose out of injuries sustained in an accident involving the operation of a hand-operated forklift manufactured by defendant.

* * *

The facts of this case are not seriously in dispute. In April of 1970, plaintiff John Prentis, who was employed as foreman of the parts department at an automobile dealership, sustained a hip injury in an accident involving the use of a forklift manufactured by defendant Yale Manufacturing Company and sold to plaintiff's employer in 1952. The forklift was a stand-up or walking type, termed by defendant a "walkie hi-lo" model, rather than a riding or sit down variety. It was operated by lifting its handle up, much like the handle of a wagon. The forklift was estimated by plaintiff to weigh about two thousand pounds and was powered by a large battery, which had to be recharged every night. The machine was equipped with a hand controlled "dead-man" switch which normally prevented it from moving if the operator let go of the handle or controls. * * *

The accident in which Mr. Prentis was injured occurred late in the day, and he testified that he was aware at the time that the battery charge on the forklift was running low. After using the machine to assist him in placing an engine inside the cargo area of a delivery van, while the forklift was in tow behind him on a slightly inclined ramp leading from the delivery bay, Mr. Prentis attempted to start the machine by working the handle up and down. When the machine experienced a power surge, he lost his footing and fell to the ground. It appears that plaintiff's injuries were a result of the fall only, as the machine did not hit or run over him, but continued past him and stopped when it ran into a parked car. Mr. Prentis received extensive treatment for multiple fractures of his left hip. * * *

The focus of plaintiffs' proofs at both trials was an alleged defect in the design of the forklift, and the substance of the expert witness's testimony was that the design of the forklift failed to properly incorporate the operator as a "human factor" into the machine's function, specifically because it did not provide a seat or platform for the operator. * * *

The development of the law of tort liability for physical injury caused by products is perhaps the most striking and dramatic of all the numerous stories in the portfolio of modern tort scenarios. When the societal goal of holding manufacturers accountable for the safety of their products has been threatened by the interposition of technical rules of law, it has been the rules that have gradually given way.

However, this has never meant that courts have been willing to impose absolute liability in this context and from their earliest application, theories of products liability have been viewed as tort doctrines which should not be confused with the imposition of absolute liability. * * *

Thus while courts have accepted the social policy rationale that those injured by defective products should be compensated for their injuries without being subject to the contractual intricacies of the law of sales, and have agreed that manufacturers can most effectively distribute the costs of injuries, they have never gone so far as to make sellers insurers of their products and thus absolutely liable for any and all injuries sustained from the use of those products.

Like the courts in every other state, whether a suit is based upon negligence or implied warranty, we require the plaintiff to prove that the product itself is actionable—that something is wrong with it that makes it dangerous. This idea of "something wrong" is usually expressed by the adjective "defective" and the plaintiff must, *in every case, in every jurisdiction,* show that the product was defective. [C]

As a term of art, "defective" gives little difficulty when something goes wrong in the manufacturing process and the product is not in its intended condition. In the case of a "manufacturing defect," the product may be evaluated against the manufacturer's own production standards, as manifested by that manufacturer's other like products.

However, injuries caused by the condition of a product may also be actionable if the product's design, which is the result of intentional design decisions of the manufacturer, is not sufficiently safe. Conscious design defect cases provide no such simple test. The very question whether a defect in fact exists is central to a court's inquiry. It is only in design defect cases that a court is called upon to supply the standard for defectiveness. Thus, the term "defect" in design cases is "an epithet—an expression for the legal conclusion rather than a test for reaching that conclusion." See Wade, On product "design defects" and their actionability, 33 Van. L.R. 551, 552 (1980).

At present, questions related to "design defects" and the determination of when a product is defective, because of the nature of its design, appear to be the most agitated and controversial issues before the courts in the field of products liability. A number of appellate courts, aware that they are engaged in the conscious task of molding the law of products liability, have become concerned that they are not differentiating with sufficient clarity between various theories of recovery in design defect cases. In response, they have sought to devise significant and well-articulated distinctions. At the same time, other courts have become concerned that the differentiation is too great, and have attempted to devise means of keeping the broad scope of liability in check. The result has been several cases in which the standard for liability in the design area has been very carefully examined by courts and often vigorously debated by the judges themselves. A survey of the important recent cases in neighboring jurisdictions suggests something of the creative ferment underlying what has been described as the "rich tapestry" of the developing common law of products liability.

The approaches for determination of the meaning of "defect" in design cases fall into four general categories. The first, usually associated with Dean Wade, employs a negligence risk-utility analysis, but focuses upon whether the manufacturer would be judged negligent if it had known of the product's dangerous condition at the time it was marketed. The second, associated with Dean Keeton, compares the risk and utility of the product at the time of trial. The third focuses on consumer expectations about the product. The fourth combines the risk-utility and consumer-expectation tests. While courts have included many other individual variations in their formulations, the overwhelming consensus among courts deciding defective design cases is in the use of some form of risk-utility analysis, either as an exclusive or alternative ground of liability. Risk-utility analysis in this context always involves assessment of the decisions made by manufacturers with respect to the design of their products. * * *

The risk-utility balancing test is merely a detailed version of Judge Learned Hand's negligence calculus. See United States v. Carroll Towing Co., 159 F.2d 169, 173 (2d Cir.1947). As Dean Prosser has pointed out, the liability of the manufacturer rests "upon a departure from proper standards of care, so that the tort is essentially a matter of negligence."

Although many courts have insisted that the risk-utility tests they are applying are not negligence tests because their focus is on the *product* rather than the manufacturer's *conduct,* [c] the distinction on closer examination appears to be nothing more than semantic. As a common-sense matter, the jury weighs competing factors presented in evidence and reaches a conclusion about the judgment or decision (*i.e.*, *conduct*) of the manufacturer. The underlying negligence calculus is inescapable. As noted by Professor Birnbaum:

"When a jury decides that the risk of harm outweighs the utility of a particular design (that the product is not as safe as it *should* be) it is saying that in choosing the particular design and cost tradeoffs, the manufacturer exposed the consumer to greater risk of danger than he should have. Conceptually and analytically, this approach bespeaks negligence." Birnbaum, Unmasking the test for design defect: From negligence [to warranty] to strict liability to negligence, 33 Van.L.R. 593, 610 (1980) * * *

The competing factors to be weighed under a risk-utility balancing test invite the trier of fact to consider the alternatives and risks faced by the manufacturer and to determine whether in light of these the manufacturer exercised reasonable care in making the design choices it made. Instructing a jury that weighing factors concerning conduct and judgment must yield a conclusion that does not describe conduct is confusing at best.

The Model Uniform Product Liability Act (UPLA) was published in 1979 by the Department of Commerce for voluntary use by the states. The act adopts a negligence or fault system with respect to design defects. It is important to examine the rationale underlying the UPLA's adoption of negligence as the criteria for liability in design defect cases. The drafters rejected, as a reason for application of strict liability to design defect cases, the theory of risk distribution wherein the product seller distributes the costs of all product-related risks through liability insurance. They believe that a "firmer liability foundation" than strict liability is needed in a design defect case because the whole product line is at risk. Furthermore, the drafters believed that a fault system would provide greater incentives for loss prevention.

The approach of the UPLA has been approved by several commentators, whose analysis is also instructive. First, unlike manufacturing defects, design defects result from deliberate and documentable decisions on the part of manufacturers, and plaintiffs should be able to learn the facts surrounding these decisions through liberalized modern discovery rules. Access to expert witnesses and technical data are available to aid plaintiffs in proving the manufacturer's design decision was ill considered.

Second, to the extent that a primary purpose of products liability law is to encourage the design of safer products and thereby reduce the incidence of injuries, a negligence standard that would reward the careful manufacturer and penalize the careless is more likely to achieve that purpose. A greater incentive to design safer products will result from a fault system where resources devoted to careful and safe design will pay dividends in the form of fewer claims and lower insurance premiums for the manufacturer with a good design safety record. The incentive will result from the knowledge that a distinction is made between those who are careful and those who are not.

Third, a verdict for the plaintiff in a design defect case is the equivalent of a determination that an entire product line is defective. It usually will involve a significant portion of the manufacturer's assets and the public may be deprived of a product. Thus, the plaintiff should be required to pass the higher threshold of a fault test in order to threaten an entire product line. The traditional tort law of negligence better serves this purpose.

Fourth, a fault system incorporates greater intrinsic fairness in that the careful safety-oriented manufacturer will not bear the burden of paying for losses caused by the negligent product seller. It will also follow that the customers of the careful manufacturer will not through its prices pay for the negligence of the careless. As a final bonus, the careful manufacturer with fewer claims and lower insurance premiums may, through lower prices as well as safer products, attract the customers of less careful competitors.

We find the formula adopted by the UPLA on the question of defective design to have the merit of being clear and understandable. We recognize that in products liability cases against manufacturers based upon alleged defects in the design of a product, the courts of this state have attempted to avoid both the notion of fault implicit in negligence and the harshness of no-fault implicit in absolute liability. Thus, on the basis of the heritage of contract and sales law underlying concepts of implied warranty, we have in the past approved instructions that attempted to focus a jury's attention on the condition of a product rather than on the reasonableness of the manufacturer's conduct or decision. We are persuaded that in so doing in the context of cases against the manufacturers of products *based upon allegations of defective design,* we have engaged in a process that may have served to confuse, rather than enlighten, jurors, who must ultimately apply understandable guidelines if they are to justly adjudicate the rights and duties of all parties. Imposing a negligence standard for design defect litigation is only to define in a coherent fashion what our litigants in this case are in fact arguing and what our jurors are in essence analyzing. Thus we adopt, forthrightly, a pure negligence, risk-utility test in products liability actions against manufacturers of products, where liability is predicated upon defective design.

We hold that in this products liability action against a manufacturer for an alleged defect in the design of its product, where the jury was properly instructed on the theory of negligent design, the trial judge's refusal to instruct on breach of warranty was (not) reversible error. Such instructions could have created juror confusion and prejudicial error. Indeed, such an instruction would have been repetitive and unnecessary and could have misled the jury into believing that plaintiff could recover on the warranty count even if it found there was no "defect" in the design of the product. [C]

This opinion is limited solely to its facts. We do (not) suggest that implied warranty and negligence are not separate and distinct theories of recovery; [c] or that the Michigan products liability statute, M.C.L.

§ 600.2945; M.S.A. § 27A.2945, has merged all former products liability theories or causes of action into a single unified "products liability theory." * * *

This holding is based upon the recognition that under the common law of products liability, in an action against the manufacturer of a product based upon an alleged defect in its design, "breach of implied warranty and negligence involve identical evidence and require proof of exactly the same elements." * * *

Applying these principles to the facts of this case, although plaintiffs alleged that their injuries were proximately caused by defendant's negligence and breach of an implied warranty, their evidence and proofs at trial focused on the single claim that the defendant *defectively designed* the "walkie hi-lo" forklift, because it failed to provide a seat or platform for the operator. Thus, recovery under either theory required the jury to determine that the forklift was defectively designed by defendant. [C] The factual inquiry was whether the design of defendant's forklift was "unreasonably dangerous" because it did not contain a seat or platform for the operator. [C]

The trial court properly recognized that the standards of liability under the theories of implied warranty and negligence were indistinguishable and that instructions on both would only confuse the jury. Accordingly, the trial judge's instructions regarding the standard of care and theories of liability properly informed the jury of defendant's legal duties as the manufacturer of the forklift. The court set forth the necessary elements for determining whether defendant defectively designed the forklift when it stated:

"A manufacturer of a product made under a plan or design which makes it dangerous for uses for which it is manufactured is, [however,] subject to liability to others whom he should expect to use the product or to be endangered by its probable use from physical harm caused by his failure to exercise reasonable care in the adoption of a safe plan or design.

"A manufacturer has a duty to use reasonable care in designing his product and guard it against a foreseeable and unreasonable risk of injury and this may even include misuse which might reasonably be anticipated."

In essence, the jury was instructed to consider whether the manufacturer took reasonable care in light of any reasonably foreseeable use of the product which might cause harm or injury. [C]

Therefore we hold that in a products liability action against a manufacturer, based upon defective design, the jury need only be instructed on a single unified theory of negligent design.

The judgment of the Court of Appeals is reversed, and the judgment of the trial court is reinstated.

WILLIAMS, C.J., and BRICKLEY and RYAN, JJ., concur.

CAVANAGH, J., concurring in result.

LEVIN, JUSTICE (dissenting) [with opinion].

NOTES AND QUESTIONS

1. When is a product to be regarded as "defective" for the purposes of imposing strict liability? Many courts and commentators have struggled with this broad issue and the principal case presents a thorough judicial discussion of the topic. See also Caterpillar Tractor Co. v. Beck, 593 P.2d 871, 880 (Alaska 1979) ("Design defects present the most perplexing problems in the field of strict products liability because there is no readily ascertainable external measure of defectiveness. While manufacturing flaws can be evaluated against the intended design of the product, no such objective standard exists in the design defect context.")

2. As indicated in the notes to Greenman v. Yuba Power Prods. Inc., page 729, the great majority of the states adopted the rule of § 402A of the Restatement. Most of them utilized the language of § 402A and spoke of the requirement that the product be unreasonably dangerous, but there were some that espoused strict liability but refused to accept the Restatement terminology. As the states developed their tests for design defect, many of them appeared to be requiring negligence or at least some showing of fault, despite their explicit adoption of strict liability. See Restatement (Third) of Torts: Products Liability § 2 cmt. a (1998), which recognizes this phenomenon and recommends a balancing of risk-utility to determine liability in design and warnings cases.

3. "_Crash-Proof Cars._" A strong dispute existed at one time on the issue whether an automobile was "defective" if it had not been designed to minimize injury to occupants during a collision. In Evans v. General Motors Corp., 359 F.2d 822 (7th Cir.1966), a new X-frame design for a car body turned out to be less safe than a conventional rectangular frame when the car was hit from the side. The court held, however, that the company was under no duty to design an accident-proof or crash-proof car, since the intended purpose of automobiles did not include its participation in a collision. Two years later another federal court in Larsen v. General Motors Corp., 391 F.2d 495 (8th Cir.1968), disagreed, holding that the risk of collisions was foreseeable and the design must reflect that. Today, the _Larsen_ view has swept the field. See Blankenship v. General Motors Corp., 185 W.Va. 350, 406 S.E.2d 781 (1991) (court noted unanimous support for _Larsen_ rule) and Restatement (Third) of Torts: Products Liability § 16 cmt. a (1998). Assuming the manufacturer owes a duty to protect the occupant of a vehicle in an accident, how far does it extend? A four-door hardtop leaves the road and turns over and lands on its top. A corner of the roof collapses on the driver and paralyzes him. Plaintiff's expert testifies that a roll bar or roll cage would have prevented the disabling injury, that roll cages were technically feasible at the time the car was manufactured and in use on race cars. Roll cages would eliminate convertibles and no mass-produced automobile had ever been built this way. Liability? Cf. Turner v. General Motors Corp., 584 S.W.2d 844 (Tex.1979). Although most of the crashworthiness or enhanced injuries cases involve automobiles, not all of them do. See, e.g., Smith v. Ariens Co., 375 Mass. 620, 377 N.E.2d 954 (1978) (snowmobile); Camacho v. Honda Motor Co. Ltd., 741 P.2d 1240 (Colo.1987) (motorcycle); Tafoya v. Sears, Roebuck & Co., 884 F.2d 1330 (10th Cir.1989) (riding lawnmower); Hillrichs v. Avco Corp., 478 N.W.2d 70 (Iowa 1991) (corn picker).

4. _Whiskey, Tobacco, and Butter._ The Restatement (Second) § 402A (1965) cautioned that products whose inherent characteristics made them dangerous were not to be considered "unreasonably dangerous." In language frequently quoted by the courts that adopted § 402A strict liability, comment _i_ provides that "Good whiskey is not unreasonably dangerous merely because it will make some people drunk, and is especially dangerous to alcoholics.... Good tobacco is not unreason-

ably dangerous merely because the effects of smoking may be harmful; . . . . Good butter is not unreasonably dangerous merely because, if such be the case, it deposits cholesterol in the arteries and leads to heart attacks; . . . ." See also Buckingham v. R.J. Reynolds Tobacco Co., 713 A.2d 381 (N.H.1998) (in context of second-hand smoke case, dismissing strict liability claim against cigarette manufacturers, citing comment *i*).

5. Unlike Michigan in the principal case, many jurisdictions instruct the jury on all available causes of action, negligence, breach of warranty, and strict liability. See, for example, Castro v. QVC Network, Inc., 139 F.3d 114 (2d Cir.1998) (under New York law, jury should be instructed separately on strict liability and breach of warranty in case involving roasting pan). See also Restatement (Third) of Torts: Products Liability § 2 cmt. n (1998) (rules are stated functionally rather than in terms of traditional doctrinal categories so that as long as the requisites set forth are met, doctrinal categories such as negligence or strict liability may be used to bring claim).

➤ O'Brien v. Muskin Corp.

Supreme Court of New Jersey, 1983.
94 N.J. 169, 463 A.2d 298.

POLLOCK, J. Plaintiff, Gary O'Brien, seeks to recover in strict liability for personal injuries sustained because defendant, Muskin Corporation, allegedly marketed a product, an above-ground swimming pool, that was defectively designed and bore an inadequate warning. In an unreported decision, the Appellate Division reversed the judgment for defendants and remanded the matter for trial. We granted certification, [c] and now modify and affirm the judgment of the Appellate Division. * * *

O'Brien sued to recover damages for serious personal injuries sustained when he dove into a swimming pool at the home of Jean Henry, widow of Arthur Henry, now Jean Glass. Ultimately, plaintiff sued as defendants not only Muskin Corporation, the manufacturer, but also Kiddie City Inc., the distributor of the pool, charging them with placing a defectively designed pool in the stream of commerce. * * *

Muskin, a swimming pool manufacturer, made and distributed a line of above-ground pools. Typically, the pools consisted of a corrugated metal wall, which the purchaser placed into an oval frame assembled over a shallow bed of sand. This outer structure was then fitted with an embossed vinyl liner and filled with water.

In 1971, Arthur Henry bought a Muskin pool and assembled it in his backyard. The pool was a twenty-foot by twenty-four-foot model, with four-foot walls. An embossed vinyl liner fit within the outer structure and was filled with water to a depth of approximately three and one-half feet. At one point, the outer wall of the pool bore the logo of the manufacturer, and below it a decal that warned "DO NOT DIVE" in letters roughly one-half inch high.

On May 17, 1974, O'Brien, then twenty-three years old, arrived uninvited at the Henry home and dove into the pool. A fact issue exists whether

O'Brien dove from the platform by the pool or from the roof of the adjacent eight-foot high garage. As his outstretched hands hit the vinyl-lined pool bottom, they slid apart, and O'Brien struck his head on the bottom of the pool, thereby sustaining his injuries.

In his complaint, O'Brien alleged that Muskin was strictly liable for his injuries because it had manufactured and marketed a defectively designed pool. In support of this contention, O'Brien cited the slippery quality of the pool liner and the lack of adequate warnings.

At trial, both parties produced experts who testified about the use of vinyl as a pool liner. One of the plaintiff's witnesses, an expert in the characteristics of vinyl, testified that wet vinyl was more than twice as slippery as rubber latex, which is used to line in-ground pools. The trial court, however, sustained an objection to the expert's opinion about alternative kinds of pool bottoms, specifically whether rubber latex was a feasible liner for above-ground pools. The expert admitted that he knew of no above-ground pool lined with a material other than vinyl, but plaintiff contended that vinyl should not be used in above-ground pools, even though no alternative material was available. A second expert testified that the slippery vinyl bottom and lack of adequate warnings rendered the pool unfit and unsafe for its foreseeable uses.

Muskin's expert testified that vinyl was not only an appropriate material to line an above-ground pool, but was the best material because it permitted the outstretched arms of the diver to glide when they hit the liner, thereby preventing the diver's head from striking the bottom of the pool. Thus, he concluded that in some situations, specifically those in which a diver executes a shallow dive, slipperiness operates as a safety feature. Another witness, Muskin's customer service manager, who was indirectly in charge of quality control, testified that the vinyl bottom could have been thicker and the embossing deeper. A fair inference could be drawn that deeper embossing would have rendered the pool bottom less slippery.

At the close of the entire case, the trial court instructed the jury on the elements of strict liability, both with respect to design defects and the failure to warn adequately. The court, however, then limited the jury's consideration to the adequacy of the warning. That is, the court took from the jury the issue whether manufacturing a pool with a vinyl liner constituted either a design or manufacturing defect.

Strict liability law, a relatively recent but rapidly growing legal phenomenon, has received uneven treatment from scholars, legislatures and courts. Underlying the various responses is a shared concern about the allocation of the risk of loss upon manufacturers, distributors and others in the stream of commerce for injuries sustained by the public from unsafe products.

One of the policy considerations supporting the imposition of strict liability is easing the burden of proof for a plaintiff injured by a defective product, a policy that is achieved by eliminating the requirement that the plaintiff prove the manufacturer's negligence. [C] Generally speaking, a plaintiff has the burden of proving that (1) the product was defective; (2) the defect existed when the product left the hands of the defendant; and (3) the defect caused injury to a reasonably foreseeable user. [C] Proof that the product was defective requires more than a mere showing that the product caused the injury. The necessity of proving a defect in the product as part of the plaintiff's *prima facie* case distinguishes strict from absolute liability, and thus prevents the manufacturer from also becoming the insurer of a product. [Cc]

Fundamental to the determination of a products liability case, including one predicated on a defective design or inadequate warning, is the duty of the manufacturer to foreseeable users. The duty includes warning foreseeable users of the risks inherent in the use of that product, [c] and not placing defective products on the market. [Cc] A manufacturer who breaches these duties is strictly liable to an injured party. That liability reflects the policy judgment that by marketing its product, a manufacturer assumes responsibility to members of the public who are injured because of defects in that product. Restatement (Second) of Torts § 402A comment c (1965). * * *

Critical, then, to the disposition of products liability claims is the meaning of "defect". The term is not self-defining and has no accepted meaning suitable for all strict liability cases. Implicit in the term "defect" is a comparison of the product with a standard of evaluation; something can be defective only if it fails to measure up to that standard. [C] Speaking generally, defects may be classified as design defects or manufacturing defects. In cases alleging manufacturing defects, as distinguished from design defects, defining the standard, and thus the meaning of "defect," is relatively easy. For example, the injury-causing product may be measured against the same product as manufactured according to the manufacturer's standards. If the particular product used by the plaintiff fails to conform to those standards or other units of the same kind, it is defective. An apt illustration is a mass-produced product that comes off the assembly line missing a part. The question in those cases becomes whether the product as produced by the manufacturer conformed to the product as intended. [C]

The considerations are more subtle when a plaintiff alleges that a product is defective due to any feature of its design, including the absence or inadequacy of accompanying warnings. In design defect or failure-to-warn cases, the product has been manufactured as intended and cannot be "defective" by comparison to a standard set by the manufacturer. [C] Rather, the standard to measure the product reflects a policy judgment that some products are so dangerous that they create a risk of harm outweighing their usefulness. From that perspective, the term "defect" is a conclusion rather than a test for reaching that conclusion. [C]

Although the appropriate standard might be variously defined, one definition, based on a comparison of the utility of the product with the risk of injury that it poses to the public, has gained prominence. To the extent that "risk-utility analysis," as it is known, implicates the reasonableness of the manufacturer's conduct, strict liability law continues to manifest that part of its heritage attributable to the law of negligence. [Cc] Risk-utility analysis is appropriate when the product may function satisfactorily under one set of circumstances, yet because of its design present undue risk of injury to the user in another situation.

Another standard is the consumer expectations test, which recognizes that the failure of the product to perform safely may be viewed as a violation of the reasonable expectations of the consumer. [C] In this case, however, the pool fulfilled its function as a place to swim. The alleged defect manifested itself when the pool was used for diving.

* * * [S]ome factors relevant in risk-utility analysis are:

(1) The usefulness and desirability of the product—its utility to the user and to the public as a whole.

(2) The safety aspects of the product—the likelihood that it will cause injury, and the probable seriousness of the injury.

(3) The availability of a substitute product which would meet the same need and not be as unsafe.

(4) The manufacturer's ability to eliminate the unsafe character of the product without impairing its usefulness or making it too expensive to maintain its utility.

(5) The user's ability to avoid danger by the exercise of care in the use of the product.

(6) The user's anticipated awareness of the dangers inherent in the product and their avoidability, because of general public knowledge of the obvious condition of the product, or of the existence of suitable warnings or instructions.

(7) The feasibility, on the part of the manufacturer, of spreading the loss by setting the price of the product or carrying liability insurance. [C] * * *

By implication, risk-utility analysis includes other factors such as the "state-of-the-art" at the time of the manufacture of the product. [C] The "state-of-the-art" refers to the existing level of technological expertise and scientific knowledge relevant to a particular industry at the time a product is designed. [C] Although customs of an industry may be relevant, [c] because those customs may lag behind technological development, they are not identical with the state-of-the-art. [Cc] A manufacturer may have a duty to make products pursuant to a safer design even if the custom of the industry is not to use that alternative. [C] * * *

Although state-of-the-art evidence may be dispositive on the facts of a particular case, it does not constitute an absolute defense apart from risk-utility analysis. [C] The ultimate burden of proving a defect is on the plaintiff, but the burden is on the defendant to prove that compliance with state-of-the-art, in conjunction with other relevant evidence, justifies placing a product on the market. Compliance with proof of state-of-the-art need not, as a matter of law, compel a judgment for a defendant. State-of-the-art evidence, together with other evidence relevant to risk-utility analysis, however, may support a judgment for a defendant. In brief, state-of-the-art evidence is relevant to, but not necessarily dispositive of, risk-utility analysis. That is, a product may embody the state-of-the-art and still fail to satisfy the risk-utility equation.

The assessment of the utility of a design involves the consideration of available alternatives. If no alternatives are available, recourse to a unique design is more defensible. The existence of a safer and equally efficacious design, however, diminishes the justification for using a challenged design.

The evaluation of the utility of a product also involves the relative need for that product; some products are essentials, while others are luxuries. A product that fills a critical need and can be designed in only one way should be viewed differently from a luxury item. Still other products, including some for which no alternative exists, are so dangerous and of such little use that under the risk-utility analysis, a manufacturer would bear the cost of liability of harm to others. That cost might dissuade a manufacturer from placing the product on the market, even if the product has been made as safely as possible. Indeed, plaintiff contends that above-ground pools with vinyl liners are such products and that manufacturers who market those pools should bear the cost of injuries they cause to foreseeable users.

A critical issue at trial was whether the design of the pool, calling for a vinyl bottom in a pool four feet deep, was defective. The trial court should have permitted the jury to consider whether, because of the dimensions of the pool and slipperiness of the bottom, the risks of injury so outweighed the utility of the product as to constitute a defect. In removing that issue from consideration by the jury, the trial court erred. To establish sufficient proof to compel submission of the issue to the jury for appropriate fact-finding under risk-utility analysis, it was not necessary for plaintiff to prove the existence of alternative, safer designs. Viewing the evidence in the light most favorable to plaintiff, even if there are no alternative methods of making bottoms for above-ground pools, the jury might have found that the risk posed by the pool outweighed its utility.

In a design-defect case, the plaintiff bears the burden of both going forward with the evidence and of persuasion that the product contained a defect. To establish a *prima facie* case, the plaintiff should adduce sufficient evidence on the risk-utility factors to establish a defect. With respect to above-ground swimming pools, for example, the plaintiff might seek to establish that pools are marketed primarily for recreational, not therapeutic purposes; that because of their design, including their configuration, inadequate warnings, and the use of vinyl liners, injury is likely; that, without impairing the usefulness of the pool or pricing it out of the market, warnings against diving could be made more prominent and a liner less dangerous. It may not be necessary for the plaintiff to introduce evidence on all those alternatives. Conversely, the plaintiff may wish to offer proof on other matters relevant to the risk-utility analysis. It is not a foregone conclusion that plaintiff ultimately will prevail on a risk-utility analysis, but he should have an opportunity to prove his case. * * *

We modify and affirm the judgment of the Appellate Division reversing and remanding the matter for a new trial.

CLIFFORD, J., concurring in result. SCHREIBER, J., concurring and dissenting [with opinion].

For affirmance as modified—CHIEF JUSTICE WILENTZ, and JUSTICES CLIFFORD, HANDLER, POLLOCK and O'HERN.

NOTES AND QUESTIONS

1. *Risk Utility Balancing Test for Design Defect.* Most jurisdictions use some form of risk utility analysis for design defect cases. See, e.g., Phipps v. General Motors Corp., 278 Md. 337, 363 A.2d 955 (1976); Miller v. Todd, 551 N.E.2d 1139 (Ind.1990); Armentrout v. FMC Corp., 842 P.2d 175 (Colo.1992). See also, Birnbaum, Unmasking the Test for Design Defect: From Negligence [to Warranty] to Strict Liability to Negligence, 33 Vand.L.Rev. 539 (1980); Wade, On Product "Design Defects" and Their Actionability, 33 Vand.L.Rev. 551 (1980); Restatement (Third) of Torts: Products Liability § 2 cmt. a (1998). Should the test be the utility to the individual who was injured or to society as a whole?

2. *Consumer Expectations Test for Design Defect.* Some jurisdictions use the consumer expectations test for design defect cases. See, e.g., Rojas v. Lindsay Mfg., Co., 108 Idaho 590, 701 P.2d 210 (1985); Ritter v. Narrangansett Elec. Co., 109 R.I. 176, 283 A.2d 255 (1971). See also, Hubbard, Reasonable Human Expectations: A Normative Model for Imposing Strict Liability for Defective Products, 29 Mercer L.Rev. 465 (1978); Montgomery & Owen, Reflections on the Theory and Administration of Strict Liability for Defective Products, 27 S.C.L.Rev. 803 (1976).

3. Some jurisdictions use both. See, e.g., Barker v. Lull Engineering Co., 20 Cal.3d 413, 573 P.2d 443, 143 Cal. Rptr. 225 (1978) (liability may be found under either of two tests) and Soule v. General Motors Corp., 8 Cal.4th 548, 882 P.2d 298 (1994) (applicable test depends on circumstances); Caterpillar Tractor Co. v. Beck, 593 P.2d 871 (Alaska 1979) and General Motors Corp. v. Farnsworth, 965 P.2d 1209 (Alaska 1998) (reaffirming viability of consumer expectations test in crashworthiness case); Ray v. BIC Corp., 925 S.W.2d 527 (Tenn.1996) (both tests generally available to plaintiffs, although some circumstances may be inappropriate for consumer expectations test). Some jurisdictions use consumer expectations as one of the factors to be considered in a risk utility analysis. See e.g., Aller v. Rodgers Machinery Mfg. Co., Inc., 268 N.W.2d 830 (Iowa 1978); Lamkin v. Towner, 138 Ill.2d 510, 563 N.E.2d 449, 150 Ill.Dec. 562 (1990). See also Restatement (Third) of Torts: Products Liability § 2 cmts. f and g (1998) (consumer expectations one factor, among many, in risk-utility balancing).

4. *Reasonable Alternative Design.* Unlike the principal case, most jurisdictions require that the plaintiff prove an alternative feasible design in order to prove design defect. See, e.g., Beech v. Outboard Marine Corp., 584 So.2d 447 (Ala.1991) (defect must be shown by safer, practical, alternative design). See also Restatement (Third) of Torts: Products Liability § 2(b) (1998) ("is defective in design when the foreseeable risks of harm posed by the product could have been reduced or avoided by the adoption of a reasonable alternative design") and Reporters' Note to § 2 cmt. d (survey of cases dealing with requirement of reasonable alternative design). But see Potter v. Chicago Pneumatic Tool Co., 241 Conn. 199, 694 A.2d 1319 (1997) (alternative feasible design is one factor to be considered, citing principal case).

5. Note that the court in the principal case appears to suggest that the plaintiff may be able to prove at the trial on remand that the defendant is liable even if there is no alternative feasible design if the product was so dangerous and of such little use that the risk utility test suggests that the product should never have been marketed. Thus, the decision to market it could subject the manufacturer to liability for harms arising from its use even in the absence of a manufacturing or design flaw in the product. Courts in two other jurisdictions have expressed similar views. See Kelley v. R.G. Indus., 304 Md. 124, 497 A.2d 1143 (1985) (cheap handguns); Halphen v. Johns–Manville Sales Corp., 484 So.2d 110 (La.1986) (asbestos). What would happen if courts in different states were to have conflicting views about whether a particular product was "too dangerous to be placed on the market"? Could the manufacturer avoid liability by selling the product in only those states that do not think the product should be taken off the market? Are there other ways to ban products that are unacceptably dangerous in light of their limited utility to product users and society? The legislatures in all three states have overruled or limited these holdings. See N.J.Rev.Stat. § 2A:58C–3(3) (1987); Md. Crim.Law Code Ann. art. 27, § 36–I (1992); La.Rev.Stat.Ann. § 9:2800.56(1) (1991). See also, Restatement (Third) of Torts: Products Liability § 2 cmts. d and g and Reporters' Notes thereto (1998); Henderson and Twerski, Closing the American Products Liability Frontier: the Rejection of Liability Without Defect, 66 N.Y.U.L.Rev. 1263 (1991); Turley, Manufacturers' and Suppliers' Liability to Handgun Victims, 10 N.Ky.L.Rev. 41 (1982).

6. Are there products that are so dangerous and of such low social utility that liability should be imposed even if there is no reasonable alternative design? What about ammunition that is designed in a way that dramatically increases the wounding power of the bullet? Victims of the shooting spree on the Long Island Railroad brought claims against the manufacturer of the "Black Talon" bullets that were used. McCarthy v. Olin Corp., 119 F.3d 148, 155 (2d Cir.1997) (applying New York law) ("the risk of injury to be balanced with the utility is a risk not intended as the primary function of the product. There is no reason to search for an alternative safer design where the product's sole utility is to kill and maim"). New Jersey, the home of the principal case, also has a statute imposing such liability. N.J. Stat. Ann. § 2A:58C–3(b) (practical and technically feasible alternative design not necessary if product is egregiously unsafe or ultra-hazardous and product has little or no usefulness). Acknowledging that there is only scant authority for such a position, Restatement (Third) of Torts: Products Liability (1998) recognizes the possibility of such liability through a comment. See § 2 comment e. Judge Calabresi, dissenting in *McCarthy*, suggested that the Black Talon bullets would qualify as "manifestly unreasonable" products under the Restatement formulation.

c. State of the Art. A key issue in design liability cases is whether a defendant can avoid liability by showing compliance with the "state of the art" at the time the product was made. The concept of "state of the art" for products has become muddled because different courts ascribe different meanings to the term. Sometimes the term is confused with evidence of compliance with "industry customs," which is introduced to show the defendant's reasonableness or to rebut allegations of product defect. The better use of the term is as a label for the requirement that the best scientific and medical technology that is practically and economically feasible at the time the product was made or marketed be utilized by the manufacturer. The product is evaluated in light of knowledge and technology that were available at the time of manufacture rather than at the time of trial. Most jurisdictions allow state of the art evidence to be considered in the determination of design defect, either by case law or statute. See, e.g., Beech v. Outboard Marine Corp., 584 So.2d 447

(Ala.1991); Voss v. Black & Decker Mfg. Co., 59 N.Y.2d 102, 450 N.E.2d 204, 463 N.Y.S.2d 398 (1983); Sturm, Ruger & Co. v. Day, 594 P.2d 38 (Alaska 1979); Colo.Rev.Stat. § 13–21–403(1)(a) (1987); Ky.Rev.Stat. § 411.310(2) (1978) (rebuttable presumption); Mich.Comp.Laws Ann. § 600.2946 (1986). But see Sternhagen v. Dow Chem. Co., 282 Mont. 168, 935 P.2d 1139 (1997); Johnson v. Raybestos– Manhattan, Inc., 69 Haw. 287, 740 P.2d 548 (1987); Carrecter v. Colson Equip. Co., 346 Pa.Super. 95, 499 A.2d 326 (1985). Other jurisdictions view state of the art as a defense to be plead and proved by the defendant. See, e.g., Ind.Code § 33–1–1.5– 4(b)(4) (1992); N.J.Stat.Ann. § 2A:58C–3 (1987). Do you understand the significance of the difference in approaches? See also Symposium, The Passage of Time: The Implications For Products, 58 N.Y.U.L.Rev. 733 (1983); Restatement (Third) of Torts: Products Liability § 2 cmt. d (1998).

8. *Open and Obvious Danger.* A few courts have held that an ''open and obvious'' or ''patent'' danger is an absolute defense to a design defect case. See e.g., Weatherby v. Honda Motor Co., 195 Ga.App. 169, 393 S.E.2d 64 (1990); Elliott v. Brunswick Corp., 903 F.2d 1505 (11th Cir.1990) (applying Alabama law); McCollum v. Grove Mfg., 58 N.C.App. 283, 293 S.E.2d 632 (1982). Most jurisdictions, however, have rejected the obviousness of the danger as a bar to recovery and instead consider it as one factor in the risk utility balancing test. See e.g., Perkins v. Wilkinson Sword, Inc., 83 Ohio St.3d 507, 700 N.E.2d 1247 (1998) (in case where children were killed in fire they started while playing with cigarette lighter, court ruled that obvious danger of cigarette lighter was factor to be considered in riskutility analysis, but was not determinative). Gann v. International Harvester Co., 712 S.W.2d 100 (Tenn.1986); Owens v. Allis–Chalmers Corp., 414 Mich. 413, 326 N.W.2d 372 (1982); Thibault v. Sears, Roebuck & Co., 118 N.H. 802, 395 A.2d 843 (1978); Micallef v. Miehle Co., 39 N.Y.2d 376, 348 N.E.2d 571, 384 N.Y.S.2d 115 (1976). See also, Darling, The Patent Danger Rule: An Analysis and Survey of its Vitality, 29 Mercer L.Rev. 583 (1978); Marschall, An Obvious Wrong Does Not Make a Right: Manufacturer's Liability for Patently Dangerous Products, 48 N.Y.U.L.Rev. 1065 (1973); Restatement (Third) of Torts: Products Liability § 2 cmt. d (1998).

9. *Applicability to Prescription Drugs and Medical Devices.* Most jurisdictions have declined to apply strict liability to prescription drugs, following comment *k* to § 402A, which provided for no liability in the case of unavoidably unsafe products. Comment *k* used prescription drugs as an example of such products, noting that ''The seller of such products, again with the qualification that they are properly prepared and marketed, and proper warning is given, . . . is not to be held to strict liability for unfortunate consequences attending their use, merely because he has undertaken to supply the public with an apparently useful and desirable product, attended with a known but apparently reasonable risk.'' See e.g., Brown v. Superior Court, 44 Cal.3d 1049, 751 P.2d 470, 245 Cal.Rptr. 412 (1988); Grundberg v. Upjohn, 813 P.2d 89 (Utah 1991); Coyle v. Richardson–Merrell, Inc., 526 Pa. 208, 584 A.2d 1383 (1991); Young v. Key Pharmaceuticals, 130 Wash.2d 160, 922 P.2d 59 (1996). But see West v. Searle & Co., 305 Ark. 33, 806 S.W.2d 608 (1991) (requiring defendant to demonstrate that drug is unavoidably unsafe using risk/utility analysis); Shanks v. Upjohn, 835 P.2d 1189 (Alaska 1992) (declining to follow *Brown*); Allison v. Merck & Co., 878 P.2d 948 (Nev.1994) (strict liability appropriate even when overall benefits of drug outweigh risks). Restatement (Third) of Torts: Products Liability has a separate section governing liability for sellers and distributors of prescription drugs and medical devices. It would impose liability for harm caused by defective design, whether grounded in negligence or strict liability, only if ''the foreseeable risks of harm posed by the drug or medical device are sufficiently great in relation to its therapeutic benefits that reasonable health-care providers,

knowing of such foreseeable risks and therapeutic benefits, would not prescribe the drug or medical device for any class of patients." Restatement (Third) of Torts: Products Liability § 6(c) (1998). For a discussion of comment *k* issues, see Schwartz, Unavoidably Unsafe Products: Clarifying the Meaning and Policy Behind Comment K, 42 Wash. & Lee L.Rev. 1139 (1985) (referred to in the *Brown* case); Ausness, Unavoidably Unsafe Products and Strict Products Liability: What Liability Rule Should Be Applied to Sellers of Pharmaceutical Products? 78 Ky.L.J. 705 (1989–90). For a discussion of Restatement (Third)'s position, see Cupp, Rethinking Conscious Design Liability for Prescription Drugs: The Restatement (Third) Standard Versus a Negligence Approach, 63 GEO. WASH. L. REV. 76 (1994); Schwartz, Prescription Products and the Proposed Restatement (Third), 61 TENN. L. REV. 1357 (1994); Henderson, Prescription Drug Design Liability Under the Proposed Restatement (Third) of Torts: A Reporter's Perspective, 48 RUTGERS L. REV. 471 (1996).

10. *Applicability to Food.* Courts have struggled with whether to impose strict liability to vendors of food when suit is based on an injury-producing substance in food. One group of cases has applied a "foreign-natural" test. Under this theory, strict liability is only applicable if the injury-causing substance is a piece of glass, wire, or other substance "foreign" to the food. If the substance is natural, like bone fragments in meat, pits in cherries, or shells in nuts, the plaintiff must prove negligence in the preparation of the food in order to recover. See, e.g., Mexicali Rose v. Superior Court, 1 Cal.4th 617, 4 Cal.Rptr.2d 145, 822 P.2d 1292 (1992) (no strict liability for throat injury from chicken bone in chicken enchilada). Another line of cases provides that regardless whether the injury-producing substance is natural or foreign, strict liability will lie if the consumer of the product would not reasonably have expected to find the substance in the product. See, e.g., Jackson v. Nestle–Beich, Inc., 147 Ill.2d 408, 589 N.E.2d 547, 168 Ill.Dec. 147 (1992) (broken tooth from biting pecan shell from can of chocolate-covered pecan-caramel candy). The Restatement (Third) endorses the latter position. Restatement (Third) of Torts: Products Liability § 2 cmt. h and § 7 (1998).

11. *Allergic Reaction.* An allergic reaction to a drug or product may occur because of an individual's unusual susceptibility to an ingredient. Since the product is reasonably fit for the ordinary user, it might be said that there is no defect and thus no recovery for any allergic reaction. Most jurisdictions have handled this as a failure to warn issue and imposed a duty on the manufacturer to warn of possible adverse reactions only if it knew or should have known of the risk. See, e.g., D'Arienzo v. Clairol, Inc., 125 N.J.Super. 224, 310 A.2d 106 (1973) (good discussion of duty). What if the allergy is common to a number of potential users? See, e.g., Braun v. Roux Distributing Co., 312 S.W.2d 758 (Mo.1958) (3–4%); Simeon v. Doe (Sweet Pepper Grill), 618 So.2d 848 (La.1993) (no strict liability against bar owner for serving oysters containing a bacteria common to Gulf region, which was not harmful to most people; plaintiff entitled to try to prove failure to warn if plaintiff could show that owner knew or had reason to know that individuals like plaintiff with a pre-existing liver or kidney disease could become ill from consuming oysters in which the bacteria was present).

(C) WARNINGS DEFECT

Asbestos case

Anderson v. Owens–Corning Fiberglas Corp.

Supreme Court of California, 1991.
53 Cal.3d 987, 810 P.2d 549, 281 Cal.Rptr. 528.

PANELLI, J.

In this case we consider the issue "whether a defendant in a products liability action based upon an alleged failure to warn of a risk of harm may present evidence of the state of the art, i.e., evidence that the particular risk was neither known nor knowable by the application of scientific knowledge available at the time of manufacture and/or distribution.'' (Order on grant of review, May 3, 1990.) As will appear, resolution of this evidentiary issue requires an examination of the failure-to-warn theory as an alternate and independent basis for imposing strict liability and a determination of whether knowledge, actual or constructive, is a component of strict liability on the failure-to-warn theory. It is manifest that, if knowledge or knowability is a component, state-of-the-art evidence is relevant and, subject to the normal rules of evidence, admissible.

We conclude that * * * the California courts, either expressly or by implication, have to date required knowledge, actual or constructive, of potential risk or danger before imposing strict liability for a failure to warn. The state of the art may be relevant to the question of knowability and, for that reason, should be admissible in that context. Exclusion of state-of-the-art evidence, when the basis of liability is a failure to warn, would make a manufacturer the virtual insurer of its product's safe use, a result that is not consonant with established principles underlying strict liability.

Defendants are or were manufacturers of products containing asbestos. Plaintiff Carl Anderson filed suit in 1984, alleging that he contracted asbestosis and other lung ailments through exposure to asbestos and asbestos products (i.e., preformed blocks, cloth and cloth tape, cement, and floor tiles) while working as an electrician at the Long Beach Naval Shipyard from 1941 to 1976. Plaintiff allegedly encountered asbestos while working in the vicinity of others who were removing and installing insulation products aboard ships. * * * [After a verdict for defendants, the trial court granted a new trial and the parties argued on appeal the admissibility of state of the art evidence in a failure to warn case.]

Defendants contend that, if knowledge or knowability is irrelevant in a failure-to-warn case, then a manufacturer's potential liability is absolute, rendering it the virtual insurer of the product's safe use. Plaintiff, on the other hand, argues that to impose the requirement of knowledge or knowability improperly infuses a negligence standard into strict liability in contravention of the principles set out in our decisions from Greenman v. Yuba Power Products, Inc. (1963) 59 Cal.2d 57 [27 Cal.Rptr. 697, 377 P.2d 897, 13 A.L.R.3d 1049] to Brown v. Superior Court (1988) 44 Cal.3d 1049 [245 Cal.Rptr. 412, 751 P.2d 470]. Plaintiff also urges that, although some courts have assumed that knowledge or knowability is a condition of strict liability for failure to warn, the issue has not been definitively resolved in this court.

Greenman v. Yuba Power Products, Inc., supra, 59 Cal.2d 57, established the doctrine of strict liability in California: "[a] manufacturer is strictly liable in tort when an article he places on the market, knowing that it is to be used without inspection for defects, proves to have a defect that causes injury to a human being." [C] "The purpose of such liability is to insure that the costs of injuries resulting from defective products are borne by the manufacturers that put such products on the market rather than by the injured persons who are powerless to protect themselves." [Cc] The strict liability doctrine achieves its goals by "reliev[ing] an injured plaintiff of many of the onerous evidentiary burdens inherent in a negligence cause of action." [Cc]

Strict liability, however, was never intended to make the manufacturer or distributor of a product its insurer. "From its inception, * * * strict liability has never been, and is not now, absolute liability. * * * [U]nder strict liability the manufacturer does not thereby become the insurer of the safety of the product's user. [Citations.]" * * *

* * *

Whatever the ambiguity of *Brown*, we hereby adopt the requirement, as propounded by the Restatement Second of Torts and acknowledged by the lower courts of this state and the majority of jurisdictions, that knowledge or knowability is a component of strict liability for failure to warn.

One of the guiding principles of the strict liability doctrine was to relieve a plaintiff of the evidentiary burdens inherent in a negligence cause of action. [C] Indeed, it was the limitations of negligence theories that prompted the development and expansion of the doctrine. The proponents of the minority rule, including the Court of Appeal in this case, argue that the knowability requirement, and admission of state-of-the-art evidence, improperly infuse negligence concepts into strict liability cases by directing the trier of fact's attention to the conduct of the manufacturer or distributor rather than to the condition of the product. Similar claims have been made as to other aspects of strict liability, sometimes resulting in limitations on the doctrine and sometimes not. * * *

However, the claim that a particular component "rings of" or "sounds in" negligence has not precluded its acceptance in the context of strict liability. * * * [T]he doctrine of strict liability was a judicial creation and, in reaching our conclusion, we blended or accommodated the "theoretical and semantic distinctions between the twin principles of strict products liability and traditional negligence." [C] * * *

[T]he strict liability doctrine has incorporated some well-settled rules from the law of negligence and has survived judicial challenges asserting that such incorporation violates the fundamental principles of the doctrine. It may also be true that the "warning defect" theory is "rooted in negligence" to a greater extent than are the manufacturing—or design-defect theories. The "warning defect" relates to a failure extraneous to the product itself. Thus, while a manufacturing or design defect can be evaluated without reference to the conduct of the manufacturer [c], the giving of a warning cannot. The latter necessarily requires the communicating of something to someone. How can one warn of something that is unknowable? If every product that has no warning were defective per se and for that reason subject to strict liability, the mere fact of injury by an unlabelled product would automatically permit recovery. That is not, and has never been, the purpose and goal of the failure-to-warn theory of strict liability. Further, if a warning automatically precluded liability in every case, a manufacturer or distributor could easily escape liability with overly broad, and thus practically useless, warnings. [C]

We * * * reject the contention that every reference to a feature shared with theories of negligence can serve to defeat limitations on the doctrine of strict liability. Furthermore, despite its roots in negligence, failure to warn in strict liability differs markedly from failure to warn in the negligence context. Negligence law in a failure-to-warn case requires a plaintiff to prove that a manufacturer or distributor did not warn of a particular risk for reasons which fell below the acceptable standard of care, i.e., what a reasonably prudent manufacturer would have known and warned about. Strict liability is not concerned with the standard of due care or the reasonableness of a manufacturer's conduct. The rules of strict liability require a plaintiff to prove only that the defendant did not adequately warn of a particular risk that was known or knowable in light of the generally recognized and prevailing best scientific and medical knowledge available at the time of manufacture and distribution. Thus, in strict liability, as opposed to negligence, the reasonableness of the defendant's failure to warn is immaterial.

Stated another way, a reasonably prudent manufacturer might reasonably decide that the risk of harm was such as not to require a warning as, for example, if the manufacturer's own testing showed a result contrary to that of others in the scientific community. Such a manufacturer might escape liability under negligence principles. In contrast, under strict liability principles the manufacturer has no such leeway; the manufacturer is liable if it failed to give warning of dangers that were known to the scientific community at the time it manufactured or distributed the product. Whatever may be reasonable from the point of view of the manufacturer, the user of the product must be given the option either to refrain from using the product at all or to use it in such a way as to minimize the degree of danger. [C] "When, in a particular case, the risk qualitatively (e.g., of death or major disability) as well as quantitatively, on balance with the end sought to be achieved, is such as to call for a true choice judgment, medical or personal, the warning must be given. [Fn. omitted.]" [C] Thus, the fact that a manufacturer acted as a reasonably prudent manufacturer in deciding not to warn, while perhaps absolving the manufacturer of liability under the negligence theory, will not preclude liability under strict liability principles if the trier of fact concludes that, based on the information scientifically available to the manufacturer, the manufacturer's failure to warn rendered the product unsafe to its users.

The foregoing examination of the failure-to-warn theory of strict liability in California compels the conclusion that knowability is relevant to imposition of liability under that theory. Our conclusion not only accords with precedent but also with the considerations of policy that underlie the doctrine of strict liability.

We recognize that an important goal of strict liability is to spread the risks and costs of injury to those most able to bear them.[14] However, it was never the intention of the drafters of the doctrine to make the manufacturer or distributor the insurer of the safety of their products. It was never their intention to impose absolute liability.

Conclusion

Therefore, in answer to the question raised in our order granting review, a defendant in a strict products liability action based upon an alleged failure to warn of a risk of harm may present evidence of the state of the art, i.e., evidence that the particular risk was neither known nor knowable by the application of scientific knowledge available at the time of manufacture and/or distribution. The judgment of the Court of Appeal is affirmed with directions that the matter be remanded to the trial court for proceedings in accord with our decision herein.

[The concurring and dissenting opinions are omitted.]

NOTES AND QUESTIONS

1. Would you have predicted this decision from the jurisdiction that was the first to adopt strict liability less than thirty years before in *Greenman v. Yuba Power Products, Inc.*, page 729, 27 Cal.Rptr. 697, 377 P.2d 897?

2. Justice Mosk in a concurring and dissenting opinion to the principal case noted the convergence of strict liability and negligence theories of liability in failure-to-warn cases and urged the court to consider "the possibility of holding that failure-to-warn actions lie solely on a negligence theory." 810 P.2d at 563. Is the distinction between the two worth preserving? Why? See also Henderson & Twerski, Doctrinal Collapse in Products Liability: The Empty Shell of Failure to Warn, 65 N.Y.U.L.Rev. 265, 278 (arguing that mixing of negligence and strict liability concepts engenders confusion). Note that the approach of Restatement (Third) of Torts: Products Liability § 2 (1998) eliminates this potential confusion by its approach of organizing liability by type of alleged defect (manufacturing, design, warning) rather than by theory of recovery (negligence, breach of warranty, strict liability).

3. In warnings cases, most courts still apply a fault-based standard by requiring the plaintiff to show that the manufacturer knew or should have known of risks that injured plaintiff. See, e.g., Vassallo v. Baxter Healthcare Corp., 428 Mass. 1,

---

14. The suggestion that losses arising from unknowable risks and hazards should be spread among all users to the product, as are losses from predictable injuries or negligent conduct, is generally regarded as not feasible. Not the least of the problems is insurability. (See Henderson, Coping with Time Dimension in Products Liability (1981) 69 Cal.L.Rev. 919, 948–949; Wade, On the Effect in Product Liability of Knowledge Unavailable Prior to Marketing (1983) 58 N.Y.U.L.Rev. 734.) Dean Wade stated the dilemma, but provided no solution:

"How does one spread the potential loss of an unknowable hazard? How can insurance premiums be figured for this purpose? Indeed, will insurance be available at all? Spreading the loss is essentially a compensation device rather than a tort concept. Providing compensation should not be the sole basis for imposing tort liability, and this seems more emphatically so in the situation where the defendant is no more able to insure against unknown risks than is the plaintiff." (58 N.Y.U.L.Rev. at p. 755.)

696 N.E.2d 909, 923 (1998) ("In recognition of the clear judicial trend regarding the duty to warn in products liability cases, and the principles stated in Restatement (Third) of Torts: Products Liability § 2(c) and cmt. m, we hereby revise our law to state that a defendant will not be held liable under an implied warranty of merchantability for failure to warn or provide instructions about risks that were not reasonably foreseeable at the time of sale or could not have been discovered by way of reasonable testing prior to marketing the product."); Fibreboard Corp. v. Fenton, 845 P.2d 1168 (Colo.1993) (risks known to it or knowable in light of the generally recognized scientific and technical knowledge available); Owens–Illinois v. Zenobia, 325 Md. 420, 601 A.2d 633 (1992); Woodill v. Parke Davis & Co., 79 Ill.2d 26, 402 N.E.2d 194, 37 Ill.Dec. 304 (1980). But see Ayers v. Johnson & Johnson Baby Prods. Co., 117 Wash.2d 747, 818 P.2d 1337 (1991) (foreseeability not an element of a warnings defect claim); In re Hawaii Federal Asbestos Cases, 960 F.2d 806 (9th Cir.1992) (applying Hawaii law); Dambacher v. Mallis, 336 Pa. Super. 22, 485 A.2d 408 (1984).

4.   Often a case involves claims based on both defective design and inadequate warnings. Should the fact that a product contains a good warning overcome the effect of a design problem—i.e., should a warning about a design hazard preclude liability, or should the manufacturer be required to eliminate the defective design condition? See, e.g., Uniroyal Goodrich Tire Co. v. Martinez, 977 S.W.2d 328 (Tex.1998) (warning on tire did not relieve manufacturer of liability for defective design); Rogers v. Ingersoll–Rand Co., 144 F.3d 841 (D.C.Cir.1998) (applying District of Columbia law) (warning is one factor to consider in risk-utility analysis, but warnings alone will not save a product from being unreasonably dangerous, citing Restatement (Third)). Klopp v. Wackenhut Corp., 113 N.M. 153, 824 P.2d 293 (1992) (defect in product cannot be overcome by warning); Robinson v. G.G.C., Inc., 107 Nev. 135, 808 P.2d 522 (1991) (adequate warning cannot cure design defect); Restatement (Third) of Torts: Products Liability § 2 cmt. l (1998) (warnings are not a substitute for a reasonably safe design).

5.   *Obvious Dangers and Generally Known Risks*. Most jurisdictions have found no duty to warn of obvious dangers or of risks that are generally known. See e.g., Glittenberg v. Doughboy Recreational Indus., 441 Mich. 379, 491 N.W.2d 208 (1992) (diving into shallow water of above ground swimming pool) (collecting cases); American Tobacco Co. v. Grinnell, 951 S.W.2d 420 (Tex.1997) (defendant established that health risks of smoking cigarettes were commonly known when plaintiff began smoking, but did not establish that addictive quality of cigarettes was commonly known); Joseph R. Seagram & Sons, Inc., v. McGuire, 814 S.W.2d 385 (Tex.1991) (danger of developing alcoholism from prolonged and excessive consumption of alcoholic beverages is within ordinary knowledge common to the community). See also Restatement (Third) of Torts: Products Liability § 2(c) and cmt. j (1998) (no duty because warning will not reduce risk and may diminish significance of warnings about non-obvious risks).

6.   In which of these situations is there a duty to warn? Should a manufacturer of a perfume have to warn that the product is highly inflammable and should not be poured on a lit candle? See Moran v. Faberge, Inc., 273 Md. 538, 332 A.2d 11 (1975). Should a manufacturer of pointed darts have to warn that they might injure someone's eye? See Atkins v. Arlans Dept. Store of Norman, Inc., 522 P.2d 1020 (Okl.1974). Should a manufacturer have to warn a hockey player that his helmet will not protect him from all blows to the head? Durkee v. Cooper of Canada, 99 Mich.App. 693, 298 N.W.2d 620 (1980). Should the manufacturer of a Jeep CJ have to warn the driver not to ride with his bare foot outside of the vehicle while travelling on a highway? See Smith v. American Motors Sales Corp., 215 Ill.App.3d

951, 576 N.E.2d 146, 159 Ill.Dec. 477 (1991). Should the manufacturer of a pickup truck have to warn of the dangers involved in riding unrestrained in the cargo bed of the pickup truck? See Josue v. Isuzu Motors, 87 Haw. 413, 958 P.2d 535 (1998). Should the manufacturer of a hot water heater have to warn that hot water could cause burns or scalds? See National Bank of Bloomington v. Westinghouse Electric Corp., 235 Ill.App.3d 697, 600 N.E.2d 1275, 175 Ill.Dec. 817 (1992). Who decides? See Liriano v. Hobart Corp., 170 F.3d 264 (2d Cir.1999) (applying New York law) (jury must decide whether obviousness of danger of operating meat grinder without guard is such that warning is not required) and Restatement (Third) of Torts: Products Liability § 2 cmt. j (1998) (when reasonable minds may differ as to whether risk is obvious or generally known, jury decides).

7. *Allergic Reactions and Hypersensitivity*. If a product is dangerous only to hypersensitive persons, do manufacturers have a duty to provide warnings if they know or should know of such dangers? See D'Arienzo v. Clairol, Inc., 125 N.J.Super. 224, 310 A.2d 106 (1973) (good discussion of duty). Most jurisdictions impose a duty to warn if the ingredient is one to which a substantial number of persons are allergic. Proving that a substantial number are affected is the plaintiff's burden. Just as in other determinations of duty, courts will consider the severity of the harm as a factor. Simeon v. Doe (Sweet Pepper Grill), 618 So.2d 848 (La.1993) (magnitude of the possible harm—serious illness or death—as a result of eating raw oysters for people with certain specific underlying conditions is factor in determining duty to warn on part of restaurant). See also Restatement (Third) of Torts: Products Liability § 2 cmt. k (1998).

8. Why not always require a warning? They cost the manufacturer very little to provide in most circumstances. Might the proliferation of warnings in obvious danger situations dilute the impact of necessary warnings? See Cotton v. Buckeye Gas Prods. Co., 840 F.2d 935 (D.C.Cir.1988) (criticizing overuse of warnings); Restatement (Third) of Torts: Products Liability § 2 cmt. j (1998) (recognizing that requiring warnings of obvious or generally known risks could reduce efficacy of warnings generally). If the manufacturer chooses to supply a warning that the law would not have required, has the manufacturer exposed itself to additional liability by assuming a duty? See May v. Defoe, 25 Wash.App. 575, 611 P.2d 1275 (1980).

9. *Adequacy of Warning*. The determination whether the warning was adequate is usually left to the jury who in turn rely on expert testimony. Manufacturer warned that its adhesive was highly flammable, that it should be used only in a well-ventilated area, and that all open flames should be extinguished before use. Plaintiff was injured when the pilot light of a gas stove ignited fumes from the adhesive. Was the warning defective if it did not specifically mention "pilot lights" as examples of open flames? Cf. Burch v. Amsterdam Corp., 366 A.2d 1079 (D.C.1976).

10. *Sophisticated Users.* Should the extent of expertise of the known user be taken into account? See Garrett v. Nissen Corp., 84 N.M. 16, 498 P.2d 1359 (1972) (experienced trampoline user landed on his head and suffered a paralyzing spinal injury); In re Asbestos Litigation (Mergenthaler), 542 A.2d 1205 (Del.Super.1986) (observing that most jurisdictions employ some form of the "sophisticated user" defense in failure to warn cases); Kennedy v. Mobay Corporation, 84 Md.App. 397, 579 A.2d 1191 (1990), aff'd, 325 Md. 385, 601 A.2d 123 (1992) (users of chemicals to manufacture Gore Tex waterproof fabric); Lawley v. Chevron Chem. Co., 720 So.2d 922 (Ala.1998) (plastic pipe manufacturer did not have duty to warn gas company or its employees because it was common knowledge among workers that failure to take certain precautions would greatly increase danger from static electricity build up).

warning must be adequate & conspicuous

"catch the eye of the user"

- must clearly delineate the danger - has to be specific

11. *Learned Intermediary Rule.* In cases involving pharmaceuticals, a key issue often is whether the pharmaceutical manufacturer should provide its warnings to the prescribing physician or directly to the patient. Most courts hold that warnings and instructions should be provided to the physician, who is a "learned intermediary" and is the best person to understand the patient's needs and assess the risks and benefits of a particular course of treatment. It is assumed that the physician will decide which warnings to pass on to the patient, taking into consideration the patient's well-being. See, e.g., Basko v. Sterling Drug., Inc., 416 F.2d 417 (2d Cir.1969) (duty to warn of risks associated with prescription drug is fulfilled by adequate warning to those authorized to prescribe drug); West v. Searle & Co., 305 Ark. 33, 806 S.W.2d 608 (1991) (health care provider is best assessor of relevant risks and benefits). See also Restatement (Third) of Torts: Products Liability § 6(d)(1) and cmt. b (1998). Many jurisdictions do not apply the learned intermediary rule in situations where the manufacturer is aware that there will be no medical provider to provide learned advice or where the patient is expected to take an active role in the selection of the product. See, e.g., Reyes v. Wyeth Labs., 498 F.2d 1264 (5th Cir.1974) (oral polio vaccine administered in "clinic-like" setting); Mazur v. Merck & Co., 964 F.2d 1348 (3d Cir.1992) (in case involving MMR vaccination at public school, court noted "mass immunization exception" to learned intermediary rule where prescription drugs are dispensed without an individualized medical balancing of the risks and benefits to the user); MacDonald v. Ortho Pharmaceutical Corp., 394 Mass. 131, 475 N.E.2d 65 (1985) (manufacturer of oral contraceptive must warn consumers directly because they often are actively involved in the decision to use the birth control pill and the physician usually has a relatively passive role). See also Restatement (Third) of Torts: Products Liability § 6(d)(2) and cmts. b and e (1998) (warning must be given directly to patient in situation where health-care provider's role is diminished by circumstances).

12.   What if the Federal Food and Drug Administration required that the patient be provided with information in patient package inserts? See MacDonald v. Ortho Pharmaceutical Corp., 394 Mass. 131, 475 N.E.2d 65 (1985) (noting fact of FDA requirement of direct patient warning in finding duty to warn patient in case involving oral contraceptive); Edwards v. Basel Pharmaceuticals, 933 P.2d 298 (Okla.1997) (same, nicotine patch). But see Lacy v. G.D. Searle & Co., 567 A.2d 398 (Del.1989) (learned intermediary rule applies even where patient provided with separate brochure pursuant to FDA regulations). What if the manufacturer of a prescription drug or medical device, like baldness remedies, allergy treatments, or Viagra markets the product directly to the general public rather than to physicians or health care facilities? Does that affect the use of the learned intermediary doctrine? Perez v. Wyeth Labs. Inc., 161 N.J. 1, 734 A.2d 1245 (1999) (learned intermediary doctrine does not apply when product is marketed directly to consumers because it belies the premises upon which the doctrine is based). Restatement (Third) of Torts: Products Liability § 6 cmt. e (1998) (leaves to developing law whether warnings must be given directly to patients in circumstances where governmental regulation mandates direct information or where manufacturer is advertising to public).

13.   The "learned intermediary" rule also arises in cases involving harm from products used in the workplace. There the issue is whether the employer should be responsible for warning and instructing its employees about use of the product because of the employer's control of the worksite, its knowledge of the hazards associated with products it has purchased, and its ability to instruct its employees on how to protect against those hazards. See, e.g., Adams v. Union Carbide Corp., 737 F.2d 1453 (6th Cir.1984), cert. denied, 469 U.S. 1062 (1984). Sometimes the

product is unpackaged or in a liquid or dust form, sold to the employer in bulk containers, so it would be difficult for the manufacturer to attach its warnings directly onto the product. See, e.g., Beale v. Hardy, 769 F.2d 213 (4th Cir.1985) (silica dust). Also, a communications expert has noted that the employer's oral communication of warnings to employees may be more effective than written information because the employer can adapt its message to particular employees of different experience, education and conceptual levels, and can answer questions, and because it is easier to demand the employee's attention with oral instruction. See Schwartz & Driver, Warnings in the Workplace: The Need for a Synthesis of Law and Communication Theory, 42 U.Cin.L.Rev. 38 (1983). What if the manufacturer relies upon an employer to warn its employees of the risks associated with the use of its product and the employer fails to so warn? Must the manufacturer's reliance be reasonable? See Willis v. Raymark Indus., Inc., 905 F.2d 793 (4th Cir.1990) (reasonableness of manufacturer's reliance on the employer prior to and during the time the workers were exposed). Restatement (Third) of Torts: Products Liability § 2 cmt. i (1998) (no general rule whether manufacturer must warn users directly or can rely on intermediary to relay warning; standard is one of reasonableness under the circumstances).

14. _Presumption that Warning Will Be Read and Heeded._ In most jurisdictions plaintiff is entitled to a presumption that the user would have read and heeded an adequate warning. See, e.g., Coffman v. Keane Corp., 133 N.J. 581, 628 A.2d 710 (1993) (collecting cases). This presumption, based on language in comment *j* to Restatement (Second) § 402A (1965), assists the plaintiff in proving causation after the plaintiff has proved an inadequate warning. See, e.g., Eagle–Picher Industries, Inc. v. Balbos, 326 Md. 179, 604 A.2d 445 (1992); Butz v. Werner, 438 N.W.2d 509 (N.D.1989). But see Potthoff v. Alms, 41 Colo.App. 51, 583 P.2d 309 (1978) (finding no indication that comment *j* creates a heeding presumption); Thomas v. Hoffman–LaRoche, Inc., 949 F.2d 806 (5th Cir.1992) (applying Mississippi law) (plaintiff not entitled to presumption in context of prescription drug case but must prove that physician would not have prescribed drug if aware of additional risk).

15. _The Presumption is Rebuttable._ Suppose defendant introduces evidence in an asbestos case that plaintiff smoked despite warning labels on cigarettes? That plaintiff never wore a seatbelt? That plaintiff was indifferent to matters of personal health? Is this enough to rebut the presumption? Cf. Theer v. Philip Carey Co., 133 N.J. 610, 628 A.2d 724 (1993); Bushong v. Garman Co., 311 Ark. 228, 843 S.W.2d 807 (1992) (plaintiff admitted he had never read a label on a cleaning product in his three years of employment at the warehouse where he was injured); Nelson v. Ford Motor Co., 150 F.3d 905 (8th Cir.1998) (applying Missouri law) (plaintiff admitted that he had not read instructions before using jack to change tire because he thought he already knew how to use it); Sharpe v. Bestop, Inc., 158 N.J. 329, 730 A.2d 285 (1999) (plaintiff, who had argued that he would have worn a seatbelt if the manufacturer of the soft top installed on his Jeep CJ had warned him to do so, admitted that he had not followed the warning on the sun visor of the Jeep to wear seatbelts at all times). What if defendant demonstrates through empirical evidence that there is no common experience on which the courts can premise the creation of a presumption that the general public reads and heeds warnings? See Coffman v. Keene Corp., 133 N.J. 581, 628 A.2d 710 (1993) (recognizing validity of defendant's argument, bolstered by "a plethora of data and studies," but adopting the presumption anyway, based on public policy considerations). How does the presumption operate in a workplace environment? James v. Bessemer Processing Co., Inc., 155 N.J. 279, 714 A.2d 898, 908 (1998) (plaintiff enjoys presumption that both he and his employer would have heeded adequate warnings and defendant may rebut by

showing that "plaintiff-employee with meaningful choice would not have heeded warning" or that "employer itself would not have heeded the warning by taking reasonable precautions for safety of its employees").

16. *Post–Sale Duty to Warn.* In addition to the duty to provide warnings at the time a product is marketed, many courts impose a duty on the manufacturer to provide post-sale warnings about risks that are discovered after the sale. See, e.g., Lovick v. Wil–Rich, 588 N.W.2d 688 (Iowa 1999); Owens–Illinois, Inc. v. Zenobia, 325 Md. 420, 601 A.2d 633 (1992); Hodder v. Goodyear Tire & Rubber Co., 426 N.W.2d 826 (Minn.1988); Walton v. Avco Corp., 530 Pa. 568, 610 A.2d 454 (1992). But see Anderson v. Nissan Motor Co., 139 F.3d 599 (8th Cir.1998) (concluding that Nebraska would not impose either a post-sale duty to warn or a duty to retrofit). Courts generally have held manufacturers to a reasonableness standard for post-sale warnings and may consider a number of factors. See, e.g., Melancon v. Western Auto Supply Co., 628 F.2d 395 (5th Cir.1980) (obviousness of the danger); Davis v. Wyeth Laboratories, Inc., 399 F.2d 121 (9th Cir.1968) (seriousness of the potential harm); Chappuis v. Sears, Roebuck & Co., 358 So.2d 926 (La.1978), writ denied, 366 So.2d 576 (1979) (whether the danger is generally known to users); Cover v. Cohen, 61 N.Y.2d 261, 461 N.E.2d 864, 473 N.Y.S.2d 378 (1984) (burden on the manufacturer in locating those to be warned). See also Restatement (Third) of Torts: Products Liability § 10 and cmts. a-i (1998) (post-sale duty to warn determined by balancing factors, including those listed above).

17. *Post–Sale Duty to Recall.* Very few courts have extended a manufacturer's post-sale obligations beyond a duty to take reasonable steps to provide warnings. Traditionally, product recall has been a function of federal administrative agencies rather than of the tort system. See Consumer Product Safety Act, 15 U.S.C. § 2064; National Traffic and Motor Vehicle Safety Act of 1966, 15 U.S.C. § 1414. Most courts that have considered the issue have declined to impose such a duty. See, e.g., Gregory v. Cincinnati, Inc., 450 Mich. 1, 538 N.W.2d 325 (1995); Patton v. Hutchinson Wil–Rich Mfg. Co., 253 Kan. 741, 861 P.2d 1299 (1993) (recognizing post-sale duty to warn, but leaving product recall decisions to administrative agencies as suggested by federal statutes). See also Restatement (Third) of Torts: Products Liability § 11 (1998) (liability for failure to act as reasonable person would in recalling product only if governmental directive requires or manufacturer voluntarily undertakes recall). For a general discussion of manufacturers' post-sale obligations, see Schwartz, The Post–Sale Duty to Warn: Two Unfortunate Forks in the Road to a Reasonable Doctrine, 58 N.Y.U.L.Rev. 892 (1983).

3. PROOF

Friedman v. General Motors Corp.

Supreme Court of Ohio, 1975.
43 Ohio St.2d 209, 72 Ohio Ops.2d 119, 331 N.E.2d 702.

[Plaintiff Morton Friedman alleged that he turned the ignition key on his 17–month-old 1966 Oldsmobile while the gearshift selector was in the "drive" position. Although he did not expect the vehicle to start, it did and the car "leaped forward, and so startled [him] that he could not regain control before the automobile ran wild * * *." Morton and three members of his family were injured in the crash.

Morton brought a claim against General Motors, the manufacturer of the vehicle. At the close of his case, the trial court granted General Motor's *trial court - directed verdict for Defendant*

motion for a directed verdict on the ground that plaintiff had not proved that the vehicle was defective. The intermediate appellate court reversed the trial judge's decision and General Motors appealed to the Supreme Court of Ohio.]

- appellate court reversed

PAUL W. BROWN, JUSTICE. The single issue presented by this appeal is whether the evidence introduced by the plaintiffs was of sufficient quality to overcome the defendant's motion for a directed verdict. The Court of Appeals, having thoroughly examined the entire record, concluded that reasonable minds could differ upon the evidence presented and reversed the judgment directing a verdict for the defendant. We affirm.

Issue

To sustain their allegation against General Motors, the plaintiffs were required to prove that the Oldsmobile Toronado, manufactured and sold by the defendant, was defective; that the defect existed at the time the product left the factory; and that the defect was the direct and proximate cause of the accident and injuries. [Cc]

Rule

A defect may be proven by circumstantial evidence, where a preponderance of that evidence establishes that the accident was caused by a defect and not other possibilities, although not all other possibilities need be eliminated. [Cc]

In our judgment, the evidence presented by the plaintiffs established a prima facie case of defect for which defendant General Motors would be liable.

From the testimony of [the retailer-dealer] and Morton Friedman, the jury could have found that the linkages and adjustments existing at the time of the accident were the original, factory set, adjustments, and that the defective condition, if the evidence established defect, was a defect created by the manufacturer and not by some third person after delivery.

Based upon the testimony of Morton Friedman, his wife, and his son, the jury might have concluded that the Toronado had always been started in Park, thus affording no opportunity for discovery of the alleged defect. Further, because the gear shift indicator and transmission had always operated properly, the jury might have inferred that when the gear shift indicator registered in Drive after the accident, it accurately reflected the position of the transmission.

Facts!

From the testimony of eye witnesses to, and participants in, the accident, the jury might have concluded that, when Friedman started the Toronado at the Sohio station, it accelerated immediately upon ignition; that the automobile's transmission was therefore in a forward position; and that the transmission jammed, upon impact, in that same forward position.

From the testimony of [expert witnesses produced by plaintiff,] the jury could have found that, subsequent to the accident, the Toronado started with the gear shift indicator in Drive position. Based upon English's testimony, the jury might have concluded further that, upon ignition, the front wheels accelerated to a speed of 30 miles per hour in five seconds.

Finally, the record clearly established that the Toronado could not have started unless the contacts in the neutral start switch were in Neutral or Park position. Even though the transmission gears and gear shift indicator were in Drive, if the contacts in the neutral start switch were in Neutral or Park, the ignition key would start the automobile, and the front wheels would immediately rotate. In light of other facts presented, this possibility approaches probability.

Because the trial court granted the defendant's motion for a directed verdict, we must construe the evidence most strongly in favor of the plaintiffs, so as to determine if reasonable minds could differ. From the evidence heretofore summarized, we believe the jury might reasonably have concluded that the defendant was guilty of manufacturing a defective automobile, which directly and proximately caused the accident. For that reason, the judgment of the Court of Appeals is affirmed.

Judgment affirmed.

STERN, JUSTICE (dissenting). * * * In products liability cases, proof that a defect existed is often difficult and complex. Frequently the product in dispute will have been destroyed, beyond any possibility of analysis, or be so complex that a plaintiff would have a greater difficulty in determining the presence of a defect than would the manufacturer. In most cases, proof of the defect must necessarily be by circumstantial evidence and inference. No general rule can adequately apply to the wide range of such cases, each involving a different mixture of fact and inference, but fundamental to any such case is that some defect must be proved. As Prosser states, in Strict Liability to the Consumer in California, 18 Hastings L.J. 9, 52–54:

"The mere fact of an accident, as where an automobile goes into the ditch, does not make out a case that the product was defective; nor does the fact that it is found in a defective condition after the event, when it appears equally likely that it was caused by the accident itself. The addition of other facts, tending to show that the defect existed before the accident, may make out a case, and so may expert testimony. So likewise may proof that other similar products made by the defendant met with similar misfortunes, or the elimination of other causes by satisfactory evidence. In addition, there are some accidents, as where a beverage bottle explodes or even breaks while it is being handled normally, as to which there is human experience that they do not ordinarily occur without a defect. As in cases of res ipsa loquitur, the experience will give rise to the inference, and it may be sufficient to sustain the plaintiff's burden of proof."

Although plaintiff's evidence may be sufficient to permit an inference that something was wrong with the car, that alone is not sufficient to establish a defect, except perhaps in cases, analogous to res ipsa loquitur, in which ordinary human experience tells us that the event could not happen without a defect. The instant case is not such a case, for driver error, failure of some part, accidental or unwitting damage to the car, and other possibilities do provide other explanations. * * *

The particular defect that plaintiff alleges is that the indicator and the transmission gear linkages were both malaligned in a similar fashion, relative to the neutral starter switch, so that the car as manufactured could start in Drive rather than, as intended, only in Park and Neutral. There are various ways in which that particular fact could be proved, by means of several types of evidence. Keeton, Manufacturer's Liability: The Meaning of Defect in the Manufacture and Design of Products, 20 Syracuse L.Rev. 559, for example, suggests five ways by which the particular fact could be proved. [C]

(1) Plaintiff might introduce evidence by an expert based upon an examination of the product in question following the happening of the damaging event. Expert evidence would be direct evidence of an identifiable defect. * * *

(2) There may simply be evidence of a damaging event occurring in the course of or following use of a product, whether by the testimony of the user or otherwise. * * *

(3) A plaintiff may produce both evidence of a damaging event occurring in the course of or following the use of a product and expert evidence that the most likely probable cause was attributable to a defect in the product being used at the time. * * *

(4) In addition to evidence of an accident and the probable cause of such accident, evidence could be introduced to negate the existence of "probable causes" not attributable to the maker. * * *

(5) In some cases, the physical evidence of the actual condition of the product after the accident would be such that a layman could infer that it was defective. * * *

The sum of the evidence [in this case] is * * * only that something unusual happened in the car, and that a possible explanation of that happening is a defect. * * *

The same difficulty arises with regard to the issue of whether the claimed defect existed at the time the car left the hands of the defendant. * * * Here, the car was 17 months old, there was no expert testimony that the claimed defect was one which would probably have existed at the time the car was manufactured, and common experience does not permit any such inference. * * *

I agree with the trial judge that plaintiffs failed to submit sufficient evidence from which it could be inferred that a defect existed in the Friedman car at the time it left the hands of the defendant.

NOTES AND QUESTIONS

1. As the principal case reflects, problems relating to proof may be equally as important as legal theory in products liability actions. Plaintiff must be prepared to show:

A. That the product that injured him was, in fact, manufactured by defendant. Suppose an alleged manufacturer's name or trademark appeared on the product.

Should that be sufficient? Compare Keegan v. Green Giant Co., 150 Me. 283, 110 A.2d 599 (1954), with Curtiss Candy Co. v. Johnson, 163 Miss. 426, 141 So. 762 (1932). See also Restatement (Third) of Torts: Products Liability § 14 (1998) (one who sells or distributes a product as its own that was manufactured by another is subject to same liability as if it were the product's manufacturer). Suppose defendant is injured by a common instrumentality that has no trademark. How does he prove it was manufactured by defendant? See Schmidt v. Archer Iron Works, Inc., 44 Ill.2d 401, 256 N.E.2d 6 (1970) (defective eye pin in a cement scoop). Suppose an entire industry produces allegedly defective products, but plaintiff cannot identify whose product injured him? See Sindell v. Abbott Laboratories, page 282; Hall v. E.I. Du Pont De Nemours & Co., Inc., 345 F.Supp. 353 (E.D.N.Y.1972) (blasting caps). In those cases, the plaintiff was able to prove that a product caused his or her injury, but was unable to prove which manufacturer made the particular product involved. In other words, the plaintiff was unable to prove that any particular manufacturer was the cause in fact of the injury. Some courts have developed a variety of theories to get the plaintiff past the requirement of proving actual causation. Other courts have refused to take this step and have applied the traditional rule that the plaintiff must prove the particular manufacturer's product caused his or her injury. Is there a middle ground? See Schwartz & Mahshigian, Failure to Identify the Defendant in Tort Law: Towards a Legislative Solution, 73 Calif.L.Rev. 941 (1985). See note 5, at page 286.

B.   That the product was defective and he was injured as a result. The principal case and the cases in the prior section are illustrative of this problem. The crash of a plane does not make out a case until the possibility of negligent flying is eliminated. Hurley v. Beech Aircraft Corp. 355 F.2d 517 (7th Cir.1966). Saieva v. Budget Rent–A–Car, 227 Ill. App. 3d 519, 591 N.E.2d 507 (1992) (summary judgment for defendant upheld where record supported inference that plaintiff lost control of van because he was driving "at an excessive speed on a dark, wet and bumpy rural highway"); Campbell Soup Co. v. Gates, 319 Ark. 54, 889 S.W.2d 750 (Ark. 1994) ("In the absence of direct proof that the product is defective because of a manufacturing flaw, the plaintiff must negate the other possible causes of failure of the product for which the defendant would not be responsible in order to raise a reasonable inference that the dangerous condition existed while the product was still in the control of the defendant."). See also Restatement (Third) of Torts: Products Liability § 3 (1998) (permitting inference of defect based on circumstantial evidence if incident of kind that ordinarily occurs as a result of product defect and other possible causes are negated).

C.   That the defect existed in the product or was incipiently in it when it was sold by the particular defendant. United States Rubber Co. v. Bauer, 319 F.2d 463 (8th Cir.1963) (breaking of belt drive might have been due to other causes); Sharpe v. Danville Coca–Cola Bottling Co., 9 Ill.App.2d 175, 132 N.E.2d 442 (1956) (intermediate handling of bottle after it left the manufacturer).

2.   Strictly speaking, since negligence is not in question, *res ipsa loquitur* has no application to a strict liability case, but the inferences that are the core of the doctrine are no less applicable to strict liability. In other words, the fact that the product went wrong may, in a proper case, give rise to a permissible inference that it was defective and that the defect existed when it left the hands of the defendant. See Moraca v. Ford Motor Co., 66 N.J. 454, 332 A.2d 599 (1975) (six-month-old, 11,000–mile Lincoln Continental skidded off the road—strong plaintiff case with equally strong dissent); Franks v. National Dairy Prods. Corp., 414 F.2d 682 (5th Cir.1969) (shortening exploded when user drained it from fryer into a can—a well developed case). But see Trost v. Trek Bicycle Corp., 162 F.3d 1004 (8th Cir.1998)

important inference of product defect allowed by circumstan evidence

(applying Minnesota law) (bicyclist's res ipsa loquitur argument not enough to prove products liability case against manufacturer of bicycle). See Restatement (Third) of Torts: Products Liability § 3 (1998) (permitting inference of defect based on circumstantial evidence if incident of kind that ordinarily occurs as a result of product defect and other possible causes are negated). Generally, under those circumstances, plaintiff is not required to prove a specific defect. This is referred to in some jurisdictions as the "general defect" theory. See, e.g., Stewart v. Ford Motor Co., 553 F.2d 130 (D.C.Cir.1977). See also Restatement (Third) of Torts: Products Liability § 3 cmt. c (1998).

3. The most convincing evidence is a direct showing of what went wrong. This may be done by the plaintiff in an appropriate case, see Agostino v. Rockwell Mfg. Co., 345 A.2d 735 (Pa.1975) (power saw—telescopic blade guard did not function) or by an expert pinpointing the defect and giving an opinion on that basis. Good advice to a client is to "save the pieces," but often the client disposes of them before he consults an attorney. If the product is destroyed in the accident, plaintiff will be left in the uncertain sphere of circumstantial proof.

4. *Rule on Excluding Evidence of Product Improvements To Prove Defect.* Should plaintiff be able to show that defendant redesigned or repaired his product after the accident occurred? What are the policy considerations? While most courts preclude plaintiffs from introducing this evidence, some will admit it if the underlying theory of liability is strict liability rather than negligence. Compare Forma Scientific, Inc. v. Biosera, Inc., 960 P.2d 108 (Colo.1998) (exclusion does not apply to strict liability claims based on design defect) with Hyjek v. Anthony Indus., 133 Wash.2d 414, 944 P.2d 1036 (1997) (exclusion applies in strict liability cases). Federal Rule of Evidence 407 was recently amended to codify the view of the majority of federal courts, providing that such evidence is not admissible to prove product defect in the federal courts. Why would a court prohibit the introduction of evidence of product improvements in a negligence case, but permit such evidence in a strict liability case? Do you agree with these cases? Do they encourage the manufacture of safer products?

Normally NOT admissible

5. *Violation of Safety Statute or Regulation.* Paralleling the doctrine of *negligence per se*, most jurisdictions provide that violation of a product safety statute or regulation makes the product defective as a matter of law. See, e.g., Ross Labs. v. Thies, 725 P.2d 1076 (Alaska 1986). Some hold that it is merely evidence of defect. Restatement (Third) of Torts: Products Liability § 4(a) (1998) deems the product defective with respect to the risks sought to be reduced by the statute or regulation.

6. When the defect arises after purchase, plaintiff is confronted with another facet of the problem of establishing that the product was "defective" or unreasonably unsafe. It has been said often enough that the seller does not undertake to provide a product that will not wear out. McNally v. Chrysler Motors Corp., 55 Misc.2d 128, 284 N.Y.S.2d 761 (Sup.Ct.1967) (leakage in 1963, no proof hydraulic brakes were defective when sold in 1961). On the other hand, when plaintiff's intestate was killed in 1965 by the collapse of a boom crane that was manufactured in 1956, the Supreme Court of Oregon observed that "prolonged use of a manufactured article is but one factor, albeit an important one, in the determination of whether a defect in the product made it unsafe * * *." Tucker v. Unit Crane & Shovel Corp., 256 Or. 318, 473 P.2d 862 (1970).

7. Information about public health and safety issues may be developed during discovery. Judges may limit public access to this information by using protective orders under Federal Rule of Civil Procedure 26(c) or its state court equivalents. How should the courts balance the private parties' interest in litigating their

dispute in private with the public's interest in matters that may affect health and safety? For a discussion of this issue, see Miller, Confidentiality, Protective Orders, and Public Access to the Courts, 105 Harv.L.Rev. 428 (1991).

4. DEFENSES

(A) PLAINTIFF'S CONDUCT

Daly v. General Motors Corp.
Supreme Court of California, 1978.
20 Cal.3d 725, 575 P.2d 1162, 144 Cal.Rptr. 380.

[Suit for death of the driver of an Opel automobile, thrown from his car in an accident, because of an alleged defect of the door latch. There was evidence that the driver did not use the shoulder harness system or lock the door, and that he was intoxicated. The case was submitted to the jury, which found for the defendant.]

RICHARDSON, JUSTICE. The most important of several problems which we consider is whether the principles of comparative negligence expressed by us in Li v. Yellow Cab Co. (1975) 13 Cal.3d 804, 119 Cal.Rptr. 858, 532 P.2d 1226, apply to actions founded on strict products liability. We will conclude that they do. * * *

From its inception * * * strict liability has never been, and is not now, absolute liability. As has been repeatedly expressed, under strict liability the manufacturer does not thereby become the insurer of the safety of the product's user. [Cc] On the contrary, the plaintiff's injury must have been caused by a "defect" in the product. Thus the manufacturer is not deemed responsible when injury results from an unforeseeable use of its product. [Cc] Furthermore, we have recognized that though most forms of contributory negligence do not constitute a defense to a strict products liability action, plaintiff's negligence is a complete defense when it comprises assumption of risk. [Cc] As will thus be seen, the concept of strict products liability was created and shaped judicially. In its evolution, the doctrinal encumbrances of contract and warranty, and the traditional elements of negligence, were stripped from the remedy, and a new tort emerged which extended liability for defective product design and manufacture beyond negligence but short of absolute liability.

In Li v. Yellow Cab Co., supra, 13 Cal.3d 804, 119 Cal.Rptr. 858, 532 P.2d 1226, we introduced the other doctrine with which we are concerned, comparative negligence. We examined the history of contributory negligence, the massive criticism directed at it because its presence in the slightest degree completely barred plaintiff's recovery, and the increasing defection from the doctrine. * * *

We stand now at the point of confluence of these two conceptual streams, having been greatly assisted by the thoughtful analysis of the parties and the valuable assistance of numerous amici curiae. We are by no means the first to consider the interaction of these two developing principles. As with the litigants before us, responsible and respected authorities have reached opposing conclusions stressing in various degrees the different considerations which we now examine.

Those counseling against the recognition of comparative fault principles in strict products liability cases vigorously stress, perhaps equally, not only the conceptual, but also the semantic difficulties incident to such a course. The task of merging the two concepts is said to be impossible, that "apples and oranges" cannot be compared, that "oil and water" do not mix, and that strict liability, which is not founded on negligence or fault, is inhospitable to comparative principles. The syllogism runs, contributory negligence was only a defense to negligence, comparative negligence only affects contributory negligence, therefore comparative negligence cannot be a defense to strict liability. [Cc] While fully recognizing the theoretical and semantic distinctions between the twin principles of strict products liability and traditional negligence, we think they can be blended or accommodated.

The inherent difficulty in the "apples and oranges" argument is its insistence on fixed and precise definitional treatment of legal concepts. In the evolving areas of both products liability and tort defenses, however, there has developed much conceptual overlapping and interweaving in order to attain substantial justice. The concept of strict liability itself, as we have noted, arose from dissatisfaction with the wooden formalisms of traditional tort and contract principles in order to protect the consumer of manufactured goods. Similarly, increasing social awareness of its harsh "all or nothing" consequences led us in *Li* to moderate the impact of traditional contributory negligence in order to accomplish a fairer and more balanced result. We acknowledged an intermixing of defenses of contributory negligence and assumption of risk and formally effected a type of merger. "As for assumption of risk, we have recognized in this state that this defense overlaps that of contributory negligence to some extent * * *." (*Li*, supra).
* * *

We think, accordingly, the conclusion may fairly be drawn that the terms "comparative negligence," "contributory negligence" and "assumption of risk" do not, standing alone, lend themselves to the exact measurements of a micrometer-caliper, or to such precise definition as to divert us from otherwise strong and consistent countervailing policy considerations. Fixed semantic consistency at this point is less important than the attainment of a just and equitable result. The interweaving of concept and terminology in this area suggests a judicial posture that is flexible rather than doctrinaire. * * *

Given all of the foregoing, we are, in the wake of *Li*, disinclined to resolve the important issue before us by the simple expedient of matching linguistic labels which have evolved either for convenience or by custom. Rather, we consider it more useful to examine the foundational reasons underlying the creation of strict products liability in California to ascertain whether the purposes of the doctrine would be defeated or diluted by adoption of comparative principles. We imposed strict liability against the manufacturer and in favor of the user or consumer in order to relieve injured consumers "from *problems of proof* inherent in pursuing negligence

* * * and warranty * * * remedies * * *." * * * As we have noted, we sought to place the burden of loss on manufacturers rather than "injured persons *who are powerless to protect themselves.*" * * *

The foregoing goals, we think, will not be frustrated by the adoption of comparative principles. Plaintiffs will continue to be relieved of proving that the manufacturer or distributor was negligent in the production, design, or dissemination of the article in question. Defendant's liability for injuries caused by a defective product remains strict. The principle of protecting the defenseless is likewise preserved, for plaintiff's recovery will be reduced *only* to the extent that his own lack of reasonable care contributed to his injury. The cost of compensating the victim of a defective product, albeit proportionately reduced, remains on defendant manufacturer, and will, through him, be "spread among society." However, we do not permit plaintiff's own conduct relative to the product to escape unexamined, and as to that share of plaintiff's damages which flows from his own fault we discern no reason of policy why it should, following *Li,* be borne by others. Such a result would directly contravene the principle announced in *Li,* that loss should be assessed equitably in proportion to fault. * * *

A second objection to the application of comparative principles in strict products liability cases is that a manufacturer's incentive to produce safe products will thereby be reduced or removed. While we fully recognize this concern we think, for several reasons, that the problem is more shadow than substance. First, of course, the manufacturer cannot avoid its continuing liability for a defective product even when the plaintiff's own conduct has contributed to his injury. The manufacturer's liability, and therefore its incentive to avoid and correct product defects remains; its exposure will be lessened only to the extent that the trier finds that the victim's conduct contributed to his injury. Second, as a practical matter a manufacturer, in a particular case, cannot assume that the user of a defective product upon whom an injury is visited will be blameworthy. * * *

In passing, we note one important and felicitous result if we apply comparative principles to strict products liability. This arises from the fact that under present law when plaintiff sues in negligence his own contributory negligence, however denominated, may diminish but cannot wholly defeat his recovery. When he sues in strict products liability, however, his "assumption of risk" *completely bars* his recovery. Under *Li,* as we have noted, "assumption of risk" is merged into comparative principles. [Cc] The consequence is that after *Li* in a negligence action, plaintiff's conduct which amounts to "negligent" assumption of risk no longer defeats plaintiff's recovery. Identical conduct, however, in a strict liability case acts as a complete bar under rules heretofore applicable. Thus, strict products liability, which was developed to free injured consumers from the constraints imposed by traditional negligence and warranty theories, places a consumer plaintiff in a worse position than would be the case were his claim founded on simple negligence. This, in turn, rewards adroit pleading and selection of theories. The application of comparative principles to strict liability obviates this bizarre anomaly by treating alike the defenses to both negligence and strict products liability actions. In each instance the defense, if established, will reduce but not bar plaintiff's claim.

A third objection to the merger of strict liability and comparative fault focuses on the claim that, as a practical matter, triers of fact, particularly jurors, cannot assess, measure, or compare plaintiff's negligence with defendant's strict liability. We are unpersuaded by the argument and are convinced that jurors are able to undertake a fair apportionment of liability. * * *

We note that the majority of our sister states which have addressed the problem, either by statute or judicial decree, have extended comparative principles to strict products liability. * * *

Of the three decisions which have declined to apply comparative negligence to strict liability, two have noted their reliance on state comparative negligence statutes which are expressly confined to "negligence" actions. [Cc] At least three jurisdictions have applied comparative negligence statutes to strict liability actions, despite language arguably limiting the statute application to negligence. [Cc] Finally, one court has judicially extended a "pure" form of comparative fault to the traditional strict liability defense of "product misuse," despite the existence of a statutory scheme of "modified" comparative negligence. (General Motors Corp. v. Hopkins (Tex.1977) 548 S.W.2d 344, 351–352.)

Moreover, we are further encouraged in our decision herein by noting that the apparent majority of scholarly commentators has urged adoption of the rule which we announce herein. * * *

We find additional significance in the provisions of the proposed Uniform Comparative Fault Act (Act). * * * Our attention has been called to the action of the Conference [of Commissioners on Uniform State Laws] in August 1977, wherein it approved adoption of the Act by a vote of 40 states to 8 (California voting favorably). The Act is the distillation of approximately five years of discussion, analysis, and contribution by a special committee and a review committee of the Conference. We quote portions of [it] * * *.

Having examined the principal objections and finding them not insurmountable, and persuaded by logic, justice, and fundamental fairness, we conclude that a system of comparative fault should be and it is hereby extended to actions founded on strict products liability. In such cases the separate defense of "assumption of risk," to the extent that it is a form of contributory negligence, is abolished. While, as we have suggested, on the particular facts before us, the term "equitable apportionment of loss" is more accurately descriptive of the process, nonetheless, the term "comparative fault" has gained such wide acceptance by courts and in the literature that we adopt its use herein. * * *

It is readily apparent that the foregoing broad expressions of principle do not establish the duties of the jury with that fixed precision which appeals to minds trained in law and logic. Nonetheless, rather than attempt to anticipate every variant and nuance of circumstance and party that may invoke comparative principles in a strict products liability context, we deem it wiser to await a case-by-case evolution in the application of the broad principles herein expressed.

By extending and tailoring the comparative principles announced in *Li,* supra, to the doctrine of strict products liability, we believe that we move closer to the goal of the equitable allocation of legal responsibility for personal injuries. We do so by relying on what Professor Schwartz aptly terms a "predicate of fairness." In making liability more commensurate with fault we undermine neither the theories nor the policies of the strict liability rule. In *Li* we took "a first step in what we deem to be a proper and just direction, * * *." [C] We are convinced that the principles herein announced constitute the next appropriate and logical step in the same direction.

The judgment is reversed.

[TOBRINER, CLARK and MANUEL, JJ., concurred; CLARK, J. filed a concurring opinion; JEFFERSON, J. (assigned), concurred in part and dissented in part and filed an opinion in which BIRD, C.J., concurred; MOSK, J., filed a dissenting opinion.]

NOTES AND QUESTIONS

1.   Most jurisdictions have followed the lead of the principal case and extended comparative negligence principles to strict liability causes of action. See, e.g., Webb v. Navistar Int'l., 166 Vt. 119, 692 A.2d 343 (1996); Huffman v. Caterpillar Tractor Co., 908 F.2d 1470 (10th Cir.1990) (applying Colorado law); Champagne v. Raybestos–Manhattan, Inc., 212 Conn. 509, 562 A.2d 1100 (1989); Simpson v. General Motors Corp., 108 Ill.2d 146, 483 N.E.2d 1, 90 Ill.Dec. 854 (1985). A few jurisdictions, however, either have refused to recognize the doctrine of comparative fault in product liability cases or have limited it to situations in which plaintiff has assumed the risk. See, e.g., Kimco Dev. Corp. v. Michael D's Carpet Outlets, 536 Pa. 1, 637 A.2d 603 (1993) (rejecting comparative fault to reduce damages in strict products liability); Phillips v. Duro–Last Roofing, Inc., 806 P.2d 834 (Wyo.1991) (comparative negligence statute does not apply to strict liability claims).

2.   Some decisions have been in accord with the Restatement (Second) of Torts, holding that negligence, in the sense of failure to discover a defect in the product or guard against the possibility of existence, is not a defense. See, e.g., General Motors Corp. v. Sanchez, 997 S.W.2d 584 (1999) (consumer has no duty to discover or guard against a product defect, but other consumer conduct is subject to comparative responsibility); Star Furniture Co. v. Pulaski Furniture Co., 171 W. Va. 79, 297 S.E.2d 854 (1982). What is the reason for this rule? Is fault irrelevant under strict liability? Or is the rule based on the theory that a purchaser may assume the product is safe? The Restatement (Second) appeared simply to carry over the rule from the approach taken in the area of Abnormally Dangerous Activities. See pages 704–711. Restatement (Third) of Torts: Products Liability § 17 cmt. d (1998) does not limit the forms or categories of plaintiff's conduct that may be taken into account to apportion damages.

4.   *Assumption of Risk.* When plaintiff voluntarily confronts a known hazard, the Restatement (Second) and many courts would bar the claim. Barefield v. La Salle Coca–Cola Bottling Co., 370 Mich. 1, 120 N.W.2d 786 (1963) (drinking

beverage known to be full of broken glass); Ferraro v. Ford Motor Co., 423 Pa. 324, 223 A.2d 746 (1966) (driving truck with knowledge that wheels would lock on left turns and accelerator pedal tended to dislodge); Cintrone v. Hertz Truck Leasing & Rental Serv., 45 N.J. 434, 212 A.2d 769 (1965) (driving truck knowing brakes to be bad); Tafoya v. Sears Roebuck and Co., 884 F.2d 1330 (10th Cir.1989) (applying Colorado law)(lawnmower tipped over as plaintiff rode it between tree and steep slope). Others would subject the plaintiff to the same fault apportionment as in comparative negligence. Bonds v. Snapper Power Equip. Co., 935 F.2d 985 (8th Cir.1991) (applying Arkansas law); King v. Kayak Mfg. Corp., 387 S.E.2d 511 (W.Va.1989). See pages 606–613 and Restatement (Third) of Torts: Products Liability § 17 cmt. d (1998).

Ford Motor Co. v. Matthews
Supreme Court of Mississippi, 1974.
291 So.2d 169.

RODGERS, PRESIDING JUSTICE. Earnest Matthews was killed as a result of being run over by his tractor and dragged underneath a disc attachment. It was alleged that Matthews was standing beside his tractor when he started it, and the tractor was in gear at the time. The Ford tractor in question was equipped with a starter safety switch which was designed to prevent the tractor from being started in gear. It is the position of the plaintiff-administratrix that the plunger connected with the safety switch was defective and allowed the tractor to be started in gear.

[The trial court, sitting without a jury, found for the plaintiff-administratrix and entered a judgment against Ford in the amount of $74,272.65. Ford appealed.]

The appellant Ford contends that Matthews' act of standing on the ground and starting the tractor while in gear was a misuse of the product. It is argued that such misuse is an absolute limitation on Ford's liability. The basic authority for this position is Comment (h), Restatement (Second) of Torts § 402A, which reads in part: "A product is not in a defective condition when it is safe for normal handling and consumption. If the injury results from abnormal handling * * * the seller is not liable." [Restatement (Second) of Torts § 402A, at 351.] Several cases are cited by appellant to illustrate this proposition. However, in the cases cited, the court either found that there was no defect and the accident was caused by a misuse, or even if there were a defect, it played no part in the causation of the accident. Here the situation is clearly distinguishable. It is apparent that the failure of the safety switch to prevent the tractor from cranking in gear was a cause of the accident. The failure of the decedent to make sure the tractor was in neutral before starting [, if that were true] may be characterized as the omission of a customary precaution, although there is no evidence that he was warned of this danger, or that he knew of the danger. Nevertheless, this was not such a misuse of the tractor as to relieve Ford from its strict liability for the defective condition of the tractor.

Although misuse of a product that causes an injury is normally a bar to strict liability, it is said that: " * * * [T]he manufacturer is not liable for injuries resulting from abnormal or unintended use of his product, *if such use was not reasonably foreseeable. The issue is one of foreseeability and misuse may be foreseeable.*" (Emphasis added). 1 Frumer and Friedman, Products Liability § 15.01, at 351 (1973).

A recent law review writer expressed it in this manner: "In strict liability cases the same duty to foresee certain unintended uses has been recognized, and ordinarily the factual issue of the foreseeability of a particular use has been left to the jury." Noel, Defective Products: Abnormal Use, Contributory Negligence, and Assumption of Risk, 25 Vand.L.Rev. 93, 97 (1972).

It is admitted that the tractor in question was designed to prevent its starting in gear. It is apparent that it could be foreseen by Ford that one day a tractor operator might carelessly crank the engine without first making certain that it was not in gear (as recommended in the owner's manual), especially if he were aware of the purpose of the safety switch system. In short, even if Matthews were guilty of negligence, such negligence was reasonably foreseeable by Ford and is not a bar to an action based on strict liability resulting from a defective tractor. * * *

[W]e are of the opinion that the total sum determined by the trial judge to be due was not excessive and the case should be affirmed.

Affirmed.

NOTES AND QUESTIONS

1. When plaintiff uses a product in a manner unintended by the manufacturer, courts often treat this as a matter of defense. On the other hand, could the matter be viewed more logically as an issue of duty or defect? What is the obligation of a manufacturer to produce a product that will withstand misuse? Evidence concerning a misuse or alteration of the product could be used to argue that there was no defect in the product (failure of prime facie case), that any defect in the product did not cause the plaintiff's injury (no causation), or that the plaintiff's conduct in contributing to the cause of the accident should reduce the plaintiff's recovery (affirmative defense of comparative fault). See also Restatement (Third) of Torts: Products Liability § 2 cmt. p and § 18 cmt. c (1998) (product misuse, alteration, and modification, whether by third party or plaintiff, are relevant to issues of defect, causation, and comparative responsibility).

2. Whether regarded as a matter of defect or causation, the manufacturer is not subject to liability for an unforeseeable abnormal use of his product. Thus, a manufacturer was not liable in a case involving an above-ground swimming pool that was installed in the ground with a deck built around it, disguising the fact that the pool was shallow from the plaintiff who was injured while diving. Amatulli v. Delhi Construction Corp., 77 N.Y.2d 525, 571 N.E.2d 645, 569 N.Y.S.2d 337 (1991).

3. Before the advent of strict liability, there were many negligence cases holding that the seller is not liable when the injury is brought about by an abnormal use of the chattel. See, for example, McCready v. United Iron & Steel Co., 272 F.2d 700 (10th Cir.1959) (casements for use as window frames were used by workmen as ladders); Marker v. Universal Oil Prods. Co., 250 F.2d 603 (10th Cir.1957) (hot catalyst used in cold catalyst refining unit); Dubbs v. Zak Bros. Co., 38 Ohio App. 299, 175 N.E. 626 (1931) (shoes far too small for plaintiff's feet caused

blisters). Even in cases based on negligence, there are unusual uses of a product that the seller had to anticipate, and against which he was required to guard, at least to the extent of a warning. Thus standing on a chair, in Phillips v. Ogle Aluminum Furniture, Inc., 106 Cal.App.2d 650, 235 P.2d 857 (1951). Or wearing a cocktail robe in proximity to the flame of a kitchen stove, in Ringstad v. I. Magnin & Co., 39 Wash.2d 923, 239 P.2d 848 (1952). Or operating a tractor downhill at fast speed, using the engine compression as a brake, in Lovejoy v. Minneapolis–Moline Power Imp. Co., 248 Minn. 319, 79 N.W.2d 688 (1956).

4. ' As the principal decision reflects, one can discern in strict liability cases a clear extension of this trend and a willingness to let the jury decide whether the misuse was foreseeable. Are the following misuses foreseeable? An 11–year-old boy rides a vacuum cleaner as if it were a toy car and his penis slips through an opening in the casing and is seriously injured by the fan blades. See Larue v. National Union Elec. Corp., 571 F.2d 51 (1st Cir.1978) (upholding the jury verdict, the court noted that the jury could have found that the intrusion of the boy's penis into the fan was within the class of dangers foreseeable to the manufacturer even though the precise circumstances of the accident might not have been). A two-year-old was being given a ride by her great-grandmother on a riding mower in a small wooden box put on the fender of mower by the owner for her dog to ride in. When the mower hit a tree stump, the child was thrown off, the operator jumped off to pick up the child, and the mower ran over the child's leg. See Erkson v. Sears, Roebuck & Co., 841 S.W.2d 207 (Mo.App.1992) (court found the use was not intended or foreseeable). A chunk of concrete was thrown from a freeway overpass by two juveniles and crashed through the car's sunroof, severely injuring the driver. See Meyering v. General Motors Corp., 232 Cal.App.3d 1163, 275 Cal.Rptr. 346 (1990) (particular manner of injury need not be foreseeable as long as the general type of injury is). A child is injured while playing with a disposable cigarette lighter. Compare Griggs v. BIC Corp., 981 F.2d 1429 (3d Cir.1992) (no strict liability because use by children of cigarette lighter not intended or reasonably foreseeable) with Bean v. BIC Corp., 597 So.2d 1350 (Ala.1992) (whether there is a duty to design a child-proof cigarette lighter is a function of foreseeability of the harm tempered by a consideration of the feasibility of an alternative and is a question for the jury). Plaintiffs' decedent suffered cardiac arrest while inhaling butane fumes to "get high." Is this a foreseeable misuse of butane against which manufacturer should be required to warn? Cf. Pavlik v. Lane Ltd., 135 F.3d 876 (3d Cir.1998) (applying Pennsylvania law) (reversing summary judgment in favor of defendant, opinion focuses on adequacy of warning and proximate cause). See also Restatement (Third) of Torts: Products Liability § 2 cmt. p (1998) (noting that foreseeable product misuse must be considered in determining whether an alternative design should have been adopted).

5. Does it make any difference whether the "misuse" or "abnormal use" is that of the plaintiff or of a third party? Can both be either lack of duty, lack of causation, or an affirmative defense?

(B) PREEMPTION AND OTHER GOVERNMENT ACTIONS

Medtronic, Inc. v. Lohr

Supreme Court of the United States, 1996.
518 U.S. 470, 116 S. Ct. 2240, 135 L. Ed. 2d 700.

MR. JUSTICE STEVENS announced the judgment of the Court and delivered the opinion of the Court with respect to Parts I, II, III, V, and VII, and an opinion with respect to Parts IV and VI, in which JUSTICE KENNEDY, JUSTICE SOUTER, and JUSTICE GINSBURG join.

[Lora Lohr is dependent on pacemaker technology for the proper functioning of her heart. In 1987 a Medtronic pacemaker equipped with one of the company's Model 4011 pacemaker leads was implanted in her heart. Three years later, the pacemaker failed, allegedly resulting in a "complete heart block" that required emergency surgery. According to her physician, a defect in the lead was the likely cause of the failure. Lohr and her husband filed suit in a Florida state court, alleging negligence and strict liability. The negligence count alleged a breach of Medtronic's "duty to use reasonable care in the design, manufacture, assembly, and sale of the subject pacemaker" in several respects, including the use of defective materials in the lead and a failure to warn or properly instruct the plaintiff or her physicians of the tendency of the pacemaker to fail, despite knowledge of other earlier failures. The strict-liability count alleged that the device was in a defective condition and unreasonably dangerous to foreseeable users at the time of its sale. A third count alleging breach of warranty was dismissed for failure to state a claim under Florida law. Medtronic removed the case to federal court and filed a motion for summary judgment arguing that 21 U.S.C. § 360k(a) preempted the state common law claims. The trial court judge granted the motion, dismissing the entire complaint. The Eleventh Circuit affirmed in part and reversed in part. Both parties sought review by the Supreme Court.]

Congress enacted the Medical Device Amendments of 1976, in the words of the statute's preamble, "to provide for the safety and effectiveness of medical devices intended for human use." 90 Stat. 539. The question presented is whether that statute pre-empts a state common-law negligence action against the manufacturer of an allegedly defective medical device. Specifically, we must consider whether Lora Lohr, who was injured when her pacemaker failed, may rely on Florida common law to recover damages from Medtronic, Inc., the manufacturer of the device.

Throughout our history the several States have exercised their police powers to protect the health and safety of their citizens. Because these are "primarily, and historically, . . . matter[s] of local concern," [c], the "States traditionally have had great latitude under their police powers to legislate as to the protection of the lives, limbs, health, comfort, and quiet of all persons," [C].

Despite the prominence of the States in matters of public health and safety, in recent decades the Federal Government has played an increasingly significant role in the protection of the health of our people. Congress' first significant enactment in the field of public health was the Food and Drug Act of 1906, a broad prohibition against the manufacture or shipment in interstate commerce of any adulterated or misbranded food or drug. [Cc] Partly in response to an ongoing concern about radio and newspaper advertising making false therapeutic claims for both "quack machines" and legitimate devices such as surgical instruments and orthopedic shoes, in

1938 Congress broadened the coverage of the 1906 Act to include misbranded or adulterated medical devices and cosmetics. [Cc]

While the FDCA provided for premarket approval of new drugs, [C] it did not authorize any control over the introduction of new medical devices, [cc]. As technologies advanced and medicine relied to an increasing degree on a vast array of medical equipment "from bedpans to brainscans," including kidney dialysis units, artificial heart valves, and heart pacemakers, policymakers and the public became concerned about the increasingly severe injuries that resulted from the failure of such devices. * * *

In response to the mounting consumer and regulatory concern, Congress enacted the statute at issue here: the Medical Device Amendments of 1976 (MDA or Act), 90 Stat. 539. * * *

[The Court then described the rigorous premarket approval ("PMA") process for Class III devices, but noted that most Class III medical devices on the market today have not undergone that process because of two statutory exceptions to the PMA requirement. First, because Congress realized that existing medical devices could not be withdrawn from the market while the FDA completed its PMA analysis for those devices, the statute "grandfathered" pre–1976 devices, allowing them to remain on the market without FDA approval until such time as the FDA initiates and completes the requisite PMA. Second, to keep manufacturers of grandfathered devices from monopolizing the market while new devices clear the arduous PMA hurdle, and to ensure that improvements to existing devices can be rapidly introduced into the market, the Act also permits devices that are "substantially equivalent" to pre-existing devices to avoid the PMA process by doing a "premarket notification" to the FDA. If the FDA concludes on the basis of the 510(k) notification that the device is "substantially equivalent" to a pre-existing device, it can be marketed without further regulatory analysis until the FDA initiates the PMA process for the underlying pre–1976 device to which the new device is "substantially equivalent."

Although Congress had anticipated that the FDA would complete the PMA process for Class III devices relatively swiftly, it was unable to do so because of the substantial investment of time and energy necessary for the resolution of each PMA application, the ever-increasing numbers of medical devices, and internal administrative and resource difficulties. Thus, vast majority of new devices, including the one at issue in this case, were approved as "substantially equivalent" to pre–1976 devices rather than through the rigorous PMA process.

The Court then reviewed the cases interpreting other statutes in which determinations had been made whether the statute preempted state common law claims.]

As in Cipollone v. Liggett Group, Inc., 505 U.S. 504, 120 L. Ed. 2d 407, 112 S. Ct. 2608 (1992), we are presented with the task of interpreting a statutory provision that expressly pre-empts state law. While the pre-emptive language of § 360k(a) means that we need not go beyond that language to determine whether Congress intended the MDA to pre-empt at least some state law, [c], we must nonetheless "identify the domain expressly pre-empted" by that language, [c]. Although our analysis of the scope of the pre-emption statute must begin with its text, [c] our interpretation of that language does not occur in a contextual vacuum. Rather, that interpretation is informed by two presumptions about the nature of pre-emption. [C]

First, because the States are independent sovereigns in our federal system, we have long presumed that Congress does not cavalierly pre-empt state-law causes of action. In all pre-emption cases, and particularly in those in which Congress has "legislated . . . in a field which the States have traditionally occupied," [c], we "start with the assumption that the historic police powers of the States were not to be superseded by the Federal Act unless that was the clear and manifest purpose of Congress." [Cc] Although dissenting Justices have argued that this assumption should apply only to the question whether Congress intended any pre-emption at all, as opposed to questions concerning the scope of its intended invalidation of state law, [c] we used a "presumption against the pre-emption of state police power regulations" to support a narrow interpretation of such an express command in Cipollone. [C] That approach is consistent with both federalism concerns and the historic primacy of state regulation of matters of health and safety.

Second, our analysis of the scope of the statute's pre-emption is guided by our oft-repeated comment, initially made in Retail Clerks v. Schermerhorn, 375 U.S. 96, 103, 11 L. Ed. 2d 179, 84 S. Ct. 219 (1963), that "the purpose of Congress is the ultimate touch-stone" in every pre-emption case. [Cc] As a result, any understanding of the scope of a pre-emption statute must rest primarily on "a fair understanding of congressional purpose." [C] Congress' intent, of course, primarily is discerned from the language of the pre-emption statute and the "statutory framework" surrounding it. [C] Also relevant, however, is the "structure and purpose of the statute as a whole," [c] as revealed not only in the text, but through the reviewing court's reasoned understanding of the way in which Congress intended the statute and its surrounding regulatory scheme to affect business, consumers, and the law. * * *

Medtronic's argument [that Congress intended to bar all common law tort claims based on medical devices] is not only unpersuasive, it is implausible. Under Medtronic's view of the statute, Congress effectively precluded state courts from affording state consumers any protection from injuries resulting from a defective medical device. Moreover, because there is no explicit private cause of action against manufacturers contained in the MDA, and no suggestion that the Act created an implied private right of action, Congress would have barred most, if not all, relief for persons injured by defective medical devices. (Footnote omitted) Medtronic's construction of § 360k would therefore have the perverse effect of granting complete immunity from design defect liability to an entire industry that, in the judgment of Congress, needed more stringent regulation in order "to provide for the safety and effectiveness of medical devices intended for human use," 90 Stat. 539 (preamble to Act). It is, to say the least, "difficult to believe that Congress would, without comment, remove all means of judicial recourse for those injured by illegal conduct," Silkwood v. Kerr–McGee Corp., 464 U.S. 238, 251, 78 L. Ed. 2d 443, 104 S. Ct. 615 (1984), and it would take language much plainer than the text of § 360k to convince us that Congress intended that result. * * *

The legislative history also confirms our understanding that § 360(k) simply was not intended to pre-empt most, let alone all, general common-law duties enforced by damages actions. There is, to the best of our knowledge, nothing in the hearings, the committee reports, or the debates suggesting that any proponent of the legislation intended a sweeping pre-emption of traditional common-law remedies against manufacturers and distributors of defective devices. If Congress intended such a result, its failure even to hint at it is spectacularly odd, particularly since Members of both Houses were acutely aware of ongoing product liability litigation. (Footnote omitted.) Along with the less-than-precise language of § 360k(a), that silence surely indicates that at least some common-law claims against medical device manufacturers may be maintained after the enactment of the MDA. * * *

[The Court then considered Medtronic's argument that the claims in this particular case should be precluded even if some claims were permitted.]

Medtronic asserts several specific reasons why, even if § 360k does not pre-empt all common-law claims, it at least pre-empts the Lohrs' claims in this suit. In contrast, the Lohrs argue that their entire complaint should survive a reasonable evaluation of the pre-emptive scope of § 360k(a). First, the Lohrs claim that the Court of Appeals correctly held that their negligent design claims were not pre-empted because the § 510(k) pre-market notification process imposes no "requirement" on the design of Medtronic's pacemaker. Second, they suggest that even if the FDA's general rules regulating manufacturing practices and labeling are "requirements" that pre-empt different state requirements, § 360k(a) does not pre-empt state rules that merely duplicate some or all of those federal requirements. Finally, they argue that because the State's general rules imposing common-law duties upon Medtronic do not impose a requirement "with respect to a device," they do not conflict with the FDA's general rules relating to manufacturing and labeling and are therefore not pre-empted. * * *

Although we do not believe that this statutory and regulatory language necessarily precludes "general" federal requirements from ever pre-empting state requirements, or "general" state requirements from ever being pre-empted, see Part VI, infra, it is impossible to ignore its overarching concern that pre-emption occur only where a particular state requirement threatens to interfere with a specific federal interest. State requirements must be "with respect to" medical devices and "different from, or in addition to," federal requirements. State requirements must also relate "to the safety or effectiveness of the device or to any other matter included in a requirement applicable to the device," and the regulations provide that state requirements of "general applicability" are not pre-empted except where they have "the effect of establishing a substantive requirement for a specific device." Moreover, federal requirements must be "applicable to the device" in question, and, according to the regulations, pre-empt state law only if they are "specific counter-part regulations" or "specific" to a "particular device." The statute and regulations, therefore, require a careful comparison between the allegedly pre-empting federal requirement and the allegedly pre-empted state requirement to determine whether they fall within the intended pre-emptive scope of the statute and regulations. (Footnote omitted.)

Such a comparison mandates a conclusion that the Lohrs' common-law claims are not pre-empted by the federal labeling and manufacturing requirements. The generality of those requirements make this quite unlike a case in which the Federal Government has weighed the competing interests relevant to the particular requirement in question, reached an unambiguous conclusion about how those competing considerations should be resolved in a particular case or set of cases, and implemented that conclusion via a specific mandate on manufacturers or producers. Rather, the federal requirements reflect important but entirely generic concerns about device regulation generally, not the sort of concerns regarding a specific device or field of device regulation that the statute or regulations were designed to protect from potentially contradictory state requirements.

Similarly, the general state common-law requirements in this suit were not specifically developed "with respect to" medical devices. Accordingly, they are not the kinds of requirements that Congress and the FDA feared would impede the ability of federal regulators to implement and enforce specific federal requirements. The legal duty that is the predicate for the Lohrs' negligent manufacturing claim is the general duty of every manufacturer to use due care to avoid foreseeable dangers in its products. Similarly, the predicate for the failure to warn claim is the general duty to inform users and purchasers of potentially dangerous items of the risks involved in their use. These general obligations are no more a threat to federal requirements than would be a state-law duty to comply with local fire prevention regulations and zoning codes, or to use due care in the training and supervision of a work force. These state requirements therefore escape pre-emption, not because the source of the duty is a judge-made common-law rule, but rather because their generality leaves them outside the category of requirements that § 360k envisioned to be "with respect to" specific devices such as pacemakers. As a result, none of the Lohrs' claims based on allegedly defective manufacturing or labeling are pre-empted by the MDA. * * *

Accordingly, the judgment of the Court of Appeals is reversed insofar as it held that any of the claims were pre-empted and affirmed insofar as it rejected the pre-emption defense. The cases are remanded for further proceedings.

It is so ordered.

[The concurring opinion of Justice Breyer and the concurring and dissenting opinion of Justice O'Connor, joined by the Chief Justice, Justice Scalia, and Justice Thomas are omitted.]

NOTES AND QUESTIONS

1. In the principal case, the court split 4–4 over whether a jury's imposition of liability on a medical device manufacturer in a product liability suit pursuant to state common law tort duties would ever amount to a conflicting state requirement subject to federal preemption. Justice Breyer provided the fifth vote necessary to support the Court's holding that none of the plaintiffs' claims were preempted, but agreed with Justice O'Connor's dissenting opinion on the extent to which more appropriate FDA requirements might preempt state law claims. He then posed this hypothetical to illustrate why state common law claims, as well as state regulatory agency rules, should be preempted by Congress: "Imagine that, in respect to a particular hearing aid component, a federal MDA regulation requires a 2–inch wire, but a state agency regulation requires a 1–inch wire. If the federal law, embodied in the '2–inch' MDA regulation, pre-empts the state '1–inch' agency regulation, why would it not similarly pre-empt a state-law tort action that premises liability upon the defendant manufacturer's failure to use a 1–inch wire (say, an award by a jury persuaded by expert testimony that use of a more than 1–inch wire is negligent)? The effects of the state agency regulation and the state tort suit are identical. To distinguish between them for pre-emption purposes would grant greater power (to set state standards 'different from, or in addition to,' federal standards) to a single state jury than to state officials acting through state administrative or legislative lawmaking processes. Where Congress likely did not focus specifically upon the matter, . . . , I would not take it to have intended this anomalous result." Justice Breyer's concurring opinion, 518 U.S. 470, 504.

2. Note that in statutes where Congress has made its intent clear, the courts have no choice. The state law is preempted by the federal law and, as a practical matter, the manufacturer need comply only with the federal statute and the regulations issued under it. What if the plaintiff can prove that the manufacturer misrepresented or withheld critical information from the agency charged with issuing the standard? Compare Hurley v. Lederle Labs. Div. of Am. Cyanamid Co., 863 F.2d 1173 (5th Cir.1988) (issue could be presented to jury whether information allegedly withheld from FDA would have materially affected warning FDA mandated for a vaccine) with Papas v. Upjohn Co., 926 F.2d 1019 (11th Cir.1991), vacated and remanded in light of *Cipollone*, 112 S.Ct. 3020 (1992), affirmed on remand, 985 F.2d 516 (11th Cir.1993) (preemption not affected by allegations that manufacturer withheld information; those allegations should be addressed within FIFRA's regulatory scheme, not the tort system). See Ausness, Federal Preemption of State Products Liability Doctrines, 44 U.S.C.L.Rev. 187 (1993) (discussing case law and proposing model of statutory interpretation).

3. Where Congress has not made its intent clear, the courts must determine whether preemption was intended and which claims are to be preempted. This requires a case by case analysis of whether a claim is preempted, both because the statutes themselves vary and because some claims under a given statute may be preempted while others are not. See, for example, Cipollone v. Liggett Group, Inc., 505 U.S. 504 (1992) (state tort law claims for failure to warn preempted, but claims for breach of express warranty would not be). Should a plaintiff be able to bring a

state tort law claim based on damages caused by a medical device that was approved pursuant to the rigorous PMA process described by the court in the principal case? Worthy v. Collagen Corp., 967 S.W.2d 360 (Tex.1998) (claim preempted). Should a plaintiff be able to bring a suit based on the manufacturer's failure to include anti-lock brakes if federal regulation permits such an omission? Freightliner Corp. v. Myrick, 514 U.S. 280 (1995) (claim not preempted). Should a plaintiff be able to bring a crashworthiness claim based on the manufacturer's failure to include an airbag if federal regulation permits such an omission? Compare Drattel v. Toyota Motor Corp., 699 N.E.2d 376 (N.Y.1998) (federal regulation does not preempt) with Geier v. American Honda Motor Co., 166 F.3d 1236 (D.C. Cir.), cert. granted ___ U.S. ___, 144 L.Ed.2d 835, 120 S.Ct. 33 (1999) (federal regulation preempts state tort claim).

4. _Government Standards._ Federal preemption of state common law should not be confused with compliance with government standards. As is more fully discussed at page 225, most jurisdictions permit the defendant to introduce evidence of compliance with government standards on the issue whether the manufacture was negligent, or, in a strict liability case, whether the product was defective. A few jurisdictions provide that compliance with government standards creates a rebuttable presumption that the product was not defective. Should the jury be permitted to "second guess" the governmental agency that issued the standard? Most jurisdictions allow the jury to do just that. The government standards and the manufacturer's compliance with those standards are evidence that the jury may consider, but is not bound by. A regulatory standard issued by the federal government may preempt (completely preclude the bringing of) state claims only in the limited circumstance that the court determines that Congress intended such preemption. See also Restatement (Third) of Torts: Products Liability § 4(b) (1998) (providing that compliance with an applicable product safety statute or administrative regulation can be considered in determining defect, but is not determinative).

5. _Government Contractor Defense._ Suppose the government not only set the standards, but mandated the design of the product? Should a manufacturer be liable for design defects in a product manufactured to government specifications? In Boyle v. United Technologies Corp., 487 U.S. 500 (1988), the family of a Navy pilot killed in a helicopter crash during a training exercise sued the helicopter manufacturer alleging a defect in the design of the escape hatch. The manufacturer urged the court to recognize a defense based on the fact that the government itself had made the design decision. The Supreme Court ruled that a contractor could be immune from liability for an allegedly defective product if the manufacturer could show that (1) the United States approved reasonably precise specifications, (2) the equipment conformed to those specifications, and (3) the supplier warned the United States about the dangers in the use of the equipment that were known to the supplier but not to the United States. The contractor has the burden of proving each of the elements of the defense. Should the government specifications defense apply to nonmilitary contractors as well? Compare Carley v. Wheeled Coach, 991 F.2d 1117 (3d Cir.1993) (finding public policy underpinnings of _Boyle_ applied to the government contractor who supplied an ambulance to the United States for civilian use) with Nielsen v. George Diamond Vogel Paint Co., 892 F.2d 1450 (9th Cir.1990) (defense not available to contractor who supplied Army Corps of Engineers with paint, fumes from which allegedly injured plaintiff in a "purely civilian setting"). Since the defense requires the manufacturer to show conformance with the government specifications, would it be available in a manufacturing defect case? Snell v. Bell Helicopter Textron, Inc., 107 F.3d 744 (9th Cir.1997) (court suggests that

defense is not precluded by label "manufacturing defect," but that the requirements of the defense would be difficult to meet in many such cases).

5. DEFENDANTS OTHER THAN PRINCIPAL MANUFACTURERS/HARM OTHER THAN PERSONAL INJURY

(A) OTHER SUPPLIERS OF CHATTELS

Peterson v. Lou Bachrodt Chevrolet Co.

Supreme Court of Illinois, 1975.
61 Ill.2d 17, 329 N.E.2d 785.

SCHAEFER, JUSTICE. On September 3, 1971, Maradean Peterson, age 11, and her brother, Mark Peterson, age 8, were struck by an automobile while they were walking home from school. Maradean Peterson died on the day of the accident, and Mark Peterson suffered severe injuries, including the amputation of one of his legs. The automobile involved in the accident was a used 1965 Chevrolet. James A. Peterson, administrator of the estate of Maradean Peterson, and Mark Peterson, by James A. Peterson, his father and next friend, brought this action against the driver of the used car, its owners, and the defendant involved in the appeal, Lou Bachrodt Chevrolet Company.

[The circuit court dismissed two counts of the complaint and this ruling is before the supreme court on appeal.]

One of the challenged counts sought recovery for the wrongful death of the daughter, the other for the injuries to the son. Each count alleged that the defendant, Lou Bachrodt Chevrolet Company, had sold the 1965 Chevrolet on June 11, 1971, in the ordinary course of business, and that at the time the automobile left the defendant's control it was defective and not reasonably safe for driving and operation in that:

"(a) A spring or springs in the left front wheel braking system was missing at the time of its sale;

"(b) One of the left rear brake shoes was completely worn out at the time of the sale;

"(c) A part of the cylinder braking system in the left rear wheel was missing at the time of the sale."

It was alleged that the injuries and death were a direct and proximate result of the defective conditions.

* * *

In Suvada v. White Motor Co. (1965), 32 Ill.2d 612, 210 N.E.2d 182, we held that a manufacturer is liable under a theory of strict liability if the plaintiffs "prove that their injury or damage resulted from a condition of the product, that the condition was an unreasonably dangerous one and that the condition existed at the time it left the manufacturer's control." (32 Ill.2d 612, 623, 210 N.E.2d 182, 188.) In Dunham v. Vaughan &

Bushnell Mfg. Co. (1969), 42 Ill.2d 339, 247 N.E.2d 401, strict liability was imposed upon a wholesaler through whose warehouse the packaged product passed unopened. In that case we pointed out: "The strict liability of a retailer arises from his integral role in the overall producing and marketing enterprise and affords an additional incentive to safety." (42 Ill.2d 339, 344, 247 N.E.2d 401, 404.) The plaintiffs now ask that the same liability be imposed upon a defendant who is outside of the original producing and marketing chain. We decline to do so.

One of the basic grounds supporting the imposition of strict liability upon manufacturers is that losses should be borne by those "who have created the risk and reaped the profit by placing the product in the stream of commerce." (32 Ill.2d 612, 619, 210 N.E.2d 182, 186.) Imposition of liability upon wholesalers and retailers is justified on the ground that their position in the marketing process enables them to exert pressure on the manufacturer to enhance the safety of the product. [Cc] A wholesaler or retailer who neither creates nor assumes the risk is entitled to indemnity. [Cc] Therefore, although liability is imposed upon anyone who is engaged in the business of selling the product (Restatement (Second) of Torts § 402A (1965)), the loss will ordinarily be ultimately borne by the party that created the risk.

There is no allegation that the defects existed when the product left the control of the manufacturer. Nor is there any allegation that the defects were created by the used car dealer. [C] If strict liability is imposed upon the facts alleged here, the used car dealer would in effect become an insurer against defects which had come into existence after the chain of distribution was completed, and while the product was under the control of one or more consumers. See Restatement (Second) of Torts § 402A, Comment f. * * *

The judgment of the Appellate Court, Second District, is reversed.

Appellate court reversed; circuit court affirmed.

GOLDENHERSH, JUSTICE (dissenting). I dissent. The rationale underlying the application of strict liability to a manufacturer is that losses should be borne by those "who have created the risk and reaped the profit by placing the product in the stream of commerce." (Suvada v. White Motor Co., 32 Ill.2d 612, 619, 210 N.E.2d 182, 186.) In Dunham v. Vaughan & Bushnell Mfg. Co., 42 Ill.2d 339, 247 N.E.2d 401, strict liability was made applicable to a wholesaler and retailer for the reason that "these considerations apply with equal compulsion to all elements in the distribution system." (42 Ill.2d 339, 344, 247 N.E.2d 401, 404.) * * *

In Galluccio v. Hertz Corp., 1 Ill.App.3d 272, 274 N.E.2d 178, appeal denied, 49 Ill.2d 575, the appellate court held strict liability applicable to the lessor of a motor vehicle. No reason presents itself for not applying the principle to a used car dealer who places in the stream of commerce a vehicle rendered unreasonably dangerous by reason of a defect discoverable upon reasonable inspection.

I am aware of the argument made by defendant and *amici curiae* that many vehicles are sold "as is" and that the cost of repairs in some instances might exceed the value of the vehicle. These pleadings present no such issues, and assuming, *arguendo,* that in some future case they will arise, there is precedent for weighing the cost of remedying the dangerous condition against the nature and extent of the risk which it creates. [C]

I would affirm the judgment of the appellate court.

NOTES AND QUESTIONS

1. The Restatement (Second) of Torts § 402A and most courts in their initial decision implementing strict products liability on tort or warranty theories limited its reach to defendants "in the business of selling products." Part of the development of strict liability law in the next two decades focused on (1) which defendants fit within this definition and (2) whether other defendants also should be included.

2. *Used Products.* As the principal case reflects, many courts may decline to impose strict liability on sellers of used products. See also Tillman v. Vance Equipment Co., 286 Or. 747, 596 P.2d 1299 (1979) (no strict liability in absence of representation of quality beyond sale itself where used equipment dealer sold twenty-four year old crane to plaintiff's employer); Peterson v. Idaho First Nat'l Bank, 117 Idaho 724, 791 P.2d 1303 (1990) (no strict liability for mobile home sale by bank that sold it after repossessing it). But see Turner v. International Harvester Co., 133 N.J. Super. 277, 336 A.2d 62 (1975) (strict liability applies to dealer of used goods who sold tractor-trailer); Nelson v. Nelson Hardware, Inc., 160 Wis. 2d 689, 467 N.W.2d 518 (1991) (strict liability applies to hardware store that took a used shotgun in trade and resold it). See also Restatement (Third) of Torts: Products Liability § 8 (1998) (focusing on consumer expectations to limit liability in cases involving used goods). If strict liability is applied, can a seller of a used product avoid it by selling the product "as is" or "with all faults"? The jurisdictions are split on this issue. See Restatement (Third) of Torts: Products Liability § 8 cmt. k and Reporters' Notes thereto (1998) (collecting cases).

3. *Lessors and Bailors of Chattels.* Strict liability was first extended to third parties not in privity in Cintrone v. Hertz Truck Leasing & Rental Serv. Co., 45 N.J. 434, 212 A.2d 769 (1965), where, in a long but good opinion, the court extended the implied warranty to the user to apply to lessors, but denied recovery to the plaintiff because of his "contributory negligence" in driving with brakes he knew to be bad. The rule that commercial lessors of chattels should be subject to strict liability has been adopted with almost uniform consistency in other states. A common situation is where a passenger or pedestrian is injured by a rented automobile, but the cases also have included trucks, airplanes, boats, and tools. See, e.g., Price v. Shell Oil Co., 2 Cal.3d 245, 466 P.2d 722, 85 Cal.Rptr. 178 (1970); Stewart v. Budget Rent–A–Car Corp., 52 Haw. 71, 470 P.2d 240 (1970); Samuel Friedland Family Enterprises v. Amoroso, 630 So.2d 1067 (Fla.1994). See also Restatement (Third) of Torts: Products Liability § 20 cmt. c (1998) (including lessors in definition of "sells or otherwise distributes," the language that triggers liability).

4. *Retailers and Wholesaler–Distributors.* Most courts have extended strict liability to retailers and wholesaler-distributors. As Justice Traynor indicated in Vandermark v. Ford Motor Co., 61 Cal.2d 256, 391 P.2d 168, 37 Cal.Rptr. 896 (1964): "In some cases the retailer may be the only member of the enterprise reasonably available to the injured plaintiff. In other cases, the retailer himself may

play a substantial part in insuring that the product is safe or may be in a position to exert pressure on the manufacturer to that end." See also Cacico, the Strict Tort Liability of Retailers, Wholesalers, and Distributors of Defective Products, 12 Nova L. Rev. 213 (1987) (noting that a great majority of states followed *Vandemark*). Note that strict liability may produce substantially different results from negligence for a retailer or wholesaler. The dealer, for example, is ordinarily not negligent in failing to open sealed containers and inspect their contents. See Frericks v. General Motors Corp., 274 Md. 288, 336 A.2d 118 (1975) (design of automobile). Data show that retailers and wholesalers end up paying product liability judgments in less than five percent of cases. Nevertheless, they are brought into a majority of product liability claims. Who benefits from all this? The Uniform Product Liability Act would hold retailers and wholesalers liable only for their own acts of negligence unless the manufacturer was out of business or unreachable through judicial process. Do you agree with that approach? Approximately a dozen states have enacted these types of provisions limiting the liability of non-manufacturer product sellers. See, e.g., Ga.Code Ann. § 51–1–11.1 (1999); Minn.Stat. § 544.41 (1999); Wash.Rev.Code § 7.72.040 (1999). The Restatement (Third) of Torts: Products Liability § 20 (1998) includes all sellers in the chain of distribution, including retailers and wholesalers, in the same category as product manufacturers.

5. An *occasional seller* who does not hold himself out as having any knowledge or skill in the commercial sense will not be subject to strict liability. See Samson v. Riesing, 62 Wis.2d 698, 215 N.W.2d 662 (1974) (nine members of the Wauwatosa High School Band Mothers sold plaintiff turkey salad contaminated with salmonella). See also Restatement (Third) of Torts: Products Liability § 1 cmt. c (1998) (applies only to those engaged in the business of selling or otherwise distributing the type of product that injured the plaintiff).

6. *Manufacturer of Component Parts or Raw Materials.* The maker of a component part not subject to further processing or substantial change in the manufacturing process is likely to be subject to strict liability if there is a defect in that part or material. See Walton v. Avco, 530 Pa. 568, 610 A.2d 454 (1992) (manufacturer of engine that contained defective part and manufacturer of helicopter into which engine was installed both had independent duties to warn of defect); Clark v. Bendix Corp., 42 A.D.2d 727, 345 N.Y.S.2d 662 (1973) (faulty power steering mechanism); Icelandic Airlines, Inc. (Loftleidir) v. Canadair, Ltd., 104 Misc.2d 239, 428 N.Y.S.2d 393 (1980) (defective hydraulic control system in airplane). The component maker or raw material supplier also may be liable if he substantially participates in integrating the component or raw material into a defective product. See Buonanno v. Colmar Belting Co., Inc., 733 A.2d 712 (R.I. 1999) and Restatement (Third) of Torts: Products Liability § 5(b)(1) (1998).

7. *Indemnity and Contribution.* As the principal case reflects, a relevant factor in determining which class of defendants should be subject to strict liability may be contribution or indemnity rights. Courts apply indemnity and contribution principles that have been utilized in negligence law. See pages 378–387. For example, the retailer would be entitled to indemnity or full reimbursement from the manufacturer, unless the retailer also was negligent. The manufacturer would be entitled to indemnity from the maker of a defective component part unless the manufacturer also was negligent. Under those circumstances, comparative fault principles would apply. See Phillips, Contribution and Indemnity in Products Liability, 42 Tenn. L.Rev. 141 (1974); Wade, Contribution and Indemnity in Products Liability Cases, 27th Ann.Miss.L.Inst. 115 (1972).

8. *Corporate Acquisitions/Successor Liability.* An increasing business phenomenon is the acquisition of one corporation by another. How should this affect

products liability? Should the acquiring corporation be subject to claims based on products manufactured and sold before the takeover? Generally, the successor corporation is liable only if it agreed to assume liability, the transfer was a fraudulent one, the two corporations merged, or the successor is essentially a continuation of the original company. See Restatement (Third) of Torts: Products Liability § 12 (1998). Some courts have gone further, holding a corporation that acquired substantially all of the assets of another corporation liable if it continues the product line. See, for example, Mettinger v. Glove Slicing Mach. Co., Inc., 153 N.J. 371, 709 A.2d 779 (1998). See generally, Phillips, Product Line Continuity and Successor Corporation Liability, 58 N.Y.U.L.Rev. 906 (1983); Schulman, Commentary: Successor Corporation Liability and the Inadequacy of the Product Line Continuity Approach, 31 Wayne L.Rev. 135 (1984); Phillips, Reply [to Schulman]: Product Line Continuity as the Basis for Successor Corporation Liability, 31 Wayne L.Rev. 149 (1984). For an argument that the goals of internalization of costs is more adequately achieved if successor liability is adopted, see Schwartz, Products Liability, Corporate Structure, and Bankruptcy: Toxic Substances and the Remote Risk Relationship, 14 J. Legal Stud. 689 (1984).

9. *Builders of Real Property.* Strict liability first entered the picture in the early 1960's when, by analogy to the sale of chattels, an implied warranty of habitability was held to run from the builder or vendor of a newly constructed home to his immediate buyer. See, e.g., Cochran v. Keeton, 287 Ala. 439, 252 So.2d 313 (1971); Carpenter v. Donohoe, 154 Colo. 78, 388 P.2d 399 (1964); Humber v. Morton, 426 S.W.2d 554 (Tex.1968). On the other hand other jurisdictions have clung to the common law rule of *caveat emptor* and refused to imply any warranty. A few jurisdictions have extended the "implied warranty of habitability" to a third-party occupant. Schipper v. Levitt & Sons, Inc., 44 N.J. 70, 207 A.2d 314 (1965) (plaintiff scalded when he came in contact with excessively hot water drawn from the faucet in the bathroom sink). The *Schipper* court relied upon the fact that the defendant was involved in the "mass production and sale of homes," and indicated that the warranty meant only that the home would be "reasonably fit for the purpose for which it was sold." See also Restatement (Third) of Torts: Products Liability § 19(a) (1998) (including real property in definition of product if the context of distribution and use is sufficiently analogous to distribution and use of tangible personal property).

10. *Sellers of Real Property.* A distinction formally was drawn between one who sells a house that he has himself built and a vendor who sells a used house. The older rule of the common law was that a vendor was not liable to his vendee, or to other persons who might come upon the land, for harm resulting from a defective condition that he did not disclose. This rule is now severely eroded. See Chapter 9.

11. *Lessors of Real Property.* Louisiana applies strict liability by statute. California applied strict liability to landlords for injuries caused by a defects in the premises, but then repudiated that position a decade later in the face of widespread criticism of the underlying rationale for the rule and of its effects. See Becker v. IRM Corp., 38 Cal.3d 454, 698 P.2d 116, 213 Cal.Rptr. 213. (1985) and Peterson v. Superior Court, 10 Cal.4th 1185, 43 Cal. Rptr.2d 836, 899 P.2d 905 (1995).

(B) SERVICES

Hector v. Cedars–Sinai Medical Ctr.

Court of Appeals of California, 1986.
180 Cal.App.3d 493, 225 Cal.Rptr. 595.

SPENCER, J.

Plaintiff Frances J. Hector appeals from an order dismissing her second and third causes of action against defendant following the granting of defendant's motion for partial summary judgment.

Plaintiff filed a complaint against Cedars–Sinai Medical Center (Cedars–Sinai) and American Technology, Inc., alleging personal injury resulting from the implantation of a defective pacemaker. The pacemaker was manufactured by American Technology, Inc., and implanted at Cedars–Sinai by plaintiff's physician, Dr. Eugene Kompaniez.

The complaint contained three causes of action: negligence, strict liability and breach of warranty. Cedars–Sinai moved for partial summary judgment on plaintiff's second and third causes of action, strict liability and breach of warranty, alleging as a matter of law there were no triable issues of fact. The trial court granted the motion. Plaintiff subsequently requested and received dismissal of the first cause of action, negligence, against Cedars–Sinai. The trial court then issued its order dismissing the second and third causes of action.

Plaintiff contends the trial court erred in finding Cedars–Sinai was exempt from the application of the strict products liability doctrine. For the reasons set forth below, we disagree.

* * *

On appeal, the court first recalls the origin of the application of strict liability in California: Greenman v. Yuba Power Products, Inc. (1963) 59 Cal.2d 57 [27 Cal.Rptr. 697, 377 P.2d 897] held that " '[a] manufacturer is strictly liable in tort when an article he places on the market, knowing that it is to be used without inspection for defects, proves to have a defect that causes injury to a human being.' " [C] The court then notes the expansion of the doctrine to impose strict liability on others in the chain of distribution, not merely manufacturers. [C] For example, Vandermark v. Ford Motor Co. (1964) 61 Cal.2d 256 [37 Cal.Rptr. 896, 391 P.2d 168] extends strict liability to retailers since they are "engaged in the business of distributing goods to the public" and "are an integral part of the overall producing and marketing enterprise that should bear the cost of injuries resulting from defective products." * * *

After surveying the cases which expand the scope of strict liability, the Silverhart [v. Mount Zion Hosp., 20 Cal.App.3d 1022, 98 Cal.Rptr. 187 (1971)] court observes: "A significant common element running through the cases is that each of the defendants against whom the standard of strict liability has been applied played an integral and vital part in the overall production or marketing enterprise. At the very least the defendant in each case was a link in the chain of getting goods from the manufacturer to the ultimate user or consumer. * * * [para.] Plaintiff seeks to extend the doctrine of strict liability to a hospital that furnishes, in connection with the care and treatment of a patient, a product that proves to have a defect that causes injury to the patient. The theory upon which she seeks to predicate such liability is that the hospital is a 'supplier' of such product and, therefore, should be subject to the same standard of liability as any other supplier of articles or products." [C]

The court then examines two key cases in which strict liability has not been applied to the medical profession: "In Magrine v. Krasnica [(1967)] 94 N.J.Super. 228 [227 A.2d 539], affirmed 100 N.J.Super. 223 [241 A.2d 637], and 53 N.J. 259 [250 A.2d 129], the court declined to apply the doctrine of strict liability to a dentist whose drill, with a latent defect, broke while he was working on his patient, causing injury to the patient. The court stated, 'Of * * * meaningful significance is a recognition that the essence of the transaction between the retail seller and the consumer relates to the article sold. The seller is in the business of supplying the product to the consumer. It is that, and that alone, for which he is paid. A dentist or a physician offers, and is paid for, his professional services and skill. That is the essence of the relationship between him and his patient.' [C]

The foregoing statement in Magrine was cited with approval in Carmichael v. Reitz [(1971)] 17 Cal.App.3d 958, 979. * * * In Carmichael it was held that the doctrine of strict liability did not apply to a doctor who prescribed a drug which produced untoward results in a patient. In that case we find the following rationale: '[There] is a difference in status or classification between those upon whom the courts have heretofore imposed the doctrine of strict liability and a physician who prescribes an ethical drug to achieve a cure of the disorders for which the patient has sought his professional services. The former act basically as mere conduits to the distribution of the product to the consumer; the latter sells or furnishes his services as a healer of illnesses. The physician's services depend upon his skill and judgment derived from his specialized training, knowledge, experience, and skill. The physician prescribes the medicine in the course of chemotherapy only as a chemical aid or instrument to achieve a cure. A doctor diagnosing and treating a patient normally is not selling either a product or insurance. One of the requisites which the Restatement prescribes for the imposition of strict liability is that "the seller is engaged in the business of selling such product." ' [Cc]"

The Silverhart court was "persuaded that the rationale of Magrine and Carmichael applies with equal force to a hospital in the exercise of its primary function which is to provide medical services. A hospital is not ordinarily engaged in the business of selling any of the products or equipment it uses in providing such services. The essence of the relationship between a hospital and its patients does not relate essentially to any product or piece of equipment it uses but to the professional services it provides." [C] The court notes, however, that "this principle does not apply where the hospital is engaged in activities not integrally related to its primary function of providing medical services, such as the situation where the hospital operates a gift shop which sells a defective product." [C] The court concludes the rule of strict liability cannot be applied to defendant hospital. [C]

* * *

Cases dealing with blood transfusions and products reflect the same considerations when declining to apply strict liability to hospitals, although there is additional statutory justification for treating these items as services rather than sales. Shepard v. Alexian Brothers Hosp. (1973) 33 Cal.App.3d 606 [109 Cal.Rptr. 132] states: "It needs no extended discussion to perceive that a hospital is primarily devoted to the care and healing of the sick. The supplying of blood by the hospital is entirely subordinate to its paramount function of furnishing trained personnel and specialized facilities in an endeavor to restore the patient's health. Providing medicine or supplying blood is simply a chemical aid or instrument utilized to accomplish the objective of cure or treatment. The patient who enters a hospital goes there not to buy medicine or pills, not to purchase bandages, iodine, serum or blood, but to obtain a course of treatment. [Cc] It is also obvious that in the normal commercial transaction contemplated in the strict liability cases the essence of the transaction relates solely to the article sold, the seller is in the business of supplying the product to the consumer, and it is that, and that alone, for which he is paid. [C] The foregoing marked distinctions compel the conclusion that a hospital is not engaged in the business of distributing blood to the public and does not put the blood as a product on the market in order to profit therefrom." [C]

Turning to the facts in the instant case, Howard Allen, M.D., Director of the Cedars–Sinai Cardiac Noninvasive Laboratory states in his declaration that the specific model and type of pacemaker to be implanted in a patient is specified by the surgeon. The surgeon ordinarily contacts the manufacturer's representative to provide for delivery of the pacemaker to the operating room when it is to be implanted. The pacemaker may be sterilized and ready for implantation when it is delivered to the hospital; the manufacturer's representative or the surgeon may pretest the pacemaker, but the hospital employees do not.

Dr. Allen indicated Cedars–Sinai does not routinely stock pacemakers, nor is it in the business of recommending, selling, distributing or testing pacemakers. The treatment provided by Cedars–Sinai in relation to implantation of pacemakers includes pre-and post-operative care, nursing care, a surgical operating room and technicians.

* * *

The essence of the relationship between hospital and patient is the provision of professional medical services necessary to effect the implantation of the pacemaker—the patient does not enter the hospital merely to purchase a pacemaker but to obtain a course of treatment which includes implantation of a pacemaker. [Cc] As a provider of services rather than a seller of a product, the hospital is not subject to strict liability for a defective product provided to the patient during the course of his or her treatment. * * *

* * *

Unlike the products sold in a hospital gift shop, for which the hospital is strictly liable * * *, the pacemaker provided to the patient is necessary to the patient's medical treatment. While the hospital itself does not use its own medical skill or knowledge in providing its services in connection with the provision of the pacemaker for the patient, the hospital still is engaged in the process of providing everything necessary to furnish the patient with a course of treatment. In this regard, the hospital's actions concerning the provision of the pacemaker are "integrally related to its primary function of providing medical services." * * *

* * *

Of equal importance, the policy considerations behind the imposition of strict product liability would not be served by its application here. Strict liability is imposed "to insure that the cost of injuries resulting from defective products are borne by the manufacturers who put such products on the market rather than by the injured persons who are powerless to protect themselves." [Cc] Further, since the defendant profits from the sale of the products, it is in a good strategic position to protect itself by inquiring about or testing the products, promoting safety through pressure on the manufacturer, selling another product which is not defective, or insuring itself and distributing the risk of injury among the public as a cost of doing business. [Cc]

Plaintiff asserts the imposition of strict liability will result in lower costs for health care, since the hospital no longer will be able to charge high fees for processing the paperwork for pacemakers ordered by physicians for their patients. But because the overall charges to the patients must equal the overall expenditures by the hospital, any decrease in the charge on pacemakers necessarily would mean an increase in another charge, and there would be no overall decrease in the cost to the consumer of health care. Moreover, if a hospital is to be considered a seller who places a product on the market and who must bear the cost of injuries resulting from defective products, it will have to insure itself and distribute the risk of injury among the public as a cost of doing business. This necessarily will result in higher costs for health care.

In the instant case, the hospital does not select the pacemaker for the patient, but the selection is made by the treating physician. Thus, the hospital is in a poor position to protect itself by inquiring about or testing the devices, pressuring the manufacturer to promote product safety or selling a different pacemaker which is not defective. The imposition of strict liability would force the hospital to become involved in the selection process. This might provide added protection to the patient; it might also increase the cost of hospital services. But once the hospital began using its medical knowledge to aid in the selection of a pacemaker, it would be in the position of providing professional medical services, for which it could not be held strictly liable. Thus, there would be no ultimate advantage to putting the hospital in the position of having to take part in the selection process.

For the foregoing reasons, we conclude Cedars–Sinai is not "engaged in the business of selling" pacemakers, but is a provider of medical services which included the provision of the pacemaker implanted in plaintiff.

Inasmuch as the hospital is not a seller, it cannot be held strictly liable for injuries to plaintiff caused by defects in the pacemaker. Accordingly, the trial court did not err in granting the motion for partial summary judgment.

The order is affirmed.

NOTES AND QUESTIONS

1. The sales-service distinction grew out of the fact that breach of implied warranty was a basis for early strict liability cases. The distinction is perpetuated by the language of the Uniform Commercial Code, of Restatement (Second) § 402A, and of Restatement (Third) of Torts: Products Liability § 19(b) (1998). Judicial reluctance to extend strict liability to services has two underlying policy rationales. In a service transaction, there is no mass production and distribution, and hence no real ability to spread the risk of loss to consumers. Moreover, service transactions do not involve a group of consumers needing protection from a remote and unknown manufacturer. See La Rossa v. Scientific Design Co., 402 F.2d 937 (3d Cir.1968) (refusing to apply strict liability to engineering company involved in construction of chemical plant). Do you agree that this is a meaningful distinction?

2. Attempts to extend strict liability to services generally have failed. See, e.g., in Hoffman v. Simplot Aviation, Inc., 97 Idaho 32, 539 P.2d 584 (1975) (repair of airplane); Swett v. Gribaldo, Jones & Assocs., 40 Cal.App.3d 573, 115 Cal.Rptr. 99 (1974) (California court declined to impose strict liability on a soils engineer although it had applied that standard to mass builder-vendors of real estate); McKee v. American Home Products Corp., 113 Wash.2d 701, 782 P.2d 1045 (1989) (pharmacist); Dubin v. Michael Reese Hosp., 83 Ill.2d 277, 415 N.E.2d 350, 47 Ill.Dec. 345 (1980) (providing of X–ray services). Hoven v. Kelble, 79 Wis.2d 444, 256 N.W.2d 379 (1977) (surgeon performing lung biopsy). There have been several attempts in recent years to impose strict liability on health care providers whose patients were injured during the course of their treatment by various products, including breast implants, hip prosthesis, electro-surgical grounding pad, hypodermic needle, spinal rod, and temporomandibular joint implants. Almost all of these have been unsuccessful. In re Breast Implant Product Liability Litigation, 331 S.C. 540, 503 S.E.2d 445 (1998) (surgeons not subject to strict liability) (collecting cases).

3. In many situations, as in the principal case, the transaction will have characteristics of both a sale and a service. In those cases, the courts will not apply strict liability if the transaction is predominately a service, with only an incidental transfer of goods. Compare Stafford v. International Harvester Co., 668 F.2d 142 (2d Cir.1981) (repair of truck steering mechanism predominately a service transaction) with O'Laughlin v. Minnesota Natural Gas Co., 253 N.W.2d 826 (Minn.1977) (strict liability applied because installation of furnace was service incidental to sale of furnace). See generally Powers, Distinguishing Between Products and Services in Strict Liability, 62 N.C.L.Rev. 415 (1984).

4. *Blood, Blood Products, and Human Tissue.* All jurisdictions exempt the providers of blood, blood products, and human tissue from strict liability, usually by statute. This protection extends not only to the physician or other healthcare provider, but also to a commercial supplier. Blood suppliers are liable only if the plaintiff can prove negligence. The Restatement (Third) of Torts: Products Liability § 19(c) and cmt. c (1998) exempts human blood and human tissue from its coverage.

5. Consider whether the following should be held to be products, thus subjecting the defendants to strict liability.

Animals. A store that does not usually carry parrots orders one as a favor to one of its employees. The employee's spouse contracts a disease from the parrot. Strict liability? Compare Latham v. Wal–Mart Stores, Inc., 818 S.W.2d 673 (Mo.App. 1991) (animal not a product) with Beyer v. Aquarium Supply Co., 94 Misc.2d 336, 404 N.Y.S.2d 778 (1977) (hamster is a product). See also Restatement (Third) of Torts: Products Liability § 19 cmt. b (1998) (a living animal sold commercially in a diseased condition is a product).

Charts and Maps. An airplane crashes into the side of Johnson Hill on a snowy night, allegedly because the pilot was using an aeronautical chart sold by defendant that did not show Johnson Hill, elevation 2257 feet, but did show a nearby hill with an elevation of 1991 feet. Strict liability? See Fluor Corp. v. Jeppesen & Co., 170 Cal.App.3d 468, 216 Cal.Rptr. 68 (1985) and Brocklesby v. United States, 767 F.2d 1288 (9th Cir.1985) (the mass production and marketing of these charts requires Jeppesen to bear the costs of accidents caused by defects in them).

Books and Games. Plaintiff is injured while body surfing in Hawaii on his honeymoon. Does he have a strict liability action against the publisher of a guide book for failing to warn him that wave and water conditions on a particular beach were dangerous to swimmers? See Birmingham v. Fodor's Travel Publications, Inc., 73 Haw. 359, 833 P.2d 70 (1992) (declining to extend strict liability to the ideas and expressions in a book). Accord, Winter v. G.P. Putnam's Sons, 938 F.2d 1033 (9th Cir.1991) (plaintiff was poisoned by wild mushrooms collected by referring to the Encyclopedia of Mushrooms); Smith v. Linn, 386 Pa. Super. 392, 563 A.2d 123 (1989) (plaintiff died after following Last Chance Diet book); Watters v. TSR, Inc., 904 F.2d 378 (6th Cir.1990) (in case where boy allegedly committed suicide because of influence of game Dungeons and Dragons, court declined to apply strict liability, noting that the doctrine of strict liability has never been extended to words or pictures). See pages 348–349 for a discussion of proximate cause and First Amendment issues arising out of *Watters* and similar cases and pages 1030–1034 for a discussion of possible misrepresentation claims. See also Restatement (Third) of Torts: Products Liability § 19 cmt. d (1998) ("Although a tangible medium such as a book, itself clearly a product, delivers the information, the plaintiff's grievance in such cases is with the information, not with the tangible medium.") What if the plaintiff developed a rash while reading the book because the ink used was contaminated with a toxic substance?

Computer Software. The Ninth Circuit suggested in dicta that strict liability would apply to computer software that "fails to yield the result for which it was designed." Winter v. G.P. Putnam's Sons, 938 F.2d 1033, 1036 (9th Cir.1991).

Electricity. Plaintiff is injured by electricity supplied by defendant. Strict liability? See Schriner v. Pennsylvania Power & Light Co., 348 Pa.Super. 177, 501 A.2d 1128 (1985) (electricity is a service while passing through transmission lines but becomes a product when it passes through the meter) and Stein v. Southern California Edison, 7 Cal.App.4th 565, 8 Cal.Rptr.2d 907 (1992) (strict liability applied to defendant whose employees' actions while repairing a transformer caused a high-voltage arc to enter plaintiff's home, exploding their meter, and setting their house on fire). See also Restatement (Third) of Torts: Products Liability § 19 cmt. d (1998).

Who makes the determination whether something is a product for strict liability purposes? In some jurisdictions, the statute imposing strict liability provides the definition. In others, it is left to the common law. In either case, it is the judge, rather than the jury, who decides whether the situation fits within the statutory definition or is one to which strict liability should apply.

6. _Endorsers, Licensors, and Franchisors._ Courts may extend strict liability to a trademark licensor or franchiser, particularly if the licensor retains the right to control the quality of the product on which the trademark is used. See, e.g., Kasel v. Remington Arms Co., 24 Cal.App.3d 711, 101 Cal.Rptr. 314 (1972) (trademark licensor strictly liable for injuries caused by explosion of allegedly defective shotgun shell); Kosters v. Seven–Up Co., 595 F.2d 347 (6th Cir.1979) (franchisor liable under implied warranty theory for design defect in carton purchased by franchisee from vendor because of franchisor's approval of the design and its general control over system of distribution of 7–Up). Cf. Miller v. McDonald's Corporation, 150 Ore. App. 274, 945 P.2d 1107 (1997) (court discusses liability of franchisor who sets quality control standards for actions of franchisee in preparation of food). The few courts that have considered the liability of endorsers of products have not imposed strict liability. See, e.g., Hanberry v. Hearst Corp., 276 Cal.App.2d 680, 81 Cal.Rptr. 519 (1969) (consumer's reliance on Good Housekeeping's "seal of approval" may give rise to liability for negligence or negligent misrepresentation, but not strict liability).

7. _Organizations that Set Standards._ What about an organization that sets voluntary standards that have significant influence on its members? Should the organization be liable if the standards are set too low? Should strict liability apply to the organization? Cf. Snyder v. American Ass'n. of Blood Banks, 144 N.J. 269, 676 A.2d 1036 (1996) (holding association of blood banks and blood-banking professionals liable for negligence in the formulation of standards for coping with the problem of AIDS contamination of the blood supply).

8. Even if strict liability does not apply, one who renders a service to another is under a duty to exercise reasonable care in doing so and is liable for any negligence to anyone who may foreseeably be expected to be injured. If cases alleging design defects and failure to warn are based on a risk-utility analysis, how important is the classification of something as a product for the purpose of imposing strict liability? See Restatement (Third) of Torts: Products Liability § 19 cmt. a (1998) (suggesting that the distinction is less important in design and warnings cases).

9. Recall that some services may be considered "abnormally dangerous activities." See Chapter 14, pages 687–704. In this area, the two roads of strict liability come together.

(C) HARM OTHER THAN PERSONAL INJURY

1. _Economic Loss Resulting from Personal Injury._ Lost wages and diminished earning capacity are common forms of economic loss that result from personal injury to plaintiff and are recoverable, along with plaintiff's other losses in a strict liability action. Most jurisdictions also permit loss of consortium claims based on personal injury in products liability cases. See Restatement (Third) of Torts: Products Liability § 21 cmts. b and c (1998).

2. _Economic Loss Without Personal Injury._ Because product liability law was developed largely to provide compensation to plaintiffs who suffered personal injury, its applicability to other types of harm is limited. An action in strict liability does not lie when the product simply did not

perform as expected. See, e.g., Seely v. White Motor Co., 63 Cal.2d 9, 403 P.2d 145, 45 Cal.Rptr. 17 (1965) (Traynor, C.J.) (truck "galloped" and did not perform properly). Chief Justice Traynor explained, however, that if there was an express warranty (including a relevant misrepresentation regarding the quality of the product), a tort action might be maintained on that basis. The *Seely* case has been followed by a majority of courts, including New Jersey, which originally had rejected it. Alloway v. General Marine Industries, 149 N.J. 620, 695 A.2d 264 (1997). See also Bocre Leasing Corp. v. General Motors Corp., 84 N.Y.2d 685, 645 N.E.2d 1195, 1199, 621 N.Y.S.2d 497 (1995) ("Tort recovery in strict products liability and negligence against a manufacturer should not be available to a downstream purchaser where the claimed losses flow from damage to the property that is the subject of the contract. Transforming manufacturers into insurers, with the empty promise that they can guarantee perpetual and total public safety, by making them liable in tort for all commercial setbacks and adversities is not prudent or sound tort public policy. In such instances, no directly related or commensurate public interest is served or protected by holding manufacturers liable. Tort law should not be bent so far out of its traditional progressive path and discipline by allowing tort lawsuits where the claims at issue are, fundamentally and in all relevant respects, essentially contractual, product-failure controversies. Tort law is not the answer for this kind of loss of commercial bargain.") The New York court and the courts of many other jurisdictions have been strongly influenced by the United States Supreme Court opinion in an admiralty case, East River S.S. Corp. v. Transamerica Delaval, Inc., 476 U.S. 858 (1986). See Chapter 8, Section 3, Pure Economic Loss. Condom users brought suit against the condom manufacturer, seeking recovery of the costs of an unwanted pregnancy. Did the product simply fail to perform as expected or was there physical harm for which the manufacturer should be strictly liable? Cf. Miceli v. Ansell, Inc., 23 F.Supp.2d 929 (N.D.Ind.1998) (court denied motion to dismiss, finding that Indiana would consider pregnancy to be a "harm" for the purposes of its product liability statute).

3. A few courts have recognized an exception to the rule that excludes recovery for pure economic loss when the alleged defect creates an "unreasonable risk" of injury to persons. Under those circumstances, economic losses resulting from damage to the product itself may be compensable. See, e.g., Vulcan Materials Co. v. Driltech, Inc., 306 S.E.2d 253 (Ga.1983) (compensation for defective product itself if it fails in a sudden and calamitous manner). Do you agree with this distinction?

4. *Damage to Property.* Section 402A covers damage to property as well as persons and most courts have agreed with this extension. See, e.g., Morrow v. Caloric Appliance Co., 372 S.W.2d 41 (Mo.1963) (defective stove set fire to a house). When the property is itself destroyed by a defect most courts treat this as an economic loss not recoverable in tort, while some courts treat this as a "property" loss and allow recovery in strict liability. See National Crane Corp. v. Ohio Steel Tube Co., 213 Neb. 782, 332 N.W.2d 39 (1983) (strict liability permitted where damage occurred as a

result of a sudden, violent event); Gherna v. Ford Motor Co., 246 Cal. App.2d 639, 55 Cal.Rptr. 94 (1966).

5.   When the defective material is used in the process of manufacturing another product and that product is ruined as a result, this may be treated as damage to property and recovery will be allowed. See Spence v. Three Rivers Builders & Masonry Supply, Inc., 353 Mich. 120, 90 N.W.2d 873 (1958) (cinder blocks used in a house); Gladiola Biscuit Co. v. Southern Ice Co., 267 F.2d 138 (5th Cir.1959) (glass in ice used in dough). Suppose the owner of a building seeks to recover from asbestos sellers for the costs of abating asbestos insulation from its building. Is this merely the failure of the product to provide safe heat-retention or has other property (the building) been damaged by the asbestos product? See, e.g., Northridge Co. v. W.R. Grace and Co., 162 Wisc.2d 918, 471 N.W.2d 179 (1991). See also Restatement (Third) of Torts: Products Liability § 21 cmt. e (1998) and Ausness, Tort Liability for Asbestos Removal Costs, 73 OR. L. REV. 505 (1994).

6.   When a purchaser such as a retailer suffers economic loss through a tort suit brought against him by a party injured by the product, he usually may shift that loss to the manufacturer by way of an indemnity claim. Should strict liability apply in an indemnity action between the manufacturer of an allegedly defective car and the driver who was seeking reimbursement for the damages he paid to an injured passenger? Cf. Dixon v. Chicago and North Western Transportation Co., 151 Ill.2d 108, 601 N.E.2d 704 (1992) (indemnity not allowed under Illinois law because plaintiff driver was not free of fault in accident). When the manufacturer has sold a retailer bad food and this in turn has driven his customers away, there is a well aged precedent that would allow recovery. See Mazetti v. Armour & Co., 75 Wash. 622, 135 P. 633 (1913).

6.   LEGISLATION AND PRODUCTS LIABILITY

1.   *Uniform Commercial Code.* Article 2 of the Uniform Commercial Code, which governs breach of warranty for the sale of goods has been enacted in all states except Louisiana. Common law and statutory breach of warranty have had an important influence on the development of the law of product liability.

2.   *Restatement (Second) of Torts § 402A.* Beginning in the 1960's, statutes directly applicable to the tort law were enacted in some jurisdictions. For example, three states enacted Restatement (Second) of Torts § 402A through legislation while it was being adopted judicially in most jurisdictions.

3.   *Tort Reform in the 1970's.* During the latter half of the 1970's, liability insurance premiums shot up dramatically. Convinced that the prime cause of the increase in premiums was a dramatic change in the substantive law of product liability in favor of plaintiffs, manufacturers and other suppliers of products sought relief from state legislatures. Many states passed comprehensive statutory schemes, in an emergency climate,

to decrease the size and number of recoveries against manufacturers and sellers. Those changes were principally in the areas of statutes of limitation and repose, the significance of state of the art evidence, the effect of alteration or misuse of the product, and the limitation of strict liability against non-manufacturing sellers. See 17 Trial [No. 11] 92 (Nov. 1981) for a chart of state legislation in effect at that time.

4. *Uniform Product Liability Act.* The same pressures that led state legislators to change product liability law at the state level also affected the Federal government. In 1976, the Ford Administration established a Federal Interagency Task Force on product liability to study the problem. Chaired by Professor Victor Schwartz, the Task Force continued into the Carter Administration and issued a Final Report in November 1977. One of the conclusions of that Final Report was that product liability law would be more stable if, as under the Uniform Commercial Code, there was less variation in the laws of the states. Thus, the Uniform Product Liability Act ("UPLA") was offered as a model for state enactment. Some legislatures have enacted portions of UPLA. When they did, they often modified its contents. Thus, even in these few states, product liability law has retained its variety. Some courts have used UPLA as a basis for changes in common law. See Prentis v. Yale Mfg. Co., page 740.

5. *Tort Reform in the 1980's.* The 1980's saw a shift in approach away from product liability-specific statutes to more broadly applicable tort reform legislation. In 1986 and 1987, 41 states passed some type of tort reform legislation. Those changes were principally in the areas of caps on damages, modification or elimination of joint and several liability, changes in the standards for awarding punitive damages, changes in the collateral source rule, and regulation of attorney contingency fees. In some states, the reform legislation was limited to particular categories of tort liability such as product liability or medical malpractice.

Because many businesses and insurers concluded that the product liability crisis could not be solved on a state by state basis, federal legislation was introduced that would preempt state tort law in a number of areas. A predicate for federal action is that product liability insurance rates are set on a nationwide, not a state-by-state, basis. The factual basis for this rate setting is that, on average, over 70 percent of goods manufactured in a particular state are shipped beyond its borders. Therefore, legislative product liability action in one state can only provide predictability for a limited number of cases for businesses in that state. Proponents of federal legislation argued that product manufacturers need uniform rules to do business in interstate commerce so that rights and obligations with respect to the same product would not vary simply because a person was injured in one state or another. While many in Congress and the Administration agreed that there was a clear basis for federal product liability law, there was considerable controversy about the substance of the proposed legislation. Moreover, with each session of Congress, the focus of the legislation, like the reform movement in the states, drifted away from the core of product liability law—establishing the standard for design defects, manufacturing defects, and defects based on failure to warn—into areas of general tort law such as whether there should be limits or caps on punitive damages and whether the doctrine of joint and several liability should be limited.

When the Republicans took over Congress in 1994, an effort was made to expand the sections dealing with punitive damages and joint and several liability to all tort claims that arose in interstate commerce. Democratic Members found it ironic that Republicans and business groups, usually proponents of states rights, were calling for broad-based federal tort reform, and the effort was doomed. In the 104th Congress, those who supported product liability reform returned to the concept of a bill that would address only product liability claims. After vetoing a version of a new product liability bill, the Clinton Administration indicated that it could support federal product liability legislation that did not contain limits on punitive damages or joint and several liability. At that point, proponents of the legislation differed as to whether this limited legislation was "worth the effort." With the proponents divided, and the opponents united, the movement for general federal product liability reform met its end in the 104th Congress. Limited liability reforms have had more success. For example, the General Aviation Revitalization Act, which applies an 18–year statute of repose for general aviation products, was enacted into law in 1994. In 1998, President Clinton signed the Biomaterials Assurance Access Act, which limits the liability of suppliers of biomaterials to situations where they had violated contract specifications for their products. Curiously, those who made these raw materials were not the bill's strongest advocates. Medical device manufacturers and other companies that needed the raw materials argued that they were unable to obtain them because of the liability exposure of their suppliers and that the lives and well being of those who needed the devices were threatened.

6. *Tort Reform in the 1990's.* The 1990's have seen the proponents of state legislation shift from arguments relating to the availability and affordability of insurance to public policy and "fairness" issues. Arguments based on fairness have been prompted, in part, by the writings of West Virginia Supreme Court Justice Richard Neely, who has observed that elected state appellate judges are prompted to shape law to favor plaintiffs because the injured party lives within a state and the defendant corporation is from out of state. See Neely, The Product Liability Mess (1988) and Blankenship v. General Motors Corp., 185 W.Va. 350, 406 S.E.2d 781 (1991) (court notes that it cannot affect the national tort system by any action it takes in West Virginia to make the system more rational and would only punish West Virginia residents without improving the tort system for anyone else). See also Huber, Liability: The Legal Revolution and Its Consequences (1988) (arguing that the product liability system's "swing" toward the plaintiff has resulted in a chilling effect on the research and production of new and useful products); Garber, "Product Liability and the Economics of Pharmaceuticals and Medical Devices," (RAND 1993). This type of public policy argument was used to support the enactment of product liability laws in several states. This legislation did not

contain strict caps or limits on plaintiffs' rights, but instead focused on outlining the basic causes of action in product liability. Opponents of this legislation argued that there really has not been adverse effects in the product liability system or that these effects have been exaggerated by tort reform proponents. A fundamental question permeating the legislative battle is whether legislatures should have any role in formulating product liability law or whether it should be left to the courts. What are the arguments on either side of this key issue? See Chapter 23, Torts in the Age of Statutes.

7. *Tort Reform in the 21st Century.* In the 21st Century, you will be the consumers and manufacturers of products, the attorneys who represent them in litigation and counsel them in risk prevention, and the judges, regulators, and legislators who make the law relating to products liability. How will you change the law?

CHAPTER XVI

NUISANCE

The term "nuisance" is surrounded by a great deal of legal confusion. The word itself, which is taken over from the French, means nothing more than harm, annoyance or inconvenience. The courts customarily speak of "a" nuisance as if it were a type of conduct on the part of the defendant or a condition created by him. Actually it is neither. The word has reference to a kind of interest invaded, a type of damage or harm. Nuisance is a field of liability, rather than a particular tort.

Nuisance covers two fields of liability—two distinct kinds of damage or harm. The two have little in common, and are unrelated except as each involves the basic idea of causing harm or inconvenience to someone, which is common to all torts. It is only by the accident of historical development that the same word is used to cover the two; but the use of the common term has led to the application of much the same rules to both.

Public Nuisance. The earliest cases involved purprestures, encroachments upon the royal domain or the public highway. An obstruction of the public highway is still a typical public nuisance. The remedy was gradually extended to cover other miscellaneous invasions of the public right. The remedy was exclusively criminal until the 15th Century, when it was first recognized that a private individual who had suffered special damage could maintain a tort action. McRae, Development of Nuisance in the Early Common Law, 1 U.Fla.L.Rev. 27 (1948).

In the United States, public nuisances are now very largely covered by statute. There are many types of specific criminal provisions covering such things as black currant plants, buildings where narcotics are sold, or waters where mosquitoes breed. In addition, many states have broad criminal statutes covering "public nuisances" without attempting to define them, which are construed to include anything that would have been a public nuisance at common law.

Because of its historical development, the traditional view has been that for public nuisance to be a tort justifying private relief it must also be a crime—either a recognized crime at common law or a violation of a legislative provision. Concern for protection of the environment, however, has caused this assumption to be questioned. After considerable debate, the American Law Institute decided to go beyond the statement that a public nuisance is a crime and to define it in terms that would indicate both why the interference with a public right is treated as criminal and why it should be a tort.

The Restatement (Second) of Torts § 821B now defines a public nuisance as "an unreasonable interference with a right common to the general public," and then provides that "circumstances that may sustain a holding that an interference with a public right is unreasonable include the following: (a) whether the conduct involves a substantial interference with the public health, the public safety, the public peace, the public comfort or the public convenience, or (b) whether the conduct is proscribed by a statute, ordinance or administrative regulation, or (c) whether the conduct is of a continuing nature or has produced a permanent or long-lasting effect and, to the actor's knowledge, has a substantial detrimental effect upon the public right."

Private Nuisance. This form of the tort action developed as an unreasonable interference with the use or enjoyment of a property interest in land. It is essentially a tort to an owner or possessor of land. It is distinguished from trespass, in that it did not require a physical entry upon the plaintiff's premises, although it might accompany a trespass.

The interference might be with the physical condition of the premises, as by blasting or vibration that damages a house; with the health of the occupant, as by unsanitary conditions on adjoining property; with his comfort or convenience, as by smoke, odors, noise or heat; or merely with his peace of mind, as in the case of a nearby bawdy house or funeral parlor. A threat of future injury may be treated as a present menace and interference with enjoyment, as in the case of stored explosives or a vicious dog.

Particular conduct may result in both a public and a private nuisance. The plaintiff may then proceed on either ground, or both, to the extent that she can make out her cause of action. Unless the facts show an interference with a public right, or with the use and enjoyment of land, there is simply no nuisance at all.

Philadelphia Electric Company v. Hercules, Inc.

United States Court of Appeals, Third Circuit, 1985.
762 F.2d 303.

A. Leon Higginbotham, Jr., Circuit Judge. This is an appeal from a final judgment of the district court in favor of Philadelphia Electric Company ("PECO") and against Hercules, Inc. ("Hercules") in the amount of $394,910.14, and further ordering Hercules to take all appropriate action to eliminate pollution on a property owned by PECO in Chester, Pennsylvania. The case was tried to a jury on theories of public and private nuisance. For the reasons set forth in the opinion that follows, we will reverse the judgment against Hercules on PECO's claims, and vacate the injunction.
* * *

[The property in question, "the Chester site," had been owned, prior to October 1971, by the Pennsylvania Industrial Chemical Corporation ("PICCO"), where it operated a hydrocarbon resin manufacturing plant. PICCO sold the facility to "Gould" in 1971. Gould sold the site to PECO in 1974. PECO had owned an adjoining site and had full opportunity to inspect and investigate the condition of the property. Subsequently Hercules, Inc. became the successor to PICCO, expressly assuming all debts, obligations and liabilities. This action is therefore held properly brought against Hercules. The court treats the relationship between defendant Hercules and plaintiff PECO as "that of a vendor and remote vendee of land." It holds that the sale of the site was subject to the rule of caveat emptor, being between two commercial corporations with no misrepresentation or concealment and full opportunity to inspect.

In 1980 the Pennsylvania Department of Environmental Resources ("DER") discovered that resinous materials similar to those once produced by PICCO were seeping into the Delaware River and directed PECO to develop and act on a plan to eliminate the situation. In all PECO spent or lost almost $400,000.

PECO brought suit against Hercules for the damages and an injunction requiring defendant to abate any further pollution. The district court granted both. The suit is based on private nuisance, public nuisance and indemnity.]

Restatement (Second) of Torts § 821D defines a "private nuisance" as "a nontrespassory invasion of another's interest in the private use and enjoyment of land." The briefs and arguments, as well as the district court's opinion, 587 F.Supp. at 152–54, give much attention to the questions of whether the condition created by Hercules on the Chester site amounted to a nuisance, and whether Hercules remains liable for the nuisance even after vacating the land. For the purposes of our decision, we may assume that Hercules created a nuisance, and that it remains liable for this condition. See *Restatement (Second) of Torts* § 840A. The crucial and difficult question for us is *to whom* Hercules may be liable.

The parties have cited no case from Pennsylvania or any other jurisdiction, and we have found none, that permits a purchaser of real property to recover from the seller on a private nuisance theory for conditions existing on the very land transferred, and thereby to circumvent limitations on vendor liability inherent in the rule of *caveat emptor.* In a somewhat analogous circumstance, courts have not permitted *tenants* to circumvent traditional limitations on the liability of *lessors* by the expedient of casting their cause of action for defective conditions existing on premises (over which they have assumed control) as one for private nuisance. [Cc] In *Harris v. Lewistown Trust Co.,* 326 Pa. 145, 191 A. 34 (1937), [c] the Supreme Court of Pennsylvania held that the doctrine that a landlord not in possession may be liable for injuries resulting from a "condition amounting to a nuisance" is confined to "the owners or occupants of near-by property, persons temporarily on such property, or persons on a neighboring highway or other places."[6] [C] Recovery on this theory was not available to tenants or their invitees: "A breach of duty owed to one class of persons cannot create a cause of action in favor of a person not within the

---

6. *Cf. Restatement (Second) of Torts* § 840A and comment c thereto ("If the vendor or lessor has himself created on the land a condition that results in a nuisance, * * * *his responsibility toward those outside of his* land is such that he is not free to terminate his liability to them * * * by passing the land itself on to a third person.") (emphasis added).

class. A plaintiff must show that as to him there was a breach of duty." [C] 326 Pa. at 152, 191 A. at 38. Similarly, under the doctrine of *caveat emptor* Hercules owed only a limited duty to Gould and, in turn, to PECO. PECO concedes that this duty was not violated. PECO cannot recover in private nuisance for the violation of a duty Hercules may have owed to others— namely, its neighbors.

We believe that this result is consonant with the historical role of private nuisance law as a means of efficiently resolving conflicts between *neighboring,* contemporaneous land uses. * * * Neighbors, unlike the purchasers of the land upon which a nuisance exists, have no opportunity to protect themselves through inspection and negotiation. The record shows that PECO acted as a sophisticated and responsible purchaser—inquiring into the past use of the Chester site, and inspecting it carefully. We find it inconceivable that the price it offered Gould did not reflect the possibility of environmental risks, even if the exact condition giving rise to this suit was not discovered. * * *

Where, as here, the rule of *caveat emptor* applies, allowing a vendee a cause of action for private nuisance for conditions existing on the land transferred—where there has been no fraudulent concealment—would in effect negate the market's allocations of resources and risks, and subject vendors who may have originally sold their land at appropriately discounted prices to unbargained-for liability to remote vendees. * * * Such an extension of common law doctrine is particularly hazardous in an area, such as environmental pollution, where Congress and the state legislatures are actively seeking to achieve a socially acceptable definition of rights and liabilities. We conclude that PECO did not have a cause of action against Hercules sounding in private nuisance.

The doctrine of public nuisance protects interests quite different from those implicated in actions for private nuisance, and PECO's claim for public nuisance requires separate consideration. Whereas private nuisance requires an invasion of another's interest in the private use and enjoyment of land, a public nuisance is "an unreasonable interference with a right common to the general public." Restatement (Second) of Torts § 821B(1). An action for public nuisance may lie even though neither the plaintiff nor the defendant acts in the exercise of private property rights.[11] As William Prosser once wrote: "There are, then, two and only two kinds of nuisance, which are quite unrelated except in the vague general way that each of them causes inconvenience to someone, and in the common name, which naturally has led the courts to apply to the two some of the same substantive rules of law. A private nuisance is narrowly restricted to the invasion of interests in the use and enjoyment of land. It is only a tort, and the remedy for it lies exclusively with the individual whose rights have been disturbed. A public nuisance is a species of catch-all low-grade

---

11. Thus, commercial fishermen and clam diggers operating in public waters can recover on a public nuisance theory for harm to the waters and marine life caused by oil discharged from a tanker in transit. *See Burgess v. M/V Tamano,* 370 F.Supp. 247 (D.Me. 1973).

criminal offense, consisting of an interference with the rights of the community at large, which may include anything from the blocking of a highway to a gaming-house or indecent exposure. Although as in the case of other crimes, the normal remedy is in the hands of the state, a public nuisance may also be a private one, when it interferes with private land. The seeds of confusion were sown when courts began to hold that a tort action would lie even for a purely public nuisance if the plaintiff had suffered 'particular damage.' " Prosser, Private Action for Public Nuisance, 52 Va.L.Rev. 997, 999 (1966).

In analyzing the public nuisance claim, we are not concerned with the happenstance that PECO now occupies the very land PICCO occupied when it allegedly created the condition that has polluted the Delaware River waters, or that the continuing source of that pollution is located on that land. The question before us is whether PECO has *standing* to bring an individual action for damages or injunctive relief for interference with a public right.

Restatement (Second) of Torts § 821C(1) provides: "In order to recover damages in an individual action for a public nuisance, one must have suffered harm of a kind different from that suffered by other members of the public exercising the right common to the general public that was the subject of interference."

The same requirements apply to individual plaintiffs seeking injunctive relief. Restatement (Second) of Torts § 821C(2); Prosser, *supra,* 52 Va. L.Rev. at 1006. PECO argues that the expense it incurred in cleaning up the offending condition constituted the harm requisite for standing to sue for public nuisance. We disagree. Though pecuniary harm certainly may be harm of a different kind from that suffered by the general public, see Restatement (Second) of Torts § 821C comment h,[14] we find in this case no allegation or evidence that PECO suffered this harm "exercising the right common to the general public that was the subject of interference." The public right that was interfered with was the right to "pure water". [C] PECO does not allege that it used the waters of the Delaware River itself, or that it was directly harmed in any way by the pollution of those waters. Thus, this is not a case "where an established business made commercial use of the public right with which the defendant interfered." [C] If PECO— as a riparian landowner—had suffered damage to its land or its operations as a result of the pollution of the Delaware, it would possibly have a claim for public nuisance. But the condition of the Chester site was not the *result* of the pollution, it was the *cause* of it. DER required PECO, as owner of the

14. It may be that under Pennsylvania law harm of a *magnitude* greater than that suffered by the general public is sufficient to confer standing. See Pennsylvania Society for the Prevention of Cruelty to Animals v. Bravo Enterprises, 428 Pa. 350, 360, 237 A.2d 342, 348 (1968). This distinction is not, however, important in the instant case. As the discussion that follows points out, even if PECO has suffered a harm both different in kind and greater in degree than that suffered by the general public, it has not suffered that harm in the exercise of a right common to the general public. Cf. Burgess v. M/V Tamano, 370 F.Supp. 247 (D.Me.1973) (businesses operating on beach did not have standing to sue for pollution of swimming waters, even though they lost customers as a result).

Chester site, to remove the sources of the pollution. PECO has been specially harmed only in the exercise of its private property rights over the Chester site. PECO has suffered no "particular damage" in the exercise of a right common to the general public, and it lacks standing to sue for public nuisance.

* * *

We emphasize that our decision today should not be interpreted as standing for the general proposition that a party that contaminates land, or the successors to its assets, can escape liability by the expedient of selling the land. To the contrary, it would seem that there are many avenues by which such a party may be held accountable.[20] We hold only that in this case the purchaser of that land, PECO—though we recognize that it acted as a responsible corporate citizen—had no cause of action against the vendor's successor, Hercules, for private nuisance, public nuisance, or common law indemnity.

For the foregoing reasons, the injunction requiring Hercules to clean up the Chester site will be vacated, and the judgment of the district court on PECO's claims against Hercules will be reversed.

NOTES AND QUESTIONS

1. In public nuisance cases, the problem of distinguishing what is difference in "kind" and what is difference in "degree" has given courts considerable difficulty. Consider the following:

A. Defendant obstructs a public highway, forcing travelers to detour. Plaintiff, on his way to work, has to travel over the highway twice a day. Cf. Borton v. Mangus, 93 Kan. 719, 145 P. 835 (1915).

B. The same facts, except that plaintiff drives into the unguarded and unlighted obstruction, and sustains personal injury. Cf. Leahan v. Cochran, 178 Mass. 566, 60 N.E. 382 (1901); Schnitzer v. Excelsior Powder Mfg. Co., 160 S.W. 282 (Mo.App. 1912).

C. The same facts, except that the obstructed highway cuts off ingress and egress to plaintiff's land. Pilgrim Plywood Co. v. Melendy, 110 Vt. 12, 1 A.2d 700 (1938). Is it enough that there is serious interference? Gates v. Bloomfield, 243 Iowa 671, 53 N.W.2d 279 (1952).

D. Noise and smoke from defendant's factory amounting to a public nuisance also interfere seriously with plaintiff's use and enjoyment of his land. Soap Corp. of America v. Reynolds, 178 F.2d 503 (5th Cir.1949); Morris v. Haledon, 24 N.J.Super. 171, 93 A.2d 781 (1952).

2. Why should it be necessary to have an injury different in kind from that of the general public? Is it because the harm suffered by the public is so trivial? Or because there would be such a flood of suits? Why not allow a class action? Or permit one member of the public to sue for an injunction that would eliminate the

---

20. For example, Hercules could be liable to neighboring landowners in private nuisance, or to users of Delaware River waters in public nuisance. DER or the federal Environmental Protection Agency may be able to proceed directly against Hercules on statutory or public nuisance theories.

nuisance? In most states the district attorney or other official may sue for abatement. See, e.g., State ex rel. Swann v. Pack, 527 S.W.2d 99 (Tenn.1975), cert. denied, 424 U.S. 954 (1976) (snake-handling).

3. Public nuisance has had a close connection with environmental concerns, although the "difference in kind" rule has limited its use by private citizens in seeking to control environmental hazards. More recently, however, the action has been employed in contexts well beyond those usually contemplated as within the bailiwick of public nuisance. It has been used in a number of cases where the courts have permitted public nuisance claims to be brought against urban street gangs and gun manufacturers and distributors. In the former category the California Supreme Court, in People ex rel. Gallo v. Acuna, 929 P.2d 596 (1997), enjoined, at the suit of city of San Jose, a widely described number of street gang members from conducting their violent and intimidating gang-like activities in a San Jose neighborhood. The court found that citizens had suffered particular damage through the gang activities that constituted a public nuisance. Other cities have considered similar claims, including Austin, Texas and Phoenix, Arizona. In the latter category of gun liability suits, cities have brought public nuisance actions against the handgun industry seeking reimbursement for police, emergency and medical costs stemming from accidental shootings and homicides. In the Chicago suit, see 17 No. 6 Prod. Liab. L. & Strategy 6, December 1998, it was alleged that the gun manufacturers, distributors, and gun shops create a public nuisance because they "knowingly design, market, and distribute firearms in order to facilitate their illegal entry into and possession in Chicago, where they are illegal to possess, and where they are often used in the commission of crimes."

4. *Use of Other Tort Remedies for Environmental Protection.* Resort has also been made to other tort actions than nuisance, with varying degrees of success. Consider the following: Trespass, Davis v. Georgia Pacific Corp., 251 Or. 239, 445 P.2d 481 (1968) (air pollution). Negligence (adds little, since nuisance will usually lie if negligence is available), Hagy v. Allied Chemical & Dye Corp., 122 Cal.App.2d 361, 265 P.2d 86 (1953) (poisonous smog); but where the loss is purely economic, a public nuisance analysis may permit recovery where negligence would not. See State of Louisiana ex rel. Guste v. M/V Testbank, 752 F.2d 1019 (5th Cir.1985). Riparian rights (also overlaps nuisance), Parker v. American Woolen Co., 195 Mass. 591, 81 N.E. 468 (1907). Strict liability for abnormally dangerous activity (also overlaps nuisance), Young v. Darter, 363 P.2d 829 (Okl.1961) (crop dusting). Products liability, City of Chicago v. General Motors Corp., 467 F.2d 1262 (7th Cir.1972) (exhaust fumes from automobiles).

Morgan v. High Penn Oil Co.

Supreme Court of North Carolina, 1953.
238 N.C. 185, 77 S.E.2d 682.

Civil action to recover temporary damages for a private nuisance, and to abate such nuisance by injunction.

[Plaintiff owned a tract of nine acres of land, on which he had his dwelling, a restaurant, and accommodations for thirty-two trailers. Defendant owned an adjoining tract on which it operated an oil refinery, at a distance of 1,000 feet from plaintiff's dwelling. Plaintiff's evidence was that for some hours on two or three different days each week the refinery emitted nauseating gases and odors in great quantities, which invaded plaintiff's land and other tracts of land within a distance of two miles, in such density as to render persons of ordinary sensitiveness uncomfortable and sick. This substantially impaired the use and enjoyment of plaintiff's land. Defendant failed to put an end to this atmospheric pollution after notice and demand from plaintiff to abate it.

Defendant's evidence was that the oil refinery was a modern plant of the type approved, known and in general use for renovating used lubricating oils; that it was not so constructed or operated as to give out noxious gases or odors in annoying quantities, and that it had not annoyed the plaintiff or other persons save on a single occasion when it suffered a brief mechanical breakdown.

The trial judge submitted to the jury the question whether the refinery was so maintained and operated as to create a nuisance. The jury returned a special verdict saying that there was a nuisance, and assessed plaintiff's damages at $2,500. The trial court entered judgment on this verdict, and enjoined defendant from continuing the nuisance. Defendant appealed.]

ERVIN, JUSTICE. * * * [The] defendant assigns as error the disallowance of its motion for a compulsory nonsuit. * * *

The High Penn Oil Company contends that the evidence is not sufficient to establish either an actionable or an abatable private nuisance. This contention rests on a twofold argument somewhat alternative in character. The High Penn Oil Company asserts primarily that private nuisances are classified as nuisances *per se* or at law, and nuisances *per accidens* or in fact; that when one carries on an oil refinery upon premises in his rightful occupation, he conducts a lawful enterprise, and for that reason does not maintain a nuisance *per se* or at law; that in such case the oil refinery can constitute a nuisance *per accidens* or in fact to the owner of neighboring land if, but only if, it is constructed or operated in a negligent manner; that there was no testimony at the trial tending to show that the oil refinery was constructed or operated in a negligent manner; and that consequently the evidence does not suffice to establish the existence of either an actionable or an abatable private nuisance. * * *

A nuisance *per se* or at law is an act, occupation or structure which is a nuisance at all times and under any circumstances, regardless of location or surroundings. [Cc] Nuisances *per accidens* or in fact are those which become nuisances by reason of their location, or by reason of the manner in which they are constructed, maintained, or operated. [Cc] The High Penn Oil Company also asserts with complete correctness that an oil refinery is a lawful enterprise and for that reason cannot be a nuisance *per se* or at law. [Cc] The High Penn Oil Company falls into error, however, when it takes the position that an oil refinery cannot become a nuisance *per accidens* or in fact unless it is constructed or operated in a negligent manner.

Negligence and nuisance are distinct fields of liability. [Cc] While the same act or omission may constitute negligence and also give rise to a private nuisance *per accidens* or in fact, and thus the two torts may coexist and be practically inseparable, a private nuisance *per accidens* or in fact may be created or maintained without negligence. [Cc] Most private nuisances *per accidens* or in fact are intentionally created or maintained, and are redressed by the courts without allegation or proof of negligence. [Cc] * * *

Much confusion exists in respect to the legal basis of liability in the law of private nuisance because of the deplorable tendency of the courts to call everything a nuisance, and let it go at that. [Cc] The confusion on this score vanishes in large part, however, when proper heed is paid to the sound proposition that private nuisance is a field of tort liability rather than a single type of tortious conduct; that the feature which gives unity to this field of tort liability is the interest invaded, namely, the interest in the use and enjoyment of land; that any substantial nontrespassory invasion of another's interest in the private use and enjoyment of land by any type of liability forming conduct is a private nuisance; that the invasion which subjects a person to liability for private nuisance may be either intentional or unintentional; that a person is subject to liability for an intentional invasion when his conduct is unreasonable under the circumstances of the particular case; and that a person is subject to liability for an unintentional invasion when his conduct is negligent, reckless or ultrahazardous. [Cc].

An invasion of another's interest in the use and enjoyment of land is intentional in the law of private nuisance when the person whose conduct is a question as a basis for liability acts for the purpose of causing it, or knows that it is resulting from his conduct, or knows that it is substantially certain to result from his conduct. Restatement (Second) of the Law of Torts, § 825; [cc]. A person who intentionally creates or maintains a private nuisance is liable for the resulting injury to others regardless of the degree of care or skill exercised by him to avoid such injury. [Cc] One of America's greatest jurists, the late Benjamin N. Cardozo, made this illuminating observation on this aspect of the law:

"Nuisance as a concept of the law has more meanings than one. The primary meaning does not involve the element of negligence as one of its essential factors. One acts sometimes at one's peril. In such circumstances, the duty to desist is absolute whenever conduct, if persisted in, brings damage to another. Illustrations are abundant. One who emits noxious fumes or gases day by day in the running of his factory may be liable to his neighbor though he has taken all available precautions. He is not to do such things at all, whether he is negligent or careful." McFarlane v. City of Niagara Falls, 247 N.Y. 340, 160 N.E. 391.

When the evidence is interpreted in the light most favorable to the plaintiff, it suffices to support a finding that in operating the oil refinery the High Penn Oil Company intentionally and unreasonably caused noxious gases and odors to escape onto the nine acres of the plaintiff to such a degree as to impair in a substantial manner the plaintiff's use and enjoyment of his land. This being so, the evidence is ample to establish the existence of an actionable private nuisance, entitling the plaintiff to recover temporary damages from the High Penn Oil Company. [Cc] When the evidence is taken in the light most favorable to the plaintiff, it also suffices to warrant the additional inference that the High Penn Oil Company intends to operate the oil refinery in the future in the same manner as in the past; * * * and that the issuance of an appropriate injunction is necessary to protect the plaintiff against the threatened irreparable injury. * * *

For the reasons given, the evidence is sufficient to withstand the motion of the High Penn Oil Company for a compulsory nonsuit.

[A new trial was ordered, however, because of an error in instructions to the jury.]

NOTES AND QUESTIONS

1. *Intentional* nuisances include such cases as the principal case, where the defendant knows that his conduct is interfering with the plaintiff's right or that it is substantially certain to do so.

2. *Negligence* is the basis of liability when the defendant has not intentionally interfered with the interest protected but has failed to exercise reasonable care to avoid the interference. Property may be allowed to fall into disrepair, so that a private nuisance is created. Schindler v. Standard Oil Co., 207 Mo.App. 190, 232 S.W. 735 (1921) (leaking waterpipe); Rose v. Standard Oil Co., 56 R.I. 272, 185 A. 251 (1936) (percolation of petroleum products). Or the defendant may fail to discover and abate a condition created by a third party. Lamb v. Roberts, 196 Ala. 679, 72 So. 309 (1916); City of Phoenix v. Harlan, 75 Ariz. 290, 255 P.2d 609 (1953). Note that an activity carried on upon adjoining property that does not affect the use and enjoyment of plaintiff's property but makes it less marketable will not support a private nuisance claim: Golen v. Union Corporation, 718 A.2d 298 (Pa. 1998) (plaintiff could not find a buyer for its site because defendant's adjoining site was contaminated with PCB's).

3. *Strict Liability*. A leading case is Heeg v. Licht, 80 N.Y. 579 (1880), holding defendant liable for damage caused by the explosion of a powder magazine that had existed for some time. Accord: Liber v. Flor, 160 Colo. 7, 415 P.2d 332 (1966) (boxes of dynamite stored). What about a vicious dog? Browning v. Belue, 22 Ala.App. 437, 116 So. 509 (1928).

4. Recall the principle of strict liability articulated in Rylands v. Fletcher, Chapter 14 (strict liability for escape of dangerous substances from defendant's land). Strict liability has been applied, without the invocation of the *Rylands* rule, when the activity poses extreme danger to plaintiff's use and enjoyment of his property. See Prosser, The Principle of Rylands v. Fletcher, in Prosser, Selected Topics on the Law of Torts 135 (1953).

Carpenter v. The Double R Cattle Company, Inc.

Supreme Court of Idaho, 1985.
108 Idaho 602, 701 P.2d 222.

BAKES, JUSTICE. * * * Plaintiff appellants are homeowners who live near a cattle feedlot owned and operated by respondents. Appellants filed a complaint in March, 1978, alleging that the feedlot had been expanded in 1977 to accommodate the feeding of approximately 9,000 cattle. Appellants further alleged that "the spread and accumulation of manure, pollution of river and ground water, odor, insect infestation, increased concentration of birds, . . . dust and noise" allegedly caused by the feedlot constituted a nuisance. After a trial on the merits a jury found that the feedlot did not constitute a nuisance. The trial court then also made findings and conclusions that the feedlot did not constitute a nuisance. * * *

The case was assigned to the Court of Appeals which reversed and remanded for a new trial. The basis for this reversal was that the trial court did not give a jury instruction based upon subsection (b) of Section 826 of the Restatement (Second) of Torts. That subsection allows for a finding of a nuisance even though the gravity of harm is outweighed by the utility of the conduct if the harm is "serious" and the payment of damages is "feasible" without forcing the business to discontinue.

This Court granted defendant's petition for review. We hold that the instructions which the trial court gave were not erroneous, being consistent with our prior case law and other persuasive authority. We further hold that the trial court did not err in not giving an instruction based on subsection (b) of Section 826 of the Second Restatement, which does not represent the law in the State of Idaho. * * *

The Court of Appeals * * * adopted the new subsection (b) of Section 826 of the Second Restatement partially because of language in Koseris [v. J.R. Simplot Co., 82 Idaho 263, 352 P.2d 235 (1960)], which reads: "We are constrained to hold that the trial court erred in sustaining objections to those offers of proof [evidence of utility of conduct], since they were relevant as bearing upon the issue whether respondents, in seeking injunctive relief, were pursuing the proper remedy; nevertheless, on the theory of damages which respondents had waived, the ruling was correct." 82 Idaho at 270, 352 P.2d at 239.

The last phrase of the quote, relied on by the Court of Appeals, is clearly *dictum,* since the question of utility of conduct in a nuisance action for damages was not at issue in *Koseris.* It is very doubtful that this Court's *dictum* in *Koseris* was intended to make such a substantial change in the nuisance law. * * * The case of McNichols v. J.R. Simplot Co., 74 Idaho 321, 262 P.2d 1012 (1953) should be viewed as the law in Idaho that in a nuisance action seeking damages the interests of the community, which would include the utility of the conduct, should be considered in the determination of the existence of a nuisance. The trial court's instructions in the present case were entirely consistent with *McNichols*. A plethora of other modern cases are in accord. * * *

The State of Idaho is sparsely populated and its economy depends largely upon the benefits of agriculture, lumber, mining and industrial development. To eliminate the utility of conduct and other factors listed by the trial court from the criteria to be considered in determining whether a nuisance exists, as the appellant has argued throughout this appeal, would place an unreasonable burden upon these industries. We see no policy reasons which should compel this Court to accept appellant's argument and depart from our present law. Accordingly, the judgment of the district court is affirmed and the Court of Appeals decision is set aside. * * *

BISTLINE, JUSTICE, dissenting. * * * I applaud the efforts of the Court of Appeals to modernize the law of nuisance in this state. I am not in the least persuaded to join the majority with its narrow view of nuisance law as expressed in the majority opinion.

The majority today continues to adhere to ideas on the law of nuisance that should have gone out with the use of buffalo chips as fuel. We have before us today homeowners complaining of a nearby feedlot—not a small operation, but rather a feedlot which accommodates 9,000 cattle. The homeowners advanced the theory that after the expansion of the feedlot in 1977, the odor, manure, dust, insect infestation and increased concentration of birds which accompanied all of the foregoing, constituted a nuisance. If the odoriferous quagmire created by 9,000 head of cattle is *not* a nuisance, it is difficult for me to imagine what is. * * *

I agree wholeheartedly that the interests of the community should be considered in determining the existence of a nuisance. However, where this primitive rule of law fails is in recognizing that in our society, while it may be desirable to have a serious nuisance continue because the utility of the operation causing the nuisance is great, at the same time, those directly impacted by the serious nuisance deserve some compensation for the invasion they suffer as a result of the continuation of the nuisance. This is exactly what the more progressive provisions of § 826(b) of the Restatement (Second) of Torts addresses. Clearly, § 826(b) recognizes that the continuation of the serious harm must remain feasible. See especially comment on clause (b), subpart f of § 826 of the Restatement. What § 826(b) adds is a method of compensating those who must suffer the invasion without putting out of business the source or cause of the invasion. This does not strike me as a particularly adventuresome or far-reaching rule of law. In fact, the fairness of it is overwhelming. * * *

We should not be adopting a rule of preference which suggests that if the community interest is preferred any other interest must be disregarded. Instead, § 826(b) accommodates adverse interests by contemplating continuation of the facility which creates the nuisance while compensating those who suffer the direct impact of the nuisance—in the instant case the homeowners who live in the vicinity of the feedlot.

The majority's rule today suggests that part of the cost of industry, agriculture or development must be borne by those unfortunate few who have the fortuitous luck to live in the immediate vicinity of a nuisance producing facility. Frankly, I think this naive economic view is ridiculous in both its simplicity and its outdated view of modern economic society. The "cost" of a product includes not only the amount it takes to produce such a product but also includes the external costs: the damage done to the environment through pollution of air or water is an example of an external cost. In the instant case, the nuisance suffered by the homeowners should be considered an external cost of operating a feedlot and producing beef for public consumption. I do not believe that a few should be required to pay this extra cost of doing business by going uncompensated for a nuisance of this sort. * * *

The majority today blithely suggests that because the State of Idaho is sparsely populated and because our economy is largely dependent on agriculture, lumber, mining and industrial development, we should forego compensating those who suffer a serious invasion. If humans are such a rare item in this state, maybe there is all the more reason to protect them from the discharge of industry. At a minimum, we should compensate those who suffer a nuisance at the hands of industry and agriculture. What the majority overlooks is that the cost of development should not be absorbed by few, but rather should be spread out and paid by all. I am not convinced that agriculture or industry will be put out of business by requiring compensation for the nuisance they generate. * * *

The decision of the Court of Appeals is an outstanding example of a judicial opinion which comes from a truly exhaustive and analytical review. See 105 Idaho 320, 669 P.2d 643 (1983). * * *

[The decision was 3 to 2.]

NOTES AND QUESTIONS

1.   Judicial balancing of factors in the determination of liability is redolent of the central test in negligence articulated by Learned Hand. An example of this reasoning is Smith v. Staso Milling Co., 18 F.2d 736 (2d Cir.1927). The approach was adopted in Copart Industries, Inc. v. Consolidated Edison Co. of New York, Inc., 41 N.Y.2d 564, 362 N.E.2d 968, 394 N.Y.S.2d 169 (1977). But in Jost v. Dairyland Power Cooperative, 45 Wis.2d 164, 172 N.W.2d 647 (1969), the court was hostile to a balancing test when the nuisance was intentional and the damage "substantial."

2.   Liability rules in nuisance thus govern the use of property. The framework of the rules reveal this underlying objective: Michelman, Property, Utility and Fairness, 80 Harv.L.Rev. 1165 (1967); Epstein, Nuisance Law: Corrective Justice and Its Utilitarian Constraints, 8 J.Leg.Stud. 49 (1979). Note that it was the application of liability rules to competing uses of property that led Ronald Coase to his Nobel prize scholarship in The Problem of Social Cost, 3 J.L. & Econ. 1 (1960). Legal rules, however, may be of limited influence in guiding the behavior of neighbors whose use of land conflicts, see Ellickson, Order Without Law: How Neighbors Settle Disputes (1991) (informal social norms are chosen outside the shadow of the law whose content maximizes the objective welfare of group members). For a reassessment of the scholarship, see Social Norms, Social Meanings, and the Economic Analysis of Law: A Conference Sponsored by the University of Chicago Law School, 27 J. Leg. Stud. 537 (1998).

3.   Recurring circumstances establish doctrines in nuisance law:

A.   *Hypersensitivity.* It is generally held that the harm must be of a kind that would be suffered by a normal person in the community. Rogers v. Elliott, 146 Mass. 349, 15 N.E. 768 (1888) (plaintiff, in highly nervous condition from sunstroke, affected by ringing of church bell); Beckman v. Marshall, 85 So.2d 552 (Fla.1956) (noise of children playing in nursery); Venuto v. Owens–Corning Fiberglass Corp., 22 Cal.App.3d 116, 99 Cal.Rptr. 350 (1971) (allergic reactions). Jenkins v. CSX Transportation, Inc., 906 S.W.2d 460 (Tenn.App.1995) (allergic reaction to creosote).

Suppose that most people in the vicinity are hardened to the discomfort of noise, smoke, dust, vibration or odors from the defendant's factory, and do not object. Does this prevent the plaintiff from maintaining an action for a nuisance, if a normal person would be affected?

B. *Sensitive Uses of Land.* What if the defendant engages in an activity that is normally harmless to his neighbors, but the plaintiff is making an abnormally sensitive use of his land, which is adversely affected? Defendant operates a race track at night, and his flood lights, directed downward, are reflected with a light approximately equal to that of the full moon. This would be inoffensive to the ordinary landowner in the vicinity; but the plaintiff has an outdoor motion picture screen, on which his pictures are made less visible, and he loses customers. Is defendant liable on the basis of nuisance? Amphitheaters, Inc. v. Portland Meadows, 184 Or. 336, 198 P.2d 847 (1948).

Plaintiff has installed an effective solar heating system on the roof of his house. Defendant proposes to construct a house on adjoining land that will shade the heating system and impair its operation and refuses to change the location of the house sufficiently to avoid the shading. Plaintiff sues for an injunction. What problems are raised? See Prah v. Maretti, 108 Wis.2d 223, 321 N.W.2d 182 (1982) (nuisance liability), but cf. Tenn v. 889 Associates, Ltd., 127 N.H. 321, 500 A.2d 366 (1985) (nuisance liability applicable but not established).

C. *Locality.* In Euclid v. Ambler Realty Co., 272 U.S. 365, 388 (1926), the case in which the Supreme Court first upheld the constitutionality of zoning legislation, Justice Sutherland said: "A nuisance may be merely a right thing in the wrong place, like a pig in the parlor instead of the barnyard." It also is important where the barnyard is located. Thus, in William Aldred's Case, 9 Co.Rep. 576, 77 Eng.Rep. 816 (1610), one of the very first reported cases on private nuisance, the action was brought for maintaining a hogstye next to the plaintiff's house. Defendant "moved in arrest of judgment, that the building of the house for hogs was necessary for the sustenance of man; and one ought not to have so delicate a nose, that he cannot bear the smell of hogs * * * but it was resolved that the action for it is * * * well maintainable."

4. *Right to Farm Statutes.* Modern nuisance law has moved away from fault-based liability toward a utilitarian model of liability that emphasizes economic efficiency. Right to Farm Statutes have been enacted in all fifty states and represent a doctrinal return to the fault-based tradition of nuisance law. See Alexander A. Reinert, The Right to Farm: Hog-tied and Nuisance–Bound, 73 N.Y.U. L. Rev. 1694 (1998). They follow a pattern of preventing new residents from restricting established agricultural practices. See Leaf River Forest Prod., Inc. v. Ferguson, 662 So. 2d 648, 661 (Miss.1995). The intent of the legislature is to prevent the encroaching urban population from destroying farmland by placing the blame on plaintiffs who "come to the nuisance," and therefore, should not be given a remedy at law. See Spur Industries v. Del E. Webb Development Co., 494 P.2d 700 (Ariz.1972), infra page 826.

5. The judicial function of zoning via liability rules calls for an examination of its relationship with public zoning regulations and environmental agency controls. On these questions see Ellickson, Alternatives to Zoning, Covenants, Nuisance Rules, and Fines as Land Use Controls, 40 U.Chi.L.Rev. 681 (1973). Constitutional constraints apply to public land use control. See Lucas v. South Carolina Coastal Council, 505 U.S. 1003 (1992).

Winget v. Winn–Dixie Stores, Inc.

Supreme Court of South Carolina, 1963.
242 S.C. 152, 130 S.E.2d 363.

LEWIS, JUSTICE. Plaintiffs instituted this action for damages alleged to have been sustained from the location and operation by the defendants of a grocery supermarket in such a manner as to constitute a nuisance and for an order perpetually restraining the defendants from using the property where the supermarket was located for a retail grocery business or for any other business purpose. The trial of the case resulted in a judgment in favor of the plaintiffs for the sum of $5,000, actual damages, and a denial by the trial judge of injunctive relief. From the judgment entered in favor of the plaintiffs, the defendants have appealed. * * *

The home of the plaintiffs is located in Sumter, South Carolina, adjacent to a grocery supermarket operated by the defendant Winn–Dixie Stores, Inc., and managed at the time of the institution of this action by the defendant John Lloyd. The supermarket began operations on October 1, 1959 and this action was instituted about six weeks later. * * *

The plaintiffs have alleged, therefore, that the supermarket in the instant case was a nuisance because of both (1) its location and (2) the manner of its operation. In ruling upon the motion of the defendants for a directed verdict the lower court in effect held that there was no evidence to sustain the allegations that the supermarket was a nuisance because of its location, but submitted the issue to the jury as to whether the store was operated in such a manner as to cause injury or damage to plaintiffs. * * * The property of the plaintiffs is located on Baker Street immediately to the rear of the store lot. * * *

The business of the defendants is a lawful one and was located in an area which had been zoned by the City of Sumter for retail business and at a location which the Zoning Board determined to be suitable for a retail grocery. The record shows that every requirement of the municipal authorities was met in establishing the business in question, both in the location and the construction of the building. There is no evidence that the building was constructed in such manner as to interfere with the rights of others. Under such circumstances, it cannot be held that the location of the business in the area in question constituted a nuisance.

The fact, however, that one has been issued a license or permit to conduct a business at a particular location cannot protect the licensee who operates the business in such a manner as to constitute a nuisance. * * *

An owner of property even in the conduct of a lawful business thereon is subject to reasonable limitations. In the operation of such business he must not unreasonably interfere with the health or comfort of neighbors or with their right to the enjoyment of their property. If a lawful business is operated in an unlawful or unreasonable manner so as to produce material injury or great annoyance to others or unreasonably interferes with the lawful use and enjoyment of their property, it will constitute a nuisance. [C]

On the other hand, every annoyance or disturbance of a landowner from the use made of property by a neighbor does not constitute a nuisance. The question is not whether plaintiffs have been annoyed or disturbed by the operation of the business in question, but whether there has been an injury to their legal rights. People who live in organized communities must of necessity suffer some inconvenience and annoyance from their neighbors and must submit to annoyances consequent upon the reasonable use of property by others. * * *

In the instant case the conflict is between the rights of the plaintiffs who reside in a residential area adjacent to a district zoned for retail business and those of the defendants who operate a retail grocery supermarket in such business area. The supermarket was located in an area zoned by the City for the conduct of such business and the normal and necessary incidents to the operation thereof cannot be condemned as a nuisance.

The plaintiffs, among other things complain that (1) the store has attracted crowds of people, and many automobiles which caused noise, unhealthy fumes, blocked traffic and generally disturbed the peace and quiet of the community, and (2) trash trucks and street sweepers operated on the premises at late night hours.

In determining the respective rights of the parties in this case, it cannot be properly held that the normal traffic and noise caused by customers going to and from the supermarket would constitute a basis for declaring the operation of the business a nuisance. Of course, the purpose of the business of the defendants is to sell merchandise and in doing so to attract to their store as many customers as possible. It is a natural consequence and incident of the operation of the supermarket that there will be an increase in the number of people visiting the area.

The testimony shows that the store is operated only on week days, opening for business at 8:30 a.m. each day and never closing later than 7:30 p.m. While the record shows that the operation of the supermarket has caused an increase in the number of people and automobiles coming into the area, there is nothing to show that there was any mass entrance to or exodus from the store at unreasonable hours. On the contrary, the only reasonable inference from the record is that the traffic to and from the business was the normal traffic of patrons visiting such a grocery store over the usual business day. There is no basis for holding that the normal traffic and noise caused by customers going to and from the supermarket constituted a nuisance.

Neither do we think that the operation of trash trucks and street sweepers in connection with the removal of trash and garbage, under the facts here, can form the basis of a finding of a nuisance. * * * There is nothing to indicate that such acts were other than the usual and normal operations of the City in the gathering and removal of trash and garbage. * * *

However, with regard to other allegations of the complaint, we think that there was some evidence requiring the submission of those issues to the jury for determination. The record shows that the defendants erected fans on their building in connection with the air conditioning equipment. These fans were so directed as to blow against the trees and shrubbery on plaintiffs' property causing some damage and inconvenience. There was also some testimony that, at least, for a while after opening the supermarket, the floodlights on defendants' lot cast a bright glare over the property of plaintiffs until late at night so as to disturb the plaintiffs in the enjoyment of their home, that obnoxious odors were created from the garbage which accumulated at defendants' store, and that paper and trash from the defendants' garbage was permitted to escape onto plaintiffs' lot to an unusual extent. The record gives rise to a reasonable inference that such acts were not normal or necessary incidents of the operation of the business. We think that the foregoing testimony presented a jury issue and that the trial judge properly refused the defendants' motion for a directed verdict. * * *

The remaining issues arise under the defendants' motion for a new trial. It is contended that a new trial should be granted because of the refusal of the trial court to strike the testimony of the witness R.E. Graham relative to depreciation in value of the property of the plaintiffs. The witness Graham was asked to give his opinion as to the value of the plaintiffs' property before and after "the moving in of this Winn–Dixie Corporation." In answer to the question, he testified that the property had depreciated in value from about $12,000 to a value of $8,000 "by reason of the Winn–Dixie moving in this property." His testimony was directed solely to the question of the alleged depreciation in value of the plaintiffs' property from the location of the supermarket on the adjoining lot and not to damages that may have resulted from the manner of the operation of the business.

* * * As stated in 66 C.J.S. Nuisances § 19d, p. 771: "[A] use of property which does not create a nuisance cannot be enjoined or a lawful structure abated merely because it renders neighboring property less valuable. If there is no public or private nuisance created in the use of property, no recovery of damages can be allowed for the diminution in value of the property by reason of the lawful use of such property made by a near-by owner." * * *

The testimony was irrelevant to any issue in the case and should have been stricken upon the motion of the defendants. The failure to strike the testimony of the witness Graham was prejudicial and the lower court was in error in refusing the motion of the defendants for a new trial on this ground.

Reversed and remanded for a new trial.

NOTES AND QUESTIONS

1. Prior to the development of zoning programs, nuisance suits, whether brought by governmental officials or private individuals, were essentially the only way of controlling the location of certain types of activities that were undesirable to the residents in a particular area. Courts thus became concerned with the extent of the undesirability of the activity. How seriously must the activity interfere with the residents? Does the decision as to a hospital depend upon the existence of health dangers (contagions), or is it sufficient to lay emphasis on such things as traffic congestion and the fear (even though irrational) of contagion? See, e.g., Everett v.

Paschall, 61 Wash. 47, 111 P. 879 (1910) (tuberculosis sanitarium). There are numerous cases involving funeral parlors and their depressing mental effect on their neighbors. Two striking opinions are Williams v. Montgomery, 184 Miss. 547, 186 So. 302 (1939); and Saier v. Joy, 198 Mich. 295, 164 N.W. 507 (1917). For discussion of zoning versus nuisance treatment of adult entertainment businesses, see Bradley, Don't Come Around Here No More: The Regulation of Adult Businesses–Zoning or Entitlements?, 49 S.C. L. Rev. 1007 (1998).

Boomer v. Atlantic Cement Co., Inc.

Court of Appeals of New York, 1970.
26 N.Y.2d 219, 257 N.E.2d 870, 309 N.Y.S.2d 312.

BERGAN, J. Defendant operates a large cement plant near Albany. These are actions for injunction and damages by neighboring land owners alleging injury to property from dirt, smoke and vibration emanating from the plant. A nuisance has been found after trial, temporary damages have been allowed; but an injunction has been denied.

Judge Bergan

The public concern with air pollution arising from many sources in industry and in transportation is currently accorded ever wider recognition accompanied by a growing sense of responsibility in State and Federal Governments to control it. Cement plants are obvious sources of air pollution in the neighborhoods where they operate.

But there is now before the court private litigation in which individual property owners have sought specific relief from a single plant operation. The threshold question raised by the division of view on this appeal is whether the court should resolve the litigation between the parties now before it as equitably as seems possible; or whether, seeking promotion of the general public welfare, it should channel private litigation into broad public objectives.

A court performs its essential function when it decides the rights of parties before it. Its decision of private controversies may sometimes greatly affect public issues. Large questions of law are often resolved by the manner in which private litigation is decided. But this is normally an incident to the court's main function to settle controversy. It is a rare exercise of judicial power to use a decision in private litigation as a purposeful mechanism to achieve direct public objectives greatly beyond the rights and interests before the court.

Effective control of air pollution is a problem presently far from solution even with the full public and financial powers of government. In large measure adequate technical procedures are yet to be developed and some that appear possible may be economically impracticable.

It seems apparent that the amelioration of air pollution will depend on technical research in great depth; on a carefully balanced consideration of the economic impact of close regulation; and of the actual effect on public health. It is likely to require massive public expenditure and to demand more than any local community can accomplish and to depend on regional and interstate controls.

A court should not try to do this on its own as a by-product of private litigation and it seems manifest that the judicial establishment is neither equipped in the limited nature of any judgment it can pronounce nor prepared to lay down and implement an effective policy for the elimination of air pollution. This is an area beyond the circumference of one private lawsuit. It is a direct responsibility for government and should not thus be undertaken as an incident to solving a dispute between property owners and a single cement plant—one of many—in the Hudson River valley.

The cement making operations of defendant have been found by the court at Special Term to have damaged the nearby properties of plaintiffs in these two actions. The total damage to plaintiffs' properties is, however, relatively small in comparison with the value of defendant's operation and with the consequences of the injunction which plaintiffs seek.

The ground for the denial of injunction, notwithstanding the finding both that there is a nuisance and that plaintiffs have been damaged substantially, is the large disparity in economic consequences of the nuisance and of the injunction. This theory cannot, however, be sustained without overruling a doctrine which has been consistently reaffirmed in several leading cases in this court and which has never been disavowed here, namely that where a nuisance has been found and where there has been any substantial damage shown by the party complaining an injunction will be granted.

The rule in New York has been that such a nuisance will be enjoined although marked disparity be shown in economic consequence between the effect of the injunction and the effect of the nuisance.

The problem of disparity in economic consequence was sharply in focus in Whalen v. Union Bag & Paper Co., 208 N.Y. 1, 101 N.E. 805. A pulp mill entailing an investment of more than a million dollars polluted a stream in which plaintiff, who owned a farm, was "a lower riparian owner." The economic loss to plaintiff from this pollution was small. This court, reversing the Appellate Division reinstated the injunction granted by the Special Term against the argument of the mill owner that in view of "the slight advantage to plaintiff and the great loss that will be inflicted on defendant" an injunction should not be granted [c]. "Such a balancing of injuries cannot be justified by the circumstances of this case," Judge Werner noted [c]. He continued: "Although the damage to the plaintiff may be slight as compared with the defendant's expense of abating the condition, that is not a good reason for refusing an injunction" [c].

Thus the unconditional injunction granted at Special Term was reinstated. The rule laid down in that case, then, is that whenever the damage resulting from a nuisance is found not "unsubstantial," viz., $100 a year, injunction would follow. This states a rule that had been followed in this court with marked consistency. * * *

Although the court at Special Term and the Appellate Division held that injunction should be denied, it was found that plaintiffs had been damaged in various specific amounts up to the time of the trial and damages to the respective plaintiffs were awarded for those amounts. The effect of this was, injunction having been denied, plaintiffs could maintain successive actions at law for damages thereafter as further damage was incurred.

The court at Special Term also found the amount of permanent damage attributable to each plaintiff, for the guidance of the parties in the event both sides stipulated to the payment and acceptance of such permanent damage as a settlement of all the controversies among the parties. The total of permanent damages to all plaintiffs thus found was $185,000. This basis of adjustment has not resulted in any stipulation by the parties.

This result at Special Term and at the Appellate Division is a departure from a rule that has become settled; but to follow the rule literally in these cases would be to close down the plant at once. This court is fully agreed to avoid that immediately drastic remedy; the difference in view is how best to avoid it. [Footnote by Court: Respondent's investment in the plant is in excess of $45,000,000. There are over 300 people employed there.]

One alternative is to grant the injunction but postpone its effect to a specified future date to give opportunity for technical advances to permit defendant to eliminate the nuisance; another is to grant the injunction conditioned on the payment of permanent damages to plaintiffs which would compensate them for the total economic loss to their property present and future caused by defendant's operations. * * * [T]he court chooses the latter alternative.

If the injunction were to be granted unless within a short period—e.g., 18 months—the nuisance be abated by improved methods, there would be no assurance that any significant technical improvement would occur.

The parties could settle this private litigation at any time if defendant paid enough money and the imminent threat of closing the plant would build up the pressure on defendant. If there were no improved techniques found, there would inevitably be applications to the court at Special Term for extensions of time to perform on showing of good faith efforts to find such techniques.

Moreover, techniques to eliminate dust and other annoying by-products of cement making are unlikely to be developed by any research the defendant can undertake within any short period, but will depend on the total resources of the cement industry nationwide and throughout the world. The problem is universal wherever cement is made.

For obvious reasons the rate of the research is beyond control of defendant. If at the end of 18 months the whole industry has not found a technical solution a court would be hard put to close down this one cement plant if due regard be given to equitable principles.

On the other hand, to grant the injunction unless defendant pays plaintiffs such permanent damages as may be fixed by the court seems to do justice between the contending parties. All of the attributions of economic loss to the properties on which plaintiffs' complaints are based will have been redressed.

The nuisance complained of by these plaintiffs may have other public or private consequences, but these particular parties are the only ones who have sought remedies and the judgment proposed will fully redress them. The limitation of relief granted is a limitation only within the four corners of these actions and does not foreclose public health or other public agencies from seeking proper relief in a proper court.

It seems reasonable to think that the risk of being required to pay permanent damages to injured property owners by cement plant owners would itself be a reasonable effective spur to research for improved techniques to minimize nuisance.

The power of the court to condition on equitable grounds the continuance of an injunction on the payment of permanent damages seems undoubted. [Cc]

The damage base here suggested is consistent with the general rule in those nuisance cases where damages are allowed. "Where a nuisance is of such a permanent and unabatable character that a single recovery can be had, including the whole damage past and future resulting therefrom, there can be but one recovery" [c].

Thus it seems fair to both sides to grant permanent damages to plaintiffs which will terminate this private litigation. The theory of damage is the "servitude on land" of plaintiffs imposed by defendant's nuisance. * * *

The judgment, by allowance of permanent damages imposing a servitude on land, which is the basis of the actions, would preclude future recovery by plaintiffs or their grantees [c].

This should be placed beyond debate by a provision of the judgment that the payment by defendant and the acceptance by plaintiffs of permanent damages found by the court shall be in compensation for a servitude on the land.

Although the Trial Term has found permanent damages as a possible basis of settlement of the litigation, on remission the court should be entirely free to re-examine this subject. It may again find the permanent damage already found; or make new findings.

The orders should be reversed, without costs, and the cases remitted to Supreme Court, Albany County to grant an injunction which shall be vacated upon payment by defendant of such amounts of permanent damage to the respective plaintiffs as shall for this purpose be determined by the court.

JASEN, J. dissenting. I agree with the majority that a reversal is required here, but I do not subscribe to the newly enunciated doctrine of assessment of permanent damages, in lieu of an injunction, where substantial property rights have been impaired by the creation of a nuisance. * * *

I see grave dangers in overruling our long-established rule of granting an injunction where a nuisance results in substantial continuing damage. In permitting the injunction to become inoperative upon the payment of permanent damages, the majority is, in effect, licensing a continuing wrong. It is the same as saying to the cement company, you may continue to do harm to your neighbors so long as you pay a fee for it. Furthermore, once such permanent damages are assessed and paid, the incentive to alleviate the wrong would be eliminated, thereby continuing air pollution of an area without abatement.

It is true that some courts have sanctioned the remedy here proposed by the majority in a number of cases, but none of the authorities relied upon by the majority are analogous to the situation before us. In those cases, the courts, in denying an injunction and awarding money damages, grounded their decision on a showing that the use to which the property was intended to be put was primarily for the public benefit. Here, on the other hand, it is clearly established that the cement company is creating a continuing air pollution nuisance primarily for its own private interest with no public benefit.

This kind of inverse condemnation [c] may not be invoked by a private person or corporation for private gain or advantage. Inverse condemnation should only be permitted when the public is primarily served in the taking or impairment of property. [Cc] The promotion of the interests of the polluting cement company has, in my opinion, no public use or benefit.

Nor is it constitutionally permissible to impose servitude on land, without consent of the owner, by payment of permanent damages where the continuing impairment of the land is for a private use. [Cc] This is made clear by the State Constitution (art. I, § 7, subd. [a]) which provides that "[p]rivate property shall not be taken for *public use* without just compensation" (emphasis added). It is, of course, significant that the section makes no mention of taking for a *private* use.

In sum, then, by constitutional mandate as well as by judicial pronouncement, the permanent impairment of private property for private purposes is not authorized in the absence of clearly demonstrated public benefit and use.

I would enjoin the defendant cement company from continuing the discharge of dust particles upon its neighbors' properties unless, within 18 months, the cement company abated this nuisance. * * *

NOTES AND QUESTIONS

1.   Is the court applying inverse condemnation here in the case of a private defendant who does not possess the power of eminent domain? Does this amount to giving the power of eminent domain to the defendant and letting it force the plaintiffs to "sell out"? Are the damages to be assessed on the basis of the harm to the plaintiffs, including personal annoyance, or should they be confined to depreciation of the value of their land? Is the injunction an inferior remedy to an award of damages? The spectre of an injunction would encourage parties intending to establish polluting activities to obtain permits and easements before the building of the plant. At this time the polluter (Atlantic) is in the better position to avoid the costs. For discussion see V. Goldberg, Readings in the Economics of Contract Law (1989), Chapter 23. What if the costs to bargaining were too great? See Kaplow and Shavell, Property Rules Versus Liability Rules: An Economic Analysis, 109 Harv. L. Rev. 713 (1996).

2.   If an injunction is to be denied, is it wise to award permanent damages to the plaintiffs? Suppose a feasible method of controlling cement dust is later discovered. Is the defendant left with any incentive to seek to find a means of control of the dust? Suppose an injunction ordering the defendants to desist had been granted. Would this have done anything more than permit the plaintiffs to hold the defendant up and insist on a much higher price for selling out?

3.   How do the two opinions in this case fit with the two opinions in Carpenter v. The Double R Cattle Co., supra page 811? Consider again Restatement (Second) of Torts §§ 926(b), 829A (1979). What about the desirability of giving the plaintiffs the option of treating this nuisance as permanent or continuing; cf. Restatement (Second) of Torts §§ 929, 930 (1979) (damages for harm to each for past and future invasions). In Baker v. Burbank–Glendale–Pasadena Airport Authority, 39 Cal. 3d

862, 705 P.2d 866, 218 Cal. Rptr. 293 (1985), the court confirmed that plaintiff may elect whether to treat a particular nuisance as permanent or continuing: but cf. Mosk J. dissenting, id. at 874. The court held that damages will be available for airplane activity around defendant's public airport. Injunctive relief could not be awarded because the activity was authorized by statute but the deleterious results were not privileged. See also Washington Suburban Sanitary Commission v. Case–Link Corporation, 330 Md. 115, 622 A.2d 745 (1993), holding that a nuisance action would lie for loss of property values when defendant constructed a sewage sludge composting facility pursuant to a federal court order under the Federal Water Pollution Control Act, 33 U.S.C. § 1215 et seq.

Most courts do not take a categoric position on whether an injunction should be granted in general. Instead, they engage in a process designated as "balancing the equities." A good case illustrating the process is Smith v. Staso Milling Co., 18 F.2d 736 (2d Cir.1927), where the plaintiff recovered damages for the pollution of a brook and the air with slate dust and for the jarring of his house by blasting, but an injunction to prevent the defendant from continuing was denied. In this process the courts take into consideration a number of different factors, no one of which is necessarily controlling, but any one of which may control in a particular case. Among these are the character and extent of the damage inflicted or threatened; the good faith or intentional misconduct of the defendant, or his efforts to avoid injury to the plaintiff, as in Elliott Nursery Co. v. Du Quesne Light Co., 281 Pa. 166, 126 A. 345 (1924); the financial investment of each party, and the relative economic hardship that will result to either from granting or denying the injunction; and especially the interest of the general public in the continuance of the defendant's enterprise.

In Madison v. Ducktown Sulphur, Copper & Iron Co., 113 Tenn. 331, 83 S.W. 658 (1904), a $2 million copper reduction plant that destroyed all vegetation in the area but was the total basis for existence of a town was not enjoined at the behest of landowners whose property had very little value. The plant was in the southeast corner of the state, however, and the State of Georgia, seeking original relief in the Supreme Court, obtained it. Georgia v. Tennessee Copper Co., 206 U.S. 230 (1907). The injunction was conditioned on allowing a reasonable time to complete structures and make efforts "to stop the fumes." After eight years of abatement attempts and extensions of the injunction, Georgia came back to the Court. An injunction was granted preventing the operation of the plant unless pollution standards were met. Georgia v. Tennessee Copper Co., 237 U.S. 474 (1915).

4.   What should be the measure of damages? See Boomer v. Atlantic Cement Co., 72 Misc.2d 834, 340 N.Y.S.2d 97 (1972) (instant case on remand, with extensive discussion of proof and measure), aff'd sub nom. Kinley v. Atlantic Cement Co., 42 A.D.2d 496, 349 N.Y.S.2d 199 (1973). Farber, Reassessing *Boomer*: Justice, Efficiency, and Nuisance Law, Property Law and Legal Education: Essays in Honor of John E. Cribbett 7, 17 (P. Hay & M. Hoeflich eds., 1988), suggests that damages should not be recovered by the formula of value before minus value after, but rather by the market value for purchase of buffer rights.

5.   In Little Joseph Realty, Inc. v. Babylon, 41 N.Y.2d 738, 363 N.E.2d 1163, 395 N.Y.S.2d 428 (1977), the court refused to apply the *Boomer* principle when an asphalt plant was located in violation of a zoning ordinance and the lower court conditioned an injunction on payment of permanent damages and abatement of the most offensive aspects. "[W]hen a continuing use flies in the face of a valid zoning restriction it must, subject to the existence of any appropriate equitable defenses, be enjoined unconditionally."

6.   The principal case influenced the 1970 amendments to the Clean Air Act. In testimony before the Senate Committee, the majority opinion was criticized for not inducing industry to improve the state of technology. Judge Jasen's proposal of a conditional injunction was praised; S. 3229, S. 3466, and S. 3546, Subcomm. on Air and Water of the Senate Comm. on Public Works, 91st Cong., 2d Sess., part 2, at 849 (1970). Thus the Clean Air Act Amendment added strict deadlines called "technology-forcing" for industry compliance.

7.   *Hazardous Waste Disposal.* Village of Wilsonville v. SCA Services, Inc., 86 Ill.2d 1, 426 N.E.2d 824, 55 Ill.Dec. 499 (1981), gives a very thorough treatment to the total problem. The 130–acre disposal site was over two-thirds in the village and was located over an abandoned coal mine. There was much expert testimony regarding the method of conducting the site and the damages from the chemicals involved. The trial court granted a permanent injunction requiring that the wastes be removed. The ruling was affirmed by the appellate court and the Supreme Court. The holding was that there was both a public and a private nuisance, both existing and prospective, based on a careful balancing of the conflicting interests. Although the site served a valuable and necessary purpose and substantial sums of money had been expended on it, its maintenance could not be "justified on such grounds when we have substantial injury to individual rights, community rights, substantial damage to human beings and other living things." Other pertinent factors were that the nuisance came to the village, that a damage remedy would be inadequate, that an injunction is appropriate against prospective damage that need not be certain to take place if it would be severe, that it was feasible to remove the drums and that the approval given by the state agency was based on data collected by the defendant that had been proved at trial to be inaccurate. The injunction was held not to "deprive the defendant of its property without due process of law."

May it be argued that the operation of a waste disposal site is ultra-hazardous, thus avoiding the necessity of weighing the relevant factors? See State, Department of Environmental Protection v. Ventron Corp., 94 N.J. 473, 468 A.2d 150 (1983) (strict liability); Lefebvre v. Central Maine Power Company, 7 F. Supp. 2d 64 (D.Me.1998).

8.   *Federal Statutes.* The Comprehensive Environmental Response, Compensation and Liability Act (CERCLA, or Superfund Act), 42 U.S.C. §§ 9601–9675 (1999) was passed in 1980. Combined with such other federal acts as the Clean Air Act, 42 U.S.C. §§ 7401–7671, the Clean Water Act, 33 U.S.C. §§ 1251–1387 (1999), and the Toxic Substance Control Act (TSCA), 15 U.S.C. §§ 2601–2629 (1999), it establishes a comprehensive and complicated system that is necessarily beyond the scope of this casebook. Specialized courses and seminars on environmental law are offered in many law schools.

Despite, or perhaps because of, CERCLA, common law liability relating to hazardous waste sites has been resurgent recently. For a discussion of the reasons behind and the advantages and disadvantages of this movement see Kuhnle, The Rebirth of Common Law Actions for Addressing Hazardous Waste Contamination, 15 Stan. Envtl. L.J. 187 (1996).

Spur Industries, Inc. v. Del E. Webb Development Co.

Supreme Court of Arizona, 1972.
108 Ariz. 178, 494 P.2d 700.

CAMERON, VICE CHIEF JUSTICE. From a judgment permanently enjoining the defendant, Spur Industries, Inc., from operating a cattle feedlot near the plaintiff Del E. Webb Development Company's Sun City, Spur appeals. Webb cross-appeals. Although numerous issues are raised, we feel that it is necessary to answer only two questions. They are:

1. Where the operation of a business, such as a cattle feedlot is lawful in the first instance, but becomes a nuisance by reason of a nearby residential area, may the feedlot operation be enjoined in an action brought by the developer of the residential area?

2. Assuming that the nuisance may be enjoined, may the developer of a completely new town or urban area in a previously agricultural area be required to indemnify the operator of the feedlot who must move or cease operation because of the presence of the residential area created by the developer?

[Farming had existed in the general area involved (about 14 to 15 miles west of urban Phoenix) prior to 1950. The property owned by Spur was well suited for cattle feeding, and Spur's predecessors began this activity. In 1959 Del Webb began to develop Sun City, some distance from Spur. The development progressed rapidly and expanded, coming into closer proximity to Spur.]

By December 1967, Del Webb's property had extended south to Olive Avenue and Spur was within 500 feet of Olive Avenue to the north. * * * Del Webb filed its original complaint alleging that in excess of 1,300 lots in the southwest portion were unfit for development for sale as residential lots because of the operation of the Spur feedlot.

Del Webb's suit complained that the Spur feeding operation was a public nuisance because of the flies and the odor which were drifting or being blown by the prevailing south to north wind over the southern portion of Sun City. At the time of the suit, Spur was feeding between 20,000 and 30,000 head of cattle, and the facts amply support the finding of the trial court that the feed pens had become a nuisance to the people who resided in the southern part of Del Webb's development. The testimony indicated that cattle in a commercial feedlot will produce 35 to 40 pounds of wet manure per day, per head, or over a million pounds of wet manure per day for 30,000 head of cattle, and that despite the admittedly good feedlot management and good housekeeping practices by Spur, the resulting odor and flies produced an annoying if not unhealthy situation as far as the senior citizens of southern Sun City were concerned. There is no doubt that some of the citizens of Sun City were unable to enjoy the outdoor living which Del Webb had advertised and that Del Webb was faced with sales resistance from prospective purchasers as well as strong and persistent complaints from the people who had purchased homes in that area. * * *

Where the injury is slight, the remedy for minor inconveniences lies in an action for damages rather than in one for an injunction. [c]. Moreover, some courts have held, in the "balancing of conveniences" cases, that damages may be the sole remedy. * * *

We have no difficulty, however, in agreeing with the conclusion of the trial court that Spur's operation was an enjoinable public nuisance as far as

the people in the southern portion of Del Webb's Sun City were concerned.
* * *

It is clear that as to the citizens of Sun City, the operation of Spur's feedlot was both a public and a private nuisance. They could have successfully maintained an action to abate the nuisance. Del Webb, having shown a special injury in the loss of sales, had a standing to bring suit to enjoin the nuisance. [Cc] The judgment of the trial court permanently enjoining the operation of the feedlot is affirmed. * * *

In the so-called "coming to the nuisance" cases, the courts have held that the residential landowner may not have relief if he knowingly came into a neighborhood reserved for industrial or agricultural endeavors and has been damaged thereby:

"Plaintiffs chose to live in an area uncontrolled by zoning laws or restrictive covenants and remote from urban development. In such an area plaintiffs cannot complain that legitimate agricultural pursuits are being carried on in the vicinity, nor can plaintiffs, having chosen to build in an agricultural area, complain that the agricultural pursuits carried on in the area depreciate the value of their homes. The area being *primarily agricultural,* any opinion reflecting the value of such property must take this factor into account. The standards affecting the value of residence property in an urban setting, subject to zoning controls and controlled planning techniques, cannot be the standards by which agricultural properties are judged.

"People employed in a city who build their homes in suburban areas of the county beyond the limits of a city and zoning regulations do so for a reason. Some do so to avoid the high taxation rate imposed by cities, or to avoid special assessments for street, sewer and water projects. They usually build on improved or hard surface highways, which have been built either at state or county expense and thereby avoid special assessments for these improvements. It may be that they desire to get away from the congestion of traffic, smoke, noise, foul air and the many other annoyances of city life. But with all these advantages in going beyond the area which is zoned and restricted to protect them in their homes, they must be prepared to take the disadvantages." Dill v. Excel Packing Company, 183 Kan. 513, 525, 526, 331 P.2d 539, 548, 549 (1958). * * *

Were Webb the only party injured, we would feel justified in holding that the doctrine of "coming to the nuisance" would have been a bar to the relief asked by Webb, and, on the other hand, had Spur located the feedlot near the outskirts of a city and had the city grown toward the feedlot, Spur would have to suffer the cost of abating the nuisance as to those people locating within the growth pattern of the expanding city. * * *

There was no indication in the instant case at the time Spur and its predecessors located in western Maricopa County that a new city would spring up, full-blown, alongside the feeding operation and that the developer of that city would ask the court to order Spur to move because of the new city. Spur is required to move not because of any wrongdoing on the part of Spur, but because of a proper and legitimate regard of the courts for the rights and interests of the public.

Del Webb, on the other hand, is entitled to the relief prayed for (a permanent injunction), not because Webb is blameless, but because of the damage to the people who have been encouraged to purchase homes in Sun City. It does not equitably or legally follow, however, that Webb, being entitled to the injunction, is then free of any liability to Spur if Webb has in fact been the cause of the damage Spur has sustained. It does not seem harsh to require a developer, who has taken advantage of the lesser land values in a rural area as well as the availability of large tracts of land on which to build and develop a new town or city in the area, to indemnify those who are forced to leave as a result.

Having brought people to the nuisance to the foreseeable detriment of Spur, Webb must indemnify Spur for a reasonable amount of the cost of moving or shutting down. It should be noted that this relief to Spur is limited to a case wherein a developer has, with foreseeability, brought into a previously agricultural or industrial area the population which makes necessary the granting of an injunction against a lawful business and for which the business has no adequate relief.

It is therefore the decision of this court that the matter be remanded to the trial court for a hearing upon the damages sustained by the defendant Spur as a reasonable and direct result of the granting of the permanent injunction. Since the result of the appeal may appear novel and both sides have obtained a measure of relief, it is ordered that each side will bear its own costs.

Affirmed in part, reversed in part, and remanded for further proceedings consistent with this opinion.

NOTES AND QUESTIONS

1. The majority rule is that the plaintiff is not barred from recovery for either a public or a private nuisance by the sole fact that he "comes to the nuisance" by buying property adjoining it. See Restatement (Second) of Torts § 840D; Witham, First Come, First Served: An Economic View of Coming to the Nuisance, 9 J.Leg.Stud. 597 (1980).

2. The rule is not, however, an absolute one; and particularly in cases where other factors are more or less balanced, the fact that the plaintiff has come to the nuisance may be important and even decisive. An interesting case is East St. Johns Shingle Co. v. Portland, 195 Or. 505, 246 P.2d 554 (1952), where the plaintiff's shingle mill relied for its supply of logs upon rafting through a slough from the Columbia River. Defendant city discharged sewage into the river, which polluted the slough and fouled the logs, thus interfering seriously with plaintiff's business. When the plaintiff had bought its property twenty years before, the city was already polluting the slough; but with the growth of the community the condition gradually became worse. The health of the city of Portland depended in large measure upon the sewage disposal, and there was no other way to dispose of it. It was held that plaintiff was not entitled either to an injunction or to damages.

3. Defendant does not acquire a prescriptive right to continue the nuisance unless during the necessary period an action might have been maintained for it. Ireland v. Bowman & Cockrell, 130 Ky. 153, 113 S.W. 56 (1908); Holsman v. Boiling Spring Bleaching Co., 14 N.J.Eq. 335 (1862). By the majority rule, one cannot acquire a prescriptive right to maintain a *public* nuisance, no matter how long it has continued, even though plaintiff brings suit for damages personal to himself. Gundy v. Merrill, 250 Mich. 416, 230 N.W. 163 (1930); Smejkal v. Empire Lite–Rock, Inc., 274 Or. 571, 547 P.2d 1363 (1976).

4. The adjustment of the equities in the principal case by requiring indemnity is a new approach and the reverse of *Boomer*. It adds to the court's repertoire of remedies. How can these remedies be adjusted or combined to produce the fairest and most effective result? Suppose that newly arrived neighbors had obtained the injunction. How would the moving costs be apportioned? This topic has been the subject of some stimulating studies of the law of nuisance. See Calabresi & Melamed, Property Rules, Liability Rules and Inalienability: One View of the Cathedral, 85 Harv.L.Rev. 1089 (1972); Lewin, Compensated Injunction on the Evolution of Nuisance Law, 71 Iowa L.Rev. 775 (1986); Kaplow and Shavell, Property Rules Versus Liability Rules: An Economic Analysis, 109 Harv. L. Rev. 713 (1996) (asserting that many variables, besides externalities, need to be taken into account in choosing between a liability and property rule). For discussion of various rules, their implications and desirability see also Symposium: Property Rules, Liability Rules, and Inalienability: A Twenty–Five Year Retrospective, 106 Yale L.J. 2083 (1997).

Defenses

1. When there is an intentional private nuisance, contributory negligence is not a defense, as in the case of other intentional torts. Higginbotham v. Kearse, 111 W.Va. 264, 161 S.E. 37 (1931); Phillips Ranch, Inc. v. Banta, 273 Or. 784, 543 P.2d 1035 (1975).

2. When the nuisance arises out of negligence, most jurisdictions recognize that contributory negligence eliminates or reduces recovery. See Timmons v. Reed, 569 P.2d 112 (Wyo.1977); McFarlane v. Niagara Falls, 247 N.Y. 340, 160 N.E. 391 (1928) (leading case); Denny v. Garavaglia, 333 Mich. 317, 52 N.W.2d 521 (1952); Restatement (Second) of Torts § 840B.

3. The dividing line between intent and negligence has led to some difficulty in cases when the defendant has intentionally invaded the rights of the public by creating only a risk of harm to travelers on the highway, without the intent to injure the travelers. Some decisions have classified this as intentional and have held that contributory negligence is not a defense. See Delaney v. Philhern Realty Co., 280 N.Y. 461, 21 N.E.2d 507 (1939); Beckwith v. Stratford, 129 Conn. 506, 29 A.2d 775 (1942). These decisions have been criticized. See Seavey, Nuisance: Contributory Negligence and Other Mysteries, 65 Harv.L.Rev. 984 (1952).

4. When the nuisance is based on strict liability, contributory negligence of the plaintiff in failing to discover the danger is not a defense; but if he discovers the danger and deliberately proceeds to encounter it, his contributory negligence or his assumption of risk may affect his recovery. Thus if defendant is blasting in dangerous proximity to a public highway and plaintiff negligently fails to observe a warning sign, drives past it and is hurt by a blast, he may recover; but if he sees the sign, or a flagman who warns him not to proceed and he insists on doing so, he cannot recover. See Worth v. Dunn, 98 Conn. 51, 118 A. 467 (1922).

5. On the effect of comparative negligence, see V. Schwartz, Comparative Negligence, ch. 11 (3d ed. 1994) (depends upon basis of action—intent, negligence or strict liability).

Self–Help to Abate a Nuisance

6. The privilege of self-help to abate a nuisance is analogous to the privilege of using reasonable force to protect the possession of land against trespass. It is open only to those to whom the condition is a nuisance. A public nuisance may be abated by a private individual only when it causes or threatens special damage to himself, apart from that to the general public. Corthell v. Holmes, 87 Me. 24, 32 A. 715 (1894); Nation v. District of Columbia, 34 U.S.App.D.C. 453 (1910).

7. It is commonly held that the privilege of abating conditions outside the actor's premises depends upon the actual existence of a nuisance, and that an honest but mistaken belief will not justify the action. Grant v. Allen, 41 Conn. 156 (1874); Humphreys Oil Co. v. Liles, 262 S.W. 1058 (Tex.Civ.App.1924), aff'd, 277 S.W. 100 (Com.App.1925).

8. The privilege extends to reasonable force according to the necessities of the situation, and may extend to the destruction of valuable property. Amoskeag Mfg. Co. v. Goodale, 46 N.H. 53 (dam) (1865); Maryland Tel. & Tel. Co. v. Ruth, 106 Md. 644, 68 A. 358 (telephone pole) (1907).

9. It does not extend to unnecessary damage or to damage unreasonable in extent. The actor may not burn down the adjoining house merely because it is used for prostitution. Moody v. Board of Supervisors of Niagara Cty., 46 Barb. 659 (N.Y.1886).

10. The abatement of a nuisance does not justify the infliction of personal injury or a breach of the peace. Walker v. Davis, 139 Tenn. 475, 202 S.W. 78 (1918).

11. Ordinarily, when time permits, the actor must notify the wrongdoer of the existence of the nuisance and demand removal of the condition. Hickey v. Michigan Central R. Co., 96 Mich. 498, 55 N.W. 989 (1893). This is not required when it is apparent that the wrongdoer is already aware of the nuisance and that the demand would be futile. Hickey v. Michigan Central R. Co., 96 Mich. 498, 55 N.W. 989 (1893).

Other Torts Involving Invasion of Interests in Real Property

Besides Trespass and Nuisance, there are two additional commonly recognized torts arising in behalf of a landowner or possessor of real property because of damage to his interests in the land. They are

1. *Interference With the Support of Land.* This applies to both lateral support and subjacent support. If the withdrawal of the support is sufficient to cause a subsidence of the land in its natural condition—i.e., "naturally necessary support" is withdrawn—the liability is strict and no showing of fault on the part of the defendant is required. Damage to artificial additions to the land is also included. If the withdrawal of support would not have caused a subsidence of the land in its natural condition but does cause subsidence because of artificial additions to the land, then liability may still exist but it depends upon a finding that the actor's conduct was negligent. See Bonomi v. Backhouse, El.Bl. & El. 686, 120 Eng.Rep. 643 (1859), aff'd, 9 H.L. 503, 11 Eng.Rep. 825 (1861); Blake Constr. Co. v. United States, 585 F.2d 998 (Ct.Cl.1978); St. Louis–S.F.R.R. v. Wade, 607 F.2d 126 (5th Cir.1979); St. Joseph Light & Power Co. v. Kaw Valley Tunneling, 589 S.W.2d 260 (Mo.1979). On subsidence caused by withdrawal of ground water, see Friendswood

Dev. Co. v. Smith–Southwest Industries, Inc., 576 S.W.2d 21 (Tex.1978). And see Restatement (Second) of Torts §§ 817–821 (1979).

2. *Interference with the Use of Water.* This tort covers three types of water: water in a watercourse or lake in or adjoining the land ("riparian rights"), ground water (sometime called subterranean water or underground water) and surface waters (from precipitation). On the subject of riparian rights, there are three distinct legal theories for determination of the rights involved. The first, adopted in England and used by a few American states, is the natural-flow theory—the right to have the water flow as it was wont to flow in nature, qualified only by the right of each riparian owner to make a limited use of it. The second, adopted in a majority of American states, is the reasonable-use theory—the right to be free from unreasonable uses that cause harm to the proprietor's own reasonable use. The third, adopted largely in the states of the west, is the prior-appropriation rule, that beneficial use of the water is the basis of the right to it and that priority of use is the basis of the division of it between appropriators when there is not enough for all. The reasonable-use theory is the most flexible and adaptable one, and it has succeeded in adapting to both of the other two in terms of the factors affecting the determination of when a user is reasonable. It is now distinctly the majority rule. In a number of states, there are statutory provisions modifying the common law rules.

On the use of "ground water" (subsurface water), there are also several theories: (1) the English rule of absolute ownership, (2) the American rule of reasonable use, a rule of correlative rights, and (3) the rule that an "underground stream" is treated like a surface stream. Here too, the adaptable reasonable-use rule is growing in number of adherents, and there are statutory modification in some states. As for surface waters, there is general agreement that a landowner can use as much of them as he needs.

The subject is canvassed in Chapter 41 of the Restatement (Second) of Torts §§ 841–864.

CHAPTER XVII

DEFAMATION

The term "tort" deriving from the Latin *tortus,* meaning twisted, is apt for the tort of defamation in two senses. The conduct involved is twisted, or crooked; and the law governing it is twisted, or wrenched sadly out of shape by its historical development. As one commentator put it, the law of defamation was "marred in the making." 1 T. Street, Foundations of Legal Liability 273 (1906). Rules and distinctions originating from ancient controversies over jurisdiction, long since obsolete, nevertheless became frozen and crystallized.

Originally the common law courts took no jurisdiction over any defamation, leaving it to be dealt with by the local seigniorial courts. When these fell into decay, the ecclesiastical courts began to take jurisdiction over slander, regarding it as a sin and punishing it with penance. Since the cases all involved oral defamation, slander became identified with word of mouth. When the ecclesiastical courts in turn began to lose their power, there was in the sixteenth century a slow infiltration of tort actions for slander into the common law courts. The excuse for this invasion of church jurisdiction was that some "temporal" damage had been done, distinct from the mere "spiritual" offense, and that it was properly a matter for the king's courts to redress. A long conflict of jurisdiction, part of the broader contest between church and state, finally fixed this as a requirement for any slander action at common law. See Ogden v. Turner, 6 Mod.Rep. 104, 87 Eng.Rep. 862 (1703); Davies v. Gardiner, Popham 36, 79 Eng.Rep. 1155 (1593); Matthew v. Crass, Cro.Jac. 323, 79 Eng.Rep. 276 (1614). The result was that slander became actionable only in those cases where special damage of a "temporal" or pecuniary character was proved or could reasonably be assumed.

About the beginning of the seventeenth century, the Court of Star Chamber began independently to punish the crime of libel, in order to suppress the seditious publications that had multiplied with the spread of printing. In the earliest cases the libels were political, and the crime was a form of sedition. It was gradually extended to non-political libels, and still later tort damages were awarded to the person defamed, probably in order to provide a legal substitute for the duel when it was forbidden. When the Star Chamber was abolished, jurisdiction over libel in turn passed to the common law courts. Through this process, libel became identified with printed or written defamation, while slander remained oral. Instead of merging the two torts, the courts maintained their separate identity, as well as the rules that had grown up around slander.

In the sixteenth and seventeenth centuries the judges were annoyed by the flood of rather frivolous actions let loose upon them once their jurisdiction over slander was established, and were reluctant to extend the possibilities of recovery. In addition, further development of the law of defamation was arrested when it encountered the rising tide of sentiment in favor of freedom of speech and the press, which, together with the odium attached to the memory of the Star Chamber and its political prosecutions, made any action for defamation an unpopular one, and the court somewhat reluctant in dealing with it.

Few commentators have had a kind word to say about the general condition of the common law of defamation as it finally developed. Many calls have been made for its complete overhaul and reform. Some studies have been undertaken with this end in view. But they have failed to accomplish any really worthwhile results. The outstanding historical treatment is R. Helmhotz, Introduction (to Select Cases on Defamation to 1600) (Selden Society 1985).

In 1964, a new reformer entered the field. The United States Supreme Court decided the case of New York Times Co. v. Sullivan, 376 U.S. 254 (1964), infra page 867, holding that the free-speech and free-press provisions of the First Amendment (acting through the Fourteenth Amendment) affected the common law of defamation.

Since that time, the decisions under the First Amendment have produced numerous changes in the law of defamation, some of them very far ranging in effect. The Supreme Court itself is still slowly feeling its way on the course to take. The Court has wavered and changed its position on several matters, so that a good deal of uncertainty remains as to the extent of present law and future change in it. For this reason, the first part of this chapter will be primarily concerned with the common law of defamation, with only incidental references to constitutional holdings. Beginning with New York Times v. Sullivan, infra page 867, the emphasis will be placed on the constitutional developments.

The law of torts involves a careful balancing of conflicting individual and social interests, with the establishment of principles, rules and standards for the purpose of enabling the court to reach the appropriate result in the particular case. In this chapter, you will observe that the same kind of balancing of interests is followed. Social concepts about the function of reputation have shifted from protection of honor to protection of property. This individual interest has had to be reconciled with the public interest in freedom of expression, not only as developed by the common law, but more recently by dint of the First Amendment. See Post, The Social Foundations of Defamation Law: Reputation and the Constitution, 74 Cal.L.Rev. 691 (1986). This maelstrom of interests sometimes creates serious difficulties in maintaining orderly organization in the tort law of defamation. It is a stimulating and sometimes frustrating process to contemplate and study.

1. NATURE OF A DEFAMATORY COMMUNICATION

Belli v. Orlando Daily Newspapers, Inc.
United States Court of Appeals, Fifth Circuit, 1967.
389 F.2d 579, cert. denied 393 U.S. 825, 89 S.Ct. 88, 21 L.Ed.2d 96 (1968).

WISDOM, CIRCUIT JUDGE. This action for damages for libel and slander is based on a false statement relating to Mr. Melvin Belli. Belli, an attorney of national prominence, is well known in the legal profession for his pioneering in the development of demonstrative evidence as a trial tactic and his success in obtaining large judgments for plaintiffs in personal injury suits. He is well known to the general public because of his representation of Jack Ruby and others in the public eye.

In March 1964 Mr. Leon Handley, an attorney in Orlando, Florida, in a conversation with Miss Jean Yothers, a columnist for the Orlando Evening Star, repeated a story he had heard concerning Belli. Handley told Yothers that the Florida Bar Association had invited Belli to serve as a member of one of the panels on the program of the Association at its 1955 Convention in Miami Beach. Belli agreed, with the understanding that "since there were no funds provided in the budget for payment per se for his contribution as a lawyer to the program the Florida Bar instead would pick up the hotel tab for himself and his wife during their stay." According to Handley, after Mr. and Mrs. Belli left Florida, the Association discovered that the Bellis "ran up a bunch of [clothing] bills" which they charged to their hotel room. The derogatory portion of the story was admittedly false: The Bellis had not charged any purchases to their hotel account. Unfortunately for all, Jean Yothers reported, with embellishments, this nine-year old story in her gossip column in the Orlando Evening Star for March 19, 1964.[2] * * *

The district court dismissed Belli's complaint for failure to state a claim upon which relief could be granted. The court relied on the erroneous assumption that the determination whether a statement is a libel (or slander) per se is solely for the court. We consider it a close question whether the publication is so clearly defamatory that as a matter of law the case should not be submitted to the jury. We hold, however, that the publication itself, without reference to extrinsic facts, is capable of carrying a defamatory meaning. It is for a jury to determine whether it was so understood by the "common mind". We reverse and remand. * * *

2. The article appeared in the Orlando Evening Star under the title "On the Town" by Jean Yothers and headed "Florida Bar Got the Bill". The full text is as follows:

Jack Ruby's flamboyant attorney Melvin Belli of San Francisco makes an indelible impression whither he goeth.

Consider the time he and Mrs. Belli were in Miami six or so years ago and Belli was a member of a panel at a program-meeting of the Florida Bar.

Here's what happened:

In making arrangements for Belli's participation it had been pointed out to him that since there were no funds provided in the budget for payment per se for his contribution as a lawyer to the program, the Florida Bar instead would pick up the hotel tab for himself and his wife during their stay.

Belli agreed.

Oops!

A local attorney remembers, with embarrassed chagrin, how the plan backfired on the Florida Bar.

After the well-dressed Mr. Belli and his well-dressed wife left town, the hotel where they had been staying received clothing bills amounting to hundreds of $s. The Bellis had shopped in Miami stores and charged clothing bills to their hotel rooms.

The Florida Bar had been taken.

It was hard to stomach but the Board of Governors of the Florida Bar picked up the Bellis' bill.

After all, that was the plan!

In Florida and in many states * * * a libel per se is "any publication which exposes a person to distrust, hatred, contempt, ridicule, obloquy". For example, in Briggs v. Brown, 55 Fla. 417, 46 So. 325, 330 (1908) the court states the formula for libels per se as follows:

"A civil action for libel will lie when there has been a false and unprivileged publication by letter or otherwise which exposes a person to distrust, hatred, contempt, ridicule, or obloquy * * * or which has a tendency to injure such person in his office, occupation, business, or employment. If the publication is false and not privileged, and is such that its natural and proximate consequence necessarily causes injury to a person in his personal, social, official, or business relations or life, wrong and injury are presumed and implied, and such publication is actionable per se." * * *

We find that the general law and Florida law are in agreement with Dean Prosser's conclusion: "It is for the court *in the first instance* to determine whether the words are reasonably capable of a particular interpretation, or whether they are necessarily so; it is then for the jury to say whether they were in fact understood as defamatory. If the language used is open to two meanings * * * it is for the jury to determine whether the defamatory sense was the one conveyed." (Emphasis added.) Prosser, Law of Torts § 106, at 765 (1963). * * *

Both judge and jury play a part in determining whether language constitutes libel. The Supreme Court has delineated these roles in Washington Post Co. v. Chaloner, 1919, 250 U.S. 290:

"A publication claimed to be defamatory must be read and construed in the sense in which the readers to whom it is addressed would ordinarily understand it. * * * When thus read, if its meaning is so unambiguous as to reasonably bear but one interpretation, it is for the judge to say whether that signification is defamatory or not. If, upon the other hand, it is capable of two meanings, one of which would be libelous and actionable and the other not, it is for the jury to say, under all the circumstances surrounding its publication, including extraneous facts admissible in evidence, which of the two meanings would be attributed to it by those to whom it is addressed or by whom it may be read." * * *

The district court in this case completely excised the jury's role, a position it could take only on the assumption that the publication unambiguously carried no defamatory meaning. Since the court did not spell out its reasons, the defendants in their briefs have attempted to articulate the rationale for the holding below.

The defendants argue that the article did not "hurt" Belli as an attorney, did not imply that he was "losing his touch with demonstrative evidence", did not affect his ability to "obtain those 'more adequate awards' for seamen and railroad workers for which he is so justly famous". In effect, so the argument runs, the article was nothing more than caustic comment on the acuteness of the Florida Bar Association. Belli simply "showed the Florida lawyers that their agreement was somewhat more favorable to him tha[n] they—in their naiveté—contemplated". In its harshest sense, they say, "the article implies no more than that Mr. Belli 'put one over' on the Florida Bar", which is "not quite the same as conning a destitute widow out of her homestead". In short, Mr. Belli just got "a little more out of the agreement than the Bar Association contemplated".

The defendants make a case—just barely—for the view that the article is capable of being reasonably interpreted as non-defamatory. But since the article on its face is also capable of carrying a defamatory meaning, it is for the jury to decide whether the words were in fact so understood.

The plaintiff contends, in his brief, "No person reading the headline and the article *sub judice* * * * could conclude other than that Melvin Belli, both as a lawyer and as a private citizen is grasping, conniving, contemptible, dishonest; a cheat, swindler, trickster, deceiver, defrauder; a person to be avoided, shunned and distrusted." Without benefit of the defendants' cavalier reading of the article or the plaintiff's retort hyperbolic, we consider that the bare bones of the article are capable of carrying the meaning that Belli tricked and deceived the Florida Bar Association out of hundreds of dollars worth of clothes. * * *

The author's comment seems intended to insure the common reader's understanding of what purportedly happened. The common reader is likely to understand "take", just as Miss Yothers must have understood it. A recent dictionary defines it: "To cheat, deceive"; other dictionaries agree with this definition. The man in the street is likely to understand that hotel expenses do not include "hundreds of dollars worth of clothing". But any doubts the reader might have as to what purportedly happened are likely to be resolved by the reference to Belli's "plan" to "take" the Florida Bar. We hold that a jury might reasonably conclude that the conduct imputed to Belli was incompatible with the standards of an ethical lawyer and as such violated one of the four traditional categories of libel per se. A jury might also conclude that such conduct subjected Belli to contempt, and ridicule, humiliating him socially and injuring him professionally.

The Court has some doubt whether the publication in question carries a non-defamatory meaning. The Court has very little doubt that it carries a defamatory meaning. The Court has concluded however that the final determination of the issue of defamation should be made by a jury.

The story is nine years old. It was not made within the context of a discussion of an important public issue. Nevertheless, the delimiting effect of the law of libel on First Amendment rights and a free press impels the Court not to excise the role of the jury. "Since one's reputation is the view which others take of him * * * [w]hether an idea injures a person's reputation depends upon the opinions of those to whom it is published." Developments in the Law: Defamation, 69 Harv.L.Rev. 875, 881–82 (1956). Thus, because it is impractical, even unreliable, to depend upon in-court testimony of recipients of the particular publication for determining whether that publication is defamatory, a logical function of the jury is to decide whether the plaintiff has been lowered in the esteem of those to whom the idea was published. * * *

We reverse the dismissal of the district court and remand the case for further proceedings consistent with this opinion.

NOTES AND QUESTIONS

1. The older definition of defamation was that of a communication to a third person which "tends to hold the plaintiff up to hatred, contempt or ridicule or to cause him to be shunned or avoided." This appears to have originated with Baron Parke, in Parmiter v. Coupland, 6 M. & W. 105, 108, 151 Eng.Rep. 340, 342 (1840). It is still often repeated by the courts.

2. When the question has arisen, the later cases have recognized that this definition is too narrow. Defamation is rather a communication that tends to damage the plaintiff's "reputation," more or less in the popular sense—that is, to diminish the respect, good will, confidence or esteem in which he is held, or to excite adverse or unpleasant feelings about him. And this is the case even though decent citizens would regard him only with pity.

3. Which of the following are in themselves defamatory?

"He is dead." Cf. Lemmer v. The Tribune, 50 Mont. 559, 148 P. 338 (1915). "He is under treatment for mental illness." Cowper v. Vannier, 20 Ill.App.2d 499, 156 N.E.2d 761 (1959). "He refuses to pay his just debts." Thompson v. Adelberg & Berman, 181 Ky. 487, 205 S.W. 558 (1918). "His parents were never married." Cf. Harris v. Nashville Trust Co., 128 Tenn. 573, 162 S.W. 584 (1914). "He is a liar." Murphy v. Harty, 238 Or. 228, 393 P.2d 206 (1964). A motion picture portrays an identifiable woman as having been raped by Rasputin. Youssoupoff v. Metro–Goldwyn–Mayer Pictures Ltd., 50 T.L.R. 581, 99 A.L.R. 864 (1934) (C.A.). His face "resembles a hard-boiled egg," "roly-poly, like a rubber beach toy," "relentlessly small town in fashion and horizon." Raymer v. Doubleday & Co., Inc., 615 F.2d 241 (5th Cir.1980). "Sinatra's Mouthpiece." Rudin v. Dow Jones & Co., 510 F.Supp. 210 (S.D.N.Y.1981).

Grant v. Reader's Digest Ass'n

United States Circuit Court of Appeals, Second Circuit, 1945.
151 F.2d 733.

L. HAND, CIRCUIT JUDGE. This is an appeal from a judgment dismissing a complaint in libel for insufficiency in law upon its face. The complaint alleged that the plaintiff was a Massachusetts lawyer, living in that state; that the defendant, a New York corporation, published a periodical of general circulation, read by lawyers, judges and the general public; and that one issue of the periodical contained an article entitled "I Object To My Union in Politics," in which the following passage appeared:

"And another thing. In my state the Political Action Committee has hired as its legislative agent one, Sidney S. Grant, who but recently was a legislative representative for the Massachusetts Communist Party."

The innuendo then alleged that this passage charged the plaintiff with having represented the Communist Party in Massachusetts as its legislative agent, which was untrue and malicious. Two questions arise: (1) What meaning the jury might attribute to the words; (2) whether the meaning so attributed was libellous. * * * The case therefore turns upon whether it is libellous in New York to write of a lawyer that he has acted as agent of the Communist Party, and is a believer in its aims and methods.

The interest at stake in all defamation is concededly the reputation of the person assailed; and any moral obliquity of the opinions of those in whose minds the words might lessen that reputation, would normally be relevant only in mitigation of damages. A man may value his reputation even among those who do not embrace the prevailing moral standards; and it would seem that the jury should be allowed to appraise how far he should be indemnified for the disesteem of such persons. That is the usual rule. [Cc] The New York decisions define libel, in accordance with the usual rubric, as consisting of utterances which arouse "hatred, contempt, scorn, obloquy or shame," and the like. [Cc] However, the opinions at times seem to make it a condition that to be actionable the words must be such as would so affect "right-thinking" people. * * * The same limitation has apparently been recognized in England [c]; and it is fairly plain that there must come a point where that is true. As was said in Mawe v. Piggott, Irish Rep. 4 Comm.Law, 54, 62, among those "who were themselves criminal or sympathized with crime," it would expose one "to great odium to represent him as an informer or prosecutor or otherwise aiding in the detection of crime"; yet certainly the words would not be actionable. Be that as it may, in New York, if the exception covers more than such a case, it does not go far enough to excuse the utterance at bar. Katapodis v. Brooklyn Spectator, Inc., 287 N.Y. 17, 38 N.E.2d 112 * * * held that the imputation of extreme poverty might be actionable; although certainly "right-thinking people" ought not to shun, or despise, or otherwise condemn one because he is poor. Indeed, the only declaration of the Court of Appeals [c] leaves it still open whether it is not libellous to say that a man is insane. [Cc]

We do not believe, therefore, that we need say whether "right-thinking" people would harbor similar feelings toward a lawyer, because he had been an agent for the Communist Party, or was a sympathizer with its aims and means. It is enough if there be some, as there certainly are, who would feel so, even though they would be "wrong-thinking" people if they did. * * *

Judgment reversed; cause remanded.

NOTES AND QUESTIONS

1.   In accord with this decision are two excellent, and lengthy, opinions arising out of a very similar charge, in Herrmann v. Newark Morning Ledger Co., 48 N.J.Super. 420, 138 A.2d 61 (1958), second appeal, 49 N.J.Super. 551, 140 A.2d 529 (1958).

2.   The leading case is Peck v. Tribune Co., 214 U.S. 185 (1909), where defendant, by mistake, published plaintiff's picture accompanying a testimonial signed by another woman, who was a nurse, in praise of the merits of Duffy's Pure Malt Whiskey. Holmes, J.: "If the advertisement obviously would hurt the plaintiff in the estimation of an important and respectable part of the community, liability is not a question of majority vote." 214 U.S. at 190. Massachusetts courts have kept the Holmesian faith: King v. Globe Newspaper Co., 400 Mass. 705, 512 N.E.2d 241

(1987) (because statement about plaintiff governor had both a libelous and a non-libelous meaning, trial judge could not enter summary judgment for defendant).

3.   What about the statement that plaintiff is obtaining a divorce? Gersten v. Newark Morning Ledger Co., 52 N.J.Super. 152, 145 A.2d 56 (1958). Or that a business man is a "price cutter"? Meyerson v. Hurlbut, 68 App.D.C. 360, 98 F.2d 232 (1938). Or that a kosher meat dealer sells bacon? Braun v. Armour & Co., 254 N.Y. 514, 173 N.E. 845 (1930). The issue is embedded in time, place, and culture. Jones v. R. L. Polk & Co., 190 Ala. 243, 67 So. 577 (1915) (to be described as "colored" defamatory); Natchez Times Publishing Co. v. Dunigan, 221 Miss. 320, 72 So.2d 681 (1954) (to be listed as a "negro" in the telephone book is defamatory); but not so in England, Forbes v. King, (1833) 1 Dowl. 672, 2 L.J.Ex. 109 (to write that plaintiff is a "Man Friday" not defamatory). An imputation of homosexuality? Nowark v. Maguire, 22 A.D.2d 901, 255 N.Y.S.2d 318 (1964); Buck v. Savage, 323 S.W.2d 363 (Tex.Civ.App.1959); Hayes v. Smith, 832 P.2d 1022 (Colo.App.1991); Liberace v. Daily Mirror Newspapers, Ltd., The Times, June 18, 1959.

4.   There must, however, be an element of discredit or disgrace, even in the eyes of the particular segment of the community. Thus if a Democrat is called a Republican, it is quite probable that unpleasant feelings would be aroused against him in the minds of some other Democrats; but it can scarcely be regarded as defamatory. Cf. Steinman v. Di Roberts, 23 A.D.2d 693, 257 N.Y.S.2d 695 (1965) ("liberal"); Haas v. Evening Democrat Co., 252 Iowa 517, 107 N.W.2d 444 (1961) ("conservative"). What of a publication saying a woman is a "feminist"?

5.   A statement that plaintiff has informed the police about crime has been held not to be defamatory. Why? Mawe v. Piggott, Ir.R. 4 C.L. 54 (1869); Rose v. Borenstein, 119 N.Y.S.2d 288 (1953); Byrne v. Deane, [1937] 1 K.B. 818. In the last case the allegation was that the plaintiff had "ratted" to the police about fellow club members' illegal gambling on club premises. Yet the goodwill of fellow club members may be vital to a person's functioning in society. Why have a test that fails to undergird the individual's interest in being free of imputations that tend to estrange her from those with whom social intercourse is most important?

Pleading Defamation

6.   When the meaning that defames the plaintiff is clear upon the face of the words uttered, the cause of action is made out by pleading, and proving, the words themselves and their communication to a third person. If the meaning is not clear upon the face of the words, the task of the plaintiff is more difficult. For example, take the words: "He burned down his own barn." This the plaintiff would have a perfect right to do if he chose, and on its face the statement does not defame him. Here the courts very early set up quite technical rules as to the way in which the action must be pleaded; and although these have been relaxed slightly here and there, they are in the main still rather rigidly followed. In such a case the plaintiff must plead:

A.   The defamatory words, "He burned down his own barn."

B.   The publication: communication of the words to a third person. "Defendant spoke these words to X."

C.   Extrinsic facts, because of which the words were reasonably understood to convey a meaning defaming the plaintiff. This is called the "inducement." For example, X knew that plaintiff had insurance on the barn.

D.   A formal allegation that the words were spoken of and concerning plaintiff. This is called the "colloquium." "He (meaning the plaintiff) burned down his own barn."

E.   An allegation of the particular defamatory meaning conveyed by the words. This is called the "innuendo." In this case, that the words were understood by X to mean that plaintiff had burned the barn in order to defraud the insurance company, which would be the crime of arson.

F.   Special damages, when they are necessary to the cause of action.

7.   Both the colloquium and the innuendo must be reasonable in the light of the words spoken and the facts pleaded in the inducement. If the words, together with such facts, do not fairly support the defamatory meaning pleaded, no cause of action is made out. See also Davis v. R.K.O. Radio Pictures, 191 F.2d 901 (8th Cir.1951) (colloquium); Grice v. Holk, 268 Ala. 500, 108 So.2d 359 (1959) (innuendo).

Kilian v. Doubleday & Co., Inc.

Supreme Court of Pennsylvania, 1951.
367 Pa. 117, 79 A.2d 657.

HORACE STERN, JUSTICE. In this action for libel the jury rendered a verdict in favor of defendant. Plaintiff appeals from the refusal of the court below to grant him a new trial.

This is the way in which the allegedly libelous article came to be written:—At the American University in Washington a course in English was conducted by Don M. Wolfe, the students being disabled veterans of World War II. The course consisted, in part, of the writing by the students of essays or stories about their personal experiences in the war; their compositions would be submitted to Dr. Wolfe, who suggested corrections and revisions. Dr. Wolfe conceived the idea of having these stories published in book form, and, after an original publication by another concern, he entered into a contract with defendant, Doubleday & Company, for that purpose. Each student in the class, 53 in all, contributed at least one article. The book was published under the title "The Purple Testament", and it was advertised in the jacket as consisting of "the native eloquence of *absolute honesty*," and as constituting "the fragments of their [the authors'] *own intimate experiences*." Some 9000 copies were sold and distributed throughout the United States. Among the articles was one by Joseph M. O'Connell which gave rise to the present suit.

O'Connell was a soldier who had been seriously injured during the course of the Normandy invasion and was hospitalized from August to October, 1944, at a station hospital about 12 miles from Lichfield, England, where there was a large replacement depot. In the original draft of the article which he wrote he narrated incidents said to have occurred at the Lichfield camp and which, he testified at the trial, were described to him by individuals who had allegedly witnessed them. Dr. Wolfe, to whom he submitted the draft several times, stated that he "thought it was interesting, and that it was the first time he had heard about it", but twice returned it with the suggestion that O'Connell should use "more descriptive detail", that he should "make it more vivid", that it "did not have in it the sights, sounds and bits of conversation necessary to make the story readable". The result was that whereas O'Connell had originally written the article in the third person he now wrote it, in order to "make it more vivid", in the first person, purporting that the incidents he narrated occurred under his own personal observation and in his own experience.

The story, as it finally appeared in "The Purple Testament", may be condensed as follows:—I [O'Connell] and my buddy, while being transferred in an ambulance from one hospital to another in England, reached a big army camp near Lichfield. The camp was dreary and ugly; it reminded me of the rotten, filthy German prison camps I had seen in France. As we lay in the ambulance we heard a loud voice outside shouting: "Just let me catch one of you sons o'bitches loaf on this detail and you'll get twenty lashes when you get back tonight." A group of four men came to carry us into the hospital; they were all dressed in blue pants and shirts with a large letter "P" sewed on their clothes. The same loud voice I had heard a few minutes before said: "You're not supposed to talk to these _____ prisoners." A big heavy-set sergeant stepped closer to me and said, "All they are is a bunch of cowards. They are too yellow to go back to combat. They'll be glad to go back when they finish with this prison." The sergeant ordered them to carry us into the hospital; as they were placing me there in my bed I noticed that one of them had all the fingers of his right hand missing and three fingers of his left. Could such things be allowed in our army? If so, it was being covered up by the brass, and the brass were making suckers of the American people. A ward attendant limping around outside the room came in and said: "I was blown out of a tank; all the muscle of my right leg was blown away. * * * I came through this way on my way [back] to combat. One day the old man (Colonel _____) ordered us out on a ten-mile hike. After about two miles I fell flat on my face. They ordered me on, but I couldn't go. So the next day they took me before the old dictator. He ordered me before a quick court martial. I got six months of hard labor. The doctor said I was unfit for hard labor, so they assigned me to this hospital. I'm still a prisoner. The other night a guard caught me stealing a piece of bread from the kitchen, and I got fifty lashes for it." * * * In the morning the old colonel himself came along to inspect the hospital. He wasn't a big guy, but he was stockily built. Behind his glasses his eyes were mean. He looked like a man who enjoys seeing another man suffer. He was surrounded by a lot of other officers. None of them looked good to me. After one scowling glance at Red [my buddy] and me, he left. As we were being carried down the hall of the ward the big sergeant was clubbing a G.I. in a corner, while some officers looked on. I only hoped that some day I would meet up with that big sergeant and the rest of the people that ran that prison. The death chair would be too good for them. But as always, Colonel _____ and the rest of the responsible officers will be protected by the big brass. Mark my word, Colonel _____ and his bullies will get off light. That is Lichfield justice.

It is not questioned that by "Colonel _____", the "old dictator", and "the old colonel", was meant Colonel Kilian, the present plaintiff, who was the commanding officer of the Lichfield camp. At the end of the article as published there was appended a footnote which Dr. Wolfe himself had added and which stated:—"On August 29, 1946, the Associated Press reported that Colonel James A. Kilian was convicted 'of permitting cruel and unusual punishment of American soldiers.' He was reprimanded by the military court and fined $500.—Editor." This insertion was obviously intended to give the impression that what was said or implied in the article in regard to Colonel Kilian was corroborated by his conviction, and further that, as the author of the article had predicted, he "got off light".

The fact in regard to plaintiff's trial before a military court in 1946 is this:—He was charged with *authorizing, aiding and abetting* the imposition of cruel, unusual and unauthorized punishments upon prisoners in confinement at the depot of which he was the Commanding Officer. The punishments referred to were itemized in the charge. A second specification was that he *knowingly permitted* the imposition of such punishments. As to the first specification—authorizing, aiding and abetting—he was acquitted; as to the second specification—knowingly permitting—he was acquitted of *knowingly* permitting and found guilty merely of *permitting;* in other words, he was convicted of neglect, but not of actual wrongdoing or of acquiescing in what occurred. Moreover, many of the alleged punishments specified in the charge as having been "permitted" were deleted by the court because they were not supported by the evidence. * * *

As affirmative defense to the action defendant pleaded justification on the ground that the publication was "a *true and accurate account of events which were observed by the author of the article in question.*" How is that defense supported by the testimony presented at the trial? As far as O'Connell being an eye-witness of any of the alleged happenings at the camp is concerned, he admitted on the witness stand that he never was at Lichfield; therefore, his article, in that respect, was wholly false. Defendant produced as witnesses three soldiers who *were* at Lichfield, who testified to punishments inflicted on them or observed by them as imposed on others, but none of the incidents they described tended to prove that a single one of the events narrated in the O'Connell article actually occurred; therefore such testimony was not properly admissible to prove the truth of the publication. While, in order to support a defense of truth, it is necessary merely to prove that it was *substantially* true, and while, therefore, if the testimony of those witnesses had shown a variance merely in the details of the events described in the article it would nevertheless have been admissible as giving support to the plea of truth, it furnished no such support by proving that other and wholly different incidents occurred although these also may have been equally blameworthy. * * * "Specific charges cannot be justified by showing the plaintiff's general bad character; and if the accusation is one of particular misconduct, such as stealing a watch from A, it is not enough to show a different offense, even though it be a more serious one, such as stealing a clock from A, or six watches from B." Prosser on Torts, p. 855, § 95. * * * None of defendant's testimony showed any instances at the camp, as alleged in O'Connell's article, of lashing, of cursing prisoners, of having a soldier whose fingers were missing act as a stretcher bearer, of ordering a badly wounded veteran on a ten-mile hike. * * * It is obvious that there was not a shred of testimony presented at the trial to prove either that the author of the article saw any of the events he narrated, or that those events or even substantially similar ones occurred, or that plaintiff was aware of any such happenings, or that he sanctioned them, or that he was a "dictator", or that in his very appearance he looked like a man who would enjoy seeing another man suffer. The court, therefore, was in error in submitting to the jury, as it did, the question whether the publication was substantially true. * * *

Judgment reversed and new trial awarded.

NOTES AND QUESTIONS

1.   Under the common law the defense that the defamatory statement was true was not open to the defendant in a prosecution for criminal libel. That crime was originated to suppress sedition, and later extended to prevent breaches of the peace, and neither was likely to be minimized if the defamation were true. Hence the criminal courts took no account of any freedom to publish the truth. De Libellis Famosis, 5 Co.Rep. 125, 77 Eng.Rep. 250 (1605); Franklin's Case, 9 Hargrave St. Trials 255, 269 (1731). This explains the statement, usually attributed to Lord Mansfield, that "the greater the truth the greater the libel." In this country, the Supreme Court has held that a criminal libel statute is unconstitutional if it imposes a penalty for making a true statement about a public official. Garrison v. Louisiana, 379 U.S. 64 (1964).

2.   The criminal law rule never was applied to civil actions. Johns v. Gittings, Cro.Eliz. 239, 78 Eng.Rep. 495 (1590); Hilsdon v. Saunders, Cro.Jac. 677, 79 Eng.Rep. 586 (1624). At common law there has been general agreement that an action of defamation will lie only if the statement is both defamatory and false. Statutes in a few states and judicial decisions in some others have indicated that an action may lie even for a true statement if it was not made for good motives and justifiable ends. E.g., Hutchins v. Page, 75 N.H. 215, 72 A. 689 (1909). But a statute of this nature was held unconstitutional as a violation of the First Amendment in Farnsworth v. Tribune Co., 43 Ill.2d 286, 253 N.E.2d 408 (1969). This is probably the result that the United States Supreme Court would reach if the issue were presented to it.

Even where true and thus not actionable as defamation, a statement may support a cause of action for invasion of privacy. See Cox Broadcasting Co. v. Cohn, 420 U.S. 469 (1975), infra page 948, and notes following.

3.   *Burden of Proof.* It has long been customary for the plaintiff to allege in his complaint that the statement is false. The common law raised a presumption of the falsity of all statements that were defamatory. As a result truth has been consistently treated as an affirmative defense, which the defendant must raise and on which he has the burden of proof. Supreme Court decisions engendered doubt about the soundness of this common law position. In the 1985 decision of Philadelphia Newspapers, Inc. v. Hepps, infra at page 907, the Supreme Court in a 5–to–4 decision held that a "media defendant for speech of public concern," had the burden of proving falsity.

4. As the principal case indicates, the determination is whether the statement is substantially true. See, e.g., Sun Printing & Publishing Ass'n v. Schenck, 98 Fed. 925 (2d Cir.1900) (specific charge of crime not justified by proof of another and more serious crime); Crellin v. Thomas, 122 Utah 122, 247 P.2d 264 (1952) (charge that plaintiff was a "whore" not shown by evidence that she worked for a short time as a "dance hall girl" or "percentage girl"). See Restatement (Second) of Torts §§ 581A, 613, caveat; St. Surin v. Virgin Islands Daily News, 21 F.3d 1309 (3d Cir.1994) (statement indicating that plaintiff was under criminal investigation, implied by references to a "prosecutor" in the headline and the U.S. Attorney's office in the article's body, was not coextensive with the truth that he was being investigated by the Environmental Protection Agency). In *St. Surin* the sting of the article was found to be factually untrue. Whereas in Smith v. Maldonado, 72 Cal.App.4th 637, 85 Cal.Rptr.2d 397 (1999), the truth of a highlighting that a third party may be conceivably understood as having a defamatory meaning; held no liability for the republication.

In the principal case, O'Connell, the writer of the story, states that some of the "events" were told to him by other persons. Suppose that the story had been told to him, but it was untrue. Liability on his part?

5. In a gubernatorial race, defendant newspaper, supporting the candidate of one party, carried a number of stories about a land transaction involving a company of which plaintiff, the other candidate, was president. The stories were essentially accurate, but the headlines and subtitles were intentionally misleading and calculated to create a false impression on the normal reader as to plaintiff's ethical conduct. Can the stories be found to be false? Sprouse v. Clay Communication, Inc., 158 W.Va. 427, 211 S.E.2d 674 (1975).

6. Suppose the plaintiff pleads as defamatory only part of a published work. Can the nonpleaded portions of the publication be considered in determining whether the pleaded portions inflicted reputational harm? In *Masson* the 9th Circuit had relied on this "incremental harm" doctrine as an alternative basis for affirming the decision of the District Court. The court ruled that "[g]iven the * * * many provocative, bombastic statements indisputably made by Masson and quoted by Malcolm, the additional damage caused [by the pleaded imputation] was nominal or non-existent, rendering the defamation claim as to this quote nonactionable," 895 F.2d at 1541. The Supreme Court stated in *Masson* that this "incremental harm" doctrine is not part of First Amendment jurisprudence although it may be accepted under state law. The doctrine is a specific application of the law that a plaintiff's reputation may be so reduced that he is unable to show that the imputation materially worsened his reputation—that the plaintiff is "libel proof." The 9th Circuit, on remand from the Supreme Court, dealt with the "incremental harm" doctrine, among other issues. 960 F.2d 896 (1992). The Court noted that the doctrine was one of state law and quoted the words of then-Judge Scalia in Liberty Lobby, Inc. v. Anderson, 746 F.2d 1563, 1568 (D.C.Cir.1984).

The theory must be rejected because it rests upon the assumption that one's reputation is a monolith, which stands or falls in its entirety. The law, however, proceeds upon the optimistic premise that there is a little bit of good in all of us—or perhaps upon the pessimistic assumption that no matter how bad someone is, he can always be worse. * * * ("He was a liar and a thief, but for all that he was a good family man.")

See also Wall St.J. A16 (Feb. 21, 1992) (psychiatrist describing Jeffrey Dahmer as "an organized, non-social, lust murderer," but "not such a bad person"). Judge Scalia concluded that the incremental harm doctrine is simply a "bad idea." *Liberty*

Lobby, 746 F.2d at 1569. The 9th Circuit agreed it was a "bad idea" and that therefore the incremental harm doctrine was not an "element of the California libel law."

The "limited, narrow" doctrine was applied in Sharon v. Time Inc., 575 F.Supp. 1162 (S.D.N.Y.1983) (General Ariel Sharon, former Israeli Minister of Defense, brought a defamation action against *Time* for article accusing him of knowingly permitting or encouraging the murder of Palestinian refugees at the Sabra and Shatilla camps in West Beirut; *Time* argued that Sharon was "libel proof" since his reputation was so tarnished by other derogatory unchallenged allegations about him; it was held that he had a sufficient reputation capable of being impugned). In Cerasani v. Sony Corporation, 991 F.Supp. 343 (S.D.N.Y.1998), the court found that plaintiff's reputation was so "badly tarnished" that he was "libel proof." Plaintiff was, the court found, a "convicted racketeer, Mafia associate, bank robber, and drug dealer." An unsuccessful prosecution did not rehabilitate him. Defendant may plead true damaging facts, either contained in the publication or outside it, relevant to plaintiff's reputation but those must be "closely related to the false ones." The requirement of relevance guards against the introduction in the evidence of a broad and boundless litany of plaintiff's discreditable acts of all kinds: Haynes v. Alfred A. Knopf, 8 F.3d 1222, 1229 (7th Cir.1993). Note that evidence of bad reputation may reduce damages. The evidence must take the form of opinion of the plaintiff's general reputation and may not encompass specific misdeeds, Snively v. Record Publishing Co., 185 Cal. 565, 198 P. 1, 7 (1921). Rumors are admissible if shown to be sufficiently widespread to affect the plaintiff's reputation. Blickenstaff v. Perrin, 27 Ind. 527 (1867); Stuart v. News Pub. Co., 67 N.J.L. 317, 51 A. 709 (1902).

Neiman–Marcus v. Lait

United States District Court, Southern District of New York, 1952.
13 F.R.D. 311.

IRVING R. KAUFMAN, DISTRICT JUDGE. * * * The defendants are authors of a book entitled "U.S.A. Confidential". The plaintiffs are the Neiman–Marcus Company, a Texas corporation operating a department store at Dallas, Texas, and three groups of its employees. They allege that the following matter libelled and defamed them: * * *

"He [Stanley Marcus, president of plaintiff Neiman–Marcus Company] may not know that some Neiman models are call girls—the top babes in town. The guy who escorts one feels in the same league with the playboys who took out Ziegfeld's glorified. Price, a hundred bucks a night.

"The salesgirls are good, too—pretty, and often much cheaper—twenty bucks on the average. They're more fun, too, not as snooty as the models. We got this confidential, from a Dallas wolf.

"Neiman–Marcus also contributes to the improvement of the local breed when it imports New York models to make a flash at style shows. These girls are the cream of the crop. Oil millionaires toss around thousand-dollar bills for a chance to take them out.

"Neiman's was a women's specialty shop until the old biddies who patronized it decided their husbands should get class, too. So Neiman's put in a men's store. Well, you should see what happened. You wonder how all the faggots got to the wild and woolly. You thought those with talent ended up in New York and Hollywood and the plodders got government jobs in Washington. Then you learn the nucleus of the Dallas fairy colony is composed of many Neiman dress and millinery designers, imported from New York and Paris, who sent for their boy friends when the men's store expanded. Now most of the sales staff are fairies, too." * * *

[Plaintiffs sued in the following groups:]

(1) Nine individual models who constitute the entire group of models at the time of the publication * * *;

(2) Fifteen salesmen of a total of twenty-five suing on their own behalf and on behalf of the others * * *;

(3) Thirty saleswomen of a total of 382 suing on their own behalf and on behalf of the others. * * *

[T]he following propositions are rather widely accepted:

(1) Where the group or class libelled is large, none can sue even though the language used is inclusive. [Cc]

(2) Where the group or class libelled is small, and each and every member of the group or class is referred to, then any individual member can sue. [Cc]

Conflict arises when the publication complained of libels *some* or *less than all* of a designated small group. Some courts say no cause of action exists in any individual of the group. [Cc] Other courts in other states would apparently allow such an action. [Cc] * * *

[I]t is the opinion of this Court that the plaintiff salesmen, of whom it is alleged that "most * * * are fairies" have a cause of action in New York and most likely other states * * * Defendants' motion to dismiss as to the salesmen for failure to state a claim upon which relief can be granted is denied.

The plaintiff saleswomen are in a different category. The alleged defamatory statement in defendants' book speaks of the saleswomen generally. While it does not use the word "all" or similar terminology, yet it stands unqualified. However, the group of saleswomen is extremely large, consisting of 382 members at the time of publication. No specific individual is named in the alleged libelous statement. I am not cited to a single case which would support a cause of action by an individual member of any group of such magnitude. * * *

Giving the plaintiff saleswomen the benefit of all legitimate favorable inferences, the defendants' alleged libel cannot reasonably be said to concern more than the saleswomen as a class. There is no language referring to some ascertained or ascertainable person. Nor is the class so small that it follows that defamation of the class infects the individual of the class. This Court so holds as a matter of law since it is of the opinion that no reasonable man would take the writer seriously and conclude from the publication a reference to any individual saleswoman. [Cc]

While it is generally recognized that even where the group is large, a member of the group may have a cause of action if some particular circumstances point to the plaintiff as the person defamed, no such circumstances are alleged in the amended complaint. * * *

Accordingly, it is the opinion of this Court that as a matter of law the individual saleswomen do not state a claim for libel upon which relief can be granted and the motion to dismiss their cause of action is granted. * * *

The amended complaint is dismissed with leave to file separate complaints as to the two groups of individuals and the corporation, all in conformity with this opinion.

NOTES AND QUESTIONS

1. For which of the following statements may an individual member of the group or class maintain an action for defamation?

"All trading stamp concerns are engaged in dishonest practices." Watson v. Detroit Journal Co., 143 Mich. 430, 107 N.W. 81 (1906). "That jury was bribed." Byers v. Martin, 2 Colo. 605, 25 Am.Rep. 755 (1875). "The election board is crooked." Story v. Jones, 52 Ill.App. 112 (1893). "All men are liars." Psalms 116:11.

2. No recovery was allowed when defendant, addressing three men, said "One of you is a crook." Cohn v. Brecher, 20 Misc.2d 329, 192 N.Y.S.2d 877 (1959); and Ball v. White, 3 Mich.App. 579, 143 N.W.2d 188 (1966) (one out of five). But recovery was allowed in Forbes v. Johnson, 50 Ky. 48 (1850) (statement that a note had been altered by A or by B); Hardy v. Williamson, 86 Ga. 551, 12 S.E. 874 (1891) (eleven engineers employed by one company, "or some of them").

3. In McCullough v. Cities Service Co., 676 P.2d 833 (Okl.1984) the plaintiff sought to bring an action as an osteopath based upon a publication that attacked generally that branch of the medical profession. The court held that the plaintiff's action was not maintainable noting that there were 19,686 doctors of osteopathy in the United States. Although size alone was not determinative, it was an important factor in determining whether the "intensity of the suspicion" cast upon the plaintiff was sufficient to give him a right to maintain a personal action. What of an allegation that National Football League players take steroids? See Fawcett Publications, Inc. v. Morris, 377 P.2d 42 (Okl.1962), cert. denied, 376 U.S. 513 (1964). See also Church of Scientology Intern. v. Time Warner, Inc., 806 F.Supp. 1157 (S.D.N.Y. 1992) (Church of Scientology International claimed it was defamed by a *Time* article; nearly two hundred entities constituted the Church; thus general references were not "of and concerning" the plaintiff; four specific references could be so construed); and Texas Beef Group v. Oprah Winfrey, 11 F.Supp.2d 858 (N.D.Tex. 1998) (segment of program describing the dangers of Mad Cow Disease in the United States did not identify the Texas Panhandle ranchers who brought the action for the decline in their business following the program).

4. Immediately after the Second World War, social concern, resulting in some legislation, focused on group defamation directed at, among others, Jews, Catholics, and African-Americans. An Illinois Act, conferring protection on racial minorities from defamation, survived a constitutional challenge in Beauharnais v. Illinois, 343 U.S. 250 (1952). First Amendment jurisprudence has since undermined the validity of such legislation, see New York Times v. Sullivan, infra page 867 and Hustler Magazine v. Falwell, infra page 964. Racial hate speech has returned as a social issue. At the same time, pornography and sexual harassment have been perceived as

social evils. See MacKinnon, Pornography, Civil Rights, and Speech, 20 Harv.C.R.–C.L.L.Rev. 1 (1985). Again, the debate has turned to appropriate legal response within the confines of the First Amendment. See Smolla, Free Speech in an Open Society, 165 (1992). The Supreme Court in R.A.V. v. City of St. Paul, 505 U.S. 377 (1992), reviewed the constitutionality of St. Paul's Bias–Motivated Crime Ordinance that proscribed actions arousing "anger, alarm, or resentment in others on the basis of race, color, creed, religion or gender." The petitioner and others were charged with the criminal offense. They had burned a cross in the backyard of an African–American family. The legislation was found unconstitutional because it regulated only some violence-inducing speech and because it controlled content and threatened censorship of ideas. First Amendment jurisprudence, and the law of defamation, is imbued with the idea of individual rights. Is it legitimate to shift to a recognition of group rights? Why should the "victims" of this speech bear the burden of the benefit of the public's free-speech interest? See Schauer, Uncoupling Free Speech, 92 Col.L.Rev. 1321 (1992) (suggesting a public scheme for compensating victims). For discussion of these issues see Symposium, Free Speech and Religious, Racial, and Sexual Harassment, 32 Wm. & Mary L.Rev. 207 (1991); Symposium, Hate Speech After R.A.V.: More Conflict Between Free Speech and Equality?, 18 Wm.Mitchell L.Rev. 889 (1992) (a useful listing of leading articles is set forth at p. 902); Byrne, Racial Insults and Free Speech Within the University, 79 Geo.L.J. 399 (1991); and O'Callaghan, Pornography and Group Libel: How to Solve the *Hudnut* Problem, 27 New England L.Rev. 363 (1992). Elsewhere in the Common Law world the problem has been addressed without the parameters of the First Amendment but still constrained by free speech concerns, see Partlett, From Red Lion Square to Skokie to the Fatal Shore: Racial Defamation and Freedom of Speech, 22 Vand.J.Trans.L. 431 (1989).

5. *Who Can Be Defamed?* Any living person can be defamed. Even a child ten minutes old may have a cause of action if called a bastard. On the other hand, it is generally agreed that there can be no actionable defamation of the dead, since there is no living person whose reputation is affected. Bello v. Random House, Inc., 422 S.W.2d 339 (Mo.1967); Gruschus v. Curtis Pub. Co., 342 F.2d 775 (10th Cir.1965). The defamation of the dead may, however, also defame the living, as where it is said that the plaintiff's deceased mother was not married to his father. Merrill v. Post Pub. Co., 197 Mass. 185, 83 N.E. 419 (1908).

6. A corporation can have no reputation in the personal sense, and cannot be defamed, for example, by being accused of unchastity. Neither can a partnership, as such. "The venereal disease was not a partnership malady. That was individual property." Bleckey, C.J., in Gilbert v. Crystal Fountain Lodge, 80 Ga. 284, 4 S.E. 905 (1887). But a corporation can maintain an action for defamation that casts an aspersion upon its honesty, credit, efficiency, or other business character. This is true even of a charitable or benevolent corporation not operated for profit, since defamation affecting its character or operations may deprive it of gifts or other sources of revenue. Boston Nutrition Society v. Stare, 342 Mass. 439, 173 N.E.2d 812 (1961); R.H. Bouligny, Inc. v. United Steelworkers of America, 270 N.C. 160, 154 S.E.2d 344 (1967). The same is true of a partnership, or an unincorporated association, such as a labor union, to the extent that the latter is recognized as a legal entity capable of bringing suit. Kirkman v. Textile Examiners & Shrinkers' Employers' Ass'n, 137 App.Div. 655, 122 N.Y.S. 460 (1910). Should a governmental entity be entitled to maintain an action in libel for words that reflect on it in its government and administrative functions? See Derbyshire County Council v. Times Newspapers Ltd. and others, [1993] AC 534 (House of Lords) (distinguishing governmental entities as bodies that should be open to "uninhibited public criti-

cism" and thus holding that, in contrast to corporations, they should not enjoy a right to sue in libel).

Bindrim v. Mitchell

Court of Appeal of California, Second District, 1979.
92 Cal.App.3d 61, 155 Cal.Rptr. 29, hearing denied by California Supreme Court, 1979; cert. denied 444 U.S. 984, 100 S.Ct. 490, 62 L.Ed.2d 412 (1979), reh. denied 444 U.S. 1040, 100 S.Ct. 713, 62 L.Ed.2d 675 (1980).

[Plaintiff, Paul Bindrim, a Ph.D. and licensed psychologist, used what he designated as a "nude marathon in group therapy as a means of helping people to shed their psychological inhibitions with the removal of their clothes." Defendant Gwen Davis Mitchell, a successful novelist, registered in Bindrim's nude-therapy program, telling him that she was participating for therapeutic reasons only, and signing a contract "not to take photographs, write articles or in any manner disclose who has attended the workshop or what has transpired." Shortly thereafter, she contracted with defendant Doubleday for a novel based on the nude-therapy technique. The novel was written and published under the title of *Touching,* with a principal character, Dr. Simon Herford, using the technique.

Claiming that he was defamed by the depiction, plaintiff brought an action of libel against the two defendants. There was a jury verdict for the plaintiff in the trial court for substantial damages, and the court granted a motion for new trial conditioned on plaintiff's accepting a remittitur. Both plaintiff and the two defendants appealed.]

KINGSLEY, ASSOCIATE JUSTICE. * * * [Defendants] claim that, even if there are untrue statements, there is no showing that plaintiff was identified as the character Simon Herford, in the novel "Touching."

[They] allege that plaintiff failed to show he was identifiable as Simon Herford, relying on the fact that the character in "Touching" was described in the book as a "fat Santa Claus type with long white hair, white sideburns, a cherubic rosy face and rosy forearms" and that Bindrim was clean shaven and had short hair. Defendants rely in part on Wheeler v. Dell Publishing Co., 300 F.2d 372 (7th Cir.1962), which involved an alleged libel caused by a fictional account of an actual murder trial. The *Wheeler* court said (at p. 376):

"In our opinion, any reasonable person who read the book and was in a position to identify Hazel Wheeler with Janice Quill would more likely conclude that the author created the latter in an ugly way so that none would identify her with Hazel Wheeler. It is important to note that while the trial and locale might suggest Hazel Wheeler to those who knew the Chenoweth family, suggestion is not identification. In [Levey v. Warner Bros. Pictures, 57 F.Supp. 40 (S.D.N.Y.1944),] the court said those who had seen her act may have been reminded of her by songs and scenes, but would not reasonably identify her."

However, in *Wheeler* the court found that no one who knew the real widow could possibly identify her with the character in the novel. In the case at bar, the only differences between plaintiff and the Herford character in "Touching" were physical appearance and that Herford was a psychiatrist rather than psychologist. Otherwise, the character Simon Herford was very similar to the actual plaintiff. We cannot say, as did the court in *Wheeler,* that no one who knew plaintiff Bindrim could reasonably identify him with the fictional character. Plaintiff was identified as Herford by several witnesses and plaintiff's own tape recordings of the marathon sessions show that the novel was based substantially on plaintiff's conduct in the nude marathon.

Defendant also relies on Middlebrooks v. Curtis Publishing Co., 413 F.2d 141 (4th Cir.1969), where the marked dissimilarities between the fictional character and the plaintiff supported the court's finding against the reasonableness of identification. In *Middlebrooks,* there was a difference in age, an absence from the locale at the time of the episode, and a difference in employment of the fictional character and plaintiff; nor did the story parallel the plaintiff's life in any significant manner. In the case at bar, apart from some of those episodes allegedly constituting the libelous matter itself, and apart from the physical difference and the fact that plaintiff had a Ph.D., and not an M.D., the similarities between Herford and Bindrim are clear, and the transcripts of the actual encounter weekend show a close parallel between the narrative of plaintiff's novel and the actual real life events. Here, there were many similarities between the character, Herford, and the plaintiff Bindrim and those few differences do not bring the case under the rule of *Middlebrooks.* [C] There is overwhelming evidence that plaintiff and "Herford" were one. * * *

Defendants contend that the fact that the book was labeled as being a "novel" bars any claim that the writer or publisher could be found to have implied that the characters in the book were factual representations not of the fictional characters but of an actual nonfictional person. That contention, thus broadly stated, is unsupported by the cases. The test is whether a reasonable person, reading the book, would understand that the fictional character therein pictured was, in actual fact, the plaintiff acting as described. [C] Each case must stand on its own facts. In some cases, such as Greenbelt Pub. Assn. v. Bresler, 398 U.S. 6 (1970), an appellate court can, on examination of the entire work, find that no reasonable person would have regarded the episodes in the book as being other than the fictional imaginings of the author about how the character he had created would have acted. * * * Whether a reader, identifying plaintiff with the "Dr. Herford" of the book, would regard the passages herein complained of as mere fictional embroidering or as reporting actual language and conduct, was for the jury. Its verdict adverse to the defendants cannot be overturned by this court. * * *

Defendants raise the question of whether there is "publication" for libel where the communication is to only one person or a small group of persons rather than to the public at large. Publication for purposes of defamation is sufficient when the publication is to only one person other than the person defamed. [C] Therefore [it is] irrelevant whether all readers realized plaintiff and Herford were identical.

[The opinion also discusses whether the depiction was defamatory, the application of the "actual malice" test of New York Times v. Sullivan, infra page 867, the fact-opinion dichotomy, and damage issues.]

The judgment, as modified on the motion for a new trial, is further modified as [to damages.] * * *

Otherwise the judgment is affirmed. Neither party shall recover costs on appeal.

JEFFERSON, ASSOCIATE JUSTICE, concurring. * * * The dissent finds error in the instruction given the jury on the issue of identification. The use of the word "reasonably" in the instruction dissipates the dissent's view that only one person was required to understand the defamatory meaning. If one person "reasonably" understood the defamatory character of the language used, it describes what readers generally would "reasonably" understand. I see no basis for the dissent's view that the instruction had the result of mulcting defendants for the exercise of their first amendment right to comment on the nude marathon. The first amendment right to comment does *not* include the right to commit libel. * * *

"Of course the fictional setting does not insure immunity when a reasonable man would understand that the fictional character was a portrayal of the plaintiff. 'Reputations may not be traduced with impunity, whether under the literary forms of a work of fiction or in jest.'" [C]

FILES, PRESIDING JUSTICE (dissenting). * * * Defendants' novel describes a fictitious therapist who is conspicuously different from plaintiff in name, physical appearance, age, personality and profession.

Indeed the fictitious Dr. Herford has none of the characteristics of plaintiff except that Dr. Herford practices nude encounter therapy. Only three witnesses, other than plaintiff himself, testified that they "recognized" plaintiff as the fictitious Dr. Herford. All three of those witnesses had participated in or observed one of plaintiff's nude marathons. The only characteristic mentioned by any of the three witnesses as identifying plaintiff was the therapy practiced. * * *

Plaintiff's brief discusses the therapeutic practices of the fictitious Dr. Herford in two categories: Those practices which are similar to plaintiff's technique are classified as identifying. Those which are unlike plaintiff's are called libelous because they are false. Plaintiff has thus resurrected the spurious logic which Professor Kalven found in the position of the plaintiff in New York Times v. Sullivan, infra page 867. Kalven wrote: "There is revealed here a new technique by which defamation might be endlessly manufactured. First, it is argued that, contrary to all appearances, a statement referred to the plaintiff; then, that it falsely ascribed to the plaintiff something that he did not do, which should be rather easy to prove about a statement that did not refer to plaintiff in the first place. * * *" Kalven, The New York Times Case: A Note on "The Central Meaning of the First Amendment," 1964 The Supreme Court Review 191, 199.

Even if we accept the plaintiff's thesis that criticism of nude encounter therapy may be interpreted as libel of one practitioner, the evidence does not support a finding in favor of plaintiff.

Whether or not a publication to the general public is defamatory is "whether in the mind of the average reader the publication, considered as a whole, could reasonably be considered as defamatory." [C]

The majority opinion contains this juxtaposition of ideas: "Secondly, defendants' [proposed] instructions that the jury must find that a substantial segment of the public did, in fact, believe that Dr. Simon Herford was, in fact, Paul Bindrim * * * was properly refused. For the tort of defamation, publication to one other person is sufficient."

The first sentence refers to the question whether the publication was defamatory of plaintiff. The second refers to whether the defamatory matter was published. The former is an issue in this case. The latter is not. Of course, a publication to one person may constitute actionable libel. But this has no bearing on the principle that the allegedly libelous effect of a publication to the public generally is to be tested by the impression made on the average reader. * * *

From an analytical standpoint, the chief vice of the majority opinion is that it brands a novel as libelous because it is "false," i.e., fiction; and infers "actual malice" from the fact that the author and publisher knew it was not a true representation of plaintiff. From a constitutional standpoint the vice is the chilling effect upon the publisher of any novel critical of any occupational practice, inviting litigation on the theory "when you criticize my occupation, you libel me."

I would reverse the judgment.

NOTES AND QUESTIONS

1.   The colloquium, or reference to the plaintiff, need not be to him by name if it is reasonably understood as referring to him. Peagler v. Phoenix Newspapers, Inc., 114 Ariz. 309, 560 P.2d 1216 (1977); cf. Youssoupoff v. Metro–Goldwyn–Mayer Pictures, 50 T.L.R. 581, 99 A.L.R. 864 (1934) (motion picture purportedly based on historical events; plaintiff identifiable as person raped by Rasputin). But if the words are not reasonably understood to refer to the plaintiff, there is no defamatory imputation identifying plaintiff. Arnold v. Sharpe, 296 N.C. 533, 251 S.E.2d 452 (1979); Sims v. Kiro, Inc., 20 Wash.App. 229, 580 P.2d 642 (1978). When the plaintiff is not expressly identified, the issue is whether a reader with knowledge of the surrounding circumstances could have reasonably understood that the words referred to the plaintiff. The standard against which the material is read or understood changes with the medium. A daily newspaper is read loosely so that factual variations in the story may not prevent the plaintiff from being reasonably identified by the story. For a discussion of these issues see Morgan v. Odhams Press [1971] 2 All E.R. 1156 (House of Lords). The fewer the number of persons who are possessed with knowledge of the surrounding circumstances that identifies the plaintiff, the less the damages that may be awarded.

2. Look at the latter part of the opinion in New York Times v. Sullivan, infra page 867, referring to the purported reference to Police Commissioner in the advertisement. Has it any relevance here?

3. If the novel *Touching* had contained a statement after the title page that this was a work of fiction and any similarity to existing persons was unintended, would that have made a difference?

4. For other recent cases offering variations to the problem of defamation in fiction, see Pring v. Penthouse Int'l, Inc., 695 F.2d 438 (10th Cir.1982), cert. denied, 462 U.S. 1132 (1983) (salacious story about a Miss Wyoming who performed on television at a Miss America Pageant sexual feats too fantastic to be believed; decision by the trial court for the real Miss Wyoming reversed (2–1)); Giesler v. Petrocelli, 616 F.2d 636 (2d Cir.1980) (plaintiff known to defendant, with identical name to that of the major character in a novel about a transsexual tennis player, allowed to recover); Springer v. Viking Press, 90 A.D.2d 315, 457 N.Y.S.2d 246 (1st Dept.1982), aff'd, 60 N.Y.2d 916, 458 N.E.2d 1256, 470 N.Y.S.2d 579 (1983) (plaintiff, former girl friend of author of a novel, given the same name as minor character in the book and similar physical characteristics, not allowed to recover because of insufficient basis for identifying the two); Haynes v. Alfred A. Knopf, 8 F.3d 1222 (7th Cir.1993) (plaintiffs featured in book on social history of black migration from the South to the North; no recovery in defamation or breach of privacy). Do you see problems with the modern genre of television docudramas? Grunfeld, Docudramas: The Legality of Producing Fact–Based Dramas—What Every Producer's Attorney Should Know, 14 Hastings Comm./Ent.L.J. 483 (1992). For interesting comments also incorporating the invasion of privacy tort see Schwartz, Explaining and Justifying a Limited Tort of False Light Invasion of Privacy, 3 Case W.Res.L.Rev. 885, 914–918 (1991).

5. There is a symposium on Defamation in Fiction, in 51 Bklyn.L.Rev. 223 (1985), including 11 articles and covering over 200 pages. See also, on the principal case, Louis, Libel in Fiction: A Chilling Decision for Authors, 6 Art & L. 3 (1983); for an excellent article placing the issue of defamation in fictional works in context see Smolla, Let the Author Beware: The Rejuvenation of the American Law of Libel, 132 U.Pa.L.Rev. 1, 42–47 (1983).

2. Libel and Slander

The erratic and anomalous development of the law of defamation has led to the survival until the present day of two forms of action for defamatory publication. One is libel, which originally concerned written or printed words; the other is slander, which was originally oral.

The prime significance of the distinction lies in the requirement of proof of damages. It has long been the rule as to slander that it is necessary to prove "special damages" (i.e. pecuniary loss; see Terwilliger v. Wands, infra page 857), unless the words spoken come within one of the four classes of what is called slander per se. Libel, on the other hand, did not require special damages to be actionable, though there was some disagreement on whether this applied to libel which was not defamatory on its face. The distinction has been an important one. Defamatory communications often do not produce pecuniary loss, and it is often impossible to prove when it does exist. The result is that for many types of slander no relief may be available. A natural question is, why should there be a difference? Is it solely a matter of history? Since the remarks of Sir James Mansfield, in Thorley v. Lord Kerry, 4 Taunt. 355, 128 Eng.Rep. 367 (1812), there has been no real effort to defend the distinction.

So long as the difference as to the requirement of special damages continues to be applied, however, it becomes necessary to draw the distinction between what is slander and what is libel. This is itself a question not at all free from difficulty. As it took form in the seventeenth century, the distinction was one between words that were written or printed and those that were oral. But not long afterward, libel was extended to include defamatory pictures, signs, statues, motion pictures and the like, and even conduct carrying a defamatory implication, such as hanging the plaintiff in effigy, or erecting a gallows before his door. From this it was concluded that libel is communicated by the sense of sight, while slander is conveyed by the sense of hearing. On the other hand slander was soon extended to include transitory gestures, such as the signals of a deaf-mute, or, as in Bennett v. Norban, 396 Pa. 94, 151 A.2d 476 (1959), the act of a storekeeper in publicly stopping a woman and searching her shopping bag. Furthermore, it was held to be a publication of a libel to read a defamatory writing aloud, as in Bander v. Metropolitan Life Ins. Co., 313 Mass. 337, 47 N.E.2d 595 (1943); and also to speak orally words expected to be and in fact written down, as in the case of dictation to a stenographer in Ostrowe v. Lee, 256 N.Y. 36, 175 N.E. 505 (1931), or of a statement made to a newspaper reporter in Valentine v. Gonzales, 190 App.Div. 490, 179 N.Y.S. 711 (1920). This has led some authorities to conclude that the distinction turns on embodiment of the defamation in some more or less permanent physical form. A delightful piece of spoofing as to a phonograph record and words taught to a parrot is in A.P. Herbert, Uncommon Law 71–76 (7th ed. 1950).

The advent of new methods of communication such as radio and television left the courts floundering to formulate the distinction, and led the Restatement (Second) of Torts § 568, to say that

"(1) Libel consists of the publication of defamatory matter by written or printed words, or by its embodiment in physical form, or by any other form of communication which has the potentially harmful qualities characteristic of written or printed words.

(2) Slander consists of the publication of defamatory matter by spoken words, transitory gestures, or by any form of communication other than those stated in Subsection (1).

(3) The area of dissemination, the deliberate and premeditated character of its publication, and the persistence of the defamation are factors to be considered in determining whether a publication is a libel rather than a slander."

Shor v. Billingsley

Supreme Court, New York County, Special Term, 1956.
4 Misc.2d 857, 158 N.Y.S.2d 476.

[Action of defamation for a nationwide telecast. One person on the program "ad-libbed" the remark: "Want to know something? I wish I had as much money as he [plaintiff] owes * * * [to] everybody—oh, a lot of people." One count in the complaint was based on this remark.]

HECHT, JUSTICE. * * * That leaves for consideration the real problem in the case—whether the first cause of * * * action based upon a telecast not read from a prepared script sounds in libel or in slander.

This precise question has not been passed upon by our appellate courts, nor apparently in any other jurisdiction. Hartmann v. Winchell held that the "utterance of defamatory remarks, *read from a script* into a radio microphone and broadcast, constitute[s] publication of libel", 296 N.Y. [296,] at page 298, 73 N.E.2d [30,] at page 31, italics supplied. It expressly did not reach the question "whether broadcasting defamatory matter which has not been reduced to writing should be held to be libellous because of the potentially harmful and widespread effects of such defamation." [C] Fuld, J., concurring, held that it should "because of the likelihood of aggravated injury inherent in such broadcasting" [c].

Sorensen v. Wood, 123 Neb. 348, 353, 243 N.W. 82 (1932), likewise held libelous radio broadcasts read from a written script; Meldrum v. Australian Broadcasting Co. Ltd., [1932] Vict.L.R. 425, to the contrary, was specifically rejected in Hartmann v. Winchell, supra. * * *.

When account is taken of the vast and far-flung audience reached by radio today—often far greater in number than the readers of the largest metropolitan newspaper [c] it is evident that the broadcast of scandalous utterances is in general as potentially harmful to the defamed person's reputation as a publication by writing. That defamation by radio, in the absence of a script or transcription, lacks the measure of durability possessed by written libel, in nowise lessens its capacity for harm. Since the element of damage is, historically, the basis of the common-law action for defamation [c], and since it is as reasonable to presume damage from the nature of the medium employed when a slander is broadcast by radio as when published by writing, both logic and policy point the conclusion that defamation by radio should be actionable per se. * * *

It is true that "the delivery of the same speech over an amplifier to a vast audience in a stadium" would still be treated as a slander despite the fact that it may cause infinitely more damage than a writing seen by few, [c]. But such a speech falls so inescapably within the conventional definition of slander that in the foregoing situation "abolition of the line between libel and slander would * * * be too extreme a break with the past to be achieved without legislation." [C] But it does not follow that a court is equally powerless when dealing with the new media of radio and television. * * *

Our own courts experience no difficulty in applying the law of libel to the new instrumentality of the motion picture because "in the hands of a wrongdoer these devices have untold possibilities toward producing an effective libel". * * *

Accordingly, the motion to dismiss is denied as to the first three causes of action. * * *

NOTES AND QUESTIONS

1. This decision was affirmed without opinion by the Appellate Division, First Department, in 4 A.D.2d 1017, 169 N.Y.S.2d 416 (1957).

2. The matter is now primarily regulated by statute. Most of the statutes, enacted under lobbying from broadcasting companies, provide that any broadcast defamation is to be treated as slander, whether there is a script or not. See Remmers, Recent Legislative Trends in Defamation by Radio, 64 Harv.L.Rev. 727 (1951). The English Defamation Act (1952) 15 & 16 Geo. VI and Eliz. II, c. 66, provides that any broadcast is libel, as does Illinois, Ill.Ann.Stat. ch. 38, § 27–1 (1964).

3. This has been a fertile subject of controversy in the law reviews. See, e.g., Vold, The Basis of Liability for Defamation by Radio, 19 Minn.L.Rev. 611 (1935); Donnelly, Defamation by Radio: A Reconsideration, 34 Iowa L.Rev. 12 (1948). For a discussion of various possibilities see Kay, Libel and Slander—Two Tests or One, 91 L.Q.Rev. 524 (1975).

Terwilliger v. Wands

Court of Appeals of New York, 1858.
17 N.Y. 54, 72 Am.Dec. 420.

Action for slander. The plaintiff proved by La Fayette Wands that the defendant asked him, Wands, what the plaintiff was running to Mrs. Fuller's so much for; he knew he went there for no good purpose; Mrs. Fuller was a bad woman, and plaintiff had a regular beaten path across his land to Fuller's; defendant said plaintiff went there to have intercourse with Mrs. Fuller, and that plaintiff would do all he could to keep Mrs. Fuller's husband in the penitentiary so that he could have free access there. * * *

The only damages proved were that the plaintiff was prostrated in health and unable to attend to business after hearing of the reports circulated by the defendant. A motion for a nonsuit was sustained * * *.

STRONG, J. The words spoken by the defendant not being actionable of themselves, it was necessary, in order to maintain the action, to prove that they occasioned special damages to the plaintiff. The special damages must have been the natural, immediate and legal consequence of the words. * * *

The special damages relied upon are not of such a nature as will support the action. * * * It is injuries affecting the reputation only which are the subject of the action. In the case of slanderous words actionable per se, the law, from their natural and immediate tendency to produce injury, adjudges them to be injurious, though no special loss or damage can be proved. "But with regard to words that do not apparently and upon the face of them import such defamation as will of course be injurious, it is necessary that the plaintiff should aver some particular damage to have happened." (3 Bl.Com. 124.) As to what constitutes special damages, Starkie mentions the loss of a marriage, loss of hospitable gratuitous entertainment, preventing a servant or bailiff from getting a place, the loss of customers by a tradesman; and says that in general whenever a person is prevented by the slander from receiving that which would otherwise be conferred upon him, though gratuitously, it is sufficient. * * *

It necessarily follows from the rule that the words must be disparaging to character, that the special damage to give an action must flow from disparaging it. * * * In the present case the words were defamatory, and the illness and physical prostration of the plaintiff may be assumed, so far as this part of the case is concerned, to have been actually produced by the slander, but this consequence was not, in a legal view, a natural, ordinary one, as it does not prove that the plaintiff's character was injured. The slander may not have been credited by or had the slightest influence upon any one unfavorable to the plaintiff; and it does not appear that anybody believed it or treated the plaintiff any different from what they would otherwise have done on account of it. The cause was not adapted to produce the result which is claimed to be special damages. Such an effect may and sometimes does follow from such a cause but not ordinarily; and the rule of law was framed in reference to common and usual effects and not those which are accidental and occasional. * * *

Where there is no proof that the character has suffered from the words, if sickness results it must be attributed to the apprehension of loss of character, and such fear of harm to character, with resulting sickness and bodily prostration, cannot be such special damage as the law requires for the action. The loss of character must be a substantive loss, one which has actually taken place. * * *

Judgment affirmed.

NOTES AND QUESTIONS

1. When special damages must be pleaded and proved to make out a cause of action for slander, the common law rule developed that the damages must be of a pecuniary character. This was a carry-over from the old conflict of jurisdiction with the ecclesiastical courts, and the rule that the king's court could take jurisdiction only where there was "temporal," as distinguished from "spiritual," harm. Hence, if no pecuniary loss is shown, it is not enough that the plaintiff has suffered acute mental distress and serious physical illness as a result of the defamation. Allsop v. Allsop, 5 H. & N. 534, 157 Eng.Rep. 1292 (1860); Scott v. Harrison, 215 N.C. 427, 2 S.E.2d 1 (1939).

2. When the cause of action is once made out, either as libel or slander per se, or by proof of special damages of a pecuniary character, plaintiff may recover additional damages for his mental distress, wounded feelings and humiliation. Pion v. Caron, 237 Mass. 107, 129 N.E. 369 (1921); Baker v. Winslow, 184 N.C. 1, 113 S.E. 570 (1922).

3. The original rule was that the defendant was liable only for damages due to his own publication, and was not responsible for repetition by others. Vicars v. Wilcocks, 8 East 1, 103 Eng.Rep. 244 (1806); Hastings v. Stetson, 126 Mass. 329 (1879). Later decisions tend to hold that the original publisher is liable for damages due to a repetition that might reasonably have been anticipated. Elms v. Crane, 118 Me. 261, 107 A. 852 (1919); Sawyer v. Gilmers, Inc., 189 N.C. 7, 126 S.E. 183 (1925).

4. The party repeating the defamation is himself liable for its publication, even though he states the source. Haines v. Campbell, 74 Md. 158, 21 A. 702 (1891); Times Pub. Co. v. Carlisle, 94 Fed. 762 (8th Cir.1899). He is held liable even though he states that he does not believe the imputation. Morse v. Times–Republican Co., 124 Iowa 707, 100 N.W. 867 (1904); Cobbs v. Chicago Defender, 308 Ill.App. 55, 31 N.E.2d 323 (1941).

5. Liability for republication raises issues of free speech. As noted infra pages 890–891, the common law and statutes provided defenses for fair reporting. See Edwards v. National Audubon Society, Inc., 556 F.2d 113 (2d Cir.1977), cert. denied, 434 U.S. 1002 (1977).

Slander Per Se

Four special kinds of slander are exceptions to the general common law rule, and actionable without proof of special damages. These are the following:

1. *Imputations of Major Crime.* The original basis for this exception seems to have been that the plaintiff was thus exposed to criminal prosecution. Later the emphasis shifted to the social ostracism involved and the probability that the plaintiff must have suffered some pecuniary loss, even though he could not prove it. Thus, the action lay without any proof of damage, even though the words made it clear that the plaintiff had been punished or pardoned, or that prosecution was barred by the statute of limitations.

The courts struggled to define a distinction between major and minor crimes. The formula that most courts now follow is that the crime must be one involving "moral turpitude," defined as "an inherent baseness or vileness of principle in the human heart." It is not the categorization of the crime, but rather the character of the act charged, that is controlling. Not every trivial assault or battery involves "moral turpitude"; but an accusation that the plaintiff beat his mother was held in Sipp v. Coleman, 179 Fed. 997 (D.N.J.1910), necessarily to do so.

2. *Loathsome Disease.* The basis of the exception for the imputation of certain diseases appears originally to have been simply the exclusion from society that would result. It began with venereal disease and leprosy, at a time when both were regarded as permanent, lingering and incurable. It was not applied to more contagious and equally repugnant disorders such as smallpox, from which one either recovered or died in a short time. James v. Rutledge, Moore 573, 4 Co.Rep. 17a, 76 Eng.Rep. 900 (1599).

The advance of medical science and a better understanding of disease tended to freeze the exception within its original limits, and today accusations of insanity, tuberculosis or other communicable diseases are not included. Furthermore, since there would not be the same social avoidance of one who had recovered, it is well settled that the imputation that the plaintiff has had even a venereal disease in the past is not sufficient to be actionable without proof of special damage. Bruce v. Soule, 69 Me. 562 (1879). The importance of this exception has been slight, and there have been almost no cases applying it in this century. Will the situation change with the advent of AIDS?

3. *Business, Trade, Profession or Office.* If the spoken words are likely to affect the plaintiff in his business, trade, profession or office, the probability of some "temporal" damage is sufficiently obvious. Any legitimate calling is included, "be it ever so base." Terry v. Hooper, 1 Lev. 115, 83 Eng.Rep. 325 (1663); cf. Fitzgerald v. Redfield, 51 Barb. 484 (N.Y.1868) (mason); Burtch v. Nickerson, 17 Johns. 217 (N.Y.1819) (blacksmith). Even uncompensated offices of confidence or trust have

been included; and in Dietrich v. Hauser, 45 Misc.2d 805, 257 N.Y.S.2d 716 (1965), it was held slander per se to say of a club president that he was a cheat and a fraud.

The exception was limited to defamation of a kind incompatible with the proper conduct of the business, trade, profession or office itself. Thus it is actionable without proof of special damage to say of an attorney that he is a shyster. Nolan v. Standard Pub. Co., 67 Mont. 212, 216 P. 571 (1923). Or of a school teacher that he has been guilty of improper conduct with his pupils. Thompson v. Bridges, 209 Ky. 710, 273 S.W. 529 (1925). Or a chauffeur that he is habitually drinking. Louisville Taxicab & Transfer Co. v. Ingle, 229 Ky. 578, 17 S.W.2d 709 (1929). Or of a bank, that it is insolvent, or of a merchant that his credit is bad. Ridgeway State Bank v. Bird, 185 Wis. 418, 202 N.W. 170 (1925). Or of the governor of a state that he is indifferent to lynching and has approved the work of a mob. Caldwell v. Crowell–Collier Pub. Co., 161 F.2d 333 (5th Cir.1947).

4. *Serious Sexual Misconduct.* The principal application of this to date has been a charge imputing unchastity to a woman. In England this was not actionable per se, until the common law rule was changed by the Slander of Women Act in 1891. Some of the American courts got around the rule, as in Kelly v. Flaherty, 16 R.I. 234, 14 A. 876 (1888), by finding that the imputation was equivalent to a charge of the crime of adultery or fornication, which involved moral turpitude. Gradually this gave way to a recognition of the essentially damaging nature of the charge, and a fourth exception is now generally recognized. Hollman v. Brady, 233 F.2d 877 (9th Cir.1956); Gnapinsky v. Goldyn, 23 N.J. 243, 128 A.2d 697 (1957).

The assumption has always been that the imputation of unchastity is not so damaging to a man, and it is still held that this is not slander per se, unless it falls into one of the other slander exceptions. Hickerson v. Masters, 190 Ky. 168, 226 S.W. 1072 (1921); Marion v. Davis, 217 Ala. 16, 114 So. 357 (1927).

Is this consistent with constitutional law requirements and ideals of equality? See Restatement (Second) of Torts § 574; Sauerhoff v. Hearst Corp., 388 F.Supp. 117 (D.Md.1974); and King v. Tanner, 539 N.Y.S.2d 617 (1989) (suggesting that Terwilliger v. Wards, supra, would not survive equal protection scrutiny).

What about the imputation of homosexual conduct or characteristics? In Buck v. Savage, 323 S.W.2d 363 (Tex.Civ.App.1959), the statement that plaintiff was "queer on" another man was held to amount to a charge of the crime of sodomy and so to be actionable per se. Similarly, to call a person a "faggot" constitutes slander per se. Plumley v. Landmark Chevrolet, 122 F.3d 308 (5th Cir.1997). However, in Donovan v. Fiumara, 114 N.C.App. 524, 442 S.E.2d 572 (1994), defendant stated that plaintiffs were "gay" and "bisexual"; the court held that the slander was not actionable without an allegation and proof of special damages. The argument that the imputation implied the commission of a crime was rejected.

Libel Per Se and Libel Per Quod

The established rule at common law was to the effect that it is not necessary to prove special damages in order to maintain an action for libel. Some American decisions deviated from this rule, apparently through an initial mistake as to the meaning of the expression "libel per se." As applied to the requirement of proof of special damages, all libel was libel per se. But if the statement was not defamatory on its face and it was necessary to be aware of certain extrinsic (or unstated) facts in order to appreciate its defamatory implications, it was sometimes called libel per quod, meaning that the plaintiff must allege and prove those extrinsic facts in order to have a cause of action. Some American decisions, breaking away from the established rule, apparently assumed that if the communication was not defamatory on its face and was called libel per quod, it was not libel per se and required proof of special damages. But other cases deliberately adopted the rule. Case authority was divided and a vigorous debate developed between Dean Prosser and Professor Laurence Eldredge on the status of the authorities and the arguments for the two rules. The matter was rendered largely moot, however, by the decision in Gertz v. Robert Welch, Inc., infra page 892, which held (1) that strict liability is unconstitutional and a defendant is not liable unless he was at fault and (2) that the presumed damages of the common law are unconstitutional and plaintiff can recover only "actual damages." The first holding eliminates any unfairness in the original common law rule when the defendant did not know of the extrinsic fact. For a recent decision attempting to clarify the law and "strongly discouraging" the use of the term "actionable per quod," see Holtzcheiter v. Thomson Newspapers, Inc., 332 S.C. 502, 506 S.E.2d 497 (1998).

The Restatement (Second) of Torts § 569 provides that special damages are not required in any libel action. See Hinsdale v. Orange County Publications, Inc., 17 N.Y.2d 284, 217 N.E.2d 650, 270 N.Y.S.2d 592 (1966); Hinkle v. Alexander, 244 Or. 267, 417 P.2d 586 (1966).

3. PUBLICATION

Economopoulos v. A.G. Pollard Co.

Supreme Judicial Court of Massachusetts, 1914.
218 Mass. 294, 105 N.E. 896.

Action by George Economopoulos against A.G. Pollard Company. There was a verdict for defendant, and plaintiff brings exceptions.

This was an action of tort in three counts * * *; the third count charging defendant with falsely and maliciously charging plaintiff with larceny by words spoken of plaintiff, as follows: "You have stolen a handkerchief from us and have it in your pocket." There was evidence that a clerk of defendant stated in English to plaintiff, a Greek, that he had stolen a handkerchief, and that a Greek clerk stated to plaintiff in Greek that plaintiff had stolen a handkerchief. There was nothing to show that third persons heard the charge, excepting the floor walker.

LORING, J. * * * There was no evidence that anybody but the plaintiff was present when Carrier spoke to the plaintiff in English. There was no publication of this statement made in English, because on the evidence the words could not have been heard by any one but the plaintiff. [C]

Nor was there any evidence of publication of the Greek words spoken by Miralos, for although there was evidence that they were spoken in the presence of others, there was no evidence that any one understood them but the plaintiff. * * *

Exceptions overruled.

NOTES AND QUESTIONS

1. "Publication" is a word of art in defamation cases. It does not mean printing, writing or even publicity, but merely communication of the defamatory words to some one other than the person defamed. It is not enough that the words

are spoken to the plaintiff himself, even in the presence of others, if no one else overhears them. Sheffill v. Van Deusen, 13 Mass. (Gray) 304, 74 Am.Dec. 632 (1859). Cf. Barnes v. Clayton House Motel, 435 S.W.2d 616 (Tex.Civ.App.1968) (letter to the plaintiff).

2. Defendant, in the presence of others who overhear him, calls plaintiff a "cocotte," which, according to the court, is a French word meaning either a prostitute or a poached egg. What else must plaintiff plead and prove in order to establish her cause of action? Rovira v. Boget, 240 N.Y. 314, 148 N.E. 534 (1925). What if the auditors are too young to know the meaning of the words? Sullivan v. Sullivan, 48 Ill.App. 435 (1892).

3. Sometimes the court presumes that some one has read and understood the defamatory words. The presumption has been employed in respect of a publication in German in a German-language newspaper circulated among subscribers who read German. Kimm v. Steketee, 48 Mich. 322, 12 N.W. 177 (1882). This presumption has also been applied to a defamatory postcard sent through the mail. Ostro v. Safir, 165 Misc. 647, 1 N.Y.S.2d 377 (1937); Abofreka v. Alston Tobacco Co., 288 S.C. 122, 341 S.E.2d 622 (1986) (statement posted on bulletin board). Other cases hold that proof of actual reading is required in such a case. McKeel v. Latham, 202 N.C. 318, 162 S.E. 747 (1932).

4. A few courts held that there is no publication when the defamatory words are dictated to a stenographer, who was regarded as such an indispensable means of transcription in business as to be treated as merely equivalent to the defendant's own writing. Watson v. Wannamaker, 216 S.C. 295, 57 S.E.2d 477 (1950); Satterfield v. McLellan Stores Co., 215 N.C. 582, 2 S.E.2d 709 (1939). Most courts have held that there is a publication, although it may be privileged; and when the words are in fact taken down, there is publication of a libel. Ostrowe v. Lee, 256 N.Y. 36, 175 N.E. 505 (1931); Rickbeil v. Grafton Deaconess Hospital, 74 N.D. 525, 23 N.W.2d 247 (1946).

5. On the same basis, most courts have held that there is publication when the communication is from one officer, agent or office of an organization to another; Jerolamon v. Fairleigh Dickinson University, 199 N.J.Super. 179, 488 A.2d 1064 (App.Div.1985) (report by university security guards to Director of Campus Safety and Provost, a publication). But cf. Perez v. Boatmen's National Bank, 788 S.W.2d 296 (Mo.App.1990) (communication between two employees of different branches of the defendant bank, not a publication); Starr v. Pearle Vision, Inc., 54 F.3d 1548 (10th Cir.1995). But cf. Lyons v. National Car Rental Systems, Inc., 30 F.3d 240 (1st Cir.1994).

6. For a communication to a third party to be a publication, it must have been done intentionally or by a negligent act. See Restatement (Second) of Torts § 577. Thus there is no publication when words are spoken by defendant directly to plaintiff, with no reason to suppose that any one can overhear, but they are in fact overheard by a concealed listener. Hall v. Balkind, [1918] N.Z.L.Rep. 740. Thus, when the words are spoken in so loud a voice that defendant can expect that some one may overhear, the defendant has published the defamatory imputation. McNichol v. Grandy, [1931] Can.S.C.Rep. 696. Where defendant mistakenly believed he had deleted a file from his hard drive, which was later accessed by third parties, held no publication. Morrow v. II Morrow, Inc., 911 P.2d 964 (Or.App.1996).

7. If the defamatory matter is sent by defendant to plaintiff himself in a sealed letter, which is unexpectedly opened and read by a third person, there is no publication. Barnes v. Clayton House Motel, 435 S.W.2d 616 (Tex.Civ.App.1968).

But there is liability if defendant knows, or should know, that plaintiff's spouse or secretary is in the habit of reading plaintiff's mail, or in the circumstances would likely read it, and the words are in fact read by such person. Rumney v. Worthley, 186 Mass. 144, 71 N.E. 316 (1904); Roberts v. English Mfg. Co., 155 Ala. 414, 46 So. 752 (1908). Theaker v. Richardson [1962] 1 All E.R. 229 (defendant composed and typed a diatribe accusing plaintiff of a list of misdeeds, finally saying "you are nothing but a lying, low-down brothel-keeping whore and thief * * * " and placed this "billet-doux" in an envelope addressed to the plaintiff in the plaintiff's letter box; envelope opened by plaintiff's husband).

8. There is a publication when a telegraph company transmits a message or a third party orally repeats a message. The postal service does not make a publication when it delivers a letter. Nor is there a publication by the telephone company when its system is used for communication purposes. See Anderson v. New York Tel. Co., 35 N.Y.2d 746, 320 N.E.2d 647, 361 N.Y.S.2d 913 (1974).

9. *Publication by Plaintiff.* Ordinarily the defendant is not liable for any publication made by the plaintiff alone, since it is considered that it is plaintiff's responsibility and not the defendant's. Lyle v. Waddle, 144 Tex. 90, 188 S.W.2d 770 (1945). But suppose it is reasonable for the plaintiff to consult someone else about a defamatory communication made only to plaintiff and the defendant might expect this. The obvious case is that of the plaintiff who is blind or illiterate. Lane v. Schilling, 130 Or. 119, 279 P. 267 (1929); cf. Hedgpeth v. Coleman, 183 N.C. 309, 111 S.E. 517 (1922) (plaintiff is a child).

10. A discharged employee of the defendant, seeking other employment, is asked by all prospective employers why he left his last job. In response, he repeats, and denies, the defamatory charge. Is defendant liable? The courts have come to inconsistent conclusions. Recently the Tennessee Supreme Court thoroughly reviewed the law, concluding that the repetition of the defamatory statement by the plaintiff to a prospective employer is not publication by the former employer: Sullivan v. Baptist Memorial Hosp., 995 S.W.2d 569 (Tenn.1999). The Tennessee Supreme Court was concerned that to find liability in termination contexts would "chill communications in the work place, preventing employers from disclosing reasons for their business decisions, and would negatively affect grievance procedures intended to benefit the discharged employee." Id. at 573. Moreover, liability would deprive plaintiffs of an incentive to mitigate damages because plaintiffs could determine the time at which the action accrued, i.e., publication. The more general policy of flexibility in at-will contracts of employment was also implicated. See also Olivieri v. Rodriguez, 122 F.3d 406 (7th Cir.1997). In contrast, the court in Van–Go Transport Co. Inc. v. New York City Board of Education, 971 F.Supp. 90 (E.D.N.Y. 1997), held that liability would adhere where the defendant could foresee that plaintiff would be forced to transmit the information to the third party. In the Missouri case, Arthaud v. Mutual of Omaha Ins. Co., 170 F.3d 860 (8th Cir.1999), the court also found that liability would obtain, stressing requirements of defendant's utterance of a false reason for termination, her knowledge of its falsity or entertainment of serious doubts about its veracity, and her intention or high likelihood and of its transmission to the third party. See also Lewis v. Equitable Life Assurance Society, 389 N.W.2d 876 (Minn.1986).

11. *Failure to Remove Defamation.* In several cases defendant has been held liable for failure to remove defamation posted on his premises. See Tidmore v. Mills, 33 Ala.App. 243, 32 So.2d 769 (1947); Hellar v. Bianco, 111 Cal.App.2d 424, 244 P.2d 757 (1952). The courts have not agreed upon a theory, and have struggled with "republication," "ratification," and negligent breach of a duty to remove.

Ogden v. Association of the United States Army

United States District Court, District of Columbia, 1959.
177 F.Supp. 498.

HOLTZOFF, DISTRICT JUDGE. The question presented for decision in this case is whether from the standpoint of the statute of limitations in an action for libel every sale or delivery of a copy of a book, periodical, or newspaper containing an alleged defamatory statement, creates a separate cause of action; or whether only one cause of action arises which accrues at the time of the first publication of one or more copies of the offending material. To formulate this question in another form, should the so-called modern "single publication rule" be the law of the District of Columbia? [The book containing the alleged libel was published in November, 1955. This suit was filed on June 25, 1959. The District of Columbia has a 1–year statute of limitations for defamation.]

The common law was originally to the effect that every sale or delivery of libelous matter was a new publication and that, therefore, a new cause of action accrued on each occasion. * * *

A leading English case on the subject is The Duke of Brunswick v. Harmer, 14 Q.B. 185, 117 Eng.Rep. 75, decided in 1849. It involved an issue of a newspaper published in 1830. A single copy was sold by the defendant seventeen years later and a suit for libel was predicated on this sale as a publication. The plea of the statute of limitations was overruled on the theory that each sale or delivery of a copy of the offending material gave rise to a new and separate cause of action. * * *

Under modern conditions the original common-law rule would give rise to an unnecessary multiplicity of suits and would practically destroy the statute of limitations as a statute of repose in actions for libel. There is no doubt, to be sure, that the number of copies of the offending publication that have been supplied to the public is a factor to be considered in determining the amount of damages to be awarded. In order to protect the plaintiff in this respect, however, it is not necessary to hold that every sale and delivery of an additional copy is a new publication and gives rise to a new cause of action.

[The court reviews decisions from many states adopting the single-publication rule and quotes the Uniform Single Publications Act, promulgated in 1952 and adopted in a number of other states.]

There are indeed a few States that expressly adhere to the original English rule in cases that were decided a great many years ago, [cc]. They are a small minority. * * *

* * * [T]he conclusion is inescapable that the modern American law of libel has adopted the so-called "single publication" rule; and, therefore, this principle must be deemed a part of the common law of the District of Columbia. In other words, it is the prevailing American doctrine that the publication of a book, periodical, or newspaper containing defamatory matter gives rise to but one cause of action for libel, which accrues at the time of the original publication, and that the statute of limitations runs

from that date. It is no longer the law that every sale or delivery of a copy of the publication creates a new cause of action. * * *

The defendant's motion for summary judgment is granted.

NOTES AND QUESTIONS

1. American jurisdictions now generally agree with the principal case. Each edition of a newspaper, magazine or book is held to be one separate publication. Backus v. Look, Inc., 39 F.Supp. 662 (S.D.N.Y.1941). This is true of each broadcast or rebroadcast over radio or television, and each exhibition of a motion picture. But when a hundred different newspapers each publish in their own editions a news report supplied by Associated Press, there are a hundred publications. See Restatement (Second) of Torts § 577A.

4. BASIS OF LIABILITY

The early law apparently imposed strict liability for defamation, as in the case of most other torts. See Holdsworth, Defamation in the Sixteenth and Seventeenth Centuries, 41 L.Q.Rev. 13 (1925).

During the Seventeenth Century, at a time when the courts were not at all anxious to encourage actions for defamation, the rule developed that the plaintiff must plead and prove not only that the defendant intended to defame him, but that he was inspired by "malice," in the sense of spite, ill will, or a desire to do harm. Parson Prick's Case, cited in Cro.Jac. 91, 79 Eng.Rep. 78; Crawford v. Middleton, 1 Lev. 82, 83 Eng.Rep. 308 (1674). Apparently this was carried over from the ecclesiastical law of slander, which was concerned with the moral sin of speaking ill of one's neighbor, and from criminal libel, which required at least a criminal intent. Veeder, History and Theory of the Law of Defamation, 4 Colum.L.Rev. 33 (1904); Green, Slander and Libel, 6 Am.L.Rev. 593 (1872).

In 1825, the historic case of Bromage v. Prosser, 4 B. & C. 247, 107 Eng.Rep. 1051 (K.B.), was decided. It drew a distinction between "malice in fact and malice in law." Malice is necessary, it held, but in the ordinary defamation case, if the statement is false and defamatory and it was made intentionally, "the law implies such malice as is necessary to maintain the action." Factual malice, on the other hand, is not a necessary part of the plaintiff's case in an ordinary defamation action; but it may be important to refute a qualified privilege or to justify punitive damages. "Malice" has also come to be used, with a still different meaning, in the constitutional law cases set out in this Section.

Thus the malice implied in law became a pure fiction, and the effect of the case was that malice in fact was no longer a requisite to a prima facie case of defamation. But the courts continued to speak of malice, and the part that the term plays in an action for defamation has become one of profound confusion. With so many meanings and so much uncertainty, the term is best avoided.

Deriving from Bromage v. Prosser, decisions were rendered imposing liability for unintended and innocent defamation. The classic case was the

Scottish decision of Morrison v. Ritchie & Co., 4 Sess.Cas. (Fr.) 645, 39 Scot.L.Rep. 432 (1904), where defendant newspaper published in good faith a report sent to it that plaintiff wife had given birth to twins. It was held liable when the report proved false and the plaintiffs had been married only three months.

Then came Hulton v. Jones, [1910] A.C. 20. Defendant newspaper published a report from a French correspondent from the resort of Dieppe containing a passage reading: " 'Whist! there is Artemus Jones with a woman who is not his wife, who must be you know—the other thing!' whispers a fair neighbor of mine excitedly into her bosom friend's ear. 'Really, is it not surprising how certain of our countrymen behave when they come abroad?' " The name Artemus Jones was a fictitious one, coined for the occasion, after the author's conversation with an American friend who had discussed an American humorist named Artemus Ward. He had not intended to refer to anyone. But a real Artemus Jones, a North Wales barrister, appeared, sued and recovered on the ground that some of his friends understood the piece to refer to him, although, apart from the name, nothing connected him with the person parodied in the article. See Smith, Jones v. Hulton: Three Conflicting Views as to Defamation, 60 U.Pa.L.Rev. 365 & 461 (1912); Holdsworth, A Chapter of Accidents in the Law of Libel, 57 L.Q.Rev. 74 (1941).

In this country, the leading case of Corrigan v. Bobbs–Merrill Co., 228 N.Y. 58, 126 N.E. 260 (1920), was similar. An author sent in a book manuscript purporting to be fictitious, and the publisher produced it without realizing that it referred in an identifiable way to a magistrate in the city of New York. "The fact that the publisher has no actual intention to defame a particular man or indeed to injure anyone does not prevent recovery of compensatory damages by one who connects himself with the publication. * * * The question is not so much who was aimed at as who was hit." There were numerous cases in accord.

Secondary Publishers. There was one important exception. A vendor or distributor of a newspaper, magazine or book is called a "secondary publisher" and is not liable if he had no knowledge of libellous matter in the publication and had no reason to be put on guard. See Vizetelly v. Mudie's Select Library, [1907] 2 Q.B. 170 (lending library); Balabanoff v. Fossani, 192 Misc. 615, 81 N.Y.S.2d 732 (1948) (newspaper vendor); McLeod v. St. Aubuyn, [1899] A.C. 549 (private lender); Grisham v. Western Union Tel. Co., 238 Mo. 480, 142 S.W. 271 (1911) (telegram innocent on its face). The same principle applies to an internet service provider who supplies the opportunity for subscribers to post messages on a computer bulletin board. See Cubby, Inc. v. CompuServe, Inc., 776 F.Supp. 135, 140 (S.D.N.Y.1991).

A newspaper or book publishing company does not qualify as a secondary publisher and is subject to strict liability even though it innocently took the defamatory material from someone else without any reason to be put on guard. However, republication of items received from wire services will not be subject to liability if (1) the service was reputable; (2) defendant did not know of the falsity; (3) the story itself does not reveal its falsity; and (4) no substantial change was made to the story. There has been sharp disagreement as to how local radio and television networks are to be classified, when they broadcast material directly from national networks or allow someone else to supply a program without opportunity for screening it. Holding that they are primary publishers: Sorenson v. Wood, 123 Neb. 348, 243 N.W. 82 (1932); Miles v. Louis Wasmer, Inc., 172 Wash. 466, 20 P.2d 847 (1933). Holding that they are secondary publishers: Kelly v. Hoffman, 137 N.J.L. 695, 61 A.2d 143 (1948); Summit Hotel Co. v. National Broadcasting Co., 336 Pa. 182, 8 A.2d 302 (1939); Auvil v. C.B.S. "60 Minutes," 800 F.Supp. 928 (E.D.Wash.1992). A number of states have statutes, the enactment of which was supported by broadcasters, providing protection unless due care was not taken. The Restatement takes the position that a broadcasting station should be treated as an original publisher. Restatement (Second) of Torts § 581(2). Prior to the Communications Decency Act (CDA), 47 USC § 230 (1996), internet service providers (ISPs) were classified as secondary publishers. This classification provided a disincentive for ISPs to screen or monitor the content of the information published since those very actions would be sufficient to inform them of libelous material, hence exposing them to liability for defamation. Stratton Oakmont, Inc. v. Prodigy Services Co., 23 Media L.Rep. 1794 (N.Y.Sup.Ct.1995). This result was at odds with the public policy of encouraging voluntary measures to prevent objectionable material from coming before children. Therefore, in order to encourage self-regulation among ISPs, Congress enacted the Communications Decency Act in 1996. The CDA grants broad immunity to ISPs. The protection extends to ISPs that fall within the definition of secondary publishers and, even more, to those that come within the terms of primary publishers. Blumenthal v. Drudge, 992 F.Supp. 44 (D.D.C.1998). Does this immunity go too far? What incentives do ISPs have to self-regulate in light of such broad protections?

How have the Supreme Court cases in the remaining part of this Section affected all this?

New York Times Co. v. Sullivan

Supreme Court of the United States, 1964.
376 U.S. 254, 84 S.Ct. 710, 11 L.Ed.2d 686.

MR. JUSTICE BRENNAN delivered the opinion of the Court.

We are required in this case to determine for the first time the extent to which the constitutional protections for speech and press limit a State's power to award damages in a libel action brought by a public official against critics of his official conduct.

Respondent L.B. Sullivan is one of the three elected Commissioners of the City of Montgomery, Alabama. He testified that he was "Commissioner of Public Affairs and the duties are supervision of the Police Department,

Front row: Clark, Black, Warren, C.J., Douglas, Harlan
Back row: White, Brennan, Stewart, Goldberg

Fire Department, Department of Cemetery and Department of Scales." He brought this civil libel action against the four individual petitioners, who are Negroes and Alabama clergymen, and against petitioner the New York Times Company, a New York corporation which publishes the New York Times, a daily newspaper. A jury in the Circuit Court of Montgomery County awarded him damages of $500,000, the full amount claimed, against all the petitioners, and the Supreme Court of Alabama affirmed.

Respondent's complaint alleged that he had been libeled by statements in a full-page advertisement that was carried in the New York Times on March 29, 1960. Entitled "Heed Their Rising Voices," the advertisement began by stating that "As the whole world knows by now, thousands of Southern Negro students are engaged in wide-spread non-violent demonstrations in positive affirmation of the right to live in human dignity as guaranteed by the U.S. Constitution and the Bill of Rights." It went on to charge that "in their efforts to uphold these guarantees, they are being met by an unprecedented wave of terror by those who would deny and negate that document which the whole world looks upon as setting the pattern for modern freedom. * * * " Succeeding paragraphs purported to illustrate the "wave of terror" by describing certain alleged events. The text concluded with an appeal for funds for three purposes: support of the student movement, "the struggle for the right-to-vote," and the legal defense of Dr. Martin Luther King, Jr., leader of the movement, against a perjury indictment then pending in Montgomery.

The text appeared over the names of 64 persons, widely known for their activities in public affairs, religion, trade unions, and the performing arts. * * *

Of the 10 paragraphs of text in the advertisement, the third and a portion of the sixth were the basis of respondent's claim of libel. They read as follows:

Third paragraph: "In Montgomery, Alabama, after students sang 'My Country, 'Tis of Thee' on the State Capitol steps, their leaders were expelled from school, and truckloads of police armed with shotguns and tear-gas ringed the Alabama State College Campus. When the entire student body protested to state authorities by refusing to re-register, their dining hall was padlocked in an attempt to starve them into submission."

Sixth paragraph: "Again and again the Southern violators have answered Dr. King's peaceful protests with intimidation and violence. They have bombed his home almost killing his wife and child. They have assaulted his person. They have arrested him seven times—for 'speeding,' 'loitering' and similar 'offenses.' And now they have charged him with 'perjury'—a *felony* under which they could imprison him for *ten years.* * * *"

[Although plaintiff was not mentioned by name, he contended that these statements attributed misconduct to him as the Montgomery Commissioner who supervised the Police Department.]

It is uncontroverted that some of the statements contained in the two paragraphs were not accurate descriptions of events which occurred in Montgomery. Although Negro students staged a demonstration on the State Capitol steps, they sang the National Anthem and not "My Country, 'Tis of Thee." Although nine students were expelled by the State Board of Education, this was not for leading the demonstration at the Capitol, but for demanding service at a lunch counter in the Montgomery County Courthouse on another day. Not the entire student body, but most of it, had protested the expulsion, not by refusing to register, but by boycotting classes on a single day; virtually all the students did register for the ensuing semester. The campus dining hall was not padlocked on any occasion, and the only students who may have been barred from eating there were the few who had neither signed a preregistration application nor requested temporary meal tickets. Although the police were deployed near the campus in large numbers on three occasions, they did not at any time "ring" the campus, and they were not called to the campus in connection with the demonstration on the State Capitol steps, as the third paragraph implied. Dr. King had not been arrested seven times, but only four; and although he claimed to have been assaulted some years earlier in connection with his arrest for loitering outside a courtroom, one of the officers who made the arrest denied that there was such an assault.

On the premise that the charges in the sixth paragraph could be read as referring to him, respondent was allowed to prove that he had not participated in the events described. Although Dr. King's home had in fact been bombed twice when his wife and child were there, both of these occasions antedated respondent's tenure as Commissioner, and the police were not only not implicated in the bombings, but had made every effort to apprehend those who were. Three of Dr. King's four arrests took place before respondent became Commissioner. Although Dr. King had in fact been indicted (he was subsequently acquitted) on two counts of perjury, each of which carried a possible five-year sentence, respondent had nothing to do with procuring the indictment. * * *

The trial judge submitted the case to the jury under instructions that the statements in the advertisement were "libelous per se" and were not privileged, so that petitioners might be held liable if the jury found that they had published the advertisement and that the statements were made "of and concerning" respondent. * * *

Under Alabama law as applied in this case * * * once "libel per se" has been established, the defendant has no defense as to stated facts unless he can persuade the jury that they were true in all their particulars. [Cc] His privilege of "fair comment" for expressions of opinion depends on the truth of the facts upon which the comment is based. * * *

The First Amendment, said Judge Learned Hand, "presupposes that right conclusions are more likely to be gathered out of a multitude of tongues, than through any kind of authoritative selection. To many this is, and always will be, folly; but we have staked upon it our all." United States v. Associated Press, 52 F.Supp. 362, 372 (S.D.N.Y.1943). * * * Thus we consider this case against the background of a profound national commitment to the principle that debate on public issues should be uninhibited, robust and wide-open, and that it may well include vehement, caustic, and sometimes unpleasantly sharp attacks on government and public officials. [Cc] The present advertisement, as an expression of grievance and protest, on one of the major public issues of our time, would seem clearly to qualify for the constitutional protection. The question is whether it forfeits that protection by the falsity of some of its factual statements and by its alleged defamation of respondent.

Authoritative interpretations of the First Amendment guarantees have consistently refused to recognize an exception for any test of truth—whether administered by judges, juries, or administrative officials—and especially one that puts the burden of proving truth on the speaker. [C] The constitutional protection does not turn upon "the truth, popularity, or social utility of the ideas and beliefs which are offered." [C] As Madison said, "Some degree of abuse is inseparable from the proper use of everything; and in no instance is this more true than in that of the press." [C] * * *

If neither factual error nor defamatory content suffices to remove the constitutional shield from criticism of official conduct, the combination of the two elements is no less inadequate. [The Court here reviewed the history of the Sedition Act of 1798, which made it a crime to publish defamation against high officers of the United States, and reached the conclusion at this late date that the Act was unconstitutional.]

What a State may not constitutionally bring about by means of a criminal statute is likewise beyond the reach of its civil law of libel. The fear of damage awards under a rule such as that invoked by the Alabama courts here may be markedly more inhibiting than the fear of prosecution under a criminal statute. * * * Presumably a person charged with violation of [a criminal-libel] statute enjoys ordinary criminal-law safeguards such as the requirements of an indictment and of proof beyond a reasonable doubt. These safeguards are not available to the defendant in a civil action. * * *

The state rule of law is not saved by its allowance of the defense of truth. * * * A rule compelling the critic of official conduct to guarantee the truth of all his factual assertions—and to do so on pain of libel judgments virtually unlimited in amount—leads to a comparable "self-censorship." * * *

The constitutional guarantees require, we think, a federal rule that prohibits a public official from recovering damages for a defamatory false-hood relating to his official conduct unless he proves that the statement was made with "actual malice"—that is, with knowledge that it was false or with reckless disregard of whether it was false or not. An oft-cited statement of a like rule, which has been adopted by a number of state courts, is found in the Kansas case of Coleman v. MacLennan, 78 Kan. 711, 98 P. 281 (1908). The State Attorney General, a candidate for re-election and a member of the commission charged with the management and control of the state school fund sued a newspaper publisher for alleged libel in an article purporting to state facts relating to his official conduct in connection with a school-fund transaction. * * * In answer to a special question, the jury found that the plaintiff had not proved actual malice, and a general verdict was returned for the defendant. On appeal the Supreme Court of Kansas, in an opinion by Justice Burch, reasoned as follows:

"[I]t is of the utmost consequence that the people should discuss the character and qualifications of candidates for their suffrage. The impor-tance to the state and to society of such discussions is so vast, and the advantages derived are so great that they more than counter-balance the inconvenience of private persons whose conduct may be involved, and occasional injury to the reputations of individuals must yield to the public welfare, although at times such injury may be great. The public benefit from publicity is so great and the chance of injury to private character so small that such discussion must be privileged." The court thus sustained the trial court's instruction as a correct statement of the law, saying:

"In such a case the occasion gives rise to a privilege qualified to this extent. Any one claiming to be defamed by the communication must show actual malice, or go remediless. This privilege extends to a great variety of subjects and includes matters of public concern, public men, and candidates for office." [C]

We hold today that the Constitution delimits a State's power to award damages for libel in actions brought by public officials against critics of their official conduct. Since this is such an action, the rule requiring proof of actual malice is applicable. * * *

[W]e consider that the proof presented to show actual malice lacks the convincing clarity which the constitutional standard demands, and hence that it would not constitutionally sustain the judgment for respondent under the proper rule of law. The case of the individual petitioners requires little discussion. Even assuming that they could constitutionally be found to have authorized the use of their names on the advertisement, there was no evidence whatever that they were aware of any erroneous statements or were in any way reckless in that regard. The judgment against them is thus without constitutional support.

As to the Times, we similarly conclude that the facts do not support a finding of actual malice. The statement by the Times' Secretary that, apart from the padlocking allegation, he thought the advertisement was "substantially correct," affords no constitutional warrant for the Alabama Supreme Court's conclusion that it was a "cavalier ignoring of the falsity of the advertisement, [from which] the jury could not have but been impressed with the bad faith of The Times, and its maliciousness inferable therefrom." The statement does not indicate malice at the time of the publication; even if the advertisement was not "substantially correct"— although respondent's own proofs tend to show that it was—that opinion was at least a reasonable one, and there was no evidence to impeach the witness' good faith in holding it. The Times' failure to retract upon respondent's demand, although it later retracted upon the demand of Governor Patterson, is likewise not adequate evidence of malice for constitutional purposes. Whether or not a failure to retract may ever constitute such evidence, there are two reasons why it does not here. *First,* the letter written by the Times reflected a reasonable doubt on its part as to whether the advertisement could reasonably be taken to refer to respondent at all. *Second,* it was not a final refusal, since it asked for an explanation on this point—a request that respondent chose to ignore. Nor does the retraction upon the demand of the Governor supply the necessary proof. It may be doubted that a failure to retract which is not itself evidence of malice can retroactively become such by virtue of a retraction subsequently made to another party. But in any event that did not happen here, since the explanation given by the Times' Secretary for the distinction drawn between respondent and the Governor was a reasonable one, the good faith of which was not impeached.

Finally, there is evidence that the Times published the advertisement without checking its accuracy against the news stories in the Times' own files.... We think the evidence against the Times supports at most a finding of negligence in failing to discover the misstatements, and is constitutionally insufficient to show the recklessness that is required for a finding of actual malice. * * *

We also think the evidence was constitutionally defective in another respect: it was incapable of supporting the jury's finding that the allegedly libelous statements were made "of and concerning" respondent.

There was no reference to respondent in the advertisement, either by name or official position. A number of the allegedly libelous statements * * * did not even concern the police. * * *

Although the statements may be taken as referring to the police, they do not on their face make even an oblique reference to respondent as an individual. * * *

This * * * has disquieting implications for criticism of governmental conduct. For good reason, "no court of last resort in this country has ever held, or even suggested, that prosecutions for libel on government have any place in the American system of jurisprudence." City of Chicago v. Tribune Co. (1923) 307 Ill. 595, 601, 139 N.E. 86, 88.

The present proposition would sidestep this obstacle by transmuting criticism of government, however impersonal it may seem on its face, into personal criticism, and hence potential libel of the officials of whom the government is composed. * * * We hold that such a proposition may not constitutionally be utilized to establish that an otherwise impersonal attack on governmental operations was a libel of an official responsible for those operations. * * *

The judgment of the Supreme Court of Alabama is reversed, and the case is remanded to that court for further proceedings not inconsistent with this opinion.

[The concurring opinions of JUSTICES BLACK and GOLDBERG are omitted. Both would categorically deny any action of defamation by a public official insofar as his public conduct is concerned. This was variously characterized as "an absolute, unconditional constitutional right to * * * say what one pleases about public affairs," "an absolute immunity for criticism of the way public officials do their public duty," and "an absolute privilege for criticism of official conduct." JUSTICE DOUGLAS joined in both opinions.]

NOTES AND QUESTIONS

1. For fuller accounts of this case and its background, see Pierce, The Anatomy of an Historic Decision: New York Times Co. v. Sullivan, 43 N.C.L.Rev. 315 (1964); Kalven, The New York Times Case: A Note on the Central Meaning of the First Amendment, 1964 S.C.Rev. 191; Lewis, New York Times v. Sullivan Reconsidered: A Return to "The Central Meaning of the First Amendment," 83 Colum.L.Rev. 603 (1983). See also Pedrick, Freedom of the Press and the Law of Libel, 49 Corn.L.Q. 581 (1964); Berney, Libel and the First Amendment—A New Constitutional Privilege, 51 Va.L.Rev. 1 (1965); Epstein, Was New York Times v. Sullivan Wrong?, 53 U.Chi.L.Rev. 782 (1986).

2. *Fair Comment.* For many years before the principal case, the courts had developed, at common law and virtually without reference to the Constitution, a privilege of criticism of public officers and their official conduct. It usually was called the privilege of "fair comment," see Milkovich v. Lorain Journal, infra page 915.

The existence of this qualified privilege was not disputed. There was, however, a sharp division of authority on whether it was limited to "comment" or criticism, that is, the expression of opinion, or whether it extended to false statements of fact. About three-quarters of the courts that had considered the question held that the privilege was limited to the expression of opinion, and did not include misstatements of fact. This was the position taken by the Supreme Court of Alabama in the principal case. 273 Ala. 656, 144 So.2d 25 (1962).

The leading case to this effect was Post Pub. Co. v. Hallam, 59 Fed. 530, (6th Cir.1893), an opinion of Judge (later President and Chief Justice) Taft. The reason he advanced was that if public men were to be subjected to false statements of fact, good men could not be found to take the positions. A vigorous minority, headed by Coleman v. MacLennan, 78 Kan. 711, 98 P. 281 (1908), and supported by most of the commentators, contended that the privilege extended to false statements of fact, so long as they were made in good faith. For an interpretive history of political libel in the United States, see Rosenberg, Protecting the Best Men (1986).

3. *Public Officials.* Rosenblatt v. Baer, 383 U.S. 75 (1966), involved comments about the supervisor of a county recreation area. The Court held that whether he was a public official was a question of federal law, not state law. The test was held to be whether "the position in government has such apparent importance that the public has an independent interest in the qualifications and performance of the person who holds it, beyond the general public interest in the qualifications and performance of all governmental employees." Cf. Tucker v. Kilgore, 388 S.W.2d 112 (Ky.1964) (patrolman); Krutech v. Schimmel, 50 Misc.2d 1052, 272 N.Y.S.2d 261 (1966) (part time accountant for public waterworks).

The *New York Times* rule is held to apply to candidates for public office. Monitor Patriot Co. v. Roy, 401 U.S. 265 (1971); Ocala Star–Banner Co. v. Damron, 401 U.S. 295 (1971).

4. *Public Figures.* The *New York Times* rule was extended to apply to "public figures" in Curtis Pub. Co. v. Butts, and Associated Press v. Walker, 388 U.S. 130 (1967). Two cases were involved: (1) suit by Coach Wally Butts of the University of Georgia (employed by a private corporation rather than the state) for a story in the Saturday Evening Post charging him with conspiring with Coach Bear Bryant of the University of Alabama to "fix" a football game, and (2) suit by Edwin A. Walker, a well-known retired army general, against the Associated Press for a story regarding his alleged part in a student disturbance at the University of Mississippi involving enrollment of its first black student. Both were held to be public figures. Recovery below was reversed in *Walker,* but affirmed in *Butts.* For an interesting book on the fact background of the *Butts* case, see J. Kirby, Fumble (1986).

The line-up of the several justices was very confusing. Justice Harlan delivered what purported to be the opinion of the Court, concurred in by Clark, Fortas and Stewart, JJ. This opinion laid down a different standard from that in *New York Times,* which would impose liability for public figures "on a showing of highly unreasonable conduct constituting an extreme departure from the standards of investigation and reporting ordinarily adhered to by responsible publishers." Applying this standard, he and the three justices concurring would reverse *Walker* and affirm *Butts.* In a separate opinion, Chief Justice Warren held that the *Times* standard of knowledge or reckless disregard should apply to public figures as well as public officials, but he concluded that applying this standard also would reverse *Walker* and affirm *Butts.* This made five justices agreeing on the affirmance-or-reversal issue. Justice Brennan, joined by Justice White, agreed with Chief Justice Warren that the *Times* standard should apply and that *Walker* should be reversed, but concluded that *Butts* should also be reversed for a new trial with more appropriate instructions. Justice Black, joined by Justice Douglas, continued to espouse the "absolute privilege" theory set forth in his separate opinion in *New York Times.* In order, however, for the Court to reach a decision, without receding from his views, he voted for the *Times* standard as set out in the Warren opinion as being nearer to his view than the Harlan opinion; he would have reversed both *Butts* and *Walker.*

The end result was that *Butts* was affirmed; and that *Walker* was reversed and remanded to the Texas court "for further proceedings not inconsistent with the opinions that have been filed herein by The Chief Justice, Mr. Justice Black and Mr. Justice Brennan." Only one of the four opinions took the position on each of the three issues that was finally adopted by a majority vote of the Court. This was the opinion of the Chief Justice, which did not have the full concurrence of any other member of the Court. These authorities foreshadowed later cases that strove to define the terms "public officials" and "public figures." Infra pages 912–915.

5. *Matter of Public or General Interest.* Rosenbloom v. Metromedia, Inc., 403 U.S. 29 (1971), expanded the *Times* knowing-or-reckless-disregard standard beyond public officials and public figures to apply to any matter of public or general interest. Rosenbloom had been arrested in a police drive against obscene books. Defendant, operating a radio news station, reported the arrest and used the terms "smut literature racket" and "girlie-book peddlers." Following acquittal of the criminal charges, plaintiff sued for libel. He recovered $25,000 in general damages and $725,000 in punitive damages, reduced by remittitur to $250,000. The Court of Appeals reversed, holding the *Times* standard applied, though the plaintiff was not a public figure. The Supreme Court agreed.

Once again the justices divided sharply. The plurality opinion was written by Justice Brennan, joined by Burger, C.J., and Blackmun. J. Black, J., concurred in the result but adhered to his absolute-privilege view; Douglas, J., did not participate in the case. White, J., concurred in the result on the ground that the report covered the official action of public officials. Harlan and Marshall, JJ. (joined by Stewart, J.), dissented in separate opinions deprecating the ad-hoc nature of a test depending upon whether an event was a matter of public or general interest and urged that the way for the Court to take care of the recurring cases was to limit the measure of recovery to "proven, actual damages" and to eliminate strict liability.

The plurality opinion of Justice Brennan remained the binding rule of constitutional law until it was repudiated in 1974 by Gertz v. Robert Welch, Inc., infra page 892. Does its spirit still live in Dun & Bradstreet, Inc. v. Greenmoss Builders, Inc., infra page 902?

6. As with all revolutions, so with *New York Times:* many problems were left in its wake. The common law had to be reconciled with First Amendment principles. We now review the "wreckage" and subsequent "salvage" work of the courts. What is the meaning of actual malice? How does it affect the press? What of imputations concerning private persons? What of information that is purely private? What of the falsity presumption of defamatory imputations? What are public figures and officials? Do defamatory imputations in the form of opinion call forth a special analysis? The case law and academic commentary on the impact of *New York Times* and its progeny is multitudinous. Anderson, Is Libel Law Worth Reforming, 140 U.Pa.L.Rev. 487, 488 n. 2 & n. 3 (1991), gives a sampling of the debate. The flow shows no signs of diminishing.

(A) ACTUAL MALICE, BURDENS OF PROOF, AND THE PRESS

St. Amant v. Thompson

Supreme Court of the United States, 1968.
390 U.S. 727, 88 S.Ct. 1323, 20 L.Ed.2d 262 (1968).

[Defendant St. Amant made a televised political speech, in the course of which he read questions that he had put to a union member, Albin, and

Albin's answers. The answers falsely charged the plaintiff, a deputy sheriff, with criminal conduct. Plaintiff sued defendant for defamation, and was awarded damages by the trial judge. The judge then considered New York Times Co. v. Sullivan, supra page 867, decided after the trial, and denied a motion for a new trial. An intermediate appellate court reversed the judgment, finding that defendant had not acted with "actual malice" within the meaning of the New York Times rule. The Louisiana Supreme Court reversed, finding that there had been sufficient evidence that defendant had acted in "reckless disregard" of the truth. The Supreme Court granted certiorari.]

MR. JUSTICE WHITE delivered the opinion of the Court. * * *

For purposes of this case we accept the determinations of the Louisiana courts that the material published by St. Amant charged Thompson with criminal conduct, that the charge was false, and that Thompson was a public official, and so had the burden of proving that the false statements about Thompson were made with actual malice as defined in New York Times Co. v. Sullivan and later cases. We cannot, however, agree with either the Supreme Court of Louisiana or the trial court that Thompson sustained this burden.

Purporting to apply the *New York Times* malice standard, the Louisiana Supreme Court ruled that St. Amant had broadcast false information about Thompson recklessly though not knowingly. Several reasons were given for this conclusion. St. Amant had no personal knowledge of Thompson's activities; he relied solely on Albin's affidavit although the record was silent as to Albin's reputation for veracity; he failed to verify the information with those in the union office who might have known the facts; he gave no consideration as to whether or not the statements defamed Thompson and went ahead heedless of the consequences; and he mistakenly believed he had no responsibility for the broadcast because he was merely quoting Albin's words.

These considerations fall short of proving St. Amant's reckless disregard for the accuracy of his statements about Thompson. "Reckless disregard," it is true, cannot be fully encompassed in one infallible definition. Inevitably its outer limits will be marked out through case-by-case adjudication, as is true with so many legal standards for judging concrete cases, whether the standard is provided by the Constitution, statutes, or case law. Our cases, however, have furnished meaningful guidance for the further definition of a reckless publication.

In *New York Times,* the plaintiff did not satisfy his burden because the record failed to show that the publisher was aware of the likelihood that he was circulating false information. In Garrison v. State of Louisiana, 379 U.S. 64 (1964), also decided before the decision of the Louisiana Supreme Court in this case, the opinion emphasized the necessity for showing that a false publication was made with a "high degree of awareness of * * * probable falsity." Mr. Justice Harlan's opinion in Curtis Publishing Co. v. Butts, 388 U.S. 130, 153 (1967), stated that evidence of either deliberate falsification or reckless publication "despite the publisher's awareness of probable falsity" was essential to recovery by public officials in defamation actions. These cases are clear that reckless conduct is not measured by whether a reasonably prudent man would have published, or would have investigated before publishing. There must be sufficient evidence to permit the conclusion that the defendant in fact entertained serious doubts as to the truth of his publication. Publishing with such doubts shows reckless disregard for truth or falsity and demonstrates actual malice.

It may be said that such a test puts a premium on ignorance, encourages the irresponsible publisher not to inquire, and permits the issue to be determined by the defendant's testimony that he published the statement in good faith and unaware of its probable falsity. Concededly the reckless disregard standard may permit recovery in fewer situations than would a rule that publishers must satisfy the standard of the reasonable man or the prudent publisher. But *New York Times* and succeeding cases have emphasized that the stake of the people in public business and the conduct of public officials is so great that neither the defense of truth nor the standard of ordinary care would protect against self-censorship and thus adequately implement First Amendment policies. Neither lies nor false communications serve the ends of the First Amendment, and no one suggests their desirability or further proliferation. But to insure the ascertainment and publication of the truth about public affairs, it is essential that the First Amendment protect some erroneous publications as well as true ones. We adhere to this view and to the line which our cases have drawn between false communications which are protected and those which are not.

The defendant in a defamation action brought by a public official cannot, however, automatically insure a favorable verdict by testifying that he published with a belief that the statements were true. The finder of fact must determine whether the publication was indeed made in good faith. Professions of good faith will be unlikely to prove persuasive, for example, where a story is fabricated by the defendant, is the product of his imagination, or is based wholly on an unverified anonymous telephone call. Nor will they be likely to prevail when the publisher's allegations are so inherently improbable that only a reckless man would have put them in circulation. Likewise, recklessness may be found where there are obvious reasons to doubt the veracity of the informant or the accuracy of his reports. * * *

Because the state court misunderstood and misapplied the actual malice standard which must be observed in a public official's defamation action, the judgment is reversed and the case remanded for further proceedings not inconsistent with this opinion.

[JUSTICES BLACK and DOUGLAS concurred in the judgment, on the ground that there should be an absolute privilege. JUSTICE FORTAS dissented, on the ground that the defendant had a duty to check the reliability of the statement, and hence that he published it in reckless disregard of the truth.]

NOTES AND QUESTIONS

1.   Almost immediately after the *New York Times* decision, the Court discarded completely the old-fashioned meaning of "malice," so far as the constitutional restriction on defamation is concerned: "The jury might well have understood these instructions to allow recovery on a showing of intent to inflict harm, rather than intent to inflict harm through falsehood. See Garrison v. Louisiana, 379 U.S. 64, 73. 'The constitutional guarantees * * * [prohibit] a public official from recovering damages for a defamatory falsehood relating to his official conduct unless he proved that the statement was made * * * with knowledge that it was false or with reckless disregard of whether it was false or not.' New York Times Co. v. Sullivan, 376 U.S. 254, 279–280 (1964)." Henry v. Collins, 380 U.S. 356, 357 (1965).

2.   The test of serious doubt in *St. Amant* is admittedly subjective in nature. In Herbert v. Lando, 441 U.S. 153 (1979), a public officer, who was under the obligation of proving knowledge or reckless disregard as to falsity in his libel action based on a program of "60 Minutes," sought to depose the defendant at length with inquiries as to his state of mind and communications with other participants in the editorial process. The defendant resisted on First Amendment grounds and the Second Circuit held for him (568 F.2d 974 (2d Cir.1977)), declaring that the First Amendment grants him an absolute privilege regarding "his thoughts, opinions and conclusions with respect to the material gathered by him and about his conversations with his editorial colleagues." The Supreme Court reversed, holding that previous decisions did not authorize or presage an editorial privilege of this nature and that it did not construe the First Amendment to authorize it as a matter of constitutional law. The holding was unanimous regarding questions on state of mind, but three justices had somewhat varying views regarding forced disclosure of communications between participants in the editorial process. On remand, the Court of Appeals held, on the basis of evidence in the new trial, that summary judgment should be granted to the defendant Herbert v. Lando, 781 F.2d 298 (2d Cir.1986).

On state of mind, would it be better to substitute an objective test for the subjective one? This does not require a negligence test, but could be based on the language of Justice White in *St. Amant:* "publisher's allegations * * * so inherently improbable that only a reckless man would have put them in circulation."

Masson v. New Yorker Magazine

Supreme Court of the United States, 1991.
501 U.S. 496.

JUSTICE KENNEDY delivered the opinion of the Court.

In this libel case, a public figure claims he was defamed by an author who, with full knowledge of the inaccuracy, used quotation marks to attribute to him comments he had not made. The First Amendment protects authors and journalists who write about public figures by requiring a plaintiff to prove that the defamatory statements were made with what we have called "actual malice," a term of art denoting deliberate or reckless falsification. We consider in this opinion whether the attributed quotations had the degree of falsity required to prove this state of mind, so that the public figure can defeat a motion for summary judgment and proceed to a trial on the merits of the defamation claim. * * *

Petitioner Jeffrey Masson trained at Harvard University as a Sanskrit scholar, and in 1970 became a professor of Sanskrit & Indian Studies at the University of Toronto. He spent eight years in psychoanalytic training, and qualified as an analyst in 1978. Through his professional activities, he came to know Dr. Kurt Eissler, head of the Sigmund Freud Archives, and Dr. Anna Freud, daughter of Sigmund Freud and a major psychoanalyst in her own right. * * *

In 1980, Eissler and Anna Freud hired petitioner as Projects Director of the Archives. After assuming his post, petitioner became disillusioned with Freudian psychology. In a 1981 lecture before the Western New England Psychoanalytical Society in New Haven, Connecticut, he advanced his theories of Freud. Soon after, the Board of the Archives terminated petitioner as Projects Director.

Respondent Janet Malcolm is an author and a contributor to respondent The New Yorker, a weekly magazine. She contacted petitioner in 1982 regarding the possibility of an article on his relationship with the Archives. He agreed, and the two met in person and spoke by telephone in a series of interviews. Based on the interviews and other sources, Malcolm wrote a lengthy article. One of Malcolm's narrative devices consists of enclosing lengthy passages in quotation marks, reporting statements of Masson, Eissler, and her other subjects.

During the editorial process, Nancy Franklin, a member of the fact-checking department at The New Yorker, called petitioner to confirm some of the facts underlying the article. According to petitioner, he expressed alarm at the number of errors in the few passages Franklin discussed with him.

* * *

The New Yorker published Malcolm's piece in December 1983, as a two-part series. In 1984, with knowledge of at least petitioner's general allegation that the article contained defamatory material, respondent Alfred A. Knopf, Inc., published the entire work as a book, entitled In the Freud Archives.

Malcolm's work received complimentary reviews. But this gave little joy to Masson, for the book portrays him in a most unflattering light.

* * *

Petitioner brought an action for libel under California law in the United States District Court for the Northern District of California. During extensive discovery and repeated amendments to the complaint, petitioner concentrated on various passages alleged to be defamatory, dropping some and adding others. The tape recordings of the interviews demonstrated that petitioner had, in fact, made statements substantially identical to a number of the passages, and those passages are no longer in the case.

Each passage before us purports to quote a statement made by petitioner during the interviews. Yet in each instance no identical statement appears in the more than 40 hours of taped interviews. Petitioner complains that Malcolm fabricated all but one passage; with respect to that passage, he claims Malcolm omitted a crucial portion, rendering the remainder misleading.

(a) *"Intellectual Gigolo."* Malcolm quoted a description by petitioner of his relationship with Eissler and Anna Freud as follows:

> " 'Then I met a rather attractive older graduate student and I had an affair with her. One day, she took me to some art event, and she was sorry afterward. She said, "Well, it is very nice sleeping with you in your room, but you're the kind of person who should never leave the room—you're just a social embarrassment anywhere else, though you do fine in your own room." And you know, in their way, if not in so many words, Eissler and Anna Freud told me the same thing. They like me well enough "in my own room." They loved to hear from me what creeps and dolts analysts are. I was like an intellectual gigolo—you get your pleasure from him, but you don't take him out in public. * * * ' "
> In the Freud Archives 38.

The tape recordings contain the substance of petitioner's reference to his graduate student friend, App. 95, but no suggestion that Eissler or Anna Freud considered him, or that he considered himself, an " 'intellectual gigolo.' " Instead, petitioner said:

> "They felt, in a sense, I was a private asset but a public liability. * * * They liked me when I was alone in their living room, and I could talk and chat and tell them the truth about things and they would tell me. But that I was, in a sense, much too junior within the hierarchy of analysis, for these important training analysts to be caught dead with me." [C]

(b) *"Sex, Women, Fun."* Malcolm quoted petitioner as describing his plans for Maresfield Gardens, which he had hoped to occupy after Anna Freud's death:

> " 'It was a beautiful house, but it was dark and sombre and dead. Nothing ever went on there. I was the only person who ever came. I would have renovated it, opened it up, brought it to life. Maresfield Gardens would have been a center of scholarship, but it would also have been a place of sex, women, fun. It would have been like the change in *The Wizard of Oz*, from black-and-white into color.' " In the Freud Archives 33.

The tape recordings contain a similar statement, but in place of the reference to "sex, women, fun," and The Wizard of Oz, petitioner commented:

> "[I]t is an incredible storehouse. I mean, the library, Freud's library alone is priceless in terms of what it contains: all his books with his annotations in them; the Schreber case annotated, that kind of thing. It's fascinating." [C]

Petitioner did talk, earlier in the interview, of his meeting with a London analyst:

"I like him. So, and we got on very well. That was the first time we ever met and you know, it was buddy-buddy, and we were to stay with each other and [laughs] we were going to pass women on to each other, and we were going to have a great time together when I lived in the Freud house. We'd have great parties there and we were [laughs]—

* * *

". . . going to really, we were going to live it up." [C]

[The Court discusses three other defamatory imputations drawn from purported quotes made by Masson that were not supported by his taped comments.]

Malcolm submitted to the District Court that not all of her discussions with petitioner were recorded on tape, in particular conversations that occurred while the two of them walked together or traveled by car, while petitioner stayed at Malcolm's home in New York, or while her tape recorder was inoperable. She claimed to have taken notes of these unrecorded sessions, which she later typed, then discarding the handwritten originals. Petitioner denied that any discussion relating to the substance of the article occurred during his stay at Malcolm's home in New York, that Malcolm took notes during any of their conversations, or that Malcolm gave any indication that her tape recorder was broken.

Respondents moved for summary judgment. The parties agreed that petitioner was a public figure and so could escape summary judgment only if the evidence in the record would permit a reasonable finder of fact, by clear and convincing evidence, to conclude that respondents published a defamatory statement with actual malice as defined by our cases. *Anderson v. Liberty Lobby, Inc.*, 477 U.S. 242, 255–256 (1986). The District Court analyzed each of the passages and held that the alleged inaccuracies did not raise a jury question. The court found that the allegedly fabricated quotations were either substantially true, or were " 'one of a number of possible rational interpretations' of a conversation or event that 'bristled with ambiguities,' " and thus were entitled to constitutional protection.

* * *

The Court of Appeals affirmed, with one judge dissenting. 895 F.2d 1535 (C.A.9 1989). The court assumed for much of its opinion that Malcolm had deliberately altered each quotation not found on the tape recordings, but nevertheless held that petitioner failed to raise a jury question of actual malice, in large part for the reasons stated by the District Court. In its examination of the "intellectual gigolo" passage, the court agreed with the District Court that petitioner could not demonstrate actual malice because Malcolm had not altered the substantive content of petitioner's self-description, but went on to note that it did not consider the "intellectual gigolo" passage defamatory, as the quotation merely reported Kurt Eissler's and Anna Freud's opinions about petitioner.

* * *

The dissent argued that any intentional or reckless alteration would prove actual malice, so long as a passage within quotation marks purports to be a verbatim rendition of what was said, contains material inaccuracies, and is defamatory. 895 F.2d, at 1562–1570. We granted certiorari, 498 U.S. 808 (1990), and now reverse.

* * *

It matters not under California law that petitioner alleges only part of the work at issue to be false. "[T]he test of libel is not quantitative; a single sentence may be the basis for an action in libel even though buried in a much longer text," though the California courts recognize that "[w]hile a drop of poison may be lethal, weaker poisons are sometimes diluted to the point of impotency." Washburn v. Wright, 261 Cal.App.2d 789, 795, 68 Cal.Rptr. 224, 228 (1968).

The First Amendment limits California's libel law in various respects. When, as here, the plaintiff is a public figure, he cannot recover unless he proves by clear and convincing evidence that the defendant published the defamatory statement with actual malice, *i.e.,* with "knowledge that it was false or with reckless disregard of whether it was false or not." New York Times Co. v. Sullivan, supra. Mere negligence does not suffice. Rather, the plaintiff must demonstrate that the author "in fact entertained serious doubts as to the truth of his publication," St. Amant v. Thompson, 390 U.S. 727, 731 (1968), or acted with a "high degree of awareness of . . . probable falsity," Garrison v. Louisiana, 379 U.S. 64, 74 (1964).

Actual malice under the *New York Times* standard should not be confused with the concept of malice as an evil intent or a motive arising from spite or ill will. [C]

We have used the term actual malice as a shorthand to describe the First Amendment protections for speech injurious to reputation and we continue to do so here. But the term can confuse as well as enlighten. In this respect, the phrase may be an unfortunate one. [C]

In general, quotation marks around a passage indicate to the reader that the passage reproduces the speaker's words verbatim. They inform the reader that he or she is reading the statement of the speaker, not a paraphrase or other indirect interpretation by an author. By providing this information, quotations add authority to the statement and credibility to the author's work. Quotations allow the reader to form his or her own conclusions, and to assess the conclusions of the author, instead of relying entirely upon the author's characterization of her subject.

A fabricated quotation may injure reputation in at least two senses, either giving rise to a conceivable claim of defamation. First, the quotation might injure because it attributes an untrue factual assertion to the speaker. An example would be a fabricated quotation of a public official admitting he had been convicted of a serious crime when in fact he had not.

Second, regardless of the truth or falsity of the factual matters asserted within the quoted statement, the attribution may result in injury to reputation because the manner of expression or even the fact that the statement was made indicates a negative personal trait or an attitude the speaker does not hold. John Lennon once was quoted as saying of the Beatles, "We're more popular than Jesus Christ now." Time, Aug. 12, 1966, p. 38. Supposing the quotation had been a fabrication, it appears California law could permit recovery for defamation because, even without regard to the truth of the underlying assertion, false attribution of the statement could have injured his reputation. Here, in like manner, one need not determine whether petitioner is or is not the greatest analyst who ever lived in order to determine that it might have injured his reputation to be reported as having so proclaimed.

A self-condemnatory quotation may carry more force than criticism by another. It is against self-interest to admit one's own criminal liability, arrogance, or lack of integrity, and so all the more easy to credit when it happens.

* * *

Of course, quotations do not always convey that the speaker actually said or wrote the quoted material. "Punctuation marks, like words, have many uses. Writers often use quotation marks, yet no reasonable reader would assume that such punctuation automatically implies the truth of the quoted material." Baker v. Los Angeles Examiner, 42 Cal.3d, at 263, 721 P.2d, at 92. In *Baker,* a television reviewer printed a hypothetical conversation between a station vice president and writer/producer, and the court found that no reasonable reader would conclude the plaintiff in fact had made the statement attributed to him. Id., at 267, 721 P.2d, at 95. Writers often use quotations as in *Baker,* and a reader will not reasonably understand the quotations to indicate reproduction of a conversation that took place. In other instances, an acknowledgement that the work is so-called docudrama or historical fiction, or that it recreates conversations from memory, not from recordings, might indicate that the quotations should not be interpreted as the actual statements of the speaker to whom they are attributed.

The work at issue here, however, as with much journalistic writing, provides the reader no clue that the quotations are being used as a rhetorical device or to paraphrase the speaker's actual statements. To the contrary, the work purports to be nonfiction, the result of numerous interviews. At least a trier of fact could so conclude. The work contains lengthy quotations attributed to petitioner, and neither Malcolm nor her publishers indicate to the reader that the quotations are anything but the reproduction of actual conversations. Further, the work was published in The New Yorker, a magazine which at the relevant time seemed to enjoy a reputation for scrupulous factual accuracy. These factors would, or at least could, lead a reader to take the quotations at face value. A defendant may be able to argue to the jury that quotations should be viewed by the reader as nonliteral or reconstructions, but we conclude that a trier of fact in this case could find that the reasonable reader would understand the quotations to be nearly verbatim reports of statements made by the subject.

* * *

The constitutional question we must consider here is whether, in the framework of a summary judgment motion, the evidence suffices to show that respondents acted with the requisite knowledge of falsity or reckless disregard as to truth or falsity. This inquiry in turn requires us to consider the concept of falsity; for we cannot discuss the standards for knowledge or reckless disregard without some understanding of the acts required for liability. We must consider whether the requisite falsity inheres in the attribution of words to the petitioner which he did not speak.

In some sense, any alteration of a verbatim quotation is false. But writers and reporters by necessity alter what people say, at the very least to eliminate grammatical and syntactical infelicities. If every alteration constituted the falsity required to prove actual malice, the practice of journalism, which the First Amendment standard is designed to protect, would require a radical change, one inconsistent with our precedents and First Amendment principles. Petitioner concedes this absolute definition of falsity in the quotation context is too stringent, and acknowledges that "minor changes to correct for grammar or syntax" do not amount to falsity for purposes of proving actual malice. [Cc]

We agree, and must determine what, in addition to this technical falsity, proves falsity for purposes of the actual malice inquiry.

Petitioner argues that, excepting correction of grammar or syntax, publication of a quotation with knowledge that it does not contain the words the public figure used demonstrates actual malice. The author will have published the quotation with knowledge of falsity, and no more need be shown. Petitioner suggests that by invoking more forgiving standards the Court of Appeals would permit and encourage the publication of falsehoods. Petitioner believes that the intentional manufacture of quotations does not "represen[t] the sort of inaccuracy that is commonplace in the forum of robust debate to which the *New York Times* rule applies," [c] and that protection of deliberate falsehoods would hinder the First Amendment values of robust and well-informed public debate by reducing the reliability of information available to the public.

We reject the idea that any alteration beyond correction of grammar or syntax by itself proves falsity in the sense relevant to determining actual malice under the First Amendment. An interviewer who writes from notes often will engage in the task of attempting a reconstruction of the speaker's statement. That author would, we may assume, act with knowledge that at times she has attributed to her subject words other than those actually used. Under petitioner's proposed standard, an author in this situation would lack First Amendment protection if she reported as quotations the substance of a subject's derogatory statements about himself.

Even if a journalist has tape recorded the spoken statement of a public figure, the full and exact statement will be reported in only rare circumstances. The existence of both a speaker and a reporter; the translation between two media, speech and the printed word; the addition of punctuation; and the practical necessity to edit and make intelligible a speaker's perhaps rambling comments, all make it misleading to suggest that a quotation will be reconstructed with complete accuracy. The use or absence of punctuation may distort a speaker's meaning, for example, where that meaning turns upon a speaker's emphasis of a particular word. In other cases, if a speaker makes an obvious misstatement, for example by unconscious substitution of one name for another, a journalist might alter the speaker's words but preserve his intended meaning. And conversely, an exact quotation out of context can distort meaning, although the speaker did use each reported word.

In all events, technical distinctions between correcting grammar and syntax and some greater level of alteration do not appear workable, for we can think of no method by which courts or juries would draw the line between cleaning up and other changes, except by reference to the meaning a statement conveys to a reasonable reader. To attempt narrow distinctions of this type would be an unnecessary departure from First Amendment principles of general applicability, and, just as important, a departure from the underlying purposes of the tort of libel as understood since the latter half of the 16th century. From then until now, the tort action for defamation has existed to redress injury to the plaintiff's reputation by a statement that is defamatory and false. See infra *Milkovich v. Lorain Journal Co.* As we have recognized, "[t]he legitimate state interest underlying the law of libel is the compensation of individuals for the harm inflicted on them by defamatory falsehood." *Gertz v. Robert Welch, Inc.,* infra. If an author alters a speaker's words but effects no material change in meaning, including any meaning conveyed by the manner or fact of expression, the speaker suffers no injury to reputation that is compensable as a defamation.

These essential principles of defamation law accommodate the special case of inaccurate quotations without the necessity for a discrete body of jurisprudence directed to this subject alone. * * * We conclude, rather, that the exceptions suggested by petitioner for grammatical or syntactical corrections serve to illuminate a broader principle.

* * * The burden is upon petitioner to prove falsity. See *Philadelphia Newspapers, Inc. v. Hepps,* infra. The essence of that inquiry, however, remains the same whether the burden rests upon plaintiff or defendant. Minor inaccuracies do not amount to falsity so long as "the substance, the gist, the sting, of the libelous charge be justified." Heuer v. Kee, 15 Cal.App.2d 710, 714, 59 P.2d 1063, 1064 (1936). [Cc] Put another way, the statement is not considered false unless it "would have a different effect on the mind of the reader from that which the pleaded truth would have produced." [Cc] Our definition of actual malice relies upon this historical understanding.

We conclude that a deliberate alteration of the words uttered by a plaintiff does not equate with knowledge of falsity for purposes of *New York*

Times Co. v. Sullivan, supra and *Gertz v. Robert Welch, Inc.,* infra, unless the alteration results in a material change in the meaning conveyed by the statement. The use of quotations to attribute words not in fact spoken bears in a most important way on that inquiry, but it is not dispositive in every case.

Deliberate or reckless falsification that comprises actual malice turns upon words and punctuation only because words and punctuation express meaning. Meaning is the life of language. And, for the reasons we have given, quotations may be a devastating instrument for conveying false meaning. In the case under consideration, readers of In the Freud Archives may have found Malcolm's portrait of petitioner especially damning because so much of it appeared to be a self-portrait, told by petitioner in his own words. And if the alterations of petitioner's words gave a different meaning to the statements, bearing upon their defamatory character, then the device of quotations might well be critical in finding the words actionable.

The Court of Appeals applied a test of substantial truth which, in exposition if not in application, comports with much of the above discussion. The Court of Appeals, however, went one step beyond protection of quotations that convey the meaning of a speaker's statement with substantial accuracy and concluded that an altered quotation is protected so long as it is a "rational interpretation" of an actual statement, drawing this standard from our decisions in *Time, Inc. v. Pape,* 401 U.S. 279 (1971), and Bose Corp. v. Consumers Union of United States, Inc., 466 U.S. 485 (1984).

* * *

The protection for rational interpretation serves First Amendment principles by allowing an author the interpretive license that is necessary when relying upon ambiguous sources. Where, however, a writer uses a quotation, and where a reasonable reader would conclude that the quotation purports to be a verbatim repetition of a statement by the speaker, the quotation marks indicate that the author is not involved in an interpretation of the speaker's ambiguous statement, but attempting to convey what the speaker said. This orthodox use of a quotation is the quintessential "direct account of events that speak for themselves." Time, Inc. v. Pape. [c] More accurately, the quotation allows the subject to speak for himself.

The significance of the quotations at issue, absent any qualification, is to inform us that we are reading the statement of petitioner, not Malcolm's rational interpretation of what petitioner has said or thought. Were we to assess quotations under a rational interpretation standard, we would give journalists the freedom to place statements in their subjects' mouths without fear of liability. By eliminating any method of distinguishing between the statements of the subject and the interpretation of the author, we would diminish to a great degree the trustworthiness of the printed word, and eliminate the real meaning of quotations. Not only public figures but the press doubtless would suffer under such a rule. Newsworthy figures might become more wary of journalists, knowing that any comment could be transmuted and attributed to the subject, so long as some bounds of rational interpretation were not exceeded. We would ill serve the values of the First Amendment if we were to grant near absolute, constitutional protection for such a practice. We doubt the suggestion that as a general rule readers will assume that direct quotations are but a rational interpretation of the speaker's words, and we decline to adopt any such presumption in determining the permissible interpretations of the quotations in question here.

* * *

We must determine whether the published passages differ materially in meaning from the tape recorded statements so as to create an issue of fact for a jury as to falsity.

(a) *"Intellectual Gigolo."* We agree with the dissenting opinion in the Court of Appeals that "[f]airly read, intellectual gigolo suggests someone who forsakes intellectual integrity in exchange for pecuniary or other gain." 895 F.2d, at 1551. A reasonable jury could find a material difference between the meaning of this passage and petitioner's tape-recorded statement that he was considered "much too junior within the hierarchy of analysis, for these important training analysts to be caught dead with [him]."

* * * We agree with the Court of Appeals that the most natural interpretation of this quotation is not an admission that petitioner considers himself an intellectual gigolo but a statement that Eissler and Anna Freud considered him so. It does not follow, though, that the statement is harmless. Petitioner is entitled to argue that the passage should be analyzed as if Malcolm had reported falsely that Eissler had given this assessment (with the added level of complexity that the quotation purports to represent petitioner's understanding of Eissler's view). An admission that two well-respected senior colleagues considered one an "intellectual gigolo" could be as or more damaging than a similar self-appraisal. In all events, whether the "intellectual gigolo" quotation is defamatory is a question of California law. To the extent that the Court of Appeals based its conclusion in the First Amendment, it was mistaken.

* * *

(b) *"Sex, Women, Fun."* This passage presents a closer question. The "sex, women, fun" quotation offers a very different picture of petitioner's plans for Maresfield Gardens than his remark that "Freud's library alone is priceless." Petitioner's other tape-recorded remarks did indicate that he and another analyst planned to have great parties at the Freud house and, in a context that may not even refer to Freud house activities, to "pass women on to each other." We cannot conclude as a matter of law that these remarks bear the same substantial meaning as the quoted passage's suggestion that petitioner would make the Freud house a place of "sex, women, fun."

[The Court analyzed the other pleaded imputations in a similar way.]

The judgment of the Court of Appeals is reversed, and the case is remanded for further proceedings consistent with this opinion.

It is so ordered.

JUSTICE WHITE, with whom JUSTICE SCALIA joins, concurred in part and dissented in part.

* * *

[T]he Court states that deliberate misquotation does not amount to *New York Times* malice unless it results in a material change in the meaning conveyed by the statement. This ignores the fact that under *New York Times,* reporting a known falsehood—here the knowingly false attribution—is sufficient proof of malice. The falsehood, apparently, must be substantial; the reporter may lie a little, but not too much.

This standard is not only a less manageable one than the traditional approach, but it also assigns to the courts issues that are for the jury to decide. For a court to ask whether a misquotation substantially alters the meaning of spoken words in a defamatory manner is a far different inquiry than whether reasonable jurors could find that the misquotation was different enough to be libelous. In the one case, the court is measuring the difference from its own point of view; in the other it is asking how the jury would or could view the erroneous attribution.

NOTES AND QUESTIONS

1.   Do you agree with the principal case that the "actual malice" terminology is misleading and should be replaced?

2.   Jeffrey Masson's "odyssey through the federal courts" (in the words of Kozinski, J.) continued when the 9th Circuit, on remand from the Supreme Court, considered the responsibility of the publishers, The New Yorker and Alfred A. Knopf, to purge defamatory material from stories submitted by free-lance writers. Masson v. The New Yorker Magazine, Inc., 960 F.2d 896 (9th Cir.1992). The *Liberty Lobby* burden of proof rule applied, requiring that Masson show that a reasonable jury could find by clear and convincing evidence that defendants published the statements with knowledge of their falsity or reckless disregard as to whether or not they were true. See below note 4. Noting The New Yorker's fact checking system and discrepancies of which the staff was aware, it was found that Masson presented a triable issue of fact as to whether The New Yorker "in fact entertained serious doubts" as to the accuracy of the quotations but chose to publish the article anyway. However, Knopf could not be found to entertain "serious doubts" because it could rely on The New Yorker's "sterling reputation," even in the face of Masson's claims communicated to Knopf before publication of the book.

3.   After a month-long trial the jury, on June 3, 1993, handed down a verdict in which it found that, although Masson had been defamed by all the pleaded imputations, only two were published with actual malice. Of the two extracted above, the jury found only the "sex, women, fun" imputation published with actual malice. The jurors deadlocked on the assessment of damages. Judge Lynch declared a mistrial. Both sides subsequently asked for a new trial. On August 3, 1993, Judge Lynch indicated that much of the case would have to be retried but appealed for the parties to call in a mediator to put an end to the ten years of litigation. The judge's

admonition was for nought and the case was retried. After a jury verdict in favor of defendant on all five imputations, Masson appealed. Masson v. The New Yorker Magazine, 85 F.3d 1394 (9th Cir.1996). He argued that the trial court's instructions on the issue of malice were not consistent with the Supreme Court's ruling and that his refusal to admit some of the excerpts from a book of Malcolm's that purportedly cast light on her journalistic practices were incorrect. The Ninth Circuit found no error and affirmed the verdict in favor of Malcolm. Because of the jury's finding on Malcolm's liability, collateral estoppel prevented relitigating the case against the New Yorker.

4. *Actual Malice and Journalistic Enterprise.* Turning a blind eye is deliberate action sufficient to constitute actual malice. In Harte–Hanks Communications, Inc. v. Connaughton, 491 U.S. 657 (1989), a newspaper published a story about the plaintiff's dirty tricks in an election campaign. The paper failed to interview a witness that it knew could verify conflicting accounts; it did not listen to tapes of an interview; it had published an article indicating a willingness to publish regardless of credibility; and critical testimony of the newspaper staff conflicted. This was not failure to investigate (no actual malice) but was "purposeful avoidance of the truth." But cf. Tavoulareas v. Piro, 817 F.2d 762 (D.C.Cir. en banc 1987), cert. denied, 484 U.S. 870 (1987), wherein the Court stressed that insufficient investigation alone, in the absence of serious doubts about the truth of statements, will not support a finding of actual malice. Reporter's ill will and a newspaper policy to find sensational stories are relevant but not sufficient in sustaining the burden of showing actual malice. The court warned that mere accumulation of factors will not meet the burden, but cf. Ball v. E.W. Scripps, 801 S.W.2d 684 (Ky.1990). In the absence of direct proof establishing that the defendant "entertained serious doubts as to the truth of [its] publication", a jury may infer awareness of falsity if it finds "obvious reasons to doubt" the accuracy of the story, and that the defendant did not act reasonably in dispelling those doubts. Masson v. New Yorker Magazine, Inc., 960 F.2d 896 (1992). Similarly, in St. Surin v. Virgin Islands Daily News, 21 F.3d 1309 (3d Cir.1994), the court held that defendant could not obtain summary judgment where its editor was aware of changes in the article that made it false. A critical concern for the press is maintenance of confidentiality of its sources. Can plaintiff insist on disclosure of a source in discovery in fashioning her prima facie case of actual malice? Without the opportunity to depose the source, the chances of plaintiff resisting a motion for summary judgment will be slim. Southwell v. The Southern Poverty Law Center, 949 F.Supp. 1303 (W.D.Mich.1996) (holding that the confidential source need not be disclosed).

5. *Public Figure or Private Figure.* In Anderson v. Liberty Lobby, 477 U.S. 242 (1986), ruling on a motion for summary judgment, should the standard applied by the court vary according to whether the plaintiff is a public figure under *New York Times* or a private person under *Gertz?* Held, yes. White J.: "In sum, we conclude that the determination of whether a given factual dispute requires submission to a jury must be guided by the substantive evidentiary standards that apply to the case. This is true at both the directed verdict and summary judgment stages. Consequently, where the *New York Times,* 'clear and convincing' evidence requirement applies, the trial judge's summary judgment inquiry as to whether a genuine issue exists will be whether the evidence presented is such that a jury applying that evidentiary standard could reasonably find for either the plaintiff or the defendant. Thus, where the factual dispute concerns actual malice, clearly a material issue in a *New York Times* case, the appropriate summary judgment question will be whether the evidence in the record could support a reasonable jury finding either that the plaintiff has shown actual malice by clear and convincing

evidence or that the plaintiff has not." Brennan and Rehnquist, JJ., dissented in separate opinions, and the Chief Justice concurred with Rehnquist, J.

In Time, Inc. v. Pape, 401 U.S. 279 (1971), Time Magazine reported on a report of the U.S. Commission of Civil Rights entitled *Justice,* listing instances of police brutality which were alleged in complaints to have occurred. The allegations of one complaint, involving plaintiff, were stated as facts. Held: "In light of the totality of what was said in *Justice* we cannot agree that, when Time failed to state that the Commission in reporting the Monroe incident had technically confined itself to the allegations of a complaint, Time engaged in a 'falsification' sufficient to sustain a jury finding of 'actual malice.' * * * Time's omission of the word 'alleged' amounted to the adoption of one of a number of possible rational interpretations of a document that bristled with ambiguities. The deliberate choice of such an interpretation, though arguably reflecting a misconception, was not enough to create a jury issue of 'malice' under *New York Times*. To permit the malice issue to go to the jury because of the omission of a word like 'alleged' * * * would be to impose a much stricter standard of liability on errors of interpretation or judgment than on errors of historic fact. * * * Nothing in this opinion is to be understood as making the word 'alleged' a superfluity in published reports of information damaging to reputation."

In Time, Inc. v. Firestone, 424 U.S. 448 (1976), Time Magazine published in its "Milestones" Section this item: "Divorced, by Russell A. Firestone, Jr., 41, heir to the tire fortune, Mary Alice Sullivan Firestone, 32, his third wife; a one time Palm Beach schoolteacher; on ground of extreme cruelty and adultery; after six years marriage, one son; in West Palm Beach Florida. The 17–month intermittent trial produced enough testimony of extramarital adventures on both sides, said the judge, 'to make Dr. Freud's hair curl.'" The language in the decree was quite ambiguous but plaintiff demanded that Time retract the statement of adultery because she had been awarded alimony and under the Florida statutes she would not be entitled to alimony if found guilty of adultery. Time's refusal produced the libel action in which she was awarded $100,000 for mental distress. The Florida Supreme Court affirmed; but the Supreme Court reversed on the ground that there was never any intentional finding of fault by court or jury in the case. The Court distinguished *Pape* on the ground that it involved the *New York Times* standard (public figure) while *Firestone* involved the *Gertz* standard (private figure).

6. *Repetition of Defamation.* Observe that in neither *Pape* nor *Firestone* was the court concerned with the truth or falsity of the defamatory charge or the measure of defendant's fault in ascertaining it. The defendant would apparently not have been liable even if it had actually known that the plaintiff was innocent of the charge, so long as the report of the official record was fair and accurate.

One is not ordinarily relieved of liability for repeating a defamatory charge, even if he indicates the source and accurately repeats it—even if he also says that he does not believe it. Restatement (Second) of Torts § 578; Dixson v. Newsweek, Inc., 562 F.2d 626 (10th Cir.1977); Harris v. Minvielle, 48 La.Ann. 908, 19 So. 925 (1896) ("talebearers are as bad as talemakers"); Martin v. Wilson Publishing Co., 497 A.2d 322 (R.I.1985); Painter, Republication Problems in the Law of Defamation, 47 Va.L.Rev. 1131 (1961); Note, Libel and The Reporting of Rumors, 92 Yale L.J. 85 (1982).

7. *The Reporter's Privilege.* At common law, there developed a special privilege, known as the "reporter's privilege" or as "record libel." It was a privilege because it did not exempt the defendant from liability unless his report was verbatim or a fair and accurate summary. *Pape* and *Firestone* now impose a

constitutional requirement of fault in failing to make the report fair and accurate. But it is still a privilege, because there is no liability for repetition of a defamatory statement even though the defendant was at fault in regard to the truth or falsity of the charge itself. See Restatement (Second) of Torts § 611. There is a good discussion in Gobin v. Globe Pub. Co., 216 Kan. 223, 531 P.2d 76 (1975), decided prior to *Firestone.*

The remaining problem involves the scope of the privilege, both at common law and under the more recent constitutional doctrine, and whether they will differ or coincide.

8. *The Privilege at Common Law.* This began as a privilege to report all official proceedings in the public interest. Wason v. Walter, L.R. 4 Q.B. 73 (1868) (Parliament); Terry v. Fellows, 21 La.Ann. 375 (1869) (session of legislative committee); Hahn v. Holum, 165 Wis. 425, 162 N.W. 432 (1917) (proceeding before justice of the peace).

It has been extended also to republication of public reports filed by officials in the performance of their duties: Greenfield v. Courier–Journal & Louisville Times Co., 283 S.W.2d 839 (Ky.1955) (grand jury); to reports given out by public officers as official statements in the performance of their duties: Brandon v. Gazette Pub. Co., 234 Ark. 332, 352 S.W.2d 92 (1961) (governor); Short v. News–Journal Co., 58 Del. 107, 205 A.2d 6 (Del.Super.1965) (district director of Internal Revenue); and to reporting official acts of public officers, such as an arrest and the charges made. Torski v. Mansfield Journal Co., 100 Ohio App. 538, 137 N.E.2d 679 (1956) (wrong man arrested for rape).

A privilege to report often attaches to information of public concern uttered at public meetings. The meetings need not be official but should be open to a wide segment of the public. Jackson v. Record Pub. Co., 175 S.C. 211, 178 S.E. 833 (1935) (words of a candidate at a political rally); Phoenix Newspapers v. Choisser, 82 Ariz. 271, 312 P.2d 150 (1957) (same, at Chamber of Commerce "forum"); Pulvermann v. A.S. Abell Co., 228 F.2d 797 (4th Cir.1956) (speech made by candidate for President); Borg v. Boas, 231 F.2d 788 (9th Cir.1956) (mass meeting held to urge calling a grand jury to investigate local law enforcement). In all of these cases, the matter reported has been one of public concern.

On the other hand, private meetings, not open to the public, have not been included. Kimball v. Post Pub. Co., 199 Mass. 248, 85 N.E. 103 (1908) (stockholders' meeting); Lewis v. Hayes, 165 Cal. 527, 132 P. 1022 (1913).

9. *Reports of Pleadings.* A considerable majority of the courts have held that there is an exception to the reporter's privilege in the case of pleadings filed with a court but not yet acted upon in any manner. Sanford v. Boston Herald–Traveler Corp., 318 Mass. 156, 61 N.E.2d 5 (1945); Nixon v. Dispatch Printing Co., 101 Minn. 309, 112 N.W. 258 (1907). But cf. Dorsey a.k.a. Engelbert Humperdinck v. National Enquirer, Inc., 973 F.2d 1431 (9th Cir.1992) (privilege applied to publication of false statement made in affidavit filed in family court proceeding that plaintiff has "AIDS related syndrome" which was reported in article headlined "Mother of His Child Claims in Court * * * Engelbert Has AIDS Virus"); Campbell v. New York Evening Post, 245 N.Y. 320, 157 N.E. 153 (1927); Langford v. Vanderbilt University, 199 Tenn. 389, 287 S.W.2d 32 (1956).

10. *The Privilege Under the Constitution. Pape* and *Firestone* are the only Supreme Court cases on the subject. A significant issue is raised by Edwards v.

National Audubon Soc'y, Inc., 556 F.2d 113 (2d Cir.1977), cert. denied, 434 U.S. 1002 (1977), espousing a much broader privilege of "neutral reportage." The court announced as a "fundamental principle" that "when a responsible, prominent organization like the National Audubon Society makes serious charges against a public figure, the First Amendment protects the accurate and disinterested reporting of those charges, regardless of the reporter's private views regarding their validity. * * * What is newsworthy about such accusations is that they were made. We do not believe that the press may be required under the First Amendment to suppress newsworthy statements merely because it has serious doubts regarding their truth. * * * The public interest in being fully informed about controversies that often rage around sensitive issues demands that the press be afforded the freedom to report such charges without assuming responsibility for them. * * *

"Literal accuracy is not a prerequisite: if we are to enjoy the blessings of a robust and unintimidated press, we must provide immunity from defamation suits where the journalist believes, reasonably and in good faith, that his report accurately conveys the charges made."

The Second Circuit continues to espouse the principle and some other courts have relied on it. Burns v. Times Argus Ass'n, Inc., 139 Vt. 381, 430 A.2d 773 (1981). But the Third Circuit has expressly repudiated it. Dickey v. CBS Inc., 583 F.2d 1221 (3d Cir.1978). The Supreme Court has remained silent. Cf. Franklin, Libel and Letters to the Editor: Toward an Open Forum, 57 U.Colo.L.Rev. 651 (1986). The California Supreme Court in Khawar v. Globe International, Inc., 79 Cal.Rptr.2d 178, 965 P.2d 696 (1998), declined to decide the constitutional moment of the privilege, although it confirmed that it applied only to public officials or public figures. The extension of the privilege to private figures would undermine the public/private distinction delineated in *Gertz*.

11. On the reporter's privilege, see Bryan, Publication of Record Libel, 5 Va.L.Rev. 513 (1918); Barnett, The Privilege of Defamation by Private Report of Public Official Proceedings, 31 Ore.L.Rev. 185 (1952); D. Elder, The Fair Report Privilege (1988); K. Sowle, Defamation and the First Amendment: The Case for a Constitutional Privilege of Fair Report, 54 N.Y.U.L.Rev. 469 (1979).

12. A newspaper, opposing a candidate for office, carries accurate stories about his business transactions affecting the government, but deliberately prepares slanted headlines, intended to give a misleading impression to a person who did not carefully read through the story as to the candidate's ethics. Can this be found to constitute reckless disregard as to falsity? Cf. McNair v. Hearst Corp., 494 F.2d 1309 (9th Cir.1974); Sprouse v. Clay Communication, Inc., 158 W.Va. 427, 211 S.E.2d 674 (1975); Journal–Gazette Company v. Bandido's, Inc., 712 N.E.2d 446 (Ind.), cert. denied, 120 S.Ct. 499 (1999) (adopting the minority "fair index" rule, i.e., if the headline is not a "fair index" of the substance, headline must be examined independently to determine its actionability in libel).

(B) PRIVATE PLAINTIFFS

Gertz v. Robert Welch, Inc.

Supreme Court of the United States, 1974.
418 U.S. 323, 94 S.Ct. 2997, 41 L.Ed.2d 789.

MR. JUSTICE POWELL delivered the opinion of the Court. * * *

I. In 1968 a Chicago policeman named Nuccio shot and killed a youth named Nelson. The state authorities prosecuted Nuccio for the homicide

Front row: Stewart, Douglas, Burger, C.J., Brennan, White
Back row: Powell, Marshall, Blackmun, Rehnquist

and ultimately obtained a conviction for murder in the second degree. The Nelson family retained petitioner Elmer Gertz, a reputable attorney, to represent them in civil litigation against Nuccio.

Respondent publishes American Opinion, a monthly outlet for the views of the John Birch Society. Early in the 1960's the magazine began to warn of a nationwide conspiracy to discredit local law enforcement agencies and create in their stead a national police force capable of supporting a Communist dictatorship. As part of the continuing effort to alert the public to this assumed danger, the managing editor of American Opinion commissioned an article on the murder trial of Officer Nuccio. For this purpose he engaged a regular contributor to the magazine. In March 1969 respondent published the resulting article under the title "FRAME–UP: Richard Nuccio And The War On Police." The article purports to demonstrate that the testimony against Nuccio at his criminal trial was false and that his prosecution was part of the Communist campaign against the police.

In his capacity as counsel for the Nelson family in the civil litigation, petitioner attended the coroner's inquest into the boy's death and initiated actions for damages, but he neither discussed Officer Nuccio with the press nor played any part in the criminal proceeding. Notwithstanding petitioner's remote connection with the prosecution of Nuccio, respondent's magazine portrayed him as an architect of the "frame-up." According to the article, the police file on petitioner took "a big, Irish cop to lift." The article stated that petitioner had been an official of the "Marxist League for Industrial Democracy, originally known as the Intercollegiate Socialist Society, which has advocated the violent seizure of our government." It labeled Gertz a "Leninist" and a "Communist-fronter." It also stated that Gertz had been an officer of the National Lawyers Guild, described as a Communist organization that "probably did more than any other outfit to plan the Communist attack on the Chicago police during the 1968 Democratic Convention."

These statements contained serious inaccuracies. The implication that petitioner had a criminal record was false. Petitioner had been a member and officer of the National Lawyers Guild some 15 years earlier, but there was no evidence that he or that organization had taken any part in planning the 1968 demonstrations in Chicago. There was also no basis for the charge that petitioner was a "Leninist" or a "Communist-fronter." And he had never been a member of the "Marxist League for Industrial Democracy" or the "Intercollegiate Socialist Society."

The managing editor of American Opinion made no effort to verify or substantiate the charges against petitioner. Instead, he appended an editorial introduction stating that the author had "conducted extensive research into the Richard Nuccio Case." And he included in the article a photograph of petitioner and wrote the caption that appeared under it: "Elmer Gertz of Red Guild harasses Nuccio." Respondent placed the issue of American Opinion containing the article on sale at newsstands throughout the country and distributed reprints of the article on the streets of Chicago.

Petitioner filed a diversity action for libel in the United States District Court for the Northern District of Illinois.

[The District Court denied defendant's motion to dismiss. After the evidence was in, it "ruled in effect that petitioner was neither a public official nor a public figure," and it submitted the issue of damages to the jury, which awarded $50,000. On further reflection the District Court concluded that the *New York Times* standard applied and entered judgment for defendant notwithstanding the jury verdict. This action was affirmed by the Court of Appeals for the Seventh Circuit, on the basis of Rosenbloom v. Metromedia, Inc., 403 U.S. 29 (1971), supra page 875 which had been decided in the meantime.]

II.   The principal issue in this case is whether a newspaper or broadcaster that publishes defamatory falsehoods about an individual who is neither a public official nor a public figure may claim a constitutional privilege against liability for the injury inflicted by those statements. The Court considered this question on the rather different set of facts presented in Rosenbloom v. Metromedia, Inc. [c]. [The opinion describes in detail the facts and opinions in *Rosenbloom*.]

III.   We begin with the common ground. Under the First Amendment there is no such thing as a false idea. However pernicious an opinion may seem, we depend for its correction not on the conscience of judges and juries but on the competition of other ideas. But there is no constitutional value in false statements of fact. Neither the intentional lie nor the careless error materially advances society's interest in "uninhibited, robust, and wide-open" debate on public issues. [C] They belong to that category of utterances which "are no essential part of any exposition of ideas, and are of such slight social value as a step to truth that any benefit that may be derived from them is clearly outweighed by the social interest in order and morality." Chaplinsky v. New Hampshire, 315 U.S. 568, 572 (1942).

Although the erroneous statement of fact is not worthy of constitutional protection, it is nevertheless inevitable in free debate. As James Madison pointed out in the Report on the Virginia Resolutions of 1798, "Some degree of abuse is inseparable from the proper use of every thing; and in no instance is this more true than in that of the press." 4 J. Elliot, Debates on the Federal Constitution of 1787, p. 571 (1876). And punishment of error runs the risk of inducing a cautious and restrictive exercise of the constitutionally guaranteed freedoms of speech and press. Our decisions recognize that a rule of strict liability that compels a publisher or broadcaster to guarantee the accuracy of his factual assertions may lead to intolerable self-censorship. Allowing the media to avoid liability only by proving the truth of all injurious statements does not accord adequate protection to First Amendment liberties. As the Court stated in New York Times Co. v. Sullivan, supra, at 279, "Allowance of the defense of truth, with the burden of proving it on the defendant, does not mean that only false speech will be deterred." The First Amendment requires that we protect some falsehood in order to protect speech that matters.

The need to avoid self-censorship by the news media is, however, not the only societal value at issue. If it were, this Court would have embraced long ago the view that publishers and broadcasters enjoy an unconditional and indefeasible immunity from liability for defamation. [Cc] Such a rule would, indeed, obviate the fear that the prospect of civil liability for injurious falsehood might dissuade a timorous press from the effective exercise of First Amendment freedoms. Yet absolute protection for the communications media requires a total sacrifice of the competing value served by the law of defamation.

The legitimate state interest underlying the law of libel is the compensation of individuals for the harm inflicted on them by defamatory falsehood. * * * The protection of private personality, like the protection of life itself, is left primarily to the individual States under the Ninth and Tenth Amendments. But this does not mean that the right is entitled to any less recognition by this Court as a basic of our constitutional system." [C]

Some tension necessarily exists between the need for a vigorous and uninhibited press and the legitimate interest in redressing wrongful injury. * * * In our continuing effort to define the proper accommodation between these competing concerns, we have been especially anxious to assure to the freedoms of speech and press that "breathing space" essential to their fruitful exercise. [C] To that end this Court has extended a measure of strategic protection to defamatory falsehood.

The New York Times standard defines the level of constitutional protection appropriate to the context of defamation of a public person. Those who, by reason of the notoriety of their achievements or the vigor and success with which they seek the public's attention, are properly classed as public figures and those who hold governmental office may recover for injury to reputation only on clear and convincing proof that the defamatory falsehood was made with knowledge of its falsity or with reckless disregard for the truth. This standard administers an extremely powerful antidote to the inducement to media self-censorship of the common-law rule of strict liability for libel and slander. And it exacts a correspondingly high price from the victims of defamatory falsehood. Plainly many deserving plaintiffs, including some intentionally subjected to injury, will be unable to surmount the barrier of the New York Times test. Despite this substantial abridgment of the state law right to compensation for wrongful hurt to one's reputation, the Court has concluded that the protection of the New York Times privilege should be available to publishers and broadcasters of defamatory falsehood concerning public officials and public figures. [C] We think that these decisions are correct, but we do not find their holdings justified solely by reference to the interest of the press and broadcast media in immunity from liability. Rather, we believe that the New York Times rule states an accommodation between this concern and the limited state interest present in the context of libel actions brought by public persons. For the reasons stated below, we conclude that the state interest in compensating injury to the reputation of private individuals requires that a different rule should obtain with respect to them.

Theoretically, of course, the balance between the needs of the press and the individual's claim to compensation for wrongful injury might be struck on a case-by-case basis. * * * But this approach would lead to unpredictable results and uncertain expectations, and it could render our duty to supervise the lower courts unmanageable. Because an ad hoc resolution of the competing interests at stake in each particular case is not feasible, we must lay down broad rules of general application. * * *

The first remedy of any victim of defamation is self-help—using available opportunities to contradict the lie or correct the error and thereby to minimize its adverse impact on reputation. Public officials and public figures usually enjoy significantly greater access to the channels of effective communication and hence have a more realistic opportunity to counteract false statements than private individuals normally enjoy. Private individuals are therefore more vulnerable to injury, and the state interest in protecting them is correspondingly greater.

More important than the likelihood that private individuals will lack effective opportunities for rebuttal, there is a compelling normative consideration underlying the distinction between public and private defamation plaintiffs. An individual who decides to seek governmental office must accept certain necessary consequences of that involvement in public affairs.

He runs the risk of closer public scrutiny than might otherwise be the case. * * *

Those classed as public figures stand in a similar position. Hypothetically, it may be possible for someone to become a public figure through no purposeful action of his own, but the instances of truly involuntary public figures must be exceedingly rare. * * * Commonly, those classed as public figures have thrust themselves to the forefront of particular public controversies in order to influence the resolution of the issues involved. * * *

The communications media are entitled to act on the assumption that public officials and public figures have voluntarily exposed themselves to increased risk of injury from defamatory falsehood concerning them. No such assumption is justified with respect to a private individual. * * * He has relinquished no part of his interest in the protection of his own good name, and consequently he has a more compelling call on the courts for redress of injury inflicted by defamatory falsehood. Thus, private individuals are not only more vulnerable to injury than public officials and public figures; they are also more deserving of recovery.

For these reasons we conclude that the States should retain substantial latitude in their efforts to enforce a legal remedy for defamatory falsehood injurious to the reputation of a private individual. The extension of the New York Times test proposed by the Rosenbloom plurality would abridge this legitimate state interest to a degree that we find unacceptable. And it would occasion the additional difficulty of forcing state and federal judges to decide on an ad hoc basis which publications address issues of "general or public interest" and which do not—to determine, in the words of Mr. Justice Marshall, "what information is relevant to self-government." Rosenbloom v. Metromedia, Inc., 403 U.S., at 79. We doubt the wisdom of committing this task to the conscience of judges. Nor does the Constitution require us to draw so thin a line between the drastic alternatives of the New York Times privilege and the common law of strict liability for defamatory error. * * *

We hold that, so long as they do not impose liability without fault, the States may define for themselves the appropriate standard of liability for a publisher or broadcaster of defamatory falsehood injurious to a private individual. This approach provides a more equitable boundary between the competing concerns involved here. It recognizes the strength of the legitimate state interest in compensating private individuals for wrongful injury to reputation, yet shields the press and broadcast media from the rigors of strict liability for defamation. At least this conclusion obtains where, as here, the substance of the defamatory statement "makes substantial danger to reputation apparent." * * *

IV. Our accommodation of the competing values at stake in defamation suits by private individuals allows the States to impose liability on the publisher or broadcaster of defamatory falsehood on a less demanding showing than that required by New York Times. This conclusion is not based on a belief that the considerations which prompted the adoption of the New York Times privilege for defamation of public officials and its extension to public figures are wholly inapplicable to the context of private individuals. Rather, we endorse this approach in recognition of the strong and legitimate state interest in compensating private individuals for injury to reputation.

But this countervailing state interest extends no further than compensation for actual injury. For the reasons stated below, we hold that the States may not permit recovery of presumed or punitive damages, at least when liability is not based on a showing of knowledge of falsity or reckless disregard for the truth.

The common law of defamation is an oddity of tort law, for it allows recovery of purportedly compensatory damages without evidence of actual loss. Under the traditional rules pertaining to actions for libel, the existence of injury is presumed from the fact of publication. Juries may award substantial sums as compensation for supposed damage to reputation without any proof that such harm actually occurred. The largely uncontrolled discretion of juries to award damages where there is no loss unnecessarily compounds the potential of any system of liability for defamatory falsehood to inhibit the vigorous exercise of First Amendment freedoms. Additionally, the doctrine of presumed damages invites juries to punish unpopular opinion rather than to compensate individuals for injury sustained by the publication of a false fact. More to the point, the States have no substantial interest in securing for plaintiffs such as this petitioner gratuitous awards of money damages far in excess of any actual injury.

We would not, of course, invalidate state law simply because we doubt its wisdom, but here we are attempting to reconcile state law with a competing interest grounded in the constitutional command of the First Amendment. It is therefore appropriate to require that state remedies for defamatory falsehood reach no farther than is necessary to protect the legitimate interest involved. It is necessary to restrict defamation plaintiffs who do not prove knowledge of falsity or reckless disregard for the truth to compensation for actual injury. We need not define "actual injury," as trial courts have wide experience in framing appropriate jury instructions in tort actions. Suffice it to say that actual injury is not limited to out-of-pocket loss. Indeed, the more customary types of actual harm inflicted by defamatory falsehood include impairment of reputation and standing in the community, personal humiliation, and mental anguish and suffering. Of course, juries must be limited by appropriate instructions, and all awards must be supported by competent evidence concerning the injury, although there need be no evidence which assigns an actual dollar value to the injury.

We also find no justification for allowing awards of punitive damages against publishers and broadcasters held liable under state-defined standards of liability for defamation. In most jurisdictions jury discretion over the amounts awarded is limited only by the gentle rule that they not be excessive. Consequently, juries assess punitive damages in wholly unpredictable amounts bearing no necessary relation to the actual harm caused. And they remain free to use their discretion selectively to punish expressions of unpopular views. Like the doctrine of presumed damages, jury discretion to award punitive damages unnecessarily exacerbates the danger of media self-censorship, but, unlike the former rule, punitive damages are wholly irrelevant to the state interest that justifies a negligence standard for private defamation actions. They are not compensation for injury. Instead, they are private fines levied by civil juries to punish reprehensible conduct and to deter its future occurrence. In short, the private defamation plaintiff who establishes liability under a less demanding standard than that stated by New York Times may recover only such damages as are sufficient to compensate him for actual injury.

V.   Notwithstanding our refusal to extend the New York Times privilege to defamation of private individuals, respondent contends that we should affirm the judgment below on the ground that petitioner is either a public official or a public figure. * * *

Respondent admits this but argues that petitioner's appearance at the coroner's inquest rendered him a "de facto public official." Our cases recognize no such concept. Respondent's suggestion would sweep all lawyers under the New York Times rule as officers of the court and distort the plain meaning of the "public official" category beyond all recognition. We decline to follow it.

Respondent's characterization of petitioner as a public figure raises a different question. That designation may rest on either of two alternative bases. In some instances an individual may achieve such pervasive fame or notoriety that he becomes a public figure for all purposes and in all contexts. More commonly, an individual voluntarily injects himself or is drawn into a particular public controversy and thereby becomes a public figure for a limited range of issues. In either case such persons assume special prominence in the resolution of public questions.

Petitioner has long been active in community and professional affairs. He has served as an officer of local civic groups and of various professional organizations, and he has published several books and articles on legal subjects. Although petitioner was consequently well known in some circles, he had achieved no general fame or notoriety in the community. * * * Absent clear evidence of general fame or notoriety in the community, and pervasive involvement in the affairs of society, an individual should not be deemed a public personality for all aspects of his life. It is preferable to reduce the public-figure question to a more meaningful context by looking to the nature and extent of an individual's participation in the particular controversy giving rise to the defamation.

In this context it is plain that petitioner was not a public figure. He played a minimal role at the coroner's inquest, and his participation related solely to his representation of a private client. He took no part in the criminal prosecution of Officer Nuccio. Moreover, he never discussed either the criminal or civil litigation with the press and was never quoted as having done so. He plainly did not thrust himself into the vortex of this public issue, nor did he engage the public's attention in an attempt to influence its outcome. We are persuaded that the trial court did not err in refusing to characterize petitioner as a public figure for the purpose of this litigation.

We therefore conclude that the New York Times standard is inapplicable to this case and that the trial court erred in entering judgment for respondent. Because the jury was allowed to impose liability without fault and was permitted to presume damages without proof of injury, a new trial is necessary. We reverse and remand for further proceedings in accord with this opinion.

It is so ordered.

[This opinion was joined by STEWART, MARSHALL, BLACKMUN and REHNQUIST, JJ.; BLACKMUN, J., stating in a concurring opinion that he found some difficulties with the majority opinion, but that he joined in it to attain a "definitive ruling."

BURGER, C.J., dissented, disapproving the requirement of negligence for private defamation and urging remand for a reinstatement of the jury verdict below. DOUGLAS, J., dissented on the basis of his absolute-privilege theory and would at least retain the *Rosenbloom* rule. BRENNAN, J., dissented and would retain the *Rosenbloom* rule. WHITE, J., dissented and would retain strict liability for private defamation.]

NOTES AND QUESTIONS

1.   Of the new ideas adopted in *Gertz,* the one requiring a finding of fault for private defamation had been urged in the dissenting opinion of Harlan, J., in Time, Inc. v. Hill, 385 U.S. 374 (1967) ("State should be free to hold the press to a duty of making a reasonable investigation of the underlying facts"), and the dissenting opinion of Marshall, J., in Rosenbloom v. Metromedia, Inc., 403 U.S. 29 (1971) ("only constitutional caveat should be that absolute or strict liability * * * cannot be used"). Eliminating presumed and punitive damages had been urged in *Rosenbloom* in the dissenting opinion of Marshall, J. (restrict "the award of damages to proven, actual injuries" and cut down on the "jury's wide ranging discretion * * * since the award will be based on essentially objective discernable factors"), and, to a large extent, in the dissenting opinion of Harlan, J. ("legitimate function of libel law must be understood as that of compensating individuals for actual, measurable harm caused by the conduct of others").

2.   *Contracting the Coverage of the New York Times Standard.* In receding from the position taken in Rosenbloom v. Metromedia, Inc., 403 U.S. 29 (1971), that the *New York Times* standard of knowledge or reckless disregard applied to any matter of public or general interest and holding that the standard applies only to public officials and public figures, the Court was speaking only of what the Constitution requires the states to do. A state must apply the *Times* standard in a suit by a public person; it is not required to do this in a suit by a private person but is entirely free to do so if it wishes. A few courts have indicated that they will continue to require knowledge or reckless disregard where the publication touches matters of public or general interest. See, e.g., Sisler v. Gannett Co., Inc., 104 N.J. 256, 516 A.2d 1083 (1986), but interpreted in Turf Lawnmower Repair, Inc. v. Bergen Record Corp., 139 N.J. 392, 655 A.2d 417 (1995), to apply the actual malice standard "where the press's [sic] statement concerns businesses affecting the public's health and safety and businesses that are subject to substantial government

regulation." The court recognized the "public benefits from having the press act as a consumer affairs watchdog." Thus the court articulated "an actual-malice standard rather than a negligence standard, even for ordinary businesses, if the consumer fraud allegations in the article, if true, would constitute a violation of the Consumer Fraud Act." Id. at 427. For other contexts, the most appropriate standard was negligence in conformity with forty-two jurisdictions. Only Colorado and Indiana apply non-negligence standards: Walker v. Colorado Springs Sun, Inc., 188 Colo. 86, 538 P.2d 450 (1975); Journal–Gazette Company v. Bandido's, Inc., 712 N.E.2d 446 (Ind.), cert. denied, 120 S.Ct. 499 (1999) (confirming the actual malice standard for "matters of general or public concern," but against strong dissent). A majority of the courts decline to impose a requirement of knowledge or reckless disregard in an action by a private person: Mead Corporation v. Hicks, 448 So.2d 308 (Ala.1983); Stone v. Essex County Newspapers, Inc., 367 Mass. 849, 330 N.E.2d 161 (1975); Jacron Sales Co., Inc. v. Sindorf, 276 Md. 580, 350 A.2d 688 (1976); Troman v. Wood, 62 Ill.2d 184, 340 N.E.2d 292 (1975); Memphis Pub. Co. v. Nichols, 569 S.W.2d 412 (Tenn.1978); Taskett v. KING Broadcasting Co., 86 Wash.2d 439, 546 P.2d 81 (1976).

3. *Scope of Fault Requirement in Action by Private Person. Gertz* seemed to indicate that strict liability for defamation is unconstitutional. This would require fault in regard, at least, to the falsity of the statement. There still remain some unanswered questions on the scope of the requirement, however. See, in general, Restatement (Second) of Torts § 580B, Comments d to f. And on the nature of the negligence standard, see id., Comments g and h. The constitutional fault standard is probably applicable to the identification issue. What result in Hulton v. Jones, supra, under the *Gertz* test? Note that in New York Times v. Sullivan, supra, the Court found that the common law standard, turning on a reasonable reader's assumptions to identify the plaintiff, was constitutionally insufficient. Reference would have to be made to the plaintiff as an individual lest criticism of government be crimped. On the effect of the fault requirement on the whole system of conditional privileges, see id., Comment l, and the Special Note preceding § 593. And see the discussion in Jacron Sales Co. v. Sindorf, 276 Md. 580, 350 A.2d 688 (1976), infra, page 930. See Franklin & Bussel, The Plaintiff's Burden in Defamation: Awareness and Falsity, 25 Wm. & Mary L.Rev. 825 (1984).

On the standard of care, see Bloom, Proof of Fault in Media Defamation Litigation, 38 Vand.L.Rev. 247 (1985); Simon, Libel as Malpractice: News Media Ethics and the Standard of Care, 53 Ford.L.Rev. 449 (1984); Franklin, What Does Negligence Mean in Defamation Cases?, 6 Com/Ent L.J. 259 (1984); Wade, The Tort Liability of Investigative Reporters, 37 Vand.L.Rev. 301 (1984). Anderson, in Is Libel Law Worth Reforming?, 140 U.Pa.L.Rev. 487, 503 (1991) states that "suits under the negligence formula of *Gertz* have turned out to be rare." Why?

4. *Nonmedia Defendants. New York Times* and *Gertz* both involved suits against members of the news media. Were their constitutional requirements confined to suits against media defendants? Although the Supreme Court has never expressly said so, the answer for the *Times* standard seems to be clearly, "no." In *Times* itself, the suit was also against private individuals who signed the political advertisement. See also Garrison v. Louisiana, 379 U.S. 64 (1964) (press conference); Henry v. Collins, 380 U.S. 356 (1965) (letter and telephone conversation); St. Amant v. Thompson, 390 U.S. 727 (1968), supra page 875, Old Dominion Branch No. 496, Nat'l Ass'n of Letter Carriers v. Austin, 418 U.S. 264, 285 (1974) (newsletter). But cf. Hutchinson v. Proxmire, 443 U.S. 111, 133, n. 16 (1979) (Supreme Court "has never decided * * * whether the *New York Times* standard can apply to an individual defendant rather than a media defendant"), and in

Milkovich v. Lorain Journal Co., infra page 915, the court was at pains to distinguish media from nonmedia defendants, but did not decide the force of the dichotomy.

There has been less agreement about the *Gertz* standard, the cases dividing almost evenly. But the opinions in *Greenmoss,* the next principal case, indicate that some of the current members of the Court would draw no distinction between media defendants and other defendants. However, in respect of the burden of proof on the issue of the falsity of the publication, the Supreme Court in *Hepps,* infra page 907, couches its decision as applying only to media defendants.

5. *When is the Statement Defamatory?* Is this issue subject to constitutional constraint? The Supreme Court entertained the question in 1942 when it granted certiorari on the (2–1) holding in Sweeney v. Schenectady Union Pub. Co., 122 F.2d 288 (2d Cir.1941). However, the Court handed down a per-curiam memorandum affirming the judgment "by an equally divided court." The Court has not accepted any other cases raising the issue. The *Masson* case, supra, suggests that the issue should be the province of state law.

6. *Damages.* Actual damages, as required by the Constitution under the holding in *Gertz,* are broader in scope than special damages, as required at common law for oral statements that are not slanderous per se. Special damages require pecuniary loss. Actual damages may include injury to reputation or emotional distress, without showing pecuniary loss, but the injury must be proved. It initially appeared that the purpose of this requirement was to give the trial and appellate courts greater control over the amount of damages that the jury can properly award. But the opportunity has not been utilized.

7. *Public and Private Plaintiffs.* The principal case turns its analysis on the characterization of the plaintiff. This is a vexing issue touched upon infra p. ___.

8. For discussions of *Gertz* and its implications, see Anderson, Libel and Press Self–Censorship, 53 Texas L.Rev. 422 (1975); Eaton, The American Law of Defamation Through Gertz v. Robert Welch, Inc. and Beyond: An Analytical Primer, 61 Va.L.Rev. 1349 (1975); Gertz, Gertz v. Robert Welch, Inc.: The Story of a Landmark Libel Case (1992).

General treatments of the constitutional law of defamation include two important symposia: Defamation and the First Amendment: New Perspectives, 25 Wm. & Mary L.Rev. 743–968 (1983); and New Perspectives in the Law of Defamation, 74 Calif.L.Rev. 677–925 (1986). And see Smolla, Let the Author Beware: The Rejuvenation of the American Law of Libel, 132 U.Pa.L.Rev. 1 (1983).

(C) SPEECH OF PRIVATE CONCERN

Dun & Bradstreet, Inc. v. Greenmoss Builders, Inc.

Supreme Court of the United States, 1985.
472 U.S. 749, 105 S.Ct. 2939, 86 L.Ed.2d 593.

[Petitioner-defendant Dun & Bradstreet supplied confidential credit rating reports to subscribers. It sent a report to five subscribers, indicating that respondent-plaintiff Greenmoss Builders had filed a voluntary petition for bankruptcy. The report was totally false, the error resulting from petitioner's use of a 17–year–old high school student to review Vermont bankruptcy proceedings. He mistakenly attributed to respondent a bankruptcy petition filed by one of respondent's former employees, and from petitioner's failure to make routine checks of accuracy. Learning of the report, respondent called petitioner's regional office, explained the error and asked for a correction. Petitioner sent out a notice which respondent regarded as inadequate, and refused to disclose the identity of the five subscribers.

Respondent sued for libel and obtained a verdict for $50,000 in compensatory or presumed damages and $300,000 in punitive damages. The trial court granted a motion for a new trial, but respondent appealed to the Vermont Supreme Court, which reversed and reinstated the verdict on the ground that the constitutional requirements of the U.S. Supreme Court did not apply when the suit was against a non-media defendant. 143 Vt. 66, 461 A.2d 414 (1983). This court granted certiorari, and affirmed the holding, "although for reasons different from those relied on by the Vermont Supreme Court."]

Justice Powell announced the judgment of the Court and delivered an opinion, in which Justice Rehnquist and Justice O'Connor joined.

In Gertz v. Robert Welch, Inc., 418 U.S. 323, we held that the First Amendment restricted the damages that a private individual could obtain from a publisher for a libel that involved a matter of public concern. More specifically, we held that in these circumstances the First Amendment prohibited awards of presumed and punitive damages for false and defamatory statements unless the plaintiff shows "actual malice," that is, knowledge of falsity or reckless disregard for the truth. The question presented in this case is whether this rule of *Gertz* applies when the false and defamatory statements do not involve matters of public concern. * * *

In *Gertz,* we held that the fact that [an] expression concerned a public issue did not by itself entitle the libel defendant to the constitutional protections of *New York Times*. These protections, we found, were not "justified solely by reference to the interest of the press and broadcast media in immunity from liability." [C] Rather, they represented "an accommodation between [First Amendment] concern[s] and the limited state interest present in the context of libel actions brought by public persons." [C] In libel actions brought by private persons we found the competing interests different. Largely because private persons have not voluntarily exposed themselves to increased risk of injury from defamatory statements and because they generally lack effective opportunities for rebutting such statements, [c] we found that the State possessed a "strong and legitimate * * * interest in compensating private individuals for injury to reputation." [C] Balancing this stronger state interest against the same First Amendment interest at stake in *New York Times,* we held that a State could not allow recovery of presumed and punitive damages absent a showing of "actual malice." Nothing in our opinion, however, indicated that this same balance would be struck regardless of the type of speech involved. * * *

We have never considered whether the *Gertz* balance obtains when the defamatory statements involve no issue of public concern. To make this determination, we must employ the approach approved in *Gertz* and balance the State's interest in compensating private individuals for injury to their reputation against the First Amendment interest in protecting this type of expression. This state interest is identical to the one weighed in *Gertz.* There we found that it was "strong and legitimate." [C] A State should not lightly be required to abandon it. * * *

The First Amendment interest, on the other hand, is less important than the one weighed in *Gertz.* We have long recognized that not all speech is of equal First Amendment importance. It is speech on " 'matters of public concern' " that is "at the heart of the First Amendment's protection." First National Bank of Boston v. Bellotti, 435 U.S. 765, 776. * * *

In contrast, speech on matters of purely private concern is of less First Amendment concern. [C] As a number of state courts, including the court below, have recognized, the role of the Constitution in regulating state libel law is far more limited when the concerns that activated *New York Times* and *Gertz* are absent. * * *

While * * * speech on matters not of public concern is not totally unprotected by the First Amendment [cc], its protections are less stringent. In *Gertz,* we found that the state interest in awarding presumed and punitive damages was not "substantial" in view of their effect on speech at the core of First Amendment concern. [C] This interest, however, is "substantial" relative to the incidental effect these remedies may have on speech of significantly less constitutional interest. The rationale of the common law rules has been the experience and judgment of history that "proof of actual damage will be impossible in a great many cases where, from the character of the defamatory words and the circumstances of publication, it is all but certain that serious harm has resulted in fact." [Cc] As a result, courts for centuries have allowed juries to presume that some damage occurred from many defamatory utterances and publications. * * * [Cc] This rule furthers the state interest in providing remedies for defamation by ensuring that those remedies are effective. In light of the reduced constitutional value of speech involving no matters of public concern, we hold that the state interest adequately supports awards of presumed and punitive damages—even absent a showing of "actual malice." * * *

The only remaining issue is whether petitioner's credit report involved a matter of public concern. In a related context, we have held that "[w]hether * * * speech addresses a matter of public concern must be determined by [the expression's] content, form, and context * * * as revealed by the whole record." Connick v. Myers, 461 U.S., at 147–148. These factors indicate that petitioner's credit report concerns no public issue. It was speech solely in the individual interest of the speaker and its specific business audience. [C] This particular interest warrants no special protection when—as in this case—the speech is wholly false and clearly damaging to the victim's business reputation. [Cc] Moreover, since the credit report was made available to only five subscribers, who, under the terms of the subscription agreement, could not disseminate it further, it cannot be said that the report involves any "strong interest in the free flow of commercial information." [C] There is simply no credible argument that this type of credit reporting requires special protection to ensure that "debate on public issues [will] be uninhibited, robust, and wide-open." New York Times Co. v. Sullivan, 376 U.S., at 270.

In addition, the speech here, like advertising, is hardy and unlikely to be deterred by incidental state regulation. [Cc] It is solely motivated by the desire for profit, which, we have noted, is a force less likely to be deterred than others. [C] Arguably, the reporting here was also more objectively verifiable than speech deserving of greater protection. [C] In any case, the market provides a powerful incentive to a credit reporting agency to be accurate, since false credit reporting is of no use to creditors. Thus, any incremental "chilling" effect of libel suits would be of decreased significance. * * *

We conclude that permitting recovery of presumed and punitive damages in defamation cases absent a showing of "actual malice" does not violate the First Amendment when the defamatory statements do not involve matters of public concern. Accordingly, we affirm the judgment of the Vermont Supreme Court.

[CHIEF JUSTICE BURGER and JUSTICE WHITE concurred in the judgment with separate opinions. They had dissented in *Gertz* and urged it to be overruled. They also wished to reevaluate the extent of application of New York Times v. Sullivan.]

JUSTICE BRENNAN, with whom JUSTICE MARSHALL, JUSTICE BLACKMUN and JUSTICE STEVENS join, dissenting. * * *

The four who join this opinion would reverse the judgment of the Vermont Supreme Court. We believe that, although protection of the type of expression at issue is admittedly not the "central meaning of the First Amendment," [c] *Gertz* makes clear that the First Amendment nonetheless requires restraints on presumed and punitive damage awards for this expression. The lack of consensus in approach to these idiosyncratic facts should not, however, obscure the solid allegiance the principles of *New York Times v. Sullivan* continue to command in the jurisprudence of this Court. * * *

When an alleged libel involves criticism of a public official or a public figure, the need to nurture robust debate of public issues and the requirement that all state regulation of speech be narrowly tailored coalesce to require actual malice as a prerequisite to any recovery. When the alleged libel involves speech that falls outside these especially important categories, we have held that the Constitution permits states significant leeway to compensate for actual damage to reputation. The requirement of narrowly tailored regulatory measures, however, always mandates at least a showing of fault and proscribes the award of presumed and punitive damages on less than a showing of actual malice. It has remained the judgment of the Court since *Gertz* that this comprehensive two-tiered structure best accommodates the values of the constitutional free speech guarantee and the states' interest in protecting reputation. * * *

In professing allegiance to *Gertz,* the plurality opinion protests too much. As Justice White correctly observes, Justice Powell departs completely from the analytic framework and result of that case: "*Gertz* was intended to reach any false statements * * * whether or not [they] implicate a matter of public importance." [C][11]

Even accepting the notion that a distinction can and should be drawn between matters of public concern and matters of purely private concern, however, the analyses presented by both JUSTICE POWELL and JUSTICE WHITE fail on their own terms. Both, by virtue of what they hold in this case, propose an impoverished definition of "matters of public concern" that is irreconcilable with First Amendment principles. The credit reporting at issue here surely involves a subject matter of sufficient public concern to require the comprehensive protections of *Gertz.* Were this speech appropriately characterized as a matter of only private concern, moreover, the elimination of the *Gertz* restrictions on presumed and punitive damages would still violate basic First Amendment requirements. * * *

The five Members of the Court voting to affirm the damage award in this case have provided almost no guidance as to what constitutes a protected "matter of public concern." JUSTICE WHITE offers nothing at all, but his opinion does indicate that the distinction turns on solely the subject matter of the expression and not on the extent or conditions of dissemination of that expression. [C] JUSTICE POWELL adumbrates a rationale that would appear to focus primarily on subject matter.[12]

The opinion relies on the fact that the speech at issue was "solely in the individual interest of the speaker and its *business* audience," [c]

---

11. One searches *Gertz* in vain for a single word to support the proposition that limits on presumed and punitive damages obtained only when speech involved matters of public concern. *Gertz* could not have been grounded in such a premise. Distrust of placing in the courts the power to decide what speech was of public concern was precisely the rationale *Gertz* offered for rejecting the *Rosenbloom* plurality approach. [C] It would have been incongruous for the Court to go on to circumscribe the protection against presumed and punitive damages by reference to a judicial judgment as to whether the speech at issue involved matters of public concern. At several points the Court in *Gertz* makes perfectly clear the restrictions of presumed and punitive damages were to apply in all cases. [C]

Indeed, JUSTICE POWELL's opinion today is fairly read as embracing the approach of the *Rosenbloom* plurality to deciding when the Constitution should limit state defamation law. The limits imposed, however, are less stringent than those suggested by the *Rosen-* *bloom* plurality. Under the approach of today's plurality, speech about matters of public or general interest receives only the *Gertz* protections against unrestrained presumed and punitive damages, not the full *New York Times v. Sullivan* protections against any recovery absent a showing of actual malice.

12. Justice Powell also appears to rely in part on the fact that communication was limited and confidential. Given that his analysis also relies on the subject matter of the credit report, it is difficult to decipher exactly what role the nature and extent of dissemination plays in JUSTICE POWELL's analysis. But because the subject matter of the expression at issue is properly understood as a matter of public concern, it may well be that this element of confidentiality is crucial to the outcome as far as JUSTICE POWELL's opinion is concerned. In other words, it may be that JUSTICE POWELL thinks this particular expression could not contribute to public welfare because the public generally does not receive it. This factor does not suffice to save the analysis. * * *

Analogizing explicitly to advertising, the opinion also states that credit reporting is "hardy" and "solely motivated by the desire for profit." [C] These two strains of analysis suggest that JUSTICE POWELL is excluding the subject matter of credit reports from "matters of public concern" because the speech is predominantly in the realm of matters of economic concern.
* * *

Greenmoss Builders should be permitted to recover for any actual damage it can show resulted from Dun & Bradstreet's negligently false credit report, but should be required to show actual malice to receive presumed or punitive damages. Because the jury was not instructed in accordance with these principles, we would reverse and remand for further proceedings not inconsistent with this opinion.

NOTES AND QUESTIONS

1. On studying the *Gertz* case, would it have occurred to you that this case would have been decided this way? After reading *this* case, what do you think the Court will do when it reviews a case involving a private plaintiff in a matter not of public concern, when the question arises whether the *Gertz* requirement of defendant's fault is raised? What would be the effect of its decision either way?

2. Do you agree with the reasoning that the nature of this information militates against its production and dissemination being "chilled" by defamation liability? Can the hazards of liability be captured by the price charged for access to this information? How does this differ from political speech? May the susceptibility of the information to chilling describe a principled distinction between the categories of public and private concern? For a discussion see Farber, Free Speech Without Romance: Public Choice and the First Amendment, 105 Harv.L.Rev. 554 (1991).

3. The principal case does appear to settle, at least for the time being, one issue that had never been specifically decided. This is the issue of whether different standards might constitutionally be applied to media defendants and nonmedia defendants. The Vermont Supreme Court had based its decision in *Greenmoss* on the ground that the defendant was not acting as a member of the news media. Although the Supreme Court affirmed, it pointedly stated that the affirmance was not based on the reasons given by the state supreme court. Justice Brennan stated in his dissenting opinion that he counted "at least six" Justices who "agree today that, in the context of defamation law, the rights of the institutional media are no greater and no less than those enjoyed by" others.

(D) FALSITY

Philadelphia Newspapers, Inc. v. Hepps

Supreme Court of the United States, 1986.
475 U.S. 767, 106 S.Ct. 1558, 89 L.Ed.2d 783.

[Plaintiffs were Maurice S. Hepps, principal stockholder of General Programming, Inc. (GPI), a corporation engaged in franchising a chain of "Thrifty Stores" (selling beer, soft drinks and snacks), plus GPI itself and some of the franchisees. The charges were that plaintiffs "had links to organized crime and used some of those links to influence the State's governmental processes, both legislative and administrative." They were published in a series of articles by defendant, Philadelphia Newspapers, Inc., in the Philadelphia Inquirer.

Front row: Marshall, Brennan, Rehnquist, C.J., White, Blackmun
Back row: O'Connor, Powell, Stevens, Scalia

Suit was in the state court, where the court followed two statutes requiring (1) a private plaintiff to prove negligence or malice by the defendant and (2) the defendant to meet the burden of proving the truth of a defamatory statement. There was also a third statute ("a shield law") providing that no person employed by a public medium should be required to disclose the source of information obtained. Plaintiffs requested an instruction that the jury could draw a negative inference from the exercise of the shield law's privilege, and defendants requested an instruction that no reference could be drawn. The judge declined to give either instruction and the jury found for the defendants.

On appeal directly to the Pennsylvania Supreme Court, that court "held that to place the burden of showing truth on the defendant did not unconstitutionally inhibit free debate, and remanded the case for a new trial." This court granted certiorari.]

JUSTICE O'CONNOR delivered the opinion of the Court.

This case requires us once more to "struggl[e] * * * to define the proper accommodation between the law of defamation and the freedoms of speech and press protected by the First Amendment." Gertz v. Robert Welch, Inc., 418 U.S. 323, 325. In *Gertz,* the Court held that a private figure who brings a suit for defamation cannot recover without some showing that the media defendant was at fault in publishing the statements at issue. [C] Here, we hold that, at least where a newspaper publishes speech of public concern, a private-figure plaintiff cannot recover damages without also showing that the statements at issue are false. * * * [The opinion describes the holdings of *New York Times, Gertz* and *Greenmoss.*]

One can discern in these decisions two forces that may reshape the common-law landscape to conform to the First Amendment. The first is whether the plaintiff is a public official or figure, or is instead a private figure. The second is whether the speech at issue is of public concern. When the speech is of public concern and the plaintiff is a public official or public figure, the Constitution clearly requires the plaintiff to surmount a much higher barrier before recovering damages from a media defendant than is raised by the common law. When the speech is of public concern but the plaintiff is a private figure, as in *Gertz,* the Constitution still supplants the standards of the common law, but the constitutional requirements are, in at least some of their range, less forbidding than when the plaintiff is a public figure and the speech is of public concern. When the speech is of exclusively private concern and the plaintiff is a private figure, as in *Dun & Bradstreet,* the constitutional requirements do not necessarily force any change in at least some of the features of the common-law landscape.

Our opinions to date have chiefly treated the necessary showings of fault rather than of falsity. Nonetheless, as one might expect given the language of the Court in *New York Times,* a public-figure plaintiff must show the falsity of the statements at issue in order to prevail on a suit for defamation. * * *

Here, as in *Gertz,* the plaintiff is a private figure and the newspaper articles are of public concern. In *Gertz,* as in *New York Times,* the common-law rule was superseded by a constitutional rule. We believe that the common law's rule on falsity—that the defendant must bear the burden of proving truth—must similarly fall here to a constitutional requirement that the plaintiff bear the burden of showing falsity, as well as fault, before recovering damages.

There will always be instances when the factfinding process will be unable to resolve conclusively whether the speech is true or false; it is in those cases that the burden of proof is dispositive. Under a rule forcing the plaintiff to bear the burden of showing falsity, there will be some cases in which plaintiffs cannot meet their burden despite the fact that the speech is in fact false. The plaintiff's suit will fail despite the fact that, in some abstract sense, the suit is meritorious. Similarly, under an alternative rule placing the burden of showing truth on defendants, there would be some cases in which defendants could not bear their burden despite the fact that the speech is in fact true. Those suits would succeed despite the fact that, in some abstract sense, those suits are unmeritorious. Under either rule, then, the outcome of the suit will sometimes be at variance with the outcome that we would desire if all speech were either demonstrably true or demonstrably false. * * *

In a case presenting a configuration of speech and plaintiff like the one we face here, and where the scales are in such an uncertain balance, we believe that the Constitution requires us to tip them in favor of protecting true speech. To ensure that true speech on matters of public concern is not deterred, we hold that the common-law presumption that defamatory speech is false cannot stand when a plaintiff seeks damages against a media defendant for speech of public concern.

In the context of governmental restriction of speech, it has long been established that the government cannot limit speech protected by the First Amendment without bearing the burden of showing that its restriction is justified. * * * It is not immediately apparent from the text of the First Amendment, which by its terms applies only to governmental action, that a similar result should obtain here: a suit by a private party is obviously quite different from the government's direct enforcement of its own laws. Nonetheless, the need to encourage debate on public issues that concerned the Court in the governmental-restriction cases is of concern in a similar manner in this case involving a private suit for damages: placement by state law of the burden of proving truth upon media defendants who publish speech of public concern deters such speech because of the fear that liability will unjustifiably result. [Cc] Because such a "chilling" effect would be antithetical to the First Amendment's protection of true speech on matters of public concern, we believe that a private-figure plaintiff must bear the burden of showing that the speech at issue is false before recovering damages for defamation from a media defendant. To do otherwise could "only result in a deterrence of speech which the Constitution makes free." [C]

We recognize that requiring the plaintiff to show falsity will insulate from liability some speech that is false, but unprovably so. Nonetheless, the Court's previous decisions on the restrictions that the First Amendment places upon the common law of defamation firmly support our conclusion here with respect to the allocation of the burden of proof. In attempting to resolve related issues in the defamation context, the Court has affirmed that "[t]he First Amendment requires that we protect some falsehood in order to protect speech that matters." *Gertz,* 418 U.S., at 341. Here the speech concerns the legitimacy of the political process, and therefore clearly "matters." [C] To provide " 'breathing space' " [c] for true speech on matters of public concern, the Court has been willing to insulate even *demonstrably* false speech from liability, and has imposed additional requirements of fault upon the plaintiff in a suit for defamation. [Cc] We therefore do not break new ground here in insulating speech that is not even demonstrably false.

We note that our decision adds only marginally to the burdens that the plaintiff must already bear as a result of our earlier decisions in the law of defamation. The plaintiff must show fault. A jury is obviously more likely to accept a plaintiff's contention that the defendant was at fault in publishing the statements at issue if convinced that the relevant statements were false. As a practical matter, then, evidence offered by plaintiffs on the publisher's fault in adequately investigating the truth of the published statements will generally encompass evidence of the falsity of the matters asserted. * * * [T]he judgment of the Pennsylvania Supreme Court is reversed, and the case is remanded for further proceedings not inconsistent with this opinion.

JUSTICE BRENNAN, with whom JUSTICE BLACKMUN joins, concurring. * * *

JUSTICE STEVENS, with whom THE CHIEF JUSTICE, JUSTICE WHITE, and JUSTICE REHNQUIST join, dissenting. * * *

The Court, after acknowledging the need to " 'accommodat[e] * * * the law of defamation and the freedoms of speech and press protected by the First Amendment,' " [c] decides to override "the common-law presumption" retained by several states that "defamatory speech is false" because of the need "[t]o ensure that true speech on matters of public concern is not deterred." [C] I do not agree that our precedents require a private individual to bear the risk that a defamatory statement—uttered either with a mind toward assassinating his good name or with careless indifference to that possibility—cannot be proven false. By attaching no weight to the state's interest in protecting the private individual's good name, the Court has reached a pernicious result. * * *

While deliberate or inadvertent libels vilify private personages, they contribute little to the marketplace of ideas. In assaying the First Amendment side of the balance, it helps to remember that the perpetrator of the libel suffers from its failure to demonstrate the truth of its accusation only if the "private-figure" plaintiff first establishes that the publisher is at "fault," either that it published its libel with "actual malice" in the *New York Times* sense * * * or that it published with that degree of careless indifference characteristic of negligence. Far from being totally in the dark about "how much of the speech affected by the allocation of the burden of proof is true and how much is false," [c] the antecedent fault determination makes irresistible the inference that a significant portion of this speech is beyond the constitutional pale. This observation is almost tautologically true with regard to libels published with "actual malice." For that standard to be met, the publisher must come close to wilfully blinding itself to the falsity of its utterance. The observation is also valid, albeit to a lesser extent, with respect to defamations uttered with "fault." Thus, while the public's interest in an uninhibited press is at its nadir when the publisher is at fault or worse, society's "equally compelling" need for judicial redress of libelous utterances is at its zenith. * * * [C]

In my opinion deliberate, malicious character assassination is not protected by the First Amendment to the United States Constitution. That Amendment does require the target of a defamatory statement to prove that his assailant was at fault, and I agree that it provides a constitutional shield for truthful statements. I simply do not understand, however, why a character assassin should be given an absolute license to defame by means of statements that can be neither verified nor disproven. The danger of deliberate defamation by reference to unprovable facts is not a merely speculative or hypothetical concern. * * *

Even assuming that attacks on the reputation of a public figure should be presumed to be true, however, a different calculus is appropriate when a defamatory statement disparages the reputation of a private individual. In that case, the overriding concern for reliable protection of truthful statements must make room for "[t]he legitimate state interest underlying the law of libel"—"the compensation of individuals for the harm inflicted on them by defamatory falsehood." *Gertz* * * *

In my view, as long as publishers are protected by the requirement that the plaintiff has the burden of proving fault, there can be little, if any, basis for a concern that a significant amount of true speech will be deterred unless the private person victimized by a malicious libel can also carry the burden of proving falsity. The Court's decision trades on the good names of private individuals with little First Amendment coin to show for it. * * *

NOTES AND QUESTIONS

1. Who has the better of the argument? Remember, this is a decision of constitutional law, binding on both federal and state courts.

2. The term "of public concern" has often been employed in garnering protection for speech carrying "First Amendment" importance. Does an article in defendant's tourist guidebook, "Let's Go: Egypt and Israel," advising that proprietor of hostel had been sued for sexual harassment and warning readers to stay away, fall within Hepps, as a matter of "public concern" published by the "media"? Shaari v. Harvard Agencies, Inc., 427 Mass. 129, 691 N.E.2d 925 (1998). A newspaper article stating that plaintiff, a married woman, had contracted chlamydia, a sexually transmitted disease, is a matter of "public concern." Cox Enterprises, Inc. v. Thrasher, 264 Ga. 235, 442 S.E.2d 740 (1994).

3. The risk of falsity is shifted to the plaintiff under the principal case. The risk is thus moved from the enterprise to the individual. Since the enterprise is likely insured, does this make sense? See Schauer, Uncoupling Free Speech, 92 Colum.L.Rev. 1321, 1339–1343 (1992), and Anderson, Is Libel Law Worth Reforming?, 140 U.Pa.L.Rev. 487, 547–49 (1991).

(E) PUBLIC FIGURES AND PUBLIC OFFICIALS

In *New York Times* the status of the plaintiff as a public official was critical in attracting to the publication the added protection of the First Amendment. This was extended to public figures in Curtis Pub. Co. v. Butts, 388 U.S. 130 (1967). The question remained open of the protection that a "private" plaintiff could garner under the First Amendment. Putting aside the wrongturning in *Metromedia* supra, *Gertz* provided the answer that the status of the plaintiff as "private" attracted a lesser, but still substantial, protection if the publication related to a matter of public concern. Beginning in *Gertz,* through many a long decision, the courts have searched for a definition of the term "public figure." A completion of the journey will likely cause students to agree that an articulation of the distinction is much like trying to nail a jellyfish to a wall, Rosanova v.

Playboy Enterprises, 411 F.Supp. 440 (S.D.Ga.1976), aff'd, 580 F.2d 859 (5th Cir.1978). The beginning point is found in *Gertz* where two rationales were deployed for imposing a greater burden on public figures: (1) their "access to the media," and (2) their assumption of risk—you must accept the heat in the kitchen if you enter. Public figures can be (1) limited (vortex) figures or (2) universal (unlimited). Very few are universal; most have thrust themselves into a public controversy.

In deciding whether a person may be a limited public figure, it is necessary first to inquire whether a "public controversy" exists. Mere public interest is not enough: many people are interested in the divorces of the wealthy, but curiosity does not a "public controversy" make. Time, Inc. v. Firestone, 424 U.S. 448 (1976). The issue must be one publicly debated with foreseeable and substantial ramifications for nonparticipants, Waldbaum v. Fairchild Publications, Inc., 627 F.2d 1287 (D.C.Cir.1980), cert. denied, 449 U.S. 898 (1980). A public controversy exists over the accreditation of a law school, Avins v. White, 627 F.2d 637 (3d Cir.1980). It does not exist in respect of a bank's expenditures despite a great public interest in its wealth, Blue Ridge Bank v. Veribanc, 866 F.2d 681 (4th Cir.1989). Dicta in one leading case, Wolston v. Reader's Digest Association, 443 U.S. 157 (1979), suggests that a public controversy requires a division of opinion; the plaintiff could not have thrust himself into a "controversy" about communist espionage "because all responsible United States citizens understandably were and are opposed to it." (Id. at 166 n. 8.) Really?

Once a public controversy is identified, the issue then becomes whether the plaintiff's role was such that he is a limited public figure in the context of that controversy. In *Wolston,* Justice Rehnquist, citing the two *Gertz* rationales, announced that the second—the assumption of risk—was the more important. The plaintiff, the nephew of a couple who had pleaded guilty to espionage charges, had failed to answer a subpoena. Sixteen years later he was listed by the defendant as a Soviet agent who had been convicted. He had never "voluntarily thrust" or "injected" himself into the controversy concerning investigations of Soviet espionage in the United States. A similar basis was relied upon in Hutchinson v. Proxmire, 443 U.S. 111 (1979), where the plaintiff, a director of a state mental hospital and adjunct professor at a state university, had applied for and obtained federal grants to study aggression in animals. Senator Proxmire, in order to illustrate his claim that federal funds were wasted on frivolous research, invented the "Golden Fleece of the Month Award," and gave it to the Navy and NASA for their grant to Hutchinson. Hutchinson was not a public figure because he had not thrust himself or his views into public controversies to influence others. Any controversy was of the Senator's making: he could not manufacture his own defense. The twin *Gertz* rationales were referred to in Khawar v. Globe International, Inc., 19 Cal.4th 254 (1998), where plaintiff was featured in a Globe article as a person implicated in the assassination of Senator Robert Kennedy. The Globe with embellished headlines and an enhanced photograph had lifted the story from a book written by Robert Morrow alleging that the Iranian Secret Police at the time of the Shah had colluded with the Mafia in the assassination. Plaintiff at the time was a photographer and had placed himself on the stage to be photographed with the Senator. The California Supreme Court reasoned he was not a vortex public figure, particularly as he had not acquired such public prominence in relation to the controversy as to permit him media access to counter the defamatory statements.

Although an important factor, voluntary assumption of risk is not essential. Some persons may be deemed to be public figures even if they were drawn involuntarily into a public controversy: Johnny Carson's wife, Carson v. Allied News Co., 529 F.2d 206 (7th Cir.1976); the leading prosecution witness in the Scottsboro case (1931), in which black youths were accused of raping the plaintiff and another white woman, Street v. N.B.C., 645 F.2d 1227 (6th Cir.1981); and the only air traffic controller on duty in 1974 at Dulles Airport when a plane crashed, Dameron v. Washington Magazine, Inc., 779 F.2d 736 (D.C.Cir.1985), cert. denied, 476 U.S. 1141 (1986). (The court in *Dameron* opined that these involuntary cases would be "few and far between.") Stern, Unresolved Antithesis of the Limited Public Figure Doctrine, 33 Hous.L.Rev. 1027 (1996).

General purpose or universal public figures are a select group. In Hustler Magazine v. Falwell, infra page 964, the Reverend Jerry Falwell was found to be one. See Post, The Constitutional Concept of Public Discourse: Outrageous Opinion, Democratic Deliberation and Hustler Magazine v. Falwell, 103 Harv.L.Rev. 601 (1990). Wells v. Liddy, 186 F.3d 505 (4th Cir.1999), confirmed that "instances of truly involuntary public figures must be extremely rare." In this case Wells had been a secretary at the Democratic National Committee (DNC) for a short period in 1972 during the Watergate break-in. She had been mentioned by Liddy, commenting on Watergate many years afterwards, as a person connected with the organization of a prostitution ring and in possession of embarrassing information relating to John Dean, the White House Counsel. In determining the status as a *voluntary* public figure the court applied five necessary elements for defendant to prove:

(1) the plaintiff has access to channels of effective communication;

(2) the plaintiff voluntarily assumed a role of special prominence in the public controversy;

(3) the plaintiff sought to influence the resolution or outcome of the controversy;

(4) the controversy existed prior to the publication of the defamatory statement; and

(5) the plaintiff retained public-figure status at the time of the alleged information.

Although Wells had made the contacts with the media, she had not tried to influence the merits of the controversy or thrust herself to the forefront of it. Time had changed the Watergate controversy and she was not a voluntary public figure in respect of its contemporary aspect.

In respect to the *involuntary* public figure the District Court had applied *Dameron*. The Court of Appeals articulated a test attempted to avoid resurrecting *Rosenbloom*. Accordingly, it defined an "involuntary public figure" as a person who has "pursued a course of conduct from which it was reasonably foreseeable, at the time of conduct, that public interest would arise." The person must have been recognized as a "central figure" during the debate over the public controversy. On this criterion Wells was not a public figure: she was not a central figure, she was peripheral, a "footnote." Without a limiting criterion, the court was concerned that all persons connected with large public controversies would be swept up, treated as public figures, and "an individual's interest in privacy and protecting her reputation would be erased from the balance of defamation law."

Public officials are more easily identified. They are persons "who have, or appear to the public to have, substantial responsibility for or control over the conduct of governmental affairs," Rosenblatt v. Baer, 383 U.S. 75 (1966). See Elder, Defamation, Public Officialdom, and the *Rosenblatt v. Baer* Criteria—A Proposal for Revivification Two Decades After New York Times Co. v. Sullivan, 33 Buffalo L.Rev. 579 (1985).

In *Wolston,* the Court emphasized the requirement of an objective approach in fashioning clear rules for those participating in public debate. Do you have a sense of clear rules prevailing? Given the absence of common law strict liability, how would you have fashioned the rules?

Although the classification is intensely factual—the person's position and responsibilities (public official) or the scope of the person's fame or connection with public affairs (public figures)—the courts regard it as a question of law, Kassel v. Gannett Co., 875 F.2d 935 (1st Cir.1989) (staff psychologist for Veteran's Administration not a public official); White v. Mobile Press Register, Inc., 514 So.2d 902 (Ala.1987) (former E.P.A. official who was officer in corporation transporting hazardous waste is limited purpose public figure).

(F) OPINION

Milkovich v. Lorain Journal Co.

Supreme Court of the United States, 1990.
497 U.S. 1.

CHIEF JUSTICE REHNQUIST delivered the opinion of the Court.

Respondent J. Theodore Diadiun authored an article in an Ohio newspaper implying that petitioner Michael Milkovich, a local high school wrestling coach, lied under oath in a judicial proceeding about an incident involving petitioner and his team which occurred at a wrestling match. Petitioner sued Diadiun and the newspaper for libel, and the Ohio Court of Appeals affirmed a lower court entry of summary judgment against petitioner. This judgment was based in part on the grounds that the article constituted an "opinion" protected from the reach of state defamation law by the First Amendment to the United States Constitution. We hold that the First Amendment does not prohibit the application of Ohio's libel laws to the alleged defamations contained in the article.

This case is before us for the third time in an odyssey of litigation spanning nearly 15 years. [Cc]

Petitioner Milkovich, now retired, was the wrestling coach at Maple Heights High School in Maple Heights, Ohio. In 1974, his team was involved in an altercation at a home wrestling match with a team from Mentor High School. Several people were injured. In response to the incident, the Ohio High School Athletic Association (OHSAA) held a hearing at which Milkovich and H. Don Scott, the Superintendent of Maple Heights Public Schools, testified. Following the hearing, OHSAA placed the Maple Heights team on probation for a year and declared the team ineligible for the 1975 state tournament. OHSAA also censored Milkovich for his actions during the altercation. Thereafter, several parents and wrestlers sued OHSAA in the Court of Common Pleas of Franklin County, Ohio, seeking a restraining order against OHSAA's ruling on the grounds that they had been denied due process in the OHSAA proceeding. Both Milkovich and Scott testified in that proceeding. The court overturned OHSAA's probation and ineligibility orders on due process grounds.

The day after the court rendered its decision, respondent Diadiun's column appeared in the News–Herald, a newspaper which circulates in Lake County, Ohio, and is owned by respondent Lorain Journal Co. The column bore the heading "Maple beat the law with the 'big lie,' " beneath which appeared Diadiun's photograph and the words "TD Says." The carryover page headline announced " * * * Diadiun says Maple told a lie." The column contained the following passages:

" ' * * * a lesson was learned (or relearned) yesterday by the student body of Maple Heights High School, and by anyone who attended the Maple–Mentor wrestling meet of last Feb. 8.

" 'A lesson which, sadly, in view of the events of the past year, is well they learned early.

" 'It is simply this: If you get in a jam, lie your way out.

" 'If you're successful enough, and powerful enough, and can sound sincere enough, you stand an excellent chance of making the lie stand up, regardless of what really happened.

" 'The teachers responsible were mainly Maple wrestling coach, Mike Milkovich, and former superintendent of schools, H. Donald Scott.

* * *

" 'Anyone who attended the meet, whether he be from Maple Heights, Mentor, or impartial observer, knows in his heart that Milkovich and Scott lied at the hearing after each having given his solemn oath to tell the truth.

" 'But they got away with it.

" 'Is that the kind of lesson we want our young people learning from their high school administrators and coaches?

" 'I think not.' " [C]

* * *

Superintendent Scott had been pursuing a separate defamation action through the Ohio courts. Two years after its *Milkovich* decision, in considering Scott's appeal, the Ohio Supreme Court reversed its position on Diadiun's article, concluding that the column was "constitutionally protected opinion." Scott v. News–Herald, 25 Ohio St.3d 243, 254, 496 N.E.2d 699, 709 (1986). Consequently, the court upheld a lower court's grant of summary judgment against Scott.

The *Scott* court decided that the proper analysis for determining whether utterances are fact or opinion was set forth in the decision of the United States Court of Appeals for the D.C. Circuit in Ollman v. Evans, 242 U.S.App.D.C. 301, 750 F.2d 970 (1984), cert. denied, 471 U.S. 1127, 105 S.Ct. 2662, 86 L.Ed.2d 278 (1985). Under that analysis, four factors are considered to ascertain whether, under the "totality of circumstances," a statement is fact or opinion. These factors are: (1) "the specific language used"; (2) "whether the statement is verifiable"; (3) "the general context of the statement"; and (4) "the broader context in which the statement appeared." [C] The court found that application of the first two factors to the column militated in favor of deeming the challenged passages actionable assertions of fact. [C] That potential outcome was trumped, however, by the court's consideration of the third and fourth factors. With respect to the third factor, the general context, the court explained that "the large caption 'TD Says' * * * would indicate to even the most gullible reader that the article was, in fact, opinion." [C] As for the fourth factor, the "broader context," the court reasoned that because the article appeared on a sports page—"a traditional haven for cajoling, invective, and hyperbole"—the article would probably be construed as opinion. [C]

Subsequently, considering itself bound by the Ohio Supreme Court's decision in *Scott,* the Ohio Court of Appeals in the instant proceedings affirmed a trial court's grant of summary judgment in favor of respondents, concluding that "it has been decided, as a matter of law, that the article in question was constitutionally protected opinion." Milkovich v. News–Herald, 46 Ohio App.3d 20, at 23, 545 N.E.2d at 1324. The Supreme Court of Ohio dismissed petitioner's ensuing appeal for want of a substantial constitutional question. App. 119. We granted certiorari [c] to consider the important questions raised by the Ohio courts' recognition of a constitutionally-required "opinion" exception to the application of its defamation laws. We now reverse. [Cc]

* * * As the common law developed in this country, apart from the issue of damages, one usually needed only allege an unprivileged publication of false and defamatory matter to state a cause of action for defamation. See, *e.g.,* Restatement of Torts § 558 (1938); Gertz v. Robert Welch,

Inc., supra. The common law generally did not place any additional restrictions on the type of statement that could be actionable. Indeed, defamatory communications were deemed actionable regardless of whether they were deemed to be statements of fact or opinion. See, *e.g.,* Restatement of Torts, *supra,* §§ 565–567. As noted in the 1977 Restatement (Second) of Torts § 566, Comment *a:*

> "Under the law of defamation, an expression of opinion could be defamatory if the expression was sufficiently derogatory of another as to cause harm to his reputation, so as to lower him in the estimation of the community or to deter third persons from associating or dealing with him. * * * The expression of opinion was also actionable in a suit for defamation, despite the normal requirement that the communication be false as well as defamatory. . . . This position was maintained even though the truth or falsity of an opinion—as distinguished from a statement of fact—is not a matter that can be objectively determined and truth is a complete defense to a suit for defamation."

However, due to concerns that unduly burdensome defamation laws could stifle valuable public debate, the privilege of "fair comment" was incorporated into the common law as an affirmative defense to an action for defamation. "The principle of 'fair comment' afford[ed] legal immunity for the honest expression of opinion on matters of legitimate public interest when based upon a true or privileged statement of fact." 1 F. Harper & F. James, Law of Torts § 5.28, p. 456 (1956) (footnote omitted). As this statement implies, comment was generally privileged when it concerned a matter of public concern, was upon true or privileged facts, represented the actual opinion of the speaker, and was not made solely for the purpose of causing harm. See Restatement of Torts, *supra,* § 606. "According to the majority rule, the privilege of fair comment applied only to an expression of opinion and not to a false statement of fact, whether it was expressly stated or implied from an expression of opinion." Restatement (Second) of Torts, *supra,* § 566 Comment *a.* Thus under the common law, the privilege of "fair comment" was the device employed to strike the appropriate balance between the need for vigorous public discourse and the need to redress injury to citizens wrought by invidious or irresponsible speech.

[The court canvassed the authorities incorporating First Amendment safeguards.]

Respondents would have us recognize, in addition to the established safeguards discussed above, still another First Amendment-based protection for defamatory statements which are categorized as "opinion" as opposed to "fact." For this proposition they rely principally on the following dictum from our opinion in *Gertz:*

> "Under the First Amendment there is no such thing as a false idea. However pernicious an opinion may seem, we depend for its correction not on the conscience of judges and juries but on the competition of other ideas. But there is no constitutional value in false statements of fact." [C]

Judge Friendly appropriately observed that this passage "has become the opening salvo in all arguments for protection from defamation actions on the ground of opinion, even though the case did not remotely concern the question." *Cianci v. New Times Publishing Co.,* 639 F.2d 54, 61 (C.A.2 1980). Read in context, though, the fair meaning of the passage is to equate the word "opinion" in the second sentence with the word "idea" in the first sentence. Under this view, the language was merely a reiteration of Justice Holmes' classic "marketplace of ideas" concept. See Abrams v. United States, 250 U.S. 616, 630, 40 S.Ct. 17, 22, 63 L.Ed. 1173 (1919) (Holmes, J., dissenting) ("[T]he ultimate good desired is better reached by free trade in ideas * * * the best test of truth is the power of the thought to get itself accepted in the competition of the market").

Thus we do not think this passage from *Gertz* was intended to create a wholesale defamation exemption for anything that might be labeled "opinion." [C] Not only would such an interpretation be contrary to the tenor and context of the passage, but it would also ignore the fact that expressions of "opinion" may often imply an assertion of objective fact.

If a speaker says, "In my opinion John Jones is a liar," he implies a knowledge of facts which lead to the conclusion that Jones told an untruth. Even if the speaker states the facts upon which he bases his opinion, if those facts are either incorrect or incomplete, or if his assessment of them is erroneous, the statement may still imply a false assertion of fact. Simply couching such statements in terms of opinion does not dispel these implications; and the statement, "In my opinion Jones is a liar," can cause as much damage to reputation as the statement, "Jones is a liar." As Judge Friendly aptly stated: "[It] would be destructive of the law of libel if a writer could escape liability for accusations of [defamatory conduct] simply by using, explicitly or implicitly, the words 'I think.' " [C] It is worthy of note that at common law, even the privilege of fair comment did not extend to "a false statement of fact, whether it was expressly stated or implied from an expression of opinion." Restatement (Second) of Torts, *supra,* § 566 Comment *a.*

Apart from their reliance on the *Gertz* dictum, respondents do not really contend that a statement such as, "In my opinion John Jones is a liar," should be protected by a separate privilege for "opinion" under the First Amendment. But they do contend that in every defamation case the First Amendment mandates an inquiry into whether a statement is "opinion" or "fact," and that only the latter statements may be actionable. They propose that a number of factors developed by the lower courts (in what we hold was a mistaken reliance on the *Gertz* dictum) be considered in deciding which is which. But we think the " 'breathing space' " which " 'freedoms of expression require in order to survive' " *Hepps,* supra (quoting *New York Times,* supra), is adequately secured by existing constitutional doctrine without the creation of an artificial dichotomy between "opinion" and fact.

Foremost, we think *Hepps* stands for the proposition that a statement on matters of public concern must be provable as false before there can be liability under state defamation law, at least in situations, like the present, where a media defendant is involved.[6] Thus, unlike the statement, "In my opinion Mayor Jones is a liar," the statement, "In my opinion Mayor Jones shows his abysmal ignorance by accepting the teachings of Marx and Lenin," would not be actionable. *Hepps* ensures that a statement of opinion relating to matters of public concern which does not contain a provably false factual connotation will receive full constitutional protection.[7]

Next, the *Bresler–Letter Carriers–Falwell* line of cases provide protection for statements that cannot "reasonably [be] interpreted as stating actual facts" about an individual. *Falwell,* 485 U.S., at 50, 108 S.Ct., at 879. This provides assurance that public debate will not suffer for lack of "imaginative expression" or the "rhetorical hyperbole" which has traditionally added much to the discourse of our Nation. [C]

The *New York Times–Butts* and *Gertz* culpability requirements further ensure that debate on public issues remains "uninhibited, robust, and wide-open," *New York Times,* supra. Thus, where a statement of "opinion" on a matter of public concern reasonably implies false and defamatory facts regarding public figures or officials, those individuals must show that such statements were made with knowledge of their false implications or with reckless disregard of their truth. Similarly, where such a statement involves a private figure on a matter of public concern, a plaintiff must show that the false connotations were made with some level of fault as required by *Gertz.* [Cc] Finally, the enhanced appellate review required by *Bose Corp.,* provides assurance that the foregoing determinations will be made in a manner so as not to "constitute a forbidden intrusion of the field of free expression." Bose, 466 U.S., at 499, 104 S.Ct., at 1959 (quotation omitted).

We are not persuaded that, in addition to these protections, an additional separate constitutional privilege for "opinion" is required to ensure the freedom of expression guaranteed by the First Amendment. The dispositive question in the present case then becomes whether or not a reasonable factfinder could conclude that the statements in the Diadiun column imply an assertion that petitioner Milkovich perjured himself in a judicial proceeding. We think this question must be answered in the affirmative. * * * This is not the sort of loose, figurative or hyperbolic language which would negate the impression that the writer was seriously maintaining petitioner committed the crime of perjury. Nor does the general tenor of the article negate this impression.

---

6. In *Hepps* the Court reserved judgment on cases involving nonmedia defendants, see 475 U.S., at 779, n. 4, 106 S.Ct., at 1565, n. 4, and accordingly we do the same. Prior to *Hepps,* of course, where public-official or public-figure plaintiffs were involved, the *New York Times* rule already required a showing of falsity before liability could result. *Id.,* at 775, 106 S.Ct., at 1563.

7. We note that the issue of falsity relates to the *defamatory* facts implied by a statement. For instance, the statement, "I think Jones lied," may be provable as false on two levels. First, that the speaker really did not think Jones had lied but said it anyway, and second that Jones really had not lied. It is, of course, the second level of falsity which would ordinarily serve as the basis for a defamation action, though falsity at the first level may serve to establish malice where that is required for recovery.

We also think the connotation that petitioner committed perjury is sufficiently factual to be susceptible of being proved true or false. A determination of whether petitioner lied in this instance can be made on a core of objective evidence by comparing, *inter alia*, petitioner's testimony before the OHSAA board with his subsequent testimony before the trial court. As the *Scott* court noted regarding the plaintiff in that case, "[w]hether or not H. Don Scott did indeed perjure himself is certainly verifiable by a perjury action with evidence adduced from the transcripts and witnesses present at the hearing. Unlike a subjective assertion, the averred defamatory language is an articulation of an objectively verifiable event." 25 Ohio St.3d, at 252, 496 N.E.2d, at 707. So too with petitioner Milkovich. [Cc]

The numerous decisions discussed above establishing First Amendment protection for defendants in defamation actions surely demonstrate the Court's recognition of the Amendment's vital guarantee of free and uninhibited discussion of public issues. But there is also another side to the equation; we have regularly acknowledged the "important social values which underlie the law of defamation," and recognize that "[s]ociety has a pervasive and strong interest in preventing and redressing attacks upon reputation." Rosenblatt v. Baer, 383 U.S. 75, 86, 86 S.Ct. 669, 676, 15 L.Ed.2d 597 (1966). Justice Stewart in that case put it with his customary clarity:

> "The right of a man to the protection of his own reputation from unjustified invasion and wrongful hurt reflects no more than our basic concept of the essential dignity and worth of every human being—a concept at the root of any decent system of ordered liberty.

* * *

> "The destruction that defamatory falsehood can bring is, to be sure, often beyond the capacity of the law to redeem. Yet, imperfect though it is, an action for damages is the only hope for vindication or redress the law gives to a man whose reputation has been falsely dishonored." [C]

We believe our decision in the present case holds the balance true. The judgment of the Ohio Court of Appeals is reversed and the case remanded for further proceedings not inconsistent with this opinion.

Reversed.

JUSTICE MARSHALL joined JUSTICE BRENNAN in dissenting.

NOTES AND QUESTIONS

1. Has the Supreme Court eroded protection of free speech?

(a) Will the jury play a larger part under the rule in the principal case, than it did when opinion was constitutionally protected? The interpretation of whether the statement was a factual assertion is judged by the reasonable listener or reader. Yetman v. English, 168 Ariz. 71, 811 P.2d 323 (1991) (a politician calling another a "Communist"). It is for the court, and not the jury, to determine as a matter of law whether an alleged defamatory statement is one of fact or opinion. Williams v. Garraghty, 249 Va. 224, 455 S.E.2d 209 (1995). But cf. Greenbelt Cooperative Publishing Association v. Bresler, 398 U.S. 6 (1970) (use of word "blackmail," reviewing court deciding the word could be understood as "no more than rhetorical hyperbole . . ."). Is expert evidence admissible on the question how the average person would understand the statement? Weller v. American Broadcasting Corporation, 232 Cal.App.3d 991, 283 Cal.Rptr. 644 (1991) (evidence of linguistics expert to assist jury in determining how certain rhetorical devises or patterns of speech convey implied meanings).

(b) Will courts be encouraged to engage in close literal interpretation, deemphasizing the context of the statement? Cf. Immuno AG. v. Moor–Jankowski, 77 N.Y.2d 235, 567 N.E.2d 1270, 566 N.Y.S.2d 906 (1991), cert. denied, 500 U.S. 954 (1991), vacated and remanded by the Supreme Court after its decision in the principal case. The New York court held that the letter to the scientific magazine was protected under the principal case but also found under the state constitution, that context played a larger part: "analysis * * * begins by looking at the content of the whole communication, its tone and apparent purpose." See Wachtel v. Storm, 796 F.Supp. 114 (S.D.N.Y.1992) for decision focusing on the interpretation of the statement alone. Factual assertions were implied by the statement "outrageous overhead and unrelated business expenses." Context has re-emerged in the case law, at least in publications where a wide license is necessary to encourage vigorous public debate. In a letter to the editor assertions about the state of a farm were construed as opinion, Rudnick v. McMillan, 31 Cal.Rptr.2d 193 (Cal.Ct.App.1994). Likewise in book reviews, assertions referable to the text of the book being evaluated are, although factually based, protected commentary. Moldea v. New York Times Co., 22 F.3d 310 (D.C.Cir.), cert. denied, 513 U.S. 875 (1994), wherein plaintiff was accused of "sloppy journalism." In remarkable fashion the court admitted a mistake in its earlier ruling in *Moldea I*, 15 F.3d 1137 (D.C.Cir.1994). The turnabout has been criticized, see Logan, Of "Sloppy Journalism," "Corporate Tyranny," and Mea Culpas: The Curious Case of *Moldea v. New York Times*, 37 Wm. & Mary L.Rev. 161 (1995).

2. "Jones is a contemptuous fellow." A non-factual assertion which cannot be proved false? What if the utterer of the statement did not in fact have this opinion of Jones but was motivated to destroy him socially? How is this to be distinguished from the *Falwell* case where Flynt, the publisher, intended to destroy Falwell's character? What of a statement that plaintiff is "a very poor lawyer"? In Sullivan v. Conway, 157 F.3d 1092 (7th Cir.1998), Posner J. held this to be an expression of opinion; no "reasonable listener" would take defendant to base the "opinion" on "knowledge of facts of the sort that can be evaluated in a defamation suit." Id. at 4. But in Armstrong v. Simon & Schuster, Inc., 610 N.Y.S.2d 503 (1994), aff'd, 85 N.Y.2d 373 (1995), defendants published a book "Den of Thieves" about Michael Milken's financial dealings. Plaintiff, a well-known criminal defense attorney complained that a passage in the book described plaintiff as presenting a perjurious affidavit for execution. Referring to the nature of the book, its tone and purpose, the court held that the assertions were of fact and not opinion.

3. Restaurant reviews have prompted litigation. Even if review statements could be reasonably regarded as asserting fact, the restaurant is a public figure and thus the plaintiff must show actual malice. Mr. Chow of New York v. Ste. Jour Azur S.A., 759 F.2d 219 (2d Cir.1985).

4. A humorous context will not prevent an interpretation that the statement constituted an assertion of fact. See Unelko v. Rooney, 912 F.2d 1049 (9th

Cir.1990). Andy Rooney on "60 Minutes," in discussing the "junk" he received in the mail, mentioned that the plaintiff's product "Rain-ex" which was designed to shed rain from windshields "didn't work." The court found this to be an implied assertion of objective fact; unlike the *Falwell* case it was not couched in base, figurative, or hyperbolic language. Are dry humorists in jeopardy?

5. PRIVILEGES

The common law developed a number of defenses in order to protect the interest of free speech and political and public debate. The defense of fair comment has now been constitutionalized, in the manner just observed. The common law recognized that some speech was essential for the functioning of representative government and the administration of justice and hence gave precedence to this speech by according it an absolute privilege. In essence the nature of this speech could not be judicially reviewed. Other speech attracted a qualified or conditional privilege. This speech was not actionable, although defamatory, if it was communicated by the publisher to the recipient where both parties had a reciprocal duty and interest to communicate and receive it. A letter of reference is an example. If the purpose for the communication is outside the purpose of the privilege, the defense is lost. Similarly, if the communication is transmitted to persons who have no duty or interest to receive it, there is no privilege.

Despite the overwhelming bulk of constitutional law, these privileges remain important in defamation law.

(A) ABSOLUTE PRIVILEGE

NOTES AND QUESTIONS

1. *Judicial Privilege.* A judge has absolute immunity for defamatory words published in the course of judicial proceedings. An attorney says the plaintiff was not truthful and was "lower than a rattlesnake because a rattlesnake gives warning before it strikes." The trial is broadcast. Privilege attaches to the judge, the attorney and the radio station. The attorney's statement may be false and malicious but will be privileged if relevant and pertinent to the issues in the litigation. See Irwin v. Ashurst, 158 Or. 61, 74 P.2d 1127 (1938). Absolute privilege, or immunity, has been applied also to petit juries and grand juries. It makes no difference that, as in the case of a grand jury, the proceeding is not open to the public. Schultz v. Strauss, 127 Wis. 325, 106 N.W. 1066 (1906).

2. The privilege extends also to witnesses, even though they testify voluntarily, and not under subpoena. It extends to a defamatory statement in a pleading filed in the action, as in Taliaferro v. Sims, 187 F.2d 6 (5th Cir.1951), and Di Blasio v. Kolodner, 233 Md. 512, 197 A.2d 245 (1964); and also to affidavits filed in a judicial proceeding, or filed for the purpose of reopening it after judgment, as in Fleming v. Adams, 153 N.Y.S.2d 964 (Sup.Ct.1956). It makes no difference that the judicial proceeding is ex parte, and only one side of the case is heard. Beiser v. Scripps–McRae Pub. Co., 113 Ky. 383, 68 S.W. 457 (1902). For privilege attaching to report of pleadings, see supra note 9, page 891.

3. The privilege applies to the hearing of a sanity commission. Jarman v. Offutt, 239 N.C. 468, 80 S.E.2d 248 (1954). Compare, for hearings before a

grievance committee of the state bar association, Wiener v. Weintraub, 22 N.Y.2d 330, 292 N.Y.S.2d 667, 239 N.E.2d 540 (1968); Ramstead v. Morgan, 219 Or. 383, 347 P.2d 594 (1959). When the proceedings of administrative agencies are found to be judicial in character, the same privilege applies to them. Robertson v. Industrial Insurance Co., 75 So.2d 198 (Fla.1954) (revocation of insurance license).

Once the privilege is found to exist, the only limitation on it is that what is said must be found to have some reasonable bearing upon or relation to the subject of inquiry. Even the judge cannot seize upon the occasion of a judicial proceeding to voice entirely unrelated defamation. La Porta v. Leonard, 88 N.J.L. 663, 97 A. 251 (1916); Stahl v. Kincade, 135 Ind.App. 699, 192 N.E.2d 493 (1963). Of course, the privilege does not extend to what is said outside of court. Kennedy v. Cannon, 229 Md. 92, 182 A.2d 54 (1962) (attorney stating his client's contentions to the press).

But the required "relevance" or "pertinence" does not mean that what is said must come within the rules of evidence as to relevancy: and a great deal of latitude is allowed. Thus when a witness answers a question asked him and not objected to, he is privileged although both the question and the answer are entirely irrelevant to the proceeding. Greenberg v. Ackermann, 41 N.J.Super. 146, 124 A.2d 313 (1956). And if he speaks under an honest, but mistaken belief as to what is called for, as when he misunderstands the question, he is privileged. Johnson v. Dover, 201 Ark. 175, 143 S.W.2d 1112 (1940).

4. The result of the absolute privilege is that there is no civil remedy at all against the witness who gives perjured testimony in court, even though he does so in furtherance of a conspiracy to injure the plaintiff. Ginsburg v. Halpern, 383 Pa. 178, 118 A.2d 201 (1955). On the other hand, it has been held that the privilege does not protect one not himself involved in the proceeding, who procures the false testimony. Bailey v. McGill, 247 N.C. 286, 100 S.E.2d 860 (1957).

5. *Legislative Proceedings.* A similar absolute privilege is applied to members of Congress and of the state legislatures, in the performance of their legislative functions. See Cochran v. Couzens, 42 F.2d 783 (D.C.Cir.1930); and U.S. Const. Art. I, § 6, cl. 1 (the speech and debate clause).

6. The common law rule was that the defamation, to be privileged, must have some relation to the business of the legislature. Coffin v. Coffin, 4 Mass. 1, 3 Am.Dec. 189 (1808). Federal and state constitutional provisions have been construed, however, to extend the privilege to anything whatever said in the course of legislative proceedings themselves. Kilbourn v. Thompson, 103 U.S. 168 (1880); Cole v. Richards, 108 N.J.L. 356, 158 A. 466 (1932).

7. The Supreme Court in Hutchinson v. Proxmire, 443 U.S. 111 (1979), focused on the scope of immunity under the speech and debate clause. Senator Proxmire gave "Golden Fleece of the Month Awards" to highlight what he considered wasteful federal spending. Hutchinson had been given federal grants for research on aggressive behavior in primates, for which the Senator gave a Golden Fleece Award. In a speech on the Senate Floor written by an aide, he demeaned Hutchinson's work. The speech was published in a press release and a summary distributed to Wisconsin constituents. The Supreme Court held that the Senator was "wholly immune" for his statements on the Senate Floor, but not immune for statements in the press releases and newsletters because they were not "essential to the deliberations of the Senate" and were not "part of the deliberative process." See also Brooks v. Muldoon [1973] 1 N.Z.L.R. 1 (statement by Prime Minister to reporters outside Parliament).

8. The privilege extends to the hearings of the legislative body, and to witnesses testifying at such hearings. Kelly v. Daro, 47 Cal.App.2d 418, 118 P.2d 37 (1941); Logan's Super Markets v. McCalla, 208 Tenn. 68, 343 S.W.2d 892 (1961). In the last case, it was held that the testimony of the witness was subject to the same rules as to pertinence to the proceeding as in the case of the judicial proceeding immunity.

9. There is disagreement on whether the legislative privilege extends to local legislative bodies, such as city councils. The majority view grants an absolute privilege. See Noble v. Ternyik, 273 Or. 39, 539 P.2d 658 (1975).

10. A person petitioning the government for relief of grievances was held not entitled to an absolute privilege, but to the *New York Times* privilege of "actual malice," in In re IBP Confidential Business Document Litigation, 755 F.2d 1300 (8th Cir.1985).

See Veeder, Absolute Privilege in Defamation: Judicial Proceedings, 9 Colum.L.Rev. 463, 600 (1909); Veeder, Absolute Immunity in Defamation: Legislative and Executive Proceedings, 10 Colum.L.Rev. 131 (1910); Yankwich, The Immunity of Congressional Speech—Its Origin, Meaning and Scope, 99 U.Pa.L.Rev. 960 (1951). Notes, 16 U.Chi.L.Rev. 544 (1949), 18 U.Chi.L.Rev. 591 (1951).

11. *Public Officials: Federal.* The Supreme Court in Barr v. Matteo, 360 U.S. 564 (1959), decided that the immunity the Court had previously given to executive officers of the Cabinet in Spalding v. Vilas, 161 U.S. 483 (1896) (Postmaster General), from defamation liability while acting as their duties required or inherently permitted, also extended to federal agents of lower standing. Rank is not the determinant, rather it is the scope of the official's duties. The lower the rank, however, the less the scope of the duty to afford an absolute immunity, Doe v. McMillan, 412 U.S. 306 (1973).

12. If the publication took place within the scope of the federal official's office, or employment, no cause of action in defamation is available against the officer or the United States. A statutory immunity is granted to the official under amendments to the Federal Torts Claims Act (FTCA): Federal Employees Liability Reform and Tort Compensation Act of 1988, Pub.L. 100–694, 102 Stat. 4563. This immunity subsists even though the plaintiff is precluded from suing the United States: United States v. Smith, 499 U.S. 160 (1991) (Federal Employees Liability Reform Act immunized federal government physicians from malpractice liability even when the FTCA precludes recovery against the United States). It follows that no action in defamation is available since the United States has not waived sovereign immunity in respect of defamation (slander and libel). This has led to attempts to frame the action in negligence, thus permitting the action against the United States. Success has been mixed: Quinones v. United States, 492 F.2d 1269 (3d Cir.1974) (claim of negligent record keeping accepted). Cf. Ross v. Gallant, Farrow & Co., 27 Ariz.App. 89, 551 P.2d 79 (App.1976) (claim of negligent recordkeeping rejected).

13. *Public Officers: State.* High state officials have an absolute immunity in the discharge of their official duties. Blair v. Walker, 64 Ill.2d 1, 349 N.E.2d 385 (1976) (governor). This has been held to include press releases to inform the public of what they are doing. Matson v. Margiotti, 371 Pa. 188, 88 A.2d 892 (1952) (state attorney general); Hackworth v. Larson, 83 S.D. 674, 165 N.W.2d 705 (1969) (state secretary of state but must not be extraneous to this informational purpose, Hutchinson v. Proxmire, supra).

14. Some state courts have adopted the federal position and extended the absolute privilege to officials of lower rank. See, e.g., McNayr v. Kelly, 184 So.2d

428 (Fla.1966), 185 So.2d 194 (Fla.App.1966); Sheridan v. Crisona, 14 N.Y.2d 108, 198 N.E.2d 359, 249 N.Y.S.2d 161 (1964). Many state courts, however, hold that minor officials are entitled only to a qualified privilege. E.g., Ranous v. Hughes, 30 Wis.2d 452, 141 N.W.2d 251 (1966); Gardner v. Hollifield, 96 Idaho 609, 533 P.2d 730 (1975); and Chamberlain v. Mathis, 151 Ariz. 551, 729 P.2d 905 (1986) (doubting the efficacy of extending absolute immunity to minor officials and recommending an objective malice test for discharging the qualified immunity defense).

(B) CONDITIONAL OR QUALIFIED PRIVILEGE

Sindorf v. Jacron Sales Co., Inc.

Court of Special Appeals of Maryland, 1975.
27 Md.App. 53, 341 A.2d 856.

[Plaintiff Sindorf worked as salesman for Jacron Sales Co., Inc., (the parent company resident in Pennsylvania). He resigned after 18 months, as a result of a dispute over his sales practices. Jacron contended that he was selling to people without adequately checking their credit ratings and apparently held up payment of his commissions until they received payment for the sales. On resigning, Sindorf kept some of his inventory, "as partial payment of the commissions due me." He soon went to work as a salesman for Tool Box Corporation of Maryland.

At the suggestion of Langton, President of Pennsylvania Jacron, a call was made to William Brose, President of Tool Box, by Bob Fridkis, Vice President of Virginia Jacron, a subsidiary of Pennsylvania Jacron, to see whether Sindorf had started working for Tool Box before leaving Jacron. Fridkis and Brose, though competitors, were friends and had had similar conversations about employees before. In a long conversation, Fridkis learned that Sindorf had not gone to work for Tool Box until after his resignation from Jacron. Fridkis told Brose that "a few cash sales and quite a bit of merchandise was not accounted for" by Sindorf, and suggested that Brose had better "watch your stock real, real carefully on trucks and things." There were other derogatory insinuations.

The trial court held that Fridkis' conversation was conditionally privileged and that no malice was shown. It granted a motion by Jacron for a directed verdict.]

ORTH, CHIEF JUDGE. * * * The first * * * question to be resolved is whether Jacron enjoyed a conditional privilege to defame Sindorf. * * *

"In an action for defamation, the plaintiff's prima facie case is made out when he has established a publication to a third person for which the defendant is responsible, the recipient's understanding of the defamatory meaning, and its actionable character. It is then open to the defendant to set up various defenses, which to some extent have moderated the rigors of the law of libel and slander." W. Prosser, Law of Torts, 776 (4th ed., 1971). One of these defenses is privilege. "It rests upon the * * * idea, that conduct which otherwise would be actionable is to escape liability because the defendant is acting in furtherance of some interest of social importance, which is entitled to protection even at the expense of uncompensated harm to the plaintiff's reputation. The interest thus favored may be one of the defendant himself, of a third person, or of the general public. If it is one of paramount importance, considerations of policy may require that the defendant's immunity for false statements be absolute, without regard to his purpose or motive, or the reasonableness of his conduct." Id. This is absolute privilege. [C] "If it has relatively less weight from a social point of view, the immunity may be qualified, and conditional upon good motives and reasonable behavior. The defendant's belief in the truth of what he says, the purpose for which he says it, and the manner of publication, all of which are immaterial when no question of privilege is involved, may determine the issue when he enters the defense of such a conditional privilege." Prosser, at 776–777. In the words of Baron Parke in Toogood v. Spyring, 1 C.M. & R. 181, 149 Eng.Rep. 1044 (1834), a publication is conditionally privileged when it is "fairly made by a person in the discharge of some public or private duty, whether legal or moral, or in the conduct of his own affairs, in matters where his interest is concerned." * * * The types of interest which are protected by a qualified privilege are classified by Prosser, at 786, as interest of the publisher, interest of others, common interest of publisher and recipient, communications made to one who may act in the public interest, and fair comment on matters of public concern. [C] "The condition attached to all such qualified privileges is that they must be exercised in a reasonable manner and for a proper purpose. The immunity is forfeited if the defendant steps outside of the scope of the privilege, or abuses the occasion. * * * [It does not] include publication to any person other than those whose hearing of it is reasonably believed to be necessary or useful for the furtherance of that interest. * * * Any reasonable and appropriate method of publication may be adopted which fits the purpose of protecting the particular interest. The dictation of a business letter to a stenographer * * * may be privileged on proper occasion. * * * [T]he fact that the communication is incidentally read or overheard by a person to whom there is no privilege to publish it will not result in liability, if the method adopted is a reasonable and appropriate one under the circumstances." Prosser, at 792–794.

The burden is upon the defendant in the first instance to establish the existence of a privileged occasion for the publication, by proof of a proper interest or duty justifying the utterance of the words. "Whether the occasion was a privileged one, is a question to be determined by the court as an issue of law, unless of course the facts are in dispute, in which case the jury will be instructed as to the proper rules to apply." Id., at 796.

The rules of law as to conditional privilege followed in Maryland generally reflect the views of the authorities above discussed. [Cc]

Thus, the law of this State is that a defamatory publication is conditionally privileged when the occasion shows that the communicating party and the recipient have a mutual interest in the subject matter, or some duty with respect thereto. [Cc] Over seventy-five years ago the Court of Appeals established that where an employer gives a character of an employee the communication is conditionally privileged under the principle that the party communicating has a duty owed, even though such duty is not a legal one, but only a moral or social duty of imperfect obligation. This is so even though the defamatory information was given voluntarily rather than upon request. Fresh v. Cutter, 73 Md. 87, 92–94, 20 A. 774. * * * The authorities are in general agreement that where a former employer communicates with a new or prospective employer about a former employee, a conditional privilege arises from a discharge of duty owed to the new or prospective employer. * * *

The circumstances here * * * were that the defamer was the vice-president of the subsidiary of the corporation which was Sindorf's former employer, and that the communicator and recipient, even though competitors, had a close personal and business relationship. Whether based on a duty owed or a common interest, we think that a qualified privilege arose. In the absence of a dispute as to the facts, the existence *vel non* of a common interest or duty giving rise to a qualified privilege is a matter of law for the court. [Cc] There was no dispute here as to such facts. We conclude that the trial court did not err in holding as a matter of law that Fridkis, and therefore Jacron, had a conditional privilege to communicate the defamatory utterance to Brose.

The second * * * question is whether Jacron lost the privilege to defame. * * *

Because a conditional or qualified privilege is conditioned upon publication in a reasonable manner and for a proper purpose, it is defeasible. * * * The Court of Appeals said in Orrison v. Vance, 262 Md. at 295, 277 A.2d at 578: * * * "In determining an abuse of privilege all relevant circumstances are admissible, [c] including the defendant's reasonable belief in the truth of his statements, [c] the excessive nature of the language used, [c] whether the disclosures were unsolicited, id., and whether the communication was made in a proper manner and only to proper parties [c]."[7]

"Malice may be a jury question." [C] It is a jury question unless only one conclusion can be drawn from the evidence. Prosser, at 796. In other words, it is only when the evidence and all inferences fairly deducible therefrom lead to conclusions from which reasonable minds could not differ, that the issue of malice is one of law for the court and not one of fact for the jury. * * *

The motion for a directed verdict was primarily based on the theory that there was no sufficient showing by Sindorf of malice within the meaning of that word as defeating a conditional privilege. It appears that

---

7. "Prosser said that the qualified privilege will be lost if the defendant publishes the defamation 'in the wrong state of mind.' At 794. He thought that the statement that the privilege is defeated if the publication is 'malicious' is misleading and discounted malice in this context as a 'meaningless and quite unsatisfactory term.' At 795. He concluded, at 796: 'Probably the best statement of the rule is that the defendant is required to act as a reasonable man under the circumstances, with due regard to the strength of his belief, the grounds that he has to support it, and the importance of conveying the information.' "

the grant of the motion was substantially bottomed on that reason. We think that the grant of the motion was wrong. We believe that the evidence, when viewed as required by the rule pertaining to the grant *vel non* of a directed verdict, led to conclusions from which reasonable minds could differ. We start with the rule that the publisher's motive will be more carefully scrutinized if his statements are volunteered than if they are in response to an inquiry, in which latter instance, greater latitude is permitted. We observe that Fridkis clearly indicated that Sindorf had been fired, whereas, as far as the record shows, he resigned. It does not appear that Langton told Fridkis that Sindorf was fired, and if Fridkis did not in fact know that Sindorf was not fired, stating that he was fired could be found to be a reckless disregard of truth. * * *

We observe that the publisher will be liable if he publishes his statement to accomplish a distinct objective, which may be legitimate enough in itself but is not within the privilege. [C] We think that a reasonable person could conclude from the evidence that Fridkis's communication to Brose was an effort to pressure Sindorf into returning the material he was holding, or, perhaps, simply to ascertain, as Langton requested, the date of employment of Sindorf by Tool Box. Neither would be within the privilege. The short of it is that we cannot find, assuming the truth of all credible evidence on the issue of malice and of all inferences fairly deducible therefrom, and considering them in the light most favorable to Sindorf, that they lead to the conclusions, from which reasonable minds could not differ, that Fridkis, and through him, Jacron, did not abuse the privilege to defame by excessive publication or by use of the occasion for an improper purpose, or by lack of grounds for belief in the truth of what was said. Therefore, the question of malice was properly for the jury and the trial judge erred in granting the motion for a directed verdict. The issue of malice should have gone to the jury with appropriate instructions. We reverse the judgment and remand the case for a new trial. * * *

NOTES AND QUESTIONS

1. *Protection of Publisher's Own Interests.* A person has a qualified privilege to make defamatory statements in a reasonable effort to recover goods stolen from him; to collect money due him or prevent others from collecting it; to protest against the mismanagement of a concern in which he has a financial interest; to protect his own business against unfair competition; or to defend any other legitimate interest. See, e.g., Teichner v. Bellan, 7 A.D.2d 247, 181 N.Y.S.2d 842 (1959) (response to doctor's bill that bill was unjustified); Montgomery Ward & Co. v. Watson, 55 F.2d 184 (4th Cir.1932) (employer accuses one employee, before others, of stealing from him); Gardner v. Standard Oil Co., 179 Miss. 176, 175 So. 203 (1937) (employer warns employees that plaintiff is of bad character and they are not to deal with him).

2. Included in the privilege of protecting the defendant's own interest is the protection of his reputation against defamation on the part of others. The privilege is not limited merely to publication of the statement that the plaintiff is an unmitigated liar and the truth is not in him. The defendant may go further and

attack the plaintiff's motives, to explain the defamation. Mencher v. Chesley, 193 Misc. 829, 85 N.Y.S.2d 431 (1948). On the other hand, the privilege does not extend to an irrelevant matter, as, for example, a statement that the plaintiff beats his wife. Cf. Sternberg Mfg. Co. v. Miller, DuBrul & Peters Mfg. Co., 170 Fed. 298 (8th Cir.1909).

3. *Protection of Interests of a Third Person.* The third person is usually the recipient of the communication but need not be. The privilege exists when the publisher reasonably believes that there is information that affects a sufficiently important interest of the third party and that he publishes the information under a legal duty or in accordance with "generally accepted standards of decent conduct." Restatement (Second) of Torts § 595. Thus, there is a privilege to answer the inquiry of a prospective employer of the plaintiff concerning his character or fitness for the position. Child v. Affleck, 9 B. & C. 403, 109 Eng.Rep. 150 (1839); Zeinfeld v. Hayes Freight Lines, Inc., 41 Ill.2d 345, 243 N.E.2d 217 (1968). And a bank is privileged to answer an inquiry about the plaintiff's credit from one who has been asked to sell him goods. Melcher v. Beeler, 48 Colo. 233, 110 P. 181 (1910).

4. In determining whether the privilege should be granted, weight is given to the question of whether the information was requested by the recipient or was volunteered. Thus, volunteered statements were held not privileged in such cases as Watt v. Longsdon, [1930] 1 K.B. 130, and Burton v. Mattson, 50 Utah 133, 166 P. 979 (1917), involving personal gossip. But there are occasions when it is appropriate to volunteer the information. De Van Rose v. Tholborn, 153 Mo.App. 408, 134 S.W. 1093 (1911) (landlord informed that his tenant was undesirable).

5. *Common Interest.* The existence of a common interest between the publisher and the recipient gives rise to a privilege to speak regarding the common interest. Here there is more freedom to volunteer information. See Restatement (Second) of Torts § 596. Representative cases include Bereman v. Power Pub. Co., 93 Colo. 581, 27 P.2d 749 (1933) (labor union); Hayden v. Hasbrouk, 34 R.I. 556, 84 A. 1087 (1912) (club); Slocinski v. Radwan, 83 N.H. 501, 144 A. 787 (1929) (church members); Smith Bros. & Co. v. W.C. Agee & Co., 178 Ala. 627, 59 So. 647 (1912) (common creditors). A family relationship is given similar treatment. See Restatement (Second) of Torts § 597; Kroger Co. v. Young, 210 Va. 564, 172 S.E.2d 720 (1970); Watt v. Longsdon, [1930] 1 K.B. 130.

6. Commercial credit agencies, such as Dun & Bradstreet, are sometimes denied any privilege at all. MacIntosh v. Dunn, [1908] A.C. 390; Pacific Packing Co. v. Bradstreet Co., 25 Idaho 696, 139 P. 1007 (1914). A majority of the American courts take the view that these agencies perform a legitimate function in providing a business service to those who have a proper interest in obtaining the information. Barker v. Retail Credit Co., 8 Wis.2d 664, 100 N.W.2d 391 (1960); Retail Credit Co. v. Garraway, 240 Miss. 230, 126 So.2d 271 (1961).

7. Recall that under *Gertz* liability could not attach to the defendant unless the plaintiff proved that the defendant was "at fault." If the plaintiff discharges her burden of proving that the defendant was negligent in the publication, can defendant, nevertheless, raise the defense of qualified privilege? In other words, does negligence under *Gertz* subsume malice in discharging the defense of conditional or qualified privilege? The issue arose on appeal from the preceding, Jacron Sales Co., Inc. v. Sindorf, 276 Md. 580, 350 A.2d 688 (1976), finding that the malice standard was stricter than negligence (under *Gertz*). It requires at least a "reckless disregard for the truth." The Virginia Supreme Court in Gazette, Inc. v. Harris, 229 Va. 1, 325 S.E.2d 713 (1985), in adopting the *Gertz* negligence standard, maintained the defense of conditional or qualified immunity. (Id. at 727)

8. Courts all agree that the defendant cannot claim a qualified privilege if he knows that his defamatory statement is false or does not believe it to be true. Lawless v. Muller, 99 N.J.L. 9, 123 A. 104 (1923); Russell v. Geis, 251 Cal.App.2d 560, 59 Cal.Rptr. 569 (1967).

Prior to the *Gertz* revolution, a majority of American courts held that malice was evaluated by an objective criterion—did defendant have reasonable grounds for believing his statement to be true. A sizeable minority followed the English rules adopting the subjective criterion—defendant does not lose his privilege if he acted in good faith and not in reckless disregard as to the falsity of the statement. A.B.C. Needlecraft v. Dun & Bradstreet, 245 F.2d 775 (2d Cir.1957). Because the requirements of *Gertz* would make the defense useless under the majority/objective criterion, the Restatement (Second) of Torts has adopted reckless-disregard as to the test for determining whether the privilege is lost. See § 600 and the Special Note preceding § 593. This position has been adopted in numerous cases. See Luster v. Retail Credit Co., 575 F.2d 609 (8th Cir.1978); British American & Eastern Co. v. Wirth Ltd., 592 F.2d 75 (2d Cir.1979); Moore v. Smith, 89 Wash.2d 932, 578 P.2d 26 (1978). What will be the consequence if Dun & Bradstreet v. Greenmoss, supra page 902, is held to apply to the fault requirement?

9. This necessarily means that "courts will find it desirable to reassess the circumstances under which it is appropriate to grant a conditional privilege. If a proper adjustment of the conflicting interests of the parties indicates that a publisher should be held liable for failure to use due care to determine the truth of the communication before publishing it, a conditional privilege is not needed and should not be held to apply." Restatement (Second) of Torts § 593, Comment c. For application of this viewpoint to a privilege for credit-rating agencies, see § 595, Comment h. If a plaintiff, as a public official, is already subject to the *New York Times* standard, a conditional privilege can have no significance and is not held to exist. Wright v. Haas, 586 P.2d 1093 (Okl.1978).

Can you envisage situations where a person unreasonably believing a statement to be true is justified in reporting it to others?

10. At common law there were two types of privileges that were unlike the others in that they did not depend upon the measure of fault on the part of the defendant regarding falsity of the defamatory communication. A defendant might successfully rely on the privilege even though he was aware of the fact that the statement was false. Instead the privilege was controlled by other restrictions. These are:

A. The *"Reporter's Privilege."* This privilege is to report public proceedings, public records and official acts. The restriction is that the report must be accurate and fair or disinterested. This has been treated supra, at pages 890–891.

B. *Privilege to Provide Means of Publication.* When the author of the defamatory utterance is in fact privileged to publish it, those who provide him with the appropriate means of publication are likewise privileged to do so. Otherwise, of course, he would have great difficulty in making his communication. Thus if the author is privileged to publish his statement in a newspaper, the newspaper itself can be no less privileged; and the same is true of a stenographer taking dictation. See Israel v. Portland News Pub. Co., 152 Or. 225, 53 P.2d 529 (1936); Western Union Tel. Co. v. Lesesne, 182 F.2d 135 (4th Cir.1950); Restatement (Second) of Torts § 612; Smith, Liability of a Telegraph Company for Transmitting a Defamatory Message, 20 Colum.L.Rev. 30 (1920).

C. *Fair Comment.* The media relied heavily upon this privilege prior to the imposition of constitutional limits on the tort. It allowed the publisher to offer criticism on matters of public concern including activities of public officials and figures and on subjects scientific, artistic, literary, and dramatic. The "freer the criticism is, the better it will be for the aesthetic welfare of the public." Lyon v. Daily Telegraph [1943] K.B. 746 at 752 per Scott L.J. The criticism must be comment or opinion, not a misstatement of fact. It must be *fair* in that it must be based upon true facts and express, within wide bounds, what an honest-minded person might conclude. The opinion, however, need not be reasonable. The privilege might be abused and lost if the criticism did not represent the actual opinion of the critic, or if it were made solely for the purpose of causing harm to the person criticized. See generally the Restatement of Torts §§ 606–610 (1938) and Titus, Statement of Fact Versus Statement of Opinion—A Spurious Debate in Fair Comment, 15 Vand.L.Rev. 1203 (1962). The holding in *Milkovich,* supra, may revivify the common law fair comment jurisprudence as constrained by the First Amendment.

6.   REMEDIES

(1) Damages. As with most other torts the prime remedy for defamation is damages. For libel and for slander per se, it was presumed at common law that there were "general damages," the damages were "at large," and thus the jury were permitted to estimate the harm to plaintiff's reputation that they thought the defamation had caused, without the need of evidence to support the conclusion. This meant that there was little control by the court over the amount that the jury assessed. As a result of the holding in Gertz v. Robert Welch, Inc., supra page 892, damages were confined to "compensation for actual injury." But see Dun & Bradstreet v. Greenmoss, supra page 902, where the common law position of presumed damages is arguably restored for publications which are not of public concern.

To the extent that damages cover pecuniary, or out-of-pocket loss, an award of money damages is entirely appropriate, as it purports to make the plaintiff whole. These are the special damages that must be proved in the case of slander, if it is not actionable per se. The Supreme Court has explained, however, that "actual injury," may include "impairment of reputation and standing in the community, personal humiliation, and mental anguish and suffering," so long as there is adequate proof of these matters. This gives the court some control over the action of the jury and it remains to be seen whether the Supreme Court will take further steps to prevent the award of very large verdicts against news media in a manner that makes them a figurative sand bag. Significantly, most of the cases that the Court has entertained have involved large sums of money that can constitute a heavy burden on the news media.

There is something anomalous in attempting to convert general impairment of standing in the community, personal humiliation and mental anguish into a money award. What kind of conversion standard can there be? Would a better approach be to limit recovery to pecuniary loss but include within this concept the plaintiff's litigation expenses, including reasonable attorney's fees? This would utilize a much more objective standard and would pay the out-of-pocket costs to the plaintiff in vindicating his name. It might also have the effect of discouraging efforts to make the prosecution of the suit so expensive as to force the plaintiff to discontinue it. For a criticism of defamation law's preoccupation with money damages as a vindication of reputation, see J.C. Fleming, Retraction Reply: Alternative Remedies for Defamation, 12 U.B.C. L.Rev. 15 (1978).

Mitigation of Damages. Provocation by the plaintiff is generally regarded as admissible for the purpose of mitigating punitive damages. Palmer v. Mahin, 120 Fed. 737 (8th Cir.1903). Under a minority holding, it may also be considered in mitigation of compensatory damages. Craney v. Donovan, 92 Conn. 236, 102 A. 640 (1917); Conroy v. Fall River Herald News Co., 306 Mass. 488, 28 N.E.2d 729 (1940). Evidence that the plaintiff's reputation is bad is also admissible in mitigation. Even rumors are admissible if they are shown to be sufficiently widespread to affect his general reputation. Blickenstaff v. Perrin, 27 Ind. 527 (1867); Stuart v. News Pub. Co., 67 N.J.L. 317, 51 A. 709 (1902). A report not so widespread as to affect the plaintiff's reputation is not admissible, however. Utah State Farm Bureau Fed. v. National Farmers Union Service Corp., 198 F.2d 20 (10th Cir.1952). And some courts have held that a person's reputation may be so bad that he is "libel-proof." See, e.g., Cardillo v. Doubleday & Co., 518 F.2d 638 (2d Cir.1975); Guccione v. Hustler Mag., Inc., 800 F.2d 298 (2d Cir.1986); Note, The Libel–Proof Plaintiff, 98 Harv.L.Rev. 1909 (1985). Note the affinity of this doctrine with the "incremental harm" doctrine, discussed in *Masson* supra. Under this doctrine, since rejected by the 9th Circuit, the defamatory impact of an imputation is measured by the state of the plaintiff's reputation once the nonactionable and nonpleaded portion of the publication is taken into account. See note 7, page 845.

Punitive Damages. Punitive damages were freely awarded at common law, if "malice" in the literal sense of that term were shown. Gertz v. Robert Welch, Inc., supra page 892, has placed some limitations on this. It seems clear that in the absence of "malice" in the constitutional sense— i.e., knowledge or reckless disregard as to falsity—they cannot be awarded. The Court did not expressly hold whether they can be awarded then, but it seems later to have assumed that they can and *Dun and Bradstreet* permits such an award in the private figure/private speech context. Herbert v. Lando, 441 U.S. 153, 162 n. 7 (1979). See, awarding punitive damages, Davis v. Schuchat, 510 F.2d 731 (D.C.Cir.1975); Maheu v. Hughes Tool Co., 569 F.2d 459 (9th Cir.1977); Buckley v. Littell, 539 F.2d 882 (2d Cir.1976), cert. denied, 429 U.S. 1062 (1977); Newspaper Pub. Corp. v. Burke, 216 Va. 800, 224 S.E.2d 132 (1976). See generally Note, Punitive Damages and Libel Law, 98 Harv.L.Rev. 847 (1985). The Supreme Court in Pacific Mutual Life Ins. Co. v. Haslip, 499 U.S. 1 (1991), upheld as constitutional Alabama's scheme for awarding punitive damages in a case outside the defamation and First Amendment arena. The court required an articulation of principles for reviewing the size of such awards. The principles are broad and flexible, see TXO Production Corp. v. Alliance Resources Corp., 509

U.S. 443 (1993). Are these principles likely to differ in the defamation context?

Nominal Damages. Gertz v. Robert Welch held that a plaintiff cannot recover unless he proves "actual injury." If he proves that the statement is both defamatory and false, but does not prove actual injury, can he recover nominal damages? The Supreme Court has not ruled, nor does it indicate whether he can bring the initial action for the purpose of recovering only nominal damages and thus vindicating his name. It would seem, however, that the latter action ought to be allowed, and even favored. See discussion in Hearst Corp. v. Hughes, 297 Md. 112, 466 A.2d 486 (1983).

(2) Declaratory Relief. The action brought solely for nominal damages, referred to immediately above, essentially seeks declaratory relief. Its purpose is to obtain a judicial determination that the statement about the plaintiff is false, and thus to vindicate his reputation—to make him whole, as far as the law can. Declaratory-judgment proceedings, if available, may accomplish the same purpose. See Franklin, Good News and Bad Law: A Critique of Libel Law and a Proposal, 18 U.S.F.L.Rev. 1 (1983); Note, The Defamed Reputation: Will Declaratory Judgment Bill Provide Vindication?, 13 J.Legis. 72 (1986). See also the description of the Arkansas "lie bill," found in Leflar, Legal Remedies for Defamation, 6 Ark.L.Rev. 423 (1952). A so-called vindication remedy was included in the March 23, 1993 Discussion Draft of the Uniform Defamation Act drafted under the auspices of the National Conference of Commissioners on Uniform State Laws. The remedy was harshly attacked and was omitted from a final version. Robert M. Ackerman, Bringing Coherence to Defamation Law Through Uniform Legislation: The Search for an Elegant Solution, 72 N.C. L.Rev. 291, 308–11 (1994).

In a declaratory proceeding of this sort, should all of the requirements of an action for compensatory damage be imposed? If the plaintiff is not seeking to recover damages, but only a ruling that the statement was false, should he have to show that defendant was at fault regarding its falsity? Do privileges serve a useful purpose here? Would it be feasible to have the trial judge pose two separate questions to the jury—(1) was the statement false, and (2) was the defendant at fault regarding its falsity?

Judge Leval, who presided over Westmoreland v. CBS Inc., 596 F.Supp. 1170 (S.D.N.Y.1984), has strongly supported a form of "no-money, no-fault suit," as "enhancing the primary object of the law of defamation: the restoration of a falsely damaged reputation." Leval, The No–Money, No–Fault Libel Suit: Keeping *Sullivan* in its Proper Place, 101 Harv.L.Rev. 1287 (1988).

There were a number of trial innovations used in the famous *Westmoreland* and *Sharon* trials. One of special interest here was the use of "tripartite verdicts" in *Sharon*. Judge Sofaer instructed the jury to render separate special verdicts on whether the communication was defamatory, whether it was false, and whether the defendant was motivated by "actual malice." The verdicts were returned on separate days. Uses of this technique should be easily apparent. For discussion see Smolla, Suing the Press (1986).

(3) Self-help. "The first remedy of any victim of defamation is self-help—using available opportunities to contradict the lie or correct the error and thereby to minimize its adverse impact or reputation." Gertz v. Robert Welch, Inc., 418 U.S. 323, 344 (1974). Thus, the defamed party may make a response to the defamatory statement about him—provided he can find a suitable medium for making the response. In making response, the defamed person is given a conditional privilege. He is not liable to the original defamer unless he abuses the privilege by making irrelevant charges, or charges of his own in reckless disregard of their truth or falsity. Phifer v. Foe, 443 P.2d 870 (Wyo.1968).

Right-of-Response Statutes. Several states have passed statutes requiring a public communications medium to give a right of response to a person who claims that he has been defamed by it. A Florida statute to this effect was held unconstitutional in Miami Herald Pub. Co. v. Tornillo, 418 U.S. 241 (1974). While the particular statute was overly broad and did not limit the requirement to cases in which there was a claim of actual defamation, the holding seems broad enough to cover a more limited statute. What about a statute requiring a newspaper to publish a news item of a defamation judgment obtained against it? See generally Danzinger, The Right of Reply in the United States and Europe, 19 N.Y.U.J.Int.L. & Pol. 171 (1986).

The person claiming to have been defamed may also go to the person publishing the defamation, explain that there has been a mistake and request a correction or a retraction. Resistance by media to informal remedial action is reported by R. Bezanson et al., see infra. On the effect of refusal to retract after notice of falsity as evidence of "malice," see Morgan v. Dun & Bradstreet, Inc., 421 F.2d 1241 (5th Cir.1970).

Retraction Statutes. There are retraction statutes in about thirty states. They vary considerably in their provisions, as to the types of defamation covered, the requirement of notice, the types of plaintiffs and defendants covered, and the effect of compliance. They are collected and analyzed in R. Sack, Libel, Slander, and Related Problems, § VIII.2 (1980). Some may be outdated as a result of constitutional developments, as in applying only to "innocent misrepresentation," or in limiting recovery to "actual damages."

A retraction, to be effective, must be unequivocal and not partial or hesitant and hypothetical, as, for example, "We do not know whether our defamatory statement was true, but if it was not, we are sorry we published it." Cf. Monaghan v. Globe Newspaper Co., 190 Mass. 394, 77 N.E. 476 (1906); Goolsby v. Forum Printing Co., 23 N.D. 30, 135 N.W. 661 (1912). A statement that the plaintiff does not have the manners of a hog is obviously not retracted by saying he has the manners of a hog. Indeed, an "evasive" and "incomplete" retraction may be grounds for punitive damages. Burnett v. National Enquirer, Inc., 144 Cal.3d App. 991, 193 Cal.Rptr. 206 (1983), *appeal dismissed,* 465 U.S. 1014 (1984).

To the effect that the *Tornillo* case on right-of-reply statutes does not indicate the unconstitutionality of retraction statutes, see Brennan, J., concurring, in Miami Herald Pub. Co. v. Tornillo, 418 U.S. 241, 258 (1974). The Uniform Correction or Clarification of Defamation Act of 1993 (National Conference of Commissions on Uniform State Laws) proposed mechanisms for correction and clarification to mend the "flaws in current law by providing strong incentives for parties in a defamation as an alternative to costly litigation." For discussion see Ackerman, supra, at 314–28.

(4) Injunctive Relief. Ever since the decision in Near v. Minnesota, 283 U.S. 697 (1931), it has been recognized that prior restraint of a publication runs afoul of the First Amendment. (On the *Near* case, see the thorough study in F. Friendly, Minnesota Rag (1981)). Nevertheless, it remains possible that injunctive relief might become a suitable supplement to other relief when it has been formally determined in court that a statement is both defamatory and false, and the defendant persists in continuing to publish it. An injunction, carefully worded so as not to be too broad, might be both appropriate and constitutional.

See in general R. Bezanson et al., Libel Law and the Press: Myth and Reality (1987); LeBel, Reforming the Tort of Defamation: An Accommodation of the Competing Interests Within the Current Constitutional Framework, 66 Neb.L.Rev. 249 (1987); Gannett Center for Media Studies, The Cost of Libel: Economic and Policy Implications (1986).

The Report of the Libel Reform Project of the Annenberg Washington Program, Proposal for Reform of Libel Law (1988) sets forth a proposed Libel Reform Act that incorporates, among other reforms, retraction and reply, a declaratory judgment option and abolition of punitive damages. Anderson, Is Libel Law Worth Reforming?, 140 U.Pa.L.Rev. 487, 550–554 (1991), views the present law as a failure in that it denies defamation victims any remedy, but at the same time chills speech by encouraging high litigation costs and occasional large judgments. Anderson calls on the Supreme Court to instigate reform that would bring uniformity and reduce even more the role of the jury by a greater resort to summary judgment and judicial review, and perhaps take the assessment of damages out of the jury's hands.

CHAPTER XVIII

PRIVACY

The recognition and development of the "right of privacy" is perhaps the outstanding illustration of the influence of legal journals upon the courts. Prior to 1890, no English or American court had ever granted relief expressly based upon the invasion of this right, although there were cases that seem in retrospect to have been groping in that direction, and Judge Cooley had coined the phrase "the right to be let alone." See, e.g., DeMay v. Roberts, supra, page 96; Hardin v. Harshfield, 12 S.W. 779 (Ky.1890) (loss of marriage engagement caused by defendant's spreading a true tale of plaintiff's embarrassing combination of expelling *flatus* in a public place and her *lapsus lingua*—treated as slander).

In 1890 there appeared in 4 Harvard Law Review 193 a noted article, "The Right to Privacy," written by Samuel D. Warren and Louis D. Brandeis, which reviewed a number of older cases in which relief had been afforded on the basis of defamation, or breach of confidence or of an implied contract, in the publication of letters, portraits and the like. The article concluded that these cases were in reality founded upon a broader principle entitled to separate recognition. This principle it stated to be the right of a private individual to be let alone and protected from unauthorized publicity in essentially private affairs.

One of the first states to consider the doctrine advanced by Warren and Brandeis was New York. After two lower courts apparently had accepted the article and recognized the right of privacy, it fell into the unfriendly hands of the Court of Appeals in Roberson v. Rochester Folding Box Co., 171 N.Y. 538, 64 N.E. 442 (1902), where the defendant had made an unauthorized use of the picture of an attractive young lady to advertise its flour. The court proceeded to reject the entire doctrine, denying the existence of any "right of privacy" at common law, and expressing a fear of a "vast amount of litigation" that would involve not only pictures, but "a comment upon one's looks, conduct, domestic relations or habits." It said that any such change in the law must be left for the legislature to make.

The immediate result of this decision was a lively public disapproval, leading to the enactment in 1903 of a statute, now New York Civil Rights Law §§ 50–51. This statute prohibits the use of the name, portrait or picture of any living person without prior written consent for "advertising purposes" or for "purposes of trade." Similar statutes were adopted in Virginia, Oklahoma, and Utah.

Three years later the same question was presented in Pavesich v. New England Life Ins. Co., 122 Ga. 190, 50 S.E. 68 (1905), when the defendant's insurance advertising made use of plaintiff's name and picture, together with a spurious testimonial purportedly from him. The court rejected the

Roberson case, accepted the views of Warren and Brandeis, and recognized the existence of a distinct right of privacy. This became the leading case. For a time authority was divided; but in the 1930's the tide set in strongly in favor of recognition.

At the present time, the right of privacy is clearly recognized, in one form or another, in all but two or three states. It is limited by statute to commercial uses of the plaintiff's name or likeness in some states.

This has been a fertile field for legal writing. Two classic articles are Larremore, The Law of Privacy, 12 Colum.L.Rev. 693 (1912); Prosser, Privacy, 48 Calif.L.Rev. 383 (1960).

Flake v. Greensboro News Co.

Supreme Court of North Carolina, 1938.
212 N.C. 780, 195 S.E. 55.

Action by Nancy Flake, by her next friend, Mrs. W.F. Flake, against the Greensboro News Company and others for damages allegedly sustained as the result of a publication of the plaintiff's photograph or likeness in connection with an advertisement which appeared in a newspaper. From an adverse judgment, the defendants appeal.

Folies de Paree was a vaudeville or stage show and advertised its performance through a system of "tie up" advertising. Under this system, some merchant and the local theatre join in the advertisement and it advertises both the product or the merchandise of the merchant and the theatre performance. Pursuant to this plan, the agent of the "Folies de Paree" solicited the defendant L. Melts, who conducted a bakery in Greensboro under the name of "Melts Bakery" and the defendant North Carolina Theatres, Inc., to join in such an advertisement and as a result a two-column advertisement was published in the Greensboro Daily News, issue of March 11, 1936. In the right portion of the advertisement there was a cut from the plaintiff's photograph showing her standing and wearing a bathing suit. To the left was the following wording, so arranged as to make four distinct statements, as follows:

"Keep that Sylph–Like Figure by eating more of Melts' Rye and Whole Wheat Bread, says Mlle. Sally Payne, exotic red haired Venus—

" 'Folies de Paree' sparkling Parisian Revue, Stage Production, National Theatre two days only, March 11 and 12.

" 'Melts' Rye and Whole Wheat Bread will give you the necessary energy, pep and vitality without adding extra weight,' says Miss Payne. Melts Bakery, 314 N. Elm St., 1829 Spring Garden St.

" 'Ask for Melts' Bread—Melts in Your Mouth.' "

In publishing this advertisement, the photograph or mat made therefrom was used without the consent of the plaintiff and was used by mistake—the defendants intending to use a cut of Sally Payne, the leading lady of Folies de Paree.

The mistake having been called to the attention of the defendant Greensboro News Company, it immediately published a full explanation of the mistake and an apology.

BARNHILL, JUSTICE. * * * The defendants were entitled to a judgment of nonsuit on the cause of action for alleged libel.

Plaintiff's second cause of action is based upon the right of privacy, so termed. It is clear that the first issue when considered in connection with the charge of the court was submitted upon the theory of this cause of action. * * *

The question of the existence of this right is a relatively new field in legal jurisprudence. In respect to it the courts are plowing new ground and before the field is fully developed unquestionably perplexing and harassing stumps and runners will be encountered.

In determining to what extent a newspaper may publish the features of an individual under any given circumstances necessarily involves a consideration of the constitutional right of free speech and of a free press. People do not live in seclusion. When a person goes upon the street or highway or into any other public place, he exhibits his features to public inspection. Is a newspaper violating any right of the individual, or doing more than exercising the right of a free press, when it publishes a correct image of such features? Must a distinction be drawn between those in private life and those in public office or public life, and if so, when does a person cease to be a private citizen and become a public character? If a newspaper may publish the features of an individual in connection with an article that is laudatory, does it not also possess the right to publish the same in connection with an article that is critical in its nature so long as it speaks the truth? If the people are entitled to know what their Governor, or their President, or other public servant, is doing and saying, is it reasonable to hold that they are not entitled as a matter of course to ascertain and know through the newspapers his physical features and appearance? These and many other questions which may hereafter arise, in connection with this type of litigation, are not now before us for decision.

So far as we have been able to ascertain, no court has yet held that it constitutes a tort for a newspaper to publish an image of an individual when such publication is not libelous, except when such publication involves the breach of a trust, the violation of a contract, or when the photograph is used in connection with some commercial enterprise, and we are presently called upon to decide only the right of an individual to prohibit the unauthorized use of an image of her features and figure in connection with and as a part of an advertisement. * * *

The subject is * * * dealt with at length in Pavesich v. New England Life Insurance Co., 122 Ga. 190, 213, 50 S.E. 68, 78. All former decisions are likewise fully discussed in this opinion, in which the court holds that the unauthorized publication of plaintiff's photograph in connection with an advertising enterprise gives rise to a cause of action. In the opinion Cobb, J., quoting at length and with approval from the dissenting opinion of Gray, J., in Roberson v. Rochester Folding Box Co., 171 N.Y. 538, 64 N.E. 442, said in part: "Instantaneous photography is a modern invention, and affords the means of securing a portraiture of an individual's face and form in invitum [of] their owner. While, so far as it merely does that, although a species of aggression, I conceded it to be an irremediable and irrepressible feature of the social evolution. But if it is to be permitted that the portraiture may be put to commercial or other uses for gain, by the publication of prints therefrom, then an act of invasion of the individual's privacy results, possibly more formidable and more painful in its consequences than an actual bodily assault might be. Security of person is as necessary as the security of property, and for that complete personal security which will result in the peaceful and wholesome enjoyment of one's privileges as a member of society there should be afforded protection, not only against the scandalous portraiture and display of one's features and person, but against the display and use thereof for another's commercial purposes or gain. The proposition is to me an inconceivable one that these defendants may unauthorizedly use the likeness of this young woman upon their advertisement as a method of attracting widespread public attention to their wares, and that she must submit to the mortifying notoriety, without right to invoke the exercise of the preventive power of a court of equity. * * *

"It would be, in my opinion, an extraordinary view, which while conceding the right of a person to be protected against the unauthorized circulation of an unpublished lecture, letter, drawing, or other ideal property, yet would deny the same protection to a person whose portrait was unauthorizedly obtained and made use of for commercial purposes. * * * Whether, as incidental to that equitable relief, she should be able to recover only nominal damages, is not material, for the issuance of the injunction does not, in such a case, depend upon the amount of the damages, in dollars and cents."

We are of the opinion that the reasoning in the Pavesich Case, supra, is sound and establishes the correctness of the conclusion that the unauthorized use of one's photograph in connection with an advertisement or other commercial enterprise gives rise to a cause of action which would entitle the plaintiff, without the allegation and proof of special damages, to a judgment for nominal damages, and to injunctive relief, if and when the wrong is persisted in by the offending parties.

One of the accepted and popular methods of advertising in the present day is to procure and publish the endorsement of the article being advertised by some well-known person whose name supposedly will lend force to the advertisement. If it be conceded that the name of a person is a valuable asset in connection with an advertising enterprise, then it must likewise be conceded that his face or features are likewise of value. Neither can be used for such a purpose without the consent of the owner without giving rise to a cause of action.

We conclude therefore, that there was error in the judgment below and that the motion of the defendants for a judgment of nonsuit should have been sustained as to the plaintiff's cause of action sounding in libel, and that there should be a new trial on the cause of action alleging the unauthorized use of plaintiff's features and person in connection with said advertisement. Upon the present record, from which it appears that said photograph was used by mistake and without malice and that the defendants immediately desisted from the use thereof upon the discovery of the mistake and made due apology therefor, the plaintiff would be entitled to a judgment for nominal damages only. As the defendants have not and did not persist in the wrong complained of, the right to injunctive relief is not here involved.

New trial.

NOTES AND QUESTIONS

1.   This was the first type of invasion of privacy to be recognized by the courts. Should an action be available where Sears photographs a three and a half month old child in its studio and uses, without parental consent, the photograph for its own promotion? Slocum v. Sears Roebuck & Co., 542 So.2d 777 (La.App.1989) (invasion of infant's privacy occurred but the limited exhibition of the photograph, its flattering quality, and the age of the infant did not reach a threshold of seriousness to make the invasion actionable). Statutes in some states are limited to commercial appropriations of name or likeness. Other courts, not restricted by statute, have allowed recovery for appropriations of the plaintiff's name for non-commercial purposes. Hinish v. Meier & Frank Co., 166 Or. 482, 113 P.2d 438 (1941) (plaintiff's name signed to telegram to governor urging him to veto a bill); State ex rel. Lafollette v. Hinkle, 131 Wash. 86, 229 P. 317 (1924) (use of name as candidate for office by political party); Hamilton v. Lumbermen's Mutual Cas. Co., 82 So.2d 61 (La.App.1955), (advertising in name of plaintiff for witnesses to an accident); Vanderbilt v. Mitchell, 72 N.J.Eq. 910, 67 A. 97 (1907) (providing father for child on birth certificate).

2.   Most of the cases have involved advertising, or pictures accompanying an article sold; but other forms of commercial appropriation have resulted in liability. Edison v. Edison Polyform Mfg. Co., 73 N.J.Eq. 136, 67 A. 392 (1907) (use of name in title of corporation); Goodyear Tire & Rubber Co. v. Vandergriff, 52 Ga.App. 662, 184 S.E. 452 (1936) (impersonation to obtain secret information); Binns v. Vitagraph Co. of America, 147 App.Div. 783, 132 N.Y.S. 237 (1911), aff'd, 210 N.Y. 51, 103 N.E. 1108 (1913) (motion picture based on incident in life of plaintiff, in which an actor represented him).

3.   It is the value of plaintiff's name that must be appropriated, rather than the name itself. Thus, there is no liability for the mere use of the same name as that of the plaintiff. Swacker v. Wright, 154 Misc. 822, 277 N.Y.S. 296 (1935) (novel); Nebb v. Bell Syndicate, Inc., 41 F. Supp. 929 (S.D.N.Y.1941) (comic strip).

4.   Right of Publicity: The right of common law protects a person's "name and likeness from unwarranted intrusion or exploitation...." Lugosi v. Universal Pictures, 25 Cal.3d 813, 603 P.2d 425, 431 (1979). In an era of media celebrity the right has been widely litigated, especially in California before the Ninth Circuit Court of Appeals. California and eleven other states supplement, or displace in few instances, the common law right with statutory protections. Cal. Civ. Code § 3344(a) (1971). The right is not confined to "appropriation of name or likeness" but extends to identity, Eastwood v. Superior Court, 149 Cal.App.3d 409, 198 Cal.Rptr. 342 (1983)

(also distinguishing right of publicity cases from "false-light" cases). Thus to use in commercial advertising: a well-known race car driver's car to promote cigarettes (Motschenbacher v. R.J. Reynolds Tobacco Co., 498 F.2d 821 (9th Cir.1974)); a soundalike voice (Midler v. Ford Motor Co., 849 F.2d 460 (9th Cir.1988); a robot redolent of Vanna White (White v. Samsung Electronics America, Inc., 971 F.2d 1395 (9th Cir.1992)), rehearing en banc denied, 989 F.2d 1512 (9th Cir.1993)); and a birthname of a famous athlete (Abdul–Jabbar v. General Motors Corporation, 75 F.3d 1391 (9th Cir.1996)) may state in California a cause of action at common law or under statute. Courts elsewhere have taken the same approach, Carson v. Here's Johnny Portable Toilets, Inc., 698 F.2d 831 (6th Cir.1983) (holding actionable under Michigan common law distributor's use of "Here's Johnny" in conjunction with promotion of a portable lavatory); Ali v. Playgirl, Inc., 447 F.Supp. 723 (S.D.N.Y. 1978) (holding publication of drawing of nude black man labeled "the greatest" entitled plaintiff to preliminary injunction under New York statutory and common law right of action); Onassis v. Christian Dior–New York, Inc., 472 N.Y.S.2d 254, aff'd, 110 A.D.2d 1095 (1985) (holding plaintiff entitled to injunction under New York law for posing a look-alike of plaintiff in advertisement of defendant's product).

5. The jurisprudential, and sometimes practically important issue is the nature of the right of publicity. Is it a right of action to vindicate the privacy rights of the person, or is it a recognition of a separate property right—a form of intellectual property? If a property right, it is alienable and survives the death of the person. The authorities are divided. Memphis Development Foundation v. Factors Etc., Inc., 616 F.2d 956 (6th Cir.1980), cert. denied, 449 U.S. 953 (1980) (holding that the right does not survive death), but compare Factors Etc., Inc. v. Pro Arts, Inc., 579 F.2d 215 (2d Cir.1978), cert. denied, 440 U.S. 908 (1979). Even if fame is not exploited in lifetime it may survive death and be passed on through the estate as a property right. Martin Luther King, Jr. Center for Social Change v. American Heritage Products, Inc., 250 Ga. 135, 296 S.E.2d 697 (1982) (holding heirs of the civil rights leader could injoin the sale of busts of his likeness). In Jim Henson Productions, Inc. v. John T. Brady & Associates, Inc., 867 F.Supp. 175 (S.D.N.Y.1994), the court reviewed the law, holding under Connecticut law that the right is descendable on death. A claim for post-mortem right in the estate is governed by the law of the decedent's domicile, Lord Cairns v. Franklin Mint Company, 24 F.Supp.2d 1013 (C.D.Calif.1998) (holding that the property rights held by the estate of Princess Diana depended upon the law of her domicile at death, i.e., England). The distinction is sometimes put as one between the right of publicity and the commercial appropriation of the right of privacy. The latter centers upon damage to human dignity. See Crump v. Beckley Newspapers, 173 W.Va. 699, 320 S.E.2d 70 (1983). In Allison v. Vintage Sports Plaques, 136 F.3d 1443 (5th Cir.1998), Alabama law was interpreted to include the commercial appropriation test which, however, incorporated the elements of the right of publicity. Hence, the right as intellectual property included the first sale doctrine that prevents the property holder once having consented to the sale of his works from exercising rights over the distribution of the work. Once sports personalities had sold rights to produce cards, those cards could be presented and sold by others to the public in an enhanced form. The courts are often not careful in distinguishing, and will enforce under the right of publicity, dignatory interests. The recognition of a property right also allows for some cases to embrace unjust enrichment in justifying liability: Zacchini v. Scripps–Howard Broadcasting Co., 433 U.S. 562 (1977).

6. *Constitutional Law.* The capacious protection of the interest potentially invades First Amendment interest. Take the leading Supreme Court decision in

Zacchini v. Scripps–Howard Broadcasting Co., 433 U.S. 562 (1977). Plaintiff was an entertainer commercially performing a "human cannonball act" in which he was shot from a cannon into a net 200 feet away, the performance taking some 15 seconds. Defendant broadcasting station, though requested not to do so, took a film of the act and showed it on the evening news broadcast. Plaintiff's suit for damages was held not maintainable by the Supreme Court of Ohio because of the station's privilege to report in its newscasts matters of legitimate public interest, relying on New York Times Co. v. Sullivan, supra page 867; and Time, Inc. v. Hill, 385 U.S. 374 (1967), infra pages 959 and 963. The Supreme Court reversed.

Speaking for the majority, Justice White said: "The differences between [false-light privacy and appropriation privacy] are important. First, the State's interests in providing a cause of action in each instance are different. 'The interest protected' in permitting recovery for placing the plaintiff in a false light 'is clearly that of reputation, with the same overtones of mental distress as in defamation.' [C] By contrast, the State's interest in permitting a 'right of publicity' is in protecting the proprietary interest of the individual in his act in part to encourage such entertainment. As we later note, the State's interest is closely analogous to the goals of patent and copyright law, focusing on the right of the individual to reap the reward of his endeavors and having little to do with protecting feelings or reputation. Second, the two torts differ in the degree to which they intrude on dissemination of information to the public. In 'false light' cases the only way to protect the interests involved is to attempt to minimize publication of the damaging matter, while in 'right of publicity' cases the only question is who gets to do the publishing. An entertainer such as petitioner usually has no objection to the widespread publication of his act as long as he gets the commercial benefit of such publication. Indeed, in the present case petitioner did not seek to enjoin the broadcast of his act; he simply sought compensation for the broadcast in the form of damages. * * *

"Wherever the line in particular situations is to be drawn between media reports that are protected and those that are not, we are quite sure that the First and Fourteenth Amendments do not immunize the media when they broadcast a performer's entire act without his consent. The Constitution no more prevents a State from requiring respondent to compensate petitioner for broadcasting his act on television than it would privilege respondent to film and broadcast a copyrighted dramatic work without liability to the copyright owner [cc], or to film and broadcast a prize fight [c], or a baseball game [c], where the promoters or the participants had other plans for publicizing the event. There are ample reasons for reaching this conclusion."

Speaking for the dissenters, Justice Powell said: "In my view the First Amendment commands a different analytical starting point from the one selected by the Court. Rather than begin with a quantitative analysis of the performer's behavior—is this or is this not his entire act?—we should direct initial attention to the actions of the news media: what use did the station make of the film footage? When a film is used, as here, for a routine portion of a regular news program, I would hold that the First Amendment protects the station from a 'right of publicity' or 'appropriation' suit, absent a strong showing by the plaintiff that the news broadcast was a subterfuge or cover for private or commercial exploitation."

7. Public commentary often focuses upon personalities. That status pursued by many leaves the few who attain it open to exploitation of that fame. In the course of public speech the famous are used to sell products, influence attitudes, and affect discourse. The balance between free speech under the First Amendment on the privacy right is often at issue. In *White*, supra page 942, the court held that

Vanna White had made a supportable claim when a robot identifiable as a representation of her was featured in an ad for defendant's product. The Ninth Circuit rejected the application for rehearing en banc, 989 F.2d 1512 (9th Cir.1993). Judge Kozinski, joined by others, dissented, finding that the right to publicity had become too expansive and inconsistent with free speech notions, where actionability rests simply on the invocation of the "celebrity's image in the public's mind." Id. at 1514. The use of a bewigged robot may be a powerful way of expressing the durability of defendant's product: as the "Wheel of Fortune" has survived, so would defendant's product.

Pearson v. Dodd

United States Court of Appeals, District of Columbia Circuit, 1969.
410 F.2d 701, cert. denied 395 U.S. 947, 89 S.Ct. 2021, 23 L.Ed.2d 465 (1969).

J. SKELLY WRIGHT, CIRCUIT JUDGE. This case arises out of the exposure of the alleged misdeeds of Senator Thomas Dodd of Connecticut by newspaper columnists Drew Pearson and Jack Anderson. The District Court has granted partial summary judgment to Senator Dodd, appellee here finding liability on a theory of conversion. At the same time, the court denied partial summary judgment on the theory of invasion of privacy. Both branches of the court's judgment are before us on interlocutory appeal. We affirm the District Court's denial of summary judgment for invasion of privacy and reverse its grant of summary judgment for conversion.

The undisputed facts in the case were stated by the District Court as follows:

" * * * [O]n several occasions in June and July, 1965, two former employees of the plaintiff, at times with the assistance of two members of the plaintiff's staff, entered the plaintiff's office without authority and unbeknownst to him, removed numerous documents from his files, made copies of them, replaced the originals, and turned over the copies to the defendant Anderson, who was aware of the manner in which the copies had been obtained. The defendants Pearson and Anderson thereafter published articles containing information gleaned from these documents."

I.   The District Court ruled that appellants' six newspaper columns concerning appellee, which were attached to appellee's complaint, did not establish liability for the tort of invasion of privacy. That tort, whose historical origin lies in the famous Warren and Brandeis article of 1890, is recognized in the District of Columbia. It has always been considered a defense to a claim of invasion of privacy by publication, however, that the published matter complained of is of general public interest. The columns complained of here gave appellants' version of appellee's relationship with certain lobbyists for foreign interests, and gave an interpretive biographical sketch of appellee's public career. They thus clearly bore on appellee's qualifications as a United States Senator, and as such amounted to a paradigm example of published speech not subject to suit for invasion of privacy.

Indeed, appellee has not urged with any vigor on appeal the theory that appellants' publications in themselves tortiously invaded his privacy. Rather he has argued that the District Court misapprehended his privacy claim, which went rather to the manner in which the information in the columns was obtained than to the matter contained in them.

Appellee proceeds under a branch of privacy theory which Dean Prosser has labeled "intrusion," and which has been increasingly recognized by courts and commentators in recent years. Thus it has been held that unauthorized bugging of a dwelling, tapping a telephone, snooping through windows, and overzealous shadowing amount to invasions of privacy, whether or not accompanied by trespasses to property.

Unlike other types of invasion of privacy, intrusion does not involve as one of its essential elements the publication of the information obtained. The tort is completed with the obtaining of the information by improperly intrusive means. * * *

We approve the extension of the tort of invasion of privacy to instances of intrusion, whether by physical trespass or not, into spheres from which an ordinary man in a plaintiff's position could reasonably expect that the particular defendant should be excluded. Just as the Fourth Amendment has expanded to protect citizens from government intrusions where intrusion is not reasonably expected, so should tort law protect citizens from other citizens. The protection should not turn exclusively on the question of whether the intrusion involves a technical trespass under the law of property. The common law, like the Fourth Amendment, should "protect people, not places."

The question then becomes whether appellants Pearson and Anderson improperly intruded into the protected sphere of privacy of appellee Dodd in obtaining the information on which their columns were based. In determining this question, we may assume, without deciding, that appellee's employees and former employees did commit such an improper intrusion when they removed confidential files with the intent to show them to unauthorized outsiders.[19]

Although appellee's complaint charges that appellants aided and abetted in the removal of the documents, the undisputed facts, narrowed by the District Judge with the concurrence of counsel, established only that appellants received copies of the documents knowing that they had been removed without authorization. If we were to hold appellants liable for

---

19. Appellants have argued that appellee's employees and former employees committed neither conversion nor trespass nor invasion of privacy, because their actions are privileged by a public policy in favor of exposing wrongdoing. See Restatement (Second) of Agency § 395, Comment f (1958):

"An agent is privileged to reveal information confidentially acquired by him in the course of his agency in the protection of a superior interest of himself or of a third person. Thus, if the confidential information is to the effect that the principal is committing or is about to commit a crime, the agent is under no duty not to reveal it. * * *"

And compare Code of Ethics for Government Service, House Doc. No. 103, 86th Cong., 1st Sess. (1958): "Any person in government service should: * * * (IX) expose corruption wherever discovered."

invasion of privacy on these facts, we would establish the proposition that one who receives information from an intruder, knowing it has been obtained by improper intrusion, is guilty of a tort. In an untried and developing area of tort law, we are not prepared to go so far. A person approached by an eavesdropper with an offer to share in the information gathered through the eavesdropping would perhaps play the nobler part should he spurn the offer and shut his ears. However, it seems to us that at this point it would place too great a strain on human weakness to hold one liable in damages who merely succumbs to temptation and listens.

Of course, appellants did more than receive and peruse the copies of the documents taken from appellee's files; they published excerpts from them in the national press. But in analyzing a claimed breach of privacy, injuries from intrusion and injuries from publication should be kept clearly separate. Where there is intrusion, the intruder should generally be liable whatever the content of what he learns. An eavesdropper to the marital bedroom may hear marital intimacies, or he may hear statements of fact or opinion of legitimate interest to the public; for purposes of liability that should make no difference. On the other hand, where the claim is that private information concerning plaintiff has been published, the question of whether that information is genuinely private or is of public interest should not turn on the manner in which it has been obtained. Of course, both forms of invasion may be combined in the same case.

Here we have separately considered the nature of appellants' publications concerning appellee, and have found that the matter published was of obvious public interest. The publication was not itself an invasion of privacy. Since we have also concluded that appellants' role in obtaining the information did not make them liable to appellee for intrusion, their subsequent publication, itself no invasion of privacy, cannot reach back to render that role tortious.

[The court treated the question of whether the defendants were liable for conversion of the plaintiff's files and concluded that they were not. See page 78 supra.]

Because no conversion of the physical contents of appellee's files took place, and because the information copied from the documents in those files has not been shown to be property subject to protection by suit for conversion, the District Court's ruling that appellants are guilty of conversion must be reversed.

TAMM, CIRCUIT JUDGE (concurring). Some legal scholars will see in the majority opinion—as distinguished from its actual holding—an ironic aspect. Conduct for which a law enforcement officer would be soundly castigated is, by the phraseology of the majority opinion, found tolerable; conduct which, if engaged in by government agents would lead to the suppression of evidence obtained by these means, is approved when used for the profit of the press. There is an anomaly lurking in this situation: the news media regard themselves as quasi-public institutions yet they demand immunity from the restraints which they vigorously demand be placed on government. That which is regarded as a mortal taint on information secured by any illegal conduct of government would appear from the majority opinion to be permissible as a technique or modus operandi for the journalist. Some will find this confusing, but I am not free to act on my own views under the doctrine of stare decisis which I consider binding upon me. * * *

NOTES AND QUESTIONS

1. Physical intrusion upon seclusion or solitude has been recognized as a distinct form of invasion of privacy. Byfield v. Candler, 33 Ga.App. 275, 125 S.E. 905 (1924) (woman's stateroom on a steamboat); Welsh v. Pritchard, 125 Mont. 517, 241 P.2d 816 (1952) (landlord moving in on tenant); Sutherland v. Kroger Co., 144 W.Va. 673, 110 S.E.2d 716 (1959) (search of woman's shopping bag in store); K–Mart Corp. Store No. 7441 v. Trotti, 677 S.W.2d 632 (Tex.App.1984) (search of employee's locker).

2. As to eavesdropping, see Rhodes v. Graham, 238 Ky. 225, 37 S.W.2d 46 (1931) (wire tapping); Roach v. Harper, 143 W.Va. 869, 105 S.E.2d 564 (1958) (microphone); Hamberger v. Eastman, 106 N.H. 107, 206 A.2d 239 (1964) (landlord "bugs" tenant's bedroom). Suppose a telephone user customarily records his telephone conversations without informing the other parties? Cf. Marks v. Bell Tel. Co., 460 Pa. 73, 331 A.2d 424 (1975).

On "telephone harassment," repeated telephone calls at unreasonable hours, see Donnel v. Lara, 703 S.W.2d 257 (Tex.App.1985); cf. Ruple v. Brooks, 352 N.W.2d 652 (S.D.1984) (obscene phone calls may create liability for intentional infliction of emotional distress). And see Nader v. General Motors Corp., 25 N.Y.2d 560, 255 N.E.2d 765, 307 N.Y.S.2d 647 (1970), involving a general campaign of harassment including lengthy surveillance, probing inquiries about Nader's political, social, racial and religious views and beliefs, his sexual behavior and attempts to entrap him in illicit relationships.

3. Intrusion can take various forms. Zimmerman v. Wilson, 81 F.2d 847 (3d Cir.1936) (unauthorized prying into private bank account); Frey v. Dixon, 141 N.J.Eq. 481, 58 A.2d 86 (1948) (invalid order requiring production of books and documents); Melvin v. Burling, 141 Ill. App.3d 786, 490 N.E.2d 1011, 95 Ill.Dec. 919 (1986) (harassed by intentional ordering of merchandise without consent). Cf. Galella v. Onassis, 487 F.2d 986 (2d Cir.1973) (continued surveillance and persistent harassment by taking photographs).

4. The invasion test has two interlinking elements. The intrusion must be into a private place, conversation, or matter, and must be highly offensive to a reasonable person. The essence of the first requirement is an objective expectation of privacy and it will vary with respect to the identity of the intruder or the nature of the intrusion. In Shulman v. Group W Productions, Inc., 18 Cal.4th 200, 955 P.2d 469 (1998), a television producer had fitted a rescue nurse with a microphone allowing plaintiff's conversation to be recorded when he was severely injured; in Sanders v. American Broadcasting Companies, Inc., 20 Cal.4th 907, 978 P.2d 67 (1999), a reporter obtained access to "telepsychic" operation and recorded conversations with fellow employees including plaintiff by means of a "hat" cam. In both cases it was held that although the conversations were not exclusively private, plaintiffs had a sufficient expectation of privacy. But compare Deteresa v. American Broadcasting Companies, Inc., 121 F.3d 460 (9th Cir.1997), where plaintiff was an attendant on the flight taken by O.J. Simpson to Chicago after the murder of his former wife, Nicole Brown. Plaintiff refused an interview with ABC, but did speak

on the street with an ABC reporter and was, without her knowledge, videotaped. The court held that considering the circumstances she could not expect privacy, and defendant did not act offensively.

5. There is ordinarily no liability for taking the plaintiff's photograph in a public place. Gill v. Hearst Pub. Co., 40 Cal.2d 224, 253 P.2d 441 (1953) (Farmers' Market in Los Angeles); Berg v. Minneapolis Star & Tribune Co., 79 F.Supp. 957 (D.Minn.1948) (courtroom); Nelson v. Maine Times, 373 A.2d 1221 (Me.1977) (picture of small Indian child). But in Daily Times Democrat Co. v. Graham, 276 Ala. 380, 162 So.2d 474 (1964), where the plaintiff was photographed in a "Fun House" with her dress blown up over her head, it was held to be an invasion of privacy.

6. The aspect of the privacy tort, intrusion upon seclusion, is that closest to the concerns animating the Warren and Brandeis article cited in the principal case. Yet, as the previous note exemplifies, the scope of the tort continues to be tested as the press has engaged in newsgathering that touches this privacy interest. Dietemann v. Time Inc., 449 F.2d 245 (9th Cir.1971) (holding that secret recordings and pictures taken in plaintiff's den by defendant's employees, pretending to be patients, is actionable), but cf. H. Desnick v. American Broadcasting Companies, 44 F.3d 1345 (7th Cir.1995). In the latter case Posner C.J. referred to First Amendment protection pertaining to defamation suits. He noted that "tabloid" style reporting was "often shrill, one-sided, and offensive, and sometimes defamatory." Yet it was entitled to protection. Id. at 1355. However, limits were drawn on capacity of the press to intrude in Food Lion v. Capital Cities/ABC Holding Co., 194 F.3d 505 (4th Cir.1999) (holding that plaintiff supermarket chain had a cause of action in trespass where defendant had breached their duty of loyalty by secretly videotaping in plaintiff's non-public areas to which they had fraudulently obtained entry). The court, for First Amendment reasons, disallowed damages flowing from the publication. The *Food Lion* case has spawned considerable academic comment attempting to chart a rule that provides for ample and certain newsgathering prerogatives, but balances the privacy interests of individuals: Sims, Food for the Lions: Excessive Damages for Newsgathering Torts on the Limitations of Current First Amendment Doctrines, 78 B.U.L.Rev. 507 (1998) and Lidsky, Prying, Spying, and Lying: Intrusive Newsgathering and What the Law Should Do About It, 73 Tul.L.Rev. 173 (1998).

Members of the media accompanying law enforcement officers on ride-alongs may also be liable for invasion of a person's privacy. Liability may obtain not only under common law, but also under civil rights legislation. To be liable under the latter—42 U.S.C. § 1983—the actions of the media must have been sufficiently in concert with the officer's actions as to be "under color of law." Berger v. Hanlon, 129 F.3d 505 (9th Cir.1997) and Wilson v. Layne, 526 U.S. 603 (1999) (finding that the Fourth Amendment protection overrode a First Amendment interest stemming from the importance of "the press" in informing the general public about the administration "of justice").

Cox Broadcasting Corp. v. Cohn

Supreme Court of the United States, 1975.
420 U.S. 469, 95 S.Ct. 1029, 43 L.Ed.2d 328.

MR. JUSTICE WHITE delivered the opinion of the Court.

The issue before us in this case is whether consistently with the First and Fourteenth Amendments a State may extend a cause of action for damages for invasion of privacy caused by the publication of the name of a deceased rape victim which was publicly revealed in connection with the prosecution of the crime. * * *

On August 1971, appellee's 17–year–old daughter was the victim of a rape and did not survive the incident. Six youths were soon indicted for murder and rape. Although there was substantial press coverage of the crime and of subsequent developments, the identity of the victim was not disclosed pending trial perhaps because of Ga.Code Ann. § 26–9901 which makes it a misdemeanor to publish or broadcast the name or identity of a rape victim. In April 1972, some eight months later, the six defendants appeared in court. Five pled guilty to rape or attempted rape, the charge of murder having been dropped. The guilty pleas were accepted by the court, and the trial of the defendant pleading not guilty was set for a later date.

In the course of the proceedings that day, appellant Wassell, a reporter covering the incident for his employer, learned the name of the victim from an examination of the indictments which were made available for his inspection in the courtroom. That the name of the victim appears in the indictments and that the indictments were public records available for inspection are not disputed. Later that day, Wassell broadcast over the facilities of station WSB–TV, a television station owned by appellant Cox Broadcasting Corporation, a news report concerning the court proceedings. The report named the victim of the crime and was repeated the following day.

In May 1972, appellee brought an action for money damages against appellants, relying on § 26–9901 and claiming that his right to privacy had been invaded by the television broadcasts giving the name of his deceased daughter. Appellants admitted the broadcasts but claimed that they were privileged under both state law and the First and Fourteenth Amendments. The trial court rejecting appellants' constitutional claims and holding that the Georgia statute gave a civil remedy to those injured by its violation, granted summary judgment to appellee as to liability, with the determination of damages to await trial by jury.

On appeal, the Georgia Supreme Court, in its initial opinion, held that the trial court had erred in construing § 26–9901 to extend a civil cause of action for invasion of privacy and thus found it unnecessary to consider the constitutionality of the statute. 231 Ga. 60, 200 S.E.2d 127 (1973). The court went on to rule, however, that the complaint stated a cause of action "for the invasion of appellee's right of privacy, or for the tort of public disclosure"—a "common law tort exist[ing] in this jurisdiction without the help of the statute that the trial judge in this case relied on." [C] Although the privacy invaded was not that of the deceased victim, the father was held to have stated a claim for invasion of his own privacy by reason of the publication of his daughter's name. The court explained, however, that liability did not follow as a matter of law and that summary judgment was improper; whether the public disclosure of the name actually invaded appellee's "zone of privacy," and if so, to what extent, were issues to be determined by the trier of fact. Also, "in formulating such an issue for determination by the fact-finder, it is reasonable to require the appellee to prove that the appellants invaded his privacy with wilful or negligent disregard for the fact that reasonable men would find the invasion highly offensive." [C] The Georgia Supreme Court did agree with the trial court, however, that the First and Fourteenth Amendments did not, as a matter of law, require judgment for appellants. The court concurred with the statement in Briscoe v. Reader's Digest Association, Inc., 4 Cal.3d 529, 541, 93 Cal.Rptr. 866, 874, 483 P.2d 34, 42 (1971), that "the rights guaranteed by the First Amendment do not require total abrogation of the right to privacy. The goals sought by each may be achieved with a minimum of intrusion upon the other."

Upon motion for rehearing the Georgia court countered the argument that the victim's name was a matter of public interest and could be published with impunity by relying on § 26–9901 as an authoritative declaration of state policy that the name of a rape victim was not a matter of public concern. This time the court felt compelled to determine the constitutionality of the statute and sustained it as a "legitimate limitation on the right of freedom of expression contained in the First Amendment." The court could discern "no public interest or general concern about the identity of the victim of such a crime as will make the right to disclose the identity of the victim rise to the level of First Amendment protection." * * *

We conclude that the Court has jurisdiction and reverse the judgment of the Georgia Supreme Court. * * *

Georgia stoutly defends both § 26–9901 and the State's common law privacy action challenged here. Her claims are not without force, for powerful arguments can be made, and have been made, that however it may be ultimately defined, there is a zone of privacy surrounding every individual, a zone within which the State may protect him from intrusion by the press, with all its attendant publicity. * * *

More compellingly, the century has experienced a strong tide running in favor of the so-called right of privacy. * * *

The version of the privacy tort now before us—termed in Georgia "the tort of public disclosure," [c]—is that in which the plaintiff claims the right to be free from unwanted publicity about his private affairs, which, although wholly true, would be offensive to a person of ordinary sensibilities. Because the gravamen of the claimed injury is the publication of information, whether true or not, the dissemination of which is embarrassing or otherwise painful to an individual, it is here that claims of privacy most directly confront the constitutional freedoms of speech and press. The face-off is apparent, and the appellants urge upon us the broad holding that the press may not be made criminally or civilly liable for publishing information that is neither false nor misleading but absolutely accurate, however damaging it may be to reputation or individual sensibilities.

It is true that in defamation actions, where the protected interest is personal reputation, the prevailing view is that truth is a defense; and the message of New York Times v. Sullivan, 376 U.S. 254 (1964); Garrison v. Louisiana, 379 U.S. 64 (1964); Curtis Publishing Co. v. Butts, 388 U.S. 130 (1967), and like cases is that the defense of truth is constitutionally required where the subject of the publication is a public official or public figure. What is more, the defamed public official or public figure must prove not only that the publication is false but that it was knowingly so or was circulated with reckless disregard for its truth or falsity. Similarly, where the interest at issue is privacy rather than reputation and the right claimed is to be free from the publication of false or misleading information about one's affairs, the target of the publication must prove knowing or reckless falsehood where the materials published, although assertedly private, are "matters of public interest." Time, Inc. v. Hill, 385 U.S., at 387–388.[19]

The Court has nevertheless carefully left open the question whether the First and Fourteenth Amendments require that truth be recognized as a defense in a defamation action brought by a private person as distinguished from a public official or public figure. Garrison held that where criticism is of a public official and his conduct of public business, "the interest in private reputation is overborne by the larger public interest, secured by the Constitution, in the dissemination of truth," [c] but recognized that "different interests may be involved where purely private libels, totally unrelated to public affairs, are concerned; therefore, nothing we say today is to be taken as intimating any views as to the impact of the constitutional guarantees in the discrete area of purely private libels." [C] In similar fashion, Time v. Hill, supra, expressly saved the question whether truthful publication of very private matters unrelated to public affairs could be constitutionally proscribed. [C]

Those precedents, as well as other considerations, counsel similar caution here. In this sphere of collision between claims of privacy and those of the free press, the interests on both sides are plainly rooted in the traditions and significant concerns of our society. Rather than address the broader question whether truthful publications may ever be subjected to civil or criminal liability consistently with the First and Fourteenth Amendments, or to put it another way, whether the State may ever define and protect an area of privacy free from unwanted publicity in the press, it is appropriate to focus on the narrower interface between press and privacy that this case presents, namely, whether the State may impose sanctions on the accurate publication of the name of a rape victim obtained from public records—more specifically, from judicial records which are maintained in

---

19. In another "false light" invasion of privacy case before us this Term, Cantrell v. Forest City Publishing Co., 419 U.S. 245, 250–251 (1974), we observed that we had, in that case, "no occasion to consider whether a State may constitutionally apply a more relaxed standard of liability for a publisher or broadcaster of false statements injurious to a private individual under a false-light theory of invasion of privacy, or whether the constitutional standard announced in Time, Inc. v. Hill applies to all false-light cases. Cf. Gertz v. Robert Welch, Inc., 418 U.S. 323."

connection with a public prosecution and which themselves are open to public inspection. We are convinced that the State may not do so.

In the first place, in a society in which each individual has but limited time and resources with which to observe at first hand the operations of his government, he relies necessarily upon the press to bring to him in convenient form the facts of those operations. Great responsibility is accordingly placed upon the news media to report fully and accurately the proceedings of government, and official records and documents open to the public are the basic data of governmental operations. Without the information provided by the press most of us and many of our representatives would be unable to vote intelligently or to register opinions on the administration of government generally. With respect to judicial proceedings in particular, the function of the press serves to guarantee the fairness of trials and to bring to bear the beneficial effects of public scrutiny upon the administration of justice.

Appellee has claimed in this litigation that the efforts of the press have infringed his right to privacy by broadcasting to the world the fact that his daughter was a rape victim. The commission of crime, prosecutions resulting from it, and judicial proceedings arising from the prosecutions, however, are without question events of legitimate concern to the public and consequently fall within the responsibility of the press to report the operations of government. * * *

The Restatement of Torts, § 867, embraced an action for privacy. Tentative Draft No. 13 of the Restatement (Second) of Torts, §§ 652A–652E, divides the privacy tort into four branches; and with respect to the wrong of giving unwanted publicity about private life, the commentary to § 652D states that "[t]here is no liability when the defendant merely gives further publicity to information about the plaintiff which is already public. Thus, there is no liability for giving publicity to facts about the plaintiff's life which are matters of public record * * *." The same is true of the separate tort of physically or otherwise intruding upon the seclusion or private affairs of another. Section 652B, Comment c, provides that "there is no liability for examination of a public record concerning the plaintiff, or of documents which the plaintiff is required to keep and make available for public inspection." According to this draft, ascertaining and publishing the contents of public records are simply not within the reach of these kinds of privacy actions.

Thus, even the prevailing law of invasion of privacy generally recognizes that the interests in privacy fade when the information involved already appears on the public record. The conclusion is compelling when viewed in terms of the First and Fourteenth Amendments and in light of the public interest in a vigorous press. * * *

By placing the information in the public domain on official court records, the State must be presumed to have concluded that the public interest was thereby being served. Public records by their very nature are of interest to those concerned with the administration of government, and a public benefit is performed by the reporting of the true contents of the records by the media. The freedom of the press to publish that information appears to us to be of critical importance to our type of government in which the citizenry is the final judge of the proper conduct of public business. In preserving that form of government the First and Fourteenth Amendments command nothing less than that the States may not impose sanctions for the publication of truthful information contained in official court records open to public inspection. * * *

Appellant Wassell based his televised report upon notes taken during the court proceedings and obtained the name of the victim from the indictments handed to him at his request during a recess in the hearing. Appellee has not contended that the name was obtained in an improper fashion or that it was not on an official court document open to public inspection. Under these circumstances, the protection of freedom of the press provided by the First and Fourteenth Amendments bars the State of Georgia from making appellants' broadcast the basis of civil liability.

Reversed.

CHIEF JUSTICE BURGER concurs in the judgment.

NOTES AND QUESTIONS

1. This is the third form of the tort of unreasonable invasion of the right of privacy. As expressed in Restatement (Second) of Torts § 652D, it applies to the giving of "publicity to a matter concerning the private life of another" which is "highly offensive to a reasonable person and is not of legitimate concern to the public."

Two important questions exist in regard to it: (1) the nature of its characteristics as they have developed at common law, and (2) the extent of the restrictions that the First Amendment to the Constitution imposes upon it.

2. *Common Law: The Right to Privacy.* The cases suggest that disclosure of an embarrassing private fact to only one or just a few persons does not amount to an invasion of privacy. Thus there is no invasion of privacy when defendant merely calls the plaintiff's employer and asks his help in collecting a debt from the plaintiff. Household Finance Corp. v. Bridge, 252 Md. 531, 250 A.2d 878 (1969); Timperley v. Chase Collection Service, 272 Cal.App.2d 697, 77 Cal.Rptr. 782 (1969); Contra: Pack v. Wise, 155 So.2d 909 (La.Ct.App.1963), writ refused, 245 La. 84, 157 So.2d 231 (1963). These cases might well be explained, however, on the basis that defendant's disclosure was privileged as a legitimate means of collecting the debt. Cf. Restatement (Second) of Torts § 652G.

3. One who intentionally seeks publicity, or puts himself in the public eye, as in the case of an actor, a professional baseball player, an explorer or an inventor, is often held to become a "public figure," and to have no right to complain of a publicity that reasonably bears upon his public activity. Cohen v. Marx, 94 Cal. App.2d 704, 211 P.2d 320 (1949) (prize fighter); Koussevitzky v. Allen, Towne & Heath, Inc., 188 Misc. 479, 68 N.Y.S.2d 779 (1947), aff'd, 272 App.Div. 759, 69 N.Y.S.2d 432 (1947) (symphony conductor); Martin v. Dorton, 210 Miss. 668, 50 So.2d 391 (1951) (sheriff).

Others may be incidentally drawn into a public event, and become, in relation to that event, a public figure. Thus Jones v. Herald Post Co., 230 Ky. 227, 18 S.W.2d 972 (1929) (plaintiff's husband murdered before her eyes); Berg v. Minneapolis Star & Tribune Co., 79 F.Supp. 957 (D.Minn.1948) (plaintiff engaged in divorce litigation); Stryker v. Republic Pictures Corp., 108 Cal.App.2d 191, 238 P.2d 670 (1951) (war hero); Elmhurst v. Pearson, 153 F.2d 467 (D.C.Cir.1946) (defendant in sedition trial). See also note 9 at page 957).

Persons captured on film incidental to newsworthy reports have no cause of action: Jacova v. Southern Radio and Television Co., 83 So.2d 34 (Fla.1955) (plaintiff present in store to make a purchase was filmed being interviewed by police subsequent to a raid of the store); Mark v. KING Broadcasting, 27 Wash.App. 344, 618 P.2d 512 (1980) (plaintiff filmed for television broadcast from outside his store in relation to a story on Medicare fraud) and Heath v. Playboy Enterprises, Inc., 732 F.Supp. 1145 (S.D.Fla.1990) (plaintiff, the daughter of Christopher Carson (son of Johnny), was photographed with her mother outside a courthouse after a paternity hearing; no action available).

What if the film, featuring plaintiff, is used to promote defendant's programming? Anderson v. Fisher Broadcasting Co., 300 Or. 452, 712 P.2d 803 (1986) (plaintiff complained of publicity of private matter and appropriation for a commercial purpose). Arguably she could also have asserted a false-light claim, see Note 2, page 962.

4. *Common Law: Breach of Confidence.* A person entrusted by another with confidential information may owe that other an obligation not to disclose the information to third parties. In Humphers v. First Interstate Bank of Oregon, 298 Or. 706, 696 P.2d 527 (1985), plaintiff birth mother agreed to place for adoption her child, born out of wedlock. An anonymous adoption was effected. Later, the child approached the doctor who had delivered her seeking her birth mother's identity. The doctor gave her a letter to the hospital which enabled her to obtain release of the sealed information by falsely stating that plaintiff had taken DES during her pregnancy and that her daughter needed the records for medical reasons. The plaintiff was distressed when located and sued the doctor's estate (he had died) for invasion of privacy and for unauthorized disclosure of the confidential information. The court held no recovery for invasion of privacy, but held for the plaintiff on her confidentiality claim. Similarly, in Doe v. Portland Health Centers, 99 Or.App. 423, 782 P.2d 446 (1989), a hospital employee disclosed information about a patient's suicide attempt to a person who subsequently publicized it widely. The patient's mother sued in breach of confidentiality and invasion of privacy, among other causes of action. The court agreed that plaintiff had no action under invasion of privacy because defendant's disclosure was not made to the public or a large number of persons. She also failed in her confidentiality action, since it was not her confidence which had been breached, although her claim in breach of contract, and the duty arising therefrom, was allowed to proceed.

Not all courts have maintained the distinction between the two actions: often the action, in substance for breach of confidence, is labelled an action for invasion of privacy: Doe v. Roe, 93 Misc.2d 201, 400 N.Y.S.2d 668 (1977) (psychiatrist published a book recording the plaintiff patient's thoughts, feelings, and fantasies; actionable although patient not named). The confluence of the two actions may be observed in the following cases on disclosure of HIV (virus which causes AIDS) status. Such disclosure is a private fact that may give rise to a breach of confidentiality claim (Estate of Behringer v. Medical Center at Princeton, 249 N.J.Super. 597, 592 A.2d 1251 (1991) (hospital failed to preserve confidentiality of HIV antibody test results of patient)) or an invasion of privacy claim (Urbaniak v. Newton, 226 Cal.App.3d 1128, 277 Cal.Rptr. 354 (1991) (disclosure of HIV status by defendant physician violated privacy rights of plaintiff when information was revealed by plaintiff to protect others who may come in contact with examining instrument)). The later case was characterized as one of "public disclosure of true, embarrassing private facts * * *." But a better characterization would be as a breach of confidence claim where the information was disclosed within a relationship of confidence.

The action in breach of confidence is based on the relationship established between the person entrusting the information and the person receiving it. Often the duty is implied from the contractual relationship between the parties: Horne v. Patton, 291 Ala. 701, 287 So.2d 824 (1973) (physician's duty to patient); and Street v. Hedgepath, 607 A.2d 1238 (D.C.App.1992) (same); or with respect to industrial or business secrets: Copley v. Northwestern Mut. Life Ins. Co., 295 F.Supp. 93 (S.D.W.Va.1968) (disclosure to plaintiff's competitors of information supplied to defendant insurance company to qualify for insurance). In English law, the relationship is viewed as one of trust, from which the fiduciary obligation of confidentiality arises: F. Gurry, Breach of Confidence (1984). In the United States, the accumulating law may be conceptualized as providing a new action in tort: the relationship establishes a duty of confidentiality: Note, Breach of Confidence: An Emerging Tort, 82 Colum.L.Rev. 1426 (1982). See Bullion v. Gadaleto, 872 F.Supp. 303 (W.D.Va. 1995) (finding that a duty is recognized where defendant psychologist revealed patient's confidences to patient's wife to initiate a sexual liaison). In McGuire v. Shubert, 722 A.2d 1087 (1998), the Superior Court of Pennsylvania considered the English law on confidentiality in holding that a bank was bound by a duty to keep customer account information confidential. An employee had allegedly accessed plaintiff's account information, which was fed to an attorney representing the employee and her husband against plaintiffs in a land dispute. The duty was implied by the contractual relationship between banker and customer. The duty was imposed upon the bank and its employees.

The action for breach of confidence is a species of privacy interest since privacy is, in part, an individual's interest in controlling information about himself: see A.F. Westin, Privacy and Freedom (1967). It has been argued that the modern object of privacy should be to give persons control over disclosure of confidential personal information and that this will lead to the recognition of the action for "tortious breach of confidence." Bezanson, The Right to Privacy Revisited: Privacy, News, and Social Change, 1890–1990, 80 Calif.L.Rev. 1133 (1992) and Gilles, Promises Betrayed: Breach of Confidence as a Remedy for Invasions of Privacy, 43 Buff. L.Rev. 1 (1995) (suggesting that a breach of confidence is an appropriate vehicle to further privacy interests eroded by the narrowness of the modern disclosure tort).

Two important issues remain. First, the information must be confidential. If the information is in the public domain, there is nothing to protect. Messinger v. United States, 769 F.Supp. 935, 937 (D.Md.1991) ("It is axiomatic that in order to bring suit for breach of confidentiality, the information allegedly published without consent cannot have previously been made public in a legitimate manner"). Second, even confidential information may be disclosed to appropriate parties on occasion. Thus, in Bryson v. Tillinghast, 749 P.2d 110 (Okla.1988), the plaintiff, while committing a rape, had been bitten on his penis. He sought medical treatment. No cause of action was maintainable against the physician who provided information to investigating police. The recipient of the confidential information also may owe a duty to warn or protect persons who may be injured at the hands of the provider of the information: recall *Tarasoff,* supra (duty of mental health professionals to warn or protect third parties of dangers posed by patients). Presumably, if there is a tort duty to disclose information, there is no liability for doing so. See Simonsen v. Swenson, 104 Neb. 224, 177 N.W. 831 (1920) (disclosure by physician that patient had venereal disease when he, in fact, did not was not actionable provided disclosure was necessary to prevent spread of disease and was made in good faith). Do the cases provide a dilemma for some classes of defendants?

5.   As in breach of confidentiality, no liability for breach of privacy will arise for disclosure if the facts were in the public domain: Meetze v. Associated Press, 230 S.C. 330, 95 S.E.2d 606 (1956) (dates of birth and marriage); Stryker v. Republic Pictures Corp., 108 Cal.App.2d 191, 238 P.2d 670 (1951) (military service record); Bell v. Courier–Journal & Louisville Times Co., 402 S.W.2d 84 (Ky.1966) (tax delinquency); cf. Rome Sentinel Co. v. Boustedt, 43 Misc.2d 598, 252 N.Y.S.2d 10 (1964) (death certificate).

6.   Defendant, an exasperated creditor, put up a placard in the show window of his garage, on the public street, stating that "Dr. W.R. Morgan owes an account here of $49.67. This account will be advertised as long as it remains unpaid." Brents v. Morgan, 221 Ky. 765, 299 S.W. 967 (1927). Cf. Hamilton v. Crown Life Ins. Co., 246 Or. 1, 423 P.2d 771 (1967).

Compare Banks v. King Features Syndicate, 30 F.Supp. 352 (S.D.N.Y.1939) (newspaper publication of X-rays of woman's pelvic region); Feeney v. Young, 191 App.Div. 501, 181 N.Y.S. 481 (1920) (public exhibition of films of caesarean operation); Griffin v. Medical Society, 7 Misc.2d 549, 11 N.Y.S.2d 109 (1939) (publication in medical journal of pictures of plaintiff's deformed nose); Hawkins v. Multimedia, Inc., 288 S.C. 569, 344 S.E.2d 145 (1986), cert. denied, 479 U.S. 1012 (1986) (plaintiff identified as teenage father of illegitimate child in news item). But cf. Justice v. Belo Broadcasting Corp., 472 F.Supp. 145 (N.D.Tex.1979) (*parents have no cause of action for disclosure that murdered son was a homosexual*).

7.   On the requirement that the publicity be highly offensive to a person of ordinary sensitivities, see Bitsie v. Walston, 85 N.M. 655, 515 P.2d 659 (1973), cert. denied, 85 N.M. 639, 515 P.2d 643 (1973) (holding that traditional beliefs of the Navajo about taking a child's photograph were not sufficient to make the action highly offensive where defendant newspaper did not know of the beliefs).

8.   *Constitutional Law.* The common law restrictions on invasion of privacy constitute, at a minimum, the constitutionally permissible boundaries of the tort. The question, however, remained after the principal case: was a tort that punished the publication of true, if private, facts constitutionally valid? The Supreme Court in a number of cases has addressed the question. In Oklahoma Publishing Co. v. District Court, 430 U.S. 308 (1977), a state court's pretrial order enjoining the media from publishing the name or photograph of a boy connected with a juvenile proceeding was struck down: reporters had attended an open court proceeding where the identity of the boy was revealed. In Smith v. Daily Mail Publishing Co., 443 U.S. 97 (1979), the Court found unconstitutional the indictment of two newspapers for breaching a state statute prohibiting the publication of the identity of youths charged with juvenile offenses. The papers had gleaned the information lawfully. In a third case, Landmark Communications, Inc. v. Virginia, 435 U.S. 829 (1978), the court struck down a state regulation prohibiting the publication of truthful information that a judge was under investigation.

In a case that rounds out the circle, the Supreme Court in The Florida Star v. B.J.F., 491 U.S. 524 (1989), addressed the issue of civil liability of a newspaper which had published the name of the victim of a sexual offense in violation of a Florida statute. The newspaper reporter had copied the police report which mistakenly included the victim's name. Unlike the principal case, the protected nature of accurate reports of *judicial* proceedings was not implicated. Nevertheless, the Court found the publication was not actionable because it was of "truthful information about a matter of public interest." Such publication could be proscribed only where it served to "further a state interest of the highest order."

The Court, however, did not completely eliminate the tort. Justice Marshall, delivering the Court's opinion, announced:

> Our holding today is limited. We do not hold that truthful publication is automatically constitutionally protected, or that there is no zone of personal privacy within which the State may protect the individual from intrusion by the press, or even that the State may never punish publication of the name of a victim of a sexual offence. We hold only that where a newspaper publishes truthful information which it has lawfully obtained, punishment may lawfully be imposed, if at all, only when narrowly tailored to a state interest of the highest order * * *.

Justice White, joined by the Chief Justice and Justice O'Connor, dissented. He was not sanguine about the future of the tort. Citing, Time, Inc. v. Hill, 385 U.S. 374 (1967), and the principal case, he concluded:

> [T]he trend in "modern" jurisprudence has been to eclipse an individual's right to maintain private any truthful information that the press wished to publish. * * * Today, we hit the bottom of the slippery slope.

9. Should individuals be given privacy protection to allow them to "make a new start in life?" Judicial attitudes have changed. Melvin v. Reid, 112 Cal.App. 285, 297 P. 91 (1931), is a widely cited privacy case. Gabrielle Darley, a prostitute, had been tried for murder and acquitted in a famous case. She subsequently married, left the state and "thereafter at all times lived an exemplary, virtuous, honorable and righteous life." Defendant produced and released a movie entitled "The Red Kimono" based on plaintiff's experiences, using her true maiden name and advertising the film as a true account. In another case, Briscoe v. Reader's Digest Ass'n, Inc., 4 Cal.3d. 529, 483 P.2d 34 (1971), plaintiff, a rehabilitated truck hijacker, had a good cause of action for a true story about him. The cases, however, are exceptional. Johnson v. Harcourt, Brace, Jovanovich, Inc., 43 Cal.App.3d 880, 118 Cal.Rptr. 370 (1974), and the modern trend is to confine them: Haynes v. Alfred A. Knopf, 8 F.3d 1222, 1231 (7th Cir.1993). In *Haynes*, Posner J. trenchantly discusses the case law. Plaintiff's early married life had been described at length in a book about African–American migration to the North. Plaintiff had reformed and was involved in community and church affairs when the book publicized his early and wayward ways. Posner J. found the publication was not actionable because although the disclosure may have deeply offended plaintiff, the facts were of a kind in which the public has a legitimate interest. Id. at 1232. The question turns on two criteria, "offensiveness and newsworthiness." Publications, particularly photographs that gratuitously ridicule, especially with a connotation, are actionable. Beyond this, the state may have an interest to prevent the publication of true facts in vindication of a paramount social interest, Capra v. Thoroughbred Racing Ass'n of North America, Inc., 787 F.2d 463 (9th Cir.1986), cert. denied, 479 U.S. 1017 (1986) (disclosures of identity of persons in witness protection program).

10. In *The Florida Star,* as in other cases, the court emphasizes that the information could have been kept secret. Once it reached the "public domain," however, the media can publish it. What constitutional law restrictions apply to breach of confidence? In Cohen v. Cowles Media Company, 501 U.S. 663, (1991), the plaintiff gave information about a political candidate to reporters of the defendant newspapers, conditioned upon the promise that his identity remain confidential. The defendant newspapers published stories identifying the plaintiff as the source

of the information. The plaintiff was fired by his employer. The majority found the plaintiff to have a good cause of action for the loss occasioned by the breach. The Court's opinion distinguished *The Florida Star* line of cases. Minnesota law "simply requires those making promises to keep them." In Ruzicka v. Conde Nast Publications, Inc., 999 F.2d 1319 (8th Cir.1993), Glamour magazine published a story about therapist-patient sexual abuse. Plaintiff gave information to the story's author on condition that she not be identified or identifiable. Story was published changing her name but supplying details allowing a reasonable recipient of the communication to identify her. (She was the only female law student or lawyer serving on the Minnesota Task Force Against Sexual Abuse.) Liability was based on a promissory estoppel theory.

Is protection of confidentiality consistent with the tenets of the First Amendment? The government contracts with its employees to keep information secret. An employee subject to such a contract discloses the information. Is the employee (or former employee) liable for breach of confidence? Can a publisher of the information, knowing of its confidential nature, be held liable? May that publisher be enjoined from publication? These issues were aired in United States v. Marchetti, 466 F.2d 1309 (4th Cir.1972), cert. denied, 409 U.S. 1063 (1972) (former CIA agent revealed secrets in book in violation of agreement) and United States v. Snepp, 897 F.2d 138 (4th Cir.1990) (similar facts). The English and Commonwealth courts in the Spycatcher litigation wrestled with the same issues when a former M.I.5 agent in retirement in Tasmania wrote a book disclosing intelligence secrets. The British Government waged a global campaign to suppress the publication: Attorney–General v. Guardian Newspapers (No. 2), [1990] 1 A.C. 109.

Cantrell v. Forest City Publishing Co.

Supreme Court of the United States, 1974.
419 U.S. 245, 95 S.Ct. 465, 42 L.Ed.2d 419.

Mr. Justice Stewart delivered the opinion of the Court.

Margaret Cantrell and four of her minor children brought this diversity action in a federal district court for invasion of privacy against the Forest City Publishing Company, publisher of a Cleveland newspaper, The Plain Dealer, and against Joseph Eszterhas, a reporter formerly employed by The Plain Dealer, and Richard Conway, a Plain Dealer photographer. The Cantrells alleged that an article published in The Plain Dealer Sunday Magazine unreasonably placed their family in a false light before the public through its many inaccuracies and untruths. The District Judge struck the claims relating to punitive damages as to all the plaintiffs and dismissed the actions of three of the Cantrell children in their entirety, but allowed the case to go to the jury as to Mrs. Cantrell and her oldest son, William. The jury returned a verdict against all three of the respondents for compensatory money damages in favor of these two plaintiffs.

The Court of Appeals for the Sixth Circuit reversed, holding that, in the light of the First and Fourteenth Amendments, the District Judge should have granted the respondents' motion for a directed verdict as to all the Cantrells. Cantrell v. Forest City Publishing Co., 484 F.2d 150. We granted certiorari, 418 U.S. 909.

I.   In December 1967, Margaret Cantrell's husband Melvin was killed along with 43 other people when the Silver Bridge across the Ohio River at Point Pleasant, West Virginia, collapsed. The respondent Eszterhas was assigned by The Plain Dealer to cover the story of the disaster. He wrote a "news feature" story focusing on the funeral of Melvin Cantrell and the impact of his death on the Cantrell family.

Five months later, after conferring with the Sunday Magazine editor of The Plain Dealer, Eszterhas and photographer Conway returned to the Point Pleasant area to write a follow-up feature. The two men went to the Cantrell residence, where Eszterhas talked with the children and Conway took 50 pictures. Mrs. Cantrell was not at home at any time during the 60 to 90 minutes that the men were at the Cantrell residence.

Eszterhas's story appeared as the lead feature in the August 4, 1968, edition of The Plain Dealer Sunday Magazine. The article stressed the family's abject poverty; the children's old, ill-fitting clothes and the deteriorating condition of their home were detailed in both the text and accompanying photographs. As he had done in his original, prize-winning article on the Silver Bridge disaster, Eszterhas used the Cantrell family to illustrate the impact of the bridge collapse on the lives of the people in the Point Pleasant area.

It is conceded that the story contained a number of inaccuracies and false statements. Most conspicuously, although Mrs. Cantrell was not present at any time during the reporter's visit to her home, Eszterhas wrote, "Margaret Cantrell will talk neither about what happened nor about how they are doing. She wears the same mask of non-expression she wore at the funeral. She is a proud woman. She says that after it happened, the people in town offered to help them out with money and they refused to take it." Other significant misrepresentations were contained in details of Eszterhas' descriptions of the poverty in which the Cantrells were living and the dirty and dilapidated conditions of the Cantrell home.

The case went to the jury on a so-called "false light" theory of invasion of privacy. In essence, the theory of the case was that by publishing the false feature story about the Cantrells and thereby making them the objects of pity and ridicule, the respondents damaged Mrs. Cantrell and her son William by causing them to suffer outrage, mental distress, shame, and humiliation.

II.   In Time, Inc. v. Hill, 385 U.S. 374, the Court considered a similar false light, invasion of privacy action. The New York Court of Appeals had interpreted New York Civil Rights Law, McKinney's Consol.Laws, c. 6, §§ 50–51 to give a "newsworthy person" a right of action when his or her name, picture or portrait was the subject of a "fictitious" report or article. Material and substantial falsification was the test for recovery. [C] Under this doctrine the New York courts awarded the plaintiff James Hill compensatory damages based on his complaint that Life Magazine had falsely reported that a new Broadway play portrayed the Hill family's experience in being held hostage by three escaped convicts. This Court, guided by its decision in New York Times Co. v. Sullivan, 376 U.S. 254, which recognized constitutional limits on a State's power to award damages for libel in actions brought by public officials, held that the constitutional protections for speech and press precluded the application of the New York statute to allow recovery for "false reports of matters of public interest in the absence of proof that the defendant published the report with knowledge of its falsity or in reckless disregard of the truth." [C] Although the jury could have reasonably concluded from the evidence in the *Hill* case that Life had engaged in knowing falsehood or had recklessly disregarded the truth in stating in the article that "the story re-enacted" the Hill family's experience, the Court concluded that the trial judge's instructions had not confined the jury to such a finding as a predicate for liability as required by the Constitution. [C]

The District Judge in the case before us, in contrast with the trial judge in Time, Inc. v. Hill, did instruct the jury that liability could be imposed only if it concluded that the false statements in the Sunday Magazine feature article on the Cantrells had been made with knowledge of their falsity or in reckless disregard of the truth. No objection was made by any of the parties to this knowing-or-reckless-falsehood instruction. Consequently, this case presents no occasion to consider whether a State may constitutionally apply a more relaxed standard of liability for a publisher or broadcaster of false statements injurious to a private individual under a false-light theory of invasion of privacy, or whether the constitutional standard announced in Time, Inc. v. Hill applies to all false-light cases. Cf. Gertz v. Welch, Inc., 418 U.S. 323. Rather, the sole question that we need decide is whether the Court of Appeals erred in setting aside the jury's verdict.

III. At the close of the petitioners' case-in-chief, the District Judge struck the demand for punitive damages. He found that Mrs. Cantrell had failed to present any evidence to support the charges that the invasion of privacy "was done maliciously within the legal definition of that term." The Court of Appeals interpreted this finding to be a determination by the District Judge that there was no evidence of knowing falsity or reckless disregard of the truth introduced at the trial. Having made such a determination, the Court of Appeals held that the District Judge should have granted the motion for a directed verdict as to all respondents. 484 F.2d, at 155.

The Court of Appeals appears to have assumed that the District Judge's finding of no malice "within the legal definition of that term" was a finding based on the definition of "actual malice" established by this Court in New York Times Co. v. Sullivan, 376 U.S. 254, 280: "with knowledge that [a defamatory statement] was false or with reckless disregard of whether it was false or not." As so defined, of course, "actual malice" is a term of art, created to provide a convenient shorthand for the standard of liability that must be established before a State may constitutionally permit public officials to recover for libel in actions brought against publishers. As such, it is quite different from the common-law standard of "malice" generally required under state tort law to support an award of punitive damages. In a false-light case, common-law malice—frequently expressed in terms of either personal ill will toward the plaintiff or reckless or wanton disregard of the plaintiff's rights—would focus on the defendant's attitude toward the plaintiff's privacy, not towards the truth or falsity of the material published. See Time, Inc. v. Hill, 385 U.S., at 396 n. 12. See generally W. Prosser, Law of Torts 9–10 (4th ed.).

Although the verbal record of the District Court proceedings is not entirely unambiguous, the conclusion is inescapable that the District Judge was referring to the common-law standard of malice rather than to the *New York Times* "actual malice" standard when he dismissed the punitive damages claims. For at the same time that he dismissed the demands for punitive damages, the District Judge refused to grant the respondents' motion for directed verdicts as to Mrs. Cantrell's and William's claims for compensatory damages. And, as his instructions to the jury made clear, the District Judge was fully aware that the Time, Inc. v. Hill meaning of the *New York Times* "actual malice" standard had to be satisfied for the Cantrells to recover actual damages. Thus, the only way to harmonize these two virtually simultaneous rulings by the District Judge is to conclude, contrary to the decision of the Court of Appeals, that in dismissing the punitive damages claims he was not determining that Mrs. Cantrell had failed to introduce any evidence of knowing falsity or reckless disregard of the truth. This conclusion is further fortified by the District Judge's subsequent denial of the respondents' motion for judgment N.O.V. and alternative motion for a new trial.

Moreover, the District Judge was clearly correct in believing that the evidence introduced at trial was sufficient to support a jury finding that the respondents Joseph Eszterhas and Forest City Publishing Company had published knowing or reckless falsehoods about the Cantrells. There was no dispute during the trial that Eszterhas, who did not testify, must have known that a number of the statements in the feature story were untrue. In particular, his article plainly implied that Mrs. Cantrell had been present during his visit to her home and that Eszterhas had observed her "wear[ing] the same mask of nonexpression she wore [at her husband's] funeral." These were "calculated falsehoods," and the jury was plainly justified in finding that Eszterhas had portrayed the Cantrells in a false light through knowing or reckless untruth.

The Court of Appeals concluded that there was no evidence that Forest City Publishing Company had knowledge of any of the inaccuracies contained in Eszterhas' article. However, there was sufficient evidence for the jury to find that Eszterhas' writing of the feature was within the scope of his employment at The Plain Dealer and that Forest City Publishing Company was therefore liable under traditional doctrines of *respondeat superior.* Although Eszterhas was not regularly assigned by The Plain Dealer to write for the Sunday Magazine, the editor of the magazine testified that as a staff writer for The Plain Dealer, Eszterhas frequently suggested stories he would like to write for the magazine. When Eszterhas suggested the follow-up article on the Silver Bridge disaster, the editor approved the idea and told Eszterhas the magazine would publish the feature if it was good. From this evidence, the jury could reasonably conclude that Forest City Publishing Company, publisher of The Plain Dealer should be held vicariously liable for the damage caused by the knowing falsehoods contained in Eszterhas' story.

For the foregoing reasons the judgment of the Court of Appeals is reversed and the case is remanded to that court with directions to enter a judgment affirming the judgment of the District Court as to the respondents Forest City Publishing Company and Joseph Eszterhas.

[JUSTICE DOUGLAS dissented, with opinion.]

NOTES AND QUESTIONS

1.   This branch of the tort of invasion of privacy can be described as placing the plaintiff in an objectionable false light in the public eye. It goes back as far as Lord Byron v. Johnston, 2 Mer. 29, 35 Eng.Rep. 851 (1816), when Byron succeeded in enjoining the circulation of a bad poem that had been attributed to his pen. See Restatement (Second) of Torts § 652E.

Representative cases include Leverton v. Curtis Pub. Co., 192 F.2d 974 (3d Cir.1951) (picture of child, hurt in automobile accident, used to illustrate article, "They Ask to be Killed"); Peay v. Curtis Pub. Co., 78 F.Supp. 305 (D.D.C.1948) (picture of honest taxi driver illustrating article on the cheating propensities of taxi drivers); Gill v. Curtis Pub. Co., 38 Cal.2d 273, 239 P.2d 630 (1952) (picture of embracing couple illustrating article on the "wrong kind of love"); Douglass v. Hustler Magazine, Inc., 769 F.2d 1128 (7th Cir.1985), cert. denied, 475 U.S. 1094 (1986) (plaintiff allowed Playboy to run nude picture of her, but Hustler did it without permission; false light lies for implying that she would allow that magazine to carry the picture); Lerman v. Flynt Distributing Co., Inc., 745 F.2d 123 (5th Cir.1984), cert. denied, 471 U.S. 1054 (1985) (plaintiff identified as actress in photographs topless and in "orgy" scene in defendant's magazine); Peoples Bank and Trust Co. of Mountain Home v. Globe International Publishing, Inc., 978 F.2d 1065 (8th Cir.1992), aff'g 786 F.Supp. 791 (W.D.Ark.1992) (plaintiff, a ninety-five-year-old woman, had her photograph featured in defendant's tabloid reporting that an Australian woman of 101 had been forced to quit her job because an affair with a millionaire had left her pregnant; award of $850,000 in punitive damages); Kolegas v. Heftel Broadcasting Corp., 154 Ill.2d 1, 607 N.E.2d 201, 180 Ill.Dec. 307 (1992) (plaintiff placed in false light by defendant's disc jockey stating that plaintiff and his wife were in shotgun wedding and his wife and son had abnormally large heads; the imputations were highly offensive).

2.   In Samuel v. Curtis Pub. Co., 122 F.Supp. 327 (N.D.Cal.1954), a woman stood on the edge of the Golden Gate bridge in San Francisco, about to jump. Plaintiff was photographed while trying to dissuade her. Two years later defendant published in its magazine an article on suicide, and used the picture as an illustration. This was held not to invade the plaintiff's privacy. In accord are Sarat Lahiri v. Daily Mirror, Inc., 162 Misc. 776, 295 N.Y.S. 382 (1937) (picture of Hindu illusionist illustrating article on the Indian rope trick); Oma v. Hillman Periodicals, 281 App.Div. 240, 118 N.Y.S.2d 720 (1953) (picture of boxer illustrating article on boxing); Kline v. Robert M. McBride & Co., 170 Misc. 974, 11 N.Y.S.2d 674 (1939) (picture of strike-breaker, book on strike-breaking). How are the two groups of cases to be distinguished?

3. In the privacy action, what becomes of the various safeguards thrown about the freedom of the press in defamation cases, such as the necessity of a defamatory innuendo, the requirement of proof of special damage when what is published is not actionable per se, the retraction statutes, and those requiring the filing of a bond for costs? See Prosser, Privacy, 48 Calif.L.Rev. 383, 422–23 (1960); Wade, Defamation and the Right of Privacy, 15 Vand.L.Rev. 1093 (1962). In Werner v. Times–Mirror Co., 193 Cal.App.2d 111, 14 Cal.Rptr. 208 (1961), the court recognized the problem, and applied a retraction statute even to false statements about the plaintiff that were not defamatory.

4. At least 20 states and the District of Columbia expressly recognize false light invasion of privacy. Seven states reject the tort. They are Massachusetts: Elm Medical Laboratory, Inc. v. RKO General, Inc., 403 Mass. 779, 532 N.E.2d 675, 681 (1989); Minnesota: Hendry v. Conner, 303 Minn. 317, 226 N.W.2d 921, 923 (1975); Markgraf v. Douglas Corporation., 468 N.W.2d 80 (Minn.App.1991); Ruzicka v. Conde Nast Publications, Inc., 939 F.2d 578 (8th Cir.1991); Lake v. Wal–Mart Stores, Inc., 582 N.W.2d 231, 235 (Minn.1998) (pointing out the tension between a false light cause of action and the First Amendment); North Carolina: Renwick v. News and Observer Publishing Co., 310 N.C. 312, 312 S.E.2d 405 (1984); Hall v. Post and the Post Publishing Co., Inc., 323 N.C. 259, 372 S.E.2d 711 (1988); Ohio: Yeager v. Local Union 20, 6 Ohio St. 3d 396, 453 N.E.2d 666 (1983); Angelotta v. ABC, 820 F.2d 806 (6th Cir.1987); South Carolina: Snakenberg v. Hartford Casualty Ins. Co., Inc., 299 S.C. 164, 383 S.E.2d 2, 5 (1989); Texas: Cain v. Hearst Corporation., 878 S.W.2d 577 (Tex.1994) (plaintiff, a prison inmate with a shocking criminal record, claimed defendant's article actionable because it claimed he was a member of the "Dixie Mafia" and had killed as many as eight people; held tort should not be recognized, but against strong dissent). In Missouri, no action is available where a defamation action would be adequate to afford relief: Sullivan v. Pulitzer Broadcasting Co., 709 S.W.2d 475 (Mo.1986); Renner v. Donsbach, 749 F.Supp. 987 (W.D.Mo.1990).

5. *Constitutional Law.* As indicated in the principal case, Time, Inc. v. Hill, 385 U.S. 374 (1967), laid down the constitutional rule that in the false-light cases, the plaintiff must prove that the defendant knew of the falsity or acted with reckless disregard of it. Gertz v. Robert Welch, Inc., supra, page 892, repudiated Rosenbloom v. Metromedia, Inc., supra, page 875, and limited the reckless-disregard formula of New York Times v. Sullivan to statements about public officials or public figures. This has given rise to speculation that the same thing will be done to Time, Inc. v. Hill and its application to the false-light cases. The principal case leaves this question undecided. See, applying the negligence standard to a false-light case, Wood v. Hustler Mag., Inc., 736 F.2d 1084 (5th Cir.1984); Jones v. Palmer Communications, Inc., 440 N.W.2d 884, 894 (Iowa 1989) (the "false light" cases are subject to the same constitutional constraints as defamation cases); Crump v. Beckley Newspapers, Inc., 173 W.Va. 699, 320 S.E.2d 70 (1983) (holding that the inconsistency will be resolved in favor of *Gertz*; photograph of woman coal miner was used to illustrate an article about sexual harassment in mines). But cf. Lovgren v. Citizens First Nat'l Bank, 126 Ill.2d 411, 534 N.E.2d 987, 128 Ill.Dec. 542 (1989) (ruling that at common law a false light action requires a showing of at least reckless falsification). If the tort requires intentional or reckless publication, it approaches extreme and outrageous conduct required under the tort of intentional infliction of emotional distress. For a case distinguishing the torts and resisting a merger see Godbehere v. Phoenix Newspapers, Inc., 162 Ariz. 335, 783 P.2d 781 (1989). The next principal case highlights the affinity of the two torts and their overriding constitutional restraints.

Hustler Magazine v. Falwell

Supreme Court of the United States, 1988.
485 U.S. 46, 108 S.Ct. 876, 99 L.Ed.2d 41.

CHIEF JUSTICE REHNQUIST delivered the opinion of the Court.

Petitioner Hustler Magazine, Inc., is a magazine of nationwide circulation. Respondent Jerry Falwell, a nationally known minister who has been active as a commentator on politics and public affairs, sued petitioner and its publisher, petitioner Larry Flynt, to recover damages for invasion of privacy, libel, and intentional infliction of emotional distress. The District Court directed a verdict against respondent on the privacy claim, and submitted the other two claims to a jury. The jury found for petitioners on the defamation claim [on the ground that the "ad parody could not 'reasonably be understood as describing actual facts' about plaintiff or actual events in which he participated." It also] found for respondent on the claim for intentional infliction of emotional distress and awarded damages [of $200,000, including punitive damages]. We now consider whether this award is consistent with the First and Fourteenth Amendments of the United States Constitution.

The inside front cover of the November 1983 issue of Hustler Magazine featured a "parody" of an advertisement for Campari Liqueur that contained the name and picture of respondent and was entitled "Jerry Falwell talks about his first time." This parody was modeled after actual Campari ads that included interviews with various celebrities about their "first times." Although it was apparent by the end of each interview that this meant the first time they sampled Campari, the ads clearly played on the sexual double entendre of the general subject of "first times." Copying the form and layout of these Campari ads, Hustler's editors chose respondent as the featured celebrity and drafted an alleged "interview" with him in which he states that his "first time" was during a drunken incestuous rendezvous with his mother in an outhouse. The Hustler parody portrays respondent and his mother as drunk and immoral, and suggests that respondent is a hypocrite who preaches only when he is drunk. In small print at the bottom of the page, the ad contains the disclaimer, "ad parody—not to be taken seriously." The magazine's table of contents also lists the ad as "Fiction; Ad and Personality Parody." * * *

On appeal [from the District Court,] the United States Court of Appeals for the Fourth Circuit affirmed the judgment against petitioners. Falwell v. Flynt, 797 F.2d 1270 (C.A.4 1986). The court rejected petitioners' argument that the "actual malice" standard of New York Times Co. v. Sullivan, 376 U.S. 254 (1964), must be met before respondent can recover for emotional distress. The court agreed that because respondent is concededly a public figure, petitioners are "entitled to the same level of first amendment protection in the claim for intentional infliction of emotional distress that they received in [respondent's] claim for libel." 797 F.2d, at 1274. But this does not mean that a literal application of the actual malice rule is appropriate in the context of an emotional distress claim. In the court's view, the *New York Times* decision emphasized the constitutional importance not of the falsity of the statement or the defendant's disregard for the truth, but of the heightened level of culpability embodied in the requirement of "knowing * * * or reckless" conduct. Here, the *New York Times* standard is satisfied by the state-law requirement, and the jury's finding, that the defendants have acted intentionally or recklessly.[3] The Court of Appeals then went on to reject the contention that because the jury found that the ad parody did not describe actual facts about respondent, the ad was an opinion that is protected by the First Amendment. As the court put it, this was "irrelevant," as the issue is "whether [the ad's] publication was sufficiently outrageous to constitute intentional infliction of emotional distress." [C] Petitioners then filed a petition for rehearing en banc, but this was denied by a divided court. Given the importance of the constitutional issues involved, we granted certiorari.

This case presents us with a novel question involving First Amendment limitations upon a State's authority to protect its citizens from the intentional infliction of emotional distress. We must decide whether a public figure may recover damages for emotional harm caused by the publication of an ad parody offensive to him, and doubtless gross and repugnant in the eyes of most. Respondent would have us find that a State's interest in protecting public figures from emotional distress is sufficient to deny First Amendment protection to speech that is patently offensive and is intended to inflict emotional injury, even when that speech could not reasonably have been interpreted as stating actual facts about the public figure involved. This we decline to do.

At the heart of the First Amendment is the recognition of the fundamental importance of the free flow of ideas and opinions on matters of public interest and concern. "[T]he freedom to speak one's mind is not only an aspect of individual liberty—and thus a good unto itself—but also is essential to the common quest for truth and the vitality of society as a whole." Bose Corp. v. Consumers Union of United States, [c] Inc., 466 U.S. 485, 503–504 (1984). We have therefore been particularly vigilant to ensure that individual expressions of ideas remain free from governmentally imposed sanctions. The First Amendment recognizes no such thing as a "false" idea. *Gertz v. Robert Welch, Inc.,* 418 U.S. 323, 339 (1974). * * *

The sort of robust political debate encouraged by the First Amendment is bound to produce speech that is critical of those who hold public office or those public figures who are "intimately involved in the resolution of important public questions or, by reason of their fame, shape events in areas of concern to society at large." [C] Justice Frankfurter put it succinctly in Baumgartner v. United States, 322 U.S. 665, 673–674 (1944), when he said that "[o]ne of the prerogatives of American citizenship is the right to criticize public men and measures." Such criticism, inevitably, will

---

3. Under Virginia law, in an action for intentional infliction of emotional distress a plaintiff must show that the defendant's conduct (1) is intentional or reckless; (2) offends generally accepted standards of decency or morality; (3) is causally connected with the plaintiff's emotional distress; and (4) caused emotional distress that was severe. 797 F.2d, at 1275, n. 4 (citing Womack v. Eldridge, 215 Va. 338, 210 S.E.2d 145 (1974)).

not always be reasoned or moderate; public figures as well as public officials will be subject to "vehement, caustic, and sometimes unpleasantly sharp attacks," *New York Times,* supra, at 270. "[T]he candidate who vaunts his spotless record and sterling integrity cannot convincingly cry 'Foul!' when an opponent or an industrious reporter attempts to demonstrate the contrary." Monitor Patriot Co. v. Roy, 401 U.S. 265, 274 (1971).

Of course, this does not mean that *any* speech about a public figure is immune from sanction in the form of damages. Since *New York Times Co. v. Sullivan,* supra, we have consistently ruled that a public figure may hold a speaker liable for the damage to reputation caused by publication of a defamatory falsehood, but only if the statement was made "with knowledge that it was false or with reckless disregard of whether it was false or not." Id., at 279–280. False statements of fact are particularly valueless; they interfere with the truth-seeking function of the marketplace of ideas, and they cause damage to an individual's reputation that cannot easily be repaired by counterspeech, however persuasive or effective. See *Gertz,* 418 U.S., at 340, 344, n. 9. But even though falsehoods have little value in and of themselves, they are "nevertheless inevitable in free debate," id., at 340, and a rule that would impose strict liability on a publisher for false factual assertions would have an undoubted "chilling" effect on speech relating to public figures that does have constitutional value. "Freedoms of expression require 'breathing space.'" Philadelphia Newspapers, Inc. v. Hepps, 475 U.S. 767, 772 (1986) (quoting *New York Times,* 376 U.S., at 272). This breathing space is provided by a constitutional rule that allows public figures to recover for libel or defamation only when they can prove *both* that the statement was false and that the statement was made with the requisite level of culpability.

Respondent argues, however, that a different standard should apply in this case because here the State seeks to prevent not reputational damage, but the severe emotional distress suffered by the person who is the subject of an offensive publication. Cf. Zacchini v. Scripps–Howard Broadcasting Co., 433 U.S. 562 (1977) (ruling that the "actual malice" standard does not apply to the tort of appropriation of a right of publicity). In respondent's view, and in the view of the Court of Appeals, so long as the utterance was intended to inflict emotional distress, was outrageous, and did in fact inflict serious emotional distress, it is of no constitutional import whether the statement was a fact or an opinion, or whether it was true or false. It is the intent to cause injury that is the gravamen of the tort, and the State's interest in preventing emotional harm simply outweighs whatever interest a speaker may have in speech of this type.

Generally speaking the law does not regard the intent to inflict emotional distress as one which should receive much solicitude, and it is quite understandable that most if not all jurisdictions have chosen to make it civilly culpable where the conduct in question is sufficiently "outrageous." But in the world of debate about public affairs, many things done with motives that are less than admirable are protected by the First Amendment. In Garrison v. Louisiana, 379 U.S. 64 (1964), we held that even when a speaker or writer is motivated by hatred or ill-will his expression was protected by the First Amendment: "Debate on public issues will not be uninhibited if the speaker must run the risk that it will be proved in court that he spoke out of hatred; even if he did speak out of hatred, utterances honestly believed contribute to the free interchange of ideas and the ascertainment of truth." Id., at 73.

Thus, while such a bad motive may be deemed controlling for purposes of tort liability in other areas of the law, we think the First Amendment prohibits such a result in the area of public debate about public figures.

Were we to hold otherwise, there can be little doubt that political cartoonists and satirists would be subjected to damages awards without any showing that their work falsely defamed its subject. [The court discusses a number of well-known cartoon caricatures.]

Respondent contends, however, that the caricature in question here was so "outrageous" as to distinguish it from more traditional political cartoons. There is no doubt that the caricature of respondent and his mother published in Hustler is at best a distant cousin of the political cartoons described above, and a rather poor relation at that. If it were possible by laying down a principled standard to separate the one from the other, public discourse would probably suffer little or no harm. But we doubt that there is any such standard, and we are quite sure that the pejorative description "outrageous" does not supply one. "Outrageousness" in the area of political and social discourse has an inherent subjectiveness about it which would allow a jury to impose liability on the basis of the jurors' tastes or views, or perhaps on the basis of their dislike of a particular expression. An "outrageousness" standard thus runs afoul of our longstanding refusal to allow damages to be awarded because the speech in question may have an adverse emotional impact on the audience. * * * [A]s we stated in FCC v. Pacifica Foundation, 438 U.S. 726 (1978): "[T]he fact that society may find speech offensive is not a sufficient reason for suppressing it. Indeed, if it is the speaker's opinion that gives offense, that consequence is a reason for according it constitutional protection. For it is a central tenet of the First Amendment that the government must remain neutral in the marketplace of ideas." Id., at 745–746. See also Street v. New York, 394 U.S. 576, 592 (1969) ("It is firmly settled that ... the public expression of ideas may not be prohibited merely because the ideas are themselves offensive to some of their hearers").

Admittedly, these oft-repeated First Amendment principles, like other principles, are subject to limitations. We recognized in Pacifica Foundation, that speech that is " 'vulgar,' 'offensive,' and 'shocking' " is "not entitled to absolute constitutional protection under all circumstances." 438 U.S., at 747. In Chaplinsky v. New Hampshire, 315 U.S. 568 (1942), we held that a state could lawfully punish an individual for the use of insulting " 'fighting' words—those which by their very utterance inflict injury or tend to incite an immediate breach of the peace." Id., at 571–572. These limitations are but recognition of the observation in Dun & Bradstreet, Inc. v. Greenmoss Builders, Inc., 472 U.S. 749, 758 (1985), that this Court has "long recognized that not all speech is of equal First Amendment importance." But the sort of expression involved in this case does not seem to us to be governed by any exception to the general First Amendment principles stated above.

We conclude that public figures and public officials may not recover for the tort of intentional infliction of emotional distress by reason of publications such as the one here at issue without showing in addition that the publication contains a false statement of fact which was made with "actual malice," *i.e.*, with knowledge that the statement was false or with reckless disregard as to whether or not it was true. This is not merely a "blind application" of the *New York Times* standard, [c] it reflects our considered judgment that such a standard is necessary to give adequate "breathing space" to the freedoms protected by the First Amendment.

Here it is clear that respondent Falwell is a "public figure" for purposes of First Amendment law. [He cannot recover in libel and] is thus relegated to his claim for damages awarded by the jury for the intentional infliction of emotional distress by "outrageous" conduct. But for reasons heretofore stated this claim cannot, consistently with the First Amendment, form a basis for the award of damages when the conduct in question is the publication of a caricature such as the ad parody involved here. The judgment of the Court of Appeals is accordingly

Reversed.

JUSTICE WHITE, concurring in the judgment. As I see it, the decision in New York Times v. Sullivan, 376 U.S. 254 (1964), has little to do with this case, for here the jury found that the ad contained no assertion of fact. But I agree with the Court that the judgment below, which penalized the publication of the parody, cannot be squared with the First Amendment.

NOTES AND QUESTIONS

1. Why is New York Times v. Sullivan, supra, invoked?

2. Once the plaintiff is identified as a public figure and the speech is directed toward public debate in which the public figure is involved, the courts, consistent with the principal case, have permitted robust and vitriolic attack: Dworkin v. Hustler Magazine Inc., 867 F.2d 1188 (9th Cir.1989) (ad hominem attack on feminist who had advocated suppression of pornography). It follows that the principal case does not protect the publisher or utterer of statement from liability where the attack is directed to a private individual: Esposito–Hilder v. SFX Broadcasting, 654 N.Y.S.2d 259 (1996) (plaintiff, who worked for a rival radio station, was identified by defendants in an "Ugliest Bride Contest"; held action for intentional infliction of emotional distress could lie, although no defamation action would lie since it asserted no facts about plaintiff).

3. Should limits be applied to speech in order to protect the viability of community norms that "inculcate the ideal of rational deliberation"? See Post, The Constitutional Concept of Public Discourse: Outrageous Opinion, Democratic Deliberation, and *Hustler Magazine v. Falwell*, 103 Harv.L.Rev. 601, 684 (1990). For another view see LeBel, Emotional Distress, The First Amendment, and "This Kind of Speech": A Heretical Perspective on *Hustler Magazine v. Falwell*, 60 U.Colo. L.Rev. 315 (1989) (arguing that the emotional distress tort claim should retain a more expanded role than the principal case allows).

4. Another commentary exploring the parameters of the principal case and attempting a resolution is Smolla, Emotional Distress and the First Amendment: An Analysis of *Hustler v. Falwell*, 20 Ariz.St.L.J. 423 (1988).

CHAPTER XIX

CIVIL RIGHTS

Ashby v. White

Court of King's Bench, 1702; House of Lords, 1703.
2 Ld.Raym. 938, 92 Eng.Rep. 126; 1 Brown P.C. 62, 1 Eng.Rep. 417.

HOLT, CHIEF JUSTICE. The single question in this case is, whether, if a free burgess of a corporation, who has an undoubted right to give his vote in the election of a burgess to serve in Parliament, be refused and hindered to give it by the officer, if an action on the case will lie against such officer.

Chief Justice Holt

I am of opinion that judgment ought to be given in this case for the plaintiff. My brothers differ from me in opinion, and they all differ from one another in the reasons of their opinion; but notwithstanding their opinion, I think the plaintiff ought to recover, and that this action is well maintainable, and ought to lie.

But to proceed, I will do these two things: first, I will maintain that the plaintiff has a right and privilege to give his vote: secondly, in consequence thereof, that if he be hindered in the enjoyment or exercise of that right, the law gives him an action against the disturber, and that this is the proper action given by the law. * * *

If the plaintiff has a right, he must of necessity have a means to vindicate and maintain it, and a remedy if he is injured in the exercise or enjoyment of it; and indeed it is a vain thing to imagine a right without a remedy; for want of right and want of remedy are reciprocal. * * * Where a new Act of Parliament is made for the benefit of the subject, if a man be hindered from the enjoyment of it, he shall have an action against such person who so obstructed him. * * * If then when a statute gives a right, the party shall have an action for the infringement of it, is it not as forcible when a man has his right by the common law? This right of voting is a right in the plaintiff by the common law, and consequently he shall maintain an action for the obstruction of it. * * *

And I am of opinion, that this action on the case is a proper action. My brother Powell indeed thinks, that an action upon the case is not maintainable, because here is no hurt or damage to the plaintiff; but surely every injury imports a damage, though it does not cost the party one farthing, and it is impossible to prove the contrary; for a damage is not merely pecuniary, but an injury imports a damage, when a man is thereby hindered of his right. * * *. So here in the principal case, the plaintiff is obstructed of his right, and shall therefore have his action. And it is no objection to say, that it will occasion multiplicity of actions; for if men will multiply injuries, actions must be multiplied too; for every man that is injured ought to have his recompence. Suppose the defendant had beat forty or fifty men, the damage done to each one is peculiar to himself, and he shall have his action. So if many persons receive a private injury by a publick nusance, every one shall have his action. * * *

But in the principal case my brother says, we cannot judge of this matter, because it is a Parliamentary thing. O! By all means be very tender of that. Besides it is intricate, and there may be contrariety of opinions. But this matter can never come in question in Parliament; for it is agreed that the persons for whom the plaintiff voted were elected; so that the action is brought for being deprived of his vote; and if it were carried for the other candidates against whom he voted, his damage would be less. To allow this action will make publick officers more careful to observe the constitution of cities and boroughs, and not to be so partial as they commonly are in all elections, which is indeed a great and growing mischief, and tends to the prejudice of the peace of the nation. But they say, that this is a matter out of our jurisdiction, and we ought not to inlarge it. I agree we ought not to incroach or inlarge our jurisdiction; by so doing we usurp both on the right of the Queen and the people: but sure we may determine on a charter granted by the King, or on a matter of custom or prescription, when it comes before us without incroaching on the Parliament. And if it be a matter within our jurisdiction, we are bound by our oaths to judge of it. This is a matter of property determinable before us. Was ever such a petition heard of in Parliament, as that a man was hindred of giving his vote, and praying them to give him remedy? The Parliament undoubtedly would say, take your remedy at law. It is not like the case of determining the right of election between the candidates. * * *

Therefore my opinion is, that the plaintiff ought to have judgment. * * *

[The opinions of GOULD, POWYS and POWELL, JJ., constituting the majority in the Court of King's Bench and reversing the jury verdict for the plaintiff, are omitted.

The report of the proceeding in the House of Lords concludes: "After hearing counsel on this writ of error, a debate ensued; and the question being put, Whether this judgment should be reversed? it was resolved in the affirmative. * * * It was therefore ordered and adjudged, that the said judgment should be reversed, and that the plaintiff should recover his damages assessed by the jury; and also, the further sum of 10£. for his costs, in this behalf sustained."]

NOTES AND QUESTIONS

1. Accord: Lane v. Mitchell, 153 Iowa 139, 133 N.W. 381 (1911); Valdez v. Gonzales, 50 N.M. 281, 176 P.2d 173 (1946).

"The objection that the subject matter of the suit is political is little more than a play upon words. Of course the petition concerns political action but it alleges and seeks to recover for private damage. That private damage may be caused by such political action and may be recovered for in a suit at law hardly has been doubted for over two hundred years. * * * If the defendants' conduct was a wrong to the plaintiff the same reasons that allow a recovery for denying the plaintiff a vote at a final election allow it for denying a vote at the primary election that may determine the final result." Holmes, J., in Nixon v. Herndon, 273 U.S. 536, 540 (1927).

2. A similar action lies for depriving a person of the right to hold political office. See, e.g., Hill v. Carr, 186 Ill.App. 515 (1914), and Goetcheus v. Matthewson, 61 N.Y. 420 (1875), both indicating a right to emoluments. Cf. Sutton v. Adams, 180 Ga. 48, 178 S.E. 365 (1934); Judd v. Polk, 267 Ky. 408, 102 S.W.2d 325 (1937). On both of these torts, see Restatement (Second) of Torts § 865. The decision of Lord Holt was to influence the course of British constitutional history in its transformation to representative democracy. Cornish & Clark, *Law and Society in England 1750–1950*, 12 (1989).

3. In Morningstar v. Lafayette Hotel Co., 211 N.Y. 465, 105 N.E. 656 (1914), plaintiff was publicly refused service at the restaurant of the hotel where he resided. The reason was his refusal to pay a disputed bill of $1 for special service. Judgment had been given for the defendant. In reversing, Cardozo, J., said: "It is no concern of ours that the controversy at the root of this lawsuit may seem to be trivial. The

fact supplies, indeed, the greater reason why the jury should not have been misled into the belief that justice might therefore be denied to the suitor. To enforce one's rights when they are violated is never a legal wrong, and may often be a moral duty. It happens in many instances that the violation passes with no effort to redress it— sometimes from praiseworthy forbearance, sometimes from weakness, sometimes from mere inertia. But the law, which creates a right, can certainly not concede that an insistence upon its enforcement is evidence of a wrong.'' On a common law action for refusal to serve, see Restatement (Second) of Torts § 866.

4.   Interference with performance of a civil duty or responsibility may give rise to a tort cause of action. In Nees v. Hocks, 272 Or. 210, 536 P.2d 512 (1975), plaintiff, who was discharged from her position for failing to comply with her employer's direction that she seek to evade jury duty, was allowed to recover damages.

5.   Should these torts be confined to an intentional interference with civil rights and duties, or should they extend to a negligent interference? Should they perhaps be restricted to a purposive interference?

6.   Despite the remarks of Judge Cardozo in note 3 supra, the tort action for damages sometimes proves not adequate and other remedies are needed. Thus, if a person is wrongfully prevented from voting and recovers in an action of tort, what is the measure of damages? Would it justify the plaintiff in bringing suit or the attorney in taking the case? How might this be handled?

For these reasons, in both the voting and refusal-of-service situations, statutory provisions for injunctive, criminal and administrative relief have largely replaced the common law action. As to voting rights, federal and state statutes control: Voting Rights Act of 1965, 42 U.S.C.A. § 1971. As to refusal of service, see particularly 42 U.S.C.A. § 2000a. Congress has enacted legislation relying, for its enforcement, on private rights of action. Two examples are the Sherman Act (Title 15, §§ 1–3, 104 Stat. 2880, Pub.L. 101–588) and RICO (Racketeer Influenced and Corrupt Organizations Act) (Title 18, §§ 1961–1968, 84 Stat. 941). Both pieces of legislation provide an incentive to promote their aims by allowing private litigants to bring enforcement actions and garner supercompensatory damages. The Supreme Court in Sedima, S.P.R.L. v. Imrex Co., 473 U.S. 479 (1985), gave a broad interpretation to civil RICO. The parameters of the action are still in flux, see Reves v. Ernst & Young, 507 U.S. 170 (1993) and notes, infra page 1176.

7.   Tort law, either alone or arising out of statute, provides a way for the individual to assert rights against government. In this way it can be said to empower the individual in his relations with the state: thus the law functions as an ombudsman, see Wade, Tort Law as Ombudsman, 65 Or.L.Rev. 309 (1986).

8.   The most pervasive cause of action arises from the Ku Klux Klan Act of 1871 wherein Congress, acting under the newly ratified Fourteenth Amendment, responded to the violence and lawlessness during Reconstruction. See Eisenberg, Section 1983: Doctrinal Foundations and An Empirical Study, 67 Cornell L.Rev. 482 (1982). Section 1 of the Act is now codified as 42 U.S.C.A. § 1983 and provides:

> Every person who, under color of any statute, ordinance, regulation, custom, or usage of any State or Territory, subjects, or causes to be subjected, any citizen of the United States or other person within the jurisdiction thereof to the deprivation of any rights, privileges, or immunities secured by the Constitution and laws, shall be liable to the party injured in an action at law, suit in equity, or other proper proceeding for redress.

Very few actions were brought until the Supreme Court decision in Monroe v. Pape, 365 U.S. 167 (1961), which made it clear that the term "every person" included state officers such as state police. The late start has not diminished the power of the section; in fact, the courts have struggled to define its limits. Much of the debate turns on balancing the need to vindicate rights with the conviction that not every wrong needs to be remedied by a federal (as opposed to state) cause of action. See Eisenberg and Schwab, The Reality of Constitutional Tort Litigation, 72 Cornell L.Rev. 641 (1987) (empirical survey showed burden of § 1983 litigation was not excessive). For an articulation of limits see Sunstein, Section 1983 and the Private Enforcement of Federal Law, 49 U.Chi.L.Rev. 394 (1982).

9. If the term "every person" included state officers such as state police, did it include local government? In Monell v. New York City Department of Social Services, 436 U.S. 658 (1978), the Supreme Court held, overruling *Monroe* in part, that a municipality may be held liable for a "policy" or "custom" that causes a constitutional violation. Given this liability requirement, could a municipality be liable for a single instance of a civil rights violation? Board of the County Commissioners of Bryan County, Oklahoma v. Brown, 520 U.S. 397, (1997) (holding that the *Monell* test should apply to a basis of liability resting upon a failure to train employees.) Note the strong dissent of Justices Breyer, Stevens, and Ginsberg arguing for "reexamination" of the *Monell* holding as it relates to the "continued viability" of the "distinction between vicarious municipal liability and municipal liability based upon policy and custom."

10. The construction of the section, among other things, has concerned the meaning of the words "rights * * * secured by the Constitution and law." In Golden State Transit Corp. v. City of Los Angeles, 493 U.S. 103 (1989), the Court prescribed a three-pronged test:

1. The provision must create obligations incumbent on the governmental unit;

2. the interest must not be so vague and amorphous as to be beyond the court's competence to enforce it; and

3. the provision must have been for the benefit of the plaintiff.

A section 1983 cause of action may be expressly excluded by Congress or impliedly precluded by an alternative remedial scheme. Wilder v. Virginia Hosp. Ass'n, 496 U.S. 498 (1990). The right under legislation must "unambiguously" confer "an enforceable right upon the Act's beneficiaries." Suter v. Artist M, 503 U.S. 347, 362 (1992) (holding that the Adoption Assistance child Welfare Act did not create such a right through the obligation imposed on states to provide "reasonable efforts" to maintain and reunify families.) It is necessary to ascertain whether the claim arises under a specific constitutional provision, say the Fourth or Eighth Amendment or, more generally, under the rubric of substantive due process. If the violative activity falls into a specific constitutional provision, it must be analyzed within the purview of that constitutional provision and not under substantive due process. U.S. v. Lanier, 520 U.S. 259 (1997). It follows that an abuse of governmental power that does not violate an individual's constitutional or federal legal rights is not actionable under § 1983: Collins v. City of Harker Heights, Tex., 503 U.S. 115, (1992) (failure of public employer to provide a safe working environment does not violate the 14th Amendment and is thus not actionable under § 1983). The official conduct must be egregious or "arbitrary in a constitutional sense." Id. at 129.

11. Federal officers may be liable in tort for violations of the plaintiff's constitutional rights. See Bivens v. Six Unknown Named Agents of the Federal Bureau of Narcotics, 403 U.S. 388 (1971), infra page 1159.

12. Expanding liability has per force placed an emphasis on the defense of governmental immunity. See Chapter 12(3). See Imbler v. Pachtman, 424 U.S. 409 (1976) (absolute immunity for certain legislative and judicial officials); Butz v. Economou, 438 U.S. 478 (1978) (good-faith immunity for executive officials performing discretionary functions); Monell v. Department of Social Services, 436 U.S. 658 (1978) (governmental immunity); Pembaur v. City of Cincinnati, 475 U.S. 469 (1986) (municipal immunity, single act); Anderson v. Creighton, 483 U.S. 635, 637 (1987) (F.B.I. officials making a warrantless search of house have "a qualified immunity, shielding them from civil damages liability as long as their actions could reasonably have been thought consistent with the rights they are alleged to have violated"); Mireles v. Waco, 502 U.S. 9 (1991) (judge enjoyed absolute immunity when ordering that plaintiff be taken from another courtroom to appear before him). Harlow v. Fitzgerald, 457 U.S. 800 (1982) (officials shielded from liability if conduct does not "violate clearly established statutory or constitutional rights of which a reasonable person would have known"). The immunity enjoyed by public officials cannot be invoked by private defendants acting under "color of state law" threatened with a § 1983 suit: Wyatt v. Cole, 504 U.S. 158 (1992). Private prison guards were not entitled to qualified immunity from suit by prisoners charging a § 1983 violation. Richardson v. McKnight, 521 U.S. 399 (1997). Recall the discussion of media liability and breach of privacy, based on Fourth Amendment violations, for media ride-alongs with law enforcement officers. Chapter 18, page 948, Note 6.

Camp v. Gregory

United States Court Of Appeals For The Seventh Circuit, 1995.
67 F.3d 1286.

ROVNER, CIRCUIT JUDGE. Anthony Young died on his sixteenth birthday. At the time of his death, Anthony was under the guardianship of the Illinois Department of Children and Family Services ("DCFS"). His aunt and former guardian, Elnora Camp, brought this suit contending that George Gregory, the DCFS caseworker assigned to Anthony, had denied Anthony substantive due process by failing to ensure that Anthony was placed in a safe living environment. The district court dismissed the suit, believing that the Supreme Court's decision in DeShaney v. Winnebago County Dep't of Social Services, 489 U.S. 189 (1989), shielded Gregory from liability for his decision where to place Anthony. Because the DCFS had assumed guardianship over Anthony, we do not think *DeShaney* necessarily bars Camp's due process claim. However, we do conclude that Gregory is entitled to qualified immunity, as prior caselaw did not make clear that a state official could be liable under facts analogous to those alleged here.

FACTS

* * *

The DCFS became Anthony's guardian on June 25, 1991, by order of the Circuit Court of Cook County, Illinois. Prior to that time, Camp had assumed guardianship of Anthony from his mother, whose medical condition rendered her unable to care for him. Camp ultimately sought appointment of another guardian, however, after concluding that she could not provide the highly structured and closely supervised environment necessary to assure Anthony's safety and well-being. The state court granted her request and by agreement appointed the DCFS Anthony's guardian. Gregory was subsequently assigned to be Anthony's caseworker.

A DCFS referral form completed by a probation officer assigned to the Cook County Juvenile Court recommended that Anthony be placed in a highly structured environment. Despite knowing that Camp could not provide the degree of supervision and care that Anthony required and that Anthony faced a greater than normal risk of physical harm while living in her home, Gregory returned him to Camp's care. Subsequently, he neglected to make any referral or application for any appropriate educational or guidance program and failed to follow up on Anthony's progress. Yet, on September 20, 1991, he represented under oath to the state court (which had retained jurisdiction over Anthony's case to monitor his progress) that Anthony had been returned to Camp at the request of the Camp family, that Anthony was attending school, and that he was "doing fine." [C] Each of these representations was false and Gregory knew as much.

Ten days later, on September 30, 1991, Camp wrote to Gregory noting that her previous telephone calls to him had gone unanswered. She requested information concerning appropriate referrals and advised Gregory that Anthony was not attending school and was "placing himself in situations jeopardizing his physical safety as well as his education." [C] She also reiterated that she could not ensure Anthony's safety.

Anthony remained in Camp's care until he died on December 30, 1991. Camp contends that his death resulted directly from Gregory's failure to arrange for Anthony to be placed in an appropriate environment and to be given the types of services he required in order to ensure his safety and well-being.

* * *

SUBSTANTIVE DUE PROCESS CLAIM

Relying on the Supreme Court's decision in DeShaney v. Winnebago County Dep't of Social Servs., 489 U.S. 189 (1989), Gregory argues that "Anthony had no constitutional right to have his DCFS caseworker protect him from being killed in a gang-related incident in his neighborhood." [C] * * * [T]he precise circumstances of Anthony's death are not at all clear at this juncture. Yet, it does seem reasonable, in light of what has been alleged, to assume that Anthony's death occurred outside of his home at the hands of someone other than a family member. The essence of Camp's claim, after all, is not that she or someone else in the Camp household posed a danger to Anthony, but that she was unable to protect him from dangers posed by others. And, indeed, Camp's counsel represented to us at oral argument that Anthony was shot and killed two blocks from Camp's home. Having this in mind, we take up two questions: first, whether, by virtue of it being appointed Anthony's guardian, the DCFS (and thus Gregory) acquired any duty to protect Anthony that it otherwise would not have under *DeShaney*; and second, whether that duty extends to dangers beyond the household in which the DCFS and Gregory placed Anthony. We understand Gregory to answer "no" to both inquiries. Our analysis begins with review of *DeShaney*.

A.   DeShaney

In *DeShaney*, the Court held that due process did not require the state to protect a child from the abuse he suffered at the hands of his father. Joshua DeShaney had repeatedly been taken to the local emergency room with injuries that physicians suspected were due to physical abuse. At one point Joshua was temporarily placed in the custody of the hospital while a "Child Protection Team" evaluated his situation; however, the Team determined there was insufficient evidence that he was being abused to retain custody. Joshua was returned to his father's custody and, despite subsequent hospital admissions for injuries indicative of abuse, local officials failed to intervene. Ultimately, his father beat Joshua so severely that he was expected to spend the remainder of his life in an institution for the profoundly retarded.

Despite the fact that local officials had suspected ongoing abuse, the Court rejected the contention that they had deprived Joshua of his liberty in violation of due process by taking no action:

> Nothing in the language of the Due Process Clause itself requires the State to protect the life, liberty, and property of its citizens against invasion by private actors. The Clause is phrased as a limitation on the State's power to act, not as a guarantee of certain minimal levels of safety and security. It forbids the State itself to deprive individuals of life, liberty, or property without "due process of law," but its language cannot fairly be extended to impose an affirmative obligation on the State to ensure that those interests do not come to harm through other means. Nor does history support such an expansive reading of the constitutional text.... Its purpose was to protect the people from the State, not to ensure that the State protected them from each other. The Framers were content to leave the extent of governmental obligation in the latter area to the democratic political processes.

The Court acknowledged that "in certain limited circumstances the Constitution imposes upon the State affirmative duties of care and protection with respect to particular individuals." 489 U.S. at 198. Thus, when someone is incarcerated, the Eighth Amendment (via the Fourteenth) requires the State to provide him with adequate medical care. Estelle v. Gamble, 429 U.S. 97, 97 S. Ct. 285, 50 L. Ed. 2d 251 (1976). Similarly, substantive due process compels the State to take reasonable steps to ensure the safety of individuals involuntarily committed to its mental facilities. Youngberg v. Romeo, 457 U.S. 307, 102 S. Ct. 2452, 73 L. Ed. 2d 28 (1982).

But these cases afford petitioners no help. Taken together, they stand only for the proposition that when the State takes a person into its custody and hold[s] him there against his will, the Constitution imposes upon it a corresponding duty to assume some responsibility for his safety and general well-being. The rationale for this principle is simple enough: when the State by the affirmative exercise of its power so restrains an individual's liberty that it renders him unable to care for himself, and at the same time fails to provide for his basic human needs—e.g., food, clothing, shelter, medical care, and reasonable safety—it transgresses the substantive limits on state action set by the Eighth Amendment and the Due Process Clause. The affirmative duty to protect arises not from the State's knowledge of the individual's predicament or from its expressions of intent to help him, but from the limitation which it has imposed on his freedom to act on his own behalf. In the substantive due process analysis, it is the State's affirmative act of restraining the individuals's freedom to act on his own behalf—through incarceration, institutionalization, or other similar restraint of personal liberty—which is the "deprivation of liberty" triggering the protections of the Due Process Clause, not its failure to act to protect his liberty interests against harms inflicted by other means.

The *Estelle-Youngberg* analysis simply has no applicability in the present case. Petitioners concede that the harms Joshua suffered occurred not while he was in the State's custody, but while he was in the custody of his natural father, who was in no sense a state actor. While the State may have been aware of the dangers that Joshua faced in the free world, it played no part in their creation, nor did it do anything to render him any more vulnerable to them. That the State took temporary custody of Joshua does not alter the analysis, for when it returned him to his father's custody, it placed him in no worse position than that in which he would have been had it not acted at all; the State does not become the permanent guarantor of an individuals's safety by having once offered him shelter. Under these circumstances, the State had no constitutional duty to protect Joshua.

B.   Gregory's Duty to Protect Anthony Generally

In essence, Gregory argues that this case is on all fours with *DeShaney*, and that he bore no duty to protect Anthony from a danger that neither he nor the State played any role in creating. Likewise, although it was Gregory who made the decision to return Anthony to the Camp household after a court had made the DCFS his guardian, Gregory reasons that in doing so he placed Anthony in no worse position than if he had taken no action whatsoever.

We believe the fact that the DCFS had been made Anthony's guardian represents a key point of distinction from *DeShaney*, however. Camp had sought to surrender her own guardianship responsibilities because she believed she could not provide him adequate care and supervision. With the agreement of both Camp and the state, the complaint tells us, the court made the DCFS Anthony's guardian. At that juncture, whether the DCFS had a duty to intervene on Anthony's behalf was moot; it had already assumed a role that made it constitutionally liable (at least to some extent) for Anthony's well-being.

That the DCFS had a cognizable duty to protect Anthony as his guardian is reflected in a series of cases holding government officials liable for placing minors in foster homes where they suffered abuse or neglect. Prominent among these is our opinion in K.H. through Murphy v. Morgan, 914 F.2d 846 (7th Cir.1990), which post-dates *DeShaney*. In that case, an abused child who had been removed from the custody of her parents was then shuffled among a series of foster homes in which she continued to suffer abuse and was deprived of the special care she required in view of her history. The child sued DCFS officials, contending that they had deprived her of due process by placing her in foster homes that they knew to be either abusive or unable to care for her properly. We agreed that the plaintiff might have a viable claim in this circumstance. We noted at the outset that the Due Process Clause quite clearly prohibits a public officer from intentionally harming an individual physically without justification, citing, inter alia, K. H. v. Morgan, 914 F.2d at 848. "The extension [of this principle] to the case in which the plaintiff's mental health is seriously impaired by deliberate and unjustified action is," we observed, "straightforward." Id. We proceeded to distinguish *DeShaney*:

> This is not a "positive liberties" case, like *DeShaney*, where the question was whether the Constitution entitles a child to governmental protection against physical abuse by his parents or other private persons not acting under the direction of the state.... Here, in contrast, the state removed a child from the custody of her parents; having done so, it could no more place her in a position of danger, deliberately and without justification, without thereby violating her rights under the due process clause of the Fourteenth Amendment than it could deliberately and without justification place a criminal defendant in a jail or prison in which his health or safety would be endangered, without violating his rights either under the cruel and unusual punishments clause of the Eighth Amendment (held applicable to the states through the Fourteenth Amendment) if he was a convicted prisoner, or the due process clause if he was awaiting trial. In either case the state would be a doer of harm rather than merely an inept rescuer, just as the Roman state was a doer of harm when it threw Christians to the lions.

> The Roman analogy is sound even if one concedes, as one must in the light of *DeShaney*, that the State of Illinois has no constitutional obligation to protect children from physical or sexual abuse by their parents. The state could have left K.H. to the tender mercies of her parents without thereby violating her rights under the Constitution. But having removed her from their custody the state assumed at least a limited responsibility for her safety.... The Illinois Department of

Children and Family Services could not have subjected K.H. to sexual abuse and then defended on the ground that by doing this it did not make her any worse off than she would have been had she been left with her parents.... Once the state assumes custody of a person, it owes him a rudimentary duty of safekeeping no matter how perilous his circumstances were when he was free. The distinction follows the lines of tort law. There is no duty to rescue a bystander in distress, but having rescued him from certain death you are not privileged to kill him. This is not to say that you assume responsibility for his future welfare. You do not. Our point is only that the absence of a duty to rescue does not entitle the rescuer to harm the person whom he has rescued.

Consistent with our analysis in *K.H.*, cases from our sister circuits also recognize that public officials may be held liable for damages when they place a child in a foster home knowing or having reason to know that the child is likely to suffer harm there. Doe v. New York City Dep't of Social Servs., 649 F.2d 134 (2d Cir.1981). [Cc]

Indeed, the Supreme Court in *DeShaney* was itself careful to acknowledge and distinguish this line of authority. Although the Court expressed no view on the validity of these cases, it did note that the state's placement of a child in a foster home presented a question distinct from the state's obligation to intervene in the first instance. [C] Thus, as our opinion in *K.H.* reflects, *DeShaney* does not preclude liability when the state, as guardian of a child, places that child in an environment where harm results. [Cc]

To be sure, there are differences between this case and *K.H.* First among them is that Gregory is not alleged to have placed Anthony in an abusive home, at least not one we would normally think of as abusive. The complaint does not suggest that anyone in the Camp household was prone to strike Anthony, or to molest him, or to deprive him of food or clothing, or to denigrate him emotionally. The focus of *K.H.* was confined to this realm: "The only right in question in this case is the right of a child in state custody not to be handed over by state officers to a foster parent or other custodian, private or public, whom the state knows or suspects to be a child abuser." 914 F.2d at 852. Camp moves a step beyond this narrow right; her theory is that Gregory knowingly returned Anthony to a household that could not supervise and guide Anthony to the degree he required. This is a theory that *K.H.* neither addressed nor endorsed. Yet, it is not one we are prepared to reject out of hand. It is no great leap to suggest that the adult custodian of a child is obligated not only to feed and clothe the child and refrain from hurting him either physically or mentally, but to monitor his activities and to step in to prevent him from harming himself. The examples spring easily to mind when the child in question is particularly young—keeping him away from electrical sockets and out of medicine cabinets, for example. As a child grows older we presume, barring some disability, that he is increasingly able to exercise his own judgment and keep himself out of harm's way. Yet, the custodial duty of supervision continues—ensuring that the child returns home at a safe hour, that he attends school, and that he does not abuse drugs or alcohol. Thus, we do not suppose that anyone would think it appropriate for the DCFS to knowingly place a child with adults who provided food, shelter, and clothing, but who routinely left the child unattended and unsupervised—be that child six years old or sixteen. [Cc] Indeed, DCFS regulations explicitly incorporate the responsibility of supervision in the criteria for foster parents. [C] Thus, we believe a child placed in the guardianship of the state has a due process right not to be placed by the state with a custodian whom the state knows will fail to exercise the requisite degree of supervision over the child. This is precisely the right that Camp alleges Gregory denied to Anthony; and it is the denial of that right, she further alleges, which resulted in Anthony's death.

In this case, of course, Gregory did not place Anthony with a stranger, but returned him to his aunt. That fact is important for two reasons. First, our cases acknowledge a difference between the state placing a child with a relative and placing him with a foster home. Second, *DeShaney* emphasized that although the state may have been aware of the danger that Joshua faced in his family's home, it had done nothing to create those dangers nor had it done anything rendering Joshua more vulnerable to them. Neither of these points necessarily bars Camp's claim, however, in view of the facts alleged.

In *K.H.*, we acknowledged that "there is indeed a difference between placing a child with a member of her family and placing the child with a foster parent" [c], explaining that "state employees who withhold a child from her family run the risk of being sued by the family for infringing their liberty of familial association, and we do not want to place child welfare workers on a razor's edge—damned if they return the child to its family and damned if they retain custody of the child or place him in a foster home or institution" [C]. That concern is not implicated here, however. Camp, after all, had affirmatively sought to terminate her guardianship over Anthony because she believed herself unable to provide the degree of care and supervision he required, and the state court apparently agreed. Thus, Gregory faced no peril in removing Anthony from the Camp household—that is exactly what Camp wanted, and it was a desire she unequivocally reiterated when she wrote to Gregory just prior to Anthony's death. Moreover, the DCFS did not relinquish its guardianship over Anthony when Gregory decided to return Anthony to the Camp household rather than seek an alternate placement immediately. Thus, to the extent Gregory and the DCFS bore a duty for Anthony's safety when it was appointed guardian, that duty did not terminate when Anthony was placed again with Camp.

Moreover, given the circumstances leading to the appointment of the DCFS as Anthony's guardian, we believe that the alleged danger he encountered in the Camp household due to Camp's inability to care for him adequately is one that may be attributed to Gregory. Again, we must distinguish this case from *DeShaney*. Had the state simply turned a deaf ear to Camp's pleas in the first instance, it would have no constitutional liability under *DeShaney*. But once the DCFS became Anthony's guardian, Gregory shouldered a responsibility to provide Anthony with a safe environment. When he returned Anthony to an environment he allegedly knew to be inadequate, Gregory might be said to have resurrected the danger that had motivated Camp to surrender guardianship in the first place.

Gregory maintains nonetheless that he could not have violated Anthony's liberty interest because he did nothing to interfere with Anthony's ability to avoid or extricate himself from dangerous situations or with Camp's ability to help him do so. This argument derives from a series of cases recognizing that state officials who might not otherwise have a cognizable duty to rescue a person from harm expose themselves to liability when they prevent others from coming to that individual's aid. See Ross v. United States, 910 F.2d 1422, 1432–33 (7th Cir.1990) (collecting cases) [Cc]. Arguing the converse of that principle here, Gregory suggests that because he did nothing to confine Anthony in a physically harmful situation, and because nothing he did prevented Camp from coming to Anthony's aid and extricating him from danger, he in no way deprived Anthony of liberty. This argument is misplaced. Even if we assume that Gregory's conduct in no way interfered with the ability of any private citizens (including Camp and Anthony himself) to ''rescue'' Anthony from the dangers that culminated in his death, that assumption does not detract from the affirmative duty to intervene on Anthony's behalf which sprang from the DCFS being made his guardian.

This is not a case in which a public official is charged with hampering private efforts to aid a victim, but rather one based on the official's failure, as his appointed guardian, to come to that victim's aid himself. At the same time, the notion that Gregory did nothing which interfered with Camp's efforts to protect Anthony or that precluded Anthony from helping himself is not necessarily accurate. As far as Anthony is concerned, it is not at all implausible to assume that as a minor, and particularly one with special educational and custodial needs, he may not have possessed the degree of maturity necessary to extricate himself from potentially harmful situations. And, indeed, that is the crux of Camp's claim—that Anthony required a heightened level of supervision, guidance, and instruction that she could not provide. Furthermore, if what Anthony really needed was a different caretaker, then Camp's own attempts to secure him one presumably were halted once the court appointed the DCFS Anthony's guardian. At that juncture, we assume, Camp was not free simply to relocate Anthony to a different household; nor, needless to say, was Anthony himself able to do so as an unemancipated minor. That ability had been officially turned over to Gregory; and at a minimum, we may suppose that Camp believed he would shoulder the burden of either finding a different placement for Anthony or supplementing Camp's efforts by providing the educational and counseling references she sought.

Camp did relinquish her guardianship over Anthony voluntarily, whereas a number of foster care cases have stressed the involuntary character of the change in guardianship as key to recognizing a due process claim. [Cc] But in this case Camp sought to surrender guardianship allegedly because she was unable to care for Anthony adequately, the court presumably agreed when it granted her request, and the state did assume guardianship. We are unwilling to decree that simply because Camp, as opposed to the state, initiated the transfer of guardianship, under no set of facts could a state official be liable for a subsequent deprivation of due process. [C]

We also find it significant that Gregory allegedly misrepresented to the Illinois court that all was well with Anthony's continued residence in the Camp household. If, in fact, he did so, he may have effectively prevented any independent assessment by that court of whether the concerns that had led to the DCFS' guardianship were being addressed. Camp's entreaties to Gregory suggest that nothing had changed; but Gregory allegedly concealed that fact from the court. Thus, in a very real sense, it could be said (if the facts bear out the complaint) that Gregory did frustrate the efforts of other private persons and public officials to improve Anthony's situation.

C.   Duty to Protect Anthony from Violence Outside of the Home

Whether Gregory's duty extended to dangers outside of the household to which he had returned Anthony is a more novel and difficult question. Gregory argues that this aspect of Camp's claim makes the case even more compelling for him than DeShaney. In one sense he is no doubt correct. Government officials can and routinely do make assessments of the adults with whom children under the state's guardianship are placed. Thus, as we recognized in *K.H.*, if a DCFS caseworker places a child in a foster home where he knows the child will likely suffer abuse, he can be held liable. But to place on the caseworker a duty to evaluate and protect a child from dangers outside of the household is a great step beyond that. Given the widespread escalation of violence we have witnessed over the years, many a child may be in danger of injury at the hands of strangers when he is outside of his home, and public officials cannot be deemed constitutionally obligated to shield a child from all such dangers beyond the reasonable control of his parent or foster parent any more than the parents themselves can be.

Even so, a parent does not relinquish all responsibility once a child leaves the house. No one would think it reasonable, for example, for a parent to knowingly permit a toddler to wander the streets at will, confronting a gamut of risks from inattentive motorists to Mr. or Ms. Stranger Danger. We expect, instead, that the parent will have the child in hand, protecting him from danger that the child is otherwise unequipped to avoid. As the child matures, the degree to which his parent is expected to supervise his activities lessens, but it does not cease altogether. We still expect parents to see to it that their children attend school, obey statutory curfews, and stay out of trouble. Parents are not the insurers of their children's conduct, but when they fail to exercise a reasonable degree of supervision, they can be held liable for their omissions. See, e.g., Restatement (Second) of Torts § 316 (1965).

Commensurate with the parental obligation to supervise a child's activities outside the home is a duty on the part of the state not to place one of its charges with an adult that it knows will not or cannot exercise that responsibility. The DCFS regulations governing placement with relative caretakers recognize that responsibility, specifying as a pre-condition to approval that the DCFS staff must find that "supervision of the related child(ren) can be assured at all times including times when the related caregiver is employed or otherwise engaged in activity outside of the home." [C] Thus, we believe that when a DCFS caseworker places a child in a home knowing that his caretaker cannot provide reasonable supervision, and the failure to provide that degree of supervision and care results in injury to the child outside of the home, it might be appropriate, depending upon the facts culminating in the injury, for the caseworker to be held liable for a deprivation of liberty.

Liability must, nonetheless, be confined to what we believe will be a very narrow range of cases. Without attempting to identify all of the factors that might limit this category, we mention a few that come readily to mind. First, before a DCFS worker or other state official can be held liable for a placement decision, he must, as we indicated in *K.H.*, have failed to exercise bona fide professional judgment. [C] Second, a caretaker can be expected only to provide a reasonable degree of supervision to a minor in her care. Extraordinary efforts to protect a child from dangers outside of the home might save the child from injury when reasonable measures would not, but only when the caretaker's efforts fall short of the reasonable could the official responsible for placing the child with that caretaker be held liable for the resulting injury. Moreover, the injury suffered must, we believe, be one reasonably foreseeable to the official. A caseworker who is aware that the caretaker he selects will not supervise the child appropriately may not be able to foresee the particular injury that will result from the lack of supervision. If that is the case, then it would be inappropriate to impose liability on the caseworker. But here, Camp alleges that she had placed Gregory on notice of the particular problems resulting from her inability to supervise and guide Anthony to the degree necessary. Finally, we stress that there must be a sufficient causal link between the failure to provide reasonable supervision and the injury. If Anthony were killed at random in a drive-by shooting while he was out for a walk after curfew, for example, there would be no basis to impose liability on Gregory even if he knew Camp was unable to supervise him reasonably. Likewise, if Anthony was so bent on engaging in dangerous activity that even reasonable efforts to restrain him from doing so would not have prevailed, it would be untenable to hold Gregory liable for his decision to leave him with Camp.

Because the complaint does not detail the particular circumstances of Anthony's death, we cannot say one way or another whether this case would fit the criteria we have articulated. In light of our conclusion below that Gregory is entitled to qualified immunity, it does not matter; no factual development of the case is required.

* * *

[W]e cannot say that the amended complaint failed to state a claim upon which relief could be granted.

D.   Qualified Immunity

A public official who has deprived someone of his constitutional right may nonetheless enjoy immunity from an award of damages if his actions were "objectively reasonable, meaning that [if] '[his] conduct does not violate clearly established statutory or constitutional rights of which a reasonable person would have known,' " he is immune from an action for civil damages. Supreme Video, Inc. v. Schauz, 15 F.3d 1435, 1438–39 (7th Cir.1994) (quoting Harlow v. Fitzgerald, 457 U.S. 800, 818 (1982)).

* * *

CONCLUSION

Although we believe that Camp's complaint alleged facts sufficient to state a claim for the deprivation of Anthony's liberty in violation of his Fourteenth Amendment right to substantive due process, we also conclude that Gregory is entitled to qualified immunity. Because Camp did not argue below that her complaint stated a separate procedural due process claim, we deem any such argument waived and need not consider its merits.

AFFIRMED

NOTES AND QUESTIONS

1.   The theatres of litigation began with prisons but have vigorously moved to state child services and to the schoolhouse. In Daniels v. Williams, 474 U.S. 327 (1986), the Court held that an official negligently causing loss or injury to life, liberty or property does not violate due process rights. The Due Process Clause does not extend a duty of due care to prisoners: Davidson v. Cannon, 474 U.S. 344 (1986). Much litigation has attended the protection of school pupils from sexual harassment and other abuse while in school. The questions in these cases are whether the student is in a special relationship denoted by control and whether the school has maintained a policy, practice, or custom of deliberate indifference: Stoneking v. Bradford Area School Dist., 882 F. 2d 720 (3d Cir.1989) (finding liability); but cf. Maldonado v. Josey, 975 F. 2d 727 (10th Cir.1992) (no liability); and Johnson v. Dallas Independent School Dist., 38 F.3d 198 (5th Cir.1994), cert. denied 514 U.S. 1017 (1995) (no liability). The courts are reluctant to extend liability beyond sexual abuse: Abeyta v. Chama Valley Independent School Dist., 77 F. 3d 1253 (10th Cir.1996) (no liability for constantly calling a student a "prostitute"). Concerns about the prevalence and incidence of sexual abuse have spurred litigation in an area where the courts have historically exercised protective jurisdiction. For a case in contrast, see Wooten v. Campbell, 49 F.3d 696 (11th Cir.1995) (no state custody therefore no liability). In claims based on denial of substantive due process as in the principal case, the courts require that the behavior of the officer is so egregious, so outrageous, that it may be said to "shock the contemporary

conscience." The need for this high threshold is dictated by the need to "preserve the constitutional proportions of constitutional claims, lest the Constitution be demoted to what [the Court has] called a font of tort law." County of Sacramento v. Lewis, 523 U.S. 833, 847, footnote 8 (1998) (holding that a high-speed police chase, albeit unreasonable, did not "shock the conscience" to found an action).

2.   In Stevens v. Umsted, 131 F.3d 697 (7th Cir.1997), plaintiff brought an action under § 1983 against the superintendent of the Illinois School for the Visually Impaired. The plaintiff's father complained that his son, while under the care of the School, was repeatedly sexually assaulted by other students. The court found no claim could be established because, unlike the principal case, no custody had been given over by the state.

3.   Many ills of modern society are catalogued in these claims. In Pinder v. Johnson, 54 F.3d 1169 (4th Cir.1995), plaintiff's children died in a fire. The perpetrator of the arson had been taken into custody earlier in the evening for an attempted arson. Plaintiff asked defendant, a police officer, whether it would be safe to leave her children and go to work in view of this attempted arson and others in the past. Defendant assured plaintiff that the perpetrator would be held in custody. He was not. He returned and carried out his plan. Judge Wilkinson, recounting the "genuinely tragic" circumstances and applying *DeShaney*, could not find the sufficient "custodial relationship" upon which to base an "affirmative constitutional duty." Promises alone do not create the required "special relationship." Moreover, it was held that an immunity covered defendant's acts because of the embryonic quality of the law.

4.   Section 1983 is not the only source of private right of action. Title IX, 20 U.S.C. § 1681(a) provides: "no person in the United States shall, on the basis of sex, be excluded from participation in, be denied the benefits of, or be subjected to discrimination under any education program or activity receiving Federal financial assistance." 20 U.S.C. § 1681(a).

In Gebser v. Lago Vista Independent School Dist., 524 U.S. 274 (1998), the Court held that a school district may be liable for damages under Title IX where it is deliberately indifferent to known acts of teacher-student sexual harassment. Pointing out that the common law holds liable those put on notice of the tortious actions of third parties, the Court in Davis v. Monroe County Board of Education, 526 U.S. 629 (1999) held that Title IX liability could obtain where the abuse or harassment was "student-on-student." "Deliberate indifference," intentional breach of a clear right, and control must be established.

5.   The principal case utilizes causation rules and duty of care analysis canvassed in Chapter 8. The *Davis* case supra note 4 also draws on common-law duty of care. Do you agree that the common law would fix a school board with liability in the circumstances in *Davis*? Title IX extends to universities. Do you see a problem?

Memphis Community School Dist. v. Stachura

Supreme Court of the United States, 1986.
477 U.S. 299, 106 S.Ct. 2537, 91 L.Ed.2d 249.

[Respondent, a tenured teacher in the Memphis, Michigan, public schools, was suspended following parents' complaints about his teaching methods in a 7th–grade life science course that included the showing of allegedly sexually explicit pictures and films. While respondent was later reinstated, he, before being reinstated, brought suit in Federal District Court under 42 U.S.C. § 1983 against petitioner School District, Board of Education, Board Members, school administrators, and parents, alleging that his suspension deprived him of liberty and property without due process of law and violated his First Amendment right to academic freedom. He sought both compensatory and punitive damages. The District Court instructed the jury on the standard elements of compensatory and punitive damages and also charged the jury that additional compensatory damages could be awarded based on the value or importance of the constitutional rights that were violated. The jury found petitioners liable, awarding both compensatory and punitive damages. The Court of Appeals affirmed. (Facts from official syllabus.)]

JUSTICE POWELL delivered the opinion of the Court. * * *

We granted certiorari limited to the question whether the Court of Appeals erred in affirming the damages award in the light of the District Court's instructions that authorized not only compensatory and punitive damages, but also damages for the deprivation of "any constitutional right." 474 U.S. 918, 106 S.Ct. 245, 88 L.Ed.2d 254 (1985). We reverse, and remand for a new trial limited to the issue of compensatory damages. * * *

We have repeatedly noted that 42 U.S.C. § 1983 creates " 'a species of tort liability' in favor of persons who are deprived of 'rights, privileges, or immunities secured' to them by the Constitution." Carey v. Piphus, 435 U.S. 247, 253 (1978). [Cc] Accordingly, when § 1983 plaintiffs seek damages for violations of constitutional rights, the level of damages is ordinarily determined according to principles derived from the common law of torts. [Cc]

Punitive damages aside, damages in tort cases are designed to provide "*compensation* for the injury caused to plaintiff by defendant's breach of duty." 2 F. Harper & F. James, Law of Torts § 25.1, p. 1299 (1956) (emphasis in original), quoted in Carey v. Piphus, supra. [Cc] To that end, compensatory damages may include not only out-of-pocket loss and other monetary harms, but also such injuries as "impairment of reputation * * *, personal humiliation, and mental anguish and suffering." Gertz v. Robert Welch, Inc., 418 U.S. 323, 350 (1974). See also Carey v. Piphus, supra, 435 U.S., at 264 (mental and emotional distress constitute compensable injury in § 1983 cases). Deterrence is also an important purpose of this system, but it operates through the mechanism of damages that are *compensatory*—damages grounded in determinations of plaintiffs' actual losses. * * * Congress adopted this common-law system of recovery when it established liability for "constitutional torts." Consequently, "the basic purpose" of § 1983 damages is "to *compensate persons for injuries* that are caused by the deprivation of constitutional rights." Carey v. Piphus, 435 U.S., at 254 (emphasis added). See also *id.*, at 257 ("damages awards under § 1983 should be governed by the principle of compensation").

Carey v. Piphus represents a straightforward application of these principles. * * * Where no injury was present, no "compensatory" damages could be awarded.

The instructions at issue here cannot be squared with *Carey,* or with the principles of tort damages on which *Carey* and § 1983 are grounded. The jurors in this case were told that, in determining how much was necessary to "compensate [respondent] for the deprivation" of his constitutional rights, they should place a money value on the "rights" themselves by considering such factors as the particular right's "importance * * * in our system of government," its role in American history, and its "significance * * * in the context of the activities" in which respondent was engaged. These factors focus, not on compensation for provable injury, but on the jury's subjective perception of the importance of constitutional rights as an abstract matter. *Carey* establishes that such an approach is impermissible. The constitutional right transgressed in *Carey*—the right to due process of law—is central to our system of ordered liberty. We nevertheless held that *no* compensatory damages could be awarded for violation of that right absent proof of actual injury. *Carey,* 435 U.S., at 264. *Carey* thus makes clear that the abstract value of a constitutional right may not form the basis for § 1983 damages.[11]

Respondent nevertheless argues that *Carey* does not control here, because in this case a *substantive* constitutional right—respondent's First Amendment right to academic freedom—was infringed. The argument misperceives our analysis in *Carey.* That case does not establish a two-tiered system of constitutional rights, with substantive rights afforded greater protection than "mere" procedural safeguards. We did acknowledge in *Carey* that "the elements and prerequisites for recovery of damages" might vary depending on the interests protected by the constitutional right at issue. [C] But we emphasized that, whatever the constitutional basis for § 1983 liability, such damages must always be designed "to *compensate injuries* caused by the [constitutional] deprivation." [Cc] That conclusion simply leaves no room for noncompensatory damages measured by the jury's perception of the abstract "importance" of a constitutional right.

Nor do we find such damages necessary to vindicate the constitutional rights that § 1983 protects. See n. 11, *supra.* Section 1983 presupposes that damages that compensate for actual harm ordinarily suffice to deter constitutional violations. * * *

Moreover, damages based on the "value" of constitutional rights are an unwieldy tool for ensuring compliance with the Constitution. History

---

11. We did approve an award of nominal damages for the deprivation of due process in *Carey.* 435 U.S., at 266. Our discussion of that issue makes clear that nominal damages, and not damages based on some undefinable "value" of infringed rights, are the appropriate means of "vindicating" rights whose deprivation has not caused actual, provable injury:

"Common-law courts traditionally have vindicated deprivations of certain 'absolute' rights that are not shown to have caused actual injury through the award of a nominal sum of money. By making the deprivation of such rights actionable for nominal damages without proof of actual injury, the law recognizes the importance to organized society that those rights be scrupulously observed; but at the same time, it remains true to the principle that substantial damages should be awarded only to compensate actual injury or, in the case of exemplary or punitive damages, to deter or punish malicious deprivations of rights." *Ibid.*

and tradition do not afford any sound guidance concerning the precise value that juries should place on constitutional protections. Accordingly, were such damages available, juries would be free to award arbitrary amounts without any evidentiary basis, or to use their unbounded discretion to punish unpopular defendants. [C] Such damages would be too uncertain to be of any great value to plaintiffs, and would inject caprice into determinations of damages in § 1983 cases. We therefore hold that damages based on the abstract "value" or "importance" of constitutional rights are not a permissible element of compensatory damages in such cases. * * *

Respondent further argues that the challenged instructions authorized a form of "presumed" damages—a remedy that is both compensatory in nature and traditionally part of the range of tort law remedies. Alternatively, respondent argues that the erroneous instructions were at worst harmless error.

Neither argument has merit. Presumed damages are a *substitute* for ordinary compensatory damages, not a *supplement* for an award that fully compensates the alleged injury. When a plaintiff seeks compensation for an injury that is likely to have occurred but difficult to establish, some form of presumed damages may possibly be appropriate. [Cc]

In those circumstances, presumed damages may roughly approximate the harm that the plaintiff suffered and thereby compensate for harms that may be impossible to measure. As we earlier explained, the instructions at issue in this case did not serve this purpose, but instead called on the jury to measure damages based on a subjective evaluation of the importance of particular constitutional values. Since such damages are wholly divorced from any compensatory purpose, they cannot be justified as presumed damages.[14] Moreover, no rough substitute for compensatory damages was

---

14. For the same reason, *Nixon v. Herndon,* 273 U.S. 536 (1927), and similar cases do not support the challenged instructions. * * *

Nixon followed a long line of cases, going back to Lord Holt's decision in *Ashby v. White,* 2 Ld.Raym. 938, 92 Eng.Rep. 126 (1703), authorizing substantial money damages as compensation for persons deprived of their right to vote in particular elections. [Cc] Although these decisions sometimes speak of damages for the value of the right to vote, their analysis shows that they involve nothing more than an award of presumed damages for a non-monetary harm that cannot easily be quantified:

"In the eyes of the law th[e] right [to vote] is so valuable that damages are presumed from the wrongful deprivation of it without evidence of actual loss of money, property, or any other valuable thing, and

the amount of the damages is a question peculiarly appropriate for the determination of the jury, because each member of the jury has personal knowledge of the value of the right." *Ibid.* * * *

See also *Ashby v. White, supra,* at 955, 92 Eng.Rep., at 137 (Holt, C.J.) ("As in an action for slanderous words, though a man does not lose a penny by reason of the speaking [of] them, yet he shall have an action"). The "value of the right" in the context of these decisions is the money value of the particular loss that the plaintiff suffered—a loss of which "each member of the jury has personal knowledge." It is *not* the value of the right to vote as a general, abstract matter, based on its role in our history or system of government. Thus, whatever the wisdom of these decisions in the context of the changing scope of compensatory damages over the course of this century, they do not support awards of non-compensatory damages such as those authorized in this case.

required in this case, since the jury was fully authorized to compensate respondent for both monetary and non-monetary harms caused by petitioners' conduct.

Nor can we find that the erroneous instructions were harmless. [Cc] When damages instructions are faulty and the verdict does not reveal the means by which the jury calculated damages, "[the] error in the charge is difficult, if not impossible, to correct without retrial, in light of the jury's general verdict." [C]

The jury was authorized to award three categories of damages: (i) compensatory damages for injury to respondent, (ii) punitive damages, and (iii) damages based on the jury's perception of the "importance" of two provisions of the Constitution. The submission of the third of these categories was error. * * *

The judgment of the Court of Appeals is reversed, and the case is remanded for further proceedings consistent with this opinion.

JUSTICE MARSHALL, with whom JUSTICE BRENNAN, JUSTICE BLACKMUN, and JUSTICE STEVENS join, concurring in the judgment.

I agree with the Court that this case must be remanded for a new trial on damages. Certain portions of the Court's opinion, however, can be read to suggest that damages in § 1983 cases are necessarily limited to "out-of-pocket loss," "other monetary harms," and "such injuries as 'impairment of reputation * * *, personal humiliation, and mental anguish and suffering.' "

I do not understand the Court so to hold, and I write separately to emphasize that the violation of a constitutional right, in proper cases, may itself constitute a compensable injury. * * *

Following *Carey*, the courts of appeals have recognized that invasions of constitutional rights sometimes cause injuries that cannot be redressed by a wooden application of common-law damages rules. In Hobson v. Wilson, 237 U.S.App.D.C. 219, 275–281, 737 F.2d 1, 57–63 (1984), [c] plaintiffs claimed that defendant FBI agents had invaded their First Amendment rights to assemble for peaceable political protest, to associate with others to engage in political expression, and to speak on public issues free of unreasonable government interference. The District Court found that the defendants had succeeded in diverting plaintiffs from, and impeding them in, their protest activities. The Court of Appeals for the District of Columbia Circuit held that that injury to a First Amendment-protected interest could itself constitute compensable injury wholly apart from any "emotional distress, humiliation and personal indignity, emotional pain, embarrassment, fear, anxiety and anguish" suffered by plaintiffs. [C] The court warned, however, that that injury could be compensated with substantial damages only to the extent that it was "reasonably quantifiable"; damages should not be based on "the so-called inherent value of the rights violated."

I believe that the *Hobson* court correctly stated the law. * * * There is no reason why such an injury should not be compensable in damages. At the same time, however, the award must be proportional to the actual loss sustained.

The instructions given the jury in this case were improper because they did not require the jury to focus on the loss actually sustained by respondent. * * *

The Court therefore properly remands for a new trial on damages. I do not understand the Court, however, to hold that deprivations of constitutional rights can never themselves constitute compensable injuries. Such a rule would be inconsistent with the logic of *Carey,* and would defeat the purpose of § 1983 by denying compensation for genuine injuries caused by the deprivation of constitutional rights.

NOTES AND QUESTIONS

1.   On the availability of punitive damages, see Smith v. Wade, 461 U.S. 30 (1983) and Boulder Valley School Dist. R–2 v. Price, 805 P.2d 1085 (Colo.1991). The principal case has been applied broadly. In Heck v. Humphrey, 512 U.S. 477 (1994), the Court held that plaintiff's asserted § 1983 claim could not be established since the corresponding common law action in malicious prosecution would not lie in the circumstances. Thus a § 1983 cause of action for damages attributable to an unconstitutional conviction or sentence does not accrue until the conviction or sentence has been invalidated. Justice Souter, with whom Justices Blackmun, Stevens and O'Connor concurred, warned that while the malicious prosecution analogy was useful in starting analysis, congressional policy was the ultimate lodestar. While formal exhaustion of state remedies is not only unnecessary, but more is inconsistent with the scheme of § 1983, a court may be guided by federal principles, applying Patsy v. Board of Regents of Fla., 457 U.S. 496 (1982).

CHAPTER XX

MISUSE OF LEGAL PROCEDURE

Texas Skaggs, Inc. v. Graves

Court of Civil Appeals of Texas, 1979.
582 S.W.2d 863.

[Suit for malicious prosecution. Plaintiff-appellee, Mrs. Sharon Graves, had "worked as a checker in the Skaggs store but was fired for reasons not material to this case." She continued to purchase groceries at Skaggs and had given the store two checks totaling $34.70. The checking account was in her name, but she had left a few blank checks signed by her at home, for her husband to use. The couple had separated and, unknown to her, her husband had withdrawn all of her funds. She agreed to pay "as soon as she could get the money from the Skaggs' credit union." Over two weeks later, when she received her money from the credit union, she "purchased a money order and mailed it to Skaggs to cover the 'hot' checks."

The next day, Bill Pennington, a Skaggs manager, filed an "Incident Report" with the Texarkana, Arkansas, Police Department reporting Mrs. Graves for a violation of the Arkansas Hot Check Law. Four days later, he filed an affidavit for warrant of her arrest. Over a week later, when Mrs. Graves was shopping in the Skaggs store, a manager summoned the police, who came and arrested her. She tried to explain to police sergeant Larry Arnold that she had paid the checks, but he took her out of the store and to the police station where she was booked on a hot check charge. Arnold then telephoned Skaggs and learned that the checks had, in fact, been paid. Arnold then released Graves and returned the two checks to her (that had been attached to the Affidavit for Warrant of Arrest). Sgt. Arnold talked to an employee of Skaggs again that afternoon and when the person he was talking to learned that Graves had been released, that person (unidentified) told Arnold that he wanted Graves prosecuted and that he did not care if she had paid the checks. The next morning, March 4th, Arnold drove to Sharon Graves' home in Texas and told her that Skaggs intended to prosecute her that afternoon. Mrs. Graves immediately hired an attorney and appeared in Court. The municipal judge dismissed the case when the prosecution could not produce the "hot checks."]

RAY, JUSTICE. * * * In Arkansas, a cause of action for malicious prosecution consists of the following elements: (1) A criminal prosecution instituted or continued by the defendant against the plaintiff; (2) Termination of the proceedings in favor of the accused; (3) Absence of probable cause for the proceeding; (4) Malice; and, (5) Damages. * * *.

In response to special issues, the jury found that Graves did not know that her bank account had insufficient funds for the payment of the two checks; that Skaggs did not have probable cause to institute the prosecution of Sharon Graves; that Skaggs acted with malice; and, that the sum of $20,000.00 would reasonably compensate Graves for her actual damages.

Institution of Criminal Proceedings. The evidence is clear and undisputed that Skaggs initiated and continued the prosecution of Sharon Graves.

Termination of the Proceedings in Favor of the Accused. The record reflects that the case against Graves was dismissed in the Municipal Court of Texarkana, Arkansas, with the notation, "dismissed on basis checks not available for presentation of case." Skaggs argues that this type of termination is indecisive and is not sufficient to establish malicious prosecution. Prosser describes types of termination that are sufficient to sustain a malicious prosecution suit:

"On the other hand, it will be enough that the proceeding is terminated in such a manner that it cannot be revived, and the prosecutor, if he proceeds further, will be put to a new one. This is true, for example, of an acquittal in court, * * * the entry of a nolle prosequi or a dismissal, abandonment of the prosecution by the prosecuting attorney or the complaining witness, * * * where any of these things have the effect of ending the particular proceeding and requiring new process or other official action to commence a new prosecution. It may be said generally, that this is true whenever the charges or the proceeding are withdrawn on the initiative of the prosecution. * * *

"On the other hand, where charges are withdrawn or the prosecution is terminated at the instigation of the accused himself, or by reason of a compromise into which he has entered voluntarily, there is no sufficient termination in favor of the accused. * * * " W. Prosser, Torts Sec. 113, pp. 857, 858 (3rd ed.1964).

Prosser is in accord with the rule established by the Restatement (Second) of Torts, §§ 658, 659 (1977). The abandonment of the proceedings because a conviction has, in the natural course of events, become impossible or improbable, is a sufficient termination in favor of the accused. [C] We are of the opinion that this case was not dismissed on technical or procedural grounds, but was an abandonment of the prosecution by the prosecuting attorney and that the inferences to be drawn from the evidence support that conclusion. We are of the further opinion that because there was a dismissal for lack of incriminating evidence, Graves could have procured a finding of "not guilty" by the municipal court had the matter been pressed for a full trial by the prosecuting attorney. Closely connected with the element of successful termination is the defense that Graves was in fact guilty of the charge. This defense was available even if Graves had been acquitted of the criminal charge. The rational basis is that the law protects only the innocent and, if guilty, the plaintiff deserved the treatment complained of. Thus, Skaggs had the option to assert the defense that

Graves was in fact guilty of the charge. There was apparently some attempt to prove this defense, but the jury rejected it.

Absence of Probable Cause. Graves had the burden of proving that the criminal proceeding was initiated or continued by Skaggs without probable cause; that is, Graves had to show that Skaggs had no honest or reasonable belief in the truth of the charge however suspicious the circumstances of Graves' acts. Probable cause has been defined by the Arkansas Supreme Court in *Hitson v. Sims,* 69 Ark. 439, 441, 64 S.W. 219, 220 (1901), as follows: " * * * such a state of facts known to the prosecutor, or such information received by him from sources entitled to credit, as would induce a man of ordinary caution and prudence to believe, and did induce the prosecutor to believe, that the accused is guilty of the crime alleged, and thereby caused the prosecution * * * "

However, it is stated in 22 Ark.L.Rev. 349: "Liability is imposed on the defendant where there are sufficient facts to indicate to a reasonable man that the plaintiff was guilty but the defendant himself knew better, i.e., a subjective test. Since the test requires more than mere unfounded suspicion the courts will hold a defendant liable in cases where a reasonable man would further investigate the facts."

The facts supporting the jury's finding of lack of probable cause are that Graves was well-known by the employees of Skaggs; that the two checks were relatively small; that the checks were used to pay for groceries alone and that no cash was obtained with the checks; that Graves could have obtained large amounts of cash because she knew all of the Skaggs' employees; that she could have cashed many checks obtaining cash, but did not; that the checks were written on her regular bank account and not some fictitious bank or bank account; that once she was notified that her two checks had been returned to Skaggs, she immediately agreed to make restitution; that Graves in fact mailed her money order to Skaggs prior to the time that prosecution was instituted; that Skaggs was aware of the restitution before her arrest; that Skaggs had agreed to await restitution and to accept payment for the checks when Graves received her money from the Skaggs credit union; that Skaggs, pursuant to its agreement with Graves, had accepted restitution but issued instructions that the prosecution continue; and, that Skaggs further insisted that the prosecution continue after having been apprised of the fact that Mrs. Graves had been arrested and released by the officer after the officer had called one of Skaggs' employees and learned that restitution had been made. From the foregoing facts, and the inferences to be drawn therefrom, the jury could have reasonably concluded that Graves did not intend to defraud Skaggs and that no probable cause existed to institute or continue the prosecution proceedings. As a defense, the burden of persuasion was on Skaggs to show that the complaining witness, Bill Pennington, believed in Graves' guilt at the time the original proceeding commenced and that this belief was supported with facts which would lead a reasonable, cautious or prudent man to the same conclusion, and which in fact did lead Pennington to this conclusion. Pennington was not called as a witness. The jury apparently believed that the testimony of Sharon Graves was more plausible than that of the employees at Skaggs and that Skaggs knew or should have known or found out from further investigation that Graves did not issue the checks knowing at the time of issuing them that she did not have sufficient funds in her bank account to cover the checks. The jury could have further believed that while a reasonable person might have concluded that Graves was guilty, Skaggs' employees knew better and should have further investigated the facts.

The "Arkansas Hot Check Law", Ark.Stat.Ann. Sec. 67–720 (Supp. 1978) provides:

"It shall be unlawful for any person to procure any article or thing of value, * * * or for any other purpose to make or draw or utter or deliver, with intent to defraud, any check, * * * upon any bank, * * * knowing at the time of such making, * * * that the maker, * * * has not sufficient funds in, or on deposit with, such bank, * * * ".

Evidence of the requisite intent to defraud is supplied by Ark.Stat.Ann. Sec. 67–722 which provides that the making of a check, " * * * payment of which is refused by the drawee, shall be prima facie evidence of intent to defraud * * * ". While the statute raises the presumption of intent to defraud, such presumption may be rebutted by evidence explaining the transaction and where the evidence is sufficient to dispel any presumption of intent to defraud, the statute alone will not support a conviction under the Arkansas Hot Check Law. [Cc]. In the present case, there was no intent to defraud because there was ample evidence to support the jury finding that Graves did not know that she had insufficient funds in her bank account at the time of writing the checks with which to make payment of the two checks when they were processed for payment at her bank. And while restitution alone is not an absolute defense to the Arkansas Hot Check Law [c], the fact that Graves immediately agreed to make restitution and did in fact make restitution is some evidence that she did not intend to defraud Skaggs. Certainly, once Graves had made restitution and that fact was coupled with all the other facts known to Skaggs' employees, a conclusion that Skaggs had no probable cause to further insist upon the prosecution of Graves would be justified.

Malice. Regarding the element of malice, it is generally agreed that the lack of probable cause may give rise to an inference of malice, sufficient to carry the question to the jury. W. Prosser, Torts, Sec. 113, p. 868 (3rd ed. 1964). The courts require that malice in fact be shown in order to sustain a recovery for malicious prosecution. This is usually established by proving that the defendant had a wrongful or improper motive or was motivated by some purpose other than bringing a guilty person to justice, such as, using the prosecution as a means to recover property, to extort money, or to collect a debt. " * * * Hence, proof of malice need not be direct but may be inferred from circumstances surrounding the defendant's act. This does not mean the defendant must have acted out of hatred, ill will, spite or grudge." 22 Ark.L.Rev. 340, 353, supra. The jury could and probably did believe that Skaggs instituted the criminal proceedings without probable cause in an effort to collect the two checks. The jury finding that Skaggs acted with malice has ample support in the record. Certainly, Skaggs' insistence that the prosecution continue against Graves after she had been released by Sgt. Arnold following her arrest with the statement to the effect that Skaggs did not care if Graves had paid the checks, Skaggs wanted her prosecuted anyway, supports the inference that Skaggs continued to act maliciously.

Damages. Appellant argues that the jury verdict was so grossly excessive as to show that it was the result of passion, prejudice or other improper motives. No cases are cited to guide this Court in its determination of this issue. The general rule is as follows:

"Although the verdict is large and the trial court, in the exercise of a sound discretion, might properly have set it aside, the appellate court will not disturb the verdict, although it may seem too large, in the absence of circumstances tending to show that it was the result of passion, prejudice, or other improper motive, or that the amount fixed was not the result of a deliberate and conscientious conviction in the minds of the jury and the court, or so excessive as to shock a sense of justice in the minds of the appellate court." 17 Tex.Jur.2d Damages, Sec. 341, p. 415 (1960).

As stated in *Green v. Meadows,* 527 S.W.2d 496 (Tex.Civ.App. Houston–1st Dist. 1975, writ ref'd n.r.e.), there are no objective guidelines by which we can measure the money equivalent of mental pain.

" * * * Much discretion must be allowed the jury in fixing this amount. The trial judge refused to order a remittitur. We are unable to say that the jury's verdict is excessive to the extent that the judgment should be reversed for that reason only. * * * "

In *Green,* the jury had awarded the plaintiff $20,000.00 in a malicious prosecution suit.

The facts in the present case show that Sharon Graves has suffered substantial injury. She was arrested and paraded through the store by a uniformed policeman and the store manager in front of her friends and former fellow employees. She was taken to the police station where she was booked and suffered the humiliation of a criminal charge. She testified that because of this criminal record she was not hired by several prospective employers because of her arrest record which will follow her the rest of her life. The evidence supports the jury verdict. * * *

To recapitulate, the pleadings were adequate to support the judgment; there was sufficient evidence to establish that Skaggs had instituted and continued criminal prosecution against Sharon Graves; there was evidence that the proceeding was terminated in favor of Graves; that the evidence established an absence of probable cause for institution of the criminal proceedings against Graves; that the evidence supports the finding of malice; and, the evidence supports the jury finding of $20,000.00 in damages. * * *

NOTES AND QUESTIONS

1. *Institution of Criminal Proceedings.* This element may be met by (1) indictment or information or (2) the issuance of criminal process to bring the accused before a magistrate whose function is to determine whether he is guilty or is to be held for later determination or (3) arrest on a criminal charge. The commencement must have been either initiated or procured by the private prosecutor, or he must have played an active part in continuing the proceeding. See Wilson v. Yono, 65 Mich.App. 441, 237 N.W.2d 494 (1975); Creelman v. Svenning, 67 Wash.2d 882, 410 P.2d 606 (1966).

2. *Termination in Favor of the Accused.* This element is met by discharge by magistrate at a preliminary hearing, Tritchler v. West Virginia Newspaper Pub. Co. Inc., 156 W.Va. 335, 193 S.E.2d 146 (1972); grand jury refusal to indict, Davis v. Quille, 248 Md. 631, 237 A.2d 745 (1968); a nolle prosequi, Bickford v. Lantay, 394 A.2d 281 (Me.1978); dismissal, Green v. Warnock, 144 Kan. 170, 58 P.2d 1059 (1936); failure to prosecute for lack of evidence, Southern Farmers Ass'n v. Whitfield, 238 Ark. 607, 383 S.W.2d 506 (1964); quashing of indictment, Davis v. McCrory Corp., 262 So.2d 207 (Fla.App.1972); or acquittal, Singer Mfg. Co. v. Bryant, 105 Va. 403, 54 S.E. 320 (1906). It is not met by an indecisive termination, Weissman v. K–Mart Corp., 396 So.2d 1164 (Fla.App.1981); Hoog v. Strauss, 567 S.W.2d 353 (Mo.App.1978); or by the impossibility of bringing the accused to trial, Halberstadt v. New York Life Ins. Co., 194 N.Y. 1, 86 N.E. 801 (1909); however, the abandonment or termination must touch the merits and indicate "accused's innocence." MacFawn v. Kresler, 88 N.Y.2d 859, 666 N.E.2d 1359 (1996); O'Brien v. Alexander, 101 F.3d 1479, 1486 (2d Cir.1996). The disposition of the underlying case need not reach the merits in all circumstances. The Restatement (Second) of Torts § 674, comment *j* (1977) enunciates a test that turns on the "circumstances under which the proceedings are withdrawn." In Cult Awareness Network v. Church of Scientology International, 177 Ill.2d 267, 278–79, 685 N.E.2d 1347, 1353 (1997), the court found that the Restatement's position "best balances the right of citizens to have free access to our courts and the right of the individual to be free from being haled into court without reason, thereby better serving the interests of justice."

3. *Lack of Probable Cause.*

A. *Mistake of Fact.* The private prosecutor must have reasonable grounds for believing that the accused is guilty of the criminal charge. But if the private prosecutor does not honestly believe that the accused was guilty, there is no probable cause. Hanson v. Couch, 360 So.2d 942 (Ala.1978).

A reasonable mistake will not destroy probable cause. The standard is akin to the reasonable person in a negligence case, but the difference is that probable cause is for the court, rather than the jury, to decide. The defendant's subjective knowledge is a question of fact for the jury under proper instructions; but whether, upon established facts, there was probable cause is not left to them. See generally Smith v. Tucker, 304 A.2d 303 (D.C.App.1973); Turner v. City of Chicago, 91 Ill.App.3d 931, 47 Ill.Dec. 476, 415 N.E.2d 481 (1980). If a reasonable person would investigate further to make more certain of the facts before instituting criminal proceedings and the private prosecutor fails to do so, he may be found to have acted without probable cause. Food Fair Stores, Inc. v. Kincaid, 335 So.2d 560 (Fla.App. 1976); Lambert v. Sears, Roebuck & Co., 280 Or. 123, 570 P.2d 357 (1977).

In both Kroger Co. v. Standard, 283 Ark. 44, 670 S.W.2d 803 (1984), and Wal-Mart Stores, Inc. v. Yarbrough, 284 Ark. 345, 681 S.W.2d 359 (1984), a customer was accosted after leaving the store with an article not paid for. Disbelieving the customer's explanation, the store prosecuted for shoplifting and the jury acquitted. Suit for malicious prosecution by the customer, who obtained a jury award of compensatory damages and substantial punitive damages in each. The appellate court affirmed one case and reversed the other, by a divided vote each time.

B.   *Mistake of Law.* A layman who institutes a criminal proceeding without seeking advice of an attorney on whether the supposed facts constitute a crime may be held to have acted without probable cause if they do not; but there may be circumstances under which the conduct is reasonable. See Meadows v. Grant, 15 Ariz.App. 104, 486 P.2d 216 (1971); Ruff v. Eckerds Drugs, Inc., 265 S.C. 563, 220 S.E.2d 649 (1975). Some courts hold, however, that even a reasonable mistake of law will not support probable cause. See Thomas v. Kessler, 334 Pa. 7, 5 A.2d 187 (1939); Atkinson v. Birmingham, 44 R.I. 123, 116 A. 205 (1922).

4.   *Effect of Various Occurrences on Determination of Probable Cause.*

A.   Action of magistrate on preliminary hearing. Discharge is conclusive of lack of probable cause unless it was not on the merits or was based on testimony of the accused at the hearing. Hawkins v. Hawkins, 32 N.C.App. 158, 231 S.E.2d 174 (1977); Huntley v. Harberts, 264 N.W.2d 497 (S.D.1978). Contra, Hoene v. Associated Dry Goods Corp., 487 S.W.2d 479 (Mo.1972). Commitment is evidence that there was probable cause. Davis v. Quille, 248 Md. 631, 237 A.2d 745 (1968). A similar distinction is made regarding action of a grand jury.

B.   Outcome of proceedings. Abandonment by the private prosecutor is evidence of lack of probable cause. See Exxon Corp. v. Kelly, 281 Md. 689, 381 A.2d 1146 (1978). Conviction is usually held to be conclusive on existence of probable cause. Earley v. Harry's I.G.A., Inc., 223 Kan. 32, 573 P.2d 572 (1977); cf. J.C. Penney Co., Inc. v. Blush, 356 So.2d 590 (Miss.1978) (presumption). Acquittal does not have any effect, according to the majority rule. Meyer v. Nedry, 159 Or. 62, 78 P.2d 339 (1938).

C.   Advice of counsel is conclusive on the issue of probable cause, if the advice is sought in good faith and is given after a full and fair disclosure of the facts within the accuser's knowledge and information. Varner v. Hoffer, 267 Or. 175, 515 P.2d 920 (1973); Bain v. Phillips, 217 Va. 387, 228 S.E.2d 576 (1976); Murray v. Wal–Mart, Inc., 874 F.2d 555 (8th Cir.1989) (Arkansas law).

5.   *"Malice."* This troublesome word turns up again in malicious prosecution, and has given its name to the action. Here, it does not necessarily mean hatred, spite or ill will, but rather a purpose in initiating the prosecution other than that of bringing a criminal to justice. "Malice" is constituted where defendant has used the prosecution to extort money from the accused, to recover property from him, to collect a debt, or to compel performance of a contract. Dislike and ill will, which are not uncommon toward any criminal, may not be enough for "malice," if the proper purpose is also found to exist. The courts have tended, however, to look to the primary objective of the defendant. This element is usually left to the jury, unless the facts in evidence permit only one decision. See Restatement (Second) of Torts § 668. It is generally agreed that the jury are to be instructed that lack of probable cause may be evidence of the existence of malice, but that malice is not evidence of lack of probable cause.

6.   *Damages.* The plaintiff must have suffered damage from the prosecution; it is assumed by the law that some damage, such as harm to reputation, will necessarily follow. The same is true of humiliation and other mental suffering. There may, in addition, be recovery for any special damages that the plaintiff can

prove, as for example those for arrest or imprisonment, discomfort or injury to health and expenses, such as attorney's fees, in defending the criminal case. This tort is clearly one appropriate for punitive damages, and it is undisputed that they can be recovered in most jurisdictions, if the jury sees fit to award them.

Malice is an ingredient in the determination of punitive damages. For a discussion of the differences in the meaning of "malice" for the substantive cause of action and for the purposes of determining entitlement for punitive damages, see Sanders v. Daniel International Corporation, 682 S.W.2d 803 (Mo. 1984).

Friedman v. Dozorc

Supreme Court of Michigan, 1981.
412 Mich. 1, 312 N.W.2d 585.

LEVIN, JUSTICE. * * * Leona Serafin entered Outer Drive Hospital in May, 1970, for treatment of gynecological problems. A dilation and curettage was performed by her physician, Dr. Harold Krevsky. While in the hospital, Mrs. Serafin was referred to the present plaintiff, Dr. Friedman, for urological consultation. Dr. Friedman recommended surgical removal of a kidney stone which was too large to pass, and the operation was performed on May 20, 1970. During the surgery, the patient began to ooze blood uncontrollably. Although other physicians were consulted, Mrs. Serafin's condition continued to worsen and she died five days after the surgery. An autopsy was performed the next day; the report identified the cause of death as thrombotic thrombocytopenic purpura, a rare and uniformly fatal blood disease, the cause and cure of which are unknown.

On January 11, 1972, attorneys Dozorc and Golden, the defendants in this action, filed a malpractice action on behalf of Anthony Serafin, Jr., for himself and as administrator of the estate of Leona Serafin, against Peoples Community Hospital Authority, Outer Drive Hospital, Dr. Krevsky and Dr. Friedman, as well as another physician who was dismissed as a defendant before trial. * * * No expert testimony tending to show that any of the defendants had breached accepted professional standards in making the decision to perform the elective surgery or in the manner of its performance was presented as part of the plaintiff's case. The judge entered a directed verdict of no cause of action in favor of Dr. Friedman and the other defendants at the close of the plaintiff's proofs. The judge subsequently denied a motion for costs brought by codefendant Peoples Community Hospital Authority, pursuant to GCR 1963, 111.6. The Court of Appeals affirmed and this Court denied leave to appeal.

Dr. Friedman commenced the present action on March 17, 1976 in Oakland Circuit Court.

[The trial court granted summary judgment for the defendants. The Court of Appeals affirmed in part and reversed in part.]

This Court granted leave to appeal on both the plaintiff's application from that portion of the Court of Appeals decision affirming the dismissal of the causes of action sounding in negligence and abuse of process and on the defendants' application to cross-appeal from that portion of the decision

reversing the dismissal of the cause of action for malicious prosecution.
* * *

Plaintiff and amici in support urge this Court to hold that an attorney owes a present or prospective adverse party a duty of care, breach of which will give rise to a cause of action for negligence. We agree with the circuit judge and the Court of Appeals that an attorney owes no actionable duty to an adverse party.

Plaintiff and amici argue that an attorney who initiates a civil action owes a duty to his client's adversary and all other foreseeable third parties who may be affected by such an action to conduct a reasonable investigation and re-examination of the facts and law so that the attorney will have an adequate basis for a good-faith belief that the client has a tenable claim. Plaintiff contends that this duty is created by the Code of Professional Responsibility and by the Michigan General Court Rules. * * *

In a negligence action the question whether the defendant owes an actionable legal duty to the plaintiff is one of law which the court decides after assessing the competing policy considerations for and against recognizing the asserted duty. * * *

Assuming that an attorney has an obligation to his client to conduct a reasonable investigation prior to bringing an action, that obligation is not the functional equivalent of a duty of care owed to the client's adversary. We decline to so transform the attorney's obligation because we view such a duty as inconsistent with basic precepts of the adversary system. * * *

[C]reation of a duty in favor of an adversary of the attorney's client would create an unacceptable conflict of interest which would seriously hamper an attorney's effectiveness as counsel for his client. Not only would the adversary's interests interfere with the client's interests, the attorney's justifiable concern with being sued for negligence would detrimentally interfere with the attorney-client relationship. * * *

Because * * * a cause of action for negligence in favor of a client's adversary might unduly inhibit attorneys from bringing close cases or advancing innovative theories, or taking action against defendants who can be expected to retaliate, we decline to recognize a duty of due care to the adverse party. * * *

To recover upon a theory of abuse of process, a plaintiff must plead and prove (1) an ulterior purpose and (2) an act in the use of process which is improper in the regular prosecution of the proceeding. * * *

We need not decide whether plaintiff's pleadings sufficiently allege that the defendants had an ulterior purpose in causing process to issue, since it is clear that the plaintiff has failed to allege that defendants committed some irregular act in the use of process. * * * [A] summons and complaint are properly employed when used to institute a civil action, and thus plaintiff has failed to satisfy the second element required. * * *

We note that other courts that have addressed the question whether abuse of process is a possible theory of recovery in the context of a medical malpractice countersuit have found that mere commencement of an action for malpractice is not an improper use of process. [Cc]

Plaintiff relies upon the same allegations respecting defendants' conduct and their failure to meet professional standards which assertedly constitute negligence in contending that he has pled a cause of action for malicious prosecution. He argues that the question of probable cause in a malicious prosecution action against the attorney for an opposing party turns on whether the attorney fulfilled his duty to reasonably investigate the facts and law before initiating and continuing a lawsuit. If the attorney's investigation discloses that the claim is not tenable, then it is his obligation to discontinue the action. * * *

We agree with defendants that under Michigan law special injury remains an essential element of the tort cause of action for malicious prosecution of civil proceedings. * * *

The recognition of an action for malicious prosecution developed as an adjunct to the English practice of awarding costs to the prevailing party in certain aggravated cases where the costs remedy was thought to be inadequate and the defendant had suffered damages beyond the expense and travail normally incident to defending a lawsuit. In 1698 three categories of damage which would support an action for malicious prosecution were identified: injury to one's fame (as by a scandalous allegation), injury to one's person or liberty, and injury to one's property. To this day the English courts do not recognize actions for malicious prosecution of either criminal or civil proceedings unless one of these types of injury, as narrowly defined by the cases, is present.

A substantial number of American jurisdictions today follow some form of "English rule" to the effect that "in the absence of an arrest, seizure, or special damage, the successful civil defendant has no remedy, despite the fact that his antagonist proceeded against him maliciously and without probable cause." A larger number of jurisdictions, some say a majority, follow an "American rule" permitting actions for malicious prosecution of civil proceedings without requiring the plaintiff to show special injury. * * *

The plaintiff's complaint does not allege special injury. We are satisfied that Michigan has not significantly departed from the English rule and we decline to do so today. * * *

Since this Court has not heretofore declared that an action for malicious prosecution of civil proceedings may be maintained in the absence of special injury, it remains to be decided whether we should so hold today. * * *

Most commentators appear to favor abrogation of the special injury requirement to make the action more available and less difficult to maintain. Their counsel should, however, be evaluated skeptically. The lawyer's remedy for a grievance is a lawsuit, and a law student or tort professor may be particularly predisposed by experience and training to see the preferred remedy for a wrongful tort action as another tort action. In seeking a remedy for the excessive litigiousness of our society, we would do well to cast off the limitations of a perspective which ascribes curative power only to lawsuits.

We turn to a consideration of Dean Prosser's criticisms of the three reasons commonly advanced by courts for adhering to the English rule. First, to the assertion that the costs awarded to the prevailing party are intended as the exclusive remedy for the damages incurred by virtue of the wrongful litigation, Prosser responds that "in the United States, where the costs are set by statute at trivial amounts, and no attorney's fees are allowed, there can be no pretense at compensation even for the expenses of the litigation itself." This argument is compelling, but it does not necessarily justify an award of compensation absent the hardship of special injury or dictate that an award of compensation be assessed in a separate lawsuit. Second, to the arguments that an unrestricted tort of wrongful civil proceedings will deter honest litigants and that an innocent party must bear the costs of litigation as the price of a system which permits free access to the courts, Prosser answers that "there is no policy in favor of vexatious suits known to be groundless, which are a real and often a serious injury." But a tort action is not the only means of deterring groundless litigation, and other devices may be less intimidating to good-faith litigants. Finally, in response to the claim that recognition of the tort action will produce interminable litigation, Prosser argues that the heavy burden of proof which the plaintiff bears in such actions will safeguard bona fide litigants and prevent an endless chain of countersuits. But if few plaintiffs will recover in the subsequent action, one may wonder whether there is any point in recognizing the expanded cause of action. If the subsequent action does not succeed, both parties are left to bear the expenses of two futile lawsuits, and court time has been wasted as well.

* * *

[S]uccessful defense of the former action is no assurance of recovery in a subsequent tort action, but the unrestricted availability of such an action introduces a new strategic weapon into the arsenal of defense litigators, particularly those whose clients can afford to devote extensive resources to prophylactic intimidation.

* * * If the instant plaintiff's approach is adopted, all plaintiffs and their attorneys henceforth must also weigh the likelihood that if they persevere in the action and receive an unfavorable decision, they will not only take nothing but also be forced to defend an action for malicious prosecution of civil proceedings. * * * [T]his would push the pendulum too far in favor of the defense, more than is necessary to rectify the evil to which this effort is directed. * * *

The cure for an excess of litigation is not more litigation. Meritorious as well as frivolous claims are likely to be deterred. There are sure to be those who would use the courts and such an expanded tort remedy as a retaliatory or punitive device without regard to the likelihood of recovery or who would seek a means of recovering the actual costs of defending the first action without regard to whether it was truly vexatious. * * *

Apart from special injury, elements of a tort action for malicious prosecution of civil proceedings are (1) prior proceedings terminated in favor of the present plaintiff, (2) absence of probable cause for those proceedings, and (3) "malice," more informatively described by the Restatement as "a purpose other than that of securing the proper adjudication of the claim in which the proceedings are based."

The following discussion addresses the chief concern of this case: the conditions under which the attorney for an unsuccessful plaintiff may be held liable. * * *

The absence of probable cause in bringing a civil action may not be established merely by showing that the action was successfully defended. To require an attorney to advance only those claims that will ultimately be successful would place an intolerable burden on the right of access to the courts.

The Court of Appeals adopted, and plaintiff endorses, the standard for determining whether an attorney had probable cause to initiate and continue a lawsuit articulated in Tool Research & Engineering Corp. v. Henigson, 46 Cal.App.3d 675, 683–684, 120 Cal.Rptr. 291 (1975): "The attorney is not an insurer to his client's adversary that his client will win in litigation. Rather, he has a duty 'to represent his client zealously * * * [seeking] any lawful objective through legally permissible means * * * [and presenting] for adjudication any lawful claim, issue, or defense.' (ABA, Code of Professional Responsibility, EC 7–1, DR 7–101[A][1], * * *.) So long as the attorney does not abuse that duty by prosecuting a claim which a reasonable lawyer would not regard as tenable or by unreasonably neglecting to investigate the facts and law in making his determination to proceed, his client's adversary has no right to assert malicious prosecution against the attorney if the lawyer's efforts prove unsuccessful. * * *

"The attorney's obligation is to represent his client honorably and ethically, and he may, without being guilty of malicious prosecution, vigorously pursue litigation in which he is unsure of whether his client or the client's adversary is truthful, so long as that issue is genuinely in doubt."

The *Henigson* court also said: "An attorney has probable cause to represent a client in litigation when, after a reasonable investigation and industrious search of legal authority, he has an honest belief that his client's claim is tenable in the forum in which it is to be tried."

In our view, this standard, while well-intentioned, is inconsistent with the role of the attorney in an adversary system.

Our legal system favors the representation of litigants by counsel. Yet the foregoing standard appears skewed in favor of non-representation; the lawyer risks being penalized for undertaking to present the client's claim to a court unless satisfied, after a potentially substantial investment in investigation and research, that the claim is tenable.

* * *

Moreover, the *Henigson* standard suggests rather ominously that every time a lawyer representing, say, a medical malpractice plaintiff encounters a fact adverse to the client's position or an expert opinion that there was no malpractice, he must immediately question whether to persevere in the action. An attorney's evaluation of the client's case should not be inhibited by the knowledge that perseverance may place the attorney personally at risk; the next fact or the next medical opinion may be the one that makes the case, and such developments may occur even on the eve of trial.

Indeed, a jury-submissible claim of medical malpractice may sometimes be presented even without specific testimony that the defendant physician violated the applicable standard of care. Thus, a lawyer may proceed in the good-faith belief that his proofs will establish a prima facie case of medical malpractice without expert testimony, only to find that the court disagrees. Such conduct is not the equivalent of proceeding without probable cause. * * *

This Court has said, in opinions addressed to the tort of malicious prosecution, that malice may be inferred from the facts that establish want of probable cause, although the jury is not required to draw that inference. This rule, developed in cases where damages were sought from a lay person who initiated proceedings, fails to make sufficient allowance for the lawyer's role as advocate and should not be applied in determining whether a lawyer acted for an improper purpose.

A client's total lack of belief that the action he initiates or continues can succeed is persuasive evidence of intent to harass or injure the defendant by bringing the action. But a lawyer who is unaware of such a client's improper purpose may, despite a personal lack of belief in any possible success of the action, see the client and the claim through to an appropriate conclusion without risking liability. * * *

The Restatement defines the mental element of the tort of wrongful civil proceedings as "a purpose other than that of securing the proper adjudication of the claim in which the proceedings are based." A finding of an improper purpose on the part of the unsuccessful attorney must be supported by evidence independent of the evidence establishing that the action was brought without probable cause.

We affirm that portion of the Court of Appeals decision which upheld summary judgment in favor of defendants on plaintiff's claims sounding in negligence and abuse of process. With respect to plaintiff's claim for malicious prosecution, we reverse the decision of the Court of Appeals and affirm the trial court's grant of summary judgment; we do so on the ground that an action for malicious prosecution of a civil action may not be brought absent special injury and the plaintiff failed to plead special injury.

[Levin, Justice concurred separately, suggesting that the Court devise a new rule authorizing the judge "to order payment of the prevailing party's actual expenses, including reasonable attorneys' fees and limited consequential damages, where the action was wrongfully initiated, defended or continued."]

NOTES AND QUESTIONS

1. The title of malicious prosecution is often expanded to cover not only criminal prosecutions but also frivolous or unwarranted civil actions. To avoid confusion the latter action is sometimes called malicious civil prosecution. The Restatement gives it the title of wrongful civil proceedings.

2. In general, the elements of the cause of action are the same for both criminal and civil prosecutions. As the principal case indicates, the major variance involves the element of damages. In the case of a civil prosecution, damages are not presumed and must be proved. The American rule is that each party to a civil action bears his own expenses of litigation, including attorney's fees. In England, attorney's fees are normally awarded to the winning party, and as a result there is no occasion for awarding them in a subsequent tort action, as part of the damages. Around a third of the American states follow the so-called "English rule"—not in awarding attorney's fees to the winner, but only in declining to allow recovery of attorney's fees as damages in the subsequent tort action. This result is distinctly anomalous: the damages that are an inevitable result of the tortious conduct and that always arise cannot be recovered, and the only recoverable damages are the abnormal special damages that are specifically proved. The Torts Restatement meets this persistent anomaly by providing expressly for certain types of injuries, such as civil proceedings involving arrest of person or deprivation of property, or repetitive actions. See §§ 677–680. But see Johnson v. Calado, 159 Wis.2d 446, 464 N.W.2d 647 (1991), reaffirming adherence to the English rule.

3. Note the differences in the elements of probable cause and "malice." The courts pride themselves in being open to the public to settle civil disputes. What is required is not a better-than-even chance that the suit will be won but a finding by the court that there was a reasonably good chance that it would. How does this concept apply when the original plaintiff was trying to persuade the court to change the law judicially?

If "malice" means bringing a civil action with an ulterior motive, how does this apply? Does it mean that the plaintiff brought the action with a subjective awareness that he had no actual chance of prevailing? Can the attorney be held liable? What is the effect of his failure to make an adequate investigation?

Is there real basis for requiring both lack of probable cause and "malice," or should either one be sufficient?

4. Is it feasible to arrange for award of appropriate litigation expenses in the original action, rather than requiring a second action in tort, with a different judge and jury? The cases have held that a countersuit, rather than a counterclaim in the same suit is required, because there must have been a termination in favor of the plaintiff at the time the tort claim is filed. A few states have provided by statute for allowing counterclaims.

5. If the case is filed in federal court, another remedy may be available through Rule 11 of the Federal Rules of Civil Procedure. Rule 11 establishes the standards that attorneys and parties must meet when filing pleadings, motions, or

other documents in court and the circumstances under which a court may impose sanctions for the violation of those standards. Essentially, the rule requires that representations made to the court be based on the best of the person's knowledge, information, and belief, formed after an inquiry reasonable under the circumstances. Violations of the standard of conduct may subject the attorney or client to various sanctions designed to deter repetition of the conduct. If the principal case had been filed in federal court under the current version of Rule 11, defendants might have served motions for summary judgment (based on the absence of proof of violation of the standard of care) and for sanctions under Rule 11. The rule specifies that the plaintiffs would then have had twenty-one days to withdraw their complaint to avoid the imposition of sanctions. Rule 11 permits the trial court judge to sanction conduct without the filing of another action. Its primary purpose, however, is to streamline litigation and not to compensate the aggrieved party. Michigan enacted a statute responding to the principal case. For discussion see Wade, On Frivolous Litigation: A Study of Tort Liability and Procedural Sanctions, 14 Hofstra L.Rev. 433 (1986).

Grainger v. Hill

Court of Common Pleas, 1838.
4 Bing.N.C. 212, 132 Eng.Rep. 769.

TINDAL C.J. This is a special action on the case, in which the Plaintiff declares that he was the master and owner of a vessel which, in September 1836, he mortgaged to the Defendants for the sum of 80£, with a covenant for repayment in September 1837, and under a stipulation that, in the mean time, the Plaintiff should retain the command of the vessel, and prosecute voyages therein for his own profit: that the Defendants, in order to compel the Plaintiff through duress to give up the register of the vessel, without which he could not go to sea, before the money lent on mortgage became due, threatened to arrest him for the same unless he immediately paid the amount: that, upon the Plaintiff refusing to pay it, the Defendants, knowing he could not provide bail, arrested him under a capias, indorsed to levy 95£ 17s. 6d., and kept him imprisoned, until, by duress, he was compelled to give up the register, which the Defendants then unlawfully detained; by means whereof the Plaintiff lost four voyages from London to Caen. * * * The Defendants pleaded the general issue; after a verdict for the Plaintiff, the case comes before us * * * under an application for a nonsuit. * * *

The * * * ground urged for a nonsuit is, that there was no proof of the suit commenced by the Defendants having been terminated. But the answer to this * * * namely, the omission to allege want of reasonable and probable cause for the Defendants' proceeding, is * * * that this is an action for abusing the process of the law, by applying it to extort property from the Plaintiff, and not an action for a malicious arrest or malicious prosecution, in order to support which action the termination of the previous proceeding must be proved, and the absence of reasonable and probable cause be alleged as well as proved. * * * If the course pursued by the Defendants is such that there is no precedent of a similar transaction, the Plaintiff's remedy is by an action on the case, applicable to such new and special circumstances; and his complaint being that the process of the law has been abused, to effect an object not within the scope of the process, it is immaterial whether the suit which that process commenced has been determined or not, or whether or not it was founded on reasonable and probable cause. * * *

Judgment for Plaintiff.

NOTES AND QUESTIONS

1. A more contemporary case on abuse of process is Board of Education of Farmingdale Union Free School District v. Farmingdale Classroom Teachers Association, Inc., 38 N.Y.2d 397, 343 N.E.2d 278, 380 N.Y.S.2d 635 (1975), where, in litigation between the School District and the Teachers Association, the latter served subpoenas on all the teachers in the school system, requiring them to report to court at the same time. This harassment of the District was held to give rise to tort liability. See also Bell v. Icard, 986 S.W.2d 550 (Tenn.1999) (filing of conservatorship proceedings to "scuttle" an allied lawsuit); Ash v. Cohn, 119 N.J.L. 54, 194 A. 174 (1937) (body execution); Ginsberg v. Ginsberg, 84 A.D.2d 573, 443 N.Y.S.2d 439 (2d Dep't 1981) (in divorce action, defendant charged with using subpoena process "for the unjustified purpose of harassing [wife] and exhausting her financial resources in order to win a collateral advantage in the legal struggle over custody of the child").

The tort of abuse of process is not available for merely filing a frivolous action, absent proof that the claim was filed for a collateral or ulterior purpose. Wells v. Orthwein, 670 S.W.2d 529 (Mo.App.1984); Martin v. Trevino, 578 S.W.2d 763 (Tex.Civ.App.1978) and In re Burzynski, 989 F.2d 733 (5th Cir.1993) (Texas law setting forth elements of claim). The tort of abuse of process is not delimited by the requirements of malicious prosecution: Brownsell v. Klawitter, 102 Wis.2d 108, 306 N.W.2d 41 (1981) (action for abuse of process may proceed without termination of action in favor of defendant, an essential element in malicious prosecution).

2. *The Tort of Spoliation of Evidence.* The integrity of the litigation process depends upon the availability of accurate and reliable information being made available in evidence. The California Supreme Court in Smith v. Superior Court, 151 Cal.App.3d 491 (1984), implied a cause of action for failure to preserve evidence where a car dealership, accused of negligence in installing the wheels of a van, lost or destroyed parts of the vehicle. The van wheels had spun off the van injuring plaintiff as she drove past the van. The actions of the dealership relating to the van after the accident made investigation of the cause of the accident impossible.

The Court of Appeals recognized a cause of action. It found that the expectation of preservation of evidence was akin to a "probable expectancy that the court must protect from the kind of interference alleged here." Id. at 502. In the later case of Velasco v. Commercial Building Maintenance Co., 169 Cal.App.3d 874 (1985), the court applied *Smith* to recognize a tort of negligent spoliation. In this case, the defendant's janitorial staff had disposed of a broken bottle kept by plaintiff's attorney in a paper bag in his office. Although the tort was recognized, the court held that it would not apply in the circumstances.

In Willard v. Caterpillar, Inc., 40 Cal.App.4th 892 (1995), the court enunciated the elements of the tort of intentional spoliation of evidence

(1) pending or probable civil litigation, (2) defendant's knowledge that litigation is pending or probable, (3) willful destruction of evidence, (4) intent to

interfere with plaintiff's prospective civil suit, (5) a casual relationship between the evidence destruction and the inability to prove the lawsuit, and (6) damages. Id. at 911.

The development of the tort has, however, been arrested in Cedars–Sinai Medical Center v. Superior Court, 18 Cal. 4th 1 (1998). The California Supreme Court held that:

> when the alleged intentional spoliation is committed by a party to the underlying cause of action to which the evidence is relevant and when the spoliation is or reasonably should have been discovered before the conclusion of the underlying litigation, it is preferable to rely on existing nontort remedies rather than creating a tort remedy. Id. at 4.

In a footnote, the court explicitly overruled *Smith* and *Willard* "to the extent they are inconsistent with [this holding]." Id. at 18 n.4.

In *Cedars–Sinai*, a hospital could not locate fetal monitoring strips that were allegedly critical to a plaintiff "prevailing in his malpractice action." Id. at 4–5. In response to the hospital's inability to produce these records, the guardian ad litem of the infant plaintiff attempted to amend his complaint to include an intentional spoliation of evidence claim. The trial court granted the motion to amend precipitating the California Supreme Court's review of the writ of mandate, and subsequent holding that scaled back the tort remedy for the intentional spoliation of evidence.

The court ironically decried intentional spoliation of evidence as "a grave affront to the cause justice ... deserv[ing] of [the court's] unqualified condemnation." Id. at 4. Despite the effect that the destruction of evidence has on "fairness and justice," the Court cited three concerns with the tort liability it originally created.

The first concern addressed by the Court involved "the conflict between a tort remedy for intentional first party spoliation and the policy against creating derivative tort remedies for litigation-related misconduct." Id. at 8. Deciding this conflict in favor of denying an independent tort remedy, the Court cited its traditional presumption against creating new derivative torts, the "spiral[ing]" burden of lawsuits, and other jurisdictions emphasis on the "finality of adjudication." Id. at 9–10. In addition, the court analogized the lack of an independent civil remedy for perjury as support for its conclusion.

The second concern for the Court was "the strength of existing nontort remedies for spoliation." Id. at 8. "Chief among these is the evidentiary inference that evidence which one party has destroyed or rendered unavailable was unfavorable to that party." Id. at 11. Other nontort remedies include the sometimes crippling sanctions imposed for violating discovery laws, id. at 12 (such as "dismissing part or all of the action, or granting a default judgment against the offending party"), and local bar associations' authority to firmly discipline lawyers that participate in the "suppression or destruction of evidence." Id. at 13 ("Lawyers are subject to discipline, including suspension and disbarment...."). The deterrent effect of criminal penalties imposed on persons found guilty of intentionally destroying evidence provides more support for relying on the strength of existing nontort remedies.

The third and final concern for the *Cedars–Sinai* court was "the uncertainty of the fact of harm in spoliation cases." Id. at 8. In other words, "even if the jury infers from the act of spoliation that the spoliated evidence was somehow unfavorable to the spoliator, there will typically be no way of telling what precisely the evidence would have shown and how much it would have weighed in the victim's favor." Id. at 13–14. Furthermore, "if evidence would not have helped to establish plaintiff's case[,] an award of damages for its destruction would work a windfall for the plaintiff." Id. at 14.

The California courts' experience with the tort of spoliation of evidence has been volatile. In the space of fifteen years, California courts have gone from an expansive recognition of both intentional and negligent spoliation of evidence causes of action, to a narrow, uncertain toleration of the tort in only the rarest cases. A recent law review note reports: "Over twenty-six jurisdictions have considered the issue of whether to adopt this emerging tort. Of these jurisdictions, only five have adopted a tort for the intentional spoliation of evidence." Rubin, Note, Tort Reform: A Call for Florida to Scale Back Its Independent Tort for the Spoliation of Evidence, 51 Fla. L. Rev. 345, 354 (1999).

CHAPTER XXI

MISREPRESENTATION

1. INTRODUCTION

"Misrepresentation runs all through the law of torts, as a method of accomplishing various types of tortious conduct which, for reasons of historical development or as a matter of convenience, usually are grouped under categories of their own. Thus a battery may be committed by feeding the plaintiff poisoned chocolates, or by inducing his consent to a physical contact by misrepresenting its character; false imprisonment may result from a pretense of authority to make an arrest, a trespass to land from fraudulent statements inducing another to enter, or a conversion from obtaining possession of goods by false representations; and a malicious lie may give rise to a cause of action for the intentional infliction of mental suffering. A great many of the common and familiar forms of negligent conduct, resulting in invasions of tangible interests of person or property, are in their essence nothing more than misrepresentation, from a misleading signal by a driver of an automobile about to make a turn, or an assurance that a danger does not exist, to false statements concerning a chattel sold, or non-disclosure of a latent defect by one who is under a duty to give warning. In addition, misrepresentation may play an important part in the invasion of intangible interests, in such torts as defamation, malicious prosecution, or interference with contractual relations. In all such cases the particular form which the defendant's conduct has taken has become relatively unimportant, and misrepresentation has been merged to such an extent with other kinds of misconduct that neither the courts nor legal writers have found any occasion to regard it as a separate basis of liability.

"So far as misrepresentation has been treated as giving rise in and of itself to a distinct cause of action in tort, it has been identified with the common law action of deceit. * * *

"The law of misrepresentation is thus considerably broader than the action for deceit. Liability in damages for misrepresentation, in one form or another falls into the three familiar divisions with which we have dealt throughout this book—it may be based upon intent to deceive, upon negligence, or upon a policy which requires the defendant to be strictly responsible for his statements without either. For the most part, the courts have limited deceit to those cases where there is an intent to mislead, and have left negligence and strict liability to be dealt with in some other type of action. * * * " W. Prosser, Torts 683 (4th ed. 1971).

Misrepresentation is thus a very complex field. The complexity results primarily from the existence of numerous alternative remedies. They include:

1. The tort action of deceit.

2. An action for breach of contract, when the representation is found to be an express or implied term of the contract itself. In the case of the sale of chattels, this may take the form of an action for breach of warranty, which has definite tort characteristics of its own. The contract liability is of course a strict one, and requires no intent to deceive, negligence, or other fault than the breach of the contract itself.

3. A negligence action for negligent misrepresentation or misstatement. This is now recognized by nearly all courts where tangible injury to person or property results, and by most of the American jurisdictions where the only damage is financial loss.

4. A suit in equity to rescind the transaction or for other relief such as an equitable lien or a constructive trust.

5. An action at law for restitution to recover back what the plaintiff has parted with, or the unjust enrichment which the defendant has received from it.

History. The action of deceit is of very ancient origin. There was an old writ of deceit known as early as 1201, which lay only in cases of what we would now call malicious prosecution. At a later period this writ was superseded by an action on the case in the nature of deceit, which became the general common law remedy for any misrepresentation, whether fraudulent or not, which resulted in actual damage. It was used to afford a remedy for many wrongs that we should now regard as breaches of contract, such as false warranties in the sale of goods. Its use was limited almost entirely to direct transactions between the plaintiff and the defendant, and it was treated as inseparable from some contract relation. In other words, tort and contract were not at all clearly distinguished.

"Caveat emptor"—let the buyer beware—was the rule. The buyer could garner protection by exacting a warranty from the seller. Thus in the picturesque old case of Chandelor v. Lopus, Cro.Jac. 4, 79 Eng.Rep. 3 (1603), a goldsmith sold a stone to the plaintiff, falsely stating that it was a bezar stone—a "calcareous concretion in the stomach of a goat," believed to have medicinal properties, particularly as a remedy against snake-bite. It was held that there was no liability, even though the seller knew his statement to be false, in the absence of an express undertaking to be bound. The only exception was in the sale of food and drink.

In 1789, in Pasley v. Freeman, 3 T.R. 51, 100 Eng.Rep. 450, the action of deceit was held to lie in a case where the plaintiff had had no dealings with the defendant, but had been induced by his misrepresentation to extend credit to a third person. After that date deceit was recognized as purely a tort action, and not necessarily founded upon a contract. At about the same time, in Stuart v. Wilkins, 1 Doug. 18, 99 Eng.Rep. 15 (1778), the remedy for breach of warranty was taken over into the action of assumpsit, and it was thus established that it had a contract character. Thereafter the two lines of recovery slowly diverge, although some vestige of confusion between the two still remains, even today.

At the beginning of the 19th Century the elements were in place to provide a wide liability for misrepresentations. These developments were put asunder by the momentous case of Derry v. Peck, infra. Deceit was established as the basis of tortious liability and deceit required an actual "intention to cheat." Norton v. Ashburton, [1914] A.C. 932, at 953. Dishonesty rather than negligence was the lodestar of liability. The tort requires a fraudulent misrepresentation relied upon by the plaintiff to his detriment. What is a "misrepresentation"?

2. CONCEALMENT AND NONDISCLOSURE

Swinton v. Whitinsville Savings Bank

Supreme Judicial Court of Massachusetts, 1942.
311 Mass. 677, 42 N.E.2d 808.

Action by Neil W. Swinton against Whitinsville Savings Bank to recover damages for alleged fraudulent concealment by defendant in sale of a house to plaintiff. From an order sustaining a demurrer to plaintiff's declaration, the plaintiff appeals.

QUA, JUSTICE. The declaration alleges that on or about September 12, 1938, the defendant sold the plaintiff a house in Newton to be occupied by the plaintiff and his family as a dwelling; that at the time of the sale the house "was infested with termites, an insect that is most dangerous and destructive to buildings"; that the defendant knew the house was so infested; that the plaintiff could not readily observe this condition upon inspection; that "knowing the internal destruction that these insects were creating in said house", the defendant falsely and fraudulently concealed from the plaintiff its true condition; that the plaintiff at the time of his purchase had no knowledge of the termites, exercised due care thereafter, and learned of them about August 30, 1940; and that, because of the destruction that was being done and the dangerous condition that was being created by the termites, the plaintiff was put to great expense for repairs and for the installation of termite control in order to prevent the loss and destruction of said house.

There is no allegation of any false statement or representation, or of the uttering of a half truth which may be tantamount to a falsehood. There is no intimation that the defendant by any means prevented the plaintiff from acquiring information as to the condition of the house. There is nothing to show any fiduciary relation between the parties, or that the plaintiff stood in a position of confidence toward or dependence upon the defendant. So far as appears the parties made a business deal at arm's length. The charge is concealment and nothing more; and it is concealment in the simple sense of mere failure to reveal, with nothing to show any peculiar duty to speak. The characterization of the concealment as false and fraudulent of course adds nothing in the absence of further allegations of fact. * * *

If this defendant is liable on this declaration every seller in liable who fails to disclose any nonapparent defect known to him in the subject of the sale which materially reduces its value and which the buyer fails to discover. Similarly it would seem that every buyer would be liable who fails to disclose any nonapparent virtue known to him in the subject of the purchase which materially enhances its value and of which the seller is ignorant. [C] The law has not yet, we believe, reached the point of imposing upon the frailties of human nature a standard so idealistic as this. That the particular case here stated by the plaintiff possesses a certain appeal to the moral sense is scarcely to be denied. Probably the reason is to be found in the facts that the infestation of buildings by termites has not been common in Massachusetts and constitutes a concealed risk against which buyers are off their guard. But the law cannot provide special rules for termites and can hardly attempt to determine liability according to the varying probabilities of the existence and discovery of different possible defects in the subjects of trade. The rule of nonliability for bare nondisclosure has been stated and followed by this court. * * * It is adopted in the American Law Institute's Restatement of Torts § 551. See Williston on Contracts, Rev. Ed., §§ 1497, 1498, 1499.

The order sustaining the demurrer is affirmed, and judgment is to be entered for the defendant. * * *

So ordered.

NOTES AND QUESTIONS

1.   The classic statement of the effect of nondisclosure is that of Lord Cairns in Peek v. Gurney, L.R. 6 H.L. 377, 403 (1873): "Mere nondisclosure of material facts, however morally censurable, however that nondisclosure might be a ground in a proper proceeding at a proper time for setting aside an allotment or a purchase of shares, would in my opinion form no ground for an action in the nature of an action for misrepresentation. There must, in my opinion, be some active misstatement of fact, or, at all events, such a partial and fragmentary statement of fact, as that the withholding of that which is not stated makes that which is stated absolutely false." Perhaps the leading case espousing the view is Keates v. Earl of Cardogan, 10 C.B. 591, 138 Eng.Rep. 234 (1851).

2.   What is the foundation of the "general rule" that an action of deceit will not lie for tacit nondisclosure, as distinguished from active misrepresentation?

3.   Three different rules modifying the harshness of the common law position developed quite early:

A.   The courts followed a much more liberal attitude when the plaintiff sought rescission of the contract, or other equitable relief. Even mutual mistake as to a basic fact affecting the transaction is ordinarily held to be sufficient grounds for such relief; and the position of the defendant is not improved if he has knowledge of the plaintiff's mistake, failed to make disclosure, and took advantage of the situation. See, for example, Simmons v. Evans, 185 Tenn. 282, 206 S.W.2d 295 (1947).

B. Even in actions at law, the defendant was held liable for nondisclosure if the parties were in some confidential or fiduciary relation to one another, so that reliance upon good faith and full disclosure was justified. McDonough v. Williams, 77 Ark. 261, 92 S.W. 783 (1905); Brasher v. First Nat. Bank of Birmingham, 232 Ala. 340, 168 So. 42 (1936). "For instance, the relations of trustee and cestui que trust, principal and agent, attorney and client, physician and patient, priest and parishioner, partners, tenants in common, husband and wife, parent and child, guardian and ward, and many others of like character." Farmers' State Bank of Newport v. Lamon, 132 Wash. 369, 231 P. 952 (1925). As to banker and customer, see Klein v. First Edina Nat'l Bank, 293 Minn. 418, 196 N.W.2d 619 (1972) and Medley v. SouthTrust Bank of the Quad Cities, 500 So. 2d 1075 (Ala.1986).

C. In addition, certain types of contracts, such as those of suretyship and guaranty, joint adventure, or insurance, were recognized as in themselves creating or involving something of a confidential relation, and hence as requiring the utmost good faith, and full and fair disclosure of all material facts.

4. An active concealment may constitute an act sufficient to base liability. The leading American case is Croyle v. Moses, 90 Pa. 250 (1879), where defendant, selling a horse to plaintiff, hitched him up short for the purpose of concealing the fact that the horse was a cribber and a windsucker.

5. Are words necessary to a misrepresentation? In addition to Jones v. West Side Buick Auto Co., 231 Mo.App. 187, 93 S.W.2d 1083 (1936), stated in the principal case, see Chapman v. Zakzaska, 273 Wis. 64, 76 N.W.2d 537 (1956), and Kuelling v. Roderick Lean Mfg. Co., 183 N.Y. 78, 75 N.E. 1098 (1905), where defendant sold a road roller with its defects concealed with putty and paint.

6. Defendant, selling plaintiff sheets of aluminum, placed good undamaged sheets on top of bundles of sheets that were corroded or otherwise damaged. The bundles were bulky and heavy, and plaintiff did not take them apart. Is this deceit? Salzman v. Maldaver, 315 Mich. 403, 24 N.W.2d 161 (1946).

7. Suppose the defendant, in possession of the facts, denies all knowledge in response to plaintiff's inquiry, and thereby discourages him from investigating further? Smith v. Beatty, 37 N.C. 456, 40 Am.Dec. 435 (1843).

Griffith v. Byers Constr. Co. of Kansas, Inc.

Supreme Court of Kansas, 1973.
212 Kan. 65, 510 P.2d 198.

FROMME, JUSTICE. The purchasers of new homes in Woodlawn East Addition, City of Wichita, Kansas, brought separate actions for damages because of the saline condition of the soil of their homesites. These actions were filed on alternative theories, (1) breach of an implied warranty of fitness and (2) fraud in the concealment of a material matter. The actions were brought against the developer. This appeal is from an order granting summary judgments in favor of the developer, Byers Construction Co. of Kansas, Inc. (Byers).

The petitions allege that Byers developed and advertised the addition as a choice residential area. Prior to the time of development the addition was part of an abandoned oil field which contained salt water disposal areas which Byers knew or should have known would not sustain vegetation because of the saline content of the soil. It was alleged that Byers graded and developed the whole addition for homesites in such a manner that it became impossible for a purchaser to discover the presence of these salt areas. It further appears from allegations in the petitions and testimony in depositions that each of the plaintiffs selected a homesite which was located within a salt water disposal area. After houses were constructed attempts to landscape the homesites failed. Grass, shrubs and trees were planted and died because of the saline content of the soil. * * * No inquiry was made and no assurance was given by Byers on soil fertility.

The facts of this case appear to be unique for, although many cases can be found on a vendor-builder's liability for the sale of a defective home no cases are cited and we find none which discuss a developer's liability for defects arising from sterility of soil. The saline content of the soil of these homesites does not affect the structural qualities of the homes. The allegations of the petitions and deposition testimony indicate that landscaping is either impossible or highly expensive.

A real estate developer by subdividing and offering lots for sale as choice residential homesites does not by implication warrant the fertility of the soil of said lots. Liability on an implied warranty of soil fertility cannot reasonably be imposed upon the real estate developer in this case. * * *

Our next inquiry is directed to the claims based on fraud. The trial court held as a matter of law no claims for fraud could be maintained because of lack of privity between the developer and these appellants. The residential lots were sold to the builders who in turn constructed the houses and then deeded the improved lots to the appellants. * * *

The allegations of fraud appear to be viable issues for trial if nondisclosure of a known material defect in the lots constitutes actionable fraud as to the appellants.

This court has held that the purchaser may recover on the theory of fraud from a vendor-builder for nondisclosure of defects. In Jenkins v. McCormick, 184 Kan. 842, 339 P.2d 8, it is stated:

"Where a vendor has knowledge of a defect in property which is not within the fair and reasonable reach of the vendee and which he could not discover by the exercise of reasonable diligence, the silence and failure of the vendor to disclose the defect in the property constitutes actionable fraudulent concealment." * * *

This *Jenkins* rule approximates that stated in Restatement (Second) of Torts, § 551:

"(1) One who fails to disclose to another a thing that he knows may justifiably induce the other to act or refrain from acting in a business transaction is subject to the same liability to the other as though he had represented the nonexistence of the matter that he has failed to disclose, if, but only if, he is under a duty to the other to exercise reasonable care to disclose the matter in question.

"(2) One party to a business transaction is under a duty to disclose to the other before the transaction is consummated. * * *

"(e) Facts basic to the transaction, if he knows that the other is about to enter into it under a mistake as to them, and that the other, because of the relationship between them, the customs in the trade or other objective circumstances, would reasonably expect a disclosure of those facts."

* * * We see no reason why the rule in *Jenkins* should not be extended in the present case to a developer of residential lots.

The appellee Byers next contends, without agency, there can be no privity and without privity there can be no duty to disclose. Here, of course, appellants never dealt with the appellee, Byers. The duty to disclose the saline nature of the soil must extend to appellants if their fraud claims are to be upheld. However, the doctrine of privity provides no defense to appellee Byers if appellants were within a class of persons appellee intended to reach. * * *

Under the alleged facts of our present case, accepting the same in the light most favorable to the appellants, we must assume the appellee, Byers, had knowledge of the saline content of the soil of the lots it placed on the market. After the grading and development of the area this material defect in the lots was not within the fair and reasonable reach of the vendees, as they could not discover this latent defect by the exercise of reasonable care. The silence of the appellee, Byers, and its failure to disclose this defect in the soil condition to the purchasers could constitute actionable fraudulent concealment under the rule in Jenkins v. McCormick, supra. One who makes a fraudulent misrepresentation or concealment is subject to liability for pecuniary loss to the persons or class of persons whom he intends or has reason to expect to act or to refrain from action in reliance upon the misrepresentation or concealment.

Of course, the fraudulent concealment to be actionable has to be material to the transaction. A matter is material if it is one to which a reasonable man would attach importance in determining his choice of action in the transaction in question. (Restatement (Second) of Torts, § 538.) There is little doubt in this case a prospective purchaser of a residential building site would consider the soil condition a material factor in choosing a lot on which to build his home. It materially affected the value and acceptability of the homesite.

As to privity we do not believe it is important to categorize its existence under a particular legal theory. Suffice it to say the appellants were in that class of persons desiring building lots in a choice residential area whom appellee intended and had reason to expect would purchase and build their homes. The fact that title was first taken in the names of the builders did not change the identity of those who would be ultimately affected by any fraudulent misrepresentations or nondisclosure of material defects in the lots. The building contractors were acting on behalf of their respective purchasers as a conduit or temporary way station for the legal title which, it was understood, would pass on completion of the homes to the appellants. There is no lack of privity in this case which would prevent causes of action based on fraud, and, in this, the district court erred in entering summary judgments for the appellee, Byers. * * *

The order of the district court entering summary judgment in favor of the appellee is affirmed as to those claims based on implied warranty but reversed as to the alternative claims based on fraud, and these cases are remanded with instructions to proceed in accordance with the views expressed herein.

NOTES AND QUESTIONS

1.   The principal case was applied in Ensminger v. Terminix Intern. Co., 102 F. 3d 1571 (10th Cir.1996), where the buyers of a home, found to be infested with termites, brought an action in fraudulent misrepresentation against the termite company that, at the request of the seller, had inspected the house prior to its sale. The court stressed the unequal access to information in the hands of a specialist on whom reliance is rested.

2.   The duty to disclose material information is much debated and replete with contradictory law. The information may be possessed exclusively by the buyer or by the seller. Sellers knowing of a termite infestation are often obligated to disclose; buyers knowing of particularly valuable gold deposits on the properties are generally found not to owe duty to disclose that information to the seller. When is it that parties assume the risk that information will not be disclosed?

3.   A person in the contemplation of the provider of the information who will act upon the information as given, although not directly given to that person, may have an action against the information provider in both fraudulent and negligent misrepresentation. Thus, the issuer of a letter of credit intended to be acted upon for a third party in a transaction may be liable for a fraudulent and negligent misrepresentation. See Banca Del Sempione v. Provident Bank of Maryland, 75 F. 3d 951 (4th Cir.1996) (applying Maryland law). The scope of liability is more narrowly circumscribed for fraudulent misrepresentation because of the intentional core of the tort. Thus, in the classic case of Peek v. Gurney, [1893] 6H.L. 377, corporate directors prepared a prospectus to induce the public to buy stock in the company. It was held that no liability would attach to persons who bought the stock from a stockholder. With the more expansive definition of intent in the modern law, the courts, as in *Banca Del Sempione*, have extended the range of persons able to recover in fraudulent misrepresentation. Note Cardozo's recognition of the limits of liability in *Ultramares*, infra page 1043.

3.   Basis of Liability

(A) To the Recipient

Derry v. Peek

House of Lords, 1889.
14 App.Cas. 337.

[This action on the case was brought by Sir Henry William Peek against William Derry, chairman, and four directors of the Plymouth, Devonport and District Tramways Company, for the fraudulent misrepresentations of the defendant; whereby the plaintiff was induced to take shares in the company.

By Section 34 of the Tramways Act, 1870, which section was incorporated in the special Act, "all carriages used on any tramway shall be moved by the power prescribed by the special Act, and where no such power is prescribed, by animal power only."

Under Section 35 of the same Act, the vehicles used on the tramways might be moved by steam or mechanical power, with the consent of the Board of Trade, for fixed periods and subject to the regulations of the Board. In February, 1883, the defendants as directors of the company issued a prospectus.

The heading, which was in large type, was as follows: "Incorporated by special Act of Parliament authorizing the use of steam or mechanical motive power." It also contained the following paragraph: "One great feature of this undertaking to which considerable importance should be attached, is, that by the special Act of Parliament obtained the company has the right to use steam or mechanical motive power, instead of horses, and it is fully expected that by means of this a considerable saving will result in the working expenses of the line as compared with other tramways worked by horses," and there were other paragraphs further setting forth the advantages to be derived from steam as compared with horse power.

Soon after the issuing of the prospectus, a copy of which the plaintiff received, he applied for and was allotted shares in the company relying, as he alleged, upon the representations of this paragraph, believing the company had an absolute right to use steam and other mechanical power.

The company proceeded to construct its tramways, but the Board of Trade refused to consent to the use of steam or mechanical power except on certain portions of the tramway, and the corporations of Devonport refused their consent to the company opening the completed part of their lines until the remainder was ready for use. In consequence the company was wound up, and immediately thereafter the plaintiff brought this action against the defendants.

At the trial the defendants all testified that they knew that consent of the Board of Trade was required for the use of steam, but that they either thought that it had been obtained, or assumed that it was assured as a matter of course once the company had been incorporated by Act of Parliament with power to use steam.

Stirling, Justice, dismissed the action, having come to the conclusion that the directors all believed that the company had the rights stated in the prospectus and that their belief was not unreasonable, nor was their conduct so reckless or careless that they ought to be held liable in an action of deceit.

On appeal the judgment of Stirling, J., was reversed on the ground that while the defendants honestly believed that the statements in the prospectus were true, the statements were made without any reasonable grounds for believing them. The defendants appealed to the House of Lords. The House of Lords unanimously reversed the decisions of the Court below and unanimously restored the opinion of Stirling, J.]

LORD HERSCHELL. * * * "This action is one which is commonly called an action of deceit, a mere common-law action." This is the description of it given by Cotton, L.J., in delivering judgment. I think it important that it should be borne in mind that such an action differs essentially from one brought to obtain rescission of a contract on the ground of misrepresentation of a material fact. The principles which govern the two actions differ widely. Where rescission is claimed it is only necessary to prove that there was misrepresentation; then, however honestly it may have been made, however free from blame the person who made it, the contract, having been obtained by misrepresentation, cannot stand. In an action of deceit, on the contrary, it is not enough to establish misrepresentation alone; it is conceded on all hands that something more must be proved to cast liability upon the defendant, though it has been a matter of controversy what additional elements are requisite. I lay stress upon this because observations made by learned judges in actions for rescission have been cited and much relied upon at the bar by counsel for the respondent. Care must obviously be observed in applying the language used in relation to such actions to an action of deceit. * * *

Lord Herschell

I think the authorities establish the following propositions: First, in order to sustain an action of deceit there must be proof of fraud, and nothing short of that will suffice. Secondly, fraud is proved when it is shown that a false representation has been made (1) knowingly, or (2) without belief in its truth, or (3) recklessly, careless whether it be true or false. Although I have treated the second and third as distinct cases, I think the third is but an instance of the second, for one who makes a statement under such circumstances can have no real belief in the truth of what he states. To prevent a false statement being fraudulent there must, I think, always be an honest belief in its truth. And this probably covers the whole ground, for one who knowingly alleges that which is false has obviously no such honest belief. Thirdly, if fraud be proved, the motive of the person guilty of it is immaterial. It matters not that there was no intention to cheat or injure the person to whom the statement was made. * * *

In my opinion making a false statement through want of care falls far short of, and is a very different thing from, fraud, and the same may be said of a false representation honestly believed though on insufficient grounds. * * *

At the same time I desire to say distinctly that when a false statement has been made the questions whether there were reasonable grounds for believing it, and what were the means of knowledge in the possession of the person making it, are most weighty matters for consideration. The ground upon which an alleged belief was founded is a most important test of its reality. I can conceive of many cases where the fact that an alleged belief was destitute of all reasonable foundation would suffice of itself to convince the Court that it was not really entertained, and that the representation was a fraudulent one. So, too, although means of knowledge are * * * a very different thing from knowledge, if I thought that a person making a false statement had shut his eyes to the facts, or purposely abstained from inquiring into them I should hold that honest belief was absent, and that he was just as fraudulent as if he had knowingly stated that which was false. * * *

I quite admit that the statements of witnesses as to their belief are by no means to be accepted blindfolded. The probabilities must be considered. Whenever it is necessary to arrive at a conclusion as to the state of mind of another person, and to determine whether his belief under given circumstances was such as he alleges, we can only do so by applying the standard of conduct which our own experience of the ways of men has enabled us to form; by asking ourselves whether a reasonable man situated as the defendants were, with their knowledge and means of knowledge, might well believe what they state they did believe, and consider that the representations made were substantially true. * * *

I think the judgment of the Court of Appeals should be reversed. * * *

Order of the Court of Appeal reversed; order of Stirling, J., restored.

NOTES AND QUESTIONS

1. Lord Bramwell in his speech approved the remark of Stirling J. in the lower court: "[M]ercantile men dealing with matters of business would be the first to cry

out if I extended the notion of deceit into what is honestly done * * *." Liability was confined to deceit (fraud), breach of contract, and breach of fiduciary obligation. It was not until 1964 that the House of Lords in Hedley Byrne & Co. v. Heller & Partners [1964] A.C. 465 extended liability to the situation where a person relied upon information supplied by another in a "special relationship."

2. The principal case has influenced American courts. See Lambert v. Smith, 235 Md. 284, 201 A.2d 491 (1964). In many of these states, however, a negligence action will lie for the pecuniary loss. See International Products Co. v. Erie R. Co., infra page 1020.

3. The unreasonableness of the defendant's belief may be strong evidence that it does not in fact exist, and that conclusion may be reached as an inference of fact. For example, Kimber v. Young, 137 Fed. 744 (8th Cir.1905); Palmacci v. Umpierrez, 121 F.3d 781 (1st Cir.1997).

4. It is generally agreed that a bad motive, as distinguished from an intent to mislead, is not essential to the tort of deceit. The defendant is liable if he intended to deceive, notwithstanding the fact that he meant no harm, was disinterested or intended to do the plaintiff a kindness. Polhill v. Walter, 3 B. & Ald. 114, 110 Eng.Rep. 43 (1832). The presence or absence of bad motive may, however, affect the issue of punitive damages for deceit. Thompson v. Modern School of Business and Correspondence, 183 Cal. 112, 190 P. 451 (1920); Laughlin v. Hopkinson, 292 Ill. 80, 126 N.E. 591 (1920).

5. Section 526 of the Restatement (Second) of Torts reads as follows:

"A misrepresentation is fraudulent if the maker

"(a) knows or believes that the matter is not as he represents it to be,

"(b) does not have the confidence in the accuracy of his representation that he states or implies, or

"(c) knows that he does not have the basis for his representation that he states or implies."

How does this fit with the definition of Lord Herschell in Derry v. Peek?

6. Suppose the plaintiff knows that the matter represented is one upon which the defendant could not have any definite knowledge? Thus a representation that there is water under land, and it will be found when a well is drilled. Harris v. Delco Products, Inc., 305 Mass. 362, 25 N.E.2d 740 (1940).

7. Suppose the defendant makes a statement that can reasonably be understood in two ways, one true and the other false. Plaintiff understands it in the false sense, and is misled, but defendant believes that plaintiff has understood in the true one. Will an action for deceit lie? Nash v. Minnesota Title Insurance & Trust Co., 163 Mass. 574, 40 N.E. 1039 (1895).

International Products Co. v. Erie R.R. Co.

Court of Appeals of New York, 1927.
244 N.Y. 331, 155 N.E. 662.

[Plaintiff, an importer, was expecting a valuable consignment of goods to arrive on the steamer Plutarch, and had made arrangements with defendants to receive and store the goods until they could be reshipped. The shipment was covered by insurance until it reached the warehouse, and plaintiff desired to insure it after that time. Giving this reason for its question, it inquired of defendant where the goods would be stored. Defendant, taking time to obtain the information, replied that the goods were docked at Dock F, Weehawken. From this reply, plaintiff reasonably inferred that the goods were already received and stored, and obtained its insurance on this basis. The goods arrived later and were stored at Dock D. They were destroyed by fire, and plaintiff was unable to collect any insurance payments because of the misdescription. Plaintiff seeks to recover from defendant the sum it would have received if defendant's statement had been correct. The trial court directed a verdict for plaintiff, which was affirmed by the Appellate Division. Defendant appeals.]

ANDREWS, J. * * * Confining ourselves to the issues before us, we eliminate any theory of fraud or deceit. * * * [C] We come to the vexed question of liability for negligent language. In England the rule is fixed. "Generally speaking there is no such thing as liability for negligence in words as distinguished from act." Pollock on Torts (12th Ed.) p. 565; [c]. Dicta to the contrary may be found in earlier cases. * * * But since Derry v. Peek, L.R. 14 App.Cas. 337, although what was said was not necessary to the decision, the law is clearly to the effect "that no cause of action is maintainable for a mere statement, although untrue, and although acted upon to the damage of the person to whom the statement is made unless the statement be false to the knowledge of the person making it," [c] or, as said elsewhere, "we have to take it as settled that there is no general duty to use any care whatever in making statements in the way of business or otherwise, on which other persons are likely to act" [c]. * * *

These cases have not been without criticism. The denial, under all circumstances, of relief because of the negligently spoken or written word, is, it is said, a refusal to enforce what conscience, fair dealing, and the usages of business require. The tendency of the American courts has been towards a more liberal conclusion. The searcher of a title employed by one who delivers his abstract to another to induce action on the faith of it must exercise care. [C] So must a physician who assures a wife that she may safely treat the infected wound of her husband [c], or hired by another, examines a patient, and states the result of his diagnosis [c]. So of a telegraph company stating that a telegram was delivered when in fact it was not. [C] And the liability of such a company to the receiver for the erroneous transcription of a telegram has also sometimes been placed on this ground. [C]

In New York we are already committed to the American as distinguished from the English rule. In some cases a negligent statement may be the basis for a recovery of damages. A reference is made to the question in Carpenter v. Blake, 75 N.Y. 12. We intimated that a physician would be liable for negligent advice given to a patient after his discharge, but this suggestion was not decisive of the point we now consider. * * * Then came Glanzer v. Shepard, 233 N.Y. 236, 135 N.E. 275. A public weigher, hired by the seller to weigh goods, realizing that the buyer would rely on his certificate in paying therefor, was held liable for erroneous statements contained therein. * * *

The negligence was inferred from the issuance of a false certificate. That was the wrong for which a recovery was allowed. "Diligence was owing, not only to him who ordered, but to him also who relied."

Obviously, however, the rule we have adopted has its limits. Not every casual response, not every idle word, however damaging the result, gives rise to a cause of action. * * * Liability in such cases arises only where there is a duty, if one speaks at all, to give the correct information. And that involves many considerations. There must be knowledge, or its equivalent, that the information is desired for a serious purpose; that he to whom it is given intends to rely and act upon it; that, if false or erroneous, he will because of it be injured in person or property. Finally, the relationship of the parties, arising out of contract or otherwise, must be such that in morals and good conscience the one has the right to rely upon the other for information, and the other giving the information owes a duty to give it with care. [C] An inquiry made of a stranger is one thing; of a person with whom the inquirer has entered, or is about to enter into a contract concerning the goods which are, or are to be, its subject, is another. Even here the inquiry must be made as the basis of independent action. We do not touch the doctrine of caveat emptor. But in a proper case we hold that words negligently spoken may justify the recovery of the proximate damages caused by faith in their accuracy.

When such a relationship as we have referred to exists may not be precisely defined. All that may be stated is the general rule. In view of the complexity of modern business, each case must be decided on the peculiar facts presented. The same thing is true, however, in the usual action for personal injuries. There whether negligence exists depends upon the relations of the parties, the thing done or neglected, its natural consequences, and many other considerations. No hard and fast line may be drawn.

Here, as we view the facts, the duty to speak with care, if it spoke at all, rested on the defendant. We have [defendant] about to become the bailee of the plaintiff's goods; the inquiry made by [plaintiff] with whom [defendant] was dealing for the purpose as it knew of obtaining insurance; the realization that the information it gave was to be relied upon, and that, if false, the insurance obtained would be worthless. We have an inquiry such as might be expected in the usual course of business made of one who alone knew the truth. We have a negligent answer, untrue in fact, actual reliance upon it, and resulting proximate loss. True, the answer was not given to serve the purposes of the defendant itself. This we regard as immaterial.

If there was negligence justifying a recovery, we cannot hold the plaintiff guilty of contributory negligence as a matter of law. Whether or not it should have discovered the error by an inspection of the bill of lading when it received it was a question of fact. * * *

The judgment appealed from should be affirmed, with costs.

NOTES AND QUESTIONS

1. A few of the American courts have held that the action for deceit itself will lie for negligent misrepresentations resulting in pecuniary loss. They have either declared outright that the fault of a negligent defendant is equivalent to that of a defendant intending to deceive, or have resorted to the obvious fiction that a duty to learn the facts is the equivalent of knowledge of their existence. See, for example, Mullen v. Eastern Trust & Banking Co., 108 Me. 498, 81 A. 948 (1911); Shoefield Gear & Pulley Co. v. Shoefield, 71 Conn. 1, 40 A. 1046 (1898).

2. As to the dictum in the principal case that "not every casual response, not every idle word * * * gives rise to a cause of action," see Renn v. Provident Trust Co., 328 Pa. 481, 196 A. 8 (1938) (gratuitous supplying of copy of will, wrong will supplied by mistake); Vartan Garapedian, Inc. v. Anderson, 92 N.H. 390, 31 A.2d 371 (1943) (casual statement about credit of prospective buyer). Is an attorney or a physician, liable to one who is not his client or his patient for "curbstone advice," when it is negligently given? Fish v. Kelly, 17 C.B. (N.S.) 194, 144 Eng.Rep. 78 (1864); Buttersworth v. Swint, 53 Ga.App. 602, 186 S.E. 770 (1936); DiMarco v. Lynch Homes, 525 Pa. 558, 583 A.2d 422 (1990) (liability of physician for negligent advice given to sexual partner of plaintiff) but cf. D'Amico v. Delliquadri, 114 Ohio App. 3d 579, 683 N.E. 2d 814 (1996) (holding that plaintiff contracting genital warts from boyfriend could not sue boyfriend's physician for negligent advice regarding the communicability of the disease).

3. What if the information, although not volunteered and given without consideration, is supplied in the course of the defendant's business or professional relations? For example, the lessor of a truck gratuitously tells the lessee, in good faith but negligently, that it is covered by insurance? Manock v. Amos D. Bridge's Sons, Inc., 86 N.H. 411, 169 A. 881 (1934). Cf. Virginia Dare Stores v. Schuman, 175 Md. 287, 1 A.2d 897 (1938) (owner to invitee). The duty may attach to the provider of information who, although not in the business of supplying information, had a pecuniary interest in the transaction contemplated by the parties. See Hawaii v. United States Steel Corporation, 919 P.2d 294 (Hawaii 1996); but cf. Fry v. Mount, 554 N.W. 2d 263 (Iowa 1996) (duty limited to those in the business of supplying information). Note that if a duty has been breached, plaintiff must still prove that, given competent advice, on the balance of probabilities, he would have secured effective insurance to cover the loss. Norwest Refrigeration Services Proprietary Ltd. v. Bain Dawes (W.A.) Proprietary Ltd., 157 C.L.R. 149 (1984) (Austl.).

4. Representations of fact made in precontractual negotiations may be actionable. Weisman v. Connors, 312 Md. 428, 540 A.2d 783 (1988) (representations about employment prospects). But cf. Onita Pacific Corp. v. Trustees of Bronson, 315 Or. 149, 843 P.2d 890 (1992) (duty dependent upon professional relationship and could not be generated in arms-length, pre-contractual negotiations).

Winter v. G.P. Putnam's Sons

United States Court of Appeals, Ninth Circuit, 1991.
938 F.2d 1033.

Before SNEED, TANG and THOMPSON, CIRCUIT JUDGES.

SNEED, CIRCUIT JUDGE: * * *

I.

FACTS AND PROCEEDINGS BELOW

The Encyclopedia of Mushrooms is a reference guide containing information on the habitat, collection, and cooking of mushrooms. It was written by two British authors and originally published by a British publishing company. Defendant Putnam, an American book publisher, purchased copies of the book from the British publisher and distributed the finished product in the United States. Putnam neither wrote nor edited the book.

Plaintiffs purchased the book to help them collect and eat wild mushrooms. In 1988, plaintiffs went mushroom hunting and relied on the descriptions in the book in determining which mushrooms were safe to eat. After cooking and eating their harvest, plaintiffs became critically ill. Both have required liver transplants.

Plaintiffs allege that the book contained erroneous and misleading information concerning the identification of the most deadly species of mushrooms. In their suit against the book publisher, plaintiffs allege liability based on products liability, breach of warranty, negligence, negligent misrepresentation, and false representations. Defendant moved for summary judgment asserting that plaintiffs' claims failed as a matter of law because 1) the information contained in a book is not a product for the purposes of strict liability under products liability law; and 2) defendant is not liable under any remaining theories because a publisher does not have a duty to investigate the accuracy of the text it publishes. The district court granted summary judgment for the defendant. Plaintiffs appeal. We affirm.

II.

DISCUSSION

A book containing Shakespeare's sonnets consists of two parts, the material and print therein, and the ideas and expression thereof. The first may be a product, but the second is not. The latter, were Shakespeare alive, would be governed by copyright laws; the laws of libel, to the extent consistent with the First Amendment; and the laws of misrepresentation, negligent misrepresentation, negligence, and mistake. These doctrines applicable to the second part are aimed at the delicate issues that arise with respect to intangibles such as ideas and expression. Products liability law is geared to the tangible world.

A.   Products Liability

The language of products liability law reflects its focus on tangible items. In describing the scope of products liability law, the Restatement (Second) of Torts lists examples of items that are covered. All of these are tangible items, such as tires, automobiles, and insecticides. The American Law Institute clearly was concerned with including all physical items but gave no indication that the doctrine should be expanded beyond that area.

The purposes served by products liability law also are focused on the tangible world and do not take into consideration the unique characteristics of ideas and expression. * * *

Although there is always some appeal to the involuntary spreading of costs of injuries in any area, the costs in any comprehensive cost/benefit analysis would be quite different were strict liability concepts applied to words and ideas. We place a high priority on the unfettered exchange of ideas. We accept the risk that words and ideas have wings we cannot clip and which carry them we know not where. The threat of liability without fault (financial responsibility for our words and ideas in the absence of fault or a special undertaking or responsibility) could seriously inhibit those who wish to share thoughts and theories. As a New York court commented, with the specter of strict liability, "[w]ould any author wish to be exposed * * * for writing on a topic which might result in physical injury? e.g. How to cut trees; How to keep bees?" *Walter v. Bauer,* 109 Misc.2d 189, 191, 439 N.Y.S.2d 821, 823 (Sup.Ct.1981) (student injured doing science project described in textbook; court held that the book was not a product for purposes of products liability law), aff'd in part & rev'd in part on other grounds, 88 A.D.2d 787, 451 N.Y.S.2d 533 (1982). One might add: "Would anyone undertake to guide by ideas expressed in words either a discrete group, a nation, or humanity in general?"

Strict liability principles even when applied to products are not without their costs. Innovation may be inhibited. We tolerate these losses. They are much less disturbing than the prospect that we might be deprived of the latest ideas and theories.

* * *

Plaintiffs * * * assert that *The Encyclopedia of Mushrooms* should be analogized to aeronautical charts. Several jurisdictions have held that charts which graphically depict geographic features or instrument approach information for airplanes are "products" for the purpose of products liability law. See Brocklesby v. United States, 767 F.2d 1288, 1294–95 (9th Cir.1985) (applying Restatement for the purpose of California law), *cert. denied,* 474 U.S. 1101, 106 S.Ct. 882, 88 L.Ed.2d 918 (1986); Saloomey v. Jeppesen & Co., 707 F.2d 671, 676–77 (2d Cir.1983) (applying Restatement for the purpose of Colorado Law). Plaintiffs suggest that *The Encyclopedia of Mushrooms* can be compared to aeronautical charts because both items contain representations of natural features and both are intended to be used while engaging in a hazardous activity. We are not persuaded.

Aeronautical charts are highly technical tools. They are graphic depictions of technical, mechanical data. The best analogy to an aeronautical chart is a compass. Both may be used to guide an individual who is engaged in an activity requiring certain knowledge of natural features. Computer software that fails to yield the result for which it was designed may be another. In contrast, *The Encyclopedia of Mushrooms* is like a book on how to *use* a compass or an aeronautical chart. The chart itself is like a physical "product" while the "How to Use" book is pure thought and expression.

Given these considerations, we decline to expand products liability law to embrace the ideas and expression in a book. We know of no court that has chosen the path to which the plaintiffs point.

B. *The Remaining Theories*

As discussed above, plaintiffs must look to the doctrines of copyright, libel, misrepresentation, negligent misrepresentation, negligence, and mistake to form the basis of a claim against the defendant publisher. Unless it is assumed that the publisher is a guarantor of the accuracy of an author's statements of fact, plaintiffs have made no case under any of these theories other than possibly negligence. Guided by the First Amendment and the values embodied therein, we decline to extend liability under this theory to the ideas and expression contained in a book.

* * * The plaintiffs urge this court that the publisher had a duty to investigate the accuracy of *The Encyclopedia of Mushrooms'* contents. We conclude that the defendants have no duty to investigate the accuracy of the contents of the books it publishes. A publisher may of course assume such a burden, but there is nothing inherent in the role of publisher or the surrounding legal doctrines to suggest that such a duty should be imposed on publishers. Indeed the cases uniformly refuse to impose such a duty. Were we tempted to create this duty, the gentle tug of the First Amendment and the values embodied therein would remind us of the social costs.

Finally, plaintiffs ask us to find that a publisher should be required to give a warning 1) that the information in the book is not complete and that the consumer may not fully rely on it or 2) that this publisher has not investigated the text and cannot guarantee its accuracy. With respect to the first, a publisher would not know what warnings, if any, were required without engaging in a detailed analysis of the factual contents of the book. This would force the publisher to do exactly what we have said he has no duty to do—that is, independently investigate the accuracy of the text. We will not introduce a duty we have just rejected by renaming it a "mere" warning label. With respect to the second, such a warning is unnecessary given that *no* publisher has a duty as a guarantor.

For the reasons outlined above, the decision of the district court is AFFIRMED.

NOTES AND QUESTIONS

1.   Restatement (Second) of Torts, § 311 states:

(1) One who negligently gives false information to another is subject to liability for physical harm caused by action by the other in reasonable reliance upon such information, where such harm results

   (a) to the other, or

   (b) to such third persons as the actor should expect to be put in peril by the action taken.

(2) Such negligence may consist of failure to exercise reasonable care

   (a) in ascertaining the information, or

(b) in the manner in which it is communicated.

Comment b to section 311 provides that "[t]he rule ... extends to any person who, in the course of an activity which is in furtherance of his own interests, undertakes to give information to another, and knows or should realize that the safety of the person of others may depend upon the accuracy of the information."

2. Plaintiff fraudulently misrepresented the safety and lack of danger of white lead pigment. Plaintiff could not prove that it directly relied on the representation, but could prove that the representation led to the injury foreseeably caused to consumers of the white lead pigment. In City of New York v. Lead Industries Association, 660 N.Y.S. 2d 422 (N.Y.App.Div.1997), the court found that reliance in cases of bodily injury, in contrast to economic loss, may be indirect.

3. Alm v. Van Nostrand Reinhold Co., Inc., 134 Ill.App.3d 716, 480 N.E.2d 1263, 89 Ill.Dec. 520 (1985), finding no duty to insure the accuracy of instruction manual; plaintiff was injured when tool shattered while following manual's instructions. No duty was found in the following cases: Jones v. J.B. Lippincott, 694 F.Supp. 1216 (D.Md.1988) (self treatment of constipation following textbook) and Smith v. Linn, 386 Pa.Super. 392, 563 A.2d 123 (1989) (plaintiff's decedent died of malnutrition following diet set forth in defendant's book).

4. The opinion in the principal case distinguished Weirum v. RKO General, Inc., 15 Cal.3d 40, 539 P.2d 36, 123 Cal.Rptr. 468 (1975) (en banc) wherein defendant ran a promotional contest involving the location of a roving disc jockey. Plaintiff's decedent was killed in an accident caused by teenager speeding to meet the disc jockey. Court found liability. The principal case commented at n. 8: "A publisher's role in bringing ideas and information to the public bears no resemblance to the Weirum scenario."

5. Other cases have distinguished Weirum where the communication, albeit not a misrepresentation or misstatement, has caused the plaintiff physical injury. Bill v. Superior Court for the City and County of San Francisco, 137 Cal.App.3d 1002, 187 Cal.Rptr. 625 (1982) (plaintiff shot by gang member after viewing movie "Boulevard Nights"); Yakubowicz v. Paramount Pictures, 404 Mass. 624, 536 N.E.2d 1067 (1989) (sixteen-year-old boy knifed to death by another youth after viewing a violent movie, "The Warriors"); Herceg v. Hustler Magazine, 814 F.2d 1017 (5th Cir.1987), cert. denied, 485 U.S. 959 (1988) (fourteen-year-old boy died while engaged in "autoerotic asphyxiation" described in defendant magazine). But cf. cases where Soldier of Fortune Magazine has been sued for deaths and injuries resulting from advertisements for "Gun for Hire": Norwood v. Soldier of Fortune Magazine, 651 F.Supp. 1397 (W.D.Ark.1987); Eimann v. Soldier of Fortune Magazine, 880 F.2d 830 (5th Cir.1989), cert. denied, 493 U.S. 1024 (1990); Braun v. Soldier of Fortune Magazine, 968 F.2d 1110 (11th Cir.1992), cert. denied, 506 U.S. 1071, 113 S.Ct. 1028 (1993); Rice v. Paladin Enterprises Inc., 128 F. 3d 233 (4th Cir.1997) (liability for advice on how to commit a murder).

6. Plaintiff, a female high school student, was sexually molested by her teacher. The teacher had been employed by the school after the school board had received a detailed recommendation by the teacher's former employer. The report did not mention the teacher's sexual proclivities known to the former employer. In Randi W. v. Muroc Joint Unified School District, 929 P. 2d 582 (Calif. 1997), the court held that the "writer of a letter of recommendation owes third persons a duty not to misrepresent the facts in describing the qualifications and character of a former employee, if making the representations would present a substantial and

foreseeable risk of physical injury to the third persons." Id. at 591. The half-truths amounted to misrepresentation.

7. In M.H. & J.L.H. v. Caritas Family Services, 488 N.W.2d 282 (Minn.1992), an adoption agency owed a duty of care to disclose information to adoptive parents about the incestuous parentage of a child. However, the courts have drawn back from imposing an affirmative duty to investigate. Meracle v. Children's Service Society of Wisconsin, 149 Wis.2d 19, 437 N.W.2d 532 (1989); Mallette v. Children's Friend and Service, 661 A.2d 67 (R.I.1995) (holding agency liable for nondisclosure of genetic or medical information when information of this nature is volunteered; agency must act with reasonable care or refuse to disclose any information); Jackson v. State, 956 P.2d 35 (Mont.1998) (recognizing a common law duty to disclose concurrent with a statutory obligation). An agency is liable for fraudulent misrepresentation. See Burr v. Board of County Comm'rs, 23 Ohio St.3d 69, 491 N.E.2d 1101 (1986) (knowing misrepresentations as to the background and health risks of child who subsequently became disabled by Huntington's Disease).

Hanberry v. Hearst Corp.

Court of Appeal of California, 1969.
276 Cal.App.2d 680, 81 Cal.Rptr. 519.

[Plaintiff-appellant purchased from defendant Akron a pair of shoes manufactured by defendant Handal. She alleges that the shoes were defective in being "slippery and unsafe" when used on vinyl floor coverings, and that "she stepped on the vinyl floor of her kitchen, slipped, fell and sustained several physical injuries."

She also sues defendant Hearst Corporation on the ground that it had negligently given a Good Housekeeping seal of approval to the shoes as "good ones." Hearst demurred to the causes against it, and the court granted judgment of dismissal to Hearst. Plaintiff appealed from this judgment.]

AULT, ASSOCIATE JUSTICE, PRO TEM. * * * Appellant further alleges respondent Hearst publishes a monthly magazine known as Good Housekeeping in which products, including the shoes she purchased, were advertised as meeting the "Good Housekeeping's Consumers' Guaranty Seal." With respect to this seal the magazine states: "This is Good Housekeeping's Consumers' Guaranty" and "We satisfy ourselves that products advertised in Good Housekeeping are good ones and that the advertising claims made for them in our magazine are truthful." The seal itself contained the promise, "If the product or performance is defective, Good Housekeeping guarantees replacement or refund to the consumer." * * *

In the second and eighth causes of action, appellant seeks to recover on the theory of negligent misrepresentation. * * *

The basic question presented on this appeal is whether one who endorses a product for his own economic gain, and for the purpose of encouraging and inducing the public to buy it, may be liable to a purchaser who, relying on the endorsement, buys the product and is injured because it is defective and not as represented in the endorsement. We conclude such liability may exist and a cause of action has been pleaded in the instant case. * * *

In both the second and eighth causes of action of the complaint under consideration, appellant has alleged respondent extended it certification and permitted the use of its seal in connection with the shoes she purchased without test, inspection or examination of the shoes, or a sample thereof, or if it tested, inspected or examined, it did so in a careless and negligent manner which did not reveal their dangerous and defective condition. If either of the alternative allegations is true, respondent violated its duty of care to the appellant and the issuance of its seal and certification with respect to the shoes under that circumstance would amount to a negligent misrepresentation.

Hearst urges its representation the shoes were "good ones" was a mere statement of opinion, not a statement of a material fact, and therefore not actionable. Since the very purpose of the seal and its certification the shoes were "good ones" was to induce and encourage members of the public to buy the shoes, respondent is in poor position to argue its endorsement cannot legally be considered as the inducing factor in bringing about their sale. [C] Respondent was not the seller or manufacturer of the shoes; it held itself out as a disinterested third party which had examined the shoes, found them satisfactory, and gave its endorsement. By the very procedure and method it used, respondent represented to the public it possessed superior knowledge and special information concerning the product it endorsed. Under such circumstance, respondent may be liable for negligent representations of either fact or opinion. [C]

Respondent argues no basis for liability has been shown because, "It is a matter of common knowledge that brand new soles on brand new shoes have a tendency of being slick and slippery until the shoes have been worn sufficiently long thereafter." The argument may well have merit [c], but it is one addressed properly to the trier of fact. The case is presented to us in the pleading context. We are unwilling to hold as a matter of law that liability will not attach under any circumstance based upon a defectively designed shoe. * * *

The judgment of dismissal is * * * reversed as to the second and eighth causes of action (negligent misrepresentation).

Richard v. A. Waldman and Sons, Inc.

Supreme Court of Connecticut, 1967.
155 Conn. 343, 232 A.2d 307.

COTTER, ASSOCIATE JUSTICE. The plaintiffs, owners of a house and lot in Vernon which they purchased from the defendant corporation, instituted an action * * * for damages for alleged false representations in connection with the sale of land. * * * [Plaintiff obtained] a judgment for damages from which the defendant has appealed. * * *

At the time of the closing, the defendant delivered to the plaintiffs a plot plan prepared by a registered engineer and land surveyor. This plan showed a sideyard of twenty feet on the southerly boundary of the lot which was in compliance with the minimum requirements for this lot according to the zoning regulations on file with the town clerk of Vernon. A permit had previously been granted for the construction of the building, consisting of a house with an attached garage, and the survey submitted at the time the defendant made the application indicated that the structure was to be located twenty feet more or less from the southerly property line. Subsequently, a certificate of occupancy was erroneously issued based on the survey submitted by the defendant. Approximately four months after the delivery of the deed to the plaintiffs, the defendant discovered, when it set pins defining the boundaries of the premises, that the southeast corner of the foundation of the plaintiffs' house was only 1.8 feet from the southerly boundary of the lot. At this time, it was found that trespass upon adjoining property occurred in entering and leaving the plaintiffs' back door and stoop. Prior to this discovery, the parties were unaware that there was a violation of the zoning regulations as to sideyard requirements. The defendant, under a mistaken assumption, had represented by the plot plan that the structure on the lot was twenty feet from the southerly boundary. Unaware of the true fact, the plaintiffs relied on this representation.

The court concluded (1) that the defendant falsely and recklessly represented to the plaintiffs, for the purpose of inducing action, that the premises had a southerly sideyard of twenty feet and that there was no violation of the zoning regulations, and (2) that the plaintiffs were induced to rely on these representations, which were the result of a mistake on the part of the defendant but were not innocent.

The defendant claims that "[a]t most, there was an innocent misrepresentation of fact by the defendant." An innocent misrepresentation may be actionable if the declarant has the means of knowing, ought to know, or has the duty of knowing the truth. [C]

The facts, as properly found, clearly show that the plaintiffs had reasonable grounds upon which to attribute to the defendant accurate knowledge of what it represented as to the location of the structure on the lot. This was a statement of fact about which the defendant as a developer of residential real estate, had special means of knowledge, and it was a matter peculiarly relating to its business and one on which the plaintiffs were entitled to rely. [Cc] The defendant was commercially involved in and responsible for the preliminary and final plans for building and locating the structure which was then constructed on the lot by the defendant in a manner which violated the zoning ordinance. Thereafter, the defendant undertook to provide the plaintiffs with a survey and plot plan which erroneously showed a southerly sideyard of twenty feet. Actual knowledge of the falsity of the representation need not be shown under the circumstances, nor must the plaintiffs allege fraud or bad faith. They have alleged all the facts material to support their claim and demand for damages. It is immaterial whether the wrong which can be legally inferred from the facts arises in contract or in tort. The plaintiffs may seek damages resulting from the defendant's misrepresentation and at the same time retain title to the property. [C] Such a misrepresentation was "in the nature of a warranty" entitling them to a recovery under the contract "as for a breach of warranty." It would be unjust to permit the defendant under these circumstances to "retain the fruits of a bargain induced by" a material misrepresentation upon which the plaintiffs relied. * * *

There was sufficient evidence which supported the court's finding that the plaintiffs were entitled to a recovery based on the rule that the measure of damages was the difference between the actual value of the property and the value of the property had it been as represented. * * *

[In *Rich v. Rankl*, 6 Conn.Cir. 185, 269 A.2d 84 (1969), the court says: "The relief granted in the Richard case was the cost of the construction work and the moving of the house to relocate it on the plaintiffs' lot."]

The facts necessary to establish the defendant's liability were alleged in the complaint, and the conclusions of the trial court are amply supported by the facts found.

There is no error.

NOTES AND QUESTIONS

1. If the plaintiff is seeking to rescind the contract, an innocent misrepresentation that is material is basis for relief. Neither scienter nor negligence is necessary. The action is not in tort, but for restitution. See Seneca Wire & Mfg. Co. v. A.B. Leach & Co., 247 N.Y. 1, 159 N.E. 700 (1928); Ross v. Harding, 64 Wash.2d 231, 391 P.2d 526 (1964).

2. The principal case allows recovery for innocent misrepresentation in a tort action. It follows a minority position. The earliest case to carry the strict liability over to a tort action for damages for the misrepresentation was Holcomb v. Noble, 69 Mich. 396, 37 N.W. 497 (1888), where the court appears to have confused equitable relief with an action at law. But Michigan now fully and consciously follows the "doctrine of innocent misrepresentation." United States Fidelity and Guaranty Co. v. Black, 412 Mich. 99, 313 N.W.2d 77 (1981).

3. This minority position has been adopted in the Restatement (Second) of Torts. Section 552C reads as follows:

"(1) One who, in a sale, rental or exchange transaction with another, makes a misrepresentation of a material fact for the purpose of inducing the other to act or to refrain from acting in reliance upon it, is subject to liability to the other for pecuniary loss caused to him by his justifiable reliance upon the misrepresentation, even though it is not made fraudulently or negligently.

"(2) Damages recoverable under the rule stated in this Section are limited to the difference between the value of what the other has parted with and the value of what he has received in the transaction.

"*Caveat:* The Institute expresses no opinion as to whether there may not be other types of business transactions, in addition to those of sale, rental and exchange, in which strict liability may be imposed for innocent misrepresentation, under the conditions stated in this Section."

4. Is the remedy of rescission adequate to take care of the plaintiff's needs, or should he be able to keep the property and sue for damages? Is a tort action needed if an action for breach of warranty is available? Is the rule in § 552C really a development of the law of torts, or one of the law of restitution, eliminating the requirement of restoring the status quo as a condition for relief?

(B) To Third Persons

Credit Alliance Corporation v. Arthur Andersen & Co.

Court of Appeals of New York, 1985.
65 N.Y.2d 536, 483 N.E.2d 110, 493 N.Y.S.2d 435.

JASEN, JUDGE. The critical issue common to these two appeals is whether an accountant may be held liable, absent privity of contract, to a party who relies to his detriment upon a negligently prepared financial report and, if so, within what limits does that liability extend.

[In Credit Alliance Corp. v. Andersen & Co., the defendant accountants prepared consolidated financial statements for L.B. Smith, Inc. Credit Alliance had provided financing to Smith for some time, insisting in 1978 upon audited financial statements. Smith supplied statements that had been prepared by defendant. "These statements contained an auditor's report prepared by Andersen stating that it had examined the statements in accordance with generally accepted auditing standards ('GAAS') and found them to reflect fairly the financial position of Smith in conformity with generally accepted accounting principles ('GAAP')." Plaintiff alleged that the statements were inaccurate because of failure to conduct investigations in accordance with proper auditing standards. Special Term denied defendant's motion to dismiss causes of action, based on negligence and fraud. A divided Appellate Division affirmed, 101 A.D.2d 231, 476 N.Y.S.2d 539, and certified to the Court of Appeals the question, "Was the order of the Supreme Court, as affirmed by this court, properly made?"

In European Am. Bank & Trust Co. v. Strahs & Kaye, ("S. & K."), the bank ("EAB") made substantial loans to Majestic Electro Industries. Majestic having become bankrupt, EAB sued S. & K. for seriously exaggerating Majestic's solvency assets. Special Term dismissed the complaint and Appellate Division reversed but certified a similar question to the Court of Appeals. EAB specifically alleges that S. & K. at all relevant times knew that EAB was Majestic Electro's principal lender, was familiar with the terms of the lending relationship and was fully aware that EAB was relying on the statements, and that S. & K. and Majestic were in communication during the entire course of the lending relationship.]

In the seminal case of Ultramares Corp. v. Touche, 255 N.Y. 170, 174 N.E. 441 [1931], this court, speaking through the opinion of Chief Judge Cardozo more than 50 years ago, disallowed a cause of action in negligence against a public accounting firm for inaccurately prepared financial statements which were relied upon by a plaintiff having no contractual privity with the accountants. This court distinguished its holding from Glanzer v. Shepard, 233 N.Y. 236, 135 N.E. 275 [1922], a case decided in an opinion also written by Cardozo nine years earlier. We explained that in *Glanzer*, an action in negligence against public weighers had been permitted, despite the absence of a contract between the parties, because the plaintiff's intended reliance, on the information *directly transmitted* by the weighers, created a bond so closely approaching privity that it was, in practical effect, virtually indistinguishable therefrom. This court has subsequently reaffirmed its holding in *Ultramares* which has been, and continues to be, much discussed and analyzed by the commentators and by the courts of other jurisdictions. These appeals now provide us with the opportunity to reexamine and delineate the principles enunciated in both *Ultramares* and *Glanzer*. Inasmuch as we believe that a relationship "so close as to approach that of privity" [c] remains valid as the predicate for imposing liability upon accountants to noncontractual parties for the negligent preparation of financial reports, we restate and elaborate upon our adherence to that standard today.

The doctrine of privity is said to have had its source in the classic enunciation of its rationale in Winterbottom v. Wright, 10 M. & W. 109, 152 Eng.Rep. 402, [supra page 401]. From *Winterbottom,* the privity doctrine developed into a general rule prevailing well into the Twentieth Century. [Cc]

By the time 90 years had passed, however, this court could note in *Ultramares* that the "assault upon the citadel of privity is proceeding in these days apace." [C] We acknowledged that inroads had been made, for example, where third-party beneficiaries or dangerous instrumentalities were involved. [C] Indeed, we referred to this court's holding in MacPherson v. Buick Motor Co., 217 N.Y. 382, [supra page 403] where it was decided that the manufacturer of a defective chattel—there an automobile—may be liable in negligence for the resulting injuries sustained by a user regardless of the absence of privity—a belated rejection of the doctrine of privity as applied to the facts in *Winterbottom*. Nevertheless, regarding an accountant's liability to unknown parties with whom he had not contracted, the considerations were deemed sufficiently dissimilar to justify different treatment.

Although accountants might be held liable in fraud to nonprivy parties who were intended to rely upon the accountants' misrepresentations, we noted that "[a] different question develops when we ask whether they owed a duty to these to make [their reports] without negligence." Ultramares Corp. v. Touche, supra. Disputing the wisdom of extending the duty of care of accountants to anyone who might foreseeably rely upon their financial reports, Cardozo, speaking for this court, remarked: "If liability for negligence exists, a thoughtless slip or blunder, the failure to detect a theft or forgery beneath the cover of deceptive entries, may expose accountants to a liability in an indeterminate amount for an indeterminate time to an indeterminate class. The hazards of a business conducted on these terms are so extreme as to enkindle doubt whether a flaw may not exist in the implication of a duty that exposes to these consequences." [C]

In *Ultramares,* the accountants had prepared a certified balance sheet for their client to whom they provided 32 copies. The client, in turn, gave one to the plaintiff company. The latter, relying upon the misinformation contained in the balance sheet, made loans to the accountants' client who, only months later, was declared bankrupt. This court, refusing to extend the accountants' liability for negligence to their client's lender, with whom they had no contractual privity, noted that the accountants had prepared a report on behalf of their client to be exhibited generally to "banks, creditors, stockholders, purchasers or sellers, *according to the needs of the occasion".* [C] In reciting the facts, we emphasized that: "*Nothing was said as to the persons to whom these [copies] would be shown or the extent or number of the transactions in which they would be used.* In particular there was no mention of the plaintiff, a corporation doing business chiefly as a factor, which till then had never made advances to the [accountants' client], though it had sold merchandise in small amounts. The range of the transactions in which a certificate of audit might be expected to play a part was as indefinite and wide as the possibilities of the business that was mirrored in the summary." [C]

The accountants' report was primarily intended as a convenient instrumentality for the client's use in developing its business. "[O]nly incidentally or collaterally" was it expected to assist those to whom the client "might exhibit it thereafter". [C] Under such circumstances, permitting recovery by parties such as the plaintiff company would have been to impose a duty upon accountants "enforce[able] by any member of an indeterminate class of creditors, present and prospective, known and unknown." [C]

By sharp contrast, the facts underlying *Glanzer* bespoke an affirmative assumption of a duty of care to a specific party, for a specific purpose, regardless of whether there was a contractual relationship. There, a seller of beans employed the defendants who were engaged in business as public weighers. Pursuant to instructions, the weighers furnished one copy of the weight certificate to their employer, the seller, and another to the prospective buyer. In reliance upon the inaccurately certified weight, the buyer purchased beans from the seller and, thereby, suffered a loss.

Explaining the imposition upon the weighers of a "noncontractual" duty of care to the buyer, this court held: "We think the law imposes a duty toward buyer as well as seller in the situation here disclosed. The [buyer's] use of the certificates was *not an indirect or collateral consequence* of the action of the weighers. It was a consequence which, to the weighers' knowledge, was the *end and aim of the transaction.* [The seller] ordered, but [the buyer was] to use. The defendants held themselves out to the public as skilled and careful in their calling. They knew that the beans had been sold, and that on the faith of their certificate payment would be made. *They sent a copy to the [buyer] for the very purpose of inducing action.* All this they admit. In such circumstances, assumption of the task of weighing was the assumption of a duty to weigh carefully for the benefit of all whose conduct was to be governed. We do not need to state the duty in terms of contract or of privity. Growing out of a contract, it has none the less an origin not exclusively contractual. Given the contract and the relation, the duty is imposed by law." [C]

The critical distinctions between the two cases were highlighted in *Ultramares,* where we explained: "In Glanzer v. Shepard * * * [the certificate of weight], which was made out in duplicate, one copy to the seller and the other to the buyer, *recites that it was made by order of the former for the use of the latter* * * * Here was something more than the rendition of a service in the expectation that the one who ordered the certificate would use it thereafter in the operations of his business as occasion might require. Here was a case where *the transmission of the certificate to another was* not merely one possibility among many, but *the 'end and aim of the transaction,'* as certain and immediate and deliberately willed as if a husband were to order a gown to be delivered to his wife, or a telegraph company, contracting with the sender of a message, were to telegraph it wrongly to the damage of the person expected to receive it * * * The *intimacy of the resulting nexus* is attested by the fact that after stating the case in terms of legal duty, we went on to point out that * * * we could reach the same result by stating it in terms of contract * * * The bond was *so close as to approach that of privity, if not completely one with it.* Not so in the case at hand [i.e., *Ultramares*]. No one would be likely to urge that there was a contractual relation, or *even one approaching it,* at the root of any duty that was owing from the [accountants] now before us to the indeterminate class of persons who, presently or in the future, might deal with the [accountants' client] in reliance on the audit. In a word, the service rendered by the defendant in Glanzer v. Shepard was primarily for the information of a third person, *in effect, if not in name, a party to the contract,* and only incidentally for that of the formal promisee." [C]

Several years subsequent to the decision in *Ultramares,* this court reiterated the requirement for a "contractual relationship or its equivalent" (State St. Trust Co. v. Ernst, 278 N.Y. 104, 111, 15 N.E.2d 416), and more recently, in *White v. Guarente,* 43 N.Y.2d 356, 401 N.Y.S.2d 474, 372 N.E.2d 315, such an equivalent was presented for our consideration. There, the accountants had contracted with a limited partnership to perform an audit and prepare the partnership's tax returns. The nature and purpose of the contract, to satisfy the requirement in the partnership agreement for an audit, made it clear that the accountants' services were obtained to benefit the members of the partnership who, like plaintiff, a limited partner, were necessarily dependent upon the audit to prepare their own tax returns. After outlining the principles articulated in *Ultramares* and *Glanzer,* this court observed that: "[T]his plaintiff seeks redress, not as a mere member of the public, but as one of a settled and particularized class among the members of which the report would be circulated *for the specific purpose of fulfilling the limited partnership agreed upon arrangement."* [C]

Because the accountants knew that a limited partner would have to rely upon the audit and tax returns of the partnership, and inasmuch as this was within the specific contemplation of the accounting retainer, we held that, "at least on the facts here, an accountant's liability may be so imposed." [C] The resulting relationship between the accountants and the limited partner was clearly one "approach[ing] that of privity, if not completely one with it." (*Ultramares Corp. v. Touche, supra*).

Upon examination of *Ultramares* and *Glanzer* and our recent affirmation of their holdings in *White,* certain criteria may be gleaned. Before accountants may be held liable in negligence to noncontractual parties who rely to their detriment on inaccurate financial reports, certain prerequisites must be satisfied: (1) the accountants must have been aware that the financial reports were to be used for a particular purpose or purposes; (2) in the furtherance of which a known party or parties was intended to rely; and (3) there must have been some conduct on the part of the accountants linking them to that party or parties, which evinces the accountants' understanding of that party or parties' reliance. While these criteria permit some flexibility in the application of the doctrine of privity to accountants' liability, they do not represent a departure from the principles articulated in *Ultramares, Glanzer* and *White,* but, rather, they are intended to preserve the wisdom and policy set forth therein.

We are aware that the courts throughout this country are divided as to the continued validity of the holding in *Ultramares*. Some courts continue to insist that a strict application of the privity requirement governs the law of accountants' liability except, perhaps, where special circumstances compel a different result. * * *

In all of [these] cases, the courts found the facts amenable to the imposition of accountants' liability under the principles of *Ultramares–Glanzer* or extended those principles to permit a more liberalized application. To the extent that the holdings in those cases are predicated upon certain criteria—to wit, a particular purpose for the accountants' report, a known relying party, and some conduct on the part of the accountants linking them to that party—they are consonant with the principles reaffirmed in this decision. To the extent, however, that those cases were decided upon the ground that *Ultramares* should not be followed and, instead, a rule permitting recovery by any foreseeable plaintiff should be adopted, the law in this State, as reiterated today, is clearly distinguishable. * * *

In the appeals we decide today, application of the foregoing principles presents little difficulty. In *Credit Alliance,* the facts as alleged by plaintiffs fail to demonstrate the existence of a relationship between the parties sufficiently approaching privity. Though the complaint and supporting affidavit do allege that Andersen specifically knew, should have known or was on notice that plaintiffs were being shown the reports by Smith, Andersen's client, in order to induce their reliance thereon, nevertheless, there is no adequate allegation of either a particular purpose for the reports' preparation or the prerequisite conduct on the part of the accountants. While the allegations state that Smith sought to induce plaintiffs to extend credit, no claim is made that Andersen was being employed to prepare the reports with that particular purpose in mind. Moreover, there is no allegation that Andersen had any direct dealings with plaintiffs, had specifically agreed with Smith to prepare the report for plaintiffs' use or according to plaintiffs' requirements, or had specifically agreed with Smith to provide plaintiffs with a copy or actually did so. Indeed, there is simply no allegation of any word or action on the part of Andersen directed to plaintiffs, or anything contained in Andersen's retainer agreement with Smith which provided the necessary link between them.

By sharp contrast, in *European American,* the facts as alleged by EAB clearly show that S. & K. was well aware that a primary, if not the exclusive, *end and aim* of auditing its client, Majestic Electro, was to provide EAB with the financial information it required. The prerequisites for the cause of action in negligence, as well as in gross negligence, are fully satisfied. Not only is it alleged, as in *Credit Alliance,* that the accountants knew the identity of the specific nonprivy party who would be relying upon the audit reports, but additionally, the complaint and affidavit here allege both the accountants' awareness of a particular purpose for their services and certain conduct on their part creating an unmistakable relationship with the reliant plaintiff. It is unambiguously claimed that the parties remained in direct communication, both orally and in writing, and, indeed, met together throughout the course of EAB's lending relationship with Majestic Electro, for the very purpose of discussing the latter's financial condition and EAB's need for S. & K.'s evaluation. Moreover, it is alleged that S. & K. made repeated representations personally to representatives of EAB, on these occasions, concerning the value of Majestic Electro's assets. It cannot be gainsaid that the relationship thus created between the parties was the practical equivalent of privity. The parties' direct communications and personal meetings resulted in a nexus between them sufficiently approaching privity under the principles of *Ultramares, Glanzer* and *White* to permit EAB's causes of action.

Finally, disposition of the second cause of action alleged in *Credit Alliance* need not detain us long. The cause of action for fraud repeats the allegations for the negligence cause of action and merely adds a claim that Andersen recklessly disregarded facts which would have apprised it that its reports were misleading or that Andersen had actual knowledge that such was the case. This single allegation of scienter, without additional detail concerning the facts constituting the alleged fraud, is insufficient under the special pleading standards required under CPLR 3016(b), and, consequently, the cause of action should have been dismissed. [Cc].

Accordingly, in *Credit Alliance* both causes of action should be dismissed, the order of the Appellate Division reversed, with costs, and the certified question answered in the negative. In *European American,* the order of the Appellate Division should be affirmed, with costs, and the certified question answered in the affirmative.

Citizens State Bank v. Timm, Schmidt & Co.

Supreme Court of Wisconsin, 1983.
113 Wis.2d 376, 335 N.W.2d 361.

[For the years 1973–76, defendant Timm, Schmidt & Co. (Timm), an accounting firm, prepared financial statements for Clintonville Fire Apparatus, Inc. (CFA), including statements of financial condition, yearly income, retained income and changes in financial condition. These were accompanied by an opinion letter to CFA stating that "the financial statements fairly presented the financial condition of CFA and that the statements were prepared in accordance with generally accepted accounting principles."

In 1975 and 1976 CFA obtained loans from Citizens State Bank amounting to $380,000, relying on Timm's statements. In 1977 Timm discovered mistakes in its statements totaling over $400,000. It notified Security, which called in all of its loans due. CFA went into receivership and was ultimately liquidated and dissolved. Still due to Citizens was $152,214. Citizens sued Timm for that amount.

Timm moved for summary judgment. All persons in the Timm firm who had worked on the CFA statements filed affidavits that they had no knowledge that CFA intended to obtain or had any loans from Citizens. There were some contradictory affidavits, especially from the CFA president, Dando, indicating that he believed that Timm knew of the dealing. The trial court granted the motion for summary judgment, and the court of appeals affirmed. The case is now before the state supreme court.]

DAY, JUSTICE * * * The question on review is whether accountants may be held liable for the negligent preparation of an audit report to a third party not in privity who relies on the report.

This is a question of first impression in this state. However, the issue has received wide consideration in both courts and law journals.

Accountants have long been held not liable for their negligence to relying third parties not in privity under an application of Judge Cardozo's decision in *Ultramares v. Touche,* 255 N.Y. 170, 174 N.E. 441 (1931). In *Ultramares,* Judge Cardozo absolved the defendant accountants from liability for overvaluing the assets of a company in an audit report to a plaintiff who had loaned money in reliance on a certified balance sheet in the report. Judge Cardozo expressed the concern that "if liability exists, a thoughtless slip or blunder * * * may expose accountants to a liability in an indeterminate amount for an indeterminate time to an indeterminate class." [C]

[At one time] *Ultramares* was relied on by every jurisdiction to consider this question to deny accountant liability to third parties. However, in recent years, *Ultramares* has received new attention and courts have started to find accountants liable to third parties.

In Rusch Factors, Inc., v. Levin, 284 F.Supp. 85 (D.C.R.I.1968), the court, citing section 552 of the Restatement, imposed liability on an accountant to a relying third party not in privity. In *Rusch Factors,* the accountant knew the statements he prepared were to be used by his client for the purpose of obtaining credit from a third party even though they did not know of the specific relying third party. Nevertheless, the court allowed liability to be imposed. 284 F.Supp. at 93.

Similarly, in Ryan v. Kanne, 170 N.W.2d 395 (Iowa 1969), the Iowa Supreme Court applying Restatement section 552, determined that an accountant could be held liable to a foreseen third party who had relied upon a negligently prepared audit report. Because the relying third party was "actually known," the court did not address the extent of foreseeability that would be necessary before an accountant could be held liable to a third party not actually known. 170 N.W.2d at 403.

In this state, although the liability of accountants to third parties not in privity has not been examined, the liability of an attorney to one not in privity was recently examined in Auric v. Continental Casualty Co., 111 Wis.2d 507, 331 N.W.2d 325 (1983). This court concluded that an attorney may be held liable to a will beneficiary not in privity for the attorney's negligence in supervising the execution of a will. 111 Wis.2d at 514. Part of the rationale for this decision was that the imposition of liability would make attorneys more careful in the execution of their responsibilities to their clients. [C]

That rationale is applicable here. Unless liability is imposed, third parties who rely upon the accuracy of the financial statements will not be protected. Unless an accountant can be held liable to a relying third party, this negligence will go undeterred.

There are additional policy reasons to allow the imposition of liability. If relying third parties, such as creditors, are not allowed to recover, the cost of credit to the general public will increase because creditors will either have to absorb the costs of bad loans made in reliance on faulty information or hire independent accountants to verify the information received. Accountants may spread the risk through the use of liability insurance.

We conclude that the absence of privity alone should not bar negligence actions by relying third parties against accountants.

Although the absence of privity does not bar this action, the question remains as to the extent of an accountant's liability to injured third parties. Courts which have examined this question have generally relied upon section 552 of the Restatement to restrict the class of third persons who could sue accountants for their negligent acts. Under section 552(2)(a) and (b), liability is limited to loss suffered:

"(a) By the person or one of a limited group of persons for whose benefit and guidance he [in this case the accountant] intends to supply the information or knows the recipient intends to supply it; and

"(b) Through reliance upon it in a transaction that he [the accountant] intends the information to influence or knows the recipient so intends or in a substantially similar transaction."

Under section 552, liability is not extended to all parties whom the accountant might reasonably foresee as using the information. Rather, as one commentator noted, "The Restatement's formulation of 'a limited group of persons' extends causes of action to a limited number of third parties who are expected to gain access to the financial statement information in an expected transaction." This limitation is stressed in comment h to section 552, where it is noted that:

"It is not required that the person who is to become the plaintiff be identified or known to the defendant as an individual when the information is supplied. It is enough that the maker of the representation intends it to reach and influence either a particular person or persons, known to him, or a group or class of persons, distinct from the much larger class who might reasonably be expected sooner or later to have access to the information and foreseeably to take some action in reliance upon it."

The fundamental principle of Wisconsin negligence law is that a tortfeasor is fully liable for all foreseeable consequences of his act except as those consequences are limited by policy factors. [Cc] The Restatement's statement of limiting liability to certain third parties is too restrictive a statement of policy factors for this Court to adopt.

We conclude that accountants' liability to third parties should be determined under the accepted principles of Wisconsin negligence law. According to these principles, a finding of non-liability will be made only if there is a strong public policy requiring such a finding. [Cc]

Liability will be imposed on these accountants for the foreseeable injuries resulting from their negligent acts unless, under the facts of this particular case, as a matter of policy to be decided by the court, recovery is denied on grounds of public policy. [C] This Court has set out a number of public policy reasons for not imposing liability despite a finding of negligence causing injury:

"(1) The injury is too remote from the negligence; or (2) the injury is too wholly out of proportion to the culpability of the negligent tort-feasor; or (3) in retrospect it appears too highly extraordinary that the negligence should have brought about the harm; or (4) because allowance of recovery would place too unreasonable a burden on the negligent tort-feasor; or (5) because allowance of recovery would be too likely to open the way for fraudulent claims; or (6) allowance of recovery would enter a field that has no sensible or just stopping point." *Ollerman* [v. O'Rourke Co., 94 Wis.2d 17, 48, 288 N.W.2d 95 (1980).]

Although in some cases this court has decided at the motion-to-dismiss stage that policy factors preclude the imposition of liability for negligent acts, [c] it has generally been found to be better practice to have a full factual resolution before evaluating the public policy considerations involved. *Ollerman*, [cc].

In this case we conclude that a determination of the public policy questions should be made after the facts of this case have been fully explored at trial. The question of the proper scope of these accountants' liabilities to the third party bank cannot be determined upon the information contained in the record. A full factual resolution is necessary before it can be said that public policy precludes Timm's liability for its allegedly negligent conduct.

The pleadings, affidavits and other information in the record before this court do not establish that Timm was entitled as a matter of law to summary judgment. Under the accepted principles of Wisconsin negligence law, Timm could be liable to Citizens if Timm's actions were the cause of Citizens' injuries and if the injuries were reasonably foreseeable unless public policy precluded recovery.

Timm's affidavits do not dispute that Citizen's reliance upon the financial statements led to the making of the loans and ultimately to the losses which were incurred. Each affidavit recites that Timm employees had no knowledge that the financial statements would actually be used by CFA to apply for a new bank loan or to increase existing loan indebtedness. However, the affidavit of Elmer Timm stated that "as a certified public accountant, I know that audited statements are used for many purposes and that it is common for them to be supplied to lenders and creditors, and other persons."

These affidavits and other information contained in the record do not dispose of the issue of whether it was foreseeable that a negligently prepared financial statement could cause harm to Citizens.

Therefore, Timm having failed to establish a *prima facie* case for summary judgment, we conclude the trial judge erred in granting the motion for summary judgment.

Decision of the court of appeals is reversed and cause remanded to the trial court for further proceedings not inconsistent with this opinion.

NOTES AND QUESTIONS

1. The scope of auditors' liability has been a vexed issue. The two principal cases represent the ends of the spectrum. *Credit Alliance* was thoroughly reexamined and reaffirmed by the Court of Appeals of New York in Security Pacific Business Credit, Inc. v. Peat Marwick, Main & Co., 79 N.Y.2d 695, 597 N.E.2d 1080, 586 N.Y.S.2d 87 (1992) (requisite relationship is not established by plaintiff calling auditor and announcing reliance). Elsewhere, the English courts have insisted upon a narrow scope of liability, see Caparo Industries P.L.C. v. Dickman, [1990] 2 A.C. 605. The duty is limited to where defendant, giving advice or information, was fully aware of the nature of the transaction which the plaintiff had in contemplation, knew that the advice or information would be communicated to him directly or indirectly, and knew that it was very likely that the plaintiff would rely on that advice or information in deciding whether or not to engage in the transaction in contemplation.

2. As quoted in the Citizens State Bank case, the Second Restatement takes an intermediate position, confining recovery to a "limited group of persons" and to a transaction or "substantially similar transaction" intended by the defendant. In Bily v. Arthur Young & Co., 3 Cal.4th 370, 834 P.2d 745, 11 Cal.Rptr.2d 51 (1992), the California Supreme Court adopted the Restatement test. The opinion, like that of the House of Lords, supports the criterion of knowledge of the class of persons and transactions that the supplier of the information "intends the information to influence." Unlimited liability is avoided and the scope of liability regulated by the supplier of the information. The court observes that the test is applicable to other professionals supplying information and evaluations for the use and benefit of others, including "attorneys, architects, engineers, title insurers and abstracters." The court formulated the following jury instructions: "The representation must have been made with the intent to induce plaintiff, or a particular class of persons

to which plaintiff belongs, to act in reliance upon the representation in a specific transaction, or a specific type of transaction, that defendant intended to influence. Defendant is deemed to have intended to influence [its client's] transaction with plaintiff whenever defendant knows with substantial certainty that plaintiff, or the particular class of persons to which plaintiff belongs, will rely on the representation in the course of the transaction. If others become aware of the representation and act upon it, there is no liability even though defendant should reasonably have foreseen such a possibility."

The California Supreme Court expressly rejected the approaches exemplified in *Credit Alliance* and *Citizens State Bank*. Other cases adopting the Restatement position after close examination of the vying authorities and the policies at play are First National Bank of Commerce v. Monco Agency, 911 F.2d 1053 (5th Cir.1990) (applying Louisiana law); Nycal v. KPMG Peat Marwick LLP, 426 Mass. 491, 688 N.E.2d 1368 (1998); and ML–Lee Acquisition v. Deloitte and Touche, 463 S.E.2d 618 (S.C.App.1995).

3.   Managers of a corporation engaged in a fraudulent scheme whereby the valuations of inventories were inflated to give a misleading picture of the corporation's wealth. Auditor failed to uncover the fraud. Eventually a corporation officer unmasked the fraud. Should the corporation have a good cause of action against the auditors? Any other person or persons? See Cenco Incorporated v. Seidman & Seidman, 686 F.2d 449 (7th Cir.1982).

4.   As suggested, other professionals who proffer advice upon which third parties rely are subject to the same liability as in the auditor cases. Vereins–Und Westbank, AG v. Carter, 691 F.Supp. 704 (S.D.N.Y.1988) (liability of attorney for opinion letter within the principles in *Ultramares*); Prudential Ins. Co. v. Dewey, Ballantine, et al., 80 N.Y.2d 377, 605 N.E.2d 318, 590 N.Y.S.2d 831 (1992) (opinion letter by borrower's lawyers to lender creates a duty of care). But cf. Ackerman v. Schwartz, 733 F.Supp. 1231 (N.D.Ind.1989) (no liability for opinion letter relied on by non-client). In Robinson v. Omer, 952 S.W.2d 423 (Tenn.1997), defendant attorney advised his client that to videotape secretly his sexual encounters would be legally permissible. Plaintiff, after being informed of this advice by the client, agreed to help him videotape the encounters. Plaintiff was sued by a number of the women who had been videotaped and settled the claims at considerable cost. The Tennessee Supreme Court held that no duty was established since the advice was not relied on for a contemplated commercial or business transaction.

5.   In M. Miller Co. v. Contra Costa Sanitary Dist., 198 Cal.App.2d 305, 18 Cal.Rptr. 13 (1961), an engineering company was hired to prepare a soil report, knowing that it would be used by bidders for work on a sewer system. The report was negligently done and inaccurate, and the successful bidder lost money. He was allowed to recover damages although the report was not made directly to him. But cf. Texas Tunneling Co. v. Chattanooga, 329 F.2d 402 (6th Cir.1964), rev'g, 204 F.Supp. 821 (E.D.Tenn.1962). Barrie v. V.P. Exterminators, Inc., 625 So. 2d 1007 (La.1993) (duty owed by termite inspector to third parties.)

6.   Another line of cases concern the liability of attorneys to disappointed beneficiaries of wills. Does the attorney who negligently causes a testamentary gift to fail owe a duty of care to the disappointed donee? See cases referred to in notes 3 and 4, supra (page 411) following Clagett v. Dacy, 47 Md. App. 23, 420 A.2d 1285 (1980), supra (page 409). The duty was narrowly construed in Noble v. Bruce, 349 Md. 730, 709 A.2d 1264 (1998) (no duty owed to beneficiaries for negligence leading to large tax liability).

Ultramares Corporation v. Touche

Court of Appeals of New York, 1931.
255 N.Y. 170, 174 N.E. 441.

[The opinions of Judge Cardozo in Glanzer v. Shepard and Ultramares Corp. v. Touche have been well described in the opinion of Judge Jason in Credit Alliance Co., supra page 1032. The description of *Ultramares* there, however, covered only the holding regarding the accountants' liability to a third person for negligent preparation of financial statements. The *Ultramares* opinion went on to discuss liability in fraud or deceit under the American doctrine of Sovereign Pocahontas Co. v. Bond, 120 F.2d 39 (D.C.Cir.1941). That part of the *Ultramares* opinion is set forth here.

Touche, Nivens' certificate in the case had stated: "We have examined the accounts of Fred Stern & Co. * * * and hereby certify that the annexed balance sheet is in accordance therewith and with the information and explanations given us. We further certify that * * * the said statement in our opinion presents a true and correct view of the financial condition of Fred Stern & Co. * * *."]

CARDOZO, C.J. * * * Our holding [on liability for negligence] does not emancipate accountants from the consequences of fraud. It does not relieve them if their audit has been so negligent as to justify a finding that they had no genuine belief in its adequacy, for this again is fraud. It does no more than say that, if less than this is proved, if there has been neither reckless misstatement nor insincere profession of an opinion, but only honest blunder, the ensuing liability for negligence is one that is bounded by the contract, and is to be enforced between the parties by whom the contract has been made. We doubt whether the average businessman receiving a certificate without paying for it, and receiving it merely as one among a multitude of possible investors, would look for anything more.

The defendants certified as a fact, true to their own knowledge, that the balance sheet was in accordance with the books of account. If their statement was false, they are not to be exonerated because they believed it to be true. [Cc] We think the triers of the facts might hold it to be false.

Correspondence between the balance sheet and the books imports something more, or so the triers of the facts might say, than correspondence between the balance sheet and the general ledger, unsupported or even contradicted by every other record. The correspondence to be of any moment may not unreasonably be held to signify a correspondence between the statement and the books of original entry, the books taken as a whole. If that is what the certificate means, a jury could find that the correspondence did not exist, and that the defendants signed the certificates without knowing it to exist and even without reasonable grounds for belief in its existence. The item of $706,000, representing fictitious accounts receivable, was entered in the ledger after defendant's employee Siess had posted the December sales. He knew of the interpolation, and knew that there was need to verify the entry by reference to books other than the ledger before the books could be found to be in agreement with the balance sheet. The evidence would sustain a finding that this was never done. By concession the interpolated item had no support in the journal, or in any journal voucher, or in the debit memo book, which was a summary of the invoices, or in any thing except the invoices themselves. The defendants do not say that they ever looked at the invoices, seventeen in number, representing these accounts. They profess to be unable to recall whether they did so or not. They admit, however, that, if they had looked, they would have found omissions and irregularities so many and unusual as to have called for further investigation. When we couple the refusal to say that they did look with the admission that, if they had looked, they would or could have seen, the situation is revealed as one in which a jury might reasonably find that in truth they did not look, but certified the correspondence without testing its existence.

In this connection we are to bear in mind the principle * * * that negligence or blindness, even when not equivalent to fraud, is none the less evidence to sustain an inference of fraud. At least this is so if the negligence is gross. Not a little confusion has at times resulted from an undiscriminating quotation of statements in Kountze v. Kennedy, [147 N.Y. 124, 41 N.E. 414 (1895)] statements proper enough in their setting, but capable of misleading when extracted and considered by themselves. "Misjudgment, however gross," it was there observed, "or want of caution, however marked, is not fraud." This was said in a case where the trier of the facts had held the defendants guiltless. The judgment in this court amounted merely to a holding that a finding of fraud did not follow as an inference of law. There was no holding that the evidence would have required a reversal of the judgment if the finding as to guilt had been the other way. Even Derry v. Peek, as we have seen, asserts the probative effect of negligence as an evidentiary fact. We had no thought in Kountze v. Kennedy, of upholding a doctrine more favorable to wrongdoers, though there was a reservation suggesting the approval of a rule more rigorous. * * * No such charity of construction exonerates accountants, who by the very nature of their calling profess to speak with knowledge when certifying to an agreement between the audit and the entries.

The defendants attempt to excuse the omission of an inspection of the invoices proved to be fictitious by invoking a practice known as that of testing and sampling. A random choice of accounts is made from the total number on the books, and these, if found to be regular when inspected and investigated, are taken as a fair indication of the quality of the mass. * * * Verification by test and sample was very likely a sufficient audit as to accounts regularly entered upon the books in the usual course of business. It was plainly insufficient, however, as to accounts not entered upon the books where inspection of the invoices was necessary, not as a check upon accounts fair upon their face, but in order to ascertain whether there were any accounts at all. If the only invoices inspected were invoices unrelated to the interpolated entry, the result was to certify a correspondence between the books and the balance sheet without any effort by the auditors, as to $706,000 of accounts, to ascertain whether the certified agreement was in accordance with the truth. * * * The defendants were put on their guard by the circumstances touching the December accounts receivable to scrutinize with special care. A jury might find that, with suspicions thus awakened, they closed their eyes to the obvious, and blindly gave assent.

We conclude, to sum up the situation, that in certifying to the correspondence between balance sheet and accounts the defendants made a statement as true to their own knowledge, when they had, as a jury might find, no knowledge on the subject. If that is so, they may also be found to have acted without information leading to a sincere or genuine belief when they certified to an opinion that the balance sheet faithfully reflected the condition of the business. * * *

Upon the plaintiff's appeal as to the second cause of action, the judgment [for the defendants in the lower courts] should be reversed, and a new trial granted, with costs to abide the event.

NOTES AND QUESTIONS

1. This part of the *Ultramares* case involves liability for fraudulent, as distinguished from negligent, misrepresentation. The defendant's conduct being more reprehensible, the opinion indicates that a wider circle of liability is required. When the defendant's conduct is not only reckless but also intended to deceive, it would appear that the scope of liability would be even broader.

2. The central requirement of intent in fraudulent misrepresentation or deceit avoids the expansiveness of reasonable foreseeability employed in negligence. The scope of deceit has broadened as the notion of intent has become more liberal but nevertheless, the nexus, as Cardozo recognized, will be close and the duty more narrowly drawn. The Siren call of reasonable foreseeability is thus nicely avoided. For the scope of liability in deceit see note 3 (page 1016).

4. RELIANCE

Williams v. Rank & Son Buick, Inc.

Supreme Court of Wisconsin, 1969.
44 Wis.2d 239, 170 N.W.2d 807.

[Plaintiff went to defendant's used car lot on March 19 and looked at a Chrysler automobile. Plaintiff testified that he was looking for an air-conditioned car; that the salesman told him the car was air-conditioned, and that the particular car had been so described in an advertisement on which he relied. The evidence was, however, that the advertisement was first published two days after plaintiff bought the car, and defendant contended that plaintiff "seized upon an error in the ad to seek a reduction in the price previously paid for the automobile." Plaintiff was invited to take the car out for a test run, and did so, driving it for about an hour and a half. According to plaintiff, however, it was not until several days after the purchase that he discovered that the knobs marked "AIR" were for ventilation, and that the car was not air-conditioned. Plaintiff brought an action for fraud, and received a judgment for $150 damages. Defendant appeals.]

HANLEY, JUSTICE. * * * [T]here is ample evidence to warrant the trial court's finding that the oral misrepresentation of the appellant's salesman was in fact made. * * *

The question of reliance is another matter. Many previous decisions of this court have held that one cannot justifiably rely upon obviously false statements. In Jacobsen v. Whitely (1909), 138 Wis. 434, 436, 437, 120 N.W. 285, 286, the court said:

" * * * It is an unsavory defense for a man who by false statements, induces another to act to assert that if the latter had disbelieved him he would not have been injured. * * * Nevertheless courts will refuse to act for the relief of one claiming to have been misled by another's statements who blindly acts in disregard of knowledge of their falsity or with such opportunity that by the exercise of ordinary observation, not necessarily by search, he would have known. He may not close his eyes to what is obviously discoverable by him. * * * "

It is apparent that the obviousness of a statement's falsity vitiates reliance since no one can rely upon a known falsity. Were the rule otherwise a person would be free to enter into a contract with no intent to perform under the contract unless it ultimately proved profitable. On the other hand, a party who makes an inadvertent slip of the tongue or pencil would continually lose the benefit of the contract.

The question is thus whether the statement's falsity could have been detected by ordinary observation. Whether the falsity of a statement could have been discovered through ordinary care is to be determined in light of the intelligence and experience of the misled individual. Also to be considered is the relationship between the parties. [Cc] In several cases this court has held that the above factors negated the opportunity to inspect and the obviousness of the statement's falsity. [C]

In the instant case, however, no such negating factors exist. The respondent specifically testified that, being a high school graduate, he was capable of both reading and writing. It is also fair to assume that he possessed a degree of business acumen in that he and his brother operated their own business. No fiduciary relationship existed between the parties. They dealt with each other at arms' length. The appellant made no effort to interfere with the respondent's examination of the car, but, on the contrary, allowed him to take the car from the premises for a period of one and one-half hours.

Although the obviousness of a statement's falsity is a question of fact, this court has decided some such questions as a matter of law. [Cc]

In the instant case the respondent had ample opportunity to determine whether the car was air-conditioned. He had examined the car on the lot and had been allowed to remove the car from the lot unaccompanied by a salesman for a period of approximately one and one-half hours. This customers were normally not allowed to do.

No great search was required to disclose the absence of the air conditioning unit since a mere flip of a knob was all that was necessary. If air conditioning was, as stated by the respondent, the main reason he purchased the car, it is doubtful that he would not try the air conditioner. * * *

We conclude that as a matter of law the respondent under the facts and circumstances was not justified in relying upon the oral representation of the salesman. This is an action brought in fraud and not an action for a breach of warranty.

Order reversed [by a vote of 4 to 3].

WILKIE, JUSTICE (dissenting). * * * I would hold that the falsity of the representation was not so obvious that it could be held as a matter of law that the respondent had no right to rely on it. It was for the finder of fact and by finding reliance the trial court, by implication, found respondent had a right to rely thereon. * * *

NOTES AND QUESTIONS

1. In H. Hirschberg Optical Co. v. Michaelson, 1 Neb.Unof. 137, 95 N.W. 461 (1901), plaintiff, buying a pair of glasses, testified that he was told by defendant's salesman that the glass used in them had a special quality which would make them adapt themselves to his eyes. On this evidence, can the plaintiff recover for deceit? See also that foremost classic of legal humor, the sad but fascinating tale of the land of Shalam. Ellis v. Newbrough, 6 N.M. 181, 27 P. 490 (1891). In Hitachi Credit America Corp. v. Signet Bank, 166 F.3d 614 (4th Cir., 1999), Hitachi was persuaded by Signet Bank to participate in the financing of a highly secret, off-shore cigarette venture that had been represented as a venture sponsored by Philip Morris with the cooperation of the United States government. In fact, the venture was a fraud. A former Philip Morris employee falsely represented to Signet and other original parties that he acted for Philip Morris in the venture, but that the venture was so secret it would be denied by Philip Morris. Hitachi was found to have reasonably relied on Signet Bank's representatives about the secret off-shore venture. The touchstone of reasonableness in reliance was "prudent investigation." The case also discusses contractual provisions relevant to reliance. In this case there was no express disclaimer of responsibility for representations. Cf. Hoover Universal, Inc. v. Brockway Imco, Inc., 809 F.2d 1039 (4th Cir.1987). A prudent investigation will encompass mounting evidence that a takeover target's financial statements represents a ridiculous overvaluation: Atari Corp. v. Ernst & Whinney, 970 F.2d 641 (9th Cir.1992).

2. What if it is made clear by the evidence that plaintiff knew that the representation made to him was false? Cox v. Johnson, 227 N.C. 69, 40 S.E.2d 418 (1946). Or that he paid no attention to it, and acted for other reasons entirely? McIntyre v. Lyon, 325 Mich. 167, 37 N.W.2d 903 (1949); Tsang v. Kan, 78 Cal.App.2d 275, 177 P.2d 630 (1947).

3. Suppose that A and B each make the same false statement to C, and his decision to act is substantially influenced by both. Strong v. Strong, 102 N.Y. 69, 5 N.E. 799 (1886); Shaw v. Gilbert, 111 Wis. 165, 86 N.W. 188 (1901). Does it make any difference that either statement alone would have been sufficient to induce the action? What case does this resemble?

4. Does the fact that plaintiff has made an inspection, examination or investigation of his own establish:

A. That he did not believe the representation, and so did not rely on it, but relied instead on his own investigation? See McNabb v. Thomas, 88 U.S.App.D.C. 379, 190 F.2d 608 (1951); Savings Bank Retirement System v. Clarke, 258 Md. 501, 265 A.2d 921 (1970).

In Enfield v. Colburn, 63 N.H. 218 (1884), defendant made statements to plaintiffs. Plaintiffs made an expensive investigation, and found that they were false. They sought to recover the expenses of the investigation. Recovery was denied, since "if they relied upon the representations, they did not investigate them; if they investigated them they did not rely upon them. It is a perversion of language to say they did both." Is this right?

B. That he believed the representation, and relied upon it, but sought verification before acting, and in the end relied upon both? John Hancock Mut. Life Ins. Co. v. Cronin, 139 N.J.Eq. 392, 51 A.2d 2 (1947); Fausett & Co. v. Bullard, 217 Ark. 176, 229 S.W.2d 490 (1950).

5. Purchasers expressed concern about the house's roof, had notice of water spots on its carpet and had personally inspected the roof. Representation was made by sellers, that the roof was in good repair. Sellers' assurances that the roof was in good repair were reasonably relied on since the spots were irrelevant to present state of roof and the inspection could not have uncovered the structural defects. Sellers' assurances of repair reasonably precluded the necessity for an independent inspection. Sippy v. Cristich, 4 Kan.App.2d 511, 609 P.2d 204 (1980).

6. *Materiality.* Suppose that defendant, as agent, is selling plaintiff a tract of land on behalf of a principal whom plaintiff never has seen. Defendant falsely states that his principal is left-handed. No other false statements are made. Can plaintiff recover in deceit after he buys the land? Farnsworth v. Duffner, 142 U.S. 43 (1891) (social, religious and political affiliation); Haverland v. Lane, 89 Wash. 557, 154 P. 1118 (1916) (identity of party).

7. Defendant induces plaintiff to send his daughter to a particular school by false representations that it is attended by her former classmates. Is this a material representation? Brown v. Search, 131 Wis. 109, 111 N.W. 210 (1907). What if plaintiff is induced to buy pictures by a false statement that his wife likes them? Washington Post Co. v. Sorrells, 7 Ga.App. 774, 68 S.E. 337 (1910). Or he is induced to give money to a college by a statement that it is to be named after one of his friends? Collinson v. Jeffries, 21 Tex.Civ.App. 653, 54 S.W. 28 (1899). See Restatement (Second) of Torts § 538(1)(b).

8. *Contributory Negligence.* Contributory negligence does not bar recovery when the misrepresentation is intentional, Yorke v. Taylor, 332 Mass. 368, 124 N.E.2d 912 (1955); and Judd v. Walker, 215 Mo. 312, 114 S.W. 979 (1908) ("the laws of hospitality seem to require that strangers should be taken in in a good sense, but courts should be astute not to permit such a 'taking in' as appears here").

9. What if the defendant's representation is made without scienter or intent to deceive, but is made negligently and the action is one for negligent misrepresentation? Is contributory negligence then a defense? How can plaintiff have reasonably relied if he has failed to take reasonable precautions to protect himself? Does the scope of the defense differ according to whether plaintiff and defendant may interact with one another? Maxwell Ice Co. v. Brackett, Shaw & Lunt Co., 80 N.H. 236, 116 A. 34 (1921); Gould v. Flato, 170 Misc. 378, 10 N.Y.S.2d 361 (1938); Grand Restaurants of Canada v. City of Toronto, [1982] 140 D.L.R.3d 191. Does comparative negligence apply here?

10. The great majority of the cases now hold that the plaintiff has no duty to make inquiry or investigation as to the truth of an apparently reliable statement made to him. This is held even though investigation could be made quickly, with little effort, by means readily at hand. Buckley v. Buckley, 230 Mich. 504, 202 N.W. 955 (1925).

11. "No rogue should enjoy his ill-gotten plunder for the simple reason that his victim is by chance a fool." Chamberlin v. Fuller, 59 Vt. 247, 9 A. 832 (1887).

12. Plaintiff, a "gullible young man," whose occupation was that of playing the piano in resorts of ill repute, inherited $40,000 from his mother. On learning this, defendant promptly offered to sell him a disreputable roadhouse, representing that it was worth $35,000. Defendant advised plaintiff not to ask questions of others, because if it got out that the place was for sale other purchasers would probably come and get the bargain away from him. Relying upon these representations, plaintiff made no inquiry, and bought the roadhouse for $35,000. It proved to be practically worthless, and had to be closed down when its license was not renewed. Plaintiff recovered from defendant. Adan v. Steinbrecher, 116 Minn. 174, 133 N.W. 477 (1911).

5. OPINION

Saxby v. Southern Land Co.

Supreme Court of Appeals of Virginia, 1909.
109 Va. 196, 63 S.E. 423.

Action to recover damages for alleged false and fraudulent representations made in regard to the sale of a certain farm known as "Winslow." A demurrer to the declaration was sustained and the suit dismissed. Plaintiff brings error.

HARRISON, J. * * * The second and third grounds of fraud alleged are that the farm contained at least 150 acres of pine timber of which about 20 acres had been burned over; whereas, there was about 120 acres in timber, of which 60 acres had been burned over.

It is well settled that a misrepresentation, the falsity of which will afford ground for an action for damages, must be of an existing fact, and not the mere expression of an opinion. The mere expression of an opinion, however strong and positive the language may be, is no fraud. Such statements are not fraudulent in law, because * * * they do not ordinarily deceive or mislead. Statements which are vague and indefinite in their nature and terms, or are merely loose, conjectural or exaggerated, go for nothing, though they may not be true, for a man is not justified in placing reliance upon them. An indefinite representation ought to put the person to whom it is made on inquiry. [C]

The declaration states that the farm in question contained 444 acres, 1 rood and 26 poles. It is manifest that the vendor was not asserting a fact in stating the number of acres in timber and the number burned over, but was merely expressing his opinion from appearances. The declaration does not charge him with saying more than that there was about 150 acres in timber and about 20 acres burned over. These expressions indicate that the defendant in error was not making statements of ascertained facts, but was merely expressing his opinion of the acreage in timber and the portion thereof which was burned over. The statements were sufficiently indefinite to have put the plaintiffs in error on their guard to make further inquiry if they regarded the matter as material.

The last two grounds of fraud alleged are that the defendant in error stated that the timber, when cut into cordwood, would readily sell at the local stations on the railroad for $4 per cord, whereas it could be sold only for a much smaller price, and that the land was specially adapted to potato culture, and would by the use of fertilizer yield 100 bushels of potatoes to the acre, whereas, by actual experiment, the land failed to produce anything like that yield by the use of fertilizers.

There is no allegation that the land had produced 100 bushels of potatoes to the acre, or that cordwood had brought $4 per cord at local stations. The production of land in the future and the price of cordwood in the future are dependent upon so many conditions that no assertion of an existing fact could be made with respect thereto.

The statements relied on as grounds of fraud cannot be regarded otherwise than as speculative expressions of opinion—mere trade talk—with respect to matters of an equally uncertain nature. * * *

We are of opinion that the demurrer to the declaration was properly sustained. The judgment complained of must, therefore, be affirmed.

NOTES AND QUESTIONS

1.   Suppose that defendant had said that the farm contained "at least 444 acres" when there were only 210? Should it make any difference whether plaintiff saw the land? Is it significant that the plaintiff filed the suit two years after the transaction took place?

2.   Which of the following statements, made by a seller to a buyer, are to be regarded as opinion, and which as fact? "This land is worth $5,000." "I paid $5,000 for this land two years ago." Medbury v. Watson, 6 Metc. (Mass.) 246, 39 Am.Dec. 726 (1843). "Property exactly like this is selling for $5,000." Brody v. Foster, 134 Minn. 91, 158 N.W. 824 (1916). "I have been offered $5,000 for this land by another party." Kabatchnick v. Hanover–Elm Building Corp., 328 Mass. 341, 103 N.E.2d 692 (1952). "The lowest price at which this land can be purchased from my principal is $5,000." Hokanson v. Oatman, 165 Mich. 512, 131 N.W. 111 (1911).

3.   Suppose the statement of opinion as to value is made by the buyer to the seller? The seller has had her car wrecked. She is told by the buyer that in its present condition it is worth only $200, and she sells it for that. Fossier v. Morgan, 474 S.W.2d 801 (Tex.Civ.App.1971).

4.   The statement of any opinion is a statement of at least one fact—the fact that the defendant does have such an opinion. If this is false and dishonest, why should the defendant not be held liable? See Keeton, Fraud—Misrepresentation of Opinion, 21 Minn.L.Rev. 643 (1937).

5.   Does a statement of opinion ever imply any other facts? In Simpson v. Western Nat'l Bank of Casper, 497 P.2d 878 (Wyo.1972), a banker, when asked about the financial condition of a customer for whose benefit the person inquiring

was depositing a check, replied that he would come out all right and there was nothing wrong with his financial condition. Held, this "was an implied statement and representation that he knew of no fact incompatible with his opinion." In Wink Enterprises v. Dow, 491 S.W.2d 451 (Tex.Civ.App.1973), an opinion was expressed to a prospective investor that a bank was "a good sound one and will continue to make money." Held, the statement "means that facts exist which lead the maker to believe the statement, or facts actually exist that the bank is in sound condition."

6. Some statements clearly in the form of an opinion are actionable: Hanberry v. Hearst Corp., 276 Cal. App. 2d 680, 81 Cal. Rptr. 519 (1969), supra page 1028. Take the following:

A. What about the opinion of an attorney on a point of law, given to a layman with whom he is dealing? Security Savings Bank v. Kellems, 321 Mo. 1, 9 S.W.2d 967 (1928).

B. Suppose a violin expert, selling a violin, gives his opinion to a purchaser who knows nothing about such instruments that it is a genuine Stradivarius? Powell v. Flechter, 45 N.Y.St.Rep. 294, 18 N.Y.S. 451 (1892). What if the purchaser is another expert? Banner v. Lyon & Healy Co., 249 App.Div. 569, 293 N.Y.S. 236 (1937). Suppose a so-called "impartial expert" misleads the plaintiff into believing that he is actually impartial? Cf. Oltmer v. Zamora, 94 Ill.App.3d 651, 49 Ill.Dec. 652, 418 N.E.2d 506 (1981).

C. What if the disparity in bargaining power does not arise from any expert knowledge or special information of the defendant, but from the unusual ignorance, inexperience, illiteracy or lack of intelligence of the plaintiff? Ellis v. Gordon, 202 Wis. 134, 231 N.W. 585 (1930).

D. Why is reliance upon statements of opinion, including value, always held to be justified where there is a special relation of trust and confidence between the parties? See, e.g., Jekshewitz v. Groswald, 265 Mass. 413, 164 N.E. 609 (1929) (affianced); Allen v. Frawley, 106 Wis. 638, 82 N.W. 593 (1900) (attorney and client).

Vulcan Metals Co. v. Simmons Mfg. Co.

United States Circuit Court of Appeals, Second Circuit, 1918.
248 Fed. 853.

[Two actions tried together. The Vulcan Metals Company brought action against the Simmons Manufacturing Company for deceit, by reason of misrepresentations in the sale by Simmons to Vulcan of machinery for the manufacture of vacuum cleaners, together with the patents covering their manufacture. The Simmons Company brought action against the Vulcan Company upon notes given for the purchase price, and in this action Vulcan counterclaimed for the same alleged misrepresentations.

The misrepresentations included "commendations of the cleanliness, economy and efficiency of the machine, that it was absolutely perfect in even the smallest detail; that water power, by which it worked, marked the most economical means of operating a vacuum cleaner with the greatest efficiency; that the cleaning was more thoroughly done than by beating or brushing; that, having been perfected, it was a necessity which every one could afford; that it was so simple a child of six could use it; that it worked completely and thoroughly; that it was simple, long-lived, easily operated, and effective; that it was the only sanitary portable cleaner on the market; that perfect satisfaction would result from its use; that it would last a lifetime; that it was the only practical jet machine on the market, and that perfect satisfaction would result from its use, if properly adjusted. The booklet is in general the ordinary compilation, puffing the excellence and powers of the vacuum cleaner, and asserting its superiority over all others of a similar sort." There were further representations that the vacuum cleaner never had been put on the market.

The trial court directed a verdict on each action for the Simmons Company. The Vulcan Company appeals.]

LEARNED HAND, DISTRICT JUDGE. The first question is of the misrepresentations touching the quality and powers of the patented machine. These were general commendations, or, in so far as they included any specific facts, were not disproved; e.g., that the cleaner would produce 18 inches of vacuum with 25 pounds water pressure. They raise, therefore, the question of law how far general "puffing" or "dealers' talk" can be the basis of an action for deceit.

The conceded exception in such cases has generally rested upon the distinction between "opinion" and "fact"; but that distinction has not escaped the criticism it deserves. An opinion is a fact, and it may be a very relevant fact; the expression of an opinion is the assertion of a belief, and any rule which condones the expression of a consciously false opinion condones a consciously false statement of fact. When the parties are so situated that the buyer may reasonably rely upon the expression of the seller's opinion, it is no excuse to give a false one. [C] And so it makes much difference whether the parties stand "on equality." For example, we should treat very differently the expressed opinion of a chemist, to a layman about the properties of a composition from the same opinion between chemist and chemist, when the buyer had full opportunity to examine. The reason of the rule lies, we think, in this: There are some kinds of talk which no sensible man takes seriously, and if he does he suffers from his credulity. If we were all scrupulously honest, it would not be so; but, as it is, neither party usually believes what the seller says about his own opinions, and each knows it. Such statements, like the claims of campaign managers before election, are rather designed to allay the suspicion which would attend their absence than to be understood as having any relation to objective truth. It is quite true that they induce a compliant temper in the buyer, but it is by a much more subtle process than through the acceptance of his claims for his wares.

So far as concerns statements of value, the rule is pretty well fixed against the buyer. * * * It has been applied more generally to statements of quality and serviceability. * * * But this is not always so. * * * As respects the validity of patents it also obtains. * * * Cases of warranty present the same question and have been answered in the same way. * * *

In the case at bar, since the buyer was allowed full opportunity to examine the cleaner and to test it out, we put the parties upon an equality.

It seems to us that general statements as to what the cleaner would do, even though consciously false, were not of a kind to be taken literally by the buyer. As between manufacturer and customer, it may not be so; but this was the case of taking over a business, after ample chance to investigate. Such a buyer, who the seller rightly expects will undertake an independent and adequate inquiry into the actual merits of what he gets, has no right to treat as material in his determination statements like these. * * *

As respects the representation that the cleaners had never been put upon the market or offered for sale, the rule does not apply; nor can we agree that such representations could not have been material to Freeman's decision to accept the contract. The actual test of experience in their sale might well be of critical consequence in his decision to buy the business, and the jury would certainly have the right to accept his statement that his reliance upon these representations was determinative of his final decision. We believe that the facts as disclosed by the depositions of the Western witnesses were sufficient to carry to the jury the question whether those statements were false. It is quite true, as the District Judge said, that the number of sales was small, perhaps not 60 in all; but they were scattered in various parts of the Mountain and Pacific states, and the jury might conclude that they were enough to contradict the detailed statements of Simmons that the machines had been kept off the market altogether. * * *

[New trial ordered in the action of deceit.]

NOTES AND QUESTIONS

1. What about a statement that "there is no better land in Vermont"? Nichols v. Lane, 93 Vt. 87, 106 A. 592 (1919). Or that a machine is "the pride of our line," and "the best on the American market"? Prince v. Brackett, Shaw & Lunt Co., 125 Me. 31, 130 A. 509 (1925). Or that shares of stock are "hot stock," "very good," and "with unlimited possibilities"? Ryan v. Collins, 496 S.W.2d 205 (Tex.Civ.App.1973). Or that a prospect for dancing lessons had "exceptional potential to be a fine and accomplished dancer," that he was a "natural dancer" and a "terrific dancer"? Parker v. Arthur Murray, Inc., 10 Ill.App.3d 1000, 295 N.E.2d 487 (1973). And see Letellier v. Small, 400 A.2d 371 (Me.1979), on "dealer talk." Schott Motorcycle Supply v. American Honda Motor Co., 976 F.2d 58 (1st Cir.1992) (defendant's assurance of Honda's future commitment to motorcycle business "puffing" and "track talk").

2. In Bertram v. Reed Automobile Co., 49 S.W.2d 517 (Tex.Civ.App.1932), the seller of a second-hand automobile described it as a "dandy," a "bearcat," a "good automobile," a "good little car," and a "sweet job." The court said: "Common experience and observation causes one to marvel at the moderation of the selling agent in making his trade talk to appellant. * * * These are relative terms, they may mean anything the orator or the listener wants, and neither may be penalized if the one exaggerates or the other is disappointed. There may be something more definite in the representations that the car had been well taken care of, had good rubber on it, had been driven but 19,000 miles, had not been mistreated, that mechanics had found it in perfect condition."

3.   "In Buckingham v. Thompson, 135 S.W. 652 (1911) an enterprising Texas realtor, evidently feeling that even the great state of Texas was too small a territory of operations, sent out literature to various parts of the United States concerning a particular ranch property he had listed, and described it as: richer than the valleys of Southern California; that it could not be kept from becoming a land of gold; that it was a land of fruit and flowers and happy homes; that independence was to be had there for the asking; that all eyes were on Texas, particularly Southwest Texas. * * * Due reference was made to the Garden of Eden, Monte Cristo and Aladdin's lamp. This the Texas court held to be statements 'so extraordinary that no man of ordinary sense could be supposed to take them * * * at their face.'

"When engaged in the analysis of this case we inquired of our uncle, a Texan and lawyer of note, what he thought of the decision. Barely able to control himself he gave it as his opinion that the judge who held the statements to be exaggerated ought to be hanged, and the real estate man who wrote them ought to be shot for understatement tantamount to treason. Thus we must report that (unofficially at least) the law of Texas on this point is unsettled." Obiter Dicta, 25 Ford L.Rev. 395 (1957).

4.   "The rule of law is hardly to be regretted when it is considered how easily and insensibly words of hope or expectation are converted by an interested memory into statements of quality or value when the expectation has been disappointed." Holmes, J., in Deming v. Darling, 148 Mass. 504, 20 N.E. 107 (1889).

6.   LAW

Sorenson v. Gardner

Supreme Court of Oregon, 1959.
215 Or. 255, 334 P.2d 471.

LUSK, JUSTICE. This is an action for deceit in which the plaintiffs recovered a judgment for $2,000 and the defendants have appealed.

The action grows out of the sale of a dwelling house. * * * The complaint alleges that the defendants falsely represented to the plaintiffs that the house was well constructed in a workmanlike manner and met all minimum code requirements, particularly with respect to electric wiring, plumbing, septic tank and sewage disposal arrangement. * * * The plaintiff introduced evidence in support of these allegations and evidence tending to show that the representations were false. * * *

* * * [The] general rule [is] that fraud cannot be predicated upon misrepresentations of law or misrepresentations as to matters of law. [C] Thus, misrepresentations concerning the legal effect of an instrument have been held to be not actionable. * * * [Conflicting] reasons [for this] have been repeated, sometimes in the same decision: first, that every man is presumed to know the law, and hence the plaintiff cannot be heard to say that he reasonably believed the statement made to him; and second, that no man, at least without special training, can be expected to know the law, and so the plaintiff must have understood that the defendant was giving him nothing more than an opinion." [C] The basis of the rule has been criticized by courts and textwriters. * * *

The rule of the Restatement of Torts upon this subject is as follows:

"§ 545. Misrepresentation of Law

"(1) If a representation as to a matter of law in a business transaction is a representation of fact the recipient is justified in relying upon it to the same extent as though it were a representation of any other fact.

"(2) If the representation as to a matter of law in a business transaction is a representation of opinion as to the legal consequences of facts known to the maker and the recipient or assumed by both to exist, the recipient is justified in relying upon it to the same extent as though it were a representation of any other opinion as stated in §§ 542, 543."

In the comment on Subsection (1) of the foregoing, it is said, "If a representation concerns the legal effect of facts not disclosed or not otherwise known to the recipient, it may justifiably be interpreted as implying that there are facts which substantiate the statement * * *. So, too, the assertion of title to a particular tract of land asserts the existence of those conveyances or relationships which are necessary to vest the title in the alleged owner. On the other hand, if all the facts believed by the maker to exist are stated to the recipient or otherwise known by him and from these facts the maker of the representation asserts that title vests in the person in question as a legal consequence, the representation is an expression of opinion and the case falls within Subsection (2)." * * *

Here we are dealing with a number of alleged misrepresentations to the effect that the house in question complied with the minimum requirements of state law. * * * There was evidence that in certain particulars the requirements of the code were not met, and evidence from which the jury could find that the defendants knew and the plaintiffs did not what the facts were in this regard. Under the rule as formulated by the Restatement, had the plaintiffs been aware of these facts and had the defendants represented to them that the facts as so known constituted a compliance with the law, then the misrepresentation in question would have been one of law and not of fact. But, the plaintiffs being ignorant of the facts, the representation in the circumstances was one of fact and the case is covered by Subsection (1) of Section 545 of the Restatement of Torts. * * * The plaintiffs are not relying on their ignorance of the law but of the facts, and the alleged representations carried with them the implication that the facts were otherwise than the evidence shows them to have been. They concerned "the legal effect of facts not disclosed or otherwise known to the recipient." * * *

Our own conclusion, which accords with the rule of the Restatement, is that such representations may, and in this case do, relate to matters of fact. Therefore, the contention of the defendants in support of the first ground of the motion for a directed verdict cannot be sustained. * * *

[Reversed, however, and new trial ordered, on the ground of error in instructions to the jury as to the measure of damages.]

NOTES AND QUESTIONS

1. Defendant, a layman, is seeking to settle a claim against plaintiff, and assures him that he is legally liable for his conduct. Plaintiff, relying upon the

assurance, settles the claim. He was not in fact liable. Has he a cause of action? Williams v. Dougherty County, 101 Ga.App. 193, 113 S.E.2d 168 (1960).

2. Defendant, a layman, sold plaintiff beverages containing 18 to 25 per cent alcohol, assuring him that the local law would permit him to sell them in unbroken packages at retail. In fact, the law did not permit such sales, and plaintiff was arrested and convicted for the unlawful sale of intoxicating liquor. Defendant was held not liable. Ad. Dernehl & Sons Co. v. Detert, 186 Wis. 113, 202 N.W. 207 (1925). Cf. Gibson v. Mendenhall, 203 Okl. 558, 224 P.2d 251 (1950) (representation that plaintiff could easily obtain a license).

3. Representations as to the law of another state are treated as statements of fact, upon which the plaintiff may justifiably rely. See, for example, Hembry v. Parreco, 81 A.2d 77 (Mun.App.D.C.1951); Fireman's Ins. Co. v. Jones, 245 Ark. 179, 431 S.W.2d 728 (1968) (deception as to foreign statute of limitations).

4. What about a statement that defendant's hospital is legally accredited? Myers v. Lowery, 46 Cal.App. 682, 189 P. 793 (1920). Or that the defendant's title is good? Barnett v. Kunkle, 256 F. 644 (8th Cir.1919).

5. What about a statement of law made by an attorney to his client? By one member of a family to another? By an insurance company to its policy-holder? Some relationships will demand a disclosure of material facts. Thus fraudulent misrepresentation may be constituted in the absence of an affirmative statement misrepresenting existing fact. Stiley v. Block, 130 Wash.2d 486, 925 P.2d 194, 208 (1996) (Talmadge, J., concurring). Stark v. Equitable Life Assurance Society, 205 Minn. 138, 285 N.W. 466 (1939).

7. PREDICTION AND INTENTION

McElrath v. Electric Investment Co.

Supreme Court of Minnesota, 1911.
114 Minn. 358, 131 N.W. 380.

BROWN, J. Appeal from an order overruling a general demurrer to plaintiffs' complaint. It appears from the complaint that the defendant was the owner of a certain summer hotel property, including the land upon which the building was situated, and certain personal property used in connection with the operation of the hotel, situated at Antlers Park, in Dakota county. On the 15th day of April, 1909, the parties to the action entered into a contract by the terms of which defendant leased the property to plaintiffs for a term of years. * * *

The action is for damages occasioned by the alleged false and fraudulent representations made by defendant for the purpose of inducing plaintiffs to enter into the contract. The complaint alleges: "That for the purpose of inducing said plaintiffs to enter into said contract, Exhibit A, this defendant wrongfully, falsely, and fraudulently stated and represented to these plaintiffs that the Minneapolis, St. Paul, Rochester and Dubuque Electric Traction Company would complete its electric railroad, and would run electric cars over said road from the city of Minneapolis to and beyond said Antlers Park during the summer of 1909, and about July 1st of that year; and said defendant further stated and represented to said plaintiffs that said defendant would, during said summer of 1909 and as soon as said electric railroad should run to said Antlers Park, make of said Antlers Park and surrounding ground an important summer resort for people living at said city of Minneapolis, and further stated and represented to plaintiffs that if they would enter into said contract, Exhibit A, they would make, through the assistance and efforts of said defendant, not less than fifteen hundred dollars ($1,500.00) per annum clear above all expenses of running and management. * * *

It is contended by defendant that the alleged false representations do not constitute a cause of action, for the reason that, when made, they had reference to the future intentions of the traction company, and were not representations of present existing facts, and further, that the complaint contains no allegations that the electric road was not constructed and in operation according to the representations.

We * * * hold that the complaint, in so far as it alleges the making of false representations for the purpose of inducing plaintiffs to enter into the contract, knowing the same to be false, to the effect that the electric road would be completed and in operation by July 1, 1909, states a cause of action. While it is true as a general rule that false representations, upon which fraud may be predicated, must be of existing facts, and cannot consist of mere promises or conjectures as to future acts or events, yet, [c] if in making the representations defendant "intended to create in plaintiffs the belief that it was, as a fact, the then intention of the" traction company to complete the road at the time represented, and "the representations might be understood and were understood by plaintiffs as asserting that fact," then a charge of fraud may be based thereon, though the represented event was to occur in the future. Upon this theory, the complaint, as against a demurrer, states a cause of action. [Cc]

Upon the question of the sufficiency of the other allegations of fraud, the case comes within the general rule that promises or assurances as to future events cannot be made the basis of an action of fraud. In this respect the complaint alleges that defendant represented that it would, as soon as the electric road reached Antlers Park, "make of said Antlers Park and surrounding ground an important summer resort for people living at said City of Minneapolis." This, aside from being a mere promise to do something in the future, namely, "make an important summer resort," rests wholly in conjecture and speculation, depending for its accomplishment upon many facts, of which both parties had, presumptively, equal notice, and depending upon conditions over which neither had control. Whether an important or other summer resort may be established at a particular place depends in the main upon its location and the disposition of the public to make it a place of recreation or pleasure. * * * The naked allegation is of a promise to create a particular condition in the future, a condition surrounded with known uncertainty and beyond defendant's control, and the general rule applies. The other allegations, namely, that plaintiffs would, in the conduct of the leased property, make a specified profit during the season, also rests in conjecture and opinion, and therefore is not open to the charge of actionable fraud.

Affirmed.

NOTES AND QUESTIONS

1. The following have been held not to justify reliance: A prediction that prices will remain unchanged. Coe v. Ware, 271 Mass. 570, 171 N.E. 732 (1930). That plaintiff will be able to obtain a job. Schwitters v. Des Moines Commercial College, 199 Iowa 1058, 203 N.W. 265 (1925). That building lots next to a highway will prove to be profitable. Campbell County v. Braun, 295 Ky. 96, 174 S.W.2d 1 (1943). That stock will triple in value within a year. Kennedy v. Flo–Tronics, Inc., 274 Minn. 327, 143 N.W.2d 827 (1966). That plaintiff will be successful in purchasing property in a foreclosure sale. Spragins v. Sunburst Bank, 605 So.2d 777 (Miss.1992). That certain adverse consequences would flow from a failure to enter a new agreement and that representor stood to make nothing from the new agreement. Fuller v. Perry, 223 Ga., App. 129, 476 S.E.2d 793 (1996).

2. In Trustees of Columbia University v. Jacobsen, 53 N.J.Super. 574, 148 A.2d 63 (1959) cert. denied, 363 U.S. 808, plaintiff, a university student, claimed that the University represented to him that he would acquire "wisdom, truth, character, enlightenment, understanding, justice, liberty, honesty, courage, beauty and similar virtues and qualities; that it would develop the whole man, maturity, well-roundedness, objective thinking and the like * * *" He failed to graduate because of poor scholastic standing. What result?

3. Contrast Steinberg v. Chicago Medical Sch., 69 Ill.2d 320, 13 Ill.Dec. 699, 371 N.E.2d 634 (1977). Plaintiff applied for admission to defendant medical school, paying the application fee, and was rejected. He alleges fraud in the catalog statements regarding selection standards to be applied, and the use of "nonacademic criteria, primarily the ability of the applicant or his family to pledge or make payment of large sums of money to the school." Held, cause of action stated and class action permitted. Recovery allowed "where the false promise or representation of future conduct is alleged to be the scheme employed to accomplish the fraud." See also Campbell v. Bettius, 244 Va. 347, 421 S.E.2d 433 (1992) (attorney's representation that plaintiffs "would be able" to collect on guarantee was not a prediction of future events; it was a representation of the present effect of contract language).

Burgdorfer v. Thielemann

Supreme Court of Oregon, 1936.
153 Or. 354, 55 P.2d 1122.

Action on the case for deceit by Charles Burgdorfer against Carl Thielemann. From a judgment in favor of plaintiff, defendant appeals.

[Plaintiff charges that defendant fraudulently induced him to exchange a $2,000 note and mortgage (plus two notes totaling $323) for two lots in the Collins View tract, by falsely promising that he would pay a $500 mortgage on the Collins View lot.]

Kelly, Justice. * * * It is further alleged in plaintiff's second amended complaint:

" * * * that the defendant had no intention at the time of making the said promise, or at any time at all, of performing the promise to plaintiff hereinabove set out; * * * that the plaintiff did believe and rely on the said representations and promise of the defendant and did act thereon to his great damage; * * * "

Defendant's first assignment of error imputes error upon the part of the court in allowing plaintiff to testify as to appellant's alleged promise to pay off the mortgage on the Collins View property.

The precise objection which defendant makes is that the alleged promise could not have been performed within one year and, therefore, to be enforceable [under the statute of frauds] it must have been reduced to writing and signed by the party sought to be charged. * * *

We think that, in an action for deceit, [the] provision of the statute [of frauds] does not have the effect of rendering inadmissible testimony of an oral promise made with the fraudulent intent on the part of the promisor at the time the promise was made not to fulfill or perform the same.

One of the reasons leading to this conclusion is that the purpose of such oral testimony is not to establish an agreement, but to prove fraud. The gist of the fraud consists in the false representation of the existence of an intention which in truth and in fact has no existence. * * *

"To profess an intent to do or not to do, when the party intends the contrary, is as clear a case of misrepresentation and of fraud as could be made." Herndon v. Durham & S.R. Co., 161 N.C. 650, 656, 77 S.E. 683, 685. * * *

As stated by Bowen, L.J., in Edgington v. Fitzmaurice, Law Reports, 29 Chancery Division, 459: "There must be a misstatement of an existing fact; but the state of a man's mind is as much a fact as the state of his digestion. It is true that it is very difficult to prove what the state of a man's mind at a particular time is, but if it can be ascertained it is as much a fact as anything else. A misrepresentation as to the state of a man's mind is, therefore, a misstatement of fact." * * *

No error was committed by allowing plaintiff to testify as to defendant's alleged promise to pay off the mortgage on the Collins View property. * * *

The judgment of the circuit court is affirmed.

NOTES AND QUESTIONS

1. Suppose the proof is merely that the defendant made a contract, and after a time broke it. Is this enough for an action of deceit? Williams v. Williams, 220 N.C. 806, 18 S.E.2d 364 (1942). What if the promise is broken immediately after it is made, with no intervening change in the situation? Guy T. Bisbee Co. v. Granite City Investing Corp., 159 Minn. 238, 199 N.W. 14 (1924). What about a promise to pay made by one who is completely insolvent at the time? California Conserving Co. v. D'Avanzo, 62 F.2d 528 (2d Cir.1933).

2. Consider the following possible advantages of the action in deceit over a contract action for breach of the promise itself:

A.   The deceit action may avoid the statute of frauds. Channel Master Corp. v. Aluminum Limited Sales, Inc., 4 N.Y.2d 403, 151 N.E.2d 833 (1958). Contra, Cassidy v. Kraft–Phenix Cheese Corp., 285 Mich. 426, 280 N.W. 814 (1938). However, to couch a breach of contract claim as a fraudulent misrepresentation claim by alleging that the promisor had no intention, at the time of contract formation, to perform its obligations is impermissible. Best Western Int'l, Inc. v. CSI Int'l Corporation, 1995 WL 505565 (S.D.N.Y.1995).

B.   It may avoid the difficulties of the parol evidence rule, which prevents any promise not integrated into a written contract from being regarded as a part of the contract. Sabo v. Delman, 3 N.Y.2d 155, 143 N.E.2d 906 (1957). Contra: McCreight v. Davey Tree Expert Co., 191 Minn. 489, 254 N.W. 623 (1934). In Pinnacle Peak Developers v. TRW Invest. Corp., 129 Ariz. 385, 631 P.2d 540 (1980), Judge Sandra Day O'Connor drew a distinction between contractual parties' "expertise and business sophistication" in the issue of whether the parol evidence rule should be displaced.

C.   It may avoid the defense that the promise was without consideration. Daniel v. Daniel, 190 Ky. 210, 226 S.W. 1070 (1921). But see: Rankin v. Burnham, 150 Wash. 615, 274 P. 98 (1929).

D.   It may avoid the defense that the contract was an illegal one, if the parties are not in pari delicto. See Keeton, Fraud—Statements of Intention, 15 Texas L.Rev. 185, 213–216 (1937).

E.   It may avoid the defense of the statute of limitations, since a longer period may be applicable in the deceit action, or the statute may run only from the plaintiff's discovery of the fraud. Fidelity–Philadelphia Trust Co. v. Simpson, 293 Pa. 577, 143 A. 202 (1928). But see: Brick v. Cohn–Hall–Marx, 276 N.Y. 259, 11 N.E.2d 902 (1937).

F.   It may avoid a limitation of liability contained in the contract itself.

G.   It may avoid a defense against the contract action, such as infancy. Wisconsin Loan & Finance Corp. v. Goodnough, 201 Wis. 101, 228 N.W. 484 (1930). Contra: Slayton v. Barry, 175 Mass. 513, 56 N.E. 574 (1900).

H.   It may avoid the necessity of joining parties to a joint contract in one action. Cf. Elliott v. Hayden, 104 Mass. 180 (1870).

8.   DAMAGES

Hinkle v. Rockville Motor Co., Inc.

Court of Appeals of Maryland, 1971.
262 Md. 502, 278 A.2d 42.

BARNES, JUDGE. The appellant, Donald Hinkle (Hinkle), purchased a 1969 Ford Galaxie automobile from the appellee, Rockville Motor Company, Inc. (Rockville), in January of 1970. * * * Hinkle alleged that Rockville fraudulently represented to him at the time of sale that the 1969 Galaxie was a new car when, in fact, it had over 2,000 miles on the speedometer and had been involved in an accident in the State of Tennessee. Hinkle discovered the mileage recorded on the speedometer while driving home on the day of the sale. He brought this to the attention of Rockville and an adjustment was made whereby he was compensated in the amount of $109.86, the amount of his first payment, in exchange for a release from any further claims except for those falling within his standard new car warranty. The adjustment for mileage was made on January 27, 1970. Hinkle maintains that it was not until April, 1970, that he learned the automobile had been involved in an accident in Tennessee in July of 1969. It is alleged in the declaration that the front and rear portions of the automobile had been welded together after having been severed in the accident. Hinkle alleged that Rockville had knowledge of the accident but that it "willfully concealed the true circumstances" and "willfully, maliciously and fraudulently misrepresented the quality and condition of the aforesaid Ford vehicle" and that he relied on these misrepresentations to his detriment. Damages were claimed in the amount of $100,000.

At the close of Hinkle's case, Rockville moved for a directed verdict. In granting the directed verdict, the trial court only found it necessary to consider Rockville's argument that Hinkle's failure to produce evidence in regard to the automobile's actual value at the time of sale deprived the jury of the only permissible standard by which the jury could determine the existence or amount of damages. The trial court determined this to be a correct statement of the law and directed a verdict in favor of Rockville notwithstanding the fact that Hinkle had produced expert testimony that the effects of the accident could be remedied and the car returned to new car condition by the expenditure of $800 for repairs. * * *

A majority of States will allow the plaintiffs to recover the "benefit of his bargain" if sufficiently proved. The theory is to compensate the plaintiff as though the transaction had been carried out as represented. [Cc]

Other States restrict the plaintiff to his "out of pocket" losses. The classic formula is the value of the object as represented less its actual value at the time of sale. The theory is to return the plaintiff economically to the position he was in prior to the fraudulent transaction thus allowing him recoupment of actual losses but not expected gain. This rigid limitation on the nature of recovery is often explained as being required because the action is one of tort rather than contract and that it has always been recognized that tort remedies are designed to compensate for actual harm suffered. * * * Maryland is one of those States which has not adopted a rigid stand as far as adopting one of the above theories to the exclusion of the other. Both theories have been used and approved in Maryland. * * *

In summary, the review of the Maryland cases on this question of the proper measure of damages in fraud and deceit cases demonstrates that this Court has applied the so-called "flexibility theory" without heretofore expressly stating the factors to be considered in its application. Selman v. Shirley, 161 Or. 582, 609, 85 P.2d 384, 394 (1938) the first case to define expressly this flexible approach, set forth the following four rules as a guide for the proper measure of damages in these cases.

"(1) If the defrauded party is content with the recovery of only the amount that he actually lost, his damages will be measured under that rule;

"(2) if the fraudulent representation also amounted to a warranty, recovery may be had for the loss of the bargain because a fraud accompanied by a broken promise should cost the wrongdoer as much as the latter alone;

"(3) where the circumstances disclosed by the proof are so vague as to cast virtually no light upon the value of the property had it conformed to the representations, the court will award damages equal only to the loss sustained; and

"(4) where * * * the damages under the benefit-of-the-bargain rule are proved with sufficient certainty, that rule will be employed." * * *

This position was advocated by Professor McCormick who wrote, "In the first place, it seems that in every case the defrauded plaintiff should be allowed to claim under the 'out of pocket' loss theory if he prefers. In the second place, the plaintiff should be allowed to choose the other theory, and recover the value of the bargain as represented, if the trial judge in his discretion considers that, in view of the probable moral culpability of the defendant and of the definiteness of the representations and the ascertainability of the represented value, the case is an appropriate one for such treatment." McCormick, Damages § 122 (1935) at p. 454. Williston on Contracts § 1392 (Rev.Ed.1937) at p. 3886 and Sutherland on Damages § 1172 (4th ed. 1916) at p. 4409 both indicate a preference for allowing the plaintiff to recover the benefit of his bargain in these cases. Sedgewick on Damages § 781 (9th ed.1912) at pp. 1629–31, while recognizing that the majority rule allows "benefit of bargain" recovery, favors a strict adherence to the "out of pocket" remedy in accordance with English common law as set forth in Peek v. Derry, 37 Ch.Div. 541 (1888). The Restatement of Torts, § 549 (1938) also sets forth the "out of pocket" rule of damages.

After the above review of cases and texts on the subject, it is concluded that the trial court erred in directing the verdict against Hinkle for failure to produce evidence upon which damages could be awarded. Hinkle's evidence in regard to the cost of necessary repairs demonstrated the existence of damages and provided an adequate measure upon which they could be predicated.

Judgment reversed and case remanded for new trial, the appellee to pay the costs.

NOTES AND QUESTIONS

1. Does the court in the principal case correctly state the test for the "tort" or "out of pocket" test?

2. "It is the very essence of an action of fraud or deceit that the same shall be accompanied by damage, and neither damnum absque injuria nor injuria absque damnum by themselves constitute a good cause of action." Casey v. Welch, 50 So.2d 124 (Fla.1951). In an action for rescission, it may not be necessary to show pecuniary loss and plaintiff can prevail if he did not receive what he was promised. See Hirschman v. Healy, 162 Minn. 328, 202 N.W. 734 (1925); Nance v. McClellan, 89 S.W.2d 774 (Tex.Comm.App.1936).

3. Auditors' accounts are relied on by plaintiff in taking over a company. The accounts are negligently audited. It is proved that plaintiff would have paid less for the company if the accounts had been accurate. Is this difference recoverable? Or has plaintiff suffered no loss because control of the company has brought an overall benefit? For differing views see opinions in Scott Group v. McFarlane [1978] 1 N.Z.L.R. 553 (C.A.).

4. Of the two "normal" measures of damages discussed here, the contract or "benefit-of-the-bargain" measure will usually result in greater damages. Thus: Price paid $5,000; Value of property purchased $3,000; Value as represented $7,000. Here the tort, or "out-of-pocket" measure results in damages of $2,000, while the "benefit-of-the-bargain" measure is $4,000.

There may, however, be cases in which the out-of-pocket measure is higher. For example, Estell v. Myers, 56 Miss. 800 (1879), where plaintiff paid $62,500 for land actually worth $27,500, and the value if the representations had been true would have been $50,000. Also Erde v. Fenster, 141 N.Y.S. 943 (1913), where plaintiff was induced to sell a claim for less than it was worth by the buyer's representation that the debtor was totally insolvent.

5. The out-of-pocket measure of damages is adopted in all deceit actions by the English courts, and by a minority of about a dozen American jurisdictions. The "benefit-of-the-bargain" rule has been adopted by about two-thirds of the American courts that have considered the question. Neither group has followed either rule with entire consistency in all cases.

6. The compromise formula, first stated in Selman v. Shirley, 161 Or. 582, 85 P.2d 384 (1938), reh'g granted as affirmed, 91 P.2d 312 (1939), has met general approval by legal writers, and has been followed in some other states. Salter v. Heiser, 39 Wash.2d 826, 239 P.2d 327 (1951); Rice v. Price, 340 Mass. 502, 164 N.E.2d 891 (1960). It has been accepted, in a simplified form, by § 549 of the Restatement (Second) of Torts.

7. In addition to the "normal" measure of damages, whether it is under the tort or the contract rule, plaintiff can recover for consequential damages resulting from the misrepresentation. Thus one who buys a horse represented to him as gentle may recover for personal injuries if he is kicked by the horse. Vezina v. Souliere, 103 Vt. 190, 152 A. 798 (1931). And one who buys infected bees, represented to be healthy, may recover for damage to his other bees when the infection spreads to them. Sampson v. Penney, 151 Minn. 411, 187 N.W. 135 (1922). Plaintiff may recover for expenses to which he has been put, as when he is induced to employ an architect by misrepresentations as to his skill and compelled to incur extra expenses in completing the building as a result. Edward Barron Estate Co. v. Woodruff Co., 163 Cal. 561, 126 P. 351 (1912). In Brooks v. Doherty, Rumble & Butler, 481 N.W.2d 120 (Minn.Ct.App.1992), the court warned of the possible overlap of contract and tort damages, allowing damages against plaintiff's law firm employer for emotional distress, damage to personal and professional reputation, lost income, and expenses in moving across the country to find a job.

8. Questions of proximate cause can arise in misrepresentation cases, too. Plaintiff is induced to buy stock in a company by defendant's fraudulent statement. The treasurer of the company subsequently absconds with funds that he had been embezzling over a period of time and the company turns out to be insolvent. Defendant knew nothing about the treasurer's misconduct and the misrepresentation did not relate to the value of the stock. Can plaintiff recover in deceit for his loss? Fottler v. Moseley, 185 Mass. 563, 70 N.E. 1040 (1904), would indicate that the

answer is yes. But a majority of the courts would apparently disagree. See Boatmen's Nat'l Co. v. M.W. Elkins & Co., 63 F.2d 214 (8th Cir.1933); Morrell v. Wiley, 119 Conn. 578, 178 A. 121 (1935). Plaintiff would be able to prevail if he sued in rescission. Seneca Wire & Mfg. Co. v. A.B. Leach & Co., 247 N.Y. 1, 159 N.E. 700 (1928).

9.   Damages recoverable as consequential loss under deceit may be broader than those under negligent misrepresentation. See Doyle v. Olby (Ironmongers) Ltd., [1969] 2 Q.B. 158 at 167: "[I]t does not lie in the mouth of a fraudulent person to say [damages] could not reasonably have been foreseen." Can an analogy be drawn with proximate cause in relation to the intentional torts? Cf. Restatement Second of Torts § 548A, damages recoverable if loss might reasonably be expected to result from reliance on the representation. Punitive damages may be awarded. Warner Communications, Inc. v. Keller, 888 S.W.2d 586 (Tex.App.1994); Roboserve, Inc. v. Kato Kagaku Co., Limited, 78 F.3d 266, 277 (7th Cir. 1996) (stating the necessity of a showing of "intent to injure constituting gross misconduct or malicious behavior").

10.   The measure of damages depends on the scope of the duty and rules of causation. The problem is exemplified in South Australia Asset Management Corporation v. York Montague Ltd. (*sub nom.* Banque Bruxelles Lambert SA v. Eagle Star Insurance Co. Ltd.) [1997] A.C. 191 and Kenny & Good Pty. Ltd. v. MGICA (1992) Ltd. 163 A.L.R. 611 (H.C. Aust. 1999). The English House of Lords and the Australia High Court respectively struggled to establish the correct principle in the following situation. A lends money to B on security of certain real estate. Valuer V is retained by B to value the real estate, knowing that A will rely on the valuation as a basis for advancing the money. V is negligent and the land is worth a fraction of its valuation. A recovers but a fraction of the money loaned to B. It is easy to establish a duty of care owed by V to A, but what is the measure of damages? If A would not have entered the transaction but for the high valuation, could it be said that A should recover from B all the losses necessary to put him back in the position he enjoyed prior to the transaction? That is, the amount of the loan less the money received on foreclosure. (Interest would be calculated.) This measure of damages includes any drop in the market value of the real estate after the loan contract. Should damages, however, incorporate a drop in the market? The House of Lords, describing the scope of the duty, argued that the damages are those caused by the wrongfulness of the valuation: the responsibility extends only to the risk of the negligent advice. To make V liable for the drop in the market would hold him liable for an event that would have occurred even if the valuation had been correct. Thus, the measure should turn on the consequences of the wrong valuation—the difference between the wrong valuation and the correct value. Similar reasoning was employed by the Supreme Court of Connecticut in First Federal Svgs. & Loan Assn. v. Charter Appraisal Co., Inc., 247 Conn. 597, 724 A.2d 497 (1999).

The Australian High Court found that the market drop should be included because the scope of the duty (the undertaking) included the assumption of the risk of a drop in the market value of the real estate.

In the cases, the analysis is the same whether the action is in tort or contract. The *Doyle* case, Note 9, may be justified because fraud requires a strong restitutionary remedy.

CHAPTER XXII

INTERFERENCE WITH ADVANTAGEOUS RELATIONSHIPS

1. BUSINESS RELATIONS

(A) INJURIOUS FALSEHOOD

Ratcliffe v. Evans

Court of Appeal, 1892.
[1892] 2 Q.B. 524.

[Plaintiff alleged that he and his father had carried on the business of engineer and boiler maker for many years under the name Ratcliffe & Sons, that the father died but plaintiff carried on the business and that defendant, publisher of the County Herald, "falsely and maliciously" published "certain words" importing "that the plaintiff had ceased to carry on his business * * * and that the firm of Ratcliffe & Sons did not then exist."]

BOWEN, L.J. This was a case in which an action for a false and malicious publication about the trade and manufactures of the plaintiff was tried at the Chester assizes, with the result of a verdict for the plaintiff for 120l. Judgment having been entered for the plaintiff for that sum and costs, the defendant appealed to this Court for a new trial, or to enter a verdict for the defendant, on the ground, amongst others, that no special damage, such as was necessary to support the action, was proved at the trial. The injurious statement complained of was a publication in the *County Herald,* a Welsh newspaper. It was treated in the pleadings as a defamatory statement or libel; but this suggestion was negatived, and the verdict of the jury proceeded upon the view that the writing was a false statement purposely made about the manufactures of the plaintiff, which was intended to, and did in fact, cause him damage. The only proof at the trial of such damage consisted, however, of evidence of general loss of business without specific proof of the loss of any particular customers or orders, and the question we have to determine is, whether in such an action such general evidence of damage was admissible and sufficient. That an action will lie for written or oral falsehoods, not actionable per se nor even defamatory, where they are maliciously published, where they are calculated in the ordinary course of things to produce, and where they do produce, actual damage, is established law. Such an action is not one of libel or of slander,

Lord Justice Bowen

but an action on the case for damage wilfully and intentionally done without just occasion or excuse, analogous to an action for slander of title. To support it, actual damage must be shown, for it is an action which only lies in respect of such damage as has actually occurred. It was contended before us that in such an action it is not enough to allege and prove general loss of business arising from the publication, since such general loss is general and not special damage, and special damage, as often has been said, is the gist of such an action on the case.

In an action like the present, brought for a malicious falsehood intentionally published in a newspaper about the plaintiff's business—a falsehood which is not actionable as a personal libel, and which is not defamatory in itself—is evidence to shew that a general loss of business has been the direct and natural result admissible in evidence, and, if uncontradicted, sufficient to maintain the action? In the case of a personal libel, such general loss of custom may unquestionably be alleged and proved. Every libel is of itself a wrong in regard of which the law, as we have seen, implies general damage. By the very fact that he has committed such a wrong, the defendant is prepared for the proof that some general damage may have been done. * * * "It is not special damage, [c] it is general damage resulting from the kind of injury the plaintiff has sustained." [C]

In the case before us to-day, it is a falsehood openly disseminated through the press—probably read, and possibly acted on, by persons of whom the plaintiff never heard. To refuse with reference to such a subject-matter to admit such general evidence would be to * * * involve an absolute denial of justice and of redress for the very mischief which was intended to be committed. * * *

Appeal dismissed.

NOTES AND QUESTIONS

1. This is the leading case giving sufficient scope to the "action on the case for words" to justify the use of the term "injurious falsehood"—a name suggested by Sir John Salmond in his treatise on Torts. Earlier cases had involved "slander of title" or "trade libel," which had developed as isolated torts of a limited scope. Sometimes they were joined together and the term "disparagement" was used. "Injurious falsehood" now denotes a broad general principle of liability for any false and malicious statement resulting in pecuniary loss to another. The principle is generally recognized at the present time, but the courts have been slow to adopt the name.

2. The elements necessary to the cause of action usually have been stated as follows:

(a) A false statement of a kind calculated to damage a pecuniary interest of the plaintiff.

(b) Publication to a third person.

(c) "Malice" in the publication. This element has received much the same treatment, and has caused about as much confusion, as in defamation.

(d) Resulting special damage to the plaintiff, in the form of pecuniary loss.

3. As illustrations of the broader scope of the general principle, see: Statements that the plaintiff is dead or is not in business or is going out of business. Davis v. New England Railway Pub. Co., 203 Mass. 470, 89 N.E. 565 (1909); McRoberts Protective Agency, Inc. v. Lansdell Protective Agency, Inc., 61 A.D.2d 652, 403 N.Y.S.2d 511 (1978). Or that he does not deal in certain goods. Jarrahdale Timber Co. v. Temperley, 11 T.L.R. 119 (1894). Or that another similar business is "unique," the only one in existence. Dale System v. Time, Inc., 116 F.Supp. 527 (D.Conn.1953). Or that plaintiff is employed by defendant, as a result of which he loses an independent sale and a commission. Balden v. Shorter, [1933] Ch. 427.

See also Gale v. Ryan, 263 App.Div. 76, 31 N.Y.S.2d 732 (1941); and Penn–Ohio Steel Corp. v. Allis–Chalmers Mfg. Co., 7 A.D.2d 441, 184 N.Y.S.2d 58 (1959) (defendant made false reports to Internal Revenue of payments made to plaintiff, as a result of which plaintiff had income-tax trouble); Al Raschid v. News Syndicate Co., 265 N.Y. 1, 191 N.E. 713 (1934) (defendant gave false information that plaintiff was not a citizen, subjecting him to deportation proceedings); Bartlett v. Federal

Outfitting Co., 133 Cal.App. 747, 24 P.2d 877 (1933) (forged assignment of wages presented to an employer, in consequence of which the employee was discharged); Owens v. Mench, 81 Pa.D. & C. 314 (1953) (false report of a physician on a worker's injury necessitated suit to recover workers' compensation); and Cooper v. Weissblatt, 154 Misc. 522, 277 N.Y.S. 709 (1935) (false statements to church authorities forced the plaintiff to defend a suit).

4. *Special Damage.* Pleading and proof of special damage are held to be essential to any cause of action for injurious falsehood. The damage must consist of pecuniary loss, and personal elements of damage such as mental distress, which are recoverable for defamation, are not sufficient to sustain this action.

5. When the damages claimed consist only of loss of prospective contracts or customers, the older and still prevailing rule is that the plaintiff must identify the particular customers who have refrained from dealing with him, and specify the transactions of which he claims to have been deprived. Wilson v. Dubois, 35 Minn. 471, 29 N.W. 68 (1886); Barquin v. Hall Oil Co., 28 Wyo. 164, 201 P. 352 (1921). It is not enough merely to show a general decline in plaintiff's business following the false publication. Ward v. Gee, 61 S.W.2d 555 (Tex.Civ.App.1933); Shaw Cleaners & Dyers v. Des Moines Dress Club, 215 Iowa 1130, 245 N.W. 231 (1932); Amerinet, Inc. v. Xerox Corporation, 972 F.2d 1483 (8th Cir.1992), cert. denied, 506 U.S. 1080 (1993); but cf. Imperial Developers, Inc. v. Seaboard Surety Co., 518 N.W.2d 623 (Minn. 1994) (finding *Amerinet* not persuasive because it did not distinguish between product and business disparagement; the former is not actionable per se while the latter is).

6. The modern tendency, deriving from the principal case, is to require the plaintiff to be specific only when it is reasonable to expect him to do so, and to allow recovery for a general decline in business if all other reasonably possible causes are excluded. Thus in Craig v. Proctor, 229 Mass. 339, 118 N.E. 647 (1918), a general allegation in the complaint was upheld, but it was said that the defendant might compel the plaintiff to furnish before trial such information as he had. In view of the reasonable impracticability of showing specific losses, plaintiff may present sufficient evidence by using detailed statistical and expert proof to exclude the influence of other factors causing the loss of general business. Teilhaber Manufacturing Company v. Unarco Materials Storage, 791 P.2d 1164 (Colo.App.1989).

Title

Horning v. Hardy

Court of Special Appeals of Maryland, 1977.
36 Md.App. 419, 373 A.2d 1273.

["The Hardys" filed suit in trespass and ejectment against "the Hornings," claiming that they owned certain real property that the Hornings were developing. The Hornings filed a counterclaim seeking to recover damages on the two bases of slander of title and tortious interference with contract. The trial court held for the Hornings on the initial suit and for the Hardys on the counterclaim, thus allowing neither party to recover. This court agrees with the holding in the suit for trespass and ejectment, on the ground that the Hardys had failed to establish ownership through either deed descriptions or adverse possession.

On the counterclaim, the trial court regarded slander of title and interference with contract as raising the same issues and analyzed the case in terms of slander of title. The Hornings were developing land in the disputed area and had one house ready for sale. On the morning of the settlement, a phone call from the Hardys' attorney advised the parties to the settlement that the Hardys had filed suit claiming ownership on the previous day. The settlement "was immediately aborted and no sales or settlements have been consummated since that day."]

LISS, JUDGE. * * * Prosser * * * suggests that the tort we are here discussing has been incorrectly designated as "slander of title." Such nomenclature derives from the earliest cases—decided before 1600—where it applied primarily to oral aspersions on the plaintiff's ownership of land, which aspersions prevented the owner from leasing or selling the land. Prosser points out that from the beginning the tort was recognized as being only loosely allied to defamation of the person and was considered instead to be an action on the case for the special damage resulting from the defendant's interference. As the years progressed, the tort was expanded to include written aspersions on property, whether land or personalty, and the disparagement of the quality of property. The tort has, therefore, been known as "disparagement of property," "slander of goods," and "trade libel." * * *

A * * * valuable contribution to the clarification of the tort in Maryland was made by Judge Wilson K. Barnes in the case of Beane v. McMullen, 265 Md. 585, 291 A.2d 37 (1972). Quoting extensively from Prosser, Judge Barnes said:

"Injurious falsehood or disparagement, then, may consist of the publication of matter derogatory to the plaintiff's title to his property, or its quality, or to his business in general, or even to some element of his personal affairs, of a kind calculated to prevent others from dealing with him, or otherwise to interfere with his relations with others to his disadvantage. The cause of action founded upon it resembles that for defamation, but differs from it materially in the greater burden of proof resting on the plaintiff, and the necessity for special damage in all cases. The falsehood must be communicated to a third person, since the tort consists of interference with the relation with such persons. But the plaintiff must plead and prove not only the publication and its disparaging innuendo, as in defamation, but something more. There is no presumption, as in the case of personal slander, that the disparaging statement is false, and the plaintiff must establish its falsity as a part of his cause of action. Although it has been contended that there is no essential reason against liability where even the truth is published for the purpose of doing harm, the policy of the courts has been to encourage the publication of the truth, regardless of motive.

"In addition, the plaintiff must prove in all cases that the publication has played a material and substantial part in inducing others not to deal with him, and that as a result he had suffered special damage. * * *

"There is liability when the defendant acts for a spite motive, and out of a desire to do harm for its own sake; and equally so when he acts for the purpose of doing harm to the interests of the plaintiff in a manner in which he is not privileged so to interfere. There is also liability when the defendant knows that what he says is false, regardless of whether he has an ill motive or intends to affect the plaintiff at all. The deliberate liar must take the risk that his statement will prove to be economically damaging to others; and there is something like the 'scienter' found in an action of deceit. Any of these three is sufficient to constitute 'malice' and support the action. But in the absence of any of the three there is no liability, where the defendant has made his utterance in good faith, even though he may have been negligent in failing to ascertain the facts before he made it." Id. at 607–09, 291 A.2d at 49.

* * *

[S]tate law [following *Gertz,* supra page 892, adopts] the standard of negligence as set forth in Restatement (Second) of Torts, § 580B (Tentative Draft #21, 1975), which states that liability may accrue only if the defendant a) knows that the statement is false and that it defames the other, b) the defendant acts in reckless disregard of these matters, or c) acts negligently in failing to ascertain them. The opinion further held that the quantum of proof required of the plaintiff was the usual negligence standard of the preponderance of the evidence.

In the case here being considered, there is one further complicating factor: the assertion of a qualified privilege by the appellees. Prosser * * * states the privilege to be as follows: "If [the defendant] has a present, existing economic interest to protect, such as the ownership or condition of property * * * he is privileged to prevent performance of the contract of another which threatens it; and for obvious reasons of policy he is likewise privileged to assert an honest claim, or bring or threaten a suit in good faith, to exercise the right of petition to public authorities or to settle his own case out of court."

Further justification for the recognition of the conditional privilege is stated in 1 Harper and James, The Law of Torts, § 6.2 (1956): "If, knowing that another is offering or about to offer land or other thing for sale as his own, he fails to take advantage of a readily available opportunity to inform the intending purchaser, or those likely to become purchasers, as where the sale is by auction, of his claim to the thing, he may preclude himself from afterwards asserting it against the purchaser. Therefore, he must be permitted without fear of liability to protect the enforceability of his claim by asserting it before the purchase is made."

Jacron, supra, makes it clear that the adoption of the negligence standard of fault in defamation cases does not make obsolete the defense of conditional privilege. In a case where a common law conditional privilege is asserted and found as a matter of law to exist, "the negligence standard of *Gertz* is logically subsumed in the higher standard for proving malice, reckless disregard as to truth or falsity * * *." Id. at 600, 350 A.2d at 700. If the plaintiff, faced with a conditional privilege, is unable to prove the malice necessary to overcome that defense, the proof of the lesser standard of negligence would not permit a recovery. [C] In conditional privilege cases, the privilege may be lost either by proof of "constitutional malice" in the form of reckless disregard for truth or falsity or knowing falsehood or by proof of common law malice in the form of spite or ill-will.

The question of whether a conditional privilege exists is a matter of law for the court. Whether the privilege has been abused or forfeited by malice is a question of fact for the trier of the facts. [C] The trial court found as a matter of law that the interference by Hardy with the Hornings' title was privileged. It concluded that the "original plaintiffs asserted an honest claim to the land in question which they had reason to believe was part of their property and they therefore had a present economic interest to protect." We hold this conclusion to be correct * * *.

Appellants urge strenuously that the failure of the appellees to act in good faith to verify the boundaries of the land which they claimed and in their failure to secure expert opinion as to the validity of their claim is evidence of a reckless disregard for the truth. This contention ignores, however, our holding in *Kapiloff* [v. Dunn, 27 Md.App. 514, 343 A.2d 251 (1975)], where we said:

"Although the test for reckless disregard does not avail itself of easy application, one point is clear: mere failure to investigate, in and of itself, is not sufficient evidence under the *New York Times* privilege. * * * Since failure to investigate cannot satisfy the constitutional test of reckless disregard, we cannot perceive how mere failure to seek assistance of educational experts, without more, could satisfy that standard." * * *

The trial court found as a fact that there was no abuse of the conditional privilege and we find no plain error in its conclusions. * * *

Judgments affirmed.

NOTES AND QUESTIONS

1. This was the first form of injurious falsehood. See, e.g., Gerard v. Dickenson, Cro.Eliz. 196, 76 Eng.Rep. 903 (1590), which is remarkably like the present case except that it was alleged that the defendant knew that her claim to the castle was based on forgery.

2. Any type of legally protected property interest that can be sold may be the subject of disparagement, including remainders, leases, mineral rights, trademarks, copyrights, patents, corporate shares and literary productions. A common form of "slander of title" is the assertion, as by filing for record, of a false claim to a mortgage or other lien on the property. See, e.g., Gudger v. Manton, 21 Cal.2d 537, 134 P.2d 217 (1943), where defendant levied and recorded execution on plaintiff's property, to force plaintiff to pay a debt contracted by his wife before their marriage.

3. *Privileges.* It appears that any absolute or qualified privilege that applies to defamation under the common law applies also to injurious falsehood. Whenever the defendant is privileged to publish a false statement that is personally defamatory, he must be no less privileged to publish one that is not. See Davis v. Union State Bank, 137 Kan. 264, 20 P.2d 508 (1933) (absolute privilege for statements in pleading filed); Stewart v. Fahey, 14 Ariz.App. 149, 481 P.2d 519 (1971) (persons

connected with judicial proceeding); Bearce v. Bass, 88 Me. 521, 34 A. 411 (1896) (criticism of public building as badly constructed); Mack Miller Candle Co. v. MacMillan Co., 239 App.Div. 738, 269 N.Y.S. 33 (1934), aff'd, 266 N.Y. 489, 195 N.E. 167 (1934) (report of judicial proceeding).

4. The defendant has a qualified privilege to protect his own interests by the assertion of a bona fide claim to any kind of property. This includes, for example, an assertion that plaintiff is infringing defendant's patent, copyright or trademark rights by the sale of his product. Oil Conservation Engineering Co. v. Brooks Engineering Co., 52 F.2d 783 (6th Cir.1931); Alliance Securities Co. v. De Vilbiss, 41 F.2d 668 (6th Cir.1930). The privilege is, however, a qualified one and it is defeated if the defendant's motive is shown to be actual malice, in the sense of a desire to do harm. Sinclair Ref. Co. v. Jones Super Service Station, 188 Ark. 1075, 70 S.W.2d 562 (1934); A.B. Farquhar Co. v. National Harrow Co., 102 Fed. 714 (3d Cir.1900). It is also defeated if the defendant has acted in bad faith, as where it is found that he did not honestly believe his assertions to be true. Hopkins v. Drowne, 21 R.I. 20, 41 A. 567 (1898); Ezmirlian v. Otto, 139 Cal.App. 486, 34 P.2d 774 (1934).

As in the case of other qualified privileges, the defendant will be liable if there is excessive publication to persons whom it is not reasonably necessary to reach or if he includes statements that he knows to be untrue. Donovan v. Wilson Sporting Goods Co., 285 F.2d 714 (1st Cir.1961). See generally Restatement (Second) of Torts §§ 635, 646A.

Goods and Trade

More common, and controversial, is the application of the disparagement tort to goods and trade. An early instance of trade disparagement is Dickes v. Fenne, March N.R. 59, 82 Eng.Rep. 411 (1639) ("Defendant having communication with some of the Customers of the Plaintiff, who was a Brewer, said, That he would give a peck of malt to his mare and she should pisse as good beare as Dickes doth Brew"; no recovery because no allegation of special damages).

In Bose Corp. v. Consumers Union of United States, Inc., 466 U.S. 485 (1984), the Supreme Court entertained an action by Bose against the defendant's magazine "Consumer Reports" commenting adversely on Bose's 901 speakers. The court applied the reasoning derived from *New York Times* in deciding that, since Bose was a public figure, it had the burden of showing "actual malice" by "clear and convincing proof" and that an appellate court must exercise independent judgment on this issue. This displaced the usual standard that findings of fact shall not be set aside unless "clearly erroneous." See discussion supra page 889. It remains unclear how far constitutional jurisprudence will influence the action for disparagement of a product. The Supreme Court in Central Hudson Gas and Elec. Corp. v. Public Serv. Comm'n of N.Y., 447 U.S. 557 (1980), and in 44 Liquormart, Inc. v. Rhode Island and Rhode Island Liquor Stores Ass'n, 517 U.S. 484 (1996), has clarified the extent to which the state may regulate advertising. Bans on truthful, nonmisleading information require the state to show not merely that they promote a legitimate state interest, but do so "to a material degree." Liability under a disparagement action will tend to promote the reliability and accuracy of information, and unlike the regulation in *Central Hudson* and *44 Liquormart*, it does not, by its intent, suppress truthful and nonmisleading commercial messages. As in defamation, however, that liability may chill the production of information. Political and commercial speech both attract First Amendment scrutiny and the disparagement action is therefore subject to examination under *New York Times*.

Intentional Infliction of Harm

It has been said that recovery for injurious falsehood requires malice involving showing of knowledge that the statement was false, or intent to harm the plaintiff or affect his interests in an unprivileged manner. Prosser, Injurious Falsehood: The Basis of Liability, 59 Colum.L.Rev. 425 (1959). See Advance Music Corp. v. American Tobacco Co., 296 N.Y. 79, 70 N.E.2d 401 (1946) (sufficient to allege that defendants "wantonly caused damage to the plaintiff by a system of conduct [that] warrants an inference that they intend harm of that type"); Remick Music Corp. v. American Tobacco Co., 57 F.Supp. 475 (S.D.N.Y.1944) ("defendants deliberately and wilfully indulged in such unfairness"); Dale System v. General Teleradio, 105 F.Supp. 745 (S.D.N.Y.1952) ("intentional publication for the sake of injuring the plaintiff"); Shapiro v. La Morta, 40 The Times L.R. 201 (Cit.App.1923) (statement must be "not bona fide"); Hahn v. Duveen, 133 Misc. 871, 234 N.Y.S. 185 (1929) (no liability "if in good faith"); cf. Demuth Development Corp. v. Merck & Co., 432 F.Supp. 990 (E.D.N.Y.1977) ("acts * * * solely malicious * * * done 'without legal or social justification' ").

Relationship of Injurious Falsehood to Defamation

These two torts may overlap, since the same statement may both defame a person and disparage the goods he sells. See Hatchard v. Mege, 18 Q.B.D. 771 (1887). The distinction drawn by the courts is that if the statement made reflects only upon the quality of what the plaintiff has to sell, or the character of his business as such, it is merely injurious falsehood, and proof of special damage is essential to the cause of action. Evans v. Harlow, 5 Q.B. 624 (1844); National Refining Co. v. Benzo Gas Motor Fuel Co., 20 F.2d 763 (8th Cir.1927); U.S. Healthcare, Inc. v. Blue Cross of Greater Philadelphia, 898 F.2d 914 (3d Cir.1990). On the other hand, if the statement imputes to the plaintiff reprehensible personal characteristics or misconduct, it is regarded as defamation. Merle v. Sociological Research Film Corp., 166 App.Div. 376, 152 N.Y.S. 829 (1915) (factory used as place of assignation); Kilpatrick v. Edge, 85 N.J.L. 7, 88 A. 839 (1913) (misconduct in a Turkish bath). In appropriate circumstances, if injurious falsehood is established, an injunction may be granted; but cf. defamation. Restatement (Second) of Torts § 626, Comment b (1977); id. § 942, Comment e (1979).

The difficulty lies in the fact that many statements do both. It might be possible to imply some accusation of personal inefficiency or incompetence, defaming the plaintiff in his business or trade, in nearly every imputation directed against a business or its product. Cf. Summit Hotel Co. v. National Broadcasting Co., 336 Pa. 182, 8 A.2d 302 (1939), where "a rotten hotel" was held to defame the management. See also Auvil v. CBS "60 Minutes," 800 F.Supp. 928 (E.D.Wash. 1992) (applying Washington law to action relating to story about use of alar as a growth regulator of apples). Both actions may stand together. A disparagement action requires the plaintiff to establish falsity and either scienter or recklessness in the statement about the product or business. Id. at 936. The courts, however, sometimes have gone to remarkable lengths in refusing to find any personal defamation. For example, Nonpareil Cork Mfg. Co. v. Keasbey & Mattison Co., 108 Fed. 721 (product a "fraud") (C.C.Pa.1901); Erick Bowman Remedy Co. v. Jensen Salsbery Laboratories, 17 F.2d 255 (8th Cir.1926) ("Barnum was right"). This is particularly true when the most that can be made out of the words is a charge of ignorance, incompetence or negligence. Shaw Cleaners & Dyers v. Des Moines Dress Club, 215 Iowa 1130, 245 N.W. 231 (1932) (garments "only half cleaned").

Personal defamation is found when the words are found clearly to impute dishonesty or lack of integrity to the plaintiff, or say that he is deliberately perpetrating a fraud upon the public by selling a product that he knows to be defective. Tobin v. Alfred M. Best Co., 120 App.Div. 387, 105 N.Y.S. 294 (1907) ("fake" insurance policy); Rosenberg v. J.C. Penney Co., 30 Cal.App.2d 609, 86 P.2d 696 (1939) (fraud in sale).

See Restatement (Second) of Torts §§ 623A–652.

Testing Systems, Inc. v. Magnaflux Corp.

United States District Court, Eastern District of Pennsylvania, 1966.
251 F.Supp. 286.

[Plaintiff and defendant were competing manufacturers of equipment, devices and systems for use in testing industrial and commercial materials. The complaint alleged that defendant circulated to plaintiff's current and prospective customers a false report to the effect that the United States Government had tested plaintiff's product, and found it to be only about 40% as effective as that of the defendant. Plaintiff also claimed that at a manufacturers' convention in Philadelphia defendant's agent, in the presence of plaintiff's current and prospective customers, "did in a loud voice state that * * * [plaintiff's] * * * stuff is no good," and that "the government is throwing them out."]

LORD, DISTRICT JUDGE. This is an action for trade libel or disparagement of property. * * * The matter is now before this Court on defendant's motion to dismiss for failure to state a claim upon which relief can be granted.

For the purposes of this motion, defendant admits the truth of the allegation, but asserts that the action must nevertheless be dismissed because (1) the defendant did no more than make an unfavorable comparison of plaintiff's product with its own; and (2) even assuming that the statements were actionable, plaintiff has failed to allege his damages with the required specificity. * * *

It would serve no useful purpose to dwell at length on the issue of unfavorable comparison. Suffice it to say, as the defendant properly points out, that a statement which takes the form of an unfavorable comparison of products, or which "puffs" or exaggerates the quality of one's own product is not ordinarily actionable. [Cc] This has long been the rule in England, where the action originated, and is now well established in the vast majority of United States jurisdictions. [Cc]

However, this Court is not convinced by the defendant's arguments that his comments amounted to mere unfavorable comparison. The modern history of the doctrine of unfavorable comparison and its permissible use in the conduct of business traces its origin to the leading English case of White v. Mellin [1895] A.C. 154. There the defendant had advertised his product as being far more healthful than plaintiff's. In refusing relief the Court established the precedent that irrespective of their truth or falsity, statements by one competitor which compare his product with that of another are not actionable.

It does not follow from this, however, that every trade disparagement is protectible under the guise of unfavorable comparison merely because the perpetrator was canny enough to mention not only the product of his competitor but also his own. The decision in White v. Mellin, supra, was founded on the near impossibility of ascertaining the truth or falsity of general allegations respecting the superiority of one product over another. To decide otherwise, explained Lord Herschell, would turn the courts "into a machinery for advertising rival productions by obtaining a judicial determination [as to] which of the two was better. [C] One is expected to believe in the superiority of his wares, and he may properly declare his belief to interested parties. It has even been said that he may 'boast untruthfully of his wares.'" Phila. D. Prod. v. Quaker City I. Co., 306 Pa. 164, 172, 159 A. 3 (1932). * * *

The fine line that separates healthy competitive effort from underhanded business tactics is frequently difficult to determine. Apart from the tradesman's right of free speech, which must be vigorously safeguarded, the public has a genuine interest in learning the relative merits of particular products, however that may come about. * * *

Nonetheless, there is an outer perimeter to permissible conduct. The tradesman must be assured that his competitors will not be suffered to engage in conduct which falls below the minimum standard of fair dealing. "[I]t is no answer that they can defend themselves by also resorting to disparagement. A self-respecting business man will not voluntarily adopt, and should not be driven to adopt, a selling method which he regards as undignified, unfair, and repulsive. A competitor should not, by pursuing an unethical practice force his rival to choose between its adoption and the loss of his trade." Wolfe, Unfair Competition, 47 Yale L.J. 1304, 1334–35 (1938).

The defendant's comments in the case presently before this Court do not entitle him to the protection accorded to "unfavorable comparison." There is a readily observable difference between saying that one's product is, in general, better than another's * * * and asserting, as here, that such other's is only 40% as effective as one's own. The former, arguably, merely expresses an opinion, the truth or falsity of which is difficult or impossible of ascertainment. The latter, however, is an assertion of fact, not subject to the same frailties of proof, implying that the party making the statement is fortified with the substantive facts necessary to make it. This distinction has never been seriously questioned. See e.g. Restatement, Torts, §§ 626, 627, 628. The defendant in this case admittedly circulated to plaintiff's present and prospective customers false statements to the effect that the government had tested both products and found the defendant's to be 60% more effective than plaintiff's. This is not the sort of "comparison" that courts will protect.

Apart from this, there is at least one additional factor which withdraws the defendant's comments from the category of unfavorable comparison. Not content with making the admittedly false statements and allowing them to be evaluated independently of any extraneous influence, the defendant here gave added authenticity to its assertions, by invoking the reputation of a third party, the United States Government. It is unnecessary to speculate on the additional force the defendant's remarks must have had when coupled with the purported approval of so highly credible a source. This, of course, is to say nothing of the statements to the effect that plaintiff had been "thrown out," which by no stretch of the imagination could be termed mere comparison.

For all of the above reasons, it is the judgment of this Court that the defendant's remarks are actionable.

NOTES AND QUESTIONS

1.   How does this case compare with Vulcan Metals Co. v. Simmons Mfg. Co., supra page 1051?

2.   The competitor's "puffing" privilege permits statements of comparison, that the defendant's goods are the best in the market, that they are better than the plaintiff's, or other boasting or exaggeration, even though the defendant is fully aware that what he says is false, and the publication is made for the purpose of injuring the plaintiff by taking business away from him. One of the leading cases is White v. Mellin, [1895] A.C. 154, where the defendant sold packages of plaintiff's baby food with a wrapper affixed to them which stated that defendant's was better. This was held to be privileged. In this respect, there is an obvious difference from personal defamation, which would not be privileged under the same circumstances.

3.   Competition for business does not, however, justify intentional false statements of fact concerning the competitor's business or product, when they are not confined to comparing the product or conduct of the competitor with that of the plaintiff, and this unfair competition is not privileged. U.S. Healthcare, Inc. v. Blue Cross of Greater Philadelphia, 898 F.2d 914 (3d Cir.1990); Hopkins Chemical Co. v. Read Drug & Chemical Co., 124 Md. 210, 92 A. 478 (1914). Sometimes the courts have leaned quite far to avoid finding an assertion to be a misstatement of fact. Thus in Nonpareil Cork Mfg. Co. v. Keasbey & Mattison Co., 108 Fed. 721 (E.D.Pa.1901), a statement that cork covering for steam pipes was a "fraud" was held to be "really but the expression of an unfavorable opinion of the goods" of its competitor. Dairy Stores, Inc. v. Sentinel Pub. Co., 104 N.J. 125, 516 A.2d 220 (1986) (applying the distinction between fact and opinion in defamation law). But such expressions are not uncommon among rivals in trade, and their correctness in each instance is for determination by those whose custom is sought, and not by the courts. Is the standard too tolerant of commercial conduct that misleads consumers in the modern marketplace? See Hayden, A Goodly Apple Rotten at the Heart: Commercial Disparagement in Comparative Advertising as Common Law Tortious Unfair Competition, 76 Iowa L.Rev. 67 (1990).

(B) INTERFERENCE WITH EXISTING OR PROSPECTIVE CONTRACTUAL RELATIONS

Lumley v. Gye
Queen's Bench, 1853.
2 El. & Bl. 216, 118 Eng.Rep. 749.

[The declaration alleged: Plaintiff, manager of the Queens Theatre for performing operas, contracted with Johanna Wagner for her to perform in his theatre for a designated time. She agreed not to perform elsewhere during the contract term. Defendant, "knowing the premises and maliciously intruding to injure plaintiff * * *, enticed and procured Wagner to refuse to perform." Defendant demurred.]

ERLE, J. The question raised upon this demurrer is, Whether an action will lie by the proprietor of a theatre against a person who maliciously procures an entire abandonment of a contract to perform exclusively at that theatre for a certain time; whereby damage was sustained? And it seems to me that it will. The authorities are numerous and uniform, that an action will lie by a master against a person who procures that a servant should unlawfully leave his service. The principle involved in these cases comprises the present; for, there, the right of action in the master arises from the wrongful act of the defendant in procuring that the person hired should break his contract, by putting an end to the relation of employer and employed; and the present case is the same. If it is objected that this class of actions for procuring a breach of contract of hiring rests upon no principle, and ought not to be extended beyond the cases heretofore decided, and that, as those have related to contracts respecting trade, manufactures, or household service, and not to performance at a theatre, therefore they are no authority for an action in respect of a contract for such performance; the answer appears to me to be, that the class of cases referred to rests upon the principle that the procurement of the violation of the rights is a cause of action, and that, when this principle is applied to a violation of a right arising upon a contract of hiring, the nature of the service contracted for is immaterial.

It is clear that the procurement of the violation of a right is a cause of action in all instances where the violation is an actionable wrong, as in violations of a right to property, whether real or personal, or to personal security: he who procures the wrong is a joint wrongdoer, and may be sued, either alone or jointly with the agent, in the appropriate action for the wrong complained of. * * * He who maliciously procures a damage to another by violation of his right ought to be made to indemnify; and that, whether he procures an actionable wrong or a breach of contract. He who procures the non-delivery of goods according to contract may inflict an injury, the same as he who procures the abstraction of goods after delivery; and both ought on the same ground to be made responsible. The remedy on the contract may be inadequate * * *.

The result is that there ought to be, in my opinion, judgment for the plaintiff.

[The concurring opinion of CROMPTON, J., and dissenting opinion of COLERIDGE, J., are omitted.]

NOTES AND QUESTIONS

1. The companion case of Lumley v. Wagner, 1 De G.M. & G. 604, 42 Eng.Rep. 687 (1852), a landmark in the law of equitable relief, affirmed injunctions preventing Miss Wagner from breaking the negative covenant in her contract with Lumley by singing for Gye at Covent Garden or elsewhere during the period of her

contractual obligation to Lumley. This was a battle in a long war between Lumley and Guy, rival London impresarios. Johanna Wagner, a cantatrice to the King of Prussia and niece of Richard Wagner, finally returned to the London stage five years later, but London audiences were deprived of her voice at its zenith.

2.   The principle announced in the principal case was received at first with a great deal of hesitation and disapproval. It was reaffirmed thirty years later in Bowen v. Hall, 6 Q.B.D. 333 (1881), and then by degrees was extended—first to contracts other than those for personal services, and then to a holding that ill-will on the part of the defendant was not essential to the tort. The present English law gives full acceptance to the proposition that intentional improper interference with any type of contract is a tort. Jasperson v. Dominion Tobacco Co., [1923] App.Cas. 709.

3.   Defendant's tortious conduct is not confined to inducing the third person to break the contract. It may apply to other means of preventing the third person from performing. See, e.g., Phez Co. v. Salem Fruit Union, 103 Or. 514, 205 P. 970 (1922) (D refuses to carry out his contract to supply goods to T, to prevent T from supplying them to P).

4.   The plaintiff must prove that the defendant knew of the contract. Imperial Ice Co. v. Rossier, 18 Cal.2d 33, 112 P.2d 631 (1941); Continental Research, Inc. v. Cruttenden, Podesta & Miller, 222 F.Supp. 190 (D.C.Minn.1963) (circumstantial evidence of knowledge); Mid–Continent Tel. Corp. v. Home Tel. Co., 319 F.Supp. 1176 (D.C.Miss.1970) (reason to know and reasonable ignorance).

5.   A third party beneficiary will be able to recover in tort for interference with the contract if he could have recovered in an action on the contract. Reynolds v. Owen, 34 Conn.Sup. 107, 380 A.2d 543 (1977).

6.   If the third party has already broken the contract or decided to do so, and offers to contract with the defendant, defendant has not induced the breach. See Middleton v. Wallichs Music & Entertainment Co., 24 Ariz.App. 180, 536 P.2d 1072 (1975); Northern Wis. Coop. Tobacco Pool v. Bekkedal, 182 Wis. 571, 197 N.W. 936 (1923).

7.   Does the tort interfere with the freedom of a party to a contract to breach and pay contract damages as a result? The theory of efficient breach holds that the freedom to breach and recontract more favorably, allows resources to be allocated to a higher valued use. Dean Perlman, Interference with Contract and Other Economic Expectancies: A Clash of Tort and Contract Doctrine, 49 U.Chi.L.Rev. 61 (1982), formulates the tort to avoid this flouting of the efficiency goal of contract law.

But the subject contracts of the tort are relational contracts—employment, leases, professional, and long-term business relationships—where the goal of efficient breach is remote and the goal of maintenance of cooperation more important. Thus the question is whether the tort supports that relational goal. See BeVier, Reconsidering Inducement, 76 Va.L.Rev. 877 (1990) (viewing the tort as promoting parties' value-enhancing behavior) and Partlett, From Victorian Opera to Rock and Rap: Inducement to Breach of Contract in the Music Industry, 66 Tulane L.Rev. 771 (1992) (viewing the tort as filling gaps in contract relationship and obliging the dissemination of information about the existence of the contract). But see Dobbs, Tortious Interference with Contractual Relationships, 34 Ark.L.Rev. 335 (1980) (criticizing the tort for its authoritarian and anti-autonomy tendencies) and Gergen, Tortious Interference: How it is Engulfing Commercial Law, Why This is Not Entirely Bad, and a Prudential Response, 38 Ariz. L. Rev. 1175 (1996) (criticizing economic analysis and supporting application of the tort to avoid unforeseen opportunistic behavior).

8. Two classic articles on the subject of this section are Sayre, Inducing Breach of Contract, 36 Harv.L.Rev. 663 (1923); and Carpenter, Interference with Contract Relations, 41 Harv.L.Rev. 728 (1928).

Bacon v. St. Paul Union Stockyards Co.

Supreme Court of Minnesota, 1924.
161 Minn. 522, 201 N.W. 326.

[Plaintiff's complaint alleges that he was employed by the Drover Livestock Commission Co., engaged in buying, selling and dealing in livestock in the defendant's stockyards, but that the defendant "wrongfully, unlawfully, and willfully excluded plaintiff from its said stockyards, and barred and prevented him from carrying on his occupation therein, and forbade any person, firm, or corporation to employ him in or about" the stockyards. Defendant's demurrer to the complaint was sustained. Plaintiff appealed.]

PER CURIAM. * * * The wrongful interference with the contract relations of others causing a breach is a tort. We are of the opinion that the complaint states a cause of action for wrongful interference with plaintiff's employment. It appears from the complaint that the plaintiff had steady employment, and that defendant wrongfully, willfully, and unlawfully prevented him from continuing in that employment. We think such conduct is in violation of plaintiff's rights. [C] The defendant may have reasons to justify its conduct, but such reasons do not appear in the complaint. * * *

Reversed.

NOTES AND QUESTIONS

1. See Restatement (Second) of Torts § 766A. Also Harber v. Ohio Nat'l Life Ins. Co., 512 F.2d 170 (8th Cir.1975) (restricting sales of plaintiff's employee); White v. Massee, 202 Iowa 1304, 211 N.W. 839 (1927) (excluding plaintiff from place of performance); Yankee Network v. Gibbs, 295 Mass. 56, 3 N.E.2d 228 (1936) (fraudulently inducing plaintiff to break his own contract); Lichter v. Fulcher, 22 Tenn.App. 670, 125 S.W.2d 501 (1938) (depriving plaintiff of necessary labor).

2. The principle also applies to conduct making plaintiff's performance of his contract more burdensome or expensive, as by deliberate damage to a highway he is under a duty to repair. McNary v. Chamberlain, 34 Conn. 384, 91 Am.Dec. 732 (1867); Cue v. Breland, 78 Miss. 864, 29 So. 850 (1901); Piedmont Cotton Mills v. H.W. Ivey Constr. Co., 109 Ga.App. 876, 137 S.E.2d 528 (1964).

3. In these "hinderance" cases, under § 766A, the bulk involve a physical interference with person or property and the commission of an independent tort. This duplication of protection and the uncertain dimensions of liability, grounded the court's reluctance to adopt § 766A liability in Windsor Securities, Inc. v. Hartford Life Ins. Co., 986 F.2d 655 (3d Cir.1993) (plaintiff investment advisor claim against mutual fund sponsor for restrictions by defendant on investor's ability to transfer investments between accounts finding no liability on the basis that the action was not "wrongful"). The interference must cause plaintiff to lose a right

under a contract or make contract rights more costly or less valuable. Thus no action available where defendant induced plaintiff's tenant to vacate premises but lease was not breached. Sampson Investments v. Jondex Corp., 176 Wis.2d 55, 499 N.W.2d 177 (1993).

Della Penna v. Toyota Motor Sales, U.S.A., Inc.
Supreme Court of California, 1995.
11 Cal. 4th 376; 902 P.2d 740

ARABIAN, J. We granted review to reexamine, in light of divergent rulings from the Court of Appeal and a doctrinal evolution among other state high courts, the elements of the tort variously known as interference with "prospective economic advantage," "prospective contractual relations," or "prospective economic relations," and the allocation of the burdens of proof between the parties to such an action. We conclude that those Court of Appeal opinions requiring proof of a so-called "wrongful act" as a component of the cause of action, and allocating the burden of proving it to the plaintiff, are the better reasoned decisions; we accordingly adopt that analysis as our own, disapproving language in prior opinions of this court to the contrary. Such a requirement, incorporating the views of several other jurisdictions, much of the Restatement Second of Torts, the better reasoned decisions of the Court of Appeal, and the views of leading academic authorities, sensibly redresses the balance between providing a remedy for predatory economic behavior and keeping legitimate business competition outside litigative bounds. We do not in this case, however, go beyond approving the requirement of a showing of wrongfulness as part of the plaintiff's case; the case, if any, to be made for adopting refinements to that element of the tort—requiring the plaintiff to prove, for example, that the defendant's conduct amounted to an independently tortious act, or was a species of anticompetitive behavior proscribed by positive law, or was motivated by unalloyed malice—can be considered on another day, and in another case.

In this case, after the trial court modified the standard jury instruction to require the plaintiff automobile dealer to show that defendant Toyota's interference with his business relationships was "wrongful," the jury returned a verdict for Toyota. The Court of Appeal reversed the ensuing judgment and ordered a new trial on the ground that plaintiff's burden of proof did not encompass proof of a "wrongful" act and that the modified jury instruction was therefore erroneous. Given our conclusion that the plaintiff's burden does include proof that the defendant's conduct was wrongful by some measure other than an interference with the plaintiff's interest itself, we now reverse the Court of Appeal and direct that the judgment of the trial court be affirmed.

I

John Della Penna, an automobile wholesaler doing business as Pacific Motors, brought this action for damages against defendant Toyota Motor Sales, U.S.A., Inc., and its Lexus division, alleging that certain business conduct of defendants both violated [the] state antitrust statute [c], and constituted an intentional interference with his economic relations. The impetus for Della Penna's suit arose out of the 1989 introduction into the American luxury car market of Toyota's Lexus automobile. Prior to introducing the Lexus, the evidence at trial showed, both the manufacturer, Toyota Motor Corporation, and defendant, the American distributor, had been concerned about the possibility that a resale market might develop for the Lexus in Japan. * * * Fearing that auto wholesalers in the United States might reexport Lexus models back to Japan for resale, and concerned that, with production and the availability of Lexus models in the American market limited, reexports would jeopardize its fledgling network of American Lexus dealers, Toyota inserted in its dealership agreements a "no export" clause, providing that the dealer was "authorized to sell [Lexus automobiles] only to customers located in the United States. [Dealer] agrees that it will not sell [Lexus automobiles] for resale or use outside the United States. [Dealer] agrees to abide by any export policy established by [distributor]."

Following introduction into the American market, it soon became apparent that some domestic Lexus units were being diverted for foreign sales, principally to Japan. To counter this effect, Toyota managers wrote to their retail dealers, reminding them of the "no-export" policy and explaining that exports for foreign resale could jeopardize the supply of Lexus automobiles available for the United States market. In addition, Toyota compiled a list of "offenders"—dealers and others believed by Toyota to be involved heavily in the developing Lexus foreign resale market—which it distributed to Lexus dealers in the United States. American Lexus dealers were also warned that doing business with those whose names appeared on the "offenders" list might lead to a series of graduated sanctions, from reducing a dealer's allocation to possible reevaluation of the dealer's franchise agreement.

During the years 1989 and 1990, plaintiff Della Penna did a profitable business as an auto wholesaler purchasing Lexus automobiles, chiefly from the Lexus of Stevens Creek retail outlet, at near retail price and exporting them to Japan for resale. By late 1990, however, plaintiff's sources began to dry up, primarily as a result of the "offenders list." Stevens Creek ceased selling models to plaintiff; gradually other sources declined to sell to him as well.

In February 1991, plaintiff filed this lawsuit against Toyota Motor Sales, U.S.A., Inc., alleging both state antitrust claims * * * and interference with his economic relationship with Lexus retail dealers. At the close of plaintiff's case-in-chief, the trial court granted Toyota's motion for nonsuit with respect to the remaining [antitrust] claim (plaintiff had previously abandoned a related claim—unfair competition—prior to trial). The tort cause of action went to the jury, however, under the standard BAJI instructions applicable to such claims with one significant exception. At the request of defendant and over plaintiff's objection, the trial judge modified BAJI No. 7.82—the basic instruction identifying the elements of the tort and indicating the burden of proof—to require plaintiff to prove that defendant's alleged interfering conduct was "wrongful."

The jury returned a divided verdict, nine to three, in favor of Toyota. After Della Penna's motion for a new trial was denied, he appealed. In an unpublished disposition, the Court of Appeal unanimously reversed the trial court's judgment, ruling that a plaintiff alleging intentional interference with economic relations is not required to establish "wrongfulness" as an element of its prima facie case, and that it was prejudicial error for the trial court to have read the jury an amended instruction to that effect. The Court of Appeal remanded the case to the trial court for a new trial; we then granted Toyota's petition for review and now reverse.

II

A

Although legal historians have traced the origins of the so-called "interference torts" as far back as the Roman law, the proximate historical impetus for their modern development lay in mid–19th century English common law. (See, e.g., Sayre, Inducing Breach of Contract (1923) 36 Harv. L.Rev. 663; Note, Tortious Interference With Contractual Relations in the Nineteenth Century: The Transformation of Property, Contract, and Tort (1980) 93 Harv. L.Rev. 1510.) The opinion of the Queen's Bench in Lumley v. Gye (1853) 2 El. & Bl. 216 [118 Eng. Rep. 749], a case that has become a standard in torts casebooks, is widely cited as the origin of the two torts–interference with contract and its sibling, interference with prospective economic relations[1]—in the form in which they have come down to us. * * *

The opinion in Lumley v. Gye [c] dealt, of course, with conduct intended to induce the breach of an existing contract, not conduct intended to prevent or persuade others not to contract with the plaintiff. That such an interference with prospective economic relations might itself be tortious was confirmed by the Queen's Bench over the next 40 years. In Temperton v. Russell (1893) 1 Q.B. 715 (Temperton), a labor union, embroiled in a dispute with a firm of builders, announced what today would be called a secondary boycott, intended to force a resolution of the union's grievances by pressuring suppliers of the builder to cease furnishing him construction materials. A failure to comply with the union's boycott demands, suppliers were warned, would result in union pressure on those who bought their supplies not to deal with them.

One such supplier of the builder, Temperton, sued the union's leadership, alleging that his business had been injured by breaches of supply contracts and the refusal of others to do business with him, all as a result

---

1. Throughout this opinion, in an effort to avoid both cumbersome locutions and clumsy acronyms ("IIPEA"), we use the phrase "interference with economic relations" to refer to the tort generally known as "intentional interference with prospective contractual or economic relations" and to distinguish it from the cognate form, "intentional interference with contract."

of the union's threats. A unanimous Queen's Bench upheld the jury's verdict for the plaintiff, reasoning in part on the authority of Lumley v. Gye, supra, 2 El. & Bl. 216, that in the words of Lord Esher, the Master of the Rolls, "the distinction ... between the claim for inducing persons to break contracts already entered into ... and ... inducing persons not to enter into contracts ... can[not] prevail." (*Temperton*, supra, 1 Q.B. at p. 728.)

"There was the same wrongful intent in both cases, wrongful because malicious," Lord Esher wrote. "There was the same kind of injury to the plaintiff. It seems rather a fine distinction to say that, where a defendant maliciously induces a person not to carry out a contract already made with the plaintiff and so injures the plaintiff, it is actionable, but where he injures the plaintiff by maliciously preventing a person from entering into a contract with the plaintiff, which he would otherwise have entered into, it is not actionable." (*Temperton*, supra, 1 Q.B. at p. 728.)

As a number of courts and commentators have observed, the keystone of the liability imposed in Lumley v. Gye, supra, 2 El. & Bl. 216, and *Temperton*, supra, 1 Q.B. 715, to judge from the opinions of the justices, appears to have been the "malicious" intent of a defendant in enticing an employee to breach her contract with the plaintiff, and in damaging the business of one who refused to cooperate with the union in achieving its bargaining aims. While some have doubted whether the use of the word "malicious" amounted to anything more than an intent to commit an act, knowing it would harm the plaintiff (see, e.g., Dobbs, Tortious Interference With Contractual Relationships (1980) 34 Ark. L.Rev. 335, 347, fn. 37), Dean Keeton, assessing the state of the tort as late as 1984, remarked that "[w]ith intent to interfere as the usual basis of the action, the cases have turned almost entirely upon the defendant's motive or purpose and the means by which he has sought to accomplish it. As in the cases of interference with contract, any manner of intentional invasion of the plaintiff's interests may be sufficient if the purpose is not a proper one." (Prosser & Keeton on Torts (5th ed. 1984) Interference with Prospective Advantage, § 130, p. 1009.)

It was, legal historians have suggested, this early accent on the defendant's "intentionality" that was responsible for allying the interference torts with their remote relatives, intentional torts of a quite different order—battery, for example, or false imprisonment. More than one account of the rise of the tort has relied on Lord Bowen's statement in an interference with contract case that "intentionally to do that which is calculated in the ordinary course of events to damage, and which does, in fact, damage another in that person's property or trade, is actionable if done without just cause or excuse." (Mogul Steamship Co. v. McGregor, Gow & Co. (1889) 23 Q.B.D. 598, 613.)

One consequence of this superficial kinship was the assimilation to the interference torts of the pleading and burden of proof requirements of the "true" intentional torts: the requirement that the plaintiff need only allege a so-called "prima facie tort" by showing the defendant's awareness of the economic relation, a deliberate interference with it, and the plaintiff's resulting injury. [C] By this account of the matter—the traditional view of the torts and the one adopted by the first Restatement of Torts—the burden then passed to the defendant to demonstrate that its conduct was privileged, that is, "justified" by a recognized defense such as the protection of others or, more likely in this context, the defendant's own competitive business interests. (See, e.g., Restatement, Torts (1939) § 766, coms. B–m, pp. 50–63 * * *)

These and related features of the economic relations tort and the requirements surrounding its proof and defense led, however, to calls for a reexamination and reform as early as the 1920's. Tracing the origins and the current status of the two interference torts in 1923, Francis Sayre concluded that "a somewhat uncertain law has resulted. .... Courts still punctiliously repeat the well-known formula which requires 'malice,' or 'without just cause' ... as one of the requirements of the tort; but there has been such a lack of agreement as to what constitutes 'malice' or 'absence of justification' that such words are becoming little more than empty phrases .... Is it not time to formulate the problem of what these worn phrases mean?" (Sayre, Inducing Breach of Contract, supra, 36 Harv. L.Rev. at pp. 672, 674–675, fn. Omitted.) The nature of the wrong itself seemed to many unduly vague, inviting suit and hampering the presentation of coherent defenses. More critically in the view of others, the procedural effects of applying the prima facie tort principle to what is essentially a business context led to even more untoward consequences.

Because the plaintiff's initial burden of proof was such a slender one, amounting to no more than showing the defendant's conscious act and plaintiff's economic injury, critics argued that legitimate business competition could lead to time consuming and expensive lawsuits (not to speak of potential liability) by a rival, based on conduct that was regarded by the commercial world as both commonplace and appropriate. The "black letter" rules of the Restatement of Torts surrounding the elements and proof of the tort, some complained, might even suggest to "foreign lawyers reading the Restatement as an original matter [that] the whole competitive order of American industry is prima facie illegal." (Statement of Professor Carl Auerbach at ALI Proceedings, quoted in Perlman, Interference With Contract and Other Economic Expectancies: A Clash of Tort and Contract Doctrine (1982) 49 U. Chi. L.Rev. 61, 79, fn. 89 * * *)

Calls for a reformulation of both the elements and the means of establishing the economic relations tort reached a height around the time the Restatement Second of Torts was being prepared for publication and are reflected in its departures from its predecessor's version. Acknowledging criticism, the American Law Institute discarded the prima facie tort requirement of the first Restatement. A new provision, section 766B, required that the defendant's conduct be "improper," and adopted a multifactor "balancing" approach, identifying seven factors for the trier of fact to weigh in determining a defendant's liability. The Restatement Second of Torts, however, declined to take a position on the issue of which of the parties bore the burden of proof, relying on the "considerable disagreement on who has the burden of pleading and proving certain matters" and the observation that "the law in this area has not fully congealed but is still in a formative stage." (See Rest.2d Torts (1965 ed.) Introductory Note, ch. 37, pp. 5–6.) In addition, the Restatement Second provided that a defendant might escape liability by showing that his conduct was justifiable and did not include the use of "wrongful means." (Id., § 768–771.)

B

In the meantime, however, an increasing number of state high courts had traveled well beyond the Restatement Second's reforms by redefining and otherwise recasting the elements of the economic relations tort and the burdens surrounding its proof and defenses. In Top Serv. Body Shop, Inc. v. Allstate Ins. Co. (1978) 283 Ore. 201 [582 P.2d 1365] (Top Service), the Oregon Supreme Court, assessing this " 'most fluid and rapidly growing tort,' " noted that "efforts to consolidate both recognized and unsettled lines of development into a general theory of 'tortious interference' have brought to the surface the difficulties of defining the elements of so general a tort without sweeping within its terms a wide variety of socially very different conduct." [C]

Recognizing the force of these criticisms, the court went on to hold in *Top Service* [c] that a claim of interference with economic relations "is made out when interference resulting in injury to another is wrongful by some measure beyond the fact of the interference itself. Defendant's liability may arise from improper motives or from the use of improper means. They may be wrongful by reason of a statute or other regulation, or a recognized rule of common law, or perhaps an established standard of a trade or profession. No question of privilege arises unless the interference would be wrongful but for the privilege; it becomes an issue only if the acts charged would be tortious on the part of an unprivileged defendant." [C]

Four years later, the views of the Oregon Supreme Court in *Top Service* [c] were adopted by the Utah Supreme Court. In Leigh Furniture and Carpet Co. v. Isom (Utah 1982) 657 P.2d 293, that court underlined the same concerns that had moved the Oregon Supreme Court in *Top Service*: "The problem with the prima facie tort approach is that basing liability on a mere showing that defendant intentionally interfered with plaintiff's prospective economic relations makes actionable all sorts of contemporary examples of otherwise legitimate persuasion, such as efforts to persuade others not to ... engage in certain activities, or deal with certain entities. The major issue in the controversy—justification for the defendant's conduct—is left to be resolved on the affirmative defense of privilege. In short, the prima facie approach to the tort of interference with prospective economic relations requires too little of the plaintiff." [C]

The Utah Supreme Court went on, however, to reject the alternative, multifactor approach adopted by the Restatement Second: "We concur in the Restatement (Second)'s rejection of the prima facie tort approach because it leaves too much uncertainty about the requirements for a recognized privilege and the defendant's burden of pleading and proving these and other matters. [C] But we also reject the Restatement (Second)'s definition of the tort because of its complexity. We seek a better alternative." [C] That alternative, the court concluded, was the one advanced by the Oregon Supreme Court in *Top Service*, [c], a "middle ground" that requires "the plaintiff to allege and prove more than the prima facie tort, but not to negate all defenses of privilege." [Cc]

Over the past decade or so, close to a majority of the high courts of American jurisdictions have imported into the economic relations tort variations on the *Top Service* line of reasoning, explicitly approving a rule that requires the plaintiff in such a suit to plead and prove the alleged interference was either "wrongful," "improper," "illegal," "independently tortious" or some variant on these formulations. * * *

III

* * *

[O]ur early economic relations cases were principally of two types, either the classic master and servant pattern of the pre-Lumley v. Gye cases (see, e.g., Buxbom v. Smith (1944) 23 Cal. 2d 535, 548 [145 P.2d 305] [hiring away of plaintiff's employees by defendant after plaintiff had built up his business to distribute defendant's publication and defendant had breached distribution contract held actionable as "an unfair method of interference with advantageous relations"]) or those involving circumscribed kinds of business relations in which the plaintiff, typically a real estate broker or attorney working on a contingency, sued to recover fees after defendant had refused to share property sales proceeds or a personal injury recovery (see, e.g., Buckaloo v. Johnson (1975) 14 Cal. 3d 815 [122 Cal. Rptr. 745, 537 P.2d 865] [defendant refused to pay plaintiff his broker's commission on the sale of beach property after plaintiff had discussed sale with buyers and directed them to defendant; held, the complaint stated a claim for relief for intentional interference with prospective economic relations].)

California cases thus reflected the historical origins and development of the tort, especially as it stood prior to the revisions of the Restatement Second and the concurrent evolution in the case law. In Zimmerman v. Bank of America (1961) 191 Cal. App. 2d 55 [12 Cal. Rptr. 319], for example, the plaintiff real estate agent alleged that the defendant bank had "maliciously" induced third parties to breach an oral agreement with him to broker the sale of their property. In holding that the statute of frauds did not bar the plaintiff's interference claim, the Court of Appeal discussed the relationship between the two interference torts. Writing for the court, Justice Tobriner both aligned the source of the economic relations tort with its contractual sibling and employed language that bears a striking symmetry with Lord Esher's statement in *Temperton*, supra, 1 Q.B. 715, 728: "The history of the tort," he wrote, "discloses its essence. It contemplates, basically, a disruption of a relationship, not necessarily the breach of a contract. . . . * * * We cannot conceive how the action for interference with an existing lawful contract, even though unenforceable, could occupy a status lower than that of interference with negotiations contemplating a contract. If interference with the negotiations constitutes the tort, interference with the contract in which the negotiations fructify must necessarily constitute the tort." (*Zimmerman*, supra, 191 Cal. App. 2d at pp. 57, 60.)

This court endorsed the reasoning of Zimmerman v. Bank of America, supra, 191 Cal. App. 2d 55, in *Buckaloo*, supra, 14 Cal. 3d at p. 822, a case in which the plaintiff sued the seller and buyers of beachfront property to recover damages for the loss of his commission from the sale of the land. Among other claims, plaintiff alleged that defendants had intentionally interfered with an expectancy arising out of the seller's open invitation to brokers and his preliminary discussions regarding the sale of the property with the buyers. Upholding the allegations of the complaint as sufficient to survive a demurrer, we characterized the economic relations tort as one "infrequently invoked" but a "more inclusive wrong" than its relative, intentional interference with contract. [c]

Our opinion in *Buckaloo* [c] reviewed a number of Court of Appeal decisions upholding the applicability of the tort to real estate brokerage situations (id. at pp. 823–826) and concluded by identifying the following elements of the cause of action. "In a real estate brokerage context these are: (1) an economic relationship between broker and vendor or broker and vendee containing the probability of future economic benefit to the broker, (2) knowledge by the defendant of the existence of the relationship, (3) intentional acts on the part of the defendant designed to disrupt the relationship, (4) actual disruption of the relationship, (5) damages to the plaintiff proximately caused by the acts of the defendant." (Id. at p. 827.)

"In California," we went on to observe, "privilege or justification is an affirmative defense, and the lack thereof need not be shown by the original pleader." [C] A note of caution, however, crept into our formulation of principles at this point. "Perhaps the most significant privilege or justification for interference with a prospective business advantage is free competition," we wrote, "Ours is a competitive economy in which business entities vie for economic advantage. In a sense, all vendees are potential buyers of the products and services of all sellers in a given line, and success goes to him who is able to induce potential customers not to deal with a competitor." [C]

In Seaman's Direct Buying Service, Inc. v. Standard Oil Co. (1984) 36 Cal. 3d 752 [206 Cal. Rptr. 354, 686 P.2d 1158] (Seaman's), overruled in part by Freeman & Mills, Inc. v. Belcher Oil Co. (1995) 11 Cal. 4th 85 [44 Cal. Rptr. 2d 420, 900 P.2d 669], relying on the first Restatement and without reviewing or even mentioning intervening revaluations of the tort by the Restatement Second, other state high courts and our own Court of Appeal, we again endorsed the prima facie tort pleading and burden of proof format, noting that "[o]nly if and when plaintiff establishes an 'intent to interfere' does the issue of 'justification' come into play. [C] '[W]hile defendant's culpable intent is an element of the cause of action to be pleaded and proved by plaintiff, defendant's justification is an affirmative defense . . . .' " [C] We went on to observe that "[defendant] is mistaken when it implies that an improper 'motive' is an element of plaintiff's cause of action rather than a factor in defendant's affirmative defense. It is not." [C]

Although our opinions following *Seaman's*, [c] to the extent they addressed the question at all, continued to enumerate the same prima facie elements of the economic relations tort, the cases consistently denied the plaintiff recovery. * * *

Meanwhile, developments in the Court of Appeal and in the practical administration of such claims in the trial courts had, if anything, outdistanced our own formulations of the elements of the tort and the allocation of the burden of proof in at least two respects. First, several Court of Appeal opinions appeared to engraft onto the elements of the plaintiff's cause of action allegations and proof that the defendant's conduct was "wrongful." * * *

Second, in 1990, BAJI, the Book of Approved Jury Instructions widely used by trial judges in civil cases, relying on the Restatement Second of Torts and Mr. Witkin's account of the tort, included an instruction providing that a defendant in an economic relations tort case could defeat liability by showing that its conduct was not independently "wrongful." [C]

These developments, of course, closely reflect a nearly concurrent change in views both within the American Law Institute and in other jurisdictions. In the face of those twin lines of development, we are thus presented with the opportunity to consider whether to expressly reconstruct the formal elements of the interference with economic relations tort to achieve a closer alignment with the practice of the trial courts, emerging views within the Court of Appeal, the rulings of many other state high courts, and the critiques of leading commentators. We believe that we should.

IV

In searching for a means to recast the elements of the economic relations tort and allocate the associated burdens of proof, we are guided by an overmastering concern articulated by high courts of other jurisdictions and legal commentators: the need to draw and enforce a sharpened distinction between claims for the tortious disruption of an existing contract and claims that a prospective contractual or economic relationship has been interfered with by the defendant. Many of the cases do in fact acknowledge a greater array of justificatory defenses against claims of interference with prospective relations. Still, in our view and that of several other courts and commentators, the notion that the two torts are analytically unitary and derive from a common principle sacrifices practical wisdom to theoretical insight, promoting the idea that the interests invaded are of nearly equal dignity. They are not.

The courts provide a damage remedy against third party conduct intended to disrupt an existing contract precisely because the exchange of promises resulting in such a formally cemented economic relationship is deemed worthy of protection from interference by a stranger to the agreement. Economic relationships short of contractual, however, should stand on a different legal footing as far as the potential for tort liability is reckoned. Because ours is a culture firmly wedded to the social rewards of commercial contests, the law usually takes care to draw lines of legal liability in a way that maximizes areas of competition free of legal penalties.

A doctrine that blurs the analytical line between interference with an existing business contract and interference with commercial relations less than contractual is one that invites both uncertainty in conduct and unpredictability of its legal effect. The notion that inducing the breach of an existing contract is simply a subevent of the "more inclusive" class of acts that interfere with economic relations, while perhaps theoretically unobjectionable, has been mischievous as a practical matter. Our courts should, in short, firmly distinguish the two kinds of business contexts, bringing a greater solicitude to those relationships that have ripened into agreements, while recognizing that relationships short of that subsist in a zone where the rewards and risks of competition are dominant.

Beyond that, we need not tread today. It is sufficient to dispose of the issue before us in this case by holding that a plaintiff seeking to recover for alleged interference with prospective economic relations has the burden of pleading and proving that the defendant's interference was wrongful "by some measure beyond the fact of the interference itself." [C] It follows that the trial court did not commit error when it modified BAJI No. 7.82 to require the jury to find that defendant's interference was "wrongful." And because the instruction defining "wrongful conduct" given the jury by the trial court was offered by plaintiff himself, we have no occasion to review its sufficiency in this case. The question of whether additional refinements to the plaintiff's pleading and proof burdens merit adoption by California courts—questions embracing the precise scope of "wrongfulness," or whether a "disinterested malevolence," in Justice Holmes's words (Amer. Bank & Trust Co. v. Federal Bank (1921) 256 U.S. 350, 358 [65 L. Ed. 983, 990, 41 S. Ct. 499, 25 A.L.R. 971]), is an actionable interference in itself, or whether the underlying policy justification for the tort, the efficient allocation of social resources, justifies including as actionable conduct that is recognized as anticompetitive under established state and federal positive law [c]—are matters that can await another day and a more appropriate case.

Conclusion

We hold that a plaintiff seeking to recover for an alleged interference with prospective contractual or economic relations must plead and prove as part of its case-in-chief that the defendant not only knowingly interfered with the plaintiff's expectancy, but engaged in conduct that was wrongful by some legal measure other than the fact of interference itself. The judgment of the Court of Appeal is reversed and the cause is remanded with directions to affirm the judgment of the trial court.

MOSK, J. I concur in the judgment.

* * *

[T]he only reasonable choice is reformulation. Indeed, an undertaking of this sort is compelled by the almost unanimous agreement * * * that the interfering party should not be allowed to interfere with impunity at all times and under all circumstances.

To this end, we should clearly define the tort, basing it on stable and circumscribed ground, and eschewing the prima facie tort doctrine, the "protectionist" premise, and the interfering party's motive. Our focus should be on objective conduct and consequences. Further, our concern should be with such conduct and consequences as are unlawful.

General considerations of a formal nature counsel us to take this path. As noted, the tort's rules are "admittedly vague" and their applications "difficult to classify." An objective definition based on unlawfulness, cast in understandable and usable terms, would reduce or remove such weaknesses.

Specific concerns of a substantive kind operate as well. It is plain from the above discussion that the tort is based on the problematic prima facie tort doctrine. In addition, it implicates the "protectionist" premise, which carries internal inconsistency and also threatens the common law's policy of freedom of competition and the First Amendment's guaranty of freedom of speech, freedom of association, and right of petition. Lastly, it has a tendency to yield untoward results, both in individual cases and generally, through its focus on the interfering party's motive. An objective definition based on unlawfulness, developed in light of such facts, would cure or mitigate the deficiency of the doctrine, lessen or eliminate the flaw attributable to the premise, and decrease or neutralize the danger to the policy and the guaranty.

Thus reformulated, the tort requires objective, and unlawful, conduct or consequences.

It follows that the tort may be satisfied by intentional interference with prospective economic advantage by independently tortious means. [Cc]

The interfering party is properly liable to the interfered-with party in such a situation. That is most plainly true when the independently tortious means the interfering party uses are tortious as to the interfered-with party himself. By the tort's very nature, the interfered-with party is an intended (or at least known) victim of the interfering party. [C] But it is true as well when the independently tortious means the interfering party uses are independently tortious only as to a third party. Even under these circumstances, the interfered-with party remains an intended (or at least known) victim of the interfering party—albeit one that is indirect rather than direct. (See Rest.2d Torts, § 767, com. C, pp. 29–30.) In this situation, the means in question are independently tortious as to the third party "if those elements that pertain to" the interfering party "are present" even if those that pertain to the third party are not. [C]

It also follows that the tort may be satisfied by intentional interference with prospective economic advantage through restraint of trade, including monopolization. [C]

* * *

So reformulated, the tort can be distinctly stated and consistently applied.

The independently tortious means that commonly appear in this context, including assault and battery, defamation, and fraud and deceit. [Cc] Surely, one would not be left to the scant "guidance" of the so-called " 'business ethics' standard" [Cc] which presupposes that "[t]he nature of the conduct which is acceptable today may ... prove unacceptable tomorrow." [C]

Also, restraints of trade may be "measured by objective economic criteria." [Cc]

Moreover, the tort's internally inconsistent "protectionist" premise is now removed. The interfered-with party is not favored over the interfering party by virtue of their respective status: the former is merely protected against the latter's use of independently tortious means and restraints of trade.

Furthermore, the tort itself does not now impair the common law's policy of freedom of competition. By its very terms, the freedom in question does not extend to the use of independently tortious means or restraints of trade.

Neither does the tort now undermine the First Amendment's guaranty of freedom of speech, freedom of association, or right of petition. That is because, to the extent that speech or association or petitioning is involved, the federal constitutional provision itself limits liability. (See, e.g., NAACP v. Claiborne Hardware Co., 458 U.S. at pp. 907–920 [73 L. Ed. 2d at pp. 1232–1241] [dealing with speech and association]; Blatty v. New York Times Co., 42 Cal. 3d at pp. 1045–1048 [dealing with speech]; Matossian v. Fahmie, 101 Cal. App. 3d at pp. 135–137 [dealing with petitioning].)

Finally, in any action based on the tort, it is the interfered-with party as plaintiff who should bear the burden of pleading and the burden of proof as to whether there has been intentional interference with prospective economic advantage either by independently tortious means or through restraint of trade by the interfering party as defendant.

* * *

Under the tort as reformulated, it is plain that the Court of Appeal erred. To be sure, the instructions appear erroneous. They did not expressly require objective, and unlawful, conduct or consequences. Neither, it seems, did they do so impliedly. Any error, however, was not prejudicial.

The reason is manifest. To the extent that they were satisfied by mere "wrongfulness"—which, at Della Penna's request, was defined under a kind of " 'business ethics' standard" as behavior "outside the realm of legitimate business transactions" because of "method" or "motive"—they were satisfied by far too little. For to that extent they did not demand the use of independently tortious means or restraints of trade. It is true that their focus on motive—"[w]rongfulness may lie . . . by virtue of an improper motive"—might threaten an arbitrary and capricious outcome in a given case. The same is true of their use of the term "wrongful" and its cognates, which are inherently ambiguous. [c] But, in spite of the foregoing, there is simply no basis to conclude that the outcome here was either arbitrary or capricious.

It is evident in the analysis presented above that, on many points, I agree with the majority's discussion of the tort of intentional interference with prospective economic advantage and Della Penna's claim against Toyota asserting such a cause of action.

On two major points, however, I am compelled to state my disagreement.

First, I would not adopt the "standard" of "wrongfulness." As I have noted, the term and its cognates are inherently ambiguous. They should probably be avoided. They should surely not be embraced. That is the course we followed in *Buckaloo*. It should be followed here as well.

Second, if I were to adopt such a "standard," I would not allow it to remain undefined. * * * Any definition of the "standard," of course, should avoid suggesting that the interfering party's motive might be material for present purposes. As I have explained, the focus on this issue is inappropriate. [c] A position of this sort, one must acknowledge, would result in the imposition of no liability on a person who is purely, but merely, "malicious"—who acts, to quote Justice Holmes, with "disinterested malevolence" (Amer. Bank & Trust Co. v. Federal Bank (1921) 256 U.S. 350, 358 [65 L. Ed. 983, 990, 41 S. Ct. 499, 25 A.L.R. 971]). Although such a person might be held responsible in conscience, he should not be made answerable in tort. * * *

NOTES AND QUESTIONS

1. The principal case represents a modern articulation of a tort with ancient roots. Has the court formulated the tort in a way that avoids the vices identified in former formulations?

2. The English courts soon after permitting a cause of action for interference with prospective contractual relations throttled the tort. In Allen v. Flood, [1898] App.Cas. 1, 121, Lord Herschell stated that there was a "chasm" between inducing a breach of contract and inducing a person not to enter a contract.

3. Justice Mosk's challenge in the principal case that wrongful conduct ought to be defined and could not include conduct motivated by malice alone, addresses a long-lingering issue. It relates to the "prima facie tort doctrine." The genesis of this tort is the action on the case. The elements were expressed by Lord Justice Bowen in the English Court of Appeal in Mogul Steamship Co. v. McGregor, Gow & Co.,

(1889) 23 Q.B.D. 598, 613: "[I]ntentionally to do that which is calculated in the ordinary course of events to damage, and which does, in fact, damage another in that person's property or trade, is actionable if done without just cause or excuse." Defendant had engaged in predatory pricing to squeeze plaintiff out of the lucrative China tea trade. Lord Justice Bowen's espousal of tortious liability for such conduct was repudiated nine years afterwards by Lord Herchell in Allen v. Flood, supra. However, it was Lord Bowen's formulation that resonated with Justice Holmes in launching the "prima facie tort doctrine."

4. Earlier case law had found liability where the plaintiff had a business or legal right intentionally interfered with by the defendant's unlawful activities. In Garret v. Taylor, Cro.Jac. 567, 79 Eng.Rep. 485 (1621), the defendant made threats of mayhem and vexatious suits against customers and workmen, and in Tarleton v. McGawley, Peake N.P. 270, 170 Eng.Rep. 153 (1793), where the defendant fired upon Africans with whom the plaintiff was about to trade. The best early statement of the principle is found in Keeble v. Hickeringill, 11 East 574, 103 Eng.Rep. 1127 (1707), where the defendant, inspired by pure malice, fired guns to frighten ducks away from the plaintiff's pond, and so prevented him from taking them.

5. A leading American case is Tuttle v. Buck, 107 Minn. 145, 119 N.W. 946 (1909). Plaintiff's complaint alleged that the defendant, a banker and a man of wealth and influence in the community, maliciously established a barber shop, employed a barber to carry on the business, and used his personal influence to attract customers from the plaintiff's barber shop, not for the purpose of serving any legitimate purpose of his own, but for the sole purpose of maliciously injuring the plaintiff; and that as a result of this conduct the plaintiff's business was ruined. The trial court overruled a demurrer to this complaint, and the supreme court affirmed, saying:

"When a man starts an opposition place of business, not for the sake of profit to himself, but regardless of loss to himself, and for the sole purpose of driving his competitor out of business, and with the intention of himself retiring upon the accomplishment of his malevolent purpose, he is guilty of a wanton wrong and an actionable tort. In such a case he would not be exercising his legal right, or doing an act which can be judged separately from the motive which actuated him. To call such conduct competition is a perversion of terms. It is simply the application of force without legal justification, which in its moral quality may be no better than highway robbery."

6. The development of a prima facie liability was possible once the "forms of action" at common law were abolished. The common law had required that every cause of action be pleaded strictly in conformity with one of the traditional forms of action–trespass, trespass on the case, assumpsit, etc. The demise of this rigid structure prompted a search to provide an organizing framework for the diffuse body of law that is called "Torts." Holmes's ideas influenced legal thought throughout the common law world. His fault principle as "the fulcrum of liability" led to the formulation of the general principle governing the law of negligence. If there were a general principle for negligence, should there be a general principle for all liability based upon intentional wrongdoing? After some shifting in his original position, Holmes accepted the prima facie liability theory as an overarching principle. This theory would account for otherwise separate torts such as interference with business relations and malicious prosecution. The separate status of the tort is doubtful even in a bastion of prima facie tort, for example, in Missouri. The Missouri Court of Appeals in Porter v. Crawford & Co., 611 S.W.2d 265 (1980), thoroughly discussed the tort confirming its application. But the supreme court has

spoken of the "misty shroud of prima facie tort." Dake v. Tuell, 687 S.W.2d 191 (1985) (en banc). In Brown v. Missouri Pacific Railroad Co., 720 S.W.2d 357, 361 (1986) (en banc), the same court noted that "[n]o case resulting in a verdict for the plaintiff on a prima facie tort theory has been affirmed by the Missouri appellate courts."

7. *Restatement of Torts.* Restatement (Second) of Torts § 870 provides: "One who intentionally causes injury to another is subject to liability to the other for that injury, if his conduct is generally culpable and not justifiable under the circumstances. This liability may be imposed although the actor's conduct does not come within a traditional category of tort liability."

The comments spell out in detail the considerations to be balanced by a court in determining whether to declare the existence of a new cause of action or to extend the parameters of an existing cause.

8.   The prima facie tort doctrine where recognized and applied has protected economic interests. However, in Morrison v. National Broadcasting Co., 24 A.D.2d 284, 266 N.Y.S.2d 406 (1965), Breitel J. extended it to protect the reputational interest of an innocent academic caught within disclosures and prosecutions flowing from NBC's rigged quiz show.

9.   As noted in the principal case, the extension of the tort to protect "prospective advantage," concern has been voiced about the clash of the tort with the assumptions of the competitive free-market system. In the A.L.I. debate on § 766, Restatement (Second) of Torts, Professor Auerbach opined that there was a "fundamental question involved, as to whether we can say in 1969 that all cases decided over more than a 100–year period reach the astounding result that the competitive order which we hold out to the world as a model is prima facie illegal." William L. Prosser, Presentation of Restatement of the Law, Second, Torts, Tentative Draft No. 14, 46 A.L.I. 201 (1969).

10.   Dean Wade, after Dean Prosser's proposal was recommitted for further consideration, proposed that the tort was actionable upon proof of the element of "impropriety" measured by a thorough fact balancing test. John W. Wade, Discussion of Restatement of the Law, Second, Torts, Tentative Draft No. 23, 54 A.L.I. 394, 394–435 (1977).

11.   Is the tort applicable to a contract terminable at the will of either party? The Restatement § 768 classifies it as prospective advantage. See Roy v. Woonsocket Instit. for Saving, 525 A.2d 915 (R.I.1987) (bank employee an at will employee, having, at best, an action for interference with prospective advantage); Duggin v. Adams, 234 Va. 221, 360 S.E.2d 832 (1987) (at will employment contract requires proof of (1) knowledge of contract and (2) improper conduct; if for definite term knowledge would suffice).

12.   Contracts that are illegal or against the public interest, as in the case of agreements intended to stifle competition in restraint of trade, are not protected against interference. Fairbanks Morse & Co. v. Texas Elec. Serv. Co., 63 F.2d 702 (5th Cir.1933), cert. denied 290 U.S. 655.

13.   Contracts to marry have received special treatment. Almost without exception, the courts have refused to hold that it is a tort to induce the parties to break them. Nelson v. Melvin, 236 Iowa 604, 19 N.W.2d 685 (1945); Brown v. Glickstein, 347 Ill.App. 486, 107 N.E.2d 267 (1952). The reason usually given is that contracts to marry are highly personal agreements, and anyone should be free to advise the parties to change their minds.

14. Inducement not to enter into a contract is normally of a third party, not the plaintiff. See Goldstein v. Kern, 82 Mich.App. 723, 267 N.W.2d 165 (1978). But preventing entry into the prospective relation may apply to either the plaintiff or a third person. See Byars v. Baptist Medical Centers, Inc., 361 So.2d 350 (Ala.1978) (hospital refused to permit nurse to be certified in nurses' registry).

Adler, Barish, Daniels, Levin and Creskoff v. Epstein

Supreme Court of Pennsylvania, 1978.
482 Pa. 416, 393 A.2d 1175, cert. denied 442 U.S. 907.

ROBERTS, JUSTICE. Appellant, the law firm of Adler, Barish, Daniels, Levin and Creskoff, filed a Complaint in Equity in the Court of Common Pleas of Philadelphia. It sought to enjoin appellees, former associates of Adler Barish, from interfering with existing contractual relationships between Adler Barish and its clients. The court of common pleas entered a final decree granting the requested relief, but a divided Superior Court dissolved the injunction and dismissed Adler Barish's complaint. We granted allowance of appeal. We now reverse and direct reinstatement of the decree of the court of common pleas. * * *

Appellee Alan Epstein's employment relationship with Adler Barish terminated on March 10, 1977. At his request, Epstein continued to use offices of Adler Barish until March 19. During this time, and through April 4, when Adler Barish filed its complaint, Epstein was engaged in an active campaign to procure business for his new law firm. He initiated contacts, by phone and in person, with clients of Adler Barish with open cases on which he had worked while a salaried employee. Epstein advised the Adler Barish clients that he was leaving the firm and that they could choose to be represented by him, Adler Barish, or any other firm or attorney.

Epstein's attempt to procure business on behalf of the firm did not stop with these contacts. He mailed to the clients form letters which could be used to discharge Adler Barish as counsel, name Epstein the client's new counsel and create a contingent fee agreement. Epstein also provided clients with a stamped envelope addressed to Epstein. [Similar actions were taken by other appellees.] * * *

On April 4, the court of common pleas granted Adler Barish preliminary relief, enjoining appellees' campaign to obtain the business of Adler Barish clients. One month later, on May 5, the court entered its final decree, which [enjoined defendants from communicating with Adler Barish clients who had active legal matters up until a certain date, except to announce the formation of the new firm. Those clients, however, were not prevented from voluntarily discharging Adler Barish and employing defendants or any other attorney. The Superior Court reversed, and the Supreme Court allowed an appeal.]

Adler Barish argues that appellees' conduct constitutes an intentional interference with existing contractual relationships between Adler Barish and its clients. According to Adler Barish, appellees' conduct is "deserving of censure, not encouragement." Appellees, on the other hand, contend that their conduct was "privileged," and that therefore no right of action for intentional interference lies. Moreover, they argue that their conduct is protected under the first and fourteenth amendments to the Constitution of the United States.

"[S]peech which does 'no more than propose a commercial transaction'" is no longer outside the protection of the first and fourteenth amendments to the Constitution of the United States. Virginia Pharmacy Board v. Virginia Consumer Council, 425 U.S. 748, 762 (1976) (striking down state statute deeming licensed pharmacists' advertising of prescription drugs "unprofessional conduct"); see Pennsylvania State Board of Pharmacy v. Pastor, 441 Pa. 186, 272 A.2d 487 (1971) (invalidating Pennsylvania statute prohibiting advertising of "dangerous drugs" dispensible only with a physician's prescription). Accordingly, states are barred from imposing blanket prohibitions against truthful advertising of "routine" legal services. Bates v. State Bar of Arizona, 433 U.S. 350 (1977). Such a blanket prohibition "serves to inhibit the free flow of commercial information and to keep the public in ignorance." Id., 433 U.S. at 365.

Nothing in the challenged decree prohibited appellees from engaging in the truthful advertising protected under *Bates*. Appellees could inform the general public, including clients of Adler Barish, of the availability of their legal services, and thus the "free flow of commercial information" to the public is unimpaired. Moreover, the injunction expressly permitted appellees to announce "formation of their new professional relationship in accordance with the requirements of DR 2–102 of the Code of Professional Responsibility." Appellees therefore were permitted to mail announcements to "lawyers, clients, former clients, personal friends, and relatives." Code of Professional Responsibility, DR 2–102(A)(2). This would include the very clients of Adler Barish whose business appellees sought. See Committee on Professional Ethics of the American Bar Association, Informal Decision No. 681 (August 1, 1963) (permitting departing attorney to send announcements "to those clients of the old firm for whom he had worked").

What the injunction did proscribe was appellees' "contacting and/or communicating with those persons who up to and including April 1, 1977, had active legal matters pending with and were represented by the law firm of Adler, Barish, Daniels, Levin and Creskoff." Our task is to decide whether the conduct of appellees is constitutionally subject to sanction.

The Code of Professional Responsibility, DR 2–103(A) (as adopted, 1974), provides: "A lawyer shall not recommend employment, as a private practitioner, of himself, his partner, or associate to a non-lawyer who has not sought his advice regarding employment of a lawyer." See also Code of Professional Responsibility, DR 2–104(A). Appellees clearly violated this "proscription against self-recommendation." [C] They recommended their own employment, even though clients of Adler Barish did not seek appellees' advice "regarding employment of a lawyer."

Ohralik v. Ohio State Bar Association, 436 U.S. 447 (1978), makes plain that, after *Bates,* states may constitutionally impose sanctions upon attorneys engaging in conduct which violates these disciplinary rules, even though the conduct involves "commercial speech." In *Ohralik,* the state bar association suspended an attorney who "solicited" persons injured in an automobile accident by making visits to the hospital room where the persons were recovering. Mr. Justice Powell, speaking for the Court, emphasized that commercial speech does not enjoy the same constitutional protections traditionally afforded other forms of speech:

"In rejecting the notion that such speech 'is wholly outside the protection of the First Amendment,' Virginia Pharmacy, 425 U.S., at 761, we were careful not to hold 'that it is wholly undifferentiable from other forms' of speech. Id., at 771 n. 24. We have not discarded the 'common-sense' distinction between speech proposing a commercial transaction, which occurs in an area traditionally subject to government regulation, and other varieties of speech. Ibid. To require a parity of constitutional protection for commercial and noncommercial speech alike could invite dilution, simply by a leveling process, of the force of the Amendment's guarantee with respect to the latter kind of speech. Rather than subject the First Amendment to such a devitalization, we instead have afforded commercial speech a limited measure of protection, commensurate with its subordinate position in the scale of First Amendment values, while allowing modes of regulation that might be impermissible in the realm of noncommercial expression. * * *

"[T]he State does not lose its power to regulate commercial activity deemed harmful to the public whenever speech is a component of that activity. Neither *Virginia Pharmacy* nor *Bates* purported to cast doubt on the permissibility of these kinds of commercial regulation." Id., 436 U.S. at 455–456. In rejecting the attorney's constitutional claim, the Court determined that the state's interests were important enough to support regulation of the attorney's conduct. * * * * " [The conduct involved solicitation in person.]

Just as in *Ohralik,* appellees' conduct frustrates, rather than advances, Adler Barish clients' "informed and reliable decisionmaking." After making Adler Barish clients expressly aware that appellees' new firm was interested in procuring their active cases, Epstein provided the clients the forms that would sever one attorney-client relationship and create another. Epstein's aim was to encourage speedy, simple action by the client. All the client needed to do was to "sign on the dotted line" and mail the forms in the self-addressed, stamped envelopes. * * *

Thus, appellees were actively attempting to induce the clients to change law firms in the middle of their active cases. Appellees' concern for their line of credit and the success of their new law firm gave them an immediate, personally created financial interest in the clients' decisions. In this atmosphere, appellees' contacts posed too great a risk that clients would not have the opportunity to make a careful, informed decision. * * * [W]e must reject appellees' argument and conclude that, just as in *Ohralik,* the Constitution permits regulation of their conduct. * * *

Thus, we turn to whether the court of common pleas properly concluded that Adler Barish is entitled to relief. In Birl v. Philadelphia Electric Co.,

402 Pa. 297, 167 A.2d 472 (1960), this Court adopted Restatement of Torts § 766 and its definition of the right of action for intentional interference with existing contractual relations. There, we stated:

"At least since Lumley v. Gye [supra], the common law has recognized an action in tort for an intentional, unprivileged interference with contractual relations. It is generally recognized that one has the right to pursue his business relations or employment free from interference on the part of other persons except where such interference is justified or constitutes an exercise of an absolute right: Restatement, Torts, § 766. * * *

In its continuing effort to provide the judicial system orderly and accurate restatements of the common law, the American Law Institute has reviewed each section of the Restatement of Torts, including Section 766. Restatement (Second) of Torts § 766 (Tent.Draft No. 23, 1977), states the Institute's present view of what constitutes the elements of the cause of action before us:

"*Intentional Interference with Performance of Contract by Third Person.* One who intentionally and improperly interferes with the performance of a contract (except a contract to marry) between another and a third person by inducing or otherwise causing the third person not to perform the contract, is subject to liability to the other for the pecuniary loss resulting to the other from the third person's failure to perform the contract." * * *

An examination of this case in light of Restatement (Second) of Torts § 766, reveals that the sole dispute is whether appellees' conduct is "improper." There is no doubt that appellees intentionally sought to interfere with performance of the contractual relations between Adler Barish and its clients. While still at Adler Barish, appellees' behavior, particularly their use of expected fees from Adler Barish clients' cases, indicates appellees' desire to gain a segment of the firm's business. This pattern of conduct continued until the court of common pleas enjoined it. Indeed, appellees' intentional efforts to obtain a share of Adler Barish's business were successful. The record reveals that several clients signed the forms Epstein prepared on behalf of appellees notifying Adler Barish that the clients no longer wished the services of Adler Barish. Likewise, the record reveals that Adler Barish and its clients were parties to valid, existing contracts.

In assessing whether appellees' conduct is "improper," we bear in mind what this Court stated in Glenn v. Point Park College, 441 Pa. [474,] 482, 272 A.2d [895,] 899, where we analyzed "privileges" in conjunction with the closely related right of action for intentional interference with prospective contract relations:

"The absence of privilege or justification in the tort under discussion is closely related to the element of intent. As stated by Harper & James, The Law of Torts, § 6.11, at 513–14: ' * * * where, as in most cases, the defendant acts at least in part for the purpose of protecting some legitimate interest which conflicts with that of the plaintiff, a line must be drawn and the interests evaluated. This process results in according or denying a privilege which, in turn, determines liability.' What is or is not privileged conduct in a given situation is not susceptible of precise definition. Harper & James refer in general to interferences which 'are sanctioned by the' rules of the game 'which society has adopted', and to 'the area of socially acceptable conduct which the law regards as privileged,' id. at 510, 511, and treat the subject in detail in §§ 6.12 and 6.13."

We are guided, too, by Restatement (Second) of Torts § 767, which focuses on what factors should be considered in determining whether conduct is "improper:"

"In determining whether an actor's conduct in intentionally interfering with an existing contract or a prospective contractual relation of another is improper or not, consideration is given to the following factors:

"(a) The nature of the actor's conduct,

"(b) The actor's motive,

"(c) The interests of the other with which the actor's conduct interferes,

"(d) The interests sought to be advanced by the actor,

"[(e) The social interests in protecting the freedom of action of the actor and the contractual interests of the others,]

"[(f)] The proximity or remoteness of the actor's conduct to the interference and

"[(g)] The relations between the parties."[17]

We find nothing in the " 'rules of the game' which society has adopted" which sanctions appellees' conduct. Indeed, the rules which apply to those who enjoy the privilege of practicing law in this Commonwealth expressly disapprove appellees' method of obtaining clients. * * * We find such a departure from "[r]ecognized ethical codes" "significant in evaluating the nature of [appellees'] conduct." Restatement (Second) of Torts,

---

17. Thus, new Restatement (Second) of Torts focuses upon whether conduct is "proper," rather than "privileged." Compare Restatement of Torts, § 766 (1939) ("[e]xcept as stated in Section 698 [(relating to contracts to marry)], *one who without a privilege to do so,* induces or otherwise purposely causes a third person not to ¶ (a) perform a contract with another, or ¶ (b) enter into or continue a business relation with another ¶ is liable to the other for the harm caused thereby" (emphasis added)). Comment b to Restatement (Second) of Torts, supra at § 767, explains the shift in inquiry:

"*Privilege to Interfere, or Interference not Improper.* Unlike other intentional torts such as intentional injury to person or property, or defamation, this branch of tort law has not

developed a crystallized set of definite rules as to the existence or non-existence of a privilege to act in the manner stated in §§ 766, 766A or 766B. Because of this fact, this Section is expressed in terms of whether the interference is improper or not rather than in terms of a specific privilege to act in the manner specified. The issue in each case is whether the interference is improper or not under the circumstances; whether, upon a consideration of the relative significance of the factors involved, the conduct should be permitted without liability, despite its effect of harm to another."

[The bracketed material in the list of the factors indicates changes in the section between the Tentative Draft and the published volume. (Ed.)]

supra at § 767 comment c.[19] All the reasons underlying our Disciplinary Rules' "proscription against [appellees'] self-recommendation," *Berlant Appeal*, 458 Pa. at 443, 328 A.2d at 474, especially the concern that appellees' contacts too easily could overreach and unduly influence Adler Barish clients with active cases, are relevant here.

Appellees' conduct adversely affected more than the informed and reliable decisionmaking of Adler Barish clients with active cases. Their conduct also had an immediate impact upon Adler Barish. Adler Barish was prepared to continue to perform services for its clients and therefore could anticipate receiving compensation for the value of its efforts. Moreover, * * * Adler Barish's fee agreements with clients were a source of anticipated revenue protected from outside interference.

It is true that, upon termination of their employment relationship with Adler Barish, appellees were free to engage in their own business venture. * * * But appellees' right to pursue their own business interests is not absolute. "[U]nless otherwise agreed, after the termination of the agency, the agent * * * has a duty to the principal not to take advantage of a still subsisting confidential relation created during the prior agency relation". Restatement (Second) of Agency, supra at § 396(d).

Appellees' contacts were possible because Adler Barish partners trusted appellees with the high responsibility of developing its clients' cases. From this position of trust and responsibility, appellees were able to gain knowledge of the details, and status, of each case to which appellees had been assigned. In the atmosphere surrounding appellees' departure, appellees' contacts unduly suggested a course of action for Adler Barish clients and unfairly prejudiced Adler Barish. No public interest is served in condoning use of confidential information which has these effects. Clients too easily may suffer in the end.[21] * * *

---

19. Restatement (Second) of Torts, supra at § 767 comment c, provides in full:

"*Business Ethics and Customs.* Recognized ethical codes for a particular area of business activity and established customs or practices regarding approved or disapproved actions or methods may also be significant in evaluating the nature of the actor's conduct as a factor in determining whether his interference with the plaintiff's economic relations was improper or not."

21. Moreover, appellees neither occupied the same status, nor pursued the same goals, as the defendants in Watch Tower Bible & Tract Society v. Dougherty, 337 Pa. 286, 11 A.2d 147 (1940). There, we concluded that defendants, leaders of their church, "cannot be mulcted in damages for protesting against the utterances of one who they believe attacks their church and misrepresents its teachings or for inducing their adherents to make similar protests." 337 Pa. at 288, 11 A.2d at 148. * * *

Appellees suggest that injunctive relief was inappropriate. "It is well settled that equity will act to prevent unjustified interference with contractual relations." Neel v. Allegheny County Memorial Park, 391 Pa. 354, 357, 137 A.2d 785, 787 (1958). Accord, Restatement (Second) of Torts, supra at § 766 comment t (approving injunctive relief "in appropriate circumstances"). Given appellees' interest in maintaining the line of credit established on the basis of Adler Barish cases, and appellees' express intent to continue their effort to gain Adler Barish clients, we believe the court of common pleas could properly conclude that equitable relief was necessary to protect all the interests at stake in this case.

In *Ohralik,* MR. JUSTICE POWELL emphasized:

"[T]he state bears a special responsibility for maintaining standards among members of the licensed professions. * * * 'The interest of the States in regulating lawyers is especially great since lawyers are essential to the primary governmental function of administering justice, and have historically been' officers of the courts.' [C] While lawyers act in part as 'self-employed businessmen,' they also act 'as trusted agents of their clients, and as assistants to the court in search of a just solution to disputes.' " Ohralik v. Ohio State Bar Association, 436 U.S. at 460. Our "special responsibility" includes the obligation to assure that persons seeking professional legal assistance receive the quality advocacy and fair treatment they justifiably expect. Our responsibility also includes the duty to provide an atmosphere conducive to proper attorney-client relationships, including those situations where, as here, associates assist other members of a firm in rendering legal services. Consistent with these jurisprudential concerns, our supervisory authority over practitioners in our courts, prior decisions, the Code of Professional Responsibility, and Restatement (Second) of Torts, it must be concluded that the court of common pleas correctly determined that Adler Barish is entitled to relief.

Order of the Superior Court reversed and court of common pleas directed to reinstate its final decree. Each party pay own costs.

MANDERINO, J., filed a dissenting opinion.

NOTES AND QUESTIONS

1. Knowing interference with a valid enforceable contract is usually itself improper. Duggin v. Adams, 234 Va. 221, 360 S.E.2d 832 (1987). The burden then rests on the defendant to justify the interference. The element of impropriety looms when the claim is based on interference with prospective advantage.

In light of the California Supreme Court's opinion in *Della Penna,* consider the following broad grounds for wrongfulness or impropriety:

A. *Violating Ethical Standards.* See Sustick v. Slatina, 48 N.J.Super. 134, 137 A.2d 54 (1957) (ultimate question is whether the conduct was "both injurious and transgressive of generally accepted standards of common morality or of law," whether it was "sanctioned by the rules of the game," and constituted "right and just dealing"); Leonard Duckworth, Inc. v. Michael L. Field & Co., 516 F.2d 952 (5th Cir.1975) ("sharp dealing or overreaching or other conduct below the behavior of fair men similarly situated"); Herron v. State Farm Mut. Ins. Co., 56 Cal.2d 202, 363 P.2d 310, 14 Cal.Rptr. 294 (1961) (rules of Nat'l Conf.Comm. on Adjusters).

B. *Other Kinds of Wrongful Conduct.* Physical violence, threats and intimidation: South Central Livestock Dealers, Inc. v. Security State Bank, 551 F.2d 1346 (5th Cir.1977); Williams v. Maloof, 223 Ga. 640, 157 S.E.2d 479 (1967). Misrepresentation: Gold v. Los Angeles Democratic League, 49 Cal.App.3d 365, 122 Cal.Rptr. 732 (1975); Johnson v. Gustafson, 201 Minn. 629, 277 N.W. 252 (1938). Defamation: Wild v. Rarig, 302 Minn. 419, 234 N.W.2d 775 (1975); Woody v. Brush, 178 App.Div. 698, 165 N.Y.S. 867 (1917). Threats of suit: Pratt Food Co. v. Bird, 148 Mich. 631, 112 N.W. 701 (1907); Gresh v. Potter–McCune Co., 235 Pa.Super. 537, 344 A.2d 540 (1975).

2.   Many cases involve conduct designed to prevent or hinder a person entering into a contractual or business relationship. Where a number of persons combine, it is called a boycott, a term that immortalizes a pariah during the Irish "troubles":

"Captain Boycott, an Englishman, who was agent of Lord Earne and a farmer of Lough Mask, served notices upon the lord's tenants, and they in turn, with the surrounding population, resolved to have nothing to do with him, and, as far as they could prevent it, not to allow anyone else to have. His life appeared to be in danger, and he had to claim police protection. His servants fled from him, and the awful sentence of excommunication could hardly have rendered him more helplessly alone for a time. No one would work for him, and no one would supply him with food. He and his wife were compelled to work their own fields with the shadows of armed constabulary ever at their heels; Justin MacCarthy's England Under Gladstone." Bouvier's Law Dictionary, summarizing statement in State v. Glidden, 55 Conn. 46, 8 A. 890 (1887).

3.   Boycotts are "primary," where the defendant himself refuses to deal with the plaintiff, or "secondary," where he seeks to compel third persons to refuse to deal, by refusing to have dealings with them if they do.

Competition in business was held under the common law to be a sufficient justification for a primary boycott on the part of a single defendant. This has been extensively limited by statute in many jurisdictions. Discrimination in competition has been penalized by the Robinson–Patman Act, and by various acts in the states, which are beyond the scope of this book.

Secondary boycotts open up whole areas of law, particularly as to restraints of trade, antitrust acts, and labor disputes, where many complex problems have arisen, also beyond the scope of this book. They are usually dealt with in courses on unfair competition, antitrust or restraint of trade, or labor law. See Smith v. American Guild of Variety Artists, 349 F.2d 975 (8th Cir.1965).

4.   In Bear v. Reformed Mennonite Church, 462 Pa. 330, 341 A.2d 105 (1975), plaintiff alleged that his business collapsed after bishops of the Mennonite Church ordered all members to "shun" him. "Shunning" was a church practice that had been traditionally applied to persons who violated church rules and were excommunicated. Defendant contended that plaintiff fell within that group. Should plaintiff have a claim in tort?

5.   When the defendant has no legitimate purpose and acts for a purpose that the law does not accept, he becomes liable if he interferes with a contractual relation of the plaintiff. Thus, there is liability when the defendant procures the discharge of a workman to prevent him from bringing a suit, as in Johnson v. Aetna Life Ins. Co., 158 Wis. 56, 147 N.W. 32 (1914); to force him to settle it, as in London Guarantee & Accident Co. v. Horn, 206 Ill. 493, 69 N.E. 526 (1903); to force him to pay a debt, or to extort money from him, as in Warschauser v. Brooklyn Furniture Co., 159 App. Div. 81, 144 N.Y.S. 257 (1913); Hill Grocery Co. v. Carroll, 223 Ala. 376, 136 So. 789 (1931). There also is liability when the defendant uses a termination clause in a contract solely for the purpose of injuring subcontractor, without other justification. Alyeska Pipeline Serv. Co. v. Aurora Air Serv., 604 P.2d 1090 (Alaska 1979).

6.   The law of civil conspiracy provides that two or more persons will be liable when they act in combination in order to cause harm to another and that harm results. The significance of the action, and a source of criticism, is that the act, if done alone, would not be actionable. The Restatement (First) of Torts § 765 (1939) provides an action for concerted refusal to deal:

Persons who cause harm to another by a concerted refusal in their business to enter into or to continue business relations with him are liable to him for that harm, even though they would not be liable for similar conduct without concert, if their concerted refusal is not justified under the circumstances.

The section sets forth a wide array of criteria under which the refusal may be justified. In Margolin v. Morton F. Plant Hospital Assn., Inc., 342 So.2d 1090 (Fla.App.1977), the court recognized the action where all the anesthesiologists in a hospital refused to provide services to a particular surgeon, making it impossible for him to practice. It was open to the defendant anesthesiologists to justify by establishing legitimate reasons for their actions. Is the concerted action appropriate considering the potential overlap with antitrust laws? Considering the width of the tortious interference action, the potential overlap with statutory and other common law actions, and the paucity of authorities, some courts have denied the existence of a separate conspiracy tort: e.g., Bloom v. Hennepin County, 783 F. Supp. 418 (D.Minn.1992).

7. Patent claims and state law claims of interference with contract and interference with prospective economic advantage are often pleaded together. Litton Systems, Inc. v. Honeywell, Inc., 87 F.3d 1559 (Fed.Cir.1996) (finding liability under each claim, and, particularly in respect to the claim for interference with prospective economic advantage, finding relevant defendant's "motive and purpose, and the means by which he has sought to accomplish [the interference]" drive the cases).

Brimelow v. Casson

Chancery Division, 1923.
[1924] 1 Ch. 302.

[The case deals with the misfortunes of a burlesque troupe known as the King Wu Tut Tut Revue, which was touring the south counties of England under the managership of one Jack Arnold. Arnold underpaid the chorus girls so badly that they were forced to eke out a living by plying another and an older trade. As the sordid tale was unfolded in court, it appeared that one of the young women had even been compelled by economic necessity to live in "immorality" with a dwarf, who was a member of the company. The secretary of the Actors' Association, named Lugg, took hold of the situation on behalf of the young women, and persuaded the owners of the theaters with which Arnold had contracts to cancel them unless higher wages were paid. This resulted in the troupe being stranded in the town of Maidenhead. A bill in equity was brought on behalf of the owners of the troupe against the representatives of the union to enjoin them from inducing the breaches of contract.]

Russell, J. It is difficult to speak of this condition of things with restraint. A young girl, almost a child, forced by underpayment to continue in sexual association with this abnormal man is, to my mind, a terrible and revolting tragedy, but the question which I have to decide is whether the acts of the defendants make them liable to an action at the suit of the plaintiff, or whether in the circumstances of this case there exists a sufficient justification for the acts which in the absence of such justification would be actionable. * * *

Prima facie interference with a man's contractual rights and with his right to carry on his business as he wills is actionable; but it is clear on the authorities that interference with contractual rights may be justified; a fortiori the inducing of others not to contract with a person may be justified. * * *

[The unions] desire in the interest of the theatrical calling and the members thereof to stop such underpayment with its evil consequences. The only way they can do so is by inducing the proprietors of theatres not to allow persons like the plaintiff the use of their theatres, either by breaking contracts already made or by refusing to enter into contracts. They adopt this course as regards the plaintiff as the only means open to them of bringing to an end his practice of underpayment which, according to their experience, is fruitful of danger to the theatrical calling and its members. In these circumstances, have the defendants justification for their acts? That they would have the sympathy and support of decent men and women I can have no doubt. But have they in law justification for those acts? As has been pointed out, no general rule can be laid down as a general guide in such cases, but I confess that if justification does not exist here I can hardly conceive the case in which it would be present. These defendants, as it seems to me, owed a duty to their calling and to its members, and, I am tempted to add, to the public, to take all necessary peaceful steps to terminate the payment of this insufficient wage, which in the plaintiff's company had apparently been in fact productive of those results which their past experience had led them to anticipate. "The good sense" of this tribunal leads me to decide that in the circumstances of the present case justification did exist. * * *

The result is that the action is dismissed with costs.

NOTES AND QUESTIONS

1. Accord, that a reasonable and disinterested motive for the protection of other individuals, or the public, will justify intentional interference with contract: Caverno v. Fellows, 300 Mass. 331, 15 N.E.2d 483 (1938) (high school supervisor, principal and superintendent reporting on conduct of teacher); Stott v. Gamble, [1916] 2 K.B. 504 (preventing improper public entertainment); Legris v. Marcotte, 129 Ill.App. 67 (1906) (mother seeking to exclude diseased person from her child's school); Porter v. King County Medical Society, 186 Wash. 410, 58 P.2d 367 (1936) (enforcing ethical rules of medical association).

2. Instances of privilege to interfere with prospective advantage, in interest of others or the public include: NAACP v. Claiborne Hardware Co., 458 U.S. 886 (1982) (picketing and boycott activity to prevent racial discrimination); Gott v. Berea College, 156 Ky. 376, 161 S.W. 204 (1913) (for protection of its students, college ordered them not to deal with plaintiff); Julie Baking Co. v. Graymond, 152 Misc. 846, 274 N.Y.S. 250 (1934) (picketing plaintiff's bakery in protest against the high price of bread); Harris v. Thomas, 217 S.W. 1068 (Tex.Civ.App.1920) (acting to protect ethical standards of medical association). The California Supreme Court in *Della Penna*, supra, canvasses the justification issue, stressing that "free competition" was tantamount.

More particularly, justification may arise from a contractual or property right of sufficient weight to take precedence. See Felsen v. Sol Café Mfg. Corp., 24 N.Y.2d 682, 249 N.E.2d 459, 301 N.Y.S.2d 610 (1969) (sole shareholder justified in attempt to protect economic interest), and Richardson v. La Rancherita La Jolla, Inc., 98 Cal. App. 3d 73, 159 Cal. Rptr. 285 (1979) (reliance upon legal advice on assertion of right). Otherwise, as in the principal case, justification springs from a public interest. Constitutional protections of free speech and assembly delimit the range of liability. See Mosk J. in *Della Penna*, supra.

3.   On asserting a bona fide claim, see Restatement (Second) of Torts § 773, McReynolds v. Short, 115 Ariz. 166, 564 P.2d 389 (App. 1977); Beane v. McMullen, 265 Md. 585, 291 A.2d 37 (1972); Allen v. Ramsey, 170 Okla. 430, 41 P.2d 658 (1935).

4.   Several cases hold that there is a privilege to give disinterested advice to withdraw from a contractual relation. See Walker v. Cronin, 107 Mass. 555 (1871); Arnold v. Moffitt, 30 R.I. 310, 75 A. 502 (1910); Coakley v. Degner, 191 Wis. 170, 210 N.W. 359 (1926). But the privilege is limited to cases where the advice is requested, or otherwise called for by the circumstances, as distinguished from officious intermeddling in matters which are not the defendant's concern. Calbom v. Knudtzon, 65 Wash. 2d 157, 396 P.2d 148 (1964). On whether the advice is disinterested if it also benefits other advisees, see Welch v. Bancorp Management Advisors, Inc., 296 Or. 208, 675 P.2d 172 (1983), and McGanty v. Staudenraus, 321 Or. 532, 901 P.2d 841 (1995).

5.   *Burden of Proof.* Some courts place the burden on the plaintiff to show that the interference was "improper," or "malicious"—i.e., without justification. M & M Rental Tools, Inc. v. Milchem, Inc., 94 N.M. 449, 612 P.2d 241 (1980); Glenn v. Point Park College, 441 Pa. 474, 272 A.2d 895 (1971). Others place the burden on the defendant to show that the interference was justified. Lowell v. Mother's Cake & Cookie Co., 79 Cal. App. 3d 13, 144 Cal. Rptr. 664 (1978). Still others suggest that it may vary, depending on the factual situation. Johnson v. Radde, 293 Minn. 409, 196 N.W.2d 478 (1972). See Restatement (Second) of Torts § 767, Comment *k*.

6.   No class of law students could be expected to ignore the principal case. At the Harvard Law School in 1938, one of the students rose to the occasion by stating the case in class as follows:

"The Ballad of Brimelow v. Casson

The ladies of the chorus of the Wututtut Revue

Through economic pressure had their virtue to eschew.

'Twas economic pressure that accounts for their proclivity

To supplement their earnings with professional activity.

That poor benighted maiden didn't say this just for fun,

'If Snow White lived with seven dwarfs, well I can live with one.'

An economic royalist, Jack Arnold was his name,

Began this competition with the houses of ill fame.

'Twas some ironic destiny by which the troupe was led

That prompted them to end their tour at England's Maidenhead.

The matter was reported to our hero, labor's Lugg,

Who vowed he'd get Jack Arnold even though it meant the jug.

He gathered up the union's most persuasive breach inducers

To tell this sad and sordid tale to Arnold's pet producers.

I'm proud to say the latter said they didn't give a damn

About Jack Arnold's contract, and they closed him like a clam.

I'm prouder of the Chancellor, who didn't bat an eye,

But calmly told Jack Arnold that his action wouldn't lie.

So here's to Merrie England, let the Union Jack unfurl,

The Chancellor and Heaven will protect the working girl."

—Published in Langdell Lyrics of 1938 by Professor W. Barton Leach, of the Harvard Law School.

Remedies

1.   The interference must cause a loss to the plaintiff. In re Alert Holdings, Inc., 148 B.R. 194 (Bkrtcy.N.Y.1992). The loss is compensable in damages. As we saw in Adler, Barish, Daniels, Levin and Creskoff, supra page 1095, in the appropriate case, such as continuing threat of interference, the court may grant an injunction. The remedy is discretionary. The plaintiff must show that damages would be inadequate. The courts are reluctant to grant an injunction if it would effectively enforce specific performance of a contract for personal services. Beverly Glen Music, Inc. v. Warner Communications, 178 Cal.App.3d 1142, 224 Cal.Rptr. 260 (1986). The courts often are slow to force persons to comply with contracts when better opportunities become available. Does this give insufficient weight to the position of the original party who has secured the defector's services?

2.   Punitive damages are available, in most jurisdictions, on the basis that the defendant's action is intentional and without justification. Duff v. Engelberg, 237 Cal.App.2d 505, 47 Cal.Rptr. 114 (1965).

3.   Recovery of damages for breach of contract will not preclude the plaintiff's action for tortious interference, although no double recovery will be allowed. Damages under the tort will include consequential losses to reputation and mental suffering. Duff v. Engelberg, supra note 2.

4.   Does the wide ambit of remedy under the tort justify its availability in addition to any contract recovery? The traditional measure of damages under contract may be inadequate, Farber, Reassessing the Economic Efficiency of Compensatory Damages for Breach of Contract, 66 Va.L.Rev. 1443, 1476–78 (1980) (arguing that the effects of transaction costs and imperfect information weaken the case for exclusive reliance on compensatory damages for breach of contract and thus supercompensatory damages may be justified). A parallel argument is made by Professor Alan Schwartz for the availability of specific performance of contracts as a matter of course, rather than to reserve the remedy for special contract and at the discretion of the court. See Alan Schwartz, The Case for Specific Performance, 89 Yale L.J. 271, 274–79 (1979).

5.   The potency of the remedy available was starkly demonstrated in the notorious *Pennzoil* case. This case involved a takeover battle for Getty Oil Co. between Pennzoil and Texaco. Pennzoil claimed that Texaco had inveigled Getty Oil Co. away from its agreement with Getty. It claimed that Texaco had known of the contract between Pennzoil and Getty at the time it made a more attractive tender offer to Getty. The jury found that Pennzoil had proved its case. The verdict stood in the Texas Court of Appeals, see Texaco, Inc. v. Pennzoil, Co., 729 S.W.2d 768–866

(Tex.App.1987), writ ref'd n.r.e., and the Texas Supreme Court declined to review it. The jury had handed down a verdict in excess of ten billion dollars, and Texaco filed for Chapter 11 bankruptcy. Numerous other legal complications arose, and the case was finally settled for the sum of three billion dollars. For succinct analyses of the central legal issues involved, see Baron and Baron, The Pennzoil–Texaco Dispute: An Independent Analysis, 38 Baylor L.Rev. 253 (1986); and Note, The $10.53 Billion Question—When Are the Parties Bound?: *Pennzoil* and the Use of Agreements in Principle in Mergers and Acquisitions, 40 Vand.L.Rev. 1367 (1987). There are fascinating treatments of the whole episode in T. Petzinger, Oil & Honor: The Texaco–Pennzoil Wars (1987); and S. Coll, The Taking of Getty Oil: The Full Story of the Most Spectacular and Catastrophic Takeover of All Times (1987). The cast of characters reads as if they came from the fertile imagination of a modern Dickens. The issue whether Pennzoil and Getty had entered a binding contract was central. There are good reasons in large financial transactions to be slow in making this conclusion until all formalities are fully executed. Arcadian Phosphates, Inc. v. Arcadian Corp., 884 F.2d 69 (2d Cir.1989). Is there a good reason to be especially wary of concluding that a contract is formed in respect of take-over transactions?

Harmon v. Harmon

Supreme Judicial Court of Maine, 1979.
404 A.2d 1020.

NICHOLS, JUSTICE. Somewhere near the frontier of the expanding field of law relating to tortious interference with an advantageous relationship we encounter the legal issue which is paramount in this appeal.

By a complaint entered November 21, 1977, in Superior Court in Cumberland County the Plaintiff, Richard Harmon, asserted that the Defendants, Harold C. Harmon and Virginia S. Harmon (who are the Plaintiff's brother and brother's wife) had by fraud and undue influence induced the Plaintiff's mother, Josephine F. Harmon, while she was 87 years old and in ill health, to transfer to the Defendants valuable property. By her 1976 will and by her more recent statements the mother had indicated her intention that the Plaintiff son should receive at least a one-half interest in this property. Thus, this transfer effectively disinherited the Plaintiff son. The mother, it appears, is still living.

Upon the Defendants' motion the Superior Court dismissed the complaint upon the grounds (a) that the complaint fails to state a claim upon which relief can be granted and (b) that the Plaintiff son lacked standing to proceed against the Defendant son and the latter's wife.

The Plaintiff son has appealed to this Court from that order of dismissal. We sustain his appeal. * * *

In Cyr v. Cote, Me., 396 A.2d 1013 (1979) we recently considered a similar question. There it was after the testator's death that certain legatees under his will commenced their action, alleging that, but for the defendants' fraud and undue influence upon the testator, they would have received the property which by such tortious conduct the Defendants obtained as an intervivos gift. In determining whether the expectancy of receiving a bequest was something which the law would protect, we had occasion to examine Perkins v. Pendleton, 90 Me. 166, 38 A. 96 (1897). There it was held that a plaintiff, employed by a company which had the right to terminate his employment at will, could bring an action against defendants who unlawfully caused the company to discharge the plaintiff. Relying upon *Perkins,* we recognized in Cyr v. Cote an action for the wrongful interference with an expected legacy or gift under a will. * * *

In *Cyr,* the interest we sought to protect was the *expectation,* and not the *certainty,* that the legatees would have received a future benefit under the will. If there had been no undue influence the testator, prior to death, could still have disinherited them or bequeathed the property to another person. Nevertheless, the wrongful conduct deprived the plaintiffs of the possibility that the testator would not have changed his mind, absent the undue influence.

Once the will has been executed an expectancy has been created in the legatee. If the legatee is injured due to some wrongful conduct on the part of a third party against the prospective testator, such act must necessarily occur within the life of the testator. The injury at this point is complete. The problem then becomes the valuation of the chance of benefit that has been lost. On this basis there may be recovery for loss of prospects falling considerably short of certainty. [C]

We find support for the precedent set by *Cyr* in a review of the historical foundations for that precedent.

The law initially proved most ready to protect commercial expectancies, such as that of entering into or continuing a business relation with another. [C] Very early cases protected a merchant whose customers were being driven away and a churchman whose donors were being harassed. [C]

Prospective or potential business relations have been protected from wrongful interference. [C]

Furthermore, it has become a settled rule in the United States that the expectancy of future contractual relations, such as the prospect of obtaining employment or employees, or the opportunity of obtaining customers, will be protected by the law from wrongful interference. [C] Tort liability for damages is the well established remedy in this situation. * * *

The law has, indeed, in the past also proved willing to protect non-commercial interests in a variety of contexts. Dean Prosser has commented:

"On this basis the earlier cases held that recovery would be denied for interference with an expected gift or a legacy under a will, even though the defendant's motives were unworthy and he had resorted to fraudulent means, because the testator might have changed his mind. There is no essential reason for refusing to protect such non-commercial expectancies, at least where there is a strong probability that they would have been realized. * * *

"*The problem appears in reality to be one of satisfactory proof that the loss has been suffered, instead of the existence of a ground to tort liability.*" W. Prosser, Law of Torts 950–951 (4th ed. 1971) (emphasis added).

Recognition of such a cause of action was made in the Restatement (Second) of Torts § 870 (1939) which declares the imposition of liability for the intended consequences of any tortious act. Comment (b), Illustration 2, is enlightening:

"A, who is zealous in the cause of labor, is about to make a gift to B, a college, when C, for the purpose of preventing the gift, falsely represents that the president of B is opposed to collective bargaining. As a result, A refuses to make the gift, which otherwise he would have made. B is entitled to maintain an action of tort against C."

The parallel between our present factual setting and this illustration is striking indeed. * * *

Likewise, the expectancy of a beneficiary in the proceeds of an insurance policy upon the life of another is an interest which the courts are ready to protect against the wrongful interference of a third person. [Cc]

Such liability in tort is recognized notwithstanding that clearly the beneficiary's interest includes no vested right, but is a "mere" expectancy. [C] The issue is not whether the interest is vested or expectant; rather the issue is whether it is legally protected so that intentional and wrongful interference causing damage to the plaintiff gives rise to liability in tort. [C]

We conclude that where a person can prove that, but for the tortious interference of another, he would in all likelihood have received a gift or a specific profit from a transaction, he is entitled to recover for the damages thereby done to him. * * *

In the case before us, we go one step further than we did in *Cyr*. Here we recognize that one may proceed to enforce this liability, grounded in tort, before the death of the prospective testatrix occurs, even as we have seen that the victim of tortious interference with a contract of employment or with a policy of life insurance has been permitted to proceed.

There are several considerations which strongly favor according the Plaintiff brother an early day in court, notwithstanding the ambulatory nature of the mother's will and the voidable nature of a trust arrangement. These include (a) the availability of witnesses to the allegedly tortious acts while their memories are relatively fresh, (b) the present availability of relevant exhibits, and (c) especially the prospect that the court may gain the testimony of the parties' aged mother, which testimony may determine the outcome here.

While delaying the adjudication until the mother's death could solidify the Plaintiff's position as allegedly a victim of fraud or undue influence, the delay might mean that important evidence would be denied the court. [Cc]

It should be noted that the claim of the Plaintiff son is to a loss of his expectancy, not to a loss of the actual property of his mother.

Having concluded that the Plaintiff son has a justiciable interest upon which he may found this action, it is clear that he has standing to proceed with this action. Therefore, the order of dismissal was in error. * * *

Remanded for further proceedings consistent with the opinion herein.

NOTES AND QUESTIONS

1. Most of the cases dealing with interference with prospective advantage have concerned future contract relations, such as the prospect of obtaining employment or hiring employees, or the opportunity of attracting customers or purchasing property. In these cases there is a background of business experience, on the basis of which it is possible to estimate with some fair amount of success both the value of what has been lost and the likelihood that the plaintiff would have received it if the defendant had not interfered. The loss of prospective profits is a familiar element of damages in cases of breach of contract.

2. When the attempt is made to extend liability for interference beyond such commercial dealings to other "expectancies," the courts have found themselves on unfamiliar ground, and frequently have refused to allow the action. The reason usually given is that there is no sufficient degree of certainty that the plaintiff would ever have received the prospective benefits.

3. Some decisions involving interference with an expected gift or legacy under a will have denied recovery on the ground that there was not sufficient certainty that the donor would not have changed his mind. Hall v. Hall, 91 Conn. 514, 100 A. 441 (1917); Cunningham v. Edward, 52 Ohio App. 61, 3 N.E.2d 58 (1936). When reasonable certainty can be found, as when the testator has become incompetent to make a change, or the will is suppressed after his death, recovery has been allowed. Creek v. Laski, 248 Mich. 425, 227 N.W. 817 (1929); Morton v. Petitt, 124 Ohio St. 241, 177 N.E. 591 (1931). Similarly, for a revocable trust after donor's death where the defendant by undue influence induces settlor to revoke the trust: Hammons v. Eisert, 745 S.W.2d 253 (Mo.App.1988).

4. Other cases have granted recovery on the basis of other evidence of a high degree of probability that the testator would have made or changed a bequest. E.g., Brignati v. Medenwald, 315 Mass. 636, 53 N.E.2d 673 (1944); Bohannon v. Wachovia Bank & Trust Co., 210 N.C. 679, 188 S.E. 390 (1936). See also, allowing equitable relief in the form of a constructive trust, Latham v. Father Divine, 299 N.Y. 22, 85 N.E.2d 168 (1949); Allen v. Leybourne, 190 So.2d 825 (Fla.App.1966); White v. Mulvania, 575 S.W.2d 184 (Mo.1978). The availability of other sufficient remedies convinced the Supreme Judicial Court of Massachusetts to reject the principal case. Labonte v. Giordano, 426 Mass. 319, 687 N.E.2d 1253 (1997).

5. The reluctance found in will cases has been carried over to cases of other non-commercial expectancies, when there is no high degree of probability. The gambling spirit dies hard as plaintiffs, over a period of a hundred years, have brought, and courts have dismissed, actions for thwarted chances of winning bets on horse racing: Western Union Tel. Co. v. Crall, 39 Kan. 580, 18 P. 719 (1888); Cain v. Vollmer, 19 Idaho 163, 112 P. 686 (1910); and Youst v. Longo, 43 Cal.3d 64, 233 Cal.Rptr. 294, 729 P.2d 728 (1987). See also: Smitha v. Gentry, 20 Ky.L.Rep. 171, 45 S.W. 515 (1898) (chance of obtaining reward); Phillips v. Pantages Theatre Co., 163 Wash. 303, 300 P. 1048 (1931) (chance of winning vaudeville contest). When the chance is attended with an ascertainable probability of success, courts in breach of contract actions have been willing to allow recovery for the loss of value of the chance itself. Wachtel v. National Alfalfa Journal, 190 Iowa 1293, 176 N.W. 801 (1920) (prize magazine subscription contest); Chaplin v. Hicks, [1911] 2 K.B. 786 (beauty contest).

(c) TORTIOUS BREACH OF CONTRACT

A party to a contract cannot be liable in tort for interfering with his own contract. Applied Equipment Corp. v. Litton Saudi Arabia Ltd., 7 Cal. 4th 503, 28 Cal. Rptr. 2d 475, 869 P.2d 454 (1994). The interfering conduct must constitute an independent tort, such as fraud. The rule underlines the distinction between tort and contract liability. As tort liability has moved beyond physical interests and focused attention on protecting economic interests, the boundary line between tort and contract has been much debated. Negligence has stretched, as witnessed in Chapter 8, to protect parties in select circumstances from negligent infliction of pure economic loss.

Contract has generally refused to provide protection for non-economic losses arising from breach. This is true despite the fact that in many contracts the parties expose themselves to the risk of the other parties' opportunistic behavior; contracts often expose parties to significant loss not conveniently and adequately measured under the usual rules of breach of contract. Consider that you have contracted with a tour company for a vacation after your first year of law school. Instead of the relaxing, rejuvenating vacation promised, you endure the hardships of Hannibal crossing the Alps. Will a return of the contract price suffice? On occasion, the relationship goes beyond contract to forge a fiduciary relationship, thus, allowing the incidents of equitable remedies. The law may also impose equitable type terms–covenants of good faith–into the contract. The remedy, however, remains in breach of contract.

The law contemplates that parties are free on pain of paying damages in breach of contract to intentionally breach a contract. The last section highlighted that third parties do not have a commensurate freedom. If they should induce a breach of contract, they will be subject to tort liability with its attendant remedies.

One question explored in this section is how far tort law, with its potent remedy of punitive damages, has invaded the domain of contract. Can a breaching party be tortiously liable for interfering with his own contract? Insurance contracts are a well-established exception. Can other contracts be brought within the fold? How is insurance contract to be defined?

Contract assumes the informed, voluntary behavior of the parties. What role does tort play in protecting the integrity of contract formation?

Neibuhr v. Gage

Supreme Court of Minnesota, 1906.
99 Minn. 149, 108 N.W. 884.

ELLIOTT, J. This action was brought to recover damages which the plaintiff claims he suffered by reason of being required while under duress to transfer to the defendant certain shares of stock in a corporation. In the court below he recovered a verdict for $8,478. The trial court denied the defendant's motion for judgment notwithstanding the verdict, but granted a new trial. Both parties appealed. * * *

[Plaintiff possessed 91 shares of stock in Gage, Hayden & Co., having a face value of $9,100. Defendant Gage accused him of the felony of grand larceny and threatened to have him convicted unless he transferred the shares to Gage. Plaintiff alleged that he was innocent and that Gage led him to believe that Gage "would produce false testimony against him, in order to establish and justify [the] false accusation." Under threat of immediate arrest and imprisonment and without opportunity for consultation, plaintiff transferred the shares.]

The defendant contends * * * that if the contract resulted from duress it was voidable, and the sole remedy of the injured party was either to rescind and to restore the benefits, and then bring his action for what he had parted with, or bring his action in equity for a rescission and for such relief as he was entitled to upon rescission. * * *

In form this is an action at law to recover damages for an injury caused by the wrongful act of the defendant Gage. It was so regarded by the trial court, and the plaintiff's evidence was offered and received upon this theory. The pleadings do not raise the question of ratification or laches. The defendant stands squarely upon the proposition that there was no duress and that the plaintiff admitted that he was an embezzler, and for the purpose of paying an acknowledged debt to Gage, Hayden & Co. freely and voluntarily transferred the stock to Gage. * * *

The remedies which are available to one who has been induced to part with his property or execute a contract by ordinary fraud are well understood. He may keep what he has received under the contract and bring an action to recover the damages which he has sustained by reason of the fraud, or he may rescind the contract by his own act, and sue at law for what he parted with by reason of the fraud, or he may sue in equity for a rescission of the contract by the court and recover what he parted with upon such conditions as the court may deem equitable. * * * If he seeks equitable relief, he must proceed promptly and comply with all the conditions which equity imposes. If he elects to rescind by his own act and sue at law for what he parted with by reason of the fraud, he must do all that he reasonably can to place the defendant in statu quo. [C]

The plaintiff abandoned his stock to the defendant. He aske [sic] no equitable relief. He ratifies and affirms the contract, but not the fraud by which it was obtained. The equitable doctrine of laches has no application in an action at law to recover damages. * * * In an action for damages where no rescission is sought a return of the consideration received under the contract is unnecessary.

But is a party who has been injured by duress entitled to the same remedies as one who has been injured by deception? We are unable to see why there should be any distinction made between these two classes of cases. Fraud is ordinarily accomplished by deceit, but it is also accomplished by many other practices. As commonly understood, fraud is a wrong accomplished by deception but * * * duress is a species of fraud in which compulsion in some form takes the place of deception in accomplishing the injury. [C]

We find no principle * * * which limits the remedy by reason of some inherent quality found in the definition of the word "deceit." The practice in either case is equally bad, and there is no reason why the remedy should not be as comprehensive and complete in one as in the other. The wrongdoer accomplishes the same wrong in each case, and does it with the same bad intent. The cases are at least analogous and on principle the remedies should be the same. It is not necessary that the law should show any special and extraordinary consideration for the wrongdoer. All he is entitled to is a fair opportunity to make good the damages resulting from his wrong without unnecessary injury to himself. It is not for him to determine the choice of remedies for the injured party. If the remedy of an action at law for damages is available to a person who has been injured by deceit, it should not lie in the mouth of the wrongdoer to say that the remedy is more restricted when the wrong is the result of the more gross and brutal acts which are known as "duress." * * * A party who has been injured by duress is entitled to the same remedies which are available in cases of deceit. * * *

The entire record has been carefully read, and we are satisfied that there is evidence to sustain the verdict. * * *

The order granting a new trial is reversed, with directions to the trial court to enter a judgment in favor of the plaintiff upon the verdict.

NOTES AND QUESTIONS

1. The principal case has not attracted a large following. In accord see Housing Authority of Dallas v. Hubbell, 325 S.W.2d 880 (Tex.Civ.App.1959) (economic pressure), and State Nat'l Bank of El Paso v. Farah Mfg. Co., 678 S.W.2d 661 (Tex.App.1984) (lender's liability). The case may suffer from its appellation as "duress" when that term is commonly used in the law of contract and restitution. The English courts have fashioned a more certain, albeit controversial tort, of "intimidation." The tort encompasses those cases in which harm is inflicted by the use of unlawful threats whereby the liberty of others to do as they please is interfered with. The wrong is of two kinds: the liberty of action interfered with may be that of the plaintiff himself or that of other persons resulting in damage to the plaintiff. Rookes v. Barnard, [1964] A.C. 1129 (appeal taken from Q.B.) (strike threats made by Union on company forcing dismissal of plaintiff employee). It is unlawful to threaten to breach contracts and thus a threat will constitute intimidation. To threaten to do what one has a legal right to do does not constitute intimidation.

2. The law of fraudulent and negligent misrepresentation plays a similar role in increasing the reliability of information upon which parties act in entering into contracts.

3. Take the following case: Silsbee v. Webber, 171 Mass. 378, 50 N.E. 555 (1898), where defendant, employer of plaintiff's son, whom he charged with embezzlement of funds, threatened to go to the father to raise the matter. As both parties know, the father was an invalid in a delicate physical condition, who might die from the interview. To prevent this, plaintiff transferred to defendant some property of her own. Should plaintiff be allowed to recover for her own emotional distress? Should it make any difference whether the son had actually embezzled funds and, if so, whether the property transferred exceeded the value? Plaintiff was not personally liable for any embezzlement.

The case raises the conundrums surrounding blackmail. Presumably the person threatened would be worse off if the information were disclosed? Is the criminal law, and therefore tort law building on it, inefficient in foreclosing the blackmailed person's choice to pay for silence? This topic has led to trenchant academic exchanges: Symposium on Blackmail, 141 U. Pa. L. Rev. 1565 (1993).

Freeman & Mills, Inc. v. Belcher Oil Company

Supreme Court of California, 1995.
11 Cal. 4th 85, 900 P.2d 669.

LUCAS, C. J. We granted review in this case to resolve some of the widespread confusion that has arisen regarding the application of our opinion in Seaman's Direct Buying Service, Inc. v. Standard Oil Co. (1984) 36 Cal. 3d 752 [206 Cal. Rptr. 354, 686 P.2d 1158] (Seaman's). We held in that case that a tort cause of action might lie "when, in addition to breaching the contract, [defendant] seeks to shield itself from liability by denying, in bad faith and without probable cause, that the contract exists." [c]

In the present case, the Court of Appeal reversed judgment for plaintiff and remanded the case for a limited retrial, but also suggested that "it is time for the Supreme Court to reexamine the tort of 'bad faith denial of contract.'" We agree, and proceed to do so here. As our order granting review stated, "the issue to be argued before this court is limited to whether, and under what circumstances, a party to a contract may recover in tort for another party's bad faith denial of the contract's existence."

* * *

[W]e have concluded that the *Seaman's* court incorrectly recognized a tort cause of action based on the defendant's bad faith denial of the existence of a contract between the parties. That holding has been widely criticized by legal scholars, has caused considerable confusion among lower courts, and has been rejected by the courts of several other jurisdictions. These critics convincingly argue that the Seaman's decision is confusing and ambiguous, analytically flawed, and promotes questionable policy. After careful review of all the foregoing considerations, we conclude that our *Seaman's* holding should be overruled.

I. Facts

* * * In June 1987, defendant Belcher Oil Company (Belcher Oil) retained the law firm of Morgan, Lewis & Bockius (Morgan) to defend it in a Florida lawsuit. Pursuant to a letter of understanding signed by Belcher Oil's general counsel (William Dunker) and a Morgan partner (Donald Smaltz), Belcher Oil was to pay for costs incurred on its behalf, including fees for accountants. In February 1988, after first obtaining Dunker's express authorization, Smaltz hired plaintiff, the accounting firm of Freeman & Mills, Incorporated (Freeman and Mills), to provide a financial analysis and litigation support for Belcher Oil in the Florida lawsuit.

In March, an engagement letter was signed by both Morgan and Freeman & Mills. At about this time, William Dunker left Belcher Oil and was replaced by Neil Bowman. In April 1988, Bowman became dissatisfied with Morgan's efforts and the lawyers were discharged. Bowman asked Morgan for a summary of the work performed by Freeman & Mills and, at the same time, directed Smaltz to have Freeman & Mills stop their work for Belcher Oil. Smaltz did as he was asked. Freeman & Mills's final statement was for $70,042.50 in fees, plus $7,495.63 for costs, a total of $77,538.13.

Freeman & Mills billed Morgan, but no payment was forthcoming. Freeman & Mills then billed Belcher Oil directly and, for about a year, sent monthly statements and regularly called Bowman about the bill, but no payment was forthcoming. In August 1989, Smaltz finally told Freeman & Mills that Belcher Oil refused to pay their bill. Freeman & Mills then wrote to Bowman asking that the matter be resolved. In September 1989, Bowman responded, complaining that Belcher Oil had not been consulted about the extent of Freeman & Mills's services and suggesting Freeman & Mills should look to Morgan for payment of whatever amounts were claimed due.

Ultimately, Freeman & Mills filed this action against Belcher Oil, alleging (in its second amended complaint) causes of action for breach of contract, "bad faith denial of contract," and quantum meruit. Belcher Oil answered and the case was presented to a jury in a bifurcated trial, with punitive damages reserved for the second phase. According to the evidence presented during the first phase, the amount owed to Freeman & Mills (as indicated on their statements) was $77,538.13.

The jury returned its first phase verdict. On Freeman & Mills's breach of contract claim, the jury found that Belcher Oil had authorized Morgan to retain Freeman & Mills on Belcher Oil's behalf, that Freeman & Mills had performed its obligations under the contract, that Belcher Oil had breached the contract, and that the amount of damages suffered by Freeman & Mills was $25,000. The jury also answered affirmatively the questions about whether Belcher Oil had denied the existence of the contract and had acted with oppression, fraud, or malice. Thereafter, the jury returned its verdict awarding $477,538.13 in punitive damages and judgment was entered consistent with the jury's verdicts.

In three post-trial motions, Freeman & Mills asked for orders (1) "correcting" the jury's verdicts and the court's judgment to reflect compensatory damages of $77,538.13 and punitive damages of $425,000 (on the ground that the jury's questions showed this was its true intent); (2) awarding attorney fees as sanctions for the litigation tactics of Belcher Oil's attorneys; and (3) awarding prejudgment interest on the compensatory damage award. Over Belcher Oil's opposition, all three motions were granted—but with some changes in the course of correcting the judgment—by giving Freeman & Mills $131,614.93 in compensatory damages (the $25,000 actually awarded by the jury, plus the $77,538.13 included in the punitive damage award, plus $29,076.80 for prejudgment interest), and $400,000 (not $425,000 as requested) in punitive damages.

Belcher Oil appealed from the "corrected" judgment. Freeman & Mills cross-appealed from a mid-trial order denying its request to amend its complaint to add a cause of action for fraud, an issue not presently before us. The Court of Appeal majority, finding no "special relationship" between the parties to justify a tort theory of recovery under Seaman's, reversed the judgment and remanded the case to the trial court for a retrial limited to the issue of damages under plaintiff's breach of contract cause of action. (The Court of Appeal dissenting justice would have sustained the tort cause of action and remanded for retrial of the damage issue as to both causes of action.) As will appear, we affirm the judgment of the Court of Appeal, concluding that a tort recovery is unavailable in this case.

II.   The Seaman's Decision

The tort of bad faith "denial of contract" was established in a per curiam opinion in *Seaman's* [C]. These were the facts before the court in that case: In 1971, Seaman's Direct Buying Service, a small marine fueling station in Eureka, wanted to expand its operation by developing a marine fuel dealership in conjunction with a new marina under development by the City of Eureka. When Seaman's approached the city about a long-term lease of a large parcel of land in the marina, the city required Seaman's to obtain a binding commitment from an oil supplier. To that end, Seaman's negotiated with several companies and, by 1972, reached a tentative agreement with Standard Oil Company of California.

Both Seaman's and Standard Oil signed a letter of intent setting forth the basic terms of their arrangement, but that letter was subject to government approval of the contract, continued approval of Seaman's credit status, and future agreement on specific arrangements. Seaman's showed the letter to the city and, shortly thereafter, signed a 40–year lease with the city. [C]

Shortly thereafter, an oil shortage dramatically reduced the available supplies of oil and, in November 1973, Standard Oil told Seaman's that new federal regulations requiring allocation of petroleum products to those that had been customers since 1972 precluded its execution of a new dealership agreement. In response, Seaman's obtained an exemption from the appropriate federal agency. Standard Oil appealed and persuaded the agency to reverse the order, but Seaman's eventually had the exemption reinstated contingent on a court determination that a valid contract existed between the parties. [C]

Seaman's then asked Standard Oil to stipulate to the existence of a contract, stating that a refusal would force it to discontinue operations. Standard Oil's representative refused the request, telling Seaman's, "See you in court." Seaman's business collapsed and it sued Standard Oil for damages on four theories—breach of contract, fraud, breach of the implied covenant of good faith and fair dealing, and interference with Seaman's contractual relationship with the city. [C]

The case was tried to a jury, which returned its verdicts in favor of Seaman's on all theories except fraud, awarding compensatory and punitive damages. Standard Oil appealed. [C] We considered "whether, and under what circumstances, a breach of the implied covenant of good faith and fair dealing in a commercial contract may give rise to an action in tort." [C] For purposes of completeness, we quote from *Seaman's* at some length:

"It is well settled that, in California, the law implies in every contract a covenant of good faith and fair dealing. Broadly stated, that covenant requires that neither party do anything which will deprive the other of the benefits of the agreement. California courts have recognized the existence of this covenant, and enforced it, in cases involving a wide variety of contracts.... In the seminal cases of Comunale v. Traders & General Ins. Co. [(1958)] 50 Cal. 2d 654 [328 P.2d 198, 68 A.L.R.2d 883], and Crisci v. Security Ins. Co. [(1967)] 66 Cal. 2d 425 [58 Cal. Rptr. 13, 426 P.2d 173], this court held that a breach of the covenant of good faith and fair dealing by an insurance carrier may give rise to a cause of action in tort as well as in contract. [C]

"While the proposition that the law implies a covenant of good faith and fair dealing in all contracts is well established, the proposition advanced by *Seaman's*—that breach of the covenant always gives rise to an action in tort—is not so clear. In holding that a tort action is available for breach of the covenant in an insurance contract, we have emphasized the 'special relationship' between insurer and insured, characterized by elements of public interest, adhesion, and fiduciary responsibility. No doubt there are other relationships with similar characteristics and deserving of similar legal treatment.

"When we move from such special relationships to consideration of the tort remedy in the context of the ordinary commercial contract, we move into largely uncharted and potentially dangerous waters. Here, parties of roughly equal bargaining power are free to shape the contours of their agreement and to include provisions for attorney fees and liquidated damages in the event of breach. They may not be permitted to disclaim the covenant of good faith but they are free, within reasonable limits at least, to agree upon the standards by which application of the covenant is to be measured. In such contracts, it may be difficult to distinguish between breach of the covenant and breach of contract, and there is the risk that interjecting tort remedies will intrude upon the expectations of the parties. This is not to say that tort remedies have no place in such a commercial context, but that it is wise to proceed with caution in determining their scope and application.

"For the purposes of this case it is unnecessary to decide the broad question which Seaman's poses. Indeed, it is not even necessary to predicate liability on a breach of the implied covenant. It is sufficient to recognize that a party to a contract may incur tort remedies when, in addition to breaching the contract, it seeks to shield itself from liability by denying, in bad faith and without probable cause, that the contract exists.

"It has been held that a party to a contract may be subject to tort liability, including punitive damages, if he coerces the other party to pay more than is due under the contract terms through the threat of a lawsuit, made ' "without probable cause and with no belief in the existence of the cause of action." ' There is little difference, in principle, between a contracting party obtaining excess payment in such manner, and a contracting party seeking to avoid all liability on a meritorious contract claim by adopting a 'stonewall' position ('see you in court') without probable cause and with no belief in the existence of a defense. Such conduct goes beyond the mere breach of contract. It offends accepted notions of business ethics. [C] Acceptance of tort remedies in such a situation is not likely to intrude upon the bargaining relationship or upset reasonable expectations of the contracting parties." [C]

Seaman's concluded that, because a good faith denial of the existence of a binding contract is not a tort [c], the trial court's failure to instruct the jury on the requirement of bad faith was error (ibid.) and that error was prejudicial. [C]

* * *

IV. Subsequent Developments

A. California Supreme Court Decisions—Subsequent opinions of this court indicate a continuing reluctance, originally reflected in *Seaman's* itself, to authorize tort recovery for noninsurance contract breaches.

In Foley v. Interactive Data Corp. (1988) 47 Cal. 3d 654 [254 Cal. Rptr. 211, 765 P.2d 373] (Foley), we considered the availability of tort damages for the wrongful termination of a discharged employee. Declining to rely on dictum in *Seaman's* [c] regarding the possible availability of tort remedies for breach of the implied covenant of good faith and fair dealing (hereafter the implied covenant) in the employment context, we refused to afford such remedies for the essentially contractual claim of breach of the implied covenant arising in that context. [C]

In reaching our conclusion in *Foley*, we relied in part on certain basic principles relevant to contract law, including the need for "predictability about the cost of contractual relationships," and the purpose of contract damages to compensate the injured party rather than punish the breaching party. [C] Focusing on the implied covenant, we observed that, with the exception of insurance contracts, "[b]ecause the covenant is a contract term, ... compensation for its breach has almost always been limited to contract rather than tort remedies." [C]

We acknowledged in *Foley* that "[t]he insurance cases ... were a major departure from traditional principles of contract law," and we stressed that the courts should take "great care" before extending "the exceptional approach taken in those cases" to "another contract setting." [C] We concluded that "the employment relationship is not sufficiently similar to that of insurer and insured to warrant judicial extension of the proposed additional tort remedies...." [C]

[The Court discusses Hunter v. Up–Right and Applied Equipment v. Litton Saudi Arabia, 6 Cal. 4th 1174, 26 Cal. Rptr. 2d 8, 864 P.2d 88 (1993), 7 Cal. 4th 503, 28 Cal. Rptr. 2d 475, 869 P.2d 454 (1994).]

* * *

Our decisions in *Foley*, *Hunter*, and *Applied Equipment* each contains language that strongly suggests courts should limit tort recovery in contract breach situations to the insurance area, at least in the absence of violation of an independent duty arising from principles of tort law other than denial of the existence of, or liability under, the breached contract. (See also White v. Western Title Ins. Co. (1985) 40 Cal. 3d 870, 901 [221 Cal. Rptr. 509, 710 P.2d 309] (conc. and dis. opn. of Kaus, J.) [observing that "our experience in *Seaman's* surely tells us that there are real problems in applying the substitute remedy of a tort recovery—with or without punitive damages—outside the insurance area," and urging a legislative solution].)

* * *

Without analyzing the particular facts of each case, it is sufficient to observe that our Seaman's holding has presented the lower courts with a number of unanswered questions, and that these courts have reached varying, and often inconsistent, conclusions in response. [Cc]

* * *

[Much] confusion and conflict has arisen regarding the scope and application of our *Seaman's* holding. For example, does the *Seaman's* tort derive from breach of the implied covenant or from some other independent tort duty? [Cc]

Confusion and conflict alone might not justify a decision to abrogate *Seaman's*, for we could attempt to resolve all the uncertainties engendered by that decision. But there are additional considerations that convince us to forgo that predictably Herculean effort. Many of the pertinent Court of Appeal decisions recognize compelling policy reasons supporting the preclusion of tort remedies for contractual breaches outside the insurance context. * * *

Similarly, in Harris [v. Atlantic Richfield Co.], 14 Cal. App. 4th 70 [(1993)], the Court of Appeal denied a tort recovery for bad faith contract breach in violation of public policy. The court elaborated on the applicable policy considerations as follows: "The traditional goal of contract remedies is compensation of the promisee for the loss resulting from the breach, not compulsion of the promisor to perform his promises. Therefore, 'willful' breaches have not been distinguished from other breaches. [C] The restrictions on contract remedies serve purposes not found in tort law. They protect the parties' freedom to bargain over special risks and they promote contract formation by limiting liability to the value of the promise. This encourages efficient breaches, resulting in increased production of goods and services at lower cost to society. [C] Because of these overriding policy considerations, the California Supreme Court has proceeded with caution in carving out exceptions to the traditional contract remedy restrictions." [C]

The *Harris* court set forth as reasons for denying tort recovery in contract breach cases (1) the different objectives underlying the remedies for tort and contract breach, (2) the importance of predictability in assuring commercial stability in contractual dealings, (3) the potential for converting every contract breach into a tort, with accompanying punitive damage recovery, and (4) the preference for legislative action in affording appropriate remedies. [Cc]

[T]he foregoing policy considerations fully support our decision to overrule Seaman's rather than attempt to clarify its uncertain boundaries. (We observe that plaintiff has asked us to take judicial notice of certain records purportedly showing there were only a few jury verdicts involving Seaman's claims during the period from 1981 to 1994. Because jury verdicts are an inconclusive indicia of excessive litigation, and because defendant has raised some doubts regarding the accuracy and completeness of the submitted materials, the application for judicial notice is denied.)

* * *

Ninth Circuit Judge Kozinski expressed his candid criticism of *Seaman's* in a concurring opinion in Oki America, Inc. v. Microtech Intern., Inc. (9th Cir.1989) 872 F.2d 312, 314–317 (Oki America). Among other criticism, Judge Kozinski found the Seaman's holding unduly imprecise and confusing. As he stated, "It is impossible to draw a principled distinction between a tortious denial of a contract's existence and a permissible denial of liability under the terms of the contract. The test ... seems to be whether the conduct 'offends accepted notions of business ethics.' This gives judges license to rely on their gut feelings in distinguishing between a squabble and a tort. As a result, both the commercial world and the courts are needlessly burdened...." [C]

Judge Kozinski also mentioned the substantial costs associated with Seaman's litigation, and the resulting interference with contractual relationships. "Perhaps most troubling, the willingness of courts to subordinate voluntary contractual arrangements to their own sense of public policy and proper business decorum deprives individuals of an important measure of freedom. The right to enter into contracts—to adjust one's legal relationships by mutual agreement [] is too easily smothered by government officers eager to tell us what's best for us." [C] Judge Kozinski concluded by observing that "Seaman's is a prime candidate for reconsideration." [C]

Similarly, in Air–Sea Forwarders, Inc. v. Air Asia Co., Ltd., supra, 880 F.2d at pages 184–185, Judge Hall observed that Seaman's *"ambiguous"* holding had caused widespread confusion among the lower courts. As Judge Hall stated, "Indeed, the *Seaman's* court's failure to explain why it was not necessary to predicate its holding on the implied covenant of good faith and fair dealing, or to justify the dramatically greater liability for the bad faith denial of the existence of a contract as compared to the bad faith dispute of a contract's terms, undoubtedly spawned the confusion in the appellate division cases discussed infra." [C]

[The Court discussed other critical case law and scholarship.]

* * *

As previously indicated, the *Seaman's* decision has generated uniform confusion and uncertainty regarding its scope and application, and widespread doubt about the necessity or desirability of its holding. These doubts and criticisms, express or implied, in decisions from this state and from other state and federal courts, echoed by the generally adverse scholarly comment cited above, convince us that *Seaman's* should be overruled in favor of a general rule precluding tort recovery for noninsurance contract breach, at least in the absence of violation of "an independent duty arising from principles of tort law" (*Applied Equipment*, supra, 7 Cal. 4th at p. 515) other than the bad faith denial of the existence of, or liability under, the breached contract.

As set forth above, the critics stress, among other factors favoring *Seaman's* abrogation, the confusion and uncertainty accompanying the decision, the need for stability and predictability in commercial affairs, the potential for excessive tort damages, and the preference for legislative rather than judicial action in this area.

Even if we were unimpressed by the nearly unanimous criticism leveled at *Seaman's*, on reconsideration the analytical defects in the opinion have become apparent. It seems anomalous to characterize as "tortious" the bad faith denial of the existence of a contract, while treating as "contractual" the bad faith denial of liability or responsibility under an acknowledged contract. In both cases, the breaching party has acted in bad faith and, accordingly, has presumably committed acts offensive to "accepted notions of business ethics." [C] Yet to include bad faith denials of liability within *Seaman's* scope could potentially convert every contract breach into a tort. Nor would limiting *Seaman's* tort to incidents involving "stonewalling" adequately narrow its potential scope. Such conduct by the breaching party, essentially telling the promisee, "See you in court," could incidentally accompany every breach of contract.

For all the foregoing reasons, we conclude that *Seaman's* should be overruled. We emphasize that nothing in this opinion should be read as affecting the existing precedent governing enforcement of the implied covenant in insurance cases. Further, nothing we say here would prevent the Legislature from creating additional civil remedies for noninsurance contract breach, including such measures as providing litigation costs and attorney fees in certain aggravated cases, or assessing increased compensatory damages covering lost profits and other losses attributable to the breach, as well as restoration of the *Seaman's* holding if the Legislature deems that course appropriate. [Cc] Thus far, however, the Legislature has not manifested an intent either to expand contract breach recovery or to provide tort damages for ordinary contract breach.

The judgment of the Court of Appeal, reversing the trial court's judgment in plaintiff's favor and remanding the case for a retrial limited to the issue of damages under plaintiff's breach of contract cause of action, and for judgment in favor of defendant on plaintiff's bad faith denial of contract cause of action, is affirmed.

Cates Construction, Inc. v. Talbot Partners

Supreme Court of California, 1999.
21 Cal. 4th 28, 980 P.2d 407.

BAXTER J. This case presents issues relating to the contract and tort liability of a commercial surety to a real estate developer under a bond guaranteeing the contract performance of a general contractor on a multimillion dollar condominium construction project. For the reasons set forth below, we conclude that the bond at issue contractually obligates the surety to pay damages attributable to the general contractor's failure to promptly and faithfully perform its contract obligations by the agreed date. We further conclude that, as a matter of law, the developer may not recover in tort for the surety's breach of the covenant of good faith and fair dealing implied in the performance bond. In light of these conclusions, we reverse the judgment of the Court of Appeal insofar as it affirmed the underlying award of tort damages for breach of the implied covenant and permitted an award of punitive damages.

FACTUAL AND PROCEDURAL BACKGROUND

In 1989, Talbot Partners (Talbot) hired Cates Construction, Inc. (Cates) to build a condominium project in Malibu on property purchased by Talbot for $1 million. The construction contract called for Cates to complete the project and have it ready for occupancy in eight months. Talbot received financing for the construction through the Bank of Montecito (the bank). The financing was secured by a deed of trust on the property and was conditioned on the issuance of a performance bond in favor of the bank.

At the time the construction contract was signed, Talbot required Cates to furnish a performance bond and a labor and materials payment bond. Transamerica Insurance Company (Transamerica), a commercial surety company, issued the bonds in favor of Talbot as obligee and the bank as co-obligee. Talbot paid the $27,000 premium on the bonds. Transamerica and Cates also executed an indemnity agreement which allowed Transamerica to recover from Cates all good faith disbursements made under the bonds.

[Various contract claims were adjudicated subsequent to a delay in construction. The delay also triggered the performance bond. The court found that Transamerica had breached the performance bond by failing to investigate Talbot's declaration that Cates was in default and by seeking to enforce a mechanic's lien without investigation of its validity. Talbot had performed and Cates had defaulted. It was further held that Transamerica's breaches of the performance bond had caused the loss of the project.]

After trial of the contract claims, Talbot tried its tort cause of action against Transamerica to a jury before the Honorable William Burby. On Transamerica's motion, the jury was not informed of the findings or the award in the breach of contract trial. The parties also stipulated to compensatory tort damages in the total amount of $1. After hearing evidence regarding the entire course of conduct between all the parties, the jury determined that Transamerica breached the implied covenant of good faith and fair dealing and was guilty of malice and oppression in doing so. The jury awarded $28 million in punitive damages.

The Court of Appeal modified the judgment to reduce the amount of punitive damages to $15 million and remanded to the trial court for a recalculation of prejudgment interest. The judgment was affirmed in all other respects. As relevant here, the Court of Appeal determined that Talbot was properly awarded $2,596,600 against Transamerica for damages attributable to Cates's failure to timely complete the construction contract. The court also determined, based on its conclusion that surety bonds are insurance, that obligees such as Talbot could recover tort damages for breaches of the implied covenant of good faith and fair dealing. Finally, the court found sufficient evidence of malice and oppression to support punitive damages, but reduced the awarded amount to $15 million on federal due process grounds.

DISCUSSION

A surety is "one who promises to answer for the debt, default, or miscarriage of another, or hypothecates property as security therefor." (Civ. Code, § 2787.) A surety bond is a " 'written instrument executed by the principal and surety in which the surety agrees to answer for the debt, default, or miscarriage of the principal.' " [C] In suretyship, the risk of loss remains with the principal, while the surety merely lends its credit so as to guarantee payment or performance in the event that the principal defaults. [C] In the absence of default, the surety has no obligation. [C]

This case presents three questions relating to the construction performance bond executed by Cates (the principal) and Transamerica (the surety) in which Transamerica agreed to answer in the event of Cates's default under its construction contract with Talbot (the obligee). First, is Transamerica contractually liable under the performance bond for damages attributable to Cates's failure to complete the project by June 1, 1990? Second, may an obligee recover in tort for a surety's breach of the covenant of good faith and fair dealing in the context of a construction performance bond? Third, if tort recovery is available, is the instant award of $15 million in punitive damages nevertheless excessive in light of the parties' stipulation at trial that Transamerica's tortious conduct resulted in actual damages of $1? We shall address these issues in order.

[The court first addressed the question of whether under a performance bond, the surety, Transamerica, could be liable for "delay damages." The court held that despite contrary Florida authority, the surety is liable for damages flowing from the delay of the project caused by contractor, Cates.]

Breach of the Implied Covenant of Good Faith and Fair Dealing

1. Current California Law regarding Tort Remedies for Breach

By now it is well established that a covenant of good faith and fair dealing is implicit in every contract. [Cc] The essence of the implied covenant is that neither party to a contract will do anything to injure the right of the other to receive the benefits of the contract. [Cc]

Because the covenant of good faith and fair dealing essentially is a contract term that aims to effectuate the contractual intentions of the parties, "compensation for its breach has almost always been limited to contract rather than tort remedies." [Cc] At present, this court recognizes only one exception to that general rule: tort remedies are available for a breach of the covenant in cases involving insurance policies. [Cc] In the insurance policy setting, an insured may recover damages not otherwise available in a contract action, such as emotional distress damages resulting from the insurer's bad faith conduct [c] and punitive damages if there has been oppression, fraud, or malice by the insurer. [C]

As our decisions acknowledge, tort recovery in this particular context is considered appropriate for a variety of policy reasons. Unlike most other contracts for goods or services, an insurance policy is characterized by elements of adhesion, public interest and fiduciary responsibility. [Cc] In general, insurance policies are not purchased for profit or advantage; rather, they are obtained for peace of mind and security in the event of an accident or other catastrophe. [Cc] Moreover, an insured faces a unique "economic dilemma" when its insurer breaches the implied covenant of good faith and fair dealing. [C] Unlike other parties in contract who typically may seek recourse in the marketplace in the event of a breach, an insured will not be able to find another insurance company willing to pay for a loss already incurred.

In addition, we have observed that the tort duty of a liability insurer ordinarily is based on its assumption of the insured's defense and of settlement negotiations of third party claims. [C] The assumption of those responsibilities obligates the insurer to give at least as much consideration to the welfare of its insured as it gives to its own interests so as not to deprive the insured of the benefits of the insurance policy. [Cc]

Significantly, this court has never recognized the availability of tort remedies for breaches occurring in the context of a construction performance bond or any other so-called "contract of suretyship." (See Pacific M. & T. Co. v. Bonding & Ins. Co. (1923) 192 Cal. 278, 285, 219 P. 972 [a bond given to guarantee the faithful performance of a contract is a "contract of suretyship"].)

* * *

It is firmly established that the insurance policy cases represent " 'a major departure from traditional principles of contract law.' " (Freeman & Mills, Inc. v. Belcher Oil Co., supra, [c] citing Foley, supra, [c]). Thus, we have cautioned courts to exercise great care in considering whether to extend " 'the exceptional approach taken in those cases' to 'another contract setting.' " In *Foley,* supra, [c] this court rejected the concept of tort recovery for an employer's breach of the implied covenant of good faith and fair dealing. We concluded that "the employment relationship is not sufficiently similar to that of insurer and insured to warrant judicial extension of the proposed additional tort remedies in view of the counter-vailing concerns about economic policy and stability, the traditional separation of tort and contract law, and ... the numerous protections against improper terminations already afforded employees." [C]

The question here is whether the exceptional approach thus far reserved for breaches in the insurance policy setting should be extended to breaches in the context of a surety bond given to assure performance on a construction contract. Talbot argues, in essence, that a performance bond is a form of insurance and that breaches in the performance bond context justify the same extraordinary remedies that are available in insurance policy cases. Transamerica, on the other hand, argues that performance bonds are fundamentally different from insurance policies and fail to warrant similar treatment. We proceed to consider these points.

Inclusion of Suretyship in the Insurance Code

* * *

Although surety is included within the Insurance Code as a class of insurance, it long has been settled that the parties in surety arrangements have certain rights and defenses that do not attend the typical insurance relationship. For instance, an insurer generally has no right of subrogation against the insured for covered losses even if the insured's negligence contributed to such losses. A surety, however, is entitled to reimbursement from its principal for amounts paid to the obligee upon the principal's default. [Cc]

Consistent with the Civil Code and the case law, regulations promulgated pursuant to the Insurance Code make special note of the "unique relationship which exists under a surety bond between the insurer [surety], the obligee or beneficiary, and the principal." (Cal. Code Regs., tit. 10, § 2695.1, subd. (c).) They also are explicit in distinguishing suretyship from traditional insurance: "In contrast to other classes of insurance, surety insurance involves a promise to answer for the debt, default or miscarriage of a principal who has the primary duty to pay the debt or discharge the obligation and who is bound to indemnify the insurer." (Ibid.; see also Cal. Code Regs., tit. 10, § 2695.2, subd. (j) [defining "insurance policy" to exclude "surety bond" or "bond"].)

In recognition of the distinctions between suretyship and traditional insurance, the regulations exempt sureties from the set of standards promoting the prompt, fair and equitable settlement of claims by insurers and instead provide that sureties are governed by a separate set of claims handling and settlement standards. (Cal. Code Regs., tit. 10, § 2695.1, subd. (c).)

Despite the fact that surety bonds have been distinguished from insurance policies in statutory, regulatory and decisional law, Talbot argues, in effect, that tort remedies for breaches in the performance bond setting are appropriate simply because surety bonds are categorized and regulated as a class of insurance under the Insurance Code. (See Ins. Code, §§ *100*, subd. (5), 105, subd. (a).) We disagree.

As one text in the surety field has observed, "the inclusion of suretyship in the Insurance Code is derived from the need for control of the surety business by a state agency and does not imply that the underlying natures of insurance and suretyship are the same." (Conners, supra, § 1.4, p. 6.) The legislative branch is free to regulate suretyship, and, assuming a rational basis, may require sureties and surety bonds to adhere to the same regulations and requirements that apply to insurers and insurance policies. Case law makes clear, however, that tort remedies for breach of the implied covenant are permitted in the insurance policy setting for policy reasons pertaining to the distinctive nature of such contracts and the relationship between the contracting parties. [Cc] Little, if any, significance has been placed on the circumstance that insurers are licensed by the Insurance Commissioner and are subject to Insurance Code regulations. Moreover, while insurers are subject to administrative sanctions for violating statutory prohibitions against unfair and deceptive claims settlement practices, statutory violations do not give rise to a private right of action for tort damages. [C]

* * *

Although suretyship is listed in the Insurance Code as a class of insurance, it does not follow that a surety bond equates to a policy of insurance under the common law or common law theories of liability. Nor does it follow that the unique policy reasons which justify extraordinary remedies in the insurance policy context are similarly implicated for bonds guaranteeing the performance of a commercial construction contract. In short, the mere inclusion of surety arrangements in the Insurance Code should not be determinative of the issue before us. Rather, we must evaluate whether the policy considerations recognized in the common law support the availability of tort remedies in the context of a performance bond. [C]

3.   Policy Considerations

As our decisions explain, tort recovery is considered appropriate in the insurance policy setting because such contracts are characterized by elements of adhesion and unequal bargaining power, public interest and fiduciary responsibility. [Cc] We now consider whether construction performance bonds are marked by such elements.

a.   Adhesion and Unequal Bargaining Power

[We] conclude that, unlike an insurance policy, the typical performance bond bears no indicia of adhesion or disparate bargaining power that might support tort recovery by an obligee.

b.   Public Interest and Fiduciary Responsibility

Our decisions observe that tort remedies are appropriate for breaches in the insurance policy context because insureds generally do not seek to obtain commercial advantages by purchasing policies; rather, they seek protection against calamity. [Cc] But while the typical insurance policy protects an insured against accidental and generally unforeseeable losses caused by a calamitous or catastrophic event such as disability, death, fire, or flood, the general purpose of a construction performance bond "is to protect the creditor [the owner/obligee] against the danger that he will be unable to collect from the debtor [the general contractor/principal] for any failure in the performance of the contract." (Regents of University of California v. Hartford Acc. & Indem. Co. (1978) 21 Cal. 3d 624, 639, 147 Cal. Rptr. 486, 581 P.2d 197). In requiring a performance bond, then, the obligee "seeks the commercial advantage of obtaining a contract with the principal which provides additional financial security." [C]

In *Foley*, supra, this court indicated that insurance is a "quasi-public" service in the sense that individuals contract with insurance companies "specifically in order to obtain protection from potential specified economic harm." [C] While our words, read in isolation, might suggest that surety-ship could qualify as a quasi-public service because a bond may be viewed as offering a form of economic protection, the context of our discussion indicates otherwise.

* * *

Contrary to Talbot's assertions, there is little basis for concluding that the relationship between a surety and an obligee is fiduciary or quasi-fiduciary in nature. Although a performance bond serves to shift the risk of the principal's nonperformance from the obligee to the surety, the conditional nature of the surety's obligations and its right to assert the defenses of the principal distinguish the surety-obligee relationship from the insurer-insured relationship. The fact that insurance regulations exempt sureties from many of the fair claims settlement standards applicable to issuers of insurance policies is consistent with and supports the conclusion that a surety does not stand in a fiduciary or quasi-fiduciary position with respect to an obligee. [Cc]

Additionally, a principal basis for recognizing tort liability in the context of liability insurance, i.e., the insurer's assumption of the insured's defense and of settlement negotiations of third party claims [Cc], is not transferable to the performance bond setting. In contrast to a liability insurer, a surety bears no responsibility to defend an obligee against third party claims and has no right to represent the obligee's interests by virtue of the surety bond. Thus, to the extent such responsibilities give rise to fiduciary or quasi-fiduciary obligations in the liability insurance setting, their absence in surety arrangements supports a different result.

c. Consequences of Allowing Tort Recovery

In Transamerica Premier v. Brighton School, supra, 940 P.2d 348, the Colorado Supreme Court held that subjecting sureties to tort liability for breach of the implied covenant "compels commercial sureties to handle claims responsibly." (940 P.2d at p. 353.) The court also determined that, when a commercial surety withholds payment of an obligee's claim in bad faith, contract damages do not compensate for the surety's misconduct and have no deterrent effect to prevent such misconduct in the future. [C] For the reasons set forth below, we are not convinced that tort remedies are necessary to achieve such objectives.

Unlike insureds, obligees possess ample bargaining power to negotiate terms that encourage timely performance of bond obligations and that provide for attorneys' fees and interest when breaches occur. [Cc] Obligees may also require a liquidated damages provision to discourage nonperformance by sureties. Accordingly, tort remedies appear largely unnecessary to induce a surety's performance or to fully compensate for a surety's breach of the covenant of good faith.

Moreover, it is generally recognized that a primary purpose of a performance bond is to protect the obligee against the risk of the principal's default on the construction contract. Where, as here, a bond is given to guarantee faithful performance of a construction contract, then contract remedies, which compensate for all damages within the contemplation of the parties at the time of contracting or at least reasonably foreseeable by them at that time (Civ. Code, § 3300), provide adequate compensation for breach of the bond.

Nor are we persuaded that tort recovery is necessary to deter misconduct by sureties. As noted, owners and developers involved in construction wield sufficient bargaining power to demand contractual provisions for interest, attorney's fees and liquidated damages.

More importantly, the Insurance Code subjects sureties to substantial administrative sanctions and penalties for violations of the Unfair Practices Act (Ins. Code, § 790 et seq.). Those sanctions include maximum civil penalties of $5,000 for each act or $10,000 for each willful act in violation of Insurance Code *section 790.03*, subdivision (h), and the issuance of cease and desist orders to enjoin further violations. Willful violations of cease and desist orders may result in an additional penalty of $55,000, while repeated violations may result in the suspension or revocation of a surety's license for up to a year.

In considering the potential consequences of allowing tort remedies in the performance bond context, we are mindful of cases and commentary indicating that, for whatever benefits might accrue from permitting such remedies, harmful economic effects appear at least as likely to occur.

Unlike insurance relationships, which involve the interests of only two parties, the surety relationship is a tripartite one implicating the separate legal interests of the principal, the obligee and the surety. When contract disputes arise between an obligee and a principal as to whether the principal is in default, it may prove difficult for the surety to determine which party is in the right and whether its own performance is due under the bond. As one text explains: "There is no simple scenario for a performance bond dispute. Most often a dispute will involve claims, counterclaims, charges, and countercharges. Seldom will any one party be altogether in the right. Often the parties are in a defensive posture when bond claims begin to surface. Usually, the project is behind schedule. Generally, prior to the time the surety is officially called upon to perform, lines have been drawn and personalities have clashed. It is no wonder that performance bond claims are fertile fields for surety litigators." (Cushman & Stamm, Handling Fidelity and Surety Claims (1984) § 6.4, p. 168.)

As the foregoing suggests, construction disputes may be complicated enough to resolve when all three parties are on a level playing field. But it is rational to assume that making tort remedies available may encourage obligees to allege a principal's default more readily than they would in the absence of such remedies. It is also reasonable to conclude that allowing obligees to wield the club of tort and punitive damages may make it easier to pressure sureties into paying questionable default claims, or paying more on properly disputed claims, because the sureties will be reluctant to risk the outcome of a tort action. [Cc] Thus, permitting obligees to sue sureties in tort may allow obligees to gain additional leverage with sureties that principals do not have in contract disputes.

With such increased leverage, obligees will have sufficient power to detrimentally affect the interests of principals when disagreements arise during construction. Claims of default by the obligee may impair the principal's ability to secure bonding on other projects, thus automatically disqualifying the principal from bidding on all public projects and many private ones. Moreover, indemnity agreements executed by principals often give sureties the right to pursue them for reimbursement of any loss, including legal expenses and the costs of investigation. In efforts to avoid bad faith liability, sureties may strive to "find" bond coverage for obligees while, at the same time, charging their investigation costs to the principal. Accordingly, even if the surety's investigation ultimately leads to the conclusion that the principal is not in default, the faultless principal may still suffer adverse consequences. These considerations, which have no parallel in disputes involving insurance policies, weigh against the recognition of extracontractual liability in the performance bond context.

Finally, allowing tort recovery in the construction bond context may open the door to increased (and sometimes successive) litigation, which in turn may increase the cost of obtaining bonds. For example, in K–W Industries v. National Sur. Corp. (Mont.1988) 231 Mont. 461, 754 P.2d 502, the subcontractor first sued in federal court on a payment bond under the Miller Act and then sued in Montana state court alleging violations of statutory prohibitions against bad faith insurance practices. But even if obligees bring their contract and tort actions in one suit, increased litigation and settlement costs are inevitable. Those costs ultimately would be passed on by contractors to obligees and may contribute to the unaffordability of bonds.

Authorities From Other States

We observe that the Texas Supreme Court recently concluded that performance bond obligees should not be permitted to recover tort damages from commercial sureties for breaches of the implied covenant of good faith and fair dealing. (Great American Ins. v. N. Austin Utility (Tex.1995) 908 S.W.2d 415; cf. U.S. ex rel. Ehmcke Sheet Metal Works v. Wausau Ins. Co., supra, 755 F. Supp. 906 [subcontractor may not sue surety in tort on a payment bond].)

As Talbot notes, however, courts in other jurisdictions have concluded otherwise. (Transamerica Premier v. Brighton School, supra, 940 P.2d 348; Loyal Order of Moose v. Intern. Fidelity (Alaska 1990) 797 P.2d 622; Dodge v. Fidelity & Deposit Co. of Md., supra, 778 P.2d 1240; Szarkowski v. Reliance Ins. Co. (N.D.1987) 404 N.W.2d 502; cf. K–W Industries v. National Sur. Corp., supra, 754 P.2d 502 [subcontractor may sue surety in tort on a payment bond].)

After carefully reviewing the foregoing authorities, we find ourselves unpersuaded by the decisions that allow tort recovery, for they fail to give appropriate consideration to the material differences between insurance policies and performance bonds and the differing relations between the parties thereto. In addition, many of the decisions place undue emphasis upon statutes regulating suretyship as a class of insurance.

Performance Bond Obligees May Not Recover In Tort

The question before us is this: Is tort recovery appropriate for a breach of the implied covenant of good faith and fair dealing in the context of a construction performance bond? In answering that question, we are reminded that "contract law exists to enforce legally binding agreements between parties; tort law is designed to vindicate social policy." (Applied Equipment Corp. v. Litton Saudi Arabia Ltd. (1994) 7 Cal. 4th 503, 514, 869 P.2d 454.)

With that guiding principle in mind, we answer the question in the negative. A construction performance bond is not an insurance policy. Nor is it a contract otherwise marked by elements of adhesion, public interest or fiduciary responsibility, such that an extracontractual remedy is necessitated in the interests of social policy. Obligees have ample power to protect their interests through negotiation, and sureties, for the most part, are deterred from acting unreasonably by the threat of stiff statutory and administrative sanctions and penalties, including license suspension and revocation.

We acknowledge that our unwillingness to recognize a new tort action may mean that isolated instances of surety misconduct may yet occur. Nonetheless, in the absence of compelling policy reasons supporting tort recovery, we leave it up to the Legislature, which is better equipped to gather data and study the effects of a significant shift in the balance of power between owner/obligees, contractor/principals and sureties, to determine whether statutorily authorized tort remedies would benefit the real estate development industry.

Accordingly, we hold that recovery for a surety's breach of the implied covenant of good faith and fair dealing is properly limited to those damages within the contemplation of the parties at the time the performance bond is given or at least reasonably foreseeable by them at that time. (See Applied Equipment Corp. v. Litton Saudi Arabia Ltd., supra, 7 Cal. 4th at p. 515; Civ. Code, § 3300 [measure of damages for breach of an obligation arising from contract].)

C. Punitive Damages

* * *

Since Talbot may not recover in tort for Transamerica's breach of the implied covenant of good faith and fair dealing, the foregoing rule compels a reversal of the award of punitive damages in its entirety.

Disposition

The judgment of the Court of Appeal is reversed insofar as it affirmed the award of tort damages for breach of the implied covenant and permitted an award of punitive damages. The matter is remanded to that court for further proceedings consistent with this opinion.

NOTES AND QUESTIONS

1. As the last two principal cases indicate, the insurance context is the only firm category in which the courts are prepared to find an action in tort for breach of the covenant of good faith. Careau & Co. v. Security Pacific Business Credit, Inc., 222 Cal. App. 3d 1371, 272 Cal. Rptr. 387 (1990) ("In insurance cases there is a well-developed history recognizing a tort remedy for a breach of the implied covenant"; noting that whether the action "has any application in noninsurance cases appears to be increasingly problematic"). However, even in the insurance context courts have been skeptical: Beck v. Farmers Insurance Exchange, 701 P.2d 795 (Utah 1985) (recognizing that "a majority of states permit an insured to institute a tort action against an insurer who fails to bargain in a * * * 'first party' [insurer] situation," but concluding that the "tort approach * * * is without a sound theoretical foundation and has the potential for distorting well-established principles of contract law"). Bad faith does not require an intention to deny insured an insurance benefit, a failure to exercise good faith in processing a claim may be constituted by a refusal to pay a claim where no reasonable grounds exist to found the refusal: Zoppo v. Homestead Insurance, 71 Ohio St. 3d 552, 644 N.E.2d 397 (1994).

2. Justice Mosk dissents in both principal cases giving the tort more ambit. He would agree with those courts that have extended to the tort to surety contracts.

3. Should tortious relief be permitted where in-house counsel is dismissed for pursuing a legal agenda that he regards as ethically binding but corporate management finds incompatible with the profit-seeking motive of the corporation? GTE Products Corp. v. Stewart, 653 N.E.2d 161 (Mass.1995).

Other "Business Torts"

There are several fields of the law in the business milieu that involve the imposition of economic injury on a person who is therefore entitled to monetary damages or an injunction against continuing the conduct. These remedies were derived essentially from the philosophy of tort law, but they have now been thoroughly merged into the legal regulation of the process of competition in business activities or the law governing the relationship of business and labor. As a result, the influence of the tort origins has decreased substantially and they have become separate fields of the law developing through statutory provisions, administrative regulations and their own independent concepts. This means that they are no longer covered in torts casebooks or treatises but have their own distinct casebooks and treatises. Only a brief reference can be made here.

1. *Copyright and Patent Infringement.* Article I, § 8, cl. 8 of the U.S. Constitution provides that Congress has the power to "promote the Progress of Science and useful Arts by securing for limited Times to Authors and Inventors the exclusive Right to their respective Writings and Discoveries." Congress has exercised this power. See 17 U.S.C.A. §§ 101 et seq. (copyright); 35 U.S.C.A. §§ 1 et seq. (patents).

There are, of course, unsettled problems. Particularly relevant is the issue of federal preemption. See, for example, the twin cases of Sears, Roebuck & Co. v. Stiffel Co., 376 U.S. 225 (1964); and Compco Corp. v. Day–Brite Lighting, Inc., 376 U.S. 234 (1964), holding that there can be no common law protection of the functional design of a product. If it is capable of being patented, compliance with the statutory procedure is necessary; if it is not, it cannot be protected by the common law. "To allow a state by use of its law of unfair competition to prevent the copying of an article which represents too slight an advance to be patented would be to permit the state to block off from the public something which federal law has said belongs to the public." However, provided the torts are not construed to offer patent-like protection, they are not pre-empted. In Rodine PLC v. Seagate Technology, Inc., 174 F.3d 1294, 1306 (Fed.Cir.1999), the court held that tortious interference and unfair competition protect separate interests: they protect business relationships from wrongful interference or attack "unethical and oppressive business practices."

2. *Trade Marks and Trade Names.* A considerable body of learning has developed regarding trade marks and trade names. Much of it has been common law, but the Lanham Act (Trademark Act of 1946, 15 U.S.C.A. §§ 1051 et seq.) has extensively revised and reorganized it.

3. *Trade Secrets.* Much of this is common law, but there are state statutes and a Uniform Trade Secrets Act. Issues of federal preemption give difficulty here, too.

4. *Unfair Competition.* The three previous topics have often been combined under the generic term "unfair competition," which is also inclusive of such matters as "passing off" of one's goods as another's or misappropriation of another's ideas, news items or unpublished writings. State statutes covering unfair trade practices, false advertising and similar matters are included.

5. *Other Statutes Involving Regulation of Business.* Federal statutes include The Sherman Antitrust Act, 15 U.S.C.A. §§ 1–7 (conspiracy in restraint of trade, attempt to monopolize), Clayton Antitrust Act, 15 U.S.C.A. §§ 12–27 (restraints and monopolies); Robinson–Patman Act, 15 U.S.C.A. §§ 12 et seq. (price discrimination); Federal Trade Commission Act, 15 U.S.C.A. §§ 41–58 et seq., and regulations. There are also various state antitrust statutes.

6. *Labor Law.* Many of the early cases on tortious interference with existing or prospective economic advantage involved contests between employers and employees. Today these have all been incorporated into the law of labor relations, both federal and state, and much of it statutory or based on administrative regulations or rulings.

7. *Civil RICO.* The Racketeer Influenced and Corrupt Organizations Act, 18 U.S.C.A. §§ 1961–1968, is primarily a criminal statute. However, Congress has provided a private cause of action for its breach under § 1964(c). Because of its potent remedies—treble damages and attorney's fees—the statutory cause of action has been increasingly asserted, especially in light of the Section's wide interpretation by the United States Supreme Court in Sedima, S.P.R.L. v. Imrex Co., Inc., 473 U.S. 479 (1985). The action is more thoroughly canvassed infra in Chapter 23.

2. FAMILY RELATIONS

Nash v. Baker

Court of Appeals of Oklahoma, 1974.
522 P.2d 1335.

ROMANG, JUDGE. The appellants, hereinafter referred to as plaintiffs, are five minor children whose mother, Marian Nash, brings this appeal as their natural guardian and next friend. The appellee is hereinafter referred to as the defendant.

Marian Nash filed the petition in her own right and as next friend of the infant plaintiffs, alleging that after Marian Nash and James Nash had been husband and wife for about 18 years and had five children (the minor plaintiffs) of that union, the defendant, a wealthy widow, who knew or should have known of the marriage and children, lured James Nash, the husband and father, away from the plaintiffs by providing said James Nash with a finer home, sexual charms, and other inducements. The plaintiff Marian Nash sought to recover actual and punitive damages in her own right for the alienation of her husband's affections, loss of consortium, and loss of a prospective increased standard of living. In addition, as next friend of her children, she sought recovery of actual and punitive damages under the common law for alienation of their father's affections, interference with their family relationships, and "loss of the society, affection, assistance, moral support and guidance" of their father. The petition also alleged adultery by the defendant with said James Nash.

The trial court sustained the defendant's demurrer as to each of the minor plaintiffs' asserted causes of action and overruled it as to Marian Nash's suit in her own right. The latter suit was tried to a jury, resulting in a verdict for the defendant. The only questions before this court deal with whether any cause of action may be maintained on behalf of the minor children of a marriage, against a woman who entices away their father from the marital home.

The sole question remaining is whether * * * a minor child has in Oklahoma a common law right to sue a third person whose luring away of the father breaks up the parents' marriage and deprives the child of the father's society and guidance. The common law recognized no such right in the child. That the injured spouse has an action for alienation of affections, loss of consortium, or criminal conversation does not require that a cause of action be given to the child. * * * The plaintiffs cite Prosser, Law of Torts 908 (3d ed. 1964) which, although recognizing that the majority of those jurisdictions which passed on the question have denied the child an action, predicts that in the future additional jurisdictions will allow his action. On the other hand, * * * modern statutes abolishing causes of action for alienation of affections, breach of promise to marry, and related actions; the increasing failure of marriages, reportedly more than one in three ending in absolute divorce or permanent separation; and the recent liberalization of divorce in several more states, including a ground or grounds not based on "fault"; and the increase in the number of children whose parents have divorced and remarried; may well prevent the future development predicted by the late Professor Prosser. In addition, there may be a growing feeling that very often the "fault" leading to the breakup of a marriage may not be readily determinable in court, and that the "fault" which caused one spouse to be attracted to a third person was not the magnetism of such third person, but that of an emotional vacuum in the home.

Affirmed.

NOTES AND QUESTIONS

1. The law of torts has been concerned not only with the protection of property and associated interests, but also with what may be called "relational" interests founded upon the relation in which plaintiff stands toward one or more third persons. W. Prosser and Keeton, Torts § 124 (5th ed. 1984); Green, Relational Interests, 29 Ill.L.Rev. 460 (1934). Much development in this area has been based on claims alleging an interference with a family relationship. At early common law, most claims were brought by husbands for loss of economic services of a wife or child. Today there is potential for a claim to be brought by any member of the family unit and the focus is more likely to be on loss of intangible matters such as companionship or affection. The concentration here is on modern remedies.

Claims Based on Intentional Interference

2. *Alienation of Affections.*

A. *Husband and Wife.* In some states today a spouse may bring a claim against a third party for alienation of affections. The plaintiff must show that the spouse's mental attitude and conjugal kindness were converted by the defendant. Although a change in the alienated spouse's state of mind must be evidenced by external conduct, most courts hold that it is not necessary to show an act of adultery. In point of fact, the defendant need not be a romantic rival. Some cases are brought against relatives who may be privileged to act when they reasonably believe it to be in the best interest of the person "alienated." See Koehler v. Koehler, 248 Iowa 144, 79 N.W.2d 791 (1956); Bishop v. Glazener, 245 N.C. 592, 96 S.E.2d 870 (1957).

B. *Parent and Child.* If a child is abducted or defendant intentionally deprives a parent of a child's economic services, precedent supports a claim. Most courts have declined, however, to create an alienation-of-affections remedy either on behalf of a parent for loss of a child or a child for loss of a parent. Bartanus v. Lis, 332 Pa.Super. 48, 480 A.2d 1178 (1984) (finding no action for parent absent proof of elements in intentional infliction of emotional distress). A father of an adult daughter is accused by that daughter of sexually molesting her many years before when she was a child. The daughter has "recovered" those memories while in psychotherapy. The father denies these accusations and asserts that the therapist has negligently implanted false memories in his child. Does the father have an action for interference with family relationship against the therapist? Doe v. McKay, 700 N.E.2d 1018 (Ill.1998) (finding no action in intentional interference).

3. *Criminal Conversation.* This is a tort in which a married person may recover both compensatory and punitive damages by proving that the spouse and the defendant engaged in sexual intercourse. The action became in the 17th Century preliminary to divorce proceedings and, thus, divorce for adultery was introduced into the Law. How should damages be computed? Where both an action for criminal conversation and alienation of affection are pleaded, the jury should be instructed not to allow recovery for the same loss under both. When the crime of adultery has been abolished by the legislature or has been reduced to a misdemeanor with a slight fine, should this affect the tort remedy? See Jasterbowski v. Michos, 44 Ohio App.2d 201, 337 N.E.2d 627 (1975); Swartz v. Steele, 42 Ohio App.2d 1, 325 N.E.2d 910 (1974); Neal v. Neal, 125 Idaho App. 627, 873 P.2d 881 (1993) (describing the action as an anachronism). Suppose the defendant shows that the plaintiff's spouse was the person who invited and procured the event. Should this be a defense? At early common law it was not, but these decisions were predicated on the outdated premise that the interest was of the husband's alone and his wife's consent could not prejudice it.

4. *Other Intentional Torts.* At common law a husband could bring an action for "enticement" or abduction of his wife. A parent could bring a claim for seduction of a minor child, an action to some extent analogous to criminal conversation. The action was not necessarily confined to claims based on an injury to female children. See White v. Nellis, 31 N.Y. 405 (1865) (alluding in dictum to "debased women who lure * * * innocent boy(s) * * * "). In general, these torts are only of historical interest today. On occasion, however, new theories of intentional interference with family relations may arise.

5. *Statutory Abolition of Actions.* Beginning in the late 1930's, legislatures in a substantial number of states have abolished tort actions based on intentional interference with family relations that carry an accusation of sexual behavior. See, e.g., Ala.Code § 6–5–330; Md.Code Ann., Cts. & Jud.Proc. § 5–801; N.Y.Civ. Rights Law § 80–a. The statutes, known as "Anti–Heart Balm" laws, have generally withstood constitutional challenge. Do you think there should be an action against a spouse or lover for intentional infliction of emotional distress? See Speer v. Dealy, 242 Neb. 542, 495 N.W.2d 911 (1993). What policy reasons support such actions? If a state has an "Anti–Heart Balm" statute, should a child's claim for alienation of affections be automatically barred? See Russick v. Hicks, 85 F.Supp. 281 (Mich. 1949). The statutes are collected in H. Clark, Domestic Relations 267 (1968).

Claims Based on Negligent Interference

6. At common law a husband was legally entitled to his wife's earnings and services. Courts protected the husband's right to these "assets" against negligent interference by third parties. The action is known as one for loss of consortium. The husband also may be able to recover general damages for loss of companionship and sexual relations. Because a wife had no legal interest in her husband's personal property, she was denied a claim.

7. With the growth of legal equality between the spouses, it might be anticipated that the cause of action for loss of consortium would disappear. Instead, beginning with Hitaffer v. Argonne Co., Inc., 183 F.2d 811 (D.C.Cir.1950), cert. denied 340 U.S. 852 (1950), courts in many states have permitted both spouses to bring a claim for loss of consortium. See, e.g., Rodriguez v. Bethlehem Steel Corp.,

12 Cal.3d 382, 525 P.2d 669, 115 Cal.Rptr. 765 (1974); Millington v. Southeastern Elevator Co., 22 N.Y.2d 498, 239 N.E.2d 897, 293 N.Y.S.2d 305 (1968). The emphasis on the damage element in the claim has shifted away from economic loss to intangibles such as loss of companionship and affection.

8.   Can the claim stand where the marriage has not been formalized? Authority is divided. For a decision insisting on the existence of a formalized marriage, see Elden v. Sheldon, 46 Cal.3d 267, 758 P.2d 582, 250 Cal.Rptr. 254 (1988).

9.   Although loss of consortium could be viewed as a wholly independent injury, most courts regard it as a derivative claim, subject to all defenses that could be asserted against the spouse who was physically injured. See Pioneer Constr. Co. v. Bergeron, 170 Colo. 474, 462 P.2d 589 (1969); Tollett v. Mashburn, 291 F.2d 89 (8th Cir.1961). However, it has been held that a statute of limitations defense relating to the underlying action does not apply to the consortium action, Barton–Malow Co., Inc. v. Wilburn, 547 N.E.2d 1123 (Ind.App.1989), affirmed on this point, 556 N.E.2d 324 (Ind.1990).

10.   Courts have generally declined to allow claims for pure loss of companionship when a child seeks a recovery of this type from a defendant who injured his parent. See Hankins v. Derby, 211 N.W.2d 581 (Iowa 1973); In re Air Crash at Dallas/Fort Worth Airport, 856 F.2d 28 (5th Cir.1988); cf. Ferriter v. Daniel O'Connell's Sons, Inc., 381 Mass. 507, 413 N.E.2d 690 (1980); Barton–Malow Co., Inc. v. Wilburn, 547 N.E.2d 1123 (Ind.App.1989) (wherein Hoffman J. dissenting, noted that since 1980 only six jurisdictions other than Massachusetts have recognized the loss of parental consortium action). Is the claim more justifiable if limited to minors or handicapped children? Belcher v. Goins, 184 W.Va. 395, 400 S.E.2d 830 (1990) (18–year–old child not entitled to consortium claim). Claims by parents solely for loss of companionship of their injured children have received similar treatment. Butler v. Chrestman, 264 So.2d 812 (Miss.1972); Ekalo v. Constructive Service Corp. of America, 46 N.J. 82, 215 A.2d 1 (1965). But see Shockley v. Prier, 66 Wis.2d 394, 225 N.W.2d 495 (1975) (medical malpractice) and Gallimore v. Children's Hosp. Med. Ctr., 67 Ohio 3d 244, 617 N.E.2d 1052 (1993) (allowing a parent to maintain an action against tortfeasor who intentionally or negligently causes physical injury to parent's minor child). Is a parent's claim more deserving?

CHAPTER XXIII

TORTS IN THE AGE OF STATUTES

The Twentieth Century saw an explosion in the number of statutes enacted by state legislatures and by Congress. The common law of torts is now riddled with statutory inroads. Legislative change has been noted in contributory negligence, contribution between tortfeasors, the abrogation of immunities, limitation periods, and many other topics touched on in the Torts course. This chapter examines those instances where statutes may impliedly or expressly provide or take away a remedy in tort. It is predictable that the century upon which we now embark will witness no diminution in the pace of legislative enactment. Accordingly, the place of tort law within that legislative explosion will continue to present a challenge.

1. IMPLIED RIGHTS OF ACTION AND STATUTORY DUTIES

Burnette v. Wahl

Supreme Court of Oregon, 1978.
284 Or. 705, 588 P.2d 1105.

HOLMAN, JUSTICE. Three identical cases have been consolidated for appeal. Plaintiffs are five minor children aged two to eight who, through their guardian, are bringing actions against their mothers for emotional and psychological injury caused by failure of defendant-mothers to perform their parental duties to plaintiffs. Plaintiffs appeal from orders of dismissal entered after demurrers were sustained to the complaints and plaintiffs refused to plead further.

Oregon Supreme Court
Seated: Holman, Denecke, C.J., Tongue
Standing: Lent, Howell, Bryson, Linde

The complaints allege that plaintiffs are in the custody of the Children's Services Division of the Department of Human Resources of the State of Oregon and are wards of Klamath County Juvenile Court.

The complaints are substantially identical, each one being in three counts. Among these counts are strewn various allegations of parental failure upon which the causes of action rest. They are:

"1. Since [date], defendant intentionally, wilfully, maliciously and with cruel disregard of the consequences failed to provide plaintiff with care, custody, parental nurturance, affection, comfort, companionship, support, regular contact and visitation.

"2. She has failed in violation of ORS 109.010[1] to maintain plaintiff, who, due to * * * age and indigency, is poor and unable to work to maintain * * * self.

"3. She has abandoned plaintiff by deserting the child with intent to abandon * * * and with intent to abdicate all responsibility for * * * care and raising, in violation of ORS 163.535.[2]

"4. She has neglected the plaintiff by negligently leaving * * * unattended in or at a place for such period of time as would have been likely to

---

1.   "ORS 109.010 Duty of Support. Parents are bound to maintain their children who are poor and unable to work to maintain themselves; and children are bound to maintain their parents in like circumstances."

2.   "ORS 163.535 Abandonment of a Child. (1) A person commits the crime of abandonment of a child if, being a parent, lawful guardian or other person lawfully charged with the care or custody of a child under 15 years of age, he deserts the child in any place with intent to abandon it.

"(2) Abandonment of a child is a Class C felony."

endanger the health or welfare of the plaintiff, in violation of ORS 163.545.[3]

"5. She has refused or neglected without lawful excuse to provide support for plaintiff, in violation of ORS 163.555.[4]

"6. Defendant has maliciously, intentionally, and with cruel disregard of the consequences, deserted and abandoned her child.

"7. Defendant has alienated the affections of the plaintiff in that she has intentionally, wilfully and maliciously abandoned, deserted, neglected and failed to maintain regular contact or visitation, or to provide for the plaintiff and has deprived plaintiff of the love, care, affection and comfort to which plaintiff is entitled."

It is apparent that the first allegation is general in nature and is intended to be all-encompassing. The second, third, fourth and fifth allege violation of statutory duties in which abandonment and desertion comprise the central theme. The sixth allegation is one of abandonment and desertion purportedly based on common law. The seventh allegation is an attempt to allege alienation of affections. Although these allegations of parental failure allege lack of support and physical care along with affectional neglect, from the allegations of injury in the complaint and the statements made in plaintiffs' brief, it appears that the injuries claimed are solely emotional and psychological.

Preliminary to a more detailed discussion, it should be noted that these claims of parental failure are different from those tort claims usually made upon behalf of children against parents. The adjudicated cases concern physical or emotional injuries resulting from physical acts inflicted upon children such as beatings and rapes and from automobile accidents. Plaintiffs admit they can cite no cases permitting them to recover from their parents for solely emotional or psychological damage resulting from failure to support, nurture and care for them.

The legislature, recognizing the necessity of parental nurture, support and physical care for children, has enacted a vast array of laws for the purpose of protecting or vindicating those rights. These are much more extensive and all-inclusive than are those statutes alleged to have been violated in plaintiffs' allegations of tortious conduct.[5]

---

3. "ORS 163.545 Child Neglect. (1) A person having custody or control of a child under 10 years of age commits the crime of child neglect if, with criminal negligence, he leaves the child unattended in or at any place for such period of time as may be likely to endanger the health or welfare of such child.

"(2) Child neglect is a Class A misdemeanor."

4. ORS 163.555 Criminal Nonsupport. (1) A person commits the crime of criminal nonsupport if, being the parent, lawful guardian or other person lawfully charged with the support of a child under 18 years of age, born in or out of wedlock, he refuses or neglects without lawful excuse to provide support for such child.

" * * *

"(3) Criminal nonsupport is a Class C felony."

5. Among these laws are ORS 108.040, providing an action against both parents for family necessities; ORS 108.110 *et seq.*, which allow a petition for the support of children to be brought against a parent by the other

ORS ch. 418 establishes extensive provisions for aid to dependent children, and it is under the provisions of this chapter and as wards of the juvenile court that plaintiffs are presently attempting to have their needs met. [The court discusses specific sections of the chapter.]

We recognize that this is not a proceeding to secure parental nurturing, support and physical care for plaintiffs, but rather an action for psychological injury claimed to have been caused by the absence of these services. However, the statutory enactments demonstrate that the legislature has put its mind to the deprivations of which plaintiff children are alleged to be victims and has attempted to remedy such situations by enacting a vast panoply of procedures, both civil and criminal, to insure that children receive proper nurturing, support and physical care. It has never undertaken to establish, however, a cause of action for damages for any emotional injury to the child which may have been caused by a parent's refusal to provide these services. This failure of the legislature to act is significant because this is not a field of recovery which has heretofore been recognized by courts and it would therefore be natural for it to have provided such a remedy if it thought it was wise in view of the social problem it attempts to solve and the statutory provisions it has enacted for that purpose. It has had no difficulty in the past in creating new causes of action for persons aggrieved by conditions which it is attempting to rectify. Examples are the creation of causes of action, including punitive damages, in aid of enforcing ethics in the marketplace, ORS 646.638; actions for compensatory and punitive damages for unlawful discrimination by places of public accommodation, ORS 30.680, and by employers, ORS 659.030 and 659.121; and actions for double and triple damages for timber trespass, ORS 105.810 and 105.815.

The establishment by courts of a civil cause of action based on a criminal or regulatory statute is not premised upon legislative intent to create such an action. It is obvious that had the legislature intended a civil action it would have provided for one, as legislatures many times do. Therefore, the underlying assumption is that it was not intended that the statute create any civil obligation or afford civil protection against the injuries which it was designed to prevent. When neither the statute nor the common law authorizes an action and the statute does not expressly deny it, the court should recognize that it is being asked to bring into existence a new type of tort liability on the basis of its own appraisal of the policy considerations involved. If a court decides to create a cause of action for the act or omission which violates the statute, the interest which is invaded derives its protection solely from the court although the legislative action in

parent or a state agency for the support of the children; ORS ch. 110, providing both criminal and civil means for reciprocal enforcement between states of the right of support for children; ORS 411.120(4), providing for assistance to dependent children; ORS ch. 416, establishing the relative responsibility law (specifically see ORS 416.090, 416.100, and 416.220 for the means of enforcement); ORS ch. 418, providing for child welfare services (specifically see ORS 418.135(1) and 418.460, concerning enforcement of parental duties); ORS ch. 419, establishing juvenile courts (specifically see ORS 419.513, 419.515, and 419.517 concerning enforcement of support of children by parents).

branding the act or omission as culpable is taken into consideration by the court in deciding whether a common law action should be established. If a civil cause of action based upon a statute is established by a court, it is because the court, not the legislature, believes it is necessary and desirable to further vindicate the right or to further enforce the duty created by statute.

Because it is plain to the legislature that it could have created the civil liability and it has not, courts must look carefully not only at the particular statute establishing the right or duty but at all statutes which might bear either directly or indirectly on the legislative purpose. If there is any chance that invasion into the field by the court's establishment of a civil cause of action might interfere with the total legislative scheme, courts should err on the side of non-intrusion because it is always possible for the legislature to establish such a civil cause of action if it desires. Courts have no omnipotence in the field of planning, particularly social planning of the kind involved here. Courts should exercise restraint in fields in which the legislature has attempted fairly comprehensive social regulation.

There is no doubt but that the statutory provisions previously cited show a strong state policy of requiring the kind of parental nurturing, support and physical care of children which the defendants here are alleged to have denied their children. As previously indicated, it does not follow as a matter of course that it would be wise or judicious to vindicate that policy by a tort action for damages by children against their mothers. The state also has other policies within its statutory plan of which such a cause of action might well be destructive, particularly the policy of reuniting abandoned children with their parents, if possible. * * *

It is recognized by the statutory scheme that in some instances the reestablishment of a biological family is impossible and it therefore provides for a proceeding to terminate parental rights in order that a new family unit for the child may be formed. * * *

It is significant that plaintiffs' complaints do not allege that proceedings for the termination of the defendants' parental rights have taken place. In such circumstances, it would be exceedingly unwise for this court to step in and to initiate a new and heretofore unrecognized cause of action in a field of social planning to which the legislature has devoted a great deal of time and effort in evolving what appears to be an all-encompassing plan. Those persons designated by statute for aiding the plaintiffs in these cases have not yet taken the step for which the plan provides when there is no longer any hope of reestablishing these children in a family unit with their mothers. Tort actions such as the present ones might well be destructive of any plans the social agencies and the juvenile court might have for these children. It is inappropriate for this court to insert a new cause of action into the picture.

* * * Plaintiffs are unable to point to any literature in the field of child care or family planning which advocates an action for money damages to vindicate a right of the kind asserted here.

In addition, there is a limitation to the extent to which use may be made of tort actions for the purpose of accomplishing social aims. If there is ever a field in which juries and general trial courts are ill equipped to do social engineering, it is in the realm of the emotional relationship between mother and child. It is best we leave such matters to other fields of endeavor. There are certain kinds of relationships which are not proper fodder for tort litigation, and we believe this to be one of them. There are probably as many children who have been damaged in some manner by their parents' failure to meet completely their physical, emotional and psychological needs as there are people. A tort action for damages by emotionally deprived persons against their parents is, in our opinion, not going to solve the social problem in the same manner in which the legislature is attempting to solve it.

In addition to the contention that defendants should be liable for civil damages because of their violation of criminal and regulatory statutes, plaintiffs also contend that defendants are responsible because of the infliction of severe emotional distress by intentional acts. Plaintiffs allege that defendants intentionally deserted and abandoned them; however, they do not contend that defendants deserted them for the purpose of inflicting emotional harm upon them. We recognize that this tort usually also encompasses the infliction of emotional harm under circumstances from which a reasonable person would conclude that harm was almost certain to result. We believe this latter rationale is inapplicable as between parents and children. If it were otherwise, the children of divorced parents would almost always have an action for emotional damage against their parents. Divorce has become a way of life with almost certain emotional trauma of a greater or lesser degree to the children from the legal dissolution of the family and the resultant absence of at least one of the parents and sometimes both.

In addition, plaintiffs contend that the common law tort of alienation of affections is applicable. They argue that because such a cause of action is intended to compensate one spouse for the intentional alienation of the other spouse's affections by a third party, and that because in one case, Daily v. Parker, 152 F.2d 174 (7th Cir.1945), this cause of action has been extended to the children, it should exist against the parent himself. The statement of the argument is its refutation. Also, the tort of alienation of affections has recently been abolished by the legislature, Oregon Laws 1975, ch. 562, § 1.

Plaintiffs generally contend that without respect to previously recognized theories of recovery, we should recognize a new tort of parental desertion. For all the reasons previously given in declining to use recognized theories of recovery, we also decline this invitation.

The judgment of the trial court is affirmed.

Tongue, Justice, concurring. * * * The doctrine of intrafamily tort immunity has been previously abandoned by this court with respect to intentional torts resulting in physical injuries. In my opinion, however, it does not follow that the doctrine should also be abandoned with respect to intrafamily torts resulting in "mental and emotional injuries" for reasons stated by the majority, although not in the context of intrafamily tort immunity.

LENT, JUSTICE, concurring in part; dissenting in part. I agree with the majority that the asserted cause of action for alienation of affections must fall. I further agree with the majority that from a technical, pleading standpoint plaintiff * * * has failed to state a cause of action for "outrageous conduct" for failure to state that defendant intended to cause the severe emotional distress described in the complaint.

In dissenting, I have joined in the dissent of Linde, J. but desire to add some additional reasons for finding that a civil cause of action for damages should obtain. * * *

At present there are over one-third of a million children in the United States who are dependent upon the community for their parental care. In Oregon during fiscal year 1976–77 the number of dependent children was over 6,000. The future is bleak for the vast majority of these children, at least those in the position of the plaintiffs, whose parents have abandoned them permanently. Only approximately five percent of such children are ever adopted and placed in a permanent parental situation.

* * *

In view of the costs, both tangible and intangible to society of caring for these dependent children who have well been termed the "orphans of the living" and the character of defendant's conduct as admitted by the demurrer, I believe defendant should shoulder so much of the financial burden as her resources permit. Further, I would hold that the emotional harm which the demurrer admits plaintiff has suffered is such as the community should conclude is monetarily compensable. As stated in Justice Linde's dissent plaintiff has alleged a cause of action.

LINDE, JUSTICE, dissenting. * * * The simple issue before us is whether a young child who allegedly has suffered severe mental and emotional injuries as a result of being deserted and abandoned by a parent acting "maliciously, intentionally, and with cruel disregard of the consequences"—conduct which the legislature has declared to be a crime—may upon proper proof hold the parent responsible in damages for these severe mental and emotional injuries. Contrary to the majority opinion, I believe that these allegations, which plead a violation of ORS 163.535, state a claim on which a child so injured may go to trial.[1]

In reaching this conclusion, I differ with the majority's treatment of its two crucial premises: (1) the source of civil liability for violation of criminal

---

1.   ORS 163.535:

(1) A person commits the crime of abandonment of a child if, being a parent, lawful guardian or other person lawfully charged with the care or custody of a child under 15 years of age, he deserts the child in any place with intent to abandon it.

(2) Abandonment of a child is a Class C felony.

Since the complaint alleges at least one cause of action, the validity of the other theories of recovery contained in the complaint need not be considered in overruling the demurrer. * * *

laws, and (2) the significance to be accorded to Oregon's child protection laws.

Liability for Damages from Prohibited Conduct. It should be noted at the outset that awarding civil damages for violations of prohibitory laws is not an uncommon or radical theory of recovery. The question when the victim of criminal or otherwise prohibited conduct may recover damages from the wrongdoer is increasingly important in many areas of law. In a number of recent cases the issue has occupied the United States Supreme Court and the federal courts, whose greater attention to statutory premises of liability probably reflects the fact that these courts are not empowered to formulate common law torts unrelated to the Constitution or laws of the United States. [C] Thus the Supreme Court has also referred to potential civil liability under state law as one factor in determining whether such liability arises implicitly from an act of Congress. [C] Apart from these differences, however, federal and state courts face the same question when prohibitory legislation implies a civil liability toward those for whose protection the legislation is enacted and when it does not. The answer depends first on whether a legislative policy to allow or to deny a civil remedy can be discerned in the text or the legislative history of the statute. If neither can be discerned, then it depends on whether the plaintiff belongs to the class for whose special protection the statute was enacted and whether the civil remedy would contribute to or perhaps detract from achieving the object of the legislation. [C]

This court has had a number of recent occasions to undertake this analysis. In Davis v. Billy's Con–Teena, Inc., Or., 587 P.2d 75 (1978), we based potential liability for damages caused by unlawfully selling alcohol to minors on a stated legislative purpose to protect the safety and health of other persons beyond the minors themselves. In Farris v. United States Fidelity, Or., 587 P.2d 1015 (1978), on the other hand, we found that the statutory penalties provided for violations of the insurance code precluded inferring a damage claim for emotional suffering or punitive damages for the violation in question. O'Toole v. Franklin, 279 Or. 513, 569 P.2d 561 (1977), recognized that a knowing violation of a provision of the Oregon State Bar act could give rise to a damage action by a member of the class for whose protection it was enacted. And only this week we found in a prohibition against discharging an employee for claiming workers' compensation a public policy that supported a civil claim for damages by a worker so discharged. Brown v. Transcon Lines, Or., 588 P.2d 1087 (1978). The American Law Institute's Restatement (Second) of Torts, Tentative Draft No. 23, 1977, lists a number of other illustrations in its discussion of proscriptive or prescriptive statutes as sources of civil liability.[2] Sometimes

---

2. Restatement (Second) of Torts § 874A (Tentative Draft No. 23, 1977):

"3. A statute makes it a crime to have sexual intercourse with a previously chaste female under the age of 17, even though she factually consents. The court may hold that the tort action of battery will lie, regardless of the consent.

"4. A federal act makes it a crime to intercept and divulge a telephone conversation. The court may 'assimilate' this conduct a common law court will assimilate the statutory duty into an existing principle of liability, as for instance the negligence action in Davis v. Billy's Con–Teena, supra, but that is not always so. See Restatement (Second) of Torts, Tentative Draft No. 23, 1977, § 874A, Comment f.[3]

Of course, the question of civil recovery for breach of a statutory duty can be an issue only when the legislation itself is silent on the point. If the legislature either provides for a civil remedy or clearly indicates that it means other provisions for enforcement to be complete and exclusive, there is nothing for a court to decide. It would help to clarify not only private rights but also the particular public policy if the legislative assembly as a routine step in the drafting of penal legislation faced the question of its civil consequences, or alternatively, if it were to enact a general formula for determining these consequences when a statute is otherwise silent.

Unfortunately legislatures do neither, but nothing can be inferred from that fact, given the existing practice of recognizing such consequences when the nature of the protective statute appears to imply them. The majority overstates the case when it equates legislative silence with an "underlying assumption * * * that it was not intended that the statute create any civil obligation or afford civil protection against the injuries which it was designed to prevent." Nor does it follow, when a court finds that the duty created or defined by the statute does imply a civil cause of action, that the court is engaged in pronouncing common law. The difference between a new common law theory of recovery in tort or otherwise and a civil claim based on a statute is obvious: The latter claim stands and falls with the statute from which it is implied, and it will disappear as soon as the amendment or repeal of the statute indicates a reconsideration of the previous public policy. Thus, while a court is often left at large to divine the implications of a statutory policy, it is equally an overstatement to say that the court simply makes its own judgment whether to "create a cause of

---

to the torts of defamation and invasion of the right of privacy and grant damages. * * *

"6. A statute makes it a crime to utter insulting and abusive language to another publicly. The court may hold that a civil action will lie, amounting to the intentional infliction of emotional distress. * * *

"8. A statute makes it a crime to seduce a woman under promises of marriage. The court may hold that this conduct gives rise to a tort action for damages. * * *

"14. A statute imposes a criminal penalty upon an employer who, upon request of a former employee, fails to supply a 'service letter' providing details of his service. The court may supply a civil action for damages for violation.

3. As early as 1934, and until 1965, the original Restatement (Second) of Torts, § 286, stated:

"The violation of a legislative enactment by doing a prohibited act, or by failing to do a required act, makes the actor liable for an invasion of an interest of another if:

"(a) the intent of the enactment is exclusively or in part to protect an interest of the other as an individual; and

"(b) the interest invaded is one which the enactment is intended to protect; and,

"(c) where the enactment is intended to protect an interest from a particular hazard, the invasion of the interests results from that hazard; and,

"(d) the violation is a legal cause of the invasion, and the other has not so conducted himself as to disable himself from maintaining an action."

action" deriving "solely" from the court's own appraisal whether additional protection for the claimed interest is "necessary and desirable."[4]

The relevance of criminal or regulatory laws to civil liability is more complex than merely being an element "taken into consideration by the court in deciding whether a common law action should be established," as the majority puts it. Such laws express distinct kinds of policies. First, the most familiar criminal laws are redefinitions of common-law crimes against private persons or property. They have equally familiar civil analogues in common-law torts. Only "victimless crimes" and crimes deemed to endanger the public as a collectivity, such as bribery, counterfeiting, or tax evasion, are likely to lack a corresponding civil liability. Violations of game laws or environmental protection laws may be other examples. Second, regulatory laws specify standards of socially responsible conduct for the protection of persons endangered by the conduct. While the tort standard may go further, we have recognized the force of the criminal or regulatory standard in negligence cases even when it was set by agencies or local governments that presumably could not themselves create civil liability whether or not they had such an intent. [Cc] Third, governmental sanctions, penal or otherwise, may be enacted to add governmental enforcement to the recognized obligations of a relationship existing apart from the legislation. In such a situation the "underlying assumption," to use the majority's phrase, is hardly that the penal sanction makes the civil obligation unnecessary. Rather, the statute shows that the obligation is considered of such importance that it deserves enforcement by public prosecution.

The Child Protection Laws. It can hardly be questioned that a statute like 163.535, which makes it a crime intentionally to desert and abandon a child, is of the third kind. It and the related sections did not enact a novel prohibition against parental neglect for the convenience of the general public or the protection of taxpayers. They enacted a legislative definition and public enforcement of certain minimal obligations of an existing relationship. Jurisprudentially it might be said that parents have a duty not to abandon and desert their young children because ORS 163.535 makes it a crime to do so, but a legislator would surely think ORS 163.535 should make it a crime to abandon and desert a child because the parent's existing duty—the duty to the child, not to the state—deserved governmental reenforcement. It is the parent's duty thus recognized under Oregon law that plaintiffs invoke in these cases.

---

4. Long ago, Chief Justice Harlan F. Stone deplored the reluctance of "modern courts [to] resort to standards of conduct set up by legislation" as sources of liability or other consequences beyond those provided by the legislation. "The statute was looked upon as in the law but not of it, a formal rule to be obeyed, it is true, since it is the command of the sovereign, but to be obeyed grudgingly, by construing it narrowly and treating it as though it did not exist for any purpose other than that embraced within the strict construction of its words. It is difficult to appraise the consequences of the perpetuation of incongruities and injustices in the law by this habit of narrow construction of statutes and by the failure to recognize that, as recognitions of social policy, they are as significant and rightly as much a part of the law, as the rules declared by judges." Stone, The Common Law in the United States, 50 Harv. L.Rev. 4 (1936).

The majority does not really deny that ORS 163.535 constitutes such a legislative recognition and reenforcement of the parent's private obligation to the child, not of some socially convenient behavior. Rather, the majority would deny a remedy for the intentional breach of this obligation on the ground that other public policies militate against such a remedy. Upon examination, the majority's statutory citations refer to the single policy of maintaining and preserving the position of the child within a functioning family as long as this is possible. Without in any way questioning that this is indeed the state's public policy, I do not agree that it supports the conclusion that the legislature meant to deny the child a remedy for injuries from a parent's unlawful acts.

First, it must be kept in mind what conduct violates ORS 163.535. The statute makes it a felony to desert one's child with intent to abandon it. Of course, we have no evidence of the actual facts in these cases, but the allegations are that defendants did desert and abandon their children "maliciously, intentionally, and with cruel disregard of the consequences." If that is true, the parents have in fact ended the family unit, so that solicitude about not impairing it by litigation may sacrifice the children's legal rights to a pious hope. Contrary to the majority, I do not believe it is this court's own judgment of the possible effects of litigation on family relations that matters (a question on which counsel was unable to enlighten us and that, if taken seriously, is hardly within judicial notice) but rather what view of these effects may be attributed to the legislature. More important for interpreting the legislative policy, however, the statute means that a district attorney or grand jury on the alleged facts could prosecute the parents for a felony. It is incongruous to hold that the legislature provided for a felony prosecution of parents who egregiously violate a duty toward their children, but that it meant to exclude civil actions on behalf of the maliciously abandoned children for fear of impairing the family unit. To hold that the plaintiffs cannot invoke this duty, one must assume a legislative policy that a deserted and abandoned child (or a guardian on its behalf) should ask a district attorney to seek the criminal punishment of the parent for this desertion, but that the child should have no claim that would be of any benefit to itself. That seems too unlikely a policy to attribute to the legislature without some showing that it was intended.

Moreover, the majority's premise proves too much. For purposes of the issue of law before us on these demurrers, it can be assumed that the plaintiffs have suffered actual, demonstrable injuries of a kind for which the law provides money damages against defendants other than parents, that defendants have assets from which these real injuries of the plaintiffs could be compensated, and that defendants caused these injuries by intentionally breaching a specific duty toward plaintiffs that is recognized in Oregon law. Perhaps the explanation for the majority's unwillingness to follow these assumptions to their conclusion is that the injuries alleged are psychological and emotional rather than physical. But if a civil remedy is denied on the majority's premise that it is precluded by a state policy of preserving family unity, that premise would apply equally to bar recovery of damages by a child crippled by physical abuse.[5] And despite the majority's reference to statutory proceedings for the termination of parental rights, it is at least questionable that a termination proceeding would create rights to a financial recovery to compensate for such very real and costly harm caused before the termination proceeding.

Although the majority does not say so, its premise is the equivalent of the doctrine of intrafamily tort immunity which Oregon has abandoned at least with respect to intentional torts, though attributed here to a supposed legislative policy subordinating legal claims of children against their parents to reliance on "protective social services." I perceive no such prescribed reliance on social services when parents who have deliberately mistreated their children in a manner made criminal by statute have the assets to be responsible for the harm caused thereby. In my view, plaintiffs have alleged at least one triable cause of action arising from an alleged intentional violation of duties recognized in ORS 163.535. Therefore, the demurrers should have been overruled.

LENT, J., joins in this dissent.

Nearing v. Weaver
Supreme Court of Oregon, 1983.
295 Ore. 702, 670 P.2d 137.

LINDE, JUSTICE: In 1977 the Legislative Assembly enacted an "Abuse Prevention Act" to strengthen legal protection for persons threatened with assault by a present or former spouse or a cohabitant. 1977 Or Laws ch 845. The means chosen for this purpose included the use of temporary restraining orders, injunctions, and temporary child custody orders, [C], and mandatory provisions for the warrantless arrest upon probable cause of a person believed to have violated such an order. [C] The present case requires us to decide whether officers who knowingly fail to enforce a judicial order under the 1977 act are potentially liable for resulting harm to the psychic and physical health of the intended beneficiaries of the judicial order, over defenses of official discretion and official immunity. We hold that these defenses do not preclude potential liability.

The case is on appeal from the circuit court's summary judgment for defendants, affirmed by the Court of Appeals. The Court of Appeals did not explain the basis for its decision.

---

5. Defendant presented a "parade of horribles" such as actions for psychological or emotional injury from receiving fewer Christmas gifts than a sibling and the like. I note this only to point out that the argument misses the point. The nature of the *breach of duty* in this case is fixed by ORS 163.535 and would not give rise to an expandable common law precedent. As far as the present issue is concerned, the case would be the same if a child had been deliberately abandoned in an unheated mountain cabin and lost a limb to frostbite or suffered other permanent injuries from lack of food or pneumonia.

Nothing is said here about claims based on other statutes invoked by plaintiffs that deal with general but unintentional neglect or nonsupport of children. The provision of alternative social services relied on by the majority may militate against implying a civil remedy for these less final and culpable violations of parental duty.

The complaint alleged the following facts. Plaintiffs are Henrietta Nearing and her two children, Robert and Jeanette, respectively 4 and 3 years old. Henrietta Nearing was separated from her husband in November 1979. On April 16, 1980, the husband entered plaintiffs' home without permission and struck Henrietta. She reported this to one of the defendant police officers, Martin Weaver, causing her husband to be arrested and charged with assault. The next day the circuit court issued an order restraining the husband from molesting plaintiffs or entering the family home. The order was served on the husband, and a copy of the order and proof of service were delivered to the police department of defendant City of St. Helens.

On May 12 and 13, 1980, the husband again entered plaintiffs' home without permission, first damaging the premises, and thereafter attempting to remove the children. Henrietta Nearing reported these incidents to defendant Weaver and asked him to arrest her husband because she was frightened of his violent proclivities. The officer confirmed the validity of the restraining order and the damage to plaintiffs' home but declined to arrest the husband on the ground that the officer had not seen the husband on the premises.

On three subsequent occasions in May, 1980, the husband returned to plaintiffs' address, sought entry to the home, and on the last occasion assaulted Henrietta's friend and damaged his van. When Henrietta reported this to defendants Weaver and Sauls on May 27, 1980, Weaver told her that the St. Helen's police would arrest the husband for violating the restraining order "because it was Robert Lee Nearing Sr.'s second offense," but no such action was taken. Two days later, on May 29, Nearing, Henrietta's husband, telephoned her and threatened to kill her friend. On June 1, Nearing intercepted the friend and plaintiffs in front of the home, repeated the threat, and assaulted the friend.

The complaint alleges the defendant officers' knowledge of the relevant facts. It further alleges that as a "proximate result" of their failure and refusal to arrest her husband, Henrietta has suffered "severe emotional distress and physical injuries" further described in the complaint and that the children have suffered "acute emotional distress," have been "upset," have had difficulty sleeping, and have suffered "psychological impairment."

Defendants denied the allegations except for the identity and status of defendants and pleaded affirmative defenses of immunity and discretion. Plaintiffs moved to strike the affirmative defenses and assigned denial of the motion as error on appeal.

Defendants' first contention in the circuit court and on appeal is that plaintiffs' action is one for damages for the negligent infliction of emotional distress, and that Oregon law does not allow recovery on this theory. Plaintiffs counter that Oregon law does allow recovery of damages for psychic or emotional harm when defendant's conduct infringes some legal right of the plaintiff independent of an ordinary tort claim for negligence. Plaintiffs are right. In a recent review of the cases, we stated:

"If there are few causes of action for psychic or emotional harm as such, the reason is not found in objections to monetary damages for harm of that nature. The reason may be found by focusing, not on the nature of the plaintiff's loss, but on the source and scope of the defendant's liability. This court has recognized common law liability for psychic injury alone when defendant's conduct was either intentional or equivalently reckless of another's feelings in a responsible relationship, or when it infringed some legally protected interest apart from causing the claimed distress, even when only negligently." Norwest v. Presbyterian Intercommunity Hospital, 293 Or. 543, at 558–59 (footnotes omitted).

The question, therefore, is whether plaintiffs pleaded an infringement by defendants of a legal right arising independently of the ordinary tort elements of a negligence action. It is clear that plaintiff did so.

The complaint alleges facts that, if proved, obliged the St. Helens police officers to respond to plaintiffs' call for protection against the exact kind of harassment by the elder Robert Nearing that is said to have occurred, and it alleges that the officers refused to enforce the restraining order in the manner prescribed by law. The duty defendants are alleged to have neglected therefore is not an ordinary common law duty of due care to avoid predictable harm to another. It is a specific duty imposed by statute for the benefit of individuals previously identified by a judicial order.

* * *

In this case a duty specifically towards these plaintiffs arises from the statute coupled with the court order. A plaintiff, of course, may plead and argue an action both under a theory of negligence and under another statutory or common law theory if he or she so chooses; actions based on injuries from defective products are a familiar example. When separate legal theories are said to require the same result on the same alleged facts, that contention should be made clear.

In this case, the issue below was the adequacy of defendants' defenses; no objection is raised to plaintiff's complaint. And plaintiff's reference to "negligence" in this case was immaterial to the alleged liability, if "negligence" is used in the sense of "carelessness" or "failure to use due care" rather than merely as a conventional legal totem, because the result would not be different if defendants had acted, or failed to act, willfully or intentionally or with some other state of mind. It must be recalled what role the allegation of "negligence" plays in an ordinary common law case. In general terms that role is to invoke a duty to take reasonable care not to cause a risk of a foreseeable type of harm to a foreseeable class of plaintiffs. Here the risk, the harm, and the potential plaintiff were all foreseen by the lawmaker and, in McEvoy and in this case, by a court. It was not left to the clerk in Brennen, the lawyer in McEvoy, or the officers in this case to foresee a possible risk and to form a "reasonable" opinion as to what "due care" might be required to avoid it. Such ad hoc judgments are exactly what the legislature meant to overcome when it enacted the obligation to enforce judicial orders.

This does not mean that the obligation creates absolute liability for resulting harm. There may be various defenses, for instance that the defendant made a good faith effort to perform, or that he was prevented from doing so by one or another obstacle, either factual or legal. The officer would not be liable, for instance, for failing to make an unconstitutional arrest. Whatever would be a defense under the statute is a defense to civil liability. But such defenses differ from a claim that failing to perform the duty created by the legislature to prevent harm by enforcing court orders is nothing other than a lack of due care toward the world at large and that liability therefore extends only to physical but not psychic or emotional injuries actually caused by that failure.

[The order] clearly gave rise to a duty of defendants toward the plaintiffs under the 1977 act. [The Act] prescribes that a peace officer "shall arrest and take into custody a person without a warrant" when the officer has probable cause to believe that an order under the statute has been served and filed and that the person has violated the order. Subsection (3) appears after two subsections that state when an officer "may" arrest a person without a warrant, and the contrasting use of "shall" in subsection (3) is no accident. The widespread refusal or failure of police officers to remove persons involved in episodes of domestic violence was presented to the legislature as the main reason for tightening the law so as to require enforcement of restraining orders by mandatory arrest and custody. Even though the arrested person is entitled to be released pending an eventual adjudication of a criminal charge or contempt, [c], the temporary removal was deemed essential to emphasize the seriousness of the court's order and to permit the victims of violence to escape further immediate danger.

Defendants argue that an officer's determination of probable cause to believe that a violation has occurred is a "discretionary function or duty" immune from liability [c]. This claim is answered by McBride v. Magnuson, 282 Or 433, 578 P2d 1259 (1978). In that case a police officer claimed immunity for her decision to take a child into custody and to make a report of child abuse. This court held that an officer or employee is not engaged in a "discretionary function or duty" whenever he or she must evaluate and act upon a factual judgment. Discretion, we stated, exists only insofar as an officer has been delegated responsibility for value judgments and policy choices among competing goals and priorities. Patently the purpose of [the section] was to negate any discretion of that kind in enforcing restraining orders issued under the Abuse Prevention Act. This conclusion does not depend on facts in the individual case. The circuit court erred in denying plaintiff's motion to strike this defense.

Defendants also claim immunity by virtue of ORS 133.315, which provides that "[n]o peace officer shall be held criminally or civilly liable for making an arrest pursuant to ORS 133.055(2) or 133.310(3) provided he acts in good faith and without malice." That section provides immunity for making good faith arrests, not for failing to do so, and its obvious purpose is to reinforce the officer's duty to arrest on probable cause. To invert this text so as to grant immunity for failing to make an arrest required by the 1977 act, as defendants propose, would fly in the face of that legislative purpose. This affirmative defense also should have been stricken.

This disposes of the issues actually raised by the parties. We add the following response to assertions introduced by the dissent.

1. The dissent asserts that we "overrule" two cases in which the court declined to find defendants liable for injury resulting from alleged conduct contrary to statutes, Bob Godfrey Pontiac v. Roloff, 291 Or. 318, 630 P.2d 840 (1981), and Burnette v. Wahl, 284 Or. 705, 588 P.2d 1105 (1978). Most of the dissent is devoted to that proposition.

Neither case was cited by defendants. Neither case holds that statutory duties never give rise to civil liability unless the legislature makes that intention explicit in the text or accompanying explanations. We do not overrule either case, as the dissent claims; children still will have no statutory civil claim under the circumstances of *Burnette* nor litigants under the circumstances in *Bob Godfrey Pontiac* unless the legislature makes a change. Those cases relate to this very different statute only because the dissent extends their holdings to a general rejection of all liability whenever the underlying duty is established by the legislature rather than by judges. That conclusion, however, must be reached for different statutes on a case-by-case basis.

The statutes in this case * * * are unique among statutory arrest provisions because the legislature chose mandatory arrest as the best means to reduce recurring domestic violence. They identify with precision when, to whom, and under what circumstances police protection must be afforded. The legislative purpose in requiring the police to enforce individual restraining orders clearly is to protect the named persons for whose protection the order is issued, not to protect the community at large by general law enforcement activity.

2. The dissent states that this decision creates "strict" liability. That is a word of uncertain meaning. It is not liability without fault. We have made it clear that the liability is not absolute; there may be defenses. The governing standard of conduct is set by the statute, not by this decision. If a statute merely calls on its addressee to exercise due care, that is the standard. This statute demands more of officers than the exercise of reasonable judgment whether to respond to requests to enforce known court orders; it mandates that they respond. That is the point of the statute.

3. The dissent asserts that the plaintiffs did not make a claim based on the statute. To the contrary, plaintiffs' argument to the circuit court covered both a common law and a statutory theory.

4. At bottom the dissent simply opposes tort liability for injuries caused by disregard of the statute on policy grounds, because it may cost local governments money. To that there are two answers. First, the same argument can be and no doubt was made against all claims under the Tort Claims Act, but the act was nevertheless enacted. This is a claim under the

Tort Claims Act. If a private defendant would be liable for harm caused by failure to carry out a mandatory duty for the benefit of a specific person protected by a court order, * * * the Tort Claims Act makes a public defendant liable in the same manner. That policy decision was made by the legislature; it is not a new policy choice to be made in this case.

The second answer is that there is in fact no liability if the statute is followed. There is here no open-ended invitation to turn courts and juries loose to second-guess local policies. That might be true if all liability can only be negligence liability for lack of "due care," as the dissent seems to argue. But here the statutory duty is too plain to create such unavoidable risks of liability. When compliance with the statute, unless prevented by good cause, will avoid exposure to liability, the argument that there should be no liability because of the potential expense actually is an argument for a privilege not to comply with the statute. But that policy choice, like the policy of the Tort Claims Act, also has been settled by the legislature.

The circuit court's letter order and the arguments made to that court show that the court was persuaded as a matter of law that plaintiff could not recover for psychic and emotional injuries, as distinct from physical injuries that might have resulted from the same inaction by defendants. Because here * * * there was a specific duty toward these plaintiffs, that proposition is incorrect. The decision of the Court of Appeals affirming the summary judgment must be reversed and the case remanded to the circuit court for further proceedings.

Reversed and remanded.

PETERSON, JUSTICE, dissenting.

The majority has, for the first time, created a strict liability tort against public bodies and their police employees because "[t]he duty defendants are alleged to have neglected * * * is not an ordinary common law duty of due care to avoid predictable harm to another. It is a specific duty imposed by statute for the benefit of individuals previously identified by a judicial order." 295 Or. at 707. I dissent, for these reasons:

1. The holding of the majority opinion is inconsistent with a number of recent decisions of this court, which it overrules without a passing glance.

2. Public bodies and their employees are responsible for the performance of many duties for the benefit of the public. Their ability to perform those duties may depend upon a number of factors including availability of resources and demands of other mandated duties. Normally, tort liability requires a showing that the putative tortfeasor is guilty of socially unreasonable conduct. We should tread warily before holding public bodies and their employees liable without fault for damages arising from the failure to perform the duty imposed by ORS 133.310(3).

3. No party in this case has ever contended that public bodies or their employees should be liable, without fault, for failure to perform the statutory duty imposed by ORS 133.310(3). The majority's utterance is the first time that any strict liability doctrine has been discussed or considered

in this case. The plaintiffs' theory of recovery has always been negligence. On its own, the majority has converted the case to one of strict liability without allowing any party the opportunity to argue or discuss the proposition, pro or con.

I

The contention that violation of a duty imposed by statute gives rise to a private right of action not known to the common law has been considered and rejected by this court several times in the last five years. Bob Godfrey Pontiac v. Roloff, [c] is the most recent case. It involved a claim for damages against two attorneys for intentionally filing a false counterclaim against the plaintiff in an earlier case. The plaintiff's theory was that the defendants were liable because they violated ORS 9.460(4), which states:

"An attorney shall: * * *

"(4) Employ, for the purpose of maintaining the causes confided to him, such means only as are consistent with truth, and never seek to mislead the court or jury by any artifice or false statement of law or fact; * * *."

The trial court sustained defendants' demurrer to the plaintiff's second amended complaint and granted summary judgment in defendants' favor after plaintiff filed a third amended complaint. On plaintiff's appeal, the Court of Appeals affirmed.

Justice Tongue, writing for the court, carefully traced our precedents concerning whether violation of a statutory duty gives rise to a new and private cause of action for damages. I quote his analysis:

"[I]t is helpful to review previous decisions by this court in deciding, in different contexts, whether violation of a duty imposed by statute will give rise to a private cause of action.

"In this court's most recent discussion of this question, Miller v. City of Portland, 288 Or 271, 604 P2d 1261 (1980), it was noted (at 276–78) that an initial distinction must be made between (1) cases in which liability would be based upon violation of a statutory duty when there is also an underlying common law cause of action, and (2) cases in which liability would be based upon violation of a statute when there is no underlying common law cause of action.

"A common example of a case of the first type is an action for damages for negligence in which it is contended that violation of a duty imposed by statute is negligence per se in that the statutory duty is the standard of conduct of a reasonably prudent person, although the other elements of a cause of action for negligence must still be shown. The test for determining whether violation of a statute constitutes negligence per se in such a case, as stated in Stachniewicz v. Mar–Cam Corporation, 259 Or. 583, 488 P.2d 436 (1971) [see supra page 202] is (1) whether the injured person is a member of the class intended by the legislature to be protected, and (2) whether the harm is of the kind which the statute was intended to prevent.

"In *Miller*, however, it is stated that the approach to be taken by this court is somewhat different in cases in which there is no underlying common law cause of action and when the court is called upon to, in effect, 'create' or 'recognize' a new tort. [C] In such a case it must still be determined whether the plaintiff is a member of the class protected by the statute and whether the harm inflicted is the type intended to be protected against. The court must undertake further analysis, however, by an examination of the statute to determine whether there exists any explicit or implicit legislative intent that a violation of a statute should give rise to a tort cause of action. [C]

"If no intent either way is evident from the statute, then, according to *Miller*, at 278, this court must attempt to ascertain how the legislature would have dealt with the problem had it been considered by the legislature. This is usually done, according to *Miller*, at 278, by 'looking at the policy giving birth to the statute and determining whether a civil tort action is needed to carry out that policy.' In *Miller*, upon application of these criteria under quite different facts, this court declined (at 279) to 'create' a new and private cause of action for damages for violation of a statute."

"In Burnette v. Wahl, 284 Or 705, 588 P2d 1105 (1978), [supra page 1137], this court also declined to 'create' or 'recognize' a new private cause of action for violation of a statute, again under quite different facts. In that case we described the question to be decided as being whether such a new tort action was 'necessary and desirable to further vindicate the right [of the aggrieved party] or to further enforce the duty created by the statute.' In employing the above analysis, this court in Burnette emphasized that in such a case it is the court, and not the legislature, which is 'creating' or 'recognizing' the new cause of action. * * *

For a number of reasons, we opted in Bob Godfrey Pontiac not to recognize a new cause of action based upon a violation of the statutory duty [c], three main reasons being: (1) that recognition of the new cause of action was not necessary to carry out the policy of the statute [c]; (2) that creation of the new cause of action would be inconsistent with long-established rules and practices [c]; and (3) that courts should go slowly in establishing new civil causes of action based upon a violation of statute because it is always possible for the legislature to establish a civil cause of action if it wishes to do so [c]."

JUSTICE LINDE concurred with the result but disagreed with the analysis quoted above. * * *

[In Burnette, the court] rejected the plaintiffs' claims saying that " * * * there is a limitation to the extent to which use may be made of tort actions for the purpose of accomplishing social aims." [C]

If stare decisis has any residual life, we should follow these cases and reject the creation of a new, strict liability tort based upon a violation of ORS 133.310(3).

II

Further reasons support my conclusion. The legislative history indicates, in clear terms, why this statute was needed. Police were chary about arresting battering spouses if the police had not witnessed the assault. Battered women were suffering as a result of police inaction. There is no question as to the need for the law or the goal of the law. But there is no suggestion in the legislative history—not a whisper—that it was contemplated that a civil cause of action would be created against police and their employers if they failed to arrest.

Of course, as the opinions cited above make clear, this court still has the power to create a new type of tort liability "on the basis of its own appraisal of the policy considerations involved." *Burnette v. Wahl*, [c]. I do not believe that we should do so today—in this case—for these reasons.

First, the rule of strict liability created in the majority opinion is at variance with the salutary principle that the basis for tort liability normally is unreasonable conduct by the tortfeasor. The common thread in almost all torts is the idea of unreasonable interference with the interests of others. W. Prosser, Torts 6 (4th ed 1971). Although this court has, in the face of manifest need, created strict liability torts, see Wights v. Staff Jennings, Inc., 241 Or 301, 405 P2d 624 (1965), we have rejected new civil torts for violation of statutes under facts similar to those at bar.

Second, this case involves public liability—the liability of the state, its cities and counties, and of peace officers employed by them. We declined to create a right of action against private persons in Burnette v. Wahl, Miller v. City of Portland, and Bob Godfrey Pontiac v. Roloff, all supra. I would tread even more gingerly in creating a new tort against public bodies and their employees. Public monies are scarce, and public responsibilities are multiplying. I do not favor compounding already hefty public problems by creating this new strict liability tort. In addition, the overwhelming weight of authority holds that a breach of duty by a police officer creates no liability on the part of the officer to an individual who is damaged by a lawbreaker's conduct. This is an extremely important question, not heretofore presented in either the trial court or the Court of Appeals, and we should not decide a question not presented.

This court is poorly equipped to make the kind of policy judgments the majority makes. We have no way of knowing how today's decision will affect the ability of municipalities and counties to enforce the law and recruit and hire competent law enforcement officers. We have no way of knowing how much today's decision will exacerbate the fiscal problems of Oregon's cities. Given the prevalence of domestic strife, the effect upon a local government budget could be considerable. Furthermore, we have no way of knowing how today's decision might affect day-to-day law enforcement practices. Although the complaint alleges serious matters for which immediate police action was appropriate, other serious matters of consequence exist. The imposition of personal liability upon officers and upon their employers for failure to arrest could result in an inefficient use of scarce police resources in a period of social crisis or high crime.

Third, this is a new law. We have no information, one way or the other, whether the creation of a strict liability remedy against public bodies and their peace officers is necessary to vindicate the statutory policy. If peace officers are not doing their duty, I favor giving the legislature a further opportunity to look into whether the creation of such a cause of action is necessary. To this day, the public bodies and their employees have not yet been heard from, either by the legislature or any court.

III

A further reason exists for rejecting the majority's analysis. This case was not brought, tried, considered or appealed as a strict liability tort case. The plaintiffs repeatedly have characterized their claims as based upon negligence. Uninvited, this court has created a new tort, a tort having farreaching [sic] consequences to cities, counties, the state, and their peace officer employees. We need not and should not reach this question without briefing or argument from any of the parties.

IV

I see this case as a negligence case, as did the plaintiffs' attorneys, the defendants' attorneys and the trial court. Considering it as a negligence case, I would affirm the trial court. * * * The mental distress sustained by the plaintiffs directly was caused by the husband and father. The participation of the peace officers alleged in the complaint is not the type of conduct which has supported the award of mental distress damages unaccompanied by physical injury. [Affirmed]

NOTES AND QUESTIONS

1. An Oregon statute provides: "Any person who is intoxicated or under the influence of controlled substances in a public place may be taken or sent home or to a treatment facility by the police. However, if the person is incapacitated, the health of the person appears to be in immediate danger, or the police have reasonable cause to believe the person is dangerous to self or to any other person, the person shall be taken by the police to an appropriate treatment facility. A person shall be deemed incapacitated when in the opinion of the police officer or director of the treatment facility the person is unable to make a rational decision as to acceptance of assistance." The statute said nothing, however, concerning what consequences could flow if the police failed to act.

The following was enacted simultaneously with the above. It provides in part: "No peace officer * * * shall be held criminally or civilly liable for actions pursuant to ORS 426.450 to 426.470 * * * provided the actions are in good faith, on probable cause and without malice."

Marilyn Scovill was killed when she walked into a city street and was struck by a car. She was badly intoxicated and a short time before had been in the City of Astoria's police station, on the floor unable to talk coherently. Police had discovered three butcher knives on her person and had assured Marilyn Scovill's friend that she would be taken care of. In Scovill v. City of Astoria, 324 Ore. 159, 921 P.2d 1312 (1996), the plaintiff's personal representative brought a claim against the city. Three grounds were alleged: negligence, statutory tort, and negligence per se. The court upheld the claim on the statutory tort ground alone.

The court recognized that a court must decide when a "tort claim for breach of a statutory duty" may be found. Id. at 1319. It is rare to find the civil action explicitly spelled out. The court reasoned that its task was to determine whether the action could be implied. Central in this inquiry was the question of whether a private right of action reinforced the statute's purpose. The court found that the statute intended to protect intoxicated persons who pose a danger to themselves. The court rejected the negligence per se argument because the statute, while it created and imposed a duty to act, did not create a standard of care. Do you agree with this reasoning?

The reasoning of the *Scovill* court appears to give no room for a court to fashion a tort—a private right of action—from a statutory provision where it is not impliedly created by the legislature. See § 874A of the Restatement (Second) of Torts. What factors should determine whether a court should provide a private tort remedy? The court may assimilate the cause of action to the nearest related tort and modify that tort under its common law authority or may create a new tort action. On factors influencing the determination of whether the court should apply a tort remedy, see Restatement (Second) of Torts § 874A, comment *h*. And see comment *1c* on the scope of the legislative purpose.

2.   Most courts have been laconic in supplying reasons for the implication of tort actions from applicable statutes: Creek v. Laski, 248 Mich. 425, 227 N.W. 817 (1929) (criminal statute on malicious destruction of a will, tort action); Laczko v. Jules Meyers, Inc., 276 Cal.App.2d 293, 80 Cal.Rptr. 798 (1969) (criminal statute against altering mileage on car odometer).

3.   Few other courts have clearly examined the statutory cause of action. The Supreme Court of New Hampshire in Marquay v. Eno, 139 N.H. 708, 662 A.2d 272 (1995), considered, among other claims, whether plaintiffs who had been sexually molested at high school by teachers had a cause of action under the New Hampshire child abuse reporting statute. The court held that the statute did not support a private right of action for its violation because it could find no "express or implied legislative intent to create such a civil liability." Id. at 715, 278. The court's reasoning is confined to express or implied rights of action, although some of the reasons for refusing to find a cause of action are more pertinent to judicially created rights of action on the statute. The court had conflated the two types of action. The courts are far from clear about the nature of these statutory actions and their relationship to negligence per se. In another reporting statute case, Kansas State Bank & Trust Co. v. Specialized Transportation Services Inc., 249 Kan. 348, 819 P.2d 587 (1991), plaintiff argued that the statutory violation was negligence per se. The court stated that a "violation of a statute alone does not establish negligence per se. The plaintiff must also establish that an individual right of action for injury arising out of the violation was intended by the legislature." Id. at 370. How should negligence per se be distinguished?

4.   In Doe v. Brainerd International Raceway, 533 N.W.2d 617 (Minn.1995), plaintiff, a minor, had become involved in a "wet T-shirt" contest at the defendant's facility. A Minnesota statute prohibited a person from allowing a minor to engage in a sexual performance. The court found that the statute may be relevant in providing a standard of care where a duty of care exists at common law or as creating a civil cause of action. The court found that the latter may arise expressly or impliedly from the construction of the statute. Principles of judicial restraint, the court stated, would preclude the court creating a new cause of action. In finding no legislative intent to imply a cause of action, the court elicited strong support from

the enactment by the legislature four years later of a provision authorizing a civil action based on the use of a minor in sexual performances.

5. Implied rights of action are not divided into accepted categories and thus the application of rules relating to defenses, damages, vicarious liability, and contribution remain problematic. For example, the tolling of the statute of limitations under Rule 10b–5 of the federal Securities Act: Lampf, Pleva, Lipkind, et al. v. Gilbertson, 501 U.S. 350 (1991) (eliciting a broad spectrum of opinion on the issue; retroactivity of limitation period overruled by Public Law 102–242 § 476 (December 19, 1991)); the right of contribution between tortfeasors under Rule 10b–5 actions: Musick, Peeler & Garrett v. Employers Insurance of Wausau, 508 U.S. 286 (1993) (contribution available). As noted in Chapter 19, pages 973–974, the nature of damages available under § 1983 remains a difficult issue.

Bivens v. Six Unknown Named Agents of Federal Bureau of Narcotics

Supreme Court of the United States, 1971.
403 U.S. 388, 91 S.Ct. 1999, 29 L.Ed.2d 619.

MR. JUSTICE BRENNAN delivered the opinion of the Court. The Fourth Amendment provides that: "The right of the people to be secure in their persons, houses, papers, and effects, against unreasonable searches and seizures, shall not be violated. * * * "

In Bell v. Hood, 327 U.S. 678 (1946), we reserved the question whether violation of that command by a federal agent acting under color of his authority gives rise to a cause of action for damages consequent upon his unconstitutional conduct. Today we hold that it does. * * *

Petitioner's complaint alleged that * * * respondents, agents of the Federal Bureau of Narcotics acting under claim of federal authority, entered his apartment and arrested him for alleged narcotics violations. The agents manacled petitioner in front of his wife and children, and threatened to arrest the entire family. They searched the apartment from stem to stern. * * *

[H]is complaint [also] asserted that the arrest and search were effected without a warrant, and that unreasonable force was employed in making the arrest, [and, by implication,] that the arrest was made without probable cause. Petitioner claimed to have suffered great humiliation, embarrassment, and mental suffering as a result of the agents' unlawful conduct, and sought $15,000 damages from each of them. The District Court, on respondents' motion, dismissed the complaint on the ground, *inter alia*, that it failed to state a cause of action.[2] 276 F.Supp. 12 (E.D.N.Y.1967). The Court of Appeals * * * affirmed on that basis. 409 F.2d 718 (C.A.2 1969). We granted certiorari. 399 U.S. 905 (1970). We reverse. * * *

---

2. The agents were not named in petitioner's complaint, and the District Court ordered that the complaint be served upon "those federal agents who it is indicated by the records of the United States Attorney participated in the November 25, 1965, arrest of the [petitioner]." * * * Five agents were ultimately served.

Respondents do not argue that petitioner should be entirely without remedy for an unconstitutional invasion of his rights by federal agents. In respondents' view, however, the rights that petitioner asserts—primarily rights of privacy—are creations of state and not of federal law. Accordingly, they argue, petitioner may obtain money damages to redress invasion of these rights only by an action in tort, under state law, in the state courts. In this scheme the Fourth Amendment would serve merely to limit the extent to which the agents could defend the state law tort suit by asserting that their actions were a valid exercise of federal power: if the agents were shown to have violated the Fourth Amendment, such a defense would be lost to them and they would stand before the state law merely as private individuals. * * *

We think that respondents' thesis rests upon an unduly restrictive view of the Fourth Amendment's protection against unreasonable searches and seizures by federal agents, a view that has consistently been rejected by this Court. Respondents seek to treat the relationship between a citizen and a federal agent unconstitutionally exercising his authority as no different from the relationship between two private citizens. In so doing, they ignore the fact that power, once granted, does not disappear like a magic gift when it is wrongfully used. An agent acting—albeit unconstitutionally—in the name of the United States possesses a far greater capacity for harm than an individual trespasser exercising no authority other than his own. [Cc] Accordingly, as our cases make clear, the Fourth Amendment operates as a limitation upon the exercise of federal power regardless of whether the State in whose jurisdiction that power is exercised would prohibit or penalize the identical act if engaged in by a private citizen. It guarantees to citizens of the United States the absolute right to be free from unreasonable searches and seizures carried out by virtue of federal authority. And "where federally protected rights have been invaded, it has been the rule from the beginning that courts will be alert to adjust their remedies so as to grant the necessary relief." Bell v. Hood, 327 U.S., at 684. * * *

Our cases have long since rejected the notion that the Fourth Amendment proscribes only such conduct as would, if engaged in by private persons, be condemned by state law. * * *

The interests protected by state laws regulating trespass and the invasion of privacy, and those protected by the Fourth Amendment's guarantee against unreasonable searches and seizures, may be inconsistent or even hostile. Thus, we may bar the door against an unwelcome private intruder, or call the police if he persists in seeking entrance. The availability of such alternative means for the protection of privacy may lead the State to restrict imposition of liability for any consequent trespass. A private citizen, asserting no authority other than his own, will not normally be liable in trespass if he demands, and is granted, admission to another's house. [Cc] But one who demands admission under a claim of federal authority stands in a far different position. [Cc] The mere invocation of federal power by a federal law enforcement official will normally render futile any attempt to resist an unlawful entry or arrest by resort to the local police; and a claim of authority to enter is likely to unlock the door as well. * * *

That damages may be obtained for injuries consequent upon a violation of the Fourth Amendment by federal officials should hardly seem a surprising proposition. Historically, damages have been regarded as the ordinary remedy for an invasion of personal interests in liberty. [Cc] Of course, the Fourth Amendment does not in so many words provide for its enforcement by an award of money damages for the consequences of its violation. But "it is * * * well settled that where legal rights have been invaded, and a federal statute provides for a general right to sue for such invasion, federal courts may use any available remedy to make good the wrong done." Bell v. Hood, 327 U.S., at 684 (footnote omitted). The present case involves no special factors counselling hesitation in the absence of affirmative action by Congress. * * * Finally, we cannot accept respondents' formulation of the question as whether the availability of money damages is necessary to enforce the Fourth Amendment. For we have here no explicit congressional declaration that persons injured by a federal officer's violation of the Fourth Amendment may not recover money damages from the agents, but must instead be remitted to another remedy, equally effective in the view of Congress. The question is merely whether petitioner, if he can demonstrate an injury consequent upon the violation by federal agents of his Fourth Amendment rights, is entitled to redress his injury through a particular remedial mechanism normally available in the federal courts. [Cc] "The very essence of civil liberty certainly consists in the right of every individual to claim the protection of the laws, whenever he receives an injury." Marbury v. Madison, 1 Cranch 137, 163 (1803). Having concluded that petitioner's complaint states a cause of action under the Fourth Amendment * * * we hold that petitioner is entitled to recover money damages for any injuries he has suffered as a result of the agents' violation of the Amendment. * * *

Judgment reversed and case remanded.

Mr. Justice Harlan, concurring in the judgment. * * * I am of the opinion that federal courts do have the power to award damages for violation of "constitutionally protected interests" and I agree with the Court that a traditional judicial remedy such as damages is appropriate to the vindication of the personal interests protected by the Fourth Amendment. * * *

[T]he interest which Bivens claims—to be free from official conduct in contravention of the Fourth Amendment—is a federally protected interest. [C] Therefore, the question of judicial power to grant Bivens damages is not a problem of the "source" of the "right"; instead, the question is whether the power to authorize damages as a judicial remedy for the vindication of a federal constitutional right is placed by the Constitution itself exclusively in Congress' hands. * * *

[I]n suits for damages based on violations of federal statutes lacking any express authorization of a damage remedy, this Court has authorized such relief where, in its view, damages are necessary to effectuate the congressional policy underpinning the substantive provisions of the statute. J.I. Case Co. v. Borak, 377 U.S. 426 (1964).[4] [Cc] * * *

Initially, I note that it would be at least anomalous to conclude that the federal judiciary—while competent to choose among the range of traditional judicial remedies to implement statutory and common-law policies, and even to generate substantive rules governing primary behavior in furtherance of broadly formulated policies articulated by statute or Constitution [cc] is powerless to accord a damages remedy to vindicate social policies which, by virtue of their inclusion in the Constitution, are aimed predominantly at restraining the Government as an instrument of the popular will. * * *

If explicit congressional authorization is an absolute prerequisite to the power of a federal court to accord compensatory relief regardless of the necessity or appropriateness of damages as a remedy simply because of the status of a legal interest as constitutionally protected, then it seems to me that explicit congressional authorization is similarly prerequisite to the exercise of equitable remedial discretion in favor of constitutionally protected interests. Conversely, if a general grant of jurisdiction to the federal courts by Congress is thought adequate to empower a federal court to grant equitable relief for all areas of subject-matter jurisdiction enumerated therein, see 28 U.S.C.A. § 1331(a), then it seems to me that the same statute is sufficient to empower a federal court to grant a traditional remedy at law. * * *

Although conceding that the standard of determining whether a damage remedy should be utilized to effectuate statutory policies is one of "necessity" or "appropriateness," [cc] the Government contends that questions concerning congressional discretion to modify judicial remedies relating to constitutionally protected interests warrant a more stringent constraint on the exercise of judicial power with respect to this class of legally protected interests. [C]

These arguments for a more stringent test to govern the grant of damages in constitutional cases seem to be adequately answered by the point that the judiciary has a particular responsibility to assure the vindication of constitutional interests such as those embraced by the Fourth Amendment. To be sure, "it must be remembered that legislatures are ultimate guardians of the liberties and welfare of the people in quite as great a degree as the courts." [C] But it must also be recognized that the

4. The Borak case is an especially clear example of the exercise of federal judicial power to accord damages as an appropriate remedy in the absence of any express statutory authorization of a federal cause of action. There we "implied"—from what can only be characterized as an "exclusively procedural provision" affording access to a federal forum [citation] a private cause of action for damages for violation of § 14(a) of the Securities Exchange Act of 1934, 48 Stat. 895, 15 U.S.C.A. § 78n(a). * * * The exercise of judicial power involved in Borak simply cannot be justified in terms of statutory construction [c]: nor did the Borak Court purport to do so. [C] The notion of "implying" a remedy, therefore, as applied to cases like Borak, can only refer to a process whereby the federal judiciary exercises a choice among traditionally available judicial remedies according to reasons related to the substantive social policy embodied in an act of positive law. [C]

Bill of Rights is particularly intended to vindicate the interests of the individual in the face of the popular will as expressed in legislative majorities * * *.

The question then, is, as I see it, whether compensatory relief is "necessary" or "appropriate" to the vindication of the interest asserted. [Cc] In resolving that question, it seems to me that the range of policy considerations we may take into account is at least as broad as the range a legislature would consider with respect to an express statutory authorization of a traditional remedy. In this regard I agree with the Court that the appropriateness of according Bivens compensatory relief does not turn simply on the deterrent effect liability will have on federal official conduct. Damages as a traditional form of compensation for invasion of a legally protected interest may be entirely appropriate even if no substantial deterrent effects on future official lawlessness might be thought to result. Bivens, after all, has invoked judicial processes claiming entitlement to compensation for injuries resulting from allegedly lawless official behavior, if those injuries are properly compensable in money damages. I do not think a court of law—vested with the power to accord a remedy—should deny him his relief simply because he cannot show that future lawless conduct will thereby be deterred.

And I think it is clear that Bivens advances a claim of the sort that, if proved, would be properly compensable in damages. The personal interests protected by the Fourth Amendment are those we attempt to capture by the notion of "privacy"; while the Court today properly points out that the type of harm which officials can inflict when they invade protected zones of an individual's life are different from the types of harm private citizens inflict on one another, the experience of judges in dealing with private trespass and false imprisonment claims supports the conclusion that courts of law are capable of making the types of judgment concerning causation and magnitude of injury necessary to accord meaningful compensation for invasion of Fourth Amendment rights. * * *

It seems to me entirely proper that these injuries be compensable according to uniform rules of federal law, especially in light of the very large element of federal law which must in any event control the scope of official defenses to liability. [C] Certainly, there is very little to be gained from the standpoint of federalism by preserving different rules of liability for federal officers dependent on the State where the injury occurs. [C]

Putting aside the desirability of leaving the problem of federal official liability to the vagaries of common-law actions, it is apparent that some form of damages is the only possible remedy for someone in Bivens' alleged position. * * *

However desirable a direct remedy against the Government might be as a substitute for individual official liability, the sovereign still remains immune to suit. * * *

The only substantial policy consideration advanced against recognition of a federal cause of action for violation of Fourth Amendment rights by federal officials is the incremental expenditure of judicial resources that will be necessitated by this class of litigation. There is, however, something ultimately self-defeating about this argument. For if, as the Government contends, damages will rarely be realized by plaintiffs in these cases because of jury hostility, the limited resources of the official concerned, etc., then I am not ready to assume that there will be a significant increase in the expenditure of judicial resources on these claims. Few responsible lawyers and plaintiffs are likely to choose the course of litigation if the statistical chances of success are truly de minimis. And I simply cannot agree with my Brother Black that the possibility of "frivolous" claims—if defined simply as claims with no legal merit—warrants closing the court-house doors to people in Bivens' situation. There are other ways, short of that, of coping with frivolous lawsuits.

On the other hand, if—as I believe is the case with respect, at least, to the most flagrant abuses of official power—damages to some degree will be available when the option of litigation is chosen, then the question appears to be how Fourth Amendment interests rank on a scale of social values compared with, for example, the interests of stockholders defrauded by misleading proxies. See J.I. Case Co. v. Borak, supra. Judicial resources, I am well aware, are increasingly scarce these days. Nonetheless, when we automatically close the courthouse door solely on this basis, we implicitly express a value judgment on the comparative importance of classes of legally protected interests. And current limitations upon the effective functioning of the courts arising from budgetary inadequacies should not be permitted to stand in the way of the recognition of otherwise sound constitutional principles. * * *

For these reasons, I concur in the judgment of the Court.

MR. CHIEF JUSTICE BURGER, dissenting. I dissent from today's holding which judicially creates a damage remedy not provided for by the Constitution and not enacted by Congress. We would more surely preserve the important values of the doctrine of separation of powers—and perhaps get a better result—by recommending a solution to the Congress as the branch of government in which the Constitution has vested the legislative power. Legislation is the business of the Congress, and it has the facilities and competence for that task—as we do not. * * * [The opinion suggests that the problem of a substitute for the "exclusionary rule" might be considered with the problem in this case and legislation recommended to Congress.]

MR. JUSTICE BLACK, dissenting. * * * Congress could create a federal cause of action for damages for an unreasonable search in violation of the Fourth Amendment. Although Congress has created such a federal cause of action against state officials acting under color of state law, it has never created such a cause of action against federal officials. If it wanted to do so, Congress could, of course, create a remedy against federal officials who violate the Fourth Amendment in the performance of their duties. But the point of this case and the fatal weakness in the Court's judgment is that neither Congress nor the State of New York has enacted legislation creating such a right of action. For us to do so is, in my judgment, an exercise of power that the Constitution does not give us.

Even if we had the legislative power to create a remedy, there are many reasons why we should decline to create a cause of action where none has existed since the formation of our Government. The courts of the United States as well as those of the States are choked with lawsuits. The number of cases on the docket of this Court have reached an unprecedented volume in recent years. A majority of these cases are brought by citizens with substantial complaints—persons who are physically or economically injured by torts or frauds or governmental infringement of their rights; persons who have been unjustly deprived of their liberty or their property; and persons who have not yet received the equal opportunity in education, employment, and pursuit of happiness that was the dream of our forefathers. Unfortunately, there have also been a growing number of frivolous lawsuits, particularly actions for damages against law enforcement officers whose conduct has been judicially sanctioned by state trial and appellate courts and in many instances even by this Court. My fellow Justices on this Court and our brethren throughout the federal judiciary know only too well the time-consuming task of conscientiously poring over hundreds of thousands of pages of factual allegations of misconduct by police, judicial, and corrections officials. Of course, there are instances of legitimate grievances, but legislators might well desire to devote judicial resources to other problems of a more serious nature. * * *

But that is not my task. The task of evaluating the pros and cons of creating judicial remedies for particular wrongs is a matter for Congress and the legislatures of the States. * * *

Should the time come when Congress desires such lawsuits, it has before it a model of valid legislation, 42 U.S.C.A. § 1983, to create a damage remedy against federal officers. * * *

NOTES AND QUESTIONS

1. In this, the first Supreme Court case implying a cause of action from a constitutional provision, the Court laid considerable reliance upon earlier cases involving actions "implied" from federal statutes, particularly J.I. Case Co. v. Borak, 377 U.S. 426 (1964) (Securities Exchange Act). Observe that *Bivens* established essentially the same cause of action against federal officers as that existing against state officers under 42 U.S.C.A. § 1983. See Chapter 19.

2. Since *Bivens* there have been other Supreme Court cases giving rise to a cause of action deriving from a constitutional provision. See, e.g., Davis v. Passman, 442 U.S. 228 (1979) (5th Amendment—due process and sex discrimination); Carlson v. Green, 446 U.S. 14 (1980) (8th Amendment—cruel and inhuman punishment). Many federal appeals court decisions may be cited. See, e.g., Dunbar Corp. v. Lindsey, 905 F.2d 754 (4th Cir.1990) (5th Amendment); Wilkins v. May, 872 F.2d 190 (7th Cir.1989) (FBI interrogation, 5th Amendment, dicta regarding 4th and 8th Amendments). But cf. Schweiker v. Chilicky, 487 U.S. 412 (1988) (cautioning that *Bivens* action is appropriate only where there are (1) no "special factors counselling hesitation in the absence of affirmative action by Congress"; (2) no explicit

statutory prohibition against relief; and (3) no exclusive statutory alternative remedy).

3. An implied cause of action may be maintained to violations of a state constitution: Brown v. New York, 89 N.Y.2d 172, 674 N.E.2d 1129 (1996).

Transamerica Mortgage Advisors, Inc. (TAMA) v. Lewis

Supreme Court of the United States, 1979.
444 U.S. 11, 100 S.Ct. 242, 62 L.Ed.2d 146.

Mr. Justice Stewart delivered the opinion of the Court. The Investment Advisers Act of 1940, 15 U.S.C.A. §§ 80b–1 et seq. was enacted to deal with abuses that Congress had found to exist in the investment advisers industry. The question in this case is whether that Act creates a private cause of action for damages or other relief in favor of persons aggrieved by those who allegedly have violated it.

The respondent, a shareholder of petitioner Mortgage Trust of America (Trust), brought this suit in a Federal District Court as a derivative action on behalf of the Trust and as a class action on behalf of the Trust's shareholders. Named as defendants were the Trust, several individual trustees, the Trust's investment adviser, Transamerica Mortgage Advisors, Inc. (TAMA), and two corporations affiliated with TAMA. * * *

The respondent's complaint alleged that the petitioners in the course of advising or managing the Trust had been guilty of various frauds and breaches of fiduciary duty. The complaint set out three causes of action, each said to arise under the Investment Advisers Act of 1940. The first alleged that the advisory contract between TAMA and the Trust was unlawful because TAMA and Transamerica were not registered under the Act and because the contract had provided for grossly excessive compensation. The second alleged that the petitioners breached their fiduciary duty to the Trust by causing it to purchase securities of inferior quality from Land Capital. The third alleged that the petitioners had misappropriated profitable investment opportunities for the benefit of other companies affiliated with Transamerica. The complaint sought injunctive relief to restrain further performance of the advisory contract, rescission of the contract, restitution of fees and other considerations paid by the Trust, an accounting of illegal profits, and an award of damages.

The trial court ruled that the Investment Advisers Act confers no private right of action, and accordingly dismissed the complaint. The Court of Appeals reversed, Lewis v. Transamerica Corp., 575 F.2d 237, holding that "implication of a private right of action for injunctive relief and damages under the Advisers Act in favor of appropriate plaintiffs is necessary to achieve the goals of Congress in enacting the legislation." Id., at 239. We granted certiorari to consider the important federal question presented. 439 U.S. 952.

The Investment Advisers Act nowhere expressly provides for a private cause of action. * * * The argument is made, however, that the clients of investment advisers were the intended beneficiaries of the Act and that courts should therefore imply a private cause of action in their favor. [Cc]

The question whether a statute creates a cause of action, either expressly or by implication, is basically a matter of statutory construction. [Cc] While some opinions of the Court have placed considerable emphasis upon the desirability of implying private rights of action in order to provide remedies thought to effectuate the purposes of a given statute, e.g., J.I. Case Co. v. Borak, [377 U.S. 426 (1964),] what must ultimately be determined is whether Congress intended to create the private remedy asserted, as our recent decisions have made clear. [Cc] We accept this as the appropriate inquiry to be made in resolving the issues presented by the case before us.

Accordingly, we begin with the language of the statute itself. [Cc] It is asserted that the creation of a private right of action can fairly be inferred from the language of two sections of the Act. The first is § 206, which broadly proscribes fraudulent practices by investment advisers, making it unlawful for any investment adviser "to employ any device, scheme, or artifice to defraud * * * [or] to engage in any transaction, practice, or course of business which operates as a fraud or deceit upon any client or prospective client," or to engage in specified transactions with clients without making required disclosures.[6] The second is § 215, which provides that contracts whose formation or performance would violate the Act "shall be void * * * as regards the rights of" the violator and knowing successors in interest.[7]

---

6. Section 206, 54 Stat. 852, as amended, as set forth in 15 U.S.C.A. § 80b–6, reads as follows:

"§ 80b–6. Prohibited Transactions by Investment Advisers

"It shall be unlawful for any investment adviser, by use of the mails or any means or instrumentality of interstate commerce, directly or indirectly—

"(1) to employ any device, scheme, or artifice to defraud any client or prospective client;

"(2) to engage in any transaction, practice, or course of business which operates as a fraud or deceit upon any client or prospective client;

"(3) acting as principal for his own account, knowingly to sell any security to or purchase any security from a client, or acting as broker for a person other than such client, knowingly to effect any sale or purchase of any security for the account of such client, without disclosing to such client in writing before the completion of such transaction the capacity in which he is acting and obtaining the consent of the client to such transaction. The prohibitions of this paragraph shall not apply to any transaction with a customer of a broker or dealer if such broker or dealer is not acting as an investment adviser in relation to such transaction;

"(4) to engage in any act, practice, or course of business which is fraudulent, deceptive, or manipulative. The Commission shall, for the purposes of this paragraph (4) by rules and regulations define, and prescribe means reasonably designed to prevent, such acts, practices, and courses of business as are fraudulent, deceptive, or manipulative." * * *

7. Section 215, 54 Stat. 856, as set forth in 15 U.S.C.A. § 80b–15 reads in part as follows:

"§ 80b–15. Validity of Contracts * * *

It is apparent that the two sections were intended to benefit the clients of investment advisers, and, in the case of § 215, the parties to advisory contracts as well. As we have previously recognized, § 206 establishes "federal fiduciary standards" to govern the conduct of investment advisers. [Cc] Indeed, the Act's legislative history leaves no doubt that Congress intended to impose enforceable fiduciary obligations. [Cc]

But whether Congress intended additionally that these provisions would be enforced through private litigation is a different question.

On this question the legislative history of the Act is entirely silent—a state of affairs not surprising when it is remembered that the Act concededly does not explicitly provide any private remedies whatever. [C] But while the absence of anything in the legislative history that indicates an intention to confer any private right of action is hardly helpful to the respondent, it does not automatically undermine his position. This Court has held that the failure of Congress expressly to consider a private remedy is not inevitably inconsistent with an intent on its part to make such a remedy available. [C] Such an intent may appear implicitly in the language or structure of the statute, or in the circumstances of its enactment.

In the case of § 215, we conclude that the statutory language itself fairly implies a right to specific and limited relief in a federal court. By declaring certain contracts void, § 215 by its terms necessarily contemplates that the issue of voidness under its criteria may be litigated somewhere. * * * Moreover, the federal courts in general have viewed such language as implying an equitable cause of action for rescission or similar relief. [Cc]

For these reasons we conclude that when Congress declared in § 215 that certain contracts are void, it intended that the customary legal incidents of voidness would follow, including the availability of a suit for rescission or for an injunction against continued operation of the contract, and for restitution. Accordingly, we hold that the Court of Appeals was correct in ruling that the respondent may maintain an action on behalf of the Trust seeking to void the investment advisers contract.

We view quite differently, however, the respondent's claims for damages and other monetary relief under § 206. Unlike § 215, § 206 simply proscribes certain conduct, and does not in terms create or alter any civil liabilities. If monetary liability to a private plaintiff is to be found, it must be read into the Act. Yet it is an elemental canon of statutory construction that where a statute expressly provides a particular remedy or remedies, a

"(b) Every contract made in violation of any provision of this subchapter and every contract heretofore or hereafter made, the performance of which involves the violation of, or the continuance of any relationship or practice in violation of any provision of this subchapter, or any rule, regulation, or order thereunder, shall be void (1) as regards the rights of any person who, in violation of any such provision, rule, regulation, or order, shall have made or engaged in the performance of any such contract, and (2) as regards the rights of any person who, not being a party to such contract, shall have acquired any right thereunder with actual knowledge of the facts by reason of which the making or performance of such contract was in violation of any such provision."

court must be chary of reading others into it. "When a statute limits a thing to be done in a particular mode, it includes the negative of any other mode." [Cc] Congress expressly provided both judicial and administrative means for enforcing compliance with § 206. First, under § 217, 15 U.S.C.A. § 80b–17, willful violations of the Act are criminal offenses, punishable by fine or imprisonment, or both. Second, § 209 authorizes the Commission to bring civil actions in federal courts to enjoin compliance with the Act, including, of course, § 206. Third, the Commission is authorized by § 203 to impose various administrative sanctions on persons who violate the Act, including § 206. In view of these express provisions for enforcing the duties imposed by § 206, it is highly improbable that "Congress absentmindedly forgot to mention an intended private action." Cannon v. University of Chicago, 441 U.S., at 742 (Powell, J., dissenting).

Even settled rules of statutory construction could yield, of course, to persuasive evidence of a contrary legislative intent. [Cc] But what evidence of intent exists in this case, circumstantial though it be, weighs against the implication of a private right of action for a monetary award in a case such as this. Under each of the securities laws that preceded the Act here in question, and under the Investment Company Act of 1940 which was enacted as companion legislation, Congress expressly authorized private suits for damages in prescribed circumstances. For example, Congress provided an express damages remedy for misrepresentations contained in an underwriter's registration statement in § 11(a) of the Securities Act of 1933, and for certain materially misleading statements in § 18(a) of the Securities Exchange Act of 1934. "Obviously, then, when Congress wished to provide a private damages remedy, it knew how to do so and did so expressly." [Cc] The fact that it enacted no analogous provisions in the legislation here at issue strongly suggests that Congress was simply unwilling to impose any potential monetary liability to a private suitor. [C]

The omission of any such potential remedy from the Act's substantive provisions was paralleled in the jurisdictional section, § 214. Early drafts of the bill had simply incorporated by reference a provision of the Public Utility Holding Company Act of 1935, which gave the federal courts jurisdiction "of all suits in equity and actions at law brought to enforce any liability or duty created by" the statute. [Cc] After hearings on the bill in the Senate, representatives of the investment advisers industry and the staff of the Commission met to discuss the bill, and certain changes were made. The language that was enacted as § 214 first appeared in this compromise version of the bill. [C] That version, and the version finally enacted into law [c] both omitted any references to "actions at law" or to "liability." The unexplained deletion of a single phrase from a jurisdictional provision is, of course, not determinative of whether a private remedy exists. But it is one more piece of evidence that Congress did not intend to authorize a cause of action for anything beyond limited equitable relief.

Relying on the factors identified in Cort v. Ash, 422 U.S. 66, the respondent and the Commission, as amicus curiae, argue that our inquiry in this case cannot stop with the intent of Congress, but must consider the utility of a private remedy, and the fact that it may be one not traditionally relegated to state law. We rejected the same contentions last term in Touche Ross & Co. v. Redington [442 U.S. 560], where it was argued that these factors standing alone justified the implication of a private right of action under § 17(a) of the Securities Exchange Act of 1934. We said in that case:

"It is true that in Cort v. Ash, the Court set forth four factors* that it considered 'relevant' in determining whether a private remedy is implicit in a statute not expressly providing one. But the Court did not decide that each of these factors is entitled to equal weight. The central inquiry remains whether Congress intended to create, either expressly or by implication, a private cause of action. Indeed, the first three factors discussed in Cort—the language and focus of the statute, its legislative history, and its purpose, [c] are ones traditionally relied upon in determining legislative intent." [C]

The statute in Touche Ross by its terms neither granted private rights to the members of any identifiable class, nor proscribed any conduct as unlawful. [C] In those circumstances it was evident to the Court that no private remedy was available. Section 206 of the Act here involved concededly was intended to protect the victims of the fraudulent practices it prohibited. But the mere fact that the statute was designed to protect advisers' clients does not require the implication of a private cause of action for damages on their behalf. [Cc] The dispositive question remains whether Congress intended to create any such remedy. Having answered that question in the negative, our inquiry is at an end.

For the reasons stated in this opinion, we hold that there exists a limited private remedy under the Investment Advisers Act of 1940 to void an investment advisers contract, but that the Act confers no other private causes of action, legal or equitable.[14] Accordingly, the judgment of the Court of Appeals is affirmed in part and reversed in part, and the case is remanded to that court for further proceedings consistent with this opinion.

Mr. Justice Powell, concurring. I join the Court's opinion, which I view as compatible with my dissent in Cannon v. University of Chicago, 441 U.S. 677, 730.[†]

---

* These four factors are quoted in note 3, of the dissenting opinion, infra page 1171. [Ed.]

14. Where rescission is awarded, the rescinding party may of course have restitution of the consideration given under the contract, less any value conferred by the other party. See 5 A. Corbin, Contracts § 1114 (1964). Restitution would not, however, include compensation for any diminution in the value of the rescinding party's investment alleged to have resulted from the adviser's action or inaction. Such relief could provide by indirection the equivalent of a private damages remedy that we have concluded Congress did not confer.

† Powell's dissenting opinion in *Cannon* said in part: "The time has come to reappraise our standards for the judicial implication of private causes of action. * * * In recent history the Court has tended to stray from the Art. III and separation-of-powers

MR. JUSTICE WHITE, with whom MR. JUSTICE BRENNAN, MR. JUSTICE MARSHALL, and MR. JUSTICE STEVENS join, dissenting.

The Court today holds that private rights of action under the Investment Advisers Act of 1940 (Act) are limited to actions for rescission of investment advisers contracts. In reaching this decision, the Court departs from established principles governing the implication of private rights of action by confusing the inquiry into the existence of a right of action with the question of available relief. By holding that damages are unavailable to victims of violations of the Act, the Court rejects the conclusion of every United States Court of Appeals that has considered the question. [Cc] The Court's decision cannot be reconciled with our decisions recognizing implied private actions for damages under securities laws with substantially the same language as the Act. By resurrecting distinctions between legal and equitable relief, the Court reaches a result that, as all parties to this litigation agree, can only be considered anomalous.

I. This Court has long recognized that private rights of action do not require express statutory authorization. [Cc] The preferred approach for determining whether a private right of action should be implied from a federal statute was outlined in Cort v. Ash, 422 U.S. 66, 78 (1975). See Cannon v. University of Chicago, 441 U.S. 677 (1979). Four factors were thought relevant,[3] and although subsequent decisions have indicated that the implication of a private right of action "is limited solely to determining whether Congress intended to create the private right of action," [c] these four factors are "the criteria through which this intent could be discerned." [C] Proper application of the factors outlined in Cort clearly indicates that § 206 of the Act, creates a private right of action.

II. In determining whether respondent can assert a private right of action under the Act, "the threshold question under Cort is whether the statute was enacted for the benefit of a special class of which the plaintiff is a member." [C] The instant action was brought by respondent as both a derivative action on behalf of Mortgage Trust of America and a class action on behalf of Mortgage Trust's shareholders. Respondent alleged that Mortgage Trust had retained Transamerica Mortgage Advisors, Inc. (TAMA), as

principle of limited jurisdiction. * * * The 'four factor' analysis of [Cort v. Ash, 422 U.S. 66] is an open invitation to federal courts to legislate causes of action not authorized by Congress. It is an analysis not faithful to constitutional principles and should be rejected. Absent the most compelling evidence of affirmative congressional intent, a federal court should not infer a private cause of action." 441 U.S. at 730, 731. [Ed.]

3. "First, is the plaintiff 'one of the class for whose especial benefit the statute was enacted,' Texas & Pacific R. Co. v. Rigsby, 241 U.S. 33, 39 (1916)—that is, does the statute create a federal right in favor of the plaintiff? Second, is there any indication of legislative intent, explicit or implicit, either to create such a remedy or to deny one? See, e.g., National Railroad Passenger Corp. v. National Assn. of Railroad Passengers, 414 U.S. 453, 458, 460 (1974) (Amtrak). Third, is it consistent with the underlying purposes of the legislative scheme to imply such a remedy for the plaintiff? See, e.g., Amtrak, supra [cc]. And finally, is the cause of action one traditionally relegated to state law, in an area basically the concern of the States, so that it would be inappropriate to infer a cause of action based solely on federal law? [Cc]" Cort v. Ash, 422 U.S. 66, 78 (1975).

its investment adviser and that violations of the Act by TAMA had injured the client corporation. Thus the question under *Cort* is whether the Act was enacted for the special benefit of clients of investment advisers.

The Court concedes that the language and legislative history of § 206 leave no doubt that it was "intended to benefit the clients of investment advisers," as we have previously recognized. [Cc] Because respondent's claims were brought on behalf of a member of the class the Act was designed to benefit, i.e., the clients of investment advisers, the first prong of the *Cort* test is satisfied in this case.

III.   The second inquiry under the *Cort* approach is whether there is evidence of an express or implicit legislative intent to negate the claimed private rights of action. As the Court noted in *Cannon:* "[T]he legislative history of a statute that does not expressly create or deny a private remedy will typically be equally silent or ambiguous on the question. Therefore, in situations such as the present one 'in which it is clear that federal law has granted a class of persons certain rights, it is not necessary to show an intention to *create* a private cause of action, although an explicit purpose to *deny* such cause of action would be controlling.' *Cort,* 422 U.S. at 82 (emphasis in original)." 441 U.S., at 694.

I find no such intent to foreclose private actions. Indeed, the statutory language evinces an intent to create such actions. In § 215(b) of the Act Congress provided that contracts made in violation of any provision of the Act "shall be void." As the Court recognizes, such a provision clearly contemplates the existence of private rights under the Act. Similar provisions in the Investment Company Act of 1940, the Securities Exchange Act of 1934, and the Public Utility Holding Company Act have been recognized as reflecting an intent to create private rights of action to redress violations of substantive provisions of those Acts. [Cc]

The Court's conclusion that § 215, but not § 206, creates an implied private right of action ignores the relationship of § 215 to the substantive provisions of the Act contained in § 206. Like the jurisdictional provisions of a statute, § 215 "creates no cause of action of its own force and effect; it imposes no liabilities." [C] Section 215 merely specifies one consequence of a violation of the substantive prohibitions of § 206. The practical necessity of a private action to enforce this particular consequence of a § 206 violation suggests that Congress contemplated the use of private actions to redress violations of § 206. It also indicates that Congress did not intend the powers given to the SEC to be the exclusive means for enforcement of the Act.

The Court's holding that private litigants are restricted to actions for contract rescission confuses the question whether a cause of action exists with the question of the nature of relief available in such an action. Last Term in *Davis v. Passman,* 442 U.S. at 239, we recognized that "the question of whether a litigant has a 'cause of action' is analytically distinct and prior to the question of what relief, if any, a litigant may be entitled to receive." Once it is recognized that a statute creates an implied right of action, courts have wide discretion in fashioning available relief. *Sullivan v.*

Little Hunting Park, Inc., 396 U.S. 229, 239. ("The existence of a statutory right implies the existence of all necessary and appropriate remedies"). As the Court stated in Bell v. Hood, 327 U.S. 678, 684 (1946), "where legal rights have been invaded, and a federal statute provides for a general right to sue for such invasion, federal courts may use any available remedy to make good the wrong done." Thus, in the absence of any contrary indication by Congress, courts may provide private litigants exercising implied rights of action whatever relief is consistent with the congressional purpose. [Cc] The very decisions cited by the Court to support implication of an equitable right of action from contract voidance provisions of a statute, indicate that the relief available in such an action need not be restricted to equitable relief. * * *

IV. The third portion of the *Cort* standard requires consideration of the compatibility of a private right of action with the legislative scheme. While a private remedy will not be implied to the frustration of the legislative purpose, "when that remedy is necessary or at least helpful to the accomplishment of the statutory purpose, the Court is decidedly receptive to its implication under the statute." * * *

Implication of a private right of action for damages unquestionably would be not only consistent with the legislative goal of preventing fraudulent practices by investment advisers, but also essential to its achievement. While the Act empowers the SEC to take action to seek equitable relief to prevent offending investment advisers from engaging in future violations, in the absence of a private right of action for damages, victimized clients have little hope of obtaining redress for their injuries. Like the statute in *Cannon,* the Act does not assure that the members of the class it benefits are able "to activate and participate in the administrative process contemplated by the statute." [C] Moreover, the SEC candidly admits that, given the tremendous growth of the investment advisory industry, the magnitude of the enforcement problem exceeds the Commission's limited examination and enforcement capabilities. The Commission maintains that private litigation therefore is a necessary supplement to SEC enforcement activity. Under the circumstances of this case, this position seems unassailable. [Cc]

V. The final consideration under the *Cort* analysis is whether the subject matter of the cause of action has been so traditionally relegated to state law as to make it inappropriate to infer a federal cause of action. Regulation of the activities of investment advisers has not been a traditional state concern. * * *

Although some practices proscribed by the Act undoubtedly would have been actionable in common-law actions for fraud, "Congress intended the Investment Advisers Act to establish federal fiduciary standards for investment advisers." [Cc] While state law may be applied to parties subject to the Act, "as long as private causes of action are available in federal courts for violation of the federal statutes, [the] enforcement problem is obviated." [C]

VI. Each of the *Cort* factors points toward implication of a private cause of action in favor of clients defrauded by investment advisers in violation of the Act. The Act was enacted for the special benefit of clients of investment advisers, and there is no indication of any legislative intent to deny such a cause of action, which would be consistent with the legislative scheme governing an area not traditionally relegated to state law. Under these circumstances an implied private right of action for damages should be recognized.

NOTES AND QUESTIONS

1.   The principal case has been taken as the leading authority in later cases dealing with the issue of implied causes of action from federal statutes. As in the principal case the federal securities laws have been a fertile field for litigation. Here, more than elsewhere, plaintiffs have had some success in arguing that the laws imply rights of action, but the scope of the action is limited. The Supreme Court, however, has confirmed the end of a period of liberal implication of private rights of action under the federal securities laws. Central Bank of Denver v. First Interstate Bank of Denver, 511 U.S. 164 (1994). The Court held that private civil liability under section 10(b) of the Securities Exchange Act (15 U.S.C.S. 78j(b)) did not extend to parties who merely aid and abet manipulative or deceptive practices. Justice Kennedy, delivering the majority opinion, insisted that the Court adhere to the text in defining the conduct covered by § 10(b). The language of that section did not in its literal terms mention "aiding and abetting." Good policy reasons for inclusion of "aiding and abetting" could not provide grounds for finding liability where the text of the provision, upon principles of construction, did not include it. Courts cannot amend statutes. Arguments importing liability into the text were dismissed. Justice Stevens was joined by Justices Blackmun, Souter, and Ginsberg in dissent. Justice Stevens found a robust common law in aid and abettor liability to which the statutory provision could be presumed to conform. Furthermore, the federal courts had long assumed the existence of this species of liability. Reluctance to imply new implied causes of action may be justified, but, the dissenting Justices stated, to "lop off" rights long recognized is not legitimate.

2.   Recall that 42 U.S.C.A. § 1983 provides a cause of action for "the deprivation of any rights, privileges, or immunities secured by the Constitution and laws" of the United States. A § 1983 action is available to a person for both violations of the Constitution and federal statutes. Maine v. Thiboutot, 448 U.S. 1 (1980). However, the statute must create (1) enforceable rights, privileges, or immunities within the meaning of § 1983 and (2) Congress must not have foreclosed such enforcement in the enactment itself. Wright v. City of Roanoke Redevelopment and Housing Authority, 479 U.S. 418 (1987). The first question canvasses a similar inquiry to that engaged by the Supreme Court in *TAMA*, page 1166. Did Congress intend to benefit the plaintiff via a private right of action? In Wilder v. Virginia Hospital Association, 496 U.S. 498 (1990), a statutory provision required health care providers to be reimbursed according to rates that were "reasonable and adequate" to meet the costs of "efficiently and economically operated facilities." The Supreme Court found that this was intended to benefit the plaintiffs via a private right of action, especially since, without a private right, the provision would be unenforceable.

3.   In LaShawn A. v. Kelly, 990 F.2d 1319 (D.C.Cir.1993), cert. denied, 510 U.S. 1044 (1994), plaintiff children brought an action against the District of Columbia for injunctive relief. The children were in foster care under the supervision of the District of Columbia Department of Human Services or had been reported to the Department as abused or neglected. They claimed that the system

was managed as to inappropriately place children or to leave them in abusive circumstances. The District Court had concluded that the children had a § 1983 action. The D.C. Circuit Court of Appeals, however, decided that "complex constitutional and federal statutory issues" (the "§ 1983 thicket") ought to be eschewed because the District's statutes and regulations provided a protective scheme for the plaintiff children. The D.C. Court of Appeals concluded that the plaintiff had a private right of action to enforce the local statutes and regulations.

4. The Court has sparingly implied rights of action from federal statutes. See Suter v. Artist M, 503 U.S. 347 (1992), finding that no cause of action could be implied from the federal Adoption Assistance and Child Welfare Act of 1980, 94 Stat. 500, 42 U.S.C.A. §§ 620–628, 670–679a. The plaintiffs failed to show under the principles enunciated in the principal case that Congress intended to create a private cause of action for breaches of the federal Act. (The Court also found that the Act did not confer an enforceable right on the plaintiffs, the infringement of which would ground a § 1983 action. The Court distinguished the *Wilder* case, supra. The presumption against implications and the predominance of Congressional intent drawn from interpretation of the statute is exemplified in Bessette v. Avco Financial Services, 240 B.R. 147 (D.R.I.1999) (holding that § 524 of the Bankruptcy Code bestowed no private right of action.)

5. In Franklin v. Gwinnett County Public Schools, 503 U.S. 60 (1992), the plaintiff high school student brought an action for damages. She claimed that, contrary to Title IX of the Education Amendments of 1972, she had been subjected to continued sexual harassment and abuse by a teacher. In Cannon v. University of Chicago, 441 U.S. 677 (1979), cited in the principal case, the Court had held that Title IX was enforceable through a private right of action. The Court then applied the principle that a right is enforceable by the full panoply of judicial remedies. Nothing in Title IX displaced this presumption. Therefore, the plaintiff was entitled to a damages remedy for violation of her private right. Justice Scalia (with whom the Chief Justice and Justice Thomas agreed) concurred but maintained his hostility, criticizing the presumption of expansive remedies. He found a remedy in damages because the legislation in issue was enacted subsequent to *Cannon,* recognizing a private right of action under Title IX.

6. What is the relationship between implied private rights of actions and private rights of action pursuant to § 1983? It is clear that despite the statute upon proper construction providing no implied private right of action, it may support an action under § 1983 by giving rise to an enforceable right by a beneficiary under the statute. Mallett v. Wisconsin Division of Vocational Rehabilitation, 130 F.3d 1245 (7th Cir.1997) (holding that the Rehabilitation Act of 1973, while providing for no implied right of action, supported a § 1983 action.)

In Harris v. James, 127 F. 3d 993 (11th Cir.1997), medicaid recipients brought a § 1983 action alleging that Alabama's Medicaid plan was not in compliance with federal regulations requiring state plans to provide transportation to and from health care providers. The court reiterated that the relevant judicial inquiry was directed to Congressional intent to create a federal right. The inquiry found only a generalized duty imposed on the State and not an individual right. Note, however, the trenchant dissent by Judge Kravitch, arguing that a § 1983 action is based on the criteria set forth in *Wilder.* It was illegitimate to import the requirement of Congressional intent under Cort v. Ash, 422 U.S.66 (1975), an authority on implied rights actions.

2.   EXPRESS RIGHTS OF ACTION: CIVIL RICO

Reves v. Ernst & Young

Supreme Court of the United States, 1993.
507 U.S. 170.

[Farmer's Cooperative of Arkansas and Oklahoma, Inc. (the Co-Op) began operations in 1946. The daily operations were conducted by the general manager, Jack White. White financed the construction of his gasohol plant with Co–Op funds. After the indictment of White and Co-Op's accountant for federal tax fraud, Co-Op acquired the company that owned the plant. Accountants were appointed to audit the Co-Op. The accounting firm changed its name on a number of occasions, although the auditors remained the same. The final appellation was Ernst & Young, but during the relevant time was Arthur Young. The value of the gasohol plant company was accepted by the auditors as about $4.5 million, the figure used by the Co–Op's convicted accountant. But if valued on a market basis the value would have been much less and the Co-Op would have been insolvent. Arthur Young also failed to relate to the Co-op directors other information about the parlous state of the Co-Op's financial health. After a run on its demand notes, the Co-Op filed for bankruptcy. The trustee in bankruptcy and note holders filed suit against Arthur Young, among others.]

JUSTICE BLACKMUN delivered the opinion of the Court.

This case requires us once again to interpret the provisions of the Racketeer Influenced and Corrupt Organizations (RICO) chapter of the Organized Crime Control Act of 1970, Pub.L. 91–452, Title IX, 84 Stat. 941, as amended, 18 U.S.C. §§ 1961–1968 (1988 ed. and Supp. II). Section 1962(c) makes it unlawful "for any person employed by or associated with any enterprise engaged in, or the activities of which affect, interstate or foreign commerce, to conduct or participate, directly or indirectly, in the conduct of such enterprise's affairs through a pattern of racketeering activity * * *." The question presented is whether one must participate in the operation or management of the enterprise itself to be subject to liability under this provision.

* * *

The District Court applied the test established by the Eighth Circuit in Bennett v. Berg, 710 F.2d 1361, 1364 (en banc), cert. denied, *sub nom.* Prudential Ins. Co. of America v. Bennett, 464 U.S. 1008, 104 S.Ct. 527, 78 L.Ed.2d 710 (1983), that § 1962(c) requires "some participation in the operation or management of the enterprise itself." The court ruled: "Plaintiffs have failed to show anything more than that the accountants reviewed a series of completed transactions, and certified the Co-op's records as fairly portraying its financial status as of a date three or four months preceding the meetings of the directors and the shareholders at which they presented their reports. We do not hesitate to declare that such activities fail to satisfy the degree of management required by Bennett v. Berg." *Id.,* at 199–200.

On remand, the Court of Appeals, affirmed the judgment of the District Court in all major respects except the damages award, which it reversed and remanded for a new trial. [C] The only part of the Court of Appeals' decision that is at issue here is its affirmance of summary judgment in favor of Arthur Young on the RICO claim. Like the District Court, the Court of Appeals applied the "operation or management" test articulated in Bennett v. Berg and held that Arthur Young's conduct did not "rise to the level of participation in the management or operation of the Co-op." [C] The Court of Appeals for the District of Columbia Circuit also has adopted an "operation or management" test. See Yellow Bus Lines, Inc. v. Drivers, Chauffeurs & Helpers Local Union 639, 286 U.S.App. D.C. 182, 188, 913 F.2d 948, 954 (1990) (en banc), cert. denied, 501 U.S. ___, 111 S.Ct. 2839 (1991). We granted certiorari, 502 U.S. ___, 112 S.Ct. 1165 (1992), to resolve the conflict between these cases and Bank of America National Trust & Savings Assn. v. Touche Ross & Co., 782 F.2d 966, 970 (C.A.11 1986) (rejecting requirement that a defendant participate in the operation or management of an enterprise).

III

"In determining the scope of a statute, we look first to its language. If the statutory language is unambiguous, in the absence of 'a clearly expressed legislative intent to the contrary, that language must ordinarily be regarded as conclusive.'" United States v. Turkette, 452 U.S. 576, 580 (1981) * * *. Section 1962(c) makes it unlawful "for any person employed by or associated with any enterprise * * * to conduct or participate, directly or indirectly, in the conduct of such enterprise's affairs through a pattern of racketeering activity * * *."

The narrow question in this case is the meaning of the phrase "to conduct or participate, directly or indirectly, in the conduct of such enterprise's affairs." The word "conduct" is used twice, and it seems reasonable to give each use a similar construction. See Sorenson v. Secretary of the Treasury, 475 U.S. 851, 860 (1986). As a verb, "conduct" means to lead, run, manage, or direct. Webster's Third New International Dictionary 474 (1976). Petitioners urge us to read "conduct" as "carry on," [C] so that almost any involvement in the affairs of an enterprise would satisfy the "conduct or participate" requirement. But context is important, and in the context of the phrase "to conduct * * * [an] enterprise's affairs," the word indicates some degree of direction.

The dissent agrees that, when "conduct" is used as a verb, "it is plausible to find in it a suggestion of control." The dissent prefers to focus on "conduct" as a noun, as in the phrase "participate, directly or indirectly, in the conduct of [an] enterprise's affairs." But unless one reads "conduct" to include an element of direction when used as a noun in this phrase, the word becomes superfluous. Congress could easily have written "participate, directly or indirectly, in [an] enterprise's affairs," but it chose to repeat the word "conduct." We conclude, therefore, that as both a noun and a verb in this subsection "conduct" requires an element of direction.

The more difficult question is what to make of the word "participate." This Court previously has characterized this word as a "ter[m] ... of breadth." [Russell v. United States, 464 U.S. 16 at 21–22 (1983)]. Petitioners argue that Congress used "participate" as a synonym for "aid and abet." [C] That would be a term of breadth indeed, for "aid and abet" "comprehends all assistance rendered by words, acts, encouragement, support, or presence." Black's Law Dictionary 68 (6th ed. 1990). But within the context of § 1962(c), "participate" appears to have a narrower meaning. We may mark the limits of what the term might mean by looking again at what Congress did *not* say. On the one hand, "to participate * * * in the conduct of * * * affairs" must be broader than "to conduct affairs" or the "participate" phrase would be superfluous. On the other hand, as we already have noted, "to participate * * * in the conduct of * * * affairs" must be narrower than "to participate in affairs" or Congress' repetition of the word "conduct" would serve no purpose. It seems that Congress chose a middle ground, consistent with a common understanding of the word "participate"—"to take part in." Webster's Third New International Dictionary 1646 (1976).

Once we understand the word "conduct" to require some degree of direction and the word "participate" to require some part in that direction, the meaning of § 1962(c) comes into focus. In order to "participate, directly or indirectly, in the conduct of such enterprise's affairs," one must have some part in directing those affairs. Of course, the word "participate" makes clear that RICO liability is not limited to those with primary responsibility for the enterprise's affairs, just as the phrase "directly or indirectly" makes clear that RICO liability is not limited to those with a formal position in the enterprise,[4] but *some* part in directing the enterprise's affairs is required. The "operation or management" test expresses this requirement in a formulation that is easy to apply.

* * *

In their comments on the floor, members of Congress consistently referred to subsection (c) as prohibiting the *operation* of an enterprise through a pattern of racketeering activity and to subsections (a) and (b) as prohibiting the *acquisition* of an enterprise.[7] Representative Cellar, who was Chairman

---

4. For these reasons, we disagree with the suggestion of the Court of Appeals for the District of Columbia Circuit that § 1962(c) requires "*significant control*" over or within an enterprise." Yellow Bus Lines, Inc. v. Drivers, Chauffeurs & Helpers Local Union 639, 286 U.S.App.D.C. 182, 188, 913 F.2d 948, 954 (1990) (en banc) (emphasis added), cert. denied, 501 U.S. ___, 111 S.Ct. 2839 (1991).

7. See, *e.g.,* 116 Cong.Rec. 607 (1970) (remarks of Sen. Byrd of West Virginia) ("to acquire an interest in businesses * * *, or to acquire or operate such businesses by racketeering methods"); *id.,* at 36294 (remarks of Sen. McClellan) ("to acquire an interest in a business * * *, to use racketeering activities as a means of acquiring such a business, or to operate such a business by racketeering methods"); *id.,* at 36296 (remarks of Sen. Dole) ("using the proceeds of racketeering of the House Judiciary Committee that voted RICO out in 1970, described § 1962(c) as proscribing the "conduct of the affairs of a business by a person acting in a *managerial* capacity, through racketeering activity." 116 Cong.Rec. 35196 (1970) (emphasis added).

Of course, the fact that members of Congress understood § 1962(c) to prohibit the operation or management of an enterprise through a pattern of racketeering activity does not necessarily mean that they understood § 1962(c) to be limited to the operation or management of an enterprise. It is clear from other remarks, however, that Congress did not intend RICO to extend beyond the acquisition or operation of an enterprise. While S. 30 was being considered, critics of the bill raised concerns that racketeering activity was defined so broadly that RICO would reach many crimes not necessarily typical of organized crime. [C] Senator McClellan reassured the bill's critics that the critical limitation was not to be found in § 1961(1)'s list of predicate crimes but in the statute's other requirements, including those of § 1962.

* * *

Thus, the legislative history confirms what we have already deduced from the language of § 1962(c)—that one is not liable under that provision unless one has participated in the operation or management of the enterprise itself.

RICO's "liberal construction" clause does not require rejection of the "operation or management" test. Congress directed, by § 904(a) of Pub.L. 91–452, 84 Stat. 947, see note following 18 U.S.C. § 1961, p. 438, that the "provisions of this title shall be liberally construed to effectuate its remedial purposes." This clause obviously seeks to ensure that Congress' intent is not frustrated by an overly narrow reading of the statute, but it is not an invitation to apply RICO to new purposes that Congress never intended. Nor does the clause help us to determine what purposes Congress had in mind. Those must be gleaned from the statute through the normal means of interpretation. The clause " 'only serves as an aid for resolving an ambiguity; it is not to be used to beget one.' " Sedima, S.P.R.L. v. Imrex Co., 473 U.S. 479, 492, n. 10 (1985), quoting Callanan v. United States, 364 U.S. 587, 596 (1961). In this case it is clear that Congress did not intend to extend RICO liability under § 1962(c) beyond those who participate in the operation or management of an enterprise through a pattern of racketeering activity.

Petitioners argue that the "operation or management" test is flawed because liability under § 1962(c) is not limited to upper management but may extend to "any person employed by or associated with [the] enterprise." [C] We agree that liability under § 1962(c) is not limited to upper management, but we disagree that the "operation or management" test is

activity to acquire an interest in businesses engaged in interstate commerce, or to acquire or operate such businesses by racketeering methods"); *id.,* at 35227 (remarks of Rep.

Steiger) ("the use of specified racketeering methods to acquire or operate commercial organizations").

inconsistent with this proposition. An enterprise is "operated" not just by upper management but also by lower-rung participants in the enterprise who are under the direction of upper management. An enterprise also might be "operated" or "managed" by others "associated with" the enterprise who exert control over it as, for example, by bribery.

The United States also argues that the "operation or management" test is not consistent with § 1962(c) because it limits the liability of "outsiders" who have no official position within the enterprise. [C] The United States correctly points out that RICO's major purpose was to attack the "infiltration of organized crime and racketeering into legitimate organizations," S.Rep. No. 91–617, at 76, but its argument fails on several counts. First, it ignores the fact that § 1962 has four subsections. Infiltration of legitimate organizations by "outsiders" is clearly addressed in subsections (a) and (b), and the "operation or management" test that applies under subsection (c) in no way limits the application of subsections (a) and (b) to "outsiders." Second, § 1962(c) is limited to persons "employed by or associated with" an enterprise, suggesting a more limited reach than subsections (a) and (b), which do not contain such a restriction. Third, § 1962(c) cannot be interpreted to reach complete "outsiders" because liability depends on showing that the defendants conducted or participated in the conduct of the *"enterprise's* affairs," not just their *own* affairs. Of course, "outsiders" may be liable under § 1962(c) if they are "associated with" an enterprise and participate in the conduct of *its* affairs—that is, participate in the operation or management of the enterprise itself—but it would be consistent with neither the language nor the legislative history of § 1962(c) to interpret it as broadly as petitioners and the United States urge.

In sum, we hold that "to conduct or participate, directly or indirectly, in the conduct of such enterprise's affairs," § 1962(c), one must participate in the operation or management of the enterprise itself.

* * *

The judgment of the Court of Appeals is affirmed.

It is so ordered.

<h2 style="text-align:center">NOTES AND QUESTIONS</h2>

1.   The principal case represents the first occasion on which the Supreme Court has taken the opportunity to narrow the application of civil RICO. Sedima, S.P.R.L. v. Imrex Co., cited in the principal case, established that RICO was to be read broadly because of its expansive language and the statute's admonition to "effectuate its remedial purposes." The Court via a footnote suggested that the construction of the language "pattern of racketeering activity" may be useful in interpreting the Act. In H.J. Inc. v. Northwestern Bell Telephone Co., 492 U.S. 229 (1989), the Court reaffirmed and amplified the pattern requirement. The Court found that the racketeering predicate acts relied on must be related *"and* that they [must] amount to or pose a threat of continued criminal activity." The crimes are those traditionally associated with racketeering—murder, kidnap, arson, robbery, bribery, extortion, drugs and pornography. But also the statutory enumeration is

expansive and includes federal offenses which may be committed by "racketeers" but which are "garden variety" fraud and would have been the subject of commercial litigation. The broadest and most troublesome are mail and wire fraud. The scope is vast and an examination of the statute leaves one "lost in a land of few signposts." Tabas v. Tabas, 47 F.3d 1280, 1290 (3d Cir. 1995) (describing the duration requirement). The relationship aspect has been relatively easy to apply: e.g., United States v. Gelb, 881 F.2d 1155 (2d Cir.1989) (concluding that multiple schemes of mail fraud directed against the same victim (the Post Office) provided sufficient evidence of relatedness to support a "pattern").

2. The principal case was followed in University of Maryland at Baltimore v. Peat, Marwick, Main & Co., 996 F.2d 1534 (1993) (finding that the provision of financial services, like auditors and computerization of accounting services relating to purchases and sales, does not form a sufficient "nexus" between "the person and the conduct of the affairs of an enterprise").

3. The principal case does not address the issue of when a person may be liable for conspiracy to violate RICO. Section 1962(d) makes it illegal "to conspire to violate," among other things, § 1962(c). Recall that subsection (c) makes it unlawful for any person employed by an enterprise engaged in interstate commerce "to conduct or participate, directly or indirectly, in the conduct of such enterprise's affairs through a pattern of racketeering activity." In Salinas v. United States, 522 U.S. 52 (1997), the Court addressed conspiracy liability and held, applying general principles of conspiracy law, that a conspirator must intend to further an endeavor which, if completed, would satisfy all the elements of the criminal offense. It suffices, however, that he adopt the goal of furthering or facilitating the crime. It may appear, then, that under subsection (d) one need not participate personally in the operation or management of the enterprise. Could such an argument avoid the nexus requirement under the principal case?

The issue is addressed in Brouwer v. Raffensperger, Hughes & Co., 199 F.3d 961 (7th Cir.2000). Investors sued a law firm and an underwriting firm for work done for a corporation that afterwards declared bankruptcy. It was alleged that the defendant firms had concealed the true financial position of the corporation and knew that investors would likely lose their investment. Admitting a conceptually difficult analysis in reconciling the principal case with *Salinas*, the court held that while it was not necessary to meet the requirements in the principal case, it was necessary to find agreement to "knowingly facilitate the activities of the operators or managers to whom subsection (c) applies [to] knowingly agree to perform services of a kind which facilitate the activities of those who are operating the enterprise in an illegal manner. It is an agreement, not to operate or manage the enterprise, but personally to facilitate the activities of those who do." The court was "painfully aware" that this was not a "bright line."

4. The provision of treble damages and attorney's fees under civil RICO provided a stimulus to include RICO counts in actions where traditional claims would lie. Can you suggest actions at common law that may have been available in the principal case?

5. A coalition of anti-abortion groups conspired to shut down abortion clinics. Can pro-abortion organizations bring a civil RICO action claiming that the coalition had thus engaged in a pattern of racketeering activity including, as a racketeering predicate act, extortion in violation of the Hobbs Act, 18 U.S.C.A. § 1951? The Supreme Court in National Organization for Women, Inc. v. Scheidler, 510 U.S. 249 (1994) held that the action would lie, finding that the "enterprise" element of the offense did not connote an "economic motive." In a separate opinion Justice Souter,

joined by Justice Kennedy, stressed that First Amendment concerns may in the appropriate case delimit the reach of RICO.

6.   Do you consider the judicial task different in respect of implied rights of action, on the one hand, and express rights of action on the other?

3.   PREEMPTION

New York Central Railroad Company v. Winfield

Supreme Court of the United States, 1917.
244 U.S. 147.

MR. JUSTICE VAN DEVANTER delivered the opinion of the court.

While in the service of a railroad company in the State of New York, James Winfield sustained a personal injury whereby he lost the use of an eye. At that time the railroad company was engaging in interstate commerce as a common carrier and Winfield was employed by it in such commerce. The injury was not due to any fault or negligence of the carrier, or of any of its officers, agents or employees, but arose out of one of the ordinary risks of the work in which Winfield was engaged. He was a section laborer assisting in the repair of the carrier's main track and while tamping cross-ties struck a pebble which chanced to rebound and hit his eye. Following the injury he sought compensation therefor from the carrier under the Workmen's Compensation Law of the State and an award was made to him by the state commission, one member dissenting. The carrier appealed and the award was affirmed by the Appellate Division of the Supreme Court, two judges dissenting, and also by the Court of Appeals. Before the commission and in the state courts the carrier insisted that its liability or obligation and the employee's right were governed exclusively by the Employers' Liability Act of Congress, c. 149, 35 Stat. 65; c. 143, 36 Stat. 291, and therefore that no award could be made under the law of the State. That insistence is renewed here.

It is settled that under the commerce clause of the Constitution Congress may regulate the obligation of common carriers and the rights of their employees arising out of injuries sustained by the latter where both are engaged in interstate commerce; and it also is settled that when Congress acts upon the subject all state laws covering the same field are necessarily superseded by reason of the supremacy of the national authority. Congress acted upon the subject in passing the Employers' Liability Act, and the extent to which that act covers the field is the point in controversy. By one side it is said that the act, although regulating the liability or obligation of the carrier and the right of the employee where the injury results in whole or in part from negligence attributable to the carrier, does not cover injuries occurring without such negligence, and therefore leaves that class of injuries to be dealt with by state laws; and by the other side it is said that the act covers both classes of injuries and is exclusive as to both. The state decisions upon the point are conflicting. The New York court in the present case and the New Jersey court in Winfield v. Erie R.R. Co., 88 N.J.L. 619, hold that the act relates only to injuries resulting from negligence, while the California court in Smith v. Industrial Accident Commission, 26 Cal. App. 560, and the Illinois court in Staley v. Illinois Central R.R. Co., 268 Illinois, 356, hold that it has a broader scope and makes negligence a test,—not of the applicability of the act, but of the carrier's duty or obligation to respond pecuniarily for the injury.

In our opinion the latter view is right and the other wrong. Whether and in what circumstances railroad companies engaging in interstate commerce shall be required to compensate their employees in such commerce for injuries sustained therein are matters in which the nation as a whole is interested and there are weighty considerations why the controlling law should be uniform and not change at every state line. Baltimore & Ohio R.R. Co. v. Baugh, 149 U.S. 368, 378–379. It was largely in recognition of this that the Employers' Liability Act was enacted by Congress. Second Employers' Liability Cases, 223 U.S. 1, 51. It was drafted and passed shortly following a message from the President advocating an adequate national law covering all such injuries and leaving to the action of the several States only the injuries occurring in intrastate employment. Cong. Rec., 60th Cong., 1st sess., 1347. And the reports of the congressional committees having the bill in charge disclose, without any uncertainty, that it was intended to be very comprehensive, to withdraw all injuries to railroad employees in interstate commerce from the operation of varying state laws and to apply to them a national law having a uniform operation throughout all the States. House Report No. 1386 and Senate Report No. 460, 60th Cong., 1st sess. Thus, in the House Report it is said: "It [the bill] is intended in its scope to cover all commerce to which the regulative power of Congress extends ... by this bill it is hoped to fix a uniform rule of liability throughout the Union with reference to the liability of common carriers to their employees.... A Federal statute of this character will supplant the numerous State statutes on the subject so far as they relate to interstate commerce. It will create uniformity throughout the Union, and the legal status of such employer's liability for personal injuries instead of being subject to numerous rules will be fixed by one rule in all the States."

True, the act does not require the carrier to respond for injuries occurring where it is not chargeable with negligence, but this is because Congress, in its discretion, acted upon the principle that compensation should be exacted from the carrier where, and only where, the injury results from negligence imputable to it. Every part of the act conforms to this principle, and no part points to any purpose to leave the States free to require compensation where the act withholds it. By declaring in § 1 that the carrier shall be liable in damages for an injury to the employee "resulting in whole or in part from the negligence of any of the officers, agents, or employees of such carrier, or by reason of any defect or insufficiency, due to its negligence, in its cars, engines, appliances, machinery, track," etc., the act plainly shows, as was expressly held in Seaboard Air Line R. Co. v. Horton, 233 U.S. 492, 501, that it was the intention of Congress to make negligence the basis of the employee's right to damages, and to exclude responsibility of the carrier to the employee for an injury not resulting from its negligence or that of its officers, agents or other employees. The same principle is seen also in § 3, which requires that where the carrier and the employee are both negligent the recovery shall be diminished in proportion to the employee's contribution to the total negligence, and in § 4, which regards injuries arising from risks assumed by the employee as among those for which the carrier should not be made to respond. The committee reports upon the bill show that this principle was adopted deliberately, notwithstanding there were those within and without the committee who looked with greater favor upon a different principle which puts negligence out of view and regards the employee as entitled to compensation wherever the injury is an incident of the service in which he is employed. A few years after the passage of the act a legislative commission drafted and the Committees on the Judiciary in the two houses of Congress favorably reported a bill substituting the latter principle for the other, Senate Report No. 553, 62d Cong., 2d Sess., House Report No. 1441, 62d Cong., 3d Sess., but that bill did not become a law.

That the act is comprehensive and also exclusive is distinctly recognized in repeated decisions of this court. Thus, in Missouri, Kansas & Texas R. Co. v. Wulf, 226 U.S. 570, 576, and other cases, it is pointed out that the subject which the act covers is "the responsibility of interstate carriers by railroad to their employees injured in such commerce"; in Michigan Central R.R. Co. v. Vreeland, 227 U.S. 59, 66, 67, it is said that "we may not piece out this act of Congress by resorting to the local statutes of the State of procedure or that of the injury," that by it "Congress has undertaken to cover the subject of the liability of railroad companies to their employees injured while engaged in interstate commerce," and that it is "paramount and exclusive"; in North Carolina R.R. Co. v. Zachary, 232 U.S. 248, 256, it is held that where it appears that the injury occurred while the carrier was engaged and the employee employed in interstate commerce the federal act governs to the exclusion of the state law; in Seaboard Air Line R. Co. v. Horton, supra, pp. 501, 503, it is said not only that Congress intended "to exclude responsibility of the carrier to its employees" in the absence of negligence, but that it is not conceivable that Congress "intended to permit the legislatures of the several States to determine the effect of contributory negligence and assumption of risk, by enacting statutes for the safety of employees, since this would in effect relegate to state control two of the essential factors that determine the responsibility of the employer;" and in Wabash R.R. Co. v. Hayes, 234 U.S. 86, 89, it is said: "Had the injury occurred in interstate commerce, as was alleged, the Federal act undoubtedly would have been controlling and a recovery could not have been had under the common or statute law of the State; in other words, the Federal act would have been exclusive in its operation, not merely cumulative [citing cases]. On the other hand, if the injury occurred outside of interstate commerce, the Federal act was without application and the law of the State was controlling."

The act is entitled, "An Act Relating to the liability of common carriers by railroad to their employees in certain cases," and the suggestion is made that the words "in certain cases" require that the act be restrictively construed. But we think these words are intended to do no more than to bring the title into reasonable accord with the body of the act, which discloses in exact terms that it is not to embrace all cases of injury to the employees of such carriers, but only such as occur while the carrier is engaging and the employee is employed in "commerce between any of the several States," etc. See Employers' Liability Cases, 207 U.S. 463.

Only by disturbing the uniformity which the act is designed to secure and by departing from the principle which it is intended to enforce can the several States require such carriers to compensate their employees for injuries in interstate commerce occurring without negligence. But no State is at liberty thus to interfere with the operation of a law of Congress. As before indicated, it is a mistake to suppose that injuries occurring without negligence are not reached or affected by the act, for, as is said in Prigg v. Pennsylvania, 16 Pet. 539, 617, "if Congress have a constitutional power to regulate a particular subject, and they do actually regulate it in a given manner, and in a certain form, it cannot be that the state legislatures have a right to interfere, and, as it were, by way of complement to the legislation of Congress, to prescribe additional regulations, and what they may deem auxiliary provisions for the same purpose. In such a case, the legislation of Congress, in what it does prescribe, manifestly indicates that it does not intend that there shall be any farther legislation to act upon the subject-matter. Its silence as to what it does not do, is as expressive of what its intention is as the direct provisions made by it." Thus the act is as comprehensive of injuries occurring without negligence, as to which class it impliedly excludes liability, as it is of those as to which it imposes liability. In other words, it is a regulation of the carriers' duty or obligation as to both. And the reasons which operate to prevent the States from dispensing with compensation where the act requires it equally prevent them from requiring compensation where the act withholds or excludes it.

It follows that in the present case the award under the state law cannot be sustained.

Judgment reversed.

MR. JUSTICE BRANDEIS, dissenting.

I dissent from the opinion of the court; and the importance of the question involved induces me to state the reasons.

By the Employers' Liability Act of April 22, 1908, Congress provided, in substance, that railroads engaged in interstate commerce shall be liable in damages for their negligence resulting in injury or death of employees while so engaged. The majority of the court now holds that by so doing Congress manifested its will to cover the whole field of compensation or relief for injuries suffered by railroad employees engaged in interstate commerce; or, at least, the whole field of obligation of carriers relating thereto; and that it thereby withdrew the subject wholly from the domain of state action. In other words the majority of the court declares, that Congress by passing the Employers' Liability Act prohibited States from including within the protection of their general Workmen's Compensation Laws employees who without fault on the railroad's part are injured or killed while engaged in interstate commerce; although Congress itself offered them no protection. That Congress could have done this is clear. The question presented is: Has Congress done so? Has Congress so willed? * * *

To ascertain the intent we must look, of course, first at what Congress has said; then at the action it has taken, or omitted to take. We look at the words of the statute to see whether Congress has used any, which in terms express that will. We inquire whether, without the use of explicit words, that will is expressed in specific action taken. For Congress must be presumed to have intended the necessary consequences of its action. And if we find that its will is not expressed, or is not clearly expressed, either in words or by specific action, we should look at the circumstances under which the Employers' Liability Act was passed; look, on the one hand, at its origin, scope and purpose; and, on the other, at the nature, methods and means of state Workmen's Compensation Laws. If the will is not clearly expressed in words we must consider all these in order to determine what Congress intended. * * *

As to origin, purpose and scope of the Employers' Liability Act and the nature, methods and means of state Workmen's Compensation Laws: The facts are of common knowledge. Do they manifest that, by entering upon one section of the field of indemnity or relief for injuries or death suffered by employees engaged in interstate commerce, Congress purposed to occupy the whole field? * * *

By the common law as administered in the several States, the employee, like every other member of the community, was expected to bear the risks necessarily attendant upon life and work; subject only to the right to be indemnified for any loss inflicted by wrongdoers. The employer, like every other member of the community, was in theory liable to all others for loss resulting from his wrongs; the scope of his liability for wrongs being amplified by the doctrine of respondeat superior. This legal liability, which in theory applied between employer and employee as well as between others, came, in course of time, to be seriously impaired in practice. The protection it provided employees seemed to wane as the need for it grew. Three defenses—the doctrines of fellow servant's negligence, of assumption of risk and of contributory negligence—rose and flourished. When applied to huge organizations and hazardous occupations, as in railroading, they practically abolished the liability of employers to employees; and in so doing they worked great hardship and apparent injustice. The wrongs suffered were flagrant; the demand for redress insistent; and the efforts to secure remedial legislation widespread. But the opponents were alert, potent and securely entrenched. The evils of the fellow-servant rule as applied to railroads were recognized as early as 1856, when Georgia passed the first law abolishing the defense. * * *

The facts showing the origin and scope of the act discussed above indicate also its purpose. It was to end the denial of the right to damages for injuries due to the railroads' negligence—a right denied under judicial decisions through the interposition of the defenses of fellow-servant, assumption of risk and contributory negligence. It was not the purpose of the act to deny to the States the power to grant the wholly new right to protection or relief in the case of injuries suffered otherwise than through fault of the railroads. * * *

In the effort to remove abuses, a study had been made of facts; and of the world's experience in dealing with industrial accidents. That study uncovered as fiction many an assumption upon which American judges and lawyers had rested comfortably. The conviction became widespread, that our individualistic conception of rights and liability no longer furnished an adequate basis for dealing with accidents in industry. It was that no system of indemnity dependent upon fault on the employers' part could meet the situation; even if the law were perfected and its administration made exemplary. For in probably a majority of cases of injury there was no assignable fault; and in many more it must be impossible of proof. It was urged: Attention should be directed, not to the employer's fault, but to the employee's misfortune. Compensation should be general, not sporadic; certain, not conjectural; speedy, not delayed; definite as to amount and time of payment; and so distributed over long periods as to insure actual protection against lost or lessened earning capacity. To a system making such provision, and not to wasteful litigation, dependent for success upon the coincidence of fault and the ability to prove it, society, as well as the individual employee and his dependents, must look for adequate protection. Society needs such a protection as much as the individual; because ultimately society must bear the burden, financial and otherwise, of the heavy losses which accidents entail. And since accidents are a natural, and in part an inevitable, concomitant of industry as now practiced society, which is served thereby, should in some way provide the protection. To attain this end, cooperative methods must be pursued; some form of insurance—that is, some form of taxation. Such was the contention which has generally prevailed. Thus out of the attempt to enforce individual justice, grew the attempt to do social justice. But when Congress passed the Employers' Liability Act of April 22, 1908, these truths had gained little recognition in the United States. Not one of the thirty-seven States or Territories which now have Workmen's Compensation Laws had introduced the system. Yet the conception and value of compensation laws was not unknown to Congress. It then had under consideration the first Compensation Law for Federal Employees which was enacted in the following month (Act of May 30, 1908, 35 Stat. 556). The need of its speedy passage had been called to the attention of Congress by the President in the same special message which urged the passage of this Employers' Liability Act.

Can it be contended that Congress by simply passing the Employers' Liability Act prohibited the States from providing in any way for the maintenance of such employees (and their dependents) for whose injuries a railroad, innocent of all fault, could not be called upon to make indemnity under that act? It is the State which is both primarily and ultimately concerned with the care of the injured and of those dependent upon him; even though the accident may occur while the employee is engaged directly in interstate commerce. Upon the State falls the financial burden of dependency, if provision be not otherwise made. Upon the State falls directly the far heavier burden of the demoralization of its citizenry, and of the social unrest, which attend destitution and the denial of opportunity. Upon the State also rests under our dual system of government the duty owed to the individual to avert misery and promote happiness so far as possible. Surely we may not impute to Congress the will to deny to the States the power to perform either this duty to humanity or their fundamental duty of self-preservation. And if the States are left free to provide compensation, what is there in the Employers' Liability Act to show an intent on the part of Congress to deny to them the power to make the provision by raising the necessary contributions, in the first instance, through employers?

The principle underlying Workmen's Compensation Laws is the same in all the States. The methods and means by which that principle is carried out vary materially. The principle is that of insurance, the premiums to which are contributed by employers generally. How the insurance fund shall be raised and administered; what the scale of compensation or relief shall be; how the contributing groups of employers shall be formed; whether or not a state fund shall be created; whether the individual employer shall be permitted to become a self-insurer; whether he shall be permitted to deal directly with the employee in making settlement of the compensation to be awarded; on all these questions the laws of the several States do and properly may differ radically.

What methods and means the State shall adopt in order to provide compensation for injuries to citizens or residents where Congress has left it free to legislate, rests (subject to constitutional limitations) wholly within the judgment of the State. It might conclude, in view of the hazard involved, that no one should engage in the occupation of railroading without providing against the financial consequences of accidents through contributing an adequate amount to an accident insurance fund. It might conclude that it was wise to make itself the necessary contributions to such a fund, out of monies raised from general taxation. Or it might conclude, as the State of Washington did, that the fairest and wisest form of taxation for the purpose was to impose upon the employer directly the duty of making the required contributions—relying upon the laws of trade to effect, through the medium of transportation charges, an equitable distribution of the burden. * * *

The practical difficulty of determining in a particular case, according to presence or absence of railroad fault, whether indemnity is to be sought under the Federal Employers' Liability Act or under a state compensation law—affords, of course, no reason for imputing to Congress the will to deny to the States power to afford relief through such a system. The difficulty and uncertainty is, at worst, no greater than which now exists in so many cases where it is necessary to determine whether the employee was, at the time of the accident, engaged in interstate or intrastate commerce. (Footnote omitted.) Expedients for minimizing inherent difficulties will doubtless be found by experience. All the difficulties may conceivably be overcome in practice. Or they may prove so great as to lead Congress to repeal the Federal Employers' Liability Act and leave to the States (which alone can deal comprehensively with it) the whole subject of indemnity and compensation for injuries to employees whether engaged in interstate or intrastate commerce, and whether such injuries arise from negligence or without fault of the employer.

We are admonished also by another weighty consideration not to impute to Congress the will to deny to the States this power. The subject of compensation for accidents in industry is one peculiarly appropriate for state legislation. There must, necessarily, be great diversity in the conditions of living and in the needs of the injured and of his dependents, according to whether they reside in one or the other of our States and Territories, so widely extended. In a large majority of instances they reside in the State in which the accident occurs. Though the principle that compensation should be made, or relief given, is of universal application, the great diversity of conditions in the different sections of the United States may, in a wise application of the principle, call for differences between States, in the amount and method of compensation, the periods in which payment shall be made, and the methods and means by which the funds shall be raised and distributed. The field of compensation for injuries appears to be one in which uniformity is not desirable, or at least not essential to the public welfare.

The contention that Congress has, by legislating on one branch of a subject relative to interstate commerce, preempted the whole field—has been made often in this court; and, as the cases above cited show, has been repeatedly rejected in cases where the will of Congress to leave the balance of the field open to state action was far less clear than under the circumstances here considered.

MR. JUSTICE CLARKE concurs in this dissent.

English v. General Electric Company

Supreme Court of the United States, 1990.
496 U.S. 72.

BLACKMUN, J., delivered the opinion for a unanimous Court.

In the particular context of this case we must decide whether federal law pre-empts a state-law cause of action for intentional infliction of emotional distress. The suit is brought by an employee of a nuclear-fuels production facility against her employer and arises out of actions by the employer allegedly taken in retaliation for the employee's nuclear-safety complaints.

I

Petitioner Vera M. English was employed from 1972 to 1984 as a laboratory technician at the nuclear-fuels production facility operated by respondent General Electric Company (GE) in Wilmington, N.C. In February 1984, petitioner complained to GE's management and to the Nuclear Regulatory Commission (NRC) about several perceived violations of nuclear-safety standards at the facility, including the failure of her co-workers to clean up radioactive material spills in the laboratory.

Frustrated by the company's failure to address her concerns, petitioner on one occasion deliberately failed to clean a work table contaminated with a uranium solution during a preceding shift. Instead, she outlined the contaminated areas with red tape so as to make them conspicuous. A few days later, petitioner called her supervisor's attention to the marked-off areas, which still had not been cleaned. As a result, work was halted while the laboratory was inspected and cleaned.

Shortly after this episode, GE charged petitioner with a knowing failure to clean up radioactive contamination, and temporarily assigned her to other work. On April 30, 1984, GE's management informed petitioner that she would be laid off unless within 90 days she successfully bid for a position in an area of the facility where she would not be exposed to nuclear materials. On May 15, petitioner was notified of the company's final decision affirming the disciplinary action taken against her. Petitioner did not find another position by July 30, and her employment was terminated.

In August, petitioner filed a complaint with the Secretary of Labor charging GE with violating § 210(a) of the Energy Reorganization Act of 1974, 92 Stat. 2951, as amended, 42 U.S.C. § 5851(a), which makes it unlawful for an employer in the nuclear industry to

"discharge any employee or otherwise discriminate against any employee with respect to his compensation, terms, conditions, or privileges of employment because the employee . . .

(1) commenced, caused to be commenced, or is about to commence or cause to be commenced a proceeding under this chapter or the Atomic Energy Act of 1954, as amended, or a proceeding for the administration or enforcement of any requirement imposed under this chapter or the Atomic Energy Act of 1954, as amended;

(2) testified or is about to testify in any such proceeding or;

(3) assisted or participated or is about to assist or participate in any manner in such a proceeding . . . or in any other action to carry out the purposes of this chapter or the Atomic Energy Act of 1954, as amended."

In her charge, petitioner alleged that GE's actions constituted unlawful employment discrimination in retaliation for her nuclear-safety complaints to GE's management and to the NRC. An administrative law judge (ALJ) to whom the matter was referred found that GE had violated § 210(a) when it transferred and then discharged petitioner. The Secretary, however, dismissed the complaint as untimely because it had not been filed, as required by § 210(b)(1), within 30 days after the May 15 notice of the company's final decision.

In March 1987, petitioner filed a diversity action against GE in the United States District Court for the Eastern District of North Carolina.

Petitioner in four counts raised two claims, one for wrongful discharge and one for intentional infliction of emotional distress. With respect to the latter, petitioner alleged that she was suffering from severe depression and emotional harm as a result of GE's "extreme and outrageous conduct." Petitioner alleged that, in addition to transferring and ultimately firing her, GE (1) had removed her from the laboratory position under guard "as if she were a criminal," id., at 14; (2) had assigned her to degrading "make work" in her substitute assignment, ibid.; (3) had derided her as paranoid; (4) had barred her from working in controlled areas; (5) had placed her under constant surveillance during working hours; (6) had isolated her from co-workers, even during lunch periods; and (7) had conspired to charge her fraudulently with violations of safety and criminal laws. [c] Petitioner sought punitive as well as compensatory damages.

Although the District Court concluded that petitioner had stated a valid claim for intentional infliction of emotional distress under North Carolina law, it nonetheless granted GE's motion to dismiss. [C] The court did not accept GE's argument that petitioner's claim fell within the field of nuclear safety, a field that, according to GE, had been completely pre-empted by the Federal Government. The court held, however, that petitioner's claim was pre-empted because it conflicted with three particular aspects of § 210: (1) a provision that bars recovery under the section to any employee who "deliberately causes a violation of any requirement of [the Energy Reorganization or of the Atomic Energy Act," § 210(g)]; (2) the absence of any provision generally authorizing the Secretary to award exemplary or punitive damages; and (3) the provisions requiring that a whistleblower invoking the statute file an administrative complaint within 30 days after the violation occurs, and that the Secretary resolve the complaint within 90 days after its filing. See §§ 210(b)(1) and (b)(2)(A). In the court's view, Congress enacted this scheme to foreclose all remedies to whistleblowers who themselves violate nuclear-safety requirements, to limit exemplary damages awards against the nuclear industry, and to guarantee speedy resolution of allegations of nuclear-safety violations—goals the court found incompatible with the broader remedies petitioner sought under state tort law.

The United States Court of Appeals affirmed the dismissal of petitioner's emotional distress claim on the basis of the District Court's reasoning. 871 F.2d 22, 23 (1989). That court concluded that Congress had intended to foreclose nuclear whistleblowers from pursuing state tort remedies, and stated its belief that the District Court "correctly identified and applied the relevant federal and state law." [C] Because of an apparent conflict with a decision of the First Circuit, see Norris v. Lumbermen's Mutual Casualty Co., 881 F.2d 1144 (1989), we granted certiorari. 493 U.S. 1055 (1990).

II

A

The sole question for our resolution is whether the Federal Government has pre-empted petitioner's state-law tort claim for intentional infliction of emotional distress. Our cases have established that state law is pre-empted under the Supremacy Clause, U.S. Const. Art. VI, cl. 2, in three circumstances. First, Congress can define explicitly the extent to which its enactments pre-empt state law. See Shaw v. Delta Air Lines, Inc., 463 U.S. 85, 95–98 (1983). Preemption fundamentally is a question of congressional intent, see Schneidewind v. ANR Pipeline Co., 485 U.S. 293, 299 (1988), and when Congress has made its intent known through explicit statutory language, the courts' task is an easy one. Second, in the absence of explicit statutory language, state law is pre-empted where it regulates conduct in a field that Congress intended the Federal Government to occupy exclusively. Such an intent may be inferred from a "scheme of federal regulation . . . so pervasive as to make reasonable the inference that Congress left no room for the States to supplement it," or where an Act of Congress "touches a field in which the federal interest is so dominant that the federal system will be assumed to preclude enforcement of state laws on the same subject." Rice v. Santa Fe Elevator Corp., 331 U.S. 218, 230 (1947). Although this Court has not hesitated to draw an inference of field preemption where it is supported by the federal statutory and regulatory schemes, it has emphasized: "Where . . . the field which congress is said to have preempted" includes areas that have "been traditionally occupied by the States," congressional intent to supersede state laws must be " 'clear and manifest.' " Jones v. Rath Packing Co., 430 U.S. 519, 525 (1977), quoting Rice v. Santa Fe Elevator Corp., 331 U.S., at 230. Finally, state law is preempted to the extent that it actually conflicts with federal law. Thus, the Court has found preemption where it is impossible for a private party to comply with both state and federal requirements, see, e.g., Florida Lime & Avocado Growers, Inc. v. Paul, 373 U.S. 132, 142–143 (1963), or where state law "stands as an obstacle to the accomplishment and execution of the full purposes and objectives of Congress." Hines v. Davidowitz, 312 U.S. 52, 67 (1941).

It is undisputed that Congress has not explicitly pre-empted petitioner's state-law tort action by inserting specific pre-emptive language into any of its enactments governing the nuclear industry. The District Court and apparently the Court of Appeals did not rest their decisions on a field pre-emption rationale either, but rather on what they considered an actual tension between petitioner's cause of action and the congressional goals reflected in § 210. In this Court, respondent seeks to defend the judgment both on the lower courts' rationale and on the alternative ground that petitioner's tort claim is located within a field reserved for federal regulation—the field of nuclear safety. Before turning to the specific aspects of § 210 on which the lower courts based their decisions, we address the field pre-emption question.

B

This is not the first case in which the Court has had occasion to consider the extent to which the Congress has pre-empted the field of nuclear safety. In Pacific Gas & Electric Co. v. State Energy Resources Conservation and Development Comm'n, 461 U.S. 190 (1983), the Court carefully analyzed the congressional enactments relating to the nuclear industry in order to decide whether a California law that conditioned the construction of a nuclear-power plant on a state agency's approval of the plant's nuclear waste storage and disposal facilities fell within a pre-empted field. Although we need not repeat all of that analysis here, we summarize briefly the Court's discussion of the actions Congress has taken in the nuclear realm and the conclusions it drew from these actions.

Until 1954, the use, control, and ownership of all nuclear technology remained a federal monopoly. The Atomic Energy Act of 1954, 68 Stat. 919, as amended, *42 U.S.C. §§ 2011* et seq., stemmed from Congress' belief that the national interest would be served if the Government encouraged the private sector to develop atomic energy for peaceful purposes under a program of federal regulation and licensing. The Act implemented this policy decision by opening the door to private construction, ownership, and operation of commercial nuclear-power reactors under the strict supervision of the Atomic Energy Commission (AEC). See Duke Power Co. v. Carolina Environmental Study Group, Inc., 438 U.S. 59, 63 (1978). The AEC was given exclusive authority to license the transfer, delivery, receipt, acquisition, possession, and use of all nuclear materials. As was observed in Vermont Yankee Nuclear Power Corp. v. Natural Resources Defense Council, Inc., 435 U.S. 519, 550 (1978), "the [Federal Government's] prime area of concern in the licensing context ... [was] national security, public health, and safety." With respect to these matters, no significant role was contemplated for the States.

In 1959, Congress amended the Atomic Energy Act in order to "clarify the respective responsibilities ... of the States and the [Federal Government] with respect to the regulation of byproduct, source, and special nuclear materials," 42 U.S.C. § 2021(a)(1), and generally to increase the States' role. The 1959 amendments authorized the NRC, by agreements with state governors, to discontinue the Federal Government's regulatory authority over certain nuclear materials under specified conditions. State regulatory programs adopted under the amendment were required to be "coordinated and compatible" with those of the NRC. § 2021(g).

In 1974, Congress passed the Energy Reorganization Act, 88 Stat. 1233, 42 U.S.C. §§ 5801 et seq., which abolished the AEC and transferred its regulatory and licensing authority to the NRC. § 5841(f). The 1974 Act also expanded the number and range of safety responsibilities under the NRC's charge. As was observed in Pacific Gas, the NRC does not purport to exercise its authority based upon economic considerations, but rather is concerned primarily with public health and safety. [C] Finally, in 1978, Congress amended both the Atomic Energy Act and the Energy Reorganization Act. Pub. L. No. 95–601, 92 Stat. 2947. Among these amendments is § 210, 42 U.S.C. § 5851, which, as discussed above, encourages employees to report safety violations and provides a mechanism for protecting them against retaliation for doing so.

After reviewing the relevant statutory provisions and legislative history, the Court in Pacific Gas concluded that "the Federal Government has occupied the entire field of nuclear safety concerns, except the limited powers expressly ceded to the States." [C] Although we ultimately determined that the California statute at issue there did not fall within the pre-empted field, we made clear our view that Congress intended that only "the Federal Government should regulate the radiological safety aspects involved in the construction and operation of a nuclear plant." [C] In the present dispute, respondent and petitioner disagree as to whether petitioner's tort action falls within the boundaries of the pre-empted field referred to in Pacific Gas.

Respondent maintains that the pre-empted field of "nuclear safety" is a large one, and that § 210 is an integral part of it. Specifically, respondent contends that because the Federal Government is better able to promote nuclear safety if whistleblowers pursue the federal remedy, the whole area marked off by § 210 should be considered part of the pre-empted field identified in Pacific Gas. Accordingly, respondent argues that all state-law remedies for conduct that is covered by § 210 are pre-empted by Congress' decision to have the Federal Government exclusively regulate the field of nuclear safety.

Petitioner and the United States as amicus curiae, on their part, contend that petitioner's claim for intentional infliction of emotional distress is not pre-empted because the Court made clear in Pacific Gas that state laws supported by non-safety rationales do not lie within the pre-empted field. They argue that since the state tort of intentional infliction of emotional distress is supported by a non-safety rationale—namely, the State's "substantial interest in protecting its citizens from the kind of abuse of which [petitioner] complains," see Farmer v. Carpenters, 430 U.S. 290, 302 (1977)—petitioner's cause of action must be allowed to go forward.

We think both arguments are somewhat wide of the mark. With respect to respondent's contention, we find no "clear and manifest" intent on the part of Congress, in enacting § 210, to pre-empt all state tort laws that traditionally have been available to those persons who, like petitioner, allege outrageous conduct at the hands of an employer. Indeed, acceptance of respondent's argument would require us to conclude that Congress has displaced not only state tort law, which is at issue in this case, but also state criminal law, to the extent that such criminal law is applied to retaliatory conduct occurring at the site of a nuclear employer. For example, if an employer were to retaliate against a nuclear whistleblower by hiring thugs to assault the employee on the job (conduct literally covered by § 210), respondent's position would imply that the state criminal law prohibiting such conduct is within the pre-empted field. We simply cannot believe that Congress intended that result. Instead, we think the District Court was essentially correct in observing that while § 210 obviously bears some relation to the field of nuclear safety, its "paramount" purpose was the protection of employees. [C] Accordingly, we see no basis for respondent's contention that all state-law claims arising from conduct covered by the section are necessarily included in the pre-empted field.

Nor, however, can we accept petitioner's position, or the reading of Pacific Gas on which it is based. It is true that the holding in that case was premised, in part, on the conclusion that the California ban on nuclear construction was not motivated by safety concerns. Indeed, the majority of the Court suggested that a "state moratorium on nuclear construction grounded in safety concerns falls squarely within the prohibited field." 461 U.S., at 213. In other words, the Court defined the pre-empted field, in part, by reference to the motivation behind the state law. This approach to defining the field had some support in the text of the 1959 amendments to the Atomic Energy Act, which provided, among other things, that "nothing in this section shall be construed to affect the authority of any State or local agency to regulate activities for purposes other than protection against radiation hazards." 42 U.S.C. § 2021(k). But the Court did not suggest that a finding of safety motivation was necessary to place a state law within the pre-empted field. On the contrary, it took great pains to make clear that state regulation of matters directly affecting the radiological safety of nuclear-plant construction and operation, "even if enacted out of non-safety concerns, would nevertheless [infringe upon] the NRC's exclusive authority." [C] Thus, even as the Court suggested that part of the pre-empted field is defined by reference to the purpose of the state law in question, it made clear that another part of the field is defined by the state law's actual effect on nuclear safety. Because it is clear that the state tort law at issue here is not motivated by safety concerns, the former portion of the field argument is not relevant. The real issue, then, is whether petitioner's tort claim is so related to the "radiological safety aspects involved in the . . . operation of a nuclear [facility]," see id., at 205, that it falls within the pre-empted field. In addressing this issue, we must bear in mind that not every state law that in some remote way may affect the nuclear safety decisions made by those who build and run nuclear facilities can be said to fall within the pre-empted field. We have no doubt, for instance, that the application of state minimum wage and child labor laws to employees at nuclear facilities would not be pre-empted, even though these laws could be said to affect tangentially some of the resource allocation decisions that might have a bearing on radiological safety. Instead, for a state law to fall within the pre-empted zone, it must have some direct and substantial effect on the decisions made by those who build or operate nuclear facilities concerning radiological safety levels. We recognize that the claim for intentional infliction of emotional distress at issue here may have some effect on these decisions, because liability for claims like petitioner's will attach additional consequences to retaliatory conduct by employers. As employers find retaliation more costly, they will be forced to deal with complaints by whistleblowers by other means, including altering radiological safety policies. Nevertheless, we believe that this effect is neither direct nor substantial enough to place petitioner's claim in the pre-empted field.

This result is strongly suggested by the decision in Silkwood v. Kerr–McGee Corp., 464 U.S. 238 (1984). The Court there held that a claim for punitive damages in a state tort action arising out of the escape of plutonium from a federally licensed nuclear facility did not fall within the pre-empted field discussed in Pacific Gas. The Court reached this result notwithstanding "the tension between the conclusion that [radiological] safety regulation is the exclusive concern of the federal law and the conclusion that a State may nevertheless award damages [including punitive damages] based on its own law of liability" governing unsafe working conditions. 464 U.S., at 256. Although the decision in *Silkwood* was based in substantial part on legislative history suggesting that Congress did not intend to include in the pre-empted field state tort remedies for radiation-based injuries, see 464 U.S., at 251–256, we think it would be odd, if not irrational, to conclude that Congress intended to include tort actions stemming from retaliation against whistleblowers in the pre-empted field but intended not to include tort actions stemming from radiation damage suffered as a result of actual safety violations. Potential liability for the kind of claim at issue in *Silkwood* will affect radiological safety decisions more directly than will potential liability under the kind of claim petitioner raises, because the tort claim in *Silkwood* attaches additional consequences to safety violations themselves, rather than to employer conduct that merely arises from allegations of safety violations. Moreover, and related, the prospect of compensatory and punitive damages for radiation-based injuries will undoubtedly affect nuclear employers' primary decisions about radiological safety in the construction and operation of nuclear power facilities far more substantially than will liability under the kind of claim petitioner asserts. It is thus not surprising that we find no evidence of a "clear and manifest" intent on the part of Congress to pre-empt tort claims like petitioner's. Cf. Goodyear Atomic Corp. v. Miller, 486 U.S. 174, 186 (1988) (increased workers' compensation award for injury caused by a safety violation at a government-owned nuclear facility is "incidental regulatory pressure" that Congress finds acceptable). Accordingly, we conclude that petitioner's claim does not lie within the pre-empted field of nuclear safety.

C

We now turn to the question whether, as the lower courts concluded, petitioner's claim conflicts with particular aspects of § 210. On its face, the section does no more than grant a federal administrative remedy to employees in one industry against one type of employer discrimination—retaliation for whistleblowing. Ordinarily, the mere existence of a federal regulatory or enforcement scheme, even one as detailed as § 210, does not by itself imply pre-emption of state remedies. The Court has observed: "Undoubtedly, every subject that merits congressional legislation is, by definition, a subject of national concern. That cannot mean, however, that every federal statute ousts all related state law.... Instead, we must look for special features warranting pre-emption." Hillsborough County v. Automated Medical Laboratories, Inc., 471 U.S. 707, 719 (1985). Here, the District Court identified three "special features" of § 210 that it believed were incompatible with petitioner's claim.

The District Court relied first on § 210(g), which provides that "Subsection (a) of this section [the prohibition on employer retaliation] shall not apply" where an employee "deliberately causes a violation of any requirement of this Act or of the Atomic Energy Act." According to the District Court and respondent, this section reflects a congressional desire to preclude all relief, including state remedies, to a whistleblower who deliberately commits a safety violation referred to in § 210(g). Permitting any state-law claim based on whistleblowing retaliation, the court reasoned, would frustrate this congressional objective. We do not agree. As an initial matter, we note that the text of § 210(g) specifically limits its applicability to the remedy provided by § 210(a), and does not suggest that it bars state-law tort actions. Nor does the legislative history of § 210 reveal a clear congressional purpose to supplant state-law causes of action that might afford broader relief. Indeed, the only explanation for any of the statute's remedial limitations is the Committee Report's statement that employees who deliberately violate nuclear-safety requirements would be denied protection under § 210(g) "in order to avoid abuse of the protection afforded under this section." S. Rep. No. 95–848, p. 30 (1978).

In any event, even if the District Court and respondent are correct in concluding that Congress wanted those who deliberately commit nuclear-safety violations, as defined under § 210(g), to be denied all remedies against employer retaliation, this federal interest would be served by preempting state law only to the extent that it afforded recovery to such violators. In the instant case, the ALJ found that petitioner had not deliberately committed a safety violation within the meaning of § 210(g), [c], and neither the Secretary nor the lower courts have suggested otherwise. Thus, barring petitioner's tort action would not even serve the federal interest the lower courts and respondent have gleaned from their reading of this section.

The District Court also relied on the absence in § 210 of general authorization for the Secretary to award exemplary damages against employers who engage in retaliatory conduct. The District Court concluded, and respondent now argues, that this absence implies a congressional intent to bar a state action, like petitioner's, that permits such an award. As the District Court put it, § 210 reflects "an informed judgment [by Congress] that in no circumstances should a nuclear whistler-blower receive punitive damages when fired or discriminated against because of his or her safety complaints." [C] We believe the District Court and respondent have read too much into Congress' decision not to authorize exemplary damages for most § 210 violations. First, even with respect to actions brought under § 210, the District Court was incorrect in stating that "in no circumstances" will a nuclear whistle-blower receive punitive damages; § 210(d) authorizes a district court to award exemplary damages in enforcement proceedings brought by the Secretary. Moreover, and more importantly, we think the District Court failed to follow this Court's teaching that "ordinarily, state causes of action are not pre-empted solely because they impose liability over and above that authorized by federal law." California v. ARC America Corp., 490 U.S. 93, 105 (1989). Absent some specific suggestion in the text or legislative history of § 210, which we are unable to find, we cannot conclude that Congress intended to pre-empt all state actions that permit the recovery of exemplary damages. Finally, we address the District Court's holding that the expeditious time frames provided by Congress for the processing of § 210 claims reflect a congressional decision that no whistle-blower should be able to recover under any other law after the time for filing under § 210 has expired. The District Court reasoned, and respondent agrees, that if a state-law remedy is available after the time for filing a § 210 complaint has run, a whistle-blower will have less incentive to bring a § 210 complaint. As a result, the argument runs, federal regulatory agencies will remain unaware of some safety violations and retaliatory behavior, and will thus be unable to ensure radiological safety at nuclear facilities. We cannot deny that there is some force to this argument, but we do not believe that the problem is as great as respondent suggests.

First, many if not most, retaliatory incidents come about as a response to safety complaints that employees register with federal regulatory agencies. The Federal Government thus is already aware of these safety violations, whether or not the employee invokes the remedial provisions of § 210. Also, we are not so sure as respondent seems to be that employees will forgo their § 210 options and rely solely on state remedies for retaliation. Such a prospect is simply too speculative a basis on which to rest a finding of pre-emption. The Court has observed repeatedly that pre-emption is ordinarily not to be implied absent an "actual conflict." See, e.g., Savage v. Jones, 225 U.S. 501, 533 (1912). The "teaching of this Court's decisions ... enjoins seeking out conflicts between state and federal regulation where none clearly exists." Huron Cement Co. v. Detroit, 362 U.S. 440, 446 (1960).

III

We conclude that petitioner's claim for intentional infliction of emotional distress does not fall within the pre-empted field of nuclear safety as that field has been defined in prior cases. Nor does it conflict with any particular aspect of § 210. The contrary judgment of the Court of Appeals is reversed, and the case is remanded for further proceedings consistent with this opinion.

It is so ordered.

NOTES AND QUESTIONS

1. The last word of the Supreme Court on the issue of preemption is Medtronic, Inc. v. Lohr, 518 U.S. 470 (1996), page 777. In this case plaintiffs, husband and wife, sought damages for injuries suffered when the wife's heart pacemaker failed. Plaintiffs claimed that the pacemaker had been negligently designed and manufactured and the defendant had omitted to warn of the tendency of the pacemaker to fail. The Food and Drug Administration had allowed the pacemaker to be marketed based on a finding that it was "substantially equivalent" to devices introduced previously into interstate commerce. Defendant argued that the claims were pre-empted by 21 U.S.C.S. § 360k(a) stating that no state may establish or "continue in effect with respect to a device intended for human use any

requirement which is different from, or in addition to, any requirement applicable" to a device. Justice Stevens announcing the judgement, joined by Justices Kennedy, Souter, Ginsberg, and Breyer, held that the negligent design claims were not pre-empted, nor were the negligent manufacture or warning claims to the extent that the statutes equilibriated those required by federal law.

The task of the Court in this instance of express preemption is to identify the domain pre-empted. Addressing itself to the purpose of Congress, the plurality opinion put weight on the unlikely intent to deprive an injured party of recourse, at least unless it was clearly enunciated. Legislative history and regulations supported an interpretation that would not preclude the common law. The common law did not impede, in the way envisioned by the legislation, the ability of the federal regulators to implement and enforce federal requirements.

2. A celebrated and notorious example of express preemption and potential preclusion of common law tort claims arises under the Employee Retirement Income Security Act (ERISA). The legislation was intended to apply federal quality control for employment benefits schemes including medical and health care schemes. The statute enacts a uniform body of law for pension and benefit plans. To effect uniformity, state tort claims are expressly preempted pursuant to § 514(a):

> Except as provided in subsection (b) ... the provisions of this [statute] ... shall supersede any and all State laws insofar as they may now or hereafter relate to any employee benefit plan ... not exempt under section 1003(b)...

Under modern health care delivery, providers of medical care often render services as part of "employee welfare benefit" plans. Thus, the prospect is created of preemption of many medical malpractice claims. Claimants are restricted to those benefits under § 502(a)(1)(B) of ERISA; these claims may be derisory.

The task of the courts has been to determine which state laws "relate to" benefit plans as to yield to § 514(a) and the preemptive scope of § 502(a)(1)(B). Bauman v. U.S. Healthcare, 193 F.3d 151 (3d Cir. 1999), exemplifies the type of case that raises the issue of how far the preemption protects HMOs and similar health care delivery entities from tort liability. Plaintiff alleged that defendant's policy of discharge from hospital after birth and its utilization review policies, discouraging readmission, had contributed to the death of Michelina Bauman. Plaintiff also claimed that defendant was liable directly and vicariously in failing to exercise due care in diagnosing and treating Michelina and the "selection, supervision, and monitoring" of the physician determining the question of discharge and readmission. The court applying authority was put to the task of line drawing. The line turned on the distinction between claims directed at the quality of the care received, on the one hand, and, on the other, claims pertaining to "erroneous withheld benefits due" or enforcement of rights under the prevailing plan. The former claims are not pre-empted; the latter are. The distinction (medical v. administrative) is sometimes conceptualized as referring to the capacity of the defendant provider as a "plan administrator" or as a "provider of health care." The *Bauman* court characterizes plaintiff's claims as related to the quality of the care and thus not within the intended preempted effect of ERISA. See also Dukes v. U.S. Healthcare, Inc., 57 F.3d 350 (3d Cir.1995). The elusiveness of the distinction has led to suggestions for Congressional reform.

Ramirez v. Plough, Inc.

Supreme Court of California, 1993.
6 Cal. 4th 539, 863 P.2d 167, 25 Cal. Rptr. 2d 97.

KENNARD, J.

We granted review in this case to determine whether a manufacturer of nonprescription drugs may incur tort liability for distributing its products with warnings in English only. Recognizing the importance of uniformity and predictability in this sensitive area of the law, we conclude that the rule for tort liability should conform to state and federal statutory and administrative law. Because both state and federal law now require warnings in English but not in any other language, we further conclude that a manufacturer may not be held liable in tort for failing to label a nonprescription drug with warnings in a language other than English.

I

Plaintiff Jorge Ramirez, a minor, sued defendant Plough, Inc., alleging that he contracted Reye's syndrome as a result of ingesting a nonprescription drug, St. Joseph Aspirin for Children (SJAC), that was manufactured and distributed by defendant. Plaintiff sought compensatory and punitive damages on theories of negligence, products liability, and fraud. The trial court granted summary judgment for defendant. On plaintiff's appeal, the Court of Appeal reversed.

* * *

In March 1986, when he was less than four months old, plaintiff exhibited symptoms of a cold or similar upper respiratory infection. To relieve these symptoms, plaintiff's mother gave him SJAC. Although the product label stated that the dosage for a child under two years old was "as directed by doctor," plaintiff's mother did not consult a doctor before using SJAC to treat plaintiff's condition. Over a two-day period, plaintiff's mother gave him three SJAC tablets. Then, on March 15, plaintiff's mother took him to a hospital. There, the doctor advised her to administer Dimetapp or Pedialyte (nonprescription medications that do not contain aspirin), but she disregarded the advice and continued to treat plaintiff with SJAC.

Plaintiff thereafter developed Reye's syndrome, resulting in severe neurological damage, including cortical blindness, spastic quadriplegia, and mental retardation.

First described by the Australian pathologist Douglas Reye in 1963, Reye's syndrome occurs in children and teenagers during or while recovering from a mild respiratory tract infection, flu, chicken pox, or other viral illness. The disease is characterized by severe vomiting and irritability or lethargy, which may progress to delirium and coma. In 1982, the Centers for Disease Control estimated that Reye's syndrome affected 600 to 1,200 children and teenagers in this country each year. The disease is fatal in 20 to 30 percent of cases, with many of the survivors sustaining permanent brain damage. The cause of Reye's syndrome was unknown in 1986 (and apparently remains unknown), but by the early 1980's several studies had shown an association between ingestion of aspirin during a viral illness, such as chicken pox or influenza, and the subsequent development of Reye's syndrome. These studies prompted the United States Food and Drug

Administration (FDA) to propose a labeling requirement for aspirin products warning of the dangers of Reye's syndrome. (See 50 Fed.Reg. 51400 (Dec. 17, 1985).) The FDA published a regulation to this effect on March 7, 1986. Unless extended, the regulation was to expire two years after its effective date. In 1988, the FDA revised the required warning to state explicitly that Reye's syndrome is reported to be associated with aspirin use, and it made the regulation permanent. [C]

Even before the federal regulation became mandatory, packages of SJAC displayed this warning: "Warning: Reye Syndrome is a rare but serious disease which can follow flu or chicken pox in children and teenagers. While the cause of Reye Syndrome is unknown, some reports claim aspirin may increase the risk of developing this disease. Consult doctor before use in children or teenagers with flu or chicken pox." The package insert contained the same warning, together with this statement: "The symptoms of Reye syndrome can include persistent vomiting, sleepiness and lethargy, violent headaches, unusual behavior, including disorientation, combativeness, and delirium. If any of these symptoms occur, especially following chicken pox or flu, call your doctor immediately, even if your child has not taken any medication. Reye Syndrome Is Serious, so Early Detection and Treatment Are Vital."

These warnings were printed in English on the label of the SJAC that plaintiff's mother purchased in March 1986. At that time, plaintiff's mother, who was born in Mexico, was literate only in Spanish. Because she could not read English, she was unable to read the warnings on the SJAC label and package insert. Yet she did not ask anyone to translate the label or package insert into Spanish, even though other members of her household could have done so. Plaintiff's mother had never heard, seen, or relied upon any advertising for SJAC in either English or Spanish. In Mexico, she had taken aspirin for headaches, both as a child and as an adult, and a friend had recommended SJAC.

Plaintiff, by and through his mother as guardian ad litem, filed suit against defendant in August 1989, alleging causes of action for fraud, negligence, and product liability, all premised on the theory of failure to warn about the dangers of Reye's syndrome.

The charging allegation as to negligence was that defendant "failed to warn" that aspirin "caused or contributed to the development of Reye's Syndrome in children suffering from the flu, chicken-pox and other viral illnesses." As to fraud, the complaint charged that defendant falsely represented that SJAC "was safe to administer to children with the flu, chickenpox and other viral illnesses," and that defendant concealed the fact that "aspirin causes or contributes to the development of Reyes [sic] Syndrome in children with the flu, chickenpox or other viral illness." As to products liability, the complaint alleged that the SJAC plaintiff ingested was defective when it left defendant's control and that the product's reasonably foreseeable use involved a substantial and not readily apparent danger of which defendant failed to adequately warn.

Defendant moved for summary judgment, submitting uncontradicted evidence of the facts as stated above. Defendant argued that it was under no duty to label SJAC with Spanish language warnings, that the English language label warnings were adequate, and that the adequacy of the English warnings was ultimately inconsequential in this case because plaintiff's mother did not read the warnings or have them translated for her. On the motion for summary judgment, the parties agreed that over 148 languages are spoken in the United States. Plaintiff adduced evidence that defendant realized that Hispanics, many of whom have not learned English, constituted an important segment of the market for SJAC, and that defendant had acted on this knowledge by using Spanish language advertisements for SJAC in Los Angeles and New York.

The court granted summary judgment. In its order granting the motion, the court stated that there was "no duty to warn in a foreign language" and no causal relationship between plaintiff's injury and defendant's activities. Plaintiff appealed from the judgment for defendant.

The Court of Appeal reversed. It reasoned that although the question of duty is an issue for the court, the existence of a duty to warn here was undisputed, the actual dispute being as to the adequacy of the warning given. The court noted that the adequacy of a product warning is normally a question of fact, and that a defendant moving for summary judgment has the burden of proving an affirmative defense or the nonexistence of an element of the plaintiff's cause of action. Given the evidence of defendant's knowledge that SJAC was being used by non-English-literate Hispanics, and the lack of evidence as to the costs of Spanish language labeling, the reasonableness of defendant's conduct in not labeling SJAC with a Spanish language warning was, the court concluded, a triable issue of fact.

II

A

Defendant concedes, as it must, that a manufacturer of nonprescription drugs has a duty to warn purchasers about dangers in its products. For purposes of the summary judgment motion, it also concedes, at least for argument's sake, that it had a duty to warn purchasers of SJAC about the reported association between aspirin use and Reye's syndrome. The issue presented, then, is not the existence of a duty to warn as such, or the class of persons to whom the duty extends, but the nature and scope of the acknowledged duty. Specifically, the issue is whether defendant's duty to warn required it to provide label or package warnings in Spanish. Issues such as this, which concern the scope of an established duty, are resolved by reference to the governing standard of care: "Once the existence of a legal duty is found, it is the further function of the court to determine and formulate the standard of conduct to which the duty requires the defendant to conform." (Rest.2d Torts, § 328B, com. f, p. 153.)

* * *

In most cases, courts have fixed no standard of care for tort liability more precise than that of a reasonably prudent person under like circumstances. [Cc] "But the proper conduct of a reasonable person under particular situations may become settled by judicial decision or be prescribed by statute or ordinance." (Satterlee v. Orange Glenn School Dist. (1947) 29 Cal.2d 581, 587 [177 P.2d 279], overruled on other grounds in Alarid v. Vanier (1958) 50 Cal.2d 617, 624 [327 P.2d 897]). [Cc]

Justice Traynor explained the rationale for using a statute to define the standard of care in the following way: "The significance of a statute in a civil suit for negligence lies in its formulation of a standard of conduct that the court adopts in the determination of such liability. (See Holmes, The Common Law, 120–129; Morris, The Relation of Criminal Statutes to Tort Liability, 46 Harv. L. Rev. 453.) The decision as to what the civil standard should be still rests with the court, and the standard formulated by a legislative body in a police regulation or criminal statute becomes the standard to determine civil liability only because the court accepts it. In the absence of such a standard the case goes to the jury, which must determine whether the defendant has acted as a reasonably prudent man would act in similar circumstances. The jury then has the burden of deciding not only what the facts are but what the unformulated standard is of reasonable conduct. When a legislative body has generalized a standard from the experience of the community and prohibits conduct that is likely to cause harm, the court accepts the formulated standards and applies them [cc], except where they would serve to impose liability without fault. [Cc]" (Clinkscales v. Carver (1943) 22 Cal.2d 72, 75 [136 P.2d 777]; accord, Casey v. Russell (1982) 138 Cal.App.3d 379, 383 [188 Cal.Rptr. 18].)

Statutory standards of conduct are commonly invoked by plaintiffs in negligence actions to establish a breach of duty by the defendant. In this setting, proof of the defendant's violation of a statutory standard of conduct raises a presumption of negligence that may be rebutted only by evidence establishing a justification or excuse for the statutory violation. [Cc]

Less common is the use of a statutory standard of conduct by a defendant to establish that no breach of duty occurred. Courts have generally not looked with favor upon the use of statutory compliance as a defense to tort liability. The Restatement Second of Torts summarizes the prevailing view in these terms: "Where a statute, ordinance or regulation is found to define a standard of conduct for the purposes of negligence actions, the standard defined is normally a minimum standard, applicable to the ordinary situations contemplated by the legislation. This legislative or administrative minimum does not prevent a finding that a reasonable [person] would have taken additional precautions where the situation is such as to call for them." (Rest.2d Torts, § 288C, com. a, p. 40; see also Elsworth v. Beech Aircraft Corp. (1984) 37 Cal.3d 540, 547 [208 Cal.Rptr. 874, 691 P.2d 630] [manufacturer's compliance with federal aircraft safety regulations does not preclude liability for defective design]; Buccery v. General Motors Corp. (1976) 60 Cal.App.3d 533, 540–541 [132 Cal.Rptr.

605] [compliance with federal motor vehicle safety standards does not preclude liability for defective design].)

But there is some room in tort law for a defense of statutory compliance. Where the evidence shows no unusual circumstances, but only the ordinary situation contemplated by the statute or administrative rule, then "the minimum standard prescribed by the legislation or regulation may be accepted by the triers of fact, or by the court as a matter of law, as sufficient for the occasion...." (Rest.2d Torts, § 288C, com. a, p. 40).

Here, defendant manufacturer argues, in substance, that the standard of care for packaging and labeling nonprescription drugs, and in particular the necessity or propriety of foreign-language label and package warnings, has been appropriately fixed by the dense layer of state and federal statutes and regulations that control virtually all aspects of the marketing of its products. To evaluate this argument, we proceed to review the applicable statutes and regulations.

B

The federal government regulates the labeling of nonprescription drugs through section 502 of the Food, Drug, and Cosmetic Act (21 U.S.C. § 352), which provides that a drug shall be considered misbranded if "its labeling is false or misleading in any particular," if any required information "is not prominently placed thereon with such conspicuousness (as compared with other words, statements, designs, or devices, in the labeling) and in such terms as to render it likely to be read and understood by the ordinary individual under customary conditions of purchase and use," or if its labeling does not bear "(1) adequate directions for use; and (2) such adequate warnings against use in those pathological conditions or by children where its use may be dangerous to health, or against unsafe dosage or methods or duration of administration or application, in such manner and form, as are necessary for the protection of users...."

The FDA has adopted detailed regulations to implement this federal statute. (21 C.F.R. § 201 et seq. (1993).) Under these regulations, drug labeling must include directions for use (, § 201.5), a statement of ingredients (, § 201.10), a statement of identity (, § 201.61), a declaration of net quantity of contents (, § 201.62), an explanation of tamper-resistant packaging (, § 211.132(c)), and indications for use or approved uses (, § 330.1(c)(2)). In addition to this required information, labeling for nonprescription drugs must contain "warnings against unsafe use, side effects, and adverse reactions in such terms as to render them likely to be read and understood by the ordinary individual, including individuals of low comprehension, under ordinary conditions of purchase and use." (§ 330.10(a)(4)(v).)

The FDA regulations specify both the subject matter of required warnings and the actual words to be used. For example, the labeling for aspirin, and for most other over-the-counter drugs, must contain a general warning on use by pregnant or nursing women ("'As with any drug, if you are pregnant or nursing a baby, seek the advice of a health professional before using this product.' "). (21 C.F.R. § 201.63(a) (1993).) Aspirin products must carry an additional warning against use during the last three months of pregnancy. (, § 201.63(e).) Aspirin products must also carry a warning to keep the product out of the reach of children (, § 201.314(a)) and a warning about Reye's syndrome (, § 201.314(h)). * * * [T]he FDA comprehensively regulates the cautionary labeling of aspirin and other nonprescription medications.

The FDA has stated that it "encourages the preparation of labeling to meet the needs of non-English speaking or special user populations so long as such labeling fully complies with agency regulations." (53 Fed.Reg. 21633, 21636 (June 9, 1988).) But the controlling regulation requires only that manufacturers provide full English labeling for all nonprescription drugs except those "distributed solely in the Commonwealth of Puerto Rico or in a Territory where the predominant language is one other than English...." (21 C.F.R. § 201.15(c)(1) (1993).) The regulation further states that if the label or packaging of any drug distributed in the 50 states contains "any representation in a foreign language," then all required "words, statements, and other information" must appear in the foreign language as well as in English. (§ 201.15(c)(2)-(3).) Finally, the regulation states that "use of label space for any representation in a foreign language" is not a basis to exempt a manufacturer from the general obligation to make required language prominent and conspicuous. (21 C.F.R. § 201.15(b)(3) (1993).)

California law parallels and reinforces federal law on the points discussed here. The Health and Safety Code mandates conspicuous English language warnings in section 25900, which provides: "Cautionary statements which are required by law, or regulations adopted pursuant to law, to be printed upon the labels of containers in which dangerous drugs, poisons, and other harmful substances are packaged shall be printed in the English language in a conspicuous place in type of conspicuous size in contrast to the typography, layout, or color of the other printed matter on the label." (See also id., § 26633, 26637.5.) Although warnings in English are expressly required, no California statute requires label or package warnings in any other language.

C

Defining the circumstances under which warnings or other information should be provided in a language other than English is a task for which legislative and administrative bodies are particularly well-suited. Indeed, the California Legislature has already performed this task in a variety of different contexts, enacting laws to ensure that California residents are not denied important services or exploited because they lack proficiency in English.

Many of these laws impose duties on government agencies to hire bilingual employees for public contact positions and to provide forms, pamphlets, and other written materials in languages other than English.

In another category are laws imposing duties on parties engaged in private commercial transactions to furnish information in a language other than English under specified conditions. [Cc]

In defining the circumstances under which a foreign language must be used, the Legislature has drawn clear lines so that affected persons and entities, in both the private and public spheres, know exactly what is expected of them.

* * *

These statutes demonstrate that the Legislature is able and willing to define the circumstances in which foreign-language communications should be mandated. Given the existence of a statute expressly requiring that package warnings on nonprescription drugs be in English, we think it reasonable to infer that the Legislature has deliberately chosen not to require that manufacturers also include warnings in foreign languages. The same inference is warranted on the federal level. The FDA's regulations abundantly demonstrate its sensitivity to the issue of foreign-language labeling, and yet the FDA regulations do not require it. Presumably, the FDA has concluded that despite the obvious advantages of multilingual package warnings, the associated problems and costs are such that at present warnings should be mandated only in English.

On this point, the FDA's experience with foreign-language patient package inserts for prescription drugs is instructive. Recognizing that "the United States is too heterogeneous to enable manufacturers, at reasonable cost and with reasonable simplicity, to determine exactly where to provide alternative language inserts," the FDA for a time required manufacturers, as an alternative to multilingual or bilingual inserts, to provide Spanish language translations of their patient package inserts on request to doctors and pharmacists. [C] But the FDA later noted that manufacturers were having difficulty obtaining accurate translations, and eventually it abandoned altogether [C] the patient-package insert requirement for prescription drugs. [C]

Were we to reject the applicable statutes and regulations as the proper standard of care, there would be two courses of action open to us. The first would be to leave the issue for resolution on a case-by-case basis by different triers of fact under the usual "reasonable person" standard of care. This was the approach that the Court of Appeal adopted in this case. As a practical matter, such an open-ended rule would likely compel manufacturers to package all their nonprescription drugs with inserts containing warnings in multiple foreign languages because, simply as a matter of foreseeability, it is foreseeable that eventually each nonprescription drug will be purchased by a non-English-speaking resident or foreign tourist proficient only in one of these languages. The burden of including warnings in so many different languages would be onerous, would add to the costs and environmental burdens of the packaging, and at some point might prove ineffective or even counterproductive if the warning inserts became so large and cumbersome that a user could not easily find the warning in his or her own language.

The other alternative would be to use our seldom-exercised power to judicially declare a particularized standard of care, giving precise guidance on this issue. But this determination would involve matters that are peculiarly susceptible to legislative and administrative investigation and determination, based upon empirical data and consideration of the viewpoints of all interested parties. A legislative body considering the utility of foreign-language label warnings for nonprescription medications would no doubt gather pertinent data on a variety of subjects, including the space limitations on nonprescription drug labels and packages, the volume of information that must be conveyed, the relative risks posed by the misuse of particular medications, the cost to the manufacturer of translating and printing warnings in languages other than English, the cost to the consumer of multilingual package warnings in terms of higher prices for, or reduced availability of, products, the feasibility of targeted distribution of products with bilingual or multilingual packaging, the number of persons likely to benefit from warnings in a particular language, and the extent to which nonprescription drug manufacturers as a group have used foreign-language advertisements to promote sales of their products. Legislation and regulations would no doubt reflect findings on these and other pertinent questions.

Lacking the procedure and the resources to conduct the relevant inquiries, we conclude that the prudent course is to adopt for tort purposes the existing legislative and administrative standard of care on this issue. The feasibility and advisability of foreign-language labeling for nonprescription drugs will, no doubt, be reviewed periodically by the FDA and other concerned agencies. Indeed, we are conscious that our decision here may prompt review of this issue by the California Legislature. That is as it should be, for further study might persuade the Legislature, the FDA, or any other concerned agency to revise the controlling statutes or regulations for nonprescription drugs.

Plaintiff and the amici curiae ("friends of the court") who have submitted briefs on plaintiff's behalf offer various arguments in support of a rule that would permit juries to award tort damages for a manufacturer's failure to provide foreign-language labeling for nonprescription drugs. None of these arguments is persuasive.

* * *

We do not, of course, foreclose the possibility of tort liability premised upon the content of foreign-language advertising. For example, we do not decide whether a manufacturer would be liable to a consumer who detrimentally relied upon foreign-language advertising that was materially misleading as to product risks and who was unable to read English language package warnings that accurately described the risks. No such issue is presented here. Although plaintiff presented evidence that defendant advertised its product in Spanish, the record contains no evidence of the content of that advertising. And, in any event, plaintiff's mother could not have relied upon defendant's advertising because she admittedly did not see or hear it.

For these reasons, we reject plaintiff's attempt to place on nonprescription drug manufacturers a duty to warn that is broader in scope and more onerous than that currently imposed by applicable statutes and regulations. The FDA has stressed that "it is in the best interest of the consumer, industry, and the marketplace to have uniformity in presentation and clarity of message" in the warnings provided with nonprescription drugs. [C] To preserve that uniformity and clarity, to avoid adverse impacts upon the warning requirements mandated by the federal regulatory scheme, and in deference to the superior technical and procedural lawmaking resources of legislative and administrative bodies, we adopt the legislative/regulatory standard of care that mandates nonprescription drug package warnings in English only.

* * *

We recognize that if a Spanish language warning had accompanied defendant's product, and if plaintiff's mother had read and heeded the warning, the tragic blighting of a young and innocent life that occurred in this case might not have occurred. Yet, as one court has aptly commented, "The extent to which special consideration should be given to persons who have difficulty with the English language is a matter of public policy for consideration by the appropriate legislative bodies and not by the Courts." (Carmona v. Sheffield (N.D.Cal.1971) 325 F.Supp. 1341, 1342, affd. per curiam (9th Cir.1973) 475 F.2d 738.) We hold only that, given the inherent limitations of the judicial process, manufacturers of nonprescription drugs have no presently existing legal duty, within the tort law system, to include foreign-language warnings with their packaging materials.

The judgment of the Court of Appeal is reversed with directions to affirm the summary judgment for defendant.

Lucas, C.J., Panelli, J., Arabian, J., Baxter, J., and George, J., concurred.

Mosk, J. delivered a separate concurring opinion.

NOTES AND QUESTIONS

1. In the Council Draft No. 1 of the Restatement of the Law, Torts: General Principles § 14 (Sept. 25, 1998), the Reporter Professor Gary Schwartz has proposed the following rule for statutory compliance:

(1) An actor's compliance with a pertinent statute, while evidence of non-negligence, does not prevent a finding that the actor is negligent when precautions in addition to those mandated by the statute are called for by § 4 [setting forth the risk factors within the reasonable standard of care in negligence].

(2) If the actor's adoption of a precaution would require the actor to violate a statute, the actor cannot be found negligent for failing to adopt that precaution.

Although compliance is usually no more than evidence of due care, the statute may dictate that the effect is conclusive of due care. Comment *f* to § 14 addresses the circumstances where conclusiveness may be found. The court may "conclude that the actor's compliance with the statute shows that his conduct does not lack reasonable care," when "the statute directly addresses the particular safety problem before the court, when the statutory scheme evidently seeks to identify all the precautions called for by the general negligence standards in § 4, and when the particular case involves no unusual circumstances."

The comment suggests that in reaching this conclusion the court take account of several factors, including, "the evident thoroughness of the statute and the desirability of a uniform liability standard that can simplify litigation and provide parties with appropriate guidance as to what precautions are expected of them." The following illustration is given:

> A state statute fixes a speed limit of 55 miles per hour for a state highway. Linda is driving her car on that highway at a speed of 50. A teenager, Dave, unexpectedly darts from the sidewalk onto the highway. Despite a proper lookout, Linda is unable to stop in time, and strikes Dave, injuring him. Had Linda been driving at 40 miles per hour, she would have been able to avoid hitting Dave. In his lawsuit, Dave alleges that Linda was negligent in driving at a speed faster than 40 miles per hour. The weather at the time had been fine, road conditions ordinary, and the traffic conditions ordinary as well. Linda was not negligent in the speed at which she operated her car.

2.   By way of review, note the institutional and substantive aspects of preemption. For the former, a court or agency may be fully or partially proscribed from regulating an activity or exercising jurisdiction. For the latter, a court (or agency) may apply but not vary a statutory standard, or it may be used by a court (agency) as a floor. The debate has mainly focused, as in *Medtronic*, on the preemptive effect of federal statistics on state product liability rules. The issue is discussed by Richard C. Ausness, The Case for a "Strong" Regulatory Compliance Defense, 55 Maryland L. Rev. 1210 (1996).

3.   How preclusive ought statutory prescriptions be when tort liability issues arise?

4.   May the United States Constitution, like a federal statutory scheme, preempt state laws claims? The argument for "complete constitutional preemption" was proposed in City of Camden v. Beretta U.S.A. Corp., 81 F.Supp.2d 541 (D.N.J.2000). The plaintiff city brought an action against 19 gun manufacturers and distributors seeking compensation for costs associated with gun violence. Actions sounded in public nuisance, among other causes of action. Defendants urged that the state claims were preempted by the operation of the Commerce Clause of the Constitution. It argued that state causes of action were in effect an interference with the freedom of interstate trade. The Commerce Clause, the court found, however, has no self-enforcing mechanism, nor does it give rise to a private right of action.

The *Camden* case also addresses whether the Gun Control Act of 1968 manifests a Congressional intent to completely preempt all state law claims touching upon the regulation of the manufacture and sale of firearms. The court on a review of the text and legislative history of the Act could find no intent to displace state laws. The Act was supplementary to state regulation.

4.   COURTS V. LEGISLATURES: WHO WILL DETERMINE TORT LAW?

Bower v. Westinghouse Corp.

Supreme Court of Appeals of West Virginia, 1999.
522 S.E.2d 424.

McGRAW, JUSTICE. This case comes to the Court on certified question from the United States District Court for the Northern District of West Virginia, and asks us to resolve the question of whether this jurisdiction recognizes a common-law cause of action for recovery of anticipated medical monitoring costs in circumstances where the plaintiffs have been tortiously exposed to toxic substances, but do not presently exhibit symptoms of any resulting disease. We conclude that West Virginia law supports such a claim for relief.

I.

BACKGROUND

Plaintiffs originally brought this action in the Circuit Court of Marion County, West Virginia, on September 15, 1997. In their complaint, they allege that they were exposed to toxic substances as a result of defendants maintaining a cullet pile containing debris from the manufacture of light bulbs. The pile covers approximately two acres and is 42 feet deep at certain points. It is uncontested that tests performed in 1994 identified the presence of 30 potentially deleterious substances. (Footnote omitted.) None of the plaintiffs presently exhibit symptoms of any disease related to the alleged exposure.

Plaintiffs have asserted the following causes of action against defendants: (1) negligent maintenance and operation of the refuse pile; (2) nuisance; (3) trespass; (4) negligent infliction of emotional distress; and (5) intentional disregard for the health and safety of plaintiffs. As relief, the complaint seeks, inter alia, consequential damages in the form of medical monitoring costs.

* * *

[The case was removed to federal court on diversity grounds and defendants moved to dismiss plaintiffs' claim for medical monitoring under Fed. R. Civ. P. 12(b)(6) or, in the alternative, Fed. R. Civ. P. 56. In support of their motion, defendants cited Ball v. Joy Mfg. Co., 755 F. Supp. 1344, 1370–72 (S.D.W.Va.1990), aff'd sub nom. Ball v. Joy Technologies Inc., 958 F.2d 36, 39 (4th Cir.1991), cert. denied, 502 U.S. 1033, 112 S. Ct. 876, 116 L. Ed. 2d 780 (1992), in which a federal court interpreting West Virginia law previously held that there is no basis for a claim of medical monitoring absent an accompanying physical injury. Plaintiffs responded by arguing that *Ball* no longer accurately reflected West Virginia law and requesting that the federal trial court judge certify the question to the West Virginia Supreme Court. The certification motion was granted and West Virginia accepted it, although it reformulated the question to be "Whether, under West Virginia law, a plaintiff who does not allege a present physical injury can assert a claim for the recovery of future medical monitoring costs where such damages are the proximate result of defendant's tortious conduct."]

IV.

DISCUSSION

Defendants argue that West Virginia law precludes the award of future medical monitoring expenses absent evidence of a present physical injury.

In the alternative, they urge the Court to impose certain requirements on claims for medical monitoring so as to reasonably narrow the universe of potential plaintiffs. We reject the former argument, but take the considered suggestions of the parties into account in formulating a standard governing medical monitoring claims.

A.

Recognizing a Claim for Medical Monitoring

A claim for medical monitoring seeks to recover the anticipated costs of long-term diagnostic testing necessary to detect latent diseases that may develop as a result of tortious exposure to toxic substances. Over the past decade, a growing number of courts have recognized this cause of action as a well-grounded extension of traditional common-law tort principles. Since the landmark decision in Askey v. Occidental Chemical Corp., 102 A.D.2d 130, 477 N.Y.S.2d 242 (1984), appellate courts in at least six other states have permitted claims for medical monitoring. (Footnote omitted.) Likewise, a growing number of federal courts sitting in diversity have interpreted state law to permit such claims. (Footnote omitted.) What these decisions uniformly acknowledge is that significant economic harm may be inflicted on those exposed to toxic substances, notwithstanding the fact that the physical harm resulting from such exposure is often latent. See In re Paoli R.R. Yard PCB Litig., 916 F.2d 829, 852 (3d Cir.1990) [hereinafter "*Paoli* I"], cert. denied sub nom. General Elec. Co. v. Knight, 499 U.S. 961, 111 S. Ct. 1584, 113 L. Ed. 2d 649 (1991).

As the Fourth Circuit correctly surmised, a claim for medical monitoring is essentially "a claim for future damages." Ball v. Joy Technologies Inc., 958 F.2d 36, 39 (4th Cir.1991). Consequently, we resort to elementary principles of tort law to determine whether medical monitoring is a proper subject of compensatory damages.

Since before the turn of the century, this jurisdiction sanctioned the recovery of future medical expenses where a plaintiff could prove with reasonable certainty that such costs would be incurred as a proximate consequence of a defendant's tortious conduct. [Cc] In Syllabus point 15 of Jordan v. Bero, 158 W. Va. 28, 210 S.E.2d 618, (1974), we stated that "to warrant recovery for future medical expenses, the proper measure of damages is ... the reasonable value of medical services as will probably be necessarily incurred by reason of the permanent effects of a party's injuries." [C] Although Jordan and cases dealing with similar subject matter sometimes speak in terms of compensating a plaintiff for the anticipated cost of treating a "permanent injury," we have never held that lasting physical harm is an absolute prerequisite for recovery of future medical expenses. Indeed, we have never before dealt with a case such as this where the plaintiff sought future medical expenses with respect to a latent disease.

We now reject the contention that a claim for future medical expenses must rest upon the existence of present physical harm. The "injury" that underlies a claim for medical monitoring—just as with any other cause of action sounding in tort—is "the invasion of any legally protected interest." Restatement (Second) of Torts § 7(1) (1964). As one of the first courts to grapple with this subject observed:

"It is difficult to dispute that an individual has an interest in avoiding expensive diagnostic examinations just as he or she has an interest in avoiding physical injury. When a defendant negligently invades this interest, the injury to which is neither speculative nor resistant to proof, it is elementary that the defendant should make the plaintiff whole by paying for the examinations." Friends for All Children, Inc. v. Lockheed Aircraft Corp., 241 U.S. App. D.C. 83, 746 F.2d 816, 826 (D.C.Cir.1984) (footnote omitted). "Although the physical manifestations of an injury may not appear for years, the reality is that many of those exposed have suffered some legal detriment; the exposure itself and the concomitant need for medical testing constitute the injury." Hansen v. Mountain Fuel Supply, 858 P.2d 970, 977 (Utah 1993) (citations omitted). A number of courts have employed similar logic to sustain claims for medical monitoring costs.[Cc]

The court in *Friends for All Children* gave the following often-quoted hypothetical to illustrate the soundness of permitting recovery for necessary diagnostic testing even in the absence of physical injury:

"Jones is knocked down by a motorbike which Smith is riding through a red light. Jones lands on his head with some force. Understandably shaken, Jones enters a hospital where doctors recommend that he undergo a battery of tests to determine whether he has suffered any internal head injuries. The tests prove negative, but Jones sues Smith solely for what turns out to be the substantial cost of the diagnostic examinations." 746 F.2d at 825. "In such circumstances it is clear that even in the absence of physical injury Jones ought to be able to recover the cost for the variety of diagnostic examinations proximately caused by Smith's negligent action.... The motorbike rider, through his negligence, caused the plaintiff, in the opinion of medical experts, to need specific medical services—a cost that is neither inconsequential nor of a kind the community generally accepts as a part of the wear and tear of daily life. Under these principles of tort law, the motorbiker should pay." Id.

Thus, it logically follows that a plaintiff asserting a claim for medical monitoring costs is not required to prove present physical harm resulting from tortious exposure to toxic substances.

Nor is the plaintiff required to demonstrate the probable likelihood that a serious disease will result from the exposure. As the Third Circuit indicated in *Paoli* I, "the appropriate inquiry is not whether it is reasonably probable that plaintiffs will suffer [physical] harm in the future, but rather whether medical monitoring is, to a reasonable degree of medical certainty, necessary in order to diagnose properly the warning signs of disease." 916 F.2d at 851. [C]

The California Supreme Court in *Potter* [v. Firestone Tire and Rubber Co., 6 Cal. 4th 965, 25 Cal. Rptr. 2d 550, 863 P.2d 795, 822–23 (1993) (in bank)] detailed a number of policy considerations that favor recognizing a right to recover medical monitoring costs:

"First, there is an important public health interest in fostering access to medical testing for individuals whose exposure to toxic chemicals creates an enhanced risk of disease, particularly in light of the value of early diagnosis and treatment for many cancer patients. [Cc] Second, there is a deterrence value in recognizing medical surveillance claims—'allowing plaintiffs to recover the cost of this care deters irresponsible discharge of toxic chemicals by defendants. . . .' [Cc]. Third, 'the availability of a substantial remedy before the consequences of the plaintiffs' exposure are manifest may also have the beneficial effect of preventing or mitigating serious future illnesses and thus reduce the overall costs to the responsible parties.' [Cc] In this regard, the early detection of cancer may improve the prospects for cure, treatment, prolongation of life and minimization of pain and disability. Finally, societal notions of fairness and elemental justice are better served by allowing recovery of medical monitoring costs. That is, it would be inequitable for an individual wrongfully exposed to dangerous toxins, but unable to prove that cancer or disease is likely, to have to pay the expense of medical monitoring when such intervention is clearly reasonable and necessary." [Cc] This Court is in agreement with these statements.

We therefore align this jurisdiction with those that have considered the issue, and conclude that cause of action exists under West Virginia law for the recovery of medical monitoring costs, where it can be proven that such expenses are necessary and reasonably certain to be incurred as a proximate result of a defendant's tortious conduct. The certified question, as reformulated, is therefore answered in the affirmative.

B.

Elements of a Claim for Medical Monitoring

Having determined that a claim for recovery of future medical monitoring costs is cognizable under West Virginia law, we are compelled to define the elements necessary to sustain such a claim.

We have consistently held that the "future effect of an injury must be proven with reasonable certainty in order to permit a jury to award an injured party future damages." [Cc] This flows from the more general rule that " 'proof of damages . . . cannot be sustained by mere speculation or conjecture.' " [Cc] Thus, as the Court stated in Syllabus point 16 of *Jordan* [v. Bero, 158 W. Va. 28, 210 S.E.2d 618 (1974)], "proof of future medical expenses is insufficient as a matter of law in the absence of any evidence as to the necessity and cost of such future medical expenses."

The various state and federal courts addressing this issue have moved toward relative consensus on the elements necessary to establish a claim for medical monitoring.* * * [The Court then reviewed the tests adopted by several courts.]

With the significant divergence of eliminating the requirement that diagnostic monitoring must be tied to the existence of a proven treatment protocol, we substantially adopt the *Paoli* test. * * * We will briefly discuss these elements in turn.

1.   Significant Exposure. Before liability can attach with respect to the cost of medical monitoring, the plaintiff must first be exposed to a hazardous substance. [C]

2.   Proven Hazardous Substance. The plaintiff must present scientific evidence demonstrating a probable link between exposure to a particular compound and human disease.

3.   Tortious Conduct. Liability for medical monitoring is predicated upon the defendant being at fault in exposing the plaintiff to a particular hazardous substance. Fault is established through application of existing theories of tort liability. "Recognition that a defendant's conduct has created the need for future medical monitoring does not create a new tort. It is simply a compensable item of damage when liability is established under traditional theories of recovery." [Cc] This is not to say that a plaintiff may not, as a matter of pleading, assert a separate cause of action based upon medical monitoring; rather, it means that underlying liability must be established based upon a recognized tort—e.g., negligence, strict liability, trespass, intentional conduct, etc.

4.   Increased Risk. Again, the plaintiff is not required to show that a particular disease is certain or even likely to occur as a result of exposure. [C] All that must be demonstrated is that the plaintiff has a significantly increased risk of contracting a particular disease relative to what would be the case in the absence of exposure. Importantly, "no particular level of quantification is necessary to satisfy this requirement." [Cc]

5.   Necessity of Diagnostic Testing. Diagnostic testing must be "reasonably necessary" in the sense that it must be something that a qualified physician would prescribe based upon the demonstrated exposure to a particular toxic agent. This Court is not entirely in accord with the statement in *Hansen* to the effect that "if a reasonable physician would not prescribe ... [medical monitoring] for a particular plaintiff because the benefits of monitoring would be outweighed by the costs, which may include, among other things, the burdensome frequency of the monitoring procedure, its excessive price, or its risk of harm to the patient, then recovery would not be allowed." [Cc] While there obviously must be some reasonable medical basis for undergoing diagnostic monitoring, factors such as financial cost and the frequency of testing should not be given significant weight. Moreover, the requirement that diagnostic testing must be medically advisable does not necessarily preclude the situation where such a determination is based, at least in part, upon the subjective desires of a plaintiff for information concerning the state of his or her health.

6.   Existence of Monitoring Procedures. Medical monitoring must be available in order to be a necessary, compensable item of damages. "If no such test exists, then periodic monitoring is of no assistance and the cost of

such monitoring is not available." [C] In the event diagnostic testing later becomes available, then a plaintiff will have the right at such later time to demonstrate the effectiveness of the test, and be compensated for utilizing it, so long as all the other elements of the cause of action are satisfied. [C]

We agree with the Pennsylvania Supreme Court that a plaintiff should not be required to show that a treatment currently exists for the disease that is the subject of medical monitoring. [C] In this age of rapidly advancing medical science, we are hesitant to impose such a static requirement. In *Bourgeois* [v. A.P. Green Indus., Inc., 716 So. 2d 355 (La.1998)], Chief Justice Calogero gave a poignant justification for permitting recovering even in instances where there is no proven treatment: "One thing that … a plaintiff might gain [even in the absence of available treatment] is certainty as to his fate, whatever it might be. If a plaintiff has been placed at an increased risk for a latent disease through exposure to a hazardous substance, absent medical monitoring, he must live each day with the uncertainty of whether the disease is present in his body. If, however, he is able to take advantage of medical monitoring and the monitoring detects no evidence of disease, then, at least for the time being, the plaintiff can receive the comfort of peace of mind. Moreover, even if medical monitoring did detect evidence of an irreversible and untreatable disease, the plaintiff might still achieve some peace of mind through this knowledge by getting his financial affairs in order, making lifestyle changes, and, even perhaps, making peace with estranged loved ones or with his religion. Certainly, those options should be available to the innocent plaintiff who finds himself at an increased risk for a serious latent disease through no fault of his own." 716 So. 2d at 363 (Calogero, C.J., concurring).

As a final matter, defendant CBS and several amici curiae argue that plaintiffs should only be compensated for medical monitoring costs through the establishment of a court-administered fund, to the exclusion of lump-sum damage awards. While there are situations where utilization of such funds may be beneficial, * * * we do not presently see a need to constrain the discretion of the trial courts to fashion appropriate remedies in cases such as these.

V.

CONCLUSION

We answer the question posed by the District Court, as reformulated, in the affirmative, and conclude that West Virginia law recognizes a cause of action for future medical monitoring costs where such necessary expenses are incurred as a proximate result of a defendant's tortious acts. Having answered the certified question, this case is dismissed from the docket of this Court.

Certified question answered; case dismissed.

MAYNARD, J. (dissenting).I dissent in this case because I believe that West Virginia law does not permit an independent cause of action to recover future medical monitoring costs absent physical injury, and this Court has no authority to create such a cause of action.

Several things about this decision trouble me. The first is the way in which the majority goes beyond the narrow question presented by the District Court in order to decide this case. I do not dispute the Court's authority under our Uniform Certification of Questions of Law Act to reformulate a question submitted by a certifying court. I do dispute, however, the necessity of doing so in the instant case. * * *

The second and obviously most troubling aspect of this decision is the majority's violation of the constitutional separation of powers doctrine by usurping the Legislature's authority to enact laws. Article V, Section 1 of the Constitution of West Virginia provides that "the legislative, executive and judicial departments shall be separate and distinct, so that neither shall exercise the powers properly belonging to either of the others[.]" According to Article VI, Section 1 of the Constitution, the legislative power is vested in the Senate and House of Delegates. This Court has described the legislative power as "the power of the law-making bodies to frame and enact laws." [C] This is in contrast to the judicial power which is, "the power which a regularly constituted court exercises in matters which are brought before it, in the manner prescribed by statute, or established rules of practice of courts, and which matters do not come within the powers granted to the executive, or vested in the legislative department of the Government." Id. This Court's jurisdiction is prescribed and limited by the constitutional provisions which create it, [C] and nowhere in the Constitution is this Court granted the power to create causes of action. See Art. VIII, § 3, W.Va. Const. This Court recognized long ago that "the legislature has the right to create new causes of action for the recovery of money." [C] We reiterated more recently that the creation, augmentation, repeal or abolishment of complete causes of action is a legislative power. [C] Up until approximately the last twenty-five years, the Court respected that fact. This decision shows just how far this Court has moved from its constitutional underpinnings and its proper role.

Finally, even if this Court did have the power to create causes of action, I would not agree with the one created by this decision. The majority rejects the fundamental 200 year old tort law principle that a plaintiff may not recover damages unless he or she has a present injury, and replaces it with the speculative and amorphous showing of "increased risk." The majority admits that "the plaintiff is not required to show that a particular disease is certain or even likely to occur as a result of exposure" (citation omitted). Because of this decision, plaintiffs will now be compensated when there is no injury, thus providing a windfall for plaintiffs. As one commentator has recently suggested, lawyers can now advertise, "Don't wait until you're hurt, call now."[1] In fact, the practical effect of this decision is to make almost every West Virginian a potential plaintiff in a

---

1. Victor Schwartz, Some lawyers ask,   July 15, 1999, at 17A.
why wait for injury? Sue now!, USA TODAY,

medical monitoring cause of action. Those who work in heavy industries such as coal, oil, gas, timber, steel, and chemicals as well as those who work in older office buildings, or handle ink in newspaper offices, or launder the linens in hotels have, no doubt, come into contact with hazardous substances. Now all of these people may be able to collect money as victorious plaintiffs without any showing of injury at all.

We recently stated, "the one area, above all, where a court should exercise caution is when it is deciding its own power." [C] The majority exercised no caution whatsoever in this case. Consequently, it exceeded its legitimate powers and usurped the function of the Legislature. As a result, its holding here is not only judge-made law, it is bad law. For these reasons, I respectfully dissent.

NOTES AND QUESTIONS

1. Is the majority or dissenting opinion correct? Is this change in the law of West Virginia a "well-grounded extension of traditional common-law tort principles" or a "rejecting of the fundamental 200 year old tort law principle" that requires plaintiff to prove present injury in favor of "the speculative and amorphous showing of 'increased risk.'"? Can you discern the difference between the breadth of the *Bower* decision and the precedent relied on by the court?

2. Other courts, including the United States Supreme Court in a Federal Employers' Liability Act case, have declined to expand tort law to cover medical monitoring costs where that is the only injury that plaintiff is claiming. Metro-North Commuter Railroad Co. v. Buckley, 521 U.S. 424 (1997): "We do not deny that the dissent paints a sympathetic picture of Buckley and his co-workers; this picture has force because Buckley is sympathetic and he has suffered wrong at the hands of a negligent employer. But we are more troubled than is the dissent by the potential systemic effects of creating a new, full-blown, tort law cause of action—for example, the effects upon interests of other potential plaintiffs who are not before the court and who depend on a tort system that can distinguish between reliable and serious claims on the one hand, and unreliable and relatively trivial claims on the other. The reality is that competing interests are at stake—and those interests sometimes can be reconciled in ways other than simply through the creation of a full-blown, traditional, tort law cause of action." Which side has the better argument? Is there some position in between the two? What do you think about the suggestion that a court-administered fund would be preferable to a lump sum award? In addition to the cases cited in the principal case, see Petito v. A.H. Robins Co. Inc., 750 So.2d 103 (Fla.App. 1999) (establishing such a fund).

3. This area of the law has attracted the interest of commentators as well as courts. See, for example, Schwartz, et. al. Medical Monitoring—Should Tort Law Say Yes?, 34 WAKE FOREST L.REV. 1047 (1999); Jordan, Medical Monitoring in Toxic Tort Cases: Another Windfall for Texas Plaintiffs?, 33 HOUS. L. REV. 473 (1996); Lee, Medical Monitoring Damages: Issues Concerning the Administration of Medical Monitoring Programs, 20 AM. J.L. & MED. 251 (1994); Blumenberg, Medical Monitoring Funds, 43 HASTINGS L.J. 661 (1992).

4. The court in the principal case seems to analyze the issue as one of harm or damages rather than one of causation. How does the analysis in the medical monitoring cases compare to the analysis in the reduced chance of recovery cases? See pages 264-268.

5.   The opinion was issued in response to a certified question. What does that mean?

6.   The court makes reference to *amici curiae*. What is their role in litigation?

7.   The dissent argues that the court does not have the power to create a new cause of action or to recognize a new form of relief. Even if it does have the power to do so, what advantages would the legislature have in addressing this issue? What are the disadvantages to waiting for the legislature? See pages 338-343. As you ponder the appropriate roles of the legislature and judiciary in recognizing new causes of action, consider their respective roles in changing the requirements of existing causes of action as you read the next two principal cases.

Williams v. Wilson

Supreme Court of Kentucky, 1998.
972 S.W.2d 260.

LAMBERT, JUSTICE. This Court granted discretionary review (CR 76.20) to consider whether KRS 411.184 violates one or more provisions of the Constitution of Kentucky, thereby rendering the statute invalid and unenforceable. To resolve this question of constitutional law, it is necessary to first determine whether, in material respects, the statute impairs the common law of this Commonwealth as it existed prior to adoption of our present Constitution, thereby implicating the doctrine of jural rights. In the event we determine that the statute does change well settled common law with respect to recovery of punitive damages, we will proceed to re-examine the doctrine of jural rights as it has been attacked in this forum as erroneous and unsound.

In 1988 the Kentucky General Assembly considered broad tort reform legislation embodied in HB 551. From among the proposals, the Legislature enacted a statute codified at KRS 411.184 intended to modify Kentucky law with respect to punitive damages. [C] In general, the intent of the Legislature was to redefine the circumstances in which punitive damages were recoverable, and toward that end a new legal standard was established. Departing from the traditional common law standard which permitted a jury to impose punitive damages upon a finding of gross negligence as measured by an objective standard, the new statutory Standard, here under review, requires a determination that the defendant acted with "flagrant indifference to the rights of the plaintiff and with a subjective awareness that such conduct will result in human death or bodily harm." It also requires proof by clear and convincing evidence. The Fayette Circuit Court and the Court of Appeals decided the constitutional question and invalidated the statute on the view that it offends Sections 14, 54 and 241 of the Constitution of Kentucky. (Footnote omitted.) Both courts below held that the statute effectively destroyed the common law right of action for punitive damages and that such was precluded by the doctrine of jural rights.

The facts which give rise to this litigation are unremarkable but not unimportant.* * * [On May 18, 1990, at 7:00 a.m., Patricia Wilson was en route to the place of her employment as a school teacher when she was struck by the vehicle being driven by Teri Williams, who was intoxicated. At the scene, Williams was arrested and charged with DUI. She subsequently pled guilty. Wilson filed a negligence action against Williams claiming both compensatory and punitive damages. At trial and after the close of all the evidence, the trial court refused to give an instruction on punitive damages because he believed the evidence did not support such an instruction due to the absence of evidence of defendant's subjective awareness that her conduct would result in death or bodily harm. In response to this ruling, plaintiff modified her position asserting that the punitive damages statute was unconstitutional and sought a punitive damages instruction based on common law gross negligence. The trial court judge declared that statute unconstitutional and gave a jury instruction based on the common law standard, "wanton or reckless disregard for the lives, safety or property of others." Williams appealed.]

THE STATUTE VERSUS COMMON LAW

Appellant contends that KRS 411.184 is not a departure from the common law standard as there was no well-established standard prior to adoption of our Constitution [in 1891]. She argues that the statute merely clarified the confusion existing in common law and codified an existing standard which would be applicable to all claims for punitive damages. Appellant also argues that pre–1891 case law and decisions in this century reveal that malice, as expressed in various forms, is no different than subjective awareness under the statute; that malice necessarily presumes actual awareness. Appellee responds that the right to recover punitive damages for gross negligence was well established prior to 1891 and that the statutory requirement of subjective awareness of death or bodily harm represents the effective abolishment of negligence-based recovery of punitive damages and substitution of a requirement of knowledge or intent.

* * *

[The court then reviewed the cases that had been decided prior to 1891.] Nevertheless, from our review of the cases, there is little doubt that prior to 1891, Kentucky law was well established that punitive damages could be recovered for negligent conduct which exceeded ordinary negligence whether such conduct was expressed as gross negligence, recklessness, wantonness, or some other such term.

* * *

Appellant asserts that "the Court will find no 'definitive statement,' 'point of recognition' or 'well-established' rule regarding liability for punitive damages at common law." We disagree. As shown by the decisions discussed hereinabove, the well established common law standard for awarding punitive damages was gross negligence. While the concept was not expressed in the same language in every opinion rendered prior to adoption of our Constitution, and while the language has not remained perfectly constant in this century, there is no doubt that unintentional conduct amounting to gross negligence, as that concept is well defined in *Horton*, was sufficient to authorize recovery of punitive damages. As the new statute requires proof of a subjective awareness that harm will result, it amounts to a vastly elevated standard for the recovery of punitive damages and a clear departure from the common law. The facts of this case well illustrate the fundamental change brought about by the statute.

By the literal language of the statute proof of "subjective awareness that such conduct will result in human death or bodily harm" is required. Ordinarily, such proof could only be obtained from the party who inflicted the harm, but in the instant case the defendant did not participate and her testimony could not be taken. As such, there was no way to prove essential elements of the statute. From this a new litigation strategy might well emerge. In cases of gross negligence, but where compensatory damages for wrongful death or personal injury would otherwise be modest, a defendant might elect to forego any participation, relying on the court to prevent an excessive award of compensatory damages, safe in the knowledge that despite his gross negligence, no award of punitive damages could be made.

* * *

JURAL RIGHTS

Appellant makes a multi-faceted attack upon the jural rights doctrine relying extensively on Lewis, Jural Rights under Kentucky's Constitution: Realities Grounded in Myth, Ky. L.Rev. 953 (1991–92). She contends that constitutional text does not support any such doctrine of law; that the Debates of the Constitutional Convention provide no support, and she effectively agrees with Professor Lewis' view that jural rights is illegitimate and "evolved from the pen of the judiciary." Id. at 973.[3] Predictably, appellee relies on this Court's decision in Ludwig v. Johnson, [243 Ky. 533, 49 S.W.2d 347 (1932)] and the virtually unbroken line of decisions following and applying it for more than sixty years. She also relies on the history and tradition in this Commonwealth of protecting the right of recovery of injured persons. With the conflict thus joined, we will weigh in.

The doctrine of jural rights was first articulated as such in this Court's 1932 decision in Ludwig v. Johnson, supra. However, language in [Louisville & Nashville R.R. v.] *Kelly's Adm'x*, 100 Ky. 421, 38 S.W. 852, an 1897 case, suggests that the idea of placing certain rights of recovery of damages for death or personal injury off-limits to legislative abolishment had been recognized much earlier. "In other words, we are of opinion that the convention intended to extend the common-law right of action to recover both compensatory and exemplary damages for injuries not resulting in death to cases in which death ensued; and a very forcible argument in favor of this construction is found in section 54 of the constitution, where it is

---

3. Illustrative of his strongly held view, Professor Lewis has written "no court is that infallible in its development of the common law. Under the jural rights doctrine, however, the Kentucky Supreme Court is infallible. Any legislative abolition or restriction of a common law right of recovery within the scope of the jural rights doctrine is invalid."

provided that 'the general assembly shall have no power to limit the amount to be recovered for injuries resulting in death or for injuries to person or property.' It seems evident that this denial of power to the legislature to limit the amount of recovery would hardly have been inserted if the intent of section 241 was to place a limit upon the amount of recovery." Kelly's Adm'x, 38 S.W. at 854.

* * *

Since its rendition, Ludwig v. Johnson has been followed many times. [The court then discussed several cases in which various statutes had been held unconstitutional violations of the jural rights doctrine.] * * *

As the foregoing authorities demonstrate, to the exclusion of any reasonable opinion to the contrary, the doctrine of jural rights is deeply ingrained in Kentucky law and to abandon it now would amount to an extraordinary change. Principles of predictability counsel against such major shifts in the law. Of course, constitutional doctrine is not immune from reconsideration [C], and indeed this Court has declared that we will refrain from "sanctification of ancient fallacy." [C] Therefore, we will reconsider the central premise of the jural rights doctrine to determine whether it is fallacious.

Sections 14, 54, and 241 have been interpreted to work in tandem and to establish a limitation upon the power of the General Assembly to limit common law rights to recover for personal injury or death.* * * [The court rejected the arguments of the defendant that the three provisions of the Constitution that plaintiff was relying upon were not intended to be bundled together. It then considered and rejected defendant's arguments that another provision of the Constitution explicitly permitted change and that punitive damages were outside the scope of the protection because they do not compensate for personal injuries.]

This cause is hereby remanded to the Fayette Circuit Court for further proceedings not inconsistent herewith.

GRAVES, LAMBERT, STUMBO, WINTERSHEIMER, JJ., and SPECIAL JUSTICE RONALD P. HILLERICH concur. STEPHENS, C.J., concurs by separate opinion. COOPER, J., dissents by separate opinion.

STEPHENS, CHIEF JUSTICE (concurring opinion). I reluctantly concur with the majority opinion.

However, for some time, I have begun to doubt the validity of the doctrine of the jural rights which "popped" into our law in 1932. Ludwig v. Johnson, 243 Ky. 533, 49 S.W.2d 347 (1932).

As the dissent points out, and as the Law Journal Article by Professor Thomas Lewis emphasizes, there is very little, if any, basis for this now routinely accepted doctrine in the Kentucky Constitution or in the Constitutional Debates. Jural Rights Under Kentucky's Constitution: Realities Grounded in Myth, 80 K.L.J. 953 (1991–92).

Perhaps even more importantly, and recent in years, this Court has moved the jural rights doctrine far beyond its original aegis, so as to restrict even the General Assembly and this Court from changing its precedents, even though created after the adoption of the present constitution.

Although, I believe this Court should carefully consider the powerful arguments set forth in Justice Cooper's dissent, reliance on precedent is a strong tenet of our common law. Precedent should not lightly be overruled.

The doctrine of stare decisis is a judicial policy implemented to maintain stability and continuity in our jurisprudence. It is based upon the belief that similar cases should be decided in a similar manner. When a court of institutional review announces a principle of law to apply to a general set of facts, the doctrine of stare decisis requires the court, in the absence of "sound legal reasons to the contrary" to adhere to that same principle in future cases where there is a similar factual pattern. [C] "Stare decisis is ordinarily a wise rule of action. But it is not a universal, inexorable command." Washington v. W.C. Dawson & Co., 264 U.S. 219, 238, 44 S. Ct. 302, 309, 68 L. Ed. 646 (1924) (Brandeis, J., dissenting).

The principle of stare decisis does not require us to adhere blindly to previous decisions when we determine those decisions were in error. [Cc] I only concur because I believe there should be extensive debate before this Court changes such an established rule of law. I hope that the logic of the dissent will be the beginning of such a process.

COOPER, JUSTICE (dissenting opinion). This case arrives in this Court in a peculiar procedural posture. Under a factual scenario clearly entitling the plaintiff/Appellee to an instruction on punitive damages, the trial court ruled first that the language of KRS 411.184(1)(c) precluded such an instruction, then that KRS 411.184 was unconstitutional because it abolished the common law right to punitive damages. Having thus discarded KRS 411.184, the trial court instructed the jury in accordance with the common law standard established in Horton v. Union Light, Heat & Power Co., Ky., 690 S.W.2d 382, 389–90 (1985), viz: conduct exhibiting a wanton or reckless disregard for the lives and safety of other persons, or a willful or malicious act. From this set of circumstances has arisen the great and unnecessary debate as to (1) whether KRS 411.184 is unconstitutional as violative of the so-called "jural rights" doctrine, and (2) whether the "jural rights" doctrine has any valid constitutional basis.

I.

There was no need to address the "jural rights" doctrine in this case, for KRS 411.184 does not abolish the common law right to punitive damages. Faced with an argument similar to that accepted by the trial court in this case, we specifically so held in Wittmer v. Jones, Ky., 864 S.W.2d 885 (1993). Justice Leibson wrote in that case: "Throughout this litigation State Farm has presented various arguments against submitting the issue of punitive damages to the jury based on its interpretation of statutory language found in the new punitive damages statute enacted in 1988, now codified as KRS 411.184. It suffices to say that this Court could not interpret KRS 411.184 to destroy a cause of action for punitive damages otherwise appropriate without fatally impaling upon jural rights guaranteed by the Kentucky Constitution, Sections 14, 54, and 241.... We shall not so interpret it." Id. at 890 (citations omitted).

KRS 411.184 and .186 did not destroy the cause of action for punitive damages, but merely established standards to guide the jury in its determination of whether such damages are appropriate and the amount to be awarded. Never before have we questioned the authority of the General Assembly to enact statutes establishing the degree of culpability necessary to entitle a litigant to recover punitive damages.* * *

The only possible argument for the proposition that KRS 411.184 "abolished" the right to punitive damages is the one rejected in Wittmer v. Jones, supra, but accepted by the trial court in this case, i.e., that the element of "subjective awareness" set forth in the definition of malice, KRS 411.184(1)(c), can be proven only by the direct testimony of the person against whom punitive damages are sought. Since the defendant/Appellant was unavailable to testify, the trial court reasoned that Appellee could not prove Appellant's "subjective awareness," thus was not entitled to an instruction on punitive damages. However, as Justice Leibson also wrote in Fowler v. Mantooth, Ky., 683 S.W.2d 250 (1984), a case addressing the requirement of proof of malice as a condition precedent to an award of punitive damages, "Malice may be implied from outrageous conduct, and need not be express so long as the conduct is sufficient to evidence conscious wrongdoing," [C] This obviously is what the Court meant by the phrase "malice implied from the facts" in Horton v. Union Light, Heat and Power Co., supra, at 390. This is also in conformance with the principle that "a plaintiff is entitled to prove a defendant's state of mind through circumstantial evidence." [Cc] Even in a criminal case, where the elements of the offense must be proven beyond a reasonable doubt, mens rea may be inferred from the act itself and/or the circumstances surrounding it. [Cc]

It is no longer arguable in this day and age that proof of the act of driving while intoxicated creates an inference of "subjective awareness" on the part of the actor of the potential consequences of the act. If that inference would satisfy the "beyond a reasonable doubt" standard of proof in a criminal case, it is sufficient to satisfy the "clear and convincing evidence" standard set forth in KRS 411.184(2).

The majority opinion also takes umbrage with the statute's use of the "clear and convincing evidence" standard as a "vastly elevated standard for the recovery of punitive damages and a clear departure from the common law." [C] Even if that were true, such would not implicate the "jural rights" doctrine, since the establishment of a heightened standard of proof would not "abolish" the right to collect punitive damages, but only establish the standard of proof to be applied by the jury in determining whether to award them. In fact, both malice and fraud have always required proof by clear and convincing evidence. [Cc] The standard recognizes the quasi-criminal nature of punitive damages by taking the middle ground between the standard ordinarily used in civil cases of proof by a "preponderance of the evidence," and the criminal law standard of proof "beyond a reasonable doubt." While holding that Due Process does not require a standard higher than the "preponderance of the evidence," if buttressed by other procedural and substantive protections, the United States Supreme Court has stated that "There is much to be said in favor of a State's requiring, as many do, . . . a standard of 'clear and convincing evidence' or, even, 'beyond a reasonable doubt.' " Pacific Mutual Life Ins. Co. v. Haslip, 499 U.S. 1, 23, n. 11, 111 S. Ct. 1032, 1046, 113 L. Ed. 2d 1 (1991). The "clear and convincing evidence" standard for punitive damages has been adopted by legislative enactment or judicial decision in twenty-nine other states and the District of Columbia, and has been recommended by each of the principal academic groups to analyze the law of punitive damages since 1979, i.e., the American Bar Association, the American College of Trial Lawyers, the American Law Institute, and the National Conference of Commissioners on Uniform State Laws. (Footnotes omitted).

The jury in this case should have been instructed on punitive damages in accordance with KRS 411.184 and .186 as initially requested by the plaintiff/Appellee. If the trial court had done so, there would have been no need to address whether the "jural rights" doctrine has any basis in our Constitution.

II.

In his well reasoned and well documented article, Jural Rights Under Kentucky's Constitution: Realities Grounded in Myth, 80 Ky. L.J. 953 (1991–92), Professor Thomas P. Lewis, a preeminent scholar of Kentucky constitutional law, makes a compelling case for the proposition that the "jural rights" doctrine is nothing more nor less than a judicial usurpation of a traditional legislative prerogative. [C] As first enunciated in the case of Ludwig v. Johnson, 243 Ky. 533, 49 S.W.2d 347 (1932), the doctrine appears to have been intended to perpetually tether the jurisprudence of this Commonwealth to nineteenth century tort principles, i.e., any common law right of action existing prior to the adoption of the 1891 Constitution is sacrosanct and cannot be abolished. [Cc] In arriving at that conclusion and in coining the phrase "jural rights," the Ludwig court relied principally upon the Oregon case of Stewart v. Houk, 127 Ore. 589, 271 P. 998, 999 (Or.1928). [C] Oregon subsequently abandoned the "jural rights" concept. [C] We, on the other hand, have expanded it to include any common law right of action, whether or not that right existed prior to the adoption of the 1891 Constitution. [Cc] Ergo, any act of the legislature abolishing any right created by judicial decision violates the "jural rights" doctrine and is, therefore, unconstitutional. (!) As if that were not expansive enough, the majority of this Court today declares that any act of the legislature which "impairs," though does not "abolish," a common law right, is also unconstitutional. [C] As Professor Lewis foresaw, this Court has now assumed for itself the sole power to make any meaningful changes in the area of tort law. [C]

If that had been the intent of the framers of the 1891 Constitution, one can only wonder why they included Section 233 and the first paragraph of the Schedule accompanying the Constitution, both of which vest in the legislature the power to alter or repeal any laws in force and effect at the time of the adoption of the Constitution. * * *

This Court has recently reiterated the maxim that public policy is within the constitutional domain of the legislature.* * *

Courts are well suited to adjudicate individual disputes concerning discrete issues and parties. The Founding Fathers recognized this when they drafted the United States Constitution to give the judiciary jurisdiction to decide "cases and controversies." [Cc] On the other hand, the judicial process is not well suited to the formulation of public policy. As Professor Lewis notes, individuals, lobbies, or other collectives cannot talk to a court. "Briefs amicus curiae may be filed, but the virtue of the judicial system is that its primary focus must be on the trial record and parties before it; judges are not generally equipped or expected to make textually generalized, interrelated rule-type decisions based on 'legislative facts.' The common law decisions of a court are law, and no better system has been devised than this technique, by which general principles of law emerge from small bits of real life experience. But the technique has worked so well not because judges have a monopoly on wisdom but because the people have always reserved the power to modify principles that in the light of mounting experience have failed to work to their satisfaction." Lewis, supra, at 983.

On the other hand, legislatures are uniquely well equipped to reach fully informed decisions about the need for broad public policy changes in the law. They have more complete access to information, including the ability to receive comments from persons representing a multiplicity of perspectives and to use the legislative process to obtain new information. If a point needs further elaboration, a witness can be recalled. The rationale for legislative preeminence in formulating broad public policy is reflective of these inherent strengths in the legislative process.

* * *

There is nothing in Section 14, 54 or 241 which expressly transfers the power to formulate public policy in the area of tort law from the legislative department to the judicial department.* * *

Nor do I subscribe to the proposition that sixty-six years of error must be perpetuated for the sake of "predictability." [C] After all, although Ludwig v. Johnson has been on the books for sixty-six years, it purported to overrule over seventy years of precedent * * * and its progeny have effectively reversed 800 years of settled Anglo–Saxon jurisprudence. * * *

NOTES AND QUESTIONS

1. You have studied the meaning of malice in tort law. Do you think the trial court judge was correct in ruling that driving while intoxicated is not evidence from which the jury could infer the "subjective awareness" required by the statute? Or is the dissent correct that because malice and state of mind can be proved by

circumstantial evidence, the defendant's driving while intoxicated was sufficient without testimony by the defendant?

2. The trial court judge's ruling on the insufficiency of the evidence, whether correct or not, set the stage for the ruling on the constitutionality of the statute. Jural rights is a doctrine you may not have been exposed to before this case. What do you think about it? Based on the opinions in this case, do you think it is what the drafters of the Kentucky constitution intended?

3. Almost all of the challenges to tort reform have focused on the state constitutions rather than the U.S. Constitution. You are probably more familiar with constitutional issues like right to jury trial, due process, and equal protection than you are with the jural rights doctrine. Why do you suppose that challenges have been based on the state constitutions rather than the U.S. Constitution?

4. Although the grounds, jural rights, is relatively unusual, the Kentucky Supreme Court is not unusual in having nullified tort reform statutes passed by its legislature. See, for example, Best v. Taylor Machine Works, 179 Ill.2d 367, 689 N.E.2d 1057, 228 Ill.Dec. 636 (1997) (declaring the Civil Justice Reform Amendments of 1995 unconstitutional under the Illinois constitution); State ex. rel. Ohio Trial Lawyer v. Sheward, 86 Ohio St.3d 451, 715 N.E.2d 1062 (1999) (civil justice reform amendments declared unconstitutional under Ohio constitution); Lakin v. Senco Products Co., 329 Ore. 62, 987 P.2d 463 (1999) (cap on noneconomic damages unconstitutional violation of Oregon right to jury trial). But see McDougall v. Schanz, 461 Mich. 15, 597 N.W.2d 148 (1999) (upholding statute setting strict requirements concerning qualifications of experts in medical malpractice cases in face of challenge brought under Michigan constitution).

5. Even though he is skeptical of the validity of the doctrine of jural rights, Chief Justice Stephens feels bound by the doctrine of stare decisis to apply it in the principal case. How does the doctrine of stare decisis affect a court's ability to rethink its own precedent? Although neither of the opinions in the *Bower* case uses the term, it is a doctrine that was applicable to the decision in that case as well. Under what circumstances should the court abandon precedent? The next principal case explores that issue in the context of another constitutional challenge to a damages cap.

Pulliam v. Coastal Emergency Svcs.

Supreme Court of Virginia, 1999.
257 Va. 1, 509 S.E.2d 307.

CARRICO, CHIEF JUSTICE. In this appeal, we are called upon to consider again the constitutionality of the medical malpractice cap imposed by Code § 8.01–581.15.[1] We previously upheld the constitutionality of the cap in Etheridge v. Medical Center Hospitals, 237 Va. 87, 376 S.E.2d 525 (1989). * * * Because we conclude that the medical malpractice cap does not violate any constitutional guarantees, we will uphold the cap's constitutionality and reaffirm *Etheridge*.

* * *

---

1. Code § 8.01–581.15 provides that "in any verdict returned against a health care provider in an action for malpractice[,] ... the total amount recoverable for any injury to, or death of, a patient shall not exceed one million dollars."

[About 3:55 a.m. on December 15, 1995, Mrs. Pulliam arrived at the emergency room of Southside Regional Hospital complaining of "legs aching." She had been diagnosed with influenza two days earlier in the office of her private physician. At Southside Regional, she was examined by Dr. DiGiovanna, who had been retained by defendant Coastal Emergency Services to staff the hospital's emergency room. About 5:00 a.m., Dr. DiGiovanna discharged Mrs. Pulliam after prescribing a muscle relaxant and giving her printed instructions on influenza and additional instructions concerning bedrest. Shortly after 11:00 a.m. the same day, Mrs. Pulliam returned to the emergency room complaining of general weakness, particularly in her lower extremities. Following a physical examination by another doctor, Mrs. Pulliam was started on intravenous fluids and subjected to a CT scan and a lumbar puncture. Thereafter, she was transferred to the intensive care unit, where her condition worsened. She was pronounced dead at 9:08 p.m. An autopsy revealed that the cause of death was bacterial pneumonia and bacteremia. She was survived by her husband, who is the executor of her estate, and a son. After a jury trial based on the medical malpractice of Dr. DiGiovanna, for whom Coastal was vicariously liable, the jury returned a verdict of $2,045,000. Pursuant to the Virginia statute quoted in note 1, the trial court judge reduced the verdict to $1,000,000 and this appeal followed.]

A. Constitutionality of Medical Malpractice Cap.

The plaintiff's assignment of error on this point states that "as a matter of law, the trial court erred in failing to conclude that the cap on medical malpractice awards is unconstitutional as applied to Coastal and to Dr. DiGiovanna." (Footnote omitted.) In considering this assignment of error, "we adhere to the well-settled principle that all actions of the General Assembly are presumed to be constitutional. This Court, therefore, will resolve any reasonable doubt regarding a statute's constitutionality in favor of its validity. Any judgment as to the wisdom and propriety of a statute is within the legislative prerogative, and this Court will declare the legislative judgment null and void only when the statute is plainly repugnant to some provision of the state or federal constitution." [C]

In *Etheridge*, we rejected challenges to the constitutionality of the medical malpractice cap based upon contentions that the cap "violates the Virginia Constitution's due process guarantee, jury trial guarantee, separation of powers doctrine, prohibitions against special legislation, and equal protection guarantee, as well as certain parallel provisions of the Federal Constitution." [C] The plaintiff makes the same challenges here, but amplifies the arguments in several respects. (Footnote omitted.)

It is clear that we cannot grant the plaintiff relief without overruling *Etheridge*. Immediately, therefore, the doctrine of stare decisis is implicated.

In Virginia, the doctrine of stare decisis is more than a mere cliche. That doctrine plays a significant role in the orderly administration of justice by assuring consistent, predictable, and balanced application of legal principles. And when a court of last resort has established a precedent, after full deliberation upon the issue by the court, the precedent will not be treated lightly or ignored, in the absence of flagrant error or mistake. [C]

The inquiry becomes, therefore, whether flagrant error or mistake exists in the *Etheridge* decision. The plaintiff contends that such error does exist and, therefore, that "the doctrine of stare decisis should not deter this Court from reversing *Etheridge*."

The plaintiff argues that the medical malpractice cap is unconstitutional on each of seven independent grounds. We will consider these grounds seriatim.

1.   Right to Trial by Jury.

Article I, § 11 of the Constitution of Virginia provides "that in controversies respecting property, and in suits between man and man, trial by jury is preferable to any other, and ought to be held sacred." In *Etheridge*, we noted that, at the time the Constitution was adopted, the jury's sole function was to resolve disputed facts, that this continues to be a jury's sole function, (footnote omitted) and that the jury's fact-finding function extends to the assessment of damages. [C] We stated, however, that "once the jury has ascertained the facts and assessed the damages, ... the constitutional mandate is satisfied [and thereafter], it is the duty of the court to apply the law to the facts." [C] The medical malpractice cap, we said, does nothing more than establish the outer limits of a remedy; remedy is a matter of law and not of fact; and a trial court applies the remedy's limitation only after the jury has fulfilled its fact-finding function. Hence, we concluded, the cap does not infringe upon the right to a jury trial. [C]

The plaintiff says, however, that the Court in *Etheridge* "erred by failing to conclude that the mandate of Article I, § 11 includes the right to receive the amount of damages awarded by a jury after a proper jury trial." In this connection, the plaintiff cites two recent Supreme Court decisions.

* * *

The plaintiff says that these two decisions support his conclusion that the medical malpractice cap violates his right to a jury trial. We do not agree. In relying on Hetzel [v. Prince William Cty., 523 U.S. 208 (1998)], the plaintiff attempts to equate remittitur with the medical malpractice cap and argues that, since remittitur without the option of a new trial violates the Seventh Amendment right to a jury trial, application of the cap likewise violates Virginia's right to a jury trial. However, the plaintiff's initial premise is faulty because remittitur and the cap are not equivalent and do not come into play under the same circumstances. Remittitur, as well as additur, is utilized only after a court has determined that a party has not received a fair and proper jury trial. [C] The cap, however, is applied only after a plaintiff has had the benefit of a proper jury trial. In the latter situation, there is no right to a new trial, and the constitutional mandate has been satisfied.

The plaintiff's reliance on Feltner [v. Columbia Pictures Television, Inc., 523 U.S. 340 (1998)] is also misplaced. There, the Court dealt primarily with whether Columbia was entitled to a jury trial even though it elected to seek statutory damages. The Court concluded that Columbia had the right to a jury trial because the common law afforded copyright owners causes of action for infringement, and these actions were tried before juries. The Court recognized that "the Seventh Amendment . . . applies not only to common-law causes of action, but also to 'actions brought to enforce statutory rights that are analogous to common-law causes of action ordinarily decided in English law courts in the late 18th century, as opposed to those customarily heard by courts of equity or admiralty.' " [C] The Court did not address the validity of a cap on the recovery of damages.

Furthermore, while it does not appear that the Supreme Court has addressed the issue of the validity of state statutory caps, it has noted the decisions of two circuit courts of appeals on the subject * * * [and those opinions] have held that district court application of state statutory caps in diversity cases, post verdict, does not violate the Seventh Amendment.

* * *

Concerning the right of trial by jury under the Seventh Amendment, the Fourth Circuit followed our reasoning that it is not the role of the jury but of the legislature to determine the legal consequences of the jury's factual findings. [C] However, the Fourth Circuit assigned this additional reason for upholding the validity of the cap against an assertion that it violated the right of trial by jury: "It is by now axiomatic that the Constitution does not forbid the creation of new rights, or the abolition of old ones recognized by the common law, to attain a permissible legislative object. Indeed, the district court conceded that a legislature's outright abolition of a cause of action would not violate the seventh amendment. If a legislature may completely abolish a cause of action without violating the right of trial by jury, we think it permissibly may limit damages recoverable for a cause of action as well." [Boyd v. Bulala, 877 F.2d 1191 (4th Cir. 1989] at 1196 (citations and interior quotation marks omitted).

* * *

Nor can it be disputed that, in addition to abolishing a cause of action, a legislature may extinguish a cause of action by the imposition of a statute of limitations, for example, two years from the date of death in the case of an action for wrongful death. Code § 8.01–244. If it is permissible for a legislature to enact a statute of limitations completely barring recovery in a particular cause of action without impinging upon the right of trial by jury, it should be permissible for the legislature to impose a limitation upon the amount of recovery as well.

The courts of other states have upheld medical malpractice caps against assertions that they violate the right to a jury trial. [Cc]

The plaintiff cites several out-of-state cases declaring medical malpractice caps unconstitutional, but we find them inapposite [due to differences between those state's constitutions and Virginia's or unpersuasive]. * * *

2. Special Legislation.

Article IV, § 14 of the Constitution of Virginia provides that "the General Assembly shall not enact any local, special, or private law . . . (18) granting to any private corporation, association, or individual any special or exclusive right, privilege, or immunity." (Footnote omitted.) In *Etheridge*, we noted that we had previously held that laws may be made to apply to a class only, even though the class may be small, provided the classification is reasonable, not arbitrary, and the law is made to apply to all persons in the class without distinction. [C] We also noted that if the classification bears a reasonable and substantial relation to the object sought to be accomplished, it will survive a special-laws constitutional challenge. Id.

We then pointed out that, in enacting the Medical Malpractice Act, the General Assembly, after a careful and deliberate study, had determined health care providers faced increasing difficulty obtaining affordable malpractice coverage in excess of $750,000, thus reducing the number of such providers available to serve Virginia's citizens. We also pointed out that the General Assembly had determined that this significant problem adversely affected the public health, safety, and welfare and necessitated the imposition of a limitation upon the liability of health care providers in medical malpractice actions. [C]

We observed that the General Assembly had decided that damage awards in medical malpractice cases should not exceed $750,000 (now $1,000,000), and we stated that the limitation applied to all health care providers and all medical malpractice patients. [C] We found that the classification was not arbitrary, that it bore a reasonable and substantial relation to the object sought to be accomplished, and that it applied to all persons belonging to the class without distinction. Id. Accordingly, we concluded that the legislation did not violate the prohibition against special legislation. Id.

* * *

[The court then considered plaintiff's argument that the cap was impermissible special legislation.] The remainder of the plaintiff's "as applied" argument is confined to the proposition that the medical malpractice cap concentrates the costs solely upon those whose losses are greatest while identifying "a specific elite class, described as 'health care providers,' to which it accords special privileges and immunities that are given to no other tortfeasors in this Commonwealth." And the plaintiff indicates his agreement with the dissent in *Etheridge* that the General Assembly acted arbitrarily in restricting the cap so that it did not apply to "all plaintiffs and all defendants regardless of their identities." [C] * * *

Here, however, we do not have to assume a set of facts that would sustain the medical malpractice cap. The actual facts were as stated in

Etheridge: "The General Assembly concluded [after careful and deliberate study] that escalating costs of medical malpractice insurance and the availability of such insurance were substantial problems adversely affecting the health, safety, and welfare of Virginia's citizens." [C] Given these facts, we think the cap bears a reasonable and substantial relation to the General Assembly's objective to protect the public's health, safety, and welfare by insuring the availability of health care providers in the Commonwealth. Accordingly, we conclude that the medical malpractice cap does not constitute special legislation.

3. Taking of Property.

Under the Fifth Amendment to the Constitution of the United States, private property shall not be taken for public use without just compensation. Under art. I, § 11 of the Constitution of Virginia, private property shall not be taken or damaged for public uses without just compensation.

Here, the argument is that the effect of the medical malpractice cap is to take the property of the plaintiff and his son in violation of these constitutional provisions. As the statutory beneficiaries of Mrs. Pulliam, the argument goes, the plaintiff and his son "had a property interest in the full measure of the jury's verdict."

We disagree. * * * [I]t is only when a right has accrued or a claim has arisen that it is subject to the protection of the due process clause * * * "for 'nobody has a vested right in the continuance of the rules of the common law.'" [quoting Hess v. Snyder Hunt Corp., 240 Va. 49, 392 S.E.2d 817 (1990) (citing Munn v. Illinois, 94 U.S. 113, 134, 24 L. Ed. 77 (1877).]. Continuing, we stated that "the fourteenth amendment does not forbid a legislature from abolishing old rights recognized by the common law in order to attain a permissible legislative objective." Id. Finally, we said that "if a legislature can abolish a cause of action for a legitimate legislative purpose, it also may prevent a cause of action from arising by enacting a statute of repose for such a purpose." Id.

This rationale applies with equal force here. The plaintiff's cause of action for wrongful death had not accrued at the time the cap was imposed upon recoveries in medical malpractice cases. One cannot obtain a property interest in a cause of action that has not accrued, and there was nothing to prevent the General Assembly from limiting the remedy, so far as unaccrued causes of action are concerned, to attain a permissible legislative objective without running afoul of the "taking" clauses of the Federal and State Constitutions. Accordingly, we find no violation of the "taking" clauses in this case.

4. Due Process.

5. Equal Protection.

In oral argument, the plaintiff combined these two subjects and attempted to convince the Court that it should apply an intermediate level of scrutiny, rather than the lower-level rational basis test, in our due process and equal protection analysis of the medical malpractice cap. (Footnote omitted.) However, we ruled in *Etheridge* that, in a due process or equal protection analysis, the rational basis test applies unless a fundamental right or a suspect class is affected.[C] And we noted that those interests that have been recognized as "fundamental" include the right to free speech, the right to vote, the right to interstate travel, the right to fairness in the criminal process, the right to marry, and the right to fairness in procedures concerning governmental deprivation of life, liberty, or property. [C] We noted further that suspect classifications are those based upon race and national origin and that classifications based upon gender, alienage, and illegitimacy are entitled to receive a level of scrutiny between strict scrutiny and the rational basis test. [C] Here, however, no fundamental right or suspect class is affected by application of the medical malpractice cap.

* * *

[The court found that *Etheridge* enunciated the correct level of scrutiny and that the rational basis test continues to provide the proper standard for determining whether there has been a denial of due process or equal protection in a case involving the medical malpractice cap, and that the statute satisfied due process.]

6.   Separation of Powers.

7.   Province of the Judiciary.

Because these two subjects are related, we will discuss them together. The plaintiff argues that the medical malpractice cap violates the separation of powers doctrine and also invades the province of the judiciary.

In rejecting a separation of powers challenge in *Etheridge*, we pointed out that under art. VI, § 1 of the Virginia Constitution, the General Assembly, subject to provisions relating to the power and jurisdiction of this Court, has "the power to determine the original and appellate jurisdiction of the courts of the Commonwealth." [C] We also noted that under art. IV, § 14 of the Constitution, the General Assembly's authority extends "to all subjects of legislation not herein forbidden or restricted," and that the common law is one area in which the General Assembly's authority has not been forbidden or restricted. Id.

Accordingly, we said that the legislature has the power to provide, modify, or repeal a remedy. [C] And we concluded that "whether the remedy prescribed in Code § 8.01–581.15 is viewed as a modification of the common law or as establishing the jurisdiction of the courts in specific cases, clearly it was a proper exercise of legislative power." [C]

* * *

Thus, we find no merit in the plaintiff's arguments concerning separation of powers and the province of the judiciary. Accordingly, we reject the arguments. * * *

[The court then ruled that the statutory cap applied to Coastal and that pre-judgment interest was included in the statutory cap.]

Affirmed.

[The concurring opinion of Justice Hassell is omitted.]

KINSER, JUSTICE (concurring opinion). I agree with the majority's rationale and decision that the medical malpractice recovery cap contained in Code § 8.01–581.15 does not violate any provision of either the Constitution of the United States or the Constitution of Virginia. (Footnote omitted.) I reach this conclusion without considering the role that stare decisis should play in this case. I write separately for the sole purpose of expressing my belief that the medical malpractice cap creates an unwarranted injustice in certain situations.

The General Assembly has the responsibility to protect the health, welfare, and safety of the citizens of this Commonwealth through appropriate legislation. However, the medical malpractice cap works the greatest hardship on those individuals who are the most severely injured by the negligence of health care providers. Nevertheless, I cannot be influenced by such concerns when deciding the constitutionality of a challenged statute. I can only express my views with the hope that the General Assembly will adopt a more equitable method by which to ensure the availability of health care in this Commonwealth.

NOTES AND QUESTIONS

1. The consideration of a catalogue of constitutional challenges by the court in the principal case is typical of the cases challenging state tort reform. Do you agree with the court's ruling on each of the challenges? There are approximately ninety decisions at various levels by state courts holding state tort reform unconstitutional under state constitutions and about a hundred and twenty upholding such laws. The Florida Civil Justice Reform legislation was under challenge as this book went to press. If Florida and others join those jurisdictions that already have nullified legislative reform, will the courts have won the day? Does this whole process have implications for federal tort reform legislation?

2. As you can see from Justice Kinser's concurring opinion in the principal case, he does not agree with the Virginia legislature's judgment on the propriety of a cap in medical malpractice cases, yet he voted to affirm the trial court's ruling. Why? As Justice Resnick noted in State ex. rel. Ohio Trial Lawyer v. Sheward, 86 Ohio St.3d 451, 715 N.E.2d 1062, 1072 (1999), "[a]ll arguments going to the soundness of legislative policy choices, however, are directed to their proper place, which is outside the door to this courthouse. This court has nothing to do with the policy or wisdom of a statute. That is the exclusive concern of the legislative branch of the government. The only judicial inquiry into the constitutionality of a statute involves the question of legislative power, not legislative wisdom." (Internal quotations and citations omitted.)

3. Note that in all of the cases in this chapter there is some discussion of the proper role of the legislature and the judiciary in declaring tort law. Sometimes the discussion is cast in terms of preference (which body is better suited to resolve the issue) and sometimes in terms of power (which body is authorized to make the decision). These are questions we have considered in other contexts as well. See pages 1137 to 1209. See also Symposium: Judges as Tort Lawmakers, 49 DePaul L.Rev. 275 (1999). The substantive issues being considered—whether medical

monitoring is a form of damage, the appropriate threshold for punitive damages, the standard for proving punitive damages, whether there should be a cap on damages—are very difficult ones, with many compelling arguments on both sides. Equally challenging is the discernment of the proper role of the two branches of government. How should they work together to make tort law? How do you see their respective roles? This struggle for power between the legislative and judicial branches of the states promises to be an important one, fervently pursued, during the next decade. What will your role in it be? How would you strike the proper balance?

CHAPTER XXIV

COMPENSATION SYSTEMS AS SUBSTITUTES FOR TORT LAW

Students come to this chapter with a close appreciation of the rambunctious and ramshackle nature of tort law. Although tort law has moved to cover more widely economic interests, its home is its protection of physical integrity. Tort lawyers are usually pictured as inhabiting courtrooms to argue personal injury claims.

This book's cases and materials show that tort law has been subject to both judicial and legislative changes, but these changes have not altered the basic picture of lawyers in the courtroom. About a century ago a more radical change occurred—no-fault workers' compensation. About thirty years ago approaches were suggested and adopted in various states for automobile no-fault compensation systems. These developments are reviewed before turning to other no-fault compensation systems, some targeting particular problems (e.g., vaccine-related injuries), others of a broader nature which would replace the entire body of tort liability for personal injury with a governmental no-fault compensation system, as was done in New Zealand in the early 1970s.

As you review these schemes ask about the nature and function of tort liability. What are its purposes and are they adequately reflected in compensation systems? Should those purposes be captured in any tort system or is it appropriate to forfeit some (for example, deterrence) in the interest of maximizing others (for example, compensation to a wide class of injured persons)? Are there ways of formulating the approaches as to preserve the benefits of tort liability while remedying its ills?

1. EMPLOYMENT INJURIES

Negligence was formed in the crucible of the Industrial Revolution. Exponential increase in speed and efficiency of transportation and industrial production resulted in an ever increasing number of personal injuries. Duties of care in negligence were imposed on employers toward their employees. Out of the numerous cases arose an elaborate doctrinal system. Thus, among others, the employer had the general duties of using due care to provide a safe place to work and to supply safe tools and appliances. There were exceptions and counter-exceptions—e.g., the simple-tool doctrine as an exception to the second duty above, and the inexperienced-employee doctrine as an exception to it. See generally Labatt, Master and Servant (1913), vols. 3 and 4.

But the most significant aspect of the doctrinal development was a group of three defenses—assumption of risk, contributory negligence and the fellow-servant rule. This "unholy trinity," added to the requirement of proving the employer's negligence meant that stumbling blocks were placed on recovery of damages by injured workers. Long, drawn-out litigation placed severe financial burdens upon workers. Even though courts cannot be said to have been uniformly hostile to workers' claims, the realities of wealth and ineffectual representational institutions for workers dictated relatively few instances of compensation.

With the incidence of industrial accidents came social pressure for a system to compensate the many injured. Sometimes the pressure was accommodated through bargains between employers and employees. More widely, Congress took note of the issue and repealed some of the common law doctrines that had frustrated the goal of more adequate compensation for railroad workers. Federal Employees' Liability Act, 1906. The Act did not survive constitutional challenge. The second attempt saw the Federal Employers' Liability Act of 1908 (45 U.S.C.A. § 51 et seq. (1908)). Congress enacted a law easing tort law burdens for longshoremen and harbor workers in 1927 (33 U.S.C.A. § 901 et seq. (as amended 1972)). These acts restructured the tort system making it easier for workers to recover damages. Much later Congress established a compensation system for coal miners commonly called the Black Lung Program (Federal Coal Mine Health and Safety Act of 1969, 30 U.S.C.A. §§ 801–962). Congress, in 1986, enacted the National Childhood Vaccine Injury Act, which provides compensation to certain injuries related to vaccines taken by children. The compensation scheme has been limited to children; the reasons for its enactment, vaccine shortages and litigation costs, were not replicated with respect to adults. U.S. Dep't of Health and Human Services, Public Health Reports No. 3, Vol. 113; p. 236 at 1 (1998).

By far, the boldest scheme is Workers' Compensation legislation that allows workers injured in the course of employment to recover compensation from the employer without having to prove employer fault. The employer is able to insure for these losses. Within each state, a large segment of common law liability was abolished, as the legislation was enacted. Compensation is now ubiquitous in the modern Western Industrial state. It was first introduced in Bismark's Germany in the late 19th Century reflecting the maturity of the industrial revolution, a rise in labor union influence, and the challenge of Marxist ideas. England and other European nations followed the German experiment. New York in 1910 was the first state to adopt workers' compensation legislation. Wisconsin's 1911 legislation was the first to withstand constitutional challenge.

The rallying theme for the movement was that the enterprise should bear the loss rather than permit it to lie on the unfortunate employee who arbitrarily had incurred the injury: "The cost of the product should bear the blood of the workman." The employer was liable to the injured employee regardless of fault, so long as the injury occurred in the course of employment. Early workers' compensation laws only protected employees from work-related injuries, but not occupational diseases. Today these also are included, with some retrenchment in the case of stress-related disease, under the workers' compensation systems. It has been argued that the systems implicitly perform the dual role of tort liability—compensation and optimal deterrence. Deterrence may operate by internalizing the costs of production, thus ensuring an optimal production of goods. The efficacy of internalization depends in part on the sensitivity of the insurance system in discriminating between safe and unsafe producers, the willingness of the political system to face producers with costs of accidents, and the impact of transaction costs, like litigation costs and uncertainty of benefits. In face of these obstacles the internalization process may be weakened as costs are spread to the public at large. Hylton & Layman, The Internalization Paradox and Workers' Compensation, 21 Hofstra L.Rev. 109 (1992). For historical background, see J. Weinstein, The Corporate Ideal in the Liberal State, 1900–1918, ch. 2 (1968); Epstein, The Historical Origins and Economic Structure of Workers' Compensation Law, 16 Ga.L.Rev. 775 (1982).

Workers' compensation has developed into a complex and highly specialized field of law. Litigation is a feature of the system as each year courts hand down many decisions that mainly concern questions about coverage. Typical questions include whether an injury fell within the scope of employment, see, e.g., Nemchick v. Thatcher Glass Mfg. Co., 203 N.J.Super. 137, 495 A.2d 1372 (App.Div.1985) (employee's injury while driving home from work after completion of an assigned off-premises task occurred in "course of employment"); or whether the injury suffered was caused by conditions of employment. See, e.g., State Accident Ins. Fund v. Noffsinger, 80 Or.App. 640, 723 P.2d 358 (1986) (psychic injury as a result of verbal harassment and horseplay at workplace); Graver Tank & Mfg. Co. v. Industrial Comm'n, 97 Ariz. 256, 399 P.2d 664 (1965) (suicide). Generally courts consider whether the injury may reasonably be regarded as an incident of employment rather than whether the injury was specifically foreseeable. See, e.g., Burns v. Merritt Eng'g Co., 302 N.Y. 131, 135, 96 N.E.2d 739, 741 (1951).

Advances in medical knowledge have established a causal connection between some diseases and exposure to toxic substances found in the work place. Claims for these diseases have challenged the limits of workers compensation coverage. Indeed, with the recognition of the influence of the workplace on the contraction of disease in general, increasing numbers of claims are brought at the very point where the difficulties of proof are greatest. Dewees, Duff, & Trebilcock, Exploring the Domain of Accident Law: Taking the Facts Seriously 351–352 (1996). For a discussion of the problem in establishing causation see Brennan, Causal Links and Statistical Links: The Role of Scientific Uncertainty in Hazardous Substance Litigation, 73 Cornell L. Rev. 469 (1988).

Perhaps the best summary of how these laws function has been provided by the author of the leading treatise in the field:

"The right to [workers'] compensation benefits depends on one simple test: Was there a work-connected injury? Negligence, and, for the most part, fault, are not in issue and cannot affect the result. Let the employer's conduct be flawless in its perfection, and let the employee's be abysmal in its clumsiness, rashness and ineptitude: if the accident arises out of and in the course of the employment, the employee receives his award. Reverse the positions, with a careless and stupid employer and a wholly innocent employee: the same award issues.

"Thus, the test is not the relation of an individual's personal quality (fault) to an event, but the relationship of an event to an employment. The essence of applying the test is not a matter of assessing blame, but of marking out boundaries.

"The typical [workers'] compensation act has these features: (a) the basic operating principle is that an employee is automatically entitled to certain benefits whenever he suffers a 'personal injury by accident arising out of and in the course of employment'; (b) negligence and fault are largely immaterial, both in the sense that the employee's contributory negligence does not lessen his rights and in the sense that the employer's complete freedom from fault does not lessen his liability; (c) coverage is limited to persons having the status of employee, as distinguished from independent contractor; (d) benefits to the employee include cash-wage benefits, usually around one-half to two-thirds of his average weekly wage, and hospital and medical expenses; in death cases benefits for dependents are provided; arbitrary maximum and minimum limits are ordinarily imposed; (e) the employee and his dependents, in exchange for these modest but assured benefits, give up their common-law right to sue the employer for damages for any injury covered by the act; (f) the right to sue third persons whose negligence caused the injury remains, however, with the proceeds usually being applied first to reimbursement of the employer for the compensation outlay, the balance (or most of it) going to the employee; (g) administration is typically in the hands of administrative commissions; and, as far as possible, rules of procedure, evidence, and conflict of laws are relaxed to facilitate the achievement of the beneficent purposes of the legislation; and (h) the employer is required to secure his liability through private insurance, state-fund insurance in some states, or 'self-insurance'; thus the burden of compensation liability does not remain upon the employer but passes to the consumer, since compensation premiums, as part of the cost of production, will be reflected in the price of the product." 1 A. Larson, The Law of Workmen's Compensation, 1–2, 5 (1991). (Copyright Matthew Bender and Company, Inc. Reprinted by permission.)

Workers' compensation law has not received the criticism leveled at the common law tort system. Yet burdens of compensation have increased for employers, from $1 billion in 1950 to $2 billion in 1960 to $5 billion in 1970 to $21 billion in 1980, reaching nearly $35 billion in 1986 (reported by the ALI Reporter Study: Enterprise Responsibility for Personal Injury, Vol. 1, p. 106 (1991)). More recently, it is estimated that the burden rose to $56 billion in 1990 and to $62 billion in 1992. Schwartz, Waste, Fraud, and Abuse in Workers' Compensation: The Recent California Experience, 52 Md. L. Rev. 983, 984 (1993). Employers have complained about the burden, especially as coverage has extended from injuries to occupational health. Thus, on July 16, 1993, California enacted legislation providing that no compensation shall be paid "for psychiatric injury if the injury was substantially caused by lawful, nondiscriminatory, good faith personnel action." Employees, in contrast, have complained about inadequacy of coverage and eroding benefits as levels of compensation are not adjusted for cost of living increases.

A significant portion of compensation dollars go to pay for hospital and medical expenses. Under the health care reforms proposed at the end of 1993 by the Clinton Administration, the question arose whether that component of the workers' compensation system should be shifted to health care plans, leaving the system to deal, in the main, with compensation for lost earnings. What do you see as the advantages or disadvantages of folding the medical expense component of workers compensation into the health care system?

The benefits provided by the workers' compensation system appear to be conspicuously modest in light of the recent developments of expanded liability for tortious conduct. Recall restriction or abolishment of the defenses of contributory negligence, assumption of the risk and the fellow servant rule. In addition, damages for non-economic loss have increased in kind and magnitude. At the same time, constraints on workers' compensation have directly inhibited extension of benefits. Some courts have responded to the disparity by circumventing the workers' compensation immunity shield.

Blankenship v. Cincinnati Milacron Chemicals, Inc.

Supreme Court of Ohio, 1982.
69 Ohio St.2d 608, 433 N.E.2d 572, cert. denied, 459
U.S. 857, 103 S.Ct. 127, 74 L.Ed.2d 110 (1982).

[Eight current or former employees of Cincinnati Milacron Chemicals, Inc. (Milacron) brought an action against Milacron, alleging that exposure to fumes of certain chemicals within the scope of their employment rendered them sick, poisoned, and permanently disabled. The employees alleged that Milacron knew that such conditions existed, failed to correct the conditions, failed to warn the employees of the damages and conditions that existed, and failed to report the conditions to various state and Federal agencies to which they were required to report by law. The employees further alleged that Milacron failed to warn the employees that certain occupational diseases were being contracted and failed to provide medical examinations as required by law, and that Milacron's omissions were intentional, malicious, and in willful and wanton disregard of the duty to protect the health of employees.

The trial court dismissed on the ground that the action was barred by relevant sections of the Ohio Constitution and the Ohio Workers' Compensation Act, which afforded an employer and his employees total immunity from civil suit. Employees appealed the trial court's holding and the Court of Appeals affirmed. The cause is now before this court pursuant to the allowance of a motion to certify the record.]

BROWN, J. * * * The sole issue raised in this appeal is whether the trial court properly granted appellees' motion to dismiss appellants' complaint on the grounds that an employee is barred by Section 35, Article II of the Ohio Constitution, and R.C. 4123.74 and 4123.741 from prosecuting an action at law for an intentional tort. * * *

The primary focus of the dispute between the parties centers upon the question of whether the Workers' Compensation Act (R.C. 4123.35 et seq.) is intended to cover an intentional tort committed by employers against their employees. Section 35, Article II of the Ohio Constitution, serves as a basis for legislative enactments in the area of workers' compensation by providing, in pertinent part:

"For the purpose of providing compensation to workmen and their dependents, for death, injuries or occupational disease, occasioned in the course of such workmen's employment, laws may be passed establishing a state fund to be created by compulsory contribution thereto by employers, and administered by the state, determining the terms and conditions upon which payment shall be made therefrom. Such compensation shall be in lieu of all other rights to compensation, or damages, for such death, injuries, or occupational disease, and any employer who pays the premium or compensation provided by law, passed in accordance herewith, shall not be liable to respond in damages at common law or by statute for such death, injuries or occupational disease. * * * "

The constitutional mandate has been implemented by R.C. 4123.74 which provides: "Employers who comply with section 4123.35 of the Revised Code shall not be liable to respond in damages at common law or by statute for any injury, or occupational disease, or bodily condition, received or contracted by any employee in the course of or arising out of his employment * * * whether or not such injury, occupational disease [or] bodily condition * * * is compensable under sections 4123.01 to 4123.94, inclusive, of the Revised Code." * * *

[W]here an employee asserts in his complaint a claim for damages based on an intentional tort, " * * * the substance of the claim is not an injury * * * received or contracted by any employee in the course of or arising out of his employment within the meaning of R.C. 4123.74 * * *." Id. No reasonable individual would equate intentional and unintentional conduct in terms of the degree of risk which faces an employee nor would such individual contemplate the risk of an intentional tort as a natural risk of employment. Since an employer's intentional conduct does not arise out of employment, R.C. 4123.74 does not bestow upon employers immunity from civil liability for their intentional torts and an employee may resort to a civil suit for damages. [C]

This holding not only comports with constitutional and statutory requirements, but it is also consistent with the legislative goals which underlie the Workers' Compensation Act.

The workers' compensation system is based on the premise that an employer is protected from a suit for negligence in exchange for compliance with the Workers' Compensation Act. The Act operates as a balance of mutual compromise between the interests of the employer and the employee whereby employees relinquish their common law remedy and accept lower benefit levels coupled with the greater assurance of recovery and employers give up their common law defenses and are protected from unlimited liability. But the protection afforded by the Act has always been for negligent acts and not for intentional tortious conduct. Indeed, workers' compensation acts were designed to improve the plight of the injured worker, and to hold that intentional torts are covered under the Act would be tantamount to encouraging such conduct, and this clearly cannot be reconciled with the motivating spirit and purpose of the Act.

It must also be remembered that the compensation scheme was specifically designed to provide less than full compensation for injured employees. Damages such as pain and suffering and loss of services on the part of a spouse are unavailable remedies to the injured employee. Punitive damages cannot be obtained. Yet, these damages are available to individuals who have been injured by intentional tortious conduct of third parties, and there is no legitimate reason why an employer should be able to escape from such damages simply because he committed an intentional tort against his employee.

In addition, one of the avowed purposes of the Act is to promote a safe and injury-free work environment. [C] Affording an employer immunity for his intentional behavior certainly would not promote such an environment, for an employer could commit intentional acts with impunity with the knowledge that, at the very most, his workers' compensation premiums may rise slightly. * * * [The court holds that the question of whether Milacron's conduct and omissions amounted to an intentional tort should have been determined by the trier of fact, and that the trial court improperly dismissed the action. Judgment of the Court of Appeals is reversed and case remanded for further proceedings].

[CELEBREZZE, C.J., and SWEENEY and CLIFFORD F. BROWN, JJ., concur. LOCHER, J., concurs in part and dissents in part. HOLMES and KRUPANSKY, JJ., dissent. The dissenting opinion of Holmes argues that tort actions should be permitted against employers only in cases of actual intent to injure the employees. Krupansky's dissent argues that there should be no judicial creation of an intentional misconduct exception to the employers' tort immunity because there is no express exception in the Ohio Workers' Compensation Act].

NOTES AND QUESTIONS

1. The subsequent evolution of the law in Ohio is tortuous and characterized by legislative initiatives and judicial counterattacks. Immediately after the principal case, the Ohio legislature enacted a statute that attempted to enfold employers' intentional torts within a provision of the Ohio code that precluded common law relief but gave enhanced compensation benefits. The benefits were to be paid from a

fund generated by levies against employers. Subsequently, this statute was declared unconstitutional. Brady v. Safety–Kleen Corp., 576 N.E.2d 722 (Ohio 1991). After more case law development, the Ohio legislature again stepped in to define the intentional tort exception more stringently than the judicial definition. Ohio Rev. Code Ann. § 2745.01. The employee must under this provision prove deliberate and intentional conduct on the employee's part.

2. The Supreme Court of West Virginia created a similar exception for employers' "willful, wanton, or reckless misconduct" in Mandolidis v. Elkins Indus., Inc., 161 W.Va. 695, 246 S.E.2d 907 (1978). Later, the West Virginia legislature modified the *Mandolidis* rule by narrowing the concept of "willful, wanton, and reckless conduct" in an attempt to create greater certainty. Two alternative methods are prescribed for proving deliberate intent. First, the employer is liable if it acts "with a consciously, subjectively and deliberately formed intention to produce the specific result of injury or death to an employee." Second, the employee may establish the requisite intent by proving: (1) unsafe working conditions violative of a statute, or otherwise firmly recognized; and (2) the employer's "subjective realization and appreciation" of that unsafe working condition. The statute is explained and applied in Handley v. Union Carbide Corp., 804 F.2d 265 (4th Cir.1986). The statute established a special "Employer's Excess Liability Fund" under which employers may voluntarily insure against this type of liability. See also Turner v. PCR, Inc., 2000 WL 232595 (Fla. March 2, 2000) (intentional tort exception to Florida worker compensation law may be shown by objective standard that employer engaged in conduct substantially certain to result in injury).

3. Other exceptions are:

(a) Successor corporations, Billy v. Consolidated Mach. Tool Corp., 51 N.Y.2d 152, 412 N.E.2d 934, 432 N.Y.S.2d 879 (1980).

(b) Third party actions for indemnity or contribution against the employer, Lambertson v. Cincinnati Corp., 312 Minn. 114, 257 N.W.2d 679 (1977).

(c) Actions for damages of a kind not covered by the statute, Foley v. Polaroid Corp., 381 Mass. 545, 413 N.E.2d 711 (1980) (injury to reputation resulting from libel).

(d) Some state statutes, reflecting recent criticism of the traditional workers' compensation scheme or its costs, allow unions and employers to provide themselves with alternative dispute resolution in some industries. The statutes are described in Moscowitz & Van Bourg, Carve–Outs and the Privatization of Workers' Compensation in Collective Bargaining Agreements, 46 Syracuse L. Rev. 1 (1995).

4. Is the result in the principal case, and the ensuing legislative reform and judicial reaction, likely to occur so long as no-fault compensation systems are islands within the tort litigation system? Ohio is among states with more limited recovery in worker compensation. Would the result have been different if worker compensation awards had been more nearly adequate? Or if, as in England, workers' compensation was not an exclusive remedy but in addition to the common law?

5. The subject of Workers' Compensation has found a separate place in the curriculum of most law schools, and this brief introduction is therefore all that is warranted in this casebook.

2. AUTOMOBILE ACCIDENT INJURIES

Motor vehicle reparation plans, or no-fault automobile insurance as they are commonly called, are of much later origin than the worker's compensation statutes, and they have been unable to obtain the widespread adoption of the worker's compensation statutes. Although Judge Marx in 1925 proposed a no-fault reparation scheme, no legislation was enacted until 1971, except in the province of Saskatchewan, Canada. The immediate impetus for automobile no-fault plans was the 1965 book by Professors Robert E. Keeton and Jeffrey O'Connell, titled Basic Protection for the Accident Victim—A Blueprint for Reforming Automobile Insurance. The plan was accompanied by a model no-fault statute. Bolstered by U.S. Department of Transportation, critical of the tort system and ultimately urging no-fault compensation, 24 states and the District of Columbia passed no-fault statutes of various types. Subsequently, a number of states repealed their statutes. As of January, 2000, thirteen states have no-fault plans that limit access to the common law liability system. Limits are expressed as either a dollar threshold—an amount that medical costs must exceed before an injured person may proceed with a common law claim—or a verbal threshold where the injured person must show his or her injuries were of a specified severity (e.g., "dismemberment"). Eight states have adopted a dollar threshold, three states have a verbal threshold, and three states offer drivers a choice between remaining in the common law system or switching to a no-fault plan either with a dollar threshold (Kentucky) or a verbal threshold (New Jersey and Pennsylvania). Eight states and the District of Columbia have adopted no-fault schemes that place no limits on access to the common law liability system. (Wisconsin may be omitted because of its derisory benefits ($1,300).) These are usually referred to as a "add-on states."

Interest in no-fault schemes has been revived with concerns about the cost of compensating victims of auto accidents. At the same time tort reform initiatives and academic advocacy has further ripened interest in auto no-fault schemes. Congress proposed the Auto Choice Reform Act of 1997 (S. 625, 105th Cong., H.R. 2021, 105th Cong.). The extent and nature of this new wave is described in Hager, No–Fault Drives Again: A Contemporary Primer, 52 U. Miami L. Rev. 793 (1998).

No-fault schemes provide insurance against economic losses (medical expenses and lost wages). No coverage is provided for noneconomic losses. For detailed coverage see Joost, Automobile Insurance and No–Fault Law (1993).

The Institute for Civil Justice: Rand published a report in 1991, No–Fault Approaches to Compensating People Injured in Automobile Accidents, by S.J. Carroll, et al. (R–4019–ICJ). No-fault plans are referred to as Personal Injury Protection (PIP). The Executive Summary in part states:

THE ICJ NO–FAULT STUDY

The argument for the traditional approach to compensation is based on widely accepted ethical norms, while the argument for the no-fault approach is based on the claim that no-fault would yield, on balance, preferable outcomes. Weighing these arguments requires consideration of whether and, if so, by how much the outcomes resulting from no-fault would actually differ from those resulting from the traditional approach. To do this, policymakers must consider the probable effects of a switch from a traditional system to a no-fault system.

The ICJ study empirically tests the assumptions made by proponents of no-fault insurance. We examine the effects of shifting from the traditional compensation system to alternative no-fault plans. The 21 alternatives studied represent a wide range of possible no-fault plans.

Because of the diverse concerns that arise in the policy debate, we examined the effects of adopting a no-fault alternative on several different outcomes:

- Total injury coverage costs;[3]
- Transaction costs—lawyer fees and claim processing costs;
- Injured parties' net compensation—after deduction of any lawyer fees;
- How compensation compares with economic loss; and
- Time to payment.

EFFECTS OF A SPECIFIC ILLUSTRATIVE NO–FAULT PLAN

The specific effects of different no-fault plans vary, depending on how they combine the critical design elements: the threshold and the PIP benefit level. To illustrate, we will begin with an examination of a no-fault plan with a verbal threshold and a $15,000 policy limit.

Effects on Total Injury Coverage Costs

The compensation provided people injured in auto accidents in the tort states, including those who received no auto insurance compensation at all, averaged $4681 in 1989 dollars.[4] Insurers' transaction costs—legal fees and claim-processing costs—averaged $793 per injured person. Overall, the total injury coverage costs of the traditional system averaged $5474 per injured person, as shown in Table S.1.

Using our models, we estimated that these same people, with the same injuries and losses, would have averaged $3764 in compensation with insurer's transaction costs of $528 had they been covered by the illustrative no-fault plan instead of the traditional system. Compared to the traditional

---

3. Injury coverage costs include total compensation paid to a claimant (including whatever the claimant may spend on legal fees) for injuries by all types of auto-insurance coverage, plus the insurers' legal fees and claim-processing costs. The study focuses exclusively on compensation for personal injuries. We do not examine compensation for

property damage resulting from auto accidents. Depending on the kinds of coverage and the policy limits purchased, roughly half the average driver's auto-insurance premium is for injury coverages.

4. All dollar amounts are adjusted for inflation and expressed in 1989 dollars.

system, the illustrative no-fault plan would have reduced the total amount spent on compensating injured people by 22 percent.[5] The plan accomplishes this partly by reducing transaction costs and partly by eliminating compensation for noneconomic loss to people below the threshold.[6]

EFFECTS ON TRANSACTION COSTS AND CLAIMANTS' NET COMPENSATION

Under the traditional system, claimants spent an average of $1036 on their legal fees and expenses. Their average net compensation was thus $3645. Adding the $793 spent by insurers on transaction costs to the $1036 incurred by claimants, total transaction costs averaged $1829 per injured person, about 33 percent of total injury coverage costs.

Figure S.1 shows the corresponding results for the illustrative no-fault plan.

The illustrative plan reduces transaction costs about 39 percent, from $1829 to $1110 (a 13–percent savings in total injury coverage costs). Under this no-fault plan, transaction costs would account for about a quarter of the total injury coverage costs. However, the plan also reduces claimant's net compensation, on average, from $3645 to $3182.

Table S.1

Effects on Total Injury Coverage Costs [a]

	Traditional system ($)	Illustrative no-fault alternative [b] ($)
Gross compensation	4681	3764
Insurers' transaction costs	793	528
Total injury coverage costs	5474	4292
Effect on total injury coverage costs	− 22%	

[a] Average per injured person; all dollar amounts have been adjusted for inflation and are expressed in 1989 dollars.
[b] Verbal threshold, $15,000 PIP benefit level.

5. Probabilistic variability leads to a 95–percent confidence interval on our estimate of total injury coverage costs of plus or minus 1 to 4 percent. Other factors, such as interstate differences for which we have limited data, would introduce additional uncertainty.

6. If the adoption of a no-fault approach to compensation reduced the frequency of claims for hard-to-verify injuries, like sprains and strains, or the medical expenses incurred by claimants with such injuries, total injury coverage costs would be an additional 3 or 4 percentage points lower than in the traditional system.

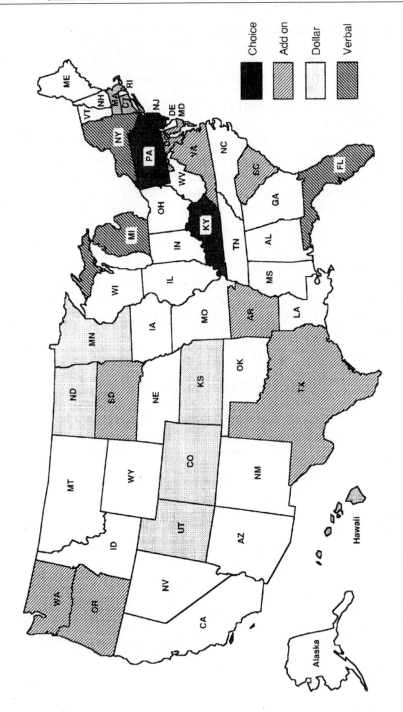

Fig. 1—Alternative Auto Insurance Compensation Systems (as of Nov. 1, 1993)

Fig. S.1—Effects on Claimants' Net Compensation and Transaction Costs

EFFECTS ON COMPENSATION RELATIVE TO ECONOMIC LOSS

Under the traditional system, people with less serious injuries tend to receive more than their economic loss, while those who had more serious injuries (economic losses of $25,000 or more) receive average compensation that is substantially less than economic loss.

A no-fault approach to compensation will narrow the gaps between compensation and economic loss, as shown in Fig. S.2. Compared to the traditional system, no-fault will reduce the amount paid in compensation in excess of their economic loss. No-fault also provides some increase in the share of economic loss compensated.

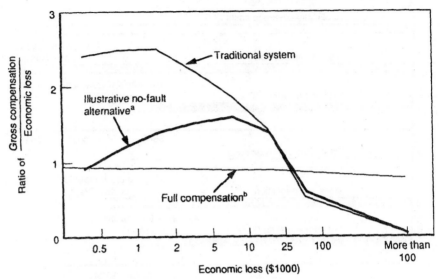

Fig. S.2—Effects on Compensation Relative to Economic Loss

In terms of the numbers of claimants affected in various ways by a no-fault approach to compensation, no-fault substantially reduces the proportion of claimants who receive compensation in excess of their economic loss and substantially increases the proportion of claimants who are fully compensated for their economic loss. Under the traditional system, 62 percent of the injured people receive compensation that exceeds their economic loss. In contrast, a no-fault plan combining a verbal threshold with a $15,000 PIP benefit level would provide more than full compensation[7] to less than a quarter of the injured. Under the traditional system, 27 percent of the people who suffered some economic loss as a result of an auto accident obtained less than full compensation from auto insurance. Under the illustrative no-fault plan, only 16 percent of these people would have ended up with less than full compensation for their economic loss (see Fig. S.3).

EFFECTS ON TIME TO PAYMENT

No-fault plans will speed the provision of compensation to injured parties, compared to the traditional system, by an average of two months. Under no-fault, the vast majority of the people injured in auto accidents receive some compensation from PIP insurance soon after the accident (see Fig. S.4). In the traditional system, MedPay auto insurance provides rapid compensation to many people. But many others lack MedPay coverage and

---

7. Full compensation equals net economic loss (medical costs, plus lost income net of taxes).

have to wait for compensation from third-party insurance, typically a much longer process.

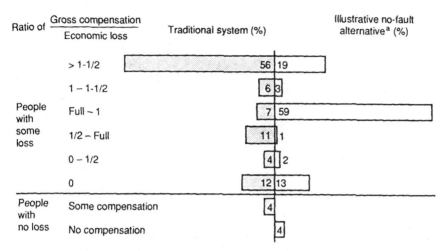

[a]Verbal threshold, $15,000 PIP benefit level.

Fig. S.3—Effects on Distribution of Compensation

*Verbal threshold, $15,000 PIP benefit level.

Fig. S.4—Time from Accident to Initial Payment, in Months

THE DESIGN OF A NO–FAULT PLAN INFLUENCES ITS EFFECTS

No-fault approaches to compensation can yield substantial savings in total injury coverage costs, compared to the traditional system. However, whether or not any particular no-fault plan will reduce injury coverage costs and, if so, how much depends on its provisions. Some no-fault plans that provide very generous PIP benefits may actually increase the total injury coverage costs of the system.

For example, Table S.2 shows the effects of eight different no-fault plans on total injury coverage costs (compared to the traditional system). One is the plan discussed in detail above ($15,000 PIP benefit level, verbal threshold). Two other plans have the same threshold but successively higher PIP benefit levels—$50,000 and $250,000. Three additional plans demonstrate the effect of adopting a $5,000 threshold at each of the three PIP benefit levels. The last two plans show the effects of an absolute ban on access to the liability system combined with either a $50,000 PIP benefit level or unlimited PIP compensation for economic loss.

Table S.2

Alternative Effects of Plan
(percent change in total injury coverage costs)

	Threshold		
PIP Benefit Level	$5,000	Verbal	Absolute Ban
$15,000	− 14	− 22	—[a]
$50,000	− 6	− 12	− 52
$250,000	+ 11	+ 5	—[a]
Unlimited	—[a]	—[a]	− 29

[a] We did not study this alternative plan.

Raising the Threshold

Other things being equal, a higher threshold tends to provide greater savings of total injury coverage costs by shifting claimants from Bodily Injury compensation, which provides compensation for both economic and noneconomic loss, to PIP, which covers only economic loss. However, by reducing the amounts paid in compensation for noneconomic loss, a higher threshold also reduces claimants' average compensation.

Higher thresholds also bring greater reductions in transaction costs. At the extreme, an absolute ban on compensation for noneconomic loss would eliminate disputes over the difficult-to-quantify noneconomic losses, eliminating over three-quarters of the transaction costs incurred in the traditional system.

Higher thresholds reduce payments in excess of economic losses. However, the height of the threshold has little effect on the share of economic loss compensated.

Raising Required PIP Policy Limits

Higher PIP benefit levels increase injury coverage costs for any given threshold. On average, more money is paid out in compensation when the PIP benefit level is higher. The PIP benefit level does not have a substantial effect on transaction costs.

Higher PIP benefit levels increase the share of economic loss compensated.

Adding a PIP Deductible

We also examined the effects of imposing a $500 deductible on PIP compensation. A PIP deductible reduces total injury coverage costs and claimants' net compensation by a small percentage. It does not have a substantial effect on transaction costs. A PIP deductible would decrease the share of economic loss compensated.

A PIP deductible has a dramatic effect on the percentage of injured people compensated by auto insurance, eliminating compensation to those whose economic losses are less than the deductible.

Offsetting PIP with Private Health Insurance

We examined the effects of mandating that injured persons covered by private health insurance collect medical costs from their health insurer rather than their auto insurer. This provision would reduce spending on auto-insurance compensation dramatically. For example, the 22 percent savings in the illustrative no-fault plan would jump to 33 percent savings with a health-insurance offset. Health-insurance offsetting would also decrease the amount that injured people take home from auto-insurance sources. However, an auto-insurance payment offset for health-insurance payments would increase health-insurance costs if it increased health-insurance claims.

INTERSTATE VARIATIONS

Our general conclusions consider the effects of no-fault plans averaged over all tort states combined. However, the effects of any particular no-fault plan will differ from state to state. These differences are sometimes very large.

These differences reflect the fact that states differ in significant ways. Comparing California and Indiana, both tort states, illustrates these fundamental differences:

- Magnitudes of loss and claim amounts vary. For example, only 41 percent of injured people in Indiana sustain medical losses above $500, while in California 67 percent exceed $500.
- Individuals in some states are much more likely to pursue a liability claim. In California, over 50 percent of injured people hire a lawyer, compared to 19 percent in Indiana.
- Claim handlers, attorneys, and juries in different states value losses differently. In Indiana, injured people with economic losses between $1000 and $2000 recover an average of $3247 per case, while in California a similar group receives $4045 per case.

These differences among states mean that the effects of any particular no-fault plan will vary from one state to another. When injuries are greater and losses higher, a larger proportion of the people injured in auto accidents will pass any given threshold. In a state characterized by extensive third-party claiming activity, the reductions in transaction costs and compensation for noneconomic loss will be much greater, and the resulting savings much larger. A no-fault plan will have a much greater effect on total injury coverage costs, and on compensation, in a state in which claimants tend to receive greater compensation for their noneconomic losses.

POLICY IMPLICATIONS

All no-fault plans have some effects that hold true from state to state, although the magnitude of the effects will vary:

- All no-fault plans reduce transaction costs, regardless of plan provisions. No-fault plans that entirely ban access to the liability system reduce transaction costs by about 80 percent. Those that would allow seriously injured people to pursue liability claims would reduce transaction costs by about 20 to 40 percent; the latter translates into a reduction in total injury coverage costs of approximately 10 percent.

- No-fault plans match compensation more closely with economic loss. No-fault plans do this by increasing the fraction of economic loss that is compensated and by reducing the amount of compensation that exceeds economic loss by reducing payouts for noneconomic loss. Injured people with smaller losses tend to recover amounts approximating their medical costs and lost wages, while those more seriously injured recover a larger share of their losses because they can collect both PIP and liability compensation.

- No-fault plans eliminate compensation for noneconomic loss, such as pain and suffering, for injured people below the threshold.

- No-fault plans generally speed up compensation. Injured people begin receiving payments on average about two months sooner under no-fault plans than under the traditional system.

However, some other effects of alternative no-fault plans are substantially different. Under different no-fault alternatives, total injury coverage costs may decrease, possibly dramatically, or may increase, possibly dramatically, depending upon the threshold and the PIP benefit level. The bottom line is that no-fault approaches to compensation can yield substantial savings over the traditional system. Whether or not any particular plan will reduce total injury coverage costs and, if so, how much depends on its provisions.

The key policy decisions in designing a no-fault plan concern the threshold, the PIP benefit level, whether private health insurance is offset, and the PIP deductible.

Because thresholds and PIP benefit levels will have different effects in different states, a state will have to tailor the threshold and benefit level to the levels of injuries and losses typically incurred by people injured in auto accidents there. A state in which people typically experience relatively small losses and in which third-party claiming activity is relatively low may find a modest threshold and modest PIP benefits sufficient. A state in which auto accidents tend to result in relatively large economic losses and in which people tend to aggressively pursue third-party claims may have to adopt a much more stringent threshold, if it wants to keep total injury coverage costs in check, and may have to adopt more generous PIP benefits, if it wants to keep benefits close to economic loss.

Our study focuses on the costs of injury coverage. However, auto-insurance premiums are based on several considerations above and beyond these costs, including property damage costs, underwriting costs, overhead costs, and market factors in the insurance industry. Without a thorough analysis of these considerations, it is impossible to estimate exactly how no-fault plans would affect premiums. However, injury costs are a large element in overall auto-insurance costs. Therefore, reduction in injury coverage costs should lead to reduction in premiums. The exact amount of this reduction remains unclear.

We make no policy recommendations about the merits of traditional versus no-fault systems. Our goal is to provide policymakers with an empirical framework for thinking about the trade-offs implicit in auto-insurance compensation systems and to clarify the difficult choices involved.

NOTES AND QUESTIONS

1. *Constitutionality of Automobile No–Fault Schemes.* The personal injury portion of automobile no-fault laws have survived attacks under the due process and equal protection clauses of the Federal Constitution in all state courts of last resort. See Montgomery v. Daniels, 38 N.Y.2d 41, 378 N.Y.S.2d 1, 340 N.E.2d 444 (1975). Most of the decisions have looked to the analogy of workers' compensation laws in order to meet the due process claim. Under those laws in most states a worker can elect to retain his common law rights, and so the analogy is not entirely congruent. (Most workers have declined to make this election).

The equal protection arguments against the no-fault thresholds have given the courts more difficulty, but the thresholds have been sustained. The first major case was Pinnick v. Cleary, 360 Mass. 1, 271 N.E.2d 592 (1971). See also Manzanares v. Bell, 214 Kan. 589, 522 P.2d 1291 (1974) ($500 medical threshold); Lasky v. State Farm Ins. Co., 296 So.2d 9 (Fla.1974) ($500 medical threshold); Fann v. McGuffey, 534 S.W.2d 770 (Ky.1975) ($500 medical threshold); Singer v. Sheppard, 464 Pa. 387, 346 A.2d 897 (1975) ($750 medical threshold). In Gentile v. Altermatt, 169 Conn. 267, 363 A.2d 1 (1975) ($500 medical threshold), the Supreme Court dismissed the appeal, 423 U.S. 1041 (1976). See also Opinion of the Justices, 113 N.H. 205, 304 A.2d 881 (1973) ($1000 medical threshold); In re Requests of the Governor and Senate, Etc., 389 Mich. 441, 208 N.W.2d 469 (1973) ("serious impairment of bodily function" and "permanent serious disfigurement" thresholds); and see Shavers v. Kelly, 402 Mich. 554, 267 N.W.2d 72 (1978).

The Supreme Court of Florida held a no-fault provision regarding damage to the insured vehicle violative of due process when it simply shifted the cost of that risk from the tortfeasor to the injured party. See Kluger v. White, 281 So.2d 1 (Fla.1973). Most no-fault plans do not cover property damage.

The Michigan Supreme Court has upheld the state's statute against numerous equal-protection objections. See O'Donnell v. State Farm Mut. Auto. Ins. Co., 404 Mich. 524, 273 N.W.2d 829 (1979).

In regard to constitutionality of no-fault statutes, see generally R. Keeton & J. O'Connell, Basic Protection for the Traffic Victim—A Blue Print for Reforming Automobile Insurance, 483–514 (1965); Hart, The Constitutionality of the New York State Comprehensive Automobile Insurance Reparations Act, 43 Ford.L.Rev. 400 (1974).

2. *Deterrence and Costs.* Does the adoption of a no-fault compensation plan for automobile accidents result in increased accident rates? See Landes, Insurance Liability and Accidents: A Theoretical and Empirical Investigation of the Effects of No–Fault Accidents, 25 J.L. & Econ. 49 (1982). Cf. O'Connell & Levmore, A Reply to Landes: A Faulty Study of No–Fault's Effect on Fault? 48 Mo.L.Rev. 649 (1983). For discussion and summation of research, A.L.I. Reporters' Study, Enterprise Responsibility for Personal Injury, Vol. 1 (1991), pp. 357–360, and Dewees and Trebilcock, The Efficacy of the Tort System and Its Alternative: A Review of Empirical Evidence, 30 Osgoode Hall L.J. 57 (1992). Are some no-fault laws "out-of-balance," in that they cause higher insurance premiums because total no-fault benefits exceed the reduction of tort liability payments? Would it be preferable to introduce a pre-or post-accident choice for the injured parties as to whether they wish to proceed under no-fault or under the common-law liability system? See O'Connell & Joost, Giving Motorists a Choice Between Fault and No–Fault Insurance, 72 Va.L.Rev. 61 (1986). For a similar scheme employing extrapolations from the Rand findings, above, see O'Connell, Carroll, Horowitz, and Abrahamse, Consumer Choice in the Auto Insurance Market 52 Mo.L.Rev. 1016 (1993); O'Connell, Carroll, Horowitz, and Abrahamse, The Costs of Consumer Choice for Auto Insurance in States Without No–Fault Insurance, 54 Md. L. Rev. 281 (1995); and O'Connell, Carroll, Horowitz, and Abrahamse, The Comparative Costs of Allowing Consumer Choice for Auto Insurance in All Fifty States, 55 Md. L. Rev. 160 (1996). The desirability of the elective no-fault scheme promoted by Professor O'Connell and his co-authors turns importantly on the cost to motorists of insurance cover under the scheme and whether the adoption of the scheme would force an increase in the premiums of those staying with traditional tort cover. In a study prepared for the Joint Economic Committee of the United States Congress by the Institute for Civil Justice: Rand (April 1997), the authors Allan Abrahamse and Stephen Carroll found that in most states the costs of compensating accident victims for drivers who select elective no-fault would be 60% less than the current system in each state. That would represent a premium savings of about 30% on average for those willing to waive tort rights. In an earlier, 1995 Rand study by the same authors (The Effects of a Choice Auto Insurance Plan on Insurance Costs, Rand, 1995), it was found that the availability of the no-fault option would have no effect on the compensation costs incurred by insurers on their behalf and hence automobile insurance premiums would be uninfluenced.

3.   OTHER NO–FAULT COMPENSATION SYSTEMS

The tort system compensates personal injuries and other losses by a system of fault assessment and liability insurance. Even in cases involving strict products liability or abnormally dangerous activities, there is a measure of moral, economic, or legal fault: the product is defective or unreasonably dangerous; the activity involves abnormal risks that outweigh its value to the community. See, e.g., Powers, The Persistence of Fault in Products Liability, 61 Tex.L.Rev. 777 (1983); J. O'Connell, Ending Insult to Injury: No–Fault Insurance for Products and Services 57 (1975); Owen, The Fault Pit, 26 Ga.L.Rev. 703 (1992); Schwartz, The Vitality of Negligence and the Ethics of Strict Liability, 15 Ga.L.Rev. 963 (1981). Litigating fault and using the court system to compensate victims involves substantial transaction costs and expenses of administration. Critics charge that, for reasons of both efficiency and fairness, a no-fault compensation system should replace the traditional tort system's method of compensating accident victims. See, e.g., J. O'Connell, Ending Insult to Injury: No–Fault Insurance for Products and Services (1975); P. Cane, Atiyah's Accidents, Compensation and the Law, 5th ed. (1993).

1.   In 1972 New Zealand adopted the first comprehensive administrative system that replaced tort claims with a new no-fault remedy for virtually all accidental injuries. The plan, administered by the government, is a social insurance system that pays limited benefits to all persons who suffer "personal injury by accident." The plan is financed through car-owner, employer, and general tax levies. See G. Palmer, Compensation for Incapacity: A Study of Law and Social Change in New Zealand and Australia (1979); Willy, The Accident Compensation Act and Recovery for Losses Arising From Personal Injury and Death by Accident, 6 N.Z.U.L.Rev. 250 (1975). The New Zealand plan does not replace the tort system in cases involving property damage, non-workplace disease, economic losses or business torts. See Henderson, The New Zealand Accident Compensation Reform, 48 U.Chi.L.Rev. 781 (1981); Franklin, Personal Injury Accidents in New Zealand and the United States, Some Striking Similarities, 21 Stan.L.Rev. 653 (1975); Phillips, In Defense of the Tort System, 27 Ariz.L.Rev. 603, 605 (1986). Under a social insurance compensation plan as in effect in New Zealand, is there a trade-off in lowered accident deterrence and diminished incentives for safety? See T. Ison, Accident Compensation 165 (1980); Love, Punishment and Deterrence: A Comparative Study of Tort Liability for Punitive Damages Under No–Fault Compensation Legislation, 16 U.C.Davis L.Rev. 232 (1983); Klar, New Zealand's Accident Compensation Scheme: A Tort Lawyer's Perspective, 33 U. Toronto L.J. 80 (1983); International Workshop: Beyond Compensation: Dealing with Accidents in the 21st Century, 15 U. Haw. L. Rev. 524 (1993). Is such a plan feasible in the United States? How much would it cost?

2.   Similar legislation was introduced into the Australian Parliament but was not enacted. The Australian scheme would have covered illness in addition to injuries. Such coverage was debated and recommended by the New Zealand Law Reform Commission. Legislation was introduced in New Zealand acting on the report, but the Government was voted out of office and the new Government was not to go ahead with the legislation. In stark contrast, rather than expanding coverage, the government amended the legislation in 1992. Since 1992, the government, through a series of measures, has shifted the scheme's social welfare objective to one focusing on risk-related insurance. In 1998, for example, employers and the self-employed were given freedom to shop for accident insurance to restrict compensable events and introduce a measure of deterrence into the system. Miller, The 1992 Changes to New Zealand's Accident Compensation Scheme, 5 Canta.L.Rev. 1 (1992) and Miller, An Analysis or Critique of the

1992 changes to New Zealand's Accident Compensation Scheme, 52 Md. L.Rev. 1070 (1993).

3.   If a comprehensive scheme is enacted, how far should the scheme adhere to tort principles? Should compensation be based, in part, on lost income? Should the scheme be wedded to the principles of social welfare and award compensation based on need alone? Should the scheme seek to adjust premiums according to risks created by the enterprise?

The tide of the comprehensive compensation scheme appears to be ebbing even in its New Zealand home. Todd & Black, Accident Compensation and the Barring of Actions for Damages, 1 Tort L.Rev. 197 (1993).

4.   In the United States, no-fault approaches to injury compensation have been applied or proposed in a number of contexts other than workers' compensation and automobile accidents:

A.   *Federal Compensation Plans.* In 1969, Congress passed the Black Lung Act, 30 U.S.C.A. §§ 901 et seq., to compensate coal miners and their dependents for the disabling respiratory disease known as "black lung." Whether viewed as a compensation system to miners, a subsidy to the mining industry, or as a type of welfare benefit, the federal black lung program represents an innovative solution to compensation in a case in which traditional tort and workers' compensation remedies proved inadequate because of the progressive nature of the disease and the effect of statutes of limitations and workers' compensation statutes that, at that time, failed to cover occupational diseases. See Ramsey & Habermann, The Federal Black Lung Program—The View From the Top, 87 W.Va.L.Rev. 575 (1985); Barth, The Tragedy of Black Lung: Federal Compensation for Occupational Disease (1987).

Political forces, focused by lawsuits, have prompted Congress to consider schemes consonant with the pattern of the Black Lung legislation. For example, some companies that manufactured products incorporating asbestos have sought legislative compensation schemes disposing with common law litigation. Vietnam veterans considering that the tort system had failed successfully lobbied for wider legislative compensation schemes. Asbestos claims procedures, for example, would have dispensed with the tort law and supplemented state workers' compensation plans. Chapter 5 observed the shortfalls of the common law in respect of Agent Orange claims. Lawsuits helped to create pressure for Congressional action. Veterans' Dioxin and Radiation Exposure Compensation Standards Act, 38 U.S.C.A. § 354. Congress, however, has been wary of expanding regulatory schemes to provide for private rights of action for personal injuries. See discussion of Superfund legislation noted in Chapter 16. For discussion of these proposals see Gaskins, Environmental Accidents: Personal Injury and Public Responsibility (1989), 253–89.

Chapter 15 noted that liability for the harmful effects of vaccines deterred their beneficial development, production, and use. In order to alleviate this concern a no-fault compensation program was introduced under the National Childhood Vaccine Injury Act of 1986 (42 U.S.C.A.

§§ 300aa–10 to 300aa–33). The fund is financed by an excise tax on each dose of vaccine. The statute covers all actual medical expenses as well as costs of rehabilitation, lost wages, if any, based on average earnings in the non-farm sector, and a capped discretionary award for pain and suffering. A claimant may opt for a common law claim but an attempt was made to make this option unappealing by the application of common law principles. (E.g., Restatement (Second) of Torts § 402A, comment *k*.)

Who are the winners and losers under these compensation schemes? Could they be the precursors of a general no-fault compensation scheme for all injuries? Would you include all incapacitating illnesses? Economic dislocation flowing from illness far outstrips that resulting from accidents. See Harris et al., Compensation and Support for Illness and Injury (1984). Remember that Congress provides a social security "safety net" covering, in varying degrees, unemployment, hospital and medical expenses, disability, retirement and survivor's benefits. Should the tort system be abolished and compensation integrated with a revamped social security system that could deliver benefits more efficiently? Sugarman, Doing Away with Personal Injury Law 114–15 (1989).

B. *Medical Malpractice.* Periods of high tort claim frequency and severity have, in certain geographical areas, like Dade County, Florida, sharply raised, for some specialties, insurance premium levels or made insurance difficult to obtain. Chapter 4 noted legislative reforms that have ensued. Often the reforms have capped damages, reduced limitation periods, abolished the collateral benefits rule, required arbitration, regulated contingent fees, and provided for periodic payments. For appraisal see Danzon, Medical Malpractice: Theory, Evidence, and Public Policy (1985).

More thoroughgoing systemic reforms have been suggested. Paul Weiler, Medical Malpractice on Trial (1991), urges the adoption of a no-fault scheme. His work derives from a large empirical study on medical malpractice in New York. Harvard Medical Malpractice Study, Patients, Doctors, and Lawyers: Medical Injury, Malpractice Litigation, and Patient Compensation in New York (1990). See also Weiler, et al., A Measure of Malpractice: Medical Injury, Malpractice Litigation, and Patient Compensation (1993). The American Medical Association has suggested an approach to take adjudication from the hands of the courts. Johnson, Phillips, Crentlicher, and Hatlie, A Fault–Based Administrative Alternative for Resolving Medical Malpractice Claims, 42 Vand.L.Rev. 1365 (1989). One study of Florida closed claims demonstrates that claimants sue for a variety of reasons, including vindication or to uncover information. What does this imply about no-fault reform? Sloan, et al., Suing for Medical Malpractice (1993).

Perhaps, as in non-medical liability, radical changes from the court-based fault liability may be expected only in pockets where liability problems seem intractable. For example, liability for birth-related neurological injuries. In Virginia obstetricians were threatened with denial of coverage for such harms. The Virginia legislature in 1987 passed the Birth–Related

Neurological Injury Compensation Act (Injured Infant Act), Va.Code Ann. §§ 38.2–5000 to 5021. The Act covers

> injury to the brain or spinal cord of an infant caused by the deprivation of oxygen or mechanical injury occurring in the course of labor, delivery or resuscitation in the immediate post-delivery period in a hospital which renders the infant permanently motorically disabled and (i) developmentally disabled or (ii) for infants sufficiently developed to be cognitively evaluated, cognitively disabled. In order to constitute a "birth-related neurological injury" within the meaning of [the act], such disability shall cause the infant to be permanently in need of assistance in all activities of daily living.

Live births only are covered; not included are disability or death caused by genetic or congenital abnormality, degenerative neurological disease, or maternal substance abuse.

Compensation is for all medical expenses not covered by other insurance. Lost wages for ages 18 to 65 are paid on a periodical basis at the rate of one-half of Virginia's average weekly earnings (non-farm). Few claims have been made so far.

Florida enacted similar legislation in 1988. Fl.Code § 766.301–316. Implementation of the Florida scheme has been problematic. The issue in this scheme, as with others, has been to confine the class of injuries and beneficiaries within the no-fault scheme. The pressure to extend common law liability principles to covered injuries is relentless. The Florida legislature in 1998, for example, amended its legislation to prevent an end run around the no-fault benefits. Sloan, et al., The Road from Medical Injury to Claims Resolution: How No–Fault and Fault Differ, 60 Law & Contemp. Probs. 35 (1997), report on aspects of the no-fault schemes finding them modestly successful.

For commentary, see 74 Va.L.Rev. 1451 (1988), articles by Professors Epstein and O'Connell. Duff, Compensation for Neurologically Impaired Infants: Medical No–Fault in Virginia, 27 Harv.J.Legis. 391 (1990); Bovbjerg & Sloan, No–Fault for Medical Injury: Theory and Evidence, 67 U. Cin. L. Rev. 53 (1998) (attempting to assess the success of the Florida and Virginia schemes and concluding that such limited no-fault schemes do not achieve the goals ascribed to no-fault).

Professor O'Connell has suggested a version of his neo no-fault model in Moore & O'Connell, Foreclosing Medical Malpractice Claims by Prompt Tender of Economic Law, 44 La.L.Rev. 1267 (1984).

C. *Products Liability*. As noted in Chapter 15, products liability has received close attention from reformers. Some have suggested a broad departure from strict liability as developed by the courts. Viscusi, Toward a Diminished Role for Tort Liability: Social Insurance, Government Regulation, and Contemporary Risks to Health and Safety, 6 Yale J. on Reg. 65 (1989); Ausness, An Insurance–Based Compensation System for Product–Related Injuries, 58 U. Pitt. L. Rev. 669 (1997) (suggesting and defending a scheme by which product sellers would be obliged to reimburse injured consumers on a no-fault basis for economic losses). Others, however, recommend absolute liability as appropriately fulfilling goals of compensation and deterrence. Hanson & Logue, The First–Party Insurance Externality: An Economic Justification for Enterprise Liability, 76 Cornell L.Rev. 129 (1990); Croley & Hanson, Rescuing the Revolution: The Revived Case for Enterprise Liability, 91 Mich. L. Rev. 683 (1993). With respect to tobacco-related diseases, Professors Hanson and Logue in The Costs of Cigarettes: The Economic Case for Ex Post Incentive–Based Regulation, 107 Yale L.J. 1163 (1998), note the lack of information available to consumers and in consequence would hold tobacco companies strictly liable in tort for tobacco-related diseases. At the same time, a compensation scheme could be established to process claims under an administrative tribunal. Their proposal is criticized by Professors LeBel and Ausness, Toward Justice in Tobacco Policymaking: A Critique of Hanson and Logue and an Alternative Approach to the Costs of Cigarettes, 23 Ga. L. Rev. 693 (1999). These professors support a tax levy that would support research, education, and health care relating to tobacco use. An immunity would be provided to the companies. They urge that their recommendations are more faithful to the moral or justice dimensions of the law. Compensation schemes for product-related injuries are bedevilled by the same requirement as for other schemes: the compensation must be triggered by a defined or compensable event. For workers' compensation the trigger is that the injury occur "in the course of employment." A much litigated question is whether the "trigger" requirement is fulfilled. How is the requirement to be defined for a scheme covering injuries caused by products? A person burns her hand on a stove? Drinks too much liquor? Drives a car off a bridge?

D. *Elective No–Fault Insurance Contracts.* To cover athletic injuries, particularly those sustained in high school football, many school districts purchase insurance contracts that oblige insurance companies to make prompt offers to pay an injured athlete's medical expenses and other economic losses set forth in the policy. But the world of politics did not treat these approaches favorably, and they were opposed by both consumer and business groups.

If the claimant accepts the payment, a release is obtained and no tort suit may be brought. If the payment is not accepted, the victim may proceed with a tort suit. See O'Connell, Elective No–Fault Liability by Contract—With or Without An Enabling Statute, 1975 U.Ill.L.Forum 59–72 (1975).

E. Additional proposals for substituting compensation plans for the tort system have been prepared and forcefully presented. See, for example, T. Ison, The Forensic Lottery (1967); Franklin, Replacing the Negligence Lottery: Compensation and Selective Reimbursement, 53 Va.L.Rev. 774 (1967).

F. Do you agree with Professor John Fleming's assessment of the American compensation picture?

The overall accident compensation landscape in America is therefore highly fragmented and lacking any systematic plan. The benefits of tort liability are not husbanded for those who are un-or under-compensated from other sources but are distributed randomly without regard to the needs or deserts of victims. Its grossly inflated transaction costs add to the remarkable inefficiency of the tort system. Only the affluence of American society has deflected serious misgivings about this wasteful arrangement and about the need to develop a more purposeful compensation policy such as that which other countries, with more limited resources, have been driven to pursue.

J.G. Fleming, The American Tort Process (1988), 30–31.

4. THE FUTURE

The fifth edition of this casebook was published 29 years ago, in 1971. The first automobile no-fault statute had just been passed by the Massachusetts legislature. No cases had been decided on the statute but the concept was being ardently pushed by its proponents and just as strongly opposed by its detractors. The subject could not then be treated in the traditional casebook fashion, but that edition contained a chapter entitled "Automobile Accidents—Tort Law or Reparation System?" The text described the alleged deficiencies in the existing systems, the steps that had been taken in some states to alleviate them, and the various proposals for extensive reform; and it identified the "policy issues" involved in the decisions to be made. It concluded with a reference to the future and presented this challenge:

"It takes more than a crystal ball to predict what the state of the law will be 20 to 40 years from now. But that is the time when you will be in your prime as a lawyer. Whatever develops, it will be a legal matter and as an attorney you are likely to be deeply involved in it. Speculate now, with the wisdom and background you presently have, both as to what will be the state of the law 30 years from now and as to what [you think] it should be. Why not do it in writing so as to make your thoughts more lucid and concrete? And then you can check yourself as the years roll by to see both how good a legal prognosticator you are and whether your viewpoints on desirable solutions have changed." Prosser and Wade, Cases and Materials on Torts 650 (5th ed. 1971).

The options are greater now than they were then but the limits of reform are more fully appreciated. The pressure for adoption of a reparation system is not as intense at present, but it is steady. We would like to repeat this challenge to you now. You will find the experience a stimulating one. What do you predict as the ultimate outcome, and what do you wish that outcome to be?

ABBREVIATIONS USEFUL FOR NOTE-TAKING IN TORT CLASSES*

π	plaintiff	Tp	trespass	kw/RD	knowledge or reckless disregard
$\triangle$	defendant	pvg	privilege		
θ	third party	Tfz	tortfeasor	Ab Dg Ak	abnormally dangerous activity
c.l.	common law	JTz	joint tortfeasor		
c/a	cause of action	lz	license		
DV/$\triangle$	directed verdict for defendant	lzc	licensee	ulhz	ultrahazardous
		$\overline{nvt}$	invitee	inj	injunction
JV/π	jury verdict for plaintiff	$\overline{tpr}$	trespasser	b.f.p.	bona fide purchaser
		nf k¢	informed consent	br/wt	breach of warranty
S/J	summary judgment			mp wt	implied warranty
R&R	reversed & remanded	$\overline{ktb}$	contribution	xp wt	express warranty
		$\overline{ndt}$	indemnity	dft	defect
Dem	demurrer	Lr	lessor	dsn	design
$	suppose	Lee	lessee	WD	wrongful death
Q	question	CN	contributory negligence	Svv	survival
O	owner			m-	mal-, mis-
axn	action	CpN	comparative negligence	m-fz	misfeasance
R2T	Restatement, Second, of Torts	LCC	last clear chance	m-pr	malpractice
stat	statute	rsb	reasonable	m-rep	misrepresentation
L	liable, liability	RPP	reasonable prudent person	n-	non-
nj	injury			n-fz	nonfeasance
Bx	Blackacre	A/R	assumption of risk	[	not, un-
JD	John Doe Jane Doe	cz	cause	[4cb	unforeseeable
		px cz	proximate cause	cov [sue	covenant not to sue
ntt	intent	cz/f	cause in fact	jdr	joinder
dmg	damages	dp iv cz	dependent intervening cause	kct	concert
dfs	defense			mut	immunity
b/p	burden of proof	ndp cz	independent cause	ndp kr	independent contractor
s/l	statute of limitations	ss cz	superseding cause		
s/f	statute of frauds	RIL	res ipsa loquitur	mp	implied
K	contract	4cb	foreseeable	mpt	imputed
T	tort	dfm	defamation	kvn	conversion
IT	intentional tort	Dct	deceit	jfc	justification
N	negligence	lbl	libel	std	standard
SL	strict liability	sld	slander	vln	violation
Az	assault			pun	punitive
Bt	battery			nom	nominal
A&B	assault & battery			nzc	nuisance
FI	false imprisonment			stfn	satisfaction
IIED	intentional infliction of emotional distress			rls	release
				pvt	privity
				rem	remedy
Sb/L	subject to liability			p.f.	prima facie

* There are only a few abbreviations that are generally conventional, like those for plaintiff, defendant and contract. Students should adopt their own system of abbreviations. These have helped some students in the past and may help you. The system should be enlarged and may vary from class to class.

INDEX

1–56662–955–1